THE OXFORD COMPANION
TO THE BIBLE

THE OXFORD

COMPANION TO THE

BIBLE

EDITED BY

BRUCE M. METZGER   MICHAEL D. COOGAN

New York   Oxford

OXFORD UNIVERSITY PRESS

1993

OXFORD UNIVERSITY PRESS

Oxford   New York   Toronto
Delhi   Bombay   Calcutta   Madras   Karachi
Kuala Lumpur   Singapore   Hong Kong   Tokyo
Nairobi   Dar es Salaam   Cape Town
Melbourne   Auckland   Madrid

and associated companies in
Berlin   Ibadan

LIBRARY OF CONGRESS CATALOGING-IN-PUBLICATION DATA
The Oxford companion to the Bible
Bruce M. Metzger, Michael D. Coogan, editors.
p.   cm.   Includes bibliographical references and index.
ISBN 0-19-504645-5
1. Bible—Dictionaries.
BS440.M434   1993   220.3—dc20
93-19315

3 5 7 9 8 6 4
Printed in the United States of America
on acid-free paper

Contents

Introduction

For nearly two millennia, the Bible has been the cardinal text for Judaism and Christianity. Its stories and characters are part of both the repertoire of Western literature and the vocabulary of educated women and men. It is, however, more than a collection of ancient tales. Even before a canonical list of books considered sacred scripture or holy writ was established, the writings we now call the Bible were considered normative: they laid down the essential principles of how human beings should deal with God and with each other. The practice of quoting from, and alluding to, earlier texts as authoritative is found within the Bible itself and has continued unabated in subsequent Jewish and Christian writings. At the same time, the Bible has also been formative; subsequent generations of believers have seen themselves as descended from, and in continuity with, those to whom God had spoken and for whom he had acted definitively in the past, and the recital of those words and events has been instrumental in shaping the religious communities of succeeding generations. The Bible has thus had an immeasurable influence on Judaism and Christianity, on the cultures of which they have formed a part, and on all those traditions in some ways derived from them, such as Islam.

Although the word "Bible" means "book," and the Bible has been treated as a single book for much of its history, it is in fact many books, an anthology of the literatures of ancient Israel, and, for Christians, also of earliest Christianity. The Bible thus speaks with many voices, and, from the time of its emergence as an authoritative sacred text, readers and interpreters have noted its many repetitions, inconsistencies, and contradictions. Since the Enlightenment especially, critical consideration of the Bible—that is, study of it insofar as possible without presuppositions—has irreversibly affected what may be called the "precritical" understanding of the Bible as simply a unified text, God's eternal, infallible, and complete word. Discoveries of ancient manuscripts (such as the Dead Sea Scrolls) and of literatures contemporaneous with, or earlier than, those preserved in the Bible (such as stories of creation and the Flood from ancient Babylonia and the gospels of Thomas and Philip from Nag Hammadi in Egypt), as well as innumerable archaeological finds, have deepened our understanding of the Bible and the historical and cultural contexts in which its constituent parts were written. This new understanding of the Bible has resulted in continuous scholarly attention and popular interest.

The Oxford Companion to the Bible is an authoritative reference for key persons, places, events, concepts, institutions, and realities of biblical times. In addition, the *Companion* provides up-to-date discussions of the interpretation of these topics by modern scholars, bringing to bear the most recent findings of archaeologists and current research methods from such disciplines as anthropology, sociology, and literary criticism. Interpretation of the Bible has of course not been consistent, and throughout history the Bible has been used to support contradictory positions on such issues as slavery, the role of women, war and peace, forms of government, and finance. The *Companion* reflects this diversity: it is consciously pluralistic, and its more than 250 contributors, as well as its editors and editorial advisory board, encompass a wide spectrum of intellectual and confessional perspectives. They represent the international community of scholars, coming from some twenty countries, on five continents. No attempt has been made by the editors to produce any dogmatic unanimity; readers should not be surprised to find differing interpretations in different entries. Contributors have been urged to present their own scholarly views while noting diverse perspectives. In general, the articles aim to present the consensus of interpretation, or its lack, attained by the most recent scholarship, and to avoid partisanship and polemic.

Recognizing that different communities of faith have different understandings of which books form their Bibles, the *Companion* has deliberately adopted a maximalist position: any book or part of a book that is recognized as canonical by any religious community is treated in this volume. A similarly inclusive and ecumenical view has led to the use of neutral terminology whenever possible; thus, following increasingly frequent scholarly practice, the term "Hebrew Bible" is used in preference to "Old Testament," and the abbreviations BCE (Before the Common Era) and CE (Common Era) are in place of BC and AD.

The *Companion* differs from comparable volumes in its sustained and systematic attention to the role the Bible has played in the ongoing life of various communities of faith, and in the development of the civilizations for which biblical traditions are in part formative. Thus, in addition to lengthy articles on the interpretation of the Bible in Jewish, Christian, and Muslim traditions, there are entries that trace the Bible's ongoing significance in such areas as the arts, law, politics, and literature. There are more than twenty lengthy entries of this type, identified by the phrase "and the Bible"; titles such as African American Traditions and the Bible, Dance and the Bible, Feminism and the Bible, Freud and the Bible, Medicine and the Bible, Music and the Bible, Popular Culture and the Bible, and Science and the Bible indicate the range of these articles. Furthermore, to show the trajectories of biblical traditions, many other entries trace the uses (and abuses) of the Bible from ancient times to the present.

The *Companion* is thus more comprehensive than the usual Bible dictionary, and provides in alphabetical sequence a broad range of more than seven hundred articles, each signed by the contributor. Articles vary in length from short summaries of what the Bible says about a topic and how biblical traditions have been interpreted and used, to major interpretive essays. The latter often take the form of composite entries, consisting of two or more articles by specialists on various periods and regions: Afterlife and Immortality; Chronology; Interpretation, History of; Literature and the Bible; Translations; and Women are just a few examples. In planning the volume, the editors used the following categories; they illustrate how the development, understanding, and influence of the Bible receive comprehensive coverage in the *Companion*:

- **The Formation of the Bible**

  The Bible is the final product of a series of stages, including orally transmitted traditions, shorter and longer written units, collections edited and in some cases translated in ancient times, and final selection by various religious communities as canonical scriptures. There is treatment of all of these processes, and detailed discussion of how the various parts of books and the books themselves were collected, passed on, edited, selected, and arranged, as well as articles on all the books of the Bible, and on the Apocrypha and the Pseudepigrapha.

- **The Transmission, Diffusion, and Circulation of the Bible**

  Once selected as an authoritative sacred text, the Bible has been continuously translated, reproduced, and disseminated. There are full entries on ancient writing, manuscripts, and bookmaking; on chapter and verse divisions; on the history and processes of printing and publishing the Bible; and on illustrated, children's, and "curious" Bibles. There are also detailed treatments of ancient, medieval, and modern translations of the Bible into hundreds of languages and into all major language groups; of the work of Bible Societies in this regard; and of the role of the translation and diffusion of the Bible in the development of linguistic theory and the spread of literacy.

- **The Biblical World**

Under this heading are included key individuals, events, dates, institutions, and realities of daily life in ancient Israel and the earliest Christian communities, understood within the larger contexts of the ancient Near East, Hellenistic Judaism, and Greco-Roman culture. There are, in addition, articles on broader topics, such as the brothers and sisters of Jesus, chronology, circumcision, the Flood, geography, rabbi, the Sabbath, and units of time; and synthetic interpretive essays on subjects such as the history of ancient Israel and Judah, feasts and festivals, kingship and monarchy, letter-writing in antiquity, medicine in biblical times, and animals and plants.

- **Biblical Concepts**

The Bible has been both the basis for and stimulus to reflection on a wide range of theological topics and human concerns. Under this rubric the *Companion* examines biblical theology as such, as well as biblical views of such perennial issues as afterlife and immortality, creation, death, faith, hope, love, monotheism, and Satan. In addition, there are detailed discussions of biblical views of numerous issues that have been the subject of contemporary attention and controversy, such as abortion, homosexuality, marriage, nature and ecology, sex, and women.

- **The Interpretation of the Bible**

Every article in the *Companion* is, of course, interpretive, and considers how biblical traditions have been understood by Jewish and Christian interpreters throughout history. The *Companion* further provides extensive separate treatments of the history, theory, and practice of the interpretation of the Bible, under such topics as the history of interpretation, quotations from the Hebrew Bible in the New Testament, typology, fundamentalism, and anti-Semitism. There are also articles on how fields such as archaeology and the social sciences, as well as methods such as structuralism, have enhanced understanding of the Bible; discussions of the uses of computers and concordances in biblical studies; and major interpretive essays on such topics as the religion of Israel, myth, and the authority of the Bible.

- **The Uses and Influence of the Bible**

Since its formation, the Bible has been a primary resource for Western culture. Its immense influence on British, North American, European, and other literatures is traced in an extensive composite entry on Literature and the Bible. There are also major interpretive surveys of the use of the Bible in art, dance, law, and music, and on the complex interplay between the Bible and such areas as feminism, medicine, politics, and science. Other articles survey the role of the Bible in African American traditions and in Eastern Orthodoxy; its significance for Islam, Mormonism, and other postbiblical religious traditions; its influence on the ideas of Freud, Jung, and Marx; the practice of reading from it in Jewish and Christian liturgical contexts; its continuing role in popular culture; and its use as family record and educational instrument.

The *Companion* is thus an authoritative and comprehensive reference for a wide audience, including general readers; students and teachers in high schools, colleges, seminaries, and divinity schools; rabbis, ministers, and religious educators; participants in religious education and Bible study programs; and scholars in the variety of disciplines for which the Bible is in some way pertinent.

The *Companion* does not aim to be an encyclopedia or encyclopedic dictionary, and is not intended as a substitute either for the Bible itself or for a concordance to the Bible. Quotations from the Bible have deliberately been kept to a minimum, and biblical references are illustrative, not exhaustive. Nor has it been thought necessary to include every name found in the Bible, but only those judged important within the biblical traditions or by later readers. This is especially true of persons and places about whom little if anything is known other than what appears in the Bible. Within the scope of one volume, then, the *Companion* is a reliable guide, from Aaron or Zion, to what the Bible says about a topic and how scholars have interpreted biblical traditions. It explores as well how those traditions have been used since the books of the Bible became scripture.

Use of the Companion

The *Companion* is arranged alphabetically. Extensive cross-references guide the reader to related entries; these cross-references are of three types:

1. Within an entry, the first occurrence of a name, word, or phrase that has its own entry, is marked with an asterisk (*).

2. When a topic treated in an entry or a related topic is discussed elsewhere in the volume, the italicized words *"see"* or *"see also"* refer the reader to the appropriate entry term(s).

3. "Blind entries," that is, entry terms that have no accompanying text but are terms that readers might expect to find discussed, appear alphabetically in the volume and refer to the entries where the topics are actually treated. Thus, the blind entry Decalogue refers readers to Ten Commandments, and Kingdom of Heaven (a term found only in the gospel of Matthew) refers readers to the more frequently used term Kingdom of God.

Further investigation of particular topics is made possible by a detailed index, which provides page references for pertinent subjects and for ancient and modern proper names. Very few volumes comparable to the *Companion* have such an index; its use will enable readers to locate topics throughout the book.

When appropriate, references are made within entries to the maps found at the end of the *Companion,* so that readers may locate places named in the text more precisely. There is also a separate index to the maps, enabling more detailed study of historical geography.

At the end of the volume, there is an extensive annotated bibliography, which will enable readers to explore in more detail topics covered in the *Companion.* The bibliography is divided into categories for easier use, such as the history, geography, and archaeology of biblical times; anthologies of nonbiblical texts; critical and popular introductions to the Bible; reference works; surveys of the history of interpretation; and methodologies used in biblical scholarship.

The translation used in the *Companion* is *The New Revised Standard Version* (NRSV), the most recent authoritative translation of the Bible into English, produced by an interfaith committee of scholars and published in 1990. The renderings of the NRSV are the basis for entry titles. Within individual entries, contributors have on occasion used other published translations or their own; in these cases, differences from the NRSV are noted.

Acknowledgments

The *Companion* has seen a long developmental process, and we wish to thank contributors for their ongoing support of the project. We are most grateful, of course, for their expert contributions, which are the essence of the volume; their names are listed after this introduction.

The advisory editors have been extraordinarily helpful in assuring that the *Companion* maintains its balanced perspective, proportion, and scope. Jo Ann Hackett, Barbara Geller Nathanson, William Propp, and Philip Sellew have been generous with their advice and time in suggesting contributors, reviewing the list of entries and individual articles, and a variety of other tasks.

Many people at Oxford University Press have been indispensable in the development and completion of the *Companion*. Invaluable support and wise counsel were provided by Linda Halvorson Morse and Claude Conyers. Stephen Chasteen and Ann Toback were project editors; their coordination of authors, editors, editorial board, copy editors, and production was characterized by skill and tact. We are also grateful to Mark Cummings, Nancy Davis, Liza Ewell, and Donald Kraus for their continuing assistance.

We especially thank Ted Byfield and Eric C. Banks for their meticulous copyediting, Vida Petronis for her diligent proofreading, and Paul Kobelski and Maurya Horgan for their detailed indexing, all of which resulted in a more consistent and accessible book.

Thanks are due to Johanna Froelich, a graduate student at Princeton University, who translated into English a number of articles written in German. Thanks are also due to Shawn Anglim, Anne Brock, Ah Seng Choo, Andrew Gilman, Julia Weaver, and Karen-Marie Yust, students at Harvard Divinity School, and Elsa Stanger, who typed the original manuscript onto disk, and to Gene McAfee, who directed that process as well as typing a great deal himself.

BRUCE M. METZGER
MICHAEL D. COOGAN
August 1993

Directory of Contributors

VALERIE ABRAHAMSEN, Waltham, Massachusetts

ELIZABETH ACHTEMEIER, Adjunct Professor of Bible and Homiletics, Union Theological Seminary, Richmond, Virginia

PAUL J. ACHTEMEIER, The Herbert Worth and Annie H. Jackson Professor of Biblical Interpretation, Union Theological Seminary, Richmond, Virginia

SUSAN ACKERMAN, Assistant Professor of Religion, Dartmouth College, Hanover, New Hampshire

PETER R. ACKROYD, Samuel Davidson Professor of Old Testament Studies, Emeritus, King's College, University of London, England

PHILIP S. ALEXANDER, Nathan Laski Professor of Post-Biblical Jewish Litertaure, University of Manchester, England

FRANCIS I. ANDERSEN, Professor of Old Testament, New College for Advanced Christian Studies, Berkeley, California

BERNHARD W. ANDERSON, Adjunct Professor of Old Testament Theology, Boston University, Massachusetts

HECTOR IGNACIO AVALOS, Carolina Postdoctoral Fellow, Departments of Religious Studies and Anthropology, University of North Carolina at Chapel Hill

E. BADIAN, John Moors Cabot Professor of History, Harvard University, Cambridge, Massachusetts

KENNETH E. BAILEY, Research Professor of Middle Eastern New Testament Studies, The Ecumenical Institute, Jerusalem, Israel

PHILIP L. BARLOW, Assistant Professor of Theological Studies, Hanover College, Indiana

WILLIAM H. BARNES, Associate Professor of Biblical Studies, Southeastern College of the Assemblies of God, Lakeland, Florida

JAMES BARR, Professor of Hebrew Bible, Vanderbilt University, Nashville, Tennessee; Regius Professor of Hebrew, Emeritus, University of Oxford, England

MARKUS K. BARTH, Professor of New Testament, Emeritus, Universität Basel, Switzerland

JOHN R. BARTLETT, Principal, Church of Ireland Theological College, Dublin; Fellow, Emeritus, Trinity College, Dublin, Ireland

JOHN BARTON, Oriel and Laing Professor of the Interpretation of Holy Scripture, University of Oxford, England

JUDITH R. BASKIN, Chair, Department of Judaic Studies, State University of New York at Albany

RICHARD J. BAUCKHAM, Professor of New Testament Studies, University of St. Andrews, Scotland

WILLIAM A. BEARDSLEE, Charles Howard Candler Professor of Religion, Emeritus, Emory University, Atlanta, Georgia

ROGER T. BECKWITH, Warden of Latimer House, Oxford, England

CHRISTOPHER T. BEGG, Assistant Professor of Theology, Catholic University of America, Washington, D.C.

ROBERT A. BENNETT, JR., Professor of Old Testament, Episcopal Divinity School, Cambridge, Massachusetts

G. E. BENTLEY, JR., Professor of English, University of Toronto, Ontario, Canada

JERRY H. BENTLEY, Professor of History, University of Hawai'i at Manoa

ADELE BERLIN, Professor of Hebrew, University of Maryland at College Park

ERNEST BEST, Professor of Divinity and Biblical Criticism, Emeritus, University of Glasgow, Scotland

OTTO BETZ, Professor and Lecturer of New Testament and Jewish Studies, Retired, Eberhard-Karls-Universität, Tübingen, Germany

PHYLLIS A. BIRD, Associate Professor of Old Testament Interpretation, Garrett Evangelical Theological Seminary, Evanston, Illinois

M. H. BLACK, Fellow, Clare Hall, University of Cambridge; former Publisher of Cambridge University Press, England

MATTHEW BLACK, Professor of Biblical Criticism, Emeritus, University of St. Andrews, Scotland

ROBERT G. BRATCHER, Translation Consultant, United Bible Societies, New York, New York

PAUL L. BREMER, Professor of Biblical Studies, Reformed Bible College, Grand Rapids, Michigan

JOHN A. BRINKMAN, Charles H. Swift Distinguished Service Professor of Mesopotamian History, University of Chicago, Illinois

S. P. BROCK, Reader in Syriac Studies, University of Oxford, England

BERNADETTE J. BROOTEN, Kraft-Hiatt Chair of Christian Studies, Near Eastern and Judaic Studies Department, Brandeis University, Waltham, Massachusetts

F. F. BRUCE, Rylands Professor of Biblical Criticism and Exegesis, University of Manchester, England, *deceased*

GEORGE WESLEY BUCHANAN, Professor of New Testament, Emeritus, Wesley Theological Seminary, Washington, D.C.

DAVID G. BURKE, Director, Translations Department, American Bible Society, New York, New York

EDWARD F. CAMPBELL, Francis A. McGaw Professor of Old Testament, McCormick Theological Seminary, Chicago, Illinois

BRUCE D. CHILTON, Barnard Iddings Bell Professor of Religion, Bard College, Annandale-on-Hudson, New York

RONALD E. CLEMENTS, Samuel Davidson Professor of Old Testament Studies, King's College, University of London, England

RICHARD J. CLIFFORD, Professor of Old Testament, Weston School of Theology, Cambridge, Massachusetts

DAVID J. A. CLINES, Professor of Biblical Studies, University of Sheffield, England

GEORGE W. COATS, Professor of Old Testament, Retired, Lexington Theological Seminary, Kentucky

AELRED CODY, O.S.B., General Editor, *Catholic Biblical Quarterly*, St. Meinrad Archabbey, Indiana

DONALD COGGAN, Archbishop of Canterbury, England, 1974–1980

RICHARD COGGINS, Senior Lecturer in Old Testament Studies, King's College, University of London, England

H. J. BERNARD COMBRINK, Professor of New Testament, University of Stellenbosch, South Africa

EDGAR W. CONRAD, Reader in Studies in Religion, University of Queensland, Australia

DEMETRIOS J. CONSTANTELOS, Charles Cooper Townsend Sr. Distinguished Professor of History and Religious Studies, Richard Stockton State College of New Jersey, Pomona

MICHAEL D. COOGAN, Professor of Religious Studies, Stonehill College, North Easton, Massachusetts

J. M. COOK, Professor of Ancient History and Classical Archaeology, Emeritus, University of Bristol, England

JAMES I. COOK, Anton Biemolt Professor of New Testament, Western Theological Seminary, Holland, Michigan

ROBIN C. COVER, Dallas, Texas

DERMOT COX, O.F.M., Professor of Old Testament Exegesis, Università Gregoriana, Rome, Italy

JAMES L. CRENSHAW, Professor of Old Testament, Duke University, Durham, North Carolina

PETER H. DAVIDS, Scholar in Residence, Langley Vineyard Christian Fellowship, British Columbia, Canada

ROBERT DAVIDSON, Professor of Old Testament Language and Literature, Emeritus, University of Glasgow, Scotland

JOËL DELOBEL, Professor of New Testament Textual Criticism and Exegesis, Katholieke Universiteit, Leuven, Belgium

ROBERT C. DENTAN, Professor of Old Testament, Emeritus, General Theological Seminary, New York, New York

J. DUNCAN M. DERRETT, Professor of Oriental Laws, Emeritus, University of London, England

ALEXANDER A. DI LELLA, O.F.M., Professor of Biblical Studies, Catholic University of America, Washington, D.C.

T. KEITH DIX, Assistant Professor, Department of Classical Studies, University of North Carolina at Greensboro

JOHN W. DRANE, Director, Center for the Study of Christianity and Contemporary Society, University of Stirling, Scotland

JOHN I DURHAM, Pastor, Greenwich Baptist Church, Connecticut

JAMES M. EFIRD, Professor of Biblical Interpretation, Duke University, Durham, North Carolina

CARL S. EHRLICH, Professor, Hochschule für jüdische Studien, Heidelberg, Germany

BARRY L. EICHLER, Associate Professor of Assyriology, University of Pennsylvania, Philadelphia

J. A. EMERTON, Regius Professor of Hebrew, and Fellow, St. John's College, University of Cambridge, England

DAVID EWERT, President, Mennonite Brethren Bible College, Winnipeg, Manitoba, Canada

GILLIAN FEELEY-HARNIK, Professor of Anthropology, The Johns Hopkins University, Baltimore, Maryland

F. CHARLES FENSHAM, Professor of Semitic Languages and Cultures, Emeritus, University of Stellenbosch, South Africa

JOSEPH A. FITZMYER, S.J., Professor of Biblical Studies, Emeritus, Catholic University of America, Washington, D.C.

DANIEL E. FLEMING, Assistant Professor, New York University, New York

PAULA FREDRIKSEN, Professor, Department of Religion, Boston University, Massachusetts

EDWIN D. FREED, Professor of Biblical Literature and Religion, Emeritus, Gettysburg College, Pennsylvania

ERNEST S. FRERICHS, Professor of Judaic Studies, Brown University, Providence, Rhode Island

SEÁN FREYNE, Professor of Theology, Trinity College, Dublin, Ireland

STEVEN FRIESEN, Fellow, Program on Cultural Studies, East-West Center, Honolulu, Hawai'i

KARLFRIED FROEHLICH, Benjamin B. Warfield Professor of Ecclesiastical History, Emeritus, Princeton Theological Seminary, New Jersey

REGINALD H. FULLER, Professor Emeritus, Virginia Theological Seminary, Alexandria, Virginia

RUSSELL FULLER, Assistant Professor of Theological and Religious Studies, University of San Diego, California

FRANCIS T. GIGNAC, S.J., Professor of Biblical Greek, Catholic University of America, Washington, D.C.

THOMAS FRANCIS GLASSON, Lecturer in New Testament Studies, Retired, University of London, England

ANDRÉ L. GODDU, Director, Program in the History and Philosophy of Science, Stonehill College, North Easton, Massachusetts

EDWIN M. GOOD, Professor of Religious Studies, Emeritus, Stanford University, California

CYRUS H. GORDON, Joseph and Esther Foster Professor of Mediterranean Studies, Emeritus, Brandeis University, Waltham, Massachusetts; Director, Center for Ebla Research, New York University, New York

ROBERT P. GORDON, Lecturer in Old Testament, University of Cambridge, England

PROSPER GRECH, O.S.A., Professor of New Testament Exegesis, Augustinianum, Rome; Lecturer in Hermeneutics, Pontificio Instituto Biblico, Rome, Italy

JOSEPH A. GREENE, Curator of Publications, Semitic Museum, Harvard University, Cambridge, Massachusetts

ROBERT A. GUELICH, Professor of Theology, Fuller Theological Seminary, Pasadena, California, *deceased*

DAVID M. GUNN, Professor of Old Testament, Columbia Theological Seminary, Decatur, Georgia

JO ANN HACKETT, Professor, Department of Near Eastern Languages and Civilizations, Harvard University, Cambridge, Massachusetts

WILLIAM W. HALLO, The William M. Laffan Professor of Assyriology and Babylonian Literature, and Curator, Babylonian Collection, Yale University, New Haven, Connecticut

BARUCH HALPERN, Professor of History, Pennsylvania State University, University Park

RAYMOND HAMMER, Professor of Theology, Emeritus, Rikkyō University, Tokyo, Japan; former Director, Bible Reading Fellowship, London, England

PHILIP C. HAMMOND, Professor of Anthropology, University of Utah, Salt Lake City

ANTHONY TYRRELL HANSON, Professor of Theology, Emeritus, University of Hull, England, *deceased*

DOUGLAS R. A. HARE, William F. Orr Professor of New Testament, Pittsburgh Theological Seminary, Pennyslvania

WALTER HARRELSON, Distinguished Professor of Hebrew Bible, Emeritus, Vanderbilt University, Nashville, Tennessee

GERALD F. HAWTHORNE, Professor of Greek, Wheaton College, Illinois

DAVID M. HAY, Professor, Department of Religion and Philosophy, Coe College, Cedar Repids, Iowa

JOHN H. HAYES, Professor of Old Testament, Candler School of Theology, Emory University, Atlanta, Georgia

PETER D. HEINEGG, Professor of English, Union College, Schenectady, New York

RONALD S. HENDEL, Associate Professor, Department of Religious Studies, Southern Methodist University, Dallas, Texas

GEORGE S. HENDRY, Professor of Systematic Theology, Emeritus, Princeton Theological Seminary, New Jersey

PAULA S. HIEBERT, Visiting Instructor, Department of Theology, Boston College, Massachusetts

THEODORE HIEBERT, Associate Professor of Hebrew Bible/Old Testament, Harvard Divinity School, Cambridge, Massachusetts

DAVID HILL, Reader in Biblical Studies, Retired, University of Sheffield, England

DELBERT R. HILLERS, W. W. Spence Professor of Semitic Languages, The Johns Hopkins University, Baltimore, Maryland

HAROLD W. HOEHNER, Chairman and Professor of New Testament Studies, and Director, Th.D. Studies, Dallas Theological Seminary, Texas

CARL R. HOLLADAY, Professor, Candler School of Theology, Emory University, Atlanta, Georgia

LATON E. HOLMGREN, General Secretary, Retired, American Bible Society, New York, New York

MORNA D. HOOKER, Lady Margaret Professor of Divinity, University of Cambridge, England

LESLIE J. HOPPE, O.F.M., Professor of Old Testament, Catholic Theological Union, Chicago, Illinois

J. L. HOULDEN, Professor of Theology, King's College, University of London, England

J. KEIR HOWARD, Diocese of Wellington Institute of Theology, New Zealand

PHILIP EDGCUMBE HUGHES, Visiting Professor, Westminster Theological Seminary, Philadelphia, Pennsylvania, *deceased*

EDWARD HULMES, Spalding Professorial Fellow, World Religions, Department of Theology, University of Durham, England

ALAN JACOBS, Associate Professor of English, Wheaton College, Illinois

JOHN FREDERICK JANSEN, Professor of New Testament, Emeritus, Austin Presbyterian Theological Seminary, Texas, *deceased*

DAVID LYLE JEFFREY, Professor of English Language and Litrature, University of Ottawa, Ontario, Canada

JOSEPH JENSEN, O.S.B., Executive Secretary, Catholic University of America, Washington, D.C.

SHERMAN ELBRIDGE JOHNSON, Dean and Professor of New Testament, Emeritus, The Church Divinity School of the Pacific, Berkeley, California, *deceased*

JAKOB JÓNSSON, Reykjavik, Iceland, *deceased*

EDWIN A. JUDGE, Macquarie University, Australia

ROBERT J. KARRIS, O.F.M., Rome, Italy

HOWARD CLARK KEE, Aurelio Professor of Biblical Studies, Emeritus, Boston University, Massachusetts; Senior Research Fellow, Religious Studies, University of Pennsylvania, Philadelphia

JACK DEAN KINGSBURY, Aubrey Lee Brooks Professor of Biblical Theology, Union Theological Seminary, Richmond, Virginia

DOUGLAS A. KNIGHT, Professor of Hebrew Bible, Vanderbilt University, Nashville, Tennessee

GEORGE A. F. KNIGHT, Professor of Old Testament Studies and Semitic Languages, Emeritus, and former Principal, Pacific Theological College, Fiji

GARY N. KNOPPERS, Assistant Professor of Religious Studies, Pennsylvania State University, University Park

DONALD KRAUS, Senior Editor, Oxford University Press, New York, New York

WILLIAM SANFORD LASOR, Professor, Fuller Theological Seminary, Pasadena, California, *deceased*

SOPHIE LAWS, Fellow, Religion and History, Regent's College, London, England

A. R. C. LEANEY, Professor of Christian Theology, Emeritus, Nottingham University, England

MARY JOAN WINN LEITH, Lecturer, Department of Literature, Massachusetts Institute of Technology, Cambridge

AMY-JILL LEVINE, Professor, Department of Religion, Swarthmore College, Pennsylvania

BARUCH A. LEVINE, Professor of Hebrew and Judaic Studies, New York University, New York

LEE LEVINE, Professor of Jewish History and Archaeology, The Hebrew University of Jerusalem; Dean and Director, The Seminary of Judaic Studies, Jerusalem, Israel

THEODORE J. LEWIS, Associate Professor of Hebrew Bible and Semitic Languages, University of Georgia, Athens

I-JIN LOH, Coordinator of Asia Opportunity Program and Translation Consultant, United Bible Societies, Asia Pacific Region, Taipei, Taiwan

JOHANNES P. LOUW, Professor of Greek, University of Pretoria, South Africa

FRANCIS LYALL, Dean of Faculty and Professor of Public Law, University of Aberdeen, Scotland

ABRAHAM J. MALHERBE, Buckingham Professor of New Testament Criticism and Interpretation, Yale Divinity School, New Haven, Connecticut

GIORA MANOR, Editor, *Israel Dance Quarterly;* Adviser, *Israel Dance Library,* Jerusalem, Israel

STEPHEN A. MARINI, Professor of Religion, Wellesley College, Massachusetts

I. HOWARD MARSHALL, Professor of New Testament Exegesis, University of Aberdeen, Scotland

RALPH P. MARTIN, Professor of Biblical Studies, University of Sheffield, England

REX MASON, University Lecturer in Old Testament and Hebrew, University of Oxford, England

ULRICH W. MAUSER, Helen H. P. Manson Professor of New Testament Literature and Exegesis, Princeton Theological Seminary, New Jersey

GENE McAFEE, Harvard Divinity School, Cambridge, Massachusetts

P. KYLE McCARTER, JR., William Foxwell Albright Professor of Biblical and Ancient Near Eastern Studies, The Johns Hopkins University, Baltimore, Maryland

PATRICK E. McGOVERN, Research Scientist, Archaeoceramics and Archaeochemistry, University Museum, University of Pennsylvania, Philadelphia

WILLIAM McKANE, Professor of Hebrew and Oriental Languages, Emeritus, University of St. Andrews, Scotland

STEVEN L. McKENZIE, Associate Professor of Old Testament, Rhodes College, Memphis, Tennessee

PAULA M. McNUTT, Assistant Professor of Religious Studies, Canisius College, Buffalo, New York

SAMUEL A. MEIER, Associate Professor of Hebrew and Comparative Semitics, Ohio State University, Columbus

WILLIAM W. MEISSNER, S.J., University Professor of Psychoanalysis, Boston College; Training and Supervising Analyst, Boston Psychoanalytic Institute, Massachusetts

BRUCE M. METZGER, George L. Collord Professor of New Testament Language and Literature, Emeritus, Princeton Theological Seminary, New Jersey

ISOBEL MACKAY METZGER, Princeton, New Jersey

CAROL L. MEYERS, Professor of Biblical Studies and Archaeology, Duke University, Durham, North Carolina

ERIC M. MEYERS, Professor of Bible and Judaic Studies, Duke University, Durham, North Carolina

ALAN MILLARD, Rankin Professor of Hebrew and Ancient Semitic Languages, University of Liverpool, England

J. MAXWELL MILLER, Professor of Old Testament Studies, Emory University, Atlanta, Georgia

PAUL S. MINEAR, Winkley Professor of Biblical Theology, Emeritus, Yale University, New Haven, Connecticut

CAREY A. MOORE, Amanda Rupert Strong Professor of Religion, Gettysburg College, Pennsylvania

LEON MORRIS, Former Principal, Ridley College, Melbourne, Australia

PAUL G. MOSCA, Professor, Department of Religious Studies, University of British Columbia, Vancouver, Canada

LUCETTA MOWRY, Professor Emerita, Department of Religion, Wellesley College, Massachusetts

JOHN MUDDIMAN, Fellow, New Testament Studies, Mansfield College, University of Oxford, England

ROLAND E. MURPHY, O. CARM., George Washington Ivey Professor of Biblical Studies, Emeritus, Duke University, Durham, North Carolina

JEROME MURPHY-O'CONNOR, O.P., Professor of New Testament, École Biblique de Jérusalem, Israel

MOGENS MÜLLER, Professor of New Testament Exegesis, Københavns Universitet, Denmark

BARBARA GELLER NATHANSON, Professor, Department of Religion, Wellesley College, Massachusetts

FRANS NEIRYNCK, Professor of New Testament, Katholieke Universiteit, Leuven, Belgium

WILLIAM B. NELSON, JR., Professor, Department of Religious Studies, Westmont College, Santa Barbara, California

JACOB NEUSNER, Distinguished Research Professor of Religious Studies, University of South Florida, Tampa

EUGENE A. NIDA, Translations Consultant, American Bible Society, New York, New York

MARK A. NOLL, Professor of History, Wheaton College, Illinois

ROBERT NORTH, S.J., Editor, *Elenchus* of *Biblica;* Professor of Archaeology, Emeritus, Pontificio Istituto Biblico, Rome, Italy

PETER T. O'BRIEN, Vice Principal and Head, New Testament Department, Moore Theological College, Newton, Australia

BEN C. OLLENBURGER, Professor of Religious Studies, Association of Mennonite Seminaries, Elkhart, Indiana

DENNIS T. OLSON, Assistant Professor of Old Testament, Princeton Theological Seminary, New Jersey

RICHARD E. OSTER, JR., Professor of New Testament, Harding University Graduate School of Religion, Memphis, Tennessee

J. ANDREW OVERMAN, Professor, Department of Religion and Classics, University of Rochester, New York

JOSEPH PATHRAPANKAL, C.M.I., Professor of New Testament and Theology, Dharmaran College, Bangalore, India

WAYNE T. PITARD, Associate Professor, Program for Study of Religion, University of Illinois at Urbana-Champaign

JAMES H. PLATT, Denver, Colorado

J. MARTIN PLUMLEY, Sir Herbert Thompson Professor of Egyptology, Emeritus, University of Cambridge, England

J. R. PORTER, Professor of Theology, Emeritus, University of Exeter, England

SCOTT F. PRELLER, Christian Science Practitioner, Andover, Massachusetts

WILLIAM H. PROPP, Associate Professor of Near Eastern Languages and History, University of California at San Diego

JAMES M. REESE, O.S.F.S., Professor, Department of Theology, St. John's University, Jamaica, New York, *deceased*

BO REICKE, Universität Basel, Switzerland, *deceased*

ERROLL F. RHODES, Editorial and Non-English Manager, Department of Translations and Scripture Resources, American Bible Society, New York, New York

JOHN RICHES, Professor of Divinity and Biblical Criticism, University of Glasgow, Scotland

HARALD RIESENFELD, Professor of Biblical Exegesis, Emeritus, Uppsala Universitet, Sweden

GUY ROGERS, Associate Professor of Greek, Latin, and History, Wellesley College, Massachusetts

J. W. ROGERSON, Professor and Head, Department of Biblical Studies, University of Sheffield, England

DAVID T. RUNIA, C. J. de Vogel Professor Extraordinarius in Ancient Philosophy, Rijksuniversiteit Utrecht, the Netherlands

D. S. RUSSELL, Baptist Union of Great Britain, Bristol

LELAND RYKEN, Professor of English, Wheaton College, Illinois

BRUCE E. RYSKAMP, Corporate Vice President, Zondervan Corporation, Grand Rapids, Michigan

LEOPOLD SABOURIN, S.J., Professor of Sacred Scripture, Emeritus, Pontificio Istituto Orientale, Rome, Italy

DENIS BAIN SADDINGTON, Professor of Roman History and Archaeology, University of the Witwatersrand, South Africa

KATHARINE DOOB SAKENFELD, William Albright Eisenberger Professor of Old Testament Literature, Princeton Theological Seminary, New Jersey

RICHARD P. SALLER, Professor of History and Classics, University of Chicago, Illinois

JAMES A. SANDERS, Professor of Biblical Studies, School of Theology at Claremont, California

NAHUM M. SARNA, Dora Golding Professor of Biblical Studies, Emeritus, Brandeis University, Waltham, Massachusetts; General Editor, Jewish Publication Society Torah Commentary

JOHN F. A. SAWYER, Professor, Department of Religious Studies, University of Newcastle upon Tyne, England

DANIEL N. SCHOWALTER, Associate Professor, Department of Religion, Carthage College, Kenosha, Wisconsin

EILEEN SCHULLER, Professor, Department of Religious Studies, McMaster University, Hamilton, Ontario, Canada

PHILIP SELLEW, Associate Professor, Department of Classical and Near Eastern Studies, University of Minnesota, Minneapolis

C. L. SEOW, Associate Professor of Old Testament, Princeton Theological Seminary, New Jersey

DRORAH O'DONNELL SETEL, Seattle, Washington

GREGORY SHAW, Professor, Department of Religious Studies, Stonehill College, North Easton, Massachusetts

MICHAL SHEKEL, Rabbi, Jewish Center of Sussex County, New Jersey

DANIEL J. SIMUNDSON, Professor of Old Testament, and Dean of Academic Affairs, Luther Northwestern Theological Seminary, St. Paul, Minnesota

STEPHEN S. SMALLEY, Dean of Chester Cathedral, England

J. A. SOGGIN, Professor of Hebrew Language and Literature, Università di Roma, Italy

WALTER F. SPECHT, Chair, Department of Religion, Retired, Loma Linda University, California.

HENDRIK C. SPYKERBOER, Professor of Old Testament Studies, Trinity Theological College, Brisbane, Australia

LYNN STANLEY, Manufacturing Controller, Oxford University Press, New York, New York

ROBERT H. STEIN, Professor of New Testament, Bethel Theological Seminary, St. Paul, Minnesota

KRISTER STENDAHL, Professor of Christian Studies, Brandeis University, Waltham, Massachusetts

PHILIP STERN, White Plains, New York

ROBERT STOOPS, Associate Professor, Department of Liberal Studies, Western Washington University, Bellingham

G. M. STYLER, Fellow, Corpus Christi College, and University Lecturer in Divinity, retired, University of Cambridge, England

JOHN N. SUGGIT, Professor Emeritus, Rhodes University, Grahamstown, South Africa

WILLARD M. SWARTLEY, Professor of New Testament, Associated Mennonite Biblical Seminaries, Elkhart, Indiana

JOHN SWEET, University Lecturer in Divinity, University of Cambridge, England

SARAH J. TANZER, Professor, McCormick Theological Seminary, Chicago, Illinois

RON TAPPY, Assistant Professor of Archaeology and Literature of Ancient Israel, Westmont College, Santa Barbara, California

ANTHONY C. THISELTON, Professor of Christian Theology, and Head, Department of Christian Theology, University of Nottingham, England

DEREK J., TIDBALL, Secretary for Mission and Evangelism, Baptist Union of Great Britain, Marcham, England

PATRICK A. TILLER, Visiting Lecturer on Greek, Harvard Divinity School, Cambridge, Massachusetts

JOHN TINSLEY, Professor of Theology, University of Leeds, 1962–1976; Bishop of Bristol, 1976–1985, England, *deceased*

ANDRIE B. DU TOIT, Professor of New Testament, University of Pretoria, South Africa

EMANUEL TOV, Hebrew University, Jerusalem, Israel

W. SIBLEY TOWNER, The Reverend Archibald McFadyen Professor of Biblical Interpretation, Union Theological Seminary, Richmond, Virginia

STEPHEN H. TRAVIS, Vice-Principal and Lecturer in New Testament, St. John's College, Nottingham, England

ALLISON A. TRITES, John Payzant Distinguished Professor of Biblical Studies, Acadia University, Wolfville, Nova Scotia, Canada

ETIENNE TROCMÉ, Professor of New Testament, Université des Sciences Humanines de Strasbourg, France

GENE M. TUCKER, Professor of Old Testament, Candler School of Theology, Emory University, Atlanta, Georgia

DAVID H. VAN DAALEN, Minister, United Reformed Church, Huntingdon, England

GERRIT E. VAN DER MERWE, General Secretary, Emeritus, Bible Society of South Africa, Cape Town

BRUCE VAWTER, C.M., DePaul University, Illinois, *deceased*

ALLEN D. VERHEY, Director, Institute of Religion, Texas Medical Center, Houston, Texas

BEN ZION WACHOLDER, Solomon B. Freehof Professor of Jewish Law and Practice; Hebrew Union College, Cincinnati, Ohio

GEOFFREY WAINWRIGHT, Robert E. Cushman Professor of Christian Theology, Duke University, Durham, North Carolina

JOHN D. W. WATTS, Donald L. Williams Professor of Old Testament, Southern Baptist Theological Seminary, Louisville, Kentucky

GORDON J. WENHAM, Senior Lecturer in Religious Studies, Cheltenham and Gloucester College of Higher Education, England

CLAUS WESTERMANN, Professor Emeritus, Universität Heidelberg, Germany

RICHARD E. WHITAKER, Information Research Specialist, Speer Library, Princeton Theological Seminary, New Jersey

JOHN L. WHITE, Professor of New Testament and Christian Origins, Loyola University of Chicago, Illinois

SIDNIE ANN WHITE, Assistant Professor of Religion, Albright College, Reading, Pennyslvania

R. N. WHYBRAY, Professor of Hebrew and Old Testament Studies, Emeritus, University of Hull, England

TIMOTHY M. WILLIS, Professor, Religion Division, Pepperdine University, Malibu, California

ROBERT McL. WILSON, Professor of Biblical Criticism, Emeritus, University of St. Andrews, Scotland

VINCENT L. WIMBUSH, Professor of New Testament and Christian Origins, Union Theological Seminary, New York, New York

WALTER WINK, Professor of Biblical Interpretation, Auburn Theological Seminary, New York

DONALD J. WISEMAN, Professor of Assyriology, Emeritus, University of London, England

DAVID F. WRIGHT, Senior Lecturer in Ecclesiastical History, and former Dean of Faculty of Divinity, University of Edinburgh, Scotland

EDWIN M. YAMAUCHI, Professor of History, Miami University, Oxford, Ohio

JOHN ZIESLER, Reader in Theology, University of Bristol, England

Transliterations

HEBREW AND ARAMAIC

Transliteration	Pronunciation		Letter
Consonants			
ʾ	(now generally not pronounced; originally a glottal stop)		א
b	b (also sometimes v)		ב
g	g		ג
d	d		ד
h	h		ה
w	v (originally w)		ו
z	z		ז
ḥ	(not found in English; approximately like German -ch)		ח
ṭ	t (originally an emphatic t)		ט
y	y		י
k	k (also sometimes like German -ch)		כ,ך
l	l		ל
m	m		מ,ם
n	n		נ,ן
s	s		ס
ʿ	(now generally not pronounced; originally a voiced guttural)		ע
p	p (also sometimes f)		פ,ף
ṣ	ts		צ,ץ
q	k (originally an emphatic k)		ק
r	r		ר
ś	s		שׂ
š	sh		שׁ
t	t		ת

Transliteration	Pronunciation	Hebrew Name	Symbol
Vowels			
ă	father	ḥāṭēp pataḥ	-ְ
a	father	pataḥ	-ַ
ā	father	qāmeṣ	-ָ

Transliteration	Pronunciation	Hebrew Name	Symbol
â	father	qāmeṣ followed by hē	
ĕ	petition	šĕwā, or ḥāṭēp sĕgôl	
e	bet	sĕgôl	
ē	they	ṣērê	
ê	they	ṣērê or sĕgôl followed by yōd	
i, ī	machine	ḥîreq	
î	machine	ḥîreq followed by yōd	
ŏ	hope	ḥāṭēp qāmeṣ	
o	hope	qāmeṣ ḥāṭûp	
o, ō	hope	ḥôlem	
ô	hope	ḥôlem with wāw	
u, ū	sure	qibbûṣ	
û	sure	šûreq	

Other Semitic

ḫ   (not found in English; approximately like German -ch)

GREEK

Transliteration	Pronunciation	Letter
a	a (father)	α
b	b	β
g	g	γ
d	d	δ
e	e (bet)	ε
z	z	ζ
ē	e (they)	η
th	th (thing)	θ
i	i (bit or machine)	ι
k	k	κ
l	l	λ
m	m	μ
n	n	ν
x	ks	ξ
o	o (off)	ο
p	p	π
r	r	ρ
s	s	σ, ς
t	t	τ
y, u	u (like German ü), or part of a diphthong	υ
ph	ph (phase)	φ
ch	ch (like German -ch)	χ
ps	ps	ψ
ō	o (hope)	ω
h	h (hope): rough breathing	ʽ

Abbreviations

Biblical Citations

Chapter (chap.) and verse (v.) are separated by a period, and when a verse is subdivided, letters are used following the verse number; thus, Gen. 3.4a = the book of Genesis, chap. 3 v. 4, the first part. Biblical books are abbreviated in parenthetical references as follows:

Acts	Acts of the Apostles	Lam.	Lamentations
Amos	Amos	Lev.	Leviticus
Bar.	Baruch	Luke	Luke
Bel and the Dragon	Bel and the Dragon	1 Macc.	1 Maccabees
1 Chron.	1 Chronicles	2 Macc.	2 Maccabees
2 Chron.	2 Chronicles	3 Macc.	3 Maccabees
Col.	Colossians	4 Macc.	4 Maccabees
1 Cor.	1 Corinthians	Mal.	Malachi
2 Cor.	2 Corinthians	Mark	Mark
Dan.	Daniel	Matt.	Matthew
Deut.	Deuteronomy	Mic.	Micah
Eccles.	Ecclesiastes	Nah.	Nahum
Eph.	Ephesians	Neh.	Nehemiah
1 Esd.	1 Esdras	Num.	Numbers
2 Esd.	2 Esdras	Obad.	Obadiah
Esther	Esther	1 Pet.	1 Peter
Exod.	Exodus	2 Pet.	2 Peter
Ezek.	Ezekiel	Phil.	Philippians
Ezra	Ezra	Philem.	Philemon
Gal.	Galatians	Pr. of Man.	Prayer of Manasseh
Hab.	Habakkuk	Prov.	Proverbs
Hag.	Haggai	Ps(s).	Psalm(s)
Heb.	Hebrews	Rev.	Revelation
Hos.	Hosea	Rom.	Romans
Isa.	Isaiah	Ruth	Ruth
James	James	1 Sam.	1 Samuel
Jer.	Jeremiah	2 Sam.	2 Samuel
Job	Job	Sir.	Sirach
Joel	Joel	Song of Sol.	Song of Solomon
John	Gospel of John	Sus.	Susanna
1 John	1 John	1 Thess.	1 Thessalonians
2 John	2 John	2 Thess.	2 Thessalonians
3 John	3 John	1 Tim.	1 Timothy
Jon.	Jonah	2 Tim.	2 Timothy
Josh.	Joshua	Titus	Titus
Jude	Jude	Tob.	Tobit
Judg.	Judges	Wisd. of Solomon	Wisdom of Solomon
Jth.	Judith	Zech.	Zechariah
1 Kings	1 Kings	Zeph.	Zephaniah
2 Kings	2 Kings		

Rabbinic Literature

To distinguish tractates with the same name, the letters *m.* (Mishnah), *t.* (Tosepta), *b.* (Babylonian Talmud), and *y.* (Jerusalem Talmud) are used before the name of the tractate.

'Abod. Zar.	*'Aboda Zara*	*Ketub.*	*Ketubot*	*Qoh. Rab.*	*Qohelet Rabbah*
'Abot R. Nat.	*'Abot de Rabbi Nathan*	*Mek.*	*Mekilta*	*Šabb.*	*Šabbat*
B. Bat.	*Baba Batra*	*Mid.*	*Middot*	*Sanh.*	*Sanhedrin*
Ber.	*Berakot*	*Midr.*	*Midrash*	*Sukk.*	*Sukkot*
'Erub	*'Erubin*	*Nez.*	*Neziqin*	*Ta'an.*	*Ta'anit*
Gen. Rab.	*Genesis Rabbah*	*Nid.*	*Niddah*	*Yad.*	*Yadayim*
Ḥag.	*Ḥagiga*	*Pesaḥ.*	*Pesaḥim*	*Zebaḥ.*	*Zebaḥim*

Other Ancient Literature

Adv. haer.	Irenaeus, *Adversus haeresis*
Ag. Ap.	Josephus, *Against Apion*
Ant.	Josephus, *Antiquities*
Apol.	Justin, *Apology*
Bapt.	Tertullian, *De baptismo*
CD	Cairo Geniza, Damascus Document
1 Clem.	1 Clement
De Dec.	Philo, *De Decalogo*
De spec. leg.	Philo, *De specialibus legibus*
Did.	Didache
Ep.	Cyprian, *Epistles*
Exhort. Chast.	Tertullian, *De exhortatione castitatis*
Geog.	Strabo, *Geographica*
GT	Gospel of Thomas
Haer.	Epiphanius, *Haereses*
Hist.	Polybius, *Histories*
Hist. eccl.	Eusebius, *Historia ecclesiastica*
Instit. Rhetor.	Quintilian, *Institution of Rhetoric*
Jov.	Jerome, *Against Jovianum*
Leg. ad Gaium	Philo, *Legatio ad Gaium*

1 Q34	Qumran Cave 1, No. 34
1 QH	Qumran Cave 1, *Hôdāyôt (Thanksgiving Hymns)*
1 QIsa[b]	Qumran Cave 1, Isaiah, second copy
1 QM	Qumran Cave 1, *Milḥāmāh (War Scroll)*
1 QpHab	Qumran Cave 1, *Pesher on Habakkuk*
1 QS	Qumran Cave 1, *Serek hayyahad (Rule of the Community, Manual of Discipline*
4Q246	Qumran Cave 4, No. 246
4Q503-509	Qumran Cave 4, Nos. 503-509
4QDeut[a]	Qumran Cave 4, Deuteronomy, first copy
4QMMT	Qumran Cave 4, *Miqsat Ma'aseh Torah*
4QpNah	Qumran Cave 4, *Pesher on Nahum*
11QMelch	Qumran Cave 11, Melchizedek text
11QTemple	Qumran Cave 11, *Temple Scroll*
Praescr.	Tertullian, *De praescriptione haereticorum*
Test. Abr.	Testament of Abraham
T. Naph.	Testament of Naphtali
War	Josephus, *Jewish War*

Other Abbreviations

ABS	American Bible Society
AV	Authorized Version
BCE	Before the Common Era (the equivalent of BC)
BCP	Book of Common Prayer
BFBS	British and Foreign Bible Society
ca.	circa
CE	Common Era (the equivalent of AD)
chap(s).	chapter(s)
D	Deuteronomist source in the Pentateuch
E	Elohist source in the Pentateuch
EB	Early Bronze
GNB	Good News Bible
Grk.	Greek
H	Holiness Code
Hebr.	Hebrew
J	Yahwist source in the Pentateuch
KJV	King James Version
L	Special Lucan material
Lat.	Latin
LB	Late Bronze
LXX	Septuagint

M	Special Matthean material
MB	Middle Bronze
MSS	Manuscripts
MT	Masoretic Text
NBSS	National Bible Society of Scotland
NEB	New English Bible
NJV	New Jewish Version
NRSV	New Revised Standard Version
P	Priestly source in the Pentateuch
par.	parallel(s), used when two or more passages have essentially the same material, especially in the synoptic Gospels
Q	from German *Quelle*, "source," designating the hypothetical common source used by Matthew and Luke
REB	Revised English Bible
RSV	Revised Standard Version
RV	Revised Version
TDH	Two Document Hypothesis
UBS	United Bible Societies
v(v).	verse(s)

THE OXFORD COMPANION
TO THE BIBLE

Aaron. A major figure in Israel's origins and the first of its high *priests. In very ancient narratives, he appears without specifically priestly features, as a leader with Hur (Exod. 17.9–16; 24.14), or as *Miriam's brother with no mention of their being related to *Moses (Exod. 15.20), to whom they even appear opposed (Num. 12). Later, but still in fairly early stages of the *Pentateuch's formation, Aaron is said to be Moses' brother and a *Levite (Exod. 4.14), and he begins to appear with features that implicitly suggest a tie with priesthood. He is with Moses when Pharaoh asks for intercession with Israel's God (Exod. 8.25; 9.27–28; 10.16–17); in Exodus 18.12, he may have been added to the account of the *covenant between *Midian and Israel because a later editor may have felt that the covenant sacrifice required a priest; his presence with his sons Nadab and Abihu, reckoned elsewhere as priestly sons, seems also to have been added to the covenant-making scene at *Sinai (Exod. 24.1, 9). The important question of Aaron's role in the episode of the *golden calf (Exod. 32) is problematic. The incident is almost certainly told with the sanctuaries in mind established by Jeroboam I at Bethel and *Dan in the northern kingdom of Israel (1 Kings 12.26–32), but in the story Aaron is not presented as a *priest or as a Levite; his guilt is brought out mainly in Exodus 32.25b, 35b, evident additions to a text in which the behavior of the people, looking to Aaron for leadership, was already contrasted negatively with the religiously correct zeal of Levites (32.25–29). In the Priestly components of the Pentateuch (*P), Aaron's role as Moses' companion in Egypt and in the *wilderness is heightened, but in P he is above all Israel's first high priest, and the other priests inaugurated with him are called his sons (Exod. 28–29; 39; Lev. 8–10; Num. 3.5–4.49; 16–18). The historical background of this development in the figure of Aaron is not clear. Although legitimate priests are called sons of *Zadok in Ezekiel (40.46; 43.19; 44.15; 48.11), with Aaron's name quite

unused in that exilic book, some suspect that the preexilic priesthood of *Jerusalem itself claimed an Aaronite origin; others believe that the first group to do so was the priesthood of Bethel, or a Levitical group in *Judah not originally identical with the priesthood of Jerusalem. In any case, the postexilic priests of Jerusalem settled peacefully into their own claim to be the sons of Aaron.   AELRED CODY, O.S.B.

Abaddon. Meaning literally "place of destruction," Abaddon refers to the realm of the dead in the Hebrew Bible. Occurring mainly in *wisdom literature, Abaddon is synonymous with Sheol (Job 26.6.; Prov. 15.11; 27.20), with Death personified (Job 28.22), and with the grave (Ps. 88.10–12). Occasionally the imagery suggests punishment; more often it indicates the inevitability and finality of death. In the New Testament, Abaddon is mentioned once (Rev. 9.11), not as the place of the dead but rather as the name of the *angel of the *abyss who leads a demonic horde of monstrous locusts against most of humanity. Rabbinic literature later describes Abaddon as part of *Gehenna.
See also Hell.   STEVEN FRIESEN

Abba. The word for "my father" or "the father." This *Aramaic word appears three times in the New Testament, followed by a translation into Greek: once in Jesus' prayer in *Gethsemane (Mark 14.36) and twice in the letters of Paul, where it is an ecstatic cry of believers in *prayer (Rom. 8.15; Gal. 4.6).
The *prayers of Jesus in the Gospels regularly address God as "Father" (Matt. 11.25, 26; 26.42; Luke 10.21; 23.34, 46; John 11.41; 12.27, 28; 17.1, 5, 11, 21, 24, 25); probably the Aramaic word *abbā* lies behind the Greek word for father in these prayers. Christian liturgical usage, which drew on reflection about the relation between the "Son" and the "Father," may have shaped

3

the language of some or even all of these passages.

Originally, *abba* was probably a child's word, but it had become an accepted way of speaking to or about one's father. It expresses a close relation to God on the part of Jesus, a relation that is also expected of the disciples, who were told by Jesus to pray, "Our Father . . ." (Matt. 6.9; *see* Lord's Prayer). Some scholars have held that the relation between God and Jesus as father and child, which this language expresses, was highly distinctive and original with Jesus, but others point to similar language in Jewish prayers of the period.

In early Christianity, this Aramaic word was retained as an address to God in prayer even after Greek had become the language of worship. It expressed the newly found relation to God as father, a relationship assured by the presence of the Spirit. The original setting for this exclamation may have been *baptism, but it probably also functioned as a response to preaching.

The word also underlies the English word "abbot" (cf. French *abbé*), a monastic title originating in Syriac Christian usage.

WILLIAM A. BEARDSLEE

Abel. *See* Cain and Abel.

Abortion. Abortion as such is not discussed in the Bible, so any explanation of why it is not legislated or commented on is speculative. One possibility is that the cultural preoccupation with procreation evident in the Hebrew Bible ruled out consideration of terminating pregnancy. Archaeological evidence indicates that in ancient Israel the infant mortality rate was as high as fifty percent. It is also possible that, given the diet and living conditions at the time, female fertility was low. Male control of reproduction and a belief that numerous decendants are a sign of divine blessing are also found in the Bible. These factors support the view that abortion would not have been common.

Alternatively, it can be argued that abortion was practiced without censure. Many women died in childbirth, a strong incentive to avoid carrying a pregnancy to term. Biblical legislation, as in Leviticus 27.3–7, indicates that the lives of children as well as women were not valued as highly as those of adult men, while no value whatsoever

was given to a child under the age of one month. There is no indication that a fetus had any status.

A key text for examining ancient Israelite attitudes is Exodus 21:22–25: "When people who are fighting injure a pregnant woman so that there is a miscarriage, and yet no further harm follows, the one responsible shall be fined what the woman's husband demands, paying as much as the judges determine. If any harm follows, then you shall give life for life, eye for eye, tooth for tooth, hand for hand, foot for foot, burn for burn, wound for wound, stripe for stripe." Several observations can be made about this passage. The Hebrew text at v. 22 literally reads "and there is no harm," implying that contrary to current sensibilities, the miscarriage itself was not considered serious injury. The monetary judgment given to the woman's husband indicates that the woman's experience of the miscarriage is not of significance, and that the damage is considered one to property rather than to human life. This latter observation is further supported by the contrast with the penalties for harm to the woman herself.

Several texts have been influential in late discussions of abortion. Both Jewish and Christian traditions have regarded the divine command "Be fruitful and multiply" (Gen. 1.28) as demanding a high rate of procreation incompatible with abortion in a non-life-threatening situation. Like Leviticus 27, later rabbinic teachings differentiated between life under and over the age of one month, while relying on biblical injunctions to respect and choose life in determining that abortions could be performed to preserve the life of the mother. Christians opposed to abortion have referred to Luke 1.41–44 as evidence that a child is cognizant in the uterus.

DRORAH O'DONNELL SETEL

Abraham. Abraham is the earliest biblical character who is delineated clearly enough to be correlated, to a limited extent, within world history. His homeland on the Fertile Crescent (possibly at Haran, at least in Gen. 12.1–5) and movements southeast toward Chaldean *Ur (Gen. 11.31), then west to *Canaan and *Egypt, correspond to known *Amorite migratory and commercial routes. He may have been a caravan merchant, though the Bible presents him only as a pastoralist. This vague relation of Abraham to history does not exclude debate as to how much of his biography might have been worked up for vividness or as retrojection of a later tribal unity. More insistent claims of historicity presume contemporaneity with *Hammurapi (despite the discredited equation of the latter with Amraphel [Gen 14.1]). An even earlier date was put forward on the basis of some premature interpretations of *Sodom at *Ebla. The name Abram (= Abiram, as Abner = Abiner), used in Genesis from 11.27 to 17.5, is there ritually changed to Abraham, a normal dialectal variant, though explained in relation to 'ab-hāmôn, "father of many."

A certain unity in the whole Abraham saga (Gen. 11.27–25.11) involves a rich variety of peoples and individuals conditioning his activity; twenty-two separate episodes are discernible (see L. Hicks, *Interpreter's Dictionary of the Bible* 1.16). Eleven are attributed to the Yahwist (*J): base around Haran, Genesis 11.28–30; call westward, 12.1–3; Canaan pause, 12.4–9; separation from Lot, 13.1–13; promise involving Mamre, 13.14–18; progeny like stars, covenant-incubation, 15.1–6, 7–24; *Hagar, 16; the three at Mamre, 18.1–15; vain plea for Sodom, 18.16–33; birth of *Isaac, 21.1–7; and old age, 24.1–25.11. Five other episodes suggest the Elohist (*E): parts of the narrative of the covenant in chapter 15, especially verses 13–16; Gerar, 20; *Ishmael expelled, 21.6–21; Abimelech 21.22–34; and the call to sacrifice Isaac, 22 (see Aqedah). The Priestly (*P) additions include: journey to Canaan, parts of Genesis 11–12; birth of Ishmael, 16.1–16; covenant of El-Shaddai and *circumcision, 17; birth of Isaac, 21.1–3; Machpelah, 23; death, 25.7–11; and, less clearly, the unique episode concerning *Melchizedek (chap. 14).

The three strands respectively see Abraham as "father of all nations" (*J); "model of faith" (E; see Rom. 4.9; Heb. 11.8); and "guarantor of Israel's survival" (P, in the context of exile). The *covenant with Abraham is also a blessing for all the peoples of the earth (Gen. 12.3; 18.18) and especially a bond of religious unity with his other descendants, the Ishmaelites (Arabs: Gen. 21.21; 25.12). Abraham's progress from (Ur or) Haran through Canaan into Egypt involves numerous theophanies (Gen. 12.6, Shechem; 12.8, Bethel; 13.18, Hebron; 21.33, Beer-sheba; 22.14, Moriah), justifying his eventual takeover of the whole area (Gen. 13.14–17) or, more sweepingly, the takeover by "his god" (El) of the cult of the local El, not clearly seen as either identical or different.

In Deuteronomy, Abraham is associated with Isaac and *Jacob (Deut. 1.8; 6.10); the three are often generalized as "your fathers" (9.18; 11.9;

NRSV: "your ancestors"), especially as those with whom God made a *covenant (7.12; 8.18), a covenant still in force (5.3). The *Deuteronomic history recalls Abraham in Joshua 24.2–3; 1 Kings 18.36; 2 Kings 13.23; but it is surprising how seldom he is mentioned there, as well as in the Psalms (only 47.9; 105.6, 9, 42) and the preexilic prophets (only Mic. 7.20, probably a late addition). The poorer classes of Judah who never were sent into exile justified their inheritance as the promise to Abraham (Ezek. 33.24), but the stronger group of returnees attributed their own liberation to God's faithfulness to Abraham "my friend" (Isa. 41.8, prominent in James 2.23 and in Muslim tradition, notably as the name of *Hebron, al-Halil). Abraham is often mentioned in the book of Jubilees and sometimes in other *pseudepigrapha.

Abraham is second only to *Moses among New Testament mentions of biblical heroes. Sometimes this is in a slightly belittling sense, when he is claimed as father of the impious (Matt. 3.9; John 8.39). More often the truly Abrahamic descent of the Jews is acknowledged as a stimulus for them to live up to their heritage (Luke 19.9; 16.24; Heb. 6.13). This true but qualified descent from Abraham forms a key factor in *Paul's anguished efforts to determine how and in what sense Christianity can claim the promises made to Israel (Rom. 4.1, 13; Gal. 3.7; 4.22). Ultimately, as father of all believers (Gal. 3.7), Abraham is to be looked to as a source of unity and harmony rather than dissent among Jews, Christians, and Muslims.

See also Abraham's Bosom; Ancestors, The; Genesis, The Book of; Pentateuch.

ROBERT NORTH

Abraham's Bosom. This expression occurs in the *parable of the Rich Man (*Dives) and Lazarus (Luke 16.19–31); after his death, Lazarus is carried by angels to Abraham's bosom (NRSV: "to be with Abraham"). One view is that the imagery is drawn from a child lying in the parent's lap (cf. John 1.18). It is more likely that Lazarus is thought of as sitting next to *Abraham at the heavenly feast. It will be recalled that in John 13.23 the beloved disciple is described as "lying close to the breast of Jesus" (NRSV: "reclining next to Jesus") at the meal. Future bliss was sometimes depicted as a banquet (Isa. 25.6), and this imagery lies behind such sayings as Matthew 8.11, where *gentiles "eat with Abraham and Isaac and Jacob in the kingdom of heaven."

Abraham was regarded as the father of the faithful, and the idea that the souls of God's people are after death welcomed by Israel's *ancestors is referred to in 4 *Maccabees, where brothers about to be martyred declare, "If we so die, Abraham and Isaac and Jacob will welcome us" (13.17).

See also Afterlife and Immortality; Heaven; Hell.   THOMAS FRANCIS GLASSON

Abram. *See* Abraham.

Absalom. Third son of King *David (2 Sam. 3.3). The story of Absalom is presented as a subplot of the life of David, a consequence of David's adultery with *Bathsheba and murder of Uriah (see 2 Sam. 12.7–12; 16.20–22). He kills David's oldest son, Amnon (Absalom's half-brother), for raping his sister, Tamar (2 Sam. 13.1–29). After a brief exile in Geshur, his mother's home, he is allowed to return to *Jerusalem (2 Sam. 14). Apparently fearful that David's judicial inactivity is creating enough discontent to endanger his—or any son's—chances to succeed his father, Absalom conspires against David. He wins a sizable following in Israel, has himself declared king in *Hebron, and chases David out of Jerusalem (2 Sam. 15–16). He soon attacks David in a wooded area of Ephraim, where he is defeated and, contrary to David's wishes, is killed by Joab, the commander of David's forces (2 Sam. 17–18). David's grief at his son's death is characteristically intense (2 Sam. 18.33–19.8).
                                       TIMOTHY M. WILLIS

Abyss. The abyss, or bottomless depth, appears in biblical tradition in several related senses. In the Hebrew Bible, *těhôm* (NRSV: "the deep") usually refers to the primordial waters upon which the ordered world of God's creation floats. Related terms are used to describe the depth of springs, the sea, or the earth. The abyss can also stand for the depth of the underworld understood as the realm of the dead. Because of its associations with *chaos and death, the abyss is identified in postbiblical Jewish literature as the realm, or more often prison, of rebellious spirits. This usage appears in the New Testament in

Luke 8.31 and throughout the book of Revelation (NRSV: "bottomless pit").
    See Hell.   ROBERT STOOPS

Acrostic. An acrostic is a poem in which the initial letters of each successive line form a word, phrase, or pattern. Acrostics are found in several ancient Near Eastern literatures; in the Bible the only poems of this type are alphabetic acrostics, in which each consecutive line or group of lines begins with a successive letter of the alphabet in the order of the letters in Hebrew. The acrostic poems in the Bible are Psalms 9–10, 25, 34, 37, 111, 112, 145; Proverbs 31.10–31; Lamentations 1, 2, 3, 4; Nahum 1.2–8 (incomplete); Sirach 51.13–30; and the most elaborate, as well as the longest chapter in the Bible, Psalm 119. Because of the structural device of the acrostic, the content of these poems is not developmental. The purpose of the acrostic may have been mnemonic; it also may have been intended to convey the idea that the entire range of sentiment is being expressed, "from A to Z," as it were. Few English translations have attempted to reproduce this formal device; one that does is by Ronald Knox.
    See also Lamentations of Jeremiah, The; Poetry, Biblical Hebrew.   MICHAEL D. COOGAN

Acts of the Apostles. The fifth book of the New Testament in the common arrangement, Acts records certain phases of the progress of Christianity for a period of some thirty years after Jesus' death and resurrection. Acts was originally written as a sequel to the gospel of *Luke; both are clearly from the same author, who apparently planned the complete work from the outset.

    Structure. Seven main divisions may be discerned in Acts: the formation and development of the church of *Jerusalem (1.1–5.42); the rise and activity of the Hellenists in the church, which led to their persecution and expulsion from Jerusalem (6.1–8.3); the dissemination of the gospel by these Hellenists, culminating in the evangelizing of *gentiles in the Syrian city of *Antioch (8.4–12.25); the extension of gentile Christianity from Antioch into Cyprus and Asia Minor (13.1–14.28); the decision reached by the Jerusalem church on problems raised by the influx of gentile converts (15.1–16.5); the carrying of the gospel by *Paul and his colleagues to the provinces bordering on the Aegean Sea (16.6–19.20);

Paul's last journey to Jerusalem, his arrest there, and his journey to Rome under armed guard to have his case heard before the emperor (19.21–28.31).

Acts, in short, is concerned with the advance of the gospel from Jerusalem to Rome; its simultaneous advance in other directions is ignored. The narrative reaches its goal when Paul arrives in Rome and, while under house arrest, preaches the gospel there without interference to all who came to visit him (28.30–31).

Authorship and Sources. For Acts, as for the gospel of Luke, the author was dependent on the information handed down by others (see Luke 1.2). But he probably made further inquiry on his own account (Luke 1.3), and he may have been present at some of the events recorded in the later part of the book of Acts. This is the prima facie inference to be drawn from the "we" sections—those sections in which the third-person pronouns "they" and "them" give way to the first-person "we" and "us." There are three such sections: Acts 16.10–17; 20.5–21.18; 27.1–28.16. All three are largely devoted to journeys by sea—from Troas to Neapolis, and then by road to Philippi; from Philippi (Neapolis) to Caesarea, and then by road to Jerusalem; from Caesarea to Puteoli, and then by road to Rome—and may have been extracted from a travel diary. The traditional view, which still has much to commend it, is that the "we" of those sections includes the "I" of Acts 1.1—that the transition from "they" to "we" is the author's unobtrusive way of indicating that he himself was a participant in the events he narrates.

Ever since the second century CE the author has been traditionally identified with the Luke mentioned in Colossians 4.14 as "Luke the beloved physician." The attribution of the twofold work to such an obscure New Testament character has been thought to speak for the genuineness of the tradition. The only question of consequence to be considered is the degree of likelihood that the author of Acts was personally acquainted with Paul, whose missionary activity forms the main subject of the second half of the book. The critical judgment of several scholars is that such personal acquaintance is highly unlikely—that the "Paulinism" of Acts is too dissimilar to the teaching of Paul's letters for the idea to be entertained that the author of Acts knew Paul or spent any time in his company. On the other hand, many authorities maintain that, when account is taken of the difference between the picture of him as seen through the eyes of an admirer and, indeed, hero-worshiper, the Paul of Acts is identical with the real Paul.

The identification of other sources than the "we" narrative is precarious. A new source is sometimes indicated by such transitional formulas as "now during these days" (6.1), "after some days" (15.36), "about that time" (19.23), or by the sudden introduction of terms or names for which no advance explanation has been given, such as Hellenists and Hebrews in 6.1 or King Herod in 12.1. The abruptness of a transition from one source to another may be made smoother by an editorial paragraph, for example, 15.1–5. Occasionally the author follows one source for some time, then breaks off to follow another, and turns back later to resume the earlier one. Thus a source relating the early Hellenistic mission is followed by 8.4–40, a section beginning: "Now those who were scattered went from place to place preaching the word." The author then leaves it to relate the conversion of Paul and *Peter's evangelistic ministry (9.1–11.18); he returns to it in 11.19, "Now those who were scattered because of the persecution that took place over Stephen," and goes on to tell of the founding of the church of Antioch.

From 15.35 on there is a continuous narrative of Paul's missionary work, broken only by occasional speeches (notably, to the Athenians, 17.22–31, and to the elders of the Ephesian church, 20.18–35). A new departure is marked in 19.21, at which Paul's plan to visit Rome is first announced; the remainder of the work tells how that plan was fulfilled in unforeseen ways.

Speeches and Letters. Luke does not appear to have been dependent on written sources for the speeches that play an important part in his work. These conform to the policy inherited by Greek historians from Thucydides (ca. 400 BCE), who explains that he has "put into the mouth of each speaker the sentiments appropriate for the occasion, expressed as I thought he would be likely to express them, while at the same time I endeavored, as nearly as I could, to give the general purport of what was actually said" (*History*, 1.20.1). Following this principle, Luke introduces speeches with proper regard for the speakers and the setting. *Stephen's defense in Acts 7.2–53, for example, presents a wholly negative appraisal of the Jerusalem Temple, whereas Luke himself, for the greater part of his narrative, treats it with respect. It is not by accident that Paul is the only speaker in Acts to call Jesus "the *Son of God" (Acts 9.20) or to mention *justification by faith (13.38, 39) or redemption by the blood of Christ (20.28). It is widely maintained that Paul's speech to the court of the *Areopagus at *Athens (Acts 17.22–31) cannot in any sense be credited to Paul. But, if the author of Romans 1–3 were brought to Athens and invited to expound the basis of the gospel to its cultured and sophisticated members in terms that they might in some degree understand, it can be argued that he was bound to say something not wholly different from what Luke represents Paul as saying on that occasion. Both here and elsewhere in Acts the speeches are appropriate to the occasion, to the speaker, and to the audience.

What is true of speeches is true also of the letters cited by Luke—the letter from the leaders of the Jerusalem church to the gentile Christians of Antioch and other places in Syria and Cilicia (Acts 15.23–29; see Apostolic Council) and the letter from the commanding officer of the Roman garrison in Jerusalem to the procurator of Judea explaining the circumstances of Paul's arrest (23.26–30). Even if Luke is the composer of those letters as we have them, their contents fit the settings in which they are placed.

Date. The latest event to be recorded in Acts is Paul's spending two years under house arrest in Rome (28.30). This period begins with his arrival in the city, probably in the early spring of 60 CE. Most of the book deals with the twenty years preceding that date, and the book as a whole is true to its "dramatic" date, that is, it reflects the situation of the middle of the first century CE, especially with regard to the administration of the *Roman empire. But the date of writing is not the same as the "dramatic" date. Some scholars have argued that it was written very shortly after that event, possibly even before Paul's appeal came up for hearing in the imperial court. Paul's death is not recorded: would it not have been mentioned (it is asked) if in fact it had taken place?

But the goal of Luke's narrative is not the outcome of Paul's appeal, whether favorable or otherwise, or the end of Paul's life: it is Paul's unmolested preaching of the gospel at the heart of the empire (Acts 28.30–31). In fact Paul's death is alluded to, by implication, in his speech to the *elders of the Ephesian church (Acts 20.24, 25), in a manner that suggests that Luke knew of it. And in general Luke appears to record the apostolic history from a perspective of one or two decades after the events. By the time he wrote, Paul, Peter, and *James had all died; and the controversies in which they were involved, while important enough at the time (as Paul's letters bear witness), had lost much of their relevance for Luke's purpose, so he ignored them.

The date of Acts cannot be considered in isolation from that of the gospel of *Luke. A date later rather than earlier than 70 CE is probable for the gospel. If we date the composition of the twofold work toward the end of Vespasian's rule (69–79 CE), most of the evidence will be satisfied.

Recipients. The one recipient of Acts named explicitly is Theophilus, to whom Luke's gospel also was dedicated (Luke 1.3). We know virtually nothing about him. His designation "most excellent" may mark him as a member of the equestrian order (the second-highest order in Roman society), or it may simply be a courtesy title.

One could regard him as a representative of the intelligent middle-class public of Rome, to whom Luke wished to present a reliable account of the rise and progress of Christianity. As late as the time when Tacitus, Suetonius, and Pliny were writing (ca. 110 CE), Christians enjoyed no good repute in Roman society; writing some decades earlier, Luke hoped to bring his readers to a less prejudiced judgment. There is much to be said for the view of Martin Dibelius that, unlike the other New Testament books, Luke and Acts were written for the book market. Perhaps there was already a positive interest in Christianity in the class of readers Luke had in mind; this could account for the substantial theological content of the work, especially its emphasis on the *Holy Spirit.

Rome is the most likely place for the first publication of the work. Not only is Rome the goal toward which it moves, but with Paul's arrival there, Rome implicitly replaces Jerusalem as the center from which the faith is to spread.

Historical Significance. Whereas the gospel of Luke has at least partial parallels in the other Gospels, all of which are concerned with Jesus' activity from his baptism to his death and resurrection, Acts is unparalleled as a record of events. Its only parallels are occasional passages in the letters of Paul (notably Gal. 1.13–2.14), in which the apostle reviews phases of his career or mentions his travel plans. Apart from Acts, we have no other continuous record of the expansion of Christianity during the thirty years after Jesus' death and resurrection. It is necessary to wait two and a half centuries for the next Christian historian—Eusebius, bishop of Caesarea in Palestine.

Even in his gospel, Luke indicates his interest

in relating the gospel to world history when he introduces the ministry of *John the Baptist with an elaborate synchronism (Luke 3.1, 2). This interest becomes more evident in Acts, when the gospel moves into the gentile world. Luke is the only New Testament writer who so much as names a Roman emperor; in addition to emperors, he introduces provincial governors, client kings, civic magistrates, and other local officials. Scholars have drawn attention to the accuracy with which these officials are designated by their correct titles—an accuracy the more noteworthy because some of those titles changed from time to time. Provinces under the nominal control of the Roman senate, for example, are governed by proconsuls, like Sergius Paulus in Cyprus and Gallio in Achaia; Philippi has praetors or duumvirs as its chief magistrates, because it is a Roman colony; Thessalonica is administered by politarchs, a title attested on a number of inscriptions as borne by the chief magistrates of Macedonian cities.

The record of Acts is interrelated with contemporary world history in a way that entitles it to be cited as an authority in its own right. Its authority has also been acknowledged in the matter of travel conditions, on land and sea, in the Roman empire in the period that it covers. Its reports of Paul's journeys in Asia Minor provide unrivaled evidence for lines of communication in that area and for the comparative ease with which they could be used. The "ease" was enjoyed more along the main roads, which were well policed; travel along other roads exposed one to hazards from robbers and others. As for travel by sea, the account of Paul's stormy voyage to Italy and shipwreck at Malta has long been recognized as a valuable document for our knowledge of seafaring in the Greco-Roman world (see Ships and Sailing).

Theological Significance. Luke is no mere chronicler: he envisages a pattern in the events he records. His interest is concentrated on the advance of the gospel: it has been launched into the world by the *resurrection of Jesus and the coming of the Spirit, and nothing can stop it. Paul and others may plan their journeys, but they would achieve little without the guidance of the Spirit of God, directing the course of events by occasionally diverting the missionaries from the path they intend to take and leading them into another (e.g., 16.6–10). Luke has been called the theologian of "salvation history"; Peter and Paul are the principal human agents, but the dominant part is played by the Spirit.

Apologetic Emphasis. In commending Christianity to the good will of his readers, Luke insists that it presents no threat to imperial law and order. He adduces in evidence the judgments expressed by officials of higher and lower degree throughout the empire. Already in the Third Gospel Pontius *Pilate, the Roman governor who hears the charges against Jesus, finds him not guilty of any capital offense (Luke 23.13–17); he sentences him to death because he gives in weakly to the chief priests and their colleagues. In the early chapters of Acts the apostles are flogged by order of the supreme court of Israel (5.40), a body dominated by the chief-priestly families; and Stephen, leader of the Hellenists, is stoned to death after their rejection of his defense (Acts 7.58). But when the heralds of Christianity move out into the gentile world, they receive fairer treatment.

Sergius Paulus, proconsul of Cyprus, gives Paul and *Barnabas a courteous hearing and is impressed by their teaching (Acts 13.7, 12). The praetors of Philippi sentence Paul and *Silas to be beaten and locked up overnight, but on learning that the two men are Roman citizens they apologize for their illegal conduct (16.22–24, 35–39). The politarchs of Thessalonica respond to the serious charge of high treason brought against Paul and his companions by making Paul's friends in the city guarantee his peaceful departure (17.6–9). At *Corinth Paul is accused before Gallio, proconsul of Achaia, of propagating an illegal form of religion, but Gallio, seeing the issue as a dispute between the local Jews and a Jewish visitor, refuses to take up the matter: so far as he is concerned, Paul must be tolerated as long as no breach of law or public morals is committed (18.12–16). In *Ephesus some leading citizens of the province of *Asia befriend Paul, and when an unruly assembly demonstrates against him, the town clerk, the chief executive officer of the city, absolves him of any offense against the cult of Ephesian *Artemis (19.23–41).

All this builds up a case in favor of Paul, who at the end of Acts, charged with offenses against public order, is about to have his appeal heard by the emperor; it also builds up a case for Christians throughout the empire, who will still be around when Paul is no longer alive.

Canonical Significance. Early in the second century CE, when the four Gospels began to circulate as one collection, Acts was detached from Luke's gospel. But when, about the middle of that century, decisions were made about the

New Testament *canon, Acts came into its own as the "hinge" that joined the gospel collection to the collection of Pauline letters. Those like Marcion, who ascribed apostolic authority to Paul alone, had no use for Acts. Acts, while not giving Paul the title *apostle in a distinctive sense, provided ample evidence that he was all that his letters claimed him to be; at the same time, it gave Peter and his colleagues full apostolic status. There is an impressive series of parallels in Acts between Paul and Peter, as though Luke planned to show that the status and ministry of both had equal divine attestation. James of Jerusalem, whose claims were exalted above those of Peter and Paul in at least one branch of second-century Christianity, plays a minor part in Acts (15.13–21).

Acts, in short, is a thoroughly catholic work, catering to all legitimate viewpoints in the church. Perhaps it was this aspect of Acts that stimulated the inclusion in the canon, alongside the Pauline collection, of another collection of letters, the catholic letters as they are traditionally called, bearing the names of James, Peter, John, and Jude. It is a matter of further interest that Acts was closely associated with these catholic letters in the copying and transmission of the New Testament, regularly sharing one codex with them or, in a more comprehensive codex, being followed immediately by them.   F. F. BRUCE

Adam. Adam (possibly meaning "ruddy" or "earth") is the common noun in Hebrew for "human(-kind)"; only in Genesis 1–5 (when used without the article) and 1 Chronicles 1.1 is it the proper name for the first man. This usage highlights the unity of humankind, leaving no special apartness for Israel or Abraham. The stylized Priestly (*P) account of the creation of humans in Genesis 1.26 and more anthropomorphic narrative of the Yahwist (*J) in Genesis 2.7 neither disprove nor suggest (the) Adam's origin by evolution, a question that simply did not arise. God's image is in "the man" in Genesis 1.26, as "the man's" in turn is in Seth (Gen. 5.3; but cf. the different perspective in 1 Cor. 11.7). Normal human toil and *death as a punishment for (the) Adam's sin is the focus in Genesis 3 rather than either its propagation or the "protoevangelium." In the New Testament, Adam is chiefly a type of Christ (Rom. 5.14; cf. "last Adam," 1 Cor. 15.45) in relation to release by resurrection from an original sin (1 Cor. 15.22, 45), perhaps taking up Adam as the ideal man (Sir. 49.16; Wisd. of Sol. 10.1).

See also Eve; Fall, The; Genesis, The Book of.   ROBERT NORTH

Additions to the Book of Esther. *See* Esther, The Book of.

Adultery. Adultery is voluntary sexual intercourse by either a married man or a married woman with someone other than his or her spouse. In ancient Israel, both the man and the woman would be considered guilty. It was prohibited by both versions of the *Ten Commandments (Exod. 20.14; Deut. 5.18) as well as by the Holiness Code of Leviticus (18.20). According to Leviticus 20.10, which prohibits adultery with the wife of one's *neighbor, the penalty for this crime was death. The mode of execution was probably the same as that specified in Deuteronomy 22.23–24, which deals with the case of a young woman, a virgin, who was engaged to be married but met and had sexual intercourse with another man in the city. Both were guilty of adultery and were to be taken to the gate and stoned to death. This punishment is also assumed in the New Testament story of Jesus and the young woman accused of adultery, where Jesus says, "Let anyone among you who is without sin be the first to throw a stone at her" (John 8.7).

Adultery was probably considered sufficient grounds for *divorce in ancient Israel. This is implied in Deuteronomy 24.1, an introduction to the law concerned with remarriage, where one interpretation of the phrase "something objectionable" has been that it refers to adultery on the part of the woman and that only this behavior justified a divorce. If a man suspected his wife of adultery but did not have any evidence, he could require her to submit to trial by ordeal, which would both determine her guilt or innocence and incorporate a physical punishment in the case of her guilt (Num. 5.11–31). In the Gospels, adultery is the only acceptable reason for divorce, although some scholars think that the phrase "except on the ground of unchastity" (Matt. 5.32) is an addition to earlier tradition (cf. Mark 10.2–12; Luke 16.18; 1 Cor. 7.10–13; Rom. 7.3).

See also Marriage; Sex; Women.

RUSSELL FULLER

Africa.

Names and Words for Africa. Africa appears throughout the Bible from Genesis 2.11–13, where the sources of the *Nile River are located in the garden of *Eden, to the apostle Philip's baptism of the African official in Acts 8.26–39. To recover these numerous references in the original Hebrew and Greek of the Bible, sometimes lost or obscured in English translation, one must first identify the key biblical names for Africa and its people.

"*Cush" in Hebrew and "Ethiopia" in Greek designate the land and people of the upper Nile River from modern southern Egypt into Sudan (Map 7:F6). The more indigenous term for this region is Nubia. "Ham" is another Hebrew term for the darker-hued people of antiquity. In Genesis 10, *Ham is son of *Noah who populates Africa, *Canaan, and *Arabia after the *Flood. In poetry, the name Ham is a synonym for Egypt (e.g., Ps. 78.51).

"Niger," the Latin word for "black," is used in Acts 13.1 to identify an African named Simeon. Simeon's companion Lucius was also African as is indicated by his place of origin, Cyrene, in Libya (Map 14:D4; see Acts 2.10). Jesus' cross is carried by Simon, also from Cyrene (Matt. 27.32).

In addition to Hebrew, Greek, and Latin terms for Africa, the Bible also uses Egyptian and Nubian names for the land and its people. The references to Africa encompass the length of the Nile Valley from the deep southern origins of the Nile down to the delta where it empties into the Mediterranean Sea. From the Lower Nile in the north to the Upper Nile in the south, the African skin color varied from brown to copper-brown to black. For the Egyptians used to these color variations, the term for their southern neighbors was *Neḥesi*, "southerner," which eventually also came to mean "the black" or "the Nubian." This Egyptian root (*nḥsj*, with the preformative *p'* as a definite article) appears in Exodus 6.25 as the personal name of Aaron's grandson Phinehas (= *Pa-neḥas*). In Acts 8.27, the first non-Jewish convert to Christianity is an African official of the Nubian queen, whose title, Candace, meaning "queen mother," is mistaken for her personal name.

Africa and Egypt. *Egypt is in Africa, and both the Bible and the early Greek and Roman explorers and historians viewed this great civilization of the Nile as African. Before the modern idea of color prejudice, the distinctions noted in antiquity between the brown Egyptians and their darker-hued neighbors to the south did not contain the racial and cultural connotations that exist today. The Bible therefore classified Egypt, along with Canaan and Arabia, as African in the Genesis account of the restored family of peoples after the Flood (Gen. 10).

This linkage between Egypt and its southern neighbor Nubia/Cush is reinforced by the presence of these darker southerners in Canaan during the ancestral period and afterward as major elements in the Egyptian army garrisoned there. The early-fourteenth-century BCE *Amarna Letters, correspondence from Canaanite kings to Pharaoh Akhnaton, testify to the early African presence there. One letter, from Abdu-heba, king of pre-Israelite *Jerusalem, complains of the rebellious Nubian troops stationed there. One can speculate that an African presence remained in the area, and that maintaining their tradition of military prowess, later generations of Nubians/Cushites either became part of *David's forces which captured Jerusalem, or remained part of Jerusalem's militia which David incorporated as his own, as he did with the older *Jebusite priesthood.

Still later in Israelite history, during the reign of *Hezekiah of Judah (727–698 BCE), Nubia ruled Egypt as its Twenty-fifth Dynasty (751–656 BCE), and forged a close alliance with Judah in a common effort to ward off capture by the *Assyrians. Even as the prophet Isaiah protested that the king should trust in God rather than in the Egyptians for the defense of Jerusalem, his oracle on the Cushite emissaries (Isa. 18.1–2) fixed in biblical tradition the Egypt/African common identity. This same equation is expressed in Nahum's lament over the fall of the Egyptian capital Thebes (Nah. 3.8–9), even as he exults over the destruction of Assyria's capital *Nineveh.

Africa at the Royal Court and in the Wisdom Tradition. The Africans who are named in the Hebrew Bible are closely aligned with the royal court and *wisdom traditions of ancient Israel. One of David's Cushite soldiers brought news of the death of his son *Absalom (2 Sam. 18.21–32), and *Solomon, already married to an Egyptian princess (1 Kings 3.1), entertained the Queen of *Sheba who had come to visit him on a trade mission (1 Kings 10.1–13). *Jeremiah was saved from death under King *Zedekiah by an African court official Ebed-melek ("servant of the king"; Jer. 38–39), while in an earlier incident under King Jehoiakim a messenger of African heritage named Jehudi communicated with the prophet

(Jer. 36.14). The prophet *Zephaniah is called "son of Cushi" (Zeph. 1.1) in his genealogy, which extends back to Hezekiah.

Solomon as patron of wisdom opened the door to Egyptian proverbs and poetry as evidenced in segments of the book of *Proverbs modeled upon the Egyptian "Instructions of Amen-em-ope" (Prov. 22.17–24.34), and in Psalm 104, which echoes an Egyptian hymn to Aton. Hezekiah, who aligned himself with the Cushite Dynasty, is also listed as a royal patron of Israel's proverbial wisdom (Prov. 25.1). The maiden in Song of Solomon 1.5 proclaims, "I am black and beautiful, O daughters of Jerusalem, like the tents of Kedar, like the curtains of Solomon." The dual imagery is clear: dark hue is paralleled by the black goat-skin tents, and beauty is matched by the sumptuous royal curtains. (The Hebrew connector wĕ is taken in its normal sense as a conjunctive "and" rather than the less usual disjunctive "but").

Africa in Israelite Worship and Messianic Thought. Among those known to God under the imagery of *Zion as mother of nations is Cush (Ps. 87.4), who also brings tribute to the Temple (Ps. 68.31). This concern for Cush and the other nations may extend from the formative experience of the *Exodus and wilderness sojourn, where Hebrews were accompanied by a "mixed multitude" (Exod. 12.38), including Phinehas (Exod. 6.25) and *Moses' Cushite wife (Num. 12.1).

In prophetic literature, after God's wrath is vindicated on the nations of the earth, God will change their speech so all can worship God, and "from beyond the rivers of Ethiopia my suppliants, the daughter of my dispersed ones, shall bring my offering" (Zeph. 3.10). This refers to the African diaspora, to Israelite exiles in Africa returning with gifts of thanksgiving to God. Africa then with its people seen as converts shall come to worship God in Zion, along with dispersed Israelite exiles. It is in this context of God's universal reign that the prophet Amos proclaims, "Are you not like the Ethiopians to me, O people of Israel? says the Lord" (Amos 9.7). God is judge and ultimately redeemer of all nations.

The New Testament proclamation of Jesus as *Messiah continues in the early mission of the apostle Philip who baptizes the African official in Acts 8.26–39. It is significant that in this incident the term "messiah" is interpreted in light of Isaiah 53.7–8 as God's suffering servant. That the African was reading Isaiah suggests that the emissary was a recent convert or a *proselyte.

In the light of the Psalms and the prophets, then, Africans can be viewed both as diaspora and as proselytes among Israel's dispersed people, and also as forerunners of the conversion of all the nations of the earth.

ROBERT A. BENNETT

African American Traditions and the Bible.

Introduction: Reading the Bible = Reading the Self and the World. African Americans' engagement of the Bible is complex and dynamic. It is a fascinating historical drama, beginning with the Africans' involuntary arrival in the New World. But as sign of the creativity and adaptability of the Africans and of the evocative power of the Bible, the drama continues to the present day, notwithstanding the complexity and controversies of intervening periods. Thus, there is in African Americans' engagement of the Bible potential not only for an interpretive history of their readings as a history of their collective self-understandings, visions, hopes, challenges, and agenda, but also—because of their singular experience at least in the United States—for significant, even singular challenges for critical biblical interpretation in the late twentieth century.

First Reading: Awe and Fear—Initial Negotiation of the Bible and the New World. From the beginning of their captive experience in what became the United States, Africans were confronted with the missionizing efforts of whites to convert slaves to the religions of the slavers. These religions or denominations—especially Anglicanism—were for the most part the establishment religions of the landed gentry; they did not appeal much to the slaves. Numerous testimonies from clerics, teachers, and missionaries of the eighteenth century register frustration and shock over the Africans' lack of understanding of and uneasy socialization into their religious cultures. The formality and the literacy presupposed by these cultures—in catechetical training and Bible study, for example—clearly frustrated the easy or enthusiastic "conversion" of the African masses. Not only were the Africans, on the whole, according to custom and law, deemed (and made) incapable of meeting the presupposed literacy requirements, but they did not seem emotionally or psychically disposed toward the customary sensibilities and orientations of the establishment religions. These missionary efforts were not very successful.

The Bible did have a place in these initial missionary efforts. But that place was not primary: its presence was indirect, embedded within catechetical materials, or muted and domesticated within doctrinaire or catechetical, and mostly formal, preaching. But it needs to be stressed that the Africans' introduction to "the Bible," or "the scriptures," by whatever agency, would have been difficult, according to available evidence. Cultures steeped in oral traditions at first generally find frightful and absurd the concept of a religion and religious power circumscribed by a book, then certainly difficult to accept and fathom; later, perhaps, they may find it awesome and fascinating.

Second Reading: Critique and Accommodation. It was not until the late eighteenth century, with the growth of nonestablishment, evangelical, and free-church and camp-meeting revivalistic movements in the North and South, that African Americans began to encounter and engage the Bible on a large scale and on a more intimate basis, minus the bewilderment. Finding themselves directly appealed to by the new evangelicals and revivalists in vivid, emotional biblical language, and noting that nearly the entire white world explained its power and authority by appeal to the Bible, the Africans could hardly fail to be drawn closer to it. They embraced the Bible, transforming it from the Book of the religion of the whites—whether aristocratic slavers or lower-class exhorters—into a source of psychic-spiritual power and of hope, a source of inspiration for learning and affirmation, and into a language capable of articulating strong hopes and veiling stinging critique. The narratives of the Hebrew Bible and the stories of Jesus, the New Testament's persecuted but victorious one, captured the collective African imagination. This was the beginning of the African American historical encounter with the Bible, and the foundation for the cultivation of the phenomenological, sociopolitical, and cultural presupposition(s) for its different, even conflicting historical readings of the Bible to come.

From the late eighteenth century through the end of slavery, the period of Reconstruction, and into the modern Civil Rights era of the 1950s and 1960s, African Americans continued their engagement with or readings of the Bible. These readings reflected major dynamics in the self-understandings and orientations of a major segment of African American culture, if not the majority. The founding of the independent churches and denominations beginning in the late eighteenth century historically postdates and logically presupposes the cultivation of certain identifiable African diaspora religious worldviews and orientations. The Bible played a fundamental role in the cultivation and articulation of such worldviews and orientations. It was discovered as a type of language world full of drama and proclamation such that the slave or freedperson could be provided with certain powerful rhetorics and visions that fired the imagination.

The most popular reading of the Bible was one in which the Protestant *canon provided the rhetorics and visions of prophetic critique, the blueprints for "racial uplift," and social and political peace (integration) as the ultimate goal, in addition to steps toward personal salvation. This reading of the Bible reflected the dominant sociopolitical views and orientations among African Americans in this period. The "reading"—both of the Bible and of American culture—expressed considerable ambivalence: it was both critical and accommodationist: on the one hand, its respect for the Protestant canon reflected its desire to accommodate and be included within the American (socioeconomic, political, and religious) mainstream; on the other hand, its interpretation of the Bible was on the whole from a social and ideological location "from below," as it were, and reflected a blistering critique of Bible-believing, slave-holding, racist America. Important personalities—from Frederick Douglass to Martin Luther King, Jr.—are among the powerful articulators of the reading. But the popular sources, some anonymous, some by not-very-well-known individuals—the songs, conversion narratives, poetry, prayers, diaries, and the like—are a truer, more powerful reflection of history.

That this reading reflected considerable ambivalence about being in America on the part of a considerable segment of African Americans over a long period of history is indisputable. That it reflects class-specific leanings within the African American population is also indisputable. Those who continued to "read" the Bible and America in this way continued to hope that some accommodation should and could be made. Those most ardent in this hope on the whole saw themselves as close enough to the mainstream to make accommodation (integration) always seem feasible.

The great interest in the dramatic narratives of the Hebrew Bible notwithstanding, it was the motifs of a certain cluster of passages from the

New Testament, especially Galatians 3:26–28 and Acts 2 and 10:34–36, that provided the hermeneutic foundation for this dominant "mainstream" African American reading of the Bible—and American culture. These passages were important because of their emphasis on the themes centering around the hope for the realization of the universality of salvation and the kinship of humanity. The passages were quoted and/or paraphrased in efforts to relate them to the racial situation in the United States by generations of African Americans—from the famous to those known only in statistics, stereotypes, and generalizations, in settings ranging from pulpits and lecture halls to nightclubs and street corners, in the rhetoric of the sermon and in the music of the streets.

That this reading continues to reflect the ethos and orientation of a considerable number, perhaps the majority, of African Americans, can be seen in its institutionalization in most African American institutions and associations—from the churches to civil rights organizations. Further, some of the most powerful and influential voices among African Americans continue to accept the ethos reflected by the reading. This suggests the continuing power of the ethos, even if it be argued that it is no longer the singular dominant ethos.

Third Reading: Critique from the Margins. Another reading was cultivated in the early decades of the twentieth century, primarily in the urban centers of the North and South. It reflected the sentiments of displaced and disoriented rural and small-town residents who moved to the big cities in search of better job opportunities. These individuals formed new religious communities that gave them a sense of belonging and solidarity missing in the established "mainline" churches and communities. A very different reading of the Bible is in evidence among such groups, one that was also reflective of a different attitude about society and culture. It was a more critical, even radical attitude about America; there was little hope of full integration into the mainstream. America was seen as racist and arrogant; its "mainstream" religious groups—including the African American groups—were seen as worldly and perfidious.

The engagement of the Bible and of religious texts in general more clearly reflects and articulates this attitude. The latter was not held by one single group; it was held by a number of groups—the Garvey Movement, Father Divine and the Peace Mission Movement, the Black Jews, the Nation of Islam, the Spiritual churches, the Pentecostal movement, among the most prominent. What they had in common were sensibilities, attitudes about the world, which were reflected not only in their more radical (Afrocentric or racialist) interpretation of the (Protestant-defined and -delimited) Bible, but also in their acceptance of other esoteric authoritative texts that, of course, justified their sensibilities and agenda. Whether through the radical reading of the (Protestant) Bible, the rejection or manipulation of its canonical delimitations, or through acceptance of other esoteric authoritative texts, these groups expressed their rejection of the racist and worldly religious ways of America and of the accommodationist and integrationist agenda of the African American religious mainstream. Many of them focused, to degrees far beyond anything on record among the African American establishment churches, on the utter perfidy and hopelessness of whites (e.g., Nation of Islam, Garvey movement) as well as the destiny and salvation of African peoples (especially Black Jews).

Fourth Reading: Leaving Race Behind. Another African American reading of the Bible and American culture is emerging as a dominant one in the late twentieth century. It is in many respects a reaction to both the integrationist/accommodationist and the separatist readings discussed above. Its use of the Bible is a sharp departure from the traditional African American engagement of the Bible. To be sure, African Americans have historically been evangelical in their religious sensibilities, including the attachment of primary importance to the Bible as guide. But there has heretofore generally been a looseness, a kind of playfulness with the Bible. The letters of the Bible and its literal sense were less important than the evocative power of the stories, poetry, and prophetic proclamations. What generally mattered most was the power of the Bible to function as a language, even a language world, into which African American visionaries, prophets, rhetors, and politicians could retreat in order to find the materials needed for the articulation of their own and their communities' views. Now there are many African Americans whose engagement to the Bible is more doctrinaire and literal, even fundamentalist. And the hermeneutic foundation or presupposition, too, has shifted from historical and cultural experience, from being race-specific (as with the mainstream groups) or radical (as with the "sects" and "cults"), to being (as it is claimed) "Bible-based," that is, focused upon true doctrine in the letters of the Bible, relativizing racial identity and experience.

In this reading of the (Protestant) Bible, which is considered the deracialized and depoliticized quest for the truth and salvation, the most radical criticism of African American religious communities and culture is expressed. Insofar as the Protestant canon is not questioned, and insofar as the foundation or presupposition for reading the canon is claimed to be other than historical experience, then a total rejection of African American existence is expressed. In much the same way that the rise of fundamentalism among whites in the early decades of the twentieth century represented a rejection of modernism, so within the world of African Americans a turn toward fundamentalism represents a rejection of African Americans' special historical experiences and claims. That in religious matters African American religious communities are being abandoned or are being transformed into fundamentalist camps on the order of white fundamentalist camps, that religious truth can now be claimed to be unrelated to experience, is a most significant development. The proliferation of new fundamentalist churches and denominational groups among African Americans, as well as the new alliances with white fundamentalist groups, is astounding.

The phenomenon begs further comprehensive investigation. But it is very clear that it represents a most significant turn in African American religious and cultural history.

Women's Reading. In evidence throughout this history of African American "readings" of the Bible are the special readings of African American women. From Phyllis Wheatley to modern "womanist" and other interpreters, women are part of each of the "readings" distinguished above. But across each of these readings, differences in historical periods, locations, classes, and other factors notwithstanding, collectively women have for the most part added special emphases. Especially poignant among them is the radical challenge of consistency in prophetic communal self-judgment as African American religious communities apply the moral imperative to define the universality of God's economy of salvation.

See also Africa; Slavery and the Bible.

VINCENT L. WIMBUSH

Afterlife and Immortality. *This entry consists of two articles on views of life after death within the historical communities of* Ancient Israel *and* Second Temple Judaism and Early Christianity. *For related discussion, see* Death; Israel, Religion of.

Ancient Israel

Israelite views of the afterlife underwent substantial changes during the first millennium BCE, as concepts popular during the preexilic period eventually came to be rejected by the religious leadership of the exilic and postexilic communities, and new theological stances replaced them. Because many elements of preexilic beliefs and practices concerning the dead were eventually repudiated, the Hebrew Bible hardly discusses preexilic concepts at all; only scant and disconnected references to afterlife and the condition of the dead appear in the texts. A few passages from late-eighth through sixth-century sources are illuminating, however, because they attack various aspects of the popular notions about the dead during that period. With these data, a general though sketchy picture of Israelite views can be proposed.

Like all cultures in the ancient Near East, the Israelites believed that persons continued to exist after *death. It was thought that following death, one's spirit went down to a land below the earth, most often called Sheol, but sometimes merely "Earth," or "the Pit" (*see* Hell). In the preexilic period, there was no notion of a judgment of the dead based on their actions during life, nor is there any evidence for a belief that the righteous dead go to live in God's presence. The two persons in the Hebrew Bible who are taken to heaven to live with God, Enoch (Gen. 5.24) and Elijah (2 Kings 2.11), do not die. All who die, righteous or wicked, go to Sheol (see Gen. 42:38; Num. 16.30–33).

The exact relationship between the body of a dead person and the spirit that lived on in Sheol is unclear, since the Bible does not discuss this issue. Many scholars assume that the Israelites did not fully distinguish between the body and the spirit, and thus believed that the deceased continued to have many of the same basic needs they had when they were alive, especially for food and drink. Unless these needs were met, the dead would find existence in Sheol to be unending misery. Such a close connection between feeding the dead through funerary offerings and their happiness in the afterlife is well attested in Mesopotamia and Egypt. It is assumed that Israelite funerary practices were similar and included long-term, regular provision of food and drink offerings for the dead.

Other scholars have pointed out the lack of evidence in the Bible for such funerary offerings. Two passages often quoted in reference to such offerings, Deuteronomy 26.14 and Psalm 106.28, are ambiguous and can be interpreted in different ways. Archaeological evidence from Iron Age tombs suggests that food and drink were provided at the tomb only when the *burial took place. There is no evidence for regular post-funeral offerings of food at tombs in Israel. It is possible that the Israelites assumed that Sheol had its own food supply, and that the food placed in the tomb was conceived as provisions for the journey of the deceased to Sheol, but this is speculative.

Virtually no discussion of what existence in Sheol was thought to be like is preserved in preexilic literature. The few datable texts in the Bible that describe Sheol tend to be late and belong to authors who opposed important aspects of the popular view. They present Sheol in negative terms, as a place of darkness and gloom, where the dead exist without thought, strength, or even consciousness (Ps. 88.3–12; Isa. 38.18–19; Job 10.21–22; Eccles. 9.10).

These texts appear to be reactions against a considerably more positive view of existence in Sheol that was held in the preexilic period. There is evidence that many Israelites thought that the dead continued to play an active role in the world of the living, possessing the power to grant blessings to their relatives and to reveal the future. This was done through the process of necromancy, the consultation of the dead by a medium, and related practices, which appear to have been quite popular in Israel. Evidence for this is found in the substantial number of vehement denunciations of necromancy in the prophetic and legal literature of the eighth through sixth centuries BCE (e.g., Lev. 19.31; 20.6, 27; Deut. 18.10–14; Isa 8.19–20). Only one narrative account of a necromantic session has been preserved in the Bible—the story of *Samuel's ghostly consultation with *Saul at Endor (1 Sam. 28), and Saul is roundly criticized by the seventh-century editor of the books of Samuel for having resorted to this practice (see Witch).

Necromancy was particularly opposed by the religious group that supported the worship of Yahweh alone. This group argued that blessings and the telling of the future were prerogatives of Yahweh, not of the dead, and that consulta-

tion with the dead for such purposes was an abomination against Yahweh. The popular views of afterlife and the dead came under increasing attack during the late eighth and seventh centuries. The laws against necromancy date to this period, and a number of outright attacks and satires on the older ideas about the nature of existence in Sheol appear in the literature of the time (e.g., Isa. 8.19–22; 14:9–11). It is interesting to note, however, that the laws against necromancy in Deuteronomy and Leviticus still assume not that it was impossible to summon the dead from Sheol but that it was inappropriate.

These laws apparently did not have the desired effect on the Judean population. During the exile, when the "Yahweh alone" party finally came to control the religious leadership of Judah, a further step was taken. Several texts appearing to date from the exilic and postexilic periods suggest that it is not only improper to consult the dead but actually impossible to do so. A new theology developed that argued there is no conscious existence in Sheol at all. At death all contact with the world, and even with God, comes to an end. This notion explicitly appears in several late Psalms (6.5; 30.8–10; 88.3–12; etc.), Job (3.11–19; 14.10–14; 21.19–21), and Ecclesiastes (9.3–10). This startling idea was not new in the Near East. Skepticism about the afterlife is found in some Egyptian texts as early as the Middle Kingdom (ca. 2000–1750 BCE), but such notions were never adopted as an official doctrine there. In postexilic Judah, however, this became the authoritative stance of the religious leadership, though it was probably not widely held by most Judeans.

WAYNE T. PITARD

Second Temple Judaism and
Early Christianity

In the postexilic period, and particularly in the Hellenistic period following the conquest of *Alexander the Great in 332 BCE, Jewish thought concerning *death and afterlife underwent a major change, owing to the widespread influence of the Platonic idea of the immortality of the soul (see Human Person). Whereas prior to the period of the Hellenistic empires the official religious stance of Israel acknowledged some form of shadowy existence in Sheol for the person after death (see Hell; also the previous article in this entry), beginning in the third century we find a flowering of literature describing the fate of the human soul after death, often in vivid and moving terms. This change is best illustrated by two passages from the *wisdom literature. The book of Ecclesiastes (ca. third century BCE) illustrates the dominant view at the end of the *exile: "Whoever is joined with all the living has hope, for a living dog is better than a dead lion. The living know that they will die, but the dead know nothing; they have no more reward, and even the memory of them is lost. . . . Whatever your hand finds to do, do with your might; for there is no work or thought or knowledge or wisdom in Sheol, to which you are going" (Eccles. 9.4–5, 10). The Wisdom of Solomon, written during the Hellenistic period, shows strong influence of Greek, especially *Stoic, thought: "God created us for incorruption, and made us in the image of his own eternity, but through the devil's envy death entered the world, and those who belong to his company experience it. But the souls of the righteous are in the hand of God, and no torment will ever touch them. In the sight of the foolish they seemed to have died, and their departure was thought to be a disaster, and their going from us to be their destruction; but they are at peace. For though in the sight of others they were punished, their hope is full of immortality" (Wisd. of Sol. 2.23–3.4).

Two ideas concerning the fate of the soul after death were held in tension during the Hellenistic and Roman periods. The first was that of resurrection, that is, that at the end of time the soul would be rejoined with the body and each person would then receive reward or punishment. The concept is found in the Hebrew Bible only at Daniel 12.2: "And many of those who sleep in the dust of the earth shall awake, some to everlasting life, and some to shame and everlasting contempt." A modification of this idea was that only the righteous dead would be resurrected to share in the messianic age.

The second idea was that the immortal soul lived on after the death of the body, and immediately received its reward or punishment. This idea is vividly illustrated in the Testament of Abraham (ca. 100 CE), which depicts the judgment of souls after death. Each soul is brought before Abel, son of *Adam, for judgment. The deeds of the soul are weighed in the balance; the righteous receive salvation, but the wicked are given over to fiery torments (Test. Abr. 12–13).

The tension between these two ideas continued in rabbinic Judaism and early Christianity. References to the rabbis' views of the afterlife are scattered, but may be summarized thus: at death, the soul leaves the body, but may return from time to time until the body disintegrates.

The righteous souls go to *paradise, but the wicked to hell. Finally, in the messianic age there will be a bodily resurrection.

In early Christianity, the tension of the "already" of immortality and the "not yet" of resurrection continued to exist, but was transformed by the death and *resurrection of Jesus. This is best illustrated by the teaching of Paul: "But if Christ is in you, though the body is dead because of sin, the spirit is life because of righteousness. If the Spirit of him who raised Jesus from the dead dwells in you, he who raised Christ from the dead will give life to your mortal bodies also through his Spirit that dwells in you" (Rom. 8.10–12). In certain groups, such as the community of John, the notion of the bodily resurrection was overridden by the spiritual life of the believer in Christ: "Very truly, I tell you, anyone who hears my word and believes him who sent me has eternal life, and does not come under judgment, but has passed from death to life" (John 5.24). Neither view has become dominant, and both continue to exist in tension in Judaism and Christianity until the present.

See also Heaven.   SIDNIE ANN WHITE

Agrapha (Extracanonical Sayings of Jesus). Since the publication of J. G. Körner's *De sermonibus Christi "agraphois"* (1778), "agrapha" (literally "unwritten things") has become the name for sayings attributed to *Jesus, but not found (i.e., "not written") in the canonical *Gospels. Interest in collecting such sayings started in the sixteenth century, but Alfred Resch was the first to present the results of a systematic research in 1889. His extensive collection of more than three hundred extracanonical sayings has been substantially enriched in the twentieth century by new manuscript discoveries.

Sources. Within the New Testament, but outside the Gospels, there are a few sayings attributed to Jesus (Acts 1.4–8; 11.16; 20.35; cf. 1 Cor. 7.10 and 1 Thess. 4.15). Some sayings, though transmitted in some manuscripts of the Gospels, have not been adopted into the *canon, and have been relegated to the critical apparatus of the various editions of the Greek New Testament (e.g., Matt. 6.13; 20.28; Mark 9.49 [codex D]; Luke 6.5 [codex D]; 9.55–56a; 11.2c [codex 700]; John 6.56 [codex D]). The fragmentary papyri (especially those from Oxyrhynchus in Egypt) discovered since the end of the nineteenth century, and the more extensive apocryphal gospels (especially the *gnostic gospels discovered in 1945 at *Nag Hammadi), contain a rich collection of "logia." The most important is the Gospel of Thomas; other gnostic writings containing revelations and hymns also provide a large range of peculiar sayings. Numerous church fathers, from the second century on, quote words of Jesus that are only partially present in the Gospels, if at all. A few words have been found in ancient liturgies and church orders. The *Talmud preserves two unparalleled sayings of Jesus ('Abod. Zar. 16b, 17a; Šabb. 116 a–b). The *Qurʾān and later Islamic writings also refer to several unknown sayings.

Origin. Oral tradition preceded and even for some time accompanied the written tradition of the Gospels. Therefore, in principle at least, some ancient sayings may have survived in oral form even after the Gospels were written, and later authors may have integrated them into their works. But it is also likely that an important figure like Jesus himself became the center of a creative tradition. Others' statements were attributed to him, and new sayings were created.

Evaluation. Taking into account the plurality of sources, spread over several centuries, there is naturally a great variety among the agrapha. They vary from possibly authentic sayings, through adaptations and combinations of sayings from the Gospels, to pure fantasy and tendentious creations. Several of them have been forged for a particular situation, for example, to support with Jesus' own authority a later (orthodox or heretical) concept or practice.

Each saying is in some way a witness to a certain concept and a particular setting. Certain collections, especially the gnostic logia, provide valuable information about various tendencies in early Christianity. In most cases, differences from the form and content of the canonical sayings, together with some evident peculiarity, clearly exclude authenticity. Among the several hundred agrapha, only a few have some chance of being really ancient and perhaps authentic. This complex documentation, therefore, adds little to a better knowledge of the historical Jesus or the earliest Christian tradition.

Examples of agrapha that have often been thought to be authentic sayings of Jesus are:

"Be approved money changers."

"The one who is near me is near the fire; the one who is far from me is far from the kingdom."

"No one can obtain the kingdom of heaven who has not passed through temptation."

"There shall be divisions and heresies."

JOËL DELOBEL

Agriculture. In the Bible agriculture and religion are intimately connected. Of the three major festivals two were clearly connected with the agricultural year. The Feast of Weeks was associated with the first fruits and the end of the grain harvest. The Feast of Booths was an occasion of joy at the completion of the harvesting of fruits. Some have connected the *Passover with the beginning of the grain harvest. (See also Feasts and Festivals.) Furthermore, the poetic imagery of the Bible is heavily freighted with agricultural *metaphors. The blessing of God was perceived in agricultural abundance and his cursing in drought. The golden age was described in terms of agricultural productivity. The singer in the *Song of Solomon uses agricultural images to portray his beloved. Renewal for the author of the later part of Isaiah (chaps. 40–66) was expressed visually in miraculous agricultural phenomena. Jesus' teachings include many agricultural metaphors. The New Testament often uses agricultural images for the church.

Water. Palestine has almost no rain for six months of the year (15 April to 15 October). In late October and November the "early rain" begins. Precipitation then slackens in December and January only to intensify again in March (the "later rain"). The *Mishnah prescribes a series of fasts if the rain fails to appear in October and November (m. Taʿan. 1.4–7). The dew in May and June triggers the final ripening process of the grain and renders the stalks soft enough to facilitate reaping.

Snow usually falls each winter on the hill country. The snow is seen as a special blessing and is called in Arabic "the salt of the earth." It kills the insects and is absorbed rather than running off. From ancient times there has been some irrigation from the *Jordan River, from its tributaries, and from the great spring of En-gedi. (See also Geography of Palestine; Water.)

Land Preparation. The soil is rich and deep in the valleys, but most of the land is rocky hills that must be terraced to be used for agriculture. Solid rock is but a few inches below the surface. A wall is built on the slope, then stones are removed and earth carried in to level the ground (see Isa. 5.1–2). Thus the rocky ground in the parable of the sower indicates an area where the soil covering is too thin to support a mature plant (Luke 8.6). Plowing is done with a light one-handled plow. The farmer's other hand holds a thin pole with a small spade on one end used for cleaning the plow point and a spike on the other end used for driving the oxen. The point of the plow is covered with iron. This metal sleeve is held together with strips of iron about the shape of a sword (cf. Isa. 2.4). After plowing, the large clods are generally broken up with heavy hoes. The land is plowed in preparation for the rain. After the first rains the seed is scattered by hand, and then the seed is covered by a second plowing. If this second plowing is done carelessly the birds will eat the seeds (see Luke 8.5). Grain is cut by hand and transported to threshing floors near the villages.

The Farmer's Enemies. Drought was an ever-present threat. A locust plague was rare (Joel 1.2–4) but devastating. There were no sprays for blight (see Amos 4.9). Fire could destroy a crop at harvest time. The hot southeast desert winds of May and June can critically damage a number of crops. Thus, remembering past losses, the farmer would "sow in tears" (Ps. 126.5–6).

Crops. Among the food-producing trees, the hardy olive bears fruit each year after six months of drought. The oil was used for food, medicine, soap, and light. Figs were a major source of sugar. The tree's deep shade was a convenient place to study (John 1.48); it symbolized peace (Mic. 4.4). The sycamore fig is small and taste-less; only the poor dress and gather them (see Amos 7.14). The tasty red pomegranate grows on a large shrub; this fruit is referred to meta-phorically in love poetry (Song of Sol. 4.3). The almond blooms first in the spring (see Jer. 1.11–12). The word apple (quince?) figures promi-nently in the Song of Solomon. A tasty molasses is boiled out of carob pods, and the remaining husks become animal feed (Luke 15.16). Date palms flourished in the Jordan valley.

The common grains were wheat, barley, and spelt (KJV: rye). The wheat was cut and trans-ported to the threshing floor where it was sys-tematically trodden by animals and flailed with sticks or crushed with a threshing sledge. The latter is made of two wide boards joined on the top with two cross arms. The bottom is embed-ded with rows of sharp-edged flint nodules. The sledge is dragged by animals in a circle over the wheat with the driver standing on the sledge to add weight. Occasionally pieces of iron were used rather than flint (Amos 1.3). The wheat was then winnowed by throwing it into the air on a windy day (Ps. 1.4; Luke 3.17). Finally the wheat was put through a sieve to remove the remaining impurities (see Luke 22.31). Flax was grown for *clothing and rope. Sesame produced cooking oil. Lentils and chick-peas supple-mented the protein available. Onions, garlic, cu-cumbers, and melons were among the vegetables cultivated. Herbs included mint and cumin. The Mishnah lists the bitter herbs to be eaten at Passover as lettuce, chicory, pepperwort, snake-root, and dandelion (*m. Pesaḥ.* 2.6).

See also Plants; Trade and Transport; Vine and Vineyard.   KENNETH E. BAILEY

Ahab. The son and successor of Omri, Ahab ruled as one of Israel's most powerful kings from roughly 873 to 851 BCE. After expanding the summit of *Samaria, his capital city, he con-structed a massive casemate fortification wall en-closing lavishly appointed royal buildings, in-cluding the "ivory house" (1 Kings 22.39). Ahab brought Israel to the fore of international poli-tics by marrying the Sidonian princess *Jezebel (1 Kings 16:31), fighting protracted wars against the *Arameans of *Damascus (1 Kings 20), struggling for hegemony over Transjordan (1 Kings 22; *Moabite Stone), and participating in the anti-Assyrian league at Qarqar in the Orontes Valley (Assyrian records). But deeply rooted north-south tensions and the Judahite perspec-tive of the final *Deuteronomic history resulted in a critical treatment of Ahab in the Bible (1 Kings 16.29–22.40); narratives describing the antagonism between Ahab and the prophet *Eli-jah (1 Kings 17–19) constitute the sharpest po-lemic against him.

See also Israel, History of.   RON TAPPY

Alexander III ("The Great"). Macedonian, born in 356 BCE. After the assassination of his father, Philip II, at Aegae in 336, Alexander ascended to the throne and took over his father's plan of a crusade to punish the *Persians for Xerxes' invasion of Greece almost a century and a half earlier. Alexander crossed the Hellespont with a total force of about fifty thousand in 334 and defeated the Persian army in three major battles, the last in 331.

These victories opened the heart of the Per-sian empire to Alexander. Persepolis was sacked and the palace of Xerxes burned. From Perse-polis and Media, Alexander conquered Bactria and Sogdiana (330–329) and then extended his eastern frontier to the Hyphasis (Beas) and the lower Indus River (327–325). At the Hyphasis, the Macedonian army refused to march farther east. From the Indus Delta, Alexander marched west with part of his army across the Gedrosian desert, where his army suffered great losses during the fall of 325. He reached Susa in March of 324, where he and ninety-one members of his court married wives from the Persian nobility. During the final year of his life, Alexander discharged ten thousand Macedonian veterans at Opis, and then at *Babylon, in 323, made plans for future conquests (especially Arabia). He died, probably of a fever following a drinking party, on 10 June 323.

Alexander undoubtedly was the greatest general in Greek history; he made the army forged by his father into an irresistible force by a combination of uncanny strategic insight, versatility, and courage beyond reason. The cities he founded (reportedly over seventy) planted pockets of Hellenism throughout the Near East. He also made monarchy central to the politics of the Greek world; his kin and generals fought to establish themselves as his heir until about 275, when there emerged the three kingdoms that dominated the eastern Mediterranean until the advance of Rome: Macedon, ruled by the Antigonids until 168 BCE; *Egypt, ruled by the Ptolemies until 31 BCE; and *Syria, ruled by the Seleucids until 64 BCE. It is against the background of the origins of the Seleucid dynasty that the author of 1 *Maccabees presents a sketch of Alexander's conquests (1.1–7) and the character of Antiochus Epiphanes (1.10–64).

GUY MacLEAN ROGERS

Alien. Also translated "sojourner," "resident alien," and "stranger," an alien (Hebr. *gēr*) is technically a person in a community who is not part of its traditional lineages. In the Hebrew Bible, "aliens" usually are non-Israelites living ("sojourning") in Israel (Exod. 12.19; Isa. 16.4; Jer. 42.15), but they can also be Israelites of one tribe "sojourning" in the territory of another tribe (Judg. 19.16; 2 Sam. 4.3; 2 Chron. 15.9). Such persons were often financially distressed, forced to be dependents of "native" residents (but see Lev. 25.45, 47). Thus, aliens are often mentioned alongside *widows, *orphans, and the *poor as typically in need of assistance (Deut. 24.17–21; Jer. 7.6; Zech. 7.10). Aliens could be subjected to manual labor (Deut 29.11); yet, special attention is given to accord them equal status with native Israelites (Num. 15.14–16; Ezek. 47.21–23), making them corecipients of God's blessings (Deut. 10.18) and curses (Num. 15.26; Deut. 31.12; Josh. 8.35). The Israelites are commanded to treat aliens well, because they were once aliens in Egypt (Exod. 22.21; 23.9; Deut.

10.19). In fact, they are to view themselves as aliens "sojourning" on God's land (Lev. 25.23; 1 Chron. 29.15; Ps. 39.12), thereby furthering their sense of dependence on God.

New Testament writers describe their Israelite ancestors as aliens in Egypt (Acts 7.6; 13.17) and the exile in Babylon as the time of "sojourning" (Matt. 1.11, 12, 17). In dealing with the problem of incorporating *gentiles into an all-Jewish community, Paul says that they are "no longer strangers and aliens, but . . . citizens . . . of the household of God" (Eph. 2.19). Any hint of separation is thereby eliminated. On the other hand, all who have become members of God's "people" must disavow allegiance to other groups, considering themselves aliens in the world around them (1 Pet. 2.11). In this regard, *Abraham is held up as an ancient model (Heb. 11.9; cf. Gen. 23.4).

TIMOTHY M. WILLIS

Allegorizing. *See* Interpretation, History of, *article on* Early Christian Interpretation; Typology.

Alleluia. *See* Hallelujah.

Alms. There is no word for "alms" or "almsgiving" in the Hebrew Bible, and there are almost no specific references to the practice of giving alms as such. Generosity to the *poor and needy was, however, required and praised (see, e.g., Deut. 15.11; Job 29.11–16). There are many commands to show benevolence to the poor, a group that included *Levites, foreigners living among Israelites (*see* Alien), *widows, and *orphans, for whom there was also a special *tithe (Deut. 14.28–29). Those who gave to the poor were thought to be blessed or happy (see Ps. 41.1; Prov. 14.21, 31; 31.20; cf. CD 6.21; 14.13–15).

The Greek word for alms is *eleēmosynē*, which comes from the basic verb *eleeō*, meaning "to pity" or "have mercy on" someone. In the *Septuagint *eleēmosynē* frequently translates the Hebrew words for "loving kindness" (*hesed*) and "*righteousness" (*ṣĕdāqâ*) (Deut. 6.25; 24.13; Prov. 3.3; 14.22). It is used of both God (Ps. 103.6; Isa. 1.27) and humans (Gen. 47.29; Prov. 20.28) having mercy toward others. Almsgiving came to be regarded as a particular form of righteousness (Tob. 1.3) and could gain merit and forgiveness of sins for the giver (Dan. 4.24; Sir. 3.30; Tob. 12.9).

In the New Testament *eleēmosynē* is always used in the sense of giving alms. In the *Sermon on the Mount piety and almsgiving are synonymous (Matt. 6.1–4). Elsewhere *eleēmosynē* occurs in the New Testament only in Luke and Acts, where it refers either to the gift or to the process of giving. In Luke 11.41 and 12.33 the expression "give alms" corresponds to the rabbinic "give righteousness" (*'Abot* 5.15; cf. Matt. 19.21; see also Acts 9.36; 10.2, 31). Paul exhorted his communities to make special efforts to remember the poor (1 Cor. 16.1–3; 2 Cor. 8–9; cf. Acts 24.17).   EDWIN D. FREED

Alpha and Omega. The first and last letters of the Greek alphabet, spoken in the book of *Revelation to John as the self-disclosure of God (Rev. 1.8; 21.6) and also of Jesus Christ (Rev. 22.13). Letters of the Greek alphabet could have numerical value, though in Revelation the focus is on the full scope of divine concern and control. "Alpha and Omega" refers to God's place at the beginning of the world, as its creator, and at the end, as its judge. John the Seer's use of these terms evokes the language of the *prophets, like Isaiah 44.6: "Thus says the LORD . . . I am the first and the last; besides me there is no god." Other New Testament writers discuss Jesus's role in the world's origin, alluding to the *creation account in Genesis (John 1; Col. 1.15–20; Phil. 2.6–11), and at its final judgment (Matt. 24).
                    PHILIP SELLEW

Altars. References to altars appear in the Bible some four hundred times, including their construction, materials (e.g., unhewn stone, wood, earth, brass/bronze, gold), types (especially for burnt offerings in the majority of cases, with a smaller number of references to incense altars), ritual acts (especially the slaughter and burning of animal sacrifices, and the sprinkling of blood), associated fixtures and paraphernalia (e.g., staves, rings, grates, horns, and vessels used), as well as more casual aspects.

The ordinary Hebrew word for altar is *mizbēaḥ*, meaning "slaughtering place"; the Greek word *thusiastērion* has a similar meaning. In biblical and nonbiblical traditions, an altar is not a natural object but rather a built structure. It is not inhabited by a supernatural force, though it attracts that force; thus, the altar is not the same as a sacred stone.

In biblical narrative, altars are built at a location where divine-human contact has been, or presumably could be, encountered. They are not habitation places; rather, they provide cultic access to the deity. They may be overturned, displaced, or rebuilt without any impact upon their use or meaning. Profaning them does not, therefore, affect the deity; instead, it precludes their use for proper ritual access, at least temporarily.

The altar in the Bible is a constructed platform, initially intended for slaughtering sacrifices for the God of Israel next to or upon its surface, who would visit the site regardless of its location (see Exod. 20.24). An altar, then, could be located anywhere needful or appropriate, and its installation and purpose would be accepted by the deity. Thus, the early proliferation of such installations posed no theological problem. It was only when, due to sociopolitical necessity, the cult was centralized at the *Temple in *Jerusalem and exclusive access to the deity was located there, that, theoretically at least, other altars were no longer permitted.

Other aspects of altars were similarly rather loosely conceived. How an altar was to be constructed—its materials, its permanency of location, and even its precise use—seem not to have been uniformly fixed. In all probability, the occasional demand for simplicity (e.g., unhewn stone for construction) can be explained only on the basis of real or fictive practice acquiring the weight of tradition, and therefore becoming proper, or on the basis of anachronistic insistence on purity.

The variation in types of altars, and the precise ritual involved for each, is perfectly explicable on both developmental and institutional grounds, as the cult developed in sophistication. However, the generic altar continued to be a point of access to the deity, regardless of the specific sacrifice made upon it to attract divine attention.

Other uses of the altar, such as a place of sanctuary or asylum place (see 1 Kings 1.50–53; 2.28–34), or for the declaration of binding oaths (Josh. 22.26–28, 34), are secondary. Since the deity could be met at altars, divine protection or divine witness could be sought at the same location.

Certain altars, especially those constructed or repaired by important people, are specifically mentioned in the Bible, either to enhance the concept, or because of the prominence of their builders. The idea of altar construction is thus carried back to *Noah (Gen. 8.20), with subsequent reinforcement of the tradition attributed to *Abraham and others of the ancestral family.

Several kings, likewise, are singled out for having performed the same pious act: *Saul, *David, *Solomon, and other monarchs are specifically noted.

Just as construction and use varied through time, the correct rituals for offering *sacrifices varied. Various references deal with sprinkling or pouring the *blood of slaughtered animals upon the altar, upon its "horns" or sides, and to burning the entire sacrifice or only the fat upon it. Uniformity developed principally with the centralization of the cult, and was read back into the time of *Moses and *Aaron in order to authenticate the practice.

The appearance of altars is complicated by references to "horns" (e.g., Exod. 29.12; 1 Kings 1.50; Amos 3.14). When these appurtenances first appear is difficult to judge, as is their precise use. On the basis of archaeological finds from somewhat later periods, these corner uprights may have served to support vessels containing the sacrifices, beneath which the coals of the altar were placed on grates. Such a utilitarian construction would have facilitated cleaning, as well as the actual placement of various kinds of offerings on separate occasions. This view is supported to some extent by references to the vessels of the altars as separate items.

PHILIP C. HAMMOND

Amalek. One of Israel's most unrelenting enemies, at least in the early periods, Amalek is first referred to in Abraham's day, in Genesis 14.7, which speaks of the Amalekite field. But later in Genesis (36.12), Amalek is made the son of Eliphaz, son of *Esau, rendering the earlier reference anachronistic.

Shortly after the *Exodus, the Amalekites attacked Israel (Exod. 17.8–16), but Israel succeeded in repulsing the attack. The enmity created is reflected in the bloodthirsty declaration "I will blot out the name of Amalek. . . . The Lord's war against Amalek is from generation to generation" (Exod. 17.14, 16; see Deut. 25.17–19).

The Amalekites raided the Israelites in the days of the judges (Judg. 3.13; 6.3, 33; etc.). Later, King *Saul made a concerted effort to destroy Amalek, following the prophet *Samuel's call for the *ban (1 Sam. 15), but enough Amalekites survived to destroy *David's city of Ziklag (1 Sam. 30.1). Nevertheless, after Ziklag the Amalekites ceased to trouble Israel. 1 Chronicles 4.42–43 depicts the tribe of *Simeon as

eradicating the remnant of Amalek, fulfilling God's earlier promise.   PHILIP STERN

Amarna Letters. Discovered in 1887, the archive of El-Amarna in *Egypt has yielded 379 cuneiform tablets that are among the most precious finds of Near Eastern archaeology. Tell el-Amarna, located about 500 km (310 mi) up the Nile from the Mediterranean, is the modern name of ancient Akhetaten, King Akhnaton's capital. The letters constitute diplomatic correspondence from the reigns of Amenophis III and Akhnaton in the first half of the fourteenth century BCE. Except for two in *Hittite and one in Hurrian (see Nuzi Tablets, The), their language is Babylonian. Some are from the rulers of the other great powers of the day—*Babylonia, *Assyria, Mitanni, and Hatti—but most are written by Egyptian vassals in *Canaan and Syria. The former group largely concerns exchanges of ambassadors and expensive gifts, but the letters from Canaanite vassals bespeak a period of unrest, as the vassal kings, caught in the power struggles of the great kingdoms, form short-lived coalitions against one another. The texts frequently refer to a disruptive group called the ḫapiru (pronounced ʿapiru), a word equated by many with the Hebrew ʿibrî, "Hebrew" (see Hebrews, The). Although the name may be the same, the nature of the ʿapiru precludes a simple identification with the Israelites. Scholars are divided on whether the term refers properly to a specific people or to a social class; most see them as militant outcasts, that is, as brigands or mercenaries. We also read of the depredations of the Syrian kingdom of Amurru, later to give its name to the *Amorites of the Bible. The Amarna letters describe the vicissitudes of cities such as *Hazor, Akko, *Megiddo, Taanach, *Shechem, *Gezer, Ashkelon, Gaza, *Lachish, and *Jerusalem in the pre-Israelite period. Because the Canaanite scribes had an imperfect command of Babylonian, their lapses have also taught scholars much about their native dialects, and thus about the prehistory of the closely related *Hebrew language.

Though they do not mention the still inchoate Israelites, the Amarna letters are an invaluable window on the world from which Israel was to emerge in the following century.

WILLIAM H. PROPP

Amen. A Hebrew word meaning "certainly" or "may it be so." In the Hebrew Bible *amen* appears as a response to someone else's statement. Sometimes it appears in a liturgical setting as a response of the people (Deut. 27.15–26; Ps. 106.48), sometimes as a solemn response to another person's statement (1 Kings 1.36; Jer. 28.6 [an ironic response]), sometimes as a response to God's word (Jer. 11.5). The doubled form, *amen, amen* (Num. 5.22; Neh. 8.6) also occurs; compare "*amen* and *amen*" (Ps. 41.13). *Amen* may be used as a substantive: "the God of *amen*" = "the God of faithfulness" (Isa. 65.16); this meaning is reflected in the New Testament (Rev. 3.14).

The Hebrew *amen* was retained among early Greek-speaking Christians as a confirmatory response to prayer, whether one's own (Rom. 16.27) or someone else's (1 Cor. 14.16). This continues in Christian liturgical usage.

In the speech of Jesus in the Gospels, *amen* often appears not as a closing response but as an opening affirmation of the validity and seriousness of what follows: "*Amen* ('Truly') I tell you . . ." (Matt. 5.18). In the Gospel of John, the *amen* that frequently introduces Jesus' speech is doubled: "*Amen, amen* ('Truly, truly' [NRSV: 'Very truly']) I say to you . . ." (John 1.51; etc.). The opening *amen* indicates the solemn claim of the speaker to authority. Many scholars see in this introductory *amen* a clear reflection of Jesus' sense of his own authority. The introductory *amen* was not completely new in the words of Jesus, however; there are a few instances of similar speech in contemporary sources. It is possible, however, that the language of early Christian worship influenced these passages.

WILLIAM A. BEARDSLEE

American Literature. *See* Literature and the Bible, *article on* North American Literature.

Ammon. A tribal state located to the east of the *Jordan River (Map 1:Y-Z4) that played a marginally significant role in the history of Palestine during the Iron Age. Relatively little is known about Ammon, its history, and its culture. Our main sources of information about it are the Bible and Assyrian inscriptions, both of which deal almost exclusively with Ammon's external affairs. Only a few substantive Ammonite inscriptions have been discovered so far, and excavations are just beginning to illuminate Ammonite culture.

The origins of the tribe of Ammon are obscure. Genesis 19:30–38 presents an artificial and satiric legend that portrays the eponymous ancestor of the Ammonites, Ben-ammi, as the offspring of the incestuous union of *Lot and his daughter. But this provides no insight into the initial development of Ammon. The region that became the land of Ammon was occupied fairly densely during the Middle and Late Bronze Ages, but there is no evidence whether the tribe of Ammon was already a distinct ethnic group during that time.

By the early part of the Iron Age (ca. 1200–1000 BCE), however, both archaeological and literary evidence indicates that a somewhat centralized state began to form around the capital city of Rabbat-bene-ammon ("Rabbah of the sons of Ammon"; modern Amman, Jordan). Conflict arose during this period between the Ammonites and the Israelites who lived to the east of the Jordan River (Judg. 11 and 1 Sam. 11). The earliest Ammonite king whose name is preserved is Nahash, who besieged the Israelite town of Jabesh-gilead and was defeated by Israelite troops rallied by the young *Saul (1 Sam. 11). Nahash's son, Hanun, provoked a war with Israel during the reign of *David, which led to Ammon's defeat and incorporation into David's empire as a vassal (2 Sam. 10; 12.26–31).

After the death of *Solomon and the breakup of the united kingdom of Israel, Ammon presumably became independent again. Little is known of the kingdom during the ninth century, but it likely came under the domination of *Aram-Damascus, especially during the reign of Hazael (ca. 842–800 BCE), as did most of Palestine. During the eighth century, Damascus declined, and Israel and Judah experienced a resurgence of political power. Ammon appears to have come under the control of Judah during the reigns of Uzziah and Jotham (2 Chron. 26.8; 27.5), but with the arrival of the Assyrian king *Tiglath-pileser III, Ammon, like the other small kingdoms, became an Assyrian vassal.

The Assyrian period (late eighth to late seventh century) was a prosperous period for Ammon. The Assyrians guaranteed its position on the international trade routes and helped protect its flanks from the various nomadic groups that threatened the security of the routes. Excavations and Assyrian texts indicate that Ammon extended its boundaries during this period, westward to the Jordan River, northward into Gilead, and southward toward Heshbon. The most substantial ruins of the Iron Age date to this period, and seals, inscriptions, and statuary indicate the kingdom's wealth. A number of stone towers found in several regions of Ammon appear to date to this period. Once thought to be a system of Ammonite fortresses, recent studies now identify most of them as agricultural towers such as the one described in Isaiah 5.2.

There is uncertainty about the situation of Ammon during the Neo-Babylonian period. It is probable that Ammon was involved in the great rebellion against *Nebuchadrezzar in 589–586 BCE, and that, as a result, it was annexed into the Babylonian provincial system. By the succeeding Persian period only the name of the kingdom of Ammon survived, largely as a geographical rather than as a political term (Map 10:Y5). Recent excavations and surveys indicate that a modest population continued to inhabit the region through this period.

Ammonite religion and culture remain little known. Even the characteristics of its patron deity, Milcom, are uncertain.

WAYNE T. PITARD

Amorites. The Amorites were among the original inhabitants of *Canaan before the Israelite *conquest, along with *Hittites, Canaanites, *Jebusites, and others (Gen. 15.18–21). The entire aboriginal population of Canaan is also called "Amorite" (Gen. 15.13–16), and *Jerusalem was perhaps an Amorite town (Ezek. 16.3). There were Amorites east of the *Jordan River at Heshbon in *Ammon (Num. 21.25–26) and at Bashan in Gilead (Josh. 2.10; 1 Kings 4.19). These were related to the Ammonites of central Transjordan, but not to the *Moabites or *Edomites in the south (Num. 21.13).

The Bible mentions Amorites as settled in Canaan and Transjordan. These were elements of an earlier, larger, more diverse Amorite group that originated apparently in the *Euphrates region of eastern Syria. Cuneiform texts of the third millennium BCE refer to a land west of the Euphrates known as MAR.TU in Sumerian or *Amurru* in Akkadian. Amurru included Syria and possibly parts of Palestine. Its inhabitants were considered foreign to Mesopotamia in language and culture. The Amorite language belongs to the linguistic family of Northwest Semitic, like *Ugaritic, *Aramaic, and *Hebrew, and Amorite material culture in Syria shows affinities with that of Palestine in the Middle Bronze Age (first half of the second millennium BCE). *Mari, a second-millennium Syrian city on the Euphrates, can be considered an Amorite town, though the

Akkadian-language Mari texts do not refer to the city's inhabitants specifically as "Amorites." Some Amorites were not town-dwellers but *nomads, and the Mari texts frequently mention one such group, the "Banu-yamina," who resembled, in name and nomadic habits, the later biblical Benjaminites (Gen. 49.27).

JOSEPH A. GREENE

Amos, The Book of. The early prophets of Israel—*Samuel, *Elijah, *Elisha, and many others—are known from stories included in the historical books of *Samuel and *Kings. Amos was the first of the prophets whose name goes with a book entirely concerned with his life and message; nothing is known about him from any other source. The composition of his prophecy represented the creation of a new kind of literature. It was followed by other books that carry the names of a succession of prophets: three large books ("major" prophets) and twelve small ones ("minor").

The authors behind these shorter books were by no means "minor" in stature. Amos himself is one of the giants of the ancient world, one of the most powerful of the biblical prophets. He brought the prophetic word against social injustice and international terrorism and he preached repentance—and, when that failed, he denounced the impenitents. As a visionary ("seer": 1.1; 7.12) he located the domestic wrongs within Israel, and the crimes within the community of nations in a global, indeed cosmic setting. He held the rulers responsible for the evils in the world (1.3–2.16) and addressed his messages primarily to them. He placed Israel, the *chosen people of Yahweh, on the same footing as other nations (3.9; 4.11; 6.2; 9.7). God expects the same morality from them all; but the words of reproach, condemnation, and judgment are addressed most directly to Israel because of its domestic wrongs.

Amos was not only a prophet of doom; he also called the people to reform, and when they failed and disaster became inescapable, he pointed to the hope of future restoration (9.11–15).

Amos's career is set in the time of two kings, Uzziah of Judah and Jeroboam II of Israel. Both monarchs had exceptionally long reigns, covering most of the first half of the eighth century BCE. Many scholars date Amos toward the end of that period (about 750 BCE), or even later; but recent research into the political situation disclosed by the book suggests that it could be earlier than that. *Assyria is nowhere recognized as a factor (except in the *Septuagint text of 3.9), and the six nations surrounding Israel are addressed in 1.3–2.3 as if they are all still independent: this more accurately describes the early decades of the eighth century.

On first reading, the literary materials in the book of Amos seem to be diverse and poorly coordinated. There is some narrative in chaps. 7–9, but the main ingredients are prophetic oracles of many different kinds. In addition, the book contains a considerable number of wisdom sayings as well as several liturgical hymns.

The vocabulary and grammar are closer to standard Hebrew prose than to the lyrical poetry of *Psalms, or even to the prophecy in *Hosea. It is, nevertheless, highly rhythmic in form and rhetorical in artistry, a distinctive medium that may be identified as "prophetic oratory." The originally oral message has been transformed into literature by skillful editing that has integrated the variegated material into a coherent composition. The result is a real book. Each constituent oracle may have had a limited application when it was originally delivered, but their arrangement brings these pieces together into a comprehensive statement about Amos's lifework, and one that is of enduring value and significance.

Scholars who expect Amos's message to be consistent, almost uniform, have doubted his authorship of some portions because they differ from the rest. Several of the oracles against the nations (Tyre, Edom, Judah) have been bracketed out by some scholars because they seem more appropriate to later times; but all eight are needed, not only for complete geographical coverage, but also to secure the intricate and remarkably symmetrical design that unifies the great speech of chaps. 1–2 and secures its total impact on ancient hearer and modern reader alike.

The three short poems that celebrate the power of Yahweh in creation and history (4.13; 5.8–9; 9.5–6) are distinct hymnal-credal statements, possibly fragments of earlier epic recitals. They have been skillfully used in the final composition of Amos's message so as to secure a vital theological component. Their scope is cosmic; God's claims on the whole world—all nations, not just Israel—are grounded in his relationship and interest as creator, owner, and judge of the universe.

The historical perspective is likewise vast. God's dealings with Israel are reviewed in the light of events that have taken place over centuries, with the *Exodus as a major point of reference (2.10; 3.1; 5.25; 9.7).

The book falls into three distinct sections, each with its own message and mood. The last, the Book of Visions (7.1–9.8) contains the only narrative material. The autobiographical report of five visions (7.1–9; 8.1–3; 9.1) provides a framework that carries the dramatic report of Amos's confrontation with Amaziah, priest of Bethel (7.10–17), as well as prophetic oracles.

In the first pair of visions (7.1–6), Amos is able to secure a reprieve for Israel by his intercession. This situation, in which there is still some hope, corresponds to the central message of the Book of Woes (5.1–6.14), which is built around the exhortation (at 5.24):

Let justice roll down like waters,
   and righteousness like an everflowing stream.

There is still time for repentance. The plagues reported in chap. 4 were intended as chastisements that would lead to contrition and reparation; but they failed to achieve this, and turned into destructive judgments.

In the second pair of visions (7.7–9; 8.1–3) the situation has completely changed. There is no intercession; rather, the Lord says twice that he will never pass by them again. This new attitude corresponds to the message of certain doom that pervades the first four chapters, and especially the opening speech, with its note of finality. The situation has become hopeless. Amos's early messages, corresponding to the intercessions of the first two visions, have been presented in the middle of the final book (chaps. 5–6); his final message comes first (chaps. 1–2), with the following material analyzing the causes and justifying the decision.

The major cause of the change in attitude between the first and second pairs of visions, the final proof that repentance will never be forthcoming, is the refusal to listen to the prophets, and worse, the attempt to silence them altogether (2.12; 3.8; 7.10–17). Amaziah's ban is the turning point: when the highest religious leader rejects the word of God and his messenger, judgment is inevitable (4.12). The fifth vision and the oracles that go with it (9.1–10) predict the total destruction of "all the sinners of my people" (9.10).

That is not the end of everything, however. As elsewhere in the Bible, death can be overcome by the miracle of resurrection; and Amos promises the recovery of Israel's life and institutions in a new age of prosperity and bliss (9.11–15).

FRANCIS I. ANDERSEN

Ananias. Three different characters in the book of Acts are named Ananias:

(1) A member of the Jerusalem church who violates its communal principles and is struck down after denying the transgression (Acts 5.1–11; cf. Josh. 7).

(2) The disciple who reluctantly restores Saul's vision after the road to Damascus experience (Acts 9.10–19; see Paul).

(3) The high *priest who presides when Paul is brought before the Council in Jerusalem (Acts 23.1–5). Later this Ananias leads a delegation from the Council to the governor in Caesarea to plead for Paul's condemnation (Acts 24.1–23).

DANIEL N. SCHOWALTER

Anathema. A Greek word corresponding to Hebr. *ḥērem* (*see* Ban) and designating an object dedicated or devoted to a deity either for consecration or to be cursed (devoted to destruction). In the former sense, objects were devoted to God and belonged to him (Lev. 27.28); offerings were given to God to adorn the Temple (Luke 21.5). Most occurrences of the term, however, describe something or someone accursed or given to God for destruction. According to Leviticus 27.29, no one who had been devoted to God for destruction could be ransomed, nor could devoted things be used by human beings (Josh. 7.11–15). According to Paul, if someone preaches a gospel contrary to the one that he preached (Gal. 1.8, 9), that person is anathema (NRSV: "cursed"; see also 1 Corinthians 16.22).

In Romans 9.3, Paul affirms his strong ties to the Jewish people and asserts that he is prepared to be "anathema from Christ" (NRSV: "accursed and cut off from Christ"), if that would benefit them—a statement similar in thought to that of Moses being willing to have his name blotted out of God's book for the sake of the Israelites (Exod. 32.32).

Individuals also invoked anathema on themselves to ensure that they would keep an oath (see Acts 23.12, 14, 21, where the Greek verb is a form of *anathema*). Such individuals called on God to curse them if they did not perform the oath they had made.

In later usage, anathema becomes virtually synonymous with excommunication.

See also Curse.   PAUL L. BREMER

Ancestors, The. Genesis 12–50 relates in the fullest form the traditions about the ancestors of Israel, frequently called the patriarchs (*Abraham, *Isaac, and *Jacob) and the matriarchs (*Sarah, *Rebekah, *Leah, *Rachel, Bilhah, and Zilpah). These chapters are part of a larger narrative that covers the period from the *creation of the world (Gen. 1) to the fall of Jerusalem in 587/586 BCE (2 Kings 24–25), and they have the specific purpose of presenting the story of the *Hebrews from their beginnings, with the call of Abraham, to their presence in Egypt following *Joseph's rise to power.

Within Genesis 12–50 can be discerned the Abraham cycle (12.7–25.11), the Isaac cycle (25.19–26.34), the Jacob cycle (27.1–35.29), and the Joseph story (37–48; 50). Each section differs markedly from the others. The Joseph story is a highly artistic and skilled narrative, leading to a climax in which Joseph, the ruler of Egypt, discloses his identity to his brothers, who had sold him into slavery. The Isaac cycle is by far the shortest, and the only one of its narratives that deals exclusively with Isaac (chap. 26) closely resembles two stories about Abraham (12.10–16; 20.1–17). While the Abraham and Jacob cycles show every sign of having been compiled from traditions that were originally separate (*see* Pentateuch), the Jacob cycle has the more integrated narrative structure.

The predominant theological theme that runs through these disparate sections is that of the fulfillment of God's purpose and promise in spite of all hindrances. After God has promised to Abraham that he will become a great nation (12.2), Abraham goes to Egypt, where God must intervene to rescue Sarah from the Pharaoh's harem. Sarah is next presented as being sterile, and in order to get offspring, Abraham considers adoption (15.1–6), only to produce a son by Sarah's Egyptian maid *Hagar (16.1–6). When Sarah finally produces a son it is in her old age (21.1–7); almost immediately (22.1–19), though, Abraham is ordered to offer the son, Isaac, as a sacrifice. Abraham's obedience is rewarded by the sparing of Isaac's life, and the first cycle ends with Rebekah being brought from Abraham's home of northeast *Mesopotamia as a wife for Isaac.

Rebekah is also sterile (25.21), so that her

children, like Sarah's child, are a special divine gift. The Isaac cycle is quickly swallowed up into the conflict between his sons Jacob and *Esau, with the latter threatening the life of Jacob, who is designated as the successor of Abraham and Isaac (chap. 28). In Haran, Abraham's original home to which Jacob flees (chap. 29), Jacob comes into conflict with his uncle Laban, and is tricked into marrying Leah before he can obtain his true love, Rachel. Like Sarah and Rebekah, Rachel turns out to be barren (29.31); the son she eventually does have, Joseph (30.23–24), will later be sold into slavery by his brothers, some of whom would have preferred to kill him (37.18–28). In the meantime Jacob, who has fled from Laban and is returning home, must survive the danger of being reunited with Esau (chaps. 32–33). Prior to this meeting, his name is changed by God to *Israel.

Joseph's words to his brothers, "It was not you who sent me here, but God" (45.8), sums up the main theological theme of the ancestral narratives: God's fulfillment of his purpose and promise. But there are subsidiary themes, prominent among which is God's rejection of parts of Abraham's family. His nephew, *Lot, has two sons who are the ancestors of the nations *Moab and *Ammon; but their rejection is indicated by their incestuous origin (19.30–38). Similarly, Esau, the ancestor of the nation of *Edom, is rejected for marrying non-Hebrew wives (28.34–5, 28.6–9, 36.1–43). Jacob's triumphs over Laban (chaps. 30–31) indicate the rejection of the northeastern branch of the family.

This subsidiary theme no doubt reflects the political realities of the time in which the narratives were being combined, the period of *David or *Solomon. In the tenth century BCE, Ammon, Moab, Edom, and kingdoms to the northeast were subject to Israelite rule (2 Sam. 8.1–14; 10.15–19; 12.26–31). This raises the question of the relation between the ancestors as historical figures and the traditions about them. Although some scholars argue that the ancestral narratives were not written until after the *exile (which is certainly when they reached their final form), a majority would accept that Abraham and Jacob were ancestors around whom traditions gathered in Israel's premonarchic period. It should be noted that Abraham is associated with *Hebron (Gen. 23) while Jacob is connected with Bethel (Gen. 28) and his sons with *Shechem (Gen. 34). This suggests that Abraham was an ancestor of the tribe of *Judah, and had migrated from northeast Mesopotamia together with

groups that later became Moab and Ammon. Jacob was the ancestor of Israel, which was originally an association of tribes, not including Judah, in the central highlands of Canaan. The odd fact that, whereas Jacob is the ancestor of Israel, the real father of the nation is the Judahite figure Abraham, is best explained by Judah's dominant position over Israel when the Abraham and Jacob traditions were united in the tenth century BCE. For a people experiencing relief from oppression for the first time in many decades, the figures of the ancestors provided the focus for stories that articulated the identity of the people, marked them off from their neighbors, and interpreted their peace and their possession of the land as the fulfillment of a divinely executed promise.

See also Genesis, The Book of.

J. W. ROGERSON

Ancient Versions. *See* Translations, *article on* Ancient Languages.

Andrew. A disciple of *Jesus and brother of *Simon Peter. The two are pictured as fishermen working beside the sea when Jesus summons them to follow him and become "fishers of people" (Mark 1.16–18; Matt. 4.18–20). In John's gospel (1.35–42) Andrew first appears as a disciple of *John the Baptist.

Although less prominent than his brother, Andrew is present for Jesus' bread miracle (John 6) and the apocalyptic speech on the Mount of Olives (Mark 13.3–37). Lists of the *Twelve name Andrew second (Matt. 10.2; Luke 6.14) or fourth (Mark 3.18; Acts 1.13). According to late medieval tradition, Andrew was martyred by being crucified on an ×-shaped cross, which later appears on the flag of Great Britain representing Scotland, whose patron is Andrew.

PHILIP SELLEW

Angels. In Israel's early traditions, God was perceived as administering the cosmos with a retinue of divine assistants. The members of this divine council were identified generally as "*sons of God" and "morning stars" (Job 1.6; 38.7), "gods" (Ps. 82) or the "host of heaven" (Neh. 9.6; cf. Rev. 1.20), and they functioned as God's vicegerents and administrators in a hierarchical bureaucracy over the world (Deut. 32.8 [LXX]; cf. 4.19; 29.26). Where Israel's polytheistic neighbors perceived these beings as simply a part of the pantheon, the Bible depicts them as subordinate and in no way comparable to the God of Israel.

The most ancient Israelites would probably have felt uncomfortable in describing all these beings as "angels," for the English word "angel" comes from the Greek *aggelos,* which at first simply meant "messenger" (as does the Hebrew term for angel, *mal'āk*). God's divine assistants were often more than mere messengers. *Cherubim and *seraphim, for example, never function as God's messengers, for their bizarre appearance would unnecessarily frighten humans. On the contrary, God is frequently depicted in early narratives as dispensing with divine messengers, for he deals directly with humans without intermediaries (*see* Theophany).

As time passed, however, an increasing emphasis on God's transcendence correlated with an increasing need for divine mediators. These beings who brought God's messages to humans are typically portrayed as anthropomorphic in form, and such a being may often be called a "man" (Gen. 18.2; Josh. 5.13; Ezek. 9.2, 11; Dan. 9.21; 12.6–7; Zech. 1.8; Luke 24.4). The members of God's council are the envoys who relay God's messages and perform tasks appropriate to their status as messengers (1 Kings 22.19–22; Job 1.6–12). In some narratives of encounters with supernatural beings, there is reluctance to identify them by name (Gen. 32.29; Judg. 13.17–18). But as these messengers become more and more frequent, they eventually are provided with individual names and assigned increasingly specific tasks that go beyond that of a messenger. The only two angels named in the Hebrew Bible are in the book of *Daniel: *Gabriel reveals the future (Dan. 8–9; cf. Luke 1) while *Michael has a more combative role, opposing the forces of evil (Dan. 10, 12; Jude 9; Rev. 12.7). The angelic hierarchy becomes more and more explicit and elaborate (Dan. 10.13; Eph. 6.12; Jude 9; 1 Pet. 3.22; *see* Archangels), and each human being has his or her own protecting angel (Matt. 18.10; Acts 12.15). The term "messenger" (Grk. *aggelos;* Hebr. *mal'āk*) is used so frequently to depict these beings in their encounters with humans that it becomes a generic term to describe all supernatural beings apart from God, whether or not they actually functioned as messengers.

Angels are depicted as having the freedom to make moral choices, for they require judicial supervision (1 Cor. 6.3; Jude 6) and God himself is reluctant to trust them (Job 4.18). The Bible records a number of angelic rebellions or perversions (Gen. 6.1–4; Ps. 82; Isa. 14.12–15; Ezek. 28; 2 Pet. 2.4; Rev. 12.4–9), as a result of which some rebel angels are already incarcerated (Jude 6).

"The Angel [or Messenger] of the Lord" is a problematic figure. The ambiguous Hebrew phrase is best translated without the definite article, that is, "an angel [messenger] of Yahweh" (as do the Septuagint and NJV; cf. Matt. 1.20; 2.13, 19; 28.2; Acts 8.26). Later Christian theology tended to see the preincarnate Christ in this figure (hence the definite article), but the phrase probably referred vaguely to any mediator sent by God. He may be human (Hag. 1.13; Mal. 2.7). When the figure is clearly referred to as superhuman, he does not always function as a messenger but instead talks and behaves as if he were God, even failing to introduce his words as the message of another who sent him. Since early stories are internally inconsistent, identifying the figure as both God and God's messenger (Gen. 16.7–13; 22.11–12; 31.11–13; Exod. 3.2–4; Judg. 6.11–23), it is probable that some of these stories originally described God at work but were modified through time to accommodate God's increasing transcendence as one who no longer casually confronted humankind.

The increasing role played by angels in the later stages of the Hebrew Bible is found everywhere in the New Testament. The voice of God (the Father) is only exceptionally heard in the New Testament, unlike earlier biblical traditions. Instead, angels bring God's message to humans (Matt. 1.20; Luke 1.11, 26; 2.9; Acts 8.26; 10.3) and assist Jesus (Matt. 4.1; Luke 22.43) and his followers (Acts 5.19; 12.7). Angels have limited knowledge (Matt. 24.36; 1 Pet. 1.12), and when they appear to human beings, they may be described as descending from heaven (Matt. 28.2; John 1.51; cf. Gen. 28.12). Although Jesus alludes to the absence of the institution of marriage among angels (Matt. 22.30), angels are sexual beings (Gen. 6.4; Zech. 5.9). Some Jews, particularly the most conservative, denied their existence (Acts 23.8). But among Jews and Christians in general, angelology continued to develop so that not only was *Satan provided with his own retinue of angels as a counterpart to God (Matt. 25.41; 2 Cor. 12.7), but hundreds of names and functions are also applied to angels in extrabiblical texts such as the books of *Enoch.

SAMUEL A. MEIER

Animals. As a modern general designation for all living creatures other than plants, "animal" does not always have a simple equivalent in the Bible. The closest equivalents in the Hebrew Bible include *ḥayyâ* ("living [creature]," Lev. 11.2), and *bĕhēmâ*, which usually refers to all quadrupeds (Gen. 6.7), or more specifically to domesticated animals (Exod. 22.9–10). Yet even these Hebrew terms do not usually include birds or fish. The *Septuagint and the New Testament frequently use *tetrapous* ("quadruped") or *thērion* to translate both Hebrew terms.

Classification Systems. Aside from problems in basic terminology, the differences between biblical and modern Linnaean systems of animal classification sometimes create uncertainties in translation. For example, the Hebrew *dîšōn* (Deut. 14.5) has been translated by different versions or scholars as "ibex," "white-rumped deer," "pygarg," or "Arabian oryx," all representing completely different genera in most modern classifications. More than one species of predatory birds (e.g., eagles and vultures) may be subsumed under the Hebrew term *nešer*.

Dietary laws in Leviticus 11 and Deuteronomy 14.3–20, as well as the sacrificial system, depended on a system of classification which distinguished clean and unclean animals. In general, a clean land animal had cloven hoofs and chewed its cud (a ruminant artiodactyl in modern zoology), thus eliminating reptiles, amphibians, rodents and carnivorous animals from the diet. Animals that only chewed their cud (e.g., the hare) or only had cloven hoofs (e.g., the pig) also were eliminated. Most insects are unclean (the locust being one exception), and only those aquatic animals with fins and scales are fit to eat (Lev. 11.9–10). The logic underlying the clean/unclean dichotomy in Leviticus remains unclear. Other ancient Near Eastern cultures had views similar to those found in Leviticus and Deuteronomy regarding unclean animals, including the pig. Not surprisingly, for the Jewish sect that became known as Christianity, Levitical animal classification was a major issue in the debate about observance of dietary laws (Acts 11.5–9). (*See also* Purity, Ritual.)

Origin, Use, and Relationship with Humans. Biblical views concerning animals are linked closely with the two principal myths of *creation. In the first account, generally ascribed to *P, all the animals were created before both man and woman (Gen. 1.20–30). In the other account (Gen. 2.7–22), usually ascribed to *J, the creation of all the animals follows that of the first man, and God creates the first woman only after none of the animals was found helpful to the man. In both accounts animals were created to serve the needs of human beings, though Genesis 9.3 (cf. Gen. 1.30) indicates that humans were not expected to use animals for food before the *Flood. Psalm 104.10–30 depicts Yahweh, not human beings, as responsible for the general welfare of the animal kingdom.

Sheep, goats, cattle, and pigs are the most extensively attested domestic animals from the Neolithic period onward in ancient Palestine. The camel may have been domesticated by the early third millennium BCE in some portions of Asia, but the geographical extent of domestication by the second millennium remains undetermined.

Aside from providing a ready reserve of fresh meat and milk, most domestic animals could provide hides, bone implements, transportation, and other commodities. Wealth and status were often measured by the number of animals that a person owned (Job 1.3). The raising and trading of horses played an important role in achieving and maintaining military power in the Near East (1 Kings 4.26; 10.28–29).

Although offering animals to appease a deity has a strong magico-religious basis, animal *sacrifice formed an important part of the economy in ancient Israel. Ordinances that required that only the best of the flock be brought to the *Temple for sacrifice (Lev. 1.2; Deut. 15.21) in effect demanded the allocation of the best animal resources (especially cattle, sheep, and goats) for the priesthood. Smaller animals such as pigeons were acceptable if the worshipper was too poor to offer larger animals (Lev. 5.7). Christian writers argued that Jesus' death nullified the need for animal sacrifice altogether (Heb. 10.1–18).

The Bible also mentions various animals that were considered harmful. Some of the *plagues sent upon Egypt (Exod. 7–11) included the uncontrolled multiplication of frogs, gnats, flies, and locusts. Locusts were particularly feared because they could destroy agriculture and so cause a famine (Joel 1.4). Rituals sometimes were devised for protection from poisonous animals (e.g., snakes in Num. 21.1–4).

Animal Imagery. Biblical authors often use animal imagery to express aspects of their culture. Sheep imagery is used to depict a future messianic utopia (Isa. 11.6–7), as well as the Israelite community (Pss. 44.11; 79.13; 80.1). In the New Testament Jesus was portrayed as a *lamb

(John 1.29), and he warned his disciples about wolves dressed in sheep's clothing (Matt. 7.15).

Lions and other ferocious animals are often used to speak of hostile armies or personal enemies (Ps. 22.21; 1 Pet. 5.8), though lions may also symbolize positive figures (e.g., Judah in Gen. 49.9). Certain birds are associated with desolation (Ps. 102.6). Dogs usually are represented negatively in the Bible (Prov. 26.11; Matt. 7.6), though a recently discovered dog cemetery from the Persian period at Ashkelon may suggest the existence of non-Israelite cults that viewed the dog positively.

The Bible is also stocked with a variety of mythological creatures such as the *cherubim (1 Kings 8.6–7) and *seraphim (Isa. 6.2), which combine human and animal traits. *Leviathan (Isa. 27.1) and *Rahab (Isa. 51.9) are primordial beasts that were believed to threaten God's creation. As was the case with El, *Baal and other Canaanite deities, Yahweh may have been depicted as a bull (Exod. 32.4–6; see Golden Calf). Bull figurines from the second and first millennia BCE have been found at, among other places, *Hazor and Ashkelon, though it is difficult to determine which deity, if any, is represented by the figurines.

Aside from biblical scholars and archaeologists, ecologists and ethicists have recently become interested in the extent to which the biblical view of animals has influenced the relationship of modern civilizations with *nature (see A. Linzey, Christianity and the Rights of Animals, 1987; and E. J. Schochet, Animal Life in the Jewish Tradition: Attitudes and Relationships, 1984).   HECTOR IGNACIO AVALOS

Anoint. To touch, smear, or rub an object or person with oil. The use of scented oils on the body was enjoyed as a cosmetic luxury in Near Eastern and Hellenistic societies (and sometimes condemned as such, Amos 6.6). It was especially used on festive occasions and, conversely, refrained from in times of *mourning (2 Sam. 14.2; Dan. 10.3) or *fasting (Matt. 6.17). The soothing qualities of oil made anointing part of medical practice (Luke 10.34), but as most *medicine involved an invoking of divine power, anointing in that context might have the character of a religious rite (Mark 6.13; James 5.14; Rev. 3.18). Similarly, the anointing of corpses for *burial (Mark 16.1) might be viewed both as a last gesture of affection toward the dead and as part of the religious ritual of burial. The woman who anointed Jesus with precious scented oil probably did so as an extravagant gesture of joy at his presence, and he receives it as such in Luke 7.36–50, while in Mark 14.8 and John 12.7 he sees it as an anticipation of his death.

Anointing has a firm place in religious practice. Objects are anointed as a sign of their dedication to the deity, such as *Jacob's pillar at Bethel (Gen. 28.18; 31.13). The book of Exodus prescribes the anointing of the *tabernacle and its furnishings, especially the *altar (Exod. 29.36; 30.22–29; 40.9–11). With the institution of *kingship in Israel, anointing rather than coronation was the ceremony in which the king took office. This rite was widely practiced in the ancient Near East; the *Amarna letters suggest that anointing was a rite of kingship in Syria-Palestine in the fourteenth century BCE, and Jotham's parable assumes its familiarity (Judg. 9.8, 15). Once kingship was established, the anointing was probably performed by a priest, as *Zadok anointed *Solomon (1 Kings 1.39). *Samuel, a prophet and probably also a priest, is said to have anointed *Saul and *David (1 Sam. 10.1; 16.13), though according to 2 Sam. 2.4; 5.3, David was anointed by the people of Judah and Israel respectively (cf. 2 Kings 23.30). According to 1 Kings 19:15–16, *Elijah the prophet is instructed to anoint Hazael as king of *Damascus and *Jehu as king of Israel; *Elisha carries out the latter task by proxy (2 Kings 9.1–13). The king's anointing symbolized his special relationship with God and was seen as the occasion when he received God's spirit; it therefore made his person sacrosanct, so that David, with Saul in his power, will not touch "the Lord's anointed" (1 Sam. 24.6,10; 26.9–11,16,23; cf. 2 Sam. 1.14–16; 19.21; Lam. 4.20).

The anointing of *priests is prescribed only in the later, Priestly, strata of the *Pentateuch. The anointing of the high priest (Exod. 29.4–7; Lev. 8.12) probably began in the postexilic period, when the high priest assumed many of the leadership functions that had belonged to the king. It was only perhaps later still extended to other priests (Exod. 28.14, 30.30, 40.12–15; Lev. 7.35–36; Num. 3.3). The ritual was not practiced in the Roman period in *Herod's Temple, where the high priest's institution was by investiture.

As anointing symbolized the special responsibility and relationship to God of king and priest, so the language might be used metaphorically of anyone thought to stand in a similar position. Thus, the prophet of Isaiah 60.1 is said to be anointed (though for the possibility that prophets were actually anointed, see 1 Kings 19.16; Ps. 105.15). King *Cyrus of Persia is God's anointed in Isaiah 45.1, as is the whole people of Israel in Habakkuk 3.13 (cf. Ps. 105.15). Jesus is described as "anointed with the Holy Spirit and with power" in Acts 10.38.

By the Roman period, some Jews had come to hope that God would restore them a king, and because anointing was remembered primarily as the sign of kingship, this hope was expressed as hope for the "anointed one," Hebr. *māšîaḥ* (English "*messiah"), Grk. *christos* (John 1.41). The *Qumran community looked for two "anointed ones," priest and king, the Messiahs of Aaron and Israel (cf. Zech. 4.14). A more generalized hope for a future leader whose precise functions were unclear might still be expressed as hope for a "Messiah," but the primary association of the title with kingship would inevitably suggest political aspirations, and it may be for this reason that Jesus appears reluctant to accept the title for himself (Mark 8.29–30; Luke 23.2–3).

Anointing remains an essential part of the English coronation ritual, in direct dependence on the Bible. SOPHIE LAWS

Anthropology and the Bible. *See* Social Sciences and the Bible.

Antichrist. The word "antichrist" occurs in the Bible only in 1 and 2 John. The prefix *anti-* in Greek means "over against," "instead of," and so may imply usurpation as well as substitution. In 1 John, the coming of Antichrist is referred to as a standard sign of the "last hour," which has already happened in people who deny that Jesus is the Christ who has come in the flesh, and have seceded from the community; they are "false prophets" who embody the "spirit of antichrist" (1 John 2.18–22; 4.1–3; 2 John 7). (*See also* John, The Letters of.)

On the other hand, 2 *Thessalonians warns, again as standard teaching, that the *day of the Lord cannot come until the "lawless one," "the one destined for destruction," has appeared. He will usurp God's place in his Temple, and deceive people with Satan-inspired signs and wonders, until the Lord Jesus appears and destroys him (2 Thess. 2.1–12). There are links with the prophecies of a desolating sacrilege in the holy place (Dan. 9.27; 12.11; Matt. 24.15; Mark 13.14), and of false messiahs and false prophets, which must precede the coming of the *Son of Man

(Mark 13.21–22; Matt. 24.23–24). Luke has historicized the picture in terms of the fall of Jerusalem in 70 CE (21.20); and John sees the "one destined for destruction" not as a future figure but as *Judas Iscariot (17.12).

The marks of the figure of Thessalonians recur in the two beasts of Revelation 13: the beast from the sea, which in its death and resurrection is a parody of Christ, and claims divine honors; and the beast from the earth, which deceives people into worshiping the first beast, and with its lamblike voice and signs and wonders is a parody of the Holy Spirit. But there is also here an element of political coercion, and the sea beast's healed wound and his number identify him as Nero, returned from the dead, the persecuting emperor who was worshiped as a god.

The antecedents of this figure lie in Daniel 7, which was immensely important for New Testament writers. This vision relates that before the coming of God's kingdom there would be a time of disasters, persecution, and apostasy, and that opposition to God and his people would be summed up in a nation or person, human or superhuman, whom God or his agent would destroy. The vision is related to the Near Eastern *myth of God's conflict with the dragon of the *chaos waters, out of which this world was created. The myth celebrated the victory of order over chaos in nature; in some biblical passages the powers of chaos were historicized as nations opposed to God and his people—*Egypt (Ezek. 29.3) and *Babylon (Jer. 51.34)—and in Daniel 7 the four beasts arising out of the sea (on which the sea beast of Rev. 13 is modeled) represent persecuting empires. They culminate in the "little horn" on the fourth beast, which represents the Greek king Antiochus Epiphanes, who tried to hellenize Judaism, and set up his statue in the Temple (the desolating sacrilege referred to at Mark 13.14 and Matt. 24.15). The book of Revelation updates this picture in terms of the Roman empire, the emperor cult, and collaborating Christians (Rev. 2.14–29; 13.1–18).

On the other hand, those who accepted the state as God's ordinance (Rom. 13.1–7) saw the expected Antichrist as the embodiment of a specious spirit of lawlessness, which the state was keeping in check (2 Thess. 2.6, 7, according to one interpretation). After the Christianization of the Roman empire, this understanding became popular and even Revelation was read in this light, but corruptions in church and state led people back to Revelation's original sense.

The Antichrist expectation, with its attendant

disasters, apostasy, and martyrdom of the faithful, dominated the Middle Ages and the sixteenth and seventeenth centuries. The myth expresses both the speciousness of evil and its apparent omnipotence, while asserting the imminence of God's final victory and the value of faithful witness in its achievement. From another point of view, it has provided a forceful way of characterizing opponents in church or state, and dignifying resistance to them.

See also Revelation, The Book of.

JOHN SWEET

Anti-Judaism. *See* Anti-Semitism.

Antioch of Syria (Map 11:G3). Present-day Antakya in Turkey, to be distinguished from the less important Antioch in Pisidia (Map 14:F3; Acts 13.14–14.28; 2 Tim. 3.11). In the first century CE, Antioch was the third-largest city of the Roman empire and capital of the proconsular province of Syria. Seleucus I Nicator founded it shortly after 300 BCE and named it for his father, Antiochus the Great. Antioch was settled by Macedonians, Greeks, native Syrians, and Jewish veterans of the army of Seleucus I. Located in the fertile Amuk plain on the Orontes River, which could be navigated to this point, it was at the junction of trade routes to *Damascus, Palestine, *Egypt, and the Aegean. By the second century BCE, it had a great public library, and under Antiochus IV Epiphanes (175–164/163 BCE) and the emperors Augustus and Tiberius fine public buildings were constructed. Excavations have disclosed splendid mosaic floors and a colonnaded main street.

The large Jewish population was generally loyal to the Seleucid monarchs and the *Roman empire. According to *Acts, a Christian mission among Antiochene Jews began when refugees from persecution arrived after the martyrdom of *Stephen (Acts 11.19). Soon gentiles were also evangelized, and here the term "*Christians" was first used (Acts 11.25–26). The new church subsequently sent *Barnabas and *Paul to Jerusalem with famine relief (Acts 11.27–30), as well as to discuss the issue of observance of the *Law by gentile converts (Acts 15; Gal. 2; *see* Apostolic Council).

For many centuries, Antioch was a great center of Christian learning. Ignatius, who was martyred early in the second century CE, was its third bishop according to tradition.

SHERMAN ELBRIDGE JOHNSON

Anti-Semitism. Anti-Semitism has become the term commonly used for attitudes and actions against Jews. It was coined in the 1870s by the German agitator Wilhelm Marr in the campaign to eradicate Jewish influences in German culture. Sometimes the valid distinction is made between anti-Semitism as a secular term built on racial and cultural thinking out of the Enlightenment, and anti-Judaism as the earlier theologically grounded forms of contempt for Jews and things Jewish. Not least with the contemporary Arab-Israeli conflict, the term anti-Semitism is a sign of the narrow Western perspective in which the term was coined—both Jews and Muslims being Semites. Yet for the victims of anti-Semitism, such distinctions, though valid, carry little weight.

The record of pre-Christian anti-Semitism in the Greco-Roman world is mixed. The Jews were seen as a people of philosophers and the wisdom of *Moses was highly respected. But there was also criticism of their rituals and their keeping to themselves, and the *Sabbath was seen as laziness. The Roman satirists especially ridiculed *circumcision. Yet on balance it seems that Cicero's reference to Judaism as a "barbarous superstition" (*Pro Flacco* 28[67]) has been wrongly taken as representative of attitudes toward the Jews. In the history of anti-Semitism the continuity between Christian and Greco-Roman anti-Semitism is often stressed in order to minimize Christian responsibility.

While at times making use of themes found in Greco-Roman writers, Christian anti-Semitism differs in one fundamental respect: Christianity claims to be the fulfillment of the prophecies and aspirations of Israel as they are expressed in Israel's own scriptures, which became the Old Testament of the church, now interpreted in the light of the life, death, and resurrection of Jesus Christ.

The Jesus-movement was a totally Jewish event—the Gospels know of few contacts of Jesus with *gentiles. Christianity begins as a Jewish reform movement, and the formative conflicts by which the Christian identity is formed are conflicts within Judaism. The very Jewishness of Jesus and the *apostles gives anti-Semitism its intensity. The scars of the intra-Jewish conflicts with *Pharisees in Galilee and the chief priests and elders of Jerusalem, and with synagogue leaders in the Jewish Diaspora, are clearly visible in the New Testament, now from the perspective of churches where the "no" of the Jewish majority to the Christian claims is often contrasted with the "yes" of gentiles.

Jesus—and *John the Baptist—speak the harsh language of the prophets, ridiculing or condemning the foibles of their contemporaries, cursing their unwillingness to listen and to repent. Woes are uttered and the listeners are called. The rhetoric is heavy: "brood of vipers" (Matt. 3.7; 12.34; 23.33; Luke 3.7), and so forth. When such words are spoken they are spoken by a Jewish prophet for a Jewish people. Jesus identifies with his people; it has been said that a true prophet of doom prays intensely that his prophecy be proven wrong, that it be a warning toward repentance.

Such discourse from within the Jewish communities fell into the hands of increasingly gentile churches when the vast majority of Jews did not accept Christian claims for Jesus of Nazareth. The gentile churches began to hurl the words of Jesus at the Jewish communities. What Jesus had said with prophetic pathos, identifying with his people, was now spoken by gentiles against "the Jews," gentiles who felt that the fall of the Jerusalem *Temple (70 CE) had proven them right and the Jewish people wrong. In that shift of setting lie the roots of Christian and New Testament anti-Semitism. For the Jewish disciples there were the sadness, the disappointment, perhaps the frustration over the "no" of the majority of their fellow Jews; hence the need for a new identity, as the Jewish communities sometimes treated them harshly. The gospel of John already lives in that perception, sharpened into a literal demonizing of "the Jews" as having the devil for father (John 8.44). Jewish Christianity—by any account the nucleus of Christianity—is marginalized and declared unacceptable by both synagogue and church. The "we and they" dichotomy does not allow such complications.

The first to have discerned the specter of gentile Christian contempt for the Jews was *Paul, the Jew who understood himself to be the apostle to the gentiles. In his final reflection on how his mission fits into God's total plan (Rom. 9–11), he warns his gentile converts against their haughty attitude toward Israel by affirming that *all* Israel shall be saved. He does so not by affirming that they will become Christians but rather refers to God's *mystery (Rom. 11.25). Perhaps Paul's sensitivity was due to his personal history: it was religious zeal that had made him a persecutor of Christians.

In spite of Paul's warning, anti-Semitism follows Christianity as its dark shadow. This anti-Semitism remains basically rhetorical until the church becomes wedded to the political power of empires and governments. About a century after the emperor Constantine's conversion to Christianity (312 CE), Augustine lays down the principles on which Jews are allowed to exist in the Christian empire, yet with inferior status (*City of God* 18.46). His interpretation of Psalm 59.11 ("Do not slay them, lest my people forget; scatter them . . .") established the status of the Jews as both protected and suppressed—a pattern that makes of the Jews a necessary negative witness to the truth of Christianity. Within this pattern of Christian anti-Semitism, two motifs become prominent, both argued on biblical grounds: the Jews are guilty of deicide, of being godkillers (of having killed God), and Judaism is the wrong way to relate to God (by law rather than by faith). While the former charge is more prominent in Catholic and Orthodox lands, the latter dominates in Protestant cultures.

How can Christians read the Bible in a manner which guards against anti-Semitism? Perhaps the majority of Christians have read and do read the New Testament's critique of Jews and things Jewish as directed to themselves: it is my hypocrisy, my boasting, my self-righteousness that is attacked; it is my sin and lack of faith that swings from "Hosanna" to "Crucify, crucify." Yet history shows that when calamities and frustrations call for scapegoats, these very texts have preconditioned Christian cultures toward anti-Semitism.

To counteract such an effect of the Christian Bible—not least after the *Holocaust—different strategies have been devised. A renewed study of the passion narratives makes it clear that Jesus was crucified by the Roman authorities. *Crucifixion was a Roman means of execution. Also in the accounts of the Gospels it is the Jerusalem establishment, not "the Jews," who collaborate. This agrees with Josephus's notes about the execution of James in 62 CE that the *Sadducees are the harsh judges, while the *Pharisees plead mercy (*Ant.* 20.9.199–202). As the story is told in the Gospels, the responsibility of the Jewish leadership is stressed and that of Pontius *Pilate minimized, as he washes his hands and the crowd accepts the responsibility: "His blood be on us and on our children" (Matt. 27.25). And Judas usually looks more Jewish than do Jesus and the other disciples in the history of Christian art; one may ask: Why? The shift of emphasis from the Romans to the Jews is often explained by the need of Christianity to present itself as acceptable to the Roman authorities. A deeper reason may well be the theological need for understanding the passion as a fulfillment of the scriptures of the Jews and thus as an inner Jewish event. Yet there can be no historical doubt that Jesus was crucified under and by Pontius Pilate as a Jewish threat to Roman law and order.

When the New Testament and especially the gospel of John gives the impression that "the Jews" are the constant enemies and opponents, we must remember that both believers and unbelievers in the Jesus story are Jews. In order to make that more clear some translators choose to use words like "Judeans" or "the Jewish leaders." One could even think of "the establishment," for there is really nothing especially Jewish in the attitudes of those leaders. While such moves help to correct the historical understanding of the events and put them into perspective, it still remains a fact that the Gospels did perceive the controversies as part of Israel's refusal to accept God's offer of redemption in Jesus Christ. Judaism, on its part, understands the Christian claim for Jesus as false, while sometimes willing to recognize Jesus as a teacher among teachers in Judaism.

But Christians burdened by the horrendous history of anti-Semitism have urgent reasons to recognize how the rhetoric of a fledgling and beleaguered minority turned into the aiding and abetting of lethal hatred when endowed with the power of being in the majority. Anti-Semitism could be branded the most persistent heresy of Christian theology and practice. To unmask it is the first step. And the second is to complete and further develop the work begun in the Second Vatican Council: a vigilant audit of Christian preaching, teaching, Bible study, and liturgy as to what perpetuates and engenders contempt for Jews and Judaism. In such a task, dialogue with Jews is indispensable. In dialogue it becomes impossible for Christians to treat Jews and Judaism as obsolete or as a nonentity after the coming of the church. Yet such patterns of so-called supersessionism have functioned as a major factor in the history of Christian anti-Semitism.   KRISTER STENDAHL

Apocalyptic Literature. The words "apocalyptic" and "apocalypse" (from a Greek root meaning "to uncover," "to reveal") are terms that came to be used from the second century CE onward to indicate a type of Jewish and Christian literature akin to the New Testament Apocalypse

(an alternative title of the book of *Revelation), which gave its name to this style of writing.

The term "apocalyptic literature" is taken to refer to a body of revelatory writing produced in Jewish circles between 250 BCE and 200 CE and subsequently taken up and perpetuated by Christianity. It includes not only the genre "apocalypse" but may also include other related types of literature, such as testaments, hymns, and *prayers, which share some of its more important characteristics and motifs; that is, it does not have a common literary form but is diverse and even hybrid in its literary expression. The apocalypse type of writing, which forms the core of this literature, is a record of divine disclosures made known through the agency of *angels, *dreams, and visions. These may take different forms: an otherworldly journey in which the "secrets" of the cosmos are made known (the so-called vertical apocalypses), or a survey of history often leading to an eschatological crisis in which the cosmic powers of evil are destroyed, the cosmos is restored, and Israel (or "the righteous") is redeemed (the so-called horizontal or historical apocalypses).

Biblical Apocalypses. The scholarly consensus sees a strong link between the apocalypse and biblical *prophecy, and regards such writings as Ezekiel 38–39, Isaiah 24–27, Zechariah 12–14, and Joel 3 if not as apocalypses per se then as forerunners of them. The *wisdom tradition undoubtedly also influenced the apocalyptic in its growth and development, but arguments that its origins lie there rather than in prophecy remain unconvincing. However closely related prophecy and apocalyptic may be, they are to be distinguished from each other in at least two respects: whereas the prophets for the most part declare God's word to his or her own generation, the apocalyptists record revelations said to have been made known by God to some great hero in earlier times and now to be revealed in a "secret" book at the end of the days; and whereas the prophets see the realization of God's purpose within the historical process, the apocalyptists see that purpose reaching its culmination not just within history but above and beyond history in that supramundane realm where God dwells.

Within the Bible itself there are two great apocalypses: *Daniel and *Revelation. In the first of these, five stories are told of a wise man, Daniel, who remained faithful to his Jewish religion during the Babylonian *exile in the sixth century BCE, and was enabled by God to interpret dreams and visions. In the second half of the book, four of Daniel's visions are recorded, along with their interpretations, which give a survey of history from the exile (when the writer is reckoned to have lived) to its denouement in the second century BCE in the time of Antiochus IV, when the book in its present form was actually written. In this sense, the book of Daniel is addressed to the writer's own contemporaries, but the method and approach are altogether different from those of the prophets. So too with his hope for the coming kingdom: in keeping with the prophets, he sees it established here on earth as the climax of history, but in no way is it to be separated from that transcendent, heavenly realm where God dwells with his holy angels.

The book of Revelation follows a somewhat similar form, for it too reveals the future course of events by means of visions and declares the triumph of God's purpose. In the course of time other Christian apocalypses appeared, some as independent works, such as the Apocalypses of Peter and Paul, and others as interpolations in or additions to existing Jewish apocalyptic books.

Extrabiblical Apocalyptic Books. A number of extrabiblical Jewish apocalypses appeared during the Greco-Roman period which, for the most part, have survived only in translation, having been preserved within the Christian tradition. They are of considerable value for the light they throw on the four hundred and fifty or so years between 250 BCE and 200 CE and not least on our understanding of the background of the New Testament. There is no agreed list of such books, but the following works are generally so regarded: 1 *Enoch (Ethiopic Apocalypse of Enoch), third century BCE to first century CE; Apocalypse of Zephaniah, first century BCE to first century CE; Apocalypse of Abraham, first to second century CE; 2 *Enoch (Slavonic Apocalypse of Enoch), late first century CE; 2 *Esdras (= 4 Ezra) 3–14, ca. 100 CE; 2 Baruch (Syriac Apocalypse of Baruch), early second century CE; 3 Baruch (Greek Apocalypse of Baruch), first to third century CE.

Besides these, there are from this period certain other Jewish writings that, though not themselves apocalypses, belong to the same milieu and are generally recognized as part of the apocalyptic literature. They are as follows: Jubilees, second century BCE; Testaments of the Twelve Patriarchs, second century BCE; Jewish Sibylline Oracles, second century BCE to seventh century CE; Treatise of Shem, first century BCE; Testa-

ment (Assumption) of Moses, first century CE; Testament of Abraham, first to second century CE.

To this list may be added material found among the *Dead Sea Scrolls: fragments of a Testament of Levi (related to a late and redacted Greek Testament of that name) and a Testament of Naphtali, and likewise fragments of the (composite) first book of Enoch and the book of Jubilees. Other writings and fragments belonging to the Qumran community indicate a close relationship between the religious outlook of the apocalyptic writers and that expressed in the scrolls, such as certain passages in the Manual of Discipline, the War Scroll, the Hymns, and such works as the book of Mysteries, the Genesis Apocryphon, and the Description of the New Jerusalem.

Literary Features. The apocalypse is recognized by many scholars as a distinct literary genre expressing itself, as we have seen, in terms of divine disclosure, transcendent reality, and final redemption. As such, it shares with other related apocalyptic books certain literary features that are worthy of note:

Revelation through visionary experience. This is a stock-in-trade of these writings, though visions may be replaced by dreams, trances, auditions, and visual/physical transference to the ends of the earth or to heaven itself. The ancient seer (in whose name the author writes) is confronted with the heavenly mysteries, either directly or as mediated by an angel, and is bidden to record what he has seen and heard.

In so doing, the writer often makes use of two literary devices that, though not confined to the apocalyptic writings, are a common feature. The first is that of secret books, in which the seer is bidden to conceal these mysteries until the end time, when he will reveal them to the wise as a sign that the end is now at hand. The second is that of pseudonymity, whereby the author writes in the name of some honored person of antiquity, such as *Adam, *Enoch, *Abraham, *Moses, or *Ezra. The intention is not to deceive but rather to strengthen the conviction that the apocalyptist is transmitting a long and authoritative tradition. The same device is followed in Christian apocalypses, such as those of Peter and Paul, but not in the book of Revelation, where it is enough that the writer should declare in his own name the revelations he himself has received directly from his risen Lord.

Symbolic imagery. Symbolism, it has been said, is the language of the apocalyptic style of writing, a code language rich in imagery culled both from biblical and from Canaanite and Babylonian traditions. Generally speaking, the code is fairly easily recognizable: wild beasts represent the gentile nations, animal horns are gentile rulers, people are angels, and so on. Elsewhere it is less easily broken, particularly where vestiges of early myths have no obvious relation to the content of the book itself.

Tracts for the times. The apocalyptic books, particularly those "historical" apocalypses of Palestinian origin, were in many cases the product of their age and its political and economic climate. As tracts for the times, they were written to encourage those who were oppressed and saw little or no hope in terms of either politics or armed might. Their message was that God himself would intervene and reverse the situation in which they found themselves, delivering the godly from the hands of the wicked and establishing his rule for all to see. Sometimes such encouragement is given in the form of discourse in which the revelation of God's sovereignty is disclosed; at other times, as in the book of Daniel, it takes the form of a story or legend concerning the ancient worthy in whose name the book is written.

Such features are not peculiar to the apocalyptic books, but their form of presentation, together with their recurring theme of revealed secrets and divine intervention, indicates an identifiable and distinct body of literature within Judaism that, though sharing the ideals of prophecy, is nevertheless markedly different from it.

Common Themes. Certain well-marked themes run through the apocalyptic writings:

History and "the end." The whole of history is a unity under the overarching purpose of God. It is divided, however, into great epochs that must run their predetermined course; only then will the end come, and with it the dawning of the messianic kingdom and the age to come when evil will be routed and righteousness established forever.

Present troubles are in fact birth pangs heralding the end. Calculations, involving the use of numerology (*see* Number Symbolism), demonstrate that soon, very soon, earth's invincible empires will disappear and be replaced by God's eternal rule: "The coming of the times is very near. . . . The pitcher is near the well and the ship to the harbor, and the journey to the city, and life to its end" (2 Bar. 85.10). The writer of Daniel tries to be more precise, interpreting Jeremiah's seventy years' captivity as seventy weeks of years, ending in the writer's own day (9.21–27; cf. Jer. 25.11–12; 29.10). The Christian expectation is no less eager, though less precise: " 'Surely, I am coming soon.' Amen. Come, Lord Jesus!" (Rev. 22.20, *see* Second Coming of Christ).

Cosmic cataclysm. The coming end will be "a time of anguish, such as has never occurred since nations first came into existence" (Dan. 12.1). Sometimes this is described in terms of political action and military struggle; at other times the conflict assumes cosmic proportions involving mysterious happenings on earth and in the heavens—earthquakes, famine, fearful celestial portents, and destruction by fire. Such things find an echo in the New Testament, where it is said that in the last days there will be an eclipse of the sun, and the stars will fall from heaven (Mark 13.24–25).

This cosmic upheaval is closely related to the concept of cosmic powers in the form of *angels and *demons. The angel hosts are drawn up in battle array against the demon hosts under the command of *Satan. In the final battle the powers of evil, together with the evil nations they represent, will be utterly destroyed.

The consummation. The coming kingdom is, generally speaking, to be established here on this earth; in some instances it has a temporary duration, and is followed by the age to come for, as 2 Esdras puts it, "The Most High has made not one world but two" (7.50). In this new divine order, the end will be as the beginning and *paradise will be restored. "Dualism" is sometimes used to describe the discontinuity between this age and the age to come, but continuity remains: generally speaking, this earth (albeit renewed or restored) is the scene of God's deliverance.

In some of these writings the figures of *Messiah and *Son of man, among others, are introduced as agents of the coming kingdom. These probably represent two originally distinct strands of eschatological expectation which, in the course of time, became intertwined.

One significant development is the prevailing belief in a resurrection, a coming judgment, and the life to come (see Dan. 12.2 for an early reference). It is by this means that the gap, as it were, between the eschatology of the nation and the eschatology of the individual is finally bridged. Both together find their fulfillment in God's final redemption when all wrongs are to be righted and justice and peace are established forever.

D. S. RUSSELL

Apocrypha. *This entry consists of two articles dealing with books or parts of books not considered canonical by every community of faith,* Jewish Apocrypha *and* Christian Apocrypha. *The first article,* Jewish Apocrypha, *surveys Jewish religious writings not recognized as part of the Bible in Jewish tradition nor by some Christian churches (see* Canon). *Among the latter these are commonly referred to as the Apocrypha of the Old Testament; those churches that do include some or all of these writings in their canon frequently refer to them as "deuterocanonical." Each of these books has a separate entry devoted to it; see also* Apocalyptic Literature *and* Pseudepigrapha. *The second article,* Christian Apocrypha, *deals with early Christian writings not included in the canon of the New Testament but which contain similar types of literature often attributed to figures of the apostolic age.*

Jewish Apocrypha

The word *apocrypha,* a Greek neuter plural (singular, *apocryphon*), is used to designate a group of important religious writings from antiquity that are not universally regarded as belonging to the authentic *canon of Scripture, though many of them have been so regarded by particular communities. The word is applied primarily to the fifteen (or fourteen) books that are included in many editions of the English Bible as a supplement, usually printed between the Hebrew scriptures and the New Testament. The name, which means "things hidden away," is inappropriate, since none of these books (with the possible exception of 2 Esdras) was ever regarded as hidden or secret. For the most part, they are simply those books found only in manuscripts of the *Septuagint (LXX), the ancient Greek translation of the Hebrew scriptures, and therefore possibly regarded as "canonical" by Greek-speaking Alexandrian Jews, though ultimately rejected by the Jewish community of Palestine and rabbinic authorities of later times (2 Esdras and the Prayer of Manasseh are not covered by this definition). Their preservation is largely due to the Christian community, which, for most of the first four centuries CE, accepted the Greek Old Testament as normative for its life and thought. In modern times the term "apocrypha" has been extended more loosely to other books from the later Hellenistic and early Roman periods but which, so far as we know, never attained even quasi-canonical status (these books are more commonly designated as *pseudepigrapha), and has also been extended by analogy to a large group of early Christian writings

excluded from the New Testament canon in its final form. In this article we shall be concerned principally with the fifteen books described at the beginning of the paragraph; for the analogous early Christian writings, see the second article in this entry.

Until recently it was commonly assumed that Jews of the period immediately before and after the beginning of the common era had two canons, one that was current in Palestine and another in Alexandria, the greatest center of Jewish life in the Hellenistic world. But newer evidence, including that from *Qumran, suggests a more complex reconstruction, and indeed the use of the word "canon" may be somewhat inappropriate, since the list of included books was not explicitly fixed until the second century CE. The contents of the first two parts (Law and Prophets) of what would ultimately be called the canon had been accepted as sacred and authoritative since at least 200 BCE, but the works that constitute the third part of the Hebrew Bible (the Writings) have a less authoritative status and have been individually evaluated in quite different ways. It is to this last class that the books of the Apocrypha belong. Their one common denominator is the fact that all are contained, in Greek, in some manuscript of the Septuagint (with the exception, once again, of 2 Esdras and Prayer of Manasseh, to which we shall return).

The definition and final closing of the Jewish canon was in large measure due to the inner restructuring of Jewish society and the tightening of standards that resulted both from the destruction of the Temple in 70 CE and from the need for self-definition in the face of the threat presented by the rise of an aggressive Christian church. Christians, increasingly of gentile origin, naturally accepted the scriptures in the form most accessible to them, the Greek Septuagint. Jews, quite as naturally, reacted by emphatically rejecting the Septuagint and insisting that only those ancient books that were written in Hebrew could be regarded as authoritative. Even such books as *Sirach and 1 *Maccabees, which had clearly been written originally in Hebrew, were rejected, since internal evidence showed that they had been composed long after the time of Ezra, when, it was believed, prophecy had ceased.

Among Christians, the Old Testament continued for a long time to be tacitly accepted in its Greek form, even though objections were occasionally voiced by theologians and other scholars who were familiar with the Jewish position. The question of the canonicity of the "extra books" became acute only with Pope Damasus's choice of Jerome, in 382 CE, to make an authoritative translation of the Bible into Latin. As he worked on the Old Testament, Jerome became convinced that the Hebrew text alone was definitive and he therefore felt obliged to reject those books found only in Greek; these books he called "apocrypha." Whatever precise meaning he attached to that word, it was certainly intended to be pejorative. Strangely, his views were not accepted, and to the present the books he designated as "apocryphal" are incorporated in the canon of the Roman Catholic church and distributed, according to their type, among the other books of the Old Testament. The formal designation for these books among Roman Catholics is "deuterocanonical," meaning books that belong to a second layer of the canon, but with no implication that they are of less worth than the others. The view of the Orthodox churches, for most of which the Septuagint continues to be the authoritative form of scripture, is substantially the same, though the list of books they regard as at least liturgically useful tends to be somewhat longer and can include such works as 1 Esdras, 3 and 4 Maccabees, and Psalm 151. (See Eastern Orthodoxy and the Bible.)

It was only with the Reformation and its emphasis upon the sole authority of scripture that Jerome's view came into its own. Protestants were unanimous in accepting the Jewish definition of the Old Testament canon. They were agreed that the extra books of the Greek canon, which was also that of the Latin *Vulgate, should be gathered together and removed from among the books of the Hebrew canon; if included in the Bible at all, they should be placed in a separate section between the Testaments clearly labeled "Apocrypha." But they were not of one opinion with regard to the value of these books. Calvinists took the most extreme view, asserting in the Westminster Confession that they were of no more value than any other human writings, and their use was discouraged. Lutherans were inclined to value them more highly and to encourage their study, though not with any sense that they were of equal value with the authoritative books of the Hebrew canon. The Church of England requires the books of the Apocrypha to be included in any edition of the Bible authorized for use in public worship, and provides for considerable use of them in its lectionary while also insisting (in Art. 3 of the Thirty-Nine Articles) that they cannot be used to prove any point

of doctrine. In the early seventeenth century some Protestant editions of the Bible were published without the Apocrypha and, since 1827, when the British and Foreign Bible Society, followed shortly by the American Bible Society, under pressure from the Calvinist (Presbyterian) churches, decided to omit the apocryphal books from all its editions, omitting them has become the common practice. In the middle of the twentieth century, however, there began a considerable revival of interest in these books among both Protestants and Jews, based partly upon a more relaxed view of the nature of the canon, but even more upon a realization of the importance of the apocryphal literature for biblical research and interpretation. As a result, numerous editions of the Apocrypha have become available and a number of significant new commentaries on the apocryphal books have been published. Newer translations (e.g., GNB, NRSV) often include them in at least some editions.

Briefly described, the books of the standard Apocrypha are as follows: 1 *Esdras is an alternative version of the Hebrew book of Ezra that includes a short extract from 2 Chronicles at the beginning and from Nehemiah at the end. It is found in manuscripts of the Septuagint, but is not considered one of the deuterocanonical books by the Latin church; in the Vulgate it is called 3 Esdras and is printed, for purely historical reasons, in an appendix after the New Testament. The *apocalyptic work traditionally called 2 *Esdras is of Jewish origin, with some Christian additions, and was never part of the Septuagint. Except for a tiny fragment, the Greek text is lost, so it is best known in the Latin version that (like 1 Esdras) is printed in an appendix to the Vulgate, where it is called 4 Esdras; it is not considered deuterocanonical. *Tobit is a romantic oriental tale, best known for its very human characters, its high ethical teaching, and its use of magic and demonology. *Judith is the fictitious story of a heroic Jewish woman who delivers her people by using feminine wiles to accomplish the assassination of the general of a pagan army that was besieging them. The Additions to the Book of *Esther consists of a series of discontinuous passages that appear only in the Greek version of that book, apparently added, for the most part, to give a religious tone to that embarrassingly secular work. Two of the apocryphal books fall into the category of wisdom literature: there is, first of all, the *Wisdom of Solomon, a patently pseudonymous work that deals with such basic themes as immortality and the nature of divine wisdom in language that is a mixture of Jewish theology and Greek philosophy; and, second, *Sirach (or Ecclesiasticus), a much more traditional work, originally composed in Hebrew, that has its closest analogue in the book of *Proverbs. The second part of the confused composition called *Baruch (3.9–4.4) also belongs to wisdom literature, being a poem in praise of wisdom as God's special gift to Israel, while the preceding prose section consists of a brief narrative introducing a lengthy confession of Israel's sins as the cause of the Babylonian exile; the concluding poem (4:5–5.9) deals with the theme of Israel's restoration. If the Letter of *Jeremiah is counted as chap. 6 of Baruch, as is often done, there are fourteen rather than fifteen apocryphal books, but it is clearly a separate work having for its theme the foolishness of idolatry. The Prayer of *Azariah and the Song of the Three Young Men, *Susanna, and *Bel and the Dragon are additions that appear in the Greek version of *Daniel, the first containing two widely used liturgical hymns, while the other two are popular tales in which Daniel is the hero. A Greek form of the *Prayer of Manasseh exists, but was not part of the original Septuagint, and it is deuterocanonical for only some eastern churches. The books called 1 and 2 *Maccabees are two entirely independent and disparate historical narratives that record the heroic struggles that led to a brief period of independence for Jews in the second and first centuries BCE.

The importance of these books arises first of all from the fact that they were composed later than the canonical books of the Hebrew Bible and, apart from 2 Esdras, before the books of the New Testament. They therefore shed a welcome light on political, religious, and cultural developments in the later Hellenistic and early Roman periods and thus on the background of the New Testament. Furthermore, when regarded for their own sake, the Wisdom of Solomon is an important theological treatise, representing the first attempt to fuse two different intellectual strains, the Israelite and the Greek; and, for most readers, Sirach is at least as interesting as Proverbs and perhaps more accessible; Tobit, Judith, and Susanna are splendid examples of narrative art; and 1 Maccabees is a fine specimen of sober historical writing.

Among other ancient works sometimes classified as "apocrypha" are 3 and 4 *Maccabees, the Psalms of Solomon, the several books of *Enoch, the Baruch apocalypse (2 Baruch), the Book of Jubilees, and the Testaments of the Twelve Patriarchs.

See also Apocalyptic Literature; Pseudepigrapha.   ROBERT C. DENTAN

Christian Apocrypha

Beyond the twenty-seven books collected in the New Testament canon, many other examples were produced of each of the four types of New Testament literature: gospels, acts, letters, and apocalypses. The intentions of the authors of these books, which are now known as New Testament Apocrypha, were diverse; some sought to supplement works already in circulation, while others sought to supplant them. In some cases, these books simply served as light entertainment for Christian believers; in others, the authors wanted to promulgate practices and ideas condemned by the church.

Apocryphal Gospels. Of the roughly two dozen gospels produced during the early centuries of Christianity, those concerning on the one hand Jesus' infancy and childhood, and on the other his *descent into hell between his death and his *resurrection clearly augment the canonical Gospels, which pass over these matters in almost total silence (Luke 2.42–51 relates one incident when Jesus was a boy of twelve). Naturally, however, early Christians were curious about both of these periods; not surprisingly, traditions grew up around each and were recorded (*see* Names for the Nameless). The Protevangelium of James and the Infancy Gospel of Thomas, two second-century infancy gospels, were developed over the following centuries into the History of Joseph the Carpenter and the Arabic Gospel of the Infancy, as well as other similar writings describing Jesus' early years and the miracles surrounding contact with the infant, his clothing, and even his bathwater.

In these works, the young Jesus is portrayed as possessing miraculous powers. The uses to which such powers are put, though, is often incompatible with the character found in the canonical Gospels. For example, while playing with other children on the Sabbath, Jesus molded twelve clay birds. When an elder reported Jesus' desecration of the Sabbath to *Joseph, Jesus clapped his hands and the birds came to life. Another time, when Jesus was walking through a crowd, someone bumped him, whereupon Jesus turned and said, "You will never get to where you are going," and the person fell down dead.

Apocryphal accounts of Christ's descent into

the underworld and his victory over its powers are more rare. One of the earliest can be found in the fourth-century Gospel of Nicodemus (also called the Acts of Pilate); another, from the next century, is the Gospel of Bartholomew.

With the discovery in 1945 of the *Nag Hammadi library, several previously unknown (or known only by name) gnostic gospels have come to light. These and related works (e.g., the Epistle of the Apostles) commonly present the risen Christ's revelations to the disciples during the period between his resurrection and *ascension (a period that the gnostics expanded from 40 days [Acts 1.3] to 550 days). Often these accounts are related as a dialogue in which the disciples question Jesus about subjects that remained obscure in his earlier teaching. Most often, however, the discussion goes beyond the Gospel traditions to speculations about cosmology, gnostic interpretations of the creation accounts of Genesis, and the fate of the different classes of humanity. Notable examples preserved at Nag Hammadi are the Apocryphon of James, the Sophia of Jesus Christ, the Book of Thomas, and the Dialogue of the Savior. Among the most significant of the Nag Hammadi documents, and very different in character, is a Coptic version of the Gospel of Thomas, a collection of 114 sayings (logia) of Jesus, many similar to logia in the synoptic Gospels and in a late second-century CE papyrus; see further Agrapha.

Still other gospels are known only by name or from brief patristic quotations. Some of these originated among early Jewish-Christian sects, as is clear from their titles (Gospel of the Hebrews; Gospel of the Ebionites; Gospel of the Nazarenes).

Apocryphal Acts. Since the canonical Acts of the Apostles record in detail the activities of only a few of the *apostles, second- and third-century Christian authors drew up narratives of the other apostles' activities. Even apostles portrayed in Acts had further exploits recounted, sometimes in minute detail. The most notable are five works from the second and third centuries, attributed to Leucius Charinus, alleged to have been a disciple of John; scholars agree, however, that the actual authors of these and all other apocryphal acts remain unknown.

The Acts of Peter (ca. 180–190 CE) describes the rivalry between *Simon Peter and Simon Magus. Among Peter's miracles are a speaking dog, a dried fish restored to life, and resurrections from the dead. The comical climax of the contest takes place in the Roman forum, when the magician attempts to fly to heaven. The document closes with an account of Peter's martyrdom by crucifixion.

The Acts of John (ca. 150–180) purports to be an eyewitness account of John's missionary travels in Asia Minor. The sermons attributed to him evince docetic tendencies: Jesus had no proper shape or body, only an appearance, so to one person he appeared in one shape, and to another in a totally different shape; when he walked, he left no footprints. Besides a droll tale about bedbugs, the work has a Hymn of Christ as well as the apostles dancing in a circle.

The Acts of Andrew (early third century?) is known chiefly through a long epitome prepared by Gregory of Tours (sixth century). To judge by the extant portions, the Acts are in essence a narrative of *Andrew's journey from Pontus to Achaia, during which he performed many miracles and delivered many lengthy, severely ascetic exhortations. The Martyrdom of St. Andrew, a variant text of part of the work, describes the apostle's death by crucifixion.

The Acts of Thomas (first half of the third century), is the only apocryphal Acts preserved in its entirety, surviving in Greek, Syriac, Ethiopic, Armenian, and Latin versions. It tells of *Thomas's missionary work in India, his healing miracles, and martyrdom. It also contains several fine liturgical hymns; the best-known is the "Hymn of the Soul" (also called the "Hymn of the Pearl"), which has suggestive allegorical overtones.

The Acts of Paul, according to Tertullian, was written by a presbyter of Asia Minor with the purpose of honoring the apostle. Despite ecclesiastical disapproval, his book become quite popular with the laity. Among the surviving episodes is one that tells of *Paul and Thecla, a noblewoman and follower of Paul who preached and administered *baptism; in this section we find the famous description of Paul: "little in stature, with a bald head and crooked legs . . . with eyebrows meeting, and a nose somewhat hooked." Another episode, discovered in 1936, gives a detailed account of Paul's encounter in the amphitheater at Ephesus with a lion to which he had earlier preached the gospel and had baptized.

These works are generally sectarian in character, whether orthodox or theologically deviant (Docetic, Gnostic, Manichean). Sectarian influence can especially be seen in emphasis on sexual asceticism and martyrdom. Other legendary Acts dating from the fourth to the sixth century are the Acts of Andrew and Matthias among the Cannibals, Acts of Andrew and Paul, Acts of Barnabas, Acts of James the Great, Acts of John by Prochorus, Acts of the Apostles Peter and Andrew, Slavonic Acts of Peter, Acts of Philip, Acts of Pilate, and Acts of Thaddaeus. This type of literature may be seen as paralleling the novels of antiquity.

Apocryphal Letters. The apocryphal epistles are relatively few in number. The spurious Third Letter of Paul to the Corinthians, with an introductory note to Paul from presbyters at Corinth, is part of the Acts of Paul, and came to be highly regarded in the Armenian and Syrian churches. It addresses doctrinal issues such as prophecy, creation, the human nature of Christ, and the resurrection of the body.

In the west, Paul's Letter to the *Laodiceans was disseminated widely and is actually included in the all eighteen printed German Bibles prior to Luther's translation. The Correspondence between Paul and Seneca, consisting of fourteen letters between the *Stoic philosopher Seneca and Paul, has come down to us in more than three hundred manuscripts; the banal content and colorless style of the letters show that they cannot come from the hands of either the moralist or the apostle. Other apocryphal letters are the Epistle of Titus and the Epistles of Christ and Abgar.

Apocryphal Apocalypses. In addition to the *Revelation of John, there are several apocalypses attributed to other apostles. The earliest is the Apocalypse of Peter (ca. 125–150 CE), preserved in part in Greek and fully in Ethiopic. Making use of beliefs about the afterlife from the *Odyssey* and the *Aeneid,* it tells of the delights of the redeemed in heaven and (at much greater length) the torments of the damned in hell. These ideas were elaborated extensively in the following century by the author of the Apocalypse of Paul, who describes how Paul is caught up to paradise (see 2 Cor. 12.1–4) and witnesses the judgment of two souls, one righteous and the other wicked. He is then led through hell, where he sees the tortures of the wicked and intercedes on their behalf, obtaining for them relief every Lord's day. A visit to paradise ensues, during which Paul meets the patriarchs, the major prophets, Enoch, and finally *Adam. Some of these themes became part of medieval beliefs given wider dissemination through Dante's *Divine Comedy.* With the discovery in 1946 of the *Nag Hammadi library, the number of apocryphal apocalypses increased: another Apocalypse of Peter, another of Paul, the First and Second Apocalypses of James, and others.

Modern Apocrypha. The urge to supplement the Bible has continued down through the ages. In modern times, fraudulent productions continue to excite the hopes of naive readers that priceless treasures have been uncovered. Despite repeated claims of authenticity, such productions invariably lack historical or literary value. Among the most often published are The Aquarian Gospel, The Archko Volume, The Letter of Benan, The Description of Christ, The Confessions of Pontius Pilate, The Gospel of Josephus, The Book of Jasher, The Lost Books of the Bible, The Nazarene Gospel, The Letter from Heaven, Cahspe, and The Twenty-ninth Chapter of Acts.   BRUCE M. METZGER

Apollos. The book of Acts records that an Alexandrian Jew named Apollos was active as a missionary in *Ephesus and Achaia (18:24–28). Although skillful in communicating and knowledgeable concerning scripture, his teaching on *baptism was incomplete. Priscilla and Aquila needed to provide him with a "more accurate" understanding, and when *Paul visited Ephesus after Apollos's departure (Acts 19.1–7), he had to rebaptize some people who had known John's baptism for repentance but not baptism in the name of Jesus.

In 1 Corinthians, Paul's references to Apollos and his teachings betray some tension between the two leaders (1 Cor 1.12; 3.4–6; 4.6; 16.12).
          DANIEL N. SCHOWALTER

Apostle. The Greek word *apostolos* ("someone who has been sent") is seldom used in classical Greek, but it occurs eighty times in the New Testament, where it means "delegate" of Jesus Christ and "messenger" of the gospel. Paul lists apostles first among the members of the body of Christ (1 Cor. 12.29; cf. Eph. 4.11).

The corresponding word in Hebrew (*šālîaḥ*) was especially used to denote someone given full authority, for some particular purpose and for a limited time, to represent the person or persons from whom the delegate comes; the rabbis said that "a man's *šālîaḥ* is as himself." The legal status of such a delegate has its roots in Semitic customs pertaining to a messenger (see 1 Sam. 25.40; 2 Sam. 10.1–5). The mission of *Paul to

*Damascus (Acts 9.1–2) and the delegation of *Barnabas and Paul by the church of *Antioch (Acts 11.30; 13.2; see 14.4, 14) are to be understood in terms of a rabbinic šālîaḥ. The same holds true for the sending of the *disciples by Jesus, who included the "apostles" (Mark 3.14 par.). They went two by two (Mark 6.7; Luke 10.1); their task of proclaiming the gospel and casting out *demons was limited as to sphere and time (Matt. 10.5–8), and they had to return to the sender and report about their task (Mark 6.30; Luke 10.17).

Although Jesus is called "apostle" only once in the New Testament (Heb. 3.1), in his "*Son of man" sayings he presents himself as the agent of God for salvation (Mark 2.17; 10.45; Luke 5.32; 7.34; 19.10; see also Matt 10.40). The divine commission of the Son is elaborated in the gospel of John, where the evangelist more than once uses the law concerning the authority of the šālîaḥ (7.33; 16.5; 17 passim).

The status of a post-Easter apostle of Christ transcends that of a Jewish šālîaḥ. In his letters, Paul often defends and defines his apostolic authority. He mentions the apostles before him (Gal. 1.17), specifying *Peter, the *twelve, James, and all the apostles (1 Cor. 15.5, 7). Though Paul was called last of all and considered himself to be the least of them (1 Cor 15.8–9), he was convinced that God had set him apart before he was born (Gal. 1.15); thus, Paul repeated the claim of the prophet Jeremiah (1.5) and of the servant of the Lord (Isa. 49.1–5). This means that the apostles of Christ had to serve during their whole lives as did the biblical *prophets, who were called by God and spoke as his messengers. Paul may have used the narrative of Isaiah's call as a key for interpreting his vision near Damascus. The motifs of Isaiah 6 can be discovered in scattered statements in which Paul speaks about the call and about the nature of his apostleship. The rhetorical questions "Am I not an apostle? Have I not seen Jesus our Lord?" (1 Cor. 9.1) get their force from Isa. 6.1, 8: "I saw the Lord . . . send me!" Moreover, Paul understood his call to apostleship as an act of the *grace of God (Rom. 1.5). As a persecutor of the Christians he was not worthy of it (1 Cor. 15.9); in a similar way, Isaiah had confessed his unworthiness (6.5–7). Isaiah had been told to bring a message of doom to the Israelites that would harden them (6.8–10); Paul experienced disobedience to the gospel by his fellow Jews (Rom. 10.16; 11.7–10), which is why he brought

it to the gentiles (see Acts 28.25–28). He felt the necessity to preach his message (1 Cor. 9.16) as Jeremiah had (20.9).

Besides the limited group of apostles (the twelve) in Jerusalem (1 Cor. 15.5, 7; Gal. 1.17, 19), Paul knew another circle of apostolic preachers (1 Cor. 9.5; 12.28; 2 Cor. 11.13; Rom. 16.7). Therefore, one may distinguish between two types of New Testament apostles in Paul's view: those called through an appearance of the risen Lord; and charismatic preachers, who were delegated by a church such as that at Antioch (see Acts 13.1–3; Rev. 2.2; Did. 11.3–6), including both men and women (Rom. 16.7; see Junia). But both types were united in a figure such as Paul. On the other hand, Luke reserves the designation "apostle" for the twelve disciples of Jesus who became the leaders of the Jerusalem church. For him, the apostle has to be a companion of Jesus and a witness to the resurrection (Acts 1.21–22). This seems to be the view of Mark (6.30; see 6.7) as well as that of Matthew (10.2).

OTTO BETZ

Apostolic Council. The gathering of the Jerusalem church under the leadership of apostles and elders reported in Acts 15.4–29. The meeting took place after unnamed Judeans raised questions in *Antioch concerning the status of converted *gentiles and the need for their *circumcision and observance of Mosaic *law. *Paul and *Barnabas came to Jerusalem as representatives of the Antiochene church, probably in 49/50 CE. A discussion among the *apostles and *elders takes place in front of the assembled church. *Peter apparently settles the question by appeal to his own experience: converted gentiles had already received the Holy Spirit apart from the Law (cf. Acts 10.1–48). *James supports this position with prooftexts from the prophets, but then suggests a set of minimum obligations that gentile Christians ought to observe. This proposal is formally adopted by the whole church and incorporated into a letter (the Apostolic Decree) addressed to the churches of Antioch, Syria, and Cilicia. The majority text tradition presents these requirements as "abstinence from idolatry, blood, meat that is strangled, and sexual immorality," which probably reflects the requirements placed on *aliens residing in Israel in Leviticus 17–18. Whether these practices would have been sufficient to facilitate fellowship between gentiles and Jews among Christians is unclear. They may represent the practices of the author's largely gentile community at a time when most Jewish Christians had been forced out of the synagogues. A later text tradition drops the reference to strangled flesh, probably takes "blood" to mean "murder," and adds the golden rule, thereby converting the requirements to a minimal moral code without reference to the issues separating Jews from gentiles within the church.

The Apostolic Council should almost certainly be identified with the events reported by Paul in *Galatians 2.1–10, although the differences between the two accounts have led some interpreters to posit distinct events. For historical reconstruction, Paul's account is to be preferred since he was a participant, though hardly a neutral observer. Paul reports a less formal meeting with Peter which settled the question of circumcision. Some scholars prefer to connect this meeting to Paul's visit to Jerusalem reported in Acts 11.29–30. Paul places the dispute concerning table fellowship in Antioch and seems to indicate that his differences with Peter on this issue were not resolved (Gal. 2.11–14).

Debate continues concerning the possibility that one or more early sources lie behind the report in Acts. The placement of the Apostolic Council at the center of *Acts underscores the importance of the theological issues raised by the success of the gentile mission. It reflects the author's interest in the relationship between Israel and the Christian church, and it integrates the Pauline mission into the larger picture of the spread of the Christian faith from Jerusalem to the rest of the world. The Apostolic Council is portrayed as affirming gentile freedom from the Mosaic law while making social relations between Jews and gentiles possible within the church.

ROBERT STOOPS

Apple of the Eye. The translation "apple of the eye" corresponds to several related phrases, all of which mean the pupil of the eye and indicate something near and dear which is to be protected. In Hebrew, these expressions (ʾîšôn ʿayin ["little man of the eye"]: Deut. 32.10; Prov. 7.2; bat ʿayin ["daughter of the eye"]: Lam. 2.18; Zech. 2.8; ʾîšôn bat ʿayin [a double reading]: Ps. 17.8) refer to the reflected human image that appears in the pupil of the eye. The same idiom is found in Sirach 17.22, in classical Greek, and in Latin (pupilla, from which the English word

"pupil" is derived). The English phrase "apple of the eye" is a periphrastic translation, using a different metaphoric idiom.   RUSSELL FULLER

Aqedah. The Hebrew word for "binding," and the common designation for Genesis 22.1–19, in which God tests *Abraham by commanding that he sacrifice his son *Isaac. Abraham binds Isaac (v. 9). When he is about to slaughter him, an angel calls to him to desist, whereupon Abraham offers a ram instead. Although the Aqedah is the climax of the Genesis narratives about Abraham, a final testimony to his faith in, obedience to, and fear of God, it is not mentioned elsewhere in the Hebrew Bible. Isaac's role in Genesis 22 is passive, but postbiblical Jewish interpretations of the first to the eighth centuries CE transform him into an adult, voluntary sacrificial offering. Some texts give reasons for the episode, including Satan's questioning of Abraham's devotion to God (b. Sanh. 89b; cf. Job 1–2) and Isaac's and *Ishmael's arguments concerning who was the more righteous (Gen. Rab. 55.4). During this period, the Aqedah became associated with the Roʾsh ha-shanah liturgy, with the shofar recalling the substituted ram. Mount Moriah, where the Aqedah took place, was identified with the site of the *Temple. Isaac emerges both as the paradigm of the martyr and as the perfect sacrifice whose act brings merit to and has redemptive value for his own descendants. Some rabbinic traditions maintain that Isaac, as a sacrificial victim, shed blood, and others conclude that he also died and was resurrected; thus wrote the twelfth-century rabbi Ephraim of Bonn, in the context of the martyrdom of many Rhineland Jews and the destruction of their communities.

The New Testament refers to the Aqedah not as an example of a redemptive sacrificial death but rather as an example of faith (James 2.21; Heb. 11.17–19; possibly Rom. 4.16–18). Echoes of the former may however be found in Paul's understanding of the significance of the death and *resurrection of *Jesus, and the *Septuagint of Genesis 22 may be alluded to in Romans 8.32, Mark 1.11, and Matthew 3.17. Early church fathers such as Clement and Tertullian understood Isaac's sacrifice as a prototype of the sacrifice of Jesus (see Typology). The divine testing of Abraham and the subsequent near sacrifice of his son also appear in the *Qurʾān (37.101–113). Early Muslim exegetes disagreed as to whether the son, unnamed in the Qur'ānic passage, is Isaac or Ishmael. Some of the earliest traditions declare him to be Isaac, but by the ninth or tenth century the consensus was that Ishmael, increasingly associated with Mecca and identified as the ancestor of the northern Arabs, was the voluntary sacrificial offering.

From antiquity to the present, the Aqedah has been portrayed in the arts. For example, it appears on a wall painting of the third-century CE synagogue at Dura-Europos and on a floor mosaic of the sixth-century synagogue at Beth Alpha. During the Renaissance, such sculptors and painters as Ghiberti, Donatello, Titian, Caravaggio, and Rembrandt included the Aqedah among their depictions of biblical subjects. Among notable modern literary treatments of the Aqedah is Søren Kierkegaard's *Fear and Trembling* (1843).
See also Suffering.

BARBARA GELLER NATHANSON

Arabia. Arabia is a large, predominately arid peninsula bounded on the east by Mesopotamia and the Persian Gulf, on the north by the Mediterranean coastal highlands of Syria and Palestine, and on the west and south by the *Red Sea and Indian Ocean (Maps 1, 2: G–K 4–6). Northwest Arabia is mountainous, stony desert. Like the neighboring *Negeb, it is desolate but habitable for sheep/goat *nomads. The sandy deserts of interior Arabia remained impenetrable until domestication of the camel allowed its scattered oases to be linked by means of caravan routes in the first millennium BCE. Southern Arabia (Yemen) is, by contrast, a well-watered highland where terraced agriculture has supported permanent settlement from at least the second millennium BCE.

The Bible reflects close familiarity with the desert places and nomadic peoples of northwestern Arabia, and southern Arabia (*Sheba, 1 Kings 10.1; Job 6.19; or Seba, Gen. 10.7; Ps. 72.10; Isa. 43.3) was also known as a source of camels, gold, *frankincense, and *myrrh. Some places, like Dumah (Josh. 15.52; Isa. 21.11; modern Jawf) and Tema (Gen. 25.15; Job 6.19; Isa. 21.14; Jer. 25.23; modern Tayma), can be identified with sites in northern Arabia; however, recent attempts to relocate the ancestral narratives wholesale from Palestine to northern Arabia must be rejected. The Hebrew word 'ărābâ means "desert," but in one form it also means "nomad" (Isa. 13.20; Jer. 3.2). The phrase "all the kings of Arabia" (1 Kings 10.15; 2 Chron.

9.14; Jer. 25.24) can mean "all the kings of the Arabs" or "all the kings of the nomads." Few of the numerous nomadic peoples mentioned in the Bible are called "Arabs," and only rarely is their territory called "Arabia." Rather, they are identified by their geographic or ethnic origin: *Amalekites (1 Sam. 15.6–8; 30.1; Judg. 6.5; 7.12), Ishmaelites (Gen. 37.25), *Midianites (Judg. 6.5; 7.12).

In the New Testament, "Arabians" (denoting probably Arabic speakers) were among the polyglot crowd gathered in Jerusalem at *Pentecost (Acts 2.5–11). For a time after his call, *Paul "went away into Arabia," perhaps to eastern Syria or Transjordan (Gal. 1.17).   JOSEPH A. GREENE

Aram. Aram is a name of both places and persons. As a place name it refers usually to Aram-Damascus (Map 1:Z2), a powerful Aramean state in southern Syria during the early first millennium BCE (*see* Damascus). Aram also designates other contemporary Aramean states along the northern border of Israel, including Aram-zobah northeast of the Anti-lebanon mountains (2 Sam. 8.3; Ps. 60.0) and Aram-maachah in the upper Jordan valley (1 Chron. 19.6). Some English translations follow the *Septuagint and put "Syria" or "Syrian" where the Hebrew text has "Aram" (place) or "Arami" (person of Aram, an Aramean). The Greek words, however, are not precise equivalents of the Hebrew (*see* Syria).

As a personal name, Aram is one of the five sons of Shem and the eponymous ancestor of the Arameans (Gen. 10.22–23). Genesis 22.20–21 identifies another Aram as son of Kemuel and grandson of Nahor, brother of the patriarch *Abraham. Abraham's son *Isaac married a granddaughter of Nahor who was sister to Laban "the Aramean" (Gen. 25.20). Abraham's grandson *Jacob wed *Rachel and *Leah, both daughters of this same Laban (Gen. 28–31). These and other accounts in Genesis that associate the *ancestors of Israel with people and places in the upper *Euphrates region (Aram-naharaim, translated "*Mesopotamia," Gen. 24.10; or Paddan-aram, Gen. 28.2) suggest a close relationship between the Israelite ancestors and the Arameans (Deut. 26.5).

Outside the Bible, Aram is mentioned in a cuneiform inscription of Naram-Sin of Akkad (ca. 2300 BCE) as a place along the upper Euphrates. Cuneiform texts from Drehem in southern Mesopotamia also name Aram as a city in the upper Euphrates region ca. 2000 BCE. Annals of the Assyrian king Tiglath-pileser I speak of punitive campaigns in his fourth year of reign (1112 BCE) against nomadic Ahlamu-Arameans who reached as far west as Tadmor (Palmyra in Syria) and the Lebanon mountains.

In the reign of *David (tenth century BCE), Aram-zobah ruled southern Syria but was eventually defeated by the Israelite king (2 Sam. 8.3–12). Aram-Damascus assumed control of southern Syria during the reign of *Solomon (1 Kings 11.23–25) and was a recurrent opponent of Israel throughout ninth–eighth centuries BCE, although it was also sometimes Israel's ally against the *Assyrians (1 Kings 22.1). Aram-Damascus and the other Aramean cities of Syria were ultimately destroyed by the Assyrians in the late eighth century BCE (Amos 1.3–5; Isa. 17.1–3; Jer. 49.23–27).

In both biblical and extrabiblical sources, Aram denotes lands occupied by speakers of *Aramaic, a Northwest Semitic language related to Hebrew and Phoenician that was widely spoken in Syria in the first millennium BCE. Aramaic language and script survived the destruction of the Aramean states in Syria. Aramaic became the lingua franca of Persian empire, and dialects of Aramaic continued to be widely spoken in Palestine and Syria into the Roman period (see Mark 5.41).   JOSEPH A. GREENE

Aramaic. A Northwest Semitic language related to *Hebrew. It was usually written in the twenty-two letters of the Phoenician alphabet, although originally some letters had to represent more than one Aramaic consonant. The shapes of the letters used for Aramaic developed into the square script, which was adopted for Hebrew too in the Persian period. Aramaic differs from Hebrew in various ways. For example: the vocabulary is different, although some words are similar (e.g., Hebrew šālôm, "peace," but Aramaic šĕlām); Hebrew uses the prefix ha- as the definite article, but Aramaic uses the suffix -ā; some consonants in Hebrew correspond to different ones in Aramaic (e.g., Hebrew hāʾāreṣ, "the land" or "earth," but Aramaic ʾarqāʾ, later ʾarʿāʾ).

A number of Old Aramaic inscriptions are known from the tenth or ninth century BCE onward from Syria and Mesopotamia, and in the latter region it replaced Akkadian (Babylonian and Assyrian) as the language of everyday speech. According to Deuteronomy 26.5, the Israelites were of Aramean descent, but the Bible nowhere represents Aramaic as their language, and Genesis 31.47–48 tells how *Jacob called a pillar Galeed ("heap of witness"), whereas his Aramean father-in-law Laban used the Aramaic equivalent, Jegar-sahadutha. In 2 Kings 18.26 (= Isa. 36.11) officials of Judah plead with an Assyrian official during the siege of Jerusalem in 701 BCE not to speak "in the language of Judah" (i.e., Hebrew) in the hearing of the ordinary people of the city, but to use Aramaic. Aramaic had thus become the language of diplomacy (one understood by Judean leaders), while ordinary people understood only Hebrew; and the Assyrian wanted such ordinary people to understand his call to surrender.

From the sixth century BCE Aramaic continued to spread as the vernacular in the Palestinian region. Jeremiah 10.11 is in Aramaic, as is Ezra 4.8–6.18; 7.12–26. The Aramaic passages in Ezra are primarily official documents, and they reflect the fact that the *Persian empire recognized the position of Aramaic by making one form of it an official language—the so-called Imperial or Official Aramaic. A Jewish colony at Elephantine (Yeb) in Upper Egypt (Map 7:F6) has left many Aramaic papyri from the fifth century BCE (including letters about the rebuilding of a Jewish temple there and about the *Passover); other documents in Aramaic from Egypt, Palestine, and other Near Eastern countries of this century and succeeding centuries have been found. Daniel 2.4b–7.28 is in Aramaic, and the book is usually dated around 164 BCE, though the author probably used earlier sources. Some scholars postulate a connection between the story of *Nebuchadnezzar's madness in Daniel 4 and the Prayer of Nabonidus, an Aramaic text from *Qumran which tells how Nabonidus, the last king of Babylon, was ill in Tema in North Arabia and was healed by the intercession of a Jew. Among other Aramaic texts from Qumran are the Genesis Apocryphon (the story of Abraham, in general dependence on Genesis), parts of 1 Enoch, and a Targum (a free translation) of Job, which differs from the Targum of later times (see Translations, article on Targums).

By the first century CE, Aramaic was in general use in Palestine, especially in Galilee, although Hebrew was also spoken as a vernacular, especially in Judea (see Hebrew). In the New Testament we find bar, the Aramaic word for "son," instead of Hebrew ben, in several personal names (e.g., *Barabbas, *Bartholomew, Bartimaeus) and in the patronymic of *Simon Peter, Bar-Jona (Matt. 16:17 [RSV]), and Aramaic words are used even in Jerusalem: *Golgotha (Mark 14.72, etc.), Gabbatha (John 19.13: "in Hebrew" probably means "in the language of the Hebrews" and can thus denote Aramaic), and Akeldama (Acts 1.19). Some of the words of Jesus are Aramaic: "Talitha cum" (Mark 5.41), and "*Eloi, Eloi, lema sabachthani" (Mark 15.34; cf. Matt. 27.46, but there is a variant reading in Hebrew); but "Ephphatha" (Mark 7.34) and "*Abba" (Mark 14.36; cf. Rom. 8.15) can be explained as either Hebrew or Aramaic. The statement in Matthew 26.73 that Peter's speech showed him to be a Galilean has been illustrated by rabbinic references to the inability of Galileans to pronounce guttural consonants correctly. As a Galilean, Jesus spoke Aramaic, and on the cross he quoted Psalm 22.1 in Aramaic, not in the Hebrew original, but he probably also spoke Hebrew. When Rabban Gamaliel wrote to Jews in Galilee—probably in the late first century CE—he wrote in Aramaic, according to the Babylonian Talmud (*Sanh.* 11b).

Many Aramaic documents from the early centuries CE have been preserved. The *Nabatean Arabs, who lived to the east and south of Palestine, used an Aramaic dialect, as did the inhabitants of Palmyra in the Syrian desert. Some letters and other documents from the Second Jewish Revolt against the Romans in 132–35 CE are written in Aramaic, some in Hebrew, and some in *Greek. They include letters from the leader of the revolt, who has usually been known as Bar Kokhba ("the son of the star" in Aramaic; cf. Num. 24.17), but whose real name was Bar or Ben Kosiba. Texts of the following centuries show differences between western and eastern dialects of Aramaic. The distinction appears, for example, in the Targums: the Jerusalem or Palestinian Targums (on the Pentateuch) are in western Aramaic, whereas the Targums of Onkelos (the Pentateuch) and Jonathan (the Former and Latter Prophets) reached their final form in the east, though they were probably originally composed in Palestine. Western dialects include Jewish Palestinian Aramaic (e.g., the Jerusalem Talmud) and Samaritan and Christian Palestinian Aramaic; and eastern dialects include Babylonian Aramaic (e.g., the Babylonian Talmud), Syriac, and Mandaic (the language used of the texts of the gnostic Mandean sect).

Syriac reached its present form ca. 200 CE. Although there are earlier, non-Christian inscriptions, most of the Syriac literature is Christian, because it became the standard language of many eastern churches. They carried its use as far as South India and even China.

Aramaic was eventually replaced by Arabic in the Near East as a result of the spread of Islam. A western form survives in a few Syrian villages, and there is still a vernacular form of Syriac.

J. A. EMERTON

Ararat. A mountainous country surrounding Lake Van in Armenia (Map 6:H3). It is commonly referred to as Urartu in *Assyrian texts, in which it first appears as a conglomeration of kingdoms in the thirteenth century BCE. A unified kingdom reached its zenith in the late ninth century under the dynasty founded by Sarduri I; its decline began when Sarduri II was defeated by *Tiglath-pileser III in 743 BCE. The end came in the early sixth century, when Urartu was conquered by the *Medes. In the Bible Ararat can be an enemy of Assyria (2 Kings 19.37; Isa. 37.38) or Babylon (Jer. 51.27). It is best known, however, as the region ("the mountains of Ararat," not "Mount Ararat"; Gen. 8.4) in which *Noah's *ark came to rest after the *Flood. In spite of later Jewish, Christian, and Muslim traditions that sought to identify the mountain on which Noah landed, all attempts to do so have ended in failure.   CARL S. EHRLICH

Archaeology and the Bible.

History of Archaeology. Archaeology is the study of the remains of ancient civilizations uncovered through excavations. It is a relatively young discipline, for the first excavations in Mesopotamia were those of Paul Emile Botta at *Nineveh in 1842 and Austin Henry Layard at Nimrud in 1845, while the first in the Aegean area were conducted by Heinrich Schliemann at Troy in 1870 and at Mycenae in 1876.

Egyptian antiquities had been brought to the attention of Europe by Napoleon's invasion in 1798. Most of the activities in Egypt in the nineteenth century, such as those by Giovanni Belzoni, were treasure hunts and not excavations. At the end of the nineteenth century, William Matthew Flinders Petrie introduced some semblance of order.

It was Petrie who was the first to excavate in Palestine at Tell el-Hesi in 1890. From his prior experiences in Egypt, Petrie recognized the value of pottery for dating the strata. The first American excavations in Palestine were at *Samaria in 1908–1910 by George A. Reisner and Clarence S. Fisher, who introduced systematic methods of recording discoveries.

William Foxwell Albright, the dean of American archaeologists in the first half of the twentieth century, established a sound basis for pottery chronology in his excavations at Tell Beit Mirsim in 1926–1932. Nelson Glueck, Albright's student, conducted extensive surface surveys in Transjordan from 1933, and in Israel's Negeb from 1952.

At excavations at *Samaria (1931–1935) and at *Jericho (1952–1958), Kathleen Kenyon introduced more precise methods of analyzing soils and debris. She later excavated in *Jerusalem (1961–1967). Significant work has also been carried on by many French and German scholars.

Since 1948, Israeli scholars have assumed leading roles in the exploration of their homeland. Yigael Yadin conducted large-scale excavations at *Hazor (1956–1958) and at Masada (1963–1965). At the latter site, Yadin initiated the practice of using volunteers rather than paid workers. After 1968, Benjamin Mazar, Nahman Avigad, and Yigal Shiloh directed major excavations in *Jerusalem.

G. Ernest Wright, in his excavations at *Shechem (1956–1964), and William G. Dever, in his work at Gezer (1964–1971), trained scores of young American excavators. It was in the 1966 season at Shechem that a geologist was first added to the staff. Since 1970, Palestinian archaeologists, influenced by New World archaeology, have also enlisted the help of architects, photographers, and pottery restorers, numerous scientific specialists such as osteologists, paleobotanists, and paleozoologists to reconstruct ancient ecologies and societies. Specialized laboratories are used for such processes as carbon-14 dating and neutron activation of pottery to determine its place of origin.

Ironically, often the most spectacular discoveries have been made by chance rather than by scientific deduction. At Ras Shamra in Syria a peasant's plow struck a tomb, which led to the discovery of ancient *Ugarit. Bedouin in search of a lost goat discovered the cave at *Qumran which contained the *Dead Sea Scrolls. Peasants seeking fertilizer in Egypt discovered the *Amarna tablets in 1887 and the Coptic Gnostic codices at *Nag Hammadi in 1945.

Archeological Methods. The first important attempt to identify sites in Palestine with biblical cities was made by Edward Robinson and Eli Smith in 1838 on the basis of modern Arabic place names. In a few cases, inscriptions have confirmed the identity of ancient sites, as at Gibeon, *Gezer, Arad, *Lachish, *Dan, and Abila.

In some cases, proposed identifications are in dispute, such as Albright's identification of Tell Beit Mirsim as Debir and Glueck's identification of Tell el-Kheleifeh as Ezion-geber. According to Yohanan Aharoni, out of the approximately 475 place names mentioned in the Bible only slightly more than half have been identified with any degree of certainty.

Recent surveys indicate how many new sites of ancient settlements may be discovered by systematic searches. Israeli surveys in 1965 in the Haifa area and the Negeb uncovered two hundred previously unknown sites. Benno Rothenberg discovered two hundred new sites in the Negeb and Arabah and a hundred in the Sinai in 1966–68. Surveys of the Golan Heights and the West Bank since 1968 have plotted hundreds of other new sites.

Most ancient Near Eastern cities have left their remains behind in stratified mounds called "tells" ("tell" is the transliteration of the Arabic, while the spelling "tel" is from Hebrew; cf. Josh. 11.13). These trapezoidal mounds are to be found in the Near East because settled urban populations have existed there for millennia, with generation after generation rebuilding upon earlier rubble; the debris was kept in a compact shape by the city wall. The height of a tell can be considerable. In Mesopotamia the tells range from 17 m (56 ft) at Kish up to 43 m (140 ft) at Tell Brak. In Palestine, the depth of debris at Jericho is about 18 m (60 ft), and at Beth-shan and *Megiddo about 21 m (70 ft).

The excavator's first step is to secure permission from the country's Department of Antiquities. The next step, if the land is privately owned, is either to purchase the area to be excavated, as at Megiddo and Dothan, or more usually to rent it with the understanding that the land will be restored to its former condition after the termination of the excavations. Not only must rent be paid for the use of the land but compensation must be given for the crops destroyed. The cost of excavating areas occupied with houses is prohibitive. Only where generous funding is available, such as for the excavations of the Athenian Agora, is this possible.

The cost of financing excavations has varied greatly. At one extreme was the luxury of the University of Chicago's expedition after World War I at Megiddo with its budget of sixteen million dollars. At the other extreme was the fabled austerity of Petrie's camp in Egypt, where a little more than a dollar per week was spent for provisions. Kenyon's excavations at Jericho cost about twelve thousand dollars per year, and her later work at Jerusalem about thirty thousand dollars per year. On average, the cost of a season's expedition now runs well over one hundred thousand dollars.

In the nineteenth century, individual subscribers in Britain supported the Palestine Exploration Fund and the Egypt Exploration Fund, which sponsored surveys, excavations, and publications. Wealthy patrons such as John D. Rockefeller, Charles Marston, Jacob Schiff, and Leon Levy have helped pay for excavations respectively at Megiddo, Lachish, Samaria, and Ashkelon.

Recent excavations have depended upon consortia of schools and other organizations. Funds for Kenyon's work at Jericho came from forty-three universities, societies, and museums. Along with securing the necessary funds the director must assemble a staff of trained supervisors and a work crew of laborers.

The site to be excavated is surveyed, both horizontally, in a grid marked with pegs, and vertically, in elevations from a benchmark. The supervisor then determines which fields should be excavated, for example, over the probable sites of the gate, the wall, the chief residences. In some recent cases, the use of a magnetometer or aerial/satellite photography has facilitated the location of such structures. Each field is then subdivided, often into a series of six-meter (ca. 20 ft) squares. Each of the square areas will be worked by an area supervisor and six or eight workers or volunteers.

The digging season varies from two weeks to six months. Most expeditions take place in the summer for the sake of participating professors and students. The exception would be work at sites such as Jericho or Susa, which are unbearably hot in the summer.

The average workday is a strenuous one, beginning long before sunrise to avoid having to work in the hot afternoon. Workers often rise before five A.M., dig for three hours, have breakfast, and then work for another three hours before lunch. After lunch, pottery is washed and sorted. The director and his staff will often work late into the night, recording their finds.

The object of the excavator is to dig stratigraphically, that is, to remove the debris and associated objects layer by layer. Bulldozers have sometimes been used to remove modern remains or ancient fill. But even those who are interested chiefly in earlier levels are obliged to record carefully later occupations, such as those of Byzantine and Islamic periods.

Since successive strata were not deposited at a uniformly level rate over a flat surface, absolute heights are not chronologically meaningful. Added complications arise from intrusions such as pits. The archaeologist often finds "robber trenches," where stones have been removed for reuse.

Picks are used to break up the soil, and large oversized hoes to scoop up the dirt into baskets. For finer work a small pick is used together with a trowel and a brush. Also essential are meter-sticks, levels, strings, tags, and labels for measuring and recording; computers are being used more and more in the field for registering excavated materials, as well as in preparing them for publication after the digging has come to an end. When a special object is found, its exact location and level are recorded. Ordinary sherds are placed in carefully labeled buckets for washing and later examination.

It is often worth sieving the soil to retrieve small objects such as coins. Most bronze coins appear as tiny spots of green in the soil. During the first three years of the Mazar excavation at Jerusalem ten thousand coins were found.

The earlier Fisher-Reisner methods had included the careful recording of objects and of building levels. But between levels their diagrams often showed empty spaces where attribution to a stratum was made according to the absolute height of the deposits. Kenyon introduced improved methods, which involved the careful cutting of balks (unexcavated strips between squares) and the minute analysis of the different types of soils that appeared in the vertical sections created by the balks. Her methods are best suited to small areas where sizable architecture is not present, although attention to stratigraphy is essential in any context.

One of the important problems facing the excavator is the location of the dump for depositing the earth that has been dug up. Care must be taken that nothing of value is thrown away. From the Chicago dump at Megiddo, for example, Israeli shepherds recovered an invaluable fragment of the Babylonian *Gilgamesh Epic.

Special difficulty attends the excavations of sites where buildings are made of stones, which are almost invariably reused. On the other hand, the detection of mud brick walls is also difficult. Tombs present special problems: they have often been reused and may be tightly packed with skeletons and objects that must be removed with special care. Tombs often reward the excavator with whole vessels and even jewelry. Caves are often packed deep with noxious bat droppings.

It is highly desirable that the areas excavated should, if possible, be tested to bedrock or to virgin soil. When, however, the water table is reached, the entire trench turns quickly into a quagmire. This is why Robert Koldewey in his work at *Babylon could explore only the later Neo-Babylonian level of *Nebuchadrezzar and not the Old Babylonian level of *Hammurapi.

The development of underwater archaeology was made possible by the invention in 1942 by Jacques-Yves Cousteau and Emile Gagnan of the aqualung and depth-compensating regulator. The advent of scuba (Self-Contained Underwater Breathing Apparatus) diving made the process much cheaper and simpler. Underwater explorations have clarified the Herodian seaport of Caesarea, and other coastal sites and harbors throughout the Mediterranean.

Archaeological Finds. The most common objects to be found are sherds of broken pottery in enormous quantities. James Pritchard estimated that four seasons at Gibeon produced in excess of two hundred thousand sherds. All the pieces of pottery are washed and sorted, but often only a fraction are saved and recorded. Of almost one hundred fifty thousand sherds washed in the first season at Dothan, Joseph Free recorded six thousand pieces.

A tiny fraction of sherds may have inscriptions on them. Over fifty thousand pieces were washed at Gibeon before an inscribed ostracon appeared. Important inscriptions have been preserved on ostraca from Samaria, Arad, and Lachish.

An ivory from Megiddo depicts nude captives being brought before a king seated on a throne. Hundreds of decorated ivory fragments have been found, fittingly enough, at Samaria in view of the reference to Ahab's "ivory house" (1 Kings 22.39). These illustrate the "beds of ivory" denounced by Amos (6.4). Carved ivories from Arslan Tash and elsewhere depict an alluring goddess or woman peering out of a window (cf. 2 Kings 9.30).

From the Assyrian siege at Lachish in 701 BCE excavators found an extraordinary assemblage of fifteen hundred to two thousand skeletons over which animal bones, mostly of pigs, had been scattered. Human skeletons can provide medical information. Three skulls from Lachish had been trephined, that is, holes had been cut into their skulls, perhaps to drain fluids resulting from trauma or disease. Evidence of gold, silver, and even bronze implants have been found in teeth from Egypt, Phoenicia, and Palestine. Measurements of skeletons found in tombs of the Herodian period indicate that the average person of that day was quite short, about 1.6 m (5 ft 3 in) tall.

Highly perishable objects, such as textiles, have been found but rarely in Palestine, and only in the dry Dead Sea region. For example, wooden boxes, coils of flax, basketry, and the oldest preserved toga were found in the caves occupied during the Second Jewish Revolt (ca. 135 CE). Even the tresses of a woman were preserved at Masada.

The many figurines found are generally interpreted as cultic, especially the nude female figurines. Representations of riders and horses found at Jerusalem may have been related to a solar cult; animal figurines from Beth-shan may have emanated from the cult of Nergal/Mekal/Seth.

Many small seals bear not only important inscriptions but also fine artistic representations. The seal of Shema found at Megiddo has a magnificent engraving of a roaring lion, the seal of Jaazaniah from Tell en-Nasbeh depicts a fighting cock, and a seal from Arad bears the outline plan of the citadel.

Metal objects vary greatly in their state of preservation. Gold objects are the best preserved; silver is usually covered with black tarnish, and bronze with a greenish patina. Iron rusts badly—often to a residue of reddish powder. Among the most significant objects in silver ever found are two amulets (ca. 600 BCE) inscribed with the priestly benediction of Numbers 6.24–26—the oldest biblical text discovered to date.

Among the most valuable metal objects are coins, usually made of silver, copper, or bronze. Coinage, which was invented in the seventh century BCE, was introduced into the Levant by the sixth century and was being minted locally by the fifth. Discoveries of coins in Palestine from the Persian period indicate that references to coins in Ezra 2.69; 8.27 and Nehemiah 7.70–72, whether they are interpreted as Persian darics or Greek drachmas, are not anachronistic. The earliest Greek coins (sixth century BCE) found in Palestine include one from Thasos found at Shechem, one from Athens, and another from Cos found at Jerusalem. (See also Money.)

Archaeological Evidence and Biblical Traditions. To appreciate the impact that archaeology has had on our understanding of biblical history and times, one must recall that pervasive skepticism about ancient traditions prevailed among biblical scholars in the nineteenth and early twentieth centuries. Working only with the literary sources, Julius Wellhausen and Ferdinand C. Baur respectively discounted the historical validity of the *Pentateuch and *Acts (*see* Interpretation, History of, *article on* Modern Biblical Criticism). Archaeological discoveries subsequently convinced scholars such as William Foxwell Albright and William M. Ramsay of the presence of sound traditions preserved in those biblical texts.

In some cases, the lack of expected archaeological data still poses problems. Often, however, excavations illuminate the background of the biblical narratives, and occasionally dramatically confirm them. But archaeology cannot "prove" the Bible: archaeological materials are for the most part rubble whose survival, discovery, and publication is fragmentary. Without inscriptional finds, the evidence is mute and requires interpretation. Furthermore, the biblical perspective is essentially religious. Archaeology may uncover the splendid structures built by *Solomon, *Ahab, or *Herod, but will not help us understand why the Bible condemns those monarchs. Archaeology may give us a better understanding of the *crucifixion and the tomb of Jesus Christ, but can say nothing of his *resurrection.

Chronological terms. Beginning with the fourth millennium BCE, the following is the usual division of eras for the Levant: Early Bronze Age (EB) = ca. 3200–2000 BCE; Middle Bronze Age (MB) = ca. 2000–1550 BCE; Late Bronze Age (LB) = ca. 1550–1225 BCE; Iron Age = ca. 1225–539 BCE; Persian Period = 539–332 BCE; Hellenistic Period = 332–363 BCE; Roman Period = 63 BCE – 324 CE.

Primeval history. Mesopotamian literature provides some parallels to the biblical stories of the *creation and the *Flood. Genesis, however, differs from the polytheistic cosmology of *Enuma Elish*, the "Babylonian creation epic" (ca. 1100 BCE), which describes how Marduk, the god of *Babylon, created the heavens and the earth from the carcass of Tiamat, the goddess of the deep.

The publication by George A. Smith in 1872 of the Babylonian flood story from the *Gilgamesh Epic created something of a sensation because of its parallels with the biblical Flood story (Gen. 6–9). In 1965, W. G. Lambert and Alan Millard published another epic, Atrahasis, which contains both a creation and a flood account. The Babylonian gods sent the flood because they could not sleep due to the noisy tumult of human beings.

Leonard Woolley believed that he had found evidence of the flood in a three m (ten ft) waterborne layer of sediment at *Ur dated to roughly 4000 BCE. But this does not correlate with other flood deposits, such as those at Fara and Kish, dated to about 2700 BCE, and flooding in the Mesopotamian river basin was a frequent occurrence. Thus, while there is general support for a background of catastrophic flooding, there is no certain correlation of a sediment layer with the biblical Flood.

Ancestral age. Although Julius Wellhausen and many later scholars have questioned the historicity of the narratives of the *ancestors of Israel as found in Genesis 12–50, evidence from Mesopotamia and Syria tends to support the antiquity and authenticity of many of the biblical traditions.

Woolley's excavations revealed the advanced civilization of *Ur in the third millennium BCE. Ur-nammu, a king at the end of the third millennium, promulgated the earliest known law code. Ur and Haran, where *Abraham and Terah are said to have sojourned, were both centers of the worship of Sin, the moon god.

The MB royal palace at *Mari on the Euphrates has yielded an archive of twenty-five thousand tablets, which provide evidence that names in Abraham's *genealogy were current in the area in the early second millennium CE. The Mari texts illustrate the system of power alliances prior to the rise of *Hammurapi, similar to the alliance related in Genesis 14.

Texts from Alalakh (eighteenth century BCE) and *Nuzi (fifteenth century BCE) have been cited to illuminate the social customs of the ancestors. *Sarah's provision of her handmaid to Abraham (Gen. 16) to procure a son was an accepted custom, also attested in the Code of Hammurapi.

Many scholars date Abraham and Isaac to the MB I period (also called EB IV and Intermediate EB/MB). A number of nonwalled villages and hundreds of smaller settlements from this period in the Negeb may illustrate the kind of seminomadic sites implied in Genesis.

The story of *Joseph (Gen. 37–50), which contains what may be called "Egyptianisms," can be set in the Hyksos period (seventeenth century BCE) or earlier. A papyrus in the Brooklyn Museum dated to the eighteenth century BCE contains a list of Semites sold as slaves to Egypt; a

Ugaritic text tells of a man who was sold by his companions to some passing Egyptians (Gen. 37.25–28). Many scholars, however, date to the first millennium the Joseph narrative because of its attestation of the personal names. But one should note the loss of papyri from the Delta region, which may have contained earlier evidence.

The Exodus. The sojourn of the Israelites in Egypt is not recorded in Egyptian documents. The sole reference to Israel comes from the stele of Merneptah (late thirteenth century BCE), which refers to them in the land of *Canaan. The storehouse of Ramesses (Exod. 1.11) has been identified with Qantir (Map 2:Q2).

Canaanite parallels have led many scholars to argue for the antiquity of the Song of the Sea (Exod. 15). Literary comparisons between the Mosaic *covenant and second-millennium treaties, especially those of the *Hittites, support arguments for its antiquity.

Two dates for the *Exodus have been proposed: an early date of about 1440 BCE, and a late date of about 1270. No definitive archaeological evidence confirms the traditional southern route through the Sinai peninsula or the location of Mount *Sinai.

The Israelites passed from the Sinai through the Transjordanian kingdoms of *Edom and of *Moab. A glistening bronze snake found at Timnah illustrates the episode recorded in Numbers 21.9. The account concerning the prophet *Balaam, called by the king of Moab to curse the Israelites (Num. 22–24), is remarkably paralleled by an Aramaic inscription from Deir 'Alla in Transjordan, dating from the late eighth century BCE.

One of the arguments for the late date of the Exodus was Nelson Glueck's conclusion from his surveys of Transjordan that there were no settled populations in Edom and Moab in the Middle and Late Bronze Ages. More recently, evidence of settlement in these periods has been found.

The conquest. Palestine before its conquest by the Israelites was occupied by the Canaanites, whose culture has been illuminated by texts from the Syrian coastal site of *Ugarit, destroyed around 1200 BCE. Ugaritic literary texts feature such Canaanite deities as *Baal, El, and *Astarte. Canaanite temples have been uncovered at many sites, including several at *Hazor, the greatest city in ancient Palestine.

The date of the *conquest of Canaan hinges on the date of the Exodus. The fourteenth-century BCE *Amarna letters discovered in Egypt include correspondence from Palestinian kings, asking for Egyptian aid against the Habiru. Although it is not possible to equate the *Hebrews with the Habiru, the former may have been a part of the larger movement of the Habiru.

Archaeological evidence for the conquest is problematic. Evidence for LB settlements at *Jericho, Gibeon, and Ai are nonexistent, scanty, eroded, or not yet discovered. The destruction in the thirteenth and twelfth centuries of strong Canaanite cities such as Hazor, Bethel, and Tell Beit Mirsim has been attributed to the Israelites. Some of the destructions of western cities at this time may have been caused by the Egyptians or invading *Philistines. The evidence of early Iron Age newcomers in Upper Galilee and in the Negeb may indicate a peaceful infiltration of Israelites in those areas. Since *Shechem shows no evidence of destruction in this period, it may have passed peacefully into Israelite hands (see Josh. 24).

The judges. The archaeological record of random destructions correlates with the picture of political chaos that prevailed in the era of the judges. The miraculous victory over Canaanite chariots celebrated in the archaic Song of *Deborah (Judg. 5) may be the explanation of the destructions around 1125 BCE of the sites of Taanach and Tel Qedesh in the Jezreel Valley. A twelfth-century ostracon with an abecedary from Izbet Sartah demonstrates the literacy of the day (cf. Judg. 8.14). The late twelfth-century destruction at Shechem may come from the violent episode of Abimelech (Judg. 9). Micah's household shrine (Judg. 17.5) may be compared to a shrine found at Tel Qiri. The destruction of the Canaanite city of Laish (Dan) may be attributed to the migration of the tribe of Dan (Judg. 18.29).

Much of Judges and 1 Samuel are occupied with the conflict between the coastal *Philistines and the Israelites over the Shephelah territory between them. The plan of the Philistine temple that Samson overthrew (Judg. 16.29) has been illuminated by the discovery of such a temple with two column bases at Tell el-Qasile. Philistine pottery from Ashdod and elsewhere, which resembles Mycenean prototypes, betrays their Aegean origins (Amos 9.7).

The united monarchy. The twelve Israelite *tribes were united briefly under three kings, *Saul, *David, and *Solomon. Saul won renown by his triumphs over the Philistines, who had dominated the Israelites by their monopoly of metallurgical technology (1 Sam. 13.19–22). An iron plow point was discovered in the excavations of Saul's fortress at Gibeah.

David succeeded in capturing the *Jebusite city of *Jerusalem. Kenyon's excavations at the base of Ophel, the city of David, uncovered a corner of the wall of the Jebusite city. A sloping, stepped structure on Ophel has been attributed to David by Shiloh. The "filling" (Hebr. millô') built both by David (2 Sam. 5.9) and by Solomon (1 Kings 9.15) was identified by Kenyon as the series of terraces on the slope of Ophel.

Earlier scholars had doubted the attribution of many of the *Psalms to David, and had dated many to a late period of Israel's history. Striking word parallels to *Ugaritic poetry now indicate that many of the Psalms may indeed date to a period as early as David's era. Ugarit has also produced the oldest musical annotation.

Solomon's celebration (1 Kings 8.65) may be compared with the feast that Ashurnasirpal II gave at Nimrud for 69,574 guests! Though Solomon built a splendid *Temple and palace in Jerusalem, no remains of these have been found. Solomonic palaces have been uncovered at *Megiddo. With brilliant insight, Yadin proved that identical triple gates were built by Solomon at Hazor, Megiddo, and *Gezer (1 Kings 9.15–17). A sanctuary at Arad was dated by its excavator Aharoni to the Solomonic period.

Solomon's trading and fame were on an international scale. An ostracon from Tell Qasile speaks of "the gold of Ophir" (1 Kings 10.11), imported by Solomon. A ninth-century South Arabian stamp seal found at Bethel may be evidence of the trade established by the queen of *Sheba. Solomon's prestige is highlighted by his marriage to the daughter of a pharaoh (1 Kings 9.16), probably Siamun.

The divided monarchy. Jeroboam I, who led the revolt against Rehoboam, Solomon's son, had taken refuge in Egypt under Shishak. In the fifth year after Solomon's death, Shishak invaded Palestine, as the Bible (1 Kings 14.25–26) and his own inscriptions at Karnak attest. A stele of Shishak has been found at Megiddo.

The polytheism that characterized popular religion in both Israel and Judah has been amply attested. A startling example from the eighth century BCE is a painting with an inscription of "Yahweh and his Asherah" found at Kuntillet 'Ajrud near Kadesh-barnea. Images of riders on horses found at Jerusalem may have belonged to a cult of the sun.

Jeroboam's northern city of Dan has yielded impressive structures, including a monumental

gate with benches, a pedestal for a throne, and a *high place. Excavators found at *Samaria magnificent buildings of *Ahab and his Phoenician wife *Jezebel, including Proto-Aeolic columns and ivory fragments.

From Ahab's reign come also the elaborate underground water system at Hazor and the "stables" at Megiddo. Ahab's military might is attested outside the Bible by texts of the Assyrian king Shalmaneser III, which credit Ahab with two thousand chariots and ten thousand infantry at the battle of Qarqar (853). One of the rare monumental inscriptions from the area is the *Moabite Stone of Ahab's enemy, King Mesha (cf. 2 Kings 3.27).

The famous Black Obelisk depicts King *Jehu (843–816 BCE) of Israel prostrating himself before Shalmaneser III. A stele of Adad-nirari III lists Joash of Samaria as offering tribute to the *Assyrians. Menahem of Israel also paid tribute to *Tiglath-pileser III (2 Kings 15.19–20).

Sargon II claimed that he captured 27,290 prisoners and "their gods," when Samaria fell in 722 BCE. The exiles were taken to places like Gozan and Calah (2 Kings 17.6); ostraca from these places list Israelite names like Menahem, Elisha, and Haggai. Sargon's army later (712) invaded Judah (Isa. 20.1), as a fragment of his stele at Ashdod confirms. The Assyrian presence is evidenced by a fortress at Tell Jemmeh, and a standard found at Tell esh-Shari'a.

The Assyrian juggernaut of *Sennacherib invaded Judah in 701 and overwhelmed city after city, including the key southern fort of *Lachish (2 Kings 18.13–17). The assault with battering rams up a ramp is illustrated in detail by reliefs from Sennacherib's palace at *Nineveh. Excavations at Lachish have uncovered the siege ramp, a counter ramp, arrowheads, the crest of a helmet, chain mail, and a chain used by the defenders against the ram.

Sennacherib, though he claims to have received tribute, does not claim the capture of Jerusalem. *Hezekiah had built the Siloam Tunnel to provide water to the city. His inscription describes how workers dug from both ends to meet in the center. Segments of the "broad wall" (Neh. 3.8), which he probably built to the west of the Temple area to enclose the "Second Quarter" (2 Kings 22.14) have been discovered. A funerary inscription from Silwan may belong to Shebna(yahu), who was rebuked by the prophet Isaiah (22.15–16) for building an ostentatious tomb.

Invasions of Judah. The early reign of *Nebuchadrezzar, including his attack on Syria and Palestine in his first year in 605 BCE, has been greatly illuminated by the publication in 1956 of the Babylonian Chronicles. These reveal a hitherto unknown battle of 601 BCE that may have misled the Judeans to rely on help from Egypt, against the advice of Jeremiah (Jer. 37.6–10). The Chronicles also describe the Babylonian attack on Jerusalem in 597 (2 Kings 24.8–17), but the portion describing the final attack in 587/586 is missing.

The advance of the Babylonian army is dramatically announced by a *Lachish ostracon, which reports "we cannot see Azekah" (see Jer. 34.7). Evidences of the devastation wrought by the Babylonians have been found at numerous Judean sites, including Jerusalem itself.

A number of seals or seal impressions probably belong to personages from this era; these bear names of such biblical figures as *Baruch, son of Neriah, Jeremiah's scribe (Jer. 36.4); Jerahmeel, Jehoiakim's son (Jer. 36.26); Jaazaniah (Jer. 40.8); and Gedaliah (Jer. 40.8).

An ostracon from Arad implies an imminent attack from the direction of *Edom. The reason *Obadiah denounced the Edomites must stem from their taking advantage of Judah during the Babylonian attack. A poignant expression in Yahweh's faithfulness even after the destruction of Jerusalem has been found at Khirbet Beit Lei (cf. Lam. 3.22–23).

Some of the splendors of the great city of *Babylon erected by Nebuchadrezzar (Dan. 4.30), such as the Ishtar Gate, have been recovered. At Babylon tablets dated 595–570 BCE explicitly confirm the biblical account that the exiled Jewish king Jehoiachin received rations from the Babylonian court (2 Kings 25.30).

The puzzling role of Belshazzar (instead of his father Nabonidus) in the book of *Daniel has been clarified by Babylonian and Aramaic documents that reveal that Nabonidus spent ten years in self-imposed exile in Arabia.

The capture of Babylon by the *Persians in 539 BCE resulted in the liberation of the Jews by *Cyrus. The magnanimity of the Persian king (Ezra 1) to other religions is fully corroborated by such documents as the Cyrus Cylinder. The Murashu texts, which list about a hundred Jewish names from the reigns of Artaxerxes I and Darius II, document the prosperity of the Jews who chose to remain in Mesopotamia.

The events recounted in Ezra-Nehemiah have been illuminated by the Elephantine papyri from Egypt, by the Xanthos inscription from Lydia, and by tablets from Persepolis. Inscriptions or papyri can be correlated with Nehemiah's opponents (Neh. 2.19)—Geshem, Tobiah, and Sanballat. Some seventy bullae acquired in 1970 reveal the names of governors of Judah who preceded Nehemiah (Neh. 5.15). Kenyon's excavations in Jerusalem clarified the line of the wall that was rebuilt (Neh. 3) and uncovered the tumble that blocked Nehemiah's donkey (Neh. 2.14).

The Hellenistic and Roman periods. The greatest discovery is the cache of *Dead Sea Scrolls, which includes our oldest manuscripts of the Hebrew Bible. In addition, Hebrew and Aramaic originals of *apocryphal works such as *Sirach and *pseudepigraphical works such as *Enoch were found.

The extensive building projects of *Herod the Great are found everywhere in Palestine: at *Jerusalem, Sebaste, Caesarea, Masada, Machaerus, *Jericho, and Herodium. The magnificent ashlars (see Mark 13.1) are visible at the *Temple platform in Jerusalem. Excavations nearby have uncovered a 64 m (210 ft) wide stairway, a limestone object inscribed *qrbn* (see Mark 7.11; *see* Corban), and debris from Titus's capture of Jerusalem. Work in the Upper City has revealed homes of the wealthy high priests, including an inscription of Bar Kathros, the head of a priestly family accused in the *Talmud of exploitation.

The magnificent remains of the synagogue at *Capernaum (Mark 1.21) have been dated to the fourth century CE on the basis of coins. Basalt remains of an earlier synagogue are visible. The second/third-century synagogue at Chorazin contains a so-called seat of Moses (Matt. 23.2). Buildings or structures identified as rare first-century CE synagogues have been found at Gamla, Herodium, and Masada. Near the Capernaum synagogue, a first-century CE fisherman's house, later venerated as Peter's house, has been uncovered.

In Jerusalem the twin pools of Bethesda (John 5.2) and the pool of Siloam (John 9.7–11) have been identified. Some scholars have placed the site of the praetorium (John 18.28), where Jesus was tried before Pilate, north of the Temple area, where flagstones under the Sisters of Zion building have been identified as the lithostraton (John 19.13) of the Fortress Antonia. The more probable site of the trial, however, is near the Jaffa Gate, where remains of Herod's palace have been found in the citadel area. In 1961, an inscription of *Pilate was found at Caesarea.

In 1968, Israeli archaeologists discovered the

first physical evidence of a victim of *crucifixion. In an ossuary, a limestone box for the redeposition of bones, were discovered a young man's *calcanei* or heel bones still pierced by an iron nail. His right *tibia* or shin bone had been fractured into slivers by a blow (cf. John 19.32). A crease in the radius indicates that the victim had been pinioned in the forearms rather than in the palms. Accordingly, the Greek word *cheiras* in Luke 24.39–40 and John 20.20, 25, 27, usually translated "hands," should perhaps be translated "arms."

Several rolling-stone type tombs may be seen in Jerusalem. Excavations in and around the Church of the Holy Sepulcher suggest that the site was outside the walls in Jesus' day. The Greek "Nazareth" inscription, thought by some to date from the reign of Claudius, warns against tampering with tombs (Matt. 28.13–15).

Many discoveries have illuminated the far-flung missions of *Paul. Excavations at Nea Paphos have uncovered an inscription of Sergius Paulus (Acts 13.7), the governor of Cyprus converted by Paul. A text dedicated to Zeus and Hermes near Lystra illustrates the episode of Acts 14.12. Inscriptions from Thessalonica confirm the accuracy of Luke's use of the term "politarchs" for rulers of that city (Acts 17.6).

Paul's speech at *Athens may have been addressed to the *Areopagus council (Acts 17.22), which met in the royal stoa recently uncovered in the agora. The reference in Paul's speech to the "*unknown God" (Acts 17.23) is illustrated by an inscription from Pergamon referring to "unknown gods."

The date of Paul's ministry in *Corinth (51 CE) has been fixed by the inscription of Gallio, the governor who tried him (Acts 18.12–17). An inscription of Erastus is probably that of one of the few wealthy members of the Corinthian church (Acts 19.22; Rom. 16.23). An inscription of a butcher marks the site of the "meat market" (1 Cor. 10.25). At Corinth, the average space available in typical *triclinia* (dining rooms) and atria not only limited the size of the house churches but could cause divisions when the wealthier Christians would be invited into the triclinium for the *love-feast, leaving the rest of the Christians outside in the atrium (1 Cor. 11.20–22).

Athletic facilities have been excavated at Isthmia, east of Corinth, the site of the Pan-Hellenic games probably observed by Paul (1 Cor. 9.24–27). A first-century harbor has been traced at Corinth's eastern harbor, Cenchreae, the home of Phoebe (Rom. 16.1).

Magnificent remains have been exposed at *Ephesus. The foundation of the temple of *Artemis, one of the seven wonders of the ancient world, was discovered after a search of six years by J. T. Wood. In front of the temple a U-shaped altar has been uncovered. Inscriptions speak about the silver images of Artemis (Acts 19.24), and the garment dedicated to the goddess. Statues of the famed goddess (Acts 19.27) have been found in thirty different places, including Caesarea. One can observe the theater that Luke gives as the scene for the assembly provoked by Paul's preaching (Acts 19.29). A fresco from a house nearby depicts scenes from Greek dramatists, including Menander, whom Paul cites (1 Cor. 15.33).

Though most New Testament cities have been excavated, there are still a number of key sites associated with Paul, such as Derbe and Colossae, which have been identified but are as yet unexcavated.   EDWIN M. YAMAUCHI

Archangels. From Greek *archaggeloi,* "chief angels" or "angels of high rank." The plural form is not found in the Bible, but in Tobit 12.15, *Raphael describes himself as "one of the seven angels who stand ready and enter before the glory of the Lord" (cf. Rev. 8.2). Further information concerning these seven angels is found in 1 *Enoch 20, whose Greek version describes them as "archangels" and lists their names as follows: Uriel, Raphael, Raguel, *Michael, Sariel, *Gabriel, and Remiel, the last name probably corresponding to the "archangel Jeremiel" of 2 Esdras 4.36. In the New Testament there are two references to individual archangels: in 1 Thessalonians 4.16 the call of the (unnamed) archangel is to herald the Lord's return, and in Jude 9 reference is made to the archangel Michael's contending with the devil over the body of Moses. But the paucity of these scriptural references is in sharp contrast to the elaborately developed angelology of the later church fathers.

See Angels.   WILLIAM H. BARNES

Areopagus. This term refers both to the "Hill of Ares" located northwest of the Acropolis in *Athens and to the Council that met on the hill until the fourth century CE. During the seventh century BCE, the Council probably watched over the laws of the city; in 462/461 BCE, the Areopagus lost its guardianship of the laws. According to the author of the Athenian Constitution, it retained the power to hear cases of deliberate wounding, homicide, poisoning that resulted in death, arson, and digging up or cutting down of the sacred olive trees of Athena. During the late fourth century BCE, the Council investigated allegations of treasonable offenses.

The judicial functions of the Council were extended during the Roman imperial period. In Acts 17.16–21, *Paul is reported to have been brought to the Hill of Ares by some *Epicurean and *Stoic philosophers because he was preaching about *Jesus and the *resurrection; there he delivered his speech about the altar of the *unknown god (17.22–32). The scene of Paul on the Areopagus constructed by the author of *Acts does not reflect an official judicial procedure or inquiry. Rather, the author of Acts has created an idealized scene of Athenian life, based upon stock motifs of Athenian topography, culture, and history, intended especially to recall the trial of Socrates. In this scene, Paul has been cast as a latter-day Socrates who discloses the true identity and plans of the unknown god to the listening *gentiles.   GUY ROGERS

Ark. The English word "ark" translates two Hebrew words that differ from each other both in form and in usage, though the *Septuagint employs one Greek word (*kibōtos*) for both.

Tēbâ means "box" or "chest." Apart from its use to designate the papyrus basket in which *Moses, as an infant, was left to float among the bulrushes of the Nile (Exod. 2.3, 5), this word is used in the Bible solely as the designation of the vessel that God commanded *Noah to construct of gopher wood (Gen. 6.14), a wood not mentioned elsewhere. It was to be large enough to contain one representative human family along with one pair of every species of animals (Gen. 6.18–21). Another form of the story speaks of seven pairs of clean animals, sufficient quantity for the sacrifice after the *Flood, and one pair of unclean animals (Gen. 7.2–3). These would ride out the rainstorm of the wrath of God. The description of Noah's ark (Gen. 6.14–16) is rather hard to understand. Its dimensions, roughly 140 m (450 ft) long, 22 m (75 ft) wide, and 12 m (45 ft) high, make it literally a very large "box." The ark had three decks (Gen. 6.16), and also natu-

rally a door. An opening, about .5 m (18 in) high, apparently ran all around the ark just below the roof and gave light and air to the vessel. There are certain points of resemblance, but more of dissimilarity, between Noah's ark and Utnapishtim's gigantic boat of the *Gilgamesh flood story.

In 1 Peter 3.20–21, Noah's ark prefigures *baptism.

'*Ārôn*, apart from its use in the sense of "coffin" (Gen. 50.26) and in the sense of "chest" for receiving money offerings (2 Kings 12.9–10; 2 Chron. 24.8, 10–11), is employed as the name of the sacred box that is variously called the ark of God, the ark of the Lord, the ark of the covenant, and so on. Data concerning this ark come from different sources and periods. It was in form a rectangular box or chest, measuring about 1 by .7 by .7 m (45 by 27 by 27 in), and made of acacia or shittim wood.

As the years went by this object became evermore venerated. It symbolized the presence of the living God at one particular spot on earth; for the God who dwelled "in the high and holy place" was also present at the ark in the midst of his people. As a result, later generations embellished descriptions of it in their traditions, seeing it as overlaid with gold both within and without (Exod. 25.10–16). The ark was transportable; it could be carried on poles overlaid with gold, which passed through rings on its side. It was considered to be of such sanctity that were an unauthorized person to touch it, even accidentally, this infraction would be punishable by death (2 Sam. 6.6).

The ark seems at one time to have contained only the two tablets of the *law (1 Kings 8.9), but according to other traditions (Heb. 9.4) it contained also *Aaron's rod that budded (Num. 17.1–10) and a golden urn holding *manna (Exod. 16.32–34).

The history of the ark parallels many of the vicissitudes of Israel. It was carried by the sons of Levi on the wilderness wanderings (Deut. 31.9); borne over the Jordan by the priests (Josh. 8.1); captured by the *Philistines (1 Sam. 4); brought to *Jerusalem by *David (2 Sam 6; 1 Chron. 13.3–14; 15.1–18). After being kept in a tentlike sanctuary (*see* Tabernacle), it was finally installed in the holiest chamber of Solomon's *Temple.

The ark had a cover or lid. Its name (Hebr. *kappōret*) is actually a theological term (cf. *kippēr*, "to purify, atone"), so we do not know what this cover looked like (Lev. 16.2, 13–15). Martin Luther described it in his German Bible as the "mercy seat" because the Lord "sat" enthroned over it in mercy, invisibly present where the wingtips of two *cherubim met above it, guarding the divine presence. So the ark represented for Israel the localized presence of God in judgment, mercy, forgiveness, and love; and because it contained the *Ten Commandments, it was a visible reminder that their life was to be lived in obedience to the expressed will of God. Since the Ten Commandments were incised on stone so as to last for all time, Israel carried in her midst God's demands for total loyalty and obedience to himself and for social justice and love of neighbor.

The ark is thought to have been captured when Jerusalem fell in 587/586 BCE, and nothing is known of its later history. Later legend reports that Jeremiah rescued it and hid it on Mount *Nebo (2 Macc. 2.4–8; but cf. Jer. 3.16).

GEORGE A. F. KNIGHT

Armageddon. A place name found only in Revelation 16.16, where it is identified as the "Hebrew" name for the location where the kings of the earth will assemble to fight against God. Scholars generally explain Armageddon (NRSV: "Harmagedon") as a Greek transliteration of the Hebrew phrase *har měgiddô* ("the mountain of Megiddo"). The city of *Megiddo, strategically located in the western part of the Esdraelon valley at the crossroads of two trade routes (Map 1:X3), was the site of several important battles in ancient times. The reference to the "mountain" of Megiddo is, however, more problematic, corresponding to no evident geographical feature in the area. Although Armageddon appears only once in the Bible, it has become a familiar designation for the future final battle between the forces of good and evil.

WILLIAM H. BARNES

Art and the Bible.

Early Art. Stories from the Bible had become the subject of a developed narrative art by the middle of the third century CE in the *synagogue discovered at Dura-Europos, where dozens of biblical scenes are depicted in frescoes; the Christian church there from the same period also has paintings representing both Old and New Testament subjects. In the sixth century, mosaics in a number of synagogues also represent biblical subjects, such as at Gerasa (modern Jerash), from the fourth or fifth century, where the procession of animals into *Noah's ark is depicted, and from the sixth century, those at Beth Alpha (the sacrifice of *Isaac), Naaran (*Daniel in the lions' den), and Gaza (*David as Orpheus). Other early illustrations of the influence of the Bible on Christian art are the mosaics in churches throughout the Near East and especially the sequence of paintings in the Roman catacombs that extend chiefly from the third to the fourth centuries CE. The purpose of these fresco paintings is not primarily to illustrate biblical material but rather to interpret them. The subjects are those that could be *typologically linked with what "fulfills" them in Christ: *Moses striking water from the rock, Noah delivered from the flood, the three men escaping from the fiery furnace, Daniel saved from the lions' den— all are juxtaposed or depicted in such a way as to indicate their anticipation of the saving, healing, releasing power of Christ as exhibited in the healing of the paralytic, the woman with the issue of blood, the Samaritan woman at the well, the miracle of the loaves, or the raising of Lazarus. No attempt is made in this painting at descriptive realism, to represent how the incident looked when it happened. Christ and the other figures are taken from contemporary art; indeed Christ is sometimes presented as a new Orpheus or Hercules, and if he appears as the good shepherd he is depicted in terms of the Hellenistic models of the day. Early Christian art is a symbolic language, and this gives it a certain indirectness; only the Christian initiate would be able to decipher in full its powerful inner meaning.

The move toward a comprehensive theological program by typological juxtapositioning of material from the Old and New Testaments is developed in the relief sculpture that began to appear on the sides of sarcophagi particularly after the Edict of Milan (313 CE). The unifying theme of these works is again salvation through Christ, and again it is treated cryptically and indirectly. On a sarcophagus in Santa Maria Antiqua in the Roman forum (third century CE) Christ appears unobtrusively as the good shepherd and as a young boy being baptized; the key to the whole work (Christianity as the new philosophy of salvation, here being pondered by a seated philosopher figure) is indicated by the extensive treatment of *Jonah, reclining like the Greek god Endymion, as a type of the saved soul. This presentation of Christian salvation does not use the *crucifixion. The same kind of typological arrangement, but more substantial and integrated into an artistic whole, is seen on the sarcophagus of Junius Bassus in the Vatican Grottoes (fourth century CE). In two panels, Christ (enthroned or entering Jerusalem) is flanked by the sacrifice of Isaac (see Aqedah), *Adam and *Eve, the sufferings of *Job, Daniel in the lions' den. The only scene from the passion of Christ is the trial before *Pilate; again, there is no crucifixion.

A particularly mature and instructive treatment of the theme of salvation, with allusions to the crucifixion, is to be seen on a Vatican sarcophagus of the middle of the fifth century CE. In the center a plain Greek equal-armed cross is surmounted by the chi-rho monogram which is encircled by a laurel victory wreath. There is no body of Christ on the cross, but on either side of it below are sleeping soldiers. To the left of the center panel are the episodes of Simon of Cyrene carrying the cross and the mock crowning of Jesus by the soldiers. To the right a double panel is devoted to the trial of Jesus before Pilate. In this sequence the artist has integrated the themes of crucifixion and *resurrection. This ability to present two themes simultaneously is one of the great strengths of visual art. The crucifixion is present in this sculptural program but only indirectly; in organic relation to the resurrection it comprises the real, though hidden, crowning of Christ in contrast to the vicarious cross-bearing of Simon, the simulated crowning of the soldiers, or the trial before Pilate—where Christ is, despite appearances, the real king who judges.

With the development of church architecture following the Edict of Milan, art soon becomes an important vehicle linking the Bible and liturgy. This is particularly the case with mosaic decoration that is organically related to its architectural setting. The best example of this is to be found in the cluster of fifth- and sixth-century Christian buildings at Ravenna, particularly the church of Sant'Apollinare Nuovo in Ravenna. In this early Byzantine church, along the north and south sides of the nave, a series of mosaic panels uses episodes from the Gospels in relation to the eucharistic celebration, which would be focused in the apse of this basilica. On the north side are scenes from the life of Jesus (including the parable of the Pharisee and the publican) leading up to the miracle at Cana of Galilee (John 2.1–12) at the edge of the sanctuary. The series on the south side starts with

the Last Supper and goes through the story of the passion (omitting the crucifixion) ending with the episode of doubting *Thomas (John 20.24–29). It is likely that the choice of these subjects was determined by the liturgical calendar in use at the time. As in the catacombs and sarcophagi, the unifying theme of the whole program is the salvation brought by Christ, with particular emphasis on martyrdom as the response to this in human life. The historiated panels just described are closely linked with two very lively processions of male and female martyrs making their way to the sanctuary; the mosaics convey a vivid sensation of movement. Martyrdom as the classic expression of following in the way of the cross is also the theme in the two baptisteries in Ravenna (of the Arians and of the Orthodox). The crucifixion is not given as a separable episode, but its meaning is diffused, so to speak, throughout the whole scheme, indicating the source of the life of the Christian martyr-follower. In the apse of the church of Sant'Apollinare in Classe (just outside Ravenna) the crucifixion is again obliquely presented, this time in the context of the transfiguration, implying that it is not an episode only of the past but is reenacted sacramentally in the eucharistic action performed in the body of the church.

Another vivid presentation in mosaic of typological themes in relation to the Eucharist is to be found in the sanctuary of the sixth-century church of San Vitale in Ravenna. On the north side, there is an integrated scene comprising *Abraham receiving the three heavenly visitors (to what looks like a eucharistic meal) and the sacrifice of Isaac, a common typological pointer to the sacrifice of Christ. Above this are Moses receiving the *law and *Jeremiah with a martyr's crown and scroll. On the south side the prefigurations of the Eucharist are *Abel offering his sacrificial lamb, and *Melchizedek. Above are Moses as shepherd and at the burning bush, and *Isaiah with martyr's crown and scroll.

The Ravenna mosaics throw light on early Christian attitudes to biblical history. The historical incidents are sketched in such a way as to suggest their permanent significance, and through the liturgy these past events become present realities.

The Middle Ages. During the Middle Ages, two very significant phases take place in the development of art: Romanesque and Gothic.

Romanesque is a term that covers the art and architecture of the eleventh and twelfth centuries, which developed from various and very different sources: classical, Byzantine, Islamic, and Mesopotamian. It thus became an art admirably equipped to express both the narrative and the symbolic requirements of a Christianity based on the Bible. Perhaps the best surviving fully articulated biblical and theological program in the Romanesque tradition is the sculpture on the royal portal of the cathedral at Chartres. The central tympanum has the seated Christ in glory surrounded by the symbols of the evangelists (Matthew: young man; Mark: lion; Luke: ox; John: eagle) and the seated elders. This derives from the visions of the book of *Revelation and is very prominent in Romanesque sculpture and painting. The adjacent bays are given over to the *ascension and the *incarnation. The latter is deliberately designed to stress the incarnation as itself God's act of self-sacrifice (the child lies on an altarlike structure and the presentation of Christ in the Temple is over an altar); no doubt this reflects eucharistic preaching of the time. As well as being a divine sacrifice, the incarnation is presented as the crown of human culture and the key to the universal meaning of all time by having the liberal arts and the signs of the zodiac in the archivolts. Somewhat in the manner of Sant'Apollinare Nuovo, a series of historiated capitals giving episodes from the life of Jesus binds the three bays together. The biblical antecedents of the New Testament story are suggested in the pillar figures of kings, queens, priests, and prophets on the columns of all three bays. Other outstanding Romanesque sculptural treatments of biblical themes in France are to be found at Vézelay, Moissac, Arles, and St. Gilles-du-Gard. The tympanum at Vézelay is especially interesting for the way it blends into one scene Christ's mission charge to the *apostles with scenes of all kinds of strange and deformed creatures drawn from early medieval fables and bestiaries, thus making a very striking interpretation of the universal Christ. In Spain, the sculptures in the cloister of Santo Domingo de Silos also relate Christ to biblical history and to a strange, somewhat surrealistic, natural world of birds with animal heads. Particularly profound at Silos is a sculptured relief that, in a way reminiscent of the Vatican sarcophagus, works into one artistic whole both crucifixion and resurrection.

The Romanesque period also saw a marked development in the use of biblical themes in painting, both in illuminated manuscripts and in fresco painting in church interiors. Some extensive examples of fresco painting are to be found in France at St. Savin-sur-Gartempe (with an impressive series of scenes from the Hebrew Bible on the ceiling of the nave), at Vicq and St. Chef; in Spain at San Isidoro in Leon; in Italy at Sant'Angelo in Formis; and in Germany on the island of Reichenau.

Extending from the thirteenth to the fifteenth centuries, the Gothic period is the high-water mark in the evolution of medieval art and architecture. In comparison with Romanesque the tendency now is toward greater realism in representation. This is well illustrated if one compares the Romanesque royal portal at Chartres with the sculpture of the north and south porches. Not that this means that the motive has become solely to illustrate the biblical narrative more strikingly by showing in more detail how the event actually happened. Rather, the typological and allegorical relating of Old and New Testament subjects still predominates, and the aim is to present as a unified whole an encyclopedia of Christian doctrine and ethics. France, where the Gothic style originated, again supplies the best examples. Chartres is the finest remaining example of this attempt to integrate architecture, sculpture, and stained glass into one comprehensive scheme. Bourges and Laon are other notable examples. The typological treatment of subjects from the Hebrew Bible remains basically that of the catacombs: biblical anticipations are juxtaposed with their fulfillment in the birth, passion, and death of Christ. The more realistic treatment of scenes from the Gospels does not indicate an interest in history for its own sake; in fact, the use of material from the Gospels in the Gothic period shows a surprising austerity compared with previous centuries. Healings, hitherto very common (the paralytic, the woman with the issue of blood, the blind man), are conspicuously absent in the Gothic period. Incidents from the life of Jesus prior to the passion story are confined to the baptism, the temptation, the sign at Cana of Galilee, and the transfiguration. This is true of illuminated manuscripts, stained glass, and sculpture. Remarkable, too, is the paucity of parables that appear in the art of this period. The emphasis falls on four parables: the good Samaritan, the ten virgins, the prodigal son, and *Dives and Lazarus—all of which were christologically interpreted in patristic and medieval preaching. Artists were not intent on giving a fully illustrated version of the biblical story, but rather on providing an accompaniment to the liturgy and on embodying the teaching of the preachers and theological commentators. The motive is still to make a doctrinal point, but not until the Italian Renaissance do we find anything like a descriptive treatment of the nativity. Throughout the Gothic period, the scene of the nativity is mysterious and troubled: the mother of Christ lies apart from her son who appears not in a manger but on a sacrificial altar.

The Renaissance and Reformation. As far as the influence of the Bible on art is concerned, the Renaissance and the Reformation are best considered together. The early Italian Renaissance led to a fresh development of the classical tradition in art, already discernible in the Gothic sculpture at Chartres, and to a renewed emphasis on humanism and textual studies. As the Reformation proceeded, the authority of the Bible became more isolated; there was also a revival of the aniconic principle found in the *Ten Commandments, so that the visual arts were regarded at best as unnecessary decoration to the biblical text and at worst as a misleading distraction. The Counter-Reformation saw a deliberate attempt to restore the position of the arts as ancillary to the Bible and subject to the rules laid down by the Council of Trent in 1563.

The great change noticeable in the use of biblical subjects at the Renaissance is the move from a largely two-dimensional hieratic art to something more realistic and more three-dimensional in perspective. Byzantine and medieval art as a whole had presented biblical subjects in their transcendental and theological perspective, especially in the light of the Last Judgment. Renaissance art, while not denying this reference, gave more prominence to the natural and the human. The change of mood is well illustrated by the sequence of biblical scenes by Giotto (1266/7–1337) in the frescoes of the Arena chapel at Padua. Such scenes as the betrayal or the lamentation have a depth of human feeling and a realism that herald developments to come in Renaissance painting. This new accent affected the treatment of New Testament subjects. One can say that a certain kind of "quest of the historical Jesus" began in art in, for example, a painter like Masaccio (1401–1428?) in his frescoes in the Brancacci chapel of Santa Maria del Carmine in Florence. These, whether the *Expulsion from the Garden of Eden* or *The Tribute Money,* show a new kind of bodily realism and a new interest in the happening for its own sake rather than its symbolic, didactic, or doctrinal significance. A compellingly realistic treatment of the resurrection by Donatello (1386–1466) in San Lorenzo, Florence, has also great

religious depth. It succeeds in linking resurrection with crucifixion; the austere Christ who emerges from the slime of the tomb is a risen Christ who has really suffered and really died. This is in great contrast to the crucifixion of Raphael (1483–1520) in the National Gallery, London, where the interest of the artist is more in classical harmony, design, and symmetry. Leonardo da Vinci (1452–1519) is more successful (e.g., in his *Madonna of the Rocks* and *The Last Supper*) in combining technique of design with religious depth. Michelangelo (1476–1564) shows the late Renaissance exuberance in the human body and composition on the grand scale. His treatment of *creation and Last Judgment in the Sistine chapel in the Vatican contrasts sharply with the handling of these themes in Romanesque art.

Something of Luther's realism in Christology ("You can't drag Christ down too deeply into our human nature") finds its way into the work of an artist who was much influenced by his teaching, Albrecht Dürer (1471–1528), especially his woodcuts and engravings. His series on the passion, in which he sees himself involved in the situation of Christ, is very Lutheran in feel. Equally striking are his woodcuts on the book of Revelation, with their realistic detail and the way Dürer contextualizes the apocalyptic scenes in contemporary society. Dürer's contemporary, Mathias Grünewald (ca. 1470/80–1528), was also influenced by Luther, and his famous Isenheim altarpiece of the crucifixion in the Unterlinden Museum in Colmar, France, marks a turning point in the iconography of that subject. It is a crucifixion that in its grim detail would not have been possible in the patristic period, when the victory of the crucified Christ was emphasized. While Luther, too, saw the atonement in terms of a great divine victory over death and sin, he felt that such a theology of glory could play down the stark realities of human life in its suffering. Grünewald's Isenheim crucifixion, with its gangrenous-looking flesh and clawlike hands, is a powerful statement of what Luther would have called a theology of the cross. Grünewald's crucifixion is not only realistic representation but it also retains symbolic elements with its unusual introduction of *John the Baptist to the scene (against a background of the text: "He must increase, but I must decrease" [John 3.30]) and the lamb with the vexillum of victory.

The Reformed tradition attains its most considerable expression in art in the work of Rembrandt (1606–1669), who must be classed as one of the great artistic commentators on the Bible. Biblical events and personalities were for Rembrandt more than a source of material for dramatic illustration, as they tended to be for Rubens. Rembrandt came to see in the biblical history his own and everyone's personal story. His painting of subjects from both testaments have a deeply felt interior quality, and his biblical work as a whole embodies a profound sense that the Bible is not only past history, but also present and universal experience. This is particularly true of the paintings and etchings of his later years, for example his crucifixions, where, like Dürer, he sees his own tribulations as a participation in those of Christ. The Hebrew Bible for Rembrandt is important in its own right and not simply as a preface to the New Testament, and no artist had hitherto entered with such intensity into the spirit of such subjects as the sacrifice of Isaac (before this time treated for the most part typologically), *Joseph interpreting his dreams, or the relations between *Saul and *David. Memorable New Testament subjects are Christ healing the sick, the return of the prodigal son, the crucifixion (especially those of his later years), and Christ at Emmaus.

The Modern Period. The eighteenth century did not produce many works of significance for appreciating the use of the Bible in art. The biblical paintings of Tiepolo (1695–1770) are on a rich and dramatic scale but remain primarily decorative. Idiosyncratic as may have been the personal religion of William Blake (1757–1827), his watercolors and etchings of biblical subjects have a sweep and intensity of great power. Especially worthy of mention are his engravings for the book of Job.

The nineteenth century, however, saw a new attempt at authentic realism and feeling in the work of the pre-Raphaelites and the painstaking attempts to reproduce accurately the Palestinian scene in the work of systematic illustrators of the Bible, such as James Tissot (1836–1902).

The twentieth century has proved to be a creative period for the use of biblical themes in art, and especially of new interpretations of the crucifixion. Graham Sutherland (1903–1980) has said that no one in the twentieth century can conceive of the crucifixion apart from Auschwitz. His crucifixions in St. Matthew, Northampton, and in Coventry Cathedral fuse event and symbol in a way that is reminiscent of Grünewald.

The two most significant artists in the twentieth century influenced by the Bible are Georges Rouault and Marc Chagall. Rouault (1871–1958), in his portraits of Christ and especially in his scenes from the passion, draws on the Byzantine tradition of the icon, and in his "biblical landscapes" he makes an innovative attempt to convey the nature of salvation in terms of landscapes, which, while they appear threatening to human life, nevertheless contain space for human beings to experience the accompanying presence of Christ.

Marc Chagall (1887–1985) is an outstanding commentator in art on biblical subjects. Drawing on both Jewish and Christian traditions and developing, like Blake, his own personal mythology, his work in painting, etching, and stained glass constitutes a uniquely important interpretation of the Bible. No painter since Rembrandt has so entered into the spirit of the Bible. Examples of how he relates, for example, creation and crucifixion are to be found in the series *Message biblique* housed in the Musée National in Nice. Chagall is also a significant figure in the evolution of the iconography of the crucifixion. He combines the suffering and hope in a new and compelling manner by relating the *Torah and the crucifixion of Christ. In a way reminiscent of Rouault's biblical landscapes, Chagall's volcanic and tumultuous scenes yet suggest the possibility of deliverance and hope, in, for instance, *Obsession* (1943), by the insertion of a green crucifix, recalling very effectively the cross as the tree of life in medieval art.

See also Illustrated Bibles.   JOHN TINSLEY

Artemis of the Ephesians. Artemis was the Greek goddess of the woods and hunting, as well as the patron of women in childbirth, identified with the Roman goddess Diana. The early background of Artemis of the Ephesians is hidden in legends and sources related to the Greek colonization of Ionia. It seems reasonable, however, to conclude that the original goddess was an amalgam of the imported Greek Artemis and an indigenous goddess, perhaps an Anatolian mother goddess.

The Ephesian Artemis functioned primarily as the tutelary deity of *Ephesus. Although she was the deity "whom all Asia and the whole world worship" (Acts 19.27), her central shrine was located in and protected by the city. Religious artifacts from this cult have been found as far west as Spain and as far east as Palestine, but only "the city of the Ephesians [was] the temple keeper of the great Artemis, and of the statue that fell from heaven" (Acts 19.35).

There has been much confusion and misunderstanding of the goddess, arising largely from a polemical Christian misnomer that labeled the egg-shaped objects attached to certain depictions of the goddess as female breasts. From the epithet "multi-breasted" it was a short, but incorrect, leap to the conclusion that the goddess was primarily a fertility goddess. In fact, there is no scholarly consensus that the egg-shaped objects attached to the goddess represented breasts. Even if they did and this mammary/fertility symbol lay at the heart of the religion, it is difficult to explain why this depiction appeared so late in the development of the cult. In addition, the Ephesians, particularly in the Greco-Roman era, associated their goddess with the chaste Greek Artemis rather than a mother goddess of Anatolia or one of the fertility goddesses of the East. The primary internal sources of the religion itself, such as texts, coins, statuary, and inscriptions, offer no cogent evidence for depicting this goddess or her cult as principally a symbol of sexuality and fecundity.

The goddess was well known for her wealth, which stemmed from two circumstances. Her temple served as a bank both for the safe deposit of others' wealth and for loans at a profitable rate of interest. The goddess also owned extensive lands and fisheries that contributed to her great wealth. Others, such as manufacturers of devotional items involving the goddess (Acts 19.23–27), received income as long as the goddess's reputation flourished.

Because of its size and wealth, the temple of Artemis was acclaimed as one of the seven wonders of the ancient world. It was constructed of marble (127 columns, each 18 m [60 ft] tall), possessed an external horseshoe-shaped altar (29 by 20 m [96 by 66 ft]) and was the largest Greek temple in antiquity (67 by 130 m [220 by 425 ft]). It was damaged by invading Gothic raiders during the mid-third century CE and finally fell into disuse because of Christian ascendancy in the fourth and fifth centuries. The temple no longer stands, and its exact location was unknown for centuries until its foundations were unearthed in the late nineteenth century.

RICHARD E. OSTER, JR.

Ascension of Christ. Despite the great importance and influence of the early church's belief in the ascension of Christ, it is described explic-itly in the New Testament only twice. In Acts, after the resurrected Christ reminded his apostles that they will be empowered by the Holy Spirit, he was "lifted up, and a cloud took him out of their sight" (Acts 1.9). The second-century CE addition to the conclusion of Mark adds that after Christ's ascension he "sat down at the right hand of God" (Mark 16.19).

In the Hellenistic world the ascent of a king, prophet, hero, or holy man to the heavens, the place of the gods, was a well-known motif signifying the divine status of the one who ascended. Heracles was deified through an ascension to heaven, and Ganymede became immortal when Zeus lifted him into heaven to serve as cupbearer to the gods. More generally, under the influence of Platonism, all human souls were believed to be immortal and returned to the heavens when cleansed of their mortal attachments. Christ's ascension similarly demonstrated his divinity, but more importantly, through the church's prophetic *interpretation of the Jewish scriptures, the ascension of Christ also signaled the beginning of a messianic kingdom and the empowerment of Christ's followers by virtue of their identification with him through the rite of *baptism.

Although rare in Jewish tradition, ascent into heaven is recorded in the case of *Enoch, who "walked with God; then he was no more, because God took him" (Gen. 5.24), and the prophet *Elijah, "who ascended in a whirlwind into heaven" (2 Kings 2.11); noncanonical writings also record the ascensions of Abraham, Moses, Isaiah, and Ezra. The ascension of Christ was unique, however, because of its eschatological significance for early Christianity. The authors of the New Testament believed that Psalm 110, celebrating the king seated at the right hand of God, referred to the ascended and victorious Christ who was exalted over all heavenly powers. The ascension was also seen as an elevated form of priestly sacrifice, for Christ is described as "the great high priest who has passed through the heavens" (Heb. 4.14), the sanctuary made by God.

The earliest kerygma of the church thus proclaimed not only Christ's *resurrection but also his ascension into heaven and enthronement at God's right hand. Christians celebrated the inauguration of this messianic kingdom and the demise of the present eon, for when Christ was given dominion over the demonic powers of this age, so were the members of his church. The letter to the *Ephesians speaks of the "immeasurable greatness of God's power for us who believe" (Eph. 1.19), for the members of the church were united with Christ who is "above all rule and authority and power and dominion" (Eph. 1.21).

The *exorcisms and miraculous cures performed by the apostles in Acts were understood to be manifestations of the *Holy Spirit that Christ "poured out" (Acts 2.33) on his apostles after his ascension, sharing his dominion over the *demons of this world with all members of his church. Thus, Paul says: "So, if you have been raised with Christ, seek the things that are above, where Christ is, seated at the right hand of God. . . . For you have died, and your life is hidden with Christ in God" (Col. 3.1–3). This "death" and hidden exaltation of Christians was effected through the ritual of baptism, which Paul compared to a burial and rebirth with Christ (Col. 2.12; Rom. 6.3–4); baptism thus elevated the members of the church into Christ's heavenly kingdom.

Among gnosticizing Christians, baptism was understood to be a rite of immortalization that deified its initiates. According to the *gnostics, if baptism initiated Christians into the death and resurrection of Christ, as Paul argued, then it also united them with Christ's ascension and enthronement, separating the baptized entirely from the mortal sphere. The gnostics' radically transcendent interpretation of baptism was opposed by Paul, who argued that Christ's exaltation was achieved through his humiliation and suffering on the cross and that the ascension of Christians would not come until the *parousia.

Nevertheless, otherworldly speculations on the ascension and immortalization of the soul developed rapidly among gnostic Christians for whom the ascension of Christ established the pattern for their visionary journeys. The gnostics' elaborate portrayals of the soul's ascent, although influenced by Hellenistic thought, in turn came to influence the understanding of the ascent and deification of the soul in Platonic, Hermetic, and other philosophical circles from the second to the fourth centuries CE.

See also Theophany.   GREGORY SHAW

Asher. The second son of *Jacob and Zilpah, *Leah's maid (Gen. 30.12), and one of the twelve *tribes of Israel. In Genesis 30.13, the name Asher is associated with the Hebrew word for blessing, but many scholars associate the name's origin with the goddess *Asherah.

According to Joshua 19.24–31, the tribe of Asher settled in northwest *Canaan (Map 3: X2–3). Biblical sources praise Asher's fertile land (Gen. 49.20; Deut. 33.24–25). The authors of Judges claim that Asher failed to occupy all of its territory (Judg. 1.31–32). *Solomon reorganized Asher's territory into an administrative district (1 Kings 4.16) and later ceded twenty Galilean cities (1 Kings 9.11–13) to the king of Tyre. After the Assyrian exile Asher's territory remained in foreign hands, but the tribe, as witnessed by its *genealogies, endured (e.g., 1 Chron. 7.30–39; cf. 2 Chron. 30.11; Luke 2.36).   GARY N. KNOPPERS

Asherah. The Canaanite mother goddess, associated with lions, serpents, and sacred trees. The word "asherah" in the Bible most often refers to a stylized wooden tree.

The biblical writers generally condemn worship of the goddess, but there is evidence that many in Israel devoted themselves to Asherah, perhaps even worshiping her as consort of Yahweh. At several times an asherah stood in Yahweh's *Temple in Jerusalem (2 Kings 18.4; 21.7; 23.6); there were in the Temple, moreover, vessels dedicated to Asherah (2 Kings 23.4) and a compound in which women wove garments for her statue (2 Kings 23.7). An asherah also stood in *Samaria, the capital of the northern kingdom of Israel (1 Kings 16.33; 2 Kings 13.6) and in Yahweh's temple in Bethel (2 Kings 23.15). Recent archaeological discoveries have confirmed that the cult of Asherah was a part of Yahwistic tradition for at least some Israelites.

SUSAN ACKERMAN

Ashtaroth; Ashtoreth. *See* Astarte.

Asia. In the Hellenistic period, Asia is a term for the Seleucid Empire (Map 11; e.g., 1 Macc. 11.13; 13.32). In the Roman period, Asia means the province of that name, in the western part of what is now Turkey (Map 14:E3; see, e.g., 2 Esd. 16.1; Acts 19.6; 1 Cor. 16.19; 1 Pet. 1.1). It was an important province, containing within its boundaries a number of wealthy cities, including *Ephesus, its capital. The *seven churches of the opening chapters of the book of *Revelation are all in the province of Asia (Rev. 1.4), as is Colossae, to whose church the letter to the *Colossians was sent.   MICHAEL D. COOGAN

Assyria. The ancient land of Assyria (Map 6: H3–4), located in what is now northeastern Iraq, drew its name from the small settlement of Assur (or Ashur) built on a sandstone cliff on the west bank of the Tigris about 35 km (24 mi) north of its confluence with the lower Zab River. Situated at a major river crossing but outside the zone for reliable annual rainfall, Assur early attracted settlements by pastoralists, since it was easily defensible and had ready access to water. Early levels of a small shrine there dating to ca. 2800–2200 BCE show affinities with *Sumerian culture to the south in furnishings and statuary.

The earliest independent ruler of the city-state of Assur attested in a contemporary inscription is Shalim-ahum, who reigned about 1900 BCE. At this time, firms of merchants in Assur established branches in several Anatolian cities and traded textiles and tin from Assur for silver.

About 1813 BCE, Shamshi-Adad I, an Amorite prince from the middle Euphrates, took possession of Assur and subsequently founded an empire with its capital at Shubat-Enlil (modern Tell Leilan in northeast Syria), with two sons reigning as subkings in *Mari and in Ekallate (just north of Assur). Under Shamshi-Adad's son Ishme-Dagan I, the empire was quickly lost; and the dynasty of Shamshi-Adad was replaced within a few decades by native Assyrians, who ruled—in relative obscurity—during the next four centuries, at times as vassals of Mitanni.

Under the dynamic Ashur-uballit I (1364–1328 BCE), Assyria reemerged as a major power, and in the next century conquered and gradually annexed much of the old heartland of Mitanni to the west, setting up an extensive provincial system and then briefly taking over much of Babylonia to the south. Its imperialist ethic was embodied in the Middle Assyrian coronation ritual, in which the officiating priest solemnly charged the king: "Expand your land!" After 1200 BCE, amid widespread upheavals and population movements in Western Asia, the Middle Assyrian empire declined both politically and territorially. An extensive if short-lived revival in the time of Tiglath-pileser I (1115–1076 BCE) dissipated under the pressure of invading Arameans, who confined Assyrian political power to a narrow strip along the Tigris until the late tenth century.

After 935 BCE, Assyrians kings reclaimed lost sections of the Assyrian heartland from the Arameans and began to expand militarily, especially to the west. Over the next three centuries, these monarchs created an extensive Neo-Assyrian empire, which at its height (ca. 660 BCE) embraced a substantial part of the ancient Near East from southern Egypt, Cyprus, and western Anatolia through Palestine-Syria and Mesopotamia to Elam and the Iranian plateau (see Map 6). The foundations of Assyrian imperial power were effectively laid by Ashurnasirpal II (884–859 BCE), who built a splendid new capital at Calah (Nimrud), restructured the Assyrian army into a fighting force without peer in southwestern Asia, reorganized the Assyrian provincial system, and earned a reputation for ruthless treatment of rebels and prisoners. His massive deportations from conquered lands, continued by his successors, brought large numbers of western Arameans into the heartland of Assyria, swelling the ranks of the court and army, influencing artistic and architectural styles, and, by the early seventh century, replacing the Assyrian language with *Aramaic as the vernacular. Ashurnasirpal's campaigns consolidated Assyrian territorial gains as far west as the Upper Euphrates and extracted tribute from these areas; his trading ventures, with military escort, succeeded in reaching the Mediterranean. His son, Shalmaneser II (859–824 BCE), began to extend Assyrian control into northern Syria; but his advance was checked temporarily at the battle of Qarqar (853 BCE) by a broad coalition of states led by *Damascus and Hamath and including Arab tribes and Israel (under *Ahab). Shalmaneser's subsequent campaigns, which reached into Cilicia, secured north Syria and brought the *Phoenician cities Tyre and Sidon into the Assyrian orbit. Despite a revolt of the major cities in Assyria (827–821 BCE) and an ensuing weakness in monarchic power, Assyria continued to be active in the west until about 785 BCE.

Meanwhile, in the late ninth and early eighth centuries in the mountains to the north of Assyria, the rival power of Urartu had risen to prominence. As the fortunes of Assyria declined after 783 BCE under weak kings and strong provincial governors, the Urartians pushed south into Iran and west across the Euphrates into northern Syria. By 745 BCE, Urartu had conquered or concluded alliances with most of the important states in south-central Anatolia and northern Syria and had assumed hegemony over the region. A revolt in Calah brought to the Assyrian throne *Tiglath-pileser III (745–727 BCE), a vigorous monarch who checked encroaching Aramean and Chaldean tribesmen in *Babylonia, restricted Urartu to its homeland, and marched across Syria and Palestine (once in response to a request from Ahaz of Judah for intervention [2 Kings 16:7–9]) as far as Gaza. His son, *Shalmaneser V (727–722 BCE), besieged Tyre and captured *Samaria, bringing the kingdom of *Israel to an end. Sargon II (722–705 BCE), a usurper, deported the population of Israel to various parts of the empire, campaigned as far as the border of Egypt, brought Babylonia under his control, and built a magnificent capital at Dur-Sharrukin (Khorsabad) in the north of the country. His son, *Sennacherib (705–681 BCE), expanded further into Anatolia. Faced with perennial unrest in Babylonia (fomented for the most part by Merodach-baladan and his fellow Chaldeans) and smarting from the murder of his crown prince, Ashur-nadin-shumi, who had been king there from 700 to 694 BCE, Sennacherib eventually sacked and depopulated Babylon. In Palestine, he received the submission of *Hezekiah, who had rebelled in collusion with Merodach-baladan, and, after a siege, extracted tribute from *Jerusalem (2 Kings 18:13–16). Assassinated by one of his sons, Sennacherib was succeeded by another son, Esarhaddon (681–669 BCE), who invaded the Iranian plateau and Egypt, but died prematurely of illness while on campaign. His empire was inherited principally by his son Ashurbanipal (669–627 BCE), who reigned in Assyria; but another son, Shamash-shum-ukin (668–648 BCE), was installed as king in Babylon. Ashurbanipal campaigned extensively in Egypt, reaching as far as Thebes, and brought the empire to its territorial apogee in about 660 BCE. In 652 BCE, Shamash-shum-ukin launched a massive revolt, which won support from Elamites, Arabs, and other disaffected Assyrian subjects. Ashurbanipal spent more than ten years defeating and wreaking reprisals on the dissidents, exhausting the empire in the process.

After Ashurbanipal's death in 627 BCE, civil war broke out in Assyria between three contenders for the throne; it took several years before Sin-shar-ishkun (623?–612 BCE) emerged as the victor. Within a decade he was faced with a coalition of *Medes and Babylonians, who invaded and destroyed the central provinces of Assyria. A final king, Ashur-uballit II (612–609 BCE), ruled briefly in the western provincial capital of Haran with the support of Egyptian armies; but he was driven out by the Babylonians. The fledgling empires of Babylon and Media divided the territories of the Assyrian empire, which disappeared with barely a trace even in its former heartland.

Assyria in the first millennium BCE, though renowned primarily as a massive military power that overwhelmed and intimidated much of southwestern Asia, had a vigorous cultural and economic life. In the decorative arts, its craftsmen displayed creative sensitivity in such diverse media as ivories, seals, and palace wall reliefs; the latter depict an astonishing variety of subjects, including formal protective deities, scenes of battlefield and siege, daily life at court, and the botanical zoological parks created in and around the Assyrian capitals. Literature also flourished, its most notable monument being the large library amassed by Ashurbanipal (669–627 BCE) at *Nineveh, whose excavation in the mid-nineteenth century led to the rediscovery of Mesopotamian literature. On the economic side, trade prospered throughout the empire as new markets were opened to entrepreneurs even from the conquered territories. Booty, tribute, and trade goods poured into the Assyrian heartland, financing the erection and renovation of resplendent urban capitals as well as the maintenance of the military machine that made the empire possible.   JOHN A. BRINKMAN

Astarte (AV: Ashtoreth, Ashtaroth). The Greek form of Ashtart, one of the three great Canaanite goddesses. Astarte was primarily a goddess of fertility and love, the counterpart of Greek Aphrodite. She was also associated with war, and, like her Mesopotamian equivalent Ishtar, had astral features.

In the Bible, worship of the goddess is repeatedly condemned: twice in the book of Judges the Israelites are punished for straying after the *Baals and Astartes (Judg. 2.13–14; 10.6–7); *Solomon is criticized for worshiping Astarte (1 Kings 11.5, 33); and Jeremiah castigates the people for making offerings to the *Queen of Heaven, a syncretism of Astarte and Ishtar (Jer. 7.16–20; 44.15–28).   SUSAN ACKERMAN

Atbash. A cryptic device in which the first letter of the Hebrew alphabet (ʾālep) is replaced by the last (tāw), the second (bêt) by the second from last (šîn), and so forth. In the *Masoretic text of the Hebrew Bible this device occurs in Jeremiah 25.26 and 51.41, where Sheshach (ššk) stands for Babylon (bbl), and in 51.1, where Leb-qamai (lb-qmy) stands for Chaldeans (kśdym). This code is apparently not original, since the *Septuagint gives the plain forms in chap. 51 (the key words in 25.26 are not found in the Greek), and both names are used frequently elsewhere in Jeremiah. The reason for the code in these cases is unknown.   MICHAEL D. COOGAN

Athens. Excavations of ancient Athens (Map 7:D3) (named after its patron goddess Athena) reveal its settlement since the Neolithic period. The easy defense of the Acropolis and the proximity of the Saronic Gulf to the south explain the importance of the site in the history of Attica. In the fifth century BCE, despite defeats in the Peloponnesian War, Athens emerged as the cultural and intellectual center of the Greek world. Innovative techniques in art and sculpture, powerful developments in Greek drama, and significant progress in political reform characterized the glory of fifth-century Athens. The wellspring for later Greek philosophical inquiry flowed from the life and thought of Socrates (ca. 470–399). Ironically, the virtual destruction of the Acropolis in the early fifth century by the Persians made way for an era of architectural creativity in the last half of the century, when the Parthenon, Erechtheion, and numerous other temples were constructed on the Acropolis.

Acts 17.16–34 contains the only extended reference in the New Testament to Athens. The plot of this narrative is structured around some of the best-known aspects of Athenian culture and local color. The city's religiousness, expressed in temples, shrines, and altars, was proverbial in both Greek and Roman thought. The travelogue composed by the Greek geographer Pausanias (second century CE) depicts a city replete with sacred edifices and statues. This facet of Athenian culture is reflected in Luke's statement that "the city was full of idols" (Acts 17.16) and *Paul's reference to the Athenians' piety (17.22) and an altar "to an *unknown god" (17.23).

From the time of Socrates until the Emperor Justinian closed the schools of philosophy in 529 CE, the name of Athens was synonymous with philosophical pursuit of truth. The city had, in fact, been the home not only for Socrates but also for Plato's Academy, Aristotle's Lyceum, the Painted Porch of Stoicism, and the Gardens of Epicurus. As a university town in Paul's time, Athens continued to attract philosophical and philhellenic intellectuals. The account of Paul's efforts there is interwoven with allusions to the city's philosophical traditions. Paul encounters "Epicurean and Stoic philosophers" (17.18), argues for the true nature of God on the basis of

natural revelation (17.24–28), and quotes the Stoic poet Aratus (17.28). (*See also* Epicureans; Stoics.) The scrutiny of Paul's doctrine of God by the council of the *Areopagus deliberately echoes the trial of Socrates for proclaiming new deities and leading the populace to question its beliefs in the traditional gods.

Beyond Acts 17, 1 Thessalonians 3.1, in which Paul mentions his stay in Athens, is the only other New Testament reference to the city. Athens was the home of several second-century Christian apologists, but otherwise did not exert much direct influence in early Christian history.   RICHARD E. OSTER, JR.

Atonement. *See* Day of Atonement.

Authority of the Bible. *This terminology is characteristic of Christian theology, and so the following entry appropriately discusses the issue from a Christian perspective. For consideration of the topic in Jewish tradition, see* Interpretation, History of, *article on* Jewish Interpretation; Torah. *For related discussion, see* Inspiration and Inerrancy *and* Revelation.

"Here is Wisdom; this is the royal Law; these are the lively oracles of God": these are the words used when the Bible, described as "the most valuable thing that this world affords," is presented to the British monarch in the course of the coronation ceremony. They illustrate the value ascribed to the Bible and indicate that its authority is ultimately the authority attributed to God. It is therefore not an authority intrinsic to the book but one linked to the conviction that the book somehow or other emanates from God. Because God was held to be holy, the Bible too is described as holy, and terms like "holy scriptures" and "sacred writings" become commonplace.

The Israelites believed that it was possible to receive a divine communication, and so the book of the Law (*see* Torah) was invested with divine authority. Later rabbinic piety came to think of the Torah as eternal in the heavens but communicated through *angels to *Moses, the divinely appointed lawgiver. The sanctity of the communication was associated with the manuscripts as well so that infinite care was demanded in copying the text. The *prophets, too, saw themselves as called into the divine council, and their utterance was consequently regarded as the very utterance of God. They were held to be

God's own mouthpieces, inspired by him, and the fulfillment of their message validated its truth.

Because they conveyed God's revelation for Israel, the writings, as collected, were revered as authoritative. As the authors had been "inspired," their writings, in turn, were held to share in the *inspiration, and it became customary to speak of them as the *word of God.

The Hebrew Bible was accepted as "holy scripture" by the early Christian communities, for *Jesus had set the seal of his authority on these writings. The early church saw them as the preparation for the coming of Jesus. It was not a matter of affirming every detail (although some would argue this) but rather the tenor and ethos of the writings that were seen as authentically indicating God's will and purpose. The early Christians saw in Jesus the climax of all that the Jewish scriptures taught. It was felt that everything had been written down in the light of the critical events associated with Jesus; hence a new interpretation came into being. While *Philo could read his own philosophical understanding and mystical experience into the scriptures, the Pharisaic rabbis (see Pharisees) see their own rules for life emanating from them, and the *Essenes reinterpret them in the light of the fortunes of the founder of their sect and the continuing destinies of their community, the Christians likewise read the scriptures in terms of their own faith and experience. Christ came to be seen as the center of scripture; he was the key to its understanding and its continuing validity. As Martin Luther (1483–1546) was to put it, "Christ is the Lord and King of the scriptures." The writer of 2 Timothy can accordingly speak of "the sacred writings that are able to instruct you for salvation through faith in Christ Jesus" (3.1) and can thus affirm that "all scripture is inspired by God" (3.16).

Gradually the same authority was granted to the New Testament writings, for they were the factual sources for his life and teaching and encapsulated the early apostolic preaching and instruction. Over against views regarded as illegitimate and later condemned as heretical, the New Testament documents were seen as pointing to an authentic faith. Fixing the *canon of the New Testament thus involved discrimination between those books seen as authoritative and so part of the sacred tradition and those that were not. It was felt to be a case not of the church's conveying authority but recognizing an intrinsic authority already present. As Origen (ca. 185–254) put it, "The sacred books were not the works of human beings; they were written by the inspiration of the Holy Spirit at the will of the Father of all through Jesus Christ" (De principiis 4.9). Just as the writings bear witness to the acts of God in history, so the church points to the Bible, preaching and teaching from its pages and subjecting itself to its guidance. But it also interprets it, providing the mainstream of tradition. The church recognizes in the scriptures the classical, normative account of Christian origins. So a sense of identity between the present and the church's roots is guaranteed and a measure of stability secured.

Inspiration. The Bible speaks of *inspiration or the divine breath as the source of vitality and power. Genesis 2.7 asserts that the Lord God "breathed into his nostrils the breath of life, and the man became a living being." Ezekiel 37.10 says of lifeless bones that "the breath came into them, and they lived, and stood on their feet." So Paul can say, "Our message of the gospel came to you not in word only, but also in power and in the Holy Spirit" (1 Thess. 1.5). The implication is that, just as divine inspiration had made the prophetic message a living one, so the words of scripture are mere signposts to something that goes beyond words.

Some have linked the notion of verbal inspiration with inerrancy and infallibility (see Inspiration and Inerrancy), but it is significant that, while Luther can speak of the Bible as "the Holy Spirit's very own book," with "God . . . in every syllable," he can also affirm that mistakes and inconsistencies do not affect the heart of the gospel. "The Holy Spirit," he affirms, "has an eye only to the substance and is not bound by words." We may agree that inspiration is no guarantee against human fallibility, nor does it affirm uniformity in quality and authority. There are levels in the scriptures: the kernel is encased in a shell; the baby lies in a manger.

Approaches to Biblical Authority. In early Christianity, the scriptures were used "for teaching, for reproof, for correction, and for training in righteousness" (2 Tim. 3.16). In the West, during the Dark Ages and the Middle Ages, the documents were viewed as the raw materials of *revelation, a veritable mine of doctrinal statements. Isolated verses could be picked at random and used for the authoritative establishment of dogma. The Bible was often used as a sourcebook for the support of ecclesiastical doctrine, but scriptural authority was largely subordinated to the authority of the church. Contradictions in the text were smoothed out by an elaborate and even overly subtle system of allegorical interpretations. (*See also* Interpretation, History of, *article on* Christian Interpretation from the Middle Ages to the Reformation.)

The Reformation saw the overthrow of ecclesiastical power structures, and scripture seemed to be substituted for the church. The revival of learning was instrumental in initiating intensive biblical study. Luther saw the Bible as "the crib in which Christ lay," a sacrament by which the living God addressed the individual soul. "All sound books agree in this, that they witness to Christ," he said. "That which does not preach Christ is not apostolic though it came from St. Peter or St. Paul. Contrariwise that which preaches Christ would be apostolic even though it came from Judas or Annas or Pilate or Herod." Luther also declared that the truth of God's self-revelation through scripture was written "inwardly in our hearts" by the Holy Spirit. This point was subsequently taken up by John Calvin (1509–64), who wrote of the "inner witness of the Holy Spirit," leading to the conviction that not only was the Bible an authentic, dependable record of God's encounter with humanity in the past but also the means of his contemporary encounter with us. At the same time, his position suggested that it is not possible to prove that God speaks through the scriptures.

It was the post-Reformation period that saw the rise of a kind of *fundamentalism, in which emphasis was laid on the very words of scripture and concerns about infallibility and inerrancy arose. Bibles were now more readily available, and "scripture alone" (*sola scriptura*) became a clarion call. What was often forgotten was that the principles of interpretation followed created a tradition of their own.

Liberal criticism of the Bible in the nineteenth century seemed to many to undermine the authority that had been attached to scripture. It appeared to turn the Bible into an ordinary collection of Near Eastern documents that had to be placed within their own historical contexts.

A different approach is undertaken by Karl Barth (1886–1968) and "*biblical theology," in which stress is laid on the act of proclamation, within which the Bible becomes the word of God. The Bible is not identified with past revelation but bears witness to a revelation in the past, as it becomes the means of hearing the voice of God today.

Contemporary thought also emphasizes the empirical test and accepts that God does speak through the scriptures and that faith is nourished by it. Charismatic movements hold that the Bible comes alive through the action of the Holy Spirit. The words become a vehicle through which a vivid awareness of the presence and activity of God is developed.

An unwarranted authority would be attributed to the Bible if the words were stressed and the human origins of the documents neglected. Just as in Christology the church rejected a docetic viewpoint that tried to support the assertion of Christ's divinity by denying the full reality of his humanity, so, with the Bible, it is important to reject an equation with the divine word, which neglects the very human character of the words of its authors. If the Bible were precisely the *word of God, questions of authority would not arise and one would expect an immediately recognizable meaning within the words of scriptures. The biblical language that speaks of the dynamic character of the word suggests that it is preferable to speak of the Bible as conveying or mediating the word of God. This then points to the experience of the community of faith through the centuries. To treat the Bible simply as a compendium of ancient literature and to limit oneself to a critical, historical analysis of its contents would be a denial of believers' experience that in the Bible they have found the word of God addressing them with "transforming and liberating power," as Thomas Merton put it. The words of scripture take on the character of the preacher who bears witness to the reality of what has been experienced. There is a need, then, for a mediating position between a fundamentalism that almost invites a worship of the Bible instead of the God of the Bible and a purely rationalistic exegesis. A claim to discover God's word and so God's own authority within the Bible must not obscure the truth of the humanity and so the limitations of its authors. Different authors have different styles, interests, and emphases and express their convictions in different ways; their language and mode of expression are not ageless. And what is true of the writers is also true of the reader. If Christianity is a religion of the spirit rather than of the letter (see 2 Cor. 3.6), we should expect a degree of variety in interpretation. There must be a subjective element in interpretation just as there was in the writing. The more one brings of human experience, spiritual sensitivity, and common sense to the Bible, the more one will get from it. And, since life is lived in community, so the experiences and insights of others illuminate the understanding of the individual reader. Finally, the biblical message is addressed to the whole person and not simply to the intellect. Hence, to recognize the authority of the Bible is to respond to the imperatives made by the God of the Bible. For ultimately what is looked for is an encounter not with language but with a person.

See also Canon; Eastern Orthodoxy and the Bible; Interpretation, History of.

RAYMOND HAMMER

Avenger of Blood. In ancient Israel, as in tribal societies in general, the members of the clan were responsible for avenging the death of innocent victims. Unavenged *blood cries out to the Lord (Gen. 4.10). Innocent blood defiles the land and must be expiated (Num. 35.31–34), and this is the duty of the avenger.

As government became more centralized, the prerogative of blood revenge was slowly taken out of the hands of the clan. Under the monarchy it appears that the king had the power to intervene and even to grant immunity from the avenger (2 Sam. 14.8–11), but the right of "blood redemption" remained a sacred duty. In Roman times the Jews were no longer permitted to carry out blood revenge (John 18.31). According to Paul, it is not the duty of the individual but that of the state to avenge evil on behalf of God (Rom. 13.4; cf. Ps. 9.12; 2 Kings 9.7; Rev. 19.2).

The execution of a criminal by the authorized authorities did not of course call for blood revenge, nor did the killing of a person in self-defense. Only *murder and involuntary homicide demanded it. Even a homicidal beast was considered bloodguilty and had to be stoned (Exod. 21.28–32). The next of kin, usually the nearest male relative, who put a person who committed homicide to death, was called "the redeemer of blood" (Num. 35.19: Hebr. gōʾēl haddām; cf. the use of gōʾel in Ruth 3.9–4.8; see Redeem).

For those who accidentally killed an innocent person there were provisions of asylum. The *altar of Yahweh was such a refuge (Exod. 21.12–14; 1 Kings 1.50–53; 2.28–34). More important were the Levitical *cities of refuge, three on either side of Jordan, to which the person who killed someone accidentally could flee (Num. 35.6–15). Those guilty of murder had no refuge but were to be executed after a judicial inquiry (Deut. 19.11–13). Since life was viewed as sacred (Gen. 9.6), no amount of money could be given as recompense for the loss of the life of an innocent person; it had to be "life for life" (Exod. 21.23; Deut. 19.21). By observing this law of retribution Israel was spared violence and endless blood feuds.

DAVID EWERT

Azariah, The Prayer of, and the Song of the Three Young Men. The Greek translation (*Septuagint) of the book of *Daniel inserts between vv. 23 and 24 of chap. 3 a section embracing sixty-eight verses, which is not found in the Semitic original; this section is seen by Protestants as one of the Apocrypha, but is considered deuterocanonical by Roman Catholics and some Orthodox churches (see Apocrypha, article on Jewish Apocrypha). It consists of a brief connecting narrative (vv. 1–2, 23–28) and two (or perhaps more correctly three) poems of liturgical character. The poems purport to be the words recited or sung by the three young men whom King *Nebuchadrezzar caused to be thrown into a fiery furnace when they refused to worship the golden image that he had set up.

The first of the poems is in the form of a *prayer and is placed upon the lips of Azariah, the Hebrew name of the youth also called by his Babylonian name, Abednego (Dan. 1.6–7). The prayer is not specifically appropriate to the situation of the fiery furnace, being simply a national lament like Psalms 74 and 79, which are petitions for the deliverance of Israel after the destruction of the Jerusalem Temple. The prayer differs from these psalms by stating that the disaster was a justified punishment for the sins of the nation (vv. 5–8), an emphasis quite incongruous with the situation of the young men, who were being punished precisely for their religious integrity. The concluding verses of the prayer (19–22) would be suitable for anyone suffering oppression and are doubtless the reason the prayer was felt to be suitable.

The much longer poem that begins in verse 29 also is irrelevant to the particular situation of the youths, except for v. 66, which may well have been added when the hymn was interpolated into the book of Daniel. It falls naturally into two parts, which may originally have constituted two separate hymns. They are known in the liturgical tradition of the Western church as, respectively, the Benedictus es and the Benedicite, from the opening words of the Latin version of each. The first consists of general words of praise addressed to God in his glory; in the second section (vv. 35–68) the various parts of creation, the heavens, the forces of nature below them, and the inhabitants of earth are summoned to join in a chorus of praise, following a pattern established by Psalm 148. The whole of verses 29–68 is unified by a refrain repeated after each line, somewhat in the manner of Psalm 136, but with an appropriately different form in each of the two parts.

It has plausibly been suggested that the reason for the introduction of this material in the middle of Daniel 3 was to correct the inartistic and perhaps religiously offensive emphasis of the original text on King Nebuchadrezzar and his reactions; the addition of the prayer and the hymns transfers the center of attention from the Babylonian king to the God of Israel and his faithful worshipers.

There are no unambiguous clues to the language in which this material was composed, but the general tone and atmosphere of the prayer and the hymn(s) suggest that it was *Hebrew, and this impression is reinforced by the fact that Hebrew was the normal language of prayer among Jews. Their lack of specific appropriateness to the situation of the three young men suggests that they were previously independent compositions arbitrarily inserted by an editor who then composed the brief narrative section, perhaps in *Aramaic, which is the language of this part of Daniel. It would follow, then, that the place of composition would likely be Palestine and the author a Palestinian Jew. The same set of suppositions would hold for the editor who introduced the poems into the book and produced the Semitic text from which the Greek translation was made.

With regard to the date of composition of the poems, there is also no clear evidence, except for v. 15, which speaks of the absence of civil government and the cessation of Temple worship. In their present context, of course, the words are intended to apply to the putative situation of the youths in the Babylonian *exile, but they would be even more appropriate in the early second century BCE when Antiochus Epiphanes desecrated the *Temple (164 BCE; 1 Macc. 1.20–61) and when, indeed, there was no prophet or native government.

For other additions to Daniel, see Susanna *and* Bel and the Dragon.   ROBERT C. DENTAN

Azazel. Appears only in the *Day of Atonement ritual in Leviticus 16. Two goats were designated by lot (16.8), one for the Lord and one for Azazel, perhaps the name of a *demon. The Lord's goat became a sacrificial sin-offering, while the scapegoat was sent into the *wilderness after *Aaron placed his hands on it and confessed the people's sins (16.21). The latter verse uses three words for *sin, but does not mention impurity (unlike 16.16). Thus, the scapegoat ritual is for sins alone, and reveals the sacrificial cult's inability to achieve complete atonement by itself.

Some scholars suspect that the scapegoat was added to the chapter; if so, it has been well integrated into the text. In 16.17, Aaron makes atonement "for the assembly of Israel," making the scapegoat seem unnecessary. Yet it was necessary: this involves the riddance of something profoundly unwanted. The sin offering could not carry the sins away like the scapegoat. The magical Azazel ritual assured that the sins were sent away.

The *Septuagint rendered Azazel as "sending away." In the Ethiopian book of *Enoch, Azazel is a fallen *angel. The Midrash and many modern commentators see Azazel as the demon to whom the scapegoat was sent. In the *Mishnah, the practice was to throw the scapegoat over a cliff; the rabbis derived from this an etymology, accepted by some (NEB: Azazel = "precipice"). Scholars have proposed other etymologies, but the origin and meaning of Azazel remain uncertain.   PHILIP STERN

✦ B ✦

Baal. A common Semitic word meaning "owner, lord, husband." As "lord" it is applied to various *Canaanite gods, such as the Baal of Peor (Num. 25.3) and the Baals (Judg. 2.11), which were largely local manifestations of the storm god Baal. Although the head of the Canaanite pantheon was El, Baal was the most important god because of his association with the storms that annually brought revival of vegetation and fertility. Baal is prominent in the great complex of fifteenth century BCE *Ugaritic epics, where he is called son of *Dagon and is named some 250 times, sometimes interchangeably with Hadad, the widely known Semitic storm god whose symbol, like Baal's, was the bull.

In art, Baal is depicted as the storm god Aliyan ("triumphant") Baal, who holds a thunderbolt in one hand and swings a mace with the other. Baal is the champion of divine order over earthly chaos—over deadly drought, represented by the deity Mot ("death"), and the unruly forces of the sea (the god Yamm). The Ugaritic epics tell how Baal defeats these powers and wins the title "rider on the clouds" (the same title ascribed to the God of Israel in Ps. 68.4).

The theme of opposition to Baal worship runs throughout the *Deuteronomic literature and the *prophets. By the ninth century BCE, Baalism had deeply pervaded Israelite life. Personal names formed with Baal appear already in the time of the Judges (6.25–32). Even *Saul and *David had sons with Baal names (1 Chron. 8.33; 14.7). Intense conflict appeared with the introduction of the Baal of Tyre into Israel by *Ahab's queen, *Jezebel, daughter of Ethbaal of Sidon (1 Kings 16.31–32; 18.17–19). Even as late as the time of *Manasseh, altars to Baal were still among the appointments in the Jerusalem *Temple (2 Kings 21.2–4).

Opposition to Baalism was led by Israel's prophets. The fertility rites associated with Baal worship corrupted the faith in Yahweh, and the *myths undergirding them wrongly deified aspects of *nature. The prophets endeavored to show Yahweh as a transcendent, universal God who provides rains and fertility yet who is no "nature god" trapped in unvarying seasonal cycles. Because *agriculture was so vital and so precariously dependent on the weather, it became important to show that Yahweh, not Baal, was the one who rode the clouds, controlled the storms, and brought freshening rains (Pss. 29; 68.4, 9; 104.3). That the struggle against Baalism was finally successful is signalled by the replacement of the Baal element in some proper names by the word *bōšet* ("shame"; 2 Sam. 2.8; cf. Hos. 9.10).

DAVID G. BURKE

Baal-zebub. The *Phoenician god at Ekron consulted by King Ahaziah (2 Kings 1.2–18). The name in Hebrew means "Lord of Flies," but no evidence exists for a *Philistine god who either drove off flies or gave oracles through their buzzing. The Hebrew form is probably a derogatory transformation of Baal-zebul, which appears in *Ugaritic texts meaning "Lord *Baal," but could also be understood as "Master of the Heavenly House" (cf. Matt. 10.25). In *Aramaic, Beel-zebul may have been construed as "Lord of Dung," Beel-zebub possibly as "Enemy." During the Greco-Roman period, Beel-zebul came to be used for a leader among the *demons opposed to God. Jesus denies that he casts out demons by authority of Beelzebul, the ruler of demons (Matt. 12.24–27 par.). Some translations employ Beelzebub in the New Testament passages, following the text of 2 Kings. Christian interpreters identified Beelzebul with *Satan on the basis of the Gospel passages.

ROBERT STOOPS

Babel, Tower of. Babel is the Hebrew word for *Babylon, which the Babylonians themselves explained as meaning "gate of God." This etymology is probably not original, but the meaning is significant for a famous city whose central temple tower was said to reach the heavens (Gen.

11.4). In Genesis 11.9 the meaning of Babel is explained by the Hebrew verb *bālal*, "to confuse, mix," and the confusion of speech.

The brief narrative in Genesis 11.1–9 also explains how there could exist such a variety of languages among the earth's people. The understanding that the earliest humans shared a common language is found in the *Sumerian Enmerkar Epic* (141–46). Genesis 11.1–9 tells how *Noah's descendants wandered to the plain of Shinar (Babylonia), where they perfected the techniques for monumental brick architecture and built the renowned tower of Babel. Building the tower is interpreted as an act of arrogance, and human history is here understood to take a decisive turn from a common thread to many strands as God descends to confuse human speech and scatter the people all over the earth.

The enormous *ziggurats of Mesopotamia could easily have symbolized the presumptuousness of the urban elite, and their ruin the judgment of God. Even as ruins their massive dimensions would have been striking. The Sumerian temple tower of the moon god Nanna at *Ur could have been the model for the tower of Babel. This huge terraced mountain of brick, with the god's temple on top, at least 21 m (70 ft) above ground level, was built ca. 2100 BCE. Of similar construction, the great temple of Marduk in Babylon, the E-sagila, is possibly the referent of the Genesis narrative; according to the Babylonian epic *Enuma Elish* (6.60–62), it took a year just to make the bricks for this colossally high structure.   DAVID G. BURKE

Babylon (Map 2:H4). Babylon is the rendering of Akkadian Babilum (Babilim), the city that for centuries served as capital of the "land of Babylon" (Jer. 50.28). Cuneiform sources interpret its name as *bāb-ilim*, "gate of the deity." The Bible rejected this popular etymology in favor of a more scurrilous one that linked the name to the confusion of tongues (Gen. 11.9, Hebr. *bālal*, "[God] confused"), and so the city is called Babel.

Not until around 1900 BCE did an independent dynasty establish itself at Babylon. Like most of their contemporaries, its rulers bore Amorite (Northwest Semitic) names, but unlike some of them, they enjoyed lengthy reigns, passing the succession from father to son without a break; this may have helped Babylon survive its rivals in the period of warring states (ca. 1860– 1760 BCE). Under the adroit *Hammurapi (ca.

1792–1750 BCE), Babylon succeeded in restoring the unity of Mesopotamia under its own hegemony.

Babylon's triumph was short-lived, though: under its next king, Samsu-iluna (ca. 1749–1712 BCE), the extreme south was lost to the new Sealand Dynasty and the north to the Kassites at Hana. About 1600 BCE, the city itself was sacked by an invading army of Hittites from distant Anatolia (modern Turkey), and these rivals took it over, the Sealanders only briefly, but the Kassites for almost half a millennium (ca. 1590– 1160 BCE).

It remained for the Second Dynasty of Isin (ca. 1156–1025 BCE) to restore Babylon to its earlier prominence. The recapture of the cult statue of Marduk from Elamite captivity by Nebuchadrezzar I (ca. 1124–1103 BCE) probably capped this development. Babylon was henceforth regarded as the heir to the millennial traditions of the ancient Sumerian centers of cult and culture. Marduk, the local patron deity of Babylon, was endowed with the attributes of the ancient Sumerian deities of those centers—notably Enki of Eridu and Enlil of Nippur—and exalted to the head of the pantheon. This exaltation was celebrated in new compositions such as *enūma elish* ("when above"; conventionally known as the "Babylonian Epic of Creation") and can be compared in certain respects with the exaltation of the God of Israel as celebrated in the roughly contemporary Song of the Sea (Exod. 15).

In the early first millennium, Babylon could not sustain a military and political posture to match these cultural and religious pretensions, and it gradually declined into the status of a vassal state to *Assyria, the powerful neighbor to the north. Occasional alliances with Elam in the east or, notably under Marduk-apal-iddina II (the biblical Merodach-baladan), with Judah in the west (2 Kings 20.12–19; cf. Isa. 39), provided brief periods of precarious independence. The city was devastated by the Assyrian king *Sennacherib (704–681 BCE) not long after his abortive siege of *Jerusalem in 701 BCE (2 Kings 18.13–19.37; cf. Isa. 36–37). It was restored by that king's son and successor Esarhaddon (680– 669 BCE), only to be caught up again in the violent civil war (652–648 BCE) between the two sons of Esarhaddon that pitted Shamash-shumukin of Babylonia against Assurbanipal of Assyria. The resultant weakening of the Assyrian empire no doubt helped clear the path for the accession of the last and in some ways greatest

Babylonian dynasty, that of the Chaldeans, sometimes referred to as the Tenth Babylonian Dynasty (625–539 BCE).

With this restoration, Babylon ranked as one of the major cities, indeed, in Greek eyes, as one or even two of the seven wonders of the ancient world, by virtue of its walls in some accounts and invariably for its famous "hanging gardens." The gardens were more likely the work of Marduk-apal-iddina II than of *Nebuchadrezzar II (as claimed by Berossos in one Hellenistic tradition), but the latter certainly rebuilt the city most grandly during his forty-four-year reign (605–562 BCE). He is remembered in biblical historiography as the conqueror of Jerusalem in 597 and 587/586 BCE (2 Kings 24–25; cf. 2 Chron. 36). The biblical record is supported and supplemented by the Babylonian Chronicle and other cuneiform documents. But the stories told in the book of Daniel about Nebuchadrezzar (especially chap. 4), as well as about *Belshazzar (chap. 5), should rather be referred to Nabonidus, who proved to be not only the last king of the dynasty (555–539 BCE) but the last ruler of any independent polity in Babylon. The city surrendered to *Cyrus the Persian in a bloodless takeover and thereafter, while continuing as a metropolis of the successive Achaemenid, Seleucid, and Parthian empires, ceased to play an independent role in ancient politics.

In the Bible, Babylon plays a dual role, positively as the setting for a potentially creative diaspora, negatively as a metaphor for certain forms of degeneracy. The "Babylonian exile" imposed by Nebuchadrezzar on the Judeans removed the center of Jewish life to Babylon for fifty or sixty years, if not the seventy predicted by the prophet Jeremiah (Jer. 29.10, cf. 2 Chron. 36.21). The exiled king Jehoiachin was released from prison by Nebuchadrezzar's son and successor Amel-Marduk, the Evil-merodach of 2 Kings 25.27 (cf. Jer. 52.31), and provided for from the royal stores, as indicated also by cuneiform sources. Jeremiah wrote to the exiles in God's name, advising them to enjoy the positive aspects of life in Babylon and to pray for its welfare (Jer. 29.4–7; contrast Ps. 122.6). Ezekiel lived among the exiles and prepared them for the restoration, while Second Isaiah welcomed the arrival of Cyrus (Isa. 44.28–45.1), which paved the way for the return of those exiles who chose to accept his proclamation (2 Chron. 36.22f.; Ezra 1.1–3).

Under Persian rule, Babylon continued to flourish as the seat of one of the most important satrapies of the Persian empire (cf. Ezra 7.16; Dan. 2.49; etc.), and the Achaemenid Artaxerxes I could still be called "king of Babylon" (Neh. 13.6). The Jews who chose to remain there enjoyed considerable prosperity, as indicated by business documents from nearby Nippur in which individuals identified as Judeans or bearing Jewish names (in Hebrew or Aramaic) engage in various agricultural and commercial activities. The foundations were thus laid for the creative role that Babylonia was to play in the Jewish life of the postbiblical period.

The Bible also reflects a negative view of Babylon. Already in the primeval history, the *tower of Babel (Gen. 11.1–9) uses the traditional *ziggurat present in each city of *Sumer as a metaphor for the excesses of human ambition that led to, and accounted for, the confusion of tongues and dispersion of peoples. The Psalmists emphasized the negative aspects of exile (Ps. 137), and the fall of the "arrogant" city (Jer. 50.31) and "its sinners" (Isa. 13.9) was predicted confidently, even gleefully, by the prophets. In the New Testament, Babylon became the epitome of wickedness (Rev. 17.5) and a symbolic name for Rome (Rev. 17–18; cf. 1 Pet. 5.13).

WILLIAM W. HALLO

Balaam. A non-Israelite *prophet who figures most prominently in the narratives of Numbers 22–24; there is also a lengthy prophecy of the same Balaam in the text from Deir ʿAllā in the Jordan Valley dating to around 700 BCE.

The Bible evaluates Balaam's character in two quite different ways. On the one hand, Balaam is often portrayed as an example of an evil diviner who would sell his prophetic powers to the highest bidder, often in conflict with God's will (Num. 31.8, 16; Deut. 23.4–5; Josh. 13.22; 24.9–10; Neh. 13.2; Mic. 6.5; 2 Pet. 2.15; Jude 11; Rev 2.14). In a particularly humorous scene, Numbers 22.21–35 makes fun of Balaam's powers as a seer; he is repeatedly unable to see the divine messenger that even his donkey can see.

On the other hand, Numbers 22–24 as a whole portrays Balaam in a favorable light. When the *Moabite king Balak hires Balaam to curse his enemy Israel as they cross his territory on the way to the *Promised Land, Balaam replies piously that as a prophet he can speak only the words that God gives to him (Num. 22.18; see also Num. 24.13).

On four occasions when Balak asks Balaam to curse the Israelites, Balaam instead obeys God and speaks only words of great blessing upon

Israel. The most famous of these oracles of blessing includes a prophecy about a great future king or *messiah of Israel. The oracle may originally have applied to *David, but later it was interpreted as the promise of a ruler who would come as a deliverer in the end time. Using royal images, Balaam proclaims, "A star shall come out of Jacob, and a scepter shall rise out of Israel" (Num. 24.17); this text probably underlies the account of the star followed by the *Magi (Matt. 2.1–12).

A passage from Balaam's final oracle was quoted in the first telegraph message: "What hath God wrought!" (Num. 23.23 KJV).

DENNIS T. OLSON

Ban. The Hebrew word *ḥērem* is generally translated "ban" or "devoted (thing)" and means something set apart as belonging to Yahweh and therefore forbidden for profane use; the English word "harem" is derived from the Arabic cognate. It may refer to something set apart for cultic use (Lev. 27.21, 28), to be used only by priests, and thus understood as being holy. The word is also used in accounts of the early wars of Israel to mean the war booty, also understood as devoted to Yahweh and therefore not to be used by the Israelites. In victory nothing is to be spared; Israel must "utterly destroy" (Hebr. *hḥrm*) everything (Deut. 7.2; 20.16–17; etc.). It is this notion of the ban that characterizes the narratives of the *conquest in *Joshua (e.g., 6.17–18).

The story of the rejection of *Saul as king of Israel in 1 Samuel 15 provides a vivid example of the ban. Yahweh commands Saul through *Samuel to utterly destroy the *Amalekites, "man and woman, child and infant, ox and sheep, camel and donkey" (v. 3). When Saul spares the king, Agag, and the best of the possessions of the Amalekites, he is pictured as having failed to obey Yahweh concerning the ban, and as a consequence Yahweh repents of having made Saul king over Israel. The story ends with Samuel taking his sword and hewing Agag to pieces, thus obeying the command to destroy utterly everything devoted to Yahweh.

The institution of the ban was not unique in Israel; the same terminology is used by the Moabite king Mesha (*see* Moabite Stone, The), and analogous practices are attested elsewhere.

See also Anathema; War.   EDGAR W. CONRAD

Baptism. A term first appearing in the New Testament as a purification ritual used by an unorthodox Jewish figure named *John (the Baptist). All four Gospels and the book of Acts describe him "preaching a baptism of repentance for the forgiveness of sins" (Mark 1.4; Luke 3.3).

Scholars have speculated how John's mission might be related to other Jewish separatist groups such as the *Qumran community, but exact origins remain unclear. There is abundant evidence that lustral bathing was an important aspect of Greco-Roman religions, especially related to healing divinities such as Asklepius. In the Hebrew Bible, cleansing with *water is an important part of purification rites, especially after sexual activity or contact with a corpse (Lev. 15.18, Num. 19.13; *see* Purity, Ritual). John the Baptist calls for a more general repentance symbolized by baptism.

The report that *Jesus himself was baptized in the *Jordan by John (Mark 1.9–11) raises the possibility that Jesus was a disciple of John who broke off and started his own movement. It is clear that later followers of Jesus were concerned about this perception. Matthew's gospel includes a dialogue in which John recognizes Jesus' spiritual superiority and baptizes him reluctantly only after Jesus insists (Matt. 3.13–17). Luke goes a step further by excluding John from the account of Jesus' baptism (Luke 3.21) and telling the story of John's imprisonment immediately before the event takes place (Luke 3.19–20). Thus, in Luke, Jesus is baptized, but the story line indicates that the baptism could not have been performed by John.

In the Gospels, John is of interest only as he is related to the ministry of Jesus (Mark 1.2–3, 7–9; Matt. 3.11–12; Luke 3.15–17), but the baptism symbol used by John becomes a central image for the developing churches. Matthew's gospel concludes with the charge to "make disciples of all nations, baptizing them in the name of the Father and of the Son and of the Holy Spirit" (Matt. 28.19). The book of Acts elaborates further when *Peter says to the crowd gathered on *Pentecost, "Repent, and be baptized every one of you in the name of Jesus Christ so that your sins may be forgiven" (Acts 2.38).

Baptism in Acts takes place immediately after someone comes to believe in Christ, and it is usually followed by receiving the *Holy Spirit. This two-stage process is founded on the contrast between John's water baptism and "being baptized by the Holy Spirit" (Acts 1.5; cf. Mark 1.8; Matt. 3.11; Luke 3.16; John 1.33). It is so important that the leaders of the Jerusalem church send Peter and John to *lay hands on believers in *Samaria who had "only been baptized in the name of the Lord Jesus," after which they receive the Holy Spirit (Acts 8.14–17). The situation is reversed when the *gentiles of Cornelius's house come to believe. They receive the Holy Spirit and speak in tongues as a sign of God's acceptance of gentile converts (see Glossolalia), so Peter asks, "Can anyone withhold the water for baptizing these people who have received the Holy Spirit just as we have?" (Acts 10.44–48).

*Paul's letters provide the earliest evidence about baptism among the Jesus followers. It is striking, therefore, that Paul makes no mention of John the Baptist or of baptism and receiving the Holy Spirit as a dual process. Paul sees that the person who has been baptized is "in Christ," no longer subject to the divisions of human society (Gal. 3.27), and part of a unified body (1 Cor. 12.13; cf. Eph. 4.5). Emphasis is on the state that has been achieved, not the way in which it has been accomplished. In fact, Paul is concerned that the Corinthians are putting too much stake in the person by whom they were baptized, and he is grateful that he baptized only a few of them: "For Christ did not send me to baptize but to proclaim the gospel" (1 Cor. 1.17).

In 1 Corinthians 15, Paul is using every possible argument to convince his readers that a resurrection of the dead will take place. In doing so he asks why people are baptized on behalf of the dead if there will be no resurrection (15.29). This brief allusion indicates that within the early churches it was possible to receive baptism in order to include in the body of Christ a friend or relative who was already dead. Paul does not specifically condemn the practice here, but it did not become an accepted part of Christian ritual.

Paul equates baptism symbolically with the death of Jesus (Rom. 6.3–4, cf. Col. 2.12), and he insists that rituals such as baptism are not spiritual guarantees, since God was not pleased with the Hebrews even though they went through a proto-baptism with *Moses at the *Red Sea (1 Cor. 10.1–5). This latter point is also made in the letter to the *Hebrews (9.9–10), while 1 *Peter contends that the story of Noah's *ark prefigures the saving value of baptism (1 Pet. 3.21).

The New Testament evidence is used in debating later Christian baptismal practice, but it is rarely definitive. Certainly the majority of people who are baptized in the New Testament are adults who are entering the community. The exception might be children included in some of the households baptized in Acts (11.14; 16.15, 33). The baptism of infants became a more routine practice within the church as the doctrine of original sin became more widely accepted.

Another controversy concerns baptism by immersion or by the sprinkling of water on the participant. The descriptions of specific New Testament baptisms indicate that the person being baptized was dipped under the water. Jesus is said to come out of the water (Mark 1.10; Matt. 3.16), while Philip and the Ethiopian eunuch go down into the water (Acts 8.38). Going under the water also fits best with the image of being buried with Christ in baptism (Col. 2.12). At the same time baptisms in the New Testament are not described in specific terms, so diverse interpretations and practices develop.

DANIEL N. SCHOWALTER

Baptist, John the. See John the Baptist.

Barabbas. Outside the Gospels nothing is known of Barabbas. His name is *Aramaic and means "son of the father" (*Abba), ironically denoting the status given exclusively to Jesus. Barabbas was imprisoned for robbery (John 18.40) or for insurrection and murder (Mark 15.7; Luke 23.19), crimes not uncommon in the turbulent Palestine of the first century CE. In the account of the trial of Jesus, the Roman prefect Pontius *Pilate is portrayed sympathetically, finding no fault in Jesus and recognizing that Jewish priests plotted his arrest. Following a *Passover custom unknown outside the Gospels, Pilate offered to free a Jewish prisoner and suggested Jesus, but the crowd (in John, "the Jews") demanded that Pilate release Barabbas and crucify Jesus. This helped establish a negative attitude toward Jews in Christian tradition (see Anti-Semitism).

GREGORY SHAW

Barnabas. Acts describes Joseph "Barnabas" as a Hellenized Jew from Cyprus who played a leading role in the gentile mission. The apostles call this Joseph "son of encouragement" when he makes a large donation to the Jerusalem church (Acts 4.36–37). Barnabas introduces Saul (*Paul) to Jesus' original apostles in Acts 9.27 and journeys to *Antioch in Acts 11.22–24 as their representative.

In the letter to the *Galatians, Paul describes how he and Barnabas were given "the right hand of fellowship" by the Jerusalem leadership and had their mission to the gentiles approved (Gal. 2.9; cf. Acts 15). Acts portrays Barnabas as Paul's senior partner in evangelizing Cyprus and Iconium (Acts 13.1–3; 14.1, 14) until their split over the role of John Mark (15.36–41: probably the Mark called Barnabas's cousin in Col. 4.10). Although Barnabas plays no further role in the New Testament, the second-century *Epistle of Barnabas* is written in his name.

PHILIP SELLEW

Bartholomew. A follower of Jesus and one of the *Twelve (Mark 3.18 par.). Other than his *Aramaic name, which means "son of Tolmai," nothing is recorded about him in the New Testament. Because Nathanael is not mentioned in the *synoptic Gospels, and Bartholomew does not occur in the gospel of John, but both are linked with *Philip, it has been suggested that they are the same person, in which case Bartholomew would be Nathanael's patronymic. Later tradition ascribes an apocryphal gospel to Bartholomew and describes his missionary activities in Egypt, Persia, India, and Armenia, where he was reportedly martyred by being flayed alive. Hence he is the patron of tanners.

MICHAEL D. COOGAN

Baruch. Son of Neriah, the scribe of *Jeremiah (see, e.g., Jer. 36.4–5, 32) and the purported author of the book of Baruch (Bar. 1.1; *see next entry*). The name is a shortened form of names like Berechiah and Barachel; all three forms are well attested in biblical and extrabiblical sources. In its full form Baruch's name also occurs on a clay seal impression (bulla) from the late seventh century BCE. The full inscription reads "[belonging] to Berechiah, son of Neriah, the scribe" and is a relatively rare example of the occurrence of the name of a biblical person in a nonbiblical source from the individual's own time. Other bullae from the same period name Seriah, Baruch's brother (Jer. 51.59), and Gemariah, son of Shaphan (Jer. 36.12).   MICHAEL D. COOGAN

Baruch, The Book of. According to the Roman Catholic and Eastern Orthodox churches, this book, which purports to be the work of *Baruch, Jeremiah's friend and secretary (Jer. 32.12–16; 36.4–32; 45), is a work of canonical scripture, but Protestants include it among the *Apocrypha. For Jews it is no more important than any other pseudepigraphical writing from antiquity. As even the casual reader will note, it is divided into at least three distinct parts (1.1–3.8; 3.9–4.4; 4.5–5.9), each with its characteristic style and point of view. This observation leads naturally to the view that Baruch is not a unified composition, but a compendium of works from several authors. The only unifying factor is the supposed common background of the Babylonian *exile.

The first part (1.1–3.8) is in prose and tells how Baruch, in Babylon, composed a prayer of confession and petition (1.15–3.8), which he read to the deposed king, Jeconiah (or Jehoiachin; 2 Kings 24.8–17), and the other exiles. The prayer was then sent to Jerusalem, with an explanatory letter (1.10–14) giving directions as to when it should be used. The second part (3.9–4.4) is a poem in the style of the *wisdom literature, in which Israel is reproached for having forsaken the wisdom that God had given her, which is then identified with the Mosaic Law, the *Torah (4.1; see Sir. 24.23). This act of apostasy is said to explain Israel's unhappy lot in exile. The third part (4.5–5.9) is a poem, partly in the style of Isaiah 40–66, encouraging the exiles to believe that God will not only deliver them but provide for them a glorious future. Characteristic of this poem is the repeated exhortation, "Take courage" (4.5, 21, 27, 30). In the first part of Baruch, the deity is frequently referred to by the title "Lord" (equivalent to Hebrew "Yahweh" or "Adonai"); the title does not occur in the rest of the book. In the third part, God is several times described as "the Everlasting" (e.g., 4.10, 14; 5.2). The *Letter of Jeremiah, although plainly a separate book, is included in Baruch as chap. 6 by the *Vulgate and by translations dependent upon it, as well as by Luther and the King James Version.

The usual critical questions of date, authorship, original language, and provenance must be raised in connection with each of the individual parts of the book, though evidence with which to answer them is on the whole rather sparse. The date of the completed work is obviously later than that of the latest of its component parts.

The explicit claim that Baruch is the author appears only in the opening verses (1.1–10), but the context in which it appears is marked by such imprecision and demonstrable error that it can hardly be taken seriously. The fact that the book was never accepted into the Jewish canon is strong evidence against any part of it being the work of Baruch, Jeremiah's companion. Modern commentators are almost unanimous in regarding this attribution as fictitious and the work as a typical *pseudepigraphon.

All extant texts and versions of Baruch are based upon the Greek of the *Septuagint. Nevertheless, scholars are generally convinced, on the basis of internal evidence, that the original language was *Hebrew or *Aramaic, most probably the former. A frequently quoted example of the kind of evidence for this is found in 3.4, where the inappropriate word "dead," if translated back into Hebrew, would be represented by a word, almost identical in appearance, that means "men" (NRSV: "people"), which is almost certainly the correct reading, the difference being a single vowel. The assumption is that the Greek translator, using a Hebrew text without vowels, misinterpreted the form. Baruch, moreover, is full of Hebrew constructions and turns of phrase.

If the book was written in Hebrew (or even Aramaic), it follows that the various authors were Palestinian Jews, and there is no evidence to controvert that supposition. The first and last sections of the book have close affinities with prophetic traditions, but the middle section (3.9–4.4) is unmistakably a product of traditional Israelite wisdom, with obvious points of contact with works such as *Job and *Sirach (Ecclesiasticus), but not with the more Hellenistic *Wisdom of Solomon. The author of this section must have been a "wise man" of the type of Ben Sira. While the dates of the various sections of the book cannot be determined with any precision, most scholars would date them within the second or early first century BCE. The parallels alleged between the prayer that begins in 2.6 and the similar prayer in Daniel 9 have sometimes been adduced to date at least this section later than the Maccabean revolt of 164 BCE, with which the book of *Daniel is certainly connected; unfortunately, through, even this evidence can be interpreted in a variety of ways.

Despite the ostensible setting of Baruch in the Babylonian exile, its purpose seems to have been to bring a message of reconciliation and hope to the worldwide Jewish community of the Hellenistic period, in which exile, in a sense, had become permanent. The book is not marked by any great originality of thought, and its language is undistinguished and filled with expressions derived from older literature. This no doubt explains the relatively few references to it in early Christian writers. The one passage that had special significance for the church is 3.37, where the subject of the words "appeared on earth" was mistakenly taken to be God rather than *Wisdom (the passage is so translated in the Vulgate and Peshitta) and the verse was therefore understood as a prophecy of the *incarnation. From the historical point of view, 4.1 provides important confirmatory evidence of the growing tendency to identify the personified *Wisdom (see Proverbs 8 and 9) with the *Torah.

In addition to this book of Baruch, several other books of that name were at one time in circulation, of which by far the most important is an apocalypse in Syriac, often designated as 2 Baruch and generally dated late in the first century CE.   ROBERT C. DENTAN

Bathsheba. Wife of King *David, mother of *Solomon. Bathsheba was the wife of Uriah the Hittite, one of David's "mighty men" (2 Sam. 23.39), but she became David's wife after David killed Uriah to cover up his affair with her (2 Sam. 11). God's displeasure over the affair is seen when the child conceived in the affair dies as an infant (2 Sam. 12.14–23). However, Solomon, David and Bathsheba's fourth child (2 Sam. 5.14; 1 Chron. 3.5), succeeds David to the throne. Solomon's successful bid for the throne is attributed in part to the efforts of Bathsheba, who apparently had risen to the status of *queen mother (1 Kings 1.11–31).

                              TIMOTHY M. WILLIS

Beelzebub. *See* Baal-zebub.

Beelzebul. *See* Baal-zebub.

Behemoth. A mythical beast described in Job 40.15–24 as the first of God's creations, an animal of enormous strength that inhabits the river valleys. Although frequently identified with the hippopotamus (as *Leviathan is with the crocodile), not all the details of the creature's physiology fit that well-known mammal. In view of the references to Behemoth in the *apocrypha and *pseudepigrapha, it is more likely that it is a form of the primeval monster of *chaos, defeated by Yahweh at the beginning of the process of creation; in fact, according to Job 40.24, the monster is represented as tamed by him and with a ring through its lip, so that like Leviathan he has become a divine pet. According to later Jewish tradition, at the end time Behemoth and Leviathan will become food for the righteous (see 2 Esd. 6.52).   MICHAEL D. COOGAN

Bel and the Dragon. This small "book" of the *Apocrypha is one of the three additions to the book of *Daniel found only in its Greek translation (the *Septuagint), but not in the original Hebrew-Aramaic text; the other two are the *Prayer of Azariah and the Song of the Three Young Men, and *Susanna. Unlike Susanna, which is a well-told, plausible story, these two tales of Daniel's detective work in exposing the fraudulent claims of the priests of Bel, and his destruction of the dragon (or, better, "snake") are obvious polemical fabrications intended to demonstrate the foolishness of Babylonian religion and the superiority of the faith of Israel. The story of Bel is at least a good story, but the story of the dragon is so preposterous as to verge on the grotesque.

Bel, equivalent to Hebrew *Baal, was another name for Marduk, the chief god of Babylon. When challenged by the king (*Cyrus!) for his failure to worship Bel, who each day proves himself to be truly a god by the enormous quantity of food he consumes, Daniel undertakes to demonstrate that Bel does nothing of the kind. After the priests have set out the regular offering of food in the temple for the god's enjoyment, Daniel sprinkles the floor with ashes in the presence of the king alone. When they return the next morning, they see in the ashes the footprints of the priests and their families who had entered by a secret trap door during the night and consumed the food. The king then, acknowledging that Daniel was right, has the priests and their families executed, and gives Daniel permission to demolish the statue and the temple.

The other story tells how Daniel destroyed the living snake (the "dragon"), though there is no evidence from antiquity that the worship of live snakes was ever a feature of Babylonian religion. Daniel feeds the snake a mixture of pitch, fat, and hair (an unpleasant but hardly lethal concoction), which, it is said, causes the snake to explode. Under compulsion from the snake's worshipers, the king has Daniel thrown into a lions' den for six days (a device borrowed from chap. 6 of the book of Daniel). While there he is fed by the prophet Habakkuk, who is miraculously transported from Judea for the purpose.

On the seventh day, an unharmed Daniel is released by the king, who immediately confesses that there is no god but the God of Daniel.

Like the other stories in Daniel 1–6, these two are examples of a partly satirical polemic against other religions, which must have been popular in the later Hellenistic period, when the attraction of Greek culture for Jews was strong. The strength of the appeal is illustrated by a passage such as 1 Maccabees 1.11–15, which describes the apostasy of a segment of the Jewish population of Jerusalem.

There is no external evidence as to the original language of the stories, but it was presumably *Hebrew, less likely *Aramaic. Palestine was probably the place of their composition, although one can point to no unambiguous clues. The time of writing is probably the second century BCE; the writer is, of course, unknown. Some critics profess to find in the stories faint echoes of the story of Marduk and his slaying of the monster Tiamat in Babylonian mythology, or of some early version of the story of Saint George and the dragon, but the points of contact are few and remote. The manner of Habakkuk's miraculous journey to Babylon is an outright borrowing from Ezekiel 8.3.

ROBERT C. DENTAN

Belial. A word that occurs two dozen times in the Hebrew Bible, frequently in the *pseudepigrapha and other Jewish literature of the Greco-Roman period, and once in the New Testament. In the Hebrew Bible it is used to characterize the wicked or worthless, such as idolaters (Deut. 13.13), the men of Gibeah (Judg. 19.22; 20.13), the sons of Eli (1 Sam. 2.12), Nabal (1 Sam. 25.17, 25), and Shimei (2 Sam. 20.1); in later literature it is a title of *Satan. The etymology of the term is unclear. The most widely held view is that it is a compound meaning "without worth." Another possibility is to understand it as a term for the underworld, literally, "[the place of] no return" (see esp. Ps. 18.4–5). More recent translations generally paraphrase the word, while older translations more often transliterated it. In the KJV, for example, "Belial" occurs fifteen times, whereas in the NRSV it is found only in 2 Corinthians 6.15, in the variant form Beliar.

MICHAEL D. COOGAN

Belshazzar. The name of the eldest son of the last Neo-Babylonian king, Nabonidus (556–539

BCE), who for ten years acted as co-regent during his father's absence in Arabia. Belshazzar (Babylonian Bēl-sharra-uṣur, "Bel has protected the kingship") follows the Aramaic form of the name; elsewhere he is referred to as Balthasar (Bar. 1.11–12) or Baltasar (Josephus), but he should not be confused with the name Belteshazzar applied to Daniel in Babylon (Dan. 1.7).

In his third regnal year, Nabonidus entrusted his army to his eldest son and put under his command troops levied from all lands. The king relinquished all control and entrusted the kingship to Belshazzar while he himself went on a long journey to Tema in the West (Persian Verse Account). Belshazzar, as crown prince and co-regent, exercised genuine royal powers; he is named in texts dated early in Nabonidus's reign (first, fifth, and seventh years) as controlling his own household and business, and he is associated with Nabonidus in oaths taken by their names in legal transactions in his twelfth-thirteenth regnal years. He issued an edict outlining a scheme in which land would be managed by specified chief revenue officials. Belshazzar's death at the time of the fall of Babylon to *Cyrus in October 539 BCE (Dan. 5.30) is likely, though not mentioned in the Babylonian (Nabonidus) Chronicle, which does refer specifically to the capture but not the death of Nabonidus (he was exiled to Carmania). Attempts to read a broken passage of the Chronicle as telling of Belshazzar's death a month after the Persian entry into Babylon in 539 BCE remain conjectural. There is no extrabiblical confirmation of Belshazzar's feast (Dan. 5).

See Daniel, The Book of.

DONALD J. WISEMAN

Ben. The Hebrew word for "son," used frequently in patronymics and also in phrases indicating quality, age, or the like. Thus, a "son of strength" is a warrior, a "son of death" is someone guilty of a capital offense, and a person or animal can be the son (or daughter) of a night (Jon. 4.10), of a year, or of any number of years. Its Aramaic equivalent is *bar*.

See also Benjamin.   MICHAEL D. COOGAN

Benjamin. The youngest son of *Jacob, by *Rachel; *Joseph's full brother; and the ancestor of the tribe of Benjamin. The name means literally "son of the right hand," and should be understood geographically, in the sense of "southern"; the same name is used of a different group in the *Mari texts. Though the smallest of the tribes (Map 3:X5), it had an importance disproportionate to its size (see Ps. 68.27). The narratives in Joshua 3–9 are all set in Benjaminite territory, and members of the tribe were reputed to be fierce warriors (Gen. 49.27; Judg. 5.14; 19–20; 1 Chron. 8.40; 12.1–2). Notable Benjaminites include Ehud the judge; *Saul, the first king of Israel; *Jeremiah the prophet; and *Paul.

See also Tribes of Israel.

MICHAEL D. COOGAN

Bethlehem (Map 1:X5). Village in Judah, ca. 10 km (6 mi) south of *Jerusalem. The site was settled in the Paleolithic era, but is first mentioned in the *Amarna letters (fourteenth century BCE); the meaning of its name is probably "house of (the deity) Lahmu" rather than the traditional "house of bread." It appears first in the Bible as home of a Levite who became a household priest in the hill country of Ephraim and was carried off by the Danites to their new city *Dan (Judg. 17–18). *Ruth came to Bethlehem with her mother Naomi, married Boaz, and became the ancestor of *David (Ruth 4.13–22).

One account of how David's career began says that he was brought to play the lyre for *Saul (1 Sam. 16.14–23), the other that he was a shepherd whom *Samuel anointed as king (1 Sam. 16.1–13). Hope for a king like David persisted in the postexilic period, and Micah 5.2–4 prophesies a shepherd king from Bethlehem. According to Matthew 2 and Luke 2, *Jesus was born in Bethlehem, and Matthew interpreted this as the fulfillment of Micah's prophecy.

Christian tradition, perhaps as early as the second century CE, identified a cave as the site of Jesus' birth. About 338 CE, Constantine had a church built over the grotto (and Justinian reconstructed it in the early sixth century). Jerome settled in Bethlehem in 386; here he made the Latin *Vulgate translation of the Bible.

Among other traditional sites in or near Bethlehem are the shepherds' field, the tomb of *Rachel (Gen. 35.19), and the well from which David's warriors brought him water (2 Sam. 23.13–17; 1 Chron. 11.15–19).

SHERMAN ELBRIDGE JOHNSON

Bible. The English word "Bible" is derived from the Greek word *biblia* (neuter plural), which means simply "books." As the collections of Jewish and Christian texts came increasingly to be considered as one unit, the same plural term in medieval Latin began to be understood in popular usage as feminine singular, no longer denoting "The Books" but "The Book." By the second century BCE the adjective "holy" had come to be used to designate some of these books (see 1 Macc. 12.9), and so now "Holy Bible" means a collection of sacred books.

Contents. The number of these sacred and/or authoritative books varies in different religious traditions. The *Samaritans recognize only five books (Genesis, Exodus, Leviticus, Numbers, and Deuteronomy) as their canon. Twenty-four books, classified in three groupings, make up the Hebrew *canon: the Law (*Torah: Genesis, Exodus, Leviticus, Numbers, Deuteronomy); the Prophets, comprising the Former Prophets (Joshua, Judges, Samuel, Kings) and the Latter Prophets (Isaiah, Jeremiah, Ezekiel, and the Twelve Prophets); the Writings (Psalms, Proverbs, Job, Song of Songs, Ruth, Lamentations, Ecclesiastes, Esther, Daniel, Ezra-Nehemiah, and Chronicles). Samuel, Kings, the Twelve, Ezra-Nehemiah, and Chronicles are each counted as one book.

Historically, Protestant churches have recognized the Hebrew canon as their Old Testament, although differently ordered, and with some books divided so that the total number of books is thirty-nine. These books, as arranged in the traditional English Bible, fall into three types of literature: seventeen historical books (Genesis to Esther), five poetical books (Job to Song of Solomon), and seventeen prophetical books. With the addition of another twenty-seven books (the four Gospels, Acts, twenty-one letters, and the book of Revelation), called the New Testament, the Christian scriptures are complete.

The Protestant canon took shape by rejecting a number of books and parts of books that had for centuries been part of the Old Testament in the Greek *Septuagint and in the Latin *Vulgate, and had gained wide acceptance within the Roman Catholic church. In response to the Protestant Reformation, at the Council of Trent (1546) the Catholic church accepted, as deuterocanonical, Tobit, Judith, the Greek additions to Esther, the Wisdom of Solomon, Sirach, Baruch, the Letter of Jeremiah, three Greek additions to Daniel (the Prayer of Azariah and the Song of the Three Jews, Susanna, and Bel and the Dragon), and 1 and 2 Maccabees (*see* Apocrypha, *article on* Jewish Apocrypha). These books, together with those in the Jewish canon and the New Testament, constitute the total of seventy-three books accepted by the Roman Catholic church.

The Anglican church falls between the Catholic church and many Protestant denominations by accepting only the Jewish canon and the New Testament as authoritative, but also by accepting segments of the apocryphal writings in the lectionary and liturgy. At one time all copies of the Authorized or King James Version of 1611 included the Apocrypha between the Old and New Testaments.

The Bible of the Greek Orthodox church comprises all of the books accepted by the Roman Catholic church, plus 1 Esdras, the Prayer of Manasseh, Psalm 151, and 3 Maccabees. The Slavonic canon adds 2 Esdras, but designates 1 and 2 Esdras as 2 and 3 Esdras. Other Eastern churches have 4 Maccabees as well. (*See* Eastern Orthodoxy and the Bible.)

The Ethiopic church has the largest Bible of all, and distinguishes different canons, the "narrower" and the "broader," according to the extent of the New Testament. The Ethiopic Old Testament comprises the books of the Hebrew Bible as well as all of the deuterocanonical books listed above, along with Jubilees, 1 Enoch, and Joseph ben Gorion's (Josippon's) medieval history of the Jews and other nations. The New Testament in what is referred to as the "broader" canon is made up of thirty-five books, joining to the usual twenty-seven books eight additional texts, namely four sections of church order from a compilation called Sinodos, two sections from the Ethiopic Book of the Covenant, Ethiopic Clement, and Ethiopic Didascalia. When the "narrower" New Testament canon is followed, it is made up of only the familiar twenty-seven books, but then the Old Testament books are divided differently so that they make up 54 books instead of 46. In both the narrower and broader canon, the total number of books comes to 81.

Format. The traditional division of chapters (previously ascribed to Hugh of St. Cher and dated about 1262) is now attributed to Stephen Langton, a lecturer at the University of Paris and subsequently Archbishop of Canterbury (d. 1228). The present method employed for verses was originated by the scholarly printer Robert Stephanus (Estienne), whose Greek New Testament with numbered verses was issued in Geneva in 1551. The first English Bible to employ Stephanus's system of numbering verses was the Geneva version (New Testament 1556; Old

Testament 1560). (*See* Chapter and Verse Divisions).

The English Revised Version of 1881–85 relinquished the separate verse division of older versions in favor of a format employing paragraphs; however, verse numbers were still provided in the margin for ease of reference. Before the employment of this modern system the many verses, or texts, of the Bible were the subject of much statistical and even superstitious research. Fortunes were divined or the "will of God" learned by random selection of biblical passages (*see* Sortes Biblicae). Some individuals undertook the daunting task of tallying the verses, words, and even the letters of the words, as though some all-important information was encoded in the result. The example below is a typical compilation, made by Thomas Hartwell Horne (1780–1862) over a three-year period. According to Horne's computations, the Authorized or King James Version of the Bible is comprised of:

	Old Testament	New Testament	Total
Books	39	27	66
Chapters	929	260	1,189
Verses	33,214	7,959	41,173
Words	593,493	181,253	774,746
Letters	2,728,100	838,380	3,566,480

This type of analysis has also brought to light miscellaneous information such as the following: the word "and" occurs in the Bible 46,227 times; the word "Lord" 1,855 times; "reverend" only once; "girl" also only once; "everlasting fire" twice; also, no words are longer than six syllables. These students of the letter of the Bible (like the Masoretes in ancient times; *see* Masorah) inform us that the middle book is that of Proverbs; the middle chapter, Job 39; the middle verse, 2 Chronicles 20.17; that the longest verse is Esther 8.9, and the shortest John 11.35 ("Jesus wept").
See also Curious Bibles.   BRUCE M. METZGER

Bible Societies. With their concern for the translation, production, and distribution of the scriptures, Bible societies are relatively recent institutions, but the concept underlying their worldwide activity is ancient. The notion that the Bible should be in the language of the people prompted the Hellenistic Jewish community of the third century BCE to produce a Greek translation (*Septuagint) of the Hebrew Bible. Inspired by this example, the early eastern Greek-speaking church began to produce translations of the Bible in a variety of languages so as to make sure that the gospel would be known as widely as possible. Likewise, the Roman church produced its own edition of the Bible, in the "vulgar" Latin of the common people, which became the most widely used translation in the western church for a thousand years, the *Vulgate.

Although there were some attempts in medieval scriptoria to mass-produce copies of the Bible, the process was slow, and the handwritten copies issued were enormously expensive. With the invention of movable type for *printing (about 1456), the situation changed, and the Bible began to be translated into vernacular languages and commercially produced for general circulation. It was, however, not until the evangelical revival in the eighteenth century and the consequent formation of missionary societies, principally in the United Kingdom, that the importance of scripture translation and publication began to be fully recognized. These missionary societies placed special emphasis on the use of the scriptures in preaching and teaching ministries, and included scripture distribution among their ongoing programs.

The organization of this period which most completely resembled the later Bible societies was a direct outgrowth of the Pietistic movement, the von Canstein Bible Institution of Halle, organized in 1710 to supply inexpensive scriptures to the poor of Germany. Although the von Canstein group confined its efforts to Germany and eastern Europe, by the end of the eighteenth century it had achieved the remarkable record of circulating over three million low-cost Bibles and New Testaments.

Meanwhile, across the English Channel a great awakening had begun, generated in large part by the preaching of John and Charles Wesley and George Whitefield. Missionary societies were formed to spread the gospel, and often their first assignment was to master the local language in order to translate the Bible. Thus William Carey (1761–1843), a shoemaker who had taught himself both Hebrew and Greek, went to India under the auspices of his Baptist Missionary Society and launched a translations program at Serampore; he participated in thirty-five translations. Robert Morrison (1782–1834), sponsored by the London Missionary Society, produced in Canton and Macao the first Chinese translation of the Bible, though he was broken in health and working against incredible odds. A bit later, Robert Moffat (1795–1883), David Livingstone's father-in-law, went to Capetown to begin his distinguished career as a pioneer missionary, his first duty being to produce a translation of the Bible in seTswana. Still others followed, and as their numbers increased and their tasks became more demanding, they and their parent societies at home found themselves, in view of their many other commitments, unable to meet the rapidly growing needs for Bible translation and production. It became clear that a new strategy was required, calling for an organization that would be concerned solely with the translation and production of scriptures for the missions in Asia, Africa, and Latin America.

The British and Foreign Bible Society. The formation of the British and Foreign Bible Society (BFBS) on 7 March 1804, was the answer. Nearly three hundred people met in the London Tavern to discuss the place of Bible distribution in Christian work and witness. Despite their deep doctrinal and ecclesiological differences they agreed to form a society whose single purpose would be to print the scriptures, without note or comment, and to distribute them without financial gain, in the British Isles and throughout the world.

The new Society grew rapidly, and within a decade there were throughout the British Isles over two hundred local groups called auxiliaries that were committed to supporting the cause. Equally important, other Bible societies, patterned after the BFBS, were being formed on the European continent and in North America.

American Bible Society. Meanwhile, in the United States, Bible societies were being organized in several states and in many county seats and principal cities of the fledgling republic. In a period of less than ten years, more than 130 such regional Bible societies were established. There were fifteen "female" Bible societies among them, the first being the Female Bible Society of Geneva, New York (1813). A similar development took place in Canada, where auxiliaries of the British and Foreign Bible Society were established.

The resulting situation was far from satisfactory, for while some communities were well served, others were destitute of scriptures. This was particularly true of the growing West in the United States, where it was reported that not a single Bible could be found in many of the new settlements and where vernacular scriptures were desperately needed in the former French and Spanish territories. The need for some kind of a central organization became increasingly evident, and a call finally went out to create a "General Bible Society." Fifty-six delegates met in New York on 8 May 1816, agreed to establish a new national organization called the American Bible Society (ABS), adopted a constitution modeled on the British one, and issued an "address" to the people of the United States in which they said of the new society that "local feelings, party prejudices, sectarian jealousies are excluded by its very nature. Its members are leagued in that, and in that alone, which calls up every hallowed, and puts down every unhallowed, principle—the dissemination of the scriptures in the received versions where they exist, and in the most faithful where they may be required." Many of the provincial societies merged at once with the new national body, but some preferred an "auxiliary" status and a few opted to remain independent, some maintaining separate organizations to the present.

Thus, by the end of the second decade of the nineteenth century, Bible societies were firmly established in Europe and North America, and their distinctive purpose and mission had become widely recognized and generally approved. As they developed, they became noted for the involvement of large numbers of lay men and women, often giving them precedence over their clergy members. They also became widely respected for the ecumenical composition of their boards and staff, for they were careful to maintain close relationships with all Protestant groups; active Roman Catholic participation in their programs did not occur until the middle of the twentieth century. They also developed an enviable reputation for careful scholarship both in publishing source texts and in providing quality translations in an incredible number of languages; they also have been (and continue to be) a significant presence in the development of linguistic theory and practice. Similarly, they maintained through the years a policy of strict impartiality in offering their services and productions to all; to that end they remained extremely cautious in avoiding the inclusion of doctrinal notes or comments in their publications. Throughout they held fast to their founding principle to present to all persons an opportunity to possess the scriptures in their own tongues, with price as no barrier to ownership.

The United Bible Societies. Throughout the

nineteenth century, most of the Bible societies confined their activities to work within their national borders. The ABS and BFBS, and to a lesser extent the National Bible Society of Scotland (NBSS) and the Netherlands Bible Society, were a conspicuous exception. These four "missionary" Societies met needs not only in their own countries but also moved out across the world to engage in scripture translation and distribution, largely following the missionaries of their own national churches, with little communication or consultation among themselves. At first there was little friction, but as the overseas outreach of these larger societies continued to expand, areas of duplication and tension began to appear. Some experimental comity arrangements were made in the early years of the twentieth century, preparing the way for a formal consultation in London in 1932 involving three of the principal societies at work in overseas areas, namely, the ABS, BFBS, and NBSS. The London meeting led to innovative cooperative efforts, particularly between the ABS and BFBS in places such as Brazil and Japan, and to a larger conference in 1939 at Amsterdam, when it was proposed to create a kind of world council of Bible societies. The outbreak of war in Europe, however, made it impossible to carry out those plans.

Following the war, in 1946 at a conference held at Haywards Heath in England, sixty-three delegates from twelve European Bible societies and the ABS brought into being the United Bible Societies (UBS), a loose federation of national societies. The UBS has flourished and serves today as a valuable center of coordination, appraisal, and strategic planning.

Working in concert through the UBS, more than seventy-five Bible societies worldwide have been able to improve their service to churches and missions through greatly improved and accelerated translation techniques, efficiently coordinated production centers, wider interconfessional relationships, and the use of more scientific marketing methods.

See also Circulation of the Bible; Translations.   LATON E. HOLMGREN

Biblical Criticism. *See* Interpretation, History of, *article on* Modern Biblical Criticism.

Biblical Theology. *This entry consists of two articles, one on the* Old Testament *and one on the* New

Testament. *(The term "Old Testament" is appropriate in this context, since biblical theology has been an almost exclusively Christian enterprise.)* For related discussion, see Interpretation, History of, *article on* Modern Biblical Criticism, *and* Israel, Religion of.

Old Testament

Strictly speaking, Old Testament theology is a Christian discipline, for it presupposes the *canon of the Christian Bible, which is divided into two parts, the Old and New Testaments. In this scriptural context, Old Testament theology is part of the larger discipline of biblical theology.

The early Christian community interpreted the life, death, and resurrection of *Jesus Christ in the perspective of the scriptures of Israel (Law, Prophets, Writings). In the New Testament, almost without exception, "scripture(s)" refers to these sacred writings. From time to time, beginning with Marcion in the second century CE, questions have been raised as to whether Israel's scriptures belong in the Christian Bible; but the church has steadfastly maintained that the Old Testament as well as the New bears witness to God's *revelation and hence has an indispensable place in Christian life, thought, and worship.

The Nature and Method of Old Testament Theology. The separation of Old Testament theology as an independent discipline occurred fairly late in the history of biblical interpretation, specifically in the period of the Enlightenment when modern views of historical development emerged. The revival of biblical theology in the twentieth century, which began in the 1920s under the leadership of such theologians as Karl Barth (dogmatic theology) and Walter Eichrodt (Old Testament theology), challenged the view of theological liberalism, in which the relation between the Testaments was understood as a unilinear historical development from lower to higher stages of spiritual evolution. Once again theologians in various ways began to address themselves to the overall theological witness of the bipartite canon of Christian scripture. Nevertheless, the earlier separation between Old Testament and New Testament theology has persisted. In part this separation is justified by the vast expansion of knowledge that requires a division of labor among biblical theologians. More important, the Old Testament has a quasi-independent role within the Christian Bible, contributing theological dimensions that supplement, enrich, and at points even qualify the witness of the New Testament. The church considers both testaments to be necessary for a full understanding of God's self-disclosure and human response to the divine initiative.

Since the Old Testament is a vast and diverse body of literature, the question immediately arises: how should one present a theology of the Old Testament? One way is to organize the material according to a structure or principle derived from the outside. This method was dominant in the late medieval and Protestant scholastic periods, when the task of biblical theology was to provide the proof texts (dicta probantia) for the support of the dogmas of the church. The method is still advocated by theologians who structure Old Testament theology according to the topics of systematic theology (God, humanity, salvation, etc.) or who interpret the Bible according to a modern philosophical perspective (evolutionary development, existentialism, Marxist social philosophy, etc.). Another approach is to try to let the Bible set the issues and determine the method, in which case theology of (subjective genitive) the Old Testament refers to what belongs to, and inheres in, the Old Testament itself.

If the latter way is followed, one immediately faces a methodological problem as to whether Old Testament theology should be presented synchronically (structurally) or diachronically (historically). The debate over method is seen in the works of two leading Old Testament theologians of the twentieth century. The Swiss theologian Walter Eichrodt (Theologie des Alten Testaments, issued 1933–1939) attempted to present the "structural unity" of Old Testament belief by using the relational model of *covenant. The German theologian Gerhard von Rad (Theologie des Alten Testaments, published 1957–1961) attempted to understand the Old Testament dynamically as a history of traditions, and in this sense a Heilsgeschichte ("salvation history"). Probably a combination of both methods is required. On the one hand much of the Old Testament is story/history; indeed it begins with a history that extends from *creation to the *exile of the Israelite people (Genesis—2 Kings). On the other hand, patterns of organization and symbolism are discernible in this historical presentation and elsewhere.

The Relationship between God and People. The starting point in an exposition of Old Testament theology is the self-disclosure of the holy God, who chooses to enter into relationship with a particular people, Israel, called to be the means through whom other peoples may know and glorify God, the creator and redeemer. The term Israel, both in biblical times and today, may be used of a political state, (e.g., the kingdoms of Israel and Judah), but basically it is a sacral term which refers to "the people of God." In its inclusive sense the term is often used in the Old Testament (e.g., Amos 3.1; Hos. 11.1), and in this larger sense *Paul could speak of the Christian community as being essentially related to, and indeed part of, Israel, the people of God (Rom. 9—11).

In the scriptures of Israel, primacy is given to the *Torah, traditionally called the "five books of Moses." In the view of the community of faith, God gave torah or instruction to the people, so that they may properly serve (worship) God and live faithfully and obediently in God's presence. This Torah has the form of an overall story or history, which includes within it commandments, or *law in the narrower sense of the term. God's self-disclosure as creator and sovereign established a relation between God and human beings, who are made in the divine image (Gen. 1.26–28), and particularly a relationship with one people, whose election is portrayed in the calling of *Abraham and *Sarah to respond in faith to the divine promise (Gen. 11.31–12.9) and the choice of *Jacob, also called Israel, over his twin brother *Esau (Gen. 25.19–28).

The heart of the Torah story, however, is found in the tradition that begins with the book of *Exodus. The disclosure of God's name, that is, identity (Exod. 6.2–9), is associated primarily with fundamental root experiences that constitute the fountainhead of the Mosaic tradition, namely Exodus and *Sinai. These core traditions, which signify the inseparably related dimensions of divine initiative and human responsibility, of *salvation and obligation, are paradigmatic for Israel's knowledge of who God is and how the people are to live faithfully in God's presence. The holy God whom Israel knows and worships is characterized as one, jealous (zealous), righteous, gracious, faithful, and trustworthy, whose judgment falls, however, upon those who betray their religious loyalty and turn to iniquity (Exod. 34.6–8). This knowledge of God is further elaborated in the preaching of *prophets, the teaching of *priests, and the counsel of sages (cf. Jer. 18.18).

Covenant History. The relationship between God and people, often expressed in the language "your God" and "my people" (e.g., Exod. 6.7; Lev. 26.12; Isa. 40.1; Jer. 31.33), is understood in the Old Testament as that of a covenant. The significance of covenant is far greater than a statistical count of the occurrences of the term would indicate. Eichrodt took this concept, understood in the broad sense of relationship, as the organizing principle in his theology. In the Reformed tradition there is precedent for this, reaching back at least to the federal (covenantal) theology of the Dutch Calvinist, Johannes Cocceius (1603–1669). In the Old Testament, however, covenant is not a univocal term, nor is it a theological umbrella that covers everything. Three major covenantal perspectives or patterns of symbolization are evident. All of these are covenants of *grace, for they rest upon the initiative and superior status of the divine covenant maker, but each nuances the relationship between God and people differently.

The Torah gives primacy to the covenant with Abraham (Gen. 17; cf. chap. 15). This covenant is based on God's gracious commitment, unconditioned by human performance. Therefore, it is designated an "everlasting covenant," one that has perpetual validity. Characteristic of this type of covenant is the giving of divine promises, not the imposition of obligations. In the priestly (see P) perspective that governs the Torah in its final form, the Abrahamic covenant belongs to a periodized history that is punctuated with three divine covenants, each of which is termed an everlasting covenant. The first period extends from creation to the covenant with *Noah after the *flood (Gen. 9), a universal, ecological covenant embracing all human beings, animals and birds, and the earth itself. The second extends from Noah to Abra[ha]m, and includes the divine promises of the land of *Canaan as an everlasting possession, a numerous posterity, and a special relationship between God and the descendants of Abraham and *Sarah ("I will be your/their God"). The third period extends from Abraham to *Moses, the mediator of the Sinai covenant, also designated as everlasting. These covenants are accompanied by three signs: the *rainbow, *circumcision, and the *Sabbath, respectively, the latter harking back to God's creation (Exod. 31.12–17). In this perspective, the Sinai covenant is regarded as the ratification or fulfillment of the ancestral covenant that God "remembers" (Exod. 2.24; Lev. 26.44–45). The special relationship with God, promised in the Abrahamic covenant, finds expression in the disclosure of the cultic name, Yahweh (see Names of God in the Hebrew Bible), and the "tabernacling presence" of God in the midst of the people (Exod. 29.45–46). The whole cult is regarded as the God-given means of grace that enables a holy people to live faithfully in the presence of the holy God. *Sacrifices are provided (the book of *Leviticus) for the expiation of sin and reconciliation to God.

A second covenantal pattern of symbolization, following the sequence of the Hebrew Bible, is associated with Moses. It is set forth classically in the book of *Deuteronomy, canonically joined to the priestly Torah discussed above, and provides the dominant theological perspective in the Former Prophets (Joshua through 2 Kings), that is, the *Deuteronomic history. In contrast to the Abrahamic covenant, which was based unilaterally on God's gracious commitment and promise, this covenant is more of a two-way affair, and places greater emphasis on human obligation. The covenantal pattern, on the analogy of ancient suzerainty treaties, includes several characteristic elements: the story of the saving deeds of the covenant initiator, the stipulations that are binding on the covenant recipient, and the sanctions of *blessing and *curse in case of obedience or disobedience. Like the Abrahamic covenant, this too is a covenant of grace, but it carries within it "the curse of the law" (cf. Gal. 3.10, 13), for the judgment of God could bring severe punishment upon the people or even annul the relationship if the people fail in their covenant responsibilities (Hos. 1.8–10).

A third covenantal pattern of symbolization is also found in the Deuteronomic history, where it is introduced as a theme secondary to the Mosaic covenant. This is the royal covenant theology, according to which Yahweh made an everlasting covenant with *David, promising perpetual divine grace (hesed) to the throne, even though particular kings performed badly in office and had to be chastised (2 Sam. 7; Ps. 89). This Davidic covenant did not supersede the Mosaic covenant; indeed, the *ark of the covenant—the sacred symbol of Mosaic tradition—was escorted into *Jerusalem and eventually was placed in the holy of holies of the *Temple (cf. Pss. 24; 132). This covenant perspective, however, moves beyond the horizon of Israel's sacred history into the cosmic dimension of God's sovereignty as creator of the universe and ruler of history. As in other religions of the ancient Near East, the two salvific institutions are *kingship and Temple (Ps. 78.67–72), both of which were alien to the Mosaic tradition. The reigning monarch is Yahweh's anointed ("*messiah") and is elected to the special role of *son of God (Ps. 2.7). When the king is gifted with wisdom, divine blessing flows into Israel's society and overflows to other nations (Ps. 72). The Temple, in Davidic theology, also has cosmic significance, for it is founded at the cosmic center—the meeting place of heaven and earth, where God is present in the midst of the people (Ps. 46.4–5). This covenantal perspective is dominant in the books of *Chronicles, and is a major factor in the *Psalms, which in their final form were issued under the aegis of David, regarded as the type of God's anointed one or messiah.

These three covenants, associated with Abraham, Moses, and David respectively, should not be understood as following one another chronologically but as existing side by side, like overlapping theological circles. In the Torah the Mosaic covenant fulfills the promissory Abrahamic covenant; the Deuteronomic history emphasizes the Mosaic covenant, but also includes the promissory Davidic covenant (1 Kings 8.23–24); and the Chronicler's history gives priority to the Davidic covenant (this historian bypasses the Mosaic period), but also includes elements of the Priestly tradition and the Mosaic torah understood in its halakic or legal sense. Indeed, to express the relationship between God and human beings all three theological perspectives are required. Each nuances in its own way polarities of the divine-human relationship: God's sovereignty and human freedom, God's transcendence (distance) and immanence (presence), and God's relation to the particular people, Israel, and God's universal sway as cosmic creator and sovereign. All three include promises and obligations, but the Abrahamic and Davidic covenants are primarily promissory, while the Mosaic covenant is primarily one of obligation.

Prophecy and Covenant. The interrelation of these covenant perspectives is evident in the second part of the canon of the Prophets: the so-called Latter Prophets, namely the books of Isaiah, Jeremiah, Ezekiel, and the Twelve. The message of the eighth-century prophet, *Isaiah of Jerusalem (Isa. 1–39), was based primarily on royal covenant theology. Virtually ignoring Exodus and Sinai, this prophet proclaimed that Yahweh is the cosmic king, whose rule is manifest on earth through the Davidic monarch and whose dwelling place is on Mount *Zion. The imminent *day of the Lord would manifest divine judgment against all presumptuous claims of earthly powers (2.6–22) and would purge Zion, the city of God, of corruption, so that it would be the center of a social order that corresponds to the order of God's cosmic rule. Later

interpreters enriched Isaiah's message with the *typology of a new exodus (Isa. 43.14–21) and transferred to the people the promises of grace made to David (55.3–5). This synthesis of covenant traditions provided the theological basis for proclaiming the coming of the *kingdom of God—a new age, indeed a new creation, in which Israel and all nations would participate.

Two of the prophets of Israel, *Hosea and *Jeremiah, stood primarily in the Mosaic covenant tradition. Both opposed the allurements of Canaanite culture, particularly the *Baal fertility religion. In the case of Hosea, however, who was active in the northern kingdom just before its fall in 722 BCE, the contact with Canaanite culture served to enrich covenant theology. He poetically portrayed the relationship between God and Israel in terms of a sacred marriage, in which the "wife," after experiencing divine discipline for her infidelity, eventually is reconciled with her "husband" in a new covenant, like the one made in "the days of her youth" (the time of the Exodus). In this restored relationship, the land will become fertile and yield abundant agricultural blessings (Hos. 2.8–15). Shifting to another family *metaphor, this poet portrayed God's relationship to the people as that of a parent who disciplines and nurtures a child (Hos. 11.1–9).

Jeremiah, at the time of the collapse of the southern kingdom of Judah, was also an interpreter of the Mosaic covenant. Portrayed as a "prophet like Moses" (Deut. 18.18; cf. Jer. 1.9), he attacked the weaknesses of royal covenant theology, as evident in the exploitative policies of Davidic kings and false confidence in the Temple. Recalling the story of Yahweh's saving action in the Mosaic period (Jer. 2.6–7), he indicted the people for their violation of the covenant commandments (7.1–15, the "Temple sermon") and summoned them, under the threat of divine judgment, to repent, that is, to turn away from false loyalties and to return to loyalty to Yahweh and the demands of the covenant. The book of Jeremiah also includes conditional promises to Davidic kings (22.1–5) and messianic hope for a coming Davidic ruler (23.5–6). The new covenant, to supersede the Mosaic covenant, which the people broke (31.31–33), would be based on God's forgiving grace and would introduce an everlasting covenant (32.36–41).

The interaction of theological perspectives is especially evident in the message of *Ezekiel. Basically this prophet stood in the priestly tradition that provided the overarching theological perspective of the Torah in its final form. This is evident in Ezekiel's sense of the divine holiness that separates God from mortal human beings, the tabernacling presence of God in the Temple, and the cultic and ethical laws designed to insure the holiness of the people. As in the priestly recension of the Torah, the Exodus tradition is important, but is invoked to demonstrate that from the very first Israel had been a sinful people under the judgment of God (Ezek. 20.6–8). The Mosaic covenant, broken by the people, will be superseded by a new covenant which, because it is based on the faithfulness and forgiveness of God and not on the people's behavior, will be an everlasting covenant (16.59–63). Portrayals of the divine restoration beyond the day of judgment include elements of royal covenant theology: the raising up of a Davidic leader who will be a "good shepherd" of the people (34.23–24; 37.24–25).

The Justice of God and the Problem of Evil. Taken together, the Torah and the Prophets (Former and Latter) portray a temporal movement from creation to final consummation under the governance of God, whose providence is evident in nature and history, and whose will is made known to, and through, Israel, the people of God. The covenantal perspectives described above accompanied Israel's sacred history, as evident in the Psalms that contain the hymns, laments, and thanksgivings of the pilgrim people.

The intensification of Israel's sufferings, owing to the fall of the nation and the exile of the people, called into question the adequacy of covenantal theology, which consistently explained *suffering as the deserved consequence of human sin or failure. The third part of the Hebrew canon, the Writings, reflects two major theological shifts of emphasis. One was the movement from torah to *wisdom. Wisdom had always been a major ingredient in covenantal theology, as evident in the Mosaic tradition with its appeal to walk in the way that yields *blessing (Deuteronomy; cf. Jer. 17.5–8), and was especially at home in royal covenant theology, which sought to align the social order with the righteousness and peace of God's cosmic kingdom. In the postexilic period the shift to the halakhic dimension of the Mosaic torah, evident in the Chronicler's writing, facilitated the identification of torah and prudential wisdom (as in torah and wisdom psalms, e.g., 1, 37, 119; see the book of *Proverbs). Facing the question of theodicy, however, some sages maintained that the divine

wisdom hidden in creation is beyond human grasp (*Ecclesiastes; *Job). *Wisdom was even accorded a cosmic role as the agent of God in creation (Prov. 8.22–31).

The other major development was the movement from prophecy to *apocalyptic, which can be traced within the book of Isaiah. Although human wisdom cannot grasp the divine secret, the mystery of God's kingdom, i.e., the time and manner of its coming, is revealed to a seer (the book of *Daniel). In apocalyptic the scene is not restricted to Israel's sacred history but unfolds into a universal drama in which the kingdom of God is triumphant over all powers of evil, including *death itself. Apocalyptic writers eclectically drew upon all of Israel's covenantal traditions, as well as extrabiblical motifs, to portray the final consummation.

The Relation between the Testaments. There is no smooth and easy transition from the Old Testament to the New, as evident from the fact that the very scriptures of Israel that nourished the early Christian community have proved to be problematic. Nevertheless, New Testament writers appropriated Israel's scriptures in various ways to interpret and elaborate the good news about Jesus, who was confessed to be the Messiah or Christ. Viewed in Christian perspective, the sacred history of Israel is part of "the story of our life"; indeed, the whole biblical narrative, extending from creation to consummation, has its center in Jesus Christ.

Accordingly, the early Christian community affirmed that God's covenants with Israel are ratified in Jesus Christ, though preference is usually given to the promissory covenants associated with Abraham and David (cf. "the covenants of promise," Eph. 2.12). To invoke the typology of Calvin, Jesus Christ is prophet, priest, and king—that is, the eschatological "prophet like Moses" of the Mosaic covenant tradition, the "son of God" of the royal or messianic tradition, and the priestly mediator who effects reconciliation with God (Letter to the Hebrews). Furthermore, in him converge the wisdom movement (cf. the *Logos of the prologue to the Fourth Gospel) and the apocalyptic expectation of the heavenly *Son of man. Finally, the Old Testament, functioning as Christian scripture, offers to the Christian community supplementary theological dimensions that are vital for a full understanding of Christian faith, such as creation theology, a healthy this-worldliness, the role of nationhood in God's economy, expostulation with God in times of human distress and perplexity, and the insistence that the command to love God and one another must be informed by God's demand for justice and *mercy in political, social, and economic relations (Mic. 6.8).

BERNHARD W. ANDERSON

New Testament

Strictly speaking there is no theology of the New Testament, but as many theologies as there are authors. Theology is systematized reflection, and only *Romans has some claim to be that. All the New Testament books are occasional in character, i.e., written for specific situations, not statements of timeless truths. Nevertheless, underlying all the books of the New Testament there is a coherent center, the proclamation (Grk. *kerygma*) of *Jesus crucified and risen. This coherent center may itself be expressed in different ways, even in the same author (e.g., in Paul, compare 1 Cor. 15.3–5; Rom. 10.9; 14.9). Sometimes only the *crucifixion is mentioned (Gal. 3.1; 1 Cor. 1.13; 2.2), sometimes only the *resurrection (1 Thess. 1.10). But each always implies the other. Sometimes *Paul gives brief statements of the kerygma, sometimes extended confessional formulae. The preaching in *Acts (Acts 2; 3; 10; 13) is similarly focused on Jesus' death and resurrection. The four Gospels are structured so as to bring out the centrality of the cross and resurrection (cf. the three passion predictions in Mark 8.31; 9.31; 10.33–34 par.) and the importance of the "hour" of Jesus' death and glorification throughout the Fourth Gospel.

This death and resurrection of Jesus constitutes the "Christ event," in which God acted definitively for the salvation (or condemnation) first of Israel, then of the human race, and finally of the whole cosmos. It is a proclamation set in the framework of Jewish *apocalyptic hope of a new heaven and a new earth. This consummation has now been inaugurated in the Christ event and will be completed when Christ returns (the *parousia).

The Doctrine of God (Theology). The New Testament offers no new doctrine of *God, but simply proclaims that the Old Testament God has now acted definitively. The God of Abraham, Isaac, and Jacob is now the God and Father of Jesus Christ. Even the fatherhood of God is not new (Isa. 64.8). Thus all Old Testament theology is implied in the New Testament: God is the creator and Lord of history, the God who acts, who calls Israel into covenant, who promises the redemption of his people. The New Testament proclaims that these promises have now

been fulfilled, or rather are now in the process of being fulfilled.

The Earthly Jesus. Although the coherent center of the New Testament focuses upon the death and resurrection of Jesus, his earthly ministry is an integral part of the Christ event. For the earthly ministry of Jesus gives shape and contours to the cross. There were hundreds of crosses in Palestine in the first century CE, but only in this cross did God act for the salvation of humankind. That is not an arbitrary claim, but is legitimated by the fact that the earthly Jesus had preached the in-breaking of God's kingdom, i.e., God's definitive salvation. Hence the four Gospels, four versions of the Good News, encapsulate the earthly ministry of Jesus in their proclamation of his death and resurrection. And although Paul seldom alludes to the earthly ministry of Jesus—only a few echoes of his sayings (1 Cor. 7.10; 9.14; 11.24–25) and an occasional reference to his character and lifestyle (2 Cor. 8.9; 10.1; Rom. 15.8; Phil. 2.8)—nevertheless Paul's frequent use of the human name "Jesus" in significant contexts is testimony to his conviction of the importance of Jesus' earthly history (see especially 1 Cor. 12.3). Moreover, the resurrection does not relegate the earthly Jesus to the archives; rather it perpetuates him, making the salvation that he offered on earth forever available through the preaching of the kerygma.

The Person of Christ (Christology). There is no single Christology in the New Testament but a variety of Christologies. But these Christologies do have a coherent center. Jesus is always interpreted christologically in the New Testament; he is always the one in whom God has decisively acted for us and for our salvation: "In Christ God was reconciling the world to himself" (2 Cor. 5.19). This coherent center of Christology is given contingent application by a variety of christological titles, patterns, and, in the Gospels, portraits. Jesus is the final prophet and servant of Yahweh; he is *Messiah (Christ, anointed one), Lord, *Son of God. In later books he is the *incarnation of the preexistent *Logos or Word of God. Some early patterns have two foci, looking back to his first coming and forward to his return (Acts 3.20–21). Some patterns depict two stages, his earthly career and his subsequent exaltation (Acts 2.36; Rom. 1.3–4). Some patterns are threefold, speaking of his preexistence, incarnate life, and exaltation (Phil. 2.6–11, though some interpret this as a two-stage Christology; Col. 1.15–20; Heb. 1.2–3; John 1.1–18, though here the exaltation is implied rather than asserted). Each Gospel has its own portrait of Jesus. *Mark emphasizes the *messianic secret; Jesus' messiahship is hidden on earth, and can be confessed only after the cross and resurrection. For *Matthew Jesus is the new *Moses; as such, he gives the definitive interpretation of the *Law and founds a church, the true Israel. For *Luke Jesus is the end-time prophet who shows human sympathy and compassion for the poor, for the outcast and the sick, and for women. For *John Jesus is the incarnate revealer whose revelation, when received, confers salvation. These various portraits are directed toward the specific situations for which the respective evangelists wrote. Some Christologies emphasize the death and resurrection (paschal Christologies); others (like the sending formula) are focused upon the beginning and purpose of Jesus' career (God sent his son, plus a statement of saving purpose; e.g., Gal. 4.4–5). The infancy stories at the beginning of Matthew and Luke (Matthew 1–2; Luke 1–2) give narrative expression to this type of Christology, and the incarnation pattern is a more developed form of it. These Christologies emphasize the divine initiative in the Christ event, of which the *virginal conception is a powerful symbolic expression.

The Work of Christ (Soteriology). At the outset, it was the total career of Jesus that was interpreted as the saving act of God (so the earliest preaching as recorded in Acts). Very soon the death of Christ was interpreted as the focal point of God's saving act. This was expressed by means of the *hyper-* (Grk. "for, on behalf of") formula, which was particularly at home in the tradition of the *Lord's Supper, in the bread and cup words (1 Cor. 11.24–25), though it also figures in some forms of the kerygma (1 Cor. 15.3). The *hyper*-formula does not mean that the death of Jesus was vicarious or substitutionary, as though the human Christ were appeasing the wrath of an angry deity and rendering him propitious toward humankind. Rather, in Christ God was acting to liberate humanity from the bondage of sin.

Often, though not invariably, combined with the *hyper*-formula is the language of "giving" or "giving up": God gave (up) his son to the death on the cross (John 3.16). Often the verb is in the passive: "he was given up," but this is a so-called divine passive (Rom. 4.25), a phrase implying that it was God who gave him up. Sometimes too the subject is Jesus himself ("who gave himself for me," Gal. 2.20). These formulae emphasize the cost of Christ's death, both to the Father and to himself. But whether God or Christ is the subject, the cross is primarily an act of God, initiated by him.

Christ's death was interpreted in earliest tradition as a sacrifice like that of the *Day of Atonement (cf. the pre-Pauline hymn in Rom. 3.25) or that of the *Passover lamb (1 Cor. 5.7). Subsequent references to *blood in connection with the death of Christ echo both of these traditions, and also the cup word in the Supper tradition (e.g., Rom. 5.9; 1 John 1.7). Blood denotes not a material substance, but the event of Christ's death in its saving significance.

Most New Testament writers are content simply to repeat or to echo such traditional formulae. Only Paul and the author of Hebrews reflect further upon the meaning of Christ's death and apply their insights to their churches' situations. Paul reflects particularly on the saving benefits of the cross in response to the judaizing (Galatians; Romans; Phil. 3) and gnosticizing (Corinthian correspondence) controversies.

Paul uses many images to describe the saving effects of Christ's death. They include *justification, reconciliation, *redemption, and expiation. These metaphors are derived from various sources. Justification originates in the law courts where it means acquittal. It denotes neither making people ethically righteous nor merely treating them as righteous, but bringing them into a right relationship with God. This sets the believer on the road to obedience. Reconciliation comes from international or personal relations. It presupposes that human beings were in a state of enmity with God and affirms that God in Christ has overcome that enmity and brought the believers into a right relationship with God. Redemption is a metaphor from the manumission of *slaves. It also occurs in the Hebrew Bible as a metaphor for salvation in connection with the *Exodus and with the powers of evil, including *sin, *death, and the devil. Expiation is a sacrificial term, not developed by Paul but occurring in the hymn whose imagery is derived from the day of atonement (Rom. 3.25). It denotes that the death of Christ covers or wipes away sin.

The letter to the *Hebrews is also a contingent application of the central affirmation of the saving death of Christ. It was written to revive the flagging enthusiasm of second- or third-generation Christians and asserts the once-and-for-all quality of Christ's saving death. There is no further sacrifice for sin and no return after apostasy. To make this point the author develops a Christology of Christ as eternal high priest (an image based on Ps. 110.4), and his sacrifice as the fulfillment of the Levitical ceremonies of the Day of Atonement with an occasional glance at the daily sacrifice.

The Holy Spirit (Pneumatology). Although only Acts casts the giving of the Holy Spirit into a story, it is the general belief of the New Testament writers that the Spirit came as a result of the Christ event. The Hebrew Bible and Jewish tradition expected an outpouring of the spirit in the last days (Ezek. 36.26; Joel 2.28–29), and the early Christian community saw in its post-Easter experiences the fulfillment of this promise (Rom. 5.5) and a foretaste of the full endtime salvation. Paul expresses this general conviction when he calls the Spirit the "first fruits" (Rom. 8.23) or "down payment" (2 Cor. 1.22 [NRSV: "first installment"]; 5.5 [NRSV: "guarantee"]) of final redemption. In the early community the presence of the Spirit was seen primarily in ecstatic phenomena, such as *miracles and speaking in tongues (*see* Glossolalia). Paul had problems in this connection at *Corinth, where the gifts of the Spirit were allowed to run riot, and he found it necessary to grade the gifts, giving priority to prophecy, and making love (Grk. *agapē*) the gift which must inform all the other gifts (1 Cor. 12—14; see also Gal. 5.22). The Fourth Gospel developed the doctrine of the Spirit (called "Paraclete"; NRSV: "Advocate") in a theological rather than ethical direction: the function of the Spirit is to lead the community into truth, not away from the truth revealed in Jesus but to an even deeper apprehension of it (John 14.16–17, 26; 15.26; 16.7, 13–14).

The Church (Ecclesiology). Jesus' intention was the end-time renewal of God's people. As a result of his saving deed in the cross and resurrection and the subsequent outpouring of the Spirit there came into being a new community that understood itself to be the *saints, the elect, and the *ekklēsia* (translating Hebr. *qāhāl*, "assembly"), the church or people of God. Sociologically the church was as yet only a sect within Judaism, but it was conscious of being the true Israel, now definitively renewed. Throughout the apostolic age the word *ekklēsia* was used primarily for the locally gathered community, especially in house-churches, but in the subapostolic period, e.g., in the deutero-Pauline *Ephesians, it was used for the universal church. But the universal church was arrived at not by

adding the local congregations together; rather, each local congregation was the visible embodiment of the one universal *ekklēsia*.

Paul developed the image of the church as the body of Christ in order to emphasize the mutual responsibility of the members for one another. The image first occurs in connection with the Eucharist (1 Cor. 10.17)—by partaking of the sacramental body the believers become the ecclesial body. The theme is developed in 1 Corinthians 12.12–31, and summarized in Romans 12.4–8. There was no formalized ministry in the apostolic age; members exercised their various gifts ministerially, though under the control of the *apostles. A more institutionalized church order first developed in the Jewish-Christian communities, beginning at Jerusalem (Acts 11.30; etc.) and in the subapostolic age was taken over in the Pauline churches (Titus, 1 Timothy; *see* Pastoral Letters, The). At this period (ca. 70–110 CE) the institutional ministry takes over the task of preserving and transmitting the apostolic tradition, encapsulated in creedal forms, together with an incipient *canon of apostolic writings (Pastorals; 2 *Peter). A reaction occurred in the Johannine community, which saw itself as a loosely gathered society of "friends," and only later accepted a more formal ministry (cf. the role played by Peter in relation to the beloved disciple in the appendix, John 21). Prior to this (John 15) the Johannine circles developed the image of Christ and the church as a vine and branches, characterized by their mutual indwelling ("I in them and they in me"), a parallel to the Pauline image of the body of Christ.

Baptism. The foundation members of the community received a direct baptism of the Spirit at *Pentecost (cf. Acts 2.1–4). But all others henceforth became members of the community and participants in the Holy Spirit through water *baptism (Acts 2.38; etc.). The community believed it had been led to this practice by the risen One, and expressed this conviction in story form by the command to baptize (Matt. 28.19; cf. Mark 16.15–16). Baptism was performed in the name of Jesus, i.e., under his authority. As a result believers were "added" (a divine passive denoting that baptism is the occasion of an act of God, i.e., in later church language a *sacrament) and became partakers of the Holy Spirit in the already established Spirit-filled community (Acts 2.38).

In response to new situations in his Hellenistic communities Paul developed the doctrine of baptism further. The believers were now baptized into Christ, made over to his ownership. For Paul this meant being baptized into Christ's death, with the hope of future *resurrection (Rom. 6.3–11). Note too that Paul carefully refrains from saying that they are already participating in his resurrection; that would not come until the end, and was conditional on their walking in newness of life. Paul also speaks of the believers as being baptized into one body (1 Cor. 12.13). Although the texts are not very clear, it appears from some New Testament writings (Acts 19.5–6; Titus 3.5.; Heb. 6.2) that the custom arose of marking the connection of baptism with the gift of the Spirit by adding to water baptism the additional act of the *laying on of hands. This was probably not a separate rite, but an attempt to underline part of the rich meaning of water baptism itself.

The Lord's Supper. The earthly Jesus had regularly celebrated meals with his disciples. These *meals were foretastes of the *kingdom of God, which was frequently depicted as a banquet. This table fellowship was renewed after Easter and some of the post-resurrectional appearances are associated with meals (e.g., Luke 24.28–32). Common meals were continued by the early community after the Easter event, and were characterized by exuberant joy (Acts 2.46), the focus being on the risen One's coming in anticipation of his coming at the end (cf. the acclamation *Maranatha ("Our Lord, come!"; 1 Cor. 16.22). Another strain in the tradition, perhaps originally associated with Passover, stressed the connection between the Supper and Christ's death (1 Cor. 11.23–26; Luke 22.19–20; Mark 14.22–24 par.). This tradition interpreted the act as a proclamation (Grk. *anamnēsis*, "memorial" [NRSV: "remembrance"]) of Christ's death. Its effect was to make the benefits of his death presently operative for the participants (*koinōnia*) in the body and blood of Christ. Paul further develops the ecclesial significance of this act: by partaking of the one loaf the believers become one body. The Johannine tradition emphasizes eternal life already here and now through eating the bread (John 6.35–51a—note the *manna *typology), while John 6.51b-58 speaks of eating the flesh and drinking the blood of the *Son of man, an act that nourishes the mutual indwelling of Christ and the believers.

The Last Things (Eschatology). Throughout the New Testament there is a tension between the "already" and the "not yet." On the one hand, the end-time kingdom has come as a result of the Christ event, while on the other hand it awaits final consummation. In Jesus' proclamation the kingdom is already breaking through (Matt. 12.28 par.) in Jesus' activity; yet his disciples are to pray, "Your kingdom come," and Jesus faces death with the conviction that after it that kingdom will shortly be consummated (Mark 14.25). The Easter event was in a sense an inauguration of the end-time rule of the kingdom of God (see above), though the final coming of the kingdom and the general *resurrection were still outstanding. This expectation was expressed in imaginative language in the hope of Christ's "parousia" or return as judge and savior (1 Thess. 1.10; Mark 14.62 par.), which the early Christians believed would take place shortly. It was the sense of what had happened already in the Christ event that enabled the early communities to weather the storm of the delay of the parousia, while maintaining the tension between the already and the not yet, though the weight placed on either side of the balance varied from writer to writer. Thus in *Ephesians and *John the emphasis is placed on the already; the future hope practically disappears, though never quite (see, e.g., Eph. 4.13; John 5.25–29; 6.39; etc.). Other writings (such as 2 *Thessalonians, *Jude, 2 *Peter and *Revelation) place the primary emphasis on the future coming, though without losing the sense that something of the end has already occurred through the Christ event.

The Normative Character of New Testament Theology. While the pluralism of New Testament theology appears to undermine its normative character, the coherent center, which we have defined as the kerygma of Christ crucified and risen, provides a criterion for the developments of theology through contingent application within the New Testament, a canon within the canon. The way in which writers like Paul move from coherent center to contingent application provides a pattern for a similar movement in contemporary theology, belief, and practice. Furthermore, the pluralism of the New Testament moves forward on certain trajectories to convergences lying beyond the New Testament period. We see that particularly with the varieties of New Testament Christology that eventually converge in the Christologies of Nicea and Chalcedon, in the doctrines of the consubstantiality of the Son with the Father, and of Christ as truly divine and truly human, with two natures and one person. The remaining problem is whether earlier Christologies, e.g., the functional Christologies of Jesus as the end-time prophet, or as the servant who is now enthroned as Christ and Lord, still have any role to play, and whether the later christological definitions represent an impoverishment. Whereas the New Testament Christologies focus upon Jesus' earthly career, his exaltation, and his parousia, and were thus concerned with God's redemptive act in the Christ event, the later definitions concentrated upon the eternal being of the Son of God and the moment of his entry as a human being into the world. The Fourth Gospel perhaps points the way for the solution of the modern dilemma in that it retains earlier christological perspectives, such as the sending of the Son for the purpose of redemption, alongside the later Christologies of preexistence and incarnation.

In short, New Testament theology does not provide a static norm, but a dynamic one, inviting the church and theology to return continually to the coherent center of the New Testament, and to move forward to its contingent application today, using the contingent applications in the New Testament as a model.

REGINALD H. FULLER

Bishop. In pre-Christian and extra-Christian usage the Greek word rendered "bishop," *episkopos*, and its cognates, refers primarily to caring for something or someone. This can involve a person's oversight of a task or a group of people, such as priests in a temple, or God's own oversight of a person or an event.

The word occurs rarely in the New Testament and only in later documents with the exception of Philippians 1.1; the other passages are Acts 1.20; 20.28; 1 Peter 2.25; 1 Timothy 3.1–2; Titus 1.7. Acts 1.20 is a citation from Psalm 109.8 used to legitimate the selection of a replacement for Judas among the disciples. Acts 20.28 is from a speech by Paul encouraging his audience to "keep watch . . . over all the flock, of which the Holy Spirit has made you overseers to shepherd the church of God." The three citations from the *Pastoral Letters have to do with requirements for the position or role of *episkopos* within the church.

Much of the debate about the usage of the term in the New Testament and early Christianity has been concerned with the evolution of an office called "bishop." Is it an authoritative role within the church that existed from apostolic times? Or should it be understood as a general term giving some measure of honor and perhaps authority to any believer? Naturally, different

Christian traditions have various stakes in how these questions are answered.

With the exception of Philippians 1.1, all of the texts cited above probably come from the very end of the first or the beginning of the second century CE. Acts 20.28 and the citations from the Pastoral Letters seem to have in mind a specific group of leaders who look out for the well-being of the larger church. Philippians 1.1 seems to have a similar sense; the overseers are mentioned together with *deacons, but there is no further indication of how they might have functioned. The Pastorals associate certain responsibilities with the office. The *episkopos* is a teacher, a good host, possesses only one wife, is above reproach, and perhaps is good in a debate (Titus 1.7); there is no evidence that this overseer had responsibility outside the local church.

The letters of Clement of Rome (ca. 95 CE) and Ignatius of Antioch (ca. 115 CE) demonstrate the development of a hierarchical office that eventually became dominant. The office of bishop is thus an indicator of the evolution of Christianity from a popular Palestinian movement to a sophisticated institution with offices, authorities, and hierarchy.

J. ANDREW OVERMAN

Blasphemy. Speech that is abusive to humans or derogatory to God. Blasphemy against humans occurs when people speak words harmful to one another (Matt. 15.19; Col. 3.8; NRSV: "slander"). Blasphemy also occurs when a person speaks against God in a way that fails to recognize the sacredness and honor of God's person and name. According to Leviticus 24.10–16, it was punishable by death.

Blasphemy was also used to describe a claim to a divine prerogative. According to Mark 2.7 (par.), Jesus was accused of blasphemy when he claimed to forgive sins; see also John 10.33–36; Mark 14.64.

The gospel writers also describe Jesus' opponents as blasphemous when they mocked him (Mark 15.29; Luke 22.65). Similarly, 1 Timothy says that Paul blasphemed Jesus when he persecuted the church (1.13), and that those who deserted the gospel were also guilty of blasphemy (1.20).

In a passage that has elicited much debate, the synoptic Gospels (Mark 3.28–29 par.) speak of blasphemy against the (Holy) Spirit as a sin that cannot be forgiven. The context indicates that this sin is not committed unintentionally by Jesus' followers, but is ascribed to the adversaries of Jesus, who had attributed his success to an evil spirit.   PAUL L. BREMER

Blessing. In most biblical texts, the associated verbs (to bless), adjectives (blessed), and nouns (blessing, blessedness) express a reciprocity pertaining between God and his chosen people. God blesses them as a mark of his *grace and favor; their blessing of God is a recognition of his presence among them. His blessing conveys to his people a share in his own vitality and ageless purpose. Their blessing of him, often in song, dance, and instrumental *music, celebrates their gratitude for his goodness and help. Each movement in this mutual activity elicits the other, so that the words point to the conjunction of two activities, especially in *worship.

This intersection is especially prominent in four types of literature. First are the historical narratives of the *Pentateuch, which describe God's choice and guidance of the *ancestors of Israel. Typical is God's promise to *Abraham, "I will make of you a great nation, and I will bless you . . . and by you all the families of the earth shall bless themselves" (Gen. 12.2–3; NRSV: "shall be blessed"); the importance of this tradition is made clear in Romans 4.6–9. The intersection is prominent, second, in *Deuteronomy, which records the *covenant sealed between God and *Moses. Here the command "You shall bless the Lord" (8.10) is linked to the promise "The Lord your God will bless you" (15.10). Third, the hymnbook used in *Temple and *synagogue shows how dominant this reciprocal action appears in regular worship. We frequently hear the injunction "Bless the Lord, O my soul" (Ps. 103.1), as well as the assurance "The Lord will bless you from Zion" (Ps 128.5). This dual motif may be found in more than a third of the *Psalms. Then there is a fourth type of literature, the writings of the *prophets and apocalyptists. The visions given to *Daniel, for instance, made him bless the name of the Lord (Dan. 2.19–20), and in response he declares as blessed by God all who persevere until "the end of the days" (Dan. 12.12–13). So too in the Christian apocalypse, the book of *Revelation, faithful *saints receive beatitudes (Rev. 1.3; 14.13; 16.15; 22.7) and join in grateful doxologies addressed to God (5.12–13; 7.12). Significant in the Christian Eucharist are the word and the cup of blessing (Matt. 14.19; Luke 24.50–51; 1 Cor. 10.16). Further, Jesus' followers are enjoined to respond to *curses

with blessings as an imitation of generous divine blessing (Matt. 5.44–48).

In the Bible the idea of blessing forms an important link between theology and liturgy, theology and ethics, theology and a way of looking at all human history and experience. Literary documents are introduced by extensive liturgical preludes that bless God for what he has done (e.g., Eph. 1.3; 1 Pet. 1.3). The beatitudes pronounced by Jesus become well-remembered clues to his entire legacy (Matt. 5.3–12; Luke 6.2–23; see Sermon on the Mount); translators of these beatitudes despair of finding equivalents in English (should "blessed" be replaced by "happy" or "fortunate"?). The problem remains: How to do justice to the conjunction of divine and human activity in a language that limits itself to human relationships.   PAUL S. MINEAR

Blindness. Due to several causes, blindness was common in the ancient world. The blind were one of the groups to whom special protection was due; it was true piety to help them (Job 29.15) and a severe violation to mislead them (Lev. 19.14; Deut. 27.18). Blindness was a ritual blemish: the blind could not function as *priests (Lev. 21.18), nor could blind animals be offered in *sacrifice (Lev. 22.22; Deut. 15.21; Mal. 1.8). Although blindness was attributed to various physical causes, including old age (1 Kings 14.4; cf. Gen. 27.1; Deut. 34.7) and trauma (Tob. 2.10), it could be interpreted as divine punishment (Deut. 28.28; John 9.2). In the Gospels, healing the blind is one of the characteristic activities of Jesus (Matt. 9.27–30 par.; 11.5; 21.14; Mark 8.22–25; John 9.1–7), and it was interpreted as a messianic sign (Matt. 11.4 par.; Luke 4.18–21; see Isa. 35.5; 61.1–2).

Blindness is also used metaphorically throughout the Bible. Isaiah 6.9 is a classical illustration, taken up repeatedly in the New Testament (Matt. 13.13–15 par.; John 12.39–41; Acts 28.26–27). The *Pharisees are denounced in Matthew 15.14 as "blind guides of the blind" (cf. John 9.40–41), but for the author of the gospel of *John, Jesus is the "light of the world" (8.12), that helps the blind see but can also blind the sighted (9.39).   PROSPER GRECH

Blood. Words translated "blood" occur nearly four hundred times in the Hebrew Bible and nearly a hundred times in the New Testament. Of these occurrences, more than half in the

Hebrew Bible and more than a quarter in the New Testament have to do with death by violence, by far the most frequent reference.

There are some passages in which life and blood are connected, principally in connection with the prohibition of eating meat with blood still in it (Gen 9.4–6; Lev. 17.11). This association has led some scholars to conclude that in the offering of *sacrifice, the death of the victim is unimportant; sacrificial atonement does not depend on an animal dying in place of the worshiper but rather on life set free from the body and offered to God. Similarly, in the New Testament it is not the death of Jesus that is the atonement, but his life.

Such a view scarcely accords with the statistical evidence summarized above, nor with the obvious fact that it is death that occurs when an animal is offered in sacrifice. Leviticus 17.11 and similar passages are to be understood in the sense that it is the life given up in death, rather than the life set free from the flesh, that is the atonement. And in the New Testament, phrases like "the blood of his cross" (Col. 1.20) cannot point to the release of life, for relatively little blood was shed in *crucifixion. Similarly, "justified by his blood" is parallel to "reconciled to God through the death of his son" (Rom. 5.9–10). In the Bible, therefore, blood normally points to the undergoing of death rather than to the release of life.

This association of blood and death partially explains the concept of blood taboo. Just as those who had contact with a corpse became unclean (Num. 11.11–13), so contact with the blood of the slain rendered a warrior ritually impure (1 Chron. 22.8; 28.3).

See also Avenger of Blood; Purity, Ritual.

LEON MORRIS

Book of Life. This symbolic phrase is parallel in meaning to other terms that the Bible associates with the phrase "of life": tree, *bread, *water, fountain, river, path, word, crown. In each case, God is the source and giver of this life, which is more than the years between birth and death.

The image of book suggests a roster of names (Neh. 7.5, 64), the names of those who through grace and obedience become members of God's family and share his life (Dan. 7.10; 12.1, 4; Luke 10.20; Phil. 4.3; Heb. 12.23; Rev. 21.27). Conversely, death is the destiny of those who have been erased from this roll call (Exod. 32.32–33; Ps. 69.28; Rev. 20.12–15). The book image also indicates the record that God keeps of human debits and credits, in preparation for a final accounting (Mal. 3.16–18; Rev. 20.12–14). Finally, the book of life can be visualized as containing the plans of God for his people, all that has happened and will happen to the community and to each of its members (Ps. 56.8; Ps. 139.16).

One reason why this image remained current was that in every service of worship from at least the *exile onward, whether in synagogue or church, the scripture would be read as God's word to his people (see Neh. 8.1–8). The act of opening and closing the scroll carried symbolic force (Rev. 5.1–5; 8.1).

See also Day of Judgment.   PAUL S. MINEAR

Books and Bookmaking in Antiquity. "This word came to Jeremiah from the Lord: Take a scroll and write on it all the words that I have spoken to you" (Jer. 36.1–2). This passage illustrates the various words in Hebrew, Greek, and Latin translated into English as "book," "scroll," or "roll." In the Hebrew phrase *mĕgillat sēper*, the word *mĕgillâ* designates a roll. While the word *sēper* seems to mean "book" in this and other passages, it can also designate a letter, a legal or private document, or even an inscription. The *Septuagint (LXX) renders the Hebrew phrase with the Greek *chartion bibliou*, "roll of a book." The word *chartēs* and its diminutive *chartion* designated paper made from the papyrus plant; both could be used for a piece of paper of any size, including a roll. *Biblos* was the Greek name for the papyrus plant; *biblos* and its diminutive *biblion* acquired the transferred meanings of a roll of paper made from the papyrus plant and the work written on a papyrus roll, that is, a book; the word "bible" is also derived from *biblos*. The *Vulgate uses the Latin phrase *volumen libri*, "roll of a book." *Volumen* comes from the verb *volvo*, "to roll," and so refers originally to the form of the writing material. *Liber* designated the bark or inner rind of a tree; thus, from the supposed use of tree bark as a primitive writing material, *liber* came to be the standard Latin word for "book."

The phrases used in all three languages point to the roll as the standard form of the "book," at least for longer and more formal texts. The reader needed both hands to handle a roll, one to unroll a new section for reading, the other to roll up the section already read. Luke's account of Jesus' visit to the *synagogue at *Nazareth mentions this procedure: "He stood up to read, and the scroll of the prophet Isaiah was given to him. He unrolled the scroll and found the place where it is written: 'The Spirit of the Lord is upon me. . .' And he rolled up the scroll, gave it back to the attendant, and sat down" (Luke 4.16–20).

A roll might be made up of sheets either of papyrus or animal skin. Papyrus is a marsh plant (*Cyperus papyrus*) which grew at various spots in Africa and the Near East, including the Sea of *Galilee in Israel; but the commercial production of paper from the papyrus plant was probably always the monopoly of the *Nile Valley of *Egypt. Two layers of strips from the soft interior of the plant, with the upper layer at a right angle to the one below, were pressed together; this pressing released a natural gummy substance which bonded together the strips and layers. Finished dried sheets of paper would then be glued together into a roll. Animal skins (primarily of sheep, goats, and cattle) might be tanned to produce leather, or they might undergo a more complicated process of washing, depilating, soaking in lime, and stretching and drying on a frame, to produce *parchment. To form a roll, the sheets of skin would be sewn together.

The Septuagint phrase *chartion bibliou* suggests that the Greeks preferred papyrus as a writing material. In Palestine, however, the preferred material seems to have been animal skin, at least for the writing of the scriptures. The great majority of the *Dead Sea Scrolls, for example, are on skin. The reasons for this preference are unclear; it may simply be that animal skins were available locally, while papyrus had to be imported from Egypt. The *Talmud apparently reflects earlier tradition when it directs that the *Torah be written on animal skin, saying this rule was given to *Moses at *Sinai.

The writing instrument used since early pharaonic Egypt was a reed that had been chewed or frayed to produce a brush. The Greeks preferred a reed pen with a split nib, resembling a modern fountain pen. The simplest form of black ink was made by mixing soot or lampblack with gum.

Other writing materials are mentioned in the Bible or are known from archaeology. Public documents that were to be preserved or displayed might be inscribed on stone (as were the *Ten Commandments) or on bronze plates (as was the decree honoring Simon the high priest, 1 Macc. 14.48). For school lessons, rough drafts, record keeping, and other temporary or personal documents, wood tablets with wax surfaces were used. The tablets consisted of two or more boards hinged to close flat. Wax filled a recess formed by a raised ridge. A stylus made of metal, wood, or bone served as the writing instrument; one end was sharpened to incise the wax, while the other end was blunt or flattened to rub out mistakes and resmooth the surface. The prophets Isaiah and Habakkuk may have recorded their oracles on such tablets (Isa. 30.8; Hab. 2.2), and the mute Zacharias, father of *John the Baptist, asked for a writing tablet to write the name of his son (Luke 1.63).

These writing tablets with their hinges and multiple leaves resembled a modern book; and the Latin name for a set of wooden writing tablets, *codex* (from *caudex*, "block of wood") became the name of the modern book form. By the late first century CE, the Romans had devised another type of notebook, consisting of sheets of parchment sewed or fastened together at the spine. The Romans called these notebooks *membranae* ("skins"). Paul seems to refer to such parchment notebooks when he asks Timothy to bring him a cloak left behind at Troas, "also the books, and above all the parchments" (2 Tim 4.13).

Two other writing materials were used in antiquity. Clay tablets were the principal medium for cuneiform, the writing system of wedge-shaped signs that originated in Mesopotamia. A broad-headed stylus was used to impress the signs on wet clay tablets; those tablets with temporary texts, such as letters and receipts, were baked in the sun, while those containing laws, history, or literary works were fired in a kiln to make them more durable. Fragments of broken pottery, called ostraca (from their Greek name) were free for the picking in ancient rubbish heaps and provided a cheap and convenient medium for writing notes or receipts.

Christianity brought with it a startling change in ancient bookmaking, namely, the rise of the codex; see Colin H. Roberts and T. C. Skeat, *The Birth of the Codex* (London, 1983). A codex— the form of modern books—is a collection of sheets fastened at the back or spine, usually protected by covers. By the second century CE, the papyrus codex had become the exclusive form for the books of the Christian Bible. For the Jewish scriptures, on the other hand, the roll continued to be the only acceptable form; in the case of Greek literature, the codex achieved parity with the roll about 300 CE and then surpassed it in popularity.

The reasons for the Christian adoption of the codex form remain a matter for speculation. The practical advantages of the codex over the roll seem obvious to the reader accustomed only to the modern book. The codex ought to have been less expensive, since it uses both sides of the writing material, while the roll rarely used both sides; for the same reason, the codex is more compact, therefore easier to store; and its compactness would allow the collection in one volume of previously separate texts. The roll seems cumbersome to read, given the need to unroll and reroll it. Such practical considerations must have played a role in the triumph of the codex in non-Christian as well as in Christian literature; yet they seem insufficient to explain (in the words of Roberts and Skeat) the "instant and universal" adoption of the codex by Christians as early as 100 CE. Pointing to the Jewish custom of committing isolated decisions of the oral law or rabbinic sayings to tablets or small rolls, Roberts and Skeat suggest that papyrus tablets similarly were used to record the oral law as pronounced by Jesus and that these tablets developed into a primitive form of codex. In whatever way the papyrus codex first came into being and came to be used for Christian texts, Christians may have favored the codex because its use differentiated them from Jews and other non-Christians.

See also Manuscripts; Writing in Antiquity. *For discussion of the production of Bibles after the invention of printing, see* Printing and Publishing.

T. KEITH DIX

Bread. Because the Bible portrays ordinary people in the round of daily life, bread is a common word in its pages from the beginning of Genesis (3.19). Every day was baking day in the homes of Palestine. Barley or wheat flour was mixed with water and salt, then baked in simple ovens. The loaves produced were such a staple of the diet that bread and food are sometimes interchangeable terms (e.g., Gen. 37.25; Judg. 13.16; Prov. 27.27). When in judgment God threatened to break the people's "staff of bread" (Lev. 26.26), it was the very basis of their life that was imperiled. Conversely, when God promised them "a land where you may eat bread without scarcity" (Deut. 8.9), it was the promise of life itself. This virtual identification of bread with existence led biblical authors to speak metaphorically about the bread of anxious toil (Ps. 127.2), of wickedness (Prov. 4.17), of idleness (Prov. 31.27), and of tears (Ps. 80.5).

Bread also occupied a significant place in biblical religion. The sacrificial system included cereal offerings (Lev. 2.4). Both *tabernacle and *Temple required the permanent display of *showbread, or "bread of the Presence" (Exod. 25.30; 1 Chron. 28.16). The festival of unleavened bread lay at the heart of Israel's remembrance of the *Exodus (*see* Feasts and Festivals; Passover). Equally linked with God's protective and providential activity was the provision of *manna, the "bread from heaven" (Exod. 16.4), which sustained Israel's life in the *wilderness.

According to the Gospels, Jesus acknowledged the importance of bread by quoting Deuteronomy 8.3, "one does not live by bread alone" (see Matt. 4.4; Luke 4.4), and then by identifying himself as the true bread from heaven that gives life to the world (John 6.33). At the Last Supper, he interpreted the breaking of the unleavened bread of Passover as symbolizing the offering of himself; this was commemorated by early Christians in the ceremony of the "breaking of the bread" (Acts 2.42; *see* Lord's Supper, The).

JAMES I. COOK

Bread of the Presence. *See* Showbread.

Brothers and Sisters of Jesus. Siblings of *Jesus are referred to collectively twice in the Gospels. In the account of the "true kindred" (Matt. 12.46–50 par.), Jesus' mother and brothers come to speak to him while he is teaching. Jesus refuses to see them, however, saying that his true sister, brother, and mother are those who do the will of God.

When Jesus teaches at the *synagogue in his hometown of *Nazareth, the listeners react angrily to his wisdom and mighty works (Matt. 13.53–58; Mark 6.1–6). The crowd doubts that a local person could be endowed with such power, and they cite the presence of his parents, brothers, and sisters as proof. The brothers are listed by name (*James, Joseph [Mark reads Joses], Simon, and Judas) but the sisters only as a group. In Luke 4.22, the crowd asks simply, "Is not this Joseph's son?"

References to brothers and sisters of Jesus conflict with some understandings of the *virgin birth. For those who feel that Jesus' mother *Mary remained a virgin for life, brothers and sisters must be read as cousins or as stepbrothers and stepsisters fathered by *Joseph in another, unmentioned, marriage.

DANIEL N. SCHOWALTER

Burial Customs. A part of the story of *Abraham is the record of his concern and care for the burying of *Sarah (Gen. 23). He buys a cave for her tomb; this purchase is his first land acquisition in the land of *Canaan. The *Hittites offered one of their sepulchers, but Abraham preferred to buy and utilize his own cave. For those outside the *Promised Land, burial in the ancestral territory continued to be important. For example, the body of *Joseph was embalmed in Egypt and returned to Canaan (Gen. 50.26). In like manner, many Jews of the *Dispersion of the Roman period preferred to be buried in the Holy Land. The burial customs and practices, as with Abraham, were carried out amid outside cultural influences but yet maintained their own distinctiveness.

Tomb construction saw considerable change and variety. Abraham, as noted above, used a cave. In later periods tombs were cut from the rock. Jesus mentions "whitewashed tombs" (Matt. 23.27), which implies buildings. One of the few monuments from the first century CE still intact in Jerusalem is the so-called Tomb of Absalom, a monument that exhibits both Greek and *Nabatean influence. Extended families often had a single connected cluster of underground tombs with niches for the various individuals or families. Often these were reused. Individual rock-cut tombs were also common. The bodies were generally not enclosed in coffins; after decomposition the remaining bones were then removed to a bone chamber in the floor or at the side of the burial ledge and the space reused. Rock tombs were sealed with a hinged door or a heavy wheel-shaped stone. Criminals were buried under a pile of stones.

With regard to the preparation of the body for burial, neither embalming (an Egyptian custom) nor cremation (called idolatry in m. ʿAbod. Zar. 1.3) was allowed. The body was washed (Acts 9.37) and enclosed (John 19.40), and finally a napkin was placed over the face (John 20.7). The Greek custom of individual coffins was occasionally followed in New Testament times; the earlier period did not use coffins.

Secondary burial, in which the remains, after decomposition, were placed in a small stone or clay box called an ossuary, gradually increased over time. A coffin (sarcophagus) averaged 1.8 m (6 ft) in length, while the ossuary was often only .8 m (2.5 ft) long. Many tombs had numerous small niches (Hebr. kôkîm) into which the ossuaries were placed. Considerable new evidence on burial customs has been gleaned from the excavations of the extensive Jewish cemetery at Beth Shearim, where secondary burials dominated. Often the ossuaries were decorated with various geometrical patterns. Roman *Jericho has yielded a significant collection of wooden coffins. It seems likely that the biblical phrase "to sleep with [or to be gathered to] one's ancestors" refers to secondary burial in the family tomb.

Burial in the Middle East has always taken place without delay; almost always the person is buried the same day. The warm climate and the lack of embalming has necessitated this practice. In the case of the burial of Jesus, the approaching *Sabbath added to the desire to complete the burial formalities before sundown (cf. Deut. 21.23).

The Middle East has long known the tradition of demonstrative *mourning. The walls of ancient Egyptian tombs often depict groups of professional women mourners as a part of the funeral procession. This profession was also known in Israel; Jeremiah explains the purpose of the presence of evocative funeral songs sung by the professionals: "that our eyes may run down with tears" (Jer. 9.18). Instruments used at funerals included the flute (Matt. 9.23); Rabbi Judah (140–165 CE) said, "Even the poorest in Israel should hire not less than two flutes and one wailing woman" (m. Ketub. 4.4).

The Bible records a number of poems composed for the deceased, the most famous being *David's lament over *Saul and *Jonathan (2 Sam. 1.18–27). The prophets use the funeral lament satirically in speaking of the ruin of nations such as *Babylon, Tyre, and *Egypt (e.g., Isa. 14.4–21; Ezek. 27; 32), and the book of *Lamentations uses the genre for *Jerusalem after its destruction in 587/586 BCE.

In biblical tradition mourning continued for seven days (Gen. 50.10). The places of burial were generally apart from the dwellings of the people; in earlier periods some burials took place within the house. While the Egyptians made elaborate preparations for the dead and placed the surroundings of life in the tomb of the deceased, these customs were kept to a minimum in Palestine. Tombs were comparatively modest and ostentation was criticized (Isa. 22.15–16). Eighty percent of the tomb inscriptions in the Beth Shearim cemetery are in Greek, yet the inscriptions themselves display a minimum of Greek ideological influence. Resurrection as a concept remains dominant over the idea of the immortality of the soul (see also Afterlife and Immortality).   KENNETH E. BAILEY

C

Caiaphas. Also named Joseph, Caiaphas was high *priest at the time of Jesus' death. According to *Josephus, he was appointed in 18 CE by Valerius Gratus, the Roman procurator before *Pilate; his father-in-law, Annas, had preceded him, as had, for very short terms, several of Annas's sons (*Ant.* 18.2.35). He was removed from office in 37 CE and replaced by another of Annas's sons (*Ant.* 18.4.95). There is some confusion in the New Testament about whether Annas or Caiaphas was high priest at the end of Jesus' life and about their role in his death, but the Gospels are consistent in their depiction of hostility toward Jesus by the high priest.

In 1990 the family tomb of Caiaphas was found in Jerusalem. It contained twelve ossuaries, one of which had inscriptions with the full name of Caiaphas in Aramaic (*yhwsp br qyp'* and *yhwsp br qp'*: Joseph, son of Caiaphas), and another with simply the family name (*qp'*).

MICHAEL D. COOGAN

Cain and Abel. Genesis 4.1–16 relates the curious story of Cain and Abel. Cain (meaning perhaps "smith," possibly related to the *Kenites), is the firstborn of *Adam and *Eve, and Abel (meaning "emptiness") is his younger brother or twin. As is generally the case among biblical siblings, they come into conflict. Cain, a farmer, offers a sacrifice of grain to Yahweh, while Abel, a shepherd, offers a sacrifice from the firstborn of his flocks. For no obvious reason, Yahweh rejects Cain's sacrifice; this appears to be a literary gap or blank. After some moral advice from Yahweh, Cain murders Abel in the field, which Yahweh discovers from Abel's blood "crying out" from the ground. Yahweh confronts Cain with Abel's absence, to which Cain feigns ignorance. As punishment, Yahweh condemns Cain to wander the earth, decreeing that the earth will no longer bear crops for him. In fear for his life, Cain pleads for mercy, which Yahweh grants by placing an unspecified sign on Cain so

that no one will murder him. Cain finally departs to wander in a land called Nod ("wandering"), east of *Eden.

Many themes appear in this story, including sibling rivalry, the attraction of sin, crime met with punishment, the futility of pretense before God, and the moral distinction between civilization and barbarism. Cain begins as a farmer, plying the fruitful earth, and because of his unchecked passion he commits a heinous crime, only to separate himself and be separated—morally, economically, and geographically—from the proper realm of civilized life. Only a plea for God's mercy (perhaps implying a degree of repentance) saves his life, signaling the small worth of life outside of civilization, where one is "hidden" from God's face.

In later interpretation, the cause of Cain's evil nature is frequently explored, with a tendency to identify Cain as the son of either *Satan (1 John 3.12), the wicked angel Sammael (Targum Pseudo-Jonathan on Gen. 4.1 and 5.3), or the serpent in Eden (4 Macc. 18.8). Other gaps in the story also receive much attention, such as the origin of Cain's wife (in Jubilees 4.9 she is his sister, Awan, meaning "Wickedness") and the fate of Cain and his offspring (identified as demons in the *Zohar* and medieval legend). An early *gnostic sect, the Cainites, may have regarded Cain as a savior figure.

In the New Testament, Abel is the prototypical martyr, who died for his faith (Matt. 23.35 par.; Heb. 11.4; 12.24).

RONALD S. HENDEL

Cain's Wife. *See* Names for the Nameless.

Calendar. *See* Time, Units of.

Calvary. *See* Golgotha.

Canaan. An ancient name for the region occupied today by Lebanon and Israel (Map 1). The origin of the term "Canaan" is obscure. It was used at *Nuzi in Upper *Mesopotamia as a term for red or purple dye, a product for which the coastal Canaanites were famous. Although it has been suggested that the geographical name Canaan was derived from the name of the dye, it is more likely that the Nuzi dyes were named for their Canaanite manufacturers. Similarly, the rare meaning "merchants" for "Canaanites" in biblical Hebrew (Zech. 14.21; Prov. 31.24) is probably a secondary development, based on the mercantile reputation of the coastal Canaanites, rather than a clue to the origin of the word.

"Canaan" was in use as a geographical designation as early as the third millennium BCE. In the latter half of the second millennium it referred to a province of the *Egyptian empire in western Asia. The province of Canaan was bordered on the north by the land of Amurru, which lay in southern *Syria west of the middle Orontes, and on the east by the province of Upe, which included the region of *Damascus and northern Transjordan. The Israelites seem to have adopted this older usage of the name when they took control of the land. The frontiers of Canaan described in Numbers 34.1–12 correspond closely to those of the Egyptian province; the eastern and western boundaries are formed by the Mediterranean coast and the Jordan rift respectively, the southern boundary extends from the southern end of the Dead Sea west to the *Wadi of Egypt near Gaza, and the northern boundary traverses the Pass of Hamath on the upper Orontes north of the Lebanon.

The biblical writers sometimes use "Canaanites" as a general designation for all indigenous inhabitants of ancient Palestine without ethnic or political distinction (Exod. 13.11; Judg. 1). Elsewhere the same peoples are collectively called "*Amorites" (Gen. 15.16; Amos 2.9, 10). This general usage of "Canaanites" was most important as a term marking ethnic boundaries, distinguishing the Israelites from the indigenous peoples with whom intermarriage was to be avoided (Gen. 24.3; 28.1). The ethnic position in which the Israelites placed the Canaanites is expressed genealogically in Genesis 10.6, 15–18, in which Canaan is said to have been a son of *Noah's second son Ham, a brother of *Cush (Ethiopia), *Egypt, and Put (Libya?), and the father of the Sidonians (the *Phoenicians), the *Hittites, the *Jebusites, the Amorites, and the other pre-Israelite inhabitants of Canaan.

Elsewhere in the Bible, the *Promised Land is thought of as having been ethnically diverse, and the Canaanites are presented as one of several peoples who lived there before the arrival of Israel (Gen. 15.18–21; Exod. 3.8, 17). According to Deuteronomy 7.1, the Canaanites were one of seven nations driven out before the Israelites. In still other passages the pre-Israelite population is said to have had regional ethnic divisions, of which the Canaanites were the coastal component (Num. 13.29; Deut. 1,7; Josh. 5.1). In this last usage the term "Canaanites" corresponds exactly to "Phoenicians."

See also Conquest of Canaan; Ugaritic.

P. KYLE McCARTER, JR.

Canadian Literature. *See* Literature and the Bible, *article on* North American Literature.

Canon. *This entry discusses how various writings and collections of writings were officially accepted by various religious authorities and communities as scripture; it consists of three articles:*

    Order of Books in the Hebrew Bible
    Canon of the Hebrew Bible
       and the Old Testament
    New Testament

The first article deals with the arrangement of books in the sacred text of Judaism, and the second article describes the processes by which those (and other) books were accepted as canonical by both Jewish and Christian communities, in the latter case as the Old Testament. The last article deals with the canonization of the New Testament.

Order of Books in the Hebrew Bible

No traditions have survived concerning the authorities who fixed the canon of Hebrew scriptures, or about the internal order of the books, or about the underlying principles that determined their sequence. It is probable, but not certain, that the three distinct collections known as the *Pentateuch, the Prophets, and the Writings (Hebr. *tôrâ* [*Torah], *něbîîm*, and *kětûbîm*, respectively, the initial letters of which form the acronym *tanak*, used in Jewish tradition for the Bible) represent the three successive stages of canonization. Apart from the Pentateuch, the order of whose five books is invariable, the arrangement of the contents of the other two corpora was not uniform in *manuscripts and printed editions until fairly recently.

An anonymous tannaitic tradition (*Bab. Bat.* 14b), no later than ca. 200 CE, lists the order of the books of the Prophets and the Writings. This presents a problem because the codex form was not adopted by Jews before the fifth century CE and because the general and favored scribal practice—with one exception—was to restrict each scroll to a single biblical book. What then is the meaning of term "order" in the rabbinic text? The most likely explanation is that it refers to the manner of storage and the system of classification and cataloguing in vogue in the libraries and schools of Palestine. The library procedures of the Hellenistic world would have required each of the three collections of canonical works to be placed in a separate armarium, with the scrolls arranged in their appropriately assigned order.

The sequence of the Former Prophets following the Pentateuch is: Joshua, Judges, Samuel, Kings. This arrangement never varies and presents one long continuous history of Israel from the beginning of the *conquest to the fall of the Judean kingdom, the Babylonian *exile, and the release of King Jehoiachin from prison in 561 BCE. (*See* Deuteronomic History.)

The variations in the order of the books occur in the Latter Prophets and particularly in the Writings. A majority of manuscripts and most printed Bibles feature Isaiah, Jeremiah, and Ezekiel, which is the proper historical order. The above-cited source, however, followed by some manuscripts, lists Isaiah in third place in juxtaposition with its contemporary Hosea. Another tradition has Jeremiah after Kings and before Isaiah and Ezekiel. This is because that prophet was active during the last years of the monarchy, and Jeremiah 39 and 52 largely duplicate 2 Kings 25.

The small prophetic books, generally known as the "Minor Prophets," were habitually transcribed onto a single scroll and were collectively designated "The Twelve" (so already in Sir. 49.10, ca. 180 BCE). Their internal arrangement is: Hosea, Joel, Amos, Obadiah, Jonah, Micah, Nahum, Habakkuk, Zephaniah, Haggai, Zechariah, Malachi. This is also the order of a scroll of the second century CE from Wadi Murabba'at (*see* Dead Sea Scrolls) containing the Hebrew Minor Prophets, and it apparently reflected traditional views about their historical sequence. The same order, but with Micah following Amos and succeeded by Joel, is given in 2 Esdras 1.39–40. This groups together three prophets of the eighth century BCE.

The order of the Writings in Hebrew printed Bibles is: Psalms, Proverbs, Job, Song of Solomon, Ruth, Lamentations, Ecclesiastes, Esther, Daniel, Ezra, Nehemiah, Chronicles. Passages like 2 Maccabees 2.13–14 and Luke 24.44 seem to attest to the great antiquity of the initial place of Psalms. The aforementioned tannaitic source has Ruth before Psalms due to the concluding genealogy of *David, the reputed author of the Psalter. The Aleppo Codex (end of ninth century CE and the Leningrad Codex of 1008 CE both open the Writings with Chronicles, probably because that work duplicates the Pentateuchal genealogies and much of the Former Prophets.

The tannaitic practice, also found in manuscripts and ultimately standardized in the printed editions, was to conclude the Hebrew scriptures with Chronicles following Ezra-Nehemiah. This must have been a very early tradition, for it is reflected in Matthew 23.35 and Luke 11.51. The inversion of the chronological order must have arisen out of a desire to close the canon on a note of consolation, and to make the statement that the fulfillment of biblical prophecy involves the return of the Jewish people to its ancestral land. Apart from this messianic exegesis, it also serves to encase the Hebrew scriptures within a framework of historical narrative, for Chronicles begins with *Adam and its last sentence contains the same two key Hebrew verbs of redemption with which Genesis concludes (*pqd*, *ʿlh*, Gen. 50.24–25; 2 Chron. 36.23).

Christian editions reverse the order of Prophets-Writings, so that the closing words of Malachi (4.5–6 [Heb. 3.23–24]) concerning *Elijah become transitional to the New Testament, and connect with the role of *John the Baptist (see Matt. 11.13–14; Mark 1.2; 9.11–13; Luke 1.16–17).

Least stable in respect of order are the small books in the corpus of the Writings. The tannaitic source follows Proverbs with Ecclesiastes and the Song of Solomon because all three are attributed to King *Solomon. Most medieval manuscripts preserve this association in one way or another. Lamentations, Daniel, and Esther are grouped together since they all belong to the period of the exile. In medieval times, the Song of Solomon, Ruth, Lamentations, Ecclesiastes, and Esther were all clustered together in that order, based upon their use as *lectionaries in the cycle of the Jewish religious calendar, commencing with *Passover. This system became the rule in the printed editions. Greek Bibles differ considerably from the Hebrew scriptures in that the books are arranged according to genres of literature. Ignoring the additional *Apocrypha that are interspersed among the canonical works, the following classification emerges. First comes a narrative-historical collection that comprises the Pentateuch and Former Prophets, with Ruth attached to Judges, and Chronicles following Kings. Second is a prophetic collection consisting of: Isaiah; Jeremiah, to which is adjoined Lamentations for thematic reasons and traditions of authorship; Ezekiel; Daniel, because he is regarded as a prophet, a contemporary of Ezekiel, and is identified with the personality of that name mentioned in Ezekiel 14.14, 20; 28.3; and the Twelve in a slightly different internal order. The two complete Greek codices, the fourth-century CE Vaticanus and the fifth-century CE Alexandrinus, share these characteristics. However, the latter has Esther and Ezra-Nehemiah immediately after the prophetical collection, while the former places Ezra-Nehemiah after Chronicles. The third part is a poetic-didactic collection. Codex Vaticanus has Psalms, Proverbs, Ecclesiastes, Song of Solomon, Job, and Esther. The order of Codex Alexandrinus is Psalms, Job, Proverbs, Ecclesiastes, and Song of Solomon. Also the sequence of the second and third collections interchanges in the two codices.

Other Greek codices feature different arrangements and there is no uniformity in the traditions of the churches. All extant Greek codices and lists are of Christian origin, and it is uncertain whether or not any represent alternative Jewish conventions about the order of the biblical books.　　　　NAHUM M. SARNA

Canon of the Hebrew Bible and the Old Testament

From the fourth century CE, the word "canon" (from a Greek word meaning "a rule") has been used to denote the correct list of the biblical books, and in consequence the collection of books thus listed. It is important to distinguish between the composition of the biblical books and their recognition as scripture. Scholars sometimes envisage a five-stage process of composition, circulation, revision, collection, and recognition as canonical, and such a long process may indeed have been involved for some books. Others of the books may have been much more rapidly acknowledged. But if we may judge from the history of the New Testament canon (see the next article in this entry), some books were probably recognized as having divine authority more slowly than others. It was at one time widely believed that the whole canon had been recognized by

the time of *Ezra, and this idea is already reflected in 2 Esdras 14.44–48, where Ezra is said to have "made public" twenty-four books (the standard Jewish count of the canonical books). The idea that Ezra knew the canon is probably not entirely without foundation, for most of it had then been written, and an older tradition speaks of Ezra's contemporary *Nehemiah, after the calamity of the *exile, gathering together in a library "the books about the kings and prophets, and the writings of David, and letters of kings about votive offerings" (2 Macc. 2.13). In addition, Ezra would have known the books of the *Pentateuch, which must also have been gathered together by this time, so most scholars agree, and which were the basis of his reforming work. A few of the latest books, however, had not yet been written, and they at least would obviously have had to be added to the sacred collection later. Moreover, there is reason to believe that *Esther and *Daniel were not finally accepted into the canon until the crisis of the second century BCE, related in the following verse of 2 *Maccabees, where we are told that "in the same way Judas also collected all the books that had been lost on account of the war that had come upon us" (2 Macc. 2.14). This would have taken place about 164 BCE. The Judas in question is Judas Maccabeus, and the war is the persecuting campaign of the Hellenistic Syrian king Antiochus Epiphanes, who attempted to destroy the scriptures (1 Macc. 1.56).

Many factors contributed to the recognition of certain books as canonical; among them are the following: the tradition that many of the books came from *Moses or one of the other acknowledged prophets; the spiritual authority of the books themselves, as it was experienced in public or private reading, and in exposition; the fact that the books had come to be laid up in the *Temple as sacred; the opinions of religious leaders and the common convictions of the people about the books. And for Christians, there was the additional consideration that Jesus himself and his apostles, in the pages of the New Testament, often refer to the Jewish scriptures in general, and to many of the individual books, as having the authority of God.

The division of the Hebrew Bible into three sections (not four or five, as in Greek, Latin, and English translations), known as the Law, the Prophets, and the Writings, can be traced back to the second century BCE, when it is three times referred to in the prologue of *Sirach, added by the Greek translator of the book in about 130

BCE. He refers to the three sections as "the Law and the Prophets and the others that have followed them," "the Law and the Prophets and the other books of our ancestors," "the Law and the Prophecies and the rest of the books." It should be noted that the third section had not yet been given a definite name, though the use of the definite article and the expression "the rest of" suggests that it already had a fixed content. In other early references to the three sections (in Luke 24.44, the *Dead Sea Scrolls, and *Philo), the third section seems to be called "the Psalms," taking its name from one of the chief books it included. The later Jewish name, the Writings (Hebr. *kĕtûbîm*, translated into Greek as *hagiographa*), is first found in rabbinic literature.

For the past hundred years it had been commonly believed that the three sections do not really have any distinct identity, but are accidents of history, reflecting the different stages at which books were accepted as canonical: the Law in the fifth century BCE, the Prophets in the third century BCE, and the Hagiographa at the "synod" of Jabneh or Jamnia, about 90 CE (an academic debate that discussed, among other things, the canonicity of Ecclesiastes and the Song of Solomon). The Law, however, clearly does have a distinct identity, consisting of the four books that comprise the life of Moses and the legislation bearing his name (Exodus to Deuteronomy), together with a historical introduction (Genesis) tracing the course of events between creation and his own day. This leads one to suspect that the other two sections may also have a logical rationale, even if it is less obvious; and, especially if one takes the books in traditional order, recorded in an early quotation in the Babylonian *Talmud, it is not too difficult to see what this rationale is. Both sections, like the Law, include narrative books (covering the two subsequent periods of history) and books of another kind, not legislative, but in the case of the prophets oracular, and in the case of the Hagiographa lyrical and sapiential (*wisdom literature). The four narrative books in the Prophets are Joshua, Judges, Samuel, and Kings, carrying on the history from the death of Moses to the end of the monarchy; these are followed by the four oracular books Jeremiah, Ezekiel, Isaiah, and the Twelve (the Minor Prophets). In the Writings the four narrative books Daniel, Esther, Ezra-Nehemiah, and Chronicles continue Jewish history by covering the period of the exile and return, Chronicles being put last probably be-cause it begins with *Adam and ends with the return, thus recapitulating the whole of Israel's history. Preceding these are the six lyrical and sapiential books in the Hagiographa, Psalms, Job, Proverbs, Ecclesiastes, Song of Solomon, and Lamentations, with Ruth prefixed to Psalms (but counted separately) because it ends with the genealogy of the psalmist *David. Thus, there is nothing irrational (as has usually been supposed) in the isolation of Chronicles from Samuel and Kings, and of Daniel from the Prophets, in a different section of the canon.

The belief that the Law was the first complete section to be recognized as canonical is very likely true, given its traditional association with Moses. It is quite possible, however, that some of the earlier books in the other two sections were recognized as canonical alongside the Law; and these may originally have been a single collection of non-Mosaic books, like Nehemiah's "library," which gradually increased and was only organized in two sections after it was complete. The view that the canon of the *Samaritans, which consists of the Law alone, shows that when their schism with the Jews took place this was all the Jewish canon consisted of, cannot be sustained. *Qumran evidence has now made it probable that the schism did not become final until the destruction of the Samaritan temple on Mount Gerizim by the Jews in about 120 BCE. So the Samaritans of that period must certainly have rejected books which were already canonical among the Jews, probably because many of those books explicitly recognized the Jerusalem Temple.

One of the main reasons for supposing that the Hagiographa were not received into the canon until a late date is that four of them (Proverbs, Ecclesiastes, the Song of Solomon, and Esther) raise serious problems that were debated among the rabbis of the first few centuries CE. We know, however, from rabbinic literature that similar problems were raised by most of the other canonical books, and that it was only because in these books they were particularly intractable that they were taken so seriously. Moreover, there was a fifth book that raised equally serious problems, Ezekiel, which is in the Prophets. If the canonicity of this book could be debated after the first century CE, clearly the question was not one of adding books to the canon but of removing books from it. Needless to say, nothing of the kind was actually done.

It has been widely supposed that certain schools of thought had divergent canons. Some of the church fathers say that the *Sadducees accepted only the Law, like the Samaritans. The Sadducees may have joined up with the Samaritans during the century after the destruction of the Jerusalem Temple (the center of their influence) by the Romans in 70 CE, but prior to that time their canon seems to have been the same as that of the *Pharisees. Again, the presence of books of the *Apocrypha in *Septuagint manuscripts has led to the suggestion that the Hellenistic Jews of Alexandria had a wider canon than that of the Jews of Palestine. However, the voluminous writings of the first-century CE Alexandrian Jew *Philo are against this theory. Moreover, the manuscripts in question were produced by Christian scribes, at a date when knowledge of the Jewish canon was becoming somewhat vague in Christian circles; and in any case they are evidence of what Christians regarded as edifying reading rather than as strictly canonical. Finally, the *Essenes have been supposed to have included in their canon congenial pseudonymous apocalypses such as 1 Enoch and Jubilees. In fact, they seem rather to have treated these as a sort of interpretive appendix to the canon, on a lower level of inspiration. Jude 14–15, which quotes 1 Enoch, is certainly not saying more than this about it, and in Jude's Christian (not Essene) context is probably saying less, that is, he may be using the quotation as an ad hominem argument.

The New Testament shows Jesus and his apostles endorsing a canon wider than that of the Samaritans and indistinguishable from that of the Pharisees, which now seems to have been the standard (if not, indeed, the only) Jewish canon. It had probably closed, in the form found in the Hebrew Bible, not later than the second century BCE. The threefold division of the canon, the traditional order of the books, and their standard Jewish numeration as twenty-four may well be due to Judas Maccabeus and his advisors (see 2 Macc. 2.14, and above); the slightly later numeration of the books as twenty-two, found in *Josephus, is based on the number of letters in the Hebrew alphabet, and appends Ruth to Judges and Lamentations to Jeremiah, thus reducing the number by two.

Today, the canon exists in two main forms: that found in the Hebrew Bible, followed by Jews, Protestants, and some Orthodox churches, and that found in the *Septuagint, which includes the *Apocrypha, followed by Roman Catholics and also some Orthodox churches. (*See also* Bible.)   ROGER T. BECKWITH

New Testament

The canon of the New Testament resulted from the interplay of various theological and historical factors. The decisive factor was the impact of the person and message of *Jesus Christ, together with the Christian conviction that in him as the Lord, God had spoken his final and authoritative word in history. As the Christian movement was confronted with philosophical and religious trends current in the Mediterranean world of its time, the need for an authentic expression and preservation of the foundation of its belief became the basic motivation toward the realization of the New Testament canon. This grew the more acute after the demise of the first generation of eyewitnesses. Certainly the idea of an Old Testament canon functioned as an analogy and, to a certain extent, as a stimulus in this regard. Few factors, however, expedited the growth of the idea of the canon more than the attacks from heterodox quarters, like those of Marcion, the *gnostics, and the Montanists (see below). Finally the need for one, universally accepted holy book for the whole church also played a role.

Historical Survey. Historical processes do not lend themselves to neat chronological delineations. Nevertheless, we can roughly divide the far-reaching process through which the twenty-seven books of the New Testament were brought into a normative, carefully delineated, and ecclesiastically accepted unit, with an authority equivalent to that of the Hebrew Bible, into four periods:

The first phase (latter part of first century CE): *Creation of various early Christian documents.* Initially the gospel message was transmitted orally. In this period the young church was guided, in addition to the Old Testament, first by the apostolic witness, which developed into the apostolic tradition, and second by early Christian *prophecy. In particular, the first of these factors was destined to play a decisive role in the eventual decisions about the extent of the New Testament canon. The authoritative writings would be those emanating from the *apostles or the circle of those standing in a not too indirect relation to them. The prophetic witness is represented in the New Testament canon by the book of *Revelation, although its ultimate recognition was determined by its association with *John the apostle. The authors of the early Christian documents did not visualize their writings as part of a future canon. Rather they intended merely to give pastoral guidance to young churches. But as foundational documents, standing so close to the origin of Christianity, they possessed the inherent possibility of later becoming part of a normative collection.

The second phase (roughly from the close of the first century to the middle of the second): *Growing recognition of the normative character and collection into groups of a basic number of writings.* This period, demarcated by Clement of Rome (ca. 96 CE) on the one hand and Justin Martyr (ca. 150 CE) on the other, finds oral tradition increasingly replaced by the written *Gospels. Initially oral tradition was used alongside and even preferred to the Gospels. But as the reliability of the former declined, it was gradually replaced by the four Gospels. In 1 Clement, the Didache, Ignatius, and Papias, the "living voice" (as Papias terms it) of the oral tradition still enjoys preference, while in Polycarp's letter to the Philippians (ca. 135 CE) the scale tips in favor of the written Gospels. In 2 Clement (ca. 140 CE) we have at least twice as many quotations from the written Gospels as from all other sources, and from the middle of the second century the written Gospels are predominant. The gnostic Gospel of Truth, for example, knows all four Gospels, while only uncertain traces of the oral tradition occur. The same holds true for Justin Martyr who makes only sporadic use of the oral tradition. Parallel to this development is the increasing use of the written Gospels for liturgical readings. Justin (*Apology* I.67.3–4) reports that the memoirs of the apostles (i.e., the Gospels) are not only read but also commented upon in public worship, which would put them on a par with the Old Testament books. The growing recognition of a substantial number of writings is also evidenced by the way references to them are made. In 2 Clement 2.4 and Barnabas 4.14 the gospel of *Matthew, for instance, is referred to as on equal footing with Old Testament writings. At this stage we also find the collecting of early Christian writings around two foci, the Pauline correspondence and the Gospels. We can reasonably accept that by the middle of the second century the Pauline corpus as well as the four gospels were available in collections. All these factors serve to illustrate that they were increasingly recognized as normative ecclesiastical documents. The idea of a New Testament canon was beginning to emerge.

The third phase (ca. mid-second century to 190 CE): *The New Testament canon becomes a reality.* Marcion was the first person, as far as we know, who actually visualized the idea of a New Testament canon. He deliberately excluded the Old Testament from his normative collection and included only *Luke and ten Pauline letters (which he purged of Jewish traits). The official church reacted by emphasizing the normative character of all four Gospels as well as all thirteen letters ascribed to *Paul. Irenaeus reflects this position. In addition he probably accepted all the other New Testament books (though he does not mention all the *Catholic letters) and, perhaps, also Hermas. His evaluation of 1 Clement and the *Wisdom of Solomon is positive, but it is doubtful whether he regarded them as "holy scripture." It is clear, however, that by now the idea of the canon has materialized; its broad base is fixed, but uncertainty still exists over the books on its periphery.

Final stage (ca. 190–400 CE): *The closing of the canon.* It was particularly the claims to having received new revelations made by the gnostics (against whom Irenaeus already had reacted) and the Montanists, members of an apocalyptic prophetic movement, that stressed the need for a clear demarcation of the canon. Whereas the canon of Clement of Alexandria was still open, Origen and Eusebius in the Eastern church, as well as the author of the Canon of Muratori, a late second-century list, in the West, were convinced of the necessity of a clearly demarcated canon. For that reason both the former two writers, each in their own way, differentiated between three groups of writings: the generally accepted, the uncertain, and those that should be definitely excluded. In the wake of the vehement anti-Montanist reaction, many Eastern churches now began to question the position of the one prophetic-apocalyptic book in the canon, namely Revelation, a question sporadically recurring until the Middle Ages. In the West the anti-Montanist reaction took another course: in reaction against their accent on passages like Hebrews 6.4–6, the authenticity of the letter to the *Hebrews became a matter of dispute which lasted until the fourth century. Uncertainty still existed in various quarters over some of the Catholic letters and also over books like the Didache, the Shepherd of Hermas, and the Wisdom of Solomon.

In the East the uncertainty was cleared up by the thirty-ninth Paschal Letter of Athanasius, metropolitan of Alexandria, written in 367 CE, which listed all the books of the present New Testament. The writings of the apostolic fathers are excluded, but allowance is made for Hermas, the Didache, and the Wisdom of Solomon (as well as certain Old Testament *apocrypha) to be read privately. It is also noteworthy that in this letter the Greek equivalent for the verb "to canonize" (in the sense of: "officially recognize as normative") is used three times of the biblical books. (Some fifteen years earlier Athanasius had used the word "canon" in a technical sense of the Bible—the first certain occurrence of this use of the word.) Although only intended for the churches under his supervision, Athanasius's influence was such that his canon was widely approved in the East, and it greatly expedited the movement towards uniformity in the whole church. In the Western church the canon of Athanasius was probably approved at the Synod of Rome in 382 CE and definitely confirmed by a papal declaration of the year 405. Under Augustine's influence the North African church followed suit at the Synods of Hippo Regius (393) and Carthage (397), and, owing to persisting uncertainties regarding Hebrews, *James, and *Jude, reiterated its decisions at Carthage (419). By now the New Testament canon, with its twenty-seven books, was almost universally accepted as the second part of the Christian Bible. The one exception was the Syrian National Church where the popular Diatessaron of Tatian, a second-century harmonization of the Gospels, had held sway for centuries at the cost of the four "separate gospels," and where initially strong resistance existed against some general epistles and Revelation. Here it would still take some time for the Peshitta, the official Syriac translation, to oust the Diatessaron. The small East-Syrian Nestorian church, however, persisted with a canon of twenty-two books (excluding 2 Peter, 2 and 3 John, Jude, and Revelation). The other exception was the Ethiopian church, which included Hermas, the two Clementine epistles, and the Apostolic Constitutions, and whose New Testament canon consists, up to our own day, of thirty-eight books (see Bible).

Criteria of Canonicity. In determining the content and scope of the canon various criteria were applied, e.g., that of apostolicity, the rule of faith (regula fidei), and the consensus of the churches. Of these the first played the most important role. It would be a mistake, however, to deduce from this that apostolicity was, at least initially, treated as a merely formal criterion. As attested, for instance, by the Canon of Muratori, the real consideration was rather that of reliability. As primary sources the apostles and their followers were seen as the trustworthy exponents of the original revelation given in *Jesus Christ.

It would also be a mistake to regard the official recognition of our present twenty-seven books by the church as the act which gave them their canonical status. The decisions of the church were in reality the acknowledgement of the intrinsic authority and power of these writings.

See also Interpretation, History of, *article on* Early Christian Interpretation.

ANDRIE B. DU TOIT

Canticle of Canticles. *See* Song of Solomon.

Capernaum. A village on the northwest shore of the Sea of Galilee (Map 12: X2). The Greek name *Kapharnaoum* evidently represents a Semitic original, "village of Nahum." It is identified as Tell Hum, a mound that has now been extensively excavated.

Jesus is reported to have settled in Capernaum (Matt. 4.13) and made his home there at the beginning of his ministry (Mark 2.1). From here he carried on his early preaching and healed many, beginning with an *exorcism in the synagogue (Mark 1.21–28). Here he healed the slave of the *centurion who had built the synagogue (Luke 7.1–10; Matt. 8.5–13). The synagogue is also the scene of the discourse on the *bread of life (John 6.22–59).

The first archaeological discovery was a magnificent *synagogue, now dated to the fourth century CE. It is constructed of limestone, enclosed by columns and adorned with fine carvings, and the facade faces Jerusalem.

More recently a large area has been excavated, in which single-story basalt dwellings were grouped in squares, with streets in between. In this complex there is an octagonal church from about 450 CE. Beneath it is a house church (about 350 CE), which was remodeled from a dwelling that the Franciscan archaeologists identify as Peter's house (Mark 1.29). Near the great synagogue there is a smaller one, built of basalt, probably from the first century CE.

Capernaum was evidently a fishing village when its houses were built in the first century BCE and had a population of not more than one thousand.   SHERMAN ELBRIDGE JOHNSON

Catholic Letters. "General" (Grk. *katholikos*) epistles written to early Christianity at large, rather than to specific congregations (like the letters of *Paul and Rev. 2–3). The New Testament contains seven catholic letters: *James, traditionally ascribed to "the brother of Jesus" (Mark 6.3; cf. Gal 1.19; 1 Cor. 9.5; Acts 1.14); 1 and 2 *Peter, ascribed to Jesus' disciple; 1, 2, and 3 *John, which are related to the gospel of John; and *Jude, ascribed to the brother of James.

PHILIP SELLEW

Centurion. A century in the *Roman army was nominally a hundred, in practice usually eighty strong. There were sixty centurions in a Roman legion. They were of officer rank, corresponding to company commanders. They were men of status in the community and had a wide range of expertise and experience. Their duties often ranged beyond the strictly regimental, even to judicial functions and the administration of small military districts.

Centurions were also found in the auxiliary regiments supplementing the legions. These were either promoted from the ranks or transferred from a legion, and they might be Roman citizens (often recently enfranchised) or noncitizens.

The centurion at *Capernaum (Matt. 8.5) was probably a member of the armed forces of the *tetrarch *Herod, organized on the Roman pattern. The centurion at the death of Jesus (Mark 15.39 par.) was serving in a Roman auxiliary unit, as were the centurions at the arrest of Paul (Acts 21.32). So too were Cornelius (10.1) and Julius (27.1), both probably Roman citizens.

DENIS BAIN SADDINGTON

Chaldeans, Ur of the. *See* Ur of the Chaldeans.

Chaos. The Hebrew word *tōhû* is generally translated in two ways. It can denote the arid *wilderness, where *wadis disappear (Job 6.18), the deranged wander (Job 12.24; cf. Isa. 40.23), and Israel was found (Deut. 32.10). It can also mean the chaotic state before *creation (Job 26.7); in this sense it can be paired with *bōhû* (Gen. 1.2; Isa. 34.11; Jer. 4.23) and by extension can mean any empty, formless reality, especially other gods (1 Sam. 12.21; Isa. 41.29; 44.9), or defeated nations (Isa. 24.10; 34.11; 40.17).

These two concepts are linked in biblical tradition (Isa. 45.18) and in underlying mythology. Ancient Near Eastern *myths of creation frequently describe a battle between the creator, generally a storm god, and primeval forces, most frequently watery; reflexes in biblical traditions include the sea, the deep, and *Leviathan, whose chaotic powers must be kept under control (see Job 9.8; 26.8–13; 38.8–11; Pss. 89.8–11; 104.6–9; Isa. 27.1). Canaanite tradition in the texts from *Ugarit and elsewhere also narrates a conflict between *Baal, the Canaanite storm god, and the god Mot (Death); the domain of the latter is the arid desert as well as the underworld. In biblical tradition creation can be depicted as the triumph of Yahweh over the sterile forces of drought (see Gen 2.4–5); this is then applied to the creation of Israel (Deut. 32.10) and to its restoration (Isa. 35.6–7; 43.20; 51.3). Thus God's defeat of the forces of chaos, both water and desert, is a necessary prelude to creation as well as an ongoing activity. (*See also* Israel, Religion of.)

The Hebrew pair *tōhû wābōhû* is also the basis of the English and French word *tohu-bohu,* meaning "chaos and confusion."

MICHAEL D. COOGAN

Chapter and Verse Divisions. The complete Bible of today is ordinarily divided into chapters and verses, but such divisions were not part of the original texts. They were developed at a much later date, primarily in the interest of facilitating reference; consequently they do not always agree with the natural development of thought in the text.

Divisions in the Hebrew Text. The earliest biblical manuscripts, from *Qumran, have certain divisions in the text, although they are not yet standardized and may occur at different places in copies of the same book. Eventually a system was developed (except in the Psalter) involving what are called open and closed paragraphs *(pārāšâ,* plural *pārāšiyyôt),* the purpose of which was to give assistance in understanding the flow of thought. An open *(petûḥâ)* paragraph is one that begins a new line after an empty or incomplete line; a closed *(setûmâ)* paragraph is separated from the preceding paragraph by a short space within the line. Later scribes ignored this distinction in the actual written format but prefixed the Hebrew letter *p* or *s* to indicate the distinction. In the Psalter the verse division depends on the parallelism *(see* Poetry, Biblical Hebrew).

Another division of the text into more lengthy sections was developed by Palestinian scholars, who provided 452 *sedārîm* (weekly lessons) for a three-year *lectionary cycle. In Babylonia, where the *Torah *(see* Canon, *article on* Order of Books in the Hebrew Bible) was read through each year, the division was made into fifty-four (or fifty-three) weekly lessons.

Divisions in the Greek Text. Division within books in *Septuagint *manuscripts was also in use at an early period. The variety in the systems used suggests that they were drawn up independently by a number of different scribes and/or editors.

In New Testament Greek manuscripts we find several different systems of division. The oldest seems to be that contained in Codex Vaticanus, in which the divisions into sections were made with reference to breaks in the sense. There are 170 in Matthew, 62 in Mark, 152 in Luke, and 80 in John.

Many manuscripts of the Gospels are provided with an ingenious system developed by Eusebius of Caesarea (ca. 260–ca. 340 CE) to aid the reader in locating parallel passages. Each gospel was divided into longer or shorter sections, depending on the relation of each section to one or more parallels in the other Gospels: 355 for Matthew, 233 for Mark, 343 for Luke, and 232 for John. Then Eusebius prepared tables, called canons. The first contains a list in which all four Gospels agree; the second, passages common to Matthew, Mark, and Luke; the third, passages in which Matthew, Luke, and John agree; the fourth, passages in which Matthew, Mark, and John agree; and so on until almost all the possible combinations were exhausted. Finally, there were references to material in each gospel alone—62 in Matthew, 19 in Mark, 72 in Luke, and 96 in John.

For the book of Acts several systems of chapter divisions are found in the manuscripts. Codex Vaticanus has two sets of chapters, one of thirty-six, the other of sixty-nine. Most of the manuscripts of the book have a system of forty chapters.

The Pauline and general letters were also divided into chapters. Codex Vaticanus has two sets of chapters—an earlier and a later. In the Pauline letters, according to the earlier division of the text, the numeration of the chapters runs continuously through the whole corpus as though the letters were regarded as constituting one book. Because of a break in the numbering between pages 70 and 93 of the codex, it is evident that in an ancestor of Vaticanus the letter to the Hebrews stood between Galatians and Ephesians.

Some manuscripts of the book of Revelation are supplied with a system of divisions that was developed by Archbishop Andrew of Caesarea in Cappadocia (ca. 600), who wrote a commentary on the book that gives a "spiritual" exegesis. He divided the book into twenty-four discourses (Gk. *logoi*) and each of these into three smaller divisions, thus making seventy-two of the latter. According to Andrew's explanation, the number of the discourses corresponds to the number of elders sitting on thrones about the throne of God (Rev. 4.4), and the three subdivisions symbolize the tripartite nature of the elders (body, soul, and spirit).

Development of Modern Chapter and Verse Divisions. The introduction of the present system of chapter divisions has sometimes been attributed to Cardinal Hugo of St. Cher (d. 1263) for use in his concordance to the Latin *Vulgate. Before Hugo, however, the system that, with small modifications, is still in use today was introduced into the Latin Bible by a lecturer at the University of Paris, Stephen Langton, later Archbishop of Canterbury (d. 1228). Even before the invention of *printing (ca. 1456) the system began to be adopted for manuscripts of the Bible in languages other than Latin.

The chapters were at first subdivided (probably by Hugo of St. Cher) into seven portions (not paragraphs), marked in the margin by the letters A, B, C, D, E, F, G. In the shorter Psalms, however, the division did not always extend to seven. This division (except in the Psalms) was modified by Conrad of Halberstadt (ca. 1290), who reduced the divisions of the shorter chapters from seven to four, so that the letters were always A–G or A–D. This subdivision continued long after the introduction of the present verses.

Numbered verses (for a Hebrew concordance to the *Masoretic text) were first worked out by Rabbi Isaac Nathan in about 1440. In the earlier printed Hebrew Bibles each fifth verse is marked with its Hebrew numeral. Arabic numerals were first added for the intervening verses by Joseph Athias at Amsterdam in 1661 at the suggestion of Jan Leusden. The first portion of the Bible printed with the Masoretic verses numbered was the *Psalterium Quincuplex* of Faber Stapulensis. The *Psalterium* was beautifully printed at Paris in 1509 by Henry, father of Robert Stephanus, each verse commencing the line with a red letter and a numeral prefixed. In 1527 (or 1528) the Dominican Sanctes Paginus of Lucca published at Lyons, in quarto, his accurate translation of the Bible into Latin from the Hebrew and Greek. The verses are marked with Arabic numerals in the margin.

The current verse division in the New Testament was introduced by Robert Stephanus (Estienne), who in 1551 published at Geneva a Greek and Latin edition of the New Testament with the text of the chapters divided into separate verses. The first whole Bible divided into the present verses, and the first in which they were introduced into the *Apocrypha, was Stephanus's Latin Vulgate issued at Geneva in 1555. In the books of the Hebrew Bible Stephanus followed Paginus, but in the New Testament and in the Apocrypha he increased the number of verses. Thus, in the gospel of Matthew, Paginus has 577 verses, and Stephanus 1071; in Tobit Paginus has but 76 verses, while Stephanus has 292. According to Stephanus's son, his father made the divisions into verses *inter equitandum* on a journey from Paris to Lyons. Although some have taken this to mean "on horseback" (and have explained occasionally inappropriate verse divisions as originating when the horse bumped his pen into the wrong place!), a better interpretation is that the task was accomplished at intervals while he rested at inns along the road.

The verse divisions devised by Stephanus were widely and rapidly adopted and first appeared, for example, in English in the Geneva Bible (New Testament, 1557; Bible, 1560). Despite its utility, the system has often been criticized not only because the division sometimes occurs in the middle of a sentence, thus breaking the natural flow of thought, but also because to the reader the text appears to be a series of separate and detached statements. While it is too late to change the system to correct unfortunate verse divisions, at least the verses should never be printed each as a separate paragraph (as in most editions of the King James or Authorized Version), but the text should be continuous, in logical paragraphs, with the numerals in the margin or printed inconspicuously in the text.

WALTER F. SPECHT

Cherethites and Pelethites. A group of mercenaries loyal to *David. As a military unit separate from the regular army, the Cherethites and the Pelethites were under the command of Benaiah (2 Sam. 8.18; 20.23). They followed David on his flight from *Absalom (2 Sam. 15.18), fought for him during the revolt of Sheba (2 Sam. 20.7), and supported Benaiah's efforts to crown *Solomon as his father's successor (1 Kings 1.38, 44). Although this personal mercenary unit seems to disappear after David's death and the elevation of Benaiah to commander-in-chief of Solomon's army (1 Kings 2.29–35), some scholars connect the Cherethites with the Carites mentioned in 2 Kings 11.4, 19.

Research on the Cherethites and the Pelethites has focused on their origins and ethnic affiliations. Most commonly, but by no means universally, the terms are understood as Cretans and *Philistines, respectively. In two later prophetic passages (Ezek. 25.16; Zeph. 2.5) the Cherethites appear in poetic parallelism with the Philistines. Oracles of doom against the Philistines also make use of word play on the Hebrew root *krt*, "to (be) cut off," with which the word for Cherethites was associated (e.g., Jer. 47.4; Amos 1.8). From 1 Samuel 30.14 it can be surmised that the Cherethites were settled in southern Philistia and were engaged by David while he was in Ziklag as a vassal to Achish, the Philistine king of Gath (1 Sam. 27; 29). Although the exact relationship between the Cherethites and the Pelethites and the Philistines is unresolved, it is likely that they were all descended from the various sea peoples of Aegean origin who first settled on the southwestern coastal strip of Palestine at the beginning of the Iron Age (twelfth century BCE).

CARL S. EHRLICH

Cherub, Cherubim. Hebrew singular and plural for hybrid supernatural creatures associated with the presence of God, and in postbiblical tradition identified as one of the choirs of *angels. Among the nearly one hundred occurrences of the word in the Bible, the usual image is that of a huge eagle-winged, human-faced bull-lion, iconographic features familiar in Assyrian and Canaanite sources. Four interrelated roles for the cherubim can be identified.

Guardians of Paradise. As guardians of the entrance to *Eden (Gen 3.24; Ezek. 28.14–16) they are the functional counterparts of the colossal, human-faced winged bulls used in Mesopotamian architecture to guard the entrance to temples and palaces.

Protective Bearers of God's Throne. In descriptions of the *ark, a three-dimensional cherub stands at either side with wings protectively outstretched over its cover (e.g., Exod. 25.18–20). Before the *Temple was built, when the ark was still a portable shrine and housed in the tent of meeting (*see* Tabernacle), the Lord spoke to Moses "from between the two cherubim" (Exod. 25.22; Num. 7.89), where he was understood to sit invisibly enthroned (1 Sam 4.4; 2 Sam 6.2; Isa. 37.16; Pss. 80.1; 99.1). Portable shrines similar to Israel's ark are known from Egypt, Mesopotamia, Canaan, and Arabia, and some also feature cherubim as a decorative motif. In Solomon's Temple the ark became a permanent fixture (1 Kings 8.4–8), and the size of the cherubim increased dramatically (1 Kings 6.23–28). Notable Canaanite parallels are the Megiddo ivory reliefs (ca. 1200 BCE) and the Ahiram sarcophagus from Phoenicia (ca. 1000), both of which depict winged cherubim supporting the throne of the local king.

Decorative Elements. The walls and doors of the Temple were carved with cherubim and palm trees (1 Kings 6.29–35). In many ways the art and symbolism of the Temple replicated the garden of Eden, where the cherubim guarded the tree of life, widely depicted as the date palm.

Means of Yahweh's Mobility. In the theophanic visions of Ezekiel 1 and 10, the cherubim become the power by which God's chariot-throne is able to fly. In 2 Samuel 22.11 (= Ps. 18.10) the Lord is said to ride on a cherub, equated in poetic parallelism with flying on the wings of the wind.

The etymology of the Hebrew word *kĕrûb* is uncertain, but some connection with Akkadian *kāribu,* the intercessor guardian creature, seems probable. The cherubim of the Bible have no relationship with the winged infants or *putti* often featured in Renaissance art.   DAVID G. BURKE

Children's Bibles. The recasting of the Bible to meet the needs of children has been a topic of increasing interest in the twentieth century. Although children were always included within the concern of the religious communities for which the Bible served as scripture, they were understood as parts of families within which the Bible would be read and explained. In Christian circles, such an assumption lies behind the widespread production of *family Bibles and their use by parents in reading to their children. But the view of the Bible as a work to be read independently by children and the accompanying challenges for a child reading an adult book reflect a recent approach to children's Bibles. Attempts to translate the Bible in language comprehensible to children have been significant only from about 1970 on.

The education of children included a knowledge of the Bible, a goal to be carried out in the home, the church, and the school, until the nineteenth century. Since it was regularly believed that the goals of education were piety, civility, and learning, children and youth were expected to be familiar with the Bible. The necessary knowledge of the Bible included not only its contents but also an affirmation of the *authority of scripture.

After the invention of *printing by movable type and the rise of vernacular Bibles, the widespread dissemination of Bibles was accompanied by significant study helps such as chapter summaries (Coverdale Bible, 1535) and marginal notes (Geneva Bible, 1560). A Puritan divine such as Cotton Mather (1663–1728), in his *Bonifacius: An Essay upon the Good,* proposed a number of methods intended to enable children to learn the contents of the Bible. These included Bible storytelling at the dinner table and rewards for Bible memorization—with appropriate attention to the age, interests, and abilities of particular children. The study of the Bible by children also included catechisms, psalters, and liturgies, intended to prepare them for a knowledge of the Christian faith and participation in public worship.

Among the ways used to teach children the Bible, one of the most important in England and the United States beginning in the late eighteenth century was the Sunday School in its own right and as a forerunner of the common school. Two of the popular texts used in Sunday Schools were *The Sunday School Spelling Book* (1822) and *The Union Spelling Book* (1838), both containing biblical texts and biblical diction.

In areas such as the United States where Protestants predominated through the middle of the nineteenth century, there was agreement that the reading of the Bible should be a central aspect of the public-school curriculum. The increasing religious pluralism of the United States would question this assumption and its accompanying presupposition that public reading of the Bible would be from the Authorized Version of 1611. In the United States the publication of both Roman Catholic and Jewish versions in the nineteenth century was intended, in part, to offset the exclusive use of the Authorized Version in public-school education.

By 1850 McGuffey's *Eclectic Readers* (1836) was the basic school reader in some thirty-seven states. Eighty percent of the schoolchildren of the United States used McGuffey's *Readers* for some seventy-five years. Although the majority of the material in McGuffey was nonbiblical, there was still a significant degree of biblical content in the six readers.

During the nineteenth century Sunday Schools evolved a systematic approach to Bible study. The need for children's Bibles received little attention when the focus of the child's Bible study was either the memorization of Bible verses or catechetical learning that had subsumed the Bible into affirmations of the Christian faith. In the case of memorization much attention was paid to the selection of particular verses, and contextual reading of the Bible played little role. When the Bible was the primary source of moral example, this became the strongest influence in the education of children in the Sunday Schools. Initially started as interdenominational agencies, these shifted in the course of the nineteenth century to a denominational basis. Their early goals had been to improve the moral life of their students as expressed in effective citizenship. Increasingly a knowledge of the Bible was viewed as essential for personal salvation and social stability; the Bible was a source of texts to be memorized. The texts might reflect moral themes drawn from Jesus' ministry or the lives of the ancestors and prophets. Lewis Baldwin's *The Bible Interrogatory* (1816) was one of the first attempts to systematize biblical study in Sunday Schools. The greatest achievement of interdenominational Sunday Schools was the creation of the International Lesson System. A post–Civil War development, these plans stressed uniform lessons for all ages. Critics of the lesson plans noted that they ignored child psychology, and in 1894 the Lesson Committee developed a separate course for younger children.

The establishment of *Bible Societies and the dissemination of Bibles, or parts of Bibles (*see* Circulation of the Bible), contributed to a consideration of the forms of Bibles for children. One result was to ensure that children have their own Bibles. This could be accomplished within the Sunday School movement by giving children Bibles as they completed one part of the Sunday School and moved to another. These presentation Bibles were usually an existing adult translation with a presentation nameplate and occasional illustrations.

Another form of children's Bible was a collection of Bible stories, selected for various emphases, and either paraphrased or completely rewritten. This has been the most popular form of children's Bible and accounts for a large part of juvenile Bibles available at any time.

A well-known example of the storybook Bible was *Child's Bible Reader* (1898), a work widely employed by three generations of Protestant Sunday School teachers in the southeastern United States. The stories in the *Reader* were attributed to the popular British writer, Charlotte M. Yonge. Thousands of southern homes owned copies of this *Reader*, distributed by door-to-door salesmen of the Southwestern Company of Nashville, Tennessee. Equally popular in a later generation was Walter de la Mare's *Stories from the Bible*.

The storybook approach to children's Bibles inevitably involves the selection of stories considered to be appealing or appropriate to children. Perennial favorites include *Noah, *Moses, *Samson, *David, *Jonah, and *Jesus. Common to these collections are also stories about birth and childhood, animals, and adventure stories. Such storybook Bibles generally avoid events, persons, or narratives seen as inappropriate or incomprehensible to children, such as the story of *Joshua, the letters of *Paul, and the book of *Revelation.

The storybook Bible has encouraged the use of illustrations to complement the biblical narratives and to increase their appeal for children. Examples that have been publicly recognized for their aesthetic achievement include E. Boyd Smith's writing and illustrating of *The Story of Noah's Ark* (1905) and Dorothy Lathrop's *Animals of the Bible* (1937). (*See* Illustrated Bibles.)

The most recent development has been the production of translations specifically for children, with considerable initiative coming from the United Bible Societies. Based on the understanding of psychological, social, and intellectual development, this movement has attempted to produce readable Bibles to match the abilities and interests of various ages. In 1983 the Sweet Publishing Company issued the pioneering *International Children's Version (New Testament)* as the first translation for children. In 1986, the Worthy Publishing Company issued the *International Children's Bible, New Century Version*, noting that this was not a storybook or a paraphrased Bible but the first translation of the whole Bible prepared specifically for children. Because of its specialized vocabulary, the publishers claim that their Bible translation can be understood by children with a grade-three reading level.

ERNEST S. FRERICHS

Chosen People. The Bible describes various individuals as "chosen" by God: *Abraham, *Jacob, *Moses, *Aaron, *Saul, *David, *Solomon, *Zerubbabel, and *Jesus; Jesus, in turn, chose his *disciples. These individuals are not chosen, so far as we know, for their previous virtue. All are depicted as fallible, except the shadowy Zerubbabel and the perfect Jesus. Election is usually linked with heredity; the chosen belongs to a dynasty, often as its founder. God may also choose a larger group, such as the tribe of *Levi.

The most common function of this election motif is the legitimation of groups: the house of David, the Aaronic *priests, the Levites, the *apostles. But what does it mean to be "chosen"? There is no sign of being chosen; the election theme is primarily an assertion of God's favor.

Another body called "chosen" is Israel itself (Isa. 41.8–9; 44.1–2; cf. 14.1; Ps. 105.6 [= 1 Chron. 16.13]; 106.5; 135.4; Rom. 9.11). Some consider this a later development; priestly and royal election are democratized, as all Israel becomes a "kingdom of priests" (Exod. 19.5).

The classic statement of Israel's election is Deuteronomy 7.6–9 (cf. 10.15; 14.2; 26.18; Mal. 3.17; Ps. 135.4): "The Lord your God has chosen you out of all the peoples on earth to be his people, his treasured possession. It was not because you were more numerous . . . it was because the LORD loved you, and kept the oath that he swore to your ancestors." Although the verb "choose" does not appear in Deuteronomy 32.8, according to that text God gave each nation its own god (thus the *Septuagint and Qumran versions; cf. Judges 11.24), keeping Israel for himself. Ideally, this election elicits reciprocity from Israel, which in turn chooses God (Josh. 24.22).

Election entails responsibility and risk as well as privilege; Deuteronomy 7.10–11 threatens punishment should Israel violate the *covenant; compare Amos 3.2. According to Amos 9:7–10, Israel's uniqueness lies in the fact that God will never utterly destroy it (cf. Lev. 26.44).

It is unclear when God chose Israel; one might cite the call of Abram (Gen. 12.1–3), Jacob's vision (Gen. 28.13–15), or the experience at *Sinai (Exod. 19, 20, 24). Ezekiel 20.5 dates Israel's election to God's revelation in Egypt (cf. Exod. 6.2–8).

Second *Isaiah's concept of chosenness poses special problems. Sometimes he explicitly calls Israel "chosen" (Isa. 41.8–9; 43.10; 44.1–2; 45.4; 48.10 [text uncertain]; 65.9, 15, 22), promising divine succor and numerous, pious offspring. But the prophet also describes one chosen to be a "light to the nations" (Isa. 42.1, 6; cf. 49.5–9), whose suffering atones for others' sins (Isa. 53). Scholars debate whether this is the nation of Israel, a segment thereof, or a particular member; Christianity traditionally applies these oracles to Jesus.

While the Bible does not associate Israel's election with its intrinsic merit, later Judaism reacted to its often dire circumstances by developing a belief in the spiritual superiority of all Jews, whether by birth or by choice. Thus, the *Torah was offered to various peoples but accepted only by Israel; the eroticism of the *Song of Solomon expresses God's unique love for Israel; only Israel's history is governed directly by God, other nations being subject to the laws of nature; Jewish souls derive directly from God, while the souls of *gentiles are of lesser matter. Such theories, however, have never been central Jewish doctrines. The basic concept of "chosenness" has remained, as in biblical terms, that of covenant: God chose the Jews by imposing certain restrictions upon them and holding them to a higher ethical and ritual standard. Many contemporary Jewish thinkers reject even this more modest claim as irrelevant or harmful in today's pluralistic society.

The early church called its adherents "chosen," implying that they succeeded Israel as God's favored. All who embrace Jesus, Jew and gentile alike, become "chosen" (Matt. 22.14; 24.22, 24, 31; Mark 13.20, 22, 27; Luke 18.7; Rom. 8.33; Eph. 1.4; 1 Thess. 1.4; 2 Tim. 2.10; Titus 1.1; 1 Pet. 1.10; 2 John 1.1; Rev. 17.14). *Paul does not infer from the Christians' election any intrinsic greatness or virtue (1 Cor. 1.26–29; cf. James 2.5), and he insists that Israel retains its special status (Rom. 9–11). Ironically, while many liberal Jewish thinkers disavow "chosenness," some Christian theologians today reaffirm the continuing election of the Jews.   WILLIAM H. PROPP

Christ. See Jesus Christ; Messiah.

Christian. According to Acts 11.26, Jesus' disciples were first called Christians in *Antioch. Elsewhere in the New Testament the word "Christian" occurs in Acts 26.28 and 1 Peter 4.14–16.

The origin of the term "Christian" is uncertain. It comprises the word "Christ," the Greek word meaning "anointed one" (see Messiah) with an ending meaning "followers of" or "partisans of." Jews who did not accept Jesus as the Messiah would hardly refer to Jesus' disciples as Christians—the Messiah's followers. According to Acts 24.5, such Jews referred to Jesus' followers as "the sect of the Nazarenes," apparently regarding Christians as a Jewish group.

Because followers of Jesus used "*saints" (2 Cor. 1.1; Rom. 12.13; Acts 9.13, 32), "brothers" (1 Cor. 1.10; Rom. 1.13; Acts 1.16), "the *Way" (Acts 9.2; 19.9), "*disciples" (often in the Gospels; Acts 6.1–2; 11.26), and other designations when referring to themselves, it is unlikely that the term "Christian" originated among Christians.

In Acts 26.28 Agrippa uses "Christian" sarcastically; in 1 Peter 4.14–16 it is a term of reproach used during persecution. Thus, the term seems to have been derogatory. The contemporary Roman historians Tacitus (*Annals* 15.44) and Suetonius (*Lives of the Caesars* 6.16) use the term that way. Tacitus refers to Christians as people hated for their evil deeds, and Suetonius calls them "a new and evil superstition."

If first applied to Jesus' followers in Antioch, Roman officials may have coined the word to distinguish the Christian group from Judaism. Perhaps "Christian" was used to designate the Christian movement as hostile toward Agrippa. No matter where the term originated, it was first a word of scorn or ridicule. But by the end of the first century CE Christians accepted the name as a comforting sign of God's glory (1 Pet. 4.14–16; Ignatius, *Romans* 3.2).   EDWIN D. FREED

Christian Science and the Bible. Christian Science began in the United States during the latter half of the nineteenth century, appearing first as a religious teaching and later as an organized denomination. Known primarily for its practice of Christian healing, Christian Science teaches that the Bible's dominant theme is the superiority of spiritual over physical power, and that this power can be reliably—even "scientifically"—demonstrated in the lives of people today. It was founded by Mary Baker Eddy (1821–1910), a New England woman with a staunch Calvinist background and a devotion to regular study of the Bible.

Several social and personal factors help to explain the emergence of Christian Science. First, much of Mrs. Eddy's early religious life was shaped by her rebellion against her Calvinist upbringing, specifically its doctine of *predestination. Also, by midcentury, society was entering a new and scientific era, where reason, experimentation, and observable results were becoming the standard means of measuring progress and assessing truth claims. Yet for Eddy, the void left by her dissatisfaction with what she called "cruel creeds," could not be fulfilled by rational advances alone. Throughout her life she retained a characteristic Puritan piety, noted by several of her biographers, which she referred to as "a hunger and thirst for divine things."

This left her satisfied neither with the doctrinal interpretation of the Bible offered by the church nor with the more scientifically based historical-critical method of Bible analysis then gaining prominence, although she insisted that she retained whatever was valid in both. But what finally impelled her to take a radically different view of the meaning of the biblical revelation was her own suffering, including the years of near invalidism that dominated the first four decades of her life.

While she initially sought relief through almost every healing or medical system that promised comfort, including the suggestive therapeutics of the Maine mental healer Phineas Quimby, her bedrock conviction was that only the Bible offered the answer to "the great problem of being." According to her own account, she was healed of the effects of a serious accident in 1866 by reading of Jesus' healing works in the Gospels. Reflecting on her experience, she felt that she had discovered something of the underlying power, or spiritual law, that was at the very root of Christianity.

The nine years following her own healing were spent studying the Bible, writing, teaching, healing—all aimed at finding ways to articulate a metaphysics that she felt would make the Bible practical in a scientific age. Central to her view was the belief that undergirding the events of the Bible was a spiritual law, which, far from being a relic of ancient history, was dynamic and applicable in all time to bring about healing of disease and redemption from sin. She explicated her metaphysical interpretation of the Bible in her major work, *Science and Health*, first published in 1875 and eventually titled *Science and Health, with Key to the Scriptures*. She would revise and edit the book throughout the rest of her life, but it would remain the definitive statement of Christian Science.

The book became an immediate source of controversy. Critics charged that *Science and Health*, written by a woman with no formal training, included language not found in the Bible and deviated from orthodox Christianity in its teachings. They charged Eddy with elevating her writing to the status of the Bible.

For her part, Eddy acknowledged that her book departed from certain church doctrines, but she maintained that these doctrines originated less in the Bible than in church councils, which were often guilty of "teaching as doctrines the precepts of men" (see Isa. 29.13 AV). She asserted that the way to validate an individual's understanding of God and the Bible was by examining the fruits of that understanding. Do they demonstrate a practical grasp of the power of God's word by healing and regenerating the individual? To her, this was the acid test of biblical interpretation.

In her view, from *Moses' commandments to have no idols and to worship God alone, to the prophets' call for *repentance, to Christ Jesus' description of the presence of the *kingdom of God "within you," the Bible presented the *word of God, revealing the supremacy of God, Spirit, and the wholly spiritual nature of God's creation. Eddy felt that faith in this supreme and infinitely good God also implied that the very existence of *evil and *suffering, so evident in the material world, could be challenged as having no God-derived cause or legitimacy.

Eddy saw the nature of Godlike as being most perfectly manifested in the life of Christ Jesus. For her, Jesus' life was itself the unique revelation of what it means to live in authentic relation to God. She saw her own work, *Science and Health*, not as a second kind of Bible or as a replacement for it but as an offering of what she saw as the Bible's permanent and continuing meaning, making Christian discipleship a practicable possibility in the modern age. She felt that her "scientific" approach to Christianity merely made explicit what was implicit in the Bible all along, opening its message in a new and powerful way.

Today, regular study of the Bible and *Science and Health* remains central to the practice of Christian Science. Each day its adherents read a lesson made up of passages from these two books. This same lesson is read as the sermon in Sunday church services, and changes weekly.

Christian Scientists tend to reject the narrow literalism of *fundamentalism, as well as the liberal tendency to reduce biblical accounts to stories with intended morals. Instead, they assert that the Bible presents what might be called a "spiritual literal" account of the supremacy of God in human history. For example, Christian Scientists regard the *crucifixion, *resurrection, and *ascension of Christ Jesus as the central events of human history, embodying the supremacy of the law of God over all mortal existence. The first of six tenets left to the church by Mrs. Eddy reads, "As adherents of Truth, we take the inspired word of the Bible as our sufficient guide to eternal Life."

SCOTT F. PRELLER

Christmas. The English word Christmas means Christ's Mass, the festival of Christ's birthday. 25 December was by the fourth century CE the date of the winter solstice, celebrated in antiquity as the birthday of Mithras and of Sol Invictus. In the Julian calendar the solstice fell on 6 January, when the birthday of Osiris was celebrated at Alexandria. By about 300 CE, 6 January was the date of Epiphany in the East, a feast always closely related to Christmas. The earliest mention of 25 December for Christmas is in the Philocalian Calendar of 354, part of which reflects Roman practice in 336. Celebration of Christ's birthday was not general until the fourth century; in fact, as late as the fifth century the Old Armenian Lectionary of Jerusalem still commemorated James and David on 25 December, noting "in other towns they keep the birth of Christ." When celebrated, the theme was the *Incarnation, and the scriptures were not confined to the birth or infancy narratives. To Luke 2.1–14 and Matthew 1.18–25 were added not only John 1.1–18 but also, for example, Titus 2.11–14.

The year of Christ's birth is hard to determine. The enrollment by Quirinius in that year according to Luke 2.1–5 is dated by Josephus as equivalent to 6–7 CE (*Ant.* 18.2.26), but this enrollment was not of "all the world" (Luke 2.1), would not have taken place under *Herod, during whose lifetime Quirinius was not governor of Syria, and would not have required the presence of *Joseph, and still less of *Mary, in *Bethlehem. Although Luke 3.1–2 suggests no exact year, the passage seems to indicate between 27 and 29 CE as the times of John's baptizing and of Jesus' being about thirty years of age (Luke 3.23). Jesus' birth would then be about 4–1 BCE. The time of year is nowhere indicated. (*See also* Chronology, *article on* Early Christian Chronology.)

The place of Jesus' birth also raises problems. If we had only the gospels of *Mark and *John we would assume that it was *Nazareth (Mark 1.9; John 1.45–46; cf. Luke 2.4, 39). Luke 2.1–

20 tells the story of the birth in Bethlehem and Matthew 2.1 follows a similar tradition, though introducing not a birth narrative but an infancy narrative, for the account of the wise men (*see* Magi) implies that Jesus might have been as much as two years old when they arrived (Matt. 2.16).

The exact place at Bethlehem is doubtful; the manger of Luke 2.7 may be rather a stall with almost no covering, or even a feeding trough in the open, the "inn" itself not being a building but a yard with partial shelter at its sides. The ox and ass of subsequent art are not in Luke's story but enter from Isaiah 1.3. Another early tradition, recorded in the second century apocryphal Protoevangelium of James (18–21) and Justin (*Trypho* 78.657), tells of a cave as the birthplace. It was apparently shown to Origen ca. 246, and by 333 Constantine had built a basilica over it, which was replaced under Justinian ca. 531. Still extant, the cave claims a stone as the manger. In early liturgies both the manger and the shepherds' fields play a part, but at the inclusive feast of the Epiphany rather than at a celebration solely of Christ's birthday.

A. R. C. LEANEY

Chronicles, The Books of.

Title. As with *Samuel and *Kings, the two books of Chronicles are in reality one: the counting of words and sections customary in the Hebrew text appears only at the end of 2 Chronicles. The division was first made in the *Septuagint and thence in the Latin *Vulgate; hence it was adopted in other translations and by the sixteenth century also in printed Hebrew Bibles. The Hebrew title is "book of the acts of the days," that is, annals, a phrase used frequently in this sense to describe royal acts or records (e.g., 1 Kings 14.29, and cf. Esther 6.1). The title is not entirely appropriate: there is much material of other kinds to be found in Chronicles. Even if it reasonably fits the larger part of the work, it too easily gives the impression that we are dealing with a work of history, which is only very partially the case. In the Greek, the title given is "the thing(s) left out" (*paralipomenon);* this is intelligible on the common assumption that Chronicles was intended to supplement the books of Samuel and Kings by providing information not given there, but it is an inaccurate description for what the work really is. Indeed, it may be recognized that this misunderstanding has often led to a use of Chronicles, for example

in simplified histories of Israel and in church *lectionaries, that does not do justice to a writing that needs to be read for its own sake and in the light of its own style of approach and not just to fill gaps in a differently conceived presentation.

Contents. Briefly, the contents are:

1 Chronicles 1.1–9.34: *Genealogies from Adam onward, culminating in lists of those who returned from exile in Babylon

1 Chronicles 9.35–29.30: The kingship of David

2 Chronicles 1–9: The kingship of Solomon

2 Chronicles 10–36: The kingdom of Judah to its destruction by the Babylonians and the beginning of restoration under Cyrus the Persian.

The outline suggests a twofold approach to the story. In the first, the opening chapters (1 Chron. 1–8), consisting almost entirely of lists of names, offer a survey from the earliest figures of Israelite tradition, through a concentration on the *tribes of Israel to the family of *Saul, the first king: this ushers in chap. 9, where there is a leap forward to *Judah's unfaithfulness that led to *exile in *Babylon, and to the return, listing family groups, priests, and other religious officials. In the second approach, the story begins over again (at 9.35), with a repetition of the Saul genealogy (cf. 8.29–40), which here serves to introduce Saul's failure as a foil to the establishment and achievements of *David in chapters 10–29. With its sequel in 2 Chronicles, this second approach offers a survey covering the whole period of the monarchy, itself to end with a short reference to *Cyrus, and the promise of a return from exile. The question whether the books of *Ezra and *Nehemiah, which continue the story, are to be regarded as part of the same work or are independent of Chronicles will be considered subsequently.

Text. Like all other biblical books, the text of Chronicles presents numerous problems resulting from errors in transmission. But the more serious difficulties here arise from the considerable degree to which these books offer duplicate texts of material found elsewhere in the Bible. The main overlaps are with sections of Samuel and Kings: a substantial part of 1 Chronicles 10 to 2 Chronicles 36 contains such parallels. The relationship is not all at one level: there are passages where the Chronicles and Samuel or Kings texts are virtually the same, but many more where numerous smaller and larger differences are to be seen. Some of these differences may derive from the simple substitution of more familiar words or forms than those found in what are clearly the older texts; some of the exact coincidences may be due to cross-influence from one text to the other at a relatively late stage. Some differences are evidently the result of exegetical activity, as indeed at least some of the additional material, unparalleled in the older texts, is likely to be due to the interpretive inventiveness of the author of Chronicles. The study of the relationship is complicated by some evidence in the *Qumran texts of Samuel which suggests that the text known to the writer of Chronicles may have been closer to those texts than to Samuel as it appears in the Hebrew Bible.

There are numerous other textual overlaps. Much of the genealogical material in 1 Chronicles 1–9 is paralleled in the *Pentateuch or elsewhere. The psalm passage in 1 Chronicles 16.8–36 is paralleled in parts of Psalms 105, 96, and 106; and there are numerous other quotations or allusions to psalms and to other works, especially to various prophetic writings (e.g., 2 Chron. 20.20; cf. Isa. 7.9). These last are usually of greater interest as representing the exegesis of earlier material than for textual relationship.

Sources and Integrity. As has just been indicated, we may recognize the books of Samuel and Kings as the major source for Chronicles, allowing for the probability that the text used was not exactly the same as that familiar to us; other materials provided further sources on which the writer drew. In addition, however, we find a substantial number of passages where no parallel is known. Thus, in 2 Chronicles 28, in relating the reign of Ahaz, the Chronicler clearly knows the parallel in 2 Kings 16; but there is additional material not found there. In this particular case, we may note the probability that some of the smaller differences—but no less important for that—are due to the Chronicler's own exposition of the already familiar material. But the whole of the war narrative in 28.5–15 is not so easy to explain. The same is true of archival material about fortifications (e.g., 2 Chron. 11.5–12) and of a good deal of what is devoted to modifications in the Jerusalem *Temple, regarded favorably or unfavorably (e.g., 2 Chron. 28.24–25: Ahaz's antireforms; 2 Chron. 29.3–31.21: *Hezekiah's reforms). These extra passages have been variously assessed. Some would regard them as genuine extracts from archival and other sources that existed alongside the books of Samuel and Kings. Others would see in such unparalleled

material evidence of the Chronicler's imaginative inventiveness; but it is not easy to see why some of this material should be pure invention. It is more important that we attempt to link such embellishments of the narratives with what may be detected of the main purposes of the work, and at the same time recognize that Chronicles does not simply reuse older material but offers exegeses of it. Thus, the portrayals of Ahaz and Hezekiah, already alluded to, may serve as examples of an interpretive process by which a bad king, according to 2 Kings, becomes the worst representative of the Judean monarchy; while a good king, again as 2 Kings describes him, has become a virtually ideal figure. For the latter, it is instructive to observe not only the enormous additional account of religious reform in 2 Chronicles 29–31 (contrast the extreme brevity of 2 Kings 18.4), but also the skilled reworking of the narrative material of 2 Kings 18–20 in 2 Chronicles 32.

It is in the light of this that the sources named in the books of Chronicles should be considered. At a number of points, in the summaries of the kings' reigns, allusion is made to the sources employed; thus 1 Chronicles 29.29–30 refers to "the records of the seer Samuel, and . . . the records of the prophet Nathan, and . . . the records of the seer Gad" (cf. the similar statement for Solomon in 2 Chron. 9.29, and for Hezekiah in 2 Chron. 32.32). In other instances, as in the books of Kings, reference is made simply to annals—"the Book of the Kings of Judah and Israel" and the like. It would appear that the Chronicler is here both following the pattern of the books of Kings in citing such annalistic works, and also developing the understanding of the earlier writings and emphasizing the relationship between their stories of kings and the activity of prophets. The earlier works, from Joshua to 2 Kings, came in time to be known as the "Former Prophets" and were to stand alongside the "Latter Prophets," namely the prophetic books, Isaiah, Jeremiah, Ezekiel, and the Twelve (see Canon, article on Order of Books in the Hebrew Bible). Such a description of the earlier writings suggests that, whatever precisely the Chronicler may have had at his disposal, he was accepting and developing a particular understanding of the writings familiar to him; whatever sources unknown to us were available, we must expect that they too were handled with the same kind of creative reinterpretation.

One further question needs a brief mention here: Does the work exist essentially as it came from its author, or has it been modified to a greater or lesser extent? Various theories of stages in its formation have been proposed, but none appears entirely convincing; there is insufficient evidence to support the idea of a "first" and a "second" Chronicler, or that of a first stage belonging to the early Persian period and second and third stages from a later date. The possibility that 1 Chronicles 1–9 is a later addition has also found some supporters; but the relationship between these chapters and what follows makes that view difficult. Perhaps, and this has been particularly argued for 1 Chronicles 24–27, some expansions have been made; but unless it is possible to see clear evidence of a shift in standpoint, it is difficult to be sure. And even with such an apparent shift, we cannot be certain how far such a different emphasis was inherent in material being taken over from another source and incorporated by the author in spite of the fact that its outlook did not agree at every point with that of the main work.

The Place of Chronicles in the *Canon. In English translations, Chronicles is placed, as in the *Septuagint and the *Vulgate, in the group of books that may be roughly described as "historical." Thus, it follows the books of Kings and is in turn followed by Ezra, Nehemiah, and Esther. (The canons of some churches include Tobit, Judith, and 1 and 2 Maccabees in this group as well). There is clear logic in this arrangement: all these writings, whatever their differences, are mainly narratives of one kind or another. The Hebrew Bible offers a different picture. As has been noted, the "historical" books from Joshua to Kings there appear as the Former Prophets. Chronicles, as also Ezra-Nehemiah (as one book) and Esther, appear in the third part of the Hebrew canon, entitled the Writings. Most commonly, in manuscripts and printed editions, Chronicles stands last, preceded by Ezra-Nehemiah; this is problematic, since clearly Ezra-Nehemiah provides a continuation of the Chronicles narrative. In some manuscripts, Chronicles stands first among the Writings, immediately before Psalms; in such a position it provides a context for the Psalter, traditionally associated with David, for much of 1 Chronicles is concerned with David and lays great stress on his organization of Temple worship and singing (for the latter, see especially 1 Chron. 16). When placed at the end of the Writings, it may be regarded as setting out by both warning and example how the true Temple and true worship must be maintained. It then follows Daniel, os-

tensibly concerned with the disasters of the sixth century BCE and the destruction of Temple and worship then—though, in reality (see especially Dan. 9), it points to the defilement and hoped-for reestablishment of the Temple in the second century BCE in the period of Antiochus IV Epiphanes; and Ezra-Nehemiah, which relates various stages in the restoration of Temple and people in the Persian period. By placing Chronicles at the end, the Hebrew Bible, which eventually reflects later concerns of the Jewish community, may be seen to look to a future restoration of Jerusalem and its shrine, beyond the still later disasters of Roman rule (especially the events of 70 and 135 CE).

A Literary Work and an Interpretation. The term "the Chronicler" is often used as a convenient shorthand to refer to the unknown author of the books of Chronicles. It has the advantage of simplicity, but it can too easily seem to imply that we know who the author was. In fact, nothing at all is known; the traditional view named Ezra, but there is no real evidence for this, and it must be regarded as part of the process by which the authority of biblical writings was associated with noteworthy biblical characters. Nor do we know when Chronicles was compiled. In part, a decision on this is connected with the relationship between Chronicles and Ezra-Nehemiah; if these together form a unity, then the final shaping must be later than the events there described, which would point to the late fifth or the fourth century BCE, or perhaps later still. It is clear that, with its dependence on Samuel and Kings, whose final form cannot be earlier than the sixth century BCE, we must look in all probability in the Persian period: there is no clear evidence of the change to Greek rule. A fourth century BCE date is reasonable, but remains a balanced guess.

There can be no certainty on whether the work is the product of a single author or was produced within a particular circle whose members shared views and ideals about the nature of their community. The very fact that so much earlier material has been reused makes the assessment of literary unity very difficult. Indeed, we may wonder how far the idea of literary unity is really appropriate to such a writing. The supposition that an ancient writer would endeavor to produce a completely unified and consistent work is too much based on modern conceptions of how an editor should update older material. We should more probably expect to find general consistency, but expressed in a variety of ways.

This is particularly relevant to the debated question of whether the books of Ezra and Nehemiah are separate or belong to the same work. They are treated as separate in the Hebrew Bible, and, as noted above, they normally stand in the reverse order from that found in the Greek and derived translations. There is a small overlap between the two (2 Chron. 36.22–23 = Ezra 1.1–3a); in the alternative form in 1 *Esdras, which covers from 2 Chronicles 35 to Ezra 10 plus Nehemiah 7.73b–8.13, the material runs continuously, but the evidence of 1 Esdras is problematic. It seems clear that, whatever the actual relationship, the reader is intended to see Ezra-Nehemiah as a sequel. Alternative views range from the assumption of unity, so that Chronicles-Ezra-Nehemiah are referred to as the Chronicler's work; to the maintenance of single authorship, but with the two parts written at different times, with either order of writing proposed; and to stress disunity, the marked differences between the two works in language, style, and ideology. Such differences of view suggest that certainty cannot be achieved. In part, the decision comes down to assessing whether and to what extent the differences within the books are too great for the books to be considered other than superficially related; to what extent unity in the literary sense demands complete unity of thought and style; and to what extent disunity is related to the use in all parts of the work of source material that has its own language and style and has often been taken over virtually unaltered. If we demand very strict unity of thought and style, then we will decide to separate them; but if we think in terms of a circle of thought, in which the main lines are shared but with differences of view on many matters of detail, then an overall unity may embrace variety of approach.

Whatever the decision in this delicate matter, it seems clear that the author of the books of Chronicles, as we know them, was setting out to give to his contemporaries an understanding of their current position as a small subject people under alien (Persian) rule, in the light of his interpretation of the past. This involved seeing that small community in the light of the whole story from *creation to the restoration under Cyrus (so in 1 Chron. 1–9); a similar approach may be seen in the *Pentateuch, which traces the story from creation to *conquest. It also involved offering an understanding of the contemporary significance of the two major institutions of that history: *kingship and Temple. The total loss of the former, with no realistic possibility of its recovery, is explained through a retelling of the story with the stress laid on *David as creator, and on his worthy successors as continuers, of the religious life of the Jerusalem Temple; in this view, the real function of the monarchy was religious. The restoration of the Temple under *Persian rule described in Ezra 1–6 is implicit in the material of 1 Chronicles 9 and set in motion in the final verses of 2 Chronicles. Whoever was responsible for Ezra-Nehemiah was providing the logical conclusion to the story. At the same time, the books of Chronicles provide an idealized picture of the true people, loyal to their God and to the law of Moses (*Torah); the story does not shirk the recognition of failures by rulers and people, from the disastrous disloyalty of *Saul (1 Chron. 10), to the secession of the north from the true inheritance (2 Chron. 10), to the apostasy of other rulers, reaching a climax in Ahaz (2 Chron. 28), and so to the final disobedience that led to the exiling of the people to Babylon, leaving an empty land to recover by observing its forgotten sabbaths (2 Chron. 36.17–21). But the author does not merely paint a gloomy picture; numerous instances of repentance are included, the most remarkable being the total reinterpretation of the reign of *Manasseh who, from being the worst of the kings of Judah in 2 Kings, now becomes an exemplar—punished for evil by captivity in Babylon, he returns in repentance and becomes a reformer (2 Chron. 33.1–20), an interpretation that clearly understands Manasseh as a symbol of Judah in exile and return. Within the broad sweep of interpretation, which gives the work a clear unity of purpose, there is a rich mixture of story and comment, of homiletic development and imaginative depiction, almost like a series of sermons, all on central themes but developed in a variety of ways.

This is not a history of Judah; attempts to prove historical accuracy are as misguided as criticisms of it as fabrication. It is a work of literary skill, significant for its theological relevance to the needs of the postexilic community and to any period that demands the rethinking of long-held beliefs.

PETER R. ACKROYD

Chronology. *This entry consists of two articles on dating systems used in the Bible and their correlation with modern historiography. The first article is on*

Israelite Chronology *and the second,* Early Christian Chronology.

Israelite Chronology

Biblical chronology may be considered under two aspects: historical or scientific chronology, which deals with the real chronology of actual events, and theoretical or theological chronology, which considers the meanings and purposes of chronological schemes used as a literary vehicle of religious conceptions. Individual statements may often be considered from either point of view; both aspects will be taken into account here.

Dating Systems. The Hebrew Bible has no universal dating system like our BCE/CE system. There are several modes in which chronological information is given:

Simple addition from the datum point of creation: For example, Adam was 130 years old when his son Seth was born, Seth was 105 when his first son Enosh was born (Gen. 5.3,6). By such addition, we can reckon that the flood began in the year 1656 AM (= Anno Mundi, i.e., from creation); however, this figure is not made explicit, and readers must do their own addition. Such reckoning can produce a clear chronology, with only some uncertainties, from creation down to the start of *Solomon's *Temple.

Regnal years of kings, often synchronically correlated with another line of kings (e.g., years of a Judean king are stated along with years of a contemporary king of Israel). Such dates are relative, not absolute; they were doubtless adequate for people of the time, but they do not tell us the actual date unless we can bring some other source to bear.

Later books used the Seleucid era, commencing 312/311 BCE, for example, "in the one hundred thirty-seventh year of the kingdom of the Greeks" (1 Macc. 1.10); this was used long and widely in Jewish life.

Modern Jewish reckoning, by years from creation: the Jewish year 5754 is 1993–1994 CE, implying that the world was created in 3761 BCE. Although figures going back to creation were important, dates are not stated in this way in the Bible; this mode of stating dates did not come into use until long after biblical times.

Basic Data. The main body of chronological material in the Hebrew Bible falls into three great segments:

From creation to Abraham's migration from Haran into Canaan. This is easily fixed by addition of the ages of the patriarchs, mainly in the *genealogies of Genesis 5 and 11. The period is split by the central event of the *flood. The figures differ in various texts, being mainly lower in the Samaritan and higher in the *Septuagint (LXX); thus the flood, which is 1656 AM in the Hebrew *Masoretic text, is 1307 AM in the Samaritan and 2242 AM in the LXX. One obscurity is the "two years after the flood" of Arpachshad's birth (Gen. 11.10), which is difficult to reconcile with the dates of his father Shem (Gen. 5.32).

From Abraham's migration to the start of Solomon's Temple. This segment falls into three smaller sections:

From Abraham's entry into Canaan to the entry of Jacob and his family into Egypt. This is easily calculated from the ages of the patriarchs and amounts to 215 years.

The period spent in Egypt is expressly given by Exodus 12.40 as 430 years. The Samaritan and the LXX, however, have the extra words "and in the land of Canaan" or the like; this means that the 430 years stretch back to Abraham's entry 215 years earlier, thus reducing the time in Egypt to 215 years. This reading, 430 years from Abraham to Moses, is followed by Paul (Gal. 3.17). According to the Hebrew text, subject to some minor uncertainties, the *Exodus was probably in 2666 AM.

The time from the Exodus to the start of the Temple (not its completion) is clearly stated as 480 years (1 Kings 6.1). This comprehensive statement bridges over the times of *Joshua, the *Judges, *Samuel, *Saul, and *David, for which there are many detailed chronological statements (e.g., the years of each of the Judges), but also many gaps (e.g., the dates of Joshua, Samuel, or Saul). The total of 480 bridges these uncertainties and provides a clear overarching connection between creation and Temple. The Temple building probably began in 3146 AM.

From Solomon onward we have figures for the years of each king. If we simply add up the figures for the Judean kings, from Solomon's fourth year, when the Temple construction began, to the destruction of Temple and kingdom, the figures in themselves are 430. Here, however, we can compare the figures with historical facts, and the period cannot have been more than about 372 years (Solomon's accession 962 BCE; start of Temple 958 BCE; destruction 587/586 BCE). The figures amounting to 430 have been accounted for through overlaps of reigns, co-regencies, textual errors, historical mistakes, and schematic periodization.

In addition, it is difficult to make the years of the Israelite kings fit exactly with those of the Judean.

After the destruction of kingdom and Temple, chronological information in the Hebrew Bible is fragmentary and sporadic. Some dates are given by the year of a *Persian emperor (e.g., Zech. 1.1; Ezra 1.1; Neh. 2.1), but the Hebrew Bible itself does not tell us how long these kings reigned or in what order they came, nor did later writers preserve an accurate memory of this. Later Jewish chronography assigned only thirty-two or fifty-two years to the entire Persian empire, which had in fact lasted over two hundred years, and similarly the number of actual Persian monarchs was unknown, hence the "four" kings of Persia (Dan. 7.6; 11.2). This leads to another aspect.

Dependence on Extrabiblical Information. Chronology cannot be worked out from biblical data alone; it depends on some synchronism with points established from sources other than the Bible. Traditional biblical chronology dovetailed biblical data into Greek and Roman history. Classical sources give a fairly exact dating of events back to the sixth century BCE, and this can be synchronized with the latest events recorded in Kings, thus providing an entry from extrabiblical history into biblical chronology. In modern times, knowledge of ancient *Egypt and *Mesopotamia, as well as *archaeological discovery, have provided a much richer network of evidence against which events reported in the Hebrew Bible can be set. Thus, an inscription of Shalmaneser III of *Assyria mentions *Ahab, king of Israel, in a battle (not mentioned in the Bible!) of 853 BCE, and *Jehu in 841; Jehu's revolt against the dynasty of Omri (2 Kings 9–10) is now placed in 842 BCE. This correlation of biblical data with extrabiblical information carries us back to about 1000 BCE, and without it we would not know the true duration of the kingdom. Key dates to remember are:

962 BCE   accession of Solomon
842   revolt of Jehu and crisis in royal house of both kingdoms
722   destruction of *Samaria and end of kingdom of *Israel
587/586   destruction of *Jerusalem and end of kingdom of *Judah

(*For a chronological table of the Kings of Israel and Judah, see* Judah, The Kingdom of.)

When we go back beyond the time of David, extrabiblical information is often not sufficiently specific to provide chronological exactitude; it may suggest nothing more precise than historical circumstances or social conditions that might have fitted with an event mentioned in the Bible. Biblical dates in the earlier stages, taken alone, leave us to question whether they rest on accurate memory or on theoretical schematism. Later, in the Persian period, though the dates of kings are well known from Persian and Greek sources, the Hebrew Bible may leave it vague as to which king of a certain name was involved—for example, whether Artaxerxes I or II, an uncertainty that affects the content of *Ezra and *Nehemiah.

Theoretical Chronology. Taken as a whole, the chronology of the Hebrew Bible, though containing true historical data, may have been theological rather than historical in its interest, a literary or legendary device that bore a religious message. Thus, the Genesis figures are part of the genealogies, in which persons live to ages like 930 or 969 years; this is true of Mesopotamian legend as well, in which a king in the beginnings of the world might reign for thirty-six thousand years or more (and eight kings might last 241,000 years down to the flood), with the figures dropping rapidly after the flood. Chronology of this sort belongs to legend or myth.

Some essential dates have strikingly round figures: 215 years from Abraham to Egypt, 430 years in Egypt, 430 for the figures of the kings when added up; 40 on the march from Egypt to Canaan, 480 from the Exodus to the Temple. Are not such figures theoretical? If, as is possible, the Exodus took place in 2666 AM, is it perhaps significant that this is almost exactly two-thirds of 4000?

While some chronological material comes from ancient legend, there are signs that figures were being adjusted and modified at a late date, such as the variations between the Masoretic, Samaritan, and Greek texts in Genesis 5. The book of Jubilees, a rewriting of Genesis and Exodus 1–14 from the second century BCE with an intense chronological interest, measures time in "jubilees" of forty-nine years, and ends at the entry of Israel into Canaan, exactly fifty jubilees or 2450 years from creation; like the Samaritan Pentateuch, it dates the flood to 1307 AM.

*Enoch, the seventh from Adam, lived 365 years—obviously a very significant number, and markedly different from others in the same genealogy—before he was taken away by God (Gen. 5.21–24). The book of Enoch has many contacts with Jubilees, and it is concerned with the calendar and the movement of the heavenly bodies; the number of days in a year was hotly debated in this period.

Eschatological expectation forms another likely aspect; it might be thought that the world would last a total round number of years. Major events like the Flood, the Exodus, and the construction of the Temple, were linked with that coming end by significant number sequences. Such sequences might also lead not to the final end of the world but to the establishment of a basic constitution (e.g., completion of Mosaic legislation and start of tabernacle worship), or to a decisive historical stage (the entry into Canaan in Jubilees). If, as has been suggested, a figure of 4000 was held in mind, the present biblical chronology might be predicated upon the rededication of the Temple (about 164 BCE) after its profanation by Antiochus, which would establish a connection with Daniel, as well as with the books of Enoch and Jubilees.

The antiquity of the Jewish people was an issue in Hellenistic times, when they were sometimes regarded as newcomers on the scene of world culture. Against this, *Josephus insisted on the ancient origins of the Jews; their possession of books that went back without interruption to the beginnings of the world could be a powerful argument. This may have motivated the higher figures of the chronology in the LXX.

Conclusion. Chronological interest is a very important element in the Hebrew Bible, though it is not obtrusive as in Jubilees and not all biblical sources were equally interested in it. The chronology formed an important part of the total shape of the Bible. New Testament authors were well aware of its details: Paul quoted the 430 years exactly, though he did not need the precise figure for his argument; Acts 7.4 is precise, though contrary to the natural sense of the Hebrew, in saying that Abraham migrated from Haran "after his father died" (cf. Gen. 11.26–32; 12.4). After New Testament times, biblical chronology continued as a normal and essential aspect of Christian culture, and was cultivated by such writers as Eusebius and Bede. Histories began with creation and continued up to what were then modern times. In the Reformation, Luther's *Supputatio annorum mundi* or chronological summary was regulative for German-speaking Protestantism. In the English-speaking world, James Ussher, Archbishop of Armagh (1581–1656), wrote his detailed chronology from creation (which he fixed in 4004 BCE) to just after the destruction of the Temple in 70 CE. In this he integrated biblical data with all known material of Greek and Roman chronology. Many English Bibles have enshrined his dates in their margins. Only in the nineteenth and twentieth centuries did biblical chronology lose its charm and come to be largely forgotten; even the more conservative and literalist reader of the Bible was no longer literal enough to take seriously the precision of biblical chronology. Now is the time for its literary and theological character to be appreciated once again.   JAMES BARR

Early Christian Chronology

No special era is used by the New Testament writers. While Jewish authors were familiar with the Syrian era, which began on 1 October 312 BCE (e.g., 1 Macc. 1.20, the year 143 = 169 BCE), no references of this kind are found in the New Testament. Here, as in the works of *Josephus, dates are given simply with regard to the number of years during which a contemporary ruler had been governing when the event in question happened. Thus, *John the Baptist is said to have begun preaching "in the fifteenth year of the reign of Emperor Tiberius" (Luke 3.1), which corresponds to 28 CE. Christian writers of subsequent centuries took over the Roman era in which the years were counted from the presumed foundation of Rome on 21 April 753 BCE (*"ab urbe condita"*). In the sixth century CE this era was replaced by the Christian era which is based on calculations of the Greek monk Dionysius Exiguus in Rome. Commissioned around 532 CE to coordinate the festival calendar of the church, he dated the *incarnation of Christ to 25 March of the Roman year 754, and this year became the year 1, starting from 1 January. Dionysius Exiguus made a slight error, since Matthew 2.1 dates the birth of Jesus to the days of King *Herod, who died in 4 BCE.

*Matthew explicitly connects the birth of Jesus with the government of King Herod (Matt. 2.1), and the reference to this ruler's successor Archelaus (2.22) proves that he meant Herod the Great (*see* Herodian Dynasty). The years during which Herod was the king of the Jews are known from Josephus. According to his colorful reports, Herod was elected king of the Jews by the Roman senate in 40 BCE (Josephus, *Ant.* 14.14.385, confirmed by Strabo, Tacitus, and Appian), and he died at springtime thirty-six years later, which gives us the year 4 BCE (*Ant.* 17.8.191; *War* 1.33.665). Matthew thus reports that Jesus was born some time before the year 4 BCE. Attempts have also been made to base a more specific dating on the star discovered by the *Magi (Matt. 2.2), but all identifications with a comet, a constellation, or a nova seem arbitrary, so that Matthew's reference to Herod remains the only fixed datum.

*Luke likewise regarded Jesus as born under Herod when he dated the birth of *John the Baptist to the days of this king (Luke 1.5) and indicated that Jesus was six months younger (1.26). In his infancy narrative, however, Luke connected the birth of Jesus with an enrollment for taxation ordered by Augustus and carried out under Quirinius (2.1–2). An enrollment arranged by Quirinius as governor of *Syria is known only from 6 CE, when Judea was made the property of Augustus to be administered by a procurator in Caesarea whose task it was to collect taxes for the emperor. This taxation of 6 CE caused a revolt in Judea (War 7.8.253–56; Ant. 18.1.3–10, 23–25), but did not involve the population of *Galilee, where *Joseph and *Mary lived and where Herod Antipas ruled as *tetrarch. Luke had probably heard of an earlier registration within the whole kingdom of Herod the Great, but was attracted by the famous taxation under Quirinius. (See Christmas; Roman Empire; Tribute and Taxation, article on Roman Empire.)

Concerning the ministries of John the Baptist and Jesus, the only chronological information available is the above-mentioned reference to John's first preaching in 28 CE (Luke 3.1) and a notice that Jesus was reproached for speaking with authority though he was not yet a senior of fifty years (John 8.57).

The capital punishment of the Baptist resulted from his criticism of the marriage between Herod Antipas and Herodias, whom he accused of adultery because the latter had been the wife of the former's brother (Matt. 14.4 par.). A further consequence of this marriage was that Antipas was attacked in the year 36 by the army of the *Nabatean king, whose daughter the tetrarch had divorced in order to marry Herodias (Josephus, Ant. 18.5.109–15). John's criticism of the tetrarch cannot have been uttered many years earlier, so that his death (ibid. 116–19) will have taken place around 32 CE.

Accordingly, the death of Jesus is preferably to be dated 33 CE, and in this year the political situation favored the trial against him. Shortly before, in 31 CE, Tiberius had deposed and executed Sejanus, who had been a cruel dictator in Rome and an especially great antagonist of the Jews; subsequently and most likely in 32 the emperor had ordered his representatives in the provinces to pay attention to Jewish interests (Philo, Legation to Gaius 161). This explains the exceptional rapport between *Pilate and the *Pharisees that led to the *crucifixion of Jesus.

As to a more exact dating of Jesus' last supper and his death, it has first to be observed that in Jewish tradition each day begins in the evening so that both events belonged to the same day (see Time, Units of). According to all four Gospels, the eucharist and the crucifixion took place just before *Passover on the so-called day of preparation (Grk. paraskeuē), which that year was a Friday, so that it served to prepare Passover and the Sabbath at the same time (Matt. 27.62; Mark 15.42; Luke 23.54; John 19.31). Contrary to what is often stated, the *synoptic and Johannine reports do not contradict each other in this point. In the Jewish calendar, the day of preparation for Passover, to which all four Gospels refer, had to be 14 Nisan. The beginning of this lunar month was established year by year according to the first visibility of the crescent moon in March, and though no exact timing was possible in those days, modern studies have shown that 14 Nisan fell on a Friday in two of the years in question: ca. 7 April in the year 30 and ca. 3 April in the year 33. The political factors mentioned above speak in favor of dating Jesus' last supper and crucifixion to an evening and the subsequent day around 3 April of the year 33. (See also Jesus Christ.)

The next New Testament events to be dated are the martyrdom of *Stephen and the conversion of *Paul (Acts 7.58; 9.4), and here the circumstances justify a dating to 36 CE. In this year, troubles with the Parthians led Vitellius, the governor of Syria, to secure Jewish goodwill: he deposed Pilate in Caesarea and appointed a dynamic high priest. He allowed the latter to rule independently, and thus created a Jewish interregnum until 37 CE, when a less powerful high priest was installed and subordinated to a new imperial procurator (Josephus, Ant. 18.4–5.88–125). Since, according to Luke, the high priest who sentenced Stephen to death is not reported to have sought consent from the Roman procurator as normally would have been required, and since he sent Paul as far as *Damascus in order to arrest dissidents, he must have had unusual political authority. Thus he can be identified with the above-mentioned high priest of 36 CE, so that Stephen's martyrdom in

Jerusalem and Paul's conversion at Damascus took place in that year.

Starting from the year 36, two later visits of Paul to Jerusalem can be dated with the aid of his letter to the *Galatians, where he refers to a first visit "after three years" and to a second "after fourteen years" (Gal. 1.18; 2.1). As usual, the initial year is included in the numbers, so that the apostle refers to visits occurring two and thirteen years after his conversion; he thus came to Jerusalem in 38 and 49 CE. The latter date is that of the *Apostolic Council, described from different perspectives by Luke and Paul (Acts 15.1–29; Gal. 2.1–10).

Before the Apostolic Council, Paul had undertaken his first missionary journey under the leadership of *Barnabas (Acts 13.1–14.28), and for this a suitable date is 47–48 CE. Paul's second journey (Acts 15.36–18.22) can be supposed to have lasted from 50 to 54 for the following reasons: He probably came in 52 to *Corinth and there met Aquila and Priscilla (Acts 18.2), who, together with other Jews, had been expelled from Rome by the emperor Claudius in 50 CE (Suetonius, Claudius 25.24). At any rate, it was in 52 that Paul was confronted with the proconsul Gallio in Corinth (Acts 18.12), because this governor of Greece is mentioned in an inscription at Delphi as holding office during that year. The eighteen months that Paul is said to have spent in Corinth (18.11) thus probably covered parts of the years 52 and 53, and so the whole second journey will have included the years 50–54.

The third journey of Paul (Acts 18.23–21.16) began shortly after his second journey, or around the year 55, and it probably ended in 58 CE. During this journey the apostle spent two years in the Roman province of *Asia (19.10), then a considerable time in Troas and Macedonia (2 Cor. 2.12–13), and three months in Greece (Acts 20.3). The subsequent captivity in Caesarea lasted for two years, as long as Felix was procurator there (Acts 24.27), and when the new procurator Festus had sent Paul to the emperor, the apostle had to spend two more years in Roman custody (28.30). Since Felix was deposed in 60 CE (when Nero had overthrown his powerful brother Pallas in Rome), Paul's captivity can be dated to parts of the years 58–60. The continuation of his trial under Festus and his journey to Rome thus probably took place in the year 60, and so the date of his custody for two years in Rome will have been 61–62.

It is also possible to give approximate dates

for the death of some early Christian leaders. The apostle *James was killed around 42 CE during a persecution arranged by King Agrippa I (called Herod in Acts 12.2). James, the brother of Jesus, who had presided at the Apostolic Council held in Jerusalem in 49 CE, was stoned in the year 62 on the initiative of the high priest (Josephus, Ant. 20.9.197–203). According to later sources, Peter and Paul were killed in Rome. This happened some time after the city's destruction by fire in 64 CE, which caused Nero to persecute the Christians there (Tacitus, Annals 15.44.4), probably at the beginning of the year 65.

Shortly before the Jewish war of 66–70 CE broke out, the Christians of Palestine are said to have emigrated to Transjordan (Eusebius, Church History 3.5.3). After the destruction of Jerusalem in 70 CE the separation of Judaism and Christianity became even more evident. Domitian's persecution of Christians (Rev. 1.9; etc.), which took place around 94–95 (1 Clement 1.1, 7.1; cf. Pliny, Epistles 10.96.6: twenty years before 114), is the last datable event referred to in the New Testament.

Since the New Testament books do not indicate when they were composed, their literary origin can be dated only approximately by such historical events as those mentioned above. Without this support all scholarly theories on the age of New Testament writings are speculative, and one should not accept any general tendency or common opinion as established truth.

BO REICKE

Church. In the Greek world, the term ekklēsia meant a group of citizens "called out" to assemble for political purposes. In the New Testament, ekklēsia signifies a group of believers in Jesus who are called together, and is translated as "church." The original Greek sense survives, however, when the author of Acts describes an assembly at *Ephesus in which citizens have a heated discussion about Paul and his preaching (Acts 19.32, 39, 41). The city clerk finally tells people to suspend their debate until the next regular ekklēsia.

In the *Septuagint ekklēsia is used interchangeably with synagogē to render Hebrew terms that mean assembly. One such occurrence from Psalm 22.22 is cited by the author of Hebrews: "in the midst of the congregation (ekklēsia) I will praise you" (Heb. 2.12).

*Paul regularly uses the term church (ekklēsia)

in his letters to address individual communities of believers (Rom. 16.1; 1 Cor. 1.2; 2 Cor. 1.1; 1 Thess. 1.1; 2 Thess. 1.1), and he uses the plural form to speak in general about groups such as "the churches of God in Christ Jesus that are in Judea" (1 Thess 2.14) and "all the churches of the saints" (1 Cor. 14.33). Paul does not have a developed sense of the church as a universal institution but rather sees local assemblies of believers functioning independently in separate locations. In a few cases, however, especially in reference to his persecution of the church of God (Gal. 1.3, 1 Cor. 15.9, Phil. 3.6), Paul's use of the term seems more generalized.

The term church appears only two times in the Gospels, both in *Matthew. One occurrence refers to a local community's role in disputes between believers (Matt. 18.17), while in the other, Jesus uses the term church in a much more expansive sense. Matthew's Jesus responds to *Peter's confession by saying "on this rock I will build my church" (Matt. 16.18). Whether the "rock" refers to Peter or to his confession is strongly debated, but either way, the verse conveys a sense of the church as a universal institution.

This universal sense is developed further in the Deutero-Pauline letters. *Ephesians and *Colossians elaborate on a Pauline image by referring to the church as the body of Christ (Eph. 1.22; Col. 1.24) and to Christ as the head of that body (Eph. 5.23, Col. 1.18). In Ephesians 5.23, Christ's headship of the church is used as justification for a husband's authority over his wife.

Ignatius of Antioch (ca. 100 CE) is the earliest known author to use the phrase "catholic church" when referring to the universality of the body of Christ (Smyrneans, 8). Unanimity becomes a key concept in later discussions of the church, as orthodox leaders stress catholicity in the face of challenges from various heterodox groups. Some versions of the Nicene Creed conclude with the formula "one holy catholic and apostolic church."   DANIEL N. SCHOWALTER

Circulation of the Bible. By the end of 1992, *translations of the entire Bible had been published in 329 languages, the New Testament in 758 additional languages, and individual books of the Bible in 910 other dialects and languages. All told, these 2,009 languages account for over eighty percent of the world's population. Yet with an estimated three thousand to six thousand languages in the world, *Bible Societies still face a major task in translating the scriptures.

The earliest translation of the Hebrew scriptures was into Greek (the *Septuagint), made in Alexandria in the third century BCE, and it was this form that New Testament writers knew and quoted. Ensuing translations followed fairly slowly in succeeding centuries. By 600 CE, the Gospels had been translated into eight languages: Latin, Gothic, Syriac, Coptic, Armenian, Georgian, Ethiopic, and Sogdian.

When Johannes *Gutenberg invented the art of printing with movable type in about 1450, a mere thirty-three languages had any translations of the scriptures. In fact, when the Bible Society movement began early in the nineteenth century, the Bible had been translated into only sixty-seven languages. Soon thereafter, however, the number skyrocketed: with the rise of the missionary movement in the nineteenth century, over four hundred languages received some part of the scriptures. By the end of the first half of the twentieth century, parts of the Bible had been published in five hundred additional languages. In many cases, the language in question had no alphabet before the Bible translator undertook to encode the language in written form.

Until relatively recently, missionaries, with the assistance of native speakers, were generally responsible for translating the Bible. Now, however, native speakers often assume primary responsibility, with missionaries sometimes serving as consultants. This has many virtues, since it is invariably easier for properly trained people to translate into their own mother tongue than into a foreign language, and the end product is likely to be more effective.

A crucial aspect of recent developments in Bible translation is the realization that cultural differences among peoples must be considered in order to assure that the text is meaningfully and accurately rendered. Often, a literal translation will result in wholly erroneous understanding; for instance, "the wicked will not stand in the judgment" (Ps. 1.6) was understood in one African language to mean that evil people will not be judged; and "smiting one's breast"—a sign of contrition and repentance in biblical times— was taken to mean self-congratulation. Alternately, a given language's syntax may be ill suited to convey, for example, rhetorical questions. In Hebrews 2.3, the writer is not actually looking for an escape when he asks, "How can we escape if we neglect such a great salvation?" Rather, he is declaring emphatically that there can be no escape whatsoever. In some languages and dialects, then, one must employ a negative formulation such as "There is no possible escape if we . . ."

In spite of such difficulties, the task of translators is to reproduce the message of the original text with the closest natural equivalent—an assignment that sounds simpler than it is. For instance, Amos 4.6, "I gave you cleanness of teeth in all your cities," is potentially perplexing, for it refers not to dental hygiene but to the results of a severe famine.

Over the past generation, biblical translators and revisers have often justified the preparation of several translations within a single language area, depending on the use that the rendering will serve. Basic types of translations to meet different needs are: simplified translations for new readers; common language translations for evangelistic purposes; standard or traditional translations to meet the needs of traditionally oriented readers; literary-liturgical translations employing the total resources of the language and intended primarily for church use.

As of the beginning of 1992, the United Bible Societies and associated groups were involved in approximately 608 language projects, of which 312 were languages in which at least one segment of the biblical text was being translated for the first time. The following statistical summary (see Table below) shows the number of different languages and dialects in which publication of at least one book of the Bible (designated "portions") had been registered as of 31 December 1992.

BRUCE M. METZGER

Circumcision. Circumcision is the ritualistic removal of the male's foreskin, practiced by many African, South American, and Middle Eastern peoples. Often performed at puberty, it may have originated as a rite of passage from childhood to adulthood; some biblical texts have been interpreted in this way (Gen. 17.25; Exod 4.24–26). In Jewish tradition, following biblical commandments (Gen. 17.12; 21.4; Lev. 12.3), males are normally circumcised at eight days of age. Proselyte males are circumcised before admission into the community.

Although some rabbis held that males who had been born Jews could maintain their status without circumcision, across the centuries others demanded excommunication for those not circumcised (e.g., Gen. 17.14). According to one passage, even Moses would have died had his son not been circumcised (Exod. 4.24–26). Nevertheless, according to Joshua 5.2–9, apparently those born in the wilderness were not circumcised until they entered Canaan. Then the Lord required that they be circumcised, presumably to enable them to celebrate *Passover (Josh. 5.10; see Exod. 12.48). Later scribes modified this tradition by improbably having them be circumcised "a second time" (Josh. 5.2).

Antiochus Epiphanes had women and their sons who had been circumcised despite his proscription killed (1 Macc. 1.60). Some Palestinian Jews managed to undo their circumcisions, stood apart from the holy contract, yoked themselves to the *gentiles, and sold themselves to do evil (1 Macc. 1.15). This does not necessarily mean that they performed some sort of surgical reconstruction, for these four items are all parallel ways of making the same statement, that liberal Jews became so completely Hellenized that orthodox Jews said they were no longer circumcised. This was probably insult rather than fact, just as male Jews who mingled with gentiles socially and in business were called "harlots," as if they had mingled sexually. There may, however, have been liberal Jews and Jewish Christians who stretched the remaining foreskin to

CIRCULATION OF THE BIBLE

Continent or Region	Portions	New Testaments	Bibles	Totals
Africa	231	223	122	576
Asia	227	167	104	498
Australia/New Zealand/Pacific Islands	160	139	26	325
Europe	105	24	60	189
North America	43	20	7	70
Mexico/Caribbean Islands/Central and South America	142	197	9	348
Constructed Languages	2	0	1	3
Totals	910	770	329	2,009

make circumcision less obvious (1 Cor. 7.18). "Circumcision" was also used metaphorically. Someone who did not accept divine teaching was said to have an uncircumcised ear (Jer. 6.10), and a stubborn person had an uncircumcised heart (Lev. 26.41; Jer. 9.25–26).

Circumcision was traced back to the *covenant or contract God made with *Abraham, and thus is widely practiced by Muslims as well as Jews. It was called the "sign of the covenant" (Gen. 17.11), the covenant in the flesh (Gen. 17.13), and the "covenant of circumcision" (Acts 7.8); the traditional European Jewish (i.e., Yiddish) term for circumcision, *bris*, is an alternate pronunciation of the word for "covenant" (Hebr. *bĕrît*). In earliest Christianity, there was considerable debate over the requirement of circumcision (Acts 15.1–21; Gal. 2.3–14); Paul, however, held that circumcision was part of the old contract that had been superseded and was therefore no longer required (Gal. 6.15), and his view ultimately became normative for Christians (*see* Law, *article on* New Testament Views).

GEORGE WESLEY BUCHANAN

Cities. A city, as distinguished from a large village, reflects a more complex social organization. It typically exhibits improved technology, manufacture for sale, international commerce, and literate *scribes who produce written records. Political power extends over a wider area and is maintained by an army; walls and towers normally protect a city. In ancient times, every city had one or more temples, and the rulers typically claimed that one or more gods supported their authority.

The Israelites were curious about the origin of a city such as *Babylon, as the legend of the tower of *Babel shows (Gen. 11.1–9). Indeed, the earliest complete cities known to us, such as *Ur, arose in Mesopotamia. Babylon had straight, narrow streets at right angles, sumptuously adorned gates, a *ziggurat (the "tower"), and a processional street.

Egyptian cities were essentially residences of the Pharaohs or storage depots for a centralized agricultural economy. All were on the *Nile or in the delta and carried on international trade. Thebes had monumental temples and sacred precincts.

*Jericho, in the Jordan valley, was fortified with walls and towers in the prepottery Neolithic period (perhaps 7000 BCE) and is thus the earliest such settlement discovered anywhere.

At the time of the Israelite entry into Canaan, there were fortified towns with local rulers. *Jerusalem was such a place when *David conquered it from the *Jebusites and made it his capital (2 Sam. 5.6–10). His son *Solomon built a temple in Syrian style, engaged in international commerce, and made Jerusalem the administrative seat of a large realm, which he divided into districts. His models were the great *Phoenician cities of Tyre and Sidon; Hiram of Tyre provided building materials and skilled workmen for the *Temple (1 Kings 5–6). At that time, Jerusalem had an area of thirteen hectares (thirty-three acres) and a population of about five thousand. *Nineveh in Assyria was more than fifty times larger.

After Solomon's death, the revolt of the northern tribes, and the founding of the kingdom of *Israel, Omri ultimately established his capital at *Samaria (1 Kings 16.23–24). The northern kings were in close commercial and cultural relations with Syria and Phoenicia, and Samaria was a small fortified city.

Beginning perhaps in the eighth century BCE, a unique type of city-state developed in Greece. The citizens normally included merchants, free workmen, and landowners in the surrounding countryside. In *Athens and some other cities, a tyrant or an oligarchy sometimes ruled, at other times a democratic assembly. The pattern is found in Asia Minor and in colonies established by the older cities. Each city-state tended to be fiercely independent and jealous of its rivals, yet in some regions cities formed themselves into leagues.

Hippodamus of Miletus, the first Greek city-planner known to us (ca. 450 BCE), seems to have established the pattern of a rectangular grid for city streets. A typical Hellenistic city had an agora or marketplace, porticoes, temples, and other public buildings, all arranged for convenience and artistic effect.

The conquests of *Alexander the Great led to the founding of many cities on the Greek model. In general, he respected the autonomy of city-states that had been loyal to him. His successors in Egypt, the Ptolemies, built Alexandria as a Macedonian-Greek city that was not only a capital but also became a great center of learning. The Seleucids of Syria founded *Antioch and made it the capital of their large empire. Older cities such as Tyre and Sidon continued to be commercially important. When Rome took control of Asia Minor in the second century BCE, the forms of city autonomy were preserved, if not the substance. At this time, *Ephesus was capital of the province of *Asia.

Palestine was affected by these changes. After the *exile, Jerusalem was ruled by high priests under *Persian overlordship; this continued under the Ptolemies and Seleucids. Judas Maccabeus and his successors made Jerusalem and Judea more or less independent from 165 to 63 BCE (see Maccabees, The Books of the). After this, Rome controlled the region and after a few years installed *Herod the Great as a client king. It was he who reconstructed Jerusalem on the model of a Greco-Roman city, with a principal north-south street (cardo) and a main east-west street (decumanus) crossing it. He built aqueducts, a theater and an amphitheater, and a magnificent new temple. By this time, nearly ten thousand people lived in Jerusalem. Caesarea on the seacoast was transformed into a commercial city and one of the greatest ports of the Mediterranean. Herod also rebuilt Samaria and named it Sebaste in honor of the emperor Augustus. Most other settlements in his realm were only large towns or villages.

After Herod's death and the deposition of his son Archelaus, Judea became a minor Roman province. *Galilee and Perea (Transjordan) went to his son Herod Antipas as tetrarch. At first his capital was at Sepphoris, north of *Nazareth, but he rebuilt Tiberias and moved his capital there.

The northeast region was ruled by Philip, another son of Herod the Great, who built the cities of Bethsaida Julias and Caesarea Philippi. Within this area there was also the *Decapolis, a league of about ten city-states, of which *Damascus was the northernmost and greatest. All but one (Scythopolis, or Bethshan) were east of the *Jordan. Gadara and Gerasa are mentioned in the Gospels (Matt. 8.28; Mark 5.1). These cities were all Hellenistic in culture, and they preserved a measure of autonomy under the Roman province of Syria.

Paul's travels took him into *Arabia, perhaps near the *Nabatean caravan city of Petra, and to many of the chief cities in Asia Minor and Greece. Among these, Antioch in Pisidia and Philippi were Roman colonies. *Corinth, like Ephesus, was a great port. It was refounded by Julius Caesar after it had been destroyed by the Romans a century before.

Rome was the center of government for the whole empire, and was its most populous city. The early emperors had magnificent public buildings constructed. Rome produced little; rather it consumed, and goods and wealth flowed there from all parts of the empire.

See also Archaeology and the Bible.

SHERMAN ELBRIDGE JOHNSON

Cities of Refuge. Six cities set aside to provide safe haven for someone guilty of an accidental killing. There is some uncertainty about who decided the fate of the manslayer, whether the *elders of his hometown (Deut. 19.11–13) or the elders of the city to which he had fled (Josh. 20.4) or "the congregation" (Josh. 20.6). In any case, if the killing was judged to be premeditated, the manslayer was returned to his hometown for execution; if it was judged accidental, he was allowed to reside in the city of refuge until the death of the high priest (which constituted, in a sense, exile).

Most scholars agree that in the Bible the basic principle of asylum (Exod. 21.12–14; 1 Kings 2.28–34) evolved into the specification of six cities of refuge (Deut. 4.41–43; 19.1–13; Josh. 20.1–9) and into the linking of these with the forty-eight levitical cities (Num. 35; Josh. 21; 1 Chron. 6.54–81). Opinions as to the historicity of the actual use of these cities of refuge vary. Some hold that these cities never actually served as cities of refuge but were part of a utopian restoration program developed by priestly circles after the destruction of Judah (ca. 550–400 BCE). Others think that they served as part of the reform of King *Josiah (ca. 640–609 BCE). A third group believes that this institution was a reality, but fully so only during the United Monarchy (ca. 1025–925 BCE), because some of the cities were lost to invaders after the kingdom split (1 Kings 22; 2 Kings 15.29). One nagging question for proponents of each view is the exclusion of *Jerusalem from the lists of cities of refuge, particularly after *David had moved the central *altar there (see Exod. 21.12–14; 1 Kings 2.28–34).

See also Murder.   TIMOTHY M. WILLIS

Clean and Unclean. See Purity, Ritual.

Clothing. The nations around Palestine in the ancient Near East have left stone monuments depicting the life of the people and their garments. From Palestine we have few such monuments. Cloth disintegrates, and thus the identification of cloth and clothing is a difficult task. Fortunately, the nations that did leave stone monuments occasionally depicted people from the region of Palestine and Syria. The clothing of the surrounding nations is instructive but not necessarily normative. Yet some significant archaeological evidence does exist, including an ivory carving from *Megiddo, from about the thirteenth century BCE, depicting a victory celebration (see J. B. Pritchard, *The Ancient Near East in Pictures* [1969], no. 332). This carving not only displays actual Palestinian dress but also exhibits the Middle Eastern cultural attitude toward clothing itself. From the court there are the king, wearing an ankle-length robe (decorated around the neck and on the lower fringe), a knee-length cloak, and a togalike shawl over one shoulder (decorated similar to a garment worn by the officer in the chariot; thus, this garment may be related to the king's position as head of the military); a prince or priest, wearing a decorated head covering (servants had to cover their heads in the presence of their masters; before the king even the naked prisoners have their heads covered), a decorated cloak that covers his arms to the wrists, a cassock-type garment that comes to just above the knees, and an embroidered long robe reaching almost to the ground; a musician, with a plain cassock and a lightly decorated long robe; and palace servants wearing a single long robe that reaches to the ankles and to the elbows. Related to the military are a military officer in a chariot wearing an elbow-length cloak, something covering his arms, and protection over his thighs; a lower-ranking officer with headgear and short kilt; an armed soldier with headgear; and naked prisoners. The higher-ranking people wore more clothes; nakedness meant humiliation. Men of dignity cover the entire body, even the legs; the shame of uncovering the legs is described, for example, in 2 Samuel 10.4–5 and Isaiah 47.2.

Materials. The earliest form of clothing in the Middle East as elsewhere was apparently leaves. Tribes in the southern highlands of Ethiopia still wear leaves for working in streams and fields. Such clothing is indicated in Genesis 3.7.

The skins of animals were used for clothing at a very early stage and continued in use as a symbol of an ascetic life-style (see Mark 1.6; cf. 2 Kings 1.8).

Before the development of metals, hair could only be plucked from animals. In spite of this, goat-hair tents were constructed and felt was pounded out for caps and other uses. Some wool was plucked during the Bronze Age for clothing, but with the coming of the Iron Age shears were invented, which greatly assisted the development of woolen cloth.

Flax, and later cotton, were grown and manufactured into clothing.

Manufacture. The spinning wheel has never reached the Middle East. Spinning was and in some isolated areas still is done by a simple handheld spindle. The wool/cotton is first "carded" to make the fibers parallel. It is then formed into long, continuous strips of fibers. These strips are then loosely wound onto a U-shaped bent stick. The spinner's hand slips through the lower part of the U and the loosely wound strips of fibers extend out of the top of the hand. The second piece of equipment is a thin dowel about 35 cm (14 in) in length, with a wooden or stone crosspiece/weight near the top. The spinner twists the end of the strip of loose fibers into a length of thread, attaches it to the lower end of the weighted spindle, and then hooks the developing thread into a metal catch on the upper end. With a deft flip of the spindle the weighted stick is set spinning and gradually feeds the loose fibers from the other hand into the thread as it forms. The spindle drops as the thread forms. In the meantime the spindle loses speed. The spinner then grasps the spindle, unhooks the thread from the metal catch at the upper end of the spindle, winds up the newly formed thread onto the lower end of that same spindle, again hooks the thread into the metal catch at the upper end of the spindle, and once more twirls the spindle between the thumb and forefinger, releasing it to spin suspended in air like a top, and starts again to feed the fibers into the twist as new thread is formed. The evenness and thickness of the thread formed is related to the style and skill of the spinner. After months of spinning the family will have enough thread to approach the village weaver for the making of a piece of cloth.

Both the vertical loom and the simpler horizontal loom seem to have been used, the latter probably being more prevalent. Four cubits seems to have been a standard width (cf. Exod. 26.1–2, 7–8). Cloth could be made in long pieces for curtains and hangings, or a single garment could be woven entirely on the loom. Thus a seamless robe (see John 19.23) could come from the loom needing only to be trimmed and finished.

Cloth was made more beautiful and attractive in a variety of ways. Patterns in the weave itself were possible. Dyeing was extensively used. Indigo on white wool produced blue, and on yellow wool, green. Madder or kermes created reds. The Tyrian purple was famous for royal robes. The robes seen in the Megiddo ivory described above demonstrate extensive use of embroidery.

Garments. Dress in different ages was inevitably influenced by the wide variety of cultures that dealt with or ruled Palestine. Furthermore, specialized clothing existed for special classes and occasions. There were garments for kings, priests, and prisoners, as well as for mourners.

The dress of men was made up of a loincloth, a shirt/robe, and a cloak. Footwear, belt, and headdress completed their attire. Women wore various types of headcovering and in certain periods veils to cover the face.

The loincloth could be cloth or leather and was common to the military (note the soldier in the Megiddo ivory). The shirt/robe was the standard indoor dress for all classes of people; all of the people around the throne in the Megiddo ivory are wearing them. The outer, heavier cloak was the basic garment of the poor; it was doubled for a blanket at night. Thus, the law demanded that such a cloak be returned before nightfall to anyone who had left such a garment in pledge for a debt (Exod. 22.26; Deut. 24.10–13; cf. Amos 2.8). A belt or sash was essential to hold in the loose-fitting robe, both to protect the garment and to allow for freedom of movement. If in danger of being soiled by menial tasks, a worker would "gird up his loins," taking the lower edge of the robe and tucking it into the belt.

Women traditionally covered their heads. Such a standard was demanded by the rabbis of the first century CE, because the hair was considered a critical part of a woman's beauty, which should not be on display to the common eye. Paul urges Corinthian women to be sensitive to the cultural traditions of the community and not give unnecessary offense (cf. 1 Cor. 11.2–16).

Across the centuries sandals have been the traditional foot covering. Lack of any such covering gradually became a sign of servanthood; hus the prodigal son was given sandals (Luke 15.22).

See also Fringes.   KENNETH E. BAILEY

Colossians, The Letter of Paul to the.
Outline.

Authenticity. The Pauline authorship of Colossians has often been challenged over the last hundred and fifty years. The grounds for this questioning concern the language and style of the letter; more recently it has been argued that there are major differences between Colossians and the theology of the main Pauline letters, particularly in relation to the person and cosmic work of Christ, the church as the body of Christ, and early Christian tradition.

But such arguments against the authenticity of Colossians are not conclusive. First of all, it must be admitted that many expressions used in Colossians show decided Pauline peculiarities of style. The similarities and points of contact extend to theological terminology, such as the expressions "in Christ" (1.2, 4, 28), "in the Lord" (3.18, 20; 4.7, 17), and "with Christ" (2.12, 20; 3.1, 3), including exposition about being united with Christ in *baptism (2.11–12). Second, the thirty-four words that occur in Colossians but nowhere else in the New Testament ought to be considered in light of the fact that such hapax legomena also turn up in considerable numbers in other letters that are acknowledged to be Pauline (*Galatians, for example, has thirty-one words that recur nowhere else in the New Testament). It is reasonable to assume that several unusual terms appear in Colossians because of the heresy that Paul is combating. Third, the theological developments are consistent with the apostle's earlier teaching.

Colossians, as well as its companion letter Philemon, is present in the Pauline corpus as far back as we can trace its existence, that is, at least as early as Marcion, about 140 CE.

Date. Colossians is one of three or four letters written by *Paul at about the same time and sent to various churches in the Roman province of *Asia. He was then in prison (probably in Rome), and so these letters are called the captivity epistles. Colossians seems to have been written fairly early in this imprisonment, about 60–61 CE.

The Church at Colossae. The Christian community at Colossae came into existence during a period of vigorous missionary activity associated with Paul's Ephesian ministry (ca. 52–55 CE), recorded in Acts 19. Paul was assisted by several coworkers through whom a number of churches were planted in the province of Asia. Among these were the congregations of the Lycus Valley, Colossae, Laodicea, and Hierapolis (Map 14:E3), which were the fruit of Epaphras's endeavor (Col. 1.7, 8; 4.12, 13). A native of Colossae (4.12) who probably became a Christian during a visit to Ephesus, Epaphras was "a faithful minister of Christ"; as Paul's representative (1.7) he had taught the Colossians the gospel.

The many allusions to the former lives of the readers suggest that most were *gentile converts. They had once been utterly out of harmony with God, enmeshed in *idolatry and slavery to sin, but God had reconciled them to himself (1.21–22). As gentiles who had previously been without God and without hope, they had been united to Christ in his death, burial, and *resurrection (2.11, 12, 20; 3.1, 3). As members of his body, they had his life within them and could look forward to the day when they would share in the fullness of his glory (3.4).

The picture is thus drawn of a Christian congregation obedient to the apostolic gospel, and for which the apostle can give heartfelt thanks to God (1.4–6). He knows of their "love in the Spirit" (1.8) and is delighted to learn of their orderly Christian lives and the stability of their faith in Christ (2.5).

Occasion of the Letter. Epaphras had paid Paul a visit in Rome and informed him of the state of the churches in the Lycus Valley. While much of the report was encouraging, one disquieting feature was the attractive but false teaching recently introduced into the congregation; if unchecked, it would subvert the gospel and bring the Colossians into spiritual bondage. Paul's letter, then, is written as a response to this urgent need.

The Colossians' "Heresy." Nowhere in the letter does Paul give a formal exposition of the Colossians' "heresy"; its chief features can be detected only by piecing together and interpreting his counterarguments. Some have questioned whether there was a "Colossian heresy" at all. But in light of 2.8–23 with its references to "fullness," specific ascetic injunctions ("Do not handle!" etc., v. 21), regulations about food and holy days, unusual phrases that seem to be catchwords of Paul's opponents, and the author's strong emphasis on what Christ has already achieved by his death and resurrection, it is appropriate to speak of a "heresy" that had just begun to make inroads into the congregation.

The teaching was set forth as "philosophy" (2.8), based on "tradition" (an expression that denotes its antiquity, dignity, and revelatory character), which was supposed to impart true knowledge (2.18, 23). Basically, the heresy seems to have been Jewish, because of the references to food regulations, the *Sabbath, and other prescriptions of the Jewish calendar. *Circumcision is mentioned (2.11) but did not appear as one of the legal requirements.

This Judaism was different from that against which the churches of Galatia had to be warned; rather, it was one in which asceticism and mysticism were featured, and where *angels, principalities, and powers played a prominent role in *creation and the giving of the *Law. They were regarded as controlling the lines of communication between God and humankind, and so needed to be placated by strict observances. This teaching is to be read against the background of ascetic and mystical forms of Jewish piety (as evidenced, for example, at *Qumran). It was for a spiritual elite who were being urged to press on in wisdom and knowledge so as to attain true "fullness." "Self-abasement" (2.18, 23) was a term used by the opponents to denote ascetic practices that were effective for receiving visions of heavenly mysteries and participating in mystical experiences. The "mature" were thus deemed able to gain spiritual entrance into heaven and join in the angelic worship of God as part of their present experience (2.18).

Paul's Reply. The apostle issues a strong warning to the Colossians to be on their guard lest the false teachers carry them off as spoil "by philosophy and empty deceit" (2.8), from the truth into the slavery of error. Although they had set forth their teaching as "tradition," Paul rejects any suggestion of its divine origin. It was a human fabrication, and in reply he sets it over against the tradition of Christ—not merely the tradition that stems from the teaching of Christ, but that which finds its embodiment in Christ (2.6). Jesus Christ is the image of the invisible God (1.15), the one who incorporates the fullness of the divine essence (2.9). In a magnificent hymnic passage in praise of Christ as the Lord in creation and in reconciliation (1.15–20), it is asserted that Christ is the one through whom all things were created, including the principalities and powers that figured so prominently in the Colossian heresy. All things have been made in him as the sphere, through him as the agent, and for him as the ultimate goal of all creation (v. 16).

Those who have been incorporated into Christ have come to fullness of life in the one who is master over every principality and power (2.10). They need not seek perfection anywhere else but in him. It is in him, the one in whose death, burial, and resurrection they have been united (2.11, 12), that the totality of wisdom and knowledge is concentrated and made available to all his people—and not just in some elite group.

The apostle's criticisms are trenchant, even devastating (2.16–23). To place oneself under rules and regulations like those of v. 21 is to return to slavery to the forces overthrown by Christ (v. 20). Any teachers who lay claim to exalted heavenly visions as a prelude to fresh revelations are puffed up. Worst of all, the arrogance in these private religious experiences comes from not maintaining contact with Christ the head: they are severed from the source of life and unity (v. 19).

Ethical Teaching. Often in Paul's letters, doctrinal instruction is followed by ethical teaching (cf. Rom. 12.1; Gal. 5.1). The same feature is evident in Colossians where the conjunction "therefore" (3.5) links the practical injunctions with the theological basis for right behavior. A lengthy hortatory section (3.5–4.6) follows, with four distinctive catchwords of early Christian catechesis at the head of each paragraph: "put to death" (3.5–11; cf. also "put away," v. 8); "put on" (3.12–17); "be subject" (3.18–4.1); and "watch and pray" (4.2–6). In the third of these, "be subject," directions about the mutual duties of members of a Christian household are given. (*See also* Ethical Lists.)   PETER T. O'BRIEN

Computers and the Bible. Just as all humanistic study of ancient texts is enhanced by the application of computing technologies, the modern study of biblical texts is increasingly being transformed by the microcomputer revolution. In particular, electronic digital media and computer programs are ideally suited to the tasks of organization, manipulation, storage, and dissemination of textual information. The democratization of "personal computer" technology enables anyone who uses a computer for writing or accounting tasks to explore scriptural texts with associated linguistic data bases and reference tools in a digital environment.

Manuscript Collation and Production of Critical Editions. Computer programs help scholars reconstruct whole "texts" from ancient manuscript fragments in the same way that programs assist archaeologists in reconstructing ceramic vessels: once the physical and textual features of manuscript fragments are described, pattern-matching programs may be used to hypothesize text reconstruction based upon groupings and physical joins. When individual texts are restored and fully encoded, programs using "genetic" knowledge may be used to suggest stemmatic (genealogical) and typological relationships, dividing texts or recensions into families. Manuscript evidence may then be manipulated programmatically to create critical editions of the text, whether on a small scale or in the production of a major edition. The advantages of creating paper critical editions from electronic data bases are great: far fewer mistakes are made in printing, and the logical and physical formats of print editions are entirely negotiable, being defined in variable sets of rules similar to electronic style sheets. (*See also* Printing and Publishing, *articles on* Production and Manufacturing *and* Economics.)

Data Bases for Linguistic and Literary Annotation. Biblical texts held in simple electronic format are immediately useful since they may be edited, queried, and displayed in various ways. More subtle inquiry into the text requires that words, clauses, sentences, paragraphs, pericopes—even individual characters within words—be supplied with linguistic and literary description. Computer programs have been used to "parse" texts, assigning lexical and grammatical features to words, but in general these annotations must be made manually. Morphological data bases have been created for the Hebrew Bible, New Testament, *Septuagint, and related corpora. Each word might be lemmatized (given a normalized spelling and dictionary form), augmented with a morphological description and similar linguistic-literary annotations. Literary structural markers are placed within the texts, in addition to markers used in canonical referencing schemes such as *chapters and verses. Once descriptive enhancements are made to the text, scholars may frame queries in terms of lexical, grammatical and syntactic textual features, not merely in terms of a fixed character stream. Of course, all assignment of literary and linguistic markup is subjective, so the results of searches, however quantified, must also be qualified. In addition to the widely accessible linguistic data bases for biblical texts, rich collections of rabbinic, Greek and Latin (classical, medieval, epigraphic-ephemeral), Muslim, and Buddhist text materials are also publicly available.

Dynamic Concording. Perhaps the most popular computer applications for general users are programs that permit dynamic "concording" of texts and user-specified displays of text in *concordance formats. Whereas printed concordances are static (i.e., based upon a dictionary form or other organizing principle), a computer concordance program is dynamic. Thus, rather than scan excerpted passages containing the single word "compassion," a user specifies the search criteria, limited only by the research goals and imagination. These are some examples of searches: all sentences containing "wine" or "strong drink," as well as "joy"; all verses in the Septuagint containing more than two imperative verb forms; all conditional clauses in the book of Exodus; all interrogative sentences in the NRSV version of the book of Job. Of course, the concordance query may address only those features supported by the data base and search program.

Hypertext and Hypermedia Displays. Because the Bible has been the object of intensive textual focus for many centuries, a rich network of commentary and linguistic annotation has grown up around it. A relatively new technology for managing this network of knowledge is called "hypertext." Hypertext, and hypermedia, which includes digitized graphic images and other media formats, exploits a primary distinguishing feature of "electronic" text: nonlinearity. An electronic document may be rearranged, compressed, expanded, split into logical subdocuments, or in other ways liberated from its linear-sequential format as determined in traditional books. The concept of linking primary text with its reference works (grammar, lexicon, encyclopedia, commentary, theological wordbook) and with "parallel" texts has led to the creation of electronic books, usually scanned or keypunched, using standard reference tools. In a hypertext computer environment, each biblical verse or single word of base text is linked to portions of documents in the associated works. A hypertext application with several windows makes it possible to enjoy synchronous scrolling of several parallel texts or text versions or synchronized display of commentary text with base text. Control and navigation within such networks are not yet perfected, but hypertext technology shows great promise for individualized and interdisciplinary study of biblical texts.

Critical Study of the Bible. Most computer applications described above are general, conceptually simple, and noncontroversial. The use of quantitative and computational linguistics methodologies for the critical study of biblical texts is still immature by comparison. Within small corners of the world of biblical studies, computing techniques have been used to study such historical- and literary-critical features as textual transmission (subtle trends in spelling), authorship (unity or composite character of texts, measuring subconscious parameters of authorial style), metrical systems, translational features in ancient versions, and syntax (word order, clause patterns). The impact on mainline biblical studies has been minimal, though not insignificant. Some of the chief obstacles to acceptance of quantitative and computational methods are the difficulty of providing formal conceptual models and text representation schemes for critical inquiry; the greater appropriateness of currently understood methods to synchronic study of texts, rather than to higher-order analytic investigation; and the preference of biblical scholars for older, proven methods of research and publishing, with concomitant slowness to embrace newer methods of working in the global electronic workspace.

Conclusion. The growing popularity of international academic networks for collaborative research, the rapidly improving software for electronic publishing, and newer conceptual models for managing multilingual text all promise a bright future for computing in biblical studies. A point of critical mass has already been reached in the popular sector among Bible enthusiasts; the equivalent threshold of scholarly involvement has nearly been crossed. As trends increase toward compact mass storage (one CD-ROM disk now contains the equivalent of 150 books) and smaller, more powerful microcomputers, the growth of humanities computing appears certain. Current reports on these developments may be found in the conference activities and publication organs of the Society of Biblical Literature's Computer Assisted Research Group (CARG) and the Association Internationale Bible et Informatique (AIBI), and in annual sections of the *Humanities Computing Yearbook* (Oxford).

ROBIN C. COVER

Concordances. The understanding of a concordance is well reflected in the title of the first concordance of the complete Bible in English, published in 1550 by John Marbeck: *A Concordance, that is to saie, a work wherein by the ordre of the letters A B C, ye maie reddly find any words conteigned in the whole Bible, so often as it is there expressed or mensioned.* A concordance lists alphabetically and in their context the words that occur in a specified writing or group of writings, with citations of where they may be found.

Concordances in general vary in what words from a corpus they include. Exhaustive concordances include every word. Some concordances exclude very frequent words, or include only words of importance for some particular purpose, or specific types of words. Thus, there can be a concordance of words that occur fewer than a hundred times, of theological terms, or of proper names.

Concordances vary in how much context they provide for each word. Works giving no context but providing citations of where the words occur have historically been called concordances, but they might more properly be called indexes.

Concordances also vary in how they list words. Graphic concordances list the form of a word as it occurs in the text. They are often satisfactory for languages that have few prefixes, like English, since most related forms of a word are listed in fairly close proximity. Lexical concordances list words by the dictionary form of the word. These are necessary for languages like Hebrew, in which the tense and person of verbs may be changed by adding prefixes.

In addition, biblical concordances vary in what books (Hebrew Bible, New Testament, Apocrypha) and what language version of the Bible (Hebrew, Greek, Latin, King James Version English, etc.) they include.

The fact that the Bible exists in many *translations has meant that users of a translation are often interested not only in a word and the contexts in which it is found, but in what word or words in the original language of the texts are being translated. A monumental work of this type is *A Concordance to the Septuagint*, begun by Edwin Hatch, completed by Henry Redpath, and

published in 1897. It included several Greek versions of the Old Testament with the Hebrew words that presumably were being translated. Such a concordance is referred to as a dual language or analytical concordance.

The earliest biblical concordance known is to the Latin Bible by Antony of Padua made in the early thirteenth century. More influential, however, was the *Concordantia S. Jacobi* compiled in 1230 under the direction of Hugo of St. Caro. It was the source on which later Latin concordances were based.

The earliest Hebrew concordance was produced by Rabbi Isaac Nathan ben Kalonymos in 1448 and published in 1523. The revision by John Buxtorf in 1632 was the basis for most later Hebrew concordances.

While earlier concordances in manuscript form are mentioned, the earliest published Greek concordance of the Old Testament is *Concordantiae Graecae versionis vulgo dictae LXX interpretum* by Abraham Trommius in 1718. The first concordance of the Greek New Testament was that of Sixtus Birck (Xystus Betulejus) in 1546.

Probably the most influential and broadly published English concordance was Alexander Cruden's *A Complete Concordance to the Holy Scriptures of the Old and New Testaments* (1737).

Because of the labor and time involved and the frequency of errors, in the past it was natural that once a concordance of a text was published, later concordances of that text tended to be based on earlier concordances. This has changed radically with the introduction of the *computer and the encoding of large numbers of texts in electronic form.

The earliest computer-generated concordances were the KWIC (KEY WORD IN CONTEXT) concordances that were generated without reference to the language of the text, except to know whether the writing goes from right to left or vice versa. The usefulness of these graphic concordances depends on the nature of the language involved.

A process called "tagging" (introducing into a text codes that give information about the individual words) has made possible the automatic production of lexical concordances. These are very similar to the KWIC concordances. In addition to information about the dictionary forms of words, tags may also include morphological and syntactic information. This creates the possibility of generating "concordances" of information other than words. One may have a concordance that arranges all the nouns in the Bible together, subdividing them by how they are used in the sentence. Subjects, objects of verbs, and objects of prepositions are listed together rather than with other occurrences of the same word.

The "aligning" of texts, in which the words in two or more texts are correlated, has made possible the automatic creation of dual language or analytic concordances. By both aligning and tagging texts, a wide range of concordances can be created.

The computer has also made it practical to produce and publish concordances of other languages and groups of texts that are important to students of the Bible. Concordances exist for the *Ugaritic literature and the nonbiblical *Dead Sea Scrolls.

With tagged and/or aligned texts available in electronic form, it is possible to develop computer programs that allow the user to define the kind of concordance desired and to have the concordances generated on the spot and displayed on the screen. Today the electronic texts created by earlier scholars, rather than their concordances, are the source for new concordances.

Concordances are useful to the casual reader who wants to know where a familiar quotation is found, to the student who wants to see Paul's use of a theological term, to the preacher who is examining a biblical theme for a sermon, and to the scholar who is interested in whether the *Dead Sea Scrolls use words with the same meaning that Jesus gave to them. The range of concordances is increasing at a tremendous rate, and this is likely to continue.

RICHARD E. WHITAKER

Conquest of Canaan. The biblical story of the conquest of *Canaan is found in Joshua 1–11 and Judges 1. The Joshua account continues the story of the conquest of the Transjordan given in Numbers 21; it depicts the conquest as quick and complete. The Israelites cross into Canaan and capture *Jericho (Josh. 6) and Ai (Josh. 8). Although tricked into an alliance with the Gibeonites (Map 3:X5; Josh. 9), they defeat a coalition of cities led by *Jerusalem (Josh. 10.1–27) and sweep through the southern part of the country, destroying everything in their path (Josh. 10.28–42). This southern campaign is followed by a victory over an alliance of northern cities led by *Hazor (Josh. 11.1–5). The subjugation of Canaan takes only five years (see Josh. 14.7, 10), and most of the indigenous population is

destroyed (Josh. 11.16–20). Judges 1, however, gives the impression that the conquest was a matter of individual tribal actions occurring over an extended period and often with inconclusive results.

Modern historians have attempted to describe the process by which Israel came into control of Canaan. It seems to have had two phases, one of peaceful settlement in the hills and one of conflict with the cities of the lowlands. Surveys of Israel and Jordan show that the central highlands were sparsely populated before 1200 BCE, when a marked expansion began. Most of the newcomers were agriculturalists, not *nomads. They seem to have been of mixed origin, arriving from several directions and settling in villages. Certain continuities in material culture, including pottery and architecture, suggest that a substantial number came from the Canaanite cities of the lowlands. These peoples made up the bulk of the population of later Israel. They aligned themselves with an existing group called Israel, who were already living in the region, as shown by a reference made to them in about 1207 BCE by the Egyptian king Merneptah. The resulting larger community developed a strong sense of ethnic identity, sharply separating themselves from the peoples of the neighboring lowland cities, whom they eventually grew strong enough to conquer or assimilate in a process that was not complete until *David's capture of Jerusalem in the tenth century BCE. It was probably the memory of this process that gave rise to the tradition of Joshua's conquest.

*Archaeology has cast doubt on the historicity of many of the specific victories described in Joshua, including especially the battle of *Jericho, which was not fortified at the time of the Israelites' arrival. The story of the crossing of the *Jordan and the first victory serves the theological purpose of presenting the conquest as a part of Yahweh's plan for Israel, the means by which the land promised to the ancestors was acquired. The crossing into the sacred realm and siege of the first Canaanite city are presented in ritual terms, while the divine participation in the war is made clear (Josh. 5.13–15; cf. 10.12).

See also Joshua, The Book of.

P. KYLE McCARTER, JR.

Conversion. Conversion refers to two different kinds of "turning" to God: the change of allegiance from one religion (or branch of a religion) to another; and the movement from lack of faith or purely formal faith to commitment, or, with a more moral emphasis, from a life of sin to one of attempted virtue in obedience to God. In trying to understand conversion in the Bible, it is temping to find modern individualism operating in situations where matters of group loyalty were in fact more salient. It is also easy for the modern reader to see certain biblical episodes as conversions when they are better taken as calls by God to new roles.

The complex play of these factors may be illustrated by several examples. The stories of God's encounters with figures such as *Abraham (Gen. 12; 17), *Jacob (Gen. 28.10–17), and *Moses (Exod. 3) may, in their origins, reflect transfers of tribal allegiance to a new deity, though in their final form they appear as calls to deeper loyalty or to a new phase in the relationship between God and his people or a particular leader. Similarly, stories such as that in Joshua 9 describe the adherence of whole groups to Israel's deity, Yahweh, inspired by what appear to us to be political and social motives. In the much later setting of the New Testament, there is evidence of people moving from other religions to Judaism, just as they moved to the Christian movement (see references to *proselytes, Acts 2.10; and to *gentiles on the edge of Judaism, such as Cornelius, Acts 10).

The story of *Isaiah of Jerusalem (Isa. 6.1–8) is best seen as a call to a more profound allegiance to Yahweh. While it is wholly personal in its reference, it nevertheless places Isaiah in a well-authenticated tradition of holy individuals, among whom *Samuel, *Elijah, and *Elisha are in many ways comparable earlier examples. Such figures, themselves "converted" in a charismatic act, become charismatic leaders, stirring the people, on the basis of their God-given authority, to military zeal (as in the case of Samuel or *Saul), to faithfulness to Yahweh as opposed to other gods (Elijah and Elisha), or to cultic and moral purity (Isaiah, Amos, Hosea, Jeremiah). It is noteworthy that in the story of Isaiah's "conversion" a moral element is explicit (6.5) as God's purity is brought home.

The so-called conversion of *Paul (described in Acts 9; 22; 26; and more intimately in his own words in Gal. 1.15–16) is in many ways comparable to such prophetic calls; indeed, "call" (Grk. *kaleō*) is Paul's own most characteristic word for the summons of God both to himself and to others (1 Cor. 1.1–2; 7.17–24). It is certainly not conversion in the sense of a move from irreligion to belief, or from a life of vice to one of virtue (Phil. 3.6), nor was it perceived by Paul as a move from one religion to another; there is scarcely any sign that Paul saw the new faith as other than the true Judaism, the realization of God's plan for his people (Rom. 9–11). Rather, it was a call from God to serve as emissary (*apostle) of Jesus Christ, whom God had sent for the purpose of drawing Jews and gentiles alike into his people.

With deep-seated origins in stories of transferred tribal allegiance and the rise of charismatic military and political leaders, there emerges in the prophetic literature—whose attitudes so deeply color the final form these stories take—a pervasive sense of God's call both to individuals and, through their activity, to his people, a call for a new loyalty to him and for a more profound moral obedience. It is evident in the preexilic prophets' summons to Israel to "turn" (*see* Repentance), as well as in the later optimistic promise of restoration in Second Isaiah (Isa. 40–55).

This tradition of God's urgent call to turn again reaches new intensity in the ministry of Jesus. In the light of the coming *kingdom of God, Jesus summons people to unconditioned and simple (Matt. 18.3) allegiance to God, brushing aside competing claims such as wealth (Mark 10.17–31) and family ties (Mark 1.16–20; Matt. 8.21–22; Luke 14.26). The outcome of his summons is *salvation, seen in terms not only of the coming new age, but also of forgiveness and healing here and now. It is likely that many of the Gospel stories of healings by Jesus and other encounters with him were told and heard in terms of conversion responses to Jesus' call. It is noteworthy that precisely the same Greek words, "Your faith has saved you," are used in relation to an act of forgiveness (Luke 7.50) and an act of healing (18.42). This activity is consciously set against the prophetic background (Luke 4.18–21), as indeed is the language in which the subsequent preaching of early Christian leaders is described (Acts 9.35; 11.21; 14.15; 26.18, 20).

Although the element of repentance and "turning" is present in much biblical material concerning people's coming to God's service, the element of "call" is more fundamental; this is clear in the portrayal of Jesus' own ministry as inaugurated by such an episode (Mark 1.9–11). Here, charisma and divine recognition are bestowed with a view to his acting as God's agent.

Adopting a perspective more keenly aware of

the social realities of the world of the first century CE, we may note that in Palestine the appeal of Jesus was akin to that of a number of leaders of reform and renewal within Judaism of that period; note especially *John the Baptist. In Greco-Roman society, where the Christian movement was unique among these Palestinian groups in its success in moving beyond its original setting, both the appeal and the process of "joining" were different. It is likely that a number of those attracted were people who, in one respect or another, were on the margins of society or felt themselves to be so. As Acts indicates, a number were "God-fearers," gentiles already attracted to Jewish *synagogues but never able to be more than fringe members. Others may have been aliens living far from their native lands; and the power to attract *women may have been linked to aspirations in earliest Christianity toward gender equality (Gal. 3.28).

Such changes of religious alliance were not common in the ancient world: the open, tolerant, and undemanding nature of Greco-Roman religion made them largely incomprehensible. But there was some parallel in decisions to adhere to philosophical groups, a decision that might involve a measure of commitment to a specific way of life, and in the adoption of some of the mystical paths available within the religious spectrum. In any case, the strong group identity of the Christians must have been a powerful force; and if we ask what it felt like to join the Christians in a Greek city, then the provision of a "home," centered on Christ, was a major factor, not unlike the similar provision which might be found in the synagogue or in the many guilds or clubs that abounded in city life.

J. L. HOULDEN

Corban. A Hebrew word meaning "gift" or "offering," *corban* is used in the Hebrew Bible in the sense of a cultic offering made as a free-will gesture (e.g., Lev. 1.2). Later writings, particularly the *Mishnah, still frequently use this substantive in just such a sense. But in rabbinic literature *corban* can also mean a form of oath that turns whatever it is applied to into a cultic offering no longer suitable for its normal purpose (see the whole tractacte *Nedarim* of the Mishnah). This reflects a common custom that the Mishnah tries to discourage because it has led to serious abuse; according to Mark 7.11 (the only occurrence of the word in the New Testament), Jesus shared this view. In a controversy

with the *scribes and *Pharisees, Jesus accuses them of declaring such oaths binding even when they conflicted with one's legal duties toward parents, thus placing their tradition higher than the commandments of the Mosaic Law.

ETIENNE TROCMÉ

Corinth (Map 7:D3). A major city in Greece, mentioned in the *Iliad* and occupied throughout most of the first millennium BCE and until 521 CE. Located on the isthmus separating the harbor towns of Lechaeum on the Corinthian Gulf from Cenchreae (see Rom. 16.1) on the Saronic Gulf, Corinth owed much to its geography. Even though efforts to connect the two gulfs by a canal failed in antiquity, Corinth was still located at a crossroads of travel and commerce. Another important geographical factor was the citadel of the Acrocorinth (elevation ca. 550 m [1,800 ft]), situated directly south of Corinth.

Among important events in the city's history were its destruction by the Roman consul Mummius in 146 BCE and its reestablishment as a Roman colony in 44 BCE by Julius Caesar. Archaeological excavations have demonstrated that the traditional picture of Corinth as a city totally deserted during the period 146–44 BCE is inaccurate. Not only was the site populated, although sparsely, but several structures (e.g., stoas, archaic temple, Asclepieum, and the sanctuary of Demeter and Kore) were still in use after the defeat of the city in 146.

Certain aspects of Corinthian culture complement our understanding of nascent Christianity there. The city was apparently the provincial capital of the Roman province of Achaia and therefore the residence of the proconsul Gallio (Acts 18.12). This explains the importance of the city in *Paul's ministry (Acts 18.1–17) and why a circular letter to "all the saints throughout Achaia" (2 Cor. 1.1) would be addressed to Corinth.

The problem of sexual immorality (incest and fornication) among Paul's converts in Corinth is noteworthy (1 Cor. 5.1–13; 6.9–20), as illustrated by the fact that one of the Greek verbs meaning "to practice fornication" was *korinthiazomai*, a derivative of the city's name. The city's reputation in this matter probably owed more to being adjacent to two bustling seaports than to its temple of Aphrodite.

The practice of certain Christian men at Corinth of wearing head coverings while praying and prophesying (1 Cor. 11.4) probably mirrors the widespread Roman custom of wearing devotional head coverings during worship. Another practice mentioned by Paul as having disruptive consequences was that "strong" Christians at Corinth would be participants at meals in an idol's temple (1 Cor. 8.10), thereby creating a scandal in the eyes of "weak" Christians. Numerous banquet halls attached to temples have been excavated at Corinth. The specific location, the physical size, and the social function of these banquet rooms associated with a "temple of an idol" shed light on Paul's discussion of the strong and weak consciences of his converts.

Against the backdrop of a plethora of cults, where claims of miracles, healings, ecstatic prophecies, interpretations of prophecies, and visions abounded, one understands how gentile Christians in Corinth could easily be ignorant and misinformed about their own spiritual gifts (1 Cor. 12.1–14.40).

Although Acts 18 refers to a *synagogue in Corinth, the famous synagogue lintel inscription found there ("Synagogue of the Hebrews") cannot be dated precisely.

See also Corinthians, The Letters of Paul to the.   RICHARD E. OSTER, JR.

Corinthians, The Letters of Paul to the. Though edited as two separate letters, the canonical letters of 1 and 2 Corinthians most likely consist of several shorter letters or notes written by Paul to the church at *Corinth in the early 50s CE. Because of their length, content, and influence they rank among the major Pauline letters. Except for certain subsections, Pauline authorship is undisputed.

The Corinthian Church. Not only do the letters contain reminiscences of his founding visit (1 Cor. 1.14–16; 2.1–5; 2 Cor. 11.9; 12.12), but the narrative account in Acts also provides independent confirmation of certain details about the church's beginning (Acts 18.1–17). Especially valuable for dating the letters is the mention in Acts of Paul's appearance before Gallio (Acts 18.12–17), whose proconsulship is reliably dated ca. 51–53 CE on the basis of an inscription discovered in 1905 at Delphi. Accordingly, Paul's founding visit, which lasted eighteen months (Acts 18.11), could have occurred as early as 50–51 CE during his ministry in the Aegean. After Paul's departure from Corinth, he remained in continual contact with the church, even though he was engaged in a mission in *Ephesus, from which he wrote 1 Corinthians and at least part

of 2 Corinthians (1 Cor. 16.8, 19; Acts 19.1–40; 2 Cor. 1.8; 7.6, 13). The letters reflect at least two different stages in Paul's relationship to the church after his founding visit.

In the first stage, Paul responds to the needs and questions of a fledgling church experiencing internal tensions (1 Cor. 1.10–13; 3.3; 11.18–19) and trying to work out the implications of Paul's gospel in a heterogenous setting. The relationship between Paul and the church is still, for the most part, amicable, even though his departure and absence seem to have diminished the church's loyalty to him. In the second stage, Paul's relationship with the church is severely strained, primarily because of the arrival in the church of outside teachers whom Paul regards as opponents of his gospel. He now has to deal with issues relating to the source, nature, legitimacy, and extent of his apostolic authority. Generally, 1 Corinthians relates to the first period, whereas 2 Corinthians relates to the second.

1 Corinthians. A letter preceded the writing of 1 Corinthians (1 Cor. 5.9, 11). This letter may be preserved in 2 Corinthians 6.14–7.1, a self-contained literary unit that calls for Christians to keep their distance from non-Christians.

Situation addressed. 1 Corinthians addresses a church divided not so much by doctrinal differences as by personal loyalties to different religious teachers and by interpersonal tensions (1 Cor. 1.10–13; 3.3; 11.18–19). Some in the church were self-confident, indeed arrogant (4.19; 5.2), probably because they claimed special knowledge and spiritual wisdom (3.18; 8.1–2). Whether this outlook is "gnostic" in the nontechnical sense that it merely placed an unusually high premium on "knowledge" (gnōsis) and "wisdom" (sophia) or in the more technical sense that it stemmed from a system of thought resembling second-century *gnosticism is a matter of ongoing debate. In any case, such a claim to spiritual superiority grounded in a higher wisdom seems to be a common denominator of several problems addressed in the letter: the fragmentation beginning to appear within the church (1.10–13), the sense of perfection some were claiming to have achieved (4.8), a blasé attitude toward *sexual immorality (5.1–2), a refusal to be conciliatory in dealing with internal disputes (6.1–8), an insistence on individual freedom (6.12; 10.23–30), an expressed preference for celibacy over *marriage (chap. 7), an inability, or refusal, to consider the needs of weaker Christians in deciding how to behave (chaps. 8–10), an urge to be unconventional (11.2–16), a lack of sensitivity to the needs of others within worship (11.17–34), and an insistence on the superiority of the more visible gifts, most notably speaking in tongues (chaps. 12–14; *see* Glossolalia). Whether there is one group within the church whose theological outlook and ethic are the underlying problem or whether there are actually several groups with different theological outlooks and ethics it is difficult to say. But it is clear that the church is faced with an almost bewildering variety of pressing questions on which it needs further instruction.

Structure and content. The letter exhibits three clear divisions: chaps. 1–4, 5–6, and 7–16.

The first section, introduced by Paul's characteristic greeting and opening prayer of thanksgiving (1 Cor. 1.1–9), is a formally constructed Pauline exhortation. It opens with an exhortation to unity (1.10–17) and closes with an exhortation to heed Paul's teaching, follow his example, and listen to his messenger Timothy (4.14–21). Within this exhortation, Paul articulates his theology of the cross as a message of divine power and wisdom (1.18–2.5), expounds the nature of the higher wisdom reserved for the mature (2.6–16), and delineates his own role and that of *Apollos as God's ministers (3.1–4.13). Throughout this first section, Paul insists on the radical priority of God and thereby undercuts the arrogant self-sufficiency that he sees within the church (1.18–2.5; 3.9, 23).

In the second section (1 Cor. 5–6), Paul provides the church with what appears to be unsolicited instruction. Two questions are treated: how the congregation should deal with a case of blatant sexual immorality (5.1–13) and how the congregation should resolve disputes that have been taken before courts (6.1–11). Paul then provides further teachings on sexual morality (6.12–20).

In the third section (1 Cor. 7–16), Paul addresses a list of questions that the church had written to him (7.1). His first response concerns marriage (7.1–40). A second extended response is given to the question of eating meat offered to *idols (chaps. 8–10). A third topic treated is congregational worship (11.2–34). Two issues are treated: the proper attire (veils) to be worn in worship (11.2–16), and the proper observance of the *Lord's Supper (11.17–34). The Corinthians had also inquired about spiritual gifts (or persons), to which Paul devotes extended treatment (chaps. 12–14). The final major topic treated is the *Resurrection (15.1–58), in which Christ's own resurrection is presented as the basis for

the resurrection of Christians (15.12–58). A final question concerned the collection for the *poor Christians in Jerusalem, about which Paul provides brief procedural instructions (16.1–4). This third major section is then concluded with miscellaneous exhortations and personal greetings (16.5–24).

2 Corinthians. Scattered references in 2 Corinthians suggest that after the writing of 1 Corinthians, the situations of both the church and Paul had changed dramatically. Their relationship became severely strained, and the resulting turbulence is mirrored within the letter itself, which is much more uneven than 1 Corinthians. Abrupt changes in style, tone, and content suggest several self-contained sections (6.14–7.1; chaps. 8–9; chaps. 10–13; perhaps 2.14–6.13), which some scholars regard as separate letters written by Paul to the church throughout this second period, as well as, in some cases, earlier. Consequently, numerous theories of composition have been suggested for this letter. The relationship between the historical situation and the literary structure of 2 Corinthians is a major question in interpreting the letter.

Situation addressed. Generally, the letter reflects a worsened situation that was directly related to the arrival of outside teachers within the church (2 Cor. 3.2; 10.2, 7–12; 11.4–6, 11–15; 12.11). So seriously was Paul alienated from the church that he made a "painful," and apparently unsuccessful, visit from Ephesus to the Corinthian church (2.1, 5–8; 13.2). This was followed by a "severe letter" sent by Paul to the church (2.4, 9; 7.9, 12).

One widely accepted reconstruction regards 2 Corinthians 10–13 as the "severe letter," written from Ephesus after the unsuccessful "painful" visit. Shortly thereafter, Paul was forced to leave Ephesus (1.8–11), and journeyed to Troas anxious about the letter's reception (2.12–13). Still unrelieved, he went to Macedonia, where he eventually learned from Titus that the letter had been well received (7.5–16). Buoyed by this good news, while still in Macedonia he wrote to the church a much more positive letter of reconciliation (1.1–6.13; 7.2–16; perhaps 6.14–7.1 and chaps. 8–9), in which one still hears echoes of the earlier controversy.

Regardless of the theory of composition one adopts, and the historical reconstruction into which it is fitted, the canonical letter of 2 Corinthians reflects different concerns from those mentioned in 1 Corinthians. Throughout the letter, Paul himself is the focus of controversy.

Criticism of Paul, which was subdued in the first letter (1 Cor. 4.3–5; 9.3), is much more open and pronounced. He is accused of being vacillating and acting inconsistently (2 Cor. 1.17; 10.1), of being intimidating (2 Cor. 10.9), crude in speech (2 Cor. 10.10; 11.6), and calculating and manipulative (12.16). "Acting according to the flesh" (2 Cor. 10.2) may serve as the general rubric for several criticisms, pointing to what his critics believed to be a boorish life-style unbecoming someone with apostolic status.

As criticisms of Paul's behavior are more explicit in 2 Corinthians, so are polemical references to his opponents, who are Christian missionaries (2 Cor. 11.4, 23, 33) of Jewish background (2 Cor. 11.22). Whether they originated in Palestine or the *Dispersion is much debated and still unresolved, as is their relationship to the original apostolic circle, most notably *Simon Peter. Because they had gained an entrance into the church, Paul viewed them as evil forces set on undermining his authority. The opponents appear not to have been judaizing teachers who insisted on *circumcision as a prerequisite to salvation, as was the case in Galatia (Gal. 5.1–12). The issue may have been one of territorial infringement (2 Cor. 10.13–16), which threatened the success of Paul's collection for the Jerusalem poor (2 Cor. 11.7–11; 12.14). In any case, what emerges from the letter is a debate about apostolic legitimacy: whether true *apostleship is more properly authenticated by dazzling signs, rhetorical ability, and displays of power (2 Cor. 12.1–7, 12), or by divine power experienced through suffering, weakness, and deprivation (2 Cor. 11.23–33; 12.8–10; 13.3–4).

Structure and content of the letter. The canonical form of the letter can be divided into three sections: chaps. 1–7, 8–9, and 10–13. Each of these sections may be a composite of smaller letters or fragments of letters.

The first section (chaps. 1–7) is introduced by a Pauline greeting and opening prayer of blessing (2 Cor. 1.1–7). This is followed by recollections of mortal threats experienced in Ephesus (1.8–11) and a defense of his recent behavior toward the church and actions on their behalf, including the "painful visit" and writing the "severe letter" (2.13).

There follows an extended set of reflections on Paul's theology of ministry (2 Cor. 2.14–6.13). The tone is apologetic (2.17–3.3; 4.2–3), but what unfolds is a positive treatment of Paul's self-understanding. Basic features include his theology of the new covenant of Christ as superior to the old, Mosaic *covenant (3.4–18), a ministry illuminated by the light of the new creation (4.1–6), Paul's suffering as manifesting the death and life of Jesus (4.7–15), outward change and inward transformation grounded in a future hope (4.16–5.10), ministry compelled by the love of Christ (5.11–15), existence in Christ and the ministry of reconciliation (5.16–21), and working with God in the new age as servants embodying the paradox of power experienced through suffering (6.1–10).

This first section concludes with Paul's final appeal for the Corinthians to receive him affectionately (2 Cor. 6.11–13; 7.2–4). His recollections of the encouraging report received from Titus and the effects of the "severe letter" (7.5–16) echo sentiments expressed earlier (1.8–2.13). Also included in this section is an arguably parenthetical set of instructions urging the separation of believers from unbelievers (2 Cor. 6.14–7.1).

The second section (chaps. 8–9) consists of instructions concerning the collection, a program of relief for poor Christians in Jerusalem.

The third section (chaps. 10–13) is marked by a conspicuous change in tone and content. The pervasive mood of the section is apologetic, as Paul defends his apostolic commission against the charges of detractors (e.g., 2 Cor. 10.1–12). Prominent within this section is the "fool's speech" (11.1–12.13), in which Paul insists that he has been motivated to act toward the Corinthians out of genuine love (11.1–6), as seen in his willingness to forfeit financial support for their sake (11.7–11). After characterizing the opponents as fraudulent apostles (11.12–15) and the church as undiscriminating hearers (11.16–21), Paul engages in "foolish boasting" by listing his vicissitudes (11.16–33). His supreme boast is of a heavenly vision (12.1–10), from which he learned the paradox of gaining strength through weakness. He concludes his defense by insisting on the adequacy of his apostolic witness within the church (12.11–13). Toward the conclusion of this section, Paul discusses his future plans with respect to the Corinthian church (12.14–13.10) and closes with miscellaneous appeals and a benediction (13.11–14).

Significance. Naturally these letters have figured prominently as sources for understanding Paul's life and thought. Because of the variety of topics treated, they touch on almost every aspect of Pauline theology, ranging from his theology of the cross to his theology of ministry, even though some major Pauline themes, such as *justification by faith, play only a minor role. While he provides concrete instructions about such matters as sexual morality, settling disputes, marriage, eating sacrificial meats, liturgical protocol, and the collection, they are intended for congregational praxis. To be sure, Pauline theology emerges in these letters, but it does so in the service of the congregation. Even in those sections in which he treats more broadly his theology of ministry, he does so in order to clarify the nature of his apostolic commission vis-à-vis a local church.

Specifically, they serve as valuable sources for reconstructing Pauline Christianity and especially Christianity at Corinth. Sociological analysis of the New Testament and efforts at constructive social history of early Christianity have found the Corinthian letters to be especially valuable as sources. (See Social Sciences and the Bible, article on Sociology of the New Testament.)

The Corinthian letters have also figured prominently in discussions about gnostic influence in the New Testament. Such passages as 2 Corinthians 1–4 and 2 Corinthians 12 have figured centrally in such discussions. Another debate in which these letters have played a central role is the identification of Paul's opponents and their relationship to early Christian heresies; in particular, the polemical section of 2 Corinthians 10–13 has received extensive attention. Because of the amount of space devoted to the collection (1 Cor. 16.1–4; 2 Cor. 8–9), these letters are a primary source for understanding this project.

CARL R. HOLLADAY

Covenant. One of the fundamental theological motifs of the Hebrew and Christian scriptures. Eventually the expressions "old covenant" and "new covenant," which once referred to two eras (Jer. 31.31–33) or dispensations (2 Cor. 3.4–11), came to designate the two parts of the Christian Bible, the Old Testament (Covenant) and the New.

The Hebrew term for covenant (běrît) seems to have the root meaning of "bond, fetter," indicating a binding relationship; the idea of "binding, putting together" is also suggested in the Greek term synthēkē. Another term used in the New Testament is diathēkē ("will, testament"), pointing more to the obligatory or legal aspect of a covenant. The meaning of covenant, however, is not determined primarily by etymology but by how these and related terms function in

various literary contexts. In general, covenant signifies a relationship based on commitment, which includes both promises and obligations, and which has the quality of reliability and durability. The relationship is usually sealed by a rite—for example, an oath, sacred *meal, blood *sacrifice, invocation of *blessings and *curses—which makes it binding.

In the Hebrew Bible, various secular covenants are mentioned: covenants between leaders of two peoples (Abraham and Abimelech, Gen. 21.25–32), between two heads of state (Ahab and Ben-hadad, 1 Kings 20.34), between king and people (David and the elders of Israel, 1 Chron. 11.3), between a revolutionary priest and the army (Jehoiada, 2 Kings 11.4), between a conquering king and a vassal (Nebuchadrezzar and a Judean prince, Ezek. 17.13–19; cf. 1 Sam. 11.1). These treaties or pacts were usually thought to be supervised by the deity. This was the case for instance, in the covenant between *Jacob and Laban, which was sealed with a sacred meal and which concluded with a prayer that God would see to it that both sides lived up to the terms of the agreement (Gen. 31.44–54). Likewise the covenant between Jonathan and David, based on the loyalty (ḥesed) of friendship, was "a covenant before Yahweh" (1 Sam. 23.18).

In the ancient world, covenants or treaties often governed the relations between peoples. There were parity treaties between two equal sovereign states, and there were overlord treaties between a powerful monarch and a vassal state. Illustrative of the latter is the suzerainty treaty form of the second and first millennia, which apparently influenced Israel's Mosaic covenant theology found in the book of *Deuteronomy. These treaties included such elements as a summary of the benevolent deeds of the overlord, the stipulations binding on the vassal who receives favor and protection, and the sanctions of blessings and curses in case of obedience or disobedience.

Covenant expresses a novel element of the religion of ancient Israel: the people are bound in relationship to the one God, Yahweh, who makes an exclusive ("jealous") claim upon their loyalty in worship and social life. In a larger sense, the relationship between all creatures and their creator is expressed in the universal covenant with *Noah (Gen. 9.1–17), which assures God's faithful pledge to humanity, to nonhuman creatures, and to the earth itself. In the *Pentateuch, however, primary emphasis is given to God's covenant with the Israelite people, portrayed in the migration of *Abraham and *Sarah in response to the divine promise (Gen. 11.31–12.7) and the special relationship between God and their descendants (Gen. 15.1–21; 17.1–22). In the biblical narrative, the covenant with Israel's *ancestors is the prelude to the crucial events of the *Exodus and the Mosaic covenant at *Sinai and is supplemented by the covenant between God and the Davidic monarch, who mediates God's cosmic rule, manifest in the anointed one (the reigning ruler) and in the Temple of *Zion (Ps. 78.67–72; 2 Sam. 7).

The covenants between God and the people are all covenants of divine favor or *grace (Hebr. *ḥesed*). They express God's gracious commitment and faithfulness and thus establish a continuing relationship. They differ from one another theologically at the point of whether the accent falls upon God's loyalty, which endows the relationship with constancy and durability, or upon the people's response, which is subject to human weakness and sin. The Abrahamic and Davidic covenants belong to the type of the "everlasting covenant" *(bĕrît ʿōlām)*, for they rest upon divine grace alone and are not conditioned by human behavior. On the other hand, the Mosaic covenant, set forth classically in the book of *Deuteronomy, has a strong conditional note, for its endurance depends on the people's obedience to the covenant commandments.

Furthermore, all of God's covenants with Israel include divine promises, as well as human obligations, though they differ as to which is emphasized. The Abrahamic covenant is primarily a promissory covenant. In it God imposes no conditions (*circumcision is a sign, not a legal condition of the relationship) but rather gives promises: the land as an everlasting possession, numerous posterity, and a special relationship between God and the descendants of Abraham and Sarah (Gen. 17.7–8). Similarly, the Davidic covenant, perhaps on the analogy of royal grants of the ancient Near East, does not impose legal conditions, but offers a gracious promise of an unbroken succession of kings upon the throne of David (2 Sam. 7). Although unfaithful kings will be chastised if they behave badly in office, God will not abrogate the covenant promises of grace made to *David (Ps. 89; *see also* Kingship and Monarchy). The Mosaic covenant, however, like the suzerainty treaties of the ancient world, is a covenant of obligation, subject to the sanctions of blessings and curses (Deut. 30.15–20). If the people are unfaithful and disobey the covenant stipulations, they will be punished for breaking the covenant. Carried to the extreme, this covenant could even be annulled, so that no longer would Yahweh be their God and no longer would Israel be God's people (Hos. 1.9). The renewal of the covenant, in this view, would be based solely on God's forgiving grace (Exod. 34.6–9; Jer. 31.31–33; Ezek. 16.59–63).

The New Testament draws upon all of these covenant traditions. In some circles, however, there was a strong preference for the promissory covenants associated with Abraham and David (cf. "the covenants of promise," Eph. 2.12). Paul's interpretation of the new relationship between God and people, shown by the display of God's grace in Jesus Christ, sent him back beyond the Mosaic covenant of obligation to the Abrahamic promissory covenant (Gal. 3.6–18). And the promissory Davidic covenant, found especially in the prophecy of the book of *Isaiah, provided a theological context for the announcement that Jesus is the *Messiah (Christ), the *Son of God.

See also Biblical Theology, *article on* Old Testament. BERNHARD W. ANDERSON

Crafts. The crafts were critical to the needs of the community. Aristocrats may have looked down on craftspersons, but they paid tribute to their necessity (cf. Sir. 38.24–34).

Carpenters or builders constructed the doors and windows of all the houses, manufactured the farm implements (yokes, plows, threshing sledges, and pitchforks; *see* Agriculture), constructed the carts, and occasionally fashioned a chest or table (*see* Houses, Furniture, Utensils). No village could function without one. *Jesus is described by the Greek word *tektōn* (Mark 6.3), better understood as a carpenter/builder than a cabinet maker; many of his *parables refer to building but none to furniture making. The carpenter's tools included the hammer, adze, ax, plane, bow-drill, chisel, and saw; see the description of carpentry in Isaiah 44.13–17.

Metal workers labored with copper, bronze, and iron, with the appropriate technologies developed in that order. For village use they shaped the cutting edges of tools. Some metal kitchen utensils, sewing equipment, and *musical instruments have been found. Most of the metal was used for weapons. King Hiram of Tyre supplied an amazing list of large items of "burnished bronze" for Solomon's temple (1 Kings 7.40–47). There are descriptions of blacksmithing in Isaiah 44.12 and Sirach 38.28. (*See also* Kenites.)

Potters produced utensils for storing, cooking,

and eating food. Water was carried, stored, and cooled in pots. Lamps, cosmetic jars, votive vessels, and small idols were all made of pottery. A simple potter's wheel came into use about 3000 BCE. A type used later was two wheels joined by an axle. This unit was mounted vertically in a shallow pit. The lower wheel was turned with the foot of the seated potter; the wares were fashioned on the upper wheel (see Sir. 38.29–30). Pottery is the primary indicator for dating in *archaeology.

Tanners made leather available for shields, helmets, quivers, and other military articles. It was used also for sandals, shoes, belts, clothing, and storage skins for wine and water. Odors from tanning obliged the tanner to live at the outskirts of the town (Acts 9.43; 10.6, 32).

Jewelers worked with gold and silver. Engravers produced scarabs, signet rings, and seals of various types (see Sir. 38.27). (See Jewelry.)

Stone masons built buildings and excavated spaces in rock. Rough-cut and dressed stones were used. Palaces incorporated pillars, stone carving, and decorative capitals. Tombs, cisterns, and community water systems required excavation. The latter are extensive and remarkable. Their purpose was to ensure access to the city water supply from within the walls. Large tunnels, pits, and passageways were carved out to achieve this goal. The tools were the hammer, chisel, saw, and adze. Hezekiah's tunnel in *Jerusalem has the long sweeping marks of the adze or pick on its walls; other notable water systems are at *Gezer, Gibeon, *Hazor, and *Megiddo.

Carving in ivory and wood produced luxury items. Glassmaking was rare before Roman times. Roman glassmakers introduced a range of delicate bottles and vials previously made of pottery or alabaster.

Fullers kept the clothes white while the dyers added color. Various shades of red, a yellow from ground pomegranate rind, and the famous purple from Tyre were the main colors available. The latter took on royal significance.

The perfumer/cosmetologist was known, and Ben Sira mentions seven types of perfume (Sir. 24.15).

See also Clothing.   KENNETH E. BAILEY

Creation. The biblical accounts of the creation of the world have their background in ancient Near Eastern mythology, in which creation is often depicted as the deity's victory over the forces of *chaos, represented by threatening waters, as a result of which the god is established as a supreme king. A large number of references (e.g., Pss. 74.12–17; 89.9–13) show that this concept was well-known in Israel also. Its immediate source was probably Canaanite mythology, and it was particularly associated with the Jerusalem *Temple, where it seems likely that God's victory over primeval chaos and his royal enthronement were celebrated in a great annual festival.

Since the extended descriptions of creation in the first chapters of Genesis similarly reflect this background (see Myth), they are not to be viewed as providing a scientific account of the origin of the universe. They are religious statements, designed to show God's glory and greatness, the result of theological reflection by which the older mythology was radically transformed to express Israel's distinctive faith. The two accounts found together in these chapters, Genesis 1.1–2.4a and 2.4b–25, both tell of the creation of the physical world and the creation of humanity, though these were originally independent elements. The first account is generally considered to be from the hand of a sixth-century BCE priestly writer (*P) who, however, depends on a much older tradition. In form it is a poem or a hymn, as the repeated refrain indicates, and its seven-day structure may be due to its having been recited during the period of the annual festival mentioned above. Although the watery chaos is still there, there is no conflict between it and God, as in ancient myth. God creates in unfettered freedom by his word or command, and creation is brought about by the separation of the elements of the universe, which produces an ordered and habitable world. Hence creation is not so much dealing with absolute beginning, creation from nothing—though this idea appears later, as in 2 Maccabees 7.28—as with the world order as perceived by human beings. An originally separate account of the creation of humankind (Gen. 1.26–30)—it does not appear as creation through the word—has been added to show human beings as the crown of creation. Humanity too is created by separation into male and female made in the image of God, a much discussed expression that probably means that God makes beings with whom he can communicate and who can respond, because, in contrast to the rest of nature, they are like him. So humanity receives the divine blessing and is given the role of God's vice-regent, in language drawn from *kingship vocabulary, to have dominion or control over the future course of the world. The final verses, which tell of God's seeing all he has made and his rest on the *Sabbath, emphasize the completeness and perfection of the created order.

The outlook of the second creation account (generally attributed to *J) is essentially similar but its form is very different. It is older and it is a folktale, reflecting the concerns and interests of a peasant society, and God is described in human terms; but behind its apparent naïveté lie profound insights. It deals primarily with the creation of humanity, and the creation of the world is directed to providing a suitable agricultural environment for human beings. God molds the first man (see Adam) from the dust of the ground, an idea found in many other cultures; that is, he is part of the natural order, but he is given a unique status when God breathes into him the divine breath and he becomes a living being. His naming of the animals means that he appropriates them, corresponding to the notion of dominion in Genesis 1, and the command about the trees in the garden implies responsibility toward his maker, which is part of what is meant by humanity as the image of God. No doubt the fact that woman (see Eve) is created secondarily from man corresponds to the position of the male in a patriarchal society. Yet even more strongly the story stresses the unity of the sexes and their mutual, complementary need. So the first creation account, with its cultic background, ends with the religious institution of the Sabbath; the second, which is directed to humankind in community, with the social institution of *marriage.

Explicit references to creation may appear to be comparatively rare in the Bible. But the creation accounts in Genesis are the starting point for the history that follows and are inseparably linked with it in the biblical narrative. The *prophets and the *wisdom literature also both presuppose a comprehensive world order to which they summon men and women to conform. There are, however, two particular developments in later texts to which special attention may be called.

First, the idea grows that the goal of history is to be a new creation, a return to the beginning when the creator's original intention, frustrated by human sin and rebellion, will be fulfilled. The visions of the end of time are pictured in terms of the first things. Such is a dominant theme in the later chapters of Isaiah (e.g., 65.17; 66.22), and it is further developed in succeeding *apocalyptic literature.

Second, in certain parts of the wisdom tradition, *Wisdom comes to be represented as already existing before the creation of the world and, parallel to the divine word in Genesis 1, the means of God's creative activity (e.g., Job 28.12–27). Wisdom can be strongly personified and viewed as God's personal agent in creation (Prov. 8.22–31); in Sirach 24.3 the figure of Wisdom is identified both with the word of Genesis 1 and the primary act of creation in Genesis 2.6.

It is these two developments that determine the way in which the idea of creation is transposed into a new key in the New Testament. The New Testament writers inherited the Jewish belief in the creation of the world by the one God and frequently appeal to the ordering of the world and human life that he established at the beginning (e.g., Mark 10.6; Rom. 1.20). But the advent of Christ inaugurates the long awaited new creation (Rev. 21.1–4), both of the universe (Rom. 8.19–21) and of humanity (2 Cor. 5.17). This comes about because, on the one hand, Jesus recapitulates the former creation: he is the new Adam (1 Cor. 15.45), and the image and likeness of God (Col. 1.15; 2 Cor. 4.4). On the other hand, Christ is the agent and sustainer of all creation (Col. 1.16) and is described as the word of God (Rev. 19.13) and the wisdom of God (1 Cor. 1.24). But it is the figure of creative Wisdom that seems to have been most influential for the understanding of Jesus; so, like Wisdom, he is preexistent (Col. 1.17) and the reflection of God's *glory (Heb. 1.3; compare Wisd. of Sol. 7.24). Most striking is the first chapter of John's gospel, the opening words of which echo the beginning of Genesis, with its picture of Jesus as the *Logos. This term unites the concept of the creative word of the Hebrew Bible and, from its use in Greek philosophy, the concept of Wisdom as the mediator in creation.   J. R. PORTER

Crucifixion. The act of nailing or binding a person to a cross or tree, whether for executing or for exposing the corpse. It was considered the cruelest and most shameful method of capital punishment.

According to ancient historians such as Herodotus and Diodorus Siculus, various kinds of crucifixion (e.g., impalement) were used by the Assyrians, Scythians, Phoenicians, and Persians (see also Ezra 6.11). The practice of crucifixion was taken over by Alexander the Great and his successors, and especially by the Romans, who reserved it for slaves in cases of robbery and rebellion. Roman citizens could be punished in this way only for the crime of high treason. In the Roman provinces crucifixion served as a means of punishing unruly people who were sentenced as "robbers." *Josephus tells of mass crucifixions in Judea under several Roman prefects, in particular Titus during the siege of *Jerusalem; the same also occurred in the Jewish quarter of Alexandria, according to *Philo. Before the execution, the victim was scourged (Mark 15.15; *War* 5.11.449–51). He then had to carry the transverse beam *(patibulum)* to the place of execution (John 19.17), and was nailed through hands and feet to the cross (see Luke 24.39; John 20.25), from which a wooden peg protruded to support the body; some of these literary details are confirmed by archaeological finds of the bones of crucifixion victims.

Crucifixion, though not mentioned in the list of death penalties in Jewish law (*m. Sanh.* 7.1), might be suggested in Deuteronomy 21.22–23, which requires that a person put to death must be hung on a tree and buried on the same day. While this is interpreted by the Mishnah (*m. Sanh.* 6.4) as the exposure of the corpse of a man who was stoned because of blasphemy or idolatry, the order of the verbs is reversed in the Temple Scroll of *Qumran: the delinquent must be hung up so that he dies (11QTemple 64.8), which amounts to crucifixion. The same source also specifies that it must be applied in a case of high treason, for example, if an Israelite curses his people or delivers it to a foreign nation. Though such a crime is not mentioned in the Hebrew Bible, it must be derived from the ambiguous term "God's curse" (Deut. 21.23). Delivering up or cursing Israel is also regarded as blasphemy, because the nation belongs to God.

The same interpretation of Deuteronomy 21.22–23 underlies 4QpNah, which mentions "hanging men up alive [on the tree]," presumably a reference to the atrocious deed of Alexander Janneus when he crucified eight hundred of his Pharisean enemies who, in his view, had committed high treason (Josephus, *War* 1.4.92–97; *Ant.* 13.14.378–81). Other references to crucifixion include the hanging of eighty "witches" (probably Sadducees) by Rabbi Shimon ben Shetah (*m. Sanh.* 6.5; see *War* 1.3.79–80), the crucifixion of Rabbi Jose ben Joezer (*Gen. Rab.* 65 [141a]), and Matthew 23.34.

In rabbinic writings crucifixion is the death penalty for "robbers" (bandits [*t. Sanh.* 9.7, *Qoh. Rab.* 7:26 (109b)]) and for martyrs (*Gen. Rab.* 65

[141a]; *Mek.* 68b). Isaac, carrying the wood for his sacrifice, was compared to a man bearing the cross on his shoulders (*Gen Rab.* 56 [118b]). Similarly, a disciple of Jesus must take up his cross and follow him (Mark 8.34 par.; Matt. 10.38).

According to Matthew 20.19 and 26.2, Jesus said that once delivered to the gentiles he would suffer crucifixion. The predictions of suffering by Jesus are not necessarily prophecies after the fact. The inscription on the cross told that Jesus was crucified as "king of the Jews" (Mark 15.26). In his trial before the high priest (Mark 14.62) and before *Pilate (15.2), Jesus had admitted to being the *Messiah of Israel and *Son of God. The members of the *Sanhedrin declared that Jesus deserved death because he had uttered blasphemy (Mark 14.63–64); they must have understood Deuteronomy 21.22–23 in a way similar to the Temple Scroll (cf. John 19.7, 15). A false messiah could deliver the people of Israel and the Temple to the gentiles (see John 11.48–50). According to the Babylonian Talmud (*b. Sanh.* 43a), Jesus was executed because he had led Israel astray, a judgment based on Deuteronomy 13.1–11.

By delivering Jesus to Pilate (Mark 15.1), the members of the Sanhedrin could expect the sentence "death by crucifixion," for the claim to be the Messiah could be understood as a rebellion against Rome. It is for this reason that Jesus was compared with the revolutionary *Barabbas (Mark 15.7). After the people had asked for Barabbas (v. 11), Pilate had no other choice than to crucify Jesus, who was scourged (v. 15), mocked by the legionaries (vv. 16–19), and crucified together with two "robbers" (vv. 25–27).

Before the crucifixion Jesus had refused wine mingled with myrrh, which was intended to ease the pain (Mark 15.23). The mockery (vv. 29–32), in which the guilt of Jesus is reiterated, may have been intended in the first place to make him understand his error and to lead him to a confession of sins (see *m. Sanh.* 6.2). While the crucifixion was carried out by Roman soldiers, the burial in the evening of this day was done by a Jew in accordance with Deuteronomy 21.23 (Mark 15.42–46; see John 19.31).

Deuteronomy 21.22–23 is also related to crucifixion by Paul in Galatians 3.13 (see Acts 5.30; 10.39). Because a person hanging on a tree is cursed by God (Deut. 21.23), the cross of Jesus became a stumbling block to Jews (1 Cor. 1.23).

See also Anti-Semitism.   OTTO BETZ

Curious Bibles. The term "curious Bibles" is used of two types of Bibles: those that are noteworthy because of a typographical error or a peculiar translation, and those with an unusual format.

Oddities in Printing and Translation. In spite of the extreme care in proofreading Bibles, typographical errors have been found in them since the beginning of *printing history. In the 1562 folio edition of the Geneva Bible of 1560, there is an error in Matthew 5.9, which reads "Blessed are the place makers" instead of "peace makers"; hence this edition has been called the "Whig Bible." The same edition has another error in its indication of the contents of Luke 21: "Christ condemneth the poore widdowe" (for "commendeth"). Several editions of the Geneva Bible, issued by Robert Barker in London from 1608 to 1611, erroneously read "Judas" for "Jesus" at John 6.67. The first octavo edition of the King James Version (1612) reads at Psalm 119.161, "Printers have persecuted me without cause," instead of "princes."

A Bible issued in London in 1631 contains one of the most well-known typographical errors to date. This edition is known as the "Adulterous Bible" because of its omission of the word "not" in the seventh (sometimes numbered sixth) commandment, which then read, "Thou shalt commit adultery" (Exod. 20.14). For this mistake the printers, Robert Barker and associates, were fined £300 and ordered to suppress the thousand copies of the edition. Ironically, the same printers in 1641 published a Bible that omitted the word "no" in Revelation 21.1, so that it read, "And there was more sea."

John Fields of London published a Bible in 1653 that is marked by many careless errors, including the omission of "not" in 1 Corinthians 6.9, so that it reads, "Know ye not that the unrighteous shall inherit the kingdom of God?" In 1795, Thomas Bensley, also of London, issued a Bible in which Mark 7.27 read "Let the children first be killed" (instead of "filled").

The 1801 "Murderers" Bible was so named because of its use of "murderers" for "murmurers" in Jude 16. In Bibles printed in 1806, "fishers" in Ezekiel 47.10 is altered so that the text reads, "It shall come to pass that the fishes shall stand upon it." An edition of 1810 was dubbed the "Wife-Hater" Bible for its substitution of the letter *w* for *l* in Luke 14.26, so that the text reads, "If any . . . hate not . . . his own wife also."

More recent editions with noteworthy typographical errors include the first printing of volume 1 of the Old Testament published by the Episcopal Committee of the Confraternity of Christian Doctrine in 1950, in which Leviticus 11.30 includes the skunk as one of the animals that swarm upon the ground. The translation read "skink," which is a type of lizard, but the typesetter mistakenly made an unauthorized "correction" and changed *i* to *u*. Psalm 122.6 of the 1966 *Jerusalem Bible* instructs its readers to "Pay for peace" instead of "Pray." A less obvious error in the New American Bible's first edition of 1970 omits the last verse of the letter to the Hebrews. Early printings of the 1990 New Revised Standard Version omitted the words "having ten horns and seven heads" from Revelation 13.1.

In addition to typographical errors, unusual or eccentric translations can make an edition noteworthy. Of course, many renderings are thought unusual because their use of archaic English strikes the modern reader as odd. For example, the traditional rendering "Is there no balm in Gilead?" (Jer. 8.22) appears with the word "treacle" in both the 1535 Coverdale Bible and the 1568 Bishops' Bible, and as "Is there noe rosin in Galaad?" in the 1609 Douay Bible. The use of the word "breeches" (for "aprons") in Genesis 3.7 earned the 1560 Geneva Bible and its later printings the name "Breeches Bible." (In fact, the fourteenth-century Wycliffe Bible used the same word.)

There are also twentieth-century English Bibles with eccentric renderings. In Ferrar Fenton's 1903 Bible, Acts 19.3 finds Paul and Apollos "by profession landscape painters" instead of tentmakers. In James Moffatt's revised edition of the New Testament (1935), two people sleep in "a single bed" [i.e., not a double bed] (Luke 17.34), while the first edition reads "the one bed." And, in the New English Bible (1970), Paul warns the Corinthian faithful to "have nothing to do with loose livers" (1 Cor. 5.9).

(*See also* Translations, *article on* English Language.)

Unusual Formats. There are many examples of printed Bibles in curious formats. One such grouping is hieroglyphic Bibles, which are children's picture books citing brief scripture verses, with some words of the passages represented by small pictures. The first English hieroglyphic Bible was printed before 1784, although similar volumes had already been published in Latin,

German, and Dutch. A second printing, entitled *A Curious Hieroglyphic Bible,* appeared in London in 1784. Its subtitle is:

"Select Passages in the Old and New Testaments, represented with Emblematical Figures, for the Amusement of Youth: designed chiefly to familiarize tender Age, in a pleasing and diverting Manner, with early Ideas of the Holy Scriptures. To which are subjoined, a short Account of the Lives of the Evangelists, and other pieces, illustrated with Cuts."

This version of the Bible must have had popular appeal since it soon appeared in a number of editions and printings.

There exist two varieties of shorthand Bibles. *The New Testament in Shorthand,* prepared by Jeremiah Rich and issued in London in about 1665, used Rich's shorthand system throughout, except for the two dedication pages and the list of subscribers at the end. Another Bible in shorthand was published in 1904 in London by Sir Isaac Pitman and Sons Ltd., using the Pitman method.

The term "Thumb Bible" has been used to designate a synopsis, an epitome, or an abridgment of the Bible. Thumb Bibles are usually meant for children and are therefore printed in miniature volumes and are decorated with pictures. The oldest recognized Thumb Bible, entitled *An Agnus Dei,* is also one of the smallest: it measures 3.3 × 2.7 cm (1 5/16 × 1 1/16 in) and was issued in London in 1601. The book is made up of 128 leaves, and on each page is set about six lines of text, along with the running title and catch word. The text of this miniature volume, a rhymed account of Christ's life, was written by John Weever (1576–1632).

The second oldest and probably most well-known Thumb Bible is the *Verbum Sempiternum,* published in London in 1614. Presenting the Old and New Testament in versified summaries, this miniature Bible was the handiwork of John Taylor (1580–1653). *Verbum Sempiternum* was still being reprinted well into the 1800s. The first American edition (labelled "The Twelvth Edition, with Amendments") of this particular miniature Bible was published in Boston in 1786, with dimensions of 5.4 × 3.8 cm (2½ × 1½ in). The page facing the title page reads:

"Reader, come buy this Book, for tho' it's small, 'Tis worthy the perusal of all."

Only in 1727 was the Thumb Bible published in prose. Printed in London by R. Wilkin and entitled *Biblia or a Practical Summary of ye Old &*

New Testaments, this edition comprises close to three hundred pages (with sixteen engraved plates) and measures 3.6 × 2.4 cm (1 7/16 × 15/16 in).

Longman and Co. of London seem to have originated the term "Thumb Bible," which is found on the title page of an 1849 edition. Most likely this name was borrowed from General Tom Thumb (Charles Stratton), the famous midget who visited England with P. T. Barnum in 1844. Thumb Bibles were also printed in the eighteenth and nineteenth centuries in France, Germany, Holland, and Sweden. In all, almost three hundred separate editions are known.

In 1896 the Glasgow University Press photographically reduced the complete Oxford Nonpareil Bible (Authorized Version). David Bryce and Son of Glasgow and Henry Frowde of London issued it in a printing of 25,000 copies. This version is made up of 876 pages, each of which measures 4.2 × 2.8 cm (1 5/8 × 1 1/8 in). In a pocket inside the front cover a magnifying glass was provided. In the same year Bryce and Frowde also published a facsimile edition of the New Testament that was even smaller, just 2 × 1.5 cm (3/4 × 9/16 in), and there have been many other miniature editions.

Two other curious Bibles deserve mention. The first, published in London in 1698 by Benjamin Harris, is best described by its title: *The Holy Bible in Verse, Containing the Old and New Testaments, with the Apocripha* [sic]. *For the Benefit of Weak Memories. The Whole Containing above one thousand lines, with Cuts.* In 1988, Tyndale House Publishers reprinted Kenneth Taylor's *The Living Bible, Paraphrased* (1971; *see* Paraphrases), with the books of the Bible arranged in alphabetical order, so that the volume begins with Acts of the Apostles, and ends with the book of Zephaniah.   BRUCE M. METZGER

Curse. A curse, the opposite of a *blessing, is the pronouncement of evil on someone or something. In the Hebrew Bible, nouns and verbs associated with the Hebrew roots 'lh, 'rr, and qll are all translated by the English word "curse." While the meanings of these three roots are related and can be interchangeable, a separate treatment of each will highlight the full range of meanings of the word "curse."

The root 'lh occurs most frequently in legal contexts, associated with an oath and the protection of legal rights. Pronouncing a curse on a potential thief will protect property (Judg. 17.2; cf. Prov. 29.24). A curse pronounced on an accused person will, if it takes effect, establish the person's guilt (Num. 5.21–28; cf. 1 Kings 8.31; 2 Chron. 6.22). Pronouncing a curse on anyone who may disobey enforces a command by persons in authority (1 Sam. 14.24; cf. Gen. 24.41). Pronouncing a curse on anyone who may break a treaty guarantees loyalty to a treaty (Gen. 26.28). It is in this last sense that curse is used in connection with Israel's *covenant with the Lord, which has similarities to a treaty (Deut. 29.18). In all these senses, the curse is understood as conditional, that is, efficacious only if some legal right or agreement has been violated. Sometimes a person may be referred to as a curse (Num. 5.21; Jer. 29.18), meaning that such a person is in so calamitous a situation that he or she embodies the consequence of a curse that one might wish on another.

The root 'rr occurs most frequently in formulas that begin "Cursed be . . ." (Deut. 27.15–25; 28.16–19). In these situations, the formula is spoken by a person in authority and is directed against a subordinate (Gen. 4.11; 1 Sam. 14.24, 28). This formula functions as a way of maintaining stability within the community. Pronouncing a curse on one who has acted in ways that violate accepted social responsibility is a way of expelling that person from the community. In this sense, curse is also related to the maintenance of the covenant that the Lord made with Israel (Jer. 11.3; Deut. 27.15–25).

The root qll occurs in less technical situations; a curse can be made by private individuals against God (Lev. 24.15; 1 Sam. 3.13) or the king (2 Sam. 16.9).

In the New Testament the general usage is similar; see Mark 14.71 par.; Luke 6.28; James 3.9. For *Paul, those who adhere to the *Law are understood as being under the curse (Gal. 3.10, quoting Deut. 27.26). Furthermore, it is Christ who, on the cross (Gal. 3.13, quoting Deut. 21.23), became a curse in order to redeem those who live under the curse of the Law.

See also Anathema.   EDGAR W. CONRAD

Cush. Often translated "Ethiopia," Cush refers principally to the land of Nubia, south of Egypt (Map 7:F6). Cush's political apex came when the Nubians conquered and ruled *Egypt as its Dynasty XXV (716–656 BCE). According to 2 Kings 19.9, the Cushites saved King *Hezekiah of Ju-

dah from the *Assyrians in 701 BCE. In Genesis 2.13, Cush probably refers to *Babylon, which was occupied by Kassites in the second half of the first millennium BCE, and in Genesis 10.6–14 Cush (Babylon) has been confused with Cush (Nubia).

If *Moses' Cushite wife (Num. 12.1) was Zipporah (Exod. 2.15–22), there may have been another Cush in *Midian (whose poetic parallel is Cushan in Hab. 3.7). But *Miriam's becoming "as white as snow" with *leprosy (Num. 12.10) seems appropriately ironic punishment for her criticism of Moses' marriage to a black woman. Jeremiah 13.23 contends that Judah can no more change its penchant to sin than a Cushite can change skin color. Amos 9.7 mentions the Cushites as an example of God's universal concern. The name of Phinehas, *Aaron's grandson, is Egyptian for "the Nubian."

See also Africa.   STEVEN L. MCKENZIE

Cyrus. Cyrus (II) "the Great" founded the Persian (Achemenid) empire in 559 BCE and controlled the ancient Near East by the time of his death in 530. "Cyrus" may have been a dynastic rather than a personal name, for his grandfather Cyrus (I) was king of Anshan and a contemporary of Ashurbanipal, king of *Assyria (669–627 BCE). Cyrus took over the territories of the *Medes around 550 BCE and united them into a strong alliance, which clashed with Croesus of Lydia and captured Sardis, thus inaugurating a prolonged war with the Greek states. Cyrus's empire, which extended far to the east as well, was administered by local district governors (satraps).

In October 539, Cyrus defeated the *Babylonians at Opis, and his troops took control of the capital into which the gods from surrounding cult centers had been withdrawn for safety. When Cyrus entered the city he was warmly welcomed as a man of peace, and he demonstrated his religious tolerance with decrees returning the exiled deities to their shrines. In an edict he allowed the exiled Judeans to return home (Ezra 1.1; 2 Chron. 36.23) and later supported the restoration of the *Temple in Jerusalem. The references to Cyrus in *Isaiah (44.28; 45.1, 13) are significant, both for the usual dating of Isaiah 40–55 ("Second Isaiah") to the mid-sixth century BCE and for their description of him as the divinely designated shepherd and as the Lord's anointed ("*messiah"), the agent of the divine plan for Israel. Parts of the narrative of the book of *Daniel are also set in the reign of Cyrus, but this has been interpreted as the use of Cyrus as a dynastic name, as is the case with Darius in the same context (Dan. 6.28).

Cyrus is depicted on sculptures in his palace at Susa. He was buried in Pasargadae in 530 BCE and succeeded by his son and co-regent, Cambyses II.

See Persia.   DONALD J. WISEMAN

D

D. Scholarly shorthand for the author of *Deuteronomy, the fourth source in the *Pentateuch. D depicts *Moses giving a series of speeches, which urge Israel to follow the "*torah." But the law of which Moses speaks represents a massive revision of earlier laws. Among the Pentateuchal sources (J, E, D, and P), D is unique in mandating the centralization of the Yahwistic cult and the suppression of all Canaanite cults (Deut. 12).

Most scholars believe that Deuteronomy achieved its final form as the result of a long process of composition. Since the nineteenth century CE, they have identified "the book of the law" (2 Kings 22.8) discovered during the eighteenth year of *Josiah's reign (ca. 621 BCE) as an early form of Deuteronomy. The books of Kings mention other reformers (e.g., *Hezekiah, 2 Kings 18.4), but Josiah's exhaustive reforms and national *Passover (2 Kings 23.4–23) explicitly conform to Deuteronomic prescriptions. Hence, dating the substance of the D source (i.e., the laws in Deut. 12–26) to the seventh century BCE seems sound. A minority of scholars view the description of Josiah's reforms as a utopian projection and date D to the exilic or early postexilic age (mid- to late sixth century).

GARY N. KNOPPERS

Dagon. The national god of the *Philistines, according to the Bible. Judges 16.23 identifies a temple of Dagon at Gaza, which *Samson pulls down; the captured *ark of Yahweh is placed in another temple of Dagon at Ashdod (1 Sam. 5.2; see also 1 Macc. 10.83). The divine name also appears in the town name Beth-dagon (Josh. 15.41; 19.27). Dagon is not mentioned in inscriptions from southern Syria or Palestine, but occurs frequently in texts from north Syria and Mesopotamia as Dagan, the chief god of the middle Euphrates region; in the *Ugaritic tablets, *Baal is often referred to by the patronymic "son of Dagan." The Philistines thus probably borrowed the Semitic deity through direct contact with the coast of Syria rather than from southern Canaan.

DANIEL E. FLEMING

Damascus. A city of *Syria (*Aram); Map 1:Z1. It lies in an oasis formed by the Nahr el-Barada, which flows through the city from the anti-Lebanon range, and the Nahr el-A'waj south of Damascus, fed by springs on Mount *Hermon. These are the Abana and Pharpar of 2 Kings 5.12. The region has been inhabited since prehistoric times, and the city is mentioned in non-biblical sources by the mid-second millennium BCE. A comprehensive history is difficult to establish because no major excavations have taken place within the city, in part because it has been continuously inhabited.

*David subjected Damascus to tribute, but only briefly (2 Sam. 5.5–8; 1 Kings 11.23–25). Several wars were fought between the Aramean kingdom and Israel and Judah, and at one time Jeroboam II conquered Damascus (2 Kings 14.28). *Tiglath-Pileser III brought it into the *Assyrian empire (732 BCE), and subsequently it was under Neo-Babylonian and *Persian rule. After *Alexander the Great's conquests it fell to his successors, the Seleucids, until in 85 BCE it became briefly the capital of a *Nabatean kingdom. Rome conquered Syria in 65 BCE. Under the *Roman empire, Damascus was considered one of the city-states of the *Decapolis.

By the mid-first century CE there was a Jewish community in Damascus, among whom were Christians (Acts 9.1–25). Damascus was evidently under the control of the Nabatean King Aretas IV when *Paul escaped from his local governor (2 Cor. 11.32–33; cf. Acts 9.25).

A temple of Jupiter Damascenus was built on the site of the old temple of Hadad-Rimmon. This was superseded by the Church of Saint John the Baptist, built by Theodosius the Great (late fourth century CE), which was remodeled to become the Great Mosque.

SHERMAN ELBRIDGE JOHNSON

Dan. The fifth son of *Jacob and one of the twelve *tribes of Israel. Dan's mother is *Rachel's maid Bilhah (Gen. 30.1–6). The name Dan seems to be derived from the Hebrew verb meaning "to judge or vindicate." The tribe of Dan's first settlement is depicted as lying between the territories of Ephraim to the north, Benjamin to the east, and Judah to the south (Josh. 19.40–48). Dan was renowned for its verve (Gen. 49.16–17; Deut. 33.22).

Already at an early time, a majority of the tribe migrated northward to a site near the source of the *Jordan river (Josh. 19.47–48; Judg. 1.34). Hence, Dan often marks the northern border of Israel (1 Sam. 3.20; 2 Sam. 24.15). If the stories of the Danite hero *Samson (Judges 13–16) and the song of *Deborah (Judg. 5.17) have a historical core, however, some members of the tribe must have remained in the south. With the rise of the monarchy, these southern clans were apparently assimilated into the kingdoms of Israel and Judah.

Dan can also refer to a city (e.g., Gen. 14.14), originally called Laish (Judg. 18.7, 27–29) or Leshem (Josh. 19.47), which was captured and renamed by the Danite tribe. Dan's northern clans were probably located around this city (Map 3:Y2). The ancient sanctuary at Dan (Judg. 18.2, 30) was designated by King Jeroboam I of Israel as one of his two national shrines (1 Kings 12.29–30; see Golden Calf). Archeological work at Dan has revealed a substantial cult center dating to the tenth century BCE, the era of Jeroboam I. During the reign of Pekah, king of Israel, the territories of Dan and *Naphtali were conquered by *Tiglath-pileser III of Assyria, who exiled many of their residents (2 Kings 15.29).

GARY N. KNOPPERS

Dance and the Bible. The Bible has provided choreographers with themes and topics for their dances, and not always in a religious context: biblical characters—heroes and heroines, kings and sinners—and stories, often those with a compelling moral, provide excellent material for stage dance. They do not require copious explanatory program notes, and carry with them overtones and associations from childhood, as material learned at home or in religious education. The terse style of storytelling found in the Bible, often abounding in physical action and illuminating philosophical or moral issues, is well suited to the artistic ways and means available to the choreographer, who must deal with human movement to express aesthetic-kinetic ideas.

*Salome, the daughter of Herodias who danced before Herod Antipas, is perhaps the biblical character most often encountered in the annals of choreography. She has danced onstage from medieval passion plays right to the advent of modern dance at the beginning of the twentieth century, and she has continued to dance ever since.

In 1462, René, the king of Provence, organized a choreographic religious procession called "Lou Gue" in which there was a "minuet of the Queen of Sheba," along with other biblical dances. In 1475, the Jews of the Italian town of Pesaro used the Queen of *Sheba as part of their choreographic presentation at the wedding feast of the ruler of the region.

There are only a few examples of biblical subject matter to be found in the early French court ballets of the sixteenth and seventeenth centuries. One is *Les balet* [sic] *de la Tour de Babel,* chosen perhaps because God does not appear in the story at all, and the various languages are easily represented by folk dances from diverse countries.

Audiences as well as creators of classical ballet regarded their art as profane, if not altogether sinful and sacrilegious, and biblical subjects are rarely found in it. The revolutionaries of modern dance—Isadora Duncan, Maud Allen, and Loie Fuller, to name a few—who brought modern dance from their native America to Europe in the first decade of the twentieth century, had no such qualms, and soon a whole flurry of Salomes occupied the dance stage.

Many other biblical figures also attracted modern choreographers. Loie Fuller used the diaphanous veils and lighting effects she invented to depict the waters in *Miriam's Dance* and *The Deluge.* Ruth St. Denis and Ted Shawn choreographed a "Salome" dance, *Jephthah's Daughter,* and their ballet *Dancer at the Court of Ahasuerus* (the story of Queen *Esther) in the 1920s.

Classical ballet choreographers of the early twentieth century also turned to biblical subjects. Michel Fokine created his *Legend of Joseph* in 1914 for Diaghilev's Ballet Russe, and George Balanchine composed *The Prodigal Son* for the same company in 1929. Kassian Goleizovsky choreographed his innovative *Joseph the Beautiful* for the Experimental Stage of the Bolshoi Ballet in 1925. Even such philosophical writings as the book of *Job served choreographers, as in Ted Shawn's *Job, a Masque for Dancing* in 1931 in the

United States, and *Job* (1931) by Ninette de Valois, the founder of the British Royal Ballet.

For many leaders of American modern dance, such as Lester Horton, José Limón, and Martha Graham, the Bible was a chief source of inspiration. In particular, Graham's *Embattled Garden* and Limon's *There Is a Time* are the most perfectly wrought biblical choreographies of our time.

Not surprisingly, Israeli choreographers make frequent use of biblical themes and characters. Since the beginning of Jewish immigration to Palestine in the early part of the twentieth century, choreographers have often turned to the Bible for subjects. In the 1930s, the Russian-born ballerina Rina Nikova founded her Biblical Ballet company in Jerusalem. Several of her students were girls who had immigrated from Yemen. She soon discovered the special dance rhythms of Yemenite Jews. The teacher thus became her pupils' student, because she realized that their movement vocabulary suited the biblical stories she endeavored to depict in her works much better than did the European *danse d'école*.

Jewish-Yemenite dance traditions were also to play a decisive role in the work of the most important Israeli choreographer of her generation, Sara Levi-Tanai. She founded the Inbal Dance Theatre in 1949, and created many works based on biblical subjects, using traditional Yemenite tunes and steps to forge a personal, modern movement style that served her biblical ballets well.

The connection between ancient Yemenite artistic tradition and biblical choreography has created a commonly held fallacy, that Yemenite dance is somehow representative of dance in biblical times, of which we know little despite the many instances of dancing in the Bible. There are no less than eleven biblical Hebrew terms for dance, but hardly any further evidence that modern choreographers could use when dealing with biblical subjects.

Biblical themes also served as a source of inspiration for Israeli choreographers who since the 1940s had staged pageants, often at the very sites of the biblical events they dealt with. They combined biblical texts, music, and mass movement, in the manner and stage techniques devised by Rudolf von Laban and influenced by the "Theater of the Masses" in Soviet Russia in the 1920s and 1930s, for the kibbutzim (collective settlements). These were biblical multimedia events, staged before the term had been coined.

There is scarcely a modern choreographer of note who has not dealt with biblical materials. In recent times these include John Neumeier, Jiri Kylian, Anna Sokolow, and Laura Dean, in addition to those already mentioned. Perhaps one of the reasons modern dance artists have turned to biblical subjects is that there are so many female dramatis personae in the Bible, providing the choreographers with roles for the women in their companies.

While the Bible provides a wide cultural common denominator for all of western culture, for Israel it is in a special sense a national heritage; hence the wealth of Israeli choreographic works based on it. The Bible is indeed an excellent libretto for choreography, providing the artist with moving metaphors, in both religious and nonreligious contexts.   GIORA MANOR

Daniel, The Book of. According to the book that bears his name, Daniel was a pious and wise Jewish youth who was deported to *Babylon by King *Nebuchadrezzar (spelled Nebuchadnezzar in the book), together with his three young friends, Shadrach, Meshach, and Abednego, the royal household, and other prominent citizens. Presumably, this was the first deportation ordered by Nebuchadrezzar in 597 BCE (2 Kings 24.10–16; the date implied in Dan. 1.1 is 606 BCE). In Ezekiel 14.14, 20, a Daniel (Hebr. *dānī'ēl*) is mentioned alongside *Noah and *Job as one of the outstandingly righteous men of history; in Ezekiel 28.3, the wisdom of the king of Tyre is said to exceed even that of this Daniel. Many commentators believe that the Daniel of the Ezekiel text is to be identified with the Canaanite Dan'il (*dn'il*) of "The Tale of Aqhat" preserved among the fourteenth-century BCE texts found at Ras Shamra (*Ugarit) in Syria. There, Dan'il is described as one who "judges the cause of the widow / tries the case of the orphan." It would therefore appear that Daniel was a legendary figure, represented in this book as a youth of outstanding wisdom and piety who matures into a seer capable of receiving visions of the future.

Content. The structure of the book of Daniel is straightforward:

I. Six tales from the Babylonian exile
   A. Daniel and his friends at the table of the king (chap. 1)
   B. Daniel interprets the king's dream of the colossal statue (chap. 2)
   C. Three young men in the fiery furnace (chap. 3)

D. Nebuchadnezzar's madness (chap. 4)
E. The handwriting on the wall (chap. 5)
F. Daniel in the lions' den (chap. 6)
II. Apocalyptic visions and Daniel's prayer
   A. The vision of "the one like a son of man" (chap. 7)
   B. The vision of the ram and the he-goat (chap. 8)
   C. Daniel's prayer and the meaning of the seventy years of "the devastation of Jerusalem" (chap. 9)
   D. The final vision and the promise of resurrection (chaps. 10–12).

The internal dates throughout the book show that the narratives of Part I partially overlap the visions of Part II. The latter culminates in the final vision dated in "the third year of King Cyrus of Persia" (10.1), 535 BCE. In effect, the book records both the external and the internal history of Daniel, the former (chaps. 1–6) consisting of the stories of his virtuous deeds and wonders, and the latter (chaps. 7–12) his visionary experiences and revelations regarding the future of the world.

It should be noted that the Daniel tradition in ancient Israel was considerably larger than what is now preserved in our canonical text. We know this from the additions to the book of Daniel found in the *Septuagint (the older Greek translation of the book of Daniel, ca. 100 BCE) and in Theodotion (a more literal Greek version of the first century CE, and the one usually included in ancient Greek manuscripts). These include the Prayer of *Azariah and Song of the Three Young Men (inserted after 3.23 of the Hebrew text); the story of *Susanna and the elders (chap. 13 in the Septuagint), and the story of *Bel and the Dragon (chap. 14 in the Septuagint). (See also Apocrypha, article on Jewish Apocrypha.) In addition, a number of extracanonical Daniel materials have appeared among the *Dead Sea Scrolls at Qumran, the most interesting of which is the "Prayer of Nabonidus." Although put in the mouth of a different Babylonian king, this text parallels the story of Nebuchadnezzar's madness and recovery found in Daniel 4.

Unity and Language. The artful arrangement of the diverse subject matter of the book might suggest a single redaction, if not a single author. But the problem is further complicated by the circumstance that the book of Daniel is written in two languages, *Hebrew and *Aramaic.

The Hebrew text of Daniel 2.4a begins: "The Chaldeans said to the king (in Aramaic)." From that point until the end of chap. 7, the *Masoretic text of Daniel is written entirely in Aramaic, in the same dialect as that found in the other Aramaic texts of the Hebrew Bible (Ezra 4.8–6.18; 7.12–26, the single verse Jer. 10.11, and two words in Gen. 31.47). Why the text of Daniel switches so suddenly from Hebrew to Aramaic and back again, no one has ever been able to determine. One obvious solution would be that another writer, living at a different time and place and more deeply rooted in the literary culture of Official Aramaic, composed these chapters. Composite authorship is not the only possible solution, though. For centuries, Aramaic, a linguistic cousin to Hebrew and possibly even the language of the ancestral period (see Gen. 31.47; Deut. 26.5), was the lingua franca of the Babylonian and Persian empires, and it continued in use throughout the Hellenistic period in Palestine. Jews knew it well and used it freely—so freely, in fact, that by the Roman period it was displacing Hebrew as the language of Palestine. Perhaps a single writer of Daniel freely moved from Hebrew to Aramaic for no reason other than to tell the stories of the Babylonian diaspora in the language that was in fact being used there at the time.

Were the Aramaic portion of Daniel exactly coequal with the narrative portion, chaps. 1–6, the case for at least dual authorship would be almost irresistible—but it is not. Not only is the first tale (down to Dan. 2.4a) written in a late biblical Hebrew enriched by Persian loan words, but chap. 7, the first of the apocalyptic visions and in many ways the most central chapter in the whole book, is written in Aramaic. Literary genre and theological intention thus do not correlate with language.

One of the most frequently offered explanations of the bilingual character of Daniel is that the entire book (except for the prayer of 9.4–20) was originally written in Aramaic, and that 1.1–2.4a and chaps. 8–12 were later translated into Hebrew, perhaps in the interest of rendering the book more acceptable and authoritative to a community whose estimate of the sacredness of the Hebrew tongue waxed even as its vernacular use of that language waned. The case is supported by the fact that the Hebrew of the last five chapters in particular contains many Aramaisms and can often be clarified by translation "back" into Aramaic. While such a view of the bilingualism of the book would certainly imply an ongoing history of development of Daniel even after the text was essentially fixed, it would not necessarily demand that the book be regarded as composite in authorship. And even this modest theory faces the difficulty that the earliest fragments of the text of Daniel among the Dead Sea Scrolls of Qumran, written perhaps little more than a century after the composition of the book itself, already exhibit the same Hebrew/Aramaic/Hebrew transitions at the same points in the book.

The strongest arguments for multiple authorship are these. First, the literary style of chaps. 1–6 differs radically from that of chaps. 7–12. The former have all the flavor of heroic tales of the kind that would emanate from courtly or *wisdom circles (compare Daniel 2 with the *Joseph story and with *Esther); the latter chapters belong to that late descendant of prophetic eschatology, *apocalyptic literature. Second, the stories about Daniel in chapters 1–6 reflect a *diaspora outlook. By their language and their knowledge of cultural details, they show considerable exposure to both Persian and Hellenistic influences. In their essentials, these stories are assumed to come from the third century BCE or even somewhat earlier. The apocalypses of Daniel 7–12, on the other hand, focus on Judah, *Jerusalem, and the sanctuary. They can be dated rather more precisely (see below) to the first quarter of the second century BCE. If they were not composed by one writer who supplemented and revised the earlier work several times during a period of two or three years, then they were composed by persons working in close proximity in time and place. The writer(s) of Daniel 7–12 knew of the earlier cycle of Daniel stories, and for reasons of their own they used that collection as a basis from which to extend its ministry into their own realm of apocalyptic dreams and visions.

Date. The book of Daniel is one of the few books of the Bible that can be dated with precision. That dating makes it the latest of all the books of the Hebrew Bible, and yet it is still early enough to have been known by the sectarian community at *Qumran, which flourished between the second century BCE and 68 CE.

The lengthy apocalypse of Daniel 10–12 provides the best evidence for date and authorship. This great review of the political maelstrom of ancient Near Eastern politics swirling around the tiny Judean community accurately portrays history from the rise of the *Persian empire down to a time somewhat after the desecration of the Jerusalem *Temple and the erection there of the "abomination that makes desolate" (Dan.

11.31) in the late autumn of 167 BCE by the Greco-Syrian king Antiochus IV Epiphanes. (The story of this first of all pogroms of the Jews is told in 1 Macc. 1.41–61; see Maccabees, The Books of the.) The portrayal is expressed as *prophecy about the future course of events, given by a seer in Babylonian captivity; however, the prevailing scholarly opinion is that this is mostly prophecy after the fact. Only from 11.39 onward does the historical survey cease accurately to reproduce the events known to have taken place in the latter years of the reign of Antiochus IV. The most obvious explanation for this shift is that the point of the writer's own lifetime had been reached. Had the writer known, for example, about the success of the Jewish freedom fighters led by Judas Maccabeus in driving the garrison of the hated Antiochus from the temple precincts (an event that occurred on 25 Kislev, 164 BCE, according to 1 Macc. 4.34–31), the fact would surely have been mentioned. But evidently it had not yet happened!

The discussion of the date of the book of Daniel can be summed up as follows. With the possible exception of minor glosses, the book reached its present canonical form approximately in the middle of 164 BCE, though the translation of 1.1–2.4a and chaps. 8–12 from Aramaic into Hebrew may have taken place later. One of the best pieces of evidence available for the rapid acceptance of the book of Daniel as scripture is the inclusion of Daniel and his three friends in the list of the heroes of the Jewish faith in 1 Maccabees 2.59–60, thought to have been written in Hebrew about 100 BCE. In contrast, in Ben Sira's similar list (Sir. 44–49), written about 180 BCE, Daniel figures not at all.

Audience. To determine to whom the book was addressed in the first place, and in what circles the author or authors might have moved, two bits of internal evidence must be taken into account. First of all, the heroes of the stories of chaps. 1–6 must represent the kind of piety that would have been considered exemplary by the book's audience. These were observant Jews, heroes of the faith who refused to compromise with idolatry or, to put it another way, to participate in the syncretizing practices of the upper classes of their people during the Hellenistic reign of Antiochus IV Epiphanes (see 1 Macc. 1.41–43). In Daniel 7–12, the heroes are "the people who are loyal to their God" (11.32), "those who are wise . . . those who lead many to righteousness" (12.3). To these "holy ones of the

Most High" (Dan. 7.18) is awarded the everlasting kingdom to be their dominion forever.

Given these clues internal to the book, modern commentators have frequently identified the authors of Daniel and the audience to which they spoke with the observant party of the "Hasideans" or *hasidim*, a title variously translated "the righteous ones," "the godly ones," or even "the saints." These people are known from 1 Maccabees 2.42 and 7.13–17, where they are presented as devout persons who reluctantly join in the war of liberation raised by the Maccabean rebels and who stay with that rebellion until they are convinced that the desecration of the Temple has been removed and that the authentic *Zadokite priestly line has been restored. According to some scholars, their descendants among the observant wing of Judaism of the first century BCE branched into the covenanters at Qumran, on the one hand, and into the *Pharisees, and perhaps even the *Zealots, on the other. For several centuries, this party in Judaism stood against syncretism and accommodation and may even have organized themselves into secret conventicles to oppose the corruptions in worship and in politics indulged in by the priestly classes.

Significance. The theological value of the book of Daniel does not lie in its ability to predict the future. According to the text of Daniel 7.9–27, the great judgment of the kingdoms of the earth and the establishment of "one like a *son of man [NRSV: human being]" (7.13)—who may be "the holy ones of the Most High" themselves (7.19)—should have occurred during the reign of Antiochus IV Epiphanes, the "little horn" with the "mouth speaking arrogantly" (7.8). Such an eschatological crisis did not, of course, happen in the reign of Antiochus. The canonizers themselves must have known this; perhaps they had already reinterpreted the four beasts who rise out of the sea in chap. 7 in such a way as to make Rome the fourth beast and the little horn some Roman emperor. By means of reinterpretation of the symbols of the apocalypse, it would have been possible to keep the timetable of events leading up to the last judgment open, and it was that openness that enabled the writer of Revelation 20 to transform Daniel 7 into a vision of the imminent worldwide crisis known as the *day of judgment.

But all attempts to discern an actual timetable in the apocalyptic scenario of Daniel finally are doomed to failure. As Jews and Christians affirm, the Bible is a human word, and therefore cannot accurately predict events of the distant future in the manner of history written in advance. As Jews and Christians also affirm, however, the book of Daniel is at the same time a word from God to God's people. It teaches that the God of justice and righteousness is not mocked by the powers of oppression that hold sway in the world. God will emerge from history as the victor, and those who choose to serve the causes of justice and righteousness are on the victor's side. In their own lives they can give a foretaste of life in the kingdom of heaven, just as Daniel and his three friends do in the stories of chaps. 1–6. In prayer and proclamation, God's people can announce the good news that those who hope for equity and the vindication of the just need not wait forever. Although our age no longer shares the confidence of an earlier age that it is possible to give a timetable or to write a historylike narrative about God's coming victory, the deep faith remains fundamental to our western theological tradition that history is meaningful. It gains its meaning from the end of history, which is God's triumphant intervention on behalf of God's own goodness. And it gains its meaning in movements along the way in which the saints have opportunities to enact in their own lives of righteousness and obedience the reality of God's coming kingdom.

W. SIBLEY TOWNER

Darius. The son of Hystaspes, an Achaemenid, Darius was ruler of the *Persian empire from 522 BCE (when he usurped the kingship in Parsa) until his death in 486 BCE. After a year spent quelling revolts in Mesopotamia, Elam, Iran, and Armenia, he conquered the Indus Valley (about 516 BCE), invaded Scythia north of the Danube without success, and conquered the southeastern corner of Europe (about 514–512 BCE). Part of Libya was subdued; but campaigns against Greece in 492 and 490 failed, and with Egypt in revolt (486) Darius died before his final expedition could be launched. Under his rule, the Persian empire reached its greatest extent.

He had a talent for administration. The empire was divided by him into twenty provinces (satrapies) whose governors (satraps) were responsible for law and order, the delivery of fixed tribute, and local military operations. A leading part was played by an elite increasingly composed of Persian nobles; but in *Egypt and *Babylonia natives could hold important offices, and in Syria and *Phoenicia city kings and local rulers were responsible to the satrap. For provincial affairs, Darius seems also to have used expert advisers whom he could keep beside him or send out as agents. To *Jerusalem *Zerubbabel seems to have been dispatched as local governor; and the *Temple, whose reconstruction had been ordered by *Cyrus and allowed to lapse, was completed under his rule in 515 BCE (Ezra 4–6). The prophets *Haggai and *Zechariah prophesied during his reign (Hag. 1.1; 2.1, 10, 18; Zech. 1.1, 7; 7.1).

In his court style, Darius seems to have set himself on a pinnacle high above his subjects. He had a script invented for his royal inscriptions (in Old Persian), in which he showed himself remarkably introspective. Presumably a Zoroastrian by upbringing, he claimed an intimate relationship with the god Ahuramazda, whose universal omnipotence was matched by his own on earth. He could be called a monotheist, but he supported the established religions of the conquered peoples (including that of Yahweh). As a ruler he was dynamic (his own words at Behistun were "What was said to them by me, night and day it was done"), and though implacable he was generally just. He molded an imperial system that his successors, who prided themselves on their descent from him, were too inclined to preserve unchanged.

He was born either about 550 BCE or some eight years earlier. His principal palace was at Susa (Map 11:J4), but his rock-cut tomb is near Persepolis (Map 11:K5).

Two later Persian kings of the same name were Darius II (423–404 BCE) and Darius III (336–330 BCE). The reference in Nehemiah 12.22 to Darius the Persian could be to either Darius II or Darius III. "Darius the Mede," mentioned only in Daniel 5.31 and 9.1, is understood by most scholars to be a composite created by the author of the book of *Daniel because, they argue, texts like Isaiah 13.17 and 21.2, as well as Jeremiah 51.11, had looked forward to a Median capture of *Babylon.   J. M. Cook

David. One of the best-known biblical characters, David is a curiously elusive figure. The Bible tells of his carving out an empire unmatched in ancient Israel's history. Elsewhere, however, in historical records from near that period (tenth century BCE), he is not so much as mentioned. He is known to generations of scripture readers as "the sweet psalmist of Israel" (2 Sam 23:1 KJV) and the man whom God had chosen (1 Sam. 16.12; 2 Sam, 10.5). Yet his story

in the books of *Samuel pivots on the episode of his adultery with *Bathsheba and murder of her husband, Uriah.

The Books of Samuel and Kings. David's story emerges primarily in the books of Samuel, concluding in 1 Kings 1–2. Scholarly attempts to reconstruct the history of the composition of these books remain highly speculative. On the one hand, there is general agreement that the final form of the work belongs to the period of *exile in the sixth century BCE. On the other hand, dates for individual component units of the work vary from near the time of the events depicted to the time of final compilation, a span of some five hundred years.

Few critics, however, would deny David a significant place in the history of the ancient Israelite state. Recent scholarship views him as a paramount chief with a genius for mediation, a man supremely able to command diverse tribal, economic, and cultic allegiances and to consolidate them into the centralized power needed for the formation of a nation-state.

According to Samuel and *Kings, this youngest son of a *Bethlehem farmer is sought out and anointed by the prophet *Samuel on behalf of the Lord (1 Sam. 16). He gains access to the court of *Saul, first king of Israel, initially by virtue of his musical prowess (1 Sam. 16.14–23) and then by defeating the Philistine champion *Goliath (1 Sam. 17)—there is some inconsistency in the plot here. Jonathan, Saul's son, loves him. A period of deadly rivalry with Saul, however, ensues. During this time, he marries Saul's daughter, Michal, and establishes his own independent military power as an outlaw in the Judean wilderness and as an ally of the *Philistines (1 Sam. 18–30).

After Saul's death (1 Sam. 31), David becomes king over *Judah in the south (2 Sam. 1–2) and then over *Israel in the north (2 Sam. 3–5), hence king over "all Israel." In 2 Samuel 5–10, he is depicted as coming to the peak of his power: he wins victories over external enemies, including the Philistines, establishes *Jerusalem as a capital and a cult center, and is assured by the prophet *Nathan of an enduring dynasty (2 Sam. 7). His dealings with *Bathsheba and Uriah (2 Sam. 11–12), however, elicit divine denunciation, conveyed by Nathan. Rape and murder now erupt within David's own house (2 Sam. 13–14), his son *Absalom rebels, and civil war ensues (2 Sam. 15–20).

A coda of short stories, anecdotes, and poetry (2 Sam. 21–24), connected to what has preceded by theme and allusion rather than by plot, caps the books of Samuel. The main plot itself is brought to a close with the story of David's death and *Solomon's succession at the beginning of the next book (1 Kings 1–2).

This story of David belongs to the larger story, told in Genesis through 2 Kings, of Israel's origins, nationhood, and eventual removal from the *Promised Land. David's story belongs with the account of the emerging nation-state's attempt to adapt religious and political institutions, especially leadership, to changing circumstances. His story is also part of the story of Yahweh's attempt to maintain or re-create a relationship of loyalty between deity and people. The people's desire for a human king is taken as a rejection of divine sovereignty. Thus Saul, designated by God at the people's insistence, must be rejected in favor of David, the one whom God has chosen freely (1 Sam. 13.14).

In a sense, the reader's first glimpse of David comes even earlier in 1 Samuel (2.1–10). The childless Hannah gives thanks for the gift of a baby (Samuel) and speaks, prophetically, of the king, the "anointed one" (see *Messiah) to whom Yahweh will give power. As the child is a special gift to the woman, so the kingdom is a special gift to David. Both gifts are freely given by God.

Giving and grasping lie at the story's heart. At critical moments David seems to allow choice to rest with others, especially Yahweh. At those moments he moves with a favorable tide; he may provoke a reader to contemplate forbearance, to consider providence as reality (e.g., 1 Sam. 14 and 26; 2 Sam. 15–16). At other times he falters, unwilling to take the risk, or to accept injured esteem issuing from rejection (e.g., 1 Sam. 25; 2 Sam. 11–12). In these instances, a reader may be confronted with a more familiar reality, the reality of deceit, greed, and violence that makes many judge the David story in Samuel realistic and plausible.

God gives David the kingdom, the house of Israel and Judah (cf. 2 Sam. 12.8). David's life, however, has a private as well as public dimension. What happens, privately, in his own house (palace and family) impinges on the nation. While his mighty men are besieging Rabbah, the *Ammonite capital, David seizes Bathsheba (2 Sam. 10–12). Thus, as the one house (the house of Israel) is secured, another (the house of David) begins to crumble. In the brutal story of Amnon, Tamar, and *Absalom that follows, first Tamar, David's daughter (2 Sam. 13), then both family and nation will be rent (2 Sam. 14–20).

The kingship arose out of the people's search for security, but security readily generates corruption. David's son, the builder of Yahweh's house, falters in turn: the great Solomon falls prey to the expanding glory of his own house (see 1 Kings 11). *Kingship—even Davidic kingship, Yahweh's gift—turns out to be no talisman (see 1 Sam. 8 and Deut. 17). In Yahweh alone, the story suggests, is true power and security to be found. The larger story (Genesis—2 Kings) ends with the house of Yahweh ruined, the people dispersed. A brief note about the house (dynasty) of David concludes the work (2 Kings 15.27–30): the exiled Davidic king sits powerless in the house of his *Babylonian conqueror, like Mephibosheth, grandson of Saul, in the house of David (2 Sam. 9.13). The wheel has turned full circle. The promise of an enduring house for David seems, in 2 Samuel 7, to be unconditional. It turns out to have limits; Yahweh, after all, is unwilling to be taken for granted.

The New Testament designation of *Jesus as "son of David" has predisposed many Christian readers to idealize the king. Yet David in Samuel and Kings is a complex character. Often, to be sure, the narrator elicits for David the admiration of readers—as the heroic slayer of Goliath (1 Sam. 17), for example, or the man who twice spares Saul, his persecutor (1 Sam. 24, 26), or the king who denounces Joab for killing Abner, the enemy general (2 Sam. 3), or who grants life to the cursing Shimei (2 Sam. 16, 19). Yet, equally, the narrator opens other possible perspectives even in these same narratives; David is a man with an eye for the main chance, adept at clothing his power-seeking and self-interest in the rhetoric of piety and morality, but exposed for all to see in the story of Bathsheba and Uriah.

The undercutting of the hero is ubiquitous. The account of his incarceration ("until the day of their death") of the ten concubines whom he abandoned to be raped on the roof of the house he fled hardly conjures a character of courage or responsibility (2 Sam. 15; 16; 20). The story of Solomon's accession in 1 Kings 1 pictures the king in gray tones as the dupe of a Solomonic faction's power play. His dying charge to Solomon (1 Kings 2.1–9) to kill Joab, his long-serving general, and Shimei, to whom he had granted pardon, evokes admiration only for its tidy ruthlessness. Or the coda to 2 Samuel (chaps. 21–24) may prompt a reader to ponder, for example, the difference between Rizpah's courage and David's compliance (2 Sam. 21), or the incongruity between David's treatment of Bath-

sheba and Uriah and the psalmist king's proclamation of his innocent righteousness ("I was
blameless before [Yahweh] and I kept myself
from guilt," 2 Sam. 22.24). Is this perhaps not
righteousness but self-righteousness, not piety
but hypocrisy? Even the tale of the slaying of
Goliath, the foundation story of the heroic David, is placed in question by the coda. Without
warning, tucked in amongst miscellaneous anecdotes, is the narrator's devastating remark that
it was Elhanan who slew the mighty Gittite (2
Sam. 21.19).

In the subsequent narrative (1 and 2 Kings)
David is viewed as a standard by which most
other kings are judged unfavorably (e.g., 1 Kings
14.8; 15.3–5, 11), yet even these passages harbor
a sardonic quality. David, the narrator informs
us, "did what was right in the sight of Yahweh
and did not turn aside from anything that he
commanded him all the days of his life, except
in the matter of Uriah the Hittite" (1 Kings 15.5).
That little word "except" is powerfully subver-
sive.

In Samuel and Kings the tensions in the depiction of David are never resolved. They are,
perhaps, what give him life.

The Books of Chronicles. 1 and 2 *Chronicles
offers quite a different version of David's life.
This work is later than Samuel-Kings, composed
perhaps in the fifth century BCE, and draws upon
a version of those books which it revises and
supplements.

After a genealogical prologue, the main story
line starts (1 Chron. 10–12) with the death of
Saul and David's crowning as king of all Israel;
gone are the divisions between north and south.
Jerusalem is taken. A great muster of mighty
men is transformed into a cultic congregation
conducting David and the *ark to the new capital
with singing and celebration (1 Chron. 12–16).
Battles (1 Chron. 14; 18–20) and plague (1 Chron.
21) are mentioned but bracketed by this greater
purpose of establishing the place where Yahweh
will be worshiped. From 1 Chronicles 22 to the
end of the book and David's death, the focus is
upon worship. David gathers the congregation
once more and issues plans for the building of
Yahweh's house and the organization of those
who will sustain it. *Priests and *Levites, musicians and gatekeepers, commanders of this, chief
officers of that, all are ordered to such an end.
It is in ordering and implementing the great
praise due to God that David finds life in the
Chronicler's narrative.

The Psalms. Elsewhere in the Bible, the theme

of a promise to continue David's line (the Davidic
covenant) surfaces, for example, in the prophecy
of Isaiah 9.7 and in Isaiah 55.3–4, a message of
hope addressed to the Judean community in
exile. Otherwise, David's presence is most marked
in the *Psalms where many of the psalm titles
use the term lĕdāwīd—of, to, or about David.

Modern scholars (and a few in ancient times)
have generally considered these psalm ascrip-
tions to be later additions to material that is itself
mostly post-Davidic. Most interpreters over the
centuries, however, have read the psalms in the
light of these Davidic titles. In western iconography, for example, David is instantly recognizable as the man with crown and harp or psaltery,
David the psalmist king; in popular culture he
is often found with these attributes as the king
of spades in playing cards. The image connects
with the story of David's coming to Saul's court
in 1 Samuel 16, but much more with 1 Chronicles, where the king's concern with the promulgation of *music in the temple worship is such a
dominant theme (see also Amos 6.5). Moreover,
one psalm is shared by both the Psalter and 2
Samuel (Ps. 18 = 2 Sam. 22).

Davidic authorship of the psalms has a special
attraction for those who would flesh out the
inner life of David, especially the David of Samuel-
Kings whose piety is so tenuously pictured. Thus
Psalm 51, linked by its title to the crucial Bathsheba episode, may be read as a window into the
soul of the great king. His repentance, indicated
in the narrative with but a few words (2 Sam.
12.13), is here paraded impressively. Problems
of interpretation remain, however. The last verses
of Psalm 51, for example, conjure a postexilic context (sixth century BCE or later) and
strain any reading that takes the poem too literally as the outpourings of the tenth-century
king.

The New Testament. The New Testament
shows little interest in the personality of David,
though the account of Jesus' plucking of the ears
of grain on the *Sabbath (Mark 2.23–28 par.)
explicitly recalls David's taking the holy bread
from the priest at Nob (1 Sam. 21) and is in
character with the David of the books of Samuel.
In the Gospels, Jesus is linked to the royal dynasty of Judah and to the Davidic covenant by
both *genealogy (Matt. 1.1–17; Luke 3.23–38)
and address—he is called son of David, mostly
in the context of healing/exorcism stories (e.g.,
Matt. 15.21–28; 20.29–34). Above all, in the
New Testament, David is author—and prophet—
of the psalms (see, e.g., Mark 12.36; Acts 1.16–

20), which are interpreted where possible as messianic prophecies fulfilled by Jesus.

See also Israel, History of; Judah, The Kingdom of.   DAVID M. GUNN

Day of Atonement. Known in Hebrew as *yôm (ha)kippūr(îm)*, the Day of Atonement is the most solemn festival in the Jewish religious calendar. It is celebrated on the tenth day of the seventh month, Tishri (= September/October). The name is found in Leviticus 23.27–28; 25.9 and is explained in Leviticus 16.30: "for on that day the Lord will make atonement (*yĕkappēr*) for you to purify you from all your sins." Leviticus 16 describes the elaborate rites performed by the high *priest in the *Temple at Jerusalem. The priest drew lots between two goats, one of which was presented as a sin offering to God, and the other dispatched to *Azazel in the *wilderness. It was only on this day that the high priest entered the holy of holies, the most sacred part of the Temple enclosure in which the *ark of the covenant was situated. He would enter bearing *incense whose fragrance symbolized God's forgiveness of the sins of Israel.

In antiquity as well as today Yom Kippur was considered a festival of spiritual accounting. Leviticus 16.29, 31 ordains that "you shall afflict yourselves." This term was interpreted to signify a day of *fasting when all food and drink were avoided. Tradition has added to these abstentions other deprivations, such as refraining from bathing, the use of cosmetics, and sexual intercourse. The people spend the day within the *synagogue reciting and chanting a specially composed liturgy, the core of which includes confessional prayers, thanksgiving hymns, and petitions to God for favor in the coming year. According to Leviticus 25.9–10, Yom Kippur was the day of the jubilee year (i.e., the fiftieth year) when slaves were freed, debts canceled, and land returned to its original owners. This aspect of the ancient festival is preserved in the modern collection of pledge contributions for the assistance of those in need.

Jewish tradition regards Yom Kippur as a day of judgment. On this day God passes judgment on the past deeds of every individual and decrees who shall live and who shall die during the ensuing year. The judgment process actually begins ten days before Yom Kippur, on the first day of Tishri, or Rosh Hashanah, the Jewish New Year, and reaches its culmination on Yom Kippur.

Even after the early Christians ceased to observe the day of fasting, some of the symbolism of Yom Kippur was retained in certain formulations. Note, for example, such New Testament expressions as "the blood of Christ" or "the *day of judgment," as well as the parallel made in Hebrews 9.1–14.

See also Feasts and Festivals.

BEN ZION WACHOLDER

Day of Judgment. The "last day," the end of the present world, when God or his agent will preside over a final, universal judgment of the living and the resurrected dead. A definitive assessment of human actions will be made, and each person rewarded or punished accordingly.

Hebrew Bible. Neither the phrase "day of judgment" nor the full-blown apocalyptic *eschatology supporting it is found in the Hebrew Bible. But the cluster of ideas and images surrounding the *day of the Lord contribute significantly to its eventual development: the forensic character of "that day" when God will judge his enemies (Joel 3.2, 1, 14); its universal perspective, with judgment directed against both Israel's enemies, "the nations," and Israel herself, or at least the enemies of God in her midst (Isa. 2.6–19); and the opposing imagery of light and darkness (Amos 5.18–20), with far greater emphasis placed on the latter (Zeph. 1.14–16; the somber medieval hymn *Dies irae* draws its opening line from the *Vulgate rendering of v. 15).

Early Judaism. The factors that lead eventually to the emergence of the idea of a final day of judgment in particular are as disputed as those that lead to apocalyptic eschatology in general. Some degree of foreign influence (Persian, Egyptian, and/or Hellenistic) is plausible, but difficult to prove. What is clear is that both the phrase "day of judgment" and its substance appear in a wide variety of Jewish texts of the Greco-Roman period, along with the first undisputed reference to the resurrection of the dead (Dan. 12.2; *see* Afterlife and Immortality, *article on* Second Temple Judaism and Early Christianity). In Daniel the link between resurrection (12.2) and judgment (7.9–27) is implicit. In becomes explicit in 1 Enoch, where the angel *Raphael shows *Enoch the places appointed for all human souls "until the day of their judgment" (22.4); this is "the great judgment" (22.5), "the great day of judgment and punishment and torment" (22.11) that will affect even the rebel angels (10.6; cf. 90.24–27). In these earlier strata of 1 Enoch, judgment will apparently come from God himself (91.7); in the later Similitudes, however, God's "chosen one" is repeatedly named as judge (45–55).

The apocryphal book of 2 Esdras (4 Ezra) contains the most coherent account of the day of judgment. Judgment day will be preceded by a temporary messianic kingdom (7.28–29), a week of "primeval silence" (7.30), and the resurrection of the dead (7.32). Only then will the Most High sit in judgment; both righteous and unrighteous deeds shall stand forth clear and unchangeable, and *paradise and *hell be disclosed (7.33–36). Without sun, moon, or stars, noon or night, this "day" will in fact last "as though for a week of years" (7.43). During it, God will judge all nations, the few righteous and the many ungodly (7.51). This "day of judgment" will be definitive because it marks "the end of this age and the beginning of the immortal age to come" (7.43 [113]).

Other early Jewish texts that speak of a day of judgment include the *Septuagint of Isaiah 34.8 (rendering the Hebrew for "day of vengeance"); Judith 16.17 (against the nations); Jubilees 5.10–14 (the great day of judgment that awaits the generation of the giants and all creation) and 22.21 (against Canaan and all his descendants); Testament of Levi 3.2–3 (the second and third heavens prepared to punish unrighteous humans and spirits at the day of judgment); and Pseudo-Philo's *Biblical Antiquities* 3.10 (following a pattern similar to that of 2 Esdras 7.30–33, 43 [113]).

New Testament. The New Testament references to the day of judgment are rooted in contemporary Jewish apocalyptic thought. This is evident from such texts as 2 Peter and Jude, in both of which the fate of the rebel angel *Azazel (1 Enoch 10.4–6) is extended to his fellow rebels. In Jude 6, these angels are enchained "in deepest darkness for the judgment of the great Day"; in 2 Peter 2.4, the rebels are to be kept in hellish pits "until the judgment" (expanded in 2.9 to "until the day of judgment"). And, as in 1 Enoch 22 and other texts, that same day of judgment will signal the "destruction of the godless."

In two noticeable respects, however, early Christian views of the last judgment tend to distance themselves from traditional Jewish apocalyptic. Judgment is now seen almost exclusively in individual rather than national terms (Matt. 10.15 is something of an exception), and

the judge is increasingly identified as Jesus, returned to serve as God's agent (Rom. 2.16; *see* Second Coming of Christ), rather than God himself. Both of these features are present in Matthew 25.31–46, where it is the *Son of man who sits on the throne of judgment, and where the nations are judged not communally but individually, based on their treatment of the needy. The second development leads also to an expansion in terminology particularly noticeable in Pauline literature. Alongside "the day" (Rom. 2.16; 1 Cor. 3.13), "that day" (2 Tim. 1.12; 4.8; cf. 4.1), and "the day of wrath" (Rom. 2.5), we find "the day of Christ" (Phil. 1.10; 2.16), "the day of Jesus Christ" (Phil. 1.6), the "day of the Lord" (1 Thess. 5.2; 2 Thess. 2.2), "the day of the Lord Jesus" (1 Cor. 5.5; 2 Cor. 1.14), and "the day of our Lord Jesus Christ" (1 Cor. 1.8). The forensic role of Jesus on the day of judgment becomes central in later Christian tradition. In the Apostles' and Nicene Creeds, Jesus "will come again (in glory) to judge the living and the dead"; and artists from Giotto and Michelangelo to William Blake have placed him at the center of their depictions of the Last Judgment.   PAUL G. MOSCA

Day of the Lord. This phrase combines a strictly temporal reference to the day and a reference to the eternal (Lord). This combination, quite typical of the Bible, is an apparent contradiction that can be resolved either by giving priority to the temporal component (whether day or year)—thus imprisoning God within the slots on human calendars—or prioritizing the eternal component by thinking of this day as chosen by God to fulfill his purposes. This second option is characteristic of the Bible. The God of Israel, having created his people by sealing *covenants with them, retained authority to set a term to the period when their truancy or faithfulness would be disclosed. Typically, he would choose a time that would surprise them, whether earlier or later than they expected. His verdicts also would be surprising, often condemnation where approval was expected, or vindication where the penitent expected punishment. The primary concern of God's spokespersons was not with the date of the accounting but with its certainty.

Often, the day of the Lord is announced as "coming." That verb denotes movement, but not a movement of Israel toward a date on the calendar, but rather movement of God toward his people in order to call them to account. Where rebellion flourishes, *prophets announce God's imminent coming to lay bare the secrets of hearts (Ezek. 30; Isa. 2.12; 3.18). Where loyalty flourishes in the midst of suffering, they provide consolation and courage by promising speedy intervention by the Most High (Isa. 11–12). The approach of the day would thus be marked by both deep darkness and the shining of the dawn.

The frequent references to God's coming explain the flexibility in the use of terms. The same event could be announced as the hour, the day, the year, or the time (see Time, Units of). The importance of the event could be indicated by articles and adjectives: the day, that day, the great day, the last day. The fearfulness of God's judgment released an array of surreal images: lightning, thunder, earthquake, tidal waves, tumults among nations, all intended to express how terrible it is to fall into the hands of the living God (Isa. 13; 22; Jer. 46.10; Lam. 2; Heb. 10.31; Rev. 16.12–21). *Sodom and Gomorrah become stock examples of destruction (Gen 13.10; Matt. 10.15; Luke 17.22–30). It is impossible to organize or harmonize all pictures of God's wrath (Joel 2). But the expectations of doom could be reversed by surprising mercies (Hos. 2; Amos 9:11–15).

In biblical as in later times, false prophets and false messiahs exploited desires to know in advance the signs of the times (Mark 13.6), but others stressed divine secrecy (Mark 13.32; 1 Thess. 5.2–3). God's reckoning of time differs completely from human calculations (Ps. 90.4; 2 Pet. 3.8). It was therefore wrong either to spread panic because of the day's nearness or to counsel despair because of its distance. The function of the references to the day was thus both to warn unsuspecting rebels to watch (e.g., Matt. 24.42–44) and to assure the faithful of the nearness of their salvation (1 Thess. 5.4–11).

Early Christians commonly identified the biblical day of the Lord with the day of the *Son of man (Matt. 24.42–44; Luke 17.24, 30; Acts 17.31; Rom. 2.16), when the risen Jesus would act as judge in the heavenly trial of his followers (Matt. 25.31–46). The *twelve are also pictured as sharing the throne of judgment (Luke 22.30). Some authors, however, understood the last days to have begun with the ministry of Jesus (John 12.31; 16.8–11; Acts 2.16–21; Heb. 1.2).

PAUL S. MINEAR

Deacon. The Greek noun *diakonos* underlying the English word "deacon" has in general usage the meaning of "servant," especially in the sense of one who waits on tables (cf. Matt. 22.13; John 2.5, 9). Perhaps the word was originally applied to early Christian leaders who assisted at celebrations of the *Lord's supper. It has often been suggested that the establishment of the diaconate is sketched in Acts 6.1–6, and this may be Luke's intention, although neither here nor elsewhere does he use the noun *diakonos* (see Seven, The).

The understanding of *Jesus as servant (e.g., Mark 10.45, using the verb *diakonein*) informs later Christian concepts of ministry, though the New Testament applies *diakonos* to Jesus in a positive sense only once (Rom. 15.8). The term occurs twenty-eight other times in the New Testament but only rarely in relation to a special church office.

In Philippians 1.1 Paul addresses a letter to all the Philippian saints "with the bishops and deacons." Generally the Pauline letters do not imply the existence of fixed church offices with distinctive functions, but in this passage "deacons" clearly refers to a particular group of church leaders. No function is specified, but perhaps Paul mentions them here (along with *bishops) because they helped provide the material assistance that partly occasions his letter (4.10–18).

In Romans 16.1–3 Paul mentions a certain Phoebe as a *diakonos* of the church at Cenchreae (a port city of *Corinth) and "benefactor" of many Christians, himself included. Nothing specific is said about her work, but there is no indication that she is a deacon in a lesser or different sense from that of the persons addressed in Philippians 1.1.

One passage in the *Pastoral letters (1 Tim. 3.8–13) follows a list of qualifications for bishops with those for deacons. Deacons must be of good character, not avaricious, and good managers of their private households. Such requirements suggest that deacons are administrators with special responsibility for money. Nothing is said about teaching ability. A sentence about *women (1 Tim. 3.11) may allude to women deacons or to the wives of male deacons.

Although the Pastoral letters seem to reflect an advanced stage in the development of church organization and differentiation of clerical roles, it is noteworthy that here and elsewhere *diakonos* can also be used as a general term for Christian "minister" (1 Tim. 4.6). Paul several times applies the term in this broad sense to himself and to other church leaders (1 Cor. 3.5; 2 Cor. 3.6; 6.4; 11.23; cf. Eph. 3.7; Col. 1.23, 25).

DAVID M. HAY

Dead Sea Scrolls. Since 1947, hundreds of Hebrew and Aramaic scrolls have been discovered near the *Dead Sea, at first in unorganized searches by Bedouins and later in orderly archaeological excavations. The main location where these scrolls were found is Qumran (Map 12:X5), roughly 16 km (10 mi) south of *Jericho; other sites still farther to the south include Murabba'ât, Seelim, and Masada (Map 12:X5). Some of these locations are more inland, so that the term "Judean Desert Scrolls" is more appropriate than "Dead Sea Scrolls." In eleven caves at Qumran, hundreds of scrolls were discovered, some in jars and almost complete, such as the large Isaiah scroll from Cave 1, but others mere fragments, often very difficult to read. Their antiquity, disputed at first by a few scholars, is now beyond doubt, and dates between 250 BCE and 70 CE have been secured by carbon-14 tests, archaeological evidence, and paleography. The scrolls are kept in the Rockefeller and Israel Museums in Jerusalem, and only the major ones are shown to the public.

The caves in which the scrolls were found are located near the ruins of a settlement near the Dead Sea. These ruins (Khirbet Qumran) have been excavated; they consist of a walled site comprising various community buildings, such as a bakery, a potter's workshop, a dining hall, and possibly a scriptorium.

No external evidence on the settlement is available, but probably there was a close link between its buildings and the scrolls found in nearby caves. Some of the artifacts found near the scrolls are identical with artifacts found in the community buildings. Furthermore, the sectarian writings found in the caves describe the lifestyle of a community that would suit the buildings.

The identity and nature of the community of the scrolls has often been discussed by scholars, and most now agree that they are the *Essenes described in ancient sources. The Essenes were an ancient Jewish sect with a status similar to that of the *Samaritans, *Sadducees, and early Christians, all of whom departed from mainstream Judaism, embodied in the *Pharisees (see Judaisms of the First Century CE). While most of the Essenes lived elsewhere in Palestine, the Qumran group decided to depart physically from society when they chose to dwell in the desert of Judea. The characteristics of the Essenes (the origin of the name is unknown), described in detail by *Philo and *Josephus, agree in general with the evidence from the scrolls. These are of three types: sectarian compositions, apocryphal works, and biblical scrolls.

The sectarian compositions found in Qumran reflect a secretive community about whose life much is still unknown. The main information is found in the so-called *Manual of Discipline* (in Hebrew, "The Rule of the Community"), detailing the daily life, behavior, and hierarchy of the sect. The principal source for the history of the community is a letter supposedly written by its leader, the "Teacher of Righteousness," to the priests of Jerusalem, outlining points of difference between both groups (4QMMT).

Other details can be learned from the *Damascus Covenant*, which tells about the beginning of the sect's existence, and from *pěšārîm*. The special laws of the community are outlined in the *Damascus Covenant* and in smaller legal collections. The sect's views are reflected especially in the *pěšārîm*, exegetical writings focusing on the relevance of biblical books to the sect. The *Temple Scroll*, the largest preserved scroll, rewrites the laws of the *Pentateuch in apparent agreement with some of the sect's views. The *War Scroll* depicts the future war of the "Sons of Light" (i.e., members of the sect) against the "Sons of Darkness." The sect's expectations and grievances are expressed in the *Thanksgiving Hymns*.

Among the scrolls found in Qumran and at Masada are several Hebrew and Aramaic *apocryphal and *pseudepigraphal works, previously known only in ancient translations or from medieval sources. Of these, the books of Jubilees, *Enoch, *Sirach, and the Testament of Levi are now known in their original Hebrew or Aramaic form.

A large group of scrolls found in Qumran and at other places in the Judean desert consists of biblical manuscripts, dating from 250 BCE until 70 CE. Similar scrolls from the beginning of the second century CE have been found in other places in the Judean Desert. These finds inaugurated a new era in the study of the text of the Hebrew Bible, previously known almost exclusively from medieval sources (see Manuscripts, *article on* Hebrew Bible; Textual Criticism).

In eleven Qumran caves, roughly 190 biblical scrolls have been found, some almost complete and others very fragmentary. Different scrolls are distinguished by their script. With the exception of Esther, all books of the Hebrew Bible are represented at Qumran, some by many scrolls (Deuteronomy, Isaiah, Psalms), others by a single copy. The great majority of the scrolls are written in the Aramaic script, while sixteen are written in the paleo-Hebrew (or Old Hebrew) script.

Most of the scrolls have the same spelling as the *Masoretic Text (MT), but a significant number are written with a previously unknown form of spelling, which frequently uses letters to indicate vowels. Some scholars argue that the scrolls displaying this special spelling were written by the Qumran scribes, for all the sectarian scrolls are written in this spelling as well. The biblical scrolls from the Dead Sea area show what the biblical text looked like in the last three centuries BCE and the first century CE.

Of similar importance are the new data about the content of the biblical scrolls, since different texts are recognizable. Some texts reflect precisely the consonantal framework of the medieval MT. Others reflect the basic framework of the MT, although their spelling is different. Still others differ in many details from the MT, while agreeing with the *Septuagint or *Samaritan Pentateuch. Some texts do not agree with any previously known text at all, and should be considered independent textual traditions. Thus, the textual picture presented by the Qumran scrolls represents a textual variety that was probably typical for the period.

Although most of the scrolls have been analyzed, the nature of the collection of scrolls found in the Qumran caves is still not known. While some scholars continue to refer to the contents of these caves as the "library" of the sect, others consider it a haphazard collection of works deposited there for posterity in the difficult days of the destruction of Jerusalem in 67–70 CE.

Because the nature of the collection is not known, it is also not clear how one should evaluate the fact that biblical, apocryphal, and sectarian works were found in the same caves. Probably this does not show anything about the sect's views, but some scholars believe that the sect's concept of scripture was more encompassing than the collection that eventually became the Jewish *canon.   EMANUEL TOV

Death. The biblical concept of death is complex, like the reality it seeks to describe. Death is both natural and intrusive; it occasions no undue anxiety except in unusual circumstances such as premature departure, violence, or childless demise, and it is the greatest enemy facing humankind. In Genesis 3, death acts as punishment for primeval rebellion (see Fall, The). In the New Testament, one special death, that of *Jesus,

cancels every claim against guilty persons; hence each negative feature regarding death is balanced by its opposite. Ultimately, death is robbed of its power, and its elimination is anticipated (see Hòs. 13.14; 1 Cor. 15.55–56).

Belief in the solidarity of the *family enabled ancient Israelites to accept death calmly, for in death a person simply slept with one's ancestors. Nevertheless, this sleep was subject to disturbance, prompting a cult of the dead and the effort to contact the departed. Official Yahwism condemned both activities (Lev. 19.31; 20.27; Deut. 18.11), while implicitly acknowledging their efficacy (1 Sam. 28; cf. 1 Chron. 10.13). The conviction that a deed was met with an appropriate consequence gained ascendancy, particularly in prophetic and *wisdom literature. This popular notion eventuated in an understanding of death as punishment (Gen. 2–3), theoretically implying that humankind could have lived forever. A *Ugaritic text, Aqhat, denies the seductive suggestion that a mortal could live forever. Such reflection about death, though rare, does occur elsewhere, especially in 2 Esdras 7 and in Paul (Rom. 5.12–21). A mythological idea of Death as combatant lies behind this development. Yahweh does battle with Mot, the Canaanite name for this foe, and subjugates the enemy. Henceforth death acts on orders from Israel's God, the ultimate source of good and evil. The result is a problem of monumental proportions, that of theodicy.

References to death in the Bible presuppose a worldview that differs from modern concepts. Life consists of well-being, and death signifies diminished life. Consequently, one must speak about degrees of death. A sick person, or a persecuted one, described the peril as death and characterized deliverance as emergence from death's grip; this convention clarifies much of the languages of the *Psalms. A symbolic meaning of death thus developed. The Deuteronomist urges Israel to choose life, not death (Deut. 30.19), and *Ezekiel denies that God desires death for anyone (Ezek. 18.31). This powerful imagery for death carries over into the New Testament, where *baptism (Rom. 6.3) and discipleship are illuminated by speech about dying (2 Cor. 4.11; 1 Pet. 2.24; Rev. 12.11).

At first Israelites assumed that death was the end, at least of life as we know it. This somber message underlies the epic of *Gilgamesh, a story about a heroic king's efforts to obtain eternal life. Once water was spilled on the ground, none could retrieve it, to use a metaphor employed by the woman of Tekoa (2 Sam. 14.14). Emerging individualism and harsh political realities forged a bold hope that a resurrection would take place, at least in rare instances (Isa. 26.19; Dan. 12.2, prefigured by Hos. 6.2 and Ezek. 37). Greek belief in body and soul as separate entities enabled this hope to become strong conviction by Roman times (see Human Person).

Israel's theologians believed that God alone had authority to terminate life; those responsible for executing criminals acted in God's behalf. Suicide is rarely mentioned in the Bible (1 Sam. 31.4; 2 Sam. 17.23; 1 Kings 16.18; Matt. 27.5; Acts. 1.18), in contrast to texts from Egypt and Mesopotamia, in which suicide occurs in dire straits occasioned by shame or impending torture. In his misery *Job entertains thoughts of suicide (Job 3.21; 7.15), and the author of *Ecclesiastes has a fascination for death (Eccles. 4.2–3), but neither opts for early departure. *Sirach recognizes that personal circumstances determine one's attitude toward death (41.1–2). Occasional death wishes occur—Elijah (1 Kings 19.4), Tobit (3.6), Jonah (4.8)—and Paul confesses to having mixed feelings about death, which held many attractive features for him, in that he would then be with Christ (Phil. 1.23).

*Apocalyptic thinking posits the dawn of a new age, a resurrection, and a final reckoning. The gospel of *John views Jesus' presence as proof of the resurrection, and the book of *Revelation proclaims the complete eradication of death (21.4), which Paul also declares (1 Cor. 15.54). Christians therefore need not fear the isolation of death, for nothing can separate the believer from God (Rom. 8.38–39). This attitude is not a denial of death, the plague of the human spirit, but a recognition of the sovereignty of the covenant of God despite the grim fact of death.

See also Afterlife and Immortality; Burial Customs.   JAMES L. CRENSHAW

Deborah. A name which means "bee" in Hebrew, Deborah is the name of two women mentioned in the Hebrew Bible. Two passages (Gen. 35.8; 24.59) call Rebekah's nurse Deborah. Much more prominent is the Deborah mentioned in Judges 4 and 5, whose fame in the biblical record emerges from her role as a military leader. With her general, Barak, she successfully led a coalition of Israelite tribal militias to victory over a superior Canaanite army commanded by Sisera. The battle was fought in the plain of Esdraelon (Map 13:X3), and the mortal blow to the Ca-

naanite general was delivered by another female figure, Jael.

The account of this war, ending with an important victory for the Israelites in their struggle to control central and northern Palestine, is recounted in two versions, a prose narrative in Judges 4 and a poetic form in Judges 5. The literary and chronological relationship of these two versions is a matter of debate; but most scholars see in the archaic language of the poem evidence that it comes from a very early stage of biblical literature and may be the oldest extant Israelite poem, perhaps dating from the late twelfth century BCE, not long after the battle it recounts.

Deborah occupies a unique role in Israelite history. Not only is she a judge in the sense of a military leader, but also she is the only judge in the law-court sense of that title (Judg. 4.5) in the book of *Judges. Of all the military leaders of the book, only Deborah is called a "prophet." She is also the only judge to "sing" of the victory, illustrating the creative role played by women as shapers of tradition (cf. Exod. 15.20–21). While some would see Deborah, a female, as an anomaly in all these roles, her contributions should be set alongside those of other women who are pivotal figures in the premonarchic period (*Miriam, Jael, Jephthah's daughter, *Samson's mother). All emerge as strong women with no negative valuation, perhaps because during the period of the judges, a time of social and political crisis, able people of any status could contribute to group efforts. In the rural, agrarian setting of the period of the judges, with the *family as the dominant social institution, the important role of *women in family life was more readily transferred to matters of public concern than during the monarchy, with its more formal and hierarchical power structures. Deborah as a strong woman reflects her own gifts as well as a relatively open phase of Israelite society.

CAROL L. MEYERS

Decalogue. See Ten Commandments.

Decapolis. The Decapolis was a league of ten cities founded by *Alexander the Great and his successors around 323 BCE. By the first century CE, according to both the Gospels (Matt. 4.25; Mark 5.20, 7.31) and Pliny (Natural History 5.16.74), the term refers both to the cities and to the region in which they were situated (Map

12:Y3–5). The earliest list of the cities appears in Pliny; most scholars agree on these ten: Scythopolis/Beth-shan, Hippo, Philadelphia (modern Amman), Gerasa (Jerash), Gadara, Pella, Dion, Canatha, Raphana, and *Damascus. According to both Josephus and Polybius, by the dawn of Seleucid rule in the region of Palestine and the Transjordan at least four of the cities were of real importance (Gadara, Scythopolis, Pella, and Abila).

This region is perhaps the paramount example of the role of urbanization in the development and dominance of the Greek East by colonial empires. In both the Ptolemaic (ca. 300–200 BCE) and the Seleucid periods (200–130 BCE) these cities were built or expanded. With the conquest of the region by Pompey on behalf of Rome (ca. 63 BCE), their importance increased. They were a vital means of Roman control, both economic and military. Pompey made the capital of the league, Scythopolis/Beth-shan, the seat of the regional court (the *Sanhedrin) and utilized other cities in the region in a similar fashion. These urban centers almost invariably sided with the colonial power in revolts by the indigenous population (whether Maccabean, resistance to Pompey, or the First Jewish Revolt against Rome in 66–70 CE) and frequently put down native resistance brutally.

A number of the cities have been excavated (Pella, Gerasa, Abila), with the most recent significant project being at Scythopolis/Beth-shan. Excavations at these sites reflect a diverse, cosmopolitan milieu. Several languages were used (*Greek, *Hebrew, and *Aramaic), temples and monuments stood almost side by side with *synagogues and early churches, and local culture and trade took place within the larger setting of Roman military and economic hegemony.

J. ANDREW OVERMAN

Demons. In all cultures, fabulous notions may be found about the work of evil spirits, more or less capricious, more or less baleful. Such concepts are also found in the Bible, at times echoing extrabiblical thinking, at times reverberating with overtones charcteristic of the Bible.

Ideas about demons in the Hebrew Bible are too diverse to be systematized. Animistic notions may be discerned in the recognition of spirits inhabiting trees, animals, mountains, rivers, and storms. Allusions are found to belief in fertility deities, or in divine beings, who, through sinning, lost their heavenly home (Gen. 6.1–4; *see*

Sons of God). More often the narratives focus upon the role of evil spirits in producing erratic and unexpected behavior; they arouse explosive jealousies (Num. 5.14), powerful desires for vengeance (Judg. 9.23), or shocking mental confusions (1 Sam. 16.14). The words of a prophet could be attributed to lying spirits sent by God (1 Kings 22.22). The worship of *idols could be explained by the influence of such spirits on the gullible (Hos. 4.12).

In the New Testament, though, the picture is different. References are much more numerous, reflecting developments in the Hellenistic and Roman periods. Attitudes are more unified, reflecting the influence of stories about *Jesus. Now demons are viewed as evil by nature, since they are obedient servants of *Satan who is the ultimate adversary of God. Their power to deceive and torment is viewed as coterminous with "this evil age," so that any restriction on their movements is viewed as an intrusion of a new age.

It was the authority of Jesus over demons that posed this possibility. According to the Gospels, that authority was first demonstrated when Jesus overcame Satan's most persuasive offers (Matt. 4.1–11 par.; *see* Temptation of Christ). This victory qualified him to begin evicting demons from their human homes (Matt. 4.24). Those spirits manifested their evil power by causing spiritual and physical *blindness, deafness, paralysis, *epilepsy, and madness. Debates over Jesus' healings centered not on whether they were real but on the authority by which they were accomplished: were they a sign of Satan's fall from heaven (Luke 10.17; cf. Rev. 12.9), of God's own intervention into human affairs, of faith in Jesus' word (Matt. 17.20), or were they rather a sign of Jesus' affilation with *Beelzebul, the ruler of demons (Matt. 9.34)?

The first option was the conviction of the Gospel narrators. And for them, the healings were not limited to Jesus. Even before his death he had shared with *disciples the power over demons (Luke 9.1); after his death they continued his work (Matt. 7.22; Acts 19.11–16). Evil spirits continued to resist the power of the Holy Spirit, but faith continued to bring liberation. As a result, a more or less standard attitude toward demons emerged: (1) Their primary activity lies in blinding and paralyzing human beings, who become captives of Satan. (2) Demons are forces external to human beings, yet their power also depends on internal forces operating at subconscious levels. (3) This conjunction of demonic and human wills creates a captivity that has been granted by God and can therefore be terminated by God. (4) That is why God's word, by evoking the faith of captives, can liberate them from their demonic captors. (5) The *exorcisms attributed to Jesus point to him as authorized to speak that word. (6) After his death and resurrection, the Holy Spirit enabled his representatives to continue that work of liberation; this gift did not, however, make them immune to demonic counterattack (2 Cor. 12.7). (7) There was a widespread expectation that this counterattack would reach its deceptive maximum in the endtime, immediately before the return of the *Messiah (1 Tim. 4.1; Rev. 16.13–14; 18.2).

PAUL S. MINEAR

Descent into Hell. The visit of a god or a hero to the underworld and the realm of death; in Christian contexts ascribed to Jesus.

Ancient Near Eastern and Greek myths know of several gods and heroes who had been in the underworld among the dead without being kept there. *Sumerian traditions include narratives of this kind about Enlil and Inanna, and in Babylonian form the motif was connected with the goddess Ishtar and the young god *Tammuz. An old Egyptian text, called Amduat, depicts the sun god's journey through the underworld in a boat every night. Greek folklore cherished descent stories about heroes such as Heracles, Odysseus, Orpheus, and the daughter of Demeter called Kore or Persephone, though their visits to Hades served different purposes. Similar stories were known in the biblical world, but none of these examples are direct sources of descent motifs in the Bible.

In the Hebrew Bible certain analogies to descent ideas appear in texts dealing with the struggle of the elect in the infernal gulfs and torrents of suffering and death. This *"de profundis"* motif is often found in the *Psalms (e.g., 18.4, 16; 42.7; 69.2, 14–15). The prophet *Jonah had reason to sing a similar psalm (Jon. 2.2–6).

In nonbiblical literature, the psalms of *Qumran develop this concept of a descent into the infernal realm of suffering and death (1QH III.6–10, 19–20, 25–27, VI. 22–24). Another form of the descent topic is found in apocalyptic teaching ascribed to *Enoch. The patriarch is said to have received this message (1 Enoch 12.4–5, following the Greek text): "Enoch, you scribe of righteousness, go and tell those heavenly watchers who have left the lofty heaven [i.e., according to 1 Enoch 10.4, the fallen angels of Gen. 6.1–4, now

bound in a dark prison] . . . . : 'You will find neither peace nor forgiveness.' " Afterward the apocalypse describes visits of Enoch to the underworld.

In the New Testament some of the relevant biblical and nonbiblical Jewish texts were applied to Jesus. He was said to have presented himself as fulfilling the sign of Jonah (Matt. 12.38–41; 16.4; Luke 11.29–32). These and other reports presuppose or indicate that Jesus was in the underworld between his death and resurrection (Matt. 12.40; Acts 2.24, 27, 31; Rom. 10.7; Eph. 4.8–9). Sometimes the descent was also described as implying a messianic activity under one of three different aspects: Hades was subdued (Rev. 1.18); righteous people were delivered (Matt. 27.51–53); Christ preached to the so-called spirits in prison and to all in the realm of death (1 Pet. 3.19; 4.6). These "spirits in prison" were meant to be understood as the fallen angels of Gen. 6.1–4, who in the Enoch tradition were treated as the initiators of paganism; the reference to Christ's going to them (1 Pet. 3.19) therefore was intended to strengthen the preceding exhortation to confess one's faith in front of Roman authorities (3.15).

These aspects inspired later theologians to develop doctrines of Christ's descent in corresponding ways. The affirmation "He descended into hell" first appears in the Aquileian Creed of Rufinus (ca. 400 CE); from there it gradually spread throughout the West and found a place in the Apostles' Creed.

See also Afterlife and Immortality; Gehenna; Hell.

BO REICKE

Deutero-Isaiah. *See* Isaiah, The Book of.

Deuteronomic History. "Deuteronomic history" is a term used by biblical scholars for a hypothetical work composed in ancient times that consisted of the books of *Deuteronomy through 2 *Kings. A variant form used by some scholars is "Deuteronomistic history."

The hypothesis was proposed by Martin Noth, who in 1943 pointed to the common phrasing and theological themes that permeated those books, and argued convincingly that these similarities were evidence of a single author. This author compiled already existing traditions and supplied his own framework and connecting material, as well as speeches for key characters (e.g., Josh. 24; 1 Sam. 8; 12), to express his view of the history of the people of Israel from the time of *Moses to the *exile in Babylon. The book of Deuteronomy forms a kind of theological preface for the history, with an introduction (chaps. 1–3) and a conclusion (31.1–13 and parts of chap. 34) supplied. Noth dated this Deuteronomic history to the exilic period because it concludes (2 Kings 25.27–30) with the release of the Judean king Jehoiachin from prison in Babylon (561 BCE). According to Noth, the purpose of the history was to show the exiles that their situation was the result of infidelity to the *covenant as set forth in the Deuteronomic laws.

Noth's theory has been widely accepted. It explains why the literary traditions (*J, *E, and *P) found in the first four books of the *Pentateuch are absent in subsequent books, and why those traditions end with some abruptness without the fulfillment of the promises made in them. As the biblical books were collected, edited, and arranged, the Deuteronomic history replaced the original endings of the Pentateuchal traditions.

Subsequent scholars have elaborated positive themes in what Noth had suggested was essentially a negative work. One of the most influential refinements of Noth's hypothesis is that of Frank Moore Cross. He began by tracing two contrasting themes throughout the books of Kings: the sin of Jeroboam (1 Kings 13.34; 15.34; 16.19; 22.52; 2 Kings 3.3; 13.2; 14.24; 15.9; etc.), which culminates in the fall of the northern kingdom of *Israel and the destruction of *Samaria (2 Kings 17), and the faithfulness of David, grounded in the covenantal theology of the southern kingdom of *Judah (1 Kings 3.6; 14.8; 15.11; 2 Kings 14.3; etc.). Only two kings meet the standard set by David: *Hezekiah (2 Kings 18.3–7) and *Josiah (2 Kings 22.2). Since the reforms of Josiah (2 Kings 22.11–23.25) are the culmination of the second theme, Cross argued that the Deuteronomic history had two editions, the first during that king's reign in the late seventh century BCE, serving as a support for his political and religious programs. After Josiah's untimely death in 609 and the fall of Jerusalem in 587/586, the first edition was rewritten to explain and even to justify the exile, as Noth had originally suggested. Other modifications of Noth's hypothesis continue to be proposed, implicitly demonstrating the strength of his original insight.   RUSSELL FULLER

Deuteronomistic History. *See* Deuteronomic History.

Deuteronomy, The Book of.

Content. The book of Deuteronomy received its title from the Greek translation of Deuteronomy 17.18, where the Hebrew word indicating "copy" has been understood as meaning "second law" (*deuteronomion*, hence "Deuteronomy"); in Hebrew it is called *dĕbārîm*, "words," from the opening verse. Despite the misunderstanding, this is a good description of a book whose main part is a second corpus of laws given to Israel through *Moses, supplementing those given at *Horeb (see 29.1). This second corpus was delivered to the Israelites in the plains of *Moab on the eve of their entry into the land of *Canaan. The central part of the book lies between 4.44 and 30.20, which must once have formed its beginning and ending. Deuteronomy 29.1 describes them as "the words of the covenant [between God and Israel]," and 4.45 describes them as made up of "decrees, statutes, and ordinances." Presenting "law" or *Torah (Hebr. *tôrâ*) is the major concern of the book as it formulates the *covenant between God and Israel, the basis for the nation's life in the land of Canaan. Because such laws are to be found primarily in chaps. 12–26, the material of 4.44–11.32 can be seen as a general introduction made up of Moses' exhortations in the form of long speeches directing Israel to obey the laws; 27.1–30.20 is an epilogue with admonitions, warnings, and curses against failing to do so. The whole of the book may be described as "preaching law": often the laws themselves take the central place, but at other times a passionate preaching and admonitory manner are foremost.

The laws at the heart of the book are in many cases laws in our familiar juridical sense, specifying offenses and defining the appropriate punishments for them. At other times, however, they are essentially religious instructions and regulations for worship, as in the festival calendar of 16.1–17, or an even broader type of ethical admonition and instruction, as in the *Ten Commandments of 5.6–21. The speeches broaden this sense of the demands for godly living still further by emphasizing the need for a right attitude toward God and society. Consequently, there is much urgent warning to remember God and his dealings with Israel, not to forget the divine gifts, and to love God with a deep love in the heart (esp. 6.5).

The book thus aims to provide both the framework for a national constitution of Israel and a basic summary of every citizen's rights and duties, as well as to exhort the proper feelings and attitudes toward God and fellow citizens; it strongly endeavors to bring all of life—its private, social, and more openly religious aspects—under an awareness of obligation and duty toward God.

Sources. The sources of the book can be determined only with a degree of probability, since in many cases there is limited evidence on which to base conclusions. Clearly, a significant part of the central law collection in chaps. 12–26 repeats, with additions and modifications, many of the laws given earlier in the Book of the Covenant (Exod. 20.22–23.19). Approximately half of the laws are covered, and in a way that shows the Deuteronomic version to be later, either fuller or adapted to a more complex economic and social order. These laws provide a handbook for administration in civil or criminal cases where wrongs have been perpetrated and society must act against the wrongdoers. Why all the cases present in the earlier laws are not dealt with remains unclear.

The book's brief historical framework presupposes an earlier *Pentateuchal narrative tradition, which scholars have usually assigned to the sources *J and *E. Where a few traces of the *P (Priestly) source are to be found, these are thought to have been added after the main book of Deuteronomy had been completed. The detailed festival calendar similarly presupposes earlier forms of this material (Exod. 23.14–17; 24.18–23), now elaborated extensively (*see* Feasts and Festivals). We must assume that much of the contents of Deuteronomy rests on far older tradition, partly oral and partly written, which has not otherwise survived in biblical tradition.

The consistency of style and continuity of dominant themes suggests strongly that there was a community of scribes and legislators, often loosely described as the Deuteronomists or the Deuteronomic School, who composed the present work. This undoubtedly took place over a long period of time, perhaps as much as a century, for the book shows signs of having been elaborated, adapted, and extended until it attained its present form.

Most important from a literary perspective is the variety of patterns of addresses to the audience, which is variously referred to in the singular and the plural. In all cases, however, the reader is assumed to be an ordinary Israelite, rather than a priest, prophet, or administrator; the book is addressed to the laity, both men and women. Furthermore, it is evident that this lawbook of Deuteronomy provided the opening part of the historical narrative of Israel's fortunes as a nation, which is continued in the books of Joshua, Judges, 1 and 2 Samuel, 1 and 2 Kings. This corpus has come to be known as the *Deuteronomic (or Deuteronomistic) History because it presupposes throughout the lawbook of Deuteronomy as the primary constitution of Israel, which is frequently referred to as the "law" and sometimes as "the covenant." Deuteronomy 1.1–4.43 can best be regarded as an introduction to the whole work consisting of both law and historical narrative. Only at a late stage was this lawbook detached from its subsequent history and combined with the other laws and traditions about Israel's origins, now found in Genesis, Exodus, Leviticus, and Numbers, in order to compose the *Pentateuch. This must have taken place after the Babylonian *exile, in order to bring together in one work all the primary instructional material about the origins, nature, and responsibilities of Israel.

Date of Composition. We read in 2 Kings 22.8–20 that a lawbook was found in the Jerusalem *Temple while the Temple was undergoing repairs in the eighteenth year of the reign of King *Josiah. The authors of this narrative and of the account of the subsequent kingdom-wide reform of worship undertaken in accordance with this lawbook (2 Kings 23) intend it to be understood as the lawbook of Deuteronomy in some form. Since 1805, when the German scholar W. M. L. de Wette briefly noted the point, scholars have recognized that the date of this reform (622 BCE) has some bearing on the date of the composition of Deuteronomy. The main part of the book was most likely composed during the previous half-century, in the reigns of *Manasseh (696–642 BCE) and Josiah (639–609 BCE). A probable time is the early years of the latter's reign, when the century-long *Assyrian domination of Judah and Israel was coming to an end. Other elements of the book were composed in the later years of Josiah, and it was undoubtedly still being supplemented after his death in 609 BCE.

This period can be viewed confidently as the time when Deuteronomy was composed, and serves to explain many of its most distinctive features. Although the book evinces an air of crisis that has not passed, it does not presuppose the catastrophes that took place in the years of Babylonian rule, when the Temple was destroyed and the Davidic dynasty removed (587/586 BCE). It regards the land of Israel, the demand for national unity ("all Israel"), the gift of *kingship, and the very "name" of God dwelling in the sanctuary as the supreme spiritual endowments of the nation. These precious institutions are threatened and may even have been neglected, but clearly they had not been lost when the major part of the book was composed. It is, when viewed comprehensively, a last appeal to Israel to regain its sense of a God-given destiny, which Mesopotamian imperialism and internal apostasy were weakening perilously.

Distinctive Feature. A distinctive feature of the book is its stress on the three great unities. First, Israel is one people, which Moses can address as such (Deut. 5.1, 6.4, etc.), and which is viewed as remaining one through all its subsequent generations. Second, it must worship one God alone, the God who reveals himself to Moses on Mount Horeb; this finds expression in the great formulation (the *Shema) "Hear, O Israel: The Lord our God is one Lord" (6.4). This should not be understood as originally implying that there is only one God (*see* Monotheism), though it later came to be interpreted in this fashion. Rather, it declares that the Lord (Yahweh) is a deity who is not to be worshipped alongside, or in conjunction with, any other deity. Furthermore, though there were many sanctuaries where the Lord God was worshipped, this was not to be taken as implying that he existed in different forms or manifestations, as was the case with *Baal. The third great unity is the sole place of worship where an altar is to be set up and sacrifices offered (12.5–14). This is described as "the place that the Lord your God will choose out of all your tribes as his habitation to put his name there" (12.5). This location is not further defined, but Jerusalem was obviously intended and is later identified by the historians of the Deuteronomic school (1 Kings 8.16–21; etc.).

These three great unities of people, God, and sanctuary form the visible and outward expression of the one purpose of God first revealed to the ancestors of Israel (6.3) and confirmed and realized through the covenant made through Moses on Horeb (5.1–5). The concern for centralization of worship and a kingdomwide consistency of religious observance provide keynotes for all that the book of Deuteronomy understands by "law" *(tôrâ)*. To tolerate, let alone to encourage, the worship of other gods is capital offense (13.1–18; 17.2–7). Thus, an insistence on the purity of religious observance pervades all the Deuteronomic legislation, and appears to have given rise to the desire to control the administration of worship. Even the king, the supreme head of the people, must subject himself and his conduct wholly to the terms laid down in the Deuteronomic law (17.18–20). This concern to regulate the administration and observance of all forms of religion is extended further to cover the activity of *prophets, who fulfill a role like that of Moses (18.15). The danger of false prophets is noted (13.1–5; 18.20–22), but the true prophet's teaching conforms to that of Moses.

Alongside this stress on purity of worship, there is a surprising and far-reaching emphasis on its essential inwardness. The primary purpose of a festival even so great and deeply rooted as *Passover, with the Feast of Unleavened Bread—which Deuteronomy now for the first time firmly conjoins with it (16.1–8)—is to serve as an occasion for remembering the great acts of God toward the people's ancestors: "so that all the days of your life you may remember the day of your departure from the land of Egypt" (16.3). Worship itself, then, is valued primarily for its spiritual and psychological potential as a remembrance of the goodness of God and a demonstration of gratitude toward him. Particularly appropriate is a special concern for the oppressed and downtrodden members of the community: "Remember that you were a slave in Egypt; and diligently observe these statutes" (16.12). This deep and religiously motivated attention to the *poor is a prominent moral feature of Deuteronomy (15.7–11).

The combination of an inward psychologizing and spiritualizing of worship with a regard for the poor leads to a remarkable desacralising of *tithes, the offering of which becomes a holy opportunity for rejoicing before God and for sharing gifts with the poor and disadvantaged (14.22–29). The entire people is conceived as a single entity, whose members are regarded as being "brothers," from the king at the head (17.20) to the slave at the bottom of the social ladder (15.12–18). Likewise, the foreigner is to be accorded a certain status providing the possibility of full entry into the people (23.7–8).

The target of the religious hostility expressed in the Deuteronomic legislation is the worship of *Baal and *Asherah, more often described as the male and female deities who represent the older forms of religion practiced by the previous inhabitants of the land (7.4–5, 16, 25; 11.28; etc.). In view of the period when the Deuteronomic legislation was probably composed, it is surprising that the book never explicitly condemns the symbols and evidence of Assyrian imperial control over Judah. To what extent there had been such visible signs of Assyrian rule is not known, but the aims of the Deuteronomic reform were established when this rule was in serious decline and had largely disappeared. Deuteronomy regards the great variety of religious traditions that had survived in the land of Israel as the cause of the divine anger that led God to punish the Israelites by bringing "a nation from far away" (28.49).

In sharp contrast with this emphasis upon the inwardness of true religion and a just and caring social order is the vehement condemnation of any deviation from absolute loyalty to God. Veneration of other gods is to be ruthlessly opposed and its practitioners exterminated (7.2, 16; 13.8–10; etc.).

The most enduring expression of concern for complete loyalty of religious practice and a just social order is to be found in the *Ten Commandments (5.6–21). Since this series of injunctions, with only minor modifications, is also found in Exodus 20.2–17, scholars have been divided in their views as to whether the collection is of Deuteronomic origin or derives from a much earlier time. Clearly, the subject matter of the commandments reflects ancient and fundamental concerns in any society, but this recognition does not itself suffice to determine the actual date when this short didactic compendium of ten basic religious and moral duties was brought together. Many think that such a brief teaching form was of early date, but underwent revision and modification over a long period of time. In any case, they wholly accord with the aim of Deuteronomy to bring as much of life as possible under a sense of obligation toward God.

Authorship and Readership. The book of Deuteronomy, formulated as an address by Moses to all Israel, presupposes a literate reading public who could benefit from a book of instruction. It also recognizes, however, the need for orally teaching the law (esp. 6.7, 31.10–13) and regards the preservation of the lawbook and its placement beside the *ark in the Temple (31:24–26) as serving primarily as a "witness." Since the Levitical *priests are made the custodians of this lawbook (31.9), it is certain that they were expected to fulfill some teaching role in promulgating its contents. Clearly, *Levites would form the bridge between the custodians of the law and the laity of Israel. This suggests that some elements of the Levitical priesthood were closely

linked to, and supportive of, the lawbook's authors.

The presumption of *literacy by the lawbook's originators, combined with the pronounced rhetorical style of persons skilled in public speech-making, also points to *scribes. There are, in addition, numerous indications of expertise in legal affairs, which leads us to conclude that the Deuteronomic authors included among their number several major state officials. It is the only law collection in the Bible to include a statute defining the office of the king (17.14–20; *see* Kingship and Monarchy). All of this suggests strongly that the authors of Deuteronomy formed a body of religiously motivated reformers, drawn from a circle close to the centers of state administration but apparently not directly associated with the king and royal household. They are, in any case, too critical of many of the basic assumptions regarding priestly service and its ritual obligations to have been priests themselves.

It is important to recognize the warm interest in prophecy and the belief that certain prophets continued to fulfill a role in Israel comparable to that of Moses. Such interest, which becomes more marked in the history that elaborates the lawbook, suggests that some prophetic element may also have contributed to the Deuteronomic movement for reform in Israel. Yet the understanding of prophecy is highly distinctive, and too removed from its most fundamental forms, for the authors of the book to have been prophets themselves. Prophecy is viewed essentially as a means of promoting the knowledge and claims of the Deuteronomic law.

As to the first readers of the book, we must assume that these were the lay men and women of Judah who so eagerly watched the decline of Assyrian control during the years of Josiah's reign. With the king's untimely death, the setbacks caused by Egyptian attempts to fill the power vacuum in Judah, and then the firm assertion of Babylonian rule over Judah from 604 BCE, the first expectation of the reformers presumably gave way to a more considered hope. There is much to indicate that this took effect by a sharp shift of emphasis from the sought-after outward political changes to striving for a basic change of heart and a renewal of faith among Judah's citizens. All of this finds expression in the numerous expansions, modifications, and exhortations that were added over a long period to the original lawbook.

The Significance of the Book. The significance of the book in the growth of biblical tradition is considerable. More than any other book, it establishes the general tone and character of the Pentateuch, and it is likely that the Deuteronomic classification of "law" *(tôrâ)* gave this title to the Pentateuch more generally. In many prominent features, it was Deuteronomy's claims to represent an embodiment of Israel's religious tradition superior to that of prophet, priest, or king that established the notion of a canon of sacred legislative tradition.

In literary influence, it is demonstrable that the historical work consisting of Joshua, Judges, 1 and 2 Samuel, and 1 and 2 Kings (the *Deuteronomic History) was a direct development of the lawbook of Deuteronomy and emanates from the same general circle of authors. Furthermore, the edited book of the prophecies of *Jeremiah, which now constitutes one of the major texts dealing with the final downfall of the state of Judah at Babylonian hands (604–587/586 BCE), has also been shaped by the Deuteronomic circle of reformers. Jeremiah's prophecies are presented as the final proof of the Deuteronomic interpretation of the reasons for the collapse of Israel as a nation; they serve also as the vehicle of hope and guidance for the nation's renewal and eventual restoration.

Deuteronomy's religious ideas, which more directly than any prior element in Israel's religious traditions express a coherent and comprehensive theology, are a milestone in Israel's intellectual development. It is surprising that when the restoration of a fully organized religious life took place in Judah and Jerusalem after the initial returns from Babylonian *exile, the Deuteronomic legislation was much altered and left aside. A staunchly priestly tradition, more conducive to the thinking and aims of a traditional pattern of ritual, merged with it, heavily modifying the relatively rational and spiritualized features of Deuteronomic religion. Among the Jews of the *dispersion, however, who formed an increasing element of the surviving Jewish people after 587/586 BCE, the currency and clarity of a simple lawbook able to embody so many aspects of the Jewish tradition was of inestimable importance. With Deuteronomy, the first major step had been taken to promote the existence of Judaism as a religion of a book. Formal worship in a temple came to be simply an adjunct to a more comprehensive code of religious attitudes and duties prescribed in an instructional text.

See also Law.   RONALD E. CLEMENTS

Devil. *See* Satan.

Diana of the Ephesians. *See* Artemis of the Ephesians.

Diaspora. *See* Dispersion.

Dinah. *Jacob and *Leah's daughter, Leah's seventh child, born after her six sons (Gen. 30.21; 46.15); her name, like that of her half-brother *Dan, is derived from a root meaning "to judge." In Genesis 34, Dinah is raped by Shechem, who then falls in love and wants to marry her. Enraged at their sister's treatment, Dinah's brothers agree to intermarriage, but only if the men of *Shechem (the city) will be circumcised. While they recuperate, *Simeon and *Levi (full brothers to Dinah) kill them, and Jacob's other sons plunder the city, taking women and children as well as wealth and livestock and risking retaliation from neighboring groups.

The narrative in Genesis 34 gives a remarkable glimpse into Israelite history and customs, including the complicated relationships between the "sons of Israel" and the inhabitants of the land of *Canaan and the association of *circumcision with marriage (cf. Exod. 4.25–26).

JO ANN HACKETT

Disciple. The term *disciple* (Grk. *mathētēs*) occurs many times in the New Testament, but only in the Gospels and Acts. It is used both of the *twelve who according to the Gospels originally followed Jesus, and also of a wide range of Jesus' followers. The Gospels speak not only of disciples of Jesus but also of *Moses (John 9.28), *John the Baptist (Mark 2.18; Luke 11.1; John 1.35), and the *Pharisees (Matt. 22.16). But above all the term refers to followers of Jesus, who are literally "learners," students of Jesus of Nazareth.

The somewhat amorphous group called disciples constitutes a vital feature of all the Gospel narratives, but the authors used the term to communicate different aspects of being a follower of Jesus. In *Mark the disciples are agents of instruction for the author, but as negative examples. They teach the audience or readers, but mostly through the things they do wrong or fail to understand. The constant questions and concerns of the disciples, particularly in the central section of Mark's gospel, provide an opportunity for the author to explain the purpose of Jesus' mission and the hidden meanings of his teaching. Discipleship in Mark involves fear, doubt, and suffering, as 8.31, 9.31, and 10.33 make explicit; nowhere is this more poignantly captured than in the character of *Simon Peter. The disciples in Mark, whomever this broad term may include, never fully understand and never quite overcome their fear and apprehensions. There is actually the hint in Mark that the disciples' fear is in some sense the beginning of wisdom.

The gospel of *Matthew on the other hand offers a rather different portrayal of the band of disciples, a term he uses with much greater frequency than the other Gospels (forty-five times without parallel in Mark or Luke). A disciple in Matthew is one who understands, teaches, and does (5.19) what Jesus taught and did. Discipleship in Matthew is not a distinctive office or role but rather describes the life of an ordinary follower of Jesus in the Matthean community. Disciples have authority to teach (5.19; 13.52; 23.8–10; 28.20), and so naturally, unlike the Marcan disciples, they understand the teachings of Jesus, himself portrayed as the authoritative teacher, as the *Sermon on the Mount illustrates. Matthew alone among the Gospel writers ascribes the authority to forgive sins to the disciples (6.15; 9.8; 16.19; 18.18). As in Mark, the figure of Peter embodies all aspects of discipleship, but in contrast to the Marcan Peter, in Matthew he understands, can teach, and is granted unusual authority (16.16–19; cf. 18.18).

The meaning and content of the term "disciple" varies in the four Gospels. Each writer uses this broad term, which tends simply to designate a follower of Jesus, in ways that support their understanding of the community of the followers of Jesus and impress on their audience the contours and complexities of the life of a contemporary disciple.   J. ANDREW OVERMAN

Dispersion, Diaspora. Diaspora is a Greek word meaning "dispersion." The first dispersion of Israel followed the *Assyrian conquest of the northern kingdom in 722 BCE; the deportees did not, however, form a living diaspora community. It was the deportation of a part of the population of Judah by the *Babylonians in 597 and 587/586 BCE that resulted in the creation of a permanent community, which later produced the Babylonian *Talmud. The prophet *Jeremiah advised the new exiles to pray for Babylon, "for in its welfare will be your welfare" (Jer. 29.7). The prophet *Ezekiel preached to Israel from the newly formed Babylonian Diaspora.

After the Babylonian empire fell, the Persian king *Cyrus allowed the Judeans to return home. A commonwealth of exiles was created. The books of *Ezra and *Nehemiah treat only the returned exiles as legitimate Israelites. Those who had remained in the land or who lived elsewhere were disenfranchised. It was at this time that Judaism in effect began. Despite the return, a Jewish community continued in Babylon. Diaspora had become a way of life, one that would continue into the Greco-Roman period, when Jews were scattered over much of the ancient world. The first book of *Maccabees records a letter of the Roman Senate that reflects Jewish habitation in Egypt, Syria, Pergamum, Parthia, Cappadocia, and many individual Greek cities and islands (1 Macc. 15.16–24). Jews had begun to take pride in diaspora, although Judith 5.19 still reflects the pain, speaking of a repentance followed by a return from all the places of the dispersion to retake Jerusalem and other places left deserted. Here the dispersion is portrayed as something to be overcome.

In the New Testament, James 1.1 identifies its recipients as "the twelve tribes in the Dispersion." This may mean Jewish Christians of the Diaspora, but may also be symbolic; 1 *Peter, a letter clearly written to *gentiles, is similarly addressed (1 Pet. 1.1).

See also Exile.   PHILIP STERN

Dives. In the *parable of the rich man and Lazarus (Luke 16.19–31), one character is named (probably to facilitate dialogue between the rich man and Abraham), but the other is not. This has led to various attempts to supply the perceived deficiency. In relatively modern times, the rich man has traditionally been called "Dives," the Latin word for "rich" used in the *Vulgate. Names assigned in antiquity include Nineves (or Neves), Finaeus, Tantalus, and Amonofis.

See also Abraham's Bosom; Names for the Nameless.   PATRICK A. TILLER

Divination. *See* Magic and Divination.

Divorce. In the Hebrew Bible the right of divorce is presupposed. However, like many other customs associated with family life (*see* Marriage; Weddings), exactly how it was done and under what circumstances is obscure. It seems likely that Israel's practice with regard to divorce was broadly similar to that of its neighbors; certainly the laws on sexual offenses were very similar, so we can use other ancient Near Eastern laws to fill in the background to the biblical statements.

Although divorce was legitimate, it was evidently disapproved of. Genesis 2.24, the formula used at weddings ("I am [your] husband . . . forever"), and the elaborateness of the wedding ceremony itself all convey the hope that marriage would be for life. Malachi 2.16 probably reflects widespread popular antipathy to divorce. In practice divorce must have been quite rare, for it was not only socially reprehensible but expensive. If a man (normally only the husband could initiate divorce proceedings; *see* Women) wanted to divorce his wife for anything short of major sexual misconduct, he had to repay the dowry. This was the bride's wedding present from her father, usually larger even than the "marriage present" given by the groom's family. The dowry was given jointly to the bride and groom, but as long as the marriage remained intact, he had the use of it. However, on divorce he had to give the dowry in full to his wife and often make other large payments as well. This must have made divorce a rarity.

Laws explicitly dealing with divorce are rare. In two cases, perhaps cases in which the man has shown himself hotheaded, divorce is permanently prohibited (Deut. 22.19, 29). Some laws limit the right of a divorcée to remarry. The rules of Leviticus 18.6–18 covering the choice of marriage partners could affect divorcées as much as widow(er)s and the unmarried. But the most interesting law of all is Deuteronomy 24.1–4.

The purpose of this law is stated in v. 4, which prohibits a divorcée who has remarried from ever going back to her first husband should her second husband die or divorce her. Why this should be forbidden is obscure. Perhaps such a return would make the second marriage look like *adultery. Or perhaps because the first marriage made the couple as closely related as brother and sister (they had become one flesh), a second marriage would appear incestuous; similar principles underlie some rules in Leviticus 18.

This law also sheds light on the practice of divorce. It was initiated by the husband for whatever reasons he saw fit: "she finds no favor in his eyes" (Deut. 24.1; NRSV: "she does not please him"). "Some indecency" (NRSV: "something

objectionable") is presumably something less than proven adultery, for which the death penalty was available. The husband had to give his wife a written statement of her divorce and put it in her hand. This protected her from an accusation of adultery should she later remarry, for the key phrase in a bill of divorce was "You are free to marry any man." Freedom to remarry is the essence of divorce, as opposed to separation.

By the first century CE this Deuteronomic law was the center of debate among the *Pharisees. Some (the Hillelites) said it warranted divorce for any reason, for example, bad cooking. Others (the Shammaites) held that it allowed divorce only for serious sexual misconduct. According to Matthew 19 and Mark 10 Jesus was asked to comment on this controversy: "Is it lawful for a man to divorce his wife?" (Mark 10.2).

Jesus' reply dismisses the Mosaic divorce law as a concession to human sinfulness (Mark 10.3–5); the ideal expressed in Genesis (2.24) is that "the two shall become one flesh" and thus "what God has joined together, let no one separate" (vv. 8–9). In other words, divorce is wrong, whatever the *Law does to regulate it. According to Mark, Jesus opposed divorce more vigorously than any of the Pharisees. This is reemphasized in Mark 10.11: "Whoever divorces his wife and marries another commits adultery against her" (cf. Luke 16.18), a revolutionary statement that puts wives on an equal basis within marriage.

Matthew's account of Jesus' teaching on divorce is geared more closely to the Jewish scene and more pointedly addresses the male chauvinism that blamed women for adultery and divorce. A man may commit adultery in the heart by looking lustfully at a woman, but by divorcing an innocent wife a man causes her to commit adultery (Matt. 5.28–32). But Matthew also includes an exception clause that apparently modifies Jesus' total rejection of divorce in Mark: "whoever divorces his wife, except for unchastity, and marries another commits adultery" (Matt. 19.9; cf. 5.32). This has generated much discussion: what constitutes "unchastity," and does divorce after it allow one to remarry? The early church (up to 500 CE) took "unchastity" to mean serious sexual sin, typically adultery, but said that this did not allow the innocent party to remarry. Many Protestants, following Erasmus (1519), have taken "unchastity" to mean adultery, but suppose that remarriage is allowed. Many modern scholars take "unchastity" to mean marriage within the forbidden degrees of Leviticus 18, or premarital unchastity. This view sees the exception clause as specifying grounds for annulling a marriage. In this case remarriage would be allowed.

All views have their difficulties. Hardest to accept is that of Erasmus, since it makes Jesus' view little different from that of the Pharisees with whom he has just disagreed. It also fails to explain the disciples' astonishment at Jesus' harsh new teaching (v. 10) and the subsequent discussion of *eunuchs, that is, single people who do not marry.

*Paul quotes a word of Jesus opposing divorce and insisting on singleness for those who do separate (1 Cor. 7.10–11; cf. Rom. 7.1–3). In the case of a marriage between a Christian and an unbeliever, Paul says the Christian may grant his or her partner a divorce, if the latter demands it (1 Cor. 7.15). But he does not say that the Christian may then remarry.

GORDON J. WENHAM

Dreams. In ancient Israel, in Judaism, in the Greek world, and in the ancient Near East generally, dreams were frequently regarded as vehicles of divine *revelation, especially the dreams experienced by priests and kings. Although there is no clear example in the Hebrew Bible of this kind of revelation being sought intentionally, dreams with divine content often occurred at sanctuaries (Gen. 28.12; 1 Sam. 3; 1 Kings 3.4–15). In the book of Job, Elihu expresses the generally held view that dreams are an authentic means of divine communication (Job 33.15–17). The dream was also a medium by which truth was conveyed to a prophet (Num. 12.6), though its value was thought to be inferior to revelation received from God at firsthand. According to Joel 2.28, the dreams of old men will form part of the universal and direct contact with God to be experienced in the last days (cf. Acts 2.17).

In most cases, the content of the divine message is conveyed to the dreamer clearly and unambiguously, but in two cycles of stories—the *Joseph stories and the *Daniel narratives, both of which include dream phenomena reported by non-Israelites—the skills of experts or professional interpreters are required. These interpretative skills are God-given (Gen. 40.8; Dan. 2.27–28) and involve an ability to construe the pattern of future events from symbolic features of the dream. In the Greek world, dreams were accorded similar respect, and subtly developed systems of interpretation were employed. Dreams and their interpretation, however, were not ac-

cepted uncritically by all. Both Jeremiah (23.32; 27.9) and Zechariah (10.2) make scathing comments on empty or false dreamers, thus implying that the "word of the Lord" that came to a prophet in his intimate communion with God was superior to communication through dreams. A dreamer whose message encourages apostasy is, in the view of the Deuteronomic law, to be put to death (Deut. 13.2–6). The fleeting and insubstantial character of the dream is occasionally remarked upon (Job 20.8; Ps. 73.20; 90.5).

In the New Testament, interest in dreams is confined almost exclusively to *Matthew's gospel, and especially its birth narratives (1.20; 2.12, 13; 2.19; 2.22). For Matthew, the dream is an illustration of divine intervention and guidance operating on Jesus' life from its outset; this emphasizes the distinctive Matthean theme that Jesus is God's chosen and anointed one. These dreams in Matthew 1 and 2 conform to the Greco-Roman dream pattern in which the contents of the dream usually are narrated as the dream takes place, whereas the standard pattern in the Hebrew Bible is to state a person "dreamed a dream" and then to give the contents only after the dreamer awakes (see Gen. 37. 5–7, 9; 40.5; Dan. 2.7). In Matthew 27.19, *Pilate's wife reports to her husband the distress she suffered in a dream on account of Jesus, but the precise content of her dream is not given. In Acts, *Paul receives instructions and encouragement in visions of the night (Acts 16.9; 18.9), but it is not certain whether these are dreams or some other form of revelatory phenomenon.   DAVID HILL

Drunkenness. A state that is almost always viewed in a negative way. *Wisdom literature associates intoxication with foolish, impractical acts (Prov. 20.1; 26.9), and the impropriety that emerges as a consequence is exemplified in the well-known stories of *Noah (Gen. 9:20–27; see Ham/Canaan, Cursing of) and *Lot (Gen. 19.30–38). Kings are sometimes portrayed as being undone by their drunkenness, as is the case with Elah (1 Kings 16.9) and Ben-hadad (1 Kings 20.16).

Drunkenness, frequently in a figurative sense, is a theme that recurs in the prophetic literature of Israel. On the one hand, the leaders of Israel (including prophets, priests, and kings) are portrayed as being drunk because their acts are viewed as irresponsible (Isa. 28.1, 3; 29.9). On the other hand, those who experience the wrath of Yahweh are depicted as staggering and dazed as a drunkard. This image is applied to Israel

(Isa. 51.21; Jer. 13.13; Ezek. 23.33; Lam. 4.21), to the nations generally (Isa. 24.20; 49.26; Ezek. 39.19), and to specific nations such as *Babylon (Jer. 51.39, 57), *Nineveh (Nah. 3.11), *Egypt (Isa. 19.24), and *Moab (Jer. 48.26). Those drunk with Yahweh's judgment are sometimes pictured as having drunk from the cup or bowl of his wrath (Isa. 51.22; Jer. 25.27; Lam. 4.21; Ezek. 23.33) and sometimes as being drunk with their own blood (Isa. 49.26; cf. Ezek. 39.19). Jeremiah 23.9 represents a unique image in the prophetic literature: Jeremiah likens himself, as a prophet of Yahweh overcome with the power of Yahweh's words, to a drunken man overcome with wine; note the daring application of the same image to Yahweh himself in Psalm 78.65.

In the New Testament references to drunkenness and drunkards often occur in lists of vices (*see* Ethical Lists), and, as in the Hebrew Bible, drunken behavior is viewed negatively (Luke 21.34; Rom. 13.13; 1 Cor. 6.10; 1 Pet. 4.3). Those awaiting the *second coming of Christ should not be drunk (1 Thess. 5.7; Luke 12.45; Matt. 24.49). Paul admonishes the Corinthians not to be drunk at the *Lord's supper (1 Cor. 11.12). In Revelation 17.2, 6 "to be drunk" is used in a figurative sense of Babylon.

See also Wine.   EDGAR W. CONRAD

E. The abbreviation for the Elohist source or tradition in the *Pentateuch. The term "Elohist" is derived from *ĕlōhîm*, a Hebrew word for God. Eighteenth-century analysis of the book of Genesis distinguished two "documents," one in which God was referred to as Elohim, and another in which he was called Yahweh (*see* J; Names of God in the Hebrew Bible); later scholars concluded that in Genesis two different sources used the name Elohim (E and *P), and that the Elohist tradition was to be found beyond the book of Genesis (all sources use Yahweh after the first revelation to Moses; see Exod. 3.13–15 [E]; 6.2–3 [P]). The Elohist tradition is generally thought to have originated in the northern kingdom of Israel in the ninth or eighth century BCE. Its characteristics include a northern setting for most of its narratives in Genesis, divine communication with humans by means of *dreams or messengers (*see* Angels), and an emphasis on *prophecy. These views are widely held by scholars, though recently some have questioned various details and even the very existence of the Elohist.   MICHAEL D. COOGAN

Easter. From Eostre, a Saxon goddess celebrated at the spring equinox. In Christianity Easter is the annual festival commemorating the *resurrection of Christ, observed on a day related to the *Passover full moon but calculated differently in eastern and western churches.

In the Bible the Passover (Hebr. *pesaḥ*, Grk. and late Lat. *pascha*, hence the adjective "paschal") is part of the divine order, Israel's annual commemoration of deliverance (Exod. 12; Deut. 16; Heb. 11.28). For New Testament writers, Christ is the Christian Passover victim (1 Cor. 5.7), and the Gospel presentation has often a Passover background; see Luke 2.41 and the *synoptic passion narrative (Matt. 26.2 par.), according to which the Last Supper appears to be a Passover. In John there are three Passovers: John 2.13, which is associated with the cleansing

of the *Temple; John 6, where the feeding of the five thousand has paschal and eucharistic echoes (the synoptic accounts may also have a paschal origin); John 11–13; 18.28, 39; and 19.23–37, where Jesus dies on the cross according to this Gospel's chronology at the time when the Passover lambs were being slaughtered in preparation (19.31) for the feast. Christ is thus the eternal paschal lamb; see John 19.36 (cf. Exod. 12.46) and John 1.29, 36; *see* Lamb of God.

Easter is therefore the Christian Passover, celebrated for some time on the night of fourteenth of the Jewish month Nisan (Passover night) on whatever day of the week that date fell. This custom continued long in Asia Minor (as in Celtic Britain), with those maintaining it being called Quartodecimans ("fourteeners"), but in Rome Easter was observed on a Sunday from a date that is difficult to determine but earlier than 154 CE, when Polycarp of Smyrna, a Quartodeciman, on a visit discussed the different observances with Anicetus, head of the Roman church.

The transfer of Easter to the first day of the week was no doubt because Sunday had become the Christian weekly day for worship. That this was owing to the Lord's resurrection on Sunday is not provable but suggested strongly by the New Testament evidence and the absence of any convincing alternative theory. The first day of the week marks the discovery of the empty tomb (Matt. 28.1 par.), while on the same evening the meal recalls the Last Supper (Luke 24.30). See also John 20.1, 19 and 26, the last being the Sunday a week later, and Acts 20.7, which again suggests the custom of a Sunday evening Eucharist. Paul calls the Eucharist the *Lord's supper (1 Cor. 11.20); the word for "Lord's" recurs in the New Testament only in Revelation 1.10 in "the Lord's day." It was probably "the Lord's" because it was the day for the Lord's supper or Eucharist, at which the Lord had been physically present before his crucifixion, and especially on the day of his resurrection and subsequent days (to which Acts 1.4 and 10.41 probably refer), and invisibly ever since, anticipating his final coming.   A. R. C. LEANEY

Eastern Orthodoxy and the Bible. The Eastern Orthodox churches consider the Bible as the written memory of God's activity in history and of God's relationship to humankind. It does not reveal everything that God is or is not; in many respects, it is a mystery, and the main purpose why it was written is so that human beings may believe and have life (John 20.30). There is much diversity in its accounts, style, chronologies, descriptions, poetry. But there is also unity, a centrality in its message and in its purpose. It introduces a linear approach to history and looks forward to fulfillments and the eschaton—the end of time.

As a partial memory recorded in history by human beings, the Bible cannot be understood divorced from the historical experience and the consciousness of the communities of believers, whether ancient Israel and Judaism or Christianity. It is for this reason that the Bible is considered the book of the community, depending on the community's authority and approval of its authenticity, its inspiration, and interpretation.

It was written for practical needs and under different historical circumstances. This means that the Bible is not the totality of God's word or *revelation. God's word has been revealed "in many and various ways" (Heb. 1.1), including the order and beauty of the cosmos, human conscience and natural law, the words of philosophers, poets, and prophets of many peoples, culminating in the words of the God-made-man, the incarnate *Logos of God. Thus, the *word of God can be discerned within but also outside the Bible. Natural revelation, however, is propaedeutic and preparatory to the supernatural, more direct revelation given through God's chosen *prophets and finally through God's Son.

The first part of the Bible reveals that God exists, creates, and intervenes through signs and symbols, individuals, prophets and priests, kings and shepherds—in particular, through a people who serve as an example of God's providence and concern for humankind. From a Christian perspective, the Old Testament points toward a goal and a fulfillment. Its role was to prepare the way for the New Testament, which is viewed as the high point of God's revelation in Jesus Christ, who is the end of an era and the beginning of a new one.

Whether in the Old or the New Testament, divine revelation was recorded under the *inspiration of God's *Holy Spirit. But inspiration is understood in a dynamic way. The writers of the biblical books were not passive receivers of messages but energetic and conscious instruments recording the revealed message in their own styles, and through their own intellectual and linguistic presuppositions. For the Orthodox, inspiration *(theopneustia)* is an elevated state of being that makes it possible to grasp and record revelation. The Holy Spirit inspires the writers, but it is the writers who write and speak, not as mechanical, passive instruments but in full control of their senses. Thus, biblical authors may display human shortcomings, broad or limited education, and their own specific intellectual backgrounds.

For the Eastern Orthodox, then, the Bible is the inspired word of God in terms of content rather than style, grammar, history, or frame. Very few if any Orthodox theologians accept the word-by-word inspiration of scripture. It is for this reason that the Orthodox church has never had serious disputes concerning the application of the historical-critical method in its approach to exegesis and *hermeneutics.

The Canon and the Authority of the Bible. The Bible includes the Hebrew Palestinian canon of thirty-nine books; ten Deuterocanonicals or *Anaginoskomena* ("books that are read"; *see* Apocrypha, *article on* Jewish Apocrypha; Canon); and the New Testament of twenty-seven books.

The Greek translation of the Old Testament (*Septuagint), including the Deuterocanonical books, was the Bible used by the early Christian community, and it remains the official text of the Eastern Orthodox church. The early church as a whole did not take a definite position for or against the Deuterocanonicals. Church leaders and ecclesiastical writers of both the Greek east and Latin west were not in full agreement. Some preferred the Hebrew canon, while others accepted the longer canon that included the Deuterocanonicals. The ambivalence of ecumenical and local synods (Nicea, 325 CE; Rome, 382; Laodicea, 365; Hippo, 393) was resolved by the Trullan Synod (692). It adopted deliberations of councils that had favored the shorter list, and decisions of other synods that had advocated the longer list. Ultimately, the Deuterocanonicals were adopted as inspired books, good for reading and spiritual edification and on occasions even as sources of doctrine. The most serious justification for the adoption of the Deuterocanonicals was their frequent use in the worship and life of the early church. Books such as *Tobit, *Judith, *Wisdom of Solomon, and *Sirach (or Ecclesiasticus) are frequently used in liturgical prayers and hymns.

The official text of the Old Testament used by the Eastern Orthodox churches includes the following Deuterocanonicals: 1 *Esdras, *Tobit, *Judith, *Wisdom of Solomon, *Sirach, *Baruch; 1–3 *Maccabees; and the Letter of Jeremiah (see Jeremiah, The Letter of). Other Deuterocanonical texts such as *Susanna, The Song of the Three Children (see Azariah, The Prayer of), and *Bel and the Dragon appear as parts of the book of *Daniel. The canonicity of the Deuterocanonical books is still a disputed topic in Orthodox biblical theology.

The question whether or not the authority of the Bible stands above the authority of the church it serves is a serious theological issue. The prevailing opinion is that once the canon of the Bible has been established, its authority becomes absolute, but the church remains its continuous and watchful guardian. The Bible's inspiration, canonicity, and authenticity depend on the church's consent. The Bible is the book of the church. Revealed truth preexisted the written word, and the community in the sense of both the old and the new Israel (synagogue and church) preceded the writing of scripture.

The Orthodox Church continues in its teaching that revealed truth is incorporated in the apostolic tradition, in the decisions of the ecumenical councils, in the theological consensus of the church fathers, and in the sacramental life and worship of the church. The Holy Spirit that reveals the word of God cannot be confined to the pages of a book. Nevertheless, all facets of belief and life of the church have been saturated with the teachings of the scriptures. Doctrines, ethical teachings, and liturgical worship have scriptural foundations and are always in agreement with the scripture.

Ecclesial Authority and Biblical Authority. The distinction between revealed truth as written word and as tradition explains the reason why Eastern Orthodoxy emphasizes the importance of ecclesial authority. The church is the "pillar and bulwark of the truth" (1 Tim. 3.14); it proclaims and guards those divine truths, written and unwritten, scripture and tradition, which coexist in complete harmony with each other. The ekklēsia as a people called out by God to be God's instrument and witness existed long before the Bible's writing and codification. Whether

as "the people of God" in ancient Israel or as "the new people of God" in the Christian church, it was God's people who first witnessed to God's mighty deeds in history through his prophets and finally his own Logos, who became human in order to save humanity. The Bible itself was produced within the ekklēsia for specific reasons and for the needs of its members. What was not incorporated in the book remained a fluid living testimony that found its way in the experience of the church as writings and commentaries of chuch fathers, prayers and liturgical texts, and decisions of ecumenical councils. The totality of that part of God's revelation necessary for salvation saturates the life of the church.

Notwithstanding this holistic understanding of revelation, the Bible still occupies the central position in the Orthodox church's faith and life. Doctrinal truths, ethical teachings, liturgical and prayer life all have biblical foundations. The Bible's *authority is not minimized by ecclesial authority. The church, however, remains the lawful custodian and authentic interpreter of revelation, whether it presents itself as holy scripture or sacred tradition. The indwelling Holy Spirit guides and directs the church, especially when it is assembled in a council (Matt. 18.20), an ecumenical council in particular, which is the supreme authority on matters of doctrinal truth.

The Bible in the Worship of the Church and the Life of the Individual. Revelation through God's word in prophecy, mighty deeds, and especially God's incarnate Logos, his teachings, death, and resurrection was relived by the early church assembled in worship. The human being is not only a rational animal but also a worshiping being. And worship has been of primary importance to Eastern Orthodoxy. Orthodox worship consists of the liturgy of the word and the liturgy of the mystery, the Eucharist.

The example was set by the early church. The believers devoted themselves to the teachings of the apostles, to prayers and the breaking of bread (Acts 2.42). It is not only symbolic that the book of the Gospels occupies the central place on the altar table; there is no service in the Orthodox church that does not include readings from the Psalms, prophets, and especially the Gospels and other New Testament books. Liturgical texts, hymns, and prayers are filled with biblical passages, or inspired and saturated with the spirit, images, and symbols of the Bible.

But on the same altar table we find the chalice, the tabernacle with sacred host. The liturgy of the word and the liturgy of the Eucharist are the basis of the sermons and catechetical instruction. Listening to the exposition of the written word and participating in the mystery within the community constitute the supreme religious experience for the Eastern Orthodox. The interpretation of scripture and the celebration of the eucharist are the two principal bonds between the ancient and the ongoing life and thought of the Eastern Orthodox church.

With very few exceptions, Eastern Orthodoxy has always encouraged individual Bible reading for inspiration, edification, and the strengthening of the individual's spiritual life. "May the sun on rising find you with a Bible in your hand": these words of Evagrius Ponticus (d. 399 CE) summarize the patristic and traditional stand of Eastern Orthodoxy toward individual reading. But reading the Bible assumes a state of prayer and presupposes a sense of humility. The word of God is at once easy to understand and mysterious.

The Bible is everyone's book but not for everyone's interpretation. Subjective interpretation, which may lead to misunderstanding and extreme individualism, should be subject to the objective interpretation of the church. Subjective interpretation, usually the task of the pastor or preacher, is expected to rely on the objective exegesis of the church's theology. And there is no authentic theology outside the historic experience of the church and its teachings. It is not possible for the modern believer and the church collectively to turn their back on past centuries of accumulated wisdom and historical investigation—hence the emphasis on the value of the patristic mind and the biblical ethos of the church.   DEMETRIOS J. CONSTANTELOS

Ebla. Tell Mardikh is located about 55 km (34 mi) south and slightly west of Aleppo in Syria (Map 6:G3). In antiquity it was called Ebla in cuneiform inscriptions. Naram-Sin, a conquering king of Mesopotamia in the twenty-third century BCE, records that he captured and burned Ebla.

The Italian archeologist Paolo Matthiae began work at the site in 1964 because of its size, monumental city walls, and prominent acropolis; in 1974–1975 he discovered about fifteen thousand cuneiform tablets dating from around 2300 BCE. The script is Mesopotamian cuneiform, but the language is, as a rule, Eblaite, a Semitic dialect intermediate between Babylonian and Northwest Semitic (which includes *Hebrew).

Ebla was a commercial city-state and cultural center that included a school of learned scribes who trained students in the arts and sciences not only to write the administrative records for the palace and temples but, more generally, to master and transmit a rich tradition. The brief "Age of Ebla" is contemporary with the dynasty of Sargon of Akkad (to which Naram-Sin belonged) in Mesopotamia and the Old Kingdom in *Egypt (hieroglyphic names and titles of Chefren of Dynasty IV and Pepi I of Dynasty VI have been unearthed at Ebla).

From Ebla students were sent abroad to cities like *Mari; and scholars, such as a mathematician from the Mesopotamian city of Kish, were also brought to Ebla. Textbooks in various subjects (including bilingual vocabularies, religion, and geography) were used at Ebla in slightly different editions than those used in Mesopotamia.

The Ebla archives have changed our concept of the background of biblical history. It used to be thought that, before the Israelites, *Canaan (or Syria-Palestine) was relatively primitive, with a nomadic, or seminomadic, population. Canaan was thus regarded as a sort of cultural backwash of Mesopotamia and Egypt. Ebla shows that this was not so: the largest library that has come down to us from this period is from Ebla. The Ebla archives show that the culture of the land was urbanized; *nomads did exist but were not the controlling factor.

Because the Ebla archives predate *Abraham, the high level of Hebrew civilization from its outset is historically explicable: the biblical Hebrews did not go through a "primitive" period in civilization or literature. Rather, they built on the high culture that had long existed in Canaan, when Abraham migrated from Haran to the *Promised Land.   CYRUS H. GORDON

Ecclesiastes, The Book of. The title of the book in Hebrew is *qōhelet* (also transliterated *qōheleth* and *koheleth*), a particular form of the verb "to assemble," which led to the *Septuagint translation *Ekklēsiastēs*, one who addresses an assembly, frequently rendered "The Preacher." The content of this short treatise, however, is less ecclesial than sapiential, displaying a skepticism and dry wit that would be incongruous in a formal religious gathering. Even the ethical theory of moderation smacks of the academic, and the editorial epilogue, by another hand (12.8–10), shows the author in the guise of a scribe-teacher, adding the definite article: *haqqōhelet,* or "The

Assembler," suggesting that it may well be a student's nickname for a well-known character.

Written probably in the third century BCE, it belongs among the *wisdom books, being one of the *Megillot. Its unity is much disputed, ranging from twofold or fourfold authorship to a loose collection of short sections or chapters attributed to different hands. However, the recurrence of idiosyncratic phrases and sophistication of language may point to a single author. In spite of what appears to be a lack of sequence and an overlapping of ideas, there is real unity in the thought pattern. It presents a running dialectic: the "vanity of things" set over against the goodness of life. Being to some extent gnomic wisdom, an extended proverb, it restructures accepted truths about life, death, pleasure, and toil, and reevaluates them realistically, holding experience up to the light and refracting it. The seeming contradictions are a deliberate teaching tool, and the heterodox atmosphere comes from this dialectical style rather than from the ideas.

Philosophical more than religious, the work consists of a sequence of reactions to the question presented in 1.2–3: "What does one gain by all one's toil?" Beginning and ending with this theme, the book falls into two parts: a philosophical treatise on life and the absurd (chaps. 1–6), and an ethical discussion on how one should live one's life as a result (chaps. 7–12). Quite often a traditional maxim of the schools serves as a launching pad for a personal observation. The thesis of 1.2–3 is the starting point: "vanity," or universal contingency, qualifies cosmos, human environment, and all human effort. The idea refers more to the way Qoheleth experiences life than to a clear metaphysic. There follows a demonstration of this thesis by a study of cosmic circularity (1.4–11). All things are in perpetual flux, ending where they began—an order presumably fixed by God but to mortals quite arbitrary. One finds oneself swept up in a flood of time and destiny that cannot be controlled. Even the human desire for knowledge is contingent. The subsequent proof of this thesis (1.12–2.26) begins in typical sapiential style, from experience. Adopting the mantle of *Solomon and thus vested with perfect wisdom (1.1, 12, 16), the author looks for meaning where traditionally it is to be found: in pleasure, in riches, in work. All end in *death. Even wisdom itself avails nothing. Absurdity remains, and not simply in personal experience but rooted in human nature: "God has given to human beings" the innate urge to reason why, but even this is "vanity."

Paradoxically, the inevitability of death focuses the mind on the "now," and so human life, with its limitations and pleasures, takes center stage. Indeed, 2.16–26 suggests that the only norm is the individual. Although time rolls around fruitlessly, again and again (3.1–9), and people can find no permanent foothold, yet they still study and inquire and dream, for God "has made everything beautiful in its time, and has put eternity into their minds, yet they cannot find out what God has done from beginning to end" (3.11). From chap. 3 on the thesis is viewed from every side, philosophical and existential (3.1–12 is answered in 3.13–15; 3.16–21 in 3.22; 4.1–5.17 in 5.18–20). The mystery of existence is seen in the pattern of the cosmos and in time, both of which impose themselves on humanity, though to some extent one can control the latter and limit its mystery by judging the propitious moment. There is further the enigma of right and wrong: good is not invariably rewarded (3.16–20; 7.15); the same end comes to all (3.19–20), and all that results from human effort is bitterness (6.2–3). Contingency is as near a rule of life as one can find.

The practical conclusion is drawn in the second half of the book (7.1–11.6) in what is effectively a moral treatise, proverbial in style. If effort and toil, if even piety and justice avail so little, the only profitable attitude to adopt is to live in the world as one finds it, to be moderate in all things (even piety), and to enjoy the good pleasure that life gives, for even this is a gift, and fulfillment may not come with success (7.15–25; 8.14–17). In these chapters many familiar themes reappear, such as human destiny, God's providence, wisdom, and folly; but now they are given a moral twist, and Ecclesiastes becomes a wisdom dialectic in the service of a humanistic ethic. The fact of death and the problematic nature of moral retribution lead to the belief that life remains the only good—as long as one recognizes its precarious nature and lives within the sane limits of prudence. The presence of God acts as a moderating influence on the harder skepticism of the contemporary scene, while a strong belief in free will and human responsibility modifies its determinism. The author does of course present an enjoyment ethic, but he is quite careful to impose restrictions on the enjoyment of life's good things, which must never exceed human limits. Abuse is never acceptable. Pleasure is a practical ideal, not an absolute. This appears to be the best solution to the vanity of things.

The final word, suitably, is found in an allegory of youth and age (11.7–12.8). Life is short, and youth in particular should enjoy it, for soon will come old age when energy fades and passions die. The editorial epilogue (12.9–14), perhaps by two hands, is an orthodox footnote, sympathetic but cautious.

Ecclesiastes represents an individual's experiential view of the world and human existence and a resultant ethic based on reason applied to that experience. Without rejecting his tradition, the author's rational, universalistic tendencies made blind allegiance to that tradition impossible. God remains the God of Judaism, but the author sees him rather as Elohim, the universal creator and sovereign who remains beyond human understanding. It is this that makes the ethic so important; in an unpredictable world one maintains human values of integrity and decency. One maintains one's humanity, and perhaps this is the only certain value.

How this book found a place in the Hebrew *canon remains a puzzle. Perhaps it is a tribute to the fact that a religious scholar, heir to a tradition, could face a world of cultural ferment and make a personal contribution by offering an intellectually valid answer to the problem of existence.   DERMOT COX, O.F.M.

Ecclesiasticus. *See* Sirach.

Ecology. *See* Nature and Ecology.

Eden, The Garden of. A garden of trees and lush vegetation planted by God and occupied by *Adam and *Eve (Gen. 2–3). The meaning of the word "Eden" in Hebrew is uncertain. Some scholars connect it with a Sumerian word meaning "wilderness" or "plain," while others have proposed a derivation from the Hebrew word for "delight" or "pleasure." Thus, Eden came to be identified as an ideal garden of delight, or *paradise.

The location of the garden of Eden that the author of Genesis had in mind is difficult to determine. Genesis 2.8 places the garden "in the east," which in general indicates *Mesopotamia. Genesis 2.10–14 appears to draw from a Near Eastern tradition of an idyllic garden from which rivers flowed. Two of the four rivers named in Genesis are known, the Tigris and the Euphrates. The other two are not known (although

Gihon, meaning "gusher," is also the name of *Jerusalem's primary spring), making any precise geographical location hypothetical.

In Genesis 2–3, the garden of Eden has at its center the tree of life and the tree of the knowledge of good and evil. The garden is not simply a luxurious paradise but a place created by God in which human beings live and eat and work (Gen. 2.15). Eden functioned as a paradigm of the unbroken relationships between God and humans, and between humans and *nature, which no longer obtained after the first couple's disobedience (*see* Fall, The).

The image of the garden of Eden reappears in somewhat altered form in the later prophets. The expulsion from Eden functions as a metaphor for the coming judgment against the nations (Tyre: Ezek. 28.11–19; Egypt: Ezek. 31.8, 9, 16, 18), and for the coming judgment of the *day of the Lord (Joel 2.3). The garden of Eden is also an image of promise: in parallel with "the garden of the Lord," Eden appears in Isaiah 51.3 as a metaphor for the renewal of the land of Israel after the Babylonian *exile (see also Ezekiel 36.35; Revelation 22.2–3).
                                                DENNIS T. OLSON

Edom. A kingdom that neighbored Judah on its southeastern border during the Iron Age. It encompassed the area southward from the Wadi Hesa in Jordan to the Gulf of Aqaba, and, during part of this period, included the area called Seir, southwest of the Dead Sea and south of Kadesh-barnea (see Map 1:Y7).

Very little is known about Edom. Virtually no Edomite inscriptions have been found, apart from some seals and a few ostraca. The primary literary source for the history of Edom is the Bible, but only the barest outline can be constructed from that source. Some information comes from Assyrian records, and archaeological excavations and surveys have enabled a general picture of the development of the region to be sketched.

The early development of Edom remains largely unknown. The stories in Genesis that describe family relationships between Israel's *ancestors and those of all the surrounding kingdoms are generally understood to be artificial. For Edom this is particularly clear, since the connection between *Isaac's brother *Esau and Edom is tenuous and awkward in the narratives of Genesis 25:19–34 and is almost certainly a later imposition on the stories.

Archaeological surveys indicate that the land

of Edom was occupied fairly sparsely during the Late Bronze Age (ca. 1550–1200 BCE), with only a few small fortified towns and some tiny villages. The geographic name Edom appears for the first time in an Egyptian document of the thirteenth century BCE.

Numbers 20.14–21 suggests that Edom was already a monarchy at the time of the *Exodus in the thirteenth century. Recent studies, however, have cast considerable doubt about the historicity of this and related stories. Even the so-called Edomite king list in Genesis 36.31–39 has been shown to be garbled and unreliable.

*Saul is said to have fought Edom successfully (1 Sam. 14:47), but it was *David who conquered it and incorporated it into his empire, setting up garrisons throughout the land (2 Sam. 8.14). Although a certain Hadad tried to rebel against *Solomon, he does not appear to have been successful (1 Kings 11.14–22). Edom remained under Israelite control, ruled by an Israelite governor until the reign of Jehoram of Judah in the mid-ninth century (2 Kings 8.20). At that time the Edomites successfully rebelled and set up their own king.

During the reigns of Amaziah of Judah (797–769) and Uzziah (769–734) Edom again came under Judean domination. Uzziah recaptured and rebuilt Elath on the Gulf of Aqaba early in his reign. But in the reign of Ahaz Edom decisively threw off Judean control and remained independent of Judah from that time on.

In Judah's place, however, came *Assyrian domination, but as was the case also for *Ammon and *Moab, the Assyrian presence appears to have been economically and politically beneficial to Edom. Excavations at Buseira (probably the Edomite capital Bozrah), Tawilan, and Tell el-Kheleifeh (Elath), show that the late eighth through the mid-sixth centuries BCE saw the peak of Edomite prosperity and expansion. It is from these centuries that monumental architecture is known, and there are indications that Edom expanded its influence into the southern hinterlands of Judah.

Edom seems to have survived the violence of the *Babylonian campaigns under *Nebuchadrezzar, and, although Buseira, Tawilan, and other sites suffered destruction later in the sixth century, the region recovered and continued to play a role in international trade during the Persian period. With the rise of the *Nabateans, a significant proportion of the Edomites seem to have moved westward, so that, by the Hellenistic period, Idumea (the Greek form of Edom) was the name of the region directly to the south of Judah (Map 10:W-X5–6; see 1 Macc. 4.29). The most famous Idumean was *Herod the Great.

Attested Edomite names suggest that the Edomites worshiped the well-known West Semitic gods, Hadad/*Baal and El. But it appears that the primary deity of Edom was a god named Qaus/Qos. Little is known of this god, and even his basic characteristics (is he a war god or a storm god?) are debated. Some scholars have speculated that in the late second/early first millennium BCE, Yahweh may have been an important deity in Edomite religion, since a few biblical passages link Yahweh closely with Edom and Seir (Judg. 5.4; Deut. 33.2; Hab. 3.3).

Although Deuteronomy 23.8 expresses a tolerant attitude toward the Edomites, most biblical passages dealing with the kingdom display a severe hostility toward it, reflecting the almost constant conflict between Judah and Edom. Considerable bitterness is evident in the biblical texts concerning Edom's attitudes and actions after the destruction of Jerusalem in 587/586 BCE (see, e.g., Jer. 49.7–22; Obad.; Isa. 34). Edom, in fact, became a symbol of Israel's enemies in postexilic literature.   WAYNE T. PITARD

Egypt (Map 6:E–F5). The name is derived from the Greek *Aiguptos,* itself a rendering of the Egyptian *Ḥwt-Ptaḥ,* "Temple of Ptah." The Egyptian name for the country was *Keme,* "the Black Land"; in Hebrew it appears as *Miṣrayim.*

Apart from the delta region, formed by silt deposited for millennia by the *Nile, the rest of Egypt consists of a narrow river valley, bounded on its eastern and western sides by vast arid and inhospitable deserts. The delta is similarly bounded on the east by the Sinai desert and on the west by the Libyan desert. In the south, the turbulent waters of the First Cataract at Aswan form a natural boundary, as does the Mediterranean Sea in the north. In ancient times these natural geographical borders effectively isolated Egypt from the rest of the Near East, thereby favoring the uninterrupted development of the civilization distinctive to the Egyptians, generally undisturbed by foreign invasions. Blessed with a stable climate and extremely fertile lands, regularly watered by the river Nile, the Egyptians developed a rich agricultural economy, producing wheat, barley, vegetables of many kinds, various fruits, and grapes (see Num. 11.5). Very early on, Egypt became the granary of the ancient Near East, especially in times of famine (see Gen. 41.57). Although rich in fine types of stone suitable for building and carving—among them, limestone, alabaster, sandstone, and granite—Egypt was poor in metal ores workable at the time. The one exception was gold from the eastern desert, Nubia, and the northern Sudan. Egypt also was and still is poor in trees suitable for woodworking. External trade in this commodity dates back to early times.

The exact origin of the Egyptians is uncertain. They themselves claimed that their ancestors migrated northward from a region bordering on the Red Sea. Their language, essentially Hamitic, nevertheless reveals certain affinities with the Semitic family of languages. The latest form of Egyptian is Coptic, developed during the early period of Christianity in Egypt. It is still used in the liturgy of the Coptic church, though since the Arab conquest in the seventh century CE the ordinary language of the people has been Arabic.

Egypt's geography, largely a river valley some six hundred miles in length, led to the development of many local dialects of the native language. During the early pharaonic era, in order to overcome the difficulties caused by this diversity of speech, a special form of *writing was developed. Based on many hieroglyphic figures, it was a kind of Mandarin written language, strictly consonantal but capable of coping with the vocalic differences of the various dialects. The work of interpreting and more particularly writing the hieroglyphs was performed by a large body of trained scribes, who might be described as forming an early civil service that maintained the successful administration of Egypt.

Both from original sources and from a history written in Greek ca. 300 BCE by an Egyptian priest, Manetho, it appears that the unification of the two ancient kingdoms of the north and the south was effected by Menes, the founder of the first historical dynasty and the builder of the city of Memphis. In his history, Manetho lists the rulers of Egypt under thirty dynasties, but many of the kings he names have left no tangible records of their reigns. A simpler scheme of the long history is provided by these divisions: the Archaic Period, ca. 3100–2700 BCE; the Old Kingdom, ca. 2700–2500 BCE; the Middle Kingdom, ca. 2134–1786 BCE; the New Kingdom, ca. 1575–1087 BCE; the Late Period, until the beginning of the Greek or Ptolemaic Period, ca. 1087–332 BCE.

The Old Kingdom was a period of remarkable building and artistic excellence. In particular, the rulers of Dynasty IV erected the immense pyramids at Giza, reckoned by classical antiquity as one of the seven wonders of the world. The drain on the kingdom's economy in building the pyramids, intended as the secure burial places of the rulers, eventually so weakened the succeeding dynasties that at the end of Dynasty VI a period of anarchy and decline occurred.

Able monarchs, originating from Thebes, during Dynasty XI established effective control over the whole of Egypt and founded the Middle Kingdom. The most powerful rulers were those of Dynasty XII, who conquered and held Nubia. During the Middle Kingdom there was a revival of artistic excellence, especially in portraiture.

As had been the case with the Old Kingdom, toward the end of the Middle Kingdom a period of weakness in the central government allowed the entry into the delta region of a group of foreigners, known as the Hyksos or "Chieftains of Foreign Lands," probably of pastoral origin. They were powerful enough to hold northern Egypt for a considerable time; some ancient and modern scholars regard this period as the setting of the *Joseph narratives in Genesis. During the same period, people from Nubia (the northern Sudan) overran most of the region south of Aswan.

Despite these reverses, the rulers of Thebes eventually succeeded in defeating the forces in Nubia and expelling the Hyksos from the delta. With the founding of the powerful Dynasty XVIII, a period of military advance into Palestine and Syria began. Under warlike kings such as Tuthmose I and his later successor Tuthmose III, greatest of all the pharaohs, Egyptian armies advanced as far as the headwaters of the Euphrates. Conquest brought vast quantities of booty into Egypt to swell the treasury of the state god, Amun-Re. This period also witnessed the entry of many foreign artisans into the country, and with them new ideas. Toward the end of the dynasty, internal religious strife and external administrative weakness followed the accession of Amenhotep IV, better known as Akhnaton (also spelled Akhenaton and Ikhnaton). He attempted to change the long-established religion, bitterly opposing the priesthood and eventually removing his capital city from Thebes to Tell el-Amarna. Opinions about Akhnaton have varied from seeing him as the first monotheist to a pleasure-loving materialist. It is not easy to form a just assessment, for after his death his capital city was abandoned, the ancient religion restored, and every possible record of him destroyed. Some correspondence with Asiatic rulers in such cities as Byblos, *Jerusalem, and *Shechem has survived and is known as the *Amarna letters; it is an important source for our understanding of Syria-Palestine in this period. Among his successors was the youthful Tutankhamun, who reigned briefly, and whose tomb, filled with splendid treasures, was found in the Valley of the Kings by Howard Carter in 1922.

A significant restoration of Egypt's former glory was achieved during Dynasty XIX under the Kings Seti I and his son Ramesses II, both of whom advanced once more into Palestine and Syria; the *Exodus of the Hebrews from Egypt is dated to this period by many scholars. Ramesses warred inconclusively with the *Hittites in northern Syria, but his greatest achievements during a long reign were his building projects, especially at Thebes, and his massive rock-cut temples at Abu Simbel in Nubia. His successor, Merneptah, had to deal with foreign invasion in the north. On a triumphal stele from his reign occurs the first mention of the name of Israel, as a defeated people (see Israel, History of). In Dynasty XX, a far more serious invasion of northern Egypt by land and sea occurred. This was crushed by Ramesses III, not generally recognized as militarily the greatest of the kings bearing that name. Among the various people who attempted the invasion by sea were the group known in the Bible as the *Philistines.

A succession of kings bearing the name Ramesses followed, but each proved weaker than his predecessor, and Egypt declined in power. The geographical barriers that in times past ensured so many centuries of isolation no longer sufficed to prevent foreign invasion. Thus, Dynasty XXII was founded by a Libyan general, Sheshonq I. Called Shishak in the Bible, he invaded Palestine during the reign of Rehoboam, ca. 920 BCE, removing some of the vessels of the Temple (1 Kings 11.40; 14.25–26). A record of some of the places he claimed to have captured appears on one of the walls of the temple at Karnak. Dynasty XXV originated from Nubia. In the time of Taharqa (the Tirhakah of 2 Kings 19.9), the fourth ruler of the Dynasty, Egypt faced invasions by the *Assyrians. During the last of the Assyrian invasions in the time of Taharqa's successor, in 663 BCE, the great city of Thebes, No-Amon, was captured and sacked (Nah. 3.8).

For a period after the withdrawal of the Assyrians, Egypt revived under a number of able

rulers only to fall eventually to the *Persians under Cambyses. In 332 BCE *Alexander the Great was welcomed by the Egyptians as their deliverer from the rule of the hated Persians. Following Alexander's death and the division of his empire among his generals, Ptolemy gained Egypt in 322 BCE, becoming the first ruler of the Ptolemaic or Greek Dynasty. The last of the Dynasty was Cleopatra, who like her lover Antony committed suicide after their defeat at the Battle of Actium (31 CE). Egypt then became part of the *Roman empire.

Under the Pharaohs, the government of Egypt was essentially theocratic, the king as a child of the gods being semidivine, and as such high priest of the land. His general title, pharaoh, meaning "the Great House," can be compared with "the Palace" or "the Sublime Porte." It is not until the time of the Pharaoh Sheshonq that the throne name of the ruler of Egypt is recorded in the Bible. Two other names of rulers recorded are So (2 Kings 17.4) and Neco (2 Kings 23.29; Jer. 46.2). The order of precedence in Egyptian society can be illustrated by the figure of a pyramid: the pharaoh at the apex, and, in descending layers, the royal family and the local princes, the priests, the scribes, the artisans, and at the base the workers of the land.

To modern minds, the religion of ancient Egypt appears to be a strange, chaotic mixture of pantheism and animal worship, frequently full of contradictory beliefs. Long isolation from the rest of the ancient Near East had tended to breed in the Egyptians a strongly conservative outlook with a deep reverence for the past, so that what might seem to be contradictory was accepted as complementary. Over the centuries, purely local deities merged into larger groupings so that the god of one locality might be regarded as the husband of the goddess of another locality. In some instances, the deity of a third locality, merged into a larger grouping, might be regarded as the child of a divine marriage, thus creating a triad. In many instances, the only clues to the former existence of local gods are their names alone. It should be noted that the many gods of Egypt were essentially deities of the Nile Valley, and that of their vast number only one, the goddess Isis, was successfully translated abroad.

The many temples, supported by great estates, were established to serve the various gods, who in their turn served humankind by preserving the physical fabric of the world. The temples were in fact state institutions and not places of individual devotion and prayer. The temples played a very practical role by training able boys, regardless of their social standing, to become scribes in the service of the state. There was a widespread belief in a resurrection and a future realm of rewards and punishments, presided over by the god Osiris, who had been slain by his evil brother Set, but who was afterward restored to life. From various writings it appears that at all times there existed a sense of personal religious morality as distinct from the state religion.   J. MARTIN PLUMLEY

Elder. The designation and role of the elder (Hebr. *zāqēn;* Grk. *presbyteros*) dates to premonarchic times in Israel. In the legislation concerning the *Passover in Exodus 12.21 Moses addresses "all the elders of Israel." Similarly, in Numbers 11.16 Moses is commanded to gather together "seventy of the elders of Israel whom you know to be the elders of the people and officers over them" and bring them to the tent of meeting. As this passage and others suggest, the elder, as head of the extended family, had authority over it and also represented it in larger assemblies. These elders functioned primarily on the local level as judges, leaders in battle, and intermediaries between the people and their leaders or God. These functions continued during the monarchy, as the story of Naboth's vineyard (1 Kings 21.8–14) and other passages (e.g., Jer. 26.17; Prov. 31.23) make clear, and in the Second Temple period as well (see Ezra 6.7–8; 10.14), both in Judea (1 Macc. 12.35) and in the Diaspora (Sus. 5).

In the New Testament, the "elders of the people" figure throughout the Gospels (e.g., Mark 15.1 par.) and Acts (5.21; 22.5) as leaders of the Judean community who frequently counsel with other leadership groups and have some role in judging capital crimes. Perhaps related to such a group is the phrase "the tradition of the elders" (Mark 7.3, 5 par.) against which Jesus argues and which is associated with the *Pharisees in both the Gospels and *Josephus.

When Christianity began to institutionalize in a formal sense, it understandably drew on Jewish tradition to accomplish this task; thus the title and office of elder make their way into New Testament history and texts. Though not found in the authentic Pauline letters, there are elders mentioned in Acts in the churches at *Antioch (14.21), *Jerusalem (15.6; 21.18), and *Ephesus (20.17). The author of 2 and 3 John identifies

himself as a *presbyteros,* as does the writer of 1 Peter (5.1). The office of elder occurs frequently in the *Pastoral Letters. 1 Timothy 5.1 uses the term in the context of one who is deserving of respect, but not necessarily as a technical term; in 5.17, however, an office is clearly meant, and an elder is defined as one who both teaches and preaches. Functions such as *laying on of hands (1 Tim 4.14), anointing the sick (James 5.14), and general governance (Tit. 1.5; 1 Pet. 5.2–3) are also mentioned. There are also repeated references to the office of elder in the apostolic fathers, but as time went on hierarchical episcopacy became the normative form of church administration (*see* Bishop); the English word "priest," however, is ultimately derived from the Greek word *presbyteros*.

The title, and to some extent the functions, of elder were revived by the sixteenth-century reformer John Calvin, and the Greek word was adopted for the name of the Presbyterian church.   J. ANDREW OVERMAN

Elect, Election. *See* Chosen People; Predestination; Saint(s).

Elijah. Elijah ("Yah[weh] is my God") was a prophet in the northern kingdom of the divided monarchy during the reigns of Ahab, Ahaziah, and Jehoram (873–843 BCE). The circumstances of his birth and early life are not recorded, nor, somewhat unusually, is the name of his father. He was a native of Tishbe in Gilead, an unknown Transjordanian site.

The stories about Elijah, which once circulated separately, have been incorporated into the *Deuteronomic history as part of its extensive account of the reign of Ahab of Israel (1 Kings 16.29–22.40) and of its briefer account of the reign of his short-lived son Ahaziah (1 Kings 22.51—2 Kings 1.18). Elijah's translation to heaven and his sucession by *Elisha in 2 Kings 2.1–18 are outside the regnal frame and are part of the Elisha cycle; they take place sometime in Jehoram's reign.

The Elijah cycle records the battle in the north for the survival of authentic Yahwism. Both Ahab and his successor Ahaziah looked not only to Yahweh but also to *Baal and to his consort *Asherah for the winter rains and summer dew that fertilized the land (1 Kings 17–19), and for healing (2 Kings 1). Elijah had to contend not only with the many prophets of Baal and Asherah but with other prophets of Yahweh; 1 Kings 20 and 22 (though not mentioning Elijah) show disagreements among prophets speaking in Yahweh's name. To Elijah, Yahwism involved more than proper worship; the king was accountable to Yahweh's word delivered through prophets such as Elijah, and was bound by Mosaic laws protecting the poor (chap. 21). The royal house, influenced by the Phoenician Queen *Jezebel, looked to non-Israelite models of kingship, in which the patron gods supported the dynasty.

The section 1 Kings 17–19 is artfully arranged from short stories into a coherent demonstration of Yahweh's control of fertility and protection of his prophet. Elijah announces a drought in 17.1, then in 17.2–24 is protected from its effects and from the king. In 18.1–40 Elijah challenged Ahab and his prophets to a contest to determine which deity could end the drought. Yahweh's consumption of the bull offered to him proves that he alone is God; the rain of vv. 40–46 is therefore from Yahweh and not from Baal.

The prophetic word ending the drought, like the word that began it (17.1), puts Elijah in danger from the king. Chap. 19 tells how Yahweh protected Elijah at *Horeb, the source of authentic Yahwism. Like Moses, he encounters God. The *theophany, however, is not in the traditional storm but in "a still small voice" (19.12; NRSV: "a sound of sheer silence"), commissioning him to anoint new kings in Syria and Israel (Hazael in place of Ben-Hadad and *Jehu in place of Ahab), and a prophetic successor, Elisha. The sole divinity of Yahweh, proved in the drought-ending storm at Carmel, is asserted in a different way at Horeb; the God of Israel has authority to reject and appoint kings and to provide for a continuing prophetic word.

Chap. 21 is another confrontation of king and prophet, this time about the judicial murder of Naboth, who, in accord with the Israelite conception of land tenure, had refused to sell his family plot to Ahab. Elijah's curse upon Ahab takes effect only in the next generation, occasioning Elijah's last recorded confrontation, with Ahaziah in 2 Kings 1. The king in his illness had sent to Baal of Ekron for healing, and so he must die.

Outside the books of Kings, the Chronicler reports a letter from Elijah condemning Jeroboam (2 Chron. 21.12–15). Malachi (4.5 [Heb. 3.23], commenting on 3.1) identifies the messenger of the last days with Elijah; taken up to heaven (2 Kings 2.11), the prophet shall return to prepare the nation for the *day of the Lord

in judgment. Elijah's role as precursor continues in Jewish tradition, with the development of messianic expectations; at the Passover table a place is set for Elijah in case he returns to inaugurate the messianic age. This belief is also present in the New Testament; Mark (6.15; 8.28; 9.11–13; pars.) and John (1.21, 25) speak of Elijah as the precursor of the last days. The Elijah of the book of Kings appears in Luke 4.25–27; Rom. 11.2; James 5.17; and is dramatically presented in Felix Mendelssohn's oratorio *Elijah*.   RICHARD J. CLIFFORD

Elisha. Elisha ("God has granted salvation"), son of Shaphat, a native of Abel-Meholah in the northern kingdom of Israel (Map 3:x4), was a prophet during the reigns of Jehoram, Jehu, Jehoahaz, and Joash (849–785 BCE). The stories about him in 2 Kings 2–9 and 13.14–21 directly continue those about his prophetic predecessor *Elijah in 1 Kings 17—2 Kings 1. The *Deuteronomic history (Deuteronomy to 2 Kings), a vast work narrating the story of Israel from Moses to Josiah and into the sixth century BCE, incorporated these stories with little editing. Most scholars assume there was once a cycle of stories about Elisha, perhaps more extensive than those preserved in 2 Kings, which was then joined to the slightly older Elijah cycle before being incorporated into the Deuteronomic history. Elisha is portrayed as a disciple of Elijah (1 Kings 19.16–21; 2 Kings 2.1–18; 3.11). Elisha, however, is quite different from the solitary Elijah with his unswerving hostility toward the house of Omri. He leads prophetic guilds, "the sons of the prophets" (NRSV: "company of prophets"; 2 Kings 2.15–18; 4.38–44; 6.1–7; 9:1), and is sometimes, though by no means always, in friendly contact with the Israelite kings.

Elisha is first mentioned in 1 Kings 19. Elijah, renewed by his visit to the source of Yahwism at Mount *Horeb, is commissioned to three momentous tasks: to anoint Hazael to be king of Syria in place of Ben-Hadad, to anoint Jehu to be king in Israel in place of Jehoram, and to anoint Elisha "as prophet in your place . . . and whoever who escapes from the sword of Jehu, Elisha shall kill" (vv. 16–17). Elijah thereupon seeks out Elisha, who is plowing, and casts his mantle, the symbol of his prophetic office, upon him; Elisha becomes his servant and eventually his successor, when Elijah's mantle definitively is given into his hands (2 Kings 2.1–18). The first two tasks given to Elijah—the anointing of Hazael in 2 Kings 8.7–15 and of Jehu in 2 Kings 9—were in fact performed by Elisha.

There are two types of Elisha stories. One type is the lengthy narratives in which the prophet, sometimes with his servant Gehazi, is involved with the great figures of the day. He advises the kings of Israel, Judah, and Edom in their war with Moab (2 Kings 3.4–27); he assists the king of Israel in the matter of Naaman the Syrian (2 Kings 5); he plays a role in wars between Syria and Israel (6.8–7.20); and he foments the rebellion of *Jehu (2 Kings 9). The other type is brief stories in which Elisha alleviates the distress of individuals: he makes a spring's water nontoxic (2 Kings 2.19–22); he punishes irreverent boys (vv. 23–25); he feeds the Shunammite widow and raises her son from the dead (2 Kings 4.8–37; 8.1–6); he detoxifies a cooking pot and multiplies loaves of bread (2 Kings 4.38–44); and he makes an ax head float (2 Kings 6.1–7). Both types of stories, especially the latter, emphasize the miraculous. Their emphasis upon the extraordinary resembles that of the Elijah stories and the *plague narratives in Exodus; biblical signs and wonders, generally, are more soberly portrayed.

Elisha is mentioned only once in the New Testament, in Luke 4.27, which cites the cure of Naaman the Syrian as an instance of God's caring for non-Israelites. The miracles of Elisha, like those of Elijah, have, however, influenced the narratives of Jesus' miracles, especially in Luke, such as the raising of the widow's son (2 Kings 4.32–37; cf. Luke 7:11–17) and the multiplication of loaves (2 Kings 4.42–44; cf. Mark 6:30–44; 8:1–10; par.).   RICHARD J. CLIFFORD

Elohist. *See* E.

Eloi, Eloi, Lema Sabachthani ("My God, my God, why have you forsaken me"). According to Mark 15.34 and Matthew 27.46, this phrase, a citation of the *Hebrew or *Aramaic text of Psalm 22.1, was uttered by Jesus from the cross after a three-hour period of darkness. The Aramaic form of the saying is more sound textually, but the Hebrew form of the address ("Eli, Eli") better explains the subsequent confusion with *Elijah. The tradition may have circulated in both a Hebrew and an Aramaic form, resulting in a corruption of the manuscripts.

This citation interprets the darkness either as a sign of God's absence from Jesus or, perhaps

more likely, as a sign of God's curse upon Jesus. It is one of several allusions to Psalm 22 in the narratives of the death of Jesus (e.g., Mark 15.24 par. = Ps. 22.18; Mark 15.29 par. = Ps. 22.7).
PATRICK A. TILLER

Emmanuel. *See* Immanuel.

Emperor. The English word "emperor" is derived from Latin *imperator,* first given by soldiers in the field to a successful general, later a permanent title of Julius Caesar (100–44 BCE) and his successors, the equivalent of "commander-in-chief." It has no exact correspondent in Greek and is not used in the New Testament. In the NRSV, "emperor" is used to translate two different terms. The most frequent is the Greek word *kaisar,* itself a transliteration of the Latin *Caesar.* This was the family name of Julius Caesar, assumed by his great-nephew Octavius (Augustus) (63 BCE–14 CE) and used as a title by subsequent Roman rulers. "Emperor" is also used for Greek *basileus,* "king," in 1 Peter 2.13, 17. In neither case is the NRSV's use of "emperor" entirely accurate.

See Roman Empire.   MICHAEL D. COOGAN

English Literature. *See* Literature and the Bible, *article on* English Literature.

Enoch and the Books of Enoch. Of Enoch, son of Jared and father of *Methuselah (not to be confused with Enoch, son of Cain, mentioned in Gen. 4.17), it is written that, after walking "with God" for 365 years, "he was no more, because God took him" (Gen. 5.22–24; cf. Sir. 44.16; 49.14). From these words has grown the Enoch legend and its literature, the books of Enoch. Traces of the legend are found in Hebrews 11.5, where Enoch has become a hero of faith. The brief reference in Genesis is further elaborated in Jewish Midrashic tradition; his wife's name was Edni, and he spent hidden years with the *angels before he was taken up to heaven. There are parallels to the latter in Greek and Near Eastern sources, and the later picture of Enoch as omniscient sage and seer probably owes more to Babylonian than to Israelite ideas.

The Ethiopic book of Enoch, or 1 Enoch, is a collection of mainly apocalyptic traditions, arranged as a pentateuch. They include the following: the Watcher Legend, the story of the fall of the angels (Gen. 6.1–4); the Parables, visions of the *son of man/elect one; Astronomica; the Dream Visions, a "zoomorphic" history; the Epistle of Enoch, the "Apocalypse of Weeks," and visions of the judgment. An appendix includes the story of the miraculous birth of *Noah.

Substantial Greek portions of the book, amounting to about one-third of the closely related Ethiopic text, have been known for many years. To them have now been added numerous fragments of an *Aramaic Enoch among the *Dead Sea Scrolls from *Qumran, attesting the existence in the second and first centuries BCE of each of the Enoch tractate collections, with the exception of the Parables. Aramaic coverage of the Ethiopic has been estimated at no more than five percent, but there are substantial pieces in all four sections. There are also fragments on "the giants," offspring of the Watchers (Gen. 6.4), the probable source of the Manichean Book of the Giants. (The view that this is the second tractate collection, ousted in the common era by the Parables, is hypothetical.) The Aramaic fragments undoubtedly represent the original Enoch, while the Greek is a primary and the Ethiopic a secondary translation, always based on a Greek text. Thus the text of 1 Enoch 1.9, quoted in Jude 14–15, is now extant in Aramaic, Greek, and Ethiopic.

The absence of the Parables in the Enoch literature found at Qumran has been used to support the theory of their Christian composition, inspired by the Gospels. This argument from silence has not been deemed conclusive; there remains the insuperable difficulty that the *son of man in the Parables is identified not with *Jesus but with Enoch, in a collection of tractates now generally dated to about the first century BCE or the first century CE.

The Slavonic Enoch, or 2 Enoch, is found only in Old Slavonic manuscripts, none earlier than the fourteenth century CE. It is extant in both a longer and a shorter, earlier recension. The tractate collection falls into three main sections. Enoch ascends thorough seven heavens, each with its own special secrets, some purely natural phenomena, others eschatological, like *paradise for the righteous in the third heaven (cf. 2 Cor. 12.2–4), and others astronomical. In the second part, Enoch is confronted by the Lord himself in the seventh heaven and is shown the secrets of creation and human history down to his own time. Finally, Enoch returns to earth to brief his

posterity before ascending again to the heavenly world. An appendix lists Enoch's priestly successors, Methuselah, Nir (younger brother of Noah), and the miraculously born *Melchizedek.

The book has clearly been profoundly influenced by 1 Enoch, and it is widely accepted that it depends on a Greek Enoch, where Hebrew or Aramaic could lie behind the Greek; other explanations of "semitisms," however, are also possible. The date of the work is uncertain, with proposals ranging from the first century CE (the prevailing view), or even earlier, down to the Middle Ages.

The Hebrew Enoch, or 3 Enoch, is a heterogeneous collection of qabbalistic materials attributed to Rabbi Ishmael (second century CE). Like Enoch in 2 Enoch, Ishmael ascends to the seventh heaven, where he is admitted by the *archangel Metatron, who informs Ishmael that he, Metatron, is really Enoch, son of Jared, translated to heaven to become a vice-regent of deity, "the lesser YHWH." The rest of the book is a miscellany of the mysteries of the heavenly world. The author is familiar with 1 and 2 Enoch, but the date of composition is uncertain. Recent research suggests the fifth to sixth century CE. The main theological contribution of the book is its identification of Enoch with the qabbalistic Metatron. MATTHEW BLACK

Ephesians, The Letter of Paul to the.

Structure and Contents. *I. God's great work is completed through Jesus Christ and his Spirit (chaps. 1–2).* (a) 1.3–14: God's love has been poured out as an abundant blessing; through *grace and forgiveness Jews and *gentiles now praise God's *glory (1.6, 12, 14). (b) 1.15–23: Thanksgiving and intercession for the congregation issue in praise of God's power, which has raised *Jesus Christ from death and made him the head over all things, especially over the church. (c) 2.1–10: Christ's *resurrection reveals the omnipotence of God's love; all were dead in their sins, but they are freed by grace to do works pleasing to God. (d) 2.11–22: Peace between the divided, hostile parts of humanity, and peace of all with God, was established by the *crucifixion of Jesus and his announcement of peace. The church, as yet the unfinished house of God, is evidence of God's presence among all peoples.

II. The publication and continuation of God's work (3.1–4.16). (a) 3.1–13: To Paul and other *apostles before him it was revealed that Jews and gentiles are common heirs of God's fulfilled promises. The suffering of the apostle in prison, for the sake of this message, is reason for joy, not despair. (b) 3.14–21: In his prayer Paul asks the Father for Christ's presence in every heart, and for increased appreciation of the love bestowed through Christ. (c) 4.1–16: A call to unity prepares the way for an outline of the constitution of the universal church. The one and only God (Deut. 6.4) has now revealed himself as Spirit, Lord (Jesus), and Father. The exalted Lord provides the church with diverse gifts to maintain its unity. The diversity of the members of his body supports its harmony.

III. The testimony of daily life (4.17–6.22). (a) 4.17–32: The only way to affirm God's full revelation in Christ is to make a radical break with non-Christian behavior and to put on Christ. (b) 5.1–20: By experience Christians will learn to discern and do God's will, being inspired by God's Holy Spirit rather than by alcoholic spirits! (c) 5.21–6.9: The so-called *Haustafeln* (home rules; *see* Ethical Lists) deal with the three essentials of the human condition: sexuality (husband-wife relationship), historicity (generation problems), and economics (owner/slave; rich/poor; strong/weak). While Greek philosophers and other teachers used to direct their moral advice to the stronger groups only (fathers, kings, slaveholders), in Ephesians the weaker are addressed more extensively than are their stronger counterparts. They are declared worthy and capable of a voluntary co-responsibility for the common good (cf. Rom. 13.1–7; 1 Cor. 7.21–23). (d) 6.10–20: Threatened by the attacks of superhuman forces, Christians can trust God to provide them with an armor first used by himself, then given to the *Messiah. Their active life and the tribulations they suffer reveal their solidarity with Paul's mission and suffering.

Date and Authorship. According to 1.1; 3.1–13; 4.1; and 6.19–22, the letter was written while the author was in prison. A very few postscripts to ancient Greek manuscripts state that Ephesians was written in Rome; if this is true, the date of the letter would be about 61–63 CE. However, the Caesarean imprisonment of the apostle (between 58 and 60?; see Acts 23–26) and an Ephesian captivity (in the mid 50s) have also been suggested.

In 1792 the English divine Edward Evanson first questioned Pauline authorship. During the nineteenth century, German scholars gathered arguments in favor of pseudonymous origin, and today most researchers treat the letter as non-Pauline, dating it between 70 and 100 CE, mainly in the 90s. Some think that the author was Onesimus, the runaway slave mentioned in Paul's letter to *Philemon, who is then further identified with the bishop of Ephesus bearing the name Onesimus (mentioned in Ignatius's letter to the Ephesians 1.3; 2.1; 6.2). The arguments against Pauline origin include the following, which are balanced with counterarguments.

Style. Ephesians has to a large extent a liturgical and/or hymnic style; it has a tendency to be heavy, baroque, if not bombastic (e.g., 1.18–19, 21; 3.5; 4.15–16, 30). Extremely long sentences frequently contain vocabulary not found in unquestioned Pauline letters; well-known words occur with a new meaning; favorite Pauline terms and phrases are missing. On the other hand, whenever in his undisputed letters (such as in Romans 8.38, 39; 11.33–36) Paul breaks out in prayer, his diction is similarly pleonastic and/or liturgical. Since Ephesians contains numerous citations of or allusions to pre-Pauline confessional and hymnic elements (see 2.4–8, 10, 14–18; 3.5, 20–21; 4.4a, 5–6, 9, 21c-24, 25b-27), it is not astonishing that its style and vocabulary differ from Pauline prose usage.

Historical reasons are spearheaded by the observation that a mutual acquaintance between Paul and the readers is denied in 1.15; 3.23; 4.21. But Acts 18.17–20.1, 17 clearly speaks of short and lengthy periods of Pauline activity in *Ephesus. The alternatives seem inescapable: either this is a genuine Pauline letter that was addressed not to Ephesus but to an unknown city that Paul never visited, or Ephesus is the correct address, as it were, but Paul is not the author. Still, even this dilemma can be resolved if one assumes that Paul wrote to only a part of the congregation in Ephesus, namely to former gentiles (2.2, 11, 19; 4.17–19; 5.8) who had joined the church after the apostle's departure. Just as Paul warns against triumphalism over the Jews in Romans 11.17–24, so Ephesians is a call to remember that the church owes its existence to inclusion of gentiles into God's people Israel.

Other arguments against authenticity are based upon historical developments. The absence of a sharp dispute with judaizers seems to presuppose that the struggle about *justification by faith, not the *Law, belongs to the past. The dynamic Pauline preaching of justification appears to be replaced by the proclamation of apostolic and church authority, transmitted in a fixed tradition. Dualistic, deterministic, and mythical *gnostic elements are said to have invaded formerly pure doctrines of *sin, Christ, *salvation, and the church. Although it is acknowledged that the letter contains elements of antignostic reaction, it is yet considered a victim of the enemy it tried to battle: since no one wants to burden Paul with such weakness and defeat, the letter is not considered Pauline. On the other hand, since about 1960 the *Nag Hammadi documents have shown that the composition and the spread of the "gnostic myth" is to be dated no earlier than the second century CE. In consequence, Ephesians could neither have fought it nor have fallen prey to it.

Personal elements in Ephesians, together with original elaborations on doctrines less developed elsewhere, discourage the notion that Ephesians is no more than a composite of quotations from genuine Pauline letters. Paul was not bound always to speak of justification, nor to lash out against misuse of the Law. In other letters he also speaks of reconciliation and peace. A development of his teaching about the church's relation to Israel cannot be excluded on historical grounds: it is certainly a long way from sharp reference to God's wrath upon the Jews in 1 Thessalonians 2.14–16, to the statement that the legalistic part of Israel was driven out (Gal. 4.30), to the proclamation of God's faithfulness to his promises, which even finally may lead to the regrafting of cut-off branches (Rom. 9–11), and finally to the irenic stance taken in Ephesians 1–3, where the gentiles are described as adopted into God's eternally beloved people, Israel. At the same time, it cannot be proven that Paul was unable to learn, to develop, even to correct himself. Paul changed his teachings about the presence of salvation, the nature of the church (universal rather than local), marriage, and other issues. A plagiarist would hardly have dared to be so independent of earlier Pauline letters.

Literary dependence of Ephesians upon the Pauline letters, especially *Colossians, revealed by many almost identically phrased sentences, seems to exclude the pen of a man who in his undisputed letters is a wellspring of ever-new ideas and formulations. Thus, 6.21–22 appears to be copied to a large extent from Colossians 4.7–9. In Colossians 1 and Ephesians 1 and 3, Christ, the head of the church and the world, is described in similar terminology, though in Colossians Christ's cosmic rulership is emphasized more than in Ephesians. The latter concentrates attention upon the universal church's function, and it contains several explicit biblical quotations, together with interpretive sentences or hints

(see 1.18–22; 2.13–17; 4.8–10; 5.31–33; 6.14–17), while Colossians never explicitly cites the Bible. Scholars tend to favor dependence of Ephesians upon Colossians, making Colossians more likely to be authentic. A secretary or a later disciple of Paul may have written the letter. Pseudonymous authorship was often a sign of respect toward the one whose name was put at the head of a document; to speak of falsification and plagiarism misses the point.

Still, not even the undisputed letters (except *Galatians) were written without secretarial help. The similarity between Ephesians and Colossians might have a simple reason: at about the same time of his life, Paul may have used the same general outline to address the Colossians in polemical terms and to send a peaceful message to the Ephesian church, a kind of encyclical to all the churches in Asia Minor.

Theology. The distinct theology of Ephesians appears to tip the scale in favor of pseudonymity. Protestant scholars point out that in this letter ecclesiology overshadows Christology; that gnosticizing knowledge and cosmological speculation encroach upon the genuine, existential faith; that institution and tradition replace trust in grace and eschatological hope; that biblical ethics have yielded to petit-bourgeois moralism. In short, though under protest by Orthodox and many Roman Catholic scholars, Ephesians is considered, together with the *Pastoral Epistles and *Acts, to expound what is called "early Catholicism." Others have dubbed it a "Marseillaise of church triumphalism."

Indeed, if the theology of Paul has been fully grasped and described by the Augustinian, Lutheran, and existentialist understanding of justification, then salvation has to do primarily with the encounter between God and the individual. Because in Ephesians salvation is a social event with cosmic dimensions, the letter is thought to contradict the core of Paul's message and to be spurious. On the other hand, even in undisputed letters Paul not only speaks of justification but also of the reconciliation and solidarity of Jews and gentiles under God's grace. He also speaks of peace, of mission, of the final liberation of the whole cosmos, though these topics often receive only minor attention. The special theological features of Ephesians may reveal how much there is still to learn of Paul's complete message.

In conclusion, Ephesians should be considered an authentic Pauline letter. Its irenic and embracing character distinguishes it among the more bellicose letters of Paul. It deserves to be called his testament.

Highlights and Influence. At least four traits distinguish Ephesians from most other Pauline writings. First, this letter speaks of only one *mystery. This *mystērion* is unlike the numerous apocalyptic-historical and theological-interpretative mysteries that will be disclosed only at the end of time. Whenever the term "mystery" occurs in this letter (1.9; 3.3–4, 9; 9.19; cf. "wisdom" in 3.10), it designates a secret that has recently been disclosed, first to a few chosen people and now to be communicated to all. Its substance is the eternal will of God to save the gentiles as well as the Jews, to whom alone he had first given the hope of an *inheritance and of the *Messiah to come. Especially in 1.10 and 2.11–12, God's means to carry out his will are described: since the time of fulfillment has come, the Messiah, long ago promised to Israel, has come and has died on the cross to make peace between formerly hostile groups. The Holy Spirit continuously confirms ("seals" 1.13–14; 4.30), based upon Christ's completed work, that all sinners are forgiven and now enjoy equal rights as children in one family and as citizens of God's kingdom (2.1–19). In this letter, the "new person" is not an individual, but two former enemies (of one another and of God) now joined together in peace by the removal of what had formed a legal wall of separation (2.14–16). Even more clearly than in Romans 3.21–31 and 9–11, Ephesians reveals that the intervention of the God-sent mediator terminates segregation, hostility, and strife. Nowhere is it denied that salvation pertains also to persons and their souls. According to Ephesians, however, the liberation of individuals takes place within the framework of God's kingdom, in the victory of his love and righteousness over all injustice and misery.

Second, together with Matthew 16.17–19 and John 17.17–22, Ephesians is, within the New Testament, the magna carta of the one, holy, apostolic, and catholic church (4.4–6). The church is the palpable evidence of the work of unification accomplished by Jesus Christ (2.20–22). It is a beacon for all the world (5.8) and is the still-incomplete structure of God's house, waiting for the insertion of the capstone, that is, Christ who will come again (2.20; 4.13, 15–16).

Since the Jews have been and remain the first members of God's people, there is no unity of the church available without them. When the church is depicted as Christ's bride (5.25–27, 31–32), and when the relationship between Christ

and his church is explained in terms of the union of a man and a woman (Gen. 2.24 is quoted), then love is shown to be the bond of unity. On the other hand, it is also made clear that an identification of Christ and the church is not in question. Further, Ephesians does not support the claim that certain sacraments are to be administered exclusively by ordained clergy, nor that the difference between clergy and laity constitutes the church. In this letter, God's love for Jews and gentiles, not the church, is the "mystery of God," "mystery of Christ," and "mystery of the gospel." Since the reconciliation of Jews and gentiles with one another and with God is the paradigm of the unification of all human groups (as the *Haustafel* in 5.21–33, compared with the text about the broken wall in 2.11–22, shows), in this letter the doctrine of the church is identified with social and personal ethics.

Third, in Ephesians, the situation of the church in the world is described in an apparently antiquated way. Above, around, and perhaps even within the church and its male and female, older and younger, free and dependent members, and in the same position over against all human beings, there are good and evil principalities and powers, and a devilish realm high up in the air (1.21; 2.2, 7; 3.10; 6.11–12; *see* Prince of the Power of the Air; Satan). Rather than imposing a mythological or demonic worldview upon the readers, the author of Ephesians probably means by these terms biological and psychological, social and political, cultural and religious forces that are unseen and yet encountered in human existence (cf. Rom. 8.38–39; also Colossians and Revelation). Ephesians intends to assure the tempted, suffering, and desperate among humankind that God has made his own cause not only the suffering that must be endured, but also the resistance, combat, and victory over the superhuman ruling powers.

Finally, traditional interpretations of the passage about husbands and wives (5.21–33) have required *women to be submissive toward men. Feminists disdain this part of Ephesians and call for removal of allusions to it in marriage liturgies. The biblical text, however, speaks first of mutual subordination (5.21), never of submission, and only of married persons. It controls and qualifies the husband's headship by making it clear that only an unselfish and self-giving love characterizes such a "head." Speaking to wives, the text is far from requiring a forced subordination: Ephesians encourages wives to place themselves at the disposition of the common good. In the same way, which has nothing to do with loss of honor and selfhood, Christ subordinates himself to the Father (1 Cor. 15.28; cf. Phil. 2.6–8), and the church to Christ when it acknowledges the love he has bestowed upon it (Eph. 5.24). Since already in 1 Corinthians 7 and Galatians 3.28 Paul has spoken of the interrelationship of equally free partners under the unifying lordship of Christ, his marriage counseling in Ephesians must not serve to substantiate male superiority; rather, it promotes the partnership of those married.   MARKUS K. BARTH

Ephesus (Map 7:E3). Commonly acknowledged to be the first and greatest metropolis of the Roman province of *Asia, Ephesus played a historic part in the movement of Christianity from Palestine to Rome. *Acts depicts Ephesus as the zenith of *Paul's missionary activity (Acts 19.1–41; 20.17–35), and it was from Ephesus that Paul wrote the *Corinthian letters (1 Cor. 16.8). The *Pastoral letters (1 Tim. 1.3) and the book of *Revelation (Rev. 2.1–7) associate the city with *Timothy and *John, respectively. Later traditions held that *Mary, the mother of Jesus, lived and died there.

From the classical into the Byzantine period, Ephesus exercised hegemony in the Ionian region. It was well known for its philosophers, artists, poets, historians, and rhetoricians. Ephesus made distinctive contributions to intellectual and religious history from the pre-Socratic period down to the philosophical revivals of the later Roman empire. Small wonder that Paul is seen teaching "daily in the lecture hall of Tyrannus" at Ephesus for two years (Acts 19.9–10), that John reportedly wrote the Fourth Gospel at Ephesus, and that this was the site of the conversion of Justin Martyr, the first Christian philosopher.

The importance of Ephesus stemmed from its location on the western coast of Asia Minor at the nexus of river, land, and sea routes. The city's size at the time of early Christianity has been estimated at 250,000, and during the early empire it was one of the fastest-growing urban and commercial centers in the Roman east. Although the harbors at Ephesus were plagued by alluvium, they were still serviceable in the later empire and early Byzantine period.

According to *Josephus there was a significant Jewish community there, although few Jewish material remains have been discovered. The city was famous as a site for *magic and thaumaturgy. The Greek phrase *Ephesia grammata* (Ephesian letters) became a generic label for all types of magical words and apotropaic incantations. The city attracted Jewish exorcists (Acts 19.11–20) as well as their gentile counterparts, such as Apollonius of Tyana.

Although the Greek and Egyptian pantheons were well represented in imperial Ephesus, the religious focal point of the city was the goddess *Artemis of Ephesus. From Ephesus her worship had spread throughout the Mediterranean basin, and her Ephesian sanctuary was widely recognized as one of the seven wonders of antiquity. The site of Ephesus is exceptionally well excavated and reconstructed. Most of the excavated areas shed light on the Roman and Byzantine city rather than the Hellenistic one. Noteworthy monuments include the foundations of the Artemis temple and its altar (see Acts 19.27), the 25,000-seat theater (Acts 19.29), temples for imperial cult, the library of Celsus, numerous baths and gymnasia, the "slope houses" dating from the early empire to the Byzantine era, and the temple of the Egyptian deities. The thousands of coins and inscriptions that have been found have illuminated many facets of the history and culture of Ephesus that was contemporary with early Christianity. Prominent Christian monuments date from the Byzantine era and include the Church of Saint John, purportedly constructed over the site of the apostle's grave, the Church of Saint Mary, traditionally claimed as the site of the Council of Ephesus in 431 CE, and the legendary Cave of the Seven Sleepers.   RICHARD E. OSTER, JR.

Ephod. For the most part, ephod refers to a garment worn by the *priests. The word has been derived from the Akkadian *epattu* (pl. *epadātu*), which was an expensive garment of some kind, and connected with Syriac *peḏtā*, a sacerdotal vestment. The *Septuagint generally renders ephod by a word meaning the shoulder strap of a tunic. In the high priest's garb, the ephod connected with the breastplate of judgment, which contained the lots of divination, the *Urim and Thummim. This association led to the ephod sometimes being spoken of as if it were the agent of divination, which it was not. (*See* Magic and Divination.)

A totally different usage comes in the book of Judges, where *Gideon (and later others) constructed a gold ephod as a *graven image (Judg. 8.27; 17.5; 18.14–20).   PHILIP STERN

Ephraim. Ephraim first appears in the Bible as the name of the younger son of *Joseph, born to him in Egypt of his wife Asenath (Gen. 41.52; 46.20). In Genesis 48 the dying patriarch *Jacob blesses Joseph's two sons, *Manasseh and Ephraim, crossing his hands and giving the birthright to Ephraim. This continues the well-known biblical pattern of the lesser inheriting before the elder (Abel, Isaac, Jacob, Joseph, etc.). In the case of Ephraim this probably reflects the eventual domination of the tribe of Manasseh by the tribe of Ephraim, both of which claimed descent from the respective sons of Joseph (*see* Tribes of Israel). The tribe of Ephraim came to inhabit the central hill country of Canaan north of Jerusalem, the so-called hill country of Ephraim (Judg. 7.24; 17.8; etc.; Map 3:X4), from which the tribe probably received its name. The ancient cities of Bethel, *Shechem, and Shiloh are all to be found in its territory. Its importance is highlighted by the use of the name of Ephraim as an alternate literary designation for the whole northern kingdom of *Israel by the mid-eighth century BCE. This pivotal position is underlined by the names of some of the tribe's leading personages: *Joshua, *Deborah, *Samuel, and Jeroboam I (1 Kings 11.26), the founder of the secessionist northern kingdom. A town by the name of Ephraim is mentioned in 2 Samuel 13.23 (Map 4:X5); it may be the same as the Ephraim to which Jesus went after raising Lazarus (John 11.54).   CARL S. EHRLICH

Epicureans. Epicurus (341–270 BCE) formed a community of friends in *Athens, who held that philosophy had the practical aim of securing happiness. Believing that pleasure is the sum total of happiness, they conceived of pleasure not as sensual indulgence, as their opponents charged, but as a tranquility like that of the gods. Contrary to the popular view, they claimed that the gods exercised no providential oversight in human affairs. People therefore need not fear the gods, nor need they fear death, for it simply marks the end of human existence and should have no bearing on one's manner of life. The Epicureans sought security in organized communities where, in the company of friends, including women and slaves, they sought to "live unnoticed" by withdrawing from society, which they held in contempt. Opposition to the Epicureans was sharp and slanderous. Because they did not believe in the popular gods they were called atheists or, at best, believers in gods who

were idle or asleep; their social attitude was regarded as misanthropic and irresponsible; and the motto "eat, drink" (because there is no life after death), became a shorthand reference to supposed Epicurean hedonism.

Epicureans were associated with Gadara, Gaza, and Caesarea, and it is not surprising that traces of Epicureanism have been detected in biblical and other Jewish writings dating from the third century BCE onward. Epicureanism was not, as some have maintained, a bridge between Greek philosophy, on the one hand, and Christianity and rabbinic Judaism, on the other; some Jews and Christians, however, were aware of the alternative options presented by Epicureans and of the polemic against them. The pessimistic view of death in *Ecclesiastes (2.14–16; 4.2–2) and the advice to eat, drink, and find enjoyment in this life (2.24–25; 3.12–13) have been thought to reflect Epicurean influence, despite the expressed conviction that it is God who makes enjoyment possible. On the other hand, *Sirach's opposition to libertinism and to the view that God does not intervene in human affairs (Sir. 5.1–7; 16.17–23) suggests that the author rejects behavior and views like those attributed to Epicureans.

The only explicit reference to Epicureans in the Bible is Acts 17.18, where Paul is described as encountering Epicureans and *Stoics in Athens. These were the two major philosophical sects of the time, and they presented radically opposed views. Paul is protrayed as more congenial to the Stoic view of divine providence, which is reflected in both his argument and the sources he quotes in the sermon that follows. Paul also uses language derived from anti-Epicurean polemic in 1 Corinthians 15.32–34, where he clarifies the hope of resurrection and opposes libertinism. The attack in 2 *Peter on teachers who reject divine providence similarly reflects such polemic, particularly in the denial that the Lord is slow (2.3) and that their destruction by God is asleep (2.3). Despite these views, Christians' emphasis on love between members of their communities, their opposition to popular religion, and their reputation for antisocial behavior caused them on occasion to be lumped together with the Epicureans.

                ABRAHAM J. MALHERBE

Epilepsy. Epilepsy in its grand mal or major form was a well-known illness of the ancient world. Its frightening and bizarre nature seemed to defy anything other than a supernatural explanation, and it was frequently put down to the influence of evil spirits. The Greeks, however, referred to it as the "divine" or "sacred disease," considering its effects to derive from the activities of the gods; the Hippocratic school of medicine, on the other hand, considered that epilepsy was as much due to natural causes as any other illness. In view of the widespread occurrence of the disease, it is surprising that there are only two clear references to epilepsy in the Bible. There is a full account of the condition in the story of the epileptic boy (Mark 9.14–29 par.) and a passing reference at Matthew 4.24. In both cases the disease is represented as being due to the influence of unclean spirits. Such a view mirrored contemporary thought, and in Palestinian Judaism in particular there was a tendency to ascribe all illness to the influence of *demons, although the rabbis were also aware of the familial nature of epilepsy and placed a ban on marrying a woman from an epileptic family (*Yebam.* 64.2).

The description of the epileptic boy at Mark 9, supplemented by the parallels in the other *synoptic Gospels, provides such a full summary of the events of a grand mal epileptic seizure that any other diagnosis is unlikely. The account notes the immediate tonic phase of the fit with collapse and rigidity, followed by the clonic phase with its jerking convulsions, and finally a flaccid phase of deep coma before the eventual recovery of consciousness. Mark also notes the loss of weight and exhaustion characteristic of the severe form of the disease, with repeated and uncontrolled seizures. The danger to life and limb from falling into the fire or into water, which so distressed the boy's father, are well documented in such cases. In the phase of deep coma even the most painful stimuli may elicit no response from the patient and severe burns may result. Other injuries are not uncommon during an unrestrained fit.

Both Mark and Luke emphasize the demonic elements of the story, but Matthew plays down this interest and uses the verb *selēniazetai*, meaning "to be moonstruck" (a word occurring only here and at Matt. 4.24 in the New Testament). The verb is derived from the concept that epilepsy was under the influence of the moon, a view that persisted at least to the seventeenth century in Europe. All three versions of the story, however, preserve the tradition that Jesus ordered an unclean spirit to leave the boy in order to effect the cure.

The Markan account provides the additional information that the boy was also deaf and dumb. It is likely that this represents a conflation of two separate incidents, but if the tradition is accurate it suggests that the boy may well have suffered from some severe congenital handicap, of which epilepsy was but one sign. Although epileptiform convulsions may sometimes be a feature of hysterical (dissociative) states, together with deafness and mutism, such a diagnosis is untenable in this case in view of the classical picture presented and the presence of the self-destructive incidents that are not found in hysterical illnesses.

The only other certain reference to epilepsy is the note at Matthew 4.24, where again the verb "to be moonstruck" is used. The text links together those who were possessed, epileptics, and those suffering from paralysis. The two latter categories should probably be construed as being descriptive of the former, so that the phrase would mean "those who were demon-possessed, such as epileptics and paralyzed persons." Although there are other references to convulsive illnesses in the synoptic Gospels (e.g., Mark 1.26), these are not presented as epilepsy and are more likely to be due to functional causes rather than organic disease.

*Paul's "thorn in the flesh" (2 Cor. 12.7) has also been identified with epilepsy by some scholars. It is unlikely that this would have been idiopathic epilepsy in view of the late onset, but its clear temporal relationship to an "out of the body" experience (2 Cor. 12.2–4), possibly induced by the severe trauma of one of his many beatings or stonings (2 Cor. 11.23–25), would suggest that posttraumatic epilepsy cannot be ruled out.

There is no clear evidence of epilepsy in the Hebrew Bible, although the reference to "moon stroke" in Psalm 121.6 may possibly relate to epilepsy, particularly as it is placed in parallel to "sun stroke," another serious, at times, fatal condition. It has been suggested that *Saul and *Ezekiel may both have suffered from epilepsy, but their abnormal behavior patterns are best explained in other ways.

See also Exorcism; Medicine; Miracles.

J. KEIR HOWARD

Epistle. *See* Letter-writing in Antiquity.

Esau. The older son of *Isaac and *Rebekah, and the twin brother of *Jacob (Gen. 25.24–26).

His ruddy and hairy appearance, as well as his preference for hunting and the outdoor life, distinguished him from his brother. Despite the apparent connection between his name and his hairiness in Genesis 25.25, the etymology of Esau remains uncertain. Esau also is considered the ancestor of the *Edomites (Gen. 36.9).

Genesis 25.29–34 relates how Esau foolishly sold his birthright to Jacob for the price of a meal whose name in Hebrew (ʾādōm) resembles Edom, another name for Esau (Gen. 36.1). Jacob, acting on the advice of Rebekah, then tricked Isaac into making him the principal heir by disguising himself as his older brother and obtaining his father's blessing (Gen. 27). Esau eventually shunned revenge, was reconciled with Jacob, and settled in Seir (Gen. 33).

Most scholars view the stories of Jacob and Esau not only as folktales about fraternal relationships and reversals of fortune but also as Israelite depictions of the ambivalent and sometimes treacherous relationship between Edomites (sons of Esau) and Israelites (sons of Jacob) over territorial claims and other ethnopolitical issues (2 Sam. 8.12–14; 2 Kings 8.20–22; Obad.). Ethnopolitical relationships are ostensibly reflected in notices about Esau's marriages to women of various ethnic origins (Gen. 26.34; 28.9) and about his progeny (Gen. 36).

Within Christianity Esau became a central example in debates concerning the right of Christians to the blessings promised by God to the descendants of Isaac (Rom. 9.6–14) and in debates about *predestination.

HECTOR IGNACIO AVALOS

Eschatology. The teaching concerning last things, such as the resurrection of the dead, the Last Judgment, the end of this world, and the creation of a new one. A fully formed eschatology with all of these features emerged only late in the development of biblical traditions.

During the period of the Israelite monarchy (tenth to sixth centuries BCE), some hoped that a descendant of *David would one day conquer all of Israel's enemies (Pss. 2; 110). They envisioned a righteous king in David's line governing a continually expanding kingdom of righteousness and peace (Isa. 9.1–7; 11.1–9; see Messiah). No Israelite king attained this messianic ideal.

The eighth-century prophet *Amos predicted the fall of the northern kingdom of *Israel, utilizing the image of the *day of the Lord. This

had been understood as a time when God defeated Israel's enemies, but Amos transformed the motif into one of judgment against Israel itself (Amos 5.18–20). The Lord indeed had a day when he would defeat his enemy, but the enemy was now his own wayward people (Amos 8.2–14). The book of Amos ends with a promise of a new era of salvation after the time of judgment (Amos 9.11–15). Amos, then, is an example of prophetic eschatology; he looked for an end—not the end of the world as in later *apocalyptic literature, but the end of Israel. Beyond this end, there would be not a new world but a new period of blessing.

In 722 BCE the *Assyrians crushed the northern kingdom, and in 587/586 BCE the *Babylonians destroyed the southern kingdom of *Judah. In the subsequent exilic period new prophetic voices arose. An anonymous prophet, known as Second Isaiah (Isa. 40–55), promised a glorious return of the Jews to the land (Isa. 43.18–21; 48.20–21; 51.9–11). Ezekiel also looked to a time when the Jews would return home (Ezek. 34.11–16). A supernatural river would flow from the rebuilt *Temple eastward into the saline waters of the Dead Sea, making it a freshwater lake where healing trees would grow (Ezek. 47). Ezekiel foretold the transformation of ruined Judah into a new *Eden (Ezek 36.35) and an eschatological battle in which the nations would gather against Israel and be defeated by God (Ezek. 38–39).

Toward the end of the sixth century the Jews were released from captivity. But in the Israel to which they returned conditions were far from paradisiacal. Yet they held on to the prophetic visions. During the postexilic period the prophets *Haggai and *Zechariah encouraged the rebuilding of the Temple. They also stimulated messianic hope by putting their confidence in *Zerubbabel, a Davidic descendant, whom they apparently expected to rule with the imminent arrival of God's kingdom (Hag. 2.6–9; 2.23; Zech. 3.8; 4.6–14; 6.9–15). But the nations were not overthrown, the *kingdom of God did not materialize, and Zerubbabel was not crowned king. Messianic hope had to be deferred.

As time went on, some persecuted members of the Jewish community became pessimistic about an earthly kingdom of God and looked for salvation from above through direct intervention from God. This led to the development of apocalyptic eschatology, found in the Isaianic apocalypse (Isa. 24–27) and Third Isaiah (Isa. 56–

66). These chapters list the following end-time events: a great cataclysm (Isa. 24.1–13); a judgment accompanied by heavenly portents (Isa. 24.21–23); the Lord's arrival as king on Mount *Zion (Isa. 24.23); an eschatological banquet (Isa. 25.6); the abolition of death and sorrow (Isa. 25.8); the resurrection of the dead (Isa. 26.19); the destruction of *Leviathan, the chaos monster (Isa. 27.1); the creation of a new heaven and a new earth (Isa. 65.17; 66.22); a return to *paradise (Isa. 65.25); and eternal punishment for God's enemies (Isa. 66.15–16, 24).

The prophet Joel's vision of the day of the Lord is likewise filled with destruction. The sun, moon, and stars will cease shining (Joel 2.10; 2.31; 3.15), and there will be a great battle involving all the nations who gather against Jerusalem (Joel 3.9–11), but the Lord will come down with his warriors to judge them (Joel 3.12). On the positive side, God's spirit will be given to all (Joel 2.28–29).

The book of *Daniel was written to encourage the oppressed Jews in the second century BCE. God's kingdom would soon appear, resulting in the deliverance of the *saints and the destruction of the evil kingdoms of the world. In a vision Daniel saw "one like a son of man" coming in the clouds (Dan. 7.13). Daniel speaks of an abomination that makes desolate, a time of great tribulation, a resurrection of the dead, and a Last Judgment (Dan. 12.1–3). But once again, the kingdom of God did not arrive (Dan. 12.5–13).

Like the prophets, apocalyptists expected an end followed by a new era of God's saving activity. But the apocalyptists saw the end as complete. The judgment would be not only on Israel but on all nations. There would be not just a restoration of Israel in the land but a resurrection from the dead and the creation of a new heaven and a new earth, not just the defeat of earthly foes but destruction of the cosmic forces of evil. Many of these elements can be found in New Testament eschatology as well.

To understand Jesus, some scholars have argued for "consistent eschatology," meaning that Jesus' eschatological teaching as presented in the Gospels refers only to what will happen at the end of the world. By contrast, "realized eschatology" holds that Jesus understood the kingdom of God to have arrived with himself. Perhaps the best viewpoint is what has been called "inaugurated eschatology." Jesus brought the dawning of the kingdom of God (Matt. 12.22–28; Luke

17.20–21). Some aspects of God's reign were present in him, but other elements of the kingdom would not appear until the very end (Matt. 26.29; Mark 14.25).

Jesus is described as announcing the near arrival of the kingdom of God (Matt. 4.17). By casting out *demons, Jesus manifested his power over *Satan and showed that the kingdom had begun (Matt. 12.22–28; Luke 11.20; 17.20–21). Yet there would also be a future arrival of the kingdom in all its fullness. In the eschatological discourse found in Matthew 24–25 (par.; also called the synoptic apocalypse), the signs of the end are given: false prophets and false messiahs (24.5, 11, 23–26), wars (24.6–7), famines and earthquakes (24.8), intense persecution of Jesus' followers (24.9), apostasy (24.10), and the worldwide preaching of the gospel of the kingdom (24.14). Daniel's predictions of the abomination that makes desolate (24.15; Dan. 11.31) and the period of great tribulation (24.21; Dan. 12.1) will be fulfilled. Joel's vision of the failure of sun, moon, and stars will also come to pass (24.29; Joel 2.10, 30–31). These signs will be followed by the appearance of the *Son of man in heaven (understood as Jesus himself) coming in the clouds with great power and glory accompanied by the gathering together of his chosen ones out of all the earth (24.30–31). According to the Gospels, Jesus' eschatological teaching also included a resurrection of the dead (Luke 20.34–40; Mark 12.18–27) and a final judgment resulting in eternal life for the righteous but eternal punishment for the unrighteous (Matt. 25.31–46).

*Paul's eschatology emphasizes the resurrection. As Jesus first rose from the dead, so his followers will be raised when he comes again (1 Cor. 15.20–28; 1 Thess. 4.15–17). As a guarantee of the coming resurrection, God has given the *Holy Spirit (Rom. 8.23; Eph. 1.14; 2 Cor. 1.22; 5.5; cf. Acts 2.1–21).

The book of *Revelation is the main eschatological work of the New Testament. From Daniel it utilizes the great tribulation (Rev. 7.9–14), the coming of the Son of man (Rev. 14.14), and the resurrection and final judgment (Rev. 20.11–15). Like Joel it contains signs of the sun, moon, and stars (Rev. 8.10–12). Third Isaiah's influence can be seen in the new heaven and new earth (Rev. 21.1). The living waters (Rev. 22.1) and the return to paradise with the tree of life (Rev. 22.2) of Ezekiel are alluded to. The eschatological battle (Rev. 20.7–10) is from the books of Ezekiel and Joel. The prophetic day of the

Lord becomes "the great day of God the Almighty" (Rev. 16.14). Revelation also draws on messianic tradition, identifying Jesus as the son of David, a conquering king (Rev. 5.5; 11.15; 17.14; 19.11–16).

For the writers of the New Testament, Jesus' followers are situated between the inauguration of the kingdom of God and its consummation. In the meantime they are to be busy preaching the gospel, doing good works, and purifying themselves (Matt. 24.36–25.46; 1 John 3.1–3).

See also Afterlife and Immortality; Biblical Theology; Day of Judgment; Jerusalem; Messiah; Second Coming of Christ.

WILLIAM B. NELSON, JR.

Esdras, The Books of. *This entry consists of two articles, on 1 Esdras and on 2 Esdras.*

1 Esdras

There is no connection between 1 and 2 Esdras of the Apocrypha (*see* Apocrypha, *article on* Jewish Apocrypha) beyond the fact that Esdras (Greek form of *Ezra) is a central figure in each. 2 Esdras is most readily characterized as an "apocalypse"; 1 Esdras is a book of history, though it has sometimes been doubted that it should be called a book at all, since it may quite plausibly be regarded as a mere torso. The nature, history, and purpose of the book are among the perennial, and perhaps insoluble, problems of apocryphal literature.

In simplest terms, the book is an alternative version of the canonical book of *Ezra, to which are prefixed and subjoined brief sections of, respectively, the books of *Chronicles and *Nehemiah; it also contains one major section (3.1–5.6) not found in the Hebrew Bible at all. In manuscripts of the Greek *Septuagint this composite book (called Esdras A) stands just before the book called Esdras B, which is in fact a literal, unexpanded translation of the canonical Hebrew Ezra-Nehemiah. In effect, then, the Septuagint contains two versions of the book of Ezra, one of which (1 Esdras) diverges considerably in matters of detail from the canonical book. Eventually, 1 Esdras was dropped from the canon of the western church and is included in the standard Apocrypha only because it appears, for purely historical reasons (under the title of 3 Esdras) in an appendix to the Latin *Vulgate. It is not counted as one of the deuterocanonical books by the Roman Catholic church, but

it is recognized as such by some Orthodox churches.

The contents of the book are as follows: (1) King *Josiah celebrates the *Passover in Jerusalem in a manner unseen since the early days of Israel; afterward, he is killed in a battle with the Egyptians, and is succeeded by Jehoiakim and Jehoiachin, both of whom are eventually exiled to *Babylonia; in the reign of *Zedekiah, the *Temple is destroyed and the Babylonian *exile begins (chap. 1; except for vv. 23–24, which are wholly original, this material is substantially identical with 2 Chron. 35.1–36.21). (2) *Cyrus of Persia issues a decree permitting the Jews to return to Jerusalem and rebuild the Temple (2.1–15; [= Ezra 1]). (3) Persian officials in Palestine and neighboring areas succeed in getting King Artaxerxes to block the efforts of the Jews to rebuild the city and the Temple (2.16–30 [=Ezra 4.7–24]; not in chronological sequence in either position). (4) In the reign of *Darius, three of his bodyguards debate the question of what is the greatest force in the world. The first says "wine," the second "the king," but the third, who is identified as *Zerubbabel, says "women," but then changes and argues for "truth." The king awards the prize to the third speaker, Zerubbabel, who is thereupon given permission to build both the city and the Temple of Jerusalem (3.1–5.6; this story is found nowhere else). (5) A list of returning exiles is given, after which is related how the Temple was in fact rebuilt in the reign of Darius, and how, in the time of Artaxerxes, Ezra the scribe came to Jerusalem with his copy of the *Torah and forced the dissolution of all marriages with non-Jews (5.7–9.36; this is a translation of Ezra 2.1–10.44, with some differences, and the omission of 4.7–24, which had been included earlier [see (3) above]. Ezra 4.6 is omitted entirely). (6) The Torah that Ezra had brought is publicly read (9.37–55; this is Neh. 7.73–8.12, plus a fragment of 8.13). Note that the name of Nehemiah, which occurs in Nehemiah 8.9, does not appear in the translation. Nothing else from the book of Nehemiah is included.

Three principal problems have concerned scholars in connection with 1 Esdras: (1) Its character and purpose: Is it indeed a book, that is, a purposeful collection of items from Chronicles, Ezra, and Nehemiah, intended to support a particular viewpoint or special cause, or is it simply a mutilated remnant of a complete translation of those books, which has survived as if by accident? (2) What is the relation of this Greek text to that of the original Hebrew? How can one explain the numerous minor differences and the two major differences—the change in position of Ezra 4.7–24, and the presence in the Greek of the story of the three guardsmen, which has no parallel in the current Hebrew text? (3) What is the relation of this work to the canonical Greek 2 Esdras (i.e., the official translation of Ezra-Nehemiah, which is also contained in the Septuagint)? Obviously, though these are three separate questions, they are interrelated and cannot be discussed in isolation.

Some scholars have maintained that 1 Esdras is a unified composition intended to give a history of the Temple from the late monarchy to its restoration in the time of Darius I, or to exalt the role of Zerubbabel over against Sheshbazzar, or of Ezra rather than Nehemiah in the life of the restored community. Reasonable arguments can be advanced in support of views such as these; but the stronger argument appears to be on the side of those, like C. C. Torrey and Robert H. Pfeiffer, who believe the book has no unity in itself and is merely the much-abbreviated torso of an originally complete translation of the entire Hebrew-Aramaic text of Chronicles and Ezra-Nehemiah. According to this view, when the present Septuagint translation (Esdras B, or the 2 Esdras of the Septuagint) was made from a later Hebrew-Aramaic edition—one that included the authentic memoirs of Nehemiah (Neh. 1.1–7.5a; 12.27–13.31) but omitted the story of the three guardsmen—the now-outmoded older translation fell into disuse and would have been lost entirely, had it not been for the preservation of one mutilated copy, which survived by accident, by someone's special interest in the events surrounding the destruction and restoration of the Temple and its ritual, or—perhaps more plausibly—by someone's desire to preserve the story of the three guardsmen. Since that story is an element alien to the original text (an improbable, garrulous oriental wisdom tale in the context of a somewhat pedestrian historical narrative), and since its connection with Zerubbabel is clearly secondary, it may have been omitted in lieu of the obviously authentic memoirs of Nehemiah, which were of enormous historical value. That no great care was taken in the work of preservation is indicated by the ragged ending of 1 Esdras, which suggests something like a tear across the face of a manuscript.

As to the literary character of the two Greek translations, there can be no doubt that they are totally independent, though occasionally some slight influence (perhaps secondary) of one upon the other may be detected. 1 Esdras is a smooth, flowing, idiomatic rendering of the underlying Semitic text, whereas the Septuagint 2 Esdras (B) is woodenly literal. They come from different scribes, different circles of interest, and, almost certainly, different historical periods.

The fact that Ezra 4.7–24 appears at an early point in 1 Esdras (where it follows 2.15) may simply be a matter of different editorial tastes, since the passage is placed out of chronological order in both books. It could be that the circumstances it describes, namely, the antagonism of Persian officials in neighboring territories to the rebuilding of Jerusalem and the consequent frustration of the Jews, is meant merely to illustrate the difficulties faced by the returned exiles throughout the period of national reconstruction, irrespective of the immediate chronological sequence.

The value the book may have for the modern reader is largely confined to the story of the three guardsmen, the only item in it not duplicated elsewhere—and the reason, perhaps, for the survival of the "book" at all. The story itself presents some quite special problems. For example, is it an originally Persian tale, written in *Aramaic, adapted to its present use by the addition of 4.43–5.6 and the identification of the hero with Zerubbabel (4.13)? This seems the most likely hypothesis, but some continue to maintain that it is of Jewish origin. The surprising, and artificial, shift of the third speaker from a defense of women to "the truth" as the strongest force in the world is taken by some scholars to be part of the Persian color of the story ("truth" being paramount in Persian religion), while others insist upon its significance also in ancient Judaism (e.g., Pss. 15.2; 51.6). The story is frequently referred to in early Christian literature and its climactic words, "Great is truth, and strongest of all" (4.41; Latin *magna est veritas et praevalet*), provide one of the great texts of the Bible.   ROBERT C. DENTAN

2 Esdras

2 Esdras, one of the Apocrypha, is commonly referred to as "4 Ezra" after the enumeration in many manuscripts and the Latin *Vulgate, where it has stood since 1560 in an appendix after the New Testament. "Esdras" is the Greek form of "Ezra"; Latin can use either form. The book was never a part of the Hebrew or Greek *canon. Our principal authority is the Latin text, of which there are several old manuscripts and many late

ones. It was translated from a Greek text, of which a few scattered verses remain, preserved on papyrus or in patristic citations.

The core of the book (chaps. 3–14) is a Jewish *apocalypse, originally written around 100 CE in Hebrew or Aramaic. The date is indicated roughly by the historical allusions in chap. 12, and more precisely by the phrase "the thirtieth year after the destruction" of *Jerusalem (3.1); this is doubtless a veiled reference to the calamity of 70 CE, though ostensibly it refers to that of 587/586 BCE. For these chapters, there are versions in several languages based on the Greek, the most important of which are the Syriac and the Ethiopic. These ancient translations frequently supply a satisfactory sense where the Latin is defective or obscure, as reference to the NRSV footnotes will show.

The first two chapters are generally held to be a Christian addition, preserved in two Old Latin recensions. The replacement of Israel by a new people is foretold in language reminiscent both of the prophets and of the New Testament (cf. 1.30, 32 with Matt. 23.34–37, and 2.42–48 with Rev. 7.9). The last two chapters (15–16) are a further addition, with dire warnings and invective against enemies of God's people; they appear to reflect a knowledge of events in the third century CE. In the manuscripts, these pairs of chapters are often designated 2 Esdras and 5 Esdras respectively, and modern scholars have sometimes advocated these or similar labels. Except for one Greek fragment preserving the text of 15.57–59, they exist only in Latin.

The Ezra-Apocalypse (chaps. 3–14) relates revelations given to Ezra in seven visions by the angel Uriel. The general theme is the suffering and restoration of Israel in light of God's justice and *mercy, but it is widened to include the sin and destiny of all humanity and the fate of individual souls. In the first three visions, these problems are examined at length. Ezra begins each time by pouring out his troubled thoughts and prayers; one of these has been particularly admired (8.20–36), and many manuscripts of the Vulgate include it among other canticles as a separate item entitled "Confession of Ezra." The angel replies with arguments and discourses, often illustrated with parables or riddles. With Ezra pressing his questions, this is the most valuable part of the book (see below).

In the fourth vision (9.26–10.59), Ezra encounters a woman mourning for her husband and son; she represents *Zion in her desolation, and is transformed into a glorious new city. The fifth vision (chaps. 11–12) is closely modeled on Daniel 7, where the fourth beast with many horns symbolizes Hellenistic kings; the image here is of an eagle with many wings and three heads, evidently representing Roman emperors and usurpers, from Julius Caesar to Domitian. The eagle's doom is pronounced by a lion, symbol of the *Messiah, who comes to destroy the godless and to deliver the righteous remnant. In the sixth vision (chap. 13), the Messiah is depicted as a man rising from the sea (some of the language reflects Dan. 7.13), and his victory is described in some detail; standing on a huge mountain, he confronts a great concourse of enemies and destroys them, not with any weapon but with a stream of fire from his mouth.

In the final vision (chap. 14), the tone changes; Ezra becomes the inspired writer who dictates ninety-four books to five scribes. Twenty-four of them are the canonical scriptures, which (it is said) had been burned when the *Temple was destroyed (14.21; cf. 10.22); these are now restored, and published in a new script (i.e., the Aramaic square characters now used for writing Hebrew); the other seventy books are esoteric writings for "the wise" alone to read, for they contain the secrets that had been revealed to Ezra.

Ezra is portrayed as a man of great piety, who prepares for his visions by seven-day fasts (5.20; 6.35; 12.51); he is called "the prophet" and is the shepherd, as it were, on whom the people depend for leadership and support (5.18; 12.42). But the picture is a conventional one, and has little in common with the historical *Ezra of the Hebrew Bible; there is perhaps one deliberate point of contact in the story of the restoration of the scriptures, since the historical Ezra was scribe of the *law of Moses (Ezra 7.6; Neh. 8.1). "Ezra" is in fact a pen name, in accordance with the custom of apocalyptic writers, who present their insights in the form of discourses to holy men of old. Like *Enoch and *Elijah (and *Moses according to postbiblical tradition), Ezra is destined not to die but to be "taken up" (8.19; 14.9).

Points of Special Interest. 2 Esdras is an important book for students of Jewish apocalyptic; it throws light on developments parallel to Christianity, and therefore, at least indirectly, on Christian origins. A few points may be mentioned here.

(1) Human sin is traced back to *Adam (3.21–2; 4.30; 7.48 [118]; cf. Rom. 5.12; 1 Cor. 15.21–22). Ezra bewails the "evil heart" implanted in Adam, and the calamitous consequences he be-

queathed, apparently inevitably. In striking contrast is the affirmation of individual responsibility found in another Jewish apocalypse, closely similar to 2 Esdras in date and character: "each of us has become our own Adam" (2 Baruch 54.19).

(2) The seventy verses that follow 7.35 in the RV (1895), RSV, NRSV, NEB, and REB give a uniquely detailed account of what happens in the seven days after death. The soul's destiny is by then irrevocably fixed, and no intercession for the dead will avail. The reader will not find this passage in the AV; one page of an archetypal Latin manuscript was deliberately cut out, presumably in an attempt to suppress this harsh doctrine. Consequently the passage is absent from later manuscripts, and remained virtually unknown until the nineteenth century, when it was rediscovered in some other old Latin manuscripts and in some ancient versions. It has a further remarkable feature of theological importance: it presents an "eschatology of the individual."

(3) In other sections, the traditional corporate *eschatology prevails: the hope that God will bring deliverance to Israel. This will be brought about by his Son, the preexistent *Messiah, "whom the Most High has been keeping for many ages" (13.26; cf. 12.32). In the eagle vision, the hope takes an almost political form. In 7.28–29, the Messiah will bring four hundred years of felicity for the righteous, after which, before the final resurrection and judgment, all will die, including the Messiah. This striking statement rules out Christian authorship. It should be noted, though, that Christians preserved the book, that there are some parallels with the language and ideas of the New Testament, and that there is one unmistakable Christian interpolation, namely at 7.28, where the Latin manuscripts read "my son Jesus."

(4) In 2 Esdras, the Messiah is son of the Most High, and is described (at 13.3) in language strongly reminiscent of Daniel 7.13—more obviously so in the versions than in the Latin. It has long been a matter of controversy whether for Daniel the "one like a son of man" is the preexistent Messiah, and whether it was so interpreted at a time earlier than Jesus and the Gospels. It is therefore important to note that this equation is made in 2 Esdras, though it and the other document that makes this equation unambiguously (the Parables of Enoch [1 Enoch 37–71]) are assigned to a date too late to settle the question whether "*Son of Man" as applied

to Jesus reflects a vocabulary that was already established. Since 2 Esdras may be composite, and may in any case incorporate older writings or traditions, the problem remains.

Value for the General Reader. What is most likely to impress the general reader is the determined way in which Ezra tries to probe the problems of human sin and destiny, and of God's mercy and justice. The far-ranging discussions with the angel, especially in the first three visions, have a depth of faith, honesty, and compassion that it is hard to express in a brief summary.

Ezra presses the questions persistently. First, the suffering of Israel: True, Israel's sins deserve punishment, but surely the other nations, Israel's oppressors, have defied God's laws far more flagrantly; in comparison, Israel is almost a model of obedience. But, even if the righteous are promised a glorious age of virtue and prosperity in the future, the fact remains that the majority are not virtuous; can God's mercy reach them? Are there, indeed, any who have escaped the corruption inherited from Adam? Ezra confesses himself a sinner, and asks what hope there can be for him. Finally, if judgment is all that the vast majority of humanity can expect, what picture of God are we left with? What has become of the mercy with which he is credited in scripture? Is intercession useless? Surely, if damnation is to be the general fate, God has wasted all his work in creation, as well as all his patient efforts to build up obedience and virtue. The problems of theodicy, of justifying God's ways, have seldom been put more vividly and honestly.

In reply, the angel makes many detailed points. His first answer is perhaps the best: These things lie beyond the limit of human experience and comprehension. But his attempts to silence Ezra with puzzling riddles fail; Ezra maintains that from our human experience we know quite enough about good and evil, right and wrong, to ask for answers. The angel assures him that deliverance will come, the reign of virtue is sure, but the harvest of good requires time to grow, and we must be patient; the time, however, is now short. Those who have died will not lose their reward. The wicked deserve their punishment, and they have had ample warning. Few will be saved—enough, however, to make God's work worthwhile; after all, precious stones are rarer than base metal. Ezra himself has a balance of good works to his credit and must stop being anxious.

The angel's answers hardly match the depth

of Ezra's questions. But though he does not succeed in reconciling God's justice and love, he will not abandon either of them. The most precious of the angel's words are the reminders (5.33; 8.47) that the creator loves Israel and the creation better than Ezra can.   G. M. STYLER

Essenes. References to the Essenes occur in a number ancient sources: in *Josephus (*War* 2.8.119–61; *Ant.* 13.5.171–2; 15.10.371–9; 18.1.11, 18–22), *Philo (*Quod omnis probus* 12–13 [75–91]; *Hypothetica*, in Eusebius, *Praeparatio evangelica* 11.1–18), and Pliny the Elder (*Natural History* 5.15.73). What Josephus and Philo describe is a quite widespread group in Palestine living in communities in towns or villages and distinguished by their love for each other, their simplicity of life, and their strict adherence to the *Law. Pliny by contrast describes a community living in the desert by the Dead Sea. Josephus also describes their strict examination of initiates, their ritual baths and meals, their strict observance of the *Sabbath, their common ownership of property, and a number of other customs.

It is widely accepted that the Essenes referred to by these ancient authors were part of the same movement whose library and the ruins of whose buildings were discovered at Khirbet *Qumran on the Dead Sea in the late 1940s and early 1950s. The name Essenes itself is obscure and does not occur in the *Dead Sea Scrolls. It is said by Philo to refer to their holiness; another view suggests that the name reflects their reputation as healers.

The origins of the Essenes are not clear but probably lie in the group of Hasideans, who sought to renew the Law at the time of the Maccabean revolt (166–59 BCE; see 1 Macc. 2.42). It was not, however, until twenty years later, according to the Damascus Document (I.10–11), that they emerged as a separate group under the leadership of the Teacher of Righteousness. The occasion of this split within the movement was probably the usurpation of the high priesthood by the Maccabean king, Jonathan (152 BCE). The buildings at Qumran date from this time. They were occupied, possibly with a short interruption after an earthquake in 31 BCE, until their destruction in the First Jewish Revolt in 68 CE.

The Essene communities were tightly structured. Each group had a leader who controlled membership, administered the common goods and property, and ruled in matters of law (see CD 13–14; 1QS 6; the leader of the community is spoken of both as a priest and a guardian, but it is not always clear whether this refers to one or two persons). The community at Qumran had a council into which members were admitted only after long schooling in the ways of the community (1QS 6–9). Ultimate authority in the community lay with the priests (1QS 6.8). The community saw itself as administering the true understanding of the Law that had been entrusted by revelation to the Teacher of Righteousness (CD 3.13–15). Only the men of the community possessed such an understanding, and as such they, and only they, were the true men of the covenant of God and Israel. They were the "sons of light"; all others, including all other Jews, were "sons of darkness" (1QS 3.13–4.26).

See also Judaisms of the First Century CE.

JOHN RICHES

Esther, The Book of.

The Hebrew Book. Deriving its title from the name of its heroine, the book of Esther presents the story of an unsuccessful attempt to kill the Jews living in the *Persian empire during the reign of a certain Ahasuerus, probably meant to be Xerxes (486–465 BCE). The threat was averted by the courage and shrewdness of Esther and her cousin Mordecai, with the aid of a series of fortuitous circumstances. Since it purports to explain the origin of the festival of Purim (*see* Feasts and Festivals), the book has been read aloud in the synagogue at that feast since antiquity.

Neither the date nor the location of the book's composition can be determined with any precision. While it is clearly one of the latest books in the Hebrew Bible, the absence of clear historical allusions or perspectives renders the questions uncertain; nor is there sufficient linguistic evidence to resolve them. It may be as late as the second century BCE, just before the Maccabean period, or as early as the late fifth century, from the Persian period. Doubtless, it contains traditions and information that go back to the Persian period. In part because of its lack of interest in Palestinian religious institutions and its concern with the problems of Jews in foreign lands, it is likely that the book was composed in the eastern Diaspora.

As a well-constructed story that creates interest by developing and resolving tension, the book of Esther's plot structure includes the following elements:

I. Exposition, or setting the scene (1.1–2.23)
   A. Life in the Persian palace: the king banishes Queen Vashti (1.1–22)
   B. Esther becomes queen, and her cousin Mordecai exposes a plot against the king (2.1–23)
II. The crises and their resolution: the lives of Mordecai and of all the Jews are in jeopardy but they are saved (3.1–8.14)
   A. Haman plots to kill Mordecai and all the Jews (3.1–4.17)
   B. Esther and Mordecai take actions that avert the threat (5.1–8.14)
III. The resolution and the results (8.15–10.3)
   A. The Jews celebrate the edict (8.15–17)
   B. The Jews' victory over their enemies (9.1–15)
   C. Date of the celebration (9.16–19)
   D. Mordecai's records and letter scheduling the feast of Purim (9.20–28)
   E. Esther's letter concerning the feast (9.29–32)
   F. Epilogue in praise of Mordecai (10.1–3)

Although the details of its setting are entirely plausible and the story may even have some basis in actual events, in terms of literary genre the book is not history. Nor is it legend, though the sequence of events is as unlikely as those in legends, and folkloristic traditions probably underlie the story. Missing are the conventional legendary features of the miraculous, as are characters who reveal the power of God in human affairs and thereby serve as models for future generations. Rather, because of the extended and well-developed plot and its point of view, the book is best understood as a novella, a type that arose not as oral tradition but as a written composition. The closest biblical parallels are the story of *Joseph (Gen. 37–50) and the books of *Ruth, *Jonah, and *Tobit.

The author sacrifices characterization and, to a lesser extent, description of setting in order to emphasize the plot. Three main characters (Esther, Mordecai, and Haman) and two lesser ones (King Ahasuerus and Queen Vashti) are set forth in the account; all lack depth and complexity. The author deals only in passing with the actors' motivations and feelings, drawing them in such sharp profile that they are almost caricatures. Haman is evil incarnate, while Esther and Mordecai are synonymous with beauty, wisdom, and

the good. The storyteller gives us no opportunity to sympathize with Haman, nor to criticize or question Mordecai and Esther. The king is shown to be something of a buffoon, always acting on the spur of the moment, at the mercy of his emotions and whims.

Most of the action transpires in the palace, and is organized in series of scenes, with relatively clear markers indicating changes of time and location. The author takes pains to provide the reader with every reason to believe in the circumstances, giving particularly detailed descriptions of the palace and the king's frequent banquets.

By means of a relatively straightforward plot, the book of Esther tells the story of how the Jews were saved from persecution and death. It is a simple story of the triumph of good over evil, but the narrator takes some care to pace the tale, keeping the outcome in doubt as long as possible. Ironic twists appear—first, when Haman hears the king ask, "What shall be done for the man whom the king wishes to honor?" and, assuming the monarch has him in mind, he answers only to discover that the king intends to honor Mordecai (6.6–11). The final irony for Haman is that he is hanged on the gallows he had built for Mordecai (7.9–10). Moreover, the story is not without humor, and possibly satire as well, particularly in the portrayal of Ahasuerus.

As the outline above indicates, the first two chapters set the scene and mood for the events of the story itself. In chap. 1, though the main characters have not yet appeared, we learn how the king behaves capriciously, how much plotting and conflict there is in the court, and that when the king banishes Vashti he will need a new queen. Two events equally important for the outcome of the story are reported in chap. 2: after an empirewide search, the Jewish girl Esther becomes the queen; and her cousin Mordecai discovers a plot against Ahasuerus and reports it.

Two distinct but related threads run through the body of the story: the threat against Mordecai and the threat against the Jewish people as a whole. The first is set in motion when Mordecai refuses to bow down before Haman (3.1–3), thus disobeying one of the king's laws. The story does not state directly why Mordecai puts his life in danger, but it implies that he does so because he is a Jew. When Haman learns this (3.4–6), he vows to kill all the Jews. Then Haman schemes to accomplish his goal, bribing the king to proclaim the destruction of the Jews (3.7–15) on a date set by the casting of a lot (Hebr. *pûr;* hence the festival is called Purim [the plural form]). The first thread of the plot is brought to a climax when Ahasuerus, finding Haman in what he takes to be a compromising position with Esther, decrees Haman's death (7.1–10). It was not just Esther's appeal but a chance encounter that brought the enemy's downfall.

Still, the terrifying danger hangs over the Jews, for the king's edict has gone out and cannot be recalled. As the book stresses more than once, royal proclamations cannot be changed (1.19; 3.12–15; 8.8). Ahasuerus can and does, however, promulgate another edict, this one authorizing the Jews to defend themselves. When this document is circulated (8.11–14), the main plot has reached its resolution. What follows, including the extermination of the Jews' enemies, is the denouement of the conclusion's results.

On the surface, the book's theme is a simple one, that good triumphs over evil. The more specific form of this theme is one of the favorites of oppressed and persecuted people everywhere, that their persecutors are defeated by their own hostile plans. Moreover, the good triumph over the evil so long as they are shrewd, courageous, and fortunate. More significant, the story encourages those who see themselves threatened by hostile oppressors, and teaches those who wield authority over the weak how contemptible they are in the eyes of the powerless.

Although the story proceeds as the conflict between a Jewish minority and others bent on genocide, the book's attitudes toward foreigners and toward power are by no means unambiguous. Neither the Persians in general nor the Persian authorities are evil, but only the "enemies of the Jews" (9.1), epitomized by Haman. On the one hand, the capricious king and the immutable Persian laws are ridiculed, but on the other, Esther and Mordecai work through the channels of power to save their people. As in the book of Ruth, intermarriage between Jews and *gentiles is not only condoned but even approved.

One of the major issues in the book concerns the relation between law and justice. Mordecai disobeys the law, and on that basis he and all his people are jeopardized; Esther likewise violates the law by entering the king's presence (4.11; 5.1). But the storyteller leaves no doubt in the minds of the readers that these laws are unjust, and not simply by the standards of the Mosaic

Law—which is never mentioned—but by common sense. Haman is held in contempt for his self-serving legalism; the king's laws are shown to be petty and capricious. Thus, the book criticizes a narrow legalism with neither heart and soul, nor justice.

Behind the story stand certain views of how human history moves. The book is optimistic about the future, for history moves in a beneficent direction. Moreover, the development of events is viewed as the interaction of human wills with chance or destiny (and the latter is not a hidden reference to the will of God, who is never mentioned in the book). On the one hand, the Jews, through the hero and heroine, take care of themselves; on the other hand, they are fortunate, as is seen most clearly in Haman's downfall, when his foolish attempt to plead with the queen is misinterpreted by the king (7.7–8). These two forces, destiny and human initiative, are explicitly linked in Mordecai's words to Esther, "Who knows? Perhaps you have come to royal dignity for just such a time as this?" (4.14). In the right time and place, human individuals can hold the destiny of their people in their hands.

Additions to the Book. Jerome, in preparing his Latin *Vulgate, recognized some 107 verses as additions to the book of Esther. Since the passages in question appeared in his Greek text but not in the Hebrew, he removed them from the body of the book and placed them at its end. A further step was taken during the Protestant Reformation, when the Apocrypha was created by placing in a separate part of the Bible those books found in the Greek Old Testament but not in the Hebrew. It was then that the Additions to the Book of Esther became a separate book (*see* Apocrypha, *article on* Jewish Apocrypha).

The traditional Greek text (Codex Vaticanus) of Esther contains six additions not found in the Masoretic Hebrew text. One appears at the beginning, another at the end, and the others are interspersed through the book at appropriate points in the narrative. Their versification is somewhat confusing because when Jerome moved the additions to the end, he left the last one in place as the book's conclusion, thus disrupting the chronology of the closing passages.

The six additions, with their traditional English chapters and verses, are:

A (11.2–12.6): The beginning of the Greek version, before Hebrew 1.1. The first unit (11.2–12) reports Mordecai's dream of what will transpire in the Esther story, and the second (12.1–

6) is a variation on the account of Mordecai's discovery of the plot against the king (Esther 2.19–23).

B (13.1–7): Following Hebrew 3.13, this addition contains the text of the king's decree ordering that the Jews be killed.

C (13.8–14.9): Following Hebrew 4.17, the first part (13.8–18) is Mordecai's prayer, and the second (14.1–19) is Esther's prayer.

D (15.1–16): Replacing Hebrew 5.1–2, this is an expanded report of Esther's appeal to the king.

E (16.1–24): Following Hebrew 8.12, this gives the contents of the king's second decree, allowing the Jews to defend themselves.

F (10.4–11.1): Following Hebrew 10.3, this addition tells how Mordecai recalls his dream, which has now come true, and interprets the meaning of the figures in it; 11.1 is a colophon validating the copy of the book, called here "The Letter of Purim," brought to Egypt in the time of Ptolemy and Cleopatra.

Four of the additions, A, C, D, and F, generally are considered to rest upon a Hebrew original, but B and E, the proclamations of the king, were composed in Greek. Therefore, if one considers only the textual differences between the traditional Hebrew (*Masoretic Text) and the Septuagint B (Vaticanus), there were three clear stages of composition: the short Hebrew text, the Hebrew with four additions, and the Greek with two further expansions. The process of the text's growth and composition would have been even more complicated than that, for another Septuagint text (A [Codex Alexandrinus]) appears to rest on a different Hebrew tradition.

It follows, then, that the Additions to the Book of Esther were composed at different times and by different persons. The original book would have been written perhaps as early as the late fifth century BCE but no later than the early second century BCE. The fullest form of the book, represented in the two Greek editions, probably was written not long before when it claims to have been brought to Egypt in the "fourth year of the reign of Ptolemy and Cleopatra" (11.1), probably 114 BCE. In any case, the additions show that the book of Esther did not stabilize until relatively late.

The additions make the book of Esther a dramatically different work, and indicate that some of those who transmitted it were uneasy with the original. What had been a tale of the triumph of good over evil through the skills and courage of the hero and heroine, assisted by fortuitous circumstances, becomes a religious story stressing piety and the will of God. Whereas the book of Esther does not mention God, the additions constantly refer to the deity, to prayer, and to the sacred traditions and practices of Judaism.

The important human qualities are not shrewdness or power or royal position, but piety and humility. If Esther is eloquent before the king, it is because God has answered her prayer (14.1–9). The exercise of genuine religion leads to the salvation of the people. The authors of the additions must have been offended by all the story's pomp and circumstance, for they present Esther belittling her royal position and apologizing for her royal garb.

In the additions, one finds a significantly different understanding of history. In the first place, the story is now set between Mordecai's almost apocalyptic dream and its interpretation. This framework tells the reader that God not only knows the future but reveals it to the elect. Second, it is not chance or heroic actions that saves the Jews from extermination, but divine intervention. To be sure, that intervention was not by means of a dramatic miracle, but through influencing the human heart. Ahasuerus issued his second proclamation because "God changed the spirit of the king to gentleness" (15.8).

GENE M. TUCKER

Ethical Lists. There is a wide variety of lists in the Bible. Some deal explicitly with behavior and with dispositions toward others, and so may be designated "ethical lists." There are lists of commandments and offenses, numerical lists of moral wisdom, lists of virtues and vices, and lists of duties in the household *(Haustafeln)* or the community *(Gemeindetafeln)*.

Among the lists of commandments or offenses are the *Ten Commandments (Exod. 20.2–17; Deut. 5.6–21), the twelve crimes that bring the curse of God (Deut. 27.15–26), twelve sexual offenses (Lev. 18.6–18), and perhaps the crimes punishable by death now scattered in the text (Exod. 21.12, 15–17; 22.18, 19; 31.15). These lists of apodictic laws are certainly older than the texts within which they are found, and they may have originated in a cultic ceremony like that described in Deuteronomy 27, in which the people solemnly take upon themselves *covenant responsibilities. The same kind of ceremony provides the context for a much later list in Nehemiah 10.28–39, which is based on the Deuter-onomic legislation and represents the whole of the Mosaic law ("all the commandments") while it focuses on items relevant to Nehemiah's reform. Other late lists shift the focus from the community to the individual (Ezek. 18.5–18; Job 31.1–40; 1 Sam. 12.2–5; and the entrance liturgies in Pss. 15.2–5; 24.3–6; Isa. 33.14–16; Mic. 6.6–8). The lists remain representative of covenant faithfulness rather than exhaustive, focusing the *law rather than displacing it.

The wisdom teachers based their moral advice on experience, not directly on law. Their stylistic fondness for numerical lists along with their pedagogical concern for the formation of character and conduct yielded a number of ethical lists, for example, four kinds of sinners (Prov. 30.11–14), seven abominations (Prov. 6.16–19), three things delightful and three persons offensive to wisdom (Sir. 25.1–2). (The prophet *Amos uses this form in his indictment of the nations [1.3–3.2].)

In the New Testament there are many lists of virtues (2 Cor. 6.6–7; Gal. 5.22–23; Eph. 4.2–3, 32; Phil. 4.8; Col. 3.12; 1 Tim. 4.12; 6.11; 2 Tim. 2.22; 3.10; 2 Pet. 1.5–7) and vices (Mark 7.21–22 par.; Rom. 1.29–31; 13.13; 1 Cor. 5.10–11; 6.9–10; 2 Cor. 12.20–21; Gal. 5.19–21; Eph. 4.31; 5.3–5; Col. 3.5, 8; 1 Tim. 1.9–10; 2 Tim. 3.2–5; Titus 3.3; 1 Pet. 2.1; 4.3, 15; Rev. 21.8; 22.15). Lists of duties in the household and in the community also occur frequently (Eph. 5.21–6.9; Col. 3.18–4.1; 1 Tim. 2.1–15; 5.1–21; 6.1–2; Titus 2.2–10; 3.1–2; 1 Pet. 2.13–3.8; 5.1–5).

Such lists were a popular form of moral instruction in diverse schools of thought in the first century CE and were evidently a common part of the Christian moral tradition. Various origins have been proposed for them: Hellenistic Judaism (cf. the lists of vices in Wisd. of Sol. 14.25–26 and Rom. 1.29–30, and their association with *idolatry); *Stoicism and other Greek philosophies (Phil. 4.8; 2 Tim. 3.2–5); *Qumran (cf. 1QS 4.3–14 and Gal. 5.19–23); and Persian mythology (note the five-member structure of the lists in Colossians and the pairing of lists of vices and virtues). The lists of duties have usually been traced to the Stoic emphasis on role responsibilities, but recently they have been attributed to the renewal in the first century CE of the Aristotelian view that in household management and politics relations between ruler and ruled are "natural."

However the question of sources might be settled, it is clear that Christian moral tradition was not created out of nothing. But preexisting traditions are transformed: they are oriented to Christ and to the *neighbor's good rather than to nature and reason, as in Greek philosophy, or to law, as in Hellenistic Judaism, or even to a cosmic battle between two equally powerful angels, as in Persian myth.

The lists of virtues and vices are not exhaustive; they point beyond themselves to other qualities (sometimes explicitly, as in Gal. 5.21), and finally to Christ. The lists are largely random, but sometimes the selection of qualities is especially relevant to the community addressed (e.g., the problems of sexual immorality and factions in the Corinthian church influence the selection of vices in 2 Cor. 12.20–21). The *Haustafeln* are not timeless codes; they bring existing relationships under the critical and transforming spirit of Christ, to whom all, both ruler and ruled, are to submit.

See also Ethics.   ALLEN D. VERHEY

Ethics. Biblical ethics is inalienably religious. Reflection on issues of moral conduct and character in scripture is always qualified by religious convictions and commitments. To abstract biblical ethics from its religious context is to distort it.

Biblical ethics is unyieldingly diverse. The Bible contains many books, and more traditions, each addressed in a specific cultural and social context to a particular community facing concrete questions of moral conduct and character. Biblical ethics does not provide an autonomous and timeless and coherent set of rules; it provides an account of the work and will and way of the one God, and it evokes the creative and faithful response of those who would be God's people. The one God of scripture assures the unity of biblical ethics, but there is no simple unitive understanding even of that one God or of that one God's will. To force biblical ethics into a timeless, systematic unity is to impoverish it.

The Torah. The one God of scripture stands behind the formation and continuation of a people as liberator and ruler. The story was told in countless recitals of faith: the God of Abraham heard our groaning when we were slaves, rescued us from Egypt, and made us a people with a covenant.

The *covenant of God and the people was like an ancient suzerainty treaty, acknowledging and confirming that God will be their great king and they will be God's faithful people. Like other suzerainty treaties, the covenant begins by identifying the great king and reciting his works (e.g., Exod. 20.2), continues with stipulations forbidding conflicting loyalties and assuring peace in the land (e.g., Exod. 20.3–17), and ends with provisions for periodic renewal of the covenant and assurances of faithful blessings upon faithful observance and curses upon infidelity (e.g., Exod. 23.22–33).

This story and covenant provided a framework for the gathering of stories and stipulations until the literary formation of the *Torah or *Pentateuch, the first five books of the Bible, and its acceptance as having Mosaic authority.

"Torah" is often translated "law," and much of it is legal material. Various collections can be identified (e.g., Exod. 20.22–23.19, the Book of the Covenant; Lev. 17–26, the Holiness Code; Deut. 4.44–28.68, the Deuteronomic Book of the Law) and associated with particular social contexts of Israel's history. The later collections sometimes included older material, but it is not the case that the whole Law was given once as a timeless code. Rather, the lawmakers were evidently both creative with, and faithful to, the legal traditions.

There are two forms of *law, casuistic and apodictic. The casuistic regulations are similar in form and content to other Near Eastern law codes. The apodictic prohibitions, rejecting other gods and marking out the boundaries of freedom (and so securing it), seem an innovation.

There is no simple differentiation in the Law between ceremonial and civil and moral laws. All of life is covenanted. Ceremonially, the Torah struggles against the temptations to commit infidelity in foreign cults and nurtures a communal memory and commitment to covenant. Civilly, the Torah is fundamentally theocratic, and the theocratic conviction that the rulers are ruled too, that they are subject to law, not the final creators of it, has a democratizing effect. Morally, the Torah protects the *family and its economic participation in God's gift of the land, protects persons and property (but persons more than property), requires fairness in settling disputes and economic transactions, and provides for the care and special protection of the vulnerable, such as *widows, *orphans, sojourners (see Alien), and the *poor. This last characteristic is perhaps the most remarkable (though it is not absent from other ancient codes), but it is hardly surprising, given the story that surrounds the stipulations.

The legal materials never escape the story and

its covenant, and "Torah" is, ultimately, better rendered "teachings." The narrative and covenant preserve the responsiveness of obedience to the Law; gratitude then stands behind obedience as its fundamental motive. The story, moreover, forms and informs the Law and its use. The concern about the vulnerable reflects the story of one God who heard the cries of slaves (e.g., Exod. 22.21–23; Lev. 19.33–34). And the stories of *Moses as the champion of the oppressed were intended to shape the use of the Law by any who honored its Mosaic authority.

The narratives of the Torah, it needs finally to be said, were morally significant in their own right; artfully told, they nurtured dispositions more effectively than the stipulations themselves. The Yahwist (see J), for example, had told the stories of the *ancestors not only to trace the blessings of *David's empire to God but to evoke the readiness to use the power of empire to bless the subject nations (e.g., Gen. 12.1–2; 18–19; 26; 30.27–28).

The Prophets. The one God who rescued and established a people visited them in the *prophets. They came always with a particular word for a particular time, but the word they brought was always related to covenant. Their "Thus says the Lord" was the familiar language of diplomacy in the ancient Near East for the announcements of a messenger of a suzerain. The prophets were not social reformers, nor were they necessarily skilled in the craft and compromise of politics; they were messengers of the great king and announced his word of judgment.

The sum of that judgment was always the same: the people have forsaken the covenant (1 Kings 19.10, 14; Hos. 8.1; etc.). Concretely—and the message of the prophet was always concrete—some specific idolatry or injustice was condemned as infidelity to the covenant. The infidelity of *idolatry was never merely religious. The claims of *Baal involved the fertility of wombs and land as well as a theory of ownership. The prophet's announcement of God's greater power freed the people to farm a land stripped of divinity but acknowledged as God's gift, and bound them to leave the edges unharvested for the poor. The infidelity of injustice was never merely moral, for faithfulness to the covenant acts justly, and the welfare of the poor and powerless is the best index of fidelity and justice. So the prophets denounced unjust rulers, greedy merchants, corrupt judges, the complacent rich, but they saved their harshest words for those who celebrated covenant in ritual and ceremony without caring about justice, without protecting the powerless, without faithfulness (e.g., Amos 5.21–24).

On the other side of God's judgment, the prophets saw and announced God's faithfulness to God's own good future. God will reign and establish both peace and justice—not only in Israel but among all the nations, and not only among the nations but in nature itself. That future is not contingent on human striving, but it already affects human vision and dispositions and actions, readying the faithful even to suffer for the sake of God's cause in the world.

Wisdom Literature. The way and will of the one God can be known not only in the great events of liberation and covenant, not only in the great oracles of God's messengers, but also in the regularities of nature and experience. The moral counsel of the sage was not founded on the Torah or the covenant; reflection on moral character and conduct among the wise was grounded and tested, rather, in experience.

Careful attention to nature and experience allowed the wise to comprehend the basic principles operative in the world, the regularities to which it was both prudent and moral to conform. The one God is the creator who established and secures the order and stability of ordinary life. So the sage could give counsel about eating and drinking and sleeping and working, the way to handle money and anger, the way to relate to friends and enemies and women and kings and fools, when to speak and when to be still—in short, about everything that was a part of experience.

The ethics of *wisdom literature tends to be conservative, for the experience of a community over time provides a fund of wisdom, but the immediacy of experience keeps the tradition open to challenge and revision. The ethics of wisdom tends to be prudential, but a little experience is enough to teach that the righteous may suffer and that there is no neat fit between morality and prudence (*Job). The ethics of wisdom tends to delight both in the simple things of life, like the love of a man and woman (*Song of Solomon), and in the quest for wisdom itself, but experience itself teaches the hard lessons that wisdom has its limit in the inscrutable (Job 28) and that the regularities of nature and experience cannot simply be identified with the cause of a covenanted god (*Ecclesiastes).

Wisdom reflects about conduct and character quite differently than the Torah and the Proph-

ets, but "the end of the matter," like "the beginning of knowledge" (Prov. 1.7), is a reminder of covenant: "Fear God, and keep his commandments" (Eccles. 12.13). That beginning and end keeps the wisdom literature in touch with the Torah; between that beginning and end, wisdom struggles mightily to keep Torah in touch with experience and covenant in touch with creation.

The New Testament. *Jesus of Nazareth came announcing that the *kingdom of God was at hand and already making its power felt in his words and deeds. He called the people to repent, to form their conduct and character in response to the good news of that coming future.

To welcome a future where the last will be first (Mark 10.31), a future already prefigured in Jesus' humble service, is to be ready to be "servant of all" (Mark 9.35). To delight in a kingdom where the poor will be blessed is now to be carefree about riches and to give *alms. To repent before a kingdom that belongs to children, that is already prefigured in table fellowship with sinners, and that is signaled in open conversation with women, is to turn from conventional standards to bless children, welcome sinners, and treat women as equals.

Because Jesus announced and already unveiled the coming reign of God, he spoke with authority, not simply on the basis of law and tradition. And because the coming reign of God demanded a response of the whole person and not merely external observance of the Law, his words made radical demands. So Jesus' radical demand for truthfulness replaced (and fulfilled) legal casuistry about oaths. The readiness to forgive and be reconciled set aside (and fulfilled) legal limitations on revenge. The disposition to love even enemies put aside legal debates about the meaning of "*neighbor." The ethics was based neither on the precepts of law nor the regularities of experience, nor did it discard them; law and wisdom were both qualified and fulfilled in this ethic of response to the future reign of the one God of scripture.

Jesus died on a Roman cross, but his followers proclaimed that God had raised him up in an act of power that was at once his vindication and the prelude to God's final triumph. Moral reflection in the New Testament always looks back to the vindicated Jesus and forward to God's cosmic sovereignty.

The Gospels used the traditions of Jesus' words and deeds to tell his story creatively and so to shape the conduct and character of the particular communities they addressed. Each has a distinctive emphasis. *Mark represents Jesus as calling for heroic discipleship, ready to suffer and die and ready as well to live in ordinary relationships with heroic confidence in God. In *Matthew, the Law holds: Jesus is presented as upholding the Law and as its best interpreter even as he demands a righteousness that "exceeds that of the scribes and Pharisees" (Matt. 5.20). *Luke's emphasis falls on care for the poor, women, and sinners, as well as on the mutual respect due Jew and *gentile in the community. *John tells the story quite differently so that his reader might "have life" (John 20.31) and might know that this entails love for one another.

The letters of *Paul make little use of the traditions of Jesus' words and deeds. Paul proclaims the gospel of the cross and *resurrection as "the power of God for salvation" (Rom. 1.16) to his churches, sometimes in the indicative mood and sometimes in the imperative. The indicative describes the power of God in the crucified and risen Christ to provide an eschatological *salvation of which Christians have the "first fruits" (Rom. 8.23) and "guarantee" (2 Cor. 5.5) in the Spirit. The imperative acknowledges that the powers of the old age still threaten Christians; so, "if we live by the Spirit, let us also be guided by the Spirit" (Gal. 5.25).

Reflection about conduct and character ought to be radically affected by God's power in the cross and resurrection. Paul provides no recipe for this new discernment, but some features are clear. Christians' self-understanding as moral agents was determined by their incorporation into Christ (Gal. 2.20; Rom. 6.1–11). Their perspective was eschatological; the *Corinthian enthusiasts who claimed to be already fully in the new age were reminded of the "not yet" character of their existence, while the *Colossians, tempted to submit again to angelic powers, were told that Christ was already Lord. Freedom (Gal. 5.1; 2 Cor. 3.17) and *love (1 Cor 13; Phil. 1.9) were values that provided tokens of the new age. The moral traditions of the church, the synagogue, and the Greek schools were not to be discarded, but selected, assimilated, and qualified by the gospel. Such discernment is applied to various moral issues: the relations of Jew and gentile, slave and free, male and female, rich and poor, the individual and the state. The judgments are not timeless truths in the style of either a philosopher or a code maker; they are timely applications of the gospel to specific problems in particular contexts.

The unyielding diversity of biblical ethics is only confirmed by other New Testament writings. The *pastoral letters use common hellenistic moral vocabulary and urge commonplace moral judgment against the *gnostics. The letter of *James is a didactic text collecting instructions into a moral miscellany. The book of *Revelation provides a symbolic universe to make intelligible both the experience of injustice at the hands of the Roman emperor and the conviction that Jesus is Lord, and to make plausible both patient endurance of suffering and faithful resistance to the values of the empire.

See also Ethical Lists.   ALLEN D. VERHEY

Ethnarch. *See* Tetrarch.

Eucharist. *See* Lord's Supper.

Eunuch. A castrated male. The Hebrew word *sārîs* is derived from an Akkadian phrase, *ša rēši*, literally, "(the one) of the head," meaning a royal attendant or official. Context largely determines whether the Hebrew should be translated "eunuch" or simply "official."

In early biblical writings, eunuchs appear as members of the royal court with no mention of their physical condition. The first references occur in texts coincident with the Davidic monarchy of the tenth century BCE (e.g., Gen. 37.36; 39.1; 40.2, 7). References increase in the seventh-century *Deuteronomic history (e.g., 1 Sam. 8.15; 1 Kings 22.9; 2 Kings 8.6; 9.32; 23.11) and are most frequent in literature of the sixth century BCE and later (e.g., Jer. 29.2; 34.19; 38.7; 41.16), especially in narratives depicting the Babylonian and Persian courts (Dan. 1; Esther). This distribution does not support the view that the use of eunuchs was a custom imported into Israel from neighboring cultures. The inclusion of eunuchs among the royal entourage (e.g., 2 Kings 24.15, in which the context implies "eunuchs" rather than NRSV's "officials") suggests that eunuchs were native to ancient Israel.

Later writings are preoccupied with the physical condition of the eunuch. In Isaiah 56.5, the eunuch who fears oblivion because of his childlessness is reassured that the eschatological commonwealth holds for him a "monument and a name *(yād wāšēm)* better than sons and daughters." In Sirach 30.20, the eunuch's inability to consummate his desire is a metaphor for an invalid's frustration in enjoying life (cf. 20.4).

In the New Testament, the eunuch is a potent ascetic symbol. Matthew 19.12 recognizes that eunuchs come from differing circumstances, including those "who have made themselves eunuchs for the sake of the kingdom of heaven." In Acts 8.27, Philip converts an Ethiopian court eunuch who is reading from the book of Isaiah; the passage may be an allusion to the eunuch of Isaiah 56.   GENE MCAFEE

Euphrates. The southernmost of the two rivers that, along with the Tigris, define *Mesopotamia. The Euphrates begins from two tributaries in mountainous eastern Turkey, crosses into Syria at Carchemish, and flows south roughly 160 km (100 mi) from the Mediterranean before turning east at Emar. It then proceeds southeast past *Mari to *Babylonia and into the Persian Gulf (see Map 6). This portion of the river served as an important trade route between Egypt, Syria-Palestine, and southern Mesopotamia.

In the Bible, the Euphrates is treated as the farthest northern horizon of Israelite territory in the promise to *Abraham (Gen 15.18; see Promised Land), in the *conquest instructions to *Moses and *Joshua (Deut. 1.7; 11.24; Josh 1.4), and in the description of *David's success in *Syria (2 Sam. 8.3). Though Israelite territory never properly extended across Syria, the ambitious ideal suggests a sense of vocation to be the major inland power between Egypt and the Euphrates, as David and *Solomon may briefly have been. The river boundary did not assume control of the northern coast, which belonged to the *Phoenicians (2 Sam. 5.11; 1 Kings 5.1). The Euphrates boundary is also evident in the Persian province in Syria-Palestine called "Beyond the River," which included the district of Yehud, in earlier Judah (see Ezra 4.11; etc.).   DANIEL E. FLEMING

European Literature. *See* Literature and the Bible, *article on* European Literature.

Evangelist. Evangelist (Grk. *euaggelistēs*) derived from the verb *euaggelizomai*, meaning "to announce good news" (*euaggelion*), is a primary New Testament concept. In the Hebrew Bible we find a similar figure in the messenger who brings good news (*mĕbaśśēr*) and proclaims peace (Nah. 1.15). The "prophet of consolation" in Second Isaiah is also a messenger of good news, announcing the deliverance of the people (Isa. 40.1–2). Consequently, Jerusalem is exhorted to convey the good news to the neighboring cities that their God is coming to take care of his flock (Isa. 40.9–11) and to bring with him peace, happiness, and salvation (52.7–8).

In the Greco-Roman world the words *euaggelion* and *euaggelizomai* had acquired technical connotations associated with important events in the *Roman empire. In the New Testament the word *euaggelistēs* occurs only three times, whereas the substantive *euaggelion* and the verb *euaggelizomai* occur seventy-six and fifty-four times respectively. In the Gospels, *Jesus is presented as a preacher of the good news of the *kingdom of God (Mark 1.14–15; Luke 20.1). He tells the disciples of *John the Baptist that the poor are being evangelized, recalling Isaiah 61.1 (Matt. 11.5; Luke 7.22); the same text is referred to in Luke 4.17–19. (*See* Gospel, Genre of.)

Outside the Gospels, the word "evangelist" has three different meanings. First, it was a title for early preachers of the gospel. In a certain sense, all *apostles were evangelists, since their duty was to preach the gospel (Gal. 1.8; Rom. 1.15). Gradually, the term came to be confined to the disciples of the apostles. In Ephesians 4.11, "evangelist" is third in a list of offices in the church, after apostles and *prophets but before pastors and teachers. Timothy is referred to as someone performing the work of an evangelist (2 Tim. 4.5), probably because of the role he played in establishing the believers in their faith (1 Thess. 3.2). Philip, one of the *seven, is also called an evangelist (Acts 21.8) because he preached the gospel to the *Samaritans and those outside Judea (Acts 8.4–40). In a more restricted sense, the word denotes the author of one of the four canonical Gospels; this usage first appears in the third century CE. Traditionally, the four evangelists are symbolized by a man, a lion, an ox, and an eagle, on the basis of Revelation 4.6–10 (cf. Ezek. 1.10). Finally, in modern times, the word has developed a more specialized meaning, referring to a traveling preacher or revivalist.   JOSEPH PATHRAPANKAL, C.M.I.

Eve. The name given to the first woman by the first man (Gen. 3.20). The Bible interprets this name to mean "the mother of all living," both because Eve is, through her sons, the female ancestor of the entire human race and because the name sounds similar to the Hebrew word for "living being." The wordplay is probably etymologically incorrect, and later rabbinic tradition proposed a connection with the *Aramaic word for "serpent." The actual linguistic derivation of the name remains uncertain.

According to the account in Genesis 2–3, the woman is created to be a companion corresponding to (not originally subordinate to) the man. Because the two of them eat the forbidden fruit (see Fall, The), the man is destined to toil as a farmer in fields of thorns and thistles, and the woman is destined to suffer pain in childbearing. It is in the aftermath of these divine pronouncements that the man names the woman as he had earlier named the animals, thus indicating dominion over her.

Both Jewish tradition and the New Testament offer a very negative view of Eve, presenting her as representative of the alleged weaknesses of women. Paul feared that the Corinthian Christians would be led astray from Christ as Eve was deceived by the serpent (2 Cor. 11.3). In 1 Timothy 2.13–15, Eve's deception by the serpent and also her creation subsequent to the man are cited as reasons that women must keep silent in church (cf. 1 Cor. 14.34–35) and hold no authority over men. Early Christian theologians contrasted Eve's sinfulness with the perfection of the "new Eve," *Mary, the mother of Jesus.

This traditional emphasis on the gullibility of Eve and her tendency toward sin is one possible interpretation of the Genesis narrative; it is not, however, inherent in the text of the narrative itself. Genesis 3 gives no indication why the serpent addressed the woman and even indicates that the man and the woman were together when the serpent spoke. It has been suggested that the serpent might have addressed the woman as provider of food or as theological thinker, not as the more gullible of the couple, and that the woman's addition to the divine prohibition about the fruit ("we may not touch it") represents not a lie, but a desirable exaggeration meant to make sure that the basic command would not be broken. The man and the woman together discover their nakedness, together make fig leaf garments, and together hide from the deity. Both are destined to a life of pain (neither is cursed) because of their actions, and together they are expelled from the garden. Thus, once the reader sets aside the portrait of Eve based on later traditions, the great skill of the Genesis narrator in presenting a character open to diverse interpretation becomes apparent.

See also Adam; Eden, The Garden of; Genesis,

The Book of; Lilith; Women.

Katharine Doob Sakenfeld

Everyday Expressions from the Bible. Over the centuries, biblical phrases and expressions have become part of the vocabulary of those for whose culture the Bible is a central text. Some idea of the Bible's influence on the English language may be gleaned from the following sample of everyday expressions, all of biblical origin, chiefly in the Authorized or King James Version (1611).

A person may be said to behave like the great I Am (Exod. 3.14), or to have "the mark of Cain" (Gen. 4:15). People are tempted to eat forbidden fruit (Gen. 2.17), desire the fleshpots of Egypt (Exod. 16.3), and give up something worth having for a mess of pottage (Gen. 25.29–34).

Yet "one does not live by bread alone" (Deut. 8.3), and finally each must go the way of all flesh (cf. Gen. 6.12; Josh. 23.14) and return to the dust (Gen. 3.19). For the moment, those who find themselves "at their wits' end" (Ps. 107.27) may still escape by the skin of their teeth (Job 19.20), but others find themselves in the position of a scapegoat (Lev. 16.8–10; see Azazel). Nevertheless, "a soft answer turns away wrath" (Prov. 15.1). Unfortunately, a leopard cannot change its spots (Jer. 13.23). The wicked sow the wind and reap the whirlwind (Hos. 8.7), and because they ignore the writing on the wall (Dan. 5.24), they are fated to "lick the dust" (Ps. 72.9). Inevitably "pride goeth . . . before a fall" (Prov. 16.18), and anything that hinders success is a fly in the ointment (Eccles. 10.1). The wise recall that life lasts "but threescore years and ten" (Ps. 90.10), and so they gird their loins (Job 38.3) and teach their children "the good and the right way" (1 Sam. 12.23). Such people know that "you can't take it with you" (cf. Eccles. 5.15), and that "there is nothing new under the sun" (Eccles. 1.9).

Everyday expressions from the New Testament are largely derived from the parables and other teachings of Jesus. Who has not known a good *Samaritan (Luke 10.30–37), a person that will "go a second mile" (Matt. 5.41)? These individuals are "the salt of the earth" (Matt. 5.13) and often "turn the other cheek" (Matt. 5.38). Some seek the "pearl of great price" (Matt. 13.46), while others, like the Prodigal Son, waste their lives "in riotous living" (Luke 15.13). "No one can serve two masters" (Matt. 6.24). "A house divided against itself will not stand" (Mark 3.25), nor can "the blind lead the blind" (Matt. 15.14).

It is useless to "cast pearls before swine" (Matt. 7.6).

In antiquity a "talent" was a unit of *weight or *money, but because of Jesus' parable of the talents (Matt. 25.14–30), the word has come to mean natural endowment or ability. To disregard these abilities is to hide one's light under a bushel (Matt. 5.15). Even those who have never opened a Bible recognize the *golden rule of doing to others as we would have them do to us (Matt. 7.12; Luke 6.31).

The letters of Paul are also a source of several expressions now in everyday use: "The letter kills, but the spirit gives life" (2 Cor. 3.6); "The love of money is the root of all evil" (1 Tim. 6.10); "to see through a glass darkly" (1 Cor. 13.12); "a thorn in the flesh" (2 Cor. 12.7).

BRUCE M. METZGER

Evil. In Israel's earliest traditions, the presence of evil in the world is taken for granted as a reality that is philosophically nonproblematic. There is no terminological distinction between moral evil and calamity, for the same Hebrew word *(raᶜ or rāᶜâ)* is used for both. Evil is anything that is unpleasant, repulsive, or distorted (Gen. 41.3–4).

Genesis 1 shows how in the beginning there already exists the darkness and the cosmic sea, pervasive symbols of evil requiring God's subjugation (cf. Job 38.8–11; Matt. 8.24–27; Rev. 21.1), and no attempt is made to explain their origin. God perceives the world as "very good" (Gen. 1.31), even though it also includes the tree of the knowledge of good and evil, along with a subtle serpent who encourages the consumption of its fruit (Gen. 2–3). Although God subdues evil in the cosmos, a number of texts in the Hebrew Bible are not reluctant to identify God as the source of evil (e.g., Isa. 45.7; Jer. 4.6; Amos 3.6; Mic. 2.3; Eccles. 1.13; Job 2.10). A standard complaint when humans suffer is that God is the one who has brought the calamity on them (e.g., 1 Kings 17.20; Job 9.17–18; 13.24; 16.7–14; 19.21–22; Pss. 39.10; 51.8; 60.1–3; Lam. 3.1–16). Since God was the undisputed master of creation, it was assumed that every occurrence was through his explicit command. It was not that God merely allowed evil to happen, for God directs evil through the mediation of supernatural beings who afflict, deceive, bring harm, and do evil in general at God's command (1 Sam. 16.14–16; 1 Kings 22.19–23; Job 1.12; Ps. 78.49). Both good and evil were in God's control, and he actively employed both to accomplish his ends. Although God is often depicted in conflict with evil (Isa. 27.1; Hab. 3.8–15), there is never really any doubt that God will be victorious. Philosophical dualism finds no place in biblical literature, for God has no equal and the cosmic order that he endorses, although often in jeopardy, must inevitably be established.

There is, however, one place where evil exasperates God: the human heart (Gen. 6.5–6; Jer. 17.9; Ezek. 6.9; Eccles. 9.3), that is, a man or woman's intellectual, emotional, and spiritual center. Even here the Bible pictures God as able to manipulate humankind (Exod. 4.21; cf. Ps. 141.4; Isa. 63.17; Ezek. 36.26; Prov. 21.1; Rom. 9.18–21), but there remains a mystery that is not further explored, namely, the freedom that human beings have to direct their own hearts for good or evil (Exod. 8.15; Jer. 18.12; Ezek. 18.31; Zech. 7.12).

Evil is not an intrinsic feature of the physical world, for everywhere in the Hebrew Bible creation is seen as good and submissive to the will of God (Gen. 1.32). The story of *Jonah is representative, for although even a prophet may stubbornly resist God, it is the fish, the winds, the plants, and the worm that dutifully cooperate. It is therefore not surprising that later *gnostic thought, which perceived the physical world as inherently evil, rejected the God of the Hebrew Bible as an evil being.

The notion that evil can characteristically be associated with a supernatural being opposed to God and God's people has roots in the Hebrew Bible (Isa. 14.12–15; Ezek. 28.11–19) but only becomes common in the New Testament. There this figure is appropriately called the "Evil One" (Eph. 6.16; 1 John 2.13–14) and bears the distinctive appellatives "Adversary" (Hebr. *śāṭān; see* Satan) and "Accuser" (Grk. *diabolos*). He is accompanied by a retinue of lesser supernatural creatures with a similar ethical orientation whose origins can be traced to rare references to "evil spirits," "deceiving spirits," or "evil angels" that do God's bidding (1 Sam. 18.10; 19.9; 1 Kings 22.22–23; Ps. 78.49; *see* Demons).

In the New Testament, these beings are more explicitly responsible for a greater share of the evil in the world. When illness, tragedy, or calamity occurred in ancient Israel, one tended to see God at work; in the New Testament Satan and demons are generally seen as responsible (Matt. 17.14–18; Acts 5.3; 2 Cor. 12.7). Humanity is locked in a struggle with these unseen beings (Eph. 6.12) who seek to crush the righteous (1 Pet. 5.8) and can manipulate human hearts (John 13.2). A climactic confrontation between the cosmic forces of good and evil at some time in the future will result in the eradication of all evil along with those creatures (human or otherwise) who aligned themselves with it (Rev. 19–21).

Evil as a philosophical problem is never really addressed in biblical literature. Attempts in Judaism and Christianity to resolve the logical problem of the existence of evil in a world created by a compassionate, just, omnipotent, and omniscient God belong to postbiblical reflections on the text.

See also Suffering.   SAMUEL A. MEIER

Exile. In biblical studies, more than in the Bible itself, "the exile" looms large as a chronological hinge around 600 BCE. The decisive "preexilic" events of *covenant, *Exodus, and *kingship occupy far more space than the scanty postexilic events, but of the latter, *Ezra, Haggai-Malachi, and the deuterocanonical books (*see* Apocrypha) are taken as the key to the final editing of the prophets and the *Pentateuch. Exile as a place was *Babylonia; the earlier exile (2 Kings 17.6) was rather an exchange of populations between the northern kingdom of Israel and subject areas of *Assyria; mistrust of "the *Samaritans" is justified by Jerusalemite biblical authors because of the "pagan" element thus mingled among them, and this mistrust is extended by postexilic returnees to those residents of Judah who had never gone into exile but had been ruled as a district of "Samaria" (Ezra 4.4).

The interchangeable Hebrew terms for exile are *gôlâ* and *gālût*, generally rendered in the *Septuagint as "captivity" or "deportation." The chief deportations took place under *Nebuchadrezzar in 597 BCE (2 Kings 24.14: ten thousand including all upper classes; different figures are given in Jer. 52.28–30) and in 587/586 (2 Kings 25.11–13: "all the rest," except the poorest). Historical details have been clarified by the *Lachish ostraca and by Babylonian chronicles; also, the language of the decree of return (Ezra 1.1–4 = 2 Chron. 36.22) conforms to usages attested in the Persian chancery. Dated oracles of *Ezekiel fall during his life in Babylonia; he was a priest and his diction contributed to the original dating and identification of the exilic Holiness Code (Lev. 17–24). Jeremiah describes the exile from within Judah (chaps. 50–51 as Babylon's downfall and the restoration; chap. 52

a historical appendix). Isaiah 40–66 is the chief biblical portrayal of the restoration insofar as its inner unity and relation to Isaiah 1–39 can be clarified. The "law" of Ezra (7.6, 26; Neh. 8.2) was either the Priestly (*P) code alone (its materials being largely early) or, more probably, its incorporation into a whole Pentateuch definitely edited toward the end of the exile. *Deuteronomy also, and with it the reedited Joshua-Judges-Samuel-Kings, are varyingly related to exilic experiences; after *Jerusalem and the *Temple were destroyed, and *David's last royal descendants executed (2 Kings 25.7), it could no longer be repeated that God's fidelity precluded abandoning his chosen people and land; but admission of guilt and of just punishment carried hope of restoration and a "new covenant" (Jer. 31.31).

See Dispersion.   ROBERT NORTH

Exodus, The. The Exodus, the escape of the *Hebrews from slavery in *Egypt under the leadership of *Moses, is the central event of the Hebrew Bible. More space is devoted to the generation of Moses than to any other period in Israel's history, and the event itself became a model for subsequent experiences of liberation in biblical, Jewish, Christian, and Muslim traditions. The Exodus is ancient Israel's national epic, retold throughout its history, with each new narration reflecting the context in which it was rendered. The Exodus entails not only the actual events in Egypt but all those encompassed within the period from Moses to Joshua, from the actual escape from Egypt to the *conquest of the land of Canaan, including the wilderness wanderings. This epic is not preserved in the *Pentateuch as such; within its boundaries the promise of land made to *Abraham remains unfulfilled. But the structure of Pentateuchal narrative presumes it, and indeed the conclusion of the story is found in the book of Joshua, the beginning of the *Deuteronomic History that has apparently displaced an earlier ending to Israel's original epic. The full story is also found in summary form in other passages (Exod. 15; Deut. 26.5–9; Josh. 24; Pss. 78; 80; 105; 114; cf. Ezek 20.6), some of which are quite old.

Historical Context. The Bible itself is virtually devoid of concrete detail that would enable the Exodus to be dated securely. It names none of the Pharaohs with whom Joseph, the "sons of Israel," and Moses and Aaron are reported to have dealt. Egyptian records are also silent about the events described in the later chapters of the book of Genesis and the first half of the book of Exodus; they make no mention of Joseph, Moses, the *Hebrews, the *plagues, or a catastrophic defeat of Pharaoh and his army. The first mention of Israel in a source other than the Bible is in an inscription written to commemorate the victory of the Egyptian Pharaoh Merneptah at the end of the thirteenth century BCE; there Israel is associated with places in Canaan rather than in Egypt. Because of this lack of direct correlation between biblical and nonbiblical sources, scholars have to resort to indirect evidence in assigning a date to the Exodus. Two principal views have been proposed. The first associates the flight of the Hebrews with the expulsion of the Hyksos kings from Egypt at the end of the Middle Bronze Age (ca. 1550 BCE). First proposed by *Josephus (Against Apion 1.103), this date approximates the figure of 480 years from the Exodus to the dedication of the *Temple by *Solomon (1 Kings 6.1; cf. Judg. 11.26) and, with some variations, is held by a minority of modern scholars. Biblical *chronology itself is, however, not consistent, and most scholars date the event to the mid-thirteenth century BCE, during the reign of Ramesses II, because of a convergence of probabilities, including the identification of the store cities of Pithom and Rameses (Exod. 1.11) with recently excavated sites in the Egyptian delta and the larger context of the history of Egypt and of the Levant.

The Narratives. The account of the Exodus in the Pentateuch is multilayered, being composed of various traditions, some very ancient, such as the "Song of the Sea" in Exodus 15, and the bulk a prose narrative combining the Pentateuchal sources *J, *E, and *P, to be dated from the tenth to perhaps as late as the sixth century BCE. The existence of these traditions enables us to observe a virtually continuous process of revision; thus, for example, the place names vary, apparently reflecting those current when a particular tradition was set down.

Embellishment, heightening, and exaggeration can also be observed. The simplest account of the event at the Sea of Reeds (see Red Sea) is found in Exodus 14.24–25. This passage may be understood in its simplest terms as a summary of how a group of Hebrew slaves escaping on foot was pursued by Egyptian guards, who were forced to give up the chase when their chariots became mired in the swampy region east of the Nile delta (see Map 2). This account is ultimately transformed into a miraculous intervention of Yahweh at the sea, when through the agency of

Moses he makes a path through the sea, with walls of water on both sides (Exod. 14.21–23). Still later, in the *Septuagint, the Hebrew phrase meaning "sea of reeds" is translated as "Red Sea," further enhancing the miracle. Likewise, the number of those escaping, according to Exodus 1.15 a small group whose obstetrical needs could be handled by only two midwives, becomes six hundred thousand men, as well as women and children (Exod. 12.37), an impossible population of several million.

Another tendency is to mythologize. The escape of the Hebrews at the sea is recast as a historical enactment of an ancient cosmogonic *myth of a battle between the storm god and the sea, found also in biblical texts having to do with *creation (Job 26.12–13; Jer. 31.35; Pss. 74.12–17; 89.9–12; 93; 104; see Israel, Religion of). This mythology is explicitly applied to the Exodus in Psalm 114, where the adversaries of the deity are the personified Sea and Jordan River, who flee at God's approach at the head of Israel (cf. Judg. 5.4–5; Ps. 68.7–8; Hab. 3.3–15); Sea and Jordan are clearly related to Prince Sea and Judge River, the parallel titles of the adversary of the Canaanite storm god *Baal in *Ugaritic mythology (note the echoes of this motif in the New Testament, in such passages as Mark 4.35–41 par.; Rev. 21.1). The adversaries of the God of Israel, however, are not cosmic but historical—the Egyptian Pharaoh and his army, and sea and river are not primeval forces but geographical realities.

The same historicizing tendency is apparent in the treatment of the *Passover, originally two separate springtime *feasts from different socioeconomic contexts now given historical etiology associated with the Exodus. The "festival of unleavened bread" was originally an agrarian pilgrimage feast in which the first spring harvest of barley was offered to a deity without being contaminated with older leaven. In the Exodus narrative, the unleavened bread is explained by the need for haste as the Hebrews left Egypt (Exod. 12.34, 39; Deut. 16.3; cf. Isa. 52.12). Similarly, the slaughter of the firstborn lamb, originally an offering by pastoralists to the deity thought responsible for their flocks' increase, is linked to the protective mark of the lamb's blood on the doorposts of the Hebrews, which spared them from the last plague.

In a similar way, other laws and institutions that developed later in Israel's history were legitimated by placing their origins in the formative period of the Exodus; the formative period thus became normative. This is one way of understanding the large amount of legal and ritual material found in the books of Exodus, Leviticus, Numbers, and Deuteronomy: set in a narrative context, these laws and religious practices are thereby linked with the central event of the Exodus and with Moses, the mediator of the divinely ordained instructions.

In view of these multiple tendencies, it is impossible to determine with any certainty what may actually have occurred to Hebrews in Egypt, probably during the thirteenth century. Literary analysis of the narratives suggests that what may in fact have been several movements out of Egypt by Semitic peoples have been collapsed into one. But whatever happened, this event was also formative in the sense that ancient Israel saw its origins here. A group of runaway slaves acquired an identity that, against all odds, they have maintained to today. It is understandable, then, that the event would be magnified in song and story, in part to praise the God thought responsible for it. It is also understandable why the Exodus became a dominant theme of later writers, who saw in the events of their times a kind of reenactment of the original Exodus.

Allusions to the Exodus. Hebrew Bible. Much of biblical narrative can be seen as shaped by or alluding to the Exodus both by anticipation and in retrospect. Thus, the division of the waters and the appearance of dry land at *creation (Gen. 1.6–10) foreshadows the division of the Reed Sea (Exod. 14.21; both passages are P); the allusion to the P account of creation in Exodus 14 is an interpretation of the Exodus itself as a new creation. Likewise, the brief story of Abram (*Abraham) and Sarai (*Sarah) in Egypt (Gen. 12.10–20) is a proleptic summary of the longer narrative of Israel in Egypt that will be told later in the Pentateuch: the two ancestors go down to Egypt as aliens because of a famine (Gen 12.10; cf. 47.4); subsequently Yahweh afflicts Pharaoh and his house with great plagues (12.17; Exod. 11.1) so that the Egyptian ruler lets them go (12.19; Exod. 12.32).

The linking of Exodus and conquest in biblical poetry (Exod. 15; Ps. 114) is elaborately developed in Joshua 3–4. The Deuteronomic narrative of the crossing of the Jordan River parallels that at the Reed Sea, as the conclusion to the narrative explicitly states (Josh. 4.23).

Biblical literature as a whole is permeated by allusions to the Exodus. The prophet *Elijah is described as returning in the darkest moment of his life to the mountain of God, called *Horeb

in Deuteronomic style, where the *theophany experienced by Moses is repeated, but with a difference: Yahweh is not in the wind, the earthquake, or the fire, all manifestations of his presence in Exodus (19.18; 24.17; cf. Deut. 4.12; etc.), but in the "still small voice" (1 Kings 19.12). The prophet Hosea sees hope for Israel's restoration in a return to the wilderness (Hos. 2.14–15), the scene of Israel's honeymoon with its God (see Jer. 2.2). Scholars have also seen echoes of the Exodus in such texts as Jonah and Psalm 23.

The most sustained set of references to the Exodus in the prophets is found in the collection of oracles attributed to Second Isaiah. Writing in the context of the Babylonian captivity in the sixth century BCE, this anonymous prophet foresaw a return of Israel to its land, describing it as a new Exodus (43.2, 19–21; 52.4–5). Yahweh, who had shown his power in the defeat of the primeval sea and at the Sea of Reeds, would act again to bring his people in joy through a wilderness to Zion (51.9–11; 40.3; 41.17–20; 44.3).

Dead Sea Scrolls. The *Essene community at *Qumran in its sectarian writings continued the interpretive tradition of applying the experience of the Exodus to itself. These self-styled "covenanters" saw themselves as the new Israel, living in camps in the wilderness at the very edge of the *promised land, preparing for the ultimate triumph of God after a war of forty years, reliving both Israel's original formative experience and that of the Babylonian exile, in fulfillment of the "new covenant" of Jeremiah 31.31.

New Testament. The appropriation of the Exodus as the model for prior and subsequent events in Israel's history was continued in the New Testament. The life of Jesus is frequently understood in the Gospels as a reenactment of Israel's experience. Luke 9.31 describes Jesus' passion, death, and resurrection as an "exodus" (NRSV: "departure"), the subject of his conversation with Moses and Elijah, both associated with the original Exodus of Israel (see above). Among the *quotations from the Old Testament in the gospel of Matthew which the evangelist explicitly describes Jesus as fulfilling, one identifies Jesus as the new Israel, come out of Egypt just as the old Israel had (Matt. 2.15; cf. Hos. 11.1; Exod. 4.22). There are many other allusions to events and figures of Israel's Exodus throughout Matthew's gospel. Jesus is represented as another Moses, rescued at an early age from persecutors (2.21; cf. Exod. 4.19). He gives his teaching in five major discourses like the five books of Moses (the *Torah), of which the first is a proclamation of the new law for the new Israel, the *Sermon on the Mount, just as Moses had proclaimed the original law at Mount Sinai. Like Israel in the wilderness, Jesus' followers are fed miraculously in a deserted place (Matt. 14.13; 15.33; par.; cf. Exod. 16.4; John 6.31–32). The gospel of John carries this *typology further by identifying Jesus with the Passover lamb (1.29; 19.36, quoting Exod. 12.46), an equation made earlier by Paul (1 Cor. 5.7) and later considerably amplified in the book of *Revelation (5.6; etc.). Paul also identifies Christ with the rock from which water miraculously flowed in the wilderness (1 Cor. 10.4; cf. Exod. 17.1–7; Num. 20.2–13).

Postbiblical traditions. It is not surprising that a similar correspondence was made between the experience of ancient Israel and the life of the Christian. *Baptism is understood as a personal exodus from slavery to sin to a new life of holiness made possible by passage through water; in the Roman liturgy the second reading of the ritual for blessing the baptismal water during the Easter vigil is Exodus 14.24–15.3. Thus, Christians, like Moses (Exod. 34.29–35), behold the "*glory of the Lord" unveiled (2 Cor. 3.16–18). Likewise, at death, a traditional prayer asks that God save the soul of the dying person as he once saved Moses from Pharaoh. The Christian Eucharist is directly descended from the Passover service, because the Last Supper of Jesus was itself a Passover meal; the bread (often unleavened; *see* Leaven) and the wine of the Passover assume a specifically Christian symbolism, but the older Exodus themes are still present (1 Cor. 10.16–18; 11.23–25; *see* Lord's Supper).

In Islam, the *Qurʾān and subsequent traditions echo the biblical account of the Exodus in their description of the Hejira, the flight of Muhammad from Mecca to Medina.

The self-identification with the ancient community of Hebrews has continued into modern times. Various groups experiencing oppression have identified themselves with the Hebrew slaves in Egypt. Throughout the centuries of persecution and attempts at extermination, Jews have seen in the original Exodus a reason for hope: the God who had saved their ancestors would also save them. In the Diaspora, since the Roman destruction of Jerusalem in 70 CE, the longing for a return to the land of Israel has been expressed by the words "Next year in Jerusalem!" at the end of the Passover meal. Exodus symbolism was also adopted by the Zionist move-

ment, especially in the aftermath of World War II and the *Holocaust, and continues to be used by Jews seeking to emigrate from oppressive situations.

In the ideology of the Puritans immigrating to the "New World," the Exodus also served as a model and a divine guarantee: once again a divinely chosen group had escaped from oppression across a body of water to a new Canaan, a "providence plantation"; note the many biblical place names used in New England and throughout the United States. This conviction has continued to shape the American self-image, notably in the notion of "manifest destiny": the view that the Americans of the United States are a chosen people is commonplace in American political discourse. Ironically, in the early nineteenth century, after the founding of Liberia, American blacks used the same imagery in their spirituals; the "river" to be crossed was the Atlantic Ocean, but in the opposite direction from the Pilgrims, and Africa became the goal of their journey, the "greener pastures on the other side."

In the latter part of the twentieth century, the Exodus has been paradigmatic for liberation theology, a radical Christian movement of Latin American origin whose goals are political and social reform. Liberation theology has been criticized for its appropriation of the Exodus as sanction for views and actions espoused for other, quite legitimate, reasons. The appeal to biblical authority is highly selective and raises complicated questions: how, for example, can a God who rescues the Hebrews from Egyptian bondage be reconciled with one who immediately thereafter gives explicit commands in which the institution of slavery is not just presumed but condoned? Still, there is no denying the power of the Exodus story as a model for hope and even action to counter oppression. (*See* Politics and the Bible.)   MICHAEL D. COOGAN

Exodus, The Book of. *Wĕʾēlleh šĕmôt* begins the book of Exodus, "And these are the names." This phrase serves as the Hebrew name for Exodus, and as a convenient linking of its narrative with the preceding narratives in the canon. Indeed, the beginning of the list of the descendants of Israel in Genesis 46.8 employs precisely the same words as does Exodus 1.1, and much as the narrative of *Genesis 12–50 is concerned with the promise of Yahweh to *Abraham, *Isaac, and *Jacob of progeny and land, the narrative of the book of Exodus is concerned with various dimensions of the fulfillment of that promise.

Contents. Most of the book of Exodus is prose, as straightforward narrative, as lists of laws in apodictic (universal) or casuistic (specific case) form, or as instructions related in one way or another to worship. One important section is *poetry (15.1b–18, 21), and there is one three-line poetic stanza at 32.18.

The subject matter of the book of Exodus is far more disparate in content than in form. There are narratives about *Moses alongside narratives of Israel's oppression, and narratives of the intransigence of the Pharaoh of *Egypt alongside narratives of rescue and provision by Yahweh. There are instructions appropriate to an agricultural setting alongside instructions appropriate to an urban life. There are dramatic accounts of the coming and appearance of Yahweh alongside the most elaborate descriptions of the objects designed to suggest and memorialize Yahweh's nearness. There are stories intended to prove that Yahweh is present alongside stories of Israel's fear of both his presence and his absence. And there are reports of the authentication of Yahweh's representative alongside the instructions for the ordination and the specifications of the vestments designed to symbolize that authority.

All these quite different sequences are set into a loose geographical and chronological framework. For roughly the first third of the book of Exodus, the setting is Egypt (1.1–13.16). For the next five chapters, the setting is the *wilderness en route to *Sinai (13.17–18.27). And for just over the second half of the book, as also for *Leviticus and nearly the first third of *Numbers (through Num. 10.11), the setting is the plain before Mount Sinai (19.1–40.38). The chronological sequence of the book extends from the rise of a new dynasty in Egypt some time after *Joseph's death to the birth of Moses in the context of a bitter oppression of Israel, through Moses' growth to maturity, his flight to *Midian, his call there and his return to Egypt to lead Israel, through the sequence of the mighty acts demonstrating Yahweh's presence with his people, through the event of the Exodus and Israel's deliverance at the sea (see Red Sea) to the subsequent journey in the wilderness to Sinai. There, after an appropriate preparation, Israel experienced the advent of Yahweh, received the revelation of the "ten words" (Exod. 34.28; see Ten Commandments) and the gift of *covenant relationship. The remainder of the sequence of

Exodus, involving special instructions for the apparatus and personnel of worship, the rebellion involving the *golden calf, Yahweh's punishment and *mercy, the renewal of the covenant relationship, and the execution of the special instructions all occurs within what is represented as a brief period of time.

Unfortunately, there is no way to locate this admittedly loose chronological sequence with any precision, either in an Egyptian setting or in a wilderness setting. A wide variety of dates has been suggested, from the first half of the fifteenth century BCE to the early part of the thirteenth century BCE.

Literary Structure. From the beginning of critical inquiry into the Bible, the disparity of the various sections of the book of Exodus has been noted, and during the latter third of the nineteenth century and the first third of the twentieth, this disparity was generally attributed to the differences in vocabulary, style, and interest of the Pentateuchal or, more recently, Tetrateuchal sources. The Yahwistic (*J) and Elohistic (*E) sources were regarded as present, usually in a kind of foundational amalgam onto which the Priestly (*P) material had been grafted or attached as extended addenda here and there. In commentaries published in the sixty years following 1875, the assignment of verses and verse fragments to these "documentary" sources was made with both assurance and precision. This procedure sometimes led, however, to an absurd fragmentation of the text of Exodus, so much so that the source hypothesis came to be put forward with more caution, and eventually to be emphasized or deemphasized according to the format of a given commentary series and the interests of individual authors.

Attention to the motifs underlying these sources has led to a larger view of the book of Exodus, both as a part of a continuing narrative and also as a whole within itself. Exodus continues a narrative begun by Genesis and provides the foundation for another continued by Numbers and *Deuteronomy (see Pentateuch). Indeed, Exodus is a foundation for the entire Bible, for it sets forth a kind of first presentation of the themes of coming and presence, relationship and responsibility, which are so much a part of the biblical message. (See Exodus, The.)

The literary structure of the book of Exodus is certainly composite, whether by that one means the joining of traditions, the weaving of sources, or the exposition of themes. There is, however, an important sense in which Exodus is in itself a whole, one that needs to be taken seriously. Whatever may lie behind the book, in a literary history that can only be speculated, the canonical text of Exodus presents a whole that cannot be denied, whether or not it can be understood. On a first reading, that whole may appear somewhat more disjointed than it really is, in part because of the prejudice of years of thinking of the book of Exodus in pieces. A closer reading reveals a literary structure that is not only deliberate but also quite effective in organization.

Composition and Compilation. The composition of the book of Exodus took place over a long period of time. That much is established by the patchwork nature of the book's literary structure. Yet just how long that period of time may have been, or just when it may have begun, can only be speculated. No assignment of any part of the book of Exodus to a definite author can be made; many minds are evident in the forty chapters that comprise the book.

Tradition has ascribed Exodus, along with the other four of the first five books of the Bible, to Moses, both because of his significant role as Yahweh's representative and also on the basis of such references as Deuteronomy 1.1; 2 Kings 14.6; Ezra 6.18; 2 Chronicles 25.4; and Mark 12.26. This tradition and such references were probably never intended to suggest a Mosaic authorship, but rather to establish a Mosaic authority, a kind of guarantee of an ancient and accurate record. From the earliest history of the Bible, the book of Exodus has been recognized as a collage of sometimes conflicting and often very different traditions. Also from an early period, both Jewish (*Philo, *Josephus, the *Talmud) and Christian literature have connected Moses with the Pentateuch, and for appropriate reasons. The historicity of Moses is the most reasonable assumption to be made about him. There is no viable argument why Moses should be regarded as a fiction of pious necessity. His removal from the scene of Israel's beginnings as a theocratic community would leave a vacuum that simply could not be explained away. Moses may be connected with the earliest substratum of the book of Exodus, specifically with the accounts of call and *theophany and perhaps also with the Ten Commandments. What cannot be said, of course, is that there are, anywhere in Exodus or in the Bible, words that can be said certainly to be Moses' own.

What may be proposed in theoretical reconstruction of the composition of the book of Exodus is a substratum of narrative, cultic instruction, covenant formulary, hymnody, authorization sequences, etiological legends, and wilderness routes, gathered across the years from the time of the Exodus itself until at least the postexilic period of Israel's history. Through that period of approximately seven centuries, the book of Exodus was being composed and, in a sense, recomposed, as the gathering strata that comprise the canonical book were created, then joined, often in new arrangement. It is through these centuries that the process of composition became a process of compilation, and the canonical book is the product of this latter process.

The compilation of Exodus was by no means the haphazard arbitrary shuffle frequently implied by literary-critical essayists and commentators. Too much attention is given to the book of Exodus that might have been, and not enough to the book that is. The discontinuity and disparity in content, style, vocabulary, and organization are the result of an inevitable variation in source material, along with the growth of the book to its present form across a lengthy period of time. By no means are they the sign of careless or ignorant editorial work. Indeed, given this inevitable variation, the book of Exodus displays a remarkable unity of purpose and wholeness of organization.

The material often regarded as intrusive and even disruptive of the sequence of Exodus, such as the "Book of the Covenant" (20.22–23.33), and the two Priestly sections dealing with the media of Israel's worship (25.1–31.18 and 35.1–40.38), may be seen as deliberately placed pieces of a whole concept. The "Book of the Covenant" functions not as a displaced collection of loosely assembled laws, but as a practical and specific application of the principles of relationship set forth in the Ten Commandments. And the section on the symbols and acts and ministers of worship in Yahweh's presence are logically located, even in a narrative sequence that they disrupt. The revelation of the instructions for the creation of the media of such worship is placed immediately after the long composite narrative describing the promise of Yahweh's presence, the demonstration of Yahweh's presence, and the advent of Yahweh's presence, brought to a climax by the establishment of the covenant between Yahweh and Israel. The report of the fulfillment of those instructions is appropriately placed after the narratives describing the breaking of the covenant relationship, the consequent judgment upon Israel, the return of Yahweh's presence, and the renewal of the covenant commitment. The places of worship and their furnishings are not to be constructed until the relationship between Yahweh and Israel has been reestablished, and only when all the work of building has been determined to be in exact accord with Yahweh's direction does his presence settle upon the *tabernacle (Exod. 39.42–43; 40.34).

An even more dramatic example of the literary and thematic unity of Exodus as a compilation is provided by Exodus 18, a chapter often considered dislocated in the narrative sequence of the book because it describes events that occur in the camp at the foot of Sinai/*Horeb before Israel is said to have reached there and because it is concerned with the administration of Yahweh's requirements before they have actually been given. These inconsistencies of narrative sequence cannot, of course, have gone unnoticed by the compilers of the book of Exodus, so some other reason must be sought for the location of Exodus 18 where it now stands in the received text instead of after chap. 24 or even after chap. 34—a reason that sets aside the advantages of logical or chronological sequence. That reason is to be found in a thematic consideration: the reunion of Moses with his *Midianite family, specifically Jethro, particularly in company with his people Israel freed from bondage in Egypt, amounts to an important reuniting of the two parts of a family divided by the expulsion of *Cain (Gen. 4.10–16), by Abraham's sending forth of Keturah's sons (Gen. 25.1–6) and his disinheriting of *Hagar and *Ishmael (Gen. 21.8–21), and by the conflict between *Jacob and *Esau (Gen. 25.19–34; 27.1–45; 28.6–9; 32.3–6; 33.1–20). The redactors who compiled the book of Exodus were eager to have a reunited family of Israel before the great theophany and covenant-making at Sinai, and so they set what is now Exodus 18 where they did, ignoring other considerations.

Theology. What makes the book of Exodus as it stands a carefully organized whole is neither literary form nor authorship, neither historical sequence nor uniformity of content. Exodus is bound together by a theological intention: the presentation by narrative, by didactic device, by song, by dialogue, by legal specification, by liturgical arrangement, by a round of festival and solemn ceremony, by high drama, by symbol, by a witty and very direct picture of human nature, and by a soaring depiction of the majesty and the mystery of God, of theological themes that are foundational to the Bible and to Judaism and Christianity, as well as to Islam.

The most important of these theological themes is the repeated assertion that Yahweh is present in the ongoing daily life of Israel, his people of promise and covenant. This theme functions as a kind of center from and to which other themes are connected, as spokes to a hub. Yahweh, who made promises to Abraham, Isaac, and Jacob, is present and hence those promises are being kept; with the development of that assertion, the book of Exodus is begun. Yahweh, to be present with his people, must come to them, must bring them to himself; thus, there are in Exodus the narratives of his advent, in chaps. 3 and 4, 19 and 20, 24, 33 and 34, and 40. Yahweh must be known to be present, by his people and by those who would oppose them alike: therefore a proof-of-the-presence sequence, dramatically moved forward by Pharaoh's recalcitrance, increasing in seriousness and brought to a climax in the deliverance at the sea, is provided.

If Yahweh is present, his people will be cared for; so there are accounts of guidance through a great and terrible wilderness, and stories of the provision of water and foodstuff in the form of the *manna and the quails. Because Yahweh is present, the enemies of his people must be bested; as a result, the Egyptian learned men are in due course frustrated, the Egyptians are humbled and despoiled, Pharaoh himself is defeated, and *Amalek is vanquished at Rephidim. Since Yahweh is present, his people should know that presence in a unique manner; hence, he prepares them and comes to them at Sinai/Horeb, having given them already through Moses his unique and descriptive name, a name suggesting his very nature as the "one who really is" (*see* Tetragrammaton). The presence of Yahweh realized can only mean a response of some kind; thus, Yahweh gives his guidance for life in his presence, in the Ten Commandments, and opens himself to his people in covenant with them. The direction of life in Yahweh's presence involves a concrete application of the broad principles of life in relationship with him; therefore the Ten Commandments are applied by a rambling collection of specific case provisions.

The living memory of Yahweh's proof of his presence to Israel is essential for the generations to come; thus, provision is made for the seasonal reenactment of event, in the ritual testimony of the requirement of the firstborn, the feast of unleavened bread, the feast of the *Passover, and perhaps even a covenant-renewal festival (see Exod. 19.4–6 and 24.3–8). (See Feasts and Festivals). A constant reminder of Yahweh present among his people is also important; hence, the lengthy and detailed chapters on the media of worship, media that symbolize the circles of nearness to Yahweh's presence in the *tabernacle of Israel's devotional life, moving from the primary symbol of Yahweh's presence, the *Ark in the holiest space, to the *altar of wholly consumed offerings in the circle of the outer court, the area of preparation for entry into Yahweh's presence in worship. The instructions for the creation of the media of worship (Exod. 25–31) are ended with the specification of the *Sabbath as a sign in perpetuity of relationship with Yahweh present. The narrative of the fulfillment of those instructions (Exod. 35–40) is begun with this emphasis on the Sabbath, and ended with an account of the settling of Yahweh's presence onto the place of worship erected in their midst. Thus, the theology of Yahweh present is asserted in the book of Exodus as a presence incarnate in both the worship and the life of Israel.

Appropriately, the extended sequence of symbol is interrupted, between instruction and fulfillment of instruction, by a narrative of disobedience and forgiveness that affords a context for still other motifs of the theology of coming and nearness. Israel's sin of the *golden calf is a fundamental violation of the covenant relationship, involving disobedience to at least the first two of the Ten Commandments. As a result, Israel falls under the threat of the cancellation of the gift of Yahweh's presence, in effect a negation of the remainder of the book of Exodus. In a narrative filled with tension, Israel is judged and forgiven, and Moses witnesses a unique revelation, by Yahweh, of his own nature and attitude (Exod. 34.6–7), a revelation that extends the earlier revelation of his unique name, at the time of Moses' call. It is a sequence that provides a setting for two additional symbols of Yahweh's nearness, the tent of promised presence (Exod. 33.7–11) and the shining face of Moses (Exod. 34.29–35).

In the book of Exodus, one is brought to the thematic beginning of the Bible. For in Exodus, the biblical story and its major themes are presented, in narrative, in symbol, in expectation, or in promise. The book that begins "And these are the names" ends with a declaration that the cloud of Yahweh's presence, filling the tabernacle, provided for all Israel a vision of Yahweh's nearness to them by day and by night. And there, given all that lies between that beginning and that ending, one is in the middle of a story that is unfolding still.   JOHN I DURHAM

Exorcism. A belief in the existence of evil spirits or *demons and their ability both to cause disease and to take possession of people has been common to most societies. Side by side with such beliefs there has usually been a recognition of the power of certain individuals to exorcise such spirits, freeing the sufferer from their malign influence. Such concepts occur in the Bible, though relatively infrequently; they are almost entirely restricted to the accounts of the ministry of Jesus in the *synoptic Gospels.

There are no unequivocal examples of exorcism in the Hebrew Bible. *David's use of music to calm *Saul, who is described as being troubled by "an evil spirit from Yahweh" (1 Sam. 16.14–23), bears none of the characteristics of the later accounts of exorcism with their essential underlying component of a violent "casting out" of an evil spirit. Saul's behavior suggests a severe manic-depressive psychosis with marked paranoid overtones that gave rise to episodes of impulsive homicidal violence. Music could be expected to have a beneficial effect on the depression (1 Sam. 16.23), but not on the manic paranoia (1 Sam. 18.10–12).

In preexilic biblical traditions, the idea of *evil cosmic forces separate from, and over against, the rule of God is not prominent. By the first century CE, however, *Satan was generally viewed as ruler of the present age, having gained temporary control of the earth and holding sway over its kingdoms (a view reflected in the New Testament at Matt. 4.8–9; Luke 4.5–6; John 14.30; 2 Cor. 4.4; Eph. 6.12). This power was exercised in individual lives through demons, either in a general malevolent influence or by direct "possession." In the latter instance, the demon had to be "cast out," and thus exorcism became a dominant feature of first-century Judaism, with the professional exorcist having a recognized status. The *Pharisees apparently played a significant role as adepts in exorcisms, and there is a passing reference to this at Mark 12.27. The approach was strongly *magical, using invocations and spells (foreshadowed as early as Tobit 6.17–18). In later rabbinic literature and other sources, individual demons responsible for specific illnesses are named.

Exorcism was an undisputed feature of the ministry of Jesus. The various references in the synoptic Gospels are little more than vague and generalized comments about the healing ministry of Jesus, often being simply editorial link statements in the narrative. Six specific cases of exorcism are mentioned: the Capernaum demoniac (Mark 1.21–28 = Luke 4.31–37); the Gerasene demoniac (Mark 5.1–20 = Matt. 8.28–34 = Luke 8.26–39); the dumb demoniac (Matt. 9.32–33); the blind and dumb demoniac (Matt. 12.22); the Syrophoenician demoniac (Mark 7.24–30 = Matt. 15.21–28); the epileptic boy (Mark 9.14–29 = Matt. 17.14–21 = Luke 9.37–43). The evangelists seem to have been selective in their use of the terminology of exorcism, reserving it for conditions inexplicable for them in other ways and outside the general categories of illness that Jesus healed. Although clinical details are meager, there is suggestive evidence that the synoptic exorcisms were restricted to *epilepsy and the abnormal behavior patterns that occur in hysterical (dissociative) states.

Outside the synoptic Gospels, exorcism is mentioned only in Acts: twice in general terms (5.16 and 8.7) and twice of specific incidents (16.16–18 and 19.11–19). There are no further references in the New Testament; it is noteworthy that the Jesus of the Fourth Gospel is not an exorcist, nor does he come into contact with "possessed" people. It should also be noted that in none of the discussions of spiritual gifts in the Pauline correspondence is mention made of exorcism. A general gift of healing is recognized, but there is no suggestion that this includes exorcism. The synoptic tradition is unique in suggesting that Jesus gave the *twelve authority to exorcise, and this appears to have been limited to his lifetime (Mark 3.16 = Matt. 10.1, 8, and also Luke 9.1).

Exorcism in the Bible is thus essentially a feature of the synoptic Gospels in which it is presented as an eschatological activity of Jesus, either as evidence of the arrival of God's *kingdom or in preparation for its immediate appearance. His own explanation of the phenomenon, that he cast out demons through the spirit of God (Matt. 12.27–28; cf. Mark 3.28–30), underlines this, pointing to the arrival of the promised endtime and the power of that age. Outside the synoptic tradition, the New Testament sees Satan and his unclean spirits as decisively and finally defeated in the Easter event (e.g., Col. 2.15).

J. KEIR HOWARD

Eye of the Needle. *See* Needle's Eye.

Ezekiel, the Book of.

Author. The book of Ezekiel tells relatively little that is explicit concerning the figure for whom it is named, and apart from brief references in Sirach (49.8–9) and 4 Maccabees (18.17) he is not mentioned by name elsewhere in the Bible. Ezekiel, whose name means "God strengthens," was of priestly lineage, son of Buzi (1.3). Along with other Judeans, he suffered deportation to *Babylon following the surrender of Jehoiachin in 598/597 BCE (1.1; cf. 2 Kings 24.12–16). Ezekiel received his prophetic calling in Babylon in 593 (1.1); his age at the time is not recorded. It is disputed whether some or even all of Ezekiel's ministry actually took place in *Jerusalem rather than in Babylonia, as various of his words could suggest. According to the book's dates, he continued to receive divine communications until at least 571 (29.17). Nothing is mentioned in the Bible concerning the circumstances of his death; much later tradition states that he was murdered by one of the leaders of the exiles whose idolatry he had denounced, and that he was buried near Babylon.

Unlike his near contemporary *Jeremiah, Ezekiel appears as an outwardly stoical, highly self-controlled and somewhat passive personality, who, for example, follows without demur Yahweh's directive not to mourn the death of his beloved wife (24.15–18). On occasion, however, he does venture a protest or appeal in the face of what is communicated to him (4.14; 9.8; 11.13). It is likewise clear that Ezekiel's call to herald Judah's doom caused him profound distress (3.14–15). The response to Ezekiel's message seems to have been much less overtly hostile than was true in the case of Jeremiah. In fact, there are several references to his being respectfully consulted by the leaders of the exiles (8.1; 14.1; 20.1). Finally, the content of Ezekiel's book reveals him as a man of wide learning.

Arrangement/Divisions. The individual units of Ezekiel's material have been arranged in their present sequence on the basis of considerations of chronology and content. First of all, more so than with any other prophetic book, there seems to have been a concern with giving the dated texts of Ezekiel—there are some fifteen of these—in their correct chronological order; only twice does a deviation occur (29.1; 29.17). The materials, however, are grouped by content into three large-scale segments. Words of doom against Judah/Jerusalem are concentrated at the beginning of the book (chaps. 1–24); oracles against various foreign nations follow (chaps. 25–32); and texts concerning the eventual restoration of Yahweh's people predominate in the concluding segment (chaps. 33–48). The intention behind this sequencing (which can be seen also in the book of *Zephaniah, Isaiah 1–35, and the *Septuagint text of Jeremiah) is for the book to culminate on an upbeat note. This principle of arrangement, however, is not followed with complete consistency; chaps. 1–24 contain promises of salvation (e.g., 17.22–24), while an oracle against *Edom (chap. 35) stands with the concluding segment (chaps. 33–48).

Within each of these three major divisions, one may readily identify various distinct blocks of material. Within chaps. 1–24, the vision sequences of 1.1–3.27 and 8.11–11.25 stand out. In chaps. 25–32, brief oracles against Judah's near neighbors (chap. 25) are followed by extensive discourses of doom concerning Tyre (chaps. 26–28) and *Egypt (chaps. 29–32). The final segment, chaps. 33–48, comprises a series of generalized promises of Jewish revival (chaps. 34–37) and a detailed blueprint for the reconstruction of the cult (chaps. 40–48), with chap. 33 serving as transition from what precedes and the *Gog oracles (chaps. 38–39) as a kind of interlude.

Literary Features. As a piece of writing, the book of Ezekiel presents a variety of noteworthy peculiarities, four of which are singled out here. First, certain fixed expressions, which are either unique to Ezekiel or especially favored by him in the Bible as a whole, recur repeatedly, thereby unifying the book terminologically. Examples include "*son of man" (NRSV: "mortal") as a title/address for the prophet (roughly one hundred occurrences: 2.1; etc.); "rebellious house" (twelve times: 2.5; etc.); "to execute judgments on" (nine times: 5.10; etc.); "set your face toward/against" (nine times: 6.2; etc.); "and they/you shall know that I am the Lord" (about fifty times: 6.7; etc.); "to bear disgrace" (eleven times: 16.52; etc.). Second, in articulating its message, the book makes use of a rich variety of literary forms: vision accounts (e.g., 37.1–14), sign narratives (e.g., 12.1–11), allegories (e.g., 17.1–24), laments (e.g., 27.1–36), judgment speeches (e.g.,

13.1–23), salvation oracles (e.g., 36.37–38), disputations (e.g., 33.10–20), legal prescriptions (e.g., 44.15–31). Frequently, too, Ezekiel's literary forms are complex entities, incorporating into themselves a number of subgenres; see, for example, chap. 17, an allegory that contains both a judgment speech (17.15–21) and a salvation oracle (17.22–24). Third, Ezekiel's style evidences a consistent tendency toward prolixity and a graphic excess in the handling of traditional imagery; see, for example, his treatment of the conjugal metaphor for Israel's relation to Yahweh in chaps. 16, 20, and 23. Last, in its heavy use of metaphorical language and avoidance of proper names for contemporary figures (curiously, "Ezekiel" occurs only twice: 1.1; 24.24), the book makes a somewhat disembodied impression. Accordingly, it is not surprising that both the locality of the prophet's ministry and the date of the book's composition—it has been dated variously from the age of Manasseh in the mid-seventh century BCE to the Hellenistic period—have long been controverted.

Theology. Ezekiel's God is above all a "holy" being (36.23), that is, one who utterly transcends human comprehension, manipulation, and calculation. This quality of Yahweh finds manifold expression throughout the book. Ezekiel refrains from any direct claims to have seen the deity (see 1.26–28; cf. Isa. 6.1). Yahweh remains free to rebuff human inquiries (14.3; 20.3); he can void the schemes of practitioners of magic (13.20–23). The movements and fates of the great world powers, such as Babylon (29.20) and Gog (38.2–3), are just as much under his control as is the destiny of Israel itself. Yahweh has the capacity to manifest himself outside the land of Israel (1.1); he is able to withdraw his presence from the *Temple (11.23), and later to return there as he wills (43.1–4). He acts, unconstrained by any human claim, for his own purposes (36.22).

At the same time, however, the holy Yahweh is also a God who has freely but passionately and irrevocably committed himself to the people of Israel. Like *Hosea and Jeremiah, Ezekiel develops this dimension of Yahweh's being and activity by using conjugal imagery (chaps. 16; 20; 23). Yahweh carefully and tenderly nourished the cast-off child Israel as his future bride (16.3–14). At present, he is punishing her for her persistent infidelities, but ultimately he will not abandon his spouse to her misery and sinfulness. Rather, he will restore her prosperity and give her the inner capacity to live in faithfulness to him (see, e.g., 36.26–30). In all of this, the transcendent God is intimately and continuously involved in human history, to the end that, finally, both Israel and the nations will know him as the sole, truly efficacious deity (39.22–23, 28).

Anthropology. Ezekiel's anthropology is characterized by an underlying unresolved tension. On the one hand, he is the Hebrew Bible's great advocate of individual responsibility (18.1–32). Ezekiel is likewise commissioned precisely in order to summon his hearers to conscious decision about their behavior options (3.16–21; 33.7–16). On the other hand, however, Ezekiel's words disclose an overwhelming pessimism concerning the people's capacity ever to choose rightly. For him, unlike Hosea (3.15) and Jeremiah (2.2–3), there never was a honeymoon period in Israel's relation to Yahweh. Already during her time in Egypt (16.26; 20.8), as well as ever since, Israel has consistently chosen other gods in preference to Yahweh. Judah learned nothing from Yahweh's punishment of the northern kingdom, only redoubling her own *idolatry in the face of that experience (23.11). Although Ezekiel's hearers may not actively persecute him, neither do they give much attention to his warnings (12.26; 20.49; 33.20–33). Such circumstances suggest that the exhortations Ezekiel is sent to deliver are futile (2.7); what is needed, rather, is a direct intervention by Yahweh that will produce a transformed, obedient heart in his people (11.18–19; 36.26–27). Ultimately, like so many theologians after him, Ezekiel is left affirming both realities, human freedom and divine *grace, without being fully able to account for their interplay.

Biblical Affinities. The book of Ezekiel manifests significant links with a wide range of other biblical traditions. Ezekiel is familiar with the *creation myths incorporated into the primeval history of *Genesis (29.16; 31.8–9; 36.35). From the historical traditions of Israel, he cites the figures of *Abraham (33.24), *Jacob (37.25), and *David (34.23; 37.24). In common with Deuteronomic tradition, he emphasizes the centrality of the *Law, its observance, and especially its nonobservance, in the unfolding of the Yahweh-Israel relationship. His affinities with the Priestly (*P) material of the *Pentateuch, above all the "Holiness Code" (Lev. 17–26), both in content and phraseology, are especially marked; compare, for example, Ezekiel 44.22 with Leviticus 21.7, 13–15, and Ezekiel 44.25–27 with Leviticus 21.1–3. Similarly, Ezekiel displays many similarities with the teachings of the contemporary prophetic figures Jeremiah and Second *Isaiah, in-

cluding marital imagery, hopes for an inner transformation of the people, renewal of their *covenant with Yahweh, and recognition by the nations of Yahweh's sole deity (*see* Monotheism). The elaborateness of the accounts of his vision and the cosmic terms in which he describes God's interventions against the enemies of his people (32.7–8; 38.19–22) anticipate later *apocalyptic writing.

The book of Ezekiel is cited directly in the New Testament only rarely; see, for example, 2 Corinthians 6.16 = Ezekiel 37.27. On the other hand, its imagery often provides a point of departure for presentations of various New Testament authors, such as the allusions to Ezekiel 34 in Jesus' contrasting of himself as good shepherd with the Jewish leadership (John 10), and the use in Revelation 22.1–2 of Ezekiel 47.1–12, which describes elements of the vision of water from the temple. Thus, the book of Ezekiel, which itself brings together so many earlier streams of tradition, came to serve as a source of still more comprehensive literary and theological developments in early Christian writing.   CHRISTOPHER T. BEGG

Ezra, The Book of. At an early stage, the books of Ezra and *Nehemiah were regarded as a unity. From the time of Origen (third century CE), they were divided as we have them today.

Historical Background. Ezra 1–6 describes the return of the Jews to *Jerusalem under Sheshbazzar (539 BCE) and the initial attempts to rebuild the *Temple; their efforts, however, were frustrated by their enemies. Later, *Zerubbabel, influenced by the prophets *Haggai and *Zechariah, resumed the building of the Temple with the permission of the Persian king, *Darius. The Temple was completed in 515 BCE.

Ezra 7–10 describes a much later situation, and tells of the return of Ezra and a certain group of Jews to Judah in the time of the Persian king Artaxerxes (presumably Artaxerxes I, 465–424 BCE). According to Ezra 7.7, this happened in the seventh year of Artaxerxes (458 BCE). However, in view of disturbed conditions early in his reign, scholars have found this reference to royal permission for the return exceedingly difficult to accept. Another problem arises with the memoir of Nehemiah, in which Ezra and his important religious activities are totally ignored. It is certainly difficult to explain why Ezra and Nehemiah, if they were contemporaries, would avoid mention of each other almost completely in their memoirs (*see* Nehemiah, The Book of). Scholars have proposed various solutions to this problem. Some have pointed out that with only a slight emendation in Ezra 7.7, where "thirty" may have fallen out as a result of haplography, one can read the "thirty-seventh" year of Artaxerxes I. Thus, Ezra would have accompanied Nehemiah on his second visit to Jerusalem about 428 BCE; this solves some of the problems created by the traditional date of 458 BCE. Other scholars, assuming that the activities of Ezra and Nehemiah must be totally separated, have held that "in the seventh year of Artaxerxes" refers to Artaxerxes II (404–359/358 BCE), which brings us to 398 BCE. However, the traditional view, that Ezra arrived in 458 BCE, is still held by a number of modern scholars. In such a case, it is likely that Ezra's initial visit to Jerusalem was only a few months long. It is possible that he later returned to Jerusalem, but particulars about this are vague. Thus, it appears that the book of Ezra describes the history of certain Jews from 539 to 516 BCE and for a short period in 458 BCE.

This description, however, presents several problems: either the author assumed too much knowledge of certain events on the part of readers, or he himself was uncertain how events developed. One problem involves the role played by Sheshbazzar during the initial return, and his relationship to Zerubbabel. At a certain stage, Sheshbazzar completely vanishes from the sources; what happened to him? No satisfactory reply can be given, and some scholars identify him with Zerubbabel. But the root of this problem lies in the nature of the author's concerns. He is interested not in giving a full account of the life and acts of individuals but in the role that God played in Jewish history, namely, in allowing the people to return to Judah where they rebuilt the Temple. Another problem involves Zerubbabel: like Sheshbazzar, he simply vanishes from the sources. Yet, that he and the high priest Jeshua were active in the second attempt to rebuild the Temple is testified also by the books of Haggai and Zechariah (in both of which Jeshua is called Joshua); Zerubbabel was instrumental in obtaining permission from Darius to continue building, but in the description of the inauguration of the Temple, no mention is made of Zerubbabel. Since the sources imply that at a certain stage Zerubbabel may have been tempted to regard himself as a messiah-king, some assume that he was forcefully removed by the Persians. Yet another problem involves the return of the exiles. Did a large number return with Sheshbazzar, or did various groups return on different occasions? Is the list in Ezra 2 (cf. Neh. 7) representative of one such group of those returning, or is it a list of several groups over a long period? Although there are indications that the list is made up from several groups, one cannot be certain.

It is clear from chaps. 7–10 that Ezra was dispatched by the Persian king Artaxerxes to Jerusalem to establish the Israelite law (*Torah) among the Jews. A number of exiles returned with Ezra, a kind of ideal group consisting of, among others, *priests and *Levites. To his dismay, Ezra discovered that there had been intermarriage with the neighboring nations, and he ordered all foreign wives to be repudiated, so as to keep the religion of Jews pure of contamination by the worship of different gods.

From a historical perspective, the book of Ezra starts with the hegemony of a new imperial force in the ancient Near East, namely, the domination of the *Persians under *Cyrus. The Persians' tolerance in religious matters is well known. The book of Ezra begins with Cyrus's decree allowing the Jews to restore their sanctuary in order to serve their God according to their prescribed laws. After Cyrus, there is a lapse of time until the description of the chaotic circumstances that took place just before *Darius I assumed full control. It was at this stage that Zerubbabel and his compatriots started in earnest to rebuild the Temple. When Darius had gained firm control in 520–519 BCE, he granted the Jews the right, according to Cyrus's decree, to continue their building activities. This culminates in the dedication of the Temple in 515 BCE.

In 458 BCE, Artaxerxes I gave permission to Ezra and certain Jews to return to Judah; this was not without political motives, for in 460 BCE a revolt had broken out in Egypt under Inarus against the Persians. Pericles, the Athenian leader who had first decided to attack Cyprus, changed his plans and assisted the Egyptians against the Persians. In 460 and 459 BCE the rebels, with the aid of the Athenians, succeeded against the Persians. The latter kept only a small strip of land under their control, but they bribed the Spartans to start a war against the Athenians. In 458, the Persian general and satrap, Megabyzus, was fighting a successful war against the Egyptians, who were subdued in 456 BCE. It was thus expedient for Artaxerxes to send Ezra out in all goodwill to the Jews so that Judah, so close to the border of Egypt, could be pacified.

Author, Composition, and Sources. The authorship of the book is difficult to determine. No doubt various persons worked on it during its long history of transmission before it reached its present form. Most scholars accept that the Chronicler (*see* Chronicles, The Books of) is responsible for the final form of the book of Ezra, for the history of Israel is not concluded at the end of 2 Chronicles (36.22–23), but continues into Ezra 1. The Chronicler is thus, from this viewpoint, responsible for editing Ezra and the commentary on the sources that he incorporated into the book.

Other scholars have held that Ezra was written and edited by an author quite different from the Chronicler, one who held a different ideology. It is true that the book of Ezra expresses some religious ideas not shared by the Chronicler. One's assessment, however, depends on how thoroughly the Chronicler edited his materials. It is probable that he did not radically change the view represented in his sources, and that this explains the differences. Although we cannot be certain, it seems likely that in the fourth century BCE the book of Ezra was edited by a later Chronicler.

In any case, it is obvious that the author of the book of Ezra used various sources and put them in chronological order. In Ezra 1–6, various documents are quoted or summarized in the final author's own words. Some of these documents are of Persian origin. Until recently, most scholars rejected the authenticity of these Persian documents, because, it was thought, no Persian king would be interested in finer details of the Jews' religious activities. However, extrabiblical texts have been discovered that show the special interest of Persian authorities in their subjects' religious activities; the edict of Cambyses on the sanctuary of Neith in Egypt and the Passover papyrus from Elephantine in Egypt are two examples. Like the Elephantine papyri, some of the official documents in Ezra are written in Imperial *Aramaic with a number of Persian loanwords. Imperial Aramaic was at that stage the chancellery language of the Persian empire. The greatest majority of Persian loanwords occur in these documents and must be regarded as a further proof of the documents' authenticity. The use of Aramaic in Ezra is not restricted to these documents, however; Ezra 4.8–6.18 and 7.12–26 are in Aramaic, providing further evidence of the book's complicated literary history.

An important source in Ezra 7–10 is the Ezra memoir, written in the first person with some parts in the third person. It is probable that we have here an actual memoir used by the Chronicler. In the sections using the first person, the Chronicler has quoted from the memoir, and in those parts using the third person he has rendered it in his own words. Scholars have pointed out that the language and style of the first-person and third-person sections are similar, and that both are in the common language of the postexilic period.

We may conclude that the book of Ezra was compiled in its present form by the later Chronicler in the fourth century BCE. All indications are that the sources used for this compilation were carefully selected and edited.

Theology. In the book of Ezra, typical religious conceptions of the postexilic period predominate. The Chronicler has not changed conceptions of Ezra to agree with his own, and this is why certain differences between the conceptions of the Chronicler and Ezra can be discerned. In the first place, the role of Yahweh as the God of history is emphasized. This is a common characteristic of Jewish thought in postexilic times. Yahweh is God not only of the Jews, but also of the whole world. He can move the heart of a mighty Persian king in favor of his own people (Ezra 9.8–9). Also, the book of Ezra clearly displays a sense of guilt for sins committed in the past by Israel. In Ezra 9.6, the Israelites' sins and guilt are represented as mounting higher than their heads and even as reaching up to heaven. This view is not present in the work of the Chronicler, but it is discernible in the work of the *Deuteronomic school. Finally, heavy emphasis is laid on the observance of the law of God. The recording of legal stipulations started before the *exile, but it was a continuous process that lasted into the time of Ezra and even later. The law was used by Ezra as a new platform to discipline the Jewish people and give them something tangible to cling to in times of distress.

See also Esdras, The Books of.

F. CHARLES FENSHAM

Faith. In the Hebrew Bible, forms of the noun *ʾĕmûnâ* or the verb *ʾmn* are usually translated as "faith" or "having faith/believing." Such faith can be expressed toward God (Jon. 3.5), toward a human being (Exod. 4.1–9), or toward both: "So the people feared the Lord and believed in the Lord and in his servant Moses" (Exod. 14.31). The terms are also used to express adherence to an idea or a set of principles, "I believe in your commandments" (Ps. 119.66).

There are other ways of expressing this kind of regard for or confidence in someone or something. In fact, forms of the verb *btḥ* are much more frequent in the Hebrew Bible but are usually translated "to trust" rather than "to have faith/believe." This difference can be explained on the basis of semantic development, but there are some instances where the meanings are very close. "He [Hezekiah] trusted in the Lord, the God of Israel" (2 Kings 18.5).

One of the best-known instances of faith in the Bible concerns Abram (*Abraham), who asks how God would make of him a great nation when he was old and his wife was sterile. The Lord asserts that Abraham will indeed have offspring that will be as numerous as the stars in the sky. In response to this promise and against all tangible evidence, Abram has faith in God and is considered to be a righteous person (Gen. 15.6; NJV: "he put his trust in the Lord").

Abram's willingness to trust God in this and other situations makes him a primary example of the biblical concept of faith. His willingness to believe and to obey God is the fulfillment of the *covenant that God had made with him. Throughout the Hebrew Bible, Abraham's descendants struggle with the issue of how to continue as a faithful people. The Psalms rejoice in the faithfulness of God (Pss. 31.5; 111.7) but lament the lack of faith shown by the people (Ps. 78.8). Isaiah warns the people, "If you do not stand firm in faith you shall not stand at all" (Isa. 7.8), and Habakkuk states that "the righteous live by their faith" (2.4).

The Greek translation of the Hebrew Bible, the *Septuagint, usually translates the *ʾmn* family of words with a form of the Greek word *pisteuein*, "to trust" or "to believe/have faith." This same family of words is used frequently in the New Testament. The author of the letter to the *Hebrews defines faith as "the assurance of things hoped for, the conviction of things not seen" (11.1) and then goes on to list the great deeds that the people of Israel had accomplished "by faith" (11.4–40).

*Paul also makes use of images of faith from the Bible, especially the faith of Abraham. In the process of justifying the mission to the *gentiles, Paul argues that Abraham was said to be righteous by having faith in God before he was *circumcised and therefore is the father of the gentiles who believe, as well as of the Jews (Rom. 4; Gal. 3).

The actual content of faith—what is believed— is described in different ways in Paul's letters. In *Romans, *righteousness will be credited to those who have faith in God who raised Jesus (Rom. 4.24) and those who believe in their hearts that God raised Jesus from the dead will be saved (Rom. 10.9). Elsewhere Paul refers to believing "in Christ Jesus" (Gal. 2.16), but it can be argued that this is an abbreviation for "faith in God who raised Jesus."

Several times Paul refers to faith with a grammatical construction that can be interpreted either as "faith in Christ" or "faith of Christ" (Gal. 2.16, 20; 3.22; Rom. 3.22, 26; Phil. 3.9). Scholarly debate centers on whether Jesus is referred to in the first sense as the object of faith or in the second as an example of faith. The NRSV translation includes footnotes that offer the latter reading as an alternative. It has also been suggested that Paul is being intentionally ambiguous with the construction, leaving both possibilities open. In this case it is interesting to note that later documents tend to specify "faith in Christ," eliminating the possibility for ambiguity (e.g., 1 Tim. 3.13; Acts 20.21).

In the *synoptic Gospels faith is the operative factor in many of Jesus' *miracles. Jesus is impressed by the faith of the centurion and so heals his son (Matt. 8.5–13 par.). Jesus marvels at the faith of those who brought the paralytic man (Matt. 9.1–8 par.) and tells the woman with a hemorrhage that her faith has made her well (Matt. 9.20–22 par.). When Jesus tells the father of a demon-possessed boy that "all things are possible to the one who believes/has faith," the man responds "I believe; help my unbelief" (Mark 9.23–24).

John's gospel emphasizes having faith (always in the verbal form) throughout and states its purpose as leading people to believe that Jesus is the *Messiah, the *Son of God (John 20.31).

"The faith" as a descriptive term for Christianity is found most clearly in *Acts and the Deutero-Pauline material (e.g., Acts 6.7; 1 Tim. 4.1).

See also Justification.

DANIEL N. SCHOWALTER

Fall, The. The Fall refers to the disobedience and the expulsion of *Adam and *Eve from the garden of *Eden. According to the *J account of *creation (Gen. 2–3), humanity—represented by Adam and Eve—initially enjoyed a life of ease and intimacy with God, but their desire to become "like gods" (Gen 3.5) led them to disobey God's prohibition against eating from the tree of knowledge. They were punished with expulsion from *paradise and condemned to a life of *suffering that was passed on to their descendants.

The biblical myth of the Fall is similar to other legends that contrast humanity's present state of suffering with an earlier time of perfection, a lost paradise or golden age. The biblical narrative is unique, however, in implying that humanity's degradation was indirectly caused by its own free choice.

The fall of divine beings played a central role in the writings of the *gnostics (second and third centuries CE), many of whom believed that creation and even human existence were caused by a precosmic error. According to the gnostics, the physical cosmos was a concrete nightmare from which the divine sparks of humanity sought to escape.

In the New Testament Paul explained that Adam, the man of flesh, brought sin and death to the world while Christ, the second Adam and the man of spirit, brought life (1 Cor., 15.21–22). Paul's view that Adam's fall introduced sin and death (Rom. 5.12) led Augustine (fifth century CE) to develop the doctrine of original sin: that Adam's fall perverted all humanity and that its effects were passed by hereditary transmission from generation to generation. The belief that Adam, as a corporate personality, was responsible for the sins of humanity was never adopted by Judaism and was resisted by Christian thinkers such as Pelagius and Julian of Eclanum (fifth century CE), but Augustine's interpretation of the Fall became the accepted doctrine of Catholic Christianity. Like all myths of a lost paradise or golden age, the story of the Fall, whether of gods or humans, is an index of humanity's yearning for a better world and an attempt to account for the problems of *evil and human suffering.

GREGORY SHAW

Family. The family in ancient Israel was a fluid and open community. The most common Hebrew terms (*mišpāḥâ* and *bêt*, "house") can designate the single household unit, the wider circle of consanguinity (Gen. 24.38), the clan, the tribe, and the nation (Amos 3.1–2). This concentric usage suggests the role of the basic family in shaping the larger community. Significantly, the *Passover, Israel's foundational ritual, was essentially a family celebration (Exod. 12.3–4, 26–27).

The basis of the family is *marriage, understood as a *covenant between the husband and wife (Prov. 2.17; Mal. 2.14). Although some texts imply a monogamous relationship (Gen. 2.18, 22–24), at least in earlier periods polygamy was an accepted practice (Deut. 21.15; 1 Sam. 1.2; 1 Kings 11.1–6), enlarging the scope of the family. And in a broader sense, the extended family included other relatives (grandparents, grandchildren, siblings) as well as slaves, servants, and resident foreigners (Gen 17.23; 46.5–7, 26–27; Exod. 20.10; Judg. 9.1).

In the extended family (the "house of the father," Hebr. *bêt 'āb*), the authority of the father was the strongest cohesive force. He arranged marriages for his children, generally within the clan (Gen 24.1–9; Deut. 7.3; Neh. 13.23–25). His patriarchal power might require drastic action against worshipers of other gods (Deut. 13.6–11). Nevertheless, the fifth commandment demanded "honor" for mother as well as father (Exod. 20.12)—perhaps very pertinent in a family that included adult offspring—and the book of Proverbs teaches the respect due equally to each parent (1.8; 6.20; 10.1; 15.20).

The family provided one of the most commonly used analogies for the relationship between Israel and God, as father (Exod. 4.22; Ps. 103.13; Prov. 3.12; Jer. 31.9; Hos. 11.1–4), and also as mother (Isa. 66.3) (see Metaphors).

In the New Testament, oikia ("house, household") is the ordinary word for family, although patria (from patēr, "father") is also used. Disobedience to parents is a sin (Rom. 1.30; 2 Tim. 3.2; see Ethical Lists), and caring for one's family is strongly inculcated (1 Tim. 3.4–5; 2 Tim. 1.5). Yet in the teaching of *Jesus, his followers must give no more than second place to even the closest family ties (Matt. 19.29; Luke 14.26); the true family of Jesus are those who do his father's will (Matt. 12.46–50 par.; cf. Luke 2.48–49).

The primary use of the word oikia is in reference to the *church. The solidarity of the family as the building block of the spiritual family of God is evident in "household" conversions and baptisms (John 4.53; Acts 11.14; 16.15, 31–34). Not only is the whole church the household of God (Eph. 2.19; 1 Tim. 3.15; 1 Pet. 4.17), but also most early Christian congregations were family or house churches, meeting in domestic buildings and led by the householders, including women and husband-and-wife joint leaders (Acts 2.46; Rom. 16.3–5; 1 Cor. 16.15, 19; Philem. 1–2). This helps explain the prominence given in the New Testament to appropriate relations between individuals in the family, including masters and slaves (Eph. 5.21–6.9; Col. 3.18–4.1; 1 Tim. 5.4, 8, 9–16; Philem. 15–16; 1 Pet. 2.18–3.7). The letters in particular are full of metaphors drawn from family life, such as childhood, adoption, sonship, and inheritance (Eph. 3.15; 1 Tim.5.1–2; Philem. 10).

See also Marriage; Women.

DAVID F. WRIGHT

Family Bible. A product of early modern Europe still in use today, a family Bible is any edition of the Bible that includes manuscript records of genealogical and other personal information specific to the owners of the book over several generations. It also symbolically associates the scriptures with the ideal of the Christian family, an association that began in the Reformation, was perfected by seventeenth-century English Puritans and German Pietists, and was furthered by eighteenth-century Anglo-American evangelicals.

Through the medieval period the costly process of copying manuscripts restricted private ownership of the Bible to only the most wealthy families. Between 1450 and 1600, however, the invention of *printing and the Reformation's vernacular *translations made it possible for many families to acquire and to read the Bible. Both Protestant and Catholic reforming theologies, moreover, emphasized biblical *authority and required a greatly increased knowledge of the Bible by the laity. So the newly available vernacular Bibles soon became objects of special veneration in which facts of family history might appropriately be inscribed.

In the seventeenth and eighteenth centuries, Puritan, Pietist, and evangelical Protestants prescribed ambitious programs of doctrinal catechesis and devotional prayer for family members. The family was viewed as a spiritual commonwealth in which parents were covenantally obligated to transmit the faith to their children. Popular devotional manuals like Philip Doddridge's On the Rise and Progress of Religion in the Soul (1745) recommended family prayer and parental exposition of the scriptures every morning and evening. This new physical presence and spiritual authority of the scriptures in daily household rituals encouraged pious families to record the events of their lives—births, baptisms, conversions, confirmations, marriages, deaths—on the pages of their Bibles.

In the nineteenth century the enormous success of the evangelical movement, especially in Victorian Anglo-America, fashioned the Bible into a cultural icon of spiritual identity, biological continuity, and family prosperity. Since 1800 virtually every English translation of the Bible has been published in a special family edition, with commemorative pages dedicated to genealogy, marriages, births, and family history, and with ornamental bindings designed for prominent display in the home. The custom of keeping a family Bible continues to be observed, especially among evangelical Protestants in the United States.

Family Bibles serve scholars as unique sources for social and religious history, but their spiritual and emotional significance was well captured by an anonymous American evangelical poet, whose popular hymn, "The Family Bible," first appeared in The Young Christian's Companion (1826):

> How painfully pleasing the fond recollection
>   Of youthful connection and innocent joy,
> While blessed with parental advice and
>   affection,

Surrounded with mercy and peace from on
  high.
I still view the chairs of my father and mother,
  The seats of their offspring, as ranged on
    each hand,
And the richest of books, which excels ev'ry
  other,
The family bible that stood on the stand.
STEPHEN A. MARINI

Fasting. Fasting in connection with prayer, penitence, and preparation for new ventures has
been practiced from early times in many cultures
and religions. The Bible recognizes it as regular
in *mourning for the dead (1 Sam. 31.13),
expressions of penitence (Neh. 9.1), intercession
(2 Sam. 12.16), and *prayer for God's aid (Judg.
20.26). Fasting was undertaken for personal reasons (Ps. 25.13), as a national act in the face of
calamity (Joel 2.15), or as a periodic liturgical
observance (Zech. 8.19); normally it involved
abstinence from all food to show dependence on
God and submission to his will. The great national and liturgical fast was that of the *Day of
Atonement (Lev. 16.29–34), but fasting was generally recognized, especially after the *exile, as
a meritorious pious practice and as a potent aid
to prayer (Tob. 12.8; Luke 2.37). Later, the
author of Isaiah 58 claimed that if fasting was
to be of value, it must be accompanied by compassion and a concern for social justice.

Jesus accepted fasting as a natural discipline,
and he is described (Matt. 4.2) as deliberately
fasting before his *temptation and the start of
his ministry, similar to the action of Moses (Exod.
24.28). Jesus' disciples, in contrast to the disciples
of *John the Baptist and those of the *Pharisees,
appear not to have fasted (Mark 2.18–19): they
were in the presence of "the bridegroom," a
parabolic reference to the *Messiah, so that fasting was inappropriate. But v. 20 envisages a time
of fasting "when the bridegroom is taken away
from them"; this verse was probably a creation
of the evangelist to justify the church's custom
of fasting on Good Friday. Certainly, fasting was
regularly observed in early Christianity, and Mark
9.29 (NRSV margin) shows how copyists reflected the commonly held view of the connection between fasting and prayer.

In Acts 9.9, Paul is described as fasting before
his baptism, and this became the usual practice
from very early times (*Didache* 7.4; Justin *Apol.*
1.61; Tertullian *Bapt.* 20), both for the candidates for baptism and for other members of the
church. As *baptism was normally celebrated at
*Easter, this prebaptismal fast was probably the
origin of the Lenten fast, which lasted forty days
in the time of Cyril of Jerusalem (late fourth
century CE), corresponding to the length of Jesus' fast at the start of his ministry.
JOHN N. SUGGIT

Fear. Throughout the Bible, references to fear
occur in nonreligious as well as in religious contexts, with two distinct areas of meaning. The
first involves emotional distress and alarm with
intense concern for impending danger or evil.
Thus, the Gibeonites excused themselves before
Joshua saying, "We were in great fear for our
lives" (Josh. 9.24). In Genesis 9.2, animals are
said to be afraid of people. The signs accompanying the coming of the *Son of Man are said
in Luke 21.26 to cause people to faint with fear.

The other area of meaning relates to allegiance to and regard for deity. Among the many
expressions in the Bible for worshiping God are
some metaphors pertaining to fear. These focus
upon *worship as an event of profound respect
with the implication of awe. In Job 15.4, Eliphaz
reprimands Job saying, "But you are doing away
with the fear of God." The fear of God involves
worshiping the Lord with deep respect and devotion. It is a religious expression and as such
implies obedience, love, and trust; see, for example, Deuteronomy 10.12–13. "People who
feared God" became an expression for the truly
religious (Mal. 3.16; Luke 18.2; Acts 10.22).
Closely related is the expression "the Fear of
Isaac" (Gen 31.42), an epithet for God, meaning
"the one whom Isaac worships" (*see* Names of
God in the Hebrew Bible).

The phrase "fear and trembling" expresses the
same two areas of meaning denoted by fear. In
Psalm 55.5 and Mark 5.33, the phrase expresses
great emotional distress, while in Psalm 2.11 and
Philippians 2.12 the phrase signifies religious
devotion.
JOHANNES P. LOUW

Feasts and Festivals. Sacred feasts and festivals
punctuated the calendar of ancient Israel. New
moons were a function of a lunar system in
which the month functioned as the basic unit for
measuring *time. The Pesaḥ festival (*Passover)
in the spring, on which unleavened bread was
eaten, was historical in character, a commemoration of the *Exodus from Egypt. By contrast,
the spring and autumn harvest festivals were

seasonal celebrations linked to the agricultural economy of ancient Israel. All three annual festivals were occasions for pilgrimage (Hebr. *ḥag*).

How feasts and new moons were celebrated depended in great measure on where *sacrifices could be offered. Israelites seeking to celebrate these occasions fully were required to do so at a proper cult site, in other words, to undertake a pilgrimage to an altar *(bāmâ)* or temple. The Bible records a protracted movement toward cult centralization and the elimination of all local and regional cult sites. The doctrine that all sacrifice should be restricted to a central temple was to have serious practical implications for the scheduling of pilgrimage festivals and all occasions when sacrifices were offered.

In 622 BCE King *Josiah of Judah issued a series of edicts, recorded in 2 Kings 22–23, forbidding all sacrificial worship outside the Temple of Jerusalem. Deuteronomy 12 restricts the offering of sacrifice to a single cult place *(māqôm)* to be selected by the God of Israel. It has recently been argued that the policy of cult centralization originated in the northern Israelite kingdom of the mid- to late-eighth century BCE before its fall to the Assyrians in 722 BCE. The Judean king *Hezekiah had attempted to implement this policy (2 Kings 18.3–4,22), but since he was succeeded by *Manasseh, the heterodox king who ruled throughout most of the seventh century BCE, no progress was made in eliminating the *bāmôt* before the time of Josiah. A young king who had returned to the Lord sincerely (2 Kings 23.25), Josiah acted effectively to eliminate places of worship throughout the land.

It is logical, therefore, to conclude that most of the significant changes in the celebration of Israelite festivals went into effect only after Josiah's edicts were promulgated and that most of them were heralded in Deuteronomy. Some scholars dispute this reconstruction, however, and date the priestly codes (*P), which reflect basic changes in worship, to an earlier period.

The New Moon. The new moon (1 Sam. 20.5, 18; 2 Kings 4.23; Isa. 1.13; Hos. 2.11) is sometimes referred to as "the head of the month" (Num. 28.11; etc.). By all indications, the celebration of the new moon was an important occasion in biblical times. This importance may have diminished in time, since the growing importance of the *Sabbath eventually reduced reliance on the lunar calendar, introducing the week as a unit of time.

The account in 1 Samuel 20, set in the early monarchy, suggests that the new moon was the occasion of a sacred feast *(zebaḥ)* celebrated by the family. Fixing the precise time of the moon's "birth" was necessary for scheduling the festivals, whose dates are formulated as numbered days of the month. According to priestly law (Num. 28.11–15), the new moon was to be celebrated in the public cult by a triad of sacrifices—the burnt offering, the grain offering, and the libation, preceded by the purificatory sin offering. The new moon of the seventh month, in the early autumn (Tishrei), enjoyed special status because it heralded the autumn ingathering festival, the main pilgrimage festival of the year (Lev. 23.23–25; Num. 29.1–16; Ps. 81.3). On that new moon, the ram's horn was sounded to announce the autumn pilgrimage. In later Judaism, the new moon of the seventh month became Roʾsh ha-Shanah, the Jewish New Year.

The Festival of Unleavened Bread and the Passover. The first pilgrimage festival in the spring commemorated the Exodus from Egypt. In the Book of the Covenant, the earliest of the law codes in the Torah, this festival is called "the pilgrimage festival of unleavened bread" (*ḥag hammaṣṣôt;* Exod. 23.15). It is preceded on the eve of the festival by the "paschal sacrifice" ([*zebaḥ*] *pesaḥ;* Exod. 12.21–13.10).

This festival began on the new moon of the month of ripening grain ears (*ʾābîb*) and lasted seven days, during which only unleavened bread was to be eaten (*see* Leaven). The pilgrimage occurred on the seventh day. On the eve of the first day the paschal sacrifice, consisting of a lamb, was offered by the family near its home. According to Exodus 12.8–9, it was roasted whole over an open fire, a practice still followed by the *Samaritans. Blood from the sacrifice was poured on the threshold and then spattered on the lintel and doorposts with a twig of hyssop. The application of the blood expressed the theme of protection. The sense of the Hebrew verb *pāsaḥ,* from which Pesaḥ derives, has been misunderstood to mean "skip, pass over" (whence the name "Passover"), whereas it more properly means "to straddle, stand over," hence "protect" (Isa. 31.5). The God of Israel was pictured as standing over the homes of the Israelites in Egypt to protect them from the plague of the firstborn.

Egyptian bondage was symbolized by the bitter herbs, eaten together with the unleavened bread and the paschal sacrifice. This festival is a *môʿēd,* "appointed time," a term that indicates its observance on the same date annually (Exod. 13.10; 23.15), and the same is true of the other annual festivals.

In Deuteronomy 16.3 a rationale is given for the unleavened bread. It symbolized affliction, and its preparation was reminiscent of the hasty departure of the fleeing Israelites. Most significant in the provisions of Deuteronomy 16.1–8 is the requirement that the paschal sacrifice be offered at the single cult place selected by God and that it be prepared in the usual manner by boiling major portions of the meat in pots (1 Sam. 2.11–17), with the rest of the victim burned on the altar.

The shift of venue from the home to the central sanctuary parallels the provisions of Josiah's edict (2 Kings 23.21–23) proclaiming the celebration of the paschal sacrifice in the Temple of Jerusalem, something that, we are told, had never occurred before (but see 2 Chron. 30). The paschal sacrifice now did double duty as the festival offering of the first day. This is indicated by the composite term, "the sacred feast of the pilgrimage festival of the Pesaḥ" (Exod. 34.25).

According to Deuteronomy 16, the pilgrimage began with the paschal sacrifice. Israelites would rise the next morning and return home, continuing to eat unleavened bread for the remaining six days of the festival, and observing the seventh day in their settlements as a solemn assembly, on which labor was prohibited. The result of the Deuteronomic legislation was a brief pilgrimage that allowed farmers to return home at the busiest time of the year.

The priestly prescriptions for this festival reveal even further changes in its celebration. The date is the fifteenth of the first month (Nisan), preceded by the paschal sacrifice on the fourteenth, in the late afternoon (Exod. 12.18; Lev. 23.5–6; Num. 28.16–17). From the formulation of these priestly laws it is clear that the paschal sacrifice, like those offered on each of the seven days of the festival, occurred in the Temple. On both the first and the seventh days there is to be a "sacred assembly," on which labor is forbidden. Numbers 28.19–24 specifies the offerings of the public cult. The difficulty implicit in ordaining a seven-day pilgrimage to a central sanctuary would be dealt with, as we will see, by deferring the second pilgrimage. Proclaiming both the first and the seventh days as sacred assemblies satisfied the earlier pilgrimage of the Book of the Covenant as well as the Deuteronomic pilgrimage of the first night.

The Spring Harvest Festival of the First Grain Yield. In the Book of the Covenant (Exod. 23.16) this festival is named "the pilgrimage festival of reaping" (*ḥag haqqāṣîr*), that is, of the first yield of the barley crop. No specific date is provided in Exodus, but we may assume that it would occur quite soon after the Pesaḥ early in Iyyar.

In Deuteronomy 16.9–12 we observe the dramatic effects of the Deuteronomic requirement of celebration at a central sanctuary: the spring festival of reaping is deferred seven weeks; thus, the festival is named "the pilgrimage festival of weeks" (*ḥag šābuʿōt*). The Israelites were to count off a period of seven weeks and then present an offering of first fruits, now consisting of wheat, not barley (Exod. 34.26; Deut. 26.1–11; Lev. 2.14–16).

The most logical reason for the deferral was the anticipated difficulty of undertaking two extended pilgrimages to a central temple at the busiest season of the agricultural year. Priestly law, represented by Leviticus 23.9–22, retains the deferral instituted by Deuteronomy. An earlier desacralization of the new barley crop is, however, ordained for the day of the original festival of reaping, soon after the Pesaḥ festival. In Leviticus 23 the spring festival of reaping is not designated a pilgrimage at all; the first fruits were merely to be delivered to the central temple from the Israelite settlements (v. 17). This celebration, on the fiftieth day of the period of counting, was rendered more elaborate by including the "sacred gifts of greeting" (*šĕlāmîm* [v. 19; NRSV: "sacrifice of well-being"]), along with loaves made of semolina wheat. The counting of seven weeks was to commence on a Sunday and end on a Sunday, seven weeks later, so that seven actual sabbatical weeks would have passed, not merely forty-nine days. The fiftieth day is designated "a sacred assembly," on which labor is prohibited. Numbers 28.26–31 prescribes a complete regimen of sacrifices to be offered in the Temple and it curiously no longer includes the "sacred gifts of greeting."

In summary, we observe major changes in the celebration, scheduling, and essential meaning of the spring festival.

The Autumn Pilgrimage Festival of Ingathering. In the Book of the Covenant (Exod. 23.16) the autumn festival is called "the pilgrimage festival of ingathering" (*ḥag hāʾāsîp*), namely, "when you gather in your products from the field." It was to occur "at the outset of the year," more precisely, soon after the start of the two-month period of ingathering, corresponding to Tishri-Marheshvan (September–October). Psalm 81.3 indicates that this festival began on the full moon, at the middle of the month, rather than on the new moon. The pilgrimage lasted one day.

Once again, Deuteronomy (16.13–15) introduces a dramatic change. There this festival is named "the pilgrimage festival of booths" (*ḥag hassukkôt*) and is scheduled to last seven days. It was to occur somewhat later than the ingathering, at the time when the produce of the fields, vineyards, and groves was processed, in the vat and on the threshing floor.

This autumn pilgrimage was the major event of the year, bringing large numbers of Israelites to the Temple. For this reason it was an appropriate time for the dedication of Solomon's Temple (1 Kings 8.2).

Leviticus 23, in two successive statements (vv. 33–36; 39–42), elaborates on the festival of booths, which was a particularly joyous occasion. A rationale is provided for living in booths, namely, the conditions characteristic of the *wilderness experience. Greenery was utilized to symbolize the fertility of the land, and an eighth day with a solemn assembly was added. Like Leviticus, Numbers 29.12–38 specifies sacrifices for all eight days, with the first and eighth days designated as days of rest.

A more realistic approach would seem to suggest that the theme of "booths" was introduced in Deuteronomy as a consequence of the restriction of pilgrimage to one central temple, which also accounts for the extension of the festival to last longer than initially intended. Dwelling in temporary booths became necessary for the numerous pilgrims arriving in the capital from all over the land and, in later times, from the Diaspora as well (Neh. 8.13–18; Zech. 14.16).

The Day of Atonement. The first reference to the *Day of Atonement (*yôm hakkippūrîm*) is found in Leviticus 16, which sets forth the rites of expiation and purification to be performed by the high *priest in the sanctuary. The principal function of this day was the purification of the sanctuary and priesthood, in advance of the autumn pilgrimage festival.

The rites of expiation were quite elaborate, and they included the dispatch of the scapegoat (*see* Azazel) into the wilderness, bearing the sins of the people. On this day, the high priest entered the Holy of Holies (*see* Temple) to seek expiation for sins. In Zechariah 7.5 this day is referred to as "the fast-day of the seventh month," and its importance seems to have increased during the exilic and postexilic periods, in the wake of the national disaster of 587/586 BCE. The postexilic prophet whose words are preserved in Isaiah 58 emphasizes that the God of Israel wants more than cultic purification and sets down eth-

ical, human goals whose pursuit alone may render the atonement process acceptable to God.

Purim. The book of *Esther relates the saga of deliverance that accounts for the annual Purim feast on the fourteenth day of Adar (and, in some areas, on the fifteenth day as well). Set in the reign of Ahasuerus (possibly Artaxerxes I), the Persian ruler of the fifth century BCE, the story emphasizes divine providence over Israel, in which Esther, the queen, and Mordecai, the court counselor, foil the conspiracy of Haman, the wicked enemy of the Jewish people residing in the far-flung provinces of the Achaemenid empire. Jewish custom is to read the Esther Scroll on this occasion and to exchange gifts in celebration of deliverance.

Hanukkah. There is an additional festival, unmentioned in the Hebrew Bible, which became part of later Judaism. The generic word *ḥănukkâ*, "dedication," occurs in such passages as Numbers 7.10–11; Psalm 30 (title); and Nehemiah 12.27; but the festival of that name is first mentioned in 1 Maccabees 4.59 in its complete form as "the Dedication of the Altar" and referred to simply as "the Dedication" in John 10.22. Hanukkah is an eight-day festival whose celebration begins on the twenty-fifth day of Chislev and which was patterned after the Tabernacles festival of the harvest season, as is indicated by statements in 2 Maccabees 1.9, 18; 2.1; 10.6–8.

Hanukkah celebrates the rededication of the Second Temple of Jerusalem in 164 BCE by the victorious *Maccabees, members of the priestly Hasmoneans of Modein, after its defilement by the Seleucid ruler Antiochus IV Epiphanes, acting with the collaboration of hellenizing Jews. It is the practice to kindle lights on Hanukkah, adding one light each day throughout the eight days of the festival, and to recite psalms of praise, the Hallel (Pss. 113–118).

Conclusion. After the Roman destruction of Jerusalem and of the Second Temple in 70 CE, when all sacrificial rites became inoperative, major changes in observance affect virtually all biblical feasts. Yet all biblical feasts continue to be celebrated to this day, both in Israel and wherever Jewish communities exist.

BARUCH A. LEVINE

Feminism and the Bible.

History. As early as 1837, the American abolitionist lecturer Sarah Grimke suggested that biblical interpretation was deliberately biased against women in order to keep them in subjection. She urged women to become trained as scholars and to investigate the sacred text for themselves. By the end of the nineteenth century, a few women had indeed become trained as biblical scholars, but they were not generally using their expertise for the purpose of challenging scriptural arguments for traditional views of women. The foremost nineteenth-century example of such a challenge, *The Woman's Bible* (1895–1898), was largely the work of nonspecialists, twenty woman suffragists under the leadership of Elizabeth Cady Stanton. Already in this work and in the responses to it, hints of the shape of the twentieth-century discussion can be seen. Some contributors emphasized the heroic character of little-known women in the Bible. Others concentrated on historical development and change as a rationale for rejecting direct application of biblical cultural norms to their own setting. Some women biblical scholars declined to become involved in an unpopular project, while some feminists urged that the whole project was unnecessary because the Bible itself was an irrelevant relic of the past.

For about seventy years after publication of *The Woman's Bible* the question of feminist biblical interpretation received little attention. Renewed interest in women's rights in the 1960s led to renewed attention to the influence of the Bible on the status and role of women in Jewish and Christian traditions. Feminists quickly recognized the need to reassess not only the Bible but also the centuries of biblical interpretation undertaken mostly by male scholars. Published literature on the topic increased exponentially, and by the 1980s the annual output of books and articles was twentyfold the total publication list of the first half of the century.

Areas of Inquiry. Recent feminist study has contributed to biblical scholarship in at least five major areas.

1. It has emphasized more systematic historical inquiry into the status and role of women in biblical cultures (e.g., Bernadette Brooten, *Women Leaders in the Ancient Synagogue;* Phyllis Bird, "The Place of Women in the Israelite Cultus," in *Ancient Israelite Religion: Essays in Honor of Frank Moore Cross,* edited by P. D. Miller et al.). Such investigations attempt to take into account not only the paucity of biblical materials pertinent to the inquiry but also the androcentrism (whether unconscious or deliberate) of the biblical writers. They recognize that the Bible gives only occasional and indirect evidence about the everyday life of the common people, and especially about the life of women. The inquiries make use of extrabiblical writings, while recognizing that the same limitations apply to many of these texts as well. *Archaeology and sociological studies of preindustrial societies provide additional evidence and controls for such investigations (*see* Social Sciences and the Bible). The variety of linguistic and other specializations required for this effort demands teamwork among scholars and the gradual building of a body of data over a period of many years.

2. A more complete and balanced picture of the actual content of the Bible has been encouraged by highlighting texts pertaining to women that were not well known even among people familiar with the Bible. Among the many examples are the inheritance and marriage of the daughters of Zelophehad (Num. 27; 36), the rape of the Levite's concubine (Judg. 19), and the frequent inclusion of women in *Luke's gospel.

3. Alternative interpretations of familiar biblical texts have been introduced to show that the texts themselves do not necessarily present a negative view of women, but that biases against women have been attributed to these texts by a long succession of androcentric interpreters. Prominent examples of such studies are those arguing that male and female are created equally in the image of God and that *Adam is equally responsible with his wife *Eve for their disobedience in the garden (Gen. 1–3; e.g., Phyllis Trible, *God and the Rhetoric of Sexuality*), and those arguing that *Paul's insistence on women's silence in church refers to a specific local problem and would not have been generalized, even by Paul, to all women in all churches (1 Cor. 14.34; e.g., Elizabeth Schüssler Fiorenza, *In Memory of Her*).

4. A more complete and balanced picture of the God portrayed in the Bible has been encouraged by emphasizing texts in which the deity is compared to a woman (e.g., a midwife [Ps. 22.9], or a woman crying out during childbirth [Isa. 42.14], or one who sweeps her home to search for a lost coin [Luke 15.3–10]). Such texts, supplemented by texts using the imagery of inanimate objects for the deity (e.g., God as rock or shield), are used to undergird and reinforce the classic teaching that God is not biologically male, but is indeed beyond male and female. The small number of texts comparing God to a woman, together with the fact that these are generally comparisons (not direct appellations), results in disagreement about the significance of

these resources, particularly whether they provide a warrant for referring to the biblical deity as "mother" in contemporary theology and prayer. (*See* Metaphors.)

5. Fresh translations of all or parts of the Bible seek to reduce the amount of gender-exclusive language in the text. Some of these versions have made such changes only where scholars considered them warranted by the original Hebrew and Greek texts (e.g., the *New Revised Standard Version*), while others have eliminated many more masculine references in the text (e.g., *The Inclusive Language Lectionary*). Debate about the relative merits of the two approaches focuses on the question of how an ancient text can and should be heard in a contemporary setting: should its androcentric character be left plainly visible so that it remains true to its own time and culture, or should the androcentrism be softened so that the presumed universal message can be heard more clearly?

Options in Feminist Hermeneutics. As in the time of Stanton and *The Women's Bible,* some feminists still conclude that the Bible's androcentrism is so deep-seated that the book can no longer be regarded as authoritative for their lives. These persons tend generally to break away openly from their tradition and to give attention to the Bible only as a document having a negative influence on western culture.

Many feminists, however, do continue to regard the Bible as authoritative and remain active in church or synagogue. The goal of these feminists is to describe how this biblical authority persists despite the unacceptable patriarchal context and androcentric bias they recognize in scripture. While there are many differences in detail and nuance among the approaches to the problem, these approaches may be broadly categorized into three types.

1. Close study of texts pertaining to women, with emphasis on showing that these texts do not support the patriarchal structures and assumptions of contemporary society. This approach incorporates both the highlighting of texts previously ignored and the reinterpretation of texts traditionally used to support patriarchal structures in society. The difficulties encountered in the approach are twofold. First, there is no unanimity among scholars as to the correct interpretation of many of the debated texts. Even the criteria by which correctness might be ascertained cannot be agreed upon, since some scholars would admit various interpretations that are

plausible as literary readings of a text, while others would insist that the interpretation be evaluated in terms of the probable intent of the original author addressing the ancient cultural context. Second, there are some texts that present a patriarchal view of women for which no positive reinterpretation seems possible. Thus, the question of criteria for choosing some texts as more important than others inevitably arises. Although the problem of selectivity is as old as theology based on the Bible, the difficulty of establishing criteria or the desire to avoid such selection leads some feminists to frustration with this approach.

2. Appeal to the Bible generally (not specifically to texts about women) for a critique of patriarchy. This approach is often closely associated with the concerns of liberation theology in its search to show that the Bible challenges any viewpoint or action that demeans, limits, or controls others because of their race, class, or—in this case—gender. The prophets' criticism of economic exploitation, for example, or Jesus' criticism of ethnic narrowness, is extended by analogy to authorize criticism of the oppression of women (e.g., Rosemary Ruether, *Sexism and God-Talk*). While this approach has many adherents, others criticize what they regard as a lack of clear criteria for such extension by analogy.

3. Study of texts about women with special attention to the ways in which their patriarchal setting or androcentric worldview continues to be reflected in contemporary culture (e.g., Trible, *Texts of Terror*). In this approach, the texts function rather like a mirror, enabling modern readers to see their own situations more accurately by focusing on similarities between attitudes toward and treatment of women in biblical times and in the twentieth century. Of course, it is precisely such similarity that leads some feminists to reject the Bible as oppressive and useless as a basis for advocating change. But for those who do not reject the Bible, the mirror is expected to lead to a value judgment, the recognition that such patriarchy is wrong. The basis for this value judgment generally lies in the resources of either the first or the second approaches above.

Feminists who continue to work with the Bible as more than a historical document generally agree that the theological problem of *authority is central to their *hermeneutic task (Letty Russell, ed., *Feminist Interpretation of the Bible*). The chief poles around which the debate is structured remain those familiar to Christian theology generally: scripture versus tradition, "canon within the canon," and letter versus spirit. A review of the areas of inquiry and hermeneutic options outlined above provides illustration of each of these themes. The scripture-versus-tradition debate, for example, takes shape in the consideration of whose interpretations of the Adam and Eve story should hold sway, whether recent feminist ones or those familiar from the New Testament and church fathers. "Canon within the canon" identifies the dilemma of those who recognize discordant perspectives on women present in scripture. The debate over Bible translation is part of the larger issue of text versus spirit. Many more illustrations could be cited. They highlight the reality that the questions posed by feminism are not peripheral, but rather are central to the understanding of the Bible by communities of faith in every generation.

See also Women.

KATHARINE DOOB SAKENFELD

Festivals. *See* Feasts and Festivals.

Flesh and Spirit. The word "flesh" literally means soft tissue, as distinguished from skin and bones (e.g., Job 19.20); by extension it can mean the human race (Isa. 40.5; Joel 2.28) and even all animal life (Gen. 6.19). "Spirit" translates words that in both Hebrew and Greek mean "wind" (Gen. 8.1; cf. 1.1) or "breath" (Gen. 6.17; Ezek. 37.5), as well as vital essence. Biblical writers do not normally combine the two terms to designate the totality of human nature. The body/soul dichotomy that so fascinated Greek philosophy is not generally presupposed, even when the two terms occur in close proximity; thus, Matthew 26.41 is not a real exception to this rule. (*See* Human Person.)

In the New Testament, particularly in the letters of Paul, "flesh" and "spirit" often appear as contrasting rather than complementary terms, representing the natural and divine spheres respectively; this usage also occurs earlier (see Isa. 31.3). Thus, for Paul "flesh" often has a negative connotation, meaning the sphere of human rebellion against God (Rom. 8.3–13; Gal. 5.16–25), as contrasted with the "spirit," which is

sometimes identified as the "spirit of God" (e.g., Rom. 8.9; *see* Holy Spirit).

DOUGLAS R. A. HARE

Flood, The. Today, as in the past, catastrophic floods are experienced universally, and stories are told about them. The stories share many features: land submerged, multitudes drowned, survivors in a boat. People living in basically similar ways in separate places will react similarly; hence, common features in flood stories are predictable and are not proof that all such ancient stories refer to one great flood.

On the other hand, the *Babylonian and Hebrew stories share so much that a connection between them can hardly be denied. Surviving copies of the Babylonian story come from the seventeenth and seventh centuries BCE (the Epic of Atrahasis and the Epic of *Gilgamesh, respectively); the age of the account in Genesis 6–9 in its present form is debated. Both narratives have a pious hero warned by his god to build a great ship (*see* Ark) and to load it with his family and selected animals in order to escape the coming deluge. Once all others have perished, the ship grounds on a mountain in Armenia (*see* Ararat), a sacrifice pleases the god, and a divine oath follows never to send another flood. The later Babylonian version describes the hero releasing birds to seek vegetation, but the clay tablets on which the earlier text is recorded have been damaged where that episode might have occurred.

Both the older Babylonian account (Atrahasis) and the Hebrew account belong to larger compositions passing from the creation of human beings to later history, the flood, and its aftermath. Other Babylonian records show a wider tradition preserving names of kings from the beginning of the human race onward, interrupted by the flood. Genesis 5 and 11 present comparable lists in a comparable context. All these similarities indicate a close connection. Scholars often claim that the Hebrew flood story depends on the Babylonian, with modifications in the interest of Israel's monotheistic faith. Consideration of certain differences, however, makes it more likely that both depend upon a common original.

Whether such a flood occurred, or not, is impossible to prove. Archaeologists finding layers of silt in three Babylonian cities associated them with the flood, but each was confined to one place and they were not contemporary. What physical traces such a flood would leave is debatable; though Genesis may imply a global flood, it need not, for the Hebrew word translated as "earth" (6.17; etc.) also means "land, country" (e.g., 10.10), so the narrative could report a deluge limited to the writer's known world.

According to Genesis 9.8–10, God promised never again to send "a flood to destroy the earth." The *covenant with *Noah (9.12–17) sets human society on a basis of individual responsibility, and Genesis goes on to trace this concept in the special revelation that God gave to the line he chose.   ALAN MILLARD

Forgiveness. The several Hebrew and Greek words translated "forgive" fall into two general and overlapping meanings. The first refers to financial matters and involves the annulment of the obligation to repay what is owed, as in Matthew 18.32 (see Loans and Interest). The other meaning is much more frequent and concerns the reestablishment of an interpersonal relationship that has been disrupted through some misdeed. Thus, in Genesis 50.17, *Joseph is implored by his brothers to forgive the evil that they did to him.

Both meanings are applied to God's gracious pardoning of people's transgressions; note how in the two versions of the *Lord's Prayer, in Matthew's version (6.12) God is asked to forgive debts, in Luke's (11.4) it is sins. Various *metaphors are used to express forgiveness of sins, such as those clustered in Psalm 51: blotting out, washing, purging, hiding the face. Even more vivid language can be used, as in Isaiah 38.17, Jeremiah 31.34, and Micah 7.19: "he will tread our iniquities under foot . . . cast all our sins into the depths of the sea." Such expressive phrasing highlights the completeness of God's forgiveness, which is to serve as a model for human conduct (Luke 6.36).
See also Mercy of God.   JOHANNES P. LOUW

Fornication. Like the Greek word *porneia* that it often translates, "fornication" means extramarital or illicit sexual intercourse; it can also mean "sexual immorality" in a broader sense (see, e.g., 1 Cor. 5.1; 6.9).

Warnings against sexual immorality occur repeatedly in the New Testament, especially in Paul and in the book of Revelation; it was apparently an issue especially for gentile Christians

(see Acts 15.20; Rev. 2.14, 20–21; 17.2; see Ethical Lists).

In Matthew 5.32 and 19.9 *porneia* (NRSV: "unchastity") is a justification for *divorce, but its meaning is not clear. Is it *adultery, or some premarital conduct discovered only after *marriage (cf. Deut. 24.1)? Whether committed before or after marriage, it might denote any of the offenses condemned in Leviticus 18. It is unlikely to be merely marriage within the forbidden degrees.
See also Prostitution; Sex.   DAVID F. WRIGHT

Fourth Gospel. See John, The Gospel According to.

Frankincense. Frankincense is an aromatic gum-resin that emits a strong, pleasant odor when burned. It is extracted from trees of genus *Boswellia* native to southern *Arabia and northern Somalia. In ancient Israel, frankincense was compounded with other aromatics to make *incense (Exod. 30.34–38), used as an element in offerings to Yahweh (Lev. 2.1–2, 14–16), and displayed with the bread of the Presence (Lev. 24.7). In the New Testament, frankincense is one of the symbolic gifts of the *Magi to the infant Jesus (Matt. 2.11). Throughout antiquity frankincense was the object of a lucrative long-distance trade between southern Arabia and the Levant (Isa. 60.6; Jer. 6.20; Pliny, *Natural History* 12.30–32).
See also Myrrh.   JOSEPH A. GREENE

Freud and the Bible. The views of Sigmund Freud (1856–1939) on religion are well known. He proclaimed to his friend Oscar Pfister, a Lutheran pastor, that he was a "godless Jew" and that only such a one would have discovered the secrets of psychoanalysis. He prided himself on being an intrepid man of science, a conquistador of the mind, who cherished his Enlightenment attitude toward religion and clung to his avowed agnosticism until the end of his life. He admired Baruch Spinoza, the seventeenth-century thinker, who in the spirit of the philosophes proclaimed that one had to read the Bible just as critically as any other book. For all that, Freud's attitudes toward religion were not so simple—the superficial view does not take into account his own ambivalent conflicts about religion and the degree of his own obsessional superstition and even credulity. His view of the Bible reflects this ambiguity and ambivalence. We can discuss the problem in terms of Freud's early exposure to the Bible, his ambivalence toward it, his use of the Bible, and finally the special problem of his treatment of Moses.

Early Familiarity with the Bible. Freud's frequent denials of any meaningful religious training were long accepted as authentic testimony and consistent with his staunch atheism and agnosticism. But recently material has come to light that casts this supposition in doubt, suggesting that Freud's exposure to traditional Judaism may have been more extensive than he implied. In fact, Freud's early religious formation was considerable. His parents both came from traditional Orthodox families and remained Orthodox believers, but they did not follow all the prescribed practices. According to Ernest Jones (1957), they tended to be freethinking, but only after their move from Freiberg in Moravia to Vienna did they dispense with dietary observances and rituals of their Hasidic life-style—presumably in the service of accommodation. The Seder on the eve of *Passover continued to be observed, along with Christmas and Easter.

Freud's father Jacob was a devoted student of the *Torah and was well versed in Jewish lore and tradition, and he had attained a position of considerable respect for his scholarly knowledge of scripture. His familiarity and mastery of biblical texts in the original Hebrew was exceptional. The picture of the family religious atmosphere remains unclear, with conflicting accounts from involved observers—the divergences probably relating to what phase of the family experience was being described. There seems little doubt, in the light of recent research, that little Sigmund had considerable exposure to religious practices and traditions and particularly that he was exposed to extensive and intensive study of the Bible. He was a pupil of Samuel Hammerschlag, a Hebrew scholar of moderate Reform views, and studied the Hebrew language and the Bible from age seven through thirteen. Study of Hebrew was featured in every class, and special emphasis was given to the Torah. Freud was not only Hammerschlag's prize pupil during those years, but he also enjoyed a close and affectionate relationship with his old mentor. Freud's later denials of any knowledge of Hebrew might have been due to a lapse of memory or even a retrospective distortion.

One of the prize possessions of the Freud family was the remarkable edition of the Bible by Ludwig Philippson—the biblical texts were accompanied by numerous discussions of biblical history and comparative religion. Freud would have been quite familiar with this work. He commented in his *Autobiographical Study* (1925) that he had been deeply engrossed in the Bible from as soon as he was able to read and that this experience had had a lasting effect on him.

But Freud took pains to minimize his early religious background and may thereby have promoted a shibboleth that has persisted through the subsequent years of Freud scholarship. Peter Gay, for example, in *A Godless Jew* (1987) dismisses the years of study with Hammerschlag as merely reinforcing the religious indifference of Freud's home—"Hammerschlag was far more interested in ethics than in theology, let alone the Hebrew language." This would support Freud's repeated claim that he knew no Hebrew and that his religious upbringing was negligible. He wrote in 1930, "My father spoke the sacred language as well as German or better. He let me grow up in complete ignorance of everything that concerned Judaism." It seems that this declaration cannot be taken at face value and must be reassessed in the light of new evidence to the contrary.

Attitude toward the Bible. Freud's attitude toward the Bible was mixed, reflecting his underlying ambivalence toward his father. When Freud turned thirty-five, his father sent him the family Bible with the following inscription:

My dear Son,

It was in the seventh year of your age that the spirit of God began to move you to learning. I would say that the spirit of God speaks to you: "Read in My book; there will be opened to you sources of knowledge and of the intellect." It is the Book of Books; it is the well that wise men have dug and from which lawgivers have drawn the waters of their knowledge.

You have seen in this Book the vision of the Almighty, you have heard willingly, you have done and have tried to fly high upon the wings of the Holy Spirit. Since then I have preserved the same Bible. Now, on your thirty-fifth birthday, I have brought it out from its retirement and I send it to you as a token of love from your old father.

Curiously, this inscription, so redolent with biblical allusions, was written in Hebrew. The puzzle remains why Jacob would have addressed such a poignant sentiment to his son who professed to have no knowledge of the language. Certainly one supposition is that Jacob would have known that his son could well understand his inscription. Study of Jacob's language has concluded that he was neither a devout nor nationalistic Jew, but one of the Haskalah who envisioned Judaism as the epitome of Enlightenment rationalism—a characteristic view of Freud himself. Moreover, among the books discovered in Freud's library after his death was just such a Bible in Hebrew and German, with copious marginal notes in Freud's hand. Clearly Freud was more of a student of the Bible than he admitted.

Freud could not reconcile his staunch scientific outlook with any credibility of the Bible. He wrote in a letter in 1939, "The way you are able to reconcile esteem for scientific research with belief in the reliability of the biblical report calls forth my fullest admiration. I could not manage the feat. . . . But whence do you take the right to monopolize the truth for the Bible? I suppose it simply means: I believe because I believe." Whether he was at ease with his disbelief is open to question. If he could bring no belief to the biblical texts, they continued to exercise a fascination over and attraction for him.

Use of the Bible. Freud tended to regard the Bible as a great book of the Western literary tradition, but he did not credit it with any validity or inspiration beyond that. The Bible took its place in his mind along with other great literary works of Western culture, and his use of it was much like his references to other literary sources. His knowledge of European literature in general, both ancient and modern, was extensive—he must have been a voracious reader throughout his life. But in this regard the Bible held no special place. He even quipped at one point that the writings of Karl *Marx seemed to have replaced the Bible and the Qur'ān as sources of revelation, even though they were no more free of contradictions than the sacred books.

Consequently, although scriptural references are scattered through Freud's writings, they are used in the same vein as his references to other literary sources—as allusions or images utilized to make a point, draw a comparison, or illustrate a conclusion. The references span both Testaments, suggesting that Freud had a ready familiarity with the biblical material. References to the *Pentateuch predominate, but occasional allusions to the historical books or the Psalms are also found. Use of other books of the Hebrew Bible, such as the Song of Solomon, is incidental. The New Testament seems to have taken a back seat. The outstanding exception to this pattern is in Freud's treatment of the Moses theme.

Freud and Moses. Freud's first mention of *Moses was in a letter to Carl *Jung in 1908 in which he refers to Jung as *Joshua, who would lead the chosen people into the Promised Land, while Freud, like Moses, would only be able to view it from a distance. The metaphor of the *Promised Land was one of Freud's favorites and was a frequent reference in his letters to Wilhelm Fliess, his longtime friend and correspondent. The meaning shifts in various contexts—at one point it is Rome, the center of Christianity; at another it becomes the meaning of dreams; and toward the end of his life it was the riddle of Moses and the birth of *monotheism.

Freud's closest engagement with the biblical texts came at the end of his life in his attempt to rewrite the Moses legend in *Moses and Monotheism* (1939). It is flawed by faulty data selection and lacks appropriate methodology and verification; its conceptual structure is built on the sand of unverifiable hypotheses. It was in fact a kind of family romance, which Freud dubbed his "historical novel." Freud had been fascinated with the figure of Moses and probably strongly identified with the great prophet who led his people into the Promised Land—a metaphor for Freud himself, who led the way into the undiscovered continent of the unconscious. In 1901, he saw Michelangelo's powerful statue of Moses and became absorbed in it; he would spend weeks studying, sketching, and analyzing the statue and finally write his essay that transformed the traditional view of Moses into Freud's own vision of restrained power—a concrete expression of Freud's own ideal of the intellectual restraint of passion. He wrote of it: "Michelangelo has placed a different Moses on the tomb of the Pope, one superior to the historical or traditional Moses. He had modified the theme of the broken tablets; he does not let Moses break them in his wrath, but makes him be influenced by the danger that they will be broken and makes him calm that wrath, or at any rate prevent it from becoming an act. In this way he has added something new and more than human to the figure of Moses; so that the giant frame with its tremendous physical power becomes only a concrete expression of the highest mental achievement that is possible in man, that of struggling successfully against an inward passion for the sake of a cause to which he has devoted himself."

Clearly his identification with the figure of Moses was a powerful theme in Freud's thinking about himself and his religious views. The writing of *Moses and Monotheism* became a final effort to resolve his ambivalent identification with the figure of Moses and through him of his deep-seated conflict and ambivalence regarding his father. It became an act of rebellion, rising up against the religion of his father and toppling its hero. He wrote, "A hero is a man who stands up manfully against his father and in the end victoriously overcomes him." Moses was the leader of his people, the prophet who brought a new revelation and founded a new religion. The image of the prophet who was without honor in his own country, yet would finally prevail and be universally accepted, was part of Freud's vision.

Freud's writing of the Moses book reflected his deep study of the Pentateuch and the critical scholarship of his day. He was strongly influenced by the higher biblical criticism of his day—Julius Wellhausen was an important influence, along with William Robertson Smith, whom Freud quotes often. In Freud's rendering, Moses became an Egyptian and the chosen people were thus deprived of one of their great cultural heroes. Freud reviewed the story of Amenhotep IV (Ahknaton), who rebelled against the gods of his father and established the monotheistic cult of Aten. Moses would have brought the monotheistic cult with him as a new revelation to the chosen people. This rendering of the origins of monotheism has been countered by subsequent biblical research.

Moreover, following the rather flimsy thesis of Ernst Sellin, who claimed to have discovered evidence of the murder of Moses, Freud advanced the hypothesis that Moses was prevented from entering the Promised Land because the Jews had rebelled against his imposition of the worship of the Egyptian god Aten and killed the prophet. Freud's Moses does not reach the Promised Land because he was murdered by his sons—the idea recapitulates Freud's fantasy of the murder of the father of the primal horde as the origin of religion in *Totem and Taboo* (1912–1913). Only later, in the reunification at Kadesh, under the leadership of a second Moses, did they take up a new religion based on the worship of the volcano god Yahweh. The result was the preservation of elements of Egyptian monotheism in the worship of Yahweh, including the practice of *circumcision.

Psychoanalysts have speculated that, in addition to his identification with Moses, this argument reflects Freud's underlying guilt for his own hostile wishes against his father. Freud would

have been struggling to overcome his guilt and ambivalence by his wish to become another messiah, another Moses, who would lead his people out of psychological bondage by the new revelation of psychoanalysis. But this required the destruction of the religion of the fathers. He wrote: "There was no place in the framework of the religion of Moses for a direct expression of the murderous hatred of the father. All that could come to light was a mighty reaction against it—a sense of guilt on account of that hostility, a bad conscience for having sinned against God and for not ceasing to sin. This sense of guilt . . . had yet another superficial motivation, which nearly disguised its true origin. Things were going badly for the people; the hopes resting on the favour of God failed in fulfillment; it was not easy to maintain an illusion . . . of being God's Chosen People. If they wished to avoid renouncing the happiness, a sense of guilt on account of their own sinfulness offered a welcome means of exculpating God: . . . they deserved no better than to be punished by him since they had not obeyed his commandments."

Acceptance of Sellin's fabricated account suggests a strong need to believe on Freud's part, deriving from his identification of Moses with his father and his own unconscious hostility. The murder of Moses thus expresses a fitting punishment for Freud's own parricidal wishes. The identification with the slain Moses-father would have been intensified by Freud's advanced age and the progressive deterioration caused by his painful cancer.

Conclusion. Freud could never resolve his ambivalence toward things religious; his attitudes toward the Bible bear eloquent testimony to this conflict. He refused to acknowledge holy writ as bearing any significance beyond its status as an ancient and traditional literary masterpiece. Yet despite his skeptical and agnostic stance, he could not leave the Bible alone. He returned at the end of his life to immerse himself in the figure of Moses and the mystery of the religion he brought to God's chosen people. He created a psychoanalytic myth of the origins of monotheistic belief in the primal murder of the father in the person of Moses. If this imaginative fiction cannot bear the weight of critical appraisal as a contribution to biblical studies, the question still remains whether Freud was touching on something more profound and meaningful about the human religious condition. Certainly, the Freudian encounter with scripture carries its own lesson—that the reading and interpretation of the biblical texts may not be divorced from the motives, sometimes hidden, of the reader.

WILLIAM W. MEISSNER, S.J.

Fringes (Hebr. *ṣîṣīt,* pl. *ṣîṣīyyôt;* RSV "tassel"). Fringes were frequently worn in the ancient Near East, although this custom's origins and purpose, which was probably protective, are obscure. Numbers 15.38–41 (and, more tersely, Deut. 22.12) ordains that Israelite males are to wear fringes including a blue cord on the four corners of their outside garments as a perpetual reminder to fulfill divine commandments rather than one's own desires. Fringes may also have indicated covenantal affiliation, serving both to differentiate male from female and to distinguish between Israelite and gentile. For later Jewish tradition, wearing ritually correct fringes daily became an important signifier of male religious obligation, equivalent to affixing a mezuzah to the doorpost (Deut. 6.9; 11.20) and placing *phylacteries on the head and arm during prayer (Exod. 13.9, 16; Deut. 6.8; 11.18).

JUDITH R. BASKIN

Fundamentalism. A twentieth-century theological movement among conservative Protestants, largely in North America. Despite its broad, amorphous, and decentralized character, fundamentalism has the following features:

1. A strong emphasis on the *inspiration and *authority of the Bible, which is to be understood "literally" and which is held to be "inerrant"—totally free from any error whatsoever, whether historical, theological, or scientific. It is not surprising that fundamentalists strongly repudiate the conclusions of modern biblical criticism, seeing them as implicitly, if not explicitly, undermining the beliefs of traditional Christianity (*see* Interpretation, History of, *article on* Modern Biblical Criticism).

2. A marked, at times militant, impulse toward separatism from the other branches of Christianity. Inasmuch as the large mainline Protestant denominations were perceived in the early twentieth century to be drifting toward "modernism" or "liberalism," fundamentalists often withdrew fellowship from them, eventually creating rival Bible colleges, seminaries, publishing houses, and even entire denominations. In 1941, for example, they founded the American Council of Christian Churches, explicitly separate from its mainline counterpart, the Federal (later National) Council of Churches of Christ.

3. With a few exceptions, mostly among some Calvinist churches, fundamentalists tend to embrace the dispensationalist school of biblical interpretation, especially as popularized by the *Scofield Reference Bible. Again understanding the Bible "literally," particularly the many prophecies concerning the land of Israel as yet seemingly unfulfilled, fundamentalists tend to be premillennialists, looking forward to a literal thousand-year future reign of the *Messiah (the *second coming of Christ) over a restored Jewish nation (see Rev. 20.4). Thus, a strong emphasis on future fulfillment of biblical prophecy usually characterizes fundamentalists. A perhaps inevitable corollary to this type of premillennialism is a strong sense of pessimism concerning contemporary human history, which is expected only to degenerate further and further until Christ's return.

4. In accord with this last point, fundamentalists tend to emphasize personal piety and holiness over against the social concerns of the mainline churches. Typically, fundamentalists promote evangelistic revivals and missionary activity, both foreign and domestic, while they heavily inveigh against smoking, drinking (*see* Wine), the theater, card playing, and the like. Somewhat paradoxical, however, is their strong sense of patriotism, often identifying American values and traditions closely with Christianity. Ever since the 1960s, for example, fundamentalists have bitterly denounced the United States Supreme Court ban on prayer in the public schools as "un-American" as well as "anti-Christian."

The term "fundamentalist" first appeared in the early 1920s to describe those who subscribed to the "fundamentals" of Christian faith, especially the tenets promulgated in a twelve-volume work, entitled *The Fundamentals,* which had been printed and mailed to thousands of ministers and laypersons during the years 1910–15 by two California oil millionaires, Lyman and Milton Stewart. These booklets took issue with a wide list of enemies of Christianity—Romanism, socialism, atheism, Mormonism, and most of all naturalism, which was held to be the basis of contemporary theological liberalism. The volumes also reaffirmed what were deemed to be "fundamental" truths of traditional Christianity, especially the inspiration and authority of scripture. Historians of fundamentalism commonly link the publishing of these volumes to the "five fundamentals" that had been previously adopted by the General Assembly of the (northern) Presbyterian Church in the U.S.A. in 1910 (later reaffirmed in 1916 and 1923), namely, the inerrancy of scripture, the deity of Jesus Christ and his *virgin birth, Christ's substitutionary atonement, his physical (bodily) *resurrection, and the historicity of his *miracles. But, as Ernest R. Sandeen has pointed out, any such listing of the "five points" of fundamentalism, and still less the twelve volumes of *The Fundamentals*, never typified the leadership of this era. Nonetheless, by the early 1920s, various lists of "the fundamentals" had indeed been drawn up, and they were meant to represent the essential, and hence nonnegotiable, doctrines of Christianity.

Throughout the 1920s, fundamentalists exerted a surprisingly powerful force on American religion and politics, especially in several of the larger Protestant denominations such as the northern Presbyterians and northern Baptists. As Sandeen notes, the origins of fundamentalism were largely to be found in the northeastern region of North America in metropolitan areas, not, as commonly argued, in agrarian or southern locales. Nonetheless, the real strength of fundamentalistic religion eventually did manifest itself among the Southern Baptists and the countless independent Bible churches that began to spring up throughout North America during this time, especially in the southern and midwestern regions of the United States. Politically the fundamentalists flexed their muscles as well, strongly opposing, for example, the teaching in public schools of Darwinian evolution (*see* Science and the Bible). This opposition led eventually to the notorious "Scopes Monkey Trial" of 1925, in which William Jennings Bryan, a Presbyterian layperson and three-time Democratic party presidential candidate, argued unsuccessfully against the teaching of evolution in the public schools of Tennessee. Other famous fundamentalists of the era included the colorful and popular evangelist Billy Sunday and Princeton seminary professor John Gresham Machen, who personally resisted being called a fundamentalist, saying that it sounded like a new religion.

By the 1940s, less militant fundamentalists were also chafing under the term, regarding it as connoting anti-intellectualism, combativeness, extremism, and paranoia. Calling themselves "evangelicals," they banded together in 1942 to found the National Association of Evangelicals as a more moderate counterpart to the fundamentalist American Council of Christian Churches founded the previous year. Evangelicals still reckoned themselves as the heirs of true, historic Christianity, but they were more willing to work within and among the mainline denominations. The well-known contemporary evangelist Billy Graham, a moderate fundamentalist, has been repeatedly and bitterly denounced by his more conservative counterparts for such compromise.

Fundamentalism is still a force within modern North American Protestant Christianity. In 1976, Jimmy Carter, a self-styled "born again" evangelical Christian, was elected president of the United States, and Ronald Reagan's 1980 and 1984 presidential victories were due in part to the votes of evangelicals and fundamentalists. Jerry Falwell, a prominent Virginia preacher and founder of the so-called Moral Majority (recently disbanded), and Pat Robertson, an influential television evangelist and 1988 Republican party presidential candidate, are two contemporary North American fundamentalists of some renown.   WILLIAM H. BARNES

Furniture. *See* Houses, Furniture, Utensils.

✣ G ✣

Gabriel. Gabriel is one of the most prominent *angels in postexilic Jewish literature and in Christian texts, especially extracanonical literature. He is portrayed as one of the seven *archangels in 1 Enoch 20.7; elsewhere he is one of the four angels close to God's throne (1 Enoch 10.9; 40.3, 9; cf. Luke 1.19). This proximity to God results in his distinctive functions. Gabriel intercedes with God for those oppressed by evil (1 Enoch 9.1–11), he brings *Enoch into God's very presence (2 Enoch 21.3–6), he explains mysteries about future political events (Dan. 8.16–26; 9.20–27), and he delivers special revelations from God to individuals (Luke 1.8–20, 26–38). Jewish and Christian interpreters have sometimes concluded that biblical texts with unnamed divine messengers (e.g., Gen. 19.1) refer to the archangels Gabriel and Michael. In general, *Michael is described as a warrior, while Gabriel more often functions as an intermediary or an interpreter of *dreams.   STEVEN FRIESEN

Gad. Son of Zilpah, *Leah's maid, and *Jacob (Gen. 30.10–11), and one of the twelve *tribes of Israel. The name Gad is associated with the Hebrew word for fortune. In early Israel Gad is both populous (Gen. 46.16; Num. 26.15–18) and adept in battle (Gen. 49.19; Deut. 33.20–21; 1 Chron. 5.18; 12.8–14). The Gadites, together with *Reuben and half of *Manasseh, settle in the Transjordan, an area suited for their abundant cattle (Num. 32.26; Map 1:Y4). The Gadites support *Saul and his family (1 Sam. 31.11–13; 2 Sam. 2.8–9), aid *David (1 Chron. 12.8–14), and participate in his administration (2 Sam. 23.36).

Gad fares poorly during the divided monarchy. King Mesha of Moab (ca. 835 BCE) claims that he dealt harshly with the Gadites of Ataroth (*see* Moabite Stone). Hazael of Damascus (Syria) devastates Gad (2 Kings 10.32–33). Subsequently, *Tiglath-pileser III of Assyria exiles the Transjordanian tribes (2 Kings 15.29).

Gad can also refer to a foreign deity (Isa. 65.11), a seer during the time of David (1 Sam. 22.5; 2 Sam. 24.11–14), or an organizer of levitical service and chronicler of David's life (1 Chron. 29.29).   GARY N. KNOPPERS

Galatians, The Letter of Paul to the. A letter addressed by *Paul to "the churches of Galatia" is fourth in the usual arrangement of the Pauline letters in the New Testament. It is a sustained and passionate expostulation with a group of churches that Paul had planted, whose members were in danger of abandoning the gospel that they had received from him. They were inclined to pay heed to certain teachers who urged them to add to their faith in Christ some distinctive features of Judaism, particularly *circumcision. These teachers also endeavored to diminish Paul's authority by insisting that he was indebted to the Jerusalem church leaders for his apostolic commission and had no right to deviate from Jerusalem practice.

Contents. The opening salutation (1.1–5) is followed immediately by an expression of indignant astonishment that the readers are so quickly departing from the gospel that brought them salvation (1.6–10).

An autobiographical account follows. Paul received his gospel not from others but when God revealed his Son to him. Before that, he had become an expert in the study and practice of Judaism; he showed his zeal by persecuting the followers of Jesus. But when he received his revelation, together with the commission to preach Christ among the *gentiles, he began to fulfill his commission at once without consulting the Christian leaders in Jerusalem. Not until three years later did he go to Jerusalem for a fifteen-day visit to Cephas (*Simon Peter), during which he also met *James, the Lord's brother. After that visit he went to Syria and Cilicia, and continued preaching the gospel there (1.11–24).

Several years later he visited Jerusalem with

*Barnabas and had a conference with the three pillars of the mother church, James, Peter, and *John. They recognized that Paul and Barnabas had been specially called to evangelize gentiles, whereas their own responsibility was rather to evangelize their fellow Jews; they agreed to an appropriate demarcation of the two spheres of missionary activity. But they conferred no authority on Paul: he was in no way commissioned by them (2.1–10).

Indeed, his independence from them was shown during a visit paid by Peter to *Antioch, when Peter withdrew from sharing meals with gentile Christians because of representations made to him by messengers from James in Jerusalem. As Paul saw it, Peter's action compromised the gospel by implying that there was some difference in principle between Jewish and gentile believers. In fact, Paul maintained, there was none; both had been accepted by God through faith in Christ, not through the Jewish law (2.11–21).

Paul wonders whether the Galatians have been hypnotized: how otherwise could they imagine that the saving work was to be completed by their own endeavors when it had begun with their reception of the spirit of God through faith (3.1–5).

Abraham in his day received the promise that through him and his offspring all the gentiles would be blessed. Since it was on account of his faith that Abraham received this promise, it is on the basis of *faith that the gentiles are to experience its fulfillment. The *Law brings no blessing; instead, it brings a *curse on those who fail to keep it, but from that curse Christ has redeemed those who have faith (3.6–14). When the promise to Abraham speaks of his offspring, Christ is meant. The promise is like a deed of covenant, whose terms cannot subsequently be modified by codicil (3.15–18). The Law was given in order to bring the latent sinful propensity of humanity into the open in the form of specific transgressions, during the interval before the coming of the expected offspring. The Law was like a guardian, keeping children under restraint until their coming of age. With the coming of Christ and the exercise of faith in him, the people of God attained their maturity and enjoy their liberty as his fully grown sons and daughters (3.19–4.7).

But the Galatian Christians are turning their backs on their liberty and placing themselves in bondage to legal ordinances. Paul appeals to them to remember the affection they showed for him when he first visited them: he is not jealous because they are listening to other teachers but concerned because those teachers are robbing them of their liberty. They are trying to make them accept circumcision, but Paul warns them that, if they submit to this demand, they must keep the whole Jewish law. Those who have seduced them into this false course will have much to answer for (4.8–5.12).

Christian liberty means liberty to live according to the spirit of Christ, to fulfill the comprehensive commandment to love one another. The way of the spirit is the way of life; the "works of the flesh" lead to destruction (5.13–26). Mutual helpfulness is the hallmark of men and women of faith. Those who do good to others reap the harvest of eternal life (6.1–10).

Let others boast of their achievements; Paul will boast of nothing but the cross of Christ. The scars he has received in his apostolic service mark him as Christ's property (6.11–17). With this he takes his leave of them (6.18).

Authorship. None of the letters bearing Paul's name is so indubitably his as Galatians. Galatians is, indeed, the criterion by which the authenticity of other letters ascribed to him is gauged.

Recipients. The "churches of Galatia" addressed in this letter were situated in the Roman province of Galatia (Map 11:F3), but which part of the province is a matter of dispute. Until 25 BCE the area had been the kingdom of Galatia. The original Galatians were Celts from central Europe who invaded Asia Minor and established themselves there in the third century BCE. But the rulers of Galatia extended their authority over neighboring territories populated by other ethnic groups; these groups were included in the province of Galatia and were Galatians in the political but not in the ethnic sense. To some of these groups belonged the cities of Pisidian Antioch, Iconium, Lystra, and Derbe, which were evangelized by Paul and Barnabas around 47 CE (Acts 13.14–14.23). One view is that the churches of those cities were recipients of the letter. Another view is that the recipients were churches established later in the northern part of the Roman province, among the ethnic Galatians. It is true that *Acts makes no mention of Paul's visiting north Galatia, but Acts does not give a complete account of his missionary activity. The precise identity of the recipients does not greatly affect the argument of the letter.

Date. The date of the letter has been fixed at various points between 48 and 55 CE. If it was sent to the churches of Pisidian Antioch, Iconium, Lystra, and Derbe, a date around 48 CE is possible, even probable; if it was sent to churches in ethnic Galatia, its date would be later. The affinity between Galatians and *Romans has been thought to point to a date not long before the writing of Romans (early in 57 CE). The affinity should not be exaggerated, however; Paul's assessment of the Law, for example, was considerably modified between Galatians and Romans. Again, wherever Galatians may be dated within the limits mentioned, one's appreciation of its argument is affected only slightly.

Opponents. The traditional view, accepted here, is that those against whom Paul polemicizes in Galatians were judaizing intruders, eager to make the churches in Galatia, which were mainly gentile in composition, conform to the Jewish way of life and probably also to bring them under the control of the church of Jerusalem.

Other features, however, have been discerned in the situation implied in the letter. If Paul warns his readers not to pervert their liberty into license (Gal. 5.13–21), it might indicate that a campaign on two fronts has been simplified by one line of interpretation, according to which the one target of Paul's attack is a form of christianized Jewish *gnosticism. If it is objected that Paul gives no clear hint of this in the letter, the answer is that he did not fully understand the nature of the teaching being urged on his converts. But this is not plausible. Our sole source of knowledge about the opponents and their propaganda is found in Paul's argument; if these references cannot be trusted, there is no other source of information.

The letter can be read against the background of revived militant nationalism in Judea in the years after 44 CE. These militants (who came to be called *Zealots) treated Jews who fraternized with gentiles as traitors. Jerusalem Christians were sensitive to the charge that some of their leaders, if not they themselves, practiced such fraternization. Hence, perhaps, the representations to Peter at Antioch, which made him break off his table fellowship with gentile Christians in that city (Gal. 2.11–14); hence too, perhaps, the judaizing mission to Galatia. For if gentile converts could be persuaded to accept circumcision and conform to Jewish customs in other ways, for example, by observing the sacred calendar (Gal. 4.10), the militants (it was hoped) would be pacified.

Immediate Sequel. What effect the letter had in the churches to which it was sent we do not know. Paul's insistence on gentile believers' equal status with Jewish believers, his refusal of any procedure that compromised his converts' liberty, isolated him in large measure from his peers in the Christian movement as a whole. He was disillusioned when "even Barnabas," hitherto his closest colleague, joined those who found it expedient to stay aloof from association with gentile Christians at Antioch (Gal. 2.13). He continued to feel affection and respect for Barnabas, but confidence was no longer possible. He made no further use of the church of Antioch as a base for his missionary work, and he and the leaders of the Jerusalem church never again felt totally at ease with each other.

As for the churches of Galatia, their response to the letter is unrecorded. Certainly, circumcision soon ceased to be an issue throughout the gentile mission field. This could have been due in part to Paul's argument, but it may have been due even more to a ruling by the church of Jerusalem that circumcision was not to be required from gentile converts (Acts 15.23–29; *see* Apostolic Council). When Paul began to organize a relief fund for the church of Jerusalem, toward the end of his Aegean mission, he sent instructions to the churches of Galatia about their participation in this effort (1 Cor. 16.1), but it is not clear whether they made a contribution. Perhaps some of them did: one of Paul's companions on the journey to Jerusalem to hand over the contributions was Gaius, a man from Derbe (Acts 20.4).   F. F. BRUCE

Galilee (Map 5:X2–3). The name for the northern region of Palestine, meaning literally either the circle or the district. According to Joshua 19, this area was allotted to the tribes of Naphtali, Zebulun, and Dan, although the accounts of the tribal settlements suggest that the older population continued in the more prosperous regions such as the valley and the coast (Judg. 1.30, 33). Archaeological data, especially from surveys, add evidence of many new settlements throughout the region in the early Iron Age, as further south in the central hill country (*see* Conquest of Canaan). Galilee, together with some of its major cities, especially *Hazor, is only sporadically mentioned in biblical and nonbiblical sources in the first half of the first millennium BCE. After the fall of the northern kingdom in 722 BCE Galilee was included in the Assyrian province of Samaria, but it is unlikely that the whole Israelite population was ever completely uprooted in this largely rural area. While drawing a distinction between Upper and Lower Galilee, later writers, such as *Josephus and Pliny, extol the fertility and the variety of its agricultural produce.

The region receives more attention beginning in the Hellenistic period, when Simon, one of the Maccabean brothers, went there to rescue some fellow Jews during the persecution that followed Antiochus IV's Hellenistic reform in the mid-second century BCE (1 Macc. 5.14–23). This episode has suggested to many scholars that Galilee was then a thoroughly gentile region, but this may not be an accurate assessment. Scattered references from the Persian period (Tob. 1.10; Judith 4.6–10) indicate a continued Jewish presence there in Persian times. Archaeological surveys suggest that the region was not densely populated in the early Hellenistic period, and the episode involving Simon seems to have been confined to the region of Ptolemais. Josephus informs us that the Hasmonean Aristobulus I forcibly circumcised the Iturean people as part of the campaign to reestablish control of the old Israelite territory (Ant. 13.12.318–19.). This episode may have involved some of those dwelling in Upper Galilee but can scarcely be considered to have involved all Galilean Jews of the first century BCE.

The population of Galilee seems to have increased under the Hasmoneans by a process of "internal colonization," giving rise to a densely populated province by the first century CE (Josephus War 3.3.41–44). This "Jewish Galilee" emerged as a separate administrative unity when Pompey, the Roman general, carved up the Hasmonean kingdom, and its identity was further enhanced by the setting up of an administrative council for the region at Sepphoris by his successor Gavinius in 57 BCE. This center, and its rival Tiberias, founded by Herod Antipas in 19 CE, continued to dominate the whole of Lower Galilee administratively, whereas Upper Galilee retained a largely village culture into late Roman and Byzantine times.

Galilee's separate identity also emerged when the Romans once again intervened to carve up *Herod the Great's kingdom on his death in 4 BCE. The region, together with Perea, was entrusted to his son Herod Antipas, whose long reign (4 BCE to 39 CE) covered the career of Jesus of Nazareth. By contrast with Judea in the south, which came under direct Roman rule in 6 CE, with the consequent deterioration of social relations there, Antipas's reign appears to have brought stability to Jewish Galilee. Galilee also came under direct Roman rule, probably on the death of Herod Agrippa in 44 CE, although part of the region—Tiberias and Tarichaeae and their territories—had been given by Nero to Agrippa's son, Agrippa II, whose territory had previously been confined to Trachonitis in Transjordan.

In the First Jewish Revolt (66–70 CE), the Jewish revolutionary council appointed *Josephus as governor of Galilee at the outbreak of hostilities with Rome, but apart from a few centers such as Giscala, Gamala (situated in the Golan, although closely associated with Galilee), and Tiberias, the campaign was quickly brought to an end by the advancing Roman legions, and Josephus was captured after his last stand at the fortress of Jotapata, an account of which is highly embellished to extol his own military prowess (War 3.4.59–3.7.306). Galilee does not seem to have been involved in the Second Jewish Revolt (132–35 CE), and as part of the Roman settlement Jews from the south were forced northward. Thus, from the second century CE on, Galilee became a home of Jewish learning and piety in the land of Israel. It was there that the great scribal schools flourished at Usha, Sepphoris, and Tiberias, producing the *Mishnah and later the Palestinian *Talmud (Yerushalmi). Jews from all over the Mediterranean world were buried at Beth Shearim in Galilee. The excavated remains of the *synagogue there suggest a thriving local community with an independent religious life down to the Arab conquests of the seventh century CE, despite the increased Christian presence after Constantine's conversion.

This sketch of Galilean political and religious history should help to correct some false impressions of Galilee and Galileans that are often found in accounts of the career of *Jesus of Nazareth. Galilean life was relatively stable politically, especially in contrast to Judea, and so it is incorrect to see Galilee as the home of the *Zealots or as a hotbed of revolutionaries, at once more radical and more charismatic in the expressions of their Jewish religious loyalties. Nor were Galileans generally socially deprived or marginalized. The natural fertility of the region, its strategic location on the caravan routes to the East, as well as its role as a hinterland for the Phoenician trading centers, meant that its inhabitants were in a position to enjoy at least some of the benefits that the Hellenistic age brought to the East.

Galilee and Galileans are associated particularly with Jesus of Nazareth and his movement. While each of the four Gospels treats the region differently within the overall purposes of its narrative and does not give us the kind of detailed information about the region that one can glean from Josephus's *Life*, for example, many of their underlying social and religious assumptions are realistic on the basis of what can be reconstructed historically from other sources. For the evangelists also Galilee is thoroughly Jewish in its religious affiliation. Tensions between the religious claims on the region from Jerusalem and the distinctive regional ethos are recognized (Mark 3.22; 7.1). The rural setting predominates, and the lake region with its busy commercial life is highlighted. This picture, highly selective in its coloring, corresponds remarkably well with a more detailed profile that can be established with the aid of other sources. Galilee did indeed function as a symbol of the newness of Jesus' vision in contrast to the more established circles of Jewish belief for the early Christians, but all the indications are that the symbolic reference was grounded in an actual ministry that was conducted in the real Galilee of the first century CE.   SEÁN FREYNE

Galilee, Sea of (Map 12:Y2–3). A large, heart-shaped expanse of water, 20 km (12.5 mi) long by 11 km (7 mi) wide at its maximum points. It forms a deep basin surrounded by mountains on both sides and a narrow, shoreline plain where several important cities and towns are located. This pattern is broken only at the northwestern corner, where this strip opens out into the plain of Gennesar, the fertility of which was extolled by Josephus (*War* 3.516–21). The lake surface itself is ca. 210 m (700 ft) below sea level, thus forming a large basin for the waters of the *Jordan River. According to Josephus and Pliny its original name was the Lake of Gennesaret, although both authors are aware that it was also called the Lake of Tiberias (Josephus) or the Lake of Tarichaeae (Pliny), after two of the more important settlements on its shores in Roman times.

The gospels of Matthew (eleven times) and Mark (seven times) call it the Sea of Galilee, a designation also found in John 6 and 21. This may reflect the Hebrew (*yam*), which can mean either a freshwater lake or the sea properly understood. It has been suggested, however, that Mark's usage (followed by Matthew) has a more symbolic significance in terms of Jesus' control of the forces of evil that are associated with the deep (Job 38.8–11; Ps. 107.23–25, 28–29). Luke

reserves the word "sea" for the Mediterranean and always speaks of the "lake of Gennesaret" (5.1, 2) or "the lake" (8.22–23, 33) when referring to the Sea of Galilee. The significance of this usage is that it suggests that Luke, although presumably not a native of Palestine, was able to project himself into that context and accurately reflect local usage in differentiating between sea and lake.

The lake provided a natural boundary between Jewish Galilee and the largely gentile territories of Gaulanitis and the *Decapolis directly across. Despite differences of religious affiliation among the population on either side of the lake, archaeological evidence suggests a real continuity in terms of life-styles, trading, and other relations. The Gospels also testify to this frequent movement, even when it is not always possible to detect accurately the points of embarkation and arrival (see Mark 6.45, 63; 8.10; John 6.22–24). Josephus too mentions fleets of boats on the lake, thus suggesting a busy and thriving subregion within Galilee and linking it with the larger region.

In addition, the lake was a natural resource for Galilee because of the fish industry. Strabo, Josephus, and Pliny, as well as the Gospels, all mention the plentiful supply of fish in the lake. Both Bethsaida and Tarichaeae are generally believed to have derived their names from the fish industry; the latter is most probably the Greek name for Magdala and is derived from the Greek term for preservation. Salting of fish, which made their export possible on a much wider scale, was, we know, a technical skill that was developed during the Hellenistic age. It is likely, therefore, that there was a genuine expansion of this industry in Palestine also. Josephus mentions (*War* 3.8.520) one type of fish, the *coracin* belonging to the eel family, which was also found in the Nile, suggesting perhaps that the early Ptolemaic rulers had expanded the fish industry to Galilee as a commercial enterprise. In this regard it is worth noting that James and John, the sons of Zebedee, would appear to have abandoned a thriving business, when they left their father and his hired servants to follow the call of Jesus (Mark 1.16–20).   SEÁN FREYNE

Gamaliel. Gamaliel the Elder was a first-century CE teacher. Although he is not often quoted in the *Mishnah, it is said that "when he died the glory of the Torah ended" (*m. Soṭa* 9.15).

Gamaliel is best known outside the Mishnah for his brief speech in Acts 5.35–39. Identified as a *Pharisee respected by the people, Gamaliel counsels the *Sanhedrin to leave the early Christian leaders alone: "If this plan or this undertaking is of human origin, it will fail; but if it is of God, you will not be able to overthrow them." He is also identified as *Paul's teacher in Acts 22.3.   J. ANDREW OVERMAN

Garden of Eden. *See* Eden, Garden of.

Gehenna. The place where, according to Jesus in the synoptic Gospels, sinners are punished after death. A few times Hades (*see* *Hell) is also treated as such a place of punishment (Matt. 11.23; Luke 10.14; 16.23), but it is cited more often as the realm of death in general. (The NRSV translates Grk. *geenna* as "hell.")

Gehenna was originally the Hebrew name of a valley just south of *Jerusalem's southwestern hill (Josh. 15.8) called "the valley of Hinnom" (*gê* *hinnōm*) or "the valley of Hinnom's son(s)" (*gê* *ben(ê) hinnōm*); Map 9. Under the influence of the Aramaic form *gêhinnā(m)*, the Greek transliteration of the word became *geenna*. "Hinnom" may be understood as the representative of a *Jebusite group that once dominated the place in question, but the Bible mentions only the valley. In boundary lists it forms the border between Judah and Benjamin south of the Jebusite city (Josh. 15.8; 18.16), implying that Jerusalem belonged to Benjamin.

The later view of Gehenna as a place of punishment, especially by fire, is anticipated in an Isaianic reference to a large *topheth, or burning place, near Jerusalem, said to be lit by the Lord to punish the *Assyrians and their king (Isa. 30.33). A further stage in the development of the relevant concepts is reached in the report concerning King *Josiah's cultic reform of 622 BCE, which implied a desecration of similar tophets in Judah, especially one found in the valley of Hinnom and dedicated to Molech for children (2 Kings 23.10; cf. 2 Chron. 28.3; 33.6). The elimination ordered by Josiah was not entirely successful, for somewhat later Jeremiah made repeated attacks on the topheth and said the valley of Hinnom would become a general burial place (Jer. 7.31; 19.11; 32.35).

On the basis of such passages and influenced by parallelism with Persian ideas of a judgment in fire, Jewish *apocalypticism made the valley of Hinnom a place of punishment within an eschatological milieu. In a vision ascribed to *Enoch a cavity was depicted, into which the faithful Jews, gathered on the holy mountain, would look down to see the righteous judgment and eternal punishment of all godless and cursed people (1 Enoch 26.4; 27.2–3). No name appears here, but since the details of the picture indicate the topography of Jerusalem, the cavity in question must have been meant as the valley of Hinnom. The joining of the eschatological perspective to Jerusalem then led to an explicit use of the name Gehenna for that place of punishment, a usage that emerges in texts of the first century CE in the New Testament (e.g., Matt. 5.22; 10.28; 23.15, 33; James 3.6) and in Jewish apocalypse (e.g., 2 Esdras 7.36, in the Latin translation "Gehenna"). In the *Mishnah and later rabbinic texts, the name Gehenna (*gê* *hinnōm*) has superseded the older term for the underworld (Sheol). Gehenna is also the ordinary term in the *Qurʾān for the place of ultimate punishment.

See also Afterlife and Immortality; Descent into Hell.   BO REICKE

Genealogies. *This entry consists of two articles, the first on genealogies in the* Hebrew Bible, *especially in the book of Genesis, and the second on genealogies in the* New Testament.

Hebrew Bible

A genealogy is a catalogue of the most important information about the successive members of a family's lineage, including their birth, marriage, offspring, age achieved, and death (with many variations). This listing of biographical facts serves to preserve the continuity of a family in its progression through time. Genesis 11.10–11 (*P) is an example of a simple genealogy: "These are the descendants of Shem. When Shem was one hundred years old, he became the father of Arpachshad two years after the flood; and Shem lived after the birth of Arpachshad five hundred years, and had other sons and daughters." Originally, genealogies simply preserved a family's generational succession; later they also came to express kinship and social, political, and religious relationships, as well as connections within larger communities.

Genealogies are an independent genre whose origins go back to nomadic tribes; evidence is found mainly among Arab nomads and African tribes, in some cases to this day. They represent the history of a "prehistoric" period and lose their function after the creation of a state, to be replaced by historical facts.

There are two main types of genealogy. In the linear form, family heads are given in a straight progression from the founder of the clan down to the last or currently living representative; this serves simply to establish the lineage of the latest descendant. The other form follows the diverging branches of a family and exhibits the divisions among the communities descended from the sons of a single ancestor (e.g., Noah in Gen. 10). Genealogies, which were transmitted orally, are intrinsically mutable; changes in the relationships of groups within a larger community are expressed as changes in their genealogies. This capacity for change explains the contradictions between some genealogies: they reflect actual developments in the history of such groups.

Genealogies are an important component of the Bible and of Genesis in particular, establishing the continuity of events through the succession of generations. The original locus of genealogy is the history of the *ancestors in Genesis 12–50, where generational succession provides the framework for the narrative; subsequently, genealogies were used in accounts of primeval history as well. In religious-historical terms, this corresponds to the depiction of cosmogony as theogony; in some religions, as in those of *Egypt and *Mesopotamia, the origin of the world and its elements is attributed to a succession of divine births. An echo of this can still be found in the Hebrew designation of creation as tôlēdôt ("generations" in the literal sense) of heaven and earth (Gen. 1.1). Genealogies, however, occur in the Bible only after the creation of humankind; primeval events have been shifted from divine to human history. The genealogies in Genesis depict all of humanity as the effect of the creator's blessing, from *Adam to *Noah (chap. 5: linear genealogy) and then branching out from Noah's sons to cover the entire known world (chap. 10: branching genealogy). These genealogies knit the individual accounts of primeval events in Genesis 1–11 into a coherent narrative.

Genealogies enclose the history of the ancestors as a whole, as well as framing each of the smaller sections (chaps. 12–25 and 25–36); they thus serve as formal elements in the composition of narrative units. Narratives sometimes begin and/or end with genealogies (e.g., Gen. 34; Ruth 1.2; 4.18–22). Genealogical information delineates the lives of *Abraham and his sons. A genealogy marks the transition from primeval times to the history of the ancestors (Shem to Terah in Gen. 11.10–26 and Terah's sons in 11.27–32). Difficulties concerning the genealogies within the ancestral history arise primarily because they reflect two stages: first, the development of a small kinship group (as in Gen. 25.19–20), and second, the formation of the *tribes (e.g., the twelve sons of Jacob as the fathers of the later twelve tribes of Israel).

In earlier stages of the development of the genre, genealogy and narrative are more tightly integrated. Genealogical information anchors the narrative in a continuous temporal progression. One can merge into the other; a narrative frequently grows out of an item in a genealogy. The proximity of genealogy to narrative is demonstrated in the short elaborations within genealogies, including references to an occupation, as in Genesis 4.2 and 10.9; mention of a contemporaneous event, as in 10.25; or a remark concerning childlessness, as in 11.30. Thus, in the early stages, genealogies contained quite a few narrative elements. In subsequent traditions (P in particular), they follow a fixed format of identical or near-identical sentences, as in Genesis 5.6–8: "When Seth had lived one hundred five years, he became the father of Enoch. Seth lived after the birth of Enoch eight hundred seven years, and had other sons and daughters. Thus all the days of Seth were nine hundred twelve years; and he died." Though limited to a few facts, this form still preserves the life histories of those making up the chain of generations. In a final, later stage, all that remains is a list of names—no longer genealogy in the true sense of the word. A variant development is illustrated by the story of *Joseph, in which genealogy has so completely merged with the narrative as to lose its independent existence.

The developmental phases of the genre of genealogy can be observed in the line of *Esau's descendants (Gen. 36), where a kinship phase (his sons) is followed by one of tribes (the chiefs) and then by one of kings; the format changes accordingly.

After the formation of a state, genealogies, having been reduced to mere lists, tend to lose their importance. In a monarchy, they serve a political function in securing the succession to the throne; for a priesthood they have religious significance in securing succession to sacred office. In these contexts, genealogies still play a role in the life of the community; the lists of names in 1 Chronicles 1–9, however, are a purely literary device.

See also Chronology, *article on* Israelite Chronology.

CLAUS WESTERMANN

New Testament

The New Testament contains two genealogies of *Jesus: one in Matthew 1.1–16, which traces his descent from *Abraham, and one in Luke 3.23–38, which reverses the order. While Matthew's genealogy is limited to the Abrahamic line, Luke's goes back to *Adam. Perhaps as a mnemonic device, Matthew or his source divided the generations from Abraham to Jesus into three groups of fourteen (1.17): fourteen generations from Abraham to *David, fourteen from David to the Babylonian *exile, and fourteen from the Babylonian exile to Jesus. In order to maintain the symmetry, the names of the kings Ahaziah, Joash, and Amaziah were dropped from the second list of fourteen between Joram (Jehoram) and Uzziah. Other omissions may have occurred in Matthew's third list of fourteen, because Luke, who presents a different lineage between *Zerubbabel and *Joseph, records nineteen names for the same period.

Matthew's genealogy seems to be intentionally formed around a predetermined number. Most likely he meant to show that Jesus is a royal descendant of Abraham and David, in fact a new David: the sum of the numerical value of the Hebrew consonants in the name "David" ($d + w + d = 4 + 6 + 4$) is fourteen, and Jesus is frequently called "son of David" throughout the gospel of Matthew.

Four women appear in Matthew's list, though they are not found in Luke's. This is notable because in biblical times lineage was traced through males. Even more surprising is that three of these women were non-Israelites: *Rahab the Canaanite, *Ruth the Moabite, and (presumably) *Bathsheba, the wife of Uriah the Hittite. Their mention anticipates the inclusion of *gentiles among Jesus' disciples (Matt. 28.19).

The genealogy in Luke 3.23–38 has variations in different textual traditions. According to most Greek manuscripts (followed by the United Bible Societies' *Greek New Testament*), there are 11×7 generations from Adam to Jesus (that is, from Adam to Abraham, 3×7 generations; from Isaac to David, 2×7 generations; from Nathan to Salathiel (preexilic), 3×7 generations; from Zerubbabel (postexilic) to Jesus, 3×7 generations). Other Greek manuscripts, the Latin *Vulgate, and the Syriac Peshitta record 76 generations, and some Latin manuscripts list 72 generations. Most likely Luke traces Jesus' genealogy back

through Abraham to Adam to show that Jesus is not only the fulfillment of the history of Israel, but also that he is the savior of the world.

Many attempts have been made to reconcile the two genealogies, which after David agree in only two names (Shealtiel [Salathiel] and *Zerubbabel). Because none of these attempts have been generally accepted, it is likely that these inconsistent genealogies serve separate literary functions and are not to be interpreted like modern registers of pedigree. Matthew's genealogy is meant to show Jesus' Davidic, royal descent, and Luke's to underscore the universal role of Jesus as *Son of God.

The word genealogy occurs twice in a disparaging sense: in 1 Timothy 1.4 ("endless genealogies that promote speculations"), and in Titus 3.9 ("avoid . . . genealogies . . . for they are unprofitable"). Because the larger contexts refer to *myths, the allusions may be to the various emanations ("aeons") between God and humankind in *gnostic belief. Or, since Titus 1.14 relates to Jewish myths and 1 Timothy 1.7 calls into question the claims of those who desire to be teachers of the *Law, the genealogies referred to may be based on biblical sources but elaborated in the same way as the Book of Jubilees and more generally *aggadah*.

BRUCE M. METZGER

Genesis, The Book of. Genesis is the book of beginnings. Its account of primeval history (chaps. 1–11) extends from the creation of the world and humankind (chaps. 1–2) through its near destruction and preservation in the Flood (chaps. 6–9) to the spread of humankind over the earth (chaps. 10–11). The subsequent history of the *ancestors extends from *Abraham to the sons of *Jacob.

Chapters 1–11: Primeval History. Chapters 1–11 of Genesis form an internally coherent unity. The *creation (chaps. 1–2) and *Flood (chaps. 6–9) belong together; the crime against a brother (chap. 4) belongs within the story of rebellion against God (chap. 3; *see* Fall, The).

The building blocks of chapters 1–11 are narratives (chaps. 1; 2–3; 4; 6–9) and *genealogies (chaps. 5; 10). The narratives recount the beginnings of the world and its people; they cover the creation of the earth and of human beings (chaps. 1–2), wrongdoing and punishment (chaps. 3; 4; 6–9; 11), the first signs of cultural development, and the scattering of tribes and tongues. It is through the genealogies that the events in Genesis 1–11 become a coherent story. The creator's blessing causes the expansion of humankind through the course of time (chap. 5: genealogy from *Adam to Abraham) and the reach of space (chap. 10: the table of nations). Between the two genealogies stands the catastrophe of the Flood (chaps. 6–9), which is caused by the corruption of humankind and threatens to destroy its existence. The accounts of wrongdoing and punishment demonstrate the many possibilities for transgression; both the individual (chaps. 3; 4; 9) and the group (6.1–4, 5–9; 11) can overstep the boundaries set for human beings.

The narratives of creation. The creation of the world and the creation of humankind are independent traditions, each found in early religions throughout the world; the creation of humankind is the earlier of the two. Creation stories did not arise out of a curiosity about origins but from a sense of the menace to human existence in an endangered world. The older narrative (chaps. 2–3) emphasizes the creation of the human race, intertwined with the story of its failure; the limits of sin and death are an integral part of human existence. Human beings themselves, formed from earthly elements, become living beings by receiving the breath of God. They are creatures in all aspects of their existence; these include territory (the garden), food (the fruit of the garden), labor (the tilling and keeping of garden), community (the creation of woman), language (the call and naming), and their relationship to God.

The later narrative (1.1–2.4) emphasizes the creation of the world. In early religions, creation occurs through action, through generation and birth, and through combat. In Genesis 1, everything that exists or becomes has its origins in God's commanding word. The distribution of creation over seven days forms a temporal unity that recalls the week and its culmination in the *Sabbath, and it suggests that the history of creation and humanity also has an aim. The creation of plants and animals according to species show that a created order can include evolution rather than excluding it. The creation of the human "in God's image" means "corresponding to God," that is, as a creature to whom God can speak and who can respond to God. Human dignity is based on this likeness to God. Human rule over the rest of creation is understood in terms of the rule of a king who is responsible for the well-being of his subjects. The growth of humankind involves human effort and the advancement of culture. The refrain, "And God saw that it was good," signifies that creation was

good in God's eyes, that it was in accord with God's purpose.

The narratives of wrongdoing and punishment: human limitations. The present human condition is explained as having emerged from the basic and polarized experiences of being at once secure in God and alienated from God. Created by God, the human creature can turn against God and thus incur guilt. This is recounted in the expulsion from the garden (chap. 3). The serpent, the source of temptation, is a creature of God; there is no explanation for the provenance of evil. But God seeks out even the guilty ("Where are you?" [3.9]), and they are able to defend themselves. The punishment is expulsion from the garden, from God's presence and from access to the tree of life (although mortality is already part of the human condition [3.19]). In chap. 4, crime against a brother augments the disobedience to God's command ("Where is your brother Abel?"). Separated from God, human beings become capable of murder and, in 9.20–28, of dishonoring their parents. To this is added the overstepping of boundaries by human communities, as in 6.1–4 (the sons of God), chaps. 6–9 (the destruction of humanity), and 11.1–9 (the *tower of Babel).

Development of the text. The development of the book of Genesis was a long process extending over centuries. The first book of Moses, or Genesis, as we know it, is only the final stage of this process. Oral tradition—narratives, genealogies, itineraries—played a large part in the evolution of this book; it was a long way to the present unity that combines all of primeval and ancestral history. The question of the identity of the author (in the modern sense) of Genesis is irrelevant. It was not writers or poets who desired and first formulated these accounts; their origins lie in the human communities to whose life they belonged. Thus they express an understanding of God, of the world, and of humanity, which did not yet make distinctions between knowledge and belief, between science, philosophy, history, and religion. This explains in part the parallels to the themes of the creation story in many other cultures. These parallels were not necessarily due to literary derivation; rather, questions about origins were asked everywhere in early human history. Therefore, primeval events cannot be understood or described as the beginning of history; it is misguided to inquire about their "historicity." The appropriate question to ask of this material is not, "Did it really happen that way?" but, "Is it our world that is being portrayed? Is this description of human beings accurate?" The essential fact is that, in describing creation, people for the first time grasped the world, and humanity, as a whole.

Chapters 12–50: History of the Ancestors. The narratives of the ancestors extend from Abraham and Sarah to the sojourn of Jacob's family in Egypt. For the most part, they are family stories, dealing with the basic relationships within a familial community: the relationship of parents and children (chaps. 12–25: *Abraham, *Sarah, and *Hagar; *Ishmael and *Isaac), of siblings (chaps. 25–36: *Jacob and *Esau), and of both (chaps. 37–50: *Joseph, his father, and brothers). In these stories the family is the paradigm of community from which all others arise. Human existence is experienced through the succession of generations. One's own identity is preserved in the tales of the ancestors, and only by telling those tales is a link with them established.

Three epochs are reflected in the three generations of Genesis. The first (chaps. 12–25) is dominated chiefly by primal events; life and death are repeatedly at stake. In the second (chaps. 26–36), institutions such as property rights, judicial practice, and sacred rites in sacred locations begin to play a role. The third (chaps. 37–50) reflects the confrontation of kin and kingship in Joseph's rule over his brothers.

The ancestral narratives grew out of oral traditions. They consist of various types of stories, genealogies, itineraries, and divine oracles. In the oral stage of transmission, these elements simply occurred in various versions and underwent many changes in the course of their existence. This is also true of the divine oracles, which trace their origins back to the ancestral period but owe their further development to a later time. Our concept of history cannot be applied to these narratives; they are not historical writing. Rather, they grew out of an interest in telling of one's own ancestors in order to preserve their memory, and this only made sense if the accounts did include true reports of actual persons: in a preliterary age, past events are narrated in order to allow their hearers to share in them.

In its written form, the text in chaps. 12–36 developed from the union of two independent texts, *J ("Yahwist," the earlier of the two) and *P ("Priestly," the more recent). The older text in chaps. 12–25 and 25–36 knits together stories and accounts from the era of the ancestors into a coherent history; the author functioned simultaneously as transmitter, poet, and theologian. This work subsequently underwent a series of expansions. The more recent work grew out of a priestly theology. In addition to its narratives, this text is dominated by genealogies and itineraries that describe the course of Abraham's life (Isaac's is only alluded to) and that of Jacob and Esau. Divine promises and calls occupy a central position in both sections (chaps. 17 and 35), and the concept of *covenant is of prime significance. Characteristic of P are the etiologies of precultic rites, such as *circumcision (chap. 17), kin *marriage (chaps. 27–28), and burial on one's own land (chap. 23), which establish the family as the basic cell of the nation. This more recent text has radically altered the history from a theological point of view. A redactor (R) created a coherent presentation of ancestral history out of these two texts. *(See *Pentateuch for more detail.)*

The time of the ancestors cannot be determined with certainty (attempts to fix its beginnings have ranged from 2200 to 1200 BCE). At any rate, it is the era before the *Exodus and the settlement of the tribes in Canaan. The individuals and the societal structures belong to the prepolitical life-style of pastoral *nomads before they become settled, lacking economic or political safeguards, and passing by walled cities at a distance. They live with elemental threats to their survival: hunger and thirst, natural catastrophes, danger from those in power. For them, temporal continuity exists only in the succession of generations; the future is embodied in their offspring.

Chapters 12–25: the Abraham cycle. These chapters contain a variety of tales about Abraham, framed by genealogies (11.27–32; 25.1–18) and connected by itineraries. The narratives follow two trajectories: one begins with Sarah's sterility (11.30) and leads to the birth of Isaac (21.1–7) through 12.10–20; 15.2–4, 16, 21; and 17.15–17; in addition there are the later accounts in chaps. 22; 23; and 24. This trajectory concerns the continuation of a family's life from one generation to another among threats and tensions. The Abraham-Lot narratives (chaps. 13; 18; and 19) form a second trajectory, which deals with a family's territory. At the center are the destruction of *Sodom and the rescue of *Lot.

Beside the narratives, an independent line of tradition is found in the divine pronouncements. Their point of departure and core is the prophecy foretelling a son (15.2–3; 16.11; 18.10–14;

17.15–21), one of the earliest Abraham stories. The prophecies of blessing, multiplying, and landowning belong to a later tradition. At the center (chaps. 15–17), prophecies accumulate and form their own narratives.

Between the first ending (chap. 21) and the final one (chap. 25), three detailed stories belonging to a late phase of the Abraham tradition have been inserted (chaps. 22; 23; and 24). Abraham's questioning of God concerning the destruction of Sodom (chap. 18.16–33) also belongs to this late phase. The account of Abraham and the kings (chap. 14) is a very late addition.

Chapters 26–36: the Jacob-Esau cycle. The heart of chaps. 26–36 is the conflict between the brothers Jacob and Esau; at its center is Jacob's indenture to Laban (chaps. 29–31) and the birth of Jacob's sons (chaps. 29.31–30.24: the quarrel between *Leah and *Rachel). These too are tales of conflict. Genealogies form the introduction and conclusion, and the theme of flight and return (chaps. 29–33) provides a larger narrative framework. The conflicts concern territory, food supply, and social standing. Accounts of holy places and encounters with God have been inserted in this context (chaps. 28, 32, and 35). Chap. 26, a remnant of the oral tradition, and chap. 34, an episode from the time of the Judges, do not belong in this context. The conflicts in the Jacob-Esau cycle take place in a familial setting and must be resolved there, since they all endanger the survival of the group; consequently, the narratives tend toward a peaceful resolution of conflict, as in the reconciliation of Jacob and Esau (chap. 33).

The religion of the ancestors. The religion of the ancestral period differs from that of Israel in later times (*see* Israel, Religion of). It is entirely determined by a personal relationship to God, which corresponds to the life-style of the ancestors. They are dependent on God's blessing; he bestows fertility on humans and their livestock, grants success in enterprise, and lets flocks increase and children mature. God is with them on their path; he helps them to find watering places, directs their journeys, and guides their departures and settlings. They are as dependent on God's promises as on his guidance, for they have no other safeguards for the future. While in chaps. 12–25 God's promises carry a vital significance for the whole, in chaps. 26–36 it is his blessing that occupies this position; God's blessing is the outcome even of the brothers' quarrel as well as of several other episodes.

God not only blesses, he is also the one who saves. He answers the lament of the childless with the promise of a child (17.15–19), which constitutes deliverance. God hears the cry of a thirsty child and leads the mother to a spring (21.15–19). In this relationship with God there is no need for laws. The *curse does not yet stand beside the *blessing, and the covenant is not yet paired with the threat of judgment. This is a prepolitical form of religion; the God of the ancestors has nothing to do with waging war.

In all these narratives, the ancestors are dealing with only one God. There is no sense of polytheistic influence from the surrounding culture. It is the single God on whom they call and in whom they trust, although one cannot describe the religion of the ancestors as a studied *monotheism. They do not yet have an institutional cult; they have no temple, no priesthood, and no cultic laws. Whatever passes between God and human beings happens directly. Only expansions such as 18.16–38 contain intellectual reflections. It is only in such later passages, and not in the ancestral period, that theological concepts, such as *faith, *righteousness, trial, and *covenant, receive significance. The later text of P begins to use language of a theological cast; and only in the later layers of tradition does one find the idealization of the ancestors and the accentuation of their merits.

Chapters 37–50: the Joseph story. The narrative begins with a quarrel between *Joseph and his brothers (chap. 37) and ends with their reconciliation and reunion (chaps. 45–46). In chaps. 46–50 as in 37, the Joseph story is connected with that of Jacob. These connections at the beginning and the end show that the Joseph narrative is meant to continue the ancestral history. The Joseph story in the narrow sense (chaps. 37–45 [except 38] along with sections of chaps. 46–50) is a unified work, complete in itself, from the hand of an unknown writer who was also a theologian. It is an extensive family history, which proceeds from an imminent rift in the family of Jacob to the healing of that rift. The story is structured around two settings: the house of Jacob and Pharaoh's court. It starts with the quarrel of Joseph and his brothers (chap. 37). Chaps. 37–41 tell of Joseph's rise in *Egypt; chaps. 42–45 take up the journeys of Joseph's brothers to Egypt and end with their reconciliation. The kingdom is incorporated into the narrative by setting parts of the story at Pharaoh's court; the restoration of peace in Jacob's family becomes possible through Joseph's high position at the Egyptian court, and at the same time, famine is averted from the Egyptian people. Thus, the Joseph story corresponds to two periods in the history of the people of Israel, that of the kings and that of the ancestors, and creates a connection between them. The end of the story concerns Jacob's testament and death, and finally the death of Joseph. Chaps. 38 (Judah and Tamar) and 49 (sayings of the tribes) are not part of the Jacob story but were inserted later.

The Joseph story is a unified literary narrative, the work of one author in the early monarchic period. The author is not the same as that of the older J tradition (chaps. 12–36); the technique and style are different, for the Joseph story is not compiled from separate narratives and contains no genealogies or itineraries. This story is meant to be heard, not read; thus, the shape of the narrative is clearly defined, both as a whole and in the individual sections. Narrative techniques include key words (three pairs of dreams, Joseph's coat, famine) and doublets (two settings, two journeys, pairs of dreams). The lively description of people and interpersonal relations is characteristic, as in Joseph's rise and fall at court and the danger of abusing power.

The Joseph story is not a didactic wisdom narrative. Only chaps. 39–41 have a connection to *wisdom literature, conditioned by their subject: the wisdom of a statesman at the royal court. Pharaoh describes Joseph as a wise statesman, but his is no artificially learned, scholastic wisdom, but instead a wisdom bestowed by God and matured by hard experience.

God is with Joseph in the low and high points of his life. The effect of his blessing is directed at an individual, but it also gains a universal scope when he averts famine from Egypt. He is the God of peace who heals the rift in the family of Jacob. The God who blesses is also the God who saves. He seeks after the guilty and makes possible forgiveness and reconciliation. The interpretation in 45.5–8 and 50.19–21 summarizes the action of God in this story: God has incorporated the evil doings of the brothers into his working of good. It is God's action that fashions the sequence of events into a whole; at the same time, the whole sequence of events is encompassed within it.

See also Interpretation, History of, *article on* Modern Biblical Criticism.

CLAUS WESTERMANN

Gentile. From the Latin *gens* (literally, "nation"; Hebr. *gôy;* Grk. *ethnos*), "gentile" refers to a non-Jew or, more broadly, anyone outside the covenant community of Israel. Postexilic times witness references to individual gentiles as opposed to nations; concurrently, the possibility of *conversion to Judaism appears. Gentiles depicted in the Bible are as diverse as are Jews: From *Rahab to *Ruth, Haman to Holofernes, they come from various locations and play various roles—helpers, oppressors, witnesses, tempters.

Joshua 24.11 mentions the seven nations from whom the covenant community is to maintain separation (see Exod. 23.23–33; Deut. 7; Josh. 23). Yet a "mixed multitude" accompanies the community escaping Egypt (Exod. 12.38), and rules for the resident *alien permit the circumcised sojourner to participate in Israel's religious life (Exod. 12.48–49). The so-called promise motif (Gen. 12.3; see Ps. 72.17; Jer. 4.2) insists that by *Abraham "all the families of the earth will bless themselves/be blessed"; Isaiah 42.6 (see 60.3) calls Israel "a light to the nations"; and *Jonah is commissioned to preach to Nineveh. Yet Ezra (9–10) and Nehemiah (10.30; 13.23–30) require *divorce of gentile wives (see also Exod. 34.15–16), and the condemnation of gentile nations is a common prophetic motif. The Hebrew book of *Esther does not decry intermarriage, and the book of Ruth celebrates the union of a Judean man to a *Moabite woman, but the Greek additions to Esther and the book of *Tobit value endogamy (*see* Marriage).

Connections between Jewish and gentile communities existed in politics, trade, and even religious practices. Some gentiles became *proselytes (Jth. 14.10; Acts 6.5); others were attracted to Jewish practices and *synagogues (the "God-fearers"). The pseudepigraphical book of Joseph and Asenath presents the Egyptian priest's daughter whom Joseph marries as the archetypal proselyte. Gentiles also participated in worship in the Herodian *Temple (Josephus, *War* 2.17.412–16; 4.4.275; 5.13.563).

Jewish reactions to gentiles are also diverse. Most Jewish groups in the Hellenistic and early Roman periods believed that the righteous among the gentiles would achieve salvation, but they would do so as gentiles and by divine decree at the end of time. Such dual soteriology may also underlie Romans 9–11. *Genesis Rabbah* 34.8 lists the Noachide commandments incumbent on gentiles. *Tosepta Sanhedrin* 13.2 mentions gentiles who receive a place in the word to come (but see

1QM; 4 Ezra 3.32–36; 'Abod. Zar. 24a). Jews were to deal honestly with gentiles ('Abod. Zar. 26a) and relieve their poor (Giṭ. 61a) even as they were warned against associating with idolaters. Neither scriptural warrant nor unambiguous historical evidence exists for an organized Jewish program to convert gentiles. Distinctions were to be kept between Jew and gentile, but the manner in which separation was maintained varied economically, socially, geographically, ritually, and philosophically.

Early Christian views of gentiles are generally positive; this is not surprising, given that the church found gentile territory fertile soil for its messages and that most of its canonical documents are addressed to gentile or partially gentile communities. Matthew's *genealogy includes gentiles, and the gospel concludes with the command to make disciples of all the nations (or gentiles, panta ta ethnē; 28.19); Luke has *Simeon predict that Jesus will be "a light for revelation to the Gentiles" (2.32). *Paul is the apostle to the gentiles both in Acts and in his own letters. How Jesus himself regarded gentiles is not clear. In Matthew 10.5b–6; 15.24, he forbids his disciples to engage in a gentile mission (see also Rom. 15.8), but Luke 4 depicts his early willingness to extend the good news to non-Jews. And both comments may be redactional inserts.

Anticipated by the conversion of Cornelius in Acts 10, behavior incumbent on gentile Christians is confirmed by the *Apostolic Council in Jerusalem (Acts 15): gentiles were to follow what was likely a combination of Noachide commandments and the laws incumbent on the resident alien (see also Gal. 2). Scholars debate whether Paul himself insisted that all ritual law was abrogated in light of the Christ event, or whether ethic Jews could retain ritual practices. Within a century, this debate ended: Christianity became predominantly gentile, and Jewish practices were labeled heresies. Today, especially in the United States, "gentile" is often viewed as synonymous with "Christian." This is not, however, the case among members of the Church of Jesus Christ of Latter-day Saints (Mormons), who refer to those outside their community (including Jews) as "gentiles."   AMY-JILL LEVINE

Geography of Palestine. *(For this article map references are not given; Map 1 and the index to the maps should be consulted.)* From the time of the Greek historian Herodotus (fifth century BCE),

the term "Palestine" (derived from the word for *Philistine) designated the western tip of the Fertile Crescent, namely, the area on both sides of the *Jordan River, limited on the north by the Litani River and Mount *Hermon, on the east by the Syrian desert, on the south by the *Negeb desert, and on the west by the Mediterranean Sea. It falls into six broad geographical regions: the coastal plain, the Shephelah, the central mountain range, the Judean desert, the Jordan Valley, and the Transjordanian plateau. These can be visualized as north-south strips set side by side.

The Coastal Plain. This strip is divided into three unequal portions by the Ladder of Tyre (Rosh ha-Niqra/Ras en-Naqura) and Mount Carmel. Above Rosh ha-Niqra, the plain widens to the north reaching its greatest width at the *Phoenician city of Tyre, which in biblical times was an island. Between Rosh ha-Niqra and Mount Carmel, the plain averages 8 km (5 mi) in width. In addition to an annual rainfall of 600 mm (24 in), it is thoroughly watered, particularly south of Ptolemais (Akko), where the alluvium deposited by the Naaman and Kishon rivers has pushed the coastline forward into the Bay of Haifa. The two tips of the bay form natural harbors at Akko and Tell Abu Hawam.

South of Mount Carmel, the smooth coastline is devoid of natural harbors, but in antiquity there were lighterage stations at Dor, Strato's Tower, and Jaffa. In this area, the plain is much broader and runs all the way to Gaza. It is characterized by three parallel kurkar ridges, the remnants of prehistoric coastlines. The sand outside the first ridge gave way to swamps within, caused by the failure of rivers and *wadis to drain completely. In biblical times, the third ridge was covered with oak, and the rich soil of the land reaching to the foothills was ideal for *agriculture. The plain is divided in two by the Yarkon River, which begins at Aphek (Rosh ha-'Ayin). The plain of Sharon north of the Yarkon receives almost twice as much rain (300 mm [12 in]) as the plain of Philistia to the south. The great commercial highway, the Way of the Sea, had to pass through the 3 km (2 mi) gap between Aphek and the hills. This became a major crossroads when *Herod the Great built the first artificial harbor at Strato's Tower and named it Caesarea Maritima.

The Shephelah. As the biblical name ("lowlands") indicates, this is an area of low, rolling hills roughly 45 km (28 mi) long and 15 km (9 mi) broad, lying south of the Aijalon valley. The soft chalk and limestone hills are cut by wide valleys running both north-south and east-west. Even the driest part in the south receives about 250 mm (10 in) of rain, and in the biblical period it was intensely cultivated. Olives, sycamore figs, and vineyards are mentioned explicitly in the Bible. The key cities were *Gezer in the north, which dominated both the plain and the easiest access to the mountains, and *Lachish in the south, which controlled the main route through the center to Beth-shemesh and also the lateral route to *Hebron.

The Central Mountain Range. This region is by far the biggest, and can be divided into three areas, *Galilee, Carmel and *Samaria, and Judea.

Galilee. This mountainous area is bordered on the north by the Litani River and on the south by the Jezreel Valley, which runs along the north side of the Carmel range and broadens out into the great plain of Esdraelon (365 km² [140 mi²]) before sloping gently to join the Jordan Valley at Beth-shean. Because ancient settlements appear only on the edges, it must have been subject to flooding in biblical times. It was, nonetheless, a very important east-west route.

The classical division into Upper and Lower Galilee is based on the simple fact that the three highest peaks of the former are all over 1000 m (3300 ft), whereas the two highest of the latter barely attain 600 m (2000 ft). Even though both benefit by an average rainfall of 800–500 mm (30–20 in), the terrain is generally unsuited to agriculture, and in the biblical period was covered by oak forests. The isolation of the perfectly rounded Mount Tabor (588 m [1929 ft]) gave it a numinous quality. Beside it ran the Way of the Sea, angling out from Hazor to the coast through the Carmel range.

Carmel and Samaria. Running southeast from the coast, the Carmel range is cut by two strategic passes, the Nahal Yoqneam and the Nahal ʿIron, the latter with *Megiddo at its northern end. South of the Dothan Valley, the ridge coalesces with the mountains of Gilboa to create a much wider range with no Shephelah on the west and a steep drop into the Jordan Valley on the east. The central core of the area is constituted by Mount Gerizim (881 m [2889 ft]) and Mount Ebal (941 m [3083 ft]). The pass between them, controlled by *Shechem (Nablus), carried the major east-west route coming from the Jordan via the verdant Wadi el-Farʿah, in which Tirzah, (Tell el-Farʿah) is located, and out to the coast just south of Samaria. This was the heartland of

the northern kingdom of Israel, and the contrast between the closed site of Tirzah and the wide prospect to the west from Samaria is symbolic of the shift in policy that took place under Omri in the ninth century BCE (1 Kings 16.23–24; see Israel, History of). In this period, the hills were heavily wooded, but the valleys, which are wider in the north, produced grain, olives, and grapes. North-south travel was difficult, except on the crest running south from Shechem. The first 20 km (12 mi) of the route lay in the fertile Michmethath Valley, but after the ascent of Lubban the road wound in narrow wadis past the sanctuaries of Shiloh and Bethel.

Judea. Geographically, the Jerusalem hills are a saddle between Ramallah and *Bethlehem, which is some 200 m (650 ft) lower than the highest points of Samaria to the north and Hebron to the south. This facilitated east-west travel, and there have always been relatively easy routes to the coastal plain and the Jordan Valley. The forests that covered the hills when the Israelites first occupied the area gradually disappeared. The demands of a growing city were intensified by the insatiable appetite for firewood of a sacrificial cult that endured almost a thousand years. After the hills had been denuded, terraces began to be built on the slopes. The small fields thus developed supported mainly olive trees, but some grain crops as well. The average rainfall is 560 mm (22 in). Enveloped by higher hills with a poor water supply and a location off the natural routes, *Jerusalem would have been doomed to insignificance had *David not given it political weight by making it a religious center.

South of Bethlehem, the hills rise toward Hebron (1000 m [3300 ft]) and then descend to the great plain around Beer-sheba. The tree cover in the biblical period was oak with patches of pine, but Genesis 49.11 attests the intense cultivation of the *vine in the valleys and on terraces. The only significant route ran north-south with only one good branch route to the coastal plain. The geographic homogeneity of the Hebron hills helps to explain why it was always the territory of a single tribe, *Judah.

The Judean Desert. This region borders the Hebron hills on the east. The rainfall decreases sharply some 5 km (3 mi) east of the watershed, and in 20 km (12 mi) the land drops 1200 m (4000 ft) to the Dead Sea. The vegetation is sufficient to support only sheep and goats. In biblical times, this was the grazing land of the settlements on the eastern edge of the hill country (see 1 Sam. 25.2). There are few springs, but runoff can be collected in cisterns to water the flocks. The character of the terrain makes travel difficult. It descends to the east in a series of steps, the most important of which is the Valley of Achor at the northern end. These are cut by the deep gorges of the Wadi Murabba'ât and Wadi Ghiar, which drain into the Dead Sea; both had extensive prehistoric occupation. In the biblical period, the only significant route was that from Tekoa to En-gedi.

The Jordan Valley. From its principal source at Banyas (303 m [995 ft]) in the foothills of Mount *Hermon, the *Jordan River runs south in a great crack in the earth's surface where two tectonic plates meet. It continues down the Gulf of Aqaba/Eilat to become the Rift Valley in Africa. In biblical times, the area south of *Dan was an impassable swamp with Lake Huleh at its center. The Sea of *Galilee (21 by 12 km [13 by 7½ mi] at its longest and widest) is a freshwater lake 210 m (700 ft) below sea-level. It contains twenty-two species of fish, and fishing has always been essential to the local economy.

Shortly after the Jordan leaves the lake it is supplemented by the waters of the Yarmuk. In the 105 km (65 mi) to the Dead Sea the valley drops 194 m (540 ft) but the river meanders through 322 km (200 mi). The river bed with its tropical undergrowth that sheltered large wild *animals is some 7 m (23 ft) below the valley, which widens to 23 km (14 mi) near *Jericho, where the rainfall averages only 150 mm (6 in).

The Jordan ends in the Dead Sea (404 m [1285 ft] below sea level), which has no outlet. Water is lost only through evaporation (in the 40°C [105°F] heat of summer about 24 mm (1 in) each day), producing a high concentration of all the chlorides (26 percent as opposed to the 3.5 percent salinity of the oceans); in Hebrew it is called the "Sea of Salt" (Gen. 14.3; etc; NRSV: "Dead Sea"). It averages 16 km (10 mi) wide, and its length was reduced to 50 km (30 mi) in 1976 when the area south of the Lynch Straits dried out. This may have been the size of the sea in the historical period, but some fifty thousand years ago the water level was 225 m (731 ft) higher, and the valley as far as Galilee was a long inlet of the Red Sea. The gradually rising continuation of the valley to the Gulf of Aqaba/ Eilat is now called the Arabah, though in the Bible that term generally means other parts of the Rift Valley.

The Transjordanian Plateau. This region is a strip roughly 40 km (25 mi) wide starting at Mount Hermon and limited on the west by the escarpment of the Jordan Valley. On the east it gradually shades into the Syrian desert. The Golan, lying north of the Yarmuk river, was biblical Bashan and is a basalt plateau characterized by the small cones of extinct volcanoes. The fertile volcanic soil of the southern part gives way to wild pastureland in the north. The center of biblical Gilead is located between the rivers Yarmuk and Jabbok (Nahr ez-Zerqa), but the term is also employed to designate the area as far south as the Arnon River (Seil el-Mojib), which is also called *Ammon. The terrain and vegetation cover is very similar to that of the hill country of Samaria. At an average of 1000 m (3300 ft) above sea level, the plateau of *Moab lying between the Arnon and the Brook Zered (Wadi el-Hesa) is higher than the land to the north. In biblical times, it was proverbial for its fertility, and 2 Kings 3.4 highlights the productivity of its sheep farming. *Edom extends south of Moab as far as the Gulf of Aqaba/Eilat. Its average height parallels that of Moab, but the central peaks rise to 1700 m (5600 ft). Winters are very cold and the snows can last until March. Due to the altitude, the tree cover of this area extends much further south than the corresponding forests west of the Jordan. The great commercial route, the King's Highway, ran the length of the plateau linking *Damascus with the ports of Elath and Ezion-geber on the Gulf of Aqaba.

See also Maps of the Biblical World.

JEROME MURPHY-O'CONNOR

Gestures. The use of gestures by human beings to denote various feelings or attitudes is a universal phenomenon. Specific gestures may vary from culture to culture; therefore gestures used by the biblical peoples must be understood in their own context. Some of these can be illustrated, however, by examining various tomb paintings, reliefs, and sculptures from the ancient Near East and the biblical texts themselves.

The most frequently mentioned gesture in the biblical writings is that of bowing the head or body, kneeling, or prostrating oneself on the ground. This gesture indicates reverence or subservience to the person or being toward whom the gesture is made. Usually this mode of action is reserved for God or a king or anyone in a position of authority. Most frequently this gesture was assumed in prayer addressed to the deity (1 Kings 8.54; Dan. 6.10; Luke 22.41). While in this position the hands were often held open and upward. This latter gesture was described as "stretching out the hands" (Isa. 1.15), obviously holding out the hands to receive what was requested.

Many other gestures are mentioned in the Bible. One was expected to rise when someone of greater age or importance entered the room (Lev. 19.32; Job 29.8). Out of respect for the scriptures it seems to have been the custom to stand while reading and perhaps hearing the holy words (Neh. 8–9; Luke 4.16–20). When teaching, however, the usual posture was sitting (Matt. 5.1; 23.2; 26.55). To express contempt for another person, one would spit in the other's face (Deut. 26.9; Matt. 26.67). *Mourning was accompanied by such gestures as tearing the garments (Josh. 7.6; Job 1.20) and at times sprinkling dust on the head (Job 2.12–13) or cutting the hair (Ezek. 27.30–31). Striking the thigh seems to have denoted grief or shame (Jer. 31.19; Ezek. 21.17).

Most gestures are accompanied by oral exclamations in the biblical texts so that the meaning of the gesture is usually quite obvious.

JAMES M. EFIRD

Gethsemane (Map 9). The name of the place in *Jerusalem where, according to Matthew 26.36 and Mark 14.32, Jesus was arrested. John does not name it but calls it a garden (18.1). This fits the name's meaning, "oil-press," as does its location on the lower slopes of the Mount of *Olives, in the general vicinity of the several churches there today.   MICHAEL D. COOGAN

Gezer. A major city in antiquity and the object of important archaeological excavations in this century, Gezer lies on the border between the Judean foothills and the Shephelah, in the tribal territory of Ephraim (Map 1:W5). Mentioned in inscriptions of Pharaohs Tuthmose III (first half of fifteenth century BCE) and Merneptah (end of thirteenth century), as well as in the *Amarna letters (mid-fourteenth century), Gezer came under Israelite control at a relatively late date. Although the Israelites had failed to conquer the Canaanite city (Josh. 16.10; Judg. 1.29), it passed to their control when it was ceded to *Solomon by Egypt, ostensibly as a dowry for his wife, the pharaoh's daughter (1 Kings 9.16). The siege of Gezer by the *Assyrians (734–732 BCE) is depicted on a relief from the palace of *Tiglath-pileser III in Nimrud (ancient Calah). During the Maccabean period Gezer (called Gazara) was an important Seleucid stronghold until its capture by Simon in 143 BCE (1 Macc. 13.43–48).

CARL S. EHRLICH

Gideon. Also called "Jerubbaal" (Judg. 6.32; 9.1; 1 Sam. 12.11), Gideon is a judge-deliverer from *Manasseh who leads the central highland tribes to victory over *Midianite raiders (Judg. 6.1–8.21). His story illustrates the theme of total dependence on God: at divine command, he reduced his army from thirty-two thousand to three hundred before attacking the enemy (Judg. 7.1–8). Gideon's story also reveals tensions in premonarchic Israel. Intertribal rivalry is evident, as the tribe of *Ephraim shows its jealousy toward Gideon's tribe of Manasseh as a result of Gideon's success (Judg. 7.24–8.3). Also, there is tension over Israel's form of government. After his victory, the people move to make Gideon king; but he refuses, saying they should look on God as their king (Judg. 8.22–23). By contrast, when Gideon's son Abimelech tries to adopt *kingship for himself (after his father's death), he is rejected by the people and killed (Judg. 9).

See also Judges, The Book of.

TIMOTHY M. WILLIS

Gideons, The. The Gideons are an organization of laypeople dedicated to Christian evangelism through the distribution of scripture. They got their start through a chance encounter between two traveling salesmen at the Central Hotel in Boscobel, Wisconsin, in 1898. John H. Nicholson and Samuel Hill, who had stumbled into a raucous convention of lumberjacks, discovered that they shared a common love of the scriptures. The next year, along with W. J. Knights, they founded the Christian Commercial Travelers Association of America. Later the organization was named after *Gideon who (according to Judg. 7) led Israel, armed only with torches and pitchers, to victory over the *Midianites. The Gideons began distributing Bibles in 1908, with their first order for twenty-five copies assigned to the Superior Hotel in Iron Mountain, Montana. Since then, they have put the Bible into hotels and motels in 140 countries. They have also distributed millions of New Testaments to school children and to men and women entering the military. Their Bibles have gone to prisons, inner-city rescue missions, hospitals (in large print), and airplanes, ships, and trains. The ubiquitous presence of the Gideon Bible in hotel rooms has been the occasion of much humor, some of it risqué, but also of reassurance to countless travelers. The organization is active in at least seventy-five countries. In 1990, the Gideons presented their 500 millionth Bible to President George Bush.   MARK A. NOLL

Gilgamesh Epic. The Gilgamesh Epic is the greatest masterpiece of literature prior to the Bible and Homer. Episodes of Gilgamesh such as the *flood (from which Genesis 6–8 is in part derived) have survived in older *Sumerian tablets, but the epic as a whole was the later creation of the Semitic *Babylonians and *Assyrians. It circulated widely in the ancient Near East, and was translated into other languages, including *Hittite and Hurrian. As the foremost classic of Mesopotamian civilization, it penetrated Palestine prior to the Israelite *conquest, and Anatolia, where it was available to the Ionian Greeks of Asia Minor.

The twelve tablets of the Gilgamesh Epic form a unified composition dealing with the serious problems of life and death as experienced by the hero Gilgamesh. The milieu of the epic is urban: Gilgamesh is the king of Uruk (biblical Erech), described as a well-planned walled city of superb construction.

The Gilgamesh Epic deals with heroic values. Gilgamesh gives up selfish tyranny for the noble but dangerous aim of eliminating evil from the face of the earth. Because he needs a friend to help him in this awesome mission, a worthy companion, named Enkidu, is created for him out of clay. Together they triumph over the forces of evil in the forms of monsters and dragons.

For offending the goddess Ishtar, Enkidu dies, which reminds Gilgamesh that he too is mortal and will someday perish. For, like *Adam, Gilgamesh has gained knowledge but not immortality. Frightened by the prospect of death, Gilgamesh undertakes a perilous journey to the hero Utnapishtim, who survived the *flood and had immortality conferred on him by the assembled gods. On the way, Gilgamesh stops at the tavern run by the goddess Siduri, who tells him to make the most of life: to eat, drink, be merry; to wed and sire children whose little hands he could hold. Such are the joys within the grasp of mortals; but the gods had reserved immortality for themselves. Nevertheless, Gilgamesh persists in traversing land and sea until he finds old Utnapishtim, who explains that the gods had made him immortal because of a unique event,

the flood, which would never be repeated. The gods could not be reconvened merely to immortalize Gilgamesh. So Gilgamesh returns to Uruk, whose magnificence he admires. If we mortals cannot have heaven, we can at least enjoy the comforts of our native city.

The final tablet tells how Gilgamesh interviews the dead Enkidu and learns that the underworld is dreary at best, but utterly wretched for those who die without progeny to offer them food and drink. One's state there is alleviated by leaving children on earth—and the more, the better.

The message is clear: Make the most of the life that is given to us. Ecclesiastes (3.22; 5.17–19; 8.15) makes the same point.

CYRUS H. GORDON

Glory of God. While *holiness expresses God's transcendence, his glory concerns rather his immanence to the world. One text can be seen to combine both concepts: "Holy, holy, holy is the Lord of hosts; the whole earth is full of his glory" (Isa. 6.3). God is invisible, but his glory (Hebr. *kābôd*) manifests itself in *theophanies, usually associated with storms, fire, and earthquake (see Hab. 3.1–19; Ps. 18.7–15). Such resplendent events both reveal God's presence and reflect his transcendence, concealing him as it were. In the Yahwist (*J) tradition, God shows himself present in a pillar of cloud or of fire (Exod. 13.21), while for the Priestly (*P) tradition "the glory of the Lord" settled on Mount *Sinai and appeared to the Israelites below "like a devouring fire" (Exod. 24.17). Also according to this tradition, the radiant glory of the Lord so transfigured *Moses' face that he had to wear a veil to conceal it (Exod. 34.23–35; cf. Matt. 17.2; 2 Cor. 3.7–18). It was this same manifestation of the divine presence which filled the *Temple when it was dedicated (1 Kings 8.11); Ezekiel described it as leaving the Temple (Ezek. 10.14), going into *exile with Israel, an exile from which it would return (Ezek. 43.2–5).

Though the universal character of the divine glory is often referred to (e.g., Pss. 97.6; 145.10–13; Hab. 2.14), in later biblical traditions this universality is particularly stressed (Isa. 35.2; 40.5; 60.1–3; 66.18–19; see also Luke 2.30–32).

When Paul speaks of "an eternal weight of glory" (2 Cor. 4.17), he is recalling the etymology of the Hebrew word (which is derived from the root *kbd*, whose primary meaning is "to be heavy"). For Paul, the "glory of Christ" (2 Cor. 4.4), particularly the risen Christ, is a manifestation of the glory of the Father (Rom. 6.4; cf. Mark 8.38 par.). In the gospel of John, on the other hand, the glory of God, possessed by Christ in his preexistence (John 17.5), now dwells in him on earth. The prologue to this Gospel continues the statement that the "Word became flesh and pitched his tent among us" with another regarding seeing the glory of the Son (1.14), and the rest of the Gospel describes particular manifestations of that glory (2.11; 13.31). Similarly, for the author of the letter to the *Hebrews, the Son "is the reflection of God's glory and the exact imprint of God's very being" (1.3), somewhat like personified *Wisdom, "a pure emanation of the glory of the Almighty" (Wisd. of Sol. 7.25).

LEOPOLD SABOURIN

describes, for he reports that some had charged those who had received the Spirit with drunkenness (Acts 2.13). But Luke interprets the tongues as known languages, and Pentecost as the reversal of *Babel (Gen. 11.1–9), where a confusion of languages had divided the human community. Each of the three passages of Acts in which explicit mention is made of tongues represents a breakthrough in the church's mission. At Pentecost, the first three thousand were baptized (Acts 2.41). The second mention (Acts 10.46) represents the beginning of the gentile mission. The third (Acts 19.6) occurs when the Christian mission is clearly differentiated from that of the followers of *John the Baptist.

JOHN FREDERICK JANSEN

Glossolalia. Glossolalia (from Grk. *glōssai,* "tongues, languages," and *lalein,* "to speak") is a phenomenon of intense religious experience expressing itself in ecstatic speech. It is found in several religions, and in Christianity is understood to be a manifestation of the *Holy Spirit.

Explicit New Testament references to speaking in tongues are confined to 1 Corinthians 12–14 and three passages in Acts (2.1–13; 10.46; 19.6). While Paul and the author of Acts both affirm that tongues are a gift of the Spirit, their portrayals of the experience are very different. Paul, who himself had shared the experience (1 Cor. 14.18), describes speaking in tongues as unintelligible to others unless a further gift of interpretation enables it to be more than private devotion, and he contrasts tongues and prophecy (1 Cor. 12.30; 14.5). Luke's description of *Pentecost understands these "other tongues" (Acts 2.4) as intelligible proclamation, and he links tongues and prophecy (Acts 2.16–18; 19.6).

Paul replies to questions and assertions put to him by the Corinthian church. As with other matters in Corinth, Paul is disturbed by the self-centeredness of those who prize and parade their piety while neglecting the love that builds up the community. Accordingly, his chapter on *love as the more excellent way (1 Cor. 13) is at the heart of his discussion, and in the list of gifts of the Spirit he places tongues and the interpretation of tongues last. He suggests that undue preoccupation with tongues represents immaturity (1 Cor. 13.11; 14.20) rather than maturity, and he limits the use of tongues in the church's assembly (1 Cor. 14.27–28).

Luke's account of Pentecost may include residual traces of the unintelligible speech that Paul

Gnosticism. A modern designation for a religious movement of the early centuries CE, though only some of the groups involved actually called themselves "gnostics" (from Greek *gnōsis,* "knowledge"). Initially it was regarded as a heresy within early Christianity, opposed by Irenaeus, Hippolytus, and others, the "falsely called knowledge" of 1 Timothy 6.20. A false knowledge, however, implies the existence of a true knowledge, and Clement of Alexandria in fact uses the term "gnostic" for a Christian who has penetrated more deeply than the ordinary believer into the knowledge of the truth (*Stromata* 7.1–2). Further complications have arisen with increasing knowledge of the religious life of the ancient world, comparative study of ancient religions, and the attempt to account for the origins of gnosticism. One common error of method has been to identify terms or concepts as "gnostic" because of their appearance in developed gnostic systems, and then to trace them back through Greek philosophy or the religions of *Egypt, *Persia, or *Babylonia. This is to ignore the fact that the gnostics adapted and transformed motifs that they borrowed; some such terms and concepts are "gnostic" only in a gnostic context. More recently, increased attention has been paid to possible Jewish origins; but while there is no doubt of the importance of the Jewish contribution, for example in gnostic use and reinterpretation of the Hebrew Bible, it is by no means certain that the movement originated within Judaism or was initiated by Jews. The *Septuagint was the Bible also of early gentile Christians.

What is now clear is that the movement did not suddenly emerge in the second century CE, when it was opposed by early church fathers. There are affinities in the writings of *Philo of Alexandria, and there is evidence that there was a good deal of "gnosticizing" thought even in the first century CE. A question still in debate is the extent of "gnostic" influence on the New Testament, since the evidence has to be found in the New Testament itself, and there is always a danger of interpreting it in light of later systems, which may be to impose on it the ideas of a later period. There is still no gnostic document that in its present form can be dated prior to the New Testament.

The chief characteristics common to all the developed systems are: (1) a radical cosmic dualism that rejects this world and all that belongs to it: the body is a prison from which the soul longs to escape; (2) a distinction between the unknown transcendent true God and the creator or Demiurge, commonly identified with the God of the Hebrew Bible; (3) the belief that the human race is essentially akin to the divine, being a spark of heavenly light imprisoned in a material body; (4) a myth, often narrating a premundane *fall, to account for the present human predicament; and (5) the saving knowledge by which deliverance is effected and the gnostic awakened to recognition of his or her true nature and heavenly origin. At one time it was thought, as the church fathers sometimes allege, that the gnostic was "saved by nature," and that morality was therefore of no importance; indeed, since ethics is largely a matter of obedience to the law of the creator, who seeks to hold the human race in slavery, it could be seen as a positive duty for the gnostic to disobey all such commands. The evidence of the *Nag Hammadi documents, however, suggests that while some gnostics may have shown libertine tendencies, the main direction of the movement was toward asceticism. Some of the characteristics listed can be identified in other systems of thought, but that does not make these gnostic; it is the combination of those ideas into a new synthesis that is gnosticism.

The classic period of gnosticism is the second century CE, with such figures as Basilides and Valentinus, and the latter's disciples Ptolemy and Heracleon, but this was the culmination of a long development. The later books of the New Testament (e.g., the Pastorals, Jude, 1 John) show signs of resistance to an incipient gnosticism, but it is a mistake to think of clear distinctions between orthodoxy and heresy at such an early stage; differing points of view may well coexist

for a period, interacting with one another, before it finally becomes clear that they are incompatible. The gospel of *John makes frequent use of the verb "to know," but never employs the noun gnōsis, which may perhaps be significant; *Paul uses the noun quite often, but we need to ask whether he is speaking of a specifically gnostic knowledge. Most religions do profess to convey some kind of knowledge! While there may be doubts about gnostic influence in the New Testament, there can be no question of the significance of New Testament influence on gnosticism; this is shown by numerous allusions and direct quotations in the sources, to which the Nag Hammadi library has added greatly.

Gnosticism has often been regarded as bizarre and outlandish, and certainly it is not easily understood until it is examined in its contemporary setting. It was, however, no mere playing with words and ideas, but a serious attempt to resolve real problems: the nature and destiny of the human race, the problem of *evil, the human predicament. To a gnostic it brought a release and joy and hope, as if awakening from a nightmare. One later offshoot, Manicheism, became for a time a world religion, reaching as far as China, and there are at least elements of gnosticism in such medieval movements as those of the Bogomiles and the Cathari. Gnostic influence has been seen in various works of modern literature, such as those of William Blake and W. B. Yeats, and is also to be found in the Theosophy of Madame Blavatsky and the Anthroposophy of Rudolph Steiner. Gnosticism was of lifelong interest to the psychologist C. G. *Jung, and one of the Nag Hammadi codices (the Jung Codex) was for a time in the Jung Institute in Zurich.

ROBERT McL. WILSON

Gog. Described in Ezekiel 38–39 as ruler of the land of Magog, Gog is also "chief prince" of the lands of two tribes in Asia Minor, Meshech (Map 6:F3) and Tubal (Map 6:G3; the specific location of Magog is unknown). Gog, leading a coalition of nations from virtually all points of the compass (Ezek. 38.5–6), is summoned by Yahweh, the God of Israel, to attack Israel itself. Yahweh nonetheless promises to intervene on Israel's behalf, destroying the enemy coalition by means of stupendous natural disasters (Ezek. 38.19–23). The book of Revelation refers to a Satanic invasion of "Gog and Magog" (20.7–10), curiously placing it after the promised millennium (the thousand-year period of the reign of the *Messiah).   WILLIAM H. BARNES

Golden Calf. Three "golden calves" appear in the Bible. The first is fashioned by *Aaron at *Sinai to replace *Moses and Yahweh (Exod. 32; Deut. 9.8–21; Ps. 106.19–20; Neh. 9.18; Acts 7.39–41), and the second and third are a pair commissioned by Jeroboam, leader of the northern secession, to replace the *ark; they were worshiped respectively at *Dan and Bethel (1 Kings 12.26–33).

Hebrew ʿēgel is generally rendered "calf," but a more mature beast may be intended. On the one hand, an ʿēgel can be a prancing (Ps. 29.6), untrained (Jer. 31.18) one-year-old (Lev. 9.3; Mic. 6.6). On the other hand, the feminine ʿeglâ can denote a three-year-old heifer (Gen. 15.9), trained (Hos. 10.11) for plowing (Judg. 14.18) or threshing (Jer. 50.11 [translation uncertain]). Hosea 10.5 calls Jeroboam's images "heifers," although the reading is uncertain; elsewhere, Hosea describes the animals as male (8.5–6; 13.2). Most likely, the golden "calves" are young bulls, as the *Septuagint renders in 1 Kings 12.

It is uncertain from 1 Kings 12.28 whether Jeroboam's images are solid gold or gold-plated wood; 2 Kings 17.16 calls them "molten." Aaron's image is "molten" (Exod. 32.4, 8; Deut. 9.16; Ps. 106.19; Neh. 9.18), yet it is destroyed by grinding and burning (Exod. 32.20), as if partly wooden. Hosea 13.2 refers to molten image(s), idols, and calves (it is unclear whether these are the same), and speaks of silver, not gold, while Hosea 8.4 mentions both silver and gold, probably the constituents of the calf in 8.5. Judges 17–18 describes a molten silver image worshiped in Dan, conceivably a forerunner of Jeroboam's calf. In 1990 a silver-coated molten bronze bull 10 cm (4 in) high dated to ca. 1550 BCE was discovered at Ashkelon.

Aaron's and Jeroboam's calves are symbols of Yahweh; Aaron declares a "festival to Yahweh" (Exod. 32.5) and, throughout its history, the northern kingdom of Israel worshiped Yahweh, even while venerating the calves (2 Kings 3:3, 10.29; etc.). But it is unclear whether the calves represent Yahweh himself or a supernatural bovine on which he stands; Jeroboam's calves may even constitute the armrests of God's throne. All three interpretations have parallels in ancient Near Eastern art and literature, and perhaps more than one was current in Israel. The nonbiblical name ʿEgel-yo appears in the *Samaria

ostraca (eighth century BCE) and could mean either "calf of Yahweh" or "Yahweh is a calf."

The calf stories in Exodus 32 and 1 Kings 12 are closely related. Both extol "your gods, O Israel, who brought you up out of the land of Egypt," and both culminate in priestly ordination. The simplest explanation is that Exodus 32 is a polemic against Jeroboam's movement; this would explain the plural "your gods" in Exodus 32.4 (contrast the singluar in Neh. 9.18). Alternatively, Exodus 32 might be a polemic against an older cult revived by Jeroboam—conceivably that of Judges 17–18.

See also Graven Image; Idols, Idolatry.
                                   WILLIAM H. PROPP

Golden Rule. Since the eighteenth century CE the familiar saying "Do unto others as you would have them do unto you" has been known as the "Golden Rule." Often cited as the sum of Jesus' ethics, the saying also occurs in ancient Greek, Roman, and Jewish writings. For example, Rabbi Hillel (first century BCE) answered a question about the Law's central teaching with the statement: "What is hateful to you, do not do to your fellow creature. That is the whole Law; the rest is commentary" (b. Sabb. 31a).

Some seek to distinguish between the more common negative form just cited and the positive form found in Jesus' teaching by attributing the former to common sense based on self-interest and the latter to Jesus' higher ethical concerns. This distinction, however, fails to hold because the positive form also occurs in extrabiblical writings (*Letter of Aristeas* 207; *T. Naph.* 1; and 2 Enoch 61.1) and the negative form appears in Christian literature, such as a variant reading in Acts 15.20, 29; and *Didache* 1.1.

By itself the rule could indeed reflect a commonsense principle of conduct based on self-interest rather than conduct based on concern for others. But a closer look at New Testament usage reveals that the Golden Rule occurs in contexts calling for *love for others. Matthew and Luke have the saying as part of Jesus' teaching in the *Sermon on the Mount. In Luke 6.31 it is integral to Jesus' teaching about love for one's enemies (6.27–35). In Matthew 7.12 it comes at the conclusion of a series of demands pertaining to one's relation with others (5.21–48) and with God (6.1–7.11). Probably, therefore, Matthew took the saying from its traditional context of love for one's enemies (5.44–47) and used it as a summary of the preceding list of Jesus' demands. By adding the phrase, "for this is the law and the prophets," Matthew places the rule in the broader context of the Sermon on the Mount as well as of his entire gospel. In 5.17 he introduces the series of Jesus' demands (5.21–7.12) by noting that Jesus had come to "fulfill the law and the prophets"; a "greater righteousness" (5.20) is now demanded in one's relationship with others (5.21–48) and with God (6.1–7.11). In 22.40 Matthew directly relates the rule to the love commandment by having Jesus declare that the "law and the prophets" depend on the love commandment.

In the context of Jesus' teaching, therefore, the Golden Rule, rather than being merely a commonsense, ethical rule of thumb, is a practical expression of the love commandment growing out of love for God and one's neighbor. The same connection between the Golden Rule and the love commandment is found in *Didache* 1.2, as well as in the variant reading in Acts 15.20, 29.   ROBERT A. GUELICH

Golgotha. The site of the *crucifixion of Jesus in *Jerusalem; the tomb in which Jesus was buried was apparently nearby (see John 19.41). The name is *Aramaic, and means "the skull," a translation given after the Aramaic in Matthew 27.33, Mark 15.22, and John 19.17. Luke 23.33 gives only the Greek translation. In the *Vulgate a Latin word for "skull," *calvaria*, is used; this is the source of the English word "Calvary," used in the KJV of Luke 23.33. The origin of the name Golgotha is obscure; suggestions include its location in a cemetery and its being a site for executions. The great biblical scholar Origen (third century CE) thought it was the burial place of *Adam; following this view, artists have frequently placed a skull at the base of the cross in representations of the crucifixion.

The precise location of Golgotha and of the tomb of Jesus are not certain, but the most likely candidate is the present site of the Church of the Holy Sepulcher (Map 9), though traditions identifying it as the place of Jesus' death and burial are apparently no earlier than the fourth century CE.   MICHAEL D. COOGAN

Goliath. The heavily armed *Philistine warrior from Gath who, according to 1 Samuel 17, was slain by *David while the latter was still a young shepherd who was armed only with a slingstone and faith in Yahweh. Goliath's height is given in the MT of 1 Samuel 17.4 as six cubits and a span (ca. 3 m [9 ft 9 in]), although textual traditions represented in the *Dead Sea Scrolls and the *Septuagint give four cubits and a span (ca. 2 m [6 ft 9 in]). 1 Samuel 21.8–10 implies, perhaps ironically, that David returned to Gath with Goliath's sword.

In 2 Samuel 21.19 a warrior named Elhanan killed Goliath, a descendant of the giants of Gath, in a battle at Gob. The AV attempts to harmonize the discrepancy by reading: "Elhanan . . . slew the brother of Goliath," following an ancient tendency already found in 1 Chronicles 20.5. However, these discrepancies suggest that the attribution of Goliath's slaying to David may not be original.   HECTOR IGNACIO AVALOS

Gomorrah. *See* Sodom and Gomorrah.

Gospel, Genre of. The term "gospel" (Grk. *euaggelion*) is used in Christian tradition to designate the canonical Gospels, *Matthew, *Mark, *Luke, and *John, presumably written between 65 and 100 CE. Some source-critical theories suggest the existence of a precanonical gospel, that is, a hypothetical primitive gospel or protogospel underlying one or more of the four canonical Gospels. Other gospels were produced in the second century (and perhaps the first), but they are not recognized as canonical. (*See also* Apocrypha, article on Christian Apocrypha; Canon, article on New Testament.)

The four Gospels are grouped together in the New Testament canon, apart from the letters and *Revelation and also distinct from the other narrative book, *Acts of Apostles. The Gospels include stories about *Jesus, sayings of Jesus, and a passion narrative; they describe the career of Jesus in a connected narrative from the preaching of *John the Baptist to Jesus' death and *resurrection. This is commonly accepted as the characteristic gospel form. Justin Martyr, about 150 CE, refers to the "gospels" (the first attestation of the term in the plural) as "the memoirs of the apostles," and this historical or biographical definition remained popular through the centuries: the gospel is the story of Jesus, the account of the life and teaching of Jesus Christ.

According to the modern critical consensus, the Gospels constitute their own literary genre: they are sui generis, sharing a distinctive form and content. Three factors seem to have been of influence. First, the study of the literary relationship among the *synoptic Gospels has led to the widely accepted view that both Matthew and Luke depend on Mark, and thus the problem of the gospel genre has become to a large extent a problem of the origin of Mark. Second, form critics emphasize, on the one hand, the role of the kerygma (preaching) in the early church, and on the other, the oral origin and the unliterary character of the pre-Markan gospel material (short anecdotes, small units, and probably a primitive passion narrative). The author of Mark, by combining this traditional material into a framework, created the gospel genre. Third, the Christian gospel form is apparently not influenced by the genres of the Hellenistic literature. The kerygmatic hypothesis has taken two opposing forms. The majority opinion ascribes the gospel framework to Markan redaction. For C. H. Dodd, on the other hand, Mark serves as a commentary on the kerygma. The basic outline of the gospel corresponds to the historical section in the traditional kerygmatic scheme of the sermons in Acts. The story of the passion is prefaced in Mark 1–8, as it is in Acts 10, by an account of the ministry of Jesus in Galilee. The debate is not closed, but Lucan redaction in Acts 10.36–43 can hardly be denied.

There is, however, a growing dissatisfaction with this form-critical approach. The definition of the gospel of Mark as a passion narrative with an extended introduction is no longer acceptable. There is a renewed interest in the search for parallels to Mark's genre, especially for possible associations with Hellenistic biographical literature, in its variegated forms, including the popular biography; a biography subtype written to dispel a false image of the teacher and to provide a true model to follow; an encomium biography; and the epideictic type of biography. For other scholars, connections with Hellenistic biography remain unproved. Yet it can be recognized that the Gospels are biographical in a broader sense. Some analogies can be found in the biblical tradition: the life of Moses, or the biography of the suffering righteous one. Biography in its various types, however, is only one of the models suggested for the gospel. The *apocalyptic genre, the *Passover haggadah, the calendrical cycles, and, in Greco-Roman literature, the Socratic dialogues, the Greek tragedy, the tragicomedy, and rhetorical conventions are other suggestions. The aretalogy deserves special consideration. Mark and John are supposed to have corrected the divine-man christology of their sources, the pre-Markan collection of miracles and the pre-Johannine signs-source. The gospel thus becomes an antiaretalogy, an adaptation of the existing aretalogical genre. On the other hand, however, the source-critical and other presuppositions of these Markan and Johannine trajectories are far from certain. John's dependence on the Synoptics, at least with regard to the gospel form, is a more likely hypothesis.

The gospel of Mark is used in Matthew and Luke in combination with a second source, the hypothetical *Q document. The narrative framework, typical of the gospel form, is lacking in this sayings collection, and designations such as "wisdom gospel" or "aphoristic gospel" are inappropriate. The Q material is blocked together with special material in three interpolations in Luke and mainly in five (or six) discourses in Matthew. The Markan gospel's general outline is preserved in both, with an expansion of the biographical element in the birth stories and the genealogies at the beginning and the appearances of the risen Lord at the end. Luke and Acts explicitly form a two-volume work by one author, and some influence of the literary conventions of Greek historiography is undeniable.

Each of the four Gospels has its own individuality. Redaction criticism and narrative analysis uncover differences of language, style, and composition, differing theological concepts, and differing authorial intentions. Their anonymity is a common characteristic. The present superscriptions (Gospel according to Matthew, etc.) were affixed at an early stage of the tradition, probably under the influence of Mark 1.1, extending the use of the term gospel proclamation to the literary form of the gospel book.

The gospel genre implies a similarity of form and content. For some of the so-called noncanonical gospels—namely for those that embody stories without kerygmatic outlook or those that present sayings and dialogues without a narrative—the term gospel is used improperly.

FRANS NEIRYNCK

Grace. In the Bible, the term grace combines ideas in tension that point to profound mystery. Grace names the undeserved gift that creates relationships and the sustaining, responding, forebearing attitude-plus-action that nurtures relationships. Grace concerns the interaction between gracious person and graced recipient, involving the wills of both. The motives of the grace giver; the acceptance, rejection, or forgetfulness of the recipient; the forbearance of the giver; the entire dynamic of forgiveness; the life-renewing impact of the gift—all these are at issue. All pertain whether the gracious one is divine or human. English translations interchange "grace," "favor," "mercy," "compassion," "kindness," and "love" in probing the theme.

There is a slight distinction among the Hebrew and Greek words translated "grace, graciousness, show grace," but more significant is the large degree of overlap in meaning. The Hebrew roots *ḥnn* ("favor, grace"), *ḥsd* ("loyalty, steadfast love"), *rḥm* ("compassion, mercy"), *rṣh* ("pleasure in, favor toward"), and *ʾhb* ("love") point to the grace theme, as do Greek *charis* ("grace"), *eleos* ("mercy"), *oiktirmos* ("pity, mercy"), and *eudokia* ("pleasure in"). Close in meaning are Hebrew *ʾmn* ("steadiness, trustworthiness"), *ḥml* and *ḥws* ("to pity, to spare").

Much of the Bible portrays grace rather than naming it. In Hosea 11.1–9, the metaphor of parenting dominates, involving compassion and anger, disappointment and chagrin, intervention and forbearance. In Matthew and Mark, Jesus' *parables and person display grace; *charis* is not used, and *eleos* appears very rarely. The prophets seldom use grace vocabulary, wrestling instead in beautiful word pictures with the past, present, and future tension between divine wrath and divine yearning love, as well as with the tension in human relationships between care and violation of neighbors. When they do employ grace vocabulary, they sometimes, as Hosea does with *ḥesed*, select a word for special probing of graced relationships.

It is often said that the *ḥnn* group pertains to the gifted initiation of relationship, while the maintenance of relationship is named by *ḥesed*. Note the *Septuagint translations: *charis* for *ḥen*, *eleos* for *ḥesed*. In lament and thanksgiving *psalms, however, frequently the poet implores divine grace/mercy with an imperative of *ḥnn* paralleling other imperatives, showing that God's gracing sustains and refurbishes the existing relationship. God is asked to turn back to the one who has lost favor (Pss. 25.16; 86.16; 119.32; cf. 67.2); to hear/answer appeals based on prior experience of God's favor (Pss. 27.7; 30.11); to heal, redeem, blot out transgressions in the one graced. Whether the worshiper is contrite about transgression or bewildered by the undeserved absence of God, continuance of a prior relationship is sought.

In virtually all instances, one who does/gives/ shows grace has a superior capacity to act, while the one imploring is in need. Hence the frequent idiom of a needy one "finding favor/grace in the eyes of" someone. A gracious one reaches out to the *poor, the needy, the oppressed, the forsaken—a movement intrinsic to God and to righteous humans.

To understand grace best one can begin with human or divine instances. Proverbs 22.9 and 19.7 display human action: a gracing (NRSV: "generous") person is blessed for sharing bread with the poor; a person gracious (NRSV: "kind") to the poor lends to the Lord and will be appropriately recompensed. But grace does not act to deserve reward; grace is intrinsic to the righteous (Ps. 37.21, 26). One senses God's graciousness by observing the best of human action, but divine and human paradigms of grace inform one another: human grace imitates and depicts God's grace; God's grace calls forth human imitation.

Yet there are heightened dimensions to God's grace. One indication is the intensity of appeal to God's grace and favor in psalms and liturgical compositions. Another is the number of proper names compounded of grace vocabulary and a divine name, such as Hananiah (Ananias), Hananel, and Hanniel, and the short forms Hanan, Hanun, Hanani, and Hannah; a dozen names contain the element *rḥm*, "compassion."

Three liturgical passages are especially expressive. Exodus 33.19, "I will be gracious to whom I will be gracious, will show mercy on whom I will show mercy," combines affirmation of God's freedom with the promise that grace and *mercy are intrinsic to God. Exodus 34.6–7, using a rich range of grace language in a divine self-affirmation, is recalled in Psalms 86.15; 103.8; 111.4; 145.8; Nehemiah 9.17; Joel 2.13; Jonah 4.2; the affirmation is echoed in part in several other passages and questioned in Psalm 77.7–9. Numbers 6.24–26, the Aaronic blessing, emphasizes the continuance of God's grace and the expected consequence: *šālôm* (NRSV: "peace").

Grace and mercy in the New Testament, as well as the combination "grace and truth" in the prologue to John (1.14–17), are deeply influenced by Hebrew usage. The noun *charis* in Luke 1.30; 2.40; 2.52; and 4.22, together with verb forms in 7.21, 42, and many Lucan uses of the term in Acts, reflect the semantic range of the Hebrew Bible. A special emphasis appears in Paul's and Peter's speeches in Acts 13.43 and 15.11 and in nearby narratives about the apostles

(14.3, 26; 15.40; 18.27; 20.24, 32). Here grace as emanating from God, with a commending and sanctifying impact on those who have received it, accords with Paul's use of *charis* in Romans (fourteen times), 1 and 2 Corinthians, Galatians, and Philippians, developed in Deutero-Pauline Ephesians and Colossians. Paul's polemical emphasis is on the free gift of God's grace, a means of salvation that ought not be resisted, which impels its recipient to new, spontaneous righteousness. Thus grace is both the gift of Jesus Christ and the gift(s) of consequent righteous living in vocation. Paul's aim is to recapture the primacy of God's yearning search for humankind and the bestowal of power to become disciples. Grace, *charis*, bestows gifts, *charismata*. Paul has moved God's initiative of relationship to such prominence that "seeking God's favor" or "imploring God's mercy" fades. But Paul will go on wrestling with human response, the use made of God's gift, and the expectation of consequential, thankful living.

The tensions in the dynamic of grace characterize much of the theological wrestling of synagogue and church across the centuries. Grace can be deemed all-sufficient ("grace alone"), but repentance, merit, and reward play their part in its dynamic. Grace can seem to be irresistible in its attractiveness and yet be resisted mightily. Humans who accept God's grace can do dastardly things in God's name. God can be perceived to have run out of favor and patience, and yet new mercy appears. The freedom of God and the perplexity of human behavior have meant that both biblical authors and theologians fail finally to penetrate the depth of mystery in grace.   EDWARD F. CAMPBELL

Graven Image. Hebrew *pesel* is variously translated as "graven image," "idol," or "statue." Three-dimensional sacred images of metal, stone, wood, or clay were ubiquitously venerated in antiquity.

The Bible misrepresents *idolatry by ascribing to worshipers the naive belief that the image is the deity. Egyptians, Canaanites, and Mesopotamians believed a god's spirit inhabited a statue after consecration, causing it to move, speak, or sweat. While the statue was the god in many respects, the god was not limited to its image. The idol's purpose was to allow the mortal a vision of the divine and to help god and worshiper focus their attention on each other. A few idols had moving parts—such as a movable jaw

or dribbling breast—enabling priests to generate "miraculous" divine responses.

Since almost all ancient gods, including Yahweh (Gen. 1.26–27; 5.1; Ezek. 1.26–27), resembled humans, most idols were anthropomorphic. Some, however, portrayed animals, and Egyptian divine images often combined human and animal aspects. While humanoid idols depicted the god him- or herself, the wholly or partly animal representations metaphorically expressed aspects of its nature: a lion for ferocity, a frog for fecundity, a ram for virility, a hawk for mobility, and so forth.

The Bible forbids idolatry to Israelites (Exod. 20.4–5, 23; 34.17; Deut. 4.15–18; 5.8; 27.15). In Roman times, this proscription prevented compliance with the state cult of worshiping the emperor's statue (Rev. 13.14–15; 14.9, 11; 15.2; 16.2; 19.20; 20.4; cf. Dan. 3). Although archaeologists have uncovered virtually no representations of male gods from Israelite times, female figurines, probably representing goddesses, are common. Some equate these statuettes with biblical *Asherah or *teraphim.

Prayers might be spoken before the idol or food set before it, later to be removed for consumption by priests and/or worshipers. Among Jews and Christians of the Roman period, such food was strictly forbidden (Acts 15.29; 21.25; 1 Cor. 8; 10.18, 28; Rev. 2.14, 20).

The avoidance of divine images is called aniconism. While there is no inevitable link between *monotheism and aniconism, it cannot be coincidence that the first monotheist, Pharaoh Akhnaton (1363–1347 BCE), abolished idolatry. Apparently both he and the biblical authors believed figurative representations limited the divine to a particular conception and place or encouraged identification of the one true God with other nonexistent deities. But while Akhnaton's god, the sun, was visible to all in the sky, Yahweh was hidden in his fiery cloud (Exod. 24.17; Deut. 4.15).

Although there were few if any images of Yahweh, Israelite shrines featured statues, carvings, and embroidery depicting celestial beasts associated with Yahweh: *cherubim (winged sphinxes) (Exod. 25.18–22; 26.1, 31; 36.8, 35; 37.7–9; Num. 7.89; 1 Kings 6.23–35; 7.29, 36; 8.6–7; Ezek. 41.18, 20, 25; 1 Chron. 28.18; 2 Chron. 3.7–14; 5.7–8), bull calves (Exod. 32; 1 Kings 7.29; 12.28–30; *see* Golden Calf), and perhaps *seraphim (winged snakes) (2 Kings 18.4). The Bible preserves vestiges of a debate over their significance: Are the cherubim God's throne or canopy? Are the calves pedestals or depictions of God? Is Nehushtan (2 Kings 18.4) a seraph sheltering Yahweh (Isa. 6) or a venomous serpent (Num. 21.4–9; cf. Isa. 14.29; 30.6)?

Jewish ritual *art, like Muslim art, has generally avoided human images, but the third-century CE *synagogue of Dura Europos features realistic illustrations of Bible scenes. Periodically, Christians have banned holy statues and pictures (iconoclasm), but they are still venerated in Roman Catholicism and Eastern Orthodoxy.

WILLIAM H. PROPP

Greek. This language belongs to the western branch of the Indo-European language group, along with the Germanic, Italic, and Celtic families. It evolved into a relatively distinct and unified language ca. 2000 BCE, when Indo-European speakers mixed with earlier inhabitants in the Aegean area, especially on the Greek mainland. Extensive contact with Minoan culture ca. 1650–1450 BCE led to the development of the Mycenaean dialect recorded in the prealphabetic Linear B syllabary. With the collapse of Mycenaean civilization ca. 1250–1200 BCE, the Mycenaean dialect was largely replaced by Doric dialects, except in the interior mountainous region of the Peloponnese and in Cyprus, to which it spread. From the Doric dialects gradually developed Northwest Greek, comprising the dialects of Phocian, Locrian, and Elean, and the West Greek dialects, or Doric proper, including Laconian, Heraclean, Argolic, Corinthian, Megarian, Rhodian, Coan, Theran, Cretan, and other lesser dialects of the west, such as Syracusan and Corcyran. In the east, a dialect akin to Mycenaean, which had already reflected innovations characteristic of the east Greek dialects of classical times, evolved in the Cycladic area into historical Ionic, from which Attic later developed; and in Thessaly another dialect, which was the origin of Aeolic, spread by migrations to Boeotia and Lesbos, where it underwent further modifications through convergence with Ionic.

Only a few dialects were used in literature, and then generally in a somewhat artificial form not corresponding exactly to the spoken language. Further, these literary dialects were associated with certain classes of literature and were so used, regardless of the author's native dialect.

First and foremost among these was the Homeric dialect (well developed before 700 BCE), an amalgam of Ionic and Aeolic, a development of centuries of epic and bardic tradition based on a substratum of Mycenaean. The language of Hesiod (seventh century BCE) is substantially that of Homeric epic but with some Aeolic forms and peculiarities found in Doric and Boeotian. The epic dialect is also used, with some modifications, by elegiac and iambic poets, and to some extent it influenced all of Greek poetry.

The melic poets Alcaeus and Sappho wrote in the Lesbian dialect, with some traces of epic forms. Their language too was imitated by later writers, including Theocritus.

The language of the choral lyric is an artificial composite of Doric characteristics with the elimination of local features and some admixture of Lesbian and epic forms. It was used by the Boeotian Pindar and the Ionians Simonides and Bacchylides as well. The first prose writers were the Ionic philosophers of the sixth century BCE, and in the fifth century the historian Herodotus and Hippocrates of Cos, a Dorian, wrote in Ionic. With the political hegemony and intellectual supremacy of *Athens, the Attic dialect became the language of drama, and by the end of the fifth century it was also used in prose, but earlier prose writers such as the historian Thucydides, the tragedians Aeschylus, Sophocles, and Euripides, and the comedian Aristophanes avoided Attic peculiarities. Among the other great Attic prose writers were the orators Lysias, Isocrates, Aeschines, and Demosthenes, the philosopher Plato, and the historian Xenophon.

Some few other dialects were cultivated in local literature, but the majority of dialects are known only from inscriptions and play no role in literature.

From the welter of classical dialects emerged the Koine. Also called Hellenistic Greek, *koinē*, "the common (dialect)," designates the prevalent form of the Greek language from the time of *Alexander the Great (late fourth century BCE) to the Byzantine period (sixth-seventh century CE). The Koine emerged largely through a process of leveling and assimilation. Based primarily upon the Attic dialect, the Koine also incorporated elements from other dialects, including Ionic, Doric, and Boeotian. Features peculiar to a single dialect tended to be lost in the formation of a universal Greek vernacular, while those shared by several important dialects left their mark on it. It was spread by the Macedonian

conquests over a vast area and became the vehicle of communication for diplomacy and commerce. With the adoption of Hellenic culture it
became established in the leading centers of Greek
civilization. Its widespread use, especially by
nonnative Greek speakers, led to extensive modifications in the living language, which is best
preserved in more than fifty thousand papyri,
ostraca, and inscriptions from the fourth century
BCE to the eighth century CE.

This largely homogenous dialect continued to
develop as a living language, but a literary form
of the Koine was created in imitation of classical
Attic idiom. Among the leading Koine authors
using this elevated language were the historians
Polybius, Diodorus Siculus, *Josephus, and Ar-
rian, the biographer Plutarch, the rhetorician
Dionysus of Halicarnassus, the geographer Strabo,
the philosophers Philodemus, *Philo, and Epic-
tetus, and the Sophists Lucian, Philostratus, and
Philostratus the Younger. The Atticistic movement, an artificial revival of the classical language, flourished especially in the second century CE as a reaction to the natural developments
and innovations of the spoken language that
impinged increasingly upon even the literary
form of the Koine.

Much more akin to the living Koine is biblical
Greek. Hardly a unity in itself, the language of
the various Greek translations of the Hebrew
scriptures (see Septuagint), the writings of the
New Testament, and the Jewish and Christian
*apocrypha and *pseudepigrapha does not con-
stitute a special Jewish dialect of the Koine, much
less a language outside the mainstream of the
development of Greek. But like the papyri, ostraca, and inscriptions from Egypt subject to
extensive bilingual interference from Egyptian
(Coptic), biblical Greek in varying degrees preserves a Semitic tone and flavor, adopts Semitic
modes of speech, and reflects Semitic interference in grammar. It diverges from the rest of
the Koine most noticeably in vocabulary, as it
coins new words to express specifically biblical
concepts or uses older terms with new Jewish or
Christian meanings.

The Koine is the direct ancestor of medieval
and Modern Greek, except for the Tsaconian
dialect descended from classical Laconian. Although the Modern Greek vernacular language
(dimotiki) contains very many Latin and especially
Turkish loanwords and is itself split into numerous dialects, it represents the latest phase in the
development of the Greek language over an

unbroken period of some four thousand years.
Alongside the Modern Greek vernacular, there
is an archaizing form of the language called the
katharevousa, which long served as the standard
learned and literary language but no longer enjoys its former official status.

FRANCIS T. GIGNAC

Gutenberg, Johannes Gensfleisch zum (ca.
1396–ca. 1468). German printer and inventor
of movable type. Gutenberg was born in Mainz
and trained as a goldsmith. Around 1430 he
moved to Strassburg, where, along with three
others, he began to experiment with printing.
By the time he returned to Mainz in about 1449
he apparently had movable metal type formed
in separate letters, and had invented a typecast-
ing machine along with an oil-based ink printer.
In Mainz he became partners with Johannes
Fust, a banker, so that he could have funding
for a large Latin Bible in two-column format,
with each page containing 42 lines. The types
he prepared comprised not only the 24 capital
and 24 lowercase letters of the Latin alphabet,
but 290 different characters (47 capitals and 243
lowercase letters). Gutenberg cast such a great
number of types because he wanted to reproduce as accurately as possible the detail of letters
in sumptuous medieval manuscripts—and, if he
could, to surpass their beauty through his new
art. According to most critics, Gutenberg's Bible
is better proportioned and harmonized than any
of the manuscripts, including those transcribed
with the greatest care. Because he printed with
an exceptional deep black ink, the Bibles retain
their fresh lustre to this day. After first trying to
print the headings and initial letters of chapters
in red, he hired artisans to illuminate these un-
adorned spaces in red and blue by hand.

Generally bound in two massive folio volumes,
the Gutenberg Bible comprises 1,282 double-
columned pages. The pages measure 39.4 ×
28.3 cm (15½ × 11⅛ in). It is believed that
approximately 150 copies were printed on paper
and about 35 on *parchment (vellum). To print
each copy, 340 sheets of four pages each were
required. Since one calfskin provided only two
good sheets of this size, almost 6,000 calves were
needed to supply enough vellum for the 35
parchment copies of this Bible. Printing of the
Bible began in approximately 1452, but financing problems, as well as the use of Gutenberg's
six presses for the production of school gram-

mars, calendars, letters of indulgence, and other small print jobs, postponed the completion of the printing of the Bible until late 1455 or early 1456. Only twelve parchment and thirty-six paper copies of the original Gutenberg Bible are known to exist worldwide; four of the parchment copies are complete, as are seventeen of the paper copies.

See Printing and Publishing, *article on* The Printed Bible.   BRUCE M. METZGER

Habakkuk, The Book of. The book of Habakkuk is an integrated whole with the following outline:

The central theme of the book has to do with God's purpose. It was composed between 609–598 BCE, when the *Babylonian armies under *Nebuchadrezzar marched into and captured the Palestinian landbridge. Habakkuk resides in the southern Israelite kingdom of *Judah, and unlike the prophets who preceded him, Habakkuk addresses his words not to his compatriots but to God. His principal question is: When will God fulfill his purpose and bring in his reign of justice, righteousness, and peace on the earth? When is the *kingdom of God going to come?

In the first oracle (1.2–4), Habakkuk raises his initial lament. He sees in Judean society around him nothing but violence and evil—the oppression of the weak, endless strife and litigations, moral wrongs of every kind. And despite Habakkuk's continual pleading with God to end the wrong, God seems to ignore him and to leave the righteous helpless to correct it.

But then God does answer his prophet (1.5–11). He tells Habakkuk that he is rousing the Babylonians to march through the Fertile Crescent and to subdue Judah, as punishment for her sin. The nation that has rejected God's order and rule will find itself subjected to the order and rule of Babylonia and her gods.

In the third section (1.12–17), the prophet acknowledges the justice of God's punishment of Judah. And because God's judgment is always finally an act on the way to salvation, Habakkuk knows that Judah will not die. But his problem remains, because the Babylonians, in their cruel conquests, are even more unrighteous than Judah has been. When will God bring that unrighteousness to an end?

To seek an answer, Habakkuk stations himself on his watchtower (2.1), a symbol of his complete openness to God. And God answers him, assuring him that the "vision"—that is, God's righteous rule, God's kingdom—will come, in faithfulness to the divine promise. Indeed, the fulfillment of God's purpose hastens to its goal. It may seem delayed to human beings, but it will surely come, in God's appointed time. In the meantime, the righteous are to live in faithfulness to God, trusting his promise, obeying his commands, and acting in a manner commensurate with the coming kingdom. Only those who live such trusting and obedient lives will have fullness of life. Those who rely on themselves and their own prowess, who are proud and self-sufficient, and who have no regard for the ways and will of God, will not prosper but will sow the seeds of their own destruction.

The "woe" oracles that follow in 2.5–20 illustrate the message of 2.4. V. 5 is corrupt, but probably should be read, "Moreover, wealth is treacherous; a mighty man is proud, and he does not abide"—a reference to the Babylonians. In the following verses, the prophet then shows the inevitable downfall of all who are unfaithful—of proud tyrants who oppress their captives, of corrupt and self-glorifying governments and military powers, and of idolaters.

The hymn of 3.3–15, with its introduction, confirms the message of 2.2–3. The prophet is granted a vision of God's final, future judgment of all, and of the establishment of God's rule over all the earth. The Lord is portrayed as a mighty warrior, marching up from the southern desert, to conquer all his foes and to give salvation to all who trust him. The portrayal presents the most extensive *theophany (description of the divine appearance) to be found in the Hebrew Bible and depicts the overwhelming glory and might of God, before whose presence and promise of judgment Habakkuk both trembles and is reassured. Some scholars hold that this hymn is an earlier, perhaps much earlier, liturgical composition, incorporated into the book in the postexilic period; if so, it has been skillfully integrated into its present context.

From such a vision of God's future triumph, Habakkuk has found his certainty. He therefore sings the magnificent song of faith (3.17–19) with which the book closes. The prophet's external circumstances have not changed. Violence and injustice still mar his community, strife still abounds, nations still rage and devour the weak, and the proud still strut through the earth. But Habakkuk has been given to see the final outcome of human history. God is at work, behind all events, fulfilling his purpose. His kingdom will come, in its appointed time, when every enemy will be vanquished, and God's order of righteousness and good will be established over all the earth. The prophet, and all the faithful like him, can therefore rejoice and exult.

Nothing more is known about the prophet, though he figures as a minor character in *Bel and the Dragon 33–39. Paul quotes the book (2.4) in both Romans (1.17) and Galatians (3.11), in his discussions of *justification by faith. Hebrews 10.37–38 identifies the coming "vision" of Habakkuk 2.2–3 with Christ, and uses it to strengthen a persecuted church. And believers throughout the years have affirmed the truth of Habakkuk's central thought: No matter what the circumstances, abundant and joyful life can be had from faithfulness to God.

ELIZABETH ACHTEMEIER

Hades. *See* Hell.

Hagar. An Egyptian servant of Sarah, featured in the Genesis narratives about *Sarah and *Abraham. According to custom, Sarah, who was sterile, presented Hagar to Abraham so that Hagar might conceive and provide Abraham with an heir.

Two Hagar stories appear in the Bible. The first (Gen. 16.1–16) describes the expulsion of the pregnant Hagar from Sarah's household, her conversation in the wilderness with a messenger of God who urges her to return to the household, and the subsequent birth of her son *Ishmael. In the second Hagar story (Gen. 21.8–21),

set more than fourteen years later, when Sarah herself had at last borne a son (*Isaac) and was celebrating the day of his being weaned, Hagar and Ishmael are cast out from Sarah's household into the wilderness. A divine messenger rescues them when their water supply runs out, and he proclaims that Ishmael will become a great nation.

The literary and chronological relationship of these two narratives is problematic, but certain themes common to both can be recognized. One is that Sarah is the dominant figure in the household with respect to management of domestic affairs, including determining the fate of household staff. In both narratives, Sarah makes a decision about Hagar's fate and Abraham acquiesces. Another theme is the tension between the main wife and a concubine or servant wife with respect to inheritance. Parallels with Babylonian laws suggest that Isaac, though born later, could still be considered firstborn. Sarah's desire to exclude Ishmael from any inheritance at all is partly to satisfy the narrative of Genesis 17, in which Sarah will be the mother of the covenantal heir; it may also reflect the difficult personal relations that arise when one son receives all.

A fourth theme involves the way in which disadvantaged individuals are portrayed as surviving and being blessed with the promise of great prominence. A final theme concerns the special role of Ishmael in biblical history. The Hagar stories establish the close relationship of the Ishmaelites ("the descendants of Hagar," according to Bar. 3:23) to the Israelites, relegating them to a separate territory but recognizing that God has protected and sustained their eponymous ancestor, the son of Hagar and Abraham. Finally, the narratives, while making Hagar a heroic figure, are also sensitive to her vulnerability as a woman, a foreigner, and a servant.

Paul interprets the Hagar stories with a tendentious allegory in Galatians 4:21–31.

CAROL L. MEYERS

Haggai, The Book of. The book tells us that Haggai prophesied in the second year of *Darius the Persian (i.e., 520 BCE), his recorded ministry spanning a period of only three months, from the sixth to the ninth month of that year. The promises of *Ezekiel and Second *Isaiah, which must have spurred on many of the returning exiles, seemed not to have been fulfilled. A series of brief oracles in chap. 1 reveal the hardship of the situation of the pioneers, who were struggling to rebuild Judah after the Babylonian *exile. They had known repeated droughts and failed harvests, with consequent famine, poverty, and inflation.

Haggai challenged the community about their priorities. He replies to their protests that they are too poor to rebuild the *Temple (1.2) by saying that it is because they have not rebuilt it that they are so poor (1.4–6, 9–11). He thus draws on the old *covenant traditions that had threatened the people, if they broke the Law, with drought, pestilence, famine, and the frustration of all their activity (Deut. 28.15–24). Similarly, the *Zion tradition had linked God's presence in his Temple at Jerusalem with peace and prosperity for the land and community (e.g., Pss. 29; 72; cf. 2 Sam. 23.1–7). He therefore calls on them to rebuild the Temple (1.8).

A short narrative section (1.12–15) tells how the whole community under the leadership of *Zerubbabel, the governor, and Joshua, the high priest (the Jeshua of Ezra and Nehemiah), was energized by Haggai's preaching to begin work, encouraged by a further assurance of Yahweh's presence by the prophet (1.13).

Evidently some grew discouraged in the work; they were not helped by the cynicism of those who had seen the grandeur of Solomon's Temple (2.3). The following verses show Haggai again encouraging them, not only by assuring them of Yahweh's presence in the task (2.4) but also with the promise that this Temple, once completed, would be the scene of Yahweh's reign as universal king (2.6–9). Earlier prophetic promises are taken up again, together with themes from the *psalms that celebrate Yahweh's rule as king (the so-called enthronement psalms). So God appears, as on Mount *Sinai (Exod. 19.16–18), accompanied by earthquake and cosmic upheavals (cf. Isa. 24.18–20; Jer. 10.10; Ps. 97.1–5); the nations come in pilgrimage to Zion (cf. Isa. 2.2–4 = Mic. 4.1–4), bringing tribute to God as king (cf. Isa. 60.6). God will fill the Temple with his "*glory" as he dwells there again (cf. Ezek. 43.1–5). That is why the new Temple will excel even the first and that is why it is worth building.

The oracle based on a priestly directive in 2.10–14 (cf. Zech. 7.1–3) shows that the postexilic prophets were seen as serving in a sanctuary setting and yet also were deeply concerned with ethical and moral purity.

In 2.15–19 the prophet describes the marked contrast in fortunes that he believed would be experienced after the Temple was rebuilt. The promises of 2.6–9 are renewed in 2.20–22, while 2.23 shows that Haggai saw Zerubbabel as continuing the line of the preexilic Davidic dynasty, which, it was believed, God had promised would last forever (2 Sam. 7.16). The picture of the Davidic king as God's "signet ring" echoes what was said of Jehoiachin earlier (Jer. 22.24). Haggai thus seems to have centered some kind of messianic hope on Zerubbabel.

We know nothing about Haggai himself. The book shows that he was seen as a prophet who assured the immediate postexilic community that earlier prophecies would be fulfilled and the hopes of the Zion/David theology of preexilic Jerusalem would be renewed. The Temple was completed in 515 BCE (Ezra 6.15), but we learn no more about or from Haggai after his three months of preaching spanning the dates given in the book (Ezra 5.1–2 adds nothing new). The addition of a gloss in 2.5 alluding to the presence of God in terms of the pillar of fire and cloud that accompanied the Israelites at the time of the *Exodus (e.g., Exod. 13.21), and the description of the response of Haggai's hearers in terms reminiscent of that of the Exodus community to *Moses (1.12–14; cf. Exod. 35.29; 36.2), suggests that his oracles were handed down among those who saw the return from exile as a second Exodus (as Second Isaiah had done) and Haggai as having exercised the ministry of a second Moses.　　　　　　　　　　REX MASON

Hallelujah (Hebr. *halĕlû yāh*). The older English translation "Praise ye the Lord" makes it clear that the verb is in the plural; the command to praise is addressed to the members of the worshiping community. The ending "jah" (also written "yah") is a shortened form of Yahweh (*see* Names of God in the Hebrew Bible; Tetragrammaton).

In the Hebrew Bible, the word occurs only in the Psalter, restricted to several groups of *Psalms (104–106; 111–113; 115–117; and 146–150). It may stand at the beginning of a psalm, as in 111–112; or at the end, as in 104, 105, 115–117; or in both positions, as in 106, 113, 135, and 146–150. In Psalm 104, it concludes the praise of God in nature, and in 105–106, of the God of Israel. Psalms 146–150 are joyful, for use in public worship. It may be that these psalms were once an independent collection. The word also occurs in the Apocrypha (Tob. 13.17; 3 Macc. 7.13).

Like other Hebrew liturgical terms (e.g., *amen), "Hallelujah" is used in the New Testament; in Revelation 19.1–8 it introduces several hymns of praise for God. Rabbinic writings use "Hallel" alone as the title for a song of praise. Christian liturgical usage employs the form "Alleluia," following the Greek and Latin transliterations of the Hebrew original.

GEORGE A. F. KNIGHT

Ham/Canaan, Cursing of. According to Genesis 9.20–27, Ham saw his father *Noah lying drunk and naked in his tent, and Noah later cursed Ham's son *Canaan, pronouncing him a slave to his brothers. Ham's precise offense has been interpreted as castration, sexual assault, and incest. But the simplest explanation seems best: in failing to cover his naked father, Ham was disrespectful. Still, it is not Ham but his son Canaan whom Noah cursed, almost certainly because the story served to legitimate Israel's *conquest of Canaan and the destruction of its inhabitants.

This passage has more recently been used to support another kind of racism. Because some of Ham's descendants, notably *Cush, are black (see Gen. 10.6–14), the "curse on Ham" has been interpreted as black (Negroid) skin color and features in order to legitimate slavery and oppression of people of African origin. This interpretation occurs first in the *Talmud and has persisted in certain circles. It is also reflected in the postbiblical Christian tradition of three *Magi, one of whom is black, in parallel to Noah's three sons. Yet it was neither Ham nor Cush who was cursed, but Canaan, the "brother" of Cush and the "son" of Ham.

STEVEN L. McKENZIE

Hammurabi. *See* Hammurapi.

Hammurapi (also spelled Hammurabi, a less correct form). Sixth in a dynasty that settled in *Babylon about 1894 BCE and continued until 1595 BCE, Hammurapi ruled ca. 1792–1750 BCE. His ancestors were seminomads from the Syrian steppe who poured into Babylonia from about 2000 BCE onward and overwhelmed the local rulers. The Babylonians knew the tribes as *Amorites or "westerners" and gave that name also to Hammurapi's line (often called the First Dynasty of Babylon). Hammurapi's father, Sinmuballit, had begun to strengthen the city's position within a network of shifting alliances, dominated by Larsa in the south. Hammurapi

continued this policy, gaining control of towns farther down the *Euphrates early in his reign. For many years he held this position, raising his kingdom's prosperity by improving irrigation systems and building temples and fortifications. In his thirtieth year he took an opportunity to use his strength and his shrewd alliances to overthrow the dominant king, Rim-Sin of Larsa, thereby obtaining the rule of all southern Babylonia. To the north were other rival states, Eshnunna and *Assyria. They fell to Hammurapi two years later; then, in his thirty-third year, *Mari on the mid Euphrates became his last major conquest. Hammurapi was now master of Mesopotamia. He enjoyed his success for a few years, but at his death the conquered states reasserted themselves, and his son, Samsu-iluna, held only the region of Babylon. In the past, Hammurapi has been identified with Amraphel, king of Shinar (Gen. 14), but current knowledge does not support this.

Babylonians remembered Hammurapi for more than a thousand years. He was first to raise Babylon to great power and so to exalt her god Marduk (biblical Merodach). He was also famous as a lawgiver. Babylonian kings customarily issued a list of new or revised laws when they came to the throne, and Hammurapi did so as well. During his long reign, local governors referred awkward problems to him, and so a considerable body of royal decisions accumulated. Toward the end of his reign, Hammurapi promulgated his famous laws. They were written on clay tablets and engraved on stone stelae, one of which survives almost complete. There is no evidence that Hammurapi's laws ever came into force, perhaps because Samsu-iluna issued his own edict soon afterward. Nevertheless, scribes continued to copy them until at least the sixth century BCE.

Hammurapi's laws are a series of regulations for various circumstances, not a comprehensive code. They are set out in casuistic form, "If a man does . . . , then . . . ," with penalties graded according to the social status of the injured party. While there is a strong emphasis on property rights, the king's claim to decree justice "in order to do away with wicked and perverse men, so that the strong might not oppress the weak," and "to give justice to the orphan and widow," is evident in laws providing for members of society who lost the protection of father or husband.

Comparing Hammurapi's laws with biblical laws shows striking similarities and strong contrasts. Kidnaping, for example, carried the death penalty, and a man who wounded another in a fight had to carry the cost of his care (Hammurapi nos. 14, 206; Exod. 21.16, 18, 19). There are cases of the law of talion, "If a man has put out another man's eye, they shall put out his eye" (nos. 196, 197, 200; see Exod. 21.24). Since in many respects Israelite society was like Hammurapi's a millennium earlier, similarities are not surprising. There are also distinctions. Babylonian law can prescribe physical penalties including execution in a variety of cases involving property (e.g., forms of theft), whereas biblical laws reserve such punishment for offenses against the person, and then with careful restrictions (Exod. 22.2–3; Deut. 25.1–3), placing a special value on human life. Hammurapi did not pretend to give a complete code of laws, so there are no general apodictic commands like "You shall not kill." Although the sun god Shamash was the source of justice, Hammurapi gave no cultic rules like those in the Mosaic code. (*See also* Law, *article on* Israelite Law.)

Within Babylonian culture, Hammurapi's laws remain the most extensive surviving statement of the principles for a just and orderly society, and of the king's role in it as shepherd of his people.   ALAN MILLARD

Hands, Laying on of. *See* Laying on of Hands.

Hardening of Heart. Hebrew expresses moral and intellectual obtuseness by calling the heart "hard" (or "strong," "firm," "fat," or "bold"). "Hardness of heart" primarily connotes inflexibility of purpose or perception, often but not necessarily leading to *sin. There is no nuance of cruelty, however, as might be inferred from English "hard-hearted." Such obtuseness hinders, for example, *Jesus' disciples from understanding his *miracles (Mark 6.52; 8.17). The rejection of the Christian movement by Jews (Matt. 13.14–15; Mark 3.5; John 12.40; Acts 7.51; 19.9; 28.25–27; Rom. 11.7, 25; 2 Cor. 3.14) and gentiles (Eph. 4.18) is also blamed upon their "hardness" and "stubbornness," as is subsequent dissension within the church (Rom. 2.5; Heb. 3.8, 15; 4.7).

A heart can be made hard by God (Deut. 2.30; Josh. 11.20; Isa. 63.17) or by sinners themselves (Deut. 15.7; Ps. 95.8; 2 Chron. 36.13). In general, the Bible attributes misconduct both to human initiative (2 Kings 17.14; 9.14; 11.8; 13.10; 15.6; 16.12; 18.12; etc.) and to divine interven-

tion (1 Sam. 2.25; 1 Kings 12.15; 18.37; 22.20–23; Isa. 6.9–10; 29.10; 63.17; Ps. 105.25; 2 Chron. 25.16). Psalm 81.12 describes God abandoning the sinful to their stubbornness. Thus, sometimes the Pharaoh of the *Exodus hardens his own heart (Exod. 8.15, 3; 9.34; 1 Sam. 6.6), sometimes it is hardened for him by Yahweh (4.21; 7.3; 9.12; 10.1, 20, 27; 11.10; 14.4, 8, 17), and sometimes it simply "becomes hard" (7.13, 14, 22; 8.15; 9.7, 35). God's intervention and Pharaoh's native stubbornness together lead the king to his doom.

In Isaiah 6.9–10, Isaiah is told that the purpose of his prophecy is to make the Israelites obtuse, lest they evade their deserved punishment. Jesus cites this verse as the reason he speaks not clearly but only in *parables (Matt. 13.10–17). In other words, God has decided that some will be impervious to his message and fated for perdition.

This may seem unfair, and the book of *Jonah in fact dramatizes the converse theory: while the prophet would deny sinners the opportunity to repent, God insists that they be given a chance. Similarly, Ezekiel (3.16–21; 18; 33.1–20) maintains that Yahweh desires each sinner's *repentance; to bring this about is the prophet's job. This more benevolent picture of God contributed in the Persian period and later to the evolution of the image of *Satan, who largely relieved Yahweh of his role of tempter. But the notion of the divine origin of human sin and obtuseness survives in the New Testament. Paul addresses the question of fairness in Romans 9 but reaches no clear conclusion, merely affirming God's absolute power and inscrutable justice: "Who indeed are you, a human being to argue with God?" (Rom. 9.20); compare the divine response to Job from the whirlwind (Job 38–41): "Where were you when I laid the foundations of the earth?" (38.4).   WILLIAM H. PROPP

Hazor (Map 1:Y2). Located north of the Sea of *Galilee, Hazor was occupied from the early third millennium to the second century BCE. The city's 12-hectare (30-acre) acropolis and 70-hectare (175-acre) "Lower City," which was enclosed by earthen ramparts, gained international prominence during the second millennium. Texts mention Hazor as an enemy of Middle Kingdom *Egypt (Execration Texts), a destination for tin shipments from the east (*Mari archives), and a military objective of New Kingdom Pharaohs (Dynasties XVIII–XIX). Destruction of those levels dating from the Late Bronze Age (1550–1200), with their successive Canaanite temples, may relate to Israelite *conquest traditions (Josh. 11.1–15; 12.19). Hazor's Iron Age acropolis continued as headquarters for Canaanite alliances (Judg. 4–5) until *Solomon (1 Kings 9.15) and *Ahab made it a garrison city. Despite damage by the Arameans in the ninth century and an earthquake in the eighth, Hazor prospered under Jeroboam II before the *Assyrians razed it in 732 BCE (2 Kings 15.29), leaving destruction debris one meter thick.   RON TAPPY

Heaven. It is important to note that in the Hebrew Bible the word (šāmayim) is plural; English translations sometimes use "heaven," sometimes "the heavens." In Genesis 1.6–8, the creation of the firmament (NRSV: "dome") is described, "and God called the firmament Heaven [NRSV: Sky]." This was regarded as an overarching vault resting on pillars at the end of the earth. Above it was the celestial ocean, and above this the dwelling of God (cf. Ps. 14.2). In the firmament were openings or "windows" through which the upper waters came down in the form of rain (Gen. 7.11). At times, the term "the heavens" refers to the expanse in which the birds fly (Gen. 1.20), at times to the starry heavens, and at other times still to the highest heaven above the firmament. The context decides which meaning is appropriate.

The starry heavens are regarded as a witness to God's being and creative power; continually they "are telling the glory of God" (Ps. 19.1). These heavens remind humans of their littleness and the wonder of God's concern for them (Ps. 8.3–4). Humans' ignorance of "the ordinances of the heavens" (Job 38.33) helps to fill them with awe.

In the course of the biblical period, more transcendent ideas of God developed, and Jeremiah declares, "Do not I fill heaven and earth? says the Lord" (23.24). But even when the concept of God's omnipresence was expressed, other expressions were retained. According to 1 Kings 8.27, *Solomon recognizes that heaven and the highest heaven cannot contain God; but later in the same prayer he repeatedly asks, "Hear in heaven your dwelling place" (8.30, etc.). Isaiah 65.17 speaks of "new heavens and a new earth"; this hope for a new, or renewed, *creation had important developments in later *apocalyptic.

With respect to heaven as the final abode of God's people, this is hardly to be found in the Hebrew Bible, where for the most part the fate of everyone, good or bad, was the shadowy realm of Sheol (see Hell). After the *exile, however, Persian and Greek ideas stimulated Jewish thinking in new directions, and this is seen in some of the apocalypses of the period. Bitter persecution also produced the conviction that God would not leave without some vindication those who had died for their faith. The doctrine of resurrection was at first associated with the hope of life on a renewed earth (see Afterlife and Immortality).

By the Roman period, a blessed future holds a sure place in Jewish thinking, particularly among the *Pharisees; the *Sadducees retained the conception of a universal Sheol. In the New Testament generally, the servants of God are encouraged to look forward to a blissful eternity with God (see Luke 20.38), but the word "heaven" is used sparingly in this connection (e.g., Mark 10.21; Matt 5.12), other terms such as "eternal life," "glory," "my Father's house," being preferred. Hebrews 11.16 speaks of those who "desire a better country, that is, a heavenly one." Paul is more concerned with the company than the place and speaks of the future life as being "with Christ" (Phil. 1.23) and as seeing "face to face" (1 Cor. 13.12).

The term "heaven" still occurs in the New Testament in the sense of "sky" (e.g., Mark 13.25; Luke 13.19 [NRSV: "air"]). In the letter to the *Hebrews, mention is made of the heavens of the present creation that are destined to perish (Heb. 1.10–11), the heavens through which Jesus passed (4.14; 7.26), and the realm beyond, where he sits at the right hand of God "in heaven" (8.1). The last of these resembles in some ways the Platonic heaven of ultimate realities, of which earthly things are copies (cf. 9.23–24 and 8.5).

The word "heaven" does not necessarily refer to a literal place, for already the Christian sits with Christ in the heavenly places (Eph. 2.6). Jesus, who has "all authority in heaven and on earth" (Matt. 28.18), shares the omnipresence of the Father; he "ascended far above all the heavens, so that he might fill all things" (Eph. 4.10).

There is more about heaven in the book of *Revelation than in any other book of the Bible, and vivid pictures are given of the throne of God and the *Lamb, with living creatures and elders, angelic hosts and multitudes of the redeemed, drawn from every nation, bringing homage and praise. Popular conceptions of heaven have been derived largely from the imagery of this book.

Two other matters need mention. Some of the noncanonical writings give detailed descriptions of multiple heavens, up to seven or more. But Paul was not necessarily thinking of these when he wrote of his mystical transport into the third heaven (2 Cor. 12.2); an alternate explanation is that the expression indicates a high degree of spiritual exaltation. Second, Jewish tradition came to have such reverence for the *name of God that "heaven" and other substitutes were used; thus, for example, the prodigal son says, "I have sinned against heaven and before you" (Luke 15.18, 21); and Matthew generally uses "kingdom of heaven" and only four times "*kingdom of God."

See also Paradise.   THOMAS FRANCIS GLASSON

Hebrew. The Hebrew language is written from right to left in an alphabet of twenty-two letters. They all originally denoted only consonants, but w, y, and h have also been used to represent certain long vowels at the end of words (w = "u"; y = "i"; h = "a," "o," and "e"; w and y were later used for "o" and "e," respectively) since at least the tenth century BCE and w and y within words since the ninth. In texts from *Qumran and in later writings, letters are used more extensively to represent vowels. The full system of representing vowels by adding points to the consonants developed much later, between the fifth and the tenth centuries CE. The present system of vocalization thus reproduces the pronunciation current about a thousand years after the end of the biblical period, though it is doubtless based on earlier traditions of reading the Bible.

Among the differences between Hebrew (along with other Semitic languages) and English are the presence in the former of the guttural consonants ʿayin and ḥēt (the latter is like "ch" in Scottish "loch"); the emphatic consonants ṭēt, and ṣādeh and qōp (kinds of "t" and "s" that do not occur in English, and a kind of "k" that is not distinguished in English from any other kind of "k"); the sibilant śîn (probably the same as a consonant in Modern South Arabian dialects) alongside sāmek (s) and šîn (š); the presence of two grammatical genders, masculine and feminine; the use of the dual form for certain nouns that go in pairs (e.g., eyes, ears, and feet); the fact that many words are derived from roots of

three consonants; and a verbal system in which the use of certain vowels and consonants denotes differences in meaning (e.g., kātab "he wrote"; niktab "it was written"; hiktîb "he caused to write"), and in which there are two forms, the so-called perfect and imperfect, which were used in later times to denote the past and the future, but were employed in earlier times in ways that are still debated.

Within the Northwest Semitic group of languages, Hebrew belongs to the *Canaanite family, which includes *Phoenician, *Moabite, and *Ammonite (some would add *Ugaritic). The other major Northwest Semitic language family is *Aramaic. The word "Hebrew" (ʿibrît) is not used of the language until the Hellenistic period, but we read of "the language of Canaan" in Isaiah 19.18; and in 2 Kings 18.26, 28 (= Isa. 36.11, 13; 2 Chron. 32.18) and Nehemiah 13.24 Jerusalemites speak yĕhûdît, that is, "Judean" (later "Jewish"). Certainly, the similarity between Biblical Hebrew and Phoenician and some Canaanite words that appear in the *Amarna letters from the fourteenth century BCE shows that the Israelites' language did not differ much, if at all, from that of the Canaanites. Some have inferred from the common characteristics of Hebrew and Canaanite, and from the words "A wandering Aramean was my father" (Deut. 26.5) that the ancestors of the Israelites spoke Aramaic and that they adopted from the Canaanites the language later known as Hebrew. It is doubtful, however, whether Deuteronomy 26.5 is intended to convey information about linguistic history, and the affinities of Hebrew with what was spoken by the Canaanites may be explained on the hypothesis that the Israelites and their ancestors already spoke a language closely related to that of the Canaanites.

While the Bible is the principal source for Classical Hebrew, the same language is used in inscriptions. Among the best known are the *Gezer Calendar (tenth century BCE), a list of months defined by the characteristic agricultural work performed in them—this text may not have been written by an Israelite; the Kuntillet ʿAjrud and Khirbet el-Qom inscriptions (late ninth or early eighth century BCE), which mention Yahweh and his *Asherah; the *Samaria ostraca (eighth century BCE) recording payments of wine, oil, and so on; the Siloam Tunnel inscription (late eighth century BCE), found in the tunnel built by *Hezekiah under the city of David to bring water from the spring of Gihon to the Pool of Siloam; the *Lachish ostraca (early sixth century BCE) with military messages before the Babylonian invasion; and the Arad ostraca (same period) recording the provisions supplied to soldiers. The *Moabite Stone (ca. 830 BCE), in which King Mesha of Moab boasts of his victories over the Israelites, is in a language almost identical with Biblical Hebrew.

There were differences of dialect among the Israelites. Judges 11.5–6 reports that the Ephraimite fugitives were unable to say "*shibboleth" but said "sibboleth" and so betrayed their origin to their Gileadite enemies. The Hebrew Bible was transmitted by people in Judah, but traces of another—presumably northern—dialect have been preserved in the Bible. The Song of Deborah (Judg. 5), which appears to be of northern origin, uses the masculine plural ending -în in v. 10, and the relative particle šă- in v. 7, where the dialect of Judah would have used -îm and ʾăšer, respectively. There were other differences between southern and northern Hebrew, as in the second-person feminine singular pronoun and pronominal suffix. A northern story such as 2 Kings 4 (in which the northern prophet *Elisha appears) has thus retained something of its northern dialect. Further, northern inscriptions show dialectal differences. For example, the Biblical Hebrew word for house is bayit, but northern inscriptions have bt, which probably reflects a pronunciation bēt, and "year" is št in contrast to the southern šnh. The book of *Hosea contains many linguistic and textual difficulties, and some of them can probably be explained as resulting from the prophet's northern dialect.

Hebrew changed with the passing of time. The language of the books of Chronicles, for example, is different from that of Kings. Aramaic became the dominant language in the Syro-Palestinian region and it influenced Hebrew and eventually displaced it in some areas. Nehemiah 13.24 complains that some children of mixed marriages could no longer speak the language of Judah but spoke "the language of Ashdod." It is possible that this refers not to a survival of the Philistine language (though that cannot be excluded) but to Aramaic. The language of *Ecclesiastes differs markedly from that of preexilic texts, and the linguistic peculiarities of the *Song of Solomon are often attributed to a late date. Some people, however, could still write in the earlier style, as may be seen in the wisdom of Jesus ben Sira, written around 180 BCE (see *Sirach), and in the sectarian writing from *Qum-

ran. Yet such essays in composition in Classical Hebrew were attempts at archaizing. The prologue to the Greek translation of Sirach also contains the earliest use of the term Hebrew for the language of ancient Israel; see also 4 Maccabees 12.7.

Rabbinical writings of the first few centuries CE use a form of Hebrew that is usually known as Mishnaic Hebrew (from the collection of legal tractates known as the *Mishnah, of ca. 200 CE). It was once widely believed that this language was never used by the common people but was a scholarly language created under the influence of Aramaic. Now it is generally recognized that the rabbis did not concoct a scholarly language but used a form of Hebrew that developed in the last few centuries BCE. This conclusion arises from a study of the nature of the language and from references in rabbinic texts to its use by ordinary people, and this vernacular use doubtless lies behind its presence in the Copper Scroll from Qumran and in some letters from the Second Jewish Revolt (132–35 CE). Although Hebrew was used in Judah in the first century CE as a vernacular, Aramaic and *Greek were also spoken, and there is evidence that Aramaic was dominant in *Galilee in the north. *Jesus came from Galilee, and normally he probably spoke Aramaic. Indeed, some of his words quoted in the Gospels are Aramaic, though some (such as "*abba" and "ephphatha") can be explained as either Hebrew or Aramaic. It is not unlikely that he also spoke Hebrew, especially when visiting Judea.

Several verses in the New Testament appear at first sight to refer to the Hebrew language, and the Greek word translated as "Hebrew" (hebraisti) does indeed refer to that language in Revelation 9.11; 10.16. But it is also used of the Aramaic words Gabbatha and *Golgotha in John 19.13, 17, and it probably denotes a Semitic (as distinct from Greek) language spoken by Jews, including both Hebrew and Aramaic, rather than referring to Hebrew in distinction from Aramaic. Similarly, the Aramaic expression Akeldema is said in Acts 1.19 to be "in their language," that is, the language of the people of Jerusalem.

Some time after the Second Jewish Revolt, Hebrew died out as a vernacular in Palestine, probably in the late second or the third century CE. It continued, however, to be used by Jews as a religious, scholarly, and literary language, and was also spoken in certain circumstances. It was revived as a vernacular only in the later nineteenth century CE, and it is now the living language of the state of Israel.

See also Hebrews.   J. A. EMERTON

Hebrews. A name applied occasionally to the early Israelites, primarily to distinguish them from other cultures and peoples of the ancient Near East. An ethnic term, it antedated the common sociopolitical names *Israel or *Judah in the monarchic period, as well as the more ethnoreligious appellative *Jew in later times. The word Hebrews, used thirty-three times in the Hebrew Bible, appears in only four texts (Jer. 34.9 [twice], 14; and Jon. 1.9) describing the period after the time of the Davidic kingdom. Contemporary sources outside the Hebrew Bible refer to the people not as Hebrews but as Israel.

The derivation of the word Hebrew (Hebr. ʿibrî) is uncertain. It may be related to the verb ʿābar, "to cross over or beyond." Thus, the Hebrews would be understood as "those who crossed over" or "the ones from beyond," meaning probably from the other side of the *Euphrates River (Josh. 24.3) or perhaps the *Jordan River (Gen. 50.10). Along this line, the *Septuagint translates "Abram the Hebrew" in Genesis 14.13 as "Abram, the one who crossed over."

A second possible etymology is based on the *genealogies (Gen. 10.21, 24–25; 11.14–17; 1 Chron. 1.18–19, 25; Luke 3.35) that identify Eber, the grandson of Shem, as one of the ancestors of *Abraham and all his descendants, thus the "Eberites." No such explicit tie, however, is made in the Bible, and this connection would suggest that other peoples who are thought to derive from Abraham, including *Edomites, *Moabites, and Arabic tribes, should also be called Hebrews. The connections with Eber on the one hand and the motif of "crossing over" on the other, as well as a third possibility mentioned below, remain suggestive but inconclusive.

Virtually every reference to the Hebrews in the Hebrew Bible occurs in a context in which the purpose is to differentiate these people from those of neighboring countries, usually the Egyptians and the Philistines. *Joseph, stemming from "the land of the Hebrews" (Gen. 40.15), is identified by this name (Gen. 39.14, 17; 41.12) in the story recounting his rise to prominence under the Pharaoh. A later Egyptian ruler charges the Hebrew midwives to kill all sons born to the Hebrews, but they refuse to do so, reporting deceitfully to the Pharaoh that "the Hebrew women are not like the Egyptian women; for they are vigorous and give birth before the midwife comes to them" (Exod. 1.19). Moses is recognized by the Pharaoh's daughter as a Hebrew child, and she calls for a Hebrew woman to nurse him (Exod. 2.6–7). Subsequently, Moses defends a Hebrew, "one of his people," from a beating at the hands of an Egyptian and then flees the land when he learns that other Hebrews have heard of it (Exod. 2.11–14). In confronting the Pharaoh to demand release of his people, Moses makes reference to "the Lord, the God of the Hebrews" (Exod. 3.18; 5.3; 7.16; 9.1). At all these points, the ethnic name serves to distinguish this people from the Egyptians, who are shown as using this designation as well. Genesis 43.32 reports that the Egyptians even considered it an "abomination" to eat with Hebrews, a custom for which there is no record in Egyptian sources.

In their dealings with the *Philistines, the people are also often called Hebrews, especially by the Philistines themselves. At times it seems to be used as a term of contempt, parallel to the tradition in Genesis 43.32. In 1 Samuel 4.6, 9, the Philistines speak derisively of their opponents in battle and urge each other to fight courageously "in order not to become slaves to the Hebrews as they have been to you." In a later episode the Philistines, considering the Hebrews to be unworthy fighters who cower in caves (1 Sam. 14.11), are easily routed by the bravery of Jonathan and his armor bearer. This story also raises the question of whether the Hebrews and the Israelites are identical groups. When Saul issues the battle cry "Let the Hebrews hear," the text states that "all Israel heard" (1 Sam. 13.3–4)—which may not be the same as saying that all the Hebrews responded. It is in fact later reported that a number of Hebrews had previously attached themselves to the Philistines, and that after Jonathan's rout they disaffected and joined the Israelites (1 Sam. 14.21). This text may retain an ancient distinction that in later periods no longer applied: Hebrews as a larger socioeconomic group extending beyond Israel, and Israelites as the particular ones who banded together in the Canaanite highlands to form a new nation. In that case, the Philistines may have simply considered the Israelites to be part of the larger class of Hebrews whom they were attempting to control, for example by restricting their access to metal-working (1 Sam.

13.19). A similar confusion occurs in 1 Samuel 29.3 when the Philistines prohibit *David, who has been living with them, from joining them in battle against the Israelites—not because he is an Israelite but because he is considered a Hebrew.

There are only two other similar references to Hebrews in the Hebrew Bible. In Genesis 14.13, a context in which numerous peoples are mentioned, "Abram [Abraham] the Hebrew" appears parallel to "Mamre the Amorite." In a much later period, the prophet *Jonah, when pressed by sailors of the boat on which he sought escape, calls himself a Hebrew and a believer in the Lord who created the sea and land (Jon. 1.9).

The ethnic and sociopolitical origin of the Hebrews remains a contested point. In many respects the ʿapiru (or Ḥabiru; in Sumerian SA.GAZ) seem to be a close counterpart, and it is often suggested that the word Hebrew is derived from ʿapiru (rather than from Eber or from the verb "to cross over," as indicated above). The ʿapiru were a diverse group of people with an inferior social status, living mostly on the fringes of settled civilizations from Mesopotamia to Egypt, and there is evidence of them in numerous sources throughout the second millennium BCE. They frequently were hired as mercenaries or sold themselves into servitude in order to survive. The *Amarna letters (fourteenth century BCE) place them in the area of Syria-Palestine and describe them as basically outlaws and raiders, but such antagonism with resident populations may not have been common.

While there is no basis for equating the Hebrews with the ʿapiru, the proto-Israelites were probably a conglomeration of various Semitic groups, of which the ʿapiru was certainly one. Another was the shasu, pastoral nomads and plunderers also known to have been dwelling in Syria-Palestine as well as elsewhere in the region. The tradition of a "mixed multitude" (Exod. 12.38 [NRSV: "mixed crowd"]) or "rabble" (Num. 11.4) led by Moses through the wilderness is consistent with this picture of the early Israelites as an amalgamation of diverse peoples. Calling them "Hebrews" is an early means of distinguishing this new entity from other existing ethnic groups.

Hebrews are mentioned in one other notable context in the Hebrew Bible. Two laws dealing with *slavery distinguish those who are Hebrews from others who are not (compare Lev. 25.39–55). Exodus 21.2–11 provides for the release of every male Hebrew slave after a seven-year period of service unless he should choose to remain

for life with his master. Special rights are also reserved for a daughter who has to be sold into slavery. Deuteronomy 15.12–18 extends the law of manumission to include both male and female Hebrew slaves, stipulating that they are to be given ample provisions for starting their new life of freedom. Immediately before the fall of Jerusalem in 587/586 BCE, according to Jeremiah 34.8–22, King Zedekiah proclaimed the release of all male and female Hebrew (here also called Judean) slaves, but after this was accomplished the Israelite masters took them back, eliciting from Jeremiah an ominous pronouncement of doom. It may be that these Hebrew slaves, especially in the earlier laws, are reminiscent of the often-enslaved ʿapiru, but the Bible perceives them as compatriot Israelites deserving of treatment better than that normally afforded foreigners.

The name Hebrew, used rarely in the Hebrew Bible, thus occurs primarily to distinguish Israelites ethnically from non-Israelites. At times it is applied by foreigners (mainly Egyptians and Philistines); in other instances, by the Hebrews themselves when addressing foreigners. Except for the slave laws, Israelites normally identify themselves to each other—and often to others as well—as the people of Israel and Judah. Similar usage continues in later literature (e.g., Jth. 10.12; 12.11; 2 Macc. 15.37).

In the New Testament, the term designates Jews, hence Jewish Christians who maintained their ties with the Jewish heritage and the Aramaic or Hebrew language. Acts 6.1 contrasts them with Hellenists, perhaps Jewish Christians who accommodated more to the Hellenistic culture by speaking Greek and following certain Greek customs. Paul, born in Tarsus, proudly identifies himself as "a Hebrew born of Hebrews" (Phil. 3.5; also 2 Cor. 11.22; and Acts 22.2–3).

In modern usage, the term Hebrew is generally applied only to the language (see Hebrew) of ancient and modern Israel and of Jewish scriptures and tradition.   DOUGLAS A. KNIGHT

Hebrews, The Letter to the.

Theme and Content. The theme of the letter to the Hebrews is the supremacy of Christ. The letter opens with the assertion that God, who spoke through the *prophets in varied ways, has in this last age spoken his final word in the person of his Son. This immediately introduces an emphasis that remains prominent throughout, namely, the uniqueness and perfection of the Son in comparison with the multiplicity and imperfection of all others. The contrast is between the many and the One, between expectation and fulfillment, between shadow and reality. Thus, the many *priests of the old order, themselves sinful and temporary, are superseded by the single person of Christ, who is without sin and whose priesthood is forever; and their innumerable *sacrifices, endlessly repeated because they were unable to achieve the redemption they portended, are replaced by Christ's one perfect sacrifice of himself, which is ever-more effective for purging sins.

It is apparent from the content of the letter that there was need to insist on the supremacy of Christ by demonstrating his superiority to *angels (1.4–2.18) and to *Moses (3.1–4.13), as well as to *Aaron (4.14–10.18), the first of the high priests of the old order. At the same time, this involved instruction regarding the superiority of the new *covenant, of which Christ is the mediator, to the old covenant under which the Mosaic system operated (8.1–9.10).

Apparently, those to whom this letter was addressed were being tempted not only to assign to angels, or to some angelic being, a position above that of Christ, but also to revert to the structure of the Mosaic dispensation with its regulations and sacrifices. The readers are solemnly warned, accordingly, of the great peril of losing hold of salvation in Christ (2.1–4), of imitating the unbelieving Israelites in the wilderness (3.6b–4.2), of spiritual stagnation and apostasy (5.11–6.8), of despising the gospel (10.26–31), and of copying *Esau, who bartered his birthright to satisfy the whim of a moment (12.15–17).

Recipients and Date. The content of the letter suggests that those to whom it was addressed were Jewish Christians, that is, Jews who had recognized Jesus as the *Messiah. This accords with the traditional designation of the letter, present in the earliest manuscripts as "to the Hebrews."

The date of the letter may confidently be placed before the destruction of *Jerusalem and its *Temple, because of the many indications that the Levitical priesthood was still performing its sacerdotal duties. Furthermore, it is impossible to believe that, had the Temple already been destroyed and its sacrifices ended, no mention of so significant a development would have been made by the author. The occurrence would have been interpreted as confirming his contention that with the coming of Christ the old order had

given way to the new. The letter may therefore be dated some time, perhaps a few years, perhaps a few months (depending on how one may discern or interpret other possible indications in the text), prior to 70 CE.

Author. The identity of the author of Hebrews is not known. Allusions in Clement of Rome's letter to the Corinthians attest to the authoritative status of Hebrews before the end of the first century. Presumably Clement knew who the author was. Later on, however, questions regarding the authorship of the letter contributed to the general neglect it suffered in western or Latin Christianity. Jerome's acceptance of the work as coming from the pen of *Paul, and in particular the title "The Epistle of Paul to the Hebrews" in the *Vulgate, was mainly responsible for the belief, unquestioned for more than a thousand years, in its Pauline authorship. But there are adequate reasons for rejecting Paul as its author. First, the writer's style is different from Paul's; second, the issue seems to be settled by his assertion that he (together, apparently, with his readers) received the gospel from those who heard the Lord (2.3).

Of many conjectures that have been offered, there are but two that merit serious consideration. The author was clearly a person in a position of leadership in the apostolic church, intellectually distinguished, theologically mature, and with a profound knowledge of the Bible; two candidates mentioned in the New Testament who meet these criteria are *Barnabas and *Apollos, both of whom were Jewish Christians. Barnabas, who is called an *apostle (Acts 14.14), was an active missionary and an early supporter and companion of Paul. He also was a member of the priestly tribe of *Levi (Acts 4.36), a consideration of interest in view of the considerable length devoted to the priesthood in the letter. That there was a traditional association of Barnabas's name with the letter to the Hebrews is evident from a reference in Tertullian, writing early in the third century (De pudicitia 20).

Apollos, the other strong candidate, was a native of Alexandria and is described as "an eloquent man, well-versed in the scriptures" and a powerful exponent of the gospel (Acts 18.24–28). The Alexandrian connection has impressed those who maintain that the terminology and even the thought of Hebrews are influenced by the culture of the Alexandrian schools, and especially by the philosophical concepts of *Philo. Martin Luther was the first to propose the name of Apollos, without any attempt at substantiation or, for that matter, any thought of philosophical influence from Alexandria or elsewhere (in a 1537 sermon on 1 Cor. 3.4–6, and again in a 1545 comment on Gen. 45.20). But in the absence of any work written by Barnabas or Apollos and of any other first-century evidence, identifying either as the author of the letter is only conjecture.

Destination. The location of the recipients of Hebrews is also unknown. A note stating that the letter was written from Rome or from Italy is found in some manuscripts from the fifth century on, but it is obviously a late gloss based on 13.24, a passage that can be read as stating that the letter was sent not from but *to* Italy. A Roman destination has been much favored in modern times. But the salutation does not necessarily indicate Italy as either the place of origin or the destination of the epistle, and many scholars now think that its recipients were situated on the eastern shores of the Mediterranean, probably in Palestine or Syria.

Occasion. Like all the letters of the New Testament, Hebrews addressed a specific situation. The discovery of the *Dead Sea Scrolls at Qumran has considerably increased our knowledge of *Judaism in the first century CE. The Qumran sect had withdrawn to the desert, isolating themselves from the Temple worship of Jerusalem, and had established a community governed by the regulations of the Mosaic dispensation, pending the arrival of the eschatological kingdom when the authentic Zadokite or Aaronic high priesthood would be restored in the city of David. The kingdom to be set up would have two messianic personages, the one priestly (Aaronic) who would be superior to the other royal (Davidic), but both would be subordinate to the archangel *Michael as the supreme head. The Qumran literature gives indications of the identification of Michael and *Melchizedek. Yigael Yadin argued that the letter to the Hebrews was intended to counteract the teachings of Qumran; but the Qumran teachings may be taken as representative of *Essenism, whose adherents were to be found throughout Palestine, and there is no need to suppose that the recipients of the letter were converts from the Qumran community. They could have been ex-Essenes or simply Jewish Christians who, attracted by Essene glamorization of a past age, were tempted to compromise the perfection of their salvation in Christ.

At least we now have a clue as to why the writer of Hebrews felt compelled to demonstrate the superiority of Christ to angels, insisting that

"God did not subject the coming world . . . to angels" (2.5), and to warn that to return to the Mosaic system with its priesthood would be to lose the gospel. We can also appreciate the need for instruction regarding the true significance of Melchizedek, who as king of Salem and priest of the Most High God portended the union of eternal kingship and eternal priesthood in the single person of Christ. The postulation of two messiahs reflected the inability of combining in one person a priest of the line of Levi with a king of the line of *David. Christ, however, was both the son of David and also a priest forever after the order not of Aaron but of Melchizedek (chap. 7; Ps. 110.4).

The Old and the New. A major purpose of the letter to the Hebrews was to explain the contrast between the old sanctuary and the new and the absolute superiority of the new order over the old. Particularly prominent is the *typology of the *Day of Atonement, which was when annual atonement would be made for the sins of the people (see Lev. 16). Since the high priest too was a sinner, he first offered up a sacrifice for his own sins. Then he killed a goat as a sin offering for the people, and while the people waited outside he disappeared from their view as he went through to the innermost sanctuary of the *tabernacle (the holy of holies), and there sprinkled the animal's blood on the mercy seat. But according to the author of the letter, the old system was unable to achieve the reality that it foreshadowed (10.1–4). The earthly sanctuary also was but "a sketch and shadow of the heavenly one" (8.5). Consequently, the same sacrifices had to be offered over and over again, and the way into the innermost chamber of God's presence was barred to the people. All this served to arouse the longing expectation of the coming of the perfect high priest who would offer up the perfect sacrifice once and for all.

This expectation was made a reality by the coming of Christ, the uniquely great high priest (4.14; 7.4), who, being entirely holy and free from sin (4.15; 7.26), had no need, like the Levitical priests, to offer any sacrifice first for his own sins (7.27), and who offered up not an animal but himself, making atonement for sin by his own blood. His sacrifice avails once for all and need never be repeated (10.10–14). This means, further, that the people, not just the Israelites but now the whole of humankind, are no longer excluded from access to God's presence. This was dramatically indicated by the rending of the curtain that blocked the way into the holy of holies at the moment of Christ's death (10.20; Mark 15.37–38). But it is not a mere earthly sanctuary that has been opened to all, but the true heavenly sanctuary of God's presence (8.2), access to which has been made possible by the triumphant *ascension of the risen Lord into heaven itself (4.14; 9.24), whence his waiting people eagerly look for his glorious reappearance (9.28).

The recipients of the letter are reminded that it is by faith that they must live and die, and that hardship and affliction should never cause them to throw away their confidence and give up the struggle (10.32–39). Chap. 11 is an encomium of faith that sets before them the saints of old, both men and women. But above all they are to set their eyes on Jesus, the pioneer and perfecter of faith, whose humiliation has become glory (12.1–3). And so they are urged to stand firm under persecution, to strive after holiness, and to associate themselves with Jesus and his cross, remembering always that their true homeland is not here but hereafter (12; 13.12–14; cf. 11.10, 13–16).   PHILIP EDGCUMBE HUGHES

Hebron (Map 1:X5). A major city of Judah, located ca. 31 km (19 mi) south of Jerusalem. In biblical traditions it is especially associated with the *ancestors of Israel. *Abraham is said to have built an altar there (Gen. 13.18), and Abraham and *Sarah, *Isaac and *Rebekah, and *Jacob and *Leah were buried there in the cave of Machpelah (see Gen. 49.29–32). An enclosure wall built by *Herod the Great surrounds the traditional burial site, now incorporated into a mosque that was originally a church. Hebron's modern Arabic name reflects this association; it is called Ḥalil, for Abraham, the "friend" of God.

Also associated with Caleb and *Samson, Hebron served as *David's first capital (2 Sam. 2.1–5.5) and continued to have symbolic importance in the early monarchy (see 2 Sam. 15.7–10). But once *Jerusalem became established as the capital of the kingdom, Hebron's importance diminished.   MICHAEL D. COOGAN

Hell. Hell (from a Germanic root meaning "to cover") is the traditional English translation of the Hebrew word Sheol, found sixty-five times in the Hebrew Bible, and of the Greek word Hades, used twenty-six times in the *Apocrypha and ten times in the New Testament. In the NRSV these words are simply transliterated into English, and the translation "hell" is reserved for *Gehenna.

Both Sheol and Hades refer to a general dwelling place of souls after *death (Gen. 37.35; Acts 2.27). Since this sphere was mainly supposed to be found in the underworld (Num. 16.30; Matt. 11.23), it was also called "the pit" (Isa. 38.18), "the bottomless place" (Luke 8.31; Rom. 10.7; see Abyss), or "the lower parts" (of the world; Ps. 63.10; Eph 4.9 [Latin inferiores partes, cf. "inferno"]).

Postexilic Judaism reserved a particular section of hell for the punishment of sinners (emphasized in 1 Enoch 22.10–11). In the New Testament, the *synoptic Gospels and *James in twelve cases name this place of pain Gehenna (Matt. 5.22; James 3.6). Among the New Testament examples of Hades, there are three in which punishment is the point, so that Hades corresponds to Gehenna (Matt. 11.23; Luke 10.15; 16.23). In the other passages where Hades occurs, however, it is used in the neutral sense of a space where all dead are kept (Matt. 16.18; Acts 2.27, 31; Rev. 1.18, 6.8; 20.13, 14; also the variant reading in 1 Cor. 15.55 [cf. Hos. 13.14]).

Concerning the location of hell, the biblical references are colored by the usual cosmology of antiquity, which divided the universe into *heaven, earth, and underworld. The concept of hell, however, did not depend on cosmology, but rather on concern for the destiny of the dead. There was a general conviction that existence continued in some way after its separation from earthly life, an event that implied separation from God, the source of all life. The connection of God with heaven and the *burial of the dead in the ground gave reason generally to localize the realm of death in the underworld, and eventually to let the souls of the wicked dwell in a deeper section than those of the righteous. Such spatial aspects of hell were meant to give the distance of the deceased from God or their nearness to God concrete expression.

In the course of time several different perspectives on hell emerge in the Bible. From a neutral viewpoint, Sheol was regarded in Israel as the dwelling place of all the dead, independent of their character. *Jacob is reported to have said when he believed his son *Joseph dead: "I shall go down to Sheol to my son, mourning" (Gen. 37.35). A similar pessimism is found in various types of literature (e.g., 2 Sam. 12.23; Isa. 14.9–11; Pss. 6.5; 88.5; 115.17; Job 7.9–10). The probable etymology of the word (from the verb *šāʾal*, "to ask") reflects this universalism: the underworld is never sated, but keeps asking for more (see Prov. 27.20; 30.16). Postexilic Judaism and the New Testament also presupposed this general place of the dead, but made it provisional because of the belief in a coming resurrection (Dan. 12.2; Acts 2.27; Rom. 10.7; Rev. 20.13).

When ethical viewpoints are involved, however, Sheol is said to be a place of punishment. Korah and his companions were swallowed up by "the earth" (a term that can also mean "the underworld"), while their supporters were burned in fire (Num. 16.31–35). Psalmists and prophets threatened the godless with destruction in hell (Ps. 9.17; 31.17; 55.15; Isa. 5.14; 28.15, 18; 66.24), and wisdom teachers warned the youth to avoid hell (Prov. 7.27; 15.24); originally, this probably meant that untimely death was the deserved fate of the wicked, but many of these texts could also be interpreted to mean punishment after death. As indicated above, Judaism also developed the idea of different sections for righteous and sinful people in hell (1 Enoch 22.1–14), and especially ascribed the punishment of blasphemers to a cursed and flaming gorge (27.1–4), later called Gehenna. In the New Testament, the story of Lazarus illustrates the different places reserved for the righteous and sinners in the realm of death (Luke 16.26; *see also* Abraham's Bosom). Parenetic concerns of Jesus and his followers dominate other passages in which hell (called Hades, the abyss, Gehenna, and, in 2 Peter also *tartaros*) is represented as an instrument of divine punishment (Matt. 5.22, 29; 11.23 par.; 18.9 par.; Luke 8.31; Heb. 10.27; 2 Pet. 2.4; Jude 6; Rev. 9.1–2, 11; 17.8; 20.3). Matthew was especially concerned with this negative aspect of hell, but neither *John in his Gospel nor *Paul in his letters developed it.

Hell was even seen as a power that endeavors to attack life on earth. This found expression in psalms dealing with *salvation from mortal danger; for example: "The cords of Sheol entangled me" (2 Sam. 22.6 = Ps. 18.5), or "The pangs of Sheol laid hold on me" (Ps. 116.3). In postexilic Judaism, the topic was further developed by the community of *Qumran, which also let the "gates" of hell represent the aggressiveness of the underworld (1QH 3.16–19). According to Matthew 16.18, these gates of hell will not be able to subdue the church. It is Gehenna that inspires false teachers (Matt. 23.15) and inflames evil tongues (James 3.6), and powers of destruction

ascend from hell to rage on earth (Rev. 9.3, 11; 11.7).

Ultimately, however, God is the one who controls hell. His own fire is able to destroy it (Deut. 32.22), and hell is never hidden from his eyes (Ps. 139.8; Job 11.8; 26.6). The almighty God of Israel is often praised for his ability to rescue a pious soul from death and hell (e.g., Ps. 16.10; 54.14).

Gradually, the conviction of God's omnipotence led to a belief in the resurrection of the dead. These expectations were prepared for by prophetic sayings like the following: God "will swallow up death" (Isa. 25.7; cf. 1 Cor. 15.54); "Your dead will live, their corpses shall rise" (26.19); "He [the Servant] shall prolong his days" (53.10); "I will open your graves" (Ezek. 37.12). Influenced to some extent by Persian religion, Judaism then developed various doctrines of a resurrection and judgment implying that hell will deliver the righteous and rearrest the sinful, for example: "Many . . . shall awake, some to everlasting life, and some to shame and everlasting contempt" (Dan. 12.2); "the king of the universe will raise us up . . . because we have died for his laws" (2 Macc. 7.9); the souls will be kept in hell "until the great judgment" (1 Enoch 22.4).

In the New Testament, a new perspective is opened by the witness of the apostles that God had raised his Christ from death, confirmed by the information that some women had found the tomb empty (Matt. 28.6 par.) and that several disciples had "seen" the risen Lord (1 Cor. 15.3–8). These experiences were understood to indicate that hell and death had already been defeated by the lord of life, as Peter was reported to have proclaimed at *Pentecost (Acts 2.24, 27, 31). Some of the righteous were also reported to have risen together with him (Matt. 28.52). The provisional and the definitive victory of Christ over death and related powers was a central point for Paul (Rom. 6.9; 8.38–39; 1 Cor. 15.4), and he exclaimed with great joy: "O death, where is your victory?" (1 Cor. 15.55 [see Hos. 13.14]). Although he avoided expressions for hell, Paul certainly reserved some place for the dead until their resurrection, describing this as a peaceful sleep (1 Thess. 4.13) or a punishment in fire (1 Cor. 3.5). Christ's final victory over hell is described in more detail by the prophet John (e.g., Rev. 1.18; 9.1; 20.1). Although the destructive powers of hell increase their attacks on humankind before the approaching end (9.2–11; 13.1–8; 20.7–9), the final conflict will lead to the complete disappearance of death and hell (20.14).

See also Afterlife and Immortality; Day of Judgment; Descent into Hell; Resurrection of Christ.   BO REICKE

Hermeneutics. Hermeneutics may be defined as the theory of interpretation. More precisely, biblical hermeneutics inquires into the conditions under which the interpretation of biblical texts may be judged possible, faithful, accurate, responsible, or productive in relation to some specified goal. Whereas exegesis involves the actual process of interpretation, biblical hermeneutics moves beyond interpretation. It entails a study of method, inviting reflection on the nature, methods, and goals of biblical interpretation. It also draws on general hermeneutic theory, that is, on traditions of scholarship—within philosophy, the social sciences, theories of literature, and semiotics—that shed light on questions about meaning and understanding. The subject embodies a proper concern to understand the biblical writings not only as particular historical documents of the past but also as texts that address the present with a living and transforming voice. This has often been described as the task of "application," though some prefer to speak of "recontextualization." Finally, theological questions about the status and nature of the Bible also shape hermeneutics. Whether or in what sense the Bible is seen as the authoritative word of God shapes the ways in which issues are explored. (*See* Authority of the Bible.)

Up to the end of the eighteenth century, three sets of issues assumed particular importance in the history of biblical hermeneutics. First, the Hebrew Bible could be seen either as part of the Christian scriptures or as Jewish scripture only. For Jesus and the earliest Christian communities, the Hebrew Bible was their only scripture, providing among other things the frame of reference within which the gospel was to be understood (1 Cor. 15.3, 4; cf. Luke 24.27). These Christians saw it as applying to their situation (1 Cor. 10.11) and interpreted it in the light of the ministry of Jesus Christ (Acts 8.32–35). In the second century CE, Marcion challenged the status of the Old Testament as part of Christian scripture. But Irenaeus and other church fathers reaffirmed the unity of the two testaments as the message of the one God, who had revealed himself preeminently in Christ (*see* Interpretation, History of, *article on* Early Christian Interpretation).

The second issue concerns allegorical interpretation. Allegory presents a meaning other (Grk. *allos*) than that which might be immediately apparent in the text. For example, John Bunyan's *The Pilgrim's Progress*, which portrays a spiritual journey through language, at first sight seems to describe physical travel from place to place. In such cases, allegorical interpretation constitutes the appropriate hermeneutic method. But this method was also used extensively in the ancient and medieval world as a device with which to seek out other meanings from biblical and classical texts. It was used in classical Greece to draw "higher" meanings from Homer's narratives about petty squabbles among the Greek deities. The Alexandrian church fathers, especially Clement and Origen, were among those who inherited and used this interpretative device. Clement of Rome allegorized the scarlet thread in Rahab's window (Josh. 2.18) into a symbol of the blood of Christ (1 Clement 12.7). More subtly, many narrative *parables were interpreted as if they had been spoken as allegories in which each element of narrative description carried some independent or self-contained spiritual meaning. The Antiochene fathers, and subsequently also Luther, used the method, though more cautiously. Calvin dismissed the approach on the ground that it allows the interpreter to shape scripture in accordance with human judgments. In this respect allegory is less constrained than *typology: whereas allegory rests on parallels between ideas, typology depends on correspondences or parallels between events.

A third persistent issue in hermeneutics concerns the role of interpretative tradition. Does the way in which the Bible is read and understood depend decisively on the tradition of expectations and assumptions in which the interpreter stands? On one side, the church fathers insisted, against the *gnostics, that the Bible can be understood rightly only when it is seen as the scriptures of the catholic or universal church. On the other side, the reformers, while respecting early tradition, insisted that the Bible could stand on its own feet (*see* Interpretation, History of, *article on* Christian Interpretation from the Middle Ages to the Reformation). Its message was not to be equated with how it might already be understood within some given ecclesiastical tradition. In the modern era, it is widely recognized that interpreters must take seriously both the right of the text to speak from within its own historical particularity and the role of traditions in shaping the horizons of interpreters and their questions.

In the modern era, several movements have profoundly influenced biblical hermeneutics. Following the rise of Romanticism in the eighteenth century, Friedrich Schleiermacher and Wilhelm Dilthey argued that to understand a text we must seek out the circumstances or creative vision that caused the author to produce it. This involves sympathetic imagination, or the capacity to place oneself in the author's shoes. The Romantic theorists rightly saw that in the process of interpretation there is a progressive interaction between understanding elements of a written text and provisionally grasping the sense of the whole. In biblical study this means interaction between an analytical study of words or phrases and an attempt to grasp the message of a book or an author as a whole.

In the mid-twentieth century, a number of writers explored existentialist models of hermeneutics. Most notably, Rudolf Bultmann insisted that a narrative or descriptive mode of writing in the Bible can mislead us into failing to notice where such material serves primarily not to describe but to evoke some practical response from the reader. Thus "myth" (a descriptive or narrative mode) needs to be "demythologized," in other words, interpreted as preaching or *kerygma*. The strength of this approach is that it takes seriously the practical function of the Bible for its writers and earliest audiences. Its weaknesses are that it makes claims about the definition and use of "myth" that are open to question, and that it underplays the importance of historical report and factual truth claims in the New Testament.

Bultmann's pupil, Ernst Fuchs, together with Gerhard Ebeling, pioneered a movement that came to be known in the 1960s as the "new hermeneutic." It had close affinities with the philosophical hermeneutics of the later Martin Heidegger and Hans-Georg Gadamer. They argued that language does not merely communicate ideas; it creates a "world." Biblical language draws the interpreter into a world within which a new reality comes to life. This creative experience is described as a "language-event."

From the late 1960s to the late 1980s, various other hermeneutic models were explored. Liberation theology has taken up the sociocritical models of the social sciences by raising questions about the use of texts for the social control of communities. Paul Ricoeur and others have seen the earliest origins of a "hermeneutic of suspicion" in *Marx, Nietzsche, and *Freud. On the other hand, Ricoeur and, from a different angle, liberation theologians also seek to bring the situation of the present to bear on the text in order to produce positive meaning. Thus, feminist hermeneutics expresses suspicion of masculine interest and have attempted to derive feminist significance from new readings (*see* Feminism and the Bible). One critical question for such movements is whether the desire for change represents any less an "interest" than does desire to perpetuate the status quo.

Reader-response criticism in literary studies represents another model in process of exploration. The capacity of biblical texts to shape, revise, or confirm readers' expectations is seen as one further aspect of hermeneutic inquiry. Each of the models explored in the modern era underlines, in different ways, the many levels at which understanding, transformation, and action may take place in the encounter between the reader and the text.

See also Interpretation, History of, *article on* Modern Biblical Criticism.

ANTHONY C. THISELTON

Hermon, Mount (Map 1:Y1). The mountain that formed Israel's northern boundary (Deut. 4.48; Josh. 12.1). With an elevation of over 2,800 m (9,200 ft), it dominates the landscape of northern *Galilee and is snow-covered virtually year-round. In antiquity it was apparently the home of lions and leopards (Song of Sol. 4.8). Its name means "set apart" (*see* Ban) and indicates its sacred character, suitable for a peak from whose base flow the sources of the *Jordan River. Hermon was associated with the Canaanite god *Baal (Judg. 3.3; 1 Chron. 5.23); just below it there is a later shrine to the Greek deity Pan (modern Banias), identified with Caesarea Philippi (Mark 8.27–33 par.). Some have proposed Mount Hermon as the setting for the transfiguration of Jesus (Mark 9.2–8 par.), although Tabor is the traditional location.   MICHAEL D. COOGAN

Herodian Dynasty. Several members of the family of Herod governed Jewish Palestine during the period of Roman domination.

Sources. The primary source for the Herods is *Josephus; for the later Herods, especially Herod Antipas, Agrippa I, and Agrippa II, the

New Testament makes a small contribution to our knowledge. Josephus's two main works, *The Jewish War* and *The Jewish Antiquities,* overlap in their coverage of the Herods. Regarding Antipater and Herod the Great, Josephus depended primarily on Nicolaus of Damascus, who was Herod's court historiographer. For the period from Herod's death (4 BCE) to the First Jewish Revolt (66–70 CE), Josephus relied for the most part on oral tradition and hence has far fewer historical particulars. There has been debate about Josephus's historical credibility, but most would grant him to be reliable, taking note, however, of his biases. Archaeological discoveries in *Jerusalem, at *Qumran, and elsewhere have supported many details of his works.

Origin of the Herodian Dynasty. After the Maccabean Revolt (167–164 BCE), in 142 BCE the Jews became politically independent under the rule of the Hasmonean family. It was the Hasmonean Alexander Janneus (103–76 BCE) who appointed the Herodian Antipater, Herod the Great's grandfather, as governor of Idumea. After Alexander's death in the struggle for power among his family members, Hyrcanus II, his eldest son, after ruling only three months as king and high priest, was forced out by his younger brother, Aristobulus II (67 BCE). In 63 BCE Antipater II, son of Antipater and father of Herod the Great, was instrumental in having Hyrcanus II reinstated and in deposing his younger brother. With Rome's intervention in Palestine (63 BCE), both brothers appealed for Roman support, and Pompey sided with Hyrcanus II, reinstating him as high priest. Later Julius Caesar, who had defeated Pompey (48 BCE), reconfirmed Hyrcanus II as high priest and granted Antipater II Roman citizenship with tax exemption, making him procurator of Judea. Antipater II appointed his sons Phasael as governor of *Jerusalem and Herod as governor of *Galilee (47 BCE).

Herod the Great (47–4 BCE). *Governor of Galilee (47–37 BCE).* Although Herod was only twenty-five years old when he became governor of Galilee, he displayed efficient leadership. After the murder of Caesar in 44 BCE, Cassius, the Roman leader of Syria, appointed him as governor of Coele-Syria. After Antony defeated Cassius (42 BCE), he appointed both Herod and Phasael as *tetrarchs of Judea.

In 40 BCE troubles arose for the two new tetrarchs. When the Parthians arrived in Syria, they joined with Antigonus (the son of Hyrcanus II's deposed brother Aristobulus II) to depose Hyrcanus II. The Parthians besieged Jerusalem and sued for peace. Herod was suspicious of the offer, but Hyrcanus II and·Phasael went to meet the Parthian king, who put them in chains. On hearing of this treachery, Herod, his family, and his troops moved to Masada and then to Petra. Antigonus mutilated his uncle Hyrcanus II's ears to prevent his being reinstated as high priest and sent him to Parthia. Phasael died of either poisoning or suicide.

Herod departed for Rome, where Antony, Octavius, and the senate declared him king of Judea. On returning to Palestine, Herod was able to regain Galilee and eventually to lay siege to Jerusalem in the spring of 37 BCE. Meanwhile, before the fall of Jerusalem he married Mariamne, niece of Antigonus, to whom he had been betrothed for five years. He did this not only to spite Antigonus but also to strengthen his claim to the throne, since she was a Hasmonean. In the summer of 37, Herod defeated Antigonus and became de facto the king of the Jews.

King of the Jews (37–4 BCE). Herod's reign can be divided into three periods: consolidation (37–25 BCE), prosperity (25–14 BCE), and domestic troubles (14–4 BCE).

To consolidate his rule, Herod had to contend with four adversaries: the Pharisees, the aristocracy, the Hasmonean family, and Cleopatra of Egypt. The *Pharisees, who disliked Herod because he was an Idumean, a half-Jew, and a friend of the Romans, had great influence over the majority of the people. Herod punished both the Pharisees and their followers who opposed him and rewarded those who were loyal to him. The Sadducean aristocracy, most of whom were members of the *Sanhedrin, were pro-Antigonus. Herod executed forty-five of them and confiscated their property in order to pay the demands that Antony placed on him. The Hasmonean family was upset because Herod had replaced the mutilated high priest Hyrcanus II with Ananel of the Aaronic line. Herod's mother-in-law Alexandra successfully connived to have Ananel replaced with her seventeen-year old son Aristobulus (late 36 or early 35 BCE). Later Herod managed to have him drowned "accidentally," and soon after he put Alexandra in chains. His last adversary was Cleopatra, who wanted to eliminate Herod and Malchus of Arabia and confiscate their lands. When civil war broke out between Octavius and Antony (32 BCE), Herod was prevented from helping Antony because Cleopatra wanted Herod to make war against Malchus, hoping to weaken both and acquire their territories.

After the defeat of Antony at the battle of Actium (31 BCE) Herod proceeded to cultivate Octavius's friendship. Convinced of his loyalty, Octavius returned Jericho to him and also gave him Gadara, Hippos, *Samaria, Gaza, Anthedon, Joppa, and Strato's Tower (later Caesarea).

The last years of consolidation saw much tension in Herod's domestic affairs. Owing to a bizarre series of events, Herod executed his wife Mariamne (29 BCE), his mother-in-law Alexandra (28 BCE) after she attempted to overthrow him, and his brother-in-law Costobarus (25 BCE). Hence, all male relatives of Hyrcanus II were now removed, leaving no rival for Herod's throne.

The period from 25 to 14 BCE was marked largely by success, although there were still occasions of stress. Herod constructed theaters, amphitheaters, and hippodromes and introduced quinquennial games in honor of Caesar, thus violating Jewish law. On the site of Strato's Tower a large urban port was built and named Caesarea. In 24 BCE he built a royal palace in Jerusalem. His crowning achievement in construction was his plan to rebuild the Jewish *Temple; work on this began ca. 20 BCE and was completed in 63 CE. Herod's territory was also greatly expanded in this period with the addition of Trachonitis, Batanea, Auranitis, the area between Trachonitis and Galilee containing Ulatha and Paneas, the area north and northeast of the *Sea of Galilee, and Perea (Map 12:Y5). To gain the good will of the people, in 20 BCE he lowered taxes by a third and in 14 BCE by a fourth.

As Herod grew older a considerable amount of intrigue engulfed his life, much of which arose from his ten wives, each of whom wanted her son(s) to become his successor. This is evident in his changing his will six times. His first wife was Doris, by whom he had Antipater; he repudiated them when he married his second wife, Mariamne (37 BCE), by whom he had five children, of whom only Alexander and Aristobulus were notable. In 24/23 BCE he married his third wife, Mariamne II, by whom he had Herod (Philip). His fourth wife was a *Samaritan, Malthace (23/22 BCE), by whom he had Archelaus and Antipas. In 22 he took as his fifth wife Cleopatra of Jerusalem, who became the mother of Philip the tetrarch. Of the other five wives, none were significant and the names of only three are known.

The main rivalry was between Mariamne's two sons Alexander and Aristobulus and Doris's son Antipater. In 22 BCE Herod made his first will

naming Alexander and Aristobulus as his successors. Because of the alleged plots of these two sons, Herod made a second will in 13 BCE, naming Antipater as sole heir. Later there was reconciliation between Herod and Alexander and Aristobulus, and in 12 BCE he made out his third will naming Antipater as the first successor and next after him Alexander and Aristobulus. Because Alexander and Aristobulus became hostile in their attitude toward Herod, he finally ordered them to be executed by strangulation in 7 BCE. Immediately after their execution Herod drew up his fourth will, naming Antipater as sole heir, and, in the event of his death, Herod (Philip) as his successor. With the discovery of Antipater's plan to kill Herod, he was tried and imprisoned. A fifth will was made in which Herod passed over the next two oldest sons, Archelaus and Philip, because Antipater had influenced him against them, and he selected Antipas as sole heir. Five days before Herod's death, he executed Antipater and made his sixth will, in which he designated Archelaus as king, his brother Antipas as tetrarch of Galilee and Perea, and their half-brother Philip as tetrarch of Gaulanitis, Trachonitis, Batanea, and Paneas. It is during this last period of Herod's life, complicated by illness and plots to obtain his throne, that the narrative of the *Magi is set (Matt. 2.1–16).

In conclusion, although Herod was a successful king who was highly regarded by the Romans, his personal life was plagued by domestic troubles. After the death of Herod the Great in the spring of 4 BCE, Antipas and Archelaus contested his last two wills before the emperor in Rome. Antipas favored the fifth will because in it he was sole heir; Archelaus, of course, preferred the sixth. After some delay the emperor made Archelaus ruler over Idumea, Judea, and Samaria with the title of ethnarch, promising that he could become king if he showed good leadership. He appointed Antipas tetrarch over Galilee and Perea and Philip tetrarch over Gaulanitis, Auranitis, Trachonitis, Batanea, Paneas, and Iturea.

Archelaus (4 BCE–6 CE). Archelaus, the son of Herod and Malthace, was made ethnarch over Idumea, Judea, and Samaria in 4 BCE. Before he left for Rome to contest his father's will he was given control of the realm and proceeded to kill about three thousand people; after this there was a prolonged revolt at the feast of Pentecost. On his return he treated both Jews and Samaritans with brutality and tyranny; this is the background of Matthew 2.20–23. Archelaus continued the building policy of his father, but his rule became intolerable. Finally, in 6 CE, the emperor deposed him and exiled him to Gaul. His domain became an imperial province governed by prefects appointed by the emperor.

Antipas (4 BCE–39 CE). Antipas, the son of Herod and Malthace and a full brother of Archelaus, was appointed tetrarch over Galilee and Perea in 4 BCE. After Archelaus had been deposed, Antipas was given the dynastic title *Herod,* which had great political significance at home and in Rome. He rebuilt what had been destroyed in the widespread revolt after his father's death, including the largest city, Sepphoris, and moved his capital to a new city, Tiberias (named in honor of the emperor Tiberius).

Herod Antipas's greatest notoriety is the imprisonment and beheading of *John the Baptist (Matt. 14.1–12 par.). This incident occurred after he had married Herodias, who was his niece and the wife of his brother Herod (Philip). John the Baptist boldly criticized the marriage, for according to the Mosaic law it was unlawful to marry a brother's wife (Lev. 18.16; 20.21), except for *levirate marriage (Deut. 25.5). As a result, John was imprisoned, and eventually, at the instigation of Herodias with *Salome's help, Herod beheaded John at Machaerus in 31 or 32 CE.

According to the Gospels, Antipas thought that Jesus was John the Baptist resurrected (Matt. 14.1–2; Mark 6.14–16; Luke 9.7–9) and desired to see him, but Jesus withdrew from his territories. Later, during Jesus' final journey to Jerusalem, the Pharisees warned him to leave Galilee because Herod wanted to kill him (Luke 13.31). According to Luke, during Jesus' trial *Pilate sent Jesus to Herod when he heard that Jesus was from Galilee (Luke 23:6–12).

In 36 CE the *Nabatean king Aretas IV defeated Antipas in retaliation for Antipas's deserting his daughter to marry Herodias. Although Antipas had hoped to get help from Rome, it was not forthcoming because of the change of emperors. On his accession, Caligula (37 CE) gave his friend Agrippa I, brother of Herodias as well as nephew of Antipas, the territories of Philip the tetrarch, who had died in 34 CE, and granted Lysanius the coveted title of king. His sister Herodias became intensely jealous and urged her husband to seek the title of king for his long, faithful service. When Antipas

and Herodias went to Rome in 39 CE to request the title, Agrippa brought charges against Antipas, and consequently Caligula banished him to Gaul. Agrippa I obtained his territories.

Philip the Tetrarch (4 BCE–34 CE). Philip was the son of Herod the Great and Cleopatra of Jerusalem. In the settlement of Herod's will, he was appointed tetrarch over northern Transjordan, including Gaulinitis, Auranitis, Trachonitis, Bananea, Paneas, and Iturea (Map 13:Y2–3). He rebuilt two cities: Paneas, which he renamed Caesarea Philippi, the site of Peter's confession of Christ (Matt. 16.16), and Bethsaida, where Jesus healed a blind man (Mark 8.22–26). Philip married Herodias's daughter Salome, but they had no offspring. When he died in 34 CE, Tiberias annexed his territories to Syria and, when Caligula became emperor (37 CE), they were given to Agrippa I, Herodias's brother.

Agrippa I (37–44 CE). Agrippa I, the son of Aristobulus (son of Herod the Great and Mariamne) and Bernice (daughter of Herod's sister, Salome, and Costobarus) and the brother of Herodias, was born in 10 BCE. He lived extravagantly and with creditors pursuing him. Sometime ca. 27–30 CE Antipas provided him with a home and a position as inspector of markets in Antipas's new capital, Tiberias. Not long afterward he went to Rome and befriended Gaius Caligula. Owing to an unwise remark favoring Caligula as emperor, Tiberius put him in prison, where he remained until Tiberius's death six months later. In 37 CE when Caligula became emperor, he released Agrippa I and gave him a gold chain equal in weight to his prison chain. He also gave him the territories of Philip the tetrarch and of Lysanius, with the coveted title king. On Caligula's death in 41 CE, Claudius confirmed the rule of Agrippa I and added Judea and Samaria to his kingdom.

Of all the Herods, Agrippa I was the most liked by the Jews and, according to Acts 2, was a persecutor of early Christians. In 44 CE he died suddenly in Caesarea (Acts 12.22–23; Josephus *Ant.* 19.8.343–52). Because Agrippa's son was only seventeen years old, his territories were reduced to a Roman province. His daughter Drusilla eventually married the Roman procurator Felix (Acts 24.24).

Agrippa II (50–100 CE). Agrippa II, son of Agrippa I and Cypros, daughter of Phasael (Herod the Great's nephew), was born in 27 CE. Because of his young age he was not allowed to rule immediately, but in 50 CE Claudius appointed him king of Chalcis. In 53 Claudius gave him Abilene, Trachonitis, and Arca in exchange for Chalcis. Shortly after the accession of Nero in 54 CE, he acquired the Galilean cities of Tiberias and Tarichea, with their surrounding areas, and the Perean cities of Julias (or Betharamphtha) and Abila, with their surrounding land.

The private life of Agrippa II was not exemplary, for he had an incestuous relationship with his sister Bernice. In his public life he was in charge of the vestments of the high priest and could appoint him. The Romans would seek his counsel on religious issues, and this may be why Festus asked him to hear Paul at Caesarea (Acts 25.13–26.32).

Agrippa II failed to quell the Jewish revolt against Rome in 66 CE and sided with the Romans throughout the war of 66–70. He died childless ca. 100 CE; with his death, the Herodian dynasty ended.

Conclusion. Herodian rule brought stability to the region. With its domination of the eastern parts of the Mediterranean Sea, it was important for Rome to have a peaceful Palestine, because it acted as a buffer state between Rome and the Parthians and was crucial for the trade routes north and south of Palestine. To be a ruler of the Jews was difficult primarily because of their religion. Although the Herods were enamored of Hellenism and adopted some of its elements, they were aware of Jewish religious sensitivities. After the deposition of Archelaus, direct Roman rule of Judea by prefects like Pilate brought instability, much of it due to lack of understanding of Judaism.

Although each of the Herods (except possibly Archelaus) contributed to this stability, it was the pioneering rule of Herod the Great that laid its foundation. As a vassal king, he made it possible for Judea to be somewhat independent. Rome allowed this because he brought stability to the area and because he had proved his loyalty to Rome both militarily and financially.

See also Roman Empire.

HAROLD W. HOEHNER

Hezekiah ("Yah[weh] strengthens"). King of Judah ("the finest": 2 Kings 18.5) 715–698 (or 727–686) BCE. Like his later successor *Josiah, while young he worked closely with the priesthood (2 Chron. 29.2–4) and sought unification with the northern kingdom of Israel (left kingless), inviting the northern tribes to an ecumenical *Passover (2 Chron. 30.1, perhaps a midrashic embroidering of his reforms summarized in 2 Kings 18.4). At first he paid tribute to *Assyria, remaining submissive until 705; but apparently as part of his revolt (2 Kings 18.7; 20.12) he set about fortifying *Jerusalem (2 Chron. 32.5). The year of *Sennacherib's punitive invasion (*see* Lachish), Hezekiah's fourteenth year in 2 Kings 18.14, was 701, whence the beginning of his reign in 715, a date incompatible with 2 Kings 18.10, in which his sixth year was that of the fall of Samaria in 722 (whence the inauguration date of 727). Assyria's general (Isa. 36.4) appealed to Jerusalem's populace in their own language over the king's head; but trouble in the army (perhaps a plague: see 2 Kings 19.35) forced Sennacherib's sudden withdrawal. A second Assyrian campaign has been proposed on the basis of 2 Kings 18.17–19.36 (duplicating 18.13–16), to collect the immense sum Sennacherib claimed from Judah (2 Kings 18.14); but *Isaiah may have induced Hezekiah just to send off the money and end his years in peace (2 Kings 20.19).   ROBERT NORTH

High Place (Hebr. *bāmâ*). A hill or elevated platform used for sacrifice; a local place of worship; or, in pejorative usage, any sanctuary other than the *Temple in *Jerusalem. The term seems originally to have referred to a natural height where sacrifices were offered. The site was often a hill outside an adjacent city. It was necessary, for example, to "go up" to reach the high place that lay outside *Samuel's hometown (1 Sam. 9.12–14, 19) and to "come down" to return to the city (1 Sam. 9.25). References to the building (1 Kings 11.7; Jer. 19.5) and destruction (2 Kings 23.8; Ezek. 6.3) of high places show that artificially raised platforms were also used. Thus, it is not surprising to find mention of high places within cities (1 Kings 13.32; 2 Kings 17.29) or even in ravines and valleys (Ezek. 6.3).

The form and structure of the high place have been illustrated archaeologically by the discovery at several sites of large, raised platforms of various sizes, often accessed by steps. Some of these are from the pre-Israelite period, including an Early Bronze Age example from *Megiddo (mid-third millennium BCE) and Middle Bronze Age examples from *Gezer and Nahariyeh, near Haifa. Other excavated high places date to the Israelite period, including examples at *Dan, *Hazor, *Megiddo, Arad (Map 1:X6), and Malha, southeast of Jerusalem.

The editors of the *Deuteronomic history (Deuteronomy—2 Kings) regarded the high places as illicit. This negative judgment stemmed from the association of high places with proscribed cultic activities and the worship of foreign gods (1 Kings 11.7) and from the Deuteronomic belief that Jerusalem was the only legitimate place of sacrifice to Yahweh. According to Deuteronomy 12.1–14, Moses instructed the people that, after they had entered the *Promised Land, they must destroy all the places where the local gods were worshiped. Instead of rebuilding these places for the worship of Yahweh, they were to seek the single place that Yahweh would choose and bring their sacrifices there. The subsequent story shows that this chosen place was Jerusalem, as *Solomon asserts in his speech in dedication of the Temple (1 Kings 8.15–53). From this point of view, sacrifice at high places was acceptable in pre-Temple times. Thus Samuel is not condemned by the Deuteronomic editors for his association with a high place (1 Sam. 9.12–25), and even Solomon is excused for his sacrifices at the Gibeonite high place (1 Kings 3.3–4). After the Temple is built, however, sacrifice at local places of worship is no longer condoned. The law of the central sanctuary, in fact, becomes the chief criterion by which subsequent kings of Judah are evaluated by the Deuteronomic editors. All of the kings of Judah before *Hezekiah are said to have permitted high places to remain in use, so that Rehoboam and his successors are condemned for tolerating shrines "on every high hill and under every green tree" (1 Kings 14.23; cf. Deut. 12.2). The northern rulers are censured for the same crime, which is a part of the final condemnation of the northern kingdom in 2 Kings 17.9–10. Hezekiah and *Josiah are said to have introduced reforms in Judah that included, among other things, the removal of the high places (2 Kings 18.4; 23.8, 13, 15, 19).

P. KYLE MCCARTER, JR.

Hittites. Among the people Israel found in *Canaan were the "sons of Heth," members of a Canaanite family (Gen. 10.15). *Esau had married two of their women (Gen. 26.34), and later Ezekiel decried Israel's religious faithlessness by calling her a descendant from a Canaanite and a Hittite (Ezek. 16.3). Ephron the Hittite sold his field and cave near *Hebron to *Abraham (Gen. 23). The names given for these Hittites are all Semitic, and it is likely that all were members of a local Canaanite tribe.

The Hittites of Anatolia (modern Turkey) were another people, forgotten until excavations at Boghazköy were begun in 1906. This was the site of their capital, Hattusha, containing a palace and temples. Clay tablets inscribed with Babylonian cuneiform *writing preserve their language, the oldest recorded member of the Indo-European family. Inscriptions show that the Hittites set up their kingdom about 1750 BCE, and that from about 1380 to 1200 BCE they rivaled the Egyptians and the Babylonians in international affairs. Their armies marched into Syria, where they faced Egyptian forces. After decades of war, the battle of Qadesh (ca. 1259 BCE) led to a treaty that established a line across northern Lebanon, the frontier between their zones of influence. This line provided the limit for Israel's territory (Josh. 1.4; 2 Sam. 24.6 [emended]).

Hittite archives include many rituals for temple services with precise instructions for kings and priests, displaying concern for ritual *purity and complexity of detail similar to the ritual laws of the *Pentateuch. Treaties made by Hittite kings with vassal kings present a formula also found in biblical *covenants, especially those made before the monarchy. Beside records in cuneiform, Hittite scribes used their own hieroglyphic script for royal monuments and perhaps on wooden tablets that have perished.

After the Hittite empire had collapsed under attacks from migrant tribes (possibly including *Philistines among the Sea Peoples), several princes held on to certain cities and created local kingdoms (e.g., Carchemish, Hamath), identified today by carved monuments with Hittite hieroglyphic inscriptions. These "neo-Hittite" states were finally overwhelmed by *Assyria in the ninth and eighth centuries BCE. Before that time they supplied wives for *Solomon (1 Kings 11.1), perhaps soldiers for *David (Uriah the Hittite, 2 Sam. 11; see Bathsheba), and presented a threat to Israel's Aramean enemies (2 Kings 7.6).

ALAN MILLARD

Holiness. When the *seraphim before God's throne cry "Holy, holy, holy" (Isa. 6.3; cf. Rev. 4.8), they are engaging in an ascriptive tautology. God is holy and by that fact defines holiness. "Hallowed be thy name" is a prayer that the intrinsic holiness of God be established and recognized within creation, that is, that God's kingdom come and God's will be done (Matt. 6.9–10 par.; see Lord's Prayer).

In *The Idea of the Holy*, Rudolph Otto argues that the experience of the holy is irreducible to other categories. What he calls "the numinous" is a *mysterium tremendum et fascinans*, an awe-inspiring phenomenon that both repels and attracts. The voice from the burning bush tells *Moses to take off his shoes, for he is standing on holy ground, and Moses hides his face (Exod. 3.5–6; cf. Josh. 5.15). In the Bible, the elementary religious experience takes on a personal and ethical tone. The "wholly other," the incomparable "Holy One" (Isa. 40.25), is also the transcendent creator (Ps. 95.6). God's holy name is vindicated by his acts in history (Ps. 98.1; Ezek. 36.22–27; John 12.28; Rev. 15.3–4). If God inspires fear, it is on account of his power and *purity; if God attracts, it is by his creating love and redeeming *grace. More precisely, God's power shows itself as love for the creature; God's purity shows itself as grace to transform the sinner. In his vision of "the King," Isaiah finds his lips touched with a burning coal and his guilt is taken away (Isa. 6.5–7). The prophet is then set in God's service.

God's active claim upon a creature consecrates it. That is preeminently true of God's elect people. Yahweh is, especially in the book of Isaiah, "the Holy One of Israel." He is "God and no mortal, the Holy One in [their] midst" (Hos. 11.9). Out of love, he has chosen this people for his own (Deut. 7.6–8). Belonging to the God who dwells among them, they are a holy nation (Exod. 19.5–6; Deut. 26.19; 28.9; Jer. 2.3). The divine gift brings an obligation: "You shall be holy for I am holy" (Lev. 11.44; 19.2; 20.7, 26).

According to the New Testament, Jesus is "the Holy One of God" (John 6.69; cf. Mark 1.24 par.; Luke 1.35; Acts 3.14), and through him God's favor has been extended to believing *gentiles (1 Pet. 2.9; cf. Rom. 15.16). The church's vocation is to holiness (Eph. 1.3–4; 5.25–27; 1 Thess. 3.13). This again entails a way of life that distinguishes its members from the world (2 Cor. 6.16–7.1; 1 Thess. 4.3–7).

The way of holiness follows God by imitation (Eph. 4.24) and even participation (Heb. 12.10). Believers are "called [to be] saints" (Rom. 1.7; 1 Cor. 1.2; Col. 3.12). Having been sanctified in *baptism (1 Cor. 6.11), Christians are to yield themselves to the righteousness of God for their sanctification to continue (Rom. 6.19–22). Their sanctification is the work within them of the Holy Spirit who has been given to them (Rom. 5.5; 1 Thess. 4.8). The promise is that of being made "partakers of the divine nature" (2 Pet. 1.3–11).

From the Exodus on, the *ark of the covenant was a sign—and a dangerous one (1 Sam. 6.19; 2 Sam. 6.6–10)—of Yahweh's presence with Israel. In the Jerusalem Temple, it belonged in the "holy of holies" (1 Kings 8.6). Divinely significant objects, places, times, and people were "holy," and the adjective became practically formulaic in the priestly documents of the postexilic period: God's holy house or Temple stood on God's holy mountain; it was served by a holy priesthood, and the feasts were holy days. A matching ethic was a prophetic concern (e.g., Mal. 3.4–5). In the New Testament, cultic terminology is turned toward conduct: "Present your bodies as a living sacrifice, holy and acceptable to God" (Rom. 12.1; cf. 1 Cor. 6.19–20; Eph. 2.21–22).   GEOFFREY WAINWRIGHT

Holocaust. The English word *holocaust* is derived from Latin *holocaustum* and Greek *holocaustos/holokautos* (*holos*, "whole," and *kaustos/kautos*, "burnt"). Forms of the latter appear more than two hundred times in the *Septuagint, generally to translate Hebrew ʿōlâ (literally, that which goes up), the burnt offering, one of the most common, multipurpose, and ancient forms of Israelite *sacrifice (Lev. 1; Num. 15; etc.). The slaughtered sacrificial *animals, birds, or unblemished male quadrupeds such as sheep, goats, or cattle were wholly burned on the *altar, with the exception of the skin, which was given to the *priest who performed the ritual (Lev. 7.8). The holocaust offering is mentioned three times in the New Testament (Mark 12.33; Heb. 10.6, 8). Although the sacrificial system ceased with the destruction of the *Temple in 70 CE, rabbinic literature includes traditions about and discussions of the burnt offering, the earliest of which is in the *Mishnah, especially tractates Zebaḥim and Tamid.

The meaning of "holocaust" has evolved from complete burnt consumption in sacrifice to include complete or massive destruction, especially of people. It was used in this context in the aftermaths of World War I and II. Since the 1950s, "The Holocaust" has come to refer to the Nazi murder of European Jewry (1941–45). By extension, "holocaust" is sometimes used to designate massive atrocities against or destruction of large numbers of people. The biblical religious-sacrificial origins and connotations of the term are troubling to some who prefer the word used most often in modern Hebrew to refer to the Nazi murder of European Jewry, *Shoʾah*, whose biblical meanings include devastation, desolation, and ruin.   BARBARA GELLER NATHANSON

Holy Spirit. There is no distinct term for spirit in the languages of the Bible; the concept was expressed by a metaphorical use of words that mean, literally, wind and breath (Hebr. *rûaḥ;* Grk. *pneuma*); the English word "spirit" is simply an Anglicized form of the Latin word for breath *(spiritus)*. Wind is an invisible, unpredictable, uncontrollable force, which bears down on everything in its path; and people found early that they are exposed to influences that affect them like the wind. Breath is a miniature wind, and from this the metaphorical use of the term acquired a more precise and positive direction, for breath is essential to life (Gen. 6.17).

The Spirit of God in the Hebrew Bible. The action of the spirit is seen in a broad range of experiences, some of which seem less than "spiritual" as we now understand the word. Thus the source of (physical) strength that enabled Samson to kill a lion is ascribed to the spirit of God (Judg. 14.6). And there are several places where it is not clear whether *rûaḥ* bears the literal sense of wind or the metaphorical sense of spirit (e.g., Gen. 1.2 [cf. 8.1]; Ezek. 1.12). The action of spirit is more often seen in inner experiences, but some of these too are ambiguous (e.g., the evil spirit from the Lord that seized Saul, 1 Sam. 16.14; the lying spirit that the Lord put in the mouth of certain prophets, 1 Kings 22.22). Among the most distinctive experiences ascribed to the action of the spirit are the raptures that drove people to ecstatic speech and behavior (e.g., Saul after his anointing, 1 Sam. 10.6–11; the seventy elders, Num. 11.25); this was the original meaning of "prophecy."

None of the *prophets of Israel before the exile ascribe their vocation to the action of the spirit or, indeed, have much to say about the spirit at all. Some references of a critical or ironical nature seem to indicate that these prophets wished to dissociate their prophetic calling from the ecstatic raptures that earlier went under the name (Hos. 9.7; Mic. 2.11; cf. 1 Sam. 9.9). It is only in the later prophets that the spirit comes into prominence, notably in *Ezekiel. Ezekiel mostly used the term *rûaḥ* without the qualification "of God," and in many cases the literal and metaphorical senses of the term are hard to disentangle. A high point in the prophecy of Ezekiel is his vision of the valley of dry bones, over which he was commanded to

invoke the life-giving breath, or wind, or spirit of God (Ezek. 37.1–14; the three words all render *rûaḥ*). The hope so dramatically envisaged here becomes a major theme in the latest phase of biblical prophecy. Recognizing that the renewal of God's people could come only from God, the prophets came to look for a general outpouring of his spirit (Isa. 32.15). In no case is the fulfillment of this hope ascribed to the mediation of an expected messianic king; but in the portrayal of this figure in the prophecy of *Isaiah, he is to be the permanent bearer of the spirit (Isa. 11.2; 61.1)—perhaps in contrast to the charismatic leaders of Israel, such as Saul, from whom the spirit departed. The distinctive mark of the messianic era will be the bestowal of God's spirit on all, high and low, old and young, male and female (Joel 2.28).

The designation "holy spirit" occurs only in Psalm 51.11 and Isaiah 63.10–11.

The Holy Spirit in the New Testament. The New Testament announces the fulfillment of the eschatological hope of the spirit proclaimed by the prophets. Two elements are emphasized: the coming of the one who is the permanent bearer of the spirit and the outpouring of the spirit on "all flesh"; and both are linked.

*Jesus is identified as the promised one on whom the Spirit will remain (John 1.33). This identification took place at his *baptism by the visible descent of the Holy Spirit on him in the form of a dove. The story need not imply that the association of the Spirit with Jesus began at his baptism and that he was at that moment adopted as *Son of God; John especially saw in the baptism of Jesus the epiphany of the preexisting Son (John 1.29–34), the one in whom the prophetic hope was fulfilled. According to Luke (4.16–21), Jesus explicitly claimed this identity in his sermon at Nazareth; and it is indicated in the nativity stories, where the emphasis is on the conception by the Holy Spirit rather than on the virginity of Mary (Matt. 1.18; Luke 1.35; *see* Virgin Birth). Further references to the Holy Spirit are not frequent in the Gospels, but they occur at significant points, especially in *Luke (4.1, 14, 16–21; 11.20 [cf. Matt. 12.28]; 12.10). It is preeminently in the presence and operation of the Holy Spirit in him that Jesus is authenticated (Matt. 12.28; cf. 1 John 5.6–12); and thus to refuse the testimony of the Spirit is a sin that is infinitely graver than the sin of refusing the testimony of Jesus to himself (Matt. 12.31; John 5.31–36). The life of Jesus is presented as wholly directed by the Holy Spirit (John 3.34), and this note recurs in the apostolic preaching in *Acts (e.g., 10.38).

Jesus is not only the permanent bearer of the Holy Spirit; he is also the one who will dispense the gift of the Holy Spirit to others. But this action of Jesus (which is expressed in the future tense in the first three Gospels) does not coincide with his manifestation as the bearer of the Spirit; it is projected into a future beyond the earthly mission of Jesus. There is a stated interval between the epiphany of Jesus and the general distribution of the Holy Spirit. Luke concludes his account of the ministry of Jesus with his command to the disciples to wait for the promise of the Father (Luke 22.49), and in the sequel he measures the period of waiting as fifty days after Easter (Acts 2.1). John expressed the same point in a different way, even though he records the promise made at the baptism of Jesus in the present tense (John 1.33), and he disagrees with the Lucan chronology in placing the gift of the Spirit to the disciples on the evening of Easter (John 20.22); early in his gospel John states that the gift of the Spirit could not be bestowed before Jesus was "glorified," that is, before he had completed his mission (John 7.39), and later, in one of the Paraclete sayings (see below), he stressed that the departure of Jesus must take place first, no matter how that grieves the disciples (John 16.7).

The five sayings about the Paraclete, perhaps a separate collection before their inclusion in the gospel according to John (14.15–17; 14.25–26; 15.26; 16.4–11; 16.12–15), contain the only formal teaching about the Holy Spirit in the New Testament. The term "Paraclete" (NRSV: "Advocate") belongs to the language of the law courts, and means a defending counsel, or attorney, as opposed to the accuser, who is called *diabolos* ("devil," Rev. 12.10; *see* Satan). Paraclete is applied directly to Jesus himself in 1 John 2.1, and, indirectly, in John 14.16, where the word "another" implies a similarity between the Paraclete and Jesus himself; the Paraclete will be to the disciples what Jesus himself has been, and the coming of the Paraclete will be equivalent to a coming of Jesus himself (John 14.18, unless this is an allusion to the return of Jesus to the disciples after the Resurrection). But there are important differences, in addition to the sequential relation. The similarities and the differences may be listed summarily: the teaching of the Paraclete will be centered on Jesus and his teaching (John 14.26; 15.26; 16.14); the Paraclete will extend the range of Jesus' teaching to the world (John 16.8); the Paraclete will advance the disciples' understanding of "the truth," which is identical with Jesus (John 16.13; cf. 14.6); the presence of the Paraclete with the disciples will be permanent, in contrast to that of Jesus, which had to be withdrawn (John 14.16; 16.7); the presence of the Paraclete will be invisible and inward (John 14.17).

The relation between Christ and the Holy Spirit is also close in *Paul. The mission of Christ and the mission of the Holy Spirit are virtually indistinguishable; the presence of the Holy Spirit is equivalent to the presence of Christ. The Christ who is designated Son of God in power according to the Holy Spirit (Rom. 1.4) is no longer to be known according to the flesh (2 Cor. 5.16).

The distinction between Christ and the Holy Spirit, where it appears in Paul, is nowhere expressed in terms of a sequence but rather as one between two sides or aspects of the same act of God; the mission of Christ presents its objective, or exterior, aspect, the mission of the Spirit its subjective, or interior, aspect (1 Cor. 2; Gal. 4.4–6). Paul's main concern is with the reality of Christ for faith; for the reality of Christ is accessible only to faith, and it is made accessible through the Holy Spirit (Rom. 8.1–15). Thus to be "in Christ" (Rom. 8.1) is the same as to be "in the Spirit" (Rom. 8.9).

The notion of the "seven gifts" of the Holy Spirit, which was developed in Christian liturgical tradition, is based on Isaiah 11.2 (where the *Septuagint and the *Vulgate add "piety" after "knowledge"), but this number does not cover the endowments granted to different members of the church for the good of the whole; lists of these gifts, called "charismata," are found at various places in the New Testament (e.g., Rom. 12.6–8; 1 Cor. 12).   GEORGE S. HENDRY

Holy War. *See* War.

Homosexuality. Leviticus 20.13 prohibits sexual relations between men, defines them as an "abomination," and places them under the death penalty (see also Lev. 18.22). Ethical considerations such as consent, coercion, or the power imbalance inherent in adult-child relations are not legally relevant in these passages (nor in the surrounding levitical laws on adultery, incest, and bestiality). Thus, regardless of the sexual relationship of the participants (a man and his consenting male partner, an adult male whom he had raped, or a child victim), all are equally culpable, since all are equally defiled (see Philo, *De spec. leg.* 3.7.37–42).

Like Leviticus, *Paul does not employ the ethical categories of consent or age for distinguishing between sanctioned and condemned sexual relations. His letters contain linguistic and conceptual parallels to the levitical laws about same-sex sexual relations. Thus, 1 Corinthians 6.9–10 states that "the ones who lie with men" (NRSV: "sodomites"; cf. Lev. 20.13) will not "inherit the kingdom of God" (see also the Deutero-Pauline 1 Tim. 1.10; *and see* Ethical Lists). Paul describes male-male sexual relations as "impurity" and asserts that such men "deserve to die" (Rom. 1.24–32). Paul extends the prohibition to include sexual relations between women (Rom. 1.26) as do other postbiblical Jewish writings. Like other writers in the Roman world such as *Philo, Ptolemy, and Martial, Paul sees same-sex sexual relations as transgressions of hierarchical gender boundaries. For example, "unnatural" (Rom. 1.26) most likely refers to the women's attempt to transcend the passive, subordinate role accorded to them by nature. Similarly, the men have relinquished the superordinate, active role (see 1 Cor. 11.13) and have descended to the level of women.

Some postbiblical Jewish and early Christian writers specifically define the sin of *Sodom and Gomorrah (Gen. 18–19.28; cf. Judg. 19) as same-sex relations rather than as rape or inhospitality; see, for example, Jude 7 and Philo, *De Abrahamo* 26.134–36 (cf. 2 Pet. 2.6; *Testament of Naphtali* 3.4–5; 4.1).

Biblical prohibitions of same-sex love directly influenced later Roman law and, indeed, Western legal statutes until the present (e.g., sodomy statutes in U.S. criminal law).

See also Sex.   BERNADETTE J. BROOTEN

Hope. An attitude toward the future, an assurance that God's promises will be kept, a confidence that what is bad will pass and that what is good will be preserved. Hope is a theme in many places in the Bible, even when specific words for hope are not used.

In the Hebrew Bible, a number of words are translated into English as hope. As in English, hope can be a verb or a noun—the act of hoping, the thing hoped for or the person or thing in whom one hopes. There is no single root word that carries the major responsibility for conveying this concept. Each word provides a slightly different nuance to the process of hoping, though

we may not be able to identify each subtle distinction. The related words *qāwâ* (verb) and *tiqwâ* (noun) may be connected with meanings like "twist," "cord," or "rope," possibly referring to the tension of a time of hoping or the rope to which one clings when in need of hope. The root of the words *yāḥal* (verb) and *tôḥelet* (noun) may mean simply "to wait," being neutral about what will happen at the end of the waiting. Similarly, the verb *śābar* means "to watch," "wait," "expect" (e.g., Ps. 104.27); it becomes hope when one waits with a positive expectation about what will come.

Two words sometimes translated as hope show the relational quality of hope. The verb *ḥāsâ* can mean "to flee for protection," "to take refuge," "to put trust." The word *bāṭaḥ* is usually translated as "trust," but it can be understood as "hope," as the *Septuagint often does.

In the New Testament, the noun *elpis* and the verb *elpizein* are virtually the only words translated as hope. They are used widely in the epistles, rarely in the Gospels, and not at all in the book of Revelation. This shows clearly that hope may be expressed by a text (such as in the words of Jesus or in Revelation) even when the specific word for hope is not present.

Hope has both an objective and subjective aspect. There are promises from God to which one clings as one faces the unknown and often forbidding future. But as suggested by a word like *bāṭaḥ*, hope is also an inner sense of confidence in God, a serenity despite terrible present circumstances. Whatever strengthens *faith will also increase hope. Experiences that bring on a crisis of faith, like the *exile or persecution of the early Christians, will also make hope more difficult.

God's promises form the basis for the content of biblical hope. From the objective side, hope is dependent on the confidence that God will provide: (1) The necessities of life—food, *water, land. Without food and water, there is no hope even for life. Land plays an important part in biblical hope—it is promised, given, removed, and promised again (*see* Promised Land). (2) Protection from danger—both as a community called by God and as individuals. God sends leaders—judges, kings—to protect the nation. When the nation falls, God promises a new and better king from the line of *David, one who will outdo his illustrious ancestor (messianic promises in Isaiah, Jeremiah, Micah, and elsewhere). God will also protect individuals from all that can hurt them (Pss. 4.8; 27.1, 5). (3)

Justice—the good will be rewarded and the wicked will be restrained and punished. (4) Community—the assurance that God will never abandon the people he has chosen, and that they will live in peace and love with other human beings.

Generally speaking, there is in the Bible a growing pessimism that God's promises will be kept within historical time; this is most clearly seen in *apocalyptic writings. Confidence in God remains and hope as relationship survives, but language that had been used to articulate hope for this world is now projected into a world beyond human experience: the land becomes a heavenly home, food and water become heavenly food and the water of life; the *Messiah becomes a divine being; heaven and *hell are the final solution to the problem of justice; communities broken by death and tragedy and sin can be restored in heaven. In spite of the failures and disillusionments of this life, however, there is still hope. God will win the heavenly battle. There will be a resurrection, life after death, and a new age where God reigns.

See also Afterlife and Immortality.

DANIEL J. SIMUNDSON

Horeb. The alternate name of the mountain of revelation more frequently referred to as *Sinai. The name is derived from a root meaning to be dry, an appropriate characterization of the Sinai desert. The designation "Horeb" is characteristic of the Elohist (*E) tradition in the *Pentateuch (e.g., Exod. 3.1; 33.6) and of the book of Deuteronomy (e.g., 1.6; 5.2) and the *Deuteronomic history (1 Kings 8.9; 19.8). The identity of Sinai and Horeb is recognized in Sirach 48.7, suggesting that an attempt to locate two different peaks is misguided.   MICHAEL D. COOGAN

Hosanna. A transliteration of the Hebrew *hôšiaʿ nāʾ*, which is an imperative meaning "Save!" It occurs in the Gospels in the narrative of Jesus' entry into Jerusalem (Matt. 21.9; Mark 11.9–10; John 12.13), in a quotation of Psalm 118.25–25 (which in the Masoretic text has the variant form *hôšîʿâ nāʾ*), one of the psalms recited in the *Passover ritual. In its Greek form, it became a part of the Christian liturgy at an early period (*Didache* 10.6), and it continues to be used in the *Sanctus* and *Benedictus* of the Roman and other rites.   MICHAEL D. COOGAN

Hosea, The Book of. Hosea is the second of the eighth-century BCE prophets whose messages became a separate book (*see also* Amos, The Book of).

The first three chapters tell the story of the prophet and his family. Hosea was instructed by God to marry a woman who is described as adulterous, either because she was already immoral or in anticipation of her unfaithfulness. The three children carry the same stigma (1.2; 2.4), and they are given bizarre names to symbolize their degraded status (chap. 1).

The similarity between Hosea's experience with his wife and Yahweh's experience with Israel is worked out in the book in all its dimensions—heartbreak, enraged rejection, efforts at reconciliation. All these are interwoven in an allegory in chap. 2. The stories are really the same, because the sin of Gomer against Hosea is identical with Israel's sin against Yahweh: unfaithfulness to the covenanted relationship by resorting to the cult of *Baal, the god of the Canaanites (2.8, 13). This rival religion provided sexual activity as part of its ritual (4.10–19), at once literal and spiritual adultery.

In spite of the hopeless situation, which called for the most drastic discipline and even for the death penalty for both the mother (2.3) and the children (2.12b; 9.12–16), the Lord was quite unwilling to give up the *covenant relationship (11.8). Strenuous efforts were made to renew the marriage, to begin all over again (2.14–23).

The story and the allegory are fairly clear in chaps. 1–3, where Hosea's concerns are uppermost. The rest of the book (chaps. 4–14) deals with Yahweh and Israel. It contains prophetic discourses composed in the language of cult poetry. This language is dense, compact, often opaque. Most translations are clearer than the original due to a considerable amount of guesswork and interpretation. This is unavoidable, because the text of Hosea is notoriously difficult, perhaps the most obscure and problematic in the entire Bible. Its difficulties have been attributed to the peculiar dialect of the northern kingdom, but this has never been demonstrated. Again, the text, because of its great age, is suspected of having suffered much damage in transmission, and numerous attempts have been made to repair these supposed corruptions by textual emendations. Doubtless the surviving text is blemished from such causes, but it is more likely that most of our perplexity arises from our failure to understand the author's use of intricate poetic patterns and sophisticated rhetorical devices.

Even when the words are familiar and the grammar seems to be correct, the discussion is often oblique and enigmatic. There are references to a priest (4.4), a prophet (4.5), a mother (4.5), a king (7.3). Priests are implicated in a murder (6.9) and in other crimes (4.1–2). But no one is named, and none of the events referred to in the book can be connected with historical facts known from other sources.

None of the oracles is dated, so we cannot attach them to the political developments of the period. The military activity described briefly in 5.8–12 has been identified as one of the *Assyrian invasions, but it could be one of the many wars between the two kingdoms of Israel and Judah.

The clue provided by the title (1.1) is curiously lopsided. The four kings of Judah cover most of the eighth century BCE, but only one king of Israel is named. The prophecy predicts judgment on Bethel and *Samaria with death or exile for the king (10.7), but it does not show any awareness of the fulfillment of these threats, notably in the fall of Samaria in 722 BCE. Many of the criticisms of the religious life of Israel could have been made at most times in its history; but the deterioration of the situation fits well with the third quarter of the eighth century, when the northern kingdom went into a rapid decline after the death of Jeroboam II (745 BCE), whom Hosea evidently regarded as the last real king of the north. The discourses reflect the chaos and lawlessness that marked the last two decades of the Samarian regime, the anarchy that set in after the death of Jeroboam II in which many of his successors lost their lives through assassination or revolution.

The international scene is dominated by *Assyria and *Egypt, who are frequently mentioned together throughout the book. Many of the references to these countries reveal diplomatic moves by both Israel and Judah to seek security ("healing," 5.13) through alliance with the great powers (7.11; 8.9). All too often, the little countries in the buffer zone between the two imperial nations tried to play one off against the other, with even more disastrous results. Such moves were roundly condemned by the prophets as apostasy from Yahweh, their true and only Lord. Their new protectors became their captors (9.3).

The northern kingdom is consistently called *Ephraim, new terminology not found in Amos

a generation earlier. It probably represents the contraction of the territory ruled from Samaria to a region corresponding to the traditional homeland of that tribe, due to loss of the eastern and northern provinces to the Assyrians and through civil war.

Hosea's messages mostly attack the northern kingdom (1.4), but Judah is frequently mentioned side by side with Ephraim and similarly condemned, especially in the all-important chaps. 4–8. Some scholars wish to delete the references to Judah as secondary additions, but such a revision would seriously injure the fabric of the whole book. The references to *Jacob in the latter part of the book secure a complementary historical perspective that shows a concern for all Israel as the covenant people. It reaches deeply into the past, and Judah could hardly be excluded from Jacob's descendants. The reference to *David in 3.5 likewise recalls the original unity of the people, and looks forward to its future restoration.

The prophecy anticipates wholesale destruction of the state and the deportation of the population. Assyria will be the prime agent of this development. Conquest by Assyria is identified as punishment by God.

Beyond that the prophet anticipates a return from exile (11.11) and reconstitution of the old regime (3.5). With the benefit of hindsight, we connect such statements with the later history of the people, the dispersal first of Israel, then of Judah, and the revival of national life after the *exile. And because the promises of a return seem to fit these later developments, some scholars suspect them of being added after the fact. Unless we recover a manuscript of Hosea of preexilic date, we shall never be able to settle such a point with certainty. But the forecasts are general, even vague, and do not betray actual knowledge of what would eventually take place. It cannot even be shown that the book has been edited with a Judean perspective of later times. It betrays no awareness of the differing fate of Judah or of the later importance of *Babylon. It does not feature *Jerusalem, let alone the *Zion mystique that begins to emerge already in Hosea's younger contemporaries, *Micah and *Isaiah.

Hosea's vision of the future sometimes breaks out into an almost *apocalyptic scenario, with echoes of the serenity and bliss of the original *paradise (2.16–23; 14.4–8). Some scholars believe that such ideas did not develop in Israel until after the exile, but they are deeply woven into the fabric of the book, and any attempt to remove them would spoil the total structure.

Hosea is a book of conflicting passions. Extremes of rage alternate with the most moving expressions of tenderness and compassion. Its themes are the goodness and the severity of God. In passages of unexceeded savagery, Yahweh describes his execution and mutilation of his sinful partner (5.14; 6.5; 9.15; 13.7–8). In other places, the unquenchable affection of God for his people is expressed as grief over their loss, and as the yearning of a father for a beloved child (11.1), or of a husband for an estranged wife (chap. 3). The prophecy reveals the heart of God torn by powerful emotions: justice demands retribution; but *grace cries out for forgiveness. How can both of these divine impulses be satisfied?

Hosea presents a radical solution to this problem. We do not know the outcome of his private tragedy and his heroic measures to recover his wife. He buys Gomer back (3.2), but we are not told how she responded. In God's parallel dealings with Israel, the book everywhere threatens and announces death as the inevitable punishment for sin (2.3, 12; 4.5, 9; 5.12; 7.2; 8.10; 9.9; 10.10; 11.6; 13.7–8, 16). But that will not be the end; once God's anger has been vented, the way of return is open. They may repent (14.1–2); then there will be healing and renewed love (14.4–8). Nothing less than resurrection from the dead can achieve this, and this is what is promised (13.14).

The story and the prophecy operate on several different levels at once, and it is impossible to separate the strands. The oracles have multiple meanings, personal and individual, national and historical. The figures of estrangement/reconciliation, sickness/recovery, death/resurrection are both literal and symbolic, realistic and fantastic. Beginning with one man's private tragedy and agony, the presentation expands to an analysis of Israel's past history and future destiny, reaching from the *ancestors (chap. 12) to the eschaton (2.21–23). As one whose love was nurtured by the love of God, and whose experience then threw more light of understanding back into the love of God, Hosea reveals the Lord as both stern and sensitive, just and compassionate. He desires kindness (Hebr. ḥesed) rather than sacrifice (6.6), because kindness is an attribute in God even deeper than his justice.

FRANCIS I. ANDERSEN

Hospitality. One of the most highly praised virtues in antiquity. In nomadic societies, hospitality was an unwritten law, and the stranger was regarded as divinely protected. This is true also of the Hebrew Bible. *Abraham, a nomad, is the prime example of someone who is blessed by extending hospitality to strangers (Gen. 18.1–8). The Law requires that because the Israelites had been strangers in Egypt, they should show hospitality to strangers (Exod. 23.9; Lev. 19.33–34), who are similarly under God's protection (Deut. 10.17–19) (see Alien). Many other people appear as examples of hospitality, including *Lot (Gen. 19.1–18), Laban (Gen. 29.13), *Rahab (Josh. 2), and the Shunammite woman (2 Kings 4.8–11). Travelers could expect hospitality as a matter of course (1 Sam. 25.8), but they could also be abused (Judg. 19–20). It is therefore not surprising that people on occasion are rebuked for not being hospitable, such as Jethro's daughters (Exod. 2.20), the men of Succoth and Penuel (Judg. 8.4–9), and the men of *Sodom (Gen. 19; cf. Wisd. 19.13–14). Jael's execution of Sisera while he was her guest is noteworthy, for her abuse of hospitality is praised (Judg. 4.17–21; 5.24–27). Nevertheless, hospitality is so highly regarded that in Isaiah 58.7 it is preferred to fasting, and Job commends himself for it (31.31–32; but see 22.7).

Hospitality was equally important among the Greeks and Romans. It was viewed as a sign of a philanthropic nature (Acts 28.2) and was given religious sanction. Zeus was the "friend of strangers" and protected them (Homer, *Odyssey* 14.283–284; cf. 2 Macc. 6.2). Hospitality was required of all people; only a fool would neglect strangers. By the first century CE, travel was relatively easy and safe, and an extensive system of inns and hostels met the needs of travelers (Luke 2.7; 10.34). Because the services they provided often were minimal and their clientele of a low class, discriminating travelers availed themselves of the hospitality of friends and associates whenever possible. Private hospitality thus continued to be important, especially among simple folk.

The New Testament accords extraordinary importance to hospitality. The Gospels frequently portray *Jesus as enjoying the hospitality of private homes, which provide the setting for much of his teaching (Mark 1.29–34; Luke 7.36–50). Hospitality, furthermore, was part of Jesus' teaching: he used it to illustrate his teaching on human mercy (Luke 10.29–37), God's invitation to accept the gospel (Luke 14.15–25), God's joy over the repentance of a sinner (Luke 15.22–24), humility (John 13.1–11), one's duty to do good without expecting repayment (Luke 14.12–14), and the eschatological gathering of the nations (Luke 13.22–30). As Jesus expected hospitality for himself, he did as well for his followers who preached the gospel. This appears especially in the mission discourses, which reflect the early church's mission practice. People who received Jesus' disciples received Jesus who had sent them (Matt. 10.40–42; 25.31–46), and their offering or withholding of hospitality signified their acceptance or rejection of the gospel (Matt. 10.9–16).

Hospitality continued to be important among early Christians, who traveled as much as other people in the society. Aquila and Prisca, for example, can be placed in Pontus, Rome, *Corinth (Acts 18.1–2), *Ephesus (Acts 18.24–26; 1 Cor. 16.19), and again in Rome (Rom. 16.3). That hospitality appears frequently in exhortations to the moral life shows that it was a matter of constant concern. Hospitality was regarded as an expression of Christian love (Rom. 13.9–13), a gift of God (1 Pet. 4.8–10), a virtue exemplified by ancient worthies (Heb. 13.1–2), and a practical means by which to share in the preaching of the gospel (3 John 5–8). Traveling Christians are not presented in the New Testament as staying in inns: rather, they are described as depending on the private hospitality of the faithful (Acts 21.4–8, 15–16; Philem. 22). Hospitality was extended to defray expenses for further travel (Rom. 15.23–24; 1 Cor. 16.6–7, 11; Titus 3.13–14). Such openness led to abuses such as guests staying too long, but a matter of greater concern was the fear that by receiving someone who propounded error a host would be supporting it (2 John 9–11). One way to guard against this was to write letters of recommendation on behalf of travelers (Acts 18.27; Rom. 16.1–2; 2 Cor. 3.1), a custom widely followed by non-Christians.

Hospitality was practiced in a special way by making available one's home for the meetings of the church. Homes were frequently the settings in which the gospel was first preached (Acts 18.1–6), and for generations they remained the place where Christians met for worship. Such house churches are frequently mentioned in the New Testament (Rom. 16.3–5; 1 Cor. 16.19; Col. 4.15; Philem. 2). Aquila and Prisca, for example, were hosts to evangelists and to the church in three of the cities where they lived. Problems often attended such house churches: religious services quite easily became disorderly (1 Cor. 14), social distinctions between members, rather than being disregarded, could be accentuated (1 Cor. 11.17–32), or a domineering host could usurp power to exclude some persons from the assembly meeting in that house (3 John 9–10). As whole households were converted, so entire households also could be led astray (2 Tim. 3.6; Tit. 1.11). And, despite hospitality's personal and social benefits, it could become a burden to be extended only grudgingly (1 Pet. 4.9). Nevertheless, toward the end of the first century, a Roman Christian still celebrated the hospitality, faith, and piety by which Abraham, Lot, and Rahab were saved (1 Clement 10.7; 11.1; 12.1).   ABRAHAM J. MALHERBE

Houses, Furniture, Utensils.

Houses. The first houses of the biblical period were the tents of the *ancestors. *Nomads in the Middle East still camp where there is a source of *water, shelter from the wind (and, if possible, from the sun), and pasture for their animals. From very early times, however, villages and walled *cities also existed. Such towns were usually 2.5 hectares (6 acres) or less in size, and the houses were small. The development of cisterns and water systems made it possible to locate villages and towns away from springs and streams.

Tents were made of woven goat hair rugs that shrink and become completely waterproof when wet, and were and still are constructed with an inner dividing curtain that provides privacy. Long ropes held the sides of the tent out and up, providing ventilation and further space (see Isa. 54.2).

Permanent homes can be divided into two general classifications, single-room houses and multiple-room houses. Single-room homes were often built in two sections, a raised terrace for the family and a lower area for its animals. The raised terrace was the living area where food was stored, cooked, and eaten, and the members of the family slept and lived. Such a house is presupposed in Matthew 5.14, where a single lamp shines on all in the house. Under the same roof, but below the raised living space, was an area for the shelter of the family's animals at night (see 1 Sam. 28.24; Luke 13.15). Mangers were dug out of the floor of the raised terrace or constructed of stone or clay and placed on the lower level. Each morning, the house animals would be taken out to the courtyard and the house cleaned. These simple houses could have a guest room on the roof or adjoining the house on the same level. This is the sense of the Greek word *kataluma* in Luke 22.11 par.; if the word has the same meaning in Luke 2.7, the setting Luke gives for the birth of *Jesus is a private one-room home with mangers in the floor: Joseph and Mary are in the family room because the guest room is full.

The second category, with many varieties, is that of rooms around a central courtyard. This courtyard may be open to the sky, or partially covered, or completely roofed, and was the setting for many activities, including cooking, *crafts, and often business. The house may have one or two floors, but rarely more. The wealthier have higher homes, and they are thus able to look down on the rooftops and courtyards of their neighbors (see 2 Sam. 11.2). Wealthy homes may also have a second courtyard, with surrounding rooms, behind the first, for the family.

Palaces are essentially variations of the second type. Those of *Herod the Great at *Jericho, Masada, and elsewhere exhibit a grand style seldom matched in ancient Palestine, with their reflecting pools, gardens, Roman baths, air conditioning, decorative stone and plaster work, swimming pools, and exquisite mosaic flooring.

The simplest homes were constructed of sundried mud bricks with a waterproofing plaster; walls built of such material could easily have been dug through by thieves (see Matt. 6.19–20). Undressed field stones, cut stone, and fired brick were used in wealthier homes. The very wealthy might panel special rooms with wood (see 2 Sam. 7.2), but wood was too scarce a commodity to be used extensively in home building.

The floors were generally of packed earth, with a waterproof lime plaster often added to seal out moisture. Flagstones were occasionally used, and mosaic pavings were introduced in the Hellenistic period.

The most common roof was constructed of thick poles laid flat across the walls about 1 m (3 ft) apart, supported by columns or vertical poles if needed. Thin branches spanned the beams. These in turn were covered with coarsely woven mats and packed clay. After every rain or snow the resulting flat roof was rolled with a stone roller to prevent leaking. Grass would spring up on the roofs, but it was short-lived, as the poets

noted (Ps. 129.6–7; Isa. 37.27). Crops were dried and stored on the roof (see Josh. 2.6); guests could be entertained there; and in the summer, the roof became an auxiliary sleeping area. Ceramic tile and stone-slab roofs are found beginning in the Roman period; in the story of the paralytic (Mark 2.1–12 par.), Mark has the bearers dig through the roof, which would suggest clay, while Luke (5.19) uses a word (Grk. *kramos*) that could mean either tile or clay.

Windows on the first floor were small and high for security reasons. This made the house dark, and could require the use of lamps even in daytime (see Luke 15.8). Window spaces were closed in with lattices so that one could look out but not in; window glass was unknown during the biblical periods. Shutters or heavy drapes were used to close the windows. Second-floor windows were considerably larger.

Metaphorically, the phrase "the house of" meant primarily a person's extended family, not the home.

Furniture. Though furniture was fairly sparse, some items were common. The room built for Elisha was furnished with a bed, a table, a chair, and a lamp (2 Kings 4.10).

For sleeping, a mat or mattress on the floor was most common. Often a raised ledge was built into the floor at one end or around the walls, on which cushions and mattresses were placed for sitting in daytime and sleeping at night. Movable beds were relatively rare. Amos condemns the wealthy who reclined on beds of ivory (Amos 6.4); the prophet asserts that only pieces of this expensive wooden furniture with ivory inlays will survive (3.12). The reference to a bed in Mark 4.21 and Luke 8.16 may reflect the Hellenistic setting of those writers; noteworthy is Matthew 5.16, where the bed is not mentioned.

Chairs were also rare; the bed could also function as a couch. Kings, of course, had thrones, and "Moses' seat" (Matt. 23.2) may have been a special place of honor in the *synagogue.

By the first century CE, the triclinium of Greco-Roman culture was in use in Palestine. This was a U-shaped wide couch with a table at its center. Diners ate reclining on their left sides. Such a dining room is probably the background of Luke 7.35–51 and of the Last Supper (see John 13.23–25).

Closets could be built into the walls to save wood, or constructed as separate pieces of furniture. Chests for storage of clothes and bedding are also attested.

Utensils. The basic utensil of the home was the clay pot or vessel, used for food, light, and cosmetics.

After the food was brought from the fields, it had to be dried and stored for the year. The three age-old enemies of food preservation—moisture, rodents, and insects—were overcome by the use of large earthenware vessels, up to 1 m (3 ft) across and 1.5 m (5 ft) high. These were used for storage of dried grains and fruits, as well as for water, *wine, and oil. Wine, and sometimes water, could also be stored in animal skins.

The staple food was *bread, whose preparation required a (stone) grinder and an oven. The flat grinding stone (the saddle quern) in time was replaced by two circular stones placed one on top of another. Ovens were round and open at the top. Flat, pancakelike loaves were baked stuck to the inside of the conical-shaped oven walls. The wealthier would have had brass or copper pots. Each family would also have had a large stone mortar for crushing meat, green wheat, salt, and other foodstuffs. Pieces of bread also served as the basic eating utensils, which could be dipped into a common dish; without it a *meal could not be served (see Luke 11.5–6).

During the biblical periods, light was produced by burning olive oil in small clay lamps; the wealthy could afford lamps of bronze. Small pitchers for refilling the lamps were part of the lighting equipment. A bowl with water in it could be placed under the lamp as a protection from a falling burning wick except on the *Sabbath (M. Šabb. 3.6). Lamp stands could be niches in walls or freestanding (see also Menorah).

Among the variety of cosmetic aids in use were thin alabaster or glass vials for perfume, palettes for eye-makeup and the like, and small, shaped stones for smoothing callouses.

KENNETH E. BAILEY

Human Person. The idea of the human person, so important in modern times thanks especially to the study of psychology, was not a focus of ancient Israelite thought. Because of the corporate identity of the people of Israel, the individual person did not receive much attention in the literature of Israel. However, as Israel moved into a later period, and particularly after its encounter with Hellenism, the nature of the individual and his or her fate became much more prominent both in Second Temple Judaism and early Christianity.

The Hebrew word for the human being is nepeš, which among its wide range of meanings connotes both flesh and soul as inseparable components of a person. A nepeš, or person, is first of all a living being, animated by breath. The life of a person is seen as residing in the *blood as well as in the breath (Deut. 12.23, 24); therefore, it is unlawful to shed or to eat blood. Thus, an essential component of the person is the flesh (Hebr. bāśār), which is separate from God and carries a connotation of weakness. All animals are composed of flesh, and the human animal is no different in this regard.

However, a person is also composed of "soul," so that less concrete attributes also belong to the person. Appetites such as hunger and thirst, emotions like desire, loathing, sorrow, joy, and love, and thought or mental activity all belong to the nepeš. This is how the human differs from animals, who are only flesh; the human, who has been animated by the breath of God (Gen. 2.7), shares in the attributes of God.

At death, the person's flesh dies, and the soul dwells in Sheol, a shadowy place for the dead (see Afterlife and Immortality; Hell). There is no notion in what may be called orthodox Israelite religion of a separate existence for the soul after death. Death is accepted as a natural part of the life cycle, but it is not welcomed, for the person who dies loses his or her being. In a prayer of thanksgiving, the psalmist says to the Lord, "What profit is there in my death, if I go down to the Pit? Will the dust praise you? Will it tell of your faithfulness?" (Ps. 30.9). Death is thus perceived to be the end of all sentient life. In later times, a doctrine of the resurrection of the dead developed, so that the best hope of the person after death lay in resurrection, when the soul and body would be reunited and live again (Dan. 12.2).

With the introduction of Hellenism into the ancient Near East, Israelite thought began to espouse the notion of a separation of soul and body. In Greek thought, body (sōma) is separate from soul (psychē), and the soul contains the true essence of a person. At death, the soul flees the prison of the body to seek a higher life, so that death is truly the liberation of the soul. As Jewish thought began to be influenced by Greek, these concepts emerge in its literature. *Philo, an Alexandrian Jewish philosopher of the first century CE, assumes throughout his works a complete separation of soul and body, with flesh the chief cause of ignorance and soul the vehicle for a higher life. *Josephus, the first-century CE Jewish historian, states that the *Pharisees believe that souls have the power to survive death (*Ant.* 18.1.14), and that the *Essenes believe that the soul is immortal (*Ant.* 18.1.18). It is probable, however, that the immortality both of these groups anticipate includes a bodily resurrection.

In the New Testament, the still prominent idea of bodily resurrection (see especially the resurrection narratives in the Gospels and also 1 Cor. 15) implies that the soul and body are inseparable, but the notion of a human being composed of a separate soul and body slowly gains ascendancy. There are several Greek words used to explain different aspects of the human person. The Greek word *sarx,* the equivalent of Hebrew *bāśār,* denotes the flesh of both animals and humans. It often appears with the word "blood," as in "flesh and blood," to signify the physical being of the human (as opposed to a supernatural being such as an *angel, which is not composed of flesh and blood). As early as Paul, the word "flesh" begins to receive negative connotations, as the vehicle for *sin in the human being (Rom. 7.5).

The body (Grk. *sōma*) is the physical being of the person animated by the soul. As such, it is both physical and spiritual, and sometimes is used as the equivalent of *nepeš.* Paul uses the term *sōma* in his metaphor of the church as the body of Christ, animated by Christ's spirit (1 Cor. 12.13).

The word *psychē,* or soul, occurs over a hundred times in the New Testament, illustrating its importance in early Christian thought. The soul is the seat and center of the inner life of the human, and the location of the feelings and emotions, especially love (1 Thess. 2.8). The soul is that part of the human person that survives after the death of the body, and receives the rewards and punishments of the afterlife (cf. Luke 16.19–31). Thus the soul is the vehicle of *salvation. It cannot be injured by human instrumentality, but God can hand it over for destruction. Therefore the soul is the most important possession a person has (Mark 8.36–37). Thus the New Testament has moved beyond the Hebrew Bible concept of an inseparable *nepeš,* to the idea of a separate soul and body. The soul survives after death, but may be reunited with the body in a physical resurrection (John 11.25).

The last word associated with the makeup of the human being in the New Testament is *pneuma,* or spirit. The spirit is the breath, that which gives life to the body; in fact, it is often used with "flesh" or "body" to denote the whole person (1 Cor. 5.3–5). The spirit is the seat of insight, often giving persons glimpses of things not visible to the naked eye (e.g., John 13.21). The spirit is also the location of feeling (particularly of love and grief) and will, so that at times the spirit and the flesh are in conflict: "the spirit indeed is willing, but the flesh is weak" (Matt. 26.41). The usage of the word "spirit" often overlaps with that of "soul," and the two together divide the inner life between them. However, the use of the term "spirit" in connection with Jesus emphasizes the most important aspect of "spirit": it is the divine attribute of the human being. God, who is spiritual, breathed his own spirit into the human at creation, and now the human spirit and the divine spirit are related. Often, it is the spirit of God that animates the life of the Christian, as at *Pentecost (Acts 2.2–4). And it is the *Holy Spirit which calls to the human spirit: "it is that very Spirit bearing witness with our spirit that we are children of God" (Rom. 8.16). Thus, early Christian writers pictured the human person as composed of flesh, soul, and spirit, with the flesh, as the vehicle of sin, as something to be tamed, and the soul and spirit, as the vehicles for salvation and participation in the divine, as those parts of the human to be emphasized and nurtured.

SIDNIE ANN WHITE

Humor. *See* Irony and Humor.

Hyssop. A wild shrub, generally identified as *Origanum syriacum* (rather than the European hyssop), belonging to the mint family and still used medicinally and as an herb in the Near East. It is an insignificant plant, contrasted with the cedar in 1 Kings 4.33. Hyssop stalks were used for sprinkling blood and water in purificatory and apotropaic rituals (Exod. 12.22; Lev. 14.4–6, 49–52; Num. 19.18; Ps. 51.7; Heb. 9.19). Its mention in John 19.29 is puzzling, since the plant on which Jesus is offered wine at the *crucifixion is called a reed in Mark 15.36 par., and hyssop would not have been entirely suitable; John's use of the hyssop may therefore be symbolic.

MICHAEL D. COOGAN

I

Idols, Idolatry. An idol is a figure or image worshiped as the representation of a deity. Idols normally take the form of figures in the round or in relief. Strictly prohibited in the Bible, idolatry was widely practiced in the religions of the ancient Near East. Because of their popular appeal, idols became the frequent object of attack in biblical literature.

More than ten different Hebrew words in the Bible designate various types of idols. Some are distinguished according to the method of their construction: "carved image" of stone, clay, wood, or metal; "cast idol" of metal; "pillar," usually an unhewn stone set erect. Other terms have a more general meaning of "shape, form," and thus "representation." The few with a distinctly pejorative sense are not technical names but terms conveying contempt for idolatry: "abominations," "dung-pellets," or "worthless things."

In the religions of ancient Israel's neighbors, idolatry constituted a primary component of public and private piety, and archaeological excavations throughout the region have recovered examples from earliest times onward. These range from crude to elaborate artistic productions of figures in human or animal form, or a mixture of both. Unworked pieces, such as a meteorite rock or a simple wood pillar, could also serve as idols. *Egyptian idols, normally kept in temples, were cultically awakened at daybreak, nourished through sacrifices, dressed and adorned with jewels, and carried about on festive occasions. In *Babylonia, idols could also serve as oracles and were placed at the entrances of homes to guard against witches and evil spirits. The *Canaanites, as did others, formed some of their idols with explicit sexual features, consistent with their fertility cult's concern to ensure the fruitfulness of the land and the womb.

It is not always easy to determine how idols were interpreted in the various religions. In an Egyptian text known as "The Theology of Memphis," the high god Ptah is said to have created not only all other gods but also the idols in which

they were to live. This notion—that the idols are not themselves the gods but rather represent them or house them—was probably present in many religions, though such a distinction may not have been made by all believers, as the various cultic practices of caring for the idols seem to suggest. Several later Greek and Roman thinkers wrote polemically to the effect that weak and ignorant people need idols to help them imagine their gods, maintain faith in them, and have the magical means for securing blessing and avoiding disaster.

Strict prohibition of idolatry is one of the most distinctive features of Israelite religion: Yahweh, the God of Israel, could not be represented in physical form and would not tolerate the idols of any other gods. This aniconic principle is articulated in the *Ten Commandments: "You shall not make for yourself an idol, or any likeness of anything. . .; you shall not bow down to them or serve them" (Exod. 20.4–5 [RSV]; see also 20.23–25 and Deut. 4.15–18, 23, 28). Historically, it is uncertain when and why this prohibition first arose. Probably it is early and is directly connected to the demand for exclusive worship of Yahweh alone. Monolatry, while implicitly recognizing the existence of other gods, did not allow for worshiping them (Exod. 20.3; 22.20), and this perhaps led to banning idolatry altogether in the official cult of Israel.

Nonetheless, there are records of the presence of idols throughout Israel's history. *Rachel's cunning theft of her father's household gods (Gen. 31.19) is perhaps less an instance of idolatry than of the usurping of the father's traditional cultic and legal powers in the family. The *golden calves erected first by *Aaron in the wilderness (Exod. 32.1–6) and later by Jeroboam I at *Dan and Bethel (1 Kings 12.28–29) were, on the other hand, regarded as flagrant violations, at least in some Judean circles. Idolatry occurred also in later periods of the monarchy (e.g., the *Asherah mentioned in 1 Kings 16.33; 2 Kings 21.3) and became the object of reforms by King *Hezekiah (2 Kings 18.4) and King *Josiah (2 Kings 23.4–15). With the impending fall of Jerusalem, Ezekiel reported that the people again reverted to idols in hope of escaping destruction (7.20; 8.10). In biting sarcasm, both Jeremiah (10.3–5) and Second Isaiah (40.18–20; 41.7; 44.9–20; 46.1–2, 5–7; cf. Ps. 115.4–8; 135.15–18) exposed the futility of worshiping the products of human hands.

The line between idol representations and permissible cultic objects may at points seem unclear; the *ark, with its gold *cherubim, was not considered an idol but a manifestation of God's presence (see Exod. 25.17–22; Num. 10.33–36; 1 Sam. 4–6; 2 Sam. 6.6–7); similarly ambiguous were the *teraphim (compare Judg. 17–18 with Zech. 10.2); the *ephod (compare Exod. 28 with Judg. 8.24–27), the Nehushtan or bronze serpent (compare Num. 21.8–9 with 2 Kings 18.4), and the oxen supporting the molten sea in Solomon's *Temple (1 Kings 7.25). The criterion for illicit use of such cultic objects apparently lay in whether they were worshiped directly as manipulable substitutes for Yahweh. Theologically, aniconism became a means for insisting that Yahweh cannot—by virtue of the chasm between creator and creation—be rendered adequately in any physical form. The nature of Israel's God must be reflected not in an image but in all aspects of the people's socioeconomic, political, legal, and domestic life. The prohibition of idolatry was thus coupled with commands for alternate types of religious and moral behavior.

The New Testament polemic against idolatry was primarily related to the opposition to Greco-Roman gods (Acts 7.43; 15.20; 17.29; Rom. 1.23). The "desolating sacrilege" in Mark 13.14 may be an allusion to the Roman emperor cult. Paul discussed at some length the problem of whether Christians should eat meat sacrificed to idols (1 Cor. 8; 10.14–22; cf. Rev. 2.14, 20), and he concluded that, while such food was untainted because the idols represented nonexistent gods, Christians should be cautious not to let this practice undermine weaker believers. Figuratively, idolatry designated a shifting of reverence to worldly things, including covetousness (Col. 3.5; Eph. 5.5) and gluttony (Phil. 3.19).

The prohibition against representation of divine or human beings has been observed in *synagogue ornamentation in most periods, and is strictly complied with in Islamic religious architecture as well. In Christianity, strict observance of the prohibition has surfaced in such movements as iconoclasm and Puritanism, and there are significant differences in practice between Roman Catholic and Orthodox churches, on the one hand, and some Protestant churches, on the other.

See also Graven Image; Monotheism.

DOUGLAS A. KNIGHT

Illustrated Bibles. The subject of illustrations to the Bible includes not only two-dimensional designs, such as paintings, drawings, engravings, photographs, stained-glass windows, and mosaics, but three-dimensional works as well, such as statues and bas-reliefs. Raphael's madonnas, Michelangelo's Moses, the windows of Chartres Cathedral, the ceiling mosaics of the Santa Sophia in Istanbul, and Ghiberti's great doors to the Baptistry in Florence are all, in a sense, Bible illustrations. Annotations to the Bible are also illustrations of it, and originally this was perhaps the primary meaning of "Bible illustrations." In at least one of these senses, there have been "illustrations" of the Bible since it was written and canonized. Not only were there biblical commentaries from the earliest times, but the interpretation of the commandment against *graven images (Exod. 20.4) as a total prohibition of visual representation of sacred (or perhaps any other) scenes was not uniform even in Jewish tradition—note, for example, the cycle of paintings of scenes from the Hebrew Bible on the walls of the Dura-Europos *synagogue, destroyed by the Persians in 256 CE.

The earliest Christian visual representations of the Bible were apparently emblematic, with *Jesus depicted as "the fish" (the Greek word for fish, *ichthus,* was understood as an acronym for "Jesus Christ, God's Son, savior"), and up to the fifth century the *crucifixion was always shown symbolically rather than literally. The first narrative cycle of biblical illustrations is the mosaics in Santa Maria Maggiore in Rome, 432–440 CE, and narrative art is much more common in the West than in the eastern churches. Often postbiblical traditions are also represented; for example, *Job is depicted as a bishop and as the patron saint of music.

We are concerned in this article with illustrations *in* Bibles, largely a Christian phenomenon. The earliest such illustrations now known, from about 400 CE, are for separate sections of the Bible, particularly the *Pentateuch, the Gospels, and the book of *Revelation. Complete illustrated Bibles first appear in the Carolingian period in the eighth century.

The visual matter in such illuminated manuscript Bibles generally consists of three kinds of work: illuminated initial letters, particularly the first word of a book, often merely formal but sometimes representing more or less relevant scenes, such as Paul preaching; decorated borders, with flowers or scrolls or beasts, usually not closely related to their texts; and miniature pictures representing a scene in the text. The illuminated Romanesque Bibles were often very fine, but in them the illustrations were generally less important than the decorations. The illuminated initials in Bibles of the seventh and eighth centuries indicate the dominance of the text over the designs. Among the best-known early illustrated Bibles are the seventh-century Lindisfarne Gospels in the British Museum and the eighth-century Book of Kells in Trinity College, Dublin.

In some cases, the illustrations were not only derived from the text but were more extensive and perhaps even more important than it. The *Bible Moralisée,* made for Louis IX about 1240, had some five thousand illustrations, now scattered among the Bodleian Library, the British Museum, and the Bibliothèque Nationale. Indeed, the *Biblia pauperum,* the Bible for the illiterate poor, consisted chiefly of illustrations. The *Biblia pauperum* was a textbook of Christian *typology, often showing two Old Testament exempla or types (such as Moses in the wilderness) flanking their New Testament echo or antitype (such as Christ in the wilderness), accompanied by appropriate quotations and an explanatory verse in Latin. These were particularly popular in Germany in the thirteenth century. Later, books printed from engraved blocks of wood (not from movable type) with biblical illustrations were also popular in Germany, though they are comparatively rare in Italy and Spain. These block books were enormously influential in the fifteenth and sixteenth centuries; their images were copied in sculpture (e.g., misericords), tapestry, stained glass, and paintings. They became the visual lingua franca of the medieval church.

The first printed Bible, that by *Gutenberg in the mid-fifteenth century, had no printed illustrations, but in some copies manuscript borders and initials were added to make the work as beautiful as the manuscript Bibles that it was imitating. There were woodcuts in a German Bible of 1478–79, and later illustrators included Hans Holbein in a Bible of 1522–23 and Hans Burgkmair in a Bible of 1523. Since then, many great artists have made at least some biblical illustrations; among the best known are those by Raphael and Gustave Doré, and, in the modern period, Georges Rouault and Marc Chagall.

In England, Winchester was the most important center for early book illustration and its artisans produced innovative and very fine work particularly about 1000, remarkable especially for depictions of the *Ascension and the creator. The Bible itself was central for Protestant reformers, and Luther's translation of the Bible was one of the most popular books ever published. Further, Luther actively encouraged illustration of the Bible, so long as the text was followed meticulously. But biblical illustration was slow to develop in England, partly because the country was aesthetically backward and partly because the English Puritans were strongly iconoclastic, deploring all visual representations of holy subjects. It was not until the Restoration of Charles II in 1660 that significant illustrated Bibles were printed in England.

The first great illustrated Bible of the Restoration is the two-volume folio of *The Holy Bible* printed at Cambridge by Field with a hundred marvelous double-page plates by Jan Visscher; a splendid copy bound by 1673 in velvet with watered silk endpages is in the Norwich Cathedral Library. As in most fine book illustration in England before 1750, the artists and even the engravers were from the Continent, chiefly from Holland and France. An equally ambitious folio edition of *The Holy Bible* was published at Oxford by John Baskett in 1716–17 with sixty-seven plates mostly designed by Louis Cheron and engraved by Michael Van der Gucht and Claude Du Bosc, as well as engraved initial letters. This was issued on two sizes of page and with two suites of designs, and the magnificent copy in the Bodleian is printed on vellum, lined in red throughout, and bound in velvet with the arms of the university in silver plaques on the covers.

Before 1750, however, the illustrations in most English Bibles came from separately published suites of designs engraved by John Sturt (1716) and James Cole (1724) and added to plain texts of the Bible by the bookseller or the purchaser. One reason for this may have been that copyright of the King James translation of the Bible belonged to the crown and was assigned only to the university presses at Oxford and Cambridge and to the royal printer in London. As John Reeves, "One of the Patentees" (*see* Printing and Publishing, *article on* Royal Printers' Patent), explained in his great, nonillustrated *Holy Bible* of 1802, "These privileged persons have confined themselves to reprinting the bare text, in which they have an exclusive right; forbearing to publish it with notes, which, it is deemed, may be done by any of the King's subjects as well as themselves." Toward the middle of the eighteenth century, enterprising publishers began publishing the King James translation with notes and with illustrations, and, to distinguish their productions from those protected by the crown's perpetual copyright, called them *The Family Bible* or even *The Royal Universal Family Bible* (1780–82). Other ways of evading the copyright were to publish a *History of the Holy Bible,* or a paraphrase, or an abridgement. Frequently, perhaps normally, these works were published in inexpensive parts, often sixpence each, in folio, with extensive illustrations, sometimes a hundred and more engravings. There were scores of these bulky publications during the eighteenth century; among the most impressive editions were those printed in Birmingham by John Baskerville (1769–72), with engravings by James Fittler (London, 1795), and with plates after Richard Corbould and Charles R. Ryley (London, 1795). But the most ambitious illustrated Bible ever published in Britain was that undertaken by Thomas Macklin and published in parts from 1791 to 1800 with seventy huge and splendid plates designed by the greatest English artists, such as Benjamin West and Sir Joshua Reynolds, and engraved by the best of the English engravers. Macklin's influence on English artists and publishers was great. For instance, in the first twenty-one years of Royal Academy exhibitions (1769–89), there had been an average of six or seven biblical illustrations per year, but in the eleven years from Macklin's announcement of his great undertaking in 1789 until its completion in 1800 seventeen biblical subjects were exhibited per year. In addition Macklin held his own exhibition of the biblical pictures he had commissioned. There were later popular Bible illustrators in England, most notably perhaps John Martin, but no illustrated edition of the Bible in England has surpassed that of Thomas Macklin.

See also Art and the Bible; Children's Bibles.

G. E. BENTLEY, JR.

Image. *See* Graven Image.

Immanuel (Emmanuel). Israelite *prophets could give *names to individuals in accord with a spe-

cific message that they were trying to communicate (e.g., Jer. 20.3–6). In the same way that *Hosea named his three children to correspond with his message (Hos. 1.2–2.1), so *Isaiah noted, "I and the children whom Yahweh has given me are for signs" (Isa. 8.18): Shear-jashub, meaning "a remnant will return" (Isa. 7.3; 10.21, 22); Maher-shalal-hash-baz, meaning "swift is the booty, speedy is the prey" (Isa. 8.1, 3); and Immanuel, meaning "God is with us" (Isa. 7.14; 8.8, 10).

The time between the birth and the maturation of Immanuel is the specific focus of Isaiah's prophecy. Isaiah claims that before the boy reaches a certain age, Judah's enemies in *Damascus and *Samaria will be driven back by *Assyria (Isa. 7.14–17; cf. 8.1–4). Assyrian sources affirm that in 732 BCE the two kings (cf. Isa. 7.1) reigning in those cities were killed and their kingdoms subdued by Assyria.

This larger context makes it probable that Immanuel was a son of Isaiah. However, because Isaiah laconically says that Immanuel will be born to "the young woman" (Isa. 7.14), some suggest that the mother is someone other than Isaiah's wife, whom he refers to elsewhere as "the prophetess" (Isa. 8.3). Some propose that the mother is a queen (a wife of King Ahaz, to whom Isaiah is speaking), an unidentified bystander to whom Isaiah points, or a cult figure. The traditional Christian interpretation that "the young woman" is an intentional reference to *Mary, the mother of *Jesus (*see* Virgin Birth), does not do justice to the immediate prophecy, which required fulfillment in the eighth century BCE.

The gospel of *Matthew (1.23) applies Isaiah 7.14 to Jesus in the same way that Matthew applies other events that had already happened in Israel's history to Jesus' life (cf. Matt. 2.15, 18; 4.15–16; 10.35–36; 12.40; 13.35; 15.8–9; *see* Quotations of the Old Testament in the New Testament). Because Immanuel is one of the few names for which Matthew supplied a translation ("God with us"), it is clear that Matthew wished to stress that in the miraculous birth of Jesus there was a dimension of Isaiah's words appropriate only to Jesus. The echo of the name Immanuel in Jesus' last words in the gospel, "I am with you" (Matt. 28.20; cf. 18.20) is a literary recapitulation of the promise of the birth.

SAMUEL A. MEIER

Immortality. *See* Afterlife and Immortality.

Incarnation. Literally meaning "enfleshment," incarnation is the entry of divinity into human form and life. In some religions this is thought of as something that happens repeatedly, but in the New Testament, incarnation is a once-and-for-all occurrence in *Jesus Christ.

The earliest Christian terms for interpreting Jesus had been drawn from the eschatological hope for a future transformation of existence. In the gospel of *John this hope became secondary, and incarnation—the bringing together of the human and divine in a specific person, Jesus—became the central way of interpreting the divine presence in him.

The effort to express the full presence of God in Jesus led to the conclusion that this specific mode of presence had existed with God prior to the life of Jesus; this preexistent figure had been God's agent in creating the world (John 1.1–3). The existence of Christ before the creation is already present in Paul's writings as they are commonly interpreted (see especially 1 Cor. 8.6; Phil. 2.6; Col. 1.16 [possibly post-Pauline]) and in the non-Pauline Hebrews 1.1–3. Some question the presence of a clear belief in the preexistence of Christ before the relatively late gospel of John. According to this view, the belief developed gradually among Christians from Jewish *wisdom theology, which was first applied to the full preexistence of Christ in John. But *wisdom and word (see Logos) were spoken of in Jewish and early Christian circles as personified entities, and most scholars hold that this imagery had already provided a way of thinking about a preexistent Christ.

Incarnation is meaningful when the distance between the divine and the human is strongly held. This dualism of *flesh and spirit and its overcoming in the incarnation opened the way for the development of later incarnational theology, which held that the goal of the incarnation was the transformation of the human into a nature compatible with the divine.

The Johannine theology of incarnation served as a focal point in the thought of the early church. It became a unifying center for the development of the doctrine of the full divinity and full humanity of Christ and the doctrine of the *Trinity.

The theology of incarnation has been actively debated in modern times. Some regard incarnation as an ancient mythological form of thought; others see in the incarnation a clue to the universal entering of God into human life; still others see the particularity of the incarnation in Jesus Christ as the distinctive core of Christianity.   WILLIAM A. BEARDSLEE

Incense. Incense is formed from the resin and gums of certain trees that, when burned, give off a fragrant odor. Incense was widely used in the ancient Near East both domestically, as a perfume, and in religious rites, as a *sacrifice or as a means of driving away *demons.

The use of incense in Israelite worship parallels its widespread use in Canaanite ritual. The prophets' denunciation of it (e.g., Jer. 6.20) relates to their denunciation of sacrifices offered by unethical persons, or because incense was being burned before *idols. The reference in Ezekiel 16.18 to "my [i.e., God's] incense" shows that the offering, which should have been made to God, was being blasphemously misused.

In the Hebrew Bible we find three main uses of incense. First, it supplemented the grain offering, for which pure *frankincense was prescribed (Lev. 2.1). Doubtless, some form of incense was used with animal sacrifices to counteract the stench of burning flesh. Second, its use in censers was part of Egyptian ritual, and was included in Israelite worship probably from an early period. Finally, as part of the sacrificial system, incense was burned on the golden altar within the sanctuary; it was burned regularly twice a day (Exod. 30.1–10). This offering was restricted to the priests who officiated according to a roster (1 Chron. 24.1–19; Luke 1.8–9). On the *Day of Atonement the high priest entered the holy of holies with a censer (Lev. 16.12–13) to cover the mercy seat with a cloud of smoke, lest he be exposed to the presence of God and die.

In the New Testament there are few references to the use of incense. Most concern Israelite practices, though Revelation 5.8 and 8.3–4, describing the worship of heaven, may reflect early Christian ritual. After the destruction of the *Temple and the cessation of the sacrificial system, however, incense is unlikely to have been used by Jews or Christians; its use in other religions, and especially in the imperial cult, would have made it suspect. There are no references to Christian use of incense in the first four centuries CE.

Its use in worship from the fifth century onward probably derived from its ordinary use to show respect for eminent persons, who were sometimes preceded by servants with censers. It is therefore significant that it has been used especially in the Eucharist to cense the ministers, the people, the gospel book, the altar, and the eucharistic elements, all of which are regarded as representations of Christ himself to whom honor is due. This conception was perhaps helped by the understanding of incense as symbolizing the prayers of God's people (Ps. 141.2; Rev. 5.8).   JOHN N. SUGGIT

Inerrancy.   *See* Inspiration and Inerrancy.

Inheritance. In its secular sense, inheritance is the transmission of property on the owner's death to those entitled to receive it. In Israel this was the right of those related by blood (Num. 27.8–11; 1 Kings 21.3), generally the sons, among whom the firstborn received a double portion (Deut 21.17). The Hebrew word for inheritance, *naḥălâ*, can also mean possession or portion. There are, however, few legal provisions concerning inheritance in the Hebrew Bible, and its meaning there is primarily theological.

Thus, the land of *Canaan is frequently mentioned as the territory that God gives to Israel (Deut 4.21; 19.14). God had promised it to the *ancestors, first to *Abra(ha)m (Gen. 12.7), then to each succeeding patriarch and to *Moses (Exod. 6.8). It was divided up among the tribes, so that each received its own inheritance (Josh 14.1). The nation too is often described as the Lord's inheritance and therefore holy (Exod 19.5–6; Deut. 7.6). Only if the people maintain their *holiness by keeping God's commandments can they keep possession of the land (Jer. 7.5–7). Thus, the inheritance of the land is a sign of God's faithfulness in fulfilling his promises and a reminder of Israel's duties toward him as the true owner of the land (see Lev. 25.23).

After the *exile various developments occur in the concept of inheritance. With the dispersion of many of the nation from the land of Israel, possession of the *Promised Land increasingly becomes a future hope (Sir. 36.16). With the full development of *monotheism, the inheritance that God gives to Israel includes all peoples and countries (Ps. 111.6). He is the portion of the individual believer as representative of the righteous *remnant that can trust only in God (Pss. 16.5–6; 142.5). In the book of *Wisdom and other writings, the inheritance of the righteous is eternal life (Wisd. of Sol. 5.5).

Various aspects of these ideas are resumed in the New Testament. The promise of inheritance to Abraham is fulfilled in Christ, so that he is the promised inheritance (Gal. 3.14). Similarly, in the parable of the evil tenants (Matt. 21.33–41 par.), Christ is the son to whom inheritance rightly belongs, and after his death it passes to his followers (see also Heb. 9.15–17; Acts 20.32).

For Paul, Christians are the real descendants of Abraham, because they share in the inheritance with Christ, to whom the promise to Abraham properly refers (Gal. 3.29). This means that the inheritance now belongs not just to Abraham's physical descendants but also to faithful non-Israelites, the gentiles (Eph. 3.6).

Finally, the concept of inheritance is eschatological. Although a present reality (1 Pet 3.7), it is more commonly viewed as something Christians will receive only in the heavenly realm beyond this world (1 Pet. 1.4). Thus, it is defined as "eternal life" or "the kingdom," which are to be possessed when the *Son of Man returns at the end of time (Matt 19.29; 25.34). Similarly, the letter to the Hebrews reinterprets the promise to Abraham to refer not to Canaan but to the heavenly city (Heb. 11.8–10). *Hope is the link between present and future (Titus 3.7), as is the sealing by the Holy Spirit that guarantees to Christians their promised inheritance until they can finally possess it (Eph. 1.13–14).

J. R. PORTER

Inspiration and Inerrancy. With regard to the Bible, inspiration denotes the doctrine that the human authors and editors of canonical scripture were led or influenced by the Deity, with the result that their writings may be designated in some sense the *word of God. The theological corollary of inspiration, inerrancy, indicates that these writings have been thereby supernaturally protected from error, thus implying that scripture is entirely trustworthy and uniquely authoritative for a given community of faith. The categories of inspiration and inerrancy derive from traditional Christian theology, although analogous conclusions concerning their scriptures would be held by most Orthodox and Conservative Jews.

By far the most comprehensive of the two terms is inspiration, which is derived from a Latin word meaning "to breathe into or upon." More focused than general usage, in which a literary or artistic work or the like is said to be inspired if it is intellectually, emotionally, or volitionally moving, the theological term designates what for the community of faith would have been an objective reality: the sacred scriptures are nothing less than authentic communication from the Deity, or, as the First Vatican Council (1868–70) simply expressed it, "they have God as their author." In Christian theology, with its traditional trinitarian understanding of the one God as three persons (Father, Son, and Holy Spirit), it is usually the third person of the *Trinity who is specified as having inspired the scriptures.

The theological category of inerrancy is of less venerable vintage; the term does not appear either in Latin or in English before the nineteenth century, and modern Protestant *fundamentalists often employ it in a separative and polemical way. Inerrancy denotes the quality of errorlessness (hence, truthfulness) in all the scripture affirms. Related theological concepts such as *authority and infallibility also seek to define the utter dependability of the Bible as uniquely the word of God. Many contemporary theologians avoid the term inerrancy on the grounds that, on the one hand, too much is claimed by it (a focus on the total exclusion of mistakes rather than on the complete absence of deception, as the early church fathers emphasized), and, on the other hand, too little (typically, only the now nonexistent autographs, or original manuscripts, are deemed inerrant; all admit that the later copies contain errors).

Nonetheless, even if the term inerrant itself is of recent and controversial pedigree, the underlying concept of the complete truthfulness and dependability of all that scripture affirms has long been a part of both Jewish and Christian tradition. (Traditional Muslims would enthusiastically categorize the *Qurʾān with the same terms.) Those books that the rabbis categorized as "defiling the hands," and hence sacred scripture, were highly revered by the late first century CE, as *Josephus indicates: "We have given practical proof of our reverence for our own scriptures. For, although such long ages have now passed, no one has ventured either to add, or to remove, or to alter a syllable; and it is an instinct with every Jew, from the day of his birth, to regard them as the decrees of God, to abide by them, and, if need be, cheerfully to die for them" (*Ag. Ap.* 1.42).

The Jewish scriptures were of course sacred for Jesus and his followers, and gospel traditions present him as regarding them as humanly inalterable (Matt. 5.18) and inviolate (John 10.35). For Jesus and the New Testament writers the sacred books were "the scriptures" par excellence, and in the words of these scriptures the Holy Spirit of God spoke through human agency (Acts 4.25; cf. 1.16). Typically, words from the mouth of Yahweh found in the Hebrew Bible are labeled "scripture" in the New Testament (e.g., Rom. 9.17; Gal. 3.8), and even quotations not originally from the mouth of God are sometimes designated as such (Rom. 15.9–12; Heb. 1.5–13). Indeed, the Hebrew Bible as a whole is twice designated the "oracles of God" (Rom. 3.2; Heb 5.12), and in the classic New Testament text concerning God's inspiration of the Hebrew scriptures, 2 Timothy 3.14–17, Paul is pictured exhorting Timothy, his Jewish convert, to remember the "sacred writings" he has known since childhood, for "all scripture" (evidently a reference to all, or nearly all, of the books now included in the Hebrew *canon) is "inspired by God" (Grk. *theopneustos,* probably meaning "breathed out by God") and therefore "useful for both doctrinal instruction and ethical guidance." Similarly, the divine origin of the scripture is clearly emphasized in 2 Peter 1.21.

To be sure, the human origins of the scriptures were not altogether ignored. The personalities of the prophets Jeremiah and Ezekiel vividly shine through much of the literature attributed to them, and few readers of any age would confuse the writings of one with those of the other, even though they were contemporaries and often spoke about the same topics. The same could be said for the eighth-century BCE Judahite prophets Micah and Isaiah. Considerably later, probably in the early first century BCE, the writer of 2 Maccabees provided a memorable description of the human cost of authorship (2.24–32), including "sweat and loss of sleep," and he concluded his book as follows: "If it is well told and to the point, that is what I myself desired; if it is poorly done and mediocre, that was the best I could do. For just as it is harmful to drink wine alone, or, again, to drink water alone, while wine mixed with water is sweet and delicious and enhances one's enjoyment, so also the style of the story delights the ears of those who read the work" (15.38–39). As for the New Testament, a roundabout and not altogether complimentary attestation of the scriptural status of Paul's letters may be found in 2 Peter 3.15–16. Likewise Luke's own efforts at research are recalled in his preface to his gospel (Luke 1.1–4; cf. Acts 1.1–2). Indeed, apostolic authorship, whether actual or pseudonymous, of the New Testament writings served as a major criterion for later acceptance into the canon. Nevertheless, the relationship between the divine and human "authors" of scripture has never been easily delineated.

The subordination of the human author to the divine is clearly assumed in the New Testament (Acts 4.25; 2 Pet. 1.21). Not surprisingly, later Christian theological speculation attempted to refine the nature of this subordination, and the early church fathers utilized images for the human author such as the mouth, finger, lyre, minister, or deacon of God. Rabbinic Judaism also recognized the heavenly origin of scripture, especially the *Torah. In a discussion of interpretations of the harsh denunciation of the "high-handed" sinner of Numbers 15.30–31, the Babylonian Talmud observes: "This refers to him who maintains that the Torah is not from Heaven. And even if he asserts that the whole Torah is from Heaven, excepting a particular verse, which [he maintains] was not uttered by God but by Moses himself, he is included in 'because he has despised the word of the Lord' " (b. Sanh. 99a).

Already in the first century CE, the Hellenistic Jewish philosopher *Philo of Alexandria proposed what may be termed the "mantic theory" of the inspiration of the scriptures, in which the human author becomes possessed by God and loses consciousness of self, surrendering to the divine spirit and its communicatory powers. The second-century Christian apologist Athenagoras also subscribed to such a theory, as did the Montanists, most notably Tertullian (d. ca. 225). But this was a minority position, with both Hippolytus (ca. 170–236) and Origen (ca. 185–254) denying that the biblical writers lost their free will under the force of divine pressure. In the Middle Ages emphasis was usually given only to the divine origin of the Bible, with little interest given to its human writers, although Henry of Ghent (d. 1293) did assert that the human authors were true, if secondary, authors of the books of scripture, not merely organs or channels for the divine message.

But it was not until the Renaissance and Reformation that serious speculation as to the nature of biblical inspiration took place. One of the principal theories popular then was what may be termed the dictation theory, in which God communicated to the human writer the very words of scripture, the human contribution merely being the exact and conscious reception of the divine message. Other views included those of Sixtus of Siena (1520–69) that hypothetically a book of scripture could have been composed by purely human means, with the later approval of the church attesting to its inspiration; and Jacques Bonfrère (1573–1642), who suggested that some parts of the Bible were written only under the negative assistance of the Holy Spirit, which kept the writers from error but otherwise exerted no influence on them. The christological emphasis of Martin Luther (1483–1546) should probably be mentioned at this point; he adopted what may be termed an incarnational view of biblical inspiration, with the divinity and power of God embedded in scripture in the same way as it was in Christ's body. Luther's scorn for the letter of *James, which in his opinion did not preach Christ sufficiently, is well known: he termed it a "right strawy epistle." John Calvin (1509–64) returned to an emphasis on the divine origin of scripture, but he also stressed the concept of accommodation, God adapting the divine message to human capacity through words that accommodated their limited understanding. Post-Reformation Protestant theologians, however, tended to return to the scholasticism of the Middle Ages, describing the inspiration of the Bible as "verbal" (the very words are those chosen by God) and "plenary" (every word, even every letter of scripture is inspired). This view is akin to that of contemporary Protestant fundamentalists.

As a result of the Enlightenment, theologians have focused on issues of biblical authority; for example, whether the Bible, the product of ancient cultures, has any claim on modern humanity. Supernatural revelation was often denied in whole or in part, with such views gaining further support from the rise of modern biblical criticism in the nineteenth century (see Interpretation, History of, article on Modern Biblical Criticism). To be sure, there were exceptions such as millenarians and pietists, but for most the overarching question became and still remains whether and to what degree the Bible is inspired by God, not by what manner such inspiration took place. Today all but the most extreme Jewish and Christian fundamentalists recognize the complicated and heterogeneous origins of the Bible and that it contains statements that in any other literary work would be considered erroneous. Modern biblical criticism has immeasurably enriched our understanding of biblical backgrounds, customs, and mores, but it has inevitably raised other issues. Most modern believers acknowledge that in the end the issue of biblical inspiration is ultimately a mystery—truly a matter of faith.

WILLIAM H. BARNES

Interest, Loans and. *See* Loans and Interest.

Interpretation, History of. *This entry consists of four articles that survey the history of the interpretation of the Bible:*

> Jewish Interpretation
> Early Christian Interpretation
> Christian Interpretation from the
>   Middle Ages to the Reformation
> Modern Biblical Criticism

For further treatment of the general topic, see Hermeneutics, *and for discussion of particulars, see* Anti-Semitism; Feminism and the Bible; Fundamentalism.

Jewish Interpretation

The Earliest Commentaries. Although the process of interpretation may be traced within scripture itself (in the reinterpretation of earlier laws and oracles, and in the reuse of earlier narratives), for practical purposes the earliest phase of commentary on the Hebrew Bible extended from ca. 250 BCE to ca. 500 CE. Commentary was the primary medium of Jewish religious discourse in this period, and ideas, both new and old, were presented in the form of comments on the Bible. The commentaries were of several types.

The "rewritten Bible" texts. Into this category fall works such as Jubilees (see below), the *Liber antiquitatum biblicarum,* the Genesis Apocryphon, and the biblical sections of *Josephus's *Antiquities of the Jews.* These offer an interpretative retelling of the Bible in the interpreter's own words, and they mirror the basic form of the original. The paradigm of this type of commentary is already found within scripture, notably in the books of *Chronicles, which rework the history of the books of *Samuel and *Kings. Certain sections of the *apocalyptic writings (e.g., 1 Enoch 6–11 = Gen. 6–9) should also, perhaps, be included here, as well as the Temple Scroll from *Qumran, which codifies Temple law.

The Qumran pesharim. These are in true commentary form, in that they quote the original in full and attach to it comments introduced by such formulae as "the interpretation of the matter is" (Hebr. *pēšer haddābār*). The interpretation is mantological: interpreters see in the text of scripture cryptic allusions to events in their own time, and they decode it in the way they would decode a dream. The interpretation itself is presented in oracular style.

The commentaries of Philo. The commentaries on the Pentateuch by the Alexandrian Jewish scholar *Philo (ca. 15 BCE–50 CE) are, like the pesharim, in true commentary form, and consist of biblical lemma plus comment. They are philosophical in content and attempt, by extensive use of allegory, to read middle Platonism into the Bible. Unlike the rewritten Bible texts or the pesharim, Philonic commentary is argumentative (i.e., it presents its exegetical reasoning, not just its conclusions), and it offers multiple interpretations of the same verse.

The Targums. These Bible translations (which are sometimes very paraphrastic) were used to render the Hebrew lections simultaneously into *Aramaic in the *synagogue. Like the rewritten Bible texts, they mirror the form of the original, but in terms of content they are close to the midrashim (see below), and clearly emanate from a rabbinic milieu. (*See* Translations, *article on* Targums.)

The midrashim. These works, products of the rabbinic schools of Palestine in the Tannaitic (ca. 70–200 CE) and Amoraic periods (ca. 200–500 CE), constitute by far the largest corpus of early Jewish biblical commentary. In form they are true commentaries, proceeding by way of lemma plus comment. They are intensely argumentative, at pains to make clear their exegetical reasoning, and quote divergent, and often contradictory, opinions of various scholars. They contain both ʾaggādâ (narrative/homiletic material) and hălākâ (legal material). Important texts belonging to this category are the Mekhilta of Rabbi Ishmael (on Exodus), Sifra (on Leviticus), Sifre (on Numbers and Deuteronomy), Genesis Rabba, and Pesiqta de Rab Kahana (on the readings for the festivals and special Sabbaths).

Classical Hermeneutics. Care must be taken in analyzing the hermeneutics of such a complex phenomenon as early Jewish biblical interpretation. Much of the theory, and indeed the practice, is not explicit, and this opens the door to guesswork and subjectivity. It is also important to distinguish between descriptions of the phenomenon from outside and from inside the tradition, since descriptions stemming from these two standpoints will not always coincide. In external description, one need not accept at face value any explicit hermeneutic statements the commentators happen to make, for what they say they are doing and what they actually do are not necessarily the same. In many cases it is clear, from an external standpoint, that the commentators are reading ideas into scripture: they are engaged in eisegesis rather than exegesis. The Jewish tradition of Bible interpretation oscillates between two contrary tendencies—one centrifugal, the other centripetal. In the centrifugal tendency, the tradition moves further and further from the text of scripture, and its links with scripture become increasingly tenuous. In the centripetal tendency, the centrifugal forces are checked and an attempt is made to reintegrate the tradition with scripture. The book of Jubilees is an early example of a centripetal text: it attempts to fuse with the biblical narrative extrabiblical traditions (e.g., legends about Noah) that had grown up in the preceding one hundred or more years, and so to halt the fragmentation of the tradition. In a similar manner, the rabbinic midrashim of the third century CE and later attempt to reintegrate *Mishnah with scripture (note especially Sifra). So, too, in the Middle Ages the Zohar checked the centrifugal movement of qabbalistic literature by reading qabbalistic ideas into scripture. From an external standpoint, eisegesis is a central feature of the tradition. From within the tradition, however, eisegesis is always presented as exegesis: in order to validate the tradition it is necessary to create the illusion that the tradition is already present in scripture, and has been discovered there through meditation.

A fruitful way to analyze early Jewish biblical hermeneutics is to use rabbinic midrash as a yardstick. Rabbinic midrash serves this purpose well because it is massively documented, its underlying worldview is accessible through the living tradition of the synagogue, and, of all the traditions, it is the most explicit as to its hermeneutical theory and practice.

Midrash can be seen as a game like chess, played to strict but complex rules: it has a field of play (the chessboard); aims and objectives (checkmating the king); forces to be deployed and strategies followed to achieve the aims and objectives (the chess pieces, their moves and set patterns of play).

Two axioms define the midrashic field of play. The first is that midrash is an activity performed on the Bible, which is regarded as a fixed, canonical text. For the rabbis, *prophecy has ceased and the *canon of scripture is closed. God no longer speaks directly to humankind; his will can be discovered only through the interpretation of scripture. The *scribe replaces the prophet as the central authority in Judaism. This is the simple, traditional view of the matter. In reality, however, the situation is rather more compli-

cated. To solve the problem of authority and to preempt readings of scripture with which they could not agree, the rabbis were forced to elevate their interpretations to the same status as scripture itself: their interpretations became Oral Torah, and were traced back in principle to *Moses. In effect, the scholar too was inspired, though care was taken to distinguish his inspiration from that of the prophet. (See, however, b. B. Bat. 12a: "Since the destruction of the Temple, prophecy has been taken from the prophets and given to the sages"!) Moreover, in actual fact the rabbis did not confine midrash to scripture. There is an element in midrashic practice that simply represents the standard hermeneutics of the Greco-Roman world, and parallels to it can easily be found in Alexandrian Greek scholarship. To a certain extent, the rabbis would have interpreted any text in the way they interpret scripture. In fact, in the Gemara they apply midrashic methods to the exegesis of the Mishnah.

The second axiom is that scripture is divine speech: it has its origin in the mind of God. The human element in scripture is minimal. The prophet was invaded by a divine power—the "holy spirit" or "spirit of prophecy"—that neutralized human imperfections. "Moses fulfilled the function of a scribe receiving dictation, and he wrote the whole Torah, its histories, its narratives, and its commandments, and that is why he is called a 'copyist' [Deut. 33.21]" (Maimonides, Commentary on Mishnah Sanhedrin, Ḥeleq; cf. b. B. Bat. 15a).

From this axiom a number of inferences were deemed to flow:

1. Scripture is inerrant: it can contain no errors of fact. Errors can be only apparent, not real.

2. Scripture is coherent: each part agrees with all the other parts. Scripture forms a harmonious, interlocking text. Contradictions can be only apparent, not real.

3. Scripture is unalterable. At one level, this means that it is inviolable: it forms a closed text, which should not be changed or rewritten in any way. Interpretation must be clearly distinguished from the actual text of scripture, not integrated with it. Elaborate techniques, culminating in the full-blown *Masorah of the early Middle Ages, were devised to ensure the exact transmission of the received text of the *Torah. At another level, the unalterability of scripture means that it remains eternally relevant: since it originated in the mind of God it can never become obsolescent or be superseded. The rabbis did not admit a

doctrine of abrogation. The contrast with Islam is instructive. Abrogation in Islam originally referred to the abrogation of both Judaism and Christianity by the superior revelation brought by Muhammad, the "seal" of the prophets. But it was also used by Islamic lawyers as a way of reconciling conflicts within the *Qur'ān and *hadith:* early laws are sometimes said to have been abrogated by laws promulgated later by the prophet. The rabbis could have used such a strategy to resolve the contradictions within scripture, but they never did. Perhaps they shied away from implying that God contradicted himself.

4. Scripture is "all music and no noise." Every minute detail is significant—even whether a word is spelled fully or defectively. Mountains of religious law can be deduced even from the "crowns" added to the letters as decorative embellishment. The language of scripture does not contain any redundancy. Repetitions are regularly nuanced to give a slightly different sense.

5. Scripture is polyvalent: it does not have one, fixed, original meaning but, rather, can mean many things at once. Even when two contradictory conclusions are drawn from it, both can be seen as "words of the living God." Although interpreters have great freedom before the text, they are not totally free: they cannot simply deduce what they like from scripture. There is a tendency to stress the primacy of the literal meaning: "no verse can ever lose its plain sense (pĕšaṭ)" (b. Šabb. 63a; Sanh. 34a). With few exceptions, the cantillation and vocalization of the biblical text reflect pĕšaṭ. Latent meanings must be congruent with the pĕšaṭ. The influential dictum that "Torah speaks according to human language" (b. Ber. 31b) implies that Torah communicates like ordinary speech, and should be interpreted like ordinary speech. Halaka (religious law) also exercised a restraining hand on midrash: it was forbidden to disclose aspects of Torah that did not accord with halaka. But the ultimate restraint was the power of tradition. Correct interpretation could be given only by the *rabbis—by scholars who had studied in the right schools, and who were recipients of a tradition going back through the ages to Moses himself.

The aims of the "game" of midrash can, from an internal standpoint, be defined as drawing out the meaning of scripture and applying it to the heart and life of the Jew. This involves resolving the obscurities and contradictions of scripture, displaying its coherence, and bringing it to bear on everyday life. From an external standpoint, the aims can be seen largely in terms of validating tradition from scripture, of finding ways of attaching contemporary custom and belief to the sacred text.

The moves in the "game" of midrash are in part laid down in "rulebooks." From an early date, the rabbis drew up lists of hermeneutical norms (middôt) by which the Torah is to be interpreted. Three of these lists were particularly influential—The Seven Middot of Hillel (t. Sanh. 7.11; 'Abot R. Nat. A 37; Sipra, Introduction); the Thirteen Middot of Rabbi Ishmael (Sipra, Introduction; Mek. R. Shimʿon ben Yoḥai to Exod. 21.1); and the Thirty-Two Middot of Rabbi Eliezer ben Yose ha-Gelili (Mishnat R. Eliezer I-II; Midr. ha-Gadol Gen., Introduction). The introduction to Eliezer's list categorically states that its norms are to be employed in the exegesis of aggada (i.e., nonlegal texts in the Torah). The lists of Hillel and Ishmael, by contrast, have always been regarded as applying to the exegesis of halaka (i.e., legal texts), though not exclusively. This distinction should not be pressed too far, for some of Eliezer's norms are employed in the interpretation of halaka. There is, however, a discernible reluctance to use some of the more fanciful aggadic techniques, such as gēmaṭriâ (computation of the numerical values of words or phrases) and nôṭārîqôn (treating biblical words as acronyms) in legal argument. Wherever possible the simple sense (pĕšaṭ) of a law prevailed.

The dates of these lists are very uncertain, for their attributions cannot be taken at face value. The Seven Middot of Hillel—almost certainly the earliest of the three lists—illustrates the nature of the rabbinic exegetical norms:

1. Qal wāḥōmer, inference from a less important case [qal] to a more important one [ḥōmer]: For example, if the perpetual offering, neglect of which is not punished by cutting off, overrides the *Sabbath, then the *Passover offering, neglect of which is punished by cutting off, will also override the Sabbath (b. Pes. 66a).

2. Gĕzērâ šāwâ, inference based on the presence in two different laws of a common term: For example, the expression "in its appointed time" is used in connection with both the Passover (Num. 9.2) and the perpetual offering (Num. 28.2). Since the expression "in its appointed time" used of the perpetual offering involves overriding the Sabbath, so the same term when used of Passover must equally involve overriding the Sabbath (b. Pesaḥ. 66a).

3. Binyan 'āb mikkātûb 'eḥād ûbinyan 'āb miššēnê

kĕtûbîm, construction of a category (literally, a "father") on the basis of one text, and construction of a category on the basis of two texts: For example, if a master intentionally knocks out a slave's tooth (Exod. 21.27), or blinds him in one eye (Exod. 21.26), the slave goes free in compensation. "Tooth" and "eye" are cited by scripture merely as examples. Their common features are that they are chief organs, they are visible, and loss of them would constitute a permanent defect. Therefore, if a master injures the slave in any of his principal organs, which are visible and loss of which would cause a permanent defect, the slave is entitled to go free (*Mek. R. Ishmael, Nez.* 9).

4. *Kĕlāl ûpĕrāṭ*, when a general term *(kĕlāl)* is followed by a specific term *(pĕrāṭ)*, the general includes only what is contained in the specific: For example, in Leviticus 1.2, "When any of you bring an offering of beasts to the Lord, even of the herd and of the flock. . . ," "beasts" (the *kĕlāl*) on its own could include "wild beasts," but the addition of "herd" and "flock" (the *pĕrāṭ*) limits sacrifice to domestic animals (*b. Zebaḥ.* 34a).

5. *Pĕrāṭ ûkĕlāl*, when a specific term is followed by a general term, the general adds to the specific, and everything contained in the general term is included: For example, Exodus 22.10 (Hebr. 22.9), "If a man deliver to his neighbor an ass, or an ox, or a sheep (the *pĕrāṭ*), or any beast (the *kĕlāl*) . . ." The bailee is liable for any animal falling within the general category of "beast," not just for the specific animals mentioned (*Mek. R. Ishmael, Nez.* 16).

6. *Kayôṣēʾ bô bĕmāqôm ʾaḥēr*, the same interpretation applies in another place: For example, consecration of the firstborn to God (Deut. 15.19) does not make them God's, since they already belong to him (Exod. 13.2). Rather, this act was instituted so that one can receive a reward for obeying a divine commandment. The same interpretation applies to kindling the fire on the altar (Lev. 6.5). This act cannot do anything for God, since "Lebanon would not provide fuel enough, nor are its animals enough for a burnt offering" to God (Isa. 40.16). Rather, it gives a person the opportunity to receive a reward for fulfilling a commandment (*Mek. R. Ishmael, Pisḥa* 16).

7. *Dābār hallāmēd mēʿinyānô*, the meaning of a statement may be determined from its context: For example, "You shall not steal" in Exodus 20.15 must denote a capital offense, since the two preceding offenses in the same verse (murder and adultery) are capital offenses. It denotes,

therefore, theft of persons (kidnapping). In Leviticus 19.11, however, "You shall not steal" must refer to theft of property, since the context there is concerned with property (*b. Sanh.* 86a).

As a description of the exegetical techniques employed in midrash, these lists of *middôt* have drawbacks: they are by no means exhaustive, and they do not include norms such as *heqqēš* (analogy) and *sĕmûkîm* (inference based on juxtaposition of verses). Sherira Gaon (tenth–eleventh centuries CE), in his famous *Epistle*, gives a list of exegetical norms (designated *ʿiqqārîn* rather than *middôt*), many of which are not found in any of our three lists. Even if all the norms articulated in rabbinic literature were gathered together, they would not necessarily give a total account of the methods of the *daršānîm*. The rabbinic norms are prescriptive as well as descriptive: they are as much concerned with what should happen in midrash as with what actually does happen. Some of them are largely academic, since examples in actual midrashic texts can be found only with difficulty. Modern analysis has detected exegetical processes at work in midrash that are nowhere formally acknowledged in rabbinic hermeneutical theory. The lists of norms are useful, but they should be supplemented by direct analysis of the midrashic texts themselves. Studying the rulebooks is no substitute for watching the game actually played.

Broadly speaking, rabbinic hermeneutics appear to hold good for the early nonrabbinic Bible commentaries as well. Many of the exegetical techniques of midrash certainly seem to apply. These are so numerous and so varied that it would be surprising if the methods of the nonrabbinic exegetes could not be paralleled from somewhere in rabbinic midrash. At two points, however, differences of emphasis may be detected. The polyvalent character of scripture is stressed less in the nonrabbinic texts: they tend to offer a unitary reading of scripture. Philo comes closest to the rabbinic position by giving a variety of interpretations of a single verse. Second, in some cases the nonrabbinic commentaries appear less committed than the rabbis to the principle of the unalterability of scripture. The way in which Jubilees and the Temple Scroll rewrite the Bible in classical Hebrew would probably have been frowned upon by the rabbis. This practice raises the suspicion that a new Torah, designed to supersede the old, is being promulgated. In general, however, the aim appears not to have been to supersede the canonical text, but rather to add to it. Jubilees claims to be of divine origin—a second Torah that supplements the first (Jubilees 6.2). The book known as 2 *Esdras also implies that it is a secret book of Moses, worthy of canonical status (14.5–6). These assertions differ perhaps in degree, but hardly in kind, from the rabbis' claim that their traditions are oral Torah, or from Pesher Habakkuk's and Philo's statements that their comments on scripture are inspired (1QpHab 2.8–10; Philo, *On the Cherubim* 27).

Medieval Developments. The aims and basic methods of rabbinic biblical interpretation as defined in the Talmudic period persisted in Judaism down to modern times. The continuity of the tradition is seen in Rashi (1045–1105), the most influential of all the medieval Jewish commentators. Living in a rather hostile Christian environment in northern France at the time of the First Crusade, Rashi had little incentive to innovate. Although he has his own approach that tends to stress the plain sense (*pĕšaṭ*) of scripture, and to introduce only "sober" *dĕraš*, the general intention of his work is to digest and conserve the tradition. The first really radical break with tradition comes with Baruch Spinoza (1632–1677), who, notably in his *Tractatus Theologico-Politicus*, adumbrates a critical, historical approach to the Bible.

Despite the broad continuity down to the time of Spinoza, significant developments occurred in a number of areas.

Philology. Karaism, founded at Baghdad ca. 765 by Anan ben David, who rejected rabbinic tradition and turned back afresh to scripture, stimulated an interest among Rabbanite scholars in philology. Especially in Spain, Jewish philologians, such as Jonah ibn Janāh (first half of eleventh century), began to clarify the grammar of classical Hebrew by using contemporary Arabic linguistic theory; for example, they established once and for all the triliteral nature of the Hebrew verb. The new philology was championed by the Spanish scholar Abraham ibn Ezra (1089–1164). In the Introduction to his Commentary on the Pentateuch, he outlines five ways to approach the Bible—the Geonic, the Karaite, the Christian, the midrashic, and the philological—and makes clear his preference for the philological: "The fifth way is the one upon which I will base my commentary. Before God, whom alone I fear, it is in my view the right way. I will defer to no one when it comes to interpreting the Torah, but, to my utmost ability, will seek out the grammar of every word and then do my best to explain it." However, the most influential

of the grammatical commentators was the French scholar David Kimḥi (ca. 1160–1235). His lucid grammatical analyses, much consulted by Christian scholars at the time of the Renaissance and Reformation, have sometimes a curiously modern ring; note, for example, his comments at Genesis 10.9 on the use of the word "God" to express the superlative in classical Hebrew.

Philosophy. Philosophical interpretation of scripture, which had remained largely dormant in mainstream Judaism since Philo, reemerged powerfully in the Middle Ages. Here, too, Karaism provided the initial stimulus. Through the influence of Saadiah Gaon (882–942), the great opponent of Karaism, the leading ideas of Arabic scholastic theology (Qalām) were made acceptable to rabbinic thought. Philosophical interpretation involved reading the Bible allegorically from a certain philosophical standpoint; thus, Maimonides interprets Ezekiel's vision of the chariot (Ezek. 1) as an allegorical account of his own Neoplatonic form of Aristotelianism (*Guide of the Perplexed* 3.1–7). The preexisting philosophical system, whatever it was, functioned as a hermeneutic key to unlock scripture.

Mysticism. The rise of the mystical system of qabbalistic literature also powerfully affected biblical interpretation. The Zohar, the most influential mystical commentary, was compiled by Moses de Leon in Spain at the end of the thirteenth century. In formal terms, mystical commentary is similar to philosophical commentary: a preexistent system of ideas is used as a hermeneutic key to determine the sense of scripture, and elements of that system (e.g., the qabbalistic doctrine of the *Sefirot:* see Zohar 2. 42b–43a) are read into scripture using allegorical methods.

Hermeneutic theory in the Middle Ages was much concerned with identifying the various types of approach to scripture. The most famous classification, known by the mnemonic "PaRDeS," probably goes back to Moses de Leon: *Pĕšaṭ* = literal interpretation; *Remez* = allegorical interpretation; *Dĕraš* = homiletic interpretation; *Sôd* = mystical interpretation. The Spanish scholar Bahya ben Asher (late thirteenth century) produced a slightly different fourfold classification: literal interpretation (*pĕšaṭ*); homiletic (*midrāš*); rational, i.e., philosophical (*sekel*); and mystical (called "the way of the Lord" = Qabbalah).

In general, the various approaches to scripture were seen not as exclusive or contradictory but as complementary; the polyvalency of scripture continued to be stressed. There was a tendency, however, to rank them in hierarchical order, depending on the interpreter's standpoint. Even Maimonides, who cautioned against trying to separate the "kernel" from the "husk" in scripture (*Commentary on Mishnah Sanhedrin, Ḥeleq*), acknowledged that there was an "apparent" and a "latent" sense in scripture (*Guide of the Perplexed,* Introduction). The Zohar (3.152a) uses the analogy of the human body to illustrate the relationship between the various levels of meaning in scripture. Foolish people look only at the tales of the Torah which are its outer garments; those who are wiser look at the commandments, which are the body of the Torah (cf. the description of the commandments as *gûfê tôrâ* [literally,"bodies of the Torah"] in *m. Ḥag.* 1.8). But the true sages look only at the inner mystical sense of the Torah, the soul of the Torah. And lest it should be supposed that the meaning of divine speech could ever be exhausted, the Zohar concludes: "and in the world to come they [the mystics] are destined to look at the soul of the soul of the Torah."   PHILIP S. ALEXANDER

Early Christian Interpretation

The Bible of the earliest Christians was identical with the Hebrew scriptures of the Jewish communities. When Jesus and the writers of the apostolic period speak of "scripture(s)," they mean the *canon of Torah, Prophets, and Writings that Jews regarded as divinely inspired, that is, written under the immediate dictate or influence of God. *Inspiration was also claimed for the Greek translation of the "Seventy" (*Septuagint [LXX]), which was endorsed by Alexandrian Jewish authorities. In Christian eyes, the legend of the Septuagint's miraculous origin, first told in the Letter of Aristeas (late second century BCE), then elaborated by *Philo, and further embellished by Christian authors such as Justin Martyr, Irenaeus of Lyons, Tertullian, and Augustine, even rendered the Septuagint superior to the Hebrew original.

Jewish interpretation of the Hellenistic and Roman periods took three forms. Midrashic exegesis as practiced by the rabbis searched the holy text for clues to authoritative rules for living (*hălākâ*) or to a broadly edifying meaning in the present (*'aggādâ*), guided by tradition. The hermeneutical center was *Torah, the Law of God. Second, Jewish scholars in the Greek-speaking diaspora, exemplified by Philo, tried to harmonize the texts with the truths of Platonic or *Stoic natural philosophy and ethics. Finally, the *Es-

sene sectarians at *Qumran, relying on the authority of their "Teacher of Righteousness," read the biblical texts as divine oracles predicting their own end-time existence in the post-Maccabean period; here, the hermeneutical center was moving away from Torah to the prophetic literature. (*See also article on* Jewish Interpretation *above.*)

Traces of all three forms can be found in the earliest Christian literature. The *synoptic Gospels portray *Jesus as a rabbinical teacher who routinely answered questions about the *Law (Mark 10.1–12, 17–31; 12.13–34; Luke 12.13–15; etc.). *Paul used both halakhic and aggadic modes in interpreting biblical texts (e.g., Rom. 10.6–8; 2 Cor. 13.1; Gal. 3.15–18), even the seven rules attributed to Rabbi Hillel (Rom. 4.1–12; 5.15–17; 13.8–10; etc.). The letter to the *Hebrews, in its vision of the Temple cult as a shadow of the heavenly reality, seems to fuse the eschatology of an earlier generation with a Platonic worldview akin to Philo (cf. Heb. 8.5; 9.23–28). Most important, the central Christian affirmation of Jesus of Nazareth as being the promised *Messiah and the hermeneutics of promise and fulfillment share the tendency to shift the hermeneutical center from the Law to the Prophets. The *prophets, including *Moses, *David, and other prophetic voices in the scriptures, predicted what was to happen "in these last days" (Heb. 1.2) and thus opened up the *apocalyptic meaning of the present in the context of the overarching plan of God, for example, "Today this scripture has been fulfilled in your hearing" (Luke 4.21; cf. Isa. 61.1). The proof from prophecy very quickly became a major tool of Christian missionaries. It appealed to Jewish hearers loyal to their divine scriptures as well as to non-Jews impressed by the antiquity of such writings. Although Christians might have discarded the Jewish scriptures and started with the experience of new revelation in the person of Jesus, they retained them as a valuable tool for Christian apologetics, which, understood as divine oracles, not only appealed to potential converts but also gave Christians themselves the interpretive categories for understanding the life, death, and resurrection of Jesus the Christ (1 Cor. 15.1–3; Luke 24.25–27; Acts 2.22–36); *see* Quotations of the Old Testament in the New Testament.

It was Paul who spelled out most powerfully the theological basis of this unified vision of God's purpose in history and the meaning of Christian practices such as *baptism and the common *meal. The old *covenant of the Law had been crowned by the revelation of the new covenant predicted by the prophets (Rom. 10.4; 1 Cor. 11.25; 2 Cor. 3.6; cf. Jer. 31.1). But this fulfillment for Paul was not only linked to the story of Jesus and the Christian present; it also included the *second coming (1 Thess. 4–5). Beyond a limited store of messianic passages that had governed the formation of the earliest Christian traditions about Jesus, Paul identified further predictions and anticipations of the new era in the scriptures. He also suggested the procedures for their apocalyptic interpretation through which later generations would continue to understand biblical passages as applicable to their own situation.

Explaining the experience of Israel as a warning to Christians of his own generation, Paul used the language of "type" or "typical" (1 Cor. 10.6, 11 [NRSV: "example"]), equating it with the "spiritual" understanding of those who have the Holy Spirit (Rom. 8.9, 23; 1 Cor. 2.13–15; 7.40). This kind of *typology, which was not without Jewish antecedents, gained an immense popularity in second-century Christian interpretation. The Greek term "antitype" for Christian baptism as the counterpart of *Noah's rescue already appears in 1 Peter 3.21 (NRSV: "prefigured"). The apostolic fathers, especially the letter of Barnabas (6.11; 7.3, 7, 10, 11; etc.), show the rapid development of the concept. 1 Clement 25 even calls on an image of classical mythology, the phoenix, as a type of Christ's *resurrection. In the middle of the second century CE, the writings of Justin Martyr reveal the wide scope of possible types: Justin not only defended the traditional Christian use of messianic passages such as Genesis 49.10–12; Isaiah 7.14; 9.6; 11.1–3; 53; Psalms 2.7; 110.4 (*Apology* 32–38); he also found "types," for example, of the cross, in almost every piece of wood mentioned in the Jewish scriptures (*Dialogue with Trypho the Jew* 86). The Easter Homily by Melito of Sardis (late second century CE) demonstrates the same wealth of imagination when the author reads the *Exodus traditions as types of Christ's death and resurrection. It is likely that second-century Christians had *testimonia*, collections that grouped together for convenience messianic predictions or other texts yielding "types." Cyprian's treatise *Ad Quirinum* provides an example; its second part contains a list of "stone" testimonies from the Jewish scriptures that are interpreted as types of Christ (cf. 1 Cor. 10.4), as well as a collection of passages that mention mountain, *lamb, or bridegroom. Typological traditions also inform the earliest representations of Christian *art, especially the funerary paintings and monuments of the catacombs. The pictures frequently can be interpreted as types of salvation using biblical figures such as Noah in the ark, *Daniel between the lions, *Susanna rescued from the elders, *Jonah saved from the fish, or New Testament stories such as the raising of Lazarus and healing *miracles as pointers to the Christian hope beyond the grave.

Paul also introduced the term "allegory" into the vocabulary of Christian exegesis. Galatians 4.21–26 refers to the story of *Sarah and *Hagar (Gen. 16) with the claim that it has to be understood "allegorically" as speaking of two covenants. The interpretation of an authoritative text as having a deeper meaning (*hyponoia*) than what its words seem to suggest was an old practice among Greeks in the appropriation of Homer and the early poets. The *Homeric Allegories* of Pseudo-Heraclitus were probably written by a contemporary of Paul. Allegory as a writer's device, an "extended metaphor" in Quintilian's definition (*Instit. Rhetor.* 9.2.46), appeared with such stories as "Heracles at the crossroads" by Prodikos the Sophist (fourth century BCE). The allegorical interpretation of Homer was the hallmark of Stoic scholarship and later dominated Jewish and Christian interpretation at Alexandria. Philo's main interpretation of the Torah was entitled "Allegories of the Law"; like other allegorizers, Philo found the key to deeper meanings in etymological phenomena, numbers, and unusual terms.

Paul's use of the technical term *allēgoroumena* in Galatians 4.24 does not clearly distinguish allegory from typology. Sarah and Hagar function here as types the same way as the *wilderness generation in 1 Corinthians 10. Hellenistic allegorization, however, was deliberately employed by other Christian writers. The author of *Hebrews interprets the key texts about the role of the high priest as speaking of Jesus Christ (Heb. 5–7). The letter of Barnabas declares the entire cultic law of Judaism superseded and moralizes all its precepts. It seems that *gnostic teachers developed the apologetic potential of allegory to the fullest extent. Christian gnosis such as that represented by Clement of Alexandria in the early third century freely used the term *allēgoria* for exegetical endeavors that included extensive reinterpretation of biblical texts as teaching general and timeless truths.

Origen of Alexandria (ca. 185–254), the most prolific exegete of the early church, gave Christian allegory its theoretical foundation. In Book 4 of his treatise *On First Principles*, he claimed total inspiration by divine providence not only for the canonical scriptures themselves but even for their textual transmission with all its variants and scribal errors. Passages that present "stumbling blocks" in content and wording alert the reader that a spiritual, not a literal meaning must be sought in the holy texts. An "inspired" text requires "spiritual" interpretation that leads the soul upward (Grk. *anagōgē*) from the realm of the flesh to that of the Spirit. Origen assumed that much of the biblical revelation concerned the fate of souls, their fallen condition, and their redemption. Thus, in his commentaries on the Jewish scriptures, he allegorized the story of Israel as speaking of the journey of the soul, which, leaving the sensual world of "Egypt," seeks the *Promised Land of blessedness. The teachings of Jesus and the apostles had the same goal: they pointed, directly or allegorically, to the *hope by which Christians live.

The wide use of allegory among gnostics, however, raised early doubts about the procedure. Marcion of Pontus, who founded a successful counterchurch in the middle of the second century CE, rejected the Jewish scriptures as the revelation of an "alien" God and based his thought on a revised Paul and a purged gospel of *Luke. Such interpretation by textual revision was not uncommon; Tatian the Syrian applied it in his *Diatessaron*, an attempt to merge the four separate gospel accounts into one. To curb gnostic "misuses" of the Bible, church writers appealed to three authorities for its proper understanding: an approved canon of the "Old" Testament together with a "New" that assembled writings believed to be of apostolic origin; the "Rule of Faith," a creedal summary of accepted teachings; and the episcopal office, which was expected to decide among competing claims to authoritative exegesis. "Apostolicity" was invoked by Irenaeus and Tertullian as a central criterion against Marcion's reduced canon, a docetic Christology, or gnostic cosmological speculations. Both accused their opponents of arbitrary interpretation and displayed their strong disapproval of unchecked gnostic allegory.

They also shared a concern to apply the apostolic norm to the expansion of the Christian canon through apocrypha. Such writings were not only part of the growing gnostic literature but were also produced and read by catholic Christians. Apocryphal gospels filled in the blanks about Jesus' family and childhood, the forty days

after his resurrection, and his journey into hell and heaven (*see* Descent into Hell). Apocryphal acts interpreted the witness of the apostles as supporting ascetic ideals, especially virginity; in this way they perpetuated the strong accent on moral exhortation that was at the heart of the biblical interpretation of the apostolic fathers (1 and 2 Clement; Didache; Ignatius; Barnabas; Shepherd of Hermas). The earliest canon list of New Testament books, the Canon Muratori (ca. 200 CE), already rejects a large number of apocrypha, but despite constant attempts at curbing the genre, apocryphal books such as the Protevangelium of James, the Acts of Pilate, the Gospel of Bartholomew, and the Apocalypses of Peter and Paul influenced biblical interpretation for centuries to come. (*See also* Apocrypha, *article on* Christian Apocrypha.)

During the first two centuries, Christian biblical interpretation was guided by practical concerns: the needs of missionary preaching, the instruction of new converts, apologetics directed at non-Christians, and polemics against "heretical" teachings. In the third and fourth centuries it came to be dominated by a conflict of "schools" analogous to the rivalry of philosophical schools in the Hellenistic world. The conflict clarified some basic options in expounding canonical scriptures in a Christian framework. An ancient but unreliable tradition claimed that Alexandria had a Christian catechetical school with a succession of famous teachers, beginning with Pantaenus in the late second century, Clement of Alexandria, and Origen. Reports by Gregory the Wonderworker, Pamphilus of Caesarea, and Eusebius suggest that Origen taught a curriculum of higher Christian studies that included classical disciplines such as grammar, Greek literature, and philosophy as a basis and the study of biblical texts as the crown. *Textual criticism was as much part of this endeavor as literary analysis and spiritual interpretation. Through Jewish converts, Origen was also aware of the exegetical traditions of rabbinic Judaism and was able to draw on them.

The Alexandrian school of the fourth century carried on the interpretive methods of Origen, including the use of allegory. Major theologians, such as Athanasius, Eusebius, Apollinaris, the Cappadocian fathers, and Cyril of Alexandria, wrote interpretations of biblical books for a broad educated public in the spirit of Origen's anagogical dynamics: scripture instructs the spiritual quest of the soul for an ascent to God who, through Christ the eternal *Logos, has revealed this "way" in the holy writings. Gregory of Nyssa's *Life of Moses* presents a reading of the Exodus story in two parts, first recounting the details in their historical sequence and then opening up their spiritual meaning as a description of the soul's journey to God in its various stages. Didymus the Blind (d. 398 CE) expounded numerous books of the Bible in a similar way. Alexandrian hermeneutics shows a keen interest in philological detail. The precise wording of a biblical passage as well as its stylistic peculiarities was of utmost importance because the inspired words themselves contained the key to their divinely intended meaning. For these scholars, allegorization was a science, not an arbitrary flight of fancy.

This understanding of Christian allegory became the polemical target of Alexandria's rival, the school of Antioch, in the fourth century. *Antioch, important for earliest Christian history (Acts 11.26), could boast of a long tradition of Hellenistic scholarship. The emphasis seems to have been on the rhetorical arts; Aristotelian and Jewish influences were important. We hear of Christian teachers in Antioch from the late third century onward: Malchion; Lucian, whose recension of the Greek Bible acquired something of a normative status; Dorotheus; Eustathius, and especially Diodore of Tarsus (d. ca. 390 CE), whose ascetic community became the seedbed of the distinctive Antiochian tradition of biblical exegesis. Diodore taught a generation of great scholars, among them Theodore of Mopsuestia, John Chrysostom, and Theodoret of Cyrrhus.

Through the association of Antiochian teachers with the names of heretics such as Arius and Nestorius, many of the works of the school have perished. From the remnants we can infer a sober appreciation of the Bible as a valuable historical document in addition to its spiritual meaning. The Antiochian exegetes took note of the times and circumstances of a particular biblical book. Diodore, for example, tried to rearrange the biblical *Psalms according to their true historical sequence, which he gleaned from internal and external clues, especially the titles. Theodore considered only four Psalms as messianic (Pss. 2; 8; 45; 110) and understood the *Song of Solomon as a love poem composed by *Solomon for the Queen of *Sheba. This did not exclude a divinely intended accommodation of the texts to later times or the need to search for a spiritual sense, which the Antiochians called *theōria*. But their respect for the historical setting nourished a deep-seated distrust of Alexandrian

allegorism. Diodore wrote a (lost) treatise "On the Difference Between Theōria and Allēgoria," and Theodore deplored the dissolution of historical reality at the hand of Alexandrian exegetes, especially in the Genesis account of *creation and *fall, on which he thought the entire Christian message of sin, salvation, and human responsibility depended.

While suspicion of Antiochian theologians remained high during the christological struggles of the fifth and sixth centuries, their moral and ascetic fervor continued to be influential, thanks to the universal reception of the work of John Chrysostom. Chrysostom's sermons on biblical books were avidly copied and were known in the West through Latin translations, the earliest of which probably go back to his lifetime. The school itself found refuge first at Ephraem's school in Edessa, where it was represented by Syrian teachers such as Ibas and Narsai the Great, and later even farther East at Nisibis between the Euphrates and Tigris, where eminent scholars such as Babi the Great and Ishoʿdad of Merv upheld the great tradition through the end of the patristic period.

The Western church did not participate directly in the war of the schools. Some of its great theologians, such as Ambrose of Milan, Hilary of Poitiers, and Jerome, studied under, or drew on, scholars of both traditions for their moral and spiritual interpretations but did not take sides: Greek learning in any form was still greatly admired. Cassiodorus's list of hermeneutical textbooks for the use of students in the early sixth century includes "Alexandrian" works such as Hilary's *Treatise of Mysteries* and Eucherius of Lyon's *Varieties of Spiritual Understanding*, as well as "Antiochian" handbooks such as those of Hadrian and Junilius Africanus. There can be no question, however, that the influence of Origen and his program of spiritual exegesis was central in giving direction to Western biblical interpretation. Translations by Jerome's erstwhile friend Rufinus toned down offensive features of Origen's *On First Principles* and several of his commentaries, and the contacts with Alexandrian exegetes were never interrupted.

The indigenous Latin tradition, especially in North Africa, reflected an emphasis on catechetical instruction and apologetics, as the writings of Tertullian demonstrate. A rich store of typological exegesis, inherited from the church of the second century, seems to have served these interests; Cyprian's biblicism drew its substance from it. Western exegesis also remained more traditional in its apocalyptic tendencies. While the expectation of an imminent end met with heavy criticism in the East after the Montanist crisis of the late second century, and the book of *Revelation was still of doubtful canonicity to Eusebius at the beginning of the fourth century because of its chiliasm, apocalyptic expectations and millennial themes remained popular in the West. At the time when Greek was still the language of the Christian community in Rome, Hippolytus (early third century) wrote on the prophet Daniel and on the *Antichrist against an upsurge of apocalyptic fervor in response to the persecutions. The first Latin exegesis of the book of Revelation was written in the early fourth century by Victorinus of Pettau in Dalmatia; it is known to us through Jerome's revision, stripped of its pronounced chiliasm.

The late fourth century saw the emergence of an independent mind among Latin exegetes in Tyconius the Donatist. His *Book of Rules* did not follow Origen's allegorical principles but gathered clues from a rational analysis of biblical language to separate fulfilled messianic prophecies from the divinely intended message of the texts for the church of his day. Tyconius was guided by a vision of history that included the beginnings, the story of Israel, Christ, and the church in one great redemptive movement, understood in terms of the final victory of good over evil. The fragments of his commentary on the book of Revelation show that, while he interpreted its apocalyptic prophecy as applicable to any age, he retained a sophisticated imminent expectation of the eschatological exodus of the true church (the Donatist) from the false.

Another feature of the Western development was a rise of interest in the Pauline letters at a time when such interest was relatively low in the East. We know of five major efforts between 365 and 410 in the West at interpreting the letter to the *Romans: those of Marius Victorinus, the so-called Ambrosiaster, the Budapest Anonymous, Pelagius, and Augustine, who wrote only two fragments on Romans, but the importance of Paul for the formation of his mature theology is amply documented. By his own admission, Augustine was indebted to Tyconius in formulating his exegetical principles. He also shared the Alexandrian emphasis on the spiritual sense, even though he tended to replace the terminology of allegorization with that of "figuration." According to Augustine, scripture speaks not only of promise and fulfillment in the person of Jesus but contains literally or figuratively the answer to all basic questions of humanity. In God's providence, it is given as a means to incite believers to the double love of God and neighbor, which is the goal of the soul's journey. Its human language with all its ambiguities requires careful work by the interpreter. Augustine's plea for competence in biblical languages and the liberal arts, especially rhetoric and logic, became the charter of early medieval monastic education in the West. His exegetical writings, circulating in numerous manuscripts, constituted one of the main patristic authorities for exegetes down to the Reformation. They stressed the priority of the spiritual goal of reading scripture without discouraging the investigation of the plain sense of its words. The medieval theory of a fourfold sense—literal, allegorical, tropological (moral), and anagogical—did not originate with Augustine, however. The first writer to mention it was John Cassian in the fifth century (*Conferences* 14.8), who used the four biblical meanings of *Jerusalem as an illustration: the actual city, the church, the human soul, and the heavenly city, our final home.

The literary forms of biblical interpretation during the early centuries show a bewildering variety. At first, biblical interpretation was a function of the missionary proclamation by *apostles and *evangelists, the instruction of converts by teachers and *elders, and the itinerant ministry of *prophets. The expansion of Christianity beyond its original Jewish context brought with it the need for apologetics and polemics and moved scriptural interpretation quite naturally into the writing of the more literate members of the church, who could serve as advocates and apologists for the movement. The basic task of interpreting scripture within the Christian congregations, however, was not so much a matter of a developing Christian literature but of the living voice of *bishop, elder, and teacher. The exegetical writings of Hippolytus consist of homiletical reflections on biblical texts, often fragmentary and incomplete, as they would relate to the life of his church members. They were not biblical commentaries. On the contrary, the bishop denounced the genre of "commentary" as an invention of the pagan schools and a heretical practice.

Literary attempts at a coherent interpretation of entire canonical books in a Christian vein were first made by Christian gnostics who took the case for their esoteric theological systems to a literate non-Christian audience through detailed analysis of authoritative texts, among which the

Bible held a special place. Even the gnostic interpretation of the Fourth Gospel by the Valentinian Heracleon (end of second century), the first such piece of which we have textual evidence, was, however, far more an apologetic treatise than an exegetical commentary. Commentaries in the strict sense were the product of the Hellenistic school tradition, as Hippolytus suggested. Christian biblical commentaries were the fruit of such traditions on Christian soil, as in Alexandria and Antioch. It seems that Origen created the genre, following classical precedent and employing the three standard forms of scholia, homilies, and *tomoi,* that is, philological explanations of an entire biblical book at a time. Wherever some form of Christian education took shape in Christian "schools," monastic communities, at the residence of bishops, or in learned circles of ascetic women, biblical interpretation as a scholarly enterprise was a highly valued activity.

The fourth and fifth centuries became the golden age of commentary writing. Jerome deliberately conveyed the impression that even earlier Christians had already produced a respectable body of "commentaries" on the scriptures. Ostensibly building on this treasure, but especially on Origen and the admired exegetes of the Eastern schools, he nourished the dream of creating a Latin Christian literature equal to that of the Romans, based on the Bible and its eternal truths but matching Virgil, Cicero, and Horace in style and form. He gave this endeavor a solid foundation by providing a new Latin translation of major parts of the Bible in his *Vulgate and adapted the forms of classical textual scholarship in his own exegetical work, drawing up tools for the study of biblical chronology, prosopography, geography, and languages, as well as commentaries, in which he made use of his vast learning.

As Jerome himself had feared, his ambitious project fell victim to the new pluralism of a barbarian age that superseded the cultural unity of the crumbling Empire. In Christianity, the syntheses of the following centuries tended to look to the past for their canons of biblical exegesis before they encouraged new attempts at taking up the task. In the East, compilations of the exegetical heritage began to appear in the sixth century with Procopius of Gaza. To this literature of "chains" *(catenae),* the gathering of patristic interpretations by biblical book and chapter, we owe the preservation of precious fragments of lost commentaries. Even the outstanding theological writers of the Byzantine age

rarely wrote fresh commentaries themselves. Similarly, the West experienced a decline in commentary writing after Jerome. The shining exceptions were Cassiodorus and Pope Gregory I in the sixth century. It was the educational zeal of the great monasteries in the British Isles and of the Carolingian rulers on the Continent in the eighth and ninth centuries that created the conditions for a new flowering of serious exegetical work.   Karlfried Froehlich

Christian Interpretation from the Middle Ages to the Reformation

During the period from 600 to 1600 CE, the interpretation of the Bible reflected the broader institutional developments and intellectual concerns of western Christianity. During the earliest part of that period, students of the scriptures relied almost exclusively on the guidance of patristic authority. As a distinctive medieval civilization developed, commentators found positions in schools and universities, where they geared their work to the educational and theological needs of their world. Toward the end of the period, biblical interpretation reflected the fresh influences of critical reason and the spiritual demands that emerged during the epoch of the Protestant and Catholic Reformations. Throughout the whole period, the scriptures helped to shape western culture in all its dimensions. Little wonder, then, that commentators continuously sought to adjust their understanding of the Bible and to expound it in the light of the most advanced information available to them.

The most advanced information available during the early Middle Ages came from the church fathers. Only rarely did Christian commentators of the late first millennium BCE understand more than a smattering of Greek or Hebrew, and even less frequently did they possess the intellectual self-confidence to develop fresh interpretations. The Venerable Bede (672–735) knew some Greek, which he employed in his exposition of Acts, and Remigius of Auxerre (d. 908) seems to have compared the Latin Psalter with the Hebrew text. John Scotus Erigena (d. 877) stood alone, however, as a commentator possessing both language skills and a powerful critical faculty. He consulted the writings of the Greek fathers and based his own commentary on John's gospel on the Greek text, and furthermore he displayed a willingness to correct Latin exegesis on the basis of Greek sources. Most other early medieval commentators, however, worked in an extremely conservative vein. Even the best known of them—Alcuin (d. 804), Claude of Turin (d. 827), and Rabanus Maurus (d. 856)—did little more than reproduce the views of the Latin fathers, particularly those of Jerome and Augustine. Most commentators of the period recognized the literal sense as the foundation of scriptural exegesis, but all of them considered a literal exposition fully compatible with one or more modes of moral, allegorical, or mystical interpretation. Indeed, given the general absence of linguistic skills and philological concern, expositors had little alternative but to develop the various spiritual senses of scripture, which they did with considerable zeal.

The establishment of monastic and cathedral schools encouraged several new developments in biblical interpretation. In the first place, they created a demand for textbooks. Masters in the schools recognized the need for standardized interpretations that could serve as a common foundation for all students. The result was the compilation of the *Glossa ordinaria*, which presented a brief exposition of the entire Bible. The chief figure in the preparation of this work was Anselm of Laon (d. 1117), master in the cathedral school at Laon, though several other twelfth-century theologians and commentators also contributed to the effort. The *Glossa* drew extracts from patristic and early medieval expositions, so that it possessed no claim to originality. It exercised an enormous influence, however, since it served for half a millennium as the basic text for students embarked on their introduction to the Bible.

More important, the medieval schools fostered an intellectual and theological creativity that deeply influenced biblical interpretation. Expertise in grammar, logic, and dialectic imparted to the masters a new self-confidence in their intellectual abilities, and equipped them with the tools to fashion a new kind of exegesis. Twelfth-century commentators progressively abandoned the patristic style of running exposition in favor of explanations that concentrated on well-defined theological issues. Exegetes such as Gilbert de la Porrée (d. 1154) and Robert of Melun (d. 1167) organized their commentaries around *quaestiones*—doctrinal issues requiring explanation on the basis of reason and grounded in some source of authority—so that exposition served the interests of theological accuracy. The culmination of this practice came in the *Sentences* of Peter Lombard (d. 1160), who organized biblical and patristic doctrine into a veritable compendium of Christian theology.

The most impressive school of interpreters of this sort was that centered in the Abbey of St. Victor in Paris. Hugh of St. Victor (d. 1141), founder of the school, called for systematic, scholarly study of the scriptures. He placed equal weight on literal and spiritual exposition: the exegete must carefully employ all the relevant arts and sciences in establishing the literal sense of the text; whenever appropriate, however, its moral or theological significance should also be developed. Hugh's successors did not take so balanced an approach as their master: Richard of St. Victor (d. 1173) devoted himself to allegorical and mystical exegesis, while Andrew of St. Victor (d. 1175) insisted on a scientifically accurate exposition of the literal and historical sense of the scriptures. In preparing himself for his work, Andrew consulted Jewish scholars and steeped himself in Hebrew, thus setting an example followed by numerous Christian exegetes through the following two centuries.

Whatever their attitude toward spiritual exegesis, expositors in the schools generally geared their work toward theological and doctrinal issues. As a result, biblical interpretation became an increasingly specialized activity. Expositors developed impressive skills in language and reasoning, which they then applied in scriptural analysis. In doing so, they emphasized the significance of the scriptures for the correct understanding of Christian doctrine—rather than seeking, for example, to develop materials for homiletic or teaching purposes—so that exegesis increasingly assumed the status of a subdiscipline of theology.

The establishment of universities in the thirteenth century strongly encouraged the further development of a professional, scientific variety of biblical interpretation. Some commentators, such as Stephen Langton (1155–1228) and Hugh of St. Cher (1200–1263), continued to expound allegorical and spiritual senses of scripture. Generally speaking, however, the universities' heavy emphasis on theology encouraged interpreters to concentrate on the literal sense and to focus their commentaries on important doctrinal issues. The introduction of Aristotelian thought and subsequent development of scholastic theology worked toward the same end. Thus, Albertus Magnus (1193–1280) and Thomas Aquinas (1225–1274) brought Aristotelian science and analysis to bear on the scriptures; both produced literal expositions that plumbed the scriptures in search of support for scholastic explanations of Christian doctrine and mysteries.

The culmination of this variety of exegesis came in the work of Nicholas of Lyra (1270–1349), best known for his monumental *Postilla litteralis*, which provided an exhaustive literal exposition of the entire Bible. Lyra by no means abandoned spiritual exposition: he set great store by accurate exegesis of the spiritual senses of scripture, and as a supplement to his *Postilla litteralis* he even prepared a work that briefly outlined the moral and allegorical significance of the entire Bible. Like Albertus and Aquinas, however, Lyra concentrated on literal exposition, and he took pains whenever possible to show that the scriptures supported the scholastic understanding of theology. Yet Lyra also considerably advanced comprehension of the Hebrew Bible in particular because of his solid command of Hebrew. Lyra also closely studied rabbinic commentaries, particularly those of Rashi (1030–1105), one of the greatest of the medieval Jewish exegetes (*see article on* Jewish Interpretation, *above*). His language skills enabled him to provide both proper translations and accurate explanations of numerous biblical passages. Similar clarification of the New Testament did not become available until the fifteenth and sixteenth centuries, when Renaissance humanists brought their newly acquired knowledge of Greek to bear on the Christian scriptures.

During the later Middle Ages, theologians such as Roger Bacon (1220–1292) and Pierre d'Ailly (1350–1421) called for increased emphasis on Hebrew and Greek as a propaedeutic for biblical interpretation. Regular instruction in biblical languages did not, however, become widely available until the sixteenth century, and by then new cultural forces ensured that scholastic theology would no longer dominate exegesis. Pico della Mirandola (1463–1494) and Johann Reuchlin (1455–1522) became enchanted not only with Hebrew, but also with qabbalistic ideas, which they sought to introduce into Christian exegesis. Meanwhile, expertise in Greek enabled the Renaissance humanists to make important contributions to the understanding of the New Testament. Lorenzo Valla (1407–1457) and especially Erasmus of Rotterdam (1466–1536) inaugurated the modern tradition of New Testament interpretation: they rejected the guidance of scholastic theology, studied the Greek text of the New Testament, and offered expositions that depended on a combination of linguistic, philological, and historical considerations. Both placed high value on the derivation of moral and theological doctrine from the scriptures. Like most

of their humanist colleagues, though, they also denied the usefulness of elaborate allegorical or spiritual exegesis, insisting instead on the primacy of literal and historical expositions. Their work made possible a vastly improved understanding of the New Testament. On the basis of their knowledge of Greek and their well-developed critical faculties, they corrected the texts of the Greek and Latin New Testament, offered new Latin translations superior to those of the *Vulgate, and clarified numerous points of history and doctrine in their exegesis of the New Testament.

The Reformation movements of the sixteenth century had deep implications for biblical interpretation, as theologians of all persuasions sought scriptural support for their religious views. To some extent, both Protestant and Catholic reformers continued to work in the tradition of Erasmus and other Renaissance scholars who had brought linguistic skills and philological analysis to bear on the scriptures. Both John Calvin (1509–1564) and Cardinal Cajetan (1468–1534), for example, produced extensive commentaries based on the study of scriptural texts in their original languages and informed by all the advances the humanists had registered in the explanation of the Bible.

Inevitably, however, sixteenth-century commentaries generally betrayed the theological, controversial, or confessional intentions of their authors. Rebels against the authority of the Roman Catholic church, including John Wycliffe (1330–1384) and John Hus (1370–1415) among many others, had traditionally appealed to scripture in justifying their defiance of the pope and the institutional church. Martin Luther (1483–1546) recognized the Bible as the ultimate authority in matters of Christian doctrine, and his expositions—especially of the *Psalms and Pauline letters—helped him to develop his understanding of *faith and *grace. All the major Protestant theologians—Ulrich Zwingli (1484–1531), Martin Bucer (1491–1551), Philip Melanchthon (1497–1560), Heinrich Bullinger (1503–1575), and especially John Calvin—followed Luther's example. Protestants generally rejected the practice of developing elaborate allegorical explanations of the scriptures, but they eagerly scrutinized both the Hebrew Bible and the New Testament in search of authoritative support for Protestant doctrine. Their lectures, sermons, and commentaries on the Bible helped all the founders of Protestant Christianity to develop and solidify their theological views.

Roman Catholic theologians, of course, did not view scriptural authority as a substitute for papal primacy, but during the sixteenth century they too turned their attention to the Bible with special urgency. Jacques Lefèvre d'Étaples (1455–1536), Gasparo Contarini (1483–1542) and Juan de Valdés (1500–1541) all produced commentaries or exegetical works of a highly spiritual character. All three responded especially warmly to the Pauline letters and sought to encourage spiritual reform within the Roman church, while incidentally rendering the scriptures an instrument of Catholic as well as Protestant controversial literature. Cardinals Reginald Pole (1500–1558) and Girolamo Seripando (1492–1563) strongly encouraged delegates at the Council of Trent (1545–1564) to reform the education of clergy: a curriculum based on humanist study of the Bible rather than scholastic theology, they argued, would lead to general reform and eventually to the religious reunion of Christianity. Meanwhile, Cardinal Cajetan (1468–1534) undertook a more direct challenge to Protestant Christianity. In long commentaries on the Gospels and Pauline letters, Cajetan depended upon the methods of humanist scholarship to argue that the New Testament proved the truth of Roman Catholic doctrine and confuted the Protestant alternative.

By the late sixteenth century, then, biblical exegesis clearly reflected the theological division of western Christianity. Although it certainly became the focal point of unpleasant disputes, the Bible also retained its status as the prime source of Christian doctrine and moral teaching. Indeed, the disputes themselves testify to the point that, just as throughout the previous thousand years, the Bible still stood at the center of Christian culture.   JERRY H. BENTLEY

Modern Biblical Criticism

Biblical criticism is a very general term, and not easy to define; it covers a wide range of scholarly activities. Its ultimate basis lies in the linguistic and literary character of the Bible. Scripture, though understood to be the word of God, is in human language (*Hebrew, *Aramaic, and *Greek) and in the literary, rhetorical, and poetic patterns of human expression, which can and must be interpreted by human understanding. God speaks through scripture, but its meanings function within the structures of ordinary human language. Criticism depends on a grasp of style, of the relation of part to whole, of expression to genre; it takes the biblical diction

very seriously and moves from the detail of language to the larger overarching themes. Approached in this way, the Bible is sometimes found to have meanings other than those that traditional or superficial interpretations have suggested. Criticism is thus "critical," not in the sense that it "criticizes" the Bible (it often reveres it as the basic and holy text), but in the sense that it assumes freedom to derive from the Bible, seen in itself, meanings other than those that traditional religion has seen in it. Biblical criticism thus uncovers new questions about the Bible, even as it offers fresh answers in place of old solutions.

Criticism and Conflict. Biblical criticism need not conflict with long-accepted understandings, but it may do so. This will mean that some traditional interpretations have been ill-grounded in scripture and that some new interpretation should be suggested if justice is to be done to the facts of scripture. Criticism has thus often disturbed existing religion; yet it is also intrinsic to the religious belief in biblical *authority. Far from being a nontheological activity, it is essential to proper theological evaluation. We momentarily suspend the existing theological conviction to see whether it stands the test of questioning against the biblical material itself.

Not surprisingly, therefore, religious conflict has been a great stimulus to critical questioning. Two groups share the same scripture but have widely differing religious convictions. Each may then appeal to the scripture and argue that it cannot mean what others have taken it to mean. According to Matthew 23.23, Jesus himself says that the "weightier matters of the law" are neglected if one concentrates on the implementation of details—an appeal to the general tenor of the text against its detailed literality. As against the Christian understanding of Isaiah 7.14 as a prediction of Christ's *virgin birth, the Jew Trypho (second century CE) insisted that the Hebrew word means simply "young woman," that no virgin birth is involved, and that the reference is to the natural birth of *Hezekiah (see Immanuel).

The religious conflicts that most stimulated the rise of biblical criticism were, however, the Catholic-Protestant conflict within Christianity and, later, the disputes among the many different directions within Protestantism, for these particularly emphasized the unique role of scripture and the implications of reading it for and from itself.

Obstacles to Criticism. The main factors with

which criticism has had to contend have included the following:

General ideas or principles concerning the Bible, such as the conviction that, being the word of God, it must necessarily be perfect and thus inerrant in all its parts (*see* Inspiration and Inerrancy). As against these theoretical convictions, criticism works with the factual realities of the Bible.

Harmonizations that universalize ideas and meanings throughout the Bible, obscuring differences between one part and another. Criticism notices these differences, such as that between documents affirming a virgin birth (Matthew, less clearly Luke) and others that appear not to do so (Mark, Paul, John).

Midrash and allegorical interpretations that decontextualize the words of scripture, ascribing to them senses that may be found elsewhere but do not fit this context. Criticism takes the actual context to be decisive.

Failure to perceive the literary form of the texts, and, in particular, failure to give weight to the silences of scripture, the absences of elements that are commonly read in; for example, the absence from the Hebrew Bible of *Adam's disobedience as an explanation for *evil, the absence of any birth narrative in Mark, the absence from other Gospels of the clause "except for unchastity" (Matt. 19.9; cf. 5.32; *see* Divorce).

Anachronistic reading into the text of meanings, ideas, and situations of a later age; for example, to understand *bishop in the New Testament as if this were identical with medieval episcopacy, or "scripture" in 2 Timothy 3.16 as if it meant exactly the same set of books that are canonical in modern Protestantism (*see* Canon). Criticism insists on starting with the words in the meanings that they had in biblical times.

Rationalistic apologetic arguments supposed to overcome discrepancies; for example, the idea that, since the ejection of merchants from the temple by Jesus is placed early in the ministry by John, late by the other Gospels, the event happened several times. Criticism, on the other hand, suggests that the differential placing of the story was for reasons of theological meaning within the narrative.

Authorship. Classical biblical criticism has been much interested in matters of authorship. The *Pentateuch was not written by *Moses himself; the book of *Isaiah contains materials from a time long after that prophet lived; the Gospels were not necessarily written by the disciples whose names they bear. This realization at once changes our picture of the sort of book the Bible is: it is not a once-and-for-all, divinely dictated report but a product of tradition developed over some time within communities of faith. Relations between documents like the *synoptic Gospels are literary relations, involving revision, change of emphasis, selection, and theological difference. The feature of pseudepigraphy must be recognized as a fact: that is, that books may be written in the name of, and attributed to, some great person of the past who presides over that genre. Thus, almost all Israelite *law, of whatever time, was attached to the name of Moses, as were *wisdom writings to that of *Solomon; some letters written in the name of *Paul or *Peter may have been written by followers, perhaps using some material from the apostle himself, rather than by him directly.

Style has been an important criterion from the beginning. Already in the ancient church it was obvious that 2 *Peter was not in a style that Peter used, that the letter to the *Hebrews differed in style from Paul, and that the book of *Revelation differed vastly in style from the gospel and letters of *John; and this observation was already used in early arguments about the canonicity of such books. These ancient observations formed a basis for similar discussions later, especially in Renaissance and Reformation (*see article on* Christian Interpretation from the Middle Ages to the Reformation, *above*), when the appreciation of ancient styles had been greatly quickened.

Sources. That books had been formed by the combination of earlier sources was an obvious corollary of these ideas. *Chronicles used Samuel-Kings, revising sometimes slightly, sometimes drastically, and adding material of its own. Mark is most commonly believed to have been used and rewritten by Matthew and Luke. And the sources used could be works that had long disappeared. The books of Kings mention other historical sources known to them. Material common to Matthew and Luke, but absent from Mark, could go back to a source now lost. Within the Pentateuch the different strata, marked by very different language, style, and ideas, could be explained if different sources from different times had been gradually combined. The detection of different sources within a book may thus explain discrepancies and divergent theological viewpoints. Source criticism of this kind is a highly characteristic form of classical biblical criticism. It, along with questions of authorship and date, is sometimes called "higher criticism," in contrast to "lower criticism," the study of text and textual variations (see Textual Criticism), but these terms are now old-fashioned. Indeed, from about the 1930s on, source criticism itself became somewhat old-fashioned and less work was done on it; uncertainties in its conclusions were noted, and rivals to the widely accepted views came to be more commonly supported. Nevertheless, source-critical results continue to be used as a normal framework of discussion by the great majority of scholars, and the broad outlines of source identification in the key areas—the Pentateuch, Isaiah, and the synoptic Gospels—are very generally accepted; such alternatives as there are are equally critical, but in a different way.

Cosmology and Miracle. The rise of biblical criticism ran parallel with changing ideas about the world we live in. New scientific knowledge made it seem impossible that the world could have originated as recently as the date (5000–3600 BCE) implied by the Bible's own *chronology, and the vast majority accepted this: the world was not exactly as Genesis had made it seem (see Science and the Bible). Similarly, it was debated just how exactly factual biblical depictions of miraculous events were. Critics noted the literary aspect: scripture is quite uneven in the degree to which it brings in miracle stories, and it may describe the same event in ways that are more sheerly miraculous or less so. This suggests that the element of miracle is again in part a matter of style. Biblical criticism is not in principle skeptical about *miracles; but it takes it as clear that not all miracle stories are to be taken literally just because they are in the Bible. On the whole, critical scholarship leaves the question aside; for, in its developed form, it concentrates mainly on the meaning or function that the miracle story had within the work of the writer. For this purpose, it finds it unnecessary either to defend or to deny the reality of miracles; the exegetical process works in the same way in either case.

History has often been looked on as the essential component in biblical criticism, though we have maintained that its foundations rest more in language and in literary form. The literary perceptions thus stimulated often could not produce solutions without a historical account of what had taken place. Thus, in the method of Julius Wellhausen (1844–1918), Pentateuchal sources identified through linguistic and literary criteria were matched with the evidence of different stages in the development of religious institutions in Israel, producing a likely sequence and dating. Dating sources and setting them within the framework of known world history thus provides a strong frame of reference for biblical study and a way in which evidence can be marshaled and ordered for discussion and theological evaluation. In particular, the knowledge, even if only approximate, of what lay before and after makes it possible to understand the presuppositions of biblical writers and the situation for which they wrote.

The centrality of this frame, and the importance of the perspective it afforded, has often caused the entire operation of biblical criticism to be understood as "historical criticism." But this exaggerates the degree to which the ideals of historical research dominate biblical study. Historical investigation is only one of the aspects of traditional criticism. Much critical work is basically the exegesis of biblical books; for this, complete historical precision is often impossible, and in any case is not attained, often hardly attempted. More important is a rough and general historical location; the gross distortion of total anachronism is to be avoided. Words must be understood to mean what they meant in the language of the texts, and that means in the time of the texts; texts should be seen against the situation in life for which they were written. In fact, biblical scholars, even when they insist on a historical approach, are often not very historical; they tend to let theological predilection overcome historical realism, and their motivation is commonly the religious scholar's devotion to texts rather than pure historical rigor. It was from traditional theology that there came the emphasis on what had "really happened" in biblical times, on the persons of authority who were behind the writings, on history as the milieu of God's activity. Conversely, the historical perspective on the Bible which biblical criticism has brought about is important primarily as a major fact within theology itself, rather than as a purely historical achievement.

The Canon. One important historical aspect is the perception of the *canon of scripture: the canon came about historically and can be understood historically. The pioneering studies of Johann S. Semler (1725–91) in this area were a vital step in the development of modern biblical studies. The boundaries of scripture are not something eternally and unchangeably established by God; what scripture included at one time and place was not entirely identical with what it included at another; the study of scripture and the study of church history are not separable. That the origins of the canon can be investigated as a human undertaking is correlative with a similar study of the books themselves. The canon can still be understood as God-given, just as the contents of scripture are God-given; but not purely and supernaturally so—rather, only indirectly and through the mediation of human intentions and meanings. Biblical critics have not rejected the canon; on the whole they have continued to uphold it, maintaining that the religious content of the Bible (i.e., the canonical books) is, broadly speaking, vastly superior in quality to that of any other set of written texts.

Theological Differentiation. Central to biblical criticism, and even more important than its historical orientation, is its use of the perception that theological views and emphases differ between one part of scripture and another. The Bible is not a monochrome and unvarying photograph of the being and will of God; it is more like a choir, each member of which has a different part to sing. Thus, in spite of much common subject matter, the *P stratum of the Pentateuch has a theology quite different from that of *Deuteronomy, and Matthew presents quite a different picture of *Jesus from that of Luke. This in itself is no novel or revolutionary insight; but, rather than being content merely to admire the complementary character of the theologies of the books, biblical criticism uses it as a valuable index for the identification of strata and their relative dating, situations, and problems. Equally, it strives to perceive, understand, and evaluate these different theologies as crucial stages in the understanding of scripture as a whole, seen in a dimension of depth.

Theological Roots of Biblical Criticism. Though biblical criticism may appear as something new, in fact it has deep theological roots. The interest in personal authorship went back to early times and was part of the argument over canonicity. Style was also known as a criterion from early times; later, on the basis of style, John Calvin doubted that Peter had written 2 Peter, just as, on grounds of content, he thought that Psalms 74 and 79 came from the Maccabean period (a view later regarded as drastically critical). The emphasis on history and actual events was also part of general Christian tradition: Christianity, people thought, was a peculiarly historical religion, and the importance of the actual words and deeds of Jesus was overwhelmingly accepted and stressed. If biblical criticism noticed and used the theological differences

within the Bible, this was an extension from the practice of all theologies; for all, even when accepting the total canon of scripture, had picked out portions as more essential and dominant, while treating others as derivative or of secondary importance. As for the canon, the first obvious fact was that theological tradition had not agreed about it; there had been variations in canons throughout the early centuries, and again as between Roman Catholic and Orthodox on one side, and Protestant on the other. This fact was accentuated when Martin Luther, impressed by theological differentiation, effectively demoted from the New Testament canon *James, Hebrews (not by Paul), and Revelation on the ground of their inadequate understanding of the essential principle of *justification. Difference in emphasis between Old Testament and New Testament was also traditional and universal in Christianity.

The impetus toward biblical criticism given by the Reformation was substantial. Stressing scripture alone—as against mediation through church tradition—meant that everything seemed to depend on scripture. The grammar and wording of the original were reemphasized and a learned ministry capable of handling these words was demanded. The Reformation rejected allegorical methods that had covered over cracks in the surface of scripture, and in the Hebrew Bible it mediated influences from medieval Jewish exegesis (seen, e.g., in the KJV), which in this respect also favored literal understanding (*see article in this entry on* Jewish Interpretation, *above*). It asserted the freedom of the interpreter to take a stand on the biblical words as against traditional and authoritative interpretations. But, despite the reformers' insistence on biblical authority, they failed to produce doctrinal agreement; on the contrary, they created a wide variety of conflicting doctrinal positions, all claiming a basis in infallible scripture. The wide variation of ideas and hypotheses within later biblical criticism is a reflection of the same situation.

Rise and Reception of Criticism. The ancient and early modern anticipations of critical views are not in themselves very important. It could be obvious enough that the statement that "at that time the Canaanites were in the land" (Gen. 12.6) was not written by Moses but was a later note; so argued Abraham ibn Ezra (1089–1164), an opinion on which Baruch Spinoza (1632–1677) later built much more. Such observations were often only minor annotations and do not amount to a critical vision of any scale. More important was the growth of the general atmosphere of thought in which it seemed permissible and even normal to argue on the basis of the language and literary form of scripture, with freedom to offer the interpretations that emerged from them. This tradition may go back to Erasmus (1466–1536), and is well represented by Hugo Grotius (1583–1645), who belonged to the Arminian current in the Dutch church. In France, Richard Simon (1638–1712) argued that uncertainties about scripture undermined the Protestant reliance upon it, while freedom in biblical study produced no clash with Catholic dogma; alongside this, his argument against Moses' authorship of the entire Pentateuch is a minor point. Jean Astruc (1684–1766) pioneered the systematic source analysis of the Pentateuch, the different documents being isolated but understood to have been combined by Moses himself.

An especially active locus of new ideas about scripture was England in the seventeenth and eighteenth centuries. In conflicts over church polity, civil government, and religious freedom there were manifold viewpoints, all of which sought legitimation from scripture, and the ensuing controversies evoked an efflorescence of new ideas and arguments. Thomas Hobbes (1588–1679) is a distinguished representative. For him there is no doubting the authority of the Bible as the law of God; but equally, in the matter of authorship and date, it is simply obvious that the only light we have must come from the books themselves, and from this it is manifest that the books of Moses were written after his time, and similarly with other books. Other important exegetical ideas come from John Locke (1632–1704), who noted, among other things, how Jesus kept secret his messianic status until late in his career (*see* Messianic Secret); Sir Isaac Newton (1642–1727), who worked on biblical chronology and also thought that the idea of the *Trinity could be disproved from the New Testament; and many others.

In Germany, these ideas were followed up in the later eighteenth century by university professors, who applied them in a much more systematic way. A typical genre was the "introduction," which would cover in turn each book of Old Testament or New Testament and discuss methodically all matters of authorship, source analysis, and dates on the basis of language and content; a pioneer of such work was by Johann Gottfried Eichhorn (published 1780–1783). Central names in Old Testament scholarship are

Wilhelm Martin Leberecht de Wette (1780–1849), noted for his work on the key book of Deuteronomy, and Julius Wellhausen, whose solution (the "P" document is the latest of the Pentateuchal sources) remains the point of reference for all discussion of the subject. In New Testament studies, a central figure was Ferdinand Christian Baur (1792–1860), who saw a conflict between Pauline and Petrine traditions as decisive for early Christianity. Of the "quest for the historical Jesus," it is hard to know whether it counts as biblical criticism or as speculative theology; the claim of Johannes Weiss (1863–1914) that Jesus' mission was dominated by eschatological expectation is a more clearly critical standpoint.

The return of this developed biblical criticism to the English-speaking world was not without conflict. W. Robertson Smith was removed from his professorship in Scotland in 1881, and Charles A. Briggs from his clerical functions in the United States in 1893. But soon after these events, critical approaches had clearly won the day in these same churches. In Oxford from 1883 the cautious and erudite scholarship of Samuel Rolles Driver commended the critical reading of the Old Testament, and *Lux mundi* (1889) aligned the Catholic tradition of Anglicanism with the same. By the early twentieth century, critical perspectives, though not always easily accepted, were overwhelmingly dominant in academic study and serious publishing throughout the western non–Roman Catholic world.

Although biblical criticism made a deep difference to the handling of the Bible, this did not have the feared serious effects on doctrine. This was partly because many traditional doctrines were not nearly as solely dependent on the Bible as had been supposed. Shifts in the mode of understanding the Bible left it possible for these same doctrines to be still maintained. Indeed, biblical criticism fitted in well with certain important doctrinal emphases: in Lutheranism with justification by faith, in Anglicanism with the centrality of *incarnation, in Calvinism with the appreciation of Israel and the Old Testament. Moreover, though much biblical criticism grew up in association with latitudinarian views, with deism, and later with liberal theology, the achievements of criticism showed themselves to be separable from these origins and to be fully maintainable by those who repudiated them. Thus "dialectical" or "neo-orthodox" theology, bitterly hostile to "liberal" theology, accepted the legitimacy of critical procedures and, though itself often cool toward biblical scholarship, on the whole created an atmosphere in which it could flourish very freely.

In the Roman Catholic world, Richard Simon's argument that critical freedom favored the Catholic position was little accepted by his superiors, and critical work was muted until the rise of Catholic modernism, especially in France in the late nineteenth century with Alfred F. Loisy (1857–1940). The modernist movement was formally condemned by Pius X in 1907, and the dogmatic necessity of traditional authorships and dates was reasserted. But since the encyclical *Divino afflante spiritu* (1943) and especially since the Second Vatican Council, the critical freedom of the Catholic exegete has been acknowledged, and today Catholic and Protestant biblical scholarship form one total constituency (*see also* Pontifical Biblical Commission).

Jewish academic scholarship has often differed from the solutions favored in Christian work; examples include opposition to Pentateuchal source criticism from Moses Hirsch Segal (1876–1968) and Umberto Cassuto (1883–1951), and different reconstruction of Israelite religious history from Yehezkel Kaufmann (1889–1963). Non-Jewish scholarship was often felt to be too much influenced by Christian theological traditions. But the alternative positions advanced by Jewish scholars are in their own way just as critical, and offer no support to a consistent anticritical mode of study.

Biblical Theology. Biblical criticism has often been understood primarily as an analytical discipline, but equally it is linked with the discipline of *biblical theology, which is the synthetic side of the same movement. Biblical theology seeks to see the common elements that run through the texts, whether through a historical or developmental scheme or through the perception of an inner structure. No serious biblical theology has arisen except in conjunction with the critical approach. Biblical theology, like criticism, is an exploratory approach; the true inner theology of the Bible is not already known, but must be discovered. For opponents of critical study, the theology of scripture is already known, fixed in older creeds and traditions. Though twentieth-century biblical theology felt itself to be in contrast with biblical criticism, they are in fact two sides of the same coin.

Religious Environment. All the above may count as a depiction of "classical" biblical criticism; there remain some more recent developments to be mentioned. The older critics worked largely from the Bible itself; later, increasing

knowledge from Mesopotamia and Syria, from Hellenistic *mystery religions, from *gnosticism was added. Clearly, there is some overlap in religious ideas and institutions, in legends, myths, and poetic forms. The "history of religions" school explored this area; a central name is that of Hermann Gunkel (1862–1932).

Form Criticism, influential from the 1920s on, is interested in the smaller literary units that have a function in their "situation in life," through which one penetrates to the underlying purpose. Thus, a gospel story might be of a form fitted for controversy with Jews, a psalm might be of a form belonging to an enthronement ceremony. Important form critics are Gunkel for the Hebrew Bible, and Rudolf Bultmann (1884–1976) for the New Testament. For the New Testament, form criticism often seemed to be skeptical in character, suggesting that stories were generated for these purposes rather than actually spoken by Jesus; in the Hebrew Bible its effects were more conservative, suggesting ways in which poems might have functioned in ancient cult and liturgy.

Tradition Criticism concentrates on the way in which traditions have altered and grown, the places to which they are attached, and the social and cultic relations within which they have been meaningful. It is less interested in documentary hypotheses, more in oral stages of tradition, and it illuminates the deep underlying forces that have molded the Bible into its present form. It has been particularly exemplified in Scandinavian scholarship.

Redaction Criticism is interested in the work of the final editors, who molded the earlier sources into the text that we now have. The method depends on some view of the sources used by the redactor, but the interest falls less on these sources in themselves and more on the way in which they have been adapted into the final text. The object is therefore the shape and structure of the book as we now have it; yet the perception of this depends on a perspective in time, going back to an earlier stage or earlier revisional activity.

Modern Literary Readings. Although the literary character of biblical criticism has been emphasized here, from about 1960 on it has been increasingly felt that it is out of step with modern trends in the appreciation of literature. Literary critics from outside the technical biblical sphere— for example, Frank Kermode, Robert Alter, and Northrop Frye—have made powerful contributions and some biblical scholars are following similar lines. Most of this literary movement is interested in the final, the present, stage of the text, not in historical reconstruction; nor does it share the theological interests characteristic of most biblical criticism. The stress is on the styles, the patterns, the narrative techniques. The text, some think, does not "refer" to anything external to itself, but operates within "the world of the text" (see also Literature, The Bible as). Some of this overlaps with ideas coming from *structuralism, a movement centered in France. Structuralism is interested in the code, the set of structures, that are used in all social and literary complexes, as they are in language itself. It stresses the synchronic, the structures visible within one text at one time, rather than its development over a span of time, though it can also be extended to deal with historical change. These types of reading, in general, differ widely from traditional biblical criticism and especially from its historical interests; on the other hand, their reluctance to say anything informative about the world "outside the text" leaves it doubtful how they can fit with the older theological needs served by biblical criticism.

Canonical Criticism. This approach, advocated principally by Brevard S. Childs, insists on the *canon of scripture as the essential key to interpretation. Canonicity is interested in the final text, not in earlier stages that have led up to it. The canon of books, which brings them all together as holy scripture of the community, means that taken together they provide a "construal" of all their contents. Traditional biblical criticism is legitimate, providing, as it does, the starting points from which Childs reasons toward the canonical sense; but its perspective and direction are basically erroneous. Common areas with redaction criticism and with modern literary readings and structuralism seem obvious; but Childs is anxious to disclaim support from these quarters, for canonical criticism is not at all literary in character, and its validation comes entirely from the theological status of scripture. Though it appears to seek a connection with much earlier exegesis, canonical criticism is a clearly modern phenomenon, working entirely from the tradition of biblical criticism even when it seeks to depart from it.

Conclusion. Biblical criticism has proved to be a dynamic field of study. New approaches and perspectives continue to appear. Areas undergoing fresh examination include the nature of Hebrew poetic form (stimulated by our knowledge of *Ugaritic poetry; see also Poetry, Biblical Hebrew); the character of Judaism at the time when Christianity originated; the character of scripture as story rather than as history. Results believed to have been established will be reconsidered. Yet some of the main positions achieved have remained as essential reference points for the discussion, and no alternatives have been proposed that have gained anything like the same degree of assent. Still more important, the general intellectual atmosphere of criticism, with its base in language and literary form, its reference grid in history, and its lifeblood in freedom to follow what the text actually says, has established itself as without serious challenge. Serious work on scripture can be done only in continuity with the tradition of biblical criticism.

See also Social Sciences and the Bible.

JAMES BARR

Irony and Humor. Irony is a mode of expression in which what is said is the opposite of what is meant; consequently, ironic statements cannot be understood without rejecting their apparent sense. Humor starts with the perception of irony or of some other inconsistency strong enough to provoke confusion or tension. Sudden release from such tension often results in a smile or in laughter; the inner feeling is of sympathetic joy or of playfulness. Things that are thus perceived and the reactions to that perception are called comical.

There are many examples of irony and humor in the Bible. Genesis 17–18 tells of *Abraham and *Sarah's laughter when they think they have a joke on God. In 1 Samuel 17 it is ironic that the young shepherd boy *David is victorious over the giant *Goliath, and in 2 Samuel 12 the prophet *Nathan ironically makes King David pass sentence on himself. The *Psalms describe God as a laughing god who finds sinners ridiculous in their pride and self-deceptions (2.4; 37.13; cf. 59.9; Prov. 1.26). The *prophets used sarcasm and satire rather than humor in the positive sense. They ridiculed the belief in *idols (Isa. 44; cf. Hos. 13.2) and drew up a ridiculously exact list of the *jewelry of luxurious women (Isa. 3.18–23). Generalizations and exaggerations are also characteristic of prophetic discourse.

The book of *Proverbs provides examples of humor and irony that are different from the biting sarcasm of the prophets and the amusing storytelling of the narrator. The sign of true wisdom is obedience to God's law; the sinner is therefore ridiculous. A lazy man wants to sleep in the morning (Prov. 6.9–10) and does not have the energy to lift his hand to his mouth when he is eating (19.24). The slothful person lying in bed is like a door on its hinges, turning back and forth (26.14). A rich fool thinks he can buy wisdom with money (17.16). *Women are generally respectfully described, unless they are brawling (21.9), contentious (27.15), or immoral (11.22).

In the *synoptic Gospels, similes, *parables, and terms used by *Jesus are often akin to similar expressions in rabbinic literature. The rabbis used humor and irony in their discussion about even the most serious matters. Since Jesus was (called) a *rabbi, it is not surprising that he uses irony and humor as well. In his sayings he describes comical people (Luke 11.5–8; 18.1–8; Matt 5.25; 25.1–12), comical ideas (Matt. 5.36; 7.6, 9–10, 16), and comical events (Matt. 5.15; 7.3–5; Luke 14.7–14). These humorous texts point toward the earliest strata of Christian tradition and probably originated from Jesus himself.

In the gospel of *John everything happens simultaneously within two frames of reference. One is mystical, sublime, heavenly: there Jesus is the eternal, divine *Logos. The other is the earthly, the temporal, that of the "flesh" (John 1.14). The incarnate Jesus and the eternal Christ are the same person, and his message is interpreted in terms that have a double meaning. This results in a certain kind of irony, and the human intellect asks questions that show its lack of understanding and insight (John 2.20; 3.4; 4.11, 15, 33; 6.15, 26, 34; 7.35; 12.16, 28–30; 13.4–11, 28–29; 16.17–18). Here two tunes are interwoven into one musical composition. Those who are attentive only to the sublime tune will hardly find humor in the narrative, but readers conscious of the earthly tune will perhaps think of the *incarnation of Logos as a metamorphosis in the Greek sense, and then the way is open to the understanding of what has been called "divine irony." Among such ironical examples are the declarations of Jewish and Roman authorities (John 11.49–53; 18.5) and Jesus' feigned ignorance (Luke 24.19).

The book of *Acts is a kind of story in which the humor often consists in amusing situations. There is something comical about *Peter's return to the congregation (12.1–19), missionaries as gods (14.1–18), and Demetrius's wonderful speech in Ephesus (19.23–41).

*Paul had rabbinical training and uses ironical questions about theological matters (Rom. 3.29; 6.1, 15; 7.7, 13). He describes himself as a fool for Christ's sake (1 Cor. 4.9–10), and even speaks of God as foolish and weak (1 Cor. 1.18–31). The letter to *Philemon is a masterpiece of sympathetic irony and gentle humor.

See also Literature, The Bible as.

JAKOB JÓNSSON

Isaac. Son of *Abraham and father of *Esau and *Jacob. The principal stories about Isaac are found in Genesis 21–28. Isaac is a more shadowy figure than the other patriarchs, and little if anything can be said of him as a historical figure. He is said to have been born when his parents were both advanced in years as a fulfillment of God's promise to Abraham to grant him posterity against all human expectation (see Rom. 4.16–22). In Genesis 22 God himself seems to challenge his own promise by demanding that Isaac be offered as a human sacrifice, but rewards Abraham's unquestioning obedience by providing a ram as a substitute at the last possible moment. This story (the *Aqedah) has been important in Judaism as a reminder of the precariousness of Israel's election and yet the sure promises of God, as well as in Christianity as a "type" of the sacrifice of Christ.

Of Isaac's maturity we learn little. Genesis 24 tells how he acquired a wife (*Rebekah), but the principal characters in this tale are Isaac's servant and Rebekah's family. In Genesis 26 Isaac and Rebekah are involved in an incident with "Abimelech king of the Philistines" (an anachronistic reference), who takes Rebekah into his harem—essentially the same incident twice reported of Abraham and *Sarah (Gen. 12 and 20). Isaac next appears as an old man, deceived by Jacob into giving him the blessing of the firstborn that should by right have been Esau's (Gen. 27). The stories about Isaac locate him at Beer-sheba in the far south of Judah (Gen. 26.23–33) and associate him with the worship of the God El-roi (Gen. 22.14; 24.62), while Jacob later swears by "the Fear of his father Isaac" (Gen. 31.53), perhaps an old divine name (see Names of God in the Hebrew Bible).

See also Ancestors, The; Genesis, The Book of. JOHN BARTON

Isaiah, The Book of. Isaiah is the first of the Major Prophets in both Jewish and Christian tradition. The book consists of sixty-six chapters that can be divided into five sections of roughly the same length (1–12; 13–27; 28–39; 40–55; 56–66). All except one begin with an attack on arrogance and an appeal for justice and culminate in a hymn or prophecy of salvation, and all except one are addressed to the people of Jerusalem. The one exception is chapters 40–55, which begins "Comfort, O comfort my people," and is addressed to an exiled community in Babylon during the sixth century BCE. The book is held together by common themes and phrases (e.g., "the Holy One of Israel," Jerusalem/Zion, justice and righteousness), by quotations from, or allusions to, earlier passages in later ones (e.g., 1.6 in 53.5; 6.1–13 in 40.1–8; 6.1 in 52.13 and 57.15; 11.6–9 in 65.25), and by other kinds of continuity, such as the life and times of the prophet (1.1; 6–9; 14.28; 20; 36–39; 40.1–8) and the downfall of Babylon (13–14; 46–47).

Contents. Chaps. 1–12 consist of prolonged and bitter attacks on the arrogance and hypocrisy of Jerusalem's leaders ("rulers of Sodom," 1.10; cf. Ezek. 16.49), interspersed with prophecies of a better age to come when swords will be beaten into plowshares (2.4; cf. Mic. 4.3) and "the wolf shall live with the lamb" (11.6). As the title suggests (1.1; 2.1), the prophet's visions place special emphasis on the role of *Jerusalem and a royal savior from the line of *David (9.2–7; 11.1–9). In such a context, it was inevitable that 7.14 would be interpreted as referring to the birth of either a royal savior, *Hezekiah, or a future *messiah.

These chapters also contain a memorable account, like those of other prophets (1 Kings 22.19–23; Jer. 23.18), of Isaiah's glimpse into the heavenly court where he was confronted by the awesome *holiness of God and commissioned to convey God's judgment to his unhearing and unseeing people (chap. 6). This judgment theme continues into the narrative of his confrontation with King Ahaz during the Syro-Ephraimite crisis (chaps. 7–8; cf. 2 Kings 16). Like other eighth-century prophets, Isaiah prophesies that the *Assyrians are the real danger and that they will sweep like a mighty river over the northern kingdoms and into Judah (8.5–8). He calls for faith (7.9; cf. 30.15) and sees beyond present gloom and anguish to future victory (9.1–5). Assyria is a tool in God's hand (10.5–7). Both the terror of a confrontation between human power and God's power, and the hope of the eventual victory of God's people, are expressed in the richly emotive term *Immanuel, "God is

with us" (7.14; 8.8; 8.10). The section ends with a short hymn of thanksgiving (chap. 12).

Chaps. 13–27 further proclaim God's sovereignty over history. Isaiah's oracles concerning the nations (cf. Jer. 46–51; Ezek. 24–32; Amos 1–2) begin with *Babylon (13–14) and end with the entire earth (24–27). In addition to the customary taunts and mock laments (e.g., "How you are fallen from heaven, O Day Star, son of Dawn!" 14.12; cf. Amos 5.1–2), this series contains some unusual material: expressions of sympathy for the survivors of *Moab (16.3–5), an unexpected blessing for *Egypt and Assyria (19.24–5), and another glimpse into the trauma of a prophet's visionary experience (21.1–10).

The oracle concerning Tyre (chap. 23), an international seaport in contact with every part of the world (see Phoenicia), leads logically into the last part of this section in which the subject is the entire earth (24–27). These four chapters are often known as the "Isaiah apocalypse": although they do not have the literary characteristics of the book of Revelation and other true apocalypses, they do contain *apocalyptic language and imagery. The whole earth is depicted as desolate, twisted, despoiled, and polluted; sun and moon are eclipsed (24.23); and the passage pictures an eschatological banquet (25.6), the resurrection of the dead (26.19; cf. 25.8), and God's ultimate victory over the host of heaven (24.21), *Leviathan, the "fleeing . . . twisting serpent," and the "dragon that is in the sea" (27.1). The passage belongs firmly to Isaianic tradition, however, as is indicated by such recurring motifs as the city (26.1; cf. 1.21–26), the mountain of the Lord (25.6; cf. 2.2; 11.9), and the vineyard (27.2; cf. 5.1–7).

In chaps. 28–39, the prophet first directs the full force of his rhetoric against Israel and Judah again (28–31), just as *Amos does after his oracles concerning the foreign nations (Amos 2.4–16). The whole preceding section (13–27) functions merely as a foil for this final condemnation of his own people. He takes up where he left off in 1–12: "Ah, the proud garland of the drunkards of Ephraim" (28.1; cf. 5.11–12). "The mighty flood" of an Assyrian invasion reappears from chap. 8, and the call for faith and courage in a city under siege is repeated (30.15; cf. 7.4, 9). This time the crisis is that of 701 BCE, when *Sennacherib invaded Judah and Hezekiah was tempted to join forces with Egypt (31.1–3). Chaps. 36–37 tell the story of a miraculous victory over the Assyrians in that year, highlighting Isaiah's role. There were two other crises in the same year, Hezekiah's illness, when the prophet performs a solar miracle reminiscent of Joshua's at Gibeon (chap. 38; cf. Josh. 10.12, 14), and the visit of Babylonian ambassadors to Jerusalem, during which he foretells the Babylonian *exile (chap. 39). Like chap. 39, the central chapters of this section, especially 34 and 35, point forward to the next section.

Chaps. 40–55 are often known as the "Babylonian chapters." They constitute the most distinctive and homogeneous part of the book, both stylistically and theologically, and are for that reason commonly referred to as "Second Isaiah" or "Deutero-Isaiah." Repetition is frequent (e.g., 40.1; 51.9; 52.1). The exiled community in Babylon is described and addressed collectively as "Zion" (feminine singular; e.g., 40.9; 51.17; 52.1–2) and "my servant" (e.g., 41.8; 44.1). The rise of Cyrus, king of the *Medes and *Persians, is described (45.1–3), as are the fall of Babylon (chap. 47) and the return of the exiles to Jerusalem in a new *Exodus (48.20–21; 51.9–11; 52.11–12). The sheer scale of God's power in history and in creation is another recurring theme in these chapters (e.g., 40.12–20; 42.5–9; 45.9–13), as are explicit *monotheism (e.g., 45.5, 6, 14, 21, 22), the ridicule of *idolatry (e.g., 40.18–20; 44.9–20; 46.1–2), and feminine images for God (42.14; 46.3; 49.15; 66.9). Finally, the concept of healing and victory through the vicarious suffering of "the servant of the Lord" (52.13–53.12) marks out this section as unique in biblical prophecy.

The final section of the book (chaps. 56–66) is mainly concerned with the return of the exiles to Jerusalem and the building of a new society there. "Justice" and "righteousness" are again key motifs here as they were at the beginning (56.1; 59; 61.8; cf. 1.17). Foreigners and *eunuchs will be admitted into the *Temple (56.1). The poor and the oppressed will be set free (58.6–7; 61.1–2), and Temple *sacrifice is finally rejected in favor of humility and *repentance (66.1). The feminine imagery, introduced in chaps. 40–55, is further elaborated (62.1–5; 66.7–14). God is addressed as father (63.16; 64.8), and a striking variation on the God-as-warrior theme is the famous "grapes of wrath" passage (63.1–6) in which he is portrayed as a somewhat reluctant victor, limping home from war, blood-stained and stooping (v. 1; NRSV: "marching"). The last verse of the book, one of the few biblical texts on which a doctrine of hellfire can be based

(66.24), is so gruesome that in Jewish custom the preceding verses about "the new heavens and the new earth" are repeated after it, to end the reading on a more hopeful and at the same time more characteristically Isaianic note.

Author. All that is known of Isaiah son of Amoz, the prophet to whom the book is attributed, is found in the book itself. He is not referred to elsewhere in the Bible apart from parallel passages in Kings and Chronicles (2 Kings 19–20; 2 Chron. 29–32). The book contains a few biographical details, which present the picture of a prophet in the traditional pattern: a glimpse into the heavenly court (chap. 6); the giving of symbolic names to his children (7.3; 8.1–4; cf. Hos. 2.1–9); dramatic appearances at the courts of kings (chaps. 7; 37–39; cf. 2 Sam. 12.1–15; 1 Kings 21.17–29; Jer. 22); prophesying through symbolic actions (20; cf. 1 Kings 22.11–12; Jer. 19; Ezek 12.1–7); the performing of miracles (38.7–8; cf. 1 Kings 18.20–46; 2 Kings 4.32–37); and the condemnation of injustice and oppression (1–5; cf. 2 Sam. 12.1–6; 1 Kings 21; Amos 5). According to an extrabiblical legend, he was martyred ("sawn in two"; cf. Heb. 11.37) in the reign of *Manasseh.

The title informs us that he lived during the reigns of four kings of Judah (Uzziah, Jotham, Ahaz, and Hezekiah), that is to say, during the second half of the eighth century BCE. This was a period during which Judah's fortunes changed from affluence under Uzziah (see 2 Chron. 26) to defeat and humiliation at the hands of the Assyrians in 701 BCE (2 Kings 18). Many passages clearly reflect those traumatic years—the approaching Assyrian army (5.26–30; 10.28–32), the devastation of the land of Judah (1.7–8), the folly of Judah's leaders (chaps. 30–31)—and were probably composed at that time. Perhaps the hopes accompanying the coronation of Hezekiah in 715 BCE are expressed in the dynastic hymn 9.1–7.

A few sections of narrative, however, clearly reflect later ideas and attitudes. The story of Jerusalem's miraculous deliverance from the Assyrian army under Sennacherib in 701 (chaps. 36–37), for example, though based on the fact that Jerusalem was not destroyed on that occasion, probably owes much to an upsurge of national confidence during the reign of Josiah (626–609) when the Assyrian empire collapsed. The annals of Sennacherib, and 2 Kings 18.14–16 (omitted from the Isaianic version), suggest that the reality was very different.

Some passages, mainly in chaps. 40–66, contain no references at all to the Assyrians, but frequently allude to events and conditions in the Babylonian period (605–538 BCE): Jerusalem and the Temple in ruins (44.28; 49.17); Babylonian idols (46.1–2); a Jewish colony at Syene (Elephantine) in Egypt (49.12); *Cyrus (45.1). The bulk of the book was thus probably composed more than a century after the lifetime of Isaiah. The popular division into three sections, First Isaiah (chaps. 1–39) dated to the eighth century BCE, Second (Deutero-) Isaiah (chaps. 40–55) to the sixth, and Third Isaiah (chaps. 56–66) to the fifth, is a crude oversimplification. The literary and theological unity of the whole book is unmistakable; and some parts of First Isaiah, notably the two Babylonian chapters (13–14) and the Isaiah apocalypse (24–27), manifestly belong to the sixth century or later. Chaps. 24–27 should probably be dated to the fourth century BCE, contemporary with *Joel. Each passage must be handled on its own, though both as a product of its age and in the context of the Isaianic corpus as a whole.

Key Concepts. Some development is evident from the earliest chapters to the latest. Different images and illustrations are used in different parts of the book, reflecting changes in historical context. But there are enough common themes running throughout the book for us to be able to discuss Isaianic tradition as a rich and distinctive entity within *biblical theology. Concepts such as *holiness, justice, *righteousness, *salvation, *faith, and *peace are brilliantly related to the two fundamental Isaianic themes, the idea of God as "the Holy One of Israel" and the centrality of the city of Jerusalem, which are epitomized in some of the most familiar biblical images and visions. Holiness, perhaps the most distinctive of these concepts, is expressed not only in the recurring epithet "Holy One of Israel" but also in the prophet's vision of God "in the year that King Uzziah died" (6.1–3). Holiness refers first to the transcendent majesty of the king of the universe, creator of all things (6.3; 40.12–23) and Lord of history (10.5–7; 45.1–7). But in Isaiah it has an ethical dimension too: the Holy One condemns moral uncleanness (6.5–7) and the holy city will be characterized by justice and peace (11.6–9; 56.1–8). Ritual *purity and cultic practices are not enough in themselves; indeed, they are savagely condemned if they take the place of social justice (1.11–17; 58) or humility (66.1–4). The Temple plays only a minor role in the visions of a new Jerusalem

(1.21–26; 2.2–4; 4.2–6; 26.1–6; 49.16–21; 65.17–25), and in those passages where it is mentioned, the emphasis is on opening its doors to foreigners (56.3–8) and to the nations of the world (2.2–4; 66.18–21).

Many of the most elaborate visions of a new age focus on an individual savior figure, champion of justice and righteousness. In some he is explicitly identified as a king from the royal lineage of David (9.2–7; 11.1–5), and this is no doubt implied in others (32.1–2; 42.1–4; cf. 55.3). In the context of the Babylonian exile, *Cyrus is hailed as the Lord's anointed (45.1–7; cf. 41.2–3), and in one passage the savior figure is represented as a prophet, anointed to "bring good news to the oppressed" (61.1–4; cf. Luke 4.18–19). This prophetic model seems to underlie two others, in which he is described as "the servant of the Lord" (49.1–6; 50.4–9), though in both these cases the story of the "servant" may be understood to refer to the experience of Israel rather than any individual (cf. 49.3).

Finally, there is the celebrated "suffering servant" passage, which seems to tell the story of an individual who heals and redeems by vicarious suffering (52.13–53.12). At one time considered the last of four autonomous "servant songs" (42.1–4; 49.1–6; 50.4–9; 52.13–53.12), it is rather to be understood as an independent hymn of thanksgiving expressing the people's confidence in the power of God to intervene on their behalf, to heal their wounds, and to forgive their sins. There is no answer to the question of who the servant is or how he achieves this. The emphasis, here as elsewhere in the Isaianic tradition (1.21–26; 9.2–7; 35; 41.14–16; 49.14–26; 52.1–2), is on a transformation from humiliation to exaltation, defeat to victory. If it reflects the release of Jehoiachin from prison in Babylon in 660 BCE (2 Kings 25.27–30; Jer. 52.31–34), or the unexpected military successes of Cyrus that eventually led to the fall of Babylon in 538 BCE; it also draws on traditional religious ideas, such as the scapegoat ritual on the Day of Atonement (53.4, 6, 12; cf. Lev. 16.20–22; *see* Azazel) and the figure of *Moses, the "servant of the Lord" (Deut. 34.5; Josh. 1.1, 2, 13; etc.), who offered to die for his people (53.7–9, 12; cf. Exod. 32.32). The *Exodus and *wilderness motifs are prominent throughout these chapters (e.g., 43.15–21; 48.20–21; 51.9–11; 52.11–12; 55.12–13).

Influence. The book of Isaiah has played a central role in Christian liturgy and theology. It is sometimes called the "Fifth Gospel" because, in the words of Jerome, Isaiah recounts the life of the *Messiah in such a way as to make one think he is "telling the story of what has already happened rather than what is still to come." Isaiah is more often quoted in the New Testament than is any other book of the Hebrew Bible apart from Psalms, and has provided the church with much of its most familiar language and imagery, including the ox and the ass (1.3), the *Sanctus* (6.3), the Immanuel prophecy (7.14), the key of David (22.22), the suffering Messiah (53), the winepress (63.3), and the New Jerusalem (65.18). The popularity of the Jesse tree motif (11.1) in Christian art, and of Handel's *Messiah* (largely based on excerpts from chaps. 7; 9; 34; 40; 52; 53; 60) have further extended the influence of Isaiah on western culture. Since the Second Vatican Council (1962–1965), which quotes 2.4 and 32.17 in an important statement on peace and social justice (*Gaudium et spes*, para. 70), Isaiah has provided liberation theologians and feminists with many of their key scriptural texts.

Isaiah is prominent in synagogue *lectionaries, and has made a profound and distinctive impression on Jewish literary and religious tradition, in particular its Zion-centered visions of justice and peace (e.g., 2.2–4; 11.6–9).

JOHN F. A. SAWYER

Ishmael. Son of *Abraham and *Hagar. A generally positive attitude toward Ishmael and thus toward his descendants is found in the Genesis traditions. He is the recipient of a special divine blessing (Gen 17.20) and is present at the burial of Abraham (25.9). Like Jacob, Ishmael is the father of twelve sons, the ancestors of twelve tribes (Gen 25.16). Another indication of the generally favorable view of this patriarch is the fact that several other later Israelites have the same name. There are, however, hints of ethnic tension in the narratives as well. Like *Cain, Ishmael is depicted as an outcast and prone to violence (Gen. 16.12), and as a wanderer (note the opening words of Melville's *Moby-Dick*). The Ishmaelites are elsewhere described as leading a typically *nomadic life (Gen. 37.25; Ps. 83.6; 1 Chron. 27.30). The story of Ishmael and Hagar's separation from Abraham's household contains the kind of scurrilous sexual innuendo found elsewhere in *J's etiological narratives concerning Israel's neighbors.

In Muslim tradition, the *Arabs trace their ancestry back to Abraham through Ishmael. Because Ishmael was circumcised (Gen. 17.25), so

are most Muslims. And, analogous to Paul's reversal of the figures of *Isaac and Ishmael (Gal. 4.24–26), Muslim tradition makes Ishmael rather than Isaac the son Abraham was commanded to sacrifice (*see* Aqedah).   MICHAEL D. COOGAN

Israel. The name Israel ("he contended with God") is conferred on *Jacob by a divine messenger after their struggle at the Wadi Jabbok (Gen. 32.28; 35.10; Hos. 12.3). The twelve sons of Jacob and their tribal descendants are therefore called "the sons of Israel" (the Israelites; *see* Tribes of Israel). The earliest nonbiblical reference to Israel occurs on the inscription of Merneptah, king of Egypt (ca. 1200 BCE).

Israel remains the normal designation for the entire nation until the division of the kingdom in 924 BCE (1 Kings 12.1–20). Biblical authors term the ten northern tribes (i.e., the northern kingdom) Israel and the two southern tribes (i.e., the southern kingdom) Judah. Hence, after the northern kingdom falls (722 BCE) and only Judah remains, its residents are called Judahites or Judeans. (*See* Israel, History of; Judah, The Kingdom of.)

In the postexilic period the residents of Judah or Yehud are regularly called *Jews, but Israel is also used. In postexilic writings (e.g., Chronicles) the term Israel can therefore denote Jacob, the united kingdom, the northern kingdom, Judah, or simply the descendants of Israel. In some cases, the meaning of Israel is, however, deliberately more restrictive (e.g., the returning exiles in Ezra 2.2, 70).

In rabbinic literature Israel refers to the Jewish people, and the land of Israel describes the country of the Israelite people. In the New Testament Israel can refer to the Jewish people (2 Cor. 3.12; Rom. 11.26) or to the church (Gal. 6.16).   GARY N. KNOPPERS

Israel, History of.
   The Biblical Story of Israel. Genesis 32.28 reports God's words to Jacob: "You shall no longer be called Jacob, but Israel, for you have striven with God and with humans, and have prevailed." As the biblical narrative continues, one reads that *Jacob/Israel immigrated with his family to *Egypt where, during a long sojourn, his twelve sons fathered twelve *tribes. Eventually, these twelve "Israelite" tribes were led out of Egypt by *Moses, wandered for forty years in the *wilderness, and finally reached the plains of *Moab east of the *Jordan River. At that point

in the biblical narrative, *Joshua succeeded Moses and led the tribes across the Jordan into *Canaan, where they took possession of the land and divided it among themselves. The book of *Judges finds the tribes settled in Canaan following Joshua's death, without stable leadership and often oppressed by surrounding peoples. "In those days there was no king in Israel; all the people did what was right in their own eyes" (Judg. 17.6).

In the time of the prophet *Samuel, when the *Philistines were oppressing Israel, the people cried out to Samuel to give them a king. Against his better judgment, Samuel accommodated their desire by anointing *Saul to be the first king of Israel. Thus Saul, followed by *David and then *Solomon, ruled over a kingdom that consisted primarily of the twelve Israelite tribes with their respective territories. When Solomon died, this Israelite monarchy split into two rival kingdoms—a northern kingdom, composed of ten tribes, which kept the name Israel, and a southern kingdom, composed of the two remaining tribes, *Judah and *Benjamin, which took the name Judah. These two kingdoms existed side-by-side for two centuries, sometimes at war with each other, sometimes at peace, until the northern kingdom was conquered by *Assyria and its territory annexed by that great empire (722 BCE). Judah also fell under Assyrian domination, but it maintained its political identity for almost a century and a half, until it fell to the *Babylonians (587/586 BCE).

Hopes of national recovery remained alive during the long years of Assyrian and Babylonian domination, however, and continued in the Jewish community (the remnant of the kingdom of Judah) that struggled for survival under *Persian rule. These hopes are expressed in the prophetical books of the Hebrew Bible. Moreover, the hope was not just for recovery of Judah but for a united Israel as it had existed in the "golden age" of David and Solomon.

Thus, the biblical writers use the name Israel in different ways. It can refer to the patriarch Jacob (Gen. 35.21–22; 43.6–11); to the twelve tribes (constantly referred to as "the children of Israel" in the books Exodus through Judges); to the early united monarchy ruled over by Saul, David, and Solomon (1 Sam. 13.1; 14.47–48; 2 Sam. 8.15; 1 Kings 4.1; etc.); to the northern kingdom after the split of the united monarchy (1 Kings 14.19; 15.25; 2 Kings 17.21–23); or to the restored nation hoped for in the future (Amos 9.13–15; Zeph. 3.14–20).

Historical Uncertainties and Extrabiblical Sources. The biblical story of Israel, when examined in detail, presents numerous internal inconsistencies—for example, the several enumerations of the Israelite tribes do not always identify the same twelve (compare Gen. 49; Num. 1.20–43; 26.5–50; Deut. 33), nor do they take into account other important tribal groups such as the Calebites and Kenizzites. Moreover, the story presupposes concepts that were generally accepted in ancient times but not today, such as the idea that each of the world's nations descended from a single individual (see Gen. 10).

An Egyptian inscription from the reign of Pharaoh Merneptah (ca. 1200 BCE) provides the earliest known nonbiblical reference to Israel, and the only such reference earlier than the ninth century BCE. The Merneptah inscription is a royal monumental text inscribed on a stele discovered at the site of ancient Thebes. Unfortunately, we learn no more from it regarding Israel than that a people known by that name was on the scene in Palestine by the end of the thirteenth century. Later texts from the ninth century are also royal inscriptions, one commissioned by King Mesha of Moab (see 2 Kings 3 and *Moabite Stone), and several others from the reign of an Assyrian king, Shalmaneser III (858–824 BCE). Israel and Judah were separate kingdoms by the ninth century, and it is Israel that figures in these texts. Mesha reports that King Omri of Israel had "humbled" Moab and claims recovery of Moabite independence among the accomplishments of his own reign. Shalmaneser reports a series of military campaigns into Syria-Palestine and mentions in that context two Israelite kings, *Ahab and *Jehu. Occasional references to Israelite and Judean kings appear in later Assyrian and Babylonian documents, usually in the context of military campaign reports. These references in extrabiblical documents are especially useful for establishing a chronological framework for the Israelite and Judean kings and for correlating biblical history with international affairs.

*Archaeological excavations at Palestinian sites provide information about the material culture of biblical times and also allow for some correlations. For example, the time of the "judges" in Israel would seem to correspond roughly to the opening centuries of the Iron Age (ca. 1200–1000 BCE), which was a period of transition and change in Palestine. Many of the old cities that had flourished during the Bronze Age, especially in the lowlands, were destroyed. Most of them were rebuilt but on a much smaller scale. At the same time, there was a marked increase in the number of small village settlements in areas such as the central hill country, which seem to have been only sparsely populated during the Bronze Age. Note that most of the stories of the book of Judges have their setting among the villages in the north-central (Ephraimite) hill country. (*See* Conquest of Canaan.)

The writer of 2 Kings 9.10–14 credits Solomon with building (or fortifying) several cities including *Hazor, *Megiddo, and *Gezer. Excavations at all three of these places have unearthed remains of buildings and fortifications that date from approximately 1000 BCE; their relatively impressive scale is suggestive of royal architecture, and for this reason archaeologists generally associate them with Solomon. A somewhat more impressive royal building program from approximately the ninth century seems to be indicated by the ruins at Hazor, Megiddo, and *Samaria. This second building program generally is associated with the Omride rulers of Israel, particularly Omri and Ahab. Remains from later phases of the cities and villages of Israel and Judah show a marked decline in material wealth, many of them ending finally with destruction in approximately the seventh and early sixth centuries BCE. No doubt these later phases correspond to the years of foreign domination by the Syrians, Assyrians, and *Babylonians.

Contemporary Views Regarding the History of Israel. Given the uncertainties that arise from the biblical story, the paucity of references to Israel or Israelites in extrabiblical documents, and the very generalized nature of evidence from artifacts, it is not surprising that present-day scholars hold widely divergent views concerning Israel's history. At one extreme are those who hold that the biblical story is an essentially accurate portrayal of Israel's past; at the other are those who see the Bible as a virtually useless source for historical information and regard it as futile even to speculate on the details of Israelite history. Most biblical scholars and ancient historians hold a moderate position between these two extremes. There seems to be a growing consensus, for example, on the following points.

Nothing can be said with certainty about the origin of the various tribes and clans that composed early Israel and Judah. For the most part, these tribal groupings probably emerged gradually from the diffuse population of Late Bronze and early Iron Age Palestine rather than having entered the land from elsewhere. The name Israel probably referred in premonarchic times primarily to the tribe of *Ephraim, settled in the north-central hill country, but would have been understood to include certain surrounding tribes (such as Benjamin, *Manasseh, and Gilead) that Ephraim dominated. This Ephraim/Israel tribal group would have been the Israel to which the Merneptah inscription refers; most of the stories in the book of Judges have to do with this tribal group; and it was the core of Saul's kingdom, which he appropriately called Israel.

One should not think of Saul's Israel as a highly organized kingdom with precisely defined boundaries. Moreover, loyalty to him probably varied from region to region, with Saul's strongest base of support being the Ephraim-Benjamin-Gilead-Manasseh zone. There is nothing to suggest that the Galilean tribes were part of his kingdom. His campaign against the *Amalekites (1 Sam. 15) implies thoroughfare through Judahite territory. Saul also received some Judean support in his attempts to arrest David (1 Sam. 23.12–13; 26.1–5). This, however, does not necessarily mean that he exercised any sort of permanent control over Judah. In Judah, as in other peripheral areas, Saul's authority probably lasted only as long as he was present with his troops or the local people needed his protection against some other threat.

The battle of Gilboa, in which Saul and Jonathan were killed, left the kingdom on the verge of collapse (1 Sam. 31.1–7). A surviving son (Ishbaal [Ishbosheth]) claimed the throne but transferred his residency to Mahanaim in Transjordan and soon was assassinated (2 Sam 2.8–10; 4.1–3). Thereupon the elders of Israel went to David, who in the meantime had established a kingdom in the south-central "Judean" hill country, and recognized him as their ruler also (2 Sam. 2.1–4; 5.1–3). Later David would make *Jerusalem his capital and expand his realm to include much of Palestine (2 Sam. 5.6–10; 8).

Thus, the Davidic-Solomonic monarchy was not exactly continuous with Saul's Israel. Moreover, the Israelites appear to have maintained their separate identity under David and Solomon—for example, there was some rivalry between the Israelites and the Judahites (2 Sam. 19.41–43), as well as ongoing opposition to Davidic rule. The Israelites played a central role in both *Absalom's and Sheba's rebellions against David (2 Sam. 15–20); Solomon subjected them to forced labor in connection with his royal building projects (1 Kings 11.28); and when Solomon died they rebelled again, this time successfully (1 Kings 12.1–20). Thus was established the northern Israelite kingdom, which the biblical writers depict as a rebel and apostate state, but which the rebels themselves no doubt regarded as a restoration of pre-Davidic Israel. At the core of the rebel (or restored) kingdom was the old Ephraim/Israel tribal area, but it included additional territories (e.g., Jezreel and *Galilee) and cities (e.g., *Shechem) that had been annexed by David. The small tribal area of Benjamin became a disputed frontier between the rival kingdoms of Israel and Judah.

The northern kingdom of Israel lasted approximately two centuries (ca. 924–722 BCE), which may be divided into four phases.

Unstable beginnings (ca. 924–885). Separation left both Israel and Judah weak, while mutual warfare drained their strength even further. Moreover, Israel suffered dynastic instability that resulted finally in civil war. (See especially 1 Kings 15.25–16.22.)

The Omride dynasty (ca. 885–843). Omri, who emerged victorious from the civil war, founded a dynasty that continued through four kings. Under Omri and his son *Ahab, Israel enjoyed a period of international prestige and internal prosperity that may have surpassed that of Solomon's day. Israel clearly overshadowed and probably dominated Judah during this period. Omri built a new capital for the kingdom, which he named *Samaria. The Omride period was remembered, however, as a time of economic and social injustice, and of conflict between Baalism and Yahwism. *Elijah and *Jezebel were colorful characters of the Omride era. (See especially 1 Kings 15.21–2 Kings 10.27.)

The Jehu dynasty (ca. 843–745). Simultaneous and related palace coups brought a new ruler to the thrones of both Israel and Judah in approximately 843 BCE. *Jehu, who seized power in Israel under the banner of Yahwism, founded a dynasty that lasted approximately a century. *Damascus, however, was already on the rise when Jehu seized the throne, and it totally dominated Israel during the reigns of Jehu and his son, Jehoahaz. Damascus, faced with problems from the direction of Assyria, eventually lost its hold on Israel, and Israel in turn enjoyed a brief period of recovery and prosperity. The moment of prosperity is to be associated especially with the reign of Jeroboam II. The *Elisha stories reflect the difficult times experienced by the people of Israel during the early years of the Jehu dynasty, the years of Syrian domination. The book of Amos reflects the situation during the later years, when Israel is enjoying a recovery of prosperity, and implies that the problems of economic and social injustice remained. Zechariah, son of Jeroboam II, was assassinated soon after coming to the throne in approximately 745 BCE, and *Tiglath-pileser III ascended the Assyrian throne the following year. Israel's end was near. (See especially 2 Kings 9–10; 12.17–13.25; 14.23–29; 15.8–12.)

Assyrian conquest and annexation (745–722). Already during the Omride era, Assyrian kings had threatened the little kingdoms of Syria-Palestine in general and Israel in particular. Now Assyria turned its attention to the west and, under *Tiglath-pileser III (744–727), secured a firm grip on the whole region. Israel, which offered some resistance at first in coordination with Damascus, was reduced to vassal status and Hoshea confirmed as king. After Tiglath-pileser's death, however, Hoshea attempted to throw off the Assyrian yoke. This was a disastrous move: Assyria conquered Samaria, annexed the kingdom's territory, exiled thousands of its leading citizens, and replaced them with foreigners from other conquered lands. (See especially 2 Kings 15.13–31; 17.)

The remnants of the kingdom of Israel usually are referred to in later literature as *Samaritans, after the name of the kingdom's chief city founded by Omri (e.g., Luke 9.52; 10.29–41; John 4.1–42). A small group of Samaritans still survives in the vicinity of Nablus.

(*For a chronological table of the Kings of Israel and Judah, see* Judah, The Kingdom of.)

J. MAXWELL MILLER

Israel, Religion of.

Ancient Israel and Its Ancient Near Eastern Setting. Scholarship on ancient Israelite religion seems to swing back and forth, as if attached to a great pendulum, between those who advocate the uniqueness of the biblical revelation (the "biblical theology" approach) and those who assert that ancient Israelite religion is cut from the same cloth as other ancient Near Eastern religions (the "history of religions" approach). Much of the swing toward the latter was occasioned by archaeological discoveries that correlate the Bible and its ancient Near Eastern setting.

Most scholars of ancient Israelite religion argue that we should no longer refer to the Bible *and* the ancient Near East, as if the former were not a part of the latter. By affirming Israel's cultural and material solidarity with its neighbors, scholars have underscored that the study of ancient Israelite religion must be anchored in its historical ancient Near Eastern moorings. This need not prevent us from affirming that ancient Israel developed uniquely; by definition, all societies form cultural configurations that are distinct. The belief system that emerged from ancient Israel, especially in its conception of the divine, was indeed radical in its context.

The Formative Period. Scholars have been able to document the Canaanite heritage of ancient Israelite religion. Ancestral religion, for example, with its worship of El (as exemplified by titles found in Genesis such as El Shadday, El Elyon, El Bethel, and El, the God of Israel), is directly related to the Canaanite deity El described in the *Ugaritic texts.

Yet scholars have found it more difficult to describe the underlying reasons that led Israel to come up with a configuration of beliefs, such as *monotheism and the absence of divine sex and death, that was radical in its West Semitic Canaanite context. A closely related debate is the date assigned to the formative period for these beliefs. Scholars such as Julius Wellhausen reconstructed an evolutionary process whereby a gradual progression from polytheism and then henotheism eventually led to the "ethical monotheism" of the prophets of the eighth century BCE and later. Others, such as W. F. Albright and Yehezkel Kaufmann, argued for an early crystallization of revolutionary beliefs such as monotheism during the time of *Moses. Such debates have continued and always involve various theories on the settlement of Palestine and the archaeological evidence for the transition from the Late Bronze to the Iron Age (*see* Conquest of Canaan).

Nature and Scope. Past treatments of ancient Israelite religion were excessively narrow, treating only the "orthodox" religion described by the majority of biblical texts. While the biblical Yahwism that eventually emerged as normative takes center stage for most people, today emphasis is also placed on religious conceptions that were very much a part of ancient Israelite society yet were eventually seen as nonnormative (e.g., Asherah, cults of the dead; see below). In other words, scholars now argue that Israelite religion must be studied from its earliest times to its latest. One should not opt for late Israelite religion (e.g., Deuteronomic or prophetic) while ignoring early forms, even if it seems that the religion of the early period cannot be easily divorced from Canaanite religion.

Sources. The Hebrew Bible is the most important document for studying ancient Israelite religion, yet it has its limitations. It must be understood as collections selected and edited according to certain criteria (e.g., Judean ideology, Deuteronomic theology). Yet this is hardly different from most other ancient Near Eastern texts or even modern literature in which writers selectively edit their material.

Current scholarship runs the full spectrum from pessimism to optimism about our ability to uncover early Israelite religion. Some scholars emphasize that the majority of texts stem from later times and are more or less useless for reconstructing the earlier stages. Others, such as Albright, Frank Moore Cross, David Noel Freedman, and Johannes C. de Moor, argue that some texts, primarily poetic ones, do contain material from the earliest periods of ancient Israel's existence. All scholars face an array of questions when working with material that has an overlay of late editing. To what degree can we unearth the earlier stages of the religion? Can we uncover nonorthodox viewpoints? Does later editing, even later reworking of material, obscure every trace of early beliefs or practices that might have been more at home in the family worship than in the cult which became normative?

*Archaeology provides windows into the diversity of ancient Israelite religion. It uncovers physical remains of temples and various cult paraphernalia regardless of whether such sanctuaries and cultic objects were considered legitimate or apostate. Household shrines, foundations deposits, funeral offerings, and *burials provide new dates on which to reconstruct practices characteristic of family worship and thus outside the scope of most biblical writers. Inscriptional evidence gives us empirical data (such as theophoric elements in personal names) free from the heavy editing of most literary works. But archaeology also has its limitations, such as a simple lack of evidence. At times the extant material remains can be just as restrictive as the biblical texts. The interpretation of the evidence is also subjective and sometimes even dogmatic. But archaeology's biggest shortcoming for reconstructing religion is that it is hard-pressed to comment on underlying causes and ideologies such as monotheism.

It has been widely assumed that a great deal can be learned about a religion by looking at theophoric elements (divine names or titles) in personal *names, for the ancients often gave their children names reflecting the deity or deities whom they worshiped. Yet because of social convention, personal names do not necessarily provide full and accurate evidence of explicit religious devotion. Even polytheists such as *Ahab, *Jezebel, and Athaliah could give their children Yahwistic names. One should ask to what degree this might have been a widespread practice among polytheists who for some reason (e.g., political motivation, fear of repression) adopted the name of the national deity yet in practice worshiped other deities. The absence of naming after goddesses, especially that of *Asherah, has been considered significant. Yet at ancient Ugarit there was a vibrant cult dedicated to Asherah but only one attestation of her name as the theophoric element in a personal name.

Key Concepts. *Monotheism.* The Israelite deity goes by the names of El/Elohim (a common Semitic noun for "god") and Yahweh. There is universal agreement that Yahweh is derived from the verb "to be," but scholars differ over whether the verb underlying the name is noncausative (see Exod. 3.14) or causative, "the one who causes to come into being," that is, a reference to the deity's role as creator; the latter seems preferable. (*See also* Names of God in the Hebrew Bible.) Scholars emphasizing the Canaanite heritage also draw parallels between Israelite El/Elohim and Yahweh and the Amorite/Canaanite deities El and *Baal. A correlative issue is the relation of the names Elohim and Yahweh and their connection to the "god of the fathers" of Israelite ancestral tradition. Some, such as Cross, see in Yahweh an original epithet of the ancestral deity El ("El, who causes the heavenly hosts to come into being"). Others, such as de Moor, have argued for Yahweh-El as a south Canaanite form of the gods of the fathers.

Tracing the development of monotheism in ancient Israel is a complex endeavor with little consensus among scholars. One can easily find an advocate for placing the origin of monotheism in every age from the ancestral down to the exilic. Often one's views of monotheism are tied to equally difficult issues, such as the historicity of the *ancestors, the person of Moses, the makeup of the tribal league, kinship relations, the settlement of the land of Israel, and the social function of the *prophets.

In the early period there are clear indications of henotheism or monolatry, the worship of a single deity though recognizing the existence of others. Ancestral religion with its focus on the worship of El seems to point to a monolatrous

El cult. Other texts emphasize the presence of other deities. In Psalm 29 we read of the beckoning of the gods to praise Yahweh, and Psalm 82 represents Yahweh judging the gods (cf. Gen 1.26; 6.2; Exod. 12.12; 15.11; Deut. 32.8–9; Josh 24.15; *see also* Sons of God).

Recently scholars have emphasized the role of the monarchy in the development of nationalistic exclusivity and corresponding monolatrous tendencies. Baruch Halpern sees in *Josiah's reform a "self-conscious monotheism" (*see* Kingship and Monarchy). Further examples of explicit monotheism can be found in relatively late texts. Thus, Jeremiah no longer describes other deities as options but rather as "cracked cisterns that can hold no water" (Jer. 2.13). Explicit monotheism finds its most articulate voice in Second Isaiah: "I am Yahweh, and there is no other; besides me there is no god" (Isa. 45.5).

The goddess Asherah. The goddess *Asherah has always been known in the Bible through curious references to some type of cult object usually translated as "asherah pole." Some scholars see hints of her in Genesis 49.25 and Amos 8.14, but these verses are textually very difficult. The absence of any destruction of the prophets of Asherah in the *Elijah narrative is intriguing. Similarly, *Jehu destroys the Baal from Israel, yet no mention is made of Asherah (2 Kings 10.18–28; cf. 13.6).

Recently, the goddess and her possible roles have been studied intensively, owing to the discovery of enigmatic inscriptions referring to "Yahweh and his/its(?) Asherah/asherah" at Kuntillet Ajrud and Khirbet el-Qom. As a result some scholars have concluded that Asherah was worshiped in ancient Israel as the consort of Yahweh. But others have argued for an understanding of the word "asherah" as a symbol within the cult of Yahweh rather than a reference to the goddess herself.

Asherah/asherah was certainly present in monarchic Israel. But ancient Israelite society was more pluralistic than we usually assume. There were probably numerous differing viewpoints, many at odds with each other, and they most likely differed from city to city. The asherah symbol in its origin is not easily divorced from the goddess Asherah. Different groups may had differing degrees of toleration when someone mentioned "Yahweh and his asherah." Some may have believed Yahweh to be the national deity, yet had no problem in worshiping local Asherah deities, especially in cults dealing with fertility and agriculture. Other circles freely appropriated mythic imagery apart from mythic content, and thus for them the symbol was a legitimate part of Yahwistic religion. For yet others, such as certain prophetic groups and the Deuteronomist, who argued for exclusive worship of Yahweh, any hint of the goddess deserved condemnation.

The break with ancient Near Eastern myth. Some scholars of Israelite religion, such as Yehezkel Kaufmann and Michael Fishbane, have been struck by the Bible's break with ancient Near Eastern mythical consciousness. This new paradigm was characterized by a "creator-creature distinction" in which an autonomous God is portrayed a distinct from the created world. In addition, sex and death are conspicuously absent when the biblical god is depicted, in contrast to the prevalence of these motifs in other ancient Near Eastern literatures. Admitting henotheism in the early period, one must still recognize that the deity of the Hebrew Bible is not part of a pantheon and is not described as having any sexual relations with any consort, nor does he impregnate animals as does Baal in one of the Ugaritic texts. He is not a "dying and rising god" like Canaanite Baal or Egyptian Osiris. The biblical deity does not imbibe, unlike Canaanite El, described in another text as a pathetic drunkard. In short, the divine is portrayed more transcendently; God is not dependent on any outside power. (*See also* Myth.)

The development of this new paradigm was part of a process whereby Israelite religion emerged from its Canaanite context and changed from polytheism to monolatry and eventually to monotheism. From all indications this differentiation appeared quite early, although this is not to say that mythic imagery, especially with regard to fertility and *death, does not permeate the Bible, as Marvin Pope has shown.

The aniconic tradition. The novelty of the absence of divine iconography in Israelite religion was not lost even on the ancients. The Roman historian Tacitus thought it bizarre that the Jews would prohibit portrayal of the divine. Modern scholars have a better footing to debate the question thanks to archaeological evidence. In addition to the biblical description of Yahweh invisibly enthroned on the *cherubim (Exod. 25.22; Ps. 80.1), scholars have also looked to data such as an incense stand from Taanach as a depiction of an unseen deity. The most relevant archaeological material is the plethora of bronze and terra cotta figurines depicting Canaanite deities. In light of these, it is remarkable how few material remains exist that document the physical portrayal of Yahweh.

The scholarly debate over the origin of the aniconic tradition goes hand in hand with the debate over the origin of monotheism. Tryvge N. D. Mettinger has noted that the theology associated with the *ark of the covenant was centered on an aniconic deity. Yet he argues that the polemic against images did not reach its full force until the prophet Hosea. Ronald S. Hendel has underscored the role of divine iconography in legitimating royalty throughout the ancient Near East, and thus he traces the origin of the aniconic tradition in Israel back to the bias against kingship.

God versus the dragon and the sea. Some of the clearest examples of mythic imagery in the Bible are the descriptions of God battling a personified sea as well as a dragonlike creature called *Leviathan and *Rahab. Cross has stressed that God's battle with Leviathan, Sea, and Death (see Isa. 25.8) are alloforms of one basic cosmogonic myth in which the Divine Warrior is victorious over the forces of *chaos, found for example in Mesopotamian (Marduk vs. Tiamat) and Canaanite (Baal and Anat vs. Sea, Lotan, and Mot) mythologies. In Psalm 74.13–14 God crushes the heads of Leviathan, a close parallel to the seven-headed dragon creature of the same name known from Ugaritic. Chaos imagery is applied to historical forces (often Egypt), which Yahweh defeats in like manner (Isa. 30.7; Ezek. 29.3–5; 32.2–8; Exod. 15), and is often projected into future eschatological battles. Isaiah 27.1 describes such a battle in which Yahweh will destroy the twisting serpent Leviathan with his mighty sword. The longevity of the theme can be seen in the account in Revelation 12–13 of the defeat of the seven-headed dragon and the seven-headed beast.

The cult and abode of the dead. The biblical idioms for death, "being gathered to one's kin" and "sleeping with one's fathers," underscore the clan solidarity within ancient Israel. Nevertheless, the Yahwism that emerged as normative condemned the worship of the deceased and any form of necromancy (Lev. 19.26–32; 20.6, 27; Deut. 14.1; 18.10–11; 26.14). On the other hand, the Hebrew Bible also gives witness to the practice of certain death rituals. Note especially 1 Samuel 28, where *Saul has a necromancer conjure the dead *Samuel from the grave; the

Deuteronomic historian used this well-known tale to underscore the demise of Saul, yet he left the efficacy of the practice intact. (*See also* Witch.)

Various Hebrew terms are used, often in parallelism, to describe the abode of the dead, including Sheol, Death, and two words meaning "the Pit." Both Sheol and Death are also used for the personified chthonic power behind death (cf. the Ugaritic god Mot, whose name means "Death"). As a location, Sheol is described as the lowest place imaginable (Deut. 32.22; Isa. 7.11), often in contrast with the highest heavens (Amos 9.2; Ps. 139.8; Job 11.8). Sheol is frequently associated with water images (Jon. 2.3–6), often echoing the stories of divine combat. The gates of the underworld frequently mentioned in Egyptian and Mesopotamian accounts are also found in the Bible (Isa. 38.10; Ps. 9.13; 107.18; Job 38.17; cf. Wisd. of Sol. 16.13; Matt. 16.18). Thus Sheol is a place of imprisonment from which one cannot escape (Job 7.9). The personification of Sheol and Death can be seen in descriptions of their insatiable appetites (Isa. 5.14; Hab. 2.5; Prov. 27.20; 30.15b–16), remarkably reminiscent of the Canaanite deity Mot's voracious appetite. (*See also* Afterlife and Immortality; Hell.)

Conclusion. Many scholars have looked to the premonarchic league period to find the origins of ancient Israel's unique configuration, and have produced an array of hypotheses dependent on their views of the conquest/settlement of ancient Israel. Recently archaeologists have reemphasized the indigenous nature of early Israel; yet outside influences certainly played a substantial role. Thus, many look for the key to unlock Israel's radical configuration in the early league (Cross), Mosaic (Freedman), or even pre-Mosaic (de Moor) periods. It will remain difficult, however, to illuminate the social and political background of this period given the paucity of textual and material evidence and the fact that the texts we do have may not constitute plausible historical witnesses.

Ancient Israelite religion encompasses the full spectrum of religious belief and practice, and in addition to the cross-references given above, the reader should look to specialized entries such as the following for a more complete picture: Altars; Apocalyptic Literature; Astarte; Circumcision; Covenant; Creation; Demons; Dreams; Ephod; Eschatology; Feasts and Festival; Graven Image; Heaven; Hell; High Place; Idols, Idolatry; Kingship and Monarchy; Magic and Divination; Mourning; Nephilim; Passover; Prayer(s); Priests and High Priest; Prophets; Queen of Heaven; Rephaim; Righteousness; Sabbath; Sacrifice; Satan; Seraph, Seraphim; Sin; Tammuz; Temple; Teraphim; Theophany; Tribes of Israel; Urim and Thummim; Women, *article on* Women in the Ancient Near East and Israel.

THEODORE J. LEWIS

Issachar. A son of *Leah and *Jacob and one of the twelve *tribes of Israel. The name combines Hebrew words for "man" and "wages"; hence Leah's exclamation "God has given me my hire" (Gen. 30.18). The territory allotted to Issachar (Josh. 17.10; 19.17–23) lies in the plain of Jezreel (Map 3:X3). References to Issachar suggest close associations between it and *Zebulun (Gen. 49.13–14; Deut. 33.18). Issachar, the probable home of *Deborah, played an essential role in her campaign against Sisera (Judg. 5.15). The territory of Issachar was conquered by the *Assyrians in 732 BCE.   GARY N. KNOPPERS

Italics. Aldus Manutius (1450–1515), the famous Venetian printer, startled literate Europe in 1501 by publishing the writings of Virgil in a new font of type, characterized by sloping letters somewhat resembling handwriting. That new font of type was called *italic*, after the ancient name of Italy. As time went on it was discovered that the new typeface was not as easy to read as roman type; hence italic is not used today for the major text of a document but is reserved for specialized uses, such as the titles of books and magazines, foreign words and phrases, scientific names of genera and species, the names of plaintiff and defendant in legal citations, and, most commonly, to point out words that demand special emphasis. None of these uses, however, accounts for the presence of italics in the text of Bibles.

Sebastian Münster (1489–1552), who devoted his lifetime to the study of Hebrew and who produced over forty books, issued the first edition of the Hebrew Bible with a fresh Latin translation. For this Latin version, Münster conceived of the novel idea of printing words not present in the original Hebrew but necessary for idiomatic Latin in small roman type so as to distinguish them from the body of the text. This idea was followed, with modifications, by Calvin's cousin Olivétan in his French Bible of 1535, by Miles Coverdale in the "Great Bible" of 1539, and in the Geneva Bible of 1557–1560, the most popular Bible of the sixteenth century, which introduced the innovation of using italic type for words supplied to complete the sense that had no equivalent in the original.

The Bishops' Bible of 1568 and the original King James Version of 1611 both resumed the use of roman type for words supplied by the revisers. But in 1612, an edition of the King James Version was printed using a small clear roman type, and italics were used for the additions. This practice became standard in subsequent editions and revisions into the twentieth century. The Revised Standard Version (1946; 1952) completely abandoned the practice of using italics for words added by translators to complete or clarify the meaning, the committee regarding such words as an essential part of the translation. Almost all other English translations of the Bible made in the twentieth century have likewise dropped this use of italics as basically misleading, since the ordinary use of italics is to show special emphasis.

See also Printing and Publishing; Translations.   WALTER F. SPECHT

J

J. The abbreviation for the Yahwist "source" in the *Pentateuch, derived from the German spelling (*Jahwe*) of the divine name Yahweh (*see* Names of God). Beginning in the eighteenth century, scholars noticed that two different names were used for the deity in the book of *Genesis, and using this as a criterion, identified separate sources or traditions or documents. As this analysis matured, the J tradition was traced in the rest of the Pentateuch (and by some in the books of Joshua and Judges and beyond), and was dated to the ninth (or perhaps the tenth) century BCE, though presumably using earlier sources. It is thought to have originated in *Jerusalem. Its characteristics include the frequent use of anthropomorphism in depictions of Yahweh (e.g., Gen. 2.7, 8, 21; 3.8, 21; 7.17b; 8.21); the theme of divine promise of land, descendants, and blessing and its fulfillment; and a focus in the ancestral narratives in Genesis on the territory later controlled by Judah. Subsequent scholars postulated the existence of multiple editions and revisions of J. More recently, several scholars have questioned much of the above analysis, particularly J's date, which has been set by some after the *exile.   MICHAEL D. COOGAN

Jacob. Son of *Isaac and *Rebekah and younger brother of *Esau. The Bible presents Jacob in a double light. On the one hand, he is the revered ancestor of the people of Israel, and indeed the name "*Israel" is said to have been given him by God after he had wrestled with God himself at Penuel (Gen. 32.28; but see also Gen. 35.10); on the other, he is a trickster, who deceives his brother into parting with his birthright (Gen. 25.29–34) and his father into giving him the blessing of the firstborn that should have belonged to Esau (Gen. 27). Hosea 12.2–6 and Isaiah 43.27 may well indicate that Jacob's acts were later regarded as sinful, although the accounts in Genesis seem to record them without censure. Jacob is presented as a pastoralist,

whereas Esau is a hunter (Gen. 25.27), and the stories about them may reflect rivalries between these two groups in later times, as with the story of *Cain and *Abel (Gen. 4.1–16); equally, they are contrasted as the ancestors respectively of Israelites and *Edomites (Gen. 32.3).

Jacob, like his father Isaac, seeks a wife in Mesopotamia (Gen. 28.1–5). On the way Jacob encamps at Bethel and there in a dream sees divine messengers ascending and descending on a staircase between earth and heaven (*see* Angels) and erects a pillar to commemorate the incident—perhaps a story to explain why Israelites worshiped at what had been a Canaanite sanctuary. Jacob the trickster is himself tricked by his uncle Laban into working fourteen years to obtain the wife he desires, *Rachel; Jacob contracts to work for seven years but at the end of that time is given *Leah, her elder sister, instead (Gen. 29.15–30). Jacob has his revenge on Laban by swindling him out of large flocks and herds (Gen. 30.25–31.21) and flees from Laban's house to return to the land of *Canaan but is finally reconciled with his uncle (Gen. 31.36–54). After the mysterious incident at Penuel there follows a reconciliation also with Esau (Gen. 33.1–16).

The remaining stories of Jacob focus on the deeds of his children, the ancestors of the twelve *tribes of Israel. Jacob appears as an old man in the story of *Joseph (Gen. 37; 39–50), where the theme of trickery recurs in the deceit by which he is robbed of his favorite son by Joseph's jealous brothers (Gen. 42.36). Eventually Jacob goes down to Egypt with his sons and dies there (Gen. 49.33), but his embalmed body (Gen. 50.2–3) is taken for burial to the land of Canaan by Joseph and his brothers (Gen 50.7–13). The blessing of Jacob (Gen. 49.2–27) is widely held to contain some of the oldest poetry in the Bible.   JOHN BARTON

Jambres. *See* Jannes and Jambres.

James. Four persons in the New Testament have the name "James" (Greek *Iakōbos*), which is one of two Greek forms of the Hebrew name Jacob (the other being the simple transliteration *Iakōb*). Since *Jacob was a revered ancestor of Israel, James was a common name among Jews in the Roman period.

James, Son of Zebedee, was a Galilean fisherman in the area of *Capernaum on the Sea of *Galilee, a partner (along with his brother *John) of *Simon Peter (Luke 5.10). He was working in the family business headed by his father when called by Jesus to be his disciple (Mark 1.19–20). James and John along with Peter formed the inner core of three among the *twelve apostles; they witnessed the raising of Jairus's daughter, were present at the transfiguration, and observed (and partially slept through) Jesus' agony in *Gethsemane.

Apparently James and John either expressed themselves explosively or expected God to bring sudden judgment on the enemies of Jesus, for they were nicknamed "Boanerges" ("sons of thunder," Mark 3.17; cf. Luke 9.51–56). Their request to sit at Jesus' right and left hand in his kingdom earned them the anger of the other apostles and a mild rebuke from Jesus (Mark 10.35–45; Matt. 20.20–28; Luke 22.24–27).

Outside the synoptic Gospels James, son of Zebedee, appears only in Acts. He was present in the upper room with the group waiting for *Pentecost (Acts 1.13). The only other reference to him in the New Testament is the cryptic note that Herod (Agrippa I) had him killed (Acts 12.2). He was thus the second recorded martyr of the church (after *Stephen) and the first of the apostolic band to die (except for *Judas Iscariot, who had been replaced as an apostle).

James, Son of Alphaeus, was a Galilean Jew and one of the *twelve (Matt. 10.3; Mark 3.18; Luke 6.15; Acts 1.13); many believe he is the same person as James the younger (Mark 15.40). The Greek term translated "the younger" can also be translated "the little," which probably gives the correct meaning (i.e., he was shorter than James, son of Zebedee). If this identification is correct, this otherwise unknown apostle had a mother named Mary who was present at the crucifixion and was a witness of the resurrection and a brother Joseph (or Joses) who was probably a well-known early Christian (Matt. 27.56; Mark 16.1; Luke 24.10).

James, Father (KJV "brother") of the Apostle Judas (not Iscariot), is mentioned only by Luke (Luke 6.16; Acts 1.13). Nothing further is known about him.

James, Brother of Jesus, is named in Matthew 13.55 and Mark 6.3 along with three other brothers of Jesus (*see* Brothers and Sisters of Jesus). The Gospels indicate that neither James nor his brothers were followers of Jesus before the *crucifixion (Mark 3.21, 1–35; Luke 8.19–20; Matt. 12–46–50; John 7.1–9). After the *Resurrection, however, these same brothers are mentioned among the group of believers at prayer before *Pentecost (Acts 1.14). *Paul explains the reason for this change of heart (at least in James) in the statement that the risen Jesus had appeared personally to James (1 Cor. 15.7). James apparently rose quickly in the ranks of the church. In Acts 15.13 it is James, not Peter, who is named as the preeminent leader who summed up the deliberations of the council at Jerusalem (49 or 50 CE; *see* Apostolic Council). Thus, he is viewed as the person who presided over the compromise that allowed Jewish and gentile Christians to remain unified without either forcing *gentiles to become Jews or violating Jewish cultural sensibilities (see also Acts 21.18–26).

In his letter to the *Galatians (2.9), Paul mentions James along with Peter and John, son of Zebedee, as "acknowledged pillars" of the church at Jerusalem. James's authority appears clearly in Galatians 2.12, for emissaries from Jerusalem are said to come "from James" and apparently therefore had authority as his official representatives. Scholars are divided over whether the effort of the emissaries to split Jewish from gentile congregations was James's position (in which case Paul and Acts give differing pictures of James) or whether he had sent them for some other purpose.

James's leadership was well enough known so that the letter of James (*see next entry*) is attributed to him with a simple "James, a servant of God and of the Lord Jesus Christ" (James 1.1), and the author of the letter of *Jude identifies himself as "Jude, a servant of Jesus Christ and brother of James" (Jude 1). While the attribution of both these letters is debated, there is reason to believe that at least the material in the letter of James, if not the writing itself, stems from the brother of Jesus, and this material reveals an authoritative leader in a Palestinian context.

In 61 CE James suffered martyrdom at the instigation of the high priest Ananus after the sudden death in office of the procurator Festus (Josephus, *Ant.* 20.9.200). In the following centuries legends about James developed. For example, Hegesippus reports that James was known as "James the Just" because of his exemplary piety (Eusebius, *Hist. eccl.* 2.23), and Jerome connects him with the lost apocryphal *Gospel according to the Hebrews* (*De viris illustribus* 2). But other than the fact of his martyrdom and its approximate date, there is little evidence that any of these legends are accurate, and most are certainly apocryphal.   PETER H. DAVIDS

James, The Letter of

Outline. The letter of James is a literary composition (i.e., a letter designed to be published rather than dispatched like a true letter) and follows the conventions of the literary letter in its structure:

  I. Greeting (1.1)
 II. Opening statement (1.2–27)
      A. Testing, wisdom, and wealth (1.2–11)
          1. Testing and faith (1.2–4)
          2. Wisdom and faith (1.5–8)
          3. Wealth and faith (1.9–11)
      B. Testing, speech, and action (1.12–27)
          1. Testing and sin (1.12–15)
          2. God's gift and sinful speech (1.16–21)
          3. Action and sin (1.22–27)
              (1.26–27 are transition verses)
III. Wealth and faith (2.1–26)
      A. Wealth and prejudice (2.1–13)
          1. Thesis (2.1)
          2. Illustration of the problem (2.2–4)
          3. Theological argument (2.5–7)
          4. Biblical passage 1 (2.8–9)
          5. Biblical passage 2 (2.10–11)
          6. Summary (2.12–13)
      B. Giving and faith (2.14–26)
          1. Thesis (2.14)
          2. Illustration of the problem (2.15–17)
          3. Theological argument (2.18–19)
          4. Biblical passage 1 (2.20–24)
          5. Biblical passage 2 (2.25)
          6. Summary (2.26)
 IV. Wisdom and speech (3.1–4.12)
      A. Danger of sinful speech (3.1–12)
      B. God's gift of wisdom (3.13–18)
      C. Repentance from sinful speech and action (4.1–10)
      D. Example of sinful speech (4.11–12)
  V. Testing and wealth (4.13–5.6)
      A. Testing through wealth (4.13–17)
      B. Testing by the wealthy (5.1–6)

 VI. Closing: Patience and prayer (5.7–20)
      A. Conclusion: patience (5.7–11)
      B. Oaths (5.12)
      C. Prayer and health (5.13–18)
      D. Purpose of the letter (5.19–20)

Authorship and Date. The letter claims in 1.1 to come from *James, the brother of Jesus, but this claim has been disputed frequently because of the theology of the letter (not that of an observant Jew) and the excellent quality of the Greek. Thus, the suggestion is frequently made that it is a pseudonymous letter from the late first century CE attributed to James because he had been a great leader of the church.

While this position is widely held, it is not the only possible one. First, the theology of the letter is not as difficult as it appears, especially if one accepts the portrait of James given in *Acts over that of later legends. These legends portray James as being observant of the *Law of Moses, but they contain so many improbable details that they cannot be trusted. On the other hand, Acts portrays him as a Jewish leader who was also a diplomat, concerned that both Jew and *gentile live together in the church. There is no evidence that his teaching in Jerusalem (where the observance of the law was not an issue) had a particularly legalistic tone.

Second, while the Greek is good, among the best in the New Testament, it does from time to time employ obvious Semitisms. Furthermore, while there is a unity to the letter, the vocabulary is inconsistent (e.g., 1.12–15 and 4.1–10 use different words for the same concept). The best explanation of these data is that the letter is a collection of sermons and sayings from James (and possibly from Jesus as well, from whom 5.12 unquestionably comes) edited into letter form. This view also explains the simple attribution (as opposed to more flowery titles used for James by the end of the first century) and the fact that the letter was first circulated in the eastern church and so is missing in some of the early *canon lists in North Africa and the West (although it was known in Rome by the end of the first century, being used by the author of the *Shepherd of Hermas*). Finally, it accounts for the absence in the letter of a knowledge of Paul's writings on the one hand and the presence of depictions of Palestinian culture on the other.

If the material comes from James and reflects his setting, then the most likely place of editing is Jerusalem or at least Judea. Some of the material probably dates from before *Paul's activity became well known in Jerusalem (49 CE or earlier), for it shows no awareness of Pauline formulations or at best knows only distorted oral reports of his teaching. But the final editing was probably triggered by the martyrdom of James and the desire to preserve and spread his teaching, that is, after 61 CE but probably before the fall of *Jerusalem in 70 CE.

Unity. The letter of James has often been regarded as a collection of miscellaneous sayings without any internal unity other than an interest in some recurring themes. To a degree this is true, for the letter does contain sayings (1.26–27; 2.13; 3.18) and homilies (2.1–12; 2.14–26) that were originally not unified. But the discovery of the literary letter form with the doubled opening (i.e., A B C, A′ B′ C′) and the realization that the three main sections of the letter take up in reverse the topics mentioned in the opening (C B A) together show that these homilies and sayings have been edited into a unified whole. Even the ending fits this form. Thus, while the editor has been conservative and preserved the integrity of the various units (and even some Semitic expressions like "doers of the word" [1.23]), James is unlike *Proverbs or similar *wisdom literature, a mere collection of sayings; it has a unified structure.

Theology. James is writing in the context of a church under pressure, not facing impending martyrdom but discrimination and economic persecution. He is concerned about two tendencies, adopting the mores of the oppressors (e.g., valuing money over community) and attacking other members of the community (e.g., gossip, criticism). Thus his chief concern is the unity of the community and turning the community back from practices that threaten to disrupt it (5.19–20). Within this overriding concern there are several major themes.

The first is testing. Only true commitment to God will resist the overtures of the devil (4.7) made through the impulses of internal cravings. But it is this patient endurance, even when *suffering, that God will reward when he comes to judge the world (5.7–8, 10). In this context James introduces the "double-minded" person (1.8; 4.8) and doubter. This is not the person who trusts in God but still struggles with doubt; it is the person who does the correct religious acts (because God might answer prayer) yet whose real trust (as seen in daily actions) is in human solutions. God does not tolerate such dual trust, for it is spiritual adultery (4.4).

The second major theme is wisdom. God offers people the gift of wisdom to help them stand firm in the test. One mark of this wisdom is the gentle attitude that it produces in speech and action (3.13–18). Conversely, conflict in the community is a mark of the love of the world rather than of God.

The third theme is wealth. In the culture in which James lives, the wealthy are by and large the oppressors of the Christians, many of whom are poor. Christians, however, must not accept the world's values or view their material poverty with concern; if they are truly committed to God, they will show it in generous charity (2.14–26) and in seeking God's will in all their business plans (4.13–17).

Throughout the letter are found the themes of prayer and maintaining the proper perspective. When one is experiencing deprivation, it is easy to focus on the suffering, but James calls for joy (1.2) because the Christian has gained the perspective of God and realizes that the suffering is temporary, the return of Christ as judge imminent, and the rewards of God eternal. With this perspective the Christian should pray in confidence. This prayer is the key to endurance (chap. 1), to the supply of real needs (chap. 4), and to physical and spiritual healing (chap. 5). When he speaks of healing (5.14–18), James assumes this to be the normal practice of the church; unlike Paul (1 Cor. 12.9, 30), he does not look to the gifted healer for help, but to the *elders.

James and Paul. Because of the famous section in 2.14–26, James has often been seen as opposing Paul's stress on *justification by faith without the deeds of the Law. This appears true until one realizes that James uses his critical terms in ways that differ from Paul; in fact, James is using terminology in its older, original sense. Works for Paul are works of the Law, that is, ritual acts such as *circumcision; works for James are deeds of charity such as, according to Jewish tradition, those that Abraham performed. Faith for Paul is a commitment to God, which produces good works; for James faith (i.e., in 2.14–26, for he uses the term in two or three different ways elsewhere in the letter) is mere intellectual belief (2.19), lacking commitment. Finally, "justified" for Paul means the pronouncing of a sinner righteous; "justified" for James means the declaration that a person did in fact act justly. Paul, of course, would have agreed with James that "faith" that does not produce appropriate deeds is a false faith (see Gal. 5.6, 16–21).

Given such differences in usage of common

terminology, how are these two authors related? Two possibilities may be mentioned: either James is reacting to a misunderstood and badly distorted Paulinism, perhaps not even knowing who had originated it; or James is speaking to the fault of making intellectual religious commitments without the corresponding amendment of life. In neither case is James opposing Paul; he is simply arguing in his own context what Paul taught in his.   PETER H. DAVIDS

Jannes and Jambres (the latter sometimes Mamre). They are mentioned in late antique Jewish, Christian, and Greco-Roman (Pliny, Apuleius, Numenius) sources as Egyptian magicians; the earliest citation is the first-century BCE "Damascus Document" of the *Dead Sea Scrolls. They are identified in Jewish midrash and the New Testament (2 Tim. 3.8) as among Pharaoh's unnamed wise men (Exod. 7.11–13) who duplicated *Moses' and *Aaron's miracles. In both traditions, they symbolize false prophecy and heretical obstruction; several Jewish sources describe them as *Balaam's sons (*Targum Jonathan* to Num. 22.22; *Yalquṭ Exod.* 168, 176). The sixth-century CE Christian work "Decree of Gelasius" mentions an apocryphal book, now lost, about their exploits and ultimate conversion.
                            JUDITH R. BASKIN

Jashar, The Book of. One of a number of ancient collections referred to in the Bible that have not survived. To the Book of Jashar (KJV "Jasher"; literally, "the Upright") are attributed the poetic fragment in Joshua 10.12–13 and the lament of *David over *Saul and Jonathan in 2 Samuel 1.18–27 and perhaps also *Solomon's prayer in 1 Kings 8.12–13 (according to the *Septuagint of v. 53 as emended by many scholars). A similar anthology was "the Book of the Wars of Yahweh," cited in Numbers 21.14. The books of *Kings and *Chronicles mention such sources as "the book of the acts of Solomon" (1 Kings 11.41), "the book of the acts of the days [NRSV: annals] of the kings of Israel" (1 Kings 14.19; etc.), "the book of the acts of the days of the kings of Judah" (1 Kings 14.29; etc.), and the written words of various prophets (1 Chron. 29.29; 2 Chron 9.29); and the titles to many of the *Psalms apparently also refer to various collections of hymns.   MICHAEL D. COOGAN

Jebusites. The Jebusites were one of several groups of people living on the land that Israel eventually conquered. According to Genesis 10.15–16 and 1 Chronicles 1.14, the Jebusites were related to the *Canaanites. But these passages may indicate a geopolitical relationship rather than an ethnic one; since the Jebusites shared the same territory as the Canaanites, they were perceived to be from the same stock, though they probably were not. In fact, the biblical writers normally distinguish the Jebusites from the Canaanites and from other peoples as well (Exod. 33.2; 34.11; Num. 13.29; Deut. 20.17; Josh. 11.3; 12.8; Judg. 3.5).

*Jerusalem is sometimes identified as Jebus (Judg. 19.10; 1 Chron. 11.4). From this one might infer that Jebus was the pre-Israelite name of the city. The name Jerusalem, however, predates the Israelite *conquest by several centuries, and the city was not appropriated by Israel until the tenth century BCE. Therefore it seems best to take Jebus as an alternate Israelite designation for Jerusalem. The people, then, were not called Jebusites because they lived in Jebus; rather, the city of Jerusalem was sometimes called Jebus because the Jebusites controlled it.

Although there is a brief account of a victory over Jerusalem in the early tribal league period (Judg. 1.8), the Israelites did not take possession of the city at that time, for it is later mentioned as still being a foreign city of the Jebusites (Judg. 19.10–13). *David captured Jerusalem from them and made it his capital (2 Sam. 5.6–10; 1 Chron. 11.4–9). Apparently he did not kill or drive out all the local inhabitants, because subsequently, when he needed land on which to build an altar, he purchased it from Araunah the Jebusite (2 Sam. 24.18–24; 1 Chron. 21.18–27 has the name Ornan for Araunah). *Solomon built the *Temple on that plot of ground (1 Chron. 22.1); he also enslaved the remainder of the Jebusites, and other non-Israelites (1 Kings 9.20–21). Ultimately, they must have assimilated into Israel; Zechariah 9.7 likens them to a Judean clan.

Some have seen Jebusite origins for the changes in Israel's political structure and religious ideology that occurred with the establishment of *kingship, but there is little evidence to support such a hypothesis.   WILLIAM B. NELSON, JR.

Jehoshaphat. The fourth king of *Judah (ca. 874–850 BCE). His reign is given only brief attention in Kings (1 Kings 22.41–50; cf. 1 Kings 22), but he is one of the Chronicler's favorite monarchs (2 Chron. 17–20). Jehoshaphat reverses the policy of his predecessors by entering into military, maritime, and marital alliances with kings of Israel. Jehoshaphat's achievements as a reformer are accentuated in Chronicles. He reorganizes the judiciary, sending ministers, *Levites, and *priests to the towns of Judah "to teach the law of the Lord" (2 Chron. 17.7–9), appoints judges for the towns of Judah, and establishes a court in Jerusalem (2 Chron. 19.5–11). Jehoshaphat also reorganizes the army and fortifies cities within his domain (2 Chron. 17.2, 13–19).

The reference to the "valley of Jehoshaphat" in Joel 3.2, 12 plays on Jehoshaphat's name ("the Lord has judged"). It is unclear whether Joel is designating geography (e.g., the Wadi Kidron) or dramatizing a future judgment.

GARY N. KNOPPERS

Jehovah. An artificially constructed name for Israel's God first attested in sixteenth-century CE Christian texts. The new construction was the result of changing attitudes toward the use of God's name. The Hebrew name "Yahweh" was not normally pronounced after about the third century BCE out of respect for its holiness. In its place, readers of the Hebrew used 'ădōnāy, "Lord." When vowels were added to the consonantal text of the Hebrew Bible (ca. 1000 CE), the consonants of Yahweh were preserved but the vowels of 'ădōnāy were used as a reminder to readers. Renaissance Christian tradition erroneously combined the consonants of Yahweh and the vowels of 'ădōnāy to produce "Jehovah," which is used occasionally in the King James Version and regularly in some revisions of it. More recent English translations tend to use "LORD" rather than "Jehovah."

See also Names of God in the Hebrew Bible; Tetragrammaton.   STEVEN FRIESEN

Jehu. The son of Nimshi, Jehu was king of Israel ca. 843–816 BCE. 2 Kings 9–10 describes how, under prophetic mandate, Jehu led a bloody military revolt to seize the throne of Israel. He killed the kings of both Israel (Jehoram) and Judah (Ahaziah), had *Jezebel executed, annihilated the dynasty of Omri, and obliterated the worship of *Baal in Israel. Yahweh rewarded Jehu's faithfulness by allowing his dynasty to last five generations.

However historical its base, the account in 2 Kings 9–10 is strongly influenced by the ideology of the *Deuteronomic historian. Quite a different perspective on Jehu's revolt is found in Hosea 1.4–5, where the house of Jehu is threatened with punishment for the bloodshed of Jezreel.

The annals of the Assyrian king Shalmaneser III mention and his "Black Obelisk" depicts a "Ia-ú-a/Ia-a-ú son of Omri" paying tribute to him. This individual is probably Jehu, though his predecessor Jehoram has also been proposed; in any case, it is the only contemporary picture we have of a king of Israel.

See also Israel, History of.

STEVEN L. MCKENZIE

Jeremiah, The Book of

The Background. The editorial introduction to the book of Jeremiah, 1.1–3, informs us that the book contains "the words of Jeremiah," that is, what Jeremiah said and did—the Hebrew term translated "words" can cover both—from the beginning of his prophetic ministry in the thirteenth year of the reign of *Josiah, 627 BCE, until the fall of *Jerusalem to the *Babylonians in 587/586 BCE. This is not strictly an accurate account of the contents of the present book since chaps. 40–44 describe the activity of the prophet both in Judah and in Egypt after the fall of Jerusalem. Nevertheless the last forty years of the independent Judean state are the stage on which Jeremiah played out his major prophetic role. Since the book is full of historical references to events in this period, it is important for our understanding of the book to sketch briefly the political factors that shaped these years. They witnessed the gradual break up of the once allpowerful *Assyrian empire and the resurgence within Judah of a religious nationalism that culminated in the reformation under King Josiah in 621 BCE (2 Kings 22–23). Although this religious nationalism must have received a jolt with the death of Josiah at the battle of *Megiddo in 609 BCE, it still had a trump card: Jerusalem, the city of God, with its *Temple where God dwelt, guaranteeing by his presence that this city could never be conquered or destroyed (see Pss. 46 and 48). Such self-confident religious nationalism clashed with the new imperial power of the day, the Neo-Babylonian empire. Under a succession of monarchs, Judah tried to play antiBabylonian power politics with other small states, aided and abetted by Egypt, in an unsuccessful attempt to postpone the inevitable. In 597 BCE Jerusalem surrendered to the Babylonians, and the cream of Judean society went into exile. The last king of Judah, *Zedekiah, came to the throne as a Babylonian nominee. But the anti-Babylonian lobby in Jerusalem prevailed until, ten years later in 587/586 BCE, the city was captured and destroyed. The curtain had fallen for the last time on the independent kingdom of *Judah. The book of Jeremiah depicts a man who consistently protested against political and religious policies that sealed the fate of his country, a prophet who in the eyes of the establishment of his day was both traitor and heretic. If the fall of Jerusalem had not vindicated his stance, we might now have been reading not the book of Jeremiah but the book of Hananiah (see chap. 28) or of some of the other prophets with whom Jeremiah clashed.

The Problem of the Book. But what do we mean by the book of Jeremiah? The prophets from Amos onward are sometimes called "the writing prophets" because in the Bible we find books to which their names are attached. If this conveys the impression that in such prophetic books we are dealing with a series of books each written by one person, then this is highly misleading, nowhere more so than in the case of the book of Jeremiah. In it we find duplicate accounts of the same events: twice we hear of Jeremiah's sermon in the Temple, once in chap. 7, once in chap. 26; and there are two versions of Jeremiah's arrest, imprisonment, and secret interview with King Zedekiah (37.11–21; 38.1–13). The same or very similar passages will appear in different contexts in the book: thus 6.13–15 reappears in 8.10b–12, and 23.19–20 in 30.23–24. A passage in 49.19–20, which occurs in the context of judgment against *Edom, is repeated with minor variations in the context of judgment against Babylon in 50.44–46. Moreover, there is material within the book that is closely paralleled in other prophetic books; chap. 48 dealing with *Moab has many similarities with Isaiah 15–16, while the section on Edom in 49.7–22 reads like a series of variations on *Obadiah. At times we come across blocks of material dealing with a common theme or linked together by catchwords or phrases. Thus 3.1–4.4 deals with the infidelity and adultery of God's people; 21.1–23.6 gives us the prophet's verdict on various kings of Judah; 23.9–40 is headed "concerning the prophets"; 30, 31, and 33 (the "book of consolation") gather together words of hope for the future, and inserted in their midst (in chap. 32) is an incident from the life of Jeremiah that illustrates this theme. Within this book of consolation, brief independent sections are placed together and introduced by the same phrase. Thus three passages, each introduced by "The days are surely coming," are placed together in 31.27–40. The largest clearly defined collection of material in the book is chaps. 46–51, which contains "oracles against the nations." Such blocks of material, however, only serve to underline the general lack of order that runs through the book as a whole. There is no clear chronological ordering of material; chap. 21, for example, deals with events during the final siege of Jerusalem, chap. 26 with an event that happened more than twenty years earlier. The book keeps jumping about disconcertingly from topic to topic and seems to be needlessly repetitive. At times we are reading poetry, at other times prose. The book makes more sense as a collection or collections of varied material rather than as a work with a coherent theme or plot or any systematic historical framework.

There is a good reason for this. The preexilic prophets are not primarily writers but preachers, messengers of God who transmit their message by word of mouth. The message often takes the form of a brief poetic oracle that begins "Thus says the Lord" and often ends in the book of Jeremiah with another phrase that the NRSV renders "says the Lord," 2.1–3 being an excellent example; see also 2.5–8; 4.27–28; 5.14–15; 6.6–9, 9–12. The present book of Jeremiah contains collections of many such prophetic sayings, almost certainly preserved originally in oral form, supplemented by the addition of biographical and other editorial material. Behind it lies, as we shall see, a long and complex history of transmission, the details of which remain obscure.

The Text. We have spoken so far of the book of Jeremiah, but what book do we mean? The book of Jeremiah has come down to us in two forms, represented by the standard Hebrew *Masoretic text (MT) and the Greek text (*Septuagint [LXX]), and these two text forms differ significantly from each other. The LXX is approximately one-eighth shorter, lacking, it has been calculated, some 2,700 words of the MT. Furthermore, some of the material is differently placed in the two text forms. The "oracles against the nations" come in the MT at chaps. 46–51; in the LXX they are placed immediately after the words "everything written in this book" in 25.13a, and the individual oracles occur in a different order. Some further light on the problem of the two texts has been shed by the *Dead Sea Scrolls. Among fragments of the book of

Jeremiah from Caves Two and Four, there are some that support the MT where it differs from the LXX. From Cave Four, however, has come a Hebrew text that follows the LXX textual tradition against the MT in Jeremiah 10 in omitting vv. 6–8 and 10. Thus in Palestine prior to the common era there is evidence for the existence of two Hebrew textual traditions of the book of Jeremiah, a longer one corresponding to what became the standard Hebrew text and a shorter one corresponding to the Greek text. Which one takes us nearer to the earliest form of the text of the book is a matter of scholarly debate. On the whole, the balance of opinion favors the shorter LXX with the MT being regarded as a secondary, expanded text. It contains, for example, many descriptive titles of God not found in the LXX, and while "the prophet" appears as a designation of Jeremiah only four times in the LXX, it occurs twenty-six times in the MT. This is not, however, to say that in every case the shorter text is the superior text or that it represents the "original text" of Jeremiah, whatever that may mean. Each case must be treated on its merits. Since English Bibles follow the standard Hebrew text we shall continue to refer to the contents of the book as in this tradition.

Content and Sources. It is generally agreed that the material in the book of Jeremiah falls into three categories, each stemming from different sources or circles.

Poetic material, to be found in the main interspersed with prose passages in chaps. 1–25. These poetic sections consist largely of oracles in which the prophet functions as God's messenger, speaking in the name of God. They cover a variety of themes, including the nation's infidelity to the Lord and the call to repentance (3.1–5; 4.13–18; 6.15–17), with attacks on the religious and political establishment of the day (2.8–9; 6.13–15; 22.13–19). These poetic passages are on the whole undated and are given no clearly defined context, but it is widely held that in such passages we are in touch with the teaching of the prophet Jeremiah, and that much of the material in chaps. 1–25 represents the earliest stage of the book of Jeremiah. Such passages may well have been part of the scroll that King Jehoiakim, according to chap. 36, insolently consigned to the flames in the winter of 604 BCE, whereupon Jeremiah redictated the scroll to the scribe *Baruch and for good measure added similar words. Certainly there is little in such poetic oracles that could not have come from the early years of the prophet's ministry between the time of his call (627 BCE according to 1.2) and 604 BCE.

In addition to these oracles in which the prophet speaks the word of God to his people, there are other poetic passages in 1–25 that are in the form of intensely personal poems that have been called Jeremiah's confessions or his spiritual diary (see 11.18–12.6; 15.10–21; 17.5–10, 14–18; 18.18–23; 20.7–18). Here we listen not to the word of God on the lips of the prophet but to a man baring his own soul and exposing some of the tensions involved in being a prophet. These passages are without parallel in prophetic literature. Attempts have been made to read them as cultic poems, modeled on the *psalms of lament, that have no real roots in the life of Jeremiah. There seems, however, little reason to doubt that they reflect Jeremiah's experience. As such they are of the highest significance and interest. They show us that behind the apparently untroubled certainty of "Thus says the Lord" there may lie a host of unresolved questions and deep inner turmoil. This is a very human prophet committed to a vocation that tears him apart, agonizing over the apparent failure of his ministry, on the verge of giving up, consumed by a savage bitterness against those who opposed or ignored what he had to say, accusing God of betraying him.

There are two other blocks of material in the book outside chaps. 1–25 that similarly contain poetic prophetic oracles, often interspersed with and expanded by prose sections.

a) Chaps. 30, 31 and 33, the so-called book of consolation, consisting of oracles whose basic theme is that of hope beyond national disaster. This material is probably of very varied origin. The influence of an earlier prophet, Hosea, is very marked in some sections (e.g., 31.1–6), while the language and thought of other passages have close links with a later prophet, the author of Isaiah 40–55 (e.g., 31.10–14). That some of the material in this section goes back to Jeremiah, however, we need not doubt.

b) Chaps. 46–51, the oracles against the nations. The tradition of oracles against other nations, particularly those that threaten the existence of Israel, is one that can be traced back to Amos 1.3–2.3. Such oracles occur also in other prophetic books: Isaiah 13–23, Ezekiel 25–32, Nahum, and Obadiah. Inasmuch as Jeremiah was called, according to 1.5, to be "a prophet to the nations," it is hardly surprising that a substantial collection of such oracles appears in the book. Such oracles affirm that the God of Israel is lord over all nations and pronounce judgment on them not only for their treatment of Israel, but for the arrogant self-confidence that assumes that might is right and for actions that sacrifice justice and human rights to imperial ambitions. It is evident from the different setting in which these oracles are placed in the Hebrew and Greek texts, and the different ordering of the oracles within this material, that they once circulated as an independent collection. How much of it can be traced back to Jeremiah himself is a highly contentious issue.

Biographical narratives that claim to recount key incidents in the life of the prophet. There are two notable features of these narratives. First, there are more such narratives in the book of Jeremiah than in any other prophetic book, and thus, if authentic, they provide us with more information about Jeremiah than is available for any other prophet. Such narratives are to be found in chaps. 26–29, 32, 34–44. Second, these narratives are usually provided with precise dating, the earliest dated to 609 BCE (26:1). If therefore we assume, following 1.2, that Jeremiah's prophetic ministry began in 627 BCE, we have no such narrative for almost the first twenty years of his ministry. This, allied to the lack of any clear evidence in the book for Jeremiah's attitude to the key religious event of this period, the reformation under King Josiah in 621 BCE, has led a variety of scholars to believe that his ministry did not begin until 612 BCE or 609 BCE, with 627 BCE being the possible date of his birth. This is not, however, a necessary inference. The biographical narratives are often linked with the scribe Baruch, who appears in Jeremiah's company in chaps. 32, 36, 43, and 45. We could argue from the lack of biographical material prior to 609 BCE that Baruch first came into contact with Jeremiah in 609; perhaps he was drawn to Jeremiah as the result of the Temple sermon that chap. 26 dates to that year. We have spoken of biographical narratives, but we must not assume from this that it is possible to write a satisfactory biography of Jeremiah, even from 609 BCE onward. The narratives do not appear in chronological sequence, nor do they do any more than highlight what are taken to be certain key incidents that reveal the prophet often locked in conflict with the religious and political establishment of the day. It is no more possible to write a satisfactory biography of Jeremiah on the basis of these narratives than it is to write a life of Jesus on the basis of the gospel narratives. If we push this analogy further we would have to say that it is the events leading up to and surrounding the destruction of Jerusalem in 587 BCE that occupy in the book of Jeremiah the central place that the passion narratives occupy in the Gospels. It is perhaps not surprising that the book of Jeremiah ends in chap. 52 with an account of the fall of Jerusalem, derived in the main from 2 Kings 24–25.

Prose passages occur throughout the book, sometimes in the form of sermons or speeches attributed to Jeremiah, which are usually called Deuteronomic (or Deuteronomistic), since they reflect the style, language, and thought of the book of *Deuteronomy and the Deuteronomic editors who shaped the history of Israel that we find in the books of Judges to 2 Kings. Typical examples of this material are the Temple sermon in chap. 7 and the covenant passage in 11.1–17. It is these Deuteronomic passages that have provoked the greatest controversy in the study of the book of Jeremiah. Some would trace them to Jeremiah himself; others argue that they reflect the characteristic rhetorical prose style of Jeremiah's day and present a tradition of Jeremiah's teaching as handed down in circles familiar with this style and sympathetic to the theology of the book of Deuteronomy. A variation of this view is to regard such passages as conventional scribal compositions and attribute them to Baruch. All such views trace the material in its present form back to the time of Jeremiah. Others, however, believe that such passages are later, either emanating from Deuteronomic preachers during the period of the *exile in Babylon in the sixth century BCE or reflecting theological issues of a still later date during the Persian period. It is doubtful whether in their present form such passages can be attributed to Jeremiah, but it is unduly skeptical to deny that they may well have their roots in a tradition that builds on what Jeremiah said and did. Nor should we think that we necessarily solve problems by speaking about the Deuteronomists. They are at best shadowy figures. We do not know with certainty either who they were or when they functioned.

How or when such varied material came together to form the book of Jeremiah, either in its shorter or its longer form, we do not know, but it must have taken many decades, or even centuries, after Jeremiah's life. The very nature of the book—its varied components, the clear evidence of editing within it, the amalgamation of different traditions—raises the question as to what extent the book provides us with reliable historical data concerning the life, words, and deeds of the prophet. Some deny that the book provides us with any access to the historical Jeremiah. Behind the editing, however, and in and through the varied material, there does seem to emerge a prophetic figure of striking individuality, God's spokesman to Judah at a major crisis point in the life of the nation, and it is hard to see why such a figure should be nothing other than the invention of later ages.

Key Religious Issues. In addition to much that the book of Jeremiah shares with other prophetic books, there are two issues to which specific attention may be briefly drawn. First is the problem of *prophecy. The book speaks not only of one prophet, Jeremiah, but of many prophets. Chap. 28 describes the clash between Jeremiah and the prophet Hananiah, a representative of the Jerusalem religious establishment. Both preface their words by "Thus says the Lord," both use the same prophetic techniques to communicate the message, both are no doubt equally sincere, and both speak a diametrically opposite message. Hananiah declares that the Lord will protect his people and break the power of Babylon, and there was much in Israel's past faith to support his view (e.g., Isa. 31.1–5; Ps. 48); Jeremiah insists that such a message of peace, that all is well with the people basking in God's favor, must be false (6.13–15). But how would anyone witnessing such a clash know who had the true prophetic word? The tests for identifying false prophecy in Deuteronomy 13.1–5 and 18.16–20 would have been little help. In Jeremiah 23.9–40 it is claimed that prophets who proclaim a word that presents no challenge to the conscience of the nation stand in no relationship to God and have no access to his word. They do no more than spout lies they themselves have invented. But how could Jeremiah know this? Did he never wonder whether he himself was mistaken when he heard the confident "Thus says the Lord" of such prophets? This may be the implication of 20.7. The book of Jeremiah highlights the difficulties that people in Judah faced in deciding what was the authentic word of God for them in their day. They had to take choices and live with the consequences.

The second issue is the message of hope. Throughout the book of Jeremiah we find oracles of judgment that insist that Jerusalem must be destroyed, its fate sealed not by the Babylonians but by God. But there are also words of hope, not hope that sidesteps disaster, but hope of a new future beyond disaster. Many of the pictures of hope beyond the richly deserved judgment are modest and homely: people returning to the towns they were once forced to leave, the renewal of life in the countryside, the resumed worship of God in Jerusalem (31.23–25; 33.10–13). But there is another strand. Again and again the prophet draws attention to the stubborn evil heart or will that grips the people (e.g., 3.17). It means that the call to repent falls on deaf ears; it turns the most serious attempt to reform the nation's life into a dead letter. If things are ever to be lastingly different, it can only come through a new initiative of God that will transform human nature. This is the theme of the new covenant passage in 31.31–34, a vision that, drawing on Israel's relationship with God in the past symbolized by the *covenant at Mount *Sinai, sees a new relationship in the future, based as was the past on God's *grace, but a relationship in which the people will be able to give the obedience for which God looks. Thus the book of Jeremiah, which draws richly on Israel's past religious traditions, reaches out to the future. In terms of the new covenant theme, the New Testament claims that that future became the present in Jesus (1 Cor. 11.25; Heb. 8.6–13).   ROBERT DAVIDSON

Jeremiah, The Letter of. One of the *Apocrypha. According to Jeremiah 29, Jeremiah wrote from Jerusalem a letter addressed to the Judeans who had been carried off to *exile in *Babylon in the first deportation in 597 BCE. In that letter Jeremiah gives the people instruction as to their conduct in Babylon and warns them against false prophets in their midst. It was no doubt this passage that inspired an unknown author, living probably rather late in the Hellenistic age, to write a similar letter in the prophet's name, to be delivered, supposedly, to those condemned to exile either in 597 BCE or the final disaster of 587/586 BCE before they departed from Jerusalem. The purpose of the letter is to warn the deportees against the temptation that would confront them in Babylon to worship other gods. The danger of apostasy was, of course, also acute in the Hellenistic period, when, presumably, the letter was actually written.

The manner in which the theme is treated was very likely suggested by Jeremiah 10.1–16, and particularly by v. 11, the only verse in Jeremiah written in *Aramaic, which says, "The gods who did not make heaven and earth shall perish from the earth and from under the heavens." The author may have been further inspired by Isaiah 44.9–20. Throughout the whole book runs the motto, first stated in v. 16 and repeated eight times with variations, "It is evident that they are not gods; so do not fear them" (cf. vv. 23, 29, 40, 44, 52, 56, 65, 69). The repetition of the refrain serves to divide the book into ten irregular parts, in each of which the writer calls attention to one or more features of the statues of deities that make worshiping them seem ludicrous.

The "letter" thus does not have a developing thesis but is simply a series of somewhat repetitious tirades directed against Babylonian religion. The modern reader may find it tiresome, but to Hellenistic Jews, it was no doubt an effective and exhilarating bit of satire, adding a touch of humor to the more serious underlying argument, and it would probably have been equally effective with potential converts to Judaism.

The book is known only in Greek and in versions based on it (Latin, Syriac, Arabic), but it is the general scholarly opinion that the original language was Hebrew (or, less probably, Aramaic). This view is based largely on the presence of apparent mistranslations of Hebrew words, the most notable of which is in v. 72, where the Greek word for "marble" seems to represent a Semitic word that could in theory be translated either "marble" or "linen" (see text note in NRSV). The translation "marble" is, however, incongruous in context.

The only clue as to the date of the book is found in v. 3, which refers to a period of seven generations that was to follow the beginning of the Babylonian exile (587/586 BCE). Understanding a generation to be about forty years, this would bring one to approximately 300 BCE, which may be taken as the earliest date possible. Some important commentators accept this as the actual date of the book; others prefer the early second century BCE, when the appeal of Hellenism for Jews was most intense, as evidenced by the events accompanying the Maccabean revolt (1 Macc. 1.11–15).

In the Latin *Vulgate and some versions dependent on it, the letter is printed as chap. 6 of *Baruch rather than as a separate book, which it unquestionably is. It is considered deuterocanonical by Roman Catholics and by some Orthodox churches.   ROBERT C. DENTAN

Jericho. Jericho, whose name probably means "Moon (City)" (Hebr. *yārēaḥ*), is located 12 km (8 mi) north of the Dead Sea at the foot of the western escarpment of the *Jordan valley (Map 1:x5). At 258 m (840 ft) below sea level it is the lowest city on earth. Today a thriving market town, its ten-thousand-year history has been documented principally by the excavations of Kathleen Kenyon at Tell es-Sultan.

Mesolithic hunters were attracted to the area in the ninth millennium BCE by the abundant perennial spring of Ein es-Sultan. By about 8000 BCE a permanent settlement of some two thousand people had been established just beside it. Its irrigation system and the large tower and defense wall imply a social organization that justifies Jericho's title as the oldest city in the world. Sometime around 6800 BCE the original settlers were displaced by another Neolithic people, whose most distinctive cultural achievement was a series of skulls with individualized features restored in plaster. This group, however, had not yet discovered pottery, which first appeared around 4500 BCE when another group took possession of the site. The site was then occupied more or less continuously until the middle of the Late Bronze Age, when the city was devastated. This destruction is too early to be attributed to *Joshua (Josh. 6; *see* Conquest of Canaan), but in harmony with his words (Josh. 6.26) the site was abandoned until the seventh century BCE, a date that is too late to coincide with the reoccupation mentioned in 1 Kings 16.34 as having occurred in the ninth century BCE. The Iron Age city visited by *Elijah and *Elisha (2 Kings 2) was known as the city of palm trees (Deut. 34.3).

After the Babylonian exile Tell es-Sultan was abandoned, but there must have been a settlement elsewhere in the oasis (cf. Ezra 2.34), because in the late sixth century BCE Jericho was a Persian administrative center, a role it retained in later periods (Josephus, *War* 1.8.170). In the Hellenistic period the area was considered a private royal domain, and this inhibited any real urbanization; its fortifications guarded the eastern frontier (1 Macc. 9.50; Strabo, *Geog.* 16.2.40).

The Hasmoneans extended the cultivated area by building an aqueduct from Ein Qilt. The agricultural wealth of the enlarged oasis is extolled by Josephus (*War* 4.8.459–475) and Strabo (*Geog.* 16.2.41). The delightful winter climate inspired Alexander Janneus to build a palace on the north bank of the Wadi Qilt. *Herod the Great had Aristobulus III, his last serious rival for the crown of Judea, drowned in its great swimming pool in 35 BCE (Josephus, *Ant.* 15.3.55). During the years 34–30 BCE, when he was forced to rent the plantations from Cleopatra to whom they had been given by Mark Antony (*War* 1.18.361), Herod built a winter residence south of the Wadi Qilt. Once Octavian (Augustus) had transferred Jericho to Herod's control in 30 BCE, the latter remodeled the Hasmonean palace, constructed the theater-hippodrome complex at Tell es-Samrat, and later erected more buildings on both sides of the Wadi Qilt (*War* 1.21.407). The vast quantities of water required by the palace were supplied by three new aqueducts, two on the south wall of the Wadi Qilt and the third coming from Ein Duk at Naaran. Security was guaranteed by Kypros, a fortress on a cliff to the west.

Herod lived in the palace during his last terrible illness, but the medicinal springs of Callirhoe on the east side of the Dead Sea gave him no relief, and he died in Jericho shortly before Passover in 4 BCE (*War* 1.33.656–673). Josephus's reports that the palace was burnt by Simeon (*War* 2.4.57) and rebuilt by Archelaus (*Ant.* 17.13.340) have not been confirmed by recent excavations.

After the dismissal of Archelaus in 6 CE, a garrison occupied Kypros (*War* 2.18.484). Burials in the cliffs north of the palace continued to 68 CE. Wealthy families from Jerusalem presumably returned each winter to their villas, some of whose foundations have been traced in the plantations south of the palace. This provides the background for the preaching of *John the Baptist in this area, for the plantation slaves who were the only permanent population are unlikely to have been his primary audience. The presence of Jesus in Jericho (Mark 10.46 par.; Luke 19.1) is explained by the fact that, to avoid passing through *Samaritan territory, Galilean pilgrims to Jerusalem followed a route down the Jordan valley to Jericho.

JEROME MURPHY-O'CONNOR

Jerubbaal. *See* Gideon.

Jerusalem. *This entry consists of two articles, the first on the* History *of Jerusalem and the second on the city's* Symbolism. *For additional discussion of these topics, see* Zion. *For the entire entry, see Map 9.*

History
Name and Description. The earliest attestation of Jerusalem's name is in the Egyptian Execration Texts of the nineteenth and eighteenth centuries BCE in a form that must be a transcription of the Semitic *Urusalim*, which appears in the *Amarna letters of the fourteenth century BCE. It is a combination of two elements meaning "the foundation of [the god] Shalem." The second element, rendered Salem, is used alone in Genesis 14.18 and Psalm 76.2. The pronunciation of the Hebrew name is reflected in the Greek *Ierousalem*, which predominates in the *Septuagint. In 1 *Esdras, *Tobit, and 1–4 *Maccabees, however, the Septuagint has the strongly Hellenized *Hierosolyma*. Both forms appear in the New Testament.

The biblical city spreads across two hills (average altitude 750 m [2500 ft]) in the central mountain range. It is limited on the west and south by the Hinnom valley, and on the east by the Kidron valley, which separates it from the *Mount of Olives. Josephus alone records that the central valley was called the Tyropoeon ("Cheesemakers"). The western hill is slightly higher than the eastern hill, and both slope to the south. There are two springs, Gihon ("gusher"; see Gen 2.13) and Ein Rogel ("the fuller's spring"), in the Kidron valley. The climate is temperate, and all the rain (annual average 560 mm [22 in]) falls during the four-month winter (December to March). It occasionally snows.

Before the Exile. The original city was on the southern extension of the eastern hill known as Ophel, excavated principally by Kathleen Kenyon and Yigal Shiloh. Scattered pottery attests occupation from the third millennium BCE and the site was defended by a heavy wall from about 1800 BCE. Houses built on artificial terraces climbed the slope to the acropolis. After the Israelite *conquest the territory of Jerusalem was absorbed by the tribe of *Benjamin, but the city of the *Jebusites, with its mixed population of *Amorites and *Hittites (Ezek. 16.3), was left alone. It thus served *David's need for a capital independent of the twelve tribes. He took it ca. 1000 BCE (2 Sam. 5.6–10) and made it an effective center by bringing into it the *ark of the covenant, to which all the tribes gave allegiance. In order to house the ark appropriately David bought a threshing floor to the north of the City of David from one Araunah (2 Sam. 24.18–25), which is both a title ("lord") in Hittite and a personal name in *Ugaritic. Here *Solomon built the First *Temple ca. 960 BCE, which he linked to the city by a palace (1 Kings 6—7), effectively doubling the size of the original Jebusite city. The Jebusite water-shaft was retained for use in military emergencies, but Solomon dug a tunnel from Gihon along the edge of the hill. Sluice gates at intervals facilitated irrigation of the King's Garden in the Kidron valley. The population of Davidic and Solomonic Jerusalem was a few thousand at most.

The excavations of Nahman Avigad in the Jewish Quarter have unearthed evidence, notably a massive wall 7 m (23 ft) wide, that the city had expanded to cover the western hill in the late eighth century BCE. When *Sennacherib menaced Jerusalem, King *Hezekiah built the wall (Isa. 22.10) to protect refugees from the northern kingdom of Israel, who had settled outside the crowded city. He thus created two new quarters, the mišneh ("second"; 2 Kings 22.14) on the western hill, and the maktēš ("mortar"; Zeph. 1.11) in the Tyropoeon valley. The City of David was given a new wall just inside the Jebusite wall that had served for a thousand years. In order to guarantee the water supply, Hezekiah dug a 533 m (1750 ft) tunnel from Gihon through the Ophel ridge to the pool of Siloam in the Tyropoeon valley (2 Chron. 32). An inscription found inside the exit details the construction technique. A new wall was built to protect the vulnerable north side of the city in the seventh century BCE. Both it and houses in the City of David bear traces of the savage attack that brought Jerusalem under *Babylonian control in 587/586 BCE.

After the Exile. The Israelites who returned from the *exile in 538 BCE rebuilt the Temple under the direction of *Zerubbabel (Ezra 5—6), but were authorized to reconstruct the walls only when the *Persians appointed the first Jewish governor, *Nehemiah, about 445 BCE. A complete description of these walls is given in Nehemiah 3, but the passage abounds in textual problems, and it has proved impossible to translate the data into a precise line on the ground. The complete absence of Hellenistic remains on the western hill, however, indicates that they encompassed an area barely equal to that of the city of David and Solomon.

Jerusalem suffered three sieges in the wars between the Ptolemies of Egypt and the Seleucids of Syria (201, 199, and 198 BCE). Sirach 50.1–4 praises the high priest Simon (220–195 BCE) for his rebuilding program, but the differences between the Hebrew and Greek versions create a certain obscurity as to what he actually achieved. After Jerusalem passed into the hands of the Seleucids in 198 BCE, the Hellenizing faction among the Jews built a gymnasium in the city (1 Macc. 1.14). In 167 BCE Antiochus IV Epiphanes forbade all Jewish religious practices. In order to forestall any resistance he threw down the walls of Jerusalem, and built a great fortress, the Akra, to hold a Syrian garrison (1 Macc. 1.29–35). Nine different sites have been proposed for the Akra, but it seems likely that it was south of the Temple. It is not to be confused with the Baris sited northwest of the Temple.

The refortification of the city was begun by Jonathan Maccabeus (1 Macc. 10.10–11) and completed by his brother Simon (1 Macc. 13.10), i.e., between 160 and 134 BCE. *Josephus's description of this line (War 5.4.142–45), which he calls the First Wall, has been given precision by excavations. It ran due west from the Temple along the southern edge of a tributary of the Tyropoeon valley, followed the rim of the Hinnom valley, and mounted the eastern edge of the Ophel ridge to join the Temple. Descriptions of the Hasmonean city appear in the Letter of Aristeas (83–106) and in Josephus (Ant. 12–14), but both must be used with great caution. The date of the information in the former is uncertain, and the latter is at times guilty of anachronism.

The Herodian City. The Romans, who asserted their authority over Palestine in 63 BCE, appointed *Herod the Great king of Judea in 40 BCE. A three-year campaign to establish his sovereignty culminated with the capture of Jerusalem in the summer of 37 BCE. The fact that he had to break two walls in order to reach the Lower City (Ant. 14.16.476–77) suggests that what Josephus calls the Second Wall (War 5.146), which ran from the Gennath Gate in the First Wall to the northwest corner of the Temple, was already in existence at this time. No certain elements of this wall have been discovered, but the section running north from the First Wall cannot be farther west than the present Suq Khan ez-Zeit. Excavations beneath the Holy Sepulcher and in the Muristan reveal that this area was not within the city of the late first century BCE or early first century CE. There is unambiguous evidence that it was an abandoned quarry. A Jewish catacomb was cut in the west wall. The six kokhim graves still visible in the Holy Sepulcher are typical of the first centuries BCE and CE. A projecting corner in the south wall, which sloped to the southeast, was called *Golgotha ("[the place of] the skull"). The relationship of these two elements corresponds perfectly with the description of Jesus' crucifixion and burial in John 19.17–42.

While he presumably repaired, and in some cases certainly strengthened, the walls of the city, Herod did not alter the lines he had inherited. The prime contemporary written source for data on the area they enclosed is Josephus's *Jewish War*. The principal passages are 5.4.136–83 and 6.4.220–442, but other topographical references are scattered throughout the work. He consistently refers to the western hill as the Upper City, and alludes to the old City of David on Ophel as the Lower City. Cemeteries bordered the city on the north and east; the tombs of the families of Herod the Great (*War* 5.108) and of the high priest *Caiaphas have been located west of the city.

Herod's Buildings. Herod's first concern was for his own security. On the site of the Hasmonean Baris at the northwest corner of the Temple he built the Antonia fortress (*War* 5.5.238–45). Since it was named for Mark Antony, it must have been completed prior to the latter's defeat in 31 BCE. Paul was imprisoned there (Acts 21.27–22.30). The Roman garrison based there after 6 CE may have influenced the growth of the healing shrine outside the walls to the east, which figures in John 5.1–9. For the entertainment of his supporters Herod built a theater and an amphitheater (*Ant.* 15.8.268). The latter has not been located, but the former was in a little valley south of the Hinnom. The hippodrome (*War* 2.3.44) must have been in the Kidron valley. The quadrennial contests for which these were built gave great offense to pious Jews. In order to further elevate his splendid palace (*War* 5.4.161–82), excavations show that Herod erected a podium at the highest point of the Upper City. It was protected by three great towers, Hippicus, Mariamne, and Phasaelis. The latter surpassed the Pharos of Alexandria, one of the seven wonders of the ancient world. Its great base (today part of the Citadel) is the only element of the palace to have survived.

After the Romans assumed direct control of Palestine in 6 CE, Herod's palace became the residence of the procurators when they came to Jerusalem (*War* 2.14.301–308); Philo calls it "the house of the procurators" (*Leg. ad Gaium* 306). It is here then that we must locate the praetorium in which Pontius *Pilate judged Jesus (John 18.28). This is confirmed by the geographic term used in John 19.13, because Gabbatha ("high point") can only apply to this part of the Hero-

dian city. At this stage the descendants of Herod used the Hasmonean palace on the western edge of the Tyropoeon valley (*Ant.* 20.8.189–90; cf. Luke 23.7–12).

Starting in 20 BCE it took Herod nine and a half years to complete rebuilding the *Temple on a much grander scale than its predecessor on the same site (*War* 5.5.184–247; *Ant.* 15.11.380–425). Nothing remains except the huge retaining walls supporting the platform, the western side of which became a site for Jewish prayer (the "Wailing Wall") after the destruction of the Temple. Such building activity inspired others, and the quality of life of the wealthy in first century CE Jerusalem is nowhere more evident than in the magnificent mansions excavated in the Jewish Quarter.

The sources make no mention of any concern on the part of Herod for the water supply of the city, but Josephus's mention of the Serpent's Pool (*War* 5.3.108; today Birkat es-Sultan), which served a large catchment area west of the city, probably implies the existence of the serpentine 67 km (42 mi) low-level aqueduct that brought water from Arrub via Solomon's Pools to the Temple. Herod certainly constructed the great reservoir, Birkat Israel, against the north wall of the Temple, and it is likely that he refurbished the Pool of Siloam (John 9.7). Other known reservoirs are Struthion (*War* 5.11.467), adjacent to the Antonia, and Amygdalon (*War* 5.11.468), just north of the palace; the latter was fed by aqueducts from Mamilla and from the north. When the water stored in house cisterns is added, it has been calculated that the population ceiling must have been about seventy thousand.

After Herod the Great. Pilate is credited with having constructed a new aqueduct soon after 26 CE (*War* 2.9.175), but it cannot be identified with the 15 km (9 mi) high-level aqueduct from Bir el-Daraj that supplied the Upper City, and which inscriptions date to 195 CE. The prosperity of Jerusalem increased the demand on space, and the climate of peace meant that there was no risk in building outside the Second Wall. Herod Agrippa I (41–44 CE) tried to wall in this New City or suburb of Bezetha, but the attempt was blocked by the Emperor Claudius (*Ant.* 19.7.326–327). This wall, completed by the rebels during the First Revolt (66–70 CE), is the famous Third Wall of Josephus (*War* 5.4.147–55), which has given rise to intense debate, because the data given by Josephus are both vague and incoherent. Only two elements have been identified archaeologically, the north gate beneath the present Damascus Gate, and the east gate, which is the Ecce Homo arch near the Antonia. When eighteen thousand men were made redundant on the completion of work on the Temple in 62–64 CE, Herod Agrippa II employed them to pave the city with white stone (*Ant.* 20.9.219–22).

The Roman siege began at Passover 70 CE, while internecine warfare raged in the city. All Jerusalem was in the hand of the legions by late August. By order of Titus it was levelled to the ground, the only exceptions being the great towers, Phasaelis, Hippicus, and Mariamne, which were left as a memorial to Jerusalem's former strength and glory (*War* 7.1.1–2).

JEROME MURPHY-O'CONNOR

Symbolism

Although the sixteenth century was a period of great scientific advances among European mapmakers, one of the best known maps of that period is more imaginative than accurate: a woodcut in the form of a cloverleaf, with Jerusalem depicted as the center of the world from which emanate the continents of Europe, Asia, and Africa. The idea of the centrality of Jerusalem has been a mainstay in Christianity, in various ways, since its inception. It has also been integral to Judaism since the time of King *David in the tenth century BCE and, together with the sacred cities of Mecca and Medina, to Islam since its beginnings in the seventh century CE. In the modern era of nation-states, Jerusalem is both the capital of Israel and, for Palestinians, the capital of the state of Palestine. Thus, Jerusalem has long been a focus of powerful and intertwined passions of religion and politics. Although its name probably originally meant "foundation of [the god] Shalem," it has often been interpreted to mean "city of peace" (Hebr.ʿîr šālōm). But peace has remained an elusive goal for most of Jerusalem's entire history.

In his meditation on this most holy and painful city (*Jerusalem: City of Mirrors*, [Boston, 1989]), the "capital of memory," the Israeli writer Amos Elon observed that it is as if the very name Jerusalem (Hebr. yĕrûšālaim) is a reflection of the city's contradictory, even dualistic nature (*aim* is the Hebrew suffix indicating a dual or pair), manifesting itself even in its location on the boundary between Israel's cultivated grasslands and arid desert regions. There has always been a tension between the present and the future, the earthly and the heavenly, the real and the ideal Jerusalem, a city of diverse peoples struggling to accomplish their daily activities and the city of religious visionaries.

The name Jerusalem occurs 660 times in the Hebrew Bible; *Zion, often used as synonymous with Jerusalem, especially in biblical poetry, occurs another 154 times. The former appears most frequently in the historical narratives of 2 Samuel, Kings, Chronicles, Ezra and Nehemiah, and in the prophetic books of Isaiah, Jeremiah, Ezekiel, and Zechariah. Except for Salem in Genesis 14.18, it is absent from the *Pentateuch, achieving importance in ancient Israel's self-understanding only after David brought the *ark of the covenant, symbol of God's presence, to the newly conquered city. The ark would find its permanent home in the Jerusalem *Temple, the house of God, completed by David's son *Solomon, and strategically situated very near to the house of God's loyal servant, the king. The belief in the inviolability of Jerusalem, the chosen dwelling place of God, was challenged by such prophets as Micah and Jeremiah, who warned that the city would be destroyed as a result of its transgressions (Mic. 3.12, quoted in Jer. 26.18). But after the *Babylonian destruction of Jerusalem and its Temple in 587/586 BCE, the exilic prophets envisioned a new Jerusalem, which was simultaneously a rebuilding and restoration of the old and also an idealized city, both grander and more enduring than its predecessor, offering its inhabitants a relationship with God and concomitant peace and prosperity. For Jeremiah, the rebuilt Jerusalem was well grounded in the old, even in its physical contours (30.18; 31.38–40). Ezekiel, who understood Jerusalem as "in the center of the nations, with countries all around her" (5.5), celebrates a new city and a new Temple, areas of radiating holiness, fruitfulness, and well-being (chaps. 40–48), where God's *glory will again reside: "And the name of the city from that time on shall be, The Lord is There" (48.35). Second Isaiah is consoling in its assertion that Jerusalem "has served her term, that her penalty is paid" (Isa. 40.2). The gates of the new city will always be open (60.11), and the Lord will be its everlasting light (60.19–20). "No more shall there be in it an infant that lives but a few days, or an old person who does not live out a lifetime" (65.20).

The hopes and expectations of the exilic prophets were realized in part with the rebuilding of the city and Temple during the latter half of the sixth century BCE, the first generation of Persian rule. Both, however, would be destroyed by the Roman army in 70 CE. The Temple was never rebuilt. In the generation before its destruction, the Alexandrian Jewish philosopher and statesman *Philo wrote that the Jews "hold the Holy City where stands the sacred Temple of the most high God to be their mother city" (*Flaccum* 46). The destruction of the Temple and "mother city" was both a great blow and a great challenge to Jews, inside and outside of Israel. Some Jewish *apocalyptic texts from this period envisioned that at the end time, the heavenly Jerusalem, fashioned by God, would descend to earth; others envisioned a heavenly Jerusalem that awaited the righteous above. In either case, the renewal of Jerusalem was integral to the vision of the end time, a role already suggested in the eschatological visions of the exilic and postexilic prophets.

The formative texts of rabbinic Judaism, which date from roughly the third to the seventh centuries CE, share with the earlier apocalyptic texts both the centrality of the renewal of Jerusalem in the messianic age, and a lack of uniformity in the description of that future, ideal city; in some texts, an earthly Jerusalem, and in others a heavenly city; in some an earthly city that ascends to heaven, and in others a heavenly city that descends to earth. What is striking, however, are the linkages and interdependencies between the earthly and the heavenly Jerusalem. In the anti-Roman messianic Palestinian Jewish revolt of Bar Kochba (132–135 CE), the rebels struck coins with the image of the Temple facade and the inscription "of the freedom of Jerusalem," indicating their hopes for the rebuilding of Jerusalem and its Temple. Similarly, the Jewish rebels of the First Revolt (66–70 CE), with their constellation of religious, nationalist, and messianic apocalyptic motivations, issued coins with the inscription, "Jerusalem the holy" (*see* Money). As noted above, however, the consequence of the first revolt was not the reinvigoration of Jerusalem, but rather its destruction.

Early rabbinic literature did not focus only on the Jerusalem of the messianic age. The *Mishnah, *Talmuds, and midrashic collections celebrated the memory of the historic Jerusalem as well. Some texts describe Jerusalem as the center or "navel" of the world; others depict in glowing language the grandeur and uniqueness of the city. Jerusalem's uniqueness was reflected also in the halakhic requirements associated with the city, most of which were not practiced, given the destruction of the Temple and city, and the banning of Jews from Jerusalem by the Roman

emperor Hadrian, in the aftermath of the war of Bar Kochba.

As if in response to the words of the psalmist of a long-gone era, "If I forget you, O Jerusalem, let my right hand wither" (Ps. 137.5), the memory of Jerusalem and its Temple and the hope for their restoration were reflected in evolving Jewish liturgy, to be evoked on occasions of joy and mourning and perhaps, most importantly, to be recited as part of the Grace after Meals and the daily Amidah prayer, which together with the *Shema, constitute, in a sense, the foundation of Jewish liturgy. The ninth of the month of Av developed as a day of fasting and mourning for the destruction of the First and Second Temples, becoming associated also with other calamitous events in Jewish history (see, e.g., *m. Taʿan.* 4.6).

It is not clear to what degree and for how long Hadrian's decree banning Jews from Jerusalem was enforced. Jews were permitted to reside in Jerusalem, however, during its many centuries of Muslim rule, beginning with its conquest by Caliph Umar in 638, interrupted only by the brief and, in many ways, violent rule of the twelfth-century Crusader Kingdom of Jerusalem. During the years of Ottoman rule (1517–1917), notwithstanding the rebuilding of Jerusalem's walls (1537–1541) by Suleiman I, Jerusalem remained a small and impoverished city. Only in the mid-to-late nineteenth century did the Jews, Latin Christians, Armenian Christians, and Muslims leave their traditional quarters in the walled city to establish new ongoing neighborhoods, the Jews settling generally to the west of the Old City.

The expansion of Jerusalem outside of the walled city developed at roughly the same time as European Zionism. Many factors contributed to the evolution of the latter, including the anti-Jewish policies of the Russian czarist governments, the overall political, social, and economic conditions of Eastern European Jewry, the evolution of anti-Semitic movements and agitation in Western Europe, and the presence and vitality of other European nationalist movements. Notwithstanding the generally nontraditional religious orientation of most of the early Zionist leaders, one cannot underestimate the significance for them of Jewish historical connections with the land of Israel and the city of Jerusalem, suggested even in the term "Zionism." Nonetheless, many of the early Zionist leaders expressed a kind of ambivalence about Jerusalem, reacting seemingly both to the physical squalor of the city and, from their perspectives, to Jerusalem's tired and outdated Jewish religious practices and passions. The ultra-Orthodox Jewish communities of Jerusalem were a counterpoint to the Zionists' visions of a transformed Jewish society. As late as 1947, the Zionist leadership was willing to accept the United Nations resolution to partition Palestine into a Jewish state and an Arab state, and to make Jerusalem a separate political entity under international administration. Following the war of 1948 and the bloody battle for Jerusalem, however, neither the internationalization of Jerusalem nor the Arab state in Palestine was established. Instead, the land fell under Israeli or Jordanian rule with western Jerusalem under Israeli control and eastern Jerusalem, including the Old City and its holy places, under Jordanian control. Jerusalem was declared the official capital of Israel in December 1949. As a result of the 1967 Six Day War, Israel began to govern formerly Jordanian-held East Jerusalem, which was later officially annexed and incorporated by the Israeli government into the state of Israel. Within the Old City stood the Western or Wailing Wall, a retaining wall from the Second Temple as renovated by *Herod in the first century BCE. It continues to function as a complex religious-national symbol, a focus of prayer, and an object of pilgrimage for Jews inside and outside of Israel. Today, even most of the significant number of Israeli Jews who support territorial compromise with the Palestinians in exchange for peace, including the establishment of a Palestinian state in the West Bank and Gaza, are reluctant to give up any portion of Jerusalem, or to see the city come under international rule or be divided again. Analogously, the significant number of Palestinians who also support a "two state solution" insist that eastern Jerusalem serve as the capital of Palestine. Thus the "city of peace" remains a stumbling block in Arab-Israeli and Palestinian-Israeli negotiations.

Although the Christian population of Jerusalem, two to three percent of the total, has been in decline for the last fifty years, the number of Christian visitors and pilgrims to Jerusalem remains very large. The roots of this fascination with Jerusalem date both to the origins of Christianity as a first-century Palestinian Jewish apocalyptic movement and to the depictions of the ministry, death, and resurrection of Jesus in the four New Testament Gospels. The Gospels mention Jerusalem sixty-seven times. Matthew refers to it as the "holy city" (4.5; 27.53). Although the texts vary, each of the Gospels depicts Jesus as moving seemingly inevitably to Jerusalem, the site of the pivotal events of the life of Jesus and of Christianity's self-understanding, that is Jesus' death and resurrection; and, for first-century Palestinian Jewry, their national and religious center.

As was the case with other kinds of Judaism of this period, early Christianity knew of both an earthly and a heavenly Jerusalem (e.g., Gal. 4.25–26; Heb. 12.22–24). The book of *Revelation, drawing heavily on Ezekiel's vision of the new Jerusalem and very reminiscent of contemporary Jewish apocalyptic texts, describes "the holy city, the new Jerusalem, coming down out of heaven from God" (21.2). Unlike Ezekiel's city, however, this Jerusalem has no Temple, "for its temple is the Lord God the Almighty and the Lamb (21.22)." As Robert Wilken has noted, speculation concerning God's future kingdom on earth with Jerusalem as its center dominated Christian eschatology of the first and second centuries, as, for example, in the writings of Justin Martyr and Irenaeus. Later church fathers, however, such as Origen, who spent more than twenty years in third-century Caesarea, disputed the teachings of Justin Martyr and Irenaeus, as well as Jewish beliefs in the future restoration of some kind of Jerusalem on earth, and spoke only of the heavenly Jerusalem, which remained above and entirely separate from the earthly city.

The fourth century was a period of tremendous change for Christianity. It entered the century as the religion of a persecuted minority, and exited as the official state religion of the Roman empire. Emperor Constantine made Christianity a legal religion in 313, and became its patron and protector. Palestine and in particular Jerusalem became a Christian showplace of sorts. From the time of Constantine, massive church building projects were undertaken to create a visible and glorious manifestation of the legitimacy and permanence of Christian rule— an outward sign of the truth and victory of Christianity. Money poured in from both the government and private persons, bringing with it increased material prosperity and cosmopolitanism for all of fourth- and fifth-century Palestine. Hadrian's Jerusalem, Roman Aelia Capitolina, named after the emperor and the gods of the Capitoline in Rome, would be transformed into a Christian Jerusalem. Constantine himself sponsored the building of three major Palestinian churches, all connected with the life of Jesus, and two of which were in Jerusalem:

the Church of the Holy Sepulcher; a church on the Mount of *Olives; and the Church of the Nativity in nearby *Bethlehem. Already, in the writings of Eusebius, the early fourth-century Caesarean church historian, one can see intimations of the Palestinian church's understanding of itself as guardian of a very earthly Christian Palestine with its center at Jerusalem—a land in which Christians lived and visited, and in which one could see and touch the very places in which the saving events of biblical history had taken place.

Christian pilgrimage to Palestine and especially Jerusalem became widespread in the fourth century. Early pilgrims included Helena, the mother of Constantine. Fourth-century Christian pilgrims, as part of their quest for perfection, would undertake the dangers of travel to Palestine to visit the holy places, and therein both confirm and strengthen their faith. As pilgrimage flourished, some church leaders questioned its value, drawing attention to the contrast between "Jerusalem the Holy" and the city that awaited the pilgrim. For example, Gregory of Nyssa in his "Letter on Pilgrimage" pointed to the "shameful practices" of the people of Jerusalem as evidence that God's grace was no more abundant in Jerusalem than elsewhere.

Echoes of early Christian speculations on the role and nature of Jerusalem in the end time, as well as an interest in the earthly city itself, can be found both in the constellation of factors that shaped the Crusades of medieval Europe, and in the voyages of Columbus who, influenced by late fifteenth-century apocalyptic thought, sought to acquire the gold to finance the final crusade, which would capture Jerusalem and place it again in Christian hands—all part of God's plan for the end time.

Columbus failed in his plans, but Christian interest in and pilgrimage to Jerusalem has endured. For many pilgrims, the Church of the Holy Sepulcher, consecrated in 335, was the highlight of their trip. Today it remains the major Christian holy place in Jerusalem, although most of what can be seen dates from the period of the Crusades, the Church having been destroyed and rebuilt several times since the time of Constantine. Several Christian denominations have rights to various sections of the Church. In their stories of conflict and cooperation, they are illustrative of the diversity within Christianity and the long, complex, and vital history of the Christian community in Jerusalem.

Although an overview of the symbolism and significance of Jerusalem for Islam is beyond the scope of this article, one must note both the importance of Jerusalem for Islam, and the importance of the city's Muslim communities since their inception in the seventh century CE for the history of Jerusalem, in Arabic "al-Quds," "the Holy." Today, Jerusalem's major Muslim holy place, the magnificent Dome of the Rock, a rotunda on an octagonal base, built by the Umayyad Caliph Abd al-Malik and completed in 691/692, dominates the Haram al-Sharif, or Noble Sanctuary, also the site of the Temple Mount of the Jews. The Dome, reminiscent on a grander scale of the nearby Church of the Holy Sepulcher, was constructed in the architectural style of the Byzantine martyrium to serve as a shrine for the holy rock beneath it—a rock which by the time of the Muslim conquest of Jerusalem in 638 was already associated with the Temple and with *Abraham, the common traditional ancestor of Judaism, Christianity, and Islam. The Dome affirmed the triumph of Islam in the midst of the Christian showplace, Jerusalem, "The Holy City," and in a place, atop the Temple Mount, which the Byzantine Christians had kept in ruins to concretize Christian beliefs that the destruction of the Jerusalem Temple was both a fulfillment of prophecy and a proof of the victory and truth claims of the "New Israel."

The sanctity for Islam of the Rock, the Haram, and Jerusalem, in general, was strengthened by the identification by early Muslim authorities of Jerusalem as the destiny of the Prophet Muhammad's night journey (Sūrah 17:1), and the Rock as the place from which he ascended to heaven (Sūrah 53:4–10). As in Judaism and Christianity, Jerusalem assumed an important role in Muslim beliefs concerning the end time and the *day of judgment. So too, Muslim sources reflect the tensions between the holy city, setting of the last judgment, and Jerusalem in its daily activities. Thus Muqaddasi, a tenth-century geographer and historian, and a native of Jerusalem, would celebrate Jerusalem as "the most illustrious of cities" where the advantages of the present and the next world meet, and also describe the city as a place oppressive to the poor, lacking in learned men, "a golden basin filled with scorpions."

Jerusalem is today a city of approximately one-half million people, a city which both celebrates and is haunted by its history, a city in which the tensions between the ideal and the real Jerusalem are lived and witnessed daily, and in which the rages and passions of religion and politics bring to mind the words of the psalmist, "Pray for the peace of Jerusalem" (Ps. 122.6).　BARBARA GELLER NATHANSON

Jesus Christ

Life and Teaching. *Introduction: critical method.* By accepting the modern critical method of studying the New Testament, we need not attempt to write a life of Jesus in the modern sense of a psychological study. We can hope only to reconstruct the barest outline of his career and to give some account of his message and teaching.

We shall assume that *Mark is the earliest of the four *Gospels and that, apart from the passion narrative (14.1–16.8), the individual units of material are arranged in an order determined more by subject matter than by historical or chronological concerns. Moreover, these units of material (stories about Jesus, pronouncement stories, *miracle stories, *parables, and aphorisms) were adapted to the needs of the post-Easter community and circulated in oral tradition for some forty years before Mark was written down. The authors of the two later *synoptic Gospels, *Matthew, and *Luke, used Mark as their primary source, plus a common source consisting mostly of sayings, unknown to Mark. This source is hypothetical and only recoverable by reconstructing the non-Marcan material common to Matthew and Luke. It is generally known as *Q, from the German word *Quelle*, "source." In addition, Matthew and Luke have their own special traditions. Like Mark, the three sources— Q, Special Matthew, and Special Luke—contain material previously passed on orally for some fifty years. The evangelists, in their use of sources and oral traditions, shaped them according to their theological interests; this editorial work is known as redaction. Thus, the synoptic Gospels contain material that developed in three stages: authentic words and memories of Jesus himself (stage I), materials shaped and transmitted in oral tradition (stage II), and the evangelists' redaction (stage III). The gospel of *John, however, is very different. It contains some stage I and stage II materials independent of the synoptics that can be used sometimes to confirm or supplement the synoptic evidence in reconstructing the career and teaching of Jesus. But the Fourth Gospel contains much more material belonging to stage III. In reconstructing our account of Jesus, we shall attempt to recover stage I materials from all four Gospels. We shall be assisted by certain tests of authenticity. We may

be reasonably certain that materials go back to stage I if they meet some or all of the following criteria: (1) have multiple attestation (i.e., are attested in more than one source or in more than one type of material); (2) are distinctive to Jesus (i.e., they are without parallel in Judaism or in the post-Easter community; this test should be used with caution and generally applied to confirm rather than exclude; principle of dissimilarity); (3) cohere with other accepted Jesus traditions (test of coherence); and/or (4) exhibit indications of originating in *Aramaic (in the case of sayings), since this was Jesus' normal language (though he probably knew some *Greek), or in a Palestinian milieu or social setting.

The birth and upbringing of Jesus. The birth stories in Matthew and Luke are relatively late, and belong to stages II and III. But they contain certain items that go back to earlier tradition. Some of these are clearly theological: Davidic descent, conception through the *Holy Spirit while his mother remained a virgin, homage at birth. Factual data in these common items include: the date of Jesus' birth in the last years of the reign of *Herod the Great (died 4 BCE); the names of Jesus' parents, *Mary and *Joseph; the fact that the child was conceived between betrothal and wedding; the birth at *Bethlehem (though this may be a theological assertion, associated with the Davidic descent). In any case, Jesus was brought up in *Nazareth. His father is said in Matthew 13.55 to have been a carpenter, and Jesus is said to have been one himself in Mark 6.3. Since sons habitually followed their father's trade, this is not improbable. Presumably, Jesus received the education of the devout poor in Israel, with thorough instruction in the Hebrew scriptures.

The beginning of Jesus' public ministry: his message. Jesus' public career began when he left home for the *Jordan River to be baptized by *John the Baptist. Jesus looked back to the Baptist as the source of his mission and authority (Mark 11.27–33). For a time, he appears to have conducted a ministry of baptizing parallel to that of the Baptist (see John 3.22; 4.1), presumably continuing the Baptist's message by demanding repentance from Israel in view of the impending advent of God's *kingdom. After the Baptist's arrest (Mark 1.14), Jesus embarked upon a new kind of ministry. The message of the kingdom acquired a new urgency, perhaps as a result of the *temptation (Mark 1.12–13), which included a vision of God's victory over *Satan (Luke 10.18).

Abandoning the practice of *baptism, Jesus went to the *synagogues for a time and then spoke in the open air, reaching out to the people instead of waiting for them to come to him; but still like the Baptist, he continued preaching the coming kingdom. Jesus never defined what he meant by the kingdom, but it means God's coming in saving power and strength, defeating the powers of evil and inaugurating salvation for Israel. It is basically future ("your kingdom come" in the *Lord's Prayer) but also presently operative in Jesus' words and works (Matt. 12.28 ‖ Luke 11.20 Q). In the *parables of the kingdom, Jesus seeks to engage his hearers, persuading them to see the present operation of the kingdom in his own words and works, and to secure from them the response of faith and confidence in its future consummation—parables of the sower, the seed growing secretly, the mustard seed (Mark 4.3–32); also the leaven (Matt. 13.33 ‖ Luke 13.20–21 Q).

An inescapable conclusion is that Jesus was influenced by the prophecies of *Isaiah 40–66, where the coming of the reign of God is a central theme (Isa. 52.7). Indeed, much of Jesus' teaching is shot through with allusions to Isaiah 40–66. Jesus is represented as quoting Isaiah 61.1–2 and 58.6 in the inaugural sermon in the synagogue at Nazareth (Luke 4.18–19), but the content of the sermon was probably shaped in stage II or III. There are, however, clear echoes of these passages in the Beatitudes (Matt. 5.3–6 ‖ Luke 6.20–23 Q) and in the answer to John (Matt. 11.5–6 ‖ Luke 7.22–23). Jesus thus appeared first and foremost as eschatological prophet, one who announced the definitive coming of God's kingly rule, the salvation of the end time.

Jesus' teaching: ethics. Jesus was also recognized as a *rabbi and teacher. Like the rabbis, he taught in synagogues, collected a band of disciples, and discussed *Torah with them as well as with inquirers and critics. The forms of his teachings were similar to those employed by Pharisaic teachers: parables and aphorisms, that is, sayings, often of a wisdom type, enunciating general truths about human life and manners (e.g., the teaching on anxiety in Matt. 6.25–34). Like the *Pharisees, Jesus took the authority of the Hebrew Bible for granted. It enunciates the demands of God: prohibition of *divorce (Mark 10.6–8; Matt 5.32; Luke 16.18); the second tablet of the *Ten Commandments (Mark 10.19); the *Shema and the summary of the law (Mark 12.29–31).

Yet there are differences between Jesus' teaching and those of the Pharisees. He emphasizes more strongly than they that God demands not just outward conformity to the *law but the whole person, and not just love of *neighbor but love of enemy (see the antitheses of the *Sermon on the Mount, Matt. 5.21–48). The rich young man must not only keep the commandments but sell all he has and follow Jesus (Mark 10.21).

For Jesus, God's demand is summed up in the double commandment of *love. This raises the question of the relationship between Jesus' preaching of the kingdom and his enunciation of God's demand, between his prophetic preaching and his wisdom teaching. Jesus never relates the two; in fact, he relates his wisdom teaching to *creation rather than to the coming of God's kingly rule. Thus, the command to love one's enemy is based on the fact that God causes the rain to fall and the sun to shine upon the just and the unjust alike (Matt. 5.45; cf. Luke 6.35). Similarly, the absolute prohibition of divorce shows that the reversion to the situation at creation is now possible because of the shift in the ages: the age of *Moses is coming to an end, and God's kingly rule is coming. Therefore, Jesus' prophetic preaching presupposes his wisdom teaching. The coming of that rule makes possible the realization of God's original intent in creation. The same unspoken presupposition operates in the double commandment of love: only the coming of God's kingly rule makes it possible for people to love God in radical obedience and to love one's neighbor, including one's enemy. For God's coming in his kingly rule is an act of mercy and forgiveness (an important aspect of Jesus' message; see, e.g., Mark 2.5; Luke 7.47; Matt. 18.23–35; also Jesus' preaching of repentance is connected with his offer of forgiveness: Mark 1.15; 6.12; Matt. 11.20); and forgiveness as a human response to God's forgiveness is the supreme expression of love. Jesus' prophetic message is the indicative and his enunciation of the will of God is the imperative that the indicative implies.

Jesus' teaching about God. Jesus brought no new teaching about God. God is the creator, though this is understood in an immediate way. God did not merely create the world in the beginning, rather, it comes from him as his creation in every moment (Matt. 6.26, 30, 32, and the fourth petition of the Lord's Prayer). For Jesus, God is also the God who acts in history, the climax of which is the coming of the kingdom (see e.g., Matt. 13.16–17 ‖ Luke 10.23–24 Q, and the tradition behind Matt. 23.34–35 ∥ Luke 11.49–50). Also, Jesus frequently adduced biblical characters whose situation in their day was analogous to the situation of his contemporaries in the face of the coming kingdom (e.g., Lot and his wife, the Queen of *Sheba, Jonah).

Although the address of God as Father is not unknown in the Hebrew Bible and Judaism, and even the familiar *abba is not completely without precedent, that usage was characteristic of Jesus. He did not enunciate the fatherhood of God as an abstract doctrine or a general truth but himself experienced God as his own Father (i.e., in his call to his unique mission mediated through his baptism and temptations), and he offered to those who responded to his prophetic message a similar experience and the privilege of addressing God as abba (note the opening address of the Lord's Prayer in its original Lucan form, Luke 11.2).

Jesus' conduct. Jesus appeared as a charismatic healer as well as a preacher and teacher. This was a further implementation of the prophetic mission set forth in Isaiah 35 and 61 (Matt. 11.5–6 ∥ Luke 7.22–23). Jesus performed *exorcisms, which he claimed were the action in him of the Spirit (Matthew) or finger (Luke) of God. To deny this spirit at work in his exorcisms was blasphemy, a sin for which there would be no forgiveness (Mark 3.29). Thus, both healings and exorcisms are related to his message. The actual miracle stories may not be direct reports, but they reflect a general memory that Jesus did do such things. More problematic are the so-called nature miracles. There are three raising stories—Jairus's daughter (Mark 5.21–24, 35–43), the widow's son at Nain (Luke 7.11–17), and Lazarus (John 11.1–44)—but all these belong to stage II. The answer to John (Matt. 11.5–6 ∥ Luke 7.22–23), however, may enable us to take back the fact of resuscitations to stage I, in which case the three stories of the raising may rest upon a general memory that Jesus did perform such deeds. Another special instance of a nature miracle is the feeding of the multitude. This miracle has multiple attestation (Mark 6.30–44, Mark 8.1–10, and John 6.1–15 represent three independent traditions). The shaping of the stories originated early in stage II, where they were modeled partly on the eucharistic tradition and partly on the *Elisha story (2 Kings 4.42–44, whence the miraculous multiplication of the loaves derives). But such a meal itself may well be historical: Jesus met with his followers in

a remote place and ate with them. This meal may have been one of a series of events constituting a crisis at the climax of the Galilean ministry (see below).

Jesus also celebrated *meals with the outcast, and for this too there is multiple attestation. In the parables of the lost (Luke 15), Jesus interprets this action as a celebration in advance of the joy of the great banquet of the kingdom of God.

Like John the Baptist, Jesus addressed his message of repentance in view of the coming kingdom to Israel as a whole. But he called some to follow him, accompany him, and share in the work of proclaiming the message. From these he selected *twelve to symbolize the restoration of Israel (Mark 3.14; 6.7; Matt. 19.28; cf. Luke 22.28–30). It would seem that much of Jesus' radical demand was intended for these followers, who constituted a band of wandering charismatic preachers and therefore had to dispense, as he did, with the normal securities of human life (Mark 6.8–9), including family ties (see Mark 3.34–35; 8.34–37; 10.28–30).

The central crisis. It is clear that at one point Jesus broke off his Galilean ministry and transferred his activities to *Jerusalem. There are indications of a series of events starting with the feeding of the multitude (Mark 6.30–52; 8.1–9.13; John 6.1–71), followed by a withdrawal from the crowds, a crossing of the lake, and a period of solitary communication with his disciples (represented by the confession of Peter and the Transfiguration), after which Jesus set out for Jerusalem. We may suppose that during this period of solitude Jesus resolved that it was now God's plan for him to go to Jerusalem and carry his message to Israel at the very center of its life. Two circumstances may have contributed to this decision. First, Jesus' ministry evoked a dangerous messianic enthusiasm among the crowds (John 6.15, clarifying Mark 6.45). Second, the execution of John the Baptist (Mark 6.14–29; cf. 9.13) made Jesus fear that Herod Antipas might arrest him before he could challenge the authorities in Jerusalem (Luke 13.31–34).

The chronology of the Galilean ministry. Since Mark mentions only one *Passover during Jesus' public career, it is often supposed that his entire ministry lasted but a few months, less than one year. True, John mentions two Passovers before the final one (2.13; 6.4), but these references belong to stage III. There are, however, indications of two springs during the Galilean ministry.

In Mark 2.23, Jesus' disciples plucked ears of grain, while in the first feeding the crowds sit on the "green grass" (6.39). If we can trust these items and if they do not refer to the same spring, it would permit us to conclude that the Galilean ministry lasted over a year, for the grainfields episode requires that Jesus should have had time to collect a band of followers, and the feeding presumes a longer ministry. According to Luke 3.1, the Baptist's ministry began in the fifteenth year of Tiberius's reign (27 CE). Jesus' baptism could have occurred in that year, his Judean ministry would have covered the intervening period, and the Galilean ministry would have begun in late 27 or early 28 and ended after the spring of 29. But this is highly speculative. (*See also* Chronology, *article on* Early Christian Chronology.)

The journey to Jerusalem. John's gospel has obscured the decisiveness of Jesus' final journey to Jerusalem by bringing him to the holy city on two earlier occasions (John 2.12; 5.1), but these episodes probably belonged to the final Jerusalem period. John may be right, though, in making the Jerusalem ministry last for several months rather than for a single week, as it does in Mark. Indeed, Luke offers some support for a longer Jerusalem ministry (Luke 13.34). This would mean that the journey would have occurred some months earlier than the final Passover, perhaps bringing Jesus to Jerusalem in time for the feast of tabernacles (John 7.2). This would be in the fall of 29 CE.

The purpose of the trip is stated in Mark's three passion predictions (8.31; 9.31; 10.33-34). It is generally agreed that these predictions in their present form are prophecies after the event and therefore reflect a knowledge of the passion story (stage II). But they may well contain an authentic nucleus (stage I), such as "the Son of man will be delivered into the hands of men" (Mark 9.31), where we have an Aramaic play on words (Son of man/ men). Jesus hardly went up to Jerusalem in order to die; that, it has been suggested, would be tantamount to suicide. But he may well have realized that death would be the inevitable outcome of his mission.

The ministry in Jerusalem. Jesus continued to preach and teach in Jerusalem as he had done in Galilee. He also engaged in conflicts with his adversaries. These conflicts, Mark indicates, were of a different kind from the earlier ones in Galilee. Jesus is now a marked man and his enemies engage him on specific issues, seeking to entrap him into self-incrimination. John likewise presents Jesus as engaged in theological conflict with the religious authorities in Jerusalem.

Jesus' challenge reached its climax in his entry to Jerusalem and the "cleansing" of the Temple (so the Synoptics; John shifts the "cleansing" for theological reasons to the beginning of the ministry). It is not at all clear what the precise issues were that led the *Sanhedrin to plot Jesus' execution (for the plot see Mark 14.1-2; 10-11; John 11.45-54). The Synoptics attribute the plot against Jesus to the Sanhedrin's reaction to the cleansing of the Temple (Mark 11.18 par.), while John, less convincingly, attributes it to the raising of Lazarus. Yet John's report of the Sanhedrin meeting (John 11.47-53) seems to be based on reliable tradition: the Sanhedrin decided to get rid of Jesus out of fear that any disturbance of the peace would lead to Roman intervention and destroy the delicate balance between Jewish and Roman power.

On the eve of Passover (following the more plausible chronology of John), Jesus celebrated a farewell meal with his disciples. In the course of it, he interpreted his impending death as the climax of his life of self-giving service (Luke 22.24-27; cf. John 13.1-11; Mark 10.42-45a may originally have belonged to this context). The exact words Jesus spoke over the bread and cup are impossible to recover, since the various accounts of the institution (1 Cor. 11.23-25; Mark 14.22-24 ‖ Matt. 26.26-28; Luke 22.19-20) have been colored by liturgical developments in the post-Easter community (*see* Lord's Supper). But they all agree that Jesus associated the bread with his body (i.e., his person) and the wine with his blood (i.e., the giving of his life in death) and with the inauguration of a (new) *covenant. He also assured his disciples that beyond his death lay the coming of the kingdom of God (Mark 14.25; Luke 22.15-18).

After the supper, Jesus and the disciples went out to the garden of *Gethsemane (Mark 14.32; John 18.1) where he was arrested by Temple police, and also, if John 18.3 is correct, by Roman soldiers. This would indicate that the priestly party and the Roman prefect *Pilate were in close collusion over the matter. A preliminary investigation was held before the Jewish authorities (Mark 14.53-64; see also John 18.12-14, 19-24, which may be more accurate). This was not a formal trial, but more like a grand jury proceeding. By this investigation they established to their satisfaction that there was sufficient ground to warrant an accusation of high treason before Pilate's court (Mark 15.1–15). There Jesus was condemned to death as a messianic pretender. He was then taken out to *Golgotha and crucified with two criminals who were guilty of sedition (Mark 15.20b-32; John 19.16b–19). Jesus died later that same day and was buried, according to the gospel tradition, by sympathizers (Mark 15.42–47 par.; John 19.38–42). This marks the end of his earthly career.

Jesus' self-understanding. While Jesus' career evoked messianic hopes among his followers and fears among his enemies, stage I material shows him reluctant to assert any overt messianic claim. The self-designation he uses is *son of man. This is so widely attested in the gospel tradition and occurs (with one or two negligible exceptions) only on the lips of Jesus himself, that it satisfies the major tests of authenticity. It occurs in all primary strata of the gospel tradition (Mark, Q, Special Matthew, Special Luke, and the pre-Gospel tradition in John). It is not attested as a messianic title in earlier Judaism and occurs only once outside the gospels (apart from citations of Psalm 8.5–7), in Acts 7.56. So there should be no reasonable doubt that it was a characteristic self-designation of the historical Jesus. It is not a title but means "human one," and it is best understood as a self-effacing self-reference. It is used in contexts where Jesus spoke of his mission, fate, and final vindication.

Jesus certainly thought of himself as a prophet (Mark 6.4; Luke 13.33), but there was a final quality about his message and work that entitles us to conclude that he thought of himself as God's final, definitive emissary to Israel. He was more interested in what God was doing through him than in what he was in himself. He did not obtrude his own ego, yet his own ego was included as part of his message: "Whoever welcomes you welcomes me, and whoever welcomes me welcomes the one who sent me" (Matt. 10.40 ‖ Luke 10.16 Q); "Follow me" (Mark 1.17; etc.); "Those who are ashamed of me . . ." (Mark 8.38); "Blessed is anyone who takes no offense at me (Matt. 11.6 ‖ Luke 7.23 Q); "If it is by the Spirit [Luke: "finger"] of God that I cast out demons . . ." (Matt. 12.28 ‖ Luke 11.20 Q). Jesus dared to speak and act for God. This is clear in the antitheses of the Sermon on the Mount (Matt. 5.21–48: "It was said to those of ancient times . . . but I say to you"), in his pronouncement of the forgiveness of sins (which only God could

do, Mark 2.5–12; Luke 7.36–50), his acceptance of the outcast and healing of *lepers who were shunned under the law. Coupled with such features is the tremendous authority with which Jesus spoke and acted, an authority for which he offers no credentials save that it is intimately bound up with the authority of the Baptist (Mark 11.27–33) and rests upon God's final vindication (Mark 8.38 and Luke 12.8 Q). Jesus does not claim overtly to be *Son of God in any unique sense. Passages in which he appears to do so belong to stage II or III of the tradition. But he does call God "abba" in an unusual way, which points to God's call to which he has responded in full obedience, and therefore we may speak of his unique sense of sonship. But we must bear in mind that in this Palestinian milieu sonship denoted not a metaphysical quality but rather a historical call and obedience. Jesus did challenge his disciples to say who they thought he was, which elicited from Peter the response that he was the Christ or *Messiah (Mark 8.27–30; cf. John 6.66–69). According to Mark, he neither accepted nor rejected Peter's assertion. What did Peter mean, and in what sense did Jesus take it? It is commonly thought that it was meant in a political-nationalist sense and that Jesus rejected this. It seems more likely, however, that Peter meant it in the sense of the anointed prophet of Isaiah 61.1. Such a response to Jesus would have been wholly appropriate as far as it went. What Peter and the other disciples did not realize, of course, was that this mission extended beyond the terms of Isaiah 61 and that it also involved rejection, suffering, and death. It is possible, though much disputed, that Jesus modeled this further insight upon the figure of the suffering servant in Isaiah 53. We could be sure of this if Mark 10.45b belongs to stage I.

A very early tradition (Rom. 1.3) asserted that the earthly Jesus was of a family descended from the royal line of David. We cannot be sure that this played any role in his self-understanding. For the post-Easter community this title was important as qualifying him for the messianic role he assumed after his exaltation.

The use of "*Rabbi" and "my Lord" in addressing Jesus during his earthly ministry did not denote majesty: these were titles of respect accorded a charismatic person. However, as the conviction grew among his followers that he was the final emissary of God, these terms would acquire a heightened meaning.

In sum, we find in the Synoptics only limited

evidence for an explicit Christology in Jesus' self-understanding, and such evidence as there is is critically suspect. He was more concerned with what God was doing in him than who he was, especially in any metaphysical sense. But what God was doing through him in his earthly ministry provided the raw materials for the christological evaluation of Jesus after the Easter event.

Person and Work. *Introduction: critical presuppositions.* In reconstructing the New Testament interpretation of the person (Christology) and work (soteriology) of Jesus, we are concerned with the Christian community's response to the Christ event in its totality. This event embraces both his earthly career, culminating in his *crucifixion, and also the Easter event, that is, the community's subsequent experiences, the empty tomb, and the appearances, together with their ongoing sense of his presence and the hope of his coming again.

The earliest Christian writings we have are those letters of *Paul that are beyond question authentic, namely, 1 *Thessalonians, *Galatians, 1 and 2 *Corinthians, *Romans, *Philemon, and *Philippians. These letters contain formulae that give us evidence of the theology of the pre-Pauline communities (e.g., 1 Thess. 1.9–10; 1 Cor. 15.3–5; Rom. 1.3–4; 3.25–26; 4.25; 10.9). Some of these formulae go back to the earliest Palestinian community, others to the Hellenistic communities (Greek-speaking communities before Paul). In addition, we have the kerygmatic speeches, proclamations of the Christ event, in *Acts; though composed by the author of Luke-Acts, they probably enshrine samples of early Christian preaching (e.g., Acts 2.22–24, 32–33, 36; 3.13–15, 21). Putting the evidence afforded by these materials together, we can form a general idea of the Christologies and soteriologies of the early communities. The letters of Paul provide ample evidence for the apostle's understanding of these matters. We have no other writings that can be said with any certainty to derive from the apostolic age, but there are a number of New Testament writings that, though ascribed to apostolic authors, were probably written in the subapostolic age (i.e., the period from ca. 70 to 110 CE). This would include the "deutero-Pauline" letters, that is, those letters which though ascribed to Paul were with varying degrees of probability written by later writers. Their purpose was to perpetuate Paul's teaching after his death. They consist of 2 *Thessalonians, *Colossians, *Ephesians, and the *Pastorals (1 and 2 Timothy and Titus). Other writings for this period are *Hebrews, together with the *catholic letters (James, 1 and 2 Peter, 1, 2, and 3 John, Jude, Revelation), and stage III of the four Gospels.

The person of Christ. The Easter event established in the first disciples the conviction that, despite Jesus' crucifixion, God had vindicated him and his message. The Christ event was indeed God's saving act. The earliest Christians expressed this conviction by ascribing to Jesus titles of majesty, such as *Messiah (Grk. *christos,* Eng. "Christ," which was originally a title and is not a proper name), Lord *(kyrios),* and *Son of God. Some of the early christological patterns suggest that Jesus was "appointed" Christ, Lord, or Son of God (Acts 2.36; Rom. 1.4; Phil. 2.9–11) at his exaltation. These patterns are often called "adoptionist," but this is misleading. The meaning is not that Jesus became something he was not before, for example, a divine person; rather, he was appointed to a new office and function, that of being the one in whom God would finally judge and save the world (Acts 3.21; 1 Thess. 1.10), and through whom he was already offering salvation after Easter in the church's proclamation (Acts 2.38). Moreover, this type of Christology does not mean that the earthly life of Jesus had no christological or salvific significance. It was not nonmessianic, for God was present and acting in the earthly Jesus (Acts 2.22). But its messianic significance was initially expressed by a different set of terms, such as the end-time prophet promised in Deuteronomy 18.15 (Acts 3.22–23; 7.37). It is notable that the emphasis of these Christologies is on the end of Jesus' career; in short, they are paschal Christologies.

Over time, the titles that were first applied to the post-Easter phase of Jesus' saving activity were pushed back into his earthly life. This was notably the case with the title *Son of God. As the story of Jesus' baptism developed in stage II, this title was featured in a heavenly voice ("You are my Son," Mark 1.11), perhaps replacing an earlier use of "servant" in this context. Later in the birth stories, the title Son of God is pushed back to the moment of Jesus' conception or birth (Luke 1.35; cf. Matt. 2.15). This does not mean that some sort of metaphysical divinity is being ascribed to Jesus. In a Jewish context, it meant that like the kings of Israel Jesus was chosen for a unique role in history. Jesus' conception through the Holy Spirit is not meant to imply any metaphysical quality; it means, rather, that Jesus was a historical person elected from the womb for his unique role through the direct intervention of God (cf. Isa. 49.5; Jer 1.4). (*See* Virgin Birth.)

A similar type of Christology is expressed in the so-called sending formulae. These follow a regular pattern: a verb of sending with God as the subject and the son as the object, followed by a purpose clause stating the saving intention behind the sending. The earliest occurrence of such a formula is: "God sent his Son . . . to redeem those . . ." (Gal. 4.4–5). From such formulae it will be clear that the title "son" denotes a historical person with a saving mission. Notice that, unlike the paschal type, this type of Christology focuses upon the beginning rather than the end of Jesus' career.

In Hellenistic Christianity, a new pattern began to develop in which Christ existed in heaven before his birth. Here is a Christology of preexistence and *incarnation. It is generally agreed that this pattern developed from the identification of Jesus with the *wisdom of God. In Judaism, especially in the Greek-speaking world, the notion of the wisdom of God had undergone a remarkable development. Originally it had been no more than the personification of a divine attribute (see, e.g., Prov. 8.22–31), like God's righteousness or salvation (Isa. 51.6; Ps. 85.10–11). In the later *wisdom literature, however, and in the writings of *Philo, the concept of the wisdom or Word (*logos) of God developed in the direction of hypostatization—it became the distinct personal entity within the being of God, something like a person in the sense in which that term was later used in the Christian dogma of the *Trinity (see, e.g., Wisd. of Sol. 18.14–15). Wisdom or "Word" was that aspect of the being of God which was God turned toward the world in creative, revelatory, and saving activity (see, e.g., Wisd. of Sol. 7.22–27).

The ground for this identification of Jesus with the hypostatized wisdom of God was the fact that Jesus himself had appeared as a sage or wise man and had used the speech forms of wisdom literature (see above). He thus came to be regarded not merely as a spokesperson of wisdom but as wisdom's final envoy who acted as the mouthpiece of wisdom (cf. Matt. 11.28–30 with Sir. 24.19 and 51.23–26). From there, it was but a short step to identify him in person with wisdom itself. This happened first in certain christological hymns (Phil. 2.6–11; 1 Cor. 8.6; Col. 1.15–18a; Heb. 1.3–4; John 1.1–18). In these hymns, the same grammatical subject, usu-

ally the relative pronoun "who," governs all the verbs that speak of wisdom's activity before the incarnation, of the activity of the incarnate one in history, and of the exalted one after Easter. Thus, we now have a three-step Christology: (1) wisdom's activity in creation, revelation, providence, and salvation history before Christ; (2) the career of the historical Jesus; (3) the exalted life of Jesus after Easter. Like the sending formulae, this Christology focuses upon the origin rather than the fate of Jesus.

Outside the Fourth Gospel and the Letters of *John, this preexistence-incarnation Christology is for the most part confined to hymns. It does not widely affect the christological thinking of Paul, the deutero-Pauline writings, or Hebrews outside the hymns. There are, however, a few exceptional passages where we do see the influence of this type of Christology. When Paul says that the rock that followed the Israelites in the *wilderness was Christ (1 Cor. 10.4), this implies the identification of Christ with a preexistent wisdom who was active in Israel's salvation history, especially in the *exodus. Again, when Paul says that God sent his Son in the "likeness of sinful flesh" (Rom. 8.3), the sending formula has apparently been widened to include the idea not just of historical sending but of preexistence and incarnation.

Hebrews also shows the influence of this incarnation Christology when the author applies Ps. 8.5–7 to Jesus' career in 2.6–9, and goes on to say "since, therefore, the children share flesh and blood, he himself [Christ] likewise shared the same things" (Heb. 2.14). There are signs in Hebrews that the three-step Christology is beginning to be integrated into the author's thinking.

It is in the gospel of John, however, that the preexistence-incarnation Christology was fully integrated into the thought of the evangelist. True, the Fourth Gospel does contain earlier materials reflecting the more primitive sending formula (e.g., John 12.44, a pre-Johannine saying with synoptic parallels). There are also passages in John where, like Matthew 11.28–30, Jesus is presented as the spokesperson of wisdom (e.g., John 6.35, 37). This may also have been the original sense of the great "I am" sayings, including John 8.58, which originally was intended not to be a personal utterance of Jesus but of God's wisdom speaking through Jesus. Other parts of the evangelist's stage III materials, however, present Christ as one who was personally preexistent. He came down from heaven (3.31). God sent him into the world (3.17).

He came into the world (3.19). At the Last Supper, Jesus prays that he may resume the glory that he had before the world was made (John 17.5; cf. 13.3). Thus, in the later phases of stage III, John moves beyond the idea of Christ as wisdom's spokesperson to the idea that he is the personal incarnation of the eternal wisdom of God. This doubtless affected the understanding of the earlier sending formulae and the sayings in which Jesus is the spokesperson of wisdom. He is now perceived to be the incarnation of wisdom in person. But never does John call Jesus the wisdom of God; rather, the titles that describe him as such are "son" and, in the prologue, Word (Grk. *logos*). The consequence is that the title Son of God, or son, which had earlier been used functionally to denote historic mission, now acquired a metaphysical sense. We may now properly speak of the divinity, or better, the deity, of Christ. In three instances the Johannine writings actually call Jesus "God" (John 1.18; 20.28; 1 John 5.20). Other instances of this in the New Testament are doubtful on textual or interpretative grounds (Rom. 9.5; Tit. 2.13). When we call Jesus God, it must be carefully nuanced: Jesus is not all that God is. He is the incarnation of that aspect of the divine being which is God going forth from himself in creative, revelatory, and saving activity. In terms of later dogma, he is the incarnation of the Second, not of the First, person of the Trinity.

We may ask what motives propelled Christian writers to such a high Christology within such a relatively short period. The God whose presence had been discerned in the Christ event was the same God they had known all along, the God who created the world, the God who was known in general human experience, and, above all, the God who was known in Israel's salvation history. The Christ event was an experience of recognition. Also *creation and *salvation were closely related. Salvation was not salvation out of the world but salvation of the world.

The work of Christ. By the work of Christ is meant the saving significance of the Christ event (soteriology). The earliest Christian preaching as recorded in Acts (chaps. 2; 3; 10) does not highlight the death of Christ, but speaks of the Christ event in its totality as God's act of salvation. These speeches do feature the death of Christ, but always in the so-called contrast scheme: the death of Christ was Israel's rejection of God's offer, and the *Resurrection was God's act of vindicating his offer (Acts 2.23–24; 3.13–15; 10.39–40). Mark's passion predictions, which in

their present form belong to stage II, have the same contrast scheme. Yet these passages also state that Israel's rejection of the Messiah was in accordance with God's purpose (Acts 2.23 and the "must" of the passion predictions). It was also explicitly predicted in scripture (Acts 3.18). Thus, the way was prepared for conceiving the death of Christ not only as Israel's active refusal but also as God's act of salvation.

It was the celebration of the *Lord's Supper which appears to have provided the context for reflection on the saving significance of Christ's death. The earliest traditions that do so consist of liturgical materials. First, we have the expansion of the cup word in the Supper tradition itself (Mark 14.24; cf. Mark 10.45b). Here we get for the first time the so-called *hyper*-formula, which asserts that the death of Christ was for (Grk. *hyper*) us. Next, the *hyper*-formula appears in creedal or catechetical traditions (1 Cor. 15.4).

Over the course of time, more precise imagery was introduced to interpret the meaning of Christ's death. One pre-Pauline hymn compares the death of Christ and its effects with the ritual of the *Day of Atonement. We are "justified . . . through the redemption that is in Christ Jesus, whom God put forward as a sacrifice of atonement by his blood. . . . He did this to show his righteousness, because in his divine forbearance he had passed over sins previously committed" (Rom. 3.24–25). "Justify" is a metaphor from the law courts referring to the judge's pronouncement of the verdict "not guilty." This is another way of saying that Christ's death conveyed the forgiveness of sins, an idea that occurs later in the hymn when it speaks of God's "passing over sins." Christ's death is then described as an act of "*redemption" (Grk. *apolytrōsis*). Although this word is often thought to derive from the manumission of slaves, it has a more likely background in salvation history. God redeemed Israel by bringing it out of the land of Egypt and by restoring it after the exile, and Israel continued to hope for redemption at the end. The Song of Zechariah announces the fulfillment of this hope (Luke 1.68). Redemption thus came to denote deliverance from all the ills of history in the messianic age.

Next we have the word translated "sacrifice of atonement" (Grk. *hilastērion*). Its precise meaning is disputed. Some translate it "propitiation," which suggests appeasing or placating an angry deity—a notion hardly compatible with biblical thought and rarely occurring in that sense in the Hebrew Bible. It requires God as its object, whereas in this hymn God is the subject: "whom God put forward." Luther translated it as "mercy seat," an item of the *Temple furniture which was sprinkled with blood on the Day of Atonement (Lev. 16.14–16). But applied to Jesus the metaphor would be confused: Jesus did not cleanse himself through his own blood as the priest did with the mercy seat on the Day of Atonement. Accordingly, the rendering "expiation" is the most probable. In Israelite sacrifices, especially those of the Day of Atonement, sins were expiated, that is, they were covered over or cleansed and thus removed (Lev. 4.1–6.7; 6.24–7.1). This seems to give the best meaning in Romans 3.24–25. There is, however, an element of truth in the idea of propitiation, for it calls attention to the fact that sin is not only a defilement but a breach of the human relationship with God. As a result of Christ's saving work, this broken relationship has been restored. The last soteriological term in this hymn is the word "blood." This comes from the cup word in the supper tradition and denotes not a substance but the death of Christ as a sacrificial and saving event. Another early formula is found in Romans 4.25: Christ "was handed over to death for our trespasses and was raised for our justification."

Paul took over these earlier traditions about the saving work of Christ and developed them significantly in two directions. He speaks both of the work of Christ in itself (the objective side) and of the work of Christ in believers (the subjective side). Here we will be concerned with the former, the objective side.

The central term in Paul's soteriology is *justification. Together with its cognates, including "*righteousness" as applied to God, it occurs some forty-eight times in the undisputed letters. It is the major focus of Paul's arguments in Galatians 3–4 and in Romans 3.21–5.11. It is almost synonymous with reconciliation (Rom. 5.11). This gives it a more personal twist, for reconciliation is a metaphor derived not from the law court but from relationships between persons and between social groups. Thus, justification comes to mean not merely to pronounce not guilty but also to bring into a right relationship with God. Paul tries to explain how this happened. On the cross Christ took upon himself the curse of the *Law (Gal. 3.10–14) and endured its consequences. God made his son to be "sin" for us (2 Cor. 5.21). Christ put himself in the place of sinners, and as the sinless one he exhausted God's wrath against sin, thus making it possible for humanity to enter into a right

relationship with God. The metaphor reconciliation also gives a social and cosmic dimension to justification (2 Cor. 5.19). These dimensions received further emphasis in the deutero-Pauline letters (Col. 1.20–22; Eph. 2.16).

Paul occasionally speaks of Christ's death as a *sacrifice but only in traditional formulae (in addition to Rom. 3.25–26, see 1 Cor. 5.8). He once uses the term "blood" as shorthand for Christ's death as a saving event, in the phrase "justified by his blood" (Rom. 5.9). Otherwise, in the genuine Pauline letters "blood" occurs only in connection with the Lord's Supper.

Christ's death is also regarded by Paul as a victory over the powers of *evil, another item that comes from earlier tradition (Phil. 2.10). In speaking about victory, however, Paul is careful to emphasize that the powers, though decisively defeated, await final subjugation at the end (1 Cor 15.25–27). The apostle includes among the powers of evil not only cosmic forces but existential realities like law, *sin, and *death. This victory-soteriology becomes more important in the deutero-Pauline letters (Col. 2.15; Eph. 1.21), which abandon Paul's reservation about its present incompleteness. All that remains is for everything to be united (NRSV: "gathered up") in Christ at the end (Eph. 1.10).

In itself, the term "*salvation," with its cognates "save" and "savior," is a rather colorless word in the Pauline writings. As with the other words we have studied, its background is found in the Hebrew Bible, where it is applied to the Exodus and to the restoration from exile (Exod. 15.2; Isa. 43.11; 52.10). Like similar words, it also became part of Israel's hope for the end. Paul uses this word group in an all-embracing way. Believers have been saved, though only in hope (Rom. 8.24–25); they are being saved (1 Cor. 1.18); and they will be saved at the end (Rom. 5.10). Once again, the deutero-Pauline letters abandon this reserve and insist that believers have already been saved (Eph. 2.5,8).

The only New Testament work to develop the doctrine of Christ's saving work is the letter to the *Hebrews. This letter makes an elaborate comparison between the levitical high *priests and their sacrifices, on the one hand, and Christ and his sacrifice, on the other. The author took up certain items from earlier Christian tradition. One was the comparison of Good Friday with the Day of Atonement, which we have already seen in Romans 3.24–25 (note the expression "sacrifice of atonement," Heb. 2.17). Another was the supper tradition with its language about blood and covenant (Heb. 8.6–13). Yet a third theme, that of Christ as high priest after the order of *Melchizedek, was suggested by Psalm 110, which led the author on to verse 4 (Heb. 5.6; etc.).

In developing his argument, the author of Hebrews had first to prove that Jesus was qualified to be a high priest despite his lack of levitical descent (Heb. 5.1–10). Then, in the central part of his work (7.1–10.18), he compares Jesus and his sacrifice point by point with the levitical high priests and their sacrifices, demonstrating at every point the superiority of Jesus and his self-offering. As the comparison with the Day of Atonement shows, Christ's sacrifice is not confined to his death but includes also his *ascension into heaven. For the action of the priest in taking the blood of the victim into the Holy of Holies was an essential part of the ritual, in which the slaying of the victim was only a preliminary. Thus, Christ's sacrifice was completed only when he entered into the presence of God and sat down at his right hand (Heb. 10.12). Henceforth, Christ lives to make intercession for us (Heb. 7.25).

How does the author of Hebrews understand Christ's sacrifice to be effective in taking away sin? He follows the biblical belief that *sin is a ritual defilement that can be cleansed only with the blood of a victim (Heb. 9.22). Yet he points beyond a merely cultic interpretation of this imagery when he observes that Christ's death was the offering of a perfect obedience of his human will (Heb. 10.5–10). On the strength of his perfect obedience, believers too can draw near to God's presence and offer the sacrifice of praise that leads to the obedience of a holy life (Heb. 10.19–25; 13.15).

The author of 1 *Peter takes over the earlier tradition that compared Christ's sacrifice to that of the Passover lamb (1 Pet. 1.19). In a remarkable hymnlike passage (1 Pet. 2.21–25), the author describes Christ's passion in terms of the suffering servant of Isaiah 53. Christ's sufferings are to serve as the example for Christian slaves to follow (v. 21). This treatment of the death of Christ as an example is characteristic of the moralism of the subapostolic age.

We turn now to the treatment of the death of Christ in stage III of the four Gospels. Each evangelist presents the death of Christ from his own perspective. For Mark, the death of Jesus was the occasion for the unveiling of the *messianic secret. Only at the crucifixion could he be publicly acknowledged as the Son of God (Mark 15.39). Mark was probably countering the view

that overemphasized the miracles as revelations of Christ's deity. The miracles are important to Mark but only as prefigurations of the supreme act of salvation on the cross.

For Matthew, the cross was Israel's rejection of the Messiah. Because of it, God's judgment came upon the nation at the fall of Jerusalem in 70 CE (Matt. 27.25). A new nation, the Christian church, would arise in Israel's place (Matt. 21.43). Meanwhile, Matthew emphasizes the saving significance of the cross by adding to the cup word at the supper the phrase "for the forgiveness of sins" (Matt. 26.28).

For Luke, the death of Jesus at Jerusalem and his consequent assumption into heaven (Luke 9.51) constituted a major turning point in salvation history, inaugurating the new period of the church and its universal mission. This period would be covered by the book of Acts. Luke is wrestling with the problem created by the delay in Christ's *second coming. The time of the church will be marked by persecution and martyrdom, and Christ's passion is presented as an example for Christian martyrs to follow, such as Stephen in Acts 6–7.

John seems to shift his interest away from the cross to the revelation that Jesus brings in his earthly life (John 1.18). The death of Jesus seems to be no more than the occasion when he returned to the Father from whom he came (John 13.3; 16.5). But this is to underestimate the importance of Christ's death in the Fourth Gospel. The words and works of Christ are all overshadowed by the hour of the passion (John 2.4, etc.). The signs or miracles point to what Christ would finally accomplish on the cross. It is there that he brings in the new order symbolized by the changing of the water into wine (2.1–11). It is there that he makes his flesh available for the life of the world (6.51–58), that he cures the blindness of human life (9.1–41), and that he confers eternal life (11.1–44). It is also in the cross that all the claims made in the great "I am" sayings are substantiated. It is because of the cross that he is the true bread that comes down from heaven (6.33), that he is the light of the world (8.12), the door of the sheep (10.7), the good shepherd (10.14), the resurrection and the life (11.25), the way, the truth, and the life (14.6), and the true vine (15.1). Moreover, it is through the cross that the Spirit-Paraclete is released which leads the Johannine community into all truth (7.39). Thus it was the death of Christ and his glorification that made it possible for the Fourth Gospel to ascribe the "I am" sayings to Jesus.

Despite the apparent preoccupation of the author of *Revelation with the events leading up to the end and with the new heaven and the new earth that lie beyond, the cross for him plays a crucial role in salvation history. The central christological image in Revelation is the *Lamb that was slain. In the cross, the Lamb has conquered and taken his seat beside the Father on the throne of heaven (3.21). Because of that victory, the Lamb alone is qualified to open the scroll and its seven seals (5.5). In other words, his victorious death determines the future course of history. It becomes clear that the cross is the central and controlling event of the whole book. Meanwhile, Christ has "ransomed" believers "from every tribe and language and people and nation, and . . . made them to be a kingdom and priests serving our God" (Rev. 5.9–10).

REGINALD H. FULLER

Jew. The English word "Jew" is derived from Hebrew *yĕhûdî* (fem. *yĕhûdît*, "Judith"; see Gen. 26.34; also the book of Judith), meaning "Judean," by way of Greek *ioudaios* and Latin *judaeus*. The term is first used for citizens of the southern kingdom of *Judah in 2 Kings 16.6; previously, male inhabitants of the kingdom, or of the tribe of Judah from which the kingdom took its name, were referred to as *'îš yĕhûdâ,* literally "man [men] of Judah" (e.g., 1 Sam. 11.8). As a consequence of the *exile of many members of the upper classes of Judah by the Babylonians in 597 and 587/586 BCE, many Jews were forcibly settled in Mesopotamia (2 Kings 24–25; Jer. 52). Others, including the prophet Jeremiah, fled to Egypt (Jer. 43). This was the beginning of the Jewish *dispersion, or Diaspora, across the globe, which continues to this day. After the exile the term Jew came to be used for all descended from or identified with this ethnic or religious group, whatever their race or nationality. Thus, in Esther 2.5, Mordecai is identified both as a Jew and as a member of the tribe of *Benjamin. The term "Jew" thus began to parallel the much more ancient designation "Israelite."

The Jews who returned from exile after 538 BCE (Ezra 2; Neh. 7.6–73) settled in the Persian province of Yehud, which eventually became the Roman province of Judea and preserved its name until it was suppressed by the Romans in reaction to Jewish revolts of 66–73 and 132–135 CE.

In the New Testament "Jew" can designate both Jesus (Mark 15.2) and many of his followers (Acts 21.39), as well as some of his adversaries (1 Thess. 2.14–16). However, the rivalry between Christianity and Judaism, coupled with the often uncomplimentary portrait of Jews in the New Testament and the similarity in sound to the name of Judas, often made the word *Jew* pejorative in the Christian world (*see* Anti-Semitism).

The question of how to define a Jew, put more simply as "who is a Jew," has engendered much discussion through the ages. Are the Jews to be understood as a social, religious, national, or ethnic community? Basically, the answer of the Jewish tradition, the *halakhah,* has been that one born of a Jewish mother or one converted to Judaism is a Jew. But this definition has been challenged in recent years. The murder of many of Jewish descent who, however, were not halakhically Jewish during the *Halocaust has raised questions regarding inclusion and exclusion in the Jewish community. The high court of Israel, in the Brother Daniel Rufeisen case, has ruled that an apostate from Judaism cannot apply for automatic citizenship as a Jew under the Law of Return. And in recent years the American Jewish Reform movement has attempted to redefine the term "Jew" to include, in addition to converts, anyone of Jewish descent, whether that descent be matrilineal (the halakhic position) or patrilineal (excluded by *halakhah*), who practices Judaism and identifies himself or herself as a Jew. A strict definition is therefore impossible to reach.

CARL S. EHRLICH

Jewelry. References to jewelry in biblical literature suggest that it served most of the functions in ancient Palestine that it has served throughout human cultural development worldwide. The aesthetic appeal of different materials, colors, and shapes with which both men and women could adorn themselves was a primary concern. In addition, jewelry was a repository of wealth or form of currency, an insignia of rank or special favor, and, perhaps most important, a focus of religious or magical sentiments.

Biblical words or phrases for various items of jewelry are often enigmatic because the terms are used infrequently and the contexts provide little information about their referents. Only by a careful appraisal of textual, archaeological, and iconographic evidence from a local Palestinian and cross-cultural perspective can the meaning and significance of a term be elucidated. Among items of jewelry clearly denoted in biblical texts are the following: anklet (Isa. 3.18); armlet (Num. 31.50; 2 Sam. 1.10; Isa. 3.20); bracelet (Gen. 24.22, 30, 47; Num. 31.50); crescent pendant (Judg. 8.21, 26; Isa. 3.10); earring (Gen. 35.4; Exod. 32.2–3; 35.22; Judg. 8.24–26; Job 42.11; Hos. 2.15); frontlet (Exod. 13.16; Deut. 6.8; 11.18); necklace (Gen. 41.42; Ezek. 16.11; Dan. 5.29); nose ring (Gen. 24.22, 30, 47; Isa. 3.21; Ezek. 16.12); ring, including signet (Gen. 28.18, 25; 41.42; Exod. 28.11, 21, 36; 35.22; 39.6, 14, 30; Num. 31.50; 1 Kings 21.8; Esther 3.10, 13; 8.2, 8, 10; Job 38.14; Isa. 3.21; Jer. 22.24; Hos. 2.15; Luke 15.22; James 2.2); pendant (Judg. 8.26; Isa. 3.19).

A number of terms are variously interpreted. The "amulets" of Isaiah 3.20 (NRSV) may be snake pendants; the word translated "headbands" in Isaiah 3.18 may mean "little suns," that is, star disc pendants (see below); and the "perfume boxes" of Isaiah 3.20 are literally "soul houses," possibly tubular containers of texts, related to the inscribed frontlet worn above the eyes and to *phylacteries (Matt. 23.5).

The star disc pendant illustrates how archaeological evidence (artifactual, iconographic, and textual) can help elucidate terms for jewelry. Numerous examples of four-rayed, six-rayed, and eight-rayed varieties of this pendant have been recovered from Late Bronze Palestinian and other Near Eastern excavations, and Assyrian kings of later Iron Age dates are depicted on reliefs wearing multistringed necklaces of such pendants. Contemporaneous textual evidence (in particular, a detailed fifteenth century BCE inventory of jewelry presented to the goddess Ningal at Qatna in Syria) identifies these pendants as "suns" in Akkadian, the four- or six-rayed variety representing the sun god (Utu/Shamash/Shapash) and the eight-rayed variety representing a female deity with an astral aspect (Inanna/Ishtar/Ningal/Astarte). Similarly, other terms of biblical jewelry can be related to specific pendant types with magical and religious significance; thus, the crescent or horns pendant is probably to be identified with a moon or war god (Yerah/Baal/Resheph in West Semitic societies). Many other pendant types from Late Bronze and Iron Age Palestinian excavations represent Egyptian hieroglyphs and deities (Bes, Horus, Ptah-Sokar, etc.), fauna (fly, frog, lion, ram, bull, cat, etc.), flora (lotus, mandrake, rosette flower, etc.), and various human and geometric forms. Some of the same motifs occur on signet rings, scarabs, and seals. Although not all are explicitly mentioned in biblical texts, the symbolic associations

of the jewelry motifs imply that the ancient inhabitants of Palestine, even during the periods of the United and Divided Monarchies, wore jewelry that had amuletic and/or polytheistic significance.

The inherent contradiction of such jewelry to normative Yahwism is reflected in diatribes against the haughty "daughters of Zion" in Isaiah 3.18–23 and Ezekiel 16.15–17; in Jacob's burial of earrings and foreign gods under a tree at *Shechem (Gen. 35.4), and in Judges 8.21–27, which describes an *ephod, made by *Gideon from the rings, crescents, and other pendants of the *Midianite kings, that became a "snare." Properly employed, however, jewelry could be an item of beauty, value, and status, as exemplified by the nose and finger rings of Rebekah (Gen. 24.22, 30, 47), the signet ring and necklace of Joseph (Gen. 41.42), the armlets and crown of Saul (2 Sam. 1.10), and the signet ring presented to Mordecai by Ahasuerus (Esther 8.2, 8, 10). These items were of gold and/or semiprecious stones, which were highly valued in antiquity. Jewelry was thus an ideal symbol of Israel's relationship to Yahweh, whether as bridal or queenly apparel (Ezek. 16.10–13; Song of Sol. 1.10–11) or the high priest's breastpiece (Exod. 28.17–20; 39.10–13).

Archaeological evidence from Palestine attests to the usage and value of jewelry in a variety of contexts. Anklets, bracelets, earrings, necklaces, frontlets, and rings have been found on the wrists and ankles and near the foreheads, ears, and necks of burials. Special types often occur together on the same individual, which suggests an elevated social status. The occurrence of similar jewelry types in domestic contexts is probably due to accidental loss or to the intentional deposition of the jewelry as hoards, the latter being concentrated in larger buildings. Deposits of jewelry under floors and walls of cultic structures are also common; the jewelry might have adorned a cult statue or represented votive or foundation offerings or taxes. While gold and other precious metals (silver and electrum) are not as prevalent as suggested by some biblical texts (e.g., 2 Chron. 3.3–10), they are well represented in the archaeological record, along with copper/bronze, silicate materials (glass, faience, and frit), bone, shell, and common and semiprecious stones (principally quartz varieties, such as carnelian, agate, and amethyst). Except for precious metals, most of the materials were locally available, and workshops existed throughout the country for fabricating jewelry.　　　PATRICK E. McGOVERN

Jezebel. Princess of Tyre who married *Ahab, king of Israel (mid ninth century BCE). Jezebel was the daughter of Ethbaal, king of Tyre ("Sidonians" in 1 Kings 16.31 is a biblical term for *Phoenicians in general); according to genealogies given in *Josephus and other classical sources, this would make her the great-aunt of Dido, the founder of Carthage. Jezebel was an ardent worshiper of *Baal and *Asherah who supported their worship from the throne in Israel (1 Kings 16.31–33; 18.4, 19; 19.1–2); her name is best understood as meaning "Where is the Prince?", the cry of Baal's divine and human subjects when he is in the underworld. Jezebel exercised royal prerogatives to acquire Naboth's vineyard for her husband (1 Kings 21) by plotting to have Naboth executed. This incident prompted *Elijah to predict that dogs would eat Jezebel's corpse in Jezreel (1 Kings 21.23; see 2 Kings 9.30–37). *Jehu, the commander of King Joram's army in Israel, was anointed king in Ramoth-gilead in order to destroy Ahab's house because of what Jezebel had done to the prophets and the faithful of Yahweh (2 Kings 9.1–10). When Jehu met King Joram, son of Ahab and Jezebel, to kill him, he remarked that there could be no peace in Israel while the "whoredoms [= apostasy] and sorceries" of Jezebel continued. After killing Joram of Israel and King Ahaziah of Judah (Ahab and Jezebel's grandson), he went to Jezreel to kill Jezebel. Adorned like a queen, she appeared to him in a window, regally defiant in the face of his violence. She was thrown out of the window by her own attendants, who sided with Jehu, and was trampled to death.

Jezebel's sons and daughter also ruled. Ahaziah was king of Israel for two years after Ahab died and Joram succeeded him (1 Kings 22.51–53; 2 Kings 1.17–18; 3.1–3; 10.12–14). Jezebel and Ahab's daughter Athaliah married Jehoram of Judah, and was the mother of Ahaziah, king of Judah (2 Kings 8.25–27). When her son was killed by Jehu (9.14–28), Athaliah set out to kill all his heirs, and she herself ruled for six years (11.1–20).

Jezebel later becomes an insulting epithet for a woman, and is used in Revelation 2.20 of a prophet in Thyatira of whose teaching and practice the author disapproves.

See also Queen and Queen Mother.

JO ANN HACKETT

Job, the Book of. The book of Job is the most consistently theological work in the Hebrew Bible, being nothing but an extended discussion of one theological issue, the question of suffering. Its chief literary feature is that it does not expound or defend a dogma from one point of view, but portrays a debate in which conflicting points of view are put forward, none of them being unambiguously presented as preferable. This makes it perhaps the most intellectually demanding book of the Hebrew Bible, requiring of its readers a mental flexibility and even a willingness, in the end, to be left with no unequivocal message.

It is not only a work of intellectual vigor, though; it is also a literary masterpiece that belongs with the classics of world literature, with the *Iliad,* the *Divine Comedy,* and *Paradise Lost.* In design it has both the form of an unsophisticated prose narrative, which nonetheless contains intriguing surprises, and that of a series of subtle speeches in poetry of great delicacy and power. The interplay between prose and poetry, between naïveté and rhetorical finesse, mirrors the interplay among the six participants in the book: Job, the four friends, God—and the narrator.

Structure. The book can be most easily analyzed as narrative framework surrounding poetic core:

1.1–2.13	Framework	prose: narrative
3.1–42.6	Core	poetry: argument
42.7–17	Framework	prose: narrative

Another way of reading the shape of the book follows the indications given by the book itself about the speakers. The whole book may be seen as speech, the narrator speaking in prologue and epilogue, and the characters in the dialogue—the three cycles of conversation between Job and the first three friends, the speeches of Elihu the interloper, and the exchanges between God and Job:

I. Prologue (1.1–2.13)
   Narrator
II. Dialogue (3.1–42.6)
   A. Job and the three friends, First Cycle
      Job (3.1–26)
      Eliphaz (4.1–5.27)
      Job (6.1–7.21)
      Bildad (8.1–22)
      Job (9.1–10.22)
      Zophar (11.1–20)
   B. Job and the three friends, Second Cycle
      Job (12.1–14.22)
      Eliphaz (15.1–35)

This analysis shows, first, that the narrator's words enclose those of all the characters, which has the effect of predisposing the reader to understand how all the speakers in the dialogue are to be understood, and at the end leaving the narrator's perspective uppermost in the reader's mind. Second, it is Job who for the most part initiates conversation; he speaks, and the friends reply to him. But when Yahweh speaks, it is he and not Job who takes the initiative; though Job has summoned Yahweh to speak, Yahweh's speeches are less a reply than a new approach. Third, all the speaking moves toward silence; Job, who has done most of the talking, in the end lays his hand on his mouth (40.4–5); the friends run out of words and do not even finish the third cycle of speeches. Does the book perhaps imply that the real resolution to the problem of suffering comes not at all through talking but only when Yahweh too stops speaking and actually restores Job's fortunes (42.10)?

Argument. Although it is generally agreed that the chief issue of the book is the problem of *suffering, we need to be clear on just what that problem is.

Sometimes it is thought that the question is why is there suffering, what is its origins and cause, or why has this suffering happened to a specific person? To these serious questions the book of Job gives no satisfactory answer. It does indeed say that suffering is sometimes punishment for sins, sometimes a warning against committing sin in the future, and sometimes, as in Job's case, for no earthly reason at all, but for some inscrutable divine reason. In the end, though, readers cannot learn from the book any one clear view about what the reason for any particular suffering, or for human suffering in general, may be.

A second problem about suffering is whether there is such a thing as innocent suffering. Against cut-and-dried theologies of retribution, the book of Job, without of course denying the possibility that sometimes suffering is richly deserved by the sufferer, denies that such is always the case. Job is an innocent sufferer, whose innocence is not only asserted by himself (6.30; 9.15) but is attested to by the narrator (1.1) and above all by God (1.8; 2.3; 42.7–8).

There is a third, and more important, problem about suffering that the book does address, however indirectly. It is more existential: In what way am I supposed to suffer, or what am I to do when I am suffering? Two different but complementary answers are given. First, in the opening two chapters, Job's reaction to the disasters that come upon him is a calm acceptance of the will of God; he can bless God not only for what he has given but also for what he has taken away (1.21; 2.10). The patient Job is thus a model for sufferers. But second, Job does not remain in that attitude of acceptance. Once we move into his poetic speeches, from chap. 3 onward, we encounter a mind in turmoil, a sense of bitterness and anger, of isolation from God and even persecution by God. Job makes no attempt to suppress his hostility toward God for what has happened to him; he insists that he will "speak in the anguish of [his] spirit" and "complain in the bitterness of [his] soul" (7.11). What makes this protesting Job a model for other sufferers is that he directs himself constantly toward God, whom he regards as responsible, both immediately and ultimately, for his suffering. It is only (we may suppose) because Job insists on response from God that God enters into dialogue with Job. Even though Job's intellectual questions about the injustice of his suffering are never adequately answered, he himself is in the end satisfied, as a sufferer, by his encounter with God.

Origins. The composition of the book of Job can be dated to some point between the seventh and the second centuries BCE, but hardly more precisely than that. Quite probably there was a much older tale of an innocent sufferer, and the general theme is found also in *Jeremiah and in the poems of the Suffering Servant of the Lord in Second *Isaiah, both of these prophetic texts stemming from the sixth century. Perhaps the inexplicable suffering of Job was intended to symbolize the suffering of the Jews in Babylonian *exile in that century.

The earliest reference to Job outside the book is found in Ezekiel 14.14, 20, where Job is mentioned along with *Noah and Danel (probably not Daniel; see Daniel, The Book of) as an ancient hero. But this sixth-century reference may well be not to the book of Job but to the more ancient folktale, so no inference about the date of the book can be drawn.

There can be little doubt that the author of the book was an Israelite. Job's homeland is depicted as north *Arabia or possibly *Edom, and in most of the book Job himself does not know God by the Israelite name Yahweh (see Names of God in the Hebrew Bible). Nor does the book refer to any of the distinctive historical traditions of ancient Israel. But these facts only mean that the author has succeeded well in disguising his own age and background in his creation of the character of his hero, who is intended to have universal significance.

In the history of scholarship on the book, several critical questions have commonly attracted attention. One is whether the prose framework of the book (the prologue and epilogue) once existed as an independent story before the poem (3.1–42.6) was composed. The tendency now is to assume that although there was a prose story of Job older than the present book, the prologue and epilogue that we have now were written for their place in the book, since the prose framework by itself does not tell a completely coherent story. The other major question is whether the present allocation of speeches in the third cycle (chaps. 21–31) is the one intended by the author—for it seems strange that there is no third speech of Zophar, that the third speech of Bildad is so short that Job is credited with three speeches in a row, and that some of what Job says seems more suitable in the mouth of one of the friends. Most scholars therefore suspect that there has been some error in the manuscripts of Job, and that, for example, 26.5–14 was originally part of Bildad's speech and 27.13–28.28 was originally Zophar's third speech. A third question often raised is whether the speeches of the fourth friend Elihu (chaps. 32–37) were originally part of the book, since

Elihu (unlike the other friends) is not referred to in either the prologue or the epilogue. But it is not possible to settle this question, and in any case these speeches need to be treated as a significant part of the present book whether or not they were contained in the original book.

Job among the *Wisdom Literature. The book of *Proverbs affirms that wisdom—which means the knowledge of how to live rightly—leads to life, while folly leads to death (e.g., Prov 1.32; 3.1–2, 13–18; 8.36). Everywhere the principle of retribution is asserted or taken for granted: that righteousness is rewarded and sin is punished (e.g., Prov. 11.5–6). And the world of humans is divided into two groups: the blessed righteous, or wise, and the unhappy wicked, or foolish.

*Ecclesiastes, while not disparaging the quest for wisdom, asks, What happens to one's wisdom at death? Since death cancels out all values, not excepting wisdom, life cannot be meaningful if it is made to consist of gaining something that will inevitably be lost.

As for Job, from the viewpoint of the book of Proverbs, he is an impossibility. If he is truly righteous, he finds life, and wealth, and health. If he is in pain, he is one of the wicked and the foolish. In the end, of course, the book of Job does not completely undermine the principle of retribution, for Job ends up pious *and* prosperous; but once the principle is successfully challenged, as it is in the book of Job, even in a single case, its moral force is desperately weakened. For once the case of Job becomes known, if a person who has a reputation for right living is found to be suffering (the fate Proverbs predicts for wrongdoers), no one can point a finger of criticism; the book of Job has established that the proper criterion for determining whether people are pious or not is the moral quality of their life and not the accidental circumstances of their material existence.   DAVID J. A. CLINES

Joel, The Book of. In both the Hebrew and the Greek canons of the Bible, the book of Joel appears in proximity to that of the eighth-century BCE prophet *Amos, a circumstance that is easily explained by the close correspondence between Joel 3.16–18 and Amos 1.2; 9.13. There can hardly be any doubt that this correspondence is the result of the dependence of the text of Joel on that of Amos; from internal evidence it seems clear that the book of Joel is the work of a late postexilic prophet who was indebted for his images and metaphors to the much older prophetic traditions to which he laid claim and in which he presumed to participate.

The Author and His Times. We know nothing about the person of Joel (whose name means "Yahweh is God") other than that he is identified as the son of an equally unknown Pethuel. All the knowledge that we can derive about him and his times comes from the examination of his prophecy. He is, on the one hand, much concerned with the proprieties of the Temple worship (1.9, 13–14; 2.14–16; etc.), a trait that connects him very closely with the anonymous prophet *Malachi, who was possibly one of the very last to appear in the Judahite prophetic tradition. This trait, however, was by no means characteristic of preexilic prophecy of either Israel or Judah. Joel presupposes, therefore, the existence of a Temple—presumably the Second Temple of *Zerubbabel, which came to be in the aftermath of the initial return from exile following the liberating decree of *Cyrus the Persian after his defeat of the Babylonian empire in 539 BCE (Ezra 1.1–4). Furthermore, contrary to the picture drawn in the preexilic *Deuteronomic history of Israel and Judah, so much concerned with kings and politics, and even contrary to that of the Chronicler's depiction of the period of Ezra and Nehemiah (ca. 458–443 BCE), when Judah and Jerusalem, still under the domination of the Persian empire, were regaining a relative political autonomy with a secular (although concomitantly religious) leadership of native governors (like Nehemiah), Joel's text seems to presuppose a polity not unlike that presupposed by *Sirach (Sir. 50.1–24) or the book of *Judith, where it is taken for granted that the political leadership of the Jews has, by default, devolved upon the high priesthood. Since there is no hint of a disruption in Joel of this peaceful coexistence between religion and alien domination, we are probably not far off the mark when we assign this work to the latter stage of the Persian period of Palestine, which was disrupted only by the conquests of *Alexander the Great beginning in 333 BCE. These considerations would date Joel about 400 BCE.

Outline. The book of Joel consists of two sharply distinguished parts. There is, first of all, the graphic and highly descriptive depiction of a locust plague and a drought (the Hebrew vocabulary for "locusts" is virtually exhausted in 1.4) that descends on Judah and Jerusalem, demanding of everyone, class by class, profession by profession, repentance and prayer as the price of the Lord's continual toleration of a recalcitrant people (1.2–2.27). In the second part (2.28–3.21 [3.1–4.21 in the Hebrew Bible]), the *Day of the Lord is announced in *apocalyptic language. There is a series of salvation prophecies: Judah and Jerusalem will be restored, Israel will triumph over her enemies, and the gentiles will be requited for their misdeeds.

Interpretation. Is Joel a prophet of judgment (against Israel) or of salvation (of Israel in the face of its gentile enemies)? It is really difficult to say. Was the locust plague of the first verses an attempt to describe a real happening, as in Amos 7.1–3, or is it merely a literary device borrowed from the text of a prophetic predecessor? Is this plague a cloak for physical invasion of Israel or simply a symbol of national disintegration? Is the lifting of the plague potential or real? How much and to what extent is the repeated "Day of the Lord" intended to apply to Israel's future destiny and its relation to the gentile world? And by no means let us forget the outpouring of the spirit foretold by this prophet (2.28–32a) and the fulfillment that was discerned by New Testament writers seeking religious continuity (Acts 2.16–19). Whether Joel is to be considered a "cult" or "nationalist" prophet, a prophet of "judgment" or of "salvation," are questions that truly indicate that we have not yet fully comprehended the phenomenon of Israelite prophecy.

BRUCE VAWTER, C.M.

John the Baptist. If John was born of priestly parentage (Luke 1.5), he must have abandoned the priesthood and taken up an ascetic mode of life in the Judean *wilderness, where he subsisted on locusts and wild honey (Mark 1.6). Those who came out to him encountered a man dressed in camel-hair homespun with a leather belt around his waist, the explicit garb of a prophet (2 Kings 1.8; Zech. 13.4). With prophetic zeal he preached a new message and offered a new rite. The message was that lineal descent from *Abraham would not guarantee salvation. Abraham's merits would not suffice, but only an act of repentance that included the renunciation of all presumptions based on election or ethnicity (Matt. 3.9). The God that had called Israel out of Egypt and led it across the *Jordan River was now creating a new people by passing them through the waters of *baptism in that same river. The twelve stones that had been set up to mark Israel's crossing of the parted Jordan (Josh. 4) would themselves be raised up into twelve new tribes if the people of Israel would not repent. John was not founding a new religion but attacking the use of all religiousness as a defense against the demand of God for authenticity and justice.

This message of radical repentance was enacted in a rite of immersion in which the sin of presumption and the whole of one's old life were washed away. Those who rose out of the waters were as newborn infants (John 3.3–8), or as those who had passed from death to life, having been buried and raised from the dead (Rom. 6.1–11). These later Christian interpretations seem to have carried forward at least Jesus' own understanding of what John was about, for he spoke of his own baptism not as an event in the past but as a metaphor for his own approaching death (Mark 10.38–39; Luke 12.50).

John himself may have shared the idea, common in that period, that the last judgment would be enacted by a river of fire through which everyone would have to walk. In anticipation of that imminent judgment, John was inviting one and all to submit to God's judgment now, and by undergoing baptism to cleanse themselves of sin now, in advance of that terrible day. Those who had surrendered themselves to this washing would be preserved through the coming tribulation. They would be wheat gathered into God's granary, while the rest would be chaff burned in unquenchable fire (Matt. 3.12 par.).

John's message fell on Israel like fire on stubble. The Gospels report that "all" went out to hear him (Mark 1.5; Matt. 3.5; Mark 11.32 par.; Luke 7.29; Acts 13.24), and *Josephus comments that he was highly regarded by the whole Jewish people (*Ant.* 18.5.116–119). The crowds that attended him included tax collectors and prostitutes (Matt. 21.32; Luke 3.12; 7.29). This simple act of immersion, unlike circumcision, made salvation accessible even to women. It was John, not Jesus, who opened a way to God for those who before had felt themselves excluded. And by his dress and diet, even by the metaphors he chose (a tree cutter, a thresher), John identified himself, and the one whom he awaited, with the lowly.

Judaism had never encountered anything quite like this, yet virtually everything recorded of John had parallels in *Isaiah. These parallels include the following: an eschatological outpouring of the Holy Spirit (Isa. 32.15; Mark 1.8 par.) associated with the wilderness (Isa. 35.1–10; 40.3; 41.18–19; 43.19–20; Mark 1.3, 8, 10

par.); a spirit-endowed one to come who will act as judge (Isa. 11.2–5; 42.1–4; 61.1; Mark 1.7–8 par.); Israelites as children of Abraham (Isa. 29.22; 41.8; 51.2; 63.16; Matt. 3.9 par.); unfaithful Israel portrayed as a brood of vipers (Isa. 59.5; 1.4; Matt. 3.7 par.) or as trees that God will hew down with an axe (Isa. 6.13; 10.15–19, 33–34; 14.8; Matt. 3.10 par.); wind/breath/spirit (Hebr. *rûaḥ*), and fire compared to a river in which one is immersed (Isa. 30.27–28, 33; 43.2; Matt. 3.12 par.); Israel as the threshed and winnowed one (Isa. 21.10; Matt. 3.12 par.); Israel washed clean (Isa. 1.16; 4.4; 52.11; Mark 1.4 par.); and works of righteousness mandated subsequent to washing (Isa. 1.16–17; Matt. 3.8 par.; Luke 3.10–14).

Despite such extensive parallels, John burst on the scene as a virtual mutant, for his rite of baptism, though outwardly similar to Temple lustrations, was wholly without precedent in its meaning. Nowhere in any Jewish source is rebirth made a metaphor for redemption. One is born a Jew. Proselytes might be "reborn" as Jews, but proselyte baptism was not practiced in the first century CE, applied only to non-Jews, lacked an eschatological setting, and did not require running water. John's rite was so unique that he was named by it ("the Baptizer"), and Jesus clearly regards it as given to John by revelation from God (Mark 11.27–33). It circumvented the Temple and its rites; perhaps John's rejection of the priesthood is related to widespread revulsion against the corruption of the Temple and its priesthood in the first century CE.

John's presence in the wilderness has suggested to some that he might have at one time belonged to the community at *Qumran, possibly even being raised by them as an orphan (Luke 1.80; his parents were elderly at his birth [Luke 1.7]). Both John and the settlers at Qumran glowed with eschatological fervor, expecting an imminent judgment and preparing for it in the wilderness. Both called on all Israel to repent, denying that mere Jewishness could save. Both used washings, broke with the Temple cultus, taught prayer and fasting, and focused on Isaiah as their guide to the future. But these qualities seem to have been shared by other sectarians who had located in the wilderness. The Jerusalem *Talmud indicates that twenty-four such distinct sects had come into existence by 70 CE (*Sanh.* 29c). And much of what John and Qumran held in common derives from Isaiah.

In key respects, moreover, John was quite

different from the community at Qumran. They wore white linen; he dressed like the poor, in homespun. His disciples did not settle a community but wandered about with him. John required no three-year period of probation but accepted whoever came, and they returned home rather than remaining with him in the wilderness. He was prophetic, public, missionary, inclusive; Qumran was exclusive, secretive, and withdrawn. His opening of salvation to prostitutes, tax collectors, and sinners must have scandalized that sacerdotal sect. Qumran's ethic applied only to its own community; John's was addressed to the entire nation, even the king (Mark 6.18). He called not for the communal sharing of goods but for sharing with the wretched who had nothing (Luke 3.11). Instead of demanding that his hearers abandon lives of moral ambiguity and move to the desert, John offered an ideal attainable in society by people unable to abandon everything (Luke 3.12–14). John's baptism, unlike Qumran's washings, was not daily, but once for all, and was not intended to achieve levitical purity, but to secure the forgiveness of sins in anticipation of the coming day of wrath. Even their common use of Isaiah 40.3 was different. Qumran interpreted it to mean that the preparation for the Lord's way was to be done in the wilderness by moving there and studying scripture. John seems to have understood the wilderness only as the place where the voice cries out. And Qumran expected a prophet, a messiah of Aaron, and a messiah of Israel; John expected only a coming judge different from all three.

The evangelists each employ the traditions about John in the service of the proclamation of Jesus. Each handles him differently, but all see him as the one who stands at the beginning of the gospel story, demanding of the hearer a beginner's mind and the jettisoning of all previous securities, so that a new word can be heard.   WALTER WINK

John, The Gospel According to.

Structure and Content. The story of *Jesus in John's gospel is presented as a drama, consisting of a prologue, two main acts, and an epilogue. By considering the gospel in this light, its distinctive character may be understood and its teaching illuminated.

The prologue (chap. 1 as a whole) introduces the main theological themes developed in the body of the gospel, such as "life," "light," and "glory." It also includes the leading characters who are to be involved in the main action. *John the Baptist is there, and so are the disciples who will form the nucleus of the early Christian community: *Andrew and *Peter, *Philip and Nathanael. But the stage is dominated by the central character of Jesus himself, whose identity begins already to be disclosed, for in this single chapter he is described as *Word, Son, Christ (*Messiah), *Son of God, King of Israel, and *Son of man. The climax of the prologue is reached in 1.51 ("you will see heaven opened, and the angels of God ascending and descending upon the Son of man"). Jesus, as the incarnate and exalted Son of man and Son of God, joins earth and heaven decisively together and makes it possible, even in this world, for every believer to share the life of eternity.

Act I (chaps. 2–12) describes the revelation of the Word of God to the world. For those with eyes to see, Jesus during his ministry reveals through his words and actions the glory of God the Father. To demonstrate this truth, John makes his own selection from the miracles, or "signs," that Jesus performed and narrates six of them dramatically. To these six signs are attached explanatory discourses, all of which deal with the leading theme of "life" through Christ, and several memorable "I am" sayings, which act as a text for each sermon. These may be set out as shown in the table on the next page.

Act 2 of John's drama (chaps. 13–20) deals with the glorification of God's Word for the world. At its heart is the story of the passion and resurrection of Jesus, prepared for by the farewell address to the disciples (John 14–17), a discourse that deals with the life of the believer.

The drama ends with an epilogue, chap. 21, which may have been written later but is now firmly related to the body of the gospel. This final section narrates the seventh sign, the catch of 153 fish, and the recalling of Peter. Together these incidents point to the unlimited scope of the Christian good news, an idea retained throughout John's gospel, and provide an agenda for the church of the future. The mission of the disciples to the world can now begin on the basis of the revelation and glorification of the messianic Word of God.

Throughout his dramatic portrayal of the ministry, death, and exaltation of Jesus, John is anxious that readers should "see" the identity of the central character as Christ and Son of God (20.29–31) and "hear" his words. Verbs of seeing and hearing are important in John and are close in meaning to the activity of believing. As in a

SIGN	DISCOURSE	"I AM" SAYING
1. Changing water into wine (2)	new life (3)	the true vine (15.1)
2. Healing the official's son (4)	water of life (4)	the way, the truth and the life (14.6)
3. Making the sick man well (5)	Son, life-giver (5)	the door of the sheep (10.7)
4. Feeding the five thousand (6)	bread and Spirit of life (6–7)	the bread of life (6.35)
5. Restoring the blind man's sight (9)	light of life (8)	the light of the world (8.12)
6. Raising Lazarus from the dead (11)	shepherd, life-giver (10)	the resurrection and the life (11.25)

courtroom, witnesses are called throughout the drama to bear testimony to the life-giving Christ; and the sources of this evidence are divine (the Father, 5.37; the Spirit, 15.26; the scriptures, 5.39) as well as human (John the Baptist, 1.29–36; the Samaritan woman, 4.29, 39–42; the blind man, 9.35–38; Martha, 11.27; and, supremely, Thomas, 20.28).

John thus moves beyond the witness of the other gospel writers in exploring the nature of Jesus in relation to God and humanity, and the grounds for Christian belief and for the spiritual life that is its consequence. Jesus, in John's portrait, is both one with the Father (10.30) and one with his church on earth (16.28).

Origin. Since roughly the middle of the twentieth century support has been growing for the view that the basic tradition underlying John's gospel may be historically more reliable than previously acknowledged. After the rise of biblical criticism in the middle of the nineteenth century, scholarly opinion tended to regard this gospel as a theological rewriting of the others. The author knew Mark, Matthew, and Luke, it was thought, but went his own way when he wished to interpret their meaning. But that conclusion and the assumption that John knew and used the other Gospels in their finished form have now been seriously questioned. It is now thought possible that John drew more or less independently on common Christian sources about the life and teaching of Jesus.

This view may be supported in three ways. First, a straight literary comparison among the four Gospels reveals that, when material in John also appears in the other Gospels (such as the feeding of the five thousand [John 6; Mark 6 par.] and the anointing at Bethany [John 12;

Mark 14 par.]), John preserves interesting points of circumstantial detail that appear to be historical rather than theological. Second, the evidence from the *Dead Sea Scrolls has shown that before the common era a literary setting existed in which Jewish and Greek religious ideas were combined in a manner that was once thought to be unique to John and of a late, second century CE, date. The scrolls now make it clear that John may well have derived from *Qumran itself his language of "truth," "knowledge," "wisdom," and "faith," as well as his theological conviction that life is a struggle between truth and perversity, the sons of light and the sons of darkness, good and evil, in which God will ultimately prevail. Third, archaeological discoveries in and around Jerusalem have indicated that, when John uses place-names hitherto unknown (such as Bethesda [John 5.2] and Gabbatha [19.13]), he was not being inventive but referring to sites now identifiable. In this case the stories associated with such sites need not be theological creations either and may well rest on an underlying historical tradition.

Composition. We have already noted that John's gospel is a literary unit, which may be analyzed in terms of its dramatic structure. But, despite the unity of the gospel as we now have it, there are some features that suggest it was composed in edited stages.

For example, there are differences of style and language in various parts of the gospel, especially chaps. 1 and 21. Second, some of the discourses contain material that seems to be largely repeated (as in 6.35–50 and 50–58; chaps. 14 and 16). Third, there are notorious breaks in sequence at a number of points in the gospel. Thus the first two signs performed by Jesus are numbered "first" and "second" (2.11; 4.54), yet in 2.23 we hear of other signs that he did, and the sequence is thus unaccountably interrupted. The geographical locations, also, do not appear to be consistently exact. So in 3.22 we read that Jesus went into Judea, whereas according to 2.23 he was already there; and in 6.1 it is implied that Jesus is in Galilee, although at the end of chap. 5 he is in Jerusalem. Similarly, there is a clear break between the setting of chaps. 20 (Jerusalem) and 21 (Galilee/Tiberias). Furthermore, the continuation of the farewell discourse in John 15–16 (17) is awkward after the command of Jesus at 14.31 ("Rise, let us be on our way").

It is possible to account for some but not all of these variations, repetitions, and breaks in continuity; the problem is thus to explain their presence in what now appears to be a carefully constructed literary whole. Some scholars have suggested that there is no problem, inasmuch as the author himself chose to write in this way. Others believe that displacements in John's material have occurred at the manuscript stage, for example, that chaps. 5 and 6 became reversed, resulting in the odd geographical sequence in John 4–7.

None of the proposed restorations, however, takes the problem seriously or resolves it adequately. A third (and more plausible) explanation suggests that behind the composition of the gospel lie a number of different sources, recording the signs, the teaching, and the passion of Jesus, that have been combined and edited at various stages in the writing of this document, until its final publication as a unified work. What follows is a suggested description of those stages.

First, John the apostle, who was traditionally identified as the "beloved disciple," transmitted orally to his followers an account of the deeds (especially the miracles, or "signs") and sayings of Jesus and of his death and resurrection. As we have already seen, these reminiscences preserved historical information about the ministry of Jesus in both Judea and Galilee.

Second, the beloved disciple and his circle of followers moved to *Ephesus (a city associated, by strong tradition, with John), where the nucleus of the Johannine church was established. While there, John's disciples committed to writing the traditions preserved in their community for the purposes of worship and instruction. In this first draft of the final gospel what may now be recognized as distinctively Johannine thought emerged, as the ideas handed on by the apostle

were dramatically treated and theologically developed by the fourth evangelist and his colleagues.

Third, after the death of John his church at Ephesus published a final edited version of the gospel. This included a summary introduction (1.1–18), based on a community hymn and now tied securely to the remainder of the chapter, some editing of the discourses, possibly the addition of the prayer of consecration in chap. 17, and an epilogue (chap. 21). The whole gospel thus assembled then carried an authenticating postscript (21.24–25).

If some such process were involved in the making of John's gospel, it explains many of the features in its composition already discussed. Thus, it accounts for the likelihood that more than one author was responsible for the writing of the gospel, at more than one stage; and also for the fact that at first the Fourth Gospel was not ascribed to John the son of Zebedee. If the witness of the beloved disciple lies behind this gospel (as the text suggests; see 19.35; 21.24) but others from his community actually wrote it, the work may be regarded as apostolic in character, even though it did not in the end come (as some would argue) from the hand of John the apostle himself.

Date. We have seen that there is good reason to regard the sources that were used in the final composition of John's gospel as early and historically reliable. But even if the Johannine tradition may be dated to the early first century CE, this still leaves open the question of the date of the gospel's publication in its final form.

An upper limit may set at 150 CE or a little earlier. Two manuscripts, written on papyrus and discovered in Egypt, are relevant to dating the gospel. One, known as the Rylands Papyrus, contains a few verses of John 18 and may be dated to 135–150 CE. A second papyrus (Egerton 2) includes part of an unknown gospel that probably used John as well as Mark, Matthew, and Luke; this manuscript dates from ca. 150 CE. The existence of these witnesses suggests that John's gospel must have been written at the very latest by the beginning of the second century CE, and probably earlier.

There are no other conclusive external grounds for an earlier date and no firm evidence that any writers before ca. 150 CE knew the gospel. We must therefore look to the contents of the gospel itself to see whether they can help us—although, here again, it is difficult to establish definite conclusions.

One important clue is provided by the reference in 9.22 and 16.2 (cf. 12.42) to the possibility of Jews who confessed Christ being "put out of the synagogue." This may be an allusion to the Test Benediction that was introduced by Rabbi Gamaliel II (ca. 85–90 CE) as a means of excluding Nazarenes and other "heretics" from Jewish worship. If so, a date in this period (ca. 85 CE) may be assigned to the gospel. Such a date is also suggested by the fact that John's theology presumably took some time to develop. It is deeper and more sophisticated than that of the other evangelists, whose texts probably emerged earlier than 85 CE.

Purpose. Various motives have been suggested for the composition of John's gospel. For example, it has been argued that John's intention was to supplement or interpret the other gospels, to restate the Christian good news in Greek terms, to issue a polemical attack on the sect of John the Baptist, to adjust the sacramental teaching prevalent in the early church, to correct understanding about the return of Jesus, and to counter gnostically inclined theology.

John himself gives us (20.30–31) a reason for writing his gospel. He wants his readers to see and to hear who Jesus is: that he is the Christ and the Son of God. But this does not give us a complete picture. Who were these readers? It is unlikely that they were Jews, since by 85 CE the mission to Israel was over. It is possible that John was addressing Jewish Christians in the *Dispersion, torn between loyalty to Judaism and their new-found faith in Jesus and increasingly pressurized by the recently introduced Test Benediction (see above). This would account for the stress in this gospel on the fulfillment of Judaism. But, once again, such an interpretation of John does not take full account of his message about Jesus; nor does it relate the Fourth Gospel directly to a living church situation, in line with current thinking about John.

Let us suppose that John was addressing the needs of his own community and see whether this will provide a reason for the dramatically shaped version of the Jesus story that he preserves in his gospel. It could be that this community of Christians, gathered initially around the beloved disciple, included believers from different backgrounds, both Jewish and gentile. Some held a balanced view of Jesus: that he was both one with God and fully human. But some from a Jewish background, who still felt a loyalty to their heritage, regarded Jesus as human rather than divine. This would have been all the more likely if, after 70 CE, they were under pressure from their compatriots in the Dispersion and were tempted to return to Judaism by denying the messiahship of Jesus, as "the Jews" do throughout this gospel. On the other hand, those in the circle from a Greek background, including possibly some Hellenistic Jewish Christians, could have thought of Jesus as divine rather than human. This would be understandable if the "divine man" tradition of their original religious environment exercised influence on the Johannine church.

These two groups, it may be presumed, had begun to perceive the real identity of Jesus, but neither had seen that his nature, both human and divine, made it possible for him to be the savior of the world. Friction may have resulted; in this case John's emphasis on mutual love (15.12) and unity within the church (17.11, 21–23) would have been entirely in place.

We can find this story anticipated in the book of *Revelation and concluded in the *Johannine letters. Evidently the appeal of the fourth evangelist did little to ease the tensions that had beset his community. But his balanced estimate of the person of Jesus was exactly suited to the needs of his own adherents, and it has provided Christians ever since with important guidelines for assessing and maintaining a crucial part of their faith.

Teaching. John's theology is a theology of life. He bears testimony not only to Jesus, but also to the possibility of life through him (1.4). The repeated symbol of light makes the same point. The life that he mediates to every believer, on the basis of his revelation to the world and his glorification for the world, is the divine life that ultimately belongs to the Father himself (5.26).

Moreover, John's gospel speaks of life through Jesus in all its fullness. The seven signs make clear that Jesus is concerned about the physical dimension of human existence as well as its spiritual possibilities. And since the Word became flesh (1.14), as the signs again illustrate, all matter (not only water, bread, and wine) can point to and convey the abundant life of the life-giver (10.10). Such is John's particular "sacramentalism."

This eternal life is available to the faithful now. John's theology of salvation includes a future tense; so, for example, Jesus promises his disciples that he will eventually "come again" for them (14.3). But his emphasis is on the blessings of eternity that can be shared by the Christian in the present, when the judgment as well as the life of God are disclosed (3.16–18).

This understanding of salvation is determined by John's concept of sin. For writers of the other Gospels sin is essentially personal and communal wrongdoing: it is disobedience to God's law. Its consequence, as throughout the Hebrew Bible, is a breakdown of the *covenant between creator and creature. Such a covenant relationship can be restored only by the sacrifice on the cross, echoed in the subsequent self-offering of obedience in the lives of the disciples (Mark 10.45; Matthew 7.21; Luke 9.23).

For the fourth evangelist sin is not, as in the other Gospels and in Paul, primarily ethical. It stems from a cosmic state of alienation from God, from a spiritual blindness, or darkness, or deadness (John 3.19; 12.35). This situation can be remedied only by restored sight (9.39) and a conscious return to the light through identification with, and incorporation into, the life of the Son who unites the dimensions of heaven and earth (12.46; 15.4). So in John's gospel the passion and crucifixion of Jesus are not seen as a sacrificial explanation for the forgiveness of sin but as glorification: the exultant transformation scene in a spiritual drama of revelation. In Johannine terminology, references to Jesus as the "*Lamb of God" (1.29, 36; see Rev. 13.8) are correspondingly cosmic in character. In John's view, the cross is a timeless manifestation, mediated through a historical event: "I, when I am lifted up from the earth, will draw all people to myself" (John 12.32).

Those who are thus "drawn" to the glorified Christ are indwelt by the Spirit–Paraclete (14.16–17) and receive new life from the vine; and this not only sustains believers individually but also unites them with every other "branch" in the Christian community (15.1–5). At this point, ethical sinfulness can be eradicated by effecting the "new commandment" of love (13.34–35). The time of eternal life in Christ has yet to come; but through him, and decisively, it has arrived already.   STEPHEN S. SMALLEY

John, The Letters of.

Situation. The three letters in the New Testament that bear the name of John form a composite unit. Although each possesses individual features, all have common characteristics of style, language, and thought and appear to belong to the same situation.

1 John, in contrast to 2 and 3 John, does not at first look like a personal letter. But it was evidently addressed to a particular church situation, in which problems of belief and behavior were being encountered. Indeed, a crisis had arisen, precipitated by some members of the Johannine circle who were spreading false teaching and encouraging secession from the community. As a result, dissident groups had already been established (1 John 2.19). In the face of division, John (as we may for convenience call the writer[s] of these three epistles) composed a "letter" that was designed to correct the inadequate and erroneous views of his readers and to recall them to the fundamental elements in the apostolic gospel.

The nature of the false teaching propounded by John's opponents is indicated in various places in 1 John. The heterodox members of the church claimed to have a special relationship with God (1.6; 2.4) and to be without sin (1.8, 10). They did not believe that Jesus was the Christ or *Son of God (2.22; 5.1, 5), and denied his being *incarnate (4.2–3; 5.6; 2 John 7). The emphasis in 1 John on right behavior (renouncing sin, rejecting worldliness, and being obedient, especially to the love command) suggests that the opponents were leading others astray regarding ethical as well as theological issues.

If we try to relate these ideas to known systems of opinion in the first century CE, a number of possibilities present themselves. The most widely accepted view is that John was confronted by some early form of *gnostic thinking. Such an outlook stemmed from a sharp, characteristically Greek, division between the spiritual, regarded as good, and the material, deemed to be evil. In such a system no place for a real incarnation of the Son of God could be found; the consequence was docetism, a system that acknowledged Jesus as Son of God but claimed that this was merely a seeming or phantom advent. Views of this nature were entertained in the first century CE by Cerinthus, and in the second century by those whom Ignatius of Antioch attacked, and by Basilides.

An alternative approach is to identify John's opponents, as in the Fourth Gospel, with Jewish denials that Jesus was Messiah and Son of God. Thus, the false teachers countered by the writer claimed to know the Father but denied the Christhood of Jesus (2.4, 22–23). Those who object to this interpretation do so on the grounds that non-Christian Jews cannot have belonged to John's church (2.19) or have claimed to be guided by the Spirit (3.24; 4.1) and to be sinless (1.8, 10). But there is no problem involved if the Jewish opposition came from Jewish Christians. If so, we may combine these two solutions and say that some of John's opponents were Jewish and some were Hellenistic. In that case the situation addressed in 1 John closely approximates that in John's gospel.

Central to the theology of the fourth evangelist is his balanced understanding of the person of Christ: that he is both one with humankind and one with God (see John 16.28). Some Johannine Christians had remained orthodox in their belief. But others, from a Jewish background, needed to be reminded of the divinity of Christ; while a third group, of *gentile origin, required assurance about his real humanity.

If this is an accurate description of the volatile setting out of which John's gospel came, it will throw light on the situation behind 1 John and account for the nature of the false teaching that this writer was trying to resist. For by the time that the Johannine letters were written (say, ten years after the gospel [see below]), friction between the two heterodox groups had developed, and a polarization had begun to emerge. Those with a low view of Jesus had moved further toward a Jewish position and denied that Jesus was the Christ (2.22). Those who espoused a high Christology had become more clearly gnostic and docetic by inclination and refused to acknowledge that the Christ was Jesus (4.2). On both sides, problems of behavior accompanied those of doctrine (2.7–8, the Law is wrongly regarded as indispensable; 3.10–11, right conduct is falsely deemed unimportant). As a result, secession from the community began to take place (2.18–19).

So the writer of 1 John recalls his followers to the fundamental truths of the Christian faith. Often appealing to the teaching of John's gospel, elements of which may have been distorted by his opponents in support of their theological position, he summarizes the claims of the heterodox, provides a balanced theology of Christ's person (divine, [2.13–14], and human, [3.16]), and refutes ethical error, not least by stressing the command to love (3.11; see John 13.34).

The plea for love and unity, however, evident in both the Fourth Gospel and 1 John, seems not to have been widely heeded. The divisions in the community, already apparent when 1 John

was written, deepened; and from 2 John we learn that "many deceivers" had gone back into the world (v. 7). Perhaps these were predominantly docetic in outlook (see 2 John 9), although, again, there is nothing in the Johannine letters to suggest that docetism is the only tendency in view.

By the time 3 John appeared, the unity of the Johannine circle seems to have been threatened from an organizational, as well as doctrinal, point of view. Diotrephes was "putting himself first" and excluding orthodox members from the church (3 John 9–10), and the writer's concern that the influence of such leaders should not increase suggests that he feared the final dissolution of the Johannine community. What actually happened we can only guess. Some of the group presumably went further into gnosticism; the Jewish secessionists may have returned to Judaism, while the orthodox adherents no doubt became absorbed into the life of the great church. At that time John's gospel, with the discussion of its doctrine provided by 1 John (supplemented by 2 and 3 John), came into its own, and the teaching of John's circle was finally secured for the cause of orthodoxy.

Character. 2 and 3 John are the shortest letters in the New Testament. They each consist of one chapter only, are roughly equal in length, and correspond to the conventionally brief length of a private letter that, at the time, would have been written on a single papyrus sheet about 20 by 25 cm (8 by 10 in) in size. Both are personal missives, written by one who describes himself as the *elder. But 2 John (addressed to a community) conforms closely to the pattern of other New Testament letters; whereas 3 John (addressed to Gaius, an individual) reflects a secular form of first-century *letter writing. Moreover, 2 John is closer than 3 John to 1 John in subject matter and style. None of these variations, however, compels us to infer that 2 and 3 John are ultimately unrelated (there are evident points of contact between them) or that 2 John was written as a first draft of 1 John. The history of the Johannine community sketched above may be traced entirely naturally from the Gospel to the letters in their present sequence, despite some attempts to assign to them a different order of composition.

The literary character of 1 John, on the other hand, is more difficult to determine. It is not epistolary in character, as are 2 and 3 John; and its style is general, even if personal. Possibly it is best described as a paper or brochure. It was written in light of John's gospel, as a comment on the fourth evangelist's teaching, for purposes of teaching and debate within a troubled and slowly disintegrating community.

Structure. The ways of analyzing the structure of 1 John are numerous. One possibility is to subdivide the two main sections of the letter, which carry exhortations to live in the light as children of God, into four subsections, which set out the basic conditions for truly Christian living. These are stated in the first half of the letter and repeated in cyclical fashion (with one expansion, exemplifying the demand for obedience in terms of the command to love) during the second half. Together with 2 and 3 John this is their outline:

1 JOHN

I. Preface (1.1–4): The word of life
II. Live in the light (1.5–2.29):
   A. God is light (1.5–7)
   B. First condition for living in the light: renounce sin (1.8–2.2)
   C. Second condition: be obedient (2.3–11)
   D. Third condition: reject worldliness (2.12–17)
   E. Fourth condition: keep the faith (2.18–29)
III. Live as children of God (3.1–5.13):
   A. God is Father (3.1–3)
   B. First condition for living as God's children: renounce sin (3.4–9)
   C. Second condition: be obedient (3.10–24)
   D. Third condition: reject worldliness (4.1–6)
   E. Fourth condition: be loving (4.7–5.4)
   F. Fifth condition: keep the faith (5.5–13)
IV. Conclusion (5.14–21): Christian confidence

2 JOHN
   Living in truth and love

3 JOHN
   A plea for help.

Composition of 1 John. The difficulties involved in determining the literary character of 1 John and analyzing the structure of its material have resulted in a number of attempts to explain the present form of the letter. Two main proposals have been put forward by scholars.

According to one view, the original order has been rearranged. There is, however, no evidence for such transposition, which in the end introduces further dislocations in the text. According to others, various sources have been used and edited; theories under this heading vary considerably. Rudolf Bultmann, for example, has argued that two different styles of writing can be identified in 1 John and that one belongs to a source that may also be detected behind John's gospel while the other derives from the author himself. Wolfgang Nauck, who is critical of Bultmann's position, has proposed that 1 John stems from an earlier composition by the writer, which in due course he rewrote as a baptismal homily. But attempts of this kind to separate an underlying tradition from its edition are unsupported by firm evidence.

It is clear, therefore, that the history of this document cannot easily be explained in terms of rearrangement or written sources. The alternative view, that 1 John is a literary unity, is just as plausible; this suggestion is strongly supported by the theological coherence and balance of the letter and by its coherent structure (see above).

Authorship. The identity of the author of the Johannine letters is a matter of considerable debate and raises the issue of the relationship between these documents and both the gospel and Revelation of John. The following scheme, which attempts to take account of all the relevant data, is only one solution to the problem.

The inspiration behind the tradition and distinctive theology of the Fourth Gospel came from John the apostle, the beloved disciple, himself. In 70 CE he wrote *Revelation in order to encourage the members of his community to remain steadfast in the faith. Some of his followers later undertook the final publication of the gospel. A leading Johannine Christian (who may possibly have been involved in the composition of John's gospel) in due course wrote 1 John. An elder, close to the author of 1 John (or possibly the same person), was then responsible for 2 and 3 John.

All the Johannine documents in the New Testament are associated in some way, even if at times the links between them seem tenuous. That association is probably best accounted for by tracing their origin to a specific community, gathered in some way around John the apostle. Whatever answers are given to the question of authorship, therefore, the origin of the letters (as of the other parts of the Johannine literature) can well be assigned ultimately to an authoritative, apostolic tradition.

Date and Place of Origin. There are conflicting opinions among scholars about when and where the Johannine letters appeared. Assuming that 1, 2, and 3 John followed the gospel of John, the letters of John may be dated to the last decade of the first century CE. This allows time for a sharpening of the heterodox opinions within John's circle and for the first moves on the part of the secessionists.

Although some scholars have suggested Syria as the place of publication, the view that 1, 2, and 3 John were addressed to Johannine communities in Asia Minor, with their center in *Ephesus, is more probable. This is the traditional setting for the birth of John's gospel; it could easily have produced the controversy with Judaism and Hellenism that may be detected in both the Johannine gospel and the letters; and its religious syncretism would readily have nurtured the tendencies in the situation behind the letters.

Postscript. The Johannine letters are often described as catholic documents. This does not mean that they were written for all in the early church but that they delivered to all believers in John's community a timeless message about the nature of Jesus in relation to God and humanity, about the importance of right behavior as well as right belief, and about the need for unity, however flexible, among all the churches. The tensions in John's community were probably not resolved by the appeal for love and unity built into his letters; but the truths that they preserve have proved indispensable for the life of the universal church ever since.

STEPHEN S. SMALLEY

Jonah, The Book of. The antihero of the book of Jonah is mentioned in 2 Kings 14.25 as a prophet of salvation during the expansionistic era of Jeroboam II. The choice of this prophet as the target of didactic satire is doubly appropriate, first because he proclaimed nationalistic oracles in behalf of Israel and second because his name means "dove [of faithfulness or truthfulness]." The author wrote a short parable characterized by fantastic events to poke fun indirectly at a little man whose inner thoughts remain virtually hidden. Although certain similarities exist between this story and the prophetic legends of *Elijah and *Elisha, a greater kinship is with 1 Kings 13. Neither Jonah nor this unnamed man of God is intended for emulation; hence the term "legend" is not entirely appropriate.

The book of Jonah resembles later *midrash, for it interprets biblical texts explicitly (Exod.

34.6) and implicitly (Num. 23.19; Ezek. 18.23). In each instance the issue is the nature of Jonah's God: Is divine *mercy a more powerful attribute than justice? Can the deity actually repent? Does God's preference to grant life rather than death extend beyond Israel's borders?

Jonah's resistance to the divine call exceeds the usual reluctance, exemplified by *Moses, *Amos, and *Jeremiah. Jonah actually flees from God, and after the deity has shown him the futility of his ways, he carries out the task with a vengeance. Then he resents the sparing of repentant Ninevites and argues that justice ought to prevail, although he has experienced undeserved compassion. This picture of Israelite prophecy is not flattering, for Jonah is unrepentant to the end. Furthermore, his manipulation of the facts in answering the sailors renders the prophet suspect and extols their superior ethics. When he does resort to prayer, Jonah exalts the ego and uses the occasion to accuse God. He is also spiteful, hoping that the sailors' repentance will be short-lived, and he eagerly awaits the destruction of *Nineveh.

When was this unflattering depiction of prophecy written? Like many biblical books, this one yields few clues about its time of origin. The supposed Aramaisms may reflect a northern or Phoenician linguistic influence, so they do not necessarily indicate a postexilic date for the book. The expression "king of Nineveh" is no different from king of Samaria (1 Kings 21.1; 2 Kings 1.3); the same usage occurs in Neo-Assyrian inscriptions. Moreover, the use of the past tense with references to Nineveh is not without stylistic precedent in Hebrew narrative (Gen. 29.17; Exod. 9.11; Num. 14.24). The literary relationship between the book of Jonah and other texts (Exod. 14; 32; Deut. 21; 1 Kings 19; Jer. 26 and 36; Ps. 139) does little to clarify the date of the book. Even the apparent citation of Joel cannot be proved, for both references may derive from a common source.

Another approach to dating the book is by searching for its probable setting. The negative attitude toward prophecy resembles Zechariah 13.1–6, but that text cannot be dated with any certainty. Furthermore, unflattering views of prophecy may have existed at various times and places. The antiparticularism is often thought to be a response to the narrow policy of *Ezra and *Nehemiah. Thus, *Ruth and Jonah function to combat the view that would exclude foreigners from divine solicitude. Others suggest that the primary purpose of the book is to encourage repentance on Israel's part, and that was an important aspect of the message proclaimed by *Jeremiah and *Ezekiel. The search for an appropriate social and religious context for the book implies that its essential message is clear; this, however, does not seem to be the case. The favorable depiction of foreigners at Jonah's expense is striking, but is this openness to non-Israelites the central theme of the book?

The strange behavior on Jonah's part is given a rationale from sacred tradition. Jonah quotes (4.2) Exodus 34.6, the cultic confession that the Lord is both compassionate and just, as the reason for his flight from the divine presence. This conscious reflection on the nature of God offers a decisive clue to the purpose of the book. The conflict between Jonah and God concerns theodicy. Is it fair for the wicked inhabitants of Nineveh to escape the deity's wrath by repenting of their sins? Linguistic features link Nineveh and the cities *Sodom and Gomorrah, a comparison in which the Israelites could concur because of the suffering inflicted on them by Assyrian hordes. Nevertheless, the object lesson involving a fast-growing plant that perished just as quickly offers a justification for God's repentance. The closing question addressed to the sulking prophet throws into relief divine compassion for all creatures in Nineveh.

The author may have had more than one purpose. The great prophets had predicted the destruction of foreign nations, but these oracles had failed to come true. Were the prophets false? No, this book suggests, for the Assyrians gained time by repenting. Again, from the perspective of several prophets, Israelites were entirely unrepentant. How could the nation escape God's wrath? By turning from their evil ways and evoking the Lord's pity. Is it too late for that? No, for God is so eager to save them that repentance even by the wicked Ninevites would result in forgiveness. Although the portrait of Israelite prophecy is troubling, the radical self-criticism goes a long way toward redeeming the profession.

Several literary features of the book have captured the imagination of modern critics. These include the repetition by God and the polytheistic sailors of key words such as "get up," "go," and "cry out/proclaim"; the presence of vivid terms like "throw," "go down," and "evil" (the last even in self-description by the people of Nineveh); and varied names for the deity, which do not appear to be used capriciously. Moreover, the book has numerous allusions to earlier biblical expressions, particularly in the psalm (chap. 2) that Jonah utters from the belly of the fish. Perhaps the grotesque and fantastic achieve their pinnacle in the attribution of thoughts to the endangered ship (1.4). The weighty message does not exclude humor: on hearing Jonah's facile confession that deliverance belongs to the Lord, the fish throws up. This entire psalm is a devastating mockery of Israelite piety as it is exemplified by the dubious prophet whose sole concern was his reputation for accuracy of prediction or a restriction of divine compassion to Israel.

JAMES L. CRENSHAW

Jordan River (Map 1:Y2–5). The major river in ancient Palestine, linking the two major inland lakes of Kinneret (the Sea of *Galilee) and the Dead Sea (also known as the Salt Sea). The principal source of the Jordan is the precipitation on Mount *Hermon and the three springs near Tel Dan, Banias, and Hasbaya. In antiquity some of the headwaters of the Jordan River flowed through the Huleh Valley, a lake until modern times, which is some 300 m (985 ft) higher than the Sea of Galilee; this rapid drop in elevation, which continues farther south, probably explains the river's name (from Hebr. *yārad*, "to go down"). These sources combine near the northern edge of the Huleh Valley, and from that point the river is called the Jordan.

The river flows out of Kinneret at its southern tip, possibly an artificial outflow; 10 km (6 mi) south the Jordan is joined by its main tributary, the Yarmuk. Another tributary from the east is the Jabbok, in the Wadi Zarqa, 56 km (35 mi) farther south. The Jordan valley receives virtually no direct rainfall south of the Yarmuk. The total annual flow of the river into the Dead Sea, another 194 m (600 ft) lower than the Sea of Galilee, is 1.2 billion m³ (3 billion gal) of water. Despite this volume, the Jordan River has rarely served as a source of irrigation. The river bluffs of the flood plain of the Rift Valley (Arabic *Ghor*), which line both sides of the Jordan, are 500–1,000 m (1,500–3,000 ft) wide and constantly crumbling and rise at least 20–50 m (60–150 ft) above the river bottom. These factors constitute a serious impediment to irrigation, since the technology of pumping is fairly recent. The flood plain (Arabic *Zor*) is called "pride of the Jordan" (NRSV: "thicket"; Jer. 12.5; 49.19; 50.44; Zech. 11.3).

Because of the intense heat of the Rift Valley and the availability of moisture from the Jordan along its river banks, much of the vegetation there has the characteristic of a tropical jungle, which is typical of regions as far south as the Sudan. One plant that grows freely there is the papyrus. In addition there is much tamarisk and *spina Christi* on the river banks. In antiquity it was a haven for many wild *animals, including lions. The river is fairly narrow and easy to cross, though the current is often swift.

Much of the importance of the Jordan River in the Bible derives from the fact that it assumes so central a place in the geographical nomenclature. It forms a natural boundary, so that *Moab is "beyond the Jordan" and hence the Israelites must cross the Jordan in order to enter the *Promised Land (Josh. 3). Although Israel often controlled territory east of the Jordan, the Jordan forms a natural eastern border, and Ezekiel's idealized nation is entirely to its west (see Ezek. 47.18). Jesus is reported to be baptized at "Bethany across the Jordan" (John 1.28). It is thus both as a primary water source, especially in the northern Ghor, and as a central feature of the Palestinian landscape that the Jordan River derives its importance.   ERIC M. MEYERS

Joseph (Husband of Mary). According to the opening chapters of the gospels of *Matthew and *Luke, *Mary, the mother of *Jesus, was engaged before his birth to Joseph, son of Jacob (Matt. 1.16) or of Heli (Luke 3.23). Matthew's infancy story is written largely from Joseph's point of view, even narrating his receiving messages from *angels in his *dreams. These dreams portray his struggle to determine how to deal justly with his fiancée's unexpected pregnancy (Matt. 1.18–25) and how to respond to threats against the infant Jesus (2.13–23).

Matthew and Luke agree in their *genealogies of Jesus that Joseph was a descendent of King *David (Matt. 1.1–16; Luke 3.23–38). These genealogies imply that Joseph was in some way Jesus' father (*see* Virgin Birth). Joseph is gone from the scene when the Gospels describe Jesus' adult life, though he was apparently remembered by those around Jesus as his father (Luke 4.22; John 1.45; 6.42) and as a carpenter (Matt. 13:55). The gospel of Mark makes no mention of Jesus' father, and calls him instead "Mary's son" (Mark 6.3). The second-century CE infancy gospel *Protevangelium of James* provides additional information of a legendary character. Later Christian tradition comes to view Joseph as an elderly widower, so that the "*brothers and sisters of Jesus" in such passages as Mark 6.3 could be understood as Joseph's children from a previous marriage, not his children with Mary; later, he came to be seen as a saintly ascetic with no interest in sex, and Jesus' siblings as "cousins."

PHILIP SELLEW

Joseph (Son of Jacob). Joseph, whose name means "May God give increase," was the son of *Jacob and *Rachel (Gen. 30.22–24), and the eponymous ancestor of the house of Joseph, one of the twelve *tribes of Israel. *Genesis 37–50 portrays Joseph as a patriarch through whom the promises to *Abraham, *Isaac, and Jacob are transmitted to later Israel. The God of the ancestors is not, however, called the God of Joseph, and Joseph the patriarch is seldom mentioned in the Bible outside Genesis.

The Joseph story begins in Genesis 37.1, "Jacob settled in the land where his father had lived as an alien, the land of Canaan," and comes to its preliminary end in 47.27, where the opening formula is transformed, "Thus Israel settled in the land of Egypt, in the region of Goshen." Its unity comes not from a single theme, but from sophisticated art, narrating the interaction of the human characters; God's direct action is hardly mentioned.

The story begins with the young, self-centered Joseph announcing to his father and brothers his double *dreams of their obeisance to him. The doubling of his dreams here and later (41.1–8) proves their divine origin. Joseph later goes out to visit his brothers who are caring for their father's flock, apparently a rare event since he does not even know where they are camped (37.12–17). As he comes upon his brothers, they decide to kill him, but at the intercession of Reuben and Judah, he is spared; he ultimately falls into the hands of traders who sell him to the Egyptian Potiphar, captain of the guard. His brothers, however, tell Jacob that his son is dead, and offer as evidence his blood-stained garment, a preferential gift from his father (37.3, traditionally, although probably erroneously, translated as "a coat of many colors"). As if to indicate the passing of time and to build suspense about Joseph's fate, chap. 38 tells the story of Judah, the ancestor of the southern kingdom, a counterbalance to Joseph, the ancestor of the northern kingdom. Chap. 39 opens with Joseph as overseer of Potiphar's house. Even in prison, to which he is unjustly condemned, God protects him. His ability to interpret dreams brings him to Pharaoh's notice (40.1–41.14). He interprets Pharaoh's dream correctly as seven years of plenty and seven years of famine, and he is put in charge of preparing for the seven years of famine (chap. 41). That famine causes Jacob to send all his sons but *Benjamin (the other son of his beloved Rachel) to Egypt to buy grain. In the first visit of his brothers (chap. 42), Joseph tests them by treating them roughly, holding Simeon as hostage, putting their money back in their grain sacks, and demanding that they return with Benjamin on their next visit. Joseph, the cool courtier, wants to learn his brothers' attitude toward him, his full brother Benjamin, and their father. The second visit of the now uneasy brothers is even more eventful (chaps. 43–45): Joseph surprises them by seating them at a banquet according to the order of their birth, Benjamin is arrested on a ruse, and, finally, Judah as spokesman for the group expresses the pain the family disunity has caused (44.18–44). Joseph, by now emotionally drawn into the family's crisis, reveals himself to his brothers, acknowledging that God, despite the selfish behavior of the family members, "sent me before you to preserve life" (45.5). The last chapters narrate Jacob's blessing of his grandsons *Ephraim and *Manasseh (chap. 48), his testament (chap. 49), his death, and Joseph's final days (chap. 50).

At one level, chaps. 37–50 explain how the sons of Jacob got to Egypt through the agency of Joseph. On a deeper level, the chapters tell movingly how God kept a disintegrating family united by the repentance and restraint of its members. The lesson is an important one for Israel because its unity is often threatened by the claims of one tribe against another.

The tribe of Joseph is divided into the tribes of Ephraim and Manasseh (Gen. 48; Num. 26.28–37; Josh. 14.4). "House of Joseph" may designate the northern kingdom as distinguished from the southern kingdom of Judah (2 Sam. 19.20; Ps. 78.67–68), or it may designate all Israel (Pss. 77.15; 80.1–2).

In the New Testament, Hebrews 11.22 lists Joseph as a hero of faith; Stephen in his speech summarizes his career in Acts 7.13–17. Some have seen in Mark's episode of the youth who left his cloak behind (Mark 14.51–52) an echo of Genesis 39.11–12. Among noteworthy modern retellings of the Joseph story is Thomas Mann's *Joseph and His Brothers*.

RICHARD J. CLIFFORD

Joseph of Arimathea. Unanticipated, Joseph enters all four passion narratives to request Jesus' body from Pilate to entomb it. Mark 15.43–46 depicts a respected council member awaiting the reign of God. His Joseph buys a linen cloth, removes the body from the cross, wraps and buries it, and rolls the stone against the tomb. Possibly a disciple, he adheres to commandments concerning burial (Deut. 21.23; Tob. 1.17–18; *B. Qam.* 81a; *Ketub.* 17a; but see Num. 19.11 on restrictions involving corpse uncleanness). Matthew's "rich disciple" displays higher righteousness by placing Jesus' body in his own new tomb (27.57–60). Luke's "good and righteous" Joseph (23.50–53) explicitly dissents from the council's action against Jesus, and John's Joseph, paired with the Pharisee Nicodemus, hides his discipleship for fear of the Jews (19.38–42). Apocryphal writings variously present Joseph as caring for *Mary after the Ascension, as the patron of Glastonbury, England, and as involved in the Grail saga.

AMY-JILL LEVINE

Josephus, Flavius. Our knowledge of the life of Josephus stems directly from his own writings, four of which have survived. These works form the most important sources of contemporary information about Jewish religious life, history, and culture during the last two pre-Christian and first post-Christian centuries.

The life of Josephus (37–ca. 100 CE) divides itself into two parts: his dramatic and controversial years in Judea and his residence in Rome as a client of the Flavian emperors. He was born in Jerusalem as Yosef ben Mattityahu. While still a teenager he spent some time in the wilderness as a member of the *Essenes, whose austere life and devotion to scripture Josephus found romantic. Later he classified himself as a member of the *Pharisees. When the great revolt against Rome began in 66 CE, Josephus was appointed as general to take charge of the defense of *Galilee in the northern part of the country. His preparations, however, were nullified when Vespasian overran the Jewish forces. This rout resulted, according to Josephus, from the martial superiority of the Roman army and the tactical skill of their commander. On the other hand, the detractors of Josephus asserted that the Roman victory derived from treachery by Josephus himself, and this suspicion of Josephus's patriotism would haunt him the remainder of his public life. Josephus and some of his companions escaped the besieged town of Jotapata and formed a suicide pact in order to escape capture by the Romans. Somehow Josephus managed to become the sole survivor of this scheme and then promptly surrendered himself to the Romans. He managed to win the attention of Vespasian by forecasting that the Roman commander would become emperor, and when this prediction proved true, Josephus became a permanent fixture in the entourage first of Vespasian and then of Titus. He played a prominent role in the eventual subjugation of Judea.

Josephus spent the remainder of his life residing in Rome as a pensioner of the imperial family. He devoted himself to writing, producing his works under the name of Flavius Josephus. His first surviving work is *The Jewish War*, a seven-book account of the great rebellion in which he played so prominent a part. Josephus exhibits his skill as a historian by beginning his account two-and-a-half centuries before the actual revolt in order to portray the historical background of the unrest in Judea. His account of the war itself veers in two directions: he manages to defend and magnify the deeds of the Roman generals while simultaneously depicting the courage and heroism of the Jewish defenders of *Jerusalem.

Josephus found in Roman society a considerable interest in Jewish history and in Judaism, and to satisfy this curiosity he wrote *The Jewish Antiquities*. This work lacks the skillful writing and dramatic excitement of the *War* but makes up for this lack in sheer comprehensiveness. The first ten of its twenty books are an expanded and embellished paraphrase of the historical writings of the Hebrew Bible. Josephus supplements the biblical narrative with Jewish lore known as *haggadah* as well as with selections from Greek and other sources relevant to the biblical story. In the second half of the *Antiquities* Josephus devotes a great deal of space to the rise and reign of *Herod the Great. This section is largely dependent on the histories of Nicolaus of Damascus, a secretary to Herod.

The most charming work of Josephus is a two-book tractate in which he defends the Jewish people and religion against their ancient detractors. Something akin to *anti-Semitism had reared its head in antiquity, and Josephus records some of these ancient slanders in this work, entitled *Against Apion*. Apion was a popular publicist whose writings featured a number of these calumnies, and the essay of Josephus was intended to be a reply.

Finally, Josephus composed an autobiography originally appended to the *Antiquities*, which now circulates independently under the title of *Life*. Much of what is contained in the *Life* was previously reported in the *War*. Yet there is some additional material here as well, such as Josephus's version of his dispute with Justus of Tiberias, a rival historian.

The writings of Josephus played an important role in the culture of the Radical Reformation. If Puritan arrivals to New England possessed a book in addition to their Bibles, it was usually Josephus.

See also Judaisms of the First Century CE.

BEN ZION WACHOLDER

Joshua, The Book of. Deriving its title from the name of its protagonist, Joshua is the sixth book of the Bible. It is a narrative that reports how Joshua, following the death of *Moses (Deut. 34), led the people of Israel in occupying the *Promised Land, apportioned it to the twelve *tribes, and led them in the renewal of their *covenant with Yahweh.

Structure and Literary Characteristics. The contents of the book may be outlined as follows:

I. Stories of Israel's occupation of the land (chaps. 1–12)
   A. Prologue, with an account of Yahweh's designation of Joshua as Moses' successor (chap. 1)
   B. The spies in Jericho (chap. 2)
   C. The crossing of the Jordan and the camp at Gilgal (chaps. 3–5)
   D. The fall of Jericho (chap. 6)
   E. Achan's sin and the conquest of Ai (7.1–8.29)
   F. A covenant on Mount Ebal (8.30–35)
   G. Treaty with the Gibeonites (chap. 9)
   H. Conflict with Amorite kings and the southern campaign (chap. 10)
   I. The northern campaign (11.1–15)
   J. Summary of the occupation (11.16–12.24)
II. Account of the division of the land (chaps. 13–21)
   A. Prologue, with an account of the unconquered lands and summary of trans-Jordanian territory (chap. 13)
   B. Allotments of Judah, Ephraim, and (Western) Manasseh (chaps. 14–17)
   C. Allotments of Benjamin, Simeon, Zebulun, Issachar, Asher, Naphtali, and Dan (chaps. 18–19)
   D. Cities of refuge and Levitical cities (chaps. 20–21)

III. Concluding events (chaps. 22–24)
   A. Dismissal of Transjordanian tribes (chap. 22)
   B. Joshua's last words (chap. 23)
   C. The covenant at Shechem (24.1–28)
   D. The graves of Joshua, Joseph, and Eleazar (24.29–33)

Although the book of Joshua is a narrative work, it does not have a carefully developed plot like the books of Ruth, Jonah, and Esther. As the outline indicates, the book is a composition made up of a great many individual and diverse elements. In terms both of contents and genre, each of the three parts of the book consists of quite different types of traditions. Most elements of the first part (Josh. 1–12) are stories of the events in the occupation of the land. With few exceptions, the elements of the second part (Josh. 13–21) are geographical descriptions or lists. Speeches and reports of ceremonies predominate in the final section (Josh. 22–24).

There is, however, narrative movement, if not an explicit and developed plot. At the beginning, the people stand on the edge of the land, poised to take it, and in the end they are in the land, making a covenant with their God. How they got there, and the details of their settlement are the questions answered by the book. What unifies the work is the movement of the people of Israel toward a particular goal, their settlement of the land. Although on close examination one finds that this goal was not fully reached, it is nevertheless the major theme of the narrative. The book is also unified in the particular leader whose name symbolizes the era. Joshua was not only the person who led Israel in the realization of the promise of the land but also the last leader considered fully acceptable to Yahweh.

History of Composition. Consideration of the literary history of the book of Joshua must begin with an examination of its relationship to its context. The fundamental question is whether the book of Joshua should be seen more as a part of what precedes or what follows. Answers to this question have in large measure shaped interpretations of the book's literary history.

On the one hand, the book of Joshua continues the story begun in Genesis and brings to full circle the traditions of the *Pentateuch, recording the fulfillment of the promises to the ancestors reported in Genesis 12–50. Thus, in the late nineteenth and early twentieth centuries, the source-critical analysis of the Pentateuch was extended into the book of Joshua, and scholars found there the same sources (*J, *E, *D, and *P) recognized in the earlier books. Later form-critical and traditio-historical study by Gerhard von Rad argued that Israel's most ancient story included the events now reported in Genesis through Joshua, that is, the Hexateuch. Whether or not there was an ancient little historical credo, as von Rad argued, certainly in a great many places Israel's past was summarized in terms of a series of saving events, including the promise to the ancestors, the Egyptian sojourn and *Exodus, the wandering in the *wilderness, and the settlement of the land. In that circle, the subject matter contained in the book of Joshua would have been the concluding part.

In terms of the organization of the *canon, however, there is a distinct break between the first five books (the Torah or Pentateuch) and the section that begins with Joshua (the Former Prophets in Jewish tradition). That organization is doubtless the last stage in a long history of development, and stems in large measure from the legal contents of the Torah and its association with the authority of Moses.

On the other hand, certainly in its present literary formulation, the book of Joshua is part of the history that begins with Deuteronomy. Whether there are traces of the other Pentateuchal documents or not, its clearest literary affinities are with the book of Deuteronomy. It was Martin Noth who recognized that the book of Joshua is the second major section of a *Deuteronomic history, the account of Israel's past that includes the books of Deuteronomy through 2 Kings as they are organized in the Hebrew canon, that is, without the book of Ruth.

The diverse evidence points to the following conclusions. At an early stage in their oral transmission, Israel's traditions about the occupation of the land would have been the concluding element in the story that began with the promise of the land to the ancestors. At the latest stage, when the Hebrew books were being recognized as canonical, the book of Joshua was part of the second group of scriptures, the Prophets. But at the dominant level of their literary formulation, Joshua belongs with the Deuteronomic historical work that begins with the book of Deuteronomy.

There is abundant evidence in the book of Joshua for the Deuteronomic historians' editorial hand. These scribes—for there must have been more than one—did not create the story but rather drew upon older written and oral materials, organized and interpreted them, and at various points tied the story together with their editorial additions. These latter, recognizable by their similarities to the style and theology of the book of Deuteronomy, tend to occur at key transitions in the history, as well as to consist of speeches by the main characters in the story. Joshua 1 and 23 are such editorial contributions.

The final edition of the history must have been written not long after the last events it reports, in an anecdote concerning King Jehoiachin in Babylon. Thus it dates from ca. 560 BCE, during the Babylonian captivity, and could have been written in either Babylon or Judah. It is highly likely that there were earlier editions of the history. Evidence for two stages is seen in the two conclusions to the book of Joshua (chaps. 23 and 24), both of which bear the clear imprint of the style and theology of Deuteronomy.

In general, the final Deuteronomic editor(s) were at once historians and theologians. In a time of national disaster it was important to preserve the story of the people, especially since the institutions that transmitted the national memory were in disarray. As theologians, they interpreted their present—the Babylonian *exile—as the results of a sinful past. Because of Israel's unfaithfulness to the covenant with Yahweh, the prophetic announcements of judgment had now come to pass.

Older Traditions. When the Deuteronomic editors began to compose the book of Joshua they had at their disposal a great many oral and written materials, some doubtless quite ancient, and some already organized into collections. Most of the individual traditions in chaps. 1–12 are etiological tales, at least in their structure and intention, that is, they tend to conclude with explanations of an existing place, practice, or name in terms of some event during the time of Joshua. Thus, twelve stones at Gilgal are to be explained to future generations as those taken from the Jordan during the crossing (4.19–24), and the name Gilgal is said to come from the first *circumcision in the Promised Land (5.2–9; cf. also 6.22–25; 7.24–26).

Most of the individual stories in Joshua 1–12 relate to events in a single region, that of the tribe of Benjamin and the area near Gilgal (see Map 3:5X), an old sanctuary. What at first glance is an account of the conquest of the entire land turns out to concern the occupation of a small region. The exceptions are the reports of a southern campaign (10.28–43) and a northern one (11.1–23). It seems very likely, then, that the traditions of the tribe of Benjamin and of

the sanctuary at Gilgal formed an old collection that became the core of other stories.

Most of the lists that form the basis for the account of the division of the land in chaps. 13–21 existed before the final edition of the book. These include a list of towns and a boundary list. The town lists (15.20–62; 18.21–28) present the names of cities belonging to various tribes. Although twelve groups are given, they do not correspond to the twelve tribes; rather, they list only cities in the southern part of the country. Thus, the town lists probably give the administrative districts of Judah during the monarchy, either from the time of *Josiah (639–609 BCE) or earlier. The boundary lists (15.1–19; 17; 18.11–20; 19.10–16) trace out the frontiers between the tribes as on a *map. Although the actual tribal holdings might have changed frequently, it appears that the boundary lists give a premonarchic version of the land claimed by each tribe. This list is the basis for most contemporary maps of the tribal boundaries in the time of the judges.

Chaps. 13–21 also contain lists of the *cities of refuge and of the Levitical cities (chap. 21) and some individual stories of specific groups such as the Calebites. Some of these, which appear also in Judges 1, concern territories not captured under Joshua; they probably reflect quite ancient tradition. In the final section of the book, chap. 24 calls for special comment. Although the account of the covenant at *Shechem has been edited by the Deuteronomic historians, it probably rests upon early Israelite practice, as does the related passage in 8:30–35.

The History of the Settlement. As a source for the history of ancient Israel, the book of Joshua is useful but limited. In particular, as evidence for the period it reports, there are several reasons why its account cannot be read uncritically. First, while the Deuteronomic editorial framework gives the impression of an invasion of all of Canaan by all of Israel under the leadership of Joshua, a careful reading of the individual sections reveals a different picture. All of the stories account for only part of the land, mainly in the central hill country, and there is even a summary of unconquered territory (13.1–6). Second, the historian of this period needs to take into account a great many other passages that deal directly or indirectly with the period and its events, especially Judges 1. Others are Genesis 34, which appears to concern the settlement of the tribes of *Levi and *Simeon in the area of Shechem, and Numbers 13–14, which seems to assume the conquest of the southern plateau by the tribe of *Judah. Third, the historian needs to take note of whatever external evidence can be brought to bear, including the results of *archaeological research. There is, for example, evidence of the destruction of several Palestinian cities ca. 1200 BCE, and the appearance of a new and materially inferior culture at about that time, but the details of Israel's emergence in her homeland remain uncertain. One of the most useful historical sources in the book is the list of tribal boundaries, reflecting the situation in the period of the judges.

One general point is quite clear. It is far more accurate, both theologically and historically, to speak of what happened in the era of Joshua as the settlement rather than the conquest of the land. Theologically, virtually all levels of the tradition insist that Israel received the land as a gift from Yahweh, in fulfillment of the promise to the ancestors. The battles were understood as episodes in a holy *war in which the conflict was won by Israel's God. Historically, Israel's movement into Canaan was not a sudden series of military campaigns but a gradual settlement over a long period of time, probably more than a century. Certainly, this settlement would have seen military conflict with the native population, but more often by individual tribes than by the entire people of Israel. (See also Conquest of Canaan.)

Theological Themes. The dominant theological perspective of the book of Joshua is that of its final editors, who wrote during the Babylonian exile to interpret that disaster for those who had experienced it. These thinkers viewed the history of Israel as a series of eras, each characterized by particular leaders. Moses was, of course, the leader without peer, the only one with whom Yahweh spoke face to face (Deut. 34.10; etc.). The period of Joshua was the last era of harmony, when an obedient people experienced the fulfillment of the promise of the land. In various ways, the life of Joshua is shown to parallel that of Moses; as Moses led the people through the sea, Joshua led them across the *Jordan River, and both men led the people in the establishment and renewal of the covenant with their God. The next era, that of the Judges, was a time of testing, and the monarchy—with the primary exception of the reigns of *David and Josiah—was a history of apostasy leading up to the exile.

In this scheme, the book of Joshua stresses the importance of the land as a divine gift, addressed finally to a people that has lost that inheritance. Thus, the lists of cities and tribal holdings in chaps. 13–21 are at least as significant as the stories of battles won in chaps. 1–12. The land belongs, ultimately, to the Lord, and the people hold it in trust as an inheritance. One message of the book is that the proper social structure for maintaining that trust is that of the family and the tribe. Land, therefore, is not a commodity to be traded.

Both directly and indirectly, the book addresses the problem of syncretism. To what extent can the people of Israel adopt the religious and cultural patterns of the Canaanites? The Deuteronomic tradition argued vigorously that any compromise with foreign religions and cultures was a betrayal of the covenant and would lead ultimately to ruin. By commanding the total destruction of the native population, the writers express the dogma of a radical means to avoid the problem. This dogma had its roots in the ancient holy war tradition, in which all captives and all booty were subjected to the *ban. But the writers of the book of Joshua knew that the native population had by no means been exterminated; for the most part, they continued to live alongside the Israelites. Thus, the book of Judges reports that the Canaanites and their religious practices were left in order to test the faith of Israel (Judg. 3.1, 4).

Another theme that runs through the book is the relationship between obedience and *blessing. Although Israel receives the land as an unmerited gift, in fulfillment of the promise to the ancestors, she will remain in the land and enjoy its fruits so long as the people are faithful to the covenant. The meaning of faithfulness is expressed in the law (even understood as the "book of the law," 1.8) and the covenant stipulations (8.30–35; 21.13–20; 23.6–13; 24.14–28). Above all, this relationship between obedience and blessing is a corporate rather than an individualistic one. As the story of Achan indicates (chap. 7), the people as a whole may suffer for the sins of some of its members.   GENE M. TUCKER

Josiah. King of *Judah (640–609 BCE). His reign is described in 2 Kings 22.1–23.30 (= 2 Chron. 34–35; see also Jer. 3.6; 22.11–16). He became king at the age of eight after the assassination of his father, Amon (2 Kings 21.24), and is hailed as the most faithful of Judah's kings (2 Kings 22.2; 23.25).

Because of the decline of the *Assyrian empire, Josiah was able to promote the interests of Judah during his reign. He is praised by the biblical writers primarily for his religious reform, in which he sought to eliminate all non-Yahwistic practices and sanctuaries in Judah. Although the reform may have begun several years earlier (see 2 Chron. 34.3–7), its major impetus was the discovery of "the book of the law" (thought to be the law code of *Deuteronomy) in 621 (2 Kings 22.8–10). Some scholars also believe that an early edition of the books of Joshua–Kings (the *Deuteronomic history) was compiled in conjunction with this reform to reinforce Josiah's measures (see 1 Kings 13.2).

In 609, Pharaoh Neco of Egypt marched through Judah on his way to Carchemish to fight alongside the *Assyrians against *Babylon. Josiah intercepted the Egyptians at *Megiddo, where he was killed. His religious reform was abandoned after his death.

See also Kings, The Books of; Kingship and Monarchy.   TIMOTHY M. WILLIS

Judah, The Kingdom of.

The Tribe of Judah. The tribe of Judah, which occupied the hill country between the vicinity of *Jerusalem and *Hebron (Map 3:x5), plays a minor role in the biblical narratives that pertain to premonarchic times. In the book of *Judges, for example, there are only occasional mentions of Judah, and this tribe seems to have been very much on the fringe of Saul's kingdom. Judah comes into prominence, however, with David's rise to power, *David himself being a Judean from the village of *Bethlehem. Before conquering Jerusalem and transferring his residency there, David ruled over a kingdom centered at Hebron and consisting primarily of the tribe of Judah. Later, the tribal territory of Judah was to be the core of the southern kingdom, which remained loyal to the Davidic dynasty following *Solomon's death.

Thus the name "Judah," like the name "Israel," is used in different ways in the Bible. It can refer to the eponymous ancestor of the tribe of Judah (Gen. 29.35; 35.23; 37.26), to the tribe itself (Num. 2.3; 7.12; 10.14; Josh. 18.5; 19.1; Judg. 1.4), and to the kingdom of Judah, which covered more extensive territory and included peoples of other tribal origins (1 Kings 14.21, 29; 15.1, 7; Isa. 1.1; Jer. 1.2). These distinctions

are not always clear in the biblical story. For example, the tribal boundaries and cities recorded for the tribe of Judah in the book of *Joshua actually represent the ideal territorial extent of the kingdom of Judah. Likewise, the biblical *genealogies tend to subsume under Judah various other southern tribal groups, such as the Calebites, which became constituents of the kingdom of Judah (see Tribes of Israel).

David's Judean Kingdom. David gained popularity as a *Philistine fighter under *Saul's command. Later he broke with *Saul and led a rebel army that operated along the frontier of Judean territory. First we hear of David and his men camped at Adullam (1 Sam. 22.1–4). When Saul learned of their presence there, David and his followers moved to the barren slopes of the hill country southeast of Hebron (1 Sam. 23–26). Apparently, they received little support from the local population in either area; on the contrary, the villagers reported their whereabouts to Saul on more than one occasion.

Eventually, David found it necessary to move to Philistine territory, where he placed himself and his army under the command of Achish, the Philistine King of Gath (1 Sam. 27). Thus it happened that David was allied with the Philistines when they defeated Saul's army at the battle of Gilboa, the battle at which Saul and Jonathan lost their lives (1 Sam. 28–31). Saul's Israelite kingdom was left on the verge of collapse and without leadership. The crown fell to Ishbaal (Ishbosheth) who, realizing that the whole central hill country was now vulnerable to Philistine encroachment, moved his residency (and accordingly the administrative center of the kingdom) to Mahanaim east of the Jordan (2 Sam. 2.8–11). Thereupon David, presumably with Philistine approval, occupied the city of Hebron and its surrounding villages (2 Sam. 2.1–3). His kingship over the region was formalized when "the people of Judah came [to Hebron] and there they anointed David king over the house of Judah" (2 Sam. 2.4).

Thus, for the next seven years, according to 2 Samuel 5.4–5 and 1 Kings 2.11, David ruled over a kingdom centered in the hill country south of Jerusalem, composed largely of the tribe of Judah, with Hebron as its capital. David's realm of influence expanded rapidly during these years of rule from Hebron, so that by the time he conquered Jerusalem and moved his residency there (2 Sam. 5.6–10), the tribe of Judah was only one constituent part of the kingdom. This was to remain true throughout the reign of *Solomon. Among other constituent elements of the Davidic-Solomonic kingdom, for example, were the Israelites.

The Post-Solomonic Kingdom of Judah. Following Solomon's death, the Israelites rebelled and established an independent kingdom of "Israel" (1 Kings 12.1–17). No doubt, many of them understood this as a restoration of the old Saulide kingdom. The people of Jerusalem and of the southern hill country, however, remained loyal to the Davidic dynasty, specifically to Solomon's son, Rehoboam, who was next in line for the throne. While Rehoboam continued to rule from Jerusalem, his realm of authority consisted essentially of the area that David had ruled from Hebron, that is, the old tribal territory of Judah and immediately adjacent regions—the southern hill country, the "wilderness" region between the hill country and the Dead Sea, some of the *Negeb, and some of the Shephelah (see Map 5:w–x5–6). Not surprisingly, this post-Solomonic kingdom came to be called Judah, even though its territory and population extended well beyond those of the tribe of Judah.

This post-Solomonic kingdom of Judah remained in existence for almost three and a half centuries, from Solomon's death in approximately 925 BCE to the destruction of Jerusalem in 587/586 BCE. During the first two hundred years of this period, the kingdoms of Israel and Judah existed side by side, sometimes at peace, sometimes at war; and for much of this time, during the Omride period for example, Judah was overshadowed by, and possibly subject to, Israel.

The article in this volume on "Israel, History of" summarizes key political developments during the two centuries that the two kingdoms existed alongside each other. The following summary covers some of the same material, but focuses on Judah and extends to the destruction of Jerusalem in 587/586.

Unstable beginnings (ca. 924–855). Rehoboam was left with a small and weak kingdom. Hostilities with Israel, whose frontier was only about 17 km (10 mi) from Jerusalem, would have drained his resources even more. As if that were not enough, the Egyptian pharaoh Shishak raided Palestine during the fifth year of Rehoboam's reign. Rather than challenge Shishak, Rehoboam paid a heavy ransom from the Temple treasury (1 Kings 14.25–28).

Apparently, Shishak's raid was a temporary episode with no lasting effect. The hostilities with Israel continued for four decades, however,

through the reign of Rehoboam's grandson, Asa (ca. 905–874). 1 Kings 15.16–24 reports that Asa negotiated an agreement with Ben-hadad, the Aramean king of *Damascus, which called for an Aramean attack on Israel's northern border. With Israel's king (Baasha, ca. 902–886) thus distracted, Asa secured his own northern frontier with fortifications at Mizpah and Geba (1 Kings 15.16–22).

In the shadow of the Omrides (ca. 885–843). Under the Omride rulers during the second quarter of the ninth century, Israel emerged as a powerful kingdom. *Jehoshaphat of Judah (ca. 874–850) was roughly contemporary with the two most outstanding of the Omride kings, Omri and *Ahab; and the biblical records suggest that he was an unwavering supporter of their military undertakings; probably he had little choice. Moreover, the two royal families were joined by the marriage of Jehoshaphat's son Jehoram (ruled ca. 850–843) to Omri's daughter (or granddaughter; compare 2 Kings 8.18 with 8.26). When the Omride dynasty fell, therefore, in approximately 843 BCE, there were significant political repercussions in Judah as well.

The circumstances are described in horrible detail in 2 Kings 8.28–10.27. On an occasion when Israel's troops were defending northern Transjordan against Aramean encroachment, *Jehu, commander of the troops, assassinated the king of Israel (also named Jehoram, a son of Ahab), seized the government, and massacred the whole Omride family. Ahaziah, who by that time had succeeded Jehoram son of Jehoshaphat to the throne in Judah, also was assassinated, while visiting his Omride relatives in Israel.

A century of instability and decline (ca. 843–745). Jehu's coup initiated a period of hard times in both Israel and Judah (2 Kings 10.32–33; 12.17–18; 13.3). In fact, all of Syria-Palestine seems to have been dominated for the next four decades by the Aramean kings of Damascus. Judah was troubled as well with dynastic instability. After Ahaziah, who had been assassinated in connection with the Omride massacre, the next three Judean rulers (Athaliah, Joash, and Amaziah) were each executed or assassinated.

Athaliah, the Omride *queen mother, seized the throne for herself at Ahaziah's death and ordered the execution of all others in Judah who could possibly have any claim to it. Her own downfall and execution, after seven years of rule, resulted from a palace coup orchestrated by a priest named Jehoiada (2 Kings 11). Joash, whom Jehoiada placed on the throne in her stead, was a seven-year-old child, supposedly a son of Ahaziah who had escaped the bloodletting at the time of his father's death. Not surprisingly, Joash was much influenced during the early years of his reign (ca. 837–?) by Jehoiada and the Jerusalem priests. Later, however, as Joash reached adulthood and especially after Jehoiada died, he began to exert more independence over the priests. Eventually he too was assassinated, apparently by persons in the royal court (2 Kings 12.1–16, 19–21).

By the time that Amaziah, the son of Joash, ascended the throne (sometime near the end of the ninth century BCE), the Aramean domination of Syria-Palestine had begun to relax. Once again, conflict erupted between Israel and Judah, with Israel overwhelmingly victorious. Not only was Amaziah unable to defend his frontier against Jehoahaz of Israel, but Jehoahaz captured Jerusalem, destroyed a large section of the city wall, and took royal Judean hostages to *Samaria (2 Kings. 14.8–14). Soon thereafter, Amaziah was assassinated by his own countrymen, and Judah probably remained essentially a vassal to Israel through the reigns of Uzziah and Jotham.

Dates for the Judean kings of this period are impossible to establish with any degree of precision. Uzziah and Jotham would have lived during the latter part of the eighth and first part of the seventh centuries BCE respectively (2 Kings 15.1–7, 32–38). The prophets *Amos and *Hosea also belong to this period, as does the early career of *Isaiah.

Assyrian domination (ca. 745–627). Judah, along with all the other little city-states and kingdoms of Syria-Palestine, succumbed to Assyrian domination during the latter half of the eighth century BCE. Unlike Israel, however, whose national existence came to an end at that time and whose territory was annexed by the *Assyrian empire, Judah survived for another quarter of a century after the Assyrian empire itself collapsed. This does not mean, however, that Judah continued to enjoy any significant degree of independence. On the contrary, *Tiglath-pileser's Palestinian campaigns in 734–732 left Judah a subject nation, and this situation remained essentially unchanged until the fall of Jerusalem in 587/586. When *Hezekiah and certain other allied kings dared to challenge Assyrian domination during the reign of *Sennacherib (705–681), the attempt failed miserably, and numerous Judean cities and villages were destroyed. Jerusalem itself narrowly escaped destruction, which was regarded as a miracle (2 Kings 18.9–

19.37). The prophets Isaiah and *Micah were active during these years of Assyrian domination.

Egyptian domination (627–605). Although the specific circumstances are not well known, it seems that the Assyrians and Egyptians established an alliance during the latter years of the Assyrian empire. As the Assyrians began to relax their grip on Syria-Palestine, the Egyptians tightened theirs. Specifically, Judah seems to have been subject to Egypt from approximately the end of the reign of Ashurbanipal (668–627 BCE) until the battle of Carchemish in 605. This was the political context of *Josiah's cultic reform, his execution by Pharaoh Neco, and *Jeremiah's early career (2 Kings 22.1–23.30; Jer. 2.18–19).

Babylonian domination and the end of the kingdom of Judah (605–587/586). The *Babylonians, by defeating the Assyrians and their Egyptian allies at the battle of Carchemish in 605 BCE, became masters of Syria-Palestine as well as of Mesopotamia. Unfortunately, the Judeans persisted in challenging the new master, which resulted in the end of their kingdom. Jehoiakim (605–598) died while Jerusalem was under Babylonian siege. Jehoiakim's son Jehoichin was on the throne when the city fell in 597 and was exiled to Babylon with many other prominent Judeans (2 Kings 24.1–17). The Babylonians placed *Zedekiah on the throne; when he too proved disloyal, they conquered Jerusalem again, sacked the city, sent many more Judeans into exile, and placed one Gedaliah in charge of the region (2 Kings 24.18–25.26).

The exact status of Gedaliah, who resided at Mizpah, is unclear—whether he was regarded as a vassal king or as a military governor over annexed territory. Apparently he was not, however, of the Davidic family; soon he was assassinated by a nationalistic group who presumably wished to restore the Davidic line. Very little is known about the situation in Palestine in the aftermath of Gedaliah's assassination, but certainly by this time Judah had ceased to exist as a kingdom.

The Hasmonean Kingdom of Judah. Mention should be made finally of the revolt of the *Maccabees against the Seleucid rulers during the second century BCE. Not only was the revolt successful in throwing off the Seleucid yoke, but it resulted in a Judean kingdom with Jerusalem as its capital, lasting for a century—from the Maccabean recovery of Jerusalem in 164 BCE to Pompey's eastern campaigns in 64–63 BCE. Ruled by the Hasmonean dynasty, the family of Judas

Saul, David, and Solomon lived ca. 1000 BCE. The following dates may be regarded as accurate within ten years for the earlier kings and within two years for the later ones.

JUDAH	ISRAEL		JUDAH	ISRAEL
Rehoboam (924–907)	Jeroboam I (924–903)		Jotham (?–742)	Shallum (745)
Abijam (Abijah) (907–906)				Menahem (745–736)
Asa (905–874)	Nadab (903–902)		Jehoahaz I (Ahaz) (742–727)	Pekahiah (736–735)
	Baasha (902–886)			Pekah (735–732)
	Elah (886–885)		Hezekiah (727–698)	Hoshea (732–723)
Jehoshaphat (874–850)	Omri (885–873)			*Fall of Samaria* (722)
	Ahab (873–851)		Manasseh (697–642)	
Jehoram (850–843)	Ahaziah (851–849)		Amon (642–640)	
Ahaziah (843)	Jehoram (849–843)		Josiah (639–609)	
Athaliah (843–837)	Jehu (843–816)		Jehoahaz II (609)	
Joash (Jehoash) (837–?)	Jehoahaz (816–800)		Jehoiachin (608–598)	
Amaziah (?–?)	Joash (800–785)		Jehoiachim (598–597)	
Uzziah (Azariah)	Jeroboam II (785–745)		Zedekiah (597–587/586)	
	Zechariah (745)		*Destruction of Jerusalem* (587/586)	

Maccabeus, this kingdom included virtually all of Palestine when it reached its greatest territorial expansion under John Hyrcanus I (134–104 BCE) and Alexander Jannaeus (103–76 BCE).

J. MAXWELL MILLER

Judaisms of the First Century CE. The title of this article indicates a change in scholarly consensus from earlier in this century. Why Judaisms and not Judaism? It has become clear that in the first century CE Judaism was not monolithic but highly variegated throughout the Greco-Roman world, and diverse and complex even within the borders of Roman Palestine. No longer valid is George Foot Moore's characterization of "normative Judaism," by which he meant that Pharisaic-Rabbinic Judaism was the dominant and legitimate expression, against which all other Judaisms were judged to be aberrations or variants. Instead, the picture that has emerged is of multiple Judaisms, distinct Jewish religious systems, yet with connecting threads, indicators that they share a common legacy. Another characterization to be rejected is "late Judaism." This turn of the century terminology was used to brand Judaism in the Greco-Roman period as a legalistic degeneration of earlier prophetic religion, moving toward the end of Judaism with its lack of acceptance of Jesus as the *Messiah. Scholars today recognize that the Judaisms of the first century are early and not late, that they are much more at the beginning than at the end. Yet another contrast that has been laid aside is that of Palestinian versus Hellenistic Judaism; this is an artificial opposition which reduces an enormously complex picture into a simplistic one. Hellenization and its attendant issues were not confined to the Diaspora (*see* Dispersion). Still, while the overlap between the Judaisms inside and outside of Palestine is significant, one should not deny the distinctive features of Diaspora Judaism, many of which were an outgrowth of two issues: the great distance between the Jerusalem *Temple and most Diaspora Jews, and the fact that Diaspora Judaism was a minority religion in a heavily hellenized and polytheistic setting. In short, it is difficult to compose a coherent picture of the Judaisms of this time because of the very diversity, complexity, and dynamic character which lead us to speak of Judaisms rather than Judaism, and also because of the nature of the sources.

Sources. The primary literary sources for the Judaisms of the first century provide only a limited picture. Those preserved are those which were important to the victors of history. From the Jewish perspective this is rabbinic literature (which dates from the third century CE on, though it may preserve earlier traditions), the foundational literature of what is known as Orthodox Judaism. It gradually came to regard itself as the heir to Pharisaic Judaism, and therefore either ignored or was hostile to other varieties of Judaism in the first century. From a Christian perspective, there is mid-first to second century evidence in the New Testament and other early Christian writings. These view first century Judaisms through the lenses of various Christian communities struggling to establish identities independent of the Judaism out of which they are emerging or with which they are competing, often polemically. Additional sources include two first-century Jewish figures, the historian Flavius *Josephus and the philosopher *Philo of Alexandria, the *Dead Sea Scrolls, the Jewish literature written between the Bible and the *Mishnah and preserved in the *apocrypha and in the *pseudepigrapha, and archeological and inscriptional evidence. Each source has its own problems of interpretation, and there are major gaps, such as data concerning *women. Nevertheless, there is a wealth and variety of sources for the Judaisms of the first century which reflect diverse socioeconomic perspectives. Ironically, it is the very diversity of these perspectives which often limits historical reconstructions, because of their disagreements with one another and the gaping holes that they leave in their wake.

Pharisees. Of the named Judaisms of the first century, the best known are the *Pharisees, attested in Josephus, the New Testament, and rabbinic literature. The evidence reveals nothing of the internal organization of this group—their criteria for membership, leadership structure, or educational system. Only two known individuals

claim that they were themselves Pharisees: Josephus and *Paul. There are reasons to question Josephus's claim that at the age of nineteen he became a Pharisee, and certainly many of his writings do not seem to be those of a Pharisee or someone who is more than neutral toward the Pharisees. Still, his later writings show a change of attitude and could support a later Pharisaic affiliation. Paul wrote from the perspective of one who had left Pharisaic Judaism. Josephus's and Paul's claims to be Pharisees open up the possibility that Pharisaic Judaism was found not only in Roman Palestine, but in the Diaspora, possibly as a way of responding to the wider world of Greco-Roman culture with a consciously Jewish way of life.

Josephus mentions the Pharisees fewer than twenty times, and the portrait that emerges is of a relatively small group (six thousand at the time of Herod the Great, *Ant.* 17.2.42) that for most of the first century played a minor role in Jewish society. They are portrayed as one of three philosophical schools of thought, alongside the Sadducees and Essenes, but seem to have been primarily a political interest group. Lacking their own political power, the Pharisees sought influence with the ruling class to achieve their goals for Jewish society, attempts that succeeded especially during the latter part of Hasmonean rule, and at other times up through the beginning of the revolt against Rome in 66 CE. Josephus' selective description of Pharisaic beliefs—they believe in fate, free will, and God, that the soul is imperishable and that the souls of the wicked will be punished—reflects the interests of his Greco-Roman audience. A hint of the Pharisees' overall goals is that they had a reputation for interpreting traditional laws not recorded in the books of Moses; unfortunately Josephus does not elaborate.

Other clues concerning the Pharisees' goals for a renewed Judaism and their own internal rules come from the Gospels and rabbinic Judaism. The depiction of the Pharisees in the Gospels as the opponents of *Jesus focuses the contention between Jesus and the Pharisees around issues of *fasting and *tithing, *purity, and *Sabbath observance, issues that overlap with the agenda of early rabbinic law. Further, the early rabbinic evidence for the Pharisees presents them as applying their own tradition of priestly piety to everyday life and business. According to Anthony Saldarini, "the Pharisees drew on an old tradition of using priestly laws concerning purity, food, and marriage in order to separate, protect, and identify Judaism" ("Pharisees," *Anchor Bible Dictionary*). Without denying that the *rabbis are the ideological descendants of the Pharisees, the precise relationship between the Pharisees and the early rabbis who came after them is problematic, and there are considerable differences between the rabbis and the Pharisees. Apparently Pharisaic Judaism's rise to prominence is gradual, beginning after the war with Rome.

Sadducees. Evidence for the *Sadducees is more meager and much more difficult to interpret than that for the Pharisees. None of the sources (Josephus, the New Testament, rabbinic literature) were written from a Sadducean point of view; the Sadducees rarely appear alone in them; and they are generally hostile in their treatment of the Sadducees. The sources agree, however, that the Sadducees were a recognized and well-established group of first-century Jews. Josephus further notes that while they had limited influence, they were respected within Jewish society. Their origins and history are obscure, though we hear of them as a political party during the Hasmonean rule of John Hyrcanus (134–104 BCE) and continue to hear of them throughout the first century CE until sometime after the war with Rome. Josephus portrays the Sadducees as drawn from the ruling class and therefore not popular with the masses. Several sources suggest some sort of connection between the Sadducees and the priestly establishment, and Acts 5 associates them with the high *priest and makes them the dominant group on the *Sanhedrin (though Acts 23 envisions the Sanhedrin as more evenly divided). Caution is needed here: the Sadducees cannot be equated with the priesthood and the ruling class. Not all Sadducees were priests and at best only a very small number of the ruling class were Sadducees. In rabbinic literature the Sadducees are identified with the even less well known Boethusians. It is unclear whether these were two distinct groups or whether the rabbis have conflated two sets of opponents. The little we can glean of Sadducean beliefs comports well with the conservative nature of a group drawn from the ruling class and with some connection to the priesthood: they rejected resurrection, the *afterlife and judgment—a position connecting them with older Israelite religion and pitting them against newer beliefs. Josephus portrays them as denying fate and the traditions of the Pharisees and accepting no observance "apart from the laws." This hardly makes them scriptural literalists, and most likely

they had their own traditions of interpretation opposed to those of the Pharisees. Certainly early rabbinic sources claim that the Sadducees differ from the Pharisees concerning ritual purity and Sabbath observance. Other beliefs concerning rituals such as those related to the Temple and the Sadducean/Boethusian method of reckoning Pentecost coincide with priestly practices.

Essenes. Largely due to the discovery of the *Dead Sea Scrolls at *Qumran, the best known group from ancient sources is the *Essenes. The identification of the Qumran community with Essenes is not found in the Scrolls; rather, the impressive agreement of the evidence in the scrolls with that of the other key sources for Essenes (the Roman geographer Pliny the Elder, Philo, and Josephus) makes highly probable the identification of the Qumran community as Essenes. Still, discrepancies remain and the portrait that emerges is far from complete. Both Philo and Josephus number the Essenes at more than four thousand and say that the Essene communities were found throughout Palestine. Pliny locates a major settlement of the Essenes on the northwest corner of the Dead Sea, between Jericho and En-gedi, which all but names the site at Qumran. That site could accommodate about two hundred members at any one time; the majority of Essenes must have lived elsewhere. Both the Scrolls and Josephus seem to provide for two orders of Essenes: celibate men and those who married and had families. It is presumed that Qumran was a celibate community of Essenes and may have served as a center for Essenes from other locations—though the evidence does not rule out other interpretations. The history of the group is only imprecisely known. The Essenes may have originated in the early second century BCE. Even though the Qumran site was destroyed in the war against Rome, because the majority of Essenes lived at other settlements it is not impossible that the group persisted after 70 CE, though evidence to support their survival is hard to find.

Both the Qumran community and the other Essene groups were tightly organized. Those living outside of Qumran offered hospitality to other members, and in general the Essenes studiously avoided contact with outsiders. The penalties were severe for those who violated the rules and purity regulations of the community and for those who denigrated the community in any way. The Essenes were hierarchically organized according to seniority, standing within the community, and "perfection of spirit," with priests at the top. Admission to the group entailed a graduated process over two to three years, which was carefully regulated; there was also provision for expulsion. Full membership involved some form of communal property (even though there appears to have been some private ownership allowed), as well as communal meals and communal funds. The Essenes rigorously kept the *Sabbath. The evidence concerning the attitude of the Essenes toward animal *sacrifice and Temple worship is confusing. Possible interpretations include: there were times in the history of the group when they sent offerings to the Temple and times when they did not; or, the Qumran community dissented from the official Temple ritual, whereas the other Essene communities did not. Among their beliefs were theological determinism, present participation in "eternal life" as well as one which extended beyond the grave, and the notion of a final and universal conflagration.

Other Groups. Philo mentions the Therapeutae, a celibate community of men and women living outside of Alexandria. Their piety and communal practices resemble those of celibate Essenes, with whom there may be some connection. The evidence for *scribes in the first century CE is at best sparse and confusing, and the portrait that emerges from the various sources is incoherent. Despite the presentation of the scribes in the New Testament, scribes do not seem to have formed an organization with its own membership. Rather, scribalism was a profession and a class of literate individuals who functioned as personal secretaries and public officials at all levels of Jewish society. Scribes who worked with the ruling class would most likely have been learned in all aspects of Judaism.

There are also first century Jewish groups whose activity seems to have been primarily political during the time leading up to and throughout the First Jewish Revolt. Josephus wrote of the *Zealots mainly as a group in Jerusalem from 68–70 CE, who spent most of their energy struggling with other Jewish revolutionary groups until Jerusalem was surrounded, when they united against the Romans and mostly died fighting. Josephus also mentions the Fourth Philosophy, a group similar to the Pharisees except for their belief that only God should be acknowledged as king and ruler. The Fourth Philosophy spawned the Sicarii, who specialized in assassinating Jews who collaborated with the Romans. They may have been moti-

vated in part by eschatological and messianic expectations.

Just as there was no "normative Judaism" in the first century CE, so too the borders of first century Judaism were not impermeable. Several groups attest to the porous nature of first century Jewish identity. Most clearly on the "outside" from all but their own perspective are the *Samaritans, yet there are many reasons to view them as among the Judaisms of the age. The Samaritans believed themselves to be the authentic representatives of Mosaic religion. They are characterized by the building of their temple on Mount Gerizim and worship there rather than in Jerusalem, and by limiting themselves to their own version of the Pentateuch, which emphasizes the divine sanctity of Gerizim as the center for Israel's cultic life. Ranging from "inside" to "just outside" from a first century perspective, and yet clearly on the outside from twentieth century Jewish and Christian perspectives are Jewish Christians, a label that encompasses a complex situation and a great variety. Examples include a number of named Jewish Christian groups mentioned in early patristic sources who share their adherence to Jewish beliefs and practices alongside their messianic understanding of Jesus and often a virulent anti-Pauline strain; the community underlying the gospel of *Matthew, who seem to have understood themselves as recently and bitterly separated from the local *synagogue because of their messianic beliefs, despite the fact that they were better at practicing their Judaism; the gospel of *John may be appealing to Jews who have a secret and incipient belief in Jesus (represented by Nicodemus, the parents of the man born blind, and *Joseph of Arimathea), urging them to grow in their understanding and not to be afraid of expulsion from the synagogue or of leaving their Jewish roots behind.

The above Judaisms present only a partial picture of the diversity of the first century. Josephus and Philo are examples of individuals who do not give us a clear sense of what, if any, Jewish group they might represent (despite Josephus's claim to have been a Pharisee from the age of nineteen). Most of the first-century Jewish writings preserved in the apocrypha and pseudepigrapha are not linked to the above-named groups, yet they add significantly to the diversity and complexity of the picture. The several apocalypses and the apocalyptic features of other writings add another substantial dimension. There seem to have been a number of small groups that placed an emphasis on *baptism, whether for ritual purification, initiation, or both. We have only glimpses of other features of the Judaisms of the first century: possible Jewish-*Gnostic tendencies, peasant social banditry groups, popular messianic movements, prophetic movements and groups which formed around a wide range of charismatic leaders.

Common Elements. What do these diverse Judaisms share? In part it is what Lester Grabbe has termed "personal Jewish identity": belief in one God; the concept of being part of the chosen people—Israel; the rejection of images in worship; the centrality of *Torah; and the practice of *circumcision. But even these characteristics are complex. Torah is a good example. The third part of Jewish *canon (the Writings) was not yet closed; in general, different Jews had different ideas about what to include, which text or translation to read, which parts of the Torah, Prophets, and Writings were more authoritative, and how they should be interpreted. Also connecting the various first century Judaisms was the Jerusalem *Temple. The Temple was central both within Roman Palestine and in the Diaspora, despite the obvious problem of distance. In Jewish writings the Temple varies from concrete reality to metaphor to idealization. Long after its destruction, the Mishnah discusses the Temple as if it were still standing. Even those who were critical of current Temple practices, such as the Qumran community, did not contemplate permanently abandoning it. There are exceptions, like the Samaritans, who rejected the Jerusalem Temple, or the community of Leontopolis in Egypt, who built another. Yet even for such dissidents, temple cult in some form was central.

See also Anti-Semitism.   SARAH J. TANZER

Judas Iscariot. Judas Iscariot is mentioned only in the Gospels and Acts. The name Iscariot probably means "man from Kerioth" (a village in southern Judea) because "from" is used with the name in John (12.4; etc.) and because similar names occur in *Josephus.

Only in John is Judas called Simon's son (6.71; 13.2, 26), and Simon is also Iscariot (6.71; 13.26). So was the name Iscariot given to Judas or to his father or to both? Only John says that Judas was "a thief" and "kept the common purse" (12.6; 13.29). Unlike the *synoptic Gospels, John does not mention the kiss to indicate the one whom the authorities sought.

Judas was remembered for his betrayal of Jesus, an incident on which the sources agree (Mark 3.19 par.; 14.10–11, 43–45 par.; Matt. 26.25; John 6.71; 12.4; Acts 1.16). The motives for Judas's behavior cannot be precisely determined. Mark and Luke report that Jewish authorities promised Judas money for his action, but Matthew says that they paid him thirty pieces of silver immediately, a particular derived from the Hebrew Bible (Matt. 26.14–16; 27.3–10; Zech. 11.12–13; Jer. 18.2–3; 32.6–15). Judas repented, returned the money, and hanged himself. The authorities used the money to buy the "Field of Blood," but Acts 1.18–19 reports that Judas himself bought the field with his blood money and that he died as the result of a fall when "all his bowels gushed out." According to Acts 1.16, 20, his end was predicted in Psalms 69.25 and 109.8.

According to John 13.18, Jesus chose Judas deliberately so that the scripture (Ps. 41.9) might be fulfilled by his betrayal. John agrees with the Synoptics that at the Last Supper Jesus predicted his betrayal by Judas; but John, unlike the Synoptics, does not leave the identity of the traitor in doubt (13.26), since "the devil had already put it into the heart of Judas . . . to betray him" (13.2, 27). Luke also attributes Judas's action to Satan's influence (Luke 22.3).

Accounts of Judas are varied, inconsistent, and influenced by theological opinions of the writers, the belief in the fulfillment of scripture, and the idea that God brings death to ungodly persons (2 Macc. 9.5–12). It is therefore difficult to assess the historicity of Judas and his action. Why, for example, does Mark not mention the name of Judas in the story of the traitor (14.17–21)? Yet all sources list him among Jesus' disciples and know him as Jesus' betrayer. Perhaps as tradition grew the name of Judas became more infamous and the details of his demise more appalling.

EDWIN D. FREED

Jude, The Letter of. The letter of Jude was written to an unknown church or group of churches to combat the danger posed by certain charismatic teachers who were preaching and practicing moral libertinism. The author seeks to expose these teachers as ungodly people whose condemnation has been prophesied, and he urges his readers to maintain the apostolic gospel by living according to its moral demands.

Despite its brevity, the letter is rich in content, owing to its masterly composition and its economy of expression, which at times achieves an almost poetic effect. An analysis of the structure of the letter is essential to an adequate understanding of it:

I. Address and greeting (vv. 1–2)
II. Occasion and theme of the letter (vv. 3–4)
    A. Appeal to contend for the faith (v. 3)
    B. Background to the appeal: the false teachers (v. 4)
III. Body of the Letter (vv. 5–23)
    B¹. Background to the appeal: a commentary on four prophecies of the doom of the ungodly (vv. 5–19)
        1. Three biblical types (vv. 5–10)
        2. Three more biblical types (vv. 11–13)
        3. The prophecy of Enoch (vv. 14–16)
        4. The prophecy of the apostles (vv. 17–18)
    A¹. Appeal to Contend for the Faith (vv. 20–23)
        1. Exhortations (vv. 20–21)
        2. Advice on dealing with offenders (vv. 22–23)
IV. Concluding doxology (vv. 24–25)

It should be noted that the initial statement of the letter's theme (vv. 3–4) contains two parts that correspond, in reverse order, to the two parts of the body of the letter. The main purpose of the letter is the appeal "to contend for the faith," announced in v. 3 and spelled out in vv. 20–23. But v. 4 explains that this appeal is necessary because the readers are in danger of being misled by false teachers. The claim in v. 4 that these teachers are people whose ungodly behavior has already been condemned by God is then substantiated by the exegetical section (vv. 5–19), which argues that these are the people to whom the scriptural types and prophecies of judgment refer. This section establishes the danger in which the readers are placed by the influence of the false teachers and so performs an essential role as background to the appeal; it is not the main object of the letter, whose climax is reached only in the exhortations of vv. 20–23. Thus, the negative polemic against the false teachers is subordinate to the positive teaching of vv. 20–23. The letter concludes with a doxology (vv. 24–25), in effect a confident prayer that God will preserve the readers and achieve his purpose for them.

The form of the exegetical section (vv. 5–19) requires further explanation. It is not mere undisciplined denunciation, but carefully composed commentary that argues for the statement made in v. 4 that the condemnation of the false teachers has long been prophesied. Both the assumption that scripture is prophetic and the exegetical methods used to apply it to the present resemble the type of commentary *(pēšer)* found in the *Dead Sea Scrolls.

Jude cites four main "texts" (vv. 5–7, 11, 14–15, 17–18) and comments on each (vv. 8–10, 12–13, 16, 19). The first two are summary references to biblical figures who are types of the ungodly of the last days. The third is a prophecy quoted from the book of *Enoch (1.9), and the fourth gives a prediction of the apostles. The commentaries contain further allusions to scripture, the most prominent being the reference to an apocryphal account of the burial of Moses in v. 9. In each case, however, the transition from text to commentary is clearly marked by the word "these," indicating that the author's opponents are the people to whom the prooftext refers, and by change in tense to the present, indicating that the type or prophecy is now being fulfilled. Another feature of the exegetical method is the use of catchwords to link prooftexts with commentary and with each other; an example is "slander" in vv. 8, 9, 10.

Jude evidently had great respect for the book of *Enoch, quoted in vv. 14–15 and echoed elsewhere (see vv. 6, 12–13). V. 9 refers to an apocryphal text no longer extant, perhaps the lost ending of the Testament of Moses. The use of such literature may locate the letter in a Palestinian Jewish context, in which these works were highly valued. Other indications that point in the direction of Palestinian Jewish Christianity as the milieu in which Jude wrote are his exegetical methods, his dependence on the Hebrew text of the Bible rather than its Greek translation (the *Septuagint), his emphasis on the importance of ethical obligation rather than doctrinal orthodoxy, and his *apocalyptic outlook, which expects the *parousia in the near future. Some scholars therefore regard Jude as a relatively early work that affords a rare glimpse of early Jewish Christianity. But many other scholars date Jude relatively late (up to ca. 120 CE) and consider it an example of the post-Pauline development of early Christianity represented by such works as the *Pastoral letters and *Luke-*Acts. In favor of this latter view, two major claims are made—that Jude's view of "the faith" (vv. 3, 20) identifies Christianity with a fixed orthodoxy, and that v. 17 looks back to the age of the apostles as past—but both claims can be contested.

Two further issues related to the disagreement about the date and character of Jude are the identity of the opponents and the identity of the author. The false teachers whom Jude denounces have often been identified as *gnostics, but there are no clear traces of gnostic teaching in what Jude says about them. What is clear is that the opponents were antinomians who understood the grace of God (v. 4) as a deliverance from moral constraints. They were evidently itinerant teachers (v. 4a) and were accepted at the churches' fellowship *meals (v. 12a), where they laid claim to charismatic inspiration. They evidently regarded themselves and their followers as the truly spiritual people, distinguished from more conventional Christians by their Spirit-inspired freedom from all external authority (see v. 19). This kind of charismatic antinomianism may represent a distortion of Paul's teaching on freedom from the *Law; it would have been possible at any time in the New Testament period.

Most scholars are agreed that the Jude (a shortened form of Judas, the author's actual name, which few English translations use because of the association with *Judas Iscariot) to whom this letter is attributed is Judas the brother of Jesus (Mark 6.3). This identification is strongly implied by the phrase "brother of James" (v. 1), which distinguishes this Judas from others of the same name by mentioning his relation to *James the brother of the Lord (see Brothers and Sisters of Jesus). A majority of modern scholars think the letter is pseudepigraphical, written by a later Christian who attributed his work to Jesus' brother, but a strong case for authenticity is made by others, who point to the features already mentioned that may place the letter in the context of Palestinian Jewish Christianity.

(*For the relation between Jude and 2 Peter, see* Peter, The Letters of, *article on* The Second Letter.)   RICHARD J. BAUCKHAM

Judges, The Book of. The book of Judges follows *Joshua and purports to cover the history of Israel from the time of the settlement until just before the establishment of the monarchy. The book's chronology is a problem since the sum of the periods mentioned in it comes to about four hundred years. The *Exodus is usually dated to the thirteenth century BCE and the anointing of *Saul to the middle of the eleventh century; consequently, the era of the judges as calculated by the book is far too long. The book

presents the subjects of its narratives as referring to all Israel when originally these figures were associated with particular *tribes. It is not possible to relate the stories of these savior-judges to each other chronologically. The book of Judges is a collection of stories about ancient tribal heroes; the chronological sequence of these stories is certainly artificial, and the fact that the total number of heroes is twelve also suggests editorial design.

The book begins with an introduction (1.1–36) that serves to connect it with the book of Joshua. This introduction, in contrast with the account in Joshua, portrays the settlement as only partially successful and still somewhat incomplete (see Conquest of Canaan). A short discourse that follows (2.1–5) explains Israel's failure to complete the settlement successfully as the result of its disobedience. The purpose of this first introduction is to contrast the period of the judges with that of Joshua. Under Joshua's strong and effective leadership, the tribes enjoyed unity and success. No leader comparable to Joshua took his place, with the result that the unity of the tribes was broken: apostasy soon followed, then military defeat. Israel was faithful to Yahweh during Joshua's lifetime; after his death it fell away. Because Israel turned to other gods, it placed itself in mortal danger. The stories of the judges show how a number of tribal heroes were able to ward off this danger—but only for a time.

A second introduction (2.6–3.6) presents the period of the judges as one during which Israel was guilty of a series of apostasies. Each apostasy was followed by divine punishment, a prayer for help, the rise of a "judge" who saved Israel from destruction, and a period of peace when Israel was ruled by its savior-judge. This pattern is not reflected in all the narratives themselves; rather, it represents the Deuteronomic interpretation of this period in Israel's life (see Deuteronomic History).

The stories about the judges themselves begin in 3.7 and conclude with 16.31. The portrait of Othniel (3.7–11) is rather ill-defined, though it follows the Deuteronomic pattern: Israel sinned by worshiping the gods of Canaan; God gave Israel into the hands of its enemies for a time; the people repented and God raised up a warrior to deliver them; then Israel had rest for forty years. The story about Ehud (3.12–30) is a coarse Benjaminite saga about one of that tribe's ancient heroes who outwitted and then killed Eglon, king of *Moab. There is no narrative connected with Shamgar but only the statement that he "delivered Israel" (3.31).

The story of the prophet *Deborah and the commander Barak is told in both prose (4.1–23) and poetry (5.1–31). The poem of chap. 5 is known as the Song of Deborah and is the most authentic literary source from the period of the judges, probably composed a short time after the victory it celebrates. The story of Deborah and Barak exposes the conflicts that took place when the Israelite tribes that originally settled in the largely unoccupied highlands attempted to make their way into the more fertile and therefore more populated valleys. The tribal forces led by Deborah and Barak defeated a Canaanite army and secured the Esdraelon Valley for Israel. Archaeology has shown that Taanach was violently destroyed about 1125 BCE, when *Megiddo was occupied (see 5.19).

The story of *Gideon (6.1–8.35), also known as Jerubbaal, describes the fear with which Israelite farmers lived. There was the constant danger of having their harvest stolen by raiders. Gideon defeated the *Midianites, whose raids threatened the Israelite population in central Canaan, but he refused the offer of *kingship that the grateful tribes made. Gideon's son Abimelech, however, was quite different; he became king of *Shechem. Abimelech was not really a judge but served as commander of the tribal militia. His story (9.1–57) describes the folly of the monarchy. When the people of Shechem withdrew their support from him, Abimelech did not hesitate to turn his army against them. The remains of ancient Shechem (Tell Balatah) give evidence of a violent destruction in the twelfth century BCE. Abimelech's story was recounted by those who considered the monarchy an infringement upon the rights of Yahweh.

Following Abimelech's story, there is a short note about Tola and Jair (10.1–4). They are credited with no military exploits. The lack of any information about their activities stands in marked contrast with the stories about the exploits of the savior-judges. The two mentioned here, along with three others cited in 12.8–15, had some type of judicial and administrative authority during the period before the monarchy and therefore were known as judges; because details of their activity are so scant, they are sometimes called "minor judges." Later their title was given to military heroes whose exploits are recounted in the major portion of the book; these are the "major judges."

The story of Jephthah (10.6–12.7) shows that social class posed no barriers to exercising leadership within the Israelite community at this period; Jephthah was a son of a prostitute. He led a mercenary army in the north and was called by the elders of Gilead to deal with the *Ammonites. Jephthah is remembered for the sacrifice of his daughter to fulfill a vow (11.34–40) and for his use of the password *shibboleth during a civil war with the tribe of Ephraim (12.1–6).

Before the stories about Samson begin, there is another note about three judges who engaged in no military exploits but who, like Tola and Jair, were famous tribal leaders: Ibzan, Elon, and Abdon (12.8–15).

*Samson hardly fits the figure of a judge. His stories (13.1–16.31) do not describe leadership he provided for the Israelite tribes against their enemies; rather, they recount a series of personal battles he fought with the *Philistines. None of Samson's adventures have anything to do with the fate of Israel as a whole; he led no organized military campaigns. Samson is a tragic figure who was consumed in a Pyrrhic victory over his enemies. He is included among the judges because his final victory over the Philistines was remembered as a reaffirmation of God's presence with Israel.

The stories about the savior-judges portray them as heroes who led single tribes or groups of tribes in military campaigns in order to liberate Israel from periodic oppression by its enemies. Their rule was temporary. They led certain tribes in a specific military campaign and then, after the military threat was removed, they returned home. None of the judges succeeded in gaining the allegiance of all the tribes. They held power briefly and the area under their effective control was limited. In the present framework, however, these stories receive greater significance. They are not simply tribal sagas about famous heroes of the past; they have become testimonies to the power of Yahweh, who frees Israel when it repents and calls out for deliverance.

The predominant motif in these stories is Yahweh's deliverance of Israel through the judges. The judges are charismatic leaders upon whom has come the "spirit of Yahweh" (6.34; 11.29; 14.6,19; 15.14). This spirit enables them to accomplish what is apparently beyond their natural abilities. In Gideon's story, this receives special emphasis through the narrative about his call (6.11–23).

The remainder of the book of Judges (chaps.

17–21) is taken up with stories that illustrate the self-destructive forces at work within the Israelite tribes. These stories along with the introductions in 1.1–3.6 provide the work's basic theme. The introductory material raises the issue of strife among the tribes; the concluding chapters illustrate the extent to which this lack of unity threatened the very existence of the people of Israel.

Chaps. 17 and 18 deal with a certain Micah who set up his own shrine and introduced a *Levite from *Bethlehem to serve as his priest. This Levite was, in turn, recruited by the migrating Danites to serve as their priest. The tribe of *Dan is depicted in a very unfavorable light. The Danites lack the courage to remain in their original place of settlement; they steal Micah's *ephod, kidnap his priest, and massacre the peaceful village of Laish. The book ends with an internecine war between the tribes that almost succeeded in destroying the tribe of *Benjamin (chaps. 19–21). The purpose of these last few chapters is to portray the period just before the emergence of the monarchy as a time of chaos. The book ends with this characterization of the era: "In those days there was no king in Israel; all the people did what was right in their own eyes" (21.25). The picture of Israel in chaps. 17–21 makes the establishment of the monarchy inevitable if Israel was to survive.

Originally, stories about the most famous of tribal heroes circulated independently of one another. At some point during the period of the monarchy they were assembled in order to underscore the power and willingness of God to save Israel from those who would destroy it. This collection of stories did not involve extensive editing, which may explain some of the repetitions and apparent contradictions in the text. Under the influence of the book of *Deuteronomy, the stories about the judges were incorporated in a much larger work that traced the story of Israel in the land from the entrance under Joshua to the exile under the *Babylonians. The comprehensive purpose of this *Deuteronomic history was to convince the people of Judah that their *exile from the land was not due to some failure on God's part but, rather, that it was their own doing. Israel's peace in the land promised and given by God was constantly threatened by its disobedience and infidelity. The political and economic roots of Israel's problems with its neighbors were ignored in favor of a religious interpretation. Foreign invasions were divine punishment for Israel's infidelities with Canaanite gods. When Israel repented of its failure, foreign domination came to an end through the agency of a judge on whom had fallen the spirit of Yahweh.

For the Deuteronomists, the period of the judges was marked by apostasy after apostasy, which caused Israel to be given into the hands of oppressors. Though God saved Israel through the judges when the people cried for deliverance, Israel always repeated its infidelities. One result of this tendency to apostasy was God's determination not to drive out the nations, in order to test Israel's fidelity and to help instruct the people regarding the bitter consequences brought on by infidelity.

The book of Judges cannot be used to reconstruct the history of Canaan in the twelfth and eleventh centuries BCE except in the broadest possible terms. It describes this period as one of anarchy when the Israelites were competing with other peoples for the rich but limited resources of *Canaan. It portrays the era of the judges as a time when Israel was in the process of achieving a sense of national unity and of laying its own claim to the land of Canaan. Both the book of Judges and archaeology have shown this time to be one of political, social, and economic disorder. The Deuteronomic history continues in the books of *Samuel to show how Israel survived this difficult time.

Sometimes the perspective of the book of Judges is considered to be cyclical. The book does describe a cycle of apostasy, oppression, repentance, and deliverance followed by new apostasy, but this cycle is not endless: the anarchy of the era of the judges leads to the establishment of the monarchy. In addition, the text seems to be posing the question: How long can this cycle of apostasy, repentance, and deliverance go on? The conclusion of the Deuteronomic history states that there is a limit to the infidelities that Yahweh will countenance from Israel before expelling it from the land that had been promised and given to it.

See also Israel, History of; Social Sciences and the Bible, article on Cultural Anthropology and the Hebrew Bible.

LESLIE J. HOPPE, O.F.M.

Judgment. See Day of Judgment.

Judith, The Book of. Named after its heroine, the book of Judith is regarded by Jews and

Protestants as apocryphal and by Roman Catholics and some Orthodox churches as deuterocanonical (*see* Apocrypha, *article on* Jewish Apocrypha). Judith is a beautiful and wealthy widow who, in defense of God and country, first captivates and then decapitates Holofernes, the Assyrian general besieging her hometown, Bethulia of Samaria. Often characterized as a type of novel, the book is best understood as a folktale about a pious widow who, strengthened by her faith in the God of Israel, courageously (and literally) took matters into her own hands and so saved Israel and Jerusalem.

The story is well-told, especially chaps. 10–13, which are a masterpiece of irony. The character and personality of the principal antagonists, as well as those of minor figures such as King *Nebuchadrezzar (called Nebuchadnezzar in the book), the Jewish elder Uzziah of Bethulia, and the Ammonite convert Achior, are all vividly drawn and take on a life of their own. Their speeches, conversations, and prayers, as well as the story's plot, clearly and effectively express the storyteller's theology and ethics. Nonetheless, the book fairly bristles with problems, as the struggles over its canonicity so clearly attest. While western church fathers routinely accepted the book as canonical, eastern fathers quite often did not.

Although the book purports to be a historical account, it abounds in serious errors concerning both history and geography, the most egregious being in 1.1, where Nebuchadnezzar (605–562 BCE) is described as king of the Assyrians with his capital at Nineveh! Moreover, in 1.13–16 he kills the great Median king Arphaxad (who is otherwise unknown to scholars) and destroys Ecbatana, the great city Arphaxad had founded (1.2–4), although in point of fact Ecbatana was founded by Deioces and was conquered by *Cyrus the Great in 554 BCE.

In chap. 2, geographical errors replace historical ones: Holofernes's army traveled from Nineveh to Northern Cilicia, some 800 km (500 mi), in three days (2.21), then fought its way through Put and Lud (2.23)—which are usually identified by scholars as being in Africa and Asia Minor, respectively—only to cross the Euphrates and proceed west through Mesopotamia (2.24) and arrive in Cilicia (2.25)! Paradoxically, the brief survey of Israel's history from the days of the ancestors into the early postexilic period by the Ammonite Achior (chap. 5), is a reasonably accurate account. So too, Holofernes's itinerary

through Palestine (chaps. 2–3) seems to be more or less geographically correct. Yet, despite a wealth of geographical and topographical clues throughout the story, the location of Bethulia, the principal scene of the action, is totally unknown to scholars.

The moral and ethical views of the storyteller have frequently been censured, especially the treatment and obvious approval of the character and conduct of the heroine who, at least in her dealings with Holofernes, showed herself to be a shameless flatterer (11.7–8), a bold-faced liar (11.12–14, 18–19), and a ruthless assassin (13.7–8) who seemingly follows two highly popular but debatable axioms: "all's fair in love and war" and "the end justifies the means."

Yet both before and after her murderous (and salvific) act, Judith is regarded by her people as a saint, that is, one who is totally devoted to the Lord: diligent both in prayer (9.1–14) and in fasting (8.4–6), observant of the dietary laws (10.5; 12.2), honoring her husband's memory by remaining forever celibate after his death (16.22) and honored by all (8.8, 28–31; 16.21), and fearing the Lord (cf. 16.16). In the eyes of the storyteller, at least, Judith was the saint who murdered for her people and her God; she is the ideal Jewish woman, as her name, which is simply the feminine form of the word for "Jewish," suggests.

No other biblical book, in either its parts or its totality, is as quintessentially ironic as Judith. Given the sexist and patriarchal character of the day, its central theme is most ironic: "The Lord Almighty has foiled them by the hand of a woman" (16.5); this echoes, probably deliberately, the story of Jael (Judg. 4.17–22; 5.24–27). The storyteller probably intended even the opening verse (1.1) to be understood as ironic, and certainly all the major scenes and characters are.

A beautiful, desirable, but childless widow, Judith lived a celibate life after her husband's death; yet she gave political and spiritual rebirth to her people. Very feminine in appearance, she herself murdered the general, praying even as she decapitated him (13.7–8)! Neither King Nebuchadnezzar, lord of the whole world (2.5), nor Holofernes, the master of the west (2.21–3.9), could master Bethulia. The Ammonite Achior, a seasoned warrior who early in the story displayed more faith in Israel's God (5.20–21) than did Uzziah, the chief elder of Bethulia (7.29–31), fainted on seeing the head that Judith had cut off with her own two hands (14.6). The Assyrian patrol that captured Judith and her maid were so captivated by their captive that they escorted her into the well-protected tent of her intended victim (10.11–16).

The scenes featuring conversations between Holofernes and Achior (5.5–6.9) and between Holofernes and Judith (11.5–12.4, 14–19) abound in punctual ironies (i.e., irony at more or less isolated points) and, when taken together, are what literary critics call "episodic irony." These episodes result in a thematic irony in the book as a whole: Achior spoke the complete truth to Holofernes but was not believed, while Judith dissimulated, equivocated, and lied—and was totally believed! Holofernes had intended to have his way with Judith, but as Judith's song so eloquently expresses it, the exact opposite happened: "Her sandal ravished his eyes; her beauty captivated his mind; and the sword severed his neck" (16.9). Not surprisingly, this dramatic climax is a favorite theme of Renaissance artists.

The opinion sometimes expressed that the book is unbalanced, that chaps. 1–3 or even 1–7 are slow-moving and irrelevant to the main story in 8–16, and that this imbalance probably results from the union of two originally separate stories—that of a Mesopotamian king's war in the east and west [chaps. 1–3] and the tale of Judith—is unjustified. A careful analysis shows that the book is a unity, with chaps. 1–7, in a variety of ways and on a number of levels, serving as an effective and indispensable foil for chaps. 8–16. Moreover, each half of the book has a threefold chiastic structure and a distinctive thematic repetition, namely, fear or its denial in chaps. 1–7, and beauty and its effects in 8–16, with Judith's triumph over Holofernes (10.11–13.10a) being the story's climax in both form and content. Moreover, in chaps. 1–7 masculine, brute force wins many a battle; but in chaps. 8–16 Judith's feminine beauty and wiles, undergirded by her faith in God, wins the war. (None of this is to deny that Judith's song [16.1–17] may be, as several scholars have suggested, an older synagogal psalm adopted and adapted by the storyteller.)

As for the book's religious ideas, neither God's titles nor attributes are in any way noteworthy. His *covenant with Israel is interpreted largely in Deuteronomic terms (5.17–18, 20–21; 8.20; 11.10), with emphasis on the importance of *Jerusalem (4.2), its *Temple (4.2–3), and ritual (4.14–15; 8.5–6; 9.1; 11.13). The efficacy of

*prayer, *fasting, and wearing sackcloth (4.10–15; 8.5–6; 9.1) is unquestioned, as is the importance of the dietary laws (10.5, 11–15; 12.2–4, 19). With the exception of *almsgiving and the baptizing of gentile converts (cf. 14.10), virtually all the traditional practices of Maccabean Pharisaism are mentioned. Clearly, the storyteller believed that courage and cleverness, Pharisaic piety and patriotism, undergirded by strong faith in the Lord, would be of benefit to Jews of any time or place.

Whatever the original language of the Judith story, the basis of the Greek version, as its many Hebraisms attest, was *Hebrew. In view of this fact, as well as the storyteller's Pharisaic theology and greater knowledge of Palestinian geography, one may infer that the author was a Palestinian *Pharisee.

As for the book's date of composition, though the story has a postexilic setting and a significant number of Persian nouns and personal names, it also has unmistakable Hellenistic features (cf. "garlands" in 3.7; reclining while eating in 12.15; "wearing garlands" in 15.13), as well as distinctively Maccabean/Hasmonean elements, notably the worshiping of a king as god (3.8), the sweeping political and military powers of the high priest (4.6–7), and the supremacy of the Jerusalem *Sanhedrin (4.6, 8; 11.14).

Other elements in the story are reminiscent of the general circumstances, terminology, spirit, and tradition of the days of Judas Maccabeus (167–161 BCE), especially of the defeat of Nicanor, the general under the infamous Antiochus Epiphanes (175–163 BCE), as narrated in 1 Maccabees 7.43–50. All this, plus the fact that the book has none of the anti-Sadducean spirit so characteristic of Pharisees in the days of Alexander Jannaeus (104–78 BCE), suggests that the book was composed in the days of John Hyrcanus I (135–105 BCE).

The *Septuagint version of the book, which appears to be a very literal translation of Hebrew syntax and idiom, nevertheless has a rich and varied Greek vocabulary. The translation was made no later than the first century CE, for Clement of Rome (ca. 96 CE) alludes to Judith (1 Clem. 55.45).

Unfortunately, the ancient versions are of little help in establishing either the Septuagint text of Judith or its Semitic basis. The Old Latin, Syriac, Coptic, and Ethiopic versions are all based upon the Septuagint, but no critical or scientific edition exists for any of them. Jerome's *Vulgate (ca.

405 CE) is a paraphrase of the then-current Aramaic text, which may be based upon the Greek rather than the Hebrew. Like Judith who stood alone to do the job, so also must the Septuagint of the book of Judith.   CAREY A. MOORE

Jung and the Bible. There would be little challenge to the proposition that Carl Jung (1875–1961) paid more attention to the Bible than any other psychoanalytic thinker or that his views of the Bible provoked more commentary from his followers and other religious scholars than those of any comparable figure. All of Jung's discussions of biblical texts bear the unique mark of his psychological views and his theories of symbolic meaning. As is so often the case, Jung's immersion in the Bible reflects aspects of his personality and life experience.

Early Development. Jung's familiarity with the Bible came at an early age. He was born in Keswill on Lake Constance in Switzerland in 1875. His father was a minister and pastor of the Lutheran church there, but within six months moved to Laufen, where Jung spent his early years. Of this early experience, Jung wrote, "In my mother's family there were six parsons, and on my father's side not only was my father a parson but two of my uncles also. Thus I heard many religious conversations, theological discussions, and sermons."

Jung's relationship with his pastor father was not the happiest. The pastor was a pious and conservative man of God, but for all his religiosity he was unable to help his son with the childhood terrors and emotional turmoil, the severe nightmares and choking fits, that made life in the parsonage all but unbearable. Theological issues became a sticking point between them. Jung's curiosity and inquisitive mind led him to question his father's traditional beliefs, to which the older Jung would reply that one should not bother about thinking in religious matters, but should devote oneself to believing. Jung's early religious doubts seem to have centered around his conflicts toward his father and his deep-seated ambivalence, both toward his father and his father's religious views. For the son the religion of the father was a doctrine about God and had little to do with the living experience of God. In Jung's view, his father "had taken the Bible's commandments as his guide; he believed in God as the Bible prescribed and as his forefathers had taught him" but without any sense of "the immediate living God who stands, om-

nipotent and free above His Bible and His Church, who calls upon man to partake of His freedom." Much of Jung's later writing about religion reflects his underlying ambivalence toward his father and his constant effort to contest approaches to religion and the Bible that resulted in no more than stale doctrines and scientific facts and did not foster the life of the spirit and the enrichment of psychic life to which Jung devoted his life.

If Jung's religiously conservative father became the object of Jung's ambivalent conflicts, his mother played an important if opposite role. Her religious views were less rigid and little concerned with conventional piety. She introduced her son to works from other religious traditions and gave him a copy of Goethe's *Faust* when he was a university student. She also seems to have encouraged Jung's interest in spiritualism and parapsychological phenomena.

Jung's Approach. One cannot help but be impressed by the extent to which Jung was steeped in biblical lore. In none of his writings is he ever very far from the discussion of biblical themes or from the use of scriptural references to make his point. In the preface of *Answer to Job*, he stated, "I do not write as a biblical scholar (which I am not), but as a layman and physician who has been privileged to see deeply into the psychic life of many people." He was not interested in the usual questions of biblical research—the meaning, origins, cultural background, and history behind biblical texts. He sought to find that meaning of the texts that would speak to modern men and women in their present historical and cultural experience. He was less concerned with the origins of the texts than with their effects on the lives of contemporary readers.

His familiarity with the Bible is impressive. References can be found from all but thirteen of the sixty-six books in the Hebrew Bible and New Testament. The gospel of John was his favorite—he cited it more than 120 times. He was well acquainted with the *Apocrypha and *Pseudepigrapha, quoting from the books of *Enoch, 2 *Esdras, *Tobit, and the *Wisdom of Solomon. He also made references to the New Testament apocryphal writings, quoting from the Gospel of the Egyptians, the book of the Apostle Bartholomew, the Gospel of Peter, the Acts of Peter, the Acts of John, the Gospel of Philip, and the Acts of Thomas. References to biblical figures and biblical phrases flowed easily from his pen. Further testimony to the significance of holy writ in Jung's life are the inscriptions on the family tomb in Küsnacht. The first reads *Vocatus atque non vocatus Deus aderit* ("Summoned or not, God will be here")—the same words were inscribed on Jung's bookplate and over the entrance to his home. The second is *Primus homo terrenus de terra; secundus homo coelestis de coelo* ("The first man was earthly, from the earth; the second man was heavenly, from heaven"; 1 Cor. 15.47). In explaining the first inscription over his doorway, he said, "I have put the inscription there to remind my patients and myself: *timor dei initium sapientiae* ['the fear of God is the beginning of wisdom']. Here another not less important road begins, not the approach to Christianity, but to God himself and this seems to be the ultimate question."

Certainly Jung's use of the Bible was idiosyncratic. For him it was a primary source of material that could be translated into terms of his psychological system—with particular emphasis on the symbolic dimension of scriptural references and events that he was able to connect with aspects of his own views about the role of myths and symbols in human psychic functioning and their connection with the collective unconscious and archetypal symbols. Myths were not mere words or stories but living truths and psychic realities that exercise their power on the human soul by their use of symbolic language. Symbols thus served as the vehicles of psychic transformation that extended beyond the communication of meaning to the level of psychic integration and spiritual revitalization.

His effort was consistently directed to viewing scripture in such a way as to make it relevant to psychic concerns. He argued that the religious propositions in the Bible had their origin in the human psyche and that their meaning was in some sense determined by psychic roots, whether conscious or unconscious. They are in effect psychic facts and relevant to psychic truths that are concerned with the illumination of the soul. Their aim and purpose are not to provide information but to bring about psychic change. Jung endorsed the view that "all scripture is inspired by God and useful for teaching, for reproof, for correction, and for training in righteousness, so that everyone who belongs to God may be proficient, equipped for every good work" (2 Tim. 3.16). Insofar as religious statements are "psychic confessions" deriving from the unconscious, they are like dreams that enter consciousness to inspire new insight and illumination. Thus, the *prophets spoke of being seized by the *word or *spirit of God. The psyche becomes the place where the divine and human interact—transcendence is replaced by immanence. The scripture becomes the vehicle and means of God's presence and action in the soul. Behind and in the words there is the Word.

Christ as Archetype of the Self. A good example of this usage is Jung's development of Christ as the symbol for the integrated self. The Self in Jung's psychology represents the unity and wholeness of the personality, embracing all psychic phenomena. It stands for the goal of integration of the total personality and individuality. This archetypal image is expressed in mandalas and in the heroes of myth and legend but above all in the image of Christ who "exemplifies the archetype of the Self." As he comments in *Answer to Job,* "Christ would never have made the impression he did on his followers if he had not expressed something that was alive and at work in their unconscious. Christianity itself would never have spread through the pagan world with such astonishing rapidity had its ideas not found an analogous psychic readiness to receive them."

He makes use of the Johannine theme of Christ as the way, the truth, and the light. Christ thus comes to symbolize the way of love (John 13.35), service (Mark 10.43), the life of the Spirit (Gal. 5.19–22), salvation, and reconciliation. Christ thus becomes the archetype of the Self—the Christ-event not only speaks to the soul but acts within it to awaken, revive, cleanse, and save. In psychological terms, the Christ-event means that to become true Selves we must acquire a broader consciousness that connects the sense of identity and wholeness with love of the neighbor. Love is the mark of the Christian. Jung observes: "The men of that age were ripe for identification with the word made flesh, for the founding of a community united by an idea, in the name of which they could love one another and call each other brothers. The old idea of . . . a mediator in whose name new ways of love would be opened, became a fact, and with that human society took and immense stride forward."

In this fashion Jung strove to bring the scripture closer to vital interests and make it a force for psychic enrichment and integration—far different from his father's stale reverence for the words of scripture rather than the relation of the Bible to real life and the God of life. As he put it, "The Bible is not the words of God, but the Word of God." As the archetype of the Self, Christ becomes a real event in the life of the soul. Christ acts in the soul to draw out real effects and changes. The Christ symbol brings with it a power through *grace to become what one could not become on one's own.

Answer to Job. Despite his frequent allusions to scripture, the *Answer*, written in 1952, was his only work based exclusively on a scriptural text. It was meant to be his interpretation of the Old Testament God-image of Judaism and its transformation into the Christian God. His portrayal of God in this work was controversial and provocative, challenging the traditional Christian view of God by its theory of the "dark side" of God. Jung's God, from one perspective, is like a reflection of *gnostic dualism, ruling the world by the forces of good, embodied in the figure of Christ, and evil, embodied in the figure of *Satan. The dualism of good and evil is integrated in the unified image of God.

From another point of view, he saw God and the *Trinity in terms of a symbolic dynamic pertaining to the individual soul and the whole of Judeo-Christian culture. In the first stage God is Yahweh of the Old Testament; in the second stage the image of the Son and behind him the loving Father dominates the New Testament and its historical developments; and finally, with the doctrine of the Holy Spirit we enter the post–New Testament era of Christian history and development. We can hear the echoes of Joachim di Fiore and his preaching of the final and consummate age of the Holy Spirit that stirred millennial visions in the twelfth century. In Jung's eyes the trinitarian doctrine was rooted in archetypal symbols that characterize the collective unconscious of humanity. Despite his disclaimer that he was only addressing the image of God as a psychological construct and not as a reality outside the mind, Jung's treatment of the subject often seems to forget or ignore his own qualifications.

To recapitulate the story of *Answer to Job:* the adversary of God, Satan, casts doubt on the faithfulness of God's mortal servant *Job. Jung puzzles as to why Yahweh accepts the testimony of the father of lies and seems not to know Job's true character. Why should God believe Satan rather than his own omniscience? In any event, God turns Job over to the torments of the devil in order to win the wager with Satan. All Job's possessions and even his children are destroyed before his face, yet he still cries out in his grief, "The Lord gave and the Lord has taken away; blessed be the name of the Lord" (Job 1.21). Satan ups the ante, and Job is subjected to fur-

ther torments and afflictions. In his misery Job turns to his friends for solace, but they are helpless to explain his poor fortune, appealing to conventional wisdom which proves inadequate.

Yahweh answers Job's appeals for mercy not by rejecting the deceptions of Satan but by majestic declarations of his omnipotence (Job 38–40). But, asks Jung, what of the missing omniscience? The compensatory outpouring of rich gifts, the thousands of head of cattle, camels, oxen, and so on, even the blessings of new sons and daughters, hardly measure up to the loss of the others whom Job had loved and cherished. This God, says Jung, has no feeling, so lost in his own omnipotence is he.

The drama progresses as the figure of Sophia, a feminine figure representing *Wisdom as found in the *wisdom literature, enters. If Yahweh had consulted her rather than Satan, he would have known Job's faithfulness. Her task is to help undo the damage caused by God's omnipotence. Under her influence, Yahweh wishes to become human in order to make recompense for the torments he inflicted on Job, to restore the moral balance, and particularly to avoid the consequence of becoming a discredited and disregarded god. Most of all, he wishes to save himself from his own terrible and heartless indifference to human fate and sufferings. He can become human only through the help of Sophia, the prototype of *Mary. Sophia helps him see that his first creation went awry because of the devices of Satan in the guise of the serpent. To avoid the taint of Satan's influence, God would have to be born of a *virgin by an immaculate conception.

Answer to Job was essentially Jung's culminating effort to join his conflictual struggle with God and at another remove his father. His view of God was transmuted into a cultural crisis of modernity. He commented: "Later generations could afford to ignore the dark side of the Apocalypse, because the specifically Christian achievement was something that was not to be frivolously endangered. But for modern man the case is quite otherwise. We have experienced things so unheard of and so staggering that the question of whether such things are in any way reconcilable with the idea of a good God has become burningly topical."

Thus, Jung argues, the insistence on the concept of God as all good has lost its meaning for contemporary men and women and has led to the abandonment of God. The result is a mechanistic view of the universe, a decline of spiritual values, and a sense of the meaninglessness of human existence. The presence of *evil in the world creates a crisis for Christian consciousness: If God is omnipotent and all good, why does evil exist? Jung's answer is that God is not all good, but that he encompasses both good and evil. We can see the reflection of Jung's father's face in the face of the God he portrays in the *Answer*. It is a face compounded of good and evil that presents itself as a mystery and an enigma, just as his own father's difficult character had been for Jung as a child.

Conclusion. The Bible was for Jung not just another book to be read critically and skeptically, as *Freud might have done. It was a book of faith, of hope, of inspiration, in which Jung found the words and images that carried him along his fevered search for meaning, psychological truth, and wholeness in his own and in his contemporaries' psychic lives. His concerns were far removed from the more scientific objectives of biblical hermeneutics and exegesis. He sought what was for him a psychological cause, a lifelong crusade, to translate the God of his father into a living God of Jung's own making. The success of his effort and the validity of his accomplishment remain enigmatic.

WILLIAM W. MEISSNER, S.J.

Junia. The only woman called an *apostle (Rom. 16.7) in the New Testament. *Paul's relative or compatriot, Junia had been in prison, perhaps for the gospel. Her name suggests that she may have been a freedwoman or a descendant of a slave freed by a member of the Junian clan. As an apostle, Junia must have claimed to have seen the risen Jesus and have engaged in missionary work (cf. 1 Cor. 9.1).

Although previous scholars intrepreted the name Junia as masculine, church fathers, including Origen, John Chrysostom, and Jerome, identified her as a woman. Further, while the hypothetical male name Junias is unattested in ancient inscriptions, the female Latin name Junia occurs over 250 times in Greek and Latin inscriptions found in Rome alone. Therefore scholars today generally interpret the name as feminine.

BERNADETTE J. BROOTEN

Justice. *See* Righteousness.

Justification. The concept of justification is based on that of *righteousness; in fact, both can trans-

late the same Greek word (*dikaiosunē*). As applied to human beings, this connotes the status of being in the right when tested or judged by God. That condition lies at the heart of the covenantal relationship between Yahweh and his people, Israel. For the maintenance of *covenant relations, righteousness on Israel's part is also required, with the prospect of attaining approval from God both in this life and, in later literature, at the final judgment.

*Paul opposed this construction for two reasons. The claim that those who keep God's law will be set right with God and given approved status before God is considered by Paul to be a vain hope, inasmuch as this class of "righteous" persons has no qualified member, for "all have sinned and fall short of the glory of God" (Rom. 3.23). There is no prospect of being set right with God as long as a person stays with nomistic religion (Gal. 5.3). Instead, the outlook on such a basis is one of universal condemnation for both Jews and gentiles, since all have become sinners (Rom. 2.17–3.20; Gal. 3.21–22). All stand under divine judgment (Rom. 1.18; 3.9,19), and must remain so unless God takes action on their behalf.

The second reason why Paul opposed nomistic religion is that he believed a new era had dawned with the coming of the *Messiah. What Judaism anticipated as God's gracious intervention at the endtime, Paul now declares as a present reality for all who are of faith (Rom. 5.1), in the sure confidence that at the future tribunal the past verdict of acceptance and amnesty will be confirmed (Gal. 5.5; Phil. 1.11; 3.9). In this way the tension of the Christian life ("already justified . . . not yet finally 'saved'") is maintained as a part of Paul's proclamation.

Justification has been defined as "the gracious action of God accepting persons as righteous in consequence of faith resting upon His redemptive activity in Christ" (Vincent Taylor). This definition needs strengthening by a recognition that Paul constantly lays a basis for what he believed about God's "redemptive activity" in Christ's obedience (Rom. 5.9) or righteousness (Rom. 5.18). Consequently, more should be said in any summary statement about Paul's insistence on "imputation" as providing a rationale for the divine enterprise in canceling human guilt and providing acceptance in his holy presence. Romans 3.21–26 and 2 Corinthians 5.18–21 stand out as central to Paul's teaching. Also, Paul's thought is as much conditioned by promises of rectification of personal relationships as by assurances of forensic acquittal. Indeed, the term acquittal is best avoided if it conjures up the notion of treating sinners as though they were not sinners. Plainly, in Paul's theology there is no room for such exonerating considerations. "Amnesty," therefore, is a term preferred by some scholars, and it recalls that justification is above all a royal act by which pardon is freely bestowed on the undeserving. God's royal rule is displayed in releasing offenders from guilt out of respect for his Son, who stands as their sponsor. Jesus Christ by his undertaking arranges a new network of divine-human relations—the element of novelty is seen by Paul's statement that God's righteousness (i.e., his saving power) is shown "apart from law" (Rom. 3.21)—and the whole enterprise springs from his free favor, his "grace" (Rom. 3.24; 11.6). The fresh start made by Christ's action ushers in a new order that consists of a whole series of events involving both forensic and dynamic acts on the part of God. The refusal to delimit justification to the initial act of acquittal and remission of guilt, thought of in exclusively legal terms and played out in a courtroom drama, paves the way for a much richer understanding of the term. It certainly will include a forensic release from sin's penalty, but will also entail the entire process of the rectification of the human relationship to God, who dynamically releases a power to set this relationship in a new orbit. For Paul, the new sphere of living is one of sonship within a family context and no longer that of slavery under the taskmaster's stern eye.

Two consequences flow from these considerations, as Ernst Käsemann has observed. First, God's righteousness is a gift that has the character of power. In fact, the actual term is associated in the Hebrew Bible with other words, such as "love," "peace," "wrath," that are used in personified form and often connote divine power. That is to say, what God does in rectifying sinners is characteristically a regal fiat, announcing a new day when past failures are put away, debts and liabilities canceled, and guilt removed from those who otherwise must pay the price. According to Romans 1.17 and 3.21, a new order has come into existence, one that sets human relationships on a different footing from that of strict justice and merit. The divine power now released and known in human experience is what the Pauline gospel is all about (Rom. 1.16; 1 Thess. 1.5).

Second, God's righteousness is characterized by universality. Paul stands directly in the tradition of the exilic prophet known as Second Isaiah (Isa. 40–55), for whom divine ṣĕdāqâ (righteousness) spills over into Yahweh's saving activity put forth on Israel's behalf and issuing in the promise of a new world. The apocalyptic dimension of Paul's thought is clear in his celebration of God's power in reaching out to capture the entire world for the sovereignty of God. What seems a limited teaching in the Jewish Christian fragment of Romans 3.24–25 is taken over editorially by Paul and enlarged to cover God's faithfulness not only to the covenant people of Israel but also to the whole creation. And that statement of a new creation brought into existence at God's command (2 Cor. 5.17) will play a significant part in Paul's developed teaching on reconciliation as Paul elaborates the cosmic scope of Christ's salvific work (2 Cor. 5.18–21; cf. Col. 1.15–20).

In summary, justification by faith is a relational term. Talk of forensic acquittal, often suggesting a sterile setting free from immediate punishment, is misplaced and merits the criticism brought by some that Paul's teaching is little short of a legal fiction. But such criticism is deflected once we recall how this terminology is basically couched in the framework of interpersonal relationships, and carries for Paul a dynamic nuance of a new attitude of God to human beings, as of humans to God, which in both instances leads to a chain of events. God, for his part, takes steps to carry through the enterprise of human recovery and renewal, while on the human side the initial act of "rightwising"—to use an old English term—begins a process of moral transformation associated with union with Christ that will ultimately reach its goal in the final homecoming of the people of God at the last day (Gal. 5.4; Phil. 1.11).

Paul's teaching was so finely balanced that it was capable of being distorted and misrepresented. The evidence for this comes in Romans 3.8; 6.1–15; Galatians 5.13, where his stress on the sufficiency of God's justifying grace was understood by some as an invitation to moral laxity. Pauline extremists are evidently the subject of James's debate on faith and works (James 2.14–26; see James, The Letter of). The need to have justification by faith set in the context of the call to a new life of obedience and the fruit of holy living (already anticipated in Gal. 5.6) led to the teachings of the Pauline school of the *Pastoral letters and possibly accounts for the stress on good works in 1 *Peter and *Matthew.   RALPH P. MARTIN

K

Kenites. The Kenites are portrayed in biblical tradition as staunch supporters of Israel and Yahwism who were never fully incorporated into Israelite society. Their status as a marginal group is implied in Judges 4.17–22 and 5.24–27, where the house of Heber the Kenite is portrayed as having peaceful relations with the tribes of Israel as well as Jabin the king of *Hazor, Israel's enemy. Some relation to Israel is also suggested in Judges 1.16, where the Kenites are said to have settled with the people of Judah in the Negeb near Arad (cf. 1 Sam. 27.10, "the Negeb of the Kenites"). The positive relationship between the Israelites and the Kenites is further affirmed in 1 Samuel 15.6; 30.29.

The Kenites may have had some connection with nomadic or seminomadic metalsmiths, although they are never explicitly identified as such. A *nomadic or seminomadic mode of life is suggested by references to their presence in various locations throughout Palestine, possibly including northern Sinai (Num. 24.17–22), a region of copper mining and smelting in ancient times. The association with metalworking has been postulated on the basis of the linguistic similarity between their name and *Cain's, the ancestor of Tubal-cain, the first "forger of all instruments of bronze and iron" (Gen. 4.22). The marginal status of the Kenites also supports this hypothesis, as marginality is characteristic of metalworking groups in many traditional societies throughout the Middle East and Africa. (*See also* Crafts.)

Some interpreters have conjectured that the Kenites were responsible for introducing Yahwism to the Israelites (the "Kenite hypothesis"). This proposal is based on the traditions that *Moses first encountered Yahweh (Exodus 3) while in the service of the priest Jethro (identified in Judges 1.16 and 4.11 as a Kenite), who praises and offers sacrifice to Yahweh and instructs Moses regarding delegation of authority (Exod. 18.10–27).

The Kenites are not mentioned in traditions about the later history of Israel. They may, however, have been related to the *Rechabites (1 Chron. 2.55), another socially marginal group that was fiercely supportive of Yahwism (2 Kings 10.15–28; Jeremiah 35), and to the *Midianites. Moses' father-in-law is identified as a Midianite in the Exodus traditions but as a Kenite in Judges 1.16 and 4.11. And in 1 Samuel 15.6, the Kenites are remembered as loyal supporters of Israel during the *Exodus, a role attributed to the *Midianites in the Pentateuchal narratives.

In Numbers 24.21–22, it is foretold that the Kenites will perish. This is the one instance in which they are viewed unfavorably.

PAULA M. McNUTT

Ketib and Qere. Aramaic terms meaning "(that which is) written" and "(that which is) to be read," respectively. Both developed as part of the reading tradition for the *Masorah of the Hebrew Bible in ancient Judaism. In seeking to preserve and to transmit the proper pronunciation of the consonantal text of the Hebrew scriptures, *ketib* and *qere* indicate the correct reading and pronunciation of the text. *Ketib* always refers to the particular reading that has been preserved as part of the received Hebrew text, both consonants and vowels as originally recorded in the *Masoretic Text. The *qere*, which is given in the margin of the text, indicates either corrected pronunciation by means of alternate vowels for the consonants preserved in the received text, or alternate spelling, that is, consonants and vowels to be read instead of the form in the received text. The *qere* may correct an error in the received text, or it may offer another reading entirely (as with the *name of God Yahweh, and in euphemistic substitutions). Some scholars have maintained that the *Qere/Ketib* system, in addition to preserving a different reading tradition, was a way to preserve variants that were eliminated when the text of the Hebrew Bible was stan-

407

dardized within Judaism in the first century CE (*see* Masoretic Text).   RUSSELL FULLER

Kingdom of God. There is clear agreement among the *synoptic Gospels that the kingdom of God was the principal theme within Jesus' message (Matt. 4.17, 23; Mark 1.15; Luke 4.42, 43), although each attests to this fact distinctively. In aggregate, they present some fifty sayings and *parables of Jesus concerning the kingdom. In the gospel of John Jesus refers only once to the kingdom expressly, though the saying is repeated (3.3, 5). In that instance, however, the kingdom is presented as something that even the *Pharisee Nicodemus is assumed to understand; the point at issue is not the nature of the kingdom but how it might be entered. It is, then, a matter of consensus within the canon that the kingdom constituted a primary focus of Jesus' theology.

The notion that God is king and as such rules, or wishes to rule, his people is evident in the scriptures of Israel. In the books of *Judges and *Samuel, the Lord's kingship is even held to exclude human monarchy as the appropriate government of the covenantal people (Judg. 8.23; 1 Sam. 8.7–9). It requires a distinctive fiat, by prophetic anointing, to establish Davidic *kingship as the seal of the divine *covenant (2 Sam. 7.5–17; cf. 1 Sam. 16.1–13). In no sense, then, does the Davidic royal house supplant God's ultimate rule. God could still be conceived of as reigning over all things (Ps. 145.13), and as about to reign on behalf of Israel (Isa. 52.7). In both Hebrew and Aramaic the verb "reigns" or "rules" is cognate with the nouns "king" and "kingdom" (all from the root *mlk*); furthermore, the noun "kingdom" refers more to the fact or force of rule than to the territory governed. The phrasing of the New Testament, although distinctive, is conceptually rooted in the Hebrew Bible.

The future orientation found in Isaiah 52.7 may be perplexing. Alongside the conviction of God's continuing, royal care, there was also the hope that God would finally—and unambiguously—be disclosed as king. Just that hope, in an ultimate and irrefutable exertion of the divine reign, is characteristic of early *eschatology (e.g., Isa. 52.7). Within that perspective, the end of time is not dreaded but is rather the object of longing. The dissolution of the present age is a frightening prospect only for those who enjoy the rewards of this world; for Israel, the chosen people who had been denied the fruits of divine

promise as a result of their sin and foreign domination, the end of this age—and the beginning of another—increasingly became an urgent hope. Only then, it was believed, would the promised peace of God reign supreme. Their hope seemed only to increase the more critical became the absence of a Davidic king, the presence of the Romans, and confusing controversies concerning the efficacy of worship in the *Temple. Eschatological urgency was a function of two collateral axioms within the faith of Israel: that God was just and that Israel is the elect people of God. Within their own understanding, the people of Israel could not agree that contemporary circumstances were consistent with either axiom. God, they felt, must be about to act in vindication of both his people and his own integrity.

"The kingdom of God" (or "the kingdom of the Lord") is precisely the phrase used in certain documents of early Judaism in order to express hope in God's ultimate disclosure as king. The Targums use the phrase chiefly to convey that eschatological hope (*Targum of Isaiah* 24.23; 31.4; 40.9; 52.7). The early (perhaps first-century CE) prayer known as the Kaddish also refers to the kingdom in that sense: "May He make his kingdom reign in your lifetime!" Later rabbinic texts conventionally use the phrase "kingdom of the heavens," as in Matthew. No difference in meaning is implied by replacing the word "God" or "Lord"; "heavens" appears to be a reverential periphrasis. In most rabbinic texts, however, the kingdom appears less as an eschatological than as a moral concept; the language refers to accepting God as one's king (by reciting the *Shema) rather than to readying oneself for his rule.

The preaching of Jesus is far closer to eschatological expectation than to the moral emphasis of later rabbis. Although, in Jesus' thinking, the kingdom "has come near" (Mark 1.15), or has made itself available (Luke 16.16 par.; Matt. 12.28; par.), it was part of his programmatic prayer that the kingdom's coming should be sought (Matt. 6.10 par.). Care must be taken, however, to do justice to Jesus' distinctiveness as a *rabbi or teacher as well as to his context within Judaism. By speaking of the kingdom, Jesus adopted the language of scripture (as used in synagogues) and of prayer and made that language his own. The kingdom in his preaching was not merely promised but announced as a divine activity that demanded repentance and that could be entered into by participating in its divine force. That stance is represented not only by the programmatic descriptions of his teaching but also by the parables. Those that involve images of growth or process (Mark 4.26–29; Matt. 13.24–30, 31–33 par.) particularly insist that the kingdom must not be limited to any single temporality, be it present or future. Such limitation would betray the dynamic unfolding such parables are designed to convey. For that reason, to describe the kingdom in Jesus' expectation as apocalyptic, in the sense of an anticipated calendar of divine unveilings in which God's rule can be dated, is misleading. The dearth of references to the kingdom in *apocalyptic literature undermines that position, and much of the teaching attributed to Jesus militates against it (Luke 17.20, 21; cf. Matt. 24.36 par.; Acts 1.7, in addition to passages cited above).

A last element of Jesus' theology of the kingdom must be mentioned, which also tells against an apocalyptic construal of his message. Jesus' teaching was not simply futuristic in its eschatological orientation; he was also known as an ethical teacher (cf. Matt. 22.34–40; Mark 12.28–34; Luke 10.25–28). Many of his parables show how, within his vision of a single kingdom, Jesus could be both expectant of the future and demanding in the present. Parables of growth or process involve expectant readiness as the appropriate attitude toward the climax (Mark 4.29; Matt. 13.30; 13.32b, c par.; 13.33d par.); a king or lord who invites people to a banquet expects those invited to be prepared (Matt. 22.8, 9, 11, 12; Luke 14.24; cf. Matt. 8.11, 12 par.); even absent rulers anticipate their subjects' willing obedience during their absence (Matt. 25.1–13; 14–30; Luke 12.35–38; 17.7–10; 19.11–27). The ethical themes implicit in such parables make sense once one appreciates that Jesus conveys by them a self-disclosing kingdom whose focus is irreducibly future and whose implications are pressingly present. Just as his claim to speak on behalf of that kingdom is perhaps the most obvious root of Christology, so his message gave to the movement that succeeded him a characteristic attitude of expectancy in respect of the future and, consequently, of responsibility within the present.   BRUCE D. CHILTON

Kingdom of Heaven. *See* Kingdom of God.

Kings, The Books of. The perception of the Greek translation of the Hebrew Bible (the *Sep-

tuagint) is that the first and second books of *Samuel and of Kings should be regarded as four books of "Kingdoms," and a similar understanding of them appears in Jerome's view that they constitute four books of "Kings." They deal with the history of the monarchy from its inception and throughout its course. The narrative recounts the false starts beginning with *Saul; the achievement of a united kingdom under *David; the division of the kingdom under Rehoboam; and thereafter the record of two separate lines of kings until the northern kingdom disappears in 722 BCE. The history up to 587/586 BCE then focuses on Judean kings.

Summary of Contents. After a detailed treatment of *Solomon's reign, an account of the circumstances in which the kingdom was divided and the early history of the two kingdoms, the emphasis falls on the northern kingdom (Israel); *Jehoshaphat, king of Judah, enters the narrative only insofar as he is associated with *Ahab (1 Kings 22) and Jehoram (2 Kings 3) in military enterprises. This latter section, which extends from 1 Kings 16.29 to 2 Kings 10.36, predominates in the books of Kings. The first part of it is taken up with the conflict between *Elijah and Ahab, the second with *Elisha's involvement in the overthrow of the house of Omri and his connection with *Jehu. A narrative of the downfall of Athaliah, a Judean counterpart of Ahab (2 Kings 11) is followed by a series of short records of kings of Israel and Judah. After the final collapse of the northern kingdom has been described, there is a transition to kings of Judah: *Hezekiah, who is praised for suppressing the *high places (2 Kings 18); *Manasseh, who is roundly condemned; and *Josiah, in whom special interest is shown, for he is portrayed as an ideal king. The final kings of Judah and the circumstances of their reigns are then reviewed, and the history ends with the fall of *Jerusalem to the *Babylonians under *Nebuchadrezzar.

The Compiler and his Criterion. Josiah is represented (2 Kings 22.1–23.30) as having suppressed all cultic centers of Yahwistic worship within his borders, on the grounds that they were infested with *idolatry, and to have concentrated the worship of Yahweh in the Jerusalem *Temple, as the only legitimate cultic site. This criterion is adopted by the compiler of 1 and 2 Kings. Consequently, when he deals with the reign of Josiah, the compiler has reached the heart of his own convictions; since the aims of the Josianic reformation correlate with some or all of the book of *Deuteronomy's contents, he is revealed as a historian belonging to the Deuteronomic school.

Apart from applying his criterion, which he does by means of introductory and concluding formulae attached to accounts of individual reigns, the Deuteronomic compiler does not interfere much with his sources. He uses this material in order to achieve his effects, but only occasionally does he compose in the interests of his Deuteronomic interpretation of the history of the monarchy in Israel and Judah. For example, the narrative concerning the reform of Josiah may be the compiler's own composition, as also may be the account of the fall of Jerusalem in 587/ 586 BCE (2 Kings 25). A difference in style has been detected between the narrative of the finding of the book of the law and its effects (2 Kings 22.3–23.3, 9, 21–25), on the one hand, and the narrative of the cultic and political measures initiated by Josiah (23.4–8, 10, 15, 19–20), on the other; it has been supposed that the latter derives from a different source, namely the Book of the Annals of the Kings of Judah (see below).

1 Kings 8 been widely regarded as a case of intervention by the Deuteronomic compiler, for in it Solomon, whose preparation for the building and furnishing of the Temple, with Tyrian cooperation, is described at length (1 Kings 5– 7), appears to take on some of the features of Josiah. He is portrayed as presiding over a great religious festival in connection with the Jerusalem Temple's completion and legitimation by dint of the *ark's installation—the ark before which he stood and sacrificed in Jerusalem after the *theophany at Gibeon (1 Kings 3.15). As with the Deuteronomic view of this cult object, it is described as "the ark of the covenant" and is regarded as essentially a container for the stone tablets of the Law. Solomon is drawn as a man of great piety, full of noble religious sentiments and capable of giving utterance to a great prayer. Other compositions by the Deuteronomic compiler in this section of the books of Kings have been detected at 1 Kings 3.2–3, 14 and 11.1–13.

The Compiler's Sources. The sources on which the compiler of 1 and 2 Kings is said to have relied are given as the Book of the Acts of Solomon (1 Kings 11.41), the Book of the Annals of the Kings of Israel (e.g., at 1 Kings 14.19), and the Book of the Annals of the Kings of Judah (e.g., at 1 Kings 14.29). The Solomonic source has a different Hebrew title, and, judging from 1 Kings 11.41, it contains a variety of material and is not correctly described as either

"annals" or "chronicles." The expression "Now the rest of the acts of Solomon, all that he did as well as his wisdom" (1 Kings 11.41) suggests that the source contained both annalistic and nonannalistic material (legends and sagas). Examples of the latter are the dream at Gibeon (1 Kings 3.4–15), the Solomonic judgment (3.16– 28), and the visit of the Queen of *Sheba (10.1– 10,13). The "Book of the Acts of Solomon" was perhaps itself a composite that had been gathered together from other sources.

The other two sources are thought by some to have been essentially annalistic in character, records of particular reigns, registers of achievements, or calendars of events. If they had this form rather than that of a fully articulated historical narrative, there is a great deal in 1 and 2 Kings that could not be fitted into them. In any case, whatever precise literary form these chronicles or annals of the kings of Israel and Judah took, prophetic stories (in which the context is not in any sense royal and national, and which are especially associated with Elijah and Elisha) must be disengaged from them. Nor can we suppose that royal archives are a source for the account of the conflict between Elijah and Ahab or the episode of Naboth's vineyard and the murder of Naboth arranged by *Jezebel, nor for the interventions of Elisha in the wars against *Aram, where he appears as a national savior and his miraculous powers are heavily emphasized. The sources used by the Deuteronomic compiler were diverse and his criterion was not applied so stringently that he shaped all of them into a homogeneous whole. He is not so consumed with his narrow criterion of acceptability that he does not allow his sources to speak with different voices and to indicate concern for other and broader issues.

The Framework Formulae. The compiler's narrowness, however, is particularly evident in the introductory and concluding formulae that bracket the accounts of individual reigns of kings of Israel and Judah. Apart from affording him an opportunity to assess each reign with an introductory formula, these formulae record the accession of individual kings, indicate death and burial, and provide a synchronic *chronology relating the accession of the kings of Israel and Judah.

This chronological element has raised the question whether the formulae in their entirety are the creation of the Deuteronomic compiler or whether he is using a preexisting source comparable to the "Synchronic History" recovered from the library of Ashurbanipal, which correlates events of Babylonian and Assyrian history. The first complete example of these formulae occurs for Rehoboam (1 Kings 14.21–24, 29–31); note that the source is referred to in the conclusion. The concluding formula is missing for Joram and Ahaziah (2 Kings 9.22–28), and the introductory formula is missing for Jehu (2 Kings 10.34–36). Both are lacking for Athaliah (2 Kings 11), and the conclusion is omitted for kings violently deposed: Jehoahaz (2 Kings 23.31–34); Jehoiachin (2 Kings 23.8–17); *Zedekiah (2 Kings 24.18–25.21).

Date of Composition. What is immediately striking about the criterion is its apparently anachronistic character. Insofar as the criterion derives from the Josianic reformation and its program, and therefore could not have been formulated before this event or series of events, it gives us some indication of the date of the Deuteronomic compilation of the books of Kings. One might attempt to date the work more precisely by appealing to individual passages, but the results thus achieved must be treated with reserve: we should not assume that the history is all of a piece, or that it was created in its entirety at one time by a single compiler.

More than this, for reasons that have been indicated, we should not expect reliable consistency from a compilation of this kind and so should not appeal to a single passage in order to reach conclusions about the date of the whole. Thus, because there is a passage (2 Kings 22.20) in which the disastrous death of Josiah at *Megiddo in 609 BCE apparently lies in an unforeseen future should not lead us to conclude that the work must have been completed before that date. Nor does the fact that the work closes with reference to an event that took place in 566 BCE demonstrate that the entire compilation cannot be earlier than that. If, however, we suppose that the *Deuteronomic history contained in 1 and 2 Kings was already under way during Josiah's reign, we have to conclude that there was a subsequent supplement that brought it down to the fall of Jerusalem in 587/586 BCE, and we should then also suppose that 2 Kings 25.27–30 is a final postscript about the fate of Jehoiachin in *exile.

Interpreting the Criterion. The stringent application of the criterion is especially difficult to accept in relation to Israelite kings (as opposed to Judean kings). Too much should not be made of its anachronistic character, though, or, in stressing its apparent illogic, we might lose sight of the endeavor to understand the point of view it represents. The Deuteronomic historian regards the centralization of worship not as a new departure in the reign of Josiah but as the restoration of an ancient legitimacy. That is why the Jerusalem cult features so prominently in the account given of Solomon's reign. Before the Temple was built "he sacrificed and offered incense at the high places" (1 Kings 3.3), and it is only in his old age (so it is represented), under the influence of his foreign wives, that he becomes an idolater (1 Kings 11.1–13). Further, his political failures, which led to the division of the kingdom, are traced to his idolatry (1 Kings 11.14–25).

From this point of view, the division into two kingdoms, a political breach, had idolatry as an inevitable consequence. The political schism can then only have disastrous consequences for Yahwism: the kings of the northern part of Israel do not have Jerusalem within their territory and will set up what they regard as legitimate Yahwistic sanctuaries, which in the Deuteronomic view constitutes idolatrous worship. The narrow point, however, must be widened, otherwise the narrative would become unbearably tedious. It is made against the first of these kings who founded what he supposed to be legitimate Yahwistic sanctuaries at Bethel and *Dan (1 Kings 12.30). The "man of God" who is represented as raising his voice against the sanctuary at Bethel, while Jeroboam is sacrificing at its altar, is expressing a Deuteronomist view (1 Kings 13.1–3).

Ahab and his successors of the house of Omri are charged with a different kind of idolatry. Ahab, on whom attention is especially focused, permits Jezebel, his Tyrian wife, to establish a cult of the Tyrian *Baal in his capital city of *Samaria (compare the case of Solomon and his foreign wives). Hence, what is involved is the importation of the cult of a foreign god into Israel; although this is distinguishable from a contravention of the law of the single sanctuary, it is no doubt regarded as an aggravation of this offense (1 Kings 16.31–33). It is this contest between Yahweh and Baal which is dramatized in 1 Kings 18, where Elijah confronts Ahab and issues his challenge in the name of Yahweh. Elijah's miraculous victory over the prophets of Baal and *Asherah is enhanced by the fact that the wood that has been set alight had been saturated with water; he then acts as a rainmaker, putting an end to the drought he enforced at his first appearance (1 Kings 17.1). Jehu, by whom foreign gods were expelled, and who is Yahwistic in his religion, politics, and cultural preferences, is condemned in terms of the law of the single sanctuary, as he was bound to be insofar as he maintained the cult of Yahweh within his own territory (2 Kings 10.31).

Elijah and Elisha Narratives. The narratives concerned with the conflict between *Elijah and Ahab (1 Kings 18; 19; 21) cannot be satisfactorily interpreted on the assumption that they deal simply with an idolatry whose existence is established by the application of a narrow criterion of religious orthodoxy. We are confronted here with a criticism of a royal regime and style of life that are morally and culturally alien and unacceptable: they cannot be reconciled with the ethos of the Israelite community and its social institutions. The excavation of *Samaria has revealed a grandeur of architecture not achieved by Ahab's predecessors, which certainly is another mark of Tyrian influence (cf. 1 Kings 5).

The story of Naboth's vineyard (1 Kings 21) focuses on a clash between Ahab's royal desires and Naboth's sense of the inalienability of his ancestral land. The way in which this is delineated is not totally unsympathetic to Ahab: he does not simply confiscate Naboth's land with a display of crude power; rather, he offers what he regards as a fair price and is distressed when Naboth refuses to bargain with him. Even so, the fact that he is represented as making an offer indicates the distance between him and an older set of Israelite social values, which separated family land from the marketplace and assumed an abiding connection between the continuation and well-being of the family and its land possessions. The villain of the piece is Jezebel, for whom a peasant's resistance to the will of the king is incomprehensible, and who removes the opposition by poisoning justice at its source and disguising murderous oppressiveness with a bogus legal process. We meet here a foreign *queen who not only has established the worship of her gods in Israel but also, utterly lacking insight into Israelite social values, holds in contempt the right of her subjects to equality under the law.

The legal aspect of this is especially interesting, because there are other passages in the books of Samuel and Kings that emphasize the special responsibility of the king to ensure that justice is done to his subjects. *Absalom fastens on to David's neglect of these matters as a prime source of public discontent (2 Sam. 15.1–6), and in connection with the praise of Solomon's wisdom his legal acumen is particularly illustrated (1 Kings 3.16–28). The relation in respect of motif between 2 Samuel 12.1–7 and 1 Kings 20.35–43 should not be missed (the latter passage stands apart from the other contents of 1 Kings 20 and 22). In both these passages, a king is appealed to as supreme legal authority and he gives a verdict in which he unknowingly passes sentence on himself (cf. 2 Sam. 14).

In a more private context, Elijah is represented as a solitary *prophet who works miracles for a widow of Zarephath, providing for her and her son when they are on the edge of starvation, and who subsequently restores the dead child to life (1 Kings 17.8–24). He is a marvelous provider and life-giver, but he is also a destroyer who calls up fire to consume soldiers sent by Ahaziah to take him, and he comes into the king's presence and tells him that he will die because he has asked guidance from *Baal-zebub, god of Ekron (2 Kings 1.9–17). He runs with such great speed that he can keep up with horse and chariot (1 Kings 18.46), but he is also a prophet who loses heart and who encounters God not in what are usually portrayed as the majestic accompaniments of a *theophany but as a "still small voice" (1 Kings 19.12: AV; NRSV: "sound of sheer silence").

Two chapters stand somewhat apart from the narratives that have just been described, even though prophets play a part in both of them (1 Kings 20.1–34; 22). The motif of provocative behavior by a king of Aram in order to provide a pretext for aggression against Israel (1 Kings 20) is repeated at 2 Kings 5, in connection with the cure of Naaman's leprosy by *Elisha. In 1 Kings 20.1–34, Ahab is portrayed as conciliatory but firm, as capable of proverbial aptness (v. 11), as adopting the strategy advised by a prophet and as magnanimous in victory. Although his conflict with Micaiah, and so with a true prophetic word, is an important factor in 1 Kings 22, the account is not informed with marked animus against him, except at v. 38, where his death is linked to a prophecy uttered against him by Elijah (1 Kings 21.19). Ahab and Jehoshaphat, king of Judah, are allies in an attempt to wrest Ramoth-gilead from Aram, an attempt that ends disastrously. In the Septuagint, 1 Kings 21 follows chap. 19, and chap. 22, which is separated from chap. 20 in the Hebrew text and the English versions, is continuous with it.

Only when he is associated with Elisha is Elijah drawn into the context of prophetic communities (2 Kings 2): there is an audience of fifty prophets and Elijah is addressed by Elisha as "father," that is, perhaps, as leader of a prophetic community who is to be succeeded by Elisha. But it is Elisha's connections with prophetic communities, perhaps at Bethel, *Jericho, and Gilgal (2 Kings 2.1–4), which are more firmly established (2 Kings 4.1–7, 38–41, 42–44; 6.1–7); and although the anointing of Hazael of *Damascus and Jehu are attributed to both Elijah (1 Kings 19.15–18) and Elisha (2 Kings 8.7–9.13), it is Elisha's involvement in political intrigue which is more evident. He lends his prophetic authority to the coup d'état by which Jehu overthrows the house of Ahab, and to the bloodbath that disposes of Jehoram, Jezebel, all the members of the royal family, and all the practitioners of Jezebel's cult (2 Kings 9.14–10.14).

Nevertheless, Elisha is represented as having used his miraculous powers to assist a king of the house of Ahab (Jehoram) in his wars against *Moab (2 Kings 3.4–27) and Aram (2 Kings 6.8–7.19), and on his deathbed he teaches Jehoash, of the line of Jehu, how to work magic against Aram (2 Kings 13.14–19). There are unpleasant features about the portrayal of Elisha: his powers can be malevolent (for example, when he calls up bears to destroy some boys who had called him names; 2 Kings 2.23–25) or sensational (he brings an axe head that had sunk in the Jordan to the surface and makes it float; 2 Kings 6.1–7). This happens in the course of building extensions to a prophetic community, and other miracles have a similar context: a flask of oil is multiplied into a great supply (2 Kings 4.7); Elisha counteracts poison in a communal pot (2 Kings 4.38–41); he feeds a company of a hundred with twenty barley loaves and fresh ears of grain (2 Kings 4.42–44). It is in the setting of a family whose hospitality he has enjoyed that he puts an end to the sterility of the Shunammite woman and then restores her child to life after he dies in the harvest field (2 Kings 4.8–37; cf. 1 Kings 17.8–24).

Conclusion. The contents of 1 and 2 Kings are varied, and there are many topics that are not narrowly related to the law of the single sanctuary. This criterion influences the portrayal of Solomon, and it is influential in the view taken of Hezekiah and, above all, Josiah. The praise of Hezekiah is mixed with a criticism of his behavior during the visit to Jerusalem of Merodach-baladan, king of Babylon (2 Kings 20.12–19). Approval of other Judean kings is mingled with the criticism that they failed the acid test by not suppressing the high places: Asa

(1 Kings 15.11–15); Jehoshaphat (1 Kings 22.43–44); Amaziah (2 Kings 14.3–4); Azariah (2 Kings 15.3–4); Jotham (2 Kings 15.34–35). The final kings of Judah, with whom the disaster of exile is linked, are condemned: *Zedekiah did what was wrong in the eyes of the Lord as Jehoiakim had done. Jerusalem and Judah so angered the Lord that in the end he banished them from his sight (2 Kings 24.19–20).

See also Israel, History of; Judah, The Kingdom of; Kingship and Monarchy.

WILLIAM McKANE

Kingship and Monarchy. Ancient Near Eastern texts almost unanimously presuppose the institution of kingship as a social organizing principle. Kingship in Mesopotamia is "lowered from heaven" or is coeval with *creation. The Assyrian King List, for example, can hypothesize a time when kings "lived in tents," but not a time before kingship. The image of the "first man" as the "image of God" and as lord over creation (Gen. 1.26–28) is not unrelated: YHWH is often portrayed in Israelite literature and iconography in solar terms; just as the sun, the "major" astral body, "rules" over the sky (Gen. 1.16–18), just as YHWH rules over creation, so the relationship between humanity and the world is modeled as one of royal domination from the very outset.

Near Eastern myths, too, principally portray the order of divine organization as monarchic. *Egyptian, Greek, *Hittite, *Ugaritic, and Mesopotamian myths all recount tales of martial conflict whereby one of the gods emerges as their king. In most instances, the monarchic order is portrayed as an innovation, replacing an earlier paternal domination of children. Interestingly, in the cases of Mesopotamian and Greek myth, the new kingship is functionally elective: the pantheon appoint a king-elect from among their number, to lead them into battle; the appointee wins the battle; and, as a result, the appointee wins confirmation on the throne. The royal ideal is thus one of elective autocracy. In Babylonian myth, the winning of the throne is also the starting point for the creation of the cosmos, which is the foundation for the heavenly structure that serves as the high god's palace, the counterpart of his earthly temple.

Kings and other administrators in the ancient Near East regularly portray themselves, like the state gods, as champions of the weak and the oppressed. The king was the upholder of the social order—much like the divine king who resisted the threats and encroachments of *chaos. But fixing the social order, to judge from Mesopotamian law codes, involved attempting to fix prices and attempting to ensure the inviolability of property. It also involved occasional amnesties, and general release from debt. Ultimately, the king presented himself as the personification and defender of what was just, the supreme judicial authority.

Near Eastern kingship was overwhelmingly an urban phenomenon. Cities lent themselves to monarchic organization precisely because of the complexity of administration involved. Kings took responsibility for, and pride in, the fortification of towns: the *Gilgamesh Epic ends with a return to the subject of the mighty walls of Uruk, which were the hero's immortality. Kings thus enjoyed the right not to tax, but to direct corvée and conscription for the public good—for defense, conquest, and the construction of irrigation and navigation systems.

Claiming the right to govern by divine election, kings also relate their temple-building activities. The completion of a temple is modeled by them as a mundane repetition of the heavenly creation myth. The building of a temple also is taken as a sign of the gods' imprimatur on the builder's royal dynasty. Likewise, the New Year ritual in *Babylon, and, later, in *Assyria, combines a rehearsal of the creation myth with a renewal of the high god's temple: the king leads the high god in procession to reoccupy the temple, and at the same time renews his own kingship, after a ritual battle against *chaos. The king consistently presents himself as warrior, builder, creator, favorite, even adoptee of the gods.

Israelite conceptions of kingship reflect both continuity with, and departure from, earlier traditions. For one thing, earliest Israel was decidedly nonurban, consisting of small agricultural settlements principally in the central hill country, Transjordan, and the upper Galilee. It is impossible to identify any major urban center as Israelite before *David's conquest of *Jerusalem. Israelite monarchy, therefore, originated as a national monarchy, not as a city-state kingship. Correspondingly, Israel is the only ancient Near Eastern culture to have preserved written memories of a time before the evolution of kingship or to have constructed any account of a transition from what later tradition would construe as a theocracy to monarchic organization. (There were, however, periods when Assyrian kings presented themselves as stewards of the gods, rather than as kings, and early *Sumerian kings adopted the same recourse.)

In this connection, a number of Israelite texts express reservations about the institution of kingship—a sentiment elsewhere unparalleled. Offered a dynasty, for example, the premonarchic warrior *Gideon makes the paradigmatic reply, "I will not rule over you, and my son will not rule over you; YHWH will rule over you" (Judg. 8.24). Although the text proceeds to condemn Gideon for appropriating priestly status and constructing an *ephod (Judg. 8.24–27), similar sentiments recur in an account of the transition to monarchy (1 Sam. 8.4–20; 10.19; 12.12): the urge to enthrone a human king conflicts on this theory with the ideal of YHWH's kingship over Israel (and Hos. 13.10).

Scholars for the most part find two sources underlying the account of the origins of Israelite kingship in 1 Samuel 8–12, but differ about their precise delineation. Nevertheless, both sources seem to replicate the pattern for divine kingship: in one (1 Sam. 8; 10.17–27; 11; 12), *Saul is elected king with YHWH's approval, defeats *Ammon, and is confirmed as king; in the other (1 Sam. 9.1–10.16; 13–14), Saul is anointed king-designate, defeats the *Philistines, and is said to have "captured the kingship" (1 Sam. 14.47). There is a homology with YHWH's kingship over Israel, said to have originated in his election in order to bring Israel out of Egypt and into *Canaan, and confirmed at the completion of the *Exodus (Exod. 3.16–17; 6.7–8; 19–23); the same pattern already occurs in the Song of the Sea (Exod. 15; twelfth–eleventh century BCE), where YHWH's perpetual kingship and acquisition of a shrine (Exod. 15.18) is predicated on his defeat of Egypt and the establishment of Israel in Canaan.

Numerous psalms follow the same pattern, praising YHWH as the creator or as the victor in some cosmic or mundane martial conflict, in the context of the celebration of his kingship. Likewise, the book of *Judges describes the pattern of mundane leadership in terms of a leader's election by YHWH, defeat of a threat or oppressor, and assumption of administrative power (Judg. 2.11–19; 3.7–12.7). And the books of Samuel-Kings let the same myth inform their historiography: kings whose succession is irregular win battles or overcome obstacles and threats, before their accession formulary (that is, their historiographic confirmation on the throne) appears. The "myth of the Divine Warrior" regularly informs Israelite views of mundane, as well as divine, leadership.

Other Near Eastern conceptions of kingship are equally pervasive among the Israelites. The first Israelite kings eschewed temple-building, no doubt out of deference to their constituents' distributed and varied cultic traditions. David did bring a central icon, the *ark, to his capital. But *Solomon was the first to build a temple, and in the capital, which articulated claims of an eternal Davidic dynasty—as well as claims that Solomon, and the later Davidides, are sons of YHWH, entrants into the court of the divine king (see Son of God). Notably, the Israelite kingdom established by Jeroboam by secession from the kingship of Solomon's successor prescinded from establishing its cultic centers in the political capital. Yet the leader of the secession, Jeroboam, was moved to erect cultic establishments at Bethel and *Dan to establish himself, too, as a temple builder (see Golden Calf). His actions implied independence from *Judah yet disavowed any unchangeable divine election of his dynasty. When Omri's son, *Ahab, later erected a temple in *Samaria, his capital, the same dynamic was in effect. The revolutionary, *Jehu, destroyed the temple in the capital, ensuring a separation of capital and temple in the northern kingdom for the rest of its duration.

In the Israelite ideal, the king is one nominated (or anointed) by YHWH, by prophetic means, and adopted by the people—YHWH proposes and the people dispose. But the opportunity exists, in the aftermath of divine designation, for popular elements responsible for confirming the king to impose conditions on the king's sovereignty. The operation of this principle is evident in 1 Kings 12, where the Israelites propose to elect Rehoboam as their king, on the condition that he lower taxes. Rehoboam refuses; the people therefore reject him as king, and elect Jeroboam. Similarly, both David (2 Sam. 2.4–9; 5.1–3) and *Absalom (2 Sam. 15.1–12) campaign for election; David actually campaigns for reelection after Absalom's revolt (2 Sam. 19.10–44). Although elements of the royal establishment laid claim to a perpetual divine dynastic grant (Ps. 89), even the laws of Deuteronomy 17.14–20 acknowledge that kingship, given divine nomination of the candidate, was elective. In practice, this often meant that the king was made by army democracy—as in the cases of Solomon, Baasha, Omri, Jehu, Uzziah, and others.

The laws of Deuteronomy 17–18 also attempt to limit the king's latitude in forming policy. They limit priesthood to "*Levites," install Levitic priests as the supreme judiciary, and protect the institution of *prophecy. They further attempt to restrict the king's ability to accumulate wealth. Scholars concur that the Deuteronomic law code is late in origin. Still, the attempt to limit the ability to tax, the urge to restrict the king's right to disenfranchise priesthoods, the urge to protect *prophets (Deut. 18.18–22; 1 Kings 22.26–28; Jer. 26.16) all reflect traditional ideals and rural views of central governmental authority.

Notwithstanding popular resistance to royal encroachments on the economy in particular, Israelite kings enjoyed the power both to tax (1 Kings 4.7–19; 12; 2 Kings 15.20; 23.35) and to conscript for warfare (2 Sam. 20.4) and for public works (1 Kings 5.27–30; 11.28; cf. 9.22). Moreover, archaeological remains at important towns, such as *Megiddo and *Hazor, indicate that the kings projected their power into the countryside in the form of massive fortifications and impressive public buildings. To date, this phenomenon is less well represented in the Israelite heartland, the hill country. However, starting in the tenth century BCE, and accelerating in the eighth century, public buildings are constructed in proximity to the gate complexes of some urban centers, such as Tell Beit Mirsim, *Lachish, and Tell el-Farʿah (biblical Tirzah).

In the same period, increasing royal intervention in local economies is documented by the standardization of *weights, and probably, by indications of incipient industrialization, as at the site of Horvat Rosh Zayit, inland from Akko. And, at the end of the eighth century, *Hezekiah of Judah was able to concentrate the rural population of his kingdom in a set of fortresses.

There had always been some tension between the royal establishment and the kinship structures—the rural lineages—which were the seat of succession and conflict resolution before the monarchy and continued to function as such after the introduction of kingship. Early on, the state acknowledged an interest in restricting the feud (2 Sam. 14.11), one of the nonstate forms of conflict resolution in the society. But as the revolt of Absalom ended with the complete triumph of the professional royal army over the irregulars of the countryside, central control could be asserted over not only the succession but other aspects of statecraft as well. As early as the time of Solomon, a system of royal administrators was set in place for the purpose of extracting taxation and corvée (1 Kings 4.7–19; 11.28), bypassing traditional tribal forms of organization. It is likely that Jeroboam and the later kings of the northern kingdom undid this innovation; the Samaria ostraca furnish evidence of at least dabblings in a system of such administrators only in the eighth century (one group of ostraca reflects administration through the lineages at that time). However, even the lineage heads through whom some kings administered taxation would have been royal appointees in some sense, and certainly familiars of the establishment (see 2 Sam. 19.32–41).

It was only in the seventh century, after Hezekiah's emergency urbanization, that the monarchy achieved complete domination over the lineages. The urban geography of that era in Judah (Israel having been deported) reflects the resettlement of Judah, after its depopulation by Assyria in 701 BCE, by state orchestration. Gone are the extended-family compounds that characterize Israelite settlements until the late eighth century. Gone are the large, rambling settlements of that earlier era. Instead, the state, and the kingship, were able to stamp the ideals of the royal cult, the Jerusalem *Temple, onto the country as a whole, resulting in a policy, under *Josiah, of centralization of worship and of power. This development, and the disappearance of the monarchy in the restoration community (538 BCE), paved the way for the detachment of the monarchic ideology from its origins in relations with the agrarian hinterlands of the capital. In the Second Temple period, the idea of YHWH's anointed—the *messiah, notionally a son of YHWH—was transferred from the human king whose election was a matter of negotiation and limitation, to a future king, not wholly human, whose reign would usher in a regime of justice, of the defense of the oppressed, and of requital of the guilty. In the myth of a kingless postexilic Judah, the old, high ideals of Near Eastern kingship took renewed hold, without the brake of political realities to restrain the ambitions or the imaginings of their adherents.

See also Queen and Queen Mother.

BARUCH HALPERN

Kiss. Biblical occurrences of "kiss" can be classified into three groups. First, reference to the kiss as a romantic *gesture is found in the *Song of Solomon (1.2; 7.9; 8.1).

Second, the kiss appears most frequently as a sign of greeting, such as *Joseph kissing his brothers (Gen. 45.15), *Aaron kissing *Moses in the wilderness (Exodus 4.27), and the prodigal son being kissed by his father (Luke 15.20). Several New Testament letters conclude with an admonition to greet one another with a holy kiss (Rom. 16.16; 1 Cor. 16.20; 2 Cor. 13.12; 1 Thess. 5.26) or a kiss of love (1 Pet. 5.14). Kissing can also be part of a ritual. Examples include the *anointing of *Saul by *Samuel (1 Sam. 10.1) and the anointing of Jesus by the woman of Bethany (Luke 7.38).

Third, a kiss can also be a sign of dishonesty and treachery. *Jacob gives a kiss as part of his deception of *Isaac (Gen. 27.26–27), and Joab kisses Amasa while killing him (2 Sam. 20.9–10). Proverbs 27.6 advises that "profuse are the kisses of an enemy," and *Judas betrays Jesus with a kiss (Mark 14.45–46; Matt. 26.48–49; Luke 2.47–48).

DANIEL N. SCHOWALTER

Know. The biblical Hebrew verb most commonly translated "to know" is yādaʿ. Besides the neutral or secular sense of being aware of or acquainted with (Gen. 30.26; Num. 11.16; Deut. 2.7; Josh. 2.9; 1 Sam. 28.24; Job 42.11), the verb and its derivatives have a complex range of meanings.

Knowledge becomes a biblical topic as early as Genesis 2.9 with the tree of the knowledge of good and evil. The tree's name is probably a merismus, a literary device to describe the totality of something by naming the first and the last in its semantic spectrum (here, the full range of knowledge).

In Genesis 4.1, sexual knowledge comes from *Adam and *Eve's experience of the greatest possible intimacy, namely *sexual intercourse. The verb in this sense may have either a man or a woman as its subject (Gen. 4.1; 19.8; Num. 31.17; cf. Matt. 1.25), includes *homosexual intercourse (Gen 19.5), and can occasionally signify rape (of women and men: Gen. 19.5, 8; Judg. 19.22, 25).

The organ of knowledge is the heart (Jer. 24.7; Ps. 49.3), which suggests that knowledge is experiential and not merely speculative. One knows war (Judg. 3.2) or God's displeasure (Num. 14.34) by experiencing it. Yahweh's special relationship with *Moses is described as knowing Moses face to face (Deut. 34.10; cf. Exod. 33). While *Samuel certainly knows who Yahweh is, he does not know God until he experiences a *theophany (1 Sam. 3.7).

Yahweh wants to be known, reaching out to Israel by revelatory acts, most importantly delivering Israel from Egyptian slavery (Exod. 1–15) and by joining with Israel in the theophanic *covenant ceremony at *Sinai (Exod. 19; 24). In biblical terminology, the response to *revelation is knowledge; knowledge is akin to what elsewhere might be called *faith.

Beginning in the book of Exodus (see especially 6.1–7), the motif of knowing Yahweh becomes a dominant biblical theme, recurring especially in Deuteronomy, Hosea (who deliberately blurs the sexual and religious meanings of knowing to illustrate God's closeness to Israel), Isaiah, Jeremiah, and Ezekiel. Knowledge and knowing in this case have a technical connection to the language of covenant-making. Hosea 4.1–6 equates knowledge with keeping the covenant laws, the *Ten Commandments: Yahweh will reject those who reject knowledge. Isaiah 5.12–13 warns that *exile, a covenant curse (Lev. 26.33), is the consequence of lack of knowledge. In Jeremiah's famous "new covenant" oracle, Yahweh declares that the law will be written on all hearts and "all shall know me" (Jer. 31.31–34).

In the New Testament, the revealed Christ becomes the source of the knowledge of God, a theme developed most notably in the gospel of John (1.10; 14.7) and in Paul's letters (Eph. 3.4–6; Phil. 3.8–11).

See also Gnosticism.

MARY JOAN WINN LEITH

Koheleth. *See* Ecclesiastes, The Book of.

Koran. *See* Qur'ān and the Bible, The.

L

Lachish (Map 1:W5). Modern Tell ed-Duweir, one of the major fortified cities in Israel in the second and first millennia BCE. It has been the focus of several excavations, which have both illuminated and been illuminated by its frequent mention in written and pictorial sources. In biblical traditions, Lachish features prominently in accounts of the *conquest (Josh. 10), and as *Sennacherib's headquarters for his campaign against Judah in 701 BCE; its capture by the Assyrian king is depicted in detail in reliefs from *Nineveh.

Among the most significant discoveries at the site are the Lachish ostraca. In the excavations of J. L. Starcky in the mid 1930s, eighteen inscribed potsherds, apparently military dispatches, were discovered in the ashy debris of a room in the city's gate. They are dated to the final months of the kingdom of *Judah. Their servile tone—for example, "who is your servant but a dog" (cf 1 Sam. 24.15; 2 Sam. 9.8; 2 Kings 8.13)—shows that they were sent from an inferior to a superior, presumably the garrison commander. Letter 3 briefly reports on a mission to *Egypt and alludes to an unnamed prophet who delivered a letter of warning from a royal official. The most famous, Letter 4, ends in pathos: "We are looking for the signals of Lachish, according to all the indications my lord has given, because we do not see Azekah." This letter must have been written just after Jeremiah 34.1–5, an oracle of doom and comfort delivered by the prophet to King *Zedekiah "when the army of the king of Babylon was fighting against Jerusalem and against all the cities of Judah that were left, Lachish and Azekah; for these were the only fortified cities of Judah that remained" (Jer. 34.7). Soon, in 587/586 BCE, *Nebuchadrezzar would take *Jerusalem and raze the *Temple. The Lachish ostraca are valuable to paleographers, since they can be precisely dated, but their chief importance is as mementos of a tragic era in Israelite history.

WILLIAM H. PROPP

Lamb of God. Lambs, being common in the Near East, were one of the most usual sacrificial animals in ancient Israel. Twice per day a lamb was slaughtered in the *Temple (Exod. 29.38–42); a lamb could be offered as a sin offering (Lev. 4.32); each family annually slaughtered a paschal lamb for *Passover (Exod. 12). Thus, the lamb is often a biblical symbol of meekness, obedience, and the need for protection (Isa. 40.11; 53.7; 2 Sam. 12.1–6). In *apocalyptic language, though—probably as an expression of the final victory promised by God to the elect despite their weakness—the lamb is occasionally a conquering figure that is to overcome all the evil beasts that symbolize sin and revolt against God (Testament of Joseph 19.8; 1 Enoch 90.38). Some scholars think that *John the Baptist, as an apocalyptic preacher (Matt. 3.1–12 par.) who announced the one who was mightier than he, may have applied the title "the Lamb of God" to this mysterious person in that sense, whatever nuances later Christian interpretations may have added (John 1.29, 36). The apocalyptic writer of the book of *Revelation used the Greek word *arnion*, meaning lamb, twenty-eight times to describe the risen Christ as ruler of the world; although in the saying of John the Baptist another term (*amnos*) is used, the idea is the same. The lamb of Revelation, however, is also a slain lamb (Rev. 5.6, 9, 12), whose death has redeeming power.

The Fourth Evangelist, who adapted to his own purposes a number of traditions concerning John the Baptist, added an extensive commentary to his first mention of the phrase "the lamb of God" (John 1.29–34). In his view, the final words of v. 29, "who takes away the sin of the world," refer to the redemption brought about by Jesus' death; but they might originally have been part of the Baptist's saying, referring to the victory over evil by the apocalyptic "lamb of God" (see Rev. 17.14). Vv. 30–31 have an apologetic flavor: they try to account for the failure of the Baptist to identify Jesus as the apocalyptic lamb and suggest that he did so after the *baptism of Jesus. The designation of Jesus as lamb of God at the beginning of his ministry is balanced by the allusion to the Passover lamb at his death (John 19.33–37; see Exod. 12.46).

See also Sacrifice.   ETIENNE TROCMÉ

Lamentations of Jeremiah, The. The book of Lamentations, also commonly known as the Lamentations of Jeremiah, consists of five poems occasioned by the siege and fall of *Jerusalem in 587/586 BCE. Beginning with very early times, perhaps not long after the events (see Jer. 41.5; Zech. 7.3–5; 8.19), these laments have been used in Jewish, and later in Christian worship, as an expression of grief at the destruction of the city and also for more generalized sorrow, as in Christian liturgies of Good Friday, as well as an appeal for divine mercy. The book has attracted special interest among biblical scholars because of its relatively strict poetic form, all the chapters being alphabetic *acrostics or related in some way to the alphabet.

The title "Lamentations" of the English Bible comes from the *Vulgate's *threni* or Greek *thrēnoi,* translating a Hebrew title *qînôôt,* "laments." In Jewish tradition the book is most often called after its first word *'êkâ,* "How!"

Contents and Plan. The contents and plan of the book are difficult to summarize, since the form of the poems is dictated more by the alphabetic acrostics than by a narrative or logical sequence. In the first two poems, there is an alternation between the viewpoint of an observer of the calamity and the personified city itself. The third chapter, formally the most elaborate, also reaches heights of poignancy. The anonymous speaker is "one who has seen affliction"; through this persona the causes of the fall of the city are explored, and then the poem moves to a tentative expression of patient hope. Chap. 4 is mostly taken up with recollection of the horrors of the final days before the collapse of the city, and chap. 5 is a kind of liturgical close to the book, ending in an appeal to God for help.

Authorship and Date. One ancient tradition ascribes the book of Lamentations to the prophet *Jeremiah, and this has even affected the traditional depiction of Jeremiah in western art as the "weeping prophet." Another ancient tradition, however, is silent as to the authorship of the book, thus implying that the author was unknown, and this is also the commonly held modern critical opinion.

The *Septuagint, the ancient Greek translation of the Hebrew Bible, groups Lamentations with the book of Jeremiah, and prefaces the book with these words: ". . . Jeremiah sat weeping and composed this lament over Jerusalem and said . . ." Other ancient versions, as well as rabbinic sources, make the same ascription to the prophet. Although there is no explicit warrant for this in the Bible, there is a kind of basis for it in the comment in 2 Chronicles 35.25 that Jeremiah produced a "lament" or "laments" for King *Josiah.

In the Hebrew scriptures themselves, Lamentations is not placed with Jeremiah. It is always placed not among the Prophets but with the Writings, the third division of the Jewish *canon. Within this division its position varies, though it is usually placed somwehre with the five short books known as the five "scrolls" (*see* Megillot). This position is significant testimony to the original anonymity of Lamentations, for it is difficult to see why the book was separated from that of Jeremiah if from the beginning it was understood to have been composed by the prophet. In modern times, scholars have pointed out elements in Lamentations that seem so much at odds with the views and personality of the prophet Jeremiah that it becomes very difficult to think of him as their author. Lamentations 1.10 refers to the enemies' entry into the *Temple as a thing forbidden by God, whereas Jeremiah (7.14) had predicted it. Jeremiah foresaw the failure of foreign alliances (2.18; 37.5–10), but the author of Lamentations 4.17 shared with his people a frustrated longing for help from "a nation that could not save." Still further evidence of this sort may be pointed out, leading to the common opinion that the book's author—or authors, since the work is not strongly unified—is best regarded as unknown.

It is clear that Lamentations was written after the fall of Jerusalem in 587/586 BCE, but otherwise the date is uncertain. Since it expresses no clear hope for relief from conditions of bondage and humiliation, it probably dates to a time well before 538, when *Cyrus permitted the Jews to return from *exile. The book may have been written in Judah (rather than Babylon or Egypt), since it displays no interest in any other locale.

Acrostic Form. Chaps. 1 and 2 are made up of three-line stanzas, with the first line of the first stanza beginning with the first letter of the alphabet (*'ālep*), the second with the second (*bêt*), and so on through the twenty-two letters of the

Hebrew alphabet. Chap. 4 follows the same scheme, but with two-line stanzas. Chap. 3 is a tour de force, having three-line stanzas with each of the three lines beginning with the proper letter. Chap. 5 is not an acrostic, but has twenty-two lines, so the alphabet still to some extent determines the form.

The purpose of this alphabetic and acrostic form is unknown. It is unlikely to have been merely a mnemonic device, but no definite meaning or symbolism can confidently be attached to this formal feature, and it is safest to say that the author seems to have aimed at some aesthetic effect. In any case, the acrostics make it possible to be relatively sure where the lines of the poems begin and end, a situation unusual in Hebrew verse, which was ordinarily copied just like prose, without regard for lines of verse (*see* Poetry, Biblical Hebrew). With this foundation, scholars have found in most of Lamentations a special "lament meter," in which the second of two parallel lines is shorter than the first. Although the complete aptness of this designation may be questioned, Lamentations continues to occupy a prominent place in the study of ancient Hebrew metrics.

Lamentations and Sumerian Laments. The *Sumerians, authors of the world's oldest written literature, cultivated a genre of composition known today as "lament over the ruined city and temple." Laments over the ancient southern Mesopotamian cities *Ur, Sumer and Ur (together), Nippur, Eridu, and Uruk were composed in the early second millennium BCE and were copied in the scribal schools. These texts have survived in whole or in part, and most have been edited and translated. As a result, it is possible to trace parallels in conception and expression between this body of laments and the biblical book of Lamentations.

The subject matter in the two cases is very similar—a holy city is destroyed by the god of that city—and could be expected to produce similarities in diction quite apart from any literary contact, so that some scholars prefer to minimize the significance of parallels between the biblical book and Sumerian laments and their Akkadian descendants. Such a view likely underestimates the force of the evidence, and it is preferable to posit that Lamentations is a representative of an Israelite city-lament genre. This genre is reflected also in the prophetic books, and is related as a genre to the Mesopotamian works, though details of this process are only conjectural.   DELBERT R. HILLERS

Laodiceans, The Letter to the. A pseudonymous letter ascribed to *Paul, contained in some early Latin Bibles and mentioned by several ancient Christian authors. The community addressed was located in west-central Asia Minor, not far from Colossae (Map 14:E4). The letter to the Laodiceans is a patchwork of phrases from other letters of Paul, primarily Philippians, Galatians, and Colossians. The reason for forging the letter is puzzling, but may be connected to Colossians 4.16: "Read the letter from Laodicea" (see also Rev. 3.14–22). Though the only surviving manuscripts of the letter to the Laodiceans are in Latin, the letter must originally have been composed in Greek sometime in the second or third century CE.   PHILIP SELLEW

Last Supper. *See* Lord's Supper.

Latin. The language of imperial Rome and ancestor of the Romance languages. Because of its use by the *Roman army and civil administration, Latin had some currency in the eastern Mediterranean in the first century CE, in such provinces as *Syria and Judea. Latin inscriptions marked mileposts on roadways, and warned *gentiles against entry into the *Temple courts in *Jerusalem. Other inscriptions survive from military camps and buildings dedicated by Roman officials, such as the aqueduct and the temple for emperor worship at Caesarea Maritima. The charge for which Jesus was condemned was written on a plaque above his cross in Latin, *Greek, and *Hebrew (*Aramaic), according to John 19.20.

Several words of Latin origin are found in the Greek New Testament. Some had become familiar through the spread of Roman influence in the East, including words like *denarius*, found in Jesus' parables (Matt. 18.28; 20.2–13; *see* Money) and in his dispute over paying taxes to Caesar (Mark 12.15 par.). Despite the presences and influence of Roman institutions, some terms of Latin origin, such as *praetorium* in Philippians 1.13, or *census, centurion, legion,* and *speculator* in the gospel of Mark (12.14; 15.39–45; 5.9; 6.27) are though by some scholars to prove that those works were written in Rome.

Most Christians of the Mediterranean basin were Greek speakers at the start (Paul wrote to the Christians of Rome in Greek). Western Christians began to write in Latin only in the third century CE.   PHILIP SELLEW

Law. *This entry consists of two articles, the first on* Israelite Law *in its ancient Near Eastern context, and the second on* New Testament Views *of what came to be known as "the Law." For discussion of the influence of the Bible on later legal systems, see* Law and the Bible.

Israelite Law

Although laws and the concept of law played an overwhelmingly important role in the Hebrew Bible and in the life of ancient Israel, the Hebrew Bible has no term exactly equivalent to the English word "law." The Hebrew word most often translated as "law," *tôrâ* (*Torah), actually means teaching or instruction. As such it expresses the morally and socially didactic nature of God's demands on the Israelite people. The misleading translation of *tôrâ* as law entered Western thought through the Greek translation (*Septuagint) of the term as *nomos,* as in the name of the book of *Deuteronomy ("the second law"). That the word *tôrâ* is a loose concept is indicated by its use for the first five books of the Hebrew scriptures, which contain the bulk of ancient Israel's purely legal material, as well as for the Hebrew Bible as a whole. The vibrant nature of the legal tradition is indicated by the later Jewish distinction between the written Torah, namely the Hebrew Bible, and the oral Torah, the legal and religious traditions which were eventually codified in the *Mishnah (ca. 200 CE) and developed in the Gemara (ca. 500 CE; together they form the *Talmud) and later commentaries. The human intermediary between the people and their God in both cases is viewed as *Moses, through the revelation at *Sinai (Exod. 19–Num. 10) and later in a valedictory address in Transjordan before his death (Deuteronomy).

Among other terms employed in the Hebrew Bible that belong to the legal sphere and refer to specific practices and enactments are *ḥoq* "statute," *mišpāṭ* "ordinance," *miṣwâ* "commandment," and *dābār* "word."

Law in the Ancient Near East. Although it was once felt that biblical Israel's legal and moral traditions were unique in the ancient world, archaeological activity over the course of the last century has brought to light a large number of texts, mainly written in cuneiform script on clay tablets, which help to place biblical law in its ancient Near Eastern context. These include texts that have erroneously been termed "law codes," in addition to international treaties, royal edicts, and documents from the daily legal sphere.

The Babylonian Laws of *Hammurapi (eighteenth century BCE, copies of which have been found dating up to a millennium later) remain the most famous and comprehensive of the ancient legal collections, and include close to three hundred laws, in addition to a lengthy prologue and epilogue in which the divine mission of providing laws for the land is given to Hammurapi. Other important "codes" include: the Laws of Urnammu, a *Sumerian collection dating to ca. 2100 BCE; the Laws of Lipit-Ishtar, also in Sumerian, ca. 1900 BCE, the Laws of the city of Eshnunna, written in Akkadian and to be dated in the nineteenth century; the *Hittite Laws, which date in their original form to ca. 1600 BCE; and the Middle *Assyrian Laws from the reign of Tiglath-pileser I, ca. 1200 BCE.

These so-called law codes are not comprehensive codices in the Roman sense. They are rather miscellaneous collections of laws, compiled in order to enhance the stature of the ruler as the originator of order in his land. Although they preserve important evidence of individual stipulations and of the legal structure of a given society, these legal compilations are best viewed as literary texts. In spite of the ancient fame of a text such as the Babylonian Laws of Hammurapi, it is significant that among the thousands of legal documents known from ancient Mesopotamia not one refers to that collection for a precedent, nor to any other.

Ancient Near Eastern treaties, while important as historical, political, and legal sources, have also played a role in understanding the nature of Israel's *covenant with God as one of vassal with suzerain. Elements in treaties that have been found in the Hebrew Bible include the identification of the parties to the treaty, a historical prologue in which God's actions on behalf of Israel are listed, the treaty stipulations (i.e., the laws), and the *blessings and *curses to be expected as a consequence of obedience or of noncompliance to the terms of the covenant. Among the most important treaties are those of the Hittite empire of the second millennium BCE, to which many scholars look for the origin of the genre as a whole, and the neo-Assyrian vassal treaties, especially those of Esarhaddon (early seventh century BCE).

By far the largest number of ancient documents come from the daily practice of law. Tens of thousands of documents have been found recording economic and social transactions of all kinds, many of which can be compared to biblical practices. The closest biblical parallel to the actual practice of documenting transactions may be found in the account of Jeremiah's purchase of a plot of land in his home town of Anathoth, a transaction recorded in duplicate as were countless cuneiform documents (Jer. 32.9–15). Although most of the documents found were written on cuneiform tablets in Mesopotamia, documents written on papyrus and other perishable materials have been found in Egypt, for example at the site of the Jewish military colony at Elephantine, and in caves in the Judean desert, near the Dead Sea (*see* Writing in Antiquity).

Israel's Laws in Modern Research. In addition to the comparative study of Israel's legal traditions, which seeks to shed light upon Israel's laws in their ancient context through a comparision of similarities and differences with nonbiblical legal materials, two major trends can be identified in modern research on ancient Israel's legal traditions. The first is form-critical and concerns itself with the classification of Israel's laws according to form and syntax. The second attempts to identify the basic principles of Israel's legal tradition that set it apart from its surrounding cultures.

Basic for the study of the forms of Israelite law is the work of Albrecht Alt. In his essay on "The Origins of Israelite Law" (1934), Alt identified two basic patterns of legal formulations in the Bible. The first he termed "casuistic" law, since it arose from the sphere of case law. These are the laws formulated in the "if . . . then . . ." pattern. Alt sought the origin of these laws in Canaanite and general ancient Near Eastern traditions, which the Israelites took over after their "*conquest" of the land. The second he termed "apodictic" law. These are laws formulated as absolute pronouncements, such as the *Ten Commandments. They are mostly formed in the imperative: "You shall (not) . . ." Alt sought the origin of these formulations in Israel's ancient Yahwistic law, from Israel's preconquest traditions. While Alt's analysis of the origins of these two types of law has not withstood the test of time, since both casuistic and apodictic laws are to be found in most ancient Semitic legal collections in varying relative percentages, his basic form-critical distinction continues to serve as the starting point of contemporary discussion.

Once it could be shown that ancient Israel belonged to the cultural milieu of the world in which it lived, the question arose whether there was any aspect of Israelite law which could be identified as distinguishing it from its neighbors. Two considerations are basic to the discussion.

First is the issue of authority. Although in ancient Mesopotamia the king was guided by divine will in the establishment of (secular) justice, the source of law was the king himself. In the Bible, on the other hand, the source of law was conceived of as God. In distinction to other ancient Near Eastern practice, in Israel the king was not conceived of as the promulgator of law. Moses and others were simply intermediaries who transmitted God's rules to the people. Thus both secular and religious law were given divine origin. Obeying laws was hence both a legal and a religious requirement. Breaking a law was not simply a secular delict, but an infraction of the will of God, hence a sin. (*See* Kingship and Monarchy.)

The second is the valuation of human life, for which the case of the goring ox (Exod. 21.28–32) may serve as example. The case of an ox that injured or killed a human being appears in a number of ancient legal collections. There are differences between the various laws regarding the liability of the owner of the goring ox according to its prior behavior and to the status of the person gored. However, only in the biblical law, upon which similar medieval European legislation was based, is the ox itself subject to the death penalty for killing a human being, its flesh not to be eaten. Since the ox murdered a human being, it became taboo and hence not fit for human consumption, in spite of the fact that that inflicted a great financial loss on its owner. To give another example, in the code of Hammurapi the death penalty is adduced for theft. The killing of another human being did not necessarily warrant such severe punishment (depending on the relative societal status of the individuals involved). In the Bible, capital punishment is reserved for cultic offenses, which included *murder (see Exod. 21.12–14; Num. 35.29–34). Theft of property, as long it was not cultic or under the *ban (see the story of Achan in Josh. 7), was not punishable by death. Theft of another human being, however, was (Exod. 21.16). Thus it is postulated by Moshe Greenberg that, whereas the protection of property belonging to the upper echelons of society was of paramount concern in Babylonian law, in Israelite law the sanctity of the individual formed in the image of God was primary.

Major Collections of Biblical Laws. Among the many legal passages in the Bible are a number that have been identified as independent units by modern scholars. These include the *Ten Commandments (Decalogue; Exod. 20.2–17;

Deut. 5.6–21), the Book of the Covenant (Exod. 20.22 [or 21.1]–23.19), the Holiness Code (Lev. 17–26), and the Deuteronomic laws (Deut. 12–26). The Ten Commandments can be understood as the heart of Israel's convenantal relationship with God, since they include an identification of the suzerain, God's acts on behalf of Israel, and Israel's obligations to God formulated in apodictic style. Most of the obligations incumbent upon Israel in the Decalogue deal not with cultic issues, but with the relations between people in an orderly society. The Book of the Covenant, containing casuistic laws with many parallels in other ancient Near Eastern traditions, is assumed by many to be the oldest collection of laws in the Bible. The Holiness Code forms the oldest core of Priestly (*P) legislation and is so named on account of its concern with Israelite ritual *purity and *holiness. The Deuteronomic laws, although presented as a speech delivered by Moses in Transjordan before his death, are associated in modern scholarship with the cultic reforms of King *Josiah of Judah (640–609 BCE; see 2 Kings 22.1–23.30; 2 Chron. 34–35). The major concern of this corpus of religious legislation is with the centralization and purification of the cult and its sacrificial system in the *Temple in Jerusalem.   CARL S. EHRLICH

New Testament Views

The modern New Testament is a fourth-century anthology of mid- to late first-century documents, composed in Greek and reflecting the social and religious stresses of a new religious movement seeking to define and eventually to distinguish itself from Greek-speaking *synagogue communities. In such a charged and changing context, "the Law" (Grk. *nomos*) received widely divergent treatments, although its definition remains constant: the Law is God's revelation through *Moses to Israel.

Paul. The earliest and most problematic source is *Paul. Written to predominantly *gentile communities, his letters often address questions of *ethics and authority. On these occasions, Paul's statements concerning the Law can only be seen as unself-consciously positive. The Law is the key to decent community life and the standard for group behavior (Gal. 5.15; 1 Cor. 14.34). Gentiles "in Christ" should strive to fulfill it and keep its commandments (1 Cor. 7.19; Rom. 8.4, 13.8–10; Gal. 5.14, authorizing his instruction by appeal to Lev. 19.18; cf. his defense of his apostolic rights by quoting from "the law of Moses," Deut. 25.4, in 1 Cor. 9.8–9). One can—

and Paul did—obtain *righteousness under the Law (Phil. 3.6). *Faith in Christ, Paul says, upholds the Law (Rom. 3.31). In the largest sense, the redemption in Christ comes to gentiles in order to confirm God's promises to Israel's *ancestors as preserved in Genesis, the first of the five books of *Torah (Rom. 15.8–9; cf. 9.4–5).

Yet elsewhere Paul virtually equates the Law with sin, death, and the flesh—the worst aspects of the "old aeon" that, through Christ's death, *resurrection, and imminent *parousia, is about to be overcome (Rom. 6.14; 7.5–6). God gave the Law on account of transgression and in order to condemn: it is the "old dispensation," inglorious and incomplete, compared to the gospel of Christ (Gal. 3.16–21, 24–26; 4.10, 19–22; 5.21–31, a particularly tortured passage; 2 Cor. 3.12–15; Rom. 3.20; 4.15; 5.20; 10.4). How then can this same author possibly maintain that "the Law is holy, and the commandment is holy and just and good" (Rom. 7.12)?

Scholars have attempted to resolve this tension. Some, at one extreme, take Paul's negative statements as definitive of his (hence, *the*) gospel and his positive statements as the measure of an unthought-out sentimental attachment to his community of origin. Some at the other end maintain that Paul preached a two-covenant theology: Torah for Jews, Christ for gentiles. On this view, his only objection to the Law would be if Christian gentiles chose it, that is, opted as Christians for conversion to Judaism. But Paul's own statements—forceful, passionate, at times intemperate—defy a consistent interpretation. He himself seems aware of the tensions in his position. As Paul saw it, however, history would soon relieve him of the necessity to make sense of God's plan in electing Israel, giving the Torah, and then sending Christ. For Christ, Paul urged, was about to return, end history, and bring all under the dominion of God. This conviction, and not his statements on the Law, is the one consistent theme in all of Paul's letters, from first to last (1 Thess. 1.10; 4.13–17; Phil. 1.10; 2.16; 4.5; 1 Cor. 7.26, 29, 31; 15; Rom. 8; 9–11; 13.11–12; 16.20). It spared him having to work out a "theology" of the Law.

The Gospels. The evangelists, writing some 40–70 years after Jesus' death, turned a negative attitude toward the Law (or the Jewish understanding of it) into the touchstone of Christian identity. This tendency makes for considerable confusion when one tries to reconstruct the views of the historical *Jesus. Jesus of Nazareth, living and working in a predominantly Jewish environment, very likely had his own views on the correct interpretation of Torah, and these views may well have differed from those of his contemporaries. Argument about the Law between Jews was and is a timeless Jewish occupation: controversy implies inclusion. Transposed to a gentile context, however, argument can seem like repudiation.

Thus Mark's Jesus turns an unexceptional observation (people are morally defiled by what they do or say, not by what they eat, 7.15–23) into a repudiation of the Law regarding kosher food ("Thus he declared all foods clean"; v. 19). John's Jesus condemns his Jewish audience as sons of the lower cosmos and children of the devil (chap. 8): the Law, characterized throughout as that "of Moses" is, implicitly, not "of God," from whom comes grace, peace, and the Son (1.16; 7.19–24). In his *Sermon on the Mount, Matthew's Jesus presents his intensification of Torah ethics as if in contradistinction to Torah and Jewish tradition ("You have heard it said . . . but I say"; chap. 5). Luke, although retaining the theme of Jewish guilt for the death of Jesus both in his Gospel and in Acts, nonetheless wishes to present the new movement as continuous with a Jewish view of biblical revelation. Consequently he edits out or softens many of Mark's anti-Law statements. And all the Gospels, no matter how strong their individual polemic against Jews and Judaism (see Anti-Semitism), and hence the Law, still present a Jesus who worships at *synagogue on the *Sabbath, observes Temple sacrifice, pilgrimage holidays, and *Passover rituals, and whose followers, honoring the Sabbath, come to his tomb only on the Sunday after his death.

Later Traditions. Both within the New Testament and without, later traditions are similarly ambivalent. Negative statements tend to occur in those passages where these new communities seek to establish their identity vis-à-vis Jews and Judaism; positive statements emerge where Christians wish to distance themselves from their Greco-Roman environment. Christian ethics are in the latter case a judaizing of gentile populations according to the principles of Torah: shunning *idols, sorcery, astrology, hetero- and *homosexual *fornication; keeping litigation within the community; supporting the *poor, especially *widows; and so on—all themes found especially in Paul's Corinthian correspondence.

In the early decades of the second century, Christian dualists such as Marcion and Valentinus took the position that the God of the Jews, the God of the Law, was a second, lower, cosmic deity; God the father of Jesus, they held, thus had nothing directly to do with material creation and, thus, with the events and legislation given in scripture. Other Christians, committed to the unity of *creation and redemption, argued that the Law was of divine origin: only their particular group, however, knew how to interpret it correctly (that is, for the most part, allegorically: see esp. Justin Martyr, *Dialogue with Trypho,* and *see* Interpretation, History of, *article on* Early Christian Interpretation). The church's ambivalence toward the Law eventually determined the structure of the Christian *canon itself. Retaining the *Septuagint even as it repudiated Judaism, the church incorporated the Law into its "Old" Testament, while maintaining that it was superseded or perfected by the "New."

PAULA FREDRIKSEN

Law and the Bible. Municipal or national law is the set of rules that, within a state, orders its affairs and those of persons under its jurisdiction, and which, when necessary, is enforced by special organs of the state. There may be more than one municipal law in a state, as in the United Kingdom, which contains the Scottish, English, and Northern Irish legal systems, or in the United States, where each state has its own legal system in addition to the federal system. Other states, such as India, have special rules for special communities (e.g., for Christians). International law is the law between states and between states and other international entities.

Municipal law can be divided into the law that regulates the affairs of the state itself and that which deals with the rights and duties, privileges, and immunities of persons within it. This division is often described as one between public and private law, though these categories overlap.

The Bible has influenced all those systems of law that can be traced, sometimes tortuously, to western European sources. By and large, the legal systems of other societies have been less subject to its influence, though sometimes that influence was historically present, as with the Russian system, in which a traditional Christianity molded society in former centuries and is still to be discerned in such rules as those regarding contract.

There are two main groups within the broad European legal tradition. Civilian legal systems form one group. These owe much to the legacy of Roman Civil Law, particularly as that Law was rediscovered and developed by scholars from the twelfth to the sixteenth century. The Civil Law lays emphasis on rationality and principle, and for that reason the civilian tradition has been adopted by many states that have consciously chosen their law. The other group, roughly encompassing the Anglo-American tradition, stems in large part from the English Common Law, and like it has tended to concentrate more on remedies. This group has spread more by conquest and imposition than by conscious adoption. There is also a third group, that of the "mixed" legal systems, which draws from both main traditions. Scots Law and that of Louisiana are examples of these.

The remote history of any legal system is obscure, for much of our understanding of particular influences at specific times is conditional upon the accidental survival of documentation, and deductions therefrom. It is, however, undeniable that the influence of the Bible on the legal systems that trace themselves to a western European root is extensive, though nowadays often diffuse. Biblical principles form a part of the foundations, which, like all good foundations, are well buried. Indeed, many in the twentieth century would deny biblical influence on many legal principles, which in former years were held to be sufficiently justified by the Bible. Much depends upon a willingness to accept parallels as indicative of influence and not a simple coincidence of result. Jews or Christians interpret the evidence differently from those who proceed from rationalist, agnostic, or atheist presuppositions.

When the modern legal systems of the European family were being formed, three main bodies of law influenced their development, namely the indigenous law of the community, Roman law, and canon law. The Bible's influence was mediated through each of these.

Indigenous law was that obtaining within a community, refined in accordance with the expectation of the community as to what was right in a given situation. Naturally, such expectations had much to do with religious belief and presuppositions. In each legal system, therefore, there came to be a body of "common law" manifested and developed through the decisions of judges and the reasoning that supported those decisions. Since the early judges in most countries were in holy orders (though they were not usually canonists), the opportunity for biblical influence was great. Specific recourse to the Bible as authority was unusual, but the principles it contained exercised their influence. Within the English tradition, the common law came to be highly significant, and it is only in comparatively recent times that the legislature has come to be considered of greater authority than the common law in the sense that what Parliament legislates takes precedence over the common law. By contrast, in the American tradition, the Constitution operates as the brake upon the lawmaking power of the Congress or of state legislatures.

Throughout Europe, indigenous law was directly influenced by Roman law, particularly as enunciated in the *Corpus Juris Civilis* (529–545 CE), the product of scholars working under instructions from the Emperor Justinian. Naturally, the empire having become Christian, there was a desire on the part of these scholars to make the civil law congruent with church teachings. Biblical influences therefore were strong. From the twelfth century onward, scholars (known collectively as the Glossators) worked on the *Corpus*, expanding its precepts through commentary, with considerable effect on their contemporary municipal law.

The indigenous law was also influenced to a greater or lesser degree by the canon law, a major contribution of the church to civilization. The Roman Catholic church had extended its authority even as the Roman empire waned and disintegrated, and it was considered by many to be the only body that could continue a tradition of universal law. The sources of church law, however, were many and various, and it was only as the church organized itself on a monarchic principle under the papacy that the need for systematization was dealt with. The eleventh-century rediscovery of Roman Law in the form of the Justinianic legislation, and notably the *Digest* of 533 CE, provided a model that eventually resulted in the *Corpus Iuris Canonici,* though that was constantly augmented by interpretation and further legislation. Much of the canon law had to do with church organization, but large portions affected the daily life of the laity and influenced the development of national laws in various areas. The aim of the canonists was to make their system of law correspond as closely as possible to right Christian conduct, and to minimize the separation of law and morals. The Bible influenced their deliberations, though its principles were often mediated through the teachings of the Roman Catholic church.

One area of law affected by the canonists was the law of *marriage, an area important in every society and subject to church procedures. Another was the law of wills, where the church rules were much more simple than those of the civil law. Naturally the canonists, keen to keep law and morals together, were concerned with matters of intention and of good and bad faith. In contract, therefore, good faith was made a major requirement, and bargains were enforced through the church courts without the insistence upon the formalities for their constitution that had grown up previously (Matt. 5.34–37). (It has to be said, however, that this development took greater hold in the civilian tradition than in the Anglo-American, which has retained certain elements of formal requirements such as the notion of "consideration," and which does not recognize a unilateral contract unless entered into under appropriate ceremonial.) Again, the canonists' stress on responsibility for the consequences of one's actions helped root the concepts of tort.

In the area of crime, intention also came to be insisted upon as a prerequisite for criminality of conduct (see Matt. 5.28), thereby bringing crime into closer association with notions of *sin and allowing actions to be differently weighed in any consideration of "blame," and therefore also of punishment. (A modern extrapolation from such concepts is the Scottish defense to a criminal charge of "diminished responsibility," which stems from that root, and was only lately taken over into English law.) The emphasis on sin also produced a change in attitude to punishment. In more and more instances, prison as a place of *repentance was accorded a higher priority than vengeance exacted through physical unpleasantness. In criminal procedure, the notion of God as judge, weighing the evidence, came to be accepted as a model, and human judges were given a greater freedom in their conduct of trials than former formalities permitted.

Finally, like the theologians and philosophers, the canonists gave consideration to such social questions as the doctrine of the "just price" and the "just wage." Price fluctuations in response to market forces alone were considered contrary to notions of intrinsic value. Such matters and their attempted solutions are, of course, still with us, and still echo Exodus 20.9; 34.21; 1 Thessalonians 4.11; 2 Thessalonians 3.7, 10–12.

The Reformation produced an interest in principles taken directly from the Bible in contrast to those mediated through church tradition and canon law. In some instances, this interest produced formal legislation. To take examples from one "reformed" jurisdiction, in 1567 in the Scots law the "degrees of relationship" within which marriage could lawfully be contracted were set out in terms of Leviticus 20 and "the Law of God," and the "prohibited degrees of relationship" for the purpose of defining incest were set out specifically in terms of Leviticus 18—though inaccurately, since the Geneva version (1560) of the Bible was the source used. Again, marriage between divorced persons and their paramours was made unlawful (Matt. 5.32; 19.9; Mark 10.11–12), though this was soon administratively avoided, and *adultery was made a crime (Exod. 20.14; Lev. 20:10). *Divorce on the grounds of adultery (Matt. 1.18–19; 5.32; 19.9) or desertion (1 Cor. 7.15) was introduced. In 1563, *witchcraft was made a capital crime in terms of Exodus 22.18, and various Sunday observance statutes were passed (Exod. 20.10–11). In 1649, 1661, and 1695 *blasphemy was made a capital offence, though the full penalty was exacted only once.

The other major element that the Reformation took from the Bible was the concept of the priesthood of all believers (Exod. 19.6; Isa. 61.6; 1 Pet. 2.9; Rev. 1.6; 5.10; 20.6), which eventually filters down to the modern institutions of democratic government.

The law books of the sixteenth to eighteenth centuries, in which the roots of much modern law are laid, contain a considerable mixture of sources for the principles that they assert. The Bible is often quoted, as is the Roman law. However, appeal is also frequently made to a "natural law," containing principles that are treated as axiomatic. At first, such "law" was said by writers to be given by God, but in 1625, in the *Prolegomena* to his *De Iure belli ac pacis* ("The Law of War and Peace"), Hugo Grotius pointed out that the legal principles so identified would have a degree of validity even if there were no God. Reason would deduce such principles from a consideration of the nature of human beings and from their needs in society. Others acted on that observation, and drove a wedge between "natural law" and any religious source. This was not, however, a sudden or a complete change of emphasis. Blackstone's *Commentaries on the Laws of England* (1765), for example, discusses law as stemming from God (Intro. s.2), but makes little appeal to biblical texts. Stair's *Institutions of the Law of Scotland* (2d ed., 1693), written from a Presbyterian background, also links law to God, making a number of biblical citations in so doing (e.g. Book I, tit. 1, 2–9), but again the bulk of the work treats such matters as a base to be acknowledged and not as an active source of law. In that train, Puritanism influenced English and American law in the seventeenth and eighteenth centuries, but since then the deduction of legal principle from biblical or theological sources has been largely abandoned by lawyers. The principles remain, but their source is usually not acknowledged or is otherwise explained on bases of social, economic, or political necessity. In Europe, anticlericalism gave that trend further impetus.

In the twentieth century, major advances in securing biblical principles have been made in international law, particularly through the United Nations' Universal Declaration of Human Rights, and other international Human Rights Covenants and Conventions following in its wake. In some measure, these have provided a statement of fundamental principles for human conduct that draw on biblical ideas among their unacknowledged sources. They provide a base from which municipal law can be criticized, and even, under certain human rights treaties, a remedy and change be obtained.

Within the municipal law of most states of the European tradition, the law generally now proceeds upon unexamined assumptions. The biblical roots acknowledged in the early texts are taken for granted, and go unmentioned in modern discussions of matters such as tort, contract, marriage, divorce, wills, and the like, where the canonists did their job well in former centuries. In some areas, however, there has been a revival of appeal to biblical notions, often with explicit citation of biblical texts. Thus medical ethics, euthanasia, *abortion, and surrogacy are controverted legal matters. Curiously, it is in the United States, where the Constitution requires a separation of church and state, that most modern legislation and court action has had a clear biblical base. The debate on such matters as school prayer, abortion, and the teaching of science in schools (creationism verses evolution; *see* Science and the Bible) has had a considerable emphasis on biblical precept. In other states, the influence of the Bible and of Christianity is left as something inarticulate but nonetheless real. The principles are there, but only those who are willing to do so acknowledge their source. Legislators and judges act on them, but without reference to their origin. As noted, effective foundations are well buried.   Francis Lyall

Lawyer. Lawyer is a term used in the gospels of Matthew and Luke for a certain portion of the Jewish leadership portrayed as hostile to Jesus. There is not enough information to determine the role of these lawyers in first-century CE Roman Palestine. Doubtless they were literate officials in or around the corridors of power in the colonial setting of the Greek East (cf. Titus 3.13). The Greek term for lawyer *(nomikos)* is found only once in Matthew (22.35), and even there it is textually uncertain. Luke seems to have replaced other stereotyped members of the opposition to Jesus, such as the *Sadducees, with the lawyers. Alongside the *Pharisees in Luke, the reader can depend on a *nomikos* to ask a question that provokes Jesus' instruction or condemnation or a *parable illustrating the nature of the *kingdom of God.   J. Andrew Overman

Laying on of Hands. The laying on of hands was a ceremonial act that conferred a special favor or function on the person for whom it was performed.

In the Hebrew Bible the ceremony often conveyed a personal blessing or function. Israel (*Jacob), with his hands crossed on their heads, blessed *Ephraim and *Manasseh (Gen. 48.14–16). Several ideas are related to this. *Aaron's outstretched hands conveyed a blessing on the people (Lev. 9.22), and the psalmist was enraptured after he felt God's hand laid on him (Ps. 139.4–6).

Sometimes the ceremony conveyed the transfer of authority from one person to another (Deut. 34.9). Witnesses laid their hands on criminals to testify against them before judgment for crime (Lev. 24.13–14; Sus. 34–40).

In sacrificial worship either officials in the *Temple or the sacrificers themselves laid their hands on the animals before they were slaughtered (Exod. 29.10; Lev. 1.1–4). The basic idea was that of dedicating the victim to God to obtain the forgiveness of sins. With the scapegoat the ceremony signified the transfer of sins from the sacrificers to the victims (Lev. 16.20–22; *see* Azazel).

In the New Testament the laying on of hands served some of the same functions. Laying his hands on them, Jesus blessed the children (Mark 10.16; cf. Gen. 48.14–16), and while lifting up his hands he blessed the *disciples (Luke 24.50; cf. Lev. 9.22).

The ceremony occurs most frequently in stories of healing, both by Jesus (Matt. 9.18; Mark

5.23; 6.5; 8.22–25; Luke 4.40; 13.13) and his followers (Acts 28.8; cf. 9.10–17), reflecting the belief that through the ritual act of a person with divine favor healing power passes to a sick person. (*See also* Medicine.)

According to Acts 8.14–19; 19.6, the ceremony was understood as supplementing *baptism by the giving of the Holy Spirit. The act also conveyed authority to persons who already had the Holy Spirit: the *seven (Acts 6.3–6) and *Barnabas and Saul (*Paul; Acts 13.2–3; cf. Rev. 1.17).

The ceremony became more formal (Heb. 6.2), and officials used it to impart spiritual gifts (1 Tim. 4.14; 2 Tim. 1.6), or, perhaps, as a reconciliation of sinners who no longer were in the church but who wanted to return (1 Tim. 5.22). It is still used in ecclesiastical ceremonies such as ordination and the sacrament of confirmation.   EDWIN D. FREED

Leah. Leah, whose name means "cow," was one of the matriarchs of Israel (see Ruth 4.11). She is said to have been buried in the cave at Machpelah (Gen. 49.31). Leah, with "weak" or "delicate" eyes, is contrasted with her younger sister *Rachel, who is "graceful and beautiful" (Gen. 29.16–17). Because of their father Laban's wedding night deception, *Jacob marries both sisters (29.18–30), but loves Rachel more than Leah (see also 33.1–2). Yahweh takes pity on Leah because she is unloved and gives her many children: *Reuben, *Simeon, *Levi, *Judah (29.31–35); *Issachar, *Zebulun, and *Dinah (30.14–21; see also the lists in 35.23; 46.8–15), as well as *Gad and *Asher, the children her maid Zilpah bears to Jacob (30.9–13; 35.26; 46.16–18). Although Leah was the first wife and had several sons, she apparently did not have automatic marital rights, since in one case she is said to bargain with Rachel for Jacob's time by giving Rachel mandrakes to promote conception (30.14–16).
                                   JO ANN HACKETT

Leaven. The translation of two Hebrew terms used in reference to the fermenting of bread dough. One word (*śĕʾōr*) designates the leavening agent, a piece of old dough set aside to ferment. This produces sourdough, which itself is inedible. The other, more frequently used word (*ḥāmēṣ*), designates the mixture of flour and water to which a piece of the old or fermented dough is added to facilitate rising.

Leaven in the Bible is most prominent in texts dealing with the annual springtime *Passover (*pesaḥ*) celebration, which incorporated an ancient and originally separate agricultural festival, the Feast of Unleavened Bread (Exod. 12.15–20; 13.6–7; 23.15; 34.18; Lev. 23.5). During this seven-day feast, a flat unleavened bread called *maṣṣâ* was to be eaten instead of leavened bread. The Pentateuchal texts historicize this practice by relating it to the *Exodus event, when the haste of the Israelites' departure precluded sufficient time for bread dough to rise.

The Passover ban on leaven can be understood in relation to other biblical rituals forbidding the use of leaven. As a rule, *sacrifices containing leaven were never to be offered (Exod. 23.18; Lev. 2.11; 6.9–10). The only exceptions were offerings meant for the offerer and priest, hence they were not offered to God (Lev. 7.13; 23.17–20). The ban on leaven in sacrifices in general and on *maṣṣâ* in particular is probably related to the association of leavening with decomposition and putrefaction. Sourdough is clearly unsavory, despite its useful role in bread preparation. Leaven may thus have come to symbolize corruption, and thus an element to be consciously omitted from a feast involving spiritual rejuvenation and also from sacrifices involving communion with God. The Hebrew Bible does not make such a notion explicit, but early Jewish sources and the New Testament (e.g., 1 Cor. 5.8) assume that leaven represents evil.

See Feasts and Festivals.   CAROL L. MEYERS

Lebanon. A range of coastal mountains with elevations up to 3,000 m (10,000 ft) stretching northward from Sidon to near Homs, Syria (Map 6:G4). The name means "white," referring probably to its snowcapped peaks in winter (Jer. 18.14). Lebanon already appears as a place name in the mid-third-millennium BCE *Ebla texts. In the Bible, Lebanon denotes both the mountains and the country around them, although it is distinct from the *Phoenician cities in the neighboring coastal plain (Josh. 13.5–6). The Lebanon and Anti-lebanon mountains (a parallel range on the east) enclose the Biqaʿ valley (the "Valley of Lebanon," Josh. 11.17; 12.7). Mount *Hermon, the highest peak in the southern Antilebanon chain, stands at the headwaters of the Jordan River. The Bible mentions Lebanon chiefly as a source of timber for large buildings. *Solomon's palace and *Temple were built with Lebanon cedar (1 Kings 4.33; 7.2; 10.17, 21). The

Egyptians and Assyrians also knew Lebanon for its cedar and cypress.　　　JOSEPH A. GREENE

Lectionaries. *This entry consists of two articles on readings from the Bible in liturgical contexts, the first in* Jewish Tradition, *and the second in* Christian Tradition.

Jewish Tradition

Though it has no lectionary in the formal sense, Jewish liturgy draws extensively on the Hebrew Bible with readings, direct quotations, and textual references to explain the significance of portions of the service.

One of the oldest uses of the biblical text within the liturgy is Deuteronomy 6.4–9, the *Shema. These verses express the essential Jewish belief in a single God and provide a course of action for demonstrating this belief. This paragraph is followed in the traditional prayer service (omitted in Reform Judaism) by two other biblical passages, Deuteronomy 11.13–21 and Numbers 15.37–41, that state the consequences both of following God and of disobeying him. The Shema is the focus of the first part of the service.

Similar to the Christian lectionary is the annual Jewish cycle of *Torah readings. The Torah is a handwritten scroll containing the *Pentateuch. The fifty-four pentateuchal readings progress weekly, with successive portions of the Pentateuch, some weeks having double readings. Special Sabbaths and holy days have their own Torah readings, conveying the meaning of the holy day and replacing the weekly reading. For example, the reading for the holiday of Shavuʿot (*Pentecost) is Exodus 19–20, which includes the *Ten Commandments. This reading emphasizes the meaning of Shavuʿot as celebrating the acceptance of the Torah by the people of Israel. The Torah is traditionally read on Monday, Thursday, and Sabbath mornings. On Sabbath afternoon, the reading for the following week is begun.

On the Sabbath and holy days there is an additional reading from the Prophets called the Haftarah. Each Torah reading has a designated Haftarah that is meant to parallel and illuminate the message of the Torah reading. Thus, the Torah portion mentioning the building of the *tabernacle in the wilderness is accompanied by a Haftarah about the building of the *Temple in Jerusalem. Holy days have special Haftarah readings.

The Torah reading, central to the Jewish service, is accompanied by Devar Torah ("word of Torah"), a sermon drawing upon the weekly portion in order to teach a lesson for daily life. The portion is also used as a focus for study during the week.

Five other biblical books, collectively known as *megillot ("scrolls") are read in full during the year. The scroll of *Esther is read on the festival of Purim, commemorating the salvation of Persian Jewry. *Song of Songs is read on *Passover. In ancient Israel, Passover took place at the early spring harvest, alluded to in Song of Songs. This book is understood as an allegory of God's relationship with the Jewish people, a relationship that began with the *Exodus celebrated on Passover. The book of *Ruth is read on Shavuʿot (Pentecost), a holiday that celebrated the late spring harvest, mentioned in Ruth. In addition, it is the holiday of accepting the Torah, and Ruth in Jewish tradition is an exemplary model of a convert who accepts God's teachings. The book of *Lamentations is read on Tishʿah BeʾAv (the ninth of Ab), the day commemorating the destruction of the First and Second Temples in Jerusalem. *Ecclesiastes is read on the holiday of Sukkot (Booths), because the holiday takes place in the fall and Ecclesiastes is written in the autumn of the preacher's life.

The service surrounding the actual reading from the Torah draws on numerous biblical verses. The introductory part of the service on Sabbath and holidays strings together verses thematically emphasizing God's eternal rule and his relationship with the people of Israel (Pss. 86.8; 145.13; 10.16; 93.1; Exod. 15.18; Pss. 29.11; 51.20 [18]). This is followed by a series of verses tied to the idea of bringing out God's teaching. Numbers 10.35 is chanted in imitation of *Moses' action when the *ark traveled. Then Isaiah 2.3 is chanted, describing the Torah as being the word of God emanating from *Zion. This is followed by the Shema (Deut. 6.4), emphasizing God's unity; Psalm 34.4 (3), a call to exalt God's name; and Psalm 99.5, 9, in response to the call. After the Torah reading, Deuteronomy 4.44 and Numbers 9.23 are sung in confirmation that the Torah was given to the people of Israel by God through Moses. As the scroll is returned to its ark, the liturgy mirrors the beginning of the service with a call to exalt God's name (Ps. 148.13–14) followed by a song of exaltation (Ps. 29: Sabbath; Ps. 24: other occasions). When the scroll is placed back in the ark, there is another selection of verses strung together thematically referring to the ark being brought to rest. This selection emphasizes the centrality of the Torah to the relation between God and Israel, reaffirming the Torah as the "tree of life" (Num. 10.36; Ps. 132.8–10; Prov. 4.2; 3.18; 3.17; Lam. 5.21).

Within the central part of the service called the Amidah (standing prayer), Isaiah 6.3, Ezekiel 3.12, and Psalms 146.10 are the focal point in the Kedushah ("sanctification"). The priestly blessing (Num. 6.24–6) appears on special occasions. Numerous other verses are interpolated into the prayers as well.

Psalms are also widely used in Jewish liturgy. There is a psalm for each day of the week, a psalm for the Sabbath day (Ps. 92), a series of psalms recited Friday evening to represent the weekdays (Pss. 95–99), psalms recited in the introductory service on the Sabbath morning (Pss. 145–150). There is also a special addition to the service on holy days called the Hallel ("praise"), consisting of Psalms 113–118. While all the psalms give word to the individual's desire to praise God, those appearing in the introductory portions of the service help prepare the individual spiritually for the service.

Often the influence of the Bible on liturgy is interpretive. The public reading of the Torah is said to be based on Exodus 24.3 and Deuteronomy 5.1 and 31.11–12, all examples of Moses reciting commandments or laws to the people of Israel. The action and wording of the call to prayer at the beginning of the service is based on Nehemiah 9.5. The essential portion of the prayer service is recited standing, attributed to Phinehas's action in Psalm 106.30, the interpretation being that the act of standing will be counted in one's favor. The prayers of supplication in the daily service are based on Daniel 9.3–19; Ezra 9.6–15; and Nehemiah 1.4–11. The inclusion of a prayer for the welfare of the government in the Sabbath service is derived from Jeremiah 29.7, where the exiles are told to seek the welfare of the country in which they reside. Even relatively late additions to the prayer book use biblical verses as their foundation.

MICHAL SHEKEL

Christian Tradition

A lectionary is a set selection of passages from the Bible to be read aloud in public worship over a fixed period of time. The designation may refer to a book in which is actually printed each assigned reading or simply to a list of chapters and verses that are then read from a Bible.

Sometimes the specific pericopes (selected passages) for the lay reader, deacon/priest, and cantor are printed in separate books (the Lectionary, the Book of Gospels, and the Gradual, respectively). A community may employ multiple lectionaries, with different sets of readings for Sunday, for weekdays, for celebrations of the Eucharist, and for Services of the Word. Not all Christian communities follow a formal lectionary.

The practice of reading scripture when Christians gather for worship can be traced back very early, and is related to some extent to the Jewish practice of continuous Torah reading in the synagogue (see previous article in this entry on Jewish Tradition). Already in the second century CE, Justin Martyr described how "the memoirs of the apostles and the writings of the prophets are read for as long as possible" (Apol. 67). The pilgrim Egeria, in recounting her visit to Jerusalem in the fourth century, noted that in the church there the biblical readings were chosen so as to be appropriate for the feast or the place. Various early tables of readings are attested from both the Eastern and Western churches and exhibit great diversity in both the number and selection of readings according to language, region, and liturgical rite. In Augustine's church of the fifth century, for instance, the bishop exercised some freedom of choice, but the readings for the major feasts were basically already fixed. More complete lists have survived from the eighth century, most notably the Comes of Wurzburg, the Liber Commicus of Spain, and the Lectionary of Luxeuil from Gaul.

After the Reformation, distinctive lectionary traditions developed in the Lutheran and Anglican communities, while most of the "Free Churches" abandoned the imposition of a lectionary. The Greek churches have largely maintained the Byzantine lectionary of the eighth century. The Roman church of the West retained the Missal of Pope Paul V from 1570, with a one-year cycle of New Testament readings.

In subsequent centuries relatively little attention was paid to the lectionary until the Second Vatican Council of the Roman Catholic church called for a major reform of the entire lectionary, with the intent that "the treasures of the Bible are to be opened up more lavishly" (Constitution on the Sacred Liturgy 51). A complete revision for Sundays, weekdays, feasts, sacraments, and other rites was completed in 1969 and prepared for worldwide use in 1971; some slight revisions and a more extensive introduction were published in 1981. Various Protestant churches, particularly in North America, quickly adopted this lectionary, usually with minor changes (especially in the structure of the liturgical year and substitutions for the apocryphal/deuterocanonical books). The most important of these adaptations of the Roman lectionary is the *Common Lectionary* of 1983 and the *Revised Common Lectionary* of 1992, prepared by the Consultation on Common Texts, an ecumenical forum of Christian churches in North America. In addition, numerous other lectionaries, independent of the Roman lectionary, have been developed in the last decades, often on a regional or denominational basis; one of the most widely used is the two-year thematic-type lectionary proposed by the Joint Working Group in Britain in 1967, revised to a four-year cycle in 1990.

Certain fundamental principles guide modern lectionary planning and revision: a desire to read extensively and widely from the Bible in public worship; assignment of the more important biblical passages to Sundays and solemnities; maintenance of certain pericopes that historically have been long associated with major feasts; and a doxological, Christocentric orientation that reflects the doxological nature of liturgy rather than an academic or didactic orientation. In the Roman lectionary and its adaptations, these principles find expression in the Sunday lectionary in the development of a three-year cycle, with one gospel read in a semicontinuous fashion over each year and the gospel of John used to supplement Mark and for much of the Lenten and Easter season. A second New Testament reading from the Epistles is also semicontinuous. The Roman lectionary has a first reading, chosen from the Old Testament (except during the Easter season when it is from Acts) on the basis of a thematic connection with the Gospel; the *Revised Common Lectionary* now offers an alternative system of semicontinuous reading of Old Testament narratives for the Sundays after Pentecost. In addition, a psalm is provided for each Sunday as a congregational response between the first and second reading. The weekday lectionary is based on a two-year cycle of two semicontinuous pericopes, except for the Advent–Christmas and Lent–Easter cycle, where the readings fit the liturgical season.

Ongoing discussion and critique have focused on the fundamental nature of a lectionary as such and on the specific choices of a certain lectionary. A lectionary implies an inherent element of selectivity; it always excludes as well as includes, and to that extent it establishes its own canon of texts that form the basis for popular knowledge, preaching, and even catechetical instruction. The most problematic issues raised about specific lectionaries are questions concerning the presence or absence of biblical passages about women; the use or nonuse of passages that speak negatively about the Jews (*see* Anti-Semitism); problems in the *typological use of the Old Testament; and the difficulty of preaching on the basis of two or three virtually independent readings. Yet for many Christians the revised Roman lectionary is recognized as one of the major achievements of the Second Vatican Council. Its adoption and adaptation by many Protestant churches, even those that traditionally had not used a lectionary, has brought an unforeseen degree of ecumenical convergence in the scriptures that are read each Sunday throughout a large portion of the Christian church.

EILEEN SCHULLER

Leprosy. The biblical disorder called "leprosy" is different from the disease known as "leprosy" in the twentieth century. The latter, called Hansen's disease (*bacillus mycobacterium leprae*), is a serious skin disease that develops over a long period of time and until 1968 was believed to be uncontrollable and incurable. Many victims of the biblical affliction (Hebr. *ṣāraʿat;* LXX *lepra,* probably vitiligo), on the other hand, were reportedly healed. Not only human beings, but objects, such as houses and garments (Lev. 13.47; 14.34), were judged "leprous." A leprous house or garment was probably covered with mildew or mold, whereas the human leper had some kind of skin disorder. Although mildew and mold are not like a skin infection, both conditions are characterized by a change in color, and both were under the jurisdiction of the *priest. After the priest determined that the person or object was healed, he offered *sacrifices following a similar liturgy for both (Lev. 14.3–32, 48–53). Some kinds of leprosy occurred when there were white spots on dark skin, and the hair in the spots was also white (Lev. 13.2–3). Swelling was another symptom. Some types of leprosy involved scales or infection, like boils or pimples.

Those who had been diagnosed as lepers by the priest were required to separate themselves from the community. This was not for medical but religious reasons. Biblical lepers were treated not as ill but as ritually unclean. The priest had no technique for healing lepers; he only determined whether or not they had been healed ("cleansed"). When he considered the affliction healed, he then offered the correct sin and guilt offerings so that the former leper might be atoned for this impurity.

Lepers had two colors of skin, which was taboo, as was plowing with two kinds of beasts, raising two kinds of grain in one field, weaving two kinds of thread into one piece of cloth, or cross-breeding two kinds of cattle (Lev. 19.19; Deut. 22.10). Those covered completely with the disease, so that they had only one color of skin, were allowed to return to the community, because they were no longer lepers (Lev. 13.12–13). Once they began to heal, however, they were classified as lepers and were isolated again.

Biblical characters, such as *Moses (Exod. 4.6–7), *Miriam (Num. 12.9–15), and Naaman (2 Kings 5.14) were all healed of leprosy. Jesus reportedly healed lepers (Matt. 8.1–4; Luke 17.17–19), and he commissioned the *twelve to do the same (Matt. 10.8).

See also Purity, Ritual.

GEORGE WESLEY BUCHANAN

Letter-writing in Antiquity. Letter-writing arose in antiquity to serve official purposes. There were three broad types of official correspondence: royal or diplomatic letters, military orders and reports, and administrative correspondence used in managing internal affairs. Most letters embedded in the Hebrew Bible, along with several other nonbiblical Israelite and Jewish letters, are official in nature. *Solomon's correspondence with King Hiram of Tyre, for example, is diplomatic (1 Kings 5.2–6, 8–9; see also 1 Kings 21.8–10; 2 Kings 10.1–6). The *Lachish letters, written when Judah was under siege by *Babylonia, are military communiqués. We may add to these the letter from the Jewish military settlement in Egypt at Elephantine, which was sent to the Persian governor of Judah, requesting his intervention against attacks on a Jewish temple.

Originally, messages were oral, carried by trusted couriers. With the passage of time, the principal message of the letter was delivered in written form, but the letter's sender continued to be identified orally by the messenger with the phrase, "Thus says . . ." (e.g., Ezra 1.1–2). A written message provided confirmation of the letter's authenticity, especially when signed with the sender's seal (1 Kings 21.8–10; Esther 8.10). The written message carried by Uriah from King

*David to the military commander Joab was clearly closed, because it commanded Uriah's own death (2 Sam. 11.14–15).

Though professional couriers were used by ancient states from the beginning of recorded history, the first organized postal system was not established until the sixth century BCE, when the Persian king *Cyrus set up a network of highways and relay stations. This postal system served as a model for *Alexander the Great and his successors, as well as for the *Roman empire.

Even when the entirety of the letter was written, the messenger often continued to play a supplemental role. This was certainly the case with *Paul, who usually employed trusted coworkers as couriers and who expected messengers to represent him to his correspondents (1 Cor. 4.17; 16.10–11; 2 Cor. 7.6–16; 8.16–18, 23–24; 12.18).

Various materials were used for written messages. Correspondence in Mesopotamia was written on clay tablets in cuneiform script by means of a reed with a wedge-shaped tip. It was common in a number of places to write with a brush or reed pen on potsherds (ostraca). *Parchment and vellum (skins) were used for more important correspondence. Papyrus was the most widely used material during the Persian and Greco-Roman periods. When Hellenistic rulers proclaimed benefactions and edicts worthy of permanent record, they were inscribed on stone after delivery. (*See* Books; Writing in Antiquity.)

Gradually, the letter was adapted to serve personal and nonofficial purposes. We know from archaeological discoveries that, at least in Greco-Roman Egypt, all levels of society sent letters. Although many were written by scribes, literacy was not as rare as was formerly believed. Nonetheless, ancient postal systems existed to serve only state business, not private correspondence. Whereas wealthy families and business firms could use employees or servants to carry their mail, ordinary people depended on those traveling on business (e.g., by ship or caravan) or on friends and passing strangers.

Greek and Roman rhetoricians regarded the cultivated letter of friendship as the most authentic form of correspondence. The letter was conceived as a substitute for the sender's actual presence. Since the recipient, however, could not ask for immediate clarification on epistolary subjects, it was recognized that the letter had to be more articulate than face-to-face talk. Despite the more studied style of letter-writing relative to conversation, theorists warned that the discussion of technical subjects was not appropriate in a letter. Nonetheless, the democratization of knowledge in late antiquity, along with the dialogic character of popular philosophy at the time, made it almost inevitable that much philosophical and religious instruction would be communicated in epistolary form.

While none of the books of the Hebrew Bible takes the form of a letter, twenty-one of the twenty-seven New Testament books are letters (also known as "epistles"). This difference stems in part from the fact that New Testament letters were written by Greek-speaking Jewish Christians who were influenced by the Hellenistic practice of writing instruction in the form of letters. Moreover, letters were often used by Christian leaders, such as Paul, to maintain contact with widely separated congregations.

The New Testament letters and patristic letters of the first three centuries CE are much longer than most pieces of ancient Greek correspondence. This length corresponds directly to their purpose as letters of instruction. In this respect, Christian letters are more like philosophical letters of instruction than like ordinary letters. On the other hand, the hortatory rhetoric used in Christian letters differs significantly from that in literary letters. For example, the emphasis on the whole community's spiritual maturation brought about by Christ's return, rather than on building one's individual character, shows that Christian letters were written by a specific religious subgroup with an *apocalyptic Jewish coloring. Their special character is evident in the way traditional Jewish materials are cited within the letter (doxologies, benedictions, hymns), as well as in the tone of familiarity and equality that frequently described Christian recipients and their senders as family members. Later, in the fourth and fifth centuries CE, letters from Christian leaders conformed much more to Greek literary models of letters. JOHN L. WHITE

Levi. Son of *Jacob and *Leah, and one of the twelve *tribes of Israel. Leah associates Levi with the verb "to join" (Gen. 29.34). Aside from his involvement with *Simeon in the attack against *Shechem (Gen. 34.25–26), Levi is best known for the sacerdotal functions of his descendants. The *Levites play a prominent role in assisting Moses quell the *golden calf rebellion (Exod. 32.25–29). Whatever Aaron's ancestry, his sons, and not Levi's, dominate the Jerusalem cult from the time of *Solomon (1 Kings 2.26–27) until

the overthrow of Onias III by the Seleucids in 174 BCE.

Biblical sources depict the Levites as porters, carrying the *ark (1 Sam. 6.15; 1 Kings 8.4) and the *tabernacle (Num. 1.47–54). Given no inheritance of their own (Num. 18.23–24; Deut. 12.12–19; 14.28–29), the Levites were to reside in forty-eight designated cities (Num 35.1–8; Josh. 21.1–8). Israelites were to support the Levites through tithes and offerings (Deut. 18.1–4).

Scholars disagree whether Levi was originally a secular tribe (Gen. 49.5–7) or whether the Levites were supposed to have secondary status. *P prescribes a rigid division of duties for the descendants of Levi's sons, Gershon, Kohath, and Merari (Num. 4.1–33). Barred as *priests, the Levites function under Aaronid supervision (Num. 3.10). Similarly, Ezekiel denounces the Levites and confirms their lesser status (44.4–14).

In contrast, Deuteronomy defines a priest as a levitical priest and accords Levites an equal share at the central shrine (18.6–8). In Deuteronomy Levites are judges (17.8–9), guardians of the torah scroll (17.18), and they assist in covenant renewal (27.9). In a postexilic context, Malachi predicts Levite renaissance, because of priestly corruption at the Jerusalem *Temple (2.1–9; 3.3–4). Chronicles strikes a mediating position, depicting cooperation between the dominant Aaronids and the Levites and stressing levitical responsibilities as Temple singers, gatekeepers, and teachers of *torah (1 Chron. 6.31–48; 9.22–27; 2 Chron. 17.7–9).

Many commentators see competition between the Levites and the Aaronids as the most plausible explanation for the different duties and kinds of status ascribed to these groups by biblical writers. GARY N. KNOPPERS

Leviathan. A mythological sea monster who is one of the primeval adversaries of the storm god. In the *Ugaritic texts, *Baal defeats Lothan (*ltn*, a linguistic variant of Leviathan), described as a seven-headed serpent, apparently identified with Baal's adversary Prince Sea. In the Bible Leviathan is also identified with the Sea (Job 3.8) and has many heads (Ps. 74.14), and his defeat by God is a prelude to creation (Ps. 74.15–17). According to *apocalyptic literature, that battle will be rejoined in the end time when the evil Leviathan will be finally defeated (Isa. 27.1; Rev. 12. 3; 17.1–14; 19.20; 21.1), and, according to later tradition, given along with *Behemoth as food to the elect (2 Esd. 6.49–52), another recalling of creation (Ps. 74.14). In Job 41, Leviathan is described as fully under God's control, a divine pet (vv. 4–5; cf. Ps. 104.26). Many commentators have equated the Leviathan of Job 41 with the crocodile, and some elements of the description seem to fit this identification. But others, like his breathing fire (vv. 19–21), do not; in light of the other biblical references as well as the Canaanite antecedents it is better to understand Leviathan as a mythological creature.

In Thomas Hobbes's work by this title (1651), Leviathan is the symbolic name for the absolute power of the political commonwealth, to whose sovereign people must be subordinate but which is ultimately subject to divine control.

MICHAEL D. COOGAN

Levirate Law (from Lat. *levir*, "brother-in-law"; the Hebr. term is *yābam*, "to perform the duty of a brother-in-law"). If a man dies without bearing offspring, his *widow is to marry the deceased's brother (her *levir*). A child born of that union is considered to be perpetuating the "name" (lineage, honor, and inheritance) of the deceased (Deut. 25.5–10). Such a practice is common in traditional societies, promoting social and economic stability. Refusal to fulfill this obligation results in public shame (Deut. 25.9–10), because it indicates a greater concern for one's personal welfare than the welfare of one's extended family.

There are two examples of levirate marriage in the Bible. In Genesis 38, Judah's son Er is killed by God. His second son, *Onan, dies too, for refusing to serve as a *levir* to Tamar, the widow. When Judah refuses to give her his third son, Tamar dresses as a *prostitute and tricks Judah himself into fathering a child. This initially evokes condemnation on Tamar, but subsequently she is regarded as "righteous" for her actions (Gen. 38.26), which demonstrates the great significance placed on fulfilling this obligation. In the book of *Ruth, Boaz fulfills the obligation of the *levir* on behalf of Ruth's first husband. A closer kinsman declines to perform this duty, apparently fearful of the economic stress it would place on him (Ruth 4.6; perhaps, too, he was unwilling to marry a foreigner). This shows that a *levir*'s obligations continue until the child he has fathered is able to assume the re-

sponsibility of defending the deceased's "name" on his own.   TIMOTHY M. WILLIS

Levites. Priests in ancient Israel were considered descendants of the tribe of *Levi, or, in a broad sense, Levites. Whether such a tribe ever existed is debated. To the tribe they are connected only by *genealogies: some perhaps ancient, one at least the product of postexilic times, drawn up in order to legitimize the existing conditions and the privileges of the *Zadokites (1 Chron. 5.30–34 and 6.35–38). For the word Levite no clear etymology has been found; the most suitable meaning is "devoted to the Lord." Levites, then, are those who are given or have given themselves for the service of the Lord; this is their role in traditions of early Israel (Exod. 32.28; Deut. 33.8–11).

Although Levitical priests are the descendants of Aaron, the Zadokites claimed and eventually obtained the Levitical priesthood. Thus, in general biblical usage, the Levites are subordinate Temple officials, who never obtained full priesthood. They are prominent in later phases of biblical tradition, especially in *Deuteronomy, *P, and *Chronicles. They were charged with the more menial tasks in the Temple cult. This secondary position seems to have started with King *Josiah's reform; after the suppression of the country shrines, where it is often assumed (but is unproven) that they officiated and from which they drew their income, they were deprived of their powers and that income, thus reducing them to poverty. In Deuteronomy they are therefore often mentioned together with *aliens, *widows, and *orphans. The Jerusalem priesthood, on the contrary, increased through the reform in power, dignity, and wealth, which they refused to share. Although Deuteronomy 18.1–8 had granted equal dignity and rights to all members of the tribe of Levi, the Jerusalem priesthood succeeded in nullifying this principle, limiting the Levites as priests of the high places (2 Kings 23.9). Such a division into an upper and a lower clergy was first codified in the reconstruction program of *Ezekiel, where the Zadokites were granted the privileges of the Temple and the *sacrifices (40.46; 44.10–14). This hierarchy is confirmed by P (see Num. 3; 18) and may explain why relatively few Levites returned from the *exile.

As to the length of their service, we have contrasting information. According to an older stratum of P (Num. 4.3; see 1 Chron. 23.3), they started at thirty years of age and finished at fifty; according to a later stratum (Num. 8.23–26) they started at twenty-five, while Ezra 3.8 (= 1 Esd. 5.56) and 1 Chronicles 23.24, 27 mention the twentieth year.

In Chronicles we find traces of a struggle by the Levites to obtain equal dignity with the Zadokites, which would have meant sharing in the sacrifices. This was not obtained, however, and the Levites had to content themselves with sharing in the liturgy only. The struggle between the two groups continued until the destruction of the Second Temple (70 CE), with the Levites trying to improve their position and the Zadokites trying to deprive them of the little they had, such as the revenues of the *tithes.

See also Priests and High Priest.

J. A. SOGGIN

Leviticus, The Book of. Leviticus is the third book of the *Pentateuch, named *wayyiqrā'* in Hebrew ("and he summoned") from its opening words. The English "Leviticus" is taken over from the Latin *Vulgate's *Liber Leviticus* derived from the Greek *Septuagint. The contents of Leviticus relate not to the tribe of *Levi but more generally to matters of concern to the *priesthood, especially the proper procedures for various sacrificial offerings, priestly ordination, determinations concerning ritual *purity, and the celebration of holy days. The Pentateuch in its final form is intended to be a single composition, and its division into five books is a later development; however apt the division may be, it should not obscure the fact that Leviticus stands in continuity with what precedes it in the Priestly code (*P) and with what follows; in some cases, it presupposes them. Thus, the ordination of *Aaron and his sons, described in Leviticus 8–9, conforms to instructions given in Exodus 29, and the relation of Aaron's line to other elements of Levi is explicated, in part at least, by the conflict stories in Numbers 16 and the assignment of contributions and *tithes in Numbers 18.

Since Leviticus pertains to P, its contents are thought to have attained a relatively fixed form only in postexilic times; the rituals described therein are basically those of the Second *Temple. Since, however, priestly circles tended to be conservative (especially the Jerusalem priesthood), much of the ritual no doubt reflects that of monarchic times, and some of it possibly even earlier periods. The priestly hierarchy of Leviticus reflects that of postexilic times, as elsewhere in P, with Aaron and his sons alone functioning as priests. Aaron is not called high priest; he is, rather, "the anointed priest" who stands apart from other priests (Lev. 4.3, 5, 16), and his prerogatives pass to another by right of succession (Lev. 6.22; 16.32; cf. Num. 20.25–29). The legal prescriptions in Leviticus, as in other parts of the Pentateuch, are generally introduced by the formula, "The Lord spoke to Moses, saying, 'Speak to the people of Israel'" (1.1–2; 4.1; 7.22–23, 28–29; 12.1–2; 18.1–2; 19.1–2; etc.; cf. Exod. 20.22; 25.1; 31.12–13; Num. 5.1–2, 5–6, 11–12; 6.1–2; 15.1–2, 37–38), but for those that pertain strictly to priests, God commands Moses to speak to Aaron or to Aaron and his sons (6.8–9, 24–25; 16.1–2; 21.1, 16–17; 22.1–2; cf. Num. 6.22–23; 8.1–2); occasionally Aaron, his sons, and all Israel are included under the same rubric (17.1–2; 22.17–18).

In a sense, such formulas bind the contents of the book together. Whether or not one holds P to be a narrative source, the action is advanced very little in Leviticus; Israel, which had already encamped at Mount *Sinai in Exodus 19, remained there through all that is recounted in Leviticus, departing thence only at Numbers 10. The only narrative portions are those that tell of the ordination of Aaron and his sons (chaps. 8–10, by the rite prescribed in Exod. 29) and of a blasphemer and his punishment (24.10–23), the latter narrative occasioning and including a number of laws (vv. 17–20). Although the materials contained in Leviticus are rather disparate in nature, a degree of coherence is provided in the way that many of them are fitted in. Thus, the first *sacrifices narrated in P after the erection of the *tabernacle (Exod. 40) are those relating to the ordination of Aaron and his sons (Lev. 8.14–9.21), and these are logically preceded by extensive instructions on the offering of sacrifice (chaps. 1–7). Thus also, the detailed rules for the distinction between clean and unclean (i.e., that which defiles; *see* Purity, Ritual) in chaps. 11–15 logically precede the instructions for the great *Day of Atonement (chap. 16), whose primary goal is the cleansing of the sanctuary, meeting tent, and altar from the defilements of the Israelites (16.16–19).

Despite the present title given the book, and despite the book's interest in priestly ritual, extensive portions were directed largely to the lay population, in particular 1.1–6.7, which describes how certain sacrifices are to be carried out; these are initiated by the offerer, who also did the slaughtering, although for the priests are reserved the offering of *blood and burning of whatever parts are to be burned. In 6.8–7.10, on the other hand, many of the same matters are covered, but now from the vantage point of priestly concerns; in the outline below in this article, these sections are labeled "supplement," though in fact they must originally have formed a separate (albeit somewhat disorganized) collection, formulated, preserved, and transmitted in priestly circles. As might be expected, most sections within this block are addressed to Aaron and his sons. (This section, extended to 7.38, is sometimes labeled "manual for the priests," and the previous sections "manual for the laity.")

The Holiness Code (H), chaps. 17–26, probably stood as a separate collection before its insertion into P; it is so named because its provisions aim at maintaining the ritual purity required of God's people, and because of the formula, "You shall be holy, for I the Lord your God am holy" (19.2; cf. 20.7). The idea of *holiness here, as in the rest of Leviticus and the Hebrew Bible generally, is that of being set apart. It is of Yahweh's nature to be apart and therefore holy, but people and even things can be set apart as Yahweh's possession and for his service, and in that sense they can be holy. Israel is to "set apart" the clean from the unclean, just as Yahweh has set Israel apart from the nations (20.25–26; cf. 22.32–33). Priests are set apart in a special way, but so is sacrificial meat, the sanctuary, veil, altar and utensils, the *Sabbath, the jubilee year, *tithes, and things vowed to the Lord—and so all these can be called holy or consecrated (8.10–11; 19.24; 21.6, 8, 15, 23; 22.9; 23.3, 20; 25.10; 27.9, 28, 30). Nevertheless, the concept of holiness is broader than separateness, for the former relates to fitting worship of the all-holy God and to what is in accord with his nature. Some of the provisions, furthermore, especially many of those in chap. 19, express high ethical ideals, for example, concern for the poor, disadvantaged, handicapped, and aged (19.9–10, 13–14, 32), honesty in action, word, and judgment (19.11–12, 15–16, 35–36), and even the command to love one's *neighbor (19.18), including the resident *alien (19.33–34). The unevenness and repetition in H is attributable to the fact that it was made up of several smaller, somewhat overlapping collections before its insertion into P; later additions, intended to bring its provisions into line with those found in P, contributed further to the unevenness. The list of rewards (for obedience) and punishments

(for disobedience) with which H concludes (chap. 26) forms an epilogue similar in form, content, and function to that contained in *D (Deut. 28). Some scholars believe that H originally had a historical prologue that was detached when H was inserted into P. In its independent form, then, H may have resembled the treaty form, which is also found in the outline of D.

Chap. 27, on the redemption of votive offerings (i.e., things vowed to God), forms an appendix containing some early material that was probably added after the rest of Leviticus had reached its present form.

The book may be outlined as follows (primary references are given according to the Hebrew text; NRSV and some other translations differ from the Hebrew in parts of chaps. 5 and 6):

I. RITUAL FOR SACRIFICES
    Chap. 1: The burnt offering (ʿōlâ)
    Chap. 2: The cereal offering (minḥâ)
    Chap. 3: The peace offering (zebaḥ šĕlāmîm)
    Chap. 4: The sin offering (ḥaṭṭāʾt) for priests (vv. 1–12)
          for the community (vv. 13–21)
          for the princes (vv. 22–26)
          for private persons (vv. 27–35)
    Chap. 5: The sin offering for special cases (vv. 1–13)
          The guilt offering ʾāšām (vv. 14–26; NRSV: 5.14–6.7)
    Chap. 6: Supplement on the burnt offering (vv. 1–6; NRSV: vv. 8–13)
          Supplement on the cereal offering (vv. 7–16; NRSV: vv. 14–23)
          Supplement on the sin offering (vv. 17–23; NRSV: vv. 24–30)
    Chap. 7: Supplement on the guilt offering (vv. 1–10)
          Supplement on the peace offering (vv. 11–21)
          Prohibitions concerning blood and fat (vv. 22–27)
          Portions for priests (vv. 28–36)
          Conclusion (vv. 37–38)
II. CEREMONY OF ORDINATION
    Chap. 8: Ordination of Aaron and his sons
    Chap. 9: Their installation
    Chap. 10: Revolt of Nadab and Abihu (vv. 1–7)

JOSEPH JENSEN, O.S.B.

Lilith. A female demon who appears in Isaiah 34.14 as part of a description of the Lord's day of vengeance. The figure of Lilith may have evolved out of Babylonian demonology. In some postbiblical Jewish midrashic texts, she is depicted as a slayer of infants and women in pregnancy and childbirth, for which reason amulets were used against her destructive powers. The early medieval *Alphabet of Ben Sira* draws on traditions that *Adam had a first wife who preceded *Eve and identifies her with Lilith. Noting that both she and Adam were created from the earth, Lilith flies away from Adam after unsuccessfully demanding that she be regarded as his equal. Feminist readings of this and other texts about Lilith have observed that the male authors of the Lilith material created an antithesis to Eve, who is often depicted as more docile and dependent and, unlike Lilith, as a begetter and nurturer of children. These readings also draw positive attention to Lilith's self-reliance and demand for equality in societies in which women were legally and socially subordinated to men.

BARBARA GELLER NATHANSON

Literacy in Ancient Israel. The invention of the alphabet in the Levant in the second millennium BCE and its subsequent adoption as the preferred *writing system in various regions by the beginning of the first millennium led to significant changes in education and literature. The use of a limited acrophonic system of graphemic representation led to relatively widespread literacy in ancient Israel, and everywhere where the originally Canaanite alphabet, spread by the *Phoenicians, was adopted. Nevertheless, the boundary between oral and literate cultures is not sharp, and there is no doubt that orality continued to be important even after literacy became widespread; in Hebrew as in other languages the verb meaning "to read" (*qārāʾ*) literally means "to say aloud."

The evidence for writing in ancient Israel is fragmentary, largely because of the use of perishable writing materials. Papyrus, leather, and occasionally wood and plaster were the surfaces most frequently used, but these materials were usually destroyed in conflagrations or by natural decomposition over the centuries. Dramatic evidence for this is found in a number of seal impressions from archaeological strata in *Jerusalem dated to the time of the Babylonian destruction of the city in 587/586 BCE. The small globs of clay with their seal impressions have survived, aided by the fire that hardened them, but the documents to which they were attached were burnt; these bullae sometimes still have the impression of the strings used to tie the papyrus and occasionally impressions of the papyrus itself. Only in relatively isolated and dry locales do leather and papyrus documents like the *Dead Sea Scrolls survive. Most of the inscriptions that have been uncovered, therefore, are on stone or pottery, and they represent only a small proportion of written materials produced at any given time.

On the basis of the surviving epigraphic evidence the democratization of literacy can be dated to about the eighth century BCE. Rapid changes in the forms of letters and a statistically significant increase in the number of extant inscriptions suggest frequent and diffuse use of the alphabet beginning in this period. Certainly by the sixth century literacy is so much a reality that, for example, a soldier can boast in a letter to his superior that he has never needed a scribe to read for him (*Lachish Letter 3). Datable references to reading and writing in the Bible also become more frequent in this period (see, e.g., Isa. 8:1; 28:10, 13; 29:11–12; Deuteronomy and Jeremiah passim).

These developments had profound effects on the formation, transmission, and reception of biblical traditions. From the mid-eighth century BCE onward, there are more and more frequent references to reading and writing in both biblical and epigraphic sources; these provide further evidence of the spread of literacy beyond a scribal and socioeconomic elite. In earlier traditions, for example, God is the writer of his commandments (Exod. 24.12; 32.16; 34.1), or *Moses is his scribe (Exod. 34.27). But by the time of the composition of the book of *Deuteronomy, the tôrâ ("teaching," or "law"; see Torah), while read aloud in the universal ancient mode (Deut. 31.11), was accessible in written form to the larger population. They are prohibited from adding to or removing any of its stipulations (Deut. 12.32) and are thus themselves capable of writing. Noteworthy in this connection is the command in Deuteronomy 6.9 (see Shema): "You [pl.] shall write them on the doorposts of your house and on your gates" (cf. 11.19–20).

It is in addition more than coincidental that the rise of "classical" *prophecy in the mid-eighth century BCE is simultaneous with the spread of writing; in other words, the rise of new forms of, literally, literature is due to the availability of writing in the process of composition. The spread of literacy may also mean that the written traditions of which the Bible preserves a sample may have been accessible not only to elite scribal and priestly groups but more and more to ordinary citizens as well; as an example there is the seventh-century letter from Yavneh Yam in which a field hand shows familiarity with the legal traditions found in Exodus 22:26, Deuteronomy 24:12–13, and Amos 2:8.

Scribal schools continued to function and to flourish, especially in the palace and *Temple, but individuals also employed *scribes, the most famous of whom is *Baruch. It is presumably to such professional writers that we should attribute the *acrostic poems in the Bible. But the teaching and learning of reading and writing would have taken place in domestic and village contexts as well. It is significant that one word meaning both "to learn" and in the causal form "to teach" is derived from the name of the first letter of the alphabet (ʾālep); it is attested from the eighth century BCE onward in both *Aramaic and Hebrew (Job 15.5; 33.33; 35.11; Prov. 22.25).

See also Books and Bookmaking in Antiquity; Wisdom Literature.   MICHAEL D. COOGAN

Literature and the Bible. *This entry consists of four articles that survey, by geographical region, the uses of the Bible in and its influences on literature:*

For discussion of the literary interpretation of the Bible, see Literature, The Bible as *and* Interpretation, History of, *article on* Modern Biblical Criticism.

English Literature

From the swift Christianization of Britain in the seventh century CE, at the beginning of which native writing of texts had not yet begun, down to the present "post-Christian" era in which textuality is almost exclusively the preserve of literary traditions, the Bible has been by far the most important of foundational texts for English literature. In the earliest days of written English, it may be said that the Bible effectively established the literary canon; and until the time of the Enlightenment, it largely continued to shape its outer contours. In the modern period, though this definitive influence has declined dramatically, we may still say that the Bible remains the most widely alluded to of all texts in works by English-speaking authors.

Anglo-Saxon Period. This vast influence is attributable in part to the formative role "free translation" of the Bible had in the development of self-conscious English narrative style. Bede (673–735), in his *Ecclesiastical History of the English People,* offers as paradigm the case of Caedmon, an unlettered cowherd who was miraculously transformed overnight into an accomplished poet: Caedmon's first composition was a hymn drawing on *Genesis in praise of *creation, and his name was subsequently attached to the relatively large body of Anglo-Saxon hexameral poetry that reflected patristic commentaries on Genesis (especially the *Hexameron* of Basil). The chief literary themes of this tradition—the six days of creation, the revolt and fall of the *angels, and the temptation and *fall of Adam and Eve—are felt in the Caedmonian versification of *Genesis* (A and B), or paraphrase-abridgement of *Exodus, Daniel* (1–5), and dramatic *Christ and Satan,* with its three-part relation of the revolt and fall of the angels, Christ's *temptation, and the harrowing of hell. Later Christian poems associated with the author Cynewulf (ninth and tenth century) tend to concern saints' lives, miracles, and lyrical parables, with the notable exception of the three-part poem, *Christ.* The third section of this poem is a powerful treatment of the contest between Christ and Satan, culminating in the Last Judgment. The Exeter *Harrowing of Hell* draws heavily on the apocalyptic gospel of Nicodemus, while another tenth-century poem, *Solomon and Satan,* applies the prevalent theme of holy war between Christ and his adversary in a debate between Christian and non-Christian wisdom. As a type of Christ, *Solomon interprets biblical narratives (e.g., the tower of *Babel) as well as *wisdom literature in such a way as to confound his opponent's resistance to the gospel. All these works, as much as the sermons of Wulfstan and Aelfric, the beautiful *Advent Lyrics* or more literal translations of the Psalter and Gospels, reflect a desire to transmit biblical knowledge. The authors of Anglo-Saxon literature were for the most part missionaries, monks, or lay brothers trained in monasteries, and much of their work can be seen as an outgrowth of the evangelization of Britain. Even in the great non-Christian epic *Beowulf*

(which occurs in the same manuscript as a retelling of the apocryphal narrative, *Judith*), biblical allusion is a significant feature.

Later Middle Ages. After 1066, with the massive cultural and linguistic upheaval occasioned by the Norman invasion, there followed a quiet period for English literature. (The great *Jeu d'Adam,* perhaps the first biblical play in the vernacular to be written in England, was written in Anglo-Norman French.) Yet in the twelfth century, revival of interest in late Roman Christian learning (especially the works of Augustine and Gregory the Great) provided an opportunity for substantial progress in the development of Christian literary theory. Initially, this was applied to reading the Bible itself. But the Augustinian notion that classical literature ought to be appropriated to Christian use, "baptized" by subordination to biblical and catechetical rewriting, had also been defended in his *On Christian Doctrine* by analogy with the divine command to the Jews exiting from Egypt to take with them vessels of Egyptian gold and silver, later to put them to ordinary uses. Under the continued tutelage of Hugh of St. Victor in France and, in England, John of Salisbury (d. 1180), "Egyptian gold" became a major emphasis in late-medieval Christian ideas about literature, and shaped the interaction of scripture and vernacular writing in England until well into the Renaissance. The principle of discrimination in all reading, non-Christian as well as Christian, was held to be the Augustinian test of *love. Richard de Bury (1287–1345) reflects these ideas in his treatise on the love of books *(Philobiblion)* in which "the fables of the poets" are integrated with a canon of humane learning whose basis is scriptural and patristic. Ovid, for example, is subjected to biblical allegory, both in vernacular *(Ovide moralisé)* and Latin versions (Petrus Berchorius). Within the context provided by these developments, as well as by the striking growth of commentary on the Bible itself reflected in central textbooks such as Peter Lombard's *Sentences on the Gospels* (1150), the *Ordinary Gloss,* and Nicholas Lyra's extensive commentaries on scripture (early fourteenth century), the influence of the Bible on vernacular English literature that began to flourish again in the fourteenth century split into two main lines of development.

As in the Anglo-Saxon period, there was still a strong tradition of narrative works that may be described as biblical paraphrase and abridgement. This includes works of biblical extrapolation and sacred tradition: *Cursor mundi,* the *South*

English Legendary, the 10,840-line *Stanzaic Life of Christ,* and also the famous biblical cycle plays of York, Chester, Wakefield, Lincoln, and Coventry. Multiday pageants covering the biblical history of salvation from creation to the Last Judgment, these plays represent the most extensive adaptation of the Bible to vernacular literary use in the history of English letters. While the Bible provides the principal content, the treatment is free, with more or less skillful interpolation or narrative and dramatic expansion effecting the historiographical or homiletic purpose of the authors. (By 1350, few priests and almost no female religious had sufficient Latin to read the *Vulgate even if available; for many, such vernacular works were accordingly a principal source of their biblical knowledge.) Other writers, sometimes with much greater skill and sophistication, might take individual Bible stories and craft them into romance narratives. Two such poems are by the anonymous "Pearl-poet," probably a north-country priest: *Patience,* a retelling of the story of *Jonah, and *Cleanness,* a fierce denunciation of sin which employs biblical narratives (Sodom and Gomorrah; the fall of Babylon; the parable of the wedding feast [Matthew 22.11–13]; Nebuchadnezzar and Belshazzar) to underscore the perils of profanation. *Pearl,* in the same verse form and by the same author, is an exquisite Gothic exposition of the parables of the pearl of great price and the penny-hire (Matt. 20.1–16), blended with material from the book of *Revelation to address the relationship between present life and future hope, time, and eternity.

The second stream of biblical influence, flowing from the revival of Christian literary theory in the twelfth to the fourteenth centuries, is illustrated well in a fourth poem by the Pearl-poet, *Sir Gawain and the Green Knight.* In it Celtic myth and the conventions of ancestral romance narrative are blended with New Testament themes. Although neither biblical narrative nor extended biblical allegory is present, biblical interpretation in the Augustinian tradition heavily flavors the treatment of non-Christian narrative.

The preeminent poet of the fourteenth century, Geoffrey Chaucer (1340–1400), reveals a rich appreciation of biblical literature, yet his poetry involves rather a "baptism" of worldly tales by Christian thought and purpose than simple allegory or biblical paraphrase. In his *Canterbury Tales,* various pilgrim narrators use biblical idiom and figure in such a way as to characterize their attitudes toward justice, mercy, love, and forgiveness. The humor and the "mor-

alite" of the Miller's use of Noah's *Flood and the *Song of Solomon, like the outrageous and funny misreadings of the gospel of *Matthew and the church fathers by the Wife of Bath, equally with the Parson's sober sermon on repentance (from Jeremiah 6), toward which the collection moves, depend both upon a veridical reading of the biblical text and also upon the more elaborate hermeneutic encoding that is the product of later biblical scholarship and commentary. That how one reads the Bible can be a subject for lively cognizance and considerably sophisticated humor in English court circles is a striking measure of biblical literacy in the fourteenth century. Further, in the deliberate superimposing of biblical text over familiar classical myth, as in Chaucer's *Maunciples's Tale* or in the anonymous Christian reversal of the Orpheus and Eurydice legend, *Sir Orfeo,* we see a dependence upon Augustinian notions of how the Bible might be expected to transform non-Christian story.

For less cultured readers, the same techniques could be adapted to biblically directed social criticism. In Langland's apocalyptic *Piers Plowman* (1369; 1378; 1386), simple moral and political allegories are projected from the Gospels and Pauline epistles onto contemporary crises in church and state. Here the reader is invited to refer both text and events of contemporary life to the Bible for understanding; Langland not only assumes biblical knowledge but, much like Richard Rolle (d. 1349) and Walter Hilton (d. 1396) among spiritual writers and John Wycliffe among Oxford academics, urges his readers toward direct, personal reading of the scriptures. The Wycliffite Bible translation (1384; 1396) by Nicholas Hereford, John Purvey, and others not only contributed to but depended upon widespread interest in the Bible among nonclerical readers.

The fifteenth century is almost as unremarkable for English literature as were the years immediately following 1066. With the stiff suppression of Lollardry and condemnation of the Wycliffite Bible, it became unfashionable to exhibit biblical influence with the freedom known in the fourteenth century; one could be arrested on suspicion of heresy even for owning a copy of *The Canterbury Tales.* With the exception of continuation, for a time, of the cycle plays and allegorical morality plays, the most notable examples of biblical influence may be two surviving saints' plays, *The Conversion of St. Paul* and *The Play of Mary Magdalene.* Although true saints' plays in form, they are from the very end of the period and probably owe their preservation in Protestant times to the fact that the principals were biblical figures; the St. Paul play is particularly careful to hew close to the account in *Acts and at pains to advertise this in its preface. Some of the religious poetry of the Scots poets, such as William Dunbar, and that of English writer John Skelton show indebtedness to biblical story, and among the first printed English works of William Caxton is included an apocryphal narrative on the *Infancy of Jesus* and another translation from Latin, *The Mirror of the Blessed Life of Jesus Christ.* But central, vital influence of the Bible upon the main fabric of English literature degenerated almost entirely until after the stormiest years of the Reformation.

Reformation and Renaissance. In the sixteenth century, with the translations of Tyndale (1525–30), Coverdale (1535), Rogers, and Taverner, the "Great Bible" (1539), the Geneva Bible (1560), and finally the Bishop's Bible (1568) (*see* Translations, *article on* English Language), the combination of controversial interest and accessibility assured a fresh infusion of literary interest. While Cranmer's *Book of Common Prayer* (1564) aided in the increase of biblical knowledge among ordinary persons, its largely liturgical organization of biblical story no longer governed patterns of influence as had its Latin predecessors. The accessible English Bible now invited reading through, like other books, and the success of the King James Version (1611), rightly regarded as the high-water mark of English literary prose, merely confirmed this new type of literary enjoyment of the Bible. Thus, though there are still examples of poet-translators of scripture, such as Sir Philip Sidney and the Countess of Pembroke in their rendition of the Psalms (1586; 1589), and Joshua Sylvester's translation (1605) of the Frenchman Du Bartas' *Divine Weeks and Works* (a highly successful Protestantized version of medieval hexameral literature), the true influence of the Bible is in this period is internalized, revealing itself not merely in the emergence of previously neglected themes and narratives (such as the stories of Jephthah, Samson, Ruth, Deborah, and the theme of the covenant) but in the actual force of idiom, phrase, and cadence of the Coverdale, Geneva, and finally King James Versions working their way into English poetic diction. Spenser's sonnets (66; 68; 70) and *Epithalamion* (1595) offer exquisite examples, as do, somewhat later, many poems of George Herbert in *The Temple* (1633); biblical idiom shapes also

the prose of Hooker's *Laws of Ecclesiastical Polity* (1593; 1597), Decker's *The Seven Deadly Sins of London* (1606), the *Devotions* of John Donne (1624), and, more extravagantly, Jeremy Taylor's *Holy Living and Holy Dying* (1650; 1651), to cite but a few luminous examples. It can truly be said of the seventeenth century in England that nowhere else has the effect of the Bible on literary language been so all-pervasive. Both writers and readers savor the flavor of "biblical" English; even playwrights are able to depend on an intimate familiarity with the Bible on the part of popular audiences. As Christopher Marlowe in the opening speeches of *Dr. Faustus* (1604) can characterize his proud and self-damning protagonist by his misquotation of key biblical texts, so also William Shakespeare is able, in *Measure for Measure,* to critique the theology of the Puritans by setting his text from Matthew 7 in a rich context of quotations from Paul's letter to the *Romans, such as were frequently featured in the Puritans' own sermons. Throughout his work, Shakespeare draws heavily on the Geneva Bible to encode and enrich his work, whether in romances like *The Winter's Tale* or history plays like *Henry IV* (Parts 1 and 2).

Biblical allusion in post-Reformation England, at least until the time of Milton and Bunyan, is ubiquitous, and it salts every kind of learned discourse. Poetry in the service of biblical interpretation or theological controversy, though more easily delineated as an expression of the influence of the Bible on the growth of humane letters, is almost as impossible to summarize; it must be kept in mind that between 1480 and 1660 more than half of all books printed in England were devoted to theological or ethical subjects, and typically copiously indebted to biblical "evidences" and discourse. Many of these works were dedicated to lay readership, and a large portion elected one or another genre of poetry as a medium. The younger Giles Fletcher's long serial poem, *Christ's Victorie and Triumph in Heaven and Earth* (1618) and, to a lesser extent, his brother Phineas's *The Locusts of Apollyonists* (1627) exemplify Protestant allegorical treatments of major biblical themes.

Such adaptations of the *agon* motif familiar from earlier English portrayals of the cosmic battle between Christ and Satan may have helped redirect the classically trained John Milton (1608–1674) in his desire to write a great English epic. Milton goes beyond Spenser, not only rejecting a plot from Greek or Roman literature but choosing the biblical story of fall and redemption over the national Arthurian myth. *Paradise Lost* (1667) and *Paradise Regained* (1671) represent a high point, then, of biblical influence on English literature, perhaps the greatest exemplar of a national culture that by this point had come to see the Bible as chief amongst its foundational texts. From the "war in heaven" to the "last battle," major epic themes from the Bible were adorned with Latinate diction and humane learning of such a high order as to reinforce the centrality of biblical influence through subsequent, much less religious periods in English letters. In his short drama *Samson Agonistes* and lesser poems as well, Milton offers a shaping of biblical influence so distinctive that many subsequent authors have effectively read their Bible in Milton's "version"—which is also to say, of course, that the Bible became strongly identified in the minds of some with Milton's brand of Protestant theology.

The once-vigorous tradition of biblical drama did not entirely die out with the Reformation but was substantially adapted to serve the emphases of Protestant interpretations of the Bible. Thus, while the saints' plays probably dominated religious drama in the fifteenth century, they now gave way entirely, to be replaced by plays about heroic figures from the Hebrew Bible; individual Tudor plays, many now lost, were dedicated to the stories of *Ruth, *Esther, *Darius, *Hezekiah, Jephthah, *Joshua, *Samson, *Absalom, and *Susanna, as well as the more familiar *Abraham and Lot, *Jacob and *Esau, and a variety of plays about *Joseph and his brothers. Common to these plays, as to those with New Testament subjects (such as *John the Baptist, Pontius Pilate,* and *The Prodigal Son*) is a movement away from salvation history to a focus on individual spiritual struggle of heroic proportions, ending either in repentance, conversion, and triumph or in hardening of the heart and tragedy. Almost the sole Tudor survival of the classical saints' play is the mediocre *Life and Repentance of Mary Magdalene* (1566) by Lewis Wager. John Bale, protégé of Thomas Cromwell, employed his Antichrist play, *King Johan,* as anti-Catholic polemic. His *God's Promises* (1577), an interesting reworking of the earlier prophet plays, concerns itself with promises to the individual believer rather than the fulfillment of salvation history in Christ. Among a smaller number of surviving Elizabethan plays on biblical subjects are *Susanna* (1578) by Thomas Carter, *Absalon* by Thomas Watson, *David and Bathsabe* (1594) by George Peele, and *Herod and Antipater*

(1622) by Markham and Sampson. After this period, until Milton, biblical influence tends to be less direct yet, as J. H. Sims (*Dramatic Uses of Biblical Allusions in Marlowe and Shakespeare* [1966]) shows, entirely pervasive.

In the late sixteenth and seventeenth centuries, the English sermon was a high art form, and some of the finest examples of biblically influenced prose from this period come from the pens of Lancelot Andrewes, Richard Baxter, Isaac Barrow, the authorized homilists of the Church of England, and from poet-preachers such as John Donne (1572–1631) and George Herbert (1593–1633). The lyric poetry of the latter is replete with biblical imagery and subject, as is Henry Vaughan's postconversion *Silex Scintillans* (1655). Also, the characteristically apologetic use of the Bible in this period led to its use in political writings too numerous to contemplate here, including those of major figures such as Parker, Baxter, and Harrington. Even Hobbes's *Leviathan* (1651) is rich in biblical quotation and allusion. In no period of English literary history is literary language in every subject and genre so thoroughly indebted to the Bible; from autobiographies like the magnificent *Religio Medici* (1642) of Thomas Browne to praises of science and progress like Abraham Cowley's poem *To the Royal Society* (1677), or Francis Bacon's essay *New Atlantis* (1627), to Isaac Walton's biography of John Donne, the images, words, and accents of the English Bible echo on nearly every page of English literature.

Enlightenment. After the dismal failure of the Puritan Commonwealth under Oliver Cromwell and the Restoration under Charles II (1660) of Anglican church-state government, there was a marked turning away from anything that resembled piety in public life and the arts. Accordingly, biblical influence upon an increasingly secular literature suffered a sharp demise; while still felt at the level of language and allusion, biblical subject matter and titles almost entirely disappear, or else, in a case like Dryden's satiric political allegory, *Absalom and Achitophel* (1681), the reference of the allegory is curiously reversed: biblical story becomes a diaphanous screen for contemporary political miscreance. The notable counterpoint in this period is John Bunyan (1628–1688), whose prison writings were directed not to fashionable taste but to persons as humble as their author, whose literacy lay almost exclusively in knowledge of the Bible. Here again the device was allegory but, after *Grace Abounding to the Chief of Sinners* (1666), characterized by moral psychomachia rooted in a pattern of familiar biblical *typology. *The Pilgrim's Progress* (1678; 1684), *The Life and Death of Mr. Badman* (1680), and *The Holy War* (1682), though enduring classics, stand apart from rather than represent the pattern of biblical influence on English literature going into the eighteenth century, in that they are undisguisedly a species of evangelical tract. An allied literary form favored by the Puritans, spiritual autobiography, was to receive its best-known popular adaption in Daniel Defoe's *Robinson Crusoe* (1719), a progenitor of the modern novel, in which the protagonist's experience is a progress from original sin and alienation through exile, wandering, and providential intervention to a discovery and reading of the Bible, which then interprets life retrospectively, bringing about repentance, conversion, and rescue.

Further erosion of biblical influence on the mainstream of English literature was occasioned not only by increasing political isolation of the Puritans, with whom it had now become so closely associated, but by the rise of religious skepticism and critical attack on the scientific reliability of the biblical texts themselves. Thus, the skeptical modernism that began as a trickle in works such as Lord Herbert of Cherbury's protodeist *De Veritate* (1623), when coupled with biblical criticism such as Richard Simon's *Critical History of the Old Testament* (translated in 1682) and the philosophical writings of John Locke, was to grow into a flood of challenges to the authority and relevance of the Bible in writers of major influence, such as Shaftesbury, Bolingbroke, and, later, David Hume and Edward Gibbon. Gibbon's *Decline and Fall of the Roman Empire* (1776–88) celebrates the reinstitution of Roman as opposed to biblical models and values, and English evolution in literature from an era dominated by Christian and biblical influences to one in which they become marginal, from the Puritan to the "Augustan" age. Oliver Goldsmith, who coined the latter term in one of his essays (1759), reflects nostalgically on the fading of core biblical values from contemporary social and literary life in his *Vicar of Wakefield* (1764); his own oratorio on the *Exodus narrative was not published in his lifetime. As in Jonathan Swift's *Tale of a Tub* (1704) and *Argument against Abolishing Christianity* (1711) or the urbane criticism of Alexander Pope's quasi-deistic *Essay on Man* (1731–35), the residual influence is institutional Christianity rather than biblical narrative or language. Throughout the period a scattering of poems inspired by

progress in science employ biblical paraphrases (e.g., passages in Job, or Psalms 8; 19; 104; 139), often in an attempt to show the correspondence of Newton and scripture, and William Broome's *A Paraphrase of Parts of Job* (ca. 1720) makes the author of Job, in turn, sound like a lecturer to the Royal Society.

Within the Established Church there was a continuing tradition of biblical verse both narrative and lyric, and though much less distinguished than their predecessors, poet-priests like the nonjuror Bishop Thomas Ken (1637–1711), John Norris (1657–1711) and, at a lesser rank, Samuel Wesley the elder, wrote moral, biblically inspired verse. Among influential poets in the biblical tradition, however, Isaac Watts, scion of the dissenting tradition, and Charles Wesley, whose work is a fusion of Puritan and Catholic sensibility, must be counted as of a higher rank. Watts, a favorite of Samuel Johnson, wrote on biblical themes in his *Horae lyricae* (1706), and is remembered for his imitation of the Psalms (1719) as well as numerous celebrated hymns. Charles Wesley, cofounder of Methodism and Watts's only peer as a writer of hymns in this period, also wrote a distinguished biblical poem, *Wrestling Jacob* (1742). In eighteenth-century poetry, however, biblical influence was often accompanied by melancholic self-absorption, as in Edward Young's *Night Thoughts* (1742–45), Robert Blair's *The Grave* (1743), James Hervey's *Meditations and Contemplations* (1747), Christopher Smart's *Jubilate Agno* and *Song to David* (1763), and, preeminent in this vein, William Cowper's *Task* (1785) and *Olney Hymns* (1779), coauthored with the Reverend John Newton. In none of this later poetry is there much of the formative power of the biblical texts so familiar to the seventeenth century and, like the biblical fictions and poems of Elizabeth Rowe (1737) or even the later ones of the considerably more crisp Hannah More (1745–1833), it pales in comparison with Milton or Herbert. As with Johnson's use of biblical allusion to fortify temperate rationalism in *Rasselas* (1759) or James Thomson's in *Aeolus' Harp* (1748) to universalize sentiment, not only the focus but also the expectation of readers' familiarity with the Bible has significantly faded. Only rarely in the eighteenth century, and that most memorably in the novel, with Henry Fielding's *Joseph Andrews* (1742) and *Tom Jones* (1749), does biblical influence extend to narrative structure, governing paradigms, themes, and substance of the discourse. When this happens, as the adaptation in *Joseph Andrews* of the *Joseph story from

Genesis applied with the aid of New Testament pericopes like the parable of the Good Samaritan, the effect is to create a text with two or more levels, in which the livelier intertextual relationships seem not merely to encode a moral but ally the novel with an earlier tradition of biblically underwritten narrative.

Romanticism and the Modern Era. With William Blake (1757–1827), English literature enters an entirely new phase of relationship with the Bible. Blake, in *Songs of Experience* (1794) as well as his *Book of Thel* (1789), *Marriage of Heaven and Hell* (1793), and the revisionist *Milton* (1808), *Jerusalem* (1820), and *The Everlasting Gospel* (1818), created his "own myth," as he put it, to avoid being "enslaved by that of another man." In Blake's reading, authority is transferred from foundational text to the poet of genius, who creates his own "reading," obliterating traditional understanding: the Bible is "rewritten" to suit his myth. (*See also* Art and the Bible.) As Northrop Frye (*The Great Code* [1982]) and others have indicated, Blake becomes in this way a harbinger not only of modernist approaches to the Bible in literature, but also of postmodernism in both literature and criticism. In his reading of Milton's *Paradise Lost*, Satan becomes the real hero. Subsequent romantic poets, such as Byron in *Manfred* (1816) and *Cain* (1821), and Shelley in *Prometheus Unbound* (1820), follow suit. Coleridge, in his "Satanic Hero," reflects on certain consequences.

Within a more conservative biblical tradition was James Hogg, the Scottish shepherd whose *Pilgrims of the Sun* (1815) and *Private Memoirs and Confessions of a Justified Sinner* (1824) afford a glimpse of prevalent tensions between a biblical view of the human condition and the intensely personalistic romantic quest for identity. Walter Scott's novel *Old Mortality* (1816) studies, in language rich with the Scottish covenanters' fluent biblicism, social strife attendant upon strict literal application of the "Calvinist" Bible to politics.

Coleridge was a theologically sophisticated reader of the Bible, as chapter 13 of his *Biographia litteraria* suggests; Wordsworth, as may be seen in "Intimations Ode" and "Westminster Bridge" (1807), comparatively naive. With the second wave of Wesleyan revival in the first part of the nineteenth century, however, and the consolidation of religious values in curriculum and canon in the early years of Queen Victoria's reign, the Bible became both more widely acceptable in literary theme or motif, and much more visible in literary language. Yet R. W.

Buchanan's "Ballad of Judas Iscariot" (1863) and Thomas Beddoe's "Old Adam the Crow" (1828), like Browning's *Saul* (1847) or "Death in the Desert," put the Bible to characteristically broad-church purposes. Tennyson's "Rizpah" prefers the Bible to Calvinist interpretations of it, though Tennyson's characteristic reading of the Bible is governed, in fact, by what he called "Higher Pantheism" and other presuppositions similar to Browning's. Browning's analysis of biblical notions of worship in "Epilogue of Dramatis Personae" reveals his interest in German biblical criticism as much as "Abt Volger" does his fascination with Feuerbachian eschatology. In the 1860s a poet like Charles Tennyson might be, as Hoxie Fairchild puts it (in his six-volume *Religious Trends in English Poetry: 1700–1965*), "much less troubled by Darwinism than by the extension of scientific method to biblical criticism and the comparative study of religion."

Some of the more peculiar adaptations of the Bible as literary influence in this period are to be found in the work of minor poets such as the spiritualist F. W. H. Myers's "St. Paul" or the medieval romanticist R. W. Dixon's *Christ's Company* (1861) with its angular and psychological poems on Mary *Magdalene, *John, and the *Stabat mater* theme. An early harbinger of liberation theology is Arthur O'Shaughnessy, especially in "Christ Will Return" from his *Songs of a Worker* (1881). The evangelical poets of earlier in the period, whose best effort is probably Elizabeth Barrett's tedious *The Seraphim* (1838) and pseudo-Miltonic *A Drama of Exile* (1844), are the only ones to contribute work of substantially biblical theme and subject. Robert Pollok's *The Course of Time* (1827), Robert Montgomery's *Satan* (1830) and *Messiah* (1832), and John Heraud's *Descent into Hell* (1830) and *The Judgement of the Flood* (1834) illustrate a continuing appetite for Miltonic adaptations of the Bible, but also, as does C. J. Wells's *Joseph and His Brethren* (1824), an exhaustion of that taste and talent.

The vital continuance of biblical influence upon English literature at the close of the century is in some ways shown less vividly in the popularity of evidently Christian works such as Francis Thompson's "Hound of Heaven" (1893) or the poems of John Cardinal Newman, Arthur Hugh Clough, and the Rossettis than in the rich mastery of biblical idiom, motif, and allusion by writers notably antagonistic to orthodox religion. Partly this owes to a substantial attempt by Matthew Arnold in his *Literature and Dogma* (1873), *St. Paul and Protestantism* (1890), and *God and the*

Bible (1899) to separate the Bible from its association with Puritan or Calvinistic religion and grant it supremely literary value in an English canon. Partly it owes to the training in these orthodox traditions, and their subsequent partial or complete rejection by numerous major authors: George Eliot's *Silas Marner* (1861) and Thomas Hardy's *Jude the Obscure* (1895), like Swinburne's "Hymn to Proserpine," are rich in biblical influence despite explicit aversion to biblical religion, and George MacDonald in *Lilith* (1895) treats Jewish apocrypha in a New Testament context in such a way as to challenge his Calvinist colleagues with a hypothesis of universal salvation.

A measure of the literary power of the "English" Bible in overcoming religious considerations is the complete dominance of the King James Version from its first publication until well into the twentieth century; even James Joyce, who makes copious use of the Bible, prefers the cadences of this English translation to facilitate his inversions. This remains the pattern through W. B. Yeats ("Adam's Curse," "The Second Coming") and the fiction of D. H. Lawrence; it is visible in Robert Graves's *King Jesus* as well as in works such as Edwin Muir's *One Foot in Eden* (1956) or, more recently, Ted Hughes's, *Crow* (1970). Blakean rewriting of biblical narrative had become by World War I perhaps the significant tradition in modern English literature. The type of fiction represented by George A. Moore's *The Brook Kerith* (1916), which interweaves the lives of a Christ who survives the cross with those of *Paul and *Joseph of Arimathea, has grown abundantly in the twentieth century; examples are too numerous to list and most lack significant literary merit. Differing literary responses to the Bible have made their mark, however, including the poems of Gerard Manley Hopkins and perhaps most notably T. S. Eliot's "Ash Wednesday" (1930), "Journey of the Magi" (1927), and the magisterial *Four Quartets* (1935–42). The *Anathemata* (1952) of David Jones and R. S. Thomas's *Stones of the Field* (1946), *Pieta* (1966), and *Laboratories of the Spirit* (1975) exemplify a revival of biblical voice in modern British poetry, and may come to be seen as part of a neo-Christian revival of biblical influence. To some extent, the novels of Joyce Carey, notably his second trilogy, *Prisoner of Grace* (1952), *Except the Lord* (1953), and *Not Honour More* (1955), reflect a dissenting tradition, while the fiction of C. S. Lewis, exemplified in his Miltonic retelling of the Eden story, *Perelandra, or Voyage to Venus* (1940), and the

plays of Dorothy Sayers, including *The Man Born to Be King* (1943) and *The Zeal of Thy House* (1948), offer explicit representations of biblical narrative. A resonant incorporation of biblical theme, motif, and language is provided by J. R. R. Tolkien's evocation of Nordic saga, *The Lord of the Rings* (1954–55). Discernably then, the shaping of biblical influence by Miltonic Puritanism, Anglo-Saxon monasticism, Anglican historicism, and Anglo-Catholic sacramentalism, all find continued expression in contemporary literature. Since World War II, however, the influence of the Bible on English literature has been markedly reduced in comparison with its influence on literature being written in America and the Commonwealth (*see the corresponding articles in this entry*). For a detailed tracing of the development of biblical allusion, narrative, and typology from Anglo-Saxon to contemporary English and American literature, as well as extensive annotated bibliography of critical studies on the use of the Bible by English authors, see D. L. Jeffrey, *A Dictionary of Biblical Tradition in English Literature* (1992).   DAVID LYLE JEFFREY

British Commonwealth Literature

The influence of the Bible on British Commonwealth literature is complicated by the relatively late development of the British empire. The rise of British control of Australia and New Zealand, India, and substantial parts of Africa, accomplished chiefly in the nineteenth century, coincided with the decline of biblical authority in the West, especially among the educated classes responsible for the production of written literature. Thus, one might expect that Commonwealth literature would owe very little to the Bible; this expectation is often, but not always, fulfilled.

In Australia, for instance, literature is dominated, well into the twentieth century, by the overriding themes of that culture's history: the experiences of the convicts who first colonized Australia and of the bushrangers who soon populated the outback. Many writers understood the Bible to have little relevance to their circumstances—but not all: A. D. Hope (b. 1907), though not a believer, often makes vivid use of biblical themes and imagery (see, for instance, his "Imperial Adam"); James McAuley (1917–1976), an adult convert to Catholicism, attempts to reconstitute in modern terms, though in traditional forms, the devotional verse of Donne and Herbert:

Since all our keys are lost or broken,

Shall it be thought absurd
If for an art of words I turn
Discreetly to the Word?
("An Art of Poetry," II. 1–4)

And the continent's most prominent novelist, Patrick White (b. 1912), is noted for his use of biblical symbolism, for instance in his novel *Voss* (1957), whose title character is gradually revealed as a Christ-figure of significant dimensions.

In Anglophone Indian literature the situation is much more complex, for three dominant reasons. First is cultural independence: the rise of this literature was simultaneous with a powerful renewal of pride among Indian (especially Hindu) intellectuals in their traditional culture, a renewal strongly encouraged by visitors from the West, especially members of the Theosophical movement. Thus, the typical Anglo-Indian novel—for example, by R. K. Narayan (b. 1907)—will use European forms to express traditionally Indian ideas and ideals. Second is familial resemblance. Some Indian literature, such as the poetry of Rabindranath Tagore (1861–1941), may closely resemble certain kinds of biblical literature, especially the poetry exemplified by the *Song of Solomon; but direct influence is a less likely explanation for this phenomenon than a shared use of sexual and natural imagery. Last is Hindu syncretism; again Tagore will provide an example. His philosophical-poetic meditations on the one God often sound like a variety of Jewish or Christian mysticism, but monotheism has always been one of Hinduism's many facets. It has never been consistently emphasized throughout India, but neither has any other facet of Hinduism. That religion's syncretic ability to absorb multifarious influences makes biblical influences upon it extremely difficult to trace or fix.

In African literature, however, the influence of the Bible has been nothing less than enormous. The oral tradition in Africa is exceptionally powerful, and written literature appeared only after the coming of the Europeans. Since those Europeans, especially the British, favored literacy in the natives chiefly for religious purposes—reading the Bible and the prayer book—it should not be surprising that the earliest written literature in Africa served evangelical aims. This age of didactic literature eventually passed, replaced by novels, plays, and poems that stand at the forefront of post–World War II literature; but the influence of the Bible has remained strong in the countries once or still associated

with the British Commonwealth. Nigeria's two best-known writers, the novelist Chinua Achebe (b. 1930) and the Nobel–Prize winning playwright Wole Soyinka (b. 1934), are of different tribes, but both were raised as Christians; biblical themes and language echo throughout their work. For instance, Achebe's second novel *No Longer at Ease* presents its protagonist Obi Oknokwo in terms of the prodigal son and of the *Magi returning to their kingdoms (as described in T. S. Eliot's poem "Journey of the Magi"); further, it skilfully presents the competing languages of the traditional Ibo proverb-oriented culture and the Christian culture of biblical quotation, sometimes seeing the two in direct conflict but often as witness to the Ibos' ability to synthesize the two. Soyinka repeatedly uses biblical archetypes; he too presents the theme of the prodigal (and the larger biblical theme of two brothers in conflict) in *The Swamp Dwellers,* and writes a profound variation on the Christ-theme of sacrificial, redemptive death in one of his finest plays, *The Strong Breed.*

Likewise, in South Africa we see writers, such as the novelist and autobiographer Peter Abrahams, who claim to have learned their prose style and, what is more important, a vocabulary of justice and injustice, power, and oppression, from the King James Bible; and we also see the prodigal once again, this time fused with elements of the *David-Absalom story, in Alan Paton's forthrightly Christian plea for compassion in his land, *Cry, the Beloved Country.* Paton is white, Abrahams what the South African regime calls "coloured"; it would appear that for South Africans of whatever color, the Bible provides a complex literary vocabulary with which to confront a harsh and difficult society.

ALAN JACOBS

European Literature

The influence of the Bible on continental European literature has been so pervasive as to be almost incalculable. Both as a collection of sacred texts and as the source of the various creeds, codes, and cults of Judaism and Christianity, the Bible is the most essential document in the Western world. To begin with, the spread of Christianity generated a gigantic (and still growing) corpus of liturgies, sermons, pamphlets, prayer books, practical guides, and every conceivable form of theology, which, supplementing and accompanying the Bible, have served as the foundation for Western Christian culture. The bulk of this corpus, as enshrined, for example, in the

383 volumes of Jacques Paul Migne's (1800–75) monumental *Patrologiae Cursus Completus,* which collects the writings of the church fathers from the apostolic era to the early thirteenth century, may be a dead letter except for historians and students of religion, but significant portions have survived and remain noteworthy.

The *Missale Romanum,* for instance, which was organized and edited by the Council of Trent (1545–63), contains—apart from many biblical texts arranged to fit the cycle of the liturgical year—some memorable poetry (e.g., the powerful symbols and ceremonies of the Easter Vigil, the "sequences," etc.) and many prayers marked by a distinctive spare eloquence. Missals, breviaries, and books of hours have made the Bible (particularly the Gospels and the Psalms) an integral part of the consciousness of both clergy and pious lay people for centuries. The liturgy, like the cathedrals (each a *Biblia pauperum*) that were its supreme setting, and the church *music (from before Palestrina to after Fauré) that expressed it, mediated the Bible to the world at large.

The Bible obviously played a key role in the work of early Christian authors. In the pre-Nicene period (i.e., up to 325 CE) perhaps only Tertullian (ca. 160–225), moralist, apologist, and fierce controversialist, has retained an important place in the Western literary canon. He is remembered for, among other things, the notorious paradox, "Certum est quia impossibile," and for asking the pregnant question, "Quid ergo Athenis et Ierosolymis?"

Jerome (ca. 342–420) not only produced the first great translation of the Bible, the *Vulgate, but some of the most brilliantly rhetorical letters in any language. He is generally considered the supreme stylist of Christian Latinity. In a famous nightmare (Letter XXII) Jerome saw himself being dragged before the judgment seat and asked about his condition. Claiming to be a Christian, he was abruptly contradicted, "You lie. You are a Ciceronian. 'Where your treasure is, there will your heart be also' [Matt. 6.21]." The scene aptly conveys Jerome's ambivalence and guilt (and that of countless Christian intellectuals like him) about his love of classical literature—which persisted, despite this warning from on high.

Although, like Tertullian, he was born in North Africa, Augustine (354–430) spent his crucial formative years (384–90) in Italy; and, like Tertullian's, his works became European classics. He is naturally best remembered for his *Confessions*

and for his great rambling encyclopedic philosophy of history, *The City of God.* Augustine is the direct progenitor of countless spiritual autobiographies, from Teresa of Avila's *Libro de su vida* (1587) to Leo Tolstoy's *A Confession* (completed in 1882) and, through Jean-Jacques Rousseau (1712–78), of modern autobiography. Beyond this, the teachings in Augustine's huge oeuvre of ninety-three works reverberated long and fatefully in Western intellectual history—to choose but one example, in the seventeenth-century Jansenist controversy, which in turn spawned such diverse masterpieces as Pascal's *Provincial Letters* (1656 and after) and Sainte-Beuve's magisterial history of *Port-Royal* (1840–1859).

One of the most remarkable offshoots of the New Testament was the cult of *Mary. After modest beginnings in early Christianity it made enormous advances once Mary was defined by the Council of Ephesus (431) as "God-bearer" (Grk. *theotokos*). By the twelfth century Bernard of Clairvaux (1090–1153) could exclaim, "De Maria numquam satis," and medieval Christian writers seem to have taken this maxim to heart. There is an enormous and varied body of Marian literature, with famous tributes from writers from all over the Christian world, from Aimar, bishop of Le Puy (ca. 1087), author of the great hymn "Salve, regina," to Dante (d. 1321), who has Bernard address Mary as, "Vergine madre, figlia di tuo figlio," in the final canto of the *Paradiso.* And the tradition was continued by many later writers, in works as diverse as Cardinal Duperron's (1556–1618) "Cantique de la Vierge Marie," Anatole France's (1884–1924) *Le Jongleur de Notre-Dame,* and Rainer Maria Rilke's (1875–1926) *Das Marien-Leben.*

On a much smaller scale than the patristic writings there is a venerable tradition of hymnology and religious poetry in Latin, from Ambrose's (339–397) "Aeterne rerum conditor" to Thomas Aquinas's (1225–74) "Lauda Sion" and "Pange, lingua, gloriosi." Other names worth recalling here include Caelius Sedulius (fl. ca. 450), Columba (521–597), Venantius Fortunatus (ca. 530–610), Peter Damian (1007–72), Bernard of Cluny (fl. 1140), Adam of St. Victor (fl. 1140), Peter Abelard (1079–1142), Philip the Chancellor (d. 1236), and Thomas of Celano (ca. 1190–1260), author of the immortal "Dies irae," which borrows from Matthew 25:31–46 and other New Testament texts to create a haunting vision of the *day of judgment. There were also many fine anonymous poets, authors of such familiar pieces as "Ave maris stella," "Veni creator spiritus," "Alma redemptoris mater," "Stabat mater," and "Dulcis Iesu memoria." This poetry is simple, direct, and unassuming. Consider the Easter sequence by Wipo (d. ca. 1050), who was chaplain to two Holy Roman Emperors: "Victimae paschali laudes/ immolent Christiani./ Agnus redemit oves:/ Christus innocens Patri/ reconciliavit peccatores./ Mors et vita duello/ conflixere mirando:/ dux vitae mortuus/ regnat vivus," etc. While not true folk art, many of these hymns, heard continually in church services and learned by heart, became an integral part of popular European culture. Some, notably the "Dies irae," which was integrated into the Mass for the Dead, were set to music by composers such as Mozart and Verdi; the Gregorian chant "Dies irae" resounds menacingly in Berlioz's *Symphonie Fantastique*. These Latin hymns also introduced the use of rhyme, which was then adopted by writers of vernacular verse.

Another vital element of European literature (in the broad sense) inspired by the Bible was the unique genre of the "rule" for monastic or religious orders, such as Benedict of Nursia's (d. ca. 543) *Regula Monachorum*, and its many successors, including the rules of the Franciscans, Dominicans, and Jesuits, along with Ignatius Loyola's (1491–1556) extremely influential *Spiritual Exercises*, with its numerous echoes in later literature, such as James Joyce's *Portrait of the Artist as a Young Man* (1914–15). This sort of Christian "torah"—with its distinctly utopian cast—was not merely, or even primarily, reading material, though many generations of religious read them over and over again, down through the centuries. They were the constitutions and codes of communities that attempted, despite repeated and inevitable failures (as lampooned, e.g., in Robert Browning's hilarious "Soliloquy of the Spanish Cloister"), to rebuild Jerusalem in the various "green and pleasant lands" of Europe.

Among the founders of religious orders Francis of Assisi (1181–1226) holds a unique literary position. The author of various important works, he is best known for the "Canticle of the Sun" (a sublime variation on Ps. 148 and similar texts), which Ernest Hatch Wilkins called "the first noble composition in an Italian dialect." Francis's idiosyncratic, stunningly literal attempt to live the "evangelical counsels" made him a dubious administrator, but his poetic celebration of "Lady Poverty" (combining the *Sermon on the Mount with courtly love) and his notion of friars as God's minstrels have fired the imagination of

countless writers and readers. The *Fioretti*, an anonymous fourteenth-century collection of Franciscan legends (e.g., how Francis tamed the man-eating wolf of Gubbio), is perhaps the most colorful and charming volume of Western hagiography.

With the rise of the vernacular languages the influence of the Bible was extended through the medieval mystery (or miracle) plays, which began as severely restrained liturgical dramas on the life of Christ and the Virgin Mary, written by clerics and performed in the churches in Latin. They later moved outdoors, shedding both their Latin and their restraint. In the twelfth century, to cite just one example, the *Jeu d'Adam* dramatized the *Fall, *Cain's fratricide, and the supposed biblical prophecies about Jesus. In the later morality plays (fifteenth century), allegorical figures representing Virtue and Vice struggled for the human soul, sometimes accompanied by crowd-pleasing horseplay. While this primitive theater is little read today (continental literature has nothing to rival the delightful Wakefield *Second Shepherds' Play*, ca. 1400–50), it served as a bridge to the splendid flowering of drama in the Renaissance.

Religion of a crude chauvinistic sort played a major role in the *chansons de geste*, with their bellicose bishops and cast-iron conviction, as in *The Song of Roland* (early twelfth century), that "Paiien ont tort et chrestiens ont dreit." In *The Poem of the Cid* (ca. 1140), the Cid addresses his Castilian vassals: "I pray to God, to our spiritual Father/ That you who for my sake have left your homes and lands/ May, before I die, get some good of me/ That you may regain double what you have lost." On the enemy side, "The King of Morocco is distressed at my Cid Don Rodrigo:/ 'He has violated my territories/ And gives thanks to no one, except Jesus Christ.' "

In the immense corpus of medieval chivalric literature, religion—that is, mystical Christianity—played a large role, especially in the Arthurian cycle. The quest for the Holy Grail (the cup in which *Joseph of Arimathea supposedly received the blood from Christ's side), which was told in the legend of Parsifal both by Chrétien de Troyes (latter half of twelfth century) and Wolfram von Eschenbach (d. ca. 1220), is one of the most famous chivalric tales. For many years Wagner's *Parsifal* (1882) was regularly performed on Good Friday. But the heart of chivalry was full of war, lust, and self-aggrandizement—Tristan and Iseult's irreproachable piety is helpless to check their adulterous desire—and hence alien to Christian ideals. This point was irrefutably made by no less a critic than Sancho Panza, who told Don Quixote (Part II, Chap. viii): "And so, my lord, it's better to be a humble little friar, of any order whatever, than a valiant and wandering knight; God gives more credit for two dozen blows with a lash than for two thousand thrusts with a lance—be they at giants, monsters, or dragons." Don Quixote feebly responds that there are many paths to heavenly glory, but Sancho has dogma on his side.

Much more directly inspired by the Bible was the richly varied medieval mystical tradition. Some of its crucial figures include Bernard of Clairvaux, Francis of Assisi, Bonaventure (ca. 1217–74), and the Germans Hildegard of Bingen (1098–1179), Meister Eckhart (ca. 1260–1327), and Nicholas of Cusa (1401–64). Germany undoubtedly had the most highly developed schools of mysticism, but the later Spanish Carmelites Teresa of Avila (1515–82) and John of the Cross (1542–91) reached a wider audience and have a more distinguished place in the literary canon. Teresa's mystical writings include *The Path of Perfection* and *The Interior Castle.* John is best known today for three of his poems, "Dark Night of the Soul," a phrase now naturalized in English; "The Spiritual Canticle," based on the Song of Solomon; and "Flame of Living Love," which, like the previous two, borrows the vocabulary of sexual passion to describe the soul's encounter with God. An Augustinian contemporary of John, Luis de León (1527–91), was perhaps an even greater poet, and like him found particular inspiration in the Song of Solomon. For translating that book from the Hebrew (and his "judaizing" tendencies) he was imprisoned for almost five years, during which time he wrote a prose masterpiece, *Los Nombres de Cristo,* a Platonic dialogue on the meaning of such titles ascribed to Christ as "Prince of Peace" and "Son of God." Fray Luis also wrote a powerful *Exposition on the Book of Job.* Mystical literature is vast and of considerable importance in the later development of individualism, religious and otherwise. But most of it belongs more properly in the realm of theology or, in some cases, philosophy.

The supreme literary work of the late Middle Ages-early Renaissance is Dante's *Divine Comedy* (finished some time before 1321), which is literally in a class by itself. Dante's poem draws upon science, philosophy, and history, as well as theology, but it is supremely indebted to the Bible. Dante works leading figures from the Bible into his vast tapestry. For example, he shows us *Judas locked in the jaws of *Satan at the frozen bottom of *hell; in the *Purgatorio* he evokes the scene of Michal scorning *David's dance before the *ark; and he populates his *Paradiso* with all sorts of biblical figures, from *Adam and *Eve to *Rachel, *Rebekah, and *Rahab. But the work as a whole is dogged by the devil's disconcerting way of having all the good tunes: just as Satan is, despite everything, the most interesting and eloquent character in *Paradise Lost,* so Dante's *Inferno* is superior to the other two *cantiche* in dramatic power. And Dante's grandest moments come when he has the damned (e.g., Francesca da Rimini, Farinata, Ulysses, and Ugolino) tell their tragic stories—with a greatness of soul not lessened by the fact that they stand under God's eternal condemnation.

The late Middle Ages also witnessed the appearance of what has been perhaps the most popular of all books inspired by the Bible, the *Imitation of Christ,* written in Latin and commonly attributed to Thomas Hammerken (ca. 1380–1471), a German Augustinian monk known to history as Thomas à Kempis. Kempis was profoundly influenced by the years (1392–97) he spent with the Brothers of the Common Life, a community of pious laymen in Deventer, near Utrecht. In a simple, pellucid style, interwoven with quotations from the New Testament, the *Imitation* champions an intensely personal love of Jesus (culminating in a quasi-erotic mystical union) that focuses on the Eucharist. The book urges its readers to seek imitation in literal adhesion to the Gospels, particularly stressing humility, self-denial, rejection of the "world," and constant prayer. Kempis's highly individualistic version of Christianity, which no doubt reflects his own retiring nature (see his famous dictum, "Cella continuata dulcescit"), seems to be oblivious of social justice and the outside world in general; and this has contributed to its current status as an unread, or seldom read, classic. Devotional literature since Kempis has been a fantastically prolific but mostly undistinguished genre. One exception to this rule is the *Introduction to the Devout Life* by Francis de Sales (1567–1622), an agreeably written and more accommodating handbook of Christian piety for the layperson.

During the Middle Ages direct access to the Bible was limited to those who knew Latin. With the coming of the Reformation and the discovery of the *printing press, this would change forever. The act of reading one's own copy of the

Bible and shaping one's own interpretation of it would eventually become a kind of sacramental symbol of intellectual freedom. In Germany Martin Luther's (1483–1546) *translation of the Bible, drawing on the chancery style of Saxony, which laid the groundwork for modern High German, was of unparalleled importance. It is partly thanks to Luther that Germany has been and still is the most biblically literate country in the world. His vigorous, earthy, impetuous prose style, in his pamphlets and controversial works, along with his fine hymns ("Ein' feste Burg," "Vom Himmel hoch," etc.) earned him a large niche in German cultural history. At the same time, the power of his pen gave broad currency to his vitriolic anti-Semitism (as in his pamphlet *On the Jews and Their Lies.*)

The more irenic Desiderius Erasmus (ca. 1469–1536), a peripatetic Dutch Augustinian, published a Greek New Testament with a Latin translation that, while beneath modern standards, helped to focus scholarly attention on the original. His wonderful *Praise of Folly* (1516) is a satirical hodgepodge, ultimately inspired by 1 Corinthians 1.18–25. And John Calvin's (1509–64) *Institutes of the Christian Religion* (1536, first written in Latin) is a radical Protestant reading of the Bible, an assault on Catholicism, and a powerful piece of French prose. Partly as the result of Calvin's influence, French Protestant writers, even such a black sheep as André Gide (1869–1951), have been better versed in the Bible than their Catholic or unbelieving counterparts. And the Calvinistic practice of relentless, lonely self-scrutiny bore autobiographical and biographical fruit in later centuries. It is no accident that both Jean-Jacques Rousseau and James Boswell (1740–95) were raised in the Calvinist fortresses of Geneva and Edinburgh.

The seventeenth century saw the last great age of biblically based religious literature. The tradition of religious theater survived in the seventeenth century in Spain, with Calderón (1600–81) and his *autos sacramentales,* and France, with such masterpieces as Corneille's (1606–84) *Polyeucte* (1641), and Racine's (1639–99) *Esther* (1689) and *Athalie* (1691). The latter, with its exquisite formal artifice and courtly grandeur ("O divine, ô charmante loi! / O justice! ô bonté suprême! / Que de raisons, quelle douceur extrême / D'engager à ce Dieu son amour et sa foi!"), seems far removed from the Bible; but Racine handles his sources in 2 Kings and 2 Chronicles with intelligence and discretion. In the seventeenth and eighteenth centuries the Jesuits wrote and staged learned, edifying Latin plays on biblical themes all over Europe. Perhaps the last surviving specimens of popular Christian drama are the Passion Play of Oberammergau (which is based in part on a sixteenth-century model and has now been sanitized of its worst anti-Semitic features) and Hugo von Hofmannsthal's *Jedermann* (1911), an effective reworking of the great fifteenth-century Dutch morality play of the same name *(Elckerlijk).*

The seventeenth century was also a great age of pulpit oratory. Jacques Bénigne Bossuet (1627–1704) is still remembered for his solemn sermons delivered at the funerals of the aristocracy, full of resonant maxims on the passing of worldly glory ("Tout ce qui se mesure finit, et tout ce qui est né pour finir n'est pas tout à fait sorti du néant, où il est sitôt replongé"). Bossuet retired just about the time that the Jesuit preacher Louis Bourdaloue (1632–1704) was coming into vogue. Bourdaloue may have been the better reasoner and rhetorician, but posterity (although not Voltaire) gave the palm to Bossuet. In Portugal (and later in Brazil and Rome) a still more gifted Jesuit, António Vieira (1608–97) wrote clear, vivid, sharply reasoned sermons that rank with the finest specimens of Portuguese prose.

The age also saw at least two great, if uneven, Protestant poets. Andreas Gryphius (1616–64) lamented the horrors of the Thirty Years War and gave moving expression to his stalwart, deeply humanistic Lutheran piety. In *Les Tragiques,* a bitterly satirical epic, Agrippa d'Aubigné (1551–1630) anticipated the Last Judgment, as he championed the long-suffering Huguenots and chastised evil Catholic rulers, especially Catherine de Médicis, who launched the St. Bartholomew's Day massacre in 1572.

Pascal's *Pensées,* one of the most brilliant instances of the French talent for treating serious philosophical questions on a level accessible to the layperson, are an undeniable masterpiece, even though its proof-text treatment of scripture is its least impressive part. Pascal argued that without the apparently irrational Pauline doctrine of original sin there is no way to understand the mysteries of human nature. Pascal's most memorable device is his dramatized figure of the *libertin*—a seventeenth-century descendant of the ungodly gentiles savaged by Paul in Romans 1:18–32—desperately fleeing thoughts of death in "diversion" and terrified by "the eternal silence of those infinite spaces." Pascal is still read enthusiastically by believers and unbelievers alike, but the fact that the fideistic and pessimistic

Pensées were a rear-guard action against an increasingly triumphant secularism did not bode well for the philosophical future of Christianity.

After more than a century of exhausting religious wars, the Enlightenment brought the first large-scale rejection of the Bible and biblical religion, along with numerous apologetic counterattacks. This had the inevitable if paradoxical effect that the *philosophes* spent a great deal of time discussing Holy Writ. Voltaire (1694–1778), a rebellious product of the Jesuit Collège Louis le Grand, devoted much of his prodigious energy to mocking "l'infâme" (well defined by George Saintsbury as "privileged and persecuting orthodoxy") and everything connected with it. *Candide* (1759) pronounces all biblical theodicy bankrupt. In one of his gentler pieces, *Ingenuous* (1767), he taunts contemporary Christians for their deviations from apostolic practice. More benign critics such as Rousseau, in his "Profession of Faith of a Savoyard Vicar" in *Émile* (1762), tried to rationalize and demythologize the God of the Bible.

In one of the greatest Enlightenment texts, *Foundations of the Metaphysics of Morals,* Immanuel Kant (1724–1804) claimed to reject all external moral authority (such as churches and scriptures) in favor of a "categorical imperative" that supposedly applied to all rational beings on earth (or anywhere else), but this "universal" ethics had deep and obvious roots in the German Pietism Kant knew from his youth and in the age-old Christian tradition of self-denial.

Even as Kant was condemning all fixed theological statements as "heteronomous," his almost exact contemporary, Friedrich Gottlieb Klopstock (1724–1803) was attempting, in a grandly anachronistic (twenty cantos in hexameter) orthodox epic, *Der Messias,* to do for Germany what Milton had done for England. Drawing mainly from the New Testament, *Paradise Lost,* and the topoi of classical and Renaissance epics, the poem recounts the passion, death, resurrection, and enthronement of Jesus at the right hand of the Father. But traditional epic and biblical narrative (as Erich Auerbach showed in *Mimesis*) are scarcely compatible, and in any case Klopstock was essentially a lyricist; and so *Der Messias,* except for the first three cantos, is generally acknowledged to be a well-intentioned failure.

The eighteenth century witnessed the Haskalah, the Jewish Enlightenment, which eventually brought millions of European Jews into the mainstream of European culture. It also led to a painful state of deracination that can be ob-

served in two of the greatest modern Jewish writers, Heinrich Heine (1797–1856) and Franz Kafka (1883–1924). Heine cynically accepted baptism, but never found a satisfactory home in Judaism, Christianity, or unbelief. His scintillating, relentlessly ironic prose records the contradiction of his love for the gods of Greece and his sometimes begrudging attachment to his Jewish roots. In his *Confessions* (1854) he explains: "In my earlier days I hadn't felt any special love for Moses, possibly because I was under the sway of the Hellenic spirit, and I couldn't forgive the Lawgiver of the Jews his hatred for image-making and the plastic arts. I failed to see that . . . he himself was nevertheless a great artist, with the true artistic spirit. Only he, like his Egyptian compatriots, turned his artistic genius exclusively toward the realm of the colossal and the indestructible." Self-exiled in Paris for a quarter-century, Heine summed up his impossible position in his oft-quoted deathbed words, "Dieu me pardonnera: c'est son métier."

Kafka, who has been hailed by some critics as the twentieth-century novelist par excellence, had a love-hate relation with Judaism characteristic of his assimilated contemporaries in Austro-Hungary. Although his work seems to be marked by a blank, uncanny lack of any frame of reference, some pieces, such as his fragment "Before the Law" (later integrated into *The Trial*) evoke explicitly, as his other stories and novels do implicitly, a haunted, absurd, Job-like demand for justice. Elsewhere in *The Trial,* Joseph K., searching for the "law books" studied by his mysterious accusers (and later executioners) can find only clumsy pornography. To the extent that Kafka's dark parables refer to the Bible ("In the Penal Colony" speaks of the old and new "Commandant," sacred but unintelligible "scripts," an impossible commandment to "BE JUST!" etc.), the tone is consistently hostile. But while he was free to carp and complain—in eerily reasonable prose—about the failure of his world to resemble the Bible's, this "religious humorist," as Thomas Mann called him, was never free to leave the subject alone.

For Marcel Proust (1871–1922), whose mother was Jewish and who strongly identified with her, religion was only a source of aesthetic sensations—and guilt. Still, *Remembrance of Things Past* (1913–28) has many biblical echoes, most obviously and painfully in its longest single section, *Sodome et Gomorrhe,* where Proust projects his own horror of "inversion" onto the doomed inhabitants of *The Cities of the Plain* (as the original three volumes are called in the Montcrieff translation; see Gen. 19.29). The famous scene of the madeleine cookie and the lime tea in *Swann's Way* is a nostalgic transformation of both the *Passover seder and the Eucharist: an attempt to redeem lost time (and create "sacred history," in the absence of God and revelation) through art.

For Isaac Bashevis Singer (1904–91), the son of a Polish rabbi, biblical faith, as preserved and embodied in the *shtetl*, is unspeakably precious (especially in the horrific light of the *Holocaust), but salvation is, at best, a leap in the dark. Singer's Gimpel the fool is a model absurdist, believing for belief's sake. One of Singer's many devout atheists, Rabbi Nechemia in "Something is There," inevitably quotes Ecclesiastes 3:19 to himself, "For the fate of the sons of men and the fate of beasts is the same; as one dies, so dies the other"—before its terrible truth breaks his heart.

The Romantic movement, with its validation of the primitive, the irrational, and the noumenal, often took a positive view of biblical religion. In Italy *Saul* (very freely adapted from 1 Samuel) by Vittorio Alfieri (1749–1803) may well be the finest modern poetic treatment of any biblical figure. Alfieri's pure, severe style proved a splendid match for his subject. Alessandro Manzoni's *I promessi sposi* (1825–26) deserves mention because, although perhaps marginally "biblical" (it recounts the successful struggle of a pious Catholic couple in early seventeenth-century Lombardy to get married despite the formidable obstacles placed in their way by a villainous aristocrat and a spineless parish priest), the grandness of its conception and the richness of its execution have led to its being ranked as the greatest Italian novel.

In the early Romantic period Germany had two outstanding poets who grappled with the conflict between the Bible and secular culture (in various guises). Friedrich Hölderlin (1770–1843) is remembered for his impassioned evocation of the gods of Greece. But in his last creative years (he went incurably insane in 1806) Hölderlin wrote enigmatic hymns to an agonizing Christ ("For suffering colors the purity of this man who is as pure as a sword"), the last of the gods, joining them in a hopeful, heretical synthesis against a cruel God the Father.

In *Christendom or Europe,* Novalis (Friedrich von Hardenberg, 1772–1801) conjured up a "new golden age with dark infinite eyes, a prophetic, wonder-working and wound-healing comforting time that sparks eternal life—a great time of reconciliation." This was not meant to be a reactionary restoration of medieval Catholicism, but a kind of sacred dream come true. Novalis also had a vision of the individual as the locus of literally divine possibilities. "The history of each person," he wrote, "should be a Bible—aims to be a Bible."

In his *Essay on Criticism* (1711) Alexander Pope mocked people who "to church repair,/ Not for the doctrine, but the music there." This stricture would apply to the many Romantics who loved the Bible primarily for its symbols. A crucial instance of this is Goethe's (1749–1832) *Faust* (1808, 1832). The "Prologue in Heaven," which frames the entire narrative, is freely adapted from the book of *Job. But "der Herr" is less the Lord than the embodiment of cosmic optimism and paternal benevolence, and Mephistopheles is emphatically not the New Testament *Satan. He represents instead a destructive, cynical antihumanism. Similarly, Goethe borrows from both the Virgin *Mary and *Mary Magdalene to create Gretchen. The "Eternal Feminine" that draws Faust upward is a universal Madonna. T. S. Eliot claimed that bad poets borrow but good poets steal; and Goethe shows no compunction about ransacking the Bible for whatever he needed. In any case, nineteenth-century literature is full of Madonna-substitutes, like Solveig in Ibsen's *Peer Gynt* (1867), and Magdalene figures, such as Sonya in Dostoyevsky's *Crime and Punishment* (1866).

Similarly, other Romantic writers could be classified as in one sense or other "religious"; but upon closer inspection the role of the Bible in their work often proves to be secondary. François René de Chateaubriand (1768–1848) was a Romantic apologist for Christianity, who celebrated its aesthetic appeal in an erstwhile classic, *The Genius of Christianity, or The Poetic and Moral Beauties of the Christian Religion* (1802). In this fervent miscellany Chateaubriand extols the Bible for its "sublimity," but his two most famous works that originally formed part of the book, *Atala* and *René*, show him on more congenial ground, describing the sexual torment, guilt, and despair, in awesomely beautiful natural settings, of young Catholic characters who are projections of himself.

One of the greatest nineteenth-century religious writers is Søren Kierkegaard (1813–55), whose work is without parallel. Although essentially a philosopher-theologian, Kierkegaard's style—passionate, prodigiously energetic, dramatic, and often ironic—qualifies him as a literary figure. A sort of Danish Don Quixote, Kierkegaard's reading of the Bible "turned his head" (cf. his famous "teleological suspension of the ethical" interpretation of the binding of Isaac in Gen. 22 [see Aqedah]), and impelled him to spend his short life campaigning against the deformation of Christianity into Christendom, and proclaiming the "contemporaneousness" of the Gospels. But as with Pascal before him and Dostoyevsky after, the secular reader may wonder why Kierkegaard's eloquence is so often fired by anxiety and doubt.

In an entirely different sense Gustave Flaubert (1821–80) found frequent inspiration in the Bible. Religion for Flaubert may be an exploded illusion, but its vivid mythology is immeasurably superior to the desiccation and meanness of contemporary life. *Madame Bovary* (1857), who has been bitterly disillusioned by her banal, soulless lovers, gives the most passionate kiss of her life to the crucifix proffered to her as she dies. In Flaubert's final masterpiece, *Three Tales* (1877), the failure of biblical religion is still an open wound. The ironically named Félicité in "A Simple Heart" is a self-immolating (and totally ignorant) believer. Enslaved by her employer, mistreated or abandoned by almost everyone in a nominally Christian society, she dies during a senile fantasy of her stuffed pet parrot as the Holy Ghost. "The Legend of St. Julian the Hospitaller" retells the mysterious, harrowing life of a sort of Christian Oedipus, but the concluding lines dismiss the story as a stained-glass fairy tale. Worst of all, in "Herodias," a skillful fictionalization of the beheading of *John the Baptist, Flaubert curses all parties—Jews, Romans, *Pharisees, *Sadducees, *Essenes, and proto-Christians—as bigoted, brutal, and deluded.

Nineteenth-century Russia produced two great instances of literature shaped by the Bible: the work of the tortured believer Fyodor Dostoyevsky (1821–81) and of the aristocratic convert to evangelical simplicity, Leo Tolstoy (1828–1910). Orthodox critics have praised Dostoyevsky's "Christ-figures," such as Prince Leo Myshkin from *The Idiot* (1868–69) and the former monk Alyosha Karamazov (1880), but the voice of his nay-sayers, such as the Underground Man (1864) or the antitheist Ivan Karamazov strikes most readers as far more compelling. Ivan, to be sure, is as God-haunted as any Dostoyevskyan character, and in his prose poem, "The Grand Inquisitor," he imagines Jesus returning to sixteenth-century Spain. Yet though he kisses the Grand Inquisitor (who wants to protect his infantilized, anesthetized, but beloved flock from the dangers of Christian freedom), Dostoyevsky's Christ has literally nothing to say.

Tolstoy's peculiar brand of deism, discarding most of Christian dogma but borrowing freely from the New Testament, preaching nonresistance to evil and exalting Christ-like self-donation to others, won followers around the world, but he suffers from the archetypal liberal Christian problem of deriving the inspiration and motivating energy of his work from a source he himself no longer believes in. In two of his best stories, "The Death of Ivan Ilych" (1886) and "Master and Man" (1895), Tolstoy creates blindly materialistic protagonists who transcend their bourgeois egoism on the point of death by imitating their altruistic servants. Tolstoy's acid depiction of the lives of Ivan Ilych Golovin and Vasili Andreevich Brekhunov has an angry prophetic power, but the vague redemption they achieve (in lieu of death Ivan Ilych finds a mysterious "light," and an unnamed "Someone" comes to visit Brekhunov) seems like a biblical deus ex machina.

Then there is the unique and paradoxical case of the "antitheists," the greatest of whom is Friedrich Nietzsche (1844–1900). Like Kierkegaard, Nietzsche has secured a place in the literary canon thanks to his unique brand of philosophizing—"with a hammer," as he put it. While grimly declaring that "God is dead," and brutally insisting that the slave morality of Jews and Christians has to give way to the master morality of "the blond beast," Nietzsche, who was the son of a Lutheran pastor, produced an epochal body of work that weirdly mirrors the Bible. His aphorisms have the alternately angry, exultant, or scornful ring of the prophets. His superman is a secular messiah. His doctrine of eternal recurrence is a fantastic substitute for an eternal afterlife. And Nietzsche's life had both the suicidal courage of the Christian martyr as well as the fierce self-denial and misogynistic celibacy of a Christian hermit.

Miguel de Unamuno (1864–1936) is a paradoxical heir of Pascal, Kierkegaard, and Nietzsche, who turns doubt into a category of religious experience, an ex-believer who cannot stop wrestling with the Bible. Early on in *The Agony of Christianity* (1924) he writes: "Agony, then, is struggle. And Christ came to bring us agony, struggle, and not peace. He told us as much. 'Do not think that I have come to bring peace on earth' [Matt. 10.34]." And he concludes, "Christ, our Christ! Why hast thou forsaken us?" In *Saint Manuel the Good* (1931) Unamuno describes an utterly devoted but unbelieving priest whose honesty forces him to keep silent as his congregation recites the Creed but who is (almost) buoyed up and borne ahead by the wave of their faith.

A number of other twentieth-century atheistic writers, such as Jean-Paul Sartre (1905–80), Albert Camus (1913–60), and the practitioners of the "Theatre of the Absurd" (e.g., Luigi Pirandello, Eugène Ionesco, Samuel Beckett), can be seen as conducting a lifelong argument with the biblical version of the world, shaking their fists at an empty heaven. The "nausea" experienced by Sartre's autobiographical hero, Antoine Roquentin (1938), is a kind of metaphysical malaise caused by the fact that "every thing in existence is born without reason, prolongs itself out of weakness, and dies by accident." Although Roquentin, like Proust, decides to seek relief from a godless universe in art, he nevertheless defines himself by what he rejects: the idea of *creation.

Beckett's play *Waiting for Godot* (1952) is full of futile nostalgia for the world of the Bible. Vladimir wonders why only one of the evangelists tells the story of the good thief, and he can't remember a verse from Proverbs: "Hope deferred maketh the something sick." Although Beckett himself defined Godot as whatever one hopes for, he is clearly a tragicomically incompetent/nonexistent biblical God with an unreliable and very nervous young boy as his angel. Like Kafka, Beckett plays endless variations on the theme of being condemned to hope. But while for Kafka hope is a sort of cruel and crazy mitzvah, for Beckett it is an incurable tic douleureux from which all humans suffer.

Nikos Kazantzakis (1885–1957) is a different and unusual case. At times resembling an incoherent Unamuno, Kazantzakis was a nihilist whose obsession with Christianity knew no bounds (see *The Greek Passion, The Last Temptation of Christ,* and *Report to Greco*), but with the passage of time his work strikes many readers as embarrassingly full of sound and fury.

The most significant influence of the Bible on modern literature (roughly from the late eighteenth century to the present) may well be the persistence of Jewish and Christian symbols and allusions—as in Ibsen's *Brand* (1866), the story of a noble, but self-destructive zealot, or in the title *The Road to Damascus* (1898–1904) by August Strindberg, who had nothing in common with Paul except a hair-trigger emotional sensitivity.

All in all, this biblical influence is so varied and complex that it is hard to assess. The texts, as we have already seen, run a staggeringly broad gamut, from *Nathan der Weise* by Gotthold Ephraim Lessing (1729–81), a Christian who idealized his friend, the great *maskil* and "Jewish Socrates," Moses Mendelssohn (1729–86), to the philo-Christian "Nazarene" novels of the Yiddish writer Sholem Asch (1880–1957). Biblical themes appear in myriad guises. Ernest Renan (1823–92) had an immense scandalous success with his *Vie de Jésus* (1863) and its vision of Jesus as the "divine charmer" and Jewish Orpheus (cf. the rapturous Hellenism of Renan's "Prayer on the Acropolis" in his *Souvenirs d'Enfance et de Jeunesse* [1883]) but, although dated, it remains the most widely read popular-scholarly life of Christ. Thomas Mann (1875–1955) created an extraordinarily ambitious, sympathetic, and thoughtful, if not always aesthetically compelling, picture of the world of the *ancestors of Israel in his immense novel *Joseph and his Brothers* (1934–42). When all is said and done, no one can predict what forms the influence of the Bible on future writers may take, but it may be safe to predict that such influence will be both continuous and attenuated.

PETER D. HEINEGG

North American Literature

American literature, in its use of the Bible, is not notably characterized by medieval or Miltonic retellings of scriptural narratives. Drawing epic and dramatic material rather from frontier life, New World authors often chose to invest immediate and local experience with eternal significance by encoding it with biblical *typology. It is this typological biblicizing of national life, and the theological worldview that such a biblical typology implies, that facilitates the connection of important individual texts to the development of a larger public "myth" in the United States. In Canada, by contrast, where the wilderness seemed more resistant to subjugation, and survival rather than triumph the visible goal, the use of the Bible by literary authors does not follow from a typological worldview; hence it is more tentative, less schematic, and, where involved with questions of identity, more concerned to relate personal rather than public experience to the transvaluation afforded by biblical references.

The United States. American literature branched off from English literature just at that point in the seventeenth century when the influence of the Bible upon secular texts was at its zenith in Britain. The Puritans who settled in New England and dominated its literary culture for several generations, were, moreover, of English speakers among the most biblically literate. Extensive mastery of the entire biblical corpus in the King James (Authorized) Version was common among ordinary people in the colonies, and individuals who had memorized entire books, or, as in the case of John Cotton, large portions of both Testaments, were far from rare.

The writing of the Puritans themselves was confined largely to diaries, chronicles, and well-wrought sermons, but a few, such as Anne Bradstreet, with her sense of struggle between "The Flesh and the Spirit" (1678), and Edward Taylor, so heavily influenced (like his English metaphysical counterparts) by the *Song of Solomon, wrote reflective and devotional poetry rich in biblical theme and idiom. Almost any kind of American text in this period, from chronicle to court judgment, might not only quote the Bible extensively but be characterized throughout by biblical diction.

Biblical typology, as Sacvan Bercovitch (*Biblical Typology in Early American Literature* [1972]) and others have shown, provided a means whereby life in the colonies became literal realization of scriptural metaphor: *Fall, *exile, *Exodus, pilgrim history, *Promised Land, and even millennial kingdom are worked almost seamlessly into the narratives of William Bradford, John Winthrop, Roger Williams, Michael Wigglesworth (*The Day of Doom* [1662]), Cotton Mather, Samuel Sewall, and Jonathan Edwards. In Wigglesworth, whose text was buttressed throughout by marginal references to precise biblical texts, or later, in Edwards's dramatic "Sinners in the Hands of an Angry God" (1741), one sees the incipient apocalypticism as well as a hellfire and brimstone call to repentance that the Puritan style of Calvinism was to bequeath to American literary consciousness. In Bradford, Winthrop, and Taylor, one observes paradoxically that America was also seen as a recovered *Eden, a new Canaan, or Promised Land in the here and now. In this early period, it is clearly typology and allusion to the Hebrew Bible that predominates: even a poem such as Edward Taylor's *Christographia* (ca. 1690), a fourteen-sermon "portrait" of Christ, each sermon preceded by a poetic meditation, tends to be structured according to types, promises, and prophecies of the Hebrew scriptures.

Bercovitch has shown that developmental typology in Puritan literature relates figures from the Hebrew Bible not only to the *incarnation but, in a form of *sensus plenior*, to the *second coming of Christ. Thus, typical narratives, such as those of the Babylonian captivity and Promised Land, come to prefigure end-time events as well as aspects of the story of Christ. America is Eden "in the last days." This historiographic view is complemented by "the static biographical parallelism offered by correlative typology, in which the focus is not primarily upon Christ but upon certain Old Testament heroes . . . as they become, *through* Christ, 'redivivus' in contemporary heroes." This second typology, visible in actual names as well as the names of literary characters, relies as much as the first on *covenant theology. Typology thus becomes a link between the concept of "a recurrent national covenant and the concept of an unchanging covenant of grace manifest in succeeding stages of the history of redemption" (Bercovitch, p. 25). Thomas Shepard's *The Covenant of Grace* (1651) reads current frontier events as if they were superimposed upon the lineated covenant history of the Bible; Cotton Mather's *Magnalia Christi Americana* (1702) looks back already to the golden age of Puritanism as a lost Eden or New Canaan, as from a pilgrim prospect from which the intervention of providence must be sought to ensure against the temptation to return—even at Harvard College—to the luxurious entrapments of Egypt. For America to realize its destiny as the land of promise, the conversion of American experience into a text about God's unfolding plan of redemption, emergent in Edward Johnson's *Wonder-Working Providence of Sion's Savior* (1654), was coupled with a tendency to read the text of the Bible itself as though it were chiefly about Americans, or, as Giles Gunn puts it in *The Bible and American Arts and Letters* (1983), as if "the Bible was proleptically American."

The American jeremiad, a political sermon that joins social criticism to spiritual renewal (as well as public dream to private identity), has come to be recognized as a foundational mythopoeic American literary genre. From the frontier outpost sermons of Peter Bulkeley in the mid-seventeenth century to the television evangelists of the late twentieth century it has tended to read contemporary events as though they were written down in an unfolding text to which the Bible is the master code and ultimate governing form. Characterized not only by biblical rhetoric and diction but also formed upon biblical narrative and dependent for its wide appeal on extensive popular knowledge of the Bible, the jeremiad has in turn had a powerful influence upon other literary genres throughout the history of American letters.

This was less apparent in the second half of the eighteenth century, however, than later. The dominant American writings in this period of consolidation continued to be political, but of a decidedly Enlightenment stripe. Allusions to the Bible occur only rarely in the works of Franklin and Jefferson; classical literature, as in England, usurped the fashion. Even in poetry, dominated by the "Yale poets" (Trumball, Dwight, Barlow, Humphreys, and Hopkins) despite their uniformly Calvinist upbringing, literary use of the Bible is as marginal as it is in the poetry of Philip Freneau who, in the spirit of his time, eulogized "On the Religion of Nature." Timothy Dwight's Miltonic allegorical epic, The Conquest of Canaan (ca. 1775), populated with eighteenth-century Americans with Hebrew names and perhaps the most self-consciously biblical poem of the period, was unsuccessfully archaic, a relic of his grandfather Jonathan Edwards's day, displaced in popularity by Dwight's own rather conventional pastoral verse. Only the black slave poet, Phillis Wheatley ("Thoughts on the Works of Providence" [1770]), wrote popular verse that adhered to the Puritan vision and its biblical themes and language, and it too looked backward, as in her most famous poem, "On the Death of the Rev. Mr. George Whitefield, 1770."

The nineteenth century brought a notable revival in biblical allusion in the works of writers of diverse religious persuasions; easily recognizable from the Calvinist William Cullen Bryant to the Quaker John Greenleaf Whittier, it is richly present in the most popular poet of the nineteenth century, Henry Wadsworth Longfellow. Each of these poets wrote verse heavily marked by biblical idiom and diction, if not always devoted to a biblical theme; Whittier, however, in his concern with *slavery, readily invoked the captivity, Exodus, and *wilderness themes in poems such as "Song of Slaves in the Desert" (1847), "Ichabod" (1850), and "First Day Thoughts" (1852), while Longfellow, author of The Divine Tragedy (1871), a Passion drama, related *Pentecost and the atonement in his verse-sermon, "The Children of the Lord's Supper." In James Russell Lowell's then famous Harvard "Oration Ode" (1810), the old Puritan vision of America as "the Promised Land / That flows with Freedom's honey and milk" buttresses both the rhetoric and Lowell's moral: " 'Tis not the grapes of Canaan that repay, / But the high faith that failed not by the way."

Side by side with these sentiments, the growth of romantic naturalism and transcendentalism expressed in Henry David Thoreau and Ralph Waldo Emerson respectively is supported by a subtle recasting of selected biblical verities. Thoreau, in the prophetic sense of mission, evidenced particularly in Walden (1854) and Civil Disobedience (1849), shows familiarity with *Genesis, *Ecclesiastes, and the gospel of *Matthew, though he characteristically edits according to his strong dislike of any emphasis on *repentance. Emerson, son of a Unitarian minister and descended from Puritans, began his career as a Unitarian preacher but, in a crisis of vocation, shortly resigned to pursue an interest in Montaigne and certain writers of the English Romantic movement. As a colloquial philosopher in an era when the popular lecture was displacing the sermon in literary importance, he perceived where his future lay: "I believe that wherever we go, whatever we do, self is the sole subject we study and learn . . . but as self means Devil, so it means God." In his pursuit of the "God within," and despite his railing at "sulphurous Calvinism," he found, in his poem "The Problem" (1839), that "Out from the heart of nature rolled / the burdens of the Bible old." Though his antinomian redefinition of those burdens, most memorably expressed in his famous essay "On Self-Reliance" (1841), is what he has most contributed to the "biblical tradition" in American literature, Emerson could on occasion quickly revert to Puritan humility before an omnipotent God, as in "Grace" (1842).

In prose fiction, the novels of James Fenimore Cooper make extended use of biblical analogy for frontier experience. In a recrudescence of the Puritan pattern, Amer of The Oak Openings (1848) thinks the Bible addresses itself particularly to him, directing that he should lead the Indians, descendants of the lost tribes of Israel, back to Palestine. In The Last of the Mohicans (1826) Gamut is a singer of psalms who idolizes King *David. Yet Cooper is critical of the Puritan instinct for typological autobiography in The Deerslayer (1841), where he rejects the appropriation to the self of divine authority on the basis of forced biblical analogy. Despite their anti-Christian stance, Nathaniel Hawthorne's novels and short stories are rich in biblical allusions, though often as parody: in "Roger Malvin's Burial," the character Reuben is not only a superficial parallel to his biblical namesake, but a type of Israel seeking redemption from "Cyrus." In Herman Melville's epic-novel Moby-Dick

(1851), notwithstanding a fierce resistance to Calvinistic religion, a rich synthesis of biblical narrative and typology reveals a knowledge of the Bible that might almost have done credit to a Puritan divine; Melville's text opens with the evocative words, "Call me Ishmael." In *Pierre* (1852), he explores the theme of failed "imitation of Christ," to which he returns in the posthumously published *Billy Budd* (1924); in *The Confidence Man* (1857) he has the prototypical beguiler, Satan himself, come on board the American ship of faith, *Fidele,* and, by arguing that there are no trustworthy texts (in that the Bible itself is a devilish beguiler), demonstrate that there are in fact no real Christians aboard. The writings of Edgar Allen Poe, who refers to the Qur'ān more approvingly than the Bible, are surprisingly rich in biblicisms, and one story, "The Cask of Amontillado" (1846), has been read as a demonic parody of the Passion.

The work of these major fiction writers illustrates that if resistance to the formidable biblical inclusiveness of Puritan views of history and writing had been largely passive in the years from the mid-eighteenth century through the first quarter of the nineteenth century, it began to take on a more strident antinomian flavor during the period known as the American Literary Renaissance. This is particularly evident in the poets, of whom (beside Poe) Walt Whitman and Emily Dickinson suffice as illustration. The debt of Whitman's prosody, rhythm, and diction to the language of the King James Bible, along with his special interest in Judaism, does not hinder his Emersonian vindication of "the plain old Adam, the simple genuine self against the whole world." In "A Backward Glance O'er Traveled Roads," he tells us that in preparation for *Leaves of Grass* (1855) he grounded himself in both testaments, and the influence is clear enough at the level of structure. His tendency to see himself as a Christ or prophet, as in the climactic thirty-third section of *Song of Myself*, "I am the man, I suffered, I was there," is reinforced by his appreciation of the role of biblical prophets as visionary denouncers of social privilege and cultural hypocrisy.

Dickinson, as Herbert Schneidau has observed, presents an extreme case of the familiar paradox so apparent in Melville: "the more antinomian the American poet, the more he or she falls back upon the traditional guidebook." Her poetry requires extensive verbal familiarity with the Bible if its full import as a rejection of conformity with received traditions is to be fully understood. Following her years at Mount Holyoke Female Seminary, she sees the Bible as "an antique volume / Written by faded men / At the suggestion of Holy Spectres," rejecting with bitter ironies the orthodox and Calvinistic appropriation of the Bible in which she had been educated.

The presence of the Bible in nineteenth-century literature is largely a function of educational formation; still living off the spiritual and literary capital of the Puritan era, and possessed thereby of a biblical literacy paralleled today only in certain parts of the English-speaking third world, American writers almost unavoidably wrote in biblical language, whatever their subject. Yet "the one serious Christian novel of the age," and most seriously biblical, was Harriet Beecher Stowe's *Uncle Tom's Cabin* (1851–52). Its actual plot turns upon a biblical treatment of the problem of evil, specifically recollected in a crisis reading of Psalm 73, and the hero Tom is made to be the paragon of the imitation of Christ in his nonviolent resistance to persecution and oppression. Yet this enormously popular work— as to a lesser extent the work of George Washington Cable and Joseph Holy Ingraham's epistolary, sensationalist and trivializing life of Christ, *The Prince of the House of David* (1855)—are, despite their success in the marketplace, exceptions that merely define the literary mainstream of the later nineteenth century, as represented by the realists Mark Twain, W. D. Howells, and Henry James. Twain (Samuel Clemens), especially in *Innocents Abroad* (1869), *Adventures of Huckleberry Finn* (1883), and *A Connecticut Yankee in King Arthur's Court* (1889), offers narrators who seem to know much about the Bible, yet for strategic purposes deploy it incorrectly. Twain's notorious antireligiosity grows steadily less covert and less comic (but note *Eve's Diary* [1906]) toward the end of his life, obliterating even this use of the Bible in the despairing cynicism of *A Mysterious Stranger* (1916). W. D. Howells, raised a Swedenborgian and matured as an agnostic, is said to have known much of the Bible by heart, and his *Rise of Silas Lapham* (1885) loosely rewords the story of *Jacob and *Esau. Henry James, whose "A Passionate Pilgrim" (1871) is heading back to the European "Egypt," makes almost no significant use of the Bible, except perhaps in the title only of *The Golden Bowl* (1904), which may be an enigmatic residue of Ecclesiastes 12.6. The Bible is largely displaced in the novels of the 1890s—in Hamlin Garland, Kate Chopin, Frank Norris, Jack London; even in the work of

Stephen Crane, son of a Methodist minister, there are few traceable echoes. Exceptions to this generalization in "serious" literature were historical novels based upon biblical times, of which General Lew Wallace's *Ben-Hur* (1880) was the most successful, followed by Henry K. Sienkiewicz's *Quo Vadis?* (1896), based upon the apostolic labors of *Peter. Even Henry Adams attempted a religious-historical novel, though his *Esther* (1884) was not popular.

Among the American poets writing between the two world wars, Robert Frost reflects an ambivalent attitude toward the Bible as a source, choosing the painful paradoxes of *Job as the material for his most overtly biblical poem, *A Masque of Reason* (1945). On the one hand, popular taste was being formed by the popular religious novels of Lloyd C. Douglas, notably *The Robe* (1942) and *The Fisherman* (1949), the first of which was made into a movie, and more thoughtfully in the novels of Scholem Asch, including *The Nazarene* (1939), *The Apostle* (1943), *Mary* (1949), and *Moses* (1951). On the other, the poetry and celebrated conversion of T. S. Eliot was prompting the renewal of intellectual interest in the Bible among poets and dramatists in some ways unprecedented since the Puritans. Marianne Moore was by 1920 the "poet's poet" in America. Her poetry, fluent in biblical story and idiom, reached the height of its achievement toward the end of World War II, and is exemplified in poems rich in allusion to *Jonah ("Sojourn in a Whale") and Job ("In Distrust of Merits"). Biblical allusions nonetheless waned in the poetry of Vachel Lindsay, after *General William Booth Enters into Heaven* (1913), and is of small consequence in the work of e. e. cummings, Edna St. Vincent Millay and Hart Crane—even John Crowe Ransome and Allen Tate—though biblical phrasing flavors the work of William Carlos Williams. In quite different accents it persists in some of the writers of the Harlem Renaissance, such as Langston Hughes and Countee Cullen.

In the drama, meanwhile, as in the popular novel, there had merged a tradition of modern retelling of biblical stories: George Cabot Lodge's *Cain* (1904), F. E. Pierce's *The World That God Destroyed* (1911), William Ford Manley's *The Mess of Pottage* (1928), Richard Burton's *Rahab* (1906), Scholem Asch's *Jephthah's Daughter* (1915), and R. G. Moulton's *The Book of Job* (1918). Marc Connelly's famous *Green Pastures* (1929), Eugene O'Neill's *Belshazzar* (1915), and Archibald MacLeish's acclaimed *J.B.*, a modernization of

the Job story (1958), along with his earlier *Nobodaddy* (1926), a verse play using *Adam, *Eve, *Cain, and Abel (cf. his volume, *Songs for Eve* [1954]), illustrate something of the diversity of dramatizations of subjects from the Hebrew Bible. Plays on New Testament subjects, though less numerous, were more influential: O'Neill's *Lazarus Laughed* (1925), Thornton Wilder's *Now the Servant's Name Was Malchus* (1928) and *Hast Thou Considered My Servant Job?* (a play about Christ, Satan, and Judas), Robinson Jeffers's dramatic poem *Dear Judas* (1929), along with Marie Doran's *Quo Vadis?* (1928), a dramatic adaptation of the novel of Sienkiewicz, highlight a flurry of activity in the 1920s. These plays with their tendency to recharacterize New Testament narratives, are a sharp contrast to the still traditional biblical drama of the prewar period, well represented in Charles Kennedy's *The Terrible Meek* (1912), and anticipate successful cinematic and musical adaptations of the Christ-Judas-Peter narrative in the 1960s and 1970s.

Biblical motif more than biblical language or narrative plot marks a residual influence of the Bible on American fiction of the modern period, often hearkening back to the old Puritan typology and theology of a "God-blessed America." In Walker Percy's *Love in the Ruins* (1971), a biblically encoded national mythology is called up nostalgically in a time when it seems actually to have lost much of its cultural and religious power. In titles that are evocative rather than indicative, biblical allusion is often used as if to borrow a mythological authority for writing unsure of how to proceed without a shareable literary foundation: F. Scott Fitzgerald's *This Side of Paradise* (1920) and *The Beautiful and the Damned* (1922), John Steinbeck's *East of Eden* (1952) and *Grapes of Wrath* (1939), Katherine Anne Porter's *Pale Horse, Pale Rider* (1939), James Baldwin's *The Fire Next Time* (1963), William Faulkner's *Go Down, Moses* (1942), Saul Bellow's *The Victim* (1947), and Walker Percy's *The Second Coming* (1980), all indicate a tendency to call upon biblical points of reference—and a specific mode— to express *apocalyptic apprehension. Elsewhere the biblical titles call up a mood of lamentation in Faulkner's *Absalom, Absalom!* (1936) or, as in Ernest Hemingway's use of Ecclesiastes, an experience of undermined foundations and lost identities in *The Sun Also Rises* (1926). James Agee's *Let Us Now Praise Famous Men* (1941), in a related vein, makes use of Sirach 44 to create a jeremiad on a lost sense of national covenant history.

The *parable has become another discernible mode in modern American fiction, with Hemingway's *The Old Man and the Sea* (1952) as perhaps the most eminent modern example. Biblical titles continue to appear, as in Wright Morris's "The Ram in the Thicket" (1951), with only a loosely allusive function; even in writers with notably religious concerns, such as Percy or Flannery O'Connor ("The Lame Shall Enter First"; *The Violent Bear It Away* [1960]), substantive use of biblical material is rare.

What Ursula Brumm describes as "the figure of Christ in American literature" (*Partisan Review* 24 [1957]), notably in Hemingway, Faulkner, and Ralph Ellison's *The Invisible Man* (1952), is in effect an attempt to give transcendent meaning to the chaotic complexity of ordinary life in which the innocent are made to suffer. Theodore Ziolkowski had identified Gore Vidal's *Messiah* (1954) and John Barth's *Giles Goat Boy* (1966) as "demonic parodies of the life of Christ," works in which "all questions of meaning aside, the events as set down immutably in the Gospels prefigure the action of the plot" (*Fictional Transfigurations of Jesus* [1972], p. 26). Such works, however much narrative analogues to the Bible, are in effect "anti-Gospels"—diametrically opposite to the imitation of Christ such as is represented in American fiction by Charles M. Sheldon's "Bible Belt" classic *In His Steps* (1896). By the second half of the twentieth century, the "Christ-figure" has often become "Antichrist."

The Bible continues, nonetheless, to shape and texture American fiction in more traditional fashion. John Updike, in novels whose protagonists bear the consistent character of the fallen Adam—*Rabbit, Run* (1960), *Rabbit Redux* (1971), *Rabbit Is Rich* (1981), and *Rabbit at Rest* (1990)—as well as *The Centaur* (1963), and *Roger's Version* (1987), uses biblical allusion and elements of ancestral saga in the shaping of narrative; in his *Couples* (1968) the hero is identified with *Lot living in the cities of the plain (the coast near Boston), fleeing *Sodom with his two daughters and leaving behind his wife turned to salt. Another writer who demands considerable biblical literacy from his readers and whose use of the Bible extends from title to precept and narrative elements as well as significant allusion, is Chaim Potok, notably in his novels of Jewish life in New York, *The Chosen* (1967) and *The Promise* (1969). American Jewish fiction born of more recent immigrant experience readily employs biblical analogue for covenant saga, jeremiad, even apocalyptic (Saul Bellows's *Mr. Sammler's Planet*

[1969]) and, in the stories of Isaac Bashevis Singer, parable. The reemergence of these biblically informed genres lends an appearance of continuity with forms of literary imagination familiar in American literature from its seventeenth-century Puritan beginnings.

Canada. Canadian literature grew up slowly at the end of the eighteenth century and the beginning of the nineteenth; thus, heavily influenced by enlightenment taste and romantic self-consciousness, it did not turn readily to the Bible as a foundational literature. The dramatic poem *Jephthah's Daughter* (1865), published by Charles Heavysege shortly after his arrival in Canada, is perhaps the only significant example of biblical influence before the twentieth century. Without any equivalent to the Puritan legacy of American writers, English Canadian authors begin to take a significant interest in the Bible only after its "rediscovery," following the influence of Matthew Arnold in Britain, as a "secular" literature, and, subsequently, the success of Jewish writers in Canada following World War II. French Canadian authors have made even less use of scriptural sources, even by way of allusion, although Yves Theriault, in *Aaron* (1954), a novel about an orthodox Jew who loses his son to gentiles, is a notable parallel to contemporary developments in English Canadian fiction.

While Morley Callaghan incorporated religious ideas and even doctrines into some of his many novels, his conspicuous use of biblical allusion is peripheral: in *Such Is My Beloved* (1934), for example, the priest-protagonist concludes his frustrated idealism in a mental hospital working on a commentary on the *Song of Solomon; other of Callaghan's suggestively biblical titles fit their plots still more loosely, as is the case in *They Shall Inherit the Earth* (1935) and *More Joy in Heaven* (1937). Howard O'Hagan's *Tay John* (1939) draws on Native American mythology as well as biblical sources in a story of suffering and self-generated attempts at atonement that contrasts sharply with E. J. Pratt's use of similar sources in his poem *Brebeuf and His Brethren* (1940). Other more or less gratuitously allusive titles include Sinclair Ross's *As For Me and My House* (1941) and W. O. Mitchell's *Who Has Seen the Wind* (1947), and, with varying degrees of apropos, Hugh MacLennan's *The Watch That Ends the Night* (1959) and Marian Engel's *The Glassy Sea* (1978).

Beyond the echoing allusions of writers such as Archibald Lampman, E. J. Pratt, P. K. Page, and James Reaney, Canadian poetry and drama have produced few examples of formative biblical influence. Among these may be counted Jay Macpherson's *The Boatman* (1957) and Margaret Avison's *Sunblue* (1980), in the latter of which the poet still gladly countenances "The Bible to be Believed." Renewal of Canadian literary interest in the Arnoldian tradition, evidenced in Northrop Frye's discussion of the Bible as foundational literature in *The Great Code* (1982) and *Words with Power* (1990), is necessarily oblique to the generative power of the Bible for those writing out of an immediate experience of it as textual authority, such as Avison, Rudy Wiebe, or, most centrally, A. M. Klein. Klein's "Five Characters" is a penetrating analysis of the book of *Esther, and his "Koheleth" is a reading back of the dark sayings of *Ecclesiastes into the mind behind the utterances. He writes in imitation of the *Psalms in *The Psalter of Avram Haketani* (1948) (a volume that has in turn influenced the prose psalms of Jubilee repentance of Leonard Cohen, *A Book of Mercy* [1984]), in whimsical parody of "Jonah," and in moving evocation of Hebrew apocalyptic in *A Voice Was Heard in Ramah* (1948).

A revival of more substantial engagement of the Bible in Canadian fiction may be traced to A. M. Klein's novel of Jewish covenant history, *The Second Scroll* (1951), a "double tale" composed of five books named for those of the *Torah and five "glosses." While Ernest Buckler's *The Mountain and the Valley* (1952), with its artist protagonist David Canaan, is recognizably influenced by New England writers, it is an exception proving the rule that Puritan covenant theology has had little impact on Canadian literary consciousness. *The Second Scroll* was followed by another novel of diaspora Jewish life, Adele Wiseman's *The Sacrifice* (1956), in which Abraham and Sarah flee pogroms in the Ukraine during which their sons Jacob and Moses are murdered at Easter (Passover) by Christians only to have their son of later years, Isaac die while saving a copy of the Torah from the flames. Rudy Wiebe's *Peace Shall Destroy Many* (1962) and subsequent *The Blue Mountains of China* (1970), with its own epic recounting of family/covenant history of the Mennonite diaspora, follow Klein and Wiseman in the way in which contemporary life is grafted directly onto biblical narrative, or made to seem an outgrowth of it. Margaret Laurence's *The Stone Angel* (1964), whose heroine Hagar is a rebel not only against her husband Bram but against God and the world, is a tale from without, a novel molded by the protagonist's sense of covenantal exclusion. It is not,

however, like Timothy Findley's grisly and angry redrafting of the story of *Noah, *Not Wanted on the Voyage* (1984), a demonic parody of the Bible, or like Wiebe's *My Lovely Enemy* (1983), a desacralization and inversion of biblical salvation history.

Resistance to the influence of the Bible, especially as represented by the American Puritan legacy in political life, reaches its zenith in Margaret Atwood's *The Handmaid's Tale* (1985), a dystopia in which American fundamentalists have erected a society based on a rigid implementation of biblical law and social custom. Atwood's apocalyptic tale is an antijeremiad, expressing Canadian fears of a biblicist America declaring itself the only "chosen," and serves to indicate much of the basis for the strikingly divergent uses of biblical tradition in Canadian and American literature.   DAVID LYLE JEFFREY

Literature, The Bible As. An appreciation for the literary artistry of the Bible began early in the history of interpretation. It reached a high water mark during the era of the Renaissance and Protestant Reformation, when poets and storytellers viewed the Bible as a literary model to be emulated, and when interpreters of the Bible were sensitive to its literary style and genres.

The idea of the Bible as literature received sporadic attention throughout the twentieth century, but its most notable revival began in the late 1960s, when high school and college courses in the literature of the Bible became popular. By the 1980s, the literary approach had attracted the allegiance of biblical scholars, whose traditional methods became strongly influenced by, and often replaced by, tools of analysis long practiced by literary critics in the humanities.

How Literary Is the Bible? Acceptance of a literary approach to the Bible has always been rendered difficult (and sometimes suspect) because of the mixed nature of biblical writing. Three impulses and three corresponding types of material exist side by side in the Bible: the didactic or theological impulse to teach religious truth, the historical impulse to record and interpret historical events, and the literary/aesthetic impulse to recreate experiences and be artistically beautiful. This combination of religious, documentary, and literary interests in the Bible has made the literary study of the Bible different from the study of other literature. Literary critics of the Bible find themselves sharing the same book with scholars who approach it with very different methods.

Despite this complexity, the literary approach to the Bible can be defined with precision. It is rooted in an awareness that literature is itself a genre with identifying traits. These include the impulse to image reality and human experience instead of conveying abstract information, the presence of literary genres, reliance on figurative language and rhetorical devices, an interest in artistry as something intrinsically valuable (with special emphasis on unity), and stylistic excellence. A literary approach to the Bible begins with these features as its agenda of concerns and proceeds to apply familiar tools of literary analysis to the parts of the Bible that are most thoroughly literary in nature.

An Imaginative Book. To say that the Bible is an imaginative book is to call attention to the most important differentia of literature—its impulse to image reality. Whereas expository or informational writing tends toward abstraction and proposition, the aim of literature is to re-create an experience as concretely as possible. Literature takes human experience rather than abstract thought as its subject, and it puts a reader through an experience instead of appealing primarily to a grasp of ideas. The truth that literature portrays is primarily truthfulness to human experience in the world.

Biblical writing as a whole exists on a continuum between the poles of the expository and the literary, or between propositions and images (including characters and events), but the literary impulse to incarnate meaning—to image experience—probably dominates. Wherever we turn in the Bible, we find appeals to our image-making and image-perceiving capacity. The Bible is consistently rooted in the concrete realities of human life in this world, and a literary approach is sensitive to this experiential dimension.

It is a truism that whereas history tells us what happened, literature tells us what happens. Literature portrays universal human experience and as a result does not go out of date. A literary approach to the Bible is therefore interested in the universal, always-recognizable human experiences that are portrayed. In the Bible, we see ourselves, not only characters and events from the past. *Adam and *Jacob, *David and *Ruth are paradigms of the human condition as well as figures in historical narrative.

Because biblical literature embodies its meanings in characters, events, and images, it communicates by indirectness. It gives example rather than precept. The result is that literature puts a greater burden of interpretation on a reader than straightforward expository prose does. Even such a simple literary form as *metaphor ("God is light") requires a reader to interpret how one thing is like another. Here, too, the Bible shows itself to be a work of imagination. Again and again we find that biblical writers entrust their utterance to a literary medium in order to achieve the memorability, affective power, and truthfulness to lived experience that are characteristic of literature.

Literary Genres in the Bible. The commonest way to define literature is by its genres or literary types. Through the centuries, people have agreed that certain genres (such as story, poetry, and drama) are literary in nature. Other types, such as historical chronicles, theological essays, and genealogies, are expository (informational). Still others can fall into either category. Letters, sermons, and orations, for example, can move in the direction of literature by virtue of experiential concreteness, figurative language, and artistic style.

The Bible is a mixture of genres, some of them literary in nature. The major literary genres in the Bible are narrative or story, *poetry (especially lyric poetry), proverb, and visionary writing (including *prophecy and *apocalypse). The New Testament *letters frequently become literary because of their occasional nature, figurative language, and rhetorical or artistic patterning. Other literary genres of note in the Bible include epic, tragedy, *gospel, *parable, satire, pastoral, oratory, encomium, epithalamion (wedding poem), elegy (funeral poem), and a host of subtypes of lyric poetry (such as nature poem, psalm of praise, lament, love poem, psalm of worship, hymn).

Genre study is central to any literary approach to the Bible because every genre has its own conventions, expectations, and corresponding rules of interpretation. A biblical story, for example, is a sequence of events, not a series of ideas. It is structured around a plot conflict, not a logical argument. It communicates by means of setting, character, and event, not propositions. In short, the literary genres of the Bible require us to approach them in terms of the conventions and procedures that they possess.

Literary Language and Rhetoric. Literature uses distinctive resources of language. This is most evident in poetry. Poets, for example, think in images and figures of speech: God is a shepherd, people are sheep, the tongue is a fire. It is noteworthy how much of the Bible is poetic in form, including books in which it dominates: Job, Psalms, Proverbs, Ecclesiastes, Song of Solomon, and most of the prophets.

The whole realm of figurative language looms large in any consideration of the Bible as literature. Figurative language in the Bible includes *metaphor, simile, symbol, hyperbole, apostrophe (address to someone or something absent as though they or it were present), personification, paradox, pun, *irony, and wordplay. These resources of language are not limited to poetry but pervade the entire Bible, including parts of it that would not be considered primarily literary. Everywhere we turn in the Bible—in narrative, in the prophecy, in the Gospels, in the New Testament epistles, in apocalypse—we find figurative language. In fact, it is hard to find a page of the Bible that does not contain figurative language.

The literary use of language also includes rhetorical devices, or language arranged by stylized patterns. Examples include parallel sentences or clauses (the standard verse form in biblical poetry), any highly patterned arrangement of clauses or words or phrases, rhetorical questions, question and answer constructions, imaginary dialogues, and the aphoristic conciseness of a proverb. These rhetorical forms pervade the Bible, lending a literary quality to the Bible as a whole, giving it qualities of conscious artistry and heightening the audience's attention.

Artistry in the Bible. Literature is an art form, and one of the criteria by which we classify something as literary is the presence of beauty, form, craft, and technique. The elements of artistic form include pattern or design, unity, theme and variation, balance, contrast, symmetry, repetition or recurrence, coherence, and unified progression. The artistic spirit regards these as having inherent value.

When judged by these criteria of aesthetic form or beauty, the Bible contains artistic and literary masterpieces. The stories of the Bible are models of concise shapeliness, with every detail contributing to the total effect. Biblical *poetry, as well as some of its prose (notably the discourses of Jesus), is composed with conscious artistry in the form known as parallelism, in which two or more lines use different words to express the same idea in similar grammatical form. Whole books of the Bible show similar evidence of artistic patterning, with the gospel according to *Matthew, for example, alternating between sections of narrative and sections of discourse.

The most basic of all artistic principles is unity, and one of the things that has set off the literary approach to the Bible from other approaches is a preoccupation with unifying patterns and literary wholes. Literary unity consists of various things: the structure of a work or passage, a dominant theme, an image pattern, or progressive development of a motif. Whatever form it takes, unity is evidence of an artistic urge for order, shapeliness, and wholeness of effect.

Several functions are served by the artistry that we find in the Bible. Artistry intensifies the impact of what is said, but it also serves the purposes of pleasure, delight, and enjoyment. These purposes are abundantly satisfied when we read the Bible, as has been repeatedly shown by literary critics, who assume and find conscious artistry and design there.

The Literary Unity of the Bible. The central protagonist in the overall story of the Bible is God. The characterization of God is the central literary concern of the Bible, and it is pursued from beginning to end. Hardly anything is viewed apart from its relation to the deity.

The Bible is also unified by its religious orientation. It is pervaded by a consciousness of the presence of God. Human experience is constantly viewed in a religious and moral light. One result is that the literature of the Bible invests human experience with a sense of ultimacy. A vivid consciousness of values pervades biblical literature.

Literary archetypes also unify the Bible. Archetypes are master images that recur throughout the Bible and throughout literature. They are either images (light, water, hill), character types (hero, villain, king), or plot motifs (journey, rescue, temptation). The Bible is filled with such archetypes or master images, which lend an elemental quality to the Bible and make its world strongly unified in a reader's imagination.

The Necessity of a Literary Approach. The foregoing discussion suggests why a literary approach to the Bible is necessary. The Bible is, in significant ways, a work of literature. It will yield its meanings fully only if explored in terms of its kinds of writing. Understanding it depends partly on the reader's ability to be receptive to concrete pictures of human experience, to know what to expect from various literary genres, to interpret figurative language and recognize rhetorical patterns. Finally, a literary approach can also enhance the enjoyment of the Bible.

LELAND RYKEN

Loans and Interest. Indebtedness arose variously, but in loans the lender had discretion whether to show "grace and favor" when approached with a request. Terms would naturally tend to depend on one's relationship with the borrower. Because of the Israelites' acceptance of God's plan for their welfare and their remembrance of him (Ezek. 22.12), they must be generous in lending, in taking and keeping any pledge (Exod. 22.25–27; Deut. 24.10–13), and in the use of landed security (Neh. 5.4, 11).

There are three main classes of loan: for use, as distinct from hire (Exod. 3.21–22; 22.14–15; 2 Kings 4.3; 6.5); for consumption (Deut. 23.19; Neh. 5.10; Luke 11.5); and for business. The Bible does not deal with the third. The others demanded attention, for the parties were seldom on equal terms. The sabbatical year (Deut. 15.2–3; Neh. 10.31) was intended to cancel all loans; but so benevolent a provision impaired borrowers' credit (Deut. 15.7–11) until Hillel invented a form of agreement to protect it. Biblical traditions extol the granting of loans, praising all who are ready to lend (Pss. 37.26; 112.5) even though the "wicked" may not repay (Ps. 37.21) or restore a loaned object. The parties' interests tended to be opposed (Isa. 24.2); a loan could sour relationships (Jer. 15.10). Accordingly, "righteous" lenders must not profit from their neighbors by charging interest (KJV "usury"), enriching themselves from others' calamities (Lev. 25.36–37; Deut. 23.19, 20; Ps. 15.5; Ezek. 18.8, 13, 17; 22.12). Usurers did charge interest (Deut. 23.20; Prov. 28.8), although a Jewish court would reject a usurious transaction between Jews. But since the lender had the upper hand (Prov. 22.7) and since "righteousness" was reputable, society favored interest-free loans. God had promised that, if his people obeyed him, they would always lend to foreigners, who would defer to them (Deut. 15.6; 28.12, 44).

The *Torah allowed lending at interest to non-Jews. It certainly protected indigent Jews from exploitation (Exod. 22.25); but all loans, including commercial loans, fell under regulation by *Pharisees. To evade this, capital was sometimes invested with entrepreneurs on the basis that the parties became partners and that the party with capital hired the other as an employee. The return on such capital was not, technically, "usury" (Matt. 25.14, 16, 27; Luke 19.13, 23).

Another scheme obliged debtors who owed rent or advances of cash to acknowledge a duty to supply commodities, the value of which incorporated, in effect, capital and interest—a device found in Egyptian papyri. It would be righteous to scale such debts down (Luke 16.4–8, 9), for concealed usury violated the spirit of the Torah.

The New Testament urges the ready granting of loans (Matt. 5.42) without speculating whether the borrower will ever reciprocate (Luke 6.34–35). The Hebrew Bible distinguishes gifts and loans, but even a loan can be a good deed. He who shows kindness to the poor lends to the Lord (Prov. 19.17). Such is the religious dimension of a legal transaction, that even a thoughtful cancellation of an insolvent's debts (Matt. 18.27; Luke 7.41–42) can prove the creditor's mindfulness of God.

J. DUNCAN M. DERRETT

Logos, Grk. "word." In the prologue of the gospel according to *John, the *logos* is the divine word, a self-communicating divine presence that existed with God and was uniquely manifested in Jesus Christ. The Johannine *logos* is strongly parallel to the concept of *wisdom in Hellenistic Jewish thought, where already wisdom and word were associated (Wisd. of Sol. 9.1–2). Wisdom or Word was God's creative presence through which the world came into being. John's gospel affirms that this same divine presence was fully and (in contrast to the usual thinking about wisdom) uniquely present in Jesus Christ. It was a redemptive presence that was necessary because the world had rejected the original creative presence. The word was not in Jesus simply as verbal communication, but entered fully into human life. The *incarnation of the word brought life to human beings, to whom it was otherwise unavailable (John 1.1–18).

The Johannine prologue is the only fully explicit statement of the theme of incarnation in the New Testament, though the rest of the gospel of John shows in narrative form what the coming of the *logos* meant. The prologue of the gospel is echoed in 1 John 1.1 ("the word of life") and in the imagery of Revelation 19.13, where Christ, "the Word of God," appears as a warrior.

In the Hebrew Bible, the *word of God is both creative (Gen. 1.; Isa. 55.10–11) and commanding (Amos 3.1). This background contributed to the general usage of the term *logos* in the New Testament, where the "word" often signifies the Christian message (2 Cor. 2.17; cf. 1 Cor. 1.18). This field of meaning was drawn into the interpretation of the *logos* of John's prologue, but was only indirectly in its background.

In Greek, *logos* meant both spoken word and pervading principle. *Stoic philosophy, using the latter meaning, saw the *logos* as the ordering principle of the universe; the wise person aims to live in harmony with it. This meaning, though not a direct background for John's *logos,* was quickly drawn into the interpretation of John as "*logos* theology" developed in the second century CE. This was a principal means of making Christian thought intelligible to its environment; but this later *logos* theology was more rationalistic than was the gospel of John.

Christ as the *logos* was an important avenue of development of the doctrine of the *Trinity, but *logos* was eventually largely replaced by other terms ("hypostasis," "person,") because *logos* appeared to make of Christ a second God.

See also Creation; Philo.

WILLIAM A. BEARDSLEE

Lord's Prayer. Also known as the "Our Father" (Latin *Pater noster*) from its first words, the Lord's Prayer occurs in the New Testament in two slightly different forms. The longer form is included in Matthew's account of Jesus' *Sermon on the Mount (6.9–13) and reads (in the NRSV):

Our Father in heaven,
hallowed be your name.
Your kingdom come.
Your will be done,
on earth as it is in heaven.
Give us this day our daily bread.
And forgive us our debts,
as we also have forgiven our debtors.
And do not bring us to the time of trial,
but rescue us from the evil one.

The doxology at the close ("For the kingdom and the power and the glory are yours forever. Amen") is absent in ancient and important Greek manuscripts, and is not mentioned in early commentaries on the Lord's Prayer by Tertullian, Cyprian, and Origen. It occurs in twofold form ("power and glory") in the Didache (8.2). In liturgical use, some kind of doxology (perhaps composed on the model of 1 Chron. 29.11–13) could have concluded such a prayer as this.

The shorter form of the Lord's Prayer is given in Luke 11.2–4, where Jesus responds to a disciple's request, "Lord, teach us to pray," with the following:

Father, hallowed be your name.
Your kingdom come.
Give us each day our daily bread.
And forgive us our sins,
for we ourselves forgive everyone
indebted to us.
And do not bring us to the time of trial.

Later manuscripts, on which the King James Version depends, include additions that assimilate the Lucan form of the Prayer to that in Matthew. Furthermore, two Greek manuscripts of the Gospels (no. 162, dated 1153 CE, and no. 700, of the eleventh century) replace the petition "Your kingdom come" with "Your holy Spirit come upon us and cleanse us." This adaptation may have been used when celebrating the rite of *baptism or the *laying on of hands.

It is likely that Luke's shorter version is closer to the original and that Matthew's is an elaboration. But, of course, Jesus may well have given the prayer in different forms on different occasions.

It would seem that the mode of address that Jesus habitually used in prayer to God was "*Abba, dear Father" (the only exception is Mark 15.34, itself a quotation from Ps. 22.1). It seems that nowhere in the literature of the *prayers of ancient Judaism does the invocation of God as "Abba" occur. Perhaps there is an intimacy of relationship implied here that others had hesitated to use. However, in teaching his followers to address God in this way, Jesus lets them share in his own communion with God. That they rejoiced to do so is apparent in the letters of Paul (see Gal. 4.6; Rom. 8.15). Ancient Christian liturgies reflect something of the sense of privilege in using this approach when they preface the Lord's Prayer with the words "We are bold to say 'Our Father.'"

But if the address "Our Father" suggests intimacy, not to say familiarity, the next words, "in heaven," speak of the "otherness," the holiness, the awesomeness of God. It is when these two aspects of approach to God are held together in creative tension that real prayer can be engaged in. Further, the plural "our" should be noted—not, at least in this instance, "my." This is the prayer that Jesus' followers as members of one family are bidden to say together (see Matt. 12.49–50 and par.); the Father presides over the family unit.

Following the invocation in the Matthean form of the prayer, the petitions fall into two parts: three "you" petitions are followed by "we" petitions. The former focus on God and his purposes in the world; the latter pertain to our provision, pardon, and protection. In other words, before any thought is given to human need ("our daily bread") or even to divine forgiveness of sins or to the problem of temptation, God's name, God's kingdom, God's will must first engage our attention. This is the order of precedence when human beings engage in communication with the God who is at once immanent and transcendent.

"Your will be done" is not a prayer of resignation, but one for the full accomplishment of the divine purpose (as in Matt. 26.42). The words "on earth as it is in heaven" may be taken with all three preceding petitions.

The Greek adjective (*epiousios*), usually translated "daily," is extremely rare; it may mean "[the bread we need] for tomorrow." In either case, the sense is that we are to pray for one day's rations, perhaps with the implied suggestion that asking for more would be to engage in needless concern for the future (cf. Matt. 6.25–34).

The petition for God's forgiveness is closely linked with our forgiveness of one another (the difference in tenses between the Matthean and Lucan versions should be noted); Matthew elaborates the teaching in the following verses (6.14–15). The *Aramaic word for "debt" is used in rabbinic writings to mean "sin," and would be so understood by Jesus' hearers.

The petition often translated "lead us not into temptation" is best understood as a prayer to be kept in the hour of severe trial; it is an acknowledgment of spiritual frailty (cf. 1 Cor. 10.12) in the face of the evil one (or evil, for the Greek can mean either; *see* Satan; Temptation).

DONALD COGGAN

Lord's Supper. In 1 Corinthians 11.20 Paul refers to a gathering of church members at Corinth to eat "the Lord's supper," complaining that the way in which they did so was not consistent with the true character of the meal. What was meant to be a proclamation of the Lord's death was being celebrated as an occasion for gluttony and even *drunkenness. This is the only passage in the New Testament where the meal is described by this name. In what is no doubt a reference to the same meal, Paul states (1 Cor.

10.16) that the Christians came together to "break bread"; hence, we can assume that "the breaking of bread" (Acts 2.46) was another name for the same occasion. The same verse, with its reference to sharing (Grk. *koinōnia*) in the body and blood of Christ, is the source of the name "(Holy) Communion" for the meal, and the association with thanksgiving (Grk. *eucharistoun*) in 1 Corinthians 11.24 is the rationale for calling it the Eucharist.

The only full discussion of this meal in the New Testament is in 1 Corinthians 11.17–34, where Paul deals with irregularities that had arisen in the congregation at *Corinth. They met, doubtless in the home of one of their members, to have a communal meal, and it is likely that the practice of meeting weekly on the first day of the week (Acts 20.7; cf. 1 Cor. 16.2) was developing. It was a full meal, but apparently each person brought his or her own food (11.21). Since the church consisted of richer and poorer members, differences in the amount and quality of the food and drink existed, so that the social differences in the church were emphasized rather than diminished by this communal occasion. At some point in the meal there was a more formal sharing in a loaf of bread and a cup of wine, which became the focus of significant symbolism.

Already in 1 Corinthians 10.16–17, Paul commented that those who shared in the loaf and the cup, for which thanks had been given to God, were participating in the body and blood of Christ. The reference must be to experiencing the benefits resulting from the death of Jesus, in which he gave himself and shed his *blood for the sake of others. At the same time Paul emphasized that those who took part in this way constituted one body; their common participation in the gift of salvation, as symbolized by the one loaf, meant that they belonged together in a way that should overcome the social and other differences that had arisen in the church. Thus, the meal was a powerful sign of unity within the local congregation.

The tradition that Paul had passed on to the church at the time of his visit there is found here in its oldest written form. We also have it in slightly divergent forms in the three *synoptic Gospels (Matt. 26.26–29; Mark 14.22–25; Luke 22.15–20, reversing the order of wine and bread). In all of these cases, we have a tradition of what Jesus said and did at his Last Supper with his twelve disciples shortly before his death. Analysis of the differences between the accounts shows that we have two basic forms of the tradition, one given by Mark (who is substantially followed by Matthew), and the other found in 1 Corinthians and Luke (though Luke has also been influenced by Mark). The major difference between the two traditions lies in the two sayings of Jesus:

MARK	1 CORINTHIANS
This is my body.	This is my body that is for you. Do this in remembrance of me.
This is my blood of the covenant	This cup is the new covenant in my blood
which is poured out for many.	(Luke: + which is poured out for you.) Do this, as often as you drink it, in remembrance of me.

There is no agreement among scholars as to which is the older form of the tradition, but the differences are not too significant.

What we have here, then, is an account of the essential elements in the Last Supper that formed the pattern for the church's meal. It has been argued that the story in the Gospels is not so much a part of the story of Jesus as a liturgical text that was preserved on its own and then inserted into the gospel narrative. Some scholars would go further and claim that the story is based on early Christian liturgies rather than on history, the accounts of what the church did having been read back into the lifetime of Jesus. Still others claim that the uncertainty in the tradition of Jesus' sayings and how they express early Christian theology suggest that they are the creation of the early church (or at least that the original form has been heavily modified in transmission), with the result that we can no longer be sure what Jesus said. For example, the presence of the command to "do this" in remembrance of Jesus, which is lacking from Mark's account, given once in Luke and twice in 1 Corinthians, could be due to the early church putting into words what it took to be the intention of Jesus. Even if this is the case, we would still be left with a tradition of Jesus' sharing a loaf and a cup with his disciples, and these actions would invite interpretation. In other words, to account for the origin of the church meal and the early Christians' appeal to Jesus we must surely postulate the historicity of some kind of meal he held.

The Gospels all suggest that the Last Supper of Jesus was associated in some way with the Jewish *Passover, though the Synoptics and John disagree on the date of that festival. Like other Jewish formal *meals, it began with the breaking and distribution of bread to the accompaniment of a prayer of thanksgiving, and it included the drinking of *wine. If it was a Passover meal, the main items of food would have been treated as symbols whose significance needed to be explained. There would then be a precedent for Jesus' explaining the significance of the loaf and the cup. Whether or not a Passover *lamb was served (as Luke 22.15 and the story of the preparations for the meal clearly imply), no record has survived of any interpretation of it. Instead, Jesus made three main comments. First, he spoke of this meal as the last that he would eat with his disciples until he ate with them in the *kingdom of God (Luke 22.16). This may suggest his imminent death. Second, he made the loaf a symbol of his body, and his distribution of the broken pieces suggests his giving of himself for others. Third, he made the cup a symbol of his blood. *Blood, however, signifies death. Jesus associated it with a new *covenant, and the echoes of Exodus 24.8 suggest a sacrificial death inaugurating a new covenant. The words "for many" are an allusion to the self-giving of the Servant of the Lord "for many" in Isaiah 53.11–12. And the way in which Jesus performed this act before his death implies that he was giving his disciples a way of remembering him and enjoying some kind of association with him after his death and during the period before they would share together in the kingdom of God. Hence, the meal that his disciples were to celebrate could be regarded as in some sense an anticipation of the meal that the *Messiah would celebrate with his disciples in the new age (cf. Matt. 8.11; Luke 14.15). Such a meal would not be merely a symbol or picture of the future meal but would be a real anticipation of it. This is clear from the language of 1 Corinthians 10.16. Here the believers who receive the loaf and the cup participate in the body and blood of Jesus. The language must not be pressed literally, since the body in fact includes the blood; rather, Paul is saying in two ways that believers have a share in Jesus who died for them. This interpretation is confirmed by his point that it is inconsistent for believers to take part also in meals at which food sacrificed to *idols was consumed: such a meal was a means of being "partners with demons" (1 Cor. 10.20), that is, having some kind of spiritual relationship to them. It is also confirmed by Luke's implication that the "breaking of bread" in Acts (2.42; etc.) was a continuation of the meals described in the appearances of Jesus after the *resurrection.

We can now see how Paul meant the meal to be celebrated at Corinth. It certainly was an occasion for joyful celebration rather than a funeral meal, but some of the Corinthian Christians carried this element to excess. But it was supremely a way of proclaiming the death of Jesus as a sacrifice on their behalf and the inauguration of the new covenant. It was an occasion for bringing believers together in unity rather than in disharmony. It was a meal for the temporary period before the Lord would return in triumph, and during that period it was one of the ways in which the union between the Lord and his people was expressed.

In Acts we have further evidence that the believers met regularly to break bread (2.42, 46; 20.7; and possibly 27.35). Since there is no reference in Acts to the cup or to any relevant sayings of Jesus, it is sometimes argued that here we have evidence of a somewhat different meal from the Pauline Lord's Supper, a joyful celebration of fellowship with the risen Lord rather than a memorial of his death. There is, however, nothing incompatible between the two types of account, and the combination of solemn remembrance of the Lord's death and joyful communion with him is entirely appropriate.

John's account of the Last Supper lacks the eucharistic elements found in the other Gospels, because for John it was not a Passover meal; John recorded elsewhere teaching ascribed to Jesus about eating his flesh and drinking his blood (6.53).

There are other allusions to the Lord's Supper in the New Testament. For example, the way in which the stories of Jesus feeding the multitudes are told (Mark 6.30–44; 8.1–10 par.) suggests that the evangelists saw a parallel between Jesus' feeding the people with bread and his spiritual nourishment of the church. And the development of the understanding of the death of Jesus that we find in the New Testament most probably had its roots in the words of institution where the basic concepts of sacrifice and covenant are to be found.

See also Love-feast; Sacrament.

I. HOWARD MARSHALL

Lot. The nephew of *Abraham and ancestor of *Moab and *Ammon. Because Abraham was the oldest son of Terah, and Lot's father, Abraham's brother Haran, had died (Gen. 11.27–28), Abraham was the head of the extended family and Lot was his dependent. As such, he traveled with Abraham to the land of *Canaan (Gen. 11.31); when a dispute arose between the two branches of the family over grazing land, Abraham arbitrated it, giving Lot first choice, and enabling him to settle in the *Jordan Valley (Gen 13.5–10), in the vicinity of *Sodom. When Lot was captured by raiding kings, Abraham led a campaign to rescue him (Gen 14.1–16), and when Sodom was about to be destroyed, Lot was spared (Gen 19.1–23), presumably because of his association with Abraham. Throughout these stories, Lot is portrayed as a less than heroic figure, who has no respect in his own family (Gen 19.14), is hesitant (19.16), and is tricked by his daughters (19.30–38).

This familial history is intertwined with etiological narratives that explain topographic features (the pillar of salt and the desolation of the Dead Sea region) and several names, especially Moab and Ammon. The account of the incestuous origin of these neighbors of Israel (Gen. 19.30–38) is both a genealogical recognition of shared ethnicity and a scurrilous rationalization of Israelite superiority.

In later literature, Lot is recalled as a righteous man, whose goodness saved him from Sodom's punishment (Wisd. of Sol. 10.6; 2 Pet. 2.7–8).

MICHAEL D. COOGAN

Love (Hebr. ʾăhābâ; ḥesed). Human loves in all their rich variety fill the passages of biblical narrative: love at first sight (Gen. 29.18–20: Jacob and Rachel); sexual obsession (2 Sam. 13: Amnon and Tamar); family affection across generations (Gen. 22.2; 37.3; Ruth 4.15: between mother and daughter-in-law); long marital intimacy (1 Sam. 1: Elkanah and Hannah); servile devotion (Exod. 21.5); intense same-sex friendship (1 Sam. 18.1, 3; 20.17: David and Jonathan); enthusiastic loyalty toward a leader (1 Sam. 18.16, 28: Israel and Judah's love of David). But the religious significance of the Bible's view of love lies preeminently with its ways of speaking about God and most particularly about God's relationship with Israel. Israel's election, their redemption from Egypt (and, eventually, Babylon), the giving of the *Torah, the promise of the land—all are ascribed in biblical narrative and later rabbinic commentary to the fundamental and mysterious fact of God's love for Israel and the people's reciprocal love of God.

Human love serves as the readiest analogy when speaking of this relationship. God loves Israel as a husband loves his wife (Hos. 3.1; Jer.

2.2; Isa. 54.5–8), a father his firstborn son (Hos. 11.1–3; Jer. 31.9), a mother the child of her womb (Isa. 49.15). God manifests his love in and through his saving acts, most especially in his bringing Israel up from Egypt (Exod. 15.13; Deut. 4.37; 33.3; Neh. 9.17; Ps. 106.7; Hos. 11.4). Narratively and theologically, this liberation culminates in the Sinai *covenant, when God gives Israel his *tôrâ* (literally, "teaching"), instructing Israel on their social and religious obligations in light of their election. Chosen by God's love (Deut. 7.7–8; 10.15), Israel is to respond in kind: loving the God who redeemed them and revealed his will to them, teaching his ways to all future generations (Deut. 6.4–7).

The covenant binding God and Israel likewise binds together society. The individual is charged to "love your neighbor as yourself," kindred and foreigner both (Lev. 19.18, 34). The Bible specifies the concrete actions through which this love is to be expressed: support for the *poor (Lev. 19.9–10); honesty in measurements and in social interactions (v. 11); prompt payment to laborers; just law courts, favoring neither rich nor poor; respect for the elderly (vv. 13, 15, 32). A system of tithes underlay the welfare both of the poor, the fatherless (*see* Orphan), and the *widowed, and of *priests and *Levites who, unendowed with land, are "the Lord's portion" (Num. 18.20; Deut. 18.1–2). Right behavior, group affection, and communal social responsibility are thus the concrete measure of Israel's commitment to the covenant. And God, in turn, "keeps" or "guards" his steadfast love for Israel (Exod. 34.7; 1 Kings 3.6; Isa. 54.10; 55.3). Ultimately, Israel's confidence in redemption rests in her conviction that God's love is unwavering, his covenant eternal, his promises sure (Ps. 119.41; 130.7; Zeph. 3.17).

Much of this tradition, both social and theological, comes into the earliest strata of New Testament writings. Paul urges his gentiles in Galatia to be "servants of one another through love [Grk. *agapē*], for the whole law is fulfilled in one word, 'You shall love your neighbor as yourself'" (Gal. 5.13–14, quoting Lev. 19.18). In powerfully poetic language, he exhorts the Corinthians to be knit together as a community through love (1 Cor. 13–14; cf. Rom. 14.15). Mark's Jesus sums up the *Torah with the first line of the *Shema (love of God) and Leviticus 19.18 (love of neighbor; Mark 12.28–31). The *Q material of the later *synoptic Gospels extends this last: followers of Jesus are to love not just their *neighbor but also and even their enemies (Matt. 5.43–48 par.). Perhaps, by the criterion of multiple attestation, this ethic of passive —indeed, even active (Matt. 5.39–41)—nonresistance may go back to the historical Jesus himself. Paul teaches similarly: persecutors should be blessed; vengeance eschewed; injustice tolerated (Rom. 12.9–13.14; cf. 1 Cor. 6.7; so too other first-century Jewish texts, such as *Joseph and Asenath* 29.3–4 [cf. Prov. 20.22]; Josephus, *Ag. Ap.* 2.30.212 [cf. Deut. 20.19–20; 21.10–14]).

Love became the theological lodestone of nascent Christianity. Christ's sacrifice on the cross was understood as the ultimate sign of God's love for humanity (John 3.16; cf. Rom. 8.39). The eucharist (a community meal celebrating this sacrifice) was referred to as the *agapē*, or "*love-feast". Christians exhorted themselves to love one another (see esp. 1–3 John), calling each other brothers and sisters. Such designations and community enthusiasms, misheard at a hostile distance, fueled dislike of the new groups, who were often accused of expressing love carnally at their convocations (Tertullian, *Apology;* Minucius Felix, *Octavius*). Yet in their care for both their own poor and the poor of the late Roman city, Christians, like their Jewish contemporaries, distinguished themselves by acts of public philanthropy—a fact noted with some irritation by the non-Christian emperor Julian (the Apostate, ca. 360; *Epistle* 22). This philanthropy was the social expression of the scriptural injunction to love the neighbor.

The Christian concept of love, in both its social and its theological applications, underwent elaborate and idiosyncratic development in the work of Augustine. In the unprecedented ecclesiastical situation after Constantine (d. 337), with the church increasingly merging with late Roman imperial culture, Augustine argued that the state coercion of heretics (by which he meant most especially his schismatic rivals, the Donatists) at the behest of the church is an act of Christian love, since it is done for their ultimate spiritual welfare. Theologically, he explored the concept of the *Trinity as a dynamic of divine (and, ultimately, of human) loves: the Trinity should be understood on the analogy of the relations between and process of human self-knowledge and self-love (*De Trinitate*). Finally, and most influentially, Augustine came to analyze all humanity (and thus, given his theological anthropocentrism, all reality) according to loves: those enabled by God's love to love God belong to the "heavenly city"; those whom God leaves to their own fallen state love carnal things and thus belong to the "earthly city."

The City of God, Augustine's great masterwork, may thus be seen as a lengthy survey of the history of love, from angels through pagan culture to Israel and finally to the ultimate revelation of God's love through Christ. Fifteen centuries of Western religious thinkers, such as Bernard, Francis, Dante, and Simone Weil, attest to the power of this essentially Augustinian notion of *caritas* and *amor Dei* as the Christian virtues par excellence.   PAULA FREDRIKSEN

Love-feast. The love-feast (Grk. *agapē,* which also means "love") is the common *meal with which Christians first followed Christ's command at the Last Supper to "do this in remembrance of me" (e.g., Luke 22.19, 1 Cor. 11.24), and later to "feed my sheep" (e.g., John 21.17). According to Paul, Christians repeat the "*Lord's supper" to "proclaim the Lord's death until he comes" (1 Cor. 11.20, 26). In Acts (2.43–47; 20.7), "breaking bread . . . with glad and generous hearts" is associated with distributing goods "to all, as any had need"; only Jude 12 uses *agapē* to refer to the meal. Most scholars agree that Paul is ironic in advising the "hungry," wealthy Corinthians to "eat at home" (1 Cor. 11.34): he sees the loving inseparably from the eating. Eating in *agapē* (1 Cor. 13), Christians will "discern" Christ's presence in themselves and others together (1 Cor. 11.29, 31), just as the elders of Israel finally "saw God, and ate and drank" in making the first *covenant (Luke 24.30–31, 35–36; John 21.12; see Exod. 24:11).

The love-feasts of early Christians draw on metaphors in Israelite scripture and sectarian practice linking food and law, commensalism, and covenanted communities, with concerns about how to see "face to face" the ineffable, imageless presence of God in daily life (e.g., Exod. 33.11; Deut. 34.10; 1 Cor. 13.12). The New Testament writers' visions of epiphany in loving-eating are inseparable from their sectarian assumptions about incarnation and universalism. Love-feasts were intended less to mark boundaries than to cross them by fostering "loving" relations among infinitely disparate people, Abraham's descendants in the "many nations" (Rom. 4.17; Gen. 17.5).

Paul shows how Corinthians, untutored in midrashic debates about the bodiliness of fleshly spirits whom God may feed or consume in a moment, and committed to their own views of commensalism and community, could be blindly indiscriminate eaters of Jewish-Christian feasts (1 Cor. 11.17–23). Reports of Jesus as "a glutton and a drunkard, a friend of tax collectors and sinners" (Matt. 11:19 par.), like Peter's vision (Acts 10.9–11.18), show how Jewish-Christian feasts could be blatantly indiscriminate to fellow Jews who shared their view of the body as a temple but not their abrogation of all the laws epitomized in the dietary rules, except "the law of love" and its new creation.

Underlying the conflicts that New Testament writers attributed to differences among and between Jews and *gentiles are deeper visions of the complexities of humans and their unions seen in the presence of Judas and Peter at Christ's table, a juxtaposition that suggests the kinds of conflicts that led to the historical separation of the "loving" meal *(agapē)* from the blessing and distribution of the bread and wine, or "thanksgiving" *(eucharistia),* as Ignatius (ca. 115 CE) called it. With the incorporation of the church into the Roman empire during the fourth century CE, those well fed enough to abstain from millennial dreams of banquets gradually replaced the feast encompassed in the bread and wine with a preparatory fast.   GILLIAN FEELEY-HARNIK

Luke. *See* Luke, The Gospel According to; Acts of the Apostles.

Luke, The Gospel According to. The third gospel is "the first volume" (Acts 1.1) of a two-part work, Luke-Acts, composed by the same author and dedicated to Theophilus. In content, this gospel is related to the Marcan and Matthean gospels; collectively, these three Gospels form the group usually called *synoptic, i.e., the tradition that developed independently of the gospel according to *John.

Content. The content of the Lucan gospel may be summarized under eight headings. (1) A brief *prologue* (1.1–4), written in a stylized periodic sentence, states the author's purpose in writing. (2) Two chapters are devoted to an *infancy narrative* (1.5–2.52), recounting in studied parallelism the birth and childhood of *John the Baptist and those of Jesus. (3) One and a half chapters (3.1–4.13) set forth the appearance of John in the desert, his preaching and baptist career, and his imprisonment by Herod Antipas as a *prelude to the events inaugurating Jesus' public career,* namely, the latter's baptism, sojourn in the desert, and temptation by the devil. (4) The story of *Jesus' Galilean ministry* (4.14–9.50) begins programmatically in a synagogue in his hometown, *Nazareth, and moves on to *Capernaum and other towns and villages, as Jesus preaches the *kingdom of God, heals those who are afflicted, and associates himself with disciples whom he gradually trains. This Galilean activity serves also as the starting point for his "*exodus," or transit to the Father through death, burial, and resurrection (9.31). (5) There follows the *travel account* (9.51–19.27), which has both a specifically Lucan form (9.51–18.14) and another form in 18.15–19.27 that parallels Mark 10.13–52. In this account, Jesus is depicted not only as moving without distraction toward *Jerusalem, the city of destiny, but also as instructing crowds of people and especially the *disciples, who would become the foreordained witnesses of his ministry, career, and destiny in Jerusalem (see Acts 10.41). (6) At the end of the travel account, Jesus is accorded a regal welcome as he enters Jerusalem itself, purges its *Temple, and initiates there a period of *ministry and teaching in the Temple* (19.28–21.38), which serves as a prelude to the events of his last days. (7) The *passion narrative* (22.1–23.56a) forms the climax of his exodus, as the Jerusalem leaders conspire with Judas against him, and as he eats his last meal with the *twelve and foretells Peter's denial of him. After praying on the Mount of *Olives, Jesus is arrested, brought before a morning session of the *Sanhedrin, delivered to *Pilate, sent to *Herod, and finally handed over for *crucifixion. This narrative ends with the notice of Jesus' death and burial. (8) The Lucan *resurrection narrative* (23.56b–24.53) tells of the women who discover the empty tomb and of Jesus' appearance as risen to followers on the road to Emmaus and in Jerusalem itself. The Lucan gospel ends with Jesus giving a final commission to the eleven and others and with his *ascension (apparently on the night of the day of the discovery of the empty tomb).

Authorship. Unlike the Pauline letters, which bear the Apostle's name, the third gospel is anonymous, as are the other gospels. Ancient church tradition attributed the third gospel to the Luke who appears in Philemon 24 as Paul's "fellow worker" and is called "the beloved physician" in Collossians 4.14 (cf. 2 Tim. 4.11).

Most modern commentators on the Lucan gospel, however, are skeptical about the validity of this traditional attribution. They regard the tradition as based largely on inferences from the text of the New Testament made when people were first beginning to wonder who had written the Gospels. They further call in question Irenaeus's description of Luke as Paul's "inseparable" collaborator (*Adv. haer.* 3.14,1), which he inferred from the "we" sections of *Acts (esp. 16.10; 20.6). The nature of these "we" sections has since been questioned. Are they fragments of a diary or notebook that the author of Acts kept as he journeyed with Paul? Or are they, rather, a literary form used by the author to enhance his narrative of sea journeys? A still larger part of the problem is the relationship of the author of Acts to *Paul. In recent decades it has become evident that only with considerable difficulty can one reconcile much of the depiction of Paul in Acts with that which emerges from Paul's own letters. Hence, was the author of Luke-Acts really the "inseparable" collaborator of Paul? The difference between the Lucan Paul and the Pauline Paul is not minor; even though it is largely an issue of Acts and the Pauline letters, it bears on the authorship of the Lucan gospel. The result is that many modern commentators are uncertain about the authorship of Luke-Acts.

A minority of commentators, however, retain the traditional attribution as substantially correct. They recognize that in this tradition one must distinguish between what could have been inferred from the text of the New Testament (Luke as a physician; as Paul's fellow worker; as one who had not personally witnessed the ministry of Jesus; Luke as an author who wrote for gentile converts; who wrote after the Marcan and Matthean gospels; who began his gospel with John the Baptist and was also the author of Acts) and what could not have been so inferred (Luke as a Syrian of Antioch; who wrote in Achaia, Bithynia, or Rome; who died in Boeotia or Thebes, unmarried, childless, and at the age of eighty-four). Many of the latter details are legendary and of no value; but the substance of the tradition—that the author of the third gospel and Acts was Luke, an inhabitant of *Antioch in Syria and a companion of Paul—is far from being untenable.

In this regard, one must read Irenaeus critically. The evidence he used, namely the "we" sections of Acts, may indeed show that the author of Luke-Acts was a companion of Paul, but not that he was "inseparably" so. If one accepts the "we" sections as excerpts from a diary or notebook of the author and reads them at face value, one finds that they reveal only that the author was a *sometime* companion of Paul. He would have traveled with Paul from Troas to Philippi (Acts 16.10–17), i.e., for a short time toward the middle of Paul's second missionary journey (49–52 CE). He would have stayed in Philippi and joined Paul again only as the latter departed from Philippi at the end of his third journey (when he returns to Jerusalem for the last time [58 CE; Acts 20.6]), and as Paul sailed for Rome to appear before Caesar (Acts 27.1–28.16). Reading the evidence thus, we see that the author was not with Paul during the main part of his evangelizing endeavors, when he faced the major crisis of his missionary activity in the eastern Mediterranean area (the judaizing problem, as he struggled against those who insisted that gentile converts must observe Jewish legal practices), or when he wrote his greatest letters. Moreover, there is no indication that the author of Luke-Acts ever read Paul's letters. Yet his brief association with Paul led him to idealize Paul and make him the hero of the second part of Acts. He has painted his own picture of Paul, which may not agree in all details with the Paul of the uncontested Pauline letters. Yet, since Luke is not prominent in the apostolic age, if the gospel and Acts were not originally written by him, there is no obvious reason why they should have been associated with him. In other words, the ancient tradition which holds that Luke is the author of the third gospel and Acts may in the long run prove to be substantially valid.

Sources. The prologue of the gospel reveals that Luke depends on other gospel narratives and on information gathered from "eyewitnesses" and "servants of the word" (who may or may not represent two distinct sources for him). From an internal analysis of the gospel, one recognizes that Luke used mainly three sources: the Marcan gospel (in a form more or less as we know it today), a postulated Greek written source, often called *Q (some 230 verses common to his and the Matthean gospel but not found in Mark), and a unique source, often designated L, either written or oral (episodes exclusive to the third gospel).

From Mark, Luke has taken over six blocks of material largely in the same order, into which he has inserted matter (from Q and L); he has also omitted some Marcan material and transposed some Marcan episodes. The use of Marcan material can best be seen thus:

(1) Mark 1.1–15   = Luke 3.1–4.15
(2) Mark 1.21–3.19   = Luke 4.31–6.19
   Luke's Little Interpolation:
      6.20–8.3 (from "Q" and "L")

(3) Mark 4.1–6.44   = Luke 8.4–9.17
   Luke's Big Omission at 9.17
      (= Mark 6.45–8.26)
(4) Mark 8.27–9.40   = Luke 9.18–50
   Luke's Little Omission at 9.50
      (= Mark 9.41–10.12)
   Luke's Big Interpolation:
      9.15–18.14 (from "Q" and "L")
(5) Mark 10.13–13.32   = Luke 18.15–21.33
(6) Mark 14.1–16.8   = Luke 22.1–24.12
The Lucan Ending: 24.13–53 (from "L")

Luke has not slavishly copied this earlier material; he frequently redacts or modifies the Marcan text, improving its Greek style and language. He has also transposed seven Marcan episodes: (1) the imprisonment of John the Baptist (Mark 6.17–18) is moved up to Luke 3.19–20 (to finish the Baptist story before Jesus appears); (2) Jesus' visit to Nazareth (Mark 6.1–6) is moved up to Luke 4.16–30 (to become the programmatic beginning of Jesus' ministry); (3) the call of the disciples (Mark 1.16–20) is postponed to Luke 5.1–11 (to develop a better psychological setting for the call of Simon the fisherman); (4) the choosing of the Twelve (Mark 3.13–19) and the report of the crowds following Jesus (Mark 3.7–12) are reversed in Luke 6.12–16, 17–19 (to improve the psychological setting for the Sermon on the Plain); (5) the episode about Jesus' relatives (Mark 3.31–35) is moved to Luke 8.19–21 (to follow the interpretation of the parable of the seed, thus making Jesus' own relatives examples of the seed sown on good soil); (6) the foretelling of Judas' betrayal of Jesus (Mark 14.18–21) becomes part of the discourse after the meal (Luke 22.21–23); (7) the order of the interrogation of Jesus, his mistreatment, and Peter's denials (Mark 14.55–64a, 64b–65, 66–72) is reversed in Luke 22.54c–62 (Peter's denials), 63–65 (mistreatment), 66–71 (interrogation).

It is often difficult to distinguish between L passages and those that Luke may have freely composed. It is also a matter of debate whether some of the L passages are related to the material in the gospel of John (e.g., the anointing of Jesus' *feet* by a woman; the single account of the multiplication of the loaves and fish; the mention of Lazarus, Martha, and Mary; one of the twelve named Judas; no night interrogation of Jesus before the high priest; three nonguilty statements of Pilate during Jesus' trial; postresurrection appearances of the risen Christ in the Jerusalem area). Although there is no real evidence that the Johannine evangelist knew the Lucan gospel, some contact in the oral traditions behind both the Johannine and the Lucan gospels is not impossible.

Attempts are sometimes made to associate L with specific persons from whom Luke would have derived information: *Mary, the mother of Jesus (see Luke 2.19, 51); the disciples of John the Baptist (Acts 19.1–3); Joanna, "wife of Chuza, Herod's steward" (Luke 8.3); Cleopas (24.18). Luke could have obtained information from such sources, but such a list of candidates is based on speculation, more pious than critical, about possible informants.

Date and Place of Composition. If the Marcan gospel is rightly included among the sources used by Luke in composing his gospel, then the latter is to be dated after Mark. The Marcan gospel is commonly dated ca. 65–70 CE. How much later is the Lucan gospel? One cannot say for certain. Luke 1.1 refers to "many" others who had previously tried to write the Jesus story; even if Mark is included among the "many," more time must be allowed for the others to whom Luke alludes. Again, since the Lucan Jesus refers to Jerusalem as an "abandoned" house (13.35), this and other references to Jerusalem (21.20, "surrounded by camps"; 19.43–44, with earthworks erected against it) would suggest a date for Luke after the fall of Jerusalem in 70 CE. Some have sought to interpret these references as merely literary imitations of biblical descriptions of the fall of Jerusalem under Nebuchadrezzar, hence lacking in historical references to the Roman destruction. But this interpretation is not without its problems. In any case, it is widely held that the Lucan gospel was composed ca. 80–85 CE, even though one cannot maintain this dating with certainty.

Nothing in the Lucan gospel hints at the place where it was composed. The author's knowledge of Palestine is at times defective, which would suggest that it was not composed there. Ancient tradition mentions Achaia, Boeotia, and Rome; modern conjectures include Caesarea, the *Decapolis, or Asia Minor. No one really knows where it was written.

Intended Readers. Details in the Lucan gospel suggest that Luke was writing for a predominantly gentile Christian community. Among such details are the dedication of his two-volume work to a patron with what is clearly a Greek name (Theophilus), his concern to relate his narrative account of the Jesus story and its sequel to a Greco-Roman literary tradition, his elimination from his source materials of items with a pro-

nounced Jewish preoccupation (e.g., the controversy about what is clean or unclean, Mark 7.1–23; the substitution of Greek titles like *kyrios*, "Lord," or *epistatēs*, "master" for *rabbi/rabbouni*, cf. Mark 9.5; 10.51 with Luke 9.33; 18.41; and the omission of other Semitic words). All such details suggest that Luke envisaged his readers as predominantly gentile Christians in a Greek-speaking setting, but who were not wholly unacquainted with the *Septuagint.

Lucan Teaching. Even a brief summary of Luke's interpretation of the Jesus story must cope with its sequel, for details in Acts sometimes bear on the message of the gospel itself. Though the Lucan picture of Jesus may not be as radical as the Pauline or the Marcan, or as sublime as the Johannine, it is nevertheless one of the major testimonies to Jesus in the New Testament.

The Lucan picture of Jesus is kerygmatic. The Christian "kerygma" has been defined by Rudolf Bultmann as the proclamation of Jesus Christ, crucified and risen, as God's eschatological act of salvation. Luke clearly depicts Jesus proclaiming himself in this way, not only as God's agent of promised salvation (4.16–21) but also as the preacher par excellence of God's kingdom: "that is what I was sent for" (4.43). Luke further depicts, no less than the other evangelists, Jesus' disciples sent out to announce the kingdom and to heal (9.1). Later, in Acts, Peter proclaims Jesus Christ not only as crucified and risen but also as "Lord and *Messiah" (2.36). Indeed, Peter announces further, "Salvation is found in no one else, for there is no other name under heaven given to human beings by which we are to be saved" (Acts 4.12). Although Luke's gospel has become more of a "Life of Christ" than either Mark's or Matthew's, it has not lost its proclamatory character. It accosts Theophilus, and other readers like him, with God's eschatological salvation achieved in Jesus Christ. Luke's picture of Jesus, now rooted in history in a way that none of the other evangelists root it, has played the kerygma in another key; but it still utters a time-transcending, ever-present, existential challenge to its readers to put personal faith in, and to make a deep commitment to, Jesus the risen Lord and "the Messiah of God" (9.20).

The Lucan picture of Jesus is also drawn in a distinctive historical perspective. Luke's concern is evident from the remark that he has Paul utter before King Agrippa, "None of these things has escaped his [the king's] notice, for this was not done in a corner" (Acts 26.26). Jesus' story and its sequel, intended by God's providence to challenge human beings to Christian faith, has been rooted in human history. This is the reason that Luke has not written a "gospel," as does Mark (1.1), a term he never uses in the first part of his work (but only in Acts 15.7; 20.24), preferring instead to designate his two-volume work as a "narrative account" (diēgēsis, Luke 1.1). In this account he roots the Jesus story in a threefold synchronization, connecting it with Roman history, Palestinian history, and church history. Its relation to Roman history is shown by the connection of Jesus' birth with a decree of Caesar Augustus ordering the registration of the whole (Roman) world during the governorship of Quirinius (Luke 2.1–2). The ministry of John the Baptist (and of Jesus, by implication) is connected with the fifteenth year of the reign of the emperor Tiberius (28–29 CE) and with the prefecture of Pontius *Pilate in Judea (26–36 CE; Luke 3.1). Luke further connects events in the early Christian community with the famine in the days of Claudius (ca. 46 CE; Acts 11.18), with Claudius's expulsion of Jews from Rome (49 CE; Acts 18.2), and with the proconsulship of Gallio in Achaia (52 CE; Acts 18.12). Again, he connects the birth of Jesus with Palestinian history by linking it with the days of King *Herod the Great (37–4 BCE; Luke 1.5); and John's and Jesus' ministry to the time of the high priesthood of Annas and *Caiaphas, to the reigns of Herod Antipas, tetrarch of Galilee, of Philip, tetrarch of Ituraea and Trachonitis, and of Lysanias, tetrarch of Abilene (3.1)—even though only Galilee further figures in the Jesus story. Finally, he connects the Jesus story with Christian history in a way that no other evangelist does, by recounting its sequel in Acts. All of this historical perspective, which is exclusively Lucan, is in the long run related to his view of salvation history. Luke sees all of human history divided into three phases: the period of Israel (see Luke 16.16), the period of Jesus (from the coming of John the Baptist to the ascension), and the period of the church under stress (from the ascension to the *parousia). This historical perspective is central to the unique Lucan presentation of the Christian kerygma.

The Lucan picture of Jesus is also drawn in a geographical perspective. Luke is preoccupied in his gospel to depict Jesus as moving resolutely from his Galilean ministry, once the travel account begins (9.51), toward Jerusalem, the city of destiny—where his "exodus" is to be achieved (13.32–33). Such a perspective gives Jerusalem a distinctive centrality; towards it, all in the gos-

pel is aimed. Then in Acts it becomes the focal point from which "the word of the Lord" (8.25) goes forth as Jesus' disciples are commissioned as "witnesses" to carry it from Jerusalem to "all Judea and Samaria" and "to the end of the earth" (1.8). Since the last expression can mean "Rome" (see Ps. Sol. 8.15), and since Rome is where the story of Acts ends (see 28.16), Paul becomes the one who in effect carries the word "about the Lord Jesus Christ openly and unhindered" (28.31) from Jerusalem to that "end." Both the historical and the geographical perspectives enhance the status of the church as the sequel to Jesus' ministry in the Roman world of its time.

The Lucan picture of Jesus' ministry and its sequel also has an apologetic perspective. This is Luke's secondary purpose in writing his "narrative account," for he wanted to show that Christianity had as much right to legitimate recognition in the Roman world as did Judaism. Hence, he was concerned from the outset of the gospel to depict Jesus, the founder of Christianity, as born into a pious Jewish family, circumcised, and faithfully observant of Jewish customs. Later on, it emerges in Luke's account that Christianity, a "sect" of Judaism (Acts 24.5, 14), is the logical outgrowth of Pharisaic Judaism. He depicts Paul as stoutly maintaining his Pharisaic connection, by siding with the *Pharisees against the *Sadducees with respect to "the resurrection of the dead" (Acts 23.6). He further portrays Paul, once he has been taken captive at the end of Acts, as being declared innocent on several occasions (23.9, 29; 25.12, 18–20, 25; 26.31–32). These declarations of innocence imply indirectly that Christianity likewise stands in the same relation to the Roman government.

The key figure in Lucan salvation history is Jesus himself, about whom the evangelist makes not only christological but also soteriological affirmations about who Jesus is and what he has done for humanity. Certain aspects of Jesus, who is otherwise portrayed as a human being, hint at his transcendent condition: his virginal conception through the power of the Holy Spirit; his ministry under the auspices of the holy Spirit; his special relation to his heavenly Father; his resurrection and exaltation to glory. Luke applies many traditional christological titles to Jesus: *Messiah (or Christ), Lord, Savior, *Son of God, *Son of man, Servant, Prophet, King, Son of David, leader, Holy One, Righteous One, Teacher. Particularly noteworthy are the distinctive Lucan use of "Savior" (2.11; Acts 5.31; 13.23), "suffering Messiah" (24.26, 46; Acts 3.18; 17.3; 26.23), and the retrojection of the title "the Lord" (originally used of the *risen* Christ) even into the infancy narrative (2.11; cf. 1.43) and the ministry account, when the evangelist himself is speaking (7.13, 19; 10.1, 39, 41; 11.39; 12.42a; 13.15; etc.). When Luke speaks of the soteriological function of Jesus Christ and the effects of what he has done for humanity, he depicts them as "salvation" (1.69, 71, 77; 3.6; 19.9; Acts 4.12; 13.26, 47; 16.17; 28.28), "forgiveness of sins" (24.47; Acts 2.38; 5.31; 10.43; 13.38; 26.18), "peace" (2.14; 19.38, 42), and "life" (10.25–28; 24.5; Acts 11.18; 13.46–48), and once even as "justification" (Acts 13.39, where the context provides the interpretation of it as "forgiveness of sins"). In a way that surpasses that of the other evangelists, Luke portrays not only the ministry of Jesus itself but even the movement begun by him as especially Spirit-guided. In at least seventeen instances in the gospel and fifty-seven in Acts the influence of the Spirit is seen both on the activity of Jesus himself and on that of his followers.

Hence, though Luke may have introduced a historical perspective in the gospel tradition, he did not simply imitate Flavius *Josephus, who composed the *Jewish Antiquities*, by writing merely annalistic *Christian Antiquities*. He has preserved the proclamatory aim of the gospel tradition, and that is why we refer to it as "the gospel according to Luke."   JOSEPH A. FITZMYER, S.J.

LXX. *See* Septuagint.

M

Maccabees, The Books of the. The four books of the Maccabees are independent works. 1 and 2 Maccabees separately record the Maccabean rebellion and the events leading up to it; 3 Maccabees is a historical novel, which became associated with 1 and 2 Maccabees for thematic reasons; and 4 Maccabees is a discourse on reason which took its cue from the story of the Maccabean martyrs. Because they were either not written or not preserved in Hebrew, they are not part of the Jewish and Protestant *canons, but are accorded varying degrees of canonicity by Roman Catholic and Orthodox churches (*see* Apocrypha, *article on* Jewish Apocrypha). They differ greatly in aims and presentation, scope and detail. They also differ in matters of chronology, so reconstructing the precise course of events and their political background has been a major scholarly pursuit. It will help to begin by outlining the history of the Maccabean rebellion.

Historical Summary. In 200 BCE, Antiochus III of *Syria defeated Ptolemy V of *Egypt at Paneion, thus finally winning the Levant, including Judah, for the Seleucid empire. He won Jewish support by granting tax concessions and the right to live in accordance with traditional Jewish law (Antiochus IV's later removal of this concession precipitated rebellion). Antiochus III then tried to extend his empire into Greece, but came into conflict with Rome, which had similar interests. He was defeated and forced in the Peace of Apamea (188 BCE) to pay ruinous indemnities. Syria's financial desperation was another factor contributing to the Jewish rebellion: it caused Seleucus IV (187–175 BCE) to send his minister Heliodorus to raid the Jerusalem *Temple for money (2 Macc. 3), and it caused his successor Antiochus IV (175–164 BCE) to accept bribes from successive candidates for the Jerusalem high priesthood. Rivalry for this office was itself a major factor in the ensuing struggle. When the high priest Onias III, slandered by his rivals, went to Syria to defend his position

before Antiochus IV, his brother Jason usurped him by offering to pay more tribute and to turn *Jerusalem into a more typical Hellenistic city-state, of the kind Antiochus favored as conducive to the unity and stability of his empire. In 171 BCE Jason himself was similarly ousted by Menelaus, who, though not of the high priestly family, offered a yet higher tribute to Antiochus and raided the Temple plate to pay it, much to the anger of the people. However, the systemic change brought about by Jason and exacerbated by Menelaus subtly affected the agreement by which the Jews were allowed to regulate their lives by their own laws; a Hellenistic Jerusalem might be expected to organize itself like other cities of the Greek world, with an assembly, a voting citizen body, a gymnasium, and an ephebeion for training young men who would take part in athletic contests at home and abroad. In short, the Jews were under pressure to conform to the life-style of the surrounding world; and this too was a factor in the Maccabean struggle.

The attempt to regularize Jerusalem's position in the Seleucid empire was important to Antiochus because Judah lay between Syria and Egypt, which Antiochus wished to annex. In 172 BCE, the guardians of the newly enthroned minor Ptolemy VI declared war on Antiochus, who sent a diplomat to Rome to meet Roman objections and invaded Egypt in 169 BCE; when he did so again in 168 BCE, the Romans ejected him. Jason meanwhile had attacked Menelaus and tried to reinstate himself in Jerusalem. Antiochus, seeing this as rebellion, attacked Jerusalem and looted the Temple (1 Maccabees dates this to 169 BCE; 2 Maccabees, probably correctly, to 168 BCE), leaving a commissioner in charge. In 167 BCE, the Syrians made an unexpected and vicious attack and established a military garrison in Jerusalem (1 Macc. 1.29–35). Clearly, Antiochus was determined to control Judah, although Egypt, for the time being, was closed to him.

Antiochus's determination led him to one further disastrous political error. In 167 BCE he tried "to compel the Jews to forsake the laws of their ancestors and no longer to live by the laws of God, also to pollute the temple in Jerusalem and to call it the temple of Olympian Zeus" (2 Macc. 6.1–2). According to 1 Maccabees 1.41–50, the king decreed the Jews "to follow customs strange to the land, to forbid burnt offerings and sacrifices and drink offerings in the sanctuary, to profane sabbaths and festivals, to defile the sanctuary and the priests, to build altars and sacred precincts and shrines for idols, to sacrifice swine and other unclean animals, and to leave their sons uncircumcised." This was followed in December 167 BCE by the erection of "a desolating sacrilege upon the altar of burnt offering" (1 Macc. 1.54), the erection of altars throughout Judah, and the proscription of the Jewish *Law. These descriptions show that in Jewish eyes the king was persecuting Jewish religion by attacking the Law and the Temple. By his "decree," however, Antiochus presumably (his original wording is not extant) was withdrawing the Jewish right of self-rule by Jewish law and opening the Jerusalem Temple to all worshipers (as any other Hellenistic city temple would be); but, worse, he was making the positive practice of Jewish law punishable. It has been argued that Antiochus saw the Jews much as the Romans saw the followers of the god Bacchus—as dangerous religious fanatics—and wished to suppress them, but Antiochus was not giving way to mere prejudice; he was punishing the Jews for political rebellion by prohibiting precisely those things that constituted Jewish independence—the concession of self-rule by ancestral laws, and the exclusivity of the Jerusalem Temple.

The result was rebellion, led by Judas called "Maccabeus" ("hammerlike"; 1 Macc. 2.4), son of Mattathias, from Modin, 20 km (17 mi) northwest of Jerusalem (Map 10:X5). The rebellion is described in detail in 1 Maccabees, and cannot be recounted in full here. In outline, however, affairs developed as follows: After several local victories in Judah, Judas occupied the Temple area, purged it of non-Jewish cultic activities, and rededicated it (December 164 BCE); this was the institution of the festival of Hanukkah (called the feast of the Dedication in John 10.22; see Feasts and Festivals). The following year he widened his military activities to Idumea, Galilee, Transjordan, and Philistia; the Seleucid army responded, but, after an initially successful campaign preempted by an attempted coup d'état in Syria, the Syrians offered Judas terms, withdrawing the edict of 167 BCE (1 Macc. 6.58), but leaving the Syrian garrison in Jerusalem and destroying Judas's Temple defenses. They also executed the high priest Menelaus. Thus, in theory the Jews had regained religious independence (with no clear leadership to exercise it), and the Syrians retained political control (with inadequate popular support to maintain it). In 162–161 BCE a new Syrian king, Demetrius, and a new high priest, Alcimus, collaborated to eliminate Judas and his supporters. Judas defeated the new general sent against him, Nicanor, but fell before the more experienced Bacchides in 160 BCE. Bacchides fortified Judah, but failed to make progress against Judas's successor Jonathan and finally withdrew. Alcimus died, and power remained de facto with Jonathan, who began to "judge" the people from his home in Michmash (Map 10: inset); the historian deliberately compares Jonathan with the rulers who preceded the monarchy in Israel. Constitutionally, however, Judah was still under Seleucid rule, symbolized by the garrison in Jerusalem.

Jonathan now proceeded to steer Judah toward independence by diplomacy, bargaining with successive Seleucid rulers for political concessions. In return for Jonathan's support, the Seleucid pretender Alexander Balas gave him the high priesthood (to which Jonathan had no hereditary right) in 152 BCE. Jonathan refused to support Demetrius I and defeated Demetrius II in 147 BCE (thus earning new honors and more territory from Balas); but when Balas was killed in 145 BCE, Jonathan shifted his allegiance to Demetrius II, for which Demetrius transferred to Jonathan three districts from *Samaria. When Antiochus VI and Trypho ousted Demetrius in 145 BCE, they confirmed Jonathan in his position and made his brother Simon governor of the coastal region. Jonathan and Simon now began rapidly to develop Judah's position. The Seleucid garrison at Beth-zur was replaced by a Jewish one, Joppa was garrisoned, Adida fortified, Gaza captured, the Seleucid garrison in Jerusalem blockaded, and the walls of Jerusalem and the fortresses of Judah repaired. Jonathan renewed both the diplomatic links with Rome initiated by Judas in 161 BCE and the links of brotherhood and friendship with Sparta which supposedly were established several generations earlier by Onias the high priest and Arius king of Sparta. Jonathan campaigned, ostensibly against Demetrius II, in Syrian territory near Hamath. Trypho, naturally anxious at this Jewish resurgence, captured Jonathan by treachery, and Simon took over the Jewish leadership. He completed Jonathan's military and diplomatic program, crowning his achievements by expelling the Seleucid garrison from Jerusalem and negotiating the formal abolition of tribute payable to Syria with Demetrius II. In effect, this meant the end of Seleucid rule of Judah, and 1 Maccabees 13.41 notes that in 142 BCE "the yoke of the gentiles was removed from Israel, and the people began to write in their documents and contracts, 'In the first year of Simon the great high priest and commander and leader of the Jews.'" This was the beginning of a new era, which was to last until 63 BCE, when Pompey the Great claimed Judah for Rome.

1 Maccabees. Synopsis. 1 Maccabees presents a coherent and well-organized account of the events just described, emphasizing throughout the leadership of the Hasmonean family. Chaps. 1 and 2 form an introductory section, explaining how Israel reached the humiliating position inflicted upon her by Antiochus. The author blames not only Antiochus but also the "lawless men" who "came forth from Israel, and misled many, saying, 'Let us go and make a covenant with the gentiles around about us, for since we separated from them many disasters have come upon us'" (1 Macc. 1.11). But chap. 2 sets against these hellenizing Jews the priest Mattathias and his sons, whose loyalty to the Law and the *covenant and whose skills in counsel and battle will bring Israel's restoration.

Chaps. 3.1–9.22 recount the first phase of the restoration under the leadership of Judas, who defeats a series of increasingly professional forces sent against him, captures and rededicates the Temple, takes the war into gentile territory, achieves the abolition of the infamous decree, and arranges a treaty with Rome before being killed in battle. Judas is presented as a latter-day Saul or David, not least at his death when Israel laments him in famous words (1 Macc. 9.21; cf. 2 Sam. 1.19):

> How is the mighty fallen,
> the savior of Israel.

Chaps. 9.23–12.53 turn to Judas's youngest brother, Jonathan, who is made "ruler and leader, to fight our battle" (1 Macc. 9.30). After some skirmishing, Jonathan concludes the war with Bacchides, and begins to "judge" Israel (1 Macc. 9.73). This judgeship is important, hinting at the Hasmonean monarchy to follow. Similarly, Jon-

athan's high priesthood was important to the author, for it provided the title and justification for the frequently challenged high priesthood assumed by the Hasmonean monarchy.

The author brings the political story to its climax with the work of Simon (chaps. 13.1–16.17), under whom "the yoke of the gentiles was removed." The particular importance of Simon is that he establishes a new era (1 Macc. 13.41–42), described in terms taken from prophecies of Israel's paradisal future:

> He established peace in the land,
> and Israel rejoiced with great joy.
> All the people sat under their own vines and
>   fig trees,
> and there was none to make them afraid.
>
> (1 Macc. 14.11–12)

But the author is at particular pains to underline Simon's position as "high priest, commander, and ethnarch [NRSV: leader] of the Jews" (cf. 1 Macc. 13.41; 14.17, 35, 38, 41, 47; 15.2) and to indicate the position of John Hyrcanus as Simon's heir (1 Macc. 13.53; 14.59; 16.1–3); the book ends with a statement of John's acts, brave deeds, and achievements "from the time that he became high priest after his father" (1 Macc. 16.23–24).

Purpose. 1 Maccabees is, in effect, an apologia for the Hasmonean monarchy, and other families are not allowed to steal the limelight. When Joseph and Azariah, two subordinate commanders, try to emulate Judas's success, they fail disastrously because "they did not belong to the family of those men through whom deliverance was given to Israel" (1 Macc. 5.62). The public citation of Simon and his brothers proclaimed that they "exposed themselves to danger and resisted the enemies of their nation, in order that their sanctuary and the law might be preserved; and they brought great glory to their nation" (1 Macc. 14.29).

Sources, dating, text, and canonicity. The author's political concerns, however, do not negate his historical value. He apparently had access to official state archives and public records (cf. 1 Macc. 14.27, 48–49), from which may derive some of the documents quoted. He refers to official annals at least for the rule of John Hyrcanus (1 Macc. 16.24), during which he probably wrote. In chronological matters he uses the official Seleucid era, dating from October 312 BCE, for events of Seleucid history, and the local Jewish calendar, whose years were dated from spring

312 or 311 BCE, when drawing upon Jewish sources. What these might have been (apart from the annals of Hyrcanus's rule) we can only guess, but an obvious possibility is some account or "acts" of Judas, whose existence has been inferred from 1 Maccabees 9.22. (This might also have been the source for the work of Jason of Cyrene abridged by 2 Maccabees.) The author of 1 Maccabees is not given to pious legend (as is 2 Maccabees), though the story of Mattathias in chap. 2 comes near this, but he does include a number of poetic laments (e.g., 2.7–13) and eulogies (e.g., 3.3–9), which are full of biblical allusions and may be his own compositions.

The style of these poems and the prose narrative, often reminiscent of the books of *Samuel and *Kings, supports Jerome's statement that 1 Maccabees was originally written in Hebrew. The book exists, however, only in a Greek translation; the oldest manuscript containing it is the fourth century CE Codex Sinaiticus. The original title is debated. Origen, quoted by Eusebius, preserved as a title the phrase *sarbēth sarbanaiel*, a corrupt Greek transliteration of the Aramaic "Book of the House of the Princes of God" (or, "of Israel"), that is, "Book of the Hasmonean Family." Some such title would be more appropriate than "Maccabees," for "Maccabee" was the nickname of Judas alone, but by the end of the second century CE Clement of Alexandria was distinguishing between "the book of Maccabean history" (1 Maccabees) and "the epitome of Maccabean history" (2 Maccabees). The book is considered part of the canon by Roman Catholics and most Orthodox churches.

2 Maccabees. *Synopsis.* 2 Maccabees is a very different book, as is clear from the prologue (2.19–30) and epilogue (15.37–39). The author intends to tell "the story of Judas Maccabeus and his brothers, and the purification of the great temple, and the dedication of the altar, and further the wars against Antiochus Epiphanes and his son Eupator, and the appearances that came from heaven to those who fought bravely for Judaism, so that though few in number they seized the whole land . . . and regained possession of the temple . . . and liberated the city and re-established the laws" (2 Macc. 2.19–22). This he has condensed from the five-volume work of the otherwise unknown Jason of Cyrene, in such a way that "the style of the story delights the ears of those who read the work" (15.39).

The book begins with two letters. The first (1.1–9) is dated 124 BCE, the second (1.10–2.18)

is undated but, if authentic, is possibly from 163 BCE, before the first anniversary of the Temple rededication of 164 BCE. Both letters are from Jerusalem, urging Jews in Egypt to celebrate the feast; the author of 2 Maccabees, by prefixing them to Jason's work, has created a book that could be read at precisely such a festival (cf. Esther; 3 Maccabees).

The account of events summarized from Jason's work differs from 1 Maccabees' account in content, order, and style. It contains more political detail at certain points as well as more legendary material. The narrative has two parallel climaxes: the first is the defeat of Nicanor, the death of Antiochus, and the celebration of the purification of the sanctuary (8.1–10.8); the second is the defeat and death of Nicanor and the decree establishing the future celebration of that day (15.6–36). The summary of Jason's work is arranged between the prologue and epilogue as follows: (1) attacks on the Jewish Temple and religion by Seleucus, Antiochus, and Jewish Hellenists (3.1–6.11); (2) martyrdom of Eleazar, the seven brothers and their mother (6.18–7.42); (3) defeat of Nicanor, death of Antiochus, celebration of the Temple purification (8.1–10.9); (4) "what took place under Antiochus Eupator" (10.10–13.26); (5) defeat and death of Nicanor, decree for future celebration of the day (14.1–15.37). The author has evidently ordered the material in sections (perhaps following the divisions of Jason's five volumes). Concern to balance the sequences of sections (3) and (5) has led to adjustments in chronology; thus, for example, Antiochus IV's death precedes the Temple purification, whereas in 1 Maccabees it follows it (in fact, both events date to December 164 BCE). Three letters from Antiochus IV's reign appear in fact to belong to Antiochus V's (11.16–21; 27–33; 34–38), possibly because the author disliked crediting peace initiatives to Antiochus IV. The work ends with Nicanor's death (cf. 1 Macc. 7.47); Judas's death a year later is unmentioned and his success unclouded. In style, 2 Maccabees is more rhetorical than 1 Maccabees, addressing readers directly and involving their sympathies (see 6.12–17).

Purpose. 2 Maccabees is less concerned with the historical order of events than with the theological opposition between the Judaism represented by "orthodox" high priests like Onias and the hellenizing Judaism of Jason and Menelaus. At the heart of the struggle lies "the most holy temple in all the world" (5.15), firmly protected by God (3.39). The author knows, however, that the nation is even more important: "the Lord did not choose the nation for the sake of the holy place, but the place for the sake of the nation" (5.19). The nation's sufferings under Antiochus are punishment for apostasy (4.13–16), but "these punishments were designed not to destroy but to discipline our people" (6.12). Punishment is often shown as fitting the crime; thus Jason "who had driven many from their own country into exile died in exile" (5.9; cf. especially 9.5–28). The Jewish nation, however, was saved by the faith and prayers of Judas and his men (8.1–5; 15.7–11), which brought victory in battle (e.g., 15.20–27). Such victories were signaled by the dramatic appearance of angelic horsemen (cf. 3.25–26; 5.2–4; 10.29–30; 11.8). Equal faith was shown by martyrs such as Eleazar, the seven brothers and their mother, and the hero Razis (6.18–7.42; 14.37–46), who might expect the reward of resurrection (cf. 7.9, 11, 14, 23, 29; Dan. 12.2–3). An extension of this belief, influential in Christian theology, appears in 12.39–45, where Judas, having discovered that some of his own battle casualties had been wearing idolatrous amulets, provided sin offerings "and made atonement for the dead, so that they might be delivered from their sin," in the expectation that those who had died fighting for the Maccabeean cause might rise again. (*See* Afterlife and Immortality.)

The author thus uses the story of Judas to affirm what he sees as the central tenets of Judaism: the importance of the Temple, the Law (especially the *Sabbath observance), loyalty under persecution, faith in God's *mercy to his covenant people and in his power of miraculous intervention. 2 Maccabees' outlook is like that of the book of *Daniel and that of the *Qumran War Scroll; these books may have a Hasidean background (cf. 1 Macc 2.42; 7.13; Judas was leader of the Hasideans, 2 Macc. 14.6). The author is more concerned with Judaism than with the monarchic nationalism of the Hasmoneans, whom he ignores, perhaps pointedly. Yet he writes in Greek, not in Hebrew, in a Hellenistic genre, and he is not totally dismissive of *gentiles; even Antiochus IV grieves at the death of Onias (4.37), and Nicanor becomes genuinely friendly toward Judas (14.18–25).

Sources, dating, text, and canonicity. For all its theological concern, 2 Maccabees is an important historical document. The underlying history of Jason shows remarkable knowledge of Jerusalem politics, and perhaps access to Temple archives (from which probably comes the correspondence of 1.1–2.18 and 11.16–38). Jason may have used a Seleucid source for some details of Seleucid history (e.g., 4.21–22, 30–31; 5.1; 9.1, 29; 10.11–13), and an "acts of Judas" (see above), together with some legendary material (6.18–7.42; 14.37–46). Much of this suggests an origin at Jerusalem, though Alexandria or *Antioch has often been proposed. Jason probably wrote in the middle-late second century BCE; 2 Maccabees must be dated between 124 BCE (1.9) and the arrival of Rome in 63 BCE. If the author is deliberately anti-Hasmonean, as some think, he probably belongs to Janneus's reign (103–76 BCE). The text of 2 Maccabees is preserved in the fifth century CE Codex Alexandrinus, and in Old Latin, Syriac, and Armenian translations, and has canonical status in the Roman Catholic and most Orthodox churches.

3 Maccabees. *Synopsis.* The book begins with Ptolemy IV Philopator's preparations to meet Antiochus III in battle at Raphia (217 BCE). A plot by one Theodotus to assassinate Philopator is thwarted by a lapsed Jew, Dositheus. Philopator wins the battle, and decides to visit his subjects with gifts for their temples. He is prevented by divine intervention from entering the Jerusalem sanctuary (the story is strongly reminiscent of 2 Macc. 3); on returning to Egypt he decrees that the Alexandrian Jews should be reduced to *laographia* (tax registration) and servitude, and be forced to accept the cult of Dionysus; those who accepted willingly would be given equal citizen rights with the citizens of Alexandria. A few apostatized, but the majority stood firm.

Philopator then ordered all the Jews of the interior to be rounded up and executed; explanations and instructions were issued to the army. The roundup is described with exaggerated pathos. Jews were registered until after forty days pens and paper ran out. The Jews were herded into the hippodrome, and five hundred elephants were excited by drink and incense to trample them to death, but when the moment came to let them loose, the executioner delayed because the king was asleep. After being woken, he dined, and, only then remembering the Jews, deferred the execution until the following day, when, again forgetful, he deferred the matter one more day. Angered by courtiers' criticism, Philopator swore he would massacre the Jews, ravage Judah, and burn the Temple. The next morning the intoxicated elephants were set on the Jews; in response to the prayer of the aged priest Eleazar, two terrible angels caused the elephants to turn in panic and trample the king's soldiers.

Philopator repented, freed the Jews, and prepared a seven-day feast to celebrate the deliverance. He repatriated the Jews, with permission to execute those who had apostatized (over three hundred people). Another seven-day feast was celebrated when the Jews reached Ptolemais in the eastern delta, where they dedicated a house of prayer. The book closes with the blessing: "Blessed be the Deliverer of Israel through all times! Amen!"

Historicity and dating. Clearly, the work postdates Ptolemy IV Philopator (221–204 BCE), who is presented much as pictured by Polybius and Plutarch: given to drinking, a devotee of the god Dionysus, and interested in architecture. The visit to Jerusalem and interest in the Temple here recorded are not impossible, and the account of the battle of Raphia (chap. 1) agrees in outline with that of Polybius (*Hist.* 5.80, 86). But the story shows no certain firsthand knowledge of events, and it shares some features with other Jewish writings of the second and first centuries BCE. There are clear parallels with the story of *Esther in Dositheus's revelation of the plot to assassinate Philopator (1.3; cf. Esther 2.21–23), in the Egyptian view of the Jews as hostile to the state (3.6–7; cf. Haman's view, Esther 3.8), and in the concluding establishment of a celebratory feast (cf. Esther 9.16–32). This last is also a feature of 2 Maccabees, with which 3 Maccabees has obvious similarities: for example, Philopator's attempt to enter the sanctuary (cf. 2 Macc. 3), the vision that terrified the elephants (3 Macc. 6.18–21; cf. 2 Macc. 3.26), the attempts to hellenize the Jews, the hostility to the Temple, the figure of the aged priest Eleazar, and the use of official correspondence.

There are also close relationships between 3 Maccabees and the *Letter of Aristeas*, which is usually dated to the mid second century BCE. Both are concerned with the sanctity of the Temple and the importance of the Law; both focus on the status of Jews in Alexandria and Egypt, and the relationship between the Ptolemaic king and the Jews. In *Aristeas*, Ptolemy II Philadelphus liberates his father's Jewish captives from servitude, and in 3 Maccabees Ptolemy IV threatens to return the Jews to it and worse. *Aristeas* presents the Alexandrian king and court as sympathetic to the Jews, and the Jews as people whose Law can be seen as rational and whose wisdom and learning can contribute to the good of the state. 3 Maccabees presents the king and court in less friendly light, accepting the Jewish right to live in Egypt only after divine intervention, and it shows the Jews as a people who must resist persecution to the death and punish all who compromise. The author of 3 Maccabees knows *Aristeas* but he reflects a much more difficult situation than that presupposed by *Aristeas*, and a much later one. The author also knew the Greek translation of Esther (probably dated 114 or 77 BCE); Philopator's edict (3 Macc. 3.12–29) may derive from Ahasuerus's edict (Esther 13.2–9).

These literary dependencies, together with the use of *laographia* (see below) suggest that 3 Maccabees is a first-century BCE or even first-century CE Jewish writing from Alexandria, drawing upon a number of stock motifs. This is confirmed by Josephus's attribution (*Apion* 2.53–54) of the same elephant story to Ptolemy VIII Physcon (145–116 BCE). The story may be exaggerated, but in essence it is historical; Physcon was hostile to the Alexandrian Jews because they had supported his sister Cleopatra against him for the throne. 3 Maccabees may be combining the tradition of this episode with other material about Jewish persecution from 2 Maccabees and the Greek Esther to make his story.

Purpose. The author's concerns are clear: to show how Jews abroad should behave when threatened with persecution. In the face of an attack on the Temple, a threat to Jewish status in Alexandria, and a threat to destroy the whole Jewish population of Egypt, the correct Jewish response is above all prayer (1.16–2.20; 6.1–17; 7.20). The Jews are to hold firm to the Law and destroy apostates (2.33; 7.10–15), to remain hopeful (2.32–33) by trusting in providence (4.20), while remaining loyal to the king despite his persecution (3.3).

The story involves the vexed question of the status of the Jews at Alexandria. The Jewish community there constituted a *politeuma* (corporation), and was allowed to live in Alexandria ruled by its own elders in accordance with its own laws. Its members were neither native Egyptians (who were forbidden residence in Alexandria) nor full citizens of Alexandria. They were "foreigners in a foreign land" (6.3), yet reasonably privileged ones. This ambiguous position often led to trouble; the Roman emperor Claudius later ruled that the Jews should live peaceably in a city not their own, and that the Alexandrians should allow them this liberty.

In 3 Maccabees, Philopator proposes that, as revenge for his own humiliation, the Jews should either be reduced to *laographia* and servitude or accept initiation into the Dionysian mysteries (*see* Mystery Religions) and be rewarded with Alexandrian citizenship (*isopoliteia*; 2.28–30; 3.21). *Laographia* originally meant "census," but came to refer to the poll tax that inevitably followed a census. Such payment would reduce the Jews to non-Greek, Egyptian status. *Laographia* in this sense, however, is otherwise unknown before the census of 24–23 BCE, and it has therefore been proposed that 3 Maccabees was written with reference to this occasion, or to the troubles of Caligula's reign (37–41 CE). In this case, Philopator would represent the unstable Caligula, and Philopator's attempt to desecrate the Temple stands for Caligula's attempt to have his statue placed there.

In short, 3 Maccabees is a historical novel, drawing on familiar material, including popular memories of Philopator and Physcon and several Jewish writings, intended to encourage Alexandrian Jews at a period of renewed trouble over citizenship. The use of *laographia* with its implications for status may suggest the period of Roman administration after 31 BCE, but does not necessarily exclude a slightly earlier date.

Text and canonicity. 3 Maccabees does not appear in most canons, though the Greek text is found in Codex Alexandrinus, and some Orthodox churches do consider it canonical. Almost certainly of Alexandrian origin, it was known under its present title by Eusebius's time, but previously, perhaps, more accurately as "Ptolemaica" ("Ptolemaic matters"). Association with the Maccabean books came through its concern with persecution of the Jews by a Hellenistic king and because of its obvious similarities with 2 Maccabees.

4 Maccabees. Synopsis. The author begins by proposing to discuss whether religious reason is master of the emotions. He aims to prove his point from the courage of the Maccabean martyrs who died for the sake of virtue. He defines his terms: "reason" is the intellect choosing to live by wisdom, which is education in the Jewish Law (so "religious reason" is in effect the underlying attitude of the Jew who lives by the Law). Such wisdom, however, comprises also the Platonic and *Stoic virtues of rational judgment,

justice, courage, and self-control (1.18); it is especially by "rational judgment" that reason rules the emotions. There follow scriptural examples of individuals who ruled themselves by reason (which is assumed to mean, by the Jewish Law). In this way, *Joseph controlled his sexual desire, *Moses his anger, and so on.

The author now turns to the Maccabean history, drawing on 2 Maccabees 3–4 to introduce the stories of Eleazar (chaps. 5–7) and the seven brothers (chaps. 8–12). Eleazar becomes a philosopher and lawgiver, and the story is dramatized by the addition of speeches. King Antiochus ridicules Eleazar for abstaining from the pleasure of eating pork, one of nature's gifts (a Stoic argument); Eleazar responds that Jews must obey the Law in small things as in great; the Law has been divinely established to meet human needs. What is appropriate for one's soul is commanded to be eaten; what is not is prohibited. Antiochus will not rule Eleazar's reason in religious matters. Antiochus meets this defiance with torture; and after refusing to save himself by pretense, Eleazar dies praying that his blood be an expiation for his people, his life a ransom for theirs.

The author adds a lengthy rhetorical eulogy to point up the moral then turns to the martyrdom of the seven brothers and their mother. Antiochus urges them to adopt the Greek way of life, and he shows them the instruments of torture. They consider the arguments for submission, but reject them, being fully in control of their emotions (8.28), commenting that Antiochus has learned nothing from Eleazar. They accept their tortures calmly and philosophically (the author reveals a macabre delight in describing the details), speaking both of their readiness to suffer for the Law's sake and of Antiochus's inability to force them to abandon reason. The author underlines the lesson with a rhetorical sermon (chaps. 13–14). In chap. 15 he praises the mother's control over her natural affections, and in chap. 16 contrasts the arguments of compassion she might have used with those she actually addressed to her children before throwing herself on the fire (17.1).

The book ends with an appeal to Israel to obey the Law, knowing that reason is master of the emotions; with a statement of what the martyrs achieved; with the mother's personal apologia underlining the woman's duty to home, husband, and family; and with a final contrast between the fates of Antiochus and the martyrs, who have "received pure and immortal souls from God, to whom be glory forever and ever. Amen."

Purpose. This lengthy discourse in rhetorical Greek addresses its readers directly, and was possibly a memorial address intended for a diaspora Jewish community, perhaps in *Antioch, on the day commemorating the rededication of the Temple or the death of the Maccabean martyrs. The author strongly approves the martyrs' readiness to die for the Law and their refusal to compromise for the sake of peace with their Hellenistic neighbors. Clearly, he writes for Jews who might be put into this difficult position. Martyrdom is highly valued; martyrs are seen as champions in an athletic contest in which the tyrant is the enemy, and the world and humanity the spectators (11.20; 17.13–14), or as soldiers of God (16.14), overcoming oppressive tyranny (1.11) by their suffering and endurance (9.8, 30). In particular, the martyr's suffering has a sacrificial and atoning value for the people as a whole; thus, Eleazar at the point of death prays, "Be merciful to your people, and let our punishment suffice for them. Make my blood their purification, and take my life in exchange for theirs" (6.28–29; cf. 17.20–21). This emphasis is striking and is underlined by the eternal blessedness promised to the martyr (13.17; 15.3; 17.5, 18; 18.27), though, in sharp contrast with 2 Maccabees 7 this eternal reward does not take the form of bodily resurrection. In the Hellenistic world, this Pharisaic doctrine was not readily accepted (cf. Acts 17.32).

That the author was writing for partly hellenized Jews is also suggested by the pervasive influence of the Stoic belief in the rule of reason over the passions. The Stoics, however, believed that reason should not merely overcome the passions and emotions but subject and destroy them, whereas 4 Maccabees expressly affirms that reason rules over the passions not with the aim of destroying them but with the aim of not yielding to them (1.6; cf. 3.2–3). The author was not a hard-line Stoic—possibly he followed the teaching of Posidonius (ca. 135–50 BCE), who agreed that passions could not be totally eradicated—but commonplace Stoic teaching can nevertheless be seen throughout. The use of the cardinal virtues of prudence (NRSV: "rational judgment"), courage, justice, and temperance (1.8) goes back to Plato and Isocrates, as does the idea that it is better to suffer wrong than to do it (9.7–9; cf. Plato *Gorgias* 472e).

The author, however, is a deeply committed Jew, whose ideal is not the Stoic philosopher but the God-fearing person who witnesses to the Law, which is the Jewish wisdom and philosophy. Reason chooses wisdom, and *wisdom is education in the Law (1.15–17). Reason and the Law become almost interchangeable. The conduct of martyrs who die for the Law is thus thoroughly reasonable and therefore entirely commendable in the Hellenistic world.

Date and canonicity. 4 Maccabees can be dated between the publication of 2 Maccabees and the fall of Jerusalem in 70 CE, of which there is no hint. The description of Apollonius in 4.2 as governor of Syria, Phoenicia, and Cilicia (cf. 2 Macc. 4.4, which mentions only Coele-Syria and Phoenicia) suggests a date between 18 and 55 CE, when Cilicia was joined with the other two regions for administrative purposes. 4 Maccabees is thus evidence for diaspora Judaism in the time of *Jesus, whose death, like that of the martyrs, was also described as having atoning significance.

4 Maccabees' obvious interest in the Maccabean tradition led to its association with similar books in Codex Sinaiticus and Codex Alexandrinus as 4 Maccabees, although it has generally not been considered canonical. Eusebius (*Hist. evang.* 3.10.6) and Jerome identify the work with one called "On the Supremacy of Reason," which they wrongly attribute to *Josephus (who would not have approved the martyrs' intransigence). The title, however, described the contents well.

Influence on Christianity. 4 Maccabees had considerable influence on Christian authors, perhaps beginning with the author of the letter to the *Hebrews, who shares with 4 Maccabees an interest in the faith of the martyrs and perhaps some vocabulary (cf. Heb. 12.1–2; 4 Macc. 17.9–10). Cyprian of Carthage stressed the martyrs' faithful relationship to God (*Epist. ad Fortunatum* 11), and Origen saw them as an example of heroic martyrdom (*Exhortation to Martyrdom* 22–27). Augustine saw them as Christian in all but name and made the day of their commemoration, 1 August, a specifically Christian festival, since those who died for the Law of Moses died also for Christ (Sermon 300, *In Solemnitate martyrum Machabaeorum*). Gregory Nazianzus (*Oratio in laudem Machabaeorum* 15.1) saw them as anticipating Christian martyrdom, and the mother as anticipating *Mary, the mother of sorrows.   JOHN R. BARTLETT

Magdalene, Mary. *See* Mary Magdalene.

Magi. The term "magi" customarily refers to the anonymous wise men who followed a star until it led them to *Bethlehem (Matt. 2.1–12). While in Luke's gospel shepherds come to worship the child, Matthew introduces mysterious figures from the east who offer gifts from their treasure boxes.

Many details about the Magi are supplied by later tradition. In western Christianity they are assumed to have been three in number since three gifts are mentioned; eastern tradition gives their number as twelve. They traveled by camel, as is normal practice in the desert regions even today. Their names (Balthasar, Melchior, and Caspar, in the west) are supplied later. The fact that they are wealthy and converse with King *Herod leads to their identification as three kings. (*See also* Names for the Nameless.)

In fact, the Greek word from which "magi" is derived does not refer to royalty but to practitioners of eastern magical arts. The connection between magic and astrology is reflected in the visitors' fascination with the star that had led them to Bethlehem. Elsewhere in the Bible the portrayal of magi is not so positive. Greek versions of the book of *Daniel refer to magi who were ineffective advisers to King *Nebuchadrezzar. In Acts, apostles interact with Simon, a magician in *Samaria (8.9–24), and Bar-Jesus who was a magician and false prophet on Cyprus (13.6–12).   DANIEL N. SCHOWALTER

Magic and Divination. Magic is based on the assumption that one can achieve desired results through the recitation of proper formulas or by the performance of certain prescribed actions. In most cases, the effect sought is something that will either harm others (especially an enemy or one who is a potential threat) or ward off harm that an opponent may be plotting. The essential feature for success is to repeat the formulaic words or actions exactly. Magic is evident in many cultures, ancient and modern, and was especially prevalent in the second century CE and subsequent centuries, as the abundance of Greek magical papyri attest.

In the Hebrew Bible, magic can be associated with disbelief in the power and purpose of Yahweh. Thus, in Genesis 41 the power and wisdom of the God of *Joseph are contrasted sharply with the inability of Pharaoh's wise men and magicians to understand his dream. The God who is in control of the world and of history discloses through Joseph what his intention is, thereby thoroughly discrediting the Egyptian magicians and diviners. A similar contest takes place in Exodus 7, where the diviners and magicians gathered by Pharaoh are able to change rods into snakes, as *Aaron did, but Aaron's rod-become-snake swallows all the others. The clear implication is that God's power and purpose are stronger than the powers of the Egyptian magicians. Magical practices are prohibited in the Law of Moses (Lev. 19.26). The contrast between Yahweh's power and the claims of the magicians is set out in *Balaam's song (Num. 23.23), where after recounting God's acts in delivering his people from Egypt, he declares, "Surely there is no enchantment against Jacob, no divination against Israel; now it shall be said of Jacob and Israel, 'See what God has done!' "

The historical and prophetic books contain occasional denunciations of those who practice magic. King *Manasseh of Judah practiced soothsaying and augury, burned his son as an offering, and consulted mediums and wizards (2 Kings 21.6; 2 Chron. 33.6). An important dimension of this kind of occult practice, as we can infer from the *prophets, was divination. This was a means of direct determination of the divine will, usually by the interpretation of some object (perceived as a sign) such as a marked stone or the entrails of a sacrificial animal. Jeremiah groups together false prophets, soothsayers, diviners, and sorcerers as those to whom Judah must not turn for counsel in the face of exile and deportation (Jer. 27.9). Similar warnings are given in Ezekiel 13 and Malachi 3.5. The frequency of references to this practice attests to the continuing appeal that magic and divination held for leaders and populace, and points up the sharp difference that the legal and prophetic traditions of Israel saw between these occult practices and Yahweh's determination of his will for his people.

In the New Testament, the prophecies, visions, and *miracles of Jesus are set within the framework of the present evidence of God's rule, rather than as performances of magic, as has sometimes been asserted. The gospel narratives are characterized by a virtual absence of the formulas and techniques of magic (with the description of the healings by Jesus in the gospel of Mark being a partial exception). Encounters with magic and magicians are explicitly mentioned only in Acts, where their work is denounced (Acts 8.9–24) and the perpetrator is struck blind (Acts 13.8–9).

In the *Law of Moses there were prescribed certain means by which the divine will could be communicated. These include the *Urim and Thummim, the *ephod and the *teraphim. The inability of scholars to agree on the translation of these terms is an indication of uncertainty as to how these items were used and understood. The Urim and Thummim (Exod. 28.30; Num. 27.21) were probably a set of dice or flat stones that were marked in such a way as to indicate "yes" or "no" when thrown down by the priest in order to ascertain God's will in a specific case. The ephod (a sacred garment, perhaps with some special adornment or attachment; 1 Sam. 14.18, 41) and the teraphim (portable representations of deities; Gen. 31; Hos. 3.4–5; Ezek. 21.21) were also consulted by priests and others in order to discover the divine plan at a crucial juncture in personal or national history. The Israelites' persistence in consulting diviners and sorcerers is given as one of the chief reasons for their being carried off to *Babylon (2 Kings 17.17). Yet Ezra 2.63 (= Neh. 7.65) seems to indicate that the use of Urim and Thummim to learn God's will was to be resumed after the return of Israel from the *exile.

The attitude toward diviners in the New Testament is unambiguous: their capacity to discern is the result of their being possessed by evil spirits, as *Paul's *exorcism of the soothsaying spirit that possessed the young slave woman in Acts 16 shows. The subsequent miracle of deliverance, whereby Paul and Silas are released from prison by divine intervention in the form of an earthquake and a loosening of their bonds, demonstrates for the author of Acts that God is the protector of his own.

See also Sortes Biblicae; Witch.

HOWARD CLARK KEE

Malachi, The Book of. Since Malachi in Hebrew means "my messenger," it is unclear whether this is the name of the prophet or a description of his office. Usually the book is dated after the time of *Haggai and *Zechariah but before the coming of *Ezra and *Nehemiah in the mid-fifth century BCE. A postexilic date is indicated by the reference to a "governor" (1.8) and the fact that the *Temple is standing. The abuses Malachi attacks are thought to show the need for the reforms that Ezra and Nehemiah were soon to carry out.

Malachi's question-and-answer style usually begins with a statement from the prophet of some theological truth followed by a question from his hearers. His answer then expounds the original theme. This is a literary device but may contain echoes of the teaching and preaching practices current in the Second Temple.

A theme prominent in the book is *covenant. The stark expression in 1.1–5 of the teaching that God chose Jacob (i.e., Israel) while rejecting *Edom, a nation that became a symbol of oppression during and after the exile, is elaborated in the manner of earlier prophets, that divine choice is not a ground for complacency but for obedience. The *priests (1.6–2.9), for all their status under the covenant (2.8; cf. Jer. 33.21; Num. 25.11–13; Neh. 13.29), have been less zealous in their duties toward God than to the governor. Malachi thinks it would be better for such Temple worship to stop altogether and even contrasts it unfavorably with the offerings of other nations (1.10–11). The whole nation has violated the covenant in their cruel treatment of each other, denying their family status as children of the one God, especially in their practice of casual *divorce (2.10–16; a warning against intermarriage with foreigners has been inserted into this section, vv. 11–12).

Later, Malachi charges them with neglect of payment of *tithes for the upkeep of the Temple and its personnel (3.6–12). Obedience here will result in material prosperity (cf. the words of Haggai about the rebuilding of the Temple, Hag. 1.9–11; 2.15–19). It is important to see that, for Malachi, proper observance of cultic worship was an expression of a true relationship to God ("Return to me," 3.7). Two passages address the despair and disillusionment of his contemporaries as they see no signs of God's activity or of the fulfillment of the old prophetic promises (2.17–3.5; 3.13–4.3). Both bring the assurance that God is about to act in righteousness and that therefore his people should hold the faith. (The passage 3.1b–4, with its switch to the third person and introduction of another figure, "the messenger of the covenant," may be a later insertion.)

The book ends with a call to keep the *Law of Moses (4.4) and a promise that God will send *Elijah the prophet to prepare the people for the final "*day of the Lord" (4.5–6) so that it may prove to be a day of salvation and not a repetition of the old judgment of the "curse" (Hebr. *ḥērem*, Josh. 6.17; Lev. 27.28; *see* Ban). Perhaps Elijah was thought of in this role because he had not died but had been taken up to heaven (2 Kings 2). This idea was repeated in Sirach 48.10 and in Mark 9.11.

Malachi shows how the postexilic prophets were deeply concerned for the Temple and its worship and yet held such concern in creative tension with a call for right ethical living. They recognized the dangers the preexilic prophets had warned against, whereby external worship could easily become a substitute for genuine relationship with God, yet challenged their hearers with the call to hold both aspects of the religious life together. Their call was not for mercy rather than sacrifice (cf. Hos. 6.6) but for mercy and sacrifice. They also held together concern for obedience to the Law and a strong eschatological hope of God's future saving action.

The final verses (4.4–6) should be seen as a conclusion not just to the book of Malachi but to the whole prophetic corpus, which ends with "The Book of the Twelve" (i.e., the so-called minor prophets). At a time when the prophetic collections were on the way to being regarded as canonical in status and authority, the function of these verses is to place such collections alongside the Torah as equally authoritative expressions of God's word.   REX MASON

Manasseh.

1. Eldest son of *Joseph, brother of *Ephraim, and ancestor of the tribe of Manasseh. According to various territorial lists, the tribe of Manasseh was settled on both sides of the Jordan River, on the east, north of the Jabbok (e.g., Num. 32.39–42; Josh. 13.29–31), and on the west, in the central hill country (Josh. 17; see Map 3:4XY). It was in its later history weaker than Ephraim; this political fact is reflected in the story of Jacob's blessing, in which he reverses the birth order (Gen. 48). Manasseh is also described as the father of Machir, a genealogical explanation of a more complicated history between two apparently separate tribal entities; note that in Judges 5.14, Machir is mentioned along with Ephraim, but Manasseh is not named. (See also Tribes of Israel.)

2. King of Judah (697 [or 687]–642 BCE). His reign was the longest of any Israelite or Judean king, and in the difficult times of Assyrian domination he achieved a measure of autonomy for Judah. This apparently involved some compromises with older ideals, for Manasseh is con-

demned by the *Deuteronomic history as the worst of the Davidic kings, whose "sin" was responsible for God's punishment of Judah (2 Kings 21.9, 17; 24.3). His portrayal in *Chronicles is less harsh.

See Manasseh, The Prayer of; Judah, The Kingdom of.   MICHAEL D. COOGAN

Manasseh, The Prayer of. The account of King *Manasseh's evil reign over Judah in 2 Chronicles 33 contains the account of an episode, almost certainly legendary, in which Manasseh was taken captive by the *Assyrians and carried off to *Babylon where, in his trouble, he became a loyal worshiper of the God of his people (2 Chron. 33.11–13). This story, which has no parallel in the older account in 2 Kings 21.1–18, was no doubt told to give a theological explanation for the length and prosperity of the career of one whose policy was to promote idolatry: for in theory, he should have been punished by God with political failure and come to a disastrous end (Deut. 29.14–21). The author of *Chronicles, having explained the king's paradoxical and puzzling success by a story of his eventual return to the worship of Yahweh, also mentions that his prayer was preserved in "the Annals of the Kings of Israel" (2 Chron. 33.18–19). A devout writer from a much later period, probably the late Hellenistic age, composed a prayer such as the king might have used. The result was the small "book" called the Prayer of Manasseh.

It is a dignified penitential prayer, in traditional Jewish liturgical language, that contains nothing specifically appropriate to Manasseh's situation except the reference to "setting up abominations" in v. 10 (see 2 Chron. 33.3–5). It begins with an address to God as all-powerful and fearsome to sinners (vv. 1–5) but also as compassionate and willing to accept repentance (vv. 6–7). While penitence is unnecessary for the righteous, such as Israel's ancestors (v. 8), the royal penitent knows that his sins are too many to be overlooked and therefore confesses his deep unworthiness, in terms that are quite general except for the phrase previously noted (vv. 9–10); he begs for divine forgiveness (vv. 11–14) and concludes with a promise, similar to those in several of the biblical *psalms of lament, to engage in a formal act of praise when his prayer is answered, as undoubtedly it will be (v. 15; cf. Pss. 22.22–31; 56.12–13).

The Prayer was not part of the original Greek

*Septuagint and is not regarded as canonical by the Roman Catholic church; some Orthodox churches, however, accord it deuterocanonical status, and so it is frequently included among the Apocrypha in English Bibles (*see* Apocrypha, *article on* Jewish Apocrypha). In the Greek Codex Alexandrinus, it is included in a collection of "odes" printed as a supplement to the book of Psalms. Jerome seems not to have been acquainted with it, though in modern editions of the *Vulgate it is printed (along with 2 Esdras [= 4 Ezra] and Ps. 151) in an appendix to the New Testament. In some ancient versions, it appears after 2 Chronicles (as it does also in the Geneva Bible of 1560), but it was never incorporated into the text of that book, perhaps because it was found only in Greek or was known for some other reason to be of recent composition. Most scholars would agree in assigning it a very late date, perhaps the first century BCE. There is no unmistakable evidence that the book was composed in any language other than Greek, and some competent scholars continue to believe the Greek text to be the original. The general style, however, suggests a Hebrew original, as does the fact that Hebrew was the normal language of prayer among Jews. This is probably the prevailing view.

The liturgical style makes it suitable for use in public worship, and its inclusion in the collection of odes added to the Psalter in some Septuagint manuscripts and other ancient versions indicates that it was so used in the ancient church. In an abridged form it has been incorporated as a Lenten canticle in the 1979 Prayer Book of the American Episcopal church.

ROBERT C. DENTAN

Manna. Of uncertain origin, in Exodus 16.15 the word "manna" is given a popular etymology by Israelites who asked, when they saw it, "What is it?" (Hebr. *mān hû'*). This was the miraculous food supplied by the Lord to the Israelites during the forty years of their wandering in the *wilderness from *Egypt to *Canaan. Manna is also called, poetically, "bread of the mighty ones [NRSV: angels]" (Ps. 78.25) and "food of angels" (Wisd. of Sol. 16.20).

Early in their *Exodus from Egypt, the Israelites came to the wilderness of Sin. There the whole congregation accused *Moses and *Aaron of bringing them into the wilderness to kill them with hunger. In response the Lord promised to rain down bread for them from heaven (Exod.

16.4). Manna came six days a week. Only one day's portion was to be gathered except on the sixth day; a double portion gathered that day permitted Israel to keep the *Sabbath rest. Each morning when the dew had vanished, "there on the surface of the wilderness was a fine flaky substance, as fine as frost on the ground" (Exod. 16.14). It was "like coriander seed, white, and the taste of it was like wafers made with honey" (Exod. 16.31). Its appearance was like "gum resin" (Num. 11.7). The people "ground it in mills or beat it in mortars, then boiled it in pots and made cakes of it; and the taste of it was like the taste of cakes baked with oil" (Num. 11.8). An urn containing a quantity of manna was kept in or in front of the *ark of the covenant as a reminder of this divine provision (Exod. 16.32–34; Heb. 9.11).

From ancient to modern times, manna has been linked with natural phenomena in the *Sinai region. The traditional identification has been with a granular type of sweet substance thought to be secreted in early summer by the tamarisk bush. More recent investigations suggest that this "manna" is produced by the excretion of two kinds of scale insects that feed on the sap of the tamarisk. Because the sap is poor in nitrogen, the insects must ingest large amounts of carbohydrate-rich sap in order to consume enough nitrogen. The excess carbohydrate is then excreted as honeydew rich in three basic sugars and pectin. The amount of the substance thus produced would, of course, fall far short of Israel's need for bread; in any case, to give a natural explanation for what the Bible describes as miraculous is perhaps to miss the point.

According to the gospel of *John, when Jesus was challenged to validate his ministry with a sign comparable to that of manna, he identified himself as the "true bread from heaven," come down to give life to the world (John 6.32–35).

JAMES I. COOK

Manuscripts. *This entry consists of two articles, the first on manuscripts of the* Hebrew Bible *and the second on manuscripts of the* Greek New Testament. *For discussion of types of manuscripts, see* Books and Bookmaking. *For discussion of the importance of individual manuscripts in establishing the text of the Bible, see* Dead Sea Scrolls *and* Textual Criticism.

Hebrew Bible

Forms. Ancient texts such as the Hebrew Bible were transmitted over the centuries in various forms, at first in scrolls, later in manuscripts of codex format, and in recent centuries in printed editions. Ancient scrolls consist of sheets of leather sewn together, resembling the *Torah scrolls still used today in synagogues. A codex consists of any number of sheets (leather, parchment) bound together into a book. Scrolls contained individual biblical books, while codices could contain most or all of the Hebrew Bible. Hebrew biblical texts were first transmitted in scrolls; after the use of codices for the New Testament and other ancient literature, the codex form began to be used as well.

Development of the Biblical Text. When the composition of a biblical book was completed, in theory there should have been only one master copy of that particular book. In practice, however, even at that stage there may have been several copies which differed from one another, often a great deal; the same is true of relatively modern works as well. These differences increased rather than diminished in the next centuries, as generations of scribes added new details to the manuscripts and scrolls they copied.

At an early stage, biblical Hebrew, like other Semitic languages, was written solely with consonants; in English this would mean that a word like "book" would be written "bk." The first type of difference between biblical texts was thus in consonants, as is still visible from a comparison of early sources such as the *Dead Sea Scrolls. More differences come to light when these texts are compared with the *Samaritan Pentateuch and the *Septuagint translation in Greek, whose underlying Hebrew text can often be reconstructed.

Many of these different texts fell out of use, especially because the religious groups supporting them ceased to exist or diminished in importance. In the Roman period, however, there were many different "families" of texts in use, as the *Qumran texts show; among these was what was to become the official version of the text of the Hebrew Bible ("the received text") in the centuries to follow, the Masoretic Text.

The Masoretic Text. After the destruction of the Second Temple in 70 CE, a particular group of texts was emerging, endorsed by and copied by the central stream of Judaism, that of the *Pharisees, later to be known as the *Masoretic Text (MT). When compared with others, this text-family had no special characteristics, and the only feature that stands out is its careful transmission, though probably other texts were also

transmitted as carefully. The antecedents of the MT, found principally at Qumran, are called proto-Masoretic, since the later components of that text had not yet been added to it.

A good example of an early proto-Masoretic source is the shorter Isaiah scroll from Cave 1 at Qumran (1QIsa^b). Comparison of this scroll with the medieval and modern printed text shows that the consonantal framework of the MT changed little after the first century BCE. This is confirmed by the fragments found from Wadi Murabbaʿât south of Qumran, dating from about 130 CE, all of which are virtually identical with the medieval text. In addition, the biblical text quoted in the *Talmud and early midrashim is virtually identical with the later texts, though owing to the imprecision of quotation and the nature of the Talmudic context occasional divergences exist. Thus, around the turn of the era there was a strong tendency to create a single unified text, but this ideal was never fully achieved owing to the vicissitudes of textual transmission. In other words, at no time did there exist one "Masoretic Text"; there always were several different "Masoretic Texts."

The Masoretic Text known to us today was created in the early Middle Ages, when other components were added to the consonantal framework. Learned scribes involved in the transmission of the biblical text developed and perpetuated in and around the text various kinds of data, including vocalization and cantillation marks as well as a Masoretic apparatus of remarks in the text. These were the Masoretes who derived their name from the *Masorah (see below).

Vocalization. The use of consonantal spelling meant that any word in Hebrew could be read in different ways; in English this would mean that the letters "sl" could be read "seal," "sill," "sell," "soul," "sale," etc. Such ambiguity was troublesome, especially for an authoritative text; as a result, certain letters (ʾalep, hē, yōd, wāw) were added to the text to indicate which vowels were to be read ("vowel letters"). Later actual vowels were added to the text in the form of newly-invented graphic symbols, so that from then on there was no confusion regarding the reading of the text. Various vocalization systems were developed, but the system finally accepted by all western Jewish communities was the Tiberian system (from Tiberias) developed by Moshe Ben-Asher (tenth century CE). A so-called Babylonian system was adopted by the oriental Jewish communities. In the course of the centuries, however, the Tiberian Ben-Asher tradition has been more or less accepted by all communities, even though traces of other systems persisted in more remote areas, especially in Yemen.

Cantillation. Other signs were added to the consonants as guidance for the liturgical reading of the text in the synagogue. These signs have both musical value and syntactic importance, since they indicate the relationship between any two words in the text in different gradations of conjunctiveness or disjunctiveness. Various cantillation systems were developed, but finally the Ben-Asher system was accepted for this purpose as well. The interpretive tradition embodied in the vocalization and cantillation system was established early, but only from the eighth century CE onward were these transmitted in a written form.

Masorah. In and around the text the Masoretes added an elaborate body of notes and signs for the preservation and correct spelling of the text. In the text itself the Masoretes perpetuated all the special elements that were present in the text when the learned scribes decided to allow no more changes and which therefore became part and parcel of it, such as large and small letters, dots under or above the letters, and suspended letters. In addition, in the margin of the text the Masoretes added an elaborate apparatus of notes (*Masorah, "transmission") on individual words in the text, especially on the number of occurrences of certain forms and spellings, meant as guidance for the scribes.

There are many differences among the various Masoretic manuscripts in all these elements. Scholars consider two manuscripts as the most authentic representatives of the Ben-Asher tradition, since one was apparently vocalized by Moshe Ben-Asher himself (the Aleppo Codex, partially preserved) and another one (the Leningrad Codex) was copied from it. The text of the Leningrad Codex has been reproduced in the modern edition of the *Biblia Hebraica Stuttgartensia*.   EMANUEL TOV

The Greek New Testament

By 1989 the Münster Institute for New Testament Textual Research had catalogued the number of manuscripts of the Greek New Testament at a total of 5488, in the customary categories: 96 papyri, 299 uncials, 2812 minuscules, and 2281 *lectionaries (containing selected passages arranged according to the liturgical year, for use in church services). Most lectionaries are in minuscule script, but the oldest are in uncial. When compared to the numbers of existing manuscripts of ancient classical writers, these numbers are extraordinarily large. However, most of the papyri are fragmentary; some consist of only one or two leaves. Moreover, only 59 manuscripts contain the entire New Testament, and of these only one (Codex Sinaiticus) is uncial; roughly 1500 contain only the Gospels, and the book of Revelation survives in only 287 copies (many of which alternate between sections of text and patristic commentary).

Date. Very few manuscripts were dated by their scribes, and the exceptions tend to be late. Fortunately, secular documents of various sorts carrying dates have survived, enabling paleographers to compare handwriting and ascertain within broad limits the date of a biblical manuscript.

The oldest known New Testament manuscript is a papyrus fragment, ca. 9 by 6.35 cm (3 1/2 by 2 1/2 in), dated to 100–150 CE, which preserves five verses from John 18. P^{52}, as it is called, is now kept at the John Rylands Library in Manchester, England. The oldest substantial portions of the New Testament are the Bodmer papyrus of John (P^{66}), now in Geneva, and the Chester Beatty papyrus (P^{46}) in Dublin and Ann Arbor, which contains ten Pauline letters; both have been dated to ca. 200 CE. The oldest *parchment New Testament copies are Codex Vaticanus and Codex Sinaiticus, both from the fourth century. From roughly 300–1000 CE, about three hundred manuscripts remain; and from about 1000–1500 (*Gutenberg invented movable-type printing around 1450), about two thousand copies have survived. Since of all these known copies only fifty-nine contain the entire New Testament, it is clear that prior to the invention of *printing relatively few individuals or even congregations possessed a complete New Testament.

Identification of Manuscripts. Previously, a manuscript was identified by the name of the owner (e.g., Codex Bezae), the place where it is now preserved (Codex Vaticanus, Codex Washingtoniensis), or the place of its purported origin (Codex Alexandrinus). A simpler, more systematic nomenclature was invented by a Swiss scholar, Johann Jakob Wettstein (1693–1754), who assigned a capital roman letter to each uncial and an arabic numeral to each minuscule. Over time, however, the letters of the alphabet proved too few for the growing number of known uncial manuscripts, so Hebrew and Greek letters came into use; eventually, however, these too proved insufficient, and Caspar René Gregory (1846–1917) proposed that each uncial manuscript be assigned a numeral prefixed by o. Only for the chief uncials (such as Vaticanus) is the earlier letter system retained.

Format. Early on, Christian communities abandoned use of the scroll in favor of the leaf-book (codex), which was less expensive and more convenient (*see* Books and Bookmaking in Antiquity). Over time, parchment slowly supplanted papyrus as the material of choice for books. Several deluxe copies of the scriptures survive from the sixth century; these were prepared for nobles and high ecclesiastics on purple-dyed parchment, in script written with silver ink (and in some cases gold for initial letters). Once scribes had finished copying the text, artists added illumination and illustrations (miniatures). The text of the Gospels—and eventually that of other New Testament books—was divided into numbered sections; Eusebius (d. ca. 342) collected these into tables that showed parallel passages in four Gospels, in three Gospels, in two, and finally in those sections unique to each gospel. In some cases, scribes provided information as to the total number of lines in a gospel or letter.

In time individual books of the New Testament were provided with a variety of prologues and other prefatory material, supplying certain information about the author, contents, and character of the work. Some prologues are anonymous, while others are attributed to patristic authors (such as Chrysostom, Theodoret, Euthalius). Occasionally, lectionary notations were entered into straight-text gospel manuscripts. Likewise, musical notations to assist readers in chanting the lessons were placed above the line of text in green or red to contrast with the text's brown or black ink.

Important Manuscripts. The following lists specify the siglum (identification), date, contents, and place of preservation:

Papyri.

P^{38}: ca. 300; portions of Acts 18.27–19.16; Ann Arbor, University of Michigan Library.

P^{45}: third century; portions of the four Gospels and Acts; part in Dublin, Chester Beatty Library, and part in Vienna, Austrian National Library.

P^{46}: ca. 200; ten letters of Paul; part in Dublin, Chester Beatty Library, and part in Ann Arbor, University of Michigan Library.

P^{47}: third century; Revelation 9.10–17.2; Dublin, Chester Beatty Library.

P^{52}: first half of second century; John 18.31–33, 37–38; Manchester, John Rylands Library.

P^{66}: ca. 200; portions of the gospel of John, part in Cologny-Geneva, Bodmer Library, and part in Dublin, Chester Beatty Library.

P^{75}: third century; most of the gospel of Luke and two-thirds of the gospel of John; Cologny-Geneva, Bodmer Library.

Uncial manuscripts.

א: fourth century; entire New Testament; London, British Library (Codex Sinaiticus).

A: fifth century; New Testament, with a few lacunae; London, British Library (Codex Alexandrinus).

B: fourth century; Gospels, Acts, letters (lacking 1 Timothy through Philemon, and Hebrews 9.14 through the end of Revelation); Rome, Vatican Library (Codex Vaticanus).

C: fifth century; New Testament (a palimpsest with many lacunae); Paris, Bibliothèque Nationale (Codex Ephraemi).

D: fifth century; Gospels and Acts in Greek and Latin (with lacunae); Cambridge University Library (Codex Bezae).

W: fifth century; four Gospels (with lacunae) in the order Matthew, John, Luke, Mark; Washington, Smithsonian Institution, Freer Gallery of Art (Codex Washingtoniensis).

Θ: ninth century; four Gospels (with a few lacunae); Tiflis, Manuscript Institute (Codex Koridethi).

0169: fourth century; Rev. 3.19–4.3; Princeton Theological Seminary Library.

0212: third century; Diatessaron, brief portions of Matthew, Mark, Luke, and John; New Haven, Yale University, P. Dura 10.

Minuscule manuscripts.

1: twelfth century; New Testament, lacking the book of Revelation; Basel, University Library. Related to manuscripts 118, 131, 209, and others as family 1, reflecting the kind of text used at Caesarea in the fourth century.

13: thirteenth century; four Gospels; Paris; Bibliothèque Nationale. Related to 69 and ten other minuscule manuscripts as family 13 (they have John 7.53–8.12 after Luke 21.38), which goes back to an archetype in Calabria.

33: ninth century; New Testament, lacking the book of Revelation; Paris, Bibliothèque Nationale. Sometimes called "the queen of the minuscules," its text is similar to that in B and א.

461: 835 CE (oldest dated New Testament Greek

manuscript); four Gospels; St. Petersburg Public Library.

565: ninth century; four Gospels; St. Petersburg Public Library; a magnificent purple parchment manuscript written in gold letters.

614: thirteenth century; Acts and letters (lacuna in Jude 3–25); Milan, Biblioteca Ambrosiana. Related to the text of Acts in Codex Bezae.

700: eleventh century; four Gospels; London, British Library. In Luke 11.2 it replaces the petition of the *Lord's Prayer, "Thy kingdom come," with "Thy holy Spirit come upon us and cleanse us."

1739: tenth century; Acts, general letters, Pauline letters; Mount Athos, Lavra. Agrees frequently with the text used by Origen (d. ca. 254).

2400: thirteenth century; New Testament but without the book of Revelation; Chicago, University of Chicago Library. A splendid manuscript with ninety-eight miniatures, in a silver case.

Editions. The earliest printed Greek New Testament was volume 5 (1514) of the Complutensian *Polyglot Bible, which was sponsored by Cardinal Ximénes of Alcalá, Spain; however, the pope did not grant permission to publish it until 1520. The first published Greek New Testament, edited by Erasmus of Rotterdam and issued by Johannes Froben of Basel in 1516, relied on only a few very late manuscripts. For the book of Revelation there was only one Greek manuscript available, and it lacked the last six verses; for them, Erasmus translated the Latin *Vulgate into what he supposed the Greek text should read. This type of New Testament text, based on late and sometimes imperfect manuscripts, became the so-called *textus receptus* ("received text"). Only toward the end of the nineteenth century, once much earlier and superior New Testament manuscripts became available, could scholars produce more accurate editions.

See Textual Criticism.   BRUCE M. METZGER

Maps of the Biblical World. Maps in the conventional sense of scale drawings based on accurate ground measurements did not exist before the modern era. There were, however, written maps that served, like drawn maps, as abstract representations of space.

The Hebrew Bible contains three kinds of written maps: administrative maps, campaign itineraries, and historical or ethnographic geographies. These distinctions are based on inferences about their differing origins and functions.

The first two concern real places and are approximately contemporary with the landscape they describe; the last are retrospective or anachronizing descriptions of places and peoples either real or imagined.

Administrative maps were either boundary maps defining territorial limits or lists of towns and/or tribes within specific districts. Boundary maps usually follow the formula "from point A to point B, then to point C," and so on, returning ultimately to point A (e.g., Gen. 10.19; 15.18; Exod. 23.31; Num. 13.21; Deut. 11.24). The simplest biblical boundary map, the familiar description of *Canaan "from Dan to Beer-sheba" (2 Sam. 24.2), has only two elements. The most complex, a detailed delineation of Canaan's boundaries in Numbers 34.1–12, enumerates multiple consecutive points. Town lists were not sequences of connected points but inclusive catalogues probably compiled by a central authority for purposes of calculating revenue or population size in a given district. These probably originated in the royal administration begun by *David (e.g. the Levitical cities in Josh. 21; 1 Chron. 6) and continued by *Solomon (1 Kings 4.7–19) (e.g., the Galilean and Transjordanian tribes and northern Benjamin in Josh. 13; 18; 19) and later kings (e.g., the districts of Judah in Josh. 15.18; the towns of Simeon and Dan in Josh. 19; 1 Chron. 4).

Itineraries of military expeditions, based probably on contemporary sources, include the campaign of Ben-hadad of Aram-Damascus into northern Israel (1 Kings 15.20), the invasion of Israel by *Tiglath-pileser III of Assyria (2 Kings 15.29), Uzziah's conquests in Philistia (2 Chron. 26.6), and the *Philistine retaliation against Judah in the reign of Ahaz (2 Chron. 28.18). *Abraham's legendary war with the kings of the east (Gen. 14) contains topographic information about the southern Dead Sea region, although the historicity and geographical details of this account are disputed.

Finally, there are historical and ethnographic geographies that depict, accurately or imperfectly, real places and peoples or portray cosmic realms outside human experience. The former include the "Table of Nations" tracing *Noah's descendants after the *Flood (Gen. 10.1–32), Israelite wanderings after their *Exodus from Egypt (Num. 33.5–49), the roster of Canaanite kings opposing the Israelite invaders (Josh. 12), tribal allotments awarded after the *conquest of Canaan (Josh. 15–19), and the land that remained unconquered (Josh. 13). Ezekiel's oracle against Tyre describes not only the city but also its far-flung trading connections (Ezek. 27). Cosmic geographies include descriptions of the rivers of the *garden of Eden (Gen. 2.10–14) and Ezekiel's vision of the new *Jerusalem coupled with the idealized boundaries of the land of Israel (Ezek. 40–48). Revelation 21 is a New Testament version of Ezekiel's visionary map of the heavenly Jerusalem. Biblical word maps of real or imagined space were perhaps accompanied originally by drawings, but none of these have survived.

Drawn maps from ancient Mesopotamia do however exist. These were inscribed on clay, like most other Mesopotamian written documents. The oldest (late third millennium BCE), excavated at *Nuzi in northeastern Iraq, depicts an agricultural estate east of Nuzi belonging to "Arzala." Two additional maps, both dated to the mid-second millennium BCE, are from Nippur in southern Iraq. One shows the city itself and its adjacent canals; another locates twelve agricultural plots in the vicinity and names their owners. These maps represent cadastral (land measurement) maps, identifying plots to record ownership and perhaps for purposes of taxation, like modern land deeds. In ancient Syria-Palestine such cadastral maps may also have existed. They were probably drawn on perishable parchment or papyrus and thus have not survived.

The existence of maps, whether written or drawn, implies an underlying notion of spatial orientation. In the biblical world that orientation was eastward, not northward as with modern maps. Others directions were related to this primary one. Since east was "front" (Gen. 2.8), west was "behind" (Job 18.20), north was "on the left hand" (Gen. 14.15), and south, "on the right hand" (1 Sam. 23.24). The etymologies of the biblical words frequently used to express cardinal directions conform to this orientation. An alternate orientation, toward the rising of the sun, also existed. East was the direction of the sun's rising (Josh. 12.1), and west, of its setting (Isa. 45.6). The two orientations, one solar and one based on an observer's position, may be connected through the sacral significance, common throughout the ancient Near East, of facing the sunrise.

The best-known extant map of the biblical world is the sixth-century CE mosaic map discovered in Madaba (Medeba), Jordan (Map 1:Y5). Even in its present fragmentary state, the Madaba map is a recognizable although schematic representation of Palestine on both sides of the

Dead Sea. Byzantine Jerusalem, labeled "the holy city," is the focal point of the map. Not coincidentally, place names written on it are intended to be read as the viewer looks east, facing the mosaic.

Medieval maps of Palestine, both Jewish and Christian, were, like the Madeba map, created after the region's religious significance had been established. Such maps were concerned primarily with locations mentioned in biblical narrative and not with precise mapping of the landscape.

Modern mapping of the biblical world began in the eighteenth century CE as biblical geographers attempted to relate word maps to contemporary locations in Palestine and neighboring lands. The first accurate topographic maps of Palestine, based on field surveys conducted by C. R. Conder and H. H. Kitchener in 1872–1877, were published by the Palestine Exploration Fund in 1880. After World War I, Britain and France established topographic surveys in Palestine and Syria, respectively, which produced maps of the region that are, with improvements, still the basis for archaeological exploration in the region. (See further R. North, *A History of Biblical Map Making*, Wiesbaden, 1979.)   JOSEPH A. GREENE

Maranatha. An *Aramaic phrase found in 1 Corinthians 16.22. Paul closes his letter with some almost stock expressions common to the genre of ancient *letters; this conclusion includes a threat against "those who do not love the Lord" ("may they be *anathema"), and the prayer or charge "maranatha."

The term *maranatha* has been variously translated as "Our Lord has come," "Our Lord will come," or "Our Lord, come!" In light of early Christian *apocalyptic expectation, the last, understood as a prayer for the imminent appearance of "the Lord" (*see* Second Coming of Christ), seems the most likely meaning. The use of Aramaic probably indicates a very early stage in the development of Christian worship. Paul is thus reiterating a liturgical expression apparently well known in early church circles (cf. Rev. 22.20; *Didache* 10.6).   J. ANDREW OVERMAN

Mari Tablets. The magnificent palace of Mari with its royal archives of cuneiform tablets is the most significant archaeological find from French excavations at Tell Hariri, which is situated about a mile west of the Middle *Euphrates in Syria.

Most of these tablets, numbering in the tens of thousands, are royal correspondence dealing with domestic and international matters and economic, administrative, and juridical records of the palace. These texts have supplied important historical, chronological, geographic, ethnolinguistic, and cultural data concerning northern Mesopotamia and Syria-Palestine from the midnineteenth to the mid-eighteenth century BCE, a period just before the rise of *Hammurapi of Babylon and culminating in the formation of his Old Babylonian Empire.

Part of the significance of the Mari tablets for the interpretation of the Bible stems from the information that they provide about the West Semitic Amurrites (see Amorites), who began a massive infiltration into Mesopotamia at the beginning of the second millennium BCE. The Mari archives document a wide spectrum of Amurrites. They depict confederacies of seminomadic West Semitic tribes such as the Yaminites, who were untouched by Mesopotamian civilization and remained hostile to the central authorities. At the other extreme, they record the rule of thoroughly Mesopotamianized West Semitic kings, such as Shamasi-addu of Assyria, Zimri-lim of Mari, and Hammurapi of Babylon, who remained Amurrite only in name. They also describe the West Semitic Haneans in the process of sedentarization, who accepted the authority of the Mesopotamian kings but retained many of the ways of the Amurrites. In recording the activities of all these Amurrites, the Mari archives provide rich documentation of West Semitic personal *names, vocabulary, tribal structure and organization, and institutions and practices, such as *covenant making and census taking. In the cultic sphere, there is a small but significant group of prophecy texts, which attest to the existence of intuitive divination by "ecstatics" and "answerers" at Mari, who inform the king of the deity's message. (See Prophets, article on Ancient Israel.)

Some scholars have sought to place the events described in Genesis 12–50 within the West Semitic context of Mari, thus dating the *ancestors of Israel to the early second millennium. While one must acknowledge the invaluable contributions of the Mari tablets in illuminating the ancient West Semitic background of biblical traditions, parallels alone cannot establish contemporaneity. Until the distinguishing particularities of Amurrite and *Aramean cultures can be clarified by new discoveries, we must be content to utilize the Mari data for the insights and perspectives they provide without drawing chronological conclusions that cannot be proved.

BARRY L. EICHLER

Mark, The Gospel According to. Mark is the shortest of the four canonical Gospels and was almost certainly the first to be written. Although the use of narrative to record God's salvation of Israel is common in the Hebrew Bible and although there is an obvious correspondence between the story told by Mark and the very brief summaries of the gospel found elsewhere in the New Testament (e.g., Acts 2.22–24), there are no parallels to this precise literary form before early Christianity. In all probability, therefore, the author of this book was responsible for creating the literary genre we know as "*gospel."

Contents. Attempts to analyze this gospel run the risk of imposing our interpretation on it. In explicating a text, it is natural to look for an overall pattern, but Mark's story was almost certainly intended to be read aloud, and the impact it made on its first hearers is more likely to be discerned by noting connections between one paragraph and the next rather than by analyzing it into sections, which may obscure such links. This gospel has been built up out of many short units, and one of the features of Mark's arrangement is the frequent sandwiching together of incidents (e.g., 11.11–25). Notable also is the way in which he builds up evidence by a series of stories (e.g., about outsiders, 1.40–2.17; uncleanness, 7.1–30) or by repetition (three passion predictions, 8.31; 9.31; 10.33; two blind men healed, 8.22–26; 10.46–52; two feeding miracles, 6.31–44; 8.1–10; cf. 8.14–21; three summaries of Jesus' activity, 1.32–4; 3.7–12; 6.56). All these devices would help to convey the significance of the story as it was read.

For convenience, the following brief summary is set out in a geographical scheme, but this was not necessarily of particular importance to Mark himself.

The first thirteen verses, which establish Jesus' identity, are set in the *wilderness. In 1.14 Jesus moves into *Galilee, where he proclaims the *kingdom, calls *disciples, teaches, exorcises evil spirits, and heals (1.15–4.34); his activity brings him into conflict with the religious authorities. A series of notable miracles follows, as Jesus moves back and forth across the lake, but they are met with unbelief (4.35–8.26). In 8.27–30 Jesus reaches Caesarea Philippi in the far north, where *Peter declares him to be the *Messiah.

As he moves south, Jesus three times foretells his death and resurrection and explains the meaning of discipleship (8.31–10.52). He reaches *Jerusalem and the *Temple (chaps. 11–13), and the passion narrative unfolds (chaps. 14–15). In the final paragraph (16.1–8), women find the tomb empty. Chapter 16.9–20 and the alternative ending given in the NRSV footnote represent attempts by later writers to "complete" the gospel.

Author and Date. The ascription of the gospel of Mark goes back at least to Papias, Bishop of Hierapolis, who in about 130 CE reported that he had been told that it was written by Mark "the interpreter of Peter"; this is presumably the Mark referred to in 1 Pet. 5.13 as "my son Mark." Traditionally, he has been identified with the John *Mark mentioned in Acts 12.12, but the latter was associated with *Paul and *Barnabas, not Peter (Acts 12.25; 15.37, 39; Col. 4.10; 2 Tim. 4.11), and the name "Mark" was one of the most common in the ancient world.

This gospel is usually dated between 65 and 75 CE. The first of these dates is set by Irenaeus (late second century CE), who said that Mark wrote after Peter's death. If we accept Marcan priority, then we must allow time between the composition of Mark and that of *Matthew and *Luke, which suggests a date before about 75 CE. The only clue in the gospel itself is chap. 13, which predicts the destruction of the Temple; many commentators contrast the vague references to the fate of Jerusalem in Mark 13 with the clear reference to the siege of the city in Luke 21.20 and suggest that this indicates that Mark was written before 70 CE. But Mark 13 is concerned to separate the disasters that are going to overwhelm Judea from the supernatural chaos at the end, and it is arguable that it was written in the period following the former to explain why the end was "still to come" (13.7). The gospel of Mark was probably written, therefore, either immediately before or immediately after the destruction of Jerusalem in 70 CE.

Tradition at least as early as Irenaeus held that it was composed in Rome, but this may have been a deduction from the association with Peter. Support for a Roman origin is sometimes found in Mark's use of Latinisms (e.g., *quadrans,* a coin, 12.42), but these were probably familiar throughout the *Roman empire. Explanations of Jewish words and customs, together with a poor knowledge of Palestinian geography, suggest that Mark was writing for *gentiles living outside Palestine, but they do not point to any particular place. The emphasis on the inevitability of suffering for Jesus' followers could well be explained if this gospel were written for a community that was suffering for its faith: although the Roman church was persecuted in the time of Nero, it was by no means alone, since persecution of Christians was common at the time.

Sources. Mark's gospel contains very little material that is not included by Matthew, and the earliest explanation, given by Augustine, was that it was an abbreviation of Matthew's gospel. But Luke has to be taken into account also, since he, too, includes a great deal of this material. According to the most commonly held solution to the *synoptic problem, Mark's gospel was used as a major source by Matthew and Luke. This solution is not without problems, and the suggestion that they used an earlier version of Mark *(Urmarkus)* is an attempt to explain some of the differences from Mark that Matthew and Luke have in common. An alternative theory (known as the Griesbach hypothesis) argues that Mark used both Matthew and Luke as sources, but careful study of the parallels suggests that the Marcan version was probably the earliest.

The belief that Mark's gospel was a record of Peter's reminiscences was challenged by the work of form critics who argued that it was based on short units of oral tradition that had been handed down to the Christian communities and had been shaped by their situations and beliefs. C. H. Dodd suggested that Mark had fitted these units into a chronological outline of the ministry of Jesus, but the supposed outline proved too vague to be of value. It is possible that some of the material used by Mark, such as the conflict stories in 2.1–3.6, had already been gathered together at the oral stage, and it is commonly believed that the passion narrative had already been written down as a continuous narrative. The rise of redaction criticism, however, with its emphasis on the evangelists as authors rather than as mere collectors, has led to the realization that Mark himself may have been responsible for almost all the arrangement of the material and that his only sources may have been the individual units of tradition.

Readers. Mark probably wrote his gospel for one specific Christian community, and the problems and situation of that community will have governed the way in which he has set out the story; but these can only be deduced from the book itself. The way in which the passion narrative dominates the story suggests that the nature of Jesus' death caused Mark's readers difficulty: Mark's answer to the scandal of the crucifixion is seen in the paradoxical revelation of Jesus as *Messiah and *Son of God through his death. The suggestion that Mark was concerned to attack a "false Christology" is an anachronistic notion; we should think rather of a community that had not yet come to terms with the idea of a crucified Messiah. Similarly, the teaching about discipleship may indicate that its members had not grasped what this entailed: warnings that it involved following in the steps of Jesus suggest that persecution was either an imminent danger or had already taken them by surprise, while those warnings in Mark 13 that the end is "still to come" and that suffering will continue, suggest that the community was puzzled by the delay in the promised arrival of the kingdom.

The portrait of the *twelve as slow to comprehend the truth about Jesus has been interpreted as an attack on the church leaders in Mark's day, but it should probably be understood in relation to the "*messianic secret" *(see below).*

Interpretation. For many centuries Mark was the least used of the gospels, being overshadowed by the longer synoptics, but the theory of Marcan priority, linked with the Petrine tradition, led to the belief that this gospel was the most reliable historically and so brought Mark into the forefront of critical study toward the end of the nineteenth century. In 1901, Wilhelm Wrede challenged this assumption in his study of the secrecy motif in the Gospels and argued that Mark was a theological presentation, not a historical record (*see* Messianic Secret). In the 1920s, the development of form criticism strengthened the realization that Mark could not be treated as an eyewitness account of Jesus' ministry; attention came to be focused on the beliefs of the community that had shaped the tradition collected by the evangelist. The subsequent growth of redaction criticism shifted scholarly interest to Mark himself and to his role in the final shaping and arranging of the material; the evangelist was now acknowledged to be a theologian rather than a historian or a collector-editor. This led in the 1970s to the recognition that Mark's gospel had to be considered in relation to the community in which Mark lived, since he was influenced by that community and sought to influence it; we may thus hope to learn about the situation and beliefs of the community through him.

In studying this book, therefore, we need to ask questions at several historical levels. We can ask, first, about the way in which Mark understood the gospel and about the circumstances of the community for whom he wrote. Moving backward, we may ask about the traditions he inherited, and about the beliefs of the earliest Christians. Only then should we move to the final stage and raise questions about what Jesus himself may have said and done.

The historical problems are so complex that some commentators have abandoned them altogether and looked for other ways of interpreting Mark. Literary analysts insist that the text itself has a meaning, and some, such as *structuralists, have no concern for the original intention of the author; since, however, the meaning discovered differs from one interpretation to another, it would seem that it is imposed by the reader rather than found in the text. In fact, all interpretation involves a large subjective element, since all readers of Mark's gospel (or any other text) inevitably interpret it in terms of their own experiences, but when historical criticism is abandoned there is no control over the process.

Mark's Presentation of the Gospel. Mark begins by setting out the identity of Jesus: he is the Messiah (1.1); his coming fulfills scripture (1.2–3), since he is the mighty one announced by *John the Baptist, the messenger of the Lord (1.4–8); he is proclaimed by God as his Son, and the Spirit of God is with him (1.9–11); in the power of the Spirit he confronts *Satan in the wilderness (1.12–13).

These first thirteen verses provide vital information that enables us to understand the rest of the story. From this point on, however, the truth about Jesus is stated only rarely, and then obscurely, until the very last chapters. If we compare these opening verses with the prologue of a Greek drama, we will realize that in reading them we have been privileged to receive information that is hidden from the characters of the story, who are bewildered by the events that follow. Although Jesus' identity is known to unclean spirits (1.24) and confirmed again from heaven (9.7), it remains hidden from the religious authorities, the crowds, and even the disciples, who only half comprehend. This is partly because of human obtuseness (8.18), but Mark also depicts Jesus as silencing anyone who comes near the truth (1.25, 34; 3.12; 8.30).

The messianic secret can no longer be explained as historical reporting; nor is it, as Wrede suggested, the result of imposing a messianic interpretation on a nonmessianic tradition. Rather, from the standpoint of Christian faith the significance of Jesus' words and deeds seem clear, and the failure of his contemporaries to recognize him as Messiah needs explanation. Mark's solution is that the truth was concealed from them, partly by divine purpose, partly by their own obstinacy; but to those with eyes to see and ears to hear, all is now plain: Mark's story is thus concerned with messianic revelation as much as messianic secrecy.

*Miracles play an important role in Mark's gospel, and he makes clear in editorial summaries that there were in fact many more healings and *exorcisms than those he describes. The miracles are greeted by onlookers with amazement and incomprehension, though their significance is recognized by unclean spirits (1.24; 3.11; 5.7) and implied by Jesus in 3.22–30: through the power of the Holy Spirit he has defeated Satan and is saving men and women from his clutches. Jesus' authority to heal encompasses not only the exorcism of unclean spirits, but restoration of all kinds: cleansing a leper (1.40–45), forgiving sins (2.1–10), raising the dead and giving new life (5.21–43). His power extends over nature, so that he is able to control the sea (4.35–41; 6.45–52) and give the people bread (6.31–44; 8.1–10), both manifestations of divine power reminiscent of the *Exodus; yet the scribes accuse him of working under Satan (3.22), his family think he is mad (3.21), he meets with disbelief in his hometown (6.1–6), the *Pharisees demand a sign from him (8.11–13), and his own disciples are unable to grasp the significance of what they have seen (8.14–21). To Mark's readers, however, the miracles demonstrate Jesus' authority, since they know the answer to the disciples' bewildered question, "Who then is this?" (4.41).

It is only those with faith who can receive healing (5.34, 36; 6.5–6; 7.29; 9.14–24), and the stories themselves become paradigms for the meaning of faith. The man who has ears but cannot hear until Jesus touches them (7.31–37), the blind man who has eyes but cannot see, and who receives his sight gradually (8.22–26), the man who cries, "I believe; help my unbelief" (9.24), and the beggar who receives his sight and follows Jesus on the way to Jerusalem (10.46–52) all tell us something of what belief in Jesus means.

Mark emphasizes also Jesus' role as teacher and makes use of a considerable amount of teaching, though less is included than in Matthew and Luke. According to Mark 1.14–15, the gospel announced by Jesus concerned the *kingdom of God. Yet by his arrangement of the material, Mark makes it plain that the gospel is about Jesus himself: the kingdom is given to those who become his *disciples. By their response to Jesus, men and women are divided into those who belong to his community and those who remain "outside" (4.11; cf. 3.31–35). Much of the teaching is thus appropriate only to those who are disciples and even they find it difficult to understand. As with the miracles, however, the significance of the teaching is plain to those readers of Mark's gospel who have eyes and ears to understand.

The major block of teaching occurs in chap. 4, in which Jesus teaches the crowd in *parables. Mark believes the teaching to be deliberately enigmatic: the disciples should have understood, yet they require an explanation (4.10–12). In 8.31–10.52, Jesus teaches the disciples about his own destiny as the *Son of man, together with the understanding of discipleship that necessarily follows, but they are unable to comprehend. The final section of teaching (chap. 13), addressed to four disciples, warns them of future judgment on Jerusalem and of persecution for themselves.

Other sayings occur in conflict stories and are thus addressed to Jesus' opponents. Notable examples are the debates about *purity (7.1–23) and *divorce (10.1–12), where Jesus challenges the Pharisees' interpretation of Mosaic teaching, and the parable of the vineyard (12.1–12). All demonstrate Jesus' authority, and because his opponents reject it, they are naturally outraged by this teaching.

Jesus acts with authority, but makes no direct claims for himself; when referring to himself he uses the enigmatic phrase "the Son of man." It is others who, with varying degrees of understanding, declare his identity. The truth is partly grasped by the disciples at Caesarea Philippi: in contrast to outsiders, who regard Jesus as some great prophet figure (8.28; cf. 6.14–16), Peter acknowledges him to be the Messiah; but the need for Jesus to suffer and die cannot yet be understood at this stage (8.27–33), and for Mark, the identity of Jesus is revealed fully only through his death and resurrection (9.9). The great irony of his story is that when we come to the passion narrative, those responsible for Jesus' death unknowingly identify Jesus. The high priest announces the truth when he asks whether he is "the Messiah, the Son of the Blessed One" (14.61); *Pilate executes him on the charge of being "King of the Jews" (15.2, 9, 12, 18, 26, 32); and when he dies, his executioner proclaims him "God's Son" (Mark 15.39). Since this title earlier came from heaven (1.11; 9.7), it may be assumed that Mark believed it to be the fullest expression of the truth about Jesus. In the mouth of the Roman centurion, the phrase is remarkable: Mark appears to be affirming that through the crucifixion Jesus is fully revealed and faith is born. For Mark, the death and resurrection of Jesus provide the key to the whole story. The cross is thus no accident, but part of the divine plan.

The declaration of faith (as Mark interprets it) by a gentile brings to a climax another of Mark's important themes. Jesus proclaims the kingdom to Israel, but he is rejected by his own people—by family (3.21–35), hometown (6.1–6), religious leaders (14.1–2), one of his disciples (14.10–11), and finally by the crowd (15.6–15). He pronounces judgment on the nation's religious leaders (3.28–30; 7.6–13; 11.11–20; 12.1–12, 38–40), and foretells destruction for Jerusalem (13). His ministry appears to end in failure. Yet he dies as "a ransom for many" (10.45; cf. 14.24) and promises future vindication for his disciples (8.35; 13.27). Who, then, are the "many"? The word probably refers to all those who belong to the people of God, and for Mark that means those men and women who have responded to Jesus. There are occasional hints that gentiles will be included: in 7.24–30, a gentile woman receives help because of her faith; in 13.10 we are told that the gospel must be preached "to all nations" (cf. also 14.9); moreover, Mark is clearly writing for gentiles (7.3). The centurion's confession, together with the rending of the Temple curtain, confirms that the vineyard has been taken away from the original tenants and given to others (12.9).

The gospel of Mark ends abruptly, at 16.8, and early attempts to add an ending show that it was felt to be incomplete. It is possible that the book was never finished or that it was damaged at an early stage. Yet it may be our knowledge of the other Gospels that makes us expect this one to end with appearances of the risen Lord. Certainly, it ends in an appropriate way for Mark—with fear, human failure, and the call to discipleship: it is those who respond and who follow the risen Lord who will see him.

MORNA D. HOOKER

Marriage.

Ancient Israel. The institution of marriage is intimately related to kinship in the Hebrew Bi-

ble. There are indications that marriage was thought of as an extension of kinship through an informal or written covenant or agreement. Language that is used in connection with the *covenant, such as "love" and "hate" (for the latter, see Deut. 24.3 [NRSV "dislike"]; Judg. 15.2 [NRSV "reject"]), is also used of the marriage relationship and its dissolution. From at least the eighth century BCE onward, the covenantal relationship between Yahweh and Israel is likened to a covenanted marriage; this analogous usage begins in Hosea 1–3 and continues in later materials (e.g., Jer. 3.1–5). By analyzing the analogy we can deduce some of the ideals concerning marriage in ancient Israel, at least for those who produced the texts. Two characteristics may be noted. First, the relationship was monogamous. Israel had only one God, and God had chosen Israel over all other peoples. Second, mutual fidelity was expected. *Adultery was accepted as grounds for dissolving the relationship (*see* Divorce). Hosea implies that the relationship should be one of mutual love, respect, and fidelity (2.19–20), and that the wife would call her husband "my man" and not "my master (Hebr. *ba'al*)" (2.16).

The status of *women in ancient Israel is an important factor in understanding the institution of marriage. A woman seems always to have been under the authority and protection of her nearest male kin; for the wife, this was the husband. Some texts may imply that the status of women changed for the better over time.

Although monogamy may have been the ideal, polygamy was accepted and practiced throughout Israel's history (see Deut. 21.15), although to what extent we cannot be sure, since the sources for the most part are derived from and describe the elite ruling and upper classes. The patriarchs took more than one wife, and the kings of Israel and Judah maintained harems, of which *Solomon's was the most notorious (1 Kings 11.1–8). By the Roman period, monogamy seems to have been the common practice.

Endogamy and exogamy. Endogamy is marriage within one's group, however that may be defined, and exogamy is marriage outside it; both are attested in the Bible. In the ancestral narratives, endogamy was apparently the dominant practice; for example, in Genesis 24 *Abraham sends his servant back to *Mesopotamia to find a wife for his son *Isaac from among his own kin (see also Gen. 28.1–2, 9). Yet exogamy is also reported, as by *Esau (Gen. 26.34) and *Joseph (Gen. 41.45). Exogamy was practiced by the kings of Israel and Judah, such as *David, few of whose marriages were endogamous (beginning with Michal, *Saul's daughter; see also 2 Sam. 3.2–5; 1 Chron. 3.1–9), Solomon, and *Ahab.

The Deuteronomic view of exogamy was hostile, expressly because of a fear of apostasy (Deut. 7.1–6; 1 Kings 11.1–8; 16.31–32), a view also found in postexilic literature (Ezra 9–10; Neh. 10.28–30; 13.23–27). The book of *Ruth, on the other hand, has been interpreted as espousing a position in which exogamy is acceptable.

New Testament. No detailed teaching concerning marriage is found in the Gospels; we may infer from discussions concerning *divorce and other passages (see John 2.1–12) that Jesus viewed it positively, with monogamy as the ideal. Paul's views are more developed, and more controversial. The most detailed discussion is in 1 Corinthians 7, where Paul argues that marriage is an antidote to sexual immorality, but that celibacy is preferable. As v. 26 makes clear, in part this view was due to Paul's belief in an imminent *second coming of Christ, but other factors no doubt were also at work, including Paul's own unmarried state (v. 8). The "household codes" (*see* Ethical Lists) of the post-Pauline letters exhibit a conventional view of marriage, and the subordinate position of *women within it (see, e.g., Col. 3.18–19; Titus 2.3–5; 1 Pet. 3.1–7).

As in the Hebrew Bible, the marriage relationship is used in the New Testament to describe the bond between the community and God, in this case expressed as the church and Christ (Eph. 5.21–33; cf. Rev. 21.2).

See also Sex; Weddings.   RUSSELL FULLER

Marx and the Bible. What did Karl Marx (1818–1883) make of the Bible? Was it a book that he knew and used? Did the Bible have any influence on him, a person who became estranged from all religion, especially from Judaism and Christianity? These two religious traditions were part of his heritage, and there is evidence that Marx knew the Bible and used it in various ways for his own purposes. But, of course, a knowledge of the Bible implies neither a regard for its teaching nor a recognition of its authority. No one who was capable of writing, as Marx did in 1844, that "the criticism of religion ends with the precept that the supreme being for man is man" is likely to have had much sympathy for a collection of writings that expresses a distinctly

different point of view. He believed that human beings must unite in a revolutionary struggle to free themselves from exploitation, from belief in God, and from the illusory comforts of religion.

Marx's Jewish and Christian Background. Born in Trier on 5 May 1818, Marx was the son of a Jewish lawyer, Heinrich (Heschel) Marx, who converted to Lutheranism in 1817. The law did not permit Jews to work as civil servants or as lawyers, and those who did not convert to Christianity were obliged to accept subordinate positions in society. Conversion was not easy for either of Marx's parents, several of whose forebears in Germany and Holland had served their communities as rabbis. It was not until August 1824 that the children, including Karl, were baptized. Out of respect for her parents, Marx's mother postponed her own baptism for another fifteen months. Marx's early upbringing thus provided him with opportunities to observe both Jewish and Christian traditions.

Like Friedrich Engels, as a young man Marx was by no means hostile to Christianity. In a youthful piece, *The Union of Believers with Christ* (1835), he speaks of how Christians are able to turn to their fellow believers because they share with them an inner bond, through the sacrificial love of Christ. Union with Christ can bring "inner elevation, comfort in sorrow, calm trust, and a heart susceptible to human love, to everything noble and great, not for the sake of ambition and glory, but only for the sake of Christ." Was this an expression of genuine Christian conviction? Or was it an early example of his ability to parody the devotional language of Christian contemporaries? If it is parody, it helps to account for the apparent shift in Marx from belief to unbelief, from Christian commitment to militant atheism. The change in Marx's beliefs came when his Promethean instincts surfaced. In his doctoral dissertation at Jena (1841) he uses the words of Aeschylus's Prometheus, "In one word—I hate all the gods." Above all, he hated the God of the Bible: the creator God, who created humans in his own image (Gen. 1.27), was, in Marx's analysis, the enemy of humanity, a human projection that served only to delay progress toward final liberation.

Approaches to Alienation. Marx's concept of *Entfremdung* (alienation) is not unknown in the Bible, although there it finds a very different focus in the estrangement of human beings from their creator. The prophets inveighed against all forms of *idolatry in which human beings rendered to lifeless images the worship due alone to the living God (Hos. 14.8). These idols were the work of human hands (Ps. 135.15–18). For Marx, God was an idol, worshiped by its creator; it distracted men and women from the realization of their own potential. Marx insisted that the alienation experienced by human beings was alienation, not from God, but from themselves. Like the biblical writers, Marx's themes were those of deliverance, liberation, justice, and equality, but his conclusions were different from theirs because he held that we live in a universe without God.

The eschatological aspects of his prophetic vision of the classless society are thus very different from those in the Bible. His was a belief in a secular eschatology, a belief that in the future the difference between human essence and human existence would be eliminated. The theology of the *incarnation would be turned on its head in the deification of the human. Marx believed that salvation lies within history, not beyond it. Insofar as he used biblical concepts, and employed stylistic devices reminiscent of the prophets, Marx was at pains to correct, if not expressly, what the Bible had to say to those looking for justice and liberation from oppression. What is missing in Marx is the biblical recognition of the individual's value in eternity as well as in time. The New Testament's emphasis on the redeeming activity of Jesus (2 Cor. 5.15), on the full life to be enjoyed by the believer (John 10.10), and on the reconciling work of God in Christ (2 Cor. 5.18–19), found neither echo nor acknowledgment in Marx. In place of this he repudiated biblical teaching by means of quotation out of context, carefully selected allusions, a tendentious use of theological interpretation, and outright parody.

All of this served Marx's purpose by diminishing the value of the Bible as a credible historical record of the events it contains or as a repository of wisdom. In this he gained support from an unexpected source. While he did not acknowledge any indebtedness to the criticism of the New Testament which came into prominence in the middle of the nineteenth century in Germany (see Interpretation, History of, *article on* Modern Biblical Criticism), there is, nonetheless, in the subsequent attention that he gave to theologians like David F. Strauss (1808–1874) and Bruno Bauer (1809–1882), a recognition of the implications of their criticism. The spirit of this criticism was congenial to Marx because it served the interests of his attack on religion.

Marx's Use of the Bible. Several of Marx's works are replete with biblical quotations and allusions. In using them, Marx attempted to expose the naïveté of any lingering religious sentiments in other writers and political activists, employing an idiom with which he presumed them to be familiar, yet in a way that destroyed the original emphasis. To this end he alluded to biblical subjects and themes such as justice, equality, and deliverance, and echoed familiar phrases from the scriptures, well-known hymns, and the language of Christian piety.

The language of the *Sermon on the Mount and of the beatitudes features in his criticism of the attitudes of the poor, who delude themselves with promises of a heavenly inheritance. Texts such as Colossians 1.26 were given an interpretation more in line with his own concept of reality for a new generation of "saints." Similarly, "the time is fulfilled" (Mark 1.15) is interpreted in terms very different from those of the realized eschatology of the gospel. The emphasis on faith rather than works in Romans 3.28 is identified as a weakness typical of those who continue to accept false views of human existence. The struggles for human liberation, and the creation of a new order foreseen in Revelation 21.1, are accommodated to Marx's own vision of the future.

Despite Marx's atheism and his despisal of all religions—Judaism and Christianity especially—because they had become instruments of oppression in the struggle between workers and capitalists, there is little doubt that from time to time biblical memories came back to his consciousness. Later, his daughter Eleanor Marx-Aveling recalled how her father dealt with her "religious qualms" after she had been to a Roman Catholic church "to hear the beautiful music," when she was about six years old. Marx "quietly made everything clear and straight, so that from that hour to this no doubt could ever cross my mind again." But she adds the following note that sheds a different light on Marx's residual memory of a religious revelation that he despised.

And how I remember his telling the story—I do not think it could ever have been so told before or since—of the carpenter whom rich men killed, and many and many a time saying, "After all we can forgive Christianity much, because it taught us the worship of the child." And Marx could himself have said, "Suffer little children to come unto me," for wherever he went, there children somehow would turn up also.

To the themes of justice, equality, and the value of labor Marx brought his own perceptions. These are also biblical themes, but when Paul, for instance, addressed himself to those in the Christian community who were content to enjoy the fruits of the labors of others (1 Thess. 2.9–12; 2 Thess. 3.6–12), he spoke in response to a different vision. Marx insisted that if anyone would not work, he should not eat, but this was a note of warning, sounded from the logic of his own dualistic anthropology. Marx held that human was set against human, as enemy against enemy, as worker against capitalist.

For the Bible's essential message Marx had only derision. Yet he was obliged to admit that the transformation of the world would require more than reliance on the processes of historical materialism. Above all, it would require a new kind of human creature with the capacity, as well as the desire, to build a society in which swords are beaten into plowshares (see Isa. 2.4).

EDWARD HULMES

Mary Magdalene. Mary Magdalene is one of the inner circle of the followers of Jesus in the Gospel narratives. Her name suggests that she came from Magdala, a large city on the western shore of the Sea of Galilee, also called Taricheae (Map 10:Y3). Magdala was known for its salt trade, for its administrative role as a toparchy, and as a large urban center that was part of the contiguous cities and large villages along the western shore of the lake from Tiberias to Bethsaida/ Chorazin.

Mary Magdalene is mentioned sparingly but at crucial points in all four Gospels. During the events surrounding the *crucifixion of Jesus, she is depicted as watching the proceedings and waiting near the tomb to attend to the body (Matt. 27.56, 61; 28.1; par.; John 19.25). She is also one of the first witnesses to the *resurrection (Matt. 28.9; John 20.11–18). These passages probably gave rise to the romantic portrayals of Mary as the devoted follower whom Jesus had saved from her errant ways.

Contrary to subsequent Christian interpretation, reflected in popular belief and recent films, there is no evidence from the Gospels that Mary Magdalene was a prostitute or for the later identification of Mary Magdalene with the women who anoint Jesus' feet (Luke 7.36–50; Matt. 26.6–13 par.) or with Mary of Bethany (Luke 10.38; John 11.1–2). In Luke 8.2 it is said that Mary Magdalene was healed of seven evil spirits by Jesus. But this is in the context of a list of women who were followers of Jesus, who had also been healed, and who supplied the material support for his mission. Since Mary Magdalene, Chuza (the wife of a steward of Herod) and Susanna are the only women mentioned, it is likely that these three were the benefactors of the Jesus movement according to Luke.

J. ANDREW OVERMAN

Mary, Mother of Jesus. According to ancient Christian sources, Mary was the child of Jewish parents Joachim and Anne and was born in Jerusalem or Sepphoris in Galilee. If, as the sources suggest, Mary's first child *Jesus was born around 4 BCE and she was espoused around the age of fourteen, as was common, then Mary was probably born in 18 or 20 BCE.

During her childhood she lived in *Nazareth, where she became engaged to the carpenter *Joseph, who was descended from King *David. The gospel of *Luke relates that an *angel of God appeared to Mary and told her that she would become pregnant with God's son by the Holy Spirit, even though she was not yet married (see Virgin Birth). Mary and Joseph traveled to *Bethlehem where Jesus was born in a stable or, according to later traditions, cave. According to Jewish custom, Jesus was circumcised and then presented at the Temple in Jerusalem. He was raised by Mary and Joseph and perhaps other relatives in Nazareth and probably learned the carpentry trade. One relative specifically mentioned by Luke is Mary's cousin Elizabeth, who in her old age gave birth to *John the Baptist shortly before Jesus' birth. Some of the sources indicate that other children were born to Mary and Joseph after Jesus (e.g., Acts 1.14; see Brothers and Sisters of Jesus).

The gospel of Luke, the principal biblical source for Mary in the narratives of Jesus' infancy and childhood, also tells how, when Jesus was twelve years old, Mary and Joseph took him to the Jerusalem Temple—again, in fulfillment of Jewish law—for initiation into the faith. On the return journey, they lost him in the crowd and subsequently found him in the Temple impressing the religious leaders with his wisdom (Luke 2.41–52).

Joseph, probably considerably older than Mary, disappears from the sources at this time, and Mary's role becomes smaller as Jesus' becomes larger. She is mentioned in the context of the marriage feast at Cana (John 2.1–12), at Jesus' crucifixion (but only by John 19.25–27), and in Acts 1.14, the story of *Pentecost. The accounts of Mary's later years, death, and assumption into heaven are found only in traditions outside the Bible, some as late as the fourth century CE. It is not known where she spent her final years, but it is generally believed that she lived with John the son of Zebedee in Jerusalem and died there. The date of her death is almost impossible to determine.

In addition to the gospel accounts, Mary is mentioned in the writings of some of the church fathers, including Justin Martyr, Ignatius, Tertullian, and Athanasius; in *apocryphal works such as the Protevangelium of James (second century); and in the deliberations of the Council of Ephesus (431 CE), where she was proclaimed Theotokos, "God-bearer." A gnostic gospel of Mary and a Latin work from the Middle Ages called *The Gospel of the Birth of Mary* also exist.

It is through these and other sources that the powerful cult of Mary was born and grew, especially in the Roman Catholic, Anglo-Catholic, and Orthodox churches. Various feast days commemorate her importance for devotees: the Immaculate Conception (8 December), her purification in the Temple (2 February), the annunciation of the angel (25 March), her visit to Elizabeth when both were pregnant (2 July), and her assumption into heaven (15 August). Throughout the centuries, Mary has been revered not only as the Mother of God but also as a pure, ever-virgin woman, the perfect mother, the intercessor between human beings and God, and one who knows the deepest of human suffering, having borne witness to the agonizing and humiliating death of her firstborn son. She has been the object of pilgrimages and visions even to the present day, and the "Magnificat," attributed to her by Luke at the time of her visit to Elizabeth (Luke 1.46–55), has been part of Christian liturgy and music for centuries. Mary has been widely honored and even worshiped as representing inner strength and the exaltation of the oppressed over the oppressor.

Non-Christian sources are instructive in tracing parallels to the cult of Mary. Virgin Birth stories (e.g., Hera, Rhea Silvia, Brigid) were circulated in other cultures, as were tales of mothers mourning lost and deceased children (e.g., Demeter and Persephone; Isis and Horus). Iconographically, just as Mary was often portrayed holding or nursing the infant Jesus, so too was the Egyptian goddess Isis depicted suckling her infant son, Horus. Even as Mary was called Queen of Heaven and sometimes depicted surrounded by the zodiac and other symbols, so too were the deities Isis, Magna Mater, and Artemis.

Such parallels show that Mary's cult had roots in the cults of the female deities of the Greco-Roman pantheon, cults ultimately eradicated by Christianity. While Mary in some ways represents qualities impossible for human beings, especially women, to emulate—ever-virgin yet motherly; always gentle and obedient to God's will—her attributes nevertheless represent for many devotees important female properties not provided by the traditional all-male *Trinity. For many, the adoration of a female figure is a vital psychological supplement to their faith.

VALERIE ABRAHAMSEN

Maskil. A Hebrew word of uncertain meaning used in the titles to thirteen *Psalms (32, 42, 44, 45, 52–55, 74, 78, 88, 89, 142) and once in context (Ps. 47.7). Although related by some to the root *śkl*, meaning "to be wise," most of the psalms in which it occurs cannot be classified as *wisdom literature. It is more likely an ancient technical classification whose precise sense is no longer known, like other words used in psalm titles such as "song," "psalm," "prayer," "*miktam," and "shiggaion" (Ps. 7.1; "lament"?).

MICHAEL D. COOGAN

Masorah. The Masorah (Hebr. "tradition") refers to the system of vowel signs, accent markings, and marginal notes devised by early medieval Jewish scribes and scholars and used in copying the text of the Hebrew Bible in order to guard it from changes. The vowel signs and accent marks were integrated by the Masoretes into the received consonantal text, while marginal notes were placed in the lateral margin (*masorah qetanah* or *masorah parva*), as well as the top and bottom margins (*masorah gedolah* or *masorah magna*) of each column of text; further notes are found at the ends of biblical books (*masorah finalis*) and often at the beginning and end of a codex. The codex began to replace the scroll after the Talmudic period (ca. 700 CE) except for liturgical purposes, such as synagogue Torah scrolls, which have no Masorah at all (*see* Books and Bookmaking).

There were three such systems, the Babylonian, Palestinian, and Tiberian, as well as schools within each. The authoritative Masorah since about 1000 CE has been the Tiberian. Of the two great Tiberian schools, the Ben Naftali and the Ben Asher, the latter, especially the Masorah culminating in the work of Aaron ben Asher (ca.

915), was apparently the one approved by Maimonides (twelfth century), which would become the basis for the printed text of the Hebrew Bible. The edition published at Venice, 1524–1525, by Jacob ben Hayyim ben Adoniyahu, using twelfth-century and later manuscripts, became the received text used for printed Bibles until 1937, when late-ninth to eleventh-century Tiberian manuscripts recovered in the nineteenth century began to be used (see Manuscripts, article on Hebrew Bible; Masoretic Text).

The effect of the Masorah was to ensure remarkably accurate transmission of the text, including its inherent anomalies and discrepancies. (The only similar effort was in Syriac manuscripts of both Old Testament and New Testament, but this was limited and ineffective in comparison.) The text was sacred, not a perceived understanding of it, and a scribe was to be neither more nor less than a scribe, no matter how creative or how careless he might be. Unique or rare formations of words or phrases, especially those vulnerable to error, were noted so that the next scribe would not change them to more familiar or more understandable forms. Variant readings for a single word were preserved by carefully guarding both the received consonants for the word (*ketîb) and the vowels for the variant (qerê) as well as by other modes of noting ancient variants, either to be respected or to be avoided. Top and bottom margins contain abbreviated lists of similar words or phrases in other passages, or references to them, thereby preserving for each its own peculiarities. The Masorah, moreover, provides statistics of the number of verses, of lectionary sections, and of words, even noting what word or letter is precisely in the middle of a book or section, so that the next scribe would have full means of guarding the integrity of each letter, each word, each particular phrase, and hence each book that was his charge to copy. While there was no "canon" of the Masorah and though mistakes were made, the masorot (pl.) of the great biblical manuscripts, though different among themselves, provide a remarkable fund of information for *textual criticism.   JAMES A. SANDERS

is the text both of rabbinic Bibles and of modern scholarship.

There are thirty-one extant Masoretic *manuscripts of the Hebrew Bible, complete or fragmentary, dating from the late ninth century to 1100 CE, and some three thousand thereafter. In the sixteenth century, Eliahu ha-Levi noted that there were thousands of Masoretes over a long period of time, neither the beginning nor the end of which is known; their work began toward the end of the Talmudic period (ca. 600 CE) and found its crown in the work of the ben Asher family at the beginning of the tenth century.

The complete MT is included in a manuscript discovered in a synagogue in Cairo during the nineteenth century and now housed in the public library in St. Petersburg (formerly Leningrad, hence called Leningradensis [L]). It dates to 1009 CE and derives from the work of Aaron ben Asher. It is the text of the third Kittel-Kahle edition of Biblia Hebraica (1937) and of Biblia Hebraica Stuttgartensia (1976), its successor. A facsimile edition was published by Maqor Press (1970). The printed edition of the Second Rabbinic Bible of Jacob ben Hayyim ben Adoniyahu (Venice, 1524–25), which was based in large part on the ben Asher tradition, had been the text of the first two editions of the Kittel Bible.

Older than L by about three-quarters of a century is the partially preserved Aleppensis (A), which was brought in 1948 to Jerusalem from Aleppo. It is believed that this represents the text of which Maimonides (twelfth century) approved; it is the text of the Hebrew University Bible (1975–).

The oldest *manuscripts of the Hebrew Bible, from the *Dead Sea Scrolls, date from the third century BCE to the beginning of the second century CE, and have only consonants; most are preMasoretic; those from other caves in the same area, dating to a period after 70 CE, are proto-Masoretic and reflect the stabilization of the consonantal text taking place at the time. It was this stabilized and exceptionally well-preserved consonantal text to which the *Masorah was later added.   JAMES A. SANDERS

Masoretic Text. The Masoretic Text (MT) refers to the textual product elaborated by schools of scholars (Masoretes) who in the early Middle Ages integrated vowel signs, accent markings, and marginal notes (the *Masorah) into the received consonantal text of the Hebrew Bible. It

Matthew. Matthew is named as one of the original *disciples (Matt. 9.9; 10.3; Mark 3.18; Luke 6.15; Acts 1.13), and he has traditionally been identified as the author of the first (but not the oldest) Gospel in the New Testament (see next entry). In the other Gospels and Acts, the name

Matthew simply appears in a list of followers of Jesus, but in the Gospel that bears his name, Matthew is mentioned twice as a tax collector. This association has stuck through subsequent Christian history, although in the parallels to Matthew 9.9 in both Mark 2.14 and Luke 5.27, the tax collector is called Levi, not Matthew.

According to Papias (ca. 130 CE), "Matthew made an ordered arrangement of the sayings in the Hebrew dialect, and each one translated it as he was able" (quoted by Eusebius, the fourth-century bishop of Caesarea, *Hist. Eccl.* 3.39.16; see also 5.8.2). This leads to the view that Matthew first wrote his Gospel in Hebrew, a view today rejected by almost all scholars. But Papias also gives us the earliest association of Matthew with the first canonical Gospel, an association that probably originated in his being mentioned twice within that Gospel, and continued in the manuscript traditions that add the superscript "according to Matthew."

J. ANDREW OVERMAN

Matthew, The Gospel According to. Matthew's gospel proclaims the message that in Jesus, *Son of God, God has drawn near with his eschatological rule to dwell to the end of time with his people, the church (1.23; 16.16; 28.20). The purpose of this message is to summon the reader or hearer to perceive that God is uniquely present in Jesus and to become Jesus' disciple. As Jesus' disciple, one becomes God's child, lives in the sphere of his end-time kingdom, and engages in mission so that all people may find him in Jesus and also become Jesus' disciples.

Structure. Matthew is a gospel story in three parts. The main divisions derive from the formula that appears in 4.17 and 16.21: "From that time Jesus began to proclaim [to show his disciples] . . ." Embedded in this story are also five great speeches of Jesus. The following outline marks off the three parts of the story and indicates the distribution of the speeches:

I. The presentation of Jesus (1.1–4.16)
II. The ministry of Jesus to Israel (4.17–11.1)
   A. The Sermon on the Mount (5.1–7.29)
   B. The missionary discourse (9.35–10.42) and Israel's repudiation of Jesus (11.2–16.20)
   C. The discourse in parables (13.1–52)
III. The journey of Jesus to Jerusalem and his suffering, death, and resurrection (16.21–28.20)

   A. The ecclesiological discourse (17.24–18.35)
   B. The eschatological discourse (24.1–25.46)

As is apparent, the story that is told is of the life and ministry of Jesus. It begins with his miraculous conception and birth and closes with his death and resurrection.

The temporal setting in which this story of Jesus takes place is the history of salvation. This begins with *Abraham, the father of Israel, and extends to the consummation of the age and the return of Jesus for judgment (1.17; 25.31–46). It divides itself into two distinct epochs. The first epoch is the time of Israel, which is the time of prophecy (e.g., 2.5–6). The second epoch is the time of Jesus (earthly-exalted), which is the time of fulfillment (e.g., 1.22–23). For its part, the time of Jesus (earthly-exalted) encompasses the ministries to Israel of John (3.1–2), of Jesus (4.17), and of the pre-Easter disciples (10.7), as well as the ministry to the nations of the post-Easter disciples (24.14; 28.19–20). Central to this time, however, is the ministry of Jesus himself, for the ministry of John prepares for it and the ministries of the pre-Easter and post-Easter disciples are an extension of it.

In combination, the twin features of structure and view of salvation history advance a weighty theological claim on behalf of Jesus. As was noted, the structure of Matthew's story focuses on the life and ministry of Jesus. The view this story projects of the history of salvation describes Jesus both as the one in whom the time of Israel attains its fulfillment (1.17) and the one who is at the center of the gospel of the kingdom that is to be proclaimed to the nations (24.14; 26.12–13). Accordingly, the theological claim these two features advance is that for the salvation of all people, Jews and *gentiles, the life and ministry of Jesus is of decisive significance.

Author, Date, Place. It is commonly held that Matthew was written about 85 or 90 CE by an unknown Christian who was at home in a church located in *Antioch of Syria. A date toward the end of the first century seems probable because the destruction of *Jerusalem, which occurred in 70 CE, appears to be an event that was rapidly receding into the past (22.7). Although the apostle Matthew may have been active in founding the church in which the gospel story attributed to him arose (9.9; 10.3), it is unlikely that he was the story's author. On the contrary, the author exhibits a theological outlook, command of Greek, and rabbinic training that suggest he was a Jewish Christian of the second rather than the first generation (cf. 13.52). Also, Antioch of Syria commends itself as the place where he may have been at home, because the social conditions reflected in his story correspond with those that seem to have prevailed there: the city was Greek-speaking, urban, and prosperous, and it had a large population of both Jews and gentiles.

Readers. Scholarly opinion holds that the church for which Matthew was written was made up of Christians of both Jewish and gentile origin. Socioculturally, this church was almost certainly living in an atmosphere of religious and social tension. Its mandate was to make disciples of all nations, and this was apparently provoking hostile reactions from both Jews and gentiles. Seemingly, Christians were being hauled into court by gentile authorities, judicially harassed, hated "by all," and even put to death (10.18, 22; 13.21; 24.9). Similar persecutions were likewise taking place at the hands of the Jews: Christians were being made to submit to such ill-treatment as verbal abuse (5.11), arraignment for disturbing the peace (10.17), perjured testimony in court (5.11), flogging in the local synagogues (10.17; 23.34), pursuit from city to city (10.23; 23.34), and even death (10.28; 23.34–35).

As a body, the church of Matthew appears to have achieved organizational autonomy and to have been materially well off. Religiously, these Christians were no longer living under the jurisdiction of contemporary Pharisaic Judaism (15.13; 16.18). Quite the opposite, they already had in place the means for making their own decisions concerning matters of church doctrine and church discipline (16.19; 18.15–20). Identifiable groups within the church were *prophets, or itinerant missionaries, and teachers (10.17–18, 41; 23.34). Socioeconomically, the way in which both monetary matters and ethical and religious questions associated with the topic of riches are treated in Matthew indicates that the church in which it arose was relatively prosperous.

But Matthew's church was also rife with dissension. Under the pressure of persecution, some Christians apostatized (13.21; 24.10), while others betrayed fellow Christians to enemies (24.10); still others fell victim to the "cares of the world and the lure of wealth" (13.22). Hatred broke out among Christians (24.10), false prophets arose who led others astray (7.15; 24.11), and disobedience to the law of God was so rampant that the "love of many was growing cold" (24.12). It

was to meet the religious and moral needs of this multiracial, prosperous, yet divided and persecuted church that the author of Matthew told afresh the gospel story.

Sources. Some scholars hold that Matthew was the first gospel story written, that Luke was the second, and that Mark is a synopsis of both Matthew and Luke. Most scholars, however, espouse the two-source hypothesis in resolving the *synoptic problem. According to this view, Mark was the first of the gospel stories, and both Matthew and Luke are based on Mark, a sayings source called "Q," and traditions peculiar to each ("M" and "L," respectively). Although the latter hypothesis is to be preferred, one ought not to be misled by source analysis into thinking that, in its final form, Matthew presents itself simply as a sum of layers of tradition. Instead, it constitutes a coherent story possessing a recognizable beginning, middle, and end.

Story of Jesus. In the first part of the gospel story (1.1–4.16), Jesus is presented to the reader. Initially, the narrator describes him as the *Messiah, son of *David, and son of *Abraham (1.1). Jesus is the Messiah, the Anointed One, Israel's long-awaited King (1.17; 2.2, 4; 11.2–3). He is the son of David because *Joseph adopts him into the line of David (1.16, 18–25), and he fulfills the eschatological expectations associated with David (9.27–31; 12.22–23; 15.21–28; 20.29–21.17). He is the son of Abraham, as well, because in him the entire history of Israel attains to its culmination, and the gentiles, too, find blessing (1.17; 8.11).

Upon Jesus' birth, the *Magi arrive in Jerusalem and ask where they might find the King of the Jews (2.1–2). To *Herod, and later to *Pilate as well, this title denotes that Jesus is a pretender to the throne or an insurrectionist. Thus, Herod plots to have Jesus found and killed (2.13), and Pilate hands him over to be crucified (27.26, 37). In Matthean perspective, Jesus is in truth the King of the Jews, but not because he aspires to the throne of Israel or foments rebellion against Rome, but because he saves his people by submitting to suffering and death (27.27–31, 37, 42).

*John the Baptist is *Elijah returned, the forerunner of Jesus (3.1–12; 11.10, 14). He prepares Israel for the coming of Jesus by calling for repentance in view of the nearness of God's endtime kingdom and the final judgment (3.2, 10–12).

The baptismal scene constitutes the climax of the first part of Matthew's story (3.13–17). After

John has baptized Jesus, God empowers Jesus with his Spirit and declares him to be his unique Son whom he had chosen for messianic ministry (3.16–17). This declaration by God reveals that the Matthean Jesus is preeminently the *Son of God. The significance of this title is that it points to the unique filial relationship that Jesus has to God: conceived and empowered by God's Spirit (1.18, 20; 3.16), Jesus is "God with us" (1.23; see Immanuel), the one through whom God reveals himself to humankind (11.25–27) and who is God's supreme agent of salvation (1.21; 21.37; 26.28; 27.54).

Guided by the Spirit, Jesus submits to testing by the *devil (4.1–11). Three times the devil endeavors to get Jesus to break faith with God. Jesus, however, rebuts the tempter and shows himself to be the Son who knows and does his Father's will (see Temptation of Christ). Returning to Galilee, Jesus is poised to begin his public activity (4.12–16).

The second part of Matthew's story (4.17–16.20) tells of Jesus' ministry to Israel (4.17–11.1) and of Israel's repudiation of him (11.2–16.20). Through his ministry of teaching, preaching, and healing (4.23; 9.35; 11.1), Jesus summons Israel to repentance (4.17; 11.20–21). Israel, however, repudiates Jesus (chaps. 11–12), yet wonders and speculates about his identity (11.3; 12.23; 13.55; 14.2; 16.14). In sharp contrast to Israel's false view that Jesus is a prophet of whatever identity (16.14), the disciples correctly confess him to be the Messiah, the Son of God (14.33; 16.16).

The third part of Matthew's story (16.21–28.20) describes Jesus' journey to Jerusalem and his suffering, death, and resurrection. The passion predictions sound this theme (16.21; 17.22–23; 20.17–19; cf. 26.2), and the motif of the journey binds together disparate materials (16.21–21.11). In *Jerusalem, Jesus makes the *Temple the site of his activity, where he teaches, debates, and speaks in parables (21.12–23.39). Addressing the parable of the wicked husbandmen to the Jewish leaders, Jesus raises the claim that he is the Son of God whom the leaders will kill (21.37–39). In wanting to arrest Jesus for telling the parable (21.45–46), the leaders show that they reject Jesus' claim.

At his trial, it is the claim that Jesus made in his parable, to be the Son of God, that the high priest uses to secure Jesus' condemnation (26.63–66). When Jesus replies to the high priest's question in the affirmative (26.64), he is sentenced to death for blaspheming God. The irony is that

God has indeed affirmed Jesus to be his Son (3.17; 17.5).

Upon Jesus' death, the Roman soldiers also affirm Jesus to be the Son of God (27.54). What the reader knows and the soldiers do not is that the death of Jesus Son of God constitutes the climax of his earthly ministry and the act whereby he atones for the sins of humankind (1.21; 26.28). Atop the mountain in Galilee, Jesus appears to the disciples as the resurrected Son of God who remains the crucified Son of God (28.5, 16–20). Seeing Jesus as such, the disciples at last perceive not only who he is (16.16) but also what he has accomplished (26.28). In consequence of this, they receive the commission to go and make of all nations Jesus' disciples (28.18–20). Matthew's story ends, therefore, with both the disciples and the reader sharing the same perception of Jesus and receiving his commission.

Story of the Opponents. Entwined with the story line of Jesus in Matthew is the story of his opponents. These are the Jewish leaders, who form a united front against him and comprise such groups as the *Pharisees, *Sadducees, chief *priests, *elders, and *scribes. Not until Jesus' arrest do the Jewish crowds turn on him (26.55).

The story of the Jewish leaders develops in close correlation with that of Jesus. In the first part of Matthew (1.1–4.16), the leaders are presented to the reader and cast in an unfavorable light. Thus, they make their debut as the supporters of King Herod who place their knowledge of scripture in his service (2.1–6). Like Herod and all Jerusalem, they are frightened at hearing the news that the Messiah, the King of the Jews, has been born. Subsequently, as John the Baptist readies Israel for the coming of Jesus (3.1–12), the Jewish leaders too go out to him. Instead of receiving them, however, John denounces them as a "brood of vipers" (3.7) and in so doing characterizes them as "evil" (cf. 12.34). How such evil is to be construed comes to light in the temptation and other pericopes. In the temptation (4.1–11), the devil, the fountainhead of all evil, three times puts Jesus to the test in order to get him to break faith with God (4.1–11). Later in Matthew's story, the Jewish leaders likewise repeatedly put Jesus to the test in order to best him in debate (16.1; 19.3; 22.18, 35). Accordingly, the Jewish leaders are evil in Matthean perspective because they have affinity with *Satan.

In the second part of Matthew's story (4.17–11.1; 11.2–16.20), conflict erupts between Jesus and the Jewish leaders (chap. 9), but it does not immediately become mortal (chap. 12). At the point it does become mortal, three features characterize it: it is sparked by a question having to do with the Mosaic *Law itself (12.1–8, 9–14); it is acutely confrontational in nature, in the sense that Jesus is himself directly attacked for an act he himself is about to perform (12.9–14); and it engenders such rancor in the Jewish leaders that they go off and conspire about how to destroy Jesus (12.15). Once the conflict takes this turn toward irreconcilable hostility, death looms as Jesus' certain fate.

As Jesus journeys toward Jerusalem in the third part of Matthew's story (16.21–28.20), only once does he clash with the Jewish leaders, and the purpose this serves is the instruction of the disciples (19.3–12). Not until after Jesus has reached Jerusalem, therefore, does his last great confrontation with the Jewish leaders prior to his passion take place (21.12–22.46). As Jesus teaches in the Temple, the various groups of Jewish leaders approach him, one after the other, in order to challenge him or, at the last, to be challenged by him (21.15, 23; 22.15–16, 23, 34–35, 41). The note on which all of these controversies end is that Jesus reduces all of the leaders to silence (22.46). The result is that they withdraw from the Temple to plot the immediate arrest and death of Jesus (26.3–5).

From their own standpoint, the Jewish leaders believe that by bringing Jesus to the cross, they are doing the will of God and purging Israel of a fraud (26.65–66; 27.63). Nevertheless, God shows, by raising Jesus from the dead and exalting him to all authority in heaven and on earth, that he puts Jesus in the right in his conflict with the Jewish leaders (28.6, 18). The upshot is that the death of Jesus becomes in Matthew not the occasion of Jesus' destruction but the means whereby God accomplishes the salvation of all humankind, Jew and gentile alike (26.28).

Story of the Disciples. The third story line in Matthew is that of the *disciples. Because Jesus gathers no followers until he begins his public ministry to Israel, it is not until the second part of Matthew's story that the disciples make their appearance (4.17–16.20).

The focus in the first half of the second part of Matthew (4.17–11.1) is on the call and the task of the disciples. As Jesus bids Peter and Andrew and James and John to come after him (4.18–22), he directs attention to the nature and the purpose of discipleship. The purpose of discipleship is as absolute as engaging in worldwide missionary activity (4.19). Its nature reveals itself

in the fact that when Jesus summons the four fishermen, they forsake nets, boat, and father (profession, goods, and family) to give him their total allegiance. Through their being "with him" (12.30), he grants them to live in the sphere of God's end-time rule and makes of them a family (12.48–50), or brotherhood (23.8; 28.10), of the "sons of God" (5.9, 45) and of his disciples (10.24–25).

In the *Sermon on the Mount, the Matthean Jesus describes the piety the disciples are to practice. As those who live in the sphere of God's end-time rule, their piety is to be that of the greater righteousness (5.20). To do the greater righteousness, they must be "perfect," that is to say, they must be single-hearted in their devotion to God (5.48). What such single-hearted devotion entails is loving God with heart, soul, and mind, and one's *neighbor as oneself (5.44–48; 7.12, 21; cf. 22.34–40).

Further interaction between Jesus and the disciples or a would-be follower provides additional insight into the significance of the call to discipleship. In turning away the scribe who would arrogate to himself the authority to become a disciple (8.19–20), Jesus shows that one cannot, apart from his enabling call, either enter upon or sustain the life of discipleship. In commanding the disciple who would go bury his father to follow him instead into the boat (8.21–22, 23), Jesus discloses that the life of discipleship brooks no suspension. In chiding the disciples for displaying cowardice in the face of a storm while at the same time calming the winds and sea, Jesus reveals that although he does not condone their succumbing to the weakness of "little faith," he nonetheless stands ever-ready to assist them as they carry out whatever mission he entrusts to them (8.23–27). And in calling the tax collector Matthew to be his disciple (9.9), Jesus teaches all the disciples that he has come to gather not only the good and upright but also the despised.

As Jesus called his first disciples, the task he set before them was that of mission (4.19). With the circle of the *twelve now closed (10.2–4), Jesus summons them for instruction in the first mission they are to undertake, to Israel (10.5–42). This mission is an extension of Jesus' own mission: like him, they too are to go "to the lost sheep of the house of Israel" (10.6; 15.24); and like him, they too are to proclaim the nearness of the kingdom and to heal the sick and exorcise *demons (10.1, 7–8).

In the latter half of the second part of Matthew's story (11.2–16.20), the disciples stand out as the recipients of divine revelation. In contrast to Israel, which repudiates Jesus and shows itself to be uncomprehending, the disciples receive from God the gift of understanding (11.25–26; 13.11, 51). This encompasses insight into the mysteries of the kingdom of heaven (13.11; see Kingdom of God) and knowledge of Jesus' identity: far from being a prophet as the Jewish public imagines, Jesus is, the disciples affirm, the Messiah, the Son of God (14.33; 16.13–16).

In the third part of Matthew (16.21–28.20), the story of the disciples describes how Jesus finally overcomes their unwillingness to accept the truth that the essence of discipleship is servanthood. Although the disciples know that Jesus is the Son of God, they do not know that the fate of the Son of God is suffering and death. In the first word Jesus speaks to the disciples in the third part, he predicts his passion (16.21). Peter takes offense at this (16.22), but Jesus rebukes Peter and solemnly warns all the disciples that only those can belong to him who are prepared to take up their cross and follow him (16.23–24). The proper response to suffering sonship is suffering discipleship or servanthood (20.25–28). Because the disciples resist this notion, they are unable to persevere with Jesus in his passion and fall away: *Judas betrays him (26.49); all desert him (26.56); and Peter denies him (26.69–75).

But though the disciples fall away, the risen Jesus again gathers all of them except Judas (27.3–10) through the word he sends to them that they should meet him in Galilee (28.7, 10, 16). In gathering his scattered disciples, Jesus reconciles them to himself. Moreover, as the disciples, standing on the mountain, see the risen Jesus bearing on his person the marks of crucifixion, they are at last able to comprehend that Jesus' sonship has indeed been suffering sonship. In comprehending this, they likewise comprehend that suffering sonship is a call to suffering discipleship or servanthood. So enlightened, they recast their lives in accord with Jesus' earlier words: "If any want to become my followers, let them deny themselves and take up their cross and follow me" (16.24).

JACK DEAN KINGSBURY

Meals. Meals—from the apple in *Eden to Ezekiel's scroll, from the *Passover to Jesus' Last Supper to the messianic wedding banquet—are still among the Bible's most powerful images, despite centuries of radical change. Indeed, as most explicitly stated in the Lord's command to the Israelites to tell their children about the Passover sacrifice (Exod. 12.26–27) and in Jesus's command "Do this in remembrance of me" (Luke 22.19), these meals embody, translate, and reinterpret scripture. They speak to an ongoing process of turning water into wine, drawing the living *Torah from daily life, but also, in the New Testament, turning the blood and wine of the *crucifixion back into the milk and water of plain speech (see 1 Cor. 3.2). Biblical meals express an intensely dialogic and historical view of religious understanding, in which human responses approach the divine status of the original revelations.

Nineteenth-century evolutionists explained the prominence of food imagery in the Bible by arguing that the ancient Israelites represented earlier stages of the development from concrete to abstract forms of reasoning; taboos on meat were alleged to be the remnants of animal worship antedating *monotheism. Subsequent research has shown that symbolic or metaphorical reasoning is basic to human cognition, and food imagery is central to most known religions. Commensalism is synonymous with community; but particular cultural evaluations of who should eat what with whom, when, where, and why take many different forms, often subject to close scrutiny and debate precisely because of their critical social role.

Most scholarship on biblical meals has focused on the dietary rules concerning "clean" and "unclean" *animals (Lev. 11; Deut.14), probably because of their salience in debates over the *Law that lead to the eventual differentiation of Judaism and Christianity. The most fruitful scholarship follows Leviticus 11.44 and Deuteronomy 14.2, 21, and some early rabbis, in seeing the rules as expressing and achieving *holiness by mandating the consumption of animals that are "clean" because they conform wholly to the cosmic order of the *creation (Gen. 1) and prohibiting the "unclean" anomalies (see e.g., Mary Douglas, *Purity and Danger*, 1966; R. Bulmer in *Man* 24 [1989]: 302–20; *see also* Purity, Ritual).

Other scholars have emphasized the need for open-ended approaches, taking into account the diversity of Israelites, the paradoxical complexity of their Law, and the ways in which the Law has been continuously reinterpreted over time. For Robert Alter (*Commentary* 68/2 [1979]: 46–52) the holiness achieved by observing the dietary rules includes "vitalism," imitation of God's life-giving powers, expressed in prohibiting blood and creatures found dead, and restricting, but not completely forbidding, the consumption of animals, especially carnivores. Samuel Cooper (in Harvey E. Goldberg, ed., *Judaism Viewed from Within and from Without,* 1987) sees the "laws of mixture" on the separation of meat and milk, linen and wool, and grain and grape as mediating similar contradictions in life giving and taking. Howard Eilberg-Schwartz (*The Savage in Judaism,* 1990) is still more comprehensive, seeing Israelite animal and plant classifications as root metaphors about a people brought into being by a God with no body.

Feeley-Harnik (*The Lord's Table,* 1981) emphasizes the need to look beyond the dietary rules at the broader significance of biblical meals in the light of participants' views of their moral dilemmas—notably, "Who is the true Israelite?" and "Who is my neighbor?"—and in terms of their own modes of analysis—notably *midrash*—in changing social and historical circumstances. Food, articulated in meals, was the embodiment of God's word, divine *Wisdom, for people who would have no *graven images. The food that God provided was the foundation of the *covenant relationship in scripture and in sectarianism; the food God prohibited was *idolatry. During and after the Babylonian *exile (sixth century BCE), as God's word became increasingly identified with the Law, food law came to represent the whole Law. Sectarianism was expressed above all through differing interpretations of the dietary rules. Christians of the first century CE, as observant Jews, used the language of meals to establish both the legitimacy of Jesus and the novelty of his interpretation of the Law, which required different kinds of relations among human beings and God from those advocated by other sectarians.

Biblical meals are part of a larger semantic field, thought-action as a landscape, laid out in Genesis 1–2. The *creation embodies not only vital categories but also vital creative, transformative processes that endow specific foods with particular social values, conveyed in meals. God, as the preeminent gardener, works to produce vital, edible wisdom-food, engendering and sustaining humans who should respond to God and each other in kind. Biblical meals express bodily processes of understanding and communicating that accompany and may even transcend words in the fullest "face-to-face" encounters (Deut. 34.10; 1 Cor. 13.12). Peter's vision of the sheet filled with clean and unclean animals (Acts 10.9–11.18) is one striking example of how early Jewish-

Christians used biblical meals to communicate their "face-to-face" understanding of the Law across the babel of tongues and stomachs that characterize humankind.

See also Lord's Supper.

GILLIAN FEELEY-HARNIK

Measures. *See* Weights and Measures.

Medes. The Medes (Map 7:J3), like the *Persians, were a people of Aryan (Iranian) speech who probably entered the ancient Near East from the north. They were first encountered by the *Assyrians about 835 BCE; they occupied the north Zagros Mountain region and far eastward. The "strong Medes" bred excellent horses and suffered frequent Assyrian incursions. Sargon II in 713 BCE received the submission of some fifty of their chieftains, but in the 670s a leader named Kashtariti (Khshathrita) of Kar-Kashshi in Media was building a formidable power. With Ecbatana (Achmetha) as capital, the Medes soon rose to be rulers of an empire that reached from the central Zagros to Turkestan and included Persis and, by 600 BCE, Armenia and eastern Anatolia as well. Under the warrior king Cyaxares, after a period of Scythian dominance, they had captured *Nineveh in 612 BCE and shared the Assyrian kingdom with the *Babylonians, thus attracting the attention of Jeremiah (51.11, 28; see also Isa. 13.17; 21.2). But in 550 BCE their elderly king Astyages was conquered by *Cyrus the Persian, whose mother was said to have been a Mede.

Under Cyrus the Medes were to some extent corulers of the empire; in fact, for several centuries the outside world continued to apply the name "Mede" to the imperial power (see, e.g., Esther 1.3). But after *Darius usurped the throne the Medes rose unsuccessfully in revolt (522–521 BCE) and lost such privileged status as they had enjoyed. There does, however, seem to have been a considerable Median legacy in the institutions and titulature of the Persian court, and the *Magi who formed the Iranian clergy were in origin a Median clan. The Medes are also mentioned as a nationality in Acts 2.9.

J. M. COOK

Medicine. Although the existence of survivable surgical procedures on the skull (trephination) is attested from the Neolithic through the Arab periods, it is particularly difficult to identify and evaluate the therapeutic value of most specific treatments mentioned in the Bible. Such healing practices include the use of "balsam" from Gilead (Jer. 46.11), "mandrakes" for infertility (Gen. 30.14), and "bandages" (Ezek. 30.21).

Archaeoparasitologists have recently established the probable existence of certain intestinal diseases (e.g., tapeworm [taenia] and whipworm [trichuris trichiura] infections) in ancient Israel, but the precise identification of most diseases in the Bible has been notoriously difficult, especially in cases of epidemics (Num. 25; 1 Sam. 5.6–12). The condition usually translated as "*leprosy" (Hebr. ṣāraʿat) receives the most attention in the Bible (Lev. 13–14), but it does not have a simple modern equivalent because it probably encompassed a large variety of diseases, especially those manifesting chronic discoloration of the skin. Infertility was viewed as an illness that diminished the social status of the afflicted woman (Gen. 30.1–20).

The Hebrew Bible has at least two principal explanations for illness. One, represented by Deuteronomy 28, affirms that health (Hebr. šālôm) encompasses a physical state associated with the fulfillment of *covenant stipulations that are fully disclosed to the members of the society, and illness stems from the violation of those stipulations. Therapy includes reviewing one's actions in light of the covenant. The book of *Job offers a contrasting yet complementary view, which argues that illness may be rooted in divine plans that may not be disclosed to the patient at all and not in the transgression of published rules. The patient must trust that God's undisclosed reasons are just.

Perhaps the most distinctive feature of the Israelite health-care system depicted in the canonical texts is the division into legitimate and illegitimate consultative options for the patient. This dichotomy is partly related to monolatry, insofar as illness and healing rest ultimately on Yahweh's control (Job 5.18) and insofar as non-Yahwistic options are prohibited. Since it was accessible and inexpensive, *prayer to Yahweh was probably the most common legitimate option for a patient. Petitions and thanksgiving prayers uttered from the viewpoint of the patient are attested in the Bible (Ps. 38; Isa. 38.10–20).

Illegitimate options included consultants designated as "healers" (2 Chron. 16.12: Hebr. rōpĕʾîm, NRSV: "physicians"), non-Yahwistic temples (2 Kings 1.2–4), and probably a large variety of "sorcerers" (Deut. 18.10–12). Warnings in the canonical texts, along with archaeological evidence for fertility cults, indicate that such "illegitimate" options were used widely in ancient Israel.

The foremost legitimate consultants in the canonical texts are commonly designated as *prophets, and they were often in fierce competition with "illegitimate" consultants. Stories of healing *miracles (e.g., 2 Kings 4; 8) may reflect an effort to promote prophets as the legitimate consultants. Their function was to provide prognoses (2 Kings 8.8) and intercede on behalf of the patient (2 Kings 5.11). Unlike some of the principal healing consultants in other Near Eastern societies, the efficacy of the Israelite prophets resided more in their relationship with God than in technical expertise. The demise of the prophetic office early in the Second Temple period probably led to the wide legitimation of the rōpĕʾîm (see Sir. 38.1–15).

Another accepted option for some illnesses, particularly in the preexilic period, was the temple. In 1 Samuel 1, Hannah visited the temple at Shiloh to help reverse her infertility. 2 Kings 18.4 indicates that, prior to *Hezekiah, the bronze serpent made by *Moses as a therapeutic device (Num. 21.6–9) was involved in acceptable therapeutic rituals in the *Temple of Jerusalem. Bronze serpents have been found in temples known to have been used for therapy during the first millennium BCE (e.g., the Asclepieion at Pergamon).

By the postexilic period the Priestly code (*P) severely restricted access to the temple for the chronically ill (e.g., "lepers" in Lev. 13–14; cf. 2 Sam. 5.7 on the blind and the lame) because of fear of "impurity." "Leprosy" alone probably encompassed a wide variety of patients. The theology of impurity, as a system of social boundaries, could serve to remove socioeconomically burdensome populations from society, the chronically ill perhaps being the most prominent. In effect, the Priestly code minimizes state responsibility for the chronically ill, leaving the eradication of illness for the future (Ezek. 47.12; cf. Isa. 35.5–6). (See Purity, Ritual.)

Thanksgiving or "well-being" offerings (Lev. 7.11–36) after an illness were probably always acceptable and economically advantageous for the Temple. Offerings after an illness also may have served as public notice of the readmission of previously ostracized patients to society (Lev. 14.1–32).

The community responsible for the *Dead Sea Scrolls added to the priestly list of illnesses that excluded from the normal community and expanded the restrictions for "leprosy," the blind, and the lame (1QSa II.4–9). Socioeconomic reasons, as well as the fear of magical contamination, may be responsible for such increased restrictions.

Perhaps the most far-reaching consequence of the Priestly code was the growth of chronically ill populations with little access to the Temple. Since *Jesus and his disciples appear to target these populations (Matt. 10.8; Mark 14.3), early Christianity may be seen, in part, as a critique of the priestly health-care system. In early Christianity illness may be caused by numerous *demonic entities who are not always acting at Yahweh's command (Matt. 15.22; Luke 11.14; see also Exorcism; Satan) and not necessarily by the violation of covenant stipulations (John 9.2). Emphasizing that the cure for illness may be found in this world, early Christianity preserved many older Jewish traditions regarding miraculous healings (Acts 5.16; 9.34) and collective health (James 5.16), although the influence of Hellenistic healing cults (e.g., the Asclepius cult) also may be seen.

K. Seybold and U. B. Mueller (*Sickness and Healing*, 1978) provide a recent study of biblical medicine, although a new comprehensive study is needed to integrate the recent work by paleopathologists (e.g., Joseph Zias, "Death and Disease in Ancient Israel," *Biblical Archaeologist* 54 [1991]: 146–59) and medical anthropologists (e.g., Arthur Kleinman, *Patients and Healers in the Context of Culture: Explorations of the Borderland Between Anthropology, Medicine and Psychiatry,* 1980).   HECTOR IGNACIO AVALOS

Medicine and the Bible. It is generally agreed that modern Western medicine takes its origin from two main sources, the Greek ideals enshrined in the Hippocratic tradition, to which was added the influence of the biblical teaching of love of one's *neighbor (Lev. 19.18; Luke 10.25–37). Thus, although Western medicine owes much to its classical heritage, especially as this has been reinterpreted since the Renaissance, it was the added dimension of a biblically based ethic that gave it a distinctive approach, centered in a profound respect for the person.

The pragmatism of Greek ideals is reflected in writings dealing with the exposure of unwanted or weak infants and with solutions to the problems of the chronically ill. The latter, being useless to themselves and to the state, should be

allowed to die without medical attention (Plato, *Republic* 407). Biblical religion, on the other hand, had the frame of reference of a transcendent God to whom humankind was ultimately answerable; this gives rise to a profound respect for the dignity and innate value of the individual, seen as created in the image of God (Gen. 1.27). The responsibilities of biblical faith, whether Jewish or Christian, in the relations of people with one another are summed up in texts like "you shall love your neighbor as yourself" (Lev. 19.18) and "Do to others as you would have them do to you" (Matt. 7.12; see Golden Rule). From the standpoint of medicine, this was admirably summed up in the prayer of the great Jewish physician Maimonides (1135–1204 CE): "May I never see in my patient anything else than a fellow creature in pain."

The influence of such biblical precepts introduces an element of moral obligation into medical ethics as it developed in parallel with the rising influence of Christianity in the later Roman empire and throughout the medieval period in Europe. It also provided the spur to the church to establish hospitals that provided care for the sick; refuges that gave shelter to the blind, sufferers from leprosy, the mentally ill, and others outcast from society; and dispensaries for the poor. This same obligation, at a much later stage, led to the development of medical missionary work in conjunction with, yet distinct from, the growth of evangelistic concern that took place in the nineteenth century.

In providing a moral base for such developments, the Bible has given to modern medicine a great deal more than it might now care to acknowledge. Nevertheless, the centrality of respect for the person that originates in the Bible has now become enshrined in modern medical codes, such as the Geneva Convention Code of Ethics (1949) and the Helsinki Convention (1964) of the World Medical Association.

On the other hand, as a result of the ways in which the Bible has been interpreted and applied, there have been times when its influence on medicine has been negative. Until there was any proper understanding of the causative factors in disease and the actual disease processes themselves, there was a tendency to see sickness as the result of divine visitations and punishment for wrongdoing. The Bible itself knows little of physicians as such (see Medicine), and in the faith of Israel it was God alone who was the healer and giver of life. Most references to physicians are uncomplimentary (as in Mark 5.25–26, more temperately put in Luke 8.43) or at best neutral. Other than the reference to Luke "the beloved physician" (Col. 4.14), the only positive remarks about medical practitioners occur in Sirach 38.1–15, where the reader is exhorted to "honor physicians for their services." Even in this passage, however, the emphasis is on the need for confession of sin before any true healing could take place and the role of God as healer. (Note the much later dictum of Ambroise Paré [1510–1590]: "I treated the patient, but God healed him.")

In the Bible itself, it is the religious component that dominates in a situation where religion and medicine are inextricably bound together. This is seen particularly in Israel's legal codes, which did not separate physical disease from ritual *purity. Thus, while the sanitary code of the *Torah contains regulations that were of major importance in the promotion of health and the prevention of epidemic diseases in the community, they are set within a religious framework. Ultimately, it was God alone who sent disease and disaster as a punishment for wrongdoing or, alternatively, rewarded the good with health and well-being (see, e.g., Exod. 15.26; Deut. 7.12–15).

The establishment of such a causal relationship between disease and a failure to meet religious and moral obligations was, in some sense, an attempt to answer the unanswerable question, "Why me?" It was seen especially with regard to contagious and disfiguring diseases, of which the best example is the disease complex unfortunately called *leprosy in most English translations. Various ritual prescriptions were applied to such diseases in order to avoid the contamination of the community, which was seen as more important than the healing of the sick person. Similar ritual restrictions were also imposed in relation to normal physiological functions (see, e.g., Lev. 12; 15.16–33). Thus, consulting a physician for help could be construed as denial of the primary role of God and evidence of lack of faith in him, as well as lack of willingness to acknowledge personal sin (2 Chron. 16.12).

Many of these concepts were perpetuated in Christianity, even though such a simplistic viewpoint was challenged in the Bible (e.g., in the book of *Job and John 9.1–3). The early church, however, undoubtedly interpreted such views too literally, and medical treatment was displaced by an emphasis on prayer and fasting in order to chasten the individual. From the Re-

naissance onward, however, medicine and theology became increasingly divorced from one another, allowing the development of medicine along the now-familiar lines of scientific principles from the sixteenth or seventeenth centuries onward. Nonetheless, there has always been in Christianity a healing ministry that has been seen as biblically based (see, e.g., Luke 10.9). In general, this has not been considered as in competition with orthodox medicine but rather as complementary to it. Some more recent developments in healing ministries derived from biblical literalism, however, seem to be an attempt to return to a prescientific worldview, and will inevitably be in conflict with modern medical practice.

J. KEIR HOWARD

Meek. The English word "meek" is now largely archaic, and recent translations of the Bible use it far less frequently than earlier versions. Its connotations of gentleness and humility are not entirely accurate representations of the word it generally translates in the Hebrew Bible, where ʿānāw and its cognates refer primarily to socioeconomic and political deprivation; the ʿānāwîm are the *poor, the oppressed, whose special protector is God. They are both individuals within the community and Israel as a totality as well: their persecutors will be defeated and they will inherit the land (Ps. 37.11). Earlier suggestions that they were an identifiable political group are now generally rejected.

On occasion the Hebrew words in question seem to refer to an inner attitude of humility as well; the "meek" are somehow closer to God (see Num. 12.3; Zeph. 2.3). This spiritual connotation is dominant in the word used to translate ʿānāw in the *Septuagint. The word *praos* and its cognates are widely used in Greek literature to describe an admirable moral quality of gentle and genial composure, and this is its dominant sense in the New Testament, where it is used of both Jesus (Matt. 11.29; 2 Cor. 10.1) and his followers (Col. 3.12; 1 Tim. 6.1; 1 Pet. 3.4).

The beatitude in Matthew 5.5 that describes the meek inheriting the earth is clearly derived from Psalm 37.11, and Jesus probably intended its original, concrete sense, but in view of Matthew's spiritualization of other beatitudes with parallels in Luke 6.20–23, the meek seem for Matthew at least to be those who are not only socioeconomically deprived but patiently accepting of their status as well. (See Sermon on the Mount.)

MICHAEL D. COOGAN

Megiddo. Situated southeast of Mount Carmel at the western approach to the Jezreel Valley (Map 1:X3), Megiddo assumed geopolitical significance throughout its long occupation (early fourth millennium to early fourth century BCE). The 5.25-hectare (13-acre) site thrived at the juncture of major international trade routes connecting the northeast (*Hazor, *Damascus), the northern Israelite and *Phoenician coasts (Acco, Tyre, Sidon), and the south-central coast of Israel (Sharon Plain, Philistia, Egypt). Several archaeological expeditions have revealed significant remains from every period, including: Early-Middle Bronze Age Canaanite temple complexes with a circular altar; a Late Bronze Age treasury containing beautifully carved ivories; and multiphased gate structures, palaces, stables (or storerooms), a sophisticated water system, and grain storage facilities from the Israelite period. Besides archaeological data, Egyptian, Assyrian, and biblical records illuminate Megiddo's history. The latter mention the Israelites' inability to control this region during the settlement period (compare Josh. 12.21 with Judg. 1.27–28); *Solomon's royal building activities here during the United Monarchy (1 Kings 9.15–19); and *Josiah's ill-fated attempt to intercept at Megiddo Egyptian military aid for *Assyria against *Babylon (2 Kings 23.28–30). Later eschatological references mention the valley around *Armageddon (Hill of Megiddo) as the site of the final battle between the forces of good and evil (Rev. 16.12–16).   RON TAPPY

Megillot. The name, meaning "scrolls," given to the collection of the five shortest books of the Writings, the third section of the Hebrew Bible. The Megillot are *Song of Solomon, *Ruth, *Lamentations, *Ecclesiastes, and *Esther. Although the current order of the books in printed Bibles follows their order in the annual Jewish liturgical cycle, in some older traditions they were arranged according to traditional chronology: Ruth, Song of Solomon, Ecclesiastes, Lamentations, Esther (see also *b. B. Bat.* 14b). The Song of Solomon is read on the feast of *Passover, as well as preceding the service welcoming the *Sabbath on Friday evenings; the love poetry of the Song is thought to represent in the former case the marriage of God and Israel and in the latter the marriage of Israel and Queen Sabbath. Ruth is read at *Pentecost (Shavu'ot); among the reasons given are the setting of Ruth at the time of the barley harvest (Ruth 1.22), the tradition

that King *David, one of Ruth's descendants, was born and died at this time, and the relationship between Israel's assumption of the *Torah at Mount Sinai seven weeks after the *Exodus and Ruth's acceptance of Judaism. Lamentations, a series of dirges commemorating the destruction of *Jerusalem and the *Temple, is read on the ninth of the month of Ab, a fast day on which these events, and the destruction of the Second Temple as well, are said to have taken place. The somber mood of Ecclesiastes, read in the fall on the Feast of Booths (Sukkot), is thought to be a reflection of the season. Esther is read on Purim, the joyous holiday celebrating the salvation of the Jews as related in the book.

See also Canon, *article on* The Order of Books in the Hebrew Bible; Lectionaries, *article on* Jewish Traditions.   CARL S. EHRLICH

Melchizedek. The king of Salem and priest of God Most High (El Elyon; *see* Names of God) who met Abram when the latter was returning victorious from battle. When Melchizedek met the patriarch, he gave Abram bread and wine, and he blessed him by God Most High. Abram in turn gave the priest a tenth of the spoils (Gen. 14.17–20).

Later tradition identified Salem with *Jerusalem (Ps. 76.2), the city that King *David conquered and transformed into his capital. Apparently David tried to unite royal and sacerdotal power by appropriating the order of Melchizedek, the king-priest (Ps. 110.4).

The author of the letter to the *Hebrews, citing Psalm 110.4, argues that *Jesus is a *priest forever after the order of Melchizedek (Heb. 5.6, 10; 6.20; 7.17). The fact that *Abraham paid him *tithes shows how great Melchizedek was (Heb. 7.4). The fact that Melchizedek blessed Abraham establishes Melchizedek's superiority, for the greater always blesses the inferior (Heb. 7.7). Jesus, being in the same order, is therefore greater than Abraham, too.

One of the *Dead Sea Scrolls (11QMelch) portrays Melchizedek as a heavenly being who will bring salvation (in fulfillment of Isa. 52.7–10 and 61.1–3) and judgment (in fulfillment of Pss. 7.7–8; 82.1–2) at the conclusion of the final jubilee (Lev. 25).

In *gnostic literature, Melchizedek is variously represented as the one who brings the baptismal waters and as one who gathers and emits light. One of the *Nag Hammadi documents describes him as a prominent heavenly priest and warrior figure who, in being baptized, offered himself in sacrifice, in a way reminiscent of Jesus.

In the Slavonic version of 2 *Enoch, Melchizedek's old and sterile mother conceived him miraculously, apart from sexual intercourse. He was taken to *paradise, where he was to be the head of all future priests. The text speaks of the last generation when a new Melchizedek will arise; greater than all his predecessors, he will work miracles and rule as king and priest.

WILLIAM B. NELSON, JR.

Mene, Mene, Tekel, and Parsin. The banquet of King *Belshazzar, described in Daniel 5, was disrupted by a divine apparition; a hand etching the words "Mene Mene Teqel Upharsin" (u being a form of the common Semitic conjunction meaning "and") on the plaster of a wall.

Ancient evidence suggests that the repetiton of "mene" in v. 25 may be scribal error (see v. 26). Others interpret the first "mene" as a verbal form meaning "he has weighed."

The inability of the various diviners to elicit sense from the inscription (Dan. 5.8) was most likely rooted in their failure to understand the meaning behind the words rather than to read the words themselves. In 1886, Charles Clermont-Ganneau suggested that the terms reflect ancient *weights or measures: mina, shekel, and half-shekel; this view is now widely held. The meaning of the inscription as interpreted by *Daniel, however, lies not in these nouns but in the verbal notions behind them: Belshazzar's kingdom was numbered *(mnh);* he was weighed *(tql);* his kingdom was divided *(prs)* between the *Medes and the *Persians.

JAMES H. PLATT

Menorah. The seven-branched candelabrum of the wilderness *tabernacle and Jerusalem *Temples, it was typical of Iron Age elevated metal structures combining the functions of lampstand and lamp. The tabernacle menorah, anachronistically described in the postexilic Priestly code (*P) (Exod. 25.31–40 and 37.17–24), was said to have been hammered, together with all of its lamps and utensils, from one whole talent (ca. 44 kg [96 lb]) of pure gold by the craftsman Bezalel. Based on a tripod, three branches curved from both sides of a vertical shaft; these, with the central stem, were decorated with cups carved in the shape of open almond blossoms, the uppermost holding the lamps. These botanical mo-

tifs may reflect tree of life symbolism, common in the ancient Near East.

According to 1 Kings 7.39 (and 2 Chron. 4.7), ten pure gold lampstands, which are not described in detail, together with gold accoutrements, adorned Solomon's Temple, five on the south side of the main hall, and five on the north. The Second Temple, following the priestly directions for the wilderness tabernacle, had one golden menorah. According to Josephus (*Ant.* 3.8.199), three of its lamps burned all day; the rest were lit in the evening. The *Talmud relates that the westernmost lamp, closest to the Holy of Holies, was never extinguished (*b. Yoma* 33a). The menorah was removed in 169 BCE by Antiochus Epiphanes IV (1 Macc. 4.49–50) during his desecration of the Temple. Judas Maccabee supplied a new menorah, together with other vessels, during the Temple's cleansing (1 Macc. 4.49–50; 2 Macc. 10.3). Josephus recounts that when Herod's Temple was destroyed in 70 CE, the menorah was carried by the Romans in Titus's triumphal march (*War* 7.5.148–9). The Temple menorah seems to be depicted on the Arch of Titus in Rome, although there is some controversy over this rendition's accuracy, particularly regarding the double octagonal pedestal, since according to all Jewish sources and considerable archeological evidence, the menorah stood on three legs. After 70 CE, the menorah became an enduring Jewish religious and national symbol, frequently appearing in synagogue, domestic, and funerary art; it appears today on the emblem of the State of Israel.

JUDITH R. BASKIN

Mercy of God. The concept of a loving and merciful god is ancient, found in hymns to Egyptian, Sumerian, and Babylonian deities. In the *Ugaritic texts, the high god El is formulaically described as merciful and compassionate, with a cognate of the same word used two millennia later in Muslim characterization of God. Several Hebrew words have traditionally been translated by the English word "mercy," including *ḥānan, ḥesed,* and especially *rāḥamîm.* The last is derived from the word for uterus *(reḥem),* and is remarkable both for its maternal nuance and for its persistence in biblical and nonbiblical descriptions of male deities. The nuance is made explicit in Isaiah 49.14–15, a rare instance of maternal *metaphor to describe the God of Israel.

One of the oldest characterizations of Yahweh is found in Exodus 34.6–7, quoted or alluded to frequently (e.g., Num. 14.18; Joel 2.13; Pss. 86.15; 103.8; 111.4; 145.8; Neh. 9.17; Jon. 4.2; Eph. 2.4; cf. Ps. 77.7–9). This ancient liturgical fragment describes Yahweh as "merciful (*raḥûm*) and gracious (*ḥannûn*), slow to anger, and abounding in steadfast love . . . forgiving iniquity and transgression and sin . . . yet by no means clearing the guilty, but visiting the iniquity of the parents upon the children and the children's children," and thus raises one of the most profound dilemmas of monotheism, the tension between divine mercy and justice. Biblical tradition itself offers a partial corrective to the theory of inherited, and thus implicitly collective, guilt, notably in Ezekiel 18. But the more profound paradox of a God believed to be merciful and forgiving on the one hand and ultimately just on the other remains unresolved. The Bible is of course not an abstract theological treatise, and so it is not surprising that there is no detailed exposition of the problem. But it is one to which biblical writers frequently return, in narratives (Jonah; Luke 15), dialogue (Job; cf. Ecclesiastes; Rom. 9), and especially in *prayers (Ps. 130.3–4; Dan. 9.7–9; cf Hab. 3.2), where the hope of the worshipper is that God's mercy will prevail over his justice (see Hos. 11.8–9; James 2.13). This hope is based on the realization of the essential unworthiness of those chosen by God; the election of Israel, and the *salvation of the Christian, were motivated by gratuitous divine love (Deut. 7.7–8; Ps. 103.6–18; Titus 3.5).

God's mercy is also a model for human conduct. "Those who fear the Lord" are characterized as "gracious (*ḥannûn*), merciful (*raḥûm*), and righteous" in Psalm 112.4, phrasing that echoes the immediately preceding description of Yahweh in the similarly *acrostic Psalm 111.4. Resuming this theme, Jesus commands his followers to imitate divine mercy according to Luke 6.36 (cf. Matt. 5.43–48). *See also* Covenant; Evil; Grace; Suffering.   MICHAEL D. COOGAN

Mesopotamia. A Greek name meaning "between the rivers." As used by Greek writers from the second century BCE, it denotes the land between the Tigris and *Euphrates rivers from roughly the northern and western borders of present-day Iraq to where the two rivers came close together near present-day Baghdad (Map 14:H3).

"Mesopotamia" occurs eight times in the NRSV (Deut. 23.4; 1 Chron. 19.6; Jth. 2:24; 5:7–8; 8:26; Acts 2:9; 7.2). In the first two cases, the

Hebrew is *'ăram nahărayim*, meaning "Aram of the two rivers"; the Hebrew transliterated as Aram-naharaim is used in the NRSV three times (Gen. 24.10; Judg. 3.8; Ps. 60:1). The *Septuagint has "Mesopotamia" at Genesis 24.10 and Deuteronomy 23.4, but "Syria of rivers" at Judges 3.8 and "Syria of Mesopotamia" at 1 Chronicles 19.6.

The phrase "Aram of the two rivers" is similar to "Aram of Bet-Rehov" (2 Sam. 10.6), "Aram of Damascus" (2 Sam. 8.5), and "Aram of Zobah" (2 Sam. 10.6); strictly, it means Aramean territory between the two rivers, that is, northwest Iraq and northeast Syria. Where the Septuagint has "Mesopotamia," this is not a translation of the Hebrew but the use of an equivalent geographical name. Because of the difference in meaning between the modern use of "Mesopotamia" and the ancient use, translations are not consistent in the use of the term, and modern tendency is to avoid the word altogether or to modify it.

For further treatment of the history and cultures of Mesopotamia, see Assyria; Babylon; Sumer.

J. W. ROGERSON

Messiah. The term denotes an expected or longed-for savior, especially in Jewish tradition, where some applied it to the revolutionary Simon Bar Kokhba (d. 135 CE), the mystic Shabbetai Zevi (1626–1676), and other "false messiahs," and in Christianity, where it is exclusively applied to *Jesus Christ.

The word is derived from the common biblical Hebrew word *māšîaḥ*, meaning "anointed." In Greek it is transcribed as *messias* and translated as *christos*. In the Hebrew Bible, the term is most often used of kings, whose investiture was marked especially by *anointing with oil (Judg. 9.8–15; 2 Sam. 5.3; 1 Kings 1.39; Ps. 89.20; Sir. 46.13), and who were given the title "the Lord's anointed" (e.g., 1 Sam. 2.10; 12.3; 2 Sam 23.1; Pss. 2.2; 20.6; 132.17; Lam. 4.20). It is even used of *Cyrus, king of the *Medes and *Persians (Isa. 45.1). There is a possibility that some prophets may have been anointed (see 1 Kings 19.16; cf. Isa. 61.1), and according to some texts the investiture of *priests includes anointing too (Exod. 29.7; Lev. 4.3, 5, 16; Sir. 45.15), though this probably reflects political developments after the fall of the monarchy; the title is not normally given to priests or prophets. In a passage from Zechariah dated 520 BCE, where king and priest are described as "the two anointed ones," the term *māšiaḥ* is avoided (Zech 4.14; cf. 6.9–14). By Maccabean times, however, it is used of the high priest (Dan. 9.26).

In its primary biblical usage, then, "anointed" is, virtually a synonym for "king," in particular *David and his descendants, and it should be understood in the context of the royal ideology documented in the books of *Samuel, *Kings, and *Psalms, even when it is applied secondarily to priests and others. The king was appointed by divine command (1 Sam 10.1; 16.1–13; Ps. 45.7), and he was adopted as *son of God (2 Sam 7.14; Ps. 2.7; cf. 89.26). His own person was sacrosanct (1 Sam 24.6), the future of his dynasty was divinely protected (2 Sam 7.12–16; 22.51; Ps. 89.4, 36–37), and he was the unique instrument of God's justice on earth (2 Sam. 23.3; 1 Kings 3.28; Pss. 45.4; 72.1–4; cf. 2 Sam. 14.4; 2 Kings 3.28). As with the ideals and the realities of *Zion, the *Temple, the priesthood, and other institutions, the gap between the ideals of Davidic *kingship and historical reality widened (e.g., 1 Kings 11.6; 2 Kings 16.1–4; 21.1–18; cf. Deut. 17.14–17), and eventually royal language and imagery came to be applied primarily to a hoped-for future king, whose reign would be characterized by everlasting justice, security, and peace (Isa. 11.1–5; 32.1; Jer. 33.14–26; Ezek. 37.24–28). Such a figure is popularly known as "the messiah," and biblical texts that describe him are known as "messianic," though the term "messiah" itself does not occur with this sense in the Hebrew Bible.

At the heart of biblical messianism is the idea that God intervenes in history by sending a savior to deliver his people from suffering and injustice. Influenced by the *Exodus tradition (e.g., Exod. 2.19; 3.7–12), the stories of *Joshua and *Judges (cf. Judg. 2.16, 18), and established religious institutions, this messianic hope crystallized into several models. The first is that of a king like David who would conquer the powers of evil by force of arms (Gen 49.10; Num. 24.17; Pss. 2.9; 18.31–42) and establish a reign of justice and peace (Isa. 9.2–7; 11.1–5). In some passages his wisdom is referred to (Isa. 9.6; 11.2; cf. 1 Kings 3.9; Prov. 8.15–16; 24.5–6), in others his gentleness and humility (Isa. 42.2–3; Zech. 9.9–10). Emphasis is on the divine initiative (2 Sam. 7.8–16; Jer. 33.14–16; Hag. 2.21–23) and on the result of the action, so that some visions of a "messianic" age make little or no mention of the messiah himself (e.g., Isa. 2.2–4; 11.6–9; 32.1, 16–20; 65.17–25; Amos 9.11–15).

Belief in a priestly messiah, son of *Aaron, who would arise alongside the Davidic messiah to save Israel, appears in the *Dead Sea Scrolls (e.g., 1QS 9.1). The mysterious figure of *Melchizedek (Gen 14.18) provides a title for one who is at the same time both king and priest (Ps. 110.4; Heb. 7). A third model is that of a prophet, anointed to "bring good news to the oppressed" (Isa. 61.1; 11Q Melch. 18; Luke 4.18). The belief that a prophet like *Moses would arise (Deut. 18.18; Acts 3.22), known as Taheb ("he who brings back"), is central to *Samaritan messianism (cf. John 4.25).

Finally, the tradition that the divinely appointed savior should suffer (Luke 24.26; Acts 3.18) has its roots in numerous *psalms attributed to David (e.g., 22; 55; 88), as well as in the traditional picture of Moses and the prophets as rejected and persecuted by their people (Exod. 16.2; 17.2–4; Jer. 11.18–19; 20.7–10; Matt. 23.37). The notion that his suffering or self-sacrifice is in itself saving (cf. Exod 32.32; Isa. 53.5, 10, 12) is given a unique emphasis in Christian messianism (e.g., Rom. 5.6–8; Gal. 3.13; cf. Acts 8.32; 1 Pet. 2.24–25).

JOHN F. A. SAWYER

Messianic Secret. The use of the term "messianic secret" arose at the beginning of the twentieth century with the publication of Wilhelm Wrede's *Das Messiasgeheimnis in den Evangelien* (1901), translated into English under the title *The Messianic Secret* (Cambridge, 1971). Wrede started from an assumption that was widely held in critical biblical studies, namely, that the historical *Jesus was not conscious of being more than a Jewish prophet, and that his claims were in no way messianic. After his *crucifixion, however, his disciples were convinced that he had risen from the dead and therefore must have been the *Messiah who was foretold in scripture.

When looking back, Christians of the first generation were, according to Wrede, puzzled by the lack of consistency between the picture of Jesus of Nazareth that was presented by the traditions of his earthly life and their own belief in a risen Lord. Therefore *Mark, the author of the oldest written gospel, removed the offense by introducing into his narrative sayings in which Jesus told his followers and people he dealt with not to disclose his true nature. The injunctions to silence in different sayings are therefore not historical reminiscences but an editorial device created by the evangelist. This means that Wrede's thesis is one of the earliest attempts to elucidate the process of redaction in the formation of the Gospels. *Matthew and *Luke have retained, though not consistently, the core of Mark's redactional scheme.

According to Wrede, the texts that have been arranged with the intention to portray Jesus as attempting to conceal his messiahship include the following: *exorcisms where Jesus silences the confessions pronounced by *demons (Mark 1.23–25, 34; 3.11–12), miraculous healings (1.43–45; 5.43; 7.36; 8.26), intentional retirement (7.24; 9.30–32), a command to keep silent addressed to a disciple (8.29–30), private teaching given to the *disciples (4.34; 7.18–23; 9.28–29; 9.31–32; 10.32–34; 13.3–37), and the saying about parabolic teaching (4.10–13). All these passages are interpreted in light of Mark 9.9: "He ordered them to tell no one about what they had seen, until the Son of Man had risen from the dead. So they kept the matter to themselves."

Since Wrede published his book it has become evident that the presentation of Jesus in the *synoptic Gospels is more complicated and cannot be explained by assuming a simple redactional pattern. In only one narrative, Peter's confession (Mark 8.29–30), does the injunction to silence refer explicitly to messiahship. On the other hand, there are numerous instances where the "messianic character" of a saying or an action is by no means being concealed: the feeding of the five thousand (Mark 6.32–44), the triumphal entry into Jerusalem (11.1–11), and, not least, the trial and condemnation of Jesus, when he was found guilty of claiming to be the king of the Jews (15.2, 9, 26; cf. 14.61). It can be said that in the public ministry of Jesus there is constant paradox of secrecy and revelation, of concealment and proclamation. Mark reports exorcisms where no command to keep silent is given (5.1–20; 7.24–30; 9.14–29).

The same paradox can be observed in narratives where miraculous healings are reported. In these cases the injunctions to silence, when given, have obviously nothing to do with a messianic secret. Not one of the healing *miracles performed publicly gives the impression that Jesus was the Messiah. When the blind Bartimaeus twice hails him as Son of David, it is not Jesus who silences him (Mark 10.47–49). When Jesus cured sick people, the injunction to secrecy was primarily a matter of privacy. The raising of Jairus's daughter shows the paradox inherent in one single narrative (5.35–43).

Teaching in *parables is another context where the motif of secrecy is apparent, yet in another

modulation and without reference to messiahship. As used in Mark 4.1–13, the quotation from Isaiah 6.9 does not simply imply that Jesus' *parables were intended to conceal a mystery. What is meant is that parables were a way by which to test the serious intention of the listeners: "To those who have, more will be given; and from those who have not, even what they have will be taken away" (4.25; cf. 4.33–34). It is a question of response, which is essentially different from concealment as a literary device.

The paradox of secrecy and publicity appears also in Jesus' sayings about the *Son of man, as they are presented by Mark. The reference to Daniel 7 is clear, and in that text a heavenly figure corresponds to the suffering saints. In the sayings that were publicly pronounced, the enigmatic symbol of the Son of man stands for authority (e.g., Mark 2.10, 28; 8.38; 14.62). In the instruction given privately to the disciples, the Son of man and his followers are to face trials, suffering, and death on their way to the final kingdom (8.31–34; 9.12, 31; 10.33–34, 45; 13.24–27; cf. Dan. 7.25–27).

In the final analysis, the paradox of secrecy and publicity is inherent in different layers of reminiscences from the earthly life of Jesus, layers that precede the christological interpretation worked out by the early church. Jesus stands out as possessing more than human authority. His words and his actions are charged with a transcendent rather than a messianic significance. This is intimated in his private teaching, but he did not want it to be proclaimed (Mark 8.29–30; cf. 9.9). When unclean spirits and demons recognized him as more than human, they were silenced and defeated (3.11–12; 5.2–13). The motif of secrecy can thus be discerned in the synoptic Gospels in different variations, apparently more original in Mark, sublimated by continuing christological reflection in Matthew and Luke. The underlying prerequisite is the essential choice by those confronted with Jesus, between belief and unbelief.

HARALD RIESENFELD

Metaphors. The principal subject of the Bible is God in his relation to his world, his people, and humanity. But the God of the Bible is holy, transcendent, other, unlike anything in all creation. It follows, then, that language about God must be figurative, because it attempts to describe in terms of this world one who is totally different from this world.

We can speak about God and our relation to

him, however, because he has revealed himself through his own words and deeds in the history recorded in the scriptures. All metaphoric language about God must be consonant with that self-revelation in order to be true.

God is known in the biblical account only in relationship. The five most frequent metaphors of his relationship with his people are king/subject, judge/litigant, husband/wife, father/child, and lord or master/servant. All are commissive metaphors, implying an obligation in the relationship described.

Yet every metaphoric term for God breaks its limits and transforms the way in which it is ordinarily understood. For example, when God is described as father, the term is filled with the meaning given it by God's self-revelation, and human fathers then become responsible for growing up into the measure of God's compassionate and loving fatherhood. In short, metaphors for God come to define the goal of human life, which is to conform to the image of God.

None of the metaphors for God are intended to be taken literally in their human sense, a fact sometimes overlooked. For example, God as father or husband is never literally male, nor does he exercise sexual functions. Similarly, the use of metaphoric language for God says nothing about the historicity of his deeds and words.

Many terms for God participate in metaphoric systems and undergo rich development in the scriptures. God as father is source of life, names, care, love, discipline, family unity, and an example to children; he feeds, clothes, gives *inheritance, legal rights, property, home, and a sense of belonging. Because such a metaphoric system is involved, God is never called mother in the Bible, though he exercises mother-like love and care for his children. Female terms for God are used in the Bible only in similes, pointing to one activity (see Feminism and the Bible). If they are interpreted as metaphors, the deity is then connected with the images of birth and suckling, and they erroneously result in the view of a goddess giving birth to all things and persons, who then participate in the divine being. The distinction that the Bible insists on between creator and creature is then lost.

Figures for God can have a high or low degree of correspondence with their referents. When God is described as like a bear, lion, leopard, moth, withering wind, devouring fire, eagle, or even dry rot, the correspondence is low, and such images are used for their shock or surprise value. More appropriate are the descriptions of

God as rock, sun, living water, fortress, refuge; similarly, the descriptions of his actions in terms of those of a healer, potter, vintner, builder, farmer, tailor, shepherd, or warrior yield vivid pictures. Indeed, God is most often portrayed in anthropomorphic terms; this prevents his identification with some diffuse soul of nature, and it expresses the fact that he meets us person to person and demands from us the full depth of our personal devotion and love.

Some metaphors for God have lost their meaning because they have lost their context, such as the metaphor "*redeemer," which originally referred to a relative who bought back a family member from *slavery. The metaphor is recovered when the original context is recalled. Similarly, some figures become objectionable to some groups, for example, those of God as mighty warrior or as judge or, for feminists, as father or lord. But such metaphors are indispensable to the canonical witness to God and should be recovered by an explication of their full biblical content.

Human beings' relation to God is also described metaphorically because it deals with that which is evident only to the eyes of the faithful and must describe the unknown in terms of the known. Thus, God's faithful people are called in the Bible his adopted sons or children, his bride, kingdom of priests, holy nation, peculiar treasure, servants, jewels, witnesses, noble vine, pleasant planting, fruitful trees, and so on.

The church, in the New Testament, is called the new *Jerusalem, the bride of Christ, the true *circumcision, the Israel of God, the body of Christ, God's temple, building, field, his covenant people, new creation, or colony of heaven. Church members are pilgrims, aliens, exiles, strangers on the earth, slaves of righteousness or of Christ, heirs, fools for Christ, citizens of heaven, or ministers of reconciliation. Christ himself is their righteousness, sanctification, redemption, first fruits, covenant, temple, high priest, sacrifice, word, or wisdom and power of God. He is called priest after the order of *Melchizedek, man of heaven, *Son of God, servant, last *Adam, *Son of man, *Messiah, and Lord.

The life of faith is described in an almost limitless stock of pictures. It is soaring or being set in a broad place or on the heights. It is enjoying freedom, light, order, joy, life. It is being granted never-failing water and food, knowing shade and rest. It is experiencing the gift of a new heart and spirit.

On the other hand, the life of faithlessness is

described as slavery to sin and death, and sinners are compared to rebels, disobedient sons, adulterous wives, whores, worms, backsliders, dead bones, waterless clouds, fruitless trees, wild waves, wandering stars, restless young camels, plunging horses, wild asses, rudderless ships, stubborn heifers, dogs, wilting grass, and choking tares. They are the old Adam, those of the flesh, cursed by God, and slaves to the principalities and powers of this present evil darkness.

Some metaphor systems permeate the Bible from beginning to end, for example, those connected with the *Exodus, or with the *Temple and sacrificial system, or the *law court. Other metaphors, such as those of light and darkness, are given expression by many different words (cf. morning star, dayspring on high), while others draw on the perennial relationships and rounds of family life, as well as birth and death.

Metaphors may change their meaning from one context to another. Thus, the *wilderness can be an expression of danger and judgment or of love and care; a yoke can be a figure of sin or of faithfulness. Meanings can be determined only by the context and by the intention of the author.

Other metaphorical forms, such as those of synecdoche, eponymy, metonomy, *parable, and allegory are frequent in the scriptures. The Bible is rich in figurative terms, of which we use only a very small portion.

See also Literature, The Bible as; Symbols.

ELIZABETH ACHTEMEIER

Methuselah. One of the long-lived ancestors before the *Flood. In the Sethite *genealogy in Genesis 5.21–27 (see also 1 Chron. 1.3; Luke 3.37), which lists one male for each of the ten generations from *Adam to *Noah, Methuselah is listed eighth, the son of *Enoch and the grandfather of Noah. Methuselah is the longest lived (969 years), but all ten live to remarkably high ages, as do the pre-Flood ancestors of Mesopotamian tradition. The name Methusaleh is very like Methushael, listed as Lamech's father and Enoch's great grandson in the similar genealogy in Genesis 4 (seven male ancestors from *Cain to Noah).   JO ANN HACKETT

Micah, The Book of.

The Author. Micah, a shortened form of Micaiah (which occurs in Jer. 26.18), means "Who is like Yah(weh)?" He was a person of whom we know practically nothing other than his place of origin, which was Moresheth (Mic. 1.1) or Moresheth-gath (1.18), a tiny village in the Judean foothills (Map 8:W5). (Mic. 1.8–16, doubtless Micah's own words, confirms the information in the title of the book supplied late by an editor at 1.1, since here he seems to be speaking of the small part of the world that he knew best.) From other internal evidence it is likely too that the other data of the opening title are valid, namely, that he spoke "in the days of Kings Jotham, Ahaz, and Hezekiah of Judah." He was, in other words, a Judahite seer or prophet, roughly contemporary with the much better known *Isaiah.

Although Micah's comments on Judean society strongly parallel those of his presumed contemporary and supplement them to a large degree, there is a pronounced difference in tone between the prophecies of Isaiah and Micah. Micah's is the voice of the countryside, of one who has empirical knowledge of the result of the evil policies that Isaiah, an aristocrat of *Jerusalem, could only surmise, however much he wanted to empathize with the suffering of his compatriots. Micah was presumably from the common people, one who felt himself called on in that age of turmoil to speak in the name of Israel's God against evils that were no longer tolerable.

The Times. Although the book of Micah may contain much material that was added to or expanded on that of the original prophetic author, its nucleus goes back to Micah of Moresheth, who, in the latter part of the eighth century BCE, was protesting the internal dissolution of his country and of its religious and national nerve. His prophetic career may have begun about 725 BCE when it had become evident that the northern kingdom of *Israel—where prophecy had begun and which had always been the "elder sister" of the kingdom of *Judah to the south (Ezek. 23.1–3)—was now doomed to disappear into the outreaches of the voracious *Assyrian empire. Judah, by a combination of cynical statecraft, collaborationism, and religiously unacceptable compromise, would still be able to hold off the inevitable for a time; indeed, it outlasted the Assyrians only to become prey to their Neo-Babylonian successors. But this was done by the sacrifice of national and religious integrity, and in the end the result was the same, as Ezekiel (chap. 23) pointed out after the fact.

The Book. The book of Micah, as has already been suggested, begins with the work of an eighth-century BCE prophet whose words have been adapted to changed conditions, added to, and amplified in later generations. This process says nothing against the transmission of the biblical word but rather enhances its integrity. The biblical word, in the mind of those who preserved and developed biblical traditions, was not dead, said for one time, but a living word that could continue to inspire the faith community in which it had been engendered to further insights into the mind of God. Accordingly, the contents of the book of Micah can be outlined as follows:

1.1	A title from a later Judahite editor
1.2–7	A judgment on *Samaria: Micah's, but later edited into a universal judgment
1.8–16	Micah's lament over Judah of his day
2.1–5	Micah's particular condemnation of the exploiters
2.6–11	Micah's retort to the "naysayers" of prophecy
2.12–13	Vision of a "new Israel" inspired by Second Isaiah or Ezekiel
3.1–4	Micah's judgment against the rulers of Judah
3.5–8	Against the "prophets of peace" (cf. Jer. 6.14; 8.11)
3.9–12	The end of Jerusalem
4.1–4	The eschatological *Zion: a postexilic hymn (= Isa. 2.2–4)
4.5–8	Yahweh and the gods; probably a postexilic fantasy
4.9–11	An exilic or postexilic realization of Judah's fate in the Babylonian period
4.11–5.1	The siege of Jerusalem: *Sennacherib's in 701?
5.2–6	The ruler to come; possibly Micah's words
5.7–9	The restoration of the *remnant of Jacob; obviously exilic or postexilic
5.10–15	An oracle of judgment, probably Micah's
6.1–8	God's lawsuit against Israel, possibly Micah's
6.9–16	God's judgment on social injustice, especially of the northern kingdom; probably Micah's, at least substantively
7.1–7	Another condemnation of social justice, probably by Micah
7.8–10	Recovery of Zion; some postexilic prophet
7.11–20	Rebuilding of Zion and Zion's prayer; some prophet after 445 BCE.

BRUCE VAWTER, C.M.

Michael. One of the *archangels, whose name is a rhetorical question meaning "Who is like God?" (or, "Who is like El?"). In *apocalyptic literature he is Israel's patron angel (Dan. 12.1), who fights for Israel against the angels of other nations (Dan. 10.13, 21). As such later tradition identifies him as the nameless divine messenger called "the prince of the army of Yahweh" in Joshua 5.13–15 (cf. Exod. 23.23; note also the spiritual "Michael, Row the Boat Ashore"). Michael also becomes the surrogate of a now transcendent storm god, leading the heavenly armies in the fight against the forces of chaos, and thus is the adversary of *Satan (Rev. 12.7; Jude 9). The battle between them becomes a favorite artistic theme and may occur in variant form in the legend of George and the dragon (see Rev. 12.9).   MICHAEL D. COOGAN

Midian. The name of a tribal group that appears to have played a significant role in the premonarchic history of Israel. Very little is known of the Midianites, and even the location and extent of their homeland is a matter of scholarly debate. The only source of information about them is the Bible. No archaeological remains can yet be attributed to them, and, with the exception of references in the inscriptions of *Tiglath-pileser III and Sargon II to Ephah, one of the subtribes of Midian (referred to as a son of Midian, Gen 25.4), they do not appear in extrabiblical inscriptions.

The Midianites are generally portrayed in the Bible as seminomadic and *nomadic shepherds and traders. Their eponymous ancestor is said to have been the son of *Abraham and Keturah and to have been sent by Abraham to the east, along with his brothers (Gen. 25.1–6). In the narratives of Genesis, Numbers, Joshua, and Judges, groups of Midianites appear all across southern Palestine and Sinai, as well as in Transjordan. This is usually interpreted as an indication of the wide range of their regular migrations.

Although the Midianites are usually portrayed as enemies of Israel (see esp. Num. 22; 25.6–18; 31; and Judg. 6–8), Midian is presented in a more positive light in passages dealing with

*Moses' sojourn with Jethro/Hobab, a priest of Midian and Moses' father-in-law (Exod. 2.15–3.1). The tradition that Moses received his revelation of Yahweh while living with the Midianites and the influential role that Jethro plays in Exodus 18 have led to speculation that the worship of Yahweh may have been adopted by Israel from the Midianites. Such speculations, however, cannot be confirmed.

The battle led by *Gideon against the Midianites in Judges 6–8 appears to have been the last time that Midian was a significant political threat to Israel. No conflicts are reported between the two in the monarchic period. Midian, however, continued to survive and play a role in the spice and gold trade from *Arabia. In Isaiah 60:6, an early postexilic poem, reference is made to Midianite and Ephaite caravans along the *Arabian trade routes. WAYNE T. PITARD

Miktam. A Hebrew word of uncertain meaning used in the titles to six *Psalms (16; 56–60), all of which are attributed to *David and are approximately equal in length, but do not belong to the same genre. Like *maskil and other terms in the headings to the psalms, it is probably a musical or literary classification.

MICHAEL D. COOGAN

Miracles. A miracle is an extraordinary event, perceived to be the result of the direct, purposeful action of a god or the agent of a god. Miracles are a common feature of literature and religious tradition in every culture, from the simplest to the most sophisticated societies, and from earliest historical times to the present. The questions raised by the occurrence of an event that is understood to be a miracle are not only "What happened?" but also "What does it mean?" or more specifically, "What is the divine message imparted through this event?"

It is inappropriate to describe miracle as a violation of natural law, since most societies, including those represented in the Bible, believed in the direct action of God (or gods) in history. What happens in the world and in human experience is seen as the outworking of the divine will rather than an immutable law running its course. Even when among the *Stoics there arose the idea of natural law as a fixed, basic process by which the universe operated, allowance was still made for the direct action of the gods. Thus, for example, in the circumstances surrounding the accession to power of Julius Caesar or in the birth and attainment of the imperial authority by Augustus, contemporary accounts by Roman historians describe the miracles that accompanied these historical developments as an indication of the active interest of the gods in human affairs.

In the Hebrew Bible, several types of miracle are reported. Among these are confirmatory miracles, through which God shows his choice and support of certain individuals or groups. Examples are the direct visions of God that are granted to *Abraham, *Jacob, and especially *Moses. Thus, Abraham is given assurance by the appearance of the smoking fire pot and flaming torch that the *covenant with Yahweh will be fulfilled (Gen. 15.17–20). *Sarah's giving birth to *Isaac after years of infertility is a confirming sign that the covenant will be established (Gen. 18). Similarly, the burning bush confirms Moses' call by God to lead his people out of slavery in Egypt (Exod. 3). The confirmation of God's promise to the covenant people is given in their safe passage through the sea (Exod. 14) and in the provision of *manna and *water for them in the *Sinai desert (Exod. 16). Or again, the power of the God whom *Elijah serves is confirmed by the fire from Yahweh that consumes the altar and the offering upon it (1 Kings 18.38).

A second type of miracle is judgmental, as in the *plagues that befall the Egyptians until the release of the Israelites (Exod. 8–12) or the fall of the walls of *Jericho when its inhabitants resist Israel's entry into the *Promised Land (Josh. 6; cf. 24.11). Another type is the act of mercy, through which some basic human need is met, as in the healings performed by *Elisha (2 Kings 3–4).

Yet another type of miracle is the divine act of deliverance of individuals, as when *Daniel and his friends are preserved from the fiery furnace, from starvation, and from the lion's den (Dan. 1–6). Of a different sort are the miracles of divine vision, in which God and his purposes for his people are disclosed to certain persons, such as *Isaiah (Isa. 6), *Ezekiel (Ezek. 1) and Daniel (Dan. 7). In each case, the miracle is described as taking place in order to reveal God's purpose for his people, or to achieve some form of deliverance or punishment in behalf of individuals, of the Israelite nation, of her enemies, or of the minority who remain faithful to God.

In the New Testament, miracle is central to the earliest understanding of who Jesus is and his role in the inauguration of God's rule in the world. In the *Q source, for example, when *Jesus is asked by the followers of *John the Baptist to explain who he is, he replies by pointing to his miracles of healing as evidences of the fulfillment of the prophetic promises of benefits to the needy and the outcasts (Luke 7.18–23; Isa. 29.18–19; 35.5–6; 61.1). He also points to his *exorcisms as the major sign of the beginning of the defeat of the evil powers and the establishment of the *kingdom of God (Luke 11.20). Indeed, he refers to his own power to heal and to expel demons by the same phrase, "the finger of God," used of God's action in delivering Israel from Egypt (Exod. 8.19). There are miracle stories in the New Testament that directly parallel those in the Hebrew Bible. For example, the feeding of the five thousand (Mark 6.30–44; Matt. 14.13–21; Luke 9.10–17; John 6.1–13) shares details and overall aim with God's miraculous feeding of Israel in the desert. In both cases, a covenant people about to be reconstituted are taken out into a barren territory, where God meets their needs and where they are joined in covenant as his special people; this connection is made explicit in John's version of the story (John 6.31–33). The covenantal significance is underscored by the use within the feeding story of what become technical terms at the Last Supper: he took, he blessed, he broke, he gave (Mark 6.41; 14.22). In the gospel of John, the emphasis of the miracle stories falls on their symbolic significance, as in the story of the healing of the man born blind, who symbolizes the *blindness of traditional Jewish piety as to who Jesus is, and the light of understanding that faith brings (John 9). And the raising of Lazarus from the dead is, of course, the symbol of the triumph over death accomplished through Jesus (John 11.25–26). The symbolic significance of Jesus' miracles for John is made explicit in John 20.30–31, where the writer tells us that he has chosen to report these particular signs in order that readers might see Jesus as the anointed one (*Messiah) of God, through whom new life is given.

In Paul's letters, his encounter with the risen Lord (Gal. 1.15) and his being taken up into the presence of God (2 Cor. 12.1–4) resemble the miracles of revelation and confirmation in the Hebrew Bible. The ability to heal, to perform miracles, and to prophesy is seen by Paul as the gift that God grants through the Spirit (1 Cor. 12.8–11; Gal. 3.5). Paul's apostolic office is confirmed through "signs and wonders and mighty works" (2 Cor. 12.12). It is surprising, therefore,

that Paul makes no reference to the miracles performed by Jesus, though the miracle of his *resurrection by God is central to Paul's gospel (1 Cor. 15.12–21).

Miracles of various kinds abound in *Acts. Foremost are the confirmatory type, as when the miraculous hearing of those speaking in tongues at the outpouring of the Spirit enables people from many lands to understand in spite of linguistic differences (Acts 2.1–11; see Glossolalia). The healing of the man at the Temple gate by Peter and John (Acts 3) is interpreted by their followers as God's attestation of the gospel (Acts 4.16, 22). Similarly, Philip's evangelization of the *Samaritans is confirmed through the many healings that accompany his preaching there (Acts 8.6, 13). And the gentile mission as a whole is acknowledged by the Jerusalem leaders to be of God, by virtue of the signs and wonders that accompanied the work of Paul and his associates (Acts 15.12; 19.11). At the same time, judgmental miracles are also depicted, as in the death of Ananias and Sapphira for their duplicity and failure to meet their obligations to the community (Acts 5.1–16). The deliverance of Paul and his associates from the shipwreck and the viper (Acts 27–28) shows God's care and concern for those doing his work, since by thus preserving Paul, he is enabled to reach with the gospel the center of the world, Rome itself.

Throughout the Bible, therefore, miracles are presented as a means by which God discloses and fulfills his purpose in the world, especially in behalf of his people and for the redemption of those who respond in faith to his activity in their behalf.   HOWARD CLARK KEE

Miriam. Sister of *Moses and *Aaron. Miriam is presumably the sister who watches over Moses in the bulrushes in the story in Exodus (2.4, 7–8; see Num. 26.59). She is called a prophet in Exodus 15.20, when she leads the women dancing with tambourines after the victory at the Sea of Reeds (cf. Jephthah's daughter in Judg. 11.34). Then in Exodus 15.21 she is said to sing the first verse of the song just attributed to Moses (15.1–18). Since both Moses and Miriam are connected in the text to this "Song of the Sea," it has been speculated that the song was originally attributed to Miriam (cf. the Song of Hannah in 1 Sam. 2.1–10; the Song of Deborah in Judg. 5:1–30; and the reports of women singing victory songs in 1 Sam. 18:7; 21:11; 29:5; 2 Sam. 1:20). The process by which the name of a dominant figure like Moses could become attached to a piece of poetry and supplant the name of a less common figure like Miriam is more easily understood than the converse.

The other major biblical story about Miriam is her and Aaron's criticism of Moses' leadership in Numbers 12. They complain for two reasons, that Moses has married a "Cushite" woman and that Yahweh has spoken through them as well as through Moses (see Exod. 4.14–16; 15.20; Mic. 6.4). The story in fact serves to affirm Moses' position as leader (vv. 6–9). Yahweh is greatly angered by their complaints and punishes Miriam (but not Aaron, despite v. 11) for speaking against Moses. She is afflicted with a skin disease that turns her skin white. Aaron asks Moses to intercede with Yahweh on her behalf, and when he does she is healed after spending seven days outside the camp (see the reference to this story in Deut. 24.9 and cf. Lev. 13–14). The reference to a father spitting in his daughter's face and the seven-day period of purification (v. 14) is obscure. If *Cush in this story is meant to refer to Ethiopia, as it often does in the Bible, then Miriam's white-as-snow skin is an ironic punishment for a complaint that would have included her objection to Moses' taking an African wife. More likely Cush here refers to *Midian (see Cushan in Hab. 3.7) and Moses' marriage to the Midianite woman Zipporah (Exod. 2.11–22) is the source of the criticism, although the reference could still also have suggested the dark skin color of Ethiopians in contrast to Miriam's disease.

Miriam died while the Israelites were at Kadesh, and she was buried there (Num. 20.1). She was remembered in Micah 6.4 as one of the leaders of the *Exodus along with Moses and Aaron.   Jo Ann Hackett

Mishnah. A law code brought to closure ca. 200 CE, the Mishnah is the first document of rabbinic Judaism. Its material is arranged by topic rather than by names of authorities; this system suggests that through order, through the reordering of Israelite life, Israel attains that sanctification which inheres in its very being. The Mishnah is presented in six divisions, embracing sixty-three tractates and 531 chapters, and it encompasses six broad topics.

Agriculture (*Zeraʿim*). The primary interest of the Mishnah regarding farming encompasses the ways in which farmers should do their work in accord with the rules of sanctification contained within the *Torah. Sanctification involved ob-

serving the rules of classification, that is, not mixing diverse seeds, substances, or species.

Appointed Times (*Moʿed*). The second division of the Mishnah deals generally with holy days in the *Temple and local village. The basic principle is that what is permitted in one place is forbidden in the other.

Women (*Našim*). The third division concerns the sanctification of the family, with special reference to the holiness of the relationship between *women and men. The basic interest is in those points in a woman's life when she passes from the domain of one man, ordinarily the father, to that of another, the husband.

Damages (*Neziqin*). The fourth division of the Mishnah deals with political questions: first, institutions of government, and second, resolving questions of conflict, aggression, and property rights so as to preserve the stability of an economy of perfection. Objects have a fixed and intrinsic value, and in commerce that intrinsic worth must govern exchange so that no one will gain more or less.

Holy Things and **Purities.** The fifth division (*Qodašim*) deals with sacrifices that are offered regularly, every day, as distinct from those that are prepared on special occasions, for appointed times. The sixth division (*Ṭoharot*) concerns purity and impurity. Both relate to the Temple and its cult, though the purview of the purity laws is the home as much as the Temple. The sixth deals with three matters: sources of uncleanness, objects and substances that are susceptible to uncleanness, and modes of purification from uncleanness. Sources of contamination, listed mainly in Leviticus 11–15, break the natural balance and order of creation. Also subject to the rules of cultic uncleanness are utensils used in the home, as well as food and drink. Tractates on what is affected by uncleanness are *Kelim*, for utensils, *Ṭoharot* and *ʿUqṣin* for food and drink; tractates on modes of purification are *Para*, on making the purification water mentioned in Numbers 19, and *Miqwaʾot*, on purification water.

See also Interpretation, History of, *article on* Jewish Interpretation; Purity, Ritual; Talmud.   Jacob Neusner

Moab. A nation whose affiliation with Israel may have been the closest of all her neighbors. This is indicated by the affinity of the Moabite language and writing tradition to *Hebrew; by *David's ancestry from the Moabite *Ruth and his sending his parents for sanctuary in Moab (1 Sam. 22.3–5); by the legend of Moab's birth through the incestuous union of *Lot and his elder daughter (Gen. 19.30–37); and by religious affinities to Yahwism portrayed in the *Moabite Stone.

Moab (Map 1:Y5–6) lay along the east side of the Dead Sea. North Moab, including the plains of Moab opposite *Jericho (Num. 22.1; 33.48–49), covered an area from just north of the top of the sea to the Arnon 40 km (25 mi) south, which is mostly well-watered tableland, 600–850 mi (2000–2800 ft) above mean sea level; here lay Heshbon, the peaks of *Nebo and Pisgah, Medeba, Beth-meon, Ataroth, and Dibon. South ("true") Moab, from the Arnon to the Zered, the boundary with *Edom, is tableland 300 m (1000 ft) higher and more marginal agriculturally. A text of Pharaoh Ramesses II (early thirteenth century BCE) designates this region by the name Moab. Topographic survey, which at first seemed to display an occupation gap from roughly 2000 to 1300 BCE, has more recently contributed evidence of settlement throughout the second millennium, even in the south. Probably Moab was first a tribal society, then a monarchy.

Relations between Moab and Israel are complex and difficult to discern from the record—whether enmity or amity. The issue is bound up with whether north Moab was under Moabite control. Thus, Numbers 21 depicts the *Amorite king Sihon as having displaced Moab from north of the Arnon and makes Sihon, not Moab, Israel's foe. The Balak/*Balaam story in Numbers 22–24, on the other hand, portrays enmity and puts the action in north Moab. Deuteronomic tradition condemns Moab for inhospitality to Israel during the Transjordanian trek (Deut. 23.34; Judg. 11.17), but asserts that Yahweh granted Moab its (southern?) territory, so Israel is not to harass Moab (Deut. 2.9). Judges 3.12–30 pictures enmity, showing Moab in possession of the north with a foothold at Jericho ("city of palms"); Judges 11, on the other hand, implies amity with Moab (11.24–27).

*Saul reportedly defeated Moab (1 Sam. 14.47–48), but it is David who subjugated it, militarily and by vassal treaty (2 Sam. 8.2). The next explicit information comes from the *Moabite Stone about 830 BCE, where Mesha, king of Moab at Dibon, asserts he liberated north Moab from the control of the Israelite northern kingdom's Omri Dynasty, dispossessing the "men of Gad" during *Ahab's reign or more probably at Ahab's death about 850 BCE (2 Kings 1.1; 3.4–8). Mesha's inscription implies that Omri had regained this control; had Moab escaped subjugation sometime between Solomon and Omri? The accounts in 2 Kings 3 (Jehoram of Israel) and 2 Chronicles 20 (Jehoshaphat of Judah) contribute contemporary episodes of conflict with Moab, further suggesting struggle for independence at the end of the Omri dynasty. And 2 Kings 10.32–33 places Hazael of Damascus in north Moab in this period; perhaps Moab gained freedom from Israel only to lose it to Syria.

Moab came under loose *Assyrian control, probably through vassal treaty, around 732 BCE. In the mid-seventh century, it functioned as loyal vassal by quelling Arab rebellion against Assyria. Moab appears as *Nebuchadrezzar's client (2 Kings 24.2), helping put down Jehoiakim's revolt around 600 BCE. This period of subservience to the great powers is the setting for Amos 2.1–3, Isaiah 15–16, and Jeremiah 48 (cf. Num. 21.27–30), which link Moab to Yahweh's international dominion. These oracles judge Moab, lament over it, and convey to it divine promises. After the Babylonian conquest of the region, Moab disappears from available records, though the *Ezra-*Nehemiah campaign against mixture with foreigners suggests that Moab still designates a people in the late fourth century BCE (Ezra 9.1–2; Neh. 13.23).   EDWARD F. CAMPBELL

Moabite Stone. A stele 1.1 m (3½ ft) high, .6–.68 m (2–2¼ ft) wide, containing thirty-four lines of text celebrating the deeds of Mesha, the Moabite king of the mid-ninth century BCE (2 Kings 3.4–5). Controversy followed its discovery in 1868 at Dhiban (biblical Dibon) in Jordan by F. A. Klein, one result of which was its reduction to fragments by Bedouin involved in its sale. While it was still intact, Charles Clermont-Ganneau had a rough impression made, with the aid of which the thirty-nine recovered fragments were pieced together and placed in the Louvre. About seven hundred of some thousand original letters are preserved.

The inscription, dating about 830 BCE, represents most of what is known of the Moabite language. The writing tradition closely resembles that of the earliest *Hebrew inscriptions, while grammar and vocabulary are also close congeners of Hebrew. In the text, Mesha portrays himself recovering northern *Moab from the successors of the Israelite king Omri. Mesha celebrates his public works in Dibon, his capital, and in its subdivision Qarhoh. He boasts of construction in Aroer, Medeba, and other Moabite towns. The final broken lines hint that he regained territory in the south, toward *Edom.

Striking is the account of Mesha's relationship to Moab's national deity Chemosh, to whom the stele dedicates a *high place in Qarhoh. Chemosh's anger with Mesha's predecessor(s) had brought on Omri's oppression of Moab; with Mesha, Chemosh's favor returns, triumph comes over all opposition, and campaigns to regain territory are commanded by the deity. Cultic equipment of Yahweh, seized in war, is presented to Chemosh. All Israelite inhabitants of Ataroth and *Nebo are "devoted"—slain for divine satisfaction (see Ban). In other instances, however, Mesha uses Israelite captives as builders (alternative reading: makes treaty relations with Israelite survivors). Clearly, the Moabite stone throws remarkable light on biblical language, history, and practices.

EDWARD F. CAMPBELL

Monarchy. See Kingship and Monarchy.

Money. As a medium of exchange, originally precious metals were used, according to fixed *weights, such as the talent, the mina, and the shekel, which later became units of currency (see below). (In the NRSV, the Hebrew word for "silver" is often translated as "money," even when the context makes such an interpretation anachronistic [e.g., Gen. 17.12–13; 42.25; 1 Kings 21.2].) Minted coinage seems to have begun in Asia Minor by the seventh century BCE, and its use was spread rapidly by the Greeks and the Persians. The oldest coins found in Palestine are a Macedonian coin from *Shechem and an Athenian coin from *Jerusalem, both dated to the sixth century BCE. By the fifth century BCE coins appear more frequently in occupational strata and are commonplace by the fourth. Coins thus become a valuable means of dating for archaeologists. They are also indices of international trade patterns and political control and provide valuable data about scripts and artistic motifs.

Units of currency in biblical and nonbiblical sources and coins found in the course of excavations are generally foreign, mainly Persian, Greek, Tyrian, and Roman, although in some periods there seem to have been local mints, in places such as Gaza and Ashkelon in the Persian period. During several relatively brief periods, however, distinctive regional coinage was produced.

In the fourth century BCE, while Judah was a province of the Persian empire, a series of coins with the inscription "Judah" (yehud) in *Aramaic

script were produced, apparently in Jerusalem; some also give the title and occasionally the name of the Persian-appointed governor. These are apparently the first Jewish coins. Distinctive coins were also minted by the Hasmoneans, beginning with Alexander Janneus in the late second century BCE. *Herod the Great and his successors also issued their own coins, as did some of the Roman procurators, including *Pilate.

During the First Jewish Revolt (66–70 CE), the rebels issued their own currency, an obvious expression of political independence. These coins, in denominations of shekels and half-shekels, are made of silver and are dated from the first to the fifth years of the revolt. Their inscriptions are in Hebrew, another expression of nationalistic sentiment, and include such phrases as "Jerusalem the holy," "the freedom of Zion," and "the redemption of Zion." The coins have such symbols as a chalice, a triple pomegranate, and palm and other branches; the absence of human and animal figures is clearly deliberate, in observance of the commandment prohibiting *graven images, and is in marked contrast with Greek and Roman coinage. Similar coins were issued during the Second Jewish Revolt (132–135 CE), some of which name the leader of the insurgents, Simeon (Simon Bar Kochba). In poignant contrast to these numismatically expressed patriotic hopes are the Roman coins issues by Vespasian and Titus to commemorate their defeat of the First Revolt; some show a mourning figure and have the inscription "Judea captured" in Greek or in Latin.

The coins named in the Bible are listed below; over the centuries, the values of various denominations fluctuated, so that the figures given are only a sample.

as (AV: "farthing"; NRSV: "penny"): Made of bronze, the as (earlier assarius) = 4 quadrans; found only in Matthew 10.29 = Luke 12.6.

daric (AV: "dram"): The standard Persian gold coin, equivalent to a Greek stater, first issued by and named after *Darius I (Ezra 8.27; 1 Chron. 29.7). NRSV also uses daric in Ezra 2.69 and Nehemiah 7.69–71 for a slightly different Hebrew word that some translate as drachma. Its use in 1 Chronicles is an anachronism.

denarius (AV: "penny"): Made of silver, the denarius was approximately a day's pay for an unskilled laborer; its value was 16 as = ¼ tetradrachma = 1/100 mina (Matt 18.28; 20.2; 22.19 par.; Mark 6.37; 14.5; Luke 10.35; Rev. 6.6).

didrachma: A coin worth two drachmas, equated by the *Septuagint with the Hebrew shekel. In Matthew 17.24–27, it apparently means the half-shekel used to pay the Temple tax and is equated with the stater.

drachma: The standard Greek silver coin, equivalent to the Roman denarius, and likewise equivalent to a day's pay (see Tob. 5.15). In the New Testament it is mentioned only in Luke 15.8–9. Larger denominations of the drachma were the didrachma (2 drachmas) and the tetradrachma (4 drachmas).

lepton (AV: "mite"; NRSV: "coin, penny"): The smallest unit of currency in the New Testament, the lepton was originally Greek; in the Roman period it had the value of ½ quadrans (Mark 12.42 par.; Luke 12.59).

mina (Grk. *mna;* AV: "pound"): As a weight, the equivalent of 50 shekels. As a coin, a mina is the equivalent of 100 drachmas, used in Nehemiah 7.71–72, and in Luke's version of the parable of the talents (Luke 19.11–27).

qesitah (NRSV: "money"): occurring only in Genesis 33.19; Joshua 24.32; Job 42.11, this is probably a weight of unknown value rather than a coin as such.

quadrans (AV: "farthing"; NRSV: "penny"): ¼ as; Matthew 5.26; Mark 12.42.

shekel: The basic unit of weight in Hebrew (from the verb *šql*, "to weigh"); its monetary value was 1 stater; 30 shekels = 1 mina = 4 denarii.

stater: The equivalent of 4 drachmas (tetradrachma), found only in Matthew 17.27.

talent: The largest weight, equivalent to 3,600 shekels; as a monetary unit it equalled 6,000 drachmas.

See also Money Changers; Weights and Measures.   Michael D. Coogan

Money Changers. Mentioned only in the account of Jesus' attack on merchants in the *Temple, which according to the *synoptic Gospels took place shortly before his arrest (Matt. 21.12–13 par.) but is set by John at the beginning of Jesus' ministry (John 2.14–22). According to Exodus 30.11–16, every adult male Israelite was to pay half a shekel annually to the sanctuary (see also Neh. 10.32; Matt. 17.24–27). In the period of the Second Temple this tax was paid at *Passover; to assist pilgrims to Jerusalem, money changers apparently functioned within the large open area known as the "Court of Gentiles" (see Map 9) or in the porticoes that framed the Temple enclosure, converting to the proper payment different currencies or those that were religiously offensive because of portraits on coins (*see* Money). Although rabbinic sources provide some evidence for complaints about profiteering by the money changers, who charged as much as eight percent for their service, the reaction of Jesus seems exaggerated, especially in its fullest form in Mark 11.15–19. It is furthermore unlikely that one person could control all activity within the vast Temple courtyard; the Gospel narratives, written after the destruction of the Temple in 70 CE, are making a theological point about Jesus, depicting him as a prophet in the tradition of Jeremiah and Isaiah, both of whom are quoted directly (see also Zech 14.21).   Michael D. Coogan

Monotheism. Discussion of monotheism in the ancient world sometimes blurs the distinction between theology and religion. In non-Western settings, religion is a complex of behaviors that mark a culture. Theology, however, involves cohesive ideological speculation to justify behaviors. A single religion can have many competing or complementary theologies.

Scholars have traditionally taken a theological and prescriptive approach to the issue of Israelite monotheism: monotheism is the conviction that only one god exists, and no others. This conviction is, however, difficult to document.

Ancient Near Eastern Background. Egyptian, Mesopotamian, Hittite, Greek, and early Canaanite myths all present developed pantheons. These texts relate how one generation of gods succeeds the next just as humans succeed one another; this succession entails war among the gods. In Mesopotamia, the creation of the universe results from this conflict. Mesopotamian, Hittite, and Canaanite myths relate how the storm god defeats the sea god (in Egypt, the battle is essentially between the *Nile and the desert): a god responsible for life-giving water wins control of the cosmos. The focus in all of these myths is the succession of a patriarchal high god's royal son.

These pantheons all have a high god, under whose direction other gods—of the sun, of pestilence, and so forth—act, often independently. The high god is usually the state god. In some cases, the subordinate gods in the state pantheon represent local high gods, of areas in an empire. Thus different states may share essentially identical pantheons but identify different high gods: in Mesopotamia, the *Babylonian high god was

Marduk; the *Assyrian high god was Ashur. *Sennacherib had the Babylonian creation epic rewritten to award Marduk's role in it to Ashur.

Yet state myths did not reflect the subjective experience of a worshiper in a god's cult. Mesopotamian literature is filled with pleas to gods and goddesses, such as Ishtar of Arbela, Ishtar of Nineveh, Shamash (the sun god), and Addu (biblical Hadad). In prayer, the god being addressed is the sole object of devotion.

Scholars refer to this phenomenon as effective henotheism, devotion to one god conceding the potency of others. This principle was elevated to state policy in *Egypt under Akhnaton (ca. 1350 BCE), the pharaoh who channeled resources into the cult of the solar disk at a cost to competing cults. A similar attempt to impose a god atop a state pantheon, under the sixth-century BCE Babylonian king Nabonidus, exhibits the same characteristics, with statues of all the other gods being brought to Babylon, possibly for the New Year. Nabonidus's attempt, like Akhnaton's, proved abortive.

These failures, however, show that the line between monotheism and polytheism should not be too precisely drawn. Akhnaton and Nabonidus, the two great religious reformers of Near Eastern antiquity, focused the cult on their respective gods. Not dissimilar are the monotheistic traditions of Judaism, Christianity, and Islam: all admit the existence of subordinate divinities—*saints, *angels, *demons, and, in Christianity and Islam, *Satan, the eternal antagonist of the high god. But if these traditions are not monotheistic, no religion (as opposed to theology) is. The term monotheism loses its meaning.

Monotheism, Yehezkel Kaufmann observed, postulates multiple deities, subordinated to the one; it tolerates myths of primordial struggle for cosmic supremacy. Two elements distinguish it from polytheism: a conviction that the one controls the pantheon, and the idea of false gods.

Ancient Israel and Its Immediate Neighbors. From the outset, Israelites identified themselves as "the people of YHWH" (Judg. 5.13). The expression implies a societal commitment to a single, national god. Israelite personal *names offer confirmation: these include either the name of a god or a divine epithet. Almost uniformly, the god in Israelite personal names is YHWH or an epithet of YHWH, such as "god" (ʾēl), "lord" (baʿal), or "(divine) kinsman" (ʿamm).

This practice resembles that of the Transjordanian nations of *Ammon, *Moab, and *Edom,

Israel's nearest neighbors and, in the folklore of Genesis 12–25, closest relations. Conversely, in Canaanite and Phoenician city-states, personal names include the names and epithets of a variety of gods and goddesses. The ethnic nations that emerged in Canaan in the thirteenth–twelfth centuries BCE, unlike the states of Syria and Mesopotamia, are early tied to national gods.

None of these cultures, however, denied the existence of divinities other than the high god. The ninth-century *Moabite Stone, though treating the national god, Chemosh, as Israel treated YHWH, nevertheless mentions sacrifice to a subordinate of his. An eighth-century inscription from Deir ʿAllā, in the Israelite-Ammonite border area, mentions a pantheon, or group of gods, called Shaddayin. Similarly, many biblical texts, from the twelfth century down to the Babylonian *exile, describe the divine court over which YHWH presides as the council of the gods: these report to and suggest strategy to YHWH, praise YHWH, and are assessed by YHWH (Deut. 32.43b [with 4QDeutᵃ]; 1 Kings 22.19–23; Isa. 6; Pss. 29.1–2; 82.1, 6; Job 1.6–2.10). In monarchic theologies, the subordinate gods administered other nations for YHWH (Deut. 32.8–9 [LXX]; Mic. 4.5; 1 Sam. 26.19). But they also received Israelite homage—the sun, moon, and host of heaven, the stars who fought as YHWH's army against Canaan (Deut. 33.2–3; Josh. 5.13–14; cf. 10.12–13; Judg. 5.20; 1 Kings 19.19–23): the host was YHWH's astral army, and YHWH was regularly represented through solar imagery.

The astral gods—the host of heaven—figure prominently in early sources. The meaning of YHWH's name has long been in dispute. However, the name associated with the *ark of the covenant, and prevalent throughout the era of the monarchy, is YHWH Sebaʾot ("Lord of Hosts"). On the most common interpretation of the name YHWH, this means, "He [who] summons the hosts [of heaven] into being." If so, the full name of Israel's god in the Pentateuch's Yahwistic source (*J), YHWH Elohim, means, "He [who] summons the gods into being." And before the revelation of the name YHWH to Moses, the Priestly (*P) source calls the high god El Shadday: originally, this, too, associated YHWH with sky gods, Shaddayin, known from the Deir ʿAllā inscription. (*See* Names of God in the Hebrew Bible.)

The Israelite cult also embraced the ancestors. Israelites invoked the ancestors for aid in matters familial, agricultural, and political. The ancestral spirits could intervene with YHWH, to the benefit of the family, the landholding corporation that inherited its resources from the fathers. (*See* Israel, Religion of.)

The Emergence of Monotheism. Starting apparently in the ninth century BCE, Israelites began to distinguish YHWH starkly from other gods. It is unknown whether the distinction originated from the opposition between YHWH and foreign high gods or between YHWH and local ancestral gods. Still, the alienation of the local gods from YHWH ensued, as subordinate gods were identified as foreign.

Our first indications of the cleavage come from a ninth-century nativist revolution against the house of Omri, the ruling dynasty of the northern kingdom of Israel. *Solomon had earlier constructed a *Temple in *Jerusalem. This Temple incorporated representations of *cherubim (1 Kings 6.23–29) and, judging from later developments, probably of YHWH's *asherah, or consort, Ashtoret (*Astarte). Opposite the Temple, Solomon also consecrated shrines to YHWH's subordinates—Ashtoret, Milkom, and Chemosh (1 Kings 11.7; 2 Kings 23.13–14). After seceding from Jerusalem under Jeroboam I, the kingdom of *Israel had maintained a more conservative separation of state shrines from the capital. *Ahab, however, installed a new temple in *Samaria (1 Kings 16.32); in the Near East, a temple in the capital signified a divine grant of dynasty. Jehu's revolt, however, destroyed the temple and reaffirmed Jeroboam's cultic policy (2 Kings 10.18–29; cf. Hos. 1.4). (*See* Kingship and Monarchy.)

The earliest biblical writer to contrast YHWH with his subordinate deities is *Hosea. This eighth-century prophet rejects calling YHWH Israel's "baal" (lord) and claims that attention to the "baals" (YHWH's subordinate gods) deflects attention from the deity responsible for their ministrations (see especially Hos. 2). The alienation of the subordinates (who in the traditional theology administer other nations for YHWH) from YHWH, who administers Israel, permits Hosea to identify pursuit of the "baals" with foreign political alliances. Intellectually, the same alienation was part of a critique of traditional culture leveled by the "classical," that is, the literary, *prophets.

In the eighth century, Israel enjoyed a trading network embracing the Assyrian empire in western Asia and Phoenician trade outposts around the Mediterranean. As a bridge on the spice trade route to the south, and as a producer of cash crops such as olives and grapes, Israel underwent incipient industrialization, developing capital reserves. Foreign goods, texts, and practices became increasingly familiar to a growing middle class. In reaction, the elite was impelled to define distinctively Israelite values and culture. Groping for its identity, the elite discovered the gap between the elite theology, in which YHWH was completely sovereign, and popular practice, with its devotions to subordinate deities and ancestors; between theology, in which repentance was increasingly individuated, and ritual repentance, a matter of behavior, not attitude; between theology, in which one worshiped an unseen god, and a cult employing icons. The critique by the literary prophets thus predicated that the symbol or manifestation—the icon, the ritual, the subordinate god—was alien from, and not to be mistaken for, the Reality—the high god, or one's own inner essence. (*See* Graven Image.)

Ahaz of Judah first implemented this critique, removing plastic imagery from the Temple nave (2 Kings 16.17). In preparation for the Assyrian invasion of 701, his successor *Hezekiah concentrated the Judahite population in fortified towns; his ideologians articulated attacks on the *high places, the centers of traditional rural worship, and on the ancestral cult, linked to the agricultural areas he planned to abandon to the aggressor (Isa. 28). Assyria then deported most of the population outside of Jerusalem; Hezekiah's spokesmen took this as YHWH's judgment on the rural cult, which they interpreted to be identical with the cult of the northern kingdom (Isa. 1–5)—Samaria had fallen prey to total deportation in 720. Jerusalem's survival, by contrast, represented YHWH's imprimatur on the state cult.

Some scholars hypothesize that Israelite monotheism was husbanded by a small, "Yahweh-alone" party until the time of Hezekiah or even *Josiah. However, no text indicates such a doctrine before Josiah's reign, and the chief indices suggest its gradual development rather than some perpetual keeping of a flame. Solomon's high places, for example, survived Hezekiah's reform, although the "Mosaic" snake-icon, Nehushtan, did not (Num. 21.5–9; 2 Kings 18.4). Child sacrifice continued in the Jerusalem *Topheth—an activity directed toward the host of heaven (Jer. 19.13). Personal seals continued to include astronomical imagery, though this was increasingly astral rather than solar as earlier.

In the seventh century, however, Josiah destroyed Solomon's shrines to gods now identified as foreign and dismantled state shrines in the countryside. Josiah's campaign against the ancestral cult included tomb desecration and the exposure of bones for the first time in Israelite history. A term previously reserved for the ancestors, *Rephaim, was now applied to the Canaanite aborigines allegedly proscribed by YHWH. Deuteronomy, the legal program of Josiah's court or of a later extension of it, enjoined the worship of YHWH alone. Deuteronomy, Jeremiah, and Zephaniah explicitly identified the host of heaven as foreign, as objects of apostasy. The Priestly source of the Pentateuch rewrote the traditional ancestral lore, suppressing all references to superhuman agencies other than YHWH; it forbids any imagery in the cult—correspondingly, seals are increasingly aniconic.

Sennacherib's deportations and the processes of industrialization and cash cropping had destroyed the effectiveness of the old kinship groups among whom the traditional religion, with its multiple divinities, was rooted. The imposition of state dogma of exclusive loyalty to the state god reflects the state's ambition to deal directly with the individual, bypassing the centers of resistance, the lineages. Thus, Deuteronomy 13.6–11 instructs the Israelite to inform on brothers, children, or wives who worship other gods, such as the host of heaven.

In this period, not in the exile as earlier scholars claimed, the notion of reliance on a single god took root. That idea survived, as a doctrine distinguishing Israel from other, polytheistic nations, through the exile and over the course of the restoration. Some of the elite, such as Second Isaiah, accepted the implications of philosophical monotheism, identifying YHWH as the source of evil as well as good (Isa. 45.7). Yet even in sources that accept the activity of subordinate deities, such as Job 1–2, the concept of exclusive loyalty to the state god had taken hold. Affirmation of the cult of the one god—the ultimate cause of events—could persist despite the assumption that other divinities existed, too. The doctrine of a *Trinity, or of angels in heaven, or of a devil, coexisted happily with the idea in Judaism, Christianity, and Islam of an enlightened community distinguished from others by its monotheism.   BARUCH HALPERN

Mormonism and the Bible. Objecting to views of the Torah as a closed world, Martin Buber wrote, "To you God is One who created once and not again; but to us God is he who 'renews the work of creation every day.' To you God is One who revealed Himself once and no more; but to us He speaks out of the burning thornbush of the present." Buber's passion parallels a quintessential dimension of Mormon thought: a deep respect for biblical revelation supporting an even-higher regard for ongoing revelation.

Mormonism came into being through a man (Joseph Smith, 1805–1844) and a culture (antebellum upstate New York) that shared a profound reverence for the Bible. This reverence was thus genetically part of the movement and has not greatly dissipated in the rapidly expanding tradition even at present. Among other things, this means that Mormons have fundamental allegiances in common with many other Christians and also with Jews. Mormons tend to take what they interpret as the Bible's essential truths for granted. They are enjoined to study the testaments regularly and, excepting errors of transmission and translation, consider them to be inspired, in some sense "the word of God." Their interpretation of the Bible informs their worship, their personal and social ethics, their polity, their theology, and their overall self-consciousness.

It was in fact Joseph Smith's attachment to the Bible that led him to seek God directly during the religious confusion of his youth. This search resulted, Mormons believe, in a vision of God and Jesus (1820) and the organization of a new (or a "restored") religious tradition: The Church of Jesus Christ of Latter-day Saints (1830). This church and its belief system would be incomprehensible without its biblically inspired basis.

Despite this enduring biblical foundation, Mormon attitudes are distinct from those of other biblically based faiths. Most centrally, Mormonism rejects the notion of a closed canon. With what he described as divine guidance, Joseph Smith translated and published (1830) the abridged records of ancient Israelites who had escaped the Babylonian captivity by traveling to the Americas around 600 BCE, spawning a civilization that flourished until about 400 CE. This record, known as the Book of Mormon (after its ancient prophet-editor), was itself scripture and was inextricably entwined with the traditional Bible: at once challenging the Bible's uniqueness and yet witnessing to the Bible's authority, echoing its themes, interpreting its passages, sharing its content, correcting its errors, filling its gaps, adopting its language, and restoring its methods, namely, the prophetic process itself.

Many of Smith's later revelations—saturated with biblical themes, phrases, and figures—were also subsequently canonized (The Doctrine and Covenants; The Pearl of Great Price). This precedent of expanding the canon quickly broadened to belief in an open-ended canon. One basic Mormon tenet is that divine-human contact is an ongoing process not subject to closure at an arbitrary point by any human council: "We believe all that God has revealed, all that he does now reveal, and we believe that He will yet reveal many great and important things."

It is, however, not simply an open canon that distinguishes Mormon biblical usage. Joseph Smith's understanding of the very nature of scripture was expansive. For instance, Smith did not believe that "scripture," despite its etymology, need necessarily be written to be true and authoritative. Thus, said one of his revelations, "Whatsoever [those who hold the priesthood] shall speak when moved upon by the Holy Ghost shall be scripture, shall be the will of the Lord, shall be the mind of the Lord, shall be the word of the Lord, shall be the voice of the Lord, and the power of God unto salvation." The idea of oral scripture contrasts with contemporary Christian practice but bears historical comparison with the treatment of sacred materials in other world religions.

Moreover, scripture for Smith was not the static, final, untouchable word of God that it was for many believers of his time. The Mormon prophet considered scripture to be sacred yet provisional, subject to refinement and addition, as both the evolving texts of his own revelations and the progressive stages of his inspired revision of the Bible (never published in his lifetime) demonstrate. For Mormons, the record of God's actions with humankind is to be highly prized, but this record is necessarily subordinate to direct experience with God—the lifespring of such records—and therefore subject to expansion, clarification, and correction. Mormon leaders further observe that not all of holy writ applies beyond the local and temporal context for which it was formulated.

Since Mormonism is not fond of creeds, Mormon perceptions of scripture are not monolithic. Many Latter-day Saints, for example, assume complete theological harmony within the Bible and between the Bible and other Mormon scriptures. Others champion the priority of modern revelation when apparent conflicts surface or attribute discrepancies to corruptions in the received biblical text. Still others give broad leeway to the human element in both ancient and contemporary revelation. Brigham Young (1801–1877) dismissed parts of the Bible as "baby stories" while remaining loyal to the biblical tradition in general. Joseph Smith, emboldened by his prophetic consciousness, solved various contradictions within the Bible and between his revelations and the biblical text by rewriting portions of the Bible. In the modern context, historical-critical studies of scripture have inspired a predominantly cool, antagonistic, or even oblivious reaction in Mormonism as a whole, particularly where those studies are controlled by naturalistic assumptions. Yet the attitudes of influential leaders and lay members toward serious biblical scholarship have been as divergent as those of any denomination, ranging from enthusiastic to scandalized.

Since the time of Joseph Smith, the Mormon use of scripture has combined a traditional faith in the Bible with more "conservative" elements (like an extra dose of literalism), some liberal components (such as Joseph Smith's insistence, anticipating the thought of Horace Bushnell, on the radical limits of human language), and some radical ingredients (an open canon, an oral scripture, the subjugation of biblical assertions to experiential truth or the pronouncements of living authorities). All of this links the Saints with other religious traditions yet separates them too. Mormons in the modern world remain Bible-believing Christians but with a difference.

PHILIP L. BARLOW

Moses. As primary leader of the Israelites in their *Exodus from *Egypt and during their wanderings in the *wilderness, and as mediator of the *Law, Moses dominates the biblical traditions from *Exodus through *Deuteronomy. In fact, Exodus–Deuteronomy appears to have been edited as a biography of Moses, reporting his birth at the beginning and his death at the end. Between these events the Bible relates many episodes about his life and work.

Born in secret during the oppression in Egypt as the younger of the two sons of a *Levite couple, Amram and Jochebed (Exod. 6.18–20), Moses was hidden away for a time to avoid slaughter at the hands of the Egyptians and then placed in a basket amid the reeds of the *Nile. Discovered by a daughter of Pharaoh who had pity on the child, he was spared and, through the intervention of his older sister (*Miriam: Exod. 15.20; Num. 26.59), was nursed by his own mother. Raised by Pharaoh's daughter as her son, the child received the name Moses (Hebr.

mōšeh, understood as a participle of the verb *māšâ*, "to draw out"; the name actually appears to be a form of the Egyptian verb *mŝw*, "to be born," or the noun *mesu*, "child, son," appearing in such names as Thut-mose and Ah-mose; Exod. 2.1–10). When grown up, Moses killed an Egyptian whom he saw beating a Hebrew and, when word of his deed spread, he fled the country to save his life (Exod. 2.11–15a). Taking refuge in *Midian (2.15b–21), he married Zipporah, the daughter of a Midianite priest who is variously referred to as Reuel (2.18), Jethro (3.1; 4.18; 18.1), or Hobab (Num. 10.29; Judg. 4.11). While in Midian, she bore him two sons, Gershom and Eliezer (Exod. 2.22; 4.20; 18.3–4).

While Moses was tending his father-in-law's flocks near *Horeb, the mountain of God, God revealed himself in a burning bush and commissioned him to return to Egypt and, with the help of *Aaron, to lead the *Hebrews out of the land of oppression (Exod. 3.1–4.17). Moses returned to Egypt (4.18–31), and he and Aaron produced signs and nine *plagues to persuade Pharaoh to allow the Hebrews to depart Egypt, either to go on a three-day journey into the wilderness to offer sacrifice to God (3.18; 5.1; 7.16; 8.28; 10.7–11, 24–26) or to leave the land for good (6.10–11). The signs and plagues failed to convince Pharaoh, who repeatedly gave and withdrew his permission to leave (5.1–10.29). With the tenth plague, the slaughter of the firstborn, Pharaoh and his people urged the Hebrews to leave (11.1–12.36).

Moses and the people departed (Exod. 12.37–14.4) only to be pursued by Pharaoh, whose army was drowned in the returning waters of the *Red Sea after the waters had parted for the Israelites to cross (14.5–15.21).

During their long stay in the wilderness and on their journey to the *Promised Land (Exod. 12.22–Deut. 34.8), Moses endured the people's recurrent murmuring and complaining. He aided in securing good drinking water (Exod. 15.22–26; 17.1–7; see Num. 20.2–11), oversaw the receipt of quails and *manna (Exod. 16.1–36; see Num. 11.4–5, 31–35), directed their war with the *Amalekites (Exod. 17.8–16), and, at the suggestion of his father-in-law, established judges to hear and adjudicate the people's disputes (18.1–27; see Num. 11.16–30).

At *Sinai (Exod. 19), Moses committed the people (19.3–8) to observe the commandments of God (20.1–23.33), communicated to him during a forty-day stay on the mountain (24.18) and then addressed to the people (24.3) and subse-

quently written down by either Moses (24.4) or God (24.12). He received instructions for constructing the *tabernacle and its accoutrements (25.1–31.17). The first tablets of the Law presented to Moses (31.18) were smashed by him (32.19) when he returned to the camp to discover that Aaron had supervised the construction of a *golden calf around which the people were celebrating (32.1–35). Moses intervened with God not to destroy the people (33.1–22), and God (34.1) or Moses (34.27–28) again wrote the words of the commandments (34.17–26) during a second forty-day period (34.28), which were again proclaimed to the people (34.29–35). Moses then supervised the construction and erection of the tabernacle (35.1–40.38), received further laws and instructions (Lev. 1–7, 11–27), and consecrated the tabernacle and ordained Aaron and his sons as *priests (Lev. 8–10).

After staying at Sinai for eleven months (Exod. 19.1; Num. 1.1), a census was taken of the non-Levitical males above the military age of twenty, totaling 603,550 (Num. 1.2–54), the Levites one month and older, totaling 22,000 (3.14–39; see 4.1–49), and the firstborn males one month and older, totaling 22,273 (3.40–43). After receiving further commandments from God (2.1–34; 5.1–6.27; 8.1–26; 19.9–14; 10.1–10), consecrating the Levites (3.5–13; 4.46–49), supervising receipt and employment of the leaders' special offerings (7.1–89), Moses and the people observed the *Passover (9.1–8) and departed from Sinai on the twentieth day of the second month of the second year after leaving Egypt (10.11–36).

For the next thirty-nine years, Moses led the people in their journeys (see the itinerary in Num. 33.1–49) in the wilderness. Kadesh (-barnea), an oasis in the northern Sinai desert (Map 2:T2), and its vicinity are the scene of many of the episodes reported in Numbers 11.1–20.21. During this period the people continued their murmuring and complaining (11.1–6; 14.1–4; 20.2–5), were fed with manna and quails (11.4–35), and were supplied with water (20.2–13). Moses was confronted with complaints about his wife (whether Zipporah or not remains uncertain) by Miriam and Aaron (12.1–16) and with a rebellion led by Korah and his associates (16.1–17.13). Spies were sent out to make a reconnaissance of *Canaan but returned with a discouraging report about the strength of the inhabitants (13.1–14.38). A belated attempt to invade the region from the south, apparently without Moses' approval, led to disaster (14.39–45). During these episodes, Moses and Aaron received further ordinances from God to be communicated to the people (15.1–41; 18.1–19.22). After the death and burial of Miriam at Kadesh (20.1), Moses sent messengers to the king of *Edom to request permission to pass through his country but was refused (20.14–21).

The last phase of Moses' life (thirty-eight years, according to Deut. 2.14) was concerned with the movement of the people into and their conquest of Transjordan. Journeying from Kadesh, they defeated the king of Arad (Num. 20.22; 21.1–3) and came to Mount Hor, where Aaron died (20.23–29). Leaving Mount Hor, Moses led the people southward to bypass the land of Edom (21.4). When God sent fiery serpents against the people because of their impatience, Moses constructed a bronze serpent as an instrument of healing (21.4–9). The people eventually arrived in the territory north of the land of *Moab, where they defeated kings Sihon of the *Amorites and Og of Bashan (21.10–35). While the Israelites encamped near the *Jordan across from *Jericho, King Balak of Moab hired *Balaam to curse Israel (22.1–24.25). After a plague ravaged the people because of their worship of the Baal of Peor (25.1–18), Moses ordered a census, which counted 601,730 males above the age of twenty fit for the military (26.1–51). After the census, Moses received instructions from God about dividing the land (26.52–65), about women's inheritance rights (27.1–11; see 36.1–12), the designation of Joshua as his successor (27.12–23), a calendar of sacrifices (28.1–29.40), and women's vows (30.1–16). A battle against the Midianites provided the occasion for divine instructions about the division of battle spoils (31.1–54). Moses allotted the captured territory in Transjordan to the *tribes of *Reuben and *Gad and half of *Manasseh (32.1–42) and transmitted divine instructions about dividing the land west of the Jordan (34.1–29) and setting aside cities for the Levites (35.1–8) and *cities of refuge for those guilty of accidental homicide (35.9–34).

On the eve of his death, the first day of the eleventh month of the fortieth year after the Exodus (Deut. 1.3), Moses delivered a series of farewell addresses to the people, expounding again the *Law and its requirements for living in the land (1.6–4.40; 5.1–29.1; 29.2–30.20), offering a personal adieu (32.1–6), a song (31.30–32.43), and blessings on the tribes (33.1–29). With Joshua properly commissioned as his successor (31.7–8, 14–15, 23), and having inscribed his song (31.16–29) and written and given directions for the reading and safekeeping of the book of the Law (31.9–13, 24–29), at the command of God (32.48–52; see Num. 17.12–23) Moses went up Mount *Nebo, viewed the Promised Land, and died at the age of 120 years, full of life and vigor. He was buried by the Lord, "but no one knows his burial place to this day" (34.1–8). God did not allow Moses to enter the land he viewed, either because of his own failure to provide proper recognition of God (Num. 20.10–13; 27.12–14; Deut. 32.48–52) or because of the sins of the people (Deut. 1.37–38; 3.18–28).

Any critical attempt to assess the historicity of the portrait of Moses presented in Exodus to Deuteronomy must take into account a number of characteristics of this literature and its presentation. First, many of the stories are legendary in character and are built on folktale motifs found in various cultures. The theme of the threatened child who eventually becomes a great figure, for example, was employed from Mesopotamia to Rome and appears in the stories about Sargon the Great, Heracles, Oedipus, Romulus and Remus, *Cyrus, and *Jesus. Second, Israel's theology located the giving of the Law and the formation of the national life outside the land it occupied and thus considered the wilderness period as its constitutional time. Hence, laws and institutions from diverse times and conditions are located in this formative era. Third, the duplications in the texts and the frequent lack of cohesion in the narratives and of consistency in details indicate that the material is composite and multilayered. Fourth, the lack of external frames of reference makes it impossible to connect any of the events depicted about Moses with the history of other cultures. The Egyptian Pharaoh of the oppression, for example, goes unnamed and no contemporary nonbiblical sources mention Moses. Finally, Moses is depicted as the archetype of several offices. Throughout he is representative not only of the good leader but also of the ideal judge and legal administrator, intercessor, cult founder, and *prophet. In all of these he excelled and thus served as the standard by which others were judged.

In biblical literature outside the *Pentateuch, Moses is most often mentioned in the phrases "the book of Moses," "the law of Moses," and "the book of the law of Moses," indicating the development of the concept of the *Torah as such and of its special authority and Mosaic authorship, themes that will become central for subsequent Jewish tradition. The same implication of the special scriptural authority of the first five books of the Bible, the books of Moses, is found in the New Testament, where there are repeated appeals to what Moses said (Matt. 8.4; 19.7; 22.24; ·Mark 7.10; John 7.22; Rom. 10.5) as well as to the "law of Moses" and the "book of Moses."

Postbiblical tradition elaborated on Moses' biography from his birth to his death in such texts as the *Testament of Moses* and in haggadic literature. Details of these embellishments are also found in the New Testament in the reference to *Jannes and Jambres (2 Tim. 3.8) and in the account of the dispute between *Michael and the devil over Moses' body (Jude 9; cf. also Acts 7.22).

These haggadic legends were also known to such Hellenistic Jewish writers as *Philo and *Josephus, who added to them the Hellenistic concept of the ideal man, so that the details of Moses' life reveal him to be the consummate human being and as such the appropriate founder of the theocratic state. This may be the background for the parallels drawn in the gospel of Matthew between the lives of Moses and Jesus. Yet for Matthew, as for the author of the letter to the Hebrews, Jesus is superior: Moses' presence at the transfiguration confirms Jesus' sonship (Matt. 17.1–8), and that sonship is clearly superior to Moses' status as God's servant (Heb. 3.1–6; cf. Num. 12.7; Deut. 34.5; Josh. 1.2; Ps. 105.26; Mal. 4.4).

The artistic tradition of depicting Moses with horns on his forehead arose from the understanding by some ancient translators of the Hebrew verb *qāran* (Exod. 34.29) as related to the noun *qeren*, "horn"; an alternative is to understand the verb as meaning "to shine" (so NRSV, and most earlier English translations).

JOHN H. HAYES

Mourning. *Death was the supreme cause for grief, and around this ultimate tragic event elaborate mourning customs and practices arose that were more or less mandatory (see 1 Kings 14.13; Jer. 16.4–6). Mourning for those who had died involved all who were immediately affected by their demise, whether family (Gen 23.2), friends (2 Sam. 1.11–12; John 11.33), or an entire nation (1 Sam 25.1; 1 Macc. 9.21).

Mourning began immediately upon death and in the presence of the body (Gen. 23.2; 2 Sam.

3.31; Mark 5.38). Expressions of grief continued along the way to the grave (Luke 7.12), at the burial place (John 11.31), and for some time after burial. The length of the period of mourning depended on prevailing customs—seven days (1 Sam. 31.13), thirty days (Num. 20.29), as many as seventy days (Gen. 50.3), or even longer (Jth. 8.4–6).

Feelings of grief were rarely suppressed. Mourners frequently vented their grief publicly in piercing, tremulous shrieks, shrill cries, wails, chants, loud lamentations, breast-beating, and tears (Gen 50.10; 2 Sam. 3.32–34; Mark 5.38). Personal adornments were removed, clothing was torn, the body was neglected, sackcloth was put on, and ashes were poured on the head (Gen. 37.34; Lev. 10.6; 2 Sam 1.2; 14.2; Jth. 8.4–6). It was customary to hire professional mourners to heighten this display of grief; usually these mourners were women who sang or wailed laments especially composed for the occasion or ones that were standard (2 Chron. 35.25; Jer. 9.17–20; Matt. 9.24). The funerary poems that have been preserved give some idea of the general form of such laments: they included a eulogy that was careful to name the deceased; a recounting of what had caused the person's death; and a word of consolation that focused not on the hope that the deceased lived beyond the grave but on the good name left behind by the deceased and the posterity to perpetuate that name (2 Sam. 1.18–27; 3.33–34; cf. Ezek. 19.1–14; 32.2–16; Rev. 18.9–24).

Musical instruments, principally the flute, were used to accompany the wailing of the mourners as they chanted their dirges (Jer. 48.36; Matt. 9.23). Occasionally, fasting was employed as a means of displaying grief (1 Sam. 31.11–13; Jth. 8.6). Some evidence exists, however, of a funeral feast designed to comfort the bereaved (Jer. 16.5–7).

Certain mourning customs were forbidden in Israel, such as lacerating the body and shaving the head (Lev. 19.28; Deut. 14.1; Jer. 16.6; but see Ezra 9.3; Job 1.20; Jer. 7.29). Such practices may have originated out of fear of the dead, that they might haunt the living to harm them if their funeral rites were not properly performed, but no such explanation is found in the Bible. Very ancient funeral customs remain, and are described, but they are interpreted only as signs of sorrow.

In the New Testament, funeral practices are more subdued, in part because of the eschatological hope of life beyond the grave by virtue of the *resurrection of Christ. Yet there is no denial of death nor any attempt to suppress feelings of grief (John 11.25–35). Christians are asked to weep with those who weep (Rom. 12.15), but they are not to sorrow as those who have not hope (1 Thess. 4.13): death has been conquered (1 Cor. 15.54–57; Heb. 2.14–15), and death and mourning will have no part in the new heavens and the new earth (Rev. 7.17; 21.4).

There are other causes for mourning recorded in the Bible besides death—personal calamities, such as those experienced by Job (Job 1.13–20; 2.11–13), national disasters such as drought (Jer. 14.1–2; Joel 1.13), even impending disasters (Esther 3.13–4.3) and the threat of divine judgment (Jer. 4.5–8). Lamentations for such experiences were often identical in form with those practiced because of death (Exod. 33.4; 2 Sam. 15.32; 2 Kings 19.1–14; Ps. 35.13; Joel 1.8, 13; 2.13). On occasion, mourners also expressed their grief by sitting or lying on the ground (Judg. 20.26; 2 Sam. 12.16; Job 1.20), placing their hands over their mouths (Ps. 39.9), bowing or covering their heads (Lam. 2.10; Esther 6.12), or walking barefoot (2 Sam 15.30). Such actions and the laments that accompanied them were not simply the expected response to pain or disappointment; they were also a way of showing submission to God's will (Job 1.20–21) and contrition before him (Jer. 9.17–19; Joel 2.12–18; Jon. 3.5–10).

See also Afterlife and Immortality; Burial Customs.   GERALD F. HAWTHORNE

Murder. The biblical concept of the image of God lay at the heart of abhorrence to the taking of a human life. However the idea of a divine image was understood—physical likeness, self-transcendence, capacity to communicate, authoritative rule—it implied that one dare not destroy another person who bore God's image. The story of the first murder, *Cain's slaying of his brother Abel, insists that spilt *blood cries out to the creator, who acts to ensure vindication but not at the expense of compassion (Gen. 4.8–16). This tension between revenge and mercy produced responses to murder that lack consistency precisely because they take mitigating circumstances into consideration.

The *Ten Commandments prohibit murder categorically (Exod. 20.13; Deut. 5.17) and without exception. Nevertheless, in Israel's day-to-day existence distinctions were made, and killing was held to be justified in at least two situations,

warfare and execution for capital offenses. The first of these was fortified by the conviction that Israelites engaged in holy wars, with Yahweh as their commander-in-chief. In these circumstances compassion had no place, particularly when the enemy was placed under *ḥērem* (the *ban). *Saul's sparing of the *Amalekite king Agag, whatever its motive, was deemed an act of disobedience, and the prophet *Samuel carried out Yahweh's execution of Agag (1 Sam. 15.33). Israel's recorders of sacred history did not balk at depicting Yahweh as sanctioning, even ordering, such action. *Elijah's slaughter of competing prophets raised no objections that were rooted in the Ten Commandments (1 Kings 18.40). The same leniency occurs with respect to cases of capital punishment. In fact, the blessing of *Noah actually contains a stipulation that murderers are to be executed (Gen. 9.6).

The practical implementing of this sentence resulted in elaborate rituals and numerous distinctions. Premeditated violence differed from an act in the heat of anger or from accidental injury. From early times an institution, the *avenger of blood (*gōʾēl*), assured vindication within each family. The next of kin assumed responsibility for avenging a death, and society sanctioned this means of obtaining revenge for grievous wrong. In time, ransom of the guilty person's life introduced the principle of monetary compensation for the loss.

In cases of accidental homicide, provision was made for the establishment of *cities of refuge, thus enabling society to combine revenge and mercy (Num. 35.9–34). Persons who accidentally caused a death or who killed another person in a fit of anger could flee to a city of refuge and, after satisfactorily convincing officials that asylum was appropriate, entered the city and remained there until the high priest's death; thereafter the individual could return home without harm. Of course, these institutions of a redeemer and of cities of refuge sometimes failed, for not everyone respected the laws governing both.

In cases in which a murder occurred but the murderer was not known, the nearest town had a special ritual by which the people were exonerated of collective guilt (Deut. 21.1–9). The problem of adjudicating responsibility for murder was no simple matter. If an owner of a dangerous ox had been warned because of its habitual goring but failed to keep the ox under control so that it killed someone, the owner was held responsible for the death (Exod 21.29). Similarly, if two persons fought and one was injured but was later able to get up and walk around, the offender could go free even though death occurred a short time later (Exod. 21.18). Owners of *slaves were not culpable if they beat them to death, provided that a day or so lapsed between beating and death (Exod. 21.20–21). Moreover, a person who killed a thief in the night was not held responsible for the action (Exod. 22.2).

The older institution of blood revenge gradually disappeared. By Ezra's time officials of the state handled such matters. The Romans seem to have restricted Jewish authority in case of capital punishment, and by insisting that the murderer had to be warned immediately before the crime, the rabbis made it virtually impossible to take human life. Jesus broadened the prohibition of murder to include anger (Matt. 5.21–22).   JAMES L. CRENSHAW

Music and Musical Instruments. The most significant survival of the music of biblical times is its lyrical material. The Bible gives no indication of the actual melodies used in ancient times by singers for the rendition of the lyrical and only random reference to the range and character of music, musical instruments, and musical patterns. In the Hebrew Bible, however, there are a variety of musical expressions during the monarchic period and a treasure house of hymns after the exile, and the New Testament contains several examples of hymns as well.

The musical tradition of Israel began in the premonarchic period. Israel's *ancestors are depicted as seminomads, traveling long distances within their territorial boundaries in search of grazing land and watering places for their herds of sheep and goats. The Song of the Well (Num. 21.17–18), for example, reveals their constant search for water, and disputes over territory are reflected in their war songs, ranging from shouts associated with the banner (Exod. 17.16) and with the *ark (Num. 10.35–36) to the skillfully composed Song of *Deborah (Judg. 5); note also the reference to the lost "Book of Wars of the Lord" mentioned in Numbers 21.14–15, where a few lines are quoted. The purpose of the brief war shouts was to enable members of a tribe to identify themselves with their own group, and that of the Song of Lamech (Gen. 4.23–24) to incite them to execute the law of blood vengeance. In the case of *Miriam's brief song of triumph (Exod. 15.21) the biblical author reports that women in her entourage danced and beat

their tambourines. This suggests a sharp, strident, staccato rendering of brief war refrains. In the case of longer war odes it seems likely that they had a more elaborate instrumental setting, and, as Genesis 4.21 suggests, such instruments as harps and pipes were used from an early time. In fact the reference in Genesis 4.21 to Jubal as the "father of all who play" these instruments is particularly important for its implication of organized guilds of professional musicians in the premonarchic period.

The centralization of the monarchy brought about changes in Israel's social, economic, and cultural life. Court musicians were remembered for their participation in such functions as coronations, weddings, funerals, and banquets; note, for example, 2 Samuel 19.35. The coronation of a king was a joyous occasion: a trumpet's blast gave the signal for the crowd's acclamation (2 Kings 1.34), and the noise of pipes and trumpets was so great that "the earth quaked" (1 Kings 1.40). For celebrations of his enthronement, musicians sang odes of praise for his just rule and victory over the nation's enemies (1 Sam. 18.7; Pss. 2; 21; 72; 110). They also sang laments for slain warriors (2. Sam. 1.19–27). Court musicians performed at royal weddings (Ps. 45; Amos 6.4–6). The summoning of *David to the court to calm *Saul's violent temper by playing the lyre (1 Sam. 16.14–23; 18.10; 19.9) was an exceptional command performance. By the time of *Hezekiah's reign, court singers and instrumentalists had been so widely acclaimed that they had the unfortunate honor of being included among the royal treasures taken from the palace of *Jerusalem by *Sennacherib to his capital at *Nineveh (701 BCE).

During the monarchic period the second important center for the development of Hebrew music was the *Temple at Jerusalem. Familiar in this connection are the stories of how David brought the ark to Jerusalem in a religious procession with dancing, shouts of joy, and the sound of the ram's horn (2 Sam. 6.12–19) and how *Solomon dedicated the sanctuary in which it was housed (1 Kings 8; 2 Chron. 5.2–14). Although the music of the Temple was undoubtedly not as elaborate in Solomonic times as the later, postexilic Chronicler imagined, it is likely that the king had a major role in organizing the musical elements of the service. The blowing of the silver trumpets both summoned the congregation to the Temple and indicated the times for the offering of *sacrifice (Num. 1.1–3, 10; Ps. 98.6). To the accompaniment of stringed instruments (Ps. 98.5) the priestly choir sang hymns, which were probably the familiar ones of praise (Pss. 145–150), petition (Pss. 44; 74; 79; 80; 83), and thanksgiving (Pss. 30; 66; 106–108).

Hymns were composed according to the metrical scheme of traditional Hebrew *poetry: that is, in couplets of two lines having an accentual rhythm of three or four beats to each line and exhibiting a "parallelism of members," whether synonymous, antithetical, or progressive (step-parallelism). A much-used variation of this metrical scheme is the extension of the three-beat line by two beats, which gives the structural unit a limping or elegiac character. The 3:3 accentual pattern of a single structural unit whose lines express an idea in synonymous parallelism may be illustrated by the passage:

> The heavens are telling the glory of God,
>   and the firmament proclaims his handiwork.
>   [Ps. 19.1]

In Psalm 150 the lyricist lists many, but not all, instruments used by musicians: among the strings, the lyre (kinnôr) and the harp with ten strings (nēbel); among the wind instruments, the ram's horn (šōpār) and the flute (ʿûgāb), but not the metal trumpet (ḥăṣōṣĕrâ) and the double oboe (ḥālîl); and among the percussion instruments, the tambourine (tōp) and cymbals (ṣelṣĕlîm), but not the sistrum (mĕnaʿanʿîm).

*Prophecy and the prophetic movement give us two interesting sidelights on the development of music that occurred apart from the king's patronage: first, on the association of religion and music, and second, on the use of secular music. In the early years of the monarchy, guilds of prophets found that the playing of such instruments as harps, lyres, tambourines, and flutes induced a trancelike state during which individuals were seized by God's spirit and prophesied ecstatically (1 Sam. 10.5–7, 11–13; 2 Kings 3.14–20); in the later period none of the prophets whose oracles are recorded is known to have used music for this purpose. This did not deter them from using effectively metrical forms of lyrics for their pronouncements. Amos, for example, used the qînâ meter of professional musicians for his lament over the imminent destruction of Israel:

> Fállen no móre to ríse
>   is maíden Ísrael;
> fórsaken ón her lánd
>   with nóne to upraíse her.
>   [Amos 5.2]

These later prophets also allude to secular music of urban and rural communities: songs associated with agricultural life (Isa. 9.3; 16.10; Jer. 25.30), *wedding songs (Jer. 7.34) and songs for feasts that were accompanied by such instruments as harps, lyres, tambourines, and flutes (Isa. 23.16). An example of a harvest song is Isaiah's famous Song of the Vineyard (Isa. 5.1–4).

We hear next of the development of music two centuries after the destruction of the Temple, the fall of the monarchy, and the taking captive of its leaders to *Babylon. In the Persian period, exiles returning to Jerusalem were given permission to rebuild the Temple and organize their corporate life under the leadership of the high *priest. It is natural, therefore, that the Temple and the Law became the two foci of Jewish existence. For the development of music during this period the two outstanding sources are the books of *Chronicles and *Psalms, the latter sometimes called the "hymn book of the Second Temple."

According to these two sources it seems that from the fourth century BCE on music became an even more important feature of worship at the Temple than in the earlier period. Vocal and instrumental music was performed by guilds of professional musicians who associated themselves by descent with Heman, Asaph, and Jeduthun (and Korah), and thus ultimately with *Levi, and claimed that they had been commissioned by David himself (1 Chron. 6.16–32). They apparently collected psalms (e.g., Pss. 73–82, attributed to Asaph) and added musical and liturgical notations, some of which are obscure, like, for example, the term *selah, which probably indicates a pause in the singing of a psalm for a brief instrumental interlude. Titles to the psalms were also added to indicate how the lyrics were to be performed and used. Some psalms were to be sung with the accompaniment of stringed instruments (Ps. 4) or flutes (Ps. 5); others sung to known tunes (e.g., "The Deer of the Dawn," Ps. 22); and still others for religious occasions (for pilgrimages, Pss. 120–134; for the dedication of the Temple, Ps. 30; for the *Sabbath, Ps. 92). So well established is the relation of Temple worship and music that the psalmists associated the act of coming to the place of God's presence with that of making "a joyful noise to him with songs of praise" (Ps. 95.2) and of "making melody to him with tambourine and lyre" (Ps. 149.3).

The development of music and its use in early Christianity can be reconstructed only tentatively from materials in the New Testament, which, in comparison with those of the Hebrew Bible, cover a very short span of time and are so closely associated with the purposes of Christian missionary activity that they contain little information about the subject. In general, it seems that the music of early Christians, like that of the *synagogue, was entirely vocal (Mark 14.26; Acts 16.25) and consisted of psalms (1 Cor. 14.26; cf. the frequent quotations from the Psalter in the New Testament) and of their own lyrics, especially those to be used for baptismal and eucharistic rites.

Examples of Christian lyrics appear to represent three types of hymnody that originated in the churches of Palestine or of the Greek world beyond Palestinian borders. For the first, we have five hymnic passages that probably came from the Jewish Christian churches, having been translated into Greek from *Aramaic and exhibiting the characteristics of biblical psalmody. Two are preserved in the infancy narrative of Luke (1.46–55; 2.29–32; cf. 1.68–79, probably sung at one time by disciples of *John the Baptist). Three in the book of Revelation are a song of thanksgiving (Rev. 5.3–4), a song in praise of the slain *Lamb (Rev. 5.9–10), and hymnic material in Revelation 19.1–7, which used responses of "*Hallelujah" and "*Amen" and is about the marriage of the Lamb. The last two were probably used during the eucharistic rite.

From the churches of the Greek world there are no examples in New Testament literature of a hymn using the quantitative metric form of the Greeks, but there is hymnic material that seems to reflect mixed forms developed from the fusion of biblical and Hellenistic elements. An example that may have been translated from Aramaic but departs slightly from Jewish tradition is the fragment of a confessional hymn preserved in 1 Timothy 3.16. Here the structure is still biblical, as probably was the music, but the parallelism is that of Hellenistic rhetorical construction.

The third type of hymn is found in lyrics in praise of Christ as Lord (Phil. 2.6–11), as the image of God (Col. 1.15–20), and as the eternal *Logos (John 1.1–18). These hymns seem to be even more remote from Jewish psalmody, for they are characterized by the absence of parallelism, the brevity and equality of the lines,

and the stanza-form. These hymns come from the Christian community in its formative years.

See also Music and the Bible.

LUCETTA MOWRY

Music and the Bible. *This entry focuses on the use of the Bible in sacred and secular Western music. For music in biblical times, see* Music and Musical Instruments.

The Bible has been used in Western music for several purposes: (1) At worship Christians and Jews frequently sing biblical passages in psalms or hymns. (2) Biblical material in liturgy is also accompanied and, in effect, interpreted by music. (3) The Bible is present in music intended not for worship but for the opera house or concert hall.

Liturgy. Both Judaism and Christianity have used biblical texts for liturgical purposes. The *Psalms were composed for ritual singing, as some of the superscriptions show: "To the Choirmaster" (NRSV: "To the leader"; Pss. 18–22; etc.) probably designates a collection of songs and also suggests organized liturgical music. Exodus 15.1–18 is a psalm concluding the narrative of the *Passover celebration. Early Christians sang "psalms and hymns and spiritual songs" (Eph. 5.19), doubtless psalms in translation and Christian hymnody, such as the Magnificat and Benedictus (Luke 1.46–55, 68–79) or musical outbursts like Revelation 11.17–18; 19.1–2, 5, 6–8.

Though Judaism and Christianity generated other texts for liturgical singing, biblical language had great importance. Not all of the canon of the Mass is derived from the Bible (e.g., *Kyrie eleison* and *Credo*), but the opening lines of the *Gloria* are from Luke 2.14, and the *Agnus Dei* augments *John the Baptist's remark in John 1.29.

We know very little about the music of late antiquity. Ambrose (Bishop of Milan, 374–397 CE) introduced antiphonal singing of psalms and hymns, and the Ambrosian liturgy strongly influenced liturgical practice in France and Spain. The great figure of medieval liturgical music was Pope Gregory I (590–604 CE), who had chants collected and assigned to liturgical occasions, bringing liturgical music into a systematic whole (hence "Gregorian" chant). Music was understood as the servant of faith; it was not intended to interpret the text. Thus, melismatic embellishments on certain syllables in the chant, far from calling attention to important religious concepts in the text, fell mostly on unstressed syllables. Music, expected to dispose the mind to truth and open the heart to pious feelings, was subordinate to words. Thus, though the psalms refer to instruments, and secular music freely used them, Christian liturgy was purely vocal until the thirteenth-century revival of the organ to accompany singing. The organ, known from Hellenistic times, had been used earlier for ecclesiastical processions, and organs were known in some European churches well before the thirteenth century.

When polyphony (Greek, "many voices") replaced the older monophony ("single voice") with more complex musical textures, around 1000 CE, greater freedom to interpret the text words became possible. Sounding several musical lines simultaneously, polyphony enlarged the expressive potential of the music and became the distinctive mark of European music. It was performed in monasteries, where the monks were trained to sing, or by choirs in churches. Congregations were not expected to sing polyphony, and its introduction made the congregation in most cases the silent partner in worship.

Early polyphony consisted of one to three voices weaving faster-moving melodic lines above a slower voice holding (Lat. *tenere*, hence "tenor") a Gregorian chant melody. In the thirteenth-century polyphony of the Notre Dame school, the quick rhythms of upper voices above the long notes of the chant produce emotional depth in the psalm text. The effect is not interpretation of the words but a more emotional aspect to the experience. Polyphonic music became even less accessible to ordinary people, and the Reformation aimed to revive congregational hymn-singing. Lutheran chorales and Reformed hymns and psalms continued to be polyphonic, in that voices sang different notes at the same time, but the melody was sung by one voice (originally the tenor), with other voices in chordal accompaniment. Interpretive scope was limited.

Since the Reformation, the liturgical settings of biblical words have been mainly hymns and anthems, the former sung by congregations, the latter by choirs. Hymn melodies are conventionally sung by the soprano, not the tenor, with the other voices accompanying in chords. Many hymns have been metrical paraphrases of psalms (some Protestant, especially Calvinist, groups would sing nothing but psalms). Metrical psalms were often stilted in wording, with the meter taking precedence over clarity of sense. They usually used standardized metrical patterns in order to fit more than one tune. Some perennially favorite hymns are psalm paraphrases. For example, "Our God, our help in ages past" derives from Psalm 90, and "A mighty fortress is our God," for which Martin Luther wrote both words and melody, is a paraphrase of Psalm 46. Tunes might be written for the words, but frequently secular melodies were employed. When a melody has become traditionally associated with certain words, the melody itself is enough to recall the words to those trained in the tradition. The hymn tune "St. Anne" brings immediately to Protestant minds "Our God, our help in ages past," and the association arouses emotional resonance in the hearers.

Since the eighteenth century, congregational singing has usually been accompanied by organs, sometimes by other instruments, though a few sects refuse instruments altogether. Pianos may appear in less formal settings. In the latter twentieth century, many churches have introduced even into major liturgical occasions unison hymns accompanied by a guitar instead of an organ. Increasingly, such hymns are contemporary religious verse and not paraphrases of the Bible.

Musical Interpretation. With polyphony came more complex interpretation in the musical settings of the Bible. Voices accompanying the chant melody (*cantus firmus*, "fixed song") of the polyphonic motet might sing different, even secular, words. In a thirteenth-century motet on *Haec dies quam fecit Dominus* ("This is the day that the Lord has made," Ps. 118.24), from a gradual for Easter Sunday, the middle voice sings of the Virgin Mary as bringer of grace, the upper one a plaintive love song about "fair Marion." Easter suggested Christ's grace mediated by the Virgin, and springtime justified a declaration of love for "fair Marion," whose name echoes Mary. Simultaneous different texts might seem confused cacophony, but they lent a symbolic and interpretive depth to the "day that the Lord has made."

Understanding such a work depended on conventional frames of reference. Those who knew the Easter reference of *Haec dies* would grasp the other symbolism. Music refined its conventions of reference, making interpretive gestures familiar to congregations. Every system of musical style has such conventions. In European-derived music of the last several centuries, a reed instrument playing slowly in a ⅝, ⅞, or ¹²⁄₈ rhythm conveys the pastoral, a shepherd's song or a meadow scene. Music featuring horns and drums in a heavily accented duple meter is recognized as a march, and so on. The music by itself cannot show whether the shepherd be Greek, Palestinian, or Scandinavian, or whether the marchers are Egyptian soldiers, English constables, or an American marching band.

Complex polyphony has been sung by choirs, which can be trained to sing expressively interpretive music, rather than by congregations. In addition to "anthems" (a word corrupted from the medieval and Renaissance "antiphon") set to biblical words—some of which are no harder than hymns, though others are extremely difficult (e.g., Charles Ives's *Psalm 90* [1923])—Christian churches developed more elaborate musical forms to present biblical texts. The term "motet" came to refer to almost any liturgical choral composition, and especially in the eighteenth and nineteenth centuries, to an unaccompanied choral work on a biblical text. Johann Sebastian Bach's *"Jesu, meine Freude"* (1723?) has no biblical text, but Johannes Brahms wrote beautiful motets (e.g., *Psalm 51* [1860]). In the late Renaissance, *cantata* meant merely something "sung" (Ital. *cantare*), whereas in northern Europe, the term came to mean a multimovement religious choral work, accompanied by organ or orchestra, often with solos. In J. S. Bach's busy hands (he wrote hundreds), the cantatas meditated musically on a theme in the lectionary reading for a given Sunday, or focused on an apt chorale (e.g., Cantata no. 140, *"Wachet auf"* [1731], alluding to Isa. 40.9). The text often refers to the prescribed biblical reading, and the recitatives and arias expand upon its religious meaning to the pious soul. This kind of cantata, especially characteristic of pietistic Lutheranism, was extended in the *Passions* by Lutheran composers. Bach probably wrote five Passion settings, though only those on *St. Matthew* (1727) and *St. John* (1724) are complete, one on *St. Mark* is reconstructed, and two are lost. They intersperse narration with chorales (possibly sung by congregation and choir), interpretive recitatives, arias, and duets set to devotional words. Solo voices sing words of the characters in recitative, and words of Jesus are always accompanied by the special timbre of the orchestral strings. The chorus sings the words of groups—disciples, priests, or the crowd—to orchestral accompaniment.

A more dramatic form, often with biblical contents, was the oratorio. Originally a musical morality play performed in an oratory, a room devoted to prayer to a saint, the form developed in the seventeenth century into something like a sacred opera. Giacomo Carissimi's *Jephtha* (1650), based on Judges 11, has recitatives, arias, duets, choruses, and a narrator. Whether oratorios were staged remains uncertain. From the seventeenth century to the present many have been biblical stories or extended comment on biblical themes. The text of George F. Handel's *Messiah* (1742), the most familiar of the latter kind, is a catena of biblical verses, and the music combines vast choruses, arias, duets, and orchestral pieces. His *Saul* (1739) and *Judas Maccabaeus* (1747) dramatically interpret the biblical stories. Hundreds if not thousands of oratorios have biblical content. Franz Joseph Haydn's *The Creation* (1798), Felix Mendelssohn's *Elijah* (1846), Hector Berlioz's *L'Enfance du Christ* (1854), César Franck's *Béatitudes* (1869–1879), John Knowles Paine's *St. Peter* (1873), and Charles Gounod's *Redemption* (1882) are examples from a list that could be extended for pages. Brahms's *A German Requiem* (1868) is an oratorio like the *Messiah*, that is, an interpretation of biblical texts about death. Many oratorios, including Handel's, were written for performance not in church but in music halls or concert rooms.

In the nineteenth century, it was sometimes argued that religious music ought to be stylistically distinct from secular music. Some composers were criticized for liturgical works indistinguishable from their operas. Gioacchino Rossini's *Stabat mater* (second version, 1841) and Giuseppe Verdi's *Requiem* (1874) are perhaps the textbook examples. The argument rested both on liturgical conservatism perceptible in a Christianity that felt beleaguered by secularity's growing self-confidence and on the theological principle, always present in Christianity, that the life of faith is distinct from the life of the world.

Secular Biblical Music. Early sacred cantatas were like small operas, and oratorios like larger ones. Opera was originally drama continuously accompanied by music, the work of Florentines around 1600 intending to revive Greek drama. As the form moved beyond Florence, we find opera on religious subjects in Rome as early as Stefano Landi's *Sant'Alessio* (1632). We might have expected North German Protestants to pioneer biblical operas, but there were only sporadic compositions. Hamburg saw such works as Johann Theile's *Der erschaffene, gefallene, und wieder aufgerichtete Mensch* ("Created, Fallen, and Restored Humanity," 1678). Paris had Marc-Antoine Charpentier's *David et Jonathan* (1688). Energy that might have gone into biblical opera in the eighteenth century was apparently put mostly into the oratorio (*Jephté* by Michel Montéclair [1732] is a rare operatic exception). Perhaps the line between "sacred" and "secular" handling of biblical matters was becoming fainter.

Biblical operas proliferated in the nineteenth century, and a long list might begin with Etienne Méhul's *Joseph* (1807) and continue through such works as Rossini's *Moses in Egypt* (1818), Verdi's *Nabucco* (Nebuchadnezzar, 1842), Gounod's *The Queen of Sheba* (1861), Camille Saint-Saëns's *Samson and Delilah* (1877), Jules Massenet's *Hérodiade* (1881), Richard Strauss's *Salome* (1905, based on Oscar Wilde's one-act play on the New Testament story), Artur Honegger's *King David* (1921), to Arnold Schoenberg's incomplete masterpiece, *Moses und Aron* (1931–1932). Carlisle Floyd's Tennessee-mountain setting of the story of *Susanna and the elders in *Susannah* (1955) is perhaps the most successful American biblical opera.

"Secular" biblical music includes such orchestral works as Ralph Vaughan Williams's *Job, A Mask for Dancing* (1931), Ernest Bloch's *Schelomo* (Solomon) for cello and orchestra (1916), and Leonard Bernstein's *Jeremiah Symphony* (1942), in which a mezzo-soprano sings part of *Lamentations in Hebrew. Some vocal works intended for the concert hall are Zoltán Kodály's *Psalmus hungaricus* (Ps. 55, an old Hungarian translation [1923]), Igor Stravinsky's *Symphony of Psalms* (1930, rev. 1948), using Vulgate texts, Aaron Copland's "In the Beginning" (1947, Gen. 1.1–2.7), Luigi Dallapiccola's remarkable *Job* (1950), and Mario Davidovsky's *Scenes from Shir Hashirim* (1975–1976, Song of Solomon). Dvořák's *Biblical Songs* (1894) and Brahms's *Four Serious Songs* (1896), for voice and piano, set biblical passages in a style not different from their other songs.

Johann Kuhnau wrote six sonatas for harpsichord (1700), dramatically narrating biblical episodes: "Saul's Madness Cured by Music," "David and Goliath," and others. Instrumental music conveying biblical atmospheres must use referential conventions or composers' programmatic titles. There are few such works. Jaromír Weinberger published *Bible Poems* (1939) for organ, and the Black American composer R. Nathaniel Dett wrote *Eight Bible Vignettes* (1941–43) for solo piano, an attractive set in a Late Romantic style.

Such a survey can only drop a few names and make a few generalities. Western music has used the Bible mostly to enrich the liturgies of Christianity and Judaism. In the past century or two, the Bible has provided composers more comfortably than before with material for music other than "religious." Twentieth-century music shows the Bible's secure place as an artifact of the culture rather than as the exclusive possession of religious associations.   EDWIN M. GOOD

Myrrh. An aromatic gum-resin of *Commiphora myrrha*, a tree native to southern *Arabia and eastern Africa. Myrrh trees of Punt (Somalia) appear in fifteenth-century BCE Egyptian royal tomb reliefs. According to the Bible, myrrh was traded from Canaan to Egypt (Gen. 37.25, 43.11). "Liquid myrrh" (myrrh-scented oil) was a cosmetic (Esther 2.12, Song of Sol. 5.5), and in special formulation was used for cultic anointing (Exod. 30.23–25). In the New Testament, myrrh was one of the gifts of the *Magi to the infant Jesus (Matt. 2.11). It was used as a painkiller (mixed with wine, Mark 15.23) and to anoint corpses before burial (with aloes, John 19.39).
    JOSEPH A. GREENE

Mystery. In the Aramaic section of *Daniel, the Aramaic word *rāz*, translated in the *Septuagint by the Greek word *mystērion*, "mystery," has a specialized meaning, denoting primarily that what God has decreed shall take place in the future, that is, the eschatological secret to be made known. This use in Daniel of "mystery" with the correlative "solution" or "interpretation" is paralleled at *Qumran. Whereas in ordinary discourse "mystery" generally means a secret for which no answer can be found, this is not its sense in Greek, in which the term "mysteries" denotes the sacred rites or teachings of the *mystery religions in which only the initiated shared.

In the New Testament, therefore, *mystērion* signifies a divine secret that is being (or has been) revealed in God's good time, an open secret in some sense. The word thus paradoxically comes close to the word for revelation, *apokalypsis*, and can almost be equivalent to the Christian gospel. The only occurrence of the word in the Gospels is Mark 4.11 (= Matt. 13.11; Luke 8.10; plural in both of the latter). It refers to the *kingdom of God, the knowledge of which is reserved for those to whom it is given; at least the Markan usage appears to mean that the secret revealed is that in some sense Jesus himself in his ministry should be identified with the kingdom of God (*see* Messianic Secret).

If "mystery" is read (instead of "testimony") in 1 Corinthians 2.1, it must mean the gospel, the subject of Paul's proclamation (see also 1

Cor. 2.7; 4.1; Eph. 6.19; Col. 4.3; 1 Tim. 3.9,16; Rev. 10.7). In Romans 11.25, the "mystery" is a special aspect of the divine plan, namely, the partial eclipse of Israel until the *gentiles are won; in Ephesians (1.9–10; 3.3, 9–10) the mystery is, in particular, that aspect of God's plan which consists of the unification of the universe, including Jews and gentiles. Romans 16.25–26 is a clear example of the meaning of "mystery" as the divine plan in the process of being divulged; and in Colossians 1.26–27 and 2.2, this seems to be daringly identified with Christ himself. Perhaps 2 Thessalonians 2.7 should be included here, if by "the mystery of lawlessness" is meant a satanic parody of God's mystery, a sort of demonic gospel to be destroyed by Jesus at his coming.

Elsewhere the word can mean a more private, exclusive, and less generally divulged religious secret (1 Cor. 15.51). According to 1 Corinthians 14.2, a person who utters unintelligible sounds is speaking "mysteries in the Spirit" (cf. 1 Cor. 13.2 *and see* Glossolalia). In Ephesians 5.32, "mystery" appears to apply to the exegesis of Genesis 2.24, quoted in the preceding verse, thus denoting the inner meaning of a passage whose more obvious sense is something other; there is an analogous sense in Revelation 1.20; 17.5, 13.

The use of the word "mystery" with reference to the *sacraments (the *Vulgate sometimes translates *mystērion* by *sacramentum*) is postbiblical, but an understandable development from the above-mentioned usage of the word to denote the inner meaning of a phrase or symbol.

DAVID HILL

Mystery Religions. Mystery religions, practiced throughout the Mediterranean from the seventh century BCE to the fifth century CE, were secret and voluntary rites of initiation entered by those seeking an intensified form of worship in addition to their inherited traditions dedicated to deities of family, community, and place.

The term "mystery" derives from the Greek *mystēria*, which described the oldest initiation rites at Eleusis. The Eleusinian and Dionysian mysteries were Greek, while those of Isis, Mithras, Kybele, and Attis came from the East. Common to each of the mysteries was the prohibition against revealing its secrets to noninitiates. They were literally unspeakable because it was not knowledge but an experience that was transmitted through specific ritual acts, with each cult offering a different experience through the performance of an initiatory rite.

The participant in the mysteries ritually reenacted the drama and suffering of the deity honored in the rites, which ensured a connection with the deity and a significant change of status for the initiate. The Eleusinian mysteries promised blessedness and a guarantee of immortality, while the mysteries of Isis promised rebirth and freedom from fate.

The influence of the mysteries can be seen in both Judaism and Christianity. Jewish scriptures of the Hellenistic era employed the terminology of the mysteries to portray the *wisdom of God that remains hidden from the ungodly (Wisd. of Sol. 2.22; 6.22). The influence in this case is terminological, as also in Daniel 2.27–30, 47.

Far more problematic is the question of how far the Greco-Roman mysteries influenced the early Christian community not only in terminology but also in the rites that secured salvation with Christ. *Paul's explanation that *baptism united the initiate with the death and *resurrection of Christ (Rom. 6.3–5) has elicited heated debate from scholars who have asserted or denied Paul's dependence on the mysteries. The terminological influence of the mystery cults on early Christianity is not disputed, but the degree to which they influenced the content of Christian baptism and celebration of the Eucharist has still not been resolved.

Like their modern counterparts, early apologists sought to distinguish the Christian rites of initiation from those celebrated by others. Justin Martyr (ca. 150 CE), for example, claimed that the pagan mysteries were demonic counterfeits of the true mysteries of Christ. Yet by the fourth century, as the church adapted to Hellenistic culture, the *mystēria* of Christ reflected both the terminology and the structure of the ancient mystery cults.

See also Mystery.   GREGORY SHAW

Myth. A story, usually originally transmitted orally, that has as its main actors superhuman beings and that is typically set in otherworldly time and space. Historians of religion, while often differing on how to interpret any specific myth, tend to agree that all myths, through the use of symbolic language, communicate transcendent meaning within a culture, revealing its cosmic dimensions. In the New Testament, however, Greek *mythos* (Engl. "myth") is used negatively to mean an invented story, a rumor, or a fable

(1 Tim. 1.4; 4.7; 2 Tim. 4.4; Titus 1.14; 2 Pet. 1.16).

Hebrew Bible. At first glance, there seems very little narrative in the Hebrew Bible that can, on the basis of the definition above, be classified as myth. Only Genesis 1.1–2.4a, the story of *creation, is set in cosmic time and space and features a superhuman being, God, as its main actor. Elsewhere biblical narratives ostensibly focus on human actors living on earth during historical time. Still, it can be argued that Genesis 2.4b–11.9, including the stories of the garden of *Eden (Gen. 2.4b–3.24), *Noah (Gen. 6.5–9.17), and the tower of *Babel (Gen. 11.1–9), is myth. Humanity's first home in Eden and the plain of Shinar, where the tower of Babel is built, cannot really be understood as this-worldly locations; the date of the expulsion from *paradise and the year of the *Flood are not points that can be fixed on a historical time line. Moreover, while *Adam, *Eve, Noah, and the people of Babel are not gods, their existence is surely not limited by the kinds of constraints that define normal human experience: they have extraordinarily long life spans, and God makes clothes for Adam and Eve and speaks directly to Noah.

This conclusion concerning the mythic nature of Genesis 1–11 is enhanced by looking at the mythologies of Israel's ancient Near Eastern neighbors: *Egypt, *Canaan, and, in particular, Mesopotamia. The story of creation in Genesis 1.1–2.4a, which begins with the wind of God hovering over a watery *chaos (Hebr. *tĕhôm*), finds parallels in the *Babylonian creation myth, *Enuma elish,* which describes a primordial battle between a goddess of watery chaos, Tiamat (etymologically related to Hebr. *tĕhôm*), and Marduk, a god of wind and storm. The story of Noah should be compared to a fragmentary third-millennium flood myth from *Sumer, the myth of Ziusudra, and to two later Akkadian versions of the same myth found in the epic of Atrahasis and in the epic of *Gilgamesh. Both the Atrahasis and Gilgamesh epics also contain parallels to the story of Eden: in Atrahasis, as in Genesis 2.7, humans are molded from the clay of the earth (this tradition can also be found in Egyptian myths about the potter god of creation, Khnum); in the Gilgamesh epic, as in Genesis 3.22, there is a magical plant that, once eaten, yields a godlike state of immortality. The story of the tower of Babel similarly finds its roots in Mesopotamian sources, as the very name Babel, the Hebrew equivalent of Babylon, suggests.

While it is difficult, beyond Genesis 1–11, to speak of myth as such in Hebrew Bible narrative, scholars have identified ways in which the language and patterns of myths from the ancient Near East are present even in seemingly historical accounts. Most significant is the common Semitic myth of a fight between a storm deity and a sea deity, the Babylonian exemplar of which, *Enuma elish,* is described above. The same basic plot is known from second-millennium BCE Canaan, in *Ugaritic texts depicting a battle between a god of the waters of chaos, called both Yamm, "Sea," and Nahar, "River," and *Baal, the god of the storm. In the Hebrew Bible, while the overt polytheism of these Mesopotamian and Canaanite prototypes is rejected, scholars have argued that the ancient mythic conception of storm versus sea stands behind Exodus 15.1–18, an account of the Israelite *Exodus from Egypt that culminates with God routing the Egyptians by sending a storm to drown them in the Reed Sea.

This same notion of a battle between Yahweh, the god of Israel, and some sort of watery enemy is also alluded to frequently in poetic passages, particularly in prophetic texts (e.g., Isa. 27.1), in certain psalms (e.g., Ps. 89.9–10), and in Job (e.g., Job 26.12–13). In these texts the foe is most often described as a primordial water monster. Again, the myths of Israel's neighbors provide crucial comparative data: the biblical sea monster is at points called *yam*, "sea," and *nāhār*, "river" (e.g., Hab. 3.8), the same names given to Baal's watery foe at Ugarit; also in Ugaritic myth Yamm/Nahar is called Lotan, cognate to Hebrew *Leviathan, and Tannin, cognate to Hebrew *tannîn*, "serpent," both terms used in biblical poetry of the primordial monster (e.g., Job 41.1; Isa. 51.9). And, as in Psalm 74.13, both Ugaritic Yamm/Nahar and Tiamat, the watery enemy of *Enuma elish,* are depicted as multiheaded dragons.

Among poetic texts the theme of Yahweh's battle with the dragon often occurs in *apocalyptic literature, both poetry and prose, in which mythological language and imagery are common. For example, the collection of apocalypses found in Daniel 7–12 is full of mythological allusions: Daniel 7.9–10, 13–14 reflects, it has been argued, myths concerning a younger god who assumes power from an older deity; also mythological is the notion that the divine patrons of the nations fight in the heavens while their earthly counterparts battle below (Dan. 10.10–21). Mythic motifs manifest themselves similarly even in protoapocalyptic texts from the exilic and postexilic periods (e.g., Isa. 24–27; 34–35;

40–66; Zech. 9–14). One notable example comes from Isaiah 25.7, which describes how Yahweh, at the eschatological banquet at the end of time, will swallow up death forever; this is an allusion to a passage found in the Baal myth from Ugarit, in which it is said that the god of death, Mot, will swallow up Baal into the underworld. Yet simultaneous with allusion, there is reversal, for in the Canaanite myth, the god of storm and fertility, Baal, is rendered a prisoner through the power of death; in Israel, however, Yahweh, who shares with Baal attributes of fertility and storm god, vanquishes death through swallowing rather than being swallowed up.

The observation concerning attributes Yahweh shares with Baal suggests one final way in which older mythic traditions are reflected in biblical literature: the characteristics of ancient Near Eastern gods, in particular the gods of Canaan, are used in Israel to describe the character of Yahweh. Thus, like Baal, Yahweh is said to ride in a chariot of clouds (Ps. 68.4), to speak with a voice of thunder (2 Sam. 22.14), and to appear in a *theophany of storm (Exod. 19.16–18; Judg. 5.4–5). Yahweh is also depicted as creator and a granter of children (Deut. 32.6), as lawgiver (Exod. 33.7–11), as judge among the divine council of the gods (Psalm 82; see Sons of God), and as a deity of graciousness and compassion (Exod. 34.6), language reminiscent of El, the high god of the Canaanite pantheon.

New Testament. While, as noted above, the term "myth" is used in New Testament literature with negative connotations, much in the New Testament is in fact mythic in character. The New Testament, for example, inherits from the Hebrew Bible a mythological conception of the universe as having three tiers: heaven, earth, and underworld. Each of these three regions, according to New Testament thought, has its proper denizens (God and the *angels, humanity, and *Satan and the *demons, respectively), and this notion of divine and demonic forces also has its antecedents in mythological patternings found in the Hebrew Bible, especially in apocalyptic literature. Apocalyptic also infuses New Testament thought with a mythological view of time, in particular with a belief that time has reached its fullness and the eschaton is imminent.

Moreover, the fundamental narrative that inspires the New Testament, the story of *Jesus, could be understood as mythic in character. Thus various New Testament writers, although they differ in details, depict a Jesus who is superhuman in nature, the product of a miraculous birth, able to effect healings and *exorcisms, and, most important, a being resurrected on the third day after his death. Moreover, according especially to Paul and to the author of the gospel of John, there is found in Jesus even before he is born a cosmic dimension that transcends this-worldly space and time (see Logos). Thus the Jesus of Paul and John is described as one who was preexistent, present in the heavens with God from the beginning of time (John 1.1–18; Phil. 2.5–11). Paul, along with the author of the book of *Revelation and others, adds an eschatological, even apocalyptic component to this cosmic description of Jesus by arguing for the return of Jesus as heavenly judge at the end of creation.

See also Israel, Religion of.

SUSAN ACKERMAN

N

Nabateans.

Origins and Growth. The consensus of modern scholarship no longer relates the Nabateans to the biblical Nebaioth, the firstborn son of *Ishmael (Gen. 25.13, 16; 28.9; 36.3), nor with the Nabatu/Nabaiati of Assyrian records. Rather, they are seen to have originated somewhere in the Arabian peninsula, emerging by at least the fourth century BCE and described by Diodorus Siculus as a sedentarized group of traders occupying the ancient *Edomite site known as Petra (Map 11:G5). Pliny adds some scant details of previous Red Sea island occupation and suggests an original tribal territory between those of the Qedar and Dedan tribes.

By the first century BCE, the group had become fully sedentary, urban, and monarchically organized, controlling the major north-south *trade routes of Coele-*Syria and northern *Arabia. As a result of commerce, their sphere of influence extended far beyond their political borders, and their trading connections embraced the major luxury suppliers and markets of both east and west. Although *frankincense and *myrrh, along with Dead Sea balsams and bitumen, appear foremost in the list of their commercial products, such items as silk, gems, spices, and pharmaceuticals were probably also traded. With the trading routes went also other installations, resulting in more than a thousand sites known to have been established by Nabateans.

Their capital city, Petra, rapidly achieved a sophisticated urbanism, prompted by competition with surrounding people. A monarchic form of government (eleven kings have thus far been identified) further advanced their position as a true political state. The Nabateans seem to have reached their height under Aretas IV (9 BCE–40 CE), whose ethnarch attempted to arrest *Paul at *Damascus (2 Cor 11.32).

Language. Although the extant examples of Nabatean are basically *Aramaic, they contain a large number of Arabisms. The script gradually developed into a semicursive, ligatured form, which ultimately served as the basis for the modern Arabic script.

Hundreds of Nabatean inscriptions have been found, including letters and contracts. No literary works, however, have as yet been recovered, leaving vast gaps in knowledge concerning the ideology, social structure, and even commercial history of the people.

Technology. Despite the lack of documentary data, the material remains of the Nabateans have furnished substantial evidence of high technological skill. Hydraulic engineering, architecture, ceramics, numismatics, metallurgy, along with sculpture and decorative art, are attested throughout Nabatene areas. Especially at Petra, such skills are seen at their best, for the capital city was embellished by succeeding rulers, in addition to being militarily secured and made more generally habitable. Likewise throughout the kingdom, different types of desert-adapted water systems for both agriculture and culinary purposes are found.

Architecturally, the Nabateans show an eclecticism to be attributed to their broad trading connections. Most obvious are the more than eight hundred funerary, cultic, and other architectural features at Petra, and the smaller number, mainly tomb façades, from Medain Selah. The vast majority of these installations are carved into cliff faces, but built structures are being uncovered by recent excavations at a variety of sites. At Petra these have included public secular and religious structures, along with private residential buildings.

Ceramics also reached an extremely high technical and decorative level by the first century CE. Most impressive was the development of a fine, thin red-painted pottery, generally used for open plates. This type has become the principal marker for identifying Nabatean sites throughout the area. Of equal importance, however, were more commercial ceramic vessels, such as *unguentaria* for oils and related products, which were developed for trade throughout the Roman empire; these have been identified as far west as Spain.

Coinage and other metal production are also noticeably represented at Petra. Coin production among the Nabateans possibly began as early as 90 BCE, and continued until the beginning of the second century CE.

Sculpture, in the round and in relief, along with castings of figurines, lamps, and other objects, appear in great quantities and types, some with marked artistic excellence, at Petra, Et-Tannur and elsewhere. Fresco, appliqué, and other decorative art examples, including the decoration of architectural orders, are also beginning to come to light.

Nabatene functioned as a virtually independent kingdom throughout the Roman period, until the need to consolidate the Near East led Trajan to incorporate the area formally into the empire. In 106 CE Roman forces entered Petra and the Nabatean kingdom ceased to exist. Nabatean life and culture were scarcely affected, however, and continued with little real evidence of Roman or Christian impact.

On the evening of May 19, 363 CE, Petra was struck by a disastrous earthquake and the city fell into ruins. With that calamity, the Nabateans, as such, disappeared from recorded history. Yet their cultural, linguistic, technological, and artistic influence continued, and permeated Near Eastern culture for generations to follow.

PHILIP C. HAMMOND

Nag Hammadi Library. Before the publication of the Berlin Codex 8502, resources for the study of *gnosticism were almost entirely limited to the refutations of the early church fathers, with such extracts and quotations as they chose to include. The only original gnostic material, in Coptic—the Pistis Sophia in the Askew Codex, the two Books of Jeu, and an anonymous treatise in the Bruce Codex—was late and from a time when the movement had long since faltered. The patristic refutations were inevitably open to suspicion as the propaganda of the winning side, while the Coptic material left the impression that the whole movement was both tedious and bizarre. The Berlin Codex, known as far back as 1896 but published only in 1955, yielded three new documents: a fragmentary gospel of Mary, the Apocryphon of John, and the Sophia Jesu Christi. In contrast, the Nag Hammadi library,

discovered in 1945 and gradually made available between 1956 and 1977, contains some forty previously unknown documents together with copies of several texts already known. Fragments used to stiffen the binding of some of the codices suggest a date of about the middle of the fourth century CE, but the Greek originals from which these Coptic texts were translated probably go back in some cases to the second century CE. Thus, the library's significance for the study of some aspects of early Christianity is comparable to that of the *Dead Sea Scrolls for the Judaism of an earlier period. The library derives its name from the modern Egyptian town of Nag Hammadi on the Nile north of Luxor, which was the nearest town to the place of the discovery.

The collection consists of twelve codices in their original bindings, plus eight leaves of a thirteenth (Codex XIII), which were apparently found inside the cover of Codex VI. The total amounts to over one thousand pages, in varying states of preservation: some are almost complete, while others are more or less fragmentary. Most of one codex (Codex I = the Jung Codex) was smuggled out of Egypt, but has now been returned for preservation with the others in the Coptic Museum in Cairo. A complete facsimile edition has been published, and translations have been made into various modern languages.

Not all the documents in the library are strictly gnostic. One (Codex VI,5) is a rather poor translation of a short section of Plato's *Republic;* another (VI,8) is part of the Hermetic tractate Asclepius, previously known from a Latin version. The Teachings of Silvanus (VII,4) is an early Christian wisdom text, while XII,1 is part of the Sentences of Sextus, already known in the original Greek and in versions in other ancient languages. The strongly ascetic tone of the latter work, with the similar ascetic emphasis in other documents, indicates that the collection belonged to a group that stressed asceticism, in contrast to the accusations of libertinism often made against the gnostics in patristic sources. Of the strictly gnostic documents, some are clearly Valentinian in character, such as the gospel of Philip (II,3), the Tripartite Tractate (I,5), and the Valentinian Exposition (XI,2), though there are often variations on the Valentinian system described by Irenaeus. It has been suggested that some texts, such as the Gospel of Truth (I,3) or the Treatise on Resurrection (I,4), may have been written by Valentinus himself, but this is at best speculation. Another major group of documents has been labeled Sethian, because of the prominence given to Seth, the third son of *Adam (Gen. 4.25). These include, among others, the Hypostasis of the Archons (II,4), the Gospel of the Egyptians (III,2), the Apocalypse of Adam (V,5), and the Three Steles of Seth (VII,5). These documents do have a number of features in common, which justifies grouping them together, but the existence of an actual sect of Sethians has been disputed and is by no means certain.

It was noted several years ago that a complete gnostic "New Testament" could be put together from the Christian gnostic texts in the library: the gospel of Thomas or of Philip, the Gospel of Truth, the Acts of Peter and the Twelve Apostles, the Letter of Peter to Philip, two Apocalypses of James, an Apocalypse of Peter, and an Apocalypse of Paul. Despite their titles, however, these texts are not comparable to those in the canonical New Testament: the gospels, for example, do not relate the life and ministry of Jesus, his death and resurrection. The Gospel of Truth is a meditation on the theme of Jesus' message, the gospel of Philip a rather rambling discourse whose continuity seems largely due to catchwords or the association of ideas. The gospel of Thomas is a collection of sayings attributed to Jesus, some parallel to sayings in the canonical Gospels, others completely new, and including all the sayings in the famous Logia papyri found at Oxyrhynchus (see Agrapha). The titles in fact are no sure guide to content: the gospel of the Egyptians and the Apocalypse of Adam have been claimed as non-Christian documents, and the former is not a gospel in the accepted sense, while the latter is more a testament than an apocalypse. Moreover, similarity of title does not mean that the documents are the same: the gospel of Thomas is completely different from the apocryphal infancy gospel of Thomas, the gospel of Philip is not the one known to Epiphanius, the gospel of the Egyptians not the one quoted by Clement of Alexandria. The Nag Hammadi library itself contains two quite different Apocalypses of James. Mention should also be made here of a group of gnostic "gospels" that report revelations given by the risen Jesus to his disciples in the period between his *resurrection and *ascension, which the gnostics extended to eighteen months (in the Pistis Sophia eleven years).

Evaluation of these texts is still in progress, and in some respects they raise as many ques-tions as they answer: the identity of the owners, the purpose of the collection, the reasons for its concealment. The discovery has not solved the problem of gnostic origins, or the vexed question of a pre-Christian gnosticism, but it has enriched our knowledge in several ways. Comparison of different versions of the same document, or different presentations of the same basic system, shows how the gnostics could develop and adapt their ideas, sometimes using older material for their own purposes. Some texts show signs of the Christianization of earlier, possibly non-Christian material, while the Christian gnostic documents often quote or allude to both the Hebrew Bible and the New Testament. The discovery has given fresh stimulus to theories of a Jewish origin for the movement, but however that may be there is no doubt of the significance of the Jewish contribution. Above all, we now have for the first time a comprehensive collection of firsthand gnostic material, from which it is possible to gain some idea of what gnosticism meant to a gnostic: it was not merely bizarre and eccentric but an attempt to deal with the human predicament, to resolve the problem of evil; not a counsel of despair but a religion of hope and deliverance.

See also Apocrypha, *article on* Christian Apocrypha.

ROBERT McL. WILSON

Nahum, The Book of. The three chapters of this book constitute a powerful poem that interprets events surrounding the fall of *Nineveh in 612 BCE in terms of the Lord's control of history on behalf of his people.

Nahum means "comfort," a name that stands in contrast with the violent vengeance portrayed in the book. He is identified as "the Elkoshite," but the location of Elkosh is unknown. We have no other information about this prophet.

This is the only prophetic work that is called a "book" in the text (1.1). It is also called an oracle or "burden," a term for a prophecy spoken against a nation under judgment, and a "vision," a description it shares with *Isaiah and *Obadiah; the latter term probably means a literary presentation of an inspired experience of being in the heavenly court of God, to observe how God deals with nations and people in history. The book contains some of the most powerful poetry in the Bible, a witness to its inspiration in another sense. The prophet-poet who wrote the book looked beyond the facts of Nineveh's destruction to discern and portray God's intentions in it.

The book may be outlined as follows:

I. Yahweh, the avenging God of his people, will destroy Nineveh and bring peace to Judah.
   A. An *acrostic poem: the Lord takes vengeance (1.2–8)
   B. The leaders of Nineveh are addressed (1.9–11)
   C. Good news for Judah: no more invaders (1.12–15)
II. Nineveh's enemies are triumphant.
   A. The last battle (2.1–12)
   B. The Lord's curse on Nineveh (2.13–3.6)
   C. A taunting song over the doomed city (3.7–19).

Israel's relation to *Assyria and its capital city Nineveh extended over more than a century, when the Assyrian empire was at the height of its power. Nineveh (Map 6:H3) was the most important city in Assyria. Its greatest period came during the last century of the empire (730–612 BCE), which coincides with Israel's contacts with it. Great buildings of that period have been excavated, constructed by the emperors *Sennacherib, Esarhaddon, and Ashurbanipal. One palace housed what was at that time the best library in the world. Fortifications included two sets of walls that protected palaces and temples. Ishtar, goddess of love and war, was the city's benefactor. The finest gate was dedicated to her and decorated with her image and symbols, and a magnificent temple housed her statue.

Assyria inherited the crumbling *Hittite and Mitanni empires in the upper Mesopotamian valley in the early second millennium. In the eighth century BCE her emperors, *Tiglath-pileser III, Sargon II, and Sennacherib, sent armies into Syria, then to Judah, and finally into Egypt. Some of the earliest of the Minor Prophets note these movements and interpret them as God's judgment on Israel and the nations (see Amos 3.9). *Samaria fell to Assyrian forces in 722 BCE (2 Kings 17). Judah and her neighbors were vassals to Assyria during the following century; this authority was enforced by Assyrian arms several times (see 2 Kings 18). But Assyrian power began to weaken in the late seventh century, and *Josiah apparently owed his relative freedom of action to this development.

By 614 BCE three powers, *Media, *Babylon, and *Egypt, were prepared to fight for succession to Assyria's empire. Media seized the section east and north of the Euphrates Valley; Babylon seized the south and eventually pushed into Syria; Egypt seized her own territory and extended her control north into Palestine. Babylon laid siege to Nineveh and finally destroyed it in 612 BCE. A small Assyrian army escaped the city and fled toward Haran; it was finally destroyed in 609 BCE.

Nahum's powerful poem portrays the last days of Nineveh. This is seen as good news for Israel, a hope that is short-lived, since Egypt and Babylon turned out to be worse masters than Assyria. But the poem is correct in marking the event as a turning point in history.

There is tension in the Minor Prophets in their views toward Nineveh: repentant and the object of God's care in *Jonah, the instrument of God's judgment on Israel and Judah in *Amos, and the symbol of ultimate evil opposed to God in Nahum. A similar tension exists in Isaiah's portrayal of Assyria as the rod of the Lord's anger against Israel in chap. 10 and God's judgment on Nineveh in 30.27–33 and 31.8–9.

In Nahum a historic event is presented as symbolic of the struggle between God and ultimate evil. In a similar way, Isaiah 47 portrays the fall of Babylon to Persian forces. The book of Revelation speaks of Babylon (or Rome) in similar fashion in chaps. 12–13 and 17–18.

JOHN D. W. WATTS

Names and Namegiving.

Significance. Throughout the Bible, names are full of meaning. Scholars have long recognized that both for ancient Israel and the ancient Near East as well as for early Judaism and Christianity, the name of a person, place, or thing was somehow connected to and descriptive of its essence and/or personality. Thus names of individuals expressed their personality and status or nature. This is reflected in those stories where an individual's name is changed in recognition of a changed nature, personality, or status. Examples include *Jacob's name being changed to Israel following his successful all-night wrestling match with an unnamed (!) divine being (Gen. 32.22–32) and Abram's name being changed to *Abraham after the institution of the *covenant (Gen. 17.1–8). The same phenomenon occurs in the name change or assumption of an additional name or throne name by kings in ancient Israel, as when Mattaniah is renamed *Zedekiah (2 Kings

24.17). The names of a newborn children seem normally to have been carefully chosen to reflect the circumstances of their birth as well as to indicate something of their personality or status.

Types of Names. Names may be divided into two categories: personal names and place names. Within these two categories we may also speak of simple names, consisting of one element, and compound names, consisting of two or more elements. Simple names for individuals may be taken from the names of plants and animals (Deborah = bee/hornet; Huldah = weasel). Compound names may be formed from nouns, but most compounds are sentence names that bring together a form of the divine name (Yo-[Jo-] or Yeho- [Jeho-] and -yah[u], all derived from "Yahweh"; or El; see Names of God in the Hebrew Bible) or a title of God (father, king, etc.) plus a verb, noun, or adjective descriptive of God (e.g., Elijah = Yah[weh] is God [ʾēl]). Names that incorporate a divine name, called theophoric names, can also occur in a short form in which the divine name is omitted; this short form is called a hypocoristicon (e.g., Jonathan/Nathan; Berechiah/Baruch).

Process of Naming. In the Hebrew Bible, children are regularly named by the mother shortly after birth (Gen. 4.1, 25; 16.11; 19.37–38; 29.32–35; 30.6–24; 35.18; 38.4–5; Judg. 13.24; 1 Sam. 1.20; 1 Chron. 4.9; 7.16), but the father or others could and frequently did also name the child (Gen. 4.26; 5; 3.28–29; 16.15; 17.19; 21.3; 35.18; 41.51–52; Exod. 2.22; Judg. 8.31; 1 Chron. 7.23; Hos. 1.4, 6, 9; Ruth 4.17). Genesis 30.6–24 preserves the stories of the births and namings of seven of the sons and one daughter of Jacob. In each case, punning or wordplay in the giving of the name is evident. Usually English translations supply the reader with notes that elucidate the wordplays found in the Hebrew text. Whether wordplay always played an important role is uncertain.

In the Hebrew Bible children were named shortly after birth, but in the New Testament the practice of waiting eight days to name a male child at his circumcision is attested (Luke 1.59; 2.21). Luke's story of the naming of *John the Baptist also attests to the development within ancient Judaism of naming a newborn boy after either his father or grandfather. In the Second Temple period the latter practice is well attested in the family of the high priests.

From at least the Persian period onward, Jews often were given a non-Hebrew (Babylonian, Greek, Latin, etc.) name in addition to their Hebrew name. Biblical examples include Hadassah/Esther (Esther 2.7), Simon Peter (Matt. 4.18; Acts 10.5), John Mark (Acts 12.12), and Saul/Paul (Acts 13.9).   RUSSELL FULLER

Names for the Nameless. Although the Bible contains many named persons, it also refers to numerous individuals who are mentioned but not named. Through the ages, readers of the Bible have felt the need to identify these anonymous figures who play a part in scripture, and so names (at times more than one) have been provided for many of these unidentified persons.

Hebrew Bible. At the very beginning of the Bible, readers are prompted to ask: Who was Cain's wife (Gen. 4.7)? An answer is provided by the apocryphal Book of Jubilees, a Jewish text also known as "The Little Genesis" and thought to have been written in the second century BCE. According to Jubilees 4.9, after giving birth to *Cain and then *Abel, *Eve bore a daughter named Awan, who eventually became Cain's wife. After the birth of his son Seth, *Adam fathered another daughter and named her Azura; she later became Seth's wife (4.10–11).

The Book of Jubilees also identifies the wives of the other antediluvian males who appear in Genesis 5.6–31. *Noah, the last of this series, is said to have married Emzara, the daughter of Rakeel, who in turn was the daughter of Noah's father's brother (Jubilees 4.33). Other apocryphal texts give more names for Noah's wife—over a hundred different names are known!

Another imaginative source for names of unidentified women in the Hebrew scriptures are postbiblical Jewish legends. For example, the story of *Joseph recorded in Genesis does not include the name of Potiphar's wife, who tried to seduce the young Joseph (Gen. 39.12). Later tradition supplies her name—Zuleika. Similarly, the book of Exodus details how the baby *Moses, abandoned in a basket and left floating among the reeds of the Nile, was found by Pharaoh's daughter, who was bathing in the river. The young woman adopted the child as her own. Different names have been ascribed to Moses' surrogate mother: one tradition calls her Thematis, while another names her Bithiah.

Postbiblical sources assign two wives to Job. His first wife, who died while Job was undergoing his trials, was named Sitis (or Sitidos), a name derived from the Greek transcription of Job's hometown, Uz. After Job regained his health, he married Jacob's daughter Dinah, with whom he had a second set of children.

The pseudo-Philonic text *Liber Antiquitatum Biblicarum* (39.8) names the Ammonite ruler with whom Jephthah negotiated (Judg. 11.13) Getal. The daughter whom Jephthah presented as a sacrifice because of his regrettable oath was named Seila (40.1), and she lamented her virginity on a mountain called Stelac (40.5). The same book identifies the medium of Endor, who conjured up *Samuel's spirit for *Saul (1 Sam. 28.7–14), as Sedecla, the daughter of Debin (or Adod) the Midianite (64.3).

New Testament. The New Testament has also been substantially embellished in later Christian tradition. The gospel of Matthew does not specify the number or the names of the *Magi who bring gifts to the infant Jesus (Matt. 2.1–12). Since three gifts were offered, three wise men are assumed. Their names, Balthasar, Melchior, and Gaspar, were assigned in the *Excerpta Latina Barbari* by as early as the sixth century. Such traditions are expanded in the *Exposition of Matthew*, thought to have been written by the Venerable Bede, where it is recorded that each of the wise men came from one of the three main continents—Asia, Africa, and Europe. Furthermore, Bede also claims that the Magi were descendants respectively of Shem, Ham, and Japheth, the three sons of Noah. The East provides yet other traditions. In an Ethiopic text known as the *Book of Adam* (4.15), the Magi are named Hor, king of the Persians, Basanater, king of Saba, and Karsudan, king of the East. A dozen Magi journey to Bethlehem according to Armenian and Syrian traditions, and their names, as well as names for their fathers, are all recorded.

The anonymous shepherds to whom an angel comes to proclaim the news of Jesus' birth (Luke 2.8–18) have also been a subject of traditional interest. A thirteenth-century Syriac compendium collected and edited by Bishop Shelemon and entitled *The Book of the Bee* declares there were seven shepherds and even lists their names: Asher, Zebulan, Justus, Nicodemus, Joseph, Barshabba, and Jose.

The twelve *apostles are identified by the four Gospels, but the seventy (or seventy-two) disciples sent out by Jesus (Luke 10.1) are unnamed. Yet, over the following centuries, many unfinished lists of their names were compiled. Of several somewhat varied lists of the full group, the first appears in the *Chronicon Paschale*, a lengthy chronological-historical text produced by about 650 CE. Matthias is the first disciple listed

(Acts 1.23–26), followed by Sosthenes and Cephas, and then Linus (2 Tim. 4.21) and Cleopas (Luke 24.18). The list continues with names of twenty-six people to whom Paul sends salutations at the end of his letter to the Romans (beginning with Aquila in Rom. 16.3 and ending with Quartus in 16.23). After these names come thirty-nine others, all compiled from the remaining Pauline letters and from Acts. Almost none of the names are Palestinian, but this did not seem to bother the compilers, who also allowed the duplication of several names on the list—the result of a somewhat mechanical combining of separate sources.

The *Book of the Bee* also names various children mentioned in the Gospels. The child whom Jesus sets in the midst of his disciples (Matt. 18.2) is identified as Ignatius, who later ruled as patriarch of *Antioch. Two of the children brought to Jesus so that he would lay his hands on them and bless them (Mark 10.13–16) were Timothy and Titus, who later became bishops.

In Luke 16.19–31, Jesus does not name the rich man who asks for Lazarus's help. An Egyptian tradition of around 200 CE names the rich man *Nineveh, which is symbolic of haughty and indulgent luxury. Nineveh is also cited in an early manuscript of Luke. In the West, a different tradition is found in the pseudo-Cyprianic treatise, *De pascha computus* (200 or 300 CE), with the identification of the rich man as Phineas. Later he is called *Dives.

Of the women in the New Testament, the one who was probably named earliest in Christian tradition was the Canaanite or Syrophoenician woman who sought out Jesus to help save her daughter who was possessed by a demon (Matt. 15.22–28; Mark 7.25–30). The pseudo-Clementine *Homilies* of the third century (2.19) call the woman Justa, and her daughter Bernice. The apocryphal *Acts of Pilate* (7), also names Bernice as the woman who endured hemorrhages for twelve years (Matt. 9.20–22 par.). However, the later Arabic apocryphal gospel of John (26) identifies her as Yusufiya (Josephia). The widow whose dead son Jesus resurrects as he was being carried by on his bier (Luke 7.11–15) is named Lia (Leah) according to the Coptic text on Christ's Resurrection, ascribed to the apostle Bartholomew. Pilate's wife, who in Matthew 27.19 forewarns her husband to have nothing to do with Jesus, is variously identified as Claudia, Procla, and Perpetua.

Similarly, the robbers crucified on either side of Jesus were also given a variety of names. In the Western tradition, an Old Latin Gospel text names them Zoatham and Camma, while another refers to them as Joathas and Maggatras. In the East, they are called Dysmas and Gestas in the *Acts of Pilate,* which also identifies the Roman soldier who pierces Jesus' side with a spear (John 19.34) as Longinus. The tenth-century Codex Egberti names the man who tried to ease Jesus' thirst with a sponge filled with sour wine (Matt. 27.48) as Stephaton.

In the second-century *Gospel of Peter,* after Jesus' burial the soldiers assigned to guard his tomb were supervised by a Roman centurion called Petronius. The *Book of the Bee,* produced much later, elaborates on the descriptions of the soldiers: "They were five in number, named Issachar, Gad, Matthias, Barnabas, and Simon; but others say they were fifteen, three centurions and their Roman and Jewish soldiers."

Many traditions name the individual who accompanies Cleopas to Emmaus on the afternoon of the first Easter (Luke 24.18); among the identifications are Nathanael, Nicodemus, someone named Simon (not Simon Peter), and the evangelist Luke.

Few if any of these traditions are based on accurate historical data. The readiness to give names to the biblical nameless is a witness to the fertile imaginations of Jewish and Christian writers and to their reluctance to accept unknown elements in biblical history.

See also Apocrypha.   BRUCE M. METZGER

Names of God in the Hebrew Bible. The Bible often refers to God by his proper name, which was probably pronounced Yahweh (*see* Tetragrammaton). In the Hebrew Bible, the consonants *yhwh* are usually to be read as Adonai (*ʾădōnāy*), "my Lord," for the sake of reverence, and English versions represent the word by "Lord" or (less often) "God" in capital letters. The Hebrew word is a plural of majesty (with a singular meaning) of *ʾādôn,* which is translated "Lord" (e.g., Isa. 1.24; 3.1). The name Yahweh often appears in the phrase "Yahweh of hosts," as the Hebrew is probably to be translated (cf. "Yahweh of Teman" or "of Samaria" in the Kuntillet ʿAjrud inscriptions of ca. 800 BCE), or the longer "Yahweh the God of hosts" (e.g., 2 Sam. 5.10). Some have thought that the hosts, Sabaoth (*ṣĕbāʾôt*), are the armies of Israel (cf. 1 Sam. 17.45), but a reference to these human armies is inappropriate in, for instance, prophetic denunciations of Israel (e.g., Isa. 1.24), and the word probably

denotes heavenly or angelic armies. Some maintain that Sabaoth is an epithet in apposition to Yahweh and that it means something like "the Mighty One," but there is no evidence in Hebrew for such a meaning.

The usual Hebrew word for God is Elohim (*ʾĕlōhîm*), another plural of majesty with a singular meaning when used of Yahweh. The singular form Eloah (*ʾĕlôah*) appears, mainly in the book of Job, but the most common singular noun for God is El (*ʾēl*), which has cognates in other Semitic languages and whose *Ugaritic counterpart is used both for the chief god and as a general word for any god. The Israelites adopted this common Semitic word (cf. Gen. 33.20: El-Elohe-Israel, "El the God of Israel"), and some of the divine names compounded with El in the Hebrew Bible were probably originally used of non-Israelite deities. In Genesis 14.18–20, 22, we find El Elyon (*ʾēl ʿelyôn*), "God Most High," whose priest is *Melchizedek but who is identified by Abram with Yahweh. The word Elyon is used of Yahweh in other places in the Bible (e.g., Pss. 18.13; 87.5). In the fourth century CE, Philo of Byblos is cited by Eusebius of Caesarea as referring to Elioun, the Most High (Greek *hupsistos*), as a *Phoenician god (*Praeparatio Evangelica* 1.10.15). The Aramaic cognate of Elyon is ʿ*lyn* (perhaps ʿ*elyān*), and a god with this name appears alongside El in a treaty of the eighth century BCE from Sefire in Syria.

The element El is found in divine names in Genesis, sometimes in connection with various places, such as Bethel, "the house of God" (cf. 28.19, 22), and we find El-Bethel, "God of Bethel" (35.7; cf. 31.13). Thus, at a place in the desert there is El-roi ("a God of seeing," 16.13), and at Beer-sheba there is El Olam ("the Everlasting God," 21.33; cf. *šps ʿlm* in a Ugaritic letter, and *šmš ʿlm* in a Phoenician text of ca. 700 BCE, both of which mean "the eternal sun" god or goddess). Another name is El Shaddai, usually translated "God Almighty," and the Priestly writer (*P) in the *Pentateuch maintains that God first made himself known by that name before revealing his name Yahweh (Exod. 6.3; cf. Gen. 17.1; 35.11; 43.14; 48.3). The name is not restricted to P, for it is found in a number of places (Num. 24.4, on the lips of *Balaam, a non-Israelite; Ruth 1.20–21; Job 5.17; etc.), and it is part of the names Zurishaddai and Ammishaddai (Num. 1.6, 12). It is perhaps related to an Akkadian word for "mountain."

It is uncertain whether El-berith ("God of the covenant") in Judges 9.46 refers to Yahweh, for this deity seems to be the same as Baal-berith in 8.33; 9.4, and may be a Canaanite god. On the other hand, Baal, which means "lord," was sometimes used of Yahweh in early times without necessarily always identifying him with the Canaanite god *Baal. In 1 Chronicles 12.6, there is the personal name Bealiah, "Yah is Baal" (cf. yhwb*l on an unpublished seal). *Saul and Jonathan, who were worshipers of Yahweh, had sons named, respectively, Esh-baal and Merib-baal (1 Chron. 8.33–34), which were changed by editors to Ish-bosheth and Mephibosheth (2 Sam. 2.8; 9.6; etc.), in which "bosheth" ("shame") was substituted for "Baal." Jerubbaal (Jerubbesheth in 2 Sam. 11.21), *Gideon's other name, is probably to be explained similarly, notwithstanding the forced explanation in Judges 6.31–32. *David also had a son named Beeliada (b*lyd*, 1 Chron. 14.7), probably identical with Eliada in other lists. Hosea 2.16 says that Israel will call God "my husband" (lit. "my man") and no longer "my Baal" (i.e., "my lord," another word for husband), which may imply that some Israelites addressed God in the latter way.

Both God's holiness and his relation to his people are reflected in the phrase "the Holy One of Israel," which is characteristic of the book of *Isaiah. Although it is not strictly a name, it is relevant to mention this title here.

Yahweh is frequently described as *melek*, "king" (e.g., Deut. 33.5; Pss. 29.10; 98.6), "a great king over all the earth" (Ps. 47.2; cf. 47.7; 48.2) or "above all gods" (Ps. 95.3), "my" or "our king" (Pss. 5.2; 47.6; 68.24; 74.12), or "the King of glory" (Ps. 24.7–10). He "reigns" or "has become king" (Pss. 47.8; 93.1; 96.10; 97.1; 99.1; Isa. 52.7), and he "will reign forever" (Exod. 15.18). Personal names include Malchiel (Gen. 46.17; Num. 26.45; 1 Chron. 7.31) and Malchiah (Jer. 21.1; 38.1, 6), meaning "El" or "Yah is king." Isaiah sees a vision of "the King, Yahweh of hosts" (6.5).

Various epithets and figures of speech are applied to God, but they cannot all be described as names or titles. In Genesis 15.1, Yahweh says to Abram "I am your shield" (cf. Ps. 84.11), but that does not prove the theory that "the Shield of Abraham" was a title. On the other hand, God is described as "the Fear of Isaac" (Gen. 31.42, 53)—the suggested alternative translation, "the Kinsman of Isaac," lacks sufficient evidence—and as "the Mighty One of Jacob" (Gen. 49.24; etc.); these may be titles reflecting the special relationship of God with particular individuals. His relationship with people is also shown by names containing the element *'āb*, "father," such as Abijah, Abiel, and *Abra(ha)m. Yet although God was viewed thus (Jer. 31.9; Mal. 2.10; cf. 1.6), and could be addressed as "my (or our) Father" (Jer. 3.4; Isa. 63.16; 64.8), it is doubtful whether the evidence suffices to justify the claim that "Father" was a title, let alone a name.

See also Jehovah.   J. A. EMERTON

Naphtali. Son of Bilhah, *Rachel's maid, and *Jacob and one of the twelve *tribes of Israel. Rachel's reference to "mighty wrestlings" with her sister *Leah (Gen. 30.7) plays on the name Naphtali ("wrestler"). The tribe is allotted much territory west of the Sea of Galilee and the upper Jordan (Josh. 19.32–39; Map 3:XY2–3). The military prowess of Naphtali is praised in the blessings of Jacob (Gen. 49.21) and Moses (Deut. 33.23). During the reign of *Solomon, Naphtali becomes an administrative district headed by Solomon's own son-in-law (1 Kings 4.15).

During the divided monarchy Naphtali undoubtedly suffered from the wars between Israel and Syria (e.g., 1 Kings 15.20). "All the land of Naphtali" was captured by the *Assyrians in 732 BCE (2 Kings 15.29).   GARY N. KNOPPERS

Nathan. The main *prophet in the court of King *David. As such, he set the pattern for the proper functioning of a royal prophet. He is introduced as the prophet through whom God establishes his *covenant with David (2 Sam. 7.5–16). Later, he pronounces God's judgment on David for David's sins against *Bathsheba and Uriah (2 Sam. 12.1–15); but then he reports God's love for *Solomon, the son of David and *Bathsheba (2 Sam. 12.24–25). This sets the stage for Nathan's role in helping Solomon succeed David to the throne (1 Kings 1.11–48). In *Chronicles, Nathan is said to be partly responsible for recording the events of the reigns of David and Solomon (1 Chron. 29.29; 2 Chron. 9.29; 29.25). Though often dismissed as pious tradition, this is not an unreasonable claim. Many of the concerns that Solomon would have faced early in his reign (e.g., defending his claim to the throne)—when Nathan was still influential—are addressed by the stories about Nathan and David.   TIMOTHY M. WILLIS

Nature and Ecology. Ecology, the study of the relations between people and their environment, has become a topic of interest within biblical studies as a result of the global environmental crisis. Standing at the beginning of Western religious, ethical, and philosophical traditions, the Bible has received considerable attention in the search for the sources of modern attitudes toward nature. The results have been paradoxical, some blaming the Bible for a human-centered ethic that legitimates the exploitation of nature for human ends, others praising it for its reverence for nature and ethic of responsible stewardship of the earth's resources.

The more negative of these assessments of biblical attitudes is based in part on the traditional treatment of biblical religion as uniquely historical. While neighboring religions have been depicted as oriented toward nature, their adherents viewing nature as the place of divine revelation and the realm with which human society had to attune itself through ritual and daily behavior, biblical religion has been described as valuing history supremely, its members seeing human society as the location of divine activity and the arena of primary concern. The result of this approach has been to regard the natural world as separate from and subordinate to human history and to consider nature and human interaction with it of little significance for understanding the genius of biblical religion.

The Bible is without question preeminently about human existence, and in this sense it may be described as historical or human centered in outlook. Yet nature and society are so interdependent in the Bible that to distinguish them sharply or subordinate one to the other misrepresents biblical thought. Biblical languages, for example, possess no terms equivalent to the Western conceptions of nature and history, suggesting that this familiar modern distinction was not a part of biblical thought. A more complex relationship between people and nature is presented in the Bible than either traditional scholarship or recent polemical debates would suggest.

Biblical views of the interrelationship between people and nature are best understood by exploring them within the context of the actual environment within which biblical writers lived and their attitudes were shaped. For the Hebrew Bible, as the texts themselves and archaeological evidence from the Iron Age (1200–587 BCE) both indicate, the ecological setting is a predominantly rural society in the Mediterranean highlands that subsisted on a mixed agricultural economy, including the cultivation of grains and fruits and the herding of sheep and goats. The literature of the Hebrew Bible is the literature of an agricultural society, and this perspective infuses the attitudes toward nature reflected in it.

The essence of the human being and the purpose of human life are both related to *agriculture in the Bible's oldest creation story (Gen. 2.4–3.24), in which the first human being (ʾādām) is made out of fertile soil (ʾădāmâ) to which it is destined to return at death, and given the primary task of cultivating—literally "serving" (ʿābad)—the soil from which it was made (Gen. 2.7, 15; 3.19, 23). Life in such an earthly setting, nourished by the agricultural bounty of the fertile soil, was believed to be the highest form of human experience, not a prelude to a better world. As the source of life, the earth and its produce were viewed as God's creation and inherently good (Gen. 1). Historians, although interested primarily in political affairs, recognized a productive land as the basis for Israelite life and identity (Deut. 8). Prophets saw natural disaster and degradation as punishment for sin and agricultural plenty as the experience of redemption (Hos. 2; Joel 1–2; Amos 4; 9). Psalmists sang of divine activity (Pss. 104; 144) and sages reflected on human wisdom (Prov. 25–29) in such an agricultural environment.

The Israelite sense of dependence on the arable land is reflected in its religious ritual which originated in the cycle of the agricultural year. In its major communal festivals, Israel celebrated the primary harvests of Mediterranean agriculture: barley and wheat in the spring and fruit in the fall (Exod. 23.14–17; 34.18, 22, 23; Lev. 23; Deut. 16). As an acknowledgment of the divine powers believed to make the land and the flock fertile and as an appeal for fertility and bounty in the future, the worshiper presented to the deity the first, best fruits of the harvest and the first, choicest specimens of the flock (Exod. 34.19, 20, 26; Lev. 1.2; Deut. 26.1, 2, 10, 15; Neh. 10.35–37). Integrated with these important seasonal celebrations were the commemorations of political events such as the *Exodus from Egypt, which were held to be formative and unifying (Exod. 23.15; Lev. 23.39–43). (See Feasts and Festivals.)

The natural phenomena on which the lives of Israelite farmers depended took on for them a kind of sacred character. Features of the landscape, believed to provide points of contact between the earth and the divine worlds above and below—springs (Gen. 16.7), rivers (Gen. 32.22–

32), and trees (Gen. 12.6–7; 18.1; Exod. 3.2–4)—marked sites of divine appearances and places of worship. Especially important to Israel were mountains, in particular *Sinai and *Zion, whose ground was considered holy (Exod. 3.5; Ps. 48.1) and whose summits were the points of Israel's great revelations (Exod. 19–24; 1 Kings 8; Ps. 48; Isa. 2; 11). The thunderstorm, the most powerful and essential natural phenomenon for highland farmers dependent on rain-fed agriculture, became one of the most common ways of picturing the presence and activity of the deity in biblical *theophanies (Exod. 19; Pss. 18; 29; Hab. 3).

The traditional village agrarian culture within which Israelite attitudes toward nature were shaped is essentially the setting within which Christianity originated. The life and ministry of *Jesus and his first followers was located in the agricultural world of village peasants who made up the bulk of the population in Roman Palestine. In the New Testament Gospels, the stories about Jesus and the *parables he told present human life in terms of the dynamics of planting and harvesting, of herding flocks, and of fishing, an occupation prominent among Jesus' followers because of the Galilean setting of his ministry. Christianity is thus rooted in the land and agrarian culture of its Hebrew scriptures, and its gospel stories reflect modes of thought about nature much like those in these scriptures.

Yet new social and intellectual forces, shared with certain groups within the Judaism of its time, modified in some significant ways the viewpoint of the first Christians toward the natural world. One of these forces was the early urbanization of the Christian movement. Within a decade or two of Jesus' crucifixion, the center of Christianity shifted from the rural villages of Palestine to the great cities of the *Roman empire. *Paul and his followers were city people and wrote to city churches, and their epistles address issues of religious life in urban settings with little reflection on the world of nature.

A second force was the development in the centuries prior to the birth of Christianity of the notion that humans could hope for a meaningful life in another world. The sources of such thinking were *apocalyptic Judaism that, in its mature form already seen in the book of *Daniel, affirmed the transcendence of *death and a life for the righteous in a better world (Dan. 12:1–4), and Hellenistic dualism, reflected in Neoplatonism and *gnosticism, in which the material world was sharply differentiated from the spiritual world and viewed as alien to authentic human experience. The implication of such thought, more prominent in certain strands of later Christianity than in later Judaism, was that the earthly environment was no longer home for humanity, no longer the setting for true human existence, and was thus dispensable if not downright evil. (*See* Afterlife and Immortality.)

Influenced by both of these movements, early Christians viewed the highest form of human experience as life beyond death in a heavenly realm free from earthly struggles (Mark 13; John 14; 1 Cor. 15; 1 Thess. 4–5). Yet the New Testament vision of the new world, rooted most deeply within apocalyptic Judaism and its ancient holistic heritage, was modeled closely on the earthly environment. The entire world of nature was to participate in the final *redemption (Rom. 8:19–23; Rev. 21–22), and the individual would not escape the prison of matter (as Neoplatonism and gnosticism held) but would experience the *resurrection of the body, as had Jesus (1 Cor. 15). Thus, even in its vision of another world, the New Testament is deeply rooted in the conceptions of the interrelatedness between people and their environment found in the Hebrew scriptures.   THEODORE HIEBERT

Nazareth (Map 12:X3). A town in southern *Galilee about fifteen miles southwest of the Sea of Galilee and twenty miles from the Mediterranean westward. It was probably located at or near the site of the town by the same name in modern Israel. References to it occur in the Gospels and Acts, and all agree that Jesus was from Nazareth (Mark 1.9; Matt. 4.13; 21.11; Luke 4.16; John 1.45; Acts 10:38).

Although not situated on any main commercial roads, Nazareth was not far from them, and it was only several miles from Sepphoris, an important city near the road from Ptolemais to Tiberias. Its secluded position may explain the absence of references to it before Roman times, and this may indicate that it was an insignificant Jewish town (John 1.46). On the other hand, *Luke's references (1.26; 2.4, 39) to it as a city rather than a village may indicate that it was not an insignificant place. Distinctions, however, between the two were not great, and they were sometimes used interchangeably; furthermore, Luke's knowledge of Palestine is not always correct.

Located on a hill in the Plain of Esdraelon, it was about 365 m (1200 ft) above sea level. From its heights one could see mountains in three directions and view the Plain of Esdraelon on the south. The moderate climate, sufficient rainfall, and fertile soil were favorable for growing fruits, grains, and vegetables. The water supply of the town itself was restricted to one spring, supplemented by cisterns. If the spring is to be identified with the "Mary's Well" shown to tourists, it is the only shrine of the many in Nazareth that may go back to Jesus' time.

EDWIN D. FREED

Nazirite (KJV: "Nazarite"). An individual who was dedicated (Hebr. *nāzîr*) to special sacred service through a vow made by the individual or by a parent. The dedication could last for a lifetime or for only a limited period.

A nazirite in Israel had to fulfill several conditions in order to remain consecrated. The man or woman had to abstain from the fruit of the vine and other intoxicants, avoid defilement by contact with a dead body (even that of a close relative), and not allow a razor to cut the hair (Num. 6.1–7). Rituals were specified to deal with a nazirite's unintentional contact with a corpse (Num. 6.9–12) and to mark the completion of a period of dedication (Num. 6.9–12; Acts 21.23–24). Nazirites could drink *wine when their term was completed, but some were tempted to do so before their vow was fulfilled (Amos 2.10–11).

The best-known nazirite is *Samson (Judg. 13.1–7). His nazirite status was announced by a divine messenger while Samson was still in his mother's womb, and was later acknowledged by Samson himself (Judg. 16.17). Part of the irony of the Samson story is that Samson appears not to keep any of his vows. He attended drinking feasts (Judg. 14.10), touched the carcass of a dead lion (Judg. 14.8–9), and allowed his hair to be cut by Delilah (Judg. 16.15–19).

*Samuel is also called a nazirite (1 Sam. 1.11, 22 in *Septuagint and *Qumran textual traditions; the *Masoretic Text does not contain the word); *Joseph is as well (Gen. 49.26; Deut. 33.16), but this may only be metaphorical in the sense of one separated from his brothers.

DENNIS T. OLSON

Nebo.

1. From Mount Nebo, perhaps modern Jebel Neba just west of Heshbon (Map 1:Y5), *Moses viewed the *Promised Land across the Jordan before he died (Num. 27.12; Deut. 32.49; 34.1;

cf. Deut. 3.27 *and see* Pisgah). Later tradition tells of Jeremiah hiding the *ark of the covenant on Mount Nebo (2 Macc. 2.4–8).

2. Nebo is also the name of a town near Mount Nebo in territory allotted to the tribe of *Reuben (Num. 32.37–38; 1 Chron. 5.8). Israel's enemy *Moab often held this region; hence the prophetic oracles against Nebo (Isa. 15.2; Jer. 48.1, 22). The *Moabite Stone hints at an important early Iron Age sanctuary of Yahweh here.

3. In Isaiah 46.1, Nebo refers to the *Babylonian god of writing, Nabu.

MARY JOAN WINN LEITH

Nebuchadnezzar. *See* Nebuchadrezzar.

Nebuchadrezzar. The king of *Babylonia (605–562 BCE), frequently named in Jeremiah, Ezekiel, and Daniel, as well as by classical writers. The name is also rendered Nebuchadnezzar, a biblical variant; the form Nebuchadrezzar is closer to the Babylonian Nabû-kudurri-uṣur, "the (god) Nabu has protected the succession." He was renowned as the most distinguished ruler of the Neo-Babylonian (Chaldean) Dynasty founded by his father, Nabopolassar, in 627 BCE, and as the conqueror of *Jerusalem who took the Judeans into *exile.

Nebuchadrezzar acted as commander in chief for his aging father when in 605 BCE he took Carchemish from the Egyptians and drove them back to their borders, thus freeing Syria and Palestine. According to the Babylonian Chronicle and Josephus, he broke off this campaign in order to return to take the throne of Babylon on hearing of his father's death. He campaigned frequently in the west, receiving tribute from many rulers and from Tyre, which he subsequently besieged for thirteen years. His vassals included Jehoiakim of Judah who, however, defected in 601, misinterpreting the fierce battle between the Babylonians and Egyptians that year as a victory for the latter. Nebuchadrezzar gained revenge by capturing Jerusalem on 16 March 597, when he set up a new king (Mattaniah/ *Zedekiah) sympathetic to him. Jehoiachin, whom he called Yaukin, king of Judah, was taken prisoner to Babylon with the Temple vessels and many Judeans (2 Kings 24.10–17). Nebuchadrezzar also fought against Elam (cf. Jer. 49.38) and the Arabs, and was present in the operations that led to the sack of Jerusalem in August 587/ 586 BCE as a reprisal for Zedekiah's activity as the focus of anti-Babylonian opposition. At that time, more Judeans were taken into exile, as they also were following a later raid, including one on Egypt attested in a fragmentary Babylonian text dated 568–567 BCE (cf. Jer. 43.8–13).

Little is known of the last thirty years of Nebuchadrezzar's rule. The tale of his madness (Dan. 4.23–33) may be a pejorative account of a period in the reign of his successor Nabonidus. Nebuchadrezzar's character may be reflected in his inscriptions, which do not emphasize his military exploits yet reflect his exercise of law, order, and justice as well as stressing moral qualities and religious devotion. He rightly claims to have rebuilt Babylon, its walls, palaces, temples, and defenses as a wonder to which all peoples came with tribute; the famous "hanging gardens" of Babylon are also attributed to him in some traditions. He died during a period that saw the seeds of economic decline resulting from the cost of his enterprises; he was succeeded by his son Amel-Marduk (Evil-Merodach of 2 Kings 25.27). DONALD J. WISEMAN

Needle's Eye. The term stands for the smallest imaginable opening in the saying attributed to Jesus (Mark 10.25 par.) which announces that the camel, largest of familiar animals, can pass through the needle's eye more easily than a rich person can enter the *kingdom of God. The shocking image is softened by the comment that with God all things are possible. The whole story draws attention to the difference between human activity and divine *grace. Some patristic interpreters eliminated the mixed metaphor by reading rope (Grk. *kamilos*) rather than camel (Grk. *kamēlos*). Talmudic parallels, however, retain the animal imagery and speak of an elephant passing through a needle's eye as something impossible. Medieval fondness for moral allegory generated the suggestion that "needle's eye" referred to a narrow pedestrian gate that a camel could squeeze through only after its burden and saddle had been removed, but there is no evidence for any gate with this name.
ROBERT STOOPS

Negeb. The Negeb is a mountainous desert south of Judah between the Arabah and the Mediterranean Sea (Map 1:V–X6–7). Its name means "dryness" but can also be synonymous with "the south" (Gen. 28.14). *Abraham and *Isaac sojourned there (Gen. 12.9; 13.1–3; 20.1; 24.62;

26.17–23). The *Amalekites (Num 13.29), Jerahmeelites, *Kenites (or Kenizzites), *Cherethites, and Calebites (1 Sam. 27.10; 30.14) dwelt there. After the *conquest of Canaan, it was allotted to *Simeon (Josh. 19.1–9; 1 Chron. 4.28–33), but eventually incorporated into Judah (1 Sam. 27.10; "Negeb of Judah at Beer-sheba," 2 Sam. 24.7). The Bible depicts it as desolate (Isa. 21.1; 30.6) although habitable (Jer. 32.44; 33.13; Obad. 1.20). Archaeological evidence shows the Negeb was settled, at times surprisingly thickly, before, during, and after the biblical period.
JOSEPH A. GREENE

Nehemiah, The Book of. It is difficult to determine the precise relationship between the persons of Ezra and Nehemiah. It is understandable that Nehemiah is not mentioned in the memoir of Ezra in Ezra 7–10, because Nehemiah had not yet begun his mission. It is, however, difficult to understand why Ezra is not explicitly referred to in the memoir of Nehemiah, especially after his activities in teaching the Law, especially as it pertained to intermarriage. Because of the paucity of evidence this problem is hard to solve. (*See also* Ezra, The Book of.)

Historical Background. It is generally accepted that Nehemiah came from Susa (Map 6:J4) in Persia to rebuild the walls of Jerusalem in 445/444 BCE. As the cupbearer of the Persian king Artaxerxes (probably Artaxerxes I, 465–424 BCE), Nehemiah held a high office of some influence at court. It is also probable that Nehemiah, serving in the presence of the queen, was a *eunuch; this may explain why he was unwilling to flee to the Temple of the Lord as protection against his enemies (Neh. 6.10–14). It is clear that Shemaiah tried to lure him to the Temple in order to get him to transgress the stipulation forbidding eunuchs to enter the sanctuary (cf. Deut. 23.1; Lev. 21.17–24). If he had done so, he could have lost his influence with the people and their trust.

After Nehemiah heard of the plight of his people in *Jerusalem and that the city was in ruins without a wall of defense against their enemies, he asked the Persian king's permission to go to Jerusalem in order to see what could be done. This was granted; Nehemiah was sent out as a governor of Judah with all the privileges pertaining to the post of governor of a province in the satrapy of Trans-Euphrates. To secure his safety he was granted an escort of soldiers to accompany him; this stands in contrast to the mission of Ezra, in which no such escort was requested. It is, however, noteworthy that the mission of Nehemiah was of a political nature while that of Ezra was religious.

Artaxerxes's friendly gesture to Nehemiah was made just after a serious revolt broke out in the satrapy of the Trans-Euphrates. Megabyzus, the Persian general in Egypt, who put down the revolt in Egypt in 456 BCE, was also the satrap of the Trans-Euphrates. Megabyzus had generously promised the captured Egyptian king Inarus and certain Greek generals their release after the war. Artaxerxes, however, listened to his mother, the wife of Xerxes, the former king, and commanded their execution. This was a heavy blow to the pride of Megabyzus, and in 449 he fomented a rebellion against the Persian king, which Artaxerxes was unable to put down. Later, however, Megabyzus stopped the revolt and once again became a loyal subject of the king. It was thus politically expedient for Artaxerxes to send out Nehemiah, obviously one of his loyal officials, to Judah, one of the smaller but important provinces of the satrapy.

The Work of Nehemiah. After Nehemiah arrived in Jerusalem he conducted a secret inspection of the walls of the city. It seems that he tried to hide his true intentions from the people so that news about his plans would not reach neighboring enemies. After the inspection Nehemiah decided to organize the Jews and to rebuild the walls. Nehemiah allotted sections of the walls to various persons and groups of persons to rebuild. Some scholars think the period of fifty-two days too brief to rebuild the walls, but if we keep in mind that a significant part of the wall needed only restoration, this time was not too short for such repairs. It has been pointed out that in similar circumstances the Athenians built a wall around Athens in just a month, and, in the face of an imminent attack on Constantinople by Attila after the wall was destroyed by an earthquake, the Eastern Romans restored it in sixty days.

With the building of the wall two serious problems developed for Nehemiah and the Jews. The first was a well-orchestrated attack of psychological warfare to stop building. This was done by neighboring nations, led by Sanballat I, governor of *Samaria, and assisted by Tobiah, probably a Persian official of the *Ammonites; somewhat later, these were joined by Geshem (Gashmu), chieftain of the *Nabateans or Arabs to the south and southeast of Judah, as well as by the Ash-

dodites of the old *Philistine territory to the west. With *Samaritans to the north and Ammonites to the east, Judah was nearly encircled by its enemies. They made use of rumors and threats to discourage Nehemiah and the Jews. But Nehemiah did not hesitate to take strong measures to ensure the safety of the workers on the walls. The last resort for his enemies was to try to divide the Jewish people by infiltrating their ranks with false rumors and to induce prophets to give false prophecies. But Nehemiah saw through all these attempts. In the end, the wall was completed and his enemies conceded that they had failed to achieve their goal.

The second problem was the poverty of the Jews. At that stage Judah had a weak economic infrastructure and the burden of *taxes was heavy. The satrap collected taxes for the royal treasury, and both the satrap and his officials from the different provinces of the satrapy had to be paid. Furthermore, the governor and his officials collected taxes for their work. (Nehemiah, however, well aware of his subjects' poverty, did not collect taxes for himself and his officials.) Beyond these expenses, there were the *tithes that the Jews were obliged to pay for the maintenance of the service in the Temple. It is thus not surprising that they had to go into debt and often were forced into debt-slavery in order to meet their obligations. After becoming aware of this problem, Nehemiah canceled all debts.

Nehemiah served for twelve years as governor of Judah and then returned to the royal court in Persia. After a few years, ca. 430 BCE, he went once more to Jerusalem, and was shocked by what he saw. The principles he had laid down during his previous service as governor had been neglected. Nehemiah was so dismayed that he took strong action (Neh. 13). Having discovered that a place was furnished in the Temple for Tobiah the Ammonite by Eliashib the priest, Nehemiah threw the furniture of Tobiah out of the room and commanded that the place be purified. As a result of heavy taxes, the paying of tithes had been neglected; Nehemiah reinstituted the levy. Another problem was the desecration of the *Sabbath by foreign traders in Jerusalem; he forbade them to do any business on the Sabbath within or outside the walls of Jerusalem. Finally, Nehemiah vehemently confronted the issue of *marriages with foreigners. He even assaulted some of the men and pulled out their hair.

The book of Nehemiah ends abruptly without

telling the reader what happened to either Nehemiah or Ezra. Nothing is said of the success of the measures taken against certain Jews described in Nehemiah 13.

Author, Composition, and Sources. As with the book of Ezra, the great majority of modern scholars consider the book of Nehemiah to have been composed by the later Chronicler sometime in the fourth century BCE. The composition of the book of Nehemiah is, however, full of problems. Nehemiah 1.1–7.5 contains part of the memoir of Nehemiah written in the first person; we may accept this as verbatim quotation by the Chronicler. In Nehemiah 7.6–72, we find a list of returnees to Judah which is essentially the same as the list in Ezra 2. Probably these lists came from the same source, but it remains unexplained why the Chronicler should have repeated it. Nehemiah 8–10 is problematic because it likely represents Ezra's memoir. Several scholars have proposed that these chapters are displaced and must be added after Ezra 10 or must be inserted between Ezra 8 and 9. From a modern point of view this is logical, but it is difficult for a modern scholar to determine what motivated the arrangement of material by an ancient compiler. Nehemiah 9 in the Ezra memoir is a hymn of praise and thanksgiving to God for his guidance of Israel through history, a typical addition of the Chronicler; however, the sense of guilt expressed in this hymn is uncharacteristic of the Chronicler.

In Nehemiah 11–13, we have a variety of sources intermixed by the Chronicler and furnished with commentary, and it is difficult to determine what precisely was taken over from Nehemiah's memoir. Among a variety of proposals made by scholars, it seems possible that Nehemiah 11.1–3; 12.31–43 and 13.4–31 are to be regarded as part of the memoir. In Nehemiah 11.1–3, the third person is used for Nehemiah, but in 12.31–43 and 13.4–31 the first person is used. In 12.31–43, we have the description of the dedication of the walls of Jerusalem. In 13.4–31, the second visit of Nehemiah to Jerusalem is described along with the measures he took to combat certain abuses. It is obvious from the work of the Chronicler in Nehemiah 11–12 that he had a preference for genealogical lists, as we also know from the books of *Chronicles. In the list of high priests in 12.10–11 (which supplements that in 1 Chron. 5.27–41), we are brought to a time well after 400 BCE. Some even regard the high priest Jaddua as a contemporary of

Alexander the Great late in the fourth century BCE. One thing, however, is clear: the late Chronicler who did the final editing of this book was active well into the fourth century BCE.

Theology of the Book. Because the book is for the most part derived from Nehemiah's memoir, one can form an excellent idea of his beliefs. The most important feature in the religion of Nehemiah is his sense of a living relationship with God. Despite his high regard for the Law, he did not regard it as the only form of mediation between humans and God. If we accept the authenticity of the prayers of Nehemiah, it becomes evident that he believed in immediate contact with God through prayer. As did other Jews in postexilic times, he believed in the dominant role of the Lord as the God of history: God could move the Persian king to give Nehemiah permission to go to Jerusalem; God determined every step that Nehemiah took after his arrival in Jerusalem. Although the work of Nehemiah was mainly political (see Sir. 49.13), a close relationship between politics and religion was presumed. Nehemiah never doubted that God was on his side and would finally grant him victory over his adversaries.

F. CHARLES FENSHAM

Neighbor. The most frequently occurring Hebrew word translated "neighbor," *rēaʿ*, has a wide range of meanings, from "lover" (Song. of Sol. 5.16; Jer. 3.1) to "friend" (2 Sam. 16.7; Job 2.11) to "neighbor" in the familiar sense of someone living nearby (Exod. 11.2; cf. 3.22; Prov. 27.10); in general, its semantic field encompasses anyone not considered either a "brother" (a kinsman) or an "enemy." In legal contexts, however, "neighbor" has the more specialized meaning of a member of the same social group, but not as close as a blood relative—in other words, a fellow Israelite. A key text is Leviticus 19.16–18, where the neighbor is grouped with one's "people," one's "brother," the "sons of one's people, one's fellow"; the passage concludes with the command "You shall love your neighbor as yourself." This command is repeated with a significant variation later in the chapter: "You shall love the alien as yourself" (Lev. 19.34), which indicates that legally at least the *alien was not subsumed under the category of neighbor, who would be the "native-born" (Lev. 19.34; NRSV: "citizen").

This sense of "neighbor" as a fellow member of the covenant-community seems also to apply to the occurrences of the word in the *Ten Commandments (Exod. 19.16–17; Deut. 5.20–21), where the Israelites are instructed not to bear false witness against a neighbor nor to plot to expropriate ("covet") a neighbor's property (house, wife, slaves, livestock). It is likely that other commandments dealing with social relations have the same restriction: premeditated murder, adultery, and kidnapping are prohibited when perpetrated by one Israelite against another; the commandments against these crimes are not necessarily universal in scope.

Varying understandings of extent of the obligations of mutual assistance are found in different legal traditions in the *Pentateuch. Thus, while Deuteronomy 22.1–4 enjoins the Israelites to return lost animals and property to their "brother" (NRSV: "neighbor"), and to assist him when a pack animal has fallen under a heavy load, in Exodus 23.4–5 this philanthropic obligation extends even to the enemy, to "one who hates you."

Given the wide range of meanings for the word "neighbor," it is not surprising that debate about its interpretation existed in Jewish tradition. The *lawyer's question to Jesus reported in Luke 10.29 seems to echo that debate: "Who is my neighbor?" Jesus' response to the question is the parable of the Good Samaritan (Luke 10:30–37), in which Jesus extends the obligations of Jews toward each other to include those outside the community as well. By choosing as the hero of the parable a *Samaritan, a member of another group (see John 4.9; cf. Matt. 10.5), Jesus implies a maximalist interpretation of the concept of "neighbor." The same view is expressed in Jesus' saying "Love your enemies, do good to those who hate you" (Luke 56.27; cf. Matt. 6.44), and is generally characteristic of the *ethic demanded of Christians, as derived from Jewish tradition: the command of Leviticus 19.18, "Love your neighbor as yourself," is cited throughout the New Testament as an essential part of, even the very essence of the *Law (Matt. 19.19; Mark 12.31 par.; Rom. 13.9; Gal. 5.14; James 2.8).

MICHAEL D. COOGAN

Nephilim. The Nephilim (from Hebr. *nāpal,* "to fall," hence probably "the fallen ones") are mentioned in Genesis 6.4 and Numbers 13.33. In Genesis, they are the children of the *sons of God and human women, and are called "heroes of old" and "men of renown." In Numbers, they are described as the giant aboriginal inhabitants of *Canaan, living at the time of Moses. It is not clear why or how the Nephilim survived the *Flood to become the original Canaanites; probably a duality of older oral traditions can be detected in the clash between these two texts. The Nephilim seem to share a common fate in Genesis and in Numbers, perhaps generated by their name—they exist only to die in a great destruction, either the Flood or the Israelite *conquest. The Nephilim seem to be related to the *Rephaim (cf. Num 13.33 and Deut. 2.11), whose name is also connected with the dead, who are also giants, and who are also wiped out by the early Israelites.

RONALD S. HENDEL

New Jerusalem. *See* Jerusalem, *article on* Symbolism.

Nile. The exact etymology of the name of the great river of *Egypt derived from the Greek *neilos* is uncertain. The Egyptian name *yoteru* (later Coptic *eiōr*) is probably the basis of Hebrew *yĕʾōr.* The Nile, the longest river in the world (6540 km [4062 mi]), rises in a number of lakes in Central Africa and is joined by a tributary, the Blue Nile, near the city of Khartoum in the Sudan. The facts of its source were unknown to the Egyptians, who imagined that this was at Aswan, where the turbulent waters of the First Cataract were thought to well up from an underground cavern to flow north into Egypt and south into Nubia.

The Nile maintained the vegetation both in the extensive marshes in the north and on the agricultural lands bordering on its banks. From early times, a system of irrigation canals led from the main stream to assist cultivation. In mid July each year the Nile began to rise, overflowing its banks and thus providing natural irrigation. This annual phenomenon, the inundation, also brought with it silt, a natural fertilizer composed of vegetable matter and red mud, largely carried down by the Blue Nile from Ethiopia. The rise of the waters and the deposit of silt accounted for the rich crops of Egypt. The actual height of the rise was important, for too small a rise was disastrous for the farmers (see Isa. 19.5–8), whereas too great a rise would lead to a breakdown of the irrigation system, the breaching of dikes, and the destruction of settlements. The levels of the inundation were carefully recorded by a series of Nilometers positioned along the course of the river. Identified with the inundation was the god Hapi, represented as a pot-bellied hybrid with pendulous breasts and colored green and blue like the flood waters and regarded as the guarantor of all life in Egypt.

In the Delta, the extensive marshes provided a natural habitat for numerous wild birds of all kinds, hunted both for food and for sport. It was in the marshes that the papyrus plant flourished, offering the essential material from which the Egyptians were able to manufacture a satisfactory and durable writing surface. A royal monopoly at one time, the product of the papyrus was exported throughout the ancient world until it was replaced in the ninth century CE by paper (a word that, while denoting a different substance, is derived from "papyrus"; see Books and Bookmaking).

Beyond maintaining ample moisture for successful crops in a land that, apart from the Delta, rarely experiences rain in any great measure, the Nile provided the main highway for travel and transport. Without the Nile it would have been impossible to convey the enormous quantity and weight of stone needed for the construction of the temples and the pyramids. Boats of all descriptions plied on the Nile: warships, cargo vessels, and seagoing ships capable of transporting cedar from Lebanon and copper from Cyprus. In addition, numerous small craft traveled the Nile, some to perform the business of ferries, for there were no bridges across the river, and others (scarcely more than bundles of papyrus plants tied together) to carry fishermen on their tasks. The normally prevailing north wind assisted the passage of sail-fitted boats upstream, while the flow of the river eased the labors of those paddling their crafts downstream.

Roads were unknown in ancient Egypt. There were, however, numerous pathways, mainly along the sides of the irrigation canals, suitable for passage by pedestrians and donkeys, the universal beasts of burden. Wheeled vehicles were almost unknown. Though the horse had been introduced during the period of the Hyksos, it was used only to draw the light war chariot. The camel arrived in the Nile valley only during the time of the Ptolemies. Hence the paramount importance of the Nile for communication and transport.

See Plagues of Egypt.   J. MARTIN PLUMLEY

Nimrod. Nimrod (literally, "we will rebel" or "let us rebel" in Hebrew) is described in Genesis 10.8–12 (cf. 1 Chron. 1.10) as a "mighty hunter

before Yahweh." The list of the cities of his vast kingdom—Babel, Erech, and Akkad in *Babylon, followed by *Nineveh and Calah in *Assyria—seems to trace Mesopotamian history up to the beginnings of the Neo-Assyrian empire, when Nineveh and then Calah served as imperial capitals. Nimrod's name is likely a polemical distortion of the name of the Mesopotamian god Ninurta, who was a mighty hunter and warrior, a culture hero, and in some texts the ruler of the universe. Ninurta, who had cult centers in Babel, Calah, and other cities, was a divine patron of Neo-Assyrian kings (including Tukulti-Ninurta I, a less likely candidate for the original Nimrod). In Micah 5.5, the "land of Nimrod" is a synonym for Assyria. In postbiblical traditions, Nimrod, the inciter of "rebellion" who ruled Babel, was often identified as a giant (see Nephilim) and as the chief builder of the tower of *Babel.   RONALD S. HENDEL

Nineveh (Map 6:H3). The capital of *Assyria in the seventh century BCE, when that empire had annexed the northern kingdom of Israel and forced Judah to pay *tribute. Most biblical references reflect this time, when Nineveh was the center of the Assyria they knew. The book of *Jonah, even if written long afterward, remembers this period of Assyrian glory and Israelite humiliation. *Nahum prophesies the destruction of this enemy (1.1; 2.8; 3.7), as does *Zephaniah (2.13). *Sennacherib is said to have withdrawn to Nineveh after Yahweh inflicted a plague on his army besieging Jerusalem (2 Kings 19.36; Isa. 37.37). Otherwise, Nineveh appears in the description of Assyria in Genesis 10.11–12, where its association with Calah reflects early-first-millennium geography, when Calah (Akkadian Kalḫu) was a major complement to Assur and Nineveh. Archaeological evidence shows that Nineveh already existed in the fifth millennium BCE, and contacts with Sumer and Akkad to the south are recorded in third-millennium texts. Nineveh remained an important Mesopotamian city for the next two thousand years, though it only became capital of Assyria under Sennacherib.   DANIEL E. FLEMING

Noah. The son of Lamech, and the father of Shem, Ham, and Japheth (Gen. 5.28–32), Noah was the hero of the biblical *Flood narrative (Gen. 6.9–9.17) and the first vintner (Gen. 9.18–28). After observing the corruption of all creation, God determined to cleanse and purify the earth through a flood (Gen 6.1–7). Noah, however, found favor with God (Gen. 6.8–9), and he, together with his family and the seed of all living creatures, entered the *ark and survived the deluge. From them the earth was then repopulated (Gen. 10).

In many respects Noah was a second *Adam. The *genealogy of Genesis 5 makes his birth the first after the death of the progenitor of humanity. Like Adam, all people are his descendants. God's first command to the primordial pair to "be fruitful, and multiply, and fill the earth" (Gen. 1.28) is echoed in God's first command to Noah and his sons after the Flood (Gen. 9.1).

Other biblical figures in turn look back to Noah and are compared to him. *Moses also had to endure a water ordeal (Exod. 2.1–10); in fact, the only other time that the Hebrew word for ark (tēbâ) is used in the Bible is for the basket in which Moses was saved (Exod. 2.3, 5). In Christian tradition, Noah is viewed as a precursor of Jesus (Luke 17.26–27), and the waters of the Flood are compared to the waters of *baptism (1 Pet. 3.18–22).

Noah has traditionally been viewed as an exemplary righteous person (Ezek. 14.14, 20; Heb. 11.7; 2 Pet. 2.5; and extensive postbiblical Jewish, Christian, and Muslim literature). However, the phrase "righteous in his generation" (Gen. 6.9) has also been interpreted to mean that at any other time Noah's righteousness would not have been viewed as extraordinary (b. Sanh. 108a).

The legend of a hero who survives an inundation to repopulate the earth is one found in many cultures. Most closely related to the biblical account are the stories from ancient Mesopotamia. In the Sumerian flood story, the pious king Ziusudra survives two to three attempts, including a flood, to destroy humanity. After his ordeal, he offers a sacrifice to the gods, repopulates the earth, is granted immortality and sent to live in paradisiacal Dilmun. The eleventh tablet of the *Gilgamesh Epic relates the story of Gilgamesh's ancestor Utnapishtim, who survived the flood to gain immortality through a capricious act of the god Ea/Enki. Many of the images and details of the story parallel the biblical account. Contextually closest to the biblical story is the Atrahasis Epic, which places the flood story in the context of a primeval history. In this version Atrahasis, the "exceedingly wise one" (also an epithet of Utnapishtim), survives three attempts to destroy humanity, the last of which is a flood. The great noise of humanity and the earth's overpopulation are given as reasons for the god Enlil's wish to bring destruction. After the flood, a divine compromise is reached on ways to limit the earth's population, an idea specifically rejected in the biblical account (Gen. 9.1).

See also Ham/Canaan, Cursing of.

CARL S. EHRLICH

Nomads. When the Israelites came before God in *Canaan, the *Promised Land, bearing the first fruits of the harvest, they were to remind themselves of their origin with the words, "A wandering Aramean was my father" (Deut. 26.5)—a reference to *Jacob who, once he left his father-in-law in Haran, had no permanent home. He moved from a settled to a partly nomadic, herder's life; leaving Egypt, his descendants after forty years in the wilderness moved to a settled, agricultural life. Exchanging one way of life for the other was not an unusual act; there were always connections between the two, for nomads always need the town or village crafts and trade.

Nomadic life leaves little trace. The Bible and virtually all other ancient records were written by townsfolk, so our information is usually colored, somewhat hostile to nomads. The Egyptians thought their life-style uncivilized, and the Babylonians about 2000 BCE despised them as those who had no permanent homes, ate their meat raw, and did not bury their dead. At that time, tribes from central Syria moved into *Babylonia. The Babylonian scribes called them *Amorites, or "westerners." They overran the ancient cities and set up new states, at first on a tribal basis. King vied with king, and the famous *Hammurapi briefly dominated them all. Babylonian urban culture overwhelmed the Amorites; apart from the language, no certain Amorite characteristics can be distinguished. Babylonian scribes marked as Amorite some names that have non-Babylonian features. Such names appear in Syria-Palestine, including some in Genesis (e.g., Jacob, Ishmael). Israel's ancestors may be reckoned among these early second-millennium people. Like Israel, other states later traced their history back to nomads "who lived in tents" (see the Assyrian King List). Interaction between townsfolk and nomads, "the desert and the sown," is illustrated by texts from *Mari on the mid-Euphrates written about 1800 BCE. Mari's kings constantly tried to control neighboring tribes by force or diplomacy, lest they overrun the town. Israel faced the same problem with *Amalekites and *Midianites (see, e.g., Judg. 6). Nomadic simplicity appealed to some, and the *wilderness period seemed to be an ideal state, unalloyed by the evils of Canaanite religion (Hos. 2.14–15; 12.9). Jehonadab son of Rechab began such a movement in Israel in the ninth century BCE (2 Kings 10.15; Jer. 35.10) lasting over two centuries, yet ending in the city's shelter (Jer. 35.11; see Rechabites).

In the New Testament, nomadic life is taken as a figure of the spiritual life (Heb. 11.8–10, 13–16), and a reminder that the physical is transitory.

See Social Sciences and the Bible, article on Cultural Anthropology and the Hebrew Bible.

ALAN MILLARD

Numbers, The Book of. The book of Numbers appears in the first major section of literature in the Bible, that section known as *Torah or, in its Greek dress, the *Pentateuch. The name of the book in English reflects the Greek title, arithmoi, and arises from various texts at the beginning of the book that refer to the numbers of people counted in a census of Israel (see 1.2). The title of the book in Jewish tradition, běmidbar ("in the wilderness"), appears as a key term in the first verse of the book and locates events about to be described. Indeed, the principal topic in the entire book is *Moses' leadership of the people of Israel "in the wilderness" under the direction of God.

Analysis. The book falls into two major sections, 1.1–10.10 and 10.11–36.13. The first section continues the tradition carried in the last part of the book of *Exodus and the entire book of *Leviticus by reporting items in the legal corpus associated with the gift of the *Law at *Sinai. The second section picks up the narrative tradition from Exodus 19, a tale that recounts the arrival of Israel at Sinai, by reporting Israel's departure from the holy mountain and the continuation of the *wilderness journey. The narrative about the wilderness wanderings does not end with the close of the book of Numbers. Rather, it continues into *Deuteronomy, ending with an account of the death of Moses while the people of Israel are poised before the *Jordan. Indeed, one must ask whether the narrative does not move beyond the classical definition of Torah or Pentateuch in order to recount traditions about Israel's entry into the land of *Canaan in the book of *Joshua. In that case, the larger literary context for the book of Numbers would be the Hexateuch.

As a part of the received text of the Bible, the final form of the book of Numbers does not demand interpretation as an independent and distinct unit. It is an intrinsic part of a larger whole. Perhaps the most important point about the position of Numbers in the canonical shape of the Pentateuch/Hexateuch is the juxtaposition of law (Num. 1.1–10.10) and narrative (Num. 10.11–36.13). For the final shape of the book of Numbers, the law carried by the traditions about the events at Sinai cannot be separated from the narrative that declares God's leadership for Israel through the wilderness. Indeed, the legal corpus appears in Numbers and its larger Pentateuchal context simply as a part of the larger theme about Israel's journey in the wilderness. There is a remarkable unity between the book of Numbers and the larger Pentateuchal/Hexateuchal context. But there is a similar mark of unity within the book itself, a unity that binds 1.1–10.10 with 10.11–36.13. Despite its character as legislation that distinguishes it generically from its larger narrative context, the legal section belongs intrinsically with the narrative. It is simply the detail that identifies the importance of Sinai in the larger narrative about events at various sites in the wilderness.

Yet, despite the formal unity in the book of Numbers, some evidence of disunity in the text can nevertheless be detected. Literary analysis of the Pentateuch/Hexateuch has identified at least four strands of narration used in the composition of the text as it now appears. These four sources, identified classically by the labels *J, *E, *D, and *P, were used by editors, according to the hypothesis, to construct the present form of the Pentateuchal/Hexateuchal text. Some evidence for such different literary sources appears in Numbers, particularly in the second major section of the book. A clear distinction between the sources J and P emerges, for example, when one considers the character of literary unity in the story about the spies sent by Moses to explore the land that lay before the Israelites (Num. 13–14). On the other hand, little if any evidence for the sources D and E appears in the book of Numbers, nor is there any evidence for J in its first section. The issue of literary unity and the sources focuses on the narrative section in 10.11–36.13. But even at this point, problems posed by an editorial combination of the two sources do not detract from the sense of theological unity in the received text, a unity created by combining the law in the first section with the narrative in the second section. That sense of theological unity resides in the sources as well as in the final edition of the Torah.

The origin of the book of Numbers must be described not only in terms of a literary process of editing that combined the sources J and P but also in terms of a process that brought the traditions as story and law over the generations to the point that produced the written sources. Storytellers must have recited the traditions about Moses or Balaam, Baal Peor or Midian through generations before the written sources appeared.

Literary Genres. The tools of the storyteller's trade appear clearly in the narratives of Numbers. The larger narrative context that connects Numbers with the story about *Moses and the people of Israel in the wilderness is a classic example of a heroic saga, an episodic narrative that moves the story of the hero from his birth (Exod. 2) to his death (Deut. 34). The episodes in the saga include tales such as those in Numbers 13–14 and 16 and legends such as those in 12 and 22–24. A tale describes an event that unfolds in the story around the dramatic structure of a plot. A legend describes a person without emphasis on the drama that embroils the person with other people in a series of events. Indeed, a legend emphasizes a virtue in the person's character that can be imitated by subsequent disciples of the hero. But in addition to the tales and legends of the saga, the narrative in the book of Numbers also contains a fable. In 22.21–35, the famous seer, *Balaam, stands under judgment for mistreating his donkey, who can see better than he can. The fable typically demolishes overblown images of the great by showing them in their true colors.

It should be clear that the saga embraces not only the narrative episodes, the tales, legends, and the fable, but also the legal units. In 1.1–10.10, legal genres build the structure of the book just as narrative genres in 10.11–36.13 do. Indeed, some narrative genres appear in the legal section (Num. 6. 21–27); and some legal genres appear in the narrative section (Num. 26.1–65).

The legal genres, like the narrative genres, contribute to the process of developing group identity. The first section in the book, for example, is a legal definition of the people, a list of names that appears as the product of a census. The census no doubt allowed the people as a whole to conscript an army in the face of a crisis. But the more significant feature of the list is its definition of structure in the organization of the people. The twelve-tribe unity of the people as a whole lies at the center of the tradition. The unit is important for the history of the tradition about the structure of the people, however, because *Levi does not appear as a constitutive part of the whole. But in order to hold the number in the organization of the people at twelve, *Ephraim takes over the position of *Joseph, his father, and *Manasseh, the brother of Ephraim, assumes the empty spot in the organization. Numbers 26 contains a parallel to the census text, another census of the people in the wilderness. Again Levi is not counted as one of the tribes in Israel, no doubt a reflection of the same stage in the history of the tradition that appears in chap. 1. In this case, Joseph remains as one of the formal units in the organization of the people. But the same entry, 26.28, breaks the tribe of Joseph into the two constitutive tribes, Ephraim and Manasseh. And 26.35 introduces the sons of Ephraim as a distinct factor in the tribal list. It is essentially the same tradition as the list in chap. 1. In both cases, the census list defines the structure of the people of Israel and thus contributes to specification of national identity, indeed, of legal structure in that national identity. (*See* Tribes of Israel.)

The concern for identity in terms of statistics continues in chaps. 3–4. Chap. 5 creates a legal structure for securing family stability. Chap. 6 defines the structure of life for the *nazirites. In 6.22–27 the series of ordinances controlling domestic life is broken with a small narrative unit that contains the Aaronic blessing for the whole people. Then, 7.1–10.10 specifies cultic ordinances for the people, a significant qualification for Israelite worship. At the heart of these ordinances are specifications for *Passover, 9.1–14, and for moving the camp, 9.15–10.36. The couplet in 10.35–36 reflects a formula for moving the *ark in whatever context, doubtlessly an ancient formula, but given the meager role for the ark in these narratives, somewhat out of place.

Significance. The historical significance of the book of Numbers belongs to the larger context that embraces the book, the historical significance of the Pentateuch/Hexateuch. For the larger context and thus for the book of Numbers, value does not reside in historical accuracy or the lack of historical accuracy. It is not possible to determine, using the standards of verification basic to scholarship, whether a prophet named Balaam really confronted the Israelites with a plan to curse them. The value for the book lies more sharply in the ability of the narrator to paint a portrait of Israel struggling with Balaam, a product that captures by its aesthetic quality a significant witness to Israel's identity. Its aesthetic quality, its ability to depict identity not only for the Israelites in the wilderness under Moses' leadership but for all future disciples of Moses, gives the story value. Indeed, that very quality confirms the claim of the story as true. The book of Numbers is historically significant not because it recounts who Moses was and what he did for the children of Israel in the wilderness but rather because it tells the descendants of Israel, or any other disciples of Moses, who they are.

That historical significance merges in the book of Numbers, as it does in the larger Pentateuchal/Hexateuchal context, with distinctive theological significance. Both story and law tell the disciples of Moses that they belong not simply to Moses, but also to God. The overall structure for the narrative derives from an itinerary that shows the movement of Israel from Egypt to the Jordan. But the itinerary documents not only the movement of Israel along the way in the wilderness but also the leadership of God in that movement (see 10.11–13).

The emphasis falls, however, not only on the presence and leadership of God but also on the obedience of the people to that divine leadership. One facet of the tradition remembers Israel in the wilderness as faithful, obedient to God and to Moses (see Jer 2.2; Hos. 2.14–15). The focus of the legends on obedience to God's word (Num. 12.22–24) highlights this facet of the tradition. But in contrast, the narrative in Numbers reports that the people in the wilderness were rebels, rejecting Moses and the God whom he served. The double picture of Israelite response to God and Moses in the wilderness reflects Israel's struggles to understand its identity.

The story does not end with the end of the book of Numbers. The itinerary structure puts the Israelites on the plains of *Moab by the Jordan, opposite *Jericho. The conclusion combines that ending of the narrative structure for Numbers with the legal dimension: "These are the commandments and ordinances that the Lord commanded through Moses to the Israelites in the plains of Moab by the Jordan at Jericho" (36.13). At the end of Numbers, the reader must ask: "Where do the people go from here? What will they do with the commandments and ordinances?" The book of Numbers necessarily depends not only on the narrative in Deuteronomy but also on the narrative in Joshua to complete the story. The ending calls for recognition of the major literary and theological context as the Hexateuch. GEORGE W. COATS

Number Symbolism. In common with most people in the ancient world, the Israelites attached symbolic significance to numbers. So whenever the biblical writers mention a number, it is likely that they had a symbolic meaning in mind; in many cases the numbers must not be taken in their literal sense at all.

One signifies uniqueness or undivided wholeness or both. "Hear, O Israel: YHWH is our God. YHWH is one" (Deut. 6.4; *see* Shema), means not only that the God of Israel is unique, but also that there is no contradiction within him. The oneness of God therefore calls for the trust and love of his people (Deut. 6.5). As God is one, so, some New Testament writers insist, Christ is one with the Father (John 10.30; 17.21); therefore his people must be one (John 17.11; Eph. 4.4–6).

Two, the smallest number larger than one, was the minimum number of witnesses required to establish the truth (Deut. 19.15; cf. Exod. 31.18; Mark 6.7; John 8.17–18; 2 Cor. 13.1; Rev. 11.3–4).

Three is widely regarded as a divine number. Many religions have triads of gods. Biblical faith has no room for a triad, and the number three is rarely connected directly with God. But in some cases this number hints that God is involved. When *Abraham was visited by three men, this meant that God was calling on him (Gen. 18). The *Temple was divided into three parts (1 Kings 6). Three days were the proper time for a work of God, which meant, by the ancient reckoning of time, that it was completed on the third day (Exod. 19.11; Josh. 1.11; 1 Kings 12.5; 2 Kings 20.5; Jonah 1.17; Luke 2.46; John 2.1; etc.). This is also true of the *resurrection of Christ (Mark 8.31; 1 Cor. 15.4). Time is divided into three parts, past, present and future, and God is he who is, who was, and who is to come (Rev. 1.8). According to Paul there are three chief gifts of the Spirit (1 Cor. 13.13). The expression "Father, Son, and Holy Spirit" is not found in the Bible (1 John 5.7b is found only in very late manuscripts); the closest is Rev. 1.4. Neither is the doctrine of the *Trinity expressed there in so many words.

Three and a half years is a strictly limited period, half the full seven of God's plan. It was regarded as significant that there were three and a half years between the desecration of the Temple and its rededication (Dan. 7.25; 1 Macc. 1.45; 4.52; see also Rev. 11.2–3). The drought under *Ahab was believed to have lasted three and a half years (Luke 4.25; cf. 1 Kings 18.1).

Four is the number of the created world. There are four corners of the earth, four wind-directions, four seasons, and four kinds of living creatures: humans, domestic animals, wild animals, and creatures of sky and sea (Gen. 1.20–27; cf. Ezek. 1.10; Rev. 4.6–7). The four horsemen of the Apocalypse (Rev. 6.1–8) were derived from the four winds, but have a different function. The four Gospels were later regarded as signifying the universality of the gospel, and the evangelists were identified with the living creatures of Revelation 4, but this was long after biblical times.

Five is the number of fingers on one hand, and could stand for a handful, that is, a few.

Six is seven minus one. It is the number of incompleteness. The six days of the *creation were not complete until the seventh day of rest had come. In the book of *Revelation six seals, trumpets, etc. represent the course of the world before God's final seventh act brings about the eternal *Sabbath. And in spite of its seven heads, the number of the beast is only *six hundred sixty-six.

Seven, the sum of three plus four, of heaven and earth, signifies completeness and perfection. There were seven chief heavenly bodies (sun, moon, and the five planets known to the ancients), seven days of the week, seven *archangels. The great festivals lasted seven days, and there were seven weeks between the *Passover and the feast of weeks (*Pentecost). Every seventh year was a sabbath year, when the land would rest and lie fallow, and *Hebrew slaves were allowed to go free; and every fiftieth year was a jubilee, when alienated property had to be returned ("jubilee" from Hebr. *yōbēl*, the ramshorn that heralded its beginning). The seventh day represented God's completed work (Gen. 2.2–3), and in the book of *Revelation the seventh seal, trumpet, bowl, etc., represent the completion of God's plan. The seven spirits of God (Rev. 1.4) represent either the seven archangels, or "all spirits," or the Holy Spirit. *Seven churches represent the universal church (Rev. 1.20). It is necessary to forgive, not just seven times, but seventy times seven times (Matt. 18.21–22; cf. Gen. 4.24), that is to say, always.

Outside Israel seven was also known as a sig-

nificant number, and the monster *Leviathan had seven heads. Later interpreters noted that the Hebrew Bible refers to God by seven different *names: *YHWH* ("the LORD"); *'ădōnāy* (Lord); *'ēl* and *'ĕlōhîm* (God); *'ehyeh 'ăšer 'ehyeh* ("I am who I am"); *šadday* ("the Almighty"); and *ṣĕbā'ôt* ("[Lord God of] Hosts"). Later Christian tradition noted that the Gospels report seven last words of Jesus in all.

Eight was later used for God's new creation, the day of the Resurrection being regarded as the eighth day rather than the first, but this plays no role in the Bible.

Ten is simply a round number, the number of fingers on both hands. Some interpreters have found a special significance in the fact that the *Ten Commandments correspond with a ten-times repeated "and God said" in the creation story (Gen. 1.1–2.4): ten words to create the world were matched by ten measures to keep it in order. Generally, however, ten, a thousand, and ten thousand simply signify small or large numbers, or are used by multiplication to enhance the significance of other numbers.

Twelve, like seven, is a number of completeness and perfection. This number in particular must not always be taken literally. Israel always comprised more *tribes than the twelve that were actually counted, and the counting of the twelve was not always uniform (Gen. 49; Josh. 13–19; Rev. 7.7–8), but the twelve meant "all Israel." It was regarded as important that there were twelve *apostles and that their number should be complete, but the lists do not quite tally (*see* Twelve, The). The twenty-four elders (Rev. 4.4) clearly represent all Israel and the whole church. The twelve cornerstones and gates of the new *Jerusalem not only link the city with the tribes of Israel and the apostles, but also signify its divine perfection, as do its measurements of 12,000 stadia square and its walls of 144 cubits. The 144,000 of Revelation 7 and 14 in each case mean that the number is complete and not one of the elect is lost; in Revelation 7 John hears the 144,000 from Israel (all Israel) being counted, but sees "a great multitude that no one could count, from every nation, from all tribes and peoples and languages" (the redeemed gentiles).

Thirty was the age at which one was believed to reach full maturity (Gen. 41.46; Num. 4.3; 2 Sam. 5.4; Luke 3.23).

Forty days was a strictly limited period of time (for six, not seven, weeks?; Gen. 7.4; Exod. 24.18; 1 Sam. 17.16; Jon. 3.4; Matt. 4.2; Mark 1.13; Luke 4.2; Acts 1.3). Forty years was the length of one generation (Exod. 16.35; Num. 14.33; 32.13; Ezek. 4.6; 29.11). It was regarded as significant if a king reigned for this number of years (2 Sam. 5.4; 1 Kings 11.42).

Seventy meant a comprehensive number, and should not normally be taken literally. Seventy descendants of *Jacob moved to Egypt (Gen. 46.8–27; an overliteral scribe added some absurd names to make up the number); seventy *elders led the Israelites in the wilderness (Exod. 24.1); the Temple lay in ruins for seventy years (Jer. 25.11; Zech. 1.12); the Greek version of the Hebrew Bible was believed to have been translated by seventy (or seventy-two) men, hence its name, the *Septuagint, and its abbreviation, LXX; there were believed to be seventy nations (see Judg. 1.7; Luke 10.1); and the *Sanhedrin had seventy members.

In spite of the significance attached by its writers to numbers, the Bible contains no speculation about numbers of the kind found among the Pythagoreans, or later in the Qabbalah.

DAVID H. VAN DAALEN

Nuzi Tablets. Dating to the second half of the fifteenth century BCE, the Nuzi tablets are some thousands of texts recovered from the Hurrian levels of Yorghan Tepe, situated about 10 mi southwest of modern Kirkuk in Iraq. During this period the site bore the Hurrian name Nuzi, and the entire area was a province of Mitanni. Other sites in the area, such as Kirkuk (ancient Arrapḫa) and Tell al-Faḫḫār (ancient Kurruḫanni), have also yielded texts of the Nuzi type, all written in the same Akkadian patois, reflecting the native Hurrian background of the scribes. Some of the Nuzi tablets comprised part of the official archives of the palace and include administrative inventories and letters. Others stemmed from private archives of wealthy Nuzi families and include business contracts involving real estate, loans, and servitude; family records of marriage, adoption, and property settlement; and transcripts of litigations and court proceedings.

It is the Hurrian setting of the Nuzi tablets that has attracted the attention of biblical scholars, for the texts, replete with Hurrian personal names and terminology, show certain affinities with biblical customs. The providing of a slave girl to one's husband by a sterile wife, the ranking of heirs and the preferential treatment of the designated eldest, the association of household gods with the disposition of family property, the conditional sale into slavery of freeborn daughters, and the institution of ḫābiru-servitude (*see* Hebrews) were some of the Nuzi customs attributed to Hurrian practice. Growing evidence from *Ugarit, *Mari, and Alalakh of a substantial Hurrian presence in the ancestral homeland of Aram-naharaim in the Middle Euphrates region further revealed strong signs of Hurrian influence. On the basis of the Nuzi data, some scholars have dated the ancestral period to the middle of the second millennium BCE.

Reexamination of the Nuzi material in the last twenty-five years has seriously challenged the validity of some proposed parallels between the Nuzi texts and the Bible and their relevance for dating the period of the *ancestors. Furthermore, the uniquely Hurrian character of Nuzi legal traditions can no longer be accepted. Nevertheless, the Nuzi tablets remain a major primary source for the study of Mesopotamian socioeconomic legal practices and thus help to illuminate biblical *law, institutions, and customs.

BARRY L. EICHLER

Obadiah, The Book of. This book of twenty-one verses, the shortest in the Hebrew Bible, is formed of three distinct parts. Vv. 1–4 announce the Lord's decision to destroy *Edom because of its pride and its betrayal of *Judah. Vv. 15–18 announce the *day of the Lord for all nations. And vv. 19–21 proclaim that the Lord's dominion will be demonstrated by the return of dispersed Israelites to live in *Canaan.

The title gives us no information about the author except a name; Obadiah means "servant of the Lord." It gives no help in dating the book, though internal references imply that the destruction of *Jerusalem of 587/586 BCE had already occurred.

The book's concentration on Edom calls for a review of the relation of that country to Judah and Israel. Biblical tradition sees the Edomites as distant relatives of Israel through a common ancestor, *Isaac. The Edomites are understood to be the descendants of *Esau, as Israelites are descendants of *Jacob (Gen. 25.19–26; 36). Already settled in Edom when *Moses led the Israelites toward Canaan, they refused the Israelites passage through their territory (Num. 20.14–19). Edom and Judah were rivals for territory and power through the period of the monarchy. Although neither 2 Kings nor 2 Chronicles mentions Edom's participation in the sack of Jerusalem in 587/586 BCE, other books imply their guilt (e.g., Ps. 137.7; Lam. 4.21–22; Isa. 63.1–6; Joel 3.19; Mal. 1.4). All mention of Edom ends during the early part of the fifth century BCE, but no account of its destruction is available.

The book is called a "vision"; the books of *Isaiah and *Nahum share that description. It apparently describes a literary form that allows the readers to hear God announcing his decisions relating to history. All the forms are highly dramatic and include insights into the happenings of the heavenly court where the Lord reigns.

Obadiah's position among the Minor Prophets is stable in most texts. It is a pivotal book in the ascending scale toward *Micah in the center. It is an exponent of the return-from-exile style of *eschatology (vv. 19–21), also found in Amos 9, *Jeremiah, and *Ezekiel. This contrasts with the view in *Hosea, *Joel, and the books after Micah, in which the future of Israel is seen as being a worshiping people among the empires, hoping for a rebuilt *Temple but not expecting a return to political power.

The first part of the book (vv. 1–18) proclaims the Lord's readiness to exact retribution from Edom for wrongs done to Judah, her neighbor.

The last section (vv. 19–21) proclaims the hope that the kingdom of God will be established, that the dispersed people of Israel and Judah will return to their homelands, and that they will have power over their neighbors, especially Edom.

The central message of the book is found in v. 21: the dominion of God is sure and secure. The book should be read in the context of the Minor Prophets and of Isaiah, for Obadiah's views are balanced by *Habakkuk and other books from Micah through *Malachi. They put much more emphasis on the future Israel's worship of the Lord in Jerusalem than on political power over others.   JOHN D. W. WATTS

Olives, Mount of. The Mount of Olives is part of a ridge east of *Jerusalem directly across the Kidron Valley in the direction of Bethany and Jericho (Map 9); the ridge's northern extension is called Mount Scopus (Josephus, *War* 2.19.527), and its lower slopes *Gethsemane. With an elevation of approximately 850 m (2,800 ft), the ridge is higher than the Temple Mount across the Kidron Valley to the west.

In the Hebrew Bible the Mount of Olives is mentioned by name twice. In 2 Samuel 15.30–32 we are told of a sanctuary there (cf. 1 Kings 11.7; 2 Kings 23.13). Zechariah 14:4 claims this is where the Lord's feet will stand on the apocalyptic *day of the Lord.

In the Gospels, the Mount of Olives is the

place where Jesus goes for rest or prayer when he is in or around Jerusalem (Matt. 24.3; 26.30 par; Luke 21.37; John 8.1). Jesus enters Jerusalem from the Mount of Olives (Matt. 21.9 par.), and it is there that the apocalyptic discourses in Mark and Matthew are set; Mark 13.3 may be an allusion to Zechariah 14.4. In Acts 1:12 the Mount is implied as the site of Jesus' *ascension. These events in the narrative of the last days of Jesus in and around the Mount of Olives has made it a site for pilgrims to Jerusalem since the fourth century CE, when a small church was founded there; this may have been the basilica built by Constantine's mother Helena, mentioned by Eusebius (*Vita Const.* 3.43).

J. ANDREW OVERMAN

Omega. *See* Alpha and Omega.

Onan. The second son of Judah and his Canaanite wife Bath-shua (or "the daughter of Shua"; Gen. 38.2; 46.12; Num. 26.19; 1 Chron. 2.3). After the death of his older brother Er without progeny, Judah ordered Onan to impregnate Er's wife Tamar. Although Onan did cohabit with Tamar, "he spilled his seed on the ground"; for this he was put to death by God (Gen. 38.6–10). Onan's effort to avoid impregnating his sister-in-law has given rise to the term "onanism," a synonym for masturbation. This passage is then employed by some to indicate divine condemnation of autoeroticism. This interpretation, however, completely misses the point of the passage. Onan's sin was not sexual. Rather, it was his refusal to fulfill the obligation of *levirate marriage (Deut. 25.5–10; see also Ruth 4), according to which a man was obligated to impregnate the wife of his brother if his brother had died without an heir, thus ensuring the continuation of his brother's line and inheritance. That fulfilling this obligation often raised additional questions regarding the apportioning of the familial inheritance is indicated by the above passages from Deuteronomy and Ruth. Thus Onan's sexual act, most probably coitus interruptus, was the means whereby he avoided his fraternal duty, in spite of the fact that he seemed to be fulfilling it by cohabiting with Tamar. For this deception he was punished.

CARL S. EHRLICH

Oracle. A communication from a deity on some particular matter. The documentation from the ancient Mediterranean world, both biblical and extrabiblical, preserves many citations of, or allusions to, such oracles. Frequently, oracles are conveyed in the setting of a sanctuary, for example, the temple of Apollo at Delphi in Greece, or the *high place of Gibeon where *Solomon received a divine message in a dream (1 Kings 3.4–15). In communicating its oracles, the deity may make use of either mechanical devices—for example, the lots known as *Urim (1 Sam. 28.6; cf. Acts 1.26)—or of a human intermediary, the "prophet." Oracles may come in response to a human "inquiry" (Jer. 21.2) or at the divine initiative. In either case, however, it is recognized that God remains free either to give or withhold the oracle (2 Sam. 14.37; 28.6; Ezek. 20.3).

In content, biblical oracles range from oneword responses to yes-or-no questions (2 Sam. 2.1) to the extended discourses mediated by prophets like *Jeremiah or *Ezekiel. Like extrabiblical oracles, the latter are characterized by an elevated, poetic style, evidencing a certain ambiguity and indeterminacy.

In terms of purpose, the oracles of the prophetic books can be classified generally as either "judgment speeches" or "oracles of salvation." The former have as their intention the announcement of the evil fate awaiting the addressee. They typically consist of an accusation that serves to motivate the following statement of the punishment that God will bring on the guilty individual, group, or nation (see, e.g., 2 Kings 2.3–4; Amos 4.1–3; 8.4–14; Mic. 3.7–12). This type predominates in the material of the preexilic prophets. The oracle of salvation, which comes to the fore during the *exile (with Second Isaiah) and afterward, announces God's coming positive interventions for those addressed. These may concern both the improvement of their external circumstances (return to the land, restoration of the Davidic line, etc.) as well as their internal purification or revitalization (see, e.g., Isa. 43.1–7; Jer. 31.31–34; Ezek. 16.59–63; 37.1–14; Hag. 2.20–23). Oracles of salvation are sometimes conditional on a prior human initiative of *repentance (Mal. 3.6–12), but more often are grounded solely on God's impenetrable *mercy.

CHRISTOPHER T. BEGG

Orphan. In biblical Israel, as in the ancient Near East in general, the socioeconomic well-being of a community depended primarily on the ability of adult males to provide financially for those around them, to protect them from physical harm, and, in general, to uphold their honor ("name"). Persons without a specific male to fulfill these obligations were at greatest risk in the community; therefore, there are many calls for the protection and proper treatment of the husbandless ("*widows") and the fatherless ("orphans"), as well as others at risk in an Israelite community. In the Hebrew Bible, "widows" are mentioned alongside "orphans" in thirty-four of the forty-two occurrences of the latter. This pairing continues into the *Apocrypha (e.g., 2 Macc. 3.10), the New Testament (James 1.27), and early church writings (e.g., 1 Clem. 8.4). Other individuals at risk mentioned less frequently with "orphans" are *aliens (Deut. 24.17, 20, 21), the weak, the needy, the *poor, the destitute (Ps. 82.3–4; Isa. 10.1–2; Zech. 7.9–10), and *Levites (Deut. 14.29; 16.11, 14). The greatest concerns of these individuals are that they will be unable to protect the property they have (Job 24.3; Prov. 23.10), unable to support themselves financially (2 Kings 4.1), and unable to maintain the "name" of their deceased husband or father (Deut. 25.5–7; 2 Sam. 14.7). They are not, however, necessarily propertyless (see Prov. 23.10; 2 Macc. 3.10).

To provide care for these individuals is to "do justice" to them (Deut. 10.18; 24.17; 27.19; Ps. 10.18). Tragically, the males in a community often shirk this responsibility (Deut. 25.5–10; Ruth 4.6) or even exploit their neighbors and relatives who are at risk (2 Sam. 14.4–11; cf. Judg. 11.1–3). Those who perpetrate such injustices are called "fools" (Prov. 23.10) and "wicked" (Pss. 82.3; 146.9). The failure or inability of "orphans" and others at risk to gain support forces them to turn to royal administrators for help (2 Kings 4.13; 8.5; Jer 22.1–3). So, a primary responsibility of Israel's kings is to care for needy persons, like orphans (Ps. 72.1–4, 12–14). Unfortunately, this responsibility is mentioned most often in prophetic condemnations of the royal bureaucracy for failing to fulfill it (Isa. 1.23; 10.2; Jer. 5.28; Ezek. 22.7). The theological foundation for these condemnations is important to recognize. God is the ultimate example of one who is concerned for the welfare of individuals like orphans (Deut. 10.18; Pss. 10.14, 18; 94.6; 146.9); he is the ultimate "*redeemer" for the orphan (Prov. 23.10–11; cf. Ps. 68.6). The king and his officials are watched and criticized more than others because they have been designated as God's overseers of the people, including orphans. The failure of the king and his officials to "do justice" to orphans not only reflects badly on them but also on the God who established them.

In the New Testament, besides the exhortation to "care for orphans and widows in their distress" (James 1.27), the only reference to "orphans" appears in John 14.18 ("I will not leave you orphaned"). The imagery suggests that Jesus' followers, by themselves, would not be able to maintain their "inheritance" from God; but Jesus is saying that he will act as their protector and provider.   TIMOTHY M. WILLIS

P

P. The abbreviation for the Priestly source in the *Pentateuch. Definitively identified in the nineteenth century, P is classically described as a creation of the exilic or postexilic period (sixth or fifth century BCE) that stresses Israelite ritual and religious observance. As such, its narratives, especially in the book of *Genesis, are often etiological, providing explanations for the *Sabbath (Gen. 2.2–3), *circumcision (Gen. 17.9–14), and dietary laws (Gen. 9.4). This priestly tradition describes in detail the *Passover ritual, the ordination ceremonies and vestments of the high *priest, and the *tabernacle and its furnishings. Much of this material is derived from older sources that have been shaped by the priestly writers; this is evident in the prominence given to *Aaron in P, in contrast with the dominant role of *Moses in *J and *E, and the legal materials in the books of *Leviticus and *Numbers. Priestly tradition unites its own contribution and the older material (including J and E) it incorporates by *genealogies and by a series of *covenants, those with *Noah, *Abraham, and finally all Israel on Mount *Sinai. P's deity is more transcendent and less anthropomorphic than J's; his *glory both reveals and conceals him.

Recently some scholars have proposed that the date of the primary work of the priestly writers was preexilic, perhaps even as early as the reign of *Hezekiah (late eighth/early seventh centuries BCE).

The most significant contribution of priestly tradition is the *Torah in its present shape: Genesis begins with the P account of creation, and Deuteronomy ends with the P account of the death of Moses.   MICHAEL D. COOGAN

Palestine, Geography of. *See* Geography of Palestine.

Parables. A parable is a picturesque figure of language in which an analogy refers to a similar but different reality. In the Hebrew Bible, the word "parable" (Hebr. *māšāl*) can refer to a proverb (Ezek. 18.2–3), taunt (Isa. 14.3–4), riddle (Ezek. 17.2–10), or allegory (Ezek. 24.2–5). Although story parables (2 Sam. 12.1–4; Isa. 5.1–7) are not specifically called parables, we should include them in any definition. It is not surprising that in the New Testament "parable" covers a broad semantic range as well, for the Greek term *parabolē* was used to translate *māšāl* in the *Septuagint in all but two instances. In the Gospels it can refer to a proverb (Luke 4.23), aphorism (Mark 9.5), metaphor (Mark 7.14–17), similitude (Mark 4.30–32), story parable (Luke 14.16–24), example parable (Luke 10.29–37), or allegory (Mark 12.1–11). In contrast to Aristotelian tradition, no sharp distinction is drawn in the Bible between simile/allegory and metaphor/parable. This is true also in rabbinic tradition. In view of the broad semantic range of the term, it is impossible to give an exact list of Jesus' parables. Although *parabolē* is used explicitly to designate thirty different sayings of Jesus, when one adds other clear examples in which the term is not used (e.g., Luke 10.29–35) and other likely possibilities, the total number is about eighty. If the instances of the *paroimia* or "figure" of John are added, the number becomes still greater. Moreover, if one includes every simile, proverb, and aphorism that Jesus taught, then almost everything Jesus said falls into the category of parable (see Mark 4.34).

Numerous attempts have been made to classify the parables. These involve the use of specific chronological periods in Jesus' ministry, distinctive subject matter, as well as literary, theological, and existential categories. None of these attempts, however, has been very successful.

In his parables Jesus repeatedly used illustrations from daily life. These often contain a distinctly Palestinian and even Galilean flavor. This was originally intended to make the parables more understandable for Jesus' audience, but today it serves also to authenticate them. It is clear, for example, that the Sower (Mark 4.2–20) reveals a Palestinian method of farming in which sowing preceded plowing. Likewise, the references to a *priest, *Levite, *Samaritan, a road going from Jerusalem to Jericho (Luke 10.19–35), as well as a *Pharisee, *publican, and *Temple (Luke 18.9–14), indicate that such parables originated in Palestine. The portrayal of a fishing environment in the parable of the Great Net (Matt. 13.47–50), where good fish are separated from bad, strongly suggests that this parable originated around the Sea of *Galilee. The example of farm laborers being paid at the end of the day (Matt. 20.8) according to biblical law (Lev. 19.14; Deut. 24.15) shows the contrast between Palestinian farming, which often employed laborers, and the farming in most of the Mediterranean world, which relied on slaves. Most scholars agree that in the parables one stands on the bedrock of authentic Jesus tradition.

Although the parables are drawn from daily life, they do not necessarily portray normal, everyday actions. On the contrary, at times one encounters both exaggeration and unexpected behavior. The forgiveness of the enormous sum of a thousand talents (Matt. 18.24–27), the fact that all ten maidens are sleeping (Matt. 25.5), and that all the invited guests refused the banquet invitation (Luke 14.18) suggests the intentional use of exaggeration. In the commendation of the Unjust Steward as well (Luke 16.1–8), the hearer is taken by surprise. These forms of exaggeration, however, are fairly specific; nowhere in the parables of Jesus does one find fables in which animals speak or trees sing.

The artistic character of the parables should be noted. Jesus' portrayal of the Prodigal Son is most memorable: Having squandered his fortune, starving and destitute in a far country, "joined" to a gentile (Luke 15.15), feeding the forbidden pigs, he wishes that he could fill his stomach by sharing the food of the pigs he feeds! And how beautifully the father's love is described. Laying aside his dignity, he runs to embrace his son, refuses to hear out his confession, reclothes him in appropriately filial garments, and joyfully celebrates having regained his lost son. The artistry and descriptive power of the parables often require only a single hearing for them to be forever remembered. Such parables as the Prodigal Son and the Good Samaritan must by any standard be recognized as literary masterpieces.

The primary reason that Jesus taught in parables appears to be self-evident: he used them to illustrate. Can one find a better illustration of the love of God for the outcast than the parable of the Prodigal Son? Some of Jesus' parables are clearly "example" parables and require no explanation. Yet Mark 4.10–12 gives a different reason why Jesus taught in parables—in order to conceal his message. The reason given for concealing his message is more difficult still: Jesus did so in order that his hearers would not believe lest they repent and be forgiven. Numerous attempts have been made to explain this difficult passage, but none is truly convincing and without problems. The most common explanation is to see the lack of understanding as being the result rather than the cause of the unbelief of those "outside" (see also Messianic Secret). That the meaning of certain parables was not in fact self-evident is clear from the various explanations associated with them (Mark 7.17; Matt. 13.36). Parables served a useful purpose in concealing Jesus' message from those hostile to him: by his parables he could publicly teach about the *kingdom of God, but the representatives of the *Roman empire could find nothing in them that was seditious. A third reason Jesus taught in parables was to disarm his listeners and allow the truth of the divine message to penetrate their resistance. Often hearers could be challenged to pass judgment on a story before discovering that in so doing they had in fact condemned themselves (cf. 2 Sam. 12.1–4; Matt 21.28–31; Luke 7.36–50). A fourth reason for the use of parables was to aid memory: since Jesus' listeners preserved his teachings by memorizing them, the memorable quality of the parables proved useful.

The early church saw in the parables (and in all scripture) three distinct levels of meaning: the literal, the moral, and the spiritual. In the Middle Ages an additional level was added, the heavenly. These deeper levels of meaning were discoverable by allegorical interpretation (see Interpretation, History of, article on Early Christian Interpretation). A famous example of this is the parable of the Good Samaritan (Luke 10.30–35), in which each detail was seen as meaningful, so that: the man going down to Jericho = Adam; Jerusalem = heaven; Jericho = our mortality; robbers = the devil and his angels; priest = the Law; Levite = the prophets; Good Samaritan = Christ; beast = the body of Christ; inn = the church; two denarii = two commandments of love; innkeeper = the apostle Paul; return of the Good Samaritan = the resurrection or the *second coming; and so on. Of course, such an interpretation lost sight of the original question of what it means to be a neighbor!

Although interpreters of the Reformation sought to end allegorical methods of interpreting scripture, the parables continued to allegorize. More recently, however, new insight has been gained as to the difference between parables and allegories. An allegory consists of a string of *metaphors that have individual meanings, whereas a parable is essentially a single metaphor possessing a single meaning. The details of parable, then, should not be pressed for meaning; rather, one should seek only its basic point of comparison. Although some parables do contain details that have allegorical significance, this distinction between allegory and parable is useful and provides an important rule for interpretation: seek the main point of the parable and do not seek meaning in details unless it is necessary.

In identifying the main point of a parable, several questions prove helpful: (1) What comes at the end? This rule of end stress recognizes that the main emphasis of a parable, as in most stories, comes at the end. (2) What is spoken in direct discourse? In a parable what is found within quotation marks is especially important. (3) To what or whom is the most space devoted? Usually the most space is given to the main point of the parable.

A second rule for interpreting the parables is to try to understand its meaning in its original setting. Jesus did not address his parables to modern readers but to a first-century Jewish audience. The parables take on new life and vitality when one tries to understand them as Jesus' original audience would have. In this regard, the following questions prove helpful: (1) What is the general theological framework of Jesus' teachings? Each parable of Jesus should be interpreted in light of the totality of his teachings. (2) To what possible audience did Jesus address this parable? If addressed to Pharisees and *scribes, its emphasis might be quite different than if addressed to publicans and sinners. The discovery of the Coptic Gospel of Thomas at *Nag Hammadi has provided additional help for ascertaining the original form and meaning of the parables. Since this collection of 114 sayings and parables of Jesus did not stem from any canonical Gospel, it offers an independent tradition for investigating the original form of numerous parables.

A parable may have a specific meaning not only for its original situation of Jesus but also for that of the evangelist. One example is the parable of the Lost Sheep: in Luke 15.3–7 the parable is addressed to Pharisees and scribes, but in Matthew 18.10–14 it is addressed to the church and the "wandering" within Matthew's community. At times the evangelists added allegorical details to the parables that reveal a particular emphasis (e.g., Matt. 21.39). This leads to a third rule of parable interpretation: Seek to understand how the evangelists interpreted Jesus' parables.

Recently, the focus in research on the parables has shifted to literary-aesthetic interpretation. Parables are seen as autonomous works that possess multiple meanings and power in themselves, completely apart from their author. Although it is important to appreciate the aesthetic quality of the parables, the parables of Jesus have been treasured and loved primarily because they are parables of Jesus.

MAJOR PARABLES OF JESUS
(GT = Gospel of Thomas)

Parables found in four gospels
  Soils   Mark 4.2–9, 13–20/Matt. 13.3–9, 18–
    23/Luke 8.4–8, 11–14/GT 9
  Mustard Seed   Mark 4.30–32/Matt. 13.31–
    32/Luke 13.18–19/GT 20
  Evil Tenants   Mark 12.1–11/Matt. 21.33–
    43/Luke 20.9–17/GT 65

Parables found in three gospels
  Divided House   Mark 3.23–26/Matt. 12.25–
    26/Luke 11.17–18
  Fig Tree   Mark 13.28–29/Matt. 24.32–33/
    Luke 21.29–31
  Leaven   Matt. 13.33/Luke 13.20/GT 96
  Marriage Feast   Matt. 22.1–10/cf. Luke
    14.15–24/GT 64
  Lost Sheep   Luke 15.3–7/Matt. 18.12–14/
    GT 107

Parables found in two gospels
  Wise and Foolish Builders   Matt. 7.24–27/
    Luke 6.47–49
  Wise and Foolish Servants   Matt. 24.45–51/
    Luke 12.42–46
  Talents   Matt. 25.14–30/cf. Luke 19.12–27
  Wheat and Weeds   Matt. 13.24–30, 36–43/
    GT 57
  Hidden Treasure   Matt. 13.44/GT 109
  Pearl   Matt. 13.45–46/GT 76
  Great Net   Matt. 13.47–50/GT 8
  Rich Fool   Luke 12.16–21/GT 63

Parables found in one gospel
  Seed Growing Secretly   Mark 4.26–29

ROBERT H. STEIN

Paraclete. *See* Holy Spirit.

Paradise. Originally a Persian word meaning "park" or "enclosure," paradise first appears in the *Septuagint with reference to the garden of *Eden (Gen. 2) and became associated with a pristine state of perfection free of suffering. In *apocalyptic literature the loss of this original paradise represented the loss of the presence of God in human experience, and therefore redemption was imagined as the recovery of paradise whether it was on earth or in heaven. At the end of the world the righteous would be rewarded by a return to paradise.

Although paradise was initially an earthly garden, New Testament writers lifted it above the evils of this world. Paul says that his visionary flight to the "third heaven" carried him into paradise (2 Cor. 12.1–4), and according to Luke 23.43 Jesus tells the penitent thief that at the moment of death they will be together in paradise. Yet Jesus also is reported to have said that the eschatological paradise described by Isaiah (35.5) was manifested in his ministry (Matt. 11.5) and that the qualities of Eden were revealed in his person (John 4.10–14). Clearly, early Christian writers believed that the traditions of paradise were fulfilled in Jesus and his ministry.

GREGORY SHAW

Paraphrases. Paraphrase is a restatement of a text or passage in another form or other words, often to clarify meaning. It is generally restricted to a restatement made in the same language, rather than in another language. As applied to Bible translation, it usually means a version that often alters the original cultural and literary setting of the original, sometimes adding or omitting material in order to make the text more intelligible and acceptable to intended readers. What is sometimes called "paraphrase" in Bible translation is actually a legitimate and necessary device to represent the meaning clearly and faithfully in the target language. As C. H. Dodd noted, the line between translation and paraphrase is a fine one: "But if the best commentary is a good translation, it is also true that every intelligent translation is in a sense a paraphrase." And Ronald Knox made the cutting comment, "The word 'paraphrase' is a bogey of the half-educated. . . . It is a paraphrase when you translate *Comment vous portez-vous?* by 'How are you?' " No self-respecting translator would translate that French question by "How are you carrying yourselves?"

The earliest scriptures in English, the oral renditions of Caedmon (seventh century CE) and the written works of Aelfric (ca. 1000), were paraphrases. In the sixteenth century, several paraphrases were produced. Jan van den Campen did a Latin paraphrase of the Psalms in 1532, which was translated into English in 1535 (perhaps by Coverdale). The English version of Erasmus's New Testament Paraphrase appeared in 1549. He begins Romans as follows: "I am Paul, though formerly Saul, that is, I have become peaceful, though formerly restless, until recently subject to the law of Moses, now freed from Moses, I have been made a servant of Jesus Christ." In 1653 Henry Hammond, president of Magdalen College, Oxford, produced a paraphrase of the New Testament, which was printed alongside the KJV.

Edward Harwood's Bible (1768) was, as he stated, "not a *verbal* translation, but a *liberal* and *diffusive* version of the sacred classics." His rendition of Luke 1.46–47 is typical: "My soul with reverence adores my Creator, and all my faculties with transport join in celebrating the goodness of God my Saviour, who hath in so signal a manner condescended to regard my poor and humble station. Transcendent goodness! Every future age will now conjoin in celebrating my happiness!" Ferrar Fenton's Bible (1903) may be considered a paraphrase, at least in some passages. It begins: "By Periods God created that which produced the Solar System; then that which produced the Earth." However, because of criticism of the rendering "periods," in the fifth edition Fenton replaced it with "ages," which is also paraphrastic.

Most paraphrases are limited to one book and are usually included by their author in the commentary on that book. Such is the case of J. B. Mayor's paraphrases in his commentaries on James (1892) and on Jude and 2 Peter (1907), and W. O. Carver's paraphrase in his commentary on Ephesians (1949).

F. F. Bruce published his paraphrase of Galatians in the *Evangelical Quarterly* (January–March 1957), and of other Pauline letters in subsequent issues. In 1965 they were all published in one volume, *An Expanded Paraphrase of the Epistles of Paul*, together with the text of the Revised Version. In light of current modern language translations, Bruce's work appears quite conservative, hardly qualifying as a paraphrase. Romans 1.16–17 reads: "Believe me, I have no reason to be ashamed of the good news which I proclaim. No indeed; it is God's effective means for the salvation of all who believe, for Jews in the first place but for the Gentiles too. Why? Because in this good news there is a revelation of God's righteousness—a way of righteousness based on the principle of faith, and offered to all men for acceptance by faith, in accordance with the words of the prophet: 'It is he who is righteous by faith that will live.'"

The most popular English Bible paraphrase of all times is Kenneth N. Taylor's *The Living Bible Paraphrased* (1971). In his preface he explains that, in attempting to be faithful in paraphrasing the text, he has been guided by "the theological lodestar [of] a rigid evangelical position." It must be stated, however, that Taylor's penchant for adding to or deleting from the text, without any justification other than what is dictated by his "rigid evangelical position," effectively removes *The Living Bible* from being regarded as a trustworthy rendering. It is not that every passage in his paraphrase is tainted (in fact, some are very well done, e.g., 1 John 2.16); it is that readers who are not acquainted with the biblical text will too often be misled by Taylor's handling of it. From dozens of examples that could be cited, two must suffice here. Whereas the Hebrew of 2 Samuel 24.1 states that Yahweh incited David to take a census of the people, Taylor exonerates Yahweh from any responsibility by editing the passage, "and David was moved to harm them." Contrary to what the

*synoptic Gospels report, John 12.14 states that Jesus himself found the donkey on which he rode into Jerusalem; Taylor takes care of that problem by eliminating the passage completely!

Paraphrases of biblical texts, responsibly made, are a legitimate and useful way of making the meaning of the text clearer to the reader. When produced by translators who are ruled by rigid tenets of whatever kind, however, they serve only to confirm the truth of the Italian aphorism, "Translators are traitors" *(Traduttori traditori)*.

See also Translations, *article on* English Language. ROBERT G. BRATCHER

Parchment. A superior quality of writing material produced from animal skins by a process of cleaning, stretching, and rubbing with chalk or pumice. Parchment is durable and holds ink well on both sides. From the second century BCE, parchment and leather were preferred for *Torah scrolls intended for public reading. Parchment gradually replaced papyrus for most purposes during the first two centuries CE, and it remained the standard writing material in Europe until the advent of mechanical printing. Thus, the great majority of biblical *manuscripts are written on parchment. The *membrana* mentioned in 2 Timothy 4.13 were parchment or leather documents of unknown content.

See also Books and Bookmaking in Antiquity. ROBERT STOOPS

Parousia. "Arrival" or "presence," a Greek word used both of ordinary persons and of an emperor or a god. The term is used in early Christianity for the anticipated return of Jesus, when he was expected to judge humankind as triumphant *Son of man (*see* Second Coming of Christ). The word parousia is found with this meaning in the eschatological *parables of Matthew 24, but otherwise chiefly outside the Gospels, as in 1 Corinthians 15.23, 1 Thessalonians 2.19, and the urgently apocalyptic 2 Peter (1.16; 3.4, 12). *Paul also uses the term to mean the arrival of an ordinary person (1 Cor. 16.17; 2 Cor. 7.6; Phil. 1.26, 2.12). PHILIP SELLEW

Passover. This festival, observed on the fourteenth day of the month of Nisan (March/April), commemorates the *Exodus of the *Hebrews from *Egypt. Of the five lists of festivals in the

Hebrew Bible (Exod. 23.14–17; 34.18–25; Lev. 23.1–37; Num. 28–29; Deut. 16.1–6), only the last three make reference to Passover (Lev. 23.5; Num. 26.16; Deut. 16.1–8), and all of these associate the celebration with the seven-day festival of unleavened bread, which commences on the fifteenth of the month. Exodus 23.14–17 and 34.18–23 mention only the festival of unleavened bread as an early spring celebration. The narrative in Exodus 12.1–36 provides an explanation of the origin of Passover as well as the features involved in its celebration; this narrative also associates Passover (12.1–14) with the festival of unleavened bread (12.15–20).

According to Exodus 12.1–13, the following were characteristic of Passover. On the tenth day of the month, the animal to be slaughtered was selected and set aside for safekeeping; according to Exodus 12.5, the animal was an unblemished, one-year-old goat or lamb, although Deuteronomy 16.2 includes calves. The animal was slaughtered on the fourteenth day late in the afternoon. Some *blood of the animal was smeared on the doorposts and lintels of the houses. The animal was roasted whole (see Exod. 12.46 and Num. 9.12; Deut. 16.7 specifies boiling, which would have required dismemberment). The flesh was eaten, along with unleavened bread and bitter herbs, by members of the household or associated households. The meal was eaten in haste, with the participants dressed for flight. Any uneaten meat, should there be any, was to be burned the next morning.

The eating of unleavened bread at the meal is explained by the haste with which the Israelites had to flee (Exod. 12.34, 39), but no biblical explanation is offered for the consumption of bitter herbs. The daubing of the blood on the doorposts, later assumed to have been part of only the original episode, is described as marking the houses of the Israelites so that God would bypass their homes in the slaughter of the firstborn. (Note the similar substitution of a ram for the firstborn in Gen. 22, and the similar use of a red marker to avoid death in Josh. 2.17–21.)

If people were ritually unclean or away on a journey when Passover was observed in Nisan, they could celebrate the festival in the second month in similar fashion (Num. 9.1–13). Foreigners and thus non-Jews who had settled among the people were allowed to keep the Passover, provided they were circumcised (Exod. 12.48–49; Num. 9.14).

Although Exodus 12 seems to imply that Passover was a home festival and thus could be observed apart from a pilgrimage to a sanctuary, Deuteronomy 16.5–7 requires that the slaughter of the animal and the meal occur at a place (sanctuary) that God would choose. The same pilgrimage requirement seems assumed by Exodus 34.25 and Leviticus 23.4–7.

The Hebrew name of the festival, Pesah, is derived from the verb that means "to protect," "to have compassion," "to pass over," and is used to describe the action of God in the Exodus narrative (12.13, 23, 27). The English designation "passover" shows the influence of the *Vulgate translation.

Most scholars assume that Passover was originally a spring festival, associated with a shepherding culture, that was secondarily related to the Exodus story (note the reference to a festival in Exod. 5.1 before the Exodus). Such a celebration would have been connected with either the annual spring change of pastures or the sacrifice of the firstborn to insure the continued fertility of the flocks (see Exod. 22.29–30) or both. Characteristics pointing to such an origin for the festival in Exodus 12 are the lamb or goat to be slaughtered, cooking by roasting, the time of the year (which coincides with the lambing season and the change of pastures), the absence of priest and altar, the lack of dedicating any part of the edible flesh to God, the family nature of the celebration, and the nocturnal observance at the time of full moon.

The tractate Pesahim in the *Mishnah provides a description of the way that the rabbis (about 200 CE) understood Passover to have been celebrated before the destruction of the Second Temple (70 CE). Many of the features reflected in Pesahim are thus characteristic of the observance at the time of Jesus (see Lord's Supper), and some have continued in Jewish tradition to the present. The following elements in the celebration are noteworthy.

The people brought their Passover animals to the *Temple in the late afternoon and, because of the numbers of worshipers, were admitted to the sanctuary in three separate groups. The worshipers slaughtered their animals and the priests caught the blood and tossed it against the altar. The animals were flayed and cleaned in the Temple courtyard, with the required fat and internal portions being burned on the *altar (Lev. 3.3–4). While each group was performing these functions, the *Levites sang the Egyptian Hallel psalms (Pss. 113–118) and repeated them if time allowed (Pesah. 5.5–10).

The animals were carried from the Temple

precincts and cooked for the Passover meal. Cooking was done by roasting so as not to break any bone in the animal (*Pesaḥ.* 7.1,11; see Exod. 12.46; John 19.36).

At the meal, everyone ate at least a portion of the Passover animal. The flesh was eaten along with varied herbs (*Pesaḥ.* 2.6), unleavened bread, a dip (*ḥărôset*) composed of pounded nuts and fruits mixed with vinegar, and four cups of wine. After the second cup, a son asked the father, "Why is this night different from all other nights?" and the father instructed the son on the basis of Deuteronomy 26.5–11. Between the second and third cups, Psalm 113 (or 113–114) was sung. After the fourth cup, the Hallel was concluded. At the conclusion of the meal, the people departed but not to join in revelry (*Pesaḥ.* 10.1–8).

The people sought to celebrate the meal as if they themselves had come out of Egypt—"out of bondage to freedom, from sorrow to gladness, and from mourning to festival day, and from darkness to great light, and from servitude to redemption" (*Pesaḥ.* 10.5).

See also Feasts and Festivals; Leaven.

JOHN H. HAYES

Pastoral Letters, The. Since the second half of the eighteenth century the two letters to Timothy and the letter to Titus have been known as the Pastoral Letters. The three are closely related in both content and form and offer advice about the exercise of the pastoral office in the care and oversight of congregations.

Outline.

1 TIMOTHY

  I. Opening (1.1–2)
  II. Body of instructions (1.3–6.21a):
    A. The authority of Paul to give instructions to Timothy in the face of false teachers (1.3–20)
    B. The instructions (2.1–6.21a):
      1. On prayer for all (2.1–7)
      2. On the inner connection between the prayer of men and women and their conduct (2.8–10)
      3. On women who are false teachers (2.9–15)
      4. On bishops (3.1–7)
      5. On deacons (3.8–13)
      6. Interlude: basis of and need for instructions for the household of God in the face of false teachers who deny the goodness of marriage and creation (3.14–4.5)

      7. To Timothy to teach Paul's instructions (4.6–5.2)
      8. On widows (5.3–16)
      9. On elders (5.17–25)
      10. To slaves (6.1–2a)
      11. To Timothy to teach the foregoing instructions in the face of greedy false teachers (6.2b–21a)
  III. Closing (6.21b)

2 TIMOTHY

  I. Opening (1.1–2)
  II. Thanksgiving (1.3–5)
  III. Body of letter: Paul's example, exhortations, and predictions form his last will and testament for Timothy (1.6–4.18):
    A. Paul bequeaths to Timothy the deposit of faith for which he suffers (1.6–18)
    B. Exhortation to Timothy to be prepared to suffer, like Paul, as a teacher (2.1–7)
    C. Example of Paul who draws strength from the gospel as he suffers (2.8–13)
    D. Exhortation to Timothy to teach faithfully in the face of the evil conduct of false teachers (2.14–26)
    E. Prediction that false teachers will abound in the last times (3.1–9)
    F. Example of Paul's life of teaching amid great persecution (3.10–17)
    G. Exhortation to Timothy to teach persistently; prediction that people will give little heed to sound teaching (4.1–5)
    H. Example of Paul, who at death's door trusts in God to save him (4.6–18)
  IV. Final greetings and closing (4.19–22)

TITUS

  I. Opening (1.1–4)
  II. Body of instructions (1.5–3.11):
    A. Instruction to Titus to appoint elders and bishops in Crete who will promote sound teaching in the face of those teaching Jewish myths (1.5–16)
    B. Instructions that accord with sound doctrine (2.1–15):
      1. On older men and women (2.1–3)
      2. On younger women and men (2.4–8)
      3. On slaves (2.9–10)
      4. Theological and christological bases of the instructions (2.11–15)
    C. Additional instructions (3.1–11):
      1. Instruction to live a harmonious, generous, and gracious life with all (3.1–7)

2. Instruction to do good deeds and to avoid idle words (3.8–11)

III. Closing (3.12–15)

Authorship. The authorship of these letters, called pastoral because they deal largely with pastoral or practical matters and grouped together because they address the same issues in a uniform style, is contested. While the Pastoral Letters have a noticeable Pauline character, there are five major areas in which they differ from the indisputedly genuine Pauline letters. First, the vocabulary (e.g., "the saying is sure" [1 Tim. 1.15; 3.1; 4.9; 2 Tim. 2.11; Titus 3.8]) and style vary greatly from those of the letters to the *Romans and *Corinthians and are closer to those of the apostolic fathers such as Polycarp. Second, the theological concepts (e.g., "the faith") and the stress on public respectability differ markedly from emphases in the undisputed Pauline letters. Third, church order—*bishops, *elders, *widows, *deacons—does not correspond to that found in the genuine Pauline letters but is more like that in evidence toward the end of the first century CE. Fourth, the author relies much more heavily on traditions, both creedal and hortatory, than the *Paul of the authentic letters; unlike Paul in *Galatians, for example, he rarely argues theologically with opponents but merely upbraids them. Finally, the Pastoral Letters do not fit into the career of Paul as detailed in *Acts and Romans. The chronology of the Pastoral Letters presupposes that Paul was freed from his imprisonment in Rome, changed his plans to go to Spain, journeyed back to the East on another missionary enterprise, was imprisoned a second time, and was then martyred.

Theories that attempt to account for these differences are as follows. First, accepting the Pastoral Letters as fully authentic, it is felt that Paul was indeed freed from his first imprisonment and returned to the East for further missionary work. 1 Timothy and Titus reflect this mission. Arrested again, Paul was imprisoned, tried, and executed in Rome. 2 Timothy issues from the time of this second imprisonment. Paul's need to establish church order in communities and to counteract false teachers accounts for the different vocabulary of the Pastoral Letters. These last letters date to ca. 65 CE, and because they stem from an aged Paul, they lack the theological acumen of a vibrant and young Paul.

Another theory also presupposes further missionary work by Paul in the East, but it accounts for the high incidence of uncharacteristic Pauline elements in the Pastoral Letters by postulating that Paul employed a secretary to whom he gave greater responsibility in creating these letters ca. 65 CE.

A third theory holds that the Pastoral Letters contain so many un-Pauline words and concepts because they were written by a later author, who, ca. 85 CE, desired to apply the teaching of Paul to new situations in the Pauline missionary territory. This author worked into his letters fragments of genuine Pauline letters, such as 2 Timothy 1.15–18, 4.6–22, and Titus 3.12–14. These authentic fragments account for the personal notes, which a later author presumably would not have invented.

A fourth theory is more radical and maintains that the letters are completely pseudonymous and are in this regard like the contemporary pseudonymous Socratic letters, which are written under Socrates' name and apply his teaching to a later time. In writing three letters, the author was influenced by the trend in evidence in Cicero, Seneca, and Pliny of publishing a collection of letters. Writing ca. 100 CE, the author uses personal notes to add verisimilitude to the letters and to present Paul as an example to be imitated. Thus, for example, the personal note of 2 Timothy 4.13, which depicts the imprisoned Paul asking that the cloak he left behind in Troas be brought to him, adds local color to the letter and also shows how Paul embodies his teaching of contentment with the basic necessities of life (1 Tim. 6.8). The view adopted here is a modification of this fourth position and dates the Pastoral Letters ca. 85 CE.

Purpose. The goal of the Pastoral Letters is to provide instructions on how the household of God should live in Paul's spirit during the post-Pauline era, when the expectation of the Lord's imminent coming has receded and teachers are propounding false doctrine in the apostle's name. In this situation the author writes to two of Paul's most trusted collaborators with a message that is actually addressed to an entire church, be it a long-standing gentile church like that of *Ephesus addressed in 1 Timothy or a new Jewish Christian church like that of Crete addressed in Titus. The instructions that are to govern the churches addressed in 1 Timothy and Titus have Paul's apostolic authority behind them (note the imperatives that run throughout the letters, e.g., 1 Tim. 2.1, 8, 12; Titus 2.1, 6; 3.1). By obeying these imperatives, the entire church, but especially its leaders, will inculcate sound teaching in the face of false teachers (1 Tim. 6.1; Titus 2.5). Paul's last will and testament in 2 Timothy requires that the church imitate Paul's example (especially his willingness to suffer for the faith, 1.8; 3.10–11), follow his instructions (4.1–5), hold on faithfully to the deposit of faith (1.13–14), and be guided by his predictions (3.1–10). In doing so, they will be able to combat false teaching (14–19).

It is somewhat difficult to ascertain the exact nature of the false teaching countered in the Pastoral Letters. This is because, unlike Paul, the author rarely argues with the false teachers but is content to hurl stereotyped charges against them, paralleled primarily in popular philosophy. These charges follow a set schema: the false teachers are greedy (1 Tim. 6.5; Titus 1.11), do not practice what they preach (2 Tim. 3.5; Titus 1.16; 3.8–9), are involved in verbal quibbles (1 Tim. 1.4, 6; 4.2; 6.4; 2 Tim. 2.14, 16, 23; Titus 1.10; 3.9), are guilty of many vices (1 Tim. 1.9–10; 2 Tim. 3.2–4), and take advantage of women (2 Tim. 3.6).

Once the stereotypical aspects of the polemic are discounted, the following picture of false teachers emerges. They are Jewish Christians who emphasize the *Law (1 Tim. 1.7; Titus 3.9; cf. Titus 1.14), Jewish myths (Titus 1.14; cf. 1 Tim. 1.4; 4.7; 2 Tim. 4.4), and *genealogies (1 Tim. 4.3–5). They teach that the resurrection has already occurred (2 Tim. 2.18). Some of the proponents of their doctrine are women (1 Tim. 2.9–15). If this false teaching with its emphasis on speculation and depreciation of the material is to be called *gnosticism, then it would be advisable to call it proto-gnosticism, for it cannot be identified with any later known gnostic system or group.

Theology. While the Pastoral Letters were not written by Paul, there is no doubt of their Pauline character. The image of Paul as a prisoner for the faith, known from *Philippians and *Philemon, is reflected throughout 2 Timothy (1.8, 12; 2.8–13; 3.11–13). The Pauline emphasis on the universality of the gospel (see Rom. 1.5) is prominent (1 Tim. 2.4–7; 3.16; 4.10; 2 Tim. 4.17; Titus 2.11). The Pauline accent of God's fidelity to promise (see Rom. 3.3) finds expression in 2 Tim. 2.13; Titus 1.2. That redemption is through Jesus Christ (see Rom. 3.24–25) is underscored (1 Tim. 2.5–6; 2 Tim. 2.11–12; Titus 2.14). The Pauline hallmark that *salvation and *justification are by faith alone and not by works (see Rom. 3.28) echoes in 1 Tim. 1.13–16; 2 Tim. 1.9–10; Titus 3.5–7. The creative theologizing of the Paul of Romans may be past, but the results of that creativity live on in tradi-

tions and are actualized by the Pastoral Letters for Pauline churches of the generation after Paul.

In combating the doctrines of the false teachers, the author develops a theology of creation. The theology of the Pastoral Letters fears a benevolent God, who wills life, goodness, and salvation for all men and women (Titus 3.4–7). All that this God has created is good: marriage (1 Tim. 2.15; 4.3), food (1 Tim. 4.3), wine (1 Tim. 5.23), possessions (1 Tim. 6.17–19), the round of humdrum daily human chores (Titus 2.1–10). The instructions that form much of 1 Timothy and Titus demonstrate that this God does not desire that chaos exist in God's world; order in human affairs is willed by the divine creator.

As a corollary of his teaching on creation, the author stresses the human side of "Christ Jesus our Savior" (Titus 1.4). He is also the mediator between God and individual men and women; he is the human being who has given himself up as a ransom for all persons (1 Tim. 2.4–6). Christ Jesus, in the face of the opposition of Pontius *Pilate in his earthly life, remained steadfastly obedient to God's will and made the good confession (1 Tim. 6.13). In Titus 2.13–14 we find dynamically juxtaposed the divinity and humanity of Jesus, the great god and savior who died to redeem men and women from all iniquity and to gather them into a people.

Some of the ethical teaching in the Pastoral Letters has been evaluated as a middle-class or bourgeois ethic, which does not challenge the status quo but strives to live by its norms. Thus, for example, the qualities required of a bishop in 1 Timothy 3.1–7 are basically those required of a general by Onosander (died 59 CE). Similarly, the norms of Titus 2.1–10 are largely those of the patriarchal model of the author's society.

The author's world-affirming ethic and desire to conform to society's standards are also evident in his great concern that the conduct of church leaders should be irreproachable in the eyes of the larger public: bishops (1 Tim. 3.7; Titus 1.6, 7), deacons (1 Tim. 3.10), and widows (1 Tim. 5.7, 10). He takes great pains to ensure that the conduct of *slaves (1 Tim. 6.1; Titus 2.10) and of young wives (Titus 2.5) should not bring discredit on the word of God or on the sound teaching.

The church order of the Pastoral Letters is not that of Ignatius of Antioch (ca. 110 CE) with his insistence of the monarchical bishop with elders and deacons under him. It reflects rather the somewhat loose structure evident in 1 Clement (ca. 95 CE), in which bishops and elders exist side by side. With their offices of bishop (1 Tim. 3.1–7; Titus 1.7–9), elders (1 Tim. 5.17–22; Titus 1.5–6), deacons, both men (1 Tim. 3.8–10, 12–13) and women (1 Tim. 3.11), and widows (1 Tim. 5.3–16), the Pastoral Letters reflect the transition period between Paul, who taught that the church was animated with diverse charismata, and Ignatius, who insisted that one individual be in charge of the churches of a distinct area. In the Pastoral Letters the leaders' task, as demonstrated by the instructions to the two representative leaders, Timothy and Titus, is to guard the deposit of faith (2 Tim. 1.14) and to be apt teachers of sound doctrine, capable of refuting false teachers and revilers (1 Tim. 3.3; 5.17; 2 Tim. 4.1–2; Titus 1.9).

ROBERT J. KARRIS, O.F.M.

Patriarchs. *This term has been used in most scholarship to designate the ancestors of Israel, especially in Genesis 12–50, and its adjectival form is also generally employed, as in "patriarchal history," "patriarchal narratives," etc. These designations, however, are misleading, for in the traditions perseved in Genesis 12–50 and elsewhere in the Bible the "matriarchs" are also prominent. The* Companion *thus uses the more inclusive terms ancestor(s) and ancestral for the biblical patriarchs and matriarchs, i.e., *Abraham, *Sarah, and *Hagar; *Isaac and *Rebekah; and *Jacob, *Leah, *Rachel, Bilhah, and Zilpah, and their children. For a discussion of the ancestral narratives, see* Ancestors, The, *and* Genesis, The Book of.

Paul. Paul was born at Tarsus in Cilicia (Map 7:F3), at about the beginning of the common era. A member of a Hellenistic Jewish family, which could trace its descent to the tribe of *Benjamin (Rom. 11.1; Phil. 3.5), he was given the Hebrew name Saul, as well as the name Paul. Unlike many Jews, he was also a Roman citizen (Acts 16.37; 22.25–28).

As a child, Paul would learn of his Jewish heritage in the local *synagogue at Tarsus. He received at least the final stages of his education in Jerusalem, though, under the guidance of Rabbi *Gamaliel (Acts 22.3; 26.4). He soon rose to a position of some eminence as a *Pharisee, perhaps even becoming a member of the *Sanhedrin (Acts 26.5; Phil. 3.5).

When Christianity first came to prominence in *Jerusalem, he was strongly opposed to it and was prepared to take personal responsibility for ensuring its extermination (Acts 9.1–2; 1 Cor. 15.9; Gal. 1.13). But while on his way to *Damascus in *Syria, chasing Jewish Christians who had fled there, he had a remarkable experience that changed the course of his life. Looking back on it twenty years later, he compared it to the appearances of *Jesus to the disciples after the *Resurrection (1 Cor. 15.1–11); as a result of that encounter, his fervent devotion to biblical faith as understood by the Pharisees was augmented by an unqualified commitment to the gospel.

From this point, his life took a new direction, as he threw himself into missionary work throughout Asia Minor and Greece. He established many churches, and saw himself as God's chosen agent to take the gospel to the *gentiles (Gal. 1.15–16, 2.7–8). The New Testament nowhere mentions his death, but reliable traditions depict him as a martyr in Rome, beheaded during the persecution of Nero in the mid 60s CE.

Sources. We have two major sources of information about Paul: his letters and the book of *Acts. There has been much debate concerning their relative worth. Paul's own writings must obviously have priority, though it is certainly not easy to reconstruct the story of someone's life on the basis of a miscellaneous and incomplete collection of occasional letters. Acts at least appears to provide a plausible framework, but is not always easy to correlate with what can be deduced from the letters.

Both sources must be treated with some caution, for neither was intended to be a biography. He features prominently in Acts, but the main focus there is on the rapid spread of Christianity from Jerusalem to Rome. The letters are mainly concerned with specific circumstances in the life of various churches, and inevitably reflect more of these than they do of Paul's own life. They contain limited personal details and report very few incidents.

Additionally, Acts and the letters deal with different aspects of Paul's life. Acts shows him as a great missionary pioneer, taking the gospel to far-flung corners of the empire. It therefore reports his initial preaching of the gospel to non-Christians and their reactions to it, but it never mentions the letters! But they were written to Christians, and show how Paul related to those already in the church. For this reason alone it is difficult to draw direct comparisons between the two sources of information.

Yet we have little alternative but to try to combine the two sources. Acts provides the one really useful clue to the *chronology of Paul's life. The reference to his encounter with Gallio at *Corinth (Acts 18.12–17) dates this incident somewhere between 1 July 51 and 1 July 52, and by judicious deductions from that it is possible to work out a general outline of Paul's life. But there are still problems. There is no agreement on the number and sequence of his early contacts with the Jerusalem Christians (Acts 11–15; Gal. 1–2). There is also doubt over the number of times he was imprisoned, with Paul apparently implying an imprisonment at Ephesus not mentioned in Acts (Rom. 16.7; 1 Cor. 15.32; 2 Cor. 1.8; 11.23).

Background. Tarsus was a typical Hellenistic city, with a cosmopolitan population and a variety of religious options for its people. Its citizens were well known for their interest in philosophy, and Tarsus was home to several prominent *Stoics, including Athenodorus, adviser to Augustus. No doubt, Paul had at least a passing acquaintance with their thinking, as well as some knowledge of the various *mystery religions and of Greek philosophy in general. He occasionally makes specific reference to *Stoic writers (1 Cor. 15.33), and some have thought his letters show influence from Stoic and Cynic debating styles. But it is unlikely that he had a formal education in such subjects. He did, however, enjoy and appreciate life in the Hellenistic cities, and his metaphors demonstrate close knowledge of urban activities (1 Cor. 3.10–15; 4.9; 9.25–27).

Throughout his letters, Paul exhibits a passionate devotion to his Jewish heritage (Rom. 11.1–6; Gal. 1.13–14; Phil. 3.4–6). He was always at pains to demonstrate that his understanding of the gospel was quite consistent with biblical faith, and that Christian believers were spiritual heirs to ancient Israel. Toward the end of his ministry, he invested much time and energy in maintaining good relations between gentile Christians and the church in Jerusalem (2 Cor. 8.1–15; Rom. 15.25–33). It was his insistence that gentile churches give financial aid to the church in Jerusalem that ultimately led to his arrest and transportation to Rome (Acts 21–28).

His thinking also owed a good deal to the beliefs of the original *disciples. Admittedly, he could declare himself independent of the Jewish *apostles (Gal. 1.11–12, 17), but that was a tactical move in the face of strident opposition. When his presentation of the gospel is compared with other parts of the New Testament, it turns out to have the same basic structure as the preaching of Peter and other leading apostles. Moreover, the practical advice he gave his converts is surprisingly similar to that of other New Testament writers.

The nineteenth-century Tübingen school dismissed this picture as a harmonization produced by the writer of Acts in the interests of the later catholic church. They thought Paul radically different from Jerusalem and Jewish Christianity. More recently, things have turned full circle and some have argued that Paul was actually under the control of the Jewish church, and took his orders from Jerusalem; that too seems unlikely. Nevertheless, Paul was concerned for the unity of Jews and gentiles in the church, and we misunderstand him if we place his life and thinking outside the mainstream of first-generation Christianity.

Missionary Activity. Paul was convinced that on the Damascus road God had commissioned him to take the gospel to the gentiles. Both tactically and theologically he felt it was important that the gospel also be proclaimed to Jews (Acts 13.46–48; Rom. 1.16; 9–11; 1 Cor. 9.20–21), and, according to Acts, his usual practice was to go first to the local synagogue. Galatians 2.7–9, however, indicates that his activity was apparently directed exclusively to gentiles.

In his travels, Paul took advantage of the fine highway system built by the Romans, and in the course of three extended tours he visited most of the key centers in Greece and Asia Minor. Although he had a physical weakness (2 Cor. 12.7–8), he must have been incredibly tough, judging from the list of hardships he survived (2 Cor. 11. 23–27).

Paul seems to have had a carefully designed strategy for evangelism. He aimed to establish churches in the largest population centers, which he could easily reach on the paved Roman roads. From there, local converts could take the message into more remote towns and villages. This was evidently successful. At least one of his letters (*Colossians) was written to a church founded in this way, and later in the first century most of the areas he visited had many flourishing congregations.

Paul's converts were a typical cross section of Roman society. Many Christians were slaves, though the gospel also attracted cultured upper-class Romans. Some were clearly influential people (Rom. 16.23), the kind who would take personal disputes to law courts (1 Cor. 6.1–11) and who could afford to make donations for good causes (2 Cor. 8.1–15; Rom. 15.25–33). Paul's coworkers also enjoyed the typically mobile lifestyle of the upper classes; in the absence of church buildings, the Christian community depended on the generosity of its richer members to provide facilities for corporate worship and *hospitality for wandering preachers (Rom. 16.3–16; Philem. 2, 22; 1 Cor. 16.19). At the same time, Paul was certain that the gospel transcended the barriers of race, sex, and class, and insisted on the equality of all believers (Gal. 3.28; 1 Cor. 12.1–31).

The Letters. Literary epistles were common in the Roman world (*see* Letter-writing). Though Paul followed the style of the day, in some ways his letters are not literary works. He was essentially a speaker, and his letters contain what he would have said had he been physically present (2 Cor. 1.15–2.4). This no doubt explains his often uneven style. It also highlights some of the problems faced by the modern reader. At least one of Paul's letters (1 *Corinthians) was clearly written in answer to previous correspondence from the church at Corinth (1 Cor. 8.1), and most of the others are a response to information that had reached him in one way or another. But of course we only have one side of the correspondence. And we may not even know that as well as we think, for ancient letter writers often entrusted significant parts of their message to the bearer of the letter to deliver orally. At best, therefore, reading Paul's letters is like overhearing one side of a telephone conversation: it is possible to pick up the general drift, but specific details are more elusive.

Not all of Paul's letters are like this. Some think *Romans a more considered statement of Paul's thinking. *Ephesians seems to have been a circular letter, sent to several churches. And in many letters, Paul shows that his writing can be sophisticated (1 Cor. 13), while his detailed arguments must have been carefully worked out before they were written down (e.g., Rom. 5–8).

Scholars disagree on whether all thirteen letters attributed to Paul are genuine. He regularly used a secretary, and wrote along with associates, so we may expect variations in style. But most doubt that the *Pastoral letters come from Paul (1–2 Timothy, Titus), while others have questioned Ephesians, Colossians, and 2 *Thessalonians, on a variety of theological, stylistic, and literary grounds.

The letters certainly give us an insight into Paul's character. He was a formidable opponent (*Galatians), but he also had a remarkable capacity for deep concern and true friendship (Rom. 16.1–6; 1 Thess. 2.6–9). He had a realistic understanding of human relationships, and was sensitive to those less robust than himself (1 Cor. 7–8). He also had an uninhibited sense of humor (Gal. 5.12).

Theology. Paul did not become a Christian because he was disillusioned with Judaism. He was totally dedicated to biblical faith, and quite certain that it made sense (Gal. 1.14; Phil. 3.6). It was his *conversion experience that changed his life and played a major part in the development of his theology.

He discovered that Jesus was no longer dead, but alive—and must be "the Son of God" (Gal. 1.15–16; 2 Cor. 4.6). He realized that the *Law was not central to salvation, for on the Damascus road God had burst into his life not because of his obedience to the Law but in spite of it. All he could do was to respond to this demonstration of God's freely given love. As he did so, Paul became aware of a moral and spiritual transformation taking place within him, a process that would ultimately remake him to be like Jesus (2 Cor. 2.18; Gal. 2.19–20).

This challenged his preconceptions, especially his attitude to the Law. How could he reconcile his previous understanding of God's will with his new perspective? He did so most eloquently in the conflict with the judaizers of Galatia, arguing from the Bible itself that the Law had always been intended as merely a temporary word from God (Gal. 3.24), and that faith had always been the true basis of salvation, as far back as the time of Abraham (Gal. 3.6–9). This was why he was prepared to argue with such force that gentile converts did not need to become Jews in order to be proper Christians.

But this was not the only way Paul described his beliefs. Elsewhere he refers to the Christian life as "a new creation" (2 Cor. 5.17), in which men and women have been "rescued from the power of darkness and transferred to the kingdom of God's beloved son" (Col. 1.13–14). The "age to come" was not locked up in the future; it had burst into the present through the life, death, resurrection of Jesus, and the coming of the *Holy Spirit.

Paul knew well enough that God's will was not yet fully effective on earth, and he expected a future divine intervention when the power of evil would finally be crushed, and when Jesus would return in glory (1 Cor. 15.20–28; 1 Thess. 4.13–5.11; *see* Second Coming of Christ). But he was certain that Christians were already a part of God's new order, and the church was to be an outpost of the kingdom in which God's will might become a reality in the lives of ordinary people. Through the work of God's Spirit, individuals (Gal. 5.22–23), society (Gal. 3.28), and the whole structure of human relationships (1 Cor. 12–14), could be radically transformed, so that in the context of a physically renewed world system (Rom. 8.18–23; Col. 1.15–20), God's people should grow to "the measure of the full stature of Christ" (Eph. 4.14). JOHN W. DRANE

Peace. The Hebrew word translated "peace," *šālôm*, occurs more than 250 times in the Bible, and its richness is shown in its many usages. It is used as a courteous greeting (Gen. 43.23; *see* Salutations), and also to refer to health or to restoration to health, to general well-being such as sound sleep, length of life, a tranquil death, and even to the physical safety of an individual (Gen. 15.15; 43.27; Exod. 18.7; Josh. 10.21; 1 Kings 22.17; Job 5.23; Pss. 4.8; 38.3; Prov. 3.2; Isa. 38.17).

Šālôm is also used to describe good relations between peoples and nations (Judg. 4.17; 1 Kings 5.26). Thus, it has important social dimensions that can also be seen from the association of peace with righteousness, law, judgment, and the actions of public officials (Isa. 48.18; 60.17; Zech. 8.16).

Šālôm is used, too, to describe quiet tranquillity and contentment (Ps. 119.165; Isa. 32.17; Isa. 48.22). It can also be almost synonymous with friendship (1 Chron. 12.17; Zech. 6.13). The root ideas of the Hebrew word are well-being, wholeness, soundness, completeness.

Šālôm also has theological dimensions. God is described as peace (Judg. 6.24), and its creator and source, who gives it to his people (Lev. 26.6; Num. 6.26; 1 Kings 2.33; 1 Chron. 22.9; Ps. 29.11; Isa. 26.12). Peace in its fullest sense thus cannot be had apart from God (Ps. 4.8; Isa. 45.7; Zech. 8.10–12), a conclusion especially prominent in exilic and postexilic literature (Isa. 54.10; Ezek. 37.26; Mal. 2.5).

The usual Greek word for "peace" is *eirēnē*. In classical literature it denoted the opposite of war or conflict; later it came to describe a harmonious state of mind, an imperturbability that could exist irrespective of external circumstances. In the New Testament, *eirēnē* has these overtones as well as meanings derived from *šālôm*.

The distinctive idea about *eirēnē* in the New Testament is its mediation through Jesus Christ. He is described as the peace which ultimately unifies humanity (Eph. 2.14–17), reconciling humanity with God (Rom. 5.1) through his death (Col. 1.20). GERALD F. HAWTHORNE

Pelethites. *See* Cherethites and Pelethites.

Pentateuch.

Form. The first five books of the Bible (*see* Genesis; Exodus; Leviticus; Numbers; Deuteronomy), known as the Pentateuch (Grk. "five-volumed work"), are essentially in the form of a narrative running from the *creation to the death of *Moses just before the entry of the Israelites into the *Promised Land. Although these books contain a great deal of *law (principally in Exod. 20–40, Leviticus, Numbers, and Deuteronomy), they are not law books in essence. The Hebrew term *Torah, by which the Pentateuch is known, is indeed conventionally translated as "law," but its meaning is better represented as "instruction" or "guidance." Thus, the narratives of the *ancestors in Genesis 12–50 are as much "torah" as are the *Ten Commandments of Exodus 20, since they too offer instruction about the nature of Israel's God, the relationship of Israel to him, and the moral behavior appropriate to life in relationship to him. The "guidance" offered by the more legal parts of the Pentateuch is explicitly directive, as in the many social laws, whether in the style of legal maxims (e.g., Exod. 21.16) or of hypothetical cases (Exod. 21.2–6). Only in a few cases, though, as in the rules governing *sacrifice (Lev. 1–7) or in the instructions for the building of the *tabernacle (Exod. 25–27), is the legislation systematic. In the book of Deuteronomy, chaps. 1–26 being represented as a farewell speech of Moses, there is indeed a distinct hortatory tone in the recollection of the nation's past history (chaps. 1–11) and in the presentation of laws for life in the Promised Land (chaps. 12–26), but the historical setting keeps before the reader the fact that a particular generation in the nation's history is here directly addressed. In the more narrative materials, the "instruction" is indirect and implicit. In some cases the reader is presented with models for imitation (as in the case of Abraham's faithfulness or Joseph's uprightness), but even here, and more especially in the stories like those of *Abraham's deceptions or *Jacob's trickery, there is little direct moralizing. So the Pentateuch does not present itself as a comprehensive set of rules for life, nor does it develop a cohesive theological system, nor does it typically narrate the past for the sake of illustrating obvious or explicit moral truths.

Authorship. Although the Pentateuch has in most centuries been known as "the five books of Moses," perhaps because he is the major human figure in the narrative, it has long been recognized that he cannot have been the author, and that the Pentateuch is in fact anonymous. The Jewish tradition of referring to everything in the Pentateuch as the work of Moses, which is reflected in the New Testament (Matt. 8.4; Luke 20.37; Acts 3.22), proves nothing about its authorship, since it had obviously become customary to refer to these books as "Moses" (Luke 24.27; 2 Cor. 3.15). Within the Pentateuch itself, *Moses is indeed credited with the authorship of a relatively small portion of its content: Exodus 21–23, the laws known as the "Book of the Covenant" (Exod. 24.4–8); Numbers 33, the itinerary of Israel in the wilderness (see Num. 33.2); Deuteronomy 5.6–21, the Ten Commandments (see Deut. 31.24). These sections are, as it happens, among the elements generally considered most ancient by historical scholars. Whether or not Moses can be called the author in a literal sense of anything in the Pentateuch, it is reasonable to hold that his work and teaching were the initial stimulus for the creation of the Pentateuch.

Origins and Date. The overwhelming tendency in biblical scholarship has been to explain the origin of the Pentateuch as the outcome of a process of compilation of various documents from different periods in Israelite history. According to the classical Documentary Theory of the Pentateuch, formulated by Julius Wellhausen and others in the nineteenth century (*see* Interpretation, History of, *article on* Modern Biblical Criticism), the oldest written source of the Pentateuch was the document *J (so-called from its author, the Jahwist or Yahwist, who used the name Yahweh for God) from the ninth century BCE. The *E document (from the Elohist, who employed the Hebrew term *ʾĕlōhîm* for God) came from the eighth century, and the J and E sources were combined by an editor in the mid-seventh century. The book of Deuteronomy, a separate source dating from 621 BCE, was added to the JE material in the mid-sixth century. The final major source, the Priestly Work (*P), was combined with the earlier sources about 400 BCE. The Pentateuch as we know it thus came into

existence no earlier than the end of the fifth century BCE.

No item in the foregoing reconstruction remains unchallenged, and indeed the theory as a whole can no longer be called the consensus view; nevertheless, no other theory has gained any wide support, so this one remains the point of departure for all study of the date and origins of the Pentateuch. Among those who still hold that it is essentially correct, there has been a tendency to date the Yahwist's work a century earlier, in the time of the united monarchy, to favor an eighth-century rather than a seventh-century date for the composition of at least the core of Deuteronomy, and to allow that the Priestly work, set down in writing during the *exile in the sixth century rather than after the exile in the fifth, may well preserve much older material. More radical revisions of the theory include the proposal that the Yahwist's work should be seen as the latest, not the earliest contribution to the Pentateuch, and that it rather than the Priestly work gave the definitive shape to the whole.

A valuable development of the theory in recent decades has been the attempt to reconstruct the intentions of the authors of the presumed sources as theologians anxious to convey by their presentation of Israel's traditional history a message to their contemporaries. Thus, the Yahwist's message has come to be seen as an address to the age of *Solomon, urging Israel to prove itself to be a blessing to the nations in accord with the command to Abraham of Genesis 12; the Elohist's work is an appeal to ninth-century Israel to live in the "fear" of God in the face of persuasive foreign cults. The Deuteronomist's work is seen as a program for national reform, emphasizing the unity of Israel despite the political reality of the divided kingdom and calling for a unified worship of Yahweh. The Priestly work, then, is addressed to the Babylonian exiles, reiterating the authenticity of Israel's religious and cultic traditions and renewing the divine promise of blessing and superabundance in the land (Gen. 1.26) to a generation who had all but given up hope for the future.

Other techniques of analysis beside the detection of sources can sometimes be integrated with the documentary analysis, and sometimes run counter to it. The form-critical approach, by which the literary forms (such as saga, tale, and moral story—sometimes called legend) are analyzed in order to discover the role they played in everyday life, has on the whole proved congenial to the documentary analysis. Its concern has been to press back behind the literary sources of the Pentateuch to reconstruct the original life settings of its diverse materials, and to postulate patterns of growth of the traditions prior to the existence of any written source. Thus, for example, one influential analysis, by Martin Noth, fully accepted the documentary reconstruction but detected behind them five major "themes" or organizing ideas around which the total material of the Pentateuch had gradually gathered: the promise to the ancestors, the *Exodus from Egypt, the guidance in the *wilderness, the giving of the Law, the guidance into the land.

On the other hand, studies in the techniques of oral composition and transmission of oral literature have tended to call into question the theory of an essentially or ultimately literary growth of the Pentateuch. It is possible, for example, to see the whole of Genesis as one large oral composition, in which differing influences have left their mark in the form of relatively minor discrepancies and disagreements in representation, but which was intended to be heard as a whole, later elements in the story deliberately reflecting and building on earlier (so, for example, with the so-called ancestress in danger stories of Gen. 12.10–20; 20.1–18; 26.1–16). Other researches on the processes of literary composition as disclosed by the present shape of the Pentateuch have suggested that we should envisage individual authors creating large blocks of its material rather than editors interweaving a number of narrative strands, as the documentary theory supposed.

Themes. The question here is, what is the organizing principle of the Pentateuch as a whole, considered as a literary entity? An initial answer is, of course, that the subject matter of the Pentateuch is sufficiently unified to create the impression of general coherence in the work. The last four books in particular, beginning as they do with the birth of Moses (Exod. 2), and ending with his death (Deut. 34), have a strong narrative connection. But it would be wrong to regard the Pentateuch as primarily a biography of Moses, for then there would be no evident connection between its last four books and Genesis, for Genesis is a narrative of the ancestors of Israel in general and not especially of Moses' forebears.

Some have suggested that certain brief summaries of the Pentateuchal narrative found at Deuteronomy 26.5–10 and 6.20–24 (cf. Josh. 24.2–13), having the character of Israelite confessions of faith in the God who had directed their history, indicate the fundamental story line of the Pentateuch as a whole. The essential elements in this "little creed" (Gerhard von Rad) are the forebears' origins and divine election, their descent into Egypt, and the entry of the people into the *promised land. This outline does indeed correspond roughly with the content of the Pentateuch, though it makes the remarkable omission of the events at *Sinai, which constitute a major section of the Pentateuchal narrative. We may perhaps seek a more conceptually unified theme in the Pentateuch than a mere summary of its narrative.

The mainspring of the action of the Pentateuch seems to be the divine promise of Genesis 12.1–3 (repeated with varying emphases in 15.4–5, 13–16, 18–21; 17.4–8; 22.16–18; and alluded to in scores of passages throughout the Pentateuch). This promise contains three elements: a posterity ("I will make of you a great nation"), a relationship ("I will bless you"), and a gift of land ("the land I will show you"). It is the fulfillment, and the partial nonfulfillment, of these promises that may be said to be the theme of the Pentateuch.

The theme of the posterity is plainly the theme of Genesis. In the Abraham cycle of stories, the theme appears mostly in the shape of anxious questions: Will there be a son at all? What will become of him? Here lies the significance of the many Genesis narratives of threats to the family's survival: the sterility of matriarchs, the strife between brothers, often with near-fatal consequences, and the repeated famines in the land of promise.

The theme of the divine-human relationship comes most strongly to expression in Exodus and Leviticus. Both at the Exodus and at Sinai it becomes plain what the words of the promise ("I will bless you," "I will make my covenant between me and you," "I will be your God") meant. The blessing comes in the form of salvation from Egypt and in the gift of the law. The *covenant of Sinai, of which the opening words are "I am Yahweh your God," formalizes the relationship adumbrated by the covenant with the forebears. Leviticus spells out how the relationship now established by Yahweh is to be maintained: the sacrificial system is to exist, not as a human means of access to God, but as the divinely ordered method whereby breaches of the covenant may be repaired and atoned for.

The theme of the land dominates Numbers and Deuteronomy. Numbers begins with preparations for the occupation of the land, and ends with the actual occupation of that part of it lying to the east of Jordan by two and a half of the tribes. Deuteronomy sets before the people laws for their life under God, explicitly "in the land which Yahweh, God of your fathers, is giving to you" (Deut. 4.1).

None of the promises is fully realized within the Pentateuch itself: the posterity as numerous as the sand on the seashore (Gen. 22.17) is a promise that has only begun to achieve fulfillment by the time the Pentateuch is over, the relationship of *blessing and of covenant is a continuing and never wholly fulfilled promise, and the land, at the end of the Pentateuch, is a promise that is only partly fulfilled. The whole structure of the Pentateuch, then, is shaped by the promises to Abraham, which are never final but always point beyond themselves to a future yet to be realized.   DAVID J. A. CLINES

Pentecost. The word Pentecost (Greek "fif-tieth") appears twice in the *Septuagint as one of the designations of the "feast of weeks" (Exod. 34.22; Deut. 16.10;), which comes between *Passover and Tabernacles (see Feasts and Festivals). In the Hellenistic period, the feast also called for renewal of the *covenant God made with *Noah (Gen. 9.8–17). Later, after the destruction of the *Temple in 70 CE, the feast began to lose its agricultural association and became linked with Israel's sacred history by celebrating the giving of the *Torah on *Sinai. In synagogue worship, it became customary to read the book of *Ruth and Exodus 19–20 (see Lectionaries, article on Jewish Tradition).

Luke gives new significance to the first Pentecost following the *resurrection and *ascension of Jesus. For Luke (Acts 2) it is the fulfillment of Jesus' promise that his followers would receive power when the Holy Spirit would come upon them (Luke 24.49; Acts 1.5, 8; and see also Acts 2.16–21, quoting Joel 2.28–32).

The narrative is replete with allusions to biblical traditions, including *creation and the *Flood, the tower of *Babel (Gen. 11.1–9), and various *theophanies, especially that at *Sinai. Luke does not tell us where the followers of Jesus were assembled when the Spirit came, but the subsequent scene seems to be in the Temple court. The Spirit's coming was attended by "a sound like the rush of a violent wind" filling the house where they were gathered, and is marked by the appearance of "tongues, as of fire"; then the

followers "were filled with the Holy Spirit and began to speak in other languages" (Acts 2.2–4). While the reported charge of drunkenness (v. 13) may suggest the kind of ecstatic speech that Paul describes in 1 Corinthians 12–14 (see Glossolalia), Luke understands these "other tongues" as foreign languages and articulate witness. Within Israel, near and distant neighbors are finding their unity in the gospel. For Luke, what happens at Pentecost is a promise of what will happen among all the nations when the gospel will be preached to the *gentiles (see Acts 1.8; 10).

For Christianity, *Easter as the new Passover and Whitsunday as the new Pentecost became the basis for the liturgical year.

JOHN FREDERICK JANSEN

Periodization. See Chronology.

Persia (Map 7:K4–5). The home territory of the ancient Persians was the mainly mountainous terrain east of the head of the Persian Gulf. They called it Parsa (Grk. Persis); it was roughly equivalent to the modern Fars. The first appearance of this name (Parsua) in history, however, on the Black Obelisk of the Assyrian king Shalmaneser III (ca. 843 BCE) and followed eight years later by a mention of twenty-seven chiefs there, indicates a position somewhere in Iranian Kurdistan; but a similar name is recorded somewhere to the southeast a generation later. In 692–691 BCE, the name is cited in an alliance of peoples against *Sennacherib, which seems to have been centered in the Zagros further to the southeast.

By about 640 BCE, when a king named Kurash (Cyrus) appears in Assyrian annals, the Persians seem to have been established in Parsa; this ruling family was Achaemenid (descended from a semilegendary ancestor Achaemenes). It has been supposed that there were two Achaemenid royal lines, one (that of *Darius) in Parsa, the other (that of *Cyrus the Great) in a land called Anshan; but in 1972 it was discovered that Anshan lay in the middle of Parsa. These Persians were Indo-Iranian speakers like the *Medes (Darius spoke of himself as Ariya, i.e., Aryan or Iranian). They may perhaps have reached Parsa in stages from beyond the Caucasus; but some at least could have gradually infiltrated by way of northeastern Iran and Carmania. They were subject to the Medes before Cyrus the Great overthrew King Astyages in 550 BCE; according to Herodotus, they had been subject for the best part of a century.

Under Cyrus and his son Cambyses great conquests occurred in rapid succession: the Median empire in 550 BCE, western Asia Minor (the Lydian kingdom of Croesus) about 546 BCE, the *Babylonian empire with Elam and the Levant in 539 BCE, and (under Cambyses) *Egypt in 525 BCE. Darius I added Sind (Hindush) about 516 BCE. Thus the three great river lands of the Tigris and *Euphrates, the Indus, and (until 402 BCE) the *Nile were subject, and the resulting empire was the most extensive that the world had known.

Efficiency in military preparations and fighting skills had given the Medes and Persians a reputation for invincibility. But the failure to subdue the Scythians about 513 BCE and serious reverses in Greece between 492 and (under Xerxes) 480–479 BCE caused a collapse in confidence. After this, the sole successful major expedition in one hundred years was that in which the heroic marshal Megabyxos reconquered the Delta after a revolt (459–454 BCE). The later kings relied largely on Greek mercenaries and even fleets in their military operations in the west, with no great success, however, until the ruthless Artaxerxes III was able to bring his revolting satraps (governors) under control and in 345–343 BCE to reconquer *Phoenicia and Egypt. In the east of the empire and the Arabian fringes, however, peace seems to have generally been maintained with little exertion of force.

The system of imperial government set up by Darius I continued with little change until the end of Persian rule. In the Iranian and Anatolian satrapies noble Persian fief-holders kept household brigades and maintained order except in mountain regions where occasional punitive expeditions would be launched. Communication with the imperial chanceries was normally in *Aramaic.

In Babylonia and Egypt, a developed administrative system was in existence and was taken over. The kings appointed fiscal overseers in the temples and normally enjoyed the cooperation of the priesthoods. Confiscation after conquest and revolts gave rise to great estates belonging to the king, royal relatives, and leading nobles or court officials. In Babylonia, many fiefs were related to obligations of military service. In what had once been *Solomon's kingdom west of the Euphrates, deportation in *Assyrian times had resulted in a mixed population with little nation-

alistic feeling except in Judah and Phoenicia; prompt acquiescence to Persian rule had saved the "people of the land" from confiscations after Cyrus's conquest of Babylon.

The Achaemenids worshiped Zoroaster's god Ahuramazda with his polarization of Justice (or Order) and the Lie; but this did not lead to religious intolerance. The deities Anahita and Mithra were hardly less revered by the Persians, and fire was worshiped as a god. The officiants were *Magi. Among gods of the subject peoples the Greek Apollo, the Syrian goddess Alilat, and Yahweh seem to have been specially favored. Thanks to Cyrus and Darius I, the new *Temple in Jerusalem was completed (515 BCE); subsequently *Nehemiah (445 BCE) and *Ezra (either 428 or 398 BCE) were sent there on special missions, and Darius II seems to have yielded to objections from the Jerusalem priesthood about the right of the Jewish garrison at Yeb (Elephantine, in Upper Egypt) to rebuild its temple and also to keep its own special feast of the *Passover.

Persian rule thus allowed considerable cultural assimilation and religious syncretism, Babylon above all becoming a cosmopolitan center. Their art was a composite in which different traditions merged. The court style, which (like the Old Persian script) was devised by Darius I, exalted the grandeur of the king in a timeless setting; as seen in the Persepolis friezes it is impressive in its composure.

After the conquest by *Alexander the Great (334–323 BCE) the lands of the empire were ruled by Macedonian successor kings, Parthians, and Romans. Persia had no further importance in biblical history.   J. M. COOK

Peter. *See* Simon Peter.

Peter, The Letters of. *This entry consists of two articles, the first on* 1 Peter *and the second on* 2 Peter.

1 Peter

Content and Structure. After opening greetings (1.1–2) the writer moves to a prayer of thanksgiving for the Christians' hope of *salvation (1.3–12). Reborn through the *resurrection of Christ (1.3–5) they can await the end in hope (1.6–9), for they know more than the prophets (1.10–12). Consequently, they are summoned to a life of holy endeavor and to the avoidance of sin against one another (1.13–21); all this they can achieve because they have been born of the Word and continue to feed on it (1.22–2.3), are members of a holy people built on Christ, and have roots lying in God's choice of Israel (2.4–10).

Building on this, the writer then details the kind of behavior that should distinguish the readers as God's people (2.11–3.12) and lead unbelievers to glorify him (2.11–12). He outlines the duties of free citizens (2.13–17), slaves (2.18–25; Christ should be their example), and wives and husbands (3.1–7), and finally reminds them of their need to hold together and to react gently to outside provocation (3.8–12).

When they suffer, however, it should be because of doing good and not because they have committed some crime (3.13–17). Christ himself, although innocent, had suffered for their salvation; God vindicated him, and they may also expect to be vindicated (3.18–22). They must therefore separate themselves from their former ways of life (4.1–6) and stay together in love, for the end is not far off (4.7–11). They ought not, however, be surprised if, before it arrives, they are persecuted; if persecuted, it must not be as criminals but as Christians (4.12–19). Finally, leaders of the church are addressed (5.1–5), and all are reminded yet once again to stand firm against outside forces (5.6–11). In 5.12–14, the writer gives the closing greetings.

Although it is structured like other letters of the period, 1 Peter contains little of a personal nature; addressed to Christians in a wide area (1.1), it reads more like an address than a letter. Some scholars have therefore viewed it as a baptismal sermon or as a letter that includes, or was derived from, such a sermon or baptismal liturgy. It is preferable to regard it as a letter of a general nature, directed to readers far distant from the writer, who is unfamiliar with the details of their situation. In writing it, he makes considerable use of existing Christian tradition in the way of creedal (3.18, 21b, 22) and catechetical (2.13–3.7) material, as well as of the *Septuagint and the traditions about Jesus.

Recipients. Paul's preaching led to the beginning of the church in the Roman province of *Asia (Acts 19.1–20) and in Galatia (see Galatians, The Letter of Paul to the). It is not known how the churches in the other areas mentioned in 1.1 came into existence. Those addressed in the letter had almost all been converted from Greco-Roman religions (1.14, 18; 4.3) and came from a wide range of social, economic, and educational backgrounds. The churches would not

have been large bodies but consisted instead of little knots of believers dispersed over a wide area. They have already been persecuted and expect to be persecuted again; these persecutions, however, were not directed by the state. Those of Nero (64 CE) and Domitian (in the last decade of the first century CE) did not affect the areas to which the letter was addressed; those described by the Roman writer Pliny the Younger as taking place in part of the area are too late (112 CE). The Christians were persecuted rather by members of their own families (3.6), neighbors, and city authorities because of their withdrawal from many common activities and because of their distinctive life-style (2.12, 20; 3.14–17; 4.3–4, 14–16). Their isolation is reflected in the many exhortations to support one another with mutual love (1.22; 2.17; 4.8) and in their feeling that they are exiles (1.1; 2.11). They need to stand firm and not to retaliate against their persecutors (2.21–24; 3.13–17; 4.12–14).

Authorship. Three views have been held. According to the first, the letter was written by the apostle Peter (see Simon Peter) because his name appears on it, it has reminiscences of the teaching of Jesus that he could have provided, and 5.1 may suggest the writer was an eyewitness to the death of Jesus. But the Greek in which the letter is written suggests an educated author rather than a simple fisherman; the Septuagint, to which Peter would not have been accustomed, is used in biblical quotations in the way someone brought up with it would use it; the account of the death of Jesus (2.22–24) is not that of an eyewitness but is drawn from Isaiah 53. So it has been suggested that Silvanus (5.12) acted as secretary to Peter; the general thought in the letter would have been that of Peter, but its actual expression that of Silvanus. Since, however, the main support for Peter's authorship comes from the detail of the letter and not its general thought, this makes difficult the idea of Silvanus as secretary. If he had been secretary, we might expect him to add his own greetings (cf. Rom. 16.22). It has been suggested that he wrote it after the death of Peter to preserve Peter's teaching, but it is hardly likely that he would then have introduced the self-praise of 5.12. Increasingly, therefore, scholars have come to believe that the letter is pseudonymous (writing in the name of another person was not unknown in the ancient world). Disciples of Peter after his death may have continued to expound the special themes of his teaching, believing it should be made known to a wider circle. Each of these theories fits with the belief that the letter was written from Rome (Babylon in 5.13 is probably a code name for Rome) where Peter died.

Date. The letter must have been written prior to 120–130 CE, for by then other writers know it. It shows the influence of Pauline ideas and terms, and this suggests it must be later than 60 CE, for it was about this time that *Paul came to Rome. If Peter himself wrote it from Rome, it was also about this time that he arrived there. The sporadic and local nature of the persecutions means they cannot help in determining the date. Their strength together with the areas to which the letter was written, most of which do not appear to have been evangelized early, suggest a period later than the death of Peter, perhaps around 80 CE.

Significant Features. In 2.13–3.7 and 5.2–5, we have an example of a type of instruction in common use among the early Christians (see Eph. 5.22–6.9; Col. 3.18–4.1; 1 Tim. 2.8–15; 5.3–8; 6.1–2; Tit. 2.1–10); a code of duties is provided for various areas of behavior in the household, society in general, and the church (see Ethical Lists). These codes came to the church from the Hellenistic world via Judaism. While the areas for which advice was required did not vary in passing from secular writers to Christian, the advice itself did. It relates necessarily to the situation and period of the letter: 2.13–17 presupposes a nondemocratic government, 2.18–25 the existence of *slaves, and 3.1–6 a male-dominated society. In each case, a strong element of subjection is present and a careful attitude toward the non-Christian world is demanded (cf. 2.11–12). Indeed, one of the main themes of the letter concerns the relation of the Christian community to secular society (2.11–12); such a concern is inevitable where a community is being persecuted.

One of the most puzzling passages in the letter is 3.19, and no agreement exists as to its precise meaning. From it and other New Testament passages (Acts 2.27; Rom. 10.7; Eph. 4.9) the phrase in the Apostles' Creed, "descended into hell" was derived (see Descent into Hell). There are many stories in ancient literature, both Greek and Jewish, of visits to the underworld. The "spirits in prison" have been understood as either the unrepentant dead of *Noah's time or the fallen *angels ("*sons of God") of Genesis 6.1–4. These angels featured largely in contemporary Jewish thought, especially in 1 *Enoch, a writing that some Christians regarded highly (see Jude, The Letter of). It is normally supposed

that Christ made the journey mentioned in 3.19 during the period between his crucifixion and resurrection, but it is possible that it is that of his *ascension. Whichever it was, on it he preached to "the spirits in prison." This preaching may have been either of judgment or salvation; if the former, it implied that the power of the spirits was finally broken (cf. v. 22); if the latter, there is no indication that they accepted it, repented, and were saved. The reference in 4.6 may or may not deal with the same event. In it, the "dead" are neither the spiritually dead nor the righteous dead of the Hebrew Bible, but either Christians who have already died (the delay in the return of Christ worried many Christians as to the fate of their dead; cf. 1 Thess. 4.13) or all the physically dead who died before Christ could be preached to them.

Although the letter does not contain the word "church," it is penetrated throughout by a strong sense of togetherness. Its recipients are being persecuted. This has estranged them from the society in which they live and forced them to cling closely to one another. To sustain them, the writer reminds them that, even if they seem small in number, they belong to a body whose roots lie in the Bible. He does so by applying to them texts that were originally written in relation to Israel (see especially 2.4–10). In an age when antiquity was revered, this gave them a standing both in their own eyes and in those of outsiders. At the same time they are also reminded that they have been chosen by God to be his people. As such, they are depicted as the stones of his temple with Christ the cornerstone, and they themselves also as priests within the temple offering the sacrifice of holy living. The realization of their new position before him should compensate for any loss of position in the secular world and enable them to withstand the physical and verbal abuse of their neighbors. Certainly they should give no offence to those outside but should be continually seeking to win them to their number by declaring God's wonderful deeds. Even the wife who is abused by her husband because she is a Christian may win him for Christ by her meek and sober behavior (3.1).

The main purpose of the letter, however, is not to encourage the recipients into missionary activity or to teach them the relation of the Christian church to non-Christian society. The letter is not primarily a handbook of Christian *ethics, although it contains much on this subject; nor is it a tract on the nature of the atoning death of Christ. Rather, it is written to give its readers *hope in a situation that may terrify them because of its hostility. The situation will not continue for long, because Christ will soon return (1.6; 4.7; 5.10). Let them then rejoice even though they suffer (1.8; 4.13), for they have been born anew to a fresh hope (1.3) in God (1.21), which will be fulfilled when Christ returns.   ERNEST BEST

2 Peter

2 Peter presents itself as a testament or farewell discourse of the apostle Peter (*see* Simon Peter), written in the form of a letter shortly before his death (1.14). Its object is to remind readers of Peter's teaching and to defend it against false teachers, who were casting doubt on the Lord's coming to judgment (the *parousia) and advocating ethical libertinism.

Structure. (For the symbols, see below, Genre.)

Address and Greeting (1.1–2)
T¹ Theme: a summary of Peter's message (1.3–11)
T² Occasion: Peter's testament (1.12–15)
A¹ First apologetic section (1.16–21)
    Reply to Objection 1: the apostles based their preaching of the parousia on myths (1.16–19)
    Reply to Objection 2: biblical prophecies were the products of human minds (1.20–21)
T³ Peter's prediction of false teachers (2.1–3a)
A² Second apologetic section (2.3b–10a)
    Reply to Objection 3: divine judgment never happens (2.3b–10a)
E¹ Denunciation of the false teachers (2.10b–22)
T⁴ Peter's prediction of scoffers (3.1–4) (including Objection 4: v. 4)
A³ Third apologetic section (3.5–10)
    Two replies to Objection 4: that the expectation of the parousia is disproved by its delay (3.5–10)
E² Exhortation to holy living (3.11–16)
Conclusion (3.17–18)

Genre. 2 Peter is clearly a letter (1.1–2). But it also belongs to the literary genre of "testament," which was well known in Jewish literature of the period. In such testaments a biblical figure, such as *Moses or *Ezra, knowing that his death is approaching, gives a final message to his people, which typically includes ethical exhortation and prophetic revelations of the future. In 2 Peter, four passages (marked T¹–T⁴

in the analysis) particularly resemble the testament literature and clearly identify the work as Peter's testament. In 1.12–15, a passage full of conventional testament language, Peter describes the occasion for writing as his awareness of approaching death and his desire to provide for his teaching to be remembered after his death. This teaching is summarized in 1.3–11, which is in form a miniature homily, following a pattern used in farewell speeches. There are also two passages of prophecy (2.1–3a; 3.1–4) in which Peter foresees that after his death his message will be challenged by false teachers.

The rest of 2 Peter is structured around the four passages belonging to the testament genre. It includes three apologetic sections (A¹–A³), which give the work a polemical character and whose aim is to answer the objections the false teachers raise against Peter's teaching. There are four such objections, only the last of which is explicitly stated as such (3.4). In the other three cases, the objection is implied in the author's denial of it (1.16a, 20; 2.3b). Finally, there are two passages (E¹, E²) that contrast the libertine behavior of the false teachers, denounced in 2.10b–22, with the holy living expected of readers faithful to Peter's teaching (3.11–16).

Author and Date. Testaments were generally pseudepigraphal, attributed to biblical figures long dead, and probably understood as exercises in historical imagination. The use of the genre suggests that 2 Peter is a work written in Peter's name by someone else after his death, though it is possible that the testament genre could have been used by Peter to write his own, real testament. But it should also be noticed how the predictive character of the testament is used in 2 Peter. Nothing in the letter reflects the situation in which Peter is said to be writing; the whole work is addressed to a situation after Peter's death. The predictions of false teachers function as pegs on which is hung the apologetic debate about the validity of Peter's message. Moreover, whereas the testamentary passages speak of the false teachers in the future tense, predicting their rise after Peter's death (2.1–3a; 3.1–4; cf. 3.17), the apologetic sections and the denunciation of the false teachers refer to them in the present tense (2.3b–22; 3.5–10, 16b). It is scarcely possible to read 2 Peter without supposing the false teachers to be contemporaries of the author. The alternation of predictive and present-tense references to them is therefore best understood as a deliberate stylistic device to convey the message that these apostolic prophecies are now being fulfilled. In other words, Petrine authorship is a fiction, but one that the author does not feel obliged to maintain throughout his work. In that case, it must be a transparent fiction, a literary convention that the author expected his readers to recognize as such.

For these and other reasons, most modern scholars consider 2 Peter to be pseudepigraphal, though some still defend Petrine authorship. The most cogent additional reasons for denying Peter's authorship are the Hellenistic religious language and ideas, and the evidence for dating the work after Peter's death in the mid-60s CE. Scholars differ widely on the date of 2 Peter, which many consider to be the latest New Testament writing, written well into the second century CE. But the clearest evidence for a postapostolic date is 3.4, which indicates that the first Christian generation has died, and this passage may well suggest that the letter was written at the time when this had only just become true, around 80–90 CE. This was the time when those who had expected the *parousia during the lifetime of the apostolic generation would face the problem of the nonfulfillment of that expectation, but there is no evidence that this continued to be felt as a problem in the second century.

The literary relationship between 2 Peter and *Jude is another consideration relevant to the date of 2 Peter. There are such close resemblances (especially between Jude 4–13, 16–18 and 2 Peter 2.1–18; 3.1–3) that some kind of literary relationship seems certain. Some scholars have held that Jude is dependent on 2 Peter or that both depend on a common source, but most conclude that 2 Peter has used Jude as a source. Of course, this requires a late date for 2 Peter only if Jude is dated late.

If 2 Peter was written not by Peter, but after his death, why did the author present his work in the form of Peter's testament? Probably because his intention was to defend the apostolic message in the period after the death of the apostles (cf. 3.4) against teachers who held that, in important respects, the teaching of the apostles was now discredited. By writing in Peter's name he claims no authority of his own, except as a faithful mediator of the apostolic message, which he defends against attacks. The form of the letter as an apostolic testament is therefore closely connected with its apologetic purpose as a vindication of the normative authority of the apostolic teaching. That the author chose to write

Peter's testament is probably best explained if he was a leader of the Roman church, which had counted Peter as the most prestigious of its leaders in the previous generation.

Opponents. The opponents have usually been identified as *gnostics, but this identification, as recent scholarship has recognized, is insecure. The only features of their teaching that are clear from our author's refutation of it are eschatological skepticism and moral libertinism. The parousia had been expected during the lifetime of the apostles, but the first generation had passed away and in the opponents' view this proved the early Christian eschatological hope mistaken (3.4, 9a). This attitude seems to have been based on a rationalistic denial of divine intervention in history (cf. 3.4b) as well as on the nonfulfillment of the parousia prophecy. But it was also related to the ethical libertinism of the opponents. Claiming to be emancipating people from fear of divine judgment, they felt free to indulge in sexual immorality and sensual excesses generally (2.2, 10a, 13–14, 18).

There is no basis in 2 Peter itself for supposing that these teachings of the opponents had a gnostic basis. They are more plausibly attributed to the influence of popular Greco-Roman attitudes. The false teachers probably aimed to disencumber Christianity of elements which seemed to them an embarrassment in their larger cultural environment: its apocalyptic *eschatology, always alien to Hellenistic thinking and especially embarrassing after the apparent failure of the parousia hope, and its ethical rigorism.

In response to this challenge the author of 2 Peter mounts a defense of the apostolic expectation of judgment and salvation at the parousia and of the motivation for righteous living which this provides. The author argues that the apostles' preaching of the parousia was soundly based on their witnessing of the transfiguration, when God appointed Jesus to be the eschatological judge and ruler (1.16–18), and on divinely inspired prophecies (1.19–21). Scriptural examples prove that divine judgment does happen and prefigure the eschatological judgment (2.3b–10a). As God decreed the destruction of the ancient world in the *Flood, so he has decreed the destruction of the present world in the fire of his eschatological judgment (3.5–7, 10). The problem of the delay of the parousia is met by arguments drawn from Jewish tradition: that the delay is long only by human standards, not in the perspective of God's eternity, and should be seen as God's gracious withholding of judgment so that sinners may repent (3.8–9). Throughout his work, the author is concerned that the hope for the vindication and establishment of God's righteousness in the future (cf. 2.9; 3.7, 13) necessarily motivates the attempt to realize that righteousness in Christian lives (3.11, 14).

Theology. The peculiar theological character of 2 Peter lies in its remarkable combination of Hellenistic religious language and Jewish *apocalyptic ideas and imagery. For example, the author summarizes Peter's teaching in a passage that, in its ethical and religious terminology, is perhaps the most Hellenistic in the New Testament (1.3–11). On the other hand, he accurately and effectively reproduces Jewish apocalyptic ideas, especially in 3.3–13. This combination of theological styles is to be explained by the author's intention of interpreting and defending the apostolic message in a postapostolic and Hellenistic cultural situation. But this is a delicate task; in the author's view, in his opponents' attempt to adapt Christianity to Hellenistic culture they were compromising essential features of the apostolic message. In order to defend the gospel against this excessive Hellenization, therefore, the author resorts to sources and ideas close to the apocalyptic outlook of early Christianity, including the letter of Jude. The author thus keeps a careful balance between a degree of Hellenization of the gospel message, and a protest, in the name of apocalyptic eschatology, against extreme Hellenization that would dissolve the substance of the message. The letter is a valuable witness to Christianity's difficult transition from a Jewish to a Hellenistic environment, and provides an instructive example of how the message of the gospel was preserved through the process of cultural translation.

RICHARD J. BAUCKHAM

Pharisees.

Sources. References to the Pharisees occur widely throughout Jewish and Christian literature of the first two centuries CE. *Josephus lists them as one of the main Jewish parties emerging during the Hasmonean period (*War* 2.8.162–63; *Ant.* 13.5.171–73; 18.1.11–15). The New Testament portrays them principally as opponents of Jesus and the early Christian movement (Mark 3.6; 7.1; 10.2; Matt. 23; John 11.47), although it is from their ranks that Paul comes (Phil 3.5; Acts 23.6; 26.5). Rabbinical literature contains many references to *pĕrûšîm*, partly as those who were opposed to the *Sadducees and partly as those opposed by the sages and the rabbis.

Name. Greek *pharisaioi* and Hebrew *pĕrûšîm* can both be loosely transliterated as "Pharisees." The root *prš* in Hebrew can mean "to separate"; this may indicate that they were seen as sectarians (but by whom?) or that they sought holiness by the avoidance of what was unclean. Possibly the name was given to them by Sadducees, who thought of them as opposed to their ways.

History. The Pharisees' origin lie in the period of the Maccabean revolt (166–159 BCE), where we hear of the emergence of a group of Jews zealous for the *Law, the Hasideans (1 Macc. 2.42), who opposed the way in which the high priests were accommodating to the intrusion of Hellenistic ways into Judaism. This renewal movement spawned not only the Pharisees but also the *Essenes. It is likely that the Pharisees saw the establishment of the Hasmonean monarchy (140 BCE) as an opportunity for national renewal and the restoration of true observance of the Law. Certainly, unlike the Essenes, they remained in Jerusalem after the usurpation of the high priesthood by the Hasmoneans (152 BCE). They probably shared the popular enthusiasm for the successful campaign for Jewish independence, recorded in 1 Maccabees 14.27–49, when a great synagogue of the Jews conferred the kingship and the high priesthood on Simon. Interestingly there is no sanction for such a synagogue, or assembly, in the *Pentateuch, and this may have been justified by the oral tradition of the elders that the Pharisees cultivated. The Pharisees thus have their origins in a popular movement based on scribal traditions for interpreting the Law. They legitimated the Hasmonean monarchy by allowing it to control the *Temple and subsequently sought to influence the monarchy both at court and in the *Sanhedrin, the council in Jerusalem that was the continuation of the great synagogue. In this they were by no means always successful, falling foul of John Hyrcanus (134–104) and Alexander Jannaeus (103–76) but being restored to favor by Salome Alexandra (76–67). As their authority at the royal court diminished they sought to influence the people through the local courts and synagogues where they enjoyed considerable success. They were not a uniform movement; over the years different schools of interpretation of the Law grew up around different teachers, notably Hillel and Shammai. After the

First Jewish Revolt (66–70 CE) they emerged as the leaders, under Jonathan ben Zakkai, of the academy at Jamnia, which laid the foundation of rabbinic Judaism.

Beliefs. Central to their teaching is the belief in the twofold Law: the written and the oral *Torah. What this in effect meant was the recognition of a continuing tradition of interpretation of the Law in the debates and sayings of the elders. Ultimately this would itself be written down in the *Mishnah; but even then there was a continuing tradition of debate that found its documentation in the *Talmud. Thus while some sources portray them as legalistic, it is perhaps fairer to say that they had a zeal for legal debate and for keeping alive the tradition of meditation and study of the Law. Importantly this also meant that they were able to relate the Laws to new areas of life not already dealt with, as well as to introduce new institutions such as the *synagogues and schools.

They also seem to have been involved in the beginning of a concentration of *purity rules and regulations that would subsequently play such an important part in the Mishnah and Talmud. In this way they began to relocate the center of holiness in the home and the local community. This prepared the way for the transition from a Temple state to a communal piety that could survive the destruction of the Temple.

The Pharisees also believed in the resurrection and in future rewards and punishments. They did not believe all received their just deserts in this age; only in a future age when God acted decisively to establish his rule would justice be done. This radical expectation of a new age indicates something of the revolutionary nature of the Pharisees that has often been overlooked. Once they themselves gained power, albeit in communities that were localized and that operated under the general protection of Rome, such radical hopes could be allowed to recede, although they would not disappear altogether.

See also Judaisms of the First Century CE.

JOHN RICHES

Philemon, The Letter of Paul to. Philemon was a Christian who lived in the Phrygian town of Colossae (Map 14:E3) in the middle of the first century CE. The chief concern of the brief letter is the fate of Philemon's slave Onesimus. That name meant "useful," and it was frequently given to slaves. It seems that this slave had at first been useful to his master, but had become useless because, having found conditions intolerable, he had fled from Colossae, probably taking with him certain valuables belonging to the owner (v. 11).

The letter speaks of what followed that escape. Making his way to a larger city, Onesimus had been arrested and thrown into prison, where he met *Paul. Here the slave was converted (v. 10) and soon made himself useful to Paul. On his release, the new Christian had to decide what to do about the claims of his defrauded master. To return to him was to risk severe punishment, for escape from *slavery was a capital offence and Philemon would have every right to select his own penalty. Encouraged by Paul, however, the slave decided to return and set out for Colossae, accompanied by Tychicus (Col. 4.9) and bearing this letter from Paul. Such a decision must have been the result of intense inner struggle; on the one hand, there was the risk of punishment, at the very least the loss of freedom; on the other, the urging of Paul and the authority of his new master, Christ.

On the delivery of the letter, the master must also have faced a difficult decision. There would have been resentment over the violation of his property rights, supported as they were by Roman law and universal custom. Yet the letter was an appeal from an *apostle through whom Philemon, as well as his slave, had been converted (v. 19). Paul asked the owner to welcome his slave as a brother, to accept restitution for former losses, and to treat him as if he were Paul himself. As master, Philemon must recognize the supreme authority of his own master, Christ. Even more than forgiveness was at stake, for Paul seems to have asked Philemon not only to free Onesimus but even to send him back to Paul to help in the mission work as a substitute for his onetime owner. Reading between the lines of the letter, we can see that each member of this triangle was taking a risk and making a sacrifice stemming from his allegiance to Christ.

For Paul this was no private matter but a communal concern. By including the greetings of his colleagues, he claimed their support for his request. In addition to Timothy (v.1), he mentioned five fellow workers, including the prisoner Epaphras, to whom the church in Colossae may have owed its origin (Col. 4.12). He also wanted the members of the church in Colossae to become involved (v. 2). To help them understand the issues at stake, Paul probably sent, in the same mail as it were, another letter, the longer *Colossians (Col. 4.7, 9), in which he made the radical claim that all social distinctions have been erased among those who belong to Christ (3.11–21).

In this letter, as in all ancient documents, many points remain uncertain. The hometown may have been Laodicea and not Colossae. The location of the prison is uncertain: Rome, or more likely *Ephesus. The slaveowner may have been Archippus and not Philemon. Nothing is known of the later history of the major characters, though it is barely possible that the onetime slave later became the bishop in Ephesus (Ignatius, *Eph.* 1.3). What is certain, however, is the radical character of conversion, not only of people but of their attitudes toward their own property, their rights, and their obligations. Brief as it is, the note gives a colorful vignette of life in a congregation in western Asia Minor.

PAUL S. MINEAR

Philippians, The Letter of Paul to the.

The Church at Philippi. The letter that bears the title "To the Philippians" was addressed to the church in Philippi, an important city in Macedonia (Map 14:D2). The emperor Octavian had made Philippi a Roman colony and gave to its citizens the rights and privileges of those born and living in Rome. According to the account in *Acts, the church in Philippi began as follows: *Paul, on his second missionary journey, left Asia Minor for Macedonia, came to Philippi, preached the gospel; Lydia, a prominent woman from that area, and a few others became Christians. The church apparently was first housed in Lydia's home (Acts 16.9–40). In spite of its small beginnings, it grew and became an active Christian community, taking an important part in evangelism (Phil. 1.3–8), readily sharing its own material possessions, even out of deep poverty (4.16; cf. 2 Cor. 8.1–5), and generously sending one of its own people to assist Paul in his work and to aid him while he was in prison (2.25–30). Paul visited this church on at least three occasions (Acts 16.12; 2 Cor. 2.13; Acts 20.6).

Author and Date. No writer in ancient times and scarcely any today question that *Paul wrote the letter to the Philippians. But from where did he write it, and when? On these questions there is divergence of opinion. Most scholars hold that Paul wrote the letter from Rome; others have suggested *Corinth or *Ephesus; a good case can also be made for Caesarea. But from wher-

ever Paul wrote, it had to be a place where he was in prison, where there was a Roman praetorium (i.e., emperor's palace, or a provincial governor's official residence; see 1.12, 13), and where there were members of Caesar's household (i.e., the royal entourage at the palace or at any provincial capital; see 4.22). Hence, Rome (ca. 60 CE) or Caesarea (ca. 58 CE) are the most likely places, since each had a praetorium with its royal staff, and in each Paul is reported to have been jailed.

Integrity. An increasing number of scholars consider Philippians to be not a single letter but several—at least two, possibly three—woven into one. The disjointed nature of the letter as it stands (note the abrupt transition in tone and content between 3.1 and 3.2); Paul's leaving his "thank you" to the end (4.10–20); and Polycarp's reference in his own letter to the Philippians (3.21) to Paul's having written them several letters, are some of the reasons for suggesting that Philippians is a composite made up of different letters, or letter fragments. But the abruptness noted above is hardly an argument against the integrity of Philippians, for it is not inconsistent with the characteristics of private speech, nor with Paul's style (cf. Rom. 16.16–18; 1 Thess. 2.13–16). And though Polycarp mentions that Paul wrote several letters to the Philippians, he apparently knew and used none other than this.

Contents of the Letter. Paul begins his letter with the typical greeting (1.1–2), and continues with thanksgiving to God and prayer for the Philippians' continued growth in love and good works (1.3–11). He makes known to them how the gospel has advanced even while he is in prison (1.12–18), and assures them that he will be released and will return to Philippi (1.19–26). He begs them to live worthily of the gospel in unity, harmony, and generosity without grumbling or complaining, keeping always before themselves Jesus Christ as the supreme model for any moral action (1.27–2.18). He exhorts them further by describing the qualities of Timothy and Epaphroditus, and he promises to send both to Philippi (2.19–30). He warns them against evangelistic Jews or judaizers, whose teaching and practices are contrary to the gospel (3.1–19), and concludes the letter by making a final appeal for unity (4.1–3), offering suggestions as to how Christians should think and act (4.4–9) and thanking the Philippians for their numerous gifts to him (4.10–20). He closes with salutations (4.21–23).

The Hymn. Philippians 2.6–11 is an exquisite

example of an early Christian hymn, used and probably modified by Paul for his purposes here. Its interpretation has long been debated. Differences in interpretation revolve primarily around two Greek words, *harpagmos* (2.6) and *kenoō* (2.7). Some understand the former to mean "a thing to be held on to," and understand Christ as possessing equality with God, but not clinging to it as something he might lose (see the Jerusalem Bible). Others understand it to mean "a snatching after" and see Christ as a second *Adam, who unlike the first refused to grasp after being equal with God (see the NEB, and cf. Gen. 3.5). More recently, some have shown that *harpagmos* is part of an idiomatic expression referring to an attitude of mind one has toward that which is already possessed. Thus, Christ is seen as not regarding his being equal with God as a condition to be used (NRSV: "exploited") for his own benefit.

The other word, *kenoō*, often translated as "to empty," also means, "to make powerless," "to pour out." Some see this as an act of the human will of Jesus, the last Adam. "He made himself powerless," that is, he deliberately chose the lot of fallen humanity. Others, however, understand this as an act of the will of the preexistent, divine Christ.

The vocabulary and tone of the hymn, as well as the context in which it is placed, argue for the interpretation that sees Jesus Christ as preexistent, divine ("in the form of God"), equal with God, but who nevertheless refused to take advantage of all this for his personal gain. Instead, in that preexistent state, he willed to pour himself out, to serve by becoming human. He considered being equal with God not as an excuse for avoiding service and redemptive suffering but as that which uniquely qualified him for these tasks. Thus, God exalted him and gave him the highest name in heaven and on earth, the name "Lord."

If the hymn is about Christ, it is also about God, making clear the true nature of God. The Christ of the hymn shows by both his attitude and actions that for him to be in the "form of God," to be "equal with God," meant that he must give and spend himself. The hymn, then, makes it clear that God's true nature is not selfishly to seize but openhandedly to give.

Understood in this way the hymn fits perfectly into the context of chap. 2. Whereas the Philippians were acting selfishly, living with a grasping attitude (2.3–4), Christ's attitude and actions were exactly the opposite. So Paul appeals to them to bring their conduct into harmony with the conduct of Christ. Here is a splendid example of Paul's method of encouraging the Christian life by presenting sublime theological truth.

GERALD F. HAWTHORNE

Philistines. A group of Aegean origin, the Philistines were one of the Sea Peoples who ravaged the eastern Mediterranean world subsequent to the collapse of Mycenean civilization at the end of the Late Bronze Age. Attempting to land in Egypt, they were repulsed in a great land and sea battle by Ramesses III (ca. 1190 BCE), after which they settled on the southwestern coastal strip of Canaan (Map 3:W5). There they established a confederation of five city-states, the pentapolis consisting of Ashdod, Ashkelon, and Gaza on the coast, and Ekron and Gath inland (Josh. 13.3; 1 Sam. 7–14). Their expansion inland brought them into conflict with the Israelite tribes (Judg. 3.31; 13–16; 1 Sam. 4–6), who attempted to counter the threat by organizing themselves into a kingdom (1 Sam. 7–14). Although the Philistines were able to prevail against *Saul, the first Israelite king (1 Sam. 31), *David, Saul's successor and an erstwhile vassal of Achish, the Philistine king of Gath (1 Sam. 27; 29), decisively defeated them and halted their expansion (2 Sam. 5.17–25; 8.1; 21.15–22; 23.9–17; 1 Chron. 11.12–19; 14.8–17; 18.1; 20.4–8). Over the next few centuries their relations with Israel were for the most part in the form of border skirmishes (1 Kings 15.27; 16.15–17; 2 Chron. 26.6–7; 28.18). In the tenth century Philistia came under loose Egyptian hegemony. As a consequence of the imperialistic ambitions of the Neo-Assyrian empire, the Philistines came under *Assyrian rule in 734 BCE. Despite occasional revolts against their overlords, they remained part of the Assyrian imperium, even prospering during the seventh century, until the fall of Assyria (612 BCE). Subsequently caught between Egypt and Babylonia, Philistia was conquered and ravaged by *Nebuchadrezzar in 604 BCE. This effectively ended the history of the Philistine people, although their name as handed down through Greek and Latin eventually became a name for the whole of the land they were never able to subdue, namely, Palestine.

Archaeological activity focusing on recovering the material remains of the Philistines has been intense in recent years. Ashdod, Ashkelon, and Ekron (Tel Miqne), as well as smaller sites such as Tel Qasile on the coast and Tel Batash (ancient Timnah) inland, have been or are still being investigated. A picture has emerged of an extremely rich and highly developed civilization, putting a lie to the modern usage of the term "philistine." CARL S. EHRLICH

Philo. Philo of Alexandria (ca. 15 BCE–50 CE), also known as Philo Judaeus, is the most important representative of the Greek-speaking variety of Judaism that flourished in Alexandria from ca. 200 BCE to 100 CE. The historian *Josephus tells us that he was highly respected in the Jewish community and was "not unskilled in philosophy." The only event of his life known to us is his leadership of an embassy of Alexandrian Jews that appeared before the Emperor Gaius Caligula in 40 CE to protest against anti-Jewish mob violence. Vivid descriptions of this event and its background are given in his treatises *In Flaccum* and *Legatio ad Gaium*.

By far the majority of his writings concentrate on the interpretation of the *Law of Moses, or *Pentateuch, as found in the *Septuagint translation. These treatises can be divided into three lengthy series: the Allegorical Commentary, the Exposition of the Law, and Questions and Answers. In the Allegorical Commentary, Philo gives a very detailed and complex exegesis of Genesis 1–17, interpreting early history and *Abraham's wanderings in terms of the moral life and religious quest of the soul. The Exposition of the Law is a more varied work, containing biographies of the patriarchs and an explanation of the *Ten Commandments and the other ordinances of Mosaic law, with emphasis both on literal observance and symbolic interpretation. The third series, imperfectly preserved in an Armenian translation, poses questions and gives answers on the text of Genesis and Exodus; most of the usually short chapters contain literal followed by figurative or allegorical exegeses.

Philo's attention centers on the interpretation of scripture, but in his exegesis he demonstrates his considerable knowledge of Greek philosophy. Through the use of allegorical and symbolic interpretation, *Moses is presented as the lawgiver, prophet, and even philosopher par excellence, who is the source of all later philosophy. The apologetic motive is clear: in his Alexandrian context Philo is eager to show that Jewish culture is not inferior to Hellenistic culture. In his doctrine of God, Platonic ideas of transcendence and immanence are prominent. God as Being (Exod. 3.14) is distinguished from his powers at work in the cosmos. Highly influential is the doctrine of the *Logos, which builds upon Hellenistic Jewish wisdom speculation. The Logos can be described as that aspect of God which stands in relation to created reality. But Philo often talks about the Logos as if it were an entity with a separate existence from God himself, that is, a divine hypostasis.

Philo's thought and writings were warmly embraced by the early Christian church. His allegorical themes and theological ideas exerted a strong influence on Clement of Alexandria, Origen, and later patristic authors. In Byzantine manuscripts Philo is often called "the Bishop." It was his popularity in Christian circles that caused his writings to be preserved.

See also Judaisms of the First Century CE; Interpretation, History of, *article on* Jewish Interpretation. DAVID T. RUNIA

Phoenicia (Map 7:G4). The Greek word *phoinix*, from which apparently the geographical region of Phoenicia is named, means, literally, "red purple." Thus, the name is derived from one product of the region, red dye, for which Phoenicia was famed throughout the ancient world. It was a shared interest in commerce and trade by the inhabitants of the region rather than any tightly knit political system that gave the Phoenicians their distinctive characteristics and ethos in the ancient world.

The territory inhabited by this people, Semitic in origin and Mediterranean in outlook and activity, was the narrow coastal plain extending from the Eleutherus river in the north to the Carmel range in the south, a distance of about 260 km (160 mi) in all, approximately the extent of modern *Lebanon with an extension to the south. From ancient times kings ruled the region centered in such cities as Byblos, Berytus (Beirut), Sidon, and Tyre. Physical features give the whole region a very distinctive character, as the coastal plain is narrow, and sometimes, as at the Ladder of Tyre, the mountains form a promontory into the sea. Elsewhere they rise sharply, separating the coast from the interior, even though at certain historical periods there was a natural tendency for the various city-states to include some of that hinterland in their territory. This was certainly true in the case of Tyre, whose territory at times included parts of Galilee (1 Kings 9.11; see also Josephus, *Ant.* 5.1.63). It was probably due to the peculiar physical layout of the region inhabited by the Phoenicians that the territory as a whole never attained a fully cohesive political structure but instead comprised a number of city-states, which left them vulnerable to the more centralized political powers in the region.

There were geographical advantages also. The coastline of the Phoenician territory had a number of excellent harbors, unlike Israel further to the south, and thus *shipping was a significant aspect of the Phoenician way of life. In the ancient world, the Phoenicians were celebrated navigators (see Ezek. 27); Herodotus also attributes to them the circumnavigation of Africa. A number of important Phoenician colonies were established in the western Mediterranean, Carthage in North Africa being the most famous. This westward orientation also led to the spread of the linear Phoenician alphabet to the west (*see* Writing). In addition the climate, though warm, had good rainfall, and there was a rich vegetation with the famous cedars of Lebanon being particularly important as a supply of timber. *Solomon's building projects benefited from such a supply from King Hiram of Tyre (1 Kings 5), and there is even older evidence of Egyptian interest. Vitreous glass has been found in the region near Ptolemais, and there appears to have been a thriving fine-ware industry in Hellenistic times in the region.

Phoenician connections with the northern kingdom of Israel were generally close, as the marriage between *Ahab and *Jezebel, the daughter of the Tyrian king Ethbaal, illustrates. A distinctive Phoenician style of masonry is also characteristic of royal and public architecture at cities such as *Samaria and *Megiddo in the period. But like Israel and other states in the region, the Phoenician cities had strained relations with the *Assyrian and Neo-Babylonian rulers, and as they attempted to assert their independence, Sidon was destroyed and Tyre defeated after a thirteen-year siege by *Nebuchadrezzar. The *Persians adopted a more tolerant attitude toward their vassal states, and they utilized the navigational skills of the Phoenicians in their various campaigns to the west, most notably against the confederation of Greek city-states, until the Persian defeat at the famous naval battle of Salamis in 481 BCE.

It was during this period of relative autonomy that the various Phoenician states achieved a greater degree of harmony among themselves, and a confederation of Tyre, Sidon, and Arvad was formed, leading to a revolt against Persian rule and the consequent destruction of Sidon in

351 BCE. As *Alexander the Great began his conquest of the East, Tyre offered stout resistance to his advance on Egypt but was eventually destroyed in 332 BCE. In line with later Hellenistic policy, however, these cities, as well as Acco/Ptolemais closer to Jewish territory, were reestablished as Greek city-states and became important centers for the diffusion of Greek culture in Palestine and Syria. The games at Tyre in honor of Zeus Olympus were highly regarded, and some Jews, contrary to their religious beliefs, were tempted to participate (2 Macc. 4.18). Nevertheless, inscriptions show that Phoenician as well as Greek was spoken in Tyre as late as the first century BCE.

In line with the process of hellenization elsewhere in the ancient world, the emerging culture was a mixture of the old and the new. Particularly in the sphere of religion, various deities that were worshiped in Hellenistic times, such as Zeus and Heracles, are the older Phoenician deities Baal Shamem (Lord of the Heavens) and Melqart in Greek dress. Both were closely associated with the older Canaanite deities such as El, known to us from discoveries at Ras Shamra (*see* Ugaritic), thus suggesting ancient and close links between the Phoenicians and the *Canaanites. Even prior to the Hellenistic age, Phoenician culture had been influenced by features from many quarters, including Greece, thus underlining the many contacts that had been established through trade and commerce. This can be seen both in their art and architecture, which apparently provided a blueprint for Solomon's *Temple.

Under the Romans, the various cities in Phoenician territory continued as they had been, but now as part of the network of urban centers that Rome utilized in controlling the east. Phoenicia is named as one of the regions to which the Christian movement spread from Jerusalem after the Hellenists had been forced out (Acts 11.19). It is doubtful, however, whether the old Phoenician culture had persisted to any great degree in the area. This combination of a memory of the ethnic background and recognition of the current cultural affiliation of the territory is found in Mark's description of the woman who came to Jesus requesting to have her daughter healed. She is described as being "Greek, Syrophoenician by birth" (Mark 7.26). The Tyrian shekel, because of its stability in a volatile currency market, remained the offering for the sanctuary in Jerusalem that every male Jew was expected to make throughout the Second Temple period (*see*

Money), and recent archaeological evidence from Upper Galilee gives abundant evidence of the trading links that a religiously conservative Jewish population continued to have with Tyre in the early centuries CE. Thus, long-established patterns of religious diversity and commercial and trading links (see Ezekiel 27) were maintained between the Jewish population and its Phoenician coastal neighbors—one example among many of human need transcending religious and cultural diversity.   SEÁN FREYNE

Phylacteries. Small receptacles, generally called *tefillin*, attached by leather thongs to the upper left arm (or right, for a left-handed person) and the forehead. Normally rectangular in shape, both *tefillin* contain tiny slips of *parchment inscribed with short portions of the Bible. There are usually four interior compartments into which the slips are placed open-side up, tied round with a goat-hair thread.

The custom of praying with phylacteries on a daily basis and not on holidays is based on Exodus 13.9, 16, and Deuteronomy 6.8; 11.18. Because no explicit or detailed injunctions are provided, divergent traditions developed very early in the postexilic period. The four texts that were originally inscribed on the parchment slips are Exodus 20.2–17 (the *Ten Commandments), Deuteronomy 6.4–9 (the *Shema), Deuteronomy 11.13–21 (the second paragraph of the Shema), and Numbers 15.37–41 (the commandment to wear tassels or *fringes). The first and last passages were ultimately excluded for fear that unorthodox views would creep into Judaism, and they were replaced by Exodus 13.2–10, 11–16.

According to rabbinic tradition, both *tefillin* and *mezuzot* (small boxes containing scrolls attached to the doorpost of a house or room; see Deut. 6.9) could be written from memory. Hence it is not surprising that many of the texts found from *Qumran and the Judean wilderness caves contain departures from the *Masoretic Text. In addition, there is great variation in the passages selected from the Bible that were inserted into the compartments.

Some have argued that in antiquity only distinguished persons put on *tefillin*, either daily or occasionally. Even though in rabbinic times it became obligatory to wear them, the practice was ignored in some countries of the Diaspora. One view holds that even women, minors, and slaves should pray with phylacteries.

The extensive archaeological evidence of *tefillin* suggests that their use was already widespread in late Second Temple times. Before prayer capsules were attached to leather thongs, as attested in the archaeological record, phylacteries probably consisted merely of inscribed scrolls attached to the head and arm in order to fulfill the biblical precept: "Keep these words that I am commanding you today in your heart. . . . Bind them as a sign on your hand, fix them as an emblem on your forehead" (Deut. 6.6, 8).
                                    ERIC M. MEYERS

Pilate, Pontius. Governor of Judea (Luke 3.1) under Tiberius Caesar, he ruled the province 26–36 CE. In addition to details about him occurring in the literary sources discussed below, he is also mentioned in an inscription found at Caesarea in 1961.

The first mention of Pilate in the Gospels concerns "the Galileans whose blood Pilate had mingled with their sacrifices" (Luke 13.1), who were presumably visiting Jerusalem for *Passover; this atrocity may explain the enmity (Luke 23.12) between him and *Herod Antipas, ruler of Galilee. At the next Passover (3 April 33 CE, rather than 7 April 30 CE?), Pilate was again in Jerusalem to keep order, when the case of *Jesus was brought before him for review (Luke 23.1). Only now is he mentioned in the other three Gospels (Matt. 27.2; Mark 15.1; John 18.29); since the last two do not even explain who he was, he must already have been fixed in the apostolic preaching (see Acts 2.23; 3.13; 4.28; 13.28; 1 Tim. 6.13) as a historical anchor.

All four gospel accounts focus on Pilate's question, "Are you the King of the Jews?" In John (18.36) Jesus claims that his kingdom was "not of this world." In Luke (23.2, 5) the Jewish authorities assert that he was a rebel. According to John, *Caiaphas, as high *priest, had long foreseen the need to act against Jesus in the political interest of the nation (John 11.48–50, 53), but only Pilate could impose the death penalty (18.30–31). Pilate's skepticism about the political charge was neatly turned into a threat to his own status as "Caesar's friend" (John 19.12). Pilate washed his hands before the crowd to make clear where the moral onus lay (Matt. 27.24) and ironically retaliated against the authorities by identifying Jesus on the cross as "King of the Jews" (John 19.19).

The New Testament has Pilate maneuvered against his better judgment into authorizing what

Jewish authorities had planned. Within two centuries he could be seen (by Tertullian) as in effect a Christian, and by the sixth century CE he had become a saint and martyr in the Coptic Church. Some modern analyses have attempted to shift responsibility back onto him: Jesus (or part of his following) was indeed revolutionary; it was a Roman detachment that arrested him (John 18.12); the *Sanhedrin was capable of carrying out a death penalty had it needed to and may not even have met formally on this occasion. The momentum of this argument arises partly from the monstrous price exacted in our age for the cry "His blood be on us and on our children," found only in Matthew (27.25) and to be understood in terms of that writer's own perspective as well as first-century politics. (*See* Anti-Semitism.)

The "procurator" (see Tacitus *Annals* 15.44) of Judea was responsible for the estates of Tiberius Caesar there and for the Roman taxes (*see* Tribute and Taxation). The Sanhedrin and other local authorities handled most other administration. In his military capacity, Pilate was also referred to as "prefect," that is, in command of the province, his powers including the supervision of justice. But being only of second (or equestrian) rank, he was subordinate to the senatorial legate of *Syria. Pilate's long term implies an understanding with the high priestly dynasty of Annas. He shares their success in keeping the peace, earning the oblique compliment of Tacitus (*Histories* 5.9), "under Tiberius nothing happened." His coinage, unlike Herod's and Caesar's (Matt. 22.20), did not offend the second commandment by carrying a human likeness. He yielded to a suicidal protest by the Jews against the medallions on the military standards even though he had veiled them when brought into Jerusalem (Josephus *War* 2.9.169–74). But when they protested against the expenditure of Temple funds on an aqueduct for the city, he showed no mercy (*War* 2.9.175–77). When similarly brutal tactics were used against the *Samaritans in 36 CE, the latter appealed to Vitellius, the legate of Syria, who ordered Pilate to Rome to explain himself (Josephus *Ant.* 18.4.85–97).

In 41 CE *Philo published a "letter" of *Herod Agrippa to Gaius Caesar, successor of Tiberius, denouncing Pilate as "inflexible, stubborn, and cruel" (*Leg.* 299–305) and citing an episode when Tiberius had ordered him to remove from the palace in Jerusalem some shields that offended Jewish scruples. Clearly in the end Pilate lost the support of the Jewish leaders. Their threat to report him to Tiberius (John 19.12) may imply that he was under suspicion as an appointee of Sejanus, the head of government whom Tiberius overturned in Rome in 31 CE. Certainly Philo's tirade would not have been possible if Pilate had been granted an honorable retirement.

EDWIN A. JUDGE

Pisgah. A ridge or mountain in *Moab, at the northeast corner of the Dead Sea (Map 1:Y5), from which *Balaam viewed Israel (Num. 23.14) and *Moses viewed the *Promised Land before his death (Deut. 3.27; 34.1–4). It is in the vicinity of, if not identical with, Mount *Nebo.

MICHAEL D. COOGAN

Plagues of Egypt. The story of the ten plagues of Egypt (Exod. 7.14–12.36) is based on the ancient Israelite tradition of the "great and awesome signs and wonders against Egypt" (Deut. 6.22) that God accomplished in order to force Pharaoh to allow the Israelites to leave that country. Each plague, except the last, has a basis in natural phenomena or diseases that occur in *Egypt, either annually or at intervals, between July and April. They form an orderly series, each related to its successor; and their rapid and cumulative severity mounts to a climax in the death of Egypt's firstborn. In these partly ordinary events, the Israelites saw the hand of God active in their behalf.

All three strands composing the book of *Exodus told of plagues, though no single source lists all the plagues; *J gives eight (1–2, 4–5, 7–10); *E, five (1, 7–10); and *P, five (1–3, 6, 10). All agree on the first and the last. Sometimes God is shown as directly effecting the plague (Exod. 9.6; 12.29); sometimes *Aaron, at *Moses' command, is the agent (7.9–10; 8.16–17); and sometimes Moses himself calls down the plague (7.14–18; 9.8, 22–23).

The ten plagues of the final form of the Exodus narrative are as follows:

1. Nile water turns to blood (7.14–15). The annual rise of the river normally brings life to Egypt's soil, but on rare occasions putrid waters carrying decaying algae from the vast swamplands of the Sudan join with the waters from Ethiopia's Blue Nile into which volcanoes—active in those days—had spewed sulphuric lava and ash. Thus, once per century or so the water of the *Nile would turn red in color and become undrinkable (Exod. 7.14–24).

2. Frogs (Exod. 7.25–8.14). When the flooding Nile subsided it left heaps of dead frogs over the land, so many that some were even piled in people's homes. The Egyptians may have believed that their magicians could prevent such a disaster from falling upon the common people.

3. Gnats (Exod. 8.16–19). Swarms of "gnats" (whatever noisome insect this name represents) had bred and multiplied in the stagnant pools of water. The magicians confess that "this is the finger of God."

4. Flies (Exod. 8.20–32). The plague of "flies" (the word simply means "insects") appears to be a variant of the preceding plague; note the poetic parallelism in Psalm 105.31. The sign was not just the coming of myriads of flies but the isolation of Goshen, so that the *Hebrews were not affected.

5. Cattle murrain (Exod. 9.1–7). Anthrax, hoof-and-mouth, or some such disease, resulting from conditions created by former plagues, struck Egypt's farm animals, a principal source of food.

6. Boils (Exod. 9.8–12). Ashes from the kiln were thrown into the air and caused boils breaking out in sores on humans and animals alike. The magicians could not stand before Moses because of the boils.

7. Hail (Exod. 9.18–35). The scourge of hail (a rare occurrence in Egypt) and thunderstorm destroyed both a whole season's crops and the mudbrick homes of the disease-ridden peasantry.

8. Locusts (Exod. 10.3–20). Always a bane of the Middle East, a plague of locusts devoured whatever was left after the storm was over. The Lord "brought" the locusts by an east wind; when Pharaoh confessed his sin (10.16) God "drove" the locusts by a west wind into the Red Sea.

9. Darkness (Exod. 10.21–23). Thick darkness that could be felt may have been brought on by the wind from the desert, carrying with it much dust and sand; but the Israelites had light. The Lord was clearly confronting Amon-Ra, the sun god, whom the Egyptians worshiped as their divine father.

10. Death of the Egyptian firstborn (Exod. 11.1–8). The announcement of the final plague, the death of the firstborn in Egyptian families, from Pharaoh's down even to those of slave girls (11.4–9), is linked with what took place at the first *Passover ceremony (12.1–32). It was then that the Lord "chose" Israel, which he had "passed over," as his firstborn son (Exod. 4.22–23).

The popular theme of the superiority of the Lord's power over that of pagan gods and magicians has here found expression in one of the most characteristic products of Israelite skill in narrative prose. The account has been the source of poetic summaries in Psalms 78.43–51; 105.28–36; of the homily on them in Wisdom of Solomon 11.1–12.2; and the general references to them elsewhere in the Bible (Deut. 6.22; 7.18–19; 11.3; 29.2–3; 1 Sam. 4.8). Several features of the Egyptian plagues reappear in the account of the "seven last plagues" in the book of Revelation (15.1–16.21; 21.9).

See also Exodus, The.   George A. F. Knight

Plants. Despite its relatively small size, ancient Israel had a rich and varied flora, a function of its topographic and climatic diversity and the associated variations in soil type and rainfall (*see* Geography of Palestine). The Bible, however, mentions only 110 names of plants, for many of which the identification is unknown or uncertain, notwithstanding the recent advances of archaeologists, botanists, and biblical scholars. Thus, the *tappûaḥ* (e.g., Song of Sol. 2.3, 5; 7.8; Prov. 25.11; Joel 1.12) has been identified as an apricot, quince, and apple, the ambiguity stemming both from the vagueness of the biblical texts and the lack of certainty concerning the dates when these fruits were present in Israel. Similarly, the famed *šôšannâ* of the Song of Solomon (2.6; 4.5; 5.13; 6.2–3; 7.2; *šôšannâ* of the valleys, 2.1) has been identified as a white lily, hyacinth, narcissus, crowfoot, chamomile, and rose; one can state with certainty only that it was a showy flower, or group of flowers, of some kind. Furthermore, there is no necessary correlation between the number of times, if any, that a plant is mentioned in the Bible and its importance in the *agriculture or ecology of Israel. For example, the foreign cedar of *Lebanon, the wood of gods and kings, topics of special interest to biblical authors, appears seventy times, more than twice the number of references to wheat, one of the major cereal crops of ancient Israel and an essential dietary staple. The probably abundant carob tree is not mentioned at all in the Bible. In general, the Bible mentions plants only in passing. It contains no system of plant classification (though such may have existed: see 1 Kings 4.33), and rarely offers descriptions of sufficient detail for identification. It is not always certain whether a plant name refers to an individual species or to a larger category such as thorns and thistles. A study of the plant terminology in such ancient *translations as the *Septuagint and the *Vulgate and in the commentaries of the rabbis and church fathers often adds to the uncertainty, since translators and commentators frequently identified biblical plant names with local flora with which they were familiar, many of which were not even found in Israel. Over the centuries, many peoples outside the region have given biblically sounding names to flora that are not native to Israel (such as the Joshua tree *[Yucca brevifolia]* of North America), again contributing to the confusion. On the other hand, the botanic data that can be derived from present-day studies, given the absence of significant climatic change in Israel since the Bronze Age, the growing body of evidence from archaeological excavations concerning the dates by which many wild and cultivated plants were present, and comparative data from Egypt and Mesopotamia have all contributed substantially to the current understanding of the biblical flora. Exhaustive compilations of biblical plant names and their possible or probable identifications can be found in a number of Bible dictionaries and encyclopedia articles and in such books as Michael Zohary's *Plants of the Bible* (Cambridge, England, 1982).

Although the biblical authors did not mention specific plants in great number or detail, they vividly portrayed the centrality of plants and their cultivation for ancient Israel, whose well-being depended on the successful harvesting of such cereal crops as wheat, barley, and emmer, as well as varieties of legumes, fruit trees, and vines (see Deut. 8.8). Plants are described as the basic food in the first creation account (Gen. 1.29). The well-watered and fruitful garden was understood as the best of all places (Gen. 2.4–3.24; Song of Sol.). This characterization is not surprising: the early Israelite community sought sustenance from land often beset by drought and composed of poor soil, with a topography that necessitated such labor-intensive forms of cultivation as terrace-farming. The challenges and frustrations of the Israelites may be reflected in the punishment meted out by God to the first man at the end of the second creation account: "Cursed is the ground because of you; in toil you shall eat of it all the days of your life; thorns and thistles it shall bring forth for you; and you shall eat the plants of the field" (Gen. 3.17–18). The biblical authors envisioned God's blessings and favor as yielding rainfall and abundant harvests. Thus, Micah 4.4 depicts peace and prosperity as all sitting "under their own vines and

under their own fig trees" (cf. 2 Kings 18.31; Zech. 3.10; 1 Macc. 14.12). But when Israel violated her *covenant with God, she experienced drought, blight, and barren fields (Deut. 28.22–24; Isa. 17.10–11; Amos 4.9; 5.11).

Israelite *law reflected a concern with and some understanding of the ways in which crop production could be well managed. Thus, the Israelite farmer was forbidden to harvest immature fruit trees (Lev. 19.19), and was expected to allow his fields to remain fallow during the sabbatical year. Vegetable and *incense offerings were an essential component of the system of *sacrifice and atonement, a central piece of Israelite religion until the destruction of the *Temple by the Roman army in 70 CE (Exod. 30.34–48; Lev. 2; 7.9–10; 16.12–13; 24.5–9; Num. 15.1–10). The Bible also abounds with similes, *metaphors, and *parables rooted in the plant world. The images are as diverse as the flora itself. Thus, in addition to fertility, abundance, and continuity, plants are used to represent life's frailty, brevity, and transitory nature (Isa. 40.6–8; Job 14.2; Ps. 90.6; 1 Pet. 1.24). Biblical symbolism draws also on the characteristics of individual plants, such as the great height and longevity of the cedar tree (Ps. 92.12; see similarly the parable of Jotham, Judg. 9.8–15, and the parable of the mustard seed, Matt. 13.31–32 par.). The New Testament is replete with agricultural imagery; see, for example, Mark 4.3–8, 26–29; Matthew 9.37–38; Luke 13.6–9.

Representations of plants adorned the columns and carvings of the Solomonic Temple (1 Kings 6.18; 7.19, 26). Plants appeared also on Hasmonean and Herodian coinage, and on the coins issued by the rebels in the anti-Roman Palestinian Jewish revolts of the first and second centuries CE (*see* Money). To commemorate the defeat of the Jewish rebels in the First Jewish Revolt, the Roman government issued coins, in circulation by 71 CE, with the inscription "*JUDAEA CAPTA*" ("Judea captured"). The coin depicts a palm tree, perhaps in recognition of the importance of the date palm in Israel. On one side of the tree is a Roman legionary, on the other a woman in mourning seated under the palm. The mosaics of the *synagogues and churches of Roman and Byzantine Palestine were rich with representations of plants, depicted both realistically and in highly stylized forms.

BARBARA GELLER NATHANSON

Poetry, Biblical Hebrew. Poetry is the elevated style in which songs, hymns, lamentations, proverbs, wisdom, and prophetic speeches are composed. Biblical poems tend to be of short or medium length, ranging from two to about sixty lines. Longer poems exist, such as Psalm 119, but they are rare, and there is no continuous poem of epic proportion. Unlike most epic traditions, the Bible contains few narrative poems: its major narratives are in prose. Nevertheless, close to one-third of the Hebrew Bible is poetry, distributed in small amounts among the narrative books, in greater amounts in the prophetic books, and predominant in the collections of *Psalms, *Proverbs, and *Lamentations, and in the wisdom books of *Job and *Ecclesiastes.

Biblical poetry is characterized by a terse, binary form of expression that is eloquent and evocative. The terseness is effected by the juxtaposition of short lines with few specific connectives between them. The connective may be lacking altogether, or may consist of the multipurpose conjunction wāw, meaning "and," "but," "or," and so forth. Thus, the exact relationship between lines is often not made explicit. The lines themselves are short, usually three or four words, and their terseness is enhanced by the omission, in many cases, of the definite article, the relative pronoun, and other grammatical particles. Two examples, the first from a narrative poem and the second from a psalm, illustrate the terseness and parataxis of biblical poetry:

Water he asked:
Milk she gave:
In a lordly cup she offered cream.
(Judg. 5.25)

You give to them, they gather:
You open your hand, they are satisfied well.
(Ps. 104.28)

These two excerpts also illustrate the most prominent feature of biblical poetry, its binary form of expression known as parallelism. Parallelism is the pairing of a line (or part of a line) with one or more lines that are in some way linguistically equivalent. The equivalence is often grammatical—that is, both parts of the parallelism may have the same syntactic structure, as in "Water he asked: Milk she gave." In many cases, however, the grammatical structure is not identical, at least on the surface level. In Judges 5.25, the third line expands and rearranges the syntax of the first two lines. Similarly, in Psalm 104.28 there is partial grammatical equivalence by virtue of the "you-they ‖ you-they" pattern, but the syntax of the lines is different. Grammar has

many facets, and any one of these facets may be brought into play in parallelism.

Another common form of equivalence is semantic equivalence; the meaning of the lines is somehow related: perhaps synonymous, perhaps reflecting the converse or reverse, or perhaps extending the meaning in any one of a number of ways. Again, equivalence does not imply identity. The second line of a parallelism rarely expresses exactly the same thought as the first; it is more likely to expand or intensify it. The relationship between "they gather" and "they are satisfied well" in Psalm 104.28 is a progression. The relationship between "water he asked" and "milk she gave" in Judges 5.25 is more than a progression—it sets up an opposition, a conflict, between the request and its fulfillment.

Grammatical and/or semantic equivalence account for most parallelisms, but because there are so many equivalent permutations for any given line, the number of potential parallelisms is enormous if not infinite. Although readers/listeners may learn to anticipate a parallelism, they cannot, except in the most formulaic of expressions, predict exactly what the parallelism will be. Each parallelism is cast to fit its context, and the effect of each must be evaluated individually.

There are, however, several general effects that parallelism has. For one thing, it helps to bind together the otherwise paratactic lines, so that the basic structure of the poem is not a single line but rather sets of lines (often called a couplet or a bicolon). Another by-product of parallelism is the rhythm or balance that it creates. Scholars have long sought metric regularity in biblical poetry, but no system—be it syllable counting, stress counting, thought-rhythm, or syntactic constraints—has met with unanimous acceptance. If there is such a metric form, it continues to elude us. It is more likely that the Hebrew poets embraced a looser system—one in which many lines of a poem are more or less the same length and partake of the rhythm of their parallelisms, but without the requirement of precise measurement.

Beyond the level of specific parallel lines it is possible to find a larger structural unit that is often called a strophe or stanza. This is identified by dividing the poem into its major sections, based on contents or on structural or lexical repetitions. Although a longer poem is likely to have more strophes, that is, more subdivisions, the strophe is less well defined than the couplet and seems less basic to the overall poetic structure. The principles whereby couplets are combined into longer segments or entire poems is not well understood, but it is clear that poems have movement and development, and that their lines and couplets cohere as unified compositions. Psalm 104, for example, portrays the creation of the world by means of a description of God's habitat, the sky, and then moves to various natural habitats and the creatures that occupy them. The progression in the poem is obvious even though its strophic divisions may not be.

In addition to their main characteristics, terseness, and parallelism, biblical poems often employ devices such as word repetition, word association, ellipsis, sound play, chiasm (an *A-B B-A* pattern of words, grammatical structures, or lines), inclusio (frame or ring composition), and imagery. Although these devices are not limited to poetry, and are not poetic requirements, they do enhance the poeticality, that is, the sense of elevated style and rhetoric associated with poetry. We draw again on Psalm 104 to illustrate:

> Wrapped in light as (in) a garment:
> Spreading the sky like a curtain.
> (Ps. 104.2)

Through similes, the first elements of creation, light, and the heavens become the personal effects of God, the glory surrounding and enhancing him. There is also a good deal of assonance in the Hebrew in these two lines, as there is elsewhere in the poem. The psalm begins and ends with "Bless the Lord, O my soul," which provides a sense of closure.

The rhetorical impact of biblical poetry is considerable and its aesthetic dimensions manifold. The prophets used it to convince, the wise to instruct, the psalmists to offer praise. In the Bible, language—that is, forms of verbal expression—takes on paramount importance; and it is in poetry that verbal expression reaches its epitome.

See also Acrostic.   ADELE BERLIN

Politics and the Bible. The Bible is not a purely religious book; its pages are full of kings and empires, armies and wars, cries for justice. Its political implications have had great influence on the way in which it has been interpreted.

The Bible does not, however, present any systematic or unambiguous teaching about political matters. Its books were written over many centuries and under widely differing political systems, from Israelite tribal society to the *Roman empire. Many remarks that have political implications are brief hints rather than clearly stated principles. Later tradition, however, has tended to draw from the Bible certain great architectonic images of political life, and many have taken one such image to be the dominant one, even when the Bible itself furnishes counterindications. This article will sketch some of these classic images.

The Theocratic Image. Perhaps the most influential such image in history has been the theocratic image. God has laid down the way in which society ought to be governed; the essential constitution for human society has been written by God. The Mosaic *law exemplifies this. Basic norms were explicitly laid down by God: how to deal with homicide, which animals might be eaten, what to do if a corpse was found in the fields. Even if such rules could not be exactly followed within the very different world of Christendom, they continued to support a theocratic image. The Middle Ages struggled with the problem of interest upon *loans because "usury" was understood to be directly forbidden by God (Deut. 23.19; Luke 6.35[?]). And not only the laws, but also the centrality of persons with divine authority—kings, judges, patriarchs—reinforced the theocratic idea. Hence came the establishment of religion, the linkage of church and state, religious sanction for *war, and the divine right of kings. Later, some of these connections were weakened: monarchy was challenged, church and state could be separated, but the force of the theocratic paradigm continued; the belief that direct divine instructions for state and politics exist enshrined in the Bible lingers on. A central text was Romans 13.1: "The powers that be are ordained of God" (KJV).

In fact, the Bible's support for the theocratic image is ambiguous. *Kingship and state were not there from the beginning; when kingship, much later, was proposed, it was regarded in some circles as a rebellion against God (1 Sam. 8.7)—a principle that might have led toward a pious anarchism. Royalty is limited in theory (Deut. 17.14–20), and in historical event it was often condemned; yet democracy is hardly considered an alternative—if monarchy was revolt against God, it was the people's voice that had demanded it.

The Alien State. The great empires could at times be seen as blessed by God and as serving his purposes, but at the best they were heathen empires and their polity did not derive from the God of Israel. In Judea in the first century CE, Roman rule was often bitterly resented, and the war of 66–70 was approaching.

Thus *Jesus, with his talk of the *kingdom of God, and people's belief that he was the son of David, might easily raise political questions. The position he takes up is depicted as a strikingly neutralist one; asked if it is lawful to pay taxes to the emperor, he commands, "Render to Caesar the things that are Caesar's, and to God the things that are God's" (Mark 12.17). He does not define what is Caesar's and what is God's, but at least there is something that is Caesar's; there is a certain dualism in society; not everything is God's, nor can everything be derived from the theocratic idea. When asked to decide about an inheritance, Jesus asked, "Who made me a judge or divider over you?" (Luke 12.14); some things are human business, and Jesus refuses to involve God in people's partisan struggles. He does not encourage nationalist yearnings for revolt against Rome. Some New Testament sources, such as Luke-Acts, seem to give a favorable picture of Rome (e.g., the Roman administration protects Paul against Jewish violence). Roman persecutions of the church, however, pointed in the other direction: is Rome the beast of Revelation 13, the *Babylon of Revelation 18?

Some have thought that the historical Jesus was much more involved in the nationalist politics of his time, as indicated by the superscription "the King of the Jews" on the cross, suggesting that Jesus was put to death for political sedition; the reality of this was then covered up in the Gospels as we have them. The New Testament, seen in this way, is sometimes taken to support involvement in political conflict and violence, contrasting with the neutralist image conveyed by the existing Gospels.

The Prophetic Image. From the nineteenth century onward, the *prophets have been seen in the context of their own times as those who demanded social justice and warned of divine judgment if this demand was not met; the heathen empires would serve God in punishing his own people. The "prophetic" task of the church was thus to protest against the evils and injustices of society. Since the New Testament had not done much of this—Paul in *Philemon touches upon *slavery but does not attack the institution as such—the example of the Israelite prophets was appealed to all the more.

The prophetic image often clashes with the theocratic: God will not hesitate to overthrow that which has theocratic legitimacy if by its inaction it favors the powerful and leaves the weak to suffer. Much progressive, reformist, politically activist religion has thus relied on the prophetic image. Yet the prophets rarely proposed reform, and after early times they did little to foster political action within the nation; God's action came rather through forces from without.

The Eschatological Image. Allied with the prophetic, and still more evident in the *apocalyptic movement, is the image of the coming of a new world in which war and evil will be no more (Isa. 2.4; 11.1–9; Rev. 21.1–5)—and one that may come to pass very soon. Political upheavals and international violence may be birth pangs of this new era (Mark 13.1–30). This vision of immediate catastrophe and a new world nourishes two hostile but related tendencies: millenarianism, which almost welcomes catastrophe because it ushers in the end, and sympathy for Marxist revolution.

The Image of Migration. The Hebrew Bible emphasizes the migrations of *Abraham, of the *Hebrews from *Egypt to the *Promised Land, of the returning exiles; the New Testament also pictures the church as a pilgrim people (Hebr. 13.14). This biblical image of migration and return was the motive power for modern Zionism. Christian nations often saw themselves in the same way: they were Israel, going out to find a land where they could build a life in the pattern ordained by God—the Puritan settlers of New England and the Afrikaners in South Africa are examples.

The Image of Liberation. New Testament passages often emphasize freedom or liberty (e.g., John 8.36; Rom. 8.21; Gal. 4.26), and modern scholarly trends have emphasized the *Exodus as the dominant event of the Hebrew Bible. In Egypt, the Hebrews were enslaved and subjected to forced labor; their male population was threatened by infanticide. They looked back on the time in Egypt with horror, and their escape from Egypt was the great event, ever afterward to be celebrated. No biblical theme has received more attention for its political importance in recent years than liberation. This theme was taken up by and on behalf of the exploited and oppressed of Latin America, Asia, and Africa, and made into the keystone of liberation theology. The church must take the side of the *poor and oppressed, stand with them in their struggle, join with their cry to God for deliverance, and read the Bible from within that context. Neutrality in relation to this situation is intolerable.

This use of the Exodus theme, powerful as it seems, has also been questioned on the ground that it implies a peculiar selectivity within the biblical traditions and a neglect of contrary aspects. Why did the Hebrews not organize politically to resist oppression? Why is their demand not a call for social justice but a request to leave Egypt in order to worship God in the wilderness? If the Exodus theme is so authoritative, what about its sequel when the liberated Hebrews enter Canaan and destroy or reduce to slavery the entire population of that land? Why should one aspect be more authoritative than the other? Liberation theologians generally answer by an appeal to the context of the interpreter: if the context is right, then it will be obvious which aspects of the biblical materials are relevant.

Conclusion. The Bible is certainly deeply interested in human political, social, and historical existence, and it presents powerful images relevant for understanding it. But all of these images have a somewhat relative character within the Bible and are limited through inner qualifications and through the coexistence of other, different images. It is doubtful therefore whether any clear and unitary political view can be derived from the Bible taken alone and as an entirety. If we appeal to the contextual situation of the interpreter, then the source is not the Bible as a whole but one's contextual selection. Or is it intrinsically mistaken to appeal so directly to the Bible at all? May the biblical images be valid and salutary only insofar as they are taken up into a total religious and philosophical position that includes, but goes beyond, the actual material of the Bible? These are fundamental questions posed by a consideration of politics and the Bible.   JAMES BARR

Polyglot Bibles. Polyglot Bibles are editions that contain the biblical text in several languages, usually in parallel columns. The term is used especially with reference to four great editions of the complete Bible published in the sixteenth and seventeenth centuries: the Complutensian, Antwerp, Paris, and London polyglots. Other editions (Nuremburg, 1599 [Hutter]; London, 1831 [Bagster]; Bielefeld, 1864 [Stier/Theile]) have since followed such a pattern, but these four spanned a critical period in the development of western biblical studies, marking the transition from an appreciation of the original languages of the Bible to the realization of the need for critical editions of the text in each of the original languages.

The Complutensian Polyglot (1514–1517). The early sixteenth century saw a growing demand for sound knowledge of the Bible, not only among the scholarly clergy but also among leaders of the commercial and political communities. Humanist scholars, seeking the authentic text of the Latin *Vulgate scriptures, began studying its original languages, *Hebrew and *Greek. Centers for the study of biblical languages were established at Oxford, Paris, Basel, Geneva, Wittemberg, and elsewhere. Cardinal Francisco Ximénes de Cisneros (1436–1517) of Toledo founded a university at Complutum (Alcalá de Henares) in 1500, and in 1502 he undertook the editing of the Complutensian Polyglot to provide the necessary texts and tools for biblical studies. Eminent scholars were assembled, including Antonio de Lebrija, Lopez de Zuñiga, and the converted Jews Alphonso of Alcalá and Alphonso of Zamora. Some biblical manuscripts were purchased, others were borrowed; even the Vatican loaned from its treasures. In 1514, the New Testament was printed, and two years later the Old Testament was completed, but the whole was not formally published until 1522. The work includes not only the text of the complete Bible in five volumes, but also a Greek-Latin lexicon of the New Testament at the end of the fifth volume, and in an appended sixth volume a Hebrew-Latin dictionary with a Latin-Hebrew index and an etymological dictionary of biblical proper names. The Old Testament page format is in three columns, with the Latin Vulgate centered and the Hebrew text (the first Christian printed edition) and Greek *Septuagint (the first printed edition) in the outer and inner columns respectively. The Septuagint is provided with a literal interlinear Latin translation, and each word in the parallel Vulgate and Hebrew columns is marked with a superscript letter to show their correspondence; Hebrew roots are indicated in the margins. In the Pentateuch, the Targum of Onkelos and its Latin translation are placed at the foot of the page. The New Testament page format is in two columns, Greek and Latin. Only six hundred copies of the polyglot were printed, and within decades copies were so scarce that Philip II of Spain commissioned the preparation of the Antwerp Polyglot.

The Antwerp Polyglot (1569–1572). Edited by Benedictus Arias Montanus (1527–1598) and printed by Christopher Plantin (1514–1589), the "Royal Polyglot" of Antwerp reproduced essentially the Complutensian text, expanding it to eight volumes. Participating scholars included Franciscus Raphelengius, Guido and Nicolaus Fabricius, and Daniel Bomberg. The biblical texts remained largely unchanged, though the Hebrew text was corrected from the Bomberg Venice edition and the Septuagint from the Aldine edition; the only significant addition is the Syriac text of the New Testament, based on Widmanstadt's 1555 edition. The Old Testament page format was changed to display four columns over two pages, with the Hebrew and Latin Vulgate texts to the left and to the right a literal Latin translation of the Septuagint followed by the Greek Septuagint text, while below them the Onkelos Targum in Chaldee (Aramaic) is on the left page and a literal Latin translation of it to the right. In the New Testament the Peshitta Syriac and its literal Latin translation are on the left and the Vulgate and Greek (Erasmus's fourth edition) are on the right; the Syriac text is repeated in Hebrew characters below, with word roots identified in the margins. Scholarly helps were considerably expanded: volume six provides grammars and lexicons for Hebrew, Chaldee, Syriac, and Greek; in volume seven the Hebrew and Greek Testaments have interlinear Latin texts from Sanctes Pagninus's version and the Vulgate respectively, with notes and alternative renderings added in the margin; volume eight contains seventeen chapters of helps on topics ranging from weights and measures, biblical geography, and priestly vestments, to accounts of the *Masorah, variant readings in the Old and New Testaments and the Psalms (four, seven, and eleven pages respectively), and a review by Louvain theologians comparing the variants in the Vulgate tradition with the other traditions. Twelve hundred copies were issued on paper, and thirteen on velum.

The Paris Polyglot (1629–1645). Preparations for the ill-fated Paris Polyglot were begun by Cardinal Du Perron in 1615, halted at his death in 1617, and resumed several years later by Guy Michel Le Jay, a Parisian lawyer, who completed it at his own expense. Among his assistants were Jean Morin and Godefridus Hermant of Blois, the Maronites Gabriel Sionita and Joannes Hesronita, and Jerome Parent of the Sorbonne. Cardinal Richelieu offered to sponsor the work under his own name, but threw his influence against it when Le Jay refused. Printed by Antoine Vitré, the ten-volume work is remarkable mainly for

its initials, maps, and plates. It expanded the range of resources for biblical scholarship with the first printed edition of not only the Samaritan Pentateuch and the Samaritan Targum but also of the Syriac Peshitta Old Testament, and even completed the Syriac New Testament with the lesser Catholic letters (from Pococke, 1630) and Revelation (from de Dieu, 1627), but ultimately it was a failure. Its text followed the Antwerp Polyglot closely for the Hebrew, Greek, and Latin texts, earning severe criticism for ignoring the officially authorized Roman editions of both the Septuagint (1586–1587) and the Latin Vulgate (1592). Although the Chaldee Targum of the Pentateuch was ostensibly revised, its Latin rendering was not. Further, the biblical text was accompanied by neither helps nor apparatus, and finally it was soon overshadowed by the London Polyglot. Suffering from both political and scholarly disfavor, the work's circulation was severely hampered; rather than offer it at a reduced price, though, Le Jay sold a large number of sheets as waste paper.

The London Polyglot (1655–1657). Brian Walton designed in 1647 a plan for an improved polyglot Bible, which would (as he described it later) "not only . . . exhibit to the reader all the ancient and chief Translations, together with the Originals, but also the chief Copies, MSS., or others, of both, so that in this Edition the reader might have all or most other editions, and the best MSS. which he might consult at pleasure." This most comprehensive and important of the great polyglots is still valuable today for biblical scholarship. Walton's preface duly acknowledges the cooperation of such scholars as James Ussher, Gilbert Sheldon, John Lightfoot, Abraham Wheelocke, Edmund Castell, and Edward Pococke, and the expense of publication was met by subscription. It was dedicated to Oliver Cromwell (the republican edition), but copies issued after the accession of Charles II (29 May 1660) have a revised dedication (the loyalist edition). The first three volumes present the texts of the Old Testament, followed by the *Apocrypha and the Pseudo-Jonathan and Jerusalem Targums in the fourth volume, and the New Testament in the fifth. The texts are printed across two pages: the Hebrew text with Pagninus's Latin revised by Arias on the left paralleled by the Clementine Latin Vulgate to the right; below these come the Greek Septuagint with its Latin translation in two columns on the left, both from the 1628 Roman authorized edition and with the variants of Codex Alexandrinus added at the foot of the

Greek column, facing on the right the Onkelos Targum with its Latin translation on the right; beneath these are the Syriac and the Arabic versions, each with its Latin translation; and in the Pentateuch there is added the Samaritan Hebrew and the Samaritan Targum, with a single Latin translation but with variations footnoted. Particularly valuable is the sixth volume, which is reserved for a critical apparatus to the texts, as well as the learned prolegomena in the first volume, which devotes nearly two hundred densely packed folio pages to such topics as biblical chronology, geography, measures, and idioms, illustrated with maps and plans, and a survey of the nature of language, of alphabets, and the history of the biblical text, its editions and versions.

See also Printing and Publishing.

ERROLL F. RHODES

Pontifical Biblical Commission. By his Apostolic Letter *Vigilantiae* (30 Oct. 1902), Pope Leo XIII established the Pontifical Biblical Commission to promote biblical studies in the Roman Catholic Church, "that God's words will both be given, everywhere among us, that thorough study that our times demand and be shielded not only from every breath of error but even from every rash opinion." The commission was to study biblical questions in the light of modern trends and recent discoveries and to disseminate for the service of all whatever was useful for biblical interpretation. The first-word title of the Apostolic Letter, "vigilance," however, sounded a note that was to mark the activity of the commission, which sought above all to safeguard the authority of the Bible against the exaggerated criticism of early-twentieth-century Modernism. Though the commission was not strictly a Roman congregation, it was organized, as were Vatican commissions of that period, with five cardinal members and thirty-nine consultors (biblical scholars from many nations).

Pope Pius X (1903–1914) furthered the work of the commission. During his reign it issued thirteen *responsa* (often popularly called "decrees"), and subsequently others (until 1933), with various other declarations about biblical studies in seminaries and requirements for ecclesiastical biblical degrees.

The *responsa* were issued in the form of brief answers (affirmative or negative) to long, intricate, often "loaded" questions. They dealt with such topics as the theory of implicit quotations in the Bible; the theory of apparently historical narratives; the Mosaic authorship of the *Pentateuch; the authorship and historicity of the Fourth Gospel; the authorship and character of the book of Isaiah; the historicity of Genesis 1–3; the authorship, date of composition, and character of the Psalms or of Matthew; of the Marcan and Lucan Gospels; the *synoptic problem; the authorship, date of composition, and historicity of Acts; the authenticity, integrity, and date of composition of the Pastoral Letters; the authorship and composition of the letter to the Hebrews; the *parousia in Pauline writings; the interpretation of two texts (Ps. 16.10–11 and Matt. 16.26 = Luke 9.25). These *responsa* caused a dark cloud of reactionary conservatism to settle over Roman Catholic biblical scholarship in the first half of the twentieth century.

The commission's *responsa* were never understood to have been infallibly issued. Pius X in his Motuproprio *Praestantia sacrae scripturae* considered them to be "useful for the proper progress and guidance of biblical scholarship along safe lines." But he did require the same submission of Catholics to these *responsa* as to similar papally approved decrees of other Roman congregations.

In 1943, Pope Pius XII issued an encyclical, *Divino afflante spiritu*, on the promotion of biblical studies. Since that time, the Biblical Commission has played a more open-minded role in encouraging such studies. Its *responsa* have given way to "letters" and "instructions," in which it has gradually assumed a more positive stance, though concern is still expressed about some errors or excessive tendencies.

To many people, however, both inside and outside the Roman Catholic Church, the *responsa* have seemed to be still in effect. This, however, is not true. In 1955, a semiofficial explanation of the character of the *responsa* was issued by the secretary and the subsecretary of the commission, distinguishing *responsa* that touched on faith and morals from those that dealt with literary questions, authorship, integrity, date of composition, and so on. The former were to be regarded as still valid, whereas the latter were recognized as time-conditioned, corresponding to a historical context that no longer existed. Both secretaries explained that in matters pertaining to the *responsa* of the second category Catholic interpreters were to pursue their research and interpretation "with full freedom." Significantly, almost all of the above-mentioned *responsa* belong to the second category.

In 1964, the Biblical Commission issued an instruction "On the Historical Truth of the Gospels," in which it dealt concretely and in a positive way with a problem that has vexed modern students of the Gospels both within and without the Roman Catholic Church. Instead of merely reiterating the historical character of the Gospels, it adopted valid aspects of form criticism and distinguished three stages of the gospel tradition: (i) what Jesus of Nazareth did and said; (ii) what his disciples preached after his death and resurrection about him, his message, and his deeds; and (iii) what the evangelists selected and synthesized from that preaching and explicated for the needs of their churches. Whereas the instruction insinuated a continuum between the first and third stages, it did not in any way (fundamentalistically) identify them. (The essential content of that instruction was briefly repeated in chapter 5 of the dogmatic constitution of Vatican Council II, *Dei verbum*.)

In 1971, Pope Paul VI revamped the commission, making it a counterpart of the International Theological Commission and associating it with the Congregation for the Doctrine of the Faith. The members of the Biblical Commission are no longer cardinals, but twenty biblical scholars from across the world, appointed for five years, most of them of widely acclaimed competence.   JOSEPH A. FITZMYER, S.J.

Poor. As the formulaic association of the poor with *widows and *orphans in ancient Near Eastern literature in general and in the Hebrew Bible in particular shows, poverty was an undesirable condition and not an ascetic discipline to be embraced for a higher goal. Protection and special care for these economically deprived members of society was a responsibility of kings, who demonstrated their power in part by their ability to help those unable to help themselves (*see* Kingship and Monarchy). This royal responsibility is found in Israel as well, as the interchange between *David and *Nathan in 2 Samuel 12.1–6 implies and the royal instruction in Proverbs 31.8–9 makes explicit; see also Psalms 72.2, 12–14; Proverbs 29.14.

In premonarchic Israel this obligation was incumbent on the nation as a whole. In some of its earliest legislation, Israel is instructed to ensure that the poor have both a fair hearing in judicial contexts and food from the harvest and sabbatical fallowness (Exod. 23.6, 11; see Lev. 19.10; 23.22), and to lend money to the poor

without interest (Exod. 22.25; *see* Loans and Interest). The prophets repeatedly reminded Israel of these obligations; see Isaiah 10.1–4; 58.7; Amos 2.6–7; 4.1; Ezekiel 18.

What was incumbent on the nation as a whole was also required of the individual. *Job's passionate declaration of innocence is a summary of the individual Israelite's moral code; as part of his assertion of complete righteousness, Job details his concern for the poor (Job 29.11–17; 31.16–22; see also Deut. 15.11). This ethical obligation continues to be stressed in the New Testament and in the Qur'ān.

Those who oppressed the poor, then, were the wicked (Ps. 37.14; Prov. 14.31), and God was the protector of the poor (Ps. 140.12). He would reward those who gave to the poor (Prov. 19.17) and would ultimately provide for them himself (Isa. 41.17).

All of these texts make it clear that poverty was an unfortunate state. Its origins are explored only in wisdom literature, where it is often attributed to moral shortcomings or at least to a lack of industry, an example of the dominant biblical view that God rewards goodness and punishes wickedness. It must be noted, however, that this point of view is found in literature originating in well-to-do circles, mainly in Proverbs (10.4; 13.18; 14.23; 20.13; 23.21; 29.19).

In the New Testament as well, poverty, especially self-impoverishment, is not an ideal in itself, but rather a condition temporarily assumed for the sake of some higher goal. Paul illustrates this when he speaks of "the generous act of our Lord Jesus Christ, that though he was rich, yet for your sakes he became poor, so that by his poverty you might become rich" (2 Cor. 8.9). The larger context of the verse is the collection for the poor of the church in Jerusalem, an effort to which Paul was committed (see Gal. 2.1–10; 1 Cor. 16.1–4; Rom. 15.25–27); Paul appeals to the Christians of Corinth to imitate the selfless love of Jesus, out of concern for their more needy brothers and sisters. This idea of the "imitation of Christ," also present in Philippians 2.5–8, is made a general ideal in later, monastic Christianity, where poverty is embraced not just or not even primarily for the sake of others but as a means of freedom from material goods that enables one to attain a higher spiritual state in union with Jesus, who in an apparently hyperbolic proverb, said to one who would follow him: "Foxes have holes and birds of the air have nests, but the Son of man has nowhere to lay his head" (Matt. 8.20; Luke 9.58).

The advice of Jesus to the rich young man to "sell all and give to the poor" (Mark 10.21 par.; cf. 10.23–31) must be interpreted in the light of the eschatological urgency felt by early Christians and probably by Jesus himself, as well as the narrative context, despite later abstraction of that command into an ideal of "evangelical poverty." Following earlier biblical descriptions of divine judgment, Jesus is apparently anticipating a reversal of fortune when the *kingdom of God appears: the undesirable conditions of the poor, hungry, mourning and persecuted will be altered (Luke 6.20–23; cf. 1 Sam. 2.4–8 and Luke 1.51–53; Isa. 61.1–4 and Luke 4.16–21).

See Alms; Meek.   MICHAEL D. COOGAN

Popular Culture and the Bible. The Bible has been a fixture in American popular culture from the first European settlements to the present. Mentioning only a few random facts is enough to suggest the breadth of the Bible's presence in American civilization. The first English book published in North America was *The Whole Booke of Psalmes Faithfully Translated into English Meter* (1640). The American Bible Society, founded in 1816, has distributed well over four billion copies of the Bible or biblical portions (*see* Bible Societies). Throughout the nineteenth century, American settlers regularly named their communities after biblical places, like Zoar, Ohio (Gen. 13.10), or Mount Tirzah, North Carolina (Josh. 12.24), as well as forty-seven variations on Bethel, sixty-one on Eden, and ninety-five on Salem. When in 1842 the Roman Catholic Bishop of Philadelphia, Francis Patrick Kenrick, petitioned city officials to allow schoolchildren of his faith to hear readings from the Douay-Rheims translation of the Bible instead of the Protestant King James Version, the city's Protestants rioted and tried to burn down Philadelphia's Catholic churches. In 1964, a thought-provoking book was published on the biblical content of a famous comic strip (Robert Short, *The Gospel According to Peanuts*). Two of the most popular rock-operas of the 1970s, *Jesus Christ Superstar* and *Godspell*, were based on the biblical Gospels. During the same decade, the best-selling book of any kind (except the Bible itself) was Hal Lindsey's *The Late Great Planet Earth*, which attempted to show how current events were fulfilling prophetic passages of scripture. In 1990, at least seven thousand different editions of the Bible were available from hundreds of publishers. However difficult it may be to define the impact of the Bible on ordinary people precisely, scripture has always been a vital element in American popular life.

From the first colonists, the Bible provided themes for Americans to define themselves as a people, and then as a nation. Puritans in New England believed they were in *covenant with God just like the ancient Israelites. The first public political campaigns of the 1830s were modeled directly on the organized enthusiasm and passionate rhetoric of the religious revival. In the intense sectional strife leading to the Civil War, the Bible became a weapon put to use by both sides. In the South, passages like Leviticus 25:45 ("the children of the strangers that do sojourn among you . . . they shall be your possession") defined the righteousness of their cause. In the North, favored passages, usually from the New Testament, like Galatians 5:1 ("Stand fast . . . in the liberty wherewith Christ hath made us free"), did the same. (*See* Slavery and the Bible.) Abraham Lincoln, in his Second Inaugural Address, put the Civil War into perspective by quoting Matthew 18:7 and Psalm 19:9, and by noting that "both [sides] read the same Bible." Biblical phrases and conceptions, particularly with politicians from the South like Woodrow Wilson or Jimmy Carter, have continued to exert a political force even in the more secular twentieth century.

If anything, the Bible has been more obviously at work in the popular culture of *African Americans than among whites. Slaves made a sharp distinction between the Bible their owners preached to them and the Bible they discovered for themselves. Under slavery, stringent regulations often existed against unsupervised preaching, and sometimes even against owning Bibles. But with or without permission, slaves made special efforts to hear black preachers. One slave left this striking testimony: "a yellow [light-complexioned] man preached to us. She [the slave owner] had him preach how we ought to obey our master and missy if we want to go to heaven, but when she wasn't there, he came out with straight preachin' from the Bible."

Blacks sang and preached about *Adam and *Eve and the *Fall, about "wrestlin' Jacob" who "would not let [God] go," about *Moses and the *Exodus from Egypt, about *Daniel in the lions' den, about *Jonah in the belly of the fish, about the birth of *Jesus and his death and future return. The slaves' profound embrace of scripture created a climate for Bible reading and biblical preaching that has continued among African Americans since the Civil War. (*See also* African American Traditions and the Bible.)

In the popular media, scripture has been as omnipresent as in politics. Fiction, hymns, and poetry employing biblical themes have always made up a huge proportion of American publishing. Composers William Billings (1746–1800), John Knowles Paine (1839–1906), and many in the twentieth century, such as Charles Ives and Aaron Copland, followed earlier precedents by writing musical settings for the psalms. Among the populace at large, the flood of sheet music, hymnals, chorus books, and gospel songs has never ebbed. In the nineteenth century, one of the most frequently reprinted sheet-music titles was "My Mother's Bible." Its first appearance (1843) evoked an emotional domestic ideal: "My mother's hands this Bible clasped, / She dying gave it me." At another level, millions of Sunday school students have learned songs like "The B-I-B-L-E, / Yes, that's the book for me, / I stand alone on the word of God, / The B-I-B-L-E." (*See also* Music and the Bible.)

American writers of popular fiction have always drawn on biblical materials. Biblical allusions feature prominently in works such as Herman Melville's *Moby-Dick* (which begins, "Call me Ishmael"), William Faulkner's *Absalom, Absalom!* (1936) and *Go Down Moses* (1942), James Baldwin's *Go Tell It on the Mountain* (1953), and Peter Devries's *The Blood of the Lamb* (1961). The American people have never been able to get enough of popular fiction inspired directly by the Bible. The first important novel of this kind was William Ware's *Julian: Or, Scenes in Judea* (1856), which described gospel events through the letters of its fictional protagonist. General Lew Wallace's *Ben Hur* (1880), which climaxed in a breathtaking chariot race, is probably the supreme example of biblical fiction. President Garfield wrote his personal thanks to Wallace from the White House, and it soon became a huge success with the public at large (in part because Sears, Roebuck printed up a million inexpensive copies). *Ben Hur* was also the inspiration for an immensely successful touring drama (complete with surging horses on a treadmill) and two motion pictures. Other similar books have had nearly as much success, including Henryk Sienkiewicz's *Quo Vadis?* (1896), Lloyd Douglas's *The Robe* (1942) and *The Big Fisherman* (1949), Marjorie Holmes's *Two from Galilee* (1972), and several novels of both Taylor Caldwell and Frank G. Slaughter. One of the most unusual examples of this fiction was written first in Yiddish by a Jewish author, Sholem Asch. When published in English in 1939, *The Nazarene* won praise from Christians for its sensitive portrayal of contemporary customs at the time of Jesus. (*See also* Literature and the Bible, *article on* North American Literature.)

Many of the blockbuster biblical novels eventually found their way to the screen. Cecil B. de Mille's *The King of Kings* from 1927 (with H. B. Warner as a diffident Jesus) and George Stevens's *The Greatest Story Ever Told* from 1965 (with Max von Sydow as a Jesus who was allowed to show traces of humor) were among the most memorable, but there have been many others.

The Bible as a theme in popular communications is hardly exhausted by songs, poems, stories, and movies. In the visual arts, biblical materials have provided inspiration for German immigrants embellishing needle work with *Fraktur* print, lithographers such as Currier and Ives, countless painters at countless levels of ability, and a few masters acclaimed by both public and critics, such as Edward Hicks, who in the mid nineteenth century painted several versions of *The Peaceable Kingdom*. (*See* Art and the Bible.) Since the beginning of mass-marketed religious objects about the time of the Civil War, both Catholics and Protestants have purchased immense quantities of pictures, statues, games, children's toys, paperweights, refrigerator magnets, jewelry, T-shirts, greeting cards, calendars, and business cards decorated with biblical motifs.

Allene Stuart Phy, editor of the best book on the subject, once observed that there is often a "ludicrous discrepancy . . . between the ancient wisdom of the scriptures and the vulgarities of American popular culture" (*The Bible and Popular Culture in America*, 1985). But Phy also saw clearly that even these "vulgarities" show the "profound ways in which the holy books of the Jewish and Christian religions relate to [the] lives of Americans."

See also Everyday Expressions from the Bible.   MARK A. NOLL

Pottery. *See* Archaeology and the Bible; Crafts; Houses, Furniture, Utensils.

Poverty. *See* Poor.

Prayer(s). The Bible both talks about prayer and gives the texts of specific prayers to God. Underlying the biblical story is the conviction, so fundamental that it rarely needs to be voiced explicitly, that it is both possible and desirable for humans to address the Divine and that the Divine both can and will respond. Indeed the God of the Bible is characterized as "you who answer prayer" (Ps. 65.2; cf. 1 Kings 9.3; Matt. 7.11).

Yet the very terminology of "prayer" is much more problematic than might seem at first glance. Sometimes, in modern usage, the term is used to include any form of address to God or even outbursts of praise about God, such as hymnic compositions in which God is not addressed directly but talked about in the third person. Furthermore, communication with God can be expressed not only in words but in acts of *sacrifice, dance, ritual bodily *gestures, and other non-verbal modes of communication, and in a broad sense all of these are often included in the category of prayer. Biblical scholars usually define the term more narrowly and precisely, distinguishing between "psalms" as sung poetic compositions in formulaic language that belong to the formal, public *worship in the Temple and "prayers" as prose compositions, usually with some component of petition. Often it is difficult to draw a line between conversation with God (e.g., Gen. 18; Exod. 3–4) and the more formalized style of address and content that should be termed a "prayer."

Both prayer and sacrifice are understood in the Bible as service (Hebr. 'ăbōdâ) rendered to God as king. It is debated whether set words of prayer may have accompanied sacrifice in the Temple; certainly no such texts have been preserved. Sometimes the language of prayer and sacrifice is brought together (e.g., Ps. 141.2), and the *Temple itself came to be called a "house of prayer" (Isa. 56.7; 1 Kings 8; Luke 18.10). Little is known about origin of the practice of set statutory prayers for the community (particularly for morning and evening), although the process certainly began in the postexilic period. Among the *Dead Sea Scrolls there are, albeit preserved only in an extremely fragmentary state, the actual texts of prayers from perhaps the mid-third century BCE, prayers for each day of the week, each month of the year, and for special feasts (1Q34; 4Q503–509); in these certain features that came to be standard in subsequent Jewish prayer are already attested (in particular the blessing formulary at beginning and end of each prayer and the practice of petitionary prayer on weekdays and prayer of praise on the *Sabbath).

When we turn to actual texts of prayers given in the Bible, much study has focused on the *Psalms and on the *Lord's Prayer; yet these are by no means the only prayers in the Bible. In the Hebrew Bible alone there are over ninety prose prayers in which individuals address God directly in a time of need. These range from a short simple petition (like that of Moses' "O God, please heal her," Num. 12.13; see also Jth. 13.8; 2 Sam. 15.31; 2 Kings 6.17), to more lengthy and formal prayers blending elements of praise and petition (2 Sam. 7.18–29; 1 Kings 8.22–61; 2 Chron. 20.6–12), to communal confession of sin and lament (Jth. 10.10). Such prayers are presented as spontaneous, unrepeatable, and arising out of the immediate situation, although as Moshe Greenberg (*Biblical Prose Prayer as a Window to the Popular Religion of Ancient Israel* [Berkeley and Los Angeles, 1983]) has shown, there are links in contact, structure, and vocabulary between these prayers of individuals and the more formal psalms and public prayers. Of special interest are those narratives that portray an individual drawing on a psalm from the cultic realm as a personal prayer in time of need (1 Sam. 2.1–10; 2 Sam. 22.2–51; Jon. 2.1–9) and, from the postexilic period, a special collection of extended prayers of confession of sin and penitence (Ezra 9.6–15; Neh. 9.5–37; Dan. 9.3–19).

The *Apocrypha is especially rich in actual prayer texts, including the prayers of Esther and Mordecai added on to the Greek text of *Esther; the prayers of *Azariah and the three youths in the fire in Daniel 3; Tobit 3.2–7, 11–15; 8.5–7, 15–17; 13; Judith 9.2–14; 13.4–5; 16.1–17; and many other short prayers (*see also* Manasseh, The Prayer of). These provide a window into the continuing development of prayer forms in the Persian and Hellenistic periods, such as the increased use of the blessing formulary to begin a prayer, and give evidence of a number of new concepts about prayer that find expression in this period, such as the introduction of an angelic intermediary who presents prayers to God (Tob. 12.12) and the possibility of prayers for the dead (2 Macc. 12.41–45).

In the New Testament we continue to find both statements about prayer and the text of prayers, especially on the lips of Jesus and Paul. Thus Jesus not only teaches his disciples about prayer and gives them words to pray "like this" (Luke 1.2–4; Matt. 6.5–13; *see* Lord's Prayer) but he himself is portrayed as praying at each of the decisive moments of his life (Luke 3.21; 6.12; 9.29; 22.39–46; 23.46; John 15–17). Much of what the New Testament says about prayer continues and reiterates what is said in earlier sections of the Bible about the necessity and efficacy of prayer and the characteristics of humility and persistence to be brought to prayer. Distinctively Christian is the emphasis that prayer, though directed to God (Rom. 1.8; 1 Cor. 1.4; Col. 1.3), is to be "through Jesus Christ" (Rom. 1.8) or in the name of Jesus (John 15.17), and the role of the Spirit in making prayer possible (Rom. 8.26–28; Gal. 4.6).

See also Lectionaries.   EILEEN SCHULLER

Predestination. The notion of predestination, God's foreknowledge and arrangement of events, has been an important doctrine in certain forms of Christianity, mostly Protestantism, and particularly in forms historically and theologically related to John Calvin, the sixteenth-century reformer from Geneva. In particular this doctrine refers to God's predetermining who is elected and therefore, naturally, who is not. In the ancient world, however, the idea of predestination and foreknowledge had a wider connotation and was common in secular as well as religious writings.

God's providence or forethought was a common feature of ancient Greek writers from the time of Plato (*Timaeus* 30b; 44c) and Xenophon (*Memorabilia* 1.4.6; 4.3.6), and later in the writings of Diogenes Laertius (3.24k) and Plutarch (*Moralia* 425f; 436d). It is therefore not surprising to find that foreknowledge (Grk. *pronoia*) figures prominently in such first-century writers as *Josephus and *Philo. Josephus claims that it may have been *pronoia* that somehow allowed him to avoid participating in the mass suicide at Jotopata at the outbreak of the Jewish revolt in 67 CE (*War* 3.8.391); while others died or killed each other, Josephus was spared, taken captive by Vespasian, and lived to write his multivolume works *The Jewish War* and *The Antiquities of the Jews*. Philo wrote an entire treatise on *pronoia*. That a person should be able to ascertain God's plan and will or enjoy the predestination of the divine was a claim to one's own influence and position. Such claims were not nearly as fanciful to ancient writers and philosophers as they may seem to many moderns.

In the New Testament the few times this concept is employed it involves trying to figure out how God's actions embodied in Jesus of Nazareth can be understood in the context of and reconciled with God's plans. The writers who took this point up were deeply steeped in the Hellenistic milieu of the cities of Asia Minor and the Greek East. The speculative and philosophical nature of this discussion accords well with the ethos of these eastern urban Greek centers. Thus, the author of 1 Peter says that the elect were chosen by the foreknowledge of God (1.2) and also claims that Jesus was foreknown before the foundation of the world (1.20). Likewise, Acts 2.23, in a speech attributed to Peter, asserts that Jesus was delivered up "by the predestined plan and foreknowledge of God."

Paul utilized this language to articulate what he believed God had done in Jesus of Nazareth and what this means for Jews, *gentiles, and current believers in Jesus. To the church in Rome he says God foreknew and predestined those whom he called to become the image of his son (Rom. 8.29). In both Romans 11.2 and Galatians 3.8 Paul tries to reconcile God's predestiny of Israel with the predestiny of believers who are not Jews. This is a difficult argument. He claims finally that God has both chosen and foreordained Israel, and God predestined non-Jews or gentiles to be included in Israel through his selection of *Abraham to be a light to the nations. God was able to foresee that the gentiles would be justified by faith through the gospel preached to Abraham beforehand when he said, "All the nations shall be blessed in you" (Gal.3.8, quoting Gen. 12.3).

In the New Testament, then, the rather common Greek notions of foreknowledge and predestiny were used by writers comfortable with the Greek philosophical milieu to reconcile the events that had taken place recently in Jesus of Nazareth with the historic events and promises of Israel's past.

Over the centuries the notion of *pronoia* itself was modified and utilized for a host of theological and social conflicts that the Greek and Jewish writers of the first century CE could not have anticipated and probably would never have imagined.   J. ANDREW OVERMAN

Priestly Writers. *See* P.

Priests and High Priest. The major cultic persons in Israel. Through the centuries documented in the Bible, priestly duties and activities varied somewhat, but primary in the early period, and always basic, was the idea that a priest is a person attached to the service of God in a sanctuary, God's house. The original concept of the priest as server or minister of God in the sanctuary was analogous to that of a king's minister in the palace. As ministers in a palace set food on the table of an earthly king, early Israelite priests set holy bread on a table before God (1 Sam. 21.4–6), a practice that underlay the provisions for the bread of the presence (see Showbread). As ministers of a king served as intermediaries for citizens wishing to ask the king what course of action to take, or what the king's mind might be, early Israelite priests, using the *Urim and Thummim in the *ephod, asked God the same sorts of questions for others, including the leaders of the people (Judg. 18.5; 1 Sam. 14.3, 36–42; 22.9–10, 13, 15, 18; 23.9–12; 30.7–8), a practice which evolved into the priestly giving of tôrâ, or law, as manifestation of the divine mind. It was as intermediary between God in his holy place and the people outside that a priest communicated God's blessing to the people (Num. 6.22–27; Deut. 10.8; 21.5).

Priests and Sacrifice. In early narratives, including *J and *E, it was perfectly right for someone who was not a priest to offer a *sacrifice on an *altar not attached to a sanctuary, without any priestly intervention. When sacrifice was offered at a sanctuary, however, the priests of that sanctuary were involved in it already in the premonarchic period (1 Sam. 2.12–17), and their sacrificial prerogatives increased during the monarchic period. In Deuteronomy 33.10, bringing *incense and burnt offerings before God is mentioned among the activities characteristic of priests, but it is in last place. In Ezekiel's prescriptions for priests as they are to function after the *exile (Ezek. 44.15–31), their sacrificial activity is in first place (44.15–16), and in Jeremiah 33.18, within a postexilic addition to the book, priests are characterized entirely in terms of sacrificial work. This extension of the sacrificial role of priests can be correlated with an extension of the high degree of *holiness proper to the interior of the sanctuary, the place where God's presence was focused, to the open-air altar in the courtyard in front of the sanctuary. The prerogatives of priests to perform all acts inside the house of God was extended to include any act entailing contact with the altar of sacrifice in the courtyard outside. In all of this the fundamental principle remained that the highest degree of holiness among human beings was that of priests, and that only they could rightly enter the spaces whose degree of spatial holiness was the highest.

Priests and the Divine Will. In early texts a priest is characterized not as a person engaged in sacrifice but as one who carries the oracular ephod (1 Sam. 22.18) containing the Urim and Thummim, which were manipulated in order to provide an expression of God's mind or will in answer to a question put to him. In the oldest part of the blessing of Moses for *Levi, the Urim and Thummim are still characteristic of a priest (Deut. 33.8), but in 33.10, generally taken as part of a later expansion of the blessing for Levi added toward the middle of the monarchic period, God's ordinances and God's law (Hebr. tôrâ) are the primary objects of priestly responsibility, mentioned before incense and burnt offering. The word tôrâ may originally have been the word designating the divine response, communicated through a priest with his Urim and Thummim, to a question put to him; the Akkadian word têrtu, akin to Hebrew tôrâ, signified the response procured in certain types of Mesopotamian divination. If so, Israelite tôrâ evolved from a simple manifestation of God's will in the form of an answer "Yes" or "No" (through the Urim and Thummim) into a more complex pronouncement expressing the divine will in cultic matters based on such questions as the distinction of the holy from the profane, the pure from the impure (see the tôrâ described in Hag. 2.10–14), and in ethical matters too, because of the divine requirement of right behavior on the part of persons approaching what is holy, or, more profoundly, persons divinely expected to be holy (Ps. 15.2, 5; Lev. 19.2). By the end of the monarchic period the meaning of tôrâ had been extended to include all divinely sanctioned law, of the types codified in the *Pentateuch, and it was then as typically associated with a priest as the word of God was with a *prophet (Jer. 18.18). In this expanded sense of "law," sacred because it was an expression of the divine will, tôrâ, something in which priests had always been the rightful experts, became something in which they were competent for deciding questions and settling disputes. Ultimately they became responsible not only for upholding all divine law but also for all casuistry and jurisprudence based on it (Lev. 10.10–11; Deut. 17.8–13; 21.5; Ezek. 44.24). This is not to say that priests became teachers or preachers, unless by that, one has in mind their communicating law and legal decisions to the people. In the postexilic centuries priestly involvement with law weakened in the general consciousness, and priests increasingly came to be associated with sacrifice. The traditional idea of priests as persons making statutes and legal judgments known to the people (i.e., as persons with judiciary duties) was alive in the second century BCE (Sir. 45.14–17), but as jurists learned in the law they were by then being supplanted by the *scribes (Sir. 39.1–11). Membership of priests in commissions having judicial duties as well as administrative ones in the Roman period may have been due in large part to their social and political connections. (*See* Law; Torah.)

Historical Evolution of Priesthood. The historical roots of early Israelite priesthood probably lie, culturally, in the cultic systems of the Canaanites and other Northwest Semitic peoples, whose usual word for priest is essentially the same as the Hebrew word. Israelite settlements in Palestine had their Yahwist sanctuaries, and throughout the land there continued to be a multitude of such sanctuaries, each with one or more priests, until the ultimate suppression of all but the *Temple in *Jerusalem in the reign of *Josiah left Jerusalem the only place where anyone could actually function as a priest (2 Kings 23.5, 8–9, 15–20). In the period of the judges and in the early monarchic period one could be a priest without being a member of the tribe of Levi (Judg. 17.5; 1 Sam. 7.1; 2 Sam. 8.18; 20.26; 1 Kings 12.31), and yet a *Levite was particularly desirable as a priest (Judg. 17–18). If the unnamed ancestor of Eli in 1 Sam. 2.27–28 is Levi, as the context strongly suggests, then the priests of the sanctuary of the *ark at Shiloh were Levites. Of the personal origins of *Zadok, the founding head of the priesthood of Jerusalem (1 Kings 2.35; 4.2), nothing at all is said in the narratives in which he appears, or in any preexilic text. In some scholarly hypotheses concerning his undocumented origins he is held to have been a Levite, in others not.

By the time of Josiah's abolition of all sanctuaries except that of Jerusalem three centuries later, there was no longer any question of anyone's functioning as a priest unless he was a Levite, and the Levitical quality of the Jerusalemite "sons of Zadok" seems at that time not to have been called into question. Later still, when all priests were considered "sons of *Aaron," the postexilic Chronicler arranged things by presenting Zadok as an aide to an Aaronite commander in David's time (1 Chron. 12.27–29), and by giving Zadok himself an Aaronite genealogy (1 Chron. 24.1–6); the purpose of this is clearly that of giving the priests of Jerusalem Aaronite legitimacy, and its historicity is dubious. In any case, while any Levite, according to Deu-

teronomy, might in principle function as a priest if he were admitted to do so at the sole remaining sanctuary, in Ezekiel 40–48 only members of traditionally priestly families of Jerusalem (the "sons of Zadok") are admitted to the exclusively priestly service of the altar; all other Levites are relegated to a lower status with functions of Temple service that, except in 40.45, were not reckoned as priestly. The distinction between priests and subordinated Levites was firmly established in the postexilic restoration, but the fact that in *P the priests are not called sons of the clearly Jerusalemite Zadok but "sons of Aaron" may indicate that some members of Levitical families not originally of Jerusalem, but of other cities in the south, were admitted to priestly service together with the "sons of Zadok" after the exile, as they had perhaps been admitted before the exile, before or after Josiah's reform. All of the cities assigned to the sons of Aaron in the final form of the lists of Levitical cities (Josh. 21.9–19; 1 Chron. 6.54–60) are indeed in the south.

In the actual division of duties between priests and Levites prescribed by P, the priests did everything that entailed contact with the altars and with the offerings after they had contracted holiness (Lev. 1–7; 10.16–20; 16; 17). They were responsible for rites of purification, because of the sacrifices and sacrificial blood involved (Lev. 11–16; Num. 19). In the Persian, Hellenistic, and Roman periods each priest did his Temple service as a member of one of twenty-four divisions (1 Chron. 24.7–19), each division functioning only during a short period of the year (see Luke 1.5, 8). When leadership in matters of piety passed largely to the *Pharisees around the second century BCE, priests retained respected and in many cases high social status. Some ordinary priests, in order to make ends meet, engaged in secular occupations, and many lived outside Jerusalem.

The High Priest. Priesthood in Jerusalem in the days of the monarchy had been hierarchically structured, under a head, usually called simply "the priest" (1 Kings 4.2; 2 Kings 11.9–11; 12.8; 16.10–12; 22.12, 14; Isa. 8.2), or, if he needed to be distinguished from the "second priest," he might be called the "chief priest" (2 Kings 25.18). The head of the priesthood of Jerusalem had always held a high place in the kingdom's administrative circles, but after the exile the high priest quickly became the head of the Jewish nation, both civilly and religiously. The presence of a Jewish civil administrator appointed by the Persian imperial government at certain times (ca. 520 BCE, and during the last half of the fifth century) did little to alter the high priest's position as far as the nation itself was concerned. Although Hasmonean rulers of the second and first centuries BCE assumed the title "king," they retained the high priesthood and its title, which was more important within the Jewish community itself. From this time on, the high priests and those close to them, rather worldly in their interests, were of the aristocratic party of the *Sadducees. With *Herod the Great (37–4 BCE) ruling power in Judah passed completely out of priestly families, life tenure in high priesthood was abolished, and each appointment to the office of high priest was thereafter made by the Herodian ruler or, between 6–41 CE, by the Roman procurator. In the New Testament the plural "the high priests" refers to high priestly families as a group, or at times (e.g., Acts 9.14) to the *Sanhedrin or some other group possessing official jurisdiction under the leadership or presidency of the high priest.

In the distribution of ritual responsibilities codified in P, on the basis of degrees of holiness, only the high priest, whose degree of holiness as a person was supreme, could enter the holy of holies, the innermost part of the Temple building and the place whose degree of spatial holiness was the highest, for the rites to be performed there on the annual *Day of Atonement (Lev. 16.2–3, 15, 32–34; see Sir. 50.5–21; Heb. 9.6–7). AELRED CODY, O.S.B.

Prince of the Power of the Air. Found only in Ephesians 2.2 (NRSV: "ruler of . . ."), this phrase reflects the common belief in the hierarchical organization of *angels and *demons. In the first century CE, "prince" generally refers to a political power, whether human or spirit. "Air" represents the region between earth and heaven, which is the traditional sphere of demonic activity. In this case, "power" refers to the realm within which power is exercised. Hence, the prince of the power of the air is the spiritual ruler over this hierarchical realm of demons, to which those who are not in Christ are also subject. PATRICK A. TILLER

Printing and Publishing. *This entry consists of five articles:*

> The Printed Bible
> Production and Manufacturing
> Economics

> Royal Printers' Patent
> Red Letter Bible

The first article surveys the history of the printed Bible. The second and third articles describe the modern processes of production and manufacturing and their cost. The remaining articles deal with particular aspects of the history and composition of printed Bibles. The reproduction of the Bible prior to the invention of printing is treated in Books and Bookmaking in Antiquity *and* Manuscripts. *For further discussion of the history of printing and the design of printed Bibles, see* Chapter and Verse Divisions; Children's Bibles; Curious Bibles; Family Bible; Gutenberg, Johann Gensfleisch zum; Illustrated Bibles; Italics; Polyglot Bibles; *and* Scofield Reference Bibles.

The Printed Bible

The Significance of Printing. The process of printing from movable types was developed in Mainz in the 1450s by a partnership that included Johannes *Gutenberg. Among the first printed books were the forty-two-line Latin Bible (folio, ?Mainz, ?1455) called the "Gutenberg" or "Mazarin," and the thirty-six-line Bible that may have followed it (folio, ?Mainz or Bamberg, ?1457–1461). Both books are in "gothic" or blackletter types, in two columns, in a single size of type; they are simplifications of contemporary manuscript formats, in that they leave headings and initials for the rubricator to fill in by hand. Printing was at first seen as a means of speedy duplication, making relative cheapness possible. Later, it was understood that printing theoretically permitted a series of editions in which each copy could be identical and each edition could improve upon the previous one; but this ideal could not be fully realized until the nineteenth century. Early printers were under severe constraints: none had enough type to set up a whole Bible, so they followed a rhythm of setting and printing one "sheet" of four or eight pages, dispersing the type, and setting the next sheet. Correction took place as the sheets were printed, so that variant states of each sheet were mixed in infinite permutations through the whole edition. In keeping with the same rhythm, early edition sizes were small—normally between 250 and 1500 copies, rarely as large as 3000 or 4000. A new biblical text (e.g., Erasmus's or Luther's) was disseminated in a rapid succession of small reprints, many of which were unauthorized, since copyright protection was rudimentary; as a result, the text was quickly corrupted. While translators were alive, they could supervise corrected editions; after their death, safeguarding the text of its version of the scriptures gradually became a concern for each church. In such supervision the Vatican (from 1590) and the Lutheran church (from 1580) were pioneers.

The Fifteenth Century. As printing spread, the international trade for the leading houses was in the *Vulgate, the Bible of the European church in the language of the educated, therefore an obvious best-seller. By the end of the century, over a hundred editions had been printed, in Germany, Switzerland, Venice, and France. Unwieldy formats and the drastically simple design originally imposed by a single size of type and primitive skills gave way to smaller formats (e.g., Froben's first octavo of 1491) and a more complex international page-layout based on the traditional manuscript two-column format, using two or three sizes of type, with marginal notes and ample prefatory matter (the *plenus apparatus*). Books were entirely reproduced from type, so the rubricator was dispensed with. For a national sale, vernacular texts were also printed: between 1466 and 1522, fourteen High German and four Low German editions, some with illustrations; Italian Bibles in Mallermi's Version from 1471; the French *Bible Historiée* from the early 1470s (complete in 1478); a Catalan version in 1478; portions of a Dutch Bible in 1477; Czech Bibles in 1488 and 1499. These versions all used a national variant of black-letter, considered appropriate to the use of the vernacular; roman type was still associated with classical learning and Latin eloquence, but was also used for Italian Bibles. Printing did not reach England until 1476; since Wycliffe, English translations had been discouraged, so readers in England (essentially scholars) could use only the Vulgate, in imported copies. (*See also* Translations.)

Hebrew printing began in Italy before 1475; a Psalter was printed at Bologna in 1477, and a Pentateuch in 1482. The Soncino press in 1488 printed the whole Hebrew Bible with vowel points and accents. Greek-Latin psalters were printed in Milan in 1481 and by Aldus at Venice before 1498.

The Sixteenth Century. Renaissance scholarship and Reformation translation coincided with the great age of scholar-printers. The new movements meant that the Bible, always a steady seller, became available in its new versions in unprecedented numbers, since it was now a burning political-religious issue as well as an article of mass consumption. By the end of the century, literate laypeople of Reformed churches of Cal-

vinist tendency would expect to possess a personal copy of the scriptures in English, French, or Italian: usually a handy octavo in roman type, in double-column for compactness, with numbered verses for easy reference, with Calvinist marginal notes, "arguments" to each book, maps, diagrams, and indexes; usually with a metrical psalter bound in, and often a form of common prayer and a catechism. In territories of Lutheran tendency—the North German territories and North America—the old black-letter continued to be used for several centuries, and the Bibles were never so portable or so adapted to study.

At the beginning of the sixteenth century, the black-letter Vulgate was the staple of a popular trade dominated by Parisian printers. Scholarship and reform came mostly from elsewhere, but one Parisian (later Genevan) stands out as the greatest of all Bible printers, Robert Stephanus (Estienne). It was he who took the standard small Vulgate and first printed it in roman type (octavo, 1534); he took the device of verse numbering first used in a whole Bible by Pagnini in 1528, and applied it to the French text of Olivetan in 1553 and to the Vulgate in 1555 (*see* Chapter and Verse Divisions). His layout for small Bibles, in some ways traditional, was above all economical. Because he moved to Geneva in 1550 as the result of opposition from the Faculty of Paris, he transferred to Calvinist printing a repertory of skills and, basically, the fundamental design of most cheap Bibles in roman type up to recent times. Before he left Paris he had also printed in 1528, 1532, and 1540 a series of noble folio Vulgates that are among the most beautiful and original ever printed, as well as important contributions to the Latin text.

In Basel in 1516, Froben printed Erasmus's Greek-Latin New Testament using roman for the Latin and Greek types for the first complete Greek New Testament. Aldus printed a complete Greek Bible in Venice in 1518/19 using the Septuagint and Erasmus's New Testament. Printed before Erasmus but issued later, the Complutensian *Polyglot (Alcalá, 6 volumes, 1514–17, issued 1522) uses Hebrew, Greek, black-letter, and roman types in an exceedingly complicated layout—the greatest achievement of printing thus far. It was not matched until 1569–72, by Plantin's Royal Polyglot, which uses two sizes of italic and roman, three sizes of Hebrew, and Greek, all with decorated initials, in a demonstration of the repertory of Europe's (by then) leading printer.

Luther's September and December Testaments (Wittenberg, 1522) were in a distinctively large format, in single-column black-letter with a characteristic arrangement of elements, including illustrations, which were at once imitated by followers and opponents. Whereas perhaps eight to ten thousand copies of the old German text had been printed since 1466, and sold at high prices, Luther's official printers at Wittenberg produced a hundred large editions of his complete Bible between 1534 and 1620—perhaps two hundred thousand copies. Another three hundred editions came from other towns. Such an output required capital; a partnership of booksellers bought the "privilege" (the sole right to sell in a defined area) and administered it until 1626.

Similar problems later affected the English Bible. Tyndale's first English New Testaments (Worms, 1526; Antwerp, 1534) would have struck the contemporary observer as obviously Lutheran because of their typography. By the time Coverdale's Bible was printed (Cologne, 1535), Luther had completed his translation, and his printers, faced with a whole Bible, were forced into a two-column design that looked archaic; Coverdale's followed this pattern, as did "Matthew" in 1537, the first Bible printed in England. The subsequent "Great" and "Bishops' " Bibles were also large double-column folios in black-letter, reflecting the desire of the authorities to provide only a lectern-sized format, for reading in church. Meanwhile, in France, Stephanus's design in roman type was developed further, and in 1559 Barbier printed in Geneva a French octavo that gives the whole Genevan apparatus, to be repeated in countless editions—Latin, French, Spanish, Italian, and especially English. When Rowland Hall printed his English Geneva Bible (quarto, Geneva, 1560), it reproduced this pattern, and rivaled official English Bibles both with a more radical text and apparatus and also an intrinsically portable, more usable commodity: a layperson's Bible for private reading and devotion, visibly more modern than the competition. The handiness of the format contributed to the popularity of the version, which went on being printed until the 1640s. The King James Version of 1611 was originally a large folio in black-letter on the antique pattern; its commercial success was in doubt until smaller formats in roman type eliminated the disadvantage.

The Seventeenth and Eighteenth Centuries. After the great period of the sixteenth century, Bible printing dwindled into a national concern,

though for a while Antwerp remained what Geneva had been—an exporter of Bibles in several languages, including the English Geneva Version. The Protestant countries now supplied themselves with their authorized version in the vernacular; in Catholic countries, the vernacular was not encouraged, and the Vulgate had been overproduced in the previous era. There are few monuments of printing skill: the London Polyglot of Roycroft (folio, 1655–7, 6 volumes) adds Arabic and Samaritan to Hebrew, Greek, and their Latin versions, and is more impressive editorially than typographically. In England, the success of the 1611 version meant that money was to be made by supplying it, and the peculiar conditions governing Bible printing led to combinations and lawsuits (*see the article in this entry on* Royal Printers' Patent). European wars, especially in Germany, led to economic decline, which affected standards of materials and workmanship. The major economic constraint, that even if printers had had enough type to set a whole Bible, they could not afford to keep the text, once set, for more than one impression, was met head-on by the philanthropist Karl Hildebrand Baron von Canstein, who founded the Cansteinsche Bibelanstalt at Halle in 1710. This was a prototype Bible Society, designed to supply very cheap Bibles at no profit or even at a loss (*see* Bible Societies). The types of the New Testament of 1712 and the Bible of 1715 were kept standing, so that subsequent impressions could be corrected. The type was replaced when it wore out, usually after some thirty impressions. By 1803 the society had circulated three million copies of the scriptures, mostly in German. A Canstein Bible was the copy text for the Bible printed by Christoph Saur at Germantown, Pennsylvania, in 1743 in twelve hundred copies— the second American Bible (the first being John Eliot's Algonquin text, printed at Cambridge, Massachusetts, in 1663).

The rise of the missionary movement, especially of the British and Foreign Bible Society (1804) and its daughter societies, meant that for a century or more England became the major manufacturer of Bibles, for a market once again conceived as European-wide, and then worldwide. Effective and economical production on that scale was the consequence of technological development. (*See the article in this entry on* Economics.)

The Nineteenth Century. For four hundred years, printing had changed very little, remaining a handcraft, and permitting limited economies of scale. Mechanization produced a dramatic increase of production and so remarkable cheapness for the first time, just when missionary activity and the spread of literacy opened a vast market. The invention of stereotyping, first applied to the Bible at Cambridge in 1805–6 in time to supply the British and Foreign Bible Society (BFBS), meant that type need no longer be kept standing: the whole surface of the page of type was molded, and a cast made from the mold. Later, electrotyping gave the cast plate a very hard surface, so that hundreds of thousands of copies could be printed before there were signs of wear.

Presses began to be made of iron before 1800, giving greater pressure over a wider area and more precision of register. But the revolutionary printing machine of König and Bauer and the application of steam power meant that from 1814 it was possible to print over a thousand copies an hour. By 1849 major Bible printers had converted to steam-driven machinery. Paper had been machine-produced since 1815, and by the 1860s wood pulp and esparto-grass had replaced linen rag as the basis of paper. Composition of type was not mechanized until the end of the century and was not universal until this century; but since a single setting could now produce millions of copies, composition had become a minor factor. By the 1860s the Oxford University Press, the world's major manufacturer, regularly produced over a million Bibles a year, of which at least half went to the BFBS. Because of the scale of production, unit costs were minimal, and the strange monopoly situation in England was countered by the charitable activity of the BFBS and competition between the privileged presses.

Modern Times. The late nineteenth and early twentieth centuries saw the ultimate development of Gutenberg's process, by which individually cast metal types were set up together to make a page, inked, and impressed onto paper. Molding the surface of the type, wrapping the paper around a reciprocating cylinder, or even running it in a continuous sheet from a roll, were just some of the developments within the process that increased speed and cheapness; mechanical composition and binding changed no basic principle. Since 1945, printing has been revolutionized, abandoning "hot metal" in favor of computerized photocomposition, so that in place of metal type photographic images of letter shapes are used. Reproduction is effected by lithography, which uses chemical reactions to transfer an ink image from a flat surface. Printing takes place on large "web-fed" machines that print both sides of the paper at great speed, many pages at a time, so that whole "book blocks"—the printed and stacked pages—are delivered, folded, and ready for simple "casing" in an uninterrupted process. The data bank in the computer memory and associated programming facilities mean that a text of almost infinite length and complexity can be stored and printed out at will in any format that the program permits. In principle, stability of the text is guaranteed, or rather a correction facility promotes constant improvement. The Bible has ceased to be what it once was, a mountain that few printers could climb. It is now merely a long text with a number of special features. The rapid succession of popular modern versions (especially in the United States) is easily permitted, and the systematic development of a classic or authorized version is greatly facilitated. (*See the article in this entry on* Production and Manufacturing.)

Aesthetics. The great age of Bible printing was the sixteenth century. Froben, Stephanus, De Tournes, Oporinus, Froschauer, Plantin—the scholar-printers—produced typographical treatments of marked originality and beauty. Greatest of them all was Stephanus, whose Latin folio Bibles of 1532 and 1540 are the most original. Paradoxically, his introduction of verse-numbers and roman type fixed Bible design in the classic Genevan format for centuries. Many verses are short and would not fill a whole line in a single-column format. Over the course of an entire Bible, this would waste much space, so for economic reasons double-column became the rule. Bibles therefore looked "like Bibles" from the late sixteenth century to the middle of the twentieth. Distinguished printers like Baskerville (Cambridge, folio, 1763) could use their own type, refine the conventions, and insist on good paper, ink, and presswork, but could not break the classic mold. During the nineteenth century the *Family Bible—that mark of respectability—often incorporated engraved illustrations and encyclopedic notes; and the elaborate bindings broke away from the standard black cloth of the early publisher's bindings. The Arts and Crafts movement of the 1890s first went back behind the sixteenth century to revive the type-designs of early printing and broke away from "Bible" typefaces. The Doves Press Bible (1903) used a mixture of old scribal and early humanist conventions to produce an eclectic result—handsome but not readable. Bruce Roger's folio lectern Bible (Oxford, 1935) modifies the classic design by using Stephanus's headings, and is worthy to stand alongside its original.

New versions in the twentieth century proclaim their newness by modifying, even rejecting, the old typography. The Library Edition of the New English Bible achieved an elegant page in a modest format. But it is the lectern bible that offers the possibility of magnificence or monumentality, and since Rogers no printer has challenged the sixteenth century.

M. H. BLACK

Production and Manufacturing

The production and manufacturing of a Bible, though in outline the same as that of any other book, is affected by its length (as much as five times longer than an average novel) and by the extra use it must withstand. These factors have their effect throughout the entire process.

A Bible's production may be conveniently divided into five parts: setting the type; manufacturing the paper; printing the pages; manufacturing the binding materials; and binding the pages into a single volume.

Setting the Type. The text of a full Bible can contain over eight hundred thousand words (for the Hebrew Bible and the New Testament), and close to one million words (if the *Apocrypha are added). In addition are nearly twelve hundred chapter numbers and over thirty-one thousand verse numbers; in editions including the Apocrypha, there are almost two thousand chapters and close to forty thousand verses.

With punctuation included, any typesetting of a Bible translation requires millions of separate keyboard entries, all of which must be checked carefully. For this reason, among others, nearly all Bible translations are now prepared in electronic form. These electronic databases include not only the letters and chapter and verse numbers, but coding to specify capitalization and other special type elements. Once a database is in final form, a given version with a specific type design can be produced relatively quickly, by specifying all of the different elements and giving the instructions to the computer typesetting machine. The machine imposes the design elements on the database, sets the type to the specified width of the type column (breaking words at the ends of lines as necessary to fit), and then produces typeset pages. The typesetting for a full Bible can now be done in a few hours.

Once this typesetting is finished, a high-contrast printout of the pages is produced on glossy paper. This reproduction proof, or "repro," is photographed and the film is laid out in "forms" of 32-, 48-, 64-, or 128-page units. From these forms the printing plates are manufactured.

Paper Manufacture. Because Bibles are so long, the paper used for them must be thin; but because Bibles must be able to withstand repeated use, it must be strong as well. Modern paper manufacturing has developed a sheet that is very thin, highly opaque, and strong. The paper begins as a wet pulp mixture that is poured over a moving fine wire mesh, which allows the water to run through but retains the pulp. After most of the water has been shaken free, the matted pulp is fed into a series of heated rollers that dry out the remaining water and smooth the surface of the paper. The paper is produced in a continuous roll and the rolls are shipped to the printing plant.

Printing. Most Bibles today are printed in 64-page or 128-page forms, to produce "signatures" of 64 pages. A 64-page signature consists of a large sheet of paper that is printed on both sides and is then folded in half, then in half again, five times in all. This results in a packet of paper that, when fastened through the middle and trimmed around the edges, will become one 64-page section of the finished Bible.

Most full Bibles are longer than one thousand pages, and many of the Bibles with study apparatus included can be longer than two thousand pages. Each Bible, therefore, will contain from 16 to over 30 separate 64-page signatures. These are printed one at a time, usually on a web offset machine, which receives the paper in a continuous roll at one end, prints it on both sides simultaneously, cuts it into individual sheets, and folds it into signatures.

After all the signatures have been printed (for a large printing of a lengthy Bible this can take over a week), they are "gathered," that is, collated in order on a gathering machine. All the gathered signatures for one book are called the "book block." Once the signatures have been gathered, the manufacturing process differs, depending on the kind of binding that will ultimately be done.

Binding Materials. There are three basic types of bindings: paperback, hardcover, and leather. Paperback covers are made of thick, coated paper. Hardcovers are made of "boards" (cardboard), either two or three pieces, that are covered with cloth or textured paper. Leather covers are made of a single piece of leather or leatherlike material. The leather is either the whole skin of an animal (genuine leather), leather fibers held together with a polymer bonding (bonded leather), or plastic textured to look like leather (imitation leather). The leather cover is stamped or cut (clicked) out of a larger piece, the edges are trimmed to allow them to be turned over at the corners, and the title and other designs are stamped (and sometimes outlined with metallic foil) onto the finished cover. At this point the covers are ready to be joined to the finished book blocks in the binding process.

Binding. In paperback and some hardcover Bible bindings, the book block itself is held together with glue. This is done in one of two ways: either the inner edges of the pages are trimmed and glue is applied to that edge ("perfect binding"), or notches are cut in the inner edge and glue is applied to that edge and forced into the notches ("burst binding"). The outer pages of the book block are then glued to the case of a hardcover book; the spine of the paper cover is glued to the spine of the book block.

In other hardcover bindings, and in most leather bindings, the signatures are "sewn"; that is, the pages are held together by thread that is passed through the central fold, and the book block itself is attached to a backing. The book block is then "smashed" (compressed to drive out the air between the pages), "trimmed," and "round cornered." The edges are sanded and burnished, and metallic foil is bonded to the edges by heat. The back of the book block is then "rounded," or curved outward by the application of pressure to the page edges. The book block itself is then attached to the board or leather cover by gluing the endpapers to it. Leatherbound books may be bound in two ways: either "glued-off," as just described, or "lined-to-the-edge." Lined-to-the-edge bindings are different in two respects. The cover is lined by turning the outer edges of the cover material over the lining, with a flap of the lining left at the inner edge, front and back. The flap is glued between a second piece of lining and the white endsheet attached to the book block. Then a hollow tube is glued to the spine of the book block on one side and to the cover on the other, which provides strength and flexibility to the binding. This is the most sturdy kind of binding, since the book block is attached to the leather cover over its entire surface, including the spine.

Books may be reinforced in several ways. Hardcovers and leatherbound books have a piece of woven material called "crash" glued to the spine, with flaps on either edge that are glued between the endpaper and the board. Leatherbound books may have the first and last signatures "whipstitched": that is, the signature is stitched along the inner edge, to provide reinforcement at the hinges of the book, which receive the most wear and tear. This stitching is visible in the finished product. Some binders, instead of whipstitching, use eight pages of heavy white endsheet (instead of four pages). A piece of cambric may also be wrapped around the endpapers and first signature.

The entire process, from the beginning of composition to the delivery of finished leatherbound books, can take over a year.

DONALD KRAUS AND LYNN STANLEY

Economics

Bibles have always been an expensive commodity. As early as 1641 a London bookseller, Michael Sparke, wrote a tract entitled "Scintilla" in which he maintained that the high cost of Bibles was due to monopolies among Bible publishers (*see the article in this entry on* Royal Printers' Patent). Some of the factors contributing to the costs over three hundred years ago continue to operate today, making the world's most popular book also one of the most difficult and costly to produce.

Bible production presents the manufacturer with some of the most exacting and unusual challenges in the book industry. It also requires of the editorial staff rigorous quality standards that are time-consuming and costly. The following analysis of the specialized process of creating printed Bibles will indicate why the costs remain high.

The Editorial Process. *Translating.* The largest expense can be the work of translating the text. If it is to be highly accurate, this may take from several years to several decades and consume millions of dollars, though an individual occasionally may pursue this task as a hobby and a "labor of love." (Translators have frequently volunteered their time and expertise, for example with the KJV, RSV, and NRSV.)

Typesetting. Computers and databases for typesetting the Bible have certainly reduced the very great amount of time ordinarily needed for composing the Bible text. Typesetting the text in various styles of type and in different sizes of page now requires hours rather than months or years. What once was costly because of the labor involved is now costly in technical equipment.

Only a few typesetting companies in the world can meet the high-volume, high-quality demands of Bible composition at a reasonable price. Composing a basic text Bible is in itself a technically exacting task. Even more difficult is the process of composing a complex study-Bible. Combining footnotes, commentary, and a reference system with the text while keeping all pertinent information together on the same page requires either a labor-intensive manual process or a highly sophisticated computerized system. Either way, the expense is high.

Proofreading. Accuracy can be accomplished only through proofreading. The use of a master database for computer typesetting has made the tedious process of word-for-word proofreading optional, yet nothing has been found as reliable as the human eye and mind for guaranteeing an accurate text. Because of the quantity of information contained in a Bible and the accuracy demanded and expected in such a book, the proofreading process takes hundreds of hours and costs thousands of dollars.

Development of new materials. Basic text Bibles will always be popular, but the most popular and bestselling editions contain some or all of the following: reference system, concordance, commentary, maps, charts, articles, dictionary, and pictures. The cost of creating, writing, and editing new materials can range from a few hundred to hundreds of thousands of dollars.

The editorial cost of Bible creation is substantial. In general, however, it is a one-time, fixed-cost investment that may be spread over several printings, several years, or even several products. The editorial expense represents, however, only the first half of the Bible publishing sequence. Once the contents of the book have been determined, the actual books must then be created.

The Production Process. The following costs vary from year to year, and are affected by inflation, labor disputes, and quality requirements. The percentage that each step in the process adds to the total cost of a Bible varies in accord with the style of binding. Each step will be described separately.

Paper. Paper that is strong, thin, lightweight, and opaque is difficult and expensive to make. The high cost of such lightweight paper, coupled with the high page count of Bibles, makes paper one of the largest factors of cost in Bible manufacturing.

Printing. High-speed, high-quality web presses

Cover Style	Paper	Printing	Binding	Packaging
softcover	55%	20%	20%	5%
hardcover	50%	15%	30%	5%
bonded leather	20%	10%	60%	10%
top grain leather	15%	5%	75%	5%

designed to handle lightweight paper are available at only a few specialized printing houses. Printing on lightweight paper is an exacting science and art requiring skilled press operators and finely tuned machines. Such factors mean that the cost of printing a Bible exceeds by a large percentage the usual cost of printing an ordinary book.

Binding. Binding involves both the cover-material used for a Bible and the actual process of putting the book blocks and covers together. Some Bibles have inexpensive paper covers, others cloth or Kivar covers. The deluxe, expensive editions are bound in imitation leather or in real leather, drastically increasing the sales price. Although modern technology has to some extent replaced the skilled artisans who bound Bibles in the past, the cost of creating a beautifully bound leather Bible is still high.

Packaging. Almost every Bible must be wrapped, boxed, slipcased, banded, or jacketed. These packaging items must not only be designed and printed, but some, such as a box, also must be assembled. Each of these items adds to the cost of a Bible.

The chart above indicates how the percentages of cost shift according to the nature and style of the cover.   BRUCE E. RYSKAMP AND STAFF

Royal Printers' Patent

In England, the printing of the Authorized or King James Version of the Bible (KJV) and the Book of Common Prayer (BCP) of 1662 is the monopoly of the Royal Printer, by virtue of a patent first granted to Christopher Barker in 1577. Only the University Presses of Cambridge and Oxford are permitted by royal charter to override this monopoly; one other publisher, originally Scottish, is an accepted interloper.

Originally the office of Royal Printer, instituted in Henry VII's reign, brought with it only the right to print statutes, proclamations, injunctions, and Acts of Parliament. The first officially sanctioned Bibles in English had the normal "privilege," granted to whomever was the printer—the original form of copyright, which protected the printer of a single title from competition, usually in a specific territory, and for a specific term. Since the Great Bible and later the Bishops' Bible were "appointed to be read in the churches," and the Geneva Bible, though officially disapproved, was very popular (*see* Translations, *article on* English Language), printing them became an attractive commercial enterprise; and the right to print them in various formats was shared in the 1560s and 1570s by important members of the Stationers' Company, the guild that regulated the English book trade. But during the reign of Elizabeth I, trading monopolies in various commodities were granted or sold by the Crown to deserving or rich individuals, and certain whole categories of books became the exclusive monopolies of individual printers. In 1577, Christopher Barker became Royal Printer, and the terms of his patent gave him the right to print all Bibles and Testaments whatsoever, and the BCP. This patent, renewed, was left to heirs, so it fell to Barker's son to finance the collation, revision, and printing of the KJV in 1609–11.

So sweeping a monopoly was contested by other printers, deprived of the market for the best-selling printed book. The weakness of the royal printers' position was that the capital required to exercise their right was very large; so they were often forced to take partners, or even to lease to the company itself, which ran a co-operative part-charitable venture called the English Stock, later the Bible Stock, which among other titles printed Bibles, by agreement (usually) with the monopolists.

By its royal charter of 1534, the University of Cambridge had acquired the perpetual right to appoint three printers, who could print "all manner of books." The right preexisted Barker's patent, and was taken to cover Bibles, so Cambridge printed a Geneva Bible in 1591 and its first KJV in 1629. Oxford acquired a similar charter in 1636, and in the 1670s printed Bibles. During a large part of the seventeenth century, there were disputes and lawsuits between Royal Printers and Stationers about the patent but the two contestants tended to combine against the interloping universities. All the rights of all the parties were more than once pronounced valid by the courts, and accommodations followed; by the end of the century, the two universities were at times either compensated for not exercising their right, or the right was leased and farmed by the richer London printers who had control

of the market. The supreme monopolist of the time was John Baskett, who bought a share of the royal printer's patent in 1710, leased the Oxford Privilege in 1711, and bought a third-share of the similar Scottish royal printer's patent. The Baskett family remained printers until 1769, when they were bought out by Eyre and Strahan, the forebears of the later patent-holders Eyre and Spottiswoode. After the mid eighteenth century, the position stabilized: the Stationers' Company ceased to trade; the monopoly was accepted, as was the overriding right of the universities. In Scotland, the royal printer's patent lapsed in 1839, and the right to print Bibles was subject to license by a supervising body. Scottish Bibles were not allowed south of the border until 1858, when William Collins set up an office in London and sold his product. Until then, the only permitted infringements of the monopoly were commentaries on the Bible that included the text, and the *polyglots of Bagster. In particular, the British and Foreign *Bible Society had had to buy its supplies from the privileged presses—though it also offered serious competition by selling at subsidized prices.

The monopoly had always been resented. It was investigated by a Parliamentary Committee in 1859–60, when the expected criticisms of principle were made. But the system was found to work well; supplies were ample, and Collins's intervention had forced prices down further. The patent was renewed in 1860, and is not now subject to review. The terms of the original patent were tested in 1961 when the New English Bible (NEB) was published by Cambridge and Oxford, who had previously financed and published the Revised Version without the opposition or participation of the royal printer. The Queen's Printer now attempted to include the NEB within the scope of the old monopoly by printing an unauthorized Gospel of John. The universities brought action for breach of copyright, and won their case. The old monopoly is now limited to the KJV and the BCP (1662) and is sometimes defended on the twin grounds that the first is perpetual Crown Copyright and the second, its use in England being required by Act of Parliament, is indeed an Act of State. The two university presses showed that the right could be operated for the public good, since for centuries Bible printing helped to provide them, as charities, with funds to finance learned publications: moreover they had, since the eighteenth century, in their own recensions of the KJV text provided standard editions of the national classic, the Bible of 1611. Stability of the text was not required or secured by the monopoly itself. With the demise of Eyre and Spottiswoode in 1990, the patent passed to Cambridge.

See also article on The Printed Bible *in this entry.* M. H. BLACK

Red Letter Bible

A Bible or New Testament with all the words spoken by *Jesus printed in red. This practice has been traced to the journalist Louis Klopsch, publisher of *The Christian Herald* in the late nineteenth century. Klopsch was inspired by the words of Jesus in Luke 22.20: "This cup that is poured out for you is the new testament in my blood." Luxurious Bible manuscripts of the Middle Ages would use specially colored inks to mark chapter headings or prominent words; Codex 16 used crimson, blue, and black inks for the words of different characters. Some Red Letter Bibles print only the words of the earthly Jesus in red, leaving the words of Jesus as heard in visions (as in the books of Acts and Revelation) in black ink. Others use red ink for those sayings of God or angels in the Old Testament that have been interpreted by Christian theology as inspired by the preexistent Christ. A modern effort to determine the authentic words of Jesus on historical-critical grounds (the Jesus Seminar) has led to the production of new Red Letter Gospel editions, beginning with Robert W. Funk, *The Gospel of Mark: Red Letter Edition* (1991).

PHILIP SELLEW

Promised Land. When God called *Abraham, one of the things promised was land (Gen. 12.1–2). Though the passage perhaps dates from the tenth century BCE, the promised territory specified in Genesis 15.18 is the land of *Canaan from the *river of Egypt to the *Euphrates River (cf. Deut. 11.24); other boundaries given for the land are more modest. Genesis also records that the promise was subsequently reaffirmed to Abraham's descendants: *Isaac (Gen. 26.3), *Jacob (Gen. 28.4, 13; 35.11–12), *Joseph (Gen. 48.4), and Jacob's other sons (Gen. 50.24).

In biblical narrative, the promise was also renewed in the time of *Moses (Exod. 6.5–8). According to Leviticus 25.23, however, the land belonged to God; the Israelites were merely tenants. Deuteronomy represents the land as a gift (Deut. 5.31; 9.6; 11.17; 6.10–11) and describes it in somewhat hyperbolic terms (8.7–9), but

continuance on the land was conditional upon obedience to the law. Both Leviticus and Deuteronomy offer the threat of *exile and scattering among the nations if the Israelites break the law (Lev. 26.21, 32–33; Deut. 28.63–64) as well as the hope of restoration to the land should they subsequently repent (Lev. 26.42; Deut. 30.1–16). The *Pentateuch thus contains different attitudes toward the land, reflecting the historical contexts of its authors, attitudes modeled in part at least on such ancient Near Eastern practices as royal grants of land as rewards to individual subjects.

*Joshua began the *conquest of Canaan. While some passages indicate complete victory in his time (Josh. 10.40; 11.16–17; 21.43–44) followed by "rest from war" (Josh. 11.23), others make it clear that it was not that quick. When Joshua was an old man, there was still much territory left to seize (Josh. 13.1; Judg. 1.21–36). It was actually *David who completed the conquest in the tenth century BCE (2 Sam. 8).

In about 921 BCE, the nation of Israel split into two kingdoms: *Israel in the north and *Judah in the south. Because of sin, prophets arose to warn the people of judgment. Amos addressed the northerners, threatening them with exile (Amos 5.27; 7.17). Israel, the northern kingdom, fell to *Assyria in 721 BCE. Many were taken away to other parts of the Assyrian empire. Jeremiah, in the last days of the kingdom of Judah, predicted exile (Jer. 25.11–12). Judah fell to Babylon in 587 BCE, with the result that many of the leaders were exiled to *Babylon. The book of Kings was written in the sixth century BCE to explain the two catastrophes: both kingdoms fell because of idolatry (2 Kgs. 17; 2 Kgs. 21.1–16). Although the prophets pronounced the judgment of land loss, they also looked beyond the disasters to future times of healing and restoration (Amos 9.14–15; Jer. 16.15 = 23.7–8; 24.6; 29.10; 32.41; Ezek. 20.41–42; 34.11–17; 36.24; 37.12–14, 21–22).

During the exile, the Jews longed to return to their land but they learned to maintain their identity without it. While they could not offer animal *sacrifice, since that could only be done in *Jerusalem, they could preserve their distinctive religion through *prayer, *Sabbath keeping, *circumcision, and observing dietary laws.

In 538 BCE, King *Cyrus of Persia, having conquered Babylon a year earlier, allowed the Jews to return and rebuild their *Temple in Jerusalem (Ezra 1.1–4; 6.3–5), yet not all the Jews returned. Some became established in Babylon, giving rise to a community that thrived there for centuries. Those in the *Dispersion contributed money to support the Temple. Land and sacrifice, now restored, were elevated in importance again, but Israelite religion was not exclusively tied to the land.

In 70 CE, the Temple was destroyed again, this time by the Romans, and the Jews were once more dispersed abroad. They survived this tragedy by maintaining their traditions wherever they went. It would be wrong to say that Judaism is indifferent to the land, however, for the devout Jew prays daily that Jerusalem will be rebuilt speedily, and part of the *Passover celebration includes the hope that next year the feast will be eaten in Jerusalem.

In the late nineteenth century, Zionism developed. Largely a secular movement, its goal of the establishment of a homeland for the Jewish people was not primarily to fulfill biblical prophecy but to have a country where Jews could live in security, safe from persecution.

In the New Testament, there is little emphasis on geography, but the imagery of the promised land is symbolically used in the letter to the Hebrews. Abraham is a paradigm for Christians: just as he left his home country by faith, seeking a new one, so Christians should seek the heavenly country or city that God is preparing for them (Heb. 11.8–16).

Hebrews also alludes to the *wilderness wandering and the conquest. A whole generation was denied entrance into the land because of rebellion, disobedience, and unbelief (Heb. 3.7–19). The admonition, then, is not to be apostate like them. Hebrews also suggests that Joshua did not really give the people rest (Heb. 4.8–9); rather, God offers rest to those who are obedient and faithful. The author then encourages his audience to enter that rest, which refers not to conquering land and enjoying the ensuing peace, as it did earlier (Josh. 11.23), but rather to trusting in God's works and ceasing from one's own (Heb. 4.9–10).

Nationhood and land are not always spiritualized in the New Testament. Though Paul viewed those Jews who did not embrace Jesus as *Messiah to be outside of God's favor (Rom. 9–11), he looked forward to a day when the Jewish people as a nation would turn back to God and be forgiven (Rom. 11.26). Jesus also affirmed that the *meek would inherit the earth (Matt. 5.5; Ps. 37.11). The book of Revelation tells of a thousand-year period when martyrs of the church would rule with Jesus (Rev. 20). It also predicts the creation of a new heaven and a new earth (Rev. 21.1–4).

Despite this spiritualization of the concept of the promised land, Christians too have on occasion seen themselves as "heirs according to the promise" (Gal. 3.29) in a territorial sense. Both the Boers of South Africa and the Puritan colonizers of New England saw themselves as a new Israel, led by God to a new Canaan, a "providence plantation."

See also Inheritance.

WILLIAM B. NELSON, JR.

Prophets. *This entry consists of two articles, the first on prophets in* Ancient Israel, *and the second on the phenomenon of prophecy in* Early Christianity. *For further discussion of this topic, see* Social Sciences and the Bible, *and for discussion of individual prophets, see the entries under their names or the books that bear their names.*

Ancient Israel

No comprehensive definition of an Israelite prophet is possible. The persons conventionally included in this category appear to have manifested great diversity of character and function. They are referred to by a number of terms that in some texts are used interchangeably, and some of these shed some light on their functions: "seer" implies a recipient of visions, and "man of God" suggests some kind of close relationship with the deity. But the most common designation; *nābî'*, usually translated as "prophet," is of uncertain derivation. The prophets of the eighth century BCE seem to have avoided terminological classification altogether.

In general, it may be said that prophets were men or women believed to be recipients through audition, vision, or dream of divine messages that they passed on to others by means of speech or symbolic action. The persons they addressed might be individuals, particular groups of Israelites, the whole nation, or foreign nations. The prophets, then, were divine messengers, as is indicated by the formula, "Thus Yahweh has said," which precedes many of their utterances. Frequently, these messages were unsolicited and were delivered under divine compulsion, though on some occasions a prophet was consulted by persons who inquired whether there was a message from God for them. Several of the prophetic books contain "call narratives" in which the prophets express their conviction that they have received a particular summons to prophesy

(Isa. 6; Jer. 1; Ezek. 1.1–3.15; Amos 7.15). Several prophets, notably Jeremiah, recorded their reluctance and even strong resistance to this divine constraint. These call narratives, however, belong to a literary genre (see also Exod. 3.1–12; Judg. 6.11–17), and may not be simply (auto)biographical.

Prophetic activity was not confined to Israel, nor were all prophets prophets of Yahweh. Although the term nābî' is not found elsewhere in the ancient Near East, activities comparable with those of the Israelite prophets are attested among other Semitic peoples, notably at *Mari in the eighteenth century BCE. In Israel an early reference to prophets (1 Sam. 10.5–11) is found in a narrative that associates their activity with the founding of the Israelite kingdom by *Saul. For the next four centuries, both in northern Israel and in Judah, prophets are mainly found in close connection with the kings and with political events generally.

It is not possible to give a systematic account of this early prophecy—or indeed of much of the prophetic activity in the ensuing period—because the information available is so diverse. One can only note certain rather disparate scraps of information. There was the solitary prophet, liable to appear suddenly to confront the king (1 Kings 18; 21.17–24), in contrast with the groups known as the "sons of the prophets" (NRSV: "company of prophets") who lived in isolated communities under a leader (2 Kings 4.38–41; 6.1–7; see also Amos 7.14); these are in turn to be differentiated from groups of prophets maintained at the royal court (1 Kings 22). Other individuals appear to have been local seers or prophets (the explanatory note in 1 Sam. 9.9 does not throw much light on the distinction) who might be consulted in cases of lost property but might also serve in some local cultic capacity (1 Sam. 9). While in some cases prophetic activity took the form of apparently insane behavior attributed to seizure by the spirit of God (1 Sam. 10.10–13) and prophets could simply be dismissed as "mad" (2 Kings 9.11), others acted as military advisers to the king (1 Kings 22; 2 Kings 3) or confronted kings with their moral or religious misdeeds (1 Kings 18; 21), condemning them in God's name; in some cases, they were even capable of fomenting a coup d'état, deposing one king and choosing and consecrating another (2 Kings 9). As miracle workers, they might make an ax head float (2 Kings 6.6) but might also call down fire from heaven (1 Kings 18.36–39; 2 Kings 1.10) or raise a dead person to life (1 Kings 17.17–24; 2 Kings 4).

Such examples of contrasting behavior and activity could be multiplied from the evidence of the books of *Samuel and *Kings and, to some extent, from the prophetic books. These stories, which represent popular views of prophets, are to a large extent legendary in character; but they show clearly that Israelite prophecy was a many-sided phenomenon. Apart from some accounts of rather trivial miracle-working, however, they have one common characteristic: they represent the true prophet as the agent and defender of Yahweh in opposition both to religious apostasy and syncretism and to the authority of kings when these failed to uphold the cause of Yahweh or flouted his moral demands. This is especially true of the ninth-century prophets *Elijah and *Elisha.

The prophets of the eighth and seventh centuries BCE stood for the same principles as their predecessors. For this period, however, our sources of information are mainly of a different kind. The prophetic books (Isaiah, Jeremiah, Ezekiel, and the books of the twelve "minor" prophets) contain far fewer stories about prophets, and consist mainly of what purport to be records of words spoken by the prophets whose names they bear. The *word of God received and transmitted by the prophet now assumes primary importance. It is, however, no easy matter to identify these words and to distinguish them from other material. In their present form, the prophetic books have all become repositories of other and later material, both prophetic and nonprophetic. This additional matter has its own importance and should not be regarded as in any way inferior to the words of the original prophet; but its presence makes it difficult to form a correct notion of his message.

The extent to which the prophecy of the eighth century BCE marks a decisive change in the character of Israelite prophecy is disputed. Two features, however, call for notice: first, the eighth- and seventh-century prophets addressed themselves not only to kings and other individuals and particular groups but also to the whole people; second, they were, as far as our information enables us to judge, the first to prophesy the destruction of the entire nation as a punishment for its sins. This prophecy of national disaster, sometimes presented as avoidable through *repentance but sometimes not, was the main feature of the message of the prophets of the eighth century BCE (Hosea, Amos, Isaiah, and Micah) and also of Jeremiah and Ezekiel in the late seventh/early sixth. The latter, however, who survived the destruction of Judah and Jerusalem in 587/586 BCE, also offered hope for the future beyond the disaster. The prophets of the *exile and the postexilic period were chiefly concerned with the hope of a restoration of the nation's fortunes and with current problems of the post-exilic community.

The prophets were not primarily theologians; but some of them, in their attempt to present their message coherently and persuasively, achieved profound insights into divine and human natures and the relationship between God and his people Israel. (The theological teachings of the individual prophets are described in more detail in the articles on each prophet.)

The prophets whose words have been pre-served were only a small and probably unrepre-sentative minority. Other prophets are fre-quently mentioned by them, usually unfavorably. It is clear that, especially in the time of Jeremiah, there were two groups of prophets opposed to one another. Jeremiah regarded his opponents, who offered the people a comforting message of national security based on the belief that God would protect them irrespective of their conduct, as false or lying prophets (Jer. 14.13–16). Pas-sages such as this reflect the problem faced by the people when two groups of prophets, each claiming to speak in Yahweh's name, proclaimed diametrically opposite messages. Attempts were made to establish criteria for identifying the gen-uine prophet (e.g., Jer. 28.8–9; Deut. 13.1–5; 18.15–22), but these were unable to resolve the problem.

Prophets who delivered unpalatable messages not only encountered difficulties in gaining ac-ceptance as authentic messengers of Yahweh but were liable to suffer humiliation (Amos 7.10–13) and even threats to their lives (Jer. 26; 36–40). Yet insofar as they were believed to have an intimate relationship with God they were feared. Even kings were unable to ignore them. On the other hand, it is unlikely that prophets generally enjoyed an official status in either the religious or the political establishment. Recently, attempts have been made to define their role in sociolog-ical terms (see Social Sciences and the Bible). Whatever results may eventually emerge from this kind of study, it can be safely asserted that the prophets about whom we have any detailed information came from a wide variety of social backgrounds, and functioned in a variety of ways.   R. N. WHYBRAY

Early Christianity

Prophecy in the New Testament is the recep-tion and subsequent communication of sponta-neous and divinely given revelations; normally, those who were designated "prophets" in early Christianity were specialists in mediating divine *revelation rather than those who prophesied occasionally or only once. The exhortation to desire earnestly to prophesy (1 Cor. 14.1) may be best explained as a call to all those who re-garded themselves as gifted with inspired utter-ance (the "spiritual" ones of 14.37) to aspire to prophesy rather than to speak in tongues: none are excluded a priori from the gift, but God will not in fact distribute any one gift to all. From what we can deduce about them from *Acts and the Letters, as well as from the book of *Reve-lation (a document that self-consciously presents itself as Christian prophecy in written form), prophets might conduct their ministry in one congregation or throughout a region (Acts 15.22, 32), singly or more often in groups (Acts 11.27; 13.1; 21.10–11 cf. Rev. 22.9). In the lists of ministries (1 Cor. 12.28–30; Eph. 4.11) they are mentioned next after *apostles; they are associ-ated with teachers in the church at Antioch (Acts 13.1).

In the context of the church meeting (1 Cor. 14.26–33) the ministry of the prophet is spoken of as "revelation," and such an utterance is as-sociated with the Spirit of God (cf. 1 Thess. 5.19). This prophetic speech is not the same as speak-ing in tongues (see 1 Cor. 14.22–25, 27–29), nor is it the interpretation of tongues (see Glosso-lalia); it is some perception of the truth of God intelligibly communicated to the congregation. In Paul's view, it is an abuse of prophecy to pretend to an ecstatic frenzy so that prophets become, so to speak, out of hand; he insists that "the spirits of prophets are subject to the proph-ets" (1 Cor. 14.32), that is to say, each is in full possession of his or her faculties and is able to restrain the impulse to speak if the interests of order so require.

Most important, prophets were not to be given undiscerning credence. The utterances required "testing" or "evaluation" by other prophets (1 Cor. 14.29); only then were they to be received as the word of the Lord. This testing is not only to distinguish the Spirit's word from the speak-er's natural impulses, but also to identify and exclude false prophecy. The most important cri-terion put forward by Paul for the evaluation of prophetic speech (or indeed for viewpoints ex-pressed through a variety of oral and written forms of communication) was the content of the message, which should agree with the generally accepted beliefs and customs of the Christian community (Rom. 12.6; 1 Cor. 12.3).

The gift of prophecy gradually fell into disuse and, in spite of occasional revivals, into a measure of disrepute because of the continuing presence of false prophecy and the difficulties or uncertainties involved in discerning it. Other factors contributing to the decline of prophecy were the increasing authority of an official ministry in a church becoming more institutionalized, and the tendency to rely more on rational and didactic forms of spiritual utterance; the latter led to the place of prophets being taken by teachers, catechists, scholars, and theologians, whose authority depended not on any revelation directly received but on the exposition of an existing authoritative tradition, especially the Bible.   DAVID HILL

Proselyte. An essentially religious term used to describe a convert from one form of belief to another. It is more appropriate to use the term only for the period when the Jews were a religious community rather than an independent nation-state, that is to say, from the postexilic period onward. The *Septuagint, the Greek translation of the Hebrew Bible, rendered the Hebrew word gēr, which means "sojourner" or "resident alien" (see Alien), as prosēlytos; in later Hebrew gēr came to have a religious rather than an ethnic meaning.

The word "proselyte" is found four times in the New Testament (Matt. 23.15; Acts 2.10; 6.5; 13.43; the first and last references are translated "convert" in the NRSV). The reference in Matthew makes it clear that some Jewish groups regarded missionary work as an important part of their practice, and the presence of proselytes at the Feast of Weeks (*Pentecost) in Jerusalem (Acts 2) implies the success of such efforts. One of the basic requirements laid upon potential converts will have been *circumcision, and some groups in the Hellenistic world condemned this as a form of mutilation incompatible with the ideal of bodily perfection. Nevertheless, the rite was almost certainly required as a means of entry to the covenant community. From roughly the first century CE (and possibly earlier) a form of water ceremony ("proselyte baptism") was also required. Our earliest descriptions of this come from rabbinic sources, though it is possible that

*John the Baptist's practice was a related rite (see Baptism).

The references in Matthew and Acts support the likely hypothesis that the great majority of proselytes will have come from the *Diaspora, attracted by the lifestyle of Jewish communities in different parts of the Greek and later Roman world. *Synagogues, which first developed in the diaspora, will have been the natural context for the beginning of an acquaintance with Judaism.

It has often been argued that alongside proselytes there existed a further group of sympathetic gentiles known as "God-fearers," who were attracted to Judaism but reluctant to be circumcised. It would probably be wrong, however, to see in this a technical term; "those who feared God" is simply a way of describing those pious people who were attracted to Judaism and subsequently to Christianity (see Acts 10.2, 22; 13.16, 26).

What kind of reception might proselytes expect among those already Jews? Rabbinic texts show that they were often regarded with suspicion, as is commonly the case with converts in many religions. It is in this light that varying traditions in the Hebrew Bible relating to converts can best be understood: the story of *Ruth, whatever its original point, clearly illustrates an open attitude to those who came to Judaism in adult life, whereas the concerns in the books of *Ezra and *Nehemiah for the dangers of mixed marriage (at least insofar as it involved non-Jewish women) show a more restrictive attitude.

See also Conversion.   RICHARD COGGINS

Prostitution. The granting of sexual access for payment is disparaged in the Bible and is associated linguistically with a variety of forms of sexual immorality. A metaphorical use of language related to prostitution dominates much of the Hebrew Bible, following *Hosea, who characterizes Israel's relations with foreign gods and nations as the actions of a promiscuous bride or a prostitute seeking lovers (Hos. 1.2; 2.2–13; cf. Lev. 20.5; Judg. 2.17; Jer. 3.1). This polemical usage often makes it impossible to determine the exact nature of the practices designated as "harlotry."

In its primary form, prostitution is an institution of patriarchal society that permits males to enjoy sexual relations outside of marriage while preserving exclusive right of access to their spouses. Hence the prostitute is normally female, and male (homosexual) prostitution is weakly, and differently, attested. While the prostitute was tolerated, she always bore a degree of opprobrium (Gen. 34.31; 1 Kings 22.38), even when praised for noble character or action (*Rahab, Josh. 2.1–21; cf. 1 Kings 3.16–26). Men are warned against the wiles and waste of prostitutes (Prov. 29.3; 7.10; 23.27; cf. Luke 15.30), and wages from prostitution are prohibited as payment of vows (Deut. 23.18). Priests were forbidden to marry a prostitute (Lev. 21.7) or to force a daughter into prostitution (Lev. 19.29).

The Hebrew term for prostitute, *zônâ* (a feminine participle with no masculine counterpart), is derived from the verb *zānâ*, which describes promiscuous sexual activity in general and more specifically *fornication by an unmarried female, a crime punishable by death (Gen. 38.24; Deut. 22.20–21; Lev. 21.9). What is tolerated for prostitutes, as a class set apart, is strictly proscribed for other *women.

It is widely assumed that some form of "sacred" or "cultic prostitution" characterized Canaanite religion; however, the language of prostitution is never used to describe cultic offices or activity in ancient Near Eastern texts outside the Bible's polemical usage. The Hebrew term sometimes rendered "sacred prostitute," *qĕdēšâ* (f.)/*qādēš* (m.), simply means "consecrated (person)" (cf. *qādôš*, "holy"). Association with prostitution, or sexual activity of any sort, is inferred from biblical contexts and has no parallel in extrabiblical texts.

New Testament texts group prostitutes (*pornē*, f.) with tax collectors as representing the lowest class in moral terms (Matt. 21.31–32; cf. Luke 15.30). The masculine form of the noun (*pornos*, meaning male prostitute in classical Greek) is used in the New Testament only in the general sense of "fornicator" or "one who practices sexual immorality" (Eph. 5.5; 1 Tim. 1.10; Rev. 21.8) and may be extended to describe immorality in general (Heb. 12.16). A similar sense is conveyed by the verb *porneuō* and the abstract noun *porneia* ("fornication"), which is frequent in *ethical lists (Mark 7.21; Gal. 5.19; cf. 1 Cor. 5.9, 11) and is often associated with gentile cults and culture. The book of *Revelation continues the figurative usage of the Hebrew Bible in characterizing *Babylon as the "great whore" and its offenses as "fornication" (Rev. 17.1; 18.3; cf. Isa. 1.21).

See also Sex.   PHYLLIS A. BIRD

Proverbs, The Book of. A teaching compendium for postexilic Judaism, Proverbs is traditionally placed among the "Writings" and considered part of the *wisdom literature. It consists in part of short sayings expressing in pithy form insights into human affairs, especially of a social and religious nature. The Hebrew word (*māšāl*) translated "proverb" can mean comparison, and many of the proverbs contain a metaphor or simile. The dates of the material within the book range over a wide period of time; while the final edition was made after the exile, probably in the fifth century BCE, much of the actual contents is earlier and some of it is even premonarchic. The oral origins are often obvious.

Most scholars recognize five separate collections in the book. The first collection (1.1–9.18), labeled "Proverbs of Solomon," is really instruction genre, a series of essays on the nature of wisdom, the meaning of life, and the path to success. *Solomon's legendary wisdom (see 1 Kings 3; 4.29–34) resulted in a number of later works being attributed to his authorship; but there is little reason to doubt the essential accuracy of the tradition (see 1 Kings 4.32–33) that he did compose proverbs, just as his father *David composed songs. This collection, however, is probably the work of the final editors who placed it at the beginning of their compilation as a statement of intent, and so it probably dates to the fifth century BCE. It presents the ideal of a fully integrated human being, one who is liberally educated and morally stable. Perhaps written for a generation that had become estranged from its cultural and religious roots, it sets out to inculcate human and religious values. To do so it presents wisdom under two guises: parental instruction (aimed at reason) and a personalized *Wisdom who appeals directly in her own name (aimed at the emotions). The key to a fruitful integration of the secular and the religious is "fear of the Lord," a sense of the divine that permeates every aspect of life and impregnates the secular. These nine chapters, more theological than the rest, present a highly sophisticated worldview with a high regard for human capacity to achieve fulfillment.

The second collection (10.1–22.16), also attributed to Solomon, is simpler in style than the first and is probably preexilic. It is a gathering of heterogeneous, semi-independent proverbs, maxims, and precepts—really a literature of the schools dealing mainly with moral life and virtue. It suggests how best to live in the world. More secular than chaps. 1–9, it inculcates control of the tongue, social awareness, and respect for the mystery of existence. In the efforts to master life one must recognize that there are limits not just of volition but to human knowledge, which is finite (16.1, 9; 19.14, 21; 21.30). Justice seems to be inspired by a concern for equity rather than religion.

The third collection (22.17–24.22), entitled "the words of the wise," is a compilation of thirty instructions probably modeled on an Egyptian source, the *Instruction of Amen-em-ope*, probably to be dated ca. 1000 BCE. Although it has the appearance of a textbook, it warms to an intimate, parental style and may date to the same period as the editorial project itself. After a brief introduction (22.17–21) comes a series of warnings, counsels, and appeals to the reader's moral sense. Integration of the secular and religious, which was evident in chaps. 1–9, appears again. Good graces, culture, and social bearing are not alien to holiness. "Fear of the Lord" is part of education (23.12–18).

The fourth collection (24.23–34), much shorter than, although similar to, the third, bears the title "these also are sayings of the wise"; it represents an addition to the previous collection and may be by the same editor. Certainly the tone remains consistent. Social awareness is its topic. It presents the practical aspects of justice in a legal maxim (24.23b–29) and appends a portrait of one who neglects his social duties (24.30–34).

The fifth collection (25.1–29.27) has a clear attribution: "proverbs of Solomon that the officials of King Hezekiah of Judah copied," which places the collection, if not the composition, of these proverbs in the late eighth or early seventh century BCE. It represents what might be called an editorial program, sophisticated and quite unified. Again there is a concern to integrate secular and religious wisdom. It deals with the structure of society—government administration (25.1–7a), social responsibility (27.11–14), and human conduct (28.1–22). To a greater extent than usual God is invoked as arbiter of morality, and the traditional concept of retribution loses its overtly dogmatic tone: the human act itself has its own repercussions.

Four appendices (30.1–31.31) close the book. Although containing older elements, these appear to be a later redactional effort, perhaps intended as a general conclusion. The first (30.1–9) is an essay on skepticism; the second (30.10–33) deals with the mysterious dimensions of life, the inexplicable and therefore the fascinating; the third (31.1–9) is a "manual for rulers" personalized by being put in the form of a *queen mother's teaching—moral rather than administrative; and the final appendix (31.10–31) is a carefully drawn portrait of the ideal woman, which leaves us with the question, "Have we arrived at the practical expression of 'Lady Wisdom' presented in chaps. 1–9?"

The book is an ambitious undertaking, offering the reader "wisdom" and opening up to the willing student a world of learning. It shows how to cope with life by organizing the range of human experience so as to evolve practical rules of comportment and to develop balanced judgment, as the editorial introduction makes clear (1.2–7). On this basis of personal and inherited experience and by means of different kinds of literature—sentence, instruction, maxim, proverb—it shows "what really works" and how to achieve success in the business of living a full life. Thus, it is didactic literature in the truest sense of the term. It represents a sage, parent, or teacher, who, out of her or his treasury of experience and knowledge of the mysteries of life, speaks to a pupil in the name of natural or social values and good sense. A frequent formula is "Hear, my child" (1.8; 2.1; 3.1, 11, 21; 4.1, 10; etc.), an indication that the teaching is seldom directly imperative; the hearer reacts on the basis of personal judgment and a personal assessment of the situation. The aim is to urge the individual to think realistically about life; it does so by making the learner personally face up to the problems that besiege humanity: ignorance and poverty (9.7–12; 22.7–8), right and wrong (16.10–15), the need to adapt oneself to life in society (22.1–4), and finally, although somewhat indirectly, the need to accommodate to a mysterious divinity (16.1–19). Sometimes, indeed, contradictory proverbs are placed side by side (26.4–5) so as to provoke thought: which applies in my situation? The different kinds of literature found here share common aims: the desire to impart knowledge (1.2–7) and to form character (1.8–19), to encourage a learner to achieve maturity. Since the pupil's experience may often differ from that of the parent or teacher, it is essential to learn how to think for oneself to survive. This is suggestive, for the verbal root from which the word "proverb" derives (*māšal*) has the significance of "dominating something." These proverbs are frequently artistic, and humor is not absent (25.11; 23.29–35), but the ultimate function of wisdom, and the dominant intention of the editors, was the mastery of the human environment by the acquisition of a personal standard of values and an effective "know-how," both of which could be derived from an appreciation of cosmic order and design.

What at first sight appears to be a collection of heterogeneous instructions, proverbs, and wise sayings in fact enjoys a certain coherence, imposed, it is true, by editorial intention, to which is due the powerful educational impact the book made on later generations. As it now stands, it represents a many-faceted ideal of religious humanism, in which many disparate kinds of teaching contribute to one purpose—the formation of a whole person by leading a student on paths of uprightness, intelligence, and conviction to human fulfillment.   DERMOT COX, O.F.M.

Psalms, The Book of.

Introduction. The book of Psalms derives its name from the ancient Greek translation, *psalmoi*, which designates instrumental music and, by extension, the words that accompany the music. In Hebrew it is known as "the book of praises." One hundred and fifty psalms were numbered consecutively in the Hebrew tradition. The same number is found in the Greek and Latin versions, though there is a variation of usually one digit within Psalms 10–147 (e.g., Ps. 72 is 71 in the Greek). One of the *Dead Sea Scrolls and many Greek manuscripts have other psalms as well, especially Psalm 151, which is recognized as canonical by some Orthodox churches. By the Hellenistic period, the psalms were provided with superscriptions indicating authorship ("by" or possibly "concerning" David), musical annotations (e.g., "with stringed instruments"), and even the setting (e.g., Ps. 51, after David's sin with Bathsheba). Titles exist for 116 psalms, but the information contained in most of them is no longer understood (e.g., Ps. 69, "according to Lilies"). Nothing much can be said about the psalms as musical compositions. There are many references to musical accompaniment, and one may infer that the words were sung, but nothing is known about melody or orchestration. (*See* Music and Musical Instruments.)

There is evidence of a complicated history behind the present form of the psalter. It seems to be divided into five "books" by the insertion of doxologies: 41.13; 72.18–19; 89.52; 106.48; 150.6 (or perhaps all of Ps. 150). Behind these stand earlier collections: Psalms of David (73 in all), of Asaph (Pss. 73–83), of the Korahites (Pss.

42; 44–49; 84; 85; 87; 88), and so on. The fact that the generic name for God, Hebrew *'ĕlōhîm*, outnumbers the sacred name (*yhwh*, probably pronounced Yahweh; *see* Tetragrammaton) by about four to one in Psalms 42–83 suggests a separate collection of psalms; hence, this section has been called the "Elohistic psalter." Another sign of earlier compilation is the presence of duplicate psalms (14 = 53; 40.13–20 = 70).

Modern English translations are irregular in verse references. Some follow the Hebrew numbering, while others, such as the New Revised Standard Version (NRSV), follow the tradition of the Authorized Version, which does not count the title as a verse. Hence, there is often a difference of one digit or more between the Hebrew and English references to the verse numbers (thus, NRSV 51.1 = Hebr. 51.3). In this article, the NRSV numbering is followed.

More significant are the differences in rendering that can be found in all translations. At many points, the traditional *Masoretic text of the Psalms is corrupt and in need of emendation. Such correction is based on the usual sources, especially the ancient *translations. But these are not always trustworthy; the rendering of the tenses in the *Septuagint is particularly misleading. In order to restore the supposedly original form of the text, scholars also have recourse to the resources of related Semitic languages, especially for the meanings of words. In modern times, the discovery of *Ugaritic language and literature has provided a window on the Hebrew text that has led to improved translation.

Literary Types. Modern scholarship is skeptical about two aspects of the traditional titles: authorship (hence dating) and setting. There is no hard evidence for Davidic authorship of any of the psalms. *David's reputation as a musician (1 Sam. 16.23; Amos 6.5) makes it reasonable to associate him with the psalms, but it is not possible to prove authorship. As regards the setting, modern scholarship is much more modest in its claims. The ancients were overspecific. Rather, one can only describe the setting in a very generic way: a lament of an individual or community, a song of praise in the *Temple, and so on. In other words, literary classification has replaced the historicizing tendency that the titles display.

Hermann Gunkel (1862–1932) originated the modern literary analysis of the psalter. His conclusions have been modified somewhat by subsequent scholars, but his classification of the psalms remains basic. Many psalms resist easy classification, but the following description is helpful.

Hymns. The hymn, or song of praise, begins on a joyful note in which the psalmist summons self (Pss. 103–104) or a community (Ps. 117) to praise the Lord. Usually two reasons are given, and they constitute the heart of the prayer: God's creative activity and saving intervention is Israel's history. The pattern is: "praise the Lord, because. . . ." As far as *creation is concerned, one must be ready for the skilled and imaginative portrayal of the divine creativity, recorded throughout the Bible. One thinks of the majestic description of the effortless activity in Genesis 1, a creation by word, but there is also the picture of the divine potter in Genesis 2.7. Another mode of representation was the battle with chaos, personified in the redoubtable *Leviathan (Pss. 74.14; 104.26; cf. Isa. 27.1; Job 3.8; 41.1–34), or *Rahab (Ps. 89.9–10; Job 9.13; 26.12–13), or characterized simply as "Sea" (probably to be understood against the background of Baal's conflict with Yamm ["Sea"] in Ugaritic literature; cf. Ps. 74.13). Attention is not limited to the action of God at the beginning; creation is also continuous (Ps. 104). The Israelites obviously were able to relish and savor the creative activity of God.

Another reason for solemn praise is the divine intervention in history on behalf of Israel, especially the *Exodus (Pss. 78; 114; cf. Exod. 15.1–18). This sacred history could also be commemorated in such a way as to teach Israel a lesson (Ps. 78) or to move the people to penitence (Ps. 106). This "history" was not antiquarianism. It was re-presented in the liturgy and re-created in the hearts of the people, for whom it also guaranteed a future.

The structure of the song of praise is simple: after the initial invocation, certain themes are developed as the reason for praising the Lord. The psalm often ends on the general note of praise. But certain hymns have received special classification due to their content.

The first of these are the "Songs of Zion" (Pss. 46; 48; 84; 87; 122). They are clearly hymns, but the praise is centered on *Jerusalem. They do not view Jerusalem apart from the Lord; the Holy City is preeminently the divine dwelling place among the people, where the divine "name" (Deut. 12.11) or presence is to be found. A frequent theme is the invincibility of *Zion (Pss. 46; 48). This attitude can turn out to be a trap for those who place a false confidence in the "city of God" (cf. Jer. 7.1–15; 24.1–10). But Israel saw truly that her greatness was connected with the Lord's presence.

The second type deals with the enthronement of the Lord: "the Lord is king" (or, "has become king"). These psalms (most clearly, 47; 93; 95–99) celebrate the Lord as king, and have as themes the divine creative power as well as the divine domination of history. The kingship of the Lord is not conceived as a recent claim; it is rooted in the past and is re-presented in the liturgical celebration itself.

Thanksgiving psalms. Gunkel regarded these as the prayers offered up after deliverance from distress—a counterpart to the laments (see next paragraph): e.g., Psalms 18; 30; 40; 66; 116; 118; cf. Jonah 2.2–9. They begin like a song of praise and then quickly acknowledge that the Lord is the rescuer. This confession is sometimes expanded into a witness directed to bystanders (see Ps. 30.4–5), who may share in the thanksgiving *sacrifice offered by the psalmist. At times there is a flashback, as the psalmist recounts the difficult period before deliverance (Ps. 116.10–11). Psalm 100 is entitled a song for thanksgiving, and vv. 4–5 (cf. Jer. 33.11) are found in variant form in Psalms 106.1; 107.1; 118.1; and 136.1.

Laments. The psalms of lament can be considered from an individual or from a collective point of view. Most of them are psalms of individual lament, and indeed this literary type is the most frequent in the psalter (some forty psalms, e.g., 22; 42–43; 69). The prayer usually begins with a cry for help to the Lord ("my God"), followed by a description of the distress of the psalmist. This can be manifold: sin (Ps. 51), sickness and death (Pss. 6; 38), false accusation (Ps. 7), and especially persecution by enemies (Pss. 38.12–20; 41.5–11). It is paradoxical but true that in most cases one cannot pinpoint the precise reason for the complaint. This is because the imagery is so extravagant; Psalm 22, for example, mentions "bulls of Bashan," dogs, the sword, the lion, and wild oxen. But this can be an advantage for modern readers, who can interpret the vivid language of the psalmist in the light of their own distress. What at first sight seems to be a disadvantage turns out to be profitable, provided the modern reader develops an appreciation for the symbolic language (the *abyss, Sheol, the pit, the "waves" and "billows" of the Lord, etc.). Biblical writers are fond of extremes. *Death is not a static mystery at the end of one's days; death is parallel to Sheol, the place of the dead (see Hell), and both are visualized as a power that affects a human being in this life. To the extent that a person experiences nonlife (suffering, etc.)—to that extent one is in Sheol. Hence, the psalmist can express joy over deliverance by saying "You brought me up from Sheol" (Ps. 30.3). There has not been a resuscitation or resurrection; the psalmist has been delivered from the nonlife of suffering and distress.

The grim portrayal of personal agony in the individual lament is lightened by frequent cries for help, and especially by motifs of why the Lord should intervene. Appeals are made to the divine "steadfast love" (Hebr. ḥesed), which binds together the Lord and the covenanted Israelite. The psalmist even alleges personal integrity and loyalty (Pss. 17; 26) and also trust (Pss. 13.5; 25.1) as motives to induce the Lord to act.

In almost all the individual laments (Ps. 88 is a significant exception) a centainty is expressed that the Lord has heard the prayer, but the explanation for the change in mood is not obvious. Is it due to the psychological strength of the psalmist's trust? Or could it be that there are two moments here: the before and the after of deliverance, which have been joined together? A promising solution, which has gathered wide support, is to recognize here the liturgical background of the prayer. When one uttered a lament in the Temple, it was followed by an oracle of *salvation from one of the Temple personnel, and then the response to this was the proclamation of certainty. There are some hints of oracular assurance in several psalms (12.5; 35.3; 85.8; 91.14–16), but the lament has not retained the oracle as part of its structure.

Gunkel regarded the motif of trust, so frequent in the individual laments, as the seed of another type of psalm, the psalms of confidence (e.g., 4; 11; 16; 23; 62; 131). The motif of trust becomes the heart of the prayer.

National laments would have been characteristic of special days of crisis, such as a drought or military defeat (cf. Joel 1.13–14; 2 Chron. 20.3–12). The community would be summoned to the rites celebrated in the Temple for a day of national *mourning. There is no fixed structure, but most of the elements that appear in an individual lament are present here: a cry for help, the challenge of "why?", a description of the distress, and often a vow to praise the Lord

(perhaps akin to the motif of certainty). Among these psalms can be included 44, 74, and 79.

Royal psalms. This classification derives from content, not from literary factors. Indeed, many settings and moods are reflected in them: a royal coronation or anniversary (Pss. 2; 72; perhaps 110); a royal thanksgiving (Ps. 18; cf. Ps. 144); prayers before (Ps. 20) and after (Ps. 21) military operations; a royal wedding (Ps. 45), a "mirror of princes" (Ps. 101). In the course of time such psalms would have become "democratized." Although originally featuring the monarch as the main figure, they came to be applied to and used by the average person (e.g., Pss. 28; 61; 63).

Why were the distinctly royal psalms preserved after the fall of Jerusalem in 587/586 BCE? Monarchy disappeared until the short-lived triumphs of Simon Maccabee and the Hasmonean rulers (142–63 BCE). The most reasonable answer is that the royal psalms were reinterpreted, always bearing in mind the promise of 2 Samuel 7 (cf. Pss. 89; 132). The temporary awakening of messianism in the time of *Zerubbabel (Hag. 2.2–9, 20–23; Zech. 3.8; 4.8–11; 6.11–12), if it met the aspirations of the people, did not receive the approval of the *Persian authorities.

The royal psalms are not predictive; in their literal historical meaning they refer to the currently reigning king. Nonetheless, they were perceived as open-ended in Jewish and Christian tradition, and from that point of view can be considered as messianic in the future sense of that word (see Messiah).

Wisdom psalms. Not all would agree that this classification is proper, and there is a wide variation in determining which of the psalms might come under this rubric. The criteria for the classification remain somewhat vague: typical wisdom language (such as "teach" and "fear of the Lord"); *acrostic patterns (e.g., Pss. 34; 37); the contrast between the just and the wicked (Ps. 1); the problem of retribution (Pss. 37; 73); a meditative style (Ps. 90). If the literary genre remains difficult to pin down, perhaps it is better to speak of wisdom influence on such psalms as 1; 32; 34; 37; 49; 73. (See also Wisdom Literature)

Liturgies. In a broad sense, most of the psalms can be considered liturgical, but certain poems capture the spirit of a liturgy more obviously, particularly those in which oracles, questions, and litany response are featured. A liturgical format (question and answer) is conspicuous in the gate or entrance liturgies of Psalms 14 and 23 (cf. Isa. 33.14–16; Mic. 6.8). Prophetic oracles appear in Psalms 50; 75; 85. Psalm 136 is virtually a litany, with the repetition of the enduring "steadfast love" in each verse.

Recent Developments. Since the pioneering work of Gunkel, certain refinements in literary classification have been proposed. Sigmund Mowinckel (*The Psalms in Israel's Worship* [1951; Engl. trans. 1967]) went beyond Gunkel's analysis in his emphasis on the liturgical background of the psalter, not merely in its use in the period of the Second Temple but in its origins as well. It seems that most of the psalms were written in the first instance for liturgical performance in the Temple. There is not sufficient evidence for the feast of Yahweh's enthronement, which Mowinckel postulated, and with which he associated about forty psalms. However, the idea of the enthronement of Yahweh certainly dominates many psalms (e.g., 47; 93; 96–99).

Claus Westermann (*Praise and Lament in the Psalms* [1977; Engl. trans. 1981]) proposed to incorporate the traditional thanksgiving psalm into the class of hymns. He regarded such psalms as declarative songs of praise (e.g., Ps. 30), as opposed to descriptive songs of praise (e.g., Ps. 136). Indeed, he regarded the hymn (praise) and lament as the dominant categories of the psalter, and he presented the psalms as a movement from lament to praise.

Walter Brueggemann (*The Message of the Psalms* [1984]) has added another dimension to the interpretation of the psalter. While recognizing the traditional literary types established by Gunkel, he placed a new grid on the classification, based upon the categories of the philosopher Paul Ricoeur. He distinguished between psalms of orientation (all is right with the world; hymns such as Pss. 8; 33; 104), or disorientation (laments such as Pss. 13, 74, 88), and of new orientation (e.g., Pss. 23; 30; 66). These three categories are not univocal, since traces of movement from one stage to another can be found in many psalms. Neither is his approach merely psychological; it helps the reader to see things that may not be seen otherwise, by underscoring the dimension of personal experience.

Importance. These prayers illustrate the theology and worship of the Israelites across the six centuries in which they were composed and collected. No other book in the Bible has this kind of origin and orientation. One learns what kind of God Israel worshiped and both the history and the mystery of the covenanted relationship. At the same time, one learns much about the warmth and dynamism of Israel's faith. An important mix of theology and anthropology is the result.

In both Jewish and Christian tradition, the psalter is one of the most treasured books. It is aptly considered a school of *prayer, not simply because it contains prayers that can be appropriated for personal use but because it also teaches one to pray. The familiarity and the frankness of the lament, the enthusiasm of the hymn, the confessional character of the thanksgiving—all these characteristics speak to the human heart before God.   ROLAND E. MURPHY, O. CARM.

Pseudepigrapha.

Definition. The term Pseudepigrapha refers to a body of diverse Jewish or Jewish-Christian writings (there are others also of specifically Christian origin) that (a) are not included in the Hebrew Bible, the New Testament, the *Apocrypha, and rabbinic literature; (b) are associated with biblical books or biblical characters; (c) are more often than not written in the name of some ancient biblical worthy; (d) convey a message from God that is relevant to the time in which the books were written; and (e) were written during the period 250 BCE to 200 CE or, if later than this, preserve Jewish traditions of that period.

The word pseudepigrapha is the transliteration of a Greek word meaning "with false subscriptions," referring to books written under an assumed name. Although it is true that many of the writings in question are indeed pseudepigraphical, the word is inappropriate and misleading for at least two reasons: there are also nonpseudepigraphical books in any such list and there are pseudepigraphical books outside it!

It is much less confusing to use the word apocryphal, commonly found in ancient Christian usage, or the rabbinic expression "the outside books" (Hebr. *ḥiṣônîm*, "external") signifying those books outside the *canon. Certain of these "apocryphal" books that found their way into Greek and Latin manuscripts of the scriptures treasured by the church are known as the *Apocrypha (among Protestants) or the Deuterocanonical books (among Roman Catholics and in Eastern Orthodox churches). Those that did not gain entry, together with others subsequently written, were much later designated "pseudepigraphical" (among Protestants) or retained the designation "apocryphal" (among Roman Catholics).

There is no agreed list of such writings if only because there are no agreed criteria by which they should be determined. The situation is all the more complex because there is no agreement concerning the content of the Apocrypha itself. It would seem best to include in the Apocrypha those "extra" books which appear in most *Septuagint manuscripts but not those which appear only in the *Vulgate.

Genres. The writings of the Pseudepigrapha are varied in both content and literary form. A number of them are apocalypses, which emphasize the revelation of divine secrets relating to the cosmos and "the end of the age" (see Apocalyptic Literature). Among these are 1 *Enoch, the Apocalypse of Zephaniah, the Apocalypse of Abraham, 2 *Enoch, 2 Esdras 3–14 (= 4 Ezra) [traditionally included in the Apocrypha in English Bibles], 2 Baruch, and 3 Baruch. Some, like 1 Enoch, are composite in character and range over a period of some centuries.

Others take the form of testaments, purporting to be the words of the ancient worthy in whose name the book was written. Some of these contain apocalyptic sections or elements. The best-known writing of this kind is the Testaments of the Twelve Patriarchs, which, though Christian in its present form, is in the opinion of many scholars a redaction of a Jewish work of the second century BCE. Other writings in this category are the Testaments of Job, Moses, Abraham, Isaac, Jacob, Adam, and Solomon, ranging from the first century BCE to the second or third century CE.

A third category comprises midrashic-type comments on scripture, often in the form of stories picking up but going beyond the Hebrew texts. The most significant of these is the book of Jubilees, which comments on *Genesis and part of *Exodus. To this can be added the Genesis Apocryphon from *Qumran, which comments on the story of *Abraham in Genesis 12 and 13, embellishing the biblical text with colorful amplifications. Other books of this type are the Letter of Aristeas, the Apocryphon of Ezekiel, the Martyrdom of Isaiah, the Life of Adam and Eve, and Lives of the Prophets, Joseph and Asenath, the Book of Biblical Antiquities, 4 Baruch, *Jannes and Jambres, Eldad and Modad, and the Ladder of Jacob.

The tradition of Israelite wisdom literature expresses itself in folklore and in philosophical musings in the story of Ahikar, 3 Maccabees, 4 Maccabees, Pseudo-Phocylides, and Syriac Menander. The religion evidenced here shows the influence of Greek thought.

Hymns and *prayers are also a medium of literary expression. Most important in this connection are the Psalms of Solomon dating from the middle of the first century BCE. To these may be added the moving Prayer of *Manasseh, five apocryphal Syriac Psalms, the Prayer of Joseph, and the Prayer of Jacob.

The influence of the surrounding Greco-Roman culture can be seen in many of these writings, not least perhaps in such books as the Sibylline Oracles (from the second century BCE onward) with their prophetlike predictions of gloom, and in the Treatise of Shem (perhaps first century BCE), which describes the characteristics of the year based on the twelve signs of the zodiac.

All these books named as "pseudepigrapha" are only part of a much larger literature produced from the second century BCE onward, including the *Dead Sea Scrolls. It is a continuing point of debate which of the latter, if any, should be considered as belonging to this classification. It may be conceded that the commentaries and other works peculiar to the life and ordering of the Qumran community ought not to be included; but there is good reason to include others that have much in common with the recognized pseudepigraphical writings. Mention has already been made of the Genesis Apocryphon, to which may well be added the Temple Scroll and the Book of Giants, together with certain other writings with an apocalyptic interest, such as the Book of Mysteries and the Description of the New Jerusalem. It is of significance that among the Dead Sea Scrolls many fragments have been found of 1 Enoch and the book of Jubilees, together with a Testament of Levi and a Testament of Naphtali. But whether or not they are to be classified as pseudepigrapha, it is clear that the scrolls and the known pseudepigraphical writings must be studied together if we are to gain a true picture of Judaism in the centuries immediately preceding and following the beginning of the common era.

Preservation. For the most part, the Pseudepigrapha were preserved within Christianity, which went on to produce its own pseudepigraphical texts based on the model of the New Testament writings. Their preservation within this setting in the course of time created two problems difficult to solve, one linguistic and the other textual. Although written originally in Hebrew, Aramaic, or Greek (in Palestine or in the *Dispersion), such was their popularity in Christianity, especially in the east, that many survived only in such languages as Ethiopic, Coptic, Syriac, Georgian, Armenian, and Slavonic. This means that in a number of cases the language in which a book now appears may be once or twice or even three times removed from the language in which it was composed.

Not a few of them, moreover, are composite in character, containing Christian interpolations or substantial additions, or representing a fundamental redrafting of the entire book. The exact dating of such writings is not always easy to determine; but it must be borne in mind that late additions or even late documents may contain elements that illuminate an earlier period of Jewish history, and so should not be summarily dismissed.

The identification of these books is helped by quotations and other references in the early church fathers and by certain stichometries that emerged in Christianity which help to differentiate between canonical and apocryphal writings. Most of the books referred to are identifiable and already available, though a few remain unknown.

Significance. It is increasingly recognized that the pseudepigraphical writings, taken in conjunction with other literature of the same period, are of considerable importance for a study of the growth of Judaism and the origins of Christianity.

The picture of Judaism presented here of the period 250 BCE–200 CE is complex, unlike the "normative" Judaism of later years when it came to be deeply influenced by rabbinic teaching. It is thus misleading to speak of heresy or of sects during this time, as if these could be set over against an accepted orthodoxy. What we have is a religion in ferment, true to the scriptures and tradition and yet open to winds of change blowing from many quarters. Alongside deep traditional piety we find a cosmopolitan concern that probes the mysteries of God's workings not only in the world but also through the whole cosmos. Indeed, one of the marks of this literature is that of cosmic speculation that reveals a surprising sophistication in religious thought and expression. The picture presented is that of a Judaism far from merely parochial and very much alive. (*See also* Judaisms of the First Century CE.)

Speculative theology is seldom systematic, and with vitality went variety. The Pseudepigrapha,

and not least those books among them of an apocalyptic kind, show certain areas of particular concern: the perennial problem of the origin of *evil and its outworking in the life of the world, the consequences of this for the Jews and indeed for the whole universe, the cataclysmic end that will result in the defeat and eradication of evil, and the final triumph of God in the coming of his kingdom and the age to come. Variety, not consistency, remains the hallmark of such speculations.

Christianity grew out of the soil of Judaism, and so the Pseudepigrapha, as expressions of Judaism, are of importance for an understanding of Christian origins also. Their relation to what came to be regarded as the *canon of scripture is a particularly intriguing one. The letter of *Jude is a case in point. There, in v. 9, allusion is made to an apocryphal story about a dispute between the devil and the archangel *Michael over the body of *Moses that may have come from a lost Assumption (or Testament) of Moses, and in vv. 5–7 and 14–15 reference is made to 1 Enoch, which is quoted as prophecy. This strongly suggests that, to Jude and no doubt to many other Christians, there was in fact no clear line of demarcation between certain of the Pseudepigrapha, regarded as inspired works, and other books that in the course of time came to be regarded as canonical. This is hardly surprising because, as we know from other sources, the limits of that part of the canon known as the Writings remained somewhat indeterminate for some time in contrast to the other two parts, the Torah and the Prophets.   D. S. RUSSELL

Publicans. The word "publicans" in some English versions of the New Testament comes from the Latin *publicani,* which is in a sense a mistranslation of the Greek *telōnai;* the NRSV translates the term as "tax collector." Both Greek states and Rome had only a rudimentary civil service and budgeting process. Hence minor taxes were regularly sold to a private company, which would pay the agreed price to the treasury and collect (in principle, at the fixed rate) from the taxpayers. These *telōnai* had long been known and disliked in the Greek East (an Alexandrian comic poet calls them "birds of prey"). Roman *publicani,* while they always performed this service, had an essentially different origin. They were state contractors who would buy at auction both performance contracts (e.g., building contracts or contracts for army supplies) and collection contracts (as for taxes or the revenues of mines or ponds or forests). During the age of Roman expansion and public building, in the Middle Republic, they made most of their money from the former and, as Polybius tells us, they widely distributed prosperity among Roman citizens. This changed when the reformer Gaius Gracchus in 123 BCE entrusted them with the collection of the principal tax (the tithe on produce) of the province of *Asia, which Rome had just acquired, and also with staffing the criminal courts, which tried senators for maladministration and, in due course, for other crimes. This vastly increased the scale of their undertakings, and made them a major power in the state, though they always narrowly defended their economic interests. Their power in the courts was temporarily removed by Sulla (81 BCE), but was soon essentially restored. As a result, governors and their staffs, instead of regulating their activities, tended to become their partners—often in collusion with the provincial upper class, which could pass the burden on to those below—in grossly exploiting the provinces, especially in the east, where Pompey introduced the Asian system to all the new provinces he organized, including Syria. On one occasion, a governor of Syria tried to take the system over for his own benefit, with some relief for the provincials, who had fewer appetites to satisfy. His enemy Cicero complains that he had handed the *publicani* over to Syrians and Jews, "nations born to be slaves." Although by no means the chief or only exploiters, they and their huge staffs were the most visible, at the point of collection, and caused most of the widespread anti-Roman feeling in the eastern provinces.

They were organized as companies of shareholders (in the late Republic shares were widely traded), under a board of directors (*magistri*) who were always equestrian in standing. In the provinces, a *promagister* (not a shareholder) was in charge of a large establishment, mostly of natives, and they were what provincials called *publicani*, the vastly better organized successors of the local *telōnai*.

In the civil wars they lost their power and their fortunes, as rival commanders freely confiscated their accumulated wealth in the provinces. Caesar removed the main tax of Asia from them, collecting it directly through state officials, and Augustus in due course extended this to other provinces. When the province of Judea was annexed, after the deposition of Archelaus in 6 CE (*see* Herodian Dynasty), the *publicani* were given only the minor taxes (chiefly tariffs, again) to collect. Such tariffs were traditionally imposed, purely for purposes of revenue, at various points along main roads, as well as in all ports, as import, export, and transit dues.

In the late Republic, the power of the *publicani* led to major abuses, which we know from Cicero's speeches. Illegal extra charges were widely added, and permitted by the governor, and violence was used to extort compliance. Although there was more control under Augustus, this is the background to what we find in Judea. The Jews soon hated the Roman occupation even more than they had hated Archelaus, whose deposition they had demanded. Native collectors of taxes were now seen as collaborators with the oppressor, using his backing for their illegal profits. The problem was apparently worse in Judea than elsewhere, presumably because of the religious element in the national resistance; it is interesting that the "publicans" appear only in the Gospels, not in the rest of the New Testament, even though they were of course active in all the provinces. They are regularly coupled with sinners (note that where Matt. 5.46 has "publicans" Luke 6.32 has "sinners"), with *prostitutes, and with *gentiles. In the parable of the Pharisee and the publican (Luke 18.9–14), the latter knows his low place, whereas the former is the type of establishment respectability, despising him as an outcast. *Talmudic literature continues this aversion, until it was forbidden even to accept *alms from a tax collector. Yet wealth clearly conferred respectability. The chief tax collector (*architelōnēs*) at Jericho (perhaps a *promagister*) who followed *Jesus was treated by him like any other wealthy man (Luke 19.1–9), and in *Josephus (*War* 2.14.287) we find a *telōnēs* who is a notable of the Jewish community at Caesarea, working for the benefit of his community and trying to use his influence and his fortune on their behalf.

Most of the time we hear of the humble and despised publicans, whom Jesus made a point of treating, as he did other outcasts, like human beings who could be saved. This astonished and shocked (especially) the *Pharisees, which suggests a religious element in the aversion: dining with Levi (Mark 2.14–17 par.) was like dining with a gentile. It seems, however, that for ordinary people it was the exactions that were most disliked. Publicans who came to be baptized were told by *John the Baptist (just as soldiers were) to do what was their duty and not to abuse their power (Luke 3.12–13). This corresponds to the injunction to sin no more (John 5.14), which was all that Jesus required of humble people.

It is interesting that Matthew (9.9) sets the story of the call of Matthew (Levi) the tax collector at *Capernaum (the other accounts do not specify the location). If so, the *telōnēs* would be in the employ of Herod Antipas and would uniquely attest precisely similar aversion to *telōnai* who were not agents of Rome. But it must be suspected that Capernaum was wrongly introduced into the story, as one of Jesus' favorite towns.

See also Roman Empire; Tribute and Taxation, *article on* Roman Empire.   E. BADIAN

Purity, Ritual. Throughout the Bible reference is made to a system of ritual purity that had both social and theological significance for the Israelites. While its specific origins are not known, it can be related to practices in other ancient Near Eastern cultures in which cultic functionaries followed similar regulations, involving, for example, ritual washing and food restrictions. What appears to be unparalleled about the biblical system, however, is its extension beyond the *priesthood to the general population.

In addition to cultic activity, texts describing ritual purity focus on food and individual status related to specific events. With regard to priestly behavior, those participating in *sacrifice are required to purify themselves beforehand. This purification is achieved through ritual immersion. In Leviticus 11 and Deuteronomy 14, detailed lists are given of *animals that are ritually pure and therefore permitted for consumption, and of those that are ritually impure and therefore prohibited. Leviticus and Numbers also contain regulations concerning the purification of individuals, regardless of cultic status, after childbirth, menstruation, ejaculation, disease, and contact with corpses.

While the regulations concerning ritual purity may be clear, their significance has been variously interpreted. The Hebrew words *ṭāhôr* and *ṭāmēʾ* are commonly translated "clean and "unclean" respectively, renderings which imply associations with dirt or hygiene not present in the original. Additional confusion results from the fact that while in our culture the difference between the human and the divine is often identified with the difference between the material and the spiritual, that was not the case in early Israel. Ritual purity and impurity could be considered spiritual states, yet they are inextricably linked to physical processes. In turn, physical acts such as sacrifice and sprinkling are used to alter relationships with the divine.

Following the lead of anthropologists such as Mary Douglas, many contemporary biblical scholars consider the status of being *ṭāmēʾ* as one of pollution resulting from a disruption of divine order. Thus, animals prohibited for food are those that cross paradigmatic boundaries of sky, earth, and sea. Shellfish, for example, live in the ocean but crawl like land animals. From this perspective, human ritual impurities are connected with disorder since they involve uncontrolled bodily emissions or death.

Another interpretation of biblical notions of ritual purity focuses on impurity as a state of power rather than pollution. Again using anthropological models, this view examines the relationships between human ritual impurity and liminal states, transitions between one status and another or between life and death. In a biblical context, it is argued, these moments are linked to the nature and power of the divine, a power that contains death and destruction as well as life and creation. They are also tied to actions, such as procreation and care for the dead, which are positive and necessary for social order. Thus, rather than being "unclean" or "impure" in a negative sense, the biblical state of ritual impurity is the result of contact with the sacred. This sense of ritual impurity is evident in the later rabbinic definition of canonical (i.e., sacred) texts as those which "render the hands ritually impure." Biblical rituals of purification may have been the result of a belief that direct contact with divine power could be dangerous if sustained too long. This conception of divinity is supported by passages such as Exodus 33.20, where God warns Moses, "You cannot see my face; for no one shall see me and live." Another possibility is that ritual purifications served as a consistent reminder that the power of life and death is not human but divine.

A third interpretation addresses the social implications of the ritual purity system. The sociologist Nancy Jay has pointed out the priestly control involved in purifications and its retribution of reproductive powers from the individual women who exhibit them in menstruation and childbirth to the male (imaged) deity represented by male priests. Food prohibitions can also be interpreted functionally as a means of social separation.

While it may be argued that legislative texts concerning ritual purity are descriptive and relational in their uses of the terms *ṭāhôr* and *ṭāmē˒*, other biblical writings imply a more polarized viewpoint. Ezekiel, for example, frequently uses *ṭāmē˒* in contexts that clearly indicate a notion of defilement not only of persons but also of places, an impurity that is rooted in apostasy. Texts such as Lamentations 1.9 associate negative concepts of defilement with female sexuality as exemplified by menstruation. These different perspectives may be due to historical change, since the legislative materials are generally dated to earlier periods than the historical and prophetic texts.

With the destruction of the First and Second Temples, the cultic basis of the system of ritual purity was first disrupted and then destroyed. Remnants of the system were preserved in rabbinic practices such as ritual immersion for conversion or following menstruation, handwashing, and the separation of implements as well as categories of food in keeping kosher. While Christianity rejected the system as a whole, it retained ritual immersion in *baptism.

See also Social Sciences and the Bible, *article on* Cultural Anthropology and the Hebrew Bible.

DRORAH O'DONNELL SETEL

Q. *From German* Quelle *("source"), the hypothetical common source used by the authors of the gospels of Matthew and Luke. It consists almost entirely of sayings of Jesus. See* Synoptic Problem.

Qere. *See* Ketib and Qere.

Qoheleth. *See* Ecclesiastes, The Book of.

Queen and Queen Mother. Although several Hebrew words are translated "queen," they denote different statuses or types of royal women. The two primary terms are *malkâ* and *gĕbîrâ*. *Malkâ* seems not to have been used, even as a descriptive title, for any Judean or Israelite ruler's wife. Instead, the Bible commonly refers to the "king's wife" or the "king's mother" (1 Kings 1.11; 2.13, 19; Prov. 31.1). *Malkâ* may connote foreignness; the queen of *Sheba, Vashti and *Esther (wives of the Persian king: Esther 1.9; 2.22), and the abominated *queen of heaven are all called *malkâ*. *Gĕbîrâ* seems to refer to the mother of the acknowledged heir to the throne or to the mother of the reigning king, hence "queen mother" (Maacah: 1 Kings 15.13; *Jezebel: 2 Kings 10.13; Nehushta: Jer. 13.18). She may also be the chief wife (1 Kings 11.19; 2 Kings 10.13).

In a dynastic succession, heredity is the crucial factor. Almost every accession notice of a Judahite king includes not only his father's but also his mother's name (e.g., 1 Kings 15.2, 10). The queen mother's identity seems to have been relevant in establishing the legitimacy of the new Davidide. The *gĕbîrâ* frequently appears to come from a rich and well-connected Israelite family. It has been suggested that important provincial power groups ("the people of the land") had a vested interest in promoting a local woman to be the king's wife and subsequently pressuring the king to make her the *gĕbîrâ*.

With a power base of sorts behind her, a *gĕbîrâ* would have been able to exert some independent, if informal authority. Underlying Asa's removal of Maacah from being *gĕbîrâ* (1 Kings 15.13) was probably a power struggle between court factions. The formal notice of the demotion suggests its unprecedented nature; it also implies that the *gĕbîrâ* enjoyed not only prestige but tangible privileges.

Several episodes have led scholars to conclude that the queen mother had official status (1 Kings 2.13–25: *Bathsheba; 1 Kings 15.13: Maacah; 2 Kings 24.15: Nehushta). But recent studies have pointed out, on the basis of extrabiblical parallels, that the queen mothers involved in these episodes were unusual in having maneuvered their own sons into power even though the son had no legitimate claim to the throne. In such cases the new king owed a debt to his mother that he could scarcely ignore, and the queen mother's power might grow even greater.

Besides marrying women from local families, Israelite kings, like their ancient Near Eastern counterparts, had an eye to advantageous alliances and often chose wives from neighboring royalty. *Solomon's foreign wives are proverbial (1 Kings 11.1–8). Jezebel was the daughter of the king of Tyre (1 Kings 16.31), and her daughter Athaliah married Jehoram of Judah (2 Kings 8.18).

Kings' daughters generally receive little mention, although a Hebrew seal inscribed "Maadanah, daughter of the king" has come to light. Michal, *Saul's daughter and *David's wife (1 Sam. 18.20–27; 19.11–17; 25.44; 2 Sam. 3.13–16; 6.16–23) is exceptional, as is Athaliah's enterprising rebel daughter Jehosheba (2 Kings 11.12).

With their status and wealth, wives of rulers throughout the ancient Near East were often able to transcend the otherwise static boundaries determined by gender and society (*see* Women, *article on* Ancient Near East and Israel). In Mesopotamia, rulers' wives supervised their own households, administered palace industries, engaged in diplomacy, and participated in religious rituals apart from their husbands. This recalls the experience of the most documented biblical queen, *Jezebel. She ran her own religious establishment (1 Kings 18.19) and used her authority to initiate and execute policy (18.4). She sent official messages (19.2; cf. Prov. 9.3), counseled her husband (1 Kings 21.5–7; cf. Esther 4.16–17; 6.14–7.6), and, although 1 Kings 21.8 says that she arranged Naboth's death in *Ahab's name, elsewhere the wording may mean that the murder was committed on Jezebel's own authority (21.11, 14–15).

Occasionally women ruled independently in the ancient Near East. The queen of *Sheba, who conducted economic negotiations with Solomon, may have belonged to a dynasty of queens who ruled in North Arabia, and during the Hasmonean period *Salome was for a brief time queen of Judea (76–67 BCE). Ancient records, however, tend to look with disfavor on women who ruled in their own name, whether it is the *Sumerian "king" KU.BAU (third millennium BCE), the Egyptian Pharaoh Hatshepsut (1486–1468 BCE), or Athaliah of Judah (843–837 BCE), whose six-year reign (2 Kings 11.3) was the only break in the Davidic succession of Judahite kings.

In its attitude toward the historical queens of Israel and Judah, the Bible is either neutral (the royal accession notices), suspiciously laconic (e.g., Bathsheba and the wife of Jeroboam I), or decidedly negative (Maacah, Jezebel, Athaliah). Only Esther, in what is essentially a morale-raising fiction, merits an unequivocally favorable portrayal. From a literary point of view, however, *Sarah seems to be a positive paradigm for the gĕbîrâ, just as *Abraham is a paradigm for David. The narrative's insistence (Gen. 17.19–21; 21.12–13) that Sarah, not *Hagar, will bear the son of the promise (cf. Rom. 9.9), is reminiscent of the attention paid to the identity of the king's mother in the royal accession notices. The gospels of Matthew and Luke may reflect this when they stress *Mary's role in bearing Jesus, another son of the promise and a future king. The later tradition of Mary as the heavenly queen, however, derives not from biblical but from imperial Roman political vocabulary.

See also Kingship and Monarchy.

MARY JOAN WINN LEITH

Queen of Heaven. A goddess who, according to the prophet Jeremiah (7.16–20; 44.15–28), was worshiped in Judah in the late seventh and early sixth centuries BCE. Jeremiah's remarks associate the goddess with fertility and, to some degree, with war; as her title "Queen of Heaven" indicates, she also has astral characteristics. Her cult is described as one that is particularly attractive to women, who bake offering cakes called *kawwānîm* in the goddess's image.

The Canaanite goddess who best fits this description is *Astarte, a goddess associated with both fertility and war and who has astral features. *Phoenician inscriptions also ascribe to Astarte the title "queen." Astarte's cult, however, is not known to be one in which women played a special role. Women on the other hand did have an important place in the cult of Astarte's Mesopotamian counterpart, Ishtar, whose female devotees ritually wept in imitation of the goddess's mourning over her dead lover, *Tammuz (see Ezek. 8.14). Ishtar's cult also involved the offering of cakes called *kamānu*, a word cognate with Hebrew *kawwānîm*. The Queen of Heaven thus should be identified as a syncretism of Canaanite Astarte and Mesopotamian Ishtar.

SUSAN ACKERMAN

Queen of Sheba. *See* Sheba, Queen of.

Qumran (Map 12:X5). Khirbet Qumran is the modern Arabic name of the site at the northwest corner of the *Dead Sea, ca. 13 km (9 mi) south of Jericho, near which the *Dead Sea Scrolls were discovered beginning in 1947. Subsequent excavations revealed occupation at the site from the mid-second century BCE until the First Jewish Revolt (66–70 CE). The structures found are generally thought to have been built by the *Essenes and are chiefly of a communal nature, such as cisterns fed by aqueducts, kitchens, a dining hall, and a large room containing long rectangular tables at which some have thought the scrolls were written. A cemetary is located nearby.

MICHAEL D. COOGAN

Quotations of the Old Testament in the New Testament. All the writers of the New Testament regarded the Old Testament as their Bible. They would not have thought of it as an *Old* Testament at all. They sought in it confirmation of their beliefs, and often used it to prove their point in argument. To a large extent, knowledge of how the New Testament writers used the Old enables one to understand their modes of thought.

New Testament writers inherited a long tradition of Jewish exegesis of the Bible (*see* Interpretation, History of, *article on* Jewish Interpretation). Although they differed in some important respects from the principles of this exegesis because they were Christians and not, or not only, Jews, this was their starting point, and they saw no reason to repudiate a great deal in that tradition. Jewish exegetical tradition was in no way monochrome: various schools of exegesis can be distinguished. There were certainly some Jews who were more open toward the *gentile world than others; they would put more emphasis on those parts of the Bible that look forward to a time when Israel's God would be made known to the whole world. Again, there was in Alexandria a school of exegesis that used very extensively the allegorical method of interpretation, which had originated in a purely Greek milieu; of these, *Philo is by far the most important representative. And contemporary with the beginning of Christianity there also existed in Palestine the *Qumran community, which produced the *Dead Sea Scrolls. This sect believed that they could discover in the scriptures, both in the *Law and in the prophets, hidden prophecies of the history of their own sect. Nor must we forget the influence of the Targums, the Aramaic paraphrases of the Hebrew Bible, used in *synagogues for the benefit of worshipers who could not understand Hebrew (*see* Translations, *article on* Targums). These writings aimed above all to make the sacred text relevant to contemporary conditions, and frequently incorporated edifying legends or elaborations of the biblical narrative. We must also bear in mind that most early Christians seem to have read their scriptures in a Greek translation (the *Septuagint), which was not always an accurate rendering of the Hebrew.

All the authors of the New Testament shared certain assumptions about the Bible. The scriptures, they held, were entirely true and infallible, internally consistent, with no contradictions. Above all, the scriptures were filled with references to, and prophecies of, *Jesus Christ. The primary feature that distinguishes New Testament interpreters of the Old Testament from Jewish exegesis is that the New Testament exegesis was christocentric.

*Paul was a master of *typology; he often takes for granted that his readers will know about and believe Jewish traditions of exegesis. For example, in Galatians 4.29, a parallel is drawn between the relations of *Isaac and *Ishmael, on the one hand, and those of Christians and Jews in Paul's day, on the other. Paul writes, "But just as at that time the child who was born according to the flesh persecuted the child who was born according to the Spirit, so it is now." Paul is referring to Genesis 21.8–14, where *Sarah sees Ishmael and Isaac playing. Some Jewish scholars, wishing to justify Sarah's harsh treatment of Ishmael and *Hagar, argued that the Hebrew word "playing" in Genesis 21.9 really meant "persecuting"; Paul takes this interpretation for granted. Paul's interpretation of scripture also helps him with the problem of the Law. In Galatians 3 and Romans 4, he appeals to the text of Genesis 15.6 in order to prove that faith came before the Law; *Abraham was justified by faith before he underwent *circumcision. Again and again Paul finds in the scriptures texts that, so he believes, identify Christ with the suffering servant of God; see, for example, Romans 15.3, where he sees a verse from Psalm 69.9 as being the utterance of Christ to the Father. Or again, in 1 Corinthians 15.45 he quotes Genesis 2.7 in order to show that Christ was the second *Adam. In fact, a great deal of Paul's doctrine about Christ is based on biblical exegesis.

The author of Matthew's gospel uses quotations from the Old Testament freely in order to prove that Jesus was the promised *Messiah. He has a set of eleven quotations that he introduces with some such phrase as, "All this was done to fulfill what was spoken by the prophet" (Matt. 1.22–23; 2.5–6, 15, 17–18, 23; 4.14–16; 8.17; 12.17–21; 13.34–35; 21.4–5; 27.9–10). This usage strikes the modern reader as rather literalistic. But in a much more general sense, Matthew represents Jesus as the fulfillment, in certain respects, of *Moses: like Moses, he has to be hidden by his parents to escape persecution; like Moses, he is a great teacher; and like Moses, he gives out his teaching on a mountain. Matthew, however, is capable of using scripture in what we would regard as a more sensitive way. Thus, in Matthew 8.17 he quotes Isaiah 53.4 of Jesus, suggesting that Jesus' healing activities were in some sense vicarious, because his healings meant that he bore our diseases.

The Fourth Gospel does not have many explicit biblical quotations, but the text is full of allusions and echoes. As well as the standard texts that all the evangelists quote, John employs several allusions in a unique way. One such is in

3.14, where the episode of the brazen serpent (Num. 21.9) is presented as a foreshadowing of the cross. In several places, John uses biblical allusions to support his contention that the preexistent Christ was present on occasions during Israel's history. Thus, in 8.40, Abraham is described as one who believed a man sent from God to tell him the truth. This alludes no doubt to Genesis 18.1–15, where three men visit Abraham, one of whom he addresses as "my Lord." When in 8.51–58 we read that Abraham saw Jesus' day and that before Abraham was Jesus is, we can have no doubt that John identifies the preexistent Christ with this angel. John's characterization of Jesus as *lamb of God also draws heavily on biblical models, even to the extent of quoting the description of the *Passover lamb (Exod. 12.46) in his account of the *crucifixion (19.36).

The usage of the Bible in the book of *Revelation is also unique. There are no explicit citations, but the symbols and images employed by John the seer are nearly all taken from the Hebrew Bible, especially from *Ezekiel and *Daniel, so that John weaves out of these materials a brilliant tapestry proclaiming the events of the new dispensation.

The way in which New Testament writers use the Old Testament is very different from the way most Christians understand it today. Where they found prophecies and foreshadowings, and even occasional appearances of the preexistent Christ, Christians today see a developing revelation of God's nature and purpose, a revelation that is complete in the life, teaching, death, and resurrection of Jesus Christ. Much in the Old Testament that they believed to be history is held today to be legend or *myth. But myth and legend are vehicles of expression for the faith of Israel, and readers cannot dispense with the evidence of the Old Testament in seeking to understand the meaning of the New.

ANTHONY TYRRELL HANSON

Qur'ān and the Bible, The. The belief that God speaks through scripture he has inspired is shared by Jews, Christians, and Muslims. In spite of the considerable differences among them, these three monotheistic communities lay claim to a common distinction that links them as "People of the Book." Each community deems itself to be in possession of a written record of God's will, revealed at moments of crisis in history, re- corded for the instruction of future generations, and constantly reinterpreted in acts of individual and corporate remembrance. Each community is founded upon a faithful response to the word it has received, using as its model of obedience to the divine call the example of *Abraham.

The Qur'ān (Koran) is the holy book of Islam. Muslims believe that it was revealed by God to the prophet Muhammad, through the agency of the angel *Gabriel. These revelations came to Muhammad between 610 CE (the year of his call to be the messenger of God) and 632, the year of his death. The Qur'ān consists of 114 sūrahs, or chapters. The length of the complete book is about two-thirds that of the New Testament. The Arabic word qur'ān most probably means "that which is to be read aloud." The first sūrah to be revealed to Muhammad starts with the command "Read! [aloud] in the name of your Lord who creates." In the Arabic the opening imperative iqra' ("Read!") contains the same consonantal elements that form the word Qur'ān.

The sūrahs are named. Some of the names are familiar to readers of the Bible: "Jonah" (10), "Joseph" (12), "Abraham" (14), "Mary" (19), "The Prophets" (21), "The Resurrection" (75). Others are unfamiliar: "The Cow" (2), "The Pilgrimage" (22), "The Pen" (68), "The Dawn" (89). Others are introduced by combinations of letters, the precise significance of which is unknown. In addition to its name, each sūrah is prefaced by an indication of the place where it was revealed, either Mecca or Medina. The language of the Meccan sūrahs is appropriate for summoning an unbelieving people to accept Islam as a matter of immediate and urgent decision. At the last day, unbelievers will be given the reward merited by their unbelief, and cast into jahannam (*Gehenna), which is graphically described. On the other hand, the reward for believers on the day of reckoning will be the *afterlife in *paradise, a place described with comparable vividness. The Medinan sūrahs are longer, and chiefly concerned with the organization of life in the developing Islamic community.

In 622 CE, Muhammad and his small group of Muslim converts were obliged to leave Mecca because of persecution; this event is called the hijrah (hegira). They moved to Yathrib, about 465 km (290 mi) to the northeast. In honor of Muhammad, the place was renamed madīnat (al-nabī), "City (of the Prophet)." Medina, the name by which it is still known, is the city in which Muhammad lies buried. The year 622 CE divides the Meccan from the Medinan period in the life of the prophet Muhammad, and is the year from which the Islamic community dates the beginning of a new era, whose dates are sometimes given the designation A.H. (Latin *Anno Hejirae*).

Unlike the Bible, which emerged over a period of centuries as the work of many different (and often unnamed) witnesses to God's redemptive activity, the Qur'ān passed from the oral tradition to its written form in just over a decade after the death of Muhammad. The revelations were passed on by Muhammad orally, and those who listened to him wrote them down on whatever materials were to hand, including dried leaves, sun-bleached animal bones, and stones. This written material was finally brought together during the caliphate of 'Uthmān (644–656 CE), the third "Rightly Guided Caliph" (Arabic *khalīfah*, "successor" of the prophet Muhammad), to form the authoritative written text of the Qur'ān. No additions or deletions have ever been permitted by Muslim authorities, though many textual variations in the manuscripts have been collected by western scholars. After the first short sūrah, which is a brief exordium of praise to God, who is both creator and guide, and which is sometimes compared to the *Lord's Prayer, the other sūrahs follow each other in an order of decreasing length. The first sūrah to be revealed is numbered 96 in the final sequence.

Both Jews and Christians were present in parts of Arabia prior to the time of Muhammad. In Mecca and in Medina (as well as in his travels north and south over the ancient caravan routes), Muhammad would have come in contact with some of them. But the internal evidence of the Qur'ān provides little evidence to support the view that Muhammad had any direct knowledge of the Jewish and Christian scriptures. According to Islamic tradition he was, in any case, unable to read or write. That such an unlettered man was able to "read" the revelations has always been accepted by Muslims as a special sign of God's favor.

The similarities between the biblical and the Qur'ānic material suggest that, even had there been any direct borrowing from the former to the latter, it was highly selective. Major prophets like *Amos and *Jeremiah, for example, do not appear in the Qur'ān. And the Qur'ānic interpretation of trinitarian orthodoxy as belief in the Father, the Son, and the Virgin Mary, may owe less to a misunderstanding of the New Testament itself than to a recognition of the role accorded by local Christians to *Mary as mother in a special sense.

The use of historical criticism in studying the Qur'ān has been resisted by Muslims. For them, the Qur'ān is the sure guide to right belief, thinking, and action. The guidance it furnishes is complemented by guidance about what constitutes knowledge, and about the way knowledge is to be attained. Knowledge consists of that which God has revealed. The path to knowledge is that of submission (*islām*) to the revealed will of God. There are limits to human speculation, precisely because of what God has revealed. Intellect, will, and reason are all to be schooled by the revelation. To study the Qur'ān according to methods developed in a non-Muslim society is not encouraged in Islam. Discussion about whether or not the Qur'ān is "the Word of God" belongs to a different intellectual tradition.

According to Islamic belief, each sacred "Book" was revealed at the appropriate time and place by God, through the agency of human messengers. The message of all scriptural revelation is essentially the same; it could not be otherwise, since God himself is the author. Thus, any differences between the scriptures of the "People of the Book" are to be attributed to human distortion, and not to divine caprice. To *Moses and his people was given the *Tawrah* (the *Torah); to *David and his people was given the *Zabūr* (the book of *Psalms); to *Jesus and his people God gave the *Injīl* (the *gospel); and finally, to Muhammad was revealed the Qur'ān, the restatement of the eternal and unchanging purposes of God, to which all the messengers originally bore witness. Muslims believe that the Qur'ān is God's authoritative final word, with a particular significance for Muhammad's own people, but also a universal message for humankind.

The designation "People of the Book," viewed from outside the Islamic community, is as much a reminder of the differences as of the similarities that exist between Jews, Christians, and Muslims in their understanding of what constitutes scripture. Yet despite this there are still points of contact between the Bible and the Qur'ān, as the references to *monotheism and to Abraham, Moses, David, and Jesus indicate. In the Bible and in the Qur'ān, the themes of God's creative and re-creative activity are taken up. The reader is confronted by the one true God, besides whom there is no other. In these different scriptures are revealed the divine will and plan for humankind, the service required by God of those whom he has created, the way of salvation, and the penalty for self-imposed separation from God.

Other names and incidents are recorded in both the Bible and the Qur'ān. Two examples can be mentioned to provide a start for further reading. The first is the story of *Joseph in Genesis 37–50 compared with the story of Yūsuf ("the fairest of stories" in the Qur'ān, sūrah 12). Common to both accounts is Joseph's rise to power and authority in Egypt after being brutally treated by his brothers, his faithfulness to God through periods of suffering, his careful use of the gifts given to him by God, and his reconciliation with his family following their appeal for food in time of famine. In the Qur'ānic account, Joseph finds favor because of his exemplary acceptance of everything that God willed for him, both in times of adversity and in times of success. His submission to the will of God is held up to succeeding generations of Muslims as an example worthy of imitation.

The second example is that of *Mary, the mother of Jesus. Sūrah 19, called Maryam (Mary), may be compared with Matthew 1.8–2.23 and Luke 1.5–2.51. To anyone familiar with the New Testament passages in which Mary appears, this holds a twofold interest. The first point of interest is that the Qur'ānic account acknowledges the *virgin birth of the child Jesus ('Īsā). The second is in the Qur'ānic denial of the implications of *trinitarian theology. In the Qur'ān, Jesus is a human being, a messenger of God, but still a creature; he is not God incarnate. In associating the creature with the Creator, Christians are, therefore, guilty of the gravest impropriety. The belief of Muslims is expressed in sūrah 4.171: "O People of the Book! Commit no excesses in your religion: nor say of God (Allāh) aught but truth. Christ Jesus, the son of Mary, was (no more than) an Apostle of Allāh, and his (Allāh's) Word, which he bestowed on Mary. And (Jesus was) a spirit proceeding from him (Allāh). So believe in Allāh and his apostles. Say not 'Trinity.' Desist, it will be better for you. For Allāh is one (Allāh). Glory be to him. He is far exalted above having a son. To him belong all things in the heavens and on earth."

EDWARD HULMES

R

Rabbi. A term that arose in the first century CE for those ordained to be authoritative in their study, exposition, and practice of Jewish law. The rabbi could be found expounding the *Torah in the *synagogue, much as Jesus did (Mark 1.21; 6.2), although the application of the title to him (Matt. 26.25, 49; Mark 9.5; 11.21; etc.) was early and preserved its etymological meaning of "my master" (see John 1.38). The rabbi functioned as an interpreter of Torah and as a judge, most often of the claims of the poor. By the third century, the rabbi was regarded as having magical powers such as the ability to communicate with the dead.

Rabbis generally worked part-time at a trade, as carpenters, cobblers, and the like. Not until the Middle Ages did the rabbinate become a profession. The rabbis were not a separate caste. They mixed with the common folk on a regular basis and usually came from the ranks of ordinary people, as in the case of the most eminent of all rabbis, Akiva. The rabbis believed that all Jews could live a holy life through observance of Torah, and they said that, if all Jews observed just two *Sabbaths completely, salvation would come. Thus, common folk played an important part in the rabbinate's scheme. Rabbis could be entrusted with great responsibilities far removed from the world of Torah study in the rabbinical schools. There are instances of rabbis assuming public health responsibilities, including disaster prevention so that buildings would not collapse in a storm, and the rabbi would act to see that no one in his village lacked food to eat. Such was the central role of rabbis in late antiquity.

The earliest literary monument of the rabbis is the *Mishnah. Completed around 200 CE, the Mishnah is basically a rambling legal compilation, striking in its ahistorical character as compared with earlier Jewish writings and in its lack of reference to scripture to support its rulings. Nevertheless, it was authoritative and became the basis for the Jerusalem *Talmud (ca. 400 CE) and the Babylonian Talmud (ca. 500 CE), which comment on the Mishnah and supply its wants, ideological as well as scriptural (e.g., the Mishnah does not talk of the *Messiah).

The rabbis essentially shared the traditions and views of the *Pharisees. They embraced an all-knowing, all-wise, just, merciful, and loving God who supervised the lives of individuals and decreed the fates, even while giving room for free will to choose between good and evil. A world to come existed where recompense for the evils of this world could be expected. Both this world and the next revolved around Torah. The religion of the rabbis exalted the holy faith, the holy man, and the pursuit of a holy way of life. A part of that holy existence involved daily prayer, and the roots of the current Jewish prayerbook are to be found in the Mishnah. It was only by pursuing the holy on a daily basis that salvation could be achieved and the Messiah would come.
PHILIP STERN

Rachel. Rachel, whose name means "ewe," was the younger daughter of Laban (brother of *Rebekah) and the wife of *Jacob. The account of the meeting and subsequent marriage of Rachel and Jacob is a love story, succinct in its narration. Jacob was charged by his father *Isaac to find a wife among his mother's people at Haran in *Mesopotamia (Gen. 27.46–28.5). At the end of his journey, he came to a well where shepherds gathered to water their flocks. When he learned that they were from Haran, he asked them if they knew Laban; the shepherds pointed out to Jacob that Laban's daughter Rachel was approaching with her father's sheep. As soon as Jacob saw Rachel, he rolled the stone from the mouth of the well and watered the flock of Laban, his uncle. He kissed Rachel and made himself known to her as a relative. She then returned home and gave her father the news of the arrival of Jacob. Laban went to Jacob, greeted him, and brought him to his house, where he stayed a month helping with the daily chores. At the end of this time, his uncle suggested that even as a relative he should not serve for nothing. When he asked Jacob what his wages should be, Jacob, who loved Rachel, said, "I will serve you seven years for your younger daughter Rachel" (Gen. 29.18); this was agreed upon. At the end of the term, which passed quickly for him because of his love, he asked Laban for her hand in marriage.

A feast was prepared and Jacob received his wife who according to custom was veiled. In the morning he discovered that he had been deceived into accepting Rachel's elder sister, *Leah. When he confronted Laban, he was told that in that country the younger daughter was not given in marriage before the elder; disappointed but undaunted, Jacob worked another seven years for Rachel. Needless to say, she was his favorite wife and eventually became the mother of *Joseph and *Benjamin.

Some time later after a quarrel between Laban and Jacob, in which Rachel took her husband's part and then stole her father's household gods (*see* Teraphim), the entire clan departed stealthily on the long journey to Canaan (Gen. 31.14–21), where she died at Ephrath giving birth to her younger son Benjamin (Gen. 35.19).

See also Ancestors, The; Genesis, The Book of.   ISOBEL MACKAY METZGER

Rahab.

1. The name (Hebr. *rāḥāb*) of the Canaanite prostitute who saved the spies sent by Joshua to *Jericho, and who, along with her extended family, was subsequently incorporated into Israel (Josh. 2; 6.22–25; Heb. 11.31; James 2.25). According to Matthew's *genealogy of Jesus, she was the mother of Boaz, who married *Ruth, and thus the ancestor of *David (Matt. 1.5).

2. A name (Hebr. *rahab*) for the primeval adversary of Yahweh in the battle prior to *creation (Isa. 51.9; Ps. 89.10; Job 9.13; 26.12; Sir. 43.23–25; *see* Israel, Religion of; Myth), also known as the sea, the deep, the dragon, the serpent, and *Leviathan; this name, unlike the others, is not found in ancient Near Eastern sources outside the Bible. It is applied by extension to Egypt as the deity's quintessential historical enemy (Ps. 87.4; Isa. 30.7).   MICHAEL D. COOGAN

Rainbow. The meteorological event called the rainbow was of course well known in ancient times, and it is referred to occasionally in the Bible. In Sirach 43.11 it is mentioned in a catalog of God's creative wonders, and elsewhere its multicolored splendor is used metaphorically (Ezek. 1.28; Rev. 4.3; Sir. 50.7). The most familiar passage in which the rainbow occurs is the conclusion to the *Flood story in *P (Gen. 9.12–16), where it is a sign of the *covenant between God and *Noah and all living creatures. The Hebrew word used here and elsewhere is *qešet*, which is also the ordinary word for the weapon called the bow. There is a mythological background to P's use of the rainbow in the Flood narrative. Like other ancient Near Eastern deities, the God of Israel was frequently depicted as a warrior-god, especially in his role as god of the storm; lightning bolts are his arrows, which he shoots from his bow (see, e.g., Pss. 18.14; 77.17; Hab. 3.9–12; Wisd. of Sol. 5.21). The rainbow after the Flood is then a sign that the deity of the storm will never again use his most powerful weapon for total destruction. He has put it in the clouds as if for storage; the bow's visible presence in the clouds is a guarantee that it is not being used.   MICHAEL D. COOGAN

Raphael. An *archangel mentioned in the Bible only in the book of *Tobit, in which he is sent to cure the blindness of Tobit and to free the hapless Sarah from the power of a demon (Tob. 3.17); to accomplish these tasks he acts as the companion and protector of Tobit's son Tobias on his journey. Raphael's name means "God has healed"; this explains his curative activity in Tobit and in postbiblical Jewish literature, such as 1 Enoch, in which he is sent to remove *Azazel and to heal the earth (1 Enoch 10.5–7) and is set over diseases and wounds (40.9). Later traditions identify Raphael as one of the divine messengers in Genesis 18.1–2, and as the angel who stirs the waters of the pool Beth-zatha (Bethesda; John 5.2–4).   MICHAEL D. COOGAN

Rebekah (in Rom. 9.10, Rebecca). A woman of insight and determination, Rebekah was the daughter of Bethuel (Gen. 24.15) and the sister of Laban the Aramean (25.20). She was brought from Haran to be the wife of *Isaac, the son of *Abraham, in the following way. After the death of *Sarah, Abraham commissioned his oldest servant to find a wife for Isaac from Abraham's kindred. The servant traveled to Haran in *Mesopotamia, the city of Abraham's brother, Nahor. On arrival outside the city in the evening about the time when the women usually came to draw water from the well, the servant made the ten camels he had brought with him kneel down nearby. He then prayed that God would guide him in making the right choice of a wife for Isaac. It so happened that Rebekah was the one thus identified. After she had given water to the camels, the servant introduced himself, gave her a gold ring and two bracelets (*see* Jewelry), inquired whose daughter she was, and discovered that she was the daughter of Bethuel, son of Nahor (Abraham's brother). She immediately ran off to tell her mother's household about her encounter at the well. Her brother Laban, on hearing the news, went out to the servant and offered him hospitality. The servant would not accept any food until he had disclosed his mission. On hearing his words, Laban and Bethuel agreed that "the thing comes from the Lord" (Gen. 24.50), so they were willing to have Rebekah go back with the servant to become Isaac's wife.

Isaac and Rebekah were married and became the parents of twin sons, *Esau and *Jacob (Gen. 25.24), who were later to vie for their father's blessing when he was old and blind (chap. 27). Rebekah favored Jacob and helped him through deceit to win the father's blessing. She died apparently while Jacob was in Mesopotamia and was buried in the cave of Machpelah (Gen. 49.31).

See also Ancestors, The; Genesis, The Book of.   ISOBEL MACKAY METZGER

Rechabites. The Rechabites were an Israelite group known for their distinctive lifestyle. Drinking *wine was proscribed. They refused houses, choosing instead to live in tents; they rejected agriculture, especially the cultivation of grapes. Jeremiah commended the Rechabites for obeying their strict rule, contrasting them with the other people of Judah who disobeyed God's laws (Jer. 35).

Biblical tradition derives their name from Rechab, the father of Jonadab, although it was the latter who imposed the regulations (Jer. 35.6; 2 Kings 10.15–28). Possibly their lifestyle manifested an idealization of the *wilderness period when the Israelites lived in tents, worshiped God in a tent (2 Sam. 7.4–7), and were faithful (Jer. 2.1–2; Hos. 2.14–15). But the Hebrew word for chariot comes from the same root as Rechab, and it may be that the Rechabites were a guild of chariot-makers. If so, their preference for tents might have resulted from their need to travel to the sources of metal ore.

In other references, we learn that the Rechabites may have been related to the seminomadic *Kenites (1 Chron. 2.55). Malchijah, the son of Rechab, governed a district in the postexilic period (Neh. 3.14). The *Mishnah indicates that in the Second Temple period a special day was set aside for the Rechabites to bring the wood offering (*Ta'an.* 4.5).   WILLIAM B. NELSON, JR.

Red Cow. Numbers 19 describes an unusual ritual, to be performed in cases of impurity resulting from contact with a corpse, requiring a red cow (Hebr. *pārâ*, whose usual translation "heifer" is probably too precise; cf. Gen. 15.9; 1 Sam. 16.2). Remarkable aspects of the passage include that it specifies not only the sex but the color of the animal, that the whole animal be burned, and that participants in the act of purification are themselves rendered ritually impure (*see* Purity, Ritual). The ashes of the sacrifice are mixed with running (literally, "living") water to produce a substance called *mê niddâ*.

Hyam Maccoby has interpreted these puzzling aspects of the ritual by focusing on the term *mê niddâ*. Usually the phrase is translated "water for cleansing" (NRSV), but it can also be rendered "water of separation." The word *niddâ* is also used for a menstruating woman, "separate" from normal spheres of activity because her physical state demonstrates her participation in the divine process of giving life. Similarly, contact with the equally sacred power of death also separates individuals from the community. The red cow ritual uses "waters of separation" to counteract the effects of such contact. The substance is a symbolic substitute for *blood, the sign of life. The requirement that the sacrifice be both red and female suggests that it represents the blood of potential life, of menstruation or birth. Like the divine, it is inherently powerful, and can therefore have a different effect on those who prepare it and those who receive it.

Other scholars have connected the ritual with a cult of the dead (cf. Homer, *Odyssey* 11.23–50; *see* Afterlife and Immortality, *article on* Ancient Israel; Israel, Religion of). The tractate *Para* of the *Mishnah is devoted to the ritual described in Leviticus 19.   DRORAH O'DONNELL SETEL

Redeem. The Hebrew verb generally translated "to redeem" is *gā'al*. Its basic idea involves doing something on behalf of others because they are unable to do it for themselves (see Jer. 31.11). The motivation to redeem someone is most often familial obligation. If no relative steps forward, however, the king (2 Sam. 14.1–11; Ps. 72.12–14) or God (Jer. 15.21; 50.33–34; Prov. 23.10–11) is expected to take up that person's duty. Whoever the redeemer is, in the act of redemption, he or she is providing for the redeemed as a man would provide for his own immediate family.

The most common situation in which redemption arises is when property or persons have been confiscated to reconcile a debt. A redeemer is one who pays the debt for the debtor, thus buying back what was confiscated (Lev. 25.24–34, 47–55; 27.13–33; Jer. 32.7–8). Similarly, a prisoner, perhaps of war (Lev. 27.28–29), can be redeemed through payment of a ransom. It is not surprising, then, to find the term pādâ ("to ransom, buy back") used in the same sense (Exod. 21.8; 34.20; Lev. 27.27, 29; Jer. 31.11).

The Hebrew idea of redemption, however, extends beyond payment of money. Redemption occurs in *levirate marriage (Ruth 4.4–7). One who seeks revenge for a man who has been murdered is a "redeemer of blood" (Num. 35.16–27; Deut. 19.1–13; Josh. 20.1–9; see Avenger of Blood). In fact, redemption is sometimes used to refer to rescue or deliverance in general. In this vein, God is the ultimate redeemer. He redeems persons from Death (Job 33.28; Ps. 103.4; Hos. 13.14). He redeems Israel from Egypt (Exod. 6.6; 15.13; Prov. 23.10–11 [gā'al]; Deut. 7.8; 9.26; Mic. 6.4 [pādā]) and Babylon (Isa. 43.1; 44.22–23; 48.20; 51.10). He also redeems in a more typical way, helping those in financial distress (Jer. 15.21; cf. Ps. 72.14). He is seen as a good husband (Isa. 54.5) and father (Isa. 63.16) when he acts as redeemer.

These ideas set the stage for the ways in which New Testament writers use the Greek verb (apo)lutromai. Redemption is most often spoken of as a ransom (Col. 1:13–14; 1 Pet. 1.18–19; Heb. 11.35); but the idea entails more than a figurative business transaction. Christ redeems by his death (1 Pet 1:18–19), in that he gives humanity the forgiveness that humanity could not give itself (Eph. 1.7; Col. 1.13–14; Titus 2.14; Heb. 9.11–14). Moreover, God redeems Christians from slavery to *sin in order to adopt them as his children (Rom. 8.12–23; Gal. 4.1–7), thus perpetuating the idea that the redeemer assumes the role of familial protector over the redeemed.   Timothy M. Willis

Red Sea. The traditional translation (beginning with the *Septuagint) of the Hebrew expression yam sûf, Red Sea is the name of the body of water crossed by the Israelites in their *Exodus from Egypt. This translation, followed by later Greek biblical tradition (Jth. 5.13; Wisd. of Sol. 10.18; 1 Macc. 4.9; Acts 7.36; Heb. 11.29) and the *Vulgate, would connect the miracle of the crossing (Exod. 14–15) with either the western (the Gulf of Suez; Map 2:R3–4) or the eastern (the Gulf of Aqaba/Eilat; Map 2:T3–4) branch of the Red Sea. But in Exodus 2.3–5 (and elsewhere in the Bible) sûf means "reed," and this is how the Septuagint and Vulgate translate it there; yam sûf refers to the eastern branch of the Red Sea in only two other texts (1 Kings 9.26; Jer. 49.21). Most contemporary scholars, and a few modern translations (e.g., NJV), therefore prefer to translate the phrase "Reed Sea" or "Sea of Reeds" (see NRSV textual notes).

The record of Israel's miraculous crossing is a complex one. According to what has been taken as the more ancient stratum of Exodus 14.21–22, perhaps from *J, "The Lord drove the Sea back by a strong east wind all night, and turned the sea into dry land." Another stratum, possibly from *P, reads: "Then Moses stretched out his hand over the sea . . . and the waters were divided. The Israelites went into the sea on dry ground, the waters forming a wall for them on their right and on their left," after which the waters enveloped the Egyptians. A third version, perhaps from *E (14.24–25), reads, "At the morning watch the Lord in the pillar of fire and cloud looked down upon the Egyptian army, and threw the Egyptian army into panic. He clogged their chariot wheels so they turned with difficulty. The Egyptians said: 'Let us flee from the Israelites, for the Lord is fighting for them against Egypt.' " In the first case we have a natural event, where the miracle lies in the synchronism of natural forces; in the second we deal with a miracle in the absolute sense, so that any explanation is immaterial; in the third we have neither water nor a miracle proper; the Egyptians realize that something is going wrong and withdraw. A variant of the second version is found in chap.15. Any connection with volcanic or seismic phenomena should therefore be excluded.

The term "Sea of Reeds" or "Reed Sea" seems to mean a marshy area or a large body of water abundant in reeds in the eastern delta. One possible localization of the event, among the many that have been proposed, is Lake Sirbonis (Map 2:R–S1), where, depending on the tides, fresh water and saltwater can be found; another is the swampy region in the vicinity of the "Bitter Lakes" (Map 2:R2). We must remember, however, that we are dealing here, as in the desert wanderings, with mythical data (see Ps. 114.3–6), so with few exceptions, the localities mentioned cannot and perhaps should not be identified. J. A. SOGGIN

Reed Sea. *See* Red Sea.

Refuge, Cities of. *See* Cities of Refuge.

Regeneration. Regeneration has played a larger role in theology than would be expected from its scant use in the Bible. In the King James Version, it is used at Matthew 19.28 and Titus 3.5 to translate the Greek *paliggenesia*, which occurs only in these two passages and literally means "rebirth." The RSV interprets the first occurrence by translating "new world," and NRSV uses "renewal" for the first and "rebirth" for the second.

The concept of a new creation is found in passages such as Isaiah 65.17; 66.22; Rev. 21.1; and it is this hope to which Matthew 19.28 alludes. Just as after the corruption of the first creation by human sin, God destroyed it and created a new world (Gen. 6–9), so apocalyptic writers looked for a similar renewal following divine judgment (see also 2 Cor. 5.17; Gal. 6.15).

The language of birth is applied to this renewal in the New Testament, as in Romans 8.22 (cf. 1 Pet. 1.3). Elsewhere the image of being born again is related to *baptism by water and by the Spirit (John 3.3–8; Titus 3.5).
DOUGLAS R. A. HARE

Religion. Narrowly understood, religion means actions, especially cultic or ceremonial, that express reverence for the gods. The usual Greek word for this is *thrēskeia*, which can also have a negative sense when used of deviant or suspect cults. The word is rare in the *Septuagint, and is never used to translate a Hebrew original. It is applied to idolatrous worship in Wisdom of Solomon 14.18, 27, but to Jewish worship in 4 Maccabees 5.6, 13 and Acts 26.5, as well as by *Josephus. (A Greek word with similar connotations is used of Judaism in Acts 25.19, and of the Athenian cult of the *unknown god in Acts

17.22.) *Thrēskeia* is also rare in the New Testament. In Colossians, the "worship of angels" is condemned (2.18; cf. 2.23), but the letter of *James speaks of "pure religion" (1.27), perhaps implying a contrast between the expression of religion in cultic forms and its expression in acts of charity and self-control.

More broadly, religion involves a complex of faith and conduct. For this the common Greek term is *eusebeia*, "piety," that is, reverence for the gods and for the social or moral order, which they uphold. This term is also rare in most of the Septuagint, though in Proverbs 1.7 and Isaiah 11.2 it translates "fear of the Lord." Ben Sira writes of the "godly" (Sir. 11.17 [NRSV: devout]; 37.12), using the adjective *eusebēs*, and the whole word group is frequent in the Hellenized 4 *Maccabees. In the New Testament, the related words are used in Acts, especially of the "god-fearer" Cornelius and his household (10.2, 7, 22), but elsewhere the language is confined to the *Pastoral Letters and 2 *Peter. In the Pastorals it is related to correct belief (e.g., 1 Tim. 3.16; 6.3; Titus 1.1), and in both to a way of life deemed to result from Christian belief (e.g., 1 Tim. 2.2, 10; 5.4; 2 Pet. 1.5–7; 3.11). In neither is it directly associated with acts of worship.

Theological conclusions are sometimes drawn from this linguistic evidence. The relative rarity of words for "religion" in the Bible, and the confining of the broader terms to what are generally considered the latest writings of the New Testament, has been used to argue that "religion," with its connotations of outward activity or generalized piety, is inappropriate language to use of ancient Israel or of earliest Christianity. "Faith," as the inner response to God's call, would be more proper. To use the term "religion" of the *Pentateuch is, however, appropriate, since there the correct performance of cultic activity, as well as ethical duty, is essential in Israel's response to God. In the New Testament there is no comparable concern with the correct performance of ritual acts, but it is clear that both *Jesus and *Paul expected that a new way of living would result from acceptance of their teaching. SOPHIE LAWS

Remnant. The various terms used to express the concept of remnant in the Bible represent two closely linked ideas. On the one hand, the word indicates those who are "left over" after some great catastrophe; on the other, those who have "escaped" the disaster and are able to continue the community's life. In a theological sense, the emphasis can fall primarily either on God's judgment on his sinful people or on his *mercy in still preserving a nucleus of them as a hope for the future, and these differing emphases are reflected in various biblical writers.

Perhaps the earliest occurrence of the idea is in the *Flood story (Gen. 7.23), where the stress is on the scale of the judgment, although with the implication that the survivors will constitute a new beginning. But it is with the prophets that the concept of remnant is really developed. In *Amos, the remnant is above all the hopeless residue of the nation's utter destruction (Amos 3.12; 5.3), although there is a faint hint that repentance may yet avert the fullness of judgment (Amos 5.15).

It is in the book of *Isaiah that the idea of remnant assumes particular prominence. In the basic message of the prophet, it is a sign of doom (Isa. 10.19; 17.5–6), and the name of his son, "a remnant shall return" (Isa. 7.3), originally signified the same. However, in what are probably postexilic supplements, the remnant is the group that returns to God and so embodies hope for the future (Isa. 10.20–21), where the son's name is reinterpreted (11.11–16). This group consists of the "needy," who trust in God alone (Isa. 14.32), as is most clearly brought out in *Zephaniah (2.3; 3.12). *Jeremiah and *Ezekiel display the same phenomenon as Isaiah, the remnant as evidence of utter destruction (Jer. 8.3; Ezek. 14.21–23) but also as a promise of a future hope (Jer. 23.3; Ezek. 11.13–20).

Hence those who survived the *exile identified themselves as the remnant (Ezra 9.15). But, in the postexilic period, dissident groups emerged, such as the *Qumran community, who saw themselves as the true remnant to be vindicated at the end (e.g., 2 Esd. 12.34). So Paul, in the long argument of *Romans 9–11, citing biblical prophecies, concludes that the Jews who follow Christ are the remnant of Israel, "chosen by grace" (Rom. 11.5).   J. R. PORTER

Repentance. Sincere contrition, involving acknowledgment of wrongdoing in the sense of both admitting guilt and feeling guilty (Lev. 5.5, 17; 6.4). The sinner might signal repentance through *fasting, weeping, rending garments, and donning sackcloth and ashes (2 Sam. 12.13–17; Jon. 3.5–10). Such emotional and even public acknowledgment of prior wrongdoing is but the first step toward forgiveness: remorse must

be accompanied by resolve to cease doing wrong and do what is right (Isa. 1.17–18, 27; Amos 5.14–15). In biblical idiom, the sinner is called on to "circumcise the heart" (Deut. 30.6; Jer. 4.4), "wash the heart" (Jer. 4.14), or become "single-hearted" (Jer. 32.39); to make a new heart (Ezek. 18.31), a heart of flesh, not stone (Ezek. 36.26). These ideas are summed up in the great prophetic concept šûb, "turn" (cf. rabbinic tĕšûbâ, "repentance"), meaning both a turning from *sin and a returning to right action, *Torah, and God.

From the earliest biblical narratives through the Roman destruction of Jerusalem in 70 CE, Jewish ideas of repentance were allied to the great system of *sacrifice detailed in the Torah and centered especially in the Temple cult. Rites of communal and national repentance were enacted on the *Day of Atonement; but at any time penitent individuals could make offerings at the Temple to atone for transgressions. Full repentance for voluntary wrongdoing against one's *neighbor required, beyond remorse, restitution (plus, where pertinent, one-fifth more of the value of the thing restored, Lev. 6.5). Only then could one make the Temple offering for remission of sin. Sources stress that these offerings did not effect atonement automatically: the sinner's inner repentance is the necessary precondition of forgiveness (see Philo, *Special Laws* 1.234–38; Josephus, *Ant.* 3.9.232; cf. Matt. 5.24–25).

In the *Septuagint, *metanoia* and *metanoeō* (literally, "a change of mind") often express "repentance" and "repent," and both appear frequently in the New Testament. Mark's Jesus begins his ministry with a call for repentance in the face of the coming *kingdom of God (1.14; cf. Matt. 3.2, where the call is transposed to *John the Baptist). Luke presents Jesus' mission as particularly a call to sinners to repent in order to receive forgiveness (e.g., 5.32).

Paul scarcely speaks of repentance at all in his letters, but his audiences were for the most part *gentiles who, unlike Jews, were under no obligation to live and worship according to the Torah. Hence Paul summons these gentiles to God: they are called not to "repent" as such, that is, to return, but to turn (Grk. *epistrephō*) for the first time. This term appears in prophetic passages both in the Septuagint and in Hellenistic Jewish literature as the anticipated response of the nations once the God of Israel reveals himself in glory at the end of days (Tobit 14.6; cf. 1 Thess. 1.9–10). In the context of Christianity, the "turning from" idols meant a "turning to" Christ, and so *epistrephō* comes to mean "to convert" (e.g., Acts 15.3); *see* Conversion.

Christian thinkers eventually expressed an elaborate theology of atonement and expiation for sin centering around the sacrifice of Christ, yet the emphasis on the importance of individual repentance remained. In his commentary on Paul's letter to the Romans, written in 395 CE, Augustine observed that the only sin against the Holy Spirit that could never be forgiven is despair. Despair, he argued, inhibits repentance; if one does not repent, he cannot repudiate his sin and so be forgiven. In taking this position, Augustine came close to the view of the rabbis: "Let the sinner repent, and he will find atonement" (*y. Mak.* 2:7, 31d). PAULA FREDRIKSEN

Rephaim. In several biblical texts (e.g., Isa. 26.14; Prov. 2.18) dead "shades" (NRSV) who inhabit the underworld; in other texts a race of fearsome giants who once lived in parts of Palestine and Transjordan (e.g., Deut. 2.20; 3.11, 13; Josh. 12.4; 13.12). Scholars have in the past considered these two meanings distinct, but texts from *Ugarit suggest they may be related. At Ugarit Rephaim most often refers to members of the aristocracy (military, political, or religious) who, as a result of their status while alive, attain some sort of superhuman, even semidivine, standing in the underworld. The probable etymology of Rephaim, from the verb meaning "to heal," also suggests that these dead Rephaim were thought to have power to help the living. The term Rephaim in the Bible likewise may refer to those among the deceased (e.g., the ancestral giants) who demonstrated extraordinary prowess during life and continue to exercise some sort of power after death. Notable in this regard is Isaiah 14.9, where the Rephaim of the underworld are described as those "who were leaders of the earth" and those "who were kings of the nations."
See also Nephilim. SUSAN ACKERMAN

Resurrection of Christ.

Biblical Background. In all but the latest parts of the Hebrew Bible, the concept of resurrection was applied not to the life of the individual after death but metaphorically to the renewal of Israel corporately after the return from *exile (see Isa. 26.19; Ezek. 37.1–14, where the resurrection language, especially in v. 13, is clearly meta-

phorical). In *apocalyptic literature, beginning with Daniel 12.2, resurrection language is applied literally, denoting coming to life again after death through an act of God in a transcendental mode of existence beyond history. This new existence, however, is not conceived in an individualistic fashion; it is the elect people of God (Dan. 12.1) who are corporately resurrected. The transcendental character of this resurrection life is indicated by such similes as "shine like the brightness of the sky" (Dan. 12.3).

*Jesus proclaimed the *kingdom of God, a concept couched in apocalyptic terms and involving a new cosmic order. It was to arrive shortly; God was already at work in Jesus' ministry to bring it about. Jesus' proclamation thus implied impending corporate resurrection of the people of God, or at least of those who responded positively to his message. In the controversy with the *Sadducees, Jesus used a simile reminiscent of Daniel 12.3 to describe the transcendental character of the resurrection life; the resurrection will be "like angels in heaven" (Mark 12.25). Critical scholarship regards the predictions by Jesus of his own resurrection (Mark 8.31; etc.) as creations of the post-Easter community after the event. Since, however, Jesus' preaching of the kingdom implied resurrection, there can be no question that he foresaw the corporate resurrection of God's people as lying beyond his own death (Mark 14.25). But there is nothing in his authentic preaching to suggest that he expected an individual resurrection for himself.

The Easter Event. It is in this framework that the Easter event should be understood. Jesus appeared alive to his disciples after his *crucifixion. The earliest record of these appearances is to be found in 1 Corinthians 15.3–7, a tradition that *Paul "received" after his apostolic call, certainly not later than his visit to Jerusalem in 35 CE, when he saw Cephas (Peter) and James (Gal. 1.18–19), who, like him, were recipients of appearances. The early community adopted three models to interpret this fact: rapture, resurrection, and exaltation. According to the first model, Jesus was "taken up" (Acts 1.11; Luke 9.51; Mark 16.19) or "received" in heaven (Acts 3.21; *see* Ascension of Christ). According to the second, God "raised Jesus from the dead" (1 Cor. 15.4, where the passive "was raised" is a divine passive denoting an act of God; cf. Acts 2.24). The third model, exaltation, is found by itself, without a preceding reference to the resurrection, in a pre-Pauline hymn (Phil. 2.6–11). The letter to the Hebrews operates almost exclusively with the exaltation model (a reference to the resurrection occurs only in the benediction at Heb. 13.20). In Acts, exaltation occurs in combination with resurrection (2.32–33; 5.30–31). In John, the exaltation language is applied both to death and to resurrection (3.14; etc.). Of these three models, resurrection is the one that proved most persistent; it either absorbed or replaced the others. Its advantage was that it brought out the corporate and cosmic significance of the Easter event. Jesus was raised by God as the first and determinative instance of the resurrection of the elect people of God and the renewal of the whole cosmos (1 Cor. 15.20, 23). His resurrection will make possible all the other resurrections that will occur at the end.

The resurrection, while a real event according to the unanimous testimony of the New Testament, is not historical in the sense that ordinary events are. It occurs at the point where history ends and God's end-time kingdom begins. And it is not in itself an observable occurrence. No one saw God raise Jesus from the dead. Nor can it be verified. In a sense, it is an inference from the disciples' Easter visions (and to a lesser degree from the empty tomb; see below).

The Easter Traditions. The early community, beyond asserting in its proclamation that God raised Jesus, further organized the appearances in lists (1 Cor. 15.3–8; cf. Mark 16.7; Luke 24.34). It did not at this stage tell stories of the appearances, probably because the recipients found themselves at a loss to find language to express the ineffable (as is probably the case with Paul). The word "appeared" denotes a visionary experience, for the same word is used of angelic appearances (Luke 1.11). On the other hand, the appearances are not to be downgraded as mere subjective experiences or hallucinations. The word "appeared" denotes a disclosure from God in heaven. The most accurate description of the appearances would be "revelatory encounters." They revealed Jesus as alive.

The appearances had several effects. First, they restored the disciples' faith and hope in Jesus (cf. Luke 24.21, which accurately captures the mood of the disciples after Good Friday). Second, this faith was expressed by means of christological titles: God had vindicated Jesus and made him Lord and *Messiah (Acts 2.36). Having deserted Jesus at his arrest, the disciples were now reassembled and welded into a community that soon described itself as the *church, that is, God's end-time people. Third, their Easter

faith impelled them to embark on a mission, first to Israel, and ultimately to the *gentile world. Fourth, the leaders of the mission became *apostles, which is to say, envoys, sent ones.

Alongside the lists of appearances there existed a story of the empty tomb (Mark 16.1–8 par.). This story apparently was part of the passion narrative, and functioned as the framework for the angelic proclamation of the resurrection at the conclusion of the reading of the passion during the Christian *passover. Its presence in at least two traditions (Mark/Matthew and John; behind the Lucan account there may lie yet another independent version) indicates that the basic nucleus of the tradition, that certain women discovered Jesus' empty tomb on the Sunday after his death, is very early, despite its absence from Paul. There is also indication that the disciples verifed the women's discovery (Luke 24.12, 24; John 20.3–10). Probably this followed the disciples' return to Jerusalem, after their visions in *Galilee; they must have welcomed the empty tomb as congruous with the Easter faith, which they had already arrived at through the visions. The empty tomb did not create the Easter faith, and in any case it is in itself an ambiguous fact, susceptible of other explanations alluded to in the New Testament itself (e.g., Matt. 27.64; John 20.15). The Gospels, however, are at pains to insist that the women took note of the tomb on Good Friday evening, and therefore did not go to the wrong tomb on Easter morning (Mark 15.47 par.).

Appearance Stories. *Mark, generally regarded as the earliest Gospel, originally contained no appearance stories, but merely pointed forward to subsequent appearances in Galilee (16.7). Appearance stories seem to have grown up as isolated units (pericopes), like the bulk of the gospel material. Inevitably, what was originally indescribable came to be described in earthly terms. The risen Christ talked, walked, and even ate with the disciples, as he had while on earth (Matt. 28; Luke 24; John 20; 21; Mark 16.9–20). Clearly, the only way the postapostolic community could construct appearance stories was to model them on the stories from the earthly ministry. These stores were more than simple narratives, though. They were expressions of the impact of the appearances, as they were first experienced by the original recipients and as the community subsequently came to understand them. This impact is expressed in the words attributed to the risen one. They include a missionary charge, a command to baptize, a promise of abiding presence or the gift of the Spirit, instruction about the fulfillment of biblical promises in his death and resurrection, the assurance of his presence in the breaking of the bread, and finally the hope of his coming again. The church and its whole faith and life are seen to have originated in the Easter event.

A particularly acute problem is created by the portrayal of the physical reality of the Lord's risen body in some of the later stories. This seems to run counter to the earlier tradition (see above), to Pauline teaching on the nature of the postresurrectional existence (1 Cor. 15.35–49), and to the categorical statement in 1 Corinthians 15.50. We must ask, however, what exactly these narratives are saying. Their purpose is to assert that, in the resurrection, Jesus did not leave his earthly life behind but took it with him. As a result, his whole "being for us," which characterized his earthly ministry and which culminated on the cross, are forever present and available to us. The wounds of the nails and the hole in his side are still there in the risen body (John 20.20, 24–29). These stories are not to be dismissed merely as later materializations, for they convey important truths about the resurrection. In the risen one, the incarnate, earthly, crucified one, with all the saving benefits that result from his being in the flesh, is present for us.

The Resurrection of Believers. With all the concentration of the later Easter narratives upon the personal fate of Jesus, it must never be forgotten that resurrection is a corporate event. Jesus was raised as the firstfruits. Believers share in his resurrection initially through *baptism. Paul is very cautious about this: believers share his death but their resurrection is conditional upon their present obedience and will not be complete until the parousia or *second coming (Rom. 6.3–11; 1 Thess. 4.15–17; see also Biblical Theology, article on New Testament).

The deutero-Pauline *Colossians and *Ephesians are less cautious. Colossians asserts that we are already risen with Christ through baptism, though this risen state carries with it present moral responsibilities and its full consummation is not realized until the end (Col. 3.1–4), while in Ephesians believers are already raised to life and made to sit at Christ's right hand in heavenly places (Eph. 2.5–6). Ethical obedience is still required in Ephesians, as the exhortation in chaps. 4–6 shows, and there is still a final consummation (Eph. 4.13). Similarly, the Fourth Gospel teaches that resurrection and eternal life are already realized for believers (John 5.24; etc.),

though here again there is a future consummation to be awaited (John 6.39; etc.). The corporate and cosmic dimensions of resurrection are thus never completely lost in the New Testament.

See also Afterlife and Immortality; Easter.

REGINALD H. FULLER

Reuben. The firstborn son of *Jacob and *Leah and one of the twelve *tribes of Israel (Gen. 29.32). Reuben's primogeniture indicates that in early Israel Reuben was a preeminent tribe (Gen. 46.8–9; Exod. 6.14–16). Reuben is guilty of incest with his mother's concubine Bilhah (Gen. 35.22) and is prominent in the rebellion against *Moses (Num. 16.1); the former is blamed for Reuben's later decline (Gen. 49.3–4; 1 Chron. 5.1–2). The Reubenites, together with Gad, settle in the Transjordan (Num 32.25–38). An early manuscript of the books of Samuel among the *Dead Sea Scrolls mentions Reuben and *Gad's subjugation by Nahash, king of the *Ammonites, elucidating *Saul's deliverance of Jabesh-gilead (1 Samuel 10.27). Scholars disagree whether Reuben was absorbed into Gad during the divided monarchy (2 Kings 10.33) or retained its identity (1 Chron. 5.22) until the *Assyrian conquest (732 BCE).

GARY N. KNOPPERS

Revelation. Revelation has to do with disclosing, uncovering, or unveiling what previously was hidden, making known what had been secret. Sometimes the biblical terms for revelation have common usages (Ezek. 13.14; 16.36, 57; Isa. 47.3; Exod. 20.26). When used theologically, however, revelation refers to God's deliberate manifestation of his plans, his character, and himself.

The Israelites were not alone in their desire to discern divine mysteries. Other ancient Near Eastern peoples sought to discover the wills of their gods, and many diverse methods were employed to this end. Looking for omens in the universe, astrologers considered the movements of sun, moon, and stars when making predictions. Significance could be found in ordinary positions of heavenly bodies, but extraordinary occurrences such as eclipses were especially noteworthy. Similarly, usual natural phenomena like the movements of birds, animals, or clouds could be interpreted, but so could the unusual, like floods, plagues, or babies born with defects. Animals were cut open so that their entrails might be examined, the livers of sheep being subject to special scrutiny. Distinguishing features such as the shape of the liver would portend future events. Certain individuals were trained to read and analyze these omens. Others were skilled in the interpretation of visions and *dreams. Sometimes people consulted the deity by casting lots: they threw bones or stones on the ground as dice are thrown today. The way they landed signified certain things. Prophecy also was practiced; gods would give oracles through human messengers, whether cultic functionaries or otherwise. Mediums were consulted to summon spirits from the underworld. Similar practices are attested in the Greco-Roman world. (*See* Magic and Divination.)

Some of the above were allowed in Israel, while others were not. The God of the Bible is one who hides himself (Isa. 45.15). There is a boundary between God and humanity, and between what God knows and what humans may know. Some things are to remain secret while others are revealed (Deut. 29.29). This line cannot be crossed, nor should humans attempt to cross it. Therefore, certain occult avenues to the transcendent were closed. *Witchcraft, necromancy, augury, soothsaying, and sorcery were forbidden to the Israelites (Lev. 19.26, 31; Deut. 18.10–12). Sometimes God revealed to his messengers secrets that could not be transmitted to others (2 Cor. 12.4), and sometimes knowledge was given which was to remain sealed until a later time (Isa. 8.16; 30.8; Dan. 12.4, 9); otherwise, the revelations were transmitted to successive generations in perpetuity (Deut. 29.29).

Knowledge of God may be gained from the natural world. *Creation implies a creator; therefore, something of the existence and power of God can be grasped by observing the universe (Ps. 19.1–6; Acts 14.8–18; 17.16–34; Rom. 1.18–32; 2.12–16). But this means of information is limited, and other ways are therefore required.

Sometimes revelation is through God's actions in history. This might involve direct intervention, as when he delivered his people from Egypt (Exod. 3.20; Deut. 26.5–9; *see* Exodus, The), or it might be more indirect, as when he used the *Assyrians (Isa. 10.5–6) and *Babylonians (Hab. 1.5–6) to punish them. In either case, the history can be ambiguous—hence the need for someone to interpret the ways of God to the people, a need filled in part by *prophets. God communicated verbally to his prophets (Deut. 18.15–19), and, according to Amos 3.7, he would not do anything without first revealing it to his human messengers.

Concerning the content of revelation, God makes known his plans, as when he told *Noah he was about to destroy the world in a *flood (Gen. 6.13–14); or when he disclosed to *Abraham that he was about to destroy *Sodom and Gomorrah (Gen. 18.16–33). He gave Daniel and John visions of the end of the world (Dan. 10.14; Rev. 21.1–5). He also reveals his nature, as when he declared his name to *Moses, proclaiming that he is Yahweh, merciful and compassionate, yet holding the guilty responsible (Exod. 34.6–7); or as when he revealed himself to Isaiah as the Holy One of Israel (Isa. 6.1–5).

Regarding modes of revelation, sometimes the casting of lots was employed: to choose a king (1 Sam. 10), or to choose a disciple to replace Judas (Acts 1.24–26). A special type of lot was the priestly *Urim and Thummim (Deut. 33.8; 1 Sam. 14.36–42; 28.6). God also communicated through visions (1 Kings 22.17–23), auditions (1 Sam. 3.1–14; Isa. 22.14), *dreams (Gen. 28.10–17), the interpretation of dreams (Gen. 40–41; Dan. 2; 10.1), and *angels (Judg. 13.15–20). Sometimes the text simply says that God revealed himself, as when he appeared to *Jacob (Gen. 35.7, 9) or *Samuel (1 Sam. 3.21). While some passages assert that no one can see God and live (Exod. 33.20), it seems that God appeared in human form to Abraham (Gen. 18.1–19.1), and Jacob wrestled with God (Gen. 32.24–30). One tradition has it that Moses saw only the back parts of God (Exod. 33.21–23) but others aver that God spoke to him "mouth to mouth" (Num. 12.8) or "face to face" (Deut. 34.10). Sometimes one can prepare oneself to receive revelation by waiting in a holy place (1 Sam. 3.2–4) or by playing *music (2 Kings 3.15).

In the New Testament revelation centers on Jesus Christ. For Matthew, Jesus controls the knowledge of God absolutely: "No one knows the Father except the Son and anyone to whom the Son chooses to reveal him" (Matt. 11.27). While many opinions abounded about who Jesus was, *Simon Peter recognized that Jesus was the *Messiah and the *Son of God. In response, Jesus told Peter that this insight did not have a human source; rather it came to him by divine revelation (Matt. 16.17).

Jesus often taught in *parables. This was partly, no doubt, to use common things around him such as plant seed and different types of soil to illustrate the truths of the *kingdom of God. But another reason may have been to conceal those truths from those who were not serious about following him. He offered the parables publicly but explained their meanings privately to his inner circle of disciples (Matt. 13.10–17, 34–35; Mark 4.10–12). (*See* Messianic Secret.)

John calls Jesus "the Word" because he is the complete revelation of God (John 1.1; *see* Logos). The *word of God came to the prophets, especially Moses (John 1.17), but now the Word has become a human being (John 1.17). Only Jesus, the Son of God, the very Word of God, has seen God; now that he has taken on flesh, he has fully explained God to the rest of humanity (John 1.18). To know Jesus is to know God (John 14.9). Likewise, the letter to the Hebrews acknowledges that God previously revealed himself in various ways, but that history of revelation has culminated in Jesus (Heb. 1.1–2).

When Jesus departed from the earth, according to John, the *Holy Spirit was sent to the Church to continue the revelatory function of the Son (John 14.25–26; 16.12–15; 1 John 2.20, 26–27; 3.24). Paul concurs. Things never before known have now been revealed by the Spirit to the church. The Spirit of God, who fully comprehends the depths of the knowledge of God, lives inside the Christian believers so that it may be said that they have the mind of Christ (1 Cor. 2.9–16).

In the early church, certain individuals were considered to be endowed with spiritual gifts, such as utterances of knowledge, utterances of wisdom, revelation, and prophecy (1 Cor. 12.8, 10; 14.26). When the New Testament *canon was completed, these special charisms became less important. Emphasis shifted to the interpretation of existing revelation. Sporadically throughout the history of Christianity, there have been those who claimed to have personal revelations. The orthodox churches have always tested these by and subordinated them to scripture. The Roman Catholic church has allowed that new revelation also exists in the form of church tradition and is as binding as scripture, while Protestants consider the Bible to be the sole *authority.

In Judaism there have been similar developments. Toward the end of the biblical period, the Jewish community came to be less interested in new revelation and more interested in studying the books that had already achieved authoritative status. There was a belief that when the messianic age arrived, it would be accompanied

by new revelation, but in the meantime prophecies, visions, and dreams were not to be trusted. The oral law in Judaism is somewhat akin to church tradition in Catholicism in that it is a later elaboration of the Bible yet is also a form of revelation and hence authoritative.

See also Inspiration and Inerrancy.

WILLIAM B. NELSON, JR.

Revelation, The Book of.

Content and Structures. The book calls itself an *apocalypse (1.1) or revelation, which Jesus gave, for his servants, through his angel to John, but it begins in letter form, "John to the seven churches that are in Asia, grace to you and peace" (1.4), and ends like a Pauline letter with the "grace" (22.21). The risen Christ appears to John on the island of Patmos, off the coast of the Roman province of *Asia, and orders him to write to the *seven churches (chaps. 2 and 3); the messages warn the complacent and the worldly, and encourage the faithful. Summoned up into heaven, John sees God enthroned, holding a sealed scroll no one can open. He hears that the lion of the tribe of *Judah has won the right to open it, and he sees standing by the throne a *lamb bearing the marks of sacrificial slaughter (chaps. 4 and 5).

The Lamb's opening of the seals unleashes the first of three series of disasters, which represent God's wrath against an idolatrous and impenitent world: seven seals opened (6; 8.1), seven trumpets blown (chaps. 8 and 9), and seven bowls poured out (chap. 16). Symbolic visions in between depict the opposing forces in cosmic war, which comes to a climax in chap. 19: the Lamb and the 144,000 who bear his name and God's seal, over against the seven-headed beast, Satan's emissary (the *Antichrist), and those who bear his mark. The beast's city, *Babylon, the "great whore," is destroyed, the beast is defeated, *Satan is bound and the *saints reign for a thousand years (the millennium), until Satan is released for his final assault (19.11–20.10). Then follows God's judgment of the world, and a new heaven and earth replace the old. The holy city, *Jerusalem, the bride, comes down from God, and all earth's splendor is gathered into it.

It is a bewildering kaleidoscope of scenes, punctuated by voices and bursts of heavenly hymnody. Scholars have seen a variety of structural patterns, based on liturgy (Jewish or Christian), or drama (each city had its theater), or astrology or numerology (both staple diet for first-century folk). Each suggestion may contain some truth, but none has won general assent. The clearest structural element is the four series of seven (letters, seals, trumpets, bowls). The background for this structure is the apocalyptic discourse of Jesus on the Mount of Olives (Matt. 24; Mark 13; Luke 21), of which John's apocalypse may be seen as an updating.

Outline.

Chaps. 1–3. Seven letters warning against deception and lawlessness (cf. Matt. 24.4, 5, 9–12)

Chaps. 4–7. Seven seals on a heavenly scroll, opened by the Lamb

6   War, famine, plague (Matt. 24.6–8; birthpangs of the new age)

7   God's servants sealed: 144,000

Chaps. 8–14. Seven trumpets of warning

8–9   Disasters modeled on the *plagues of Egypt (Exod. 7–11)

10–11   Counterpoint of witness (the little scroll)

12–13   Victory in heaven, disaster for earth—Antichrist and false prophet (Matt. 24.15–24)

14   The 144,000 over against worshipers of the beast. Judgment

Chaps. 15–22. Seven bowls of God's final wrath

16   Disasters for the beast's worshipers and city (Exod. 7–11 again)

17–18   Destruction of the whore, Babylon

19–20   Coming of Christ, the millennium, and the last judgment (Matt. 24.27–31)

21   Descent of the bride, New Jerusalem, in counterpoint with the fall of Babylon (17.1 and 21.9)

In the three series of disasters there is both recapitulation—each covers the same ground—and development. The seals serve as overture, centering on the "beginning of the birthpangs" (Matt. 24.8). The trumpets lead up to the "desolating sacrilege" (Matt. 24.15), Rome and its emperor. The bowls set out their destruction and the "coming of the Son of Man" (Matt. 24.27)—bridegroom and bride over against beast and harlot.

Two further structural points are important for interpreting the book. Enclosing the scenes of destruction are the visions of God, creator and redeemer (chaps. 4 and 5), and of the new creation (chap. 21): the destructions are not simply negative; the rebelliousness of earth is finally overcome. Enclosing all the visions is the epis-

tolary opening and ending: the whole disclosure is a message to Christians of the day in their particular situations. Scattered among the visions are calls for discernment and fidelity (13.9, 10, 18; 14.12; 16.15; 17.9).

This analysis suggests that the aim of John's revelation was to warn the churches against compromise with the religious, social, and economic values of a world heading for self-destruction because of its idolatry, and to encourage them in the witness to God and purity of life which alone could defeat the deceptions of Satan and his minions. The letters to the churches show that some were sliding into a worldly lifestyle (2.14, 20), while others were asleep (3.2), complacent (3.17), or lacking in love (2.4). There is wholehearted praise only for Smyrna (2.8–11) and Philadelphia (3.7–13), where faithful Christians were suffering on behalf of Christ.

Recipients. At first sight, John is writing to seven particular congregations; many other cities in the Roman province of Asia are known to have had Christians (see Acts 19.10, 26; 1 Cor. 16.19; 2 Cor. 1.8). But seven is the number symbolic of wholeness (see below), and these churches probably represent the whole church. The seven cities were all centers of communication, set on a circular route beginning at *Ephesus, the nearest to Patmos. The writer knows the geography and traditions of each city, and clearly is acquainted with the circumstances of each church. But the particular warnings and encouragements add up to a message for all the churches (2.23; cf. 22.16), and he claims divine authority for his book (22.18, 19).

What kind of Christians were they? The warnings against Nicolaitans and others who teach Christians to "eat food sacrificed to idols and practice fornication" (2.6, 14–15, 20) remind us of issues at *Corinth (1 Cor. 6.12–20; 8; 10.14–30). Later writers connected the Nicolaitans with *gnosticism. It looks as if there was an influential movement for compromise with the world, based perhaps on Pauline teaching about Christian freedom and the divine mandate of the state (Rom. 13.1–7), and on gnostic belief in present spiritual salvation to which behavior in the material world is irrelevant. The emphasis on Christ's imminent coming may be directed against an assumption that eternal life is already here, which might have been drawn from the teaching of the Fourth Gospel. *Paul, and later the apostle John according to tradition, had both been active at Ephesus. The book seems to be recalling Christians to the apostolic standard; there is perhaps an echo of the decree of the *Apostolic Council (Acts 15.28) in the letter to Thyatira (2.24).

Situation and Date. Irenaeus (ca. 180 CE), who came from Asia and had known Polycarp, bishop of Smyrna (ca. 70–150 CE), and others of his generation, dated the book of Revelation toward the end of the reign of Domitian (81–96 CE; cf. *Against the Heresies* 5.30.3, as usually interpreted). The picture of the *Antichrist reflects popular belief that Nero, who had stabbed himself in the throat, would return from the dead (13.3, 12, 14), and many scholars see Revelation as a response to the enforcement on Christians of Domitian's demand for worship as "Lord and God." But the evidence that he persecuted the church, as opposed to a few individuals who may or may not have been Christians, dissolves on inspection, and the letters to the churches reveal no state persecution, only Jewish "slander" (2.9; 3.9). The only martyr mentioned is Antipas (2.13—referring to a past event), and the general picture is of affluence and complacency.

On the other hand, Nero's mysterious death evoked immediate rumors that he was still alive, and would return with an army from the east; and the civil wars that followed his death (68–69 CE, the Year of Four Emperors), coinciding with the Jewish War (66–70 CE), seem to lie behind the breakup of the Roman world depicted in chaps. 6–18. Consequently, some scholars date Revelation about 68–70 CE: the intensity of hatred against Rome (17.6; 18.24; 19.2) does at first seem to demand a date close to the fire at Rome (64 CE) and Nero's massacre of Christians (Tacitus *Annals* 15.44). Irenaeus's date is open to question.

There is an apparent clue to the date in the interpretation of the beast's seven heads as emperors, "of whom five have fallen" (17.7–11), but in fact there is no telling which emperor the series starts with, and seven is probably again symbolic. The seven heads represent the empire as a whole, and the beast that "ascends from the bottomless pit" is "an eighth, but belongs to the seven"; it is the quintessence of imperial power, latent now but soon to be revealed in its true colors.

But this is not yet. The present is a time when the beast-like character of the empire is out of sight. In the Roman province of Asia, the Flavian emperors (Vespasian and his sons, Titus and Domitian) were popular, being efficient and generous administrators. Inscriptions hail them as "savior," "benefactor," "son of God," and there was a local zeal for the emperor cult. So Ire-

naeus's date in fact fits the evidence from the letters well: a time of patriotic enthusiasm, expressed in terms of religious veneration, from which Christians were not holding aloof. There was as yet no state compulsion for ordinary people to take part in the emperor cult, as long as they kept clear of law courts and the taking of oaths. Pliny's letter to the Emperor Trajan (ca. 112 CE; *Letters* 10.96), about people being accused of being Christians in the neighboring province of Bithynia, shows the danger; once accused they had the choice either of cursing Christ, worshiping the gods, and praying to the emperor's statue, or of cruel execution. Trajan agreed, but said they should not be sought out. So if Christians did not provoke their neighbors by active witness and by nonparticipation in the ordinary social and patriotic decencies, then they would come to no harm. But in John's view they would be buying temporal safety at the cost of eternal loss (14.9–11). The chief threat to the church was not physical danger, as at Smyrna, but social, economic, and religious temptation. Its chief need was discernment: "let anyone who has an ear listen to what the Spirit is saying to the churches" (2.7, 11; 13.9).

Author and Sources. Irenaeus and most later writers assumed that the author was the *John who wrote the Gospel and letters, and that he was the son of Zebedee. But some, like Dionysius of Alexandria (third century), anticipated the majority of modern scholars by questioning this identification because of differences of thought, style, and language. Dionysius relied on hints that there had been two writers named John in Ephesus; and Papias (ca. 140 CE) mentions a John who was an *elder, as well as the apostle.

Another possibility is that Revelation is pseudonymous, claiming a great figure of the past as author, like much other *apocalyptic literature. There is a later tradition that the apostle John was martyred as his brother *James had been (Acts 12.2; cf. Mark 10.39; Matt. 20.23, which may be the source of the tradition); as one of the inner circle, associated as he was with Jesus at the Transfiguration and on the Mount of Olives (Mark 13.3), he would have been a good figurehead for an apocalypse calling Christians to face martyrdom. If it was published ca. 95 CE, its later acceptance as genuine could have given rise to the widely held belief that John lived to a great age in Ephesus.

But the evidence for John's martyrdom is flimsy, and if "John" is a fiction, it is odd that no capital is made out of it; the author is simply "your brother," and mentions the twelve *apostles of the Lamb (21.14) without hint that he is one of them. The only status he claims is, by implication, that of *prophet (1.3; 22.9). This tells also against genuinely apostolic authorship, but not decisively; and Dionysius's comment concerning differences in thought and style may be due to differences in situation and genre; there are also many marks of Johannine theology and expression. John's language is indeed extraordinary, breaking all sorts of grammatical rules— but not out of incompetence; he can write correct and powerful Greek. He seems to be echoing Hebrew constructions, perhaps to give a biblical feel to the book.

The whole book purports to be what John has seen and heard, but it is clear that his visionary experience has been shaped both by canonical and apocalyptic writings like *Enoch and by the *Gospels (or the traditions on which they depend)—so much so that some see the book as a scriptural meditation, based perhaps on the Sabbath readings from the *Law and the Prophets (see Lectionaries, article on Jewish Tradition), which has been cast in visionary form. Probably it is a mixture of genuine experience and literary elaboration. Biblical metaphors and images—dragon, lamb, harlot, bride—come to new life in his imagination. There are allusions to or echoes of practically every book in the Hebrew Bible. *Daniel and *Ezekiel are particularly formative; *Isaiah, *Jeremiah, *Zechariah, and the *Psalms are pervasive influences; so too are the stories of *creation and *Exodus, and of the return from Babylon and rebuilding of Jerusalem, which Isaiah depicted as a new Exodus and act of creation. Revelation is a rereading of biblical tradition in the light of the death of Jesus, and though no doubt Jewish, the author is also a citizen of the Greco-Roman world and knows its myths and astrology (see, for example, commentaries on 12.1–6).

Unity. Visionary experience and scriptural meditation may indeed be inextricably woven together, but is the book as it stands a unity? At first sight it is full of loose ends, inconsistencies, and repetitions, and many scholars have detected interpolations, revisions, and dislocations of the text. For example, there are two "last battles" (19.9; 20.8), and two visions of the holy city coming down (21.2, 10). "See, I am coming like a thief! . . ." (16.15) seems manifestly out of place in the middle of the vision of the sixth bowl, but at home in the letter to Sardis (3.3). There are obvious glosses, interpreting the heavenly incense as "the prayers of the saints" (5.8), or the bride's fine linen as "the righteous deeds of the saints" (19.8).

But the glosses may come from the author himself. The apocalyptic genre is by nature dreamlike, and thus apparently incoherent; it is best to try to make sense of what we have on its own terms, in the absence of evidence in the manuscripts for disorder.

Symbolism and Interpretation. The symbolism of Revelation is kaleidoscopic and multivalent. One picture melts into another. God's people can appear as a woman (who can be virgin, wife, or mother) or a city, and the great city where the two witnesses are killed is "spiritually called Sodom and Egypt, where also their Lord was crucified" (11.8).

*Satan is both God's ancient enemy and has a place in heaven (12.7–9); likewise the sea is both an adornment of heaven (4.6), and the abode of the seven-headed beast, which represents the powers of chaos (13.1). Here is implicit the belief that evil is a corruption of what God has created good, a corruption that he can redeem; if Jerusalem can become the "great city" that murders the Lord and his witnesses, cannot the great city become the holy city? In the final vision, the kings of the earth bring in all the glory of the nations (21.24–26), though they have been slain by the *Word of God (19.13, 21). In the new creation, the dualism of this age, the gap between God's will and earth's obedience, has been overcome; there is no more sea (21.1).

Numbers, like places, are also symbolic (see Number Symbolism). There are twelve months, signs of the zodiac, *tribes of Israel, apostles of the lamb (21.12–14). There are seven planets, days of the week, colors of the *rainbow. These are numbers of wholeness. The slain Lamb has seven horns and seven eyes (5.6); the slain beast, the Antichrist that parodies his death and resurrection, has seven heads (13.1, 3, 14). His number is six, one short of seven. Satan was created the highest of the *angels, but the good claiming to be the best is the very devil. His number is intensified as *666 (13.18). Second, the ancients did not have Arabic numerals, but used the letters of the alphabet (A = 1, B = 2, etc.). So by adding up numerical values (gematria) a number could represent a name. Nero Caesar, written in Hebrew letters, adds up to 666; Jesus, in Greek letters, makes 888. He died on the sixth day of the week, and rose on the eighth, the first day of the new age.

John wrote to illuminate his own situation.

Later, when his specific circumstances were forgotten, some took Revelation as a literal prediction of the future; others, in reaction against crude literalism, especially with regard to the millennium, interpreted it allegorically and saw the millennium as the present age of the church. In the twelfth century, Joachim of Fiore drew from Revelation (along with the rest of scripture) an understanding of the whole movement of history; his vision came to be widely influential. At various times, people have seen Revelation as a veiled picture of the subsequent history of the world or of the church, placing themselves at the penultimate moment and identifying beast and harlot with current bogeys, whether emperor or pope, church or sect. But it is now clear that John wrote for a past situation and that to look for literal fulfillments in the events of our day is misguided.

In spite of Alexandrian doubts, Revelation has had a firm place within the New Testament *canon; it has had an immense influence on later Christianity. It can be seen as the most un-Christian book—the Judas Iscariot of the New Testament, according to D. H. Lawrence (*Apocalypse* [1931])—but, with its echoes of the beginning, the tree of life restored and no more curse (22.2, 3), it is a fitting climax to the whole Bible story.   JOHN SWEET

Righteousness. The Hebrew word translated "righteous" (*ṣādîq*) and its related nominal and verbal forms has the basic meaning of someone or something proven true, especially in a legal context. It therefore has the meaning "innocent" and is applied in the Bible especially to moral conduct and character. But the scope of righteousness is much wider than judicial procedures and embraces the whole covenanted life of the people under God. The specific meaning depends on circumstances: for a ruler, it means good government and the deliverance of true judgment (Isa. 32.1; Jer. 23.5); for ordinary people, it means treating one's neighbor as a covenant partner, neither oppressing nor being oppressed (Amos 5.6–7, 21–4); and for everyone it means keeping God's will as conveyed in the *Torah (Deut. 6.25). Sometimes human righteousness is seen as a response to or reflection of the divine righteousness or graciousness (Isa. 56.1; 58.8), and essentially it is the acknowledgment of God in worship of him alone and in living as he wants (Ezek. 18.5, 9).

God's righteousness means that he is a just and reliable judge (Ps. 9.4) who keeps his side of the *covenant and who thus delivers Israel from her enemies, so that they experience that righteousness as punishment, while Israel experiences it as *salvation and vindication (Judg. 5.11). Indeed in some places God's righteousness and salvation are virtually synonymous (Isa. 51.1–3), and from the *exile onward we find God's righteousness as an object of hope (Jer. 23.5; Dan. 9.24).

In rabbinic literature of the Tannaitic period, righteousness is often specified to mean generosity in general and almsgiving in particular. There is also development of the biblical tendency for righteous to refer to Israel, or a group within Israel, everyone else being at least relatively unrighteous; this may reflect experience of oppression. In the *Dead Sea Scrolls we find the Qumran sect regarding themselves as the only truly righteous. Righteousness is still, however, essentially conformity to the divine ordinances, that is, covenantal obedience. In the *Septuagint there is very high consistency in rendering the derivatives of the Hebrew root *ṣdq* by the Greek *dikaiosunē* and its cognates, whose semantic field overlaps considerably with that of the Hebrew words.

In the New Testament, righteousness occurs with greatest frequency in the gospel of Matthew and in Paul's letters. In the case of Matthew, there is discussion about whether he uses the word for life under God in the Christian community or reserves it for life under God before Christ came and outside the Christian community, and whether righteousness is not only a divine requirement but also a divine gift, especially in 3.25; 5.6; 6.33.

For Paul, the issues are even more widely debated. It is usually agreed that sometimes he uses righteousness in a broadly biblical fashion but in a Christian context for the life of the people of God (Phil. 4.8; 2 Cor. 5.14; 9.10). It is also usually agreed that "the righteousness of God," whether or not we can speak of a fixed formula, means God's saving activity (Rom. 1.18), characteristically seen in *justification by his *grace through *faith (Rom. 3.21–6). Indeed one of the reasons why the apostle is often held to be quoting a pre-Pauline formula in the last passage is that in v. 25 God's righteousness can be held to mean God's justice in a strictly judicial sense and not his saving activity. Under the influence particularly of Galatians 3 and Romans 4 and the terminology of reckoning, there has traditionally been a view that in justification Christ's righteousness is placed to the account of sinners (is "imputed" to them).

The question remains whether in some places righteousness and justification are synonymous in Paul or at least that righteousness can sometimes be a purely forensic or relational word. The best evidence for this is Galatians 2.21, but it is widely held for other passages as well. Nevertheless, it has also been maintained that Paul consistently uses "justify" (*dikaioō*) for the restoration and maintenance of the relationship with God and "righteousness" (*dikaiosunē*) for the consequent life as his people, with both justification and righteousness being by faith. But there is disagreement about the exact meaning of most of the relevant passages. Some scholars find the key to the whole matter in the idea of God's righteousness as a power, with the gift of righteousness being inseparable from God, the giver, so that the believer is drawn into the sphere of his power.

In the New Testament apart from Paul and Matthew, righteousness normally means life as God wants it and in relation to him. It is not surprising that righteousness is sometimes found as a particular predicate of Jesus Christ (e.g., 1 John 2.1, 29; 1 Pet. 3.18).   JOHN ZIESLER

River of Egypt. The river of Egypt is the traditional southwestern boundary of the *Promised Land (Num. 34.5; Josh. 15.4; 1 Kings 8.65; Ezek. 47.19), generally identified with the Wadi el-'Arish (Map 2:S1 ["Brook of Egypt"]), ca. 80 km (48 mi) southeast of Gaza. This "river of Egypt" is not to be confused with the *Nile, for which the word *nāhār*, which properly means "river," is employed. The Hebrew phrase *nahal misrayim* is normally used for this watercourse, and cognate wording is found in Assyrian records; it is translated by the NRSV as "the Wadi of Egypt." The only exception is Genesis 15.18, where *nāhār* is used, but this may be an error (cf. Jth. 1.9).
          MICHAEL D. COOGAN

Roman Army. The most famous units in the Roman army were the legions or divisions stationed in the frontier provinces. They were supplemented by a (numerically equal) force of auxiliaries. In the city of Rome itself, there were several forces, especially the elite praetorian guard that protected the *emperor.

The army carried out many duties in addition to those purely military; besides policing, there were bureaucratic functions (cf. the requisitioning in Matt. 5.41; 27.32; for temptation to corruption, see Luke 3.14). Officers, often assisted by small detachments of troops, performed many administrative and judicial tasks.

A legion was commanded by a senator called an imperial legate; under him were six military tribunes and sixty *centurions. The full complement of a legion consisted of 5,500 to 6,000 men, who were Roman citizens. There were between twenty-five and thirty legions, but none was stationed in Judea until the Tenth Legion was sent there in 70 CE after the First Jewish Revolt. But there were four in Syria to the north, deployed in Judea when large-scale military intervention became necessary.

Legionaries were heavy infantry and were assisted by auxiliaries, especially cavalry, light-armed troops, and archers; it is not clear which of the latter the *dexiolaboi* of Acts 23.23 were. Auxiliaries were not Roman citizens, but it became customary to give them Roman citizenship after twenty-five years of service. The *auxilia*, as they were collectively known, were grouped into regiments of five hundred (in a few special cases a thousand) strong, called *alae* if cavalry, *cohortes* if infantry. Their commanders were prefects (tribunes in the case of regiments a thousand strong), usually drawn from the second order of the Roman nobility. Subordinate officers were called decurions in the *alae*, centurions in the cohorts.

The Romans also made use of the armed forces of semi-independent local kings (called "client" kings) within the Roman ambit, such as the *Herods. Soldiers from such armies are mentioned in Matthew 2.16 and Mark 6.17. Client kings often organized their armies on the Roman pattern.

The Roman forces mentioned in the New Testament were all auxiliaries. As Jews were excused from conscription into the Roman army for religious reasons, the soldiers at the *crucifixion and in *Acts were probably Syrian, *Samaritan, or Caesarean (from the non-Jewish population in Caesarea, the administrative capital of Judea): certainly, Herod the Great had Samaritans and Caesareans in his army, who were later incorporated into the Roman forces. Two regiments are named in the New Testament, the Italian and the Augustan Cohort (Acts 10.1; 27.1). These can be compared or equated with the *Cohors II Italica Civium Romanorum* and the *Cohors Augusta I* of the eastern command at the time. Both were of higher status than other auxiliary regiments (like those of Syrians or Thracians) and were stationed in Judea, possibly because no legion was there. Claudius Lysias (Acts 21.31; 23.26) is called a *chiliarch* or tribune, implying that his cohort was a thousand strong (and part of it mounted, if the cavalry escorting Paul came from it). DENIS BAIN SADDINGTON

Roman Empire. Later Christian writers looked back to the origin of their faith and saw the work of divine providence in the coincidence of the birth of Jesus and the reign of Augustus, the first Roman emperor. Under Augustus and his successors, the empire stretched from the northwest corner of Europe to Egypt and from Mauritania to the Black Sea. It brought fifty million or more inhabitants under relatively stable rule— an ideal setting for the growth of a new religion.

Rome Before the Emperors. Roman imperial institutions and ideas of citizenship went back to the Republic and Rome's origin as a city-state. According to tradition, the city of Rome (Map 14:B2) was founded by Romulus and Remus in 753 BCE at the northern edge of the plain of Latium in central peninsular Italy. Initially, the city-state was ruled by a king with the advice of the Senate, a council of elders from Rome's leading families who served for life. Important decisions, such as declarations of war, were ratified by an assembly of citizen-soldiers. The last king was expelled in 509 BCE, and his function was assumed by a pair of consuls elected annually by the citizen assembly from the body of senators. Later political thinkers interpreted these institutions as a mixed constitution with elements of monarchy (consuls), aristocracy (senate), and democracy (assembly), but in reality the senatorial aristocracy seems to have been most influential in making decisions.

Rome began its expansion in Latium as early as the regal period, but it was not until 338 BCE that Roman hegemony there was secured. From that base Rome came to dominate Italy by 270 BCE and the western Mediterranean following the two great wars against Carthage (264–241 BCE and 218–201 BCE); then the Romans moved quickly to establish hegemony over the whole Mediterranean basin with the defeat of Philip V of Macedonia (197 BCE) and Antiochus III of the Seleucid empire in Syria (189 BCE). Rome dominated from the early second century BCE but annexed these areas as provinces only slowly over the next century and a half. Syria and parts of Asia Minor came under direct Roman rule as

a result of Pompey's eastern campaigns in the 60s BCE.

Rome's unparalleled victories yielded vast concentrations of wealth and power in the hands of some citizens. The world empire left the city-state constitution and idea of citizenship outdated. Roman citizenship, a status inherited from citizen parents, had formerly entailed privileges of participation in politics in the city and responsibility for military service. As Roman power spread, though, citizenship was diffused well beyond the city by the establishment of citizen colonies in Italy and abroad and by selective grant to the conquered (first to their Latin neighbors, then to all free Italians). Participation in voting assemblies in the city of Rome was impracticable for most of these new citizens, yet citizenship continued to bestow privileged status, legal rights to marry and make contracts under Roman law, and *provocatio* (protection of a citizen from arbitrary whipping or execution by magistrates through appeal to higher authorities).

The traditional Republican constitution was ultimately inadequate to the tasks of governing a vast empire abroad and of containing political competition at home. In striving with each other to attain the highest honors, senators resorted to escalating violence, culminating in two decades of civil war initiated by Julius Caesar in 49 BCE and finished by his adopted son, Augustus, who established himself as the first *emperor.

Roman Imperial Social Structure. Augustus sought to legitimize his new regime by claiming to restore the *Respublica* and incorporating Republican institutions and aristocratic families. He styled himself *princeps* or first citizen, a traditional title for the leader of the Senate that avoided drawing attention to his autocracy. As part of his program of restoration, Augustus reaffirmed the traditional social order and strengthened its hierarchical divisions. It was a hierarchy based on wealth, respectable birth, and citizenship. High rank was marked by special clothing, the best seats at public spectacles, and various legal privileges.

At the top of the hierarchy were six hundred senators, propertied citizens of great wealth (at least one million sesterces or about one thousand times the annual salary of a legionary) who were chosen for the traditional senatorial offices at Rome. Equestrians or knights held second rank; they were citizens of free birth who possessed a census of at least four hundred thousand sesterces. Through the centuries of the empire they were recruited to serve in the imperial administration in increasing numbers. In addition to this imperial elite, each of the thousands of cities of the empire had its own local aristocracy from which was chosen a governing council consisting of a hundred or so of the town's wealthiest men (many of whom did not have Roman citizenship). These leisured elites became collectively known by the early second century CE as the *honestiores* or "more honorable men," in contrast to the humbler masses or *humiliores,* who constituted more than 90 percent of the population.

Several important distinctions of status divided ordinary working people. There were the citizens, concentrated mainly in Italy in Augustus's day but increasingly scattered throughout the provinces by the settlement of colonies and by imperial grant to favored individuals and communities. Noncitizen free provincials formed a huge amorphous group. The empire encompassed enormous cultural variation between city and countryside, and between regions. If *Latin was spoken by the urban elites of the western empire and *Greek was the primary tongue in the eastern cities, ordinary provincials continued to speak their native tongues, whether it be *Aramaic in Palestine or the Punic language around Carthage. They also continued to worship their own gods, which in some cases were assimilated to the Roman gods. Roman emperors and officials could be sensitive to the cultural diversity: the early governors of Judea tried to avoid affronts to Jewish *monotheism, but later ones were less careful. When Florus attempted to take a large sum from the *Temple treasury in Jerusalem in 66 CE, he provoked a fierce rebellion that required seven years, the destruction of *Jerusalem, and widespread slaughter to suppress.

Beneath the free population in the social hierarchy were slaves. *Slavery as an institution was taken for granted; there were no serious abolitionist movements in antiquity. Slaves formed a substantial proportion of the population in Italy (perhaps one-third), where they were heavily involved in all aspects of economic production. In most of the provinces slaves were common only as domestic servants. By law, slaves were property who could be bought or sold, beaten or tortured at the owner's whim. As the attitudes of owners varied, so also did the living conditions of slaves.

Imperial Political and Administrative Structures. The emperor ruled the peoples of the empire from Rome with the help of men chosen from the elites; with the demise of Republican elections, the popular voice in politics was lost. The capital city had a population of about one million and encompassed extremes of wealth and poverty, lavish public monuments and filthy, cramped apartments. Much of the population, perhaps even a majority, was made up of slaves and freedmen from the eastern Mediterranean, Germany, and elsewhere. Rome was able to grow to be the largest city of pre-industrial Europe because of the privileges of conquest: provincial agriculture was taxed, and part of the grain was sent to Rome to feed the masses. To keep the urban plebs quiet, the emperor also put on various spectacles, including the gladiatorial fights and wild beast hunts, in which some Christians met their end. Despite the food distributions and public entertainment, violence occasionally broke out in the city, prompting emperors to expel foreigners or to find scapegoats. So Claudius expelled the Jews from Rome (see Acts 18.2), and Nero began the official persecution of Christians when he needed scapegoats to blame for the great fire of 64 CE.

Italy was the land of citizens. As such, it was privileged with exemption from the land tax until the late third century CE. No governors were set over Italy; administration was largely left to the municipalities, with important matters referred to imperial officials in Rome.

Beyond Italy lay the Roman *imperium,* including client kings and directly ruled provinces. The Romans were slow to annex areas around the Mediterranean as provinces because they lacked a developed administrative apparatus. It was convenient to leave the governing of some peripheral areas to local kings in return for support of Rome in matters of foreign policy through occasional *tribute and troops for Roman wars. Client kings paid heed to the authority of the emperor and the senior governors of nearby provinces. Accounts of the reign of *Herod the Great, the best-known client king, illustrate how dependent he was on the continuing goodwill of the emperor and his officials, which he curried by careful attention to their wishes as well as by gifts and bribes. Gradually, as in Palestine, the client kingdoms were added to the list of directly ruled provinces.

The several dozen provinces were administered by governors sent out from Rome. Their two principal concerns were the maintenance of law and order and the collection of taxes. Roman administration can be characterized as general oversight by a handful of imperial officials who relied on local leaders. The major provinces were governed by senators in different capacities. Provinces with legions were administered by imperial legates appointed by the emperor from among those senators he considered most reliable. *Syria, with the largest legionary army of the eastern empire, was a province of this type. Major provinces without armies, such as Achaea, where supervised by senatorial proconsuls chosen in the Senate. Judea from 6 CE was one of those lesser provinces administered by equestrians (initially army officers called prefects, then imperial agents with the title of procurator). All governors held broad authority, limited by their responsibility to the emperor, who issued some instructions for administration (*mandata*); equestrian procurators also occasionally received guidance from senatorial governors of neighboring provinces.

Governors were accompanied to their provinces by minimal staffs, including friends and relatives who acted as advisory councils. The meager staffs were supplemented by military officers and soldiers acting as major figures of authority in provincial administration (as in Acts 22.23–30; 27.1). In their judicial capacity, governors heard the cases of Roman citizens who were subject to Roman law, and also adjudicated some other serious cases. For the most part, noncitizens were subject to local law and custom, and were left to local magistrates (Acts 16.19–23). Roman governors, reluctant to become entangled in squabbles among the natives, were often content to hold local leaders responsible for the preservation of order in their noncitizen communities. This tacit arrangement explains both the worry of *Caiaphas that disorder would provoke violent suppression from Rome (John 11.49–50) and the aloofness of the Roman proconsul Gallio when Paul was brought before him (Acts 18.12–17). It also accounts for the slow and sporadic pattern of persecution of the Christians before 250 CE. Roman governors were instructed to punish with death anyone brought before them who persistently admitted to being a Christian, but they were not actively to seek out Christians. As a result, in the province of Africa the first execution on the charge of Christianity did not come until about 180 CE.

Most provincials encountered Roman government over the matter of taxes—taxes on the land, on the people who worked the land, on goods moving across provincial borders, on inheritances, on sales in the market, to name but a few. The Romans did not impose a uniform tax system on conquest, but usually took over local arrangements and contracted out the collection to private agents, the *publicani,* infamous for their rapacious methods of enrichment (*see* Publicans). Julius Caesar began to phase out these middlemen at the highest levels, but they continued into the Principate to collect indirect taxes, such as custom duties. In order to assess the main land and head taxes, imperial officials occasionally carried out censuses in which provincials were required to register themselves and their property. The imperial legate Quirinius oversaw such a census in Judea in 6 CE, which, on grounds of date and Roman administrative procedures, seems to be impossible to reconcile with the account in Luke 2.1–5 (*see* Christmas; Chronology, *article on* Early Christian Chronology).

In Augustus's day, the resources of the Roman empire were sufficient to fulfill the relatively light demands of the state, but they were limited by the agricultural base and the stagnant technology of the economy. Under the Christian emperors of the later empire, increasing demands for money and recruits to support the growing army and bureaucracy were met by more determined resistance. As the "barbarian" tribes pressed ever-harder against the frontiers, the limits left emperors unable to ward off the threats. In 410 CE, the Eternal City was sacked by Alaric and his Visigoths; the last Roman emperor of the west, Romulus Augustulus, was deposed by the German leader Odoacer in 476 CE.

See also Roman Army; Tribute and Taxation, *article on* Roman Empire.   RICHARD P. SALLER

Romans, The Letter of Paul to the.

Circumstances of the Letter. Romans, the longest of Paul's letters and the only one in which the apostle does not name a companion or coauthor, is the most carefully worked out statement of his view of the Christian faith. Although Paul had never visited the Christian community in Rome, despite his repeated hope to do so (1.11, 13), and hence cannot have been one of the founders of Christianity in the capital city of the *Roman empire, he intended to visit it soon, both to encourage the believers and be encouraged by them (1.12).

Also in Paul's mind as he dictated this letter (16.22) was his plan to carry his mission to the western half of the Mediterranean world, as far as Spain (15.24), after he had delivered a gift of money to the "poor among the saints at Jerusalem" (15.26; cf. Gal. 2.10). Paul probably hoped that the Christians in Rome would underwrite this mission (15.28–29). Acts, however, reports nothing of this mission to Spain, and the danger that Paul feared in Jerusalem from nonbelievers (15.31) in fact materialized in a different way with his arrest there (cf. Acts 21.30).

It is probable that there was more than one Christian community in Rome, since Paul refers to a "house church" (16.5); others may have been in the houses of Prisca and Aquila (16.3; cf. 1 Cor. 16.19 for the house church they sponsored in Corinth), of Aristobulus (16.10), and of Narcissus (16.11). It is also probable that the Christian community there was composed of converted Jews as well as *gentiles, despite an earlier order by the Emperor Claudius that all Jews be expelled from Rome (41 or 49 CE). That this also affected Christians is evident from the reference in Acts 18.2 to Prisca and Aquila, who were Jewish Christians. Paul's direct address to Jews (e.g., 2.17), and his concern with their history (e.g., 3.1; 4.1; 9–11), owes more to the content of his own faith and the style of his argument than to actual debates he anticipated with Jews in Rome.

Although Paul had never been to Rome, he knew many Christians who lived there, and included greetings to them at the end of his letter (chap. 16). Arguments to the effect that these greetings could not have belonged to the original letter are not persuasive, since mobility within the Roman empire was great, and there were many who migrated to Rome during this period. The extent to which *women played a key role within the early church is evident also from the same chapter: for example, Phoebe, a *deacon, 16.1; Prisca, 16.3 (cf. 1 Cor. 16.19, Acts 18.2); Mary, 16.6; *Junia, an *apostle, 16.7—all of whom, as the language indicates, were active in the Christian mission.

Specific information is not available concerning the circumstances surrounding the composition of the letter, such as the place from which it was written or the exact date of its composition. Scholars are not in agreement on a chronology of *Paul's life, and the most that can be said is that the letter seems to have been written toward the end of his life. Since it is not known how well Paul was acquainted with the circumstances of Christians in Rome, we are unable to determine whether his ethical discussions in the letter (cf. 14.1–15.13) refer to specific problems, or whether they are the kind of general admonition he thought any group of Christians might read

with profit. That the problem was not between Jewish and gentile Christians about dietary matters is clear from the fact that no Jewish dietary laws forbade the general eating of meat (14.2) or the drinking of *wine (14.21). The admonitions read like a generalized account of the problem that Paul faced in *Corinth (see 1 Cor. 8), and hence they are probably intended, as is the rest of the letter, to be a summary of Christian faith and practice.

Content of the Letter. A more detailed outline of Paul's letter to the Christian communities in Rome is the following:

I. God's lordship and the problem of the past: wrath and grace (1.1–4.22)
   A. Opening (1.1–13)
   B. The gospel and God's wrath (1.14–3.20)
   C. The gospel and God's grace (3.21–4.22)
II. God's lordship and the problem of the present: grace and law (4.23–8.39)
   A. Sin and grace: Adam and Christ (4.23–5.21)
   B. Sin, grace and law (6.1–7.25)
   C. The spirit and the surety of grace (8.1–39)
III. God's lordship and the problem of the future: Israel and God's gracious plan (9.1–11.36)
   A. God's grace and Israel's rejection (9.1–29)
   B. Grace, faith, and the purpose of the law (9.30–10.21)
   C. Israel and her future with God (11.1–36)
IV. God's lordship and the problems of daily living: grace and the structures of life (12.1–16.27)
   A. Grace and the community (12.1–21)
   B. Grace and the state (13.1–7)
   C. Grace and the neighbor (13.8–14)
   D. Grace and unity in the faith (14.1–15.13)
   E. Grace and Paul's plans (15.14–33)
   F. Conclusion (16.1–27)

The central theme of Paul's letter to the Christian communities in Rome is the universal scope of God's redemptive act in Jesus Christ, offered to all who accept it in trust. That redemption, by which God reestablishes his gracious lordship over his rebellious creation, is offered not only to Jews but also to gentiles.

First Section (1.1–4.22). Paul assumes that apart from Christ, all humanity has rebelled against God, the characteristic form of that rebellion being to set something other than God at the center of one's life. Such substitution of some part of creation for the true God, whether self or some other reality, Paul understands as *idolatry (1.22–23, 25). Because there was enough evidence from the created universe itself to warn human beings away from idolatry (1.19–20), such rebellion against God is culpable (1.21) and brings wrath (1.18, 24–31). Although gentiles show by their actions that they possess a sense of morality (2.14–16), they will not be saved by being morally pure, since moral purity cannot reconcile them to the God they have rejected. Similarly, though Jews belong to God's *chosen people (3.1) and possess the *Law (2.17–20), these features will not deliver them from divine wrath brought on by their rejection of God's act of redemption in his Son, Jesus Christ. Hence all people stand in rebellion before God (3.9–18), including those who belong to the chosen people, to whom the Law was given (3.19–20).

In Christ, however, God has come in *grace to rebellious humanity, and he offers a remedy as universal as the malady (3.23–24). That remedy is to be received in *faith (3.25), a remedy open to all, of whatever origin, since God is the God of all, and he offers a restored relationship to himself through trust in the love he has shown in his Son (3.28–30). In fact, a right relationship with God on the basis of trust is not something new, but was already the case with *Abraham (chap. 4). It was Abraham's trust in God that allowed him to stand in a positive relationship to God (4.18–22); that positive relationship is what Paul calls "righteousness." Such *righteousness, based on trust, came to Abraham before he was circumcised; hence, faith is open to all, whether uncircumcised, as Abraham was when he first trusted, or circumcised, as Abraham later became (4.9–12, 16).

The record of Abraham's trust in God has, however, more than historical interest; Paul affirms that it also bears directly on his readers (4.23). With that announcement, Paul begins the second major part of his letter.

Second Section (4.23–8.39). Turning his attention to the present, Paul explains what his readers may now experience (5.1–5) as a result of the new opportunity for forgiveness of sin and a restored relationship to God which is offered in Christ (4.24–25). That new relationship is based on God's initiative in opening the way through Christ to *righteousness in the present and to *salvation in the future (5.6–11). The divine initiative remains necessary in the present, since the present continues to suffer from the inheritance of *Adam, namely, the rebellion mentioned earlier (5.12–14): the universality of sharing in Adam's rebellion is demonstrated for Paul by the universal fate of death for all people (5.12). It was from that rebellion and its negative results that Christ has saved human beings (5.15–19).

Where does God's *law fit into all this? Paul raises that question (5.20–21) and then considers it in the next two chapters. Discussing the relationship of law, *sin, and *grace in every possible combination (6.1: sin and grace; 6.15: law and grace; 7.7: law and sin), Paul argues that *baptism into Christ's death breaks the power of sin (6.1–11), and hence Christians are now free not to sin (6.12–14). Paul next argues that everyone, whether Christian or not, is under the power of some force, whether of sin or of grace (6.16–23), and that only God's grace releases a person from the power of sin through the death of Christ (7.1–17). Third, Paul argues that the close relationship of sin and law shows that those under the Law are incapable of extricating themselves from it (7.7–23). Only Christ is able to do that (7.24), as Paul had already stated in 6.1–14.

The section 7.13–23 is thus Paul's reflection on the past, namely what life under the Mosaic law looks like from a Christian perspective; 8.1–39, on the other hand, is his reflection on the present, namely what life under Christ and freed from law looks like from a Christian perspective. Thus, a life restored under the gracious lordship of God through Christ is a life wherein the enmity between God and human beings is at an end (8.1–11), and where they, restored to the family of God (8.12–17), may look beyond present deprivation (8.18–25) to the presence of God's Spirit with them (8.26–27). Life in such a situation is safe from any hazard (8.28–39).

Third Section, 9.1–11.36. One problem remains, however, and that is the rejection by the chosen people, the Jews, of God's plan for their redemption in Jesus Christ. Since God had promised them blessing through Abraham, does not their rejection of the fulfillment of that promise in Christ mean that God's promise, and thus his word, has failed (9.6)? Paul answers this question by pointing out that since God has always worked with a *remnant in Israel, it should not be surprising that he continues to do so in the case of the small minority in Israel who believe in Christ (9.1–29). Furthermore, by putting the Law ahead of Christ as an expression of God's will, the Jews have continued to resist trust in God as the way of salvation (9.20–10.4).

Yet such trust, not limited by birth, as was the Law, is God's chosen way of the redemption of sinners (10.5–13), a way that has been proclaimed to Jews as well as gentiles (10.14–21). Despite the Jews' rejection, however, God has not rejected the Jews (11.1–10), nor will the rejection of Christ by the Jews be final. Rather, that rejection is part of God's merciful plan: by rejecting Christ, the Jews have created the opportunity for gentiles to hear the proclamation of salvation. When that proclamation has been completed, the Jews will also finally accept trust in God through Christ (11.11–16). Using the analogy of grafting branches into an olive tree (11.17–24), Paul makes the point that the hardened attitude of Jews toward Christ is not the final word; in the end, they too will share in God's gracious lordship established through trust in Christ (11.25–31). All of this is part of God's merciful plan (11.32), knowledge of which calls forth praise to God, who works in such strange yet gracious ways (11.33–36).

Fourth Section, 12.1–16.27. Having ended the third section with hymnic praise to the God whose gracious ways with sinful humanity are mysterious and past finding out, Paul gives attention to the ways in which God's gracious lordship, established through trust in Christ, relates to the structures of everyday life. Showing successively how that gracious lordship impinges on life in the community (12.1–21), in the state (13.1–7), and on one's relationship with one's *neighbor (13.8–14), Paul then considers how Christians should deal with differences among themselves (14.1–15.13). Taking as his example the distinction between the "weak" (those who have scruples about eating meat, 15.2, or observing the *Sabbath, 15.5–6, or drinking *wine, 15.14) and the "strong" (those who regard such scruples as unnecessary), Paul affirms that the personal preferences of the strong are to be laid aside lest the weak be offended, and thus be lost to the Christian community (14.15; 15.1).

In the final verses, Paul outlines his travel plans (15.14–33) and sends greetings (16.1–16, 21–23) along with final exhortations (16.17–20) and a benediction (16.25–27).

Influence. Because of the range and depth of theological topics discussed in it, the letter to the Romans has played a key role at critical junctures in the history of Christianity. Amid the crumbling institutions of a Roman empire which had embraced the church, Augustine learned from Romans a view of human nature and of the state that could survive the demise of civilization. Amid the pomp of a church grown self-important, Luther and Calvin found in this letter, particularly its treatment of *justification by faith alone, a way to construct a worshiping community that allowed God's gracious lordship to be more clearly expressed. In a period of naive identification of cultural progress with God's will, Karl Barth heard in Romans the divine "no" to any attempt to equate human accomplishment with divine grace. Paul's acknowledgement of the continuing validity of God's special relationship to the Jews (e.g., 3.1–2; 11.29) stands in the way of any Christian exaltation over the modern heirs of ancient Israel. To those who pay careful heed, Romans continues to be an important guide for all who seek to make sense of their lives in the midst of historical change and cultural conflict.

PAUL J. ACHTEMEIER

Ruth, The Book of. Ruth is a gripping short story, incorporating folkloric features that make for ease of appreciation as common human experience, as well as distinctive cultural features commending Israel's theology and ethics. Ruth stands eighth, between Judges and 1 Samuel, in the *canon of the Bible familiar to Christians, but first among the five small festival scrolls (*megillot) of the Hebrew canon, usually right after Proverbs. Ruth is the festal reading for Shavuʿot (*Pentecost) in Jewish tradition.

The book begins with a background scenario of a Bethlehemite family, two parents and their two sons, sojourning in *Moab because of famine back home. The sons marry Moabites. Father and two sons die, leaving three widows, Naomi, Orpah, and Ruth. Naomi, choosing to return home, urges her daughters-in-law to remain in Moab. Orpah does so, but Ruth cleaves to Naomi. Naomi, lamenting bitterly, arrives in *Bethlehem with Ruth accompanying her; she sees little prospect of fullness of life. Scene two (chap. 2) has Ruth initiate efforts to support herself and Naomi by gleaning at the harvest, where she chances upon the field of Boaz, a worthy Bethlehemite. Boaz notices her, at first makes minimal provision, then moves to progressively greater care for this woman who has displayed such loyalty to her family.

In scene three (chap. 3), Naomi, encouraged by the success of Ruth's first steps, directs her how to move things from a temporary to a long-term resolution: marriage and offspring for Ruth, redeemer care for Naomi. Ruth forces the matter with Boaz in a provocative scene at the threshing-floor, only to learn that the redeemer responsibility falls first upon a person other than Boaz. In the final scene (4.1–17), while Ruth and Naomi wait, Boaz maneuvers this other person to yield his role at a public forum in the town gate. The way is clear for Boaz to marry Ruth, provide an heir to Ruth's first husband, and provide a redeemer for Naomi. The redeemer is Obed, David's grandfather—this information is the striking climax of a chorus by the Bethlehem townspeople celebrating first Boaz, then Ruth and Naomi. The story closes (4.18–20) with a *genealogy connecting *David through Obed and Boaz to Perez, Judah's offspring (Gen. 38).

Scholarly efforts to reconstruct earlier stages in the development of the story or to identify additions to the original have yielded little insight into its meaning; even the conclusion that the genealogy at the end (cf. 1 Chron. 2.5–15) is an appendix is now regularly challenged, and interpreters study the book as a carefully crafted whole.

Almost two-thirds of the story is conveyed in conversation, a characteristic of biblical storytelling artistry. Both conversation and narration include captivating literary devices. For example, on the road back to Bethlehem, the hesitation of Orpah and Ruth, the combined urging and complaint of Naomi, and the commitment of Ruth are all handled with superb pacing and beautiful language. Guide words such as "return" in scene one and "glean" in scene two bind episodes internally. Key words in pairs are used to link scene to scene and connect the posing of plot problems to their resolutions (e.g., "lads" Naomi has lost in 1.5 with the "lad" Naomi gains in 4.16; Yahweh's "wings" of care in 2.12 with Boaz's "wings" of marital commitment in 3.9). The storyteller is sparing in detail, providing only the essentials and sometimes leaving gaps: we are taken by surprise in 4.3 by a field that Naomi can sell, and are not told whether Boaz and Naomi ever meet.

Emphasizing these literary characteristics follows the trend of current scholarship on Ruth, and it means playing down questions of historicity on the one hand or of the book's role as polemic on the other. In the past, Ruth was often seen as composed in the fourth century BCE to oppose the Ezra-Nehemiah effort to dissolve mixed marriages. Instead, interpretation now focuses on Ruth as historical fiction, serving as an edifying and entertaining encounter with typical events in a typical town. Clearly, care for those in danger of being left on society's margins

is a crucial concern—in the Ruth story typified by two *widows, one a foreigner. Structures exist to meet this concern: the gleaning provision (cf. Lev. 19.9–10; Deut. 24.19–22); marriage to one's husband's relative (Ruth 2.12–13; 4.5); *redeeming, which involves responsibility for property recovery and care of persons; responsibilities devolving upon members of a wider circle designated by Hebrew words translated "kinsman" in 2.1 and 3.2. The story brings all these customs to bear, assuming that the audience knows how they worked. Among these, the particular practice called *levirate marriage (Deut. 25.5–10; Gen. 38) may pertain; alternatively, Ruth 1.12–13 and 4.5 may point to some allied custom otherwise unattested in the Bible. What the story does portray clearly is the interplay of agents of care and recipients of care within society: in turn, the three principal characters both give and receive. Orpah and the potential redeemer in 4.3–6 are ready to give some help; the drama lies with the greater risk and commitment required of Ruth and Boaz to bring good out of bad, a theme expressed in the key concept ḥesed, "kindness," in 1.8; 2.20; and 3.10.

Theology is muted in Ruth. The book participates in an exploration of divine providence also seen in the *Joseph cycle (Gen. 37–50), in 2 Samuel 9–20, and in *Job. Only Ruth 1.6, 4.13, and probably 2.20 assert divine intervention, but the greetings and blessings and outcries of the characters keep deity present. The sharp outcry against God by Naomi in 1.20–21 sounds the prominent biblical theme of lament.

The climax, which comes with the note about David in 4.17, suggests that blessing of Israel's royal line is an issue here. The blessing speeches in 4.13–17 are comparable to other Near Eastern royal blessings. If the David theme is intrinsic to the book—this was often debated in the past—then it provides the historical datum that David had a Moabite ancestor. The book is quite probably part of a cycle of stories about David's ancestry, which would include Genesis 38 and other episodes now lost—for instance, about Perez and Zerah prepared for by Genesis 38.27–30, and about Obed prepared for by Ruth 4.16–17.

To decide about the date and audience of Ruth is difficult. Linguistic criteria and judgments about its place in the development of thought, invoked in the past as pointers to a late date, have lost their cogency. A date anywhere in the time of the Judean monarchy is plausible. The audience was probably village people and the storyteller a professional bard, quite possibly a wise woman (cf. 2 Sam. 14.1–20). Alternatively, the story may be a self-conscious imitation of a folktale, written at the royal court.

The universal appeal and the plausible presentation of typical Israelite life mask precise time and place, and release the story of Ruth for the pleasure and edification of all. The Targumic tradition and rabbinic commentary build the relation between Naomi and Ruth into a paradigm for the education of a *proselyte. They celebrate the portrayal of "kindness" and probe the institutions of levirate, shoe transfer (4.6–8), and redemption. Down the centuries, more modern literary allusions give us Dante's "gleaner-maid, meek ancestress" of David, Bunyan's "Mercy," Milton's chooser of the better part, Keats's recipient of the nightingale's solace "amid the alien corn," and Goethe's accolade: the most beautiful "little whole" of the Hebrew Bible.

EDWARD F. CAMPBELL

❖ S ❖

Sabbath (Hebr. *šabbāt*). The last day of the week; the only day bearing a name, the others being merely numbered. It is considered the absolute day of rest without exceptions. Its observance is probably very old but is attested only since the eighth century BCE (Amos 8.5; Hos. 2.13; Isa. 1.13, 2 Kings 4.23). An earlier date is suggested by Israelite legal traditions (Exod. 23.12; 34.21); the references in the *Ten Commandments (Exod. 20.8–11; Deut. 5.12–15) may not be older than Deuteronomy itself.

The etymology of *šabbāt* is uncertain. A relation to the verb *šbt*, to which it has naturally been connected (see Gen 2.2–3; Exod. 20.11), is questionable, since *šbt* is never attested in the intensive form or in connection with the practice of resting from work, while its meaning is "coming/bringing to an end." A connection with the Akkadian *šab/pattu*, the day of the full moon, falling on the fifteenth of the lunar month, or with the seventh, fourteenth, twenty-first, and twenty-eighth days should probably be rejected, as they are unpropitious days, the opposite of what the Sabbath seems to be. Nevertheless, the former connection is so obvious etymologically that one should ask whether the abstention from work on such a day does not lead, eventually, to the Israelite concept of rest. Sometimes the Sabbath is connected with the feast of the new moon (Amos 8.5; Hos. 2.13; Isa. 1.13); what this means we do not know.

The origins of the Sabbath are also obscure. Biblical tradition (but in late texts) attributes it to *Moses; this, however, cannot be verified and, since the practice presupposes a relatively advanced agricultural society, is improbable. In preexilic times its observance cannot have been very strict; 2 Kings 11.5–9 tells us, without any criticism, of the arrest and execution on the Sabbath of the Queen Mother Athaliah, who had been usurping the kingship, something inconceivable in later times.

By postexilic times keeping the Sabbath had become one of the distinctive practices of obser-

vant Jews. During this period detailed regulations developed so as to make its observance absolute, a tendency already evident in the explanations in the Ten Commandments. The Sabbath was also a socioeconomic institution and meant feeding humans and animals although they were not working, besides losing profit; thus attempts were made to circumvent the law, and these needed to be countered. In Maccabean times the problem of fighting on the Sabbath arose (1 Macc. 2.32–38; 2 Macc. 6.11), the faithful preferring to be killed rather than desecrate the Sabbath.

In the New Testament and in rabbinic Judaism we hear echoes of the debates that developed around the observance of Sabbath until finally a criterion was proposed: "Every case of danger of life allows for the suspension of the Sabbath" (*Yoma* 8.6). According to Rabbi Akiba, one should not desecrate the Sabbath for things that can be done the day before or the day after, but no desecration exists when such a possibility is not offered. Therefore a midwife can function and should be helped on the Sabbath. Rabbinic teaching differs from the New Testament in that healing in the New Testament is considered to fall under the principle of "danger of life," a point that later rabbinic teaching did not accept. The rabbis concluded: "Sabbath has been given to you; you have not been given to the Sabbath" (*Mekilta* to Exod. 31.13; cf. Mark 2.27). Some sectarians thought otherwise; so at *Qumran on the Sabbath one was not supposed to help an animal when it was giving birth or involved in an accident.

New Testament discussions about the Sabbath seem therefore to be inner-Jewish discussions. By the end of the first century CE, the first day of the week was celebrated as the day of the Lord, to which Christian observance of the Sabbath was transferred (see Rev 1.10; also Acts 20.7; 1 Cor. 16.2). Some Christian groups, notably the Seventh-day Adventists, following biblical legislation exactly, observe the seventh day of the week, the original (and continuing) Jewish Sabbath.   J. A. SOGGIN

Sabeans. *See* Sheba, Queen of.

Sacrament. The term is not found in the New Testament, though the *Vulgate sometimes uses *sacramentum* to render the Greek word for *mystery *(mystērion),* as in Ephesians 1.19. The word may have been suggested by its secular meaning, the oath of allegiance taken by a Roman soldier on enlistment. The Roman governor Pliny (ca. 112 CE) described Christians as those who bound themselves by an oath *(sacramentum)* not to commit crimes.

By the third century CE, the word was being used to describe *baptism and eucharist *(see* Lord's Supper) as specific acts of Christian worship, and it was later extended to include other official liturgical acts of the church. In 1564 the Council of Trent defined seven sacraments as instituted by Christ, namely, Baptism, Confirmation, Eucharist, Penance, Extreme Unction, Holy Orders, and Marriage. The Reformers with their biblical emphasis preferred to confine the term to baptism and eucharist, which are generally recognized as the two gospel sacraments.

The development of sacramental theology reflects different views found in the New Testament concerning the relation between God and human beings, where some stress God's *grace and others *faith. The Donatist controversy of the third century led to the use of the phrase *ex opere operato* to indicate that the efficacy and value of the sacrament did not depend on the worthiness of the minister but on the promise of God to the church. Therefore, as long as the church was obedient to its Lord and used the right "matter" (e.g., water in baptism, bread and wine at the eucharist) and the right "form" (the words or prayer expressing the meaning of the action), participants could be assured of God's presence and action in the sacrament. To avoid the mechanical understanding to which this view could easily lead, the Reformers emphasized faith in differing ways. Some, like Ulrich Zwingli, thought of the sacraments as signs of God's action in the past, whereas others regarded them as means of grace assured by the outward sign and the promise of Christ.

Modern theology tends to describe the sacraments as occasions of encounter between God and the believer, where the reality of God's gra-

cious actions needs to be accepted in faith to effect a true meeting. This accords with New Testament teaching, which sees God's grace focused in the person of Jesus and his death and resurrection. This is the "mystery" of Christ (Col. 4.3), in the sense that God's secret purpose has been declared and made known in Christ. The sacraments therefore are means of grace insofar as they are occasions when the gracious act of God is made present to the believer. Paul expresses this understanding with regard to both the eucharist (1 Cor. 11.26) and baptism (Rom. 6.3–4).

The use of the term "the holy mysteries" (encouraged by 1 Cor. 4.1) to refer to the sacraments, especially in the Eastern Orthodox churches, shows more clearly the connection between the redemptive acts of Christ and their liturgical representation.   JOHN N. SUGGIT

Sacrifice. The offering of some commodity to God, generally making use of the services of a cultic official, a *priest. In the Bible, the various kinds of sacrifices are presented most systematically in Leviticus 1–7 (cf. Num. 15). The different sacrifices cited there can be classified in several ways. Most prominent are those utilizing clean animals (cattle, sheep, goats, doves, pigeons). All such animal sacrifices have a number of features in common: killing/dismemberment of the victim, burning of at least some part of it (the fat in particular) on the *altar, application of the *blood to the altar by the priest in some manner (sprinkling or smearing).

The burnt offering or *holocaust is particularly distinctive (Lev. 1.3–17; 6.8–13). As the latter name implies, a complete consumption of the victim's remains (except for the skin, which was given to the priest: Lev. 7.8) by fire was involved here. The rite opened with the offerer's laying his hand on the victim's head (Lev. 1.4a); this gesture of self-identification signifies that, through the beast, he is offering himself to God. The intended purpose of the holocaust was to effect atonement with Yahweh for the offerer (Lev. 1.4b).

Another major animal sacrifice is the peace offering (NRSV: "offering of well-being"; the differently translated Hebrew word is šĕlāmîm), described in Leviticus 3.1–17; 7.11–36. In this instance, the designation employed points to the ritual's aim, that is, to (re-)establish "peace," fellowship between the divine and human parties. In line with this end, the victim's remains are divided between God (for whom the fat is burned on the altar), the assisting priest, and the offerer's household. The peace offering can further be specified, in accordance with the motive prompting it, as a thanksgiving, votive, or freewill offering. In the first instance, the victim's flesh must be consumed on the day of the sacrifice itself (Lev. 7.15); in the latter two, the time allotted for this extends through the following day (Lev. 7.16).

Two further animal sacrifices are the sin offering and the guilt offering (Lev. 4.1–6.7; 6.25–7.10). The Bible does not clearly distinguish these in terms of either their ritual or the situations that necessitate them (see Lev. 7.17). Both are designed to effect atonement in cases of a nondeliberate offense (e.g., bodily discharges, contact with the unclean), and in both it is only the victim's fat that is burned on the altar. The sin offering is, however, the more public of the two, being offered on the major *feasts of the year (Num. 28–29), while the guilt offering functions as part of a process of reparation undertaken by an individual (Lev. 5.16; 6.4).

The Bible also prescribes various nonbloody sacrifices; these utilize cereals (Lev. 2.1–15), *frankincense, and *wine. Of these, the last must accompany other sacrifices, whereas the first two may be offered separately. Finally, biblical narratives evidence familiarity with the practice of human sacrifice (see, e.g., Gen. 22; Judg. 10.30–40; 1 Kings 16.34; 2 Kings 3.27); this, however, is strongly condemned in the laws of the Pentateuch (e.g., Lev. 18.14).

Taken as a whole, the Hebrew Bible manifests a certain ambivalence regarding sacrifice. In the Pentateuch, it is solemnly enjoined as a positive divine requirement, while other passages seem to articulate God's rejection of the practice as a whole (e.g., Amos 5.21–27; Isa. 1.10–20; Ps. 51.16–17). The latter formulations are best seen as hyperbolic reminders of the truth that cultic sacrifice is pleasing to God only when offered by one whose whole life is lived in accordance with God's will.

In the New Testament, particularly in *Hebrews, the death of *Jesus is described as a sacrifice that definitively secures for the whole of humanity the effects (atonement, fellowship with God) that older sacrifices brought about only temporarily (Heb. 9.23–28). Likewise in the New Testament, the notion of a spiritual sacrifice comes to the fore (Rom. 12.1; 15.16; Phil. 2.17; 4.18; 1 Pet. 2.5). In this conception, every action of a Christian's life has the capacity, when performed in faith, to be an offering acceptable to God. CHRISTOPHER T. BEGG

Sadducees. The Sadducees were one of the Jewish parties referred to by *Josephus (*War* 2.8.164–66; *Ant.* 13.5.173; 18.1.16–17). Disputes between them and the *Pharisees are mentioned in later Jewish writings (*m. Yad.* 4.6–7; *m. 'Erub.* 6.2; *m. Para* 3.7; *m. Nid.* 4.2; *b. Yoma* 2a, 19b, 53a; *b. Sukk.* 48). They are depicted in the New Testament as opponents of *Jesus who, together with the Pharisees, tested him with questions (Mark 12.18; Matt. 16.1, 6). In *Acts they feature as opponents of the early Christians (4.1; 5.17).

The name (probably Hebr. *ṣaddûqîm*) is derived from *Zadok. The most likely association is with the high priest under David; although it is just possible, as one tradition suggests, that they were connected with a later Zadok, pupil of one of the Sages, Antigonus of Socho (early second century BCE), who, as they believed, rejected belief in the resurrection. There were of course Zadokites, descendants of the original high *priest, who controlled the *Temple in Jerusalem for many centuries before the second century BCE, which is when Josephus introduces them. Possibly the emergence of Sadducees as a party is the result of a crisis occasioned by the usurpation of the high priesthood by Jonathan in 152 BCE; possibly this is also the point at which the *Essenes broke away from the high-priestly group and moved out into the desert. In any case the Sadducees and the Pharisees both strove for influence at court and for control over the Temple, which would of course give them the power required to exercise an important role in national affairs. Fortunes changed not infrequently; doubtless the power of the Temple aristocracy was substantially limited under Roman rule, but the Sadducees were prepared to accept a measure of compromise with the Roman authorities and probably had influence with them. Once they lost their cultic function as a result of the destruction of the Temple (70 CE) they ceased to exist as a group. This may reflect the extent to which they had lost popular support.

We learn of their beliefs only from others' writings. Whereas the Pharisees accepted the authority of the Tradition of the Elders as a valuable tool for extending and interpreting the Law, the Sadducees did not (*Ant.* 18.1.16). Nor did they, as the New Testament also attests, believe in the resurrection of the dead (*Ant.* 18.1.16–17; *War* 2.8.165; Mark 12.18; Acts 23.8;

see Afterlife and Immortality, *article on* Second Temple Judaism and Early Christianity). Josephus also reports that they did not believe in fate but thought that men and women were in control of their actions. They are also said to have rejected belief in *angels and *demons (Acts 23.8).

The sense of all this is elusive. In their development of an oral tradition of legal interpretation, the Pharisees and Sages were in one way doing no more than what had been done throughout Jewish history, that is, adapting their legal traditions to changing circumstance. Why should the Sadducees oppose this? Possibly because the written Law reinforced their control over the Temple; possibly too because the Pharisees were attempting to undermine that position by transferring some of the priestly rituals and practices away from Jerusalem to the towns and villages outside. Certainly the Sadducees were concerned principally to uphold the Temple and its sacrifices: for them it was the proper observance of Temple ritual that maintained the *covenant relationship between Israel and God.

Rejection of belief in the resurrection again indicates a traditionalist stance. Jews had long believed that so long as Israel obeyed the Law then God would rule over them and reward the righteous and punish the wicked in this life. Belief in the resurrection, on the other hand, was linked to beliefs that the present age was in the grip of dark powers, so that in this life the righteous would suffer, although God would ultimately vindicate them. Those who had died would be raised so that they too could receive their due rewards (Dan. 12.2). To reject belief in the resurrection and, indeed, possibly also in demonic powers who controlled this world in the present age, was then also to reject the belief that this present age was radically corrupted; in fact, from the Sadducees' point of view, those who argued the contrary view may have appeared to deny the continued existence of the covenant between God and Israel. This may also explain their denial of fate. They believed that Jews were free to influence their destiny; if they obeyed the Law and repented and made due restitution when they sinned, then all would be well. The darker views of the world associated with belief in the resurrection also entailed beliefs in the pervasiveness of the power of sin (see Rom. 5.12–21, which may owe more than a little to Paul's Pharisaic background, although such beliefs should not be thought of as specifically Pharisaic), such that men and women were no longer in control of their fate. It is such views that the Sadducees rejected.

This may suggest a further reason why the Sadducees disappeared after 70 CE. Not only was their position as the Temple aristocracy fundamentally destroyed; their belief that the maintenance of the Temple cult would suffice to stave off real disaster for Israel had also been proven false.

See also Judaisms of the First Century CE.

JOHN RICHES

Sailing. *See* Ships and Sailing.

Saint(s). "Saint" most frequently translates some derivative of Hebrew *qādôš* and Greek *hagios*. Both words apply primarily to the gods as those beings who rightly deserved awe, or who were worthy of worship; their extended meaning includes those persons and things that had a unique relation to these gods. Because of this relationship, such persons and things were set apart from the unhallowed world about them so that they might be ceremonially clean, sufficiently pure to be of special service in the worship of the gods.

In the Hebrew Bible, the Lord God is holy (Lev. 19.2), meaning that he is set apart from, different from, and transcendent over everything in the created order, and is therefore uniquely worthy of awe and worship (Isa. 6.1–5). But because God stands in special relation to parts of his creation, certain things can be holy, such as *Jerusalem (Isa. 48.2), the *Temple (Isa. 64.10), the *Sabbath (Exod. 31.14), garments (Exod. 28.2), *water (Numb. 5.17), and oil (Exod. 30.25); and people can be holy (Lev. 19.2), even an entire nation. Israel is called holy, elect, a people separated from all other peoples, set apart to the Lord God, that is, God's own people (Exod. 19.5, 6; Lev. 11.44, 45; cf. Hos. 2.23; Ezek. 37.27).

In the Bible, therefore, the word "saints" refers to "holy people"—holy, however, not primarily in the moral sense, but in the sense of being specially marked out as God's people. Thus, just as the people of Israel are "saints," "holy ones," a nation set apart by God for the worship and service of God, so in the New Testament those who comprise the church are also called holy, "saints," because they too are set apart to God, God's own people (Rom. 1.7; Phil. 1.1; *passim*). The church is seen as the new Israel, the new community separated from the world around it and dedicated to God, the people of the end times to whom God will make good his promises (cf. Dan. 7.18, 27; see also John 17.11; Acts 9.13; 1 Pet. 2.9, 10). The term is also applied to dead members of the community (Matt. 27.52; Rev. 16.6; etc.), though this is not its primary biblical usage.

Moral or ethical ideas were never wholly absent from the word "saints," both in the Hebrew Bible (Lev. 17–26; 19.2–18) and in the New Testament (1 Pet. 1.16; cf. Matt. 5.8; 1 Tim. 1.5; 2 Tim. 2.22). Because God is holy, that is, because God is perfect in goodness and justice and love and purity (Lev. 19.2), it is expected that his special people will pattern their lives accordingly (Lev. 19.2–18; 1 Pet. 1.16). Hence, *ethics belongs together with *religion. Relationship with the God of the Bible demands a moral response in accord with the character of God.

See also Holiness. GERALD F. HAWTHORNE

Salem. *See* Jerusalem.

Salome. The name of two women appearing in the New Testament:

1. The daughter of Herodias and Herod (Philip), and thus the granddaughter of *Herod the Great, famous as the performer of the dance (Matt. 14.1–12 par.) for which, at her mother's instigation, she was rewarded with the head of *John the Baptist on a platter. She is not named in the Gospels, but Josephus identifies her and also reports her marriage to Herod's son, her uncle Philip (*Ant.* 18.5.137–38). Salome's dance is a favorite theme in *dance, art, and literature, as in Gustave Flaubert's story *Hérodias* and Richard Strauss's opera and Oscar Wilde's play, both called *Salome*.

2. A disciple of Jesus, present at the *crucifixion and at the tomb on the following Sunday (Mark 15.40; 16.1). She is identified by Matthew (27.56) as the mother of *James and John and would therefore have been the wife of Zebedee as well as Jesus' aunt (see John 19.25).

MICHAEL D. COOGAN

Salutations. A salutation is a greeting when people meet. In biblical times this greeting was understood as an actual blessing bestowed on the person(s) greeted; see, for example, Genesis 43.29; Ruth 2.4; 3.10; Daniel 6.21. While most greetings were indications of good will, there are instances when the salutation was negative, if not derogatory, as in 1 Kings 18.17.

In Hebrew (as in other Semitic languages), greetings often include the word šālôm ("*peace"). The word signifies totality and wholeness, the sum of all good things. To greet someone with peace was thus to wish for that person all good (Judg. 6.23; 1 Chron. 12.18). At times, as in modern Hebrew, šālôm was also used as a parting blessing (e.g., Exod. 4.18).

In Greek, a common greeting was *chaire* ("hail," literally, "rejoice") (e.g., Matt. 26.49; Luke 1.28). At the beginning of his *letters Paul regularly used the related noun *charis* ("*grace") in combination with the Greek word for "peace" *(eirēnē)*.

In the ancient world oral salutations were frequently accompanied by other types of physical actions to express good wishes, such as raising the hand, prostrating oneself on the ground, kissing, or embracing (*see* Gestures).

JAMES M. EFIRD

Salvation. The primary meaning of the Hebrew and Greek words translated "salvation" is non-religious. Thus, the derivatives of the Hebrew root yšʿ are used frequently in military contexts, as of victories by *Gideon (Judg. 8.22), *Samson (Judg. 15.18), Jonathan (1 Sam. 14.45), and *David (1 Sam. 23.5; 2 Sam. 19.3); of projected defeats of Aram (2 Kings 13.17) and of the enemies of Gibeon (Josh 10.6); and of victory in general. In fact, recent translations often translate nominal derivatives of yšʿ with "victory." An analogous sense is found in Deuteronomy 22.27: a woman who has been raped "in the field" is not guilty, because there would have been no "rescuer" (Hebr. môšiaʿ) to hear her cry for help. And, in poetry, synonyms used in poetic parallelism for yšʿ often mean "to rescue, to deliver, to help escape, to protect."

This sense of victory or rescue from danger, defeat, or distress is also primary when God is the agent. Thus, in the clearly military metaphors of Psalm 91, the conclusion sums up the divine promise of protection as follows: "I will satisfy him with length of days, and show him my victory (yešûʿātî)"; the NRSV is inconsistent both here and in other places where God is the source of the victory, often using the theologically weighty word "salvation." In fact, when God is the source of "salvation" in the Hebrew Bible the meaning is overwhelmingly physical rather than spiritual, and in this life rather than in some *afterlife (Exod. 14.30; 2 Sam. 8.6; Pss. 44.3; 144.10; Isa. 59.16; Zeph. 3.17). It is difficult to stress this too much, since Christian readers of the Bible especially have understandably read back into the Hebrew Bible the spiritual and eschatological nuances of the concept of salvation found in the New Testament. Despite the fact that in a great majority of the occurrences of the root *yšʿ* in the Hebrew Bible God is the agent of "salvation," it rarely if ever has an unambiguously spiritual nuance. An eschatological sense is of course present in such passages as Ezekiel 34.22 and throughout Second Isaiah, but the "salvation" prophesied is the restoration of Israel in its land, not some otherworldly bliss. Even in the New Testament salvation can be physical and this-worldly. In the healings of both the woman with the hemorrhage (Mark 5.34 par.) and the blind Bartimaeus (Mark 10.52 par.), Jesus proclaims that their faith has "saved" them; most recent translations correctly render the Greek verb *sōzō* "has made you well"; cf. Mark 3.4; 5.23, 28; 6.56; Luke 17.19; Matt. 27.42 par.). Likewise, *sōzō* is used by the disciples when they thought they were drowning (Matt. 8.25; cf. 14.30) and (in a compound form) of Paul's escape from shipwreck (Acts 27.44; 28.1).

But the majority of occurrences in the New Testament of the Greek verb *sōzō* ("to save") and its derivatives, especially the noun *sōtēria* ("salvation") have to do with the ultimate salvation of believers in Christ Jesus. The same phrase used in the stories of healing is also used of forgiveness of sin (Luke 7.48–50; cf. 18.52), and in the account of the paralytic (Matt. 9.2–8 par.) forgiveness of sin is a spiritual kind of healing concomitant with the physical restoration of health. For the one forgiven this spiritual healing is thus "salvation," in the sense of admission into the *kingdom of God understood as both a present and a future reality. The salvation of individuals is the principal focus of the earlier New Testament writings. In Paul this salvation is both present and future; the two are closely linked, in part at least because of Paul's expectation of a prompt *Second Coming (Rom. 5.8–11; 8.18–25; 13.11). So Paul can speak of those "who are being saved" (1 Cor. 1.18; 15.2; 2 Cor. 2.15), as well as those who will be "saved in the day of the Lord" (1 Cor. 5.5), both Jews (Rom. 11.26) and gentiles (1 Thess. 2.16). This same kind of "realized eschatology" is also found in the *synoptic Gospels and in Acts, though in both it is a

future salvation that dominates (Mark 8.35; 13.13 par.; Acts 15.11; contrast Luke 19.9: "Today salvation has come to this house" and cf. Acts 2.47).

In the gospel of John not only is Jesus identified as "savior," an interpretation of his name (see below), but the object of salvation is frequently identified as "the world" (Grk. *kosmos*), the created order now at enmity with God and therefore in need of salvation through Jesus (John 3.16–17; 12.47; cf. Rev. 12.10–12).

A large number of personal *names are derived from the Hebrew root *yšʿ*, including those of Moses' successor Joshua, the prophets Hosea, Isaiah, and probably Elisha, the *Moabite king Mesha, and Jesus (a Grk. form of Hebr. *yēšûaʿ*; see Matt. 1.21; John 4.42; Acts 5.31; Phil. 3.20; Eph. 5.23; Titus 1.4; 2 Pet. 1.1); in all of these names God rather than the person with the name is explicitly or implicitly the agent of salvation. The exclamation transliterated "*Hosanna" is also from this root.

MICHAEL D. COOGAN

Samaria. Omri (885–873 BCE), the sixth king of the northern kingdom of *Israel, founded his new capital Samaria (Hebr. *šōmrôn*) on land purchased for the high price of two silver talents (7,200 shekels; cf. 2 Sam. 24.24) from the family of Shemer (1 Kings 16.23–24). Archaeologists have found traces of a rural estate from the eleventh to the early ninth centuries on the hill of Samaria, on which Omri's new city was built; it was easily defended and located near important trade routes (Map 5:X4). Like the names Israel and Ephraim, Samaria may have become an alternate name for the northern kingdom as a whole (1 Kings 21.1; 2 Kings 1.3).

Although the principal temple cities of the kingdom were Bethel and *Dan (1 Kings 12.29; *see* Golden Calf), an inscriptional reference (ca. 800 BCE) from Kuntillet ʿAjrud (northern Sinai) to "Yahweh of Samaria and his Asherah" suggests that a shrine to Yahweh also stood in Samaria (cf. Hos. 8.5). Omri's son *Ahab built a temple to *Baal there (1 Kings 16.32), perhaps for his Phoenician queen *Jezebel. When *Jehu overthrew the Omride dynasty, he demolished Baal's temple and turned it into a latrine (2 Kings 10.27), but a shrine to the goddess *Asherah continued to exist (1 Kings 16.33; 2 Kings 13.6; Amos 8.14?).

Samaria flourished in the time of Omri and Ahab and again during the reign of Jeroboam

II in the mid-eighth century. During the latter period Samaria symbolized the entire northern kingdom for the prophets *Amos and *Hosea, who condemned Israel's religious and social ills. The Samaria Ostraca, a cache of sixty-three inscribed potsherds recording what may be tax receipts, illustrates the concentration of wealth that the prophets criticized.

Kings of Samaria alternately allied themselves with or fought against *Damascus (1 Kings 20.34; 2 Kings 5.5; 16.5) and *Judah (1 Kings 22.2; 2 Kings 8.26). They enjoyed trade and diplomatic relations with the *Phoenicians, whose artistic influence is apparent in references to Ahab's ivory house (1 Kings 22.39) and in the hundreds of eighth-century ivory furniture inlays (see Amos 6.4) excavated at Samaria. Splendid walls of local limestone cut in the precise Phoenician style surrounded Samaria's royal precinct. In later times pottery, bronzes, seal impressions, and locally minted coinage from the Persian period (sixth–fourth centuries) indicate that Samaria continued to be more open than Judea to foreign influences.

*Assyria conquered Samaria in 722 BCE, transforming it into the capital of the province of Samerina. The Assyrians deported Samaria's leading citizens and resettled conquered peoples from Syria and Mesopotamia there (2 Kings 17). Nevertheless, a large population of Israelites probably remained. The Judean kings *Hezekiah and *Josiah made political overtures to these surviving Israelites (2 Chron. 30.1–11, 18; 34.3–7; cf. Jer. 41.4–6), and prophets describe a future reunited Israel (Jer. 31.1–6; Ezek. 16.51–55).

After the Babylonian exile, *Samaritans led by the governor Sanballat opposed *Nehemiah's attempts to rebuild Jerusalem (Neh. 4; 6). These Samaritans were probably Jews living both in Judea and in Samaria (cf. Ezra 4.4) who had continued to worship and to administer the territory of ancient Israel in the exiles' absence; their quarrel with Nehemiah was political, not religious. It is notable that Samaritan women are not mentioned among those whom Jews have wrongfully married (Neh. 13.23), although for priests such intermarriage was unacceptable (13.28).

From the many Yahwistic names on Wadi Daliyeh papyri (375–335 BCE), it seems that ruling-class Samaritans of the Persian period revered Yahweh. Late in the fifth century, Jews living in Egypt wrote for help in rebuilding their temple at Elephantine to leaders both in Jerusalem and in Samaria. Sometime after the arrival of *Alexander the Great (332 BCE), the Samaritans constructed on Mount Gerizim near *Shechem a temple of Yahweh to rival Jerusalem's, but evidence from the *Dead Sea Scrolls suggests that the definitive religious break (the "Samaritan schism") between Samaria and Jerusalem, so apparent in the New Testament, did not occur before the Hasmonean period (second century BCE).

Alexander the Great's army destroyed Samaria in 331 after a rebellion. It was rebuilt to become a wealthy Hellenistic city surrounded by a massive wall with a series of monumental round watchtowers (one, ca. 19 m [63 ft] in diameter, still stands to a height of over 8 m [27 ft]). The Hasmonean John Hyrcanus destroyed the city in 108 BCE, but it began to revive after Rome took over Palestine (63 BCE). *Herod the Great embellished the city on a grand scale, renaming it Sebaste after the Greek title of the emperor Augustus. This magnificent city, with its colonnaded streets, stadium, theater, and temples, was demolished during the First Jewish Revolt (66–70 CE), but it soon revived and flourished until finally declining during the Byzantine period.

*Samaritans appear in key episodes in the *Gospels and in Acts. Some reject Jesus (Luke 9.52–53), but he portrays a Samaritan as a good *neighbor (Luke 10.29–37). Jesus' friendly meeting with the Samaritan woman (John 4) demonstrates his openness to women; by her testimony she becomes one of the earliest missionaries (4.39). Philip's ministry to Samaria (Acts 8) is the first by an apostle outside strictly Jewish territory; Samaria is a symbolically transitional place between Judaism and the gentile world into which the Christian movement will travel.

MARY JOAN WINN LEITH

Samaritans. The Samaritans are unique among the many religious groups described in the Bible apart from traditional Judaism and Christianity: the others have long passed into oblivion, but the Samaritans still survive in our own day, as a community preserving its ancient rites on its holy site, Mount Gerizim (Map 1:X4), near the ancient site of *Shechem and the modern city of Nablus.

The Samaritans are best understood as a conservative group within the total spectrum of Judaism. This rather clumsy definition is necessary because of the ambiguity of the word "Judaism." The word is sometimes used in a biblical context to denote the community owing allegiance to the Jerusalem authorities, with the Jerusalem *Temple its chief holy place; sometimes it refers to a broader complex of beliefs and practices, united mainly by reverence for the holy traditions enshrined in scripture. The Samaritans should be included in the Judaism of the second type but not of the first. (*See* Judaisms of the First Century CE.)

We can obtain some knowledge of the Samaritans from the Bible, but because these references are not free of polemic, it is best to begin by noting that our sources of knowledge include important material handed down by the Samaritans themselves. Chief among this is the Samaritan *Pentateuch. The scroll preserved by the present-day Samaritan community is claimed by them to date back to Abishua, the great-grandson of *Aaron mentioned in 1 Chronicles 6.4; it is actually a medieval scroll, although it certainly preserves older traditions sometimes valued by textual critics (e.g., at Deut. 27.4 the reading "Gerizim" for "Ebal" is often preferred). The fact that the scroll contains only the Pentateuch is doubly significant: it reminds us that this is the extent of the writings regarded by the Samaritans as scripture; and it illustrates the conservative nature of the group, deeply distrustful of anything that smacked of innovation and modernizing.

Other features of their religious practice illustrate this point also. They have observed the *Sabbath with great strictness, spurning those devices that Jews developed to facilitate ordinary life on the Sabbath. Ritual requirements, in particular those relating to food laws, have been understood and imposed with a greater degree of literalism than has been usual in Judaism as a whole. They claim that their holy mountain, Mount Gerizim, which is mentioned in the Pentateuch (Deut. 11.29; 27.12), has a greater claim to veneration than does Mount *Zion, for Jerusalem entered the people's history only relatively late, at the time of *David.

In these characteristic features it is possible to see the Samaritans as having a recognizable position within the spectrum of Judaism at the beginning of the common era. New Testament references, especially in *Luke and *Acts, make it clear that by that time the Samaritans were an established group.

Unambiguous earlier references are few, the clearest being found in the *Apocrypha. In Sirach 50.26, "the foolish people that dwell in Shechem" are condemned as if they were an alien group; 2 Maccabees 6.2 makes a slighting reference to their willingness to compromise their ancestral traditions. Each of these statements is polemical, a hostile comment from a rival religious position. Much the same can be said of *Josephus, who has frequent and almost invariably hostile references to the Samaritans, particularly in his *Antiquities*. Although the historicity of his description of the building of the Samaritan temple on Mount Gerizim in the time of *Alexander the Great has been much doubted, its destruction by the Jewish king John Hyrcanus late in the second century BCE is beyond serious dispute.

Samaritan origins have often been described in terms of a schism, as if there were some specific event that separated them from the Jews. The Samaritans' own Chronicles date that event as early as the time of Eli, before the establishment of the monarchy. That is unlikely to be historical; equally improbable is the Jewish version, preserved in 2 Kings 17, which pictures the Samaritans as descended from aliens of non-Yahwistic origin, from which the true Israel was bound to distance itself. (This story gave rise to the later, contemptuous name for the Samaritans, "Kuthim" [from "Cuthah" in v. 24] and is also the only place in most English translations of the Hebrew Bible where the word "Samaritans" is found [v. 29].) This is religious polemic; nothing in Samaritan practice suggests any link with *Assyrian or other foreign origin. Nor should the Samaritans be identified, as is sometimes done, with those left in the land at the time of the Babylonian *exile, or with the opponents of *Ezra and *Nehemiah. Their distinctive identity emerged later, and it is unlikely that any single event precipitated a schism.

How far they preserved characteristically northern traditions is difficult to decide. As the Hebrew Bible is a Jerusalem collection, hostile to the north, it is not easy to identify any distinctive northern traditions that the later Samaritans might have inherited. In any case, their characteristic features arise from the Judaism of the postexilic period, since all that we know of Samaritanism relates to religious rather than political or national characteristics: which books were holy, where might sacrifice properly be offered, which families might legitimately exercise the priesthood.

Some scholars have claimed to detect similarities between the Samaritans and the *Dead Sea Scrolls community, but these are also widely questioned. More striking is the obvious sympathy toward the Samaritans shown by the author of Luke-Acts, who twice in the Gospel goes out of his way to praise a Samaritan (Luke 10.33–36; 17.15–18). It has also been suggested, though this is less certain, that *Stephen, the central figure of Acts 6–7, was of Samaritan origin; certainly Simon Magus (Acts 8.9–13) came to be associated with a heterodox form of Samaritanism. It is therefore clear that in the Roman period the Samaritans were an identifiable group, comparable with, but distinct from, the larger Jewish community; John 4.9, though the accuracy of the rendering has been questioned, expresses the situation clearly. There was a Samaritan diaspora, and the community maintained its existence, with a rebuilt temple, through the changing political circumstances that affected Palestine. The fourth century CE was a time of revival, with many of their theological and literary traditions reaching definitive form at that time. In the centuries since, their numbers have declined and they have suffered persecution, but they retain something of their distinctive identity and their ancestral home, despite all the political and religious turmoil that has affected Palestine.

See also Judaisms of the First Century CE; Samaria.   RICHARD COGGINS

Samson. Samson (whose name is derived from the word for "sun") was the twelfth and last judge of Israel (Judg. 13–16) before civil war threatened to tear the tribes apart (Judg. 17–21). He harassed the *Philistines in the border country between his native *Dan, Judah, and Philistia. Besides killing thousands of Philistines, Samson ripped a lion apart with his bare hands (14.5–6) and told a riddle about it (14.14), loved two women who betrayed him for very different reasons (14.15–17; 16.5–6), burned Philistine crops (15.4–5), visited a Philistine prostitute and carried off the city gates of Gaza on the same night (16.1–3), was blinded and enslaved by the Philistines (16.21), and caused his own death by toppling the pillars of the Philistines' temple upon himself and his foes (16.28–30).

With his powerful libido, Samson resembles other judges who fell outside the behavioral norms of Israelite society (left-handed Ehud, the woman *Deborah, young *Gideon, the bastard Jephthah). Unlike other judges, however, Samson was neither an adjudicator nor (despite Judg. 13.5) a "deliverer" of his people. Personal vengeance was the motive for his single-handed forays against the Philistines. Samson's oblivious-

ness to the requirements of his *Nazirite status (Judg. 14.8–9, 10; 15.15) suggests that it is not original to the Samson legend, although it is important in the literary framework of the biblical narrative.

The Samson story reflects an early stage of actual Philistine-Israelite confrontations, but it is rooted in Danite folktales and perhaps Philistine story traditions. It resembles tales of intertribal relations told in other areas where neighboring groups borrow story lines from each other. The Philistines were related to Homer's Mycenaean Greeks, and the Samson saga has motifs in common with Greek and other Indo-European literatures. Samson also resembles *Gilgamesh, as well as tricksters like *Jacob.

*Josephus is typical of early Jewish and Christian interpreters in his verdict that Samson's heroic death transcended the sins of his life (Ant. 5.8.317). Samson's questionable morality could even be glossed over (Heb. 11.32), or, as later for Milton in Samson Agonistes, superseded by his heroic death.

Judges 13–16 is one of the most artfully composed tales in the Bible. It is framed by a prediction of Samson's birth to his barren mother (Judg. 13; cf. Gen. 17.15–19; 18; 1 Sam. 1) and his spectacular death (Judg. 16.22–30), episodes that mirror each other (e.g., in the obtuseness of both Manoah and the Philistines, and the rituals for Yahweh and Dagon). There is an exuberance of wordplay, including etiologies (15.17, 19), riddling couplets (14.12–14, 18), and ring compositions (especially Judges 13). One finds foreshadowing (13.7), crisp characterizations (Samson, his mother and father), and clever inversions from episode to episode (compare the restraining of Samson by the men of Judah and by Delilah). Most of all, the narrative presents a subtle study of deception and betrayal, by humans and by God, for good and for ill.

See also Judges, The Book of.
          MARY JOAN WINN LEITH

Samuel. The son of Elkanah and Hannah, Samuel was Israel's leader in the transition from the premonarchic to the monarchic period. The books of Samuel (see next entry) preserve various traditions about him, and he is described in several roles. He was a judge, in both the judicial (1 Sam. 7.15–8.3) and military (1 Sam. 7.13–14; 12.11 [MT]) senses of that office in the Bible; as the last of the judges, he was unable to defeat the *Philistines, and their threat to Israel's existence was the primary historical reason for the establishment of the monarchy (*see* Kingship and Monarchy). He was apparently a *priest (1 Sam. 2.11; see also Ps. 99.6; Sir. 46.13) and probably a *nazirite (1 Sam. 1.11, 22, according to LXX and Qumran texts). Most frequently, however, he is called a *prophet.

According to the *Deuteronomic historians, for whom the prophets are key actors in their narrative, Samuel illustrates some of the key roles of later prophets. He was both king maker (for *Saul and *David) and king breaker (Saul), like *Nathan, *Elijah, and *Elisha; he rebuked both kings and people for their violations of *covenant (see especially 1 Sam 15.22, a saying that would fit well into the collections of the eighth-century prophets).

Because of this idealized portrait, drawn from Israel's later institutions and traditions and shaped by the Deuteronomic historians, it is difficult to say much about Samuel historically, especially on the key issue of the monarchy: was he for or against it? Our sources give both perspectives. But of his importance in the crucial period of the mid-eleventh century BCE there can be no doubt, and he is linked with *Moses as one of Israel's preeminent leaders (Ps. 99.6; Jer. 15.1).   MICHAEL D. COOGAN

Samuel, The Books of.

Title. The two books are in reality one (cf. *Kings, *Chronicles): in the Hebrew text, they run continuously, with the counting of words and sections characteristic of the Hebrew tradition coming only at the end. The division into two appears first in the Greek translation (the *Septuagint) and then in the Latin *Vulgate: from there it came to be used in other translations, and by the sixteenth century also in printed Hebrew Bibles. The traditional title "Samuel" reflects the fact that he dominates much of the material, particularly in the establishing of the monarchy; hence he came to be seen as the author. The Greek and Latin texts use titles that cover also the following books of Kings—thus either "four books of kingdoms" or "four books of kings." Since these four books together cover the whole period of the monarchy, these latter titles are really more appropriate.

Contents. Briefly the contents are:

1 Samuel 1–15:   Samuel and Saul
1 Samuel 16–31: Saul and David
2 Samuel 1–8:   David's rise to power
2 Samuel 9–20:   David's reign
2 Samuel 21–24: narratives, psalms, and lists.

Such an outline does not show the complex interweaving of themes which the books reveal, and for a proper understanding we also need to consider both what precedes and follows, as well as the subdivisions and interlinkages within the books themselves.

What precedes in the Hebrew text is the book of *Judges. (*Ruth in that text stands in the third section of the *canon, as one of the Five Scrolls, with Song of Solomon, Ecclesiastes, Lamentations, and Esther.) The sequence in this form is clearly right for the narratives: Eli the priest at Shiloh, who appears in the first four chapters, is depicted so as to fit into the series of "judges," his activity rounded off at his death (4.18) with the statement that "he had judged Israel forty years." In addition, the refrain in Judges 17–21, "in those days there was no king in Israel; all the people did what was right in their own eyes" (17.6; 18.1; 19.1; 21.25), may be seen as an appropriate preface to the establishment of the monarchy. The order in the English text places Ruth after Judges: this derives from the Greek and Latin versions and is also intelligible—not only is the book of Ruth set "in the days when the judges ruled" (1.1), but it has its climax in the birth of a son to Ruth who was to be the grandfather of *David. The story of Ruth prepares for the appearance of David as king.

There is no break between Samuel and Kings; the story of David does not end, as we might have expected, at the end of 2 Samuel; it continues into 1 Kings 1–2. A commonly held view is that the group of chapters from 2 Samuel 9 to 1 Kings 2—ignoring for the moment 2 Samuel 21–24—forms a continuous unit, often called the "Succession Story" or the "Court History of David" (see below).

The recognition of continuity into 1 Kings and of the link back to Judges, itself continuous with *Joshua, points to the understanding of the whole group of books from Joshua to Kings. They form a "history" from the conquest of Canaan to the fall of Judah. Because of many links of language and thought with the book of *Deuteronomy, which precedes them, they are often termed the *Deuteronomic (or Deuteronomistic) history, though it is evident that the differences between the books, in particular in their style of presenting the narratives, raise many questions about the nature of this whole compilation.

Nevertheless, whatever the processes involved, we are invited to read the books as a sequence, and at many points later parts of the story can only be fully understood by reference back to earlier, as well as back to the presentation of Israel and its laws offered by Deuteronomy.

A closer look at the material within the main sections as set out above shows many different kinds of writing now woven together. The proper understanding of the books involves the recognition of these different elements and a discussion of their possible origin and significance, but also an appreciation of the overall presentation, its patterns and its functions. The date of the books of Samuel can only be determined within this broader framework: its final shaping must belong at the earliest in the sixth century BCE.

The Text of the Books of Samuel. The detailed problems of the Hebrew text and its relationship to alternative forms, attested by the early Greek translation and by the fragmentary manuscripts from *Qumran, are a matter for a full commentary. There are passages where the evidence points to the existence of more than one recension, and, as may be seen from the brief notes in NRSV and from similar notes in other modern translations, there are many instances of small variations between the alternative texts. For example, the last verses of 1 Samuel 1 differ considerably in the Greek, and the psalm in 1 Samuel 2.1–10 is there followed by the addition of a passage found also in Jeremiah 9.23–24, expounding the ideas of knowledge of God and of divine justice. In addition, some parts of the Samuel text—the death of Saul and sections of the David story—are to be found in a different form and arrangement in 1 Chronicles, and the psalm in 2 Samuel 22 appears also as Psalm 18. Textual questions arise in all such duplicate texts.

Sources. As mentioned above, various types of material are found in the final form of the books of Samuel. The psalm in 2 Samuel 22 may be set alongside that in 1 Samuel 2.1–10; the latter does not appear in the book of *Psalms, but it is clearly a psalm, used in the narrative to draw out the significance of the birth of Samuel in relation to the establishment of the monarchy. (The hymn in Luke 2.46–55 is closely related to this poem.) 2 Samuel 22 is immediately followed by another short poetic passage (2 Sam. 23.1–7), which depicts David as prophetic spokesman, though it also has considerable links with psalms relating Davidic *kingship to the rule of God.

Two poems of a quite different kind, laments over the dead, appear in 2 Samuel 1.19–27 and 3.33–34. These seem likely to be early: the first is cited from the Book of *Jashar, the second has a gnomic quality. Some material in the books is of archival character: the family and officials of Saul are noted in 1 Samuel 14.49–51; the family of David in 2 Samuel 3.2–5 and 5.13–16, distinguishing his kingship in *Hebron from that in *Jerusalem; and David's officials in two slightly variant forms in 2 Samuel 8.15–18 and 20.23–26. The *genealogical material is paralleled in the much more elaborate lists in 1 *Chronicles; the lists of officials (cf. also 1 Kings 4.1–6 and 7–20) function as markers at the end of narrative sections. Lists of David's warriors, found in 2 Samuel 21.15–22 and 23.8–39, appear also, and in part more fully, in 1 Chronicles 21.4–8 and 11.10–47.

The major part of the two books consists of narratives. These are grouped around the main characters or associated with particular themes. Thus, 1 Samuel 1–4 are associated with Eli, head of the priestly house at Shiloh and linked to a first defeat by the *Philistines and the loss of the *ark of God: in part they are more concerned with the appearance of *Samuel and the interweaving of the downfall of Eli's priesthood with the anticipation of a new and lasting priesthood alongside a royal house (2.27–36, also 3.10–18). The ark theme of 1 Samuel 4 continues in 5–6, and reappears in 2 Samuel 6: this has led to the supposition of an "ark source," though it may be doubted whether such a source existed independently of other material. Various stories, clearly not all of one piece, have gathered around the figure of *Samuel: he is depicted as a prophet (so, for example, in 1 Sam. 2; 9–12), a judge (so 1 Sam. 7.15–8.3), and a military leader (1 Sam. 7.3–14). As a prophet, he continues to appear in the narratives, or in some measure to overshadow them, not only through to his death (1 Sam. 25.1) but beyond it, in his appearance to pronounce doom on Saul in 1 Samuel 29. *Saul, as also his son Jonathan, appears in heroic stories such as 1 Samuel 11 and 13–15. They appear as foils to David in 1 Samuel 16–31, in stories gathered more closely around the figure of David as the true king increasingly recognized as designated to replace Saul, who had been divinely chosen but then divinely rejected. With the death of Saul, told in two forms in 1 Samuel 31 and 2 Samuel 1, the way is clear for David to establish his kingship, over the south at Hebron, over the north with the death of Saul's feeble son Ishbaal (Ishbosheth), and with victories over the Philistines and the surrounding lands (2 Sam. 5 and 6). The stories of his reign in 2 Samuel 9–20; 21; 24 reveal further aspects of his achievements and his weaknesses, in effect brought to a conclusion when the succession of *Solomon is defined in 1 Kings 1–2.

The two stories in 2 Samuel 21 and 24 are concerned with the consequences of religious disobedience (cf. also 1 Sam. 13 and 15): 2 Samuel 21.1–14 records a failure by Saul which had dire repercussions rectified by David; 2 Samuel 24 a failure by David resulting both in disaster and in the establishment of a new holy place.

The variety in style and level of the many stories suggests various origins. If we may judge from what is told of other heroic figures, both biblical and nonbiblical, it is likely that some are popular legends now attracted to a particular figure. Some may be early; others are evidently late, at least in their present form (so, for example, the Samuel war story in 1 Sam. 7). How much of actual history they contain is debated; precision of detail, such as is to be found in the intimate accounts of the life of David and his court, for example in 2 Samuel 12 and 13, are often thought to have eyewitness character. But this is deceptive; a good storyteller will provide the details that makes a story vivid, whether or not it is closely linked to actual events.

A Literary Work. Various theories have been propounded to account for the present shape of the books of Samuel and to describe their literary evolution. Older views saw the possibility of parallel sources combined; the stories of the establishment of the monarchy in 1 Samuel 9–12, showing both favorable and unfavorable attitudes, seem to point clearly in that direction. But there is little evidence of continuous sources; alternative traditions have been brought together (so, for example, 1 Sam. 24 and 26: David's sparing of Saul's life; and 1 Sam. 31 and 2 Sam. 1: the death of Saul). Attempting harmonization in such cases is not satisfactory. An attempt has also been made to discover blocks of material, such as the Samuel birth narratives, the ark narratives, the story of David's rise to power, the Succession Story or Court History of David. It is difficult to determine where such blocks begin and end, and to understand the function of such blocks before they were incorporated into the final work. 2 Samuel 9–20 with 1 Kings 1–2, most often recently designated the "succession story" and the one most widely ac-

cepted as an ancient source, presents substantial problems; those who have studied it most closely do not agree on its function: Is it a pro-Solomon apology or a virulent anti-Solomon polemic? Is it virtually the work of an eyewitness (with candidates for authorship from the entourage of David) or a later reflective compilation? Did it originally stand in the work, or, bearing in mind that most of it is absent in 1–2 Chronicles, was it a late insertion? It may be proper to recognize that this, sometimes hailed as the earliest piece of real historical writing in the Bible and on occasion used as evidence for a supposed period of Davidic-Solomonic enlightenment, is perhaps more a construction of modern scholarship than an actual ancient independent work.

More recently, there has been a tendency to think rather in terms of a great wealth of stories, naturally attached to that period in which monarchy came to be instituted and looking to the almost legendary characters of David and Solomon, which have been worked over to produce a now vivid literary work, highly structured and skillfully woven together, to be read as one: the unevennesses and discrepancies that exist, which a modern reader notes, reveal both something of the diversity of origin and also much of a literary technique not concerned with historical evaluation but with meaning and impact.

Discerning larger patterns in the arrangement and handling of the material has led to illuminating insights: the stories of David, for example, have been thought to be so ordered as to depict him as first under divine blessing and protection and then under a divine curse (cf. also the changing picture of Saul in 1 Sam.); but not everything fits so easily into a single pattern. *Structuralist approaches, though sometimes so elaborate as to be unconvincing, have nevertheless pointed to the literary skill of the work: the narrator anticipates, provides occasional résumes, offers comment on the meaning of events (so for example in 1 Sam. 12 and 2 Sam. 7), and, sometimes explicitly but more often implicitly, points to the significance of what is being told. The comments are often religiously based, and in some measure linked to the thought of Deuteronomy; more clearly, they show the attempt of a compiler concerned to understand the contemporary situation in which the community now exists by relating the story of the past. Some clues (so, for example, in 1 Sam. 4–6) may point to the sixth-century BCE period of Babylonian conquest and *exile for leading members of the Judean state; the victory of the captive God of the ark in a foreign land (that of the Philistines in the story) suggests hope for a defeated people, deprived of political and religious leadership and institutions: their God might be thought defeated and captive, but in reality he mocks his powerless opponents. Such an interpretation would also fit with the overall impression of the Deuteronomic history, which reflects on Israel's failures but has a climax at the end of 2 Kings in the release of the captive Davidic king, suggesting some hope of restored life.

At first sight there is a certain miscellaneous quality about the various elements in 2 Samuel 21–24, but they should not be seen merely as an "appendix": there is a similar collection in Judges 17–21. A closely knit structure is evident in 2 Samuel: two narratives (21.1–14 and 24) enclose two lists and brief anecdotes of heroes (21.15–22 and 23.8–39), which in their turn enclose two psalms (22 and 23.1–7). The first narrative finally resolves the problem of the royal family of Saul; the first hero list provides a link passage associated with the Philistine wars, which brought the downfall of Saul and the triumph of David (cf. 1 Sam. 17–18 and 31; 2 Sam. 1; 5). The first psalm is associated by its heading with the deliverance of David from "all his enemies . . . and from Saul" (22.1). The second psalm depicts the kingship of David and points to a final kingdom; its military theme is drawn out in the hero lists and stories of 23.8–39. The second narrative in chap. 24 draws together the theme of David's failures and that of his establishment of kingdom and Temple—for though the *Temple is not here mentioned, the placing of this narrative as a lead-in to the succession of Solomon is clearly designed to imply what later (1 Chron. 22.1) was regarded as established fact.

History and Interpretation. In the light of the comments already made, it is clear that questions about the actual history of the period with which it deals are difficult to answer. Estimates vary greatly. There are those who would claim that much of the material lies very close to the events, and therefore believe that reasonably firm statements can be made about events and characters. Some would see particular sections or narratives as authentic in this sense, and others, such as 1 Samuel 7, as late inventions. Other commentators, while recognizing the presence of stories based on ancient traditions, would doubt the possibility of a historical reconstruction. The work presents considerable chronological difficulties. Eli belongs within the judge style of presentation, with his forty year period of rule; Samuel

is similarly described, but without any figure given (cf. 1 Sam. 12.1–2; 25.1). The reign of Saul is problematic, since clearly the "two years" of 1 Samuel 13.1 is an error. David (like Solomon) again has forty years; the division of the reign into seven years in Hebron and thirty-three in Jerusalem does not suggest good chronological information. Problems arise when the attempt is made to order events alluded to or described: the stories of 2 Samuel 9–20, together with those of 21 and 24, do not make up a satisfactory sequence. Unlike the material of 1 Kings 15 to 2 Kings 25, there is no overall archival framework into which the individual sections are fitted. Numerous stories could derive from popular legend, now applied to particular figures. The story of *Absalom's rebellion looks like history, but is in many respects more stylized than real.

The view taken by an individual reader or by a historian will often depend on the degree to which some measure of harmonization is undertaken. But it may be doubted whether such historical uncertainty is a serious disadvantage in reading the books. What appears to be more important, for writer and reader alike, is the overall picture. We may observe the development and interpretation of a number of interrelated themes. Within the whole story, from the *conquest of Canaan to the fall of Judah, changes clearly took place in the life of Israel: the shift from tribal life with local leaders to national life under the monarchy; the question of true *kingship arose; the one shrine was established, *Jerusalem; a true priestly line emerged, to stand alongside the royal dynasty—a theme that was to become vital during the period of the exile and to result in various claims and counterclaims in the postexilic community.

All these issues are dominant in the books of Samuel. Ostensibly, the story is one of the past. But in reality, its final shaping has drawn together themes that serve not simply to describe what was believed about the past; claims are being made about the present, to depict for a community that has its own questions and uncertainties the meaning of that age which had brought into being the major institutions of the monarchical period and to invite a revaluation of these institutions in a later time of change.

PETER R. ACKROYD

Sanhedrin. The Gospels and Acts utilize this Greek term for council, which literally means "sitting together," both for the locus of opposition to Jesus and his movement, often in combination with elders and chief priests, and for the venue where both Jesus and his followers make their defense (Matt. 26.59 par.; John 11.47; Acts 4.5–22; 5.17–43; 6.12–15; 22.30–23.10).

This term for a kind of judicial and administrative body goes back in Roman Palestine at least to Pompey the Great. When Pompey was pulled into a domestic dispute between two quarreling Hasmonean brothers in 66 BCE, the Romans decided to run Palestine directly. Pompey reorganized Palestine as part of his larger project of subduing and organizing the entire Greek East for the Roman Senate, dividing it into five councils (*synedria*; Josephus, *Ant.* 14.5.91; *War* 1.8.170).

The fact that this neutral administrative term becomes firmly imbedded in the Gospel tradition as a place of local officials hostile to the Jesus movement and with the power to do something about it highlights the utilization of local elites by Rome in their ever-expanding colonial rule. The Sanhedrin was a court made up of local elite, probably with some sort of Roman oversight, that handled census, *tax, and other administrative and military responsibilities. In the divided socioeconomic context of Roman imperial rule, as time went on the Sanhedrin had a negative connotation for many who had to pay an increasing amount in taxes, stood a good chance of losing their land, and had to contend regularly with the reality of foreign occupation.

In the rabbinic period (ca. 200 CE) Sanhedrin became a technical term for the rabbinic court. This court and its leaders adjudicated many of the rulings that made their way into the *Mishnah, the first codification of rabbinic law and debate. There is an entire tractate in the Mishnah devoted to Sanhedrin.

J. ANDREW OVERMAN

Sarah. The wife of *Abraham and mother of *Isaac. Before Genesis 17.15 she is called Sarai; the two forms of the name are linguistic variants, both meaning "princess." The book of Genesis describes her as a beautiful woman (12.11, 14), a theme elaborated by later tradition, especially the *Genesis Apocryphon* from *Qumran. According to the biblical narrator, Abraham was so conscious of her beauty that before they entered Egypt at the time of a severe famine in their own land, he begged her not to reveal to the Egyptians that she was his wife but rather his

sister, lest he be killed. Indeed, as it turned out, the Egyptians thought her so beautiful that she was taken into Pharaoh's house to be his wife (Gen. 12.15), and for her sake Abraham prospered. In time, however, after great plagues had afflicted Pharaoh and his household (Gen. 12.17; cf. Exod. 7–12), the true identity of Sarah was revealed to Pharaoh, who ordered Abraham to be gone with his wife and all his possessions. A variant of this story is found in Genesis 20.1–14 (cf. also Gen. 26.6–11).

During their years of wandering, Sarah was childless, and so God's promise that she would be the ancestor of nations (Gen. 17.16) was unfulfilled. Accordingly she persuaded Abraham to take her Egyptian slave, *Hagar, as his wife. He did so, and she bore him *Ishmael. At the age of ninety, however, Sarah bore *Isaac, thus fulfilling the divine promise. Sarah lived to be 127 years old, died in the land of Canaan, and was buried at Machpelah (Gen. 23.1–20).

In Isaiah 51.2 Sarah is referred to as the great mother of the nation; in the New Testament she is held up as an example of a wife's proper respect for her husband (1 Pet. 3.6). Paul uses the account of the birth of a son to Sarah by divine promise to develop an allegory of the new covenant in Christ and the heavenly Jerusalem (Gal. 4.22–31).

See also Ancestors, The; Genesis, The Book of.   ISOBEL MACKAY METZGER

Satan. The name of the archenemy of God and the personification of *evil, particularly in Christian tradition. The name may derive from a Semitic root *śṭn*, but the primitive meaning is still debated, the most popular suggestions being "to be remote" and "to obstruct." Some alternative roots include *śwṭ* (cf. Hebr. "to rove") and *šyṭ* (cf. Arabic "to burn," especially of food).

In the Hebrew Bible *śāṭān* could refer to any human being who played the role of an accuser or enemy (1 Sam. 29.4; 2 Sam. 19.22; 1 Kings 5.4; 1 Kings 11.14). In Numbers 22.32 *śāṭān* refers to a divine messenger who was sent to obstruct *Balaam's rash journey.

Job 1–2, Zechariah 3, and 1 Chronicles 21.1 have been central in past efforts to chart an evolution of the concept of *śāṭān* that culminates in a single archenemy of God. However, such evolutionary views have not gained general acceptance because *śāṭān* in these passages does not necessarily refer to a single archenemy of God and because the relative dating of the texts remains problematic. In Job 1–2, the śāṭān seems to be a legitimate member of God's council. In Zechariah 3.1–7 śāṭān may refer to a member of God's council who objected to the appointment of Joshua as chief priest. The mention of śāṭān without the definite article in 1 Chronicles 21.1 has led some scholars to interpret it as a proper name, but one could also interpret it as "an adversary" or "an accuser" acting on God's behalf.

Most scholars agree that in the writings of the third/second centuries BCE are the first examples of a character who is the archenemy of Yahweh and humankind. Nonetheless, the flexibility of the tradition is still apparent in the variety of figures who, although not necessarily identical with each other, are each apparently regarded as the principal archenemy of God and humankind in Second Temple literature. Such figures include Mastemah (Jubilees 10.8), Semyaz (1 Enoch 6.3), and *Belial at *Qumran (Zadokite Document 4.13). Still undetermined is the extent to which the concept of the Hebrew śāṭān was influenced by *Persian dualism, which posited the existence of two primal and independent personifications of good and evil.

Although it shares with contemporaneous Jewish literature many of its ideas about demonology, the New Testament is probably more responsible for standardizing "Satan" (Greek satanas) as the name for the archenemy of God in Western culture. However, the devil (the usual translation of "Satan" in the *Septuagint), Beelzebul ("the prince of demons," Matt. 12.24; see Baal-zebub), "the tempter" (Matt. 4.3), Beliar (2 Cor. 6.15), "the evil one" (1 John 5.18), and Apollyon (Rev. 9.11) are other names for Satan in the New Testament. Lucifer, a name for Satan popularized in the Middle Ages, derives ultimately from the merging of the New Testament tradition of the fall of Satan from heaven (Luke 10.18) with an originally separate biblical tradition concerning the Morning Star (cf. Isa. 14.12).

According to the New Testament, Satan and his *demons may enter human beings in order to incite evil deeds (Luke 22.3) and to cause illness (Matt. 15.22; Luke 11.14). Satan can imitate "an angel of light" (2 Cor. 11.14), has command of the air (Eph. 2.2), and accuses the faithful day and night before God (Rev. 12.10). Jude 9 mentions the struggle between Satan and the archangel *Michael for the body of *Moses. Revelation 20.2, among other texts, equates "the Devil and Satan" with "the dragon," thus reflecting the merging of ancient myths concerning gigantic primordial beasts that wreak havoc on God's creation with the traditions concerning Satan. Satan's destiny is to be cast into a lake of fire (Rev. 20.10–15).

In 563 CE the Council of Braga helped to define the official Christian view of Satan that, in contrast to dualism, denied his independent origin and his creation of the material universe. As J. B. Russell (*Lucifer: The Devil in the Middle Ages*, 1984) notes, writers and theologians of the medieval period popularized many of the characteristics of Satan that remain standard today and that have roots in, among other sources, Greek, Roman, and Teutonic mythology. Although the Enlightenment produced explanations of evil that do not refer to a mythological being, the imagery and concept of Satan continues to thrive within many religious traditions.

See also Exorcism.   HECTOR IGNACIO AVALOS

Saul. The first king of Israel, who ruled ca. 1020–1000 BCE. His story is part of the larger account, in the books of *Samuel, of how Israel became a nation-state. Saul is one of the few biblical characters of whom the term "tragic" has often been used. Glimpsing this dimension, D. H. Lawrence in his play *David* has Saul say of himself, "I am a man given over to trouble and tossed between two winds."

His story begins in 1 Samuel 8 with the elders of Israel asking *Samuel, priestly prophet and judge, to appoint a king to judge (govern) them "like all the nations." For the people, the theocratic rule that Samuel delegates to his corrupt sons portends disaster. Only a generation earlier such corruption in the house of Eli had incurred Yahweh's anger and brought Israel defeat. For the deity, however, the request spells yet again the people's failure to see Yahweh's sovereignty and providential care. To an equally affronted Samuel, Yahweh observes that it is "not you they have rejected, but me they have rejected from being king over them" (1 Sam. 8.7). Yet, surprisingly, Yahweh decrees that the prophet obey the people and appoint for them a king. And so it transpires, much against Samuel's better judgment, which he expresses in mighty counterblasts against both king and people (1 Sam. 8; 12). Thus, the *kingship is grounded in conflict between deity, prophet, and people.

Saul (whose name means "asked for"), the handsome son of a wealthy Benjaminite, is Yahweh's "designate" (Hebr. nāgîd; NRSV: "ruler").

He goes looking for his father's livestock and finds kingship instead (1 Sam. 9–10).

Saul is made king before Yahweh at the cult center in Gilgal, and in Gilgal his kingship begins to unravel (1 Sam. 13). Pressed to act decisively when a great host of *Philistines threatens his fearful and deserting army, he refuses to wait for Samuel beyond a time previously appointed by the prophet (10.8), and he offers a sacrifice. Samuel, as though waiting in the wings, immediately appears and, ignoring the king's explanation, condemns him outright. Saul, asserts the prophet, has not kept Yahweh's commandment, and his kingdom will not continue. Yahweh has sought out another "designate," a man sought out according to the divinity's own intention ("heart").

Commentators have long debated the reason for the condemnation. Other texts in Samuel and Kings make it unlikely that it is simply a matter of cultic law, involving the king's intrusion upon a priestly or prophetic office (cf. 1 Sam. 14.33–35; 1 Kings 3.3). Rather, the immediate cause appears to be Saul's breaking of Samuel's ambiguous instruction to wait—as interpreted by Samuel. But lying behind Samuel's readiness to condemn lurks perhaps a more pertinent reason rooted in the origins of Saul's kingship. Saul, asked for by the people, represents rejection for both prophet and deity. For the sake of theocracy this king must, in turn, be rejected.

In Gilgal comes final rejection (1 Sam. 15). Returning from a campaign against the *Amalekites with the captured king, Agag, and the best of the livestock, Saul once again meets a vehement Samuel. Why, demands the prophet, has Saul not done as instructed and "devoted [by destruction]" to Yahweh all living things? Saul responds that he has done what he was commanded to do, and that the animals have been brought to Gilgal for sacrifice. The issue turns on the difference between "devotion" and "sacrifice" (see Ban). Samuel, however, ignores Saul's explanation and invokes Yahweh's judgment upon him. Before such unrelenting opposition Saul acquiesces and asks pardon. But spurning him, Samuel declares that he is rejected as king—Yahweh has chosen "a neighbor" who is "better" than he. The reader soon learns that this man is *David, son of Jesse (1 Sam. 16).

The remainder of the king's story is played out against this backdrop. Saul knows that the deity has rejected him, but he does not know his successor's identity. Yahweh, soon to be so elo-

quent for David (see 1 Sam. 23.6–14; 30.7–8), remains silent before Saul. That silence produces the irony of the young David being introduced into Saul's court in order to make him well. It also feeds the king's growing suspicion and jealousy of the successful and admired young captain (1 Sam. 17–18). Yet, as if that corrosive silence were not enough, the deity provokes Saul directly: an "evil spirit from God" goads him to violence (1 Sam. 18.10–11) and disrupts his son Jonathan's attempt at reconciliation (1 Sam. 19.1–11).

David's fortune is Saul's fate: whatever Saul attempts to turn against David rebounds against Saul. Using as bait his own daughter, Michal, Saul seeks to entice David into a suicide mission; instead, he gains two hundred Philistine foreskins and loses his daughter, who will herself later betray her father to save the husband she loves (1 Sam. 18–19); her subsequent story is poignant (1 Sam. 25.44; 2 Sam. 3; 6). Likewise, Saul's savage revenge upon the priests of Nob for having helped the fleeing David only displaces into the fugitive's hand the oracular *ephod (1 Sam. 21–22).

Both Jonathan with goodwill and Saul with resentment come to see David's succession as inevitable (1 Sam. 20.12–17, 30–33; 23.16–18; 24.16–22; 26.25). Saul, moreover, spared twice by his elusive rival (1 Sam. 24; 26), confesses publicly the superior justice of David's actions. King and competitor each forswear all hostile intent toward the other, but they keep their distance and go their own way (26.25). As David works for the Philistines and accumulates power (1 Sam. 27–29), Saul faces them in battle (chap. 28). He seeks again a word from the silent Yahweh and, in desperation, has a medium conjure up the spirit of Samuel. The word he receives is a reiteration of rejection, but with one addition: on the next day he and his sons will die. So it happens that as David carries off booty from the Amalekites (1 Sam. 30), Saul and his sons fall to the Philistines on Mount Gilboa among the slain men of Israel (1 Sam. 31).

The king asked for by the people has failed: the way is now open for the king offered by Yahweh. Yet the people's king never forfeits their loyalty. The book ends with a moving epilogue. The inhabitants of Jabesh-gilead, delivered by Saul as his reign began, now risk their lives to close his reign with dignity. Retrieving his body from the walls of Philistine Beth-shan, they claim him as their own and honor him with burial in Jabesh. David, too, pays his own homage in a poem of beauty and irony (2 Sam. 1.17–27), a poem perhaps more beautiful than honest.

See also Israel, History of; Judah, The Kingdom of.   DAVID M. GUNN

Scapegoat. *See* Azazel.

Science and the Bible. The dramatic conflicts between Galileo and the Roman Inquisition and between Darwin and his biblicist opponents have understandably dominated the perception of the relation between science and religion in the popular imagination. But this perception is distorted because it neglects the indispensable role that religious beliefs played in the Western approach to *nature that led to the rise of modern science. On the other hand, emphasis on the integration of scientific and religious beliefs has often led to facile syntheses, provoking reactions that emphasize the separation of science and religion. Even if this separation were philosophically sound, it provides little basis for understanding the historical interaction, often constructive on both sides, between science and religion.

On the relation of science to the Bible, the diversity of views and interpretations is vast, but representatives can usefully serve to indicate the variety of types of reactions found in the Judeo-Christian tradition. In *De Doctrina Christiana (DDC)* and *De Genesi ad Litteram (DGL)*, Augustine (354–430 CE) makes clear the relative insignificance of specialized sciences as compared with understanding scripture, yet Augustine does not suggest that all knowledge can be found in scripture. In *DDC*, Augustine provides general rules for the interpretation of ambiguous terms. It is a mistake to read figurative signs literally (a rule that covers anthropomorphisms) and literal signs figuratively. The method of determining whether a particular expression is literal or figurative is that an expression that does not literally pertain to virtuous behavior or to the truth of faith must be taken figuratively. If the meaning of an expression is absurd when taken verbally, then we must examine its figurative possibilities. It follows from these guidelines that the believer should not read the Bible to learn facts about the natural world unrelated to salvation. In *DGL*, however, Augustine seems to require the certain truth of a new claim about nature in order to revise the apparently plain meaning of the biblical text, but even in *DGL* Augustine reiterates the principle that God did not wish to teach men

and women things of no relevance to their salvation. It was clear to Augustine that secular knowledge was indispensable for the correct interpretation of scripture. Although not a license for the autonomy of science, the principle in Augustine's approval of secular disciplines was expanded by later authors into arguments legitimating knowledge of the natural universe as another way of honoring God. Such authors, like William of Conches (1080–1154), presumably did not foresee the developments that would contribute to the autonomy of the sciences, but they were confident that natural science would still perform its proper role when rightly interpreted.

The revival of Aristotle in the medieval Latin West prompted scholars like Thomas Aquinas (1225–1274) to construe theology by analogy with Aristotelian science. Even so, in the context of medieval society, the definitive resolution of anomalies in the understanding of the cosmos was impossible and hence generated a resignation to the limitations of human knowledge. Nicholas Oresme (1320–1382) took seriously the hypothesis of the diurnal rotation of the earth but rejected it because no confirmation seemed possible; he fell back on the Bible in this case as providing persuasive confirmation of the greater probability of the geocentric view.

In *De Revolutionibus* (1543) Copernicus's arguments for the heliocentric theory rely partly on his religious point of view. Copernicus (1473–1543) shared not only the traditional beliefs about the intrinsic rationality and harmonious design of God's creation but also another traditional belief that God had made the universe for human beings; he then concluded, perhaps originally, that it therefore must be knowable. Copernicus had no reason to believe that the heliocentric theory would ever be empirically confirmed by some neutral test or observation, but he believed that criteria already existed for preferring the heliocentric hypothesis, namely, the ordering of the planets and the spheres that arose from the mathematical coherence between period of planetary orbit and distance from the sun, and the natural relation between hypothesis and some observations. In the preface dedicated to Pope Paul III (d. 1549), Copernicus denigrates those ignorant of astronomy who distort some passage of scripture in order to censure his undertaking. The biblical texts most often cited in later controversies are Joshua 10.12–14, Ecclesiastes 1.5, and Psalms 19.4–6; 93.1; 104.5.

There is evidence of early official Catholic

opposition to Copernicus, but plans to censure the theory in the mid-1540s were supposedly frustrated by the death of the master of the Sacred Palace, Bartolomeo Spina, in 1547. Lutheran reactions to the Copernican theory permitted use of the Copernican models even as the system was rejected as a literal truth. One of Tycho Brahe's (1546–1601) reasons for rejecting the Copernican theory was its incompatibility with texts of scripture, but Tycho's other reasons were astronomical and physical. Nevertheless, there is no question that Johannes Kepler (1571–1630) shared Copernicus's beliefs in divine design, the knowability of the universe, and the clues provided by mathematical coherence and commensurability for determining the order of the planets and even the true shape of their orbital paths.

Likewise, Galileo (1564–1642) shared the views of Copernicus and Kepler on mathematical coherence, but he also felt the need to demonstrate the truth of the Copernican theory, and his personal relations with several theologians, cardinals, popes, and political leaders introduced further complications into the story.

The text in which Galileo most directly and fully addresses questions about the Bible and science is the *Letter to the Grand Duchess Christina* (1615). Galileo cites Augustine several times, and he initially adopts the traditional view, emphasizing the principle of accommodation and arguing that it is not the purpose of the Bible to teach science. Where Joshua 10.12–14, then, reports the sun standing still, we are not to read the text as a literal description of the motions of the heavenly bodies.

Almost immediately, however, Galileo apparently accepts the criterion proposed by Cardinal Robert Bellarmine (1542–1621) earlier in 1615 in a letter to Paolo Antonio Foscarini (1580–1616), a theologian who supported the Copernican theory, that only in cases in which a scientific conclusion is demonstrated, and not merely probable, are we authorized to reinterpret the plain meaning of the biblical text. Later in his letter Galileo presses the attack further. If geocentrists insist on the literal interpretation of scripture, the passage from Joshua requires that the motion of the sun be stopped. According to the Ptolemaic theory, however, the proper motion of the sun is its annual motion on the ecliptic. Stopping the sun's annual motion would shorten the day, not lengthen it, argues Galileo. Then Galileo suggests a literal interpretation of the text of Joshua consistent with the Copernican

theory. The very idea is astounding; it is hardly surprising that theologians were shocked, and even less surprising that they misinterpreted the point of Galileo's critique.

Although Galileo's intention was to demonstrate the absurd consequence of insisting on using scripture for proof of a scientific hypothesis, it does appear that Galileo got carried away by his telescopic observations, his discovery of the sunspots, the cleverness of his own literal reading of the text of Joshua, and by his conviction that he could demonstrate the truth of Copernican theory. If Galileo intended to forestall official restrictions being placed on the Copernican theory, then his acceptance of Bellarmine's challenge and the introduction of the second reading seems to have provoked the very reaction he was trying to deflect.

In 1616 the Congregation of the Index condemned Foscarini's work supporting the Copernican theory, and it suspended Copernicus's *De Revolutionibus* and Diego de Zuñiga's (1536–1597) Copernican interpretation of texts of scripture until they were corrected. The decree followed the decision of the Congregation of the Holy Office, which accepted the arguments propounded by Bellarmine, who in a letter to Foscarini had expanded the Augustinian criterion about faith and morals to include under faith any natural assertion declared by the Holy Spirit. Hence, the text of Joshua had to be interpreted plainly as asserting the geocentric view, and because it was declared by the Holy Spirit, the conclusion had to be accepted as pertaining to faith. Bellarmine's reasoning was faulty, and through adoption by the Holy Office it set a dangerous precedent. Galileo was issued a warning, but one that also confirmed that his views had not been censured.

By the end of 1616, however, the premises for the eventual case against Galileo were in place: the Copernican theory was under censure and it appears that Galileo had been warned against defending it. From a narrow, legal point of view, Galileo's *Two Chief World Systems* (1632), even with the license that he was granted, violated the spirit, if not the letter, of the earlier injunction. Historians tend to excuse the Inquisition's mistake in condemning Galileo in 1633 on the grounds that the Roman Catholic church felt itself under pressure from some Protestant critics to guard against individual interpretations of scripture, thus abandoning its traditional, sound view for a narrower, literalist interpretation of the biblical text. In spite of Pope John Paul II's public acknowledgments in 1983 of Galileo's mistreatment at the hands of church authorities in 1633, and in 1992 of the correctness of Galileo's views, the Vatican continues to refuse scholars complete access to the Vatican archival records on the Galileo case, fueling further speculation about the case.

The Catholic reaction partly provoked by Protestant literalistic criticisms lent the more open approaches of yet other Protestants an air of free inquiry. Scholars still debate the concreteness of supposed Puritan or Anglican influences on scientific activity, but there seems little question that, in England and Holland, religious ideology played a role in the advancement of empirical science. Francis Bacon's (1561–1626) appeal to the recovery of the garden of *Eden in a technological paradise, Robert Boyles's (1627–1691) efforts to Christianize Epicurean atomism, the development of a natural theology supportive of scientific activity, the legitimation of science as a profession, and other similar consequences, however diverse and however loosely connected with any official doctrine, cannot be dismissed as irrelevant. Isaac Newton's (1642–1727) religious beliefs, even if not orthodox, and his extensive biblical commentaries attest to the importance that he himself attached to the Bible and to the partly religious foundations of his own conception of the universe. The later separation of the legitimation of science from religious motivations does not argue against the importance of religion for science prior to the eighteenth century.

In the nineteenth century, the controversies provoked by Charles Darwin's (1809–1882) theory of evolution were viewed as the focal point for a much broader perception of conflicting loyalties—to the belief in a universe divinely created with purpose or to the belief that the universe is the result of chance. The notion that the human eye could be the result of millions of years of evolution seems as improbable to those who believe in a special divine *creation as the biblical story of *Eve's creation from *Adam's rib seems to the paleontologist. The official Roman Catholic response of the late nineteenth century was subordinated to the church's antimodernist reaction, constituting a position between liberal Protestantism and *fundamentalism. In 1950 Pope Pius XII declared the belief in monogenesis as a foundation for the biblical account of original sin and its universal consequences. The a priori proscription of polygenesis on theological grounds has restricted Catholic

evolutionists' options. Liberal Protestants have not seen fit to restrict God's options on this question. The impact of the theory of evolution on biblical interpretation is undeniably clear from the further developments in historical-critical method and the emphasis on the social-ethical message of scripture. Literalistic creationists have rightly pointed out problems with the theory of evolution, but to most scientists the theory remains the best available and is strongly supported by evidence from physics and astronomy. Some scientists speak of evolution dogmatically as a fact, but such a dogmatic stance seems partly provoked by the educational threat posed by fundamentalists—efforts in America to legislate the teaching of religious alternatives to the theory of evolution and the effect of such efforts on textbook publishers demonstrate the reality of such threats. Ironically, in the case of Teilhard de Chardin (1881–1955), the French Jesuit paleontologist, the Roman Catholic church was concerned with tying Christian dogma to scientific theory and hence advocated more circumspect theological discussions of evolution, thus demonstrating the caution it had painfully learned from the Galileo case.

There is always a theoretical background to empirical research, but the danger for theology lies in the use of science to advance a particular interpretation of the Bible and the danger for science lies in the use of dogma to obstruct scientific theorizing; it does not lie in the use of dogma or the Bible to promote scientific research or to question a specific interpretation of the Bible. The advance of science depends to some extent on skeptical questioning of established views. The recognition of the contingency of nature is consistent with the belief in creation and in the dependence of nature on God's sustaining and controlling presence. Contemporary theologians who advocate the revival of traditional natural theology seem unaware of its earlier fate. The preference of some cosmologists for the anthropic principle requires the theological assumption that human beings are the goal of God's creation in order for the anthropic principle to be regarded as explanatory. But even from a theological point of view, such an account is unsatisfactory for it places a priori limitations on how God could have accomplished the divine purposes. The principles enunciated by Augustine seem susceptible of a broad interpretation with modern amendments: the Bible does not teach natural science; theology makes legitimate knowledge claims; our understanding of the meaning of the Bible has changed with our growth in knowledge of the physical universe; belief in the divine origin of the universe has often motivated and sustained confidence in the ability of humans to penetrate the secrets of the universe; the failures of science and the excesses of human intervention alert us to the relevance of values for decisions in science and technology; historical experience enjoins us to admit the possibly ultimate futility of human achievements; biblical homage to the sacredness of nature and human responsibility is harmonious with the awe and wonder expressed by cosmologists and environmentalists; and the search for meaning in human existence supports the limited aim of consonance between theological and scientific interpretations of the cosmos.

ANDRÉ L. GODDU

Scofield Reference Bible. A popular and influential reference Bible published by Oxford University Press early in the twentieth century. The editor, C. I. Scofield (1843–1921), was a successful lawyer, but after his religious conversion in 1879 he devoted himself to Bible study and Christian service, eventually becoming an ordained Congregational minister of some prominence. In 1909 he published *The Scofield Reference Bible,* with a second, revised edition in 1917. By 1930, total sales of the two editions had exceeded one million copies.

Utilizing the King James Version with Scofield's notes and comments in the margins, *The Scofield Reference Bible* featured the so-called dispensational system of biblical interpretation. Dispensationalists claim that God's dealings with humankind have varied throughout the different eras or "dispensations" of biblical history. They emphasize their "literal" interpretation of the Bible, suggesting, for example, that some of the prophecies concerning the land of Israel are yet to be fulfilled. A controversial feature of this system is the nearly total separation of God's relationship with Israel and the Jewish people from that of the Christian church. Dispensationalism has been and remains a significant force in Protestant Christianity in North America.

In 1967, Oxford University Press published *The New Scofield Reference Bible* under the editorial direction of E. Schuyler English; this edition was also based on the King James Version and retained the dispensational flavor of Scofield's notes. More recently, editions based on the New

International Version and the New American Standard Bible have also been published.

See also Fundamentalism.

WILLIAM H. BARNES

Scribes. Scribes were distinguished professional people throughout the ancient world. Although they were called scribes because they could read and write, they were not only copyists. In Israel, some were officials who had authority to draw up legal documents (Jer. 32.12–15; 36.26). Some held special positions in the royal palace (2 Kings 18.18; Jer. 36.12) and functioned as ministers of finance or secretaries of state (2 Kings 22.3; Isa. 36.3). Some were academic advisers to the king. During the Diaspora (*see* Dispersion) in *Babylon, scribes became responsible for preserving and interpreting scripture. Later, scribes were also called "the wise" and described as those with special knowledge of the *Law (Dan. 11.33, 35; 12.3; Sir. 39.6–11; Ezra 7.6, 10). Early in the conflict with Antiochus Epiphanes (ca. 168 BCE), a group of Jewish scribes met with Antiochus's agents to negotiate justice (1 Macc. 7.12). They were probably local politicians with legal training.

In the New Testament, scribes are described functioning as *lawyers (Luke 5.17; 7.30) and judges (Matt. 23.2), and they are shown arguing with *Jesus over legal matters—authority to forgive (Matt. 9.3; Luke 5.21), traditions of the elders (Matt. 15.1), dietary laws (Mark 2.16; 3.22; Luke 5.30; 15.2), *purity laws (Mark 7.1–2), interpretation of scripture (Matt. 17.10; Mark 9.11; 12.28, 35; Luke 20.39; John 8.2), and *Sabbath observance (Luke 6.7). Scribes were often associated with *Pharisees, but the two were not identical. The "scribes of the Pharisees" (Mark 2.16; Luke 5.30; Acts 23.9) were probably legal counselors employed by the Pharisees. Chief priests also employed scribes (Mark 15.31; Acts 4.6) as their legal counselors.

Scribes were associated with the *Sanhedrin, probably as clerks, legal counselors for participants in trials, and judges. The fact that Jesus was reported arguing with the scribes at the same time that he was refuting the Pharisees does not prove that scribes were Pharisaic. Since the scribes whom Jesus attacked were defending the Pharisees, Jesus opposed them as well as the clients they represented.

The authority of scribes was delegated. They interpreted existing law; they did not create it. Well-trained scribes were acquainted with all kinds of law, both ancient and contemporary (Matt. 13.52). When Jesus was distinguished from the scribes as one who had authority (Matt. 7.29; Mark 1.22), the implication was that, as the *Messiah, he had authority to make law, just as *David and other kings did. This gave him authority over the Sabbath (Matt. 12.8) and all other national laws. He also had authority to pardon (Matt. 9.6), as other kings did.

Some scribes also copied biblical texts. The care with which this was done has been recognized with the discovery of the *Dead Sea Scrolls, which allow scholars to compare medieval texts with examples copied a thousand years earlier. The relatively few differences disclosed are not so often scribal errors as variant texts. At the ends of some books, the scribe gave the total number of words in the book and told which word was the exact middle, so that later scribes could count both ways to be sure they had not omitted a single letter; this tradition was continued by the *Masoretes.

See also Books and Bookmaking in Antiquity; Judaisms of the First Century CE; Textual Criticism; Writing in Antiquity.

GEORGE WESLEY BUCHANAN

Seba. *A part of the kingdom of *Sheba, perhaps a colony in northeast Africa.*

Second Coming of Christ. "He will come again to judge the living and the dead": in this way, the Apostles' Creed summarizes the Christian hope that God will complete his purpose for the world in a final, triumphant coming of Christ. The parallel terms "first coming" and "second coming" (suggested in Heb. 9.26–28) highlight the theological connection between these two chief moments of Christ's work.

The *prophets had declared that God's purpose in history would reach its goal in a future period of blessing under God's rule, a rule that would be righteous, peaceful, universal, and permanent (Isa. 11.2–5; 60; 65–66; Mic. 4.3–4). Often God was said to exercise his rule through an earthly king descended from *David (Isa. 9.6–7; Zech. 9.9–10).

*Jesus taught that this longed-for time of salvation had dawned, the *kingdom of God had drawn near (Mark 1.15). The promises were now being fulfilled in him, and his possession of God's spirit, his *miracles and *exorcisms were evidence of this (Matt. 11.2–6; 12.28). Yet God's kingdom had not fully arrived. For although

through his ministry the blessings of God were experienced with a new immediacy, still death and suffering and the ambiguities of life remained for his followers. The complete realization of the kingdom was in the future. Thus he taught his disciples to pray, "Your kingdom come" (Luke 11.2; *see* Lord's Prayer), and proclaimed that the coming of the *Son of man would mark the dividing line between the present course of history and the full realization of God's kingdom (Mark 13.26).

The so-called apocalyptic discourse of Mark 13 (and the related passages in Matt. 24; Luke 17.22–37; 21) warns of the sufferings and conflicts that Jesus' followers should expect before his final coming as Son of man. Both here (Mark 13.30) and elsewhere (Rom. 13.11–12; 1 Pet. 4.7) the nearness of Christ's coming is stressed. But there is also an expectation that certain events must take place before the end comes (Mark 13.10; 2 Thess. 2.2–8), and an insistence that the date cannot be predicted (Mark 13.32–33; Luke 17.20; Acts 1.7). So the statements about nearness are best understood as vivid assertions of the certainty that God's purpose, begun in Christ's first coming, will be completed in his second coming.

Similarly, the New Testament writers are more concerned with the purpose of Christ's coming than with its manner, which is variously described. Christ will come to complete the work of rescuing humankind, which began with his first coming (Heb. 9.26–28). He will come to pass judgment on the whole human race (Matt. 25.31–46; 1 Cor. 4.5), to welcome into his presence those who have lived by trust in him (Mark 13.27), while those who have rejected him will find themselves shut out (2 Thess 1.7–10). Thus his coming will mark his final conquest over evil (1 Cor. 15.24–25), and the realization of his kingdom of peace, righteousness, and love. This is described as "new heavens and a new earth, where righteousness is at home" (2 Pet. 3.13; cf. Rev. 21.3–4).

Not all interpreters take the New Testament's message of the second coming at face value. Some argue that Jesus' sayings about the coming of the Son of man are not authentic to him, or that he intended them as symbols of God's triumph rather than as promises of an actual future coming; in that case, the hope of the early Christians would be based on a misunderstanding of Jesus' teaching. Others argue that since the expectation of Christ's coming within a generation of his lifetime did not materialize, it must be interpreted symbolically to mean that Christ "comes to me" in my decision for him and his rule. In contrast, some understand all references to the second coming quite literally, and believe the passages about "the signs of the times" (e.g. Mark 13) enable its timing to be calculated precisely. In any case, it is possible to affirm the basic structure of Christian hope, with its emphasis on the second coming as the goal and fulfillment of God's past work in Christ, without committing oneself to any precise view about its nature or when it will be.

See also Biblical Theology, *article on* New Testament; Maranatha; Parousia.

STEPHEN H. TRAVIS

Second Isaiah. *See* Isaiah, The Book of.

Selah. A (transliterated) Hebrew word of uncertain meaning which occurs seventy-one times in the *Psalms and three times in Habakkuk 3. It often appears at the end of a psalm (Ps. 3.8), though also at the end of a section within a psalm (Ps. 3.2, 4). The word also occurs in the postcanonical Psalms of Solomon (17.29 [31]; 18.9 [10]). The *Septuagint translated selah into Greek as *diapsalma,* which may mean "interlude," though the sense of this word is also uncertain.

Selah is probably a liturgical direction, added to the original text of a psalm. It may mean "lift up," either to indicate the lifting up of the voices of the singers in a doxology, or to call for "lifted-up" instrumental music in an interlude in the singing.   WILLIAM A. BEARDSLEE

Sennacherib (Sin-aḫḫe-eriba). King of *Assyria (705–681 BCE). Sennacherib, as crown prince under his father Sargon II (722–705 BCE), served as administrator in the Assyrian heartland while his father was on campaign. After Sargon had been killed in battle, Sennacherib viewed this as a sign of divine disfavor and dissociated himself from his father. He abandoned Sargon's newly built capital and, contrary to Assyrian custom, omitted his genealogy in official inscriptions. Sennacherib chose as his capital the old city of *Nineveh, which he embellished by installing wide boulevards, bringing in mountain water by aqueduct, planting trees, and laying out parks. Sennacherib campaigned actively in foreign lands, chiefly against *Babylon (dominated at this time by Chaldeans) and Elam. His struggles with Bab-

ylon reached a crisis after the Babylonians had handed over his crown prince, Ashur-nadin-shumi, to the Elamites; Sennacherib eventually besieged, captured, and ruthlessly destroyed the city, diverting a watercourse through the ruins so that the site would be permanently obliterated.

In 701 BCE, Sennacherib led an expedition into Palestine to reinstate his ally Padi of Ekron, who had been deposed by his subjects. The siege of *Lachish during this campaign is vividly illustrated in the reliefs from the royal palace at Nineveh. After the fall of Lachish, Sennacherib besieged *Hezekiah in *Jerusalem, imprisoning him, as the Assyrian annals report, "like a bird in a cage"; Hezekiah made peace only by paying extensive tribute (cf. 2 Kings 18–19; Isa. 36–37; 2 Chron. 32). Because of apparent discrepancies in the biblical and extrabiblical accounts of Sennacherib's activities in Palestine, it has sometimes been proposed that Sennacherib mounted another, less successful expedition—not recorded in the cuneiform records—against the area at some time after 689 BCE; but this is unlikely. Nevertheless, the survival of Jerusalem was viewed as the equivalent of a victory by some biblical writers, and this led to the narrative of the city's miraculous deliverance (see Isa. 37.33–37 = 2 Kings 19.32–36), celebrated in Byron's "The Destruction of Sennacherib." Sennacherib was assassinated in 681 BCE by his son Arda-Mulishshi (cf. 2 Kings 19.36–37; 2 Chron. 32.21).

JOHN A. BRINKMAN

Septuagint. The traditional term for the translations of the Hebrew Bible into *Greek. Meaning "seventy" and often abbreviated by the Roman numeral LXX, it is derived from the second-century BCE legend that, at the request of Ptolemy II (285–246 BCE), seventy-two elders of Israel translated the Hebrew Bible into Greek in seventy-two days in Alexandria in Egypt. Most scholars accept the substance of the legend, that the earliest Greek versions of the Bible were created in the third century in Egypt for Greek-speaking Jews. The earliest manuscripts of the Septuagint are from *Qumran and are dated to the second century BCE. The relationship between the Greek and Hebrew textual traditions was complicated and fluid, with frequent revision of the Greek to bring it closer to the Hebrew as the latter developed.

The Septuagint includes a number of writings not found in the traditional Hebrew canon, some translations from Hebrew or Aramaic originals and others composed in Greek. These become the *Apocrypha, accepted by some Christian churches as canonical but not part of the Bible for Jews and Protestants.

The Septuagint was the primary form of the Bible for Hellenized Jewish communities and thus was that used by most early Christians. When the Bible is quoted in the New Testament, it is almost always from the Septuagint version, which elevated its status for Christian theologians.

See also Translations, *article on* Ancient Languages. MICHAEL D. COOGAN

Seraph, Seraphim. Hebrew singular and plural for supernatural beings associated with the presence of God, and in postbiblical tradition identified as one of the choirs of *angels. They appear only once in the Bible, in the call-vision of Isaiah (chap. 6), where they sing praise to God in the now-famous words of the "Thrice Holy" hymn. Isaiah saw the Lord on his throne, surrounded by seraphim in the same way that early rulers were surrounded by a courtly retinue. Like the derivative four living creatures of Revelation 4.8, the seraphim had three pairs of wings, one for flying, one for covering their eyes (for apparently not even these beings could look directly on God), and one to cover their feet (almost certainly a euphemism for genitalia).

The noun *śārāp* is usually related to the verb *śārap*, "to burn." Because the term appears several times with reference to the serpents encountered in the *wilderness (Num. 21.8; Deut. 8.15; Isa. 14.29; 30.6), it has often been understood to refer to "fiery serpents." From this it has also often been proposed that the seraphim were serpentine in form and in some sense "fiery" creatures or associated with fire. In Isaiah 6.6 one of the seraphs brings the prophet a live coal from the fire on the altar; note, however, that the seraph uses tongs. DAVID G. BURKE

Sermon on the Mount. In popular thought the Sermon on the Mount epitomizes Jesus' ethical teaching; it is the first of five discourses by *Jesus in *Matthew's gospel and is found in Matthew 5–7. Augustine first called this discourse the "Sermon on the Mount" because of its setting in Matthew 5.1. Matthew describes it as a speech or teaching (5.2; 7.28) given by Jesus while seated, the typical Jewish position for teaching (cf. 23.2).

The sermon shares a striking structural and material parallel with Luke 6.20–49, often called the "Sermon on the Plain" because of its setting. Each opens with a series of beatitudes (Matt. 5.3–12; Luke 6.20–23) followed by a series of demands for conduct (Matt. 5.21–7.12; Luke 6.27–42) and concludes with a series of alternatives, the last being a parable of two builders (Matt. 7.13–27; Luke 6.43–49). Although some have attributed these similarities to Jesus' use of the same "sermon" on more than one occasion, most explain them as the evangelists' use of a common tradition that had already taken its basic shape.

Why then the extensive differences between the two accounts, such as length (Matthew has over a hundred verses, Luke thirty)? Careful examination of the material indicates that some of the differences arose in the development of the tradition used by each evangelist respectively, and some, especially in wording, arose from the evangelists' adaptation of the tradition for their purposes. Much of Matthew's additional material, however, appears elsewhere in Luke's gospel (e.g., 7.7–11, 13–14, 22–23; Luke 11.2–4, 9–13, 34–36; 12.22–34; 13.23–27) and suggests that Matthew thematically combined other parts of the tradition common to Matthew and Luke (*Q) to expand the "sermon" tradition. And if Matthew has drawn from the larger, common tradition with Luke, it is likely that he also drew from other traditions to fill out this discourse (e.g., 5.17–19, 21–24, 27–28, 33–37; 6.1–8, 9–13, 16–18). Consequently Matthew's Sermon on the Mount represents an underlying "sermon" tradition expanded by the use of other traditions.

Does then the Sermon on the Mount come from Jesus? If one precisely defines the Sermon as the discourse found in Matthew 5–7, the answer is no. Matthew 5–7 as it now stands is the evangelist's final product of an oral/literary process involving several traditions. Yet analysis of the traditions found in the Sermon indicates their strong claim to being rooted in Jesus' own ministry, and to represent his teaching faithfully.

Some have drawn a parallel between Matthew's structure with five discourses (5–7; 10; 13; 18; 23–25) and the five books of Moses (the *Torah). Consequently, the mountain setting and the apparently ethical content of the Sermon have naturally led to interpreting the Sermon as a new law or the messianic Torah given by Jesus, the new *Moses. This view, however, fails to do justice to Matthew's gospel as a whole by relegating the infancy, baptism, and temptation narratives (chaps. 1–4) to the status of a preamble and the passion narrative (chaps. 26–28) to that of an epilogue. It suffers from the lack of evidence that Jesus' role either in the Sermon or in the gospel was that of a new Moses.

Others have found the clue to Matthew's structure in the transitional statement, "From that time on, Jesus began . . ." (4.17; 16.21), which divides Matthew's portrait of Jesus into three parts, the first focused on the person of Jesus Messiah, the second on the presentation of Jesus Messiah, and the third on the passion of Jesus Messiah. In this schema, the Sermon comes as part of Jesus' presentation of himself and his summons to the Kingdom in 4.17–16.20. This reading concurs with Matthew's immediate setting for the Sermon. The discourse in 5–7 and the miraculous deeds in 8–9 are enclosed by the identical programmatic summary in 4.23 and transitional summary in 9.35. These summaries point to Jesus as the promised *Messiah presenting the message of the Kingdom and effecting its work.

The audience of the Sermon is the *disciples, a group that for Matthew has a dual significance. In the context of Jesus' ministry the disciples always refers to the *twelve. But the disciples also represent a model or paradigm of the followers of Jesus in general (28.19; cf. 27.57). They are the community of the Messiah, who have responded to Jesus' message of the Kingdom, and in whose lives the Kingdom is at work. Therefore, the Sermon is also a statement about the identity of the new people of God (5.3–16; 7.13–27) and their conduct in relationship to each other (5.21–48) and to God (6.1–7.11).

The beatitudes (Matt. 5.3–12) bear witness to Jesus and identify the people of the Kingdom. Although Matthew appears to have spiritualized or ethicized the beatitudes to the *poor, the hungry, and the weeping (cf. Luke 6.20b–23), his first four beatitudes reflect a deliberate alignment in wording and order with Isaiah 61 to show Jesus to be the fulfillment of Isaiah's promised messenger anointed by the Spirit (Matt. 3.16) to proclaim the good news of God's deliverance (cf. Matt. 4.23; Luke 4.18–21).

At the same time the beatitudes identify the people of the Kingdom as those who stand before God empty-handed, vulnerable, seeking a right relationship with him and others, open to receive and express his *mercy and *forgiveness with integrity, ready to experience and to establish peace. These are the people of the Kingdom who find themselves at odds with this world. Yet they are the "salt of the earth" (5.13) and the "light of the world" (5.14–15) whose "good works" bring glory to God (5.16).

The demands of the Sermon (5.17–7.12) set forth the "greater righteousness" (5.20) of the followers of Jesus. But Matthew prefaces these demands by noting again that Jesus' coming meant the fulfillment of biblical promises, "the law and the prophets" (5.17).

The first set of demands (5.21–48), often referred to as the "antitheses," assumes a new relationship between individuals that issues in conduct that supersedes the Law. These six demands, like much biblical *law as well as other teachings of Jesus, are more illustrative than comprehensive.

The second set of demands (6.1–7.11) reflects a right relationship with God. These demands fall into two groups, the first of which has three illustrations of traditional Jewish piety (6.1–18). The second group consists of a series of apparently miscellaneous exhortations (6.19–7.11). The connecting link between these two groups of demands may lie in the petitions of the *Lord's Prayer, which was inserted (6.8–15) into the first group (6.1–18) as an example of how to pray. Each exhortation corresponds to a petition of the Lord's Prayer (6.9b–10 = 6.19–24; 6.11 = 6.25–34; 6.12 = 7.1–4; 6.13 = 7.6), and the series concludes with a promise for answered prayer (7.7–11).

Matthew rounds off the demands of the Sermon (5.21–7.11) with the *Golden Rule (7.12). Drawn most likely from the context of love for one's enemy (5.43–48; cf. Luke 6.27–35), this demand, now located after the second set of demands pertaining to one's relationship with God (6.1–7.11), resumes the first set of demands regarding one's relationship with others (5.21–48). Therefore, the heart of the Sermon defines the life of the Kingdom in terms of horizontal (5.21–28) and vertical relationships (6.1–7.11).

The Sermon concludes with three sets of alternatives—two ways, two trees, and two builders (7.13–27). One alternative offers life, the other death or destruction. Jesus' way, followed by few, is the more difficult (7.13–14) but is productive (7.16–17) and capable of weathering the storm of judgment (7.24–25).

But can one really "hear" and "do" Jesus' words as the Sermon suggests? Apart from the beatitudes that appear to bless conduct contrary to what it takes to survive in the real world, can one today love the enemy and live with anger

(5.22), evil thoughts (5.28), the guarantee of one's word (5.34–37), the recourse to legal justice (5.29–40), or even *divorce (5.32)? To understand the Sermon, one must read it in its biblical context woven into the fabric of Matthew's gospel as a statement, above all, about who Jesus is. In this initial discourse, one "hears" Jesus whose words support his preaching about the presence of the Kingdom and point to his person in whom God is acting in keeping with the promise of Isaiah 61. With these words, Jesus declares that a new day has dawned in human relationships because God is offering new relationships with those who are willing to let God be sovereign in their lives (5.3–10). Thus the Sermon is the message of the "good news," the "gospel of the kingdom," that declares "blessed" those who have nothing to claim or cling to before God.

At the same time, the Sermon does offer, in a sense, the ethic of the Kingdom. It sets forth how the people of the Kingdom live in relationship with God and others. When accepting Jesus' words of God's gracious acceptance in the beatitudes, one does not "perform" to achieve God's reward (6.1–18), but, placing one's life in God's hands (6.19–7.6), one responds to God out of gratitude and love. Furthermore, in light of the recognition of God's rule, one is free to leave one's best interest in God's hands and to respond to others out of love rather than self-interest. Only then does the prohibition of anger, lust, and use of legal justice and divorce, or the demand for total honesty and love for the enemy (5.21–48) avoid being utopian.

ROBERT A. GUELICH

Seven Churches, The. The *Revelation to John was addressed to seven churches in the Roman province of *Asia. There were other churches in the province (Colossae and Troas), but seven were chosen to represent the entire church (*see* Number Symbolism). The letters to these churches (Rev. 2–3) present a picture of diversity in Christianity. The church of *Ephesus, which had been founded by *Paul, and remained for many centuries one of the chief centers of the eastern church, was zealous in guarding against heresy (that of the Nicolaitans), but lacking in Christian love. The church of Smyrna appears to have stood up well under harassment and, sometimes, the imprisonment of its members. Pergamum was an important religious center, with a famous shrine of Zeus, a temple of Asklepios with a

renowned medical school, and a temple of Augustus; "Satan's throne" may mean any of these, but probably refers to emperor worship. The church had suffered some persecution but it had remained faithful, though there was some laxity with regard to the Nicolaitans. The church of Thyatira abounded in love and faith, service and patient endurance, but allowed the evil teachings of a prophetess *Jezebel. The church of Sardis was outwardly flourishing, but not without serious damage to its spiritual life. Philadelphia, on the other hand, was a city where Christians were isolated in the community; but the church had remained faithful. At Laodicea the church seemed to be flourishing, but was spiritually poor. (See Map 14:E3.)

Each letter is specific and contains praise and criticism, warning and encouragement as appropriate. But the plural "churches" at the end of each letter shows that they were meant to be read by every church. They are part of the opening vision of Revelation, where John saw the heavenly *Son of man surrounded by seven lampstands, which were the seven churches. The letters show that this was not meant as a picture of an ideal church, but as a means of showing the churches as they really are, with their heresies, quarrels, and weak faith, but also with their faith and hope and love. This introduction to the Revelation plays an essential part in the book's purpose of warning and comfort.

DAVID H. VAN DAALEN

Seven, The. According to Acts 6.1–6, a dispute arose between "Hellenists" and "Hebrews" over the distribution of food to *widows. The *twelve decided that "seven men of good standing" be chosen to oversee the task. In some later Christian traditions this decision is understood as the institution of the office of *deacon, though that title does not occur in the passage.

This passage has traditionally been interpreted as reflecting tension between Jewish and *gentile Christians. But recent scholarship has shown the fine line that existed between Jews and Greeks in this part of the world in the Roman period. Even Acts itself warns against too glib an approach to ethnic and religious identities. The "God-fearers" in Acts (10.2; 13.16, 36) are just such a group who stand on the border between putative Greek and Jewish culture. It is more likely then, that both groups are Jewish Christians, the Hebrews being Aramaic-speakers and the Hellenists perhaps originally from the *Dispersion but now living in Jerusalem. The episode would thus reflect tension between them, a tension resolved by the establishment of a new form of leadership in some ways parallel to the twelve; two of the seven, *Stephen and Philip, are active preachers just like the twelve (Acts 6:8–8.40). The narrative may also be inspired by the accounts of Moses' sharing of leadership (Exod. 18.123–27; Num. 11.16–25). J. ANDREW OVERMAN

Sex. An appreciation of the biblical concern with the establishment of a holy people—the "children of Abraham," variously understood—reveals the relationship between sexuality and such related issues as virginity, pre- and extramarital sexual behavior, *marriage, polygyny, concubinage, *adultery, and *homosexuality.

Sexual Behavior in the Hebrew Bible. The paradigmatic biblical statement on sexuality and sexual behavior is found in Genesis 1.26–28, the creation of human beings in God's image as male and female with the duty to "be fruitful and multiply," and it reflects the vigorous pronatalist worldview that characterized most of the period of the composition of the Hebrew Bible. From the call of *Abraham in Genesis 12 to the death of *Joseph in Genesis 50, the combined promises of land, heir, and many descendants provide the scaffolding by which the history of earliest Israel is erected (Gen. 12.2; 13.16; 22.17; 24.60; etc.). Israel shared this desire for offspring with its ancient Near Eastern neighbors, as evidenced in the fourteenth-century BCE *Ugaritic epic of Kirta. The threat of the extinction of one's biological line is a commonplace in ancient Near Eastern treaty curses, and was appropriated directly by biblical writers (Deut. 28.18, 32; Josh. 6.26; Ps. 109.13; etc.).

All sexual behavior that did not produce legitimate Israelite offspring to the holy commonwealth was, in varying degrees, censured or controlled, and there was a concomitant double standard with regard to sexual behavior. Premarital virginity, for example, was incumbent only upon females; there is no indication that males were expected to be virgins at marriage, and there is no provision in the Hebrew Bible for lifelong virginity. If a husband accused his wife of not having been a virgin at the time of her marriage, and if his charges were substantiated, the woman was stoned. If, on the other hand, the man's charges were refuted, he was merely flogged and fined (Deut. 22.13–21).

Marriage was regarded as the normal estate of adults by the biblical writers, although in actuality the closing of the Israelite frontier and concomitant laws granting patrimony to the firstborn son would almost certainly have deprived some sons and daughters of the economic resources necessary to establish families of their own. Such unmarried sons were shunted into military, bureaucratic, or clerical careers (e.g., the landless *Levites). Some unmarried women may have found a social role among the temple functionaries termed qādēš/qĕdēšâ (literally, "set apart," but usually translated "sacred prostitute" on the basis of such passages as Gen. 38.21–22 and Deut. 23.18). There is no direct evidence, however, that the wages of such persons were derived from sexual activity (see Prostitution).

The function of marriage in the Hebrew Bible was (a) social (the regulation of sexual behavior, especially of *women); (b) psychological and emotional (to provide companionship for the partners); (c) economic (through family agrarian and artisan enterprises); (d) religious (since the majority of festivals centered on household participation); and, most important, (e) theological (through the procreation, legitimation, and socialization of children, the basis of the people of God). In the majority of biblical writings, children were the supreme example of divine favor (Gen. 12.2; Deut. 28.9–11; Ps. 127.3–5), and childlessness was understood to be a curse (Gen. 15.2, Deut. 28.18, 30).

Endogamy was prescribed (Exod. 34.15–16; Deut. 7.3–6; Josh. 23.11–13), but intermarriage was routine in actuality, especially by kings. The *Samson cycle (Judg. 13–16) vividly illustrated the perceived danger of exogamy. Ezra and Nehemiah (Ezra 9–10; Neh. 10.28–30) attempted to restore ethnic endogamy after the exile, but by Hellenistic times intermarriage was again recorded as a practice among diaspora Jews (Acts 16.1–3; 24.24).

The conviction that procreation is an unqualified good is also reflected in three well-known institutions regulating sexual behavior: polygyny, concubinage, and levirate marriage.

Polygyny seems to have been practiced since the earliest periods of Israelite history, but was probably never statistically prevalent due to the relative affluence necessary to support more than one wife; note *Jacob's fourteen-year indenture for his two wives and two concubines (Gen. 29.20–29). Both *David and *Solomon practiced polygyny on a grand scale (1 Sam. 25.39–43; 27.3; 2 Sam. 3.2–5), although the Deuteronomic theologians admonished even royalty to refrain from the practice because of its religiously adulterating possibilities (Deut. 17.17; cf. 1 Kings 11.1–7).

Although concubines did not enjoy the same rights as a wife, they were socially and legally recognized in ancient Israel. A concubine's children did not share the rights of a wife's children, unless, like *Hagar, sexual contact with the concubine was for the explicit purpose of producing heirs, in which case the children became the wife's children (Gen. 21.14; 25.5–6). Wives and concubines of a deposed or conquered king were considered war booty (2 Sam. 12.8; 1 Kings 20.3). Thus, *Absalom's public intercourse with David's concubines during the latter's flight from Jerusalem was considered treasonous (2 Sam. 16.20–22), and Adonijah's request for the concubine Abishag amounted to insurrection (1 Kings 2.13–25).

Although the legislation concerning *levirate marriage (Deut. 25.5–10) specifies the brother of the deceased as bearer of the responsibility to marry his widowed sister-in-law, the story of Judah and Tamar in Genesis 38 indicates that the responsibility to the widow rested with the dead man's family, not merely with his brother (v. 26). Further, "to preserve the name" refers to the dead man's property, not merely to his nominal existence, as is clear from the account in Ruth 4. *Josephus is probably correct, then, in seeing the purpose of levirate marriage to be threefold: to continue a lineage, to prevent the alienation of family property, and to provide for the social and economic welfare of *widows (*Ant.* 4.8.254). Levirate marriage was at least known (if not actually practiced) into the Hellenistic period (cf. Matt. 22.22–33).

All sexual behavior that did not contribute to the biblical notion of "the children of Israel" was proscribed. *Homosexuality, bestiality, contraception, and masturbation were all prohibited, directly or by inference. *Adultery—sexual activity between a married woman and a man of any marital status—is consistently condemned in the biblical writings (Exod. 20.14, 17; Lev. 18.20, 20.10; Num. 5.11–31; Deut. 22.22–29; Matt. 5.32). Sexual activity by an unmarried woman, whether for hire or not, was termed *prostitution (the same Hebrew words, zānâ and its derivatives, are also translated as "to fornicate," "to be a harlot, a whore") and the response ranged from toleration (in the case of *Rahab, Josh. 2) to burning (in the case of a priest's daughter, Lev. 21.9; cf. Gen. 38.24). Harlotry as a meta-

phor for spiritual unfaithfulness was used by the prophets to denounce Israel's apostasy.

A conspicuous exception to the dominant sexual ideology of the Bible is the *Song of Solomon. The Song's frank erotic imagery, its indifference to social proprieties such as marriage and reproduction, and its lack of overtly religious sentiments have forced generations of exegetes to allegorize its sensuality to bring it into harmony with the social control of sexuality sought by most biblical authors.

Sexual Behavior in the Greco-Roman Period. Beginning in the later books of the Hebrew Bible and continuing through the New Testament, there is a general decline in the value of sexuality and a tendency toward exaggerating its sinfulness. This shift in attitude resulted less from the influence of apocalyptic religious thought than from the Greco-Roman cultural hegemony of the third century BCE to the second century CE. *Philo (ca. 20 BCE–ca. 50 CE) interpreted the *Septuagint's reordering of the *Ten Commandments to place adultery at the top of the list of sins against one's neighbor, before murder and theft (Exod. 20.13–15: LXX; Deut. 5.17–19: LXX), to indicate that adultery was the most serious of all sins (*De Dec.* 121, 131). Philo also condemned any expression of sexuality, even within marriage, that was not for the purpose of procreation (*Spec. Leg.* 3.32–36).

The *Essenes at *Qumran, who believed that they were living on the eve of the final eschatological battle between "the children of light and the children of darkness," considered themselves especially susceptible to pollution from sexual contact (1QM 7.4–7), and so some of them, according to statements of Philo (*Apol.* 14–17), Josephus (*War* 2.8.120–21; *Ant.* 18.121) and other ancient sources, renounced marriage and reproduction. The paucity of juvenile and female skeletons in the Qumran cemetery lends credence to these statements.

Early Christian attitudes toward sexuality arose from this background of Hellenistic asceticism, Jewish *apocalypticism, and *ethics inherited from the Hebrew Bible. Adultery and homosexuality are forbidden, for example (e.g., Rom. 1.26–27; 1 Tim. 1.10), and other sexual activities are proscribed, such as fornication by males as well as females (1 Cor. 6.9). We find in the *synoptic Gospels antimarital and antifamilial sentiments attributed to Jesus (Matt. 8.21–22; 10.34–37; 19.10–12; Luke 8.19–21; 11.27–28), and *Paul unambiguously counseled the Corinthian Christians that marriage represented a compromise of the spiritual life, the highest degree of which was attainable only by celibates like Paul (1 Cor. 7.1, 7–9; cf. Matt. 19.10–12; Rev. 14.4).

New Testament endorsement of marital sexuality and *family life is clearest in the Deutero-Pauline and pastoral letters, where the patriarchal household current in the Mediterranean world of the first century CE (with such modifications as premarital chastity for males) was assumed as the Christian norm (Eph. 5.22–24; 1 Tim. 2.15; 4.1–4; 5.14; cf. Heb. 13.4). The tension between sexual renunciation and full participation in married life was not decisively resolved in early Christianity, however, as both apocryphal and patristic writings attest (e.g., Acts of Paul and Thecla; Tertullian, *Exhort. Chast.* 3; Jerome, *Jov.* 1.40).

See also Know.   GENE McAFEE

Shalmaneser V. Shulmanu-ashared, King of *Assyria (727–722 BCE); otherwise known as Ululayu ("born in the month Ululu"). As son of his predecessor, *Tiglath-pileser III (745–727 BCE), Shalmaneser served as administrator in Calah, the Assyrian capital, while his father campaigned in foreign lands. After Tiglath-pileser's death, Shalmaneser inherited the dual monarchy of Assyria and *Babylonia and ruled for almost five years. Because Shalmaneser's reign was unexpectedly brief, court scribes had not drafted an official account of his campaigns and building achievements before his death; accordingly, his known royal inscriptions consist chiefly of eight Assyrian-Aramaic bilingual texts on lion weights from Calah. Thus, the events of his reign must be reconstructed at present principally from later cuneiform inscriptions, the Assur Ostracon, brief references in 2 Kings, and Hellenistic texts such as *Josephus's *Antiquities*. Shalmaneser was on the throne when *Samaria fell to the Assyrians in 722 after a three-year siege (Babylonian Chronicle, I.28; 2 Kings 17.5–6, 18.9–10); but the subsequent deportation of the Israelites probably took place in 720 under his successor, Sargon II (722–705 BCE).   JOHN A. BRINKMAN

Sheba, Queen of. A ruler of a people called the Sabeans, who occupied a territory in southwest Arabia, approximately where Yemen is today (*see* Map 6:G6). The Semitic inhabitants of Sheba built up a far-reaching trade, especially in spices and precious metals and stones; they colonized nearby parts of Africa, including the Ethiopian

coast. Sheba was a prosperous land and thus a symbol of wealth (Isa. 43.3; 45.14; Joel 3.8; Ps. 72.10).

In the tenth century BCE, Sheba's queen is said to have visited *Solomon, the king of Israel (1 Kings 10.1–13; 2 Chron. 9.1–12). She arrived with extravagant gifts and with questions to test Solomon's wisdom. Her visit reflects several important and interrelated features of Solomonic rule: internationalism, diplomacy, and sagacity. Solomon's peaceful domination of far-flung territories was sustained through his skill as a diplomat rather than through the repeated show of military force, and his close ties with foreign nations is evident in the numerous relationships he is said to have established with women from outside his native land. Such diplomatic skill, particularly on the international level, is associated throughout the ancient Near East with wisdom. The Queen of Sheba's interaction with Solomon exemplifies that connection. The report of her visit to *Jerusalem is a vehicle for the biblical author to extol Solomon's wealth and wisdom. Furthermore, the Queen of Sheba, by transporting some of her nation's wealth to Jerusalem, thus aggrandizes the capital of Solomon's empire and contributes to the assertion of Jerusalem's prominence in the Near East at that time.

According to later legend, the relationship between Solomon and the queen was more intimate, and their son was the founder of the (former) royal house of Ethiopia.

CAROL L. MEYERS

Shechem. A major Canaanite and Israelite city in the hill country of Ephraim (Map 1:X4), Shechem first appears in the historical record as an enemy of *Egypt in an execration text and on a stele of the nineteenth century BCE. During the *Amarna period (fourteenth century), Shechem, under its ruler, Labayu, and his sons, asserted itself against the other Canaanite city-states and, hence, against the weakening Egyptian hegemony in Canaan.

Shechem appears prominently in the ancestral narratives. *Abraham had a *theophany near Shechem and built an altar there (Gen. 12.6–7), as did *Jacob (Gen. 33.18–20). In Genesis 34, *Simeon and *Levi kill the inhabitants of Shechem and plunder it in retaliation for the rape of their sister Dinah by Shechem, son of Hamor (cf. Gen. 49.5–7). *Joseph's body was brought back from Egypt and buried at Shechem (Josh. 24.32; see also the somewhat erroneous Acts 7.16), and *Joshua's great *covenant renewal ceremony took place there (Josh. 24). The first abortive Israelite attempt at *kingship under Abimelech was centered at Shechem, but Abimelech exacted a terrible revenge in the city after a mutual falling out (Judg. 9). It was to Shechem that Jeroboam I went to be crowned first king of *Israel (1 Kings 12.1), and it served as his first capital (1 Kings 12.25).

Shechem has been located at the site of Tell Balatah, guarding the pass between Mount Ebal to the north and Mount Gerezim to the south, near modern Nablus. After earlier village occupation of the site in the Chalcolithic period, a large and well-fortified urban center developed at Shechem in the Middle Bronze Age (ca. 1850–1550 BCE). Of particular interest are the temples found at the site, including one designated the "fortress temple" because of its massive walls. After a violent destruction at the end of the Middle Bronze Age, presumably by one of the early pharaohs of Dynasty XVIII, Shechem lay uninhabited for close to a century. Completely rebuilt, probably with Egyptian consent, the city prospered during the first part of the Late Bronze Age, only to suffer destruction at the hands of Labayu's enemies, whether Egyptian or Canaanite or both. The subsequent Late Bronze Age city was not as prosperous, yet it managed to survive into the early Iron Age, when it probably passed peacefully into Israelite hands. The destruction of Shechem in the late twelfth century is generally attributed to Abimelech. Shechem recovered to some extent during the following centuries, becoming a town of some importance, until it was once again destroyed, this time by the *Assyrians in their campaign of conquest of the northern kingdom Israel (724–722 BCE). The habitation of Shechem remained poor and sparse throughout the remainder of the Iron Age and the first part of the Persian period. During the Hellenistic period (as of ca. 330 BCE) Shechem regained some of its ancient importance and glory as the *Samaritan rival of Jerusalem. The city was finally destroyed in 107 BCE by the Hasmonean John Hyrcanus.   CARL S. EHRLICH

Shema. The first word of Deuteronomy 6.4 in Hebrew, "Shema" is used as the name of the verse as a whole ("Hear, O Israel, YHWH is our God, YHWH alone/is one"). While acknowledging that the Shema was a central confessional statement of ancient Israel, modern scholars do not agree on its interpretation. If it is connected with the centralization of the cult in Jerusalem during the reforms of *Josiah in the late sixth century BCE, then it could mean that there is only one acceptable manifestation of YHWH, namely in Jerusalem. The Shema could also imply that among all gods Israel is to worship only YHWH (henotheism), or that YHWH is the only God (*monotheism). It is in this latter sense that the Shema has become the central Jewish declaration of faith in one God. The Shema in its expanded form includes Deuteronomy 6.5–9 (love of God); 11.13–21 (rewards and punishments for observance); and Numbers 15.37–41 (duty of remembrance). It is recited by observant Jews as part of the morning and evening prayers (Deut. 6.7), as well as before going to sleep. Deuteronomy 6.4–9 and 11.13–21, written on parchment, are also to be found in *phylacteries (Exod. 13.9, 16; Deut. 6.8; 11.18) and on doorposts (*mězûzôt;* Deut. 6.9; 11.20). Following the lead of Rabbi Akiba (died ca. 135 CE), the Shema is to be recited before death, especially in cases of martyrdom. The early and great importance of the Shema is underlined by Jesus' reference to it as the greatest commandment (Matt. 22.34–40 par.).   CARL S. EHRLICH

Sheol. *See* Hell.

Shibboleth ("flowing stream" or "ear of grain"). In Judges 12.1–4, troops from *Ephraim crossed the Jordan, angry with the east-bank Gileadites for not including them in the Ammonite war reported in Judges 11 (ca. 1100 BCE). The Gileadites fought the Ephraimites, defeated them, and secured the fords by which the surviving Ephraimites would cross back to their own land. Ephraimites who wanted to escape would simply claim not to be Ephraimites; the Gileadites discovered these impostors by having them pronounce the word written in the Hebrew text as *šibbolet.* The Ephraimites could not pronounce the word properly; the Hebrew text represents their pronunciation as *sibbolet* (Judg. 12.6). The two dialects had different pronunciations for the same word, and the story might mean that the Ephraimites simply slipped and used their own pronunciation. The text implies, however, that the Ephraimites were not able to pronounce a consonant that existed in the Gileadite dialect (the initial sibilant of the word in question).   JO ANN HACKETT

Ships and Sailing. Despite Israel's proximity to the Mediterranean, the Israelites were never a seafaring people. By contrast, Canaanites in the Late Bronze Age (ca. 1500–1200 BCE) seem to have traded extensively by sea, and the *Philistines came by sea to establish themselves in Palestine simultaneously with the emergence of Israel. In the first millennium BCE Israel's *Phoenician neighbors to the north controlled several excellent harbors and became the great maritime people of the ancient world.

Southern Palestine's coastal *geography was generally unsuited for harborage, and Israel seldom controlled the modest harbor towns of Acco, Dor, Joppa, and Ashkelon. Before the tenth century BCE the tribes of *Zebulun (Gen. 49.13) and *Dan and *Asher (Judg. 5.17) possibly went to sea, but in the Bible, ships often belong to foreigners, and Israel's attitude toward them can be wary (Isa. 33.21; Deut. 28.68; Judg. 5.17; Prov. 30.19).

Only during the reign of *Solomon in the tenth century BCE does Israel seem to have engaged in significant sea trade (1 Kings 9.26–28; 10.11, 22; 2 Chron. 8.18; 9.21). Israel and Tyre joined fleets to sail the lucrative Red Sea trade route to Ophir (southern Arabia and/or East Africa) and possibly to the Indian Ocean for such valuable commodities as spices and gold. Subsequent rulers of Judah and Israel failed to revive this maritime commerce (1 Kings 22.48, 49; 2 Chron. 20.35–37; 26.2).

The recurring phrase "ships of Tarshish" (1 Kings 10.22; Ps. 48.7; Isa. 2.16; 23.1; 60.9; cf. Jon. 1.3) seems to be a generic term referring to foreign (probably Phoenician) ships propelled by a combination of sails and oars. It derives from Phoenician trade with a place called Tarshish whose exact location was perhaps Anatolia, Cyprus, or the Mediterranean coast of Spain. Ezekiel 27 contains an elaborate description of these vessels (see also Isa. 33.23).

Many poetic references to ships and sailors relate to the ancient mythic tradition of Yahweh's power over the sea (Exod. 15; Pss. 48.7; 77.19; 104.25–26; 107.23; Ezek. 27.26; Jon. 1). Isaiah 60.9 reflects this theme in the promise that Israel will return to *Zion in ships of Tarshish (cf. Dan. 11.30). Later echoes appear in Wisdom of Solomon 14.1–4, and in the New Testament when Jesus calms the storm that threatens his disciples' boat (Mark 6.47–52; cf. Isa. 43.16). (*See also* Israel, Religion of.)

The tale of *Noah's ark (Gen 6.5–9.19) belongs to a story tradition that Israel shared with Mesopotamia, where boats and towed barges were common forms of transport. The description of the *ark, however, suggests that it was not a boat at all but a sort of enclosed box with no sail or oars and with a single window. For later Christians the ark came to symbolize the church and its salvation.

Several of Jesus' disciples sailed fishing boats on the freshwater Sea of *Galilee (Matt. 4.18–22), and Jesus often made use of these craft (Luke 5.3; Matt. 9.1). In 1986 archaeologists discovered a well-preserved example of such a boat from the first century BCE, just below shore level in the Sea of Galilee.

*Paul is the most famous sea traveler of the New Testament. His Mediterranean journeys profited from Roman domination of the seas and improvements in shipbuilding techniques. Even so, he was shipwrecked several times (2 Cor. 11.25; cf. Acts 27).

MARY JOAN WINN LEITH

Showbread. Also "shewbread" (KJV) or "bread of the Presence" (NRSV). The showbread in the *tabernacle and *Temple lay on a table in the holy place and was replaced weekly (1 Sam. 21.6; cf. Exod 25.30; 1 Chron. 9.32; 2 Chron. 13.11). Made of choice flour, topped with pure *frankincense, and arranged in two rows of six loaves each, the showbread was to be eaten only by the Aaronid *priests (Lev. 24.5–9). The giving of showbread by the priest of Nob to *David and his men was therefore exceptional (1 Sam. 21.1–6; Matt. 12.3–4 par.).   GARY N. KNOPPERS

Silas. As representatives of the church in Jerusalem, Silas and Judas/Barsabbas are sent to Antioch to report on the decree of the *Apostolic Council (Acts 15.22). They are then said to return to Jerusalem (15.33), but several verses later, Silas is chosen to accompany *Paul on a new missionary journey. Silas is described as a *prophet (15.32), but in Acts he follows Paul silently through Macedonia until Beroea, and rejoins him in Corinth (18.5), after which he is not mentioned again. Paul refers to a coworker named Silvanus in some of his letters (2 Cor. 1.19; 1 Thess. 1.1; 2 Thess. 1.1; cf. 1 Pet. 5:12), leading to the common assumption that the Silvanus named in the letters is identical with the Silas described in Acts.

DANIEL N. SCHOWALTER

Silvanus. *See* Silas.

Simeon.

1. The name given to *Jacob's second oldest son, born to *Leah (Gen. 29.33). After the *conquest, the tribe descended from Simeon was given territory in the south of *Canaan, within the land later controlled by Judah (Josh. 19.1–9).

2. In the New Testament, Simeon is the name of a devout man, said to be waiting for the "consolation of Israel," introduced by Luke (2.25–35). When he sees the infant Jesus being brought into the Temple, he gives praise for having seen God's salvation; his brief words are traditionally known by the first two words of the Latin translation, *Nunc Dimittis*. Simeon also informs *Mary that Jesus' coming would have an impact on all of Israel and that she would suffer as well.

DANIEL N. SCHOWALTER

Simon Peter. The son of Jonah (Matt. 16.17) or John (John 1.42); originally he was known as Simon (or Simeon, Acts 15.12). According to the Gospels, Jesus gave him the name Peter, the Greek translation of an Aramaic word "Cepha(s)" meaning "stone, rock" (Mark 3.16; Matt. 16.18; John 1.42). He and his brother Andrew were fishermen (Mark 1.16) of the poorer class, since apparently they did not own a boat. He was among the first disciples whom Jesus called (Mark 1.17; John 1.40–42). Married (Mark 1.29–31), his wife later traveled with him on some of his missionary journeys (1 Cor. 9.5).

An *apostle and one of the *twelve (Mark 3.14–19), he was prominent among them, belonging to a small inner group (Mark 5.37; 9.2; 13.3; 14.33). He often acted as their spokesperson (Mark 8.29; 11.21; 14.29), especially in acknowledging Jesus as the *Messiah, though he did not understand Jesus would have to suffer (Mark 8.27–33). On several other occasions he is presented in a poor light (Matt. 14.28–31; Mark 9.5–6; 14.29–31), particularly in the gospel of *Mark and especially in his denial of Jesus (Mark 14.66–72). We should, however, remember that the purpose of the Gospels is to inform us about Jesus, not to give a biography of Peter.

Peter's failures serve to highlight Jesus' courage and compassion.

After the resurrection, Peter was the first male disciple to see the risen Jesus (Luke 24.34; 1 Cor. 15.5), and he quickly took a leading position in the young church (Acts 1–12, 15; Gal. 1.18–19; 2.1–10). According to Luke, he preached (Acts 2.14–36; 3.12–26; etc.), healed the sick (Acts 3.1–10; 9.32–42), went as envoy from Jerusalem to oversee the work of other missionaries (Acts 8.14–25), and suffered for his faith (Acts 4.13–22; 5.17–41; 12.1–11). Guided by a vision, he was the first to preach to and convert *gentiles (Acts 10.1–11.18), and he supported *Paul on this matter in the council of Acts 15. Paul's own account of Peter's position in the controversy differs somewhat; in Galatians we are told that on a visit to Antioch, Peter refused to have full fellowship with gentile Christians (Gal. 2.11–14). At either the council of Acts 15 or another (Gal. 2.1–10), Paul was allotted the gentiles as his missionary concern and Peter the Jews. After this Peter disappears from the New Testament story. *James, the brother of Jesus, apparently became the sole leader of the Jerusalem church, and Peter went traveling (1 Cor. 9.5). He may have visited *Corinth and/or the areas mentioned in 1 Peter 1.1 and came to Rome shortly before his death. Extrabiblical tradition says that he was martyred when Nero persecuted the Christians there (64 CE). Yet later tradition claims that St. Peter's in Rome was built over his burial place.

The meaning of Jesus' words to Peter in Matthew 16.17–19 have been disputed. Is the rock Peter himself, his confession, or Peter as confessor? Is the power of the keys that of ecclesiastical discipline or of admitting to the church through preaching? Is binding and loosing the determination of what is correct and orthodox or the power to excommunicate? Is this power restricted to Peter alone or given to the whole church (Matt. 18.18)? Were the words of 16.17–19 spoken by the incarnate Jesus, the risen Jesus (cf. John 21.15–19), or did they come into being later to represent the position Peter actually attained?

Two of the writings of the New Testament are attributed to him (*see* Peter, The Letters of). Early tradition associates him with the gospel of *Mark. Some later *apocryphal writings were written in his name, a gospel of Peter and at least two apocalypses. There was also an Acts of Peter. Their appearance indicates his importance for the second-century church. In the first century, there was a group that strongly supported him (1 Cor. 1.12; 3.22; 9.5).

ERNEST BEST

Sin. Sin is basically an offense against God. Although by sinning people cannot do God any actual harm, they do act against God by despising him and his commandments, and by injuring others (or themselves), since the person injured is also an object of divine providence and protection. The principal Hebrew words for sin express these basic notions. The verb ḥāṭāʾ and the nouns related to it, such as its Greek translation hamartanō and its derivatives, means originally to miss a target or to fail to reach it; with the connotation "to sin," it is used most frequently in relation to God, as a violation of his law. The verb pāšaʿ and the noun pešaʿ mean rebellion, either against a human being, such as a king (1 Kings 12.19), or against God (Isa. 1.2). Both of the words just discussed are used together in Isaiah 43.27 and Job 34.37. A third main word for sin in Hebrew is ʿāwōn, which can mean an offense, the guilt resulting from it, or the punishment that follows (see Gen. 4.13).

In the *Dead Sea Scrolls and other postbiblical Jewish literature, there is a tendency to speak of sin less as an individual deed than as a power that governs men and women and inspires their conduct. This is particularly the case with the nouns ʿāwel and ʿawlâ, meaning "wickedness." Correspondingly, the role of the opposite force, the "holy spirit," is stressed in these writings. Depending on such passages as Isaiah 11.1–9; Jeremiah 31.33–34; and Ezekiel 36.26–27, several passages speak of this "holy spirit" as repairing the broken relationship between God and human beings (see, e.g., 1QS IV.20–23).

The New Testament vocabulary for sin is largely that of the *Septuagint, where the word hamartanō and its derivatives can translate all three Hebrew terms discussed above. Another important word is anomia, literally meaning lawlessness, which mainly translates ʿāwōn but can also be used for pešaʿ and rāšaʿ, "wicked." Also used to translate pešaʿ are asebeia, meaning impiety, and its derivatives.

In the Gospels, sin is often understood as a kind of debt. This metaphor is found in Jewish tradition and is developed in the *Lord's Prayer, whose fifth petition links divine forgiveness of human sins to a corresponding human forgiveness of others; see also Matthew 6.14–15; 18.23–25; and note especially Sirach 28.2. The *synoptic Gospels speak of sins to be forgiven in the plural (e.g., Mark 2.5), but this plural form is found only three times in the gospel of *John (8.24; 9.34; 20.23), probably in dependence on earlier traditions. More often hamartia, in the singular, means not just a particular sinful deed (as in Matt. 12.31), but a state or even a power that separates a person and the world as a whole from God. This power is personified as the devil, or *Satan, who is the adversary of God's Son and his followers (1 John 3.8–10; cf. 2 Thess. 2.1–12).

In Romans 5–7, *Paul elaborates the view that sin, like death, originated with *Adam; long dormant, its power emerged simultaneously with the giving of the *Law. Christ's death was the expiatory sacrifice (Rom. 8.3; cf. 2 Cor. 5.21) that liberated human beings from their enslavement to the power of sin.

See also Fall, The; Temptation.

LEOPOLD SABOURIN, S.J.

Sinai (Map 2:S–T2–4). A triangular peninsula, bordered on the north by the Mediterranean Sea, on the west by the Gulf of Suez and the Suez Canal, and on the east by the Gulf of Aqaba/Eilat. Moving from the coastland south, the terrain gradually rises to the Ijma Plateau, near the center of the peninsula. The region south of the plateau becomes mountainous before the terrain descends to a narrow coastland between the mountains and the gulfs. From the fourth millennium BCE the mountains have been mined for copper, which was exported to both Egypt and Canaan.

It is generally assumed that somewhere on this peninsula is Mount Sinai, the mountain from which Moses reputedly delivered the *Ten Commandments to the Israelites, but evidence is scant for determining which of the many mountains was called Mount Sinai during the time of the wilderness wanderings. Since Sinai is the wilderness nearest Egypt, this seems the most likely place for Mount Sinai (Num. 33.8–10; Deut. 1.1; Josephus, Apion 2.2.25), but there are problems. The mountain from which Moses received the commandments is sometimes called Sinai (generally in *J and *P) and sometimes *Horeb (*E and *D). It is also labeled "the mountain of God" (Exod. 3.1; 4.27; etc.) and simply "the mountain." It is not certain whether these were different names for the same place or different mountains. Some have thought it was initially Horeb but was renamed Sinai after the peninsula, but no one knows when the peninsula was named "Sinai"; neither Josephus nor Paul (Gal. 4.25) calls it by that name.

One of the ways scholars have tried to identify Mount Sinai has been to conjecture the route the Israelites traveled on their way to Canaan. Since the most direct route from Egypt follows the Mediterranean coastline, some have assumed that the Israelites took this route, and that one of the nearby mountains in the northern lowland or southern Canaan was Mount Sinai, but archaeological remains show that the Egyptians had this well-traveled route fortified (and see Exod. 13.17); consequently, refugees probably avoided such confrontation. It is more likely that they turned south (see Num. 33.8–10). Since they reportedly lived in this wilderness for about forty years, they may not have planned originally to settle in Canaan.

The most popular candidate for Mount Sinai is Jebel Musa ("the mountain of Moses"; Map 2:S4) near Saint Catherine's Monastery. This identification was apparently first made by Byzantine monks in the fourth century CE, and there is no evidence to show that they had any local data that are not known today for choosing the site. Most of the modern sites are named after plants, trees, and topographical features, and they provide no clues to ancient Israelite history. Other possible sites include several mountains in northwestern Arabia, and Mount Karkom in Machtesh Ramon just west of the Arabah; the latter conjecture, made in 1985, was based on art and architecture found on and around Karkom, but it depends on a date for the *Exodus in the third millennium BCE.

When Byzantine monks settled in Sinai (300–600 CE) they were able to dig wells, make terraces and direct rainfall, and raise gardens and orchards in valleys. The Emperor Justinian had a church constructed and a monastery fortified (527 CE); this was later called Saint Catherine's Convent. Within an area of two square miles is the Byzantine identification of the site of the burning bush, the place where Moses struck the rock, the mountain where God spoke to Moses, and the hill where Aaron made the golden calf. The monks apparently found an isolated location in this historic peninsula where they could survive. They then identified biblical sites with places in their immediate surroundings.

GEORGE WESLEY BUCHANAN

Sirach (Ecclesiasticus). One of the earliest of the deuterocanonical/apocryphal books (see Apocrypha, *article on* Jewish Apocrypha), Sirach is the most extensive portion of Israelite *wisdom literature preserved in the Bible. Modeled in great part on *Proverbs, Sirach is a compilation of materials that include moral and ethical maxims, folk proverbs, psalms of praise and lament, theological reflections, homiletic exhortations, and pointed observations about Jewish life and religious mores in the second century BCE. It is one of the longest books of the Bible.

Authorship and Unity. Sirach is one of the rare books of the Hebrew Bible that was actually written by the author to whom the book is ascribed. In 50.27, he identifies himself as "Jesus (Hebr. *yēšûaʿ*), son of Eleazar, son of (Hebr. *ben*) Sira (Grk. *S[e]irach*)"; hence, the name Ben Sira, or Sirach, which is found in the title of the book in Greek. Since the extant Hebrew manuscripts begin with 3.6b, we do not know what title the book had in Hebrew. The Latin title, Ecclesiasticus, probably means "the ecclesiastical (or church) [book]," because it was used so widely in the Christian liturgy.

After the introduction (1.1–10), the book opens (1.11–30) with a carefully crafted twenty-two-line nonalphabetic poem (there are twenty-two letters in the Hebrew alphabet) on the fear of the Lord as the foundation and source of true wisdom and closes, like Proverbs (31.10–31), with an elegant alphabetic *acrostic poem (51.13–30) in which Ben Sira tells how he prayed for wisdom and sought after her (here, as elsewhere in the Bible, wisdom is personified as a woman; see Wisdom), not for himself alone but also to impart her to others who came to him. This major inclusion (1.11–30 and 51.13–30) clearly suggests that all the material between the two poems is by the same author. From his youth, Ben Sira had been a pious and devoted student of the Law and of the traditions of Israel, and he became a professional *scribe, a vocation he extols in 38.34–39.11. According to 50.27 (Greek text), he lived in Jerusalem, but like many other educated persons of his day he traveled widely (34.12; cf. 39.4) and acquired "much cleverness" (34.11). Ben Sira was also willing to learn the wisdom of other nations (cf. 39.2–4). He composed his book not for personal gain (cf. 51.25) but "for all who seek instruction" (33.18). He ran a school or academy (cf. 51.23) for young men; this fact accounts for the male orientation found throughout the book (see below, Contents and Theology).

Date and Authenticity. The book was written originally in Hebrew, as Ben Sira's grandson states explicitly in the foreword to his Greek translation. But the Hebrew text, apart from some quotations in rabbinic literature, had been lost for centuries. Between 1896 and 1900, four fragmentary Hebrew manuscripts (called A, B, C, and D), which could be dated from the tenth to the twelfth centuries CE, were recovered from the Geniza (storage room) of the Qaraite synagogue in Old Cairo. A fifth manuscript (E) was discovered in 1931, a sixth (F) in 1982, and more leaves of manuscripts B and C in 1958 and 1960. Several scholars have questioned the authenticity of the Geniza text because of the presence of some retroversions from Syriac and Greek. But the common scholarly opinion favors authenticity. Further Hebrew fragments, found at *Qumran and dating from the second half of the first century BCE and the first half of the first century CE, and at Masada (first half of the first century BCE) have corroborated the substantial authenticity of the Hebrew text found in the six Geniza manuscripts. Nonetheless, since these manuscripts do contain some retroversions from Syriac and probably a few from Greek, one must take into account all the principal witnesses before deciding on the best form of a text. About two-thirds of the book is now extant in Hebrew.

The date when Ben Sira composed the book can be calculated on the basis of information provided in the foreword. The grandson writes that he "came to Egypt in the thirty-eighth year of the reign of Euergetes and stayed for some time." The year would be 132 BCE, in the reign of Ptolemy VII Physcon Euergetes who began his rule in 170 BCE as co-regent with his brother Ptolemy VI. If we allow sufficient time between grandson and grandfather, we arrive at a date ca. 180 BCE for the composition of the book. This date receives support from the book itself. In 50.1–21, Ben Sira writes a lengthy panegyric on Simeon II, who was high priest from 219–196 BCE. This poem gives the impression that Simeon had been dead for several years. The Greek translation was published in Egypt some time after 117 BCE. The Greek is the most important witness to the text whenever the Hebrew is not extant.

Canonicity. Although written in Hebrew and published in Jerusalem even before the book of *Daniel, Sirach was excluded from the Jewish *canon despite the fact that it was employed in the ancient synagogue services. The probable reason is that the *Pharisees who defined the Jewish canon near the end of the first century CE disliked some of Ben Sira's theology (e.g., his denial of retribution in the afterlife), which resembled the teachings of the *Sadducees. Nevertheless, Sirach was often cited by the later rabbis, some of whom even introduced quotations from it with the words "(as) it is written," a phrase that was used exclusively for quotations from scripture. The church from as early as the second and third centuries (e.g., Didache, Clement of Rome, Polycarp, Irenaeus, Tertullian) accepted into its canon Sirach and all the other deuterocanonical books found in the *Septuagint. In the sixteenth century, Martin Luther decided in favor of the Jewish canon of the Hebrew Bible; other Protestants followed his lead in rejecting the canonicity of the deuterocanonical books. Like the Orthodox churches, the Roman Catholic church, however, has retained the older Christian canon, which was formally defined at the Council of Trent in 1546.

Contents and Theology. Being a typical work of Hebrew wisdom, Sirach offers advice and gnomic sayings on a wide variety of topics of concern to the Jewish community. Like Proverbs, Sirach generally manifests no discernible order of subject matter, nor is there any obvious coherence. The only exception is found in chaps. 44–50, which in Hebrew manuscript B are entitled appropriately "Praise of the Ancestors of Old"; the opening line of this section is the well-known "Let us now praise famous men" (KJV). Unlike Proverbs, however, Sirach consists of larger units, generally from ten lines (or bicola) to the classic twenty-two- and twenty-three-line lengths (e.g., 1.11–30; 6.18–37; 21.1–21; 29.1–20; 38.24–34; 49.1–16 [the closing poem on Israel's great ancestors]; 51.13–30). Ben Sira learned the twenty-two- and twenty-three-line poetic convention from such compositions as Proverbs 2; 6.20–7.6; 7.7–27; 31.10–31; Psalms 9–10; 25; 33; 34; 94; 145; Lamentations 5.

In addition to several major poems extolling wisdom and the Lord as source of wisdom (1.1–10, 11–30; 4.11–19; 6.18–37; 16.24–17.23; 19.20–30; 24.1–31; 37.16–26; 39.12–35; 42.15–43.33), Ben Sira offers aphorisms and comments on such subjects as humility (3.17–24; 4.8; 7.16–17; 10.26–28), charity (3.30–4.6, 8–10; 7.32–36; 12.1–7; 29.8–13), pride, folly, and other sins (3.26–28; 10.6–18; 16.5–23; 20.2–31; 21.1–22.2), virtues and vices of the tongue (5.6–6.1; 19.5–17; 20.5–8, 13, 16–20, 24–31; 22.6, 27–23.4, 7–15; 27.4–7; 28.12–26), anger, malice, and vengeance (27.22–28.11). He also gives practical advice on such topics as one's attitude and behavior regarding parents (3.1–16; 7.27–28), children (7.23–25; 16.1–4; 30.1–13; 41.5–10), friends and associates (6.5–17; 11.29–34; 12.8–13.23; 22.19–26; 27.16–21; 37.1–15), wealth (11.10–11, 14, 18–19, 23–28; 13.15–14.10; 31.1–11), poverty (10.30–11.6, 14; 13.18–14.2; 25.2–3), enjoying life (14.11–19), loans (29.1–7, 14–20); health and physicians (30.14–20; 38.1–15), death (38.16–23), table etiquette (31.12–32.13; 37.27–31), shame (41.14–42.1d).

In various sections of the book, he writes at length about *women (3.2–6; 7.19, 24–26; 9.1–9; 19.2–4; 22.3–5; 23.22–26; 25.1, 8, 13–26.18; 28.15; 33.20; 36.26–31; 40.19, 23; 42.6, 9–14). He deals with woman as daughter, wife, mother, adulteress, or prostitute, and much of what he says is offensive to the contemporary western reader. But in the society for which he wrote, Ben Sira would not have been considered an extremist; rather, he was a typical Jewish male of the period, who lived in a patriarchal society in which women had few rights as free and autonomous human beings. A female was subject to either her father or her husband. In Exodus 20.17, a wife is even listed with a husband's property. It must be remembered that Ben Sira was writing only for young Jewish men in a male-centered society; it was not his intention to instruct women. It is in this context that his (often deplorable) statements about women are to be evaluated.

The theology of Sirach is essentially Deuteronomic; hence, it is traditional and conservative. He reflects the teachings of earlier biblical books on such subjects as God, the election of Israel, retribution, morality, kindness to the *poor and disadvantaged, the centrality of fear of the Lord. The expression "fear of the Lord/God" occurs about sixty times in Sirach, and the term "wisdom" about fifty-five times. In 1.1–2.18 there is a detailed treatise on wisdom as fear of the Lord. The fundamental thesis of Sirach is that wisdom, which is identified with the *Law (chap. 24), is bestowed only on one who fears the Lord (19.20). God grants wisdom to those who love him (1.10), that is, those who "keep the commandments" (1.26). Fear of the Lord, which is "the beginning of wisdom" (1.14; cf. Prov. 9.10), "gives gladness and joy and long life" (1.12). Fear of the Lord and wisdom make life meaningful and worthwhile (34.14–20). Sinners or fools—the terms are synonyms for Ben Sira—can never attain wisdom (15.7–8).

The doctrine of God reflects earlier biblical traditions. God is one and the same from all eternity (42.21). He created all things by simply uttering his almighty word (39.17–18; cf. Gen. 1.3–24). He knows all things, even the deepest mysteries of the universe, and sees all things even before they occur (15.18–19; 23.19–20; 39.19–20; 42.18–20). God is merciful not only to his chosen people but to other nations as well (18.13; cf. 17.29). Believers may address God as Father (23.1, 4; 51.10), confident that he will listen to their prayer. Ben Sira denies that God is responsible in any way for human sin (15.11–13, 20; cf. Exod. 11.10; 2 Sam. 24.1–10). Virtue and vice result from human free choice (15.14–17). But the origin of sin according to Genesis 3.1–6 is also alluded to in Sirach (25.24). Since human beings are free, there is hope even for sinners, for they can turn away from sin and repent (17.25–26, 29).

Ben Sira teaches the traditional doctrine of retribution: reward for fidelity to the Law (1.20; 34.14–20) or punishment for infidelity (9.12; 11.24, 26, 27–28) takes place in one's lifetime here on earth; after death saint and sinner alike are thought to go to Sheol, the nether world, where they share a dark, listless, dismal survival separated from the Lord (17.27–28). The grandson's Greek translation, however, makes definite allusions to retribution in the *afterlife (7.17b; 48.11bc), and a later recension, called Greek II, makes even more allusions (cf. 2.9c; 16.22c; 19.19) as do the still later Latin and Syriac versions. One survives in one's children (30.4–5) and in one's good name (41.11–13). Prayer, being the language of faith, is found in several places in Sirach (22.27–23.6; 36.1–22; 39.12–35; 42.15–43.33; 51.1–12). Respect for the priests and the offering of *sacrifices are enjoined (7.29–31), but these are useless if one is guilty of injustice (34.21–27). Observance of the Law, especially with regard to charity, is the best form of sacrifice and worship (35.1–5). The sacrifices of the wicked who oppress the poor are not acceptable to God (35.14–15). Ben Sira speaks emphatically of the need to practice social justice and to assist the weak and the defenseless (3.30–31; 4.2–6, 8–10); he derived this teaching from Exod. 22.22; Deut. 24.17–22; Lev. 19.9–10; Job 29.11–16; Prov. 14.13; Amos 5.10–15.

ALEXANDER A. DI LELLA, O.F.M.

Six Hundred Sixty-six. This number, mentioned in Revelation 13.18, is not, as is sometimes thought, a conundrum to be solved by readers in order to discover the identity of the beast described in that chapter. The identity of the beast is clear: it is the absolutist state as personified in the Roman Emperor Nero. The emperors claimed divine authority and their power seemed invincible. John wanted his readers to understand that the state and its rulers were neither divine nor invincible. They were human and carried the seed of their own destruction: their number is only 666, and does not reach the completion of seven (*see* Number Symbolism). The number was arrived at by presenting Nero's Greek name *Kaisar Nerōn* in Hebrew letters, which also function as numbers: *qsr nrwn;* *q* = 60, *s* = 100, *r* = 200, *n* = 50, *w* = 6, so *qsr nrwn* adds up to 666. (Some western manuscripts read "six hundred sixteen"; the scribes possibly did not understand John's usage of Hebrew numbers, and thought in terms of the Greek *kaisar theos*, the "god-emperor," which would add up to 616 using the Greek letters as numerals; but it is more likely that they simply dropped the final *n: qsr nrw* for *Kaisar Nerō*, making 616.)   DAVID H. VAN DAALEN

Slavery. The socioeconomic institution of slavery was present in both Israel and early Christianity. Slavery among the Israelites shared many of the features present in other ancient Near Eastern cultures, just as slavery among Christians was similar to the practices prevailing in the *Roman empire. Throughout the Bible, however, distinctive humanitarian impulses regulate the treatment of slaves.

Exodus 21.1–11, Leviticus 25.39–55, and Deuteronomy 15.12–18 define the status and regulate the treatment of slaves. Each text is literarily framed by Israel's moral obligations to God's order for their lives: Exodus 21 by the *Ten Commandments (20.1–17), which put the Covenant Code laws (chaps. 21–23) under sole allegiance to Yahweh (note that the rights of the slave's release are guaranteed as the code's first stipulation); Leviticus 25 and Deuteronomy 15 by *Sabbath and sabbatical regulations, which include the obligation to treat the *poor generously. Rather than viewing slavery as a divinely sanctioned institution, as proslavery writers argued over a century ago, the biblical texts accent how God's commands protect slaves from cruel and capricious treatment. (*See* Slavery and the Bible.)

Three types of servile status are identifiable in Israel's practice: an Israelite became a servant to a fellow Israelite voluntarily as security against poverty, or by birth or purchase (Exod. 21.32 sets the compensation for a slave's death at thirty shekels); Israelites took non-Israelites as slaves through capture in war or purchase; Israelites sold themselves to non-Israelites as security against debt. In the first category, servants were guaranteed both the seventh-year sabbatical and fiftieth year jubilee releases (Exod. 21.2–6; Lev. 25.10, 38–41). In the second category, slaves, though circumcised and sworn into covenant membership (Gen. 17.9–14, 23; Deut. 29.10–15), did not receive the benefit of these releases (Lev. 25.44–46), but were protected against oppression (Exod. 22.21; 23.9). In the third category, slaves were eligible for redemption by a relative at any time, and were mandatorily freed in the jubilee year (Lev. 25.47–55). Slaves in all categories enjoyed Sabbath rest and participated in Israel's religious festivals. (*See* Hebrews.)

The moral imperative that mercy and kindness be shown toward slaves was based upon God's deliverance of Israel from slavery in Egypt: "Remember that you were a slave in the land of Egypt, and the Lord your God redeemed you; for this reason I lay this command upon you today" (Deut. 15.15; see also Lev. 25.42–43). The prophets also criticized injustices in Israel's slavery: forbidding King Ahaz to enslave captives from Judah (2 Chron. 28.8–15), attributing Israel's *exile to failure to give sabbatical release to the slaves (Jer. 34.8–20), calling Israel to "let the oppressed go free and to break every yoke" (Isa. 58.6). In the eschatological vision of Joel (2.29), God's spirit would be poured out also on slaves.

Jesus' ministry and the writing of the New Testament literature occurred within the cultural practice of slavery, both Jewish and Roman. The *Talmud indicates that various types of servile status continued among Jews from around 200 BCE to 400 CE. Many events and teachings in the Gospels reflect the presence of slaves, especially in the household (Luke 7.1–10; 12.37–46; Matt. 26.51; 24.45–51; 25.14–30).

The New Testament letters frequently regulate the conduct of masters and slaves (Eph. 6.5–9; Col. 3.22–4.1; 1 Tim. 6.1–2; Titus 2.9–10; 1 Pet. 2.18–19). Although the gospel of Jesus Christ abolished distinctions between slave and free (Gal. 3.28; 1 Cor. 12.13; Col. 3.11), slaves were instructed not to presume upon their new standing to legitimate careless work or disrespect toward masters. Slaves were called to direct accountability to God for proper conduct within the existing social institution. Masters similarly were told to treat their slaves justly and kindly. Paul sent the runaway slave, Onesimus, back to his owner *Philemon, instructing Philemon to receive Onesimus as a brother "both in the flesh and in the Lord" even "as you would welcome me" (Philem. 16–17).

The biblical vocabulary for slavery, in both its noun (Hebr. *ʿebed,* Grk. *doulos*) and verb forms (*ʿābad; douloō*), carries a wide range of meaning, from domestic service to enforced labor (1 Kings 9.15–22), and is metaphorically extended to the relationship of humans to God. Thus, both *Moses (Deut 34.5; etc.) and *David (Ps. 18.1) are called the "servant [Hebr. *ʿebed*] of the Lord," and Israel and others are instructed to "serve" (*ʿābad*) the Lord (Deut. 11.12; Ps. 2.11; etc.; *see* Worship). The same imagery is found in the New Testament. Just as Jesus took upon himself "the form of a slave" (Phil. 2.7), so Jesus' followers are also to think and do (Phil. 2.5; cf. Mark 10.42–45); thus, *Paul identified himself as a slave of Christ (Rom. 1.1; Phil. 1.1).

WILLARD M. SWARTLEY

Slavery and the Bible. Slavery in the New World produced one of the great biblical controversies of early modern times. Especially in sixteenth-century Spain and in the United States between 1730 and 1860, biblical texts were used on both sides of the protracted debates over the institution of slavery. The Spanish controversy was largely about *encomienda,* a form of labor slavery imposed on the native peoples of New Spain by the Laws of Burgos (1513). Court spokesmen cited the *conquest of Canaan (Deut. 20), the destruction of *Sodom (Gen. 18.16–19.29), and Jesus' parable of the wedding feast (Matt. 22.1–14) to advocate *encomienda* as part of a just Christian war against New World "barbarians." Reform-minded missionaries led by Bartolomé de Las Casas, a Dominican friar and the bishop of Chiapas in Mexico, condemned *encomienda* as unjust and rejected its biblical defense. In his treatise *In Defense of the Indians* (1550), Las Casas insisted that all three texts were historically conditioned commands superseded by Jesus' teaching of love to neighbors and enemies.

Meanwhile, a new kind of slavery—the importation and ownership of Africans as property—spread quickly in the seventeenth century to Portuguese, Dutch, French, and British colonies in the New World. The Church of England was the legally established religion in the British col-

onies of Virginia, Barbados, and the Carolinas, but planter elites there guaranteed that Anglican priests neither opposed slavery nor missionized the slaves. Instead, the church used biblical authority to depict Africans as bearers of the mark of *Cain (Gen. 4.10–15) and as children of *Ham, cursed by Noah to be the "servants of servants" (Gen. 9.25, AV; NRSV: "lowest of slaves"). Anglican support for slavery went largely unquestioned until the 1730s, when Evangelicals in Britain and America launched a new biblical critique of slavery. John Wesley and George Whitefield, founders of Methodism, condemned slaveholding as a grave sin inconsistent with their theology of spiritual rebirth (John 3.1–8), sanctification (Matt. 5.48), and evangelism (Mark 16.15). Truly born-again Christians, they taught, will know through the Spirit to free their slaves and evangelize them.

During the Revolutionary era, the major evangelical Calvinist denominations in America—Congregationalists, Presbyterians, and Baptists—joined the antislavery cause. These churches added the argument that slavery violated America's covenant with God as the new chosen people. In his *Dialogue Concerning the Slavery of the Africans* (1776), the Congregationalist Samuel Hopkins established the scriptural ground for this contention by invoking the prophets' vision of justice and mercy (Isa. 1.16–18; 33.15–16; 58.6; Jer. 7.1–7; 22.3–5; Amos 5.24), and judgment (Jer. 21.12; Ezek. 22.29–31; Amos 2.6; Zech. 7.9–12). At the same time, the Society of Friends in America also undertook a powerful witness against slavery led by the preaching and writing of John Woolman, especially in his *Considerations on the Keeping of Negroes* (1754/1762) and his *Journal* (1774). Warning that slaveholding was disobedience to the characteristic Quaker doctrines of plainness and peace, Woolman cited Jesus' warnings against materialistic greed (Matt. 6.19) and violence toward poor strangers (Matt. 25.44) as his principal biblical evidence.

By 1825, however, thriving cotton plantations had revived American slavery, and southern evangelicals, both Methodist and Calvinist, began to construct new biblical arguments justifying Christian slaveholding. A classic example is *A Scriptural View of Slavery* (1856), a sermon by Thornton Stringfellow, a Virginia Baptist, who held that God had sanctioned slavery through Noah, Abraham, and Joseph (Gen. 9.25–27; 14.14; 16.9; 17.12–13; 24.35–36; 26.13–14; 47.14–25), that slavery was "incorporated" in the Mosaic law (Exod. 20.17; 21.2–4, 20–21; Lev.

25.39–46), and that Jesus and the apostles recognized slavery as a "lawful institution among men" (2 Cor. 11.20; Eph. 6.5; Col. 3.22).

Evangelical abolitionists answered these proslavery arguments in writings like Angelina Grimké's *Appeal to the Christian Women of the South* (1836). Grimké claimed that Hebrew slavery differed in nature and kind from American slavery and therefore could not justify it. In Mosaic law she found six warrants for Hebrew slavery, all more limited than America's chattel slave system (e.g., Exod. 21.4, 7; Lev. 25.39, 47–55; 2 Kings 4.1), along with substantial legal protections for slaves lacking in American law (e.g., Exod. 21.3–6, 20–21, 26–27). Other abolitionists contrasted Greco-Roman and American slavery to obviate the Pauline instruction that slaves obey their masters (Eph. 6.5).

Slaves and free blacks in the antebellum period created their own radical vision of evangelical Christianity, understanding their condition as analogous to Israel in Egypt. African American preachers ceaselessly proclaimed the victorious Exodus as the slaves' destiny here on earth. This oral tradition inspired some leaders, including Gabriel Prosser, Denmark Vesey, and Nat Turner—all Methodists—to lead slave rebellions in the name of God. African American protest found its classic literary voice in David Walker, whose *Appeal to the Coloured Citizens of the World* (1829) arraigned hypocritical evangelical slaveholders for not observing the Christian mandate of peace (Acts 10.36–27), calling down on them the judgment of the returning Christ (Rev. 22.11).

Britain abolished slavery peacefully in 1833, but in the United States these disputes over slavery brought Presbyterians, Methodists, and Baptists to schism by 1845, and encouraged the fratricidal Civil War that finally resolved the crisis. One of the chief ironies of the conflict over slavery was the confrontation of America's largest Protestant denominations with the hitherto unthinkable idea that the Bible could be divided against itself. But divided it had been by intractable theological, political, and economic forces. Never again would the Bible completely recover its traditional authority in American culture.

See also African American Traditions and the Bible; Exodus, The; Hebrews; Slavery.

STEPHEN A. MARINI

Social Sciences and the Bible. *This entry deals with the application of anthropology and sociology to the Bible, and consists of two articles, the first on* Cultural Anthropology and the Hebrew Bible, *and the second on* Sociology of the New Testament.

Cultural Anthropology and the Hebrew Bible

Cultural anthropology as understood in the United States, and its British counterpart social anthropology, is the study of the material culture and the beliefs and social organization of preindustrial societies. Although it did not obtain the status of a distinct discipline until the nineteenth century and did not establish methodological precision until the twentieth, it has a long prehistory, some of which deeply affected the study of the Bible.

Travelers to Palestine, Egypt, and Mesopotamia over many centuries recorded their observations of life and customs in those lands, and these were often used to help interpret biblical texts. Further, the Hebrew Bible contains material that invites speculation of an anthropological nature. How were Israelite *tribes organized? How did *sacrifices achieve their desired ends? In the second half of the nineteenth century, when general theories of the evolution of culture and religion were propounded, the Bible was fitted into the resultant schemes. Israelite religion, it was thought, had evolved from animism (belief in spirits) through polytheism to *monotheism, and there had been both a progressive elaboration of the sacrificial cult, and a spiritualization of that religion in terms of social justice.

These evolutionary schemes were largely abandoned after World War II, but until around 1970 it was commonplace to regard the people of ancient Israel as quasi primitives who knew little about scientific causality, and who thus lived in a mystical and magical world in which any event was potentially a miracle. A variation on this view was that the *Canaanites, among whom the Israelites lived, had an essentially magical worldview, whereas Israel had broken with this outlook thanks to God's revelation to them through historical events.

Since 1970 there has been a renewal of interest in social anthropology among biblical scholars, and the work done has been based upon thorough and up-to-date knowledge of anthropological literature. Special attention has been focused on the following areas, each of which will be discussed in turn: Israel's origins and social organization, Israel's classification of the world and its sacrificial system, and the social dimensions of prophecy.

Israel's Origins and Social Organization. Visitors to Arabia and Palestine in the sixteenth through the nineteenth centuries were able to observe tribes of bedouin who were predominantly camel *nomads. It was understandable that such visitors thought they were seeing people living the same kind of life as Abraham, and many comparisons were made between the bedouin and the people of biblical times. With the rise of theories about the evolution of culture, the early Israelites were described as seminomads, people some way along the road from "pure" nomadism to being fully settled. In the 1930s, it was suggested that the Israelite occupation of Canaan was in fact a largely peaceful process of sedentarization in which Israelite seminomads ceased to move from winter to summer pasturages and settled down in one area.

Recent studies have shown that "pure" nomadism is a late phenomenon in the ancient Near East, and that seminomadism is not a staging post along an evolutionary road from nomadism to being permanently settled. Indeed, settled peoples can become seminomads by being expelled from their lands, or because of small changes in the climate. There is, however, growing agreement that the Israelites were, from the mid-thirteenth century BCE, settled farmers living in villages in the central highlands of Canaan remote from the main cities and loosely associated in an acephalous society, that is, one without a central political organization.

Exactly how Israel came into being in this form is a hotly debated issue. Norman Gottwald (*The Tribes of Yahweh*, 1979) has argued that Israelite society was the result of a retribalization process that enabled groups oppressed by the Canaanite city-states to form an alternative, liberated, and egalitarian society. He has focused attention upon the nature of Israelite tribes and of their political organization. Niels Lemche (*Early Israel*, 1985) disagrees with Gottwald on anthropological grounds, arguing against the retribalization view and pointing out that acephalous societies are not necessarily egalitarian.

From the viewpoint of the evidence of the Bible, Lemche is probably correct. The lists of "minor judges" in Judges 10.1–5; 12.8–15 indicate that these "judges" (probably the heads of dominant families who arbitrated disputes) had considerable wealth and prestige in return for the responsibilities that they bore. This evidence also militates against another theory, that early Israel was a segmentary lineage society, that is, a society in which power was distributed horizontally among equally ranked segments. This theory has been adopted from the influential book by Christian Sigrist (*Regulierte Anarchie*, 1967), and has been used to explain why opposition to monarchy continued for long after that institution became established in Israel. However, segmentary lineage societies as described by Sigrist have features that can hardly have existed in early Israel, such as indifference to murder within the family groups and avoidance of the inheritance rights of the eldest son. The persistence of opposition to monarchy can best be explained in terms of Jürgen Habermas's theory of conflict between belief systems and social mechanisms of integration (*Theorie des kommunikativen Handelns*, vol. 2, 1981). Israelite tribes could well have been simple chiefdoms, ruled by dominant families. Economic and external political pressure combined to make these chiefdoms accept a form of monarchy at the close of the eleventh century BCE, but Israel's belief systems remained critical of the institution for many generations. (*See also* Conquest of Canaan; Kingship and Monarchy.)

Israel's Classification of the World and Its Sacrificial System. One of the largest changes in perception of the ancient Israelites brought about by social anthropology has been in relation to "the Hebrew mind." Studies in the early part of the twentieth century suggested that the Israelites were like contemporary "primitives," unable to distinguish clearly the limits of a group or of individuals, and attributing many natural events to supernatural causes. Attempts to explain the logic of sacrifice concentrated upon the psychology of individual Israelites: how did they think that sacrifices achieved their aims? As a result of the structural-functional study of preindustrial peoples, given classical expression in the work of E. E. Evans-Pritchard, a different picture of "primitives" emerged. They were seen to be no less rational than people in industrial societies, provided their overall framework of understanding was appreciated. This framework was articulated in sacred traditions and worked out in social networks and corporate activities.

The application of such an approach to the Hebrew Bible (Mary Douglas, *Purity and Danger*, 1967) has drawn attention to Israel's classification of reality as detailed in Genesis 1, in the prohibitions of clean and unclean animals (Lev. 11; Deut. 14.3–20; *see* Purity, Ritual), and in the regulations for dealing with the violation of sacred boundaries in Leviticus generally. It has emerged that, for Israel as for other ancient peoples, *creation meant order: the dividing of reality into distinct spheres such as sky/earth/sea, clean/unclean, life/death, Israel/other nations, holy/profane. To violate these distinctions was to run the risk of offending God, who would withhold his blessing by not sending the rains necessary for producing food. Thus, far from living in a chaotic universe where distinctions familiar to us were not made, the Israelites made distinctions and organized them into a particular worldview. Their difference from us lies not in their supposed inability to divide reality into categories, but rather in the organization of the categories. They regarded holy places and objects as the property of the deity, to be approached only by properly designated people. They had a sense that *blood was the property of the deity, that it was not to be eaten, and that it should be carefully handled. This "danger" also inhered in corpses, which no longer strictly belonged to human society, and contact with which required washing with water medicated with special ashes (Num. 19).

*Sacrifice has come to be interpreted by scholars not from the viewpoint of the psychology of individual worshipers, but as communal, symbolic action set within the framework of a strongly delineated world. Sacrifices enabled boundaries to be crossed: by *priests moving from the ordinary to the sacred (Lev. 8) and by "*lepers" moving from exclusion to acceptance in the community (Lev. 14). They removed the defilement believed to infect the sanctuary when offenses occurred for which a sin or guilt offering was required (Lev. 4—7). On the *Day of Atonement (Lev. 16), all types of moral uncleanness and social disharmony were identified with a goat, whose journey through the community and out into the desert symbolized and effected the removal of these factors from the society (*see* Azazel). The view just outlined was not, however, necessarily true for all Israelites in all periods. It is clear that in the premonarchic period there was no priesthood in Israel with exclusive rights, and that the predominant sacrifice was the burnt offering, given as a communal activity on occasions such as preparing to fight a battle (1 Sam. 13.9). The view of reality and order implied in Genesis 1 and in Leviticus is that of the postexilic community, which was a Temple-based community living in close proximity to *Jerusalem. Although the details of sacrifices no doubt contain elements much older

than the postexilic community, in their present form they take their meaning from the story of God's deliverance of Israel from slavery in Egypt. Thus, social anthropology can shed light on many details of these rituals, but cannot supply the religious ideology of the traditions in their final form.

The Social Dimension of Prophecy. We often think of *prophets as individuals with an abnormal or unusual psychology, despite the evidence that *Elijah, *Elisha, and *Samuel were the heads of prophetic guilds, that *Isaiah had a group of disciples (Isa. 8.16), and that *Jeremiah was supported by the family of Shaphan (Jer. 26.24). Research into the roles of prophets in many cultures has indicated the importance both of support groups and of the expectations that such support groups, as well as the societies in which prophets function, held. David Petersen (*The Roles of Israel's Prophets*, 1981) has suggested two main types of prophets: peripheral prophets and central morality prophets. The former operate on the margins of society, supported by their own groups, often acting amorally. Such a description fits well with Elijah, who was a marginal figure at the head of groups of prophets withdrawn from society, and whose conduct in calling down fire on those who sought to capture him was certainly amoral (2 Kings 1). A good example of a central morality prophet would be Isaiah, who moved in royal circles (Isa. 7.3–17) and who, though critical of the king, also provided support for the state when it was attacked by the *Assyrians in 701 BCE (Isa. 37.21–29). Researches of this kind illustrate the shift that has been noted above—from the study of the psychology of individual prophets to a study of the corporate functioning of social groups and activities. Whereas earlier studies were concerned with the psychology of prophecy, recent study concentrates on its social dimensions. While this is valuable, drawing upon models taken from general observations of social phenomena, it must be noted that such studies illuminate only the outer aspects of the phenomena. As with sacrifice, it is the task of theology to illuminate the distinctive beliefs that formed the basis for the social actions of prophets.   J. W. ROGERSON

Sociology of the New Testament

Although it is possible to trace earlier roots, the sociological perspective became embedded in the soil of New Testament studies in the 1970s. Sociology is the disciplined study of social relationships and the changes that occur in them over time. It will be readily seen how the application of the techniques and perspectives of sociology to the New Testament holds much promise for our understanding of it. The disciples of Jesus originated from the rural hinterland of *Galilee and served as a renewal sect within Judaism before spreading throughout the Roman world and becoming most successful in the urban environment of Greek civilization.

Sociological explanations should not supplant a theological explanation of the New Testament, rather they should complement it, enriching the theological understanding of the text by bringing the real social content and the actual social relationships to the fore. Theological explanations alone too easily become abstract and academic. For example, the tensions in the church at *Corinth are usually attributed by theologians either to the presence of incipient *gnosticism or to overrealized *eschatology. Without rejecting the value of such insights, one can also appreciate how the diversity of the social classes that rubbed closely together in a church—unusual for clubs and guilds in Roman society—illuminates the divisions that are mentioned in 1 *Corinthians. The "strong" were the socially powerful who would act as hosts at the Lord's table and would see no difficulty in eating meat offered to idols, whereas the "weak" were the poor (1 Cor. 8.1–13; see also Meals).

The application of sociology to the New Testament is not without difficulty. There is danger that the birth and growth of Christianity might be reduced purely to explanation in social terms, and theology might not be given sufficient weight as an independent factor in explanation. Sociology tends to compress unique historical events and processes into general models and recurring patterns. The data with which the sociologist must work are limited and not selected originally for the benefit of the sociologist. Given the limited data, it is tempting to draw parallels between the social behavior of early churches and other contemporary social institutions where such parallels may not be legitimate. Nonetheless, for all the caution that needs to be exercised, a sociological perspective has much value for New Testament studies.

Several major areas of interest may be identified, though they cannot be distinguished neatly from each other. One is the description of the social context in which the disciples of Jesus came together and developed into a worldwide movement. This is most akin to social history but can never be divorced completely from sociological interpretation. The Roman occupation of Palestine had major political and economic implications for the Jews of that region, many of which are evident in the Gospels (e.g., references to "a house divided against itself," the existence of beggars, robbers, and absentee landlords, and paying taxes to Caesar). But the presence of Rome also posed major questions for the Jews' self-understanding as the covenant people of God who had a unique destiny in the world. Several movements had offered solutions to that cultural crisis, including the *Herodians, the *Pharisees, the *Essenes, and the *Zealots; *Jesus offered another that was to meet with a tremendous response.

Contributions have been made to our understanding of specific aspects of Pauline Christianity by describing such features as city life, mobility, the place of *women, and the nature of urban Judaism. There is a growing consensus that early Christianity was not a proletarian movement but was very mixed in its social composition. Its members maintained their strength and purity through their leadership, through procedures for handling conflicts, rituals of initiation (*baptism) and of solidarity (communion), common beliefs, and common life.

A second major area of study has been contemporary social institutions. An understanding of the nature and functioning of the household is vital to the interpretation of the leadership, organization, mission, training, place of women, and ethical teaching of early Christianity. The household was a large inclusive unit in which freedmen, *slaves, and other dependent families grouped around a principal family. Often these people were economically dependent on the principal family and expressed their solidarity by adopting a common religion. The household structure had an impact even on the entire Roman empire, which saw itself as one vast household. In addition to the household, there were many unofficial associations, guilds, and cults through which people found personal identity and fellowship in the empire.

An extension of that area is the investigation of Christianity as a social organization. The primary understanding of Jesus, in this regard, is to see him as the founder of a millenarian movement. Such movements, frequently found among disinherited people, cater to a desire for change, offer a radically new interpretation of life and center in a prophet whose role is to bring heaven into being on earth and to vindicate his followers. Although this model when applied to the mission of Jesus has its difficulties, it largely fits and has the merit of rooting the ministry of Jesus in the real social world of his time.

After the death of the charismatic founder, the movement is usually seen in terms of a sect, that is, a small voluntary religious institution with an exclusive membership, clearly separated from the world as well as world-rejecting in outlook. This provides us with a framework for understanding not only the early church in Jerusalem but also some of the developments in structure and theology that took place as it spread and eventually became acceptable to more people.

A number of secondary issues are raised by the study of social organization. In relation to Jesus, these concern the relationship between those who leave everything to follow him and those, such as Mary and Martha, who remain settled in their homes, as well as the structure of the band of *twelve disciples. In the study of early Christianity, much has been done to explore the nature of apostolic authority and to set wandering preachers and prophets in the broader context of wandering philosophers of whose style of teaching and means of support we know. The relationship of the Pauline mission, originating in *Antioch, to the church of Jerusalem, and this, in turn, to the authority of the original *apostles is of special interest here.

The sociological insights mentioned so far aid the task of exegesis. But in addition to illuminating particular aspects of the text there is a growing body of literature concerned with sociological redaction. An excellent example is Philip Eschler's work on Luke/Acts, where he demonstrates the way in which the material has been shaped to answer questions posed by the mixed sociological situation of its readers (Jew/gentile, rich/poor, and so on).

A further major area is the tentative offering of sociological explanations for events described in the New Testament. The above-mentioned concept of the millenarian movement when applied to Jesus is not just a description but ventures toward an explanation as well. John Gager has also proposed an explanation as to why the dispirited apostles turned into zealous missionaries after the day of *Pentecost. According to the theory of cognitive dissonance, when a specific belief that many hold has been proved wrong (in the case of the early disciples, that Jesus would usher in his kingdom on earth), rather than giving up the belief people lessen their unease (dissonance) by converting others to their way of thinking. The addition of new members

suggests to them that they could not have been wrong! Such an explanation is debatable. Less controversial, but still debatable, is the explanation that many joined the Christian movement because of status inconsistency. To be a woman of wealth, or a wealthy Jew in a gentile environment, or a skilled freedman stigmatized by one's origin, involved status contradictions. These could be resolved by joining a church, for there the sufferer would find a welcoming home that would provide an emotional buttress against the loneliness of a status-ridden world. Much is also made of the process of institutionalization and its effect on the development of early Christianity. Such explanations vary in effectiveness but can prove illuminating, provided one does not resort to the view that the growth of Christianity was due to nothing but the operation of such social forces.

A final area may be identified as the sociology of knowledge. Everyone inherits as pregiven an interpretation of the world. But one's experience may raise questions, leading to modification or sometimes even to radical replacement. One's interpretation of life is formed in response to one's social location. Potentially, this is the most enriching perspective: already it has led to a deeper understanding of the way in which the gospel writers variously express the same life of Jesus, to a fuller understanding of the title "*Son of man," and to a fresh understanding of miracles. The perspective has also been used to relate the "ascent/descent" motif in *John's gospel to the social location of John's readers; the idea of homelessness in 1 *Peter to those who were literally displaced persons; and the cosmic conflicts of *Revelation to the persecuted Christians.

Others have expressed interest in the social functions of literature and in the insights of anthropology. The sociology of the New Testament is a diverse discipline and is still in a youthful stage of development. Some theologians remain skeptical of its value, preferring to tread the well-worn paths of more traditional approaches, but many have welcomed its perspective. As a youthful discipline, it will doubtless make many mistakes, not the least of which will be the mistake of thinking the traffic should all be one-way, from sociology to the New Testament, rather than two-way, enabling our understanding of the New Testament to enrich sociology in general and sociology of religion in particular. But the perspective these approaches offer will be ignored only at great cost to New Testament studies. It cannot be overstressed that the formation of earliest Christianity took place in a real social context and was inhabited by real flesh-and-blood people, not by abstract theologizers.   DEREK J. TIDBALL

Sociology and the Bible. *See* Social Sciences and the Bible.

Sodom and Gomorrah. Two cities, legendary for their incorrigible wickedness (Gen. 13.13) and for their ultimate annihilation by God in a cataclysm of "brimstone and fire" (Gen. 19.24–25). In the story of *Abraham's war against the kings of the east (Gen. 14), Sodom and Gomorrah are numbered among the "five cities" in the "Valley of Siddim," along with Admah, Zeboiim, and Zoar. Abraham's nephew *Lot sojourned for a time in Sodom but fled at divine instigation before the city's final devastation (Gen. 19.15–22). Passages mentioning Sodom and Gomorrah generally agree in locating them along the southern shore of the Dead Sea, but so far no archaeological evidence for their existence has been found there. Suppositions that their remains may yet be discovered beneath the shallow waters of the southern Dead Sea are unlikely ever to be proved. Early Bronze Age (third millennium BCE) settlements and cemeteries at Bab edh-Dhra and Numeira on the southeastern edge of the Dead Sea do, however, provide evidence for very early pre-Israelite occupation in the region. The presence of these ruins, abandoned long before the advent of the Israelites in Canaan, may have given rise much later to local legends that their destruction resulted from divine wrath. At a subsequent stage these legends may have become attached to stories of the wanderings of Abraham and Lot in Canaan.

Whatever the origin of these legends, Sodom and Gomorrah become powerful symbols of human wickedness and divine retribution. Sodom and Gomorrah together (or more frequently, Sodom alone) are held up as archetypes of sinfulness, justly deserving and finally receiving God's punishment. This theme is prominent in prophetic writings (Isa. 1.9; Jer. 23.14; Ezek. 16.44–58; Amos 4.11) and in the New Testament (Matt. 10.15; Luke 10.12; Rom. 9.29; 2 Pet. 2.6; Rev. 11.8).   JOSEPH A. GREENE

Solomon. The son of *David and *Bathsheba, Solomon ruled over Israel ca. 962–922 BCE. His exploits are detailed in 1 Kings 1–11 and 1 Chronicles 28–2 Chronicles 9. Supported by *Bathsheba, *Nathan, and Benaiah, he came to power in a coup d'état that sidetracked his older brother Adonijah and Joab. His reign was marked by prosperity and prestige, grandiose building projects, and a cultural transformation.

The prosperity is portrayed in the fulsome description given in 1 Kings 4.20–28 and 10.14–29, in the marriage with Pharaoh's daughter (and there was a considerable harem; 1 Kings 11.3), in the international role indicated by his dealings with Hiram of Tyre (1 Kings 9.26–28; 10.11–12) and the visit of the Queen of *Sheba (1 Kings 10.1–10), as well as the extensive international trade (a fleet at Ezion-geber, 1 Kings 9.26; "Tarshish" ships, 10.22; trading in horses and chariots, 10.26–29).

Solomon's building program consisted principally in the *Temple as well as the palace complex (the palace, the "House of the Forest of Lebanon"—a kind of armory—and even a palace for his Egyptian wife). In addition, he built up a corps of chariots and cavalry that functioned out of chariot cities in the realm (1 Kings 10.26). Such opulence was sustained by a revision of the administrative areas in the kingdom (1 Kings 4.7–19), which led to increased revenue for the crown, as well as to a weakening of the old tribal ties and to further assimilation of the Canaanite population. All this was obtained at a price, as is suggested by Solomon's having to cede land to Hiram of Tyre (1 Kings 9.10–14; but contrast 2 Chron. 8.2) and by the *corvée*. Despite 1 Kings 9.20–22, it appears that Israelites as well as Canaanites were involved in forced labor, and this became a major complaint against Solomon (5.13–14; cf. 4.6; 12.18).

The cultural transformation of the population must have been considerable, though it is largely a matter of historical inference. But political centralization won out over the old tribalization; a new wealthy class emerged, and cleavage between rich and poor increased. This aspect of Solomon's reign is not reflected in the tradition. Rather, his reign is acclaimed, and his personal wisdom is underlined. His wisdom is compared to that of the Egyptians (4.29–34), and is illustrated by the famous incident of the two prostitutes (3.16–28). Hence he has come down in the tradition as the wise man par excellence, to whom several works were eventually attributed: Psalms 72 and 127, the book of *Proverbs, the *Song of Solomon, and *Ecclesiastes within the Hebrew Bible; *Wisdom of Solomon among the *apocrypha; Psalms and Odes among the *pseudepigrapha. Scholars have inferred that such compositions as the Yahwist history (*J) probably date to the Solomonic period.

The theological judgment passed upon Solomon is mixed. The name Jedidiah (beloved of Yah or the Lord) was given him by the prophet Nathan ("the Lord loved him," 2 Sam. 12.24-25). The description of his sincerity and simplicity is highlighted in the sacrifice at Gibeon (1 Kings 3). He asks for a "listening heart" (1 Kings 3.9; NRSV: "understanding mind") whereby to rule the people, and the Lord assures him of this as well as of riches and glory. On the other hand, the typical Deuteronomic judgment on royalty is also passed upon Solomon (1 Kings 11), and notice is taken of the "adversaries" whom the Lord raised up: Hadad the Edomite, Rezon of Damascus, and especially Jeroboam, who was to lead the rebellion against Rehoboam, Solomon's son.

Nothing is known of "the Book of the Acts of Solomon" (1 Kings 11.41), which might have cast a fuller light on the reign of the fabled monarch. But the immediate dissolution of the united monarchy in the lifetime of his son is surely suggestive of the inadequacies of Solomon's reign (1 Kings 12.14).

ROLAND E. MURPHY, O. CARM.

Song of Solomon. The Song of Solomon follows the book of *Ruth in the Hebrew Bible and *Ecclesiastes in the *Septuagint. Also called the Song of Songs (i.e., the most excellent song) and the Canticle (of Canticles), it was divided in the Middle Ages arbitrarily into eight *chapters, which do not correspond to significant units of content. This brief composition of fewer than two hundred poetic verses has always been an enigma, and little agreement exists concerning such questions as origin, date of composition, structure, and unity.

Authorship and Date. The attribution "to *Solomon" affixed to the Song is an editorial superscription that links this poetry to Israel's famous poet and sage rather than a declaration of authorship. No hint of actual author or authors appears in the text. The intense style of poetry belongs to the genre of love lyrics found in ancient Egyptian collections. Lush, extravagant imagery appealing to the senses of smell, taste, and touch, detailed descriptions of the human body, male and female, and highly styl-

ized terms of endearment like dove, sister, and king link the Song to other ancient Near Eastern cultures.

The Song of Solomon displays striking metaphors from a variety of flora and fauna, some twenty-five species of *plants and ten of *animals, mentioned not as a display of learning but for the images they invoke. It also exploits the evocative power of place names like *Lebanon, home of fragrant cedars (3.9), Gilead, famous for its balm (4.1), snow-covered Amana (4.8), and Tirzah, ancient capital of the northern kingdom of Israel (6.4).

Nothing in the Song itself proves its date of composition. It seems to be made up of lyrics that came down in oral tradition long before they were gathered into their canonical form. The appealing subject matter and vivid imagery, like the woman being compared to a mare that throws the war stallions of the pharaoh's chariots into disorder (1.9), explain why these lyrics were preserved in the schools of the Temple of Jerusalem. They proved to be a useful teaching tool. Boldness of imagery, repetitions, and variations on erotic themes point to frequent recital before they were edited in the final form, possibly between 450–400 BCE. This date is plausible because of widespread scribal activity at that time, because the syntax exhibits *Aramaic constructions, and because the *Persian loan word for *paradise is found in 4.13.

After the destruction of the Second Temple in 70 CE, the Song of Solomon was incorporated into the Jewish *canon over the objections of some rabbis, who found its subject matter unsuitable for Israel's sacred literature. Once it became part of the official scriptures, commentators both Jewish and Christian attempted to interpret it in religious terms. Eventually it was recited as part of the services for the final day of the *Passover celebration.

Structure and Nature. Commentators are divided concerning the structure of the Song of Solomon. Three approaches persist: that it is a literary unity; that it is a systematic organization of love poems; and that it is a random collection of lyrics. Some find as many as eighty distinct units. The literal sense of the verses describes movements of passion and affection between a man and a woman, who is called "my darling" (Hebr. ra‘yātî; NRSV: "my love") nine times, a term never found elsewhere in the Bible. Poetic features like chiasm, inclusion, historical allusions, refrains, and thematic repetition provide a basis for the variety of theories about the

Song's structure. Both Jewish and Christian exegetes have found deeper meaning in its verses. Medieval qabbalists proposed a sacred code as key to its interpretation.

The theories about the nature of the Song can be divided into five headings.

Allegorical. The Aramaic *translations called Targums preserve traditions that read the Song as an allegory of the Lord's love for Israel. On this basis allusions to events in Israel's history are found throughout. Christian mystical tradition as early as Origen took a similar approach. His commentary, part of which is extant in Latin translation, interprets the Song as celebrating Christ's love for his church or for the believing soul. The most famous medieval example of the allegorical method of reading the Song is the eighty-six homilies of Bernard of Clairvaux, covering only the first two chapters.

Dramatic. A few ancient Greek manuscripts assign sections of the lyrics to specific speakers. Following that tradition, some exegetes read the Song as describing a shepherd's courtship of the Shulammite maid (6.13). They often introduce Solomon as rival suitor. They disagree about how to assign the dramatis personae and where to place the climaxes. They usually find from five to eight scenes. The dramatic theory was especially popular in the nineteenth century.

Literal-historical. By far the most common interpretation of the Song of Solomon is that it is a collection of lyrics celebrating human love. This approach, based on affinities with ancient Near Eastern love poetry, seeks to do justice to the plastic language and sensuous imagery that reveal vivid imagination and artistic skill. As lyric poetry the Song employs language that functions simultaneously on a literal and a symbolic level. The garden and vineyard are places of nurture, whether for plants or for sexual capacity. The pasture is a place for feeding the shepherd's flock and for nourishing human intimacy. Eating applies to both physical and sexual satisfaction. Such flexibility of language is the stuff of masterpieces that attract readers of every generation.

Some scholars suggest that the Song was a collection of songs assembled as a repertoire for *wedding celebrations. The vivid portrayal of the body of the woman (4.1–7; 6.4–7; 7.1–6) and of the man (5.10–16) resemble Arabic *wasfs* sung at weddings. This genre includes vivid metaphors: hair falling like descending flocks of mountain goats; teeth sparkling like newly shorn goats; cheeks glistening like the inside of a pome-

granate covered by a thin veil. Stylized royal imagery explains the designation of the lover as king.

Other scholars search for the origin of these lyrics in dream fantasy, because the woman speaks of having a dream in 5.2, and possibly in 3.1–4. Such an origin could account for the stream-of-consciousness succession of events from city streets to wine cellars to country landscapes to remote deserts and mountain tops inhabited by hostile animals.

Other students of the Song of Solomon feel that the nature of these lyrics does not point to a specific point of origin. Rather, they share the universal language of love poetry with such commonplace themes as the excitement of seeking and finding or the terror of seeking and not finding the loved one. Their appeals to such a wide range of smells and shapes and colors are ways of portraying the universal presence of love. The scribe who finally brought these lyrics together proclaims love to be "strong as death" (8.6), so powerful that even floods cannot drown it. That comment encouraged efforts to find deeper meaning in the Song.

Cultic or ritualistic. The mention of death as well as unusual situations pictured have led some commentators to see the Song as originating in an ancient ritual, possibly a sacred marriage or fertility rite or in ceremonies to ward off death. They find cultic origins for the elaborate procession of 3.6–11 and the phrase "house of my mother" (3.4; 8.2).

Parabolic or typological. Some commentators have made ingenious efforts to tie these lyrics, which never mention God, closer to his saving plan. They read the Song of Solomon in terms of certain topics of Israelite theology, like the *covenant relationship between Yahweh and Israel, which was compared to marriage in the prophetic tradition. This interpretation finds a variety of second-level meanings in the imagery: for example, the man signifies the Lord and the woman Israel; their coming together portrays the restoration of intimacy lost in the garden of *Eden; the woman's spontaneity recalls original innocence.

Significance. The Song of Solomon embodies a surplus of meaning in its artistic unfolding of lyrics that portray a poetic genius and emotional warmth of universal impact and appeal. Its unusual vocabulary (almost fifty words appear nowhere else in the Bible) adds excitement to the swift pace and evocative scenes. A minority of critics read it as containing some kind of narrative or thematic unity reflected in repetitions like "caresses sweeter than wine" (1.2 and 4.10) and the refrain in 2.7; 3.5; 5.8; 8.4. But most modern editors present it as a collection of related lyrics loosely united, composed not to teach but to touch, to please, and to delight. The power of its beauty is its celebration of and appeal to love.

No apparent order governs the flow of its verse, except perhaps the final verses that point to the reflective bent of the sage inviting readers to resonate to the power of love. The New Testament contains no reference to the Song.

JAMES M. REESE, O.S.F.S.

Song of Songs. *See* Song of Solomon.

Son of God. The Hebrew *ben and Aramaic *bar,* "son," designate not only a male descendant but also a relationship to a community, a country, a species (e.g., animals), etc. "Son of God" can thus mean both a mythological figure of divine origin, a being belonging to the divine sphere (such as an *angel), or a human being having a special relationship to a god. In antiquity, son of god was used predicatively of kings begotten by a god (in Egypt) or endowed with divine power (in Mesopotamia). In the Roman period, it also was used in the East as a title for the emperor.

In the Hebrew Bible, *sons of God occur in Genesis 6.1–4, where they marry human women and became fathers of the giants (KJV) or *Nephilim (NRSV); in Job 1.6; 2.1 (NRSV: "heavenly beings"), where they make up the court of God; and also in Deuteronomy 32.8 (NRSV: "gods"); Psalms 29.1 and 89.6 (NRSV: "heavenly beings"); cf. Psalm 82.6 "sons of the Most High" (NRSV: "children of the Most High"). Elsewhere, the designation son of God is used especially of the king. Thus, in the primary passage of the Israelite ideology of divine *kingship, it is said of *Solomon, "I will be his father, and he will be my son" (2 Sam. 7.14; cf. 1 Chron. 17.13). Neither in 2 Samuel 7.12–14 nor in Psalm 89.26–29 does the designation son of God express anything more than a special relationship; there is no question of deification. This also applies to Psalm 2.7, where God says to the king, "You are my son; today I have begotten you"; "today" rules out a mythological interpretation. The title son of God indicates that the king has his kingdom from God, and the saying belongs to the coronation day or its anniversary. (*See also* Kingship and Monarchy; Messiah.)

This manner of speaking of God as a father and the correlative usage, son or sons of God, has also been extended to cover the people of God. In Exodus 4.22 and Jeremiah 31.9, God calls Israel his firstborn son; in Exodus 4.23 and Hosea 11.1 his "son." Correspondingly, in Deuteronomy 32.6, 18 and Jeremiah 3.4, God is called the people's "father," and in Deuteronomy 14.1; 32.5, 19 the Israelites appear as "sons" (and "daughters") of God. Finally, the plural form may designate a special group, like the pious (Ps. 73.15) or the priests (Mal. 1.6).

In postbiblical literature, "son of God" designates either the pious (Sir. 4.10) or the suffering righteous (Wisd. of Sol. 2.18; cf. 2.13, 16; 5.5; cf. also Psalms of Solomon 13.9), while the plural denotes the elect people (Wisd. of Sol. 9.7; 12.19, 21; Psalms of Solomon 17.27). Obviously, son of God was not a common messianic title in Judaism before Roman times. Passages like 2 Esd. 7.28–29; 13.32, 37, 52; 14.9, which speak of "my son [the Messiah]," and 1 Enoch 105.2, do not alter this, since both are influenced by the "servant of the Lord" in Second *Isaiah. Messianic usage of the expression outside the New Testament from this period does occur in the *Dead Sea Scrolls, as in a fragment of a Daniel Apocryphon from Qumran (4QpsDan Aᵃ) and in 4Q246, another fragment, which has a close parallel in Luke 1.32, 35. But the fact that the title was used for the king makes it understandable that it could also be applied to the Messiah.

In the New Testament, Son of God (and its abbreviated form, "the Son") is a title often used in christological confessions. From the beginning it seems to have been used in connection with the belief in the *resurrection and exaltation of *Jesus. The confessional fragment in Romans 1.3–4 speaks of the gospel "concerning his Son, who was descended from David according to the flesh and was declared to be Son of God with power according to the spirit of holiness by resurrection from the dead." The originally exchangeable expressions Son of David and Son of God are here conferred on the earthly Jesus and the risen Lord, it being presupposed that before his death Jesus was Messiah-designate, and that the resurrection implied a new position (cf. Acts 2.36). The authors of Acts 13.33 and Hebrews 1.5; 5.5 also quote Psalm 2.7 in this connection. Yet it is still possible to speak of a special "Son of God" Christology insofar as the designation expresses Jesus' unique relationship to God. From an early stage, this belief included the idea of a preexistence and the sending of Jesus to the world (cf. Gal. 4.4 and also Phil. 2.6–11; John 1.1). The title seems to have attracted to it ideas connected with *wisdom as well.

In the *synoptic Gospels we may observe how the title Son of God has penetrated into the traditions about the life of Jesus. In *Mark, it is used only by God and the demons (cf. 1.11; 9.7; 3.11; 5.7); the one time it is used by a human (15.39), the past tense ("was") suggests a distinction between the confession of the centurion to the deceased Jesus, and later on, to the risen Lord. In *Matthew we also find it in the confessions of the disciples (14.33; 16.16; cf. also 26.63), in the story of the *temptation (4.3, 6), and the story of the mocking at the cross (27.43; cf. also Matt. 11.27). In *Luke, it is mostly found in traditional material; the idea of a *virgin birth probably does not belong here. In *John, the Son of God, together with the title the Son, plays a central role in depicting Jesus as being one with the Father (e.g., 3.35–36 and 1.18; 10.30).

The origin of the title seems, in the first place, to be Jesus' unique addressing God as father (see especially Mark 14.36, where the Aramaic *abba is preserved), and second, its connection with kingship ideology in view of the conviction that Jesus was the anticipated son of David. Yet characteristically in the New Testament it stands beside the usage of the phrase sons of God, referring to those whom Jesus has brought to salvation (Rom. 8.14–21; 9.8, 26; Gal. 3.26; Matt. 5.9, 45; John 1.12; 1 John 3.1). In the apostolic fathers, the designation describes the divine nature of Jesus as apart from his human nature (e.g., Ignatius, *Ephesians* 20.2; *Epistle of Barnabas* 12.10, where it corresponds to son of man).

To summarize the evidence in the New Testament, it might be said that the title Son of God primarily expresses Jesus' unique relation to God, while the Lord, the christological title preferred by *Paul (see 1 Cor. 12.3; Phil. 2.11), emphasizes his position in the church and in the world.

MOGENS MÜLLER

Son of Man. The self-designation most often used by *Jesus in the Gospels. It occurs seventy-two times in the *synoptics; two passages (Matt. 18.11; Luke 9.56) are, however, textually uncertain, and if parallels are not counted, the number of different Son of man sayings is forty-three. To these may be added thirteen in the Fourth Gospel. John 12.34, like Luke 24.7, is only an apparent exception to the rule that the expression is always uttered by Jesus himself, the only

genuine exception being Acts 7.56. Apart from John 5.27, the designation in all these passages is literally "the son of the man." In the New Testament the undetermined form, "a son of man," is found in Hebrews 2.6 (quoting Ps. 8.5) and in Revelation 1.13 (the exalted Christ) and 14.14 (an angel).

The Son of man sayings in the synoptics fall into two groups, those about the Son of man's mission and his fate on earth (e.g., Mark 2.10 par.; 2.28 par.; 10.45 par.) together with the passion predictions (Mark 8.31 par.; 9.31 par.; 10.33 par.), and those concerning the position and role of the risen and exalted Son of man and his *parousia (e.g., Mark 8.3 par.; 13.26 par.; 14.62 par.). All Son of man sayings are christologically significant. Nevertheless, in the synoptics there are many passages without the expression where textually and linguistically there could be no objection to it (e.g., Mark 2.17 par.), and such passages sometimes have synoptic parallels containing the expression (e.g., Luke 22.27; cf. Mark 10.45 and Matt. 20.28). In the synoptics, there seems to be an increasing monopolization of the expression in sayings of Jesus about his mission, his fate, and his position beyond the resurrection. In the Fourth Gospel the situation is different: here Son of man sayings compete with the "I am" sayings and the self-designation "the Son." The distinction in usage is always significant; "Son of man" is always used in major statements.

Being central in the Gospel tradition, then, it is no wonder that Son of man is one of the most debated expressions in the New Testament. Its seemingly enigmatic character can be measured by the endless attempts to find an acceptable solution as to its meaning, and despite tendencies apparent in more recent research, it is not accurate to speak of a growing consensus. It is possible, however, to distinguish between two main views: (1) The expression was current and, under certain circumstances, understandable as a messianic title at the time of Jesus. (2) Such usage must be excluded on linguistic grounds alone. There is also the question whether the expression as it now stands in the Gospels is to be understood as a messianic title or not. And in the case of the former, are we to presume a development in meaning from Jesus to the Gospel tradition?

The New Testament itself does not give us the slightest hint as to the meaning of the expression, and there is no evidence for the double-determined form ("the Son of the man") before it appears in the New Testament. In the *Greek of the *Septuagint it appears only in the undetermined form, which, similar to the *Hebrew original *ben ʾādām*, conveys a generic meaning synonymous with "man," that is, human being (Ps. 8.5; Ezek. 2.1; Dan. 8.17). In the Hebrew Bible, the expression occurs 108 times, 93 of which are in Ezekiel as God's way of addressing the prophet. The *Aramaic equivalent, *bar ʾĕnāš*, occurs only once, in Daniel 7.13, which speaks of "one like a (son of) man." This saying has had a decisive impact on the understanding of Son of man in the New Testament, and it is quoted or alluded to many times (see Mark 13.26 par.; 14.62 par.; but also Rev. 1.7, which does not actually mention any son of man). The imagery of Daniel 7.13–14 may be the foundation of the Son of man sayings relating to the status of the exalted Christ.

Now, "one like a man" in Daniel 7.13 is by no means a messianic figure, but a symbol of the victorious Israel, the kingdom of the saints of the Most High, which succeeded the four world empires (Dan. 7.18, 22, 25, 27). Thus, when we find in 1 Enoch 46–71 and 4 Ezra 13 similar imageries of a son of man or simply a man, these cannot be independent witnesses of a special concept, but uses of the imagery of Daniel to describe a messianic figure. The comprehensive attempt earlier this century to verify the existence of a special son of man conception, sometimes assumed to be a variant of the ancient Near Eastern myth of the primeval man, universal and transcendent in its outlook (in contrast to the nationalistic and earthly expectation of a Davidic messiah), has obviously failed.

Another question is whether the expression in the Gospels and Acts 7.56 is to be understood as a title. With the exception of Matthew 16.13 and John 9.35, this is possible. On the other hand, the title never occurs in confessions (e.g., Jesus is the Son of man), nor is it used predicatively (Jesus, the Son of man). The determined form must not be taken as a reference to the expression "like a son of man" in Daniel 7.13.

There is, however, yet another possibility. Granted that the Greek form of the expression originates in Aramaic, it may be explained as a direct extension of the idiomatic use of the expression *bar ʾĕnāš*. It is now almost universally agreed that at Jesus' time this expression was in general usage in Galilean Aramaic both as a noun (meaning "a human being") and as a substitute for the indefinite pronoun and as a peri-

phrasis for "I," the actual meaning depending on the context. The double entendre may express a generalization, meaning "one," "a human," or it may be a self-reference provoked by awe, modesty, or humility, in accord with the content of the actual saying. In that case, the double entendre is deceptive, a near parallel being Paul's way of speaking of himself in 2 Corinthians 12.2–3. It is possible to understand the Gospel Son of man sayings in accordance with this Aramaic idiom. But the double entendre has been done away with by the Greek rendering with its awkward literalness ("the son of the man"), which substitutes an explicit indication of the identity of the subject speaking. This does not mean, however, that the expression has become a title. In the Gospels it is, at the same time, Jesus' periphrasis for "I" and a way to emphasize who is speaking. In other words, it is not the expression "son of man" that tells us who Jesus is, but on the contrary, it is Jesus who tells us who the Son of man is.

It is thus reasonable to suppose that the usage of the expression in the Gospels originates in the way in which Jesus spoke of himself. The question of the genuineness of the individual Son of man sayings must therefore depend on their content: are they understandable in the mouth of the historical Jesus or not? Naturally, the answer will depend upon the individual interpreter's idea of what Jesus believed and preached about himself, and what may be referred to the early community. It seems probable that the sayings about the risen and exalted Son of man and his parousia, depending on Daniel 7.13–14 for their imagery, were created in the process of interpreting the faith in the *resurrection of Jesus, and that they were shaped in analogy to other sayings of Jesus about himself. As indicated by 1 Thessalonians 4.15–17, this interpretation is early and reflects the same tradition expressed later in Mark 13.26 and especially Matthew 24.30–31.

The uncomplicated way in which the expression is used in the Gospels indicates an early foothold in the Greek gospel tradition, which is confirmed by its occurrence also in the Fourth Gospel. In this gospel, one can perceive a beginning of reflection upon its wording, which transcends the purely idiomatic meaning it had in Aramaic (see especially John 5.27). In the apostolic fathers, it is understood as a statement of Christ's human nature and corresponds to the title *Son of God (see Ignatius *Ephesians* 20.2;

cf. Epistle of Barnabas 12.10). Later, it is seen as a reference to the figure in Daniel 7.13 and is read as a messianic prophecy (Justin, *Apology* I.51). Not until the nineteenth century do we find an attempt to see a specific conception behind the expression.   MOGENS MÜLLER

Sons of God. The sons of God (or children of God; Hebr. *běnê ʾĕlōhîm,* and variants) are divine members of God's heavenly assembly. They are depicted in many roles: praising God at the dawn of creation (Job 38.7); praising God in heaven (Ps 29.1); meeting in the heavenly assembly before God (Job 1.6, 2.1; cf. Pss. 82.1, 6; 89.6–8); representing the foreign nations (Deut. 32.8, following a text from *Qumran and the *LXX); and, most curiously, marrying and having offspring with human women (Gen. 6.1–4). Other terms, such as *seraphim, *angels (i.e., "messengers"), and hosts of heaven also refer to these members of God's heavenly assembly (see 1 Kgs. 22.19; Isa. 6; Ezek. 13.25). The sons of God are also identified with the stars in heaven (Job 38.7; cf. Judg. 5.20). The title "sons/children of God" is familiar from *Ugaritic mythology, in which the gods collectively are called the "children of El (literally, God)" *(bn ʾil).* One of El's titles is "Father of the Children of God," indicating that the term refers to the gods as his physical offspring, with *Asherah (called "Creatress of the Gods") as their mother. The sons/children of God are also found in Phoenician and Ammonite inscriptions, referring to the pantheon of subordinate deities, indicating that the term was widespread in West Semitic religions. Beginning in the seventh and sixth centuries BCE, several Israelite writers (especially Jeremiah, the Deuteronomist, and Second Isaiah) explicitly rejected the notion that there were gods other than Yahweh, and depicted the "hosts of heaven" as a foreign intrusion in Israelite *monotheism.
                                RONALD S. HENDEL

Sortes Biblicae. In the ancient world, a method of fortune-telling called sortilege was performed by randomly choosing one of several slips on which were written verses of a poet, such as Homer or Virgil *(sortes Homericae* or *sortes Vergilianae).* Another soothsaying system involved randomly opening a copy of Homer's *Iliad* or Virgil's *Aeneid* and interpreting as prophetic the first line upon which the eye settled. Even though

Christianity denounced augury and the related practice of sortilege, many continued to use such practices in the early church. A specific type of soothsaying *(sortes biblicae)* pursued by Christians involved using the Bible to divine their destiny by "sacred lots." After randomly opening the Bible and selecting the first line their eye fell upon, early Christians considered the passage a divine message to be applied to the problem that had caused them to employ such means of divination. The widespread use of *sortes biblicae* is confirmed by its repeated condemnation. For example, in France, the Gallican synods of Vannes (465 CE), Agde (506), Orléans (511), and Auxerre (570–590) passed ordinances vowing to excommunicate any Christian who "should be detected in the practice of this art, either as consulting or teaching it."

Along with gleaning messages from randomly chosen texts of scripture, early Christians also sometimes consulted specially prepared copies of the Bible, especially the Gospels, to learn their fortunes. In the lower margin of successive manuscript pages there occasionally appear brief comments, before each of which the Greek word *hermēneia* ("interpretation") is written. And so early Christians opened the Bible at random, or even cast dice to determine page numbers, in order to divine their fortunes. Such "interpretations" are found, for example, on eight Greek manuscript copies of John's gospel from the third or fourth century to the eighth century. Similarly, the fifth-century Codex Bezae bears such comments written in the lower margins of the gospel of Mark. Dating perhaps from the ninth or tenth century, these sixty-nine successive short statements include "You will be saved from danger," "Expect a great miracle," "You will receive joy from God," "Seek something else," "After ten days it will happen," and "What you seek will be found." An Old Latin codex of the Gospels of the eighth century is also inscribed along the margins of the gospel of John with a similar collection of sayings.

Sortilege was the influencing factor of St. Augustine's conversion; Augustine himself, however, credits a providential calling. His account *(Confessions* 8.12) reveals that, upon hearing a child's voice urging *Tolle, lege; tolle lege* ("Take up, read; take up, read"), he opened up a copy of the scriptures and his eyes were drawn to Romans 13.13–14, a passage that caused him to repudiate his former life. Later Augustine looked unfavorably on using the scriptures for divination: "As to those who read futurity by taking at random a text from the pages of the Gospels, it is better that they should do this than go to consult spirits of divination; nevertheless I am displeased with this custom, which turns the divine oracles, which were intended to teach us concerning the higher life, to the business of the world and the vanities of the present life" (*Epistle* 55.20.37).

Undoubtedly, the use of the lot to select Matthias as the twelfth *apostle after Judas' suicide (Acts 1.26), along with the verse "The lot is cast into the lap, but the decision is wholly from the Lord" (Prov. 16:33), stimulated the practice of biblical sortilege. John Wesley and early Methodists were known to take seriously this method of consulting the scriptures, and it is still practiced from time to time in various places.

See Magic and Divination.

BRUCE M. METZGER

Spirit, Flesh and. *See* Flesh and Spirit.

Spirit, Holy. *See* Holy Spirit.

Stephen. The first Christian martyr, Stephen appears only in *Acts. He is first mentioned as one of the *seven appointed to ensure equitable distribution of food between "Hebrews" and "Hellenists" (Acts 6.1–6). The seven were probably leaders of the Hellenistic group in the Jerusalem church.

According to Acts 6, in an explicit literary parallel to Luke's story of Jesus, Stephen was charged with blasphemy and summoned to defend himself before the supreme *Sanhedrin (Acts 6.8–15).

His defense (Acts 7.2–53) is a detailed exposition of the teaching that had provoked the charges against him. The speech may be regarded as a manifesto of early Hellenistic Christianity or at least of one phase of it. It does not represent Luke's point of view: for most of Luke's narrative, his appraisal of the *Temple is much more positive than Stephen's. Quoting the scriptures in support of his position, Stephen argues that to speak of the Temple as an institution to be destroyed or superseded was not to commit blasphemy, because God is independent of any building. It was commonly held by many early Christians that in Christ the Temple order had given way to something better, but Stephen's

assertion that the Temple was a mistake from the beginning is without parallel in the New Testament. The position nearest to it is in the letter to the *Hebrews, but its author simply ignores the Temple and bases his exposition of the high-priestly ministry of Christ on the biblical account of the wilderness *tabernacle.

Stephen was apparently found guilty of *blasphemy and sentenced to death. His execution took the form of a judicial stoning, carried out in accordance with the Law (Lev. 24.15–16). Those who bore witness against him had the duty of throwing the first stones (see Deut 17.7); on this occasion "a young man named Saul" guarded their cloaks as they did so, and thus *Paul makes his first appearance.

Analogies have been found to Stephen's position among the *Samaritans, the *Qumran community, and the Ebionites. These groups, for various reasons, expressed a negative attitude to the Jerusalem Temple and its ceremonial. But Stephen's critique is distinctive; not only is it rooted in the preexilic prophets but it has a new basis in the Christ event. The radical Hellenistic theology represented by his speech survived particularly in Alexandrian Christianity, where its best-known expression is the letter of Barnabas (late first/early second century CE).

Stephen's impeachment and execution are said to have precipitated a persecution of the Jerusalem church, especially its Hellenistic members, who were forced to leave Jerusalem and Judea. But they preached the gospel wherever they went. Stephen's fellow-almoner Philip preached it in *Samaria; others, unnamed, preached it to the Greeks of *Antioch. Stephen's blood proved to be the seed of gentile Christianity.

F. F. BRUCE

Stoics. A philosophical school founded in Athens by Zeno of Citium (335–263 BCE) which became the most influential philosophic sect in the Greco-Roman world. Stoics conceived of philosophy as the knowledge of things divine and human, and its goal as a life in harmony with nature. They thought that the universe was permeated by the *Logos or Reason, also referred to as God or Providence. Human beings, they held, are particles of God, for divine Reason is manifested in a special way in human reason. As one rationally develops those conceptions of the divine that are innate in all people, one more clearly discerns the nature of things, including oneself. Stoics who make progress in this manner advance from ignorance, which is responsible for vice, to knowledge of reality, which makes virtue possible. Virtue and vice they delineated in extensive lists. Stoics disregarded all matters external to themselves, and cultivated an impassivity which made them self-sufficient or content (autarkēs). Hardships that befell them therefore did not affect their true selves, but merely showed their true character. Their view of divine kinship gave a devotional cast to their language, and their doctrine that all things in the universe are in harmonious relationship to each other accommodated much of popular religion, including the veneration of religious images. As a messenger of the divine, the Stoic sage sought to show others their error and to lead them to the good. This included instruction in civic responsibility, which Stoics, as did other philosophers, summarized in lists of duties of members of a household (see Ethical Lists).

In Jewish thought, *wisdom was personified and increasingly related to the doctrine of *creation. Stoic echoes of the cosmic wisdom are present in the *Septuagint translation of Proverbs 8.22–31, and other Stoic elements begin to appear in Jewish literature, partly, perhaps, in reaction to Epicurean tendencies in such works as *Ecclesiastes. *Sirach advances a Stoic-like view of God as "the all" (43.27) who is responsible for every human experience (11.14), yet differs from Stoic pantheism in deeming God greater than his works (43.28). Wisdom, like the Stoic Logos, permeates the universe (24.5–6), but is identified with the *Law of Moses (24.23), which is thus elevated to something suprahistorical and rational. The *Wisdom of Solomon similarly describes all-pervading Wisdom as the agent of *creation (7.22–26), which is directed by divine providence (6.7; 14.3). Using the Stoic notion of natural theology, Wisdom of Solomon argues that, while knowledge of God is possible by observing creation, human failure to attain this knowledge resulted in an unpardonable ignorance (13.8) that plunged humanity into idolatry and immorality (14.12). Stoic influence is also clearly discernible in 4 *Maccabees, which defines wisdom as the knowledge of divine and human things (1.16–17) and sets out to determine whether devout reason is master of the passions (1.1). Unlike the Stoics, however, the author advocates the mastery, not eradication, of the passions (1.30–35; 3.2).

Stoics are mentioned explicitly in the Bible only in Acts 17.18, where, according to Luke, in company with their opponents the *Epicureans they encounter *Paul. The sermon that follows (17.22–31) has Paul making extensive use of popular Stoicism: the veneration of images as an expression of human religiosity, providence, kinship with the creator God, and the quotation of writers who represent Stoic views. Since Stoics focused on the material world, Paul's reference to the resurrection is mocked by his audience. Similar Stoic thought, perhaps mediated by Jewish wisdom traditions, is used in Romans 1.18–32. But, where in Acts 17 Paul is represented as using Stoicism positively, excusing former ignorance, in Romans he uses it to indict, as Wisdom 13 does: God had granted knowledge of himself in creation, but that knowledge was rejected and humanity was therefore given over to immorality. The Stoic interpretation of Wisdom as the agent of creation may also have influenced the view of the Logos in John 1.1–2. Paul further uses Stoic lists, many of which may have come to him by way of Hellenistic Judaism, such as lists of virtues and vices (1 Cor. 6.9–10; Gal. 5.19–23) and of hardships (1 Cor. 4.9–13; 2 Cor. 6.4–10). Paul christianizes such lists, as he does the Stoic view of self-sufficiency. In Philippians 4.11–13, he claims to be content (autarkēs), which does not mean that he is impassive or had attained self-sufficiency on his own; on the contrary, he is able to experience all things fully because God empowers him. The Stoic lists of social responsibilities are similarly christianized (Eph. 5.22–6.9; Col. 3.18–4.1). God's initiative and the eschatological perspective also place the Stoic-sounding language of 2 Peter 1.3–4 in a different Christian perspective.

ABRAHAM J. MALHERBE

Structuralism.

Characteristics. Structuralism is interdisciplinary, involving a variety of methods. It is not concerned with the intent of the author, the observable phenomena, or the organization of the text (rhetorical criticism), but with constraints and cultural codes that impose themselves on any speaker or author (deep structures). It studies structure as a totality in which the whole and the parts are integrally related; the fundamental structures are those "below" the surface of the empirical manifestation.

The dichotomy expression/content (signifier/signified) is basic. Structuralism emphasizes the synchronic dimension (the timeless aspect of a text), as opposed to the diachronic aspect, which focuses on its historical development; modern biblical studies have traditionally emphasized the diachronic dimension. The syntagmatic and paradigmatic features of a text are also important. The syntagmatic order, the chainlike manifestation of what precedes and what follows, primarily reflects the intention of the author. A paradigmatic reading presupposes various systems, but manifests only a certain section of these systems or paradigms. Further essential features are the emphasis on fundamental binary oppositions, as well as the challenge to penetrate through the surface structure of spoken discourse *(la parole)* in order to reach the basic laws of language *(la langue)*.

Background and Proponents. The roots of structuralism go back to the linguistic theories of Ferdinand de Saussure (1915) and the influence of the Russian formalists, with their emphasis on linguistics and the poetics of the text, how it is made. Roman Jakobson was influential in the shift in European criticism from Russian formalism to structuralism; he placed the study of poetics within the context of linguistics by describing six basic external factors and corresponding internal functions.

The roots of structuralism can further be traced to anthropology, especially to the pioneering work of Claude Lévi-Strauss. The influence of de Saussure (culture as a generalized version of language-as-system model) and Jakobson (binary opposition) can be detected in his work. He claims that literature gives evidence of the unconscious structuring patterns of society. In myths, the binary oppositions of life are mediated and transformed. So, for example, the opposition between life and death is mediated by the concept of hunting (to kill in order to live). Myth consists of both *langue* (reversible time, the synchronic element) as well as *parole* (nonreversible time, the diachronic element). The meaning of myth is to be found not in the intrinsic content of the actions but rather in the combination of the synchronic and diachronic elements.

Structuralism is also related to three different streams of literary studies: Russian (Vladimir Propp), French (Roland Barthes and A. J. Greimas), and American. Barthes was one of the most important proponents of structuralism, though he later abandoned this approach. For him there is no antithesis between history and structure: the structure of the sentence serves as a model for the structure of discourse. Barthes abandons the inductive model, and opts for a deductive approach, seeing a text as a homogeneous unit. He proceeds with a sequential analysis (division of the text into basic units), as well as a structural analysis of sequences. Barthes distinguishes three levels of narrative structure: functions (Propp), actions (Greimas), and narration (Tzvetan Todorov). He concentrates on a specific text, underlining its plurality of meanings, rather than inferring common structures from a number of texts.

Greimas, with his deductive and scientific methodology, is concerned not with the meaning of the text as such but rather with the semantic structures underlying the narrative. Three levels of text are to be distinguished. The level of manifestation concentrates on performance, the competence of the author as it is realized in the empirical text. The level of narrative structure deals with functions (Propp) and actants, as well as the axes of communication, volition, and power. On the discursive or thematic level, isotopies as levels of coherence constructed from classemes allow the reader to discern the interaction of various levels of meaning. Paradigmatic meaning is related not in a syntagmatic manner to the context of the rest of the sentence but rather, in a binary or ternary fashion, to oppositions of meaning.

Structuralism and Biblical Studies. In 1961 Edmund Leach was the first to apply the approach of Lévi-Strauss to the text of Genesis 1–3, explicating myths that are the product of universal structures of human thought, involving binary oppositions and their reconciliation. Lévi-Strauss himself did not consider this exercise to be successful. In a comparison made by Leach of *Jesus and *John the Baptist, he points out various parallel and opposite features. Beneath the surface structure of the text, which seems to deal with Jesus, the geological substratum of universal structure deals with humankind.

Roland Barthes addressed the account of Jacob's struggle with the angel (Gen. 32.22–32). He emphasizes the element of ambiguity and paradox in the Genesis account, and shows how imagining a countertext can illuminate the narrative. He also uses the actantial model of Greimas: Barthes takes this narrative to be typical of a common Russian folk-narrative in which a hostile spirit guards a difficult passage over a ford.

Jean Calloud applied the methodology of Greimas to Matthew 4.1–11. First, a syntactic or narrative analysis is given of the lexies of the text, as well as its functional and actantial schemes. Jesus is the Receiver of a mandate given by the Spirit. The devil as Sender then sends tests to

Jesus. The Word as Helper gives assistance to Jesus. In the glorifying test Jesus proves to be the Hero. The consequent semantic analysis deals with the paradigmatic aspect of the text. The functioning of the semantic contents, skillfully woven around the two main actors Jesus and Satan, is then interrelated with the analysis of the narrative structure.

Robert C. Culley is more interested in the "syntagmatic" narrative structures, the linear and rhetorical tradition, the repetition of patterns in seven miracle stories from the Hebrew Bible. Jean Starobinski's analysis of Mark 5.1–20 is also an example of a purely synchronous reading of the text from a literary point of view. He demonstrates the oppositions in the text between the unchanging singularity of Jesus and the pluralization of the demoniac.

The approach of Erhardt Güttgemanns is called generative poetics or linguistic theology. He sees a particular text as the result of grammatical rather than historical forces. Generative poetics is a deductive method, which aims to free theology from its traditional confinement by means of a scientific and interdisciplinary approach. The narrative analysis is interested not in the performance text but in the deep text, the underlying semantic content of the narrative. This is arrived at by way of two separate analyses, a motifemic and an actantial analysis.

Daniel Patte, applying the methodology of Lévi-Strauss to biblical texts, aims to study the symbolic and connotative dimension of language, which should be distinguished from the informational dimension of language. By describing the system of convictions and symbolic values of the authors of biblical texts, structural exegesis aims to open up hermeneutic possibilities.

In his analysis of Galatians 1.1–10, Patte shows that mythical structures can be discovered in nonmythical texts. In Galatia there is a conflict between two mythical structures—the gospel of Paul and the antigospel of his opponents. By a syntagmatic reading, the text is tentatively deconstructed into elements of a mythical system. By a subsequent paradigmatic reading, the structure that governs these mythical elements is discerned: through the mediating of the oppositions of this mythical structure, it becomes clear that Christ is the mediation of the fundamental opposition between the divine and the human.

In his structural introduction to the letter, Patte deals with Paul's faith as a system of convictions. Faith and theology are to be distinguished in the light of semiotic and structural research. In order to describe Paul's faith, attention is given to the convictional pattern that underlies and validates his arguments, as well as to the motivating factors presupposed.

Discourse Analysis. Besides analyzing the universal "deep" structures of a text (as described above), more attention should be given to the "surface" structure, and to the function of a text's stylistic, organizational, and rhetorical features. This implies an awareness of the importance of different discourse patterns in the text as a whole. The text must therefore be mapped in a way that will allow us to discern the syntactic, semantic, and pragmatic relationships of the various constituent parts. This approach includes attention to the inter- and extratextual dimensions of the text.

Building on the metatheory of structural semiotics of Greimas, Patte has recently proposed a six-step method incorporating the main features of different structural exegetical methods. Through a multiplicity of underlying structures, the reader is guided to a close reading of the surface structure of the text. In this way, the specific features of a discourse unit as well as the basic convictions of the author are conveyed.

Evaluation. On the negative side, one can point to the lack of unity and clarity among proponents, their neologisms, and the methodological complexity. Although the universal dimensions and internal relations of a text are emphasized, the more specific forms of a given culture or of the biblical text are often played down. The message becomes only a quotation of the underlying code, and specific saving acts of God are reduced to general truths. The methodology of Propp, devised for the description of Russian folktales, cannot simply be applied to the Bible, for the folktales do not have universal validity. Lévi-Strauss himself had reservations about applying his approach to the Bible. Without detracting anything from the grammaticality and literality of the text, the specific context of the Bible should also be taken into account.

On the positive side, structuralism can be an aid to biblical exegesis and *hermeneutics within the context of semiotics. A text and its structural analysis collectively form a sign-system. Codes should not be deemed more important than the message itself; therefore adequate emphasis should be given to the surface structure of the text. Attention to deep structures underlines the depth of meaning and the coherence of different books. The synchronic approach serves as a corrective to the one-sided emphasis of the genetic (diachronic) paradigm. The integrity of the text as object is emphasized.

The critic/reader acquires a new role in the process of reading the text. Structuralism and *hermeneutics can be complementary when the text is seen again as message, *parole*. While structuralism reveals the multiplicity of readings, it also controls them by means of a structural analysis of the text. Hermeneutics limits the possibilities by confronting the vertical aspect of meaning (diachronic) with the synchronic coexistence of meanings.

See also Interpretation, History of, *article on Modern Biblical Criticism.*

H. J. Bernard Combrink

Suffering. Like prosperity, suffering introduces a test into human lives, both disclosing and forming character. For religious people, suffering comes as a special trial, particularly its unjust distribution. Belief in the goodness and power of God implies a just distribution of misery. When good persons experience undeserved suffering, it becomes difficult to maintain the conviction that God controls a universe that operates on a principle of reward and retribution. One biblical response to this dilemma was daring: chosen individuals voluntarily take upon themselves the suffering of the guilty. Less bold, but also significant, is the view that suffering offers an opportunity to learn something worthwhile, especially patience (James 1.2–4).

The world of suffering is special, causing everyone to think that the experience of pain is unique and consequently focusing the ego inward, which heightens self-centeredness. Suffering takes place in solitude, isolating one from the community and generating a sense of alienation. At the same time, suffering strives toward the building of community, for its power extends from the greatest to the least. Genuine sympathy is possible precisely because others have felt pain and isolation. Hence the language of suffering is readily comprehended by all who are searching for meaning in a hostile world.

In ancient literature suffering was often expressed in lyrical poetry. Emotion-laden speech tends to exaggerate, but even such hyperbole fails to evoke the full range of feelings in suffering. Personal pronouns abound in laments, focusing remembered joy and present pain, individualizing both in a powerful manner. Simile and *metaphor call attention to language's poverty in describing the misery resulting from invasion from outside by hostile forces.

Drawing on ancient insights from Mesopotamia to some degree, biblical attempts to explain suffering throw considerable light on the problem, although failing to clarify the mystery altogether. An early explanation seized the partial truth (well articulated much later by Paul in Rom. 7.15) that most individuals do evil even when willing good, and hence suffering is in a very real sense punishment for sin. The book of *Proverbs regularly insists on this retributive understanding of *evil, and the same view is shared by the *Deuteronomic history and by Israel's *prophets. When reportedly offered an opportunity to endorse this view of suffering, *Jesus refused to do so (John 9.3). Job's friends appealed to parental discipline of children, assuming by analogy that God punishes those who enjoy divine favor. The profound story about the divine test of Abraham (Gen. 22.1–18; *see* Aqedah) and the prologue to the book of *Job suggest that adversity may indicate a divine test to which God's "favorites" are submitted.

Confidence in God's integrity and character resulted in an *eschatological hope that deliverance would come in the end, setting all things right. *Apocalyptic literature found this view compatible because of the extreme suffering of the periods in which it arose. Injustice could elicit the daring hope in survival beyond earthly existence (Dan. 12.2; *see* Afterlife and Immortality). In some circles suffering was seen as redemptive, both for self and for others. Doxologies of judgment dared to praise God in the face of execution (Josh. 7.19), and the "servant poems" in Second *Isaiah (especially Isa. 53) envisioned the death of their leader as vicarious, a view that Christians shared in reflecting on Jesus' passion.

In some instances biblical writers thought of suffering as transitory, resulting from an illusion that resembles a dream, while others believed that God's revelatory presence in suffering compensated adequately for any amount of misery (Ps. 73). The astonishing conclusion to the dialogue in the book of Job acknowledges a seeing of God that corrects hearsay information and leaves the sufferer speechless but content (42.5–6). At the same time, the poet admits that an adequate answer to Job's suffering cannot be offered, and hence the mystery remains. A wholly different response occurs in *Ecclesiastes, in which the author accuses the distant, divine despot of indifference to the human suffering that distresses him, a mere human being (4.1).

Both Judaism and Christianity find the problem of suffering especially acute because of their elevated view of God as ethical, that is, their belief in theodicy. These religions further suggest that suffering is not merely a human phenomenon, for God also suffers because of rebellion on the part of men and women. The prophets emphasized divine pathos, and Christianity adopted this understanding of God. The suffering of Christ manifests the divine response to evil, culminating in victorious *resurrection. Christians are called on to enter into the suffering of Christ for the sake of the Kingdom.

Suffering, therefore, is rooted in divine mystery, and at the same time it is profoundly human. God's redemption of the world employs suffering in its numerous forms to enable persons to recognize their own humanity and to acknowledge their true selves. As a result of this divine pedagogy, suffering offers potential for enriching faith and life itself. Nevertheless, some suffering, by its very intensity, lacks this positive dimension, introducing destructive powers that ultimately triumph over its victim. In the face of this kind of suffering, believers find their faith tested to the limit. Neither Judaism nor Christianity has denied the existence of such suffering, nor did they trivialize it by offering simple answers. Instead, moving beyond tragedy, they insisted that evil is under the dominion of God.   JAMES L. CRENSHAW

Sumer (Map 6:J4). Shumer (conventionally: Sumer) is the name given to the lower Mesopotamian plain by its Akkadian neighbors; in its own Sumerian language, the land was called Kengir. It occupied the area between the city of Nippur in the northwest and the shoreline of the Persian (or Arabian) Gulf in the southeast; upstream from Nippur lay the land of Akkad. Together, Sumer and Akkad occupied all the land between the rivers *Euphrates and Tigris below their nearest convergence around modern Baghdad. In this relatively constricted area (the later *Babylonia), there arose not only the world's first civilization but also one of its great ancient cultures, destined to influence all Near Eastern cultures, including Israel, and to bequeath a lasting legacy to civilization as a whole.

The origin of the Sumerians is uncertain. They themselves looked to Dilmun, that is, the islands

and Arabian shore of the Persian Gulf, as a kind a paradise, and may have originated from there, or even further east. They regarded Eridu, then on the northern edge of the Gulf, as their first city, and perhaps this was indeed their first foothold in Mesopotamia. Traces of this tradition survive in Genesis 4.17b, which may be understood thus: "And he [Enoch] became the [first] builder of a city, and he named it after his son [i.e., Irad], did Enoch."

The basic ingredients of civilization as it emerged in Sumer at the end of the fourth millennium BCE included cities, *writing, and the formation of capital. Building on the earlier agricultural revolution and its domestication of plants and animals (symbolized in the biblical account by *Cain and Abel respectively; cf. Gen. 4.2), the urban revolution in Sumer soon brought in its train such secondary developments as craft specialization, metallurgy, and the emergence of *kingship. A rich documentation in cuneiform preserves the records of these achievements as well as the Sumerians' own interpretation of them in literary texts. Long after Sumerian itself had ceased to be spoken, these literary texts continued to be studied and translated in the scribal schools of Babylonia and the rest of the Near East. Some of them are thus echoed in the Bible, whose primeval history (Gen. 1–11) is situated in Sumer.

The centerpiece of Sumerian historiography is the "Sumerian King List," perhaps better described as a Sumerian city list, which records the eleven cities that exercised hegemony over all of Sumer and Akkad, together with the names of their kings, their length of rule, and occasional biographical notes. It begins in legendary times, when kingship "descended from heaven," and ends with the destruction of the city of Isin in 1794 BCE, one year before the accession of King *Hammurapi of Babylon. Its antediluvian rulers, in most recensions eight in number, and the wise counselors associated with them (in other sources), bear an undeniable resemblance to the lines of Seth and Cain in Genesis 5 and 4 respectively.

The Sumerian story of the *flood is preserved in a single fragmentary tablet that, via various Akkadian intermediaries, no doubt helped shape the biblical version in Genesis 6–8. After the flood, kingship was believed to have come down from heaven again, first to the city of Kish and then to Uruk, the Erech of the "table of nations" (Gen. 10.10). Its fourth ruler, Dumuzi, is celebrated in poems about his sacred marriage with the goddess Inanna, and passed into Akkadian—and Hebrew (cf. Ezek. 8.14)—as the deified *Tammuz. The epic of "Enmerkar and the lord of Aratta" includes a passage reminiscent of the biblical tale of the confusion of tongues that, in Genesis 11, is linked to the building of "a city and a tower" clearly modeled on the *ziggurat (stepped temple tower) characteristic of Sumerian cities (see Tower of Babel). The end of the "Early Dynastic Period" in Sumer (ca. 2900–2300 BCE) is marked by the conflict of two other city-states (Lagash and Umma) over the *edin*, a fertile area lying between them that may have inspired the biblical tale of the garden of *Eden (Gen. 2–3).

There followed an interval of subjugation to the Semitic-speaking Akkadians (ca. 2300–2150 BCE), so named after the city of Akkad whose greatest rulers, Sargon and especially his grandson Naram-Sin, may conceivably have provided the model for Nimrod and Akkad in Genesis 10.8–12. Then the Sumerians reasserted themselves under local rulers such as Gudea of Lagash, who left a magnificent legacy of both literary and sculptural remains, and under the hegemony of *Ur, which reunited all of Sumer and Akkad for a century (ca. 2100–2000 BCE) under the city recalled in the Bible as the birthplace of *Abraham (Gen. 11.28, 31; etc.).

After the fall of Ur (ca. 2000 BCE), Sumerian traditions were preserved intact by the dynasty of Isin (ca. 2000–1800 BCE) and thereafter by the schools and temples of Babylonia and *Assyria. Among the Sumerian innovations thus passed on to later ages are the sexagesimal system of counting and computation (using the base 60), irrigation agriculture, and a variety of literary genres.

The Akkadian language, and the civilization of the Babylonians and Assyrians who inherited and preserved Sumerian culture, transmitted the Sumerian legacy, or portions of it, to posterity. Among the heirs of this legacy was biblical Israel. While the name of Sumer itself is no longer thought to lurk behind the biblical Shinar (Gen. 10.10; etc.), other Hebrew words and names can be traced to Sumerian, such as *hêkāl* ("palace, temple"), *ṭipsār* ("scribe"), *mallāḥ* ("sailor"), and numerous names of spices, plants, minerals, and other commodities whose names traveled with the products they identified. Many ideas too can be traced from their biblical formulation back to Sumerian origins, for example the casuistic (conditional) formulation of precedent *law. When the Bible placed the origins of (civilized) humankind, and of Israelite prehistory, in the lower valley of the Tigris and Euphrates, it was anticipating the modern rediscovery of the Sumerians and their formative contributions to civilization.   WILLIAM W. HALLO

Susanna. A devout and beautiful Jewish woman, whose name means "lily." She was falsely accused of adultery, but saved from sentence of death by the young Daniel, who presented in court an unorthodox but clever defense; and she is the heroine of the small book of the Apocrypha that goes by her name. (*See* Apocrypha, *article on* Jewish Apocrypha.)

In Theodotion's edition of the Greek and in several ancient versions based upon it, Susanna appears as a prefix to chap. 1 of the book of *Daniel, but in the older Greek *Septuagint and the Latin *Vulgate it is placed in an appendix after chap. 12 along with the story of *Bel and the Dragon. It seems almost certain that it was originally an independent work, since neither the style and setting of the story nor the character of Daniel, its hero, seem to harmonize with the rest of the book. Other independent stories about Daniel were current in antiquity, as is evidenced by the discovery of fragments of Daniel legends among the *Dead Sea Scrolls.

The story is interesting and well told. Susanna, the wife of Joakim, a wealthy and highly respected Jew who lived in Babylonia during the *exile, used to walk every afternoon in the garden of her house, and attracted the lecherous interest of two elders of the community who had been appointed judges and were frequent visitors to Joakim's home. Separately bent on seducing her, they met by chance in the hiding place where each had her under observation, and concocted a plot against her virtue. One day when she was bathing in the garden and the doors to the house had been shut by her two maids, the elders rushed out of their place of concealment and demanded that she lie with them; otherwise they would publicly accuse her of committing adultery with a young man, and would declare that they had witnessed the act. Susanna, true to her principles, refused their request and said she was willing to accept the consequences. When the inevitable trial began, they carried out their threat and, as a result, she was condemned to die. But at the critical moment God inspired the youthful Daniel to protest against the sentence and to undertake to cross-examine the two elders separately. In an anticipation of the technique of the classic detective story, he caught them in a clear contradiction about the kind of tree under which the alleged crime was committed, with the result that Susanna was acquitted and the accusers suffered the fate they had intended for her (cf. the similar ironic reversal in *Esther).

The tale is commonly accepted as fiction, but there has been no general agreement on its purpose. Some scholars have thought the story a kind of midrash dealing with the fate of the two false prophets, Ahab and Zedekiah, who were the objects of a curse by Jeremiah, and were accused by him, incidentally, of adulterous conduct (Jer. 29.21–23). Others regard it as a partisan polemic calling for an improvement in the commonly accepted procedures of the rabbinic courts. The prevailing view, however, sees it as simply a popular tale, probably secular, and perhaps even non-Jewish in origin, which has been provided with edifying religious motifs and adapted for Jewish readers. Some scholars who assert that specific elements in the story have been taken from traditional folklore, notably the theme of the "wise child"—the youth who displays more insight than his elders and is able to correct some flagrant injustice—but the evidence is vague and indecisive.

Until comparatively recent times, it was the common view that the original language was Greek; this seems especially persuasive because of the puns on the names of the two trees in vv. 54–55 and 58–59 (see text notes b and c in NRSV), which make sense only in Greek. Recently, however, the book has increasingly been thought a translation from an original Semitic text, probably Hebrew but possibly Aramaic, though there is no supporting external evidence. The book does, however, contain a number of apparent Hebraisms, and the social ambience suggests a Palestinian origin. The puns could have been introduced by the Greek translator. The date could be as early as the Persian period and certainly no later than ca. 100 BCE, when the Septuagint translation was completed. The story of Susanna was a popular subject of later Christian art and literature, and poetic versions of the tale are known in several European languages.

For other additions to Daniel, see Azariah, The Prayer of and Bel and the Dragon.

ROBERT C. DENTAN

Symbols. A symbol entails the use of a specific entity to represent or parallel an idea, concept, or reality. Usually there is some likeness between the object used as a symbol and its intended parallel. Symbols in the Bible are drawn from everyday life or from a specific cultural setting and are especially frequent in *apocalyptic literature.

Symbols drawn from everyday life are easily illustrated. A person who observes the *Law and with whom God is pleased can be described as a tree or garden that grows and blossoms. The struggle against evil can be viewed as warfare (Wisd. of Sol. 5.17–20; Eph. 6.11–17; 1 Tim. 6.12; 2 Tim. 4.7; Rev. 12.17). Fire is used in various ways, most significantly perhaps in *theophany narratives, in which God's presence is symbolized by fire (e.g., Exod. 3.1–6; 19.16–19; 1 Kings 18.38; Acts 2.1–4; see Metaphors).

In Judaism and Christianity certain symbols are drawn from their historical and cultural backgrounds. Thus, *circumcision is the sign of entrance into the community for Jews, as *baptism is for Christians. The seven-branched lampstand or *menorah used in the Temple can symbolize the Jewish community, while the cross can stand for the Christian community.

Finally, symbols are used extensively in apocalyptic literature. Animals and fantastic beasts can represent other nations; *numbers and colors have symbolic importance.

Ancient writers assumed that their audience would correctly interpet a symbol by making the necessary comparison. Later interpreters, however, can read too much (or too little) into a symbol, applying to it an anachronistically modern understanding. Thus, knowledge of the actual setting and of the literary genres used by ancient writers is necessary for interpretation of the Bible's many and marvelous symbols.

See also Number Symbolism.

JAMES M. EFIRD

Synagogue. The emergence of the synagogue constituted a revolutionary development in the history of Judaism. The synagogue represented not only a wholly new concept of religious observance but also a new form of communal institution. With the synagogue the nature of official worship shifted dramatically, with *prayer, study, and exhortation replacing sacrifice as the way to serve God. Officiating on behalf of the community was no longer confined to a small coterie of *priests but was open to all. Ceremonies were conducted in full view of the participants, with the masses of people no longer being relegated to outer courtyards, as was the case in the Jerusalem *Temple. Moreover, the synagogue was a universal institution and not confined to any one specific locale.

Despite its importance in Jewish history, the origins of the synagogue and its early development are shrouded in mystery. Only during and after the first century CE does literary and archaeological evidence appear for Palestine. As for the Roman Diaspora, references before then are practically nonexistent (and what does exist refers to the Diaspora). Synagogue inscriptions from third- and second-century BCE Egypt have been preserved, as have remains of a Delos synagogue building dating from the first century BCE.

Owing to the paucity of sources, opinions have varied widely as to when, where, and why the synagogue developed. Theories have ranged from the late First Temple period (eighth-seventh century BCE), through the exilic (sixth century) and postexilic (fifth century) eras, and down to the late Persian (fourth century) and Hellenistic times (third or second century). Most scholars have assumed a midway position, one that posits the emergence of the synagogue closely following the destruction of the First Temple in 587/586 BCE, either during the Babylonian *exile or soon after, when the Jews returned to Judea during the era of restoration.

Over the centuries the synagogue became a fully developed communal institution and apparently the central one in most communities. It served as a place for study, sacred meals, court proceedings, depositing communal funds, and political and social meetings, as a hostel, and as a residence for certain synagogue officials. Of central importance, of course, were the religious services. At first these consisted primarily of the Torah-reading ceremony and its accompanying activities: translation of the *Torah into the vernacular, be it Aramaic (Targums) or Greek (see Translations, articles on Ancient Languages and Targums), the haftarah or a selected reading from the prophets, and a sermon. The sources from the Second Temple period—*Josephus, *Philo, rabbinic writings, and the Theodotus inscription—point to this centrality. The existence of regular communal prayers at this time is unclear. While prayer appears to have been an integral part of the religious service in the Diaspora, its presence in Palestinian synagogue settings before 70 CE is unattested. Only after this date are we on firm ground in assuming the importance and centrality of public prayer in all synagogue settings.

These two components of the religious service—Torah reading and prayer—were characterized in antiquity by their fluidity no less than their uniformity. While Torah reading was accepted as normative on *Sabbaths and holidays and later on Mondays and Thursdays as well, the division into weekly portions varied considerably. In Palestine the Torah was read over a three- or three-and-a-half-year period with a plethora of local traditions on the precise divisions of the weekly portions (141, 154, 161, 167, and 175). Moreover, the practice in Babylonian communities living in late Roman and Byzantine Palestine only added to this diversity: They concluded the Torah reading in one year. How widespread the custom was of translating the Torah portion into the vernacular is unknown, but the use of Greek in addition to Aramaic cannot be denied. The place of the sermon in the synagogue service was likewise diverse. The content, of course, might have varied considerably from one of an expository nature to one of ethical, political, halakhic, or even eschatological dimensions. When sermons were delivered on the Sabbath (Friday evening, Saturday morning, or Saturday afternoon), or when during the service (before or after the Torah reading), might differ widely from one congregation to another.

The diversity is found also with regard to prayer. Undoubtedly by the post-70 era the two main foci of the prayer service had crystallized. The *Shema prayer (Deut. 6.4–9) with its accompanying paragraphs (Deut. 11.13–21; Num. 15.37–41) had been adopted from Temple practice and was now supplemented by three blessings, each focusing on a central theme, respectively—*creation, *revelation, and *redemption. Together this unit provided the central ideational portion of the prayer experience and was recited in the synagogue twice daily, during the morning and evening services. The second focus of the prayer service was the Shemoneh Esreh (literally, "eighteen" blessings, although a nineteenth was added some time in late antiquity) or the Amidah (standing prayer). When precisely this prayer came into usage is unknown, but by the second century CE it held a central position. Recited three times daily, no special prayer service, be it on the Sabbath, Holiday, or High Holiday, was complete without it. The Amidah consisted of three parts: the first three benedictions were in praise of God, the last three were expressions of thanks, while the middle section changed each day. On a weekday, twelve (later thirteen) petionary blessings were recited; on Sabbaths and holidays this section expressed the unique message of that particular day. During the early centuries CE prayers were added to the morning service, such as prayers of supplication, morning blessings, psalms of praise, and others.

During the Byzantine period, the recitation of liturgical poems—*pîyyûṭîm*—was added to the service, particularly those for the Sabbath and holidays. When and from where the *pîyyûṭ* developed has been a subject of scholarly debate. Some claim it evolved from earlier midrashim, prayers, or songs recited in the Temple and synagogue, others see it as the adoption and adaptation of liturgical poems recited in Byzantine churches, and still others as a protest against organized, fixed prayers. Whatever the explanation, the *pîyyûṭ* made its appearance in fourth- and fifth-century Palestine, and today we know of at least twenty poets who functioned in the pre-Muslim era. These *pîyyûṭîm* were recited during the morning service, either in addition to or in place of the fixed liturgy.

Archaeological remains of the ancient synagogue abound. In Palestine alone traces of over a hundred structures have been identified, and in the Diaspora some fifteen. The latter stretch from Dura Europos on the Euphrates River in the east, to Tunisia on the North African coast in the west. The overwhelming majority of synagogue remains in Palestine are located in the *Galilee and Golan regions; others are to be found in Beth–shean, coastal areas, and Judea. Architecturally, these synagogues can be divided into three types. The Galilean type, characterized by a monumental and richly decorated facade, was oriented towards Jerusalem, often with three entrances. Fine ashlar masonry of either limestone or basalt was characteristic of these buildings, and their rectangular interiors were simple, with two or three colonnades dividing the hall into a central nave with two or three aisles. Entablatures, pilasters, and friezes typical of Roman art of late antiquity decorated the buildings, along with molded stucco and painted plaster. With but few exceptions, no permanent shrines for the Torah scrolls have been found.

The second type of synagogue modelled itself after the basilical plan used extensively in Byzantine churches, and was modest on the exterior, reserving its splendor for the interior. In contrast to the Galilean type with its splendid entrance on the facade facing Jerusalem, the entrance in the basilica type shifted to the wall opposite the direction of prayer. A round or square apse was set in the wall facing Jerusalem in which the Torah ark rested on a raised platform (*bîmâ*). Only two rows of columns lined the elongated character of the prayer hall. Most notable in the basilica type of synagogue was its richly decorated mosaic floor, often in clear imitation of regnant Byzantine patterns and not infrequently with unique Jewish symbols, such as a *menorah, Torah ark, lulav, ethrog, and shofar. Such symbols were practically nonexistent in buildings of the Galilean type. Finally, a third type of building which appears in but a few locales of Palestine and the Diaspora is the broadhouse synagogue. The uniqueness of these buildings is that their focus of worship, either an apse, *bîmâ*, or shrine—which is located along the long wall of the synagogue. These buildings share features common to the other types in most other respects.

Aside from the Jewish symbols mentioned above, Jewish figural art is represented in only a few synagogues: the *Aqedah (Genesis 22) at Beth Alpha, *Noah at Gerasa, *David at Gaza, and *Daniel at Naʿaran and Susiya. Of an entirely different order is the third-century CE synagogue of Dura Europos, whose walls are covered from floor to ceiling with decorated panels. These panels depict scenes from the Bible, using Greek and Persian artistic motifs and incorporating a significant amount of *midrash* (rabbinic or otherwise) in their interpretations and representations. One of the most striking examples of synagogue art, at Hammath Tiberias and elsewhere, represents Helios, the zodiac signs, and the four seasons. Interpretations of these motifs vary considerably. The first reaction was to interpret them as the gift of the emperor or as an expression of some fringe group in Judaism. With the discovery, however, of such pavements all over Israel, it became clear that this was a popular and accepted form of artistic expression. Among the interpretations proposed of the zodiac motif are: it was simply a decorative motif; it reflects the importance of the Jewish calendar; it represents the power of God in creating the world each day; it stands for the Divine himself; it reflects belief in *angels, especially Helios, who was well known within certain Jewish circles of the period. Of these several explanations, none has won general acceptance. (*See also* Art and the Bible.)

Owing to the centrality of the synagogue as

the primary Jewish communal institution and to the extensive remains that have survived, the study of this institution is of paramount importance for those wishing to gain as complete a picture of ancient Judaism as possible. Patterns of Jewish settlements, the diversity of religious practices, the influence of surrounding cultures, Jewish artistic expression, Jewish prosography, titles and professions among synagogue donors are areas well attested in synagogue remains.

See also Lectionaries, *article on* Jewish Tradition.   LEE LEVINE

Synoptic Problem.

Synoptic Problem. The synoptic Gospels are those of *Matthew, *Mark, and *Luke. They are called "synoptic" ("seen together") because of their close similarities, which enable the texts to be set out in parallel for comparison. It is generally agreed that there is a literary relationship among them, but the phenomena are complex and judgments on them are conflicting. Dominant in modern critical scholarship is the Two Document Hypothesis (TDH), namely, that Mark was the first gospel and was one of two sources used by both Matthew and Luke, the other being "Q" (German *Quelle*, "source"). But the TDH has not shaken off challenges from the older view that the earliest gospel was that of Matthew.

All four Gospels reflect a common tradition about *Jesus. But *John is sharply distinguished—in style and wording, structure, and especially theological emphasis. It may show knowledge of the synoptics; but the "Johannine problem" is a separate one. This article will summarize the synoptic phenomena, the leading hypotheses, and the main arguments. For a detailed study, readers should use one of the various synopses or harmonies that print the texts in parallel columns and highlight the verbal similarities by positioning the words skillfully or using distinctive type or colors. They are available in Greek and in translation; some include John as well as the synoptics. Details of content and order can be checked by reference to their analytic index.

The Phenomena. It is convenient to take the shortest gospel (Mark) as the norm, and use words like "agree" and "omit" when making comparisons, but the question of relative priority must not be prejudged thereby.

Content. It has been calculated that of Mark's 661 verses all except 31 (six sections or pericopes) are paralleled—over 600 in Matthew and

at least 350 in Luke. There are some 200 verses common to Matthew and Luke, but absent from Mark. These are commonly labelled "Q material," but some scholars restrict the symbol "Q" to the hypothetical source. "M" and "L" are used to denote material peculiar (or special) to Matthew and Luke.

Structure and order. Mark's structure is simple: *John the Baptist, Jesus' baptism and *temptation, his Galilean ministry, the journey to Judea, and the climax in *Jerusalem, culminating with the narrative of the passion and the discovery of the empty tomb.

Matthew and Luke share this framework, with some differences. Both preface their works with infancy narratives (but these are strikingly different) and conclude with appearances of the risen Christ (again, very different). Both have much non-Marcan material. Matthew inserts most of his Q and M material in five blocks of discourse at appropriate points, the most notable being the *Sermon on the Mount (Matt. 5–7). Luke omits Mark 6.45–8.26 (his "great omission") and concentrates Q and L material into two sections (6.20–8.3; 9.51–18.14), dubbed his "lesser" and "greater interpolations." The latter begins at the point where Jesus sets out for Judea (Luke's route is different), and is called his "travel narrative."

Luke scarcely deviates from Mark's order in his closer parallels, though he makes omissions. But he has a number of remote parallels, remote both in context and in substance (4.16–30; 5.1–11; 11.17–23; 13.18–19; 22.24–30); this group plays a significant part in synoptic criticism. Luke's passion narrative raises special problems: much of it resembles Mark, much differs strikingly.

Matthew follows Mark's order from Mark 6.14 onward, but his earlier chapters contain an almost unbroken sequence of miracle stories (8.1–9.34), some of which occur elsewhere in Mark.

Mark's order is always supported by at least one of the others; that is, Matthew and Luke never agree against Mark with respect to the order of the pericopes. To this there are only tiny exceptions.

The order of the Q material is harder to define; much of it comes in different places in Matthew and Luke. Nevertheless, of 23 pericopes some 13 come in the same relative order. For the first two of these (John's preaching and Jesus' temptations), the Marcan framework supplies a fixed place. But after that, Matthew and Luke never again coincide in choosing the same

Marcan context for the same piece of Q material. Any Q order is thus distinguishable from the Marcan order.

Wording. Select list of representative passages:

MATTHEW	MARK	LUKE
I. ——	1.23–26	4.33–35
9.6	2.10	5.24
16.24–28	8.34–9.1	9.23–27
21.12–13	11.15–17	19.45–46
II. 17.1–8	9.2–8	9.28–36
28.1–8	16.1–8	24.1–9
III. 16.13–15	8.27–29	9.18–20
22.23	12.8	20.27
IV. 11.2–22	——	7.18–35;10.13–
		15, 21–22
V. 10.34–36	——	12.51–53
22.2–14	——	14.6–24

Verbal similarity varies greatly: from near identity in groups I and IV to a low degree in II and V. It is in group IV, that is, non-Marcan passages, that the highest degree of sustained identity occurs. We have, then, the paradox (aptly named "the Marcan cross-factor") that, whereas the presence of a passage in Mark makes agreement in order more likely, identity of wording is most striking in some Q passages, that is, passages absent from Mark.

In Marcan passages, wording tends to follow the same pattern as order: it is exceptional to find Matthew and Luke in agreement against Mark. But there are exceptions, dubbed "the minor agreements," a label that must not be allowed to disguise their importance and extent. Very different are Luke's remote parallels; they provide the major agreements with Matthew, which heavily outweigh Luke's agreement with Mark.

The examples in groups I and IV put it beyond reasonable doubt that the Gospels have some close literary connection, and those in III put it beyond any doubt whatever that the connection is in Greek, since the identity extends to the Greek syntax and sentence structure. Only here does Mark use the accusative and infinitive construction for indirect statement—a construction used in these passages by all three Gospels. Notice especially that Mark 8.28 and Luke 9.19 both switch to the alternative construction, with the conjunction "that" at precisely the same point.

Leading Hypotheses. Independent knowledge of a common tradition and independent translation from Hebrew or Aramaic originals have doubtless contributed to the synoptic Gos-

pels. But neither will suffice as a hypothesis to account for the close similarities. Equally inadequate is the hypothesis supported at one time that all the synoptics draw on a single basic gospel; this fails to account for the Marcan cross-factor.

Leaving aside more complicated reconstructions, we may pick out three hypotheses that have had wide support and do justice to many of the phenomena. For the first two the earliest gospel is Matthew, for the third it is Mark.

The hypothesis of Augustine (AH) put the gospels in their canonical order; Mark is an abbreviation of Matthew, and Luke writes with knowledge of both. AH has had backing from ecclesiastical authority; in modern times it has been powerfully advocated by, for example, B. C. Butler and, more recently, by John Wenham. A modified form of it assigns priority to an Aramaic Matthew, used by Mark, but allows that Mark influenced our Greek Matthew. The arguments about relative priority are summarized below. But even if the direct arguments for Marcan priority are dismissed, AH has difficulty with the Marcan cross-factor.

The hypothesis of J. J. Griesbach (1789) (GH) was accepted in the nineteenth century and revived in modern times by William R. Farmer, Bernard Orchard, and others: the order is Matthew, Luke, Mark; Mark, the latest, utilizes both Matthew and Luke, sometimes preferring one and sometimes the other. Arguments for and against GH are summarized below.

The Two-Document hypothesis (TDH), widely accepted by modern scholars, holds that the two documents, namely Mark and Q, were utilized independently by Matthew and Luke. B. H. Streeter gave classical expression to it in English (1924), along with some refinements, especially that L and Q had already been combined in Proto-Luke before the Marcan material was added; a full discussion would require detailed examination of the passion narratives. Other variants of TDH are that one document was an earlier edition of Mark ("Ur-Markus") and that the Q material comes from more than one document.

Leading Arguments. The only second-century statements about the Gospels early enough to have any weight are the traditions transmitted through Papias (Eusebius, *Hist. Eccl.* 3.39): that Matthew "composed the oracles in Hebrew," and that Mark reproduced the firsthand testimony of Peter. This evidence is obscure (what are "the oracles"?—one speculation among many is that the original reference might be to Q) and also ambivalent. Argument must therefore rest on the internal evidence of the Gospels.

The main arguments for Marcan priority. The priority of Mark, advocated since the eighteenth century, came to be hailed as the one assured result of criticism. That claim was excessive, but though challenged it has retained majority support.

Content. Mark is the shortest gospel, and omits much striking teaching; if the author had been drawing on Matthew and Luke, would he have omitted Matthew's Sermon (chaps. 5–7), and Luke's most famous parables?

Vividness. Mark is rich in circumstantial detail, and has a vividness compatible with eyewitness testimony (e.g., 2.2–4; 4.35–8). Matthew is less vivid; although his accounts sometimes include extra points of substance, these often look like insertions of alien material (e.g., 15.12–14; 16.17–19).

Wording. When variations in language are examined, it is usually easy to suggest why Matthew or Luke might want to alter Mark: to improve the Greek, to eliminate criticism of disciples (Mark 10.35) or apparent disrespect toward Jesus (4.38; 10.18), to simplify or clarify (8.21; 9.12–13). Sometimes a distortion or improbability is introduced (Matthew 9.18; Luke 8.51); and sometimes—a weighty argument—Matthew retains a Marcan phrase incompatible with a change he has made, and thus betrays knowledge of Mark (Matt. 14.9; cf. 14.5).

General character. These arguments have considerable force, for example, from Christology, Matthew's apologetic and ecclesiastical interests, and Luke's literary quality. But not every passage points the same way; discussion would be lengthy and inconclusive.

Order. These arguments are both controversial and important. Because Mark's order is always supported by at least one of the others, many have argued that Mark's priority is immediately proved. But that is not so: the same formal relationships could result if Mark were the middle or last of the three. But the argument gains weight when combined with the Marcan cross-factor: why should Luke (according to AH) sometimes follow Matthew's wording slavishly but not his order, and at other times his order but not his wording? Or why should Mark (according to GH) omit just those verses where Matthew and Luke are almost identical (see especially Matt. 12.27–28, 30)?

The case for Q. The simplest explanation of similarities in so-called Q material is direct use of Matthew by Luke, or vice versa. But to this there are two series of objections, and these ipso facto constitute arguments for the alternative explanation, a common source (or sources) used independently by both—in other words, the case for Q.

If Matthew is Luke's source, there seems to be no commonsense explanation for his order and procedure. True, it is possible to suggest interesting and subtle—perhaps overly subtle—reasons why he might rearrange material to bring out his distinctive themes. But the question remains, why should he do so for only part of the time, or adhere most closely to wording when he is showing least respect for order?

If Luke were Matthew's source, this difficulty would be less acute, for Matthew seems in any case to conflate and rearrange his material. Advocates of Lucan priority have been few, though, and space forbids further discussion. The second objection would still hold.

If one gospel were the source for the other, the older gospel would presumably be closer to the original wording, though arguments on relative originality are often disputed. Matthew's wording is often conceded to be the older; but there are a number of sayings where the verdict is commonly given in favor of Luke (e.g., 6.20; cf. Matt. 5.9)—and it must surely be Luke who gives the original setting for the parable of the lost sheep (15.2; cf. Matt. 18.10–14). Q accounts for these phenomena perfectly. True, it is hypothetical; but, in any case, Luke 1.1 is evidence that written documents now lost once existed.

It should be noted that acceptance of Q does not rule out the further possibility that one evangelist may have known, and made some use of, the other gospel.

Counterarguments. First, Matthew seems to have been the best-known gospel. Second, Matthew has a conspicuously Jewish and conservative character (see 5.17–20), in contrast with Mark's hints that the *Law is no longer binding (e.g., 7.19, 27). Third, Mark sometimes is clearly abbreviating a fuller version (e.g., 1.8, 12–13). This may be in Q; it undoubtedly is in Matthew.

Above all, there are the minor agreements of Matthew and Luke against Mark in passages where no appeal to Q can legitimately be made. Many can be explained away as obvious grammatical improvements, others as the result of textual corruptions. But some contain points of substance (not always in identical wording, e.g.,

Matt. 14.17; Luke 9.13), and these are too numerous to be lightly dismissed, especially if account is taken of negative agreements (i.e., agreements in omitting some Marcan words) and agreements in word order (see also below).

The Griesbach hypothesis. According to GH, the minor agreements of Matthew and Luke, and the more frequent agreements of Mark with one or the other, are easily explained as the result of Mark's editorial activity.

In some passages, Mark (e.g., 1.32) may be conflating Matthew and Luke; but there are none that demand this explanation.

The fact that either Matthew or Luke always supports Mark's order can be construed as a strong argument for GH, since according to TDH there should be a statistical expectation that both of them, if acting independently, would sometimes coincidentally make a change at the same point. The statistics that result from a study of some 32 pericopes in Mark 1.16–6.44 are striking, particularly if it is assumed, per TDH, that the changes made by Matthew and Luke were random. But that would be unwarranted: Matthew's changes of order are a single operation, and create his sequence of miracle stories. Furthermore, Matthew and Luke do occasionally coincide in making the same omission.

Against GH stand all the arguments given above for Marcan priority, including the strange procedure implied for Mark in, for example, 3.23–30. In addition, though, it faces extreme difficulty in supplying a credible reason why anyone, given Matthew and Luke, ever wrote Mark.

Concluding Comments. AH, GH, and TDH all meet the conditions that there must be a literary connection between the Greek texts, and that Mark has a position in the middle: chronologically (AH), or a pendant from Matthew and Luke (GH), or a peg from which both hang (TDH). Both AH and GH have difficulty in meeting the strong arguments for Marcan priority, which remain strong even if Q stands under question.

TDH is more satisfactory. Q is hypothetical and might be one source or many; though embarrassing, this is not a fatal objection. The chief difficulty comes from the minor agreements, only partially met by appeal to linguistic improvements and textual corrections. Some further explanation seems necessary, and can be only be speculative—an alternative parallel tradition, or even secondary knowledge and use of, say, Matthew by Luke. The once-popular "Ur-Markus"

theory unfortunately fails to account for the fact that Matthew's and Luke's changes are often improvements.

If none of this is acceptable, the remaining possibility is that a plurality of documents were used and combined in successive stages. Such theses are complicated and speculative, hard either to establish or to disprove. The synoptic "problem" therefore remains.   G. M. STYLER

Syria (Map 6:G4). Syria is a geographical area bounded by the *Euphrates River on the east, Palestine on the south, and the Mediterranean Sea on the west. It has been assumed that the name Syria derived from Tyre, which was the port of entry for Romans, Greeks, and others who explored or expanded eastward. Syria's major centers were *Damascus, *Antioch on the Orontes, and the region of the two rivers, the Tigris and the Euphrates.

In the Hebrew Bible, *David extends his kingdom up to Damascus in Syria (2 Sam. 8.6; 1 Chron. 18.6). Syria, generally called *Aram, is clearly a foreign country, but close enough to go in and out of, know quite a lot about, and seriously compete with, both religiously and economically. Syrian gods are criticized (Judg. 10.6; Isa. 7.1), and there are wars with numerous Syrian kings and cities.

The region was captured by *Tiglath-pileser III in the eighth century BCE, conquered by *Alexander the Great, and later became a center for the Seleucid dynasty that ultimately provoked the Maccabean revolt in Palestine in 165 BCE. Roman writers could frequently lump Palestine and Syria together without distinction under the name Coele-Syria. Pompey and leaders after him, including *Herod the Great, used Damascus as a center for military and bureaucratic expansion. It was from Damascus that Pompey launched his pacification of Palestine in 66 BCE in the wake of the Hasmonean civil war. Both cities were among the leading cultural, religious, and economic centers of the entire Roman empire.

Syria is rarely mentioned by name in the New Testament. On several occasions, Syria is referred to as proof that Jesus' fame is spreading (e.g., Matt. 4.24); in Acts, Syria is mentioned in the context of the spread of Christianity.

There were numerous and sizable Jewish communities in Syria. The Jews of Antioch are singled out by *Josephus as a vibrant community who were constantly attracting *gentiles to their religious ceremonies (*War* 7.3.43–45). In the fourth century CE, the sermons delivered by John Chrysostom against the Jews make it clear that the Jewish community in Antioch was still large, popular, and a threat to Christians like Chrysostom.

Similarly Syria and its larger cities became centers for early Christianity. The early second-century writer Ignatius of Antioch emerged as an important figure in the early church, as did Chrysostom, and many early Christian texts, including some of the Gospels, have been associated with Syria.

Syria in history and today remains an intriguing if enigmatic country and culture, which represents and joins city and village, east and west, Jew, Christian, and Muslim. It has played a pivotal role in the development and definition of Jewish and Christian belief and identity.

J. ANDREW OVERMAN

T

Tabernacle. The portable sanctuary constructed by *Moses at *Sinai and primarily associated with the people's wilderness wandering. Various expressions are used in referring to this sanctuary—"tent," "tent of meeting," "tabernacle," "tabernacle of the testimony [NRSV: covenant]." Conceived as a movable shrine, the tabernacle was constructed so that it could be assembled, dismantled, and reassembled as the people moved from one place to another.

The account of the construction of the tabernacle is found in the book of *Exodus: in chaps. 25–31, God provides instructions to Moses for its construction, and chaps. 35–40 report how these were carried out. Included in these texts are directions for the construction of the cultic furniture used in conjunction with the tabernacle. These include the *ark (25.10–22; 37.1–9), table of *showbread (25.23–30; 37.10–16), the lampstand or *menorah (25.31–40; 37.17–24), the altar of burnt offering (27.1–8; 38.1–7), the altar of *incense (30.1–10; 37.1–10), and the bronze basin (30.17–21; 38.8). In addition, directions are given for preparing priestly garments (28.1–43; 39.1–31), for ordaining *Aaron and his sons as *priests (29.1–46; see Lev. 8), for collecting the sanctuary tax (30.11–16), for mixing the anointing oil and incense (30.22–38; 37.29), and for other matters associated with the ritual of the tabernacle.

The tabernacle and its furnishings were made of materials and with labor contributed voluntarily by members of the community (25.2–7; 35.4–36.7) under the supervision of Bezalel of the tribe of Judah and Oholiab of the tribe of Dan (31.1–11; 35.30–36.1). The tabernacle complex was rectangular in shape, measuring 100 by 50 cubits (27.9–18). The exact dimensions expressed in modern equivalents are uncertain, since the length of the ancient cubit (the distance from the point of the elbow to the end of the middle finger) remains in doubt; estimates range from 45 to 52 cm (17.5 to 20.4 in). The approximate dimensions of the sanctuary were 32 by

23 m (105 by 75 ft). The complex was oriented so that the short sides faced east and west with a 20-cubit entrance on the east protected by the embroidered screen (26.36–37; 27.16).

The tabernacle was divided into three distinct zones of increasing *holiness: the courtyard, the holy place, and the holy of holies. The courtyard was divisible into two 50-cubit squares. The eastern square contained the *altar of burnt offering where *sacrifices and offerings were burned (5 × 5 × 3 cubits), located at its center, and the basin, to the west of the altar, which held water for the priests to wash their hands and feet before officiating. The western square contained the tent of meeting or tabernacle proper. This was a separate enclosure measuring 30 × 30 × 10 cubits subdivided into the holy place (20 × 10 × 10 cubits) and the holy of holies (10 × 10 × 10 cubits).

Located within the holy place were the table of showbread (2 × 1 × 1.5 cubits) situated on the north side; the menorah on the south side, and the altar of incense or holden altar (1 × 1 × 2 cubits) located between the table and lampstand immediately in front of the veil to the holy of holies. Every *Sabbath twelve freshly baked loaves were placed on the table, arranged in two rows (Lev. 24.5–9; Exod. 25.30). The lamps on the menorah were lit each evening by the high priest and allowed to burn all night (Lev. 24.1–4). Every morning and evening, at the time when the lamps of the menorah were tended, the high priest burned incense on the golden altar (Exod. 30.7–9).

The holy of holies, separated from the holy place by an embroidered curtain (Exod. 26.31–33), housed only the ark (2.5 × 1.5 × 1.5 cubits) containing the "testimony" (25.21; 40.20), assumed to be the tablets of the *Law. A special lid or "mercy seat" covered the top of the ark and was ornamented with two *cherubim whose outspread wings overarched the cover and touched one another (25.17–20; 26.34; 37.6–9). The covering of the ark was the place where

God promised to meet and communicate with the representative of the community (25.22). Only the high priest was to enter the holy of holies (30.10; Lev. 16.2, 29–34).

The entire courtyard of the enclosure with its perimeter of 300 cubits, with the exception of the entryway, was surrounded by hangings of twisted linen, 5 cubits high, hung on upright posts placed at intervals of 5 cubits (Exod. 27.9–19). The inner rectangle, the tabernacle proper, was enclosed, except on the eastern end, by forty-eight wooden frames (Exod. 26.15–29; 36.20–34). The assembled frames were overlaid first by a covering of sheets of linen (26.1–6) and then by a covering of goats' hair curtains (26.7–13), which was overlaid by a covering of tanned ram skins (26.14).

Gradations of holiness are reflected in the layout, building materials, and use of the tabernacle enclosure. The less holy area, the outer courtyard, was open to the laity, and the metal associated with its construction was bronze. Only priests and *Levites were admitted to the holy place in which the items were overlaid with gold (except for the menorah, which was of pure gold). The contents of the holy of holies were gold plated outside and inside (the ark) or else were of pure gold (the mercy seat). The sacredness of the entire precinct is evident from the command that the priests and Levites should camp between the tabernacle and the tents of the tribes on their journeys in the wilderness (Num. 1.53; 2.1–34).

The tabernacle was the place where God was present among his people (Exod. 25.8), where he met with them and communicated with them (25.22; 29.43–46). The symmetry and wholeness of the tabernacle (see 26.6, 11; 36.13, 18) were reflective of the unity and perfection of God and of the divine relationship to *creation. Note the association of the construction of the tabernacle with the Sabbath (31.12–17; 35.1–3) and the presence of six formulas of divine address to Moses dividing the material into six units (25.1; 30.11, 17, 22, 34; 31.1), thus paralleling the six days in the account of creation in Genesis 1.1–2.3.

Questions have been raised about whether an edifice as elaborate as the tabernacle existed in the *wilderness. Scholars have pointed to a number of difficulties. Could the Israelites, newly out of slavery in Egypt, have possessed the necessary artistic skills to produce such a structure when later Solomon had to hire the *Phoenicians to build the Jerusalem *Temple (1 Kings 5.1–6)?

Would they have had sufficient precious metals, gems, and fabrics to make the cultic furniture and priestly garments? (Estimates indicate the need for at least 1,000 kg [1 ton] of gold, 3,000 kg [3 tons] of silver, and 2,500 kg [2.5 tons] of bronze.) Could such a massive and heavy structure have been dismantled and reassembled with any practicability? Why is there no mention of carrying the tabernacle across the *Jordan in the account of the entry into the *Promised Land (Josh. 3) and such infrequent reference to the structure in the narratives after the entry (see Josh. 18.1; 1 Sam. 2.22; 1 Kings 8.4; 2 Chron. 1.3)? How is the tabernacle, situated in the center of the tribal camp and guarded by thousands of Levites, related to the wilderness tent that was pitched outside the camp, guarded by a single individual, and used to communicate with the deity (Exod. 33.7–11)? Such questions have led to the theory that the tabernacle was an idealized version of the Jerusalem Temple projected back into the wilderness and that the portable shrine was much simpler.

In support of the historicity of the tabernacle or at least some modified version of it, scholars have pointed to the use of portable shrines among other cultures, especially Arab Bedouin cultures, to the fact that Egyptian armies camped encircling the sacred tent and artifacts associated with the Pharaoh, and to the "despoiling of the Egyptians" as a source of the wealth required for the tabernacle (see Gen. 15.13–14; Exod. 11.2; 12.35–36; Ps. 105.37).

See also Hebrews, The Letter to the.

JOHN H. HAYES

Talmud. The Talmuds are systematic commentaries on the *Mishnah, the law code of Judaism formulated in the late second century CE. Two Talmuds developed, one in the land of Israel ca. 400 CE, the other in Babylonia, between ca. 500 and 600 CE. The Palestinian Talmud comments on the divisions of the Mishnah that concern Agriculture, Appointed Times, Women (family law and personal status), and Damages, but it ignored Holy Things. The Babylonian Talmud covers Appointed Times, Women, Damges, and Holy Things (Temple Law) but omits reference to Agriculture. Neither Talmud deals with Purities, excluding the tractate Niddah, on the woman's menstrual period. The first Talmud stresses Mishnah exegesis, with 90 percent of its volume devoted to that task. The second Talmud is not continuous with the first, although it does follow a shared program of exegesis of the Mishnah. In addition to Mishnah exegesis, the Babylonian Talmud devotes substantial attention to the explanation of blocks of biblical materials. In Mishnah exegesis both Talmuds take up words and phrases, the biblical sources of the Mishnah's laws, contradictions in cases and rules that require harmonizations, and similar problems. They engage in speculation on principles behind case laws of the Mishnah and bring into harmony diverse cases that present contradictions in the application of those unifying principles. The Babylonian Talmud differs from the Palestinian in one important respect. In the Palestinian Talmud the fundamental editorial structure derives solely from the Mishnah, but in the Babylonian Talmud, not only the Mishnah but also long passages of scripture serve to organize and unify discourse.

The Talmuds fill vast gaps in the Mishnah's discourse. They account for the authority of the Mishnah by systematically linking its rules and laws to scripture. The need to explain the standing and origin of the Mishnah led sages to posit, first, that God's revelation of the *Torah at *Sinai encompassed the Mishnah as much as scripture, and second, that the Mishnah was handed on through oral formulation and oral transmission from Sinai to the framers of the document as we have it. Consequently, the two Talmuds, along with a variety of other books of exegesis of the Mishnah and of scripture, came to be called the oral Torah. The twin explanations for the status of the Mishnah first surfaced in the Palestinian Talmud, which contains clear allusions to the dual Torah, one part in writing, the other, oral, and now in the Mishnah.

The two Talmuds make use of further documents that fall into the classification of (oral) Torah. They cite and regularly explain the Tosefta, a collection of supplements to the laws of the Mishnah. The Tosefta presents materials of three types: citation and gloss of a passage of the Mishnah; amplification of a Mishnah passage not cited verbatim; and a small amount of material essentially unrelated to the Mishnah. The Talmuds further know commentaries to the written Torah by sages of the time, such as Sifra to Leviticus, Sifre to Numbers, another Sifre, this one to Deuteronomy, Genesis Rabbah, Leviticus Rabbah, and the like. All of these other documents, but especially the Mishnah and its two great Talmuds, contain the teachings of the sages of late antiquity, from the first through the sixth centuries CE. The final statement of the whole is in the Talmud of Babylonia, the encyclopedia of Judaism that from the sixth century CE to the present has provided the focus for authoritative opinion.   JACOB NEUSNER

Tammuz. Tammuz corresponds to the *Sumerian deity Dumuzi, who figures prominently in myths, sacred marriage texts, and laments. Largely a tragic figure, he is the lover of the goddess Inanna who consigned him to the netherworld. The presence of two kings named Dumuzi in the Sumerian King List, one before the flood and one after, suggests that there may have been a historical person with that name.

Much of the early scholarly attention concerning Tammuz focused on James G. Frazier's interpretation *(The Golden Bough),* in which Tammuz was connected to the motif of the dying god. In this understanding, now largely abandoned, the death and resurrection of the god corresponds to the seasonal cycle with its alternation of decay and revival of plant life.

In the single biblical occurrence of Tammuz (Ezek. 8.14), the prophet sees women at the Temple court weeping for Tammuz. The ample first-millennium BCE cuneiform documentation pertaining to mourning rites for Dumuzi provides a suitable backdrop for the passage in Ezekiel.

In Judaism, the fourth month of the year (June/July) is called Tammuz.

                    JAMES H. PLATT

Targums. *See* Translations, *article on* Targums.

Taxation. *See* Tribute and Taxation.

Tax Collectors. *See* Publicans.

Temple. A building or place symbolizing the presence of a deity or deities, intended for the purpose of worship. In the Bible, "temple" usually refers to the Temple erected by *Solomon or the Temple of *Zerubbabel that was enlarged and refurbished by *Herod.

Terminology. Hebrew *hêkāl* comes from Akkadian *ekallu,* which in turn is derived from *Sumerian É.GAL, "great house." The term is generic, and can apply to the house of a god (a temple) or to the house of a king (a palace). It is used of Ahab's palace (1 Kings 21.1) and that of the king of Babylon (2 Kings 20.18). As Israel's king, Yahweh dwelt in a palace, seated on a throne (Isa. 6.1). The word is also used of the house of Yahweh at Shiloh (1 Sam. 1.9; 3.3); of Solomon's Temple (2 Chron. 3.17); of the Second Temple, built by Zerubbabel (Zech. 8.9); of the Temple of Ezekiel's vision (Ezek. 40–48); and of God's heavenly dwelling place (Ps. 11.4).

Hebrew *bayit*, "house," by itself, is used very often of the Temple, or in combination, "house of God" (1 Chron. 9.11), and especially "house of Yahweh" (1 Kings 6–8). This word was also used of the tent of worship (Judg. 18.31), of a local shrine (1 Chron. 9.23), and of temples of other gods (Judg. 9.4; 1 Sam. 5.5). The term "house," referring to the Temple at Jerusalem, is a broader term, including the nave (strictly speaking, the *hêkāl*) and the inner sanctuary (the holy of holies). The Temple mount is known as "the mountain of the Lord's house" (Isa. 2.2) or even "the mountain of the house" (Jer. 26.18; Mic. 3.12).

Greek *hieron*, "sanctuary, temple," in the New Testament is used once of the temple of Artemis (Acts 19.27), but otherwise of the Temple at Jerusalem. The term includes the whole Temple complex. Unfortunately, both this and the next term *(naos)* are translated "temple," which leads to confusion. Jesus, who was not a priest, could not enter the "temple" *(naos)*, nor could the money changers (Matt. 21.12), nor could Paul (Acts 21.26). The word used in each instance is *hieron*, which might be more accurately translated "temple mount."

Greek *naos*, "temple," is used in the New Testament of Herod's Temple, that is, the sanctuary itself and not the entire Temple area (Matt. 27.51; Luke 1.21; John 2.20), and of the heavenly sanctuary (Rev. 11.19; 14.17; but there is no temple in the New Jerusalem, for the Lord God himself is the temple, Rev. 21.22). The word is also used of sanctuaries of other gods (Acts 17.24; 19.24, translated "shrines"; *hieron* is used in 19.27). Used figuratively, *naos* refers to the human body (John 2.21; 1 Cor. 3.16–17; 6.19) and to the church (Eph. 2.21).

Greek *oikos*, "house" (referring to the Temple), except for Luke 11.51 and Hebrews 10.21, occurs only in quotations in the New Testament of passages in the Hebrew Bible where *bayit* is used.

Solomon's Temple. The *tabernacle had served as the center of worship from the time of *Moses to *David (2 Sam. 6.17; 7.6). David wanted to build a more permanent structure, but the Lord forbade it (1 Chron. 22.7–8). David set about collecting materials and making plans for the building to be built by his son, Solomon (2 Sam. 7.13; 1 Chron. 22.2–5; 28.11–19).

The Temple was located on the eastern hill, north of the city of David, where the Dome of the Rock is located today. (*See* Jerusalem; Map 9.) At that time the Temple mount was considerably smaller, Solomon having enlarged it somewhat (Josephus, *War*, 5.5.185) and Herod having enlarged it still more to the present size of the platform known as Haram esh-Sharif. This is "the threshing floor of Araunah the Jebusite" (2 Sam. 24.18), "Mount Moriah" (2 Chron. 3.1), and probably the *Zion of the Psalms and the prophets (Pss. 110.2; 128.5; 134.3; Isa. 2.3; Joel 3.16 [MT 4.16]; Amos 1.2; Zech. 8.3) although the term belonged to the city of David (1 Kings 8.1).

The general plan of the Temple was similar to that given for the tabernacle: rectangular, with a porch or vestibule (*'ûlām*, 1 Kings 6.3) facing east, a nave *(hêkāl)*, and an inner sanctuary (*dĕbîr*, 6.5) or holy of holies (8.6). The dimensions were double those of the tabernacle: 60 cubits by 20 (1 cubit = 0.5 m [19.7 in]), but triple its height (30 cubits). The building was of hewn stone, dressed at the quarry (1 Kings 6.7). The porch was 10 cubits deep (1 Kings 6.3) and 120 cubits high (2 Chron. 3.4)—a numeral that may have suffered textual corruption. Two columns, Jachin and Boaz, made of hollow bronze, 35 or 40 cubits high, stood at each side of the entrance (2 Chron. 3.15–17). The inner walls of the *hêkāl* were lined with cedar brought from *Lebanon (1 Kings 5.6–10; 6.15–16), and the entire structure was lined with gold (v. 22). The holy of holies was overlaid with "pure" gold (v. 20). The skilled work was done by Tyrian artisans supplied by King Hiram (5.1) and under the supervision of a person also named Hiram (7.13) or Huram-Abi (2 Chron. 2.13).

The holiest place contained the *ark of the covenant (1 Kings 6.19) and two winged figures (*cherubim) of olive wood overlaid with gold (v. 23) that stretched from wall to wall. Doors of olive wood, covered with gold, separated the holy of holies from the nave (v. 31), and similar doors separated the nave from the porch (v. 33). The nave contained the golden altar (7.48, to distinguish it from the bronze altar in the courtyard) made of cedar (6.20) or the "altar of incense" (1 Chron. 28.18), which stood before the holy of holies; the golden table for the bread of the Presence ("*showbread"); the golden lampstands and other items (1 Kings 6.48–50).

The building was surrounded by two courts, the inner one constructed of three courses of stone and one of cedar beams (v. 36; also called the court of the priests, 2 Chron. 4.9), and the great court (1 Kings 7.9), which probably also enclosed the royal buildings. The size of the inner court is not given, but if it was double the size of the court of the tabernacle, it would have been 200 by 100 cubits. The inner court contained the bronze altar (2 Chron. 4.1) where sacrifices were offered, the ten bronze basins on ten stands, five on each side of the house, and the great sea (the molten or bronze sea) on the southeast corner of the house. The bronze work was cast in the Jordan valley (1 Kings 7.46), the most impressive being the great sea, 10 cubits in diameter and 5 cubits high, with a capacity of 2,000 baths (approximately 40,000 liters [10,000 gal]). The water was used for supplying the lavers for washing the parts of the sacrificial victims and for the priests' ablutions (2 Chron. 4.6).

The First Temple, having been plundered several times, was finally destroyed by *Nebuchadrezzar in 587/586 BCE (2 Kings 25.8–17; Jer. 52.12–23).

Ezekiel's Temple. The Temple in Ezekiel 40–48 is presented as a vision, and so the details may be assumed to be symbolic rather than material. The plan in general follows closely that of Solomon's Temple, although it is markedly symmetrical. Some of the description is more detailed than that given in Kings or Chronicles, and such details as the plan and dimensions of the gates (Ezek. 40.6–16) have been indirectly confirmed by archaeological discoveries at *Gezer, *Hazor, and *Megiddo.

Zerubbabel's Temple. When the Jews returned from *exile (538 BCE) there was an effort to rebuild the Temple (2 Chron. 36.23; Ezra 1.1–4). The work was begun (Ezra 3) but languished until 520, when as a result of the encouragement of *Haggai and *Zechariah, it was resumed and the Temple was finished on the third day of Adar in the sixth year of *Darius (12 March 515; Ezra 6.15). It was comparable in size to Solomon's Temple (6.3) and probably also in its ground plan, with the holy of holies and the sanctuary with the golden altar, table lampstand, and other furnishings (1 Macc. 1.22; 4.48–51). It was surrounded by an inner court with the altar of burnt offering and an outer court. According to *Josephus, reporting Hecateus, the outer court was approximately 150 by 45 m (500 by 150 ft), and the altar of unhewn stones was 20 cubits square and 10 cubits in height (*Ag. Ap.* 1.198). According to the *Talmud (*Yoma* 21b), five things were missing from the Second Temple: the ark, the sacred fire, the *shekinah*, the holy spirit, and the *Urim and Thummim.

Herod's Temple. Herod did not tear down the Second Temple—that would surely have instigated a revolt, as Herod recognized (Josephus, *Ant.* 15.11.387). He rebuilt and refurbished it by preparing materials for parts, using priests as carpenters and masons in the sacred areas, and doing the work by sections. The building was made new without ever destroying the old and without interrupting the sacred offerings and sacrifices. Begun in Herod's twentieth year (20 BCE), it was finished in a year and a half (*Ant.* 15.11.420).

Work on the Temple platform may have begun in Herod's fifteenth year (Josephus, *War* 1.21.401), and it continued until ca. 64 CE (*Ant.* 20.9.219). The Kidron valley was partially filled, shifting its bed eastward; likewise the central (Tyropoeon) valley was partially filled, shifting it several hundred feet to the west. Using huge ashlars ("Herodian" stones, ca. 1 m [40 in] high, 1–3 m [3 to 10 ft] long [one measures 12 m (39 ft) in length!], and 4 m [13 ft] wide), the western, southern, and eastern walls were built, and the Temple mount was extended to a width of 280 m (915 ft) across the southern end, 310 m (1,017 ft) across the northern, and approximately 450 m (1,500 ft) north to south. At the southeastern corner, the wall rose 48 m (158 ft) above the Kidron valley. A stoa or portico was built along all four sides, with marble columns 25 cubits high, and ceiled with cedar panels; the royal stoa at the south had four rows of columns, the others had double rows of columns. The stoa along the eastern side was attributed by Josephus (*Ant.* 20.9.221) to Solomon (see John 10.23; Acts 3.11; 5.12).

The Temple itself (Map 9) was surrounded by a wall or balustrade, 3 cubits high, separating the holy place from the court of the gentiles. It was 322 cubits east to west by 135 cubits north to south, raised by 14 and 5 steps (all steps were 1/2 cubit). The holy place was not in the center of the Temple mount, but more to the north and west. On the surrounding wall were warnings, some in Greek, others in Latin, forbidding the entry of any gentile under penalty of death; two of these have been found. Ten cubits inside the balustrade a wall of 25 cubits high surrounded the sacred area, with seven gates: three each on the north and south sides, one on the east (*Mid.* 1.4).

Within this holy place, there were increasingly sacred areas: the court of the women at the east, the court of the Israelites (i.e., males only), the court of the priests, then the Temple (*naos*). This area was separated from the Women's Court, being 15 steps higher, and could be entered through the Nicanor Gate. The Temple was still higher by another 12 steps; it consisted of the porch (100 by 100 cubits, 11 cubits wide), the nave (40 by 20 cubits) containing the table of the Presence, the lampstand or *menorah (taken to Rome by Titus and portrayed on the Arch of Titus), and the altar of incense, and behind that the holy of holies (20 by 20 cubits), which was empty except for a sacred stone. Built into the wall around the Temple were rooms or chambers, increasing the size of the Temple by 70 to 100 cubits. To the east and south of the Temple was the altar, 32 cubits square, and north of the altar the place of slaughtering.

Only the priests could enter the Temple, and only the high priest could enter the holy of holies, and that only on the *Day of Atonement (*m. Kelim* 1.9; cf. Heb. 9.25). The priests were divided into twenty-four "courses," each course serving twice a year for a week (see Luke 1.8). A veil of Babylonian tapestry hung in the opening to the nave (*War* 5.5.212); a second veil separated the nave from the holy of holies (219). It would seem that it was the outer veil that was torn at the time of the death of Jesus (Mark 15.38), since the inner veil would not be seen by bystanders.

There were eight gates leading into the Temple mount: one on the north, four on the west, two on the south, and one on the east (*Ant.* 15.11.410); the Mishnah says five [*Mid.* 1.3], naming only one on the west). Along the western wall was the deep central valley, with a paved walk that continued around the southern end of the Temple. A great staircase led up to the triple Huldah gate, and next to the stairs was a structure containing a large number of immersion pools for ceremonial cleansing (Hebr. *miqwā'ôt*). The worshiper, after his or her purification, entered the right of the two double gates and passed through a tunnel leading upward into the Temple area. A second entrance could be made by a large staircase that led to the royal

stoa ("Robinson's Arch" marks this entrance), but no purification was available here. Leading from the western hill to the Temple mount was a bridge ("Wilson's Arch" marks this). Details of the other entrances are not clear; they were possibly located where Barclay's and Warren's Gates are now. The Tadi Gate was in the northern wall; possibly the sacrificial animals were brought in by this entrance, since it was near the Sheep Pool and Market. The Susa gate in the eastern wall was used only by the high priest and priests in connection with the ceremony of burning the *red cow at a location on the Mount of *Olives from which the high priest could look directly into the entrance of the sanctuary.

Destruction of the Temple. There is a full account of the capture of Jerusalem in *War* 5–6, according to which Titus commissioned Josephus to urge the Jews to surrender in order to spare the Temple, but to no avail. The Antonia was razed to the ground in August 70 CE, and the continual sacrifice ceased to be offered. Josephus made a second appeal. Titus then decided to destroy the Temple. This occurred on the tenth day of the fifth month (Ab; according to Jewish tradition, the ninth of Ab), the same day on which the First Temple had been burned by the king of Babylon. Josephus portrays the Romans as trying to extinguish the fire that had been started by the insurgents. Widespread plundering, murder, and finally the burning of all structures on the Temple mount ended the history of the Temple.

WILLIAM SANFORD LaSOR

Temptation. In biblical traditions, temptation is generally a test or trial to which the tempter subjects another person, often by confusing what is good with what is evil. Along with strength of will, the capacity to discern good is being tested, and the tester is usually the God of Israel or occasionally the adversary, *Satan. Less frequent is the understanding of temptation as the conscious desire of individuals to do what they know to be wrong, though this does occur (Gal. 6.1; James 1.14).

In the Hebrew Bible, the most famous example of God's setting a specific trial for an individual is the testing of Abraham (Gen. 22; *see* Aqedah). Another is God's permission to Satan to put *Job to the test (Job 1.6–12). In the New Testament, God is likewise the ultimate initiator of the temptation of Jesus (*see next entry*), for it is the Spirit that drove Jesus into the wilderness, where Satan's offers would serve as a maximum test of Jesus' discernment and courage (Mark 1.12–13; Matt. 4.1–11 par.). Similarly, God is pictured as setting tests for Jesus' followers (Luke 22.28; James 1.2; 1 Pet. 1.6).

The Bible also speaks of putting God to the test. Israel presumes that because God has delivered it from earlier crises, he will do so again (Exod 17.2–7; Num. 14.20–25; Deut. 6.16; Pss. 78.18; 95.9). Evildoers challenge God to punish them, but they escape unscathed (Mal. 3.15). The same language is used in the New Testament, where Jesus refuses to test God (Matt. 4.7; cf. 26.53); Christians may test him by their improper conduct (Acts 5.9; 15.10; 1 Cor. 10.9).

A larger role is assigned to Satan in the New Testament than in the Hebrew Bible. God uses Satan to tempt people; Satan uses them to tempt God. The afflictions believers suffered because of their faith were often understood as an opportunity for the tempter (Mark 4.14–17 par.; 1 Thess. 3.4–5). This provides a background for interpreting the climactic petitions designed by Jesus for his followers as they faced persecutions (Matt. 6.13). These petitions can be understood as asking, "Father . . . do not bring us to the time of trial by the Evil One, but rescue us from his power" (*see* Lord's Prayer). It was because Jesus had also been tempted that he was able to help those struggling against the same foe (Heb. 2.14–18; 4.15).   PAUL S. MINEAR

Temptation of Christ. Each of the *synoptic Gospels gives an account of the temptation of Christ (Matt.4.1–11; Mark 1.13; Luke 4.1–13), and all three place the temptation within the same sequence, following Jesus' *baptism by John, and preceding the first statement of Jesus' preaching of the *kingdom of God (Matt. 4.17; Mark 1.14–15; Luke 4.14–15, 43). Luke has interrupted the sequence with the insertion of Jesus' *genealogy (3.23–38), but the common themes of Spirit and Sonship together with the geographical reference establish the close connection between Luke's baptism story (3.2, 21–22) and his account of the temptation.

This agreement in sequence should not hide the fact that we have two very different types of narrative in *Mark, on the one hand, and in *Matthew and *Luke, on the other. Mark includes the temptation in a single sentence that is more a cryptogram than a narrative, while Matthew and Luke write of three scenes in which a minimum of action provides the setting for three

verbal exchanges between *Jesus and *Satan, all of which center in quotations from Deuteronomy 6 and 8 (from the *Septuagint). The quotations are the climax of each scene so that the narrative as a whole resembles a midrash. The stories cannot be derived one from the other; they represent the literary result of two different traditions about Jesus' temptation, and efforts to interpret them should refrain from harmonizing one version with the other.

Both narratives combine topics that had grown through centuries of Israelite and early Jewish tradition. They had, therefore, become so rich in associations with traditional themes that the expositor is faced with a wide array of interpretive possibilities, and no single governing theme can do justice to them.

Mark includes the temptation in a single, terse statement (1.13): "He was in the wilderness forty days, tempted by Satan; and he was with the wild beasts; and the angels waited on him." There is no narrative or dialogue; no fasting is mentioned; but Jesus is placed in the presence of wild beasts, which goes beyond the record of Matthew and Luke. The forms of the four verbs are sufficiently ambiguous to leave unclear whether they comprise a sequence of episodes or are simultaneous aspects of one event. There are two major interpretations of Mark's cryptic sentence: Jesus as the second *Adam who restores *paradise, and Jesus as the protagonist in God's struggle against Satan. Both rely on Jewish adaptations of biblical themes.

According to the first, the temptation is only one motif alongside others, which renders it doubtful whether Mark 1.13 is exclusively a temptation story. The picture of a peaceful coexistence of humans with wild animals is a well-attested eschatological theme (e.g., Isa. 11.6–9; 65.25), and the idea of service of *angels to Adam and Eve in paradise is found in Jewish tradition (e.g., *b. Sanh.* 59b). According to the principle that the world to come would restore the conditions of the original creation, ideas about creation and about the end time became interchangeable. The introduction of the *wilderness and the temptation by Satan does not necessarily provide a discordant note to the image of paradise restored, because satanic temptation is an element of the story of Adam and Eve (Gen. 3; the identification of the serpent with Satan had already been made), and the wilderness is a place not only of horror and judgment but also of ultimate restoration. The coordination of three (or four?) equal motifs therefore provides a reading of Mark 1.13 that sees Jesus, in consequence of his declaration as God's Son in his baptism and prior to the beginning of his public activity, as the new Adam who triumphs over Satan (in contrast to the first Adam) and thereby inaugurates a promised new condition in which wild animals are no longer a threat and the angels render service.

The alternate understanding of Mark 1.13 relies more on a similarity to the accounts of the temptation in Matthew and Luke: the forty days are part of a *typology alluding to Israel's forty years in the desert (Deut. 8.2), the wilderness is the haunt of demons and terrifying animals, and the service of the angels is regarded (as in Matt. 4.11) as the resolution of the conflict after the devil's departure. This assumes that the motifs of the wild animals and the angels are subordinate to that of the wilderness, which represents the time and the place controlled by powers hostile to God. Mark 1.13 thus presents Christ as the protagonist of God's fight against satanic forces, who invades the stronghold of the enemy and thus overcomes him (see Mark 3.27).

Matthew and Luke differ in the order of the second and third temptations and in some details, but generally the content of their three temptation scenes is the same, so that a common tradition behind them (*Q?) must be assumed. Since the vocabulary in Luke, where he differs from Matthew, shows clear traces of Lucan style, and since Luke's sequence of the scenes can be explained by his tendency to emphasize the crucial role of Jerusalem, it is probable that Matthew preserves the more original order and wording. The following comments are therefore based on the Matthean order. Matthew's scenes shift from the wilderness to the *Temple and finally to a very high mountain, each culminating in Jesus's quoting Deuteronomy (8.3, 6.16, and 6.13, respectively, all close in content and position to the *Shema, whose first part contains Deut. 6.4–9).

Attempts have been made to understand the whole temptation story in Matthew as a logically constructed unit with one organizing idea. This has been variously described as: the demand of Deuteronomy 6.5 to love God with one's whole heart, soul, and might, so that the tripartite division of human faculties is explicated in the three episodes of Jesus' temptation, describing him as one who lives in total dedication to the one God of Israel; or the fullness of the messianic office, which combines a prophetic *messiah (*Moses in the wilderness, the prophet par excellence according to Deut. 18.18), a priestly

messiah (the Temple as center of the priestly office), and a political messiah (world dominion offered on the mountain), each episode containing a strong antithesis to popular conceptions of these messianic offices; or a thoroughgoing Israel-typology that coordinates the climactic quotation in each scene of the temptation with an analogous situation in Israel's wilderness sojourn, patterned after the textual sequence in the Exodus story (Deut. 8.3 – Manna – Exod. 16; Deut. 6.16 – provocation of God at Massah – Exod. 17; Deut. 6.13 – promise of land, warning against idolatry – Exod. 23.20–33; 34.11–14), portraying Jesus as the true Israelite who did not yield to temptation precisely at the point of Israel's failure.

Each of these unifying interpretations draws on a wealth of pertinent evidence in Jewish tradition, but none is conclusive. A variety of complex motifs coalesce, forming a confessional narrative in which four intentions merge. First, the title *Son of God binds together baptism and temptation (3.17; 4.3, 6); the baptism of Jesus culminates in his being declared Son of God, the temptation describes the cost of this Sonship. Second, in the temptation narrative Jesus is presented as the authentic interpreter and doer of God's will in scripture. Third, the dominance of the title Son of God marks the temptation as a christologically and soteriologically oriented narrative. Finally, factually, and perhaps intentionally, the story implies a radical criticism of popular conceptions about the eschatological agent of God. The true Son of God does not abuse his status for self-preservation, he refrains from using his power for protection against death (cf. Matt. 26.53; 27.42–43), and he refuses to exercise world dominion in any form other than that bestowed on him by God in consequence of his death and resurrection (Matt. 28.18).

ULRICH W. MAUSER

Ten Commandments. Also called the Decalogue ("the ten words"; see Exod. 34.28), the Ten Commandments comprise a short list of religious and ethical demands laid by the Deity on the people of ancient Israel and are of continuing authority for the religious Jewish community and the Christian community. They appear in two places in the Bible (Exod. 20.1–17 and Deut. 5.6–21) and are alluded to or quoted in part in several places in the Hebrew Bible and in the New Testament.

The commandments prohibit the worship of

any God other than Israel's God, held to be the true God of the other nations as well (*see* Monotheism). They rule out the making of images of the Deity in any plastic form (*see* Graven Image; Idols); the misuse of the divine Name and the power associated with it; and they require observance of the *Sabbath day and the honoring of one's parents (especially in view are the elderly parents of adults, not the parents of young children). They also prohibit *murder, *adultery, stealing, false testimony (not primarily the telling of untruths in general), and the coveting of the life and goods of others.

The enumeration of the commandments varies among the religious communities. Worshiping other Gods and making images of the Deity are placed together in a number of religious communities (Jewish, Roman Catholic, Lutheran), while Reformed and Orthodox Christian communities treat these as the first two commandments. For the Jewish community, the first commandment is "I am the LORD your God who brought you out of the land of Egypt, out of the house of bondage," while the ninth and tenth commandments for Roman Catholic and Lutheran communions are the two prohibitions of coveting: the household (commandment 9) and the remainder of the list in Exod. 20.17 (commandment 10). The contents of the Ten Commandments are, however, the same for all of the religious communities, despite the differences in their enumeration. The differences between the contents of Exodus 20 and Deuteronomy 5 are quite small, reflecting changes over time in the way in which the commandments were understood and applied.

The commandments are of enormous value and influence—on the community of Israel, within the Christian community, and throughout the entire world today. The commandments fall into four groups. The first three, the commandments demanding the worship of God alone, against image-making, and against the use of God's name to do harm, are commandments stressing God's exclusive claim over the lives of the people. God will brook no rivalry; as Israel's savior, God demands a commitment that preserves the people from divided loyalties, protects them from supposing that anything in the whole of creation could adequately represent the Deity, the Creator of all, and also protects persons from the religious community's misuse of divine power to serve its own ends.

The next two commandments, calling for observing every seventh day as a day of rest and for honoring parents even when they might no longer be of significant economic value within the community, are special institutions for the protection of basic realities in society—human need for rest from labor as well as for labor and the preservation of human dignity against any kind of exploitation.

The next three commandments focus especially on the life of the individual or the family in the larger community. They insist on the sanctity of human life, the sanctity of marriage and of sexual life, and the necessity to maintain a community in which the extension of the self into one's property is recognized and respected.

The last two commandments are more social and public, calling for speaking the truth before the courts or the community's elders and for living a life not distorted or corrupted by the lust for other persons' goods or lives.

*Moses is identified as the great lawgiver in ancient Israel. The Ten Commandments are understood by the community to have been handed down from God through Moses. It is clear, however, that the legal materials of the Hebrew Bible have developed over centuries, reflected changes in religious understanding and practice, and incorporated those changed perspectives into the legal heritage assigned to Moses and to Moses' God.

The substance of the Ten Commandments probably does originate in the work and discernments of Moses. The unique understanding of idolatry reflected in the Ten Commandments, and the requirement that one day in seven be characterized by an absolute break with the other days—by cessation from normal pursuits for a full day—these are without precedent in the ancient Near Eastern world. Other commandments are not unique, but this tenfold collection of short, primarily negative, statements is unique. It stems from a person of extraordinary religious discernment—and Moses was such a person.

The Ten Commandments probably had a place in family life, as a means by which the young were introduced to the fundamental requirements of the covenant between God and people. They also had a place in public religious life and in the great festivals when the bond between people and God was regularly reaffirmed and confirmed (*see* Feasts and Festivals).

The Ten Commandments were of great value as summations of the demands of God, easily remembered by reference to the ten fingers of the hand. As negative statements, they helped shape the community's recognition of those kinds of conduct that simply ruined life in community and so could not be allowed. They were not intended to be legalistic in character or in effect; they were to ward off conduct from the community that could be its ruin. Positive law must develop in association with these pithy, negatively put demands. Rather than such "dos and don'ts" encouraging oppressive control of a society by its leaders, they are a summons to a life freed to enjoy existence in community.

See also Neighbor.   WALTER HARRELSON

Teraphim. A cult object or objects, mentioned fifteen times in the Bible, generally translated "household god(s)." The word can be either singular (1 Sam 19.13, 16) or plural (Gen 31.32, 34; Zech 10.2) in meaning. A plausible etymology is from *Hittite *tarpi(š)*, which means some sort of benevolent or malevolent spirit, perhaps analogous to the *penates* of Roman religion. On occasion they apparently have human shape and are apparently life-size (1 Sam. 19.13–16), though in Genesis 31 the teraphim are small enough so that Rachel can sit on them; they may have been statues or perhaps only masks. The function of the teraphim is also not entirely clear; often it seems to be divinatory (1 Sam. 15.23; Ezek. 21.21; Zech. 10.2; note the association with the *ephod in Judg. 17.5; 18.14–20; Hos. 3.4); but in Genesis 31 it has been suggested on the basis of Hurrian parallels from *Nuzi that they were the equivalent of deeds or legal title to property. In most contexts the use of teraphim is at least implicitly condemned, although it was apparently known from premonarchic times to at least the sixth century BCE.

See Magic and Divination.

MICHAEL D. COOGAN

Tetragrammaton. A Greek word meaning "four letters," used to designate the consonants of the divine name Yahweh. This *name of God is so sacred that Jews traditionally do not pronounce it but use a substitute, and the vowels of Adonai (*ădōnāy*), "my Lord," are written in the Hebrew Bible (with "e" as the first vowel instead of "a") with the four letters *yhwh* (whence "Jehovah"), though they are not pronounced with those consonants. (*See* Jehovah.)

Outside the Bible, *yhwh* is first found in the *Moabite Stone (ca. 830 BCE) and in inscriptions from Khirbet el-Qom and Kuntillet ʿAjrud (late ninth or early eighth century BCE). In the Bible, we also find the related form *yāh*, and the elements *yĕhô-*, *yô-*, *-yāhû*, and *-yâ* in personal names. Jews in Egypt in the fifth century BCE wrote *yhw* (*yāhû*) and *yhh* (*yāhōh*).

It is probable that the first part of *yhwh* was pronounced *yah-* (cf. the "a" vowel in related forms and in Greek transcriptions in Christian times), and the second *-eh* (cf. the assonance with *'ehyeh* ["I AM" in the NRSV] in Exod. 3.14), hence *yahweh*. If *yahweh* is shortened by the omission of *-eh*, the natural result in Hebrew is *yāhû*, whereas the former cannot easily be derived from the latter. The name *yahweh* looks like the third-person singular of the verb *hāwâ*, a rare alternative to the usual *hāyâ*, "to be." The "a" vowel suggests the causative theme of the verb ("he causes" or "will cause to be"), but that theme is not used with this verb in the Bible. If, however, the name is archaic or of non-Israelite origin, then another meaning is possible, and some have sought a meaning found in Aramaic ("to fall" [cf. Job 37.6] as well as "to be") or in Arabic ("to fall, blow," etc.), but firm evidence is lacking.

Some have suggested a connection with the element *ya* in cuneiform personal names at *Ebla and in Mesopotamian texts, but this interpretation is disputed, and a connection with *yw* in a *Ugaritic name is also questionable. More plausible—though still uncertain—is a connection with *yhw* (perhaps *yahweh*) in Egyptian texts from ca. 1400–1200 BCE, which may be a place (the site of a shrine?) associated with pastoral nomads in or near the *Sinai peninsula. What is important, however, is not the origin of the name but the nature of the God who bore it in the Bible.

J. A. EMERTON

Tetrarch. A title originating in Greece, the only place where its literal meaning of "ruler of a fourth (part)" applied, and used throughout the Near East in the Hellenistic and Roman periods for subordinate rulers. In the *Roman empire a tetrarch was of lower rank than an ethnarch ("ruler of a people"), who in turn was lower than a king. According to *Josephus, *Herod the Great was first appointed tetrarch over Judea in 42 BCE by Mark Antony (*Ant.* 14.13.326) and shortly thereafter named king. On Herod's death, his sons Philip and Antipas were named tetrarchs over *Galilee and Perea, and Gaulanitis (the modern Golan), respectively (see Luke 3.1 and

Map 13), while Archelaus was promised that his rank of ethnarch over Judea would be elevated to king if he proved worthy (*War* 2.6.93).

Both the New Testament and other ancient sources use these titles inconsistently; for example, Herod Antipas is called tetrarch in Matthew 14.1 but king in 14.9 and in the parallels in Mark 6. The NRSV uses "ethnarch" in 1 Maccabees (14.47; 15.1–2) but "governor" for the same term in 2 Corinthians 11.32, and it always translates "tetrarch" by the generic "ruler."   MICHAEL D. COOGAN

Textual Criticism. Because at times the word "criticism" can mean "finding fault with," it is important to note that when it is used here it means "evaluation," the analysis of something with the intent of determining its value. The wording of the *manuscripts of the Hebrew Bible and of the Greek New Testament varies here and there to a greater or lesser degree. It is necessary, therefore, to employ the criteria of textual criticism in order to evaluate the various readings so as to determine, if possible, the original author's text prior to the modifications that appear in extant manuscripts—for the original autographs were lost long ago. There are three classes of sources that scholars use in textual criticism of biblical texts: the Hebrew or Greek manuscripts; ancient *translations in other languages; and quotations made by rabbis and church fathers.

The first step in the determination of the original text involves a scrupulous comparison of all the witnesses (or, at least, the important witnesses) in these three classes of texts, and then producing a compilation of the differing readings. Such a compilation is known as a critical apparatus. At times this process sheds light on how and why a scribe introduced a textual variation. The majority of differing readings occurred because of unintentional error; in other instances, the text may have been intentionally altered. Accidental variations can result from one letter being mistaken for another; from the reversal of the sequence of two letters (metathesis); from exchanging letters and words that sound similar; from confusing two successive lines that begin with the same letters or words (homoeoarchton) or that end with the same letters or words (homoeoteleuton), by allowing the eye to skip from the first to the second line (parablepsis), thus omitting the intermediate text

(haplography); and from the eye accidently processing the same word or groups of words twice so that the scribe writes for a second time a text that was meant to be read only once (dittography).

Oddly enough, scribes who thought about the text were more likely to make emendations than those who simply wanted to produce an accurate copy. Deliberate changes include correcting spelling and grammar; conforming a reading to a parallel passage; expanding or polishing the text by adding a familiar word or phrase where one seemed to be called for; combining similar phrases; clarifying historical and geographical problems; substituting synonymous words or expressions; and modifying or deleting expressions considered objectionable by the scribe.

The textual critic's fundamental considerations when assessing variant readings involve both external and internal evidence. External evidence relates to the date of the witnesses, the geographical distribution of the witnesses that agree, and the family relationship (if determinable) of manuscripts and groups of witnesses. Internal evidence is concerned with transcriptional probabilities, which require analysis of paleographical details and the scribe's habits, and intrinsic probabilities, which necessitate examination of the author's style and vocabulary throughout the book.

The differing conclusions of textual critics can usually be traced to one's judgment as to which criteria are deemed most significant. For example, for the Hebrew Bible most scholars use the *Masoretic text as a point of departure for textual criticism because it is a complete, established text that was scrupulously transcribed. In some cases, however, readings in the *Qumran Hebrew manuscripts are considered superior to the Masoretic text by virtue of their agreement with ancient translations. The Qumran manuscripts, however, are not complete, and some were negligently copied.

As a general rule, the more difficult reading is usually to be preferred, as is also the less smooth or unassimilated reading—since in both instances scribes resisted the urge to produce a more polished, harmonious text. The shorter reading is also favored by the majority of textual scholars (unless specific omissions can be traced to homoeoteleuton, or unless the shorter reading does not conform to the character, style, or scope of the author), since scribes tended to supplement the text with explanations or material from parallel passages rather than to abridge it. Simply stated, the reading that best explains the origin of the other readings should be preferred as the original.   BRUCE M. METZGER

Theology. *See* Biblical Theology.

Theophany. A deity's physical manifestation that is seen by human beings. The appearance of gods and their involvement with humans are common motifs in ancient Near Eastern and classical mythology. That similar phenomena are found in the Bible seems problematic at first, for a persistent tradition in the Hebrew Bible affirmed that death comes to any human who sees God (Gen. 16.13; 32.30; 24.10–11; 33.20; Deut. 5.24–26; 18.16; Judg. 6.22–23; 13.22; cf. Exod. 20.19; Isa. 6.5). In most of these contexts, however, the narration undermines this sentiment by depicting the pleasant surprise of those who survive. The text presents this perspective as a misperception to which human beings subscribe, for no humans in the Bible ever die simply because they have seen God. On the contrary, throughout the Bible God wants to communicate intimately with humans. The problem of how God can adequately show himself to humankind without harm is a conundrum that is never really resolved in the Bible.

The ease and frequency with which God visits and talks with humans in the early biblical narratives underscore how comfortable ancient Israelites were in depicting God's confrontation with humanity. Such theophanies are unspectacular, for God appears in form as an undistinguished human being (Gen. 18.1–2) who walks (Gen. 3.8) and stands (1 Sam. 3.10). Humans speak freely of seeing God's face (Gen. 33.10; Pss. 11.7; 17.15), and it is possible that the phrase used to describe a pilgrimage to the Temple ("to appear in the presence of Yahweh") has been modified by later tradition from an original vocalization that should be translated as "to see the face of Yahweh" (e.g., Exod. 23.15; 34.23; Deut. 16.16; 31.11; 1 Sam. 1.22; Ps. 42.2). In the scores of cases where the text simply reads, "God said," it is not clear if a theophany is to be presumed. Only when the narrative clarifies that "God appeared" is a theophany explicit (Gen. 12.7; 17.1; 26.24; 35.9; 48.3). Occasionally, God is described as descending when the theophany begins (Exod.

19.11, 18–20; 34.5) and/or ascending when it ends (Gen. 17.22; 35.13).

Although God may reveal himself whenever and to whomever he wishes, it is only to select individuals and in isolated places that God repeatedly appears. *Moses, for example, is depicted as having a unique relationship with God, who knew and spoke with Moses face to face (Num. 12.6–8; Deut. 34.10). The most common types of places where theophanies occur are near trees (Gen. 12.6–7; 13.18; 18.1) and mountains (Gen. 12.8; 22.2, 14; Ex. 19.2–3; Num. 23.3; Deut. 33.2; Ps. 3.4; Joel 3.16; Hab. 3.3; Mic. 1.3).

Because God characteristically reveals himself at such places, they become places of pilgrimage for humans seeking divine guidance or assistance. Shrines and temples, along with their sacred objects (such as the *ark), are built to formalize, protect, and regulate the approach to the divine presence. Those who enter such sacred precincts may experience a dramatic revelation of God's presence (Isa. 6.1), particularly those who spend the night (1 Sam. 3.1–15; 1 Kings 3.4–5). God's presence in this institutionalized framework can be confirmed by the theophanic cloud inside the shrine (Exod. 33.9; 40.34; 1 Kings 8.10–11). Here it is common to find people dying not because they have seen God but because they have not followed the rules in approaching him (1 Sam. 6.19; Lev. 10.2; 16.2; 2 Sam. 6.7).

As in other ancient Near Eastern traditions, one of the common forms in which God is depicted as appearing is as a warrior (Exod. 15.1–3; Judg. 5.4–5), garbed with battle armor and weapons (Isa. 34.5–6; 59.17; Zeph. 2.12; Hab. 3.9–15; Zech. 9.13–14), smiting his foes and saving his people (Isa. 42.13; Zeph. 3.17; Zech. 14.3). He may go into battle alone (Isa. 59.16; 63.3, 5) or he may be accompanied by an army or entourage (Isa. 5.26–30; 13.3–5; Joel 2.1–11; Hab. 3.5) as he rides upon horses and chariot (Hab. 3.8, 15; Zech. 10.3). He returns from battle drenched in the enemy's blood (Isa. 63.1–6). When God makes such a dramatic appearance, characteristic visible phenomena that accompany his presence include clouds, lightning, earthquakes, and fire (Gen. 15.17; Exod. 13.21; 19.9, 16; Nah. 1.3; Zech. 9.14; Job 38.1). Particularly when God marches into battle, he rocks creation with convulsions that shatter rocks and mountains (Isa. 13.3; Joel 2.10; 3.16; Mic. 1.4; Nah. 1.5–6; Hab. 3.6, 10; Zech. 14.4–5), creating an upheaval and diminution of sun, moon, stars, and heavens (Isa. 13.10; 37.4; Joel 2.10; 3.15; Hab. 3.11; Zech. 14.6); *see* War.

The book of Kings explains why earlier manifestations of God were dramatic in contrast to the more subdued revelation of the later writing *prophets. In 1 Kings 19.8–13, the ninth-century BCE prophet *Elijah returns to Mount *Horeb and witnesses the typical convulsions of nature that accompany a theophany (storm, earthquake, fire), but this time God is in none of them. Instead, it is only a subdued, calm voice that testifies to God's presence. This narrative accounts for the gradual cessation of the classical theophanies and a rise in importance of the prophetic word as the medium of God's self-revelation. It is in the following century that the first of the known so-called writing prophets, *Amos, appears in Israel.

The New Testament affirms that *Jesus is the only adequate manifestation of God (John 1.1, 14–18; Col. 1.15; 2.9). Jesus' transfiguration (Mark 9.2–8 par.) and *ascension (Acts 1.9–12) correspond to theophanies of the Hebrew Bible (on a mountain, voice from a cloud, radiance) in order to stress the continuity of God's self-revelation (Matt. 17.1–8).   SAMUEL A. MEIER

Thessalonians, The Letters of Paul to the. The New Testament includes two letters ascribed to *Paul and addressed to the church at Thessalonica in Macedonia (Map 14:D2).

The first follows the normal pattern of Pauline letters in beginning with a formal greeting (1.1), followed by a report of how Paul remembers the church in his prayers; he thanks God for the positive response of its members to his initial preaching of the gospel (1.2–10). He then discusses this work in the town, claiming that he and his companions acted uprightly and lovingly (2.1–12). He returns to the topic of the church's warm response despite disincentives caused by those opposed to the spread of the gospel (2.13–16); his defense of his own conduct may be a reply to slanders current in the town. The continuation of opposition to the church since his departure had worried him so much that he had wished to go back to see how things were; finding this impossible for reasons that he does not divulge, beyond saying that "Satan blocked our way" (2.18), he sent Timothy as his representative, and the latter has now returned full of enthusiasm for the healthy state of the church (2.17–3.13). In the remainder of the letter, Paul gives the church the kind of teaching and prac-

tical advice that he would have liked to share with them in person. He encourages the believers to live holy lives—with special reference to the avoidance of sexual immorality—and to continue to grow in love (4.1–12). He gives instruction to comfort Christians who are fearful about the fate of those of their number who had died and assures them that, when the Lord returns, the resurrection of the dead will take place, so that those who "fell asleep" (NRSV: "died") will come with Christ and be united with those still alive. Believers need not worry when this will take place; if they are truly "awake," they will not be taken by surprise (4.13–5.11). Finally, Paul commends brotherly love and encourages the use of spiritual gifts (5.12–24), closing the letter with personal greetings (5.25–28).

The second letter follows the same pattern. The opening greeting (1.1–2) is followed by a prayer report, which also functions as encouragement and teaching: the church is still suffering from opposition, but is bearing it steadfastly, and Paul assures the believers that God will judge those who oppose them and will prepare the church to share in his glory when Christ comes (1.3–12). The center of the letter is teaching about the return of Christ, directed against people who were claiming Paul's authority for asserting that the *day of the Lord had begun and that the return of Christ could be expected immediately. Paul replies by stating that a period of Satanic opposition to God on an unparalleled scale must first happen, and then Christ will come to bring it to an end; meanwhile, the church must hold firm (2.1–17). The final part of the letter is exhortation: the church is asked to pray for Paul, and attention is drawn to some Christians who had abandoned their daily work and were living off the generosity of their good-natured friends. Paul condemns this idleness and the consequent nuisance of the idlers strongly (3.1–16). There is a brief closing greeting (3.17–18).

Thessalonica was one of the towns in Macedonia that was visited by Paul, *Silas, and Timothy during the second of the missionary tours described by Luke in Acts 16–18. It was in fact the capital of the Roman province, an important commercial center situated on the major highway, the Via Egnatia. Not surprisingly, its population included Jews (Acts 17.1, 5). Paul and his companions spent a brief time here after leaving Philippi, but sufficiently long to gain a number of converts from Jewish and Greek attenders at the *synagogue and so to establish a church. According to Luke, Jewish opposition forced the missionaries to leave precipitately. They moved into Achaia and worked briefly at *Athens and then for a longer period at *Corinth. It was during this period that Timothy paid the visit mentioned in 1 Thessalonians 3.1–6, and that Paul wrote the first letter, doubtless from Corinth.

The history of the church between its foundation and the composition of the letter is known only from allusions in the letter. The picture that emerges is of a church free from groups opposed to Paul, and developing in faith and love. Certainly, Paul was worried about whether the church could stand up to attacks from outside, but this concern arose more from the recent foundation of the congregation than because of any inherent defects.

The major point where Paul felt the need to give instructions was the future advent (or *parousia) of the Lord Jesus. It is unlikely that there were any false teachings; it appears rather that the Thessalonian Christians had not fully understood Paul's teaching about the parousia and the resurrection of the dead. The *second coming of the Lord played a prominent part in Paul's preaching, for he refers to it with remarkable frequency in the letter (1.10; 2.19; 3.13; 4.13–5.11; 5.23). Otherwise, the letter reflects the typical characteristics of Paul's thought, including the distinctive use of the phrase "in Christ" to characterize the nature of the Christian life.

There is no doubt that Paul was the author of this letter. Theories that it is a forgery need not be taken seriously. Some scholars have argued that the letter has a peculiar shape, and attempt to explain it as a combination of two or more documents or as a document that had been subjected to interpolations, but these theories are more ingenious than convincing.

The second letter raises problems to which there are no generally agreed answers. Its language and content are sufficiently similar to those of 1 Thessalonians to indicate that, if authentic, it was probably written not long after the first letter. Yet it lacks concrete references to the situation of the readers or of the writer. From chap. 1, it appears that attack from outside must have worsened. The pungency of Paul's language may also suggest that he himself was the object of particular attack from people outside the church (see 3.2).

The situation behind chap. 2 is difficult to reconstruct. There must have been a group in the church who believed that they were living in the very last days. They appear to have been encouraged in this view by some statement that was alleged to have come from Paul himself. Paul, however, stopped short of affirming that the end had actually arrived, and he referred to other events that must happen before the return of the Lord. There is no unanimity as to what Paul envisaged by the apostasy and the man of lawlessness, or what he meant by the force that was at present restraining the lawless one from appearing (2 Thess. 2.9; see Antichrist). The language used has a mythological character and may reflect *apocalyptic literature in which a heavenly force restrains the powers of evil. But whether Paul used this language to refer to specific persons or beings is not certain. One view is that Paul saw the Roman emperor and/or empire as embodying the forces of law and order that restrained the forces of chaos from taking over. Another view, perhaps more persuasive, sees God himself or the preaching of the gospel as the force holding back the full impact of the forces of evil. Paul wrote allusively, even for his first readers, and therefore it is not surprising that we are at a loss to know precisely what he had in mind.

In the final part of the letter we find evidence that some members of the church were living in idleness at others' expense. Although no explicit connection is made, it is hard not to believe that the apocalyptic excitement reflected in chap. 2 contributed to this situation. It called forth strong censure from Paul, who firmly believed that Christians should work for their living. Apparently, discipline in the church consisted of exclusion from the privileges of fellowship.

These comments on 2 Thessalonians have been made in terms of the ostensible historical context of the document as a genuine letter from Paul to the church at Thessalonica. In this view, we must assume that in the period after the writing of 1 Thessalonians a kind of apocalyptic fervor, whose origins can be detected in the earlier letter, developed in the church. Paul does not deal with it in terms of castigating a group of opponents, as in other letters; rather, he writes to believers who may have been misled by a misinterpretation of his teaching.

Such a situation appears to be quite plausible. Yet it does not appear so to some commentators, for whom there is sharp contrast between the nearness of the parousia in 1 Thessalonians and its delay in 2 Thessalonians. This alerts them to other odd features in the latter, such as the lack of personal, concrete allusions, the peculiar repetition of phraseology from 1 Thessalonians, and some differences in language and thought. In the judgment of numerous scholars these differences are incompatible with the traditional understanding of the letter as authentically Pauline. Attempts to solve the problem by arguing that the letters were written in reverse chronological order or that they are compositions of fragments originally written in a different order have not commanded assent. So it is argued that 2 Thessalonians is a later composition by another writer who wished to use Paul's name to correct his teaching or false inferences from it, perhaps even to claim that this letter alone was authentic (cf. 3.17) and that 1 Thessalonians was to be rejected. A solution of this kind can be defended by concentrating on the unusual features of 2 Thessalonians. Its major weakness, however, is the lack of a convincing and plausible reconstruction of the circumstances in which such a letter could have been composed—and directed to Thessalonica in particular. The letter, for example, appears to assume that the *Temple in Jerusalem is still standing (2.4). The language refuting the claim that the *day of the Lord had already arrived is so cryptic that it is hard to envisage a later writer expressing himself in this fashion if he wanted to persuade his readers. The brazenness of the hypothetical author in writing 2 Thessalonians 3.17 is also remarkable. Although it must be granted that there are some oddities in the language, structure, and thought of the letter, the difficulties in considering it pseudonymous are greater.

I. HOWARD MARSHALL

Third Isaiah. *See* Isaiah, The Book of.

Thomas. An *apostle, named in all lists of the *twelve, but a major character only in the gospel of John. Mentioned in John 11.16 and 14.5, Thomas is prominent in John 20.24–29, where his insistence on physical proofs for Jesus's *resurrection has led to the phrase "doubting Thomas." Several *apocryphal works are ascribed to or are about Thomas, including the *gnostic gospel of Thomas and the Acts of Thomas. In the latter, his name, which means "twin" in Aramaic, is the basis for his identification as Jesus' twin brother. He is also said to have preached the gospel as far east as India.

MICHAEL D. COOGAN

Three Young Men, Song of the. *See* Azariah, The Prayer of, and The Song of the Three Young Men.

Thummin. *See* Urim and Thummin.

Tiglath-Pileser III. Tukulti-apil-Esharra, King of *Assyria 745–727 BCE, sometimes known by the hypocoristic Pul or Pulu. Having risen to power after a revolt against Ashur-nirari V (755–745 BCE), Tiglath-pileser reversed decades of Assyrian political decline and ousted Urartu as the principal power in Western Asia. He laid the foundations for the most expansive phase of the Neo-Assyrian empire by a prolonged series of annual campaigns, by reorganizing and geographically extending the Assyrian provincial system, and by massive deportations of troublesome subject populations.

After early campaigns against Arameans in *Babylonia and against western Iran (745–744 BCE), Tiglath-pileser turned his attention to the more crucial northern and western fronts. He defeated Urartu in 743 and 735 BCE and crushed its Syrian allies, particularly Arpad (742–740 BCE). He invaded Syria and Palestine in 738 and 734 BCE, reaching almost to the border of Egypt and receiving the submission of Zabibe, queen of Arabia. Menahem of Israel paid tribute to Tiglath-pileser, who withdrew from his kingdom (2 Kings 15.19). When Pekah had succeeded to the throne, Tiglath-pileser captured part of the northern section of Israel (2 Kings 15.29) and later deported some of the population to Assyria (1 Chron. 5.26). On behalf of Ahaz of Judah, who had sent him munificent gifts, Tiglath-pileser campaigned against *Damascus and Israel (2 Kings 16.7–9). After Tiglath-pileser had captured Damascus, Ahaz met him there; Ahaz was subsequently accused of changing cult paraphernalia because of the Assyrian king (2 Kings 16.10–18).

Tiglath-pileser campaigned in Babylonia in 731 and 729 BCE and then himself became king of Babylonia in 728. After his death in 727 BCE, he was succeeded by his son, *Shalmaneser V.

JOHN A. BRINKMAN

Time, Units of. The universal division of time into past, present, and future is expressed in Hebrew (as in other Semitic languages) by a spatial metaphor. Contrary to Western usage, the past is what lies ahead (Hebr. *qedem*) and is therefore known; the future is unknown and is behind (Hebr. *ʾāḥôr; ʾaḥărôn*).

There is no clear evidence for division of the day into smaller, equal parts in ancient Israel, though such systems were known elsewhere in the ancient Near East (and see perhaps Neh. 9.3). By the Roman period, a system of twelve hours of daylight was in use (3 Macc. 5.14; Matt. 20.3–6). Generally in the Bible the term "hour" is used in a nonspecific sense. The day was either the period of sunlight, contrasted with the night (see John 11.9) or the whole period of twenty-four hours, although not defined as such in the Bible. In earlier traditions a day apparently began at sunrise (e.g., Lev. 7.15–17; Judg. 19.4–19), but later its beginning was at sunset and its end at the following sunset. Thus, in Genesis 1, the six days of *creation are each described as follows: "there was evening, and there was morning." It should be stressed that this clear description makes impossible any understanding of the days of creation in Genesis 1 as longer periods, such as geological eras. This system became normative (see Exod. 12.18; Lev. 23.32; Neh. 13.19) and is still observed in Jewish tradition, where, for example, the *Sabbath begins on Friday evening at sunset and ends Saturday at sunset. The word "day" can also be used metaphorically, referring to a critical time, such as the day of birth or death (Eccles. 7.1), the *day of the Lord, and the day of Christ (Phil. 1.10). The plural form can be used in a looser sense, equivalent to the general notion of time, as in phrases like "in those days" and "days of old."

The night was apparently divided into watches, three of which are implied in Judges 7.19 and four apparently named in Mark 13.35.

The week consisted of seven days, the last of which was the *Sabbath, the only one to be named. The first six days are designated by ordinal numbers.

The two Hebrew words for month (*yeraḥ* and *ḥodeš*) are both related to the moon and its cycle (cf. *yārēaḥ* "moon" and *ḥādāš* "new"). Different names are used for the months in different periods, as follows (those in parentheses are not attested in the Bible but are found in other ancient sources):

CANAANITE NAME	BABYLONIAN NAME	MODERN EQUIVALENT
Abib	Nisan	March/April
Ziv	(Iyyar)	April/May
	Siwan	May/June
	(Tammuz)	June/July
	(Ab)	July/August
	Elul	August/September
Ethanim	(Tishri)	September/October
Bul	(Marheshvan)	October/November
	Chislev	November/December
	Tebeth	December/January
	Shebat	January/February
	Adar	February/March

Four of the months have Canaanite names: Abib, used only in connection with the *Exodus and its commemoration in the festival of unleavened bread or *Passover (Exod. 13.4; 23.15; Deut. 16.1), and the remaining three in the account of the dedication of the *Temple in 1 Kings (6.1, 37–38; 8.2). The Babylonian names are used in texts dating from the sixth century BCE on. Often months are simply indicated by their ordinal number, with Abib/Nisan being the first (Exod. 12.2), at the time of the vernal equinox. But this also seems to be a relatively late innovation, patterned after the Babylonian system; earlier traditions imply that the new year was celebrated in the fall, at the autumnal equinox (see Exod. 23.16; 34.22), apparently in agreement with Canaanite practice. A tenth-century BCE calendar from *Gezer lists the agricultural activities characteristic of twelve months, beginning with the fall harvest.

The year was apparently based on the lunar cycle and consisted of twelve months (1 Chron. 27.15; Rev. 22.2), apparently of twenty-nine or thirty days each. The use of an intercalary month is disputed but may have occurred (see 1 Kings 12.33). It is possible that there was also use of a true solar year, although the evidence is fragmentary.

No absolute system of *chronology is used in the Bible, most systems referring either to the regnal years of various rulers or to key events (e.g., 1 Kings 6.1), although the figures given in various sources are frequently inconsistent. Contrary to modern practice, in totaling units both the first and the last were usually counted.   MICHAEL D. COOGAN

Timothy, The Letters to. *See* Pastoral Letters, The.

Tithe. Attested in ancient Near Eastern sources apart from the Bible, in Israel the development of the practice of tithing (Hebr. *ma'ăśēr*, meaning a tenth) is unknown and not all the particulars are mutually reconcilable. According to Genesis, tithes were voluntarily offered by *Abraham to *Melchizedek and accepted by him on God's behalf, long before the *Temple (Gen. 14.20; Heb. 7.4–10). This was confirmed as an obligation by *Jacob in his vow (Gen. 28.22): "Of all that you give me, I will surely give one tenth to you," God being the universal donor. In other traditions, the chief purpose of tithe was to maintain *priests and *Levites, who had not been allotted a share in realty in *Canaan (Num. 18.21–24; Josh. 14.3–4). Tithe was assessed on the fruits of the land of Israel and (see Jubilees 32.15) herds and flocks there, such tithes not being redeemable for money (Lev. 27.30–33). The Levites at one time received tithe and passed on a tenth to the priests or for the use of the Temple (Num. 18.25–32; Neh. 10.37–39); but by the first century CE priests collected for themselves. It is not unknown for some priests to forestall others forcibly. The king no longer collected tithes, if he ever did (cf. 1 Sam. 8.15).

Particularity about tithing, as required in the *Mishnah, was not inconsistent with neglect of other commandments not so easily quantified (Matt. 23.23; Luke 11.42). Priests obtained income from other sources, but failure to pay tithes (cf. Neh. 13.10) was a spiritual offense (Deut. 12.6), so as to excite God's anger (Mal. 3.8, 10). A perfect Israel would proudly contribute to the cult with its tithes (2 Chron. 31.5–6; Neh. 12.44–47), and *Pharisees could boast of their reliability (Luke 18.12). But there was a discrepancy between such observances and spirituality (Amos 4.4–5). What accretions and what gains, natural and otherwise, must be submitted to Pentateuchal tithe could be argued, but the Mishnah declares all cultivated and edible growths liable. Pharisees regarded food that might not have been tithed as unfit for consumption by the righteous.

Another tithe of produce is required at Deuteronomy 14.22–23 to be realized by its owners and spent in Jerusalem to subsidize the city, its Temple, and the Levites. This may refer to the first fruits or the money received from their sale, which the producers had to take to Jerusalem (cf. Deut. 26.1–15), but this is doubtful. It is important that that "second tithe" was to be spent on servants, *orphans, *widows, and *aliens as well as Levites (cf. Deut. 12.17–19; 14.22–

29). A regular collection for the *poor was known by the second century BCE (Tob. 1.8), and the Mishnah speaks of a tithe for the poor even though payment of it was voluntary (cf. Sir. 7.32). On the other hand it rules that the animals of Leviticus 27.30–33 are subject to the "second tithe."

Luke 11.41–42 suggests the probability that, in at least some churches, the Pentateuchal precepts were applied by analogy for the benefit of the Christian poor. Matthew 23.23 suggests that the custom of tithing was preserved somehow. The New Testament nowhere explicitly requires tithing to maintain a ministry or a place of assembly.   J. DUNCAN M. DERRETT

Titus, The Letter to. *See* Pastoral Letters, The.

Tobit, The Book of. The book of Tobit, regarded by Jews and Protestants as apocryphal and by Roman Catholics and some Orthodox churches as deuterocanonical (*see* Apocrypha, article on Jewish Apocrypha), is named after its alleged author Tobit, a generous and God-fearing Jew whose blindness and poverty in *Nineveh (Map 6:H3) are the direct result of his performing one of his most characteristic good deeds, namely, burying an executed compatriot.

But thanks to the courageous efforts of his devoted son, Tobias (who unknown to both of them was assisted by the angel *Raphael masquerading as Azariah), Tobit ultimately recovers his sight and fortune and also gains a virtuous daughter-in-law, Sarah, a Medean relative from whom Tobias has exorcised Asmodeus, the demon who had claimed the lives of each of her seven previous husbands on their wedding night. Shortly before his death as a very old man, Tobit has Tobias and his large family move from Nineveh to Ecbatana (Map 6:J4), where Tobias lives to a very rich old age.

Although the book has all the outer trappings of a historical account, including mention of well-known historical personages (e.g., *Shalmaneser V in 1.13; *Sennacherib in 1.15) and places (e.g., Nineveh, 1.3; Ecbatana, 3.7; and Rages, 4.1), the narrative is best understood as a novella or, more specifically, a Diaspora romance, centering on a successful quest. The story is intended to edify and to inspire faith in God and human effort; for without Tobias's own devotion and courage (5.1–8; 6.2–3, 14–18; 7.9–13; 8.1–3), neither his father nor his wife would have been delivered, the help of the angel Raphael notwithstanding (6.4–9; 8.3).

In creating this charming pastiche about everyday Jewish "saints" in the *Dispersion, the ancient narrator utilized as his basic fabrics three well-known folktales: the ubiquitous story of the Grateful Dead, the tale about a man who was at first impoverished but ultimately was rewarded for burying an abused corpse; the Monster in the Bridal Chamber, a widespread tale featuring an evil creature who is in love with a beautiful maiden and kills her husband on their wedding night; and the Ahiqar Story, the last-named being a wise courtier who, though betrayed by his adopted son, is ultimately vindicated.

Although the author of Tobit wove these folktales together quite skillfully, their seams are occasionally discernable in certain loose or incompatible threads: e.g., the gratuitous mention of Tobias's dog, an unclean animal (Tob. 6.2 and 11.4); and Tobit's injunction to his son to pour his wine on the grave of the righteous (4.17), which, while contrary to biblical teaching (Deut. 26.14), is included in the counsels of the nonbiblical Ahiqar.

Even though the basic fabrics of the book are secular folktales, their designs and colors are distinctly biblical, being patterned after stories in Genesis (e.g., the story of Joseph [Gen. 37 and 39–50] and the betrothal stories of Isaac and Jacob [cf. Tob. 5.17–22; 7.1–16; 10.7–13 with Gen. 24 and 29]) and colored by the theology of the book of Deuteronomy in general, and its doctrine of just deserts in particular. The author of Tobit subscribed to the Deuteronomic equation (cf. Deut. 28) that righteousness ultimately results in material prosperity (so Tob. 11.14–18; 13.10–11; 14.1–2), while wickedness always brings punishment and material disaster (so Tob. 1.21; 3.3–6; 13.12; 14.4, 10).

The author of Tobit also used the biblical *Job as the model for Tobit; the two characters are both men of outstandingly good deeds and piety who, though they suffered and were tested (cf. Job. 1.6–2.10 and Tob. 12.14), did not lose their faith (so Job 31.37 and Tob. 3.2–6) and ultimately were rewarded with even greater blessings (so Job 42.10–16 and Tob. 14.1–2). While the author of Tobit expressly mentions Amos (2.6) and Nahum (14.4), it is prophets who are not mentioned by name, notably Jeremiah, Ezekiel, and Third Isaiah, who exerted the strongest influence on him, especially in Tobit 13–14, where Israel's *exile and return are predicted.

The book of Tobit, like the meaning of his name ("[God] is my good"), is essentially ironic. Although Tobit fed the hungry, clothed the naked, and buried exposed corpses (cf. 1.16–18)—all of which he insisted delivers one from death and keeps one "from going into the Darkness" (Tob. 4.10)—he lost both his wealth *and* his sight. Sarah, too, is an ironic figure: a virtuous, loving, and level-headed young maiden, she was plagued by an evil that almost drove her to suicide (3.10–15).

The story has little tension or suspense, for quite early in the narrative the reader learns not only that Sarah and Tobit will be healed (3.16–17) but even how (6.6–9). But this special knowledge also enables the reader better to appreciate various ironies in the story, including Tobit's assurance to his son that "an angel" will accompany him and Azariah (5.17), Raguel furtively digging a grave for the apparently doomed Tobias (8.9–12), and the conviction of Tobias's mother that her long-delayed son is dead (10.4–7).

Given the tragic circumstances of Tobit and Sarah at the height of their miseries, many of the names in the story are highly ironic. Tobit's father was Tobiel ("God is my good"); Tobit's sharp-tongued wife (2.14; 5.18–20; 10.7) is called Anna ("Grace"); the angel Raphael ("God heals") poses as Azariah ("Yahweh has helped"); the mother of the demon-possessed Sarah is Edna ("Pleasure").

The narrator's theological views are clearly and effectively expressed in the book's plot as well as in its characters' monologues (e.g., 1.3–3.6, 10), conversations (e.g., 2.11–14; 5.18–22; 6.16–18), speeches (4.3–21; 12.6–15, 17–20; 14.3–11), and especially their prayers (3.1–6, 11–15; 8.5–8; 13.1–17).

The century-long debate by scholars as to whether the book was originally composed in Greek or in a Semitic language has been resolved by the discovery of one Hebrew and four Aramaic manuscripts of the book among the *Dead Sea Scrolls at Qumran. Because the manuscripts are very fragmentary and not fully published, certainty is denied us; but it would appear that *Aramaic was the original language of the book, though the Septuagint may be based upon a Hebrew version. In the Qumran texts, Tobit's name is Tobi; his son's name, Tobiyah.

In spite of Tobit's obvious literary and theological merits, it was excluded from the Jewish canon, probably because of the late date of its composition (see below), though it does also contradict the rabbinic halakah on marriage, whereby the groom, not the bride's father as in Tobit 7.12–13, writes out the marriage contract.

As for the Christian canon, more often than not Eastern church fathers denied Tobit canonicity, while Western councils and fathers, starting with Pseudo-Clement (2 Clem. 16.4) ca. 150 CE, nearly always accepted the book.

Converging lines of evidence suggest that the book was composed sometime ca. 225–175 BCE. The phrase "the law/book of Moses" (Tob. 6.13; 7.11, 12, 13) is late, occurring first in 2 Chronicles (23.18); and not until ca. 200 BCE were the prophetic books regarded as the word of God (cf. Tob. 14.4). A date of composition later than 175 BCE is precluded by the total absence from the book of any of the strife and turmoil associated with the days of Antiochus IV Epiphanes (175–164 BCE) and the Maccabees (164–135 BCE). Then too, by the first century BCE, Jewish concern for endogamy, which is so prominent in Tobit (4.12–13; 6.10–12, 16; 7.8–15), had diminished. The book's presence at Qumran virtually rules out a first-century BCE date.

Whether the book originated in Mesopotamia, Egypt, or Palestine is unclear, though arguments for a Palestinian provenance may be gaining support.

Of the three major versions of Tobit used by Christian churches down through the millennia, the so-called longer recension (longer by 1700 Greek words as preserved by Codex Sinaiticus, and the Old Latin version) is the most authentic and is the basis for the NEB and the NRSV; the "shorter recension," used by the RSV, is an abbreviation of the longer, while, as Jerome himself reports, his Vulgate was based upon an Aramaic text.   CAREY A. MOORE

Tongues, Speaking in. *See* Glossolalia.

Topheth. A site southwest of *Jerusalem in the Valley of Hinnom (*see* Gehenna) where, according to Jeremiah, worshipers burned their sons and daughters as offerings (Jer. 7.31; 19.5). Jeremiah associates this ritual of child sacrifice with the god *Baal; elsewhere the god to whom children are sacrificed at the Topheth is called Molech (2 Kings 23.10). Inscriptional evidence from cemeteries of infants and young children found at Carthage and elsewhere in the Phoenician world, however, suggests that Molech may be a common noun meaning "sacrificial offering"; also, Jeremiah's prophecies associating the cult with

Baal may not be historically accurate. At least some people apparently sacrificed their children to Yahweh, including Kings Ahaz (2 Chron. 33.6) and *Manasseh (2 Chron. 33.6). The great reformer king of Judah, *Josiah (ca. 640–609 BCE), is said to have destroyed the Topheth as part of his purification of the Yahwistic cult (2 Kings 23.10).   SUSAN ACKERMAN

Torah. One of the basic concepts of biblical religion and rabbinic literature. The meaning of "torah" (Hebr. *tôrâ*) is "instruction, teaching." "Torah" is often rendered "law," as consistently in the *Septuagint, although Greek *nomos* had broader meaning than simply "law." This rendering has been deplored, but it has validity. For example, Exodus 12.49 reads, "There shall be one torah for the native and for the resident alien." Clearly the translator must render "torah" here as "law." "Law" is an extension of the basic meaning of "torah," for divine instruction assumes the force of law. In Leviticus and Numbers particularly, the individual divine laws are referred to as "torahs" (Hebr. *tôrôt*). Underlying the biblical concept of Torah is another concept, one of these being a way of God that had to be followed, a concept that finds its fullest expression in the prophets and in the Psalms.

If the divinity is the promulgator of Torah as law, Torah in its broadest sense may be promulgated by kings, *priests, wise men, and even wise *women (Prov. 1.8; 6.20). Most significant historically is the promulgation of Torah through *Moses, an idea found already in the *Pentateuch, as in Deuteronomy 4.44: "This is the torah that Moses set before the Israelites." The tractate of the *Mishnah known as "the Ethics of the Fathers" *(Pirqe ʾAbot)* begins with the statement "Moses received the Torah at Mount Sinai," one of the fundamental precepts of rabbinic Judaism. Not only were the *Ten Commandments given at *Sinai, but, as we shall see, the Torah in a wider sense.

The development of the concept of Torah proceeded as follows: (1) the promulgation of individual divinely directed *tôrôt*; (2) the Torah of the divinely inspired figure of Moses; (3) a definite idea of Torah as the book of the Torah, which by the days of Ezra and Nehemiah meant the Pentateuch in an early form; (4) in the rabbinic period, the Torah as Pentateuch, in a form not unlike the Pentateuch of the present day (*see* Canon). Rabbinic usage of the term was quite broad. It could refer to the five books of Moses or to the totality of divine revelation. It included two basic types of materials: legal (halakhic) and literary (aggadic), with the latter including everything from stories to poetry to nonlegal interpretation of biblical texts and more. The rabbis extended Torah to include another dichotomy: the written Torah and the oral Torah, the latter consisting of traditions that were transmitted orally until they were given written expression in the Mishnah, the basis of the *Talmud (cf. the "Temple Scroll" from *Qumran, which may have functioned as an additional book of Torah). Both Torahs were considered to have descended from heaven; there was even a rabbinic tradition that the Torah preexisted *creation, and another that through it God effected creation (cf. Sir. 24.1–23; Prov. 9.22–31). Rabbinic Judaism stressed the joy of fulfilling the Torah's commandments; Torah observance ensured salvation. It is difficult to overstate the importance of Torah in early Judaism, an emphasis that has continued to the present.

In biblical tradition the role of the king in relation to Torah is specified in Deuteronomy 17.18: "When he [the king] is seated on his royal throne, he shall have written for himself a copy of this torah on a book before the levitical priests." No king of Israel or Judah is known to have followed this law, with the partial exception of *Josiah, who read the book without actually having it written out (2 Kings 23.3). The king's role in relation to Torah is hinted at in the lament of Lamentations 2.9: "Her king and her princes are among the nations; there is no torah." Priests as well are upholders of God's Torah and its interpreters as part of their everyday functions (Jer. 18.18; Hag. 2.11–13). The *prophets too were greatly concerned with Torah, especially when the people failed to follow the divine way (Isa. 1.10; 5.24; Jer. 2.8; 9.12). Malachi 4.4 is the only prophetic reference to the Torah of Moses, showing that the early conception of Torah as direct divine teaching had precedence for the prophets over the concept of the Mosaic Torah.

The earliest Christian attitudes toward Torah were ambivalent. One view is found in Jesus' saying in Matthew 5.17: "Do not think that I have come to abolish the law or the prophets; I have come not to abolish but to fulfill. For truly I tell you, until heaven and earth pass away, not one letter, not one stroke of a letter, will pass from the law until all is accomplished." But this clear-cut and positive view is not that of the entire New Testament. *Paul, though expressing

the belief that the law may be fulfilled through love (Rom. 13.8–10), also asserts that "a person is justified not by the works of the law but through faith in Jesus Christ" (Gal. 2.16) and that "the power of sin is the law" (1 Cor. 15.56); see Justification. With these radical doctrines, Paul was able to sever the Judaic umbilical cord and to set Christianity on its present track.

See Interpretation, History of, article on Jewish Interpretation; Law; Lectionaries, article on Jewish Tradition; Synagogue.   PHILIP STERN

Tower of Babel. See Babel, Tower of.

Trade and Transport.

Trade. Palestine is a bridge between Africa and Asia as well as a land passage between Europe and Egypt. Thus local trade in Palestine has been supplemented across the millennia by international trade, and archaeological evidence of imported goods is found from the Neolithic period onward. Biblical authors generally take notice of trade as they comment on ethics and theology related to it.

Ezekiel's informative summary of the trading patterns of his day (27.12–25) lists the products of Judah and Israel as "wheat from Minneth, millet, honey, oil, and balm" (v. 17). Wheat and millet are easily transportable. Olive trees need little water, and the oil can be extracted and traded easily. The Hebrew word for "honey" is děbaš, which means both honey and syrup. Grape juice was and is made into *wine or boiled into a tasty syrup. The "land flowing with milk and honey" thus means a land with extensive pasture for flocks of sheep and goats and with hillsides where grapes can be grown that will produce large quantities of syrup/honey. Wool and wool products also became exportable merchandise.

*Solomon developed copper mining in the south of the country, and from *David onward the Philistine restriction of blacksmithing was ended, but the extent of iron technology in Palestine is uncertain. In the Hellenistic period asphalt was gathered and marketed from the Dead Sea. In Roman times trade was widespread but was not very significant to the authors of the New Testament.

The prophets are especially interested in speaking to the human problems created by manufacturing and trade. *Amos cries out against merchants who make the grain measure (the ephah) small and the payment ingot (the shekel;

see Money) large, and who are eager for the *Sabbath to be over so that they may return to their trading (8.4–6). The injustice caused by accumulated wealth is a major topic throughout his prophecy. Metallurgy becomes a parable for Isaiah as he describes how God will refine the people through punishment (1.25). The oppression of workers is sharply criticized (Isa. 58.3–8), a passage partially quoted in Luke 4.17–20. Then, in the parables of Jesus, trading becomes a framework within which to discuss faithfulness to an absent master (Luke 19.11–27). The kingdom of God is not compared to a "pearl of great price" but rather to a merchant searching for such a pearl (Matt. 13.44–45).

Barter as a means of exchange gradually gave way to payment in gold and silver ingots, bars, and rings. Coins began to circulate during Persian times but came into common uses only after *Alexander the Great (*see* Money). Banking flourished in the Roman period and is mentioned in Luke 19.23. From David and Solomon onward the authorities in Palestine could collect significant sums of money in customs charges on goods passing through the country. Much of *Herod the Great's considerable wealth may have come from such sources. The neighboring *Nabateans and Palmyra flourished because of their dominant positions along trade routes.

Transport. Transport during the biblical periods was facilitated by means of porters, donkeys, camels, carts, and ships.

Porters have been a major part of the transport system in the Near East since ancient times, carrying goods of any kind from one place to another. This was and is done on the back, often with a strap around the bottom of the burden up over the top of the head to keep the weight from slipping. A second method of carrying goods was with the use of a yoke across the shoulders. Jesus' often-quoted saying "My yoke is easy" (Matt. 11.30) refers to a yoke for porters, not for oxen.

The lowly donkey was in extensive use by the second millennium BCE and remains a basic means of transport in villages all across the Middle East. Egyptian tomb paintings in Beni Hassan (ca. 1890 BCE) depict travelers from Palestine with goods arriving by donkey. The donkey is surefooted, patient, and easy to manage. It can carry over 135 kg (300 lb) and as a riding animal can easily travel more than 32 km (20 mi) a day.

The camel was domesticated at least by the second millennium BCE and was known in Palestine before the first. It has been used exten-sively for transport ever since (cf. Gen. 37.25; Job 6.18–19; Isa. 21.13; 60.6). The camel can carry up to 225 kg (500 lb) and is able to travel long distances without food or water. Its greatest weakness is its need for smooth footing. Yet for long distances and/or heavy loads, over smooth ground, the camel is superb and has remained a primary method of transport in the Middle East.

Crude carts from Palestine are depicted on the walls of the temple of Ramesses III (early twelfth century BCE) at Medinet Habu in Luxor, Egypt. Carts are mentioned in historical narratives (e.g., 1 Sam. 6.7; 2 Sam. 6.3) and in the prophets (e.g., Amos 2.13). With the building of the Roman road system carts came into their own as an important transport alternative.

The *ships of the ancient world were small craft that usually hugged the coasts and beached each night. Gradually navigational skills and boat construction made it possible for larger ships to venture across the Mediterranean (Jon. 1.3; Acts 27). The *Phoenicians were famous for their skill and daring in the art of sailing (cf. Ezek. 27.1–9). Because the Palestinian coast has no natural harbors and because it was frequently under the control of others, the Israelites generally relied on the Phoenicians for maritime commerce (see 1 Kings 9.26–28; 10.11, 22).

Horses were used for war and as a means of travel for the upper classes but rarely for transport. There is no record of the use of elephants for transportation in the Middle East.

KENNETH E. BAILEY

Translations. *This entry deals with translations, or "versions," of the Bible from the original *Hebrew, *Aramaic, and *Greek, and consists of ten articles:*

>Theory and Practice
>Ancient Languages
>Targums
>Medieval Versions
>English Language
>Modern European Languages
>African Languages
>Asiatic Languages
>Australian Aboriginal Languages
>Native American Languages

The first article deals with general theories and problems of translation. The second article discusses all ancient versions, except for the Targums, which are the subject of the third article. The remaining articles survey medieval versions and translations into other languages, first English, then groups of languages ordered by continent. Related discussion is found in Circulation of the Bible; Paraphrases; Polyglot Bibles; Septuagint; Vulgate; *and* Wycliffe Bible Translators.

Theory and Practice

The theory and practice of scripture translation represent three different traditions with distinctive but largely complementary sets of principles. These three primary approaches to translating may be designated as philological, linguistic, and communicative.

The Philological Approach focuses on such features as the author's background, distinctive features of style, literary genres, the history of text transmission, literary criticism, and the manner in which a text has been interpreted through the years. The first Bible translator to deal overtly with these issues was Jerome, who in accordance with the best classical tradition realized that the sense must have priority over the words. This represented a radical departure from the Old Latin practice.

Luther's translation of the Bible into German also broke with tradition and the dominance of the *Vulgate by translating directly from Greek and Hebrew and by using the ordinary words of common people. In the English language, Tyndale likewise insisted that the message of the scriptures should be understood by everyone, and with this intent he produced what later proved to be a major contribution to the King James Version.

The committee that produced the King James Version was especially concerned for the stylistic quality of a text for public reading, and they were surprisingly successful in producing a translation that not only dominated the use of scriptures in English for almost two centuries but greatly influenced the production of early translations by missionaries in Asia, Africa, and the Americas.

The latter part of the nineteenth century and the beginning of the twentieth century were marked by intense interest in archaeological finds and the discovery of many ancient manuscripts, which inevitably led to new insights in interpretation of many biblical passages. The English Revised Version (1885) and the corresponding American Standard Version (1901) represented the best in nineteenth-century biblical scholarship, but the many awkward literalisms in these translations greatly limited their acceptability for English-speaking people.

During this same period certain individual translators produced versions that were stylistically more in line with present-day usage in English, such as Weymouth's *New Testament in Modern Speech* (1902), Moffatt's *The Bible: A New Translation* (1928), and Goodspeed's *The New Testament: An American Translation* (1935). Such translations inevitably influenced the demand for more standard texts that would have a wider range of acceptance, including the Revised Standard Version (1946, 1952), the New English Bible (1970), and the New American Bible (1970). Similar developments occurred in a number of other major languages, for example, La Bible de Jérusalem (1956), Die Einheitsübersetzung (1974), and Nueva Biblia Española (1975).

The Linguistic Approach became an important factor after 1945, when there was a rapid expansion of missionary work in hundreds of minor languages without any written literary tradition or even system of writing. Most missionary translators had little to guide them in formulating alphabets, analyzing complex grammars, determining the meanings of words in quite different cultures, and learning to appreciate some of the remarkable stylistic features of oral literatures.

To determine what could and should be done, the Netherlands Bible Society organized for the United *Bible Societies the first international conference of Bible translators held in Woudschoten, Netherlands, in 1946. The journal *The Bible Translator* began publication the next year, and this was followed by a number of books: *Bible Translating* (1947), *Toward a Science of Translating* (1964), *The Theory and Practice of Translation* (1969), and *From One Language to Another* (1986), as well as a series of *Translators' Handbooks* providing detailed information on exegetical and cultural problems. The Summer Institute of Linguistics, also known as the *Wycliffe Bible Translators, has also published a number of helps for Bible translators.

A major problem in producing revisions or new translations in languages having a long biblical tradition is the change of meaning that has often taken place in words and idioms. For example, most English speakers understand the terms "justify" and "justification" as meaning "using questionable means for making something seem right or correct, even when it is not." Accordingly, some English translations now use expressions such as "to be put right with" or "to make acceptable to." Some of the most creative attempts to express the meaning of the scriptures in present-day language are *The New Tes-*

tament in Modern English (J. B. Phillips, 1958), *La Version Popular* in Spanish (1979), *Today's English Version* (1976), *Gute Nachricht* in German (1982), *La Bonne Nouvelle d'Aujourd'hui* in French (1982), and *The Contemporary English Version* (New Testament, 1991).

The linguistic approach to translating may be viewed as a four-phase process: analysis (determining the meaning of the biblical text on the most explicit level), transfer (shifting from the source to the target language on this explicit level), restructuring (reproducing the message on the appropriate language level for the intended audience), and testing (to determine the accuracy and degree of natural equivalence based on readers' responses).

The Communicative Approach to translating (based in large measure on communication theory) has been a natural outgrowth of the linguistic orientation. The key factors in communication are source (for the Bible, both divine and human), message (form and content), receptors (addressees and the wider audience), noise (anything altering the text in the process of transmission, e.g., copyist errors), feedback (how people have reacted to the message), and setting (the original, as well as present-day circumstances of communication). Such an approach to Bible translation depends heavily on insights from cultural anthropology.

The concept of closest natural equivalence has sometimes been discussed in terms of "dynamic equivalence," but unfortunately some have assumed that any dynamic expression can be an equivalence. Accordingly, it is better to speak of "functional equivalence" in order to specify more clearly the relation between an original text and its translation into another language. Interlingual equivalence can never be an absolute or mathematical equivalence. There can, however, be a communicative equivalence, something that is effective in obtaining an appropriate response.

A definition of translation on a maximal level of communicative equivalence may be stated as follows: "The readers of a translation should understand and appreciate the text in essentially the same way as the original audience understood and appreciated it." But since no two cultures or languages are ever identical, a maximal level is unattainable, even though it can be a helpful theoretical goal. The more practical minimal definition of equivalence would be the following: "The readers or hearers of a translation should be able to comprehend how the original readers or hearers of a text must have under-

stood and appreciated it." Bible translating should fall somewhere between these maximal and minimal levels.

The practical implications of these complementary philological, linguistic, and communicative approaches to scripture translation can be readily seen on the three levels of language: words, grammar, and discourse. Translation problems are more conspicuous on the lexical level, because the boundaries of meaning of words and idioms are almost always uncertain and fuzzy. For most speakers of English the term "grace" represents pleasing form or movement, the name of a girl, or a period of time before a bill must be paid. Accordingly, some translations of the Bible employ "kindness" or "goodness" in order to more accurately represent the meaning of the Hebrew and Greek terms traditionally rendered by "*grace."

In some languages relative clauses always precede rather than follow, and many languages have two forms of "we," inclusive and exclusive of the audience, while a number of languages do not specify a subject when it is evident from the context. All such grammatical features require extensive formal adjustments in translating, as is also evident in most present-day renderings of Ephesians 1.3–14, which in Greek is one sentence but in an English translation must normally be broken up into six to ten different sentences.

On the level of discourse some languages require the order of clauses and sentences to follow the historical sequence. This requires considerable restructuring of Mark 6.16–18. A literal rendering of Hebrew poetic parallelism is regarded in some languages as an insult to hearers because it suggests that the people are not intelligent enough to understand the first expression, but in other languages the lack of parallelism is regarded as a serious mistake. Some languages require rhetorical questions to be changed into emphatic statements and indirect discourse to be altered into direct discourse.

Because Bible translations serve quite distinct purposes for different audiences under varying circumstances, most major languages with marked social-class dialects require at least three different kinds of scripture texts: a traditional type of translation to meet the needs of those whose religious experience has been deeply influenced by a particular kind of "holy language"; a common-language translation (a modern koine) representing a relatively narrow overlapping of literary and colloquial usage; and a translation that fully exploits the total resources of a language and in this way does justice to the literary diversities of the Greek and Hebrew texts.

See also Circulation of the Bible.

EUGENE A. NIDA

Ancient Languages

The Hebrew Bible. In antiquity, the Hebrew Bible was translated into Greek (Septuagint [= LXX]), Syriac, Jewish Aramaic (the Targums), and Latin (Vulgate). The earliest of these was into Greek, where no precedent existed for any large-scale translation of a Near Eastern religious text. These ancient versions were to exert an enormous and enduring cultural and linguistic influence, above all in Christianity (though two, and perhaps three, of them began as Jewish undertakings). From them a large number of daughter versions were produced. Since the Septuagint in particular dates from a time prior to the stabilization of the Hebrew text (late first century CE), it serves as an important witness, alongside the biblical manuscripts from Qumran (*see* Dead Sea Scrolls), to early textual forms of the Hebrew Bible (*see* Manuscripts, *article on* Hebrew Bible).

After an initial period of experimentation, "word for word" translation soon came to be regarded as the ideal for biblical texts (whereas literary translations from Greek into Latin were "sense for sense"). This norm, formulated by Jerome, influenced all subsequent translation until the end of the Middle Ages; a different approach only came in during the Reformation, partly as a result of the invention of printing (*see* Printing and Publishing, *article on* The Printed Bible).

Greek: The *Septuagint*. According to tradition, recorded first in the Letter of Aristeas to Philocrates (late second century BCE) the translation of the Pentateuch into Greek was commissioned by Ptolemy II (282–246); for this purpose an accurate Hebrew manuscript was sent from Jerusalem to Alexandria where the work was undertaken by seventy-two elders from the twelve tribes (rounded off to seventy, whence the term LXX, later extended to cover the entire Greek translation of the Hebrew Bible). Though a direct connection with Ptolemy II is implausible, it is likely that the first group of books to be translated was the *Pentateuch, and that this took place in the early third century BCE in Egypt, probably as a result of the liturgical and educational needs of the large Jewish community

there. The translation of other books was carried out piecemeal over the next two centuries and included books of the *Apocrypha whose Hebrew original has been either lost, or recovered in part only in modern times (e.g., *Sirach). The style of translation varies from book to book, and some books (notably 1 Samuel and Jeremiah) were translated from editions of the Hebrew text that differ from those surviving in the *Masoretic text.

Two attitudes developed among Hellenistic Jews with regard to the Greek translation once it had come into existence. Some (probably mainly in Palestine), considering the original translations to be too free, undertook to correct and revise them, bringing them into closer line with the current Hebrew text (itself developing); the culmination of this approach was the ultraliteral version by Aquila (early second century CE). Others (notably *Philo) held that the Greek translators were themselves inspired, and so for them the LXX shared equal authority with the Hebrew (thus obviating any need for correction).

Early Christianity inherited from Hellenistic Judaism both the LXX and Philo's attitude to it; Greek-speaking Jews as a result abandoned the LXX in favor of various revised versions, above all that of Aquila. The resulting differences between Jewish and Christian texts of the Greek Old Testament led Origen to undertake a massive revision of the LXX, bringing it into line with the Hebrew and the Jewish Greek versions, and producing the Hexapla. Although Origen probably intended his revised LXX only for scholarly use, it came to exercise an extensive influence, thanks to its propagation by Eusebius and Pamphilus. Other Christian recensions of the fourth century, attributed to Lucian and Hesychius, were primarily stylistic in character.

The LXX remains to this day the authoritative biblical text of the Greek Orthodox church (*see* Eastern Orthodoxy and the Bible).

As regards manuscripts of the Septuagint, the earliest fragments, on papyrus, date from the second century BCE. Manuscripts normally contain groups of books, rather than the whole Bible; notable exceptions are three fourth- and fifth-century CE codices, Vaticanus, Alexandrinus, and Sinaiticus (Old Testament and New Testament, all nearly complete, each with slightly different contents). The order of books differs from that of the Hebrew Bible (*see* Canon).

Syriac: The *Peshitta*. The origins of the Syriac version are shrouded in uncertainty. As was the case with the LXX, different books were translated at different times (probably first and second centuries CE), and perhaps at different places (Edessa, Nisibis, and Adiabene have been suggested). At least some books were translated by Jews, and there are links with the Targum tradition especially in the Pentateuch; the Targum of Proverbs actually derives from the Peshitta. Although the translators worked basically from the Hebrew, in some books they evidently occasionally consulted the LXX. Apart from some stylistic improvement, there appear to have been no subsequent revisions of the Peshitta text, which is remarkably stable (unlike the LXX where there are many variations between manuscripts). With the exception of Sirach, based on Hebrew, the books of the Apocrypha were translated from Greek.

The Peshitta remains the authoritative biblical text of the Syriac churches (Syrian Orthodox, Church of the East, Maronite). The oldest manuscripts are of fifth and sixth centuries CE; these normally contain groups of books, and only five complete Bibles earlier than the seventeenth century are known, the earliest being Codex Ambrosianus of the sixth/seventh century. The term "Peshitta," meaning "simple," distinguishes this version (made from Hebrew) from the Syrohexapla (made from Greek; see below).

Latin: The *Vulgate. Jerome's earliest biblical translations were made from Origen's revision of the LXX (a few books, notably the Gallican Psalter, survive), but in ca. 393 he boldly turned to the Hebrew original as a better source, and in the course of a dozen years he produced a Latin version that quickly became the standard version of the Western church (hence the term *Vulgata*), replacing the Old Latin, translated from the LXX. Jerome's undertaking was both remarkable and revolutionary: remarkable in that he achieved a knowledge of Hebrew unique for a Christian at that period (it went well beyond Origen's), revolutionary in that he successfully overthrew the authority of the LXX within the Latin church. Of the many Vulgate manuscripts, the Codex Amiatinus, a complete Bible of the early eighth century, is one of the most important.

Daughter translations. Since LXX, Peshitta, and Vulgate became the official Old Testament texts for the Greek-, Syriac-, and Latin-speaking churches, they became the bases for subsequent translations into many other languages for the use of daughter churches. The most important are:

1. From the Septuagint (in approximate chronological order): Old Latin, Coptic, Ethiopic, Armenian, Georgian, Christian Palestinian Aramaic, Syriac (the Syrohexapla, translated ca. 616 from Origen's revised LXX text), Arabic, and Slavonic. Not all of these are preserved complete.

2. From the Peshitta: Persian and Sogdian (mostly lost), Arabic.

3. From the Vulgate: the medieval western vernacular translations and some of the earlier Reformation translations (*see article below on* Medieval Versions).

The New Testament. The most important translations of the Greek New Testament are the Latin and the Syriac, both of which go back to the second century CE.

Old Latin. The earliest translations that constitute the Old Latin were probably made in the second half of the second century CE, and perhaps in North Africa rather than Rome. They are of considerable textual interest. The extant manuscripts (mostly fragmentary and some going back to the fourth century) exhibit many variations among themselves, and the version was subject to constant sporadic revision from the Greek. Jerome's revision of the Old Latin New Testament, known as the Vulgate, was completed ca. 384; the gospel text was the most revised. The oldest Vulgate gospel manuscript may belong to the fifth century.

Syriac. The oldest Syriac version is probably the Diatessaron (Gospel Harmony), made by Tatian ca. 160. In Syriac (which may even be its original language), the Diatessaron at first enjoyed wide popularity, but as a result of its suppression in the early fifth century only quotations survive. The subsequent translation of the four Gospels (late second–early third centuries), known as the Old Syriac, survives in two early manuscripts, the Curetonianus and Sinaiticus; the translation was made from an early Greek text form with many "western" features (*see* Manuscripts, *article on* New Testament; Textual Criticism). In due course, the rather free translation of the Old Syriac was revised on the basis of an early form of the Koine, or Byzantine, Greek text; this revision, eventually called the Peshitta (to distinguish it from the Harclean), emerged ca. 400 to become the standard New Testament text of the Syriac churches. The Peshitta covers the whole New Testament, apart from 2–3 John, 2 Peter, Jude, and Revelation (none of which formed part of the early Syriac canon). It is preserved in many manuscripts (some of the fifth century), and the text is very stable.

A further revision of the Syriac New Testament was sponsored by Philoxenus of Mabbug in 507/8, but of this only quotations survive (a sixth-century translation of the minor Catholic Epistles and Revelation may also belong). The Philoxenian was itself revised in 616 by Thomas of Harkel, who produced a mirror version of the Greek. Surprisingly, this version, known as the Harclean, was often used for *lectionary purposes. The oldest manuscripts of the Harclean Gospels date to the eighth or even the seventh century.

Other versions. Other ancient versions of the New Testament include translations into Coptic, Gothic, Ethiopic, Armenian, Georgian, Slavonic, and Arabic.

Coptic. The translations into various Coptic dialects were first made in the third or fourth century CE and subsequently revised. Several gospel manuscripts of the fourth century survive.

Gothic. This was made by Ulfilas (fourth century), and the earliest manuscripts date from the sixth century.

Ethiopic. The version probably goes back to the fifth century, but the earliest manuscripts date to about the fourteenth century.

Armenian. The translation is traditionally associated with the patriarchs Mesrop and Sahak (early fifth century); though it was made from Greek, some use may have been made of an earlier translation from Syriac, now lost. The oldest dated manuscripts are of the ninth century.

Georgian. It is not certain whether the original translation, which may go back to the fifth century, was made from Greek, Armenian, or Syriac; subsequently, it was thoroughly revised on the basis of the Greek. The oldest dated manuscripts are of the ninth and tenth centuries, though earlier fragments exist.

Arabic. The earliest translations probably date from the eighth century (some were made from Syriac or Coptic, rather than Greek). The oldest manuscripts are of the ninth century.

Slavonic. The translation goes back to Cyril and Methodius (ninth century). The oldest manuscripts (written in Glagolitic rather than Cyrillic script) are of late tenth/eleventh century.

Several of these translations continue in liturgical use.   S. P. BROCK

Targums

The Targums are interpretive renderings of the books of the Hebrew Bible into *Aramaic;

the Aramaic word *targûm* means "translation" or "interpretation." The origin of Targum as institution is to be traced to the Second Temple period, when Jews living in Palestine and elsewhere in the Near East were no longer familiar with their ancestral tongue, having adopted Aramaic, the official language of the *Persian administration. The Targums cover the whole of the Hebrew Bible, with the exception of the books of *Ezra, *Nehemiah, and *Daniel. In general, their place of origin is Palestine, though in the form in which we have them, Targums Onqelos to the Pentateuch and Jonathan to the Prophets bear signs of substantial revision in Babylonia, where by the second or third century CE they were recognized as "official" Targums. During the same period, the Targum tradition continued to flourish in Palestine, so that there are extant two complete Palestinian Targums to the Pentateuch (Neofiti and Pseudo-Jonathan) and a substantial number of fragments representing other Palestinian Pentateuchal Targums (or, as some would have it, other versions of the one Palestinian Targum). In addition to the "Babylonianized" Targum to the Prophets, there are in later writings many references to and quotations from a "Jerusalem" Targum to the Prophets, but whether these point to the existence at one time of a complete Palestinian version is debatable. The *Dead Sea Scrolls include substantial fragments of a Targum to the book of *Job, in a version significantly different from that already known. There are also small fragments of a Targum to Leviticus.

Talmudic tradition traces the institution of Targum to the occasion described in Nehemiah 8.8 when the law of Moses was read "with interpretation" so that the assembled congregation might understand. Whether or not translation into Aramaic was involved, the need for such a provision in *synagogues will have become apparent at an early stage. The *Mishnah (ca. 200 CE) lays down rules in connection with the reading and translation of scripture in the synagogue; these include a ban on written Targum texts, evidently lest the authority of the original be compromised. Thus, the developing Targum corpus owed much to synagogal traditions of interpretation, but depended for its literary crystallization and transmission upon other means of support. Some evidence points to the Jewish schools, which often shared buildings and personnel with the synagogue, as the preservers of this written Targum tradition.

All translations of the Bible are necessarily

interpretive to a degree, but the Targums differ in that they are interpretive as a matter of policy, and often to an extent that far exceeds the bounds of "translation" or even "paraphrase." Even the "Babylonian" Targums, which over long stretches give the appearance of being fairly literal, often compress in a word or short phrase an allusion to a tradition of interpretation represented elsewhere in rabbinic (usually Talmudic or Midrashic) literature. At those points in the Pentateuch and the historical books where prose gives way to poetry (e.g., Gen. 49; Deut. 32; 33; Judg. 5; 1 Sam. 2) the Targums tend to be more expansive and more pronouncedly "targumic" in the doctrines and views they superimpose upon the biblical text. Basically, the Targums set themselves to inculcate reverence for God (witness the frequent introduction of the *mêmrā* ["Word"] of God to avoid any derogation of the truth of divine transcendence); to resolve discrepancies in the sacred text; to contemporize in matters of geography, law, or theology; and to promote teachings beloved of rabbinic authorities but not necessarily present in the biblical text or not as prominent as was wished (e.g., *prayer, meritorious deeds, messianism, resurrection). The tone is often moralistic and the intention obviously pedagogical, as would befit either a synagogal or school constituency. Another feature characteristic of the Targums perhaps more than of any other Bible translation ancient or modern is their reliance upon a number of stock words and expressions that are especially likely to occur where the underlying Hebrew text is obscure. Words like "strong," "strength," "destroy," and "plunder" are very common and often have been the basis of reconstructed readings of the Hebrew text where no such variant readings actually existed. Recurrent expressions like "the rich in possessions" or "cause the Shekinah to dwell" may likewise be translational ciphers, as well as having sociological or theological significance in inner Targumic terms.

There is an extensive literature on the contribution of the Targums to the understanding of the New Testament. The extent of such influence can easily be exaggerated, and the theory has depended to a considerable extent upon the assumption of an early (not later than the first century CE) date of origin for the Palestinian Targum(s) to the Pentateuch in particular. It is not possible, however, to date the Targums with any such degree of precision; the extant texts are probably best viewed as the product of several centuries of development. Thus the grounds for distinguishing between the Targums and other types of rabbinic literature as potential sources of light on the New Testament are questionable. There are nevertheless occasional points of contact, such as Mark 4.12 where "and be forgiven" interprets the reference to healing in Isaiah 6.10 exactly as does the Targum. Similarly, the exposition of Psalm 68.18 in Ephesians 4.8 reflects an interpretation that is represented in Targum but is scarcely deducible from the standard Hebrew text.

See also Interpretation, History of, *article on* Jewish Interpretation.   ROBERT P. GORDON

Medieval Versions

Latin was the universal language of learning in the West during the Middle Ages, and the principal version of the Bible was the Latin *Vulgate. Yet the common people of the period were not limited to the art and drama of the church, or to homilies and mystery plays, for a knowledge of the Bible in their vernaculars. Educational and devotional needs both of monastic schools and of the laity were served by the glossing of Latin texts. The first books to be glossed or translated were usually the Psalter, the Gospels, and some Old Testament narratives. Before the fourteenth century, complete Testaments were rare, but by the middle of the fifteenth century, when the art of printing from movable type was developed, vernacular versions of the Bible were no longer uncommon. These were generally not translations of the Bible in the modern critical sense, but were either extremely literal or free renderings, frequently paraphrased or expanded with explanations for the reader. The stages of this development in several major European languages are reviewed in the following paragraphs in alphabetical order.

Dutch. The earliest surviving fragment of the scriptures in a Dutch vernacular version is of a paraphrase of the Psalms that dates from the early part of the tenth century. In the twelfth century, the religious revival of the Beguines and the Beghards in the Netherlands and Belgium, which subsequently spread to Germany and France, led to other biblical translations. The Liège Diatessaron, a vernacular translation of Tatian's harmony, was one of the earliest biblical translations in Dutch. It has been compared with Luther's German version for its vigorous idiomatic quality. Other Dutch translations include the book of Revelation in West Flemish (ca. 1280), a Southern Dutch Psalter, and by 1300 the New Testament Gospels and Epistles. In 1271 the poet Jacob van Maerlant published his *Rijmbijbel,* a free translation that was based on Comestor's *Historia scholastica* and enjoyed considerable popularity. While paraphrases and adaptations continued to appear, the fourteenth and fifteenth centuries showed an increasing demand for more precise biblical versions, with comments and additions clearly distinguished from the biblical text.

English. The earliest surviving examples of Old English literature are the poetic paraphrases attributed by tradition to Caedmon, the seventh-century cowherd, who sang of the creation of the world, the wanderings of the Israelites, and of the gospel stories he learned from the monks of Whitby. This school of poetry survived to the tenth century. King Alfred's (849–899) educational policies and monastic reforms undoubtedly did much to promote the status of the vernacular as well as the level of learning among the clergy. The ninth-century *Vespasian Psalter,* the earliest known English gloss on a biblical text, was followed by the continuous gloss by Aldred in the *Lindisfarne Gospels* (ca. 950). The Rushworth Gloss (ca. 975), based in part on the Lindisfarne gloss, is in a continuous prose form and is probably the earliest surviving example of English biblical translation. Although Aelfric (955–1020), the most important English biblical writer before Wycliffe, wrote homilies, *Lives of the Saints,* and a free rendering of the Heptateuch, he remained a biblical expositor and not a translator. An anonymous contemporary produced the West-Saxon Gospels, a literal but readable translation of the four Gospels.

With the Norman conquest, a new Anglo-Norman vernacular developed with a more sophisticated literature. From the twelfth and thirteenth centuries, several versions of the Psalter and a number of passion narratives are known. The medieval Latin Psalter had three forms: the Vulgate, or Old Latin text based on the Greek Septuagint, the Roman revision of it by Jerome, and Jerome's fresh translation made from the Hebrew. The *Eadwine Psalter* (ca. 1160) contained all three, accompanying the Vulgate with the *glossa ordinaria,* the Roman with an interlinear Old English gloss, and the Hebrew with an interlinear Old French gloss. But the homily cycles and biblical versifications of the period (especially the *Cursor mundi*) reflect a general withdrawal from direct biblical study and an increased dependence on scholastic theology, especially the *Glossa ordinaria* and the theological schemes of Peter Comestor's *Historia scholastica,* a digest of biblical history.

In the fourteenth century, when the Franciscan emphasis on spiritual activity gave rise to a demand among lay contemplatives for vernacular scriptures as a guide and ground for private mystical experience, the *English Psalter* of Richard Rolle (1300–1349) proved the vernacular an adequate medium of religious expression. Several decades later (about 1382), the Lollard John Wycliffe (1329–1384) and his colleagues at Oxford began work on the first complete translation of the Bible from the Latin Vulgate into English. The first form of the translation was a quite literal rendering of the Latin Vulgate, and it was soon revised to conform more nearly to idiomatic English usage. In 1407, Archbishop Arundel issued a "constitution" against Lollardy, condemning the private translation of scripture "into English or any other language," and specifically forbidding the use of any translation associated with Wycliffe under pain of excommunication. The popularity of the version, however, may be gauged from the fact that nearly two hundred copies of it have survived.

French. In the twelfth century, the Psalter was widely known in a very literal French vernacular gloss; it is found in a continuous form in the *Montebourg Psalter* and the *Arundel Psalter,* among others. Not until the *Metz Psalter* (ca. 1300) and the Psalter of Raoul de Presles (ca. 1380) does the gloss become more idiomatic in its syntax and vocabulary. In contrast, there was a late-twelfth-century prose version of Samuel and Kings in an excellent style, though quite free and with considerable commentary added to the biblical text. In Provence, the followers of Peter Waldo (d. 1217), who claimed the scriptures as their sole rule of life and faith, translated the Psalms and other books of the Old Testament and the complete New Testament into Provençal by the early thirteenth century. Pope Innocent III attempted to suppress the movement, but their influence was felt not only in France but also in the Netherlands and Germany and in Italy. Vernacular translations of Judges and other books were being made, and by the mid-thirteenth century, compilations of these were assembled and illuminated for wealthy patrons and royalty—examples are the *Acre Bible* of Saint Louis (1250–1254), which contained over a dozen Old Testament books (including the earliest vernacular version of Job in a European language), and the *De Thou Bible* (ca. 1280), with a different selection of Old Testament books and parts of the New Testament (Gospels, Acts, and Catholic Epistles). The complete thirteenth-century French vernacular of the whole Bible survives in very few copies (British Library, Pierpont Morgan Library, Chantilly). It was a compilation, uneven in its glossing, its style, and its quality; but the translation movement it inaugurated climaxed in the *Biblia historiale* (1291–1295) of Guyart des Moulins. This expanded translation of Comestor's *Historia scholastica* incorporated versions of many biblical books and developed into a veritable medieval biblical encyclopedia. It appeared in many editions, and was both abridged and revised. The Renaissance scholar Jacques Lefèvre d'Etaples, who published the first printed French Bible in 1530, made use of the text of the *Biblia historiale*, revising it literally and eliminating its medieval glosses.

German. Apart from fragments of a Gothic version of the scriptures, translated by Ulfilas in the second half of the fourth century and probably revised under Latin influences during the next two centuries, Germanic theological literature dates from the Carolingian Renaissance. Fragments of the gospel of Matthew written in the Bavarian dialect and surviving in an eighth-century manuscript written at the monastery of Monsee, near Salzburg, have been associated with Charlemagne's reputed concern that Latin works be translated into the German vernacular. In the reign of his successor, Louis the Pious, an East Frankish dialect version of Tatian's *Diatessaron* was made at Fulda about 830, written together with its Latin base in parallel columns, but it was so literal a translation as to be nearly interlinear in character. The contemporary versified Old Saxon epic *Heliand* ("Savior") of about six thousand alliterative lines was also based on the *Diatessaron,* freely combined with material from commentaries, apocrypha, and legend. The *Liber evangeliorum* of Otfrid of Weissenberg in Alsace was based on gospel lessons from a *lectionary and written in South Rhine Frankish; it expanded the lectionary lessons liberally, adding whole chapters of commentary to them. Notker Labeo (950–1022), one of the founders of German vernacular literature, translated the *Psalter,* adding the Latin text, a German translation, and a German commentary in sequential rather than interlinear arrangement. The paraphrase of the Vulgate *Song of Songs* by Williram of Ebersburg (ca. 1060), arranged in parallel columns of Latin hexameters and a German prose rendering mixed with Latin, was remarkably popular and was copied and emulated through the fifteenth century.

By the end of the fourteenth century, German possessed a complete vernacular New Testament (1350, "Augsburg Bible") and Old Testament (ca. 1389–1400, "Wenzel Bible"). The *Codex Teplensis* (ca. 1400), a New Testament written in Bohemia, may reflect Waldensian associations. Opposition to the vernacular scriptures was not altogether lacking. In 1369, Charles IV issued an edict prohibiting the translation of religious books, and a papal rescript in 1375 forbade vernacular scriptures in Germany. Although the tide of scripture circulation could not be stemmed, creative efforts were discouraged, and the first printed German Bible, published by Mentel in 1466, still reflected the language and translation techniques of the early fourteenth century.

Italian. In Italy, vernacular translations of the Gospels and the Psalter may have existed by the mid-thirteenth century if not earlier, and of the entire Bible in the fourteenth century, though the earliest biblical manuscripts are from the fourteenth century, and the earliest surviving complete Bible is from the fifteenth century. Almost invariably these versions were in the Tuscan dialect, made from Latin, usually from the Vulgate text. The Gospels were mostly harmonies based on the Latin translation of Tatian's *Diatessaron* found in the Codex Fuldensis, but a freely glossed Venetian version of the Gospels has survived based on an earlier form of the Latin *Diatessaron*. A Venetian version of the *Psalter* is also known. There is evidence of a thirteenth-century Jewish-Italian version of substantial parts of the Hebrew Bible preserved in manuscripts of the fifteenth or sixteenth century written in Hebrew characters. Vernacular biblical translations otherwise show dependence on the Latin Vulgate text current in southern France in the twelfth and thirteenth centuries and traces of contact with French and Provençal translations. Although they may originally have been the work of Waldensians, they were adopted by the Dominicans and Franciscans and freely glossed for doctrinal instruction. It is interesting that Dante (1265–1321), when referring to the scripture versions, never mentions any in Italian, and that when he cites the scriptures he makes his own translation from the Vulgate. The first printed Italian Bible, attributed to the Venetian monk Nicolo Malermi, was essentially a compilation of fourteenth-century Tuscan texts adapted to Venetian usage.

Spanish. The existence of Spanish vernacular

texts in the early thirteenth century need not be inferred from the edict issued by Juan I of Aragon at the Council of Tarragona in 1233 forbidding the possession of a vernacular Bible by anyone, cleric or lay: this edict simply repeats a similar decree of the Council of Toulouse in 1229 directed against the Albigensians. Alfonso X of Castille (1221–1284) is said to have authorized a vernacular translation of the Bible in the 1270s as part of a *Grande e general estoria,* designed as an expanded and monumental *Bible historiale.* In its execution some portions were literal translations of the Vulgate while others were freely paraphrased, with commentary drawn from both Christian and non-Christian sources. The fourteen extant biblical manuscripts, mostly from the fourteenth and fifteenth centuries, reflect a varied and complex tradition of translation. The *Osuna Bible* is patterned after the French *Bibles moralisées illustrées.* Many translations of the Hebrew Bible were based not on the Latin Vulgate but on the Hebrew *Masoretic Text, observing the Hebrew *canonical arrangement of the Law, followed by the Former and Latter Prophets, yet preserving reminiscences of the Vulgate. The Alba Bible, commissioned in 1422 by Luis de Guzman and completed in 1433, included a fresh version of the Hebrew Bible made from the Hebrew by Rabbi Moses Arragel, and is remarkable for combining Jewish and Christian exegetical lore in its commentary. Scripture versions in Catalan are known from references in the thirteenth and fourteenth centuries, but the earliest surviving copies are from the fifteenth century.   ERROLL F. RHODES

English Language

Beginnings. As was the case with other languages, the translation of the scriptures into English was at first an oral process. The Venerable Bede tells how Caedmon (seventh century CE) retold Bible stories in alliterative verses in Anglo-Saxon: "He sang of the world's creation, the origin of the human race, and all the story of Genesis; he sang of Israel's Exodus from Egypt and entry into the promised land, of very many other stories from Holy Writ, of our Lord's incarnation, passion, resurrection, and ascension into heaven, of the coming of the Holy Spirit and the apostles' teaching."

Bede himself (d. 735) is said to have translated the gospel of John into Anglo-Saxon, which may be the earliest written translation in English of any portion of the Bible. Alfred the Great (reigned 871–901) is credited with having translated part

of the *Ten Commandments and other passages from Exodus 21–23. The *Lindisfarne Gospels* are interlinear glosses written in the Northumbrian dialect around 950 on a seventh-century Latin manuscript. The *Wessex Gospels,* a tenth-century translation into West Saxon, is the earliest extant Old English version of the Gospels.

The first complete translation of the Bible into English (1382; New Testament 1380) is credited to John Wycliffe (Wyclif) (ca. 1330–84). His translation work was part of his larger task of reforming the church, for which he earned the title "Morning Star of the Reformation." It was his contention that the church could be reformed only if everyone knew God's law, and this required that the Bible be translated into the language of the people. Said Wycliffe: "No man was so rude a scholar but that he might learn the Gospel according to its simplicity." There are two Wycliffite versions, the second of which appeared after Wycliffe's death. It is uncertain how much of either version is the work of Wycliffe himself and how much is the work of his colleagues, John Purvey and Nicholas of Hereford. Although the later version is more idiomatic than the earlier one, the Wycliffe Bible is almost a word-for-word equivalent of the Vulgate. For 150 years this was the only Bible in English, and some 107 manuscript copies have survived. In 1415 the Wycliffe Bible was condemned and burned. Purvey and Nicholas were jailed and forced to recant their Lollard principles; and in 1428 Wycliffe's body was exhumed and burned. The earliest printed edition of Wycliffe's New Testament was published in 160 copies at London in 1731; the first printed edition of the complete Wycliffite version was issued at Oxford in 1850.

Tyndale and His Successors. William Tyndale, "the Father of the English Bible," was born (1494?) in Gloucestershire and educated at Oxford (B.A. 1512, M.A. 1515), and at Cambridge, where he may have studied Greek. As chaplain and tutor in the household of Sir John Walsh, he got into debates with various clergy and other "learned men," and was soon accused of espousing heretical ideas. His opponent in one dispute argued that Christians were better off without God's law (the scriptures) than without the Pope's laws (Canon Law), to which Tyndale replied, "If God spare my life, ere many yeares I wyl cause a boye that dryveth the plough shall know more of the scripture than thou doest!"

Unable to get authorization in England to produce his translation, Tyndale went to the Continent (April or May 1524), staying in Wittenberg for almost a year, after which he moved to Hamburg and finally to Cologne (August 1525). There he gave his translation to Peter Quentel, a printer, but the city senate forbade the printing. Tyndale got the printed sheets, went up the Rhine to Worms, and toward the end of February 1526 the complete New Testament was published. About a month later copies began to appear in England.

Tyndale's translation was the first printed New Testament in English and was also the first English New Testament translated from the original Greek. About eighteen thousand copies of the original 1526 edition and the revisions of 1534 and 1535 were printed, of which only two are known to survive. Cuthbert Tunstall, Bishop of London, bought copies in great numbers and burned them publicly, and Sir Thomas More, the Lord High Chancellor, published a *Dialogue* in which he denounced Tyndale's translation as "not worthy to be called Christ's testament, but either Tyndale's own testament or the testament of his master Antichrist."

Tyndale next began the work of translating the Hebrew Bible: the Pentateuch was published in 1530, and Jonah in 1531. During this time he was living in Antwerp, and many attempts were made to lure him back to England. He was betrayed on 21 May 1535, arrested by agents of Emperor Charles V, and taken to Vilvorde, six miles north of Brussels, where he was imprisoned in a fortress. In August 1536 he was tried, found guilty of heresy, and turned over to the secular power for execution. On 6 October 1536, he was strangled and burned at the stake. According to John Foxe his last words were, "Lord, open the King of England's eyes!"

Before Tyndale's death a complete English Bible, dedicated to Henry VIII, was edited by Miles Coverdale and published on the continent in 1535. The New Testament was essentially a revision of Tyndale's New Testament, and his translation of portions of the Old Testament was used. The first authorized Bible was published in 1537, the so-called Thomas Matthew Bible, edited by John Rogers, a friend of Tyndale. The New Testament and Pentateuch were Tyndale's, and his manuscripts of Joshua through 2 Chronicles were used. In 1539 Richard Taverner, a lawyer, published a revision of the Matthew Bible, the first to be completely printed in England. Coverdale's revision of the Matthew Bible, known as the Great Bible (its pages measured 23 × 38 cm [9 × 15 in]), was printed in Paris in 1539

and was enthusiastically received by Tunstall, now bishop of Durham.

In the reign of Queen Mary (1553–1558) all printing of English Bibles in England was stopped, and the English Bible could not be used in church services. Many Protestant leaders sought refuge on the Continent. William Whittingham, pastor of the English Church in Geneva, translated the New Testament (published 1557) and served as editor of the Old Testament translation; the Geneva Bible of 1560 was dedicated to Queen Elizabeth (whose reign began in 1558). It was printed in roman type, bound in small octavo size, and was the first English Bible to have verse numbers. It became immensely popular: it was the Bible of Shakespeare and Bunyan, of the pilgrims to the New World and the Mayflower Compact, of Oliver Cromwell and his army. It was the first Bible published in Scotland (1579) and was dedicated to James VI, King of Scotland. Over 150 editions were published, and it remained popular for nearly a hundred years. Its extremely Protestant notes were offensive to the bishops, and in 1568 a revision of the Great Bible was published, which became known as the Bishops' Bible, owing to the great number of bishops on the committee. In 1570 the Convocation of Canterbury ordered it to be placed in all cathedrals, and so it became the second Authorized Version. It ran through twenty editions before 1606, but did not replace the Geneva Bible in popular esteem.

The King James Version (KJV) and Its Revisions. When James VI of Scotland ascended to the throne of England in 1603 as James I, there were two competing Bibles: the Bishops' Bible, preferred by the church authorities, and the Geneva Bible, the favorite of the people.

At a conference of theologians and churchmen at Hampton Court in January 1604, called by King James "for the hearing, and for the determining, things pretended to be amiss in the Church," the Puritan leader John Reynolds proposed that a new translation be made, which would replace the two Bibles. The king approved of the plan and on 10 February he ordered that "a translation be made of the whole Bible, as consonant as can be to the original Hebrew and Greek, and this is to be set out and printed without any marginal notes and only to be used in all Churches of England in time of Divine Service." Fifty-four "learned men" were divided into six panels: three for the Old Testament, two for the New Testament, and one for the Apocrypha. They began their work in 1606, meeting at Oxford, Cambridge, and Westminster Abbey. A list of fifteen rules to guide the translation was drawn up, the first of which was, "The ordinary Bible read in the Church, commonly called the Bishops' Bible, to be followed, and as little altered as the truth of the original will permit." Rule fourteen listed the translations that could be followed "when they agree better with the Text than the Bishops' Bible": Tyndale, Matthew, Coverdale, Whitchurch [that is, the Great Bible], and Geneva.

The translation was published in 1611 and rapidly went through several editions, nearly all of which had changes in the text. The edition of 1614, for example, differs from the original in over four hundred places. The most careful and comprehensive revision was made in 1769 by Dr. Benjamin Blayney of Oxford, who worked for nearly four years on the task. Although never formally authorized by King or Parliament, it became known as "the Authorized Version."

It took some forty years before the 1611 Bible replaced the Geneva Bible in the affection of the people. But once established it became *the* Bible of the English-speaking people. In its various forms and editions it continues to be one of the most widely read Bibles in English.

In 1870, the Church of England authorized a revision of the King James Bible. The work was entrusted to fifty scholars, most of whom were Anglicans, but it included Baptists, Congregationalists, Methodists, Presbyterians, and one Unitarian. They were divided into two companies for the revision of the two Testaments. Of the eight rules drawn up to guide their work, the first specified that changes were to be made only if required by the need to be faithful to the original text. American scholars were invited to participate, by correspondence, with the proviso that an American edition not be published until fourteen years after the publication of the British edition.

The work was done carefully, and in the New Testament alone about thirty thousand changes were made, over five thousand of them on the basis of a better Greek text. The New Testament was published in May 1881 and was enthusiastically received. In the first year three million copies of the New Testament were sold in Great Britain and the United States. In 1885 the complete Revised Version appeared, with an appendix that listed the changes preferred by the American scholars. The Apocrypha appeared in 1895. In 1901 the Americans published their edition, the American Standard Edition of the

Revised Version, popularly known as the American Standard Version. It removed many archaisms, replaced a large number of obsolescent words, and substituted American English terminology for words and expressions peculiarly British.

Rheims-Douai Bible. While not conceding the right of the laity to read the Bible in the vernacular without ecclesiastical sanction, Roman Catholic authorities felt the need for an officially approved English version for Catholics. In 1565, William Allen, a fellow of Oriel College, Oxford, like many other Roman Catholics, was forced to leave England. In Douai, Flanders, he founded a college for the purpose of training priests who would eventually go to England, and it was there that the translation of the Bible from the Latin *Vulgate was begun. In 1578, the college moved to Rheims, where the New Testament was completed in 1582; eventually the college returned to Douai, and the Old Testament was published there in 1609–10. In 1738 Bishop Challoner of London assisted in a thorough revision of the New Testament and made extensive revisions of the whole Bible in his 1749–52 editions. The Challoner revision of the Rheims-Douai Bible was authorized for use in the United States in 1810.

Translations Independent of the KJV. Many Bibles and more than 250 translations of the New Testament in English have appeared since 1611. Robert Young, an Edinburgh bookseller who is famous for his *Analytical Concordance* to the Bible, in 1862 published a literal translation of the Bible, which is practically a word-for-word equivalent of the original. In the United States Charles Thomson, Secretary of the Continental Congress, translated the Greek Septuagint and the New Testament after retiring at the age of sixty from politics and business. After almost twenty years' work his translation was published in 1808. Thomson holds the distinction of having made the first English translation of the Septuagint and of having produced the first English New Testament to be translated and published in America. Ferrar Fenton, an English businessman, published his translation of the Bible in 1903 (New Testament 1895). He claimed it was the most accurate translation ever made, "not only in words, but in editing, spirit, and sense." It enjoyed considerable success, and as late as 1944 a new edition was published. In 1876 Julia E. Smith, an American, produced a translation of the whole Bible, in which she attempted to use one and the same English word or phrase for every Hebrew and Greek word. One odd principle she followed was that of rendering the imperfect tense of the Hebrew verbs by the future tense in English, even in the account of creation. Genesis 1.3 reads: "And God will say there shall be light, and there will be light." In 1885 Helen Spurrel, of London, translated the Hebrew Bible. She began her study of Hebrew after turning fifty, and in her translation she kept to the unpointed consonantal text, disregarding the vowel points of the Masoretic text.

Modern Translations. The modern era of Bible translation into English began with the *Twentieth Century New Testament,* which was first issued as a tentative edition in separate parts in 1898–1901 and appeared in its definitive form in 1904. The translators, mostly laywomen and laymen, included Anglicans, Methodists, Congregationalists, Presbyterians, and Baptists. The project was begun through the efforts of Mary K. Higgs, the wife of a Congregational minister, and Mr. Ernest Malan, a signal and telegraph engineer, both of whom were troubled by the fact that the language of the KJV was so difficult for young people to understand. One of their advisors was Richard Francis Weymouth, a classical scholar, fellow of University College, London; his *New Testament in Modern Speech* was published posthumously in 1902. His purpose was to produce a translation that lay people could understand. "Alas, the great majority of even 'new translations,' so called, are in reality only Tyndale's immortal work a little—and often very little—modernized!" He intended his translation to be used for private reading, not for public worship.

The translation that made the greatest impact upon the Bible-reading public, though, was that of the Scottish scholar James Moffatt. He began with a rendering included in his textbook, *The Historical New Testament* (1901), and in 1913 published *The New Testament: A New Translation.* His translation of the Old Testament appeared in 1924 and the whole Bible was revised in 1935. He spent the last years of his life as Professor of Church History at Union Theological Seminary, New York, and at the time of his death (1944) he was working on a translation of the Apocrypha.

Edgar J. Goodspeed, of the University of Chicago, answered the long-felt need for a New Testament in American English. "For American readers . . . who have had to depend so long upon versions made in Great Britain," he wrote, "there is room for a New Testament free from

expressions which . . . are strange to American ears." His *New Testament, An American Translation* appeared in 1923. In 1927 a group of scholars headed by J. M. Powis Smith produced a translation of the Old Testament, which in 1935 was published with Goodspeed's New Testament as *The Bible, An American Translation.* In 1938 Goodspeed translated the Apocrypha, and *The Complete Bible: An American Translation* appeared in 1939.

Two important translations of the New Testament in the twentieth century are those of J. B. Phillips and William Barclay. As rector of a church in London, Phillips first translated Paul's epistles into modern English under the title *Letters to Young Churches* (1947). Eventually, his complete New Testament appeared, *The New Testament in Modern English* (1958). In 1972, Phillips brought out a thoroughly revised second edition. All translators of the Bible into modern English owe an incalculable debt to Phillips. For clarity of thought, vividness of language, and imaginative use of figures, he is rarely equaled and never surpassed. Professor Barclay's *The New Testament: A New Translation* (two vols., 1968, 1969) is more traditional in language, but embodies a wealth of scholarship from which all readers can profit. Mention should also be made of Hugh J. Schonfield's *Authentic New Testament* (1955), which was reissued, with very few changes in the text, in 1985 under the title *Original New Testament.* Schonfield's translation claims to be the first one made into English by a Jew. The footnotes, with a wealth of information for the careful reader, are the best feature of his work.

In 1961, the Jehovah's Witnesses (Watch Tower Bible and Tract Society) published a translation of the Bible under the title *New World Translation of the Holy Scriptures,* which reflects the unitarian bias of the Witnesses, most vividly displayed in John 1.1, "and the Word was a god." In 1972, the Watch Tower Bible and Tract Society posthumously published a translation by Steven T. Byington, mainly, it appears, because Byington used *Jehovah as the proper name of God.

An attempt to make the English text accessible to all who speak or read English was made in *The New Testament in Basic English* (1941). The term "basic" is an acronym for "British American Scientific International Commercial" (English), which consists of a vocabulary of 850 words compiled by the linguist C. K. Ogden as an international auxiliary language and as an aid in learning English. A committee chaired by S. H. Hooke, of the University of London, used this vocabulary with the addition of another hundred words, plus fifty special Bible words. The complete Bible appeared in 1949.

The latest Bible in the Tyndale–King James tradition is the *Revised Standard Version*. In 1937, the International Council of Religious Education authorized a revision of the American Standard Version, stating that it should "embody the best results of modern scholarship as to the meaning of the scriptures, and express this meaning in English diction which is designed for use in public and private worship and preserves those qualities which have given to the King James Version a supreme place in English literature." The work was done by thirty scholars, headed by Luther A. Weigle. The New Testament appeared in 1946, the Old Testament in 1952, and the Apocrypha in 1957. In 1977 an "Expanded Edition" appeared, which included not only the Roman Catholic deuterocanonical books, but also 3 and 4 Maccabees and Psalm 151, thus making it acceptable to Eastern Orthodox churches. The *New Revised Standard Version* (NRSV), published in 1990, is a model of what a revision of an existing translation should be. In matters of text, exegesis, and language it goes a long way toward becoming *the* Bible of English-speaking readers for generations to come. It has dropped archaic terms and obsolete language, including the pronouns and verb forms used in addressing God. With notable success it has tackled the difficult task of making the English text inclusive where the original is not exclusive. The revisers did their work remarkably well; at times, however, one wishes that in the application of their guiding maxim "as literal as possible, as free as necessary," they had more often favored freedom over literalism.

The *New King James Bible* (1982), falsely claiming to be "the first major revision of the KJV since 1867," aims to maintain the supremacy of the KJV as the Bible of conservative Protestants.

What may justly be called a landmark in Bible translation was achieved with the publication, in 1970, of the *New English Bible* (NEB; New Testament 1961). Representing nearly all major Christian denominations in Great Britain and Ireland, this translation broke away completely from the Tyndale–King James tradition. As explained by the Chairman, Prof. C. H. Dodd, in the introduction to the New Testament: "We have conceived our task to be that of understanding the original as precisely as we could (using all available aids), and then saying again in our own native idiom what we believed the author to be saying in his." Using all resources of the English language, the translators produced an English Bible whose language is fresh and natural, but not slangy or undignified. Passage after passage may be read with pleasure and profit. At times the vocabulary is a bit too British for Americans, and many of its textual decisions, especially in the Hebrew Bible, have been criticized as idiosyncratic. The *Revised English Bible* (REB) was published in 1989 with the aim of providing a translation that would be even more faithful and understandable. In textual matters the revision is considerably more conservative than the original NEB, especially in the Old Testament. The same conservative restraint is detectable in exegetical and linguistic decisions. The NEB rendering of Genesis 1.1 was fresh and vivid; the REB rendering is hardly distinguishable from that of the King James version. The delicate and frustrating task of trying to make the English text inclusive seems not to have ranked as high with the revisers as it did with the revisers of the NRSV. In comparison with the stunning achievement of the NEB in 1970, the 1989 revision is a disappointment.

In 1966 *Good News for Modern Man* (the New Testament in Today's English) was published by the American Bible Society. Its main features were the use of "common language," easily accessible to all who read English, whether as their own tongue or as an acquired language, and the systematic application of the principles of "dynamic equivalence" translation (as opposed to "formal equivalence"). The translator, Robert G. Bratcher, was assisted in his task by a panel of specialists. One novel feature of this translation was the imaginative line-drawings by the Swiss artist, Annie Vallotton. A committee of seven translated the Hebrew Bible, and the *Good News Bible* was published in 1976. The deuterocanonical books (Apocrypha) were added in 1979.

When the Revised Standard Version was published in 1952, it was received not only with appreciation and gratitude but also with bitter criticism and condemnation, especially from conservative Protestants. Because of its sponsorship by the National Council of Churches, this Bible was seen by some as tainted by liberal, if not heretical, beliefs. It was even said that the translation committee included Communist sympathizers. Conservatives felt a strong need for a modern translation that they could trust. Several appeared, among them *The Amplified Bible* (1965) and *The Modern Language Bible* (The New Berkeley Version) in 1969 (New Testament 1945). In

1971 the *New American Standard Bible* was offered (New Testament 1963), intending to preserve and perpetuate the American Standard Version as the most faithful Bible translation in English. All were well received, but none achieved the status of *the* Bible acceptable to a majority of conservative Protestants, most of whom were still using the KJV. (For *The Living Bible, see* Paraphrases.) Finally in 1978 the *New International Version* was published (New Testament 1973), the culmination of a process that had begun in 1956–1957. The intense advertisement campaign focused on the trustworthiness of the translators, all of whom, it was claimed, had "a high view of Scripture," believing that the Bible, in its entirety, "is the Word of God written and is therefore inerrant in the autographs." In its various editions this Bible is now widely used, and bids fair to become *the* Bible for those who still view the RSV (and other modern translations) with suspicion.

Roman Catholic Translations. Roman Catholics have produced their share of modern translations. In 1955 Monsignor Ronald Knox, of Great Britain, published a translation of the Bible from the Latin Vulgate, "in the light of the Hebrew and Greek originals." It was a remarkable tour de force and may possibly be the last translation of the Bible into English made by one individual. In 1966, the English version of *La Bible de Jérusalem* (one-volume edition) was published under the title *The Jerusalem Bible;* a revised edition, *The New Jerusalem Bible,* based on the 1973 revised French edition, appeared in 1985. American Roman Catholics began a fresh translation of the Vulgate in 1937, and in 1941 the New Testament was printed. Work was being done on the Old Testament, but with the publication in 1942 of the encyclical *Divino afflante spiritu,* authorizing vernacular translations made directly from the original Hebrew, Aramaic, and Greek texts, the translation was begun anew, and in 1970 *The New American Bible* was published, the first English Bible translated directly from the original texts by American Catholic scholars. The first step for producing a revision of this translation was taken in 1989 with the publication of the revised edition of the New Testament. One of its main purposes was to eliminate exclusive language in passages that are not exclusive in the original text. Somewhat ingenuously, however, the revisers claim that "brothers," which is retained, still has its inclusive sense. Of greater significance is the deliberate return to the principle of formal equivalence in translation, in place of dynamic equivalence. So now Jesus says "Amen, amen, I say to you" (John 3.3) and the obsolete "behold" is found. After the bold step forward in 1970, this revision represents a timorous step backward.

Jewish Translations. One of the earliest Jewish translations of the Pentateuch into English (1785) was the work of Alexander Alexander, of Great Britain. In 1861, Abraham Benisch published a translation of the Hebrew Bible that was called *Jewish School and Family Bible,* and in 1881 the translation by Michael Friedlander, also of England, was published. In the United States the earliest translation of the Hebrew Bible was done by Isaac Leeser (1854), which became the accepted version in all synagogues in the United States; a revised edition was published in London in 1865. Under the sponsorship of the Jewish Publication Society of America, a group of Jewish scholars headed by Marcus Jastrow produced a new translation, which became known as the *Jewish Publication Society Bible* (1917). This translation became the standard Bible of the American Jewish community until the appearance of what is known as the *New Jewish Version,* which was published in stages. A committee headed by Harry M. Orlinsky translated the *Torah* (1962); the final volume, *The Writings,* appeared in 1981. The complete translation, under the title *Tanakh,* was published in one volume in 1985.

At no other time in history have English-speaking people had such a variety of good translations of the Jewish and Christian scriptures, and those who care to read them will be able clearly to see "the process, order, and meaning of the text," in fulfillment of Tyndale's fervent desire.

See also Paraphrases.   ROBERT G. BRATCHER

Modern European Languages

Modern versions of the Bible date from the Renaissance and the Reformation, when humanistic studies brought a fresh appreciation of the Greek and Hebrew languages to biblical scholarship. By 1500, the Bible had been printed in four languages besides Latin and Hebrew: German, Italian, Catalan, and Czech. As national languages developed, Bibles were translated and revised. From the sixteenth to the twentieth centuries, discoveries of biblical manuscripts led to new critical editions of the biblical texts with new generations of translations and revisions. In the twentieth century, rapid cultural change has prompted "common language" translations, using a range of vocabulary and style common to all speakers of a language, regardless of their social class or formal education, while the pace of linguistic change now requires that standard versions be reviewed every thirty-five years. Interconfessional versions also witness to growing ecumenical cooperation in Bible translating.

Today the complete Bible is read in more than forty European languages other than English, as listed in the table below in the chronological order of their first published Bibles. The following paragraphs sketch this history by the major language groups represented, though limitation of space precludes consideration of all the languages individually.

Germanic. *German.* The first fourteen editions of the German Bible (1466–1518) printed a version based on the Latin *Vulgate that had circulated in manuscripts since the fourteenth century. Martin Luther's translation of the New Testament in September 1522 marked the beginning of a new era characterized by a commitment to translating from the original languages of the scriptures. Relying on the Greek New Testament edited by Desiderius Erasmus (sec-

ond edition, 1519), the Soncino edition of the Hebrew Bible (Brescia, 1495), and the linguistic counsel of his scholarly colleagues Philipp Melanchthon and Matthäus Aurogallus, in twelve years Luther translated the entire Bible into a vigorous popular German. Revised eleven times during his lifetime, Luther's Bible established the Reformation, created literary German, and became the model for translations in many other languages. With significant revisions in 1581, 1695, 1883, 1912, 1956, and 1984, it remains the standard Bible of German Protestant churches.

Independent Protestant versions were few. The Zwingli Bible (Zürich, 1524–29) adapted Luther's version to Swiss usage, supplementing it with an independent version of the Prophets; in successive revisions it deviated increasingly from Luther. Johann Piscator's Bible (1602–06) was based on the Latin Vulgate and was replete with Latinisms. J. Friedrich Haug's pietistic eight-volume Bible (Berlenberg, 1726–48) drew on Luther, but included New Testament apocrypha and other postapostolic books. Twentieth-century Protestant Bibles include versions by Franz Eu-

1466	German	1584	Slovenian	1739	Estonian	1875	Russian
1471	Italian	1588	Welsh	1751	Portuguese	1889	Tréguier Breton
1478	Catalan	1590	Hungarian	1796	Lower Sorbian	1895	Norwegian Saami
1488	Czech	1642	Finnish	1801	Gaelic	1903	Ukrainian
1526	Dutch	1679	Ladin Sut Romansch	1804	Serbo-Croatian	1921	Nynorsk
1530	French	1685	Irish	1811	Swedish Saami	1943	Frisian
1541	Swedish	1688	Romanian	1832	Slovak	1948	Faroese
1550	Danish	1689	Latvian	1834	Norwegian	1958	Guipuzcoan Basque
1553	Spanish	1718	Sursilvan Romansch	1840	Modern Greek	1973	Byelorussian
1561	Polish	1728	Upper Sorbian	1865	Labourdin Basque	1990	Macedonian
1581	Slavonic	1733	Manx	1866	Léon Breton		
1584	Icelandic	1735	Lithuanian	1871	Bulgarian		

gen Schlachter (1905), Hermann Menge (1926), Hans Bruns (1962), and the common language translation *Die gute Nachricht* (1967).

Roman Catholic versions have been numerous. Hieronymus Emser's New Testament (1527) altered Luther's text only slightly. Johann Dietenberger (1534) relied heavily on Emser's New Testament and Luther's Old Testament, modifying them according to the Vulgate. Johann Eck (1537) used Emser's New Testament and the pre-Luther Old Testament, with unfortunate results. Caspar Ulenberg's revision of Dietenberger (1630), further revised in Mainz (1662), became known as the "Catholic Bible of Mainz." A version begun by Heinrich Braun (1788–1807) and revised by J. F. Allioli (1830–37) became the standard Catholic version, and was further revised by B. Weinhart (1865) and S. Weber (1911). This and a New Testament by J. H. Kistemacher (1825) were widely circulated by the British and Foreign Bible Society. Twentieth-century Catholic versions include Bibles by Konstantin Rösch and Eugen Henne (1934), Pius Parsch "Klosterneuberg," (1934), the Herder Bible (1966), and the Bishops' Bible "Einheitsübersetzung" (1980).

The first Jewish biblical translation into German was Moses Mendelssohn's Pentateuch (1783). This was opposed at first by Orthodox Jews, but Mendelssohn's colleagues completed the Hebrew Bible in Moses Israel Landau's edition of 1833–37. Further versions were produced by Leopold Zunz (1837) and Ludwig Philippson (1854). Significant twentieth-century versions include those of Martin Buber and Franz Rosenzweig (1925–29) and Harry Torczyner (Tur-Sinai; 1935–58).

Dutch and Frisian. The first printed Dutch New Testament (1522) was based on the Latin Vulgate. Anonymous translations of Luther's German New Testament appeared the following year, and in 1526 the first complete Dutch Bible was published by J. van Liesveldt, based on what had been published of Luther's German version, supplementing it at first with a translation of the Prophets from the Vulgate. Revised in 1558 ("Biestkins Bible"), in 1648 (by Adolf Visscher), in 1750 (by Nicholas Haas), and in 1823 (by J. T. Plüschke), it remained the Bible of Dutch Lutherans until the Netherlands Bible Society version of 1951.

The Bible edited by J. Gheylliaert in 1556, based on the German Zürich version, was popular in the Dutch Reformed Church, but Govaert van Wingen's version of 1561–62 ("Deux Aes Bible") became the Bible of the Reformed

Church until 1637. The States-General version of 1637 commissioned by the Synod of Dort (1618–19) is still in use today, most recently revised in 1977 by a committee under the direction of W. L. Tukker and P. den Butter.

Nicholas van Winghe and his colleagues at Louvain found M. Vorsterman's (1528) adaptation of the Liesveldt Bible inadequate, and prepared a revision of the 1477 Delft Bible for the use of Roman Catholics. Revised in 1599 to accord with the 1592 Clementine Vulgate text, the Louvain Bible served Dutch Catholics for centuries. The Peter Canisius Society version by B. Alfrink, R. Jansen, J. Cook, and others (1929–39) enjoyed several printings; the 1939 Bible by Laetus Himmelreich and Crispinus Smits was less successful. The present standard text for Dutch Catholics is a fresh translation in modern Dutch published at Boxtel in 1961–73, with notes patterned after the French Jerusalem Bible. A joint Catholic–Protestant publication of the complete Bible in a common language version (1982), edited by A. W. G. Jaakke and a committee, should also be noted.

The earliest modern scripture portion in Frisian was a metrical Psalter begun by Gijsbert Japiks (1668) and completed by Simon and Jan Althuysen (1755). In the twentieth century, a Protestant translation of the New Testament by G. A. Wumkes and E. B. Folkertsma was published in 1933, followed by the complete Bible in 1943. In 1978, a common language version of the entire Frisian Bible was prepared and published jointly by Catholics and Protestants.

Scandinavian: Swedish, Danish, Norwegian, Faroese, Icelandic. The first Swedish Bible ("Gustavus Vasa's"), translated by Laurentius Petri, archbishop of Uppsala, assisted by his brother Olaus and others (1541), was based primarily on Luther's German Bible. Official revisions commissioned by Gustavus Adolphus (1618) and Charles XII (1703) achieved only minor changes in format and orthography, with few other alterations. The Charles XII Bible remained the standard text until 1917 when the Royal Commission of Gustavus V, working from critical editions of the Hebrew and Greek texts, produced a completely new version that was approved as the Swedish Church Bible. A new official version of the New Testament was translated by David Hedegard in 1965, and work on a new revision of the Old Testament is under way.

The earliest Danish New Testament (1524), commissioned by King Christian II, was translated by Hans Mikkelsen and Christiern Vinter from the Vulgate and Luther's German in a mixture of Danish and Swedish. Christiern Pedersen, the "Father of Danish literature," produced the first truly Danish New Testament (1529), based on the Latin Vulgate, and also a draft of the entire Bible (1543). Pedersen's work probably underlay the Reformation Bible (1550), which was commissioned by Christian III with instructions to follow Luther's text as closely as possible. Revised in 1589 (Frederick II Bible), and in 1633 (Christian IV Bible), with further editions into the nineteenth century, this remained the standard Bible of the Danish church. Meanwhile Hans Poulsen Resen, bishop of Zealand, prepared a Danish version of the Bible (1607) based on Hebrew and Greek texts; revised by Hans Svane (later archbishop) in 1647, the Svaning-Resen Bible was a "scholarly" Bible, with further revisions in 1712 and 1732 (Orphan House "Mission Bible"), 1824, and 1829. The 1907 Danish Bible Society revision of the Svaning-Resen New Testament served as the standard church text until 1948, when a new revision was issued with the Old Testament revision of 1931. This remained the official Bible of the National Danish Church until February 1992, when Queen Margarethe II gave official authorization to a new version of the complete Bible prepared by the Danish Bible Society under the direction of Neils Jørgen Cappelørn. The religious revival of the nineteenth century produced a number of individual translations, such as the Bible by J. C. Lindberg (1837–56), and the annotated New Testament by Bishop Skat Rørdam (1885). Roman Catholic New Testaments include versions by J. V. L. Hansen (1893) and Peter Schindler (1953).

When Norway became independent of Denmark in 1814, there were two Norwegian languages: the Riksmål or Bokmål of the majority, a kind of "Danish-Norwegian" spoken in urban areas and the southeast, and the Landsmål or Nynorsk (New Norwegian) or the rural regions in central and western Norway. The first Riksmål Bible was a revision of the Danish Svaning-Resen version by W. A. Wexels (1834), which the Norwegian Bible Society issued in further revised editions (Old Testament 1869, 1887, 1891; New Testament 1873, 1904). A new revision of the Bible was issued in 1930. A Roman Catholic version of the Bible in Riksmål was published in 1902 (revised 1938 from the original texts).

The first New Testament in New Norwegian (1889) was translated by J. Belsheim, E. Blix, and M. Skard; the complete Bible followed in 1921. In 1938 the Bible was revised, corrected by R. Indrebø to the 1930 Riksmål revision. The present standard Bibles in both Riksmål and New Norwegian were both prepared for the Norwegian Bible Society by committees headed by Magne Saebø and Sverre Aalen, and were published simultaneously (New Testament 1975, Old Testament 1978).

The first scripture publication in Faroese was a diglot gospel of Matthew with Danish (Randers, 1823), prepared by J. H. Schroeter, a Faroese pastor. Jacob Dahl undertook a translation of the Bible from the original languages, but completed only the New Testament (1937) and several books of the Old Testament. His work was completed by a group of pastors and published by the Danish Bible Society in 1961. Meanwhile, Victor Danielsen aided by a committee prepared a Faroese Bible based on a number of modern European versions (New Testament 1937, Bible 1948).

The first Icelandic New Testament (1540) was translated by Oddur Gottskalksson from the Vulgate and Luther's German. Parts of the Old Testament were translated by Gissur Einarsson (1580). These were revised and the Old Testament completed by Gudbrandur Thorlaksson to produce the Reformation Bible (1584), an outstanding example of Icelandic literary and book production. The Gudbrand Bible was replaced by Thorlakur Skulason's revision (1644), based on the Danish Svaning-Resen version, which became popular through the eighteenth century. The Icelandic Bible Society revision of 1841 was further revised in 1866 by Petur Petursson, and further again in 1912 by Haraldur Nielsson and others from the original languages. The present Church Bible of Iceland was published in 1981, prepared by Thorir Thordarsson, Jon Sveinnjørnsson, and others.

Romance. *Italian.* The first printed Italian Bible (Venice 1471) was translated from the Latin Vulgate by Nicolo Malermi (or Malerbi). Antonio Brucioli, a Catholic layman with Protestant tendencies, published a Bible (Venice 1532) based on the original languages which was widely influential and often reprinted. In Geneva in 1562, Filippo Rustici revised the Brucioli Old Testament and the Massimo Teofilo 1551 New Testament (translated from Greek) for the first Italian Protestant Bible. In 1564 Pope Pius IV prohibited the use of vernacular scriptures, effectively discouraging further translations until 1757, when Pope Benedict XIV gave them a qualified approval and prompted Antonio Martini to prepare a vernacular translation (1769–81). The Martini version became the standard Catholic Bible, an Italian classic. Meanwhile in Geneva, the scholar Giovanni Diodati published a Bible (1607, revised 1641) that gained immediate popularity and through many revisions (d'Erberg 1711, G. Muller 1744, G. Rolandi 1819, T.P. Rosetti 1850) has remained the standard Italian Protestant Bible.

Twentieth-century Catholic versions have been issued by the Cardinal Ferrari Society (1929), the Pontifical Biblical Institute (Old Testament 1958, New Testament 1965), and the Italian Episcopal Conference (1971), and there are individual translations by Marco Sales (1931) and Eusebio Tintori (1931); Protestant versions include a revision of Diodati by the Waldensian scholar Giovanni Luzzi and others (1924; Luzzi published his own version independently in 1930); ecumenical versions include the Italian Bible Society's Bibbia Concordata (1968), translated by a committee of Catholic, Orthodox, Protestant, and Jewish scholars, and a common language Bible (1985) produced by Catholic and Protestant scholars.

Romansch. The first scripture publication in Romansch was a New Testament translated by J. Bifrum from the Latin Vulgate (1560) in Ladin Sura of the Upper Engadine Valley. Later translations were made from the Greek text by J. L. Griti (1640) and J. Menni (1861). The first complete Romansch Bible, translated into Ladin Sut of the Lower Engladine Valley by Jacob Dorta and J. A. Vulpius (1679), was later revised by J. Andreer and N. Vital (1867–70). A new version of the Bible by J. U. Gaudenz and R. Filli appeared in 1953. The Sursilvan Romansch Bible comprising the New Testament by L. Gabriel (1648, revised 1856) and the Old Testament of P. Saluz, was revised by J. M. Darms and L. Candrian for the British Bible Society in 1869–70.

French. The first printed French Bible (Antwerp, 1530), a literalistic version by Jacques Lefèvre d'Étaples based on the *Biblia historiale,* was printed abroad because of suspicions of a Protestant bias aroused by his earlier New Testament (Paris, 1523). The first Protestant French Bible (Geneva, 1535) was translated by Pierre Robert Olivétan. The 1553 edition was the first modern version to incorporate *chapter and verse numbers throughout. Constantly revised by the Geneva pastors, the definitive Geneva Bible was edited by Theodore Beza (1588). Revisions were made in the seventeenth century by Jean Diodati

(1644) and Samuel de Marets (1669), more significantly in the eighteenth by David Martin (Amsterdam, 1707) and J.-F. Ostervald (Amsterdam, 1744). The Synodal version (Paris, 1910) of the Synod of Reformed Churches is a revision of Ostervald, while the widely popular version of Louis Segond (Geneva, 1874 Old Testament, 1880 New Testament) was based on Martin and Ostervald, and was further revised in 1975 and 1978.

The first French Catholic Bible (Louvain, 1550), which was edited by Nicholas de Leuze and François de Larben and which reproduced the text of Lefèvre slightly revised with some borrowings from Olivétan, was often revised and reprinted. The Port-Royal version (1667–95), prepared by Antoine and his brother Louis Isaac Lemaistre (de Sacy, pseudonym), was a masterpiece of French literary classicism, achieving popularity among both Catholics and Protestants. Richard Simon's translation of the New Testament (Trévoux, 1702) from the Vulgate deserves mention for its nonsectarian scholarship. Among twentieth-century Catholic Bibles should be noted those of Abbé Crampon (Tournai, 1894–1904), revised by J. Touzard and E. Levesque in 1939, by J. Bonsirven and A. Tricot in 1952; the Pieuse Société Saint Paul (1932); Paul George Passelecq and the monks of Maredsous (1950, revised 1968); A. Liénart (Ligue Catholique de l'Évangile, 1951); and especially that by the École Biblique of Jerusalem (Paris, 1954, revised 1973; the *Bible de Jérusalem* ["Jerusalem Bible"]), whose concise scholarly and exegetical notes have inspired similar editions in many other languages. Other versions of interest include the scholarly Pléiade version (Paris, 1959 Old Testament, 1971 New Testament), the *Traduction oecuménique* (Paris, 1975) of A. Bea and M. Boegner, and the common language *Français Courant* (Paris, 1982) by Jean-Claude Margot.

A Jewish version of the Hebrew scriptures was produced by Samuel Cahen (1831–51), which was superseded by *La Bible du rabbinat français* (1899–1906, revised 1966). An independent version of both Testaments was published by André Chouraqui (Paris, 1975–77).

Spanish; Catalan. Although the Spanish Inquisition allowed biblical themes in the classical Spanish theater of the sixteenth and seventeenth centuries, it acted as an effective check on the spread of vernacular Bibles in Spain. Yet the influence of the Reformation was felt. The first Spanish New Testament (1543), translated in Wittenberg by Francisco Enzinas from Erasmus's

Greek text, was published in Antwerp; the second (1556) by Juan Perez de Pineda, a refugee monk from Seville, was published in Geneva. Meanwhile, in 1553 a literal translation of the Hebrew Bible into Spanish, which Protestant and Catholic translators found useful, was printed by a Jewish press at Ferrara, translated by Abraham Usque and published by Yomtob Atias under ducal patronage.

The first complete Spanish Bible (Basel, 1569, the "Bear Bible") was translated by Cassiodoro de Reina. Revised by Cipriano de Valera (Amsterdam, 1602), this text has been frequently revised (in 1960 by the Bible Societies) and is still a standard Protestant Bible today. The first complete Bible printed in Spain was translated from the Latin Vulgate by Felipe Scio de San Miguel (Valencia, 1793). Another Catholic version (Madrid, 1825) was translated by Felix Torres Amat, who probably revised an unpublished translation by the Jesuit J. M. Petisco. Twentieth-century Catholic versions of the complete Bible include revisions of the Amat text (by Severiano del Paramo in 1928, by Serafin de Ausejo in 1965), and new versions by E. Nacar Fusta and A. Colunga (Madrid, 1944), José Maria Bover and F. Cantera Burgos (Madrid, 1947, revised 1966), Juan Straubinger (Buenos Aires, 1951), E. Martin Nieto (Madrid, 1961), Pedro Franquesa and Jose M. Sole (Barcelona, 1966), Jose Angel Ubieta on the basis of the French Jerusalem Bible (Brussels, 1967), Ramon Ricciardi (Madrid, 1971), and Luís Alonso Schökel and others (1975, revised 1982).

Mention is also due an ecumenical version (Barcelona, 1975) prepared by S. de Ausejo and F. de Fuenterrabia and revised by Catholic and Protestant scholars, and, *Dios habla hoy* (1979), a Bible Society common language version.

The first printed Bible in Catalan, the dialect of northeastern Spain and the official language of Andorra, was translated by Bonifacio Ferrer from the Latin Vulgate (Valencia, 1478); it was so thoroughly destroyed by the Spanish Inquisition that only the last page of one copy has survived. The next scripture publication was the New Testament (London, 1832) translated by J. Prat, which enjoyed several reprints. In the twentieth century three complete Bibles have appeared: two by Benedictines of Montserrat (Barcelona, 1926–66, with commentary; and Andorra, 1970), and one by the Catalan Biblical Foundation (Barcelona, 1968).

Portuguese. The first printed Portuguese New Testament (1681) was translated by João Ferreira d'Almeida in the East Indies and published in Amsterdam; his translation of the Old Testament remained unpublished until it was revised by Danish missionaries at Tranquebar (1751). It was repeatedly revised (1753–73 by J. M. Mohr, 1847 by G. Bush, 1875 by Manoel Soares), and remains a popular Protestant version today, especially in Brazil, where it was revised first in 1917 (based on the 1901 American Standard Version) and again in 1958. The earliest Portuguese Bible published in Portugal (Lisbon, 1781), translated by Anton Pereira de Figueiredo from the Latin Vulgate, has also been frequently revised and widely circulated. In the twentieth century, the Bible Society of Brazil published a common language Bible in 1988, and Roman Catholic versions of the complete Bible have been produced by Matos Soares (Porto, 1930–34) based on the Latin Vulgate, the Catholic Biblical Center of São Paolo (1959) based on the French Maredsous version, and L. Garmus (Petropolis, 1983) based on the New American Bible.

Romanian. The first printed book in Romania was a catechism (1541?) containing scripture selections; the second was the Gospels (1561), translated by Coresi, a Wallachian deacon. The first New Testament (1648) was begun by the monk Silvestru and completed by others. The complete Bible (1688) by Nicolae Milescu is considered the supreme achievement of seventeenth-century Romanian literature. Revised by Samuil Micu Clain (1795), it was reprinted even into the nineteenth century. Further translations of the complete Bible, sponsored by the British and Foreign Bible Society, were made by Ion Eliade Radulescu (1858), N. Balasescu and others (1867–73), and D. Cornilescu (1921). A new version by Vasile Radu and Grigorie Pisculescu (Gala Galaction) was published by the Romanian Orthodox church in 1938, and further revised in 1968 and 1975. Romanian was written in the Cyrillic alphabet until 1860, when the Roman alphabet was adopted. In 1984, however, the Cornilescu version was printed also in Cyrillic for use in Moldavia.

Slavonic. The first printed (Old Church) Slavonic Bible (Ostrog, 1581) was prepared for Prince Konstantin of Ostrog from a manuscript Bible dated 1499 and attributed to Archbishop Gennadius of Novgorod. Revised successively in 1633, in 1712 for Peter the Great, and in 1751 for the Tsarina Elizabeth, this remains the standard Slavonic Bible of the Russian Orthodox church.

East Slavic: Byelorussian, Ukrainian, Russian.
The earliest scripture printed in East Slavic was an incomplete Bible in Byelorussian (Prague, 1517–25) translated from Slavonic, Latin, and Czech sources by Franciscus Skoryna to supply the laity with a vernacular version. The next Byelorussian scripture publications to appear were the New Testament and Psalms of L. Dziekuć-Malej and A. M. Luckiewič (Helsinki, 1931), and the complete Bible by Moses Gitlin and J. Stankievič (New York, 1970–73).

Ukrainian versions of the Bible were first based on the Russian Synodal text of 1751 (Pochayev, 1798; Peremyshl, 1859). Modern versions have been translated from the original languages by Ivan Ohienko (London, 1962), and Ivan Khomenko (Rome, 1963).

The earliest scripture portion in modern Russian was Archbishop Mefodiy's translation of Romans (Moscow, 1792). The New Testament was published in 1821 and the Old Testament through Ruth in 1825 by the Russian Bible Society (founded 1814, dissolved 1826), translated by a committee appointed by the Holy Synod at the request of Tsar Alexander I. The complete Bible was published by the Holy Synod in 1875, translated by E. I. Lovyagin, D. A. Khvolson, and others; this remains the standard Bible of the church in Russia. Jewish versions of the Pentateuch were published by Leon I. Mandelstamm (Berlin, 1862), J. Herstein and J. L. Gordon (1875), and J. Steinberg (Vilna, 1899), and the complete Hebrew Bible by D. Yosippon (Jerusalem, 1978).

West Slavic: Czech, Slovak, Polish. The first printed Czech New Testament (Plzeň, 1475) was based on a Hussite revision of the Church Slavonic text by the Latin Vulgate, as was also the first complete Bible (Prague, 1488; revised in Venice 1506). The Moravian bishop Jan Blahoslav translated the New Testament (Ivančice, 1564) from Greek with concern for both scholarly accuracy and practical clarity; the complete Bible produced by his successors (Kralice, 1579–94) became the standard Protestant Bible, and a definitive influence in the history of the Czech language. Through successive revision it has remained the standard Czech Bible. The Wenceslaus Bible (1677–1715) of the Counter-Reformation, prepared by Jesuits J. Barner, J. Constantius, and M. V. Steyer, was based on the 1506 Venice revision and the Latin Vulgate but influenced also by the Kralice text. Modern versions which should be noted include a Catholic Bible (1917–25) translated by Jan Hejč and Jan

Sýkora from the Vulgate (New Testament revised by R. Col, 1947, 1970), a Catholic Old Testament (1955–58) based on the Hebrew by J. Heger, a Catholic New Testament (1948) based on the Greek by Pavel Škrábal; an ecumenical Bible (1979) prepared by M. Bič and J. B. Souček of the Czech Brethren Evangelical church, and a literary Jewish trnaslation of the Hebrew Bible (1947–51) by Vladimír Šrámek.

The earliest Bible printed in Slovak (1829–32) was translated by Jiří Palkovič, Catholic canon of Gran, from the Latin Vulgate. This was superseded by a new translation from the Vulgate made by Jan Donoval (Trnava, 1926). Modern Protestant versions of the complete Bible include a translation from the original languages by Josef Rohaček (1936) and the Tranoscius version (1978), based on the Czech Kralice text.

The first printed New Testament in Polish (Königsberg, 1553) was translated from Greek by Jan Seklucjan, a Lutheran pastor, but the first complete Bible (Krakow, 1561) was attributed to the Roman Catholic theologian Jan Leopolita (of Lwów) and ostensibly based on the Latin Vulgate. A scholarly Protestant Bible (Brest, 1563) translated from Hebrew and Greek by Jan Laski, F. Stankarus, and others under the patronage of Nicolas Radziwill was criticized for Socinianism in its notes, but revised by Daniel Mikolajewski and Jan Turnowski (Danzig, 1632) it became the standard Bible of Polish Protestants. Meanwhile, a Bible translated by Jakub Wujek from the Vulgate (Krakow, 1599) was accepted by the Synod of Piotrkow in 1607 as the official Polish Catholic version. Modern editions include revisions of the Wujek version (1935 by S. Styś and J. Rostworowski; 1962 by S. Styś and W. Lohn), two new Catholic versions (1965 "Millennium Bible," revised 1971, now the official Catholic text; and 1975, by M. Peter and M. Molniewicz); and an ecumenical "Millennium Bible" (1975) prepared by scholars of the Lutheran, Reformed, Orthodox, Old Catholic, and Protestant Free churches.

South Slavic: Bulgarian, Serbo-Croatian, Slovenian. The first biblical portion in modern Bulgarian was the Russian Bible Society edition of Matthew (St. Petersburg, 1823) from the New Testament translated by Archimandrite Theodosius from Church Slavonic; the project was discontinued when the Russian Bible Society was suppressed. The first printed New Testament based on the Slavonic (Smyrna, 1840) by Neophyt Rilski and revised from the Greek (1849), as well as the first complete Bible (Istanbul, 1871), were sponsored by the British and Foreign Bible Society, with revisions prepared by Robert Thomson (1914, 1923), and Gavrail Tsetanov (1940). The Bulgarian Synod version begun in 1891 was issued in 1925, the work of five successive translation committees. The first New Testament in Macedonian was published in 1967 in the Bulgarian usage, prepared by a committee of the Macedonian Orthodox Church including Georgi Milošev. Protestant and Roman Catholic scholars participated in its revision in 1976, and in 1980 the Bible was completed with a translation of the Old Testament prepared under the supervision of Archbishop Gavril.

Although Serbo-Croatian is linguistically homogeneous, the Serbs are mainly Eastern Orthodox and use the Cyrillic script, while the majority of the Croats are Roman Catholic and use the Roman alphabet. However, the first New Testament in Serbo-Croatian (1563), translated by Antun Dalmatin and Stipan K. Istrianin from Erasmus's Latin version and Luther's German, was printed in Glagolitic characters. A second printing (1563) was in Cyrillic, and the Prophets (1564) was printed in Roman letters. The translator of the first complete Bible in Serbian (Budapest, 1804) is unknown; the first Bible in Croatian (Budapest, 1831) was a literal translation made from the Latin Vulgate by M. P. Katančić. The linguistic reformer Vuk S. Karadžić sought to promote a common literary language with his Serbian translation of the New Testament (1847); although not approved by the Serbian church, it was later issued together with an Old Testament prepared by his colleague G. Daničić (1868) simultaneously in both Serbian and Croatian. The Vuk-Daničić Bible remains popular in both scripts. Other significant Bibles were issued by Lujo Bakotić (Belgrade, 1933), I. E. Šarić (Sarajevo, 1942, New Testament revised by an ecumenical committee in 1969), and the Stvarnost edition (Zagreb, 1968) based on the French Jerusalem Bible.

The first Slovenian Bible (Wittenberg, 1584) combined the New Testament of the Reformed preacher Primus Truber (Tübingen, 1582) with the Old Testament of the Lutheran Juri Dalmatin, both translated from the original languages with close reference to Luther's German version. The first Roman Catholic Bible (Ljubljana, 1784–1802), was translated from the Vulgate by Juri Japel, Blaz Kumerdey, and others; a second Catholic version (1859) was based on the German Allioli version. Renewed interest in the Slovenian language in the early twentieth century led to a revision of the Truber-Dalmatin version by Anton Chraska (Bible, 1914; New Testament, 1946), and a new Catholic version of the Bible (New Testament, 1929; Old Testament, 1961), which was revised by Lutheran and Roman Catholic scholars and issued as an ecumenical Bible in 1974.

Others. Greek. The first modern Greek New Testament (Geneva, 1638) was translated by a monk from Gallipoli, edited by Cyril Lucar, Patriarch of Constantinople, and published at the expense of the Dutch States General. It has often been revised and reprinted: by Seraphim of Mitylene (London, 1703), Anastasius Michael (Halle, 1710), Demetrius Schinas (1827), and others. The Bible translated by N. Bambas (London, 1840 Old Testament, 1844 New Testament) has become the standard Protestant Modern Greek Bible. A vernacular version of the Gospels by Alexander Pallis from the fourth century Codex Vaticanus (Liverpool, 1902) provoked legislation prohibiting all modern versions (repealed in 1924). Modern editions include a Bible translated by Athanasios Chastoupis and Nikolaos Louvaris (Athens 1955, a paraphrase), and New Testaments by B. Vellas (Athens, 1967) and S. Agourides, J. Karavidopoulos, and others (Athens, 1985; an interconfessional version).

Uralic: Hungarian, Estonian, Finnish, Saami. The first printed Hungarian New Testament (Új Sziget, 1541) was translated by Janos Erdösi (Sylvester), a pupil of Melanchthon. The first complete Bible (Vizsoly, 1590), translated by Caspar Karoli, Reformed pastor at Göncz, played a decisive role in the national life and literature of Hungary comparable to that of Luther's Bible in Germany. Through successive revisions, most recently by Kalman Kallay and Jozsef Pongracz for the Joint Bible Commission of Lutheran and Reformed Churches (Budapest, 1975), it has remained the standard Protestant Bible of Hungary. The first Catholic Bible (Vienna, 1626) was an excellent rendering of the Vulgate by György Csipkes (revised by Bela Jozsef Tarkanyi, 1865). Modern Hungarian translations of the complete Bible were made by the Reformed scholar Sandor Czgledy (Gyor, 1938), and the Roman Catholic scholars A. Szöreny, Ferenc Gal, and Istvan Kosztolanyi (Budapest, 1976), translated from the original languages and based on the Jerusalem Bible.

The first Estonian New Testament (Riga, 1686) was in the southern dialect of Tartu (Dorpat), begun by Johann Gutsleff and completed by N. von Hardungen, Adrian Virginius, and Marco

Schütz. Revisions were made by Ferdinand Meyer (Mitau, 1836) and Uku Masing (Dorpat, 1896). The first Estonian Bible (Tallinn, 1739) was in the northern dialect of Tallinn (Reval), translated by Anton Thor Helle, Heinrich Gutsleff, and others; it was later revised by C. Malm (Berlin, 1878), then by Uku Masing and John V. Veski (Tallinn, 1938). After World War II, a new version of the Old Testament and a further revision of the New Testament (London, 1968) was sponsored by the Swedish church, prepared by Endel Köpp and Toomas Pöld for Estonian refugees in Sweden.

The first Finnish New Testament (Stockholm, 1548) was translated by Michael Agricola on the basis of Luther's German text. The complete Bible (Stockholm, 1642) was published under the patronage of Queen Christina of Sweden, translated from the original languages by M. Martin Stodius, Gregory Matthaei, and Heinrich J. Hoffman. Frequently revised (Turku, 1685, the "War Bible," by Henrik Florinus; 1776, by Anders Lizelius; Helsinki, 1932–38, by E. Stenij, J. Schwartzberg, and others), this version remains the standard Finnish Bible. The Finnish Bible Society has published a common language translation of the New Testament (Turku, 1972), translated by Esko Rintala, R. Huikuri, and H. Räisänen.

The earliest scripture portion in Saami (Stockholm, 1648) was an edition of Psalms, Proverbs, Ecclesiastes, and Ecclesiasticus (Sirach), translated in Swedish Saami by J. J. Tornaeus. The first New Testament (Stockholm, 1755) was translated by Pehr Fjellström, and the first complete Bible (Hernösand, 1811) by S. Öhrling, E. J. Grönlund, E. Öhrling, and N. Fjellström. The first New Testament in Norwegian Saami (Christiania, 1840) was the work of N. J. C. V. Stockfleth, which was revised for the first complete Bible (Christiania, 1895), prepared by L. J. Haetta, J. A. Friis, and J. K. Qvigstad.

Baltic: Latvian, Lithuanian. The first Latvian Bible (Riga, 1689) was translated by the Lutheran scholars Ernst Glück and C. B. Witten. Revised often (Königsberg, 1739; Mitau, 1877 and 1898; Riga, 1960 New Testament; London, 1965), it remains the standard Bible of the Latvian church. In 1937, a New Testament was published in Latgalian, the Eastern dialect of Latvian, translated from the Latin Vulgate by Aloizijs Broks.

The earliest biblical publication in Lithuanian was a Psalter (Königsberg, 1625), revised by J. Rhesa from an unpublished 1590 version of the Bible by J. Bretken which was based on Luther's German. Samuel B. Chyliński's version of Genesis to Job (London, 1662) was based on the Polish Danzig version; his translation of the New Testament was discovered in 1934 and published by C. Kudzinowski in 1958. The first complete Bible (Königsberg, 1735) was translated by J. J. Quandt and P. Ruhig; a revision by L. J. Rhesa in 1816 was often reprinted. A Roman Catholic version of the New Testament was published in 1816, and a new version of the complete Bible (Kaunas, 1936) was translated from the original languages by Juozapas Skvireckas.

Celtic: Breton. The first Breton New Testament (Angoulême, 1827) was translated from the Latin Vulgate in the Léon dialect by Jean François Le Gonidec, who later completed the Bible (St. Brieuc, 1866). A revision of this New Testament (Brest, 1847) by J. Jenkins, who corrected it from the Greek, was often revised and reprinted (1866, 1870, 1885, 1897). More recently, a new Catholic New Testament (Guingamp, 1971) was translated by Maodez Glanndour. Meanwhile a New Testament (Guingamp, 1853) appeared in the Tréguier dialect under the patronage of the Catholic bishop of St. Brieuc, and a Bible (Tremel, 1889) was translated by G. Le Coat, the Protestant pastor at Tremel.

Basque. One of the earliest publications in Basque was the New Testament in Labourdin Basque (La Rochelle, 1571), translated by Jean Leiçarraga under the patronage of Jeanne d'Albret, the Protestant Queen of Navarre (reprinted by the Trinitarian Bible Society, 1908). A Roman Catholic New Testament was translated from the Vulgate by Jean Haraneder, but only the Gospels were published (Bayonne, 1855), edited by Abbé Maurice Harriet of Halsou. The complete Bible (London, 1865) was translated by Captain Duvoisin for Louis-Lucien Bonaparte. In Guipuzcoan Basque, the gospel of Luke (Madrid, 1838) was translated by Oteiza, a physician, and edited by George Barrow; the first New Testament (Bilbao, 1931) and Bible (Bilbao, 1958) were translated by Raimondo Olabide and José F. Echeverria.   ERROLL F. RHODES

African Languages

African translations of the Bible are used in the most complex ethnic, linguistic, and culturally diverse human mosaic on earth. About two thousand languages are spoken in fifty-nine different countries by five hundred million people. Scripture versions (of which over a hundred are complete Bibles) in five hundred languages are available to the seven thousand denominations on the African continent. Arabic scriptures are available in some five different script forms. The Tuareq people of Niger Republic speak the language they themselves call Tayrt, but it is part of the Tamahaq language of nomads in the Sahara; several portions of scriptures in at least three alphabetic systems are available in this complex language. In about eight hundred places on the continent, linguistic groups are separated by political boundaries. This creates special challenges for translators; for example, portions of the scriptures for the Borana people living in Kenya are written in Roman characters while the same version for the Boranas living in Ethiopia requires Amharic characters.

By the end of the eighteenth century the complete Bible was available in two African languages, namely Ge'ez (Ethiopic) and Arabic, while a New Testament was available in Coptic. During the nineteenth century, growing Christian missionary activity generated a steady stream of versions of the Bible, or parts thereof, in the indigenous languages of Africa. Pioneering missionaries used available European versions to reach unevangelized Africans. For example, a Dutch New Testament (printed in the Netherlands in 1692) provided the foundation for the work of the Lutheran church in Southern Africa. Georg Schmidt left this Testament in the early eighteenth century with five converts in a valley some eighty miles from the Cape of Good Hope. The Khoisan speaking community used it for nearly fifty years without any missionaries present, because Schmidt had to go back to Europe. The only complete Bible available in a Khoisan language, namely Nama—still the living language of some fifty thousand people in Namibia—was published in 1966. It took more than 140 years to complete this translation.

In the 1980s the complete Bible (sixty-six books) became available in 121 indigenous versions in Africa, amounting to 38 percent of complete Bible versions available around the globe. Many of these versions also contain the expanded *canon used by the Roman Catholic and other churches. The first Bible in Africa published by *Bible Societies that was accepted in unaltered form and sanctioned for use by Roman Catholics was the Afrikaans version, in 1965, with the chiChewa version approved shortly afterward.

Some eighteen indigenous languages in Africa (and offshore islands) are spoken by five million people or more. These languages (in alphabetical order) are: Afrikaans, Amharic, Arabic, chiShona, Fulfulde, Hausa, isiXhosa, isiZulu, kinyaRwanda, kiRundi, kiSwahili (Central), kiSwahili (Zaire), liNgala, Malagasy, Oromo (Western), Somali, Yoruba. Complete Bibles are available in all these languages. Because of language development and refinement of translation techniques, retranslations continue to be made in most of these languages, mostly by indigenous speakers.

A noteworthy trend in linguistic development in Africa has been the merging of languages used in Bible versions into the "Union Versions." For example, in the Xhosa version elements of some seven dialects are merged. By the middle of the twentieth century, there were at least fourteen union language versions available, namely in chiChewa, chiShona, chiTonga, ichiMambwe, Igbo, Kalenjin, kiSwahili (Ngwana—Zaire), loMongo, Nuer, oluLuyia, Omyene, runyaNkore, isiXhosa, seTswana. In kiSwahili—the lingua franca of East Africa—a complete Bible was published in 1914.

The first complete Bible version translated and printed by movable type on the continent of Africa itself was the seTswana Bible, published in 1857 at Kuruman, Southern Africa. Space allows more extended discussion of only a few versions.

Arabic. Although various complete Bible versions in this language already existed, the translation by Eli Smith and Cornelius van Dyck attained the status of a standard edition after its publication in 1865. The complex dialectal, orthographical, and denominational needs within Arabic-speaking communities provide an ongoing challenge for the various geographical areas. The spread of Islam south of the Sahara, especially in the twentieth century, with its emphasis on its scripture, the *Qur'ān, has stimulated the program for Bible versions in Arabic.

Hausa. The Hausa Bible is available in both Arabic and roman script. This version had a complex translation history from 1857 to 1932, when the complete Bible was published. Missionaries of Sudan Interior Mission, with the help of Hausa-speaking Christians under the guidance of the British and Foreign Bible Society (BFBS), produced a version that has maintained record levels of distribution over the years.

Malagasy. The Malagasy Bible, published by the BFBS in 1835, was the first version of the Bible for an African country that was printed by movable type—although in England.

Tiv. Although the Tiv people (of Northern Nigeria) numbered only about two million, the publication of the New Testament in this language in 1936 provided a stimulus for this language group to convert from Islam to Christianity; in 1940, less than 1 percent of the people were Christian, but by 1972, 95 percent were Christian.

Amharic. Amharic is the official language of Ethiopia and has been in existence as a literary language since the fourteenth century. Parts of the Bible have been published since 1824 in a diglot version together with the ancient language of Ethiopia, Ge'ez. An official version of the Bible was published in 1961 through the work of a joint committee appointed by Emperor Haile Selassie and the BFBS.

seTswana. In 1830 the gospel of Luke in seTswana was published. Through the perseverance of Robert Moffat and his Batswana helpers during the early part of the nineteenth century, the translation was completed and ten thousand copies of the Old Testament printed on a hand press at Kuruman in 1857. These copies of the Old Testament were attached to available printed New Testament sections. The press used by Moffat was carted by ox wagon over more than eight hundred miles of the most difficult terrain from the Cape of Good Hope into the interior.

isiZulu. The complete Bible was published in 1883 by the American Bible Society. The people speaking the related Nguni languages of siSwati and Ndebele (both Southern and Northern) have used this version for many years. Translation into these related languages of various individual books of the Bible has been in progress during the twentieth century. The complete Bible in Ndebele (Northern) was published in 1978, while versions of the New Testament and Psalms in siSwati and in Ndebele (Southern) were published in 1986. The complete Bible in isiZulu was retranslated and published in 1959. In 1986, a new version of the New Testament and Psalms in isiZulu was published. This edition is unique because the type was set in such a way that hyphenation was eliminated and lines were carefully segmented into meaningful sentences and word clusters.

Afrikaans. This Indo-Germanic language came into being on the African continent over the last three centuries and has generated an extensive literature. The complete Bible was published in 1933, and some six million copies were distributed in fifty years. It is the only African version in which the translation directly from the original Hebrew and Greek was done exclusively by native speakers. In 1983, a new translation was

published, of which one million copies were distributed within a period of three years.

GERRIT E. VAN DER MERWE

Asiatic Languages

In addition to the Syriac, Armenian, Georgian, and Arabic versions (*see the article on* Ancient Languages *earlier in this entry*) there are also other, less well known, early versions of the Bible in Asia, some still extant. For example, in China a version of the Gospels, prepared by Nestorian missionaries for Emperor Taizong of the Tang Dynasty, is known to have existed as early as 640 CE. When the Jesuit missionary Francis Xavier arrived in Japan in 1549, he reportedly brought with him a translation of Matthew prepared by a Japanese convert in India. The Dutch traders were instrumental in translating several early versions: examples include the gospel of Matthew in High Malay (1629), which was the first translation in a non-European language made expressly for the purpose of evangelism; the gospels of Matthew and John (1661) in the now extinct Sinkang dialect of Taiwan; and the Gospels in Sinhalese (1739). Ziegenbalg, the first missionary sent to India by the Danish-Halle Mission, published the Tamil New Testament in 1715, and, assisted by B. Schultz, the Bible in 1727.

A flurry of Bible translation followed on the heels of the great missionary movement inspired by Pietism and the Great Awakening. Starting from the Middle East, the Arabic "Smith–Van Dyck Version" (New Testament 1860, Bible 1865), which has gone through successive revisions, is still in use today. Franz Delitzsch's New Testament in Hebrew (1877) has appeared in several revised editions. The first complete Turkish Bible (New Testament 1819, Bible 1827), known as the "Ali Bey Version," was originally translated in the mid-seventeenth century. Ali Bey, a Pole sold at Constantinople as a slave, was requested by the Dutch ambassador to Constantinople to translate the Bible because of his exceptional linguistic skills. Henry Martyn translated the most influential Persian version; his New Testament (1815), translated in Calcutta, has remained the basis of subsequent revisions. The common-language Persian New Testament appeared in 1973. Martyn also translated the first New Testament into Urdu (1814), the state language of Pakistan. The first Urdu Bible, translated by the Benares Committee, appeared in 1843. Pashto, one of the official languages of Afghanistan, had its first New Testament in 1818, and a full Bible in 1895. Dari, the other official language of Afghanistan, had its first New Testament published in 1982.

India has the Bible or a portion of it in 142 of its languages and dialects. William Carey is reported to have translated the Bible into six languages, and parts of it into twenty-nine more. The Serampore Press, which he established, has published scriptures in no fewer than forty-five languages, of which thirty-five are languages of India. The first Bengali New Testament, which he translated, appeared in 1801, and the complete Bible in 1809. It was due largely to his work and influence that most of the major languages in India got their first Bible in the early nineteenth century—for example, Oriya (1815), Marathi (1821), Sanskrit (1822), Gujarati (1823), Kannada (1831), Assamese (1833), Hindi (1835), Malayalam (1841), Urdu (1843), Telugu (1854). Although Panjabi had the first New Testament in 1815, the Bible did not appear until 1959. Common-language Bibles include Hindi (1978), Panjabi (1985), Sema Haga (1985), Marathi (1987), Rongmei Naga (1989), Boro (1991), and Gangte (1991). Nepali, a language used both in Nepal and India, had its first New Testament in 1821 and Old Testament in 1914. The common-language New Testament was published in 1981, and the complete Bible is expected in 1992. A notable version from Bangladesh is the common language New Testament (1980) in Musalmani Bengali, a form of language spoken by its Muslim population.

Adoniram Judson translated the first Burmese New Testament in 1832 and the Bible in 1835. Due to Burmese hostility to Europeans, he spent twenty-one months in prison while translating the New Testament. The first Hwa Lisu New Testament (1938), by J. O. Fraser in the syllabic script that he developed, is an example of the Bible translator as an inaugurator of vernacular literature. The new common-language Lisu Bible appeared in 1987. In Thailand, the gospel of Luke (1834), translated by Karl Gutzlaff, was the first scripture published in Thai. The first New Testament appeared in 1843, the Bible in one volume 1891–96, and an interconfessional common-language Bible in 1981. In Laos, the first Lao New Testament was released in 1926, the Bible in 1932, and the common-language New Testament in 1975 and Shorter Old Testament in 1980. In Kampuchea, the first Khmer scripture was the gospel of Luke (1899), translated by a king's interpreter, and the next publication, Luke-Acts (1900), by a Buddhist monk.

The first New Testament appeared in 1929, and the Bible in 1954. The first Vietnamese Bible (1913–16) was translated from the Latin Vulgate by a Catholic priest. A Protestant version followed, the New Testament in 1923, and the Old Testament in 1925; the New Testament, revised in 1954, is still in circulation. In Malaysia, the first complete Malay Bible (1733), translated by Melchior Leidekker, was the basis for several subsequent revisions. Another version, consisting of the 1879 Old Testament and 1938 New Testament, is still in use today. The common-language New Testament was published in 1976, and the Bible in 1987.

In Indonesia, the Bible or a portion of it has been translated into seventy-two languages and dialects. The first language of Indonesia to have the complete Bible was Javanese (1854). Another version by P. Jansz (New Testament 1890, Old Testament 1893) has undergone several revisions and appeared in Javanese, Arabic, and Roman scripts. Indonesian, the national language, had its first New Testament only in 1968, and the Bible in 1974; the common-language New Testament followed in 1977, and the Bible in 1985. Other major language versions include Bugis and Makassar (New Testament 1888, Old Testament 1891–1901), Sundanese (New Testament 1877, Bible 1891), and Toba (New Testament 1878, Old Testament 1894). In addition to Indonesian, other common-language Bibles published include Batak Koro (1987), Batak Toba (1989), Bali (1990), Batak Angkola (1991), and Sunda (1991).

In the Philippines, the Bible or a portion of it has been translated into eighty-three languages and dialects. The Pangasinan Luke (1887) was the first portion to appear. Pilipino, or Tagalog, the national language, had its first New Testament in 1902 and Old Testament in 1905. Most of the major languages had their first Bible in the first half of the twentieth century: Bikol (1914), Cebuano (1917), Hiligaynon (1912), Ilokano (1909), Pampango (1917), Pangasinan (1915), and Samarenyo (1937). Being a dominantly Roman Catholic country, it is very active in interconfessional translations. Thus far, interconfessional Bibles in common language have appeared in Tagalog, Bikol, Cebuano, Hiligaynon, Ilokano, Pangasinan, and Samarenyo.

In China, the Bible or a portion of it has been translated into fifty-eight languages and dialects. Marshman and Lassar produced the first Chinese literary Wenli Bible in 1822; however, the 1823 Bible by Morrison and Milne made a greater impact. W. H. Medhurst, Karl Guszlaff, and Elijah Bridgman also exerted considerable influence when they produced the 1838 Bible; they left their mark on several subsequent versions, some of which bear their names. The 1855 Delegates' Version is still in circulation. Among the Easy Wenli versions, the 1902 Bible by Joseph Schereschewsky deserves special mention. Stricken with paralysis in 1881 and unable to hold a pen, he continued to work on the translation of the entire Bible, typing with one finger of each hand. Hence this Bible is known as the "Two-finger Edition." Important Mandarin versions include the 1878 Bible (Old Testament by Schereschewsky and New Testament by Peking Committee) and the 1919 Union Version, which continues to be the standard Bible today. The Today's Chinese Version in common language, translated entirely by Chinese scholars, appeared in 1985. The Bible (Old Testament 1946–52, New Testament 1957–59), translated by Franciscan Fathers, is widely used by Roman Catholics. Schereschewsky was also involved in producing the first Bible portion (Matthew, 1872) in Khalka Mongolian (the official language of the People's Republic of Mongolia), based on the literary Mongolian New Testament published in 1846. The common-language New Testament, in Cyrillic script, appeared in 1990. In Taiwan, the Amoy Bible (1882–84), revised by Thomas Barclay in 1933, remains the standard Bible for Taiwanese speakers in Taiwan. Common-language translation is in progress in Taiwanese and Hakka. For the tribal people, the common-language Old Testament with a shorter New Testament has appeared in Amis (1981) and Taroko (1988), and the New Testament in Bunun (1973), Paiwan (1973), and Tayal (1974).

In Korea, the first portion (Luke and John) appeared in 1882, the New Testament in 1887. This translation, in Hankul characters, was done by John Ross in Manchuria. The 1911 Bible, revised in 1938 and 1956, is still in use today. Korea is also the first country in the world to have published the common-language and interconfessional Bible (1977). In Japan, Karl Gutzlaff, an influential figure in the history of Chinese and Thai Bible translation, in 1837 translated the first ever portions (John and 1–3 John). J. C. Hepburn, the originator of the Hepburnian system of romanization, translated the first New Testament (1880), which formed the basis of the Standard Version Bible (1887). In 1917 a revised New Testament was released. The Colloquial Version Bible (1955), translated entirely by Japanese scholars, is still the standard Bible. However, the circulation of the New Interconfessional Translation Bible (1987) has passed one million copies.

In Micronesia, Hildegard Thiem and Harold Hanlin made an outstanding contribution. The former translated the Palauan New Testament (1964), Shorter Old Testament (1985), and the Yapese Shorter Bible (1981); the latter, the Trukese New Testament (1957) as well as the Ponapean New Testament (1972) and Shorter Old Testament (1977). Hanlin also helped in the preparation of the Marshallese Shorter Bible (1983). In Papua New Guinea, the Bible or a portion of it has been translated into 198 languages and dialects. The first Bible in the national language (Tok Pisin) was published in 1989. Translation in Pijin, the lingua franca of the Solomon Islands, is in progress. In the rest of the Pacific Islands, most of the major areas had their first Bible by the mid-nineteenth century—for example, Tahitian (1838), Hawaiian (1839), Rarotongan (1851), Samoan (1855), and Maori (1858). Bislama, the national language of the new Republic of Vanuatu, had its first New Testament in 1980, and is expected to have the Bible in 1993. Because of their expertise, the translators were called upon to help translate the Constitution of the new republic.

According to a report compiled by the United Bible Societies, as of the end of 1991, complete Bibles, New Testaments, and portions of the Bible have been published in 811 different languages and dialects from Asia and the Pacific Islands, comprising 125 Bibles, 304 New Testaments, and 382 portions.   I-JIN LOH

Australian Aboriginal Languages

At the time of the arrival of the Europeans in Australia at the end of the eighteenth century, there were at least three hundred thousand aborigines speaking more than five hundred languages and dialects; the present aboriginal population (tribal and other, including many with European blood) is about half that, or one percent of the total population of Australia. Portions of the Bible have been translated over the last century into approximately thirty Australian languages. Most translations cover only small parts of scripture; no full Bible has been published as yet and only a few full New Testaments. This selective approach is because the number of speakers of most aboriginal languages is lower than one thousand, often far less.

One reason for the activity of Bible translators

is, of course, their desire to evangelize. Among churches and missionary organizations, however, a much greater appreciation of aboriginal culture has replaced earlier attitudes that were intent on eradicating tribal customs and traditions. The aborigines themselves are aware of their non-European position in relation to scripture. Although most tribal aborigines have received a traditional Christian education from white ministers and teachers at aboriginal mission stations, as aboriginal people become more assertive they discover the similarity between their own position and that of the people of God in the Bible. The stories of *creation, of the *ancestors, of the oppression under Pharaoh, of the *Exodus, the *conquest, the *exile, and the return have a special appeal. In their struggle for land rights they discover that the biblical concept of land as a gift from God and as something with which humanity is inseparably united is much more closely related to their own aboriginal understanding than to the European understanding of land as a commodity to be bought and sold. Similarly, the concept of *covenant, with its strong emphasis on community and on corporate life, appeals to them much more than the individualistic thinking of Europeans.

Djiniyini Gondarra, a prominent aboriginal United Church Minister, the first aboriginal theologian and vice president of the United and Islander Christian Congress, provides a good illustration of the new assertiveness of aboriginal Christians. Two important addresses given by him in 1983 and 1985 were entitled, respectively, "Let my people go" and "Overcoming the captivities of the western church context" (the latter being based on Galatians 5.1). Djiniyini, as a black theologian, sees God as black, and he is most conscious of the European wrapping in which the aborigines have received Christianity and the Bible. He is therefore a strong supporter of the movement to translate the biblical message into aboriginal cultural forms.

It would be incorrect to assume that all aboriginal Christians are critical of the Western wrapping in which the biblical message is received. Many aborigines still receive the biblical message as it was presented fifty and even a hundred years ago. Until very recently, the destruction of all aboriginal culture was propagated, and in some cases this may still occur. Nevertheless, the new developments may be the sign of a new era in biblical interpretation: they will influence not only aborigines, as they try to understand Christianity in their own cultural setting, but also European traditional understandings. The latter may be noted in two particular points.

First, the biblical and theological interpretation of land has stimulated aboriginal Christians to new understandings. Is it valid, some ask, to use the Hebrew Bible in the current debate on land rights? Does this not impose the life and thought of an ancient culture upon modern times? Should the Old Testament not be interpreted in the light of the New Testament, and if this cannot be done (because the New Testament does not offer any thought on the matter in discussion), should we then not abandon all attempts to make connections between the Old Testament and our present world? Others argue that the Old Testament is not subservient to the New Testament, that the difference in culture does not necessarily mean a difference in ethos, and that it is this ethos with which the church has to wrestle when it interprets the biblical message.

Second, a significant outcome of the new developments in aboriginal biblical understandings for the Europeans is that they are forced to reconsider some of their own assumptions. The thought that there is only one way of understanding scripture is challenged, and the question is raised whether Western biblical interpretations are not more influenced by prejudices related to Western civilization and culture than has often been thought. The newer aboriginal understandings challenge and stimulate those whose prerogative it has been for many centuries to interpret scripture.

HENDRIK C. SPYKERBOER

Native American Languages

At the end of 1990, 399 native American languages (Indian, Eskimo, and Aleut) had at least one book of the scriptures in published form. One hundred ninety-seven of these languages have complete New Testaments, and fifteen have complete Bibles. Out of a total population of approximately twenty million, some ninety-eight percent have at least something of the Bible in a form meaningful to them, provided they can read. In addition to these strictly native American languages, there are publications in seven creole languages, including an entire Bible in Haitian Creole, based on French and spoken by more than six million people, a New Testament in Sranan, an English-based creole spoken by some 300,000 people in Surinam, and a New Testament in Papiamento, a Portuguese-based creole with heavy Spanish borrowings spoken in the Netherlands West Indies by more than 250,000 people.

Evaluating this important development in the translation of the scriptures is extremely difficult in view of a number of crucial factors: (1) in many instances lack of adequate field surveys for determining the degrees of mutual intelligibility between languages and dialects; (2) extreme differences in population sizes (e.g., in Ecuador, Peru, and Bolivia six million Quechuas are divided into some twenty different dialects, while in Brazil 77 languages out of 136 have less than 200 speakers); (3) extent of literacy (e.g., 600,000 literate Aymaras out of a total population of 1.7 million in contrast with ninety percent illiteracy in some other language areas); (4) ninety-two percent bilingualism in the Mexican Indian population and less than forty percent in a number of the Quechua dialects of Peru; and (5) significant differences in the quality of translations depending on the linguistic training of missionaries and the theological training of indigenous translators.

The majority of translations published in the languages of North America took place prior to 1900, while in Latin America and the Caribbean only thirteen out of 337 translations were published by that date, and most of the translations have appeared in print since World War II.

The first Bible to be translated and published in the Western Hemisphere was in the Massachusetts Indian language, spoken by a tribe of Indians settled along the Atlantic Coast north of Boston. John Eliot, a Roxbury minister originally from England, spent fifteen years learning the Indian language before beginning to translate. Genesis and Matthew were published in 1655 and the entire Bible in 1663. Eliot's decision to translate the Bible for the Indians living nearby was without precedent in modern times. Not since the eighth century CE had anyone undertaken to translate the entire Bible primarily for missionary purposes. Unfortunately, there are no Indians who still speak this language. But in Mohawk, an Iroquoian language, the gospel of Mark was first published in 1787, and later in the nineteenth century the rest of the New Testament appeared. These scriptures continue to be used by Mohawk Indians, many of whom live in New York City.

A fascinating story of biblical translation in North America concerns the Cherokee language and an orthography designed to represent the many distinctive sounds. Although an Indian named Sequoya could not read or write in English, he was deeply impressed by the power of written words. "If I could make things fast on paper, it would be like catching a wild animal and taming it," he said. Finally, he devised a remarkably accurate syllabary, completed in 1821 and subsequently used by missionaries to translate the New Testament in a version still widely used and cherished by Cherokees, who constitute the second-largest tribe in the United States.

In Latin America and the Caribbean the translation of the scriptures has been carried out by Christian missionaries representing a number of denominations as well as several so-called Faith Missions, such as the South American Indian Mission, New Tribes Mission, and the *Wycliffe Bible Translators, also known as the Summer Institute of Linguistics. The Wycliffe Bible Translators have been responsible for the production of New Testaments in 180 languages and have plans to undertake translations of the New Testament in twenty more languages and to complete work in thirty-five other languages in which work was begun but not completed.

Because of the limited educational opportunities for most native people in the Americas, Bible translating has generally been carried out by missionaries, but in some cases translation committees consist entirely of indigenous people. An example is the manuscript of the New Testament in the Inuktitut dialect of Eskimo (Eastern Arctic), which went to the printers in 1992; almost forty percent of the Old Testament is in first draft for some 20,000 Inuktitut speakers, of whom ninety percent are members of the Anglican church.

The languages of the Americas are remarkably diverse and in many instances are structurally very complex. Linguists have classified these languages into more than thirty families, each with distinctive structural features and different vocabularies. A number of languages in southern Mexico have even more tones than Cantonese Chinese and must employ a complex system of tone marks to indicate crucial differences of meaning. Some languages, like Eskimo and Quechua, have exceptionally long words, consisting of as many as a dozen syllables. Verbs in Quechua begin with a root and may be followed by a number of different suffixes and clitics in as many as eight positions in some dialects, with the result of many verbs having more than ten thousand forms.

Because of the linguistic problems faced by translators working in languages not previously reduced to writing, missionary translators have generally invested a great deal of time and effort in the development of scientific alphabets, the analysis of unusual grammatical constructions, and the study of oral literature. The Summer Institute of Linguistics has been particularly active and creative in this area of research.

Because of the linguistic and cultural differences between the biblical text and the indigenous ways of life, some people have seriously doubted the possibility of effective functional equivalence in translating, but the resources of language and culture are generally adequate. In fact, in one language there are two expressions for the ambiguous English expression "love of God." God's love for people is expressed as "God hides them in his heart" and people's love for God is "their hearts go away with God."

But for a full understanding of the biblical message there are serious cultural differences. Many Indians in South America see no reason "to fear God." He is generally regarded as being too far away to be of any real concern for people. What they fear are the malicious spirits of the forests, streams, and caves, which must be placated with gifts.

A traditional syncretistic Christopaganism also poses real problems for communication. In many areas a name such as *Tata Dios*, literally, "Father God," is really a name for the sun, and *Mama Dios*, literally "Mother God," is in some places a triple reference to the moon, the earth, and the Virgin Mary.

For a variety of reasons the publication of the scriptures in some Indian languages has not been a success, but where there have been missionaries or leaders of national churches who have encouraged literacy, instructed people in the meaning and relevance of the Bible message, and trained local leadership, the response has been remarkable.

The production of the scriptures in indigenous languages of the Americas has produced three important byproducts: literacy by believers anxious to learn to read the scriptures; concern for further education in their own language as well as in the dominant language of the area (Spanish, Portuguese, English, or French); and a sense of ethnic pride, so important for socially and economically exploited people. As one Totonac Indian said when he first purchased a New Testament in his own language, "Now we are a people because we have a book."

EUGENE A. NIDA

Tribes of Israel. The Hebrew Bible in its final form takes it for granted that the Israelite people is descended from the twelve sons of *Jacob, each being the ancestor of the tribe named after him (1 Kings 18.31). This tradition has persisted into later times. The book of Genesis records the births of Jacob's twelve sons (chaps. 29–35), and then provides a list of them arranged under the names of their mothers: *Reuben, *Simeon, *Levi, *Judah, *Issachar, and *Zebulun were the sons of *Leah; *Joseph and *Benjamin the sons of *Rachel; *Dan and *Naphtali the sons of Jacob's concubine Bilhah; *Gad and *Asher the sons of his concubine Zilpah (35.22–26). After Joseph, in Egypt, brought his family from Canaan (Gen. 46–47), the twelve brothers and their families continued to reside in Egypt and there increased in numbers, becoming the people of Israel, literally the "sons of Israel" (Exod. 1.1–7), Jacob's name having been changed by God to *Israel (Gen. 32.28; 35.10). This united people, after many vicissitudes, took possession of the land of Canaan and established their home there, with each tribe assigned its own territory (Josh. 13–19; Map 3).

The Bible is, however, not consistent with regard to either the number or the names of the tribes. In the numerous tribal lists found in the various books of the Bible, the number varies from eleven to thirteen. These variations are mainly due to the appearance in some lists of the two sons of Joseph, *Ephraim and *Manasseh (Gen. 48.8–20) as separate tribes, and to the omission of Simeon or Levi from others. In the Song of Deborah (Judg. 5), which is not necessarily a complete roll call of the tribes, Judah and Gad are missing, while Machir, the son of Manasseh (Josh. 17.1) appears to take the place of his "father." The variations are presumed to reflect fluctuations in the constitution and history of the tribes and their relative size and importance.

Very little is known of the early history of the tribes. The "blessing of Jacob" (Gen. 49) and the "blessing of Moses" (Deut. 33) contain some very ancient, but also very cryptic, allusions to early tribal events and characteristics, but these passages have also undergone later expansions and editing, especially in the blessing of Judah (Gen. 49.8–12), which is a "prophecy" of the kingdom of *David, and that of Joseph (Deut. 33.13–17), which reflects the special prominence at some time of the tribes of Ephraim and Manasseh. Parts of the books of Joshua and Judges preserve traditions of the early history of some of the tribes during and after their settlement in Canaan. Some of these passages (especially Judg. 1) suggest that the tribes, rather than conquering and settling the entire country as a united people (the impression given by the book of Joshua in its present form), possessed no military or political unity at the time of the settlement, but were independent units each making its way into the country, in some cases encountering opposition from the local population. (*See* Conquest of Canaan; Social Sciences and the Bible, *article on* Cultural Anthropology and the Hebrew Bible.)

There can be little doubt that the concept of Israel as a close-knit family of twelve tribes acting in concert before, during, and after the settlement in Canaan is an elaboration of a later period. Although the tribes probably entered the country from outside, they did so for the most part in a piecemeal way, over a long period of time; the people of Israel was in fact constituted for the first time on Canaanite soil. Indeed, some of the tribes, such as Ephraim and Judah, appear to have acquired their names after their arrival in Canaan.

Little is known of the lives of the tribes after their arrival in Canaan, and of the process by which they may have moved toward some kind of national consciousness before the institution of the monarchy; scholarly opinions differ widely. Two groups, Judah (which seems to have been composed of several originally distinct elements) in the south, and the "house of Joseph" (which at some point constituted two distinct tribes, Ephraim and Manasseh) in the central highlands, seem to have been especially prominent. Less is known of the history of the other tribes further north and to the east of the Jordan, with the exception of Dan, which moved, probably under *Philistine pressure, from its original territory to the extreme north of the country (Judg. 18; compare chaps. 13–16). The tribe of Levi is an enigma. According to some traditions (Num. 1.47–54; Deut. 10.8–9; 18.1–2; 33.8–11; Josh. 13.14, 33) it was distinguished from all other tribes in that it was given no territorial rights but had special sacerdotal functions that entitled it to material support from the other tribes, among whom its members moved. In other passages (Gen. 34.25–31 and 49.5–7), however, it is portrayed as being on the same footing as the other tribes. (*See* Levites.)

It is important to realize that the word "tribe" does not necessarily suggest a nomadic or semi-nomadic existence or origin: in the ancient Near East and elsewhere, it frequently denotes a territorial group of settled agricultural or even urban people who claim a common ancestry. Moreover, despite the impression given by many passages in the Bible, the tribe was not the basic social or economic unit in Israel in either pre-monarchic or later times; the basic units were the family and the village, which were bound together by local agricultural and other common concerns. The larger body, the tribe, was a much looser unit whose main function was apparently, in the period before the monarchy, to provide a militia in times of danger. With the advent of the monarchy, the tribes lost this function and were henceforth little more than a means of genealogical identification. The division of the kingdom after the death of *Solomon was a political rather than a tribal matter.

See Israel, History of.

R. N. WHYBRAY

Tribute and Taxation.

Tribute and Taxation. *This entry deals with payments exacted upon subject populations by imperial powers, and consists of two articles, the first on the* Ancient Near East, *and the second on the* Roman Empire.

Ancient Near East

Tribute and taxation encompass all obligations in precious metals, other goods, or service imposed by a central government on its own people, on visiting traders, or on regions that submitted to it. Tribute generally refers to payments made by one state to another dominant state to prevent attack or in ongoing submission. Taxation would then describe obligations within a state, including payments by visiting merchants. In the empires conquered by *Assyria (ninth to seventh centuries BCE), *Babylon (605–539 BCE), and *Persia (539 to the late fourth century BCE), payments by distant territories incorporated into the realm as provinces might still be called tribute, but with sovereignty lost this simply represented the highest stage in a pyramid of taxation required to support the central authority.

In the biblical portrayal of Israel's *conquest of the *Promised Land, the defeated peoples are annihilated when possible in holy *war, without negotiation. This extreme policy only applied where the goal was to occupy the land (see Deut. 20.16–18). When the *Canaanites managed a negotiated settlement, the obligation was not tribute but forced labor (Deut. 20.11; Josh. 9.26; 16.10; 17.13; Judg. 1.28). In the period of the judges, Israel repeatedly suffered defeat and is once said to have paid tribute, to Eglon of *Moab (Judg. 3.15–18).

By contrast, *David (ca. 1000–961 BCE) carved out a small empire that brought a flow of booty and tribute to the new capital at *Jerusalem, from Moab, *Aram, and Hamath (2 Sam. 8.2–10). This income continued under *Solomon (ca. 961–922; 1 Kings 4.21), supplemented by gifts and taxes received from foreign trade (1 Kings 10.14–15). David's new dynasty not only brought Israel great wealth but building projects, a standing army, and a palace bureaucracy, all of which required support by internal taxation along with the foreign revenue. There is no mention of civil taxation before the monarchy, although legal traditions provide for support of the religious institutions by payments such as offerings of first fruits (Exod. 23.19; Deut. 26.2–10) and *tithes (Lev. 27.30; Num. 18.21–32; Deut. 14.22–29).

The institution of *kingship in Israel is remembered by this negative side of success (1 Sam. 8), and the Bible acknowledges painful new taxation while boasting of Solomon's wealth. Solomon divided Israel into twelve (nontribal) districts to supply the monthly needs of the palace (1 Kings 4.7–19, 22–23, 27–28) and appointed high-ranking administrators (v. 56). He made the Israelites contribute forced labor for building the palace (1 Kings 5.13–14). 1 Samuel 8.11–17 lists further demands of royal taxation, including military conscription to support a chariot army and forced service as craftsmen, palace workers, and farmers. The burden of taxation is remembered as the principal cause of the separation by the northern tribes after Solomon, under Jeroboam I (922–901; 1 Kings 12). Even under David, a census for possible conscription of fighting men is treated as a crime (2 Sam. 24.1–17).

After the split into two kingdoms, there is little mention of internal taxation, although the kings surely continued the system at some level, in order to sustain palace and army. The Bible's depiction of the divided monarchy focuses once more on tribute, this time paid by Israel and Judah to hold off foreign attack. In the ninth century this consisted of one-time payments to the Aramean kingdom centered at *Damascus by Asa (913–873) and Joash (837–800) of Judah (1 Kings 15.19; 2 Kings 12.18), and *Ahab (869–850) of Israel (1 Kings 20.3–7). Aram gave way to the more distant but more serious threat from Assyria. Menahem (745–737) of Israel paid "Pul" (*Tiglath-pileser III, 745–727) to withdraw (2 Kings 15.19–20), and one-time payments are recorded for Ahaz (735–715) and *Hezekiah (715–687) of Judah to Tiglath-pileser and *Sennacherib (704–681; 2 Kings 16.8; 18.14–16). Assyrian royal annals also claim such tribute from *Jehu (843–815) of Israel to Shalmaneser III (858–824) and from Israel to Adad-nirari III (809–782).

Traumatic as it was, one-time payment represented the least of obligations in a hierarchy that proceeded to annual tribute and finally incorporation as a province of the empire. The first biblical indication of annual tribute occurs just before the fall of the north, when Hoshea (732–724) pays *Shalmaneser V (726–722; 2 Kings 17.4; cf. 18.9–11). Before their revolts, Johaiakim (609–598) and *Zedekiah (597–587) of Judah probably paid annual tribute in becoming vassals of Babylon (cf. 2 Kings 24.1, 17–18).

Detailed records from Assyria show us the system into which Israel and Judah were drawn. The Assyrian king received payments from foreign rulers as "tribute" (Akkadian *maddattu*) and *namurtu*, originally a gift brought for a royal audience. Payments from territories annexed to the empire were no longer called *maddattu*, but obligations increased, including various taxes on agricultural produce, animals, and other materials, along with the *ilku*, or personal service to the state. The *ilku* might involve military service or forced labor for public projects (canals, building repair, etc.), and it could be avoided by paying and supplying a replacement.

The provincial administration of the Assyrian empire was taken over by *Nebuchadrezzar (605–562) of Babylon, who could not otherwise have consolidated his new realm. Innovation was left to the Persians, who further expanded the empire. *Darius I (522–486) set up twenty satrapies, which combined existing provinces into larger units, including "Across-the-(Euphrates) River," or Syria-Palestine (Herodotus 3.89). Each satrapy then made a fixed payment according to its productive capacity, which actually protected the populace from local officials who might curry favor by promising higher revenue. Persian regulation of taxation was designed to produce stable submission, and complemented the measured local autonomy allowed in matters of religion and administration. Within each satrapy, however, enforcement of obligations for payments or service was handled mainly by local lords.

The sum of tax obligations in the district of Yehud (Judea) is described as "tribute, custom, and toll" in the complaint to the king by those who opposed reconstruction of Jerusalem, with the claim that a revolt would stop payment (Ezra 4.13, 20). The one concern of the empire was that its authority be recognized by an uninterrupted flow of revenue. There was ample opportunity for oppressive local taxation, as Nehemiah acknowledged when he refused the standard governor's levy for maintaining his household (Neh. 5.14–15).

Persian rule was brought to an abrupt end with *Alexander's sweep across the empire, but he simply took over the existing administrative systems. The dynasties of his generals, the Ptolemies in Egypt and the Seleucids in Mesopotamia and Syria, competed for control of Palestine, and eventual Seleucid domination in the second century BCE brought increased taxation, with collection rights sold to whomever promised the highest revenue (Josephus *Ant.* 12.4.1–5). Standard taxes are described in 1 Maccabees 10.29–30 as tribute, salt tax, crown levy, one-third of grain, and one-half of fruit.

DANIEL E. FLEMING

Roman Empire

Rome acquired its first province (part of Sicily) in the middle of the third century BCE after defeating the Carthaginians, and took over the system of taxation they had instituted there. Similarly, as more provinces were added during the next two centuries, local systems were for the most part taken over without any attempt to introduce uniformity. A new general tax was instituted only where there had been no previous control or systematic taxation by any power. The chief purpose of direct taxation was to pay the costs of the wars of conquest and of continuing control. Thus, the tax in Spain was called *stipendium*, that is, "soldiers' pay." Although government monopolies and indirect taxes, farmed out to *publicans, were often profitable, and although a great deal of wealth flowed in various ways from the provinces both to Roman individuals and to the state, no major profit seems to have been derived from direct taxation before the annexation of the kingdom of Pergamum.

The gradual annexation of the kingdoms around the eastern Mediterranean, from Pergamum (133 BCE) to Egypt (30 BCE), produced a major change. Most of them had been thoroughly organized by their Hellenistic monarchs for their own profit, and Rome inherited both the organization and the profits, often simplifying collection by using the experienced *publicani*. In the 60s BCE, Pompey annexed some of these territories and reorganized others, greatly increasing public revenues. He also initiated the practice of imposing tribute on minor client rulers, thus increasing public profit without assuming any direct administration of intractable populations.

The result, by the end of the Republic, was an aggregate of provinces in which direct taxes were levied at different rates and collected in different ways (either by officials or by *publicani*), and each province was a mosaic of political entities of varying degrees of administrative and fiscal subjection. Extortion and dissatisfaction increased as the state proved unable to control either its administrators (members of its governing body, the Senate) or the powerful corporations of *publicani*, and the civil wars of the 40s and 30s BCE greatly increased the financial burdens of the provinces while disrupting their administration and economy.

Augustus tried to tighten control and begin some systematization. Censuses of people were taken in new and in some old provinces (thus the famous one of Sulpicius Quirinius in Syria and Judea: see Luke 2.1–4, with some chronological confusion, and cf. Acts 5.37; *see also* Chronology, *article on* Early Christian Chronology); and, following a limited example set by Caesar, he continued the removal of *publicani* from the collection of direct taxes and had them collected instead by officials in new provinces. His immediate successors completed these measures, but the large variety of local statuses and the farming of the numerous indirect taxes (see below) by *publicani* were only very slowly reduced. On the whole these changes benefited the government and not the taxpayers.

In Palestine, *Herod paid a fixed tribute to Rome and could collect his own taxes as he saw fit. We know little about how he did so, and the protests to Augustus after his death about his administration do not dwell on fiscal oppression. His sons inherited his obligations and his privilege, and although we are told the total of their revenues (Josephus, *Ant.* 17.11.318–20), we do not know much about their method of collection. In outline, though, their system did not differ much from that introduced by Augustus into Judea after its annexation (6 CE) or from that of Roman Syria, since both were descended from Hellenistic models.

In Judea there were two regular direct taxes: a tax on agricultural produce, still levied in kind, but during the early empire converted into a fixed amount of money as in all other provinces; and a poll tax, about which we know little in detail. Perhaps paid only by those not liable to the produce tax, it consisted of a flat-rate personal tax on all men from age fourteen and women from age twelve to age sixty-five and was levied at least at the rate of one denarius (about a day's wage) per year (see the tribute *money of the Gospels: Matt. 22.15–22 par.). Later (we do not know when) it was combined with a percentage tax on property. These were paid to Roman officials, but we do not know who collected them from the taxpayers. (Income taxes were unknown in antiquity.) By 17 CE they were so burdensome that a joint deputation from Syria and Judea asked Tiberius for relief (Tacitus, *Annals* 2.42.5). We casually hear of other taxes, for example, a house tax in Jerusalem, and we must assume the impositions known from other provinces: the notorious *aurum coronarium,* originally a contribution to a governor's Roman triumph, but later demanded by emperors on various occasions; lavish free hospitality for governors and their staffs and friends; perhaps quartering of soldiers; and—an item subject to unsuccessful regulation ever since Augustus— responsibility for the transport of official parties by communities along the roads. The incidence of the total of direct taxation was thus uneven and unpredictable.

Indirect taxes were probably worse. Government monopolies (such as salt, the produce of lakes and rivers, and the famed Judean balm) were farmed out to *publicani,* as were the Roman customs duties and road tolls at provincial boundaries (and perhaps elsewhere) and harbor dues. On top of these, cities were free to impose charges for their own revenues. The result was great disparity in the cost of the same products between communities, as well as the usual bribery at the point of collection, and the highest cost of living in the Near East. The poor naturally suffered most, and this social and economic component merged with religious and nationalist feelings in the revolts against Rome. Each failed revolt resulted in harsher exactions and an increase in distress and dissatisfaction.

E. BADIAN

Trinity. Because the Trinity is such an important part of later Christian doctrine, it is striking that the term does not appear in the New Testament. Likewise, the developed concept of three coequal partners in the Godhead found in later creedal formulations cannot be clearly detected within the confines of the *canon.

Later believers systematized the diverse references to God, *Jesus, and the Spirit found in the New Testament in order to fight against heretical tendencies of how the three are related. Elaboration on the concept of a Trinity also serves to defend the church against charges of di- or tritheism. Since the Christians have come to worship Jesus as a god (Pliny, *Epistles* 96.7), how can they claim to be continuing the *monotheistic tradition of the God of Israel? Various answers are suggested, debated, and rejected as heretical, but the idea of a Trinity—one God subsisting in three persons and one substance— ultimately prevails.

While the New Testament writers say a great deal about God, Jesus, and the Spirit of each, no New Testament writer expounds on the relationship among the three in the detail that later Christian writers do.

The earliest New Testament evidence for a tripartite formula comes in 2 Corinthians 13.13, where Paul wishes that "the grace of the Lord Jesus, the love of God, and the communion of the Holy Spirit" be with the people of Corinth. It is possible that this three-part formula derives from later liturgical usage and was added to the text of 2 Corinthians as it was copied. In support of the authenticity of the passage, however, it must be said that the phrasing is much closer to Paul's understandings of God, Jesus, and the Holy Spirit than to a more fully developed concept of the Trinity. Jesus, referred to not as Son but as Lord and Christ, is mentioned first and is connected with the central Pauline theme of *grace. God is referred to as a source of love, not as father, and the Spirit promotes sharing within the community. The word "holy" does not appear before "spirit" in the earliest manuscript evidence for this passage.

A more familiar formulation is found in Matthew 28.19, where Jesus commands the disciples to go out and baptize "in the name of the Father and of the Son and of the Holy Spirit." The phrasing probably reflects baptismal practice in churches at Matthew's time or later if the line is interpolated. Elsewhere Matthew records a special connection between God the Father and Jesus the Son (e.g., 11.27), but he falls short of claiming that Jesus is equal with God (cf. 24.36).

It is John's gospel that suggests the idea of equality between Jesus and God ("I and the Father are one"; 10.30). The Gospel starts with the affirmation that in the beginning Jesus as Word (*see* Logos) "was with God and . . . was God" (1.1), and ends (chap. 21 is most likely a later addition) with Thomas's confession of faith to Jesus, "My Lord and my God!" (20.28). The Fourth Gospel also elaborates on the role of the Holy Spirit as the Paraclete sent to be an advocate for the believers (John 14.15–26).

For the community of John's gospel, these passages provide assurance of the presence and power of God both in the ministry of Jesus and in the ongoing life of the community. Beyond this immediate context, however, such references raise the question of how Father, Son, and Spirit can be distinct and yet the same. This issue is debated over the following centuries and is only resolved by agreement and exclusion during the christological disputes and creedal councils of the fourth century and beyond.

While there are other New Testament texts where God, Jesus, and the Spirit are referred to in the same passage (e.g., Jude 20–21), it is important to avoid reading the Trinity into places where it does not appear. An example is 1 Peter 1.1–2, in which the salutation is addressed to those who have been chosen "according to the foreknowledge of God the Father in holiness of spirit." This reference may be to the holiness of spirit of the believers, but translators consistently take it as the Holy Spirit in order to complete the assumed trinitarian character of the verse: "who have been chosen and destined by God the Father and sanctified by the Spirit" (NRSV). This translation not only imposes later trinitarian perspectives on the text but also diminishes the important use of the spirit of human beings elsewhere in 1 Peter (e.g., 3.4, 19).

DANIEL N. SCHOWALTER

Twelve, The. "The twelve" is an expression employed by all the Gospel writers, and once by Paul (1 Cor. 15.5), to denote an inner, more intimate circle of followers of Jesus. They are listed by name in Matthew 10.2–4, Mark 3.16–19, Luke 6.14–16, and Acts 1.13, and although these lists do not always agree in either the names or their order, the reader is always told that Jesus chose twelve disciples in particular. While these twelve are *disciples, they are further distinguished by the designation "the twelve." This is especially the case in Acts 6.1–2, where the disciples and the twelve are juxtaposed; the latter are clearly the authorities in the story. As readers, we know who the twelve are, including *Judas Iscariot—a point stressed by all the authors, and we see that they are the recipients of

special instruction, have certain expectations from Jesus, and bear the burden of gathering the community of his followers together after the upheaval of the *crucifixion and *resurrection.

Whether the names and the widespread agreement among the Gospel writers about the number twelve are historical facts is difficult to say. Did Jesus really call twelve followers initially who then called others? This is possible. Did Jesus consciously act as if he were establishing the new Israel by selecting twelve representatives? The symbolic significance of the number twelve is difficult to miss. But there are others in the story who are just as close or closer to him than the twelve, such as some women and others who are called disciples. The twelve do get special teaching; perhaps Jesus was training leaders to carry on in his stead. In Mark, however, the twelve hardly understand anything (see Messianic Secret); the special teaching apparently does not pay off. The roles of the disciples and the twelve are so important in the stories, and they have received so much attention from both the authors and the interpreters, that what actually transpired historically is impossible to retrieve. Matthew himself, for example, uses the terms disciple, *apostle, and the twelve interchangeably in chap. 10, as if these were all equivalent or the distinctions were needless.

The symbolism of the number twelve was certainly clear to the authors, and it has not been lost on subsequent interpreters (see Number Symbolism). A program of the renewal if not the reconstitution of Israel by the Jesus movement is strongly suggested by the number itself, as well as the collection of twelve baskets at the multiplication of the loaves and fishes (Matt. 14.20 par; John 6.13), the portrayal of the disciples sitting on twelve thrones judging Israel (Matt. 19.28; cf. Luke 22.30), and the repeated use of the number twelve in the book of *Revelation (7.5–8; 12.1; 21.12–14; 21.21; 22.2). The usurpation of Israel's symbols and heroic figures (see Tribes of Israel) along with Israel's scriptures and myths, and in particular use of the potent symbol twelve, points in this direction for early Christianity. Ultimately, however, the church claimed through Melito, Justin, and others to be a "third race" and not the renewed Israel the number twelve suggested.

J. ANDREW OVERMAN

Typology. The practice in the New Testament and the early church whereby a person or a series of events occurring in the Old Testament is interpreted as a type or foreshadowing of some person (almost invariably Christ) or feature in the Christian dispensation. For example, in 1 Peter 3.19–21 the story of *Noah's *ark is taken as a type of *baptism, and in Hebrews 11.17–19 *Abraham's willingness to sacrifice his son *Isaac (see Aqedah) is understood as a type of Christ's resurrection. These two examples also show that the word "type" need not be used for a typological comparison to be made.

The very possibility of such typology depends on the Christian assumption that the Bible recounts the course of salvation history. By this is meant the Bible as a record of the long development by which God, with a redemptive purpose always in mind, called Israel into being out of Egypt, led her through the *wilderness, made a *covenant with her, brought her into *Canaan, guided and admonished her through her troubled history (including the traumatic experience of the Babylonian *exile), and consummated his relationship by sending his Son in Jesus Christ—thereby effecting an eternal salvation by establishing a people of God whose membership is open to all. What justifies understanding the Bible typologically (if it can be justified) is the conviction that God is always the same. If he is fully known in Jesus Christ, then when he revealed himself under the old dispensation, he must in some sense have been known as the God of Jesus Christ. It is, therefore, justifiable to seek in his revelation of himself under the old dispensation some similarity with his revelation under the new. In fact, a sort of typology can be found in the Hebrew Bible itself: see, for example, Isaiah 43.1–19; 51.9–11, where God's action of old in creation and redemption from Egypt are treated as types of the new deliverance from exile about to occur (see Exodus, The).

Clear examples of typology occur in 1 Corinthians 10.1–11, where the events of the crossing of the *Red Sea, the giving of the *manna, and the water issuing miraculously from the rock are taken as types of baptism and of the bread and wine in the Eucharist. What is more, the presence of the preexistent Christ with Israel in the wilderness is implied.

If used excessively or indiscriminately, typology can pass over into allegory. Allegory means using any person, event, or object in the Old Testament arbitrarily to signify a corresponding event or thing in the New Testament. The difference lies in the authenticity of the analogy. Allegory does sometimes appear in the New Testament; in Galatians 4.21–30, for example, *Paul launches into an elaborate comparison of *Ishmael and Isaac, on the one hand, with Judaism and Christianity, on the other. But he brings in so many terms of comparison that the meaning merges into an unconvincing allegory. Again, in 1 Corinthians 9.9–10 Paul argues that apostles have a right to be supported because, according to the Law, an ox is allowed to eat the grain as it treads it out. The comparison fails to carry much conviction, however, because oxen are not apostles.

Some modern Roman Catholic scholars have used the medieval concept of *sensus plenior* to justify a modern use of typology. This was the idea that the words of inspired writers in the Old Testament might bear a deeper or fuller sense than they were aware of, and that this deeper sense can be perceived in the New Testament. This can be a helpful and illuminating way of reading the Bible as long as it is kept within reasonable bounds. For example, in Psalm 119.105 the psalmist exclaims, "Your word is a lamp to my feet." A Christian, who knows of the Word made flesh, may reasonably and profitably apply this to Christ, as long as one does not claim that the psalmist knew about Christ in writing the words.

See also Interpretation, History of, *article on* Early Christian Interpretation.

ANTHONY TYRRELL HANSON

Ugaritic. In 1928 a Syrian farmer accidentally uncovered ancient tombs on the Mediterranean coast, directly opposite the northeastern tip of Cyprus. This led to the excavation of the main city at nearby Ras Shamra, which yielded one of the most sensational archaeological finds of the twentieth century: the political and religious texts of archives of the ancient kingdom of Ugarit. The French excavators uncovered numerous cuneiform tablets, many of which were written in a hitherto unknown alphabetic script. On decipherment of that alphabet, it was seen that the language of Ugarit belongs, with *Hebrew and *Aramaic, to the family of Northwest Semitic languages. Dating roughly from the fifteenth to the thirteenth centuries BCE, these tablets now include a large collection of various kinds of texts: literary, religious, epistolary, administrative, and economic. Together they form the single most important archaeological contribution in the twentieth century to our knowledge of the language and symbol world of ancient Israel.

In the first place, the discovery of the Ugaritic tablets has greatly enhanced, and at times corrected, our understanding of biblical Hebrew. Many Hebrew words whose meanings had been unknown or merely conjectured have been clarified by Ugaritic cognates. The close relationship of Hebrew with Ugaritic, moreover, allows one to reconstruct still more accurately the early history of the Hebrew language and to discern some early linguistic features in (and hence the relative dates of) parts of the Hebrew Bible. The identification of certain grammatical elements in Northwest Semitic languages has greatly facilitated the task of translating the Hebrew Bible; texts that were hitherto grammatically awkward, if not impossible, can now be explained (e.g., Pss. 29.6; 68.2; 89.18; Isa. 9.19; 10.2). On the basis of Ugaritic literature too, scholars have been able to make advances in the study of Hebrew prosody, for the two languages apparently share the same poetic structures and utilize the same stylistic devices (*see* Poetry, Biblical Hebrew).

Beyond the details of language and prosody, the tablets also contribute to our knowledge of Canaanite religion. The Ugaritic pantheon includes many of the gods already known to us from the Hebrew Bible as Canaanite deities against whom the prophets inveighed. Much more is now known, for example, about *Baal and *Asherah (Athirat in Ugaritic) and the fertility cult with which they are associated. Thus, in *Elijah's encounter with the prophets of Baal (1 Kings 18), the failure of the latter to bring rain demonstrates the impotence of Baal even in what was thought to be his domain; instead, it is Yahweh who controls nature. But the value of the Ugaritic texts goes beyond the horizons of Canaanite faith. The evidence suggests that Israelite theology was not as radically discontinuous with Canaanite religions as was once thought. Yahweh was imbued with characteristics associated with El and Baal. Like El, the chief deity of the Ugaritic pantheon, Israel's God is regarded as the Most High (Pss. 47.2; 97.9; Deut. 32.8; Gen. 14.19) who presides over the divine council and judges other gods (cf. Ps. 82; 89.5–7). The Ugaritic descriptions of El's abode (a tent) in "the far north" (*see* Zaphon) and "at the source of the two-rivers" correspond to the biblical depiction of the divine abode (Isa. 14.13; 33.20–22; Ezek. 47.1–12; Joel 4.18; Zech. 14.8), which, according to Judean theology, was on Mount *Zion (2 Sam. 6–7; Ps. 46.4). Like the storm-god Baal, Yahweh is portrayed as a divine warrior who sets out to fight the cosmic forces of chaos most commonly depicted as the flood(s) (e.g., Pss. 29.10; 93.3; 98.8) and "mighty waters" (Pss. 29.3; 77.19; 93.4; Hab. 3.15), as sea and river (corresponding to the Ugaritic synonymous parallelism Prince Sea/Judge River; Pss 24.2; 89.25; 114.3; Isa. 50.2; Hab. 3.8), and as sea monsters, including *Leviathan (Ugaritic *ltn*). Accordingly, the manifestation of divine presence is often couched in the language of a storm *theophany (Ps. 29; 97.1–6; 2 Sam. 22.8–16). Indeed, the language and content of Psalm 29 are so reminiscent of Ugaritic that scholars are generally agreed that it was originally a Canaanite hymn to Baal adapted for Yahwistic worship. As in the Ugaritic myths and hymns, the divine warrior in the Bible is enthroned in the sanctuary as a consequence of the victory over enemies. It has also become clear that Isaiah's metaphor of the fallen "Day Star" (Isa. 14.12–15) is to be located in the Ugaritic myth of the fallen astral deities, notably Athtar, who presumed to usurp the throne of Baal; the persistence of this theme is seen in the later development of traditions about *Satan (Luke 10.18).

From the Ugaritic tablets, much can also be learned about the social institutions and structure of the region. The legends and administrative texts provide insights into the Israelite understanding of divine and human *kingship. Among other things, it was the king's task to "decide the case of the widow" and to "judge the suit of the orphan"; failure to do so was tantamount to surrender of royal prerogative. Besides the king, one learns about various cultic functionaries, military personnel, and people of various social strata. Among the military elite and powerful nobility are people designated "bulls," "gazelles," "boars," and the like (cf. Exod. 15.15; Isa. 14.9; Ezek. 34.17; Amos 4.1; 2 Sam. 1.19). In the Ugaritic texts, one encounters a respected group known as the *nqdm*, a class or guild to which Mesha the king of *Moab and *Amos belong, calling into question the traditional translation of *nqd* as "shepherd" (Amos 1.1).

In minute details of the Hebrew language as well as in our understanding of broad themes and literary forms in the Bible, Ugaritic has had an impact. Several commentaries and numerous reference works have been written with the explicit purpose of elucidating the biblical text through the advances made possible by the discoveries at Ras Shamra. Although the correspondences between the Ugaritic texts and the Bible have at times been exaggerated in scholarly works, the study of Ugaritic is an indispensable discipline in biblical scholarship.

See also Canaan; Israel, Religion of; Myth.

C. L. SEOW

Unknown God. A dedication found on an Athenian altar according to Acts 17.23. Altars belonging to unknown gods (plural) at Olympia and elsewhere were probably aimed at satisfying divinities who had been overlooked, but they do not explain the singular formulation in Acts. Because votive offerings were connected to specific prayers, it is unlikely that an individual who had received aid would make a dedication to an unknown divinity. There is no evidence that either *Stoics or *gnostics addressed or worshiped the supreme being as an unknown god. The most likely reference is to the anonymous altars (i.e., bearing no inscription) erected to local divinities throughout *Athens under Solon. In Roman literature, these altars are sometimes cited as dedications to unknown gods (always plural). Whatever the source, the *Areopagus speech reveals both the importance of relating the Christian message to broader cultural assumptions and the distinctiveness of Christian *monotheism.   ROBERT STOOPS

Urim and Thummim. These two words usually occur together (Exod. 28.30; Lev. 8.8; Deut. 33.8; Ezra 2.63; Neh. 7.65; 1 Esd. 5.40; Sir. 45.10; and the LXX of 1 Sam. 14.41); in Numbers 27.21 and 1 Samuel 28.6 only the word Urim occurs. The meaning of the words is not certain. Although both are plural in form, they seem to refer to single objects that functioned as sacred lots and may have had the form of dice, pebbles, or sticks. Another possibility is that they were two stones, one white and the other black. According to the texts in Exodus and Leviticus Moses put the Urim and Thummim into Aaron's breastpiece, a small square pocket attached to the *ephod, an outer covering. Uncertainty about the meaning and function of the ephod complicates the matter further. What is clear is that they were associated with the priestly office and were used when people came to seek divine consultation. Apparently, therefore, it was thought possible for the high priest and the Levites to give a divine oracle with the help of the Urim and Thummim. From 1 Samuel 14.41 we may conclude that these sacred lots provided a "yes" or "no" answer. Saul's inquiry of the Lord in 1 Samuel 28.6 shows that a positive or negative answer was not guaranteed, and it may mean that the procedure followed was not as simple as our "heads or tails" method.

The contexts where the Urim and Thummim are mentioned seem to indicate that these lots fell into disuse when the monarchy was established. The parallel texts in Ezra 2.63, Nehemiah 7.65, and 1 Esdras 5.40 may imply that a return to the use of the Urim and Thummim was not expected.

In Hebrew letters the words are the motto of Yale University.

See Magic and Divination.

HENDRIK C. SPYKERBOER

Ur of the Chaldeans. The homeland of *Abraham and the starting point of his *migration to Canaan (Gen. 11.28, 31; 15.7; Neh. 9.7), Ur of the Chaldeans (AV: Chaldees) is traditionally identified with the southern Mesopotamian site Tell el-Muqayyar (Maps 6, 7:J4), on the *Euphrates river. The site was systematically excavated from 1922 to 1934 by Sir Leonard Woolley. Among his discoveries were the *ziggurat constructed by Ur-nammu, the founder of the Ur III Dynasty, in the late third millennium BCE

and, in the royal cemetery, the burial of queen Pu-abi, whose grave had never been robbed.

The identification of "Ur of the Chaldees" with Tell el-Muqayyar is not universally accepted. Some scholars have suggested that it is Urfa (Edessa), while others have proposed a connection with a city named Ura. It has also been suggested that Ur in this context may reflect the generic Sumerian word for city, URU; note that in the *Septuagint "Ur of the Chaldeans" is translated "land of the Chaldeans" (cf. Acts 7.4).

The Chaldeans were a group of five tribes who became dominant in *Babylonia during the late sixth century BCE. They are not mentioned by name in any source before the ninth century, which makes the biblical phrase "Ur of the Chaldeans" relatively late.

JAMES H. PLATT

Utensils. *See* Houses, Furniture, Utensils.

Vengeance. In biblical thought, God's vengeance is an expression of his *holiness. Rendering vengeance to his adversaries is essentially a response to evil. Vengeance is punishment in retribution for injury and so is often linked with the wrath of God (Isa. 59.17; 63.4; Nah. 1.2). Vengeance was understood as God's way of redressing wrongs, and the word seldom has a connotation of vindictiveness. Cries to Yahweh for vengeance (Jer. 11.20; 15.15; 20.12; 50.15; Ps. 94.1–3) are cries for healing and redemption—even though a restoration may call for retributive justice. God's vengeance is balanced by his *mercy (Ps. 103.10). Vengeance, then, is very much a part of God's character and does not contradict his love.

God's vengeance is directed at those who oppose him and who refuse to acknowledge his commands. These include his enemies (Deut. 32.41, 43; Nah. 1.2), who are often other nations (Ps. 149.7; Mic. 5.15), or a single nation that has done evil (Ezek. 25.14, 17), especially toward Israel, God's people (Deut. 32.35, 36). When, however, Israel becomes unfaithful to Yahweh and breaks *covenant, God's vengeance exacts punishment also on Israel (Lev. 26.25; Isa. 1.24; Jer. 5.9,12). In the absence of justice in the land, God puts on his "garments of vengeance" (Isa. 59.17), ready to punish Israel, ready to display his wrath. Vengeance, then, is a sign of God's working in history, fulfilling his purposes. Although vengeance belongs to him alone (Deut. 32.35; Rom. 12.19; Heb. 10.30), God can authorize people to act as agents of his vengeance (Num. 31.2–3; 2 Kings 9.7; Ezek. 25.14).

Since wrongs are not always righted in the present and God's vengeance is delayed because of his patience, later prophets look forward to a "day of vengeance" in the future—an apocalyptic day that will mark the beginning of a new age (Isa. 34.8; 35.4; Jer.46.10; *see* Day of the Lord).

Although the Hebrew Bible has little to say about life after death (*see* Afterlife and Immortality), the hope that sin will be punished and faithfulness be rewarded in the life to come is stated in Daniel 12.2, 3. In the New Testament divine vengeance is closely tied to the *day of judgment at the end of the age, when Christ will return in glory (*see* Second Coming of Christ). For the wicked he appears "in flaming fire, inflicting vengeance" (2 Thess. 1.8; Jude 7), but innocent sufferers who wonder why God does not act on their behalf (Rev. 6.10) have the assurance that in the end he will vindicate his servants (Rev. 19.2).

Vengeance as a principle of *law was well established in ancient Israel: "life for life, eye for eye, tooth for tooth" (Exod. 21.23–24; cf. Deut. 19.21); this is known as the *lex talionis* (the law of equivalent retribution). On its face it seems brutal, but it was an advance in legal thinking. It shut the door to unlimited revenge and kept the punishment from exceeding the crime. It established the principle of equity in punishment and allowed for no favoritism. The law functioned under the jurisdiction of judges (Exod. 21.22; Deut. 19.17–18).

The New Testament upholds the right of the governing authorities to avenge wrongs, acting as God's servants for the well-being of the community (Rom. 13.4; 1 Pet. 2.14). As in ancient Israel, personal vengeance was forbidden (Lev. 19.18; Rom. 12.19); indeed, doing an enemy good was considered to be a part of wisdom (Prov. 25.21; Rom. 12.20). Jesus not only taught nonretaliation, exhorting his followers to suffer loss rather than resort to personal vindictiveness (Matt. 5.38–48 par.), but he also modeled it (1 Pet. 2.23).

See also Avenger of Blood.   DAVID EWERT

Verse Division. *See* Chapter and Verse Divisions.

Versions. *See* Translations.

Vine and Vineyard. The "Song of the Vineyard" (Isa. 5.1–7) describes the different steps that were required to plant a vineyard and successfully harvest its grapes. First the soil had to be cleared of stones before planting the vine stocks in it. The stones could be used to build a wall to keep out animals such as boars (Ps. 80.13) and foxes (Song of Sol. 2.15). A watchtower might also be constructed to ensure the safety of the crop, especially at harvest time (Isa. 5.2). The vinedresser would prune away the new small shoots so that the main fruit-bearing stems would obtain greater nourishment (Lev. 25.3; Isa. 18.5; John 15.2). A wine press would be constructed (usually hewn of rock), for the main purpose of raising grapes in ancient times was for the making of *wine.

The symbolic use of the vine occurs throughout the Bible. In Psalm 80.8 Israel is identified as a vine: "You brought a vine out of Egypt; you drove out the nations and planted it." While this imagery is used positively to indicate how Israel will bear fruit as a vine (Hos. 14.7; cf. Ps. 128.3), more commonly Israel is described as an unproductive vine (Jer. 8.13; cf. 6.9), a vine that is plucked up and left to wither away (Ezek. 19.12), a choice vine that has become wild (Jer. 2.21). Closely related to this imagery is the portrayal of Israel as a vineyard, as in Isaiah 5.1–7. Here Israel, whom Yahweh planted looking for choice grapes, has yielded wild grapes (Jer. 12.10–11). Many have understood John's image of Jesus as "the true vine" (John 15.1) as a deliberate contrast to the portrayal of Israel as a vine/vineyard that has not proved fruitful.

In the Gospels, Jesus is quoted as using the vineyard in two *parables: the parable of the laborers in the vineyard who were hired at different hours of the day (Matt. 20.1–16), and the parable of the wicked vinedressers (Matt. 21.33–41 par.); the description in the latter of the work done in the vineyard is derived from Isaiah 5.1–7.   EDGAR W. CONRAD

Virgin Birth of Christ. As a major tenet of Roman Catholic teaching and a foundation for fundamentalist belief, the virgin birth remains an essential doctrine for many Christians. Since the advent of modern historical criticism, however, others have been skeptical about the virgin birth. Ultimately, the issue will be decided by a person's faith stance and view of scripture.

Belief in the virgin birth of Christ is based on the stories of Jesus' birth found in the gospels of Matthew and Luke. In Luke 1.5–38, shortly after Elizabeth miraculously conceives in her old age, the angel *Gabriel appears to *Mary who is specifically described as a virgin (Grk. *parthenos*). He tells Mary that she will conceive and bear a son who will inherit the throne of *David. Mary, surprised by this news, asks "How can this be, since I do not know a man?" Gabriel reassures her that she will be impregnated by the Holy Spirit and cites as proof the fact that Elizabeth is now with child. There is no confusion possible in Luke's account. The author wants it to be clear that this is a miraculous impregnation of a woman who had not had sexual relations. The detailed nature of this dialogue between Mary and Gabriel suggests that the author of Luke was responding to specific questions about the virgin birth of Christ. Luke also alludes to the virgin birth in his *genealogy of Jesus when he says that Jesus was "the son (as was supposed) of Joseph" (Luke 3.23).

Matthew 1.18–25 takes the tradition about Jesus' miraculous conception and develops it in a slightly different way. The angel, who is not named, appears not to Mary but to *Joseph, who has discovered that Mary is pregnant. Although Joseph plans to break off his engagement, the angel commands him to go through with the marriage since the child is from the Holy Spirit. As in Luke, Matthew wishes to make it clear that Mary and Joseph had not had sexual relations prior to this announcement (1.18). In fact, the author stresses that Joseph "did not know her until she had borne a son" (Matt. 1.25).

The author of Matthew often attempts to prove that Jesus is the *Messiah by showing how the details of his life fulfill the Hebrew scriptures. In this case, Matthew presents a passage from Isaiah 7 in which the prophet is speaking to Ahaz, king of Judah. Ahaz faces attack from the forces of *Syria and Israel (734 BCE), and so he is contemplating an alliance with the king of *Assyria. God makes it clear to Ahaz that such an alliance should not take place. Isaiah declares that the Lord will provide a sign that will make known the Lord's will in spite of Ahaz's recalcitrance. A young woman who is pregnant will bear a son, and before that child is old enough to tell the difference between good and evil, the powers that threaten Judah will be defeated. Ahaz refuses to believe the sign and sends tribute to the Assyrian king who destroys *Damascus and kills the king of Syria (2 Kings 16.9). The other threatening force, Israel, is conquered by Assyria twelve years after the occasion of this sign at about the time that the child mentioned in the sign would have reached the age of maturity.

Isaiah's intent in discussing this child is clearly to set a time frame for the destruction of Israel. There is nothing miraculous about the mother or the conception process. The Hebrew word used, ʿalmâ, means simply "young woman," without any implication of virginity. The Greek word parthenos used to translate ʿalmâ can mean either a young woman or a virgin. Matthew used a Greek Bible, so he naturally reinterpreted Isaiah 7:14 as a prophecy referring to the virgin birth of Jesus. For the evangelist, Isaiah's original meaning was superseded by the identification of Jesus as *Immanuel (Grk. Emmanouēl).

One of the most frequently raised objections to the virgin birth is that, with the exception of Matthew and Luke, New Testament authors do not make explicit mention of it. Other alleged references are at best vague allusions (Mark 6.3; John 1.13–14; 6.42). Such an argument from silence cannot be determinative, but it is an important consideration for people who see the virgin birth as a feature created within the early traditions about Jesus rather than a historical occurrence.

Those who doubt the historicity of the virgin birth argue that it was created by the early church as a way of honoring the coming of Jesus as the *Son of God or of explaining the idea of God becoming flesh. Miraculous human birth stories are common in biblical tradition, going back to Abraham and Sarah (Gen. 17.15–19, 18.9–15, 21.1–7), and numerous references to deities impregnating women are found within the Greco-Roman tradition. The mother of Heracles, for instance, was said to have been impregnated by Zeus (Diodorus Siculus, 4.9,1–10).

Affirmation of the virgin birth by the apostolic father Ignatius (Smyrneans 1) confirms that the concept was an early and strongly held belief. As Christian doctrine developed, the virgin birth became a preeminent statement of faith and the ultimate test of belief in biblical inerrancy. It was also expanded in several directions. The veneration of Mary is related to the virgin birth, as is the tradition that Mary was ever virgin. Belief in this latter concept requires that the *brothers and sisters of Jesus mentioned in the New Testament must have been stepbrothers and stepsisters or cousins. Mary's virginity also becomes an important factor in ascetic Christianity and in the promotion of a life of celibacy.

DANIEL N. SCHOWALTER

Vulgate. The translation of the Bible into Latin by Jerome. Pope Damascus commissioned the work in 382 CE because previous Latin translations had been piecemeal, inelegant, and sometimes unreliable. Jerome spent twenty years on the project. For the Old Testament he produced an entirely fresh translation, taking the revolutionary step of relying largely on the original *Hebrew and *Aramaic, rather than the customary Greek version, the *Septuagint (except in the Psalms). Jerome's work on the New Testament followed his predecessors much more closely. The whole project was complete in 405 CE.

Pious tradition prevented Jerome's version from entirely supplanting the older Latin translations for many years, but the Vulgate eventually gained broad acceptance among the Latin-speaking Christian public. It thus came to be called the versio vulgata, the "common translation," and to this day remains the official scriptural text of the Roman Catholic church. The first printed book was the Vulgate Bible (see Gutenberg). The Renaissance, with its interest in Greek antiquity, and then later the Enlightenment, with its interest in historical inquiry, were ultimately to challenge the primacy of the Vulgate in the Western church for purposes of critical biblical scholarship.

See also Translations, article on Ancient Languages.

PHILIP SELLEW

W

Wadi. An Arabic word meaning a deep gully or streambed that is dry except during the winter rains. These gullies are ubiquitous in the Palestinian landscape and are similar to the arroyos of the American Southwest. The word "wadi" is used, inconsistently and somewhat inappropriately, in the NRSV, to translate Hebrew *naḥal,* especially in the names of individual valleys; but when the term is generic, NRSV uses words like "valley," "brook," "river," and "torrent" for the same Hebrew word, following the practice of other translations for all its occurrences.

See also River of Egypt.

MICHAEL D. COOGAN

War. In the Hebrew Bible war almost always refers to armed struggle between nations; in the New Testament the word more often refers to spiritual or cosmic conflict against evil.

Hebrew Bible. It is important to recognize that Israel was both a nation and a people of Yahweh its God. As a nation, it lived among other nations and was subject to the struggles—military, economic, social, and political—that are common to all nations. As a people of God, the Israelites were constantly being reminded that they were to put their trust in the Lord (cf. Ps. 20.7).

Since God had chosen them to be his "treasured possession" (Deut. 14.2) and had entered into *covenant with them (Exod. 19.5–6), he fought their battles and drove out the enemy before them (Deut. 9.4–6). Yahweh is called a warrior (Exod. 15.3), and the expression "the Lord of hosts" (1 Sam. 17.45; Isa. 1.24; "God of hosts," Amos 5.27) is sometimes interpreted to mean that he leads an army or wages a war; another interpretation conveys the idea of heavenly hosts, either the sun, moon, and stars (Deut. 4.19) or the heavenly beings (1 Kings 22.19). For theological or sentimental reasons, this concept is repulsive to many moderns. Yet, according to treaties from the ancient Near East, the ruler who made such a covenant with a people was obligated to protect and defend them. On another line of reasoning, the only way Yahweh could preserve the identity of this small nation against the more powerful nations surrounding them was by fighting their battles for them.

Particularly objectionable to many are the wars in which the Israelites were commanded by Yahweh to exterminate (or "devote"; *see* Ban) a people, "men and women, young and old, oxen, sheep, and donkeys" (Josh. 6.21) with the sword; this command is explained in Deuteronomy 20.16–18 as a safeguard against idolatry. It must also be noted that Yahweh punished his people similarly for their transgressions against him. Accordingly, *Amos grouped the rebellions of Judah and Israel with those of other nations (Amos 1.3–2.16).

War, both in Israel and in the ancient Near East, was in some respects a religious act. God was to be consulted before going to war (1 Kings 22.5). Perhaps this was the reason for God's anger when *David held a census, the method of mustering an army for war (2 Sam. 24.2–9), without first seeking God's will. The leader was possessed of "the spirit of the Lord" (Judg. 6.34), and when the spirit departed, the leader was powerless before the enemy (16.20). Sacrifice was offered before the conflict began (1 Sam. 7.8–10). War was "sanctified" (Hebr. *qiddaš;* NRSV "prepare"). The camp was a holy place where God himself was present (Deut. 20.4; 23.14), therefore there was to be nothing unclean (e.g., a nocturnal emission or human excrement; Deut. 23.10, 13). The warrior refrained from sexual intercourse (1 Sam. 21.4–5), which is why Uriah refused to comply with David's devious request (2 Sam. 11.6–12). The priest gave counsel and encouragement (Deut. 20.2), and those who could not devote themselves fully to the conflict were sent back home (vv. 5–8). Terms of peace were to be offered, but if rejected, then the Israelite army was to carry out the Lord's judgment (vv. 10–14; cf. 20.19–21.9).

After the return from *exile, Israel was no longer an independent nation—although there was a tolerated independence resulting from the wars of the *Maccabees for about a century. The idea of war became more eschatological: it represented freedom from the oppressor. Two ways to this freedom were envisaged; the one was by the *Messiah, the son of David, who would lead the armies to victory (Pss. Sol. 17.23–27); the other was by divine intervention, a heavenly "*son of man" and his angels (Dan. 7.13; Enoch 37–71). The *Apocrypha and *Pseudepigrapha furnish many and varied details of this hope for deliverance.

A remarkable picture is drawn in the War of the Sons of Light with the Sons of Darkness (the "War Scroll," 1QM), one of the *Dead Sea Scrolls. In this document, dating from the first century BCE, there are detailed plans for the final battle, including the location of the tribes in the camp, the standards, and many other points. The son-of-man concept is apparently not found in the Qumran documents, but the final battle is suddenly ended by the appearance of the archangel *Michael (1QM 17.6).

In the New Testament. Contrary to a widely held view, the position of the New Testament is not total pacifism: that was the product of church fathers, principally Tertullian, Origen, and Cyprian. According to Matthew, Jesus stated that "wars and rumors of wars" are part of the present world order (Matt. 24.6–7) and said bluntly that he had not come to "bring peace to the earth, but a sword" (Matt. 10.34). According to Luke (3.14), John the Baptist did not forbid the soldiers to participate in war. When Jesus' disciples were about to face the hostile world, he advised them to sell their robes to buy a sword (Luke 22.35–36, 38). Paul recognized that the governing authorities maintain order with the sword and urged his readers to be subject to such authorities (Rom. 13.1–7).

At the same time, Jesus is not reported to have commanded his followers to use warfare as a means of conquest (contrary to the method of the emperor Constantine). He apparently rejected the implication that he lead a messianic war (John 6.15; Acts 1.6); he rebuked the disciple who used the sword against those who had come to arrest him (Matt. 26.51–53); he pointedly told *Pilate that, if his kingdom "were from this world," his soldiers would be fighting to defend him (John 18.36).

Like ancient Israel, the church is composed of the people of God and is under attack from enemy forces. Unlike Israel, the church is not one of the nations of the world; rather it is transnational, composed of peoples from all nations. Its warfare was not against "enemies of blood and flesh" but rather against demonic forces intent on destroying God's redemptive work (Eph. 6.12); hence its defense must be spiritual (vv. 11–17). The author of 1 *Peter urged his readers to "abstain from the desires of the flesh that wage war against the soul"; yet at the same time they were told to submit "for the Lord's sake" to "every human institution," whether emperor or governor (1 Pet. 2.11–14).

According to the apocalyptic view of the book of *Daniel, the kingdoms of this world—each more terrible than the preceding—would be defeated by the action of God himself (Dan. 2.36–45). The book of *Revelation likewise proclaims that the final triumph will be brought about by One who is called Faithful and True, who comes with the armies of heaven to smite the nations (Rev. 19.11–15). At last the dreams of the prophets of old will come true: "they shall beat their swords into plowshares, and their spears into pruning hooks; nation shall not lift up sword against nation, neither shall they learn war any more" (Isa. 2.4; Mic. 4.3).

WILLIAM SANFORD LASOR

Water. Compared to the alluvial plains of *Egypt and *Mesopotamia, hilly Syria-Palestine relies more upon ground- and rainwater for its fertility (Deut. 11.10–11). Its peoples venerated storm gods, among them Yahweh, often accompanied by the tempest (Exod. 14.21; 15.8, 10; 19.16, 19; Judg. 5.4–5; 1 Sam. 12.17–18; 2 Sam. 22.8–16; Isa. 66.15–16; Ezek. 1; Zech. 9.14; Pss. 29.3–9; 68.7–9; 77.16–18; 97.2–5; 144.5–6; Job 38.1). Water is God's gift par excellence (Gen. 27.28; Isa. 30.23; 44.3–4; Jer. 5.24; 14.22; Ezek. 34.26; Hos. 6.3; Joel 2.23; Pss. 68.9; 104.10–13; Job 5.10; 12.15; 36.27–28; 37.2–11; 38.25–30), which he may withhold in punishment (Lev. 26.19; Deut. 11.17; 28.23–24; 1 Kings 8.35 [= 2 Chron. 6.26]; 17.1; Isa. 5.6; Jer. 3.3; Ezek. 22.24; Amos 5.28; Hag. 1.10–11; Zech. 14.17; Job 12.15; 2 Chron. 7.13). Running water is called "living" in Hebrew; in the New Testament this image becomes "water of life" (John 4.7–15; 7.37–38; Rev. 21.6; 22.17).

In the Israelite conception, boundless water was the original constituent of the universe (Gen. 1.2; 2 Pet. 3.5), perhaps coeval with God himself (Gen. 1.1, by one interpretation); compare Egyptian Nun, Sumerian Nammu, Babylonian Apsu and Tiamat, all personifying primordial waters. God's first act of *creation was to suffuse a diurnally pulsating light through the aqueous void (Gen. 1.3–5). Next he restricted the waters, creating a bubble bounded by water below and the firmament above (Gen. 1.6–8; cf. Amos 9.6; Pss. 104.3, 5–9; 148.4; Job 26.8). The lower waters were restricted, and the flat earth emerged, surrounded by seas and floating upon the deep (Gen. 1.9–10; cf. Pss. 24.2; 136.6). The dry land and the crystalline firmament were semipermeable, penetrated by springs and precipitation (Gen. 7.11; 8.2; Deut. 8.7; Isa. 24.18; Mal. 3.10; Pss. 74.15; 104.10–13; Prov. 3.20).

Water has four primary connotations in the Bible: birth, fertility, danger, and cleansing. More than one aspect can operate in any given passage.

Birth imagery is dimly present in Genesis 1, with the world emerging from the grammatically feminine "Deep." *Moses is drawn from water by his foster mother (Exod. 2.1–10). The Israelite nation is "born" in the *Red Sea (Exod. 14–15). After crossing the *Jordan, the Israelites *circumcise themselves (Josh. 3.1–5.9), a rite that is associated with birth (Gen. 17.10–14).

The fertility motif is clear in Genesis 2.6, 10–14, where Yahweh moistens the earth with ground water and rivers. Similarly, a fertilizing river will one day flow from *Jerusalem (Ezek. 47.1–12; Joel 4.18; Zech. 14.8; Pss. 36.8–10; 46.4; cf. Rev. 22.1), granting Israel prosperity comparable to that of Egypt and Mesopotamia; compare the *Temple's bronze sea (1 Kings 7.23–26), and also the Canaanite image of El's dwelling "at the source of the two rivers, in the midst of the channels of the two deeps." Yahweh's gift of drinking water in the desert (Exod. 17.1–7; Num. 20.1–13; cf. Deut. 8.15; Isa. 48.21; Pss. 78.15–16; 105.41; 114.8; Neh. 9.15) seems also to symbolize fructification (Deut. 32.13–14, Isa. 35; 41.17–19; 43.19–20; Pss. 107.35–38).

The waters treated so far are passive or benign, but other texts describe a hostile Sea or aquatic monster that God kills, tramples, or confines (Isa. 51.9–10, Nah. 1.4; Hab. 3.8, 10, 15; Pss. 74.13–15; 77.16–18; 89.9–10; 93.3–4; Job 7.12; 9.13; 26.12–13) and will one day defeat anew (Isa. 27.1; Dan. 7; Rev. 12–13; 21.1; see Leviathan). This story has antecedents in Mesopotamian and Canaanite *myths of creation, wherein a storm god defeats the Sea. The image of Jesus mastering the wind (Matt. 8.23–27 par.) and treading upon the sea (Matt. 14.22–33; Mark 6.45–52; John 6.16–21) may echo these motifs.

We see the danger of water in the *Flood (Gen. 6–9), likewise a popular Near Eastern myth. Israelite fear of the water is also reflected in awestruck descriptions of the sea and navigation (Jon. 1–2; Ps. 107.23–30; Prov. 30.19; see Ships and Sailing).

Water cleanses actually and symbolically, as when *Pilate washes his hands (Matt. 27.24). Water is a key ingredient in purification and healing rites in both the Bible (Exod. 19.10; 29.4; 30.17–21; 40.12, 30–32; Lev. 6.27–28; 11.25, 28, 32, 40; 14–15; 16.4, 24, 26, 28; Num. 8.6–7; 19; 31.23–24; Deut. 23.11; Matt. 15.2; Mark 7.2–4; John 2.6; 5.2–7) and the *Dead Sea Scrolls; some writers refer metaphorically to spiritual cleansing (Isa. 1.16; Ezek. 36.25; Ps. 51.2, 7; Eph. 5.26; Titus 3.5).

Purification imagery combines readily with (re)birth imagery. Naaman immerses himself and his leprous skin becomes "like that of a small child" (2 Kings 5.10, 14). *Baptism, like the Jewish conversion rite of immersion, signifies spiritual rebirth (Mark 1.9–11; Luke 3.21–22; John 1.33–34; 3.5; Rom. 6.4; Gal. 3.26–27); note the reference to "water and blood" in 1 John 5.6, 8. And the images of birth and cleansing are combined with danger when God rescues a sufferer from metaphorical drowning (Jon. 2.2–9, Pss. 18.16; 88.17). WILLIAM H. PROPP

Way, The. As a word having literal, metaphorical, and theological connotations, "way" is used in the Bible with a variety of meanings. The specific term "the Way," though, can be attributed to *Luke, who used it in *Acts to designate the early Christian movement (9.2; 19.2, 23; 22.4; 24.14, 22); according to Luke it was known in both Palestine and Ephesus and also to the Roman procurator, Felix (24.22). The theology of the Way is further developed by Luke in the form of a travel narrative in two stages, first from Galilee to Jerusalem (Luke 9.51–19.27), and from Jerusalem to the end of the earth (Acts 1.8).

The specific use of the Way as another name for Christianity seems to have its background in various sources, including the *Qumran community. In the document known as the Manual of Discipline, the *Essene way of life is referred to as "the Way" (1QS 8.13–16; 9.16–21), and it consists in the strict observance of the *law. The inspiration for this comes from Isaiah 40.3, with its invitation to prepare the way of the Lord in the wilderness, used also by the synoptic Gospels as the starting point of the New Testament preaching by *John the Baptist. Later *John identifies Jesus as the way, the truth, and the life (John 14.6).   JOSEPH PATHRAPANKAL, C.M.I.

Weapons. Almost every kind of weapon known in the ancient Near East is mentioned in the Bible, largely owing to its origin in a region where armies from the north and from the south marched and fought. Mentioned most frequently is the sword, a word that from Genesis to Revelation occurs over four hundred times. The names of several weapons are also used figuratively with political or religious significance (e.g., Rom. 13.4, 12).

Weapons are of two main kinds, defensive and offensive, with some overlap in actual use. Defensive weapons, used to protect the body, include the shield, helmet, and armor of various kinds. Offensive weapons include those for battering, piercing, throwing or hurling, or shooting (in antiquity meaning the bow and arrow). The horse and chariot may be included as an instrument (a mobile platform) that in effect becomes a weapon.

Defensive Weapons. To protect the entire body, the large, oblong shield was used. *Goliath's shield was so large that a shield bearer went before him (1 Sam. 17.41). The small, round shield or buckler was held in the left hand (by right-handed warriors; note the apparent strategic advantage in being left-handed [Judg. 3.15; 20.16]). The large shield was protection against javelin and arrows; the buckler was more useful for hand-to-hand combat. Yahweh's faithfulness is both a shield and a buckler (Ps. 91.4)—however, the unusual word here translated "buckler" is built on a root that suggests something like a cuirass, a protection that encircles the body. Shields and bucklers were made of leather stretched on wooden frames; hence few have been found in excavations.

The helmet protected the head and was made of cloth, felt, wood, leather, or bronze. The body was protected with armor, most likely a breastplate made of plates of leather or bronze fastened together by thongs (1 Kings 22.34). Greaves protected the legs from the knee to the ankle (1 Sam. 17.6); they were made of wood, leather, or bronze. The belt around the loins supported the sheath in which the sword was kept (2 Sam. 20.8). Normally the sheath was on the left side, but Ehud, who was left-handed, wore his on the

right thigh (Judg. 3.16). The "whole armor of God" (Greek *panoplia*) in Ephesians 6.11–17 consisted of defensive weapons, except for the "sword of the Spirit, which is the word of God."

Offensive Weapons. Some could be used only at short range. The warclub was used to shatter heads (Jer. 51.20). The sword or dagger was used to slash, cut, or stab the enemy. A very short sword is a dirk or dagger, usually shorter than .25 m (10 in). Because of the relative weakness of bronze, longer swords did not come into use until the Iron Age. They varied in shape, some having two sharp edges (Judg. 3.16), either straight or curved, narrow or broad. The sword is symbolic of the word of God (Eph. 6.16; Heb. 4.12; Rev. 1.16; 19.15).

Other weapons could be used at longer range. The staff was used by shepherds, as was the rod, but both could also be used as a club or lance against an enemy (2 Sam. 23.21; Isa. 10.5). The spear or lance was used to pierce an enemy (1 Sam. 18.10; Judg. 5.8). Strictly speaking, the spear was held while piercing, whereas the javelin was hurled; the distinction, however, is not observed in the Hebrew Bible or in some English translations.

An effective middle-distance weapon was the sling and slingstones (Job 41.28). The sling consisted of a piece of cloth or leather with strings into which (the "hollow," 1 Sam. 25.29) a small stone was placed. The strings were held by the fingers and the sling was whirled around several times; one string was released and the stone flew rapidly at the target. Such was *David's weapon against Goliath (1 Sam. 17.49). The accuracy of some slingers was remarkable (Judg. 20.16). For greater distance the bow and arrows were used. The bow, made of wood shaped in a single or double arc, was strung by holding the lower end with the foot while pulling down the upper, hence to "tread" the bow (Isa. 5.28; NRSV "bent"). Arrows were made of reeds, usually with a stone or metal head.   WILLIAM SANFORD LaSOR

Weddings. Given the importance of *marriage, the rituals marking it must have been both splendid and complex. But since everyone in biblical times knew how weddings should be celebrated, biblical authors do not bother to describe them in detail. So we are forced to build up a composite picture from bits of information scattered throughout the Bible and to fill in the gaps on the basis of customs attested in parallel cultures.

This means that it is impossible to say how wedding ceremonies changed over the biblical period, and even some key aspects of the ceremony remain obscure.

The wedding itself represented the culmination of long discussions between the two families involved. When at last the issues of the "marriage present," dowry, and the terms of the marriage contract were agreed, and both parties thought that the time was right for the bride to set up house with her husband, the wedding took place. In comparison with modern Western weddings, the ceremonies were more elaborate and took much longer.

Both bride and groom bathed, anointed themselves with oil and perfume and dressed in special clothes (Ps. 45.7–14). *Jewelry and garlands were also worn. In the New Testament the *kingdom of God is compared to a marriage feast, and it is possible that the white robes of the *saints reflect the practice of wearing white at weddings (Rev. 19.8). Throughout the ceremony the bride was veiled (Gen. 24.65).

The bride was accompanied by bridesmaids (Ps. 45.14) and the groom had attendants too; the chief of these, the friend of the bridegroom, acted as best man (Judg. 14.20; John 3.29).

The public ceremonies began with the groom and his companions processing to the bride's home. After greeting her family, giving and receiving presents, and some drinks, all returned to the groom's house in a lively processional dance accompanied by music, and lanterns if night had already fallen (Ps. 45.15; 1 Macc. 9.39; Matt. 25.1–10).

Sometime before the meal was eaten, the marriage contract was read out and a public declaration made by the groom. One formula may be preserved in Hosea 2.19–20a; another is found in a fifth-century BCE Aramaic document from the Jewish community at Elephantine in Egypt: "She is my wife and I am her husband from this day and forever." Whether the woman had to make any declaration is uncertain. Then all the guests blessed the couple with words such as "May the God of heaven keep you safe and give you peace and prosperity" (Tob. 7.13).

There followed the wedding breakfast, a great meal attended by all the friends and relatives of the families involved. They too came in their best clothes; it was an insult to decline a wedding invitation or not to dress properly for the occasion (Matt. 22.7, 11–12). At the feast *wine flowed freely (John 2.1–11) and songs were sung in honor of marriage and the wedded couple.

Finally, the evening concluded with the groom symbolically wrapping his cloak around the bride (Ezek. 16.8) and, escorted by the parents and bridal attendants, leading her to the specially prepared marriage chamber. Presumably this was usually an inner part of the bridegroom's house, though the word used (cf. Ps. 19.5; Num. 25.8) suggests a special tent. There at last the bride removed her veil and the marriage was consummated (Gen. 29.23–25).

This, however, was not the end of the celebration. Festivities continued for another week, or sometimes two. These consisted of eating, drinking, making music, and telling riddles (Gen. 29.27; Judg. 14.12–18). The *Song of Solomon may reflect songs sung at these occasions.

Both the Hebrew Bible and the New Testament view marriage as an image of the relationship between God and his people. It is therefore appropriate that the prophets, Jesus, and the book of *Revelation use the imagery of weddings to describe the end of time, when God will be united with his people forever (Isa. 25.6–9; Matt. 22.1–13; 25.1–12; Rev. 18.6–10; 21.1–4).

GORDON J. WENHAM

Weights and Measures. See tables on pages 796 and 797.

Widows. The term "widow," the usual translation of Hebrew 'almānâ and Greek chēra, has a more specific meaning in the biblical texts than the English word conveys. The woman designated by these terms was not merely someone whose husband had died; she lived outside of the normal social structure in which every female lived under the authority of some male; she was responsible to and for herself.

The structure of ancient society was kinship-based and patriarchal. *Marriage within this society represented a contract made between two families rather than between two individuals. When a woman married, she passed from the authority of her father's household to the authority of her husband's household. When her husband died, her status was determined in relation to the surviving members of his household.

Biblical *law provided for a woman of childbearing age whose husband had died without male issue. By means of a *levirate marriage (Deut. 25.5–10) the dead man's wife was given to a relative of the husband's family in order that a child be produced to inherit the dead

Weights and Measures in the Bible

I. HEBREW MEASURES OF LENGTH

Hebrew	NRSV	Equivalence	U.S. Measures	Metric Units
'ammâ	cubit	2 spans	17.49 in	.443 m
zeret	span	3 handbreadths	8.745 in	.221 m
ṭōpaḥ, ṭepaḥ	handbreadth	4 fingers	2.915 in	.074 m
'eṣba'	finger		0.728 in	.019 m

The cubit described in Ezekiel (40.5; 43.13) is equal to seven (not six) handbreadths, namely 20.405 inches.

II. MEASURES OF LENGTH IN THE NEW TESTAMENT

Greek	NRSV	U.S. Measures	Metric Units
pēchus	cubit	about 1 ½ ft	.456 m
orguia	fathom	about 72.44 in	1.839 m
stadion	stadia, or the equivalent in miles	about 606 ft	184.7 m
milion	mile	about 4,854 ft	1.482 km

III. HEBREW MEASURES OF CAPACITY

DRY MEASURES

Hebrew	NRSV	Equivalence	U.S. Measures	Metric Units
ḥōmer	homer	} 2 lethechs	6.524 bu	229.7 l
kōr	measure, cor			
letek	lethech	5 ephahs	3.262 bu	114.8 l
'êpâ	ephah, measure	3 seahs	20.878 qts	22.9 l
šĕ'â	measure	3⅓ omers	6.959 qts	7.7 l
'ōmer	omer	1⅘ kabs	2.087 qts	2.3 l
'iśśārôn	tenth part (of ephah)			
qab	kab		1.159 qts	1.3 l

LIQUID MEASURES

Hebrew	NRSV	Equivalence	U.S. Measures	Metric Units
kōr	measure, cor	10 baths	60.738 gallons	230 l
bat	bath	6 hins	6.073 gallons	23 l
hîn	hin	3 kabs	1.012 gallons	3.829 l
qab	kab	4 logs	1.349 quarts	1.276 l
lōg	log		0.674 pint	.32 l

IV. MEASURES OF CAPACITY IN THE NEW TESTAMENT

Greek	NRSV	Equivalence	U.S. Measures	Metric Units
batos	measure	(Hebrew) bat		
koros	measure	(Hebrew) kōr	see Table III	
saton	measure	(Hebrew) šĕ'â		
metrētēs	measure		10.3 gallons	39 l

IV. MEASURES OF CAPACITY IN THE NEW TESTAMENT

Greek	NRSV	Equivalence	U.S. Measures	Metric Units
choinix	quart		0.98 dry quart	1.079 l
modios	bushel	(Latin) modius	7.68 dry quarts	8.458 l
xestēs	pot	(Latin) sextarius	0.96 dry pint, or 1.12 fluid pints	.53 l

V. HEBREW WEIGHTS

Hebrew	NRSV	Equivalence	U.S. Avoirdupois	Metric Units
kikkār	talent	60 minas	75.558 pounds	34.3 kg
māneh	mina	50 shekels	20.148 ounces	571.2 g
šéqel	shekel	2 bekas	176.29 grains	11.42 g
pîm (or payim)	pim	⅔ shekel	117.52 grains	7.61 g
beqa'	beka, half a shekel	10 gerahs	88.14 grains	5.71 g
gērâ	gerah		8.81 grains	.57 g

The practice of weighing unmarked ingots of metal used in commercial transactions prior to the invention of *money explains that the names of the units of weight were used later as indications of value, and as names for monetary standards. There is, however, no direct relation between the shekel-weight and the weight of a shekel piece.

VI. WEIGHTS IN THE NEW TESTAMENT

Greek	NRSV	Equivalence	U.S. Avoirdupois	Metric Units
talenton	talent	(Hebrew) talent	see Table V	
mna	pound	(Hebrew) mina	see Table V	
litra	pound	(Latin) libra	0.719 pound	326.4 g

husband's estate. This practice not only provided for inheritance rights but also secured the well-being of the woman. However, a man could legally refuse to carry out this obligation. For example, concern for the diminution of his own inheritance might prompt the dead husband's relative to forgo a levirate marriage. The stories of Tamar, Judah's daughter-in-law who was temporarily an 'almānâ, and *Ruth illustrate the implementation of levirate marriage (Gen. 38; Ruth).

While the Hebrew Bible identifies certain women as 'almānôt (plural of 'almānâ; 1 Kings 7.14; 11.26; 17) and specifies their distinctive clothing (Gen 38.19; 2 Sam. 14.5), its depiction of them is sketchy. Laws from ancient Mesopotamia provide some details. In the Middle Assyrian Laws, the almattu (cognate with 'almānâ) emerges as a woman whose husband and father-in-law were deceased, and who had no son capable of providing for her. A woman in this state was issued a document verifying her new status,

and henceforth could act on her own. Presumably, the document gave her access to a society that normally excluded women from the public sphere.

There is evidence that the biblical 'almānâ may have been similar to the Mesopotamian almattu. That she was a woman living beyond male authority is illustrated by the law regarding women's vows (Num. 30.1–15): while the validity of a vow made by a woman depended ordinarily upon the approval of either her father or her husband, the validity of an 'almānâ's vow stood on its own (Num. 30.10).

The 'almānâ's independence from male authority was at the same time a sign of her precarious social position. In more than half of its occurrences, the 'almānâ is linked with the *orphan or with the orphan and the client (see Alien). Existing outside of the normal social structure, these three groups were susceptible to oppression, injustice, and exploitation. Because the 'almānâ had no male protector, Yahweh was pictured as her primary defender and every Israelite was supposed to treat her justly. The Bible legislates the protection and support of the 'almānâ and exhorts against oppressing her. Prophetic texts claim that the welfare of the defenseless 'almānâ, orphan, and alien was the measure by which Yahweh determined the moral fiber of his people. The vulnerability and isolation of the 'almānâ suggested a metaphorical use of the term, and prophetic texts (Isa. 47.8–9; 54.4; Jer. 51.5; Lam. 1.1) describe a vulnerable city (Babylon, Jerusalem) or land (Israel, Judah) as an 'almānâ.

The vulnerable and unconventional social position of the 'almānâ is also evident in laws regulating the priesthood. The affiliation of a *priest with such a woman was a source of concern. While Leviticus 21.14 implicitly permits a priest to marry an 'almānâ but forbids a high priest from doing so, in Ezekiel 44.22 no priest is allowed to marry an 'almānâ unless her husband had been a priest. Other legislation (Lev. 22.13) permits a priest's daughter who is an 'almānâ to eat at his table.

From the mention of the widow (Grk. chēra) in the Gospels (Mark 12.40, 42–44 par.; Luke 7.12; 18.3–5), it is evident that the Hebrew 'almānâ's precarious and threatened existence persisted into the first century CE. Early Christianity singled out widows as recipients of social welfare, establishing an organized means of caring for this group of women. In the Jerusalem church, a food distribution program is specified (Acts 6.1). 1 Timothy 5 mentions an official list of widows with eligibility requirements that included age and certain religious and moral behavior in addition to the absence of a responsible family member (see Ethical Lists).

See also Poor; Women.   PAULA S. HIEBERT

Wilderness. Hebrew *midbār*, "wilderness, desert," originally meant "place of herding." Since many wilderness areas of Palestine were sparsely vegetated, in contrast to the barren Syro-Arabian desert, *nomads could traverse them with asses and flocks (1 Sam. 17.28; 25.4, 21; Isa. 27.10; Jer. 23.10; Joel 2.22; Ps. 65.12). Oases sustained concentrated settlements of pastoralists and agriculturalists.

The wilderness has mostly negative associations in the Bible. It is a bad place (Num. 20.5; Prov. 21.19) of hunger, thirst, and deprivation (Ps. 107.4–5; Job 30.3); it is unsettled (Jer. 2.6; Job 38.26), nonarable (Jer. 2.2), windswept (Isa.

21.1; Hos. 13.15; Job 1.19), haunted by noxious beasts and demons (Deut. 8.15; Isa. 13.21; 34.14), and echoing with frightful noises (Deut. 32.10). It is the domain of *Cain (Gen. 4.12–16), *Ishmael (Gen. 16.12; 21.20–21; 25.6, 18), *Esau (Gen. 27.39–40), and raiders (Luke 10.30; Acts 21.38) such as the *Arabs (Jer. 3.2), *Midianites (Judg. 6–8), and *Amalekites (Exod. 17.8–16; Deut. 25.17–19; Judg. 6.3, 33; 7.12; 10.12; 1 Sam. 15). Apart from nomads and the lawless, only the mad inhabit the wilderness (Luke 8.29), or those with no other recourse (Gen. 16.6–14; Exod. 2.15; 1 Sam. 22.2; 1 Kings 19; Jer. 9.1; 48.6; Ps. 55.7–8; Rev. 12.6). The wilderness is figuratively dark (Jer. 2.6, 31), recalling the primordial state of the universe (cf. Deut. 32.10). To punish a people God may "uncreate" a country, converting arable land to wilderness (Isa. 6.11–12; 14.17; 34; Jer. 9.11; 22.6; 50.39–40; 51.43; Ezek. 6.6; Hos. 2.3, 6; Joel 2.3; Zeph. 2.13; Ps. 107.33–34).

On the other hand, there is nostalgia for aspects of the seminomadic lifestyle of the ancestral and *Exodus periods. The *Rechabites continue to build no houses, plant no fields, and live in tents (Jer. 35.6–7). The tent in particular remains a powerful symbol: God's proper dwelling is a tent (Exod. 26; 33.7–11; 36; 40.34–38; Josh. 18.1; 2 Sam. 6.17; 7.2, 6; cf. Pss. 27.5; 74.7; 1 Chron. 6.32; 9.23); the cry of secession from the Davidic kingdom is "To your tents, O Israel" (2 Sam. 20.1; 1 Kings 12.16), and Hosea predicts a return to tents (Hos. 12.9). Pastoralism, too, has positive associations. Both God (Isa. 40.11; Jer. 23.1, 3; Ezek. 34; Pss. 23; 78.52; Rev. 7.17) and the king (1 Sam. 16.11–13; 17.34–37; 2 Sam. 7.8; Jer. 23.2, 4; Ezek. 34; 37.24; Ps. 78.70–72) are shepherds, a common royal epithet in antiquity. As divine king, *Jesus, too, is shepherd (John 10.1–30; Heb. 13.20).

The wilderness is also a place for spiritual renewal. *Hagar (Gen. 16.7; 21.19), *Moses (Exod. 3.1–4.17), and *Elijah (1 Kings 19) flee there and meet God. Jesus similarly seeks solitude in the desert (Matt. 4.1 par.; Mark 1.35 par.; Luke 5.16; John 11.54). The wilderness is above all associated with the wanderings of Israel narrated in Exodus-Deuteronomy. Most texts recall this as a time of tension between God and his people (Exod. 15.22–26; 16; 32; Lev. 10; Num. 11–14; 16–17; 20.1–13; 21.4–9, Deut. 1.19–46; 6.16; 9.7–10.11; Jer. 7.24–26; Ezek. 20; Pss. 78; 106; Neh. 9; Acts 7.39–43; 1 Cor. 10.5–12; Heb. 3–4), but Jeremiah 2.2–3 and Hosea 2.15 idealize it as a time of piety. Some sources maintain that God simply found Israel in the desert and brought them to the land (Deut. 32.10; Ezek. 16; Hos. 9.10), apparently ignoring the Exodus proper. It was in this wilderness, at Mount *Sinai/Horeb, that God entered into a *covenant with Israel (Exod. 19.1 – Num. 10.10), a covenant reaffirmed on the wilderness borders of the *Promised Land (Deuteronomy).

Nostalgia for desert life and the negative associations of the wilderness are, ironically, compatible. Israel is forced to rely upon God in the most inhospitable of climates, and God shows his power to sustain them (Exod. 16; 17.1–7; Num. 11; Deut. 8.3–4, 15–16; 29.5–6; Ps. 78.19–20, 23–29; 1 Cor. 10.3–4); just as *Jesus feeds the multitudes in the desert (Mark 6.30–44; 8.1–10; par.). The desert is also God's crucible, in which he tests Israel (Exod. 15.25–26; Deut. 8.2–3, 5, 16; 33.8) and eliminates the unwanted.

Some prophets believe that Israel must return to the desert for renewal and purification (Hos. 2.14–15; 12.9; Isa. 35.3–4, 8–10; 40.3–4, 41.17; 43.19–20; 48.21; 49.9–12; Jer. 31.2–3, 9; Ezek. 20.35; 34.25). Second *Isaiah, encouraging Babylonian Jews to cross the desert and rebuild Judah (Isa. 49.8; 51.3), envisions the desert negated, turned into a *paradise (Isa. 35.1–2, 6–7; 41.18–19; cf. Isa. 32.15; Ps. 107.35).

The *Qumran community conceived of itself as fulfilling the call of Isaiah 40.3 (1QS 8.13–14; 9.19–20), to make a way in the desert in preparation for a national rebirth. *John the Baptist was viewed in the same light (Matt. 3.3 par.; John 1.23). The tradition of desert monasteries continues to this day.　　WILLIAM H. PROPP

Wine. The cultivation of the grape *vine and the fermentation of grape juice into wine seem to have occurred in prehistoric times in Eurasia; the Semitic words related to the word "wine" are apparently loanwords from ancient *Greek or its predecessors. Cultivated (rather than wild) grapes are found in deposits from the fourth millennium BCE onward throughout the Near East, and there is archaeological evidence for wine making by the third millennium. In biblical times, the production and consumption of wine were familiar aspects of everyday life, to which the Bible refers repeatedly and, for the most part, positively.

To produce wine, harvested grapes were placed in a wine vat, often carved out of bedrock for that purpose (Isa. 5.2), where the juice was squeezed from the grapes by foot (Isa. 16.10; 63.1–3; Amos 9.13). From this first vat the juice was drained into a lower vat, where the pulpy liquid could be pressed again, often with a stone weight. The juice was then placed in skins or in large storage jars; the latter may have a capacity of 40 liters (10 gallons) or more and are often inscribed with the name of the place of origin. A well-preserved winery with most of these features was excavated at Gibeon (el-Jib). Stamped jar handles attest to wine production (and standard royal measurement) in the kingdom of Judah and to the import of wine from Rhodes and other Greek islands, beginning in the Persian period; wine jars from Italy have been found in a late first-century BCE house in Jerusalem.

Wine is metaphorically called "the blood of grapes/the grape" (Gen. 49.11; Deut. 32.14; Sir. 39.26; 50.15), and so the trampling of grapes can be a figure for destructive divine fury (Isa. 63.1–6; Rev. 19.15; cf. Julia Ward Howe's biblicizing phrasing "He is trampling out the vintage where the grapes of wrath are stored").

Wine was a staple of life (Sir. 39.26), as the formula "grain, wine, and oil" shows (Deut. 11.14; Joel 1.10). It was a source of pleasure for both humans (Eccles. 10.19; Sir. 31.27–28; 32.5–6; 40.20) and the gods (Judg. 9.13) and was thus a regular component of ritual (Exod. 29.40; Lev. 23.13). Wine was a divine gift (Deut. 7.13; Ps. 104.15; Hos. 2.8) and would be provided abundantly in the end time (Jer. 31.12; Joel. 3.18; Amos 9.13–14).

Overindulgence in wine is condemned in the Bible by both precept and example (*see* Drunkenness). Total abstinence, however, is not advanced as a general ideal, although it was practiced, either for a time, by *nazirite vow (Num. 6.2–4), or as a lifelong commitment, as by the *Rechabites (Jer. 35; see also 1 Sam 1.11 LXX).

The generally positive attitude of biblical writers toward moderate consumption of wine posed a problem for modern advocates of total abstinence ("temperance") as both a personal and a social ideal. How could those who accepted the Bible as supreme authority reject its teaching that wine was good, a teaching exemplified by the practice of Jesus (Luke 7.34; Mark 14.23 par; John 2.1–11) and others? Was the use of wine at the Christian Eucharist defensible? Some made a distinction between naturally fermented wines and distilled spirits, including fortified wines, although biblical support for such a distinction was questionable. Others argued that social changes since biblical times made the legal prohibition of any alcoholic beverage necessary, citing not only general biblical norms but also such passages as Romans 14.21.

One curious influence of the Bible on the use of wine is in the names given to ascending sizes of bottles used for champagne. After a magnum (the equivalent of two bottles [1.5 liters]), the sizes are as follows: Jeroboam (four bottles), named for the first king of the northern kingdom of Israel; Rehoboam (six bottles), *Solomon's son and successor as king of Judah (see especially 1 Kings 12.10–12); *Methuselah (eight bottles) (Gen. 5.21–27); and the three largest for kings of Assyria and Babylon: Salmanazar (*Shalmaneser, 2 Kings 17.3; twelve bottles), Balthazar (*Belshazzar, Dan. 7.1; sixteen bottles), and Nebuchadnezzar (see Nebuchadrezzar; twenty bottles), who destroyed *Jerusalem.

Along with wine, "strong drink" (Hebr. šēkār, probably beer or ale made from barley and other grains) is mentioned in the Bible (e.g., Lev. 10.9; Prov. 20.1) and is well attested in both archaeological and literary sources throughout the Near East.   MICHAEL D. COOGAN

Wisdom. Biblical *wisdom literature emphasizes the desirability and the elusiveness of true wisdom (Hebr. hokmâ, a feminine noun). Job 28.25–27 even locates wisdom with God at *creation. Thus it is of interest that a series of poems in Proverbs 1–9 metaphorically personifies wisdom as a woman in a variety of positive female roles; see Women, article on Ancient Near East and Israel.

The female figure of Wisdom first appears in Proverbs speaking as a *prophet (Prov. 1.20–33), a profession to which both men and women were called. In Proverbs 9.1–6, Wisdom is a high-ranking woman who can employ a messenger (cf. 1 Kings 19.2; 21.8–11); on her own initiative (cf. Esther 5.4) she invites the "simple" to a banquet in her substantial seven-pillared house.

Wisdom is also a "sister" (Prov. 7.4), a word with two connotations: a literal sister with whom a man may associate on the intimate level of family, or alternately a wife or lover (as in the *Song of Solomon). In the book of Proverbs, both the ideal wife (31.10) and the woman Wisdom (3.15; 8.11) are "more precious than jewels," and Proverbs 4.6 enjoins the listener not to forsake Wisdom just as Proverbs 5.15–17 demands marital fidelity. Like wives and mothers in ancient Israel (Prov. 1.8; 4.6–9; 6.20; 31.1,

26), Wisdom is a counsellor and teacher (8.6–10, 14). Interestingly, she is not a child-bearer, although she is regularly described as a life-giver or life-preserver (Prov. 3.16, 18, 22; 4.13; 9.6).

The dividing line between Wisdom the woman and God can grow hazy. Without the introductory verses to Proverbs 1.22–33 one might easily assume that the speaker is not Wisdom but God! Theologians have observed that Wisdom functions as a mediator between God and humanity. She is God's companion (Prov. 3.19; 8.22–31) before the beginning of creation; yet God offers her, as she offers herself, to God's human subjects. If they accept her, they will find that God is protecting and guiding them (Prov. 3.26). Scholarly consensus places the book of *Proverbs in the postexilic period (fifth-fourth centuries BCE), although it is generally agreed that Proverbs contains motifs and themes that were part of preexilic Israelite culture. Wisdom's mediating role may have answered a spiritual need earlier fulfilled by the king (see Ps. 72; 1 Kings 8.22–53).

Scholars have pursued the theory that Wisdom the woman is in some way related to an ancient Near Eastern goddess or goddesses. Evidence is lacking for the suggestion that a goddess, Wisdom, was worshiped in preexilic times in Israelite scribal schools. She does however share some attributes with the Egyptian goddess Maat, "Truth," and with certain ancient Near Eastern goddesses who protected the king and his officials (cf. Prov. 8.1–21).

Wisdom the woman's most striking affinities, however, are with *Asherah, the Canaanite fertility goddess. Wisdom is the tree of life (Prov. 3.8), and Asherah's primary symbol was a tree of life. Wisdom's banquet invitation (Prov. 9.1–6) recalls Asherah's banquet in the *Ugaritic myth of *Baal. Proverbs 9 may consciously play on the ambiguities of the word "house," which can also mean temple (see 2 Sam. 7.5–6); in ancient Near Eastern mythology, the construction of a house/temple for the gods is often the climax of cosmogony, notably also the theme of Wisdom's preceding address in Proverbs 8.22–31.

At the same time, there are clearly similarities between Wisdom's corrupt counterpart, the "foolish woman" of Proverbs 9.13–18, and several goddesses in ancient Near Eastern myths whose seductive blandishments and promises of life to the young male hero can lead to death (cf. Prov. 9.18; also 2.18–19; 5.5; 6.26; 7.26–27). It has been suggested that throughout Proverbs 1–9, in a particularly Israelite twist, the description of the evil seductive/adulterous woman (Prov. 2.16; 5.3–20; 6.24–35; 7.5–27) may deliberately employ Canaanite goddess imagery in order to undercut it.

It is not impossible that Lady Wisdom represents an irruption in the Bible of the persistent but biblically suppressed Israelite worship of a female counterpart to Yahweh (*see* Israel, Religion of). In the book of Proverbs, however, both Wisdom the woman and the "foolish woman" seem to be literary creations in which goddess language has been artfully transformed and recombined with imagery from other elements of Israelite female experience.

The motif of Wisdom the woman subsequently played a notable part in Jewish and Christian thought. She appears, for example, in the *Wisdom of Solomon, in *Sirach, in *Baruch 3:9–4:4, and in the nonbiblical texts from *Qumran, and her words are echoed in the New Testament (e.g., Matt. 11.28). Perhaps most resonant of all was Wisdom's speech in Proverbs 8.22–31, stressing her presence at the beginning of creation. *Sirach equates Wisdom with the creative word of God (24.3) and with *Torah (24.23). Readers of the Jewish philosopher *Philo of Alexandria (first century CE) have found it difficult to disentangle the properties of God's word (*logos) from wisdom (*sophia*). *Paul calls Christ the wisdom (*sophia*) of God (1 Cor. 1.24). The mini-creation story in John 1.1–3 consciously evokes Proverbs 8. And for *gnostic Jews and Christians, the female principle Sophia was a figure of great complexity and primary importance.

Mary Joan Winn Leith

Wisdom Literature. The scope of biblical wisdom is disputed, but three books are almost universally included in this category: *Proverbs, *Job, and *Ecclesiastes. To these are added *Sirach (Ecclesiasticus) and *Wisdom of Solomon from the Deutero-canon, often called the *Apocrypha. These five books resemble an extensive literary corpus in Egypt identified by the expression *seboyet* ("instruction") and in Mesopotamia. Some significant Instructions from Egypt are those of Ptahhotep, Merikare, Ani, Amenemopet, Insinger, and Onksheshonky. Mesopotamian wisdom includes instructions of Shuruppak, proverbs (Sumerian and Akkadian), and reflections on life's meaning (the Sumerian "Man and his God," and the Babylonian "I Will Praise the Lord of Wisdom," "The Babylonian The-

odicy," and "The Dialogue between a Master and Slave"). In addition, omen texts, onomastica (name lists), and scribal texts can be classified as wisdom literature.

Other biblical texts contain vocabulary and ideas similar to those found in wisdom literature. This common usage has prompted some modern interpreters to enlarge the wisdom corpus or to magnify its influence greatly. Many canonical books have been placed under the sage's domain, including Genesis 1–11, 37–50; Exodus 32; Deuteronomy; Amos; Micah; Isaiah; Jonah; Habakkuk; Esther; 2 Samuel 9–20; 1 Kings 1–2; Song of Solomon; and Psalms. The result of this effort is unclear, although many claims are exaggerated or lack adequate criteria to be persuasive.

It therefore remains fundamentally correct to label wisdom literature as an alien body within the Hebrew scriptures. That judgment rests partly on what is missing in these texts: the promises to the *ancestors, the *Exodus from Egypt and the Mosaic *covenant, the centrality of *Jerusalem and the Davidic dynasty, and much more. The situation changed when Sirach and Wisdom of Solomon entered the picture, for with them a decisive transition occurred as a result of the combination between wisdom and traditional Yahwism. However, the assessment of alienness also arises from a consideration of the unique form and content of Proverbs, Job, and Ecclesiastes. These books represent a human search for knowledge that enriches life or makes existence bearable. A self-revealing deity manages one brief appearance (Job 38–41), and Ecclesiastes rejects revelation on principle.

Wisdom literature can be divided into four categories: natural, experiential, judicial, and theological. Encyclopedic name lists did not survive in Israel, although 1 Kings 4.33 (MT 5.13) may allude to them. The widespread folktale about *Solomon's judgment (1 Kings 3.16–28) exemplifies judicial wisdom. The distinction between theological wisdom and experiential is not an absolute one, for some lessons from experience use religious reinforcements. The difference is therefore one of degree, and certain texts (Job and Ecclesiastes) are more theological than others. In Egypt the wisdom corpus aimed at training courtiers and equipping pharaohs for effective leadership. Mesopotamian wisdom was in part an attempt to manipulate the gods to ensure prosperity; cult and magic thus lay at the heart of some of these nonbiblical texts.

When did Israel's wisdom literature come into

existence? Centuries of observations went into the compilation of the book of Proverbs, a process that probably began in the early monarchy and ended in postexilic times. The probable sequence of the several collections is as follows: chaps. 25–29; 10.1–22.16; 22.17–24.22; 24.23–34; 30.1–9; 30.10–33; 31.1–9; 1–9; 31.10–31. The book of Job dates from the late sixth or fifth century BCE, although the prose tale existed much earlier. Ecclesiastes best fits in the mid- or late third century, Sirach at the beginning of the second (ca. 190), and Wisdom of Solomon in the first century BCE.

What was the occasion for writing these texts? The collections in Proverbs were the accumulation of valuable insight within various settings, particularly the family. Ecclesiastes and Sirach, on the other hand, comprise the teaching of scholars to pupils, presumably young men from wealthy families. Both Job and Wisdom of Solomon may also have functioned to expand the horizons of students. However, the appeal of such school texts as these four books certainly reached beyond the academy, and even Proverbs may have assisted in training professional courtiers during *Hezekiah's reign (see Prov. 25.1). It is noteworthy that the first epilogist in Ecclesiastes states that Qoheleth taught the people, which may suggest a democratization of learning in his day (12.9–12). Certain themes come to prominence within these five books: *creation as an ordering of the universe, the *fear of Yahweh as the beginning and end of knowledge, the contrast between fools and wise persons as an ethical distinction, and the literary expression of personified wisdom and folly. The universal character of wisdom requires a grounding of its theology in creation rather than in Israel's particularistic traditions. *Revelation occurred at creation, and individuals drew analogies between the natural realm and the social. This search for analogies presupposed an ordering principle of the universe that manifested itself in reward for virtue and punishment for base action. All knowledge rested on a religious commitment, at least for the collection in Proverbs 1–9. But the most radical thinkers, Job and Ecclesiastes, did not dispense with the theistic assumption. The adjective "wise" was an ethical term rather than a cognitive judgment. Fools were not ignorant: they were scoundrels—lazy, hot-headed, disrespectful, lustful. The personification of wisdom, demanded by her active role at creation, enabled her to address young men and to woo them away from her rival, Dame Folly. This symbolism

also mediated between a searching humanity and a transcendent deity. In Sirach a correlation between *Torah and Wisdom brought God closer to human subjects and introduced the category of *mercy where strict justice had prevailed as a desideratum. (*See* Wisdom.)

If one takes content into consideration, the wisdom corpus used its own distinctive literary forms. These include aphoristic sayings and instructions (in Proverbs mainly), dispute (in Job), reflection (in Ecclesiastes), a school text (Sirach), and a diatribe (Wisdom of Solomon). Within these broader types many other categories exist, for example, royal fiction, autobiographical narrative, numerical proverb, allegory, *prayer, hymn, and *midrash*-like interpretation. Three settings for the resulting literature were the family, court, and school. Little is known about any of these sociological contexts, although the clan was probably the earliest, followed by the royal court and finally the scribal (priestly?) school.

Of course, some of the above literary types also occur in prophetic and narrative literature (e.g., disputes, allegory, prayer, hymn). What then is distinctive about the wisdom corpus? Answering this question is complicated by concepts that the sages shared with prophets and the priestly guilds, especially the principle of reward and punishment. The mere allusion to this principle cannot identify wisdom, nor can a reference to creation.

The first identifying characteristic of wisdom literature is its anthropocentric base. The sages asked about human good, which they perceived to rest in long life, health, wealth, children, and reputation. Furthermore, the focus was on each individual rather than on larger groups or the nation itself. Indeed, truth was believed to be universal, which ruled out exclusive claims by special interest groups. Insights from abroad were equally valid, and membership in the Jewish nation was not a prerequisite for contributing to the wisdom corpus. Hence a small portion of the Egyptian Instruction of Amenemopet was included in the book of Proverbs (22.17–24.22), together with two collections by foreign authors (30.1–4; 31.1–9). Even the hero of the book of Job is probably depicted as a non-Jew. Because of the individualistic emphasis, wisdom placed no stress on historical events as the arena of divine disclosure. The primary concern was existential, often expressing itself in self-gratification but also asking hard questions about life's meaning in the face of undeserved *suffering and the oppressive shadow of *death.

A second feature of wisdom literature is its reliance on the intellect to cope with every eventuality. Hidden within the natural universe and the behavior of animals and people were secrets that enriched human existence. The goal of wisdom was to discover these insights and to draw correct analogies that would enable one to live long and well. It follows that such a quest presupposes a cosmos, a reliable order from which to draw lessons with predictable outcomes. Insights gained from nature or from the behavior of animals carried over into the human arena, and these truths perdured through the ages.

This reliance on one's ability to act and to think in a manner that yielded life's richest rewards did not last. Thus, we come to a third feature of the wisdom corpus, its conscious reflection on the injustices of earthly existence and on the limits of the human intellect. To be sure, wrestling with the issue of theodicy was the prerogative of sensitive prophets, psalmists, and historiographers as well. But the crown of theodicy is surely worn by the author of the book of Job, and the radical exposure of life's enigmas in Ecclesiastes brooks no rival. A bankrupt morality and intellect yielded opposite responses in these two masterpieces. Job fell to his knees in repentance and submission before a mystery that defied understanding, and the author of Ecclesiastes ventured the conclusion that life was utterly absurd because the deity's will and actions escaped detection in a world where death and probable extinction were sovereign.

Some emphases of wisdom literature are present in the New Testament and in *gnosticism. *Jesus' teachings take the form of aphorisms; he invites disciples to take his yoke on them in the same way that Dame Wisdom issues an invitation for her subjects to accept the statutes of the Torah. The Fourth Gospel describes Jesus in the language of the divine *logos, just as wisdom was equated with the logos. In addition, *Paul uses the language of traditional wisdom in hymns about Jesus as the agent of creation, and the letter of *James resembles wisdom literature in form and substance. Within *gnosticism, three texts belong to the category of wisdom: the gospel of Thomas, the Sentences of Sextus, and the Teachings of Silvanus (see Nag Hammadi Library).   JAMES L. CRENSHAW

Wisdom of Solomon. The Wisdom of Solomon, a Greek work of a Hellenistic Jewish author, is not found in the Hebrew Bible. In the *Septu-

agint it follows the book of *Job; in the *Vulgate it follows the *Song of Solomon. The book is thus considered one of the *Apocrypha by Jews and Protestants but is accepted as canonical by the Roman Catholic and most Orthodox churches. It is never quoted in the New Testament, but some commentators find allusions to the vocabulary of Wisdom 7.26 in Hebrews 1.3 and to its description of the "son of God" mocked and persecuted by his enemies (2.18–20) in the passion narratives of the Gospels.

Scholars have dated the work from 100 BCE to 100 CE on the basis of links to Hellenistic philosophy, literature, and science. Cultured readers of that period would have been familiar with its terminology, such as "intelligent spirit" that "pervades" and "penetrates" all (7.22, 24), "living spirit" (15.11), with its description of the human body as an "earthly tent" (9.15), and with references to the cosmic god Aeon. They would applaud the use of compound terms, including over seventy beginning with the negative prefix equivalent to the English "non-."

Allusions to Jewish scripture, especially the *Psalms and *Isaiah, show that the author used the Septuagint rather than a Hebrew text. The style is that of a writer familiar with textbook rhetoric and literary figures like balance, personification, irony, and ring style; he is skillful in making plays on words, even to the point of creating new compounds. A good example of rhetoric appears in the vivid contrasts between true and apparent sterility, true and apparent fruitfulness, and true and apparent stability (3.1–5.1) In translation the style at times appears heavy and prolix.

Content and Structure. The overall literary form of the work was popular in Hellenistic Greek, namely, the protreptic or rhetorical exhortation. This complex form served the author's purpose, which was to glorify traditional faith and to encourage Israel's future leaders to commit themselves to God's saving presence in history. The opening address to "rulers of the earth" is a literary fiction in keeping with the goal of arousing enthusiasm for Israel's covenant-God and for its historical mission.

The author uses this literary form, which goes back as far as Aristotle, with great flexibility, skillfully integrating a variety of minor literary genres. Its four major developments are connected by interweaving them to avoid abrupt breaks in continuity. Part I (1.1–6.11) begins with a carefully structured and tightly argued prologue urging readers to seek that divine "righteousness" that is "immortal" (1.1–15). Motivation to do so is steeped in biblical tradition and assumes familiarity with values of the Mosaic *covenant. The appeal is further developed by a series of descriptions contrasting persons who faithfully pursue uprightness with the conduct of their arrogant foes. Such polemical contrasts identify those who seek God's will as the truly wise, for they will reign with God forever.

This identification of righteousness with wisdom leads into Part II of the book (6.12–10.21), which is devoted to singing the praises of Lady Wisdom, partner of both God and the author (6.14; 9.4). It is in this part that the author assumes the person of King *Solomon and builds on his famous dream asking for a listening heart to serve God's people (1 Kings 3.6–9).

In an extended explanation of his life, Solomon tells how, while praying for prudence, Lady Wisdom came to him as his bride. She is God's craftswoman who gave him such gifts as scientific knowledge, her own spirit with its twenty-one desirable qualities, the four cardinal virtues prized by Hellenistic philosophy, and even immortality (7.1–8.2). This lyrical celebration of Lady Wisdom recalls the Greek aretalogies or prose poems honoring the Egyptian goddess Isis, patron of wisdom, who was worshiped in many Hellenistic shrines. With good reason, then, Part II of the book has been called "the Book of Wisdom proper." (*See* Wisdom.)

After praising Lady Wisdom, Solomon offers a fervent prayer to God to continue to let her be the delight of his life, guide of his reign, and teacher of salvation to all on earth (9.1–18). The conclusion of the prayer employs for the first time the verb "save" that will dominate the activity portrayed in the rest of the book. A long description of the saving work of Lady Wisdom on behalf of biblical heroes from *Adam to *Moses, although none are mentioned by name, brings Part II to a close (10.1–21).

The power of God's saving presence dominates the rest of the book, but in ways that enfold its relation to the entire universe. This shift in perspective mirrors the author's preoccupation with the relation of the *chosen people to all creation. He starts to reflect on God's saving intervention for Israel in the *Exodus, which he presents in a series of seven contrasts. God's activity in rescuing the chosen people took the form of using elements of creation to favor them and to punish their enemies. But after describing God's first intervention, the author interrupts the contrasts to formulate a polemic that makes up the third part of the book, its richest theological development (11.15–15.19).

Part III of the book serves a double purpose. First, it provides an apologia for God's justice in ruling the world (11.15–12.27). God's way of punishing sinners is not capricious or vindicative but displays how he manages all events "by measure and number and weight" (11.20). God shows wisdom by allowing the effects of sin to take place, because sin includes its own punishment (11.16). Second, Part III appeals to Jewish readers to reject false religions. The elaborate condemnation of various forms of *idolatry warns readers not to be trapped by such foolish practices that have harmed the gentiles.

Nature worship is a display of ignorance in that it refuses to recognize the world as handiwork of a wise creator (13.1–9). Idol worship is still worse in that it places hope in the weak works of mortals and seeks salvation in helpless objects (13.10–14.8). The *Egyptians, identified only as enemies of the chosen people, merit special condemnation because they worship gods in the form of animals (15.14–19). Included in this polemic is an explanation of the origin of idolatry according to the theory of Euhemerus (ca. 300 BCE), namely, that the first gods were deified mortals (14.9–15.6).

Part IV of the book begins at 16.1 with the second of the seven contrasts based on the Exodus. These are remarkable for their poetic descriptions portraying God's care for his chosen people amid the *plagues sent against Egypt. These contrasts are addressed to God to remind him how he once used the same creatures and situations, such as water, animals, sudden death, light, and darkness, to save the Israelites and punish their foes. The author updates the biblical narratives by introducing psychological details that captured the Hellenistic religious imagination. For example, he describes darkness as creating a prison of fear for the Egyptians (17.2–21).

Teaching and Significance. An analysis of the content of the Wisdom of Solomon reveals that, as the book progresses, its style shows less clear-cut parallel phrasing. The contrasts based on the Exodus become overloaded and obscure. For this reason some scholars have postulated a different author for the latter part. Yet the large number of flashbacks and deliberate allusions to earlier chapters point to composition by the same author. The complexity results from the double polemic: against unbelieving gentiles and against Jewish apostates falling under the spell of Hellenism. Possibly the author was unable to revise and polish the final chapters.

The book is pseudonymous: its author's identity is hidden by the literary technique of writing in the person of Israel's great wisdom-figure, Solomon. This approach fit the author's purpose: to compose an apologia for Israel's traditional religious beliefs in a cosmopolitan setting. Such a procedure would not have misled the cultured audience to whom this sophisticated composition was directed. Omission of proper names assumes that readers were familiar with Israelite tradition. The style and religious intensity identify its author as a pious teacher.

The "autobiography" of the idealized Solomon, whose life was a search for Lady Wisdom, describes the plan of action necessary for Israel's future leaders. Wisdom's gifts to the devout include qualities and skills valued in Hellenistic Alexandria. Enthusiasm for Israel's tradition is no barrier to cultural progress. The author believed that Israel's role as God's chosen people was as important as ever and guaranteed by constant divine protection (19.22). The Wisdom of Solomon preserves the carefully planned appeal of a learned and imaginative Jewish teacher to his cultured students to cultivate loyalty to their revealed faith in an environment threatening their religious identity. Only fidelity to their received revelation wins eternal life with God (1.15; 15.3).   JAMES M. REESE, O.S.F.S.

Wise Men, The Three. *See* Magi.

Witch. Biblical references to witches reflect a category of ritual specialist whose status and function are now virtually unknown. Texts from other ancient Near Eastern cultures provide evidence of a variety of both male and female cultic functionaries, and there is evidence of ritual practitioners, such as oracular speakers, who were not part of a temple cult. The Hebrew Bible, by contrast, accords official cultic status to only two related categories of males, *Levites (temple functionaries) and sacrificial *priests, while portraying all other ritual experts pejoratively.

Several Hebrew terms are associated with the English word "witch." These can also be translated "sorcerer," "sorceress," "medium," or "necromancer." Most appear in references to prohibited practices (e.g., Deut. 18.9–11; 2 Kings 23.24) and seem to be concerned with divination or necromancy. *Women may have been especially involved in such activities since they were excluded from those of the official cult. Specific association with women is found in Exodus 22.18, Leviticus 20.27, and 2 Kings 9.22. A phrase meaning "a woman proficient in necromancy" is used in 1 Samuel 28.7; commonly known as "the witch of Endor" (wording not found in the Bible), this woman is able to make the dead prophet *Samuel appear before *Saul, even though he had prohibited the practice.

The strong condemnation of witches and other ritual specialists with whom they are often grouped may be the result of an attempt by ancient Israelites to distinguish their religious practices and beliefs from those of surrounding cultures, as well as to provide central state control of all forms of religious observance. But both the legal prohibitions and the prophetic attacks (Jer. 27.9; Mic. 5.11; Mal. 3.5) on various forms of *magic, sorcery, divination, and necromancy indicate that they were a perennial aspect of popular religion in ancient Israel, as they have been in postbiblical Jewish and Christian traditions.

The injunction "Thou shalt not suffer a witch to live" (Exod. 22.18, KJV) was invoked in enforcing the death penalty against women accused of witchcraft in Europe and England from the sixteenth to the eighteenth centuries, and in Salem, Massachusetts, in 1692.

See also Afterlife and Immortality, *article on* Ancient Israel; Israel, Religion of.
                              DRORAH O'DONNELL SETEL

Witness. As a juridical term, a witness is one who has direct knowledge about certain facts and can declare before a court of law what he or she has seen or heard. In the Bible, witnesses are used to attest contracts and to certify proceedings (Jer. 32.10, 12; Ruth 4.9–11; Isa. 8.2). Sometimes, inanimate objects provide the evidence that an agreement has been concluded (Gen. 31.44–54; Josh. 24.27). The tables of the law in the *ark are described as the "tables of testimony," for they are inscribed with God's commandments; sometimes the ark itself is termed "the testimony" (Exod. 25.16; 31.18; Num. 17.4).

False or malicious witness was prohibited, and sanctions were imposed against it (Exod. 20.16; 23.1–3; Deut. 19.15–19). False witnesses are mentioned in the New Testament in the trials of Jesus and Stephen (Matt. 26.60; Acts 6.13; 7.58).

Israelite law required the evidence of several

witnesses to convict a person of a capital offense (Deut. 17.6–7; 19.15; Num. 35.30). This principle is alluded to in the New Testament (John 8.13–18; 1 John 5.7–8), and was apparently honored in questions of church discipline (Matt. 18.16; 2 Cor. 13.1; 1 Tim. 5.19).

An important use of this terminology is its application to the role of Israel and of Jesus and his followers as God's witnesses before the world. Israel's mission is to bear witness to God as his chosen servant: "You are my witnesses," Yahweh emphatically declares (Isa. 43.10, 12; 44.8). Israel is to take God's side and bear witness to him as the lord of history, the only true God, and her redeemer and savior. Here the controversy language comes alive with freshness and power.

In the New Testament the witness theme is central in the gospel of John, Acts, and Revelation. In John's gospel, God in Christ has a controversy with the world. A cosmic lawsuit is underway, and each side presents its evidence and argues its case. The different witnesses to Jesus present their testimony to refute the hostile charges of his enemies (5.31–47). Jesus himself bears witness to the truth (3.31–33; 18.37), as will the *Holy Spirit as the "Advocate" (15.26).

In Acts the witness of the apostles is of prime importance (1.8, 21–22; 4.33; 10.38–43), as is that of *Paul (22.14–15; 26.16). The center of their witness is the resurrection (2.32; 3.15; 5.30–32; cf. 1 Cor. 15.3–11).

In the book of Revelation, witness is set against the background of persecution. The seer of Patmos presents Jesus as the model witness, whose example Christians must follow. "The testimony of Jesus" probably refers not to the testimony concerning him but to the testimony borne by him (Rev. 1.9; 12.17). Jesus is "the faithful and true witness" (1.5; 3.14), and loyalty to him may mean martyrdom (2.13). Here one traces the first steps of the process by which the Greek word for witness (martys) developed into the later sense of "martyr." ALLISON A. TRITES

Women. *This entry on the roles and status of women consists of four articles:*

　　An Overview
　　Ancient Near East and Israel
　　Second Temple Period
　　Early Christianity

The introductory article is an overview of the status of women in biblical times, and the remaining articles are more detailed discussions of women in the Ancient Near East and Israel, *in Judaism of the Second*

Temple Period, *and in* Early Christianity. *Related discussion is found in entries on individual women named in the Bible, and the impact of the Bible's images of women on modern views is discussed in* Feminism and the Bible.

An Overview

Before the Babylonian *exile in 587/586 BCE, women in Israel enjoyed a status and freedom comparable to that of men. Israel lived in a patriarchal world, but her society was always informed by a faith that gave equality to women in the eyes of God. Thus, the woman is understood in the tenth-century BCE story of Genesis 2.18 as the necessary complement of the man and as his helper in a relationship of mutual companionship (cf. Mal. 2.14) and assistance, just as male and female both are necessary to the image of God in the sixth-century BCE account of Genesis 1.27. The subordination of women to men is considered to be the result of human sin (Gen. 3), and the subsequent practice of polygamy (Gen. 4.19) is a manifestation of the spread of sin.

Women are found serving as *prophets (Exod. 15.20; 2 Kings 22.14–20), judges (Judg. 4–5), and *queens (1 Kings 19; 2 Kings 11) in preexilic Israel. They are never excluded from the worship of God (Deut. 16.13–14; 1 Sam. 1–2). They are sometimes honored as models of wisdom (2 Sam. 14; 20.16–22). The honor of mothers ranks with that of fathers in Israel's basic law, the *Ten Commandments (Exod. 20.12; Deut. 5.16). The family rights of wives and mothers are protected by law (Gen. 16.5–6; 38). The woman who engages in profitable commercial enterprises, who teaches with wisdom, and who serves the community through deeds of charity is honored as an ideal (Prov. 31.10–31).

Though single females lived under the authority of their fathers in Israel, love and choice in *marriage were known (Gen. 24.57, 67; 29.20), and the woman was never considered a piece of property to be bartered. Sexual love was celebrated as a gift of God (Gen. 2.23; *Song of Solomon), and the marital relationship was so prized that it could serve as a metaphor of the love between God and his covenant people (Jer. 2.2; Hos. 2.14–20)—an impossibility if marriage had been a repressive relationship for the woman.

Those preexilic stories in the Bible that exhibit cruelty toward women and treat them as objects of degradation reflect the environment in which Israel lived and are intended as protests against it (Gen. 19.8; Judg. 11; 19.22–30).

When Israel was carried into Babylonian exile, her priests in exile determined that they would draw up a plan for Israel's life that would ensure that she would never again be judged by God. They therefore collected together and wrote priestly legislation that would ensure Israel's ritual and social *purity. At the same time, they emphasized the importance of *circumcision as a sign of the covenant (Gen. 17). This emphasis brought sexuality into the realm of the cult and related females to the covenant community only through their males. The blood of the sacrifice on the altar became the means of atonement for sin (Lev. 10.17–18; 16; 17.10–11), and blood outside of the cult became ritually unclean (Gen. 9.4). Thus, women were excluded from the cult during their menstruation (Lev. 15.19–31) and childbirth (Lev. 12.2–5). Indeed, they were increasingly segregated in worship and society. They had access to the holy only through their males. A woman's court was added to the *Temple to distance them from the sanctuary. Their vows to God were no longer considered as valuable as those of males (Num. 27.1–8), and a husband could annul the vow of his wife (Num. 30.1–5). In the Second Temple period, women were excluded from testifying in a court trial; they were not to be seen in public or to speak with strangers, and outside their homes they were to be doubly veiled. They could not even teach or be taught the *Torah in their homes— a far cry from that time when Huldah the prophet interpreted *Deuteronomy for King *Josiah (2 Kings 22.14–20)—and they were not to be educated. They had become second-class Jews, excluded from the worship and teaching of God, with status scarcely above that of slaves.

The actions of *Jesus of Nazareth toward women were therefore revolutionary. He did not hesitate to engage even unclean foreign women in public conversation (John 4.27). He ignored all strictures of ritual impurity (Mark 5.25–34, 35–43). He himself taught women (Luke 10.38–42), gave them an equal rank with men as daughters of *Abraham (Luke 13.10–17), openly ministered to them as "children of wisdom" (Luke 7.35–50), and afforded them the highest respect as persons (Matt. 5.28). Women belonged to the inner circle of the disciples (Luke 8.1–3), and they are attested as the first witnesses of the *resurrection (Luke 24.1–11; John 20.18). The Fourth Gospel begins and ends with the testimony of a woman to the Christ (John 4.29; 20.18).

Women therefore played a leading role in earliest Christianity, being baptized and receiving the Spirit (Acts 2.17; 5.14; 8.12; 16.15), doing acts of charity (9.36), suffering imprisonment for their faith (8.3; 9.1–2), and serving as ministers of the church (Rom. 16.1–7). They were allowed to preach and to pray in worship (1 Cor. 11.5), as well as to prophesy (Acts 21.8–9) and to teach (18.25–26). Their equal status in Christ was strongly affirmed by Paul, who considered the ancient subordination of women in Genesis 3.16 to have been overcome by Christ (Gal. 3.27–28). When Paul was faced with the misuse of Christian freedom in his churches, however, he could revert to his Pharisaic background to silence both contentious men and women in his congregations (1 Cor. 14.28, 33–36).

As Christianity spread through the Roman world of the late first and early second centuries CE, it faced the necessity of consolidating its doctrine and regularizing its polity, over against judaizers and *gnostics. Unfortunately, in an alien environment, the church bought these developments at the price of the freedom of females. Because some women fell prey to gnostic teachings, they were forbidden leadership in some churches, on the basis of rabbinic interpretations of the scriptures (1 Tim. 2.11–15; 2 Tim. 3.6–9; Tit. 2.1–10). Patriarchal patterns of marriage reasserted themselves (1 Pet. 3.1–6; Col. 3.18), though these were often tempered by a high view of marriage and of the mutual subjection of both husband and wife to Christ (Eph. 5.21–33). Most importantly, political power struggles for control of ecclesiastical districts (cf. 3 John) led to the formation of a male hierarchy in the church that often continues to this day, in opposition to the witness of much of the Bible.

ELIZABETH ACHTEMEIER

Ancient Near East and Israel

The images of women in the Bible were shaped by literary genres and colored by historical circumstances and political ideologies. Furthermore, over the last two and a half millennia the Bible has accumulated additional resonances from the religious traditions that take it as a foundation. In essence, however, the Bible is an ancient Near Eastern document and can best be studied and understood in that context.

Women and the Family. Family and family ties determined the status and fate of women as well as men. An Israelite man or woman's formal name customarily included the name of the father (2 Sam. 20.1; 21.8); alternatively, a woman might be referred to as "PN (personal name) the wife of PN" (Judg. 4.4). Children were subject to their father (but see Deut. 21.18–21; Exod. 21.15) until the parents arranged for their *marriage (e.g., *Isaac in Gen. 24; *Rachel and *Leah in Gen. 29). Nevertheless, love poetry from Mesopotamia, Egypt, and Israel (the *Song of Solomon) implies that children may have had some influence on their parents' selection. At her marriage the Israelite bride moved to her husband's household (Gen. 24) and was thenceforth subject to him.

The strains in a society so rooted in the family are occasionally apparent in the Bible. The outrages against *Hagar (Gen. 16; 21), *Dinah (Gen. 34), and the two Tamars (Gen. 38; 1 Kings 13) arise partly out of the sexual dynamics of the family. A childless *widow had little autonomy and was supposed to return to her father's house (Lev. 22.13; but cf. Ruth 1.8). Widows with sons, *divorced women (Num. 30.9), and *prostitutes (Josh. 6.22) were probably less dependent on male authority, but if they were poor, their lives could become precarious in the absence of a related male protector (Ruth 1.4–6).

The Bible reflects Israel's double standard in its attitude toward male and female *sexuality. Virginity was required of the bride but not of the groom (Deut. 22.13–21); by contrast, in Babylon before the sixth century BCE the bride's virginity was not an important part of marriage agreements. Husbands were free to visit prostitutes even as they enjoyed exclusive rights to their wives' sexuality. In Israel *adultery with a married woman meant death for both offenders (Lev. 20.10; Exod. 20.14; Deut. 22.22), but a man who raped an unbetrothed virgin was simply compelled to marry her (Deut. 22.28–29; Exod. 22.16–17; cf. 2 Sam. 13.15–16). Deuteronomy 24.1–4 implies that only men initiated divorces (cf. Jer. 3.8; Isa. 50.1). In only one book of the Bible, the *Song of Solomon, are male and female sexuality described in an equally positive manner.

The limitations placed on ancient Near Eastern women can be regarded in part as a function of patrilineal systems that try to keep children and property within the family, rather than as an example of low female status. Families usually traced their *genealogies through the male line, with sons inheriting the bulk of the father's property. The biblical term for the family household, "the father's house" (Exod. 6.14; Num. 1.2), reflects the priority of the paternal family line. A wife suspected of infidelity thus threatened more than just the husband's honor; the identity of her children could no longer be securely tied to the husband and his lineage.

When there were no sons, daughters could play a role in preserving the integrity of the family property. At *Nuzi in eastern Assyria and at Emar in Syria, a father without sons could declare his daughter legally a son and heir. Similarly, Numbers 36 provides for the daughters of Zelophehad to inherit their father's estate (cf. Job 42.15), but with the qualification that they must marry within their father's clan. The fact that the patriarchs were related to their spouses may be a reflex of these sorts of concerns.

It is not surprising that most biblical references to women concern mothers. Whereas *Abraham's servant enumerates his master's greatness in terms of property (Gen. 24.35), *Sarah's prominence comes from being potentially, then actually, *Isaac's mother. Rachel (Gen. 29.31–30.24; 35.16–20) and Hannah (1 Sam. 1) suffer for their apparent sterility. The only stipulation in the *Ten Commandments that treats women and men equally is the command to honor both father and mother (Exod. 20.12; Deut. 5.16; cf. Lev. 20.9; Prov. 30.17).

The Bible's focus on male-dominated institutions and values ignores the details of a woman's everyday life in the home. Although the Bible portrays men and women preparing food (Gen. 18.6–7; Gen. 27), it is assumed that women did the cooking for their families. Mothers provided the primary care and nurture for children until they were weaned at about three years old (1 Sam. 1.22, 24). From Proverbs 1.8 and 31.1 and by ethnographic analogy, it appears that mothers were also responsible for the socialization and much of the moral education of their small children (Prov. 6.20).

Mothers are particularly prominent in one of the most familiar biblical stories, that of the miraculous birth of a son to a sterile mother. Despite its primary focus on God and the child, the genre is careful to mark the mother as special. For example, Pharaoh, the most powerful man in the world, cannot resist Sarah's beauty (Gen. 12.12–20; cf. the similar stories of Rachel, Gen. 29.10–30; 31.19, 34–37; *Samson's mother, Judg. 13.1–20; and Hannah, 1 Sam. 1.9–2.10). This theme reappears in the Gospel accounts of Elizabeth (Luke 1) and of *Mary (Luke 1.26–56; Matt. 1.18–25), whose virginity, rather than sterility, serves to imply that *Jesus' birth is the most miraculous of all.

Social Patterns and Female Power. By combining ethnography and archaeology, scholars are reassessing the nature of the premonarchic Israelite community (1200–1000 BCE) and of women's roles in this period. The pattern of complex households in small villages was probably a response to the labor needs generated by early Israel's agrarian environment. Micah's household (Judg. 17–18), with living units occupied by Micah, his mother, his sons (and perhaps their wives), a hired priest, and servants, mirrors the archaeological evidence. Because each household member made a crucial contribution to the household, there was greater scope for women to exercise informal authority (Gen. 25.28; 27.5–17, 42–46; 28.4, 6–7; 1 Sam. 1.22–28; 2 Sam. 25; 2 Kings 4.8–10; 8.8). Indeed, the Bible accepts as normative the phenomenon of wives counseling and influencing their husbands (e.g., *Eve; Samson's mother; Abigail; the Shunammite woman; Job's wife).

*Samuel is reported to have predicted in the late eleventh century BCE that *kingship would break up the rural family and disrupt old patterns of formal and informal family authority (1 Sam. 8.11–13). And, in fact, small freeholds did give way to landed estates (1 Sam. 8.14; 1 Kings 21; Isa. 5.8), although Israel's economy remained agriculturally based, and rural women probably influenced their families more than their urban counterparts. Urban male-dominated royal, military, economic, and religious institutions took the lead in shaping Israelite culture and defining its norms and values. The Bible is rooted in these institutions; this explains why so much of Israelite women's lives, experiences, and values have remained hidden and inaccessible.

Women's Legal Status. Cuneiform tablets show that wealthy Mesopotamian wives and widows throughout history made business contracts and appeared in court as plaintiffs, defendants, and witnesses. They borrowed and lent money, and bought and sold property. Almost always, however, the woman is acting in concert with or on behalf of her husband or another male family member. In Egypt, women from different social strata engaged in litigation and owned houses and fields, which they seem to have been able to bequeath as they liked (but usually within the family).

Israelite seals and seal impressions with women's names provide important evidence that in Israel, as in Mesopotamia and Egypt, women had the right to sign documents, a fact that the Bible never hints at. Relatively egalitarian ideals underlie the old *laws of Exodus 21.26–32, where

a value is placed on an injury irrespective of the sex of the injured party. But casuistic laws that begin "If a man . . ." usually refer to the man with the Hebrew word ʾîš ("a male") rather than with the generic ʾādām ("human being"). When an occasional law clearly applies to both men and women, ʾiššâ ("woman") may be added (Lev. 13.38; Num. 6.2). Apodictic laws are declared in second person masculine verb forms and may implicitly exclude women, as do many collective social terms. For example, in Exodus 19.14 Moses returns to "the people," who in the next verse are ordered to stay away from women (cf. 2 Sam. 5.1; 19.15; 1 Kings 12.1; 2 Kings 21.24).

Women's Activities Outside the Home. Besides being wives, concubines, and mothers, the Bible shows women working in the fields (Ruth 2.21–23), fetching water (Gen. 24.11, 15), and tending flocks (Gen. 29.9; Exod. 2.16, 21). They were midwives (Gen. 35.17; Exod. 1.15) and nurses (Ruth 4.16; 1 Kings 1.2, 4). Royal establishments employed women as perfumers, bakers, cooks (1 Sam. 8.13), and singers (2 Sam. 19.35). Although only men are mentioned as potters in the Bible, ethnographic analogies suggest that women were skilled in this important craft, and in weaving as well. There are references to enslaved women, some of whom would have been debt-slaves (Deut. 15.12) or war-captives (Deut. 20.14). Prostitutes were tolerated but, as in Mesopotamia, they were relegated to the margins of society (Deut. 23.17 outlaws only prostitutes associated with non-Yahwistic cults).

Wives of rulers, *queens, and women of the nobility were able to act with a relative degree of autonomy (1 Kings 21.1–16). The queen of *Sheba, who may have belonged to a dynasty of Arabian queens, negotiated with King *Solomon (1 Kings 10). Biblical accession formulas in 1 and 2 Kings are careful to note the name of each new Judahite king's mother (e.g., 1 Kings 15.2, 10), and the queen mother may have had quasi-official status.

Women's Religious Practice and Experience. All biblical evidence for women's religious experience has been filtered through male eyes; thus much remains hidden. The description of the ideal wife (Prov. 31.10–31), for example, mentions her wise advice, but is mute about religious activity. Men and women incurred temporary ritual impurity, and thus exclusion from the cult, for genital emissions (Lev. 12.2–5; 15.1–33), but menstruation especially penalized women. A woman after the birth of a son was impure for seven days, but for fourteen after a daughter's birth (Lev. 12.2–5).

Biblical laws obliged only men to attend the three primary pilgrimage *feasts (Exod. 23.17; 34.23; Deut 16.16), but women such as Hannah clearly participated as well. During the festival she prays and makes a vow (1 Sam. 1–13, 27), and when Samuel is born she praises God with a song of thanksgiving (1 Sam. 2.1–10; cf. Exod. 15.20–21). The detailed legislation regarding women's vows (Num. 30) suggests that this was a significant form of female piety. The personal piety of several women appears in accounts of wives or widows consulting or helping prophets (1 Kings 14.1–6; 17.8–16; 2 Kings 4.1–37). The motif in the Gospels of women appealing to and following Jesus (e.g., Mark 7.24–30; John.11.1–44) derives in part from these stories.

Monotheistic Israel differed from Mesopotamia and Egypt, where women served many deities as priestesses and even as high priestesses. The Israelite *priesthood consisted of men who inherited the office from their fathers. Some women in Israel, called qedēšôt (formerly translated as "sacred *prostitutes") were apparently consecrated to non-Yahwistic cults (Hos. 4.14; Deut. 23.19–20), but their function is unclear. Women served in some unexplained capacity at the tent shrine (Exod. 38.8; 1 Sam. 2.22), and after the *exile the *Temple employed female singers (Ezra 2.65; Neh. 7.67.).

What Israelite women did at the pilgrim feasts and how their worship differed from that of men is unclear, but it is an instructive question. Recognizing that gender differentiation—in tandem with the preconceptions of the observer—plays a role in determining what is considered "religious," scholars are beginning to reassess the ancient forms of women's piety. For example, Hannah stays home from the feast to nurse Samuel (1 Sam. 1.22), which might suggest that women's spirituality was contingent upon and secondary to men's. Is she temporarily cutting herself off from God, or were there compensatory home-centered rituals?

Besides the preparation of the corpse (cf. Mark 16.1; Luke 23.55–24.1) and funerary lamentations (Jer. 9.17), Israelite women no doubt participated in additional rituals related to the lifecycle. One suspects that midwives performed birth rituals (Gen. 35.17). The tradition of mourning for Jephthah's daughter (Judg. 11.37–40) may have been a rite of passage for adolescent girls. Zipporah performs a marriage-related *circumcision (Exod. 4.24–26). The prophets

*Deborah (Judg. 4.4) and Huldah (2 Kings 22.14) were married women; perhaps they should be compared to postmenopausal women in other societies who become religious practitioners.

*Miriam (Exod. 15.20), Deborah (Judg. 4.4), Huldah (2 Kings 22.14), and Noadiah (Neh. 6.14) are called *prophets (see also Ezek. 13.17; Joel 2.28). Deborah's and Huldah's prophecy seems to differ in no way from male prophecy. Contemporaneously with Huldah (seventh century BCE), the *Assyrians were very interested in and influenced by prophecy; texts mention female prophets, many of whom apparently operated independently of any temple cult.

Power struggles among priestly families may underlie the account in Numbers 12 of Miriam's and *Aaron's revolt. Micah 6.4 is mute on the subject of any wrongdoing, and equally commends Miriam, *Moses, and Aaron as deliverers. Miriam's very presence in the account of the *Exodus (Exod. 15.20–21) and *wilderness wanderings, complete with death notice in Numbers 20.1, suggests that she was an important cultic leader in Israelite memory.

Certain practices that the Bible considers abhorrent may at times have constituted mainstream Israelite religious activity. Significant female participation may be sought in lost, hidden, or forbidden categories of worship. The Bible condemns *Saul for consulting Samuel's ghost through the female medium at Endor (1 Sam. 28; see Witch), and disapproves of what seems to be a cult of the dead (Isa. 65.4); yet recent research has shown that the cult of dead ancestors was important to many Israelites (see Afterlife and Immortality). In the two biblical episodes involving *teraphim (household gods related to the cult of dead ancestors), the persons handling them are women (Gen. 31.19; 1 Sam. 19.13).

The numerous female clay figurines (often called Asherah figurines) found in Israelite domestic and tomb contexts must have had a religious function, perhaps related to a mother-goddess cult. Evidence from Kuntillet Ajrud in the Sinai and elsewhere, in combination with reassessments of the biblical text, suggests that many Israelites during the monarchy worshiped the Canaanite goddess *Asherah, possibly even as a consort of Yahweh.

It is worth noting two exceptions to the Bible's tendency to treat women as lesser members of the religious congregation; both mark the inauguration in *Jerusalem of a new religious era. When *David installs the *ark in Jerusalem, women and men share in the ritual meal (2 Sam.

6.9), and when Ezra conducts his public reading of the *Torah (Neh. 8.2–3), the text stresses that his audience consists of understanding men and women. Reminiscent of the latter passage is Genesis 1's assumption of the equal status of male and female (v. 27); the gender-inclusiveness of this text (generally dated to the exilic period) may reflect the importance of women among the exiles in maintaining the cohesion of family, community, and religion in the absence of male-dominated institutions such as the *kingship and the Temple *priesthood, which could no longer be regarded as keepers of the national identity.

Female Symbolism. Women play an important role in the Bible's symbolic repertory. One of the most striking and influential *metaphors in the Bible is the personification of *Wisdom as a woman (Prov. 1; 8; 9). Jeremiah 31.15 describes war-ravaged Israel as a mother, Rachel, weeping for her dead children. In a familiar biblical metaphor, God too becomes a parent who feels exasperation but also compassion—literally "womb-feeling" (Hos. 2.23; Jer. 31.20; see Mercy of God)—for the child Israel. Israel, Jerusalem, and even foreign nations and cities may be personified as daughters (see Isa. 1.8; 23.12; Lamentations). Marriage becomes a central metaphor to describe the past and future intimacy of God the husband and Israel the wife (e.g., Hos. 2.14–20; Ezek. 16.1–4; Jer. 2.2), who all too often turns into an adulteress ("playing the harlot") with other gods (Hos. 2; Jer. 3.6–10; Ezek 16.15). Political considerations help to explain the function of some women in the Bible. Abishag is actually a symbolic pawn, first of the northern tribes (1 Kings 1.3), then of Adonijah (1 Kings 2.17). The story of *Rahab (Josh. 2; 6.22–25) and the presence of women in *genealogies (1 Chron. 1–9; cf. Matt. 1.1–16) served to imply that the descendants of these women belonged to kinship groups considered subordinate by more dominant Israelite tribes.

Biblical laws against a man lying "with a male as with a woman" (Lev. 18.22) and against cross-dressing (Deut. 22.5) suggest that the borders between male and female realms are not to be crossed. Women are not warriors; thus it is ultimate humiliation for Sisera and Abimelech to die at the hands of a woman (cf. Judith). Jeremiah's oracle against Babylon even threatens Babylonian mercenaries with becoming women (Jer. 50.37). At the same time, in the deliberately shocking imagery that characterizes prophetic discourse, Jeremiah epitomizes the newness of the era when Jerusalem will be restored by suggesting some sort of gender reversal (Jer. 31.22).

Negative Views of Women. Women in the Bible are generally less important than men and subject to male authority, but paradoxically women are also very powerful in one respect, their seductive persuasiveness. The Bible singles out foreign women as dangerous, liable to lead their partners away from exclusive Yahwism (Deut. 7.1–4; 23.17–18; Num. 25; 1 Kings 11.1–6; Ezek. 8.14–15; Ezra 9.2–10.44; Neh. 13.23–27). The Bible condemns Phoenician *Jezebel for persuading Ahab to neglect the Israelite *covenant with Yahweh (1 Kings 16.31–33; 21). Canaanite *Rahab (Josh. 2.9–11) and *Ruth the Moabite are exceptions as good foreign women who take Yahweh as their God. The opposite phenomenon—Israelite women led to apostasy by foreign men—is addressed only metaphorically, when Israel is personified as a adulterous wife who has been unfaithful to her husband, Yahweh (Hos. 1–3; Ezek. 16).

The prophets denounce vain and selfish women (Isa. 3.16–23; Amos 4.1), and Proverbs scorns contentious and headstrong women (Prov. 21.19; 27.15; 11.22). The "strange" woman of Proverbs 1–9, a combination of every possible negative female type (an adulteress, a cult-related prostitute, a goddess, a foreign woman), is a literary creation who functions rhetorically as the exact opposite of a positive female figure, Lady *Wisdom.

The Bible's negative assessment of several women may arise from an unspoken political or rhetorical subtext (e.g., Michal, Jezebel, Athaliah, Gomer). Potiphar's wife (Gen. 39.6–21) and Delilah (Judg. 16.4–21) are bad women indeed, but folklorists recognize that these "evil" women play a crucial role in propelling the central character toward hero status, a story pattern repeated in countless folktales.

Genesis never refers to a woman as the cause of the human condition (see Eve). The earliest biblical reference to this concept occurs in Sirach 25.24 (early second century BCE). It is a doctrine, like the related ones of original sin and *Satan, that developed during the Second Temple Period (ca. 500 BCE – 70 CE), to be taken up in turn by early Christianity (1 Tim. 2.12–14; cf. Rom. 5.12).

Social Reality and Narrative Patterns. Investigators of women's history view with interest the intersection between religious symbols and narrative patterns on the one hand and social reality on the other. The fact that Ishtar or Hathor is an authoritative female deity does not mean that real-life women could achieve comparable power in Egyptian or Mesopotamian society.

Nevertheless, in actual society and in literature, women who function on the upper or lower margins of normative society—queens, wealthy widows, priestesses, prostitutes—may transcend otherwise static boundaries determined by gender. As high priestess of the Sumerian moon god, the princess Enheduanna (twenty-third century BCE) composed hymns which may have provided a model for later hymnists. The prostitute Rahab negotiates successfully for the common good of her family and Israel (Josh. 2; 6). In the *Gilgamesh Epic, the prostitute Shamhat is pivotal in bringing Enkidu from bestiality to civilization; her role may usefully be compared to that of *Eve in Genesis 3. Anthropologists have observed that this mediating quality is often a distinctive aspect of femaleness.

A recurrent pattern in biblical stories about women is their use of indirection, even subterfuge, to achieve divinely sanctioned ends (e.g., *Rebekah, Gen. 27; Tamar, Gen. 38; Shiphrah and Puah, Exod. 1.15–21; *Esther). By seemingly devious actions which invert or overthrow established but restrictive social hierarchies, women often bring about a new order of life and freedom.   MARY JOAN WINN LEITH

Second Temple Period

Interest in the role and status of women in Second Temple Judaism (and generally in Judaism and Christianity) has increased exponentially in the past twenty-five years. As research has progressed, however, the difficulty of reclaiming women's voices from a largely silent patriarchal textual tradition has been acknowledged. The major groups of texts of the Second Temple period are androcentric in focus, written by male authors for a male audience, and they mention women only rarely and usually in peripheral contexts. A second body of evidence that can be utilized in the search for women's lives is archaeological, the material remains of society both in Palestine and in the Diaspora. But material remains are generally silent as to the gender of their owners, and so are subject to the potentially biased interpretation of the excavator. These limitations make the recovery of women's lives from the Second Temple period fraught with difficulty.

Women's Daily Lives. The beginning of the Second Temple period was the era of *Persian domination of the ancient Near East (538–332

BCE). During this time Jewish settlement was concentrated in Babylon, Judea, and to a more limited extent in Egypt. Judea in this period was poor, with a rural, agrarian economy. Extended families (the "father's house") worked their own fields and were self-reliant in most matters of daily existence. Both women's and men's work was essential to the survival of the family unit. Women's tasks included agricultural labor, food processing, textile manufacture, and child care (women would often have ten or more pregnancies to insure that a minimum number of children survived to adulthood). Because of the interdependent nature of the family unit, gender roles were not sharply defined except for biological function.

As Greek culture spread over the ancient Near East, especially in the Hellenistic period (332 – ca. 200 BCE), the mingling of the two worlds produced the unique blend of culture called Hellenism. Hellenism created a more urban, mobile society, and also saw the rise of an extensive Diaspora community, particularly in Alexandria in Egypt and in Asia Minor. Urban life brought with it smaller families and specialized economic roles, so that women's roles became more circumscribed. While men performed their tasks in the public sphere, women became more confined to the home, limited to their maternal and housekeeping roles (this is primarily true for upper- and middle-class women). Spinning and weaving continued to be women's work. Upper-class women evidently could and did play active roles in the Greco-Roman Jewish Diaspora, but for the vast majority of women such occasions were limited. Educational opportunities expanded for women in this period, but a good part of the population remained illiterate. The visual arts reveal a new interest in the eroticism of women. So women as women are both more visible, in art and literature, and less visible, being more and more confined to the home. This created a tension in Hellenistic society's view of women, reflected in Jewish literature of the period.

Women in Postexilic Biblical Literature. The group of canonical works from the Persian period is small, and few of those are concerned with women; notable exceptions are the books of Esther, Ruth, and the Song of Solomon, all of which contain positive portrayals of women.

The book of *Esther, written in the late Persian–early Hellenistic period, is a fictional account of events leading up to the Jewish festival of Purim. Set in the eastern Diaspora, the book describes how a young Jewish girl named Esther became the consort of the Persian king and saved her people from destruction by her resourcefulness and courage. Notorious for its lack of interest in religious matters (it never mentions God, although the author clearly believes in a divine providence at work in human affairs), the book focuses on the Jews as an ethnic group and on Esther as a human heroine who saves her people by her own actions and thus as a role model for Jews in the Diaspora.

The date of the book of *Ruth is disputed, but sometime in the fifth century BCE is reasonable, understanding the book as a response to the postexilic decrees by Ezra and Nehemiah against intermarriage. The main character is Ruth the Moabite, who accompanies her Israelite mother-in-law Naomi back to Judea after the death of their husbands, and eventually, through her own praiseworthy actions, becomes the ancestress of king *David. The book concerns itself with the mundane things of life: food, *marriage, offspring, and particularly the covenant-loyalty of one (foreign) woman for another. Ruth becomes the paradigm of loyalty for all women and men, and her attachment to Naomi resembles the marriage vow: "Where you go, I will go; where you lodge, I will lodge; your people shall be my people, and your God my God. Where you die, I will die—there will I be buried. May the Lord do thus and so to me, and more as well, if even death parts me from you!" (1.16–17).

The *Song of Solomon (of uncertain date, but with final redaction in the Second Temple period) is the only book in the Bible partly written in a woman's voice. It is a series of love songs that are frankly erotic in character, celebrating the sexual life between an unnamed woman and a man, with the woman acting as a free agent, pursuing her lover, initiating their encounters, and glorying in their physical love. Conspicuously absent are the usual biblical roles for women, those of wife and mother. The couple functions as equals in their erotic union, resulting in an unusual and compelling portrayal of the woman.

Women in the Apocrypha. The *Apocrypha are writings considered canonical by the Roman Catholic and Eastern Orthodox churches, but not by Judaism and the Protestant churches. Like the Hebrew Bible, the Apocrypha comprise various types of literature, and also like the Hebrew Bible, they are androcentric, mentioning women only occasionally, when their lives impinge on the activities of men. Two important

portraits of women are found in the Additions to Esther and the book of Judith.

The Additions to *Esther are six major blocks of material added to the Hebrew book of Esther, along with minor changes in the text, when it was translated into Greek, probably in 78 BCE. The Additions attempt to remedy problems perceived in the Hebrew book: the lack of mention of God and Esther's non-Jewish lifestyle. The changes make Esther a pious but passive girl, relying on God instead of herself, so that God becomes the true hero of the story. Esther's beauty is emphasized and her brains and skill downplayed. The changes may have rendered Esther more palatable as a heroine to a Hellenistic audience accustomed to passive romantic heroines. This, then, is an example of conscious downgrading of the role of a woman.

The book of *Judith, probably composed in the second century BCE, presents an unambiguous female hero. In this fictitious narrative, Judith (whose name is a feminine form of the word for "Jew"), a beautiful, wealthy, and pious widow, leaves her quiet existence to save her town of Bethulia from the besieging Assyrians. She does this by pretending to desert to the enemy and then seducing the Assyrian general Holofernes; when he is drunk, she cuts off his head and returns to Bethulia in triumph. Thus "one Hebrew woman has brought disgrace on the house of King Nebuchadnezzar" (14.18). However, this behavior by a woman is acceptable only in national emergencies; after the Assyrians are defeated, Judith returns to her quiet existence, remaining a widow until her death. Women's power is expressed in Judith, but only within the confines of patriarchy.

Women in the Pseudepigrapha. Similarly ambivalent attitudes toward women also exists in the eclectic collection of Jewish writings known as the *Pseudepigrapha. The Conversion of Asenath and The Testaments of the Twelve Patriarchs are two examples of the wide variety of portraits of women in this literature.

The Conversion of Asenath was written to answer the question of how *Joseph, the quintessential man of God, could have married an Egyptian, "Asenath daughter of Potiphera, priest of On" (Gen. 41.45). According to the story, Joseph does indeed refuse to marry Asenath at first, because she is an idol worshipper. But Asenath, who the text emphasizes is a virgin, is so stricken by Joseph's refusal that she repents and converts to the worship of Joseph's God. The bulk of the story is the account of Asenath's conversion. She retires to her chamber, puts on mourning garments, and laments and fasts for seven days. On the eighth day she repents of her idolatry and confesses to God. In response an archangel appears to her, declares that her repentance has been accepted, and gives her a mysterious honeycomb to eat. Her marriage to Joseph follows, and she lives (basically) happily ever after. Asenath is the prototype for all future proselytes, an important role for a woman. However, once again her prominence is within the context of patriarchy, for the purpose of her conversion is to enable her to marry Joseph.

The Testaments of the Twelve Patriarchs are part of the genre of pseudepigraphical literature known as testaments, which are the deathbed words of prominent figures from Israel's past, in this case the eponymous ancestors of the twelve *tribes. Each testament is concerned with particular virtues or vices, which the patriarch instructs his offspring to practice or ignore. The theme of chastity enjoys special prominence in the Testaments. Therefore in the Testaments women exist chiefly as temptations for pious men, their lewdness often coupled with drunkenness as an aid to fornication. For example, Judah, telling of his intercourse with his daughter-in-law Tamar, says, "Since I was drunk with wine, I did not recognize her and her beauty enticed me because of her manner of tricking herself out" (12.3; *The Old Testament Pseudepigrapha* [ed. James H. Charlesworth, Doubleday, 1983] 1, 798). *Reuben, while discussing his sin with his father's concubine Bilhah, says, "Do not devote your attention to a woman's looks, nor live with a woman who is already married, nor become involved in affairs with women" (3.1; ibid., 783). In the Testaments, women exist only as objects to trip up heedless men.

All of the above examples are from literature that in some way features women prominently. But we know almost nothing about the communities that produced this literature and their relation to one another. With classical sources, we are on firmer ground, for we know more about the authors and their audiences.

Women in the Classical Sources. *Josephus and *Philo are the main sources for Jewish thought about women in classical literature. Josephus, who wrote in Rome under the patronage of the Flavian emperors after the First Jewish Revolt (66–70 CE), wrote several works, including *The Antiquities of the Jews*, which is essentially a rewriting of the biblical text for apologetic purposes. In attempting to present Jews and Judaism in a favorable light to his Greco-Roman audience, Josephus makes many changes in the presentation of biblical narratives, including their portrayals of women. One example will suffice. When Josephus rewrites the story of Esther, he has before him both the Hebrew and the *Septuagint versions of the book. He chooses to retain most of the changes introduced by the latter, heightening the erotic aspect even more, and downplaying Esther's active role in the story. Thus, the Jewish people are saved, but mainly because Esther is beautiful and the king desires her sexually, not because of her intelligence and resourcefulness.

Philo, a first-century CE Alexandrian Jew with an extensive knowledge of Greek philosophy and literature, undertakes an allegorical interpretation of the biblical text that is a fusion of Jewish thought and Greek philosophy. Therefore, the women and men in the biblical stories become symbols for higher philosophical realities. In the process the women are completely denigrated. Philo draws his dichotomy of male/female from Pythagorean and Aristotelian schemes. Man is *nous* or "mind," the higher intellectual capacity; woman, on the other hand, is *aisthēsis* or "sense-impression," the lower form of perception. Man *(nous)* is immortal, in the image of God, while woman is mortal, closely connected with *sōma*, "body." Since the goal of *nous* is to be free of the troubles of the body, woman is automatically placed in the category of undesirable and wrong. Philo's are the most systematically misogynist of all the writings we have surveyed.

Conclusion. A pattern has emerged in this survey. The earlier literature, stemming from a period when gender roles were more egalitarian and both men and women had essential economic and social roles to play, allows women greater freedom of action and a louder voice (Esther, Ruth, Song of Solomon). The later literature, influenced by Hellenistic culture with its more restricted view of women's roles, allows women to act only in relation to men, or in situations of crisis (Asenath, Judith). Finally, in literature written by men on whom the influence of Greek thought is clear, women are more thoroughly denigrated and swept from the stage of an all-male world (Josephus, Philo).

SIDNIE ANN WHITE

Early Christianity

Information on early Christian women is found in the New Testament, writings of the early church fathers, apocryphal and gnostic literature, and archaeological finds such as inscriptions and papyri. In recent years, these sources, historically overlooked for data on women, have been exploited by scholars, resulting in dozens of important secondary works. While the evidence must be treated carefully by the historian and theologian, it furnishes proof that data on the women of antiquity do exist; in fact, the study of women in the New Testament and early church constitutes one of the liveliest and most fruitful areas of biblical scholarship today.

The Greco-Roman and Jewish Heritage. Like Christians in general, women in the early church were products of the wider culture. In general, women were dependent both financially and legally on the men in their lives—fathers, husbands, uncles, brothers, and sons. Women generally married while still teenagers, bore one or more children, and died young (the average life expectancy was thirty-four years), often in childbirth. If a girl survived childhood (i.e., was not exposed), and a woman survived childbirth, she might live a long life and bury her husband: women were the primary caretakers of the graves of family members, including those of in-laws. It was also women who passed on the household (usually the men's) religious practices such as ancestor worship to their descendants.

Except in the most outlying rural areas, women were not isolated from each other or from other men. Middle- and upper-class women living in villas or in urban areas often functioned as chief household managers, especially when their husbands were absent for long periods of time on commerce or at war. While there is considerable evidence for independent and wealthy women, most women lived in slavery, near poverty, or middle-class stability; therefore, most worked for wages for their own economic survival and that of their families, even if they were married to a merchant or freedman. In some cases, women may have been secluded in their homes, but for the most part they moved freely in many spheres of the Greco-Roman world—the agora, baths, businesses, and religious associations.

With regard to religious background, some early Christian women were Jewish, since Christianity was a sect of Judaism for a time. Other women converted from Greco-Roman cults, while still others, often in the same family or neighborhood, remained non-Christian. This coexistence of adherents of different religions systems was often peaceful but could lead to conflict, often over the issue of appropriate roles of women in the various groups.

Evidence from both Jewish and Greco-Roman circles shows that women held leadership roles in these groups. In Judaism, archaeological and other evidence demonstrates that some women in the first few centuries CE held positions such as head of a synagogue (*archisynagōgis*), leader (*archēgissa*), elder (*presbytis*), "mother of the synagogue" (*mater synagogae*), and priest (*hiereia*). The exact functions of these women are difficult to ascertain, but they were probably equivalent to the functions of men bearing parallel titles. The evidence further demonstrates that women were integrated into regular services, not segregated in "women's galleries" or separate rooms, and that some were major financial contributors to local synagogues.

Similarly, women held leadership roles in many, if not most, of the myriad Greco-Roman cults that allowed women members. Some of their functions included priest, musician, stolist, prophet, torchbearer, dancer, and mourner. Outside of religion, women worked as midwives, lawyers, merchants, artists, teachers, physicians, prostitutes, and laborers and professionals of all sorts.

Women in positions of authority in religion and society did not constitute a majority: the culture was still patriarchal, that is, controlled primarily by men. However, the fact that women did play some leadership roles in both Judaism and the larger society became significant for the growth of Christianity: women who were drawn to it undoubtedly would have expected to be active participants in the new cult if not leaders. Their presence had a definite effect on the development of the *canon, the emerging role of the *priest and *bishop, as well as liturgy, theology, and battles with heresy and *gnosticism.

Women in the Early Christian Movement. The New Testament and early church fathers provide preliminary data on women. The earliest evidence, from *Paul's letters, suggests that women functioned as dynamic leaders of the movement (Phil. 4.2–3; Rom. 16), *deacons (Rom. 16.1–2), *apostles (Rom. 16.7), and missionaries (1 Cor. 16.19; Rom. 16.3–4). The Gospels relate that Jesus had women followers as well as men (Mark 15.40–41; Matt. 27.55; Luke 8.1–3) and treated women as equals (cf. John 4.9, 27; Luke 10.38–42); it was also women who were the first to bear witness to his *resurrection. The Acts of the Apostles mention the four daughters of Philip who prophesied (21.9); Lydia from Thyatira, a merchant and the head of her household (16.14–

15); the missionary couple, Priscilla and Aquila (chap. 18); house-church leaders (12.12); and prominent converts (17.4, 12).

Thus, in pre-Pauline and Pauline Christian communities, women appear to have functioned almost identically to men. In fact, it is possible that more women than men were house-church leaders, hosting vital prayer meetings that became the kernel of the movement. At least one woman deacon, Phoebe, is recorded in the New Testament (Rom. 16.1–2), and she functioned as an official teacher and missionary in the church of Cenchreae. Euodia and Syntyche from Philippi (Phil. 4.2–3) were prominent leaders of that community, and *Junia served the church at Rome as an apostle (Rom. 16.7). The most prominent woman in the New Testament is Prisca/Priscilla, who worked alongside her husband and was probably the more renowned of the pair (1 Cor. 16.19; Rom. 16.3–4; Acts 18). The women Mary, Tryphaena, Tryphosa, and Persis in Romans 16 are described as having labored (kopian) for the Lord, the same term Paul used to describe his own evangelizing and teaching activities. (See Elizabeth Schüssler Fiorenza, In Memory of Her, New York, 1983.)

Celibacy became a major life-style choice for both men and women early in the Christian movement, and by the third and fourth centuries men and women were living in houses and monasteries (a term that includes convents) segregated by gender. Renunciation by men was not deemed problematic, but the popularity of female celibacy led to fears that women's independence would undermine the very fabric of home and society. Early attestations of this popularity and the subsequent social tensions it created are found in many of the apocryphal Acts of the second and third centuries, including the Acts of Paul and Thecla, the Acts of Andrew, the Acts of Peter, and the Acts of Thomas (see Apocrypha, article on Christian Apocrypha). In the stories in these Acts, celibacy was idealized, and many women were portrayed as heroines for breaking off engagements and leaving husbands and traditional home situations for the sake of the gospel. While many of the stories in the Acts may be fictitious, they probably originated in oral form in circles of independent women and reflect actual people, events, and trends.

Other threats to the survival of the young church in the eyes of male leaders included the leadership of independent women in gnostic and heretical groups. Two prophets, Priscilla and Maximilla, were prominent in the Montanist sect of the second century, and women in those groups may have baptized and celebrated the Eucharist (Cyprian, Ep. 75[74].10; Epiphanius, Haer. 49.2). Some gnostic sects also allowed women to serve as priests and to baptize (Hippolytus, Haer. 6.35; Irenaeus, Haer. 1.13.1–2; Epiphanius, Haer. 42.4; Tertullian, Praescr. 41). Bishop Atto of Vercelli (ca. 885–961) wrote in several tracts that women were ordained just like men in the ancient church, were leaders of communities, were called elders (presbyterae), and fulfilled the duties of preaching, directing, and teaching.

Female celibacy and other acts of independence led male leaders to disseminate countertreatises in which they prescribed strict behavior for all women and attempted to bring the entire Christian movement more in line with the overall culture's ideal of the patriarchal family and household. The New Testament "household codes" (Eph. 5.21–6.9; Col. 3.18–25; 1 Peter 2.18–3.7; see Ethical Lists), written by followers of Paul, not Paul himself, clearly urged women's subordination to men. The so-called *Pastoral letters (1 and 2 Timothy and Titus) are also early works accepted into the New Testament canon. 1 Timothy 2.11–12 forbade women from speaking in church, and Titus 1.7–9 assumed that only men would be bishops.

Retrenchment and Later Trends. The church fathers of the second through fourth centuries, being among those who agitated against women's independence, decreed that women could only minister to other women as deacons or be enrolled as virgins or *widows. Women deacons as described in third- and fourth-century documents were at least fifty or sixty years of age, ministered to sick and poor women, were present at interviews of women with (male) bishops, priests, or deacons, and instructed women catechumens. Before the decline of adult *baptism, women deacons assisted at the baptisms of women, probably their most important role. Women deacons may have been the only women admitted into ministry in the orthodox church by the laying-on of hands by the bishop. In the earliest church, however, female deacons may have functioned much more similarly to male deacons, since the sources are not always clear.

Widows and virgins, while not ordained, had recognized status and privileges in the early church. However, there were restrictions placed on them. Widows in New Testament times had to be at least sixty years of age and married only once; younger widows were expected to remarry. The references to virgins in the New

Testament are more vague (Acts 21.9; 1 Cor. 7.1, 8, 25–38), but the order seems to be closely linked to that of widows.

Meanwhile, the male leaders reserved for themselves the right to serve the whole church in the more important and powerful roles such as *elder (*presbyteros*) and *bishop (*episkopos*) and adhered to the ideal of the monarchical episcopate: the high reverence due the bishop and the subordination of others to that office. Bishops in these fathers' minds could, of course, only be fellow men, and the directives they set down toward women could be stringent.

Polycarp, bishop of Smyrna, writing to the Philippians around 110 CE, attempted to limit women's behavior by clearly delineating their roles as virgins, widows, and ever-faithful wives. Ignatius of Antioch urged Polycarp to be the "protector" of widows and exhorted women to be "altogether contented with their husbands" (*Ep. Polycarp* 4,5). Libanius (314–95) complained that women distract men from their religious duties (*Ep.* 1057). Canons from the Council of Gangra in 340 declare *anathema women who wear male attire, who leave their husbands, and who cut off their hair, a sign of their subjection.

Tertullian, perhaps the most misogynist of all the early fathers, wrote four lengthy treatises dealing with women: *On the Apparel of Women* (ca. 202), *On the Veiling of Virgins* (ca. 204), *To His Wife* (ca. 207), and *On Monogamy* (ca. 208). In *On the Apparel of Women* 1.1, he described women as "the gateway of the devil" and blamed them for leading men astray through their sexual wiles. In chap. 9 of *On the Veiling of Women*, he wrote, "It is not permitted to a woman to speak in the church; but neither is it permitted her to teach, nor to baptize, nor to offer, nor to claim to herself a lot in any manly function, not to say in any sacerdotal office." To Tertullian's way of thinking, the ideal woman was a totally subservient being, completely regulated by strict rules governing every facet of her life—a far cry from the autonomous woman of many of the nascent Christian communities.

One early church leader who was more positive toward women in some ways was Jerome (342–420). In a number of letters between him and the many women of his social circle, Jerome appears as a sort of mentor and father figure to upper-class women who had chosen the celibate life-style. One of his Roman disciples, Paula, founded a monastery near *Bethlehem.

However, even some of Jerome's saintly women were admired for leading lives that followed strict rules of behavior, rules not generally applied to men. Fabiola, a young Christian woman from Rome, divorced her husband because he was a sinner; this was applauded by other Christians. However, these same Christians, including Jerome, condemned her for subsequently remarrying: "She did not know that the rigor of the gospel takes away from women all pretext for remarriage, so long as their former husbands are alive." When she finally realized her "mistake," she publically confessed and was restored to communion. Then, being wealthy, she sold her property and, with the money, founded a hospital to nurse the poor and sick (*Ep.* 77).

Monasticism became increasingly important for women in the face of these restrictions and the eradication of heretical and gnostic groups that had promoted women's independence. A number of women besides Paula, mostly from the upper strata of society, founded or cofounded all-women houses, communities, and nunneries where young women learned to read, write, paint, and draw. Such houses, like those of men, followed rules of order and were self-supporting and devoted to prayer and good works. At first the houses were independent of local church authorities, but over time they were brought under the jurisdiction of the bishop.

While female monasteries may have been centers of opportunity primarily for members of the upper classes, thereby restricting most other women to marriage in patriarchal households or to lives as virgins and widows dependent on men, these communities nevertheless made important contributions to the entire church that have historically been overlooked. While the evidence is meager, especially compared with evidence from all-male enclaves, it suggests that all-women groups produced high-quality illuminated manuscripts; wove many of the tapestries that adorned the great basilicas, as well as the ornate robes worn by clergy; crafted at least some of the silver Communion ware and jewelry used in the liturgy; and contributed to sketch books that served imperial architects as blueprints for exquisite mosaics that decorated many basilicas. Also, women in some communities taught men reading, writing, and drawing; dispensed wisdom to male leaders; and became renowned as leaders of centers of learning.

Significantly, despite attempts by the hierarchy through the ages to conceal the evidence, there is attestation for women priests into the Byzantine era. An epistle of Pope Gelasius I (492–96) to bishops in Italy and Sicily mentions in annoyance that women were officiating at the sacred altars and taking part in ecclesiastical affairs imputed only to men. An inscription from Bruttium dating to the end of the fifth century mentions the presbytera Leta (*Corpus incriptionum latinarum* 10.8079), and another from Salona in Dalmatia (425 CE) mentions the presbytera Flavia Vitalia. While these attestations are rare, they confirm that women functioned sacerdotally—and that male bishops occasionally ordained them.   VALERIE ABRAHAMSEN

Word. *See* Logos.

Word of God. "The Word of God" is a common expression for *revelation. In biblical tradition, the term is first applied to prophecy and later comes to describe the *Law as communication from God; in the New Testament, it is used for scripture and also for the gospel and the person of Jesus Christ. In Christian tradition, the expression occurs in a loose, popular sense that implies the *inspiration of the Bible, and in a stricter way, particularly in modern Protestant *hermeneutics (see below).

In preexilic Israel, the phrase "the word of Yahweh" denotes the source of prophetic inspiration, not necessarily its character as verbal or rational. The word may be received in visionary form by a prophet whose own mental processes are temporarily suspended (Num. 24.4). In the exilic prophets and exilic redaction of earlier traditions, however, the transcendence of the divine self-disclosure comes into sharper focus. Thus, Jeremiah can speak of his struggle with God's word (Jer. 20.8–9), and Second Isaiah contrasts its effective purpose with the transience of human nature (Isa. 40.8). While for Jeremiah the prophetic word and the Law remain distinct (Jer. 18.8), in Deuteronomy they are brought into closer conjunction (Deut. 30.14). In the postexilic period, the word of God becomes an overarching concept comprising revelation through abidingly valid legal commandments, through prophetic interpretation of historical experience, and through creation (Ps. 147.15). The latter two understandings are especially prominent in *apocalyptic literature and in Hellenistic Judaism, respectively.

In the New Testament, the word of God, along with equivalents like "God says," "it was spoken," and so on, is used in connection with biblical *quotations (e.g., John 10.35; Rom. 15.10, and

Mark 7.13, where the phrase implies the idea that written law is superior to the oral tradition of the scribes). Echoing prophetic language, in the prologue to Luke's gospel, the motif of a new era of active prophecy is evoked by the coming of the word of God to *Simeon and *John the Baptist (Luke 2.29; 3.2). Moreover, the word of God, or variants such as "the word of the Lord" or "the Word," is applied especially in Luke-Acts (but frequently elsewhere as well) to the gospel message of salvation through Jesus (Mark 4.14, cf. Luke 8.11; Acts 4.31; 8.25; 11.19; 1 Thess. 1.6; 1 Cor. 14.36; 1 Tim. 1.15). Because of this it is occasionally difficult to decide whether the word refers to Jewish scripture or to the gospel (e.g., Heb. 4.12; Eph. 6.17). The word in the sense of the gospel message is closely paralleled with the person of Christ as the content of preaching (Rom. 10.8, 1 Cor. 1.23). It is therefore but a small step to identify Jesus himself as the divine Word or *Logos incarnate (John 1.14; cf. Rev. 19.9).

Throughout postbiblical tradition, the word of God is regularly found as a pious periphrasis for the Bible. At the Reformation, however, the phrase acquired a new, controversial emphasis, and often carries the implication of the supremacy of scripture over both tradition and the sacraments in the theology and practice of the church. Whereas Luther, following Augustine, still maintained a distinction between the transcendent Word of God and the biblical text, holding the preaching of the gospel to be its essential mediation, other reformers tended to identify the two more closely and saw revelation as conveyed inwardly to the individual through the text itself. As a result, in the following centuries, the word of God came to be understood in terms of a propositional view of revelation and the verbal inspiration of scripture. In the twentieth century, this understanding was challenged by dialectical theology, which is sometimes known as "the Theology of the Word of God," associated especially with Karl Barth and Rudolf Bultmann. They emphasized the contrast between God's Word as sovereign address and human response to it in faith. While Barth attempted a complex system of interrelation between the Word of God in three senses, Jesus Christ, the witness of scripture, and preaching, Bultmann's existentialist philosophy led him to stress preaching as the occasion for actualizing the divine word. Recent developments have tended in different directions, emphasizing variously the historical and eschatological or the linguistic and symbolic aspects of revelation, so that it is no longer possible to speak of a coherent concept of the word of God in Protestant thought.   JOHN MUDDIMAN

Worship. In teaching that "man's chief end is to glorify God and to enjoy him forever," the Westminster Catechism of 1647 faithfully captured the developed biblical vision. As creator and redeemer, God calls for worship on the part of humankind. Human salvation consists in communion with the beneficent God. The first commandment is to worship the Lord God alone (Exod. 20.1–6 = Deut. 5.6–10; Matt. 4.10 = Luke 4.8). The content of that worship, according to the *Shema, is total devotion: "You shall love the Lord your God with all your heart, soul, and might" (Deut. 6.5; Mark 12.30 par.). The idolatry of the *golden calf epitomizes the perennial human tendency to turn from the creator and worship the creature (Ps. 96.5; Rom. 1.21–25). Nevertheless, God visits and redeems his people. The prophets picture the future time of salvation as a flocking of the nations to the *Temple (Zech. 14.16–21; cf. Isa. 2.2–4), a banquet on God's holy mountain when death will have been destroyed (Isa. 25.6–9). According to the book of Revelation, salvation will be marked by worship in the heavenly city where there is no temple apart from the Lord God Almighty and the Lamb (Rev. 21.22; 19.6–10).

When the Lord called on Pharaoh to let his people go, it was so that they might "worship" or "serve" him (Exod. 3.13). The Lord who commissioned *Moses to lead Israel out of Egypt was the God who had appeared to the *ancestors as God Almighty and had been worshiped by them (Exod. 3.6, 15; 6.2–3; cf. Gen. 12.7; 13.18; 22.1–14; 28.10–22). Safely delivered through the *Red Sea, Israel worshiped the Lord on Mount *Sinai and there received the terms of the Lord's *covenant with them, including their sole obligation to Yahweh, their "jealous" God (Exod. 19–31). The deliverance was to be commemorated each year in the *Passover rite (Exod. 12–13; Lev. 23.5–8; Deut. 16.1–8), and the covenant would be renewed regularly as under Joshua at *Shechem (if Gerhard von Rad is correct in his interpretation of Josh. 24; cf. Deut. 31.10–13). In the *Promised Land, agricultural festivals would be related to the events of Israel's history, for example, the feast of weeks (Lev. 23.15–21; Deut. 16.9–12) to the whole ancestral story as far as the entry into the land flowing with milk

and honey (cf. Deut. 26), and the feast of booths or tabernacles (*sukkôt:* Deut. 16.13–15; Neh. 8.13–18) to the dwelling in tents in the wilderness (Lev. 23.33–36, 39–43; *see* Feasts and Festivals). Nevertheless, the gods of the land remained a permanent temptation to Israel; the conflict between *Elijah and the prophets of Baal is emblematic (1 Kings 18.20–42). The book of *Deuteronomy records an attempt to reform, purify, and control Israel's worship by centering it in one place, presumably the Jerusalem Temple, which had been built under *Solomon as a focus of the Lord's presence amid the nation (1 Kings 5–8). *Prophets kept reminding the nation of the unacceptability of worship that was not matched by the performance of God's will in daily living (Amos 5.21–24; Hos. 6.6; Isa. 1.10–17; Jer. 7).

The Babylonian *exile, itself seen as divine punishment for infidelity, affected the worship of Israel in various ways. The nation's experience led it to recognize Yahweh as the one, universal God (Isa. 45). The older *sacrifices had been the whole burnt offering (*ʿōlâ* or *kālîl*), symbolizing total consecration, and the communion sacrifice (*zebaḥ šĕlāmîm*), in which the meal was shared by God and the worshipers with the intention of either thanksgiving or a vow or a freewill offering. To these were added, in the rebuilt Temple, the sin offering (*ḥaṭṭāʾt*) and the guilt offering (*ʾāšām*). The *Day of Atonement (Lev. 16) is also postexilic. The Psalter has been called "the hymnbook of the second Temple." Doubtless much of its material is older, and the *Psalms have continued in liturgical use among Jews and Christians: the praises, thanksgivings, confessions, complaints, and prayers are suited to recurrent events and situations in the life of a people and of individuals.

From its earliest days, Christianity interpreted the Psalms christologically, seeing in them messianic prophecies and prayers that could be addressed either to Christ or, with Christ, to the God he addressed as "*Abba, Father." The dispute between Jews and Christians as to whether Jesus was the Messiah is at heart a dispute about worship, since it concerns the identity of God. Christians believed that the God of Israel, the one true God, had acted decisively in Jesus, and indeed in such a personal way that Jesus was not only the mediator of salvation but did himself, as "the Word made flesh" (John 1.14), call forth worship ("My Lord and my God!" John 20.28). "Worship in spirit and in truth" (John 4.19–26) would no longer take place in the Temple in

Jerusalem (itself destroyed in 70 CE), but the temple was now Christ's body (John 2.19–22), into which believers were incorporated and themselves became temples of the Holy Spirit (1 Cor. 6.19–20). The letter to the *Hebrews argues that Jesus' death fulfilled the sacrifices of the old covenant by achieving what its foreshadowings were not able to deliver (Heb. 7–10). After Jesus' self-offering (Heb. 9.14), believers now approach "the throne of grace" through him as their great high priest in the heavens (Heb. 4.14–16; cf. Eph. 2.18). In several hymnic passages of the New Testament, Jesus is included in the worship rendered to God (Phil. 2.5–11; Rev. 1.5–6; 5.13; cf. 2 Pet. 3.18).

The earliest Christians in Jerusalem continued to worship in the Temple (Luke 24.53; Acts 2.46). Fairly soon, however, Christian worship took on a clearly independent character, marked particularly by the fact that Christians assembled "in the name of Jesus" (cf. Matt. 18.20). When Christians gathered together as a church, the most characteristic thing they did was to celebrate the *Lord's Supper (1 Cor. 11.17–34), the rite that Paul and the *synoptic Gospels (Mark 14.22–25 par.) describe Jesus as instituting at the Last Supper. It is debated whether or not the Last Supper was a Passover meal, but it seems clear from the narratives that the Christian meal was intended to commemorate the "exodus" and the new "covenant" inaugurated by the death of Jesus; the word "*exodus" is used of Jesus' death at Luke 9.31, and the Gospels speak of his covenant blood poured out for the many. At their liturgical assemblies, the early Christians hailed the presence of the risen Jesus and called for his return: "*Maranatha" (1 Cor. 16.22; cf. Rev. 22.20; 1 Cor. 11.26).

The earliest deliberate description we have of Christian worship dates from the second century. Justin Martyr in his *First Apology* (66.1–3) describes Christians as gathering from town and country on "the first day of the week," the day of Christ's resurrection and so the beginning of a new creation. They would listen to "the writings of the prophets" and "the memoirs of the apostles." The president of the assembly interpreted these scriptures (the sermon). Prayers were said for church and world. Bread and a cup of mixed wine were brought to the president, who gave thanks to God over them for creation and redemption. The bread and the wine, signs of the body and the blood of Christ, were distributed and consumed. *Deacons took them to the absent. In light of this description,

it may be possible to see already the reflections of such a "service of word and sacrament" in such passages as Luke 24.13–32, where the risen Jesus expounds the scriptures to the two travelers on the road to Emmaus and is made "known to them in the breaking of the bread," and Acts 20.7–12, where the Christians of Troas gather on the first of the week and Paul preaches all night to them before they break bread.

In fact, little is known about the "service of the word" in New Testament times. Later evidence suggests influence from the *synagogue, in the form of readings and prayers. Christians sang "hymns, psalms, and spiritual songs" (Eph. 5.18; Col. 3.16), and 1 Corinthians 14 includes some ecstatic elements among "prophecy," "revelations," "speaking in tongues," "interpretations," and "teaching."

Since for Paul the greatest spiritual gift was love (1 Cor. 13), like the prophets he implied an ethical test for true worship. He used cultic language to exhort Christians to appropriate conduct: "I appeal to you . . . to present your bodies as a living sacrifice, holy and acceptable to God, which is your spiritual worship" (Rom. 12.1; cf. 1 Cor. 6.18–20; 2 Cor. 6.6–7.1). Paul also spoke of his apostolic labors in liturgical terms (Rom. 15.15–16; Phil. 2.17; cf. 2 Tim 4.6).

Twentieth-century scholarship has rediscovered how much material in the Bible arose from and was shaped by the worship practiced by the Israelite, Jewish, and Christian communities. It is the continuing use of the Bible in worship that preserves it as a sacred and "living" book.

See also Lectionaries; Prayers; Priests and High Priest.   GEOFFREY WAINWRIGHT

Writing in Antiquity. The invention of writing in the strict sense of the word was preceded by a series of earlier developments that gradually led up to it. Soon after the invention of pottery in the neolithic period (ca. 8000 BCE) in the Near East, excavations reveal the existence of a system of clay counters and tokens that, in their earliest form, appear to have served to identify the number and kinds of goods traded, entrusted to second parties, or otherwise dealt with. By the fourth millennium BCE, such counters were being enclosed in hollow clay envelopes (bullae) which, after drying, constituted a sealed physical record of the transaction; but until and unless the envelope was broken open, this record could not be verified or retrieved. Before long it was realized that, like the seals, the counters could be impressed on the surface of the bulla before it dried, thus providing an ever-present record of the counters enclosed in it; only if their number and character needed to be verified was it necessary actually to break the bulla open. Next it must have been seen that the counters could be dispensed with altogether, and thereafter it became logical to abandon the hollow bulla format as well, in favor of a more or less flat clay tablet with an only slightly rounded writing surface. Finally, the counters themselves were abandoned and their approximate shapes reproduced instead by means of a stylus made of reed. This final development seems to have occurred first in *Sumer, where clay and reeds were both abundant; it signaled the emergence of writing in its full sense and may probably be dated about 3100 BCE.

Within a century or so, the system expanded from the depiction of concrete objects by means of pictograms to the expression of sounds or syllables by means of syllabograms, a first application of the rebus principle. An example is the name ᵈEn-lil-ti, "the god Enlil lives (or gives life)," in which the first three signs may be described as logograms (word signs) but the last is a picture of an arrow whose pronunciation in Sumerian is *ti*, as is (more or less) the pronunciation of the Sumerian word for "life, live" (actually *til*).

No further significant innovations in the inner structure of the cuneiform script were needed beyond this point, nor indeed were they forthcoming. All subsequent changes involved only phonetic adjustments to the needs of other dialects and languages, or the external forms of the signs, whose total number was stabilized at about six hundred. From their pictographic origins, they rapidly evolved into stylized linear representations. Gradually, these were replaced in turn by the wedge-shaped characters that result from the impression of a split reed (shaped like a prism) into wet clay and that justify the modern designation "cuneiform" first applied to them by Thomas Hyde in 1700 CE.

The newly invented cuneiform script remained in use in the Near East for three millennia (until ca. 100 CE), undergoing considerable changes in external appearance as it spread rapidly from its Sumerian base. In Elam (southwestern Persia) to the east and Egypt to the west, it stimulated native writing systems ("proto-Elamite" and hieroglyphics respectively) that owed no more than their basic inspiration to the orig-inal invention. Elsewhere, the borrowing was more direct. The syllabic values of the cuneiform script were taken over in their entirety for writing Akkadian by *Babylonians and *Assyrians; the Sumerian logograms were given their Akkadian equivalents; some new syllabic values were assigned to existing cuneiform signs on the basis of such equivalents, others by convention to render sounds not found in the Sumerian phonemic roster. A little later in the third millennium BCE, the Elamites also adopted the Sumerian system.

In Anatolia (central Turkey) the first attested writing, early in the second millennium BCE, consists of Old Assyrian texts and a few native inscriptions modeled on them. But the conquest of the area by the *Hittites about 1700 BCE led to the adoption of a Babylonian version of cuneiform, probably from *Mari, and its adaptation to the special requirements of their Indo-European language. A distinct script was developed by Luvian, a language (closely related to Hittite) that survived the fall of the Hittite empire about 1200 BCE, especially in northern Syria. This script is pictographic in form and essentially syllabic in structure. It is conventionally designated as Hieroglyphic Hittite, though it has nothing to do with Egyptian hieroglyphics (see below) and is not, strictly speaking, used for Hittite. Mesopotamian cuneiform also provided the vehicle for Urartian (*see* *Ararat), the language of eastern Anatolia from ca. 1300–600 BCE.

While the Elamite, Hittite, and Urartian adaptations retained the essential forms and functions of Mesopotamian writing, a wholly new cuneiform script was devised about 520 BCE to record Old Persian. Its individual characters were wedge-shaped, but beyond that they owed nothing to Mesopotamian cuneiform; they were nearly all syllabograms of the form consonant-plus-vowel (or simply vowel) and numbered no more than forty; only four of them were logograms. And while Persia thus continually experimented with new scripts inspired by Mesopotamian models, native factors predominated in the further development of writing in Egypt. From its origins before the end of the fourth millennium BCE, it quickly evolved into the elaborate logo-syllabic system known by its Greek designation as hieroglyphics (literally "sacred carvings"). Its syllabograms were indifferent as to vowels; they distinguished only the consonants and must therefore be transliterated without vowels (or with the vowel *e* conventionally inserted between the consonants). Extensive use was made of logograms and (to a greater extent than in cuneiform) of determinatives or "semantic indicators," that is, signs not pronounced in speech but alerting the reader to the meaning class of the ensuing word.

Like Mesopotamian cuneiform, Egyptian hieroglyphics survived for over three millennia, their last use dating from the Roman period. On monumental texts, the hieroglyphic signs retained their essentially pictographic character, and even elaborated on it secondarily by adding color or direction to the individual signs. But before the end of the third millennium BCE, a cursive adaptation of hieroglyphic, the hieratic script, began to evolve for use on papyrus and ostraca (potsherds). Early in the first millennium BCE, the Demotic dialect of Egyptian developed its own cursive script, while, at the end of the millennium, twenty-three hieroglyphic signs and their Demotic equivalents were adopted for the unrelated Meroitic language of Nubia, south of Egypt. The various Coptic dialects of Egyptian were written in a modified Greek alphabet.

The internal development of hieroglyphic also continued. By the side of the traditional logo-syllabic script, there developed in the second millennium a so-called syllabic orthography, particularly for foreign names, which attempted to indicate vowel quality by means of semiconsonants. It is this form of syllabic hieroglyphic writing which is generally thought to have inspired the first attempts at the written recording of Northwest Semitic speech, beginning in the Sinai peninsula, where speakers of Canaanite (or proto-Canaanite) came in contact with Egyptian culture in the middle of the second millennium BCE. At the Sinaitic site of Serabit el-Khadim, where Canaanite laborers (or slaves) worked copper and turquoise mines under Egyptian overseers, graffiti and other inscriptions in the "proto-Sinaitic" script employed clearly pictographic characters (which in some cases may have been conventionalized replicas of hieroglyphic signs) to represent the Northwest Semitic roster of phonemes. According to the acrophonic theory advocated by many scholars, the Canaanite word represented by the sign provided its name, and the first syllable of that word became the pronunciation of the sign. This principle works better for some signs than for others; it may therefore be best to regard the decipherment of proto-Sinaitic as provisional and the assignment of letter names as a later development.

Meantime Northwest Semitic also came into contact with the cuneiform tradition of writing, knowledge of which had spread through the Near East in the Late Bronze Age (ca. 1550–1200 BCE), at least among scribes trained at scribal schools on the Babylonian model that are known from El-*Amarna in Egypt to Hattusha in Anatolia and along the entire Levantine littoral in between, especially at Ugarit on the north Syrian coast. Here, some time after 1400 BCE, thirty cuneiform signs were newly devised to represent the consonantal phonemes of *Ugaritic (which represents another early form of Canaanite), its three basic vowels (when preceded by the glottal stop) and a Hurrian phoneme for words and names in that non-Semitic language. Outside Ugarit itself, scattered examples of the new script have been found as far away as Israel. The spread of the invention was helped by the mnemonic device of arranging the signs in a conventional sequence and inscribing them in this sequence on practice tablets today referred to (like their later Latin counterparts) as abecedaries (from a-b-c-d-arium); allowing for the intervening reduction in the number of signs, this sequence already equals that of the subsequent Hebrew and Greek alphabet (from the latter's first two letters, alpha, beta), the former attested in the alphabetic *acrostics-poems of the Bible (Pss. 9–10; 25; 34; 37; 111; 112; 119; 145; Prov. 31.10–31; Lam. 1–4).

Both Ugaritic and proto-Sinaitic served as prototypes and possibly as inspirations of the earliest forms of what is loosely called *Phoenician script, the ancestor of all later alphabets. This script was not, however, a true alphabet, but more properly a syllabary, which continued to ignore vocalic quality in favor of syllables of the type consonant-plus-(any or no)-vowel. It was adopted without essential modifications for the writing of such Northwest Semitic languages as *Hebrew and *Aramaic as well as Phoenician, the last probably responsible for spreading its knowledge westward as early as the beginning of the first millennium BCE to Greece and beyond, as *Greek sources state. The Greek world had evolved an earlier system of writing in the Late Bronze Age, the Linear B known from archival texts found on Crete and the Greek mainland. These texts were written on clay and thus may represent a response to a Mesopotamian, or at least a cuneiform, stimulus. (The contemporary Linear A and the Phaistos Disc have not yet been satisfactorily deciphered.) But the greater simplicity of the new script recommended itself to the Greeks as it had to the Phoenicians.

The Greeks, moreover, turned the new invention into a true alphabet by employing some of the otiose consonantal phonemes into signs for vowels; they also took advantage of the fixed order of the letters to assign them numerical values. Both of these ideas were subsequently adopted, with modifications, for the original Northwest Semitic signs, notably in Hebrew. But the vowel signs (*matres lectionis,* or mothers of reading), never fully succeeded in distinguishing vowel quality, so that later Hebrew, Aramaic and, eventually, Arabic developed a system of (optional) diacritics for this purpose.

Via the Greeks, the alphabet was transmitted to the Romans and to the rest of the European world. Meantime the Aramaic version of the Northwest Semitic script inspired the Indic writing of Asoka and, indirectly, Sanskrit and other scripts of Asia to the east, and North Arabic, South Arabic, and Ethiopic to the south. The alphabet was thus truly ready to conquer the world, with the notable exception of China and Japan. But in antiquity, the older scripts of Mesopotamia and Egypt continued side by side with it. The last datable cuneiform text is an astronomical tablet for 75 CE. The last Egyptian texts are rock inscriptions from the island of Elephantine (Philae), below the Aswan Dam, and are dated 394 and 425 CE for hieroglyphic and hieratic respectively.

See also Books and Bookmaking in Antiquity; Literacy in Ancient Israel.   WILLIAM W. HALLO

Wycliffe Bible Translators. A nondenominational missionary agency devoted to the *translation of the Bible for those peoples who lack it in their native languages. Founded by William Cameron Townsend in 1934, Wycliffe Bible Translators (WBT) takes its name from the famous fourteenth-century British reformer John Wycliffe, who was responsible for the first complete English translation of the Bible. Wycliffe Bible Translators was incorporated in 1942 along with its sister organization, the Summer Institute of Linguistics (SIL). Although closely aligned with WBT (members of SIL must belong to WBT and vice versa), SIL presents itself as a secular linguistics institute, thus enabling it to enter countries otherwise restricted to missionary activity. This strategy, pioneered by Townsend in Mexico in the 1930s, has engendered some controversy in missiological circles in recent years. Nevertheless WBT/SIL has long been recognized as the world's largest organization for the translation of the scriptures, with more than six thousand members currently working with more that 850 different languages in fifty countries.   WILLIAM H. BARNES

Y

Yahweh. *See* Names of God in the Hebrew Bible.

Yahwist. *See* J.

Yam Suf. *See* Red Sea.

Yom Kippur. *See* Day of Atonement.

Z

Zadok, Zadokites.

Zadok was one of *David's two *priests (2 Sam. 15.24–29, 36; 17.15; 19.11; 20.25; 1 Chron. 15.11; 16.39; cf. 2 Sam. 8.17; 1 Chron. 18.16; 24.3, 6, 31). He sided with *Solomon against Adonijah in the succession struggle late in David's life and anointed Solomon king at David's request (1 Kings 1). As a result, he was the sole chief priest under Solomon, while Abiathar was banished to Anathoth (1 Kings 2.35; 1 Chron. 29.22). Zadok's descendants controlled the priesthood in *Jerusalem from this time on until the *exile (the chief priest in *Hezekiah's time is said to be from the house of Zadok, 2 Chron. 31.10), and in *Ezekiel's vision of the restoration, all the priests in charge of the altar are Zadokites (Ezek. 40.46; 43.19; 44.15; and especially 48.11, where Zadokites are separated from other Levites). While there is some controversy about Zadok's origins, his lineage in 1 Chronicles 6.1–8, 49–53 ties him to *Aaron through Eleazar, and there is a Zadok from the house of Aaron mentioned as part of David's army at *Hebron (1 Chron. 12.27–29; see also Josh. 21.9–13; 1 Chron. 6.54–57), so it would seem that he was an Aaronite priest.

After the exile, the Zadokites apparently controlled the high priesthood (1 Chron. 9.10–11 and Neh. 11.10–11, with a slightly different genealogy) until the time of Antiochus IV Epiphanes in the second century BCE. The *Qumran sect was dedicated to the Zadokite priesthood, as well, and it has been suggested that the name of the priestly *Sadducees is derived from Zadok.   JO ANN HACKETT

Zaphon.

The Hebrew word ṣāpôn is one of the ordinary words for "north"; this is its most frequent meaning in the Bible, but it is derived from its primary sense. Zaphon was the name (meaning "lookout") of a mountain on the Mediterranean coast ca. 10 km (6 mi) north of *Ugarit, later called Mount Casius and now Jebel el-ꜥAqraꜥ. As a prominent peak in the northern part of the *Canaanite world, its name was used as a synonym for the direction north, just as one of the words for "west" literally means the (Mediterranean) Sea. It is primarily identified with *Baal, as widespread references to Baal-zephon (see Exod. 14.2) indicate; it was his home and as such could also be deified.

There are several passages in the Bible in which the original sense of ṣāpôn as the mountain home of the storm god is meant. Job 26.7 and Isaiah 14.13 are both in contexts permeated with references to Canaanite mythology. Psalm 89.12 may refer to Zaphon and Amanus, rather than north and south, as parallel to Tabor and *Hermon. The usual translation "Mount Zion in the far north" in Psalm 48.2 is a geographical absurdity; but the identification of Yahweh's home, *Zion, with Baal's home, Zaphon, makes sense in light of the Canaanite origins of the Jerusalem *Temple and its ideology. The verse should therefore be rendered: "Mount Zion, the heights of Zaphon, is the city of the great king." The name of the prophet *Zephaniah is probably also derived from this meaning.

Zaphon is also the name of an important town in the Jordan Valley (Josh. 13.27; Judg. 12.1).
                                MICHAEL D. COOGAN

Zealot.

Zealot is a term that has been associated with a movement of revolutionaries active throughout the first century CE in Roman Palestine and thus during the time of Jesus' ministry. These Zealots supposedly played the major role in the social unrest which ultimately erupted in the First Jewish Revolt against Rome in 66 CE. Jesus' teaching, and in particular speeches such as the *Sermon on the Mount, have been read against the Zealots' advocacy of armed resistance against and the overthrow of the Roman occupational forces and administrators. In fact, one of Jesus' followers, Simon, was called "zealot" (Luke 6.15; Acts 1.13), but this may simply be a descriptive epithet rather than meaning a member of an organized group.

However, this older and disturbingly tidy scholarly reconstruction concerning the Zealots has recently been overturned. The Jewish revolt in 66–70 is not now viewed as the work of a longstanding group called the Zealots. A much closer reading of *Josephus reveals that such an organized group did not exist for the six decades before the revolt. The Zealots only emerge at the outset of the revolt, and then only as a coalition of popular groups seeking the overthrow of Rome, including numerous bandit groups (Grk. *lastai*), Sicarii or dagger people (urban terrorists), as well as groups lead by messianic figures and popular kings. The pioneering work of Richard A. Horsley, particularly in his work, *Bandits, Prophets, and Messiahs: Popular Movements at the Time of Jesus* (New York, 1985) has demonstrated this with great clarity. During the first century the colonial situation brought on by Roman domination and exacerbated by the ruling *Herodian dynasty escalated into a socioeconomic malaise characterized by great debt, unemployment, social division, crime, banditry, and finally revolt; the Jesus movement developed in this context, and many of Jesus' sayings are only understandable when placed in it. Josephus describes these social ills and the movements which arose in *Galilee and Judea with disdain. "Zealot" became one term to describe the brief coalition of such movements. As the coalition fragmented, some groups went to Masada in the south to await the outcome of the struggle, some killed each other, and others fought the Romans to the death. There was thus no single, monolithic group called the Zealots against whom other perspectives can be easily measured.

See Judaisms of the First Century CE.

J. ANDREW OVERMAN

Zebulun. Son of *Jacob and *Leah and one of the twelve *tribes of Israel (Gen 30.19–20). The tribe settled in the region of Galilee between *Asher and *Naphtali to the north and *Manasseh and *Issachar to the south (Map 3:X3). Zebulun figures prominently in the wars of Judges (4.6, 10; 5.14, 18; 6.35). According to the Chronicler, Zebulun continues to play a major role during *David's reign (1 Chron. 12.34). Members of this tribe seem to have survived the *Assyrian conquest (Isa. 9.1; 2 Chron. 30.6, 10–

11). King Josiah's wife, Zebidah, came from Rumah in Zebulun (2 Kings 23.36).

The Jewish community of *Galilee in the Second Temple period perhaps stemmed in part from Zebulun. After the destruction of the Second Temple, the Jewish academic centers of learning located in this area were pivotal to the survival of Jewish tradition.

GARY N. KNOPPERS

Zechariah, The Book of.

Chaps. 1–8. The first eight chapters of the book contain the teaching of Zechariah in a series of eight visions of the night (1.7–6.15) together with accompanying oracles. These are sandwiched between accounts of his preaching in 1.1–6 and chaps. 7–8. Like *Haggai, Zechariah is said to have prophesied in the second year of *Darius the Persian (520 BCE), but his ministry extended to the fourth year (518 BCE). Like Haggai, therefore, he is addressing and seeking to encourage the postexilic community in Judah in all their frustrations and difficulties.

Several visions and oracles assure the people of God's imminent action on their behalf. While the first vision, that of the horsemen (1.8–13), shows that nothing can yet be seen to be happening (v. 11), the oracle brings assurance that God is deeply concerned for the welfare of *Jerusalem, which he is about to "choose" again and to which he will come to resume his dwelling. He will punish the nations that have destroyed the city and taken its citizens into *exile, the theme also of the second vision of the "horns" and "smiths" (1.18–20). The third (2.1–5) takes up Second *Isaiah's picture of the unlimited size of the restored city (Isa. 49.19–21) and assures them that God's *glory (his presence) will be in the city (cf. Ezek. 43.1–5; Hag. 2.9). God will protect them as he did when he led the Israelites in the *wilderness by a pillar of fire (Exod. 13.21). The oracle that follows (2.6–13) calls on the exiles to return, for Yahweh is about to dwell in the city to which not only Jews, but all nations, will come. The fourth vision (3.1–10) shows the cleansing of Joshua, the high priest (called Jeshua in Ezra and Nehemiah), a sign that God is now determined to forgive and cleanse the community. The fifth (4.1–14) suggests a joint leadership of *Zerubbabel as civil governor and Joshua, and contains a promise that Zerubbabel will complete the rebuilding of the *Temple, but also a warning that he must do so only in complete reliance on God's spirit (vv. 6–10a). The two visions in chap. 5 announce the cleansing of the restored community, while a final vision (6.1–8), echoing the first, pictures horsemen and chariots patrolling the earth, reporting that God's spirit is now at rest in the north country (traditionally the direction from which Israel's enemies have come in judgment from God; see Jer. 1.14). Now, however, this is the peace, not of inaction, as in the first vision, but of the resolution of the people's problems by God's saving actions. The passage 6.9–15, along with 3.6–10, seems to describe a situation in which the priestly line has assumed preeminence, while messianic hope now attaches to an unnamed and future figure called the Branch (see Isa. 11.1)

The surrounding oracles contain warnings against repeating the sins of preexilic generations who ignored the teaching of the prophets (1.1–6; 7.7–14; 8.14–17). They reinforce the promises of the visions of an imminent new age by assuring questioners (7.1–3) that all mourning fasts for the fall of Jerusalem are about to be replaced by joyful festivals of celebration (8.18–19).

The fact that 1.1–6 and chaps. 7–8 contain echoes of some of the "sermons" in the books of *Chronicles (e.g., 2 Chron. 30.6–9) may suggest that the teaching of Zechariah was handed down by preaching and teaching personnel of the postexilic Temple. This is strengthened by the presence of teaching on such subjects as true fasting (7.4–6), found elsewhere in postexilic literature (e.g., Isa. 58). Again, oracles of Zechariah are taken up and expounded afresh in 8.1–8 (cf. 1.14, 16), while 8.9–13 appears to be exposition of Haggai 2.15–19. The universalist tone in Zechariah's teaching (2.11) is strongly and splendidly renewed in 8.20–23.

Zechariah, like Haggai, was thus remembered as a prophet who encouraged the immediate postexilic community by assuring them of God's imminent action in terms that echoed the preaching of *Ezekiel and Second Isaiah and took up themes of the preexilic *Zion/David theology expressed in many psalms. His picture of a joint messiahship of civil and religious leaders was to reappear in the teaching of the *Qumran community. The form of the teaching in a series of visions is reminiscent of one test of a true *prophet in some of the earlier literature, namely, that he had been admitted to the council of heaven (Jer. 23.18). The stronger sense here, however, that what is happening on earth is a projection of what is happening in heaven, has suggested to some that in Zechariah 1–8 we have an early hint of *apocalyptic.

Chaps. 9–14. In Zechariah 9–14 no mention is made of the building of the Temple that now is standing, nor of the time of Darius I, while there is a reference to "Yawan" (literally, Ionia; NRSV: "Greece") in 9.13. There is nothing corresponding to the visions of chaps. 1–8 or to the ethical teaching of 1.1–6 and chaps. 7–8. For these reasons most scholars assign these chapters to a later time and another hand or hands. Broad thematic features are, however, common to both parts of the book, such as a strongly Zion-centered interest, God's cleansing of the community in preparation for his final act of salvation, a marked universalism, dependance on earlier prophecy, and a concern for a true and proper leadership as one sign of the new age. These suggest that the later parts of the book came from circles that maintained the traditions of Zechariah's teaching.

Many attempts have been made to date these chapters by the supposed historical allusions found in them, but these attempts have yielded such widely differing results that we must question their validity. It is more likely that we have here exposition of earlier prophetic themes in general terms in which particular countries, personalities, and events are now seen as typical or symbolic of the clash of the forces of evil with God's universal kingship. By such means earlier prophecies are related to the writer's own time and their relevance for people of later generations demonstrated.

The material is broadly of two kinds: eschatological passages that look forward to the triumph of God over evil and controversy passages in which strong attacks are made on those who are seen as false leaders of the community, in the manner of some earlier prophetic books.

Chap. 9 speaks of the advance of an enemy, echoing oracles of *Amos and Ezekiel (vv. 1–7). God, however, defends Jerusalem, to which her king comes in triumph bringing peace among all nations (vv. 9–10), words later quoted in the New Testament and used of the triumphal entry of Jesus into Jerusalem (Matt. 21.1–9 par.) Vv. 11–17 speak of God's ultimate victory, taking up earlier prophetic themes and the imagery of the enthronement psalms, a note continued in 10.3b–12.

Chaps. 12–14 introduce new themes. In 12.1–13.6 the nations have gathered to attack Jerusalem. Yahweh, however, intervenes to defeat them and delivers both Judah and Jerusalem, this resulting in an act of divine cleansing and renewal of the whole community. Chap. 14 paints an even more cosmic picture, with God himself gathering the nations who come to lay siege to Jerusalem. Only after half the population has been exiled does God come to the aid of his stricken city (vv. 2–3). He appears on the Mount of *Olives; the mountain is connected to the city by a great earthquake so that Yahweh once more enters Jerusalem (vv. 4–5). Thereafter all nature is renewed, and God is acclaimed as universal king (v. 9). Jerusalem becomes the highest point in the land (vv. 10–11; cf. Isa. 2.2); all who oppose God's rule are defeated (vv. 12–15) and all nations come to worship him in Jerusalem (vv. 16–21). Because the *eschatology of chaps. 12–14 tends more toward that of apocalyptic and because the heading "Oracle" is found, not only at 9.1 but again at 12.1, some scholars hold that these chapters are later than chaps. 9–11. Since, however, the same degree of dependence on earlier prophecy is found in each section and controversy passages occur in both, they may be more closely connected than some have thought.

The controversy passages (10.1–3a; 11.13; 11.4–17; 13.7–9) express increasingly severe condemnation of false shepherds, presumably the priestly leaders of the community at some point, or points, in the postexilic period.

So much is obscure in these chapters that interpretation of them can be only tentative. The view that they came from a sharply eschatological party that found itself increasingly at odds with the official priesthood and Temple, and so looked for a more and more radical intervention of God, would account for much that is here. If that were so, it would mean that some of the factors that later gave rise to the Qumran community were already being felt by those from whom chaps. 9–14 came, perhaps in the third century BCE.   REX MASON

Zedekiah. Last king of *Judah (597–587/586 BCE). A younger son of *Josiah, he was placed on the throne by *Nebuchadrezzar of *Babylon to replace his uncle, Jehoiachin, whom Nebuchadrezzar had deposed. Nine years later, Zedekiah rebelled against Nebuchadrezzar, prompting him to besiege and destroy *Jerusalem (2 Kings 24.18–25.7; 2 Chron. 36.11–14).

In the book of *Jeremiah, Zedekiah's reign is described in fatalistic tones: destruction by Bab-

ylon is inevitable (Jer. 21.1–7; 24.1–10; 32.1–5; 34.1–3; 37.6–10); submission to Nebuchadnezzar is Zedekiah's only option (27.12–15); he and the people refuse to heed Jeremiah's warnings and should expect punishment (37.2); the insincerity of repentance is exposed (34.8–22). On one occasion, Zedekiah reveals his belief in the truth of Jeremiah's warnings, yet he fears certain Judahites more than God's wrath (38.14–28). In the end, he attempts to escape under cover of darkness, but is captured by the Babylonians and led away in shame (Jer. 39.1–7; see Ezek. 12.1–16).   TIMOTHY M. WILLIS

Zephaniah, The Book of. The ninth book of the Minor Prophets proclaims the coming *day of the Lord, with its judgment on Israel and the nations, to be the best hope for salvation.

The prophet's name means "Yah(weh) protects"; in an earlier form it may have been a confession, "Zaphon is Yahweh," *Zaphon being the deified Canaanite mountain who is thus identified with Israel's Yahweh. The superscription goes to unusual lengths in giving the prophet's ancestry, which is traced back to *Hezekiah, the great Judean king.

The prophecy is dated to the reign of King *Josiah (640–609 BCE), who was responsible for major reforms in Judah's worship (2 Kings 22–23; 2 Chron. 34–35). Josiah was the "son of Ammon," who was murdered by revolutionaries (2 Kings 21.23). But a group called "the people of the land" rose up to quell the revolution and put his son Josiah on the throne. This group supported Josiah in his reforms and *Jeremiah in his preaching. Zephaniah seems to be very close to their goals and aims.

Zephaniah fought against foreign influences and against the worship of other gods. His message is close to that of the great eighth-century prophets, especially *Isaiah. He taught that pride was the major sin of humankind, and that it leads to rebellion against divine authority. He understood God's judgment to be universal. Hope for him lay beyond the great *day of judgment. The book serves as a bridge between the eighth-century prophets of judgment such as *Hosea and *Amos, and the prophets after the exile, such as *Haggai and *Zechariah, who proclaimed a coming salvation of God.

The book is composed as a dramatic dialogue between Yahweh and someone else, possibly the prophet. Each of the seven parts of the book includes a speech by Yahweh and one by the prophet, except the last, which has only Yahweh's speech.

1. Yahweh's speech (1.2–6) announces a total judgment over all creation. People have stopped serving the Lord and worship other gods. The prophet calls for silence (1.7) and puts a name on the judgment: "the day of the Lord."

2. Yahweh's anger still is hot (1.8–13) as he condemns everyone in Israel, from the rulers to the skeptics. Then the prophet develops his picture of the day of the Lord (1.14–16), verses that serve as the starting point for the medieval hymn *Dies irae*.

3. Yahweh's third speech is more calm (1.17) but still insists that sin will make the people become "dust" and "dung." The prophet's speech is longer (1.18–2.7). He introduces two new themes: that there is a possible way to escape the judgment, and that other nations are to be condemned. The "humble of the land" (2.3) may escape the devastation.

4. Yahweh fills out the prophet's message (2.8–10) by announcing judgment on *Ammon and *Moab for their pride and promising that the surviving remnant of Israel will plunder their enemies. The prophet continues by noting that the nations are judged because of their *idols (2.11). This pair of speeches is a kind of pause in the action.

5. Yahweh speaks out to include Ethiopia in the judgment (2.12). His dialogue partner compares Israel with *Assyria (2.13–3.5), which will be completely devastated; Israel is also wicked and will be destroyed.

6. Yahweh's speech begins to resolve the problem (3.6–13). After judgment and destruction comes God's mercy. All the nations are offered the opportunity to "call on the name of the Lord and serve him with one accord" (3.9). Then the Lord will purify their speech; he will remove Israel's shame and forgive her sin (3.13). The prophet calls on Israel to rejoice in God's presence (3.14–17).

7. Yahweh's final speech (3.18–20) summarizes the salvation that he promises Israel, dealing with her oppressors, saving those who are lame, and restoring those in the dispersion.

The book has developed a plot that seems to promise only doom for all creation, including Israel. Such a fate is thoroughly deserved. Then a slight hope is raised for some to survive when specifically identified peoples are marked for the judgment; some hope for the "humble of the land" is disclosed. Finally the Lord's mercy offers a way of escape for the nations and for Israel.

Zephaniah makes a strong contribution to the understanding of the day of the Lord. In the Minor Prophets, this day is understood as a decisive turning point in which the Lord's judgment falls upon Israel and the nations for their idolatry and pride. The events that lead up to *Jerusalem's final destruction in 587/586 BCE are clearly in mind. Zephaniah shows that this terrible moment can bring the opportunity for a new beginning, for both Israel and the nations. The true opportunity is for those who are "humble and lowly" (3.12). The book opens the door to the messages that the following three books of the collection will bring. In Haggai and Zechariah, God leads in rebuilding the *Temple a full century after Zephaniah's time, and the final chapters of Zechariah as well as *Malachi look to the opportunities and responsibilities of the people of God in the postexilic age.

JOHN D. W. WATTS

Zerubbabel. The name, meaning "offspring of Babylon," of a descendant of *David who returned from the Babylonian *exile (Ezra 2.2) to become governor of the Persian province of Yehud (Judah) under *Darius I (522–486 BCE). He was a grandson of Jehoiachin (Jeconiah), the exiled king of Judah (1 Chron. 3.17–19). Zerubbabel and Joshua the high priest were responsible for the completion of the rebuilding of the *Temple. Hopes for the restoration of the nation were probably attached to him because of his ancestry. Haggai 2.23 calls him the "servant of Yahweh" and the one he has "chosen." The prophet Zechariah (3.8; 6.12) mentions a "branch," which also may refer to Zerubbabel. Although the Temple was only begun in 520 BCE and was finished in 515 BCE, there is no mention of Zerubbabel at its dedication (Ezra 6.16–18). It may be that he was removed from power by the Persian authorities because of the threat of rebellion in Yehud. Zerubbabel appears in the *genealogies of Jesus in Matthew 1 and Luke 3.

RUSSELL FULLER

Ziggurat. The Akkadian word *ziqqurratu* (cf. *zaqru,* "high") refers to the sacred stepped tower built of sun-baked bricks that was part of the temple complex in many Mesopotamian cities. At the top of the tower was a chapel or shrine, which was depicted with blue facing and surmounted by large horns. The earliest ziggurats were constructed during the reign of Ur-Nammu (ca. 2100 BCE). Their design transformed the older architectural tradition of temples set on platforms, and may have been influenced by the Egyptian pyramids. The most famous ziggurat of antiquity was Etemenanki ("house that is the foundation of heaven and earth") of the temple complex of Marduk at *Babylon. This seven-staged ziggurat was probably built during the First Dynasty of Babylon (ca. 1900–1600 BCE), or possibly during the reign of Nebuchadrezzar I (ca. 1100 BCE; see Enuma Elish VI.63). It is likely that the fabled *tower of Babel of Genesis 11 is a reminiscence of this ziggurat, retrojected to the dawn of human history.

RONALD S. HENDEL

Zion. A name of *Jerusalem (Map 9). The etymology of the Hebrew term is unknown. Perhaps the earliest reference to Zion is the account in 2 Samuel 5 of *David's conquest of Jerusalem, then under the control of the *Jebusites; v. 7 speaks of "the stronghold of Zion." This and other texts, as well as recent archaeological research, suggest that Zion was limited originally to the Jebusite fortress located on the crest of a hill at the southeast corner of Jerusalem, also called the Ophel (2 Chron. 27.3; etc.). After his victory, David renamed the stronghold "the city of David" (2 Sam. 5.9). With its physical features and the presence of the fresh-water spring of Gihon nearby, the site was of strategic importance. The city of Jerusalem soon expanded north along the eastern ridge to include what became the Temple mount, but even then the name Zion could be restricted to the city of David to the south. According to 1 Kings 8.1, at the dedication of the *Temple *Solomon had the *ark of the covenant brought up to the Temple from "the city of David, which is Zion."

Later, poetry recalled that it was David who had found the ark and brought it to Zion, the place Yahweh desired for "his habitation" (Ps. 132.13). Already in early texts from the book of Psalms, however, Zion refers not to David's city but preeminently to Yahweh's dwelling place, Yahweh's "holy hill" (Ps. 2.6). This extension of the term is probably connected with the transfer of the ark from the city of David to the Temple newly constructed by Solomon. The ark represented the footstool of Yahweh's royal throne, and the Temple enshrining it symbolized the presence of Yahweh as king. In this way the term Zion lost its originally precise geographic designation and came to refer to the Temple area and even to the entire city of Jerusalem (Ps.

76.1–2). In later times the name Zion was erroneously restricted to the western hill, still called Mount Zion, but this was uninhabited until the eighth century BCE (see Jerusalem). But what it lost in geographic precision Zion more than regained in the rich symbolism associated with it.

That symbolism centered on Zion as the dwelling place of Yahweh as king. Since it was viewed as the site of Yahweh's throne, Zion was portrayed as a lofty peak extending into heaven, the point at which heaven and earth meet. Thus, Psalm 48.1–2 depicts Zion as Yahweh's holy mountain "on the heights of Zaphon" (NRSV: "in the far north"). *Zaphon was the mountain home of the Canaanite god *Baal, and imagery from Canaanite religion is applied to Zion in Psalm 48 and elsewhere. True to its original designation of "stronghold," but especially because Yahweh reigned there as king, Zion was also a symbol of security. Yahweh was Zion's defender against the threats of kings and nations (e.g., Pss. 46; 48; 76). For that reason Zion was also portrayed as the place of refuge, especially for the *poor (Isa 14.32; cf. Ps. 9).

All of this seems to have given rise to a notion of Zion's inviolability, as reflected in Micah 3.9–12 and Jeremiah 7.1–15. According to these prophets, the people of Jerusalem believed the city's security against *Assyrian and *Babylonian threats to be guaranteed. The book of *Isaiah accepts the notion of Zion's inviolability (8.9–10, 16; 17.12–14) but distinguishes between the security promised to Zion and the destruction with which Yahweh threatens Jerusalem (1.21–26; 29.1–8). Zion will endure even beyond Jerusalem's destruction.

After Jerusalem and the Temple were destroyed in 587/586 BCE, hope for the future was often expressed in terms of the restoration of Zion (Isa. 51.1–6); because of this hope, the modern Zionist movement took the ancient designation as its own. In some texts from the exilic and postexilic periods, Zion/Jerusalem is addressed in royal language common to the Near East (Isa. 45.14–17; 49.22–23; 60.4–7); in others, Zion is portrayed as a mother (Isa. 66.7–11). Occasionally, Zion is identified with the community itself: "saying to Zion, 'You are my people' " (Isa. 51.16). 2 Esdras speaks of Zion in referring to the heavenly Jerusalem that would ultimately replace the earthly one (13.36; cf. Rev. 21.1–17). In Hebrews 12.22, Zion refers to the "new covenant" of Jesus. In all of these diverse ways, Zion is the "city of God" (Ps. 87.3).

BEN C. OLLENBURGER

Bibliography

To assist readers, the editors have prepared this bibliography of some important and useful books about the Bible available in English.

Critical Introductions. These provide summaries of modern scholarly research on the formation of the Bible from the smallest literary units to the final canonical arrangement, as well as a bibliographic starting point.

Childs, Brevard S. *Introduction to the Old Testament as Scripture.* Philadelphia: Fortress, 1979.

Childs, Brevard S. *The New Testament as Canon: An Introduction.* Philadelphia: Fortress, 1985.

Collins, Raymond F. *Introduction to the New Testament.* Garden City, N.Y.: Doubleday, 1983.

Hayes, John H. *An Introduction to Old Testament Study.* Nashville, Tenn.: Abingdon, 1979.

Koester, Helmut. *Introduction to the New Testament,* vol. 2: *History and Literature of Early Christianity.* Philadelphia: Fortress, 1982.

Kaümmel, Werner G. *Introduction to the New Testament,* Rev. ed. Nashville, Tenn.: Abingdon, 1975.

Popular Introductions. These are frequently used as text in undergraduate courses, and provide readable surveys of the development of the Bible and of the history of the biblical world.

Alter, Robert, and Frank Kermode. *The Literary Guide to the Bible.* Cambridge, Mass.: Belknap, 1987.

Anderson, Bernard W. *Understanding the Old Testament.* 4th ed. Englewood Cliffs, N.J.: Prentice-Hall, 1985.

Barr, David L. *New Testament Story: An Introduction.* Belmont, Calif.: Wadsworth, 1987.

Court, John M. and Kathleen M. Court. *The New Testament World.* Englewood Cliffs, N.J.: Prentice-Hall, 1990.

Crenshaw, James L. *Old Testament Story and Faith: A Literary and Theological Introduction.* Peabody, Mass.: Hendrickson, 1992 (repr. of 1986 ed.).

Freed, Edwin D. *The New Testament: A Critical Introduction.* 2d ed. Belmont, Calif.: Wadsworth, 1991.

Gottwald, Norman K. *The Hebrew Bible: A Socio-Literary Introduction.* Philadelphia: Fortress, 1985.

Harrington, Daniel J. *Interpreting the New Testament: A Practical Guide.* Wilmington, Dela.: Michael Glazier, 1979.

Harris, Stephen L. *The New Testament: A Student's Introduction.* Mountain View, Calif.: Mayfield, 1988.

Johnson, Luke T. *The Writing of the New Testament: An Interpretation.* Philadelphia: Fortress, 1986.

Kee, Howard C. *Understanding the New Testament.* 5th ed. Englewood Cliffs, N.J.: Prentice-Hall, 1993.

Metzger, Bruce M. The New Testament: Its Background, Growth, and Content. 2nd. ed. enlarged. Nashville, Tenn.: Abingdon, 1983.

Perrin, Norman, and Dennis C. Duling. *The New Testament: An Introduction.* 2d ed. New York: Harcourt Brace Jovanovich, 1982.

Rendtorff, Rolf. *The Old Testament: An Introduction.* Philadelphia: Fortress, 1986.

Rogerson, John W., and Philip Davies. *The Old Testament World.* Englewood Cliffs, N.J.: Prentice-Hall, 1989.

Sandmel, Samuel. *The Hebrew Scriptures: An Introduction to their Literature and Religious Ideas.* New York: Oxford University, 1978.

History

Bickerman, Elias J. *The Jews in the Greek Age.* Cambridge, Mass.: Harvard University, 1988.

Bright, John. *A History of Israel.* 3d ed. Philadelphia: Westminster, 1971.

Cohen, Shaye J. D. *From the Maccabees to the Mishnah.* Philadelphia: Westminster, 1987.

Edwards, I. E. S., ed. *The Cambridge Ancient History.* 3d ed. Cambridge University, 1970–.

Herrmann, Siegfried. *A History of Israel in Old Testament Times* 2 ed. Philadelphia: Fortress, 1981.

Jagersma, Henk. *A History of Israel in the Old Testament Period.* Philadelphia: Trinity, 1983.

———. *A History of Israel from Alexander the Great to Bar Kochba.* Philadelphia: Fortress, 1986.

Koester, Helmut. *Introduction to the New Testament,* vol. 1: *History, Culture, and Religion of the Hellenistic Age.* Philadelphia: Fortress, 1982.

Miller, J. Maxwell, and John H. Hayes. *A History of Ancient Israel and Judah.* Philadelphia: Westminster, 1986.

Safrai, Shmuel, and Menahem Stern, eds. *The Jewish People in the First Century: Historical, Geography, Political History, Social, Cultural and Religious Life and Institutions.* 2 vols. Philadelphia: Fortress, 1974, 1976.

Schürer, Emil. *The History of the Jewish People in the Age of Jesus Christ.* 4 vols. Rev. and ed. by Geza Vermes and Fergus Millar. Edinburgh: T. and T. Clark, 1973–87.

Shanks, Hershel, ed. *Ancient Israel: A Short History from Abraham to the Roman Destruction of the Temple.* Washington, D.C.: Biblical Archaeology Society, 1988.

———, ed. *Christianity and Rabbinic Judaism: A Parallel History of Their Origins and Early Development.* Washington, D.C.: Biblical Archaeology Society, 1992.

Soggin, J. Alberto. *A History of Ancient Israel from the Beginnings to the Bar Kochba Revolt, A.D. 135.* Philadelphia: Westminster, 1985.

de Vaux, Roland. *The Early History of Israel.* Philadelphia: Westminster, 1978.

Nonbiblical Texts. These standard anthologies and surveys provide introductions to the literatures of the ancient Near Eastern and Greco-Roman neighbors of ancient Israel and earliest Christianity, as well as to early Jewish and early Christian writings not included in the canon.

Barrett, C. K., ed. *The New Testament Background: Selected Documents.* Rev. ed. San Francisco: Harper and Row, 1989.

Cameron, Ron, ed. *The Other Gospels: Non-Canonical Gospel Texts.* Philadelphia: Westminster, 1982.

Charlesworth, James H., ed. *The Old Testament Pseudepigrapha.* 2 vols. Garden City, N.Y.: Doubleday, 1983, 1985.

Coogan, Michael D. *Stories from Ancient Canaan*. Philadelphia: Westminster, 1978.

Miller, Robert J., ed. *The Complete Gospels: Annotated Scholars Version*, Sonoma, Calif.: Polebridge, 1992.

Nickelsburg, George W. E. *Jewish Literature between the Bible and the Mishnah: A Historical and Literary Introduction*. Philadelphia: Fortress, 1981.

Pritchard, James B., ed. *Ancient Near Eastern Texts Relating to the Old Testament [ANET]; The Ancient Near East in Pictures Relating to the Old Testament [ANEP]*. Princeton: Princeton University, rev. ed., 1969. (There is an abridged version of both: *The Ancient Near East: An Anthology of Texts and Pictures [ANETP]*, 2 vols., 1958, 1975.)

Robinson, James M., ed. *The Nag Hammadi Library*. Rev. ed. San Francisco: HarperCollins, 1988

Schneemelcher, Wilhelm, ed. *New Testament Apocrypha*. Ed. Robert McL. Wilson. 2 vols. Nashville: Westminster/John Knox, 1991 (1965).

Sparks, H. F. D., ed. *The Apocryphal Old Testament*. Oxford: Clarendon, 1984.

Stone, Michael E., ed. *Jewish Writings of the Second Temple Period: Apocrypha, Pseudepigrapha, Qumran, Sectarian Writings, Philo, Josephus*. Philadelphia: Fortress, 1984.

Vermes, Geza. *The Dead Sea Scrolls in English*. 3d ed. Sheffield, Eng.: JSOT Press, 1987.

Archaeology

Aharoni, Yohanan. *The Archaeology of the Land of Israel*. Philadelphia: Westminster, 1982.

Ben-Tor, Amnon, ed. *The Archaeology of Ancient Israel*. New Haven: Yale University, 1991.

Kenyon, Kathleen M. *The Bible and Recent Archaeology*. Rev. ed. by P. R. S. Moorey. Atlanta: John Knox, 1987.

Mazar, Amihai. *Archaeology of the Land of the Bible: 10,000–586 B.C.E.* New York: Doubleday, 1990.

Stern, Ephraim, ed. *The New Encyclopedia of Archaeological Excavations in the Holy Land*. New York: Simon and Schuster, 1993.

Stillwell, Richard et al., eds. *The Princeton Encyclopedia of Classical Sites*. Princeton: Princeton University, 1976.

Wilkinson, John. *The Jerusalem Jesus Knew: An Archaeological Guide to the Gospels*. New York: Thomas Nelson, 1983.

Geography

Aharoni, Yohanan. *The Land of the Bible: A Historical Geography*. Rev. ed. Philadelphia: Westminster, 1979.

Aharoni, Yohanan, and Michael Avi-Yonah. *The Macmillan Bible Atlas*. 3d ed. New York: Macmillan, 1992.

Baly, Denis. *The Geography of the Bible*. Rev. ed. New York: Harper and Row, 1974.

May, Herbert G. *Oxford Bible Atlas*. 3rd ed. rev. by John Day, New York: Oxford University, 1984.

Orni, Ephraim, and E. Ephrat. *Geography of Israel*. 4th ed. Jerusalem: Israel Universities, 1980.

Pritchard, James B. *The Harper Atlas of the Bible*. New York: Harper and Row, 1987.

Religion and Society. All of the following are major contributions to the study of Israelite, early Jewish, and early Christian religion, literature, and culture. While the discussion is frequently technical, they will repay serious reading.

Cross, Frank Moore. *Canaanite Myth and Hebrew Epic: Essays in the History of the Religion of Israel*. Cambridge, Mass.: Harvard University, 1973.

Kaufmann, Yehezkel. *The Religion of Israel from Its Beginnings to the Babylonian Exile*. Chicago: University of Chicago, 1960.

Kraemer, Ross Shepard. *Her Share of the Blessings: Women's Religions among Pagans, Jews, and Christians in the Greco-Roman World*. New York: Oxford University, 1992.

Kraus, Hans-Joachim. *Worship in Israel: A Cultic History of the Old Testament*. Richmond, Va.: John Knox, 1966.

Noth, Martin. *A History of Pentateuchal Traditions*. Trans. Bernhard W. Anderson. Englewood Cliffs, N.J.: Prentice-Hall, 1972.

Sandmel, Samuel. *Judaism and Christian Beginnings*. New York: Oxford University, 1978.

Segal, Alan F. *Rebecca's Children: Judaism and Christianity in the Roman World*. Cambridge, Mass.: Harvard University, 1986.

Schiffman, Lawrence H. *From Text to Tradition: A History of Second Temple and Rabbinic Judaism*. Hoboken, N.J.: Ktav, 1991.

Stambaugh, John E., and David L. Balch. *The New Testament in Its Social Environment*. Philadelphia: Westminster, 1986.

de Vaux, Roland. *Ancient Israel: Its Life and Institutions*. New York: McGraw-Hill, 1965.

Weber, Max. *Ancient Judaism*. New York: Free Press, 1952.

Biblical Theology

Botterweck, G. Johannes, and Helmer Ringgren, eds. *Theological Dictionary of the New Testament*. Grand Rapids, Mich.: Eerdmans, 1977–.

Bultmann, Rudolf. *Theology of the New Testament*. New York: Scribner's, 1955.

Conzelmann, Hans. *An Outline of the Theology of the New Testament*. New York: Harper and Row, 1969.

Eichrodt, Walther. *Theology of the Old Testament*. 2 vols. Philadelphia: Westminster, 1961–1967.

Fredricksen, Paula. *From Jesus to Christ: The Origins of New Testament Images of Jesus*. New Haven: Yale University, 1988.

Fuller, Reginald H. *The Foundations of New Testament Christology*. New York: Scribner's, 1965.

Hanson, Paul D. *The People Called: The Growth of Community in the Bible*. San Francisco: Harper and Row, 1986.

Kittel, Gerhard, and Gerhard Friedrich, eds. *Theological Dictionary of the New Testament*. Grand Rapids, Mich.: Eerdmans, 1985.

Levenson, Jon D. *The Hebrew Bible, the Old Testament, and Historical Criticism*. Louisville, Ky.: Westminster/John Knox, 1993.

von Rad, Gerhard. *Old Testament Theology*. 2 vols. New York: Harper and Row, 1962–1965.

Wright, G. Ernest. *God Who Acts: Biblical Theology as Recital*. Chicago, Ill.: Regnery, 1952.

Methodology. A series of useful "Guides to Biblical Scholarship" is published by Fortress Press (Minneapolis). More detailed surveys are found in three volumes on "The Bible and Its Modern Interpreters," published by the Society of Biblical Literature and Scholars Press (Atlanta); they are:

Knight, Douglas A., and Gene M. Tucker, eds. *The Hebrew Bible and Its Modern Interpreters*. 1985.

Kraft, Robert A., and George W. E. Nickelsburg, eds. *Early Judaism and Its Modern Interpreters*. 1986.

Epp, Eldon Jay, and George W. MacRae, eds. *The New Testament and Its Modern Interpreters*. 1989.

Textual Criticism

Aland, Kurt, and Barbara Aland. *The Text of the New Testament: An Introduction to the Critical Editions and to the Theory and Practice of Modern New Testament Textual Criticism*. 2d ed. Grand Rapids, Mich.: Eerdmans, 1989.

Metzger, Bruce M. *The Text of the New Testament: Its Transmission, Corruption, and Restoration*. 3d ed. New York: Oxford University, 1992.

Tov, Emanuel. *Textual Criticism of the Hebrew Bible*. Minneapolis: Fortress, 1992.

History of Interpretation. In addition to articles in *ABD* and *IDB* and *IDPSup* (see next heading), good starting points are:

Baird, William. *History of New Testament Research*, vol. 1: *From Deism to Tübingen*. Minneapolis: Fortress, 1992.

Coggins, R. J., and J. L. Houlden. *A Dictionary of Biblical Interpretation*. Philadelphia: Trinity, 1990.

Greenslade, S. L., et al. *The Cambridge History of the Bible*. 3 vols. Cambridge University, 1963–1970.

Kümmel, Werner Georg. *The New Testament: The History of the Investigation of Its Problems*. Nashville: Abingdon, 1972.

Kugel, James L., and Rowan A. Greer. *Early Biblical Interpretation*. Philadelphia: Westminster, 1986.

Morgan, Robert, and John Barton. *Biblical Interpretation*. New York: Oxford University, 1988.

Neill, Stephen, and N. T. Wright. *The Interpretation of the New Testament, 1861–1986*. 2d ed. New York: Oxford University, 1988.

Orlinsky, Harry M., and Robert G. Bratcher. *A History of Bible Translation and the North American Contribution*. Atlanta: Scholars, 1991.

Reference

Encyclopedic Dictionaries. Of the many Bible dictionaries available, these are some of the better and most recent. All provide extensive bibliography for further reading.

Achtemeier, Paul J., ed. *Harper's Bible Dictionary*. San Francisco: Harper & Row, 1985.

Buttrick, George A., ed. *The Interpreter's Dictionary of the Bible [IDB]*, 4 vols., with *Supplementary Volume [IDBSup]* (ed. K. Crim). Nashville: Abingdon, 1963, 1976.

Freedman, David Noel et al., *The Anchor Bible Dictionary [ABD]*. New York: Doubleday, 1992.

Mills, Watson E., ed. *Mercer Dictionary of the Bible*. Macon, Ga.: Mercer University, 1990.

Myers, Allen C., ed. *Eerdmans Bible Dictionary*. Grand Rapids, Mich.: William B. Eerdman, 1987.

Concise Commentaries.

Anderson, Bernhard W., ed. *The Book of the Bible*. 2 vols. New York: Scribner's, 1989.

Brown, Raymond E., *et al.*, eds. *The New Jerome Biblical Commentary*. Englewood Cliffs, N.J.: Prentice Hall, 1990.

Laymon, Charles M., ed. *The Interpreter's One Volume Commentary on the Bible*. Nashville: Abingdon, 1971.

Mays, James L., ed. *Harper's Bible Commentary*. San Francisco: Harper and Row, 1988.

Newsom, Carol A., and Sharon H. Ringe, eds. *The Women's Bible Commentary*. Louisville: Westminster/John Knox, 1992.

Other Useful Reference Works. These more general encyclopedias have a large number of articles on the Bible and related topics.

Eliade, Mircea et al. eds. *The Encyclopedia of Religion*. New York: Macmillan, 1987.

Roth Cecil, ed. *Encyclopaedia Judaica*. New York: Macmillan, 1972.

Bibliographies

Fitzmyer, Joseph A. *An Introductory Bibliography for the Study of Scripture*. 3d ed. Rome: Pontifical Biblical Institute, 1990.

Harrington, Daniel J. *The New Testament: A Bibliography*. Wilmington, Dela.: Michael Glazier, 1985.

Stuart, Douglas. *Old Testament Exegesis: A Primer for Students and Pastors*. 2d ed. Philadelphia: Westminster, 1984.

Zannoni, Arthur E. *The Old Testament: A Bibliography*. Collegeville, Minn.: Liturgical, 1992.

Index

Hope *(cont.)*
  in Hebrew Bible, 289
  in New Testament, 289
Hoppe, Leslie J., O.F.M., *as contributor*, 397–399
Horeb, **290**
  Elijah at, 183
  identification of, with Sinai, 290
Horne, Thomas Hartwell, 80
Horns
  altars and, 22
Horsley, Richard A., 826
Hosanna, **290**
Hosanna, 290
Hosea (person), 290–292
  life and family of, 290–292
Hosea, The Book of, **290–292**
  content of, 290
  covenant tradition and, 85
  dating of, 290–291
  northern kingdom in, 291
Hospitality, **292–293**
  among early Christians, 293
  among Greeks and Romans, 292
  laws of, 292
  in New Testament, 292–293
  teaching of Jesus and, 292–293
Houlden, J. L., *as contributor*, 132–134
House church
  at Capernaum, 104
Household
  in ancient Israel, 809
Household codes
  and family, 224
Household gods
  stolen by Rachel, 642
House of David
  election and, 110
Houses
  of nomads, 293
  types of, 293–294
Houses, Furniture, Utensils, **293–295**
Howard, J. Keir, *as contributor*, 190–191, 216–217, 509–510
Hugh of St. Cher, 79
  biblical interpretation and, 316
  chapter and verse divisions of scripture, 106
Hugh of St. Victor
  biblical interpretation and, 316
Hughes, Philip Edgcumbe, *as contributor*, 274–277
Hugo of St. Caro
  concordances and, 131
Hulmes, Edward, *as contributor*, 497–499, 638–640
Human limitations
  wisdom literature and, 803
Human person, **295–296**. *See also* Afterlife and Immortality
  corporate identity of, 295
  Essenes' beliefs about, 296
  fate of, after death, 295
  Hellenistic idea of, 295–296
  in New Testament, 296
  nepeš and, 295
  Pharisees' beliefs about, 296
  soul and, 295
  spirit and, 296
Human race
  creation of, 140, 141

in gnosticism, 256
Humor. *See* Irony and Humor
Hurrian language
  Amarna Letters and, 22
Hurrians, 563
Hus, John
  biblical interpretation and, 317
Hyksos
  in Egypt, 180
Hyksos period
  and Joseph story, 50
Hymn of the Pearl
  in Acts of Thomas, 40
Hymn of the Soul
  in Acts of Thomas, 40
Hymns
  music and, 534
  Psalms as, 627
  of Qumran, and apocalyptic literature, 35
Hypermedia
  and computer technology, 130
Hypertext, 130
Hyphasis, 19
Hypostasis of the Archons, 544
Hyssop, **296**

Ibn Ezra, Abraham
  biblical interpretation and, **309**
Idolatry, 261
Idols, Idolatry, 261, **297–298**
  incense and, 301
  meat sacrificed to, in Paul, 298
Idumea
  as Greek form of Edom, 179
Ignatius of Antioch, 32, 122
Ikhnaton. *See* Akhnaton
Illness
  covenant and, 508
  demons and, 509
  offerings after, 508
Illumination of manuscripts
  and Bible illustrations, 299
Illustrated Bibles, **298–300**
Image. *See* Graven Image
Image of God
  creation and, 140
Images
  in Christianity, 262
  in Jewish ritual art, 262
Immanuel (Emmanuel), **300**
  book of Isaiah and, 326
Immortality, 17. *See* Afterlife and Immortality
  Gilgamesh and, 254
Imperial Aramaic. *See* Aramaic, Imperial
Impurity
  red cow and removal of, 643
Inanna, 163
Incarnation, **301**
  of Christ, and Christmas, 112
  depiction of, in art, 58
  Logos and, 463
Incense, **301–302**
Inclusive Language Lectionary, The
  and feminist concerns, 230
Indian Ocean, 44
Indus River, 19
Inerrancy
  authority of the Bible and, 66

Midrash and, 306
  as obstacle to criticism, 319
  virgin birth of Christ and, 790
Infallibility of the Bible
  inerrancy and, 303
Infancy Gospel of Thomas, 39
Infancy narratives, 88
  Luke and, 469
Ingathering
  Autumn festival of, 227–228
Inheritance, **302**
  women and, 808
Injustice
  wisdom literature and, 803
Ink
  and writing, 94
Inner-biblical exegesis
  and books of Chronicles, 114
Inscriptions
  Aram in, 44–45
  Assyria and, 63
  cuneiform, Ebla and, 176
  Old Aramaic, 45
Inspiration
  authority of the Bible and, 66
  Eastern Orthodoxy and, 174
  inerrancy and, 66
  infallibility and, 66
  plenary, 304
  verbal, 304
  word of God and, 818
Inspiration and Inerrancy, **302–304**
Instruction of Amen-em-ope, 12, 625
  wisdom literature and, 802
Interest, Loans and. *See* Loans and Interest
Intermarriage
  book of Esther and, 200
  book of Ezra and, 220
  sexual behavior and, 690
International Children's Bible, New Century Version, 109
International Children's Version (New Testament), 109
International Lesson System, 109
Interpretation, **305–324**. *See also* Hermeneutics
  allegorical, 67, 279
  Alexandrian school and, 279
  anachronistic reading of the Bible and, 319
  biblical theology and, 323
  canon and modern biblical criticism, 320–321
  canonical criticism, 324
  Christian interpretation from the Middle Ages to the Reformation, 315–318
  classical hermeneutics, 305–309
  cosmology and miracle, 320
  dispensational system, 684
  earliest Jewish commentaries, 305–309
  early Christian interpretation, 310–315
  form criticism, 323
  Jewish interpretation, 305–310
  literal vs. figurative, 681
  literary criticism, 323–324
  medieval developments, 309–310
  modern biblical criticism, 318–324
  obstacles to modern criticism, 318–319
  redaction criticism, 323

Malta
Paul's shipwreck at, 9
Mamre, 5
Manasseh, 226, **485**
in Chronicles, 116
Ephraim and, 190
Manasseh, The Prayer of, **485–486**
Manasseh, tribe of, 485
Mandaic
as dialect of Aramaic, 46
Mandean sect
language of, 46
Manetho
as writer of history of Egypt, 180
Manicheism, 256
Manna, 55, 90, 215, **486**
and ark, 55
Manor, Giora, as contributor, 148–149
Manual of Discipline, 159
apoclyptic literature and, 35
Manuscripts of the Bible, **486–490**
computers and collation of, 129
Dead Sea Scrolls and, 159–160
illumination and, 58
and order of biblical books, 99
Manutius, Aldus
italics and, 336
Maps of the biblical world, **490–491**
geographical orientation of, 491
medieval and modern, 491
Mesopotamia, 491
Maranatha, 90, **491**
Marbeck, John
concordances and, 131
Marcion, 82, 279
attitude of, toward Acts, 10
biblical interpretation and, 312
canon of scripture and, 102, 103
Colossians and, 128
Marduk, 50, 77, 268
temple of, in Babylon, 71
Marduk-apal-iddina II, 71, 72
Mare, Walter de la, 109
Mari, 24, 63, 268
archaeology and, 50
Mari Tablets, **491–492**
Mariamne, tower of, 351
Marini, Stephen A., as contributor,
224–225, 701–702
Mark, The Gospel According to,
492–496
author and date of, 493
contents, 492–493
interpretation, 494
Mark's presentation of the gospel,
494–495
readers, 493–494
sources of, 493
Marr, Wilhelm, 32
Marriage, 496, 795, 796. See also
Adultery
in ancient Israel, **496–497**
1 Corinthians and, 136
creation and, 141
endogamy and exogamy, 496–497
in Ephesians, 188–189
Esdras and, 194
family and, 223
imagery of, in Ezekiel, 218
and levirate law, 434
New Testament, 497

sacred, 85
and sexual behavior in the Hebrew
Bible, 690
as symbol, 811
weddings and, 794–795
women and, 808
Marshall, I. Howard, as contributor,
465–467, 741–743
Marston, Charles, 48
Martin, Ralph P., as contributor,
405–406
Martyn, Henry
as Bible translator, 773
Martyrdom of Isaiah, 630
Martyrdom of St. Andrew, 40
Martyrs, 142, 339, 714
Marx and the Bible, **497–499**
approaches to alienation, 497–498
Marx's Jewish and Christian
background, 497
Marx's use of the Bible, 498–499
Marx, Karl. See Marx and the Bible
Mary, Mother of Jesus, **499–500**
literature and, 447
in Muslim and biblical tradition, 640
role of, 636
Mary Magdalene, **499**
Masaccio (painter), 59
Masada, 53, 159
archaeology and, 47
Maskil, 500
Mason, Rex, as contributor, 266–267,
484–485, 826–828
Masonry, 140
Masorah, **500–501**
and biblical transmission, 306
Masoretes, 79
Masorah and, 500
Masoretic Text, 407–408, 501
Atbash in, 64–65
Mastemah, 679
Masturbation, 565
Maternal imagery
mercy of God and, 512
Mather, Cotton
and children's Bibles, 108
Matthew, The Gospel According to,
502–506
author, date, place, 502–503
readers, 503
sources, 503
story of Jesus, 503–504
story of the disciples, 505–506
story of the opponents, 504–505
structure, 502
Matthiae, Paolo
as excavator of Ebla, 176
Maurer, Ulrich W., as contributor,
735–736
Mazar, Benjamin, 47
Mazarin Bible, 611
McAfee, Gene, as contributor, 205–206,
690–692
McCarter, P. Kyle, Jr., as contributor,
98, 132, 284–285
McGovern, Patrick E., as contributor,
366–367
McGuffey's Readers, 108–109
McKane, W., as contributor, 409–413
McKenzie, Steven L., as contributor,
145, 268, 343

McNutt, Paula M., as contributor, 407
Meal, sacred
covenant and, 138
Meals, 506–507
Measures. See Weights and Measures
Meat offered to idols
1 Corinthians and, 136
Medes, 46, 64, 507
Medical ethics
the Bible and, 509
Medicine, 507–509
Medicine and the Bible, **509–510**
Mediterranean Sea, 11
Medium. See Witch
Meek, **510**
Megiddo, 56, 251, **511**
Amarna Letters and, 22
archaeology and, 47, 48, 49, 126
high place at, 284
ivory and clothing and, 127
Solomonic palaces at, 52
Megillot, **511**
Ecclesiastes and, 177
Meier, Samuel A., as contributor, 27–28,
208–209, 300, 740–741
Meissner, William W., S.J., as con-
tributor, 232–236, 402–405
Melchizedek, 5, 276, **511–512**
depiction of, in art, 57
Enoch and, 185
tithes and, 745
Melito of Sardis
biblical interpretation and, 311
Melqart, 593
Melville, Herman, 606
biblical typology and, 456–457
Mene, Mene, Tekel, and Parsin, **512**
Menelaus
high priesthood and, 475
Menes
founder of first dynasty of Egypt, 180
Menorah, 512
Menstruation
cult and, 807
purity and, 809–810
Mercy
vengeance and, 788
Mercy of God, **512–513**
remnant and, 646
Merneptah inscription, 51
and name of Israel, 132, 181, 329, 330,
331
Merodach-baladan, 64, 71
Mesha, inscription of
and Israel, 330
Mesha, king of Moab, 52, 73, 238
Mesopotamia, 44, 513
afterlife and, 15
ancestors and, 26
Aramaic inscriptions in, 45
archaeology and, 46
Euphrates River and, 206
Garden of Eden and, 178
laws of, 797
literature, 50
Messengers
and ancient letter writing, 432
Messiah, 31, 84, 86, 87, **513–514**
apocalyptic literature and, 36
book of Isaiah and, 326
crucifixion and, 142

THE NEW OXFORD

BIBLE MAPS

Prepared by Oxford Cartographers
and based on the Oxford Bible Atlas.

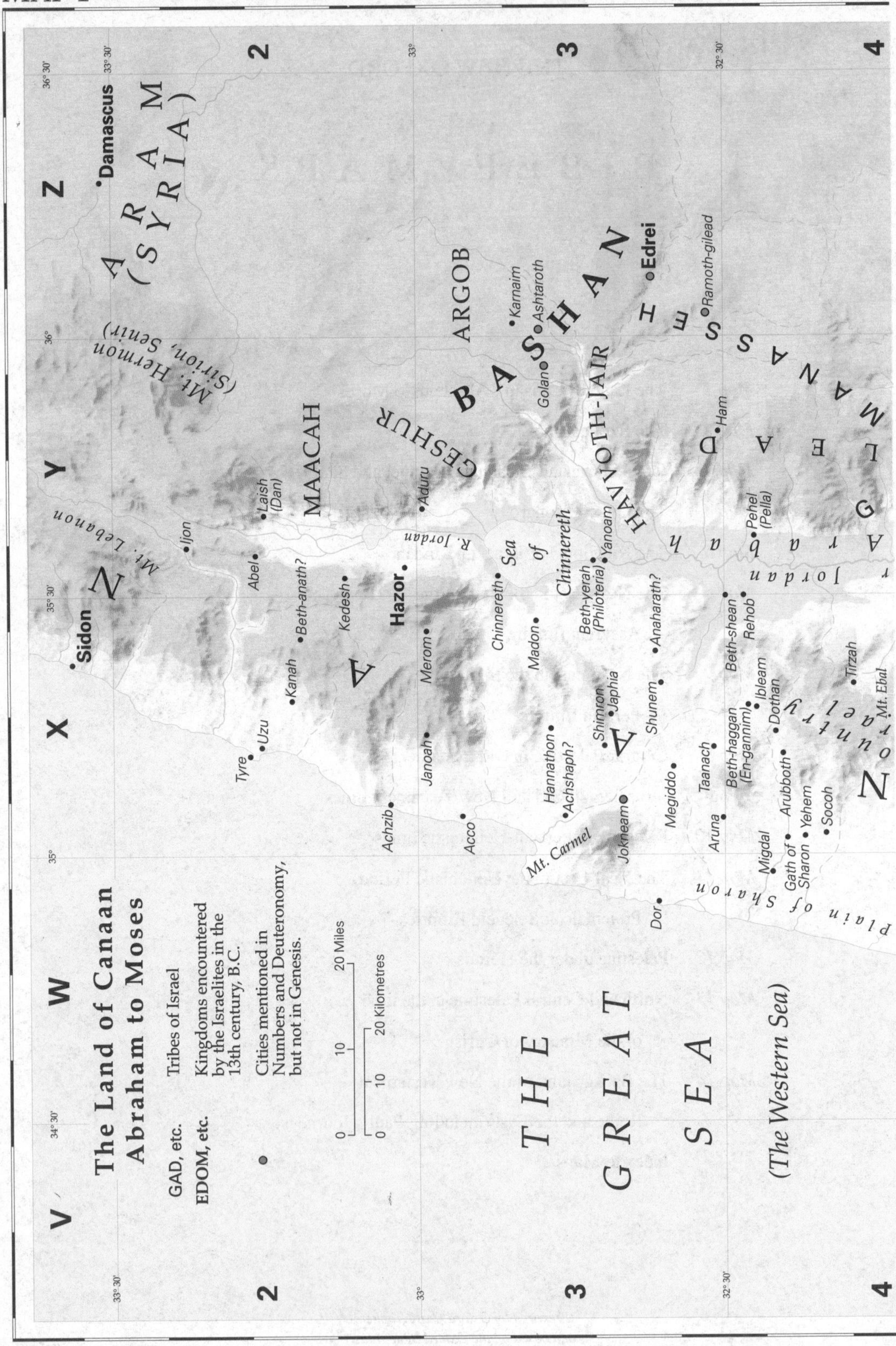

MAP 1

The Land of Canaan Abraham to Moses

GAD, etc.   Tribes of Israel

EDOM, etc.   Kingdoms encountered by the Israelites in the 13th century, B.C.

● Cities mentioned in Numbers and Deuteronomy, but not in Genesis.

20 Miles

20 Kilometres

THE GREAT SEA

(The Western Sea)

ARAM (SYRIA)

Damascus

Mt. Hermon (Sirion, Senir)

Mt. Lebanon

Sidon

Tyre

Uzu

Achzib

Acco

Mt. Carmel

Dor

Plain of Sharon

Gath of Sharon

Migdal

Aruna

Jokneam

Achshaph?

Hannathon

Janoah

Shimron

Japhia

Shunem

Taanach

Megiddo

Yehem

Socoh

Arubboth

Dothan

Ibleam

Beth-haggan (En-gannim)

Rehob

Beth-shean

Tirzah

Mt. Ebal

Anaharath?

Yanoam

Beth-yerah (Philoteria)

Madon

Chinnereth

Sea of Chinnereth

R. Jordan

Merom

Hazor

Kedesh

Beth-anath?

Kanah

Abel

Ijon

Laish (Dan)

Aduru

MAACAH

GESHUR

ARGOB

BASHAN

Karnaim

Ashtaroth

Golan

Edrei

Ramoth-gilead

Ham

Pehel (Pella)

HAVVOTH-JAIR

GILEAD

MANASSEH

Jordan

Arabah

Israel

N

N

0 10 20

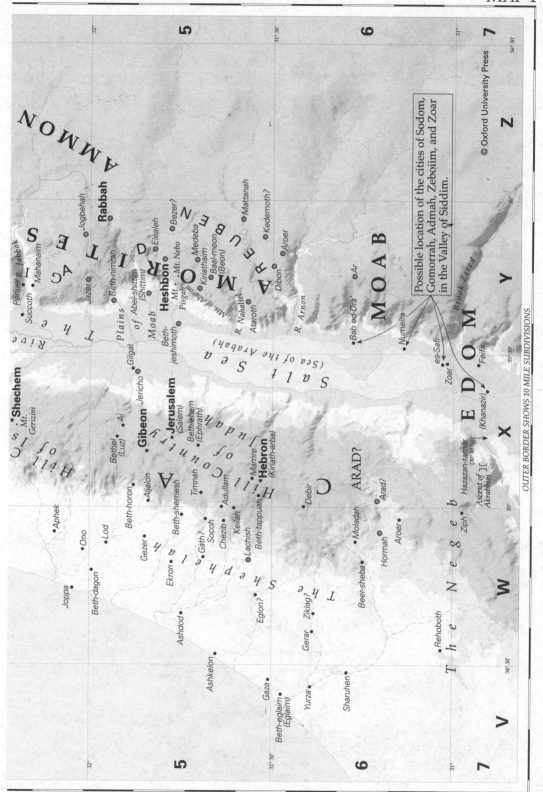

MAP 1

© Oxford University Press

Possible location of the cities of Sodom, Gomorrah, Admah, Zeboiim, and Zoar in the Valley of Siddim.

OUTER BORDER SHOWS 10 MILE SUBDIVISIONS

MAP 2

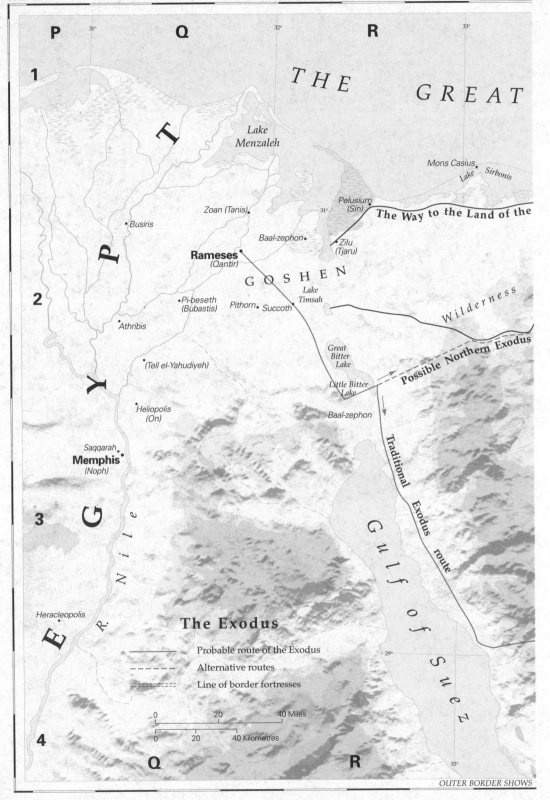

P   31°   Q   32°   R   33°

1

THE   GREAT

T

Lake
Menzaleh

Mons Casius
Lake   Sirbonis

P

Pelusium   31°
(Sin)   *The Way to the Land of the*

Zoan (Tanis)·

·Busiris   Baal-zephon·   ·Zilu
(Tjaru)

Rameses
(Qantir)   G O S H E N

P   Lake
Timsah   W i l d e r n e s s

2   ·Pi-beseth   Pithom·   ·Succoth
(Bubastis)

Possible Northern Exodus
·Athribis

Great
·(Tell el-Yahudiyeh)   Bitter
Lake

Y

Little Bitter
Lake

·Heliopolis
(On)   Baal-zephon

Saqqarah·
Memphis
(Noph)

G   *Traditional*

3

R
.
N
i
l
e

Exodus

G
u
l
f   *route*

·Heracleopolis   **The Exodus**   o
f

E   _____ Probable route of the Exodus   S   29°
u
- - - - - - Alternative routes   e
z
░░░░░░░░ Line of border fortresses

0   20   40 Miles

0   20   40 Kilometres

4
Q   R   33°

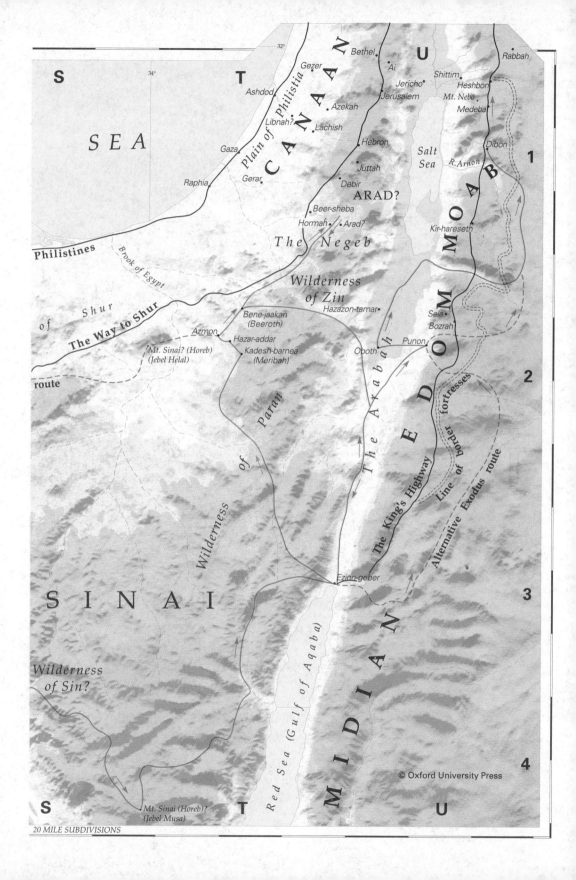

S T U

SEA

S

32°

34°

Bethel

Gezer

Ai

Rabbah

Ashdod

Jericho

Shittim

Heshbon

Jerusalem

Mt. Nebo

Azekah

Medeba

Libnah?

Lachish

Gaza

Hebron

Salt
Sea

Dibon

Raphia

Gerar

Juttah

R. Arnon

Debir

ARAD?

Beer-sheba

Kir-hareseth

Hormah

Arad?

The Negeb

Wilderness
of Zin

Brook of Egypt

Hazazon-tamar

Sela

Philistines

Bene-jaakan
(Beeroth)

Bozrah

of

Shur

The Way to Shur

Azmon

Hazar-addar

Oboth

Punon

Mt. Sinai? (Horeb)
(Jebel Helal)

Kadesh-barnea
(Meribah)

route

Paran

Line of border fortresses

Alternative Exodus route

of

Wilderness

SINAI

Ezion-geber

Wilderness
of Sin?

Mt. Sinai (Horeb)?
(Jebel Musa)

S T U

© Oxford University Press

20 MILE SUBDIVISIONS

C A N A A N

P L A I N   O F   P H I L I S T I A

M O A B

E D O M

M I D I A N

The King's Highway

The Arabah

Red Sea (Gulf of Aqaba)

1

2

3

4

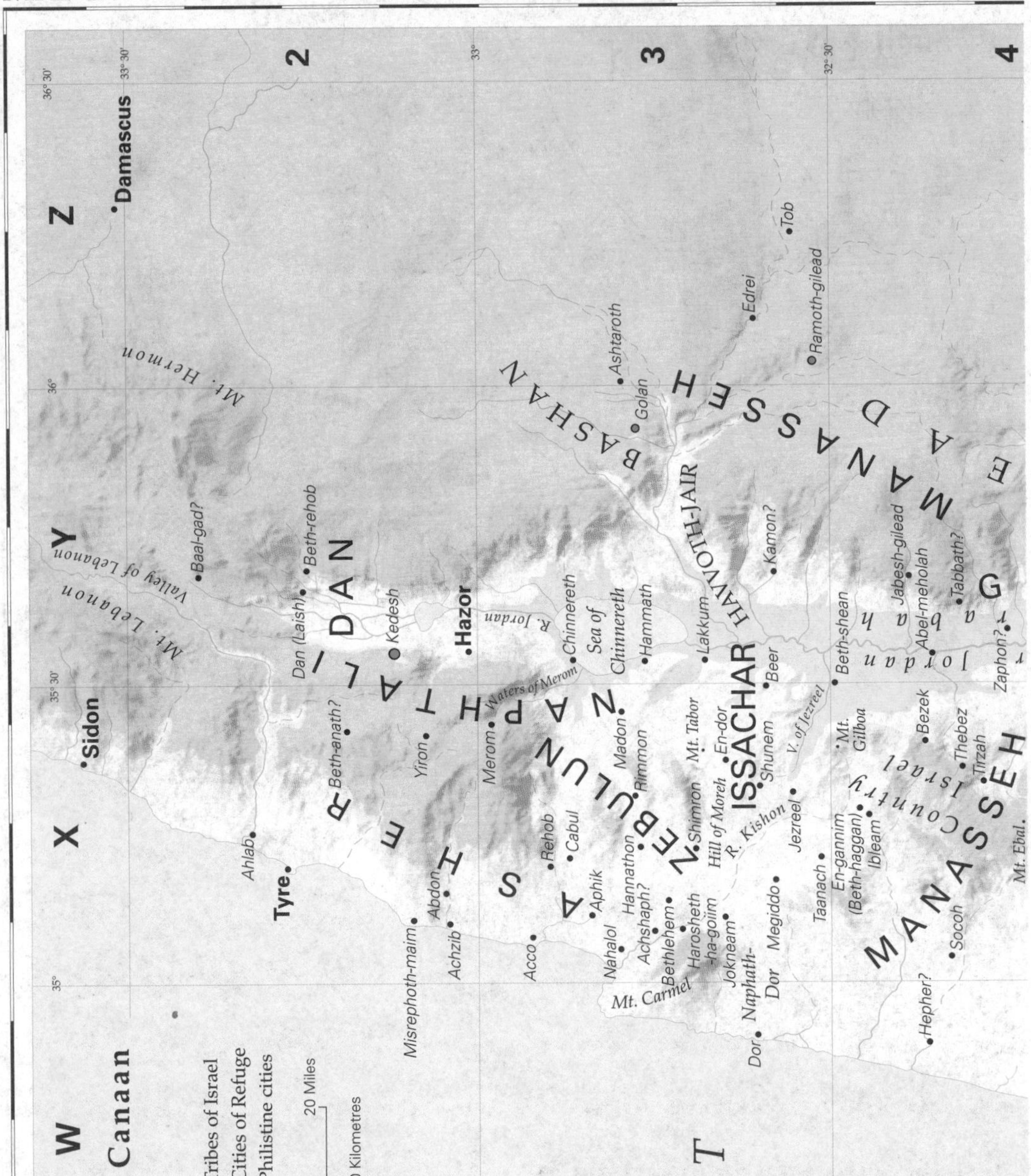

MAP 3

Israel in Canaan

ASHER, etc. Tribes of Israel
● Cities of Refuge
■ Philistine cities

20 Miles

20 Kilometres

10

10

0

THE GREAT SEA

Damascus

Sidon

Tyre

Mt. Lebanon
Valley of Lebanon
Mt. Hermon

Baal-gad?

Beth-rehob

Dan (Laish)
Kedesh
Hazor

DAN

NAPHTALI

ASHER

Ahlab
Beth-anath?
Yiron
Abdon
Achzib
Misrephoth-maim

Merom
Waters of Merom

Madon
Rimmon
Hannathon
Achshaph?
Cabul
Rehob
Aphik
Acco
Nahalol
Bethlehem
Haroshethha-goiim
Jokneam
Dor
Naphath-
Dor

Mt. Carmel

ZEBULUN

Shimron
Hill of Moreh
Mt. Tabor
En-dor
Shunem

Chinnereth
Sea of
Chinnereth
Hammath

R. Jordan

BASHAN

Ashtaroth
Golan
Edrei
Tob
Ramoth-gilead

HAVVOTH-JAIR

MANASSEH

GAD

ISSACHAR

Lakkum
Karnon?
Beer
Beth-shean

V. of Jezreel
Jezreel
R. Kishon
Taanach
En-gannim
(Beth-haggan)
Ibleam
Socoh
Hepher?

MANASSEH

Mt.
Gilboa
Bezek
Thebez
Tirzah

Mt. Ebal

Country
of Israel

Jabesh-gilead
Abel-meholah
Jabbath?
Zaphon?

Jordan

MAP 3

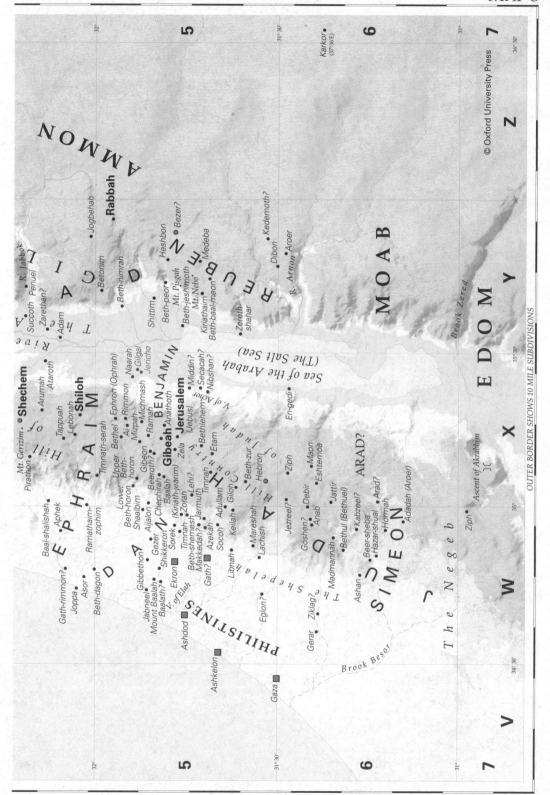

OUTER BORDER SHOWS 10 MILE SUBDIVISIONS

AMMON

GILEAD

River Jordan

The Arabah

Succoth

Penuel

R. Jabbok

Zarethan?

Adam

Betonim

Beth-nimrah

Jogbehah

Rabbah

Shechem

Mt. Gerizim

Pirathon

Baal-shalishah

Aphek

Ramathaim-zophim

Asor

Beth-dagon

Gath-rimmon?

Joppa

Jabneel

Mount Baalah

Baalath?

Gibbethon

Shikkeron?

Ekron

V. of Elah

Ashdod

Ashkelon

Gaza

PHILISTINES

Gath?

Beth-shemesh

Makkedah?

Azekah

Socoh

Libnah

Eglon?

Gerar

Ziklag?

Brook Besor

The Shephelah

The Negeb

Ziph

Ascent of Akrabbim

Adadah (Aroer)

Hormah

Arad?

Hazar-shual

Beer-sheba

Kabzeel?

Bethul (Bethuel)

Ashan

Madmannah

Goshen?

Debir

Anab

Jattir

Eshtemoa

Maon

Jezreel?

Ziph

Hebron

ARAD?

SIMEON

JUDAH

Hill Country of Judah

En-gedi

Beth-zur

Giloh

Adullam

Keilah

Jarmuth

Mareshah

Lachish

Zorah

Sorek

(Kiriath-jearim)

Baalah

Timnah

Ajalon

Shaalbim

Lower Beth-horon

Gezer

Beeroth

Upper Beth-horon

Chephirah?

Gibeon

Lehi?

Timnah

Zela

Gibeah

Jerusalem

(Jebus)

Ramah

Michmash

Mizpah

Anathoth

Bethlehem

Etam

BENJAMIN

Ai

Bethel

Ephron (Ophrah)

Naarah

Rimmon

Gilgal

Jericho

Timnath-serah

EPHRAIM

Hill of

Tappuah

Lebonah

Shiloh

Arumah

Ataroth

Zarethan?

Valley of Achor

Middin?

Secacah?

Nibshan?

Sea of the Arabah

(The Salt Sea)

REUBEN

Shittim

Beth-peor

Mt. Pisgah

Beth-jeshimoth

Mt. Nebo

Kiriathaim

Beth-baal-meon

Medeba

Zereth-shahar

Heshbon

Bezer?

Dibon

Aroer

R. Arnon

Kedemoth?

MOAB

Brook Zered

EDOM

Karkor
(37°36'E)

MAP 4

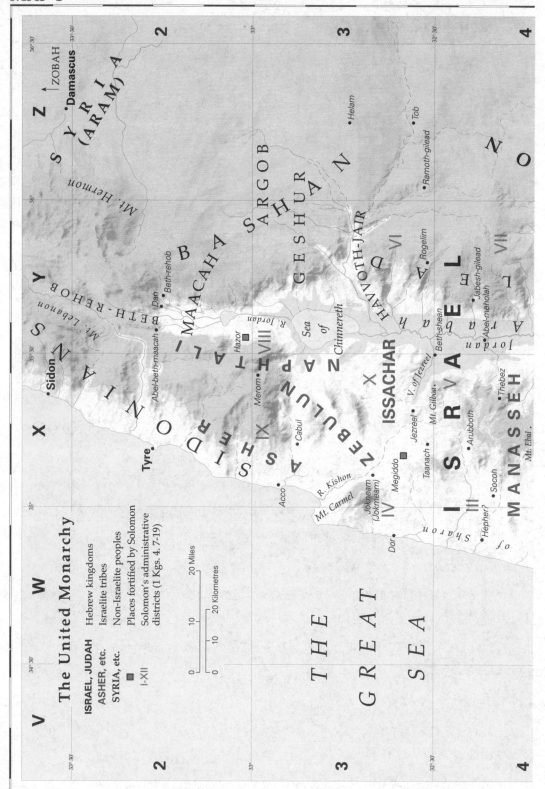

The United Monarchy

ISRAEL, JUDAH   Hebrew kingdoms
ASHER, etc.   Israelite tribes
SYRIA, etc.   Non-Israelite peoples

■ Places fortified by Solomon

I–XII   Solomon's administrative
districts (1 Kgs. 4. 7-19)

0   10   20 Miles
0   10   20 Kilometres

ZOBAH
•Damascus
S Y R I A (ARAM)
Mt. Hermon
•Helam
•Tob
•Ramoth-gilead
SARGOB
MAACAH
GESHUR
BASHAN
HAVVOTH-JAIR
Beth-rehob•
Dan•
Abel-beth-maacah•
Hazor ◻ VIII
R. Jordan
Sea of Chinnereth
VI
•Rogelim
SIDONIANS
•Sidon
Mt. Lebanon
BETH-REHOB
NAPHTALI
Merom•
ASHER IX
Cabul•
ZEBULUN
ISSACHAR
V. of Jezreel
Beth-shean
Jabesh-gilead•
•Abel-meholah
GILEAD VII
I S R A E L
Tyre•
Acco•
R. Kishon
Mt. Carmel
Jokneam (Jokmeam)
Megiddo ◻ IV
Taanach•
Jezreel•
Mt. Gilboa•
•Arubboth
•Thebez
MANASSEH
Dor•
Hepher? •
•Socoh
Mt. Ebal •
III
of Sharon
T H E
G R E A T
S E A
AMMON
Jordan
Arabah

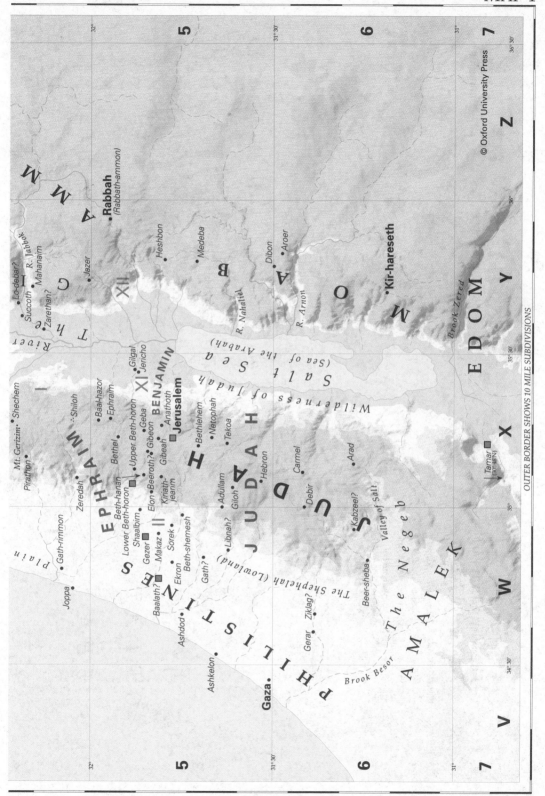

MAP 4

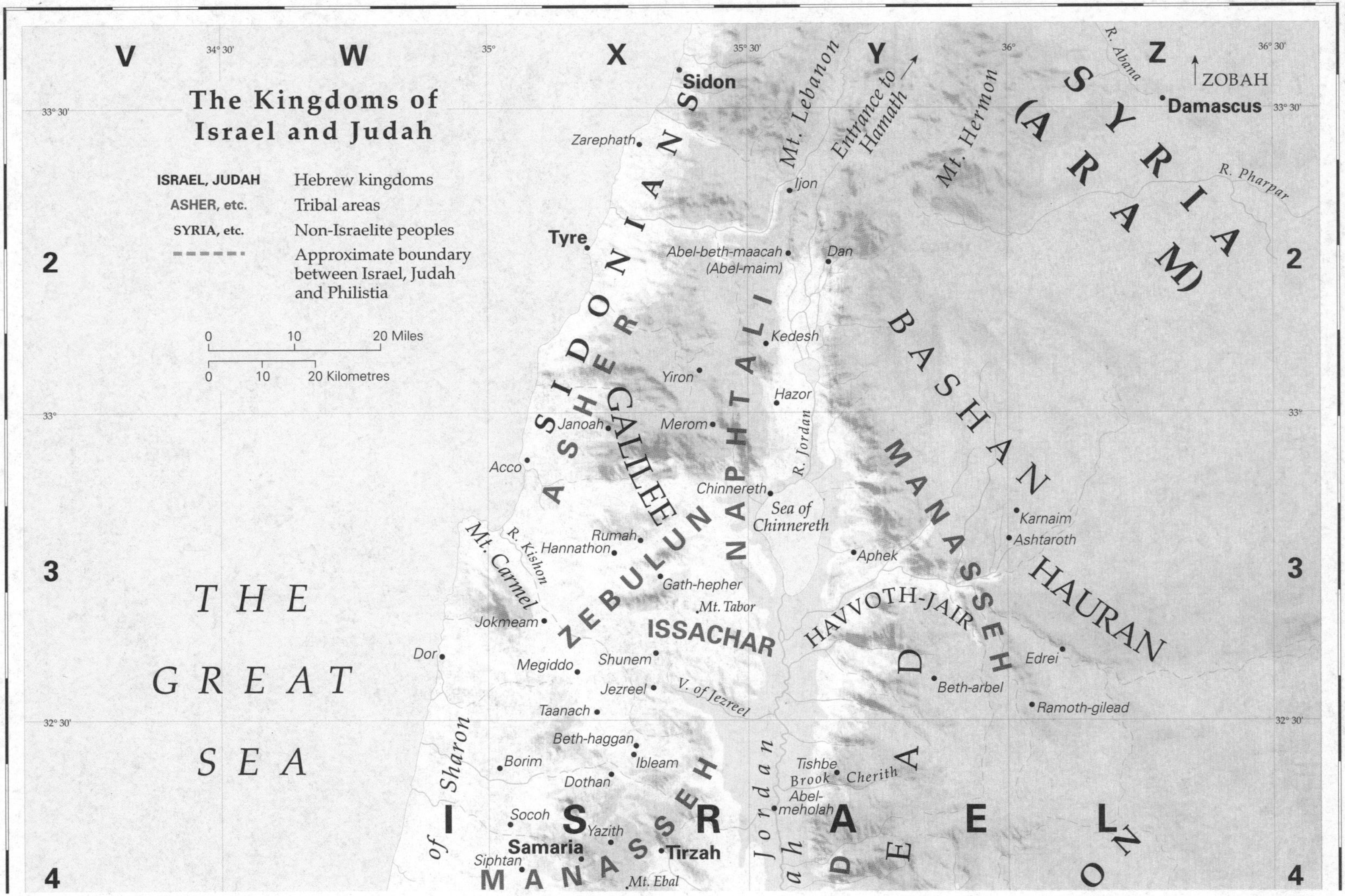

MAP 5

The Kingdoms of Israel and Judah

ISRAEL, JUDAH Hebrew kingdoms

ASHER, etc. Tribal areas

SYRIA, etc. Non-Israelite peoples

- - - - - Approximate boundary between Israel, Judah and Philistia

20 Miles

20 Kilometres

10

10

0

0

ZOBAH

Damascus

S Y R I A

Z

R. Pharpar

R. Abana

(A R A M)

Mt. Hermon

Entrance to Hamath

Mt. Lebanon

Sidon

S I D O N I A N S

X

V

W

Zarephath

Tyre

Ijon

Dan

Abel-beth-maacah (Abel-maim)

Kedesh

Yiron

Hazor

N A P H T A L I

BASHAN

HAURAN

Karnaim

Ashtaroth

Edrei

Beth-arbel

Ramoth-gilead

MANASSEH

HAVVOTH-JAIR

Aphek

R. Jordan

Sea of Chinnereth

Chinnereth

Merom

Janoah

Rumah

R. Hannathon

GALILEE

Z E B U L U N

A S H E R

Gath-hepher

Mt. Tabor

ISSACHAR

V. of Jezreel

Jezreel

Shunem

Acco

R. Kishon

Mt. Carmel

Jokmeam

Megiddo

Taanach

Beth-haggan

Dothan

Borim

Ibleam

Socoh

Yazith

Siphtan

Samaria

Tirzah

Mt. Ebal

M A N A S S E H

of Sharon

D A N

Tishbe

Brook Cherith

Abel-meholah

G A D

J o r d a n

Jabbah

I S R A E L

Z O

Dor

T H E

G R E A T

S E A

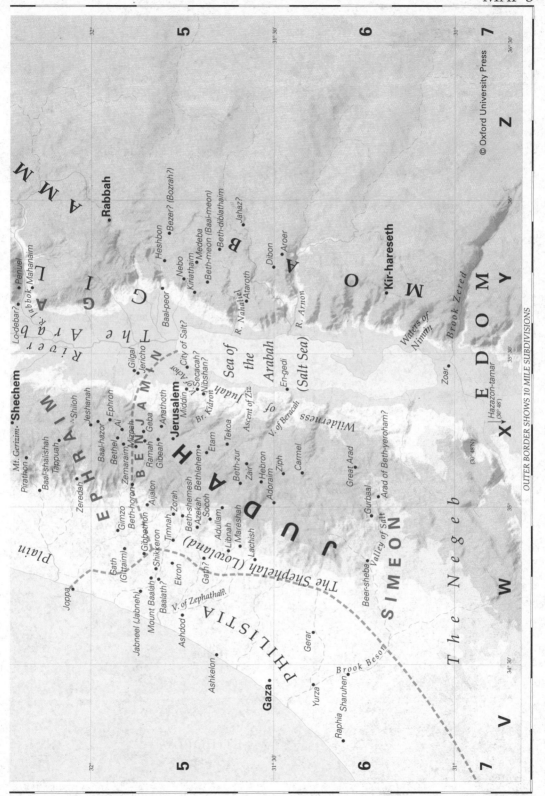

MAP 5

© Oxford University Press

OUTER BORDER SHOWS 10 MILE SUBDIVISIONS

Rabbah

Shechem
Mt. Gerizim

AMMON

GILEAD

The Arabah

River Jabbok

Lo-debar?
Panuel
Mahanaim

Heshbon
Bezer? (Bozrah?)
Nebo
Kiriathaim
Medeba
Beth-meon (Baal-meon)
Beth-diblathaim
Baal-peor
R. Nahaliel
Ataroth
Dibon
Aroer
Jahaz?
R. Arnon

MOAB

Kir-hareseth

Waters of Nimrim

Brook Zered

EDOM

Zoar
Hazazon-tamar
(30° 48'N)
X

EPHRAIM
Pirathon
Baal-shalishah
Tappuah
Shiloh
Zeredah
Baal-hazor
Bethel
Ai
Ephron
Jeshanah
Gilgal
Jericho
Ophrah
City of Salt?
Secacah?
Nibshan?
Middin?
Anathoth
Mizpah
Ramah
Gibeah
Geba

BENJAMIN

Jerusalem
Br. Kidron
Ascent of Ziz
V. of Beracah
Wilderness of Judah

Sea of the Arabah
(Salt Sea)

En-gedi

Plain

Joppa
Jabneel (Jabneh)
Mount Baalah
Balath?
Ashdod
V. of Zephathah?
Gath (Gittaim)
Gibbethon
Shikkeron
Ekron
Gath?
Gimzo
Beth-horon
Aijalon
Timnah
Zorah
Beth-shemesh
Azekah
Socoh
Adullam
Libnah
Mareshah
Lachish

JUDAH

Etam
Bethlehem
Tekoa
Beth-zur
Zair
Hebron
Adoraim
Ziph
Carmel

The Shephelah (Lowland)

Great Arad

Gurbaal
Valley of Salt
Arad of Beth-yeroham?
Arad of Bethyeroham?

SIMEON

Beer-sheba

The Negeb

Ashkelon

Gaza

PHILISTIA

Gerar
Brook Besor
Yurza
Raphia
Sharuhen

32°

31° 30'

31°

36° 30'

36°

35° 30'

35°

34° 30'

5
6
7
Z
Y
X
W
V

MAP 6

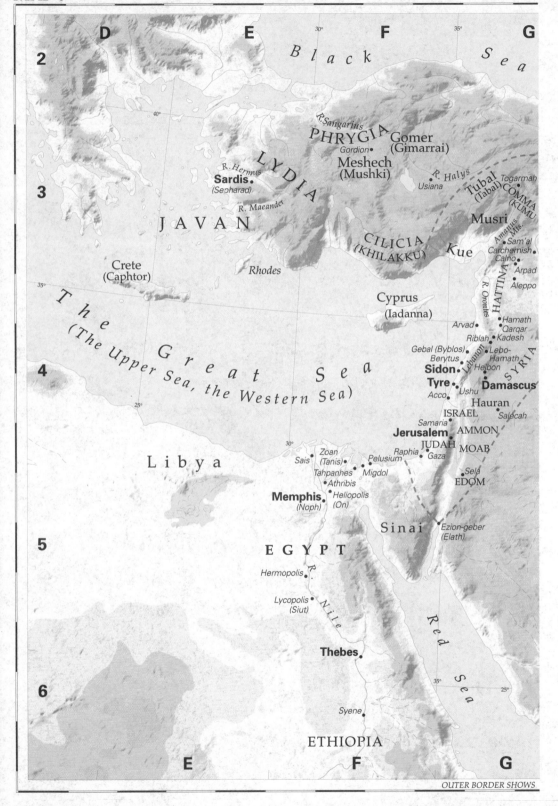

Black Sea

D E F G

2

R. Sangarius

PHRYGIA Gomer
Gordion• (Gimarrai)
Meshech
(Mushki)
R. Halys

LYDIA

Sardis• Usiana• Tubal Togarmah
(Sepharad) (Tabal) COMMA
(KUMU)

JAVAN Musri

R. Maeander Amanus
Mts.
Sam'al
CILICIA Carchemish•
(KHILAKKU) Kue Calno•
Arpad•
Rhodes Aleppo•

Crete
(Caphtor)

Cyprus
(Iadanna) Hamath
Arvad• Qarqar•
Riblah• Kadesh
Gebal (Byblos)• Lebo-
Berytus• Hamath
Sidon• Helbon•

Tyre• Damascus•
Acco• Ushu

Hauran
Salecah•
ISRAEL
Samaria• AMMON
Jerusalem•
JUDAH MOAB
Raphia•
Zoan Pelusium Gaza
(Tanis)• Sela•
Sais• EDOM
Tahpanhes• Migdol
Athribis•
Memphis• Heliopolis Sinai Ezion-geber
(Noph) (On) (Elath)

EGYPT

Hermopolis•
R.
Lycopolis•
(Siut) Nile

Thebes•

Syene•

ETHIOPIA

E F G

3 4 5 6

The Great Sea
(The Upper Sea, the Western Sea)

Libya

Red Sea

HATTINA

R. Orontes

SYRIA

Lebanon

R. Hermus

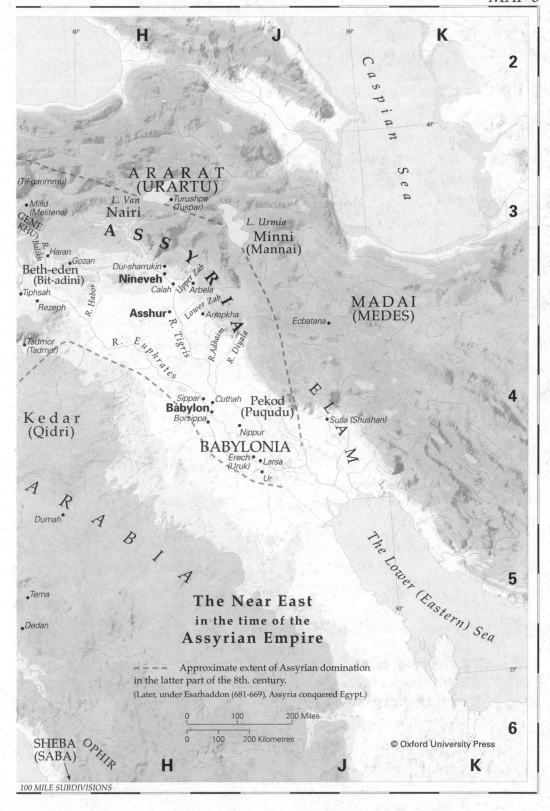

MAP 6

H   J   50°   K   2

40°   40°

C
a
s
p
i
a
n

S
e
a

(Til-garimmu)

A R A R A T
(URARTU)

•Milid
(Melitene)   L. Van   •Turushpa
(Tuspar)   3

GENE   Nairi
KHU)   L. Urmia

A   Minni
(Mannai)

R. Balikh   S   •Haran   Gozan   S   Dur-sharrukin•   Y
Beth-eden   Nineveh   R   MADAI
(Bit-adini)   •Tiphsah   Calah   Upper Zab   Arbela   I   (MEDES)
•Rezeph   Asshur•   Lower Zab   •Arrapkha   A   •Ecbatana

R. Habor   R. Tigris   R.Adhaim   R. Diyala

•Tadmor
(Tadmar)   R.   E u p h r a t e s   E   4

K e d a r   Sippar   •Cuthah   Pekod   L   •Susa (Shushan)
(Qidri)   •Babylon   (Puqudu)   A
Borsippa•   •Nippur   M

BABYLONIA
A   Erech   •Larsa
(Uruk)•
•Ur

R
A
B   •Dumah
I
A   T
h
e

L
o
w
e
r

•Tema   (E
a
s
t
e
r
n
)   •Dedan

S
e
a

The Near East
in the time of the
Assyrian Empire

50°   5

- - - Approximate extent of Assyrian domination
in the latter part of the 8th. century.

(Later, under Esarhaddon (681-669), Assyria conquered Egypt.)

25°

0   100   200 Miles

0   100   200 Kilometres

© Oxford University Press   6

SHEBA   OPHIR
(SABA)   H   J   K

100 MILE SUBDIVISIONS

MAP 7

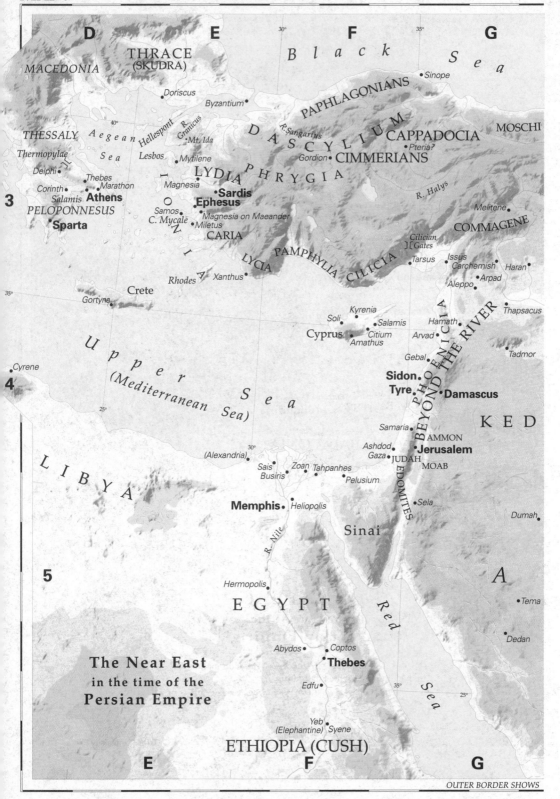

D E 30° F 35° G

Black   Sea

MACEDONIA
THRACE
(SKUDRA)

• Sinope

• Doriscus

PAPHLAGONIANS

Byzantium •

DASCYLIUM

R. Sangarius

CAPPADOCIA

MOSCHI

THESSALY

Aegean   Hellespont R. Granicus

• Mt. Ida

PHRYGIA

Gordion •

CIMMERIANS

• Pteria?

Thermopylae

Sea

Lesbos   Mytilene •

LYDIA

R. Halys

Delphi •

Magnesia

Melitene •

Thebes

Corinth •   Marathon

Sardis

COMMAGENE

Salamis   Athens

Ephesus

3

PELOPONNESUS

Samos

Magnesia on Maeander

Cilician

Sparta

C. Mycale   • Miletus

CARIA

] Gates [

Issus

Aleppo •

LYCIA

PAMPHYLIA

CILICIA

Tarsus •

Carchemish •

Haran •

Rhodes   Xanthus •

Arpad •

35°

Crete

Thapsacus •

Gortyna •

Kyrenia

Hamath •

Soli •

Salamis •

Arvad •

Cyprus

Citium

Tadmor •

Upper

Amathus •

Gebal •

4

• Cyrene

(Mediterranean   Sea)   *Sea*

Sidon •

Tyre •

Damascus •

K E D

25°

Samaria •

AMMON

LIBYA

30°

Ashdod •

Jerusalem

(Alexandria) •

Gaza •

JUDAH

MOAB

Sais •

Zoan   Tahpanhes •

Busiris •

Pelusium •

EDOMITES

Dumah •

Memphis   • Heliopolis

Sela •

Sinai

5

Hermopolis •

Red

A

EGYPT

• Tema

R. Nile

Dedan •

Abydos •   Coptos •

The Near East

Thebes

in the time of the

Edfu •

35°

25°

Persian Empire

Sea

Yeb
(Elephantine) •   Syene

ETHIOPIA (CUSH)

E F G

MAP 7

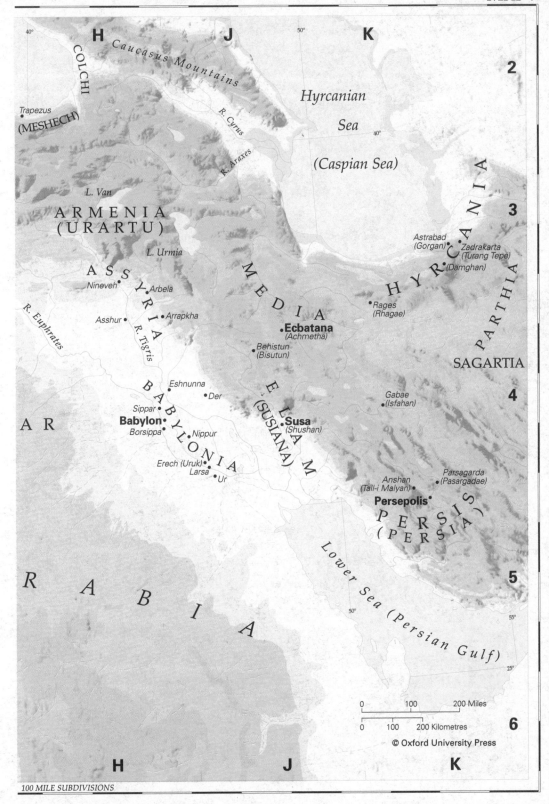

COLCHI

H

Caucasus Mountains

J

K

2

Hyrcanian

Trapezus
(MESHECH)

R. Cyrus

Sea

(Caspian Sea)

R. Araxes

L. Van

ARMENIA
(URARTU)

H
Y
R
C
A
N
I
A

3

L. Urmia

Astrabad
(Gorgan)

Zadrakarta
(Turang Tepe)

ASSYRIA

Nineveh

Arbela

(Damghan)

M
E
D
I
A

Rages
(Rhagae)

P
A
R
T
H
I
A

Asshur

Arrapkha

Ecbatana
(Achmetha)

SAGARTIA

Behistun
(Bisutun)

4

R. Euphrates

R. Tigris

BABYLONIA

Eshnunna

Der

Gabae
(Isfahan)

Sippar

E
L
A
M

A R

Babylon

Borsippa

Nippur

(SUSIANA)

Susa
(Shushan)

Erech (Uruk)

Larsa
Ur

Parsagarda
(Pasargadae)

Anshan
(Tall-i Malyan)

R

Persepolis

P E R S I S

A B I A

(P E R S I A)

5

Lower Sea (Persian Gulf)

0	100	200 Miles

0	100	200 Kilometres

© Oxford University Press

6

H

J

K

100 MILE SUBDIVISIONS

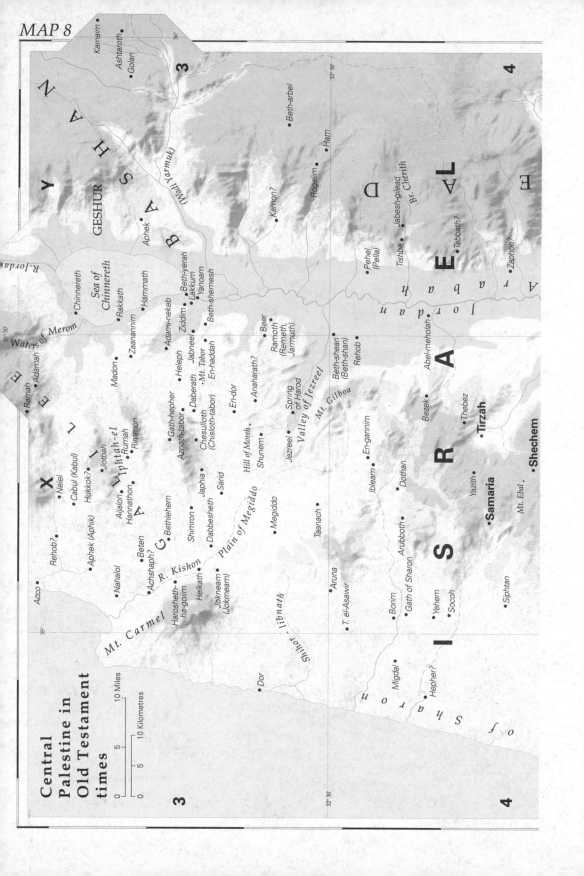

MAP 8

Central
Palestine in
Old Testament
times

10 Miles

10 Kilometres

0   5   10

0   5

3

3

4

BASHAN

GESHUR

(Wadi Yarmuk)

Karnaim

Ashtaroth

Golan

36°

32° 30'

Beth-arbel

Ham

Rogelim

Kamon?

GILEAD

Jabesh-gilead

Tishbe

Br. Cherith

Tabbah?

Pehel
(Pella)

Zaphon?

EAST

J o r d a n

A r a b a h

35° 30'

Waters of Merom

R. Jordan

Ramah

Adamah?

Chinnereth

Sea of
Chinnereth

Rakkath

Hammath

Aphek

Beth-yerah

Adami-nekeb

Ziddim

Lakkum

Yanoam

Beth-shemesh

Jabneel

Zaanannim

Heleph

En-haddah

Beer

Ramoth
(Remeth,
Jarmuth)

NAPHTALI

Madon

Rumah

Rimmon

Gath-hepher

Aznoth-tabor

Daberath

Mt. Tabor

Chesulloth
(Chisloth-tabor)

En-dor

Anaharath?

Rehob

Beth-shean
(Beth-shan)

Abel-meholah

Rehob?

Neiel

Cabul (Kabul)

Hukkok?

Jotbah

ZEBULUN

Ajalon

Hannathon

Beten

Iphtah-el

Bethlehem

Shimron

Japhia

Dabbesheth

Sand

Hill of Moreh

Shunem

Jezreel

Spring
of Harod

Valley of Jezreel

Mt. Gilboa

Bezek

Thebez

Tirzah

Aphek (Aphik)

Achshaph?

R. Kishon

Helkath

Jokneam
(Jokmeam)

Plain of Megiddo

Megiddo

Taanach

En-gannim

Ibleam

Dothan

Yazith

Mt. Ebal

Samaria

Shechem

Acco

Nahalol

Mt. Carmel

Harosheth-
ha-goiim

Shihor-libnath

Dor

Aruna

T. el-Asawir

Borim

Gath of Sharon

Arubboth

Yehem

Socoh

Siphtan

ISRAEL

P l a i n   o f   S h a r o n

Migdal

Hepher?

35°

35° 30'

32° 30'

MAP 8

AMMON

Rabbah

Jogbehah

GILEAD

(Araq el-Emir)

Jazer

Penuel (Peniel)
Lo-debar?
Mahanaim
Zarethan? (Zeredah, Zererah)
Gilead
Betonim
Succoth
R. Jabbok

Adam

(Wadi Farah)

Atoroth
Janoah

Mt. Gerizim
Pirathon
Baal-shalishah

Hill Country

of

Ephraim

Arumah
En-tappuah
Tappuah
Lebonah
Shiloh
Gilgal?
Jeshanah
Baal-hazor

Heshbon
Elealeh
Beth-peor (Baal-peor)
Bezer? (Bozrah?)
Beth-diblathaim (Almon-diblathaim?)
Mt. Nebo
Nebo
Bamoth-baal
Medeba
Beth-meon (Baal-meon, Beon)
Siбmah
Kiriathaim
Beth-meon (Baal-meon, Beth-baal-meon, Beon)
Mattanah
Jahaz?
Kedemoth?
Dibon
Kerioth
Ataroth

MOAB

© Oxford University Press

Mts. of Abarim
Mt. Pisgah
Beth-jeshimoth
R. Nahaliel
Zereth-shahar

R. Arnon

Beth-nimrah
Plains
of Moab
Abel-shittim (Shittim)
Beth-haram

Naarah
Gilgal (Beth-gilgal)
Jericho

Beth-hoglah
City of Salt?
Middin?
Secacah?
Nibshan?

Salt Sea

(Sea of the Arabah)

Wilderness of Judah

Ascent of Ziz

V. of Beracah

En-gedi

Ramathaim-zophim (Ramah)
Zeredah
Timnath-serah (Timnath)
Chephar-ammoni
Bethel (Beth-aven)
Zemaraim
Ophrah (Ephron, Ophrah)
Ai
Rimmon
Ataroth-addar
Michmash
Migron
Geba
Parah
Almon
Anathoth
Adummim
Debir

En-shemesh
Nob
Ananiah
Laishah
Br. Kidron

Upper Beth-horon
Mizpah
Ramah
Hazor
Taralah
Neptoah

Lower Beth-horon
Gibeon
Beeroth?
Chephirah
Jerusalem
Gibeah
Rabbah
Bethlehem
Etam
Tekoa

Aithaim
Chesalon
Eltekon?
Netophah
Eltam

Beth-haccherem

Kiriath-jearim
Eshtaol
Lehi?
Zanoah
Timnah
Gedor
Gilo
Maarath
Beth-zur (Zair)
Zior (Zair)
Beth-anoth

Baalah
Eton
Ajalon
Gederah
Gezer
Shaalbim
Makaz

Sorek
Ashnah
Zorah
Beth-shemesh
Jarmuth
Enam
Adullam
Nezib
Keilah
Achzib (Cheziib)?
Nebo
Iphtah Halhul
Mamre
Beth-tappuah
Hebron (Kiriath-arba)
Aphekah
Kain
Adoraim
Ipthah

Makkedah?
Azekah
Socoh (Socoh)
Harim
Mareshah
Lahmam
Cabbon
Bozkath
Aphekah

Eltekeh?
Gibbethon
Lod
Gimzo
Hadid
Neballat
Gath (Gittaim)

Brook of Kanah
Aphek
Eben-ezer

Joppa
Asor
Bene-berak
Ono
Gath-rimmon?
Beth-dagon

Plain

Jabneel
Mount Baalah
Baalath?
Shikkeron
Ekron
Timnah
Zorah
Gath?
Moresheth-gath?
Libnah?
Ether
Mizpeh
Maresh
Ashnan

Hadashah?
Lachish
Chitlish?
Eglon?
Dilean

PHILISTIA

Ashdod

JUDAH

X

Y

W

B

A

5

5

OUTER BORDER SHOWS 10 MILE SUBDIVISIONS

31° 30'
32°
35°
35° 30'
31° 30'

MAP 9

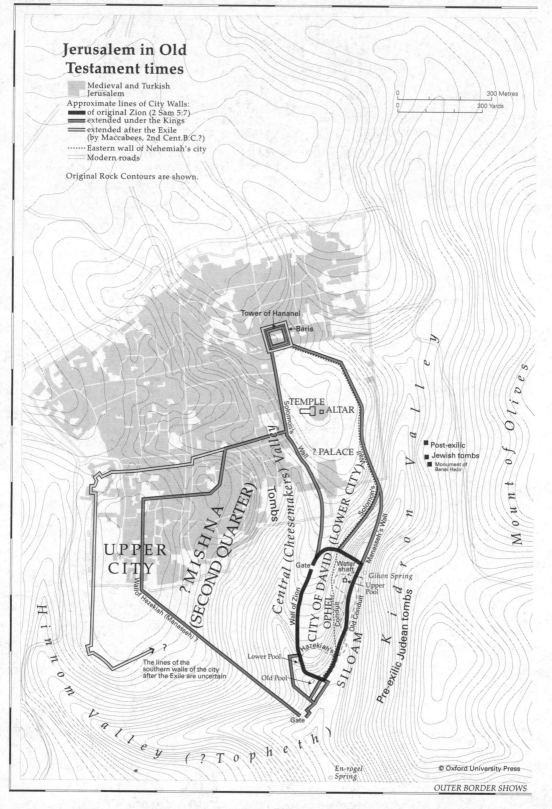

Jerusalem in Old Testament times

Medieval and Turkish Jerusalem

Approximate lines of City Walls:
- of original Zion (2 Sam 5:7)
- extended under the Kings
- extended after the Exile (by Maccabees, 2nd Cent.B.C.?)
- Eastern wall of Nehemiah's city
- Modern roads

Original Rock Contours are shown.

0 ——— 300 Metres
0 ——— 300 Yards

Tower of Hananel
←Baris

TEMPLE
☐ ALTAR

? PALACE

Solomon's Wall

Central (Cheesemakers) Valley

Tombs

Post-exilic
Jewish tombs
Monument of Benei Hezir

UPPER CITY

?MISHNA (SECOND QUARTER)

Wall of Hezekiah (Manasseh)?

Gate

Wall of Zion

Water shaft

(LOWER CITY)

Solomon's Wall

Gihon Spring
Upper Pool

Manasseh's Wall

CITY OF DAVID

OPHEL

Conduit

Old Conduit

Hezekiah's

SILOAM

Pre-exilic Judean tombs

Kidron Valley

Mount of Olives

Lower Pool

?

The lines of the southern walls of the city after the Exile are uncertain

Old Pool

Gate

Hinnom Valley (? Topheth)

En-rogel Spring

© Oxford University Press

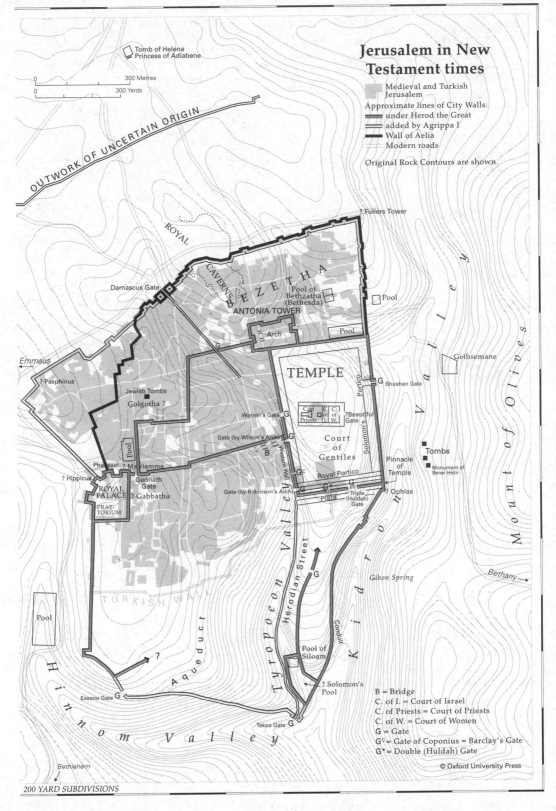

MAP 9

Tomb of Helena
Princess of Adiabene

Jerusalem in New Testament times

Medieval and Turkish
Jerusalem

Approximate lines of City Walls:
— under Herod the Great
— added by Agrippa I
— Wall of Aelia
— Modern roads

Original Rock Contours are shown.

0   300 Metres
0   300 Yards

OUTWORK OF UNCERTAIN ORIGIN

ROYAL CAVERNS

BEZETHA

?Fullers Tower

Damascus Gate

Pool of
Bethzatha
(Bethesda)

Pool

ANTONIA TOWER

Arch

Pool

Emmaus

? Psephinus

G

Gethsemane

TEMPLE

Portico

G Shushan Gate

Jewish Tombs

Golgotha ?

Warren's Gate

C. of
Priests

C. C.
of I.
W.

?Beautiful
Gate

Gate (by Wilson's Arch)

G

Court
of
Gentiles

Tombs

Monument of
Benei Hezir

Pool

B

Western Wall

Pinnacle
of
Temple

Phasael ? Mariamme

? Hippicus

Gennath
Gate

Gc

ROYAL
PALACE

? Gabbatha

Gate (by Robinson's Arch)

Royal Portico

G* G

Plaza

? Ophlas

PRAE-
TORIUM

Triple
(Huldah)
Gate

Mount of Olives

Kidron Valley

Solomon's Portico

TURKISH WALL

Herodian Street

G

Gihon Spring

Bethany

Pool

Aqueduct

Tyropoeon Valley

Conduit

Pool of
Siloam

Hinnom Valley

Essene Gate G

? Solomon's
Pool

Tekoa Gate G

B = Bridge
C. of I. = Court of Israel
C. of Priests = Court of Priests
C. of W. = Court of Women
G = Gate
Gc = Gate of Coponius = Barclay's Gate
G* = Double (Huldah) Gate

Bethlehem

© Oxford University Press

200 YARD SUBDIVISIONS

MAP 10

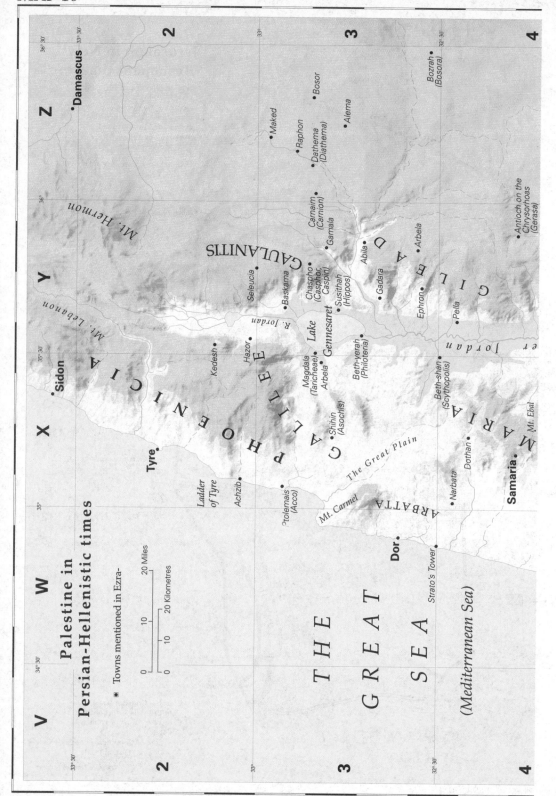

Palestine in Persian-Hellenistic times

• Towns mentioned in Ezra-

20 Miles

20 Kilometres

V   W   X   Y   Z

Damascus

Mt. Hermon

Mt. Lebanon

Sidon

Tyre

Ladder of Tyre

Achzib

Ptolemais (Acco)

Kedesh

Hazor

Seleucia

GALILEE

PHOENICIA

GAULANITIS

Baskama

Chaspho (Caspho; Caspin)

Carnaim (Carnion)

Gamala

Maked

Raphon

Dathema (Diathema)

Bosor

Alema

Bozrah (Bosora)

Antioch on the Chrysorhoas (Gerasa)

Abila

Arbela

Gadara

Susitah (Hippos)

GILEAD

Ephron

Pella

R. Jordan

Lake Gennesaret

Magdala (Taricheae)

Arbela

Shihin (Asochis)

Beth-yerah (Philoteria)

er Jordan

Beth-shan (Scythopolis)

SAMARIA

Mt. Ebal

Mt. Carmel

The Great Plain

ARBATTA

Narbata

Dothan

Samaria

Dor

Strato's Tower

THE GREAT SEA

(Mediterranean Sea)

0   10   20

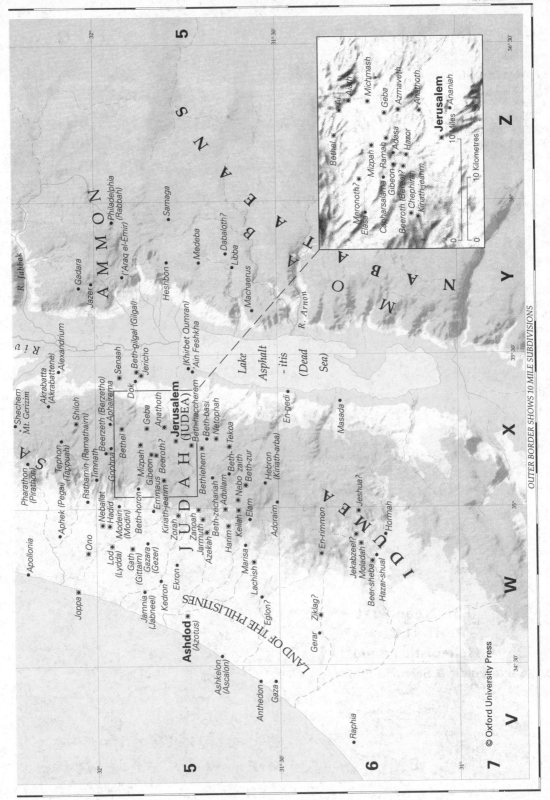

MAP 10

5

32°

R. Jabbok

A M M O N

Gadara

Jazer

('Araq el-Emir) (Rabbah)
Philadelphia

Samaga

N A B A T A E A N S

311·30'

Medeba

Heshbon

Dabaloth?

Libba

Machaerus

M O A B

N A B A T A E A N S

R. Arnon

Shechem
Mt. Gerizim

Akrabatta
(Akrabattene)

Alexandrium

R i v

Beth-gilgal (Gilgal)

Senaah

Jericho

Dok

(Khirbet Qumran)
'Ain Feshkha

Lake

Asphalt

- itis

(Dead

Sea)

S A M

Shiloh

Rathamin (Ramathaim)

Beerzeth (Berzetho)

Aphairema

Bethel

Mizpah

Gibeon

Emmaus

Kiriath-jearim

Beeroth?

Pharathon
(Pirathon)

Tephon
(Tappuah)

Aphek (Pegai)

Ono

Neballat

Hadid

Modein
(Modin)

Beth-horon

Zorah

Dok

Anathoth

Jerusalem
(JUDEA)

Beth-haccherem

Geba

Beth-basi

Netophah

Tekoa

Bethlehem

Beth-zechariah

Adullam

Nebo

Beth-zur

En-gedi

Masada

Hebron
(Kiriath-arba)

J U D A H

Zanoah

Jarmuth

Azekah

Harim

Keilah

Elam

Adoraim

I D U M A E A

En-rimmon

Jeshua?

Jekabzeel?

Moladah

Beer-sheba

Hazar-shual

Hormah

Apollonia

Joppa

Jamnia
(Jabneel)

Lod
(Lydda)

Gath
(Gittaim)

Gazara
(Gezer)

Kedron

Ekron

Marisa

Lachish

Eglon?

Ziklag?

Gerar

Ashdod
(Azotus)

LAND OF THE PHILISTINES

Ashkelon
(Ascalon)

Anthedon

Gaza

Raphia

34°30'

V

W

X

Y

Z

6

7

5

5

6

7

© Oxford University Press

Jerusalem inset

Ai

Alath

Michmash

Geba

Azmaveth

Anathoth

Ananiah

Bethel

Meronoth?

Elasa

Mizpah

Caphar-salama

Ramah

Gibeon

Adasa

Hazor

Beeroth (Bireh)?

Chephirah

Kiriath-jearim

Jerusalem

10 Miles

10 Kilometres

0

10 Kilometres

0

MAP 11

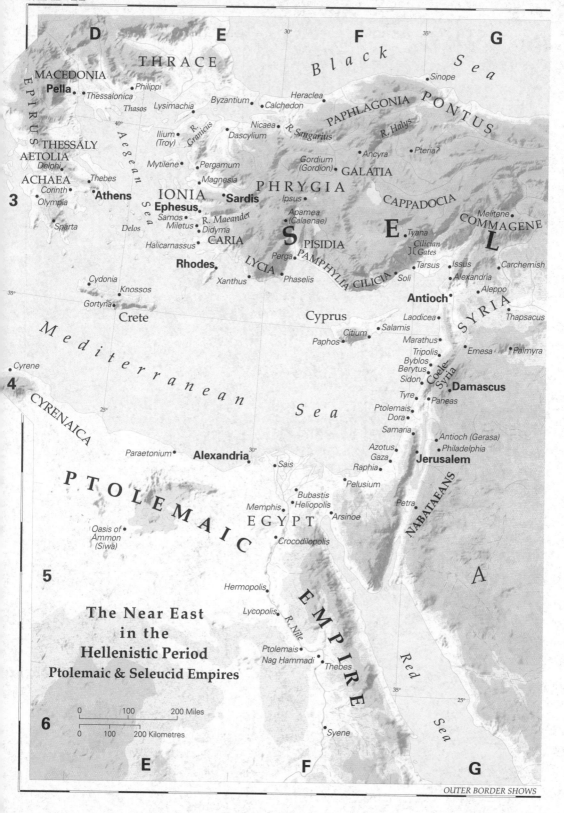

D   E   30°   F   35°   G

T H R A C E   *Black   Sea*

MACEDONIA   • *Philippi*   • *Sinope*

Pella •   • *Thessalonica*   • *Heraclea*   P A P H L A G O N I A   P O N T U S

Thasos   *Lysimachia*   *Byzantium*   • *Calchedon*

E P I R U S   *Aegean*   *Nicaea*   *R. Sangarius*   *R. Halys*

THESSALY   *Ilium*   *R. Granicus*   *Dascylium*   • *Ancyra*   • *Pteria?*

AETOLIA   *Delphi*   *Mytilene* •   • *Pergamum*   *Gordium* (*Gordion*)   G A L A T I A

ACHAEA   • *Thebes*   • *Magnesia*   P H R Y G I A   C A P P A D O C I A

Corinth •   **Athens**   I O N I A   **Sardis** •   • *Ipsus*   S

Olympia •   **Ephesus** •   *Apamea* (*Calaenae*)   E   • *Tyana*   *Melitene* •

3   *Sparta* •   *Samos* •   *R. Maeander*   *Cilician*   C O M M A G E N E

Delos   *Miletus* •   • *Didyma*   C A R I A   P I S I D I A   *Gates*   L

Halicarnassus   *Perga*   P A M P H Y L I A   *Tarsus* •   • *Issus*   *Carchemish*

Rhodes   L Y C I A   *Phaselis*   C I L I C I A   *Soli* •   • *Alexandria*   *Aleppo* •

Cydonia •   *Xanthus* •   **Antioch** •   S Y R I A   *Thapsacus* •

35°   *Knossos* •   C y p r u s   *Laodicea* •   • *Marathus*   *Emesa* •   *Palmyra* •

Gortyna •   *Paphos* •   *Citium* •   *Salamis*   *Tripolis* •

C r e t e   *Byblos* •   *Berytus* •   *Coele*

M e d i t e r r a n e a n   *Sidon* •   *Syria*   **Damascus**

4   *Cyrene* •   *Tyre* •   • *Paneas*

C Y R E N A I C A   25°   *Ptolemais* •   *Dora* •

Samaria •   *Antioch* (*Gerasa*) •

Paraetonium •   **Alexandria**   30°   *Azotus* •   • *Philadelphia*

Sais •   *Gaza* •   **Jerusalem**

P T O L E M A I C   *Raphia* •   *Pelusium* •   *Petra* •   N A B A T A E A N S

Bubastis •

Memphis •   *Heliopolis* •

Arsinoe •   E G Y P T

Crocodilopolis •

Oasis of Ammon (*Siwa*) •

5   E M P I R E

**The Near East
in the
Hellenistic Period**
Ptolemaic & Seleucid Empires

Hermopolis •

Lycopolis •   *R. Nile*   A

Red

Ptolemais •

Nag Hammadi •   *Thebes* •

Sea   35°   25°

0   100   200 Miles

6   0   100   200 Kilometres

Syene •   S e a

E   F   G

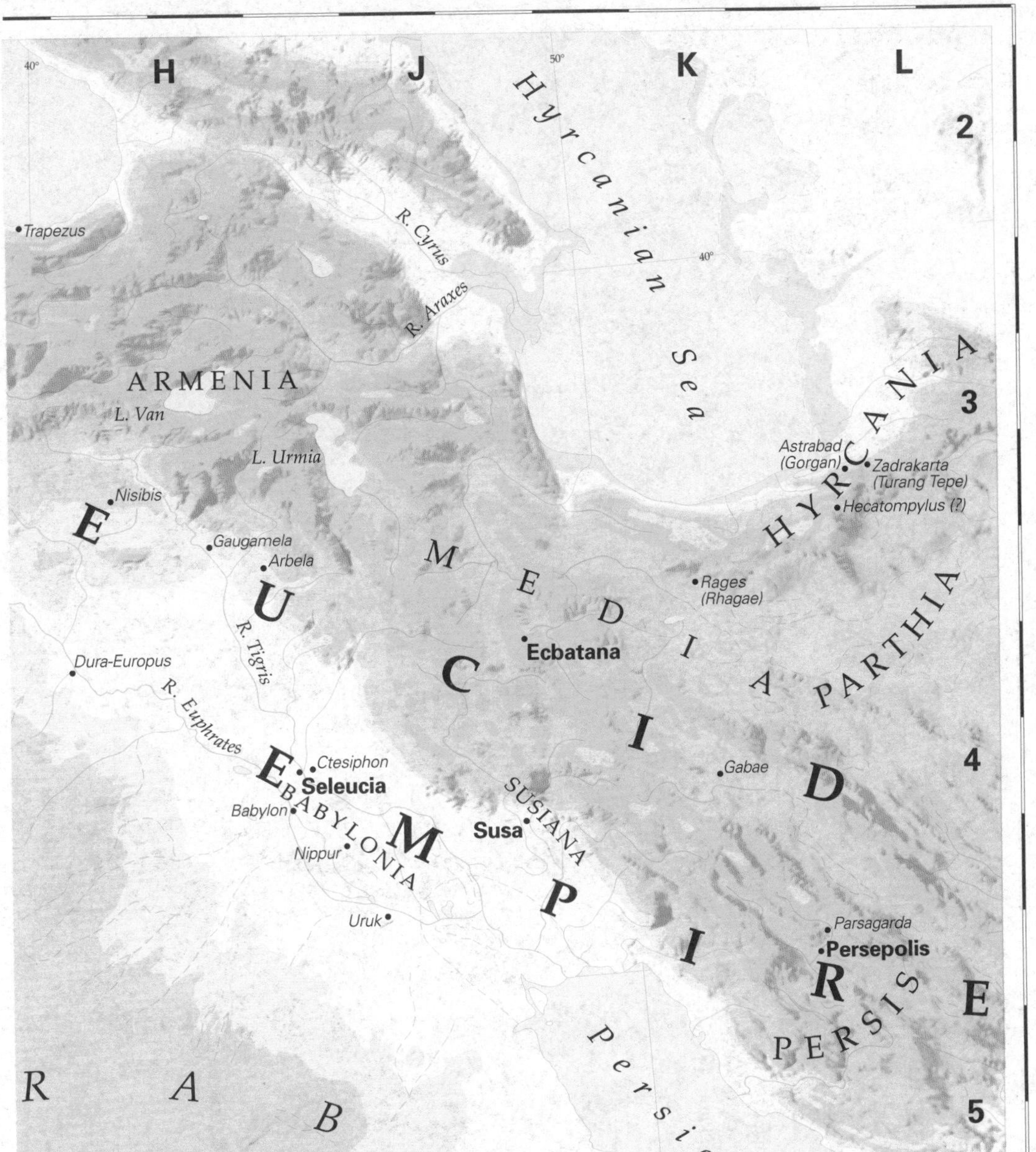

MAP 11

40°

H

J

50°

K

L

2

40°

H y r c a n i a n S e a

•*Trapezus*

R. Cyrus

R. Araxes

H Y R C A N I A

3

ARMENIA

L. Van

*Astrabad
(Gorgan)* •

•*Zadrakarta
(Turang Tepe)*

L. Urmia

•*Hecatompylus (?)*

•*Nisibis*

M

*Rages
(Rhagae)* •

P A R T H I A

•*Gaugamela*
•*Arbela*

E

U

E

D

C

•*Dura-Europus*

R. Tigris

I

Ecbatana

A

R. Euphrates

•*Ctesiphon*

Seleucia

E

BABYLONIA

Babylon •

•*Gabae*

4

M

Nippur •

SUSIANA

Susa •

P

Uruk •

I

•*Parsagarda*

•**Persepolis**

R

S

R

A

B

I

A

P E R S I S

E

5

P e r s i a n

50°

55°

25°

G u l f

© Oxford University Press

6

100 MILE SUBDIVISIONS

H

J

K

MAP 12

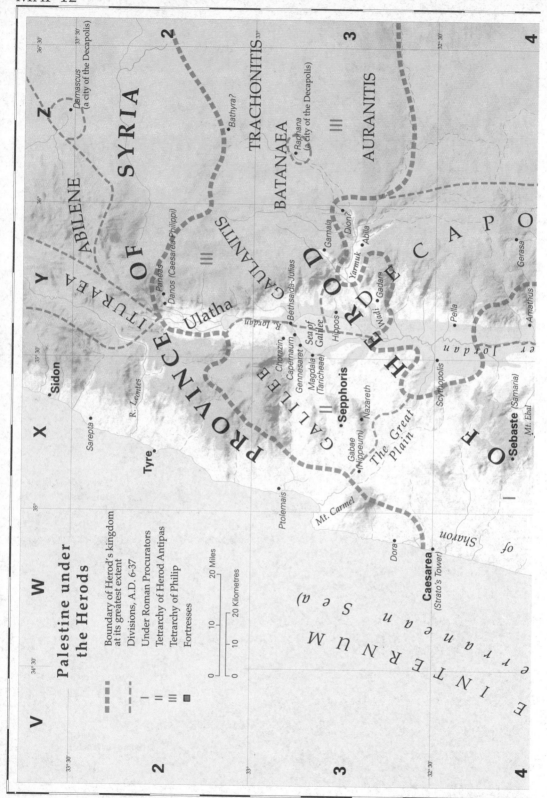

Palestine under
the Herods

Boundary of Herod's kingdom
at its greatest extent

Divisions, A.D. 6-37

Under Roman Procurators
Tetrarchy of Herod Antipas
Tetrarchy of Philip

Fortresses

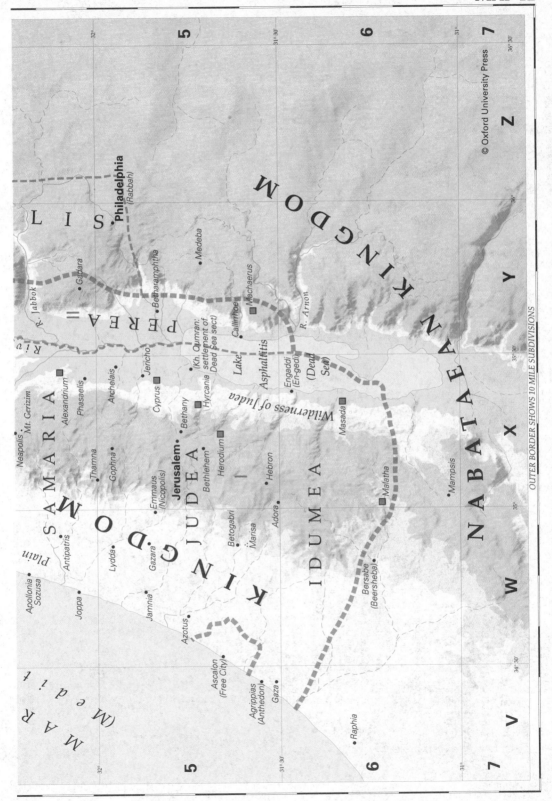

MAP 12

© Oxford University Press

OUTER BORDER SHOWS 10 MILE SUBDIVISIONS

MAR
(Medit

SAMARIA

Plain

Apollonia
Sozusa

Antipatris

Joppa

Lydda

Gazara

Jamnia

Azotus

Ascalon
(Free City)

Agrippias
(Anthedon)

Gaza

KINGDOM

Neapolis

Mt. Gerizim

Thamna

Gophna

Emmaus
(Nicopolis)

JUDEA

Jerusalem

Bethlehem

Betogabri

Marisa

Adora

Hebron

Raphia

Alexandrium

Phasaelis

Archelais

Cyprus

Bethany

Hyrcania

Herodium

Jericho

(Kh. Qumran:
settlement of
Dead Sea sect)

Wilderness of Judea

Engaddi
(En-gedi)

IDUMEA

Malatha

Bersabe
(Beersheba)

Mampsis

Lake
Asphaltitis

(Dead
Sea)

River

R. Jabbok

Gadara

PEREA =

Betharamphtha

Medeba

Callirrhoe

Machaerus

R. Arnon

Philadelphia
(Rabbah)

LIS

KINGDOM

NABATAEAN KINGDOM

5

31° 30'

6

31°

7

Z

Y

X

W

V

32°

31° 30'

31°

7

5

6

36° 30'

36°

35° 30'

35°

34° 30'

32°

5

MAP 13

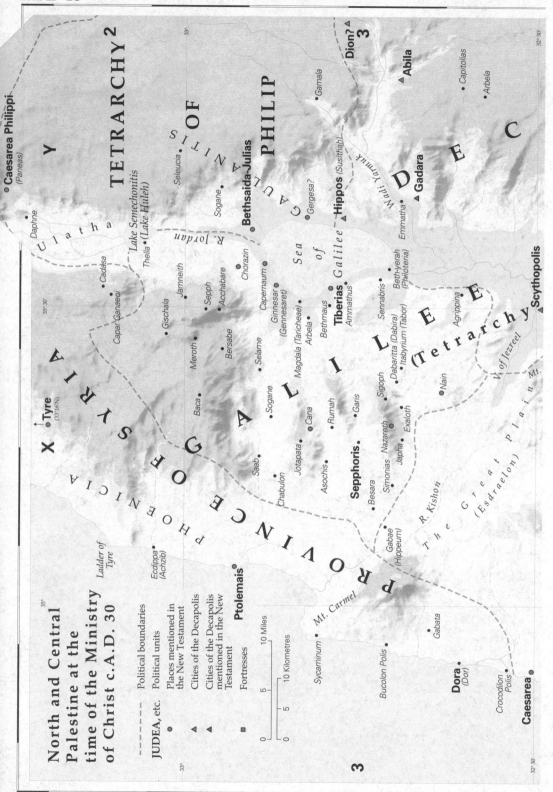

North and Central Palestine at the time of the Ministry of Christ c.A.D. 30

- – – – Political boundaries
- JUDEA, etc. Political units
- ● Places mentioned in the New Testament
- ▲ Cities of the Decapolis
- ▴ Cities of the Decapolis mentioned in the New Testament
- ■ Fortresses

0 5 10 Miles
0 5 10 Kilometres

PROVINCE OF SYRIA

X

TETRARCHY²

Y

PHILIP

TETRARCHY OF

GAULANITIS

DECAPOLIS

GALILEE (Tetrarchy)

PHOENICIA

● Caesarea Philippi (Paneas)

Daphne

Ulatha

Lake Semechonitis
Thella ●(Lake Huleh)

● Cadasa

Capar Ganaeoi ●

Tyre (33°16'N)

Ecdippa (Achzib) ●

Ladder of Tyre

Gischala ●

Jamneith ●

Seleucia ●

Sogane ●

Bethsaida-Julias

Gamala ●

● Gergesa?

Chorazin ●

Capernaum ●

Sepph ●

Acchabare ●

Bersabe ●

Meroth ●

Baca ●

Selame ●

Sea of Galilee

Hippos (Susitha) ▴

Emmatha ●

Gadara ▴

Abila ▴

Wadi Yarmuk

● Capitolias
● Arbela

Dion? ▴ 3

Ginnesar (Gennesaret) ●

Magdala (Taricheae) ●

Arbela ●

Bethmaus ●

Tiberias

Ammathus ●

Beth-yerah (Philoteria) ●

Sennabris ●

Sogane ●

Saab ●

Cana ●

Rumah ●

Jotapata ●

Asochis ●

Garis ●

Sigoph ●

Dabaritta (Dabira) ●

Itabyrium (Tabor) ▲

Agrippina ●

Scythopolis ▲

Chabulon ●

Besara ●

Simonias ●

Nazareth ●

Japha ●

Exaloth ●

Nain ●

V. of Jezreel

Mt.

Sepphoris

R. Kishon

The Great Plain (Esdraelon)

Gabae (Hippeum) ●

Gabata ●

Sycaminum ●

Mt. Carmel

Bucolon Polis ●

Dora (Dor) ●

Crocodilon Polis ●

Ptolemais

Caesarea

R. Jordan

35° 35°30'

33°

32°30'

3

MAP 13

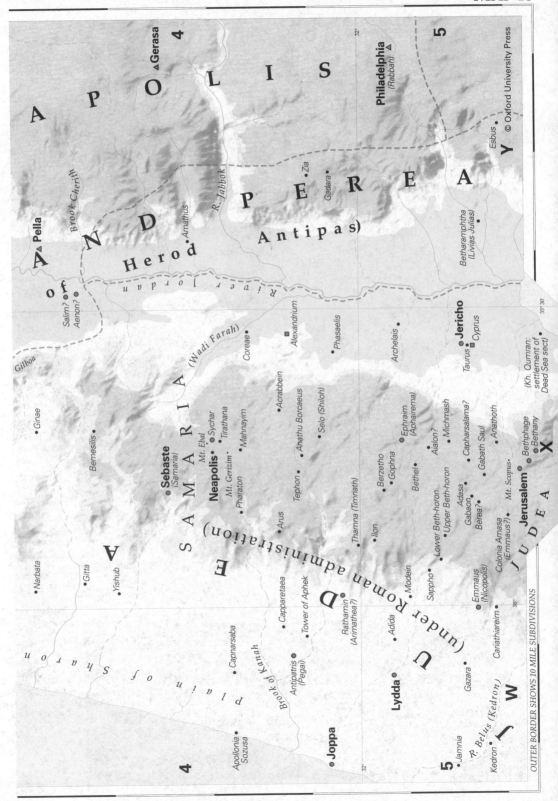

APOLIS

▲Gerasa

4

32°

Philadelphia
(Rabbah) ▲

5

© Oxford University Press

N D

P E R E A

Brook Cherith

R. Jabbok

Zia

Amathus

Gadara

▲Pella

A

Herod

Antipas)

Betharamphtha
(Livias Julias)

Esbus

of

Salim?
Aenon?

River Jordan

Gilboa

Jericho

35° 30'

Coreae

Alexandrium

Phasaelis

Taurus

Cyprus

S A M A R I A

(Wadi Farah)

Archelais

(Kh. Qumran:
settlement of
Dead Sea sect)

Ginae

Acrabbein

Anathu Borcaeus

Selo (Shiloh)

Ephraim
(Aphairema)

Anathoth

Bernesilis

Mt. Ebal

Sychar

Tirathana

Mahnayim

Berzetho

Michmash

Sebaste
(Samaria)

Neapolis

Mt. Gerizim

Pharaton

Tephon

Thamna (Timnath)

Gophna

Bethel

Adasa

Capharsalama?

Gabath Saul

Mt. Scopus

E

Arus

Ilon

Lower Beth-horon

Gabaon

Adida

Upper Beth-horon

Berea?

Colonia Amasa
(Emmaus?)

Jerusalem

Bethphage

Bethany

Narbata

A

Capparetaea

Sappho

Modein

Emmaus
(Nicopolis)

X

Gitta

Yishub

D

J U D E A

(under Roman administration)

Capnarsaba

Brook of Kanah

Tower of Aphek

Rathamin
(Arimathea?)

U

Plain of Sharon

Antipatris
(Pegai)

Adida

Cariathiarem

W

Apollonia
Sozusa

Gazara

Lydda

R. Belus (Kedron)

Joppa

Jamnia

Kedron (Kedron)

4

32°

36°

5

MAP 14

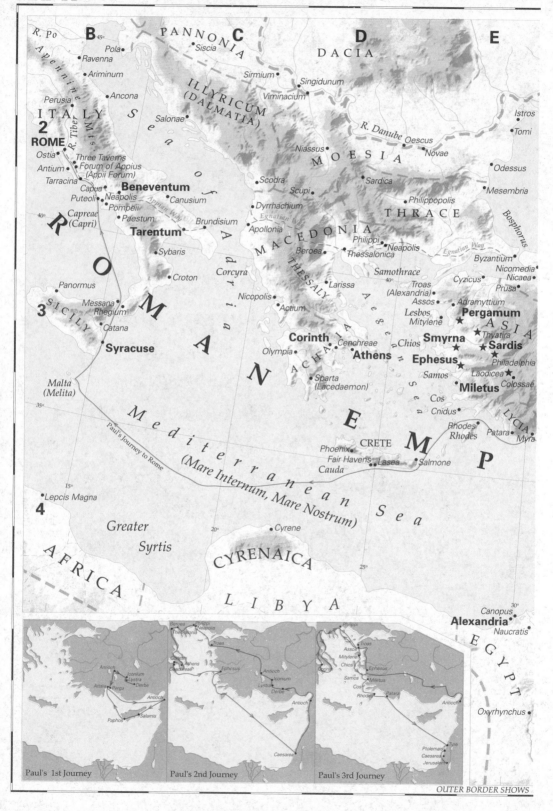

B 45°

C

D

E

PANNONIA

DACIA

R. Po

Pola

Ravenna

Ariminum

Siscia

Sirmium

Singidunum

Ancona

Viminacium

ILLYRICUM
(DALMATIA)

R. Danube Oescus

Istros

Perusia

ITALY

Salonae

Niassus

MOESIA

Novae

Tomi

2

ROME

Ostia

Antium

Three Taverns

Forum of Appius
(Appii Forum)

Scodra

Sardica

Odessus

Tarracina

Capua

Benchorus

Philippopolis

THRACE

Mesembria

40°

Capreae
(Capri)

Puteoli

Neapolis

Pompeii

Paestum

Canusium

Brundisium

Dyrrhachium

Apollonia

MACEDONIA

Philippi Neapolis

Byzantium

Nicomedia

Nicaea

ROME

Tarentum

Sybaris

Croton

Corcyra

Beroea

Thessalonica

Egnatian Way

Bosphorus

Prusa

Panormus

Messana

Rhegium

Catana

SICILY

3

Nicopolis

Actium

Larissa

THESSALY

Samothrace

40°

Troas
(Alexandria)

Assos

Lesbos

Mitylene

Cyzicus

Adramyttium

Pergamum

ASIA

Thyatira

Syracuse

Corinth

Olympia

Cenchreae

Athens

ACHAIA

Chios

Smyrna

Sardis

Ephesus

Philadelphia

Laodicea

Samos

Colossae

Miletus

Malta
(Melita)

Paul's Journey to Rome

Sparta
(Lacedaemon)

Aegean Sea

Cos

Cnidus

Rhodes

Rhodes

Patara

LYCIA

Myra

35°

Mediterranean Sea

(Mare Internum, Mare Nostrum)

CRETE

Phoenix

Fair Havens

Cauda

Lasea

Salmone

M

P

Lepcis Magna

15°

4

Greater

Syrtis

20°

Cyrene

AFRICA

CYRENAICA

25°

LIBYA

Canopus

30°

Alexandria

Naucratis

EGYPT

Oxyrhynchus

Paul's 1st Journey

Paul's 2nd Journey

Paul's 3rd Journey

OUTER BORDER SHOWS

MAP 14

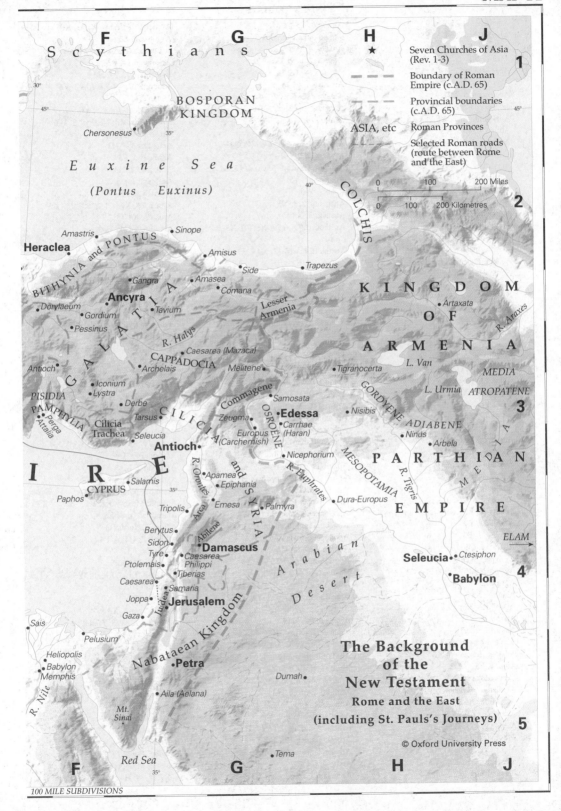

S c y t h i a n s

BOSPORAN KINGDOM

Chersonesus

E u x i n e   S e a

(Pontus   Euxinus)

COLCHIS

0   100   200 Miles

0   100   200 Kilometres

Amastris   *Sinope*

Heraclea   BITHYNIA and PONTUS

Amisus

Side   *Trapezus*

Gangra   *Amasea*

Ancyra   *Comana*

Dorylaeum   *Tavium*

Lesser Armenia

KINGDOM

Gordium   *Artaxata*

Pessinus   O F   *R. Araxes*

GALATIA   *R. Halys*

Caesarea (Mazaca)   A R M E N I A

Antioch   CAPPADOCIA   *Melitene*   *L. Van*

PISIDIA   *Archelais*   *Tigranocerta*   MEDIA

Iconium   *L. Urmia*   ATROPATENE

PAMPHYLIA   *Lystra*   Commagene   *Samosata*   GORDYENE   M E D I A

Perga   *Derbe*   C I L I C I A   *Zeugma*   **Edessa**   *Nisibis*   ADIABENE

Attalia   *Tarsus*   OSROENE   *Carrhae*   *Ninus*

Cilicia   *Seleucia*   Europus   *(Haran)*   *Arbela*

Trachea   *(Carchemish)*   P A R T H I A N

I   R   E   *Nicephorium*   MESOPOTAMIA   *R. Tigris*   M   E   D   I   A

Salamis   *Apamea*   and   *R. Euphrates*   E M P I R E

CYPRUS   R. Orontes   *Epiphania*   *Dura-Europus*

Paphos   *Tripolis*   *Emesa*   *Palmyra*   ELAM

Berytus   Abilene   S Y R I A

Sidon   A r a b i a n   **Seleucia** *Ctesiphon*

Tyre   **Damascus**

Ptolemais   *Caesarea*   D e s e r t   **Babylon**

Caesarea   Philippi

Tiberias

Samaria   Judea

Joppa   **Jerusalem**

Gaza

Sais

Pelusium

Heliopolis   Nabataean Kingdom

Babylon   **Petra**

Memphis   *Dumah*

R. Nile   *Aila (Aelana)*

The Background of the New Testament

Rome and the East

(including St. Pauls's Journeys)

Mt. Sinai

Tema   © Oxford University Press

Red Sea

INDEX TO MAPS